1973

THE READER'S ENCYCLOPEDIA
OF AMERICAN LITERATURE

THE
READER'S
ENCYCLOPEDIA
OF
AMERICAN
LITERATURE

By

MAX J. HERZBERG

and the staff of the

THOMAS Y. CROWELL COMPANY

THOMAS Y. CROWELL COMPANY

Established 1834

NEW YORK

Published in Canada by Fitzhenry & Whiteside Limited, Toronto.
*Manufactured in the United States of America
by the Vail-Ballou Press, Inc., Binghamton, N.Y.
Library of Congress Catalog Card No. 62-16546*

ISBN 0-690-67341-8
Designed by Andor Braun

6 7 8 9 10

Introduction

Literature in America has gone through many phases. It has had great decades and others that were meager, but it has at last attained a monumental development that warrants an encyclopedia wholly devoted to it. This volume, the result of many years of editing, touches on virtually every subject that is related to American literature. It includes biographical sketches of authors, bibliographies, and articles, short or long, on the social background of American writing, its schools and movements. In this encyclopedia appear entries on Canadian writers, on Latin American writers connected in some way with the United States, on magazines, editors and statesmen, famous characters in fiction, folk heroes, historical events. With entries, as well, on novels and poems, and essays on various types of writing, this comprehensive handbook covers its wide-ranging subject with remarkable thoroughness.

During the last half century there has been a great change in the appreciation of American literature. In 1909, Randolph Bourne wrote, "Emerson, Whitman and Thoreau have delighted me infinitely more than all my English official reading," yet, he added, "the professors seldom refer to them." Bourne's Columbia class in literature was making an "intensive" study of Tennyson while he himself was reading these American authors, and he presently rose in revolt against the professors and foreswore any further literary courses. At Harvard, at about this time, the situation was much the same, and Barrett Wendell, who lectured on it, said that our literature was mainly a "record of American inexperience"; it was, he added, a minor branch of the literature of England. America itself, said the critic William Crary Brownell, was a "literary dependency of England." The general feeling in colleges was that English authors were the only authors in our language who could be taken seriously. Randolph Bourne spoke for the first generation that was in rebellion against the dominance of England in the mind of this country.

That was, of course, a moment of power among living British writers, who included Hardy, Kipling, Yeats, Shaw, Wells, and Arnold Bennett. It was equally a time of weakness in American letters, when the older great men were dead and when Mark Twain was about to die, like Henry James in England and the elderly Howells. But it was not many years before the author of *Dodsworth* was to receive the first of the American Nobel prizes, a series that, within two or three decades, announced that American literature was one of the major literatures of the world. It was in the position of German literature, little known before Goethe's time, when the world-famous author of *Faust* gave it universal currency. By the end of World War II there were no authors anywhere who had more general influence than Faulkner, Hemingway, and John Dos Passos. With Emerson, Thoreau, and Whitman among the old masters, our literature had become an important subject in all American universities. This was partly because of the exhaustion of Europe in two universal wars, together with the rise of self-confidence in the American mind.

Looking back on this change now, one sees that the fusion of races here was one of the causes that produced it, the intermingling of peoples from every country that suggested the crew of Melville's ship, the *Pequod*. The Germans, the Jews, the Armenians, the Portuguese, the Swedes were represented among twentieth-century authors, where only English names had been known before, and Dreiser, Lippmann, Saroyan, Dos Passos, and Sandburg largely replaced the Anglo-Americans of old. Walt Whitman had prophesied the post-World-War America that was to be made up of many races, each bringing its own tradition and strength, and all emerging into print after two or three generations had silently browsed on the life they were to express. Nor can one doubt that the "new critics" were of service to many writers of the time, sharpening their wits, setting their ideas in order, imposing on the chaos of their minds the notion of formal perfection, a discipline that led them to make the most of their capabilities. But it might also be said that these critics over-defended an orthodoxy that was out of place in the creative world, rejecting the natural pluralism of American writers.

There have been two great periods in the history of our literature, the nineteen-twenties and the eighteen-fifties, both "heats and genial periods," to use Emerson's phrase, "by which high tides are caused in the human spirit." The decade before the Civil War produced Whitman's *Leaves of Grass*, Melville's *Moby Dick*, and *The Scarlet Letter* of Hawthorne. Much of the best work of Emerson and Thoreau appeared in this decade, along with the other eminent New England poets; or, if some wrote before this time, and several wrote after, they were all at a peak in the eighteen-fifties. It was a time of ardent faith and the study of greatness among people who were mainly of English descent, closely connected with the soil of the country, as in the "springtime" that Spengler called the high moment in culture-cycles. Before Boston became the literary capital, Irving, Fenimore Cooper, and Poe had done much of the work for which they were famous, Audubon had written about the frontier that he was exploring for birds, and John Lloyd Stephens had told us about the ruined cities of Yucatán.

After the Civil War, the great causes disappeared and the mind of the country, for a long generation, seemed to have lost its intensity and produced "idle singers of an empty day." The general energy was involved in railroad-building, in developing the West, and in the all-obsessive impulse of industry and business. Then, with the First World War, or in the years before it, the fiddles began to tune again, in the phrase of a sympathetic artist who had come from abroad, and poets appeared, new magazines, the theater of Eugene O'Neill, and presently several novelists of distinction and power. Beginning as a poetic renaissance, a movement was soon under way that spread to every corner of the West and the South, the Southwest of New Mexico, the streets of Chicago, New Orleans, San Francisco, Richmond, Charleston. Each of these centers had a moment of its own, with a cluster of unusual writers who gathered for a while, New York remaining as the general literary focus. Howells, praising Italian novels, Spanish, and Norwegian, had drawn Americans away from the novel of England, and meanwhile the so-called expatriates had resorted to Europe, to Paris, and to Rome, Geneva, Munich. Publishing little magazines, they studied in Paris the art of writing, sometimes under the tutelage of Gertrude Stein. These young men revolted against the aesthetically joyless American scene, against their humdrum world and the "genteel tradition" on which Santayana bestowed a reverberant name. The romance of the *rive gauche* captivated many, the "revolution of the word" preoccupied more, and various well-known styles, Hemingway's among them, were the outcome of that indoctrination. . . .

Regionalism had gone by the board with the Second World War, while every decade had its own note; the proletarian thirties, the forties, the fifties, each governed by its own peculiar mood. A generation had grown up that had no associations with England. The "alien" whom Henry James had found in serene and triumphant possession when he returned from England in 1905 stood in the front rank of literature as in every other sphere, and a cosmopolitan point of view dominated many for whom even the whole country seemed too small. Forgotten were the days when literary America was comprised in a little chain of cities on the Atlantic seaboard: Boston, New York, Philadelphia, Richmond, and Charleston. While they were based upon towns from which they had fled in earlier years, writers still roamed the world more freely than ever; yet, detached from society in the larger sense, not attempting to picture it, they dealt with isolated circles and restricted themes. Possessing Whitman's "orbic" mind, they had none of the immersion in a social scene that had marked the novelists of the twenties and thirties,

and they seemed to have lost touch with the common humanity of Sinclair Lewis or of Willa Cather, or, for that matter, of Robert Frost. In fiction and poetry few major talents succeeded the minds of the twenties and thirties that had influenced writers in Germany, Italy, and France —especially Faulkner and Hemingway, whose vitality and inventiveness had roused flagging spirits in war-shocked Europe.

The new time seemed like a backward leap from spring into winter, for a pessimism that was equally blind had replaced the optimism that was so obviously blind in earlier days. In the "age of anxiety" writers looked back with nostalgia to the relatively confident 1920's, whose feeling of disillusion had been slight beside theirs, for an overwhelming "power of blackness" filled many of these world-conscious later minds. A helpless fear of atomic war paralyzed certain talents that seemed to exist in a state of suspended animation, and the note of Emerson and Whitman ceased to be heard any longer in the earthquake weather after the two world wars. "I am afraid of all that has happened and all that is to come," a character says in Eliot's *The Family Reunion;* and the old belief in revolution changed to a belief that society could no longer be altered by any effort of the will. Man was never the victor but always the victim in Hemingway, Dos Passos, and Eugene O'Neill, and the faith begotten by despair was never a faith in humanity; one had to look "outside history" for one's hope. Brilliant novels, poems, and plays continued to appear, but a reversion to Calvinism had taken the place in literature of the vivid prospects of earlier years. The negativity of Henry Adams had suddenly prevailed against William James's adventurous faith in the future. But history had always shown alternating moods—expansion, for example, following tension—and it seemed, unless science came to be given a monopoly of wisdom, that literature in America would recover its buoyancy and faith.

The details, the personalities of this complex history can be found in this encyclopedia. In it are the facts, the earliest and the latest, relating to literature in America, its creators and its background. Many of the longer articles, written by eminent critics, are entertaining as well as profound. From Paul Elmer More to Marianne Moore, from Henry Miller to Joaquin Miller, from Herman Melville to William Faulkner and Elinor Wylie, one will discover in these pages the details of biography with sound and just critical appreciations. One will find answers to questions about James Thurber or Scott Fitzgerald, about *The Federalist* or *The Evergreen Review,* or about the Mississippi or the Missouri Rivers as they appear in American literature and art. This book is invaluable to every American who cares for the shape of his country, its presence and expression in literary form; and it will be extremely useful as a primary work of reference in every household library for old and young.

Van Wyck Brooks

Publisher's Preface

The Reader's Encyclopedia of American Literature, the most comprehensive reference book on its subject in existence, gives all the essential information on writers and writing in America. Covering the United States and Canada from the earliest colonial period to 1962, it includes entries on authors, titles, characters, periodicals, literary groups, historical personages, and other topics related to literature.

Author entries start with the author's birthplace, dates of birth and death (in day, month, and year, where possible), chief professions, and types of writing. Further biographical data and critical comments follow. The entries conclude with generous, though selective, bibliographies of the author's own works and of biographical or critical works about him. *Title entries* begin with the category of writing and the author's name, followed by descriptive comment. Most entries include either a definition of the theme or a brief plot synopsis, historical data, and critical remarks.

Entries for well-known *characters* from fiction give not only the author and the title of the work, but also some description and comment on their significance, if any. Particular attention is given to those who appear in more than one work, who are more important than the work itself, or whose role lies outside the main plot as sketched in the title entry. Scores of *periodicals* have entries, with mention of their principal editors and contributors. Their historical significance is further traced in general articles on newspapers and on magazines. Entries on *literary movements and groups* include such a wide variety as the Hartford Wits, the Imagists, and the Fugitives. There are many articles on such *general topics* as humor, dialect, the Yankee stereotype, and the Bible. Outside the purely literary areas are two sizable categories that increase the usefulness of this encyclopedia for the general reader: *historical figures* (presidents, explorers, distinguished statesmen) and *personages, places, and events* (Carrie Nation, Greenwich Village, the Cardiff Giant) which, as the stuff of American life, are frequently alluded to in literature.

The editors of *The Reader's Encyclopedia of American Literature* have invited well-known authorities to contribute special articles on major authors and on such broad subjects as the novel, poetry, and social criticism. In some cases these authors have written or reviewed the smaller entries on related subjects. For example, the coverage of individual Canadian authors writing in English and French was suggested by the authors of the surveys on these two subjects.

Many of the articles are illustrated with photographs or contemporary engravings of authors or of reproductions of pages from famous books or magazines. Family trees trace the genealogy of the many writers in the Adams and Mather families. A special feature are the genealogical charts of the six main families in William Faulkner's Yoknapatawpha saga. A Glossary defines literary terms that most frequently appear in this encyclopedia, but does not pretend to cover literary terminology in general.

A word about the cross-references will be helpful. Any work that appears printed in SMALL CAPITALS in the body of an entry has an entry of its own elsewhere in this encyclopedia. In the rare cases when titles to be referred to are ordinarily printed entirely in capitals or numbers (J.B., 1601), the abbreviation *q.v.* appears after them in parentheses. If the reader might profitably turn to a second entry not mentioned in the body of the text of the first entry, he is referred to it with the usual "See" or "See also." Special reference symbols used only in the Glossary are explained in a note at its head.

In authors' names appearing in boldface type in entry headings, brackets set off those names or parts of names not regularly used by the author. Bracketed names in quotation marks are pen names.

The Publisher would like to thank Professors Lewis Leary and Joseph Ridgely of Columbia University for their help and many kindnesses throughout the preparation of *The Reader's Encyclopedia of American Literature*. The late Earle W. Walbridge of New York University deserves special mention. Many researchers and writers have worked devotedly for years and to them all go appreciation and thanks. We record with sadness and a profound sense of loss the death of the chief editor and compiler, Max J. Herzberg, before the completion of this monument to his industry. We can conceive of few better memorials to a dedicated student of American literature than this pioneer *Reader's Encyclopedia of American Literature*.

Contributors of Special Articles

Gay Wilson Allen
NEW YORK UNIVERSITY, NEW YORK, NEW YORK

Quentin Anderson
COLUMBIA UNIVERSITY, NEW YORK, NEW YORK

Charles Angoff
FAIRLEIGH DICKINSON UNIVERSITY
RUTHERFORD, NEW JERSEY

George Warren Arms
UNIVERSITY OF NEW MEXICO
ALBUQUERQUE, NEW MEXICO

Margot Astrov

Cleanth Brooks
YALE UNIVERSITY, NEW HAVEN, CONNECTICUT

Oscar Cargill
NEW YORK UNIVERSITY, NEW YORK, NEW YORK

Hayden Carruth

Richard Crowder
PURDUE UNIVERSITY, LAFAYETTE, INDIANA

Robert L. Crowell

Edwin S. Fulcomer
MONTCLAIR STATE COLLEGE
MONTCLAIR, NEW JERSEY

John Gassner
YALE UNIVERSITY, NEW HAVEN, CONNECTICUT

Philip Gordon
FORMERLY AT SETON HALL COLLEGE

Paul Green
UNIVERSITY OF NORTH CAROLINA
CHAPEL HILL, NORTH CAROLINA

Allan Gates Halline (deceased)
FORMERLY AT BUCKNELL UNIVERSITY
LEWISBURG, PENNSYLVANIA

Manning Hawthorne

Eldon C. Hill
MIAMI UNIVERSITY, OXFORD, OHIO

Howard W. Hintz
BROOKLYN COLLEGE, BROOKLYN, NEW YORK

Carl F. Klinck
UNIVERSITY OF WESTERN ONTARIO
LONDON, CANADA

George Kummer
WESTERN RESERVE UNIVERSITY
CLEVELAND, OHIO

Lewis Leary
COLUMBIA UNIVERSITY, NEW YORK, NEW YORK

Ernest E. Leisy
SOUTHERN METHODIST UNIVERSITY
DALLAS, TEXAS

Max Lerner
BRANDEIS UNIVERSITY
WALTHAM, MASSACHUSETTS

Joan London

Thomas O. Mabbott
HUNTER COLLEGE, NEW YORK, NEW YORK

Frederick T. McGill, Jr.
RUTGERS UNIVERSITY AT NEWARK
NEWARK, NEW JERSEY

Margie Sornsen Malmberg

Frank Luther Mott
UNIVERSITY OF MISSOURI, COLUMBIA, MISSOURI

William Van O'Connor
UNIVERSITY OF CALIFORNIA, DAVIS, CALIFORNIA

Thomas Parkinson
UNIVERSITY OF CALIFORNIA
BERKELEY, CALIFORNIA

Vesta M. Parsons
BLOOMFIELD HIGH SCHOOL
BLOOMFIELD, NEW JERSEY

Martin Leonard Pops
HUNTER COLLEGE, NEW YORK, NEW YORK

Louise Pound (deceased)
FORMERLY AT THE UNIVERSITY OF NEBRASKA
LINCOLN, NEBRASKA

Joseph Ridgely
COLUMBIA UNIVERSITY, NEW YORK, NEW YORK

Richard C. Robey
COLUMBIA UNIVERSITY, NEW YORK, NEW YORK

Frances Clarke Sayers
UNIVERSITY OF CALIFORNIA
LOS ANGELES, CALIFORNIA

Philip A. Shelley
PENNSYLVANIA STATE UNIVERSITY
UNIVERSITY PARK, PENNSYLVANIA

R. W. Stallman
UNIVERSITY OF CONNECTICUT
STORRS, CONNECTICUT

Jean Guy Sylvestre
ASSOCIATE PARLIAMENTARY LIBRARIAN
LIBRARY OF PARLIAMENT
OTTAWA, CANADA

Charles C. Walcutt
QUEENS COLLEGE, NEW YORK, NEW YORK

Herbert Faulkner West
DARTMOUTH COLLEGE
HANOVER, NEW HAMPSHIRE

Ray B. West
SAN FRANCISCO STATE COLLEGE
SAN FRANCISCO, CALIFORNIA

Victor Weybright
THE NEW AMERICAN LIBRARY OF WORLD
LITERATURE, INC.
NEW YORK, NEW YORK

Dudley Wynn
UNIVERSITY OF NEW MEXICO
ALBUQUERQUE, NEW MEXICO

Philip Young
PENNSYLVANIA STATE UNIVERSITY
UNIVERSITY PARK, PENNSYLVANIA

CONTENTS

CONTENTS

THE READER'S ENCYCLOPEDIA
OF AMERICAN LITERATURE

A

Abbey, Henry (b. Kingston, N.Y., July 11, 1842—d. June 7, 1911), businessman, poet. Abbey wrote simple, mostly didactic verse. His first collection was *May Dreams* (1862); others are *Ballads of Good Deeds* (1872); *Poems* (1879); *Dream of Love* (1910). His best-remembered poem begins, "What do we plant when we plant a tree?"

Abbot, Willis J[ohn] (b. New Haven, Conn., March 16, 1863—d. May 19, 1934), newspaperman, historian. Abbot wrote mainly for young people; his *Blue Jackets of '76* (1888) and *Battlefields and Campfires* (1890) were especially popular. He first applied the phrase "the Great Commoner" to WILLIAM JENNINGS BRYAN.

Abbott, Eleanor Hallowell [Mrs. Fordyce Coburn] (b. Cambridge, Mass., Sept. 22, 1872—   ), novelist, short-story writer. Granddaughter of JACOB ABBOTT and niece of LYMAN ABBOTT, she wrote *Molly Make Believe* (1910), her most famous book, as well as *Sick-a-Bed Lady and Other Stories* (1911); *Fairy Prince and Other Stories* (1922); *Being Little in Cambridge When Everyone Else Was Big* (1936, autobiographical).

Abbott, George (b. Forestville, N.Y., June 25, 1889—   ), actor, playwright, producer. Originally an actor, Abbott collaborated with James Gleason on *The Fall Guy* (1925), with PHILIP DUNNING on BROADWAY (1926), with Ann Preston Bridgers on COQUETTE (1928), and then with JOHN CECIL HOLM on *Three Men on a Horse* (1935), a horse-race burlesque which was the hit of the season. Thereafter he turned to directing and producing. See BETTY SMITH.

Abbott, Jacob (b. Hallowell, Me., Nov. 14, 1803—d. Oct. 31, 1879), clergyman, teacher, author of books for children. Abbott's most famous productions were the twenty-eight "Rollo Books" (begun in 1834), stories about a boy named Rollo whose experiences on a New England farm and out in the wide, wide world (including Europe) were used by Abbott to teach lessons of self-improvement, honesty, and industry. These stories and his "Franconia Stories," "The Gay Family" series, and others helped break down the puritanic prejudice of the times against allowing children to read fiction. In all, Abbott wrote more than two hundred books, which have now become mere museum curiosities.

Abbott, John S[tevens] (b. Brunswick, Me., Sept. 18, 1805—d. June 17, 1877), clergyman, teacher, historian. Abbott collaborated with his brother Jacob on several books. His best-known work was *The History of Napoleon Bonaparte* (1855), which failed to please American critics because of his lavish praise of Napoleon.

Abbott, Lyman (b. Roxbury, Mass., Dec. 18, 1835—d. Oct. 22, 1922), clergyman, editor. This son of JACOB ABBOTT began by studying law, later became a Congregationalist minister, but in 1899 resigned to give his full time to a magazine originally called *The Christian Union* and later THE OUTLOOK. He was a liberal in both theology and politics. He wrote a *Life of Henry Ward Beecher* (1903) and *Reminiscences* (1915). Ira V. Brown wrote *Lyman Abbott, Christian Evolutionist* (1953).

Abe Lincoln in Illinois (1938), a play by ROBERT E. SHERWOOD. In this Pulitzer Prize-winning (1939) drama Sherwood shows Lincoln from his beginnings in New Salem until his departure for Washington as President. Lincoln grows in the play, becomes more certain of himself, yet remains humble. He frequently speaks actual words Sherwood culled from Lincoln's speeches and writings. One feels throughout the intensity of Sherwood's devotion to democracy, his belief in America. He prepared a movie version of the play (1939) and also a radio play that provided a sequel to it, *Abe Lincoln in Washington* (1948).

Abie's Irish Rose (produced, 1922; published, 1924), a comedy by Anne Nichols. A Jewish lad and an Irish girl fall in love. Fearing to tell their fathers about the affair, they are married by a Methodist minister. Their further attempts at concealment stirred laughter and tears in audiences to such an extent that the play made a then record-breaking run on Broadway—2,327 performances over a period of five years. Later it formed the basis for a novel (1927), a radio program (1942), and a movie (1946).

Absalom, Absalom! (1936), a novel by WILLIAM FAULKNER. *Absalom, Absalom!* is a further—albeit somewhat different—experiment with the technique Faulkner used in THE SOUND AND THE FURY. In place of the sustained interior monologue Faulkner projects his story by means of three narrators; their personalities and concerns are revealed as each tells the story of Thomas Sutpen, the central character. Miss Rosa Coldfield, Sutpen's sister-in-law, first tells the story to Quentin Compson shortly before his departure for Harvard; her story is supplemented by that of Quentin's father; and Quentin, in turn, relates the stories of the first two narrators, in addition to his own interpretation, to his Harvard roommate, Shreve McCannon.

The story centers on Thomas Sutpen and his attempts to fulfill his "grand design" to become accepted as a Southern aristocrat and the founder of a wealthy family. The son of a West Virginia poor white, he raises himself to social eminence in Jefferson, Mississippi, and, at the climax of his career, is elected Colonel of Jefferson's regiment in the Civil War. Returning to his estate, Sutpen's Hundred, after the war, he finds his daughter confirmed in spinsterhood, his son disappeared, and his plantation half ruined. He attempts to have another son to continue his name, but the poor-white girl with whom he has an affair bears a daughter, and Sutpen is murdered by her grandfather. As the Sutpen saga comes to an end in 1910, all that is left of his dream is an idiot Negro, Jim Bond, Sutpen's only living descendant, howling in the ashes of the burned house. Having accepted the social code of the Old South as a part of his grand design, Sutpen had repudiated his first part-Negro wife and their son; the consequences of this act pursue him through life and triumph over his dream after his death.

Accent. A LITTLE MAGAZINE published on the campus of the University of Illinois. Founded in 1940 and appearing quarterly, it gave as its aim from the beginning the "representative collection of the best creative and critical writing of our time, carefully balancing the work of established authors with that of comparative unknowns." It has printed the fiction of Thomas Mann, Katherine Anne Porter, Irwin Shaw, and Kay Boyle; the poetry of Horace Gregory, Wallace Stevens, Conrad Aiken, and E. E. Cummings; and critical pieces by David Daiches, Kenneth Burke, and Edwin Berry Burgum. Two editors of *Accent*—Kerker Quinn and Charles Shattuck—prepared an *Accent Anthology* (1946).

Acheson, Dean [Gooderham] (b. Middletown, Conn., April 11, 1893—   ), lawyer, author, former Secretary of State. Acheson attended Yale and Harvard and has honorary degrees from several universities. He was secretary to Louis D. Brandeis, later Justice of the U.S. Supreme Court (1919–21), was appointed Undersecretary of the Treasury in 1933 and Assistant Secretary of State in 1941. He was Secretary of State from 1949 to 1953. He has written *A Democrat Looks at his Party* (1955); *A Citizen Looks at Congress* (1957); *Power and Diplomacy* (1958).

Acres of Diamonds (1888), a lecture by Rev. RUSSELL HERMAN CONWELL. Conwell, a Baptist minister and the founder of Temple University, delivered this lecture more than six thousand times. Its effective anecdotes stress the importance of individual initiative and the responsibility of the wealthy to society. Conwell devoted the proceeds from his lecture to the education of more than ten thousand young men.

Across the Plains (1892), a travel book by ROBERT LOUIS STEVENSON. It continues the account of Stevenson's adventures in the United States begun in *The Amateur Emigrant* (1883), describing a railroad trip from New York to San Francisco.

Across the Wide Missouri (1947), a history by BERNARD DE VOTO. This Pulitzer Prize volume tells the story of the "mountain men" who, from 1832 to 1838, penetrated the unknown land between the Missouri River and the Rocky Mountains, stripped the territory of furs, destroyed its isolation, and unknowingly welded two coastlines into a continent and a nation. The text is supplemented by on-the-spot drawings and paintings by Alfred Jacob Miller, Charles

Bodmer, and GEORGE CATLIN, many reproduced for the first time in De Voto's book.

Active Service (1899), a novel by STEPHEN CRANE. The hero of this distinctly minor work is a newspaper man who, while covering the Greek War, rescues his sweetheart and her father. According to the *Bookman*, the novel was "careless and formless. Mr. Crane has a talent which he should take more seriously." The majority of the critics agreed, but the *Academy* pointed out that the book was "full of those feats of description for which the author is famous—some of them really excellent, others nothing but trickeries in which a certain effect is obtained by applying to men the epithets of things and to things the epithets of men. . . . But it quite deserves to be called a remarkable book."

Activists, The. This stimulating group of writers living mostly in the San Francisco Bay region began working in 1936 under the discipline of an idea presented by Professor Lawrence Hart. His concern was with the effectiveness of words in poetry; the group reviewed "ways in which language could be made active enough; that is, alive enough to communicate what they felt was sufficient emotion." The May, 1951, issue of *Poetry* was given over to their work and to an exposition by Hart, who edited the issue.

Actress of Padua, The (1836), a tragedy by RICHARD PENN SMITH. This play was based on one by Victor Hugo, and no copy survives. But its story is included in *The Actress of Padua and Other Tales* (published anonymously, 2 v., 1836).

Adair, James (b. England or Ireland, about 1709—d. about 1783), trader, pioneer. Adair for many years after his arrival in America in 1735 lived with Chickasaw and Cherokee Indians. In 1775 he published *History of the American Indians*, which describes Indian customs and maintains that the Indians are descendants of the ancient Jews.

Adam and Eve (1927), a novel by JOHN ERSKINE. In this free reconstruction of the myth, Erskine tells how Adam learned about women. His "social life" at the beginning is somewhat tame. Then Lilith arrives, then Eve; and he cannot decide which he prefers. Finally Eve bears him a son, and the question is settled.

Adamic, Louis (b. Yugoslavia, March 23, 1899—d. Sept. 4, 1951), novelist, writer of sociological studies. Adamic emigrated to this country when he was fifteen. He described his life as an immigrant in *Laughing in the Jungle* (1932), his impressions when he revisited Yugoslavia in *The Native's Return* (1934). *Dynamite: The Story of Class Violence in America* (1931) is a study of labor. *Grandsons* (1935) relates the saga of a Slovenian family which emigrates to America. In later years Adamic was greatly concerned with America as a melting-pot and felt that the melting was proceeding too slowly. He spoke of American society as in a state of "psychological civil war." *My America* (1938) shows his beliefs. *From Many Lands* (1940) shows the contributions made by immigrants to the greatness of the United States. Adamic in 1940 became editor of *Common Ground,* a magazine devoted to bringing together the country's diverse elements. Always a caustic critic, Adamic published in *Dinner at the White House* (1946) his account of conversations with President Roosevelt and Prime Minister Churchill, along with comments on each. Other books: *Cradle of Life* (1936); *The Eagle and the Roots* (1952), a biography of Tito.

Adams, Abigail [Smith] (b. Weymouth, Mass., Nov. 11, 1744—d. Oct. 28, 1818), wife of JOHN ADAMS [2]. Her literary fame is based on her letters, first printed by her grandson, Charles Francis Adams, Sr., in 1840. A less reti-

cent collection, edited by Stewart Mitchell, appeared as *New Letters, 1788–1801* (1947). She might have been thinking of herself when she wrote, "If we mean to have heroes, statesmen, and philosophers, we should have learned women"; in her letters, among the liveliest ever written by an American, she mixed laughter with learning. Janet Whitney wrote a biography of her in 1947.

Adams, Andy (b. Whitley Co., Ind., May 3, 1859—d. Sept. 26, 1935), author. He knew cowboy life at first hand, and his best-known book, LOG OF A COWBOY (1903), includes many autobiographical episodes. *The Outlet* (1905) describes the methods of railroad companies and politicians; *Cattle Brands* (1906) is a book of short stories. Among the most literary writers of westerns, Adams gave accurate pictures of people and social settings.

Adams, Brooks (b. Quincy, Mass., June 24, 1848—d. Feb. 13, 1927), historian, lawyer. The great-grandson of JOHN ADAMS [2], Brooks Adams was a lawyer who wrote sardonically on the prejudices and venalities of judges, a descendant of Puritans who examined with skepti-

cism the annals of their early rule in Massachusetts, and an aristocrat who analyzed history as a mere ebb and flow of greed and fear, centralization and decentralization. He developed elaborate theories of civilization, mostly based on a mechanistic analogy, and expounded them in several volumes: THE LAW OF CIVILIZATION AND DECAY (1895); *Theory of Social Revolution* (1913); and a lengthy preface to *The Degradation of the Democratic Dogma* (1919), the rest of the volume being a letter by his brother HENRY ADAMS. Brooks Adams was a reactionary nonconformist who saw in religion and capitalism the twin enemies of human progress and who felt that the modern world is plunging into degradation and destruction. Thornton Anderson has written sympathetically on *Brooks Adams: Constructive Conservative* (1951), and A. F. Beringause's biography (1955) is based on many previously inaccessible documents.

Adams, Charles Follen (b. Dorchester, Mass., April 21, 1842—d. March 8, 1918), writer of humorous verse. Although of Massachusetts birth, Adams made his reputation by writing sentimental and funny poems in the "scrapple English" spoken by the Pennsylvania Dutch and by the German immigrants he encountered while serving in the army during the Civil War. His favorite character appeared frequently in *Leedle Yawcob Strauss and Other Poems* (1878; reissued as *Yawcob Strauss and Other Poems,* 1910).

Adams, Charles Francis, Jr. (b. Boston, May 27, 1835—d. March 20, 1915), lawyer, railroad expert, historian. This brother of HENRY and BROOKS ADAMS was a successful businessman who in time became disgusted with the "low instinct" of money-getting and turned to writing history. His work in that field was honest and capable, but not brilliant. He was chiefly interested in the history of Massachusetts, and wrote *Three Episodes of Massachusetts History* (1892); *Massachusetts: Its History and Historians* (1893). Earlier he had exposed conditions of the railroads in *Chapters of Erie and other Essays* (1871) and *Railroads: Their Origins and Problems* (1878). He published lives of Richard Henry Dana (1891) and of his father (1900), as well as an *Autobiography* (1916).

Adams, Frank R[amsay] (b. Morrison, Ill., July 7, 1883—d. Oct. 8, 1963), playwright, novelist, screenwriter. Adams wrote musical comedies while still at college, in collaboration with Will M. Hough. Thirteen of these were produced, including *The Prince of Tonight* (1909). From this came the lyric (written to music by J. E. Howard) *I Wonder Who's Kissing Her Now.* Among Adams' novels are *The Long Night* (1929); *Gunsight Ranch* (1939); *Arizona Feud* (1941); *When I Come Back* (1943); *The Hearse at the Wedding* (1945); *Nothing to Lose* (1946); *Thirteen Lucky Guys* (1951). He is also known for his collaboration on nineteen motion pictures.

Adams, Franklin P[ierce] [F.P.A.] (b. Chicago, Nov. 15, 1881—d. March 23, 1960), columnist, poet, translator, editor. Adams was a newspaper columnist for several decades for the Chicago *Tribune*, the New York *Evening Mail*, the New York *Tribune* (his column was at that time called THE CONNING TOWER), the

made a new version of GEORGE M. COHAN's *Forty-five Minutes from Broadway*, a 1906 musical comedy success. He also compiled a *Book of Quotations* (1952).

Adams, George Matthew (b. Sabine, Mich.,

ADAMS FAMILY

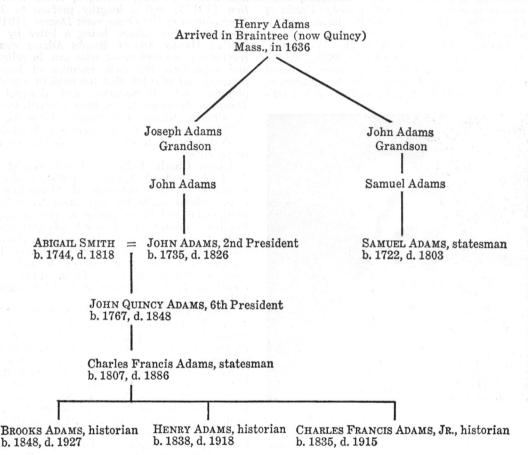

Henry Adams
Arrived in Braintree (now Quincy)
Mass., in 1636

Joseph Adams
Grandson

John Adams
Grandson

John Adams

Samuel Adams

ABIGAIL SMITH = JOHN ADAMS, 2nd President
b. 1744, d. 1818   b. 1735, d. 1826

SAMUEL ADAMS, statesman
b. 1722, d. 1803

JOHN QUINCY ADAMS, 6th President
b. 1767, d. 1848

Charles Francis Adams, statesman
b. 1807, d. 1886

BROOKS ADAMS, historian
b. 1848, d. 1927

HENRY ADAMS, historian
b. 1838, d. 1918

CHARLES FRANCIS ADAMS, JR., historian
b. 1835, d. 1915

New York *World*, the renamed *Herald Tribune*, and the New York *Post*. He also appeared for some time on the radio program INFORMATION, PLEASE, to which his contribution was mainly a mixture of dry wit and esoteric data relating to Gilbert & Sullivan, baseball, and barber-shop singing. Adams was a versifier, a diarist (in the Pepysian style which he often parodied), a connoisseur of typographical and grammatical errors, and a gifted translator from the Latin of Horace, Propertius, and others. In his "Conning Tower" appeared some of the earliest work of a long line of celebrated authors, including Edna St. Vincent Millay, Dorothy Parker, Christopher Morley, Ring Lardner, and George S. Kaufman.

Among Adams' books are *Tobogganing on Parnassus* (1911); *The Conning Tower Book* (1926); *The Second Conning Tower Book* (1927); *The Diary of Our Own Samuel Pepys* (1935); *Nods and Becks* (1944). In 1947 he

Aug. 23, 1878—d. Oct. 1, 1962), newsman. He was president of the George Matthew Adams Service and originated or took over numerous features that have been widely syndicated in newspapers all over the world. One of his own features, "Today's Talk," had a wide circulation for more than twenty years. Adams wrote *You Can* (1913); *Just Among Friends* (1928); *Better Than Gold* (1949); *The Great Little Things* (1953).

Adams, Hannah (b. Medfield, Mass., Oct. 2, 1755—d. Dec. 15, 1831), historian. Miss Adams, sometimes called the first professional woman author in America, was a relative of the great Adamses and a decided eccentric. She compiled histories of Christian sects, and wrote *History of New England* (1799) and *History of the Jews* (1812). Her *Memoirs* appeared in 1832.

Adams, Henry [Brooks] (b. Boston, Feb. 16, 1838—d. March 27, 1918), historian, novelist, memoirist. Though he was a descendant of presidents and a part of a family long used to taking an active part in the shaping of the nation, Adams' temperamental variations from the

Bettmann Archive

family norm led him first to become a special correspondent from Washington to the Boston *Daily Advertiser*. Later, while accompanying his father, who was Minister to England, he sent dispatches to the Boston *Courier* and the New York *Times*. In 1870 he was offered the editorship of the *North American Review*, to which he had contributed, and an assistant professorship of history at Harvard, both of which he accepted. He taught medieval, European, and American history for seven years, and thus laid the foundation for his later original work in the philosophy of history. His biography of Albert Gallatin (4 v., 1879) led him to study the Jefferson and Madison papers and directed him toward his nine-volume HISTORY OF THE UNITED STATES OF AMERICA DURING THE ADMINISTRATIONS OF THOMAS JEFFERSON AND JAMES MADISON (1889–91). This work presented a segment of history at the point of transition between European domination and American expansion. It seemed to Adams most fit to illustrate his naturalistic and deterministic theories, which argue that man and his acts, no matter how noble, are incapable of changing or even directing the course of the world.

In 1872 Adams married Marian Hooper of Boston; from that time until her suicide in 1885 little is known of Adams' life, for the years between 1872 and 1892 are omitted from his autobiographical writings. He wrote two anonymously published novels, DEMOCRACY (1880) and ESTHER (1884), that, although not of great literary value, reflect Adams' concerns during those years and deal respectively with the two

major problems of the day: the corruption in government resulting from a capitalistic economy and the inroads made upon religious faith by the new discoveries in science.

After the death of his wife Adams made several trips to the Orient with his friend, the artist John La Farge, gaining a knowledge of Asiatic religion, and to the high Sierras with the geologist CLARENCE KING, who furthered Adams' interest in science. He traveled to Europe and found in Mont-Saint-Michel and the cathedral at Chartres the symbols which he needed to express both his theory of history and of man's inner need and struggle for unity; accordingly, MONT-SAINT-MICHEL AND CHARTRES (privately printed, 1904; published, 1913) was subtitled *A Study in Thirteenth-Century Unity*, and THE EDUCATION OF HENRY ADAMS, *A Study in Twentieth-Century Multiplicity* (privately printed 1907; published 1918). The forces which governed the 13th century, in which Adams found man's need for inner unity most fully realized, were symbolized by the Virgin; the dynamo was his symbol for the 20th century, with its emphasis on science and reasoning and in which nature and not man was the center of the universe. Taken together, the books present the ideological conflict between man and nature, and although logically somewhat inadequate as applications of science to history, they form an aesthetic whole expressing man's inner need to create unity out of the chaos of multiplicity.

Adams is often seen at best in his letters, especially those edited by Harold Dean Cater in *Henry Adams and His Friends* (1947). Other books on Adams include W. H. Jordy's *Henry Adams, Scientific Historian* (1952); Ernest Samuels' *Young Henry Adams* (1948) and *Henry Adams: The Middle Years* (1958); Elizabeth Stevenson's *Henry Adams* (1955). See BROOKS ADAMS; PRAYER TO THE VIRGIN OF CHARTRES.

Adams, J[ames] Donald (b. New York City, Sept. 24, 1891—d. Aug. 22, 1968), editor, author, critic. Adams is best known for his weekly column, "Speaking of Books," which began to appear on page 2 of The *New York Times Book Review* in 1943. After receiving his A.B., *cum laude*, from Harvard in 1913, he served briefly as a teacher of English at the University of Washington. His journalistic career began in 1915 when he took a job as reporter for the New Bedford (Mass.) *Evening Standard*. Subsequently, he worked for a number of other newspapers, including the New York *Sun* and the *Herald*. His association with the *New York Times* began in 1924, when he was hired as assistant editor of the *Book Review*. A year later, he became editor of the *Book Review*, a position which he occupied until 1943, when he became a contributing editor. Besides his weekly column, Mr. Adams published *The Shape of Books to Come* (1944); *The Treasure Chest: An Anthology of Contemplative Prose* (1946); *Literary Frontiers* (1950); *The New Treasure Chest: An Anthology of Reflective Prose* (1953); *Triumph over Odds: An Anthology of Man's Unconquerable Spirit* (1957); *Copey of Harvard: A Biog-*

raphy of Charles Townsend Copeland (1960).

Adams, James Truslow (b. Brooklyn, N.Y., Oct. 18, 1878—d. May 18, 1949), historian. Adams engaged successfully in several business enterprises, and in World War I served on the House Commission to prepare data for the Peace Conference. On his return from France in 1919, he began writing history. His interests expanded from New England history (his *The Founding of New England*, 1921, won a Pulitzer Prize) to the general history of the United States, then to the history of the British Empire: *Revolutionary New England* (1923); *New England in the Republic* (1926); *The March of Democracy* (2 v., 1932–33); *Building the British Empire* (1938). In addition, although himself not a Boston Adams, he wrote an account of *The Adams Family* (1930) and of *Henry Adams* (1933), as well as analyses of Hamilton and Jefferson (1938). He edited the DICTIONARY OF AMERICAN HISTORY (6 v., 1940). His *Epic of America* (1931) has been rendered into nine other languages. THE AMERICAN [2] (1943) surveys American history to demonstrate "the making of a new man," with a presentation of the geographical, historical, and social forces that have made the American different from the citizen of any other nation. In *Big Business in a Democracy* (1945) he depicted our huge industrial and commercial concerns much more favorably than other historians have. He saw big business as "a function of American democracy" and as the most characteristic of our folkways. His thesis throughout was that Americans love property but hate privilege.

Adams, John [1] (b. 1704[05?]—d. Jan. 22?, 1740), clergyman, poet. Probably Nova Scotian by birth, Adams attended Harvard, served as a minister in several New England towns, was greatly esteemed by his contemporaries for his learning and his literary gifts. After his early death was published *Poems on Several Occasions* (1745), including translations from Horace and original poems in heroic couplets.

Adams, John [2] (b. Braintree [now Quincy], Mass., Oct. 19, 1735—d. July 4, 1826), pamphleteer, lawyer, statesman, second President. Adams graduated from Harvard, was admitted to the bar in 1758, and was carrying on a successful practice of law when the Stamp Act of 1765 drew him into politics. He wrote a series of articles, later collected as A DISSERTATION ON THE CANON AND FEUDAL LAW, in which he argued that the Stamp Act was contrary to the "inherent rights of mankind." He was a delegate to the first Continental Congress in 1774. His *Thoughts on Government* (1776) included a plan for the government of the colonies which is particularly notable for its insistence on a second body to act as a "mediator" between the representatives of the people and the executive. He was instrumental in the choosing of Thomas Jefferson as the author of the DECLARATION OF INDEPENDENCE, and he himself defended the Declaration when it was presented to Congress.

In 1785, after several years' service as minister to France, Britain, and Holland, he began to write his *Defence of the Constitutions of Government of the United States of America* (3 v., 1787–88), in which he discussed the history of republican government. Elected Vice-President under Washington, he became President in 1796.

He quarreled with Hamilton over a treaty with France in 1800, and the resulting split in the Federalist party contributed to his loss to Jefferson in the election of 1800.

John Adams' essentially conservative political philosophy placed him between the extreme Federalism of Hamilton and the agrarianism of Jefferson. His concept of Republicanism was based on a "balance" of power that would prevent the power-hungry from gaining control, and his awareness of the weaknesses and vices of mankind led him to put his faith in the "natural aristocracy" of a few men, who, like himself, would use the power vested in them for the good of the people rather than for their private ends.

Adams' *Works* were edited by Charles F. Adams (10 v., 1850–56), his *Selected Writings* by Adrienne Koch and William Peden (1946). Zoltan Haraszti collected comments Adams made in the margins of over a hundred books, primarily of French and English philosophers, in *John Adams and the Prophets of Progress* (1952); other studies of Adams include Gilbert Chinard's *Honest John Adams* (1933) and Catherine Drinker Bowen's *John Adams and the American Revolution* (1950). In 1961 Harvard University Press published the first volumes of *The Adams Papers: Diary and Autobiography of John Adams*, edited by L. H. Butterfield. See the FEDERALIST PARTY; DANIEL LEONARD.

Adams, John Quincy (b. Braintree [now Quincy], Mass., July 11, 1767—d. Feb. 23, 1848), lawyer, diplomat, sixth President. An extraordinarily bright child, young Adams accompanied his father JOHN ADAMS [2], a diplomat, to Europe, and studied in Paris and at the University of Leiden; he graduated from Harvard in 1787 and began to practice law in Boston in 1790.

In 1791 Adams replied to Thomas Paine's RIGHTS OF MAN in a series of articles signed PUBLICOLA, stressing the rights of the minority as opposed to Paine's doctrine that the will of the majority must prevail. The Publicola papers

were considered the best defence of the Federalist position that the violation of the "immutable laws of justice" was not within the rights of majority rule. Adams wrote two other series of articles, signed Marcellus and Columbus respectively, defending President Washington's position regarding the war between England and France, and attacking Edmond Genêt, who sought American support for France in the war. Adams' writings brought him to the attention of Washington, and in 1794 he was made minister to Holland. He served as Minister to Portugal and Prussia before returning to America in 1801. He was elected to the Senate in 1803, but often voted independently of his party, finally breaking with the Federalists and resigning from his post in 1808. He held several other diplomatic positions until 1817, when he was appointed Secretary of State under Monroe; Adams was largely responsible for the establishment of the MONROE DOCTRINE.

Although Andrew Jackson received more electoral votes than Adams (99 to 84) in the election of 1824, the election was given to the House of Representatives, no candidate having a majority. Henry Clay, the candidate who had received the least number of electoral votes, gave his support to Adams, who was elected. When Adams appointed Clay Secretary of State the followers of Jackson cried "corrupt bargain" (although it is doubtful that a bargain between Adams and Clay had been made), and the Republican party split.

In 1830, after one term as president, Adams was elected to the House of Representatives, where he served for seventeen years. He fought for free speech when a motion was made to restrict the petitions of the Abolitionists from the floor of the House and argued for the right of the government to free slaves in time of war.

Adams' diary, covering more than sixty years, was edited and published by his son, CHARLES FRANCIS ADAMS, entitled *The Memoirs of John Quincy Adams* (12 v., 1874–77); a selection of the *Memoirs* was made by Allan Nevins in 1929. Adams made a capable translation (first published in 1940) of the German poet Martin Wieland's romance *Oberon*, and wrote verse in the 18th century fashion, including *Poems* (1848) and *Poems of Religions and Society* (1859). He wrote a classic treatise *On Weights and Measures* (1821), and published his *Harvard Lectures on Rhetoric and Oratory* (delivered 1806, published 1810). Samuel F. Bemis wrote *John Quincy Adams and the Foundations of American Foreign Policy* (1949) and *John Quincy Adams and the Union* (1956).

Adams, Joseph Quincy (b. Greenville, S.C., March 23, 1881—d. Nov. 10, 1946), Shakespearean scholar. Dr. Adams published a long series of authoritative volumes on Shakespeare, including *Shakespearean Playhouses* (1917) and *Life of William Shakespeare* (1923), and edited *Chief Pre-Shakespearean Dramas* (1924). He was director of the Folger Shakespeare Library in Washington from 1931 to his death, was general editor of the *New Variorum Shakespeare* and the *Publications* of the Folger Library. See HENRY CLAY FOLGER.

Adams, Léonie [Fuller] (b. Brooklyn, N.Y., Dec. 9, 1899—   ), poet. Her poems are marked by a deeply mystical view of nature, by vigorous metrics, and by a sense of song that lends delicacy to her "tough" lines. Her books include *Those Not Elect* (1925); *High Falcon* (1929); *This Measure* (1933); *Poems: A Selection* (1954).

Adams, Maude [stage name of Maude Kiskadden] (b. Salt Lake City, Utah, Nov. 11, 1872—d. July 17, 1953), actress, drama teacher. Miss Adams made her first stage appearance in E. H. SOTHERN's theatrical company, and later appeared with John Drew and other notables. Her work was noted for a kind of elfin charm. Her greatest successes were in plays by Sir James M. Barrie, including *The Little Minister, Quality Street, Peter Pan, What Every Woman Knows, A Kiss for Cinderella*. She was less effective in Edmond Rostand's *L'Aiglon* and *Chantecler*, in both of which she played male roles. She became a teacher of dramatic art at Stephens College in 1937. Phyllis Robbins wrote *Maude Adams: An Intimate Portrait* (1956).

Adams, Oscar Fay (b. 1855—d. April 20, 1919), historian, storyteller. Adams wrote several books on American literature, including *A Dictionary of American Authors* (1897); he also wrote *The Archbishop's Unguarded Moment and Other Stories* (1899) and *Sicut Patribus and Other Verse* (1906).

Adams, Ramon F. (b. Moscow, Tex., Oct. 3, 1889—   ), businessman, collector of folklore.

A resident of Dallas, Tex., Adams for years has assembled the folklore, special language, and history of cattlemen. His books include *Cowboy Lingo* (1936); *Western Words: A Dictionary of the Range, Cow Camp, and Trail* (1944); *Six-Guns and Saddle Leather: A Bibliography of Books and Pamphlets on Western Outlaws and Gunmen* (1954); *Rampaging Herds* (1959).

Adams, Samuel (b. Boston, Sept. 27, 1722—d. Oct. 2, 1803), orator, member of the Continental Congress, pamphleteer. Adams was an incompetent businessman, but in serving his countrymen he was not only an excellent propagandist but also a good organizer, as he demonstrated in the "Boston Tea Party" of 1773. Governor THOMAS HUTCHINSON stated that Adams "was for near twenty years a writer against government in the public newspapers." In these writings Adams anticipated many American doctrines, as when he said in 1772: "Among the natural rights of the colonists are these: First, a right to life; secondly, to liberty; thirdly, to property; together with the right to defend them in the best manner they can." Adams' *Writings* (4 v., 1904–08) were edited by H. A. Cushing; his *Letters* appeared in 1917–25.

Adams, Samuel Hopkins (b. Dunkirk, N.Y., Jan. 26, 1871—d. Nov. 16, 1958), journalist, novelist, historian, biographer. While on the staffs of *McClure's* and *Collier's*, Adams was active in exposing frauds, especially in the field of medicine, and helped to bring about the enactment of the Pure Food and Drug Act. A long series of novels and short-story collections deal with the fictional recollection of American life, among them THE CLARION (1914); *Success* (1921); *The Gorgeous Hussy* (1934); CANAL TOWN (1944); *Banner by the Wayside* (1947); *Sunrise to Sunset* (1950); *Grandfather Stories* (1955); *Tenderloin* (1959). The Harding era engaged him in REVELRY (1926), where he depicted Harding as a suicide, and in *The Incredible Era: The Life and Times of Warren Harding* (1939). In 1930 Adams did a biography of Daniel Webster called *The Godlike Daniel;* a later biography, *A. Woollcott: His Life and His World* (1945), reads like a novel. *Average Jones* (1911) is a book of detective stories, and PLUNDER (1948) depicts post-World War II Washington. *The Harvey Girls* (1942) became a successful motion picture musical.

Adams, William Taylor ["Oliver Optic"] (b. Boston, July 30, 1822—d. March 27, 1897), teacher, writer of books for boys. Adams began as a teacher, but in his early thirties started writing fiction—a huge number of short stories and more than a hundred books, all arranged in series. He was in his day the chief rival of HORATIO ALGER, but his books were more manly and laid stress on character rather than on mere success. In 1865 he gave up his work as principal of the Bowditch School in Boston to devote his entire time to writing; two years later he founded *Oliver Optic's Magazine for Boys and Girls,* which continued publication for eight years. He later edited *Our Little Ones* and *Student and Schoolmate.* His books, including *The*

Boat Club Series (1854), *Army and Navy Series* (1865 onward), *Onward and Upward Series* (1870), *Yacht Club Series* (1872 onward), took his young characters through all sorts of exciting and educational experiences, at home and abroad.

Adams and Liberty (1798), a song by ROBERT TREAT PAINE, JR. It was composed to fit the old Anacreon tune which was later adapted for *The Star-Spangled Banner.* The verses appeared during the campaign of John Adams for the Presidency and presented a long, tiresome, and rhetorical harangue against the republican French.

Addams, Jane (b. Cedarville, Ill., Sept. 6, 1860—d. May 21, 1935), settlement worker, sociologist, author. The nature of Miss Addams' remarkable work and influential viewpoint, together with many of her significant experiences, are related in her widely read TWENTY YEARS AT HULL HOUSE (1910), followed two decades later by *The Second Twenty Years at Hull House.* Miss Addams' early dedication to the cause of the poor and oppressed was followed by a lifetime of beneficent activity, so that Hull House became a center of civic activity in Chicago. Also a determined worker for international peace, she published *Democracy and Social Ethics* (1902) and *Peace and Bread in Time of War* (1922), among other writings, and shared a Nobel peace prize in 1931.

Adding Machine, The (1923), a play by ELMER RICE. This satiric attack on the half-men produced by the "machine age" tells how Mr. Zero, discharged when adding machines are introduced into his office, kills his employer in a fit of insanity and is joined in suicide by a middle-aged worker in the same office, Daisy Diana Dorothea Devore. Finding his company in heaven too indecent (Swift and Rabelais, for instance), although he enjoys operating a celestial adding machine, he is consigned back to earth to become the perfect industrial slave. Known as one of the best examples of expressionistic drama in America, the play uses the techniques of fantasy to depict inner states usually hidden by surface appearances.

Addums, Mozis. See GEORGE W. BAGBY.

Ade, George (b. Kentland, Ind., Feb. 9, 1866—d. May 16, 1944), newspaperman, fabulist, playwright. Educated at Purdue, Ade joined (1890) the old Chicago *Morning News* (later the *Record*), where he wrote realistic but amusing "Stories of the Street and the Town," involving Artie, a brash but good-hearted young man. His experiences appeared in the popular *Artie* (1896). Later Ade gathered stories of a colored bootblack in *Pink Marsh* (1897) and of a gentlemanly liar in *Doc' Horne* (1899).

In 1898 Ade wrote his first "fable in slang," *The Blond Girl Who Married a Bucket Shop Man.* This fable established the formula for Ade: colloquial expressions, irregular capitalizations, characters out of everyday life, a moral frequently seasoned with impertinence. For ten years he continued to write his tales, about one a week. They went into book form: FABLES IN

SLANG (1900), *More Fables* (1900), *Forty Modern Fables* (1901), and others. Ade's use of language fascinated observers; the British called him "the Shakespeare of slang." His "slang" is not slang, however, but a picturesque prose with numerous racy colloquialisms and many luxuriant figures of speech. Ade discovered in capitals a semantic device for lifting shopworn words out of triteness.

His career as a playwright began with the successful musical comedy, *The Sultan of Sulu* (produced, 1902; published, 1903). His nonmusical plays, THE COUNTY CHAIRMAN (produced, 1903), THE COLLEGE WIDOW (produced, 1904), and *Father and the Boys* (produced, 1908) were equally popular; *The College Widow* was made into a musical comedy, *Leave It to Jane*, with music by Jerome Kern.

Adeler, Max. See CHARLES HEBER CLARK.

Adler, Felix (b. Germany, Aug. 13, 1851— d. April 24, 1933), philosopher, teacher, founder of the Ethical Culture movement. Adler came to America at sixteen and attended Columbia University. While teaching at Cornell in 1876 he founded the Society for Ethical Culture, which emphasized the need for a stronger morality to meet the problems of the time, advocated the moral education of children and various social and labor reforms. Adler established the first free kindergarten for the children of the poor in New York; this soon grew into a vocational school, the first to include manual training and ethical instruction in its curriculum. He was instrumental in the establishment of the Tenement House Commission of 1884, arranged for trained nurses to visit the poor, argued for parks and playgrounds in poor areas, and opposed child labor. Ethical Culture Societies soon appeared in several other large American cities and in Europe. Adler wrote a number of books, including *The Ethics of the Political Situation* (1884); *The Moral Instruction of Children* (1892); *Marriage and Divorce* (1905); *What the Ethical Culture School Stands For* (1910); *An Ethical Philosophy of Life* (1918); *The Reconstruction of the Spiritual Ideal* (1923).

Adler, Mortimer J[erome] (b. New York City, Dec. 28, 1902—   ), philosopher, writer, lecturer. While still a student at Columbia University, Adler began his career by teaching psychology there. In 1927 he taught psychology at the City College of New York, lectured at the People's Institute, and gave a Great Books course in the basement of a church. After receiving his Ph.D. from Columbia, he joined the faculty of the University of Chicago in 1929, where he taught philosophy until 1952. During this period he wrote *Crime, Law and Social Science* (1933, with J. Michael); *What Man Has Made of Man* (1938); *St. Thomas and the Gentiles* (1938); *Problems for Thomists* (1940). These books develop his opposition to PRAGMATISM and his affirmation of absolute values and of the moral and intellectual order he found in St. Thomas Aquinas. *How to Read a Book* (1940) and *How to Think About War and Peace* (1944) were best sellers, indictments of the modern inability to read or think properly. *Great Books of the Western World* (1952), which he edited with Robert M. Hutchins, is a monumental anthology of 54 volumes containing 443 works by 76 authors from Homer to Freud. Its two-volume master-key, called the *Syntopicon* (a new word coinage meaning "collection of topics"), is an index of ideas, covering 102 general topics, referring the reader to the passages in the books where the ideas are discussed, and to related topics. As a direct outgrowth of his work on the *Syntopicon*, in 1952 Dr. Adler became Director of the newly founded Institute for Philosophical Research in San Francisco. There he wrote *The Idea of Freedom* (1958), the first volume of the Institute's analyses of philosophical literature from the advent of philosophy in ancient Greece to the present day. The second volume came out in 1961. Other books by Mortimer Adler are: *The Capitalist Manifesto* (1958, with Louis O. Kelso), and *The Revolution in Education* (1958, with Milton Mayer).

Adrea (1904), a romantic melodrama by DAVID BELASCO and JOHN LUTHER LONG. It is laid in the fifth century, on an island in the Adriatic Sea, and depicts a conflict between two sisters, royal princesses. Based on serious historical research, it ran in New York for two seasons.

Adulateur, The: A Tragedy (1773), a satirical play by MERCY OTIS WARREN. Supposedly laid in Serbia, the play really deals with the Boston Massacre and other events preceding the Revolution. It attacks the secret loyalist THOMAS HUTCHINSON and introduces many figures of the time in disguise, including the author's brother, JAMES OTIS, who is called Brutus. The play was probably never performed.

Adventures. For narratives where this is the first principal word in the title, see the proper name instead, *e.g.*, *The Adventures of Tom Sawyer*: see *Tom Sawyer*.

Adventures in Contentment (1907), essays by David Grayson. See RAY STANNARD BAKER, who used this pseudonym for a number of volumes, including also *Adventures in Friendship* (1910), *Adventures in Understanding* (1925), and *Adventures in Solitude* (1931).

Adventures of a Young Man (1939), a novel by JOHN DOS PASSOS. See GLENN SPOTTSWOOD.

Advertisements for the Unexperienced Planters of New England, or Anywhere (1631), by Capt. JOHN SMITH. In a subtitle Smith calls his book "the Pathway to Erect a Plantation." It gives advice based on much experience and is addressed primarily to John Winthrop and the settlers of Massachusetts.

Aesop, G. Washington. See GEORGE T. LANIGAN.

Afloat and Ashore, or, The Adventures of Miles Wallingford (1844), a novel by JAMES FENIMORE COOPER. Two boys and a Negro slave run off to sea, fight Malay pirates, are shipwrecked on Madagascar, manage to reach their home in New York again. Later one of them ships again with the slave, helps to capture French privateers, sails for the Pacific, and has exciting adventures on the coast of South America and in China. Cooper has some strong passages on the evils of the impressment of sailors. The novel was reprinted (1956), with a preface by Allen Klots.

After the Ball (1891), a lyric by CHARLES K. HARRIS. One of the most popular songs ever written in America, this was first sung in a Milwaukee production of Charles H. Hoyt's famous farce, A Trip to Chinatown. John Philip Sousa played it regularly at the Chicago World's Fair. Harris, although he received an immediate offer of $10,000 for the complete rights to the song, wisely refused to sell.

After the Surprising Conversions (1944), a poem by ROBERT LOWELL. See NARRATIVE OF SURPRISING CONVERSIONS.

Agar, Herbert [Sebastian] (b. New Rochelle, N.Y., Sept. 29, 1897—   ), newspaperman, editor, author. Although he was born in the North, Agar's thinking has been largely of and in the South; his family came from Louisiana, and for a number of years he was editor of the Louisville Courier-Journal. He became a member of the "Southern Agrarians," and was frequently critical of democracy, of economic trends in the United States, and of the North. However, Agar later changed his views, particularly under the influence of New Deal ideas. He was, in addition, deeply moved by the danger of Nazi aggression. Among Agar's books the best-known is perhaps The People's Choice (1933), which won a Pulitzer Prize; it was a harsh dissection of the American Presidency. Other books by Agar are Bread and Circuses (1930); Land of the Free (1935); Pursuit of Happiness (1938); A Time for Greatness (1942); The Price of Union (1950); A Declaration of Faith (1952); Abraham Lincoln (1952); The Price of Power (1957). He has called himself a "creative conservative."

Agassiz, [Jean] Louis [Rodolphe] (b. Switzerland, May 28, 1807—d. Dec. 14, 1873), naturalist, educator, author. Agassiz had already won a notable reputation for his study of glaciers and his work on fish when, in 1846, he came to the United States as a lecturer and decided to remain permanently. He became widely known as a professor at Harvard and curator of the noted Agassiz Museum at Cambridge; he also founded the Marine Biological Laboratory (1872) at Woods Hole, Mass. He wrote fluently in the fields of zoology and geology and showed an astonishing command of English. Chief among his writings is Contributions to the Natural History of the United States of America (4 v., 1857–62). He was an influential teacher of laymen as well as students, and he epitomized his teaching in the directive: "Go to Nature; take the facts in your own hands; look, and see for yourself!" Although he opposed the Darwinian theory of evolution, he did much to arouse interest in the natural sciences and to establish methods of study and classification. His wife Elizabeth Cary Agassiz wrote his biography (2 v., 1885); Jules Marcou prepared The Life, Letters, and Works (2 v.,

1896); J. D. Teller, Louis Agassiz, Scientist and Teacher (1947).

Agee, James (b. Knoxville, Tenn., 1909—d. May 16, 1955), poet, novelist, film critic. Agee was born and raised in the Cumberland Mountain region of Tennessee, the area in which both of his novels are situated; his background con-

Florence Homolka

tributed to a deep feeling for the poetry of the land and its people which is present in most of his writing. He graduated from Harvard in 1932; in 1934 his first collection of verse, Permit Me Voyage, was published in the YALE SERIES OF YOUNGER POETS. In 1936 he was assigned by Fortune magazine to spend some weeks living with several Alabama sharecropper families in order to write a report on the "typical" sharecropper family. For various reasons the report never appeared in Fortune and Agee was later awarded the rights to the manuscript, which was published with a series of photographs by Walker Evans as Let Us Now Praise Famous Men (1941). Agee joined the staff of Time magazine in 1939, and was motion picture reviewer for the Nation from 1943 until 1948. All the film reviews he wrote for the Nation, a selection of his anonymous reviews for Time, and various film articles he wrote for Life, the Partisan Review, and Sight and Sound have been collected and published posthumously in a volume called Agee on Film (1958). Most of Agee's work after 1948 was done for motion pictures; he wrote the commentary and dialogue for the documentary film The Quiet One, an adaptation of Stephen Crane's The Bride Comes to Yellow Sky, and of C. S. Forester's The African Queen. The second volume of Agee on Film (1960) contains five of Agee's screenplays, including *Noa Noa*, based on the life of Paul Gauguin, written in 1953 but not produced; *Night of the Hunter*, based on the novel by Davis Grubb; and *Blue Hotel*, from the story by Stephen Crane, also not yet filmed.

Agee's first novel, *The Morning Watch* (1954) is a story of one day in the life of a twelve-year-old boy in a Tennessee church school. Although highly praised by critics, it did not achieve the recognition of *A Death in the Family* (1957), on which Agee was working at the time of his death in 1955. *A Death in the Family* was awarded a Pulitzer Prize and was dramatized by TAD MOSEL in 1960 as *All The Way Home*; the play also won a Pulitzer Prize, the New York Drama Critics' Circle Award, and was cited by *Life* magazine as "The Best American Play of the Season."

Age of Chivalry and **Age of Fable.** See THOMAS BULFINCH.

Age of Innocence, The (1920), a novel by EDITH WHARTON that won a Pulitzer Prize. A satirical picture of social life in New York during the 1870's, it describes the marriage of Newland Archer to May Welland, bound by her tribal code of the elite, and his attraction to her unconventional cousin, Ellen Olenska, from which he can never derive satisfaction because they are both too obedient to the code.

Age of Jackson, The (1945), a history by ARTHUR SCHLESINGER, JR. This volume immediately became a best seller and won a Pulitzer Prize. Schlesinger had written an earlier book on *Orestes A. Brownson: A Pilgrim's Progress* (1939) which led him to study the Jacksonian era in the light of documents of the time; he was convinced that traditional histories did not give a faithful picture of the era. His book had, moreover, a contemporaneous impulse, since Schlesinger perceived many parallels between the Jacksonian age and that of Roosevelt's New Deal. He stresses the fact that in the days of Jackson, as in all periods of rapid social adjustment, there was a close correspondence between the movements of politics and the movement of ideas; he therefore examines the politics in terms of the ideas. Furthermore, Schlesinger contends that contrary to the notions of many historians, who see in Jacksonianism an uprising of the West, its development was shaped much more by reasoned and systematic conceptions of society than has been generally recognized, and many of its controlling beliefs and motives came from the South and East, not the West. Readers were attracted by Schlesinger's gift for swift anecdote and sustained narrative.

Age of Reason, The (Part I, 1794; Part II, 1796), an attack on traditional religion by THOMAS PAINE. Paine wrote the book while he was helping the cause of the French Revolution in Paris. An affirmation of DEISM, not of atheism, as many thought, it asserts "I believe in one God" and contains the famous sentence: "The world is my country, all mankind are my brethren, and to do good is my religion."

Ages, The (1821), a poem by WILLIAM CULLEN BRYANT. This Phi Beta Kappa poem was delivered first at a Harvard commencement, then published in a pamphlet. It is an account of the ages of mankind in thirty-five Spenserian stanzas and includes an optimistic view of the future. Poe, while praising some of the passages, thought it should have been written in prose.

Agrarians. A number of southern writers, including HERBERT AGAR, JOHN CROWE RANSOM, ROBERT PENN WARREN, ALLEN TATE, and DONALD DAVIDSON, associated themselves under this name in a movement to set up for the South new economic (and perhaps political) ideas and goals based on agriculture that would enable it to return to its culture and attain greater independence from the North. Grant McConnell wrote of the movement in *The Decline of Agrarian Democracy* (1943). See HOWARD W. ODUM; I'LL TAKE MY STAND.

Ahab, Captain. The monomaniac one-legged ship captain in Herman Melville's MOBY DICK (1851).

Ahearn, Robert G. See WESTWARD THE BRITON.

Ahkoond of Swat, Threnody for the (1878), a humorous poem by GEORGE THOMAS LANIGAN. It was based on a headline in the London *Times* of Jan. 22, 1878, "The Ahkoond of Swat is dead," and ends "The Ahkoond of Swat/Is not." (Swat is a state in northwestern India.) Later EUGENE FIELD wrote a poem about the same character.

Ah Sin. The innocent seeming Chinese card player in BRET HARTE's *The Heathen Chinee*, also called PLAIN LANGUAGE FROM TRUTHFUL JAMES (1870). The popularity of the poem led Harte to collaborate with Mark Twain on a play called *Ah Sin*, which ran for five weeks in 1877.

Aiken, Albert W. (b. [?]—d. [?]), writer of DIME NOVELS. He managed to write about one a week over a long period of years. One of his earliest was *The Brigand Captain* (1871); later he wrote *Sol Ginger, the Giant Trapper* (1879) and *Lone Hand, the Shadow* (1889). Dates of issue are all uncertain.

Aiken, Conrad Potter ["Samuel Jeake, Jr."] (b. Savannah, Ga., Aug. 5, 1889—), poet, critic, novelist, short-story writer. Aiken wrote his first poem at the age of nine. Tragedy struck early in his life when his father, a gifted physician, killed his mother and committed suicide. The boy was sent to live with relatives in New Bedford, Mass. At thirteen he began to memorize the poems of Poe, his own work later revealing the influence of Poe's rhythms. In 1911 he became part of that famous Harvard class that included T. S. Eliot, Walter Lippmann, Robert Benchley, Van Wyck Brooks; he began to publish in 1914. The wave of French Symbolists and Imagists, surging high at the time, flowed over Aiken; from then on he strove unceasingly to create poetry that would come as close as possible to the art of music. The influences of Freud, Havelock Ellis, WILLIAM JAMES, and Bergson also touched him, affecting to some extent his fictional characterizations in the BLUE VOYAGE

(1927) and the *Great Circle* (1933). Criticism of Aiken often tends to be a catalogue of names of other writers who have supposedly influenced him, but he somehow emerges as still essentially Aiken. Undoubtedly the influence of EDGAR ALLAN POE is strongest; the similarities between the two writers are numerous. Undoubtedly, too, the influence of psychologists and psychoanalysts have strengthened Aiken's tendency toward introspection. Yet in the final analysis, Aiken should be praised for the synthesis he has achieved. He sums up his age better than almost any other writer of the past generation, and he does so less obscurely and more melodiously. He has poured intellect, sex, morbidity, and uncertainty into verse of a remarkable variety of pattern and line. He can also write a lyric of such traditional and classic clarity as *Music I Heard,* or the poem on Cleopatra beginning, "She poured cold poison." In 1930 his *Selected Poems* (1929) won a Pulitzer Prize and the Shelley Award. Houston Peterson has described Aiken as a "romanticist without hope, a realist steeped in speculative psychology." USHANT (1952) is a brilliant and difficult autobiographical novel written in the form of a poetic essay. Aiken's output of poetry continued to be prolific, and he is generally regarded as one of America's outstanding poets. He held the post of Consultant in Poetry for the Library of Congress (1950–52). His short stories, such as *Mr. Arcularis* and *Silent Snow, Secret Snow,* often anthologized, are delicate and sometimes terrifying probings of the human spirit. Other works: *King Coffin* (1935); *Brownstone Eclogues and Other Poems* (1942); *The Soldier* (1944); THE KID (1947); *Divine Pilgrim* (1949); *Skylight One* (1949); *Collected Poems* (1953); *Sheepfold Hill* (1953); *Letter From Li Po and Other Poems* (1955); *Reviewer's ABC,* collected criticism of Conrad Aiken from 1916 to the present (1958); *Collected Short Stories of Conrad Aiken* (1960).

Aiken, George L. (b. Boston, Dec. 19, 1830—d. April 27, 1876), actor, playwright. Aiken had no notable success as an actor, and in 1867 retired to devote his time to writing plays. He is remembered chiefly for his melodramatic dramatization of UNCLE TOM'S CABIN, first produced in 1852. Though not the first stage version of Mrs. Stowe's novel, it soon surpassed all its predecessors in popularity.

Airs from Arcady (1884), a collection of poems by HENRY CUYLER BUNNER, many of which had appeared originally in the humorous magazine PUCK, edited by Bunner.

Airways, Inc. (1928), a play by JOHN DOS PASSOS. It describes a group of millworkers during a strike and paints a gloomy picture of industrial conditions.

Akeley, Carl Ethan (b. Clarendon, N.Y., May 19, 1864—d. Nov. 17, 1926), explorer, sculptor, author. Akeley made numerous trips to Africa for the Field Museum and the American Museum of Natural History; he died on one of his expeditions. He was noted for his artistic skill in assembling groups of stuffed animals on a natural background, and for his bronze sculptures of animals. He wrote *In Brightest Africa* (1923), *Lions, Gorillas, and Their Neighbors* (1932), and other books. His wife Mary Jobe Akeley, also an explorer, accompanied him on his final expedition, later wrote *Carl Akeley and the Great Adventure* (1940).

Akers, Elizabeth [Chase] ["Florence Percy"] (b. Strong, Me., Oct. 9, 1832—d. Aug. 7, 1911), poet, novelist, newspaper editor. Mrs. Akers did editorial work for the Portland *Transcript* and the Portland *Daily Advertiser,* and contributed verse to the *Atlantic Monthly* and other magazines. She also wrote fiction, but this was less popular than her sentimental verse. She became renowned for the poem ROCK ME TO SLEEP, MOTHER, the most famous lines of which are: "Backward, turn backward, O Time, in your flight; / Make me a child again just for tonight." The verses first appeared in the *Saturday Evening Post* (June 9, 1860), later in her collections *Poems* (1899) and *Sunset Song and Other Verses* (1902).

Akins, Zoë (b. Humansville, Mo., Oct. 30, 1886—d. Oct. 29, 1958), poet, dramatist, screenwriter. Miss Akins won a Pulitzer Prize for her dramatization of Edith Wharton's THE OLD MAID, produced in 1935. An intelligent, sincere observer of the American scene, Miss Akins passed through several stages. She began by writing plays that were somewhat too serious and not as profound as she wished them to be, like *Déclassée* (1919), which depicts the decline of an English peeress from a secure position in England to a dubious one in this country, and won Miss Akins her first great success. Later she turned to light romantic comedies, and did some of her best work in plays like *The Varying Shore* (1921); *The Texas Nightingale* (1922; also called *Greatness*); *A Royal Fandango* (produced, 1923); *The Greeks Had a Word for It* (1930); *O Evening Star* (1936); *Another Darling* (1950); *The Swallow's Nest* (1950). In later years Miss Akins devoted herself mainly to writing screenplays, among them that of Edna Ferber's SHOW BOAT. She also wrote verse and a novel, *Forever Young* (1941).

Al Aaraaf (1829), a poem by EDGAR ALLAN POE. This was the title poem in Poe's second collection of verse, *Al Aaraaf, Tamerlane, and Minor Poems.* It is the longest poem Poe ever wrote, and into it, says Hervey Allen in ISRAFEL: THE LIFE AND TIMES OF EDGAR ALLAN POE (1926), "the young poet poured a wealth of imagination, lovely sound, and airy fancy that entitle the work to a higher consideration than it has ever received." Al Aaraaf is a region placed by Arabian poets between heaven and hell; the presiding spirit is Nesace, a beautiful maiden. As Poe conceives it, Al Aaraaf is a wondrous star, lolling on the golden air near four bright suns. Thither is brought a passionate youth, Angelo, with hope of entering heaven, but an earthly love prevents him from hearing Nesace call him.

Alamo, The. This mission building in San Antonio, Tex., was used as a church until 1793, when the building was secularized. At the time of the rebellion against Mexico (1836) it was defended gallantly by a force of Texans under William B. Travis; but the Mexican General Santa Anna, whose forces were overpoweringly larger, bombarded the enclosure, and his troops entered the building and killed all the defenders (March 6). Among those killed were DAVY CROCKETT and Col. James Bowie. "Remember the Alamo!" became an inspiring war cry in the later and victorious battles of the war. Many historical novels have dealt with the incident, among them Augusta Evans Wilson's *Inez, A Tale of the Alamo* (1855); Amelia E. Barr's *Remember the Alamo* (1888); Herbert Gorman's *The Wine of San Lorenzo* (1945); and Paul I. Wellman's *The Iron Mistress* (1951). John Myers Myers wrote a historical account, *The Alamo* (1948).

Albee, Edward (b. Washington, D.C., March 12, 1928—), playwright. Most of Albee's one-act plays, produced within a period of some three years, showed acute characterization and witty dialogue. *The Death of Bessie Smith* (1960), however, was called by the *Herald Tribune* "a heavy-handed diatribe on race relations." Among his plays: *The Zoo Story* (1958); *The Sandbox* (1959), written in memory of his grandmother; *The American Dream* (1959–60); and *Fam and Yam* (1960), an imaginary interview. Albee claimed that "the responsibility of the playwright is to comment boldly and relentlessly on his time."

Alcott, [Amos] Bronson (b. Wolcott, Conn., Nov. 29, 1799—d. March 4, 1888), peddler, philosopher, pedagogue, poet. At first an un-

successful peddler in the south, Alcott became one of the great figures of his day, an influential exponent of transcendentalism and a potent

molder of education. Van Wyck Brooks, in THE FLOWERING OF NEW ENGLAND (1936), pictured him as "a tall, mild, milky, passionless man, with a singular gift for understanding children. . . . Plato's cloudland was, for him, far more solid than the United States." In his Boston school he included in his talks to children suggestions on religion and physiology (the latter a mild approach to sex education). As a consequence he was denounced as unorthodox and indecent.

Alcott revered the mystical virtues of the Nordic race, but was also an ardent abolitionist. When he admitted a Negro girl to his classes he was forced to close the school, and he retired to Concord. For a time he ran a farm, futilely; for a time, no less futilely, a cooperative community called FRUITLANDS. Through all this time the Alcott family carried on valiantly, despite Bronson's many financial difficulties. In 1859 he became superintendent of schools in Concord. When, largely through his daughter Louisa's books, Alcott attained some degree of financial independence, he set up in Concord a School of Philosophy. His chief disciple, Dr. WILLIAM T. HARRIS, did much to disseminate Alcott's ideas of the importance of heredity as against environment, his belief in a central Mind, his emphasis on identification with God and on the soul's preexistence. At all times benevolence was the keynote of his thinking. (See IDEALISM; TRANSCENDENTALISM.)

Alcott's stock in trade was conversation (often however in the form of a monologue), although he kept long journals and published a few books: *Observations on the Principles and Methods of Infant Instruction* (1830); TABLETS (1868); *Concord Days* (1872); *New Connecticut* (privately printed, 1881; published, 1887); *Sonnets and Canzonets* (1882). He also contributed many ORPHIC SAYINGS to the DIAL. Much of what he wrote still remains unpublished. Odell Shepard wrote a biography, *Pedlar's Progress, The Life of Bronson Alcott* (1937); Dorothy McCluskey described his influence on education in *Bronson Alcott, Teacher* (1940); Sanford Salyer paid tribute to Alcott's long-suffering wife in *Marmee, the Mother of Little Women* (1949).

Alcott, Louisa May (b. Germantown, Pa., Nov. 29, 1832—d. March 6, 1888), novelist, poet. Bronson Alcott was running a school in Germantown when his Louisa May was born; she was, thereafter, to become his mainstay in life. Although educated by her father, her mind was strong and independent, and she felt pangs of conscience because she could not maintain toward him the idolatrous attitude of her sisters. Obliged to do physical labor in order to earn a pittance for the Alcott household, she was determined to write. Her first book, *Flower Fables*, written when she was sixteen, appeared when she was twenty-two. In 1863 came the widely read HOSPITAL SKETCHES, based on vivid letters she had written while serving as a volunteer nurse in the military hospital at Georgetown. Then in 1868–69 came the turning-point in her career: she published LITTLE WOMEN and was famous. She followed up her first success with a number of similar stories, all intended for young people but likely to be read by their elders too: *An Old-Fashioned Girl* (1870); *Little*

Men (1871); *Aunt Jo's Scrap-Bag* (1872–82); *Eight Cousins* (1875); *Rose in Bloom* (1876); *Under the Lilacs* (1878); *Jo's Boys* (1886); and others. She died in Boston on the day her father was buried.

Miss Alcott's fiction was autobiographical. *Little Women* portrays the Alcott household; *Little Men* tells about her nephews. Perhaps because of this authenticity, she far surpasses her contemporary Jacob Abbott as a writer of juveniles. At least eight of her books still sell steadily; millions of copies have been sold since the first of them appeared, in addition to versions in at least twelve foreign languages. *Little Women* was made into a successful drama and was later twice filmed. Madeleine B. Stern's biography, *Louisa May Alcott* (1950), is exhaustive, while Marjorie Worthington's, *Miss Alcott of Concord* (1958), is romantic and admiring. Katharine Anthony's *Louisa May Alcott* (1937) uses a Freudian approach.

Alcuin (1797), a tract in dialogue by CHARLES BROCKDEN BROWN. In this he pleaded for the legal, political, economic, and cultural freedom of women.

Alden, Betty. See BETTY ALDEN.

Alden, Henry Mills. See HARPER'S MAGAZINE and HARPER'S WEEKLY.

Alden, John (b. England, 1599?—d. Sept. 12, 1687), one of the settlers of Plymouth, a founder of Duxbury, and a leading character in H. W. Longfellow's THE COURTSHIP OF MILES STANDISH (1858). He signed the MAYFLOWER COMPACT, and in Longfellow's poem (founded on an unauthentic legend) Priscilla Mullens speaks to him the celebrated words: "Why don't you speak for yourself, John?"—words founded

on an oral tradition in the family of Longfellow, himself a descendant of the Plymouth pair. See BETTY ALDEN.

Alderbrook (1847), a collection of village sketches and poems by Fanny Forester. See ADONIRAM JUDSON.

Aldrich, Bess Streeter (b. Cedar Falls, Iowa, Feb. 17, 1881—d. Aug. 3, 1954), teacher, novelist. Mrs. Aldrich taught school for a number of years, and wrote some of her best books about pioneer life: A LANTERN IN HER HAND (1928) is laid in Nebraska, *Song of Years* (1939) in Iowa. She was particularly interested in the character of the pioneer mothers, and wrote of them with admiration and humor. Among her other books: *A White Bird Flying* (1931); MISS BISHOP (1933); *Journey Into Christmas* (1949); *The Bess Streeter Aldrich Reader* (1950).

Aldrich, Thomas Bailey (b. Portsmouth, N.H., Nov. 11, 1836—d. March 19, 1907), editor, poet, novelist, dramatist, essayist. Aldrich was forced for a time into business, but soon turned to writing verse and obtained an editorial posi-

tion on a New York magazine. When the Civil War broke out he went to the front as a correspondent. He resumed magazine work after the war. In 1881 he became editor of the ATLANTIC MONTHLY, and continued in that position until 1890, when he retired to give all his time to writing.

Aldrich was a man of brilliant wit, with a wide circle of friends. As a poet he had technical skill in the "genteel tradition." His stories are ingeniously plotted, some of them memorable for their originality and humor. His resistance to change and his exclusively literary interests made him turn in horror from colloquialism or dialect, and Dr. Oliver Wendell Holmes once said to him: "You love the fragrance of certain words so well that you are in danger of making nosegays when you should write poems. Your tendency to vanilla-flavored adjectives and patchouli-scented participles stifles your strength in cloying euphemisms."

Aldrich's best book is probably THE STORY OF A BAD BOY (1870), a novel which draws heavily on his early memories of Portsmouth. Other fiction of Aldrich's includes *Marjorie Daw and Other People* (short stories, 1873); *Prudence Palfrey* (1874); THE STILLWATER TRAGEDY (1880); and *Two Bites at a Cherry, with Other Tales* (1894). His collections of verse include THE BELLS (1855); *Cloth of Gold* (1874); *Friar Jerome's Beautiful Book* (1881); *Mercedes and Later Lyrics* (1884); *Judith and Holofernes* (1896). He dramatized MERCEDES (1894) and *Judith and Holofernes* (produced as *Judith of Bethulia*, 1904). *From Ponkapog to Pesth* (1883) and *Ponkapog Papers* (1903) are collections of essays and travel sketches. His *Writings* appeared in eight volumes (1897) and in nine volumes (1907). Ferris Greenslet wrote his life (1908). See MARJORIE DAW.

Aleichem, Sholom. See SHOLOM ALEICHEM.

Alexander's Bridge (1912), a novel by WILLA CATHER. Bartley Alexander, an American engineer, encounters an actress, a dangerous flame of his youth, on a visit to London. The conflict between his attraction to her and his loyalty to his wife is still unsolved when a bridge on which he is working crashes and he is killed. Walter Fuller Taylor notes that when she turned from this depiction of a life of which she could know little "back to the primitive West of her youth," she produced O PIONEERS! (1913).

Alger, Horatio, Jr. (b. Revere, Mass., Jan. 13, 1832—d. July 18, 1899), writer of stories for boys. Alger, the oldest child of a pompous Unitarian minister, attended Harvard College and Harvard Divinity School, but fled to Paris as a rebellious bohemian. He was finally persuaded to come back to the United States and become a minister. In 1866 he was made chaplain of a Newsboys' Lodging House, to which he devoted his time, money, and affection for the rest of his life.

Alger wished to write novels for adults; his actual literary labors resulted only in a great many series of boys' books. Herbert R. Mayes, in *Alger: A Biography Without a Hero* (1928), lists 119 titles. The heroes were bootblacks and newsboys; they were invariably smugly good, and as a result (so Alger implied) they became rich and successful. Perhaps 20,000,000 copies of his books have been sold. Among the most popular were the RAGGED DICK *Series* (1867), the *Luck and Pluck Series* (1869), and the *Tattered Tom Series* (1871). He also wrote juvenile biographies of famous men.

Russel Crouse, who undertook the task of editing an Alger omnibus (*Struggling Upward and Other Works*, 1945), admitted that he still admires Alger "because, for many years . . . he got away with literary murder." He never used a simple word where a circumlocution could be devised. A barber in his stories is "a knight of the scissors," and liquor is "a poisonous decoction." The Horatio Alger Awards are made annually by the American Schools and Colleges

LUCK and PLUCK.

Association to those Americans who, in its judgment, have risen to fame and fortune despite handicaps at the beginning.

Algerine Captive, The (2 v., 1797), a novel by ROYALL TYLER. The book, whose theme was related to the difficulties America was currently having in Tripoli, had a preface urging the production of a distinctively native fiction in response to an increasing domestic demand for novels. The narrator, Dr. Updike Underhill, satirizes college education in New England, quack medicine in the backwoods, and slavery in the southern United States and in Africa. While on his travels, he is taken into captivity as a slave in Algiers, but returns to denounce the miserable condition of all such prisoners.

Algic Researches (1839), a book by H. R. SCHOOLCRAFT. This collection of Indian tales and legends was of great assistance to Henry Wadsworth Longfellow when he came to write HIAWATHA. The subtitle described the book as "comprising Inquiries respecting the Mental Characteristics of the North American Indians."

Algonquin Hotel. See FRANK CASE; THE ROUND TABLE.

Algren, Nelson (b. Detroit, Mich., March 28, 1909—), novelist and short-story writer. Algren lived a long time in Chicago, and the slums of that city's west side have been the background for most of his novels and short stories. His first novel *Somebody in Boots* (1935) was a bitter portrayal of "depression youth." *Never Come Morning* followed in 1942. This story of poverty and crime among the Poles of Chicago's west side brought Algren recognition as a writer of importance; he was compared to JAMES T. FARRELL and RICHARD WRIGHT, both acknowledged masters of the "Chicago school of realism." Algren's most important work, THE MAN WITH THE GOLDEN ARM (1949), story of the morphine addict Frankie Machine, won the National Book Award and was made into a motion picture. Algren also published *The Neon Wilderness* (short stories 1947) and *A Walk on the Wild Side* (1956).

Alias Jimmy Valentine (1909), a play by PAUL ARMSTRONG. This was based on O. Henry's A RETRIEVED REFORMATION, included in *Roads of Destiny* (1903). The play later became a popular movie. It is said that O. Henry got the idea for the story from one of his fellow prisoners in the Ohio State Penitentiary. Armstrong also took some suggestions from a famous play, *The Ticket-of-Leave Man* (1863), by Tom Taylor. See WILSON MIZNER.

Alice Adams (1921), a novel by BOOTH TARKINGTON that was awarded a Pulitzer Prize. It is said to have been written as an answer to Sinclair Lewis' MAIN STREET; by many critics it is regarded as Tarkington's greatest novel. It deals with the disintegration of the middle-class Adams family in a small middle-western town. Virgil Adams has a minor position in a drug company, a nagging wife with overweening ambitions, a shiftless son, a daughter. Alice does her best to be pretty, vivacious, popular; the failure of her pathetic efforts makes the story. She is a wallflower at dances, she lies to win admiration, she does her best to conceal the truth about her family. At the end of the book she is seen entering the stairway that leads to Frincke's Business College. It is the end of her hopes, but she enters bravely.

Alice of Old Vincennes (1900), a historical novel by JAMES MAURICE THOMPSON. In this story of frontier days in Indiana the central figure is a girl abducted in her childhood and brought up by a French trader. She becomes strong, reliant, beautiful, expert in the use of gun and sword. She wins the love of Lieutenant Beverley, an officer in George Rogers Clark's famous expedition. See SIMON KENTON.

Alison's House (1930), a play by SUSAN GLASPELL that won a Pulitzer Prize. It is based on the life of Emily Dickinson and depicts a poet whose love poems are preserved against her wishes by her sister. The scene is an Iowa village, and the action takes place many years after the death of the poet. Miss Glaspell stresses the contrast between two generations and their attitude toward the love of a man already married.

Allatoona (1874), a play by Major General Judson Kilpatrick and J. Owen Moore. One of the earliest plays to deal with the Civil War, *Allatoona* takes the form of a chronicle in which two men, classmates at West Point, find themselves on opposite sides in the great struggle.

Allen, Ethan (b. Litchfield, Conn., Jan. 10, 1738—d. Feb. 12, 1789), leader of the GREEN MOUNTAIN BOYS, philosopher, author. Allen led a force of Vermont and Connecticut volunteers against Fort Ticonderoga during the American Revolution. Later he was captured by the British and held prisoner for two years. Before the war he had been prominent in the territorial controversy between Vermont and New York; his exacerbated Vermont patriotism led afterward to what some have regarded as treasonable correspondence with the British. He wrote a vigorous and egotistic NARRATIVE OF ETHAN ALLEN'S CAPTIVITY (1774) and an exposition of his religious (or anti-religious) views, REASON THE ONLY ORACLE OF MAN (1789). (See DEISM.) Allen appears in Daniel Pierce Thompson's *The Green Mountain Boys* (1840), F. F. Van de Water's *Reluctant Rebel* (1948), and other novels. John Pell wrote a colorful life of Allen (1929, 1954).

Allen, Fred (b. Cambridge, Mass., May 31, 1894—d. March 17, 1956), comedian. Allen's real name was John Florence Sullivan. He began as a juggler in vaudeville, appeared in several musical comedies, but earned his greatest fame in radio. His gravelly voice was notable, but his satire on the current scene was more memorable. His material was gathered from assiduous study of the newspapers. It was stated on good authority that although he had several "assistant writers," he wrote most of his shows himself. Some of his sayings were widely quoted, as when he summed up a celebrity who went to church wearing sun glasses: "He is afraid God might recognize him and ask him for an autograph." Allen's own story of his career, *Treadmill to Oblivion* (1954), was continued in *Much Ado About Me* (1956).

Allen, Frederick Lewis (b. Boston, July 5, 1890—d. Feb. 13, 1954), editor, teacher, historian. Educated at Harvard, where he taught for a time, Allen was on the editorial staffs of *Atlantic Monthly* (1914–16), *Century Magazine* (1916–17), and HARPER'S MAGAZINE (1923–53). Observing the "tremendous trifles" of the 1920's, he wrote a best seller, *Only Yesterday* (1931), followed by *Since Yesterday* (1940), *I Remember Distinctly* (with his wife Agnes Rogers, 1947), and *The Big Change* (1952), all social chronicles. He also prepared two collections of photographs with commentaries, *American Procession* (1933) and *Metropolis* (1934), and wrote *The Lords of Creation* (1935), an account of America's financial expansion, and a life of J. Pierpont Morgan (1949).

Allen, Gay Wilson (b. Lake Junaluska, N.C., Aug. 23, 1903—   ), critic, professor. After studying and teaching at a number of colleges and universities, Allen became a professor of English at New York University in 1946. He wrote *American Prosody* (1935) and *Literary*

Criticism: Pope to Croce (with H. H. Clark, 1941) before beginning to publish books in the field which made him best known. The *Walt Whitman Handbook* (1946) was welcomed as a complete guide to the mass of material on the poet then extant, including criticism in other languages. *The Solitary Singer: A Critical Biography of Walt Whitman* (1955) was acclaimed for its thorough scholarship and objectivity. Allen also wrote *Whitman Abroad* (1955) and, in collaboration with C. T. Davis, *Walt Whitman's Poems* (1955).

Allen, [William] Hervey (b. Pittsburgh, Pa., Dec. 8, 1889—d. Dec. 28, 1949), teacher, poet, novelist, biographer. Allen's first books were in verse and won much favorable comment, particularly *Wampum and Old Gold* (1921); *Carolina Chansons*, issued in 1922 with Du Bose Heyward; and *The Blindman* (1923). *Towards the Flame* (1926) is an autobiographical novel of his war service. Allen spent five years on the composition of a historical novel, *Anthony Adverse* (1933). The book, laid in the Napoleonic era, takes its hero all over the world, and for weight, length, and frank treatment of sex set the pace for numerous other novels. It also aroused a controversy regarding Allen's sources, and was called by Howard Fast "a mountain of trash." Allen then composed a series of novels, including *Action at Aquila* (1938), which failed to rival the earlier one. He began work on a quintet of novels called The Disinherited (1943–49), all historical; only three were published in his lifetime, the fourth posthumously. In 1926 Allen published Israfel, biography of Edgar Allan Poe, and in the same year wrote, with Thomas O. Mabbott, an account of *Poe's Brother*. See Brantz Mayer.

Allen, Ida [Cogswell Bailey] (b. Danielson, Conn., 1885—   ), dietician, editor, author. Mrs. Allen's contributions to the art of cooking have appeared in many magazines, and her more than fifty cookbooks have sold more than fifteen million copies. Among them are *Mrs. Allen's Cook Book* (1916); *Bride's Book* (1922); *Your Foods and You* (1926); *Pressure Cooking* (1947); *Sandwich Book* (1955); *Cook Book for Two* (1957); *Gastronomique* (1958).

Allen, James Lane (b. Lexington, Ky., Dec. 21, 1849—d. Feb. 18, 1925), teacher, essayist, novelist. Born in the heart of the blue-grass region, Allen used that setting as the background for a number of novels that were widely read at the turn of the century, particularly A Kentucky Cardinal (1894), *Aftermath* (1896), and The Choir Invisible (1897). Allen had begun by publishing a series of sketches, *The Blue-Grass Region of Kentucky* (1892), and a collection of Kentucky short stories, *Flute and Violin* (1891). He continued writing for many years; his last book was another gathering of stories, *The Landmark* (1925). But by that time he had lost his vogue, partly because of a growing mysticism and obscurity in his books, partly because his sentimentality and unreality had ceased to appeal. His Kentucky was an un-

The Macmillan Company

substantial land of imagination; he even refused to visit the real Kentucky during his later years. Grant C. Knight wrote *James Lane Allen and the Genteel Tradition* (1935).

Allen, Paul (b. Providence, R.I., Feb. 15, 1775—d. Aug. 18, 1826), poet, historian, editor. Eight years after graduating from what is now Brown University, Allen published *Original Poems, Serious and Entertaining* (1801). Under various pen names he contributed to magazines. With the help of John Neal he wrote a *History of the American Revolution* (2 v., 1819); he edited Nicholas Biddle's *History of the Expedition Under the Command of Captains Lewis and Clark* (1814). He also edited several magazines. He was a man of highly impractical, childlike nature who won many friends; they were constantly rescuing him from embarrassing financial difficulties.

Allen, Robert S[haron] (b. Latonia, Ky., July 14, 1900—   ), columnist, author. Allen first worked on Wisconsin newspapers, later for various syndicates and news services in Washington. He served in both World Wars, and received many decorations. He and Drew Pearson were among the first to exploit the growing interest of the country in the personalities of prominent men and women at the capital. They ran a syndicated column called "Washington Merry-Go-Round," which became the title of their first book in 1931; later appeared *More Washington Merry-Go-Round* (1932); in 1936, as a contribution to Franklin D. Roosevelt's attempt to enlarge the Supreme Court, *Nine Old Men* was published. Later Allen wrote *Our Fair City* (1946) and *The Truman Merry-Go-Round*

(1950), the latter in collaboration with William V. Shannon.

Allen, Steve [Stephen Valentine Patrick William] (b. New York City, Dec. 26, 1921—), television personality, composer, musician, author. Educated in journalism, he began his career as radio announcer, comedian, and disc jockey. In 1950 he achieved national recognition in television with *The Steve Allen Show.* He played leading roles in a number of films, including *The Benny Goodman Story* and *College Confidential.* In the latter he co-starred with his wife, Jayne Meadows. He has written more than two thousand songs, among them the title songs for such film successes as *Picnic; Houseboat; Sleeping Beauty; Bell, Book and Candle.* His books include: *Fourteen for Tonight* (1955); *Bop Fables* (1955); *The Funny Men* (1956); *Wry on the Rocks* (verse, 1956); *The Girls on the Tenth Floor* (1958); *Mark It and Strike It: an Autobiography* (1960).

All God's Chillun Got Wings (1924), a play by EUGENE O'NEILL. White Ella Downey marries Negro Jim Harris, who is struggling to become a lawyer. The tragic consequences of her mental inferiority are intensified by latent racial prejudice as she tries to use it in a desperate effort to gain superiority before lapsing into insanity and a regression to childhood.

Allport, Floyd H[enry] (b. Milwaukee, Wis., Aug. 22, 1890—), psychologist. A graduate of Harvard, Allport taught at several universities before joining (1924) the faculty of Syracuse University as professor of social and political psychology. He has studied human behavior closely in its social relationships, as in his *Social Psychology* (1924) and *Institutional Behavior* (1933).

Allport, Gordon W[illard] (b. Montezuma, Ind., Nov. 11, 1897—), psychologist, writer. Like his brother FLOYD ALLPORT, Gordon Allport graduated from Harvard, and he taught there from 1924 on. He has specialized on studies of personality, its growth and development, as in *Personality—A Psychological Interpretation* (1937), notable for its pioneering ideas. He also has investigated rumor and the psychology of the radio. In *Becoming* (1955) he discussed the psychology of personality in relation to democracy, human welfare, and religion. *Personality and Social Encounter* was published in 1960.

All Quiet Along the Potomac (*Harper's Weekly*, 1861), a poem by ETHEL LYNN BEERS. This famous piece about an unknown soldier of the Civil War was first published under the title "The Picket Guard," and was signed merely "E.B." The authorship was claimed by various persons, but the poem was undoubtedly Mrs. Beers'. She reprinted it in *All Quiet Along the Potomac and Other Poems*, 1879.

Allston, Joseph Blythe (b. near Georgetown, S.C., 1833—d. 1904), lawyer, soldier, poet. Allston graduated from South Carolina College, read law, and was admitted to the bar in 1854. On the outbreak of the war he volunteered immediately and served till the end, reaching the rank of captain. He then resumed the practice of law in Georgetown and Baltimore. He contributed many poems to newspapers and magazines; they have never been collected. He won fame with a single poem, *Stack Arms*, in which he gave a symbolic significance to the familiar military command.

Allston, Washington (b. Waccamaw, S.C., Nov. 5, 1779—d. July 9, 1843), painter, poet, novelist. Allston studied painting in Europe and was intimate with some of the great writers and artists of the day; one of his greatest works

was a portrait of Samuel Taylor Coleridge; another, *Dead Man Revived by Touching the Bones of the Prophet Elisha.* In 1818 he returned to America and began trying to finish a huge historical canvas, *Belshazzar's Feast*, a painful attempt still unfinished at his death. He published a volume of sentimental and satiric poems, *The Sylphs of the Seasons* (1813), and a novel with a painter hero, *Monaldi* (1841). His brother-in-law Richard Henry Dana edited his *Lectures on Art and Poems* (1850). Edgar P. Richardson has written a biography of Allston (1948).

All's Well, or The Mirror Repolished. The famous magazine, *Reedy's Mirror*, was given this name when it was taken over in 1920 by CHARLES J. FINGER. It continued publication to the end of 1935.

All the King's Men (1946), a novel by ROBERT PENN WARREN. Jack Burden, a young intellectual, narrates the story of the rise and fall of Willie Stark, a Southern demagogue obviously modeled on Huey Long. Willie starts off as a popular reformer, but degenerates into an unprincipled power-seeker. Even at his worst, however, Stark accomplishes some good things, such as building a clinic. This forces Burden to confront the problem of identifying good and evil, and leads him to a new self-understanding at the end of the book, after Stark has been assassinated. Warren adapted the Pulitzer Prize winning novel into a motion picture which received an Academy Award, and into a stage play.

All Trivia (1933, 1945), miscellanea by LOGAN PEARSALL SMITH. See TRIVIA.

almanacs. Two books were sure to be found in every early American home, a Bible and an almanac. As Paul Leicester Ford pointed out: "In our colonial period [an almanac] was the *vade mecum* of every household—a calendar, diary, meteorological bureau, jest-book, and indeed sometimes school-book." It is believed that the first American printed production in English, apart from broadsides, was *An Almanac Calculated for New England,* issued at Cambridge (1639) by WILLIAM PEIRCE or Pierce. The first humorous almanac is said to have been compiled by JOHN TULLEY, of Saybrook, Conn. (1687). Boston became a center of almanac-making, but numerous almanacs appeared in New York and Philadelphia, and one in Virginia. Among these were Samuel Danforth's *An Almanac for the Year of our Lord 1649;* Josiah Flint's *Almanac* (1666); and John Richardson's *Almanac* (1670), which anticipated BENJAMIN FRANKLIN and others with its humorous hard sense. By 1720 at least five almanac series were running concurrently; by 1765 there were thirty-one series running. Among the chief almanac-makers were Franklin, DANIEL LEEDS and his son Titan Leeds, and NATHANIEL AMES, father and son. In the 19th century almanacs became more specialized, representing not merely farmers but groups like the Free Masons, temperance enthusiasts, and religious sects. Most famous of all almanacs was Franklin's POOR RICHARD'S (begun 1733). Longest continued was THE OLD FARMER'S, first issued in 1792 and still going. Most widely circulated today is THE WORLD ALMANAC (founded 1868). See also NATHAN DABOLL; BENJAMIN WEST; COMIC ALMANACS; ANNUALS.

Alonzo and Melissa, or, The Unfeeling Father (1811), a novel by Isaac Mitchell (1759–1812). In the Gothic style, but the haunted castle is in Connecticut. Eleven editions were published.

Alsop, George (b. England, 1638?—?), traveler, writer. Alsop came to this country in 1658 and wrote in 1666 *A Character of the Province of Mary-Land.* It is written in mingled verse and prose, with alternate seriousness and jocularity.

Alsop, Joseph [Wright, Jr.] (b. Avon, Conn., Oct. 11, 1910—   ), newspaperman, columnist. With his brother **Stewart [Johonnot Oliver]** (b. Avon, Conn., May 17, 1914—   ) he ran a syndicated column, "Matter of Fact," in the New York *Herald Tribune.* It began in December, 1945, and was widely read and esteemed for its combination of accurate fact-gathering, clear thinking, and hard-hitting arguments. Someone called Joseph and Stewart Alsop "the reporter with four legs." Joseph Alsop has written three books in collaboration with his brother: *We Accuse* (1954); *The Reporter's Trade* (1958); and *Nixon and Rockefeller* (1960).

Alsop, Richard (b. Middletown, Conn., Jan.

23, 1761—d. Aug. 20, 1815), poet, satirist. Educated at Yale, Alsop was a member of the HARTFORD (or Connecticut) WITS. He wrote a good deal of verse, but not so exclusively as to

prevent his acquiring a fortune in trade. But his interest in literature was genuine and his scholarship sound. With LEMUEL HOPKINS and THEODORE DWIGHT he published THE POLITICAL GREENHOUSE FOR THE YEAR 1798, a sometimes witty blast against Jacobins and their American sympathizers. Because of the poem Alsop was accused in Congress of trying to start a war between Connecticut and France. He also collaborated with others of the Hartford Wits. A long poem in heroic couplets, *The Charms of Fancy,* was not published in book form until 1856. See THE ECHO.

Altgeld, John Peter (b. Germany, Dec. 30, 1847—d. March 12, 1902), lawyer, public official, author. As governor of Illinois (1892–96) Altgeld pardoned three anarchists who had been convicted in connection with the HAYMARKET RIOT (May 4, 1886), and this, together with his activity in behalf of labor and his early support of WILLIAM JENNINGS BRYAN, gave him a countrywide reputation as a radical. He attacked the American judicial system in *Our Penal Machinery and Its Victims* (1884) and wrote *Live Questions* (1890). Vachel Lindsay praised him warmly in a poem, THE EAGLE THAT IS FORGOTTEN (1913), and HOWARD FAST made him the hero of his novel *The American* (1946). He is the principal subject of Ray Ginger's *Altgeld's America: The Lincoln Ideal versus the Changing Realities* (1958).

Altsheler, Joseph (b. Three Springs, Ky., April 29, 1862—d. June 5, 1919), newspaperman, writer. Altsheler was a newspaperman who became an author largely by accident. For several years he worked on Louisville papers. In 1892 he became a member of the New York *World* staff, ultimately editor of its magazine section. He needed a story for boys, and since none was available, he wrote one himself. This set him off on his long and fruitful career as an author of juveniles; he wrote as many as two a year for many years, most of them historical tales. His books are sound in plot, in characterization, in their agreeable humor, in their faithfulness to history. Many of them fall into series —*The Young Trailers* (perhaps his most popular), *The Great West, The Civil War*, and others. He is still widely read.

Ambassadors, The (1903), a novel by HENRY JAMES. James makes an ironic study of the "deteriorating" influence of Europe's "wickedness" on Americans. "Chad" Newsome refuses to come back from Paris to Woollett, Mass., to take care of his legitimate business; his widowed mother, a woman of wealth and social position, suspects the worst. She sends two ambassadors to find out what's wrong and bring her son home. The first, Lambert Strether, who is about to marry Mrs. Newsome, is himself seduced by the charm of France and is convinced that Chad's relationship with Mme. de Vionnet is entirely virtuous. Then Mrs. Newsome sends her daughter Sarah, who sees through it all, demands that her brother return at once, and tells Strether that all is over between him and her mother. Although Strether, by accident, then learns that everything charged against Chad and his "friend" is true, he still believes Chad should stay, but goes back to America himself. The entire action is skillfully and slowly revealed through Strether's mind. James considered *The Ambassadors* his best book, its essence being summed in a remark by Strether, "Live all you can; it's a mistake not to."

Ambitious Guest, The (published in *The Token*, 1835; in TWICE-TOLD TALES, 1837), a story by NATHANIEL HAWTHORNE. In this striking tale, Hawthorne depicts a young man stopping for the night in a lonely cottage in the White Mountains. There he and the simpleminded, kindly members of the household discuss their ambitions and wishes. The youth himself speaks freely of his yearning for fame and fortune. Then, during the night, a great landslide destroys them all.

America (1831), a patriotic hymn by the Rev. Samuel Francis Smith (1808–1895). It was first sung at a Fourth-of-July meeting in Boston in 1831, and was published in 1832. The tune was originally English and is the music to which both the English and the Austrian national anthems are set.

American, The (1877), a novel by HENRY JAMES, dramatized by James in 1891. Christopher Newman, a wealthy "self-made" American in France, becomes involved in the intrigues of an aristocratic French circle; some of the events are melodramatic. Newman finds himself deeply interested in the types of character he finds in France; despite the callous selfishness he finds in high places, he is deeply impressed by French culture. The French aristocrats, on the other hand, are somewhat taken aback by Newman's brisk and energetic self-confidence. The story is based on one of James' favorite themes—the contrast between two ways

of life, forthright simplicity and subtle sophistication.

American, The (1943), a historical analysis by JAMES TRUSLOW ADAMS. Adams seeks to present the geographical, historical, and social forces that have made the American different from the citizen of any other country. In an epilogue he sums up the American—his individualism balanced by his passion for equality, his hospitality, his disregard of the past, his love of the practical, his amazing versatility, his sense of hurry, and his love of work. But he finds predominant in him the "dream" that has drawn people to these shores and still works like yeast within them.

American Academy of Arts and Letters. The inner circle of the National Institute of Arts and Letters. The latter, founded in 1898 by the American Social Science Association, deemed it necessary six years later to create a smaller society composed of the more distinguished members of the Institute; the first seven men elected to membership were William Dean Howells, Augustus Saint-Gaudens, Edmund Clarence Stedman, John La Farge, Samuel L. Clemens, John Hay, and Edward MacDowell. The aim of the Academy is to give "the stamp of its approval" to the best in literature and art that both the present and the past have to offer. It awards medals and prizes for distinguished work, and holds almost continuous art exhibits in its building, 633 West 155th Street, New York City.

American Anthology, An (1900), a collection edited by EDMUND C. STEDMAN. This includes selections from 1787 to 1900 and is prefaced with a twenty-page critical introduction. It was intended to serve as a companion volume to the editor's *A Victorian Anthology, 1837–95* (1895).

American Anthology, the Spirit of the Public Journals; or, Beauties of the American Newspapers for 1805 (1806). This is believed to be the first collection of extracts from American newspapers.

American Archives (1837–53), edited by PETER FORCE. Force conceived a grandiose scheme for publishing a collection of documents that would provide first-hand source material for the history of the country up to the adoption of the Constitution. Congress authorized his scheme in an unwisely drawn contract, in which no limit was set to the number of volumes. Only nine volumes were ever published, carrying the history down to 1776.

American Boy. Founded in 1899 as the Boy Scout magazine, this periodical continued for many years to publish some of our best reading for the juvenile public. It passed into private hands in 1939. In 1929 it had absorbed *Youth's Companion*, in 1953 it was joined with another magazine as *Open Road-American Boy*. Franklin M. Reck, one of its editors, in 1948 published an anthology of writings collected from the magazine. See GRIFFITH O. ELLIS.

American Caravan, The (1927–36), an annual volume edited by VAN WYCK BROOKS the first year, thereafter by LEWIS MUMFORD, ALFRED KREYMBORG, and PAUL ROSENFELD. It aimed to exhibit the best of contemporary literature, and attracted many writers of note, including Ernest Hemingway.

American Claimant, The (1892), a drama by MARK TWAIN and WILLIAM DEAN HOWELLS and a novel based on it written by Twain. In the 70's Twain had collaborated with CHARLES DUDLEY WARNER on a novel called THE GILDED AGE, later dramatized by Twain and famous for the character of Colonel Mulberry Sellers (in the novel he is called Beriah). In 1883 he and Howells wrote a play continuing the adventures of Sellers "ten years later." In 1892 Twain published this second novel, based on the play. It shows Sellers aspiring to an English earldom. The British heir, an earnest young man, comes to the United States to discover if he is really entitled to the earldom, engages in numerous strange adventures, and settles the matter happily by falling in love with the colonel's daughter. Sellers still cherishes the fantastic schemes that had amused audiences and readers in the earlier play and book. But he has become a bore; Twain is not at his best here. See BERIAH SELLERS.

American Commonwealth, The (1888; revised, 1910; 50th anniversary edition, 1939), by James Bryce (1838-1922). A classic by an English statesman and historian of the structure of American government and the character of American society, it is perhaps more widely read in the United States than in England. Bryce (later an ambassador to this country) visited the United States five times before writing his massive and comprehensive two-volume work, the most important study of this nation since DE TOCQUEVILLE's *Democracy in America*. He dealt with the Federal government, the state and municipal governments, political machinery and the party system, the workings of public opinion, the strength and weakness of democratic government, the social, intellectual, and spiritual forces operating in American life. Bryce was an enthusiastic believer in America but not blind to American faults and weaknesses. A supplementary chapter on the Tweed Ring in New York City caused the entire first edition to be suppressed.

American Crisis, The (Dec. 19, 1776—April 19, 1783), sixteen pamphlets by THOMAS PAINE. The first, published in *The Pennsylvania Journal*, was begun while Washington was retreating across New Jersey and opens with the famous sentence, "These are the times that try men's souls." Washington caused it to be read to his downhearted troops, and it had a great effect in arousing new zeal for the American cause. In succeeding years Paine continued to comment on the course of events, to inspire the colonists to continue their struggle against England, and to oppose compromise. The last pamphlet is called *Thoughts on the Peace and the Probable Advantages Thereof*, and begins, "The times that tried men's souls are over."

American Democrat, The, or Hints on the Social and Civic Relations of the United States of America (1838), one of a series of critical disquisitions by JAMES FENIMORE COOPER Cooper wrote this diatribe against his countrymen on his return from a seven-year stay in Europe. Brought up in the aristocratic Federalist tradition, Cooper while abroad had become an ardent and somewhat tactless defender of democracy. Returning home, he was repelled by much that he saw in the wild Jacksonian era, and spoke his mind freely and with a tactlessness equal to that he had shown abroad. As a result he became, as Walter Fuller Taylor has phrased it, "the most popular author and the most unpopular man in American literature." He repudiated as vicious a system of government founded on property, but refused to believe that a majority could do no wrong, or that special intelligence dwelt under a coonskin cap or in a log cabin. The fullest statement of his political principles may be found in *The American Democrat*, the title of which, he said, should have been "Anti-Cant." Other books that Cooper wrote in his attempt to reform the vulgarity and crudity of his country included A LETTER TO HIS COUNTRYMEN (1834); THE MONIKINS (1835); HOMEWARD BOUND (1838); and *Home as Found* (1838). They brought upon him such scurrilous epithets in the press of the time as "spotted caitiff" and "leprous wretch." Cooper brought libel suits against several American papers, acted as his own lawyer, and for the most part not merely won verdicts but helped to establish legal remedies against such attacks as he had suffered. But he lost a fortune in winning his point.

American Dictionary of the English Language (1828), the original title given to his monumental work by NOAH WEBSTER. He spent twenty years on the compilation of this volume, the most ambitious publication issued up to that time in America and a great scholarly achievement. As the title indicates, Webster favored usage rather than purity as his guide, and insisted that America had its own language.

American English Grammar (1940), a philological and educational treatise by Charles Carpenter Fries (1887—   ). Analyzes the grammatical structure of present-day American English, with special reference to social differences and class dialects. He proposes an educational program, based on a study of the real grammar used today, to develop a knowledge of the wide resources of the language.

American Flag, The (*New York Evening Post*, May 29, 1819), a poem by JOSEPH RODMAN DRAKE. It is said that Drake's friend, FITZ-GREENE HALLECK, contributed the final quatrain of this endlessly recited poem. William Ellery Leonard called it "a lyric full of the old-fashioned expansive and defiant Americanism."

American folklore. See FOLKLORE IN AMERICAN LITERATURE.

American Folk-Lore Society. This was founded in 1888 for "the study of folklore in general and, in particular, the collection and publication of the folklore of North America." A leading article in the first volume of the *Journal of American Folklore*, published by the Society, classifies the latter purpose under four categories: relics of Old English folklore, southern Negro lore, Indian lore, the lore of French Canada, Mexico, etc. In addition to the rich material appearing in the *Journal,* the Society has published since 1894 a series of valuable monographs.

American Frontier, The History of the (1924), by FREDERIC L. PAXSON. Paxson's influential book, which was awarded a Pulitzer Prize, endeavors to unify American history in terms of a constantly receding frontier which helped to produce in frontiersmen a common interest and a common purpose. The disappearance of the frontier, Paxson says, was to be followed by an age "likely to be shaped by industry and the pressure of the outside world."

American Guide Series. See WORKS PROGRESS ADMINISTRATION.

American Heritage. A magazine first issued in 1949 by the American Association for State and Local History. By 1954 the circulation had grown so large that it was placed in professional publishing and advertising hands to reach a still larger public. The magazine explores the highways and byways of American history, with accompanying illustrations.

American Historical Novel, The (1950), a treatise by ERNEST E. LEISY. According to Leisy, the American historical novel has been a best seller during three periods: in the years of national expansion after the War of 1812, in the early 20th century, and in the middle of the same century. Leisy is concerned entirely with novels dealing with the development of America. In themselves they give an unsurpassed picture of American history. No other literary form, Leisy points out, has more acceptably expressed the nation's origins, its ideals, its evolution. He also makes clear that the historical novel is invariably an expression of the era in which it is written rather than of that in which the scene is laid.

American Humor: A Study of the National Character (1931), a historical and critical study by CONSTANCE ROURKE. Viewing the whole development of American literary effort as a series of "continuities," Miss Rourke assembles oral and written expression in a pattern to demonstrate how "the popular arts—humor is one of them—have much to say as to underlying forces in American life." She stresses the fantastic quality of much American humor and is especially effective in her treatment of the traditional Yankee, the frontiersman, and the "comic" Negro.

American Idyl, An (1919), by Cornelia Stratton Parker (1885—   ). Parker tells the story of her marriage to a college professor. The book was widely popular and was continued in *Wanderer's Cycle* (1934).

American Indian literature. See AMERINDIAN LITERATURE.

American in the Making, An (1917), an autobiography by Marcus Eli Ravage. The author, a Rumanian, chronicles his early years in the United States, describing with particular detail the life and spirit of a Middle Western university that he attended.

Americanization of Edward Bok, The (1920). See EDWARD BOK.

American Jest-Book, The (1796). Published at Boston, this was perhaps the earliest American imitation of the English "Joe Miller" collections. Another collection with the same title was published in Philadelphia, 1833.

American Language. The (1919, 1921, 1923, 1936; *Supplement One,* 1945; *Supplement Two,* 1948), a treatise by H. L. MENCKEN. Mencken first began writing on this subject in the Baltimore *Evening Sun* in 1910. He felt at that time that the American form of the English language was plainly departing from the parent stem, and it seemed likely that the differences between American and English would increase. But from 1923 on the pull of American, in his judgment, became so powerful that it began to drag English with it, and in consequence some of the differences once visible have begun to disappear. Mencken, with infinite detail, treated the two streams of English, the beginnings of American, the period of growth, the language today, the differences between American and English, the pronunciation of American, American spelling, the common speech, proper names in America, American slang, the future of the language, and non-English dialects in America.

For many years Mencken had had endless fun with American scholars; then, in this work, to their immense astonishment (and perhaps his own) he barged into their midst, exhibiting a wealth of knowledge, unwearying delving into first sources, eager and intelligent curiosity. Mencken's humor was too fundamental a quality in his composition for him to avoid it even in these learned volumes. In fact, one imagines that what attracted him to this theme was the profound humor of the American language itself—its prankishness, irreverence, earthiness, gifts of insult and persiflage, fantastic inventiveness, effervescent energy of expression.

American Library Association. See LIBRARIES IN THE U.S.; NEWBERY AWARD.

American Magazine, The. Several periodicals have borne this title, the most notable of which were:

[1.] *The American Magazine, or, A Monthly View of the Political State of the British Colonies* was the first magazine to be issued in America. It appeared February 13, 1741 (dated "January, 1740–41"), from the press of Andrew Bradford in Philadelphia. Half its pages were occupied by the proceedings of colonial assemblies. The only belles-lettres consisted of an excerpt of "characters" from the *London Magazine.* The venture lasted only three months.

[2.] NOAH WEBSTER's *American Magazine,* which had only twelve issues, showed a variety and spirit unusual for its time. It was New York's first monthly magazine, and was issued by the printer-bookseller Samuel Loudon in December of 1787. Webster, a strong Federalist, printed much about the newly written constitution; he was also an educational leader and made schools and teaching a favorite subject. Women's interests received more attention than in any previous American magazine. Extracts from American books and some new fiction and poetry were included.

[3.] NATHANIEL PARKER WILLIS' *American Monthly Magazine* was founded in Boston in April, 1829, and lasted through twenty-seven numbers; it was one of the most entertaining magazines yet published in America. Clearly modeled upon Thomas Campbell's *New Monthly Magazine* in London, it was filled with essays, tales, criticism, and humor, a large part of which was written by the editor. Other contributors included Richard Hildreth, John L. Motley, Mrs. Lydia Sigourney, Albert Pike, and Park Benjamin. The magazine's satirical bent and disregard of Boston *mores* offended many, and in 1831 Willis turned his subscription list over to the *New York Mirror,* of which he became associate editor.

[4.] HENRY WILLIAM HERBERT, better known as "Frank Forester," founded the *American Monthly Magazine* in 1833 in New York as a competitor of the new KNICKERBOCKER; in the magazine's second year, Herbert took CHARLES FENNO HOFFMAN as partner. The two editor-publishers wrote much of the *American*'s contents, but also included the work of James K. Paulding, Gulian C. Verplanck, and James Hall. The magazine had variety, and Herbert's commentary on New York theaters, music, and art was notable. Herbert yielded his place at the end of 1835 to Park Benjamin, who made an unsuccessful effort to make a tri-city publication of the *American* through the interest of Boston and Philadelphia publishers. Each number now had an engraved plate, and special interest articles on the new West, the Indians, Latin America, German literature, and the American Lyceum. In its last year or two the magazine became more a political review, and its Whig tendencies were emphasized by the contributions of Horace Greeley. In 1838 its subscription list was turned over to Greeley's *New-Yorker.*

[5.] *Frank Leslie's Popular Monthly* (see FRANK LESLIE) was begun in New York in January, 1876, as a $2.50 general magazine in competition with the $4 monthlies. Its contributors included Joaquin Miller, Amelia E. Barr, Harriet Prescott Spofford, and Brander Matthews. Mrs. Frank Leslie, who managed the magazine after her husband's death in 1880, leased it to others in 1895, but had to take it back after three years of decline; she changed format, lowered the price to ten cents, and made it a success again. ELLERY SEDGWICK, formerly of the *Youth's Companion* and later of the *Atlantic Monthly,* brought current public affairs into *Leslie's Magazine,* as it came to be called in 1904, and recruited such contributors as Stephen Crane, Frank R. Stockton, and Stewart Edward White. Ellis Parker Butler's *Pigs is Pigs* was a hit of 1905. After 1906 the magazine was taken over by a staff seceding from *McClure's,* headed by

JOHN S. PHILLIPS as publisher and including Ida M. Tarbell, Lincoln Steffens, Ray Stannard Baker, Finley Peter Dunne, and William Allen White. The monthly, renamed the *American Magazine,* stressed serious MUCKRAKING and human-interest articles and sketches. The Crowell-Collier Publishing Company bought the *American* in 1915 and made John M. Siddall editor, and the magazine began to stress "success stories," S. S. Van Dine's detective stories, and Clarence Budington Kelland's endless "Scattergood Baines" serials. The 2,500,000 circulation which the magazine reached in the 1920's did not attract advertisers, who were disinclined to pay high rates for so generalized a mass medium, and after some floundering in policy the *American Magazine* was discontinued by the Crowell-Collier Company in 1956.

American Memoir (1947), reminiscences by HENRY SEIDEL CANBY. In 1934 Canby published *The Age of Confidence,* reminiscences of his early years; and in 1936, *Alma Mater,* memoirs of Yale. *American Memoir* includes the earlier volumes, in somewhat different form, and adds to them a section called *Brief Golden Age.* This section gives a view of the literary life in New York following World War I. The mellow but keen observations in *American Memoir* are those of an intelligent defender of the old order.

American Men of Letters Series. A series of biographies of famous American authors published in the late 1870's by Houghton Mifflin Co., under the editorship of CHARLES DUDLEY WARNER. It was revived in 1948 by William Sloane Associates.

American Mercury, The. William D'Alton Mann founded the SMART SET (1900–1930) as a monthly magazine of general literature with much the same kind of "snob appeal" that characterized his more scandalous weekly, *Town Topics* (1879–1937). The *Smart Set* was distinguished under later ownerships by the work of a number of brilliant writers. In 1908 HENRY L. MENCKEN became its book-review editor, and the next year GEORGE JEAN NATHAN its theater editor. When Nathan and Mencken became editors and part-owners in 1914, they introduced such contributors as F. Scott Fitzgerald, Maxwell Anderson, Eugene O'Neill, and Ruth Suckow, and supplied their own pungent social, literary, and dramatic criticism. By 1923 Mencken and Nathan had tired of the *Smart Set,* and readily accepted Alfred A. Knopf's offer to provide them a more impressive and dignified forum in a new monthly in which they would have a one-third interest as working editors. Thus the *American Mercury* was founded in 1924. Nathan retired from his coeditorship after one year, but remained five years longer as a departmental editor. In the new magazine Mencken found it "an agreeable duty to track down some of the worst nonsense prevailing and do execution upon it." Some of the *Mercury*'s departments were continued from the *Smart Set,* such as the always entertaining "Americana," an olio of current absurdities in popular culture and cults, arranged geographically by states. But not all of the *Mercury* was negative; there were able articles on folk literature, anthropology, the American Negro, newspapers, major literary figures, philology (with emphasis on American usages), picturesque personalities and events, and unswept corners of American history. Among contributors were Margaret Mead, Lewis Mumford, Louis Adamic, William E. Dodd, and Fred Lewis Pattee. Notable writers of fiction were Sinclair Lewis, James Stevens, and William Faulkner; among the poets were Vachel Lindsay, Edgar Lee Masters, Carl Sandburg, Countee Cullen, James Weldon Johnson, and George Sterling. The beginning of the depression of the 1930's coincided with a recession in Mencken's popularity, and he retired in 1933. Lawrence E. Spivak came into control for the next fifteen years, and the magazine soon became a pocket-size miscellany with strongly conservative tendencies in politics and economics. The price was cut from 50 to 25 cents, and the circulation (never much over 60,000 under Mencken) increased. After the Spivak regime, the magazine had its ups and downs with politics and sex, and eventually became a strong rightist organ of limited circulation owned by the oil and munitions millionaire, J. Russell Maguire.

American Myths and Legends (1903), by Charles M. Skinner (1852–1907). In this all sections of the country are covered, and a great variety of traditional tales is included.

American Note-Books (1868; ed. Randall Stewart, 1932), by NATHANIEL HAWTHORNE, notes on stories, reflections and maxims, observations of nature and life. From one of the "notes," given him freely by Hawthorne, Henry Wadsworth Longfellow obtained the idea of EVANGELINE.

American Notes for General Circulation (1842), Charles Dickens' account of his tour of the United States in 1842. He visited New York and Boston, got as far west as St. Louis, confined himself to objective description for the most part, but was so severe at times on American manners and so scathing on the subject of American piracy of English books that his book was most unfavorably received in the United States. Oliver Elton remarks that *American Notes* prepared readers for "the ghastly but specious caricature of American manners in MARTIN CHUZZLEWIT."

American Portraits, 1875–1900 (1920), biographical sketches by GAMALIEL BRADFORD. Bradford announced his intention of treating the whole of American history in a series of *psychographs*, interpretative portraits concerned with the souls of his subjects, "with their work only as their souls are illustrated in it." This volume discusses Mark Twain, Henry Adams, Sidney Lanier, James McNeill Whistler, James G. Blaine, Grover Cleveland, Henry James, and Joseph Jefferson. Bradford made many acute analyses, often epigrammatically expressed. A series of similar volumes followed.

American Primer (1904), notes by WALT WHITMAN. Among the ideas advocated by Whitman was that America should be cleared of all names smacking of Europe, with an American vocabulary enriched by many words not then in the dictionaries.

American Prose Masters (1909), by WILLIAM C. BROWNELL. These thoughtfully-written essays deal with Cooper, Hawthorne, Emerson, Poe, Lowell, and Henry James.

American Revolution, the. Literature written during the American Revolution was almost without exception political. It played on patriot pride, ridiculed the enemy at home and abroad, or addressed itself in sober argument to the task of persuasion. No masterworks appeared, except the DECLARATION OF INDEPENDENCE, its authorship probably multiple and still disputed; but much of the writing of this period is remembered with pride because it provided substantial ideological foundations on which later generations have built. It was a time for plain speaking and the reduction of thought to essentials; literary style was often sacrificed to clear simplicity which guaranteed understanding.

As the war years approached, men with literary aspirations put them aside for practical application of their talents to current events. By 1776 patriots like WILLIAM LIVINGSTON, who was to become wartime governor of New Jersey, and who as a younger man had written polite prose and verse in the manner of Pope and the London essayists, turned to the rough and tumble wrangling of pamphlet warfare. In Philadelphia the little literary group which, under the leadership of the Reverend WILLIAM SMITH, provost of the college there, had made that city merry with songs and masques and even serious drama written by FRANCIS HOPKINSON, NATHANIEL EVANS, THOMAS GODFREY, Thomas Coombe, and others, was dispersed by death or divided loyalties. Of those prominent among them only Hopkinson remained, to create in prose A PRETTY STORY (1774) and in verse THE BATTLE OF THE KEGS (1777), small, bright, patriotic pieces which have been remembered more affectionately than Hopkinson's serious or more heavily satirical contributions to patriotic newspapers.

PHILIP FRENEAU and HUGH HENRY BRACKENRIDGE, recently graduated from Princeton, both turned from purely literary ambition to become ardent propagandists. TIMOTHY DWIGHT and JOEL BARLOW, from Yale, shelved plans for epic poems in order to dedicate their talents to war. Young ALEXANDER HAMILTON left college to become a pamphleteer, then a soldier. BENJAMIN FRANKLIN, who had been writing for fifty years and who in 1771 had begun quietly to record his AUTOBIOGRAPHY, proved his pen was still sharp in such essays as EDICT BY THE KING OF PRUSSIA (1773) and "Rules by Which a Great Empire Might Be Reduced to a Small One" (1773). In Connecticut JOHN TRUMBULL, whose wit had been directed against collegiate follies in *The Progress of Dulness* (1772–73), pointed it now toward Tories and mob-directed rebels in the deft octosyllables of M'FINGAL (1772–82), which became, perhaps after the ubiquitous YANKEE DOODLE (*ca.* 1778), the most popular native poem of its time.

Most consistently active among the verse-makers was Freneau, remembered with some justification as "the poet of the American Revolution." Between 1775 and 1783 he anathematized the British or celebrated patriot triumphs in scores of partisan rhymes, many of which were collected after the war in his *Poems* (1786). Best remembered among them are THE HOUSE OF NIGHT (1779), which speaks less of war than of turmoil within the poet's mind; THE BRITISH PRISON-SHIP (1781), a long hate-filled diatribe based on its author's own experience as a captive; and "To the Memory of the Brave Americans" (1781). In "The Political Balance" (1782) Freneau hurls ridicule against defeated redcoats in anapestic lines which show better control of meter and imagery than of his uneven temper. When the war was over, Freneau turned to poetry of a less raucous kind, producing such deft and distinctive lyrics as THE WILD HONEY SUCKLE (1786) and "Neversink" (1791), until caught up again by politics as an ardent but ultimately disillusioned republican.

Freneau's wartime prose, which was never completely collected although much of it was reprinted in his *Miscellaneous Works* (1788), is less adroit and forceful than his verse. More persuasive in his prose was the urbane JOHN DICKINSON, who, until his hesitation in 1776 over the question of whether complete independence was really desirable, seemed luminously to sum up colonial grievances in such writings as LETTERS FROM A PENNSYLVANIA FARMER (1768). After the Declaration of Independence, THOMAS PAINE's pamphlet signed COMMON SENSE (1776) and the sixteen issues of *The Crisis* (1776–83) (see THE AMERICAN CRISIS) caught and held public attention. Cogent yet passionate, they expressed confidence that in those times when men's souls were tried, American freemen would prevail, aided by divine power, but also by the resolute strength of their arms and convictions. Only in later years, with THE RIGHTS OF MAN (1791–92) and THE AGE OF REASON (1794–95), did Paine, even more than Freneau, seem to conservative countrymen to carry notions of human freedom to extremes. These two voices rose, often stridently, above the clamor of other men who from press or pulpit pelted laggard neighbors or haughty foes with emotion-packed phrases. Hundreds of others contributed squibs, verses, and columns of polemic, satirical, sincere, and enthusiastic prose; but, though their cumulative influence was large, they are now forgotten. They wrote, someone has said, wisely but not often well.

The most polished and continuingly attractive prose came from the pen of HECTOR ST. JEAN DE CRÈVECŒUR, a French settler in upper New York, an observant noncombatant who was suspected and harried by both sides. During the last year of the war he made his way to London, where he published LETTERS FROM AN AMERICAN FARMER (1782), a work later translated and expanded in French. It presented idyllic descriptions but also forthright, realistic accounts of the customs and labors and pleasures of life on the American frontier, and posed and answered the tantalizing question: "What then is the American, this strange man?" More than a century later further materials, earlier suppressed by Crèvecœur or his publisher, were discovered and printed as *Sketches of Eighteenth Century America* (1925). Here tales of privation were told, of marauding attacks by patriots and loyalists alike, of house burnings and terror and slaughter, similar to that revealed in the letters of ANN ELIZA BLEECKER in her *Posthumous Works* (1792), or in Hilliard d'Auberteuil's *Mis Mac Rea* (1784).

Accounts of atrocities and captivity like Freneau's *The British Prison-Ship* played a quickening role in sustaining patriot resolution. A NARRATIVE OF COLONEL ETHAN ALLAN'S CAPTIVITY (1779), which Melville was later to use in ISRAEL POTTER, went through many hastily printed editions. *A Narrative of the Captivity and Treatment of John Dodge by the English at Detroit* (1779) and *The Old Jersey Captive* (1781) realistically reinforced contemporary convictions of the cruel barbarism of the enemy. Though not printed until 1857, the autobiographical *Narrative of the Capture of Henry Laurens, of His Confinement in the Tower of London, and So Forth, 1780, 1781, 1782*, contains, it has been said, an "unsurpassed embodiment of the proudest, finest, wittiest, most efficient, and most chivalrous Americanism" of that time. Colonials who chose the other side, daring patriot wrath by remaining loyal to England, endured their share of hardship more silently, except in letters and journals and petitions for reimbursement submitted to the Parliament in London, many of which are heart-rending and authentic personal documents, not intended as literature.

Loyalist poets and propagandists, however, were not silent. Joseph Stansbury, socially prominent in Philadelphia, filled the newspapers of that city with witty verse and playful, satirical prose until shipped off to Nova Scotia for the duration. JONATHAN ODELL, a clergyman from New Jersey, became a chaplain in the British army, under the protection of which in occupied New York he peppered his patriot neighbors with polished verses done after the satirical model of Pope, Dryden, and Juvenal. After Freneau's, his was the clearest poetic voice of those times. His *The Congratulation* (1779) and *The American Times* (1780) speak valiantly of the colonial rebellion as an uprising of unthinking men against tradition and authority. SAMUEL PETERS, an Anglican clergyman from New England who fled from the wrath of his patriot countrymen, published in London a grotesquely fabricated *General History of Connecticut* (1781), which intended to brand all Yankees as bland hypocrites, misguided in morality and politics. The former colonial governor of Massachusetts, THOMAS HUTCHINSON, a man of greater breadth and probity, completed in England the third volume of his monumental *History of the Colony and Province of Massachusetts Bay* (1764–1828).

Patriot historians were also active. William Henry Drayton, a member of the Continental Congress from South Carolina, worked in Charleston and Philadelphia over his *Memoirs of the American Revolution* (1821), printed long after his death; and DAVID RAMSAY, also of Charleston, collected materials there for his later *History of the War in South Carolina* (1791). MERCY OTIS WARREN, better remembered for her patriotic dramas, who as a woman could not participate in war, spent these years gathering materials for her *History of the Rise, Progress and Termination of the American Revolution* (1805). Opposed to conflict of any kind, Quaker Robert Proud spent the war-torn years writing his precise and ponderous *History of Pennsylvania* (1797).

Several patriot authors turned their hand to drama (see DRAMA IN THE U.S.), most of it meant to be read as propaganda or to be played by amateur groups as ardent as they. Mercy Otis Warren in Massachusetts wrote THE ADULATEUR (1773), described as "A Tragedy, as it is now Acted in Upper Servia," but which was in reality a satire directed against Tory activity in Boston. Like her later THE GROUP (1775), it is more interesting for what it reveals of dissension among colonials than for its excellence as literature. Most ambitious of the patriot dramas was THE FALL OF BRITISH TYRANNY (1776), usually ascribed to John (or Joseph) Leacock of Philadelphia. A tragicomedy in five acts, in which farce and melodrama are relieved by pastoral interludes in which shepherds comment innocently on passing events, it vigorously details supposed evil intentions abroad and braveries at home. Its final scene introduces General Washington in his first appearance as a character on the stage.

Bombastic but better were the two short plays in verse written by HUGH HENRY BRACKENRIDGE for production by students in his Maryland academy. THE BATTLE OF BUNKERS HILL (1776) celebrates the courage of patriot volunteers; *The Death of General Montgomery* (1777) denounces the cowardice and treachery of the enemy. Attributed to Thomas Paine is *A Dialogue between the Ghost of General Montgomery, Just Arrived from the Elysian Fields, and an American Delegate in a Wood near Philadelphia* (1776), which is hardly dramatic at all, but an argument cogently and forcefully reasoned. Best plotted and most finished of the dramas of these times was THE PATRIOTS (1776), by Colonel Robert Munford of Virginia, who found subjects for quiet satire among both patriots and loyalists. *The Motley Assembly* (1779), which reviles social climbing collaborators, is sometimes attributed to Mrs. Warren, but it is a coarse, indignant, slapstick affair, hardly the kind to be expected of a lady from Boston.

Tories turned to drama also. The anonymous *A Dialogue Between a Southern Delegate and His Spouse on His Return from the Grand Continental Congress* (1774) is slight but amusing: how much better, it suggests, would affairs have turned out if women had been allowed to manage them. JONATHAN SEWALL, once attorney-general of Massachusetts, wrote a sharp criticism of his countrymen in *The Americans Roused in a Cure for the Spleen* (1775), which pretended to record "the substance of a conversation on the times over a friendly tankard and a pipe" between colonials met in a tavern; the patriots among them were bumpkins of little sense or knowledge, while the loyalists included better men, like the parson and the justice of the peace. After General Burgoyne's farce, THE BLOCKADE (1776), was performed by British troops in Boston, it was countered by a scurrilous patriot reply called *The Blockheads* (1776), another topical satire sometimes said (though probably wrongly) to have been written by Mrs. Warren. Other British plays were performed, perhaps written or adapted for jubilant occasions, by officers of His Majesty's army stationed in New York or Boston. Among them was another *The Blockheads*, an opera in two acts, performed and printed in the former city, probably late in the war, and republished in London in 1782. But most writers, patriot or Tory or among the British occupation forces, were busy with other things besides drama. Many, like Freneau, who left unfinished "The Spy," a play based on the capture of Major André, must have started to write or wanted to write dialogues or dramatic sketches to celebrate these exciting, liberating times. College students, like John Smith of Dartmouth, who produced "Dialogue between an Englishman and an Indian" (1779), tried their hands hurriedly, but then quickly turned to other things.

Almost all the writing done in America during the war years was copied or adapted, sometimes parodied, from English models. Much of it was brief, written for an occasion, hurriedly or in the heat of controversy. Colonel DAVID HUMPHREYS, an aide-de-camp to General Washington, composed ponderous poems in praise of patriot victories. JOHN PARKE, also a patriot officer, composed odes about battles and American heroes which were collected after the war as *The Lyric Works of Horace, Translated into English Verse* (1786). James McClurg, a physician and collegemate of Thomas Jefferson, wrote martial songs, as did ST. GEORGE TUCKER of Williamsburg and BENJAMIN YOUNG PRIME, long known as a minor part-time poet in New York. But few of their songs have survived, nor have the battle songs and hymns of Joel Barlow and Timothy Dwight, who wrote with no less patriotic fervor.

It might almost be said that not until after the war did the literature of the American Revolution begin to appear. Then Freneau was able to collect his poems, Parke, his *Lyric Works,* and Humphreys, volume after volume of patriotic lines. Then Dwight could complete his *The Conquest of Canaan* (1785), a Biblical epic which, in spite of its author's protests, most readers thought was about Washington emblemized as Joshua, who led loyal hosts to the promised land of freedom. Joel Barlow completed and published *The Vision of Columbus* (1787), which stumbled earnestly through versified expectations of the new country's great future. Then GEORGE WASHINGTON began to emerge as a national hero in plays, poems, novels, and biographies, to reign supreme for seventy-five years, until Abraham Lincoln took his place. MASON LOCKE WEEMS, in his *Life of Washington* (1800), fixed forever the story of young George and the cherry tree, an incident which lasts longer than any detailed in the better lives by John Marshall (1804–07), James Kirke Paulding (1835), or Washington Irving (1855–59).

In drama, PETER MARKOE celebrated Washington in *The Patriot Chief* (1784). WILLIAM DUNLAP in his tragedy of *André* (1789) provided a prominent role for the former commander. But of the scores of plays which have been written about Washington (see VALLEY FORGE) or the American Revolution, none really survives. Nor have poems on these subjects been conspicuously successful. Almost every native poet, from Bryant through Holmes and Lowell to Stephen Vincent Benét, has touched on the subject, but perhaps only RALPH WALDO EMERSON's "Concord Hymn" (1837), which speaks of the "rude bridge which arched the flood" and the "shot heard round the world," convincingly combines patriotism and poetry.

In fiction, however, the situation has been quite different. Hundreds of novels and tales have been written about the Revolutionary conflict. Perhaps best known of them are James Fenimore Cooper's THE SPY (1821) and Cooper's tales of maritime adventures, such as THE PILOT (1823) and THE RED ROVER (1827). William Gilmore Simms' seven Revolutionary novels include THE PARTISAN (1834), *Woodcraft* (1853), and *The Forayers* (1855). John Pendleton Kennedy wrote of skirmishes on the Southern frontier in HORSE-SHOE ROBINSON (1835); Lydia Maria Child combined war and romance in *The Rebels* (1825), as did Catherine M. Sedgwick in *The Linwoods* (1835), JAMES KIRKE PAULDING's *The Old Continental* (1846) may seem dull beside Herman Melville's ISRAEL POTTER (1855), which tells of battles at sea and captivity on land, but both will admit precedence to S. Weir Mitchell's HUGH WYNNE, FREE QUAKER (1897), which has been called the best novel of the American Revolution, or to SARAH ORNE JEWETT's *The Tory Lover* (1901), which combines sentiment with controlled sensibility. Most popular of recent novels of the Revolution are Kenneth Roberts' ARUNDEL (1930), RABBLE IN ARMS (1933), and OLIVER WISWELL (1940); Walter D. Edmonds' DRUMS ALONG THE MOHAWK (1936); Inglis Fletcher's several novels, from *Raleigh's Eden* (1940) to *Roanoke Hun-*

dred (1948); and HOWARD FAST's *The Unvanquished* (1943).

Studies of the literature of the Revolution include: William Alfred Bryan, *George Washington in American Literature* (1952); Bruce Ingham Granger, *Political Satire in the American Revolution* (1960); Ernest E. Leisy, *The American Historical Novel* (1950); William Bradley Otis, *American Verse, 1625–1807; A History* (1909); Arthur Hobson Quinn, *A History of the American Drama from the Beginning to the Civil War* (1944); MOSES COIT TYLER, *The Literary History of the American Revolution* (1897).

LEWIS LEARY

American Rhythm, The (1923). See MARY AUSTIN.

American Scene, The (1907), a travel book and re-examination of the United States by HENRY JAMES. The volume is mainly a description of life in Saratoga, Newport, and other important American social and cultural centers, remembered as they were in the 1870's and 1880's and re-analyzed as James saw them again in 1904. James ignored the Far West, the Middle West, and the Deep South, although he visited Baltimore, Washington, Charleston, and Florida. Four chapters are devoted to New York, including one on "The Bowery and Thereabouts." In his introduction to the edition published in 1946, W. H. Auden argues that "the best way to approach this book is as a prose poem of the first order. . . . It is no more a guidebook than the *Ode to a Nightingale* is an ornithological essay." James often speaks scathingly of what Americans have done to America.

American Scholar, The (Aug. 31, 1837), an address by RALPH WALDO EMERSON delivered before the Phi Beta Kappa Society of Harvard. It was published separately in 1837, and reprinted in *Nature, Addresses, and Lectures* (1849). Oliver Wendell Holmes called it "our intellectual Declaration of Independence," although it should be noted that William Cullen Bryant, writing a critique of American literature in the *North American Review*, had anticipated Emerson's ideas by nineteen years. Emerson exhorted his listeners, and America generally, to mental independence and self-confidence. He called on scholars to "defer never to the popular cry" and "to cheer, to raise, and to guide men by showing them facts amidst appearances." The lecture established him at once as a leader of thought in New England.

American Songbag, The (1927), a collection of folk songs and ballads made by CARL SANDBURG. In tours of the country Sandburg himself has sung many of these songs, accompanying them on his banjo or guitar. A number of them have been recorded by him for the phonograph; perhaps the best-known is "The Boll-Weevil."

American Speller, The (1783), by NOAH WEBSTER. This famous textbook originally formed part of Webster's GRAMMATICAL INSTITUTE OF THE ENGLISH LANGUAGE, COMPRISING AN EASY, CONCISE, AND SYSTEMATIC METHOD OF

EDUCATION DESIGNED FOR THE USE OF ENGLISH SCHOOLS IN AMERICA. This consisted of three parts: a spelling book, a grammar, and a reader, in all of which Webster emphasized his patriotic as well as educational ideas. The speller soon took on an independent existence, and was the first American schoolbook. It continued in use throughout the 19th and into the 20th century, reaching a sale ultimately of more than 75,000,-000 copies. The book helped to standardize American spelling and pronunciation.

American Spirit, The (1942), a treatise by CHARLES A. and MARY BEARD. See THE RISE OF AMERICAN CIVILIZATION.

American Tragedy, An (1925), a novel by THEODORE DREISER. Based on a real case, that of Chester Gillette, who in July, 1906, murdered Grace Brown at Big Moose Lake in the Adirondacks, the book shows Dreiser sometimes following the "facts," at other moments transcending them in an interpretation of his own. CLYDE GRIFFITHS' boyhood reproduces some of the details of Dreiser's own earlier years.

Clyde revolts against the piety and poverty of his family life in a western city; he becomes a bellboy in a luxurious hotel, is involved in an automobile accident, and takes to flight; a distant relative, owner of a collar factory in upper New York State, gives him employment and hope for advancement. But Clyde's weak nature pulls him down. He seduces one of the working girls, then falls in love with a young woman in a higher social set. To save himself he plans to murder the working girl, who has now become pregnant. What he plans comes true by accident when a sudden lurch of the boat throws Roberta Alden into the water and she drowns. Clyde is accused of murder, and Dreiser's best pages describe his trial, conviction, and execution. Clyde is portrayed as a weakling, but Dreiser rather blames society and the industrial system for corrupting persons like Clyde.

The publication of *An American Tragedy* aroused threats of censorship, but these ultimately failed. The novel was dramatized by Patrick Kearney in 1926, again in 1936 by Erwin Piscator and Lena Goldschmidt in a version called *The Case of Clyde Griffiths;* movie versions were made in 1931 and 1951. Charles Samuels, in *Death Was the Bridegroom* (1955), retold the factual story of Chester Gillette.

America's Coming of Age (1915), by VAN WYCK BROOKS. An early and optimistic statement by Brooks, this book affirmed American cultural strength and heralded the arrival of a new generation of writers.

America's Lost Plays (1940–41), edited by BARRETT H. CLARK (1890–1953). Many dramas of the 18th and 19th centuries remain in manuscript; Clark, a noted drama critic, undertook to make twenty of them available in print.

America the Beautiful (1895; rev., 1904, 1911), by KATHARINE LEE BATES. The poem has been set to music many times, but the tune with which it is most frequently associated is *Materna,* by SAMUEL A. WARD. It has often been suggested that the poem should replace *The Star-Spangled Banner* as the national anthem.

Amerika (1927; English translation, 1938), a fragment of a novel by Franz Kafka (1883–1924). One of Kafka's last works, this story relates a fantastic, often comic adventure in America, a land Kafka had never seen. It is probably Kafka's least bitter piece of writing. It ends with the hero joining the company of "The Great Oklahoma Nature Theater," which Kafka apparently intended as a symbolic structure of universal acceptance. Throughout the novel, which developed from a short story called *The Stoker,* an atmosphere of dream-fantasy prevails, yet something of the spirit of America has been caught.

Amerindian prose and poetry. American Indian literature, like all other literature, has to be viewed from two angles if we wish to understand its essential character. First, we must consider its cultural function; second, we must analyze the structure both of poetic expression and narrative style.

The functional significance of Amerindian literature may be placed above its structural aspects. To the American Indian, song and story is inextricably interwoven with economic, social, and religio-ritual phenomena. Therefore, his literature cannot be understood outside the cultural whole.

Indian song and story almost always serve a purpose; they are thoroughly pragmatic. A song is sung, a prayer recited, a spell uttered, a mythical story related. Their purposes may be to keep the universe in motion; to promote the fertility of man, field, and animal; to restore the clan member to health and to slay the enemy; or to ward off evil and overcome death. In its broadest sense song and myth are the American Indian's tools for causing and preserving life.

The functional need of song is beautifully expressed in a Navaho myth recorded by WASHINGTON MATTHEWS. According to this legend, song was created out of the weeping of two lonely children who were forsaken not only by their own kin but by the very gods themselves. The children were sick and suffered. But none of the deities wanted to work a cure on them because the children were so poor and wretched that they owned nothing to sacrifice to the demanding gods. Thus, the legend has it, the children walked in sadness, and as they walked they wept, and their weeping turned into singing. "They cried to music and they turned their thoughts to song." This the Holy Ones heard. They marveled; they were pleased. They decided to help the children in their need, for song seemed to them more precious a sacrifice than feathers of the bluebird or long strings of turquoise beads. Ever since, song has been considered the most highly esteemed sacrifice which man in distress may offer to his gods.

Among the Fox of the Plains we find the same concept of song as a life-preserving means. In the traditions of these people Owl, the guardian of the tribe, is reported as having admonished his "children": "Well, now I shall tell you about this which we sing. As we sing the manitou hears us. The manitou will not fail to hear us. It is just as if we were singing in the manitou's dwelling. . . . We are not singing sportive songs. It is as if we were weeping, asking for life. . . ."

Among some tribes of the Northwest Coast the creation myth is ceremonially related at the memorial festival for the dead. The very act of recital is an act of restoration and has magical-functional significance: the relation of the origin myth in the very face of death is firmly believed to undo death and to restore the life of the group to its former state of wholeness.

Many other examples could be assembled to prove still more poignantly that the American Indian's literature is a religio-economic necessity.

Language and world view influence each other. The aborigine of North America believes in the creative power of the word. He is firmly convinced that he may influence his environment by describing it in terms of growth, germination, and unfolding. The mind of the inhabitant of desert and steppe naturally dwells upon clouds and rain with greatest intensity. And as it is a law pertaining to all magical practices that the more detailed the description, the more satisfying the outcome, one may expect in the vocabulary of such a people delicate nuances concerning climatological factors. Thus the Pueblo people of the Southwest discriminate between various forms of rain: fine and heavy, female and male, misty and torrential. For the ZUÑI INDIANS, poetry serves first and foremost an economic end: the growth of corn and beans largely depends on the proper handling of the *word*. It is not surprising, therefore, that Zuñi, according to Ruth Bunzel, is a poetical language per se, exceptionally rich in sensual expressions:

And yonder, wherever the roads of the rain-
     makers come forth,
Torrents will rush forth,
Silt will rush forth,
Mountains will be washed out . . .
Yonder all the mossy mountains will drip with
     water.
The clay-lined hollows of our earth-mother
Will overflow with water.
Desiring that it should be thus,
I send forth my prayer.

There is a hypnotic quality radiating from the words of this formulalike prayer. Indeed, most of the songs and prayers of the American Indian are characterized by a more or less subtle suggestiveness which intends to make nature work in the desired direction.

The magic-prophetic function of language is expressed still more strikingly in the literature of the NAVAHO Indians, shepherds of the northern deserts of New Mexico and Arizona. The following healing incantation, recorded by the present writer during a year's stay on the Navaho Reservation, illustrates well the endeavor to influence the future by way of the word:

Chief of all mountains . . .
You will make me well today.
My soles you will restore today.
My legs you will restore today.
My knee joints you will restore today.
My body you will restore today.
My mind you will restore today.
This day you will make me well.
This day you will give me power.
That which is making me sick will be taken
     away from me.

The roots of literature seem to be revealed with this archaic incantation. The word originally was used like any other tool: it was meant to shape, to influence, to bring forth, to attack, and to defend.

The word heals and restores. The chief aim of the *Midé*—the native religion of the Chippewa —was to secure health and long life to its adherents, and elaborate ceremonies and initiations were held during spring. Each initiate had his own set of songs, some of which he had composed himself and others which he had purchased for considerable sums of money or for equal values of goods. The initiates, we are told, had to go through eight degrees, which means through a succession of symbolic deaths and resurrections. The following song is a song a neophyte receives while he is passing through a painful experience of ceremonial dying:

You will recover; you will walk again.
It is I who say it; my power is great.
Through our white shell
I will enable you to walk again.

And as the initiate revives, the words of this song will forever retain their healing power.

The ESKIMO, well aware of the psychotherapeutic qualities inherent in the word, have developed an interesting literary form, the contest of the juridical drum song. Unvented anger and fixed resentment that find no egress whatsoever are capable of eating up a man's soul, step by step, very slowly and very painfully. The Iglulik Eskimo, consumed by an uncontrollable hatred toward a fellow being, will not reach for a weapon. He will sharpen another tool: the word. In the contest song he will challenge his enemy and endeavor to present him in a ridiculous light, making him the laughingstock of the assembled community. Sneers hiss like sharp arrows to and fro. Weaknesses and faults are uncovered with wit and laughter. Sometimes the opponents give vent to their anger in a most poetical form, drumming and singing against each other until all anger is evaporated and peace has been established among the enemies. Which proves again that song, at least with the American Indian, hardly exists as a pure art form. It always serves an end.

It is customary to divide the folk tales of the American Indian into sacred myths, which are related with a certain amount of ritual elaboration, and the more or less casually recited secular narratives with which the aborigine, presumably, does not associate any ceremonial significance. Experience in the field convinces one that not all tribes draw such a sharp line of demarcation. It is true that certain sacred narratives may be told only during wintertime, when the snakes are underground and the thunder asleep; other stories may be related only at the opening of the hunting season; and again others, only at the time when the seed of the corn in about to unfold. However, with many Indian groups the narration of almost any story, even if anecdotal or slightly obscene, is believed to exert a life-increasing influence on individual and group.

Because the American Indian considers song an integral and indispensable part of the cultural pattern, without which the gods would not give aid or the earth produce, the maker of songs is one of the most highly esteemed members of the group.

Since the proper use of the word, along with music and dance, has direct influence on the economic weal of the group, the status of its guardian is high economically as well as socially. The individual singer, the shaman, and the priest are likely to accumulate wealth. The man who does not own a single song by which to influence the weather, or game, or the growth of the crops is socially and economically insecure. Beyond this purely economic relationship the ownership of song and stories provides a vast network of social and supernatural securities in which the aborigine may exist. CLYDE KLUCKHOHN points out that recital of or reference to the myths of the past reaffirms the solidarity of the whole social system. "Knowing a good story," a Navaho informant told him, "will protect your home and children and property. A myth is just like a big stone foundation." This attitude toward the protecting function of the word is characteristic not only of the Navaho Indians but of all other Indian tribes.

Certain types of Indian tales are distributed all over the continent, as for instance stories dealing with the world in its various stages of evolution; myths explaining the origin of ceremonies; hero tales; trickster cycles; stories of journeys to the other world; and animal tales. Over and above continent-wide similarities of themes there are regional variations of significance.

The distinctive feature of American Indian mythology is its wide range of literary forms. Myth, legend, anecdote, and novelette often overlap and cannot be neatly classified. Or a given theme may be treated as a witty anecdote by one tribe (the Wintu of California, for instance), as an epic myth (by the Navaho), or as a piece of fiction (among the PAWNEE). Thematically, American Indian mythology stands out through its complex concept of the culture hero, who may be everything—god and man, animal and monster, benefactor and trickster—and who is as often a threat to man as he is his redeemer. In the eyes of the Indian there is nothing ever quite perfect, and nothing ever quite evil, but good may come out of evil if

only it is harnessed with a deft hand. The Indian is a realist.

Unfortunately, a thorough study of the literary style of aboriginal verse and prose has not yet been attempted. The fact that research can be carried on only through the medium of translations has not been conducive to such an undertaking. However, as more and more investigations into aboriginal culture and literature are taken up by academically trained Indians, who are naturally the best equipped to do so, it is to be hoped that such a conclusive analysis will be available in the not-too-distant future.

However, there is evidence that American Indian languages can be rendered in such a way that conclusions with reference to style and pattern may, with restraint and caution, be drawn even from translations.

A fundamental trait of poetic style is rhythmic repetition of identical or alternating units. Doubtless, rhythm is primarily a physical necessity, and corresponds to the contraction and expansion of the respiratory organs, the pulsating of the blood, the beating of the heart. But rhythmic expression also answers the elementary psychic need of organization, especially that of time. The various literary devices of repetition—preludes, refrains, burdens, iteration of motives or phrases in part or in whole—are readily reproduced in every language.

The exciting or the soothing effect of regulated motion has consciously been utilized by the American Indian in many of his verbal compositions. The following sacred song of the OSAGE, as translated by FRANCIS LAFLESCHE, is a good example of a kind of complicated repetition which may be called syncopated parallelism:

> At this place he shall appear,
> He shall appear,
> The black bird,
> The Black Hawk shall appear.

In a second verse the same words are repeated for the Red Hawk. In these lines the rhythm of the endlessly recurrent movements of the coming and going of day and night (symbolized by the Red and the Black Hawk) are well expressed by the rhythm of a fine verbal pattern.

The Navaho are unexcelled masters in the use of syncopated rhythmical movements. The following verse, though unassuming in itself, is built up with the precision of a musical motif:

> I came to the holy dwelling,
> To the black mountain
> I came.
> Like rays in the distance
> I saw the male rain.
> The power of the rain
> I saw it.

The use of rhyme is unknown to the American Indian poet. Instead of attempting to achieve an external balance through the regular recurrence of sounds, he has become a master in producing an internal balance of his cadences through the infinite echoing and re-echoing of repeated phrases.

The various methods of balance, parallel phrasing, and incremental repetition are also employed in many of the prose compositions of the American Indian. In the recital of mythical stories repetitions are utilized for magical and organization purposes. In the art of oratory, repetitions are used mainly for the sake of emphasis. How subtly this device may be employed is shown in the following fragment of an oration by a Crow warrior about to enter the warpath with the express desire to die:

"You above, if there be one who knows what goes on, repay me today for the distress I have suffered. The One Who causes things, Whoever he may be, I have had now my fill of life. Grant me death. My sorrows are overabundant. Though children are timid, they die harsh deaths. I do not wish to live long, my sorrows would be overabundant; I do not want it."

Aboriginal prose as well as poetry is, more often than not, extremely direct in expression.

A Hidatsa war song as recorded by FRANCES DENSMORE may be cited here as an example of the conciseness so characteristic of Amerindian poetry.

> If that is the enemy
> I will go.
> Here I am.

Oratorical economy marks the following address to a deceased person, a Crow text as recorded by ROBERT H. LOWIE:

"You are going. A good land reach. All Indians see, good-looking ones. Do not return. This not good land is. It is old. It is good for you to go."

Contrary to popular opinion, the Indian uses figures of speech sparingly. But when the aboriginal poet employs metaphor or simile, he does it with striking accuracy; and not infrequently his comparisons call forth startling associations. His literary strength, however, should not be sought in his use of comparison or contrast but in the direct statement, as, for instance, in the following song of the Yuma:

> The little blackbirds
> Are singing this song
> As they dance
> Around the four corners of the sky.

To the Indian, as far as I know, poetry cannot be dissociated from music. In fact, poetry, music, and dance form an inseparable unit among most of the aboriginal groups in North America.

Furthermore, few songs are complete in themselves. Often they present the psychological climax of a mythical tale in fixed formal words; as often, they are mere mnemonic summaries of events which have to be explained in a story either before or after the song.

Proverb and riddle are unknown to the American Indian.

Though it is believed by authorities that epic poetry remained limited to Europe and central Asia, a tendency toward epic elaboration may be perceived in the mythic cycles of some tribes, as for instance, the Delaware, the Winnebago, some Californian groups, and some of the Northwest Coast.

Many ceremonies contain dramatic elements, notably those of the Hako of the Pawnee Indians and the mourning ceremonies of the aborigines of California.

In whatever form and context the American Indian expresses himself, be it in song or in story, in spell or incantation, in prayer or in speech, he always presents himself as a master of the word. He is a master because he handles the word with economy and reverence and because he has the wisdom to use it against a background of silences.

In our present period of reinterpretation of American literature, much consideration has been given to the role which the first native literature of this country has played in the development of thought and culture in postconquest America. From PHILIP FRENEAU to HENRY WADSWORTH LONGFELLOW; from JAMES FENIMORE COOPER to HAMLIN GARLAND; from THOMAS JEFFERSON to HENRY DAVID THOREAU and ADOLPH BANDELIER, the Indian stands out as a favorite subject. He has been reproduced as the noble child of nature, as the treacherous savage, as the serene philosopher of the woods, as the bloodthirsty primitive roaming the prairies, and as the feather-bedecked maker of bombastic speeches. Whether misinterpreted or not, the conspicuousness of the Indian as subject matter is indisputable. But we would search in vain for traces of a direct influence of American Indian literature on white man's forms of literature. Thus far, no such influence is at work. It is only in our present generation that here and there men of literature become aware of the unused mines which America possesses in the literature of the American Indian. Only as this awareness increases, and only as more literary documents of the native of this country are made accessible, will these direct and creative influences make themselves felt, and instill, no doubt, a new strength into the white man's literary productiveness. See INDIAN (AMERINDIAN) LANGUAGES.

MARGOT ASTROV

Ames, Fisher (b. Dedham, Mass., April 9, 1758—d. July 4, 1808), statesman, essayist. The son of NATHANIEL AMES, this leading representative of New England Federalism argued that "the quintessence of good government is to protect property and its rights," and referred to "the dangerous mass of the poor and vicious." As a member of Congress and an orator on many public occasions, Ames won a wide reputation; he was offered the presidency of Harvard, but declined. His *Works* appeared in 1809, an enlarged edition in 1854.

Ames, Nathaniel (b. Bridgewater, Mass., July 22, 1708—d. July 11, 1764), physician, compiler of almanacs. Ames issued his first almanac at the age of seventeen, eight years before Franklin's POOR RICHARD'S ALMANACK. It was called *Astronomical Diary and Almanack,* and was continued until 1775 by his son, Dr. Nathaniel Ames. The almanacs were more than a collection of astronomical and weather data. They helped, says Samuel Marion Tucker, "in disseminating throughout New England a knowledge of the English poets and perhaps also in fostering a taste for humorous poetry." The elder Ames included a poem called *Essay upon the Microscope,* described by Tucker as "perhaps our first ode in irregular verse." The younger Ames was as ardent a Republican as his brother Fisher was a Federalist. In 1891 appeared *The Essays, Humor, and Poems of Nathaniel Ames, Father and Son, of Dedham, Mass., from Their Almanacks, 1726–1775,* edited with notes and comments by Samuel Briggs.

Among the Hills (1868), a narrative poem by JOHN GREENLEAF WHITTIER. Intended as a companion piece to SNOW-BOUND, this poem tells of an uncouth farmer who woos a cultured city girl; both find happiness "among the hills."

Amory, Cleveland (b. Nahant, Mass., Sept. 2, 1917—   ), social historian, journalist, novelist. Amory graduated from Harvard, became editor of the *Saturday Evening Post's* "Postscripts" page, moved to Tucson, where he worked for the *Arizona Star,* and then to Prescott, Arizona, where he was managing editor of the *Evening Courier.* He returned to the East and became a specialist in the "international" article, a sharp, humorous sketch of representative parts of American society. In 1947 Amory published THE PROPER BOSTONIANS, a history of Boston society and its first families from colonial times to the present; *The Last Resorts* followed in 1952, a study of the great society resorts of the late 19th and early 20th centuries. His novel *Home Town* (1950) is a satire on book publishing and publicity. *Who Killed Society?* followed in 1958. With Frederic Bradlee he edited *Vanity Fair: A Cavalcade of the 1920's and 1930's* (1960).

Amos Judd (1895), a novel by JOHN AMES MITCHELL. A young rajah, in a time of civil war, is smuggled out of India to Connecticut, where he is brought up as Amos Judd, in ignorance of his origin. Mitchell depicts skillfully the development of traits that make it clear how far the young Hindu's character is from that of the practical Yankees around him.

Anarchiad, The: A Poem on the Restoration of Chaos and Substantial Night (Oct. 26, 1786 —Sept. 13, 1787). This mock-heroic poem, composed in collaboration by several of the "Connecticut Wits," appeared originally in the *New Haven Gazette and Connecticut Magazine* and was widely reprinted in the newspapers of the day. It was first published as a whole in 1861. The authors chiefly concerned were Dr.

LEMUEL HOPKINS, DAVID HUMPHREYS (who probably originated the idea), JOHN TRUMBULL, and JOEL BARLOW. The 1,200 lines of the poem represented a fanatic statement of the Federalist point of view. It attacked SHAYS' REBELLION, paper money in Rhode Island, and the delay in ratifying the Constitution and setting up a strong central government. The poem was an imitation of an English production, *The Rolliad,* and included parodies of Homer, Dante, Milton, Pope, and Goldsmith. See the HARTFORD WITS.

Anderson, Margaret. See THE LITTLE REVIEW.

Anderson, Maxwell (b. Atlantic, Pa., Dec. 15, 1888—d. Feb. 28, 1959), dramatist. The son of a Baptist clergyman, Anderson was educated in Pennsylvania, Ohio, Iowa, and North Dakota; he graduated from the University of North

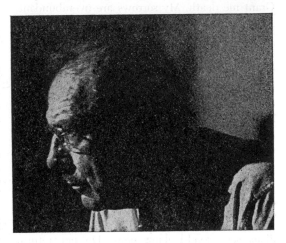

Dakota in 1911. He spent several years teaching English at Leland Stanford University and Whittier College, then turned to newspaper work in San Francisco and New York. While working on the New York *World* he met LAURENCE STALLINGS, with whom he collaborated successfully on a number of plays.

Anderson's first Broadway play was *White Desert* (1923), which attracted little attention. *What Price Glory?* (1924), however, brought fame to Anderson and Stallings, who here collaborated for the first time; a play about World War I, its outspoken language and realistic war scenes established it as a landmark in drama history—the first modern play to apply realistic techniques to war. Readers today, however, see that the play's realism is somewhat superficial, vitiated by rather sentimental comedy scenes. The authors' attempt to debunk war fails because most of the cynical lines are spoken by professional soldiers rather than draftees. Anderson and Stallings collaborated on two further plays, *First Flight* (1925), about Andrew Jackson's youth, and *The Buccaneer* (1925), a story of Capt. Morgan. Neither was a success. *Outside Looking In* (1925), by Anderson alone, is a badly constructed play based on JIM TULLY's autobiography, BEGGARS OF LIFE (1924).

Anderson's only domestic comedy is *Saturday's*

Children (1927), centering on a young couple's vain efforts to make a success of marriage in the face of immaturity, poverty, and interfering relatives. The play is notable for its spirited husband-wife quarrel and for its apparent approval of the idea that love flourishes best among unmarried couples. The play was a success. In *Gods of the Lightning* (1928, with Harold Hickerson) he used the Sacco-Vanzetti theme, but the result is more propagandistic than dramatic. Only several years later was Anderson able to make this material into a successful play.

With ELIZABETH THE QUEEN (1930) Anderson hit his stride in the historical play, and for the first time made a modern play in blank verse commercially successful. The special quality of this drama is the vitality given to historical characters through the emphasis on their emotional inwardness and the use of highly expressive language. The conflict of two indomitable wills in Elizabeth and Essex, the subtle play of feeling, and the swift etching of minor characters gives the play a tense, richly chromatic texture. *Night Over Taos* (1932), a regional drama concerned with the conflict of Montoya, a native leader among New Mexican Indians, and the United States, was a less successful work.

Anderson next turned to political satire. BOTH YOUR HOUSES (1933) is a barbed attack on bungling, rapacious, and dishonest congressmen. An idealistic newcomer to Congress tries to defeat an unsound appropriations bill by loading it with fantastic riders, but to his consternation the bill passes. The play was awarded a Pulitzer Prize. The play which first incorporated all the features of Anderson's theory of tragedy was *Mary of Scotland* (1933), a play made especially notable in performance by the acting of Helen Hayes. The struggle between Catholic Mary and imperious, Protestant Elizabeth is powerfully drawn, with sympathy for the sweet-tempered Mary, who is vilified and betrayed by the scheming Elizabeth. The ennoblement of character, so essential to tragedy in Anderson's view, is clearly presented in Mary's deeply moral faith. Another historical play, VALLEY FORGE (1934), an attempt to interpret George Washington as a product of the general revolutionary fervor, failed to carry conviction.

One of Anderson's most notable achievements, *Winterset* (1935), is a tragedy in verse which uses as background the Sacco-Vanzetti case. The central character, the son of a man put to death for another's crime, seeks to clear his father's name and wreak vengeance upon the actual murderers. His motives are upset by his falling in love with the sister of one of the criminals he wishes to expose. He succeeds in clearing his father's name to his satisfaction, and discovers that the girl's love has redeemed him from the necessity of revenge. The verse of *Winterset* is modern in diction and rhythm yet retains in its highest moments great power, and it has won wide acclaim. The theme of the play has invited comparison with *Hamlet*.

Less important plays of the mid-1930's include: *Wingless Victory* (1936); *The Masque of Kings* (1936); *The Star Wagon* (1937); and HIGH TOR (1937). KNICKERBOCKER HOLIDAY (1938) is a musical comedy based on Irving's account of the early Dutch in New York; the score is by Kurt Weill.

Key Largo (1939) conforms to Anderson's theory of tragedy. In the memorable first scene an American volunteer in the Spanish Civil War deserts his post and comrades to save his own life; in the rest of the play he seeks to redeem himself by telling the story of his comrades' heroism and by sacrificing himself in a situation where he has no personal attachment. *Key Largo* is one of Anderson's most searching plays in its probing of the bases of man's ethical faith.

With the advent of World War II Anderson wrote *Candle in the Wind* (1941) which exposes Nazi duplicity and cruelty in the story of a love affair between an American girl and a French officer in occupied Paris. *The Eve of St. Mark* (1942) combines the comedy of a training camp, the high tragedy of youthful sacrifice, and the fantasy of legend; the chief scene of the play is that in which the young soldiers voluntarily choose death in order to gain a military advantage. *Storm Operation* (1944) is a technically sound account of military maneuvers in the Mediterranean, but fails of its own documentary weight.

Truckline Café (1946) was another failure, but Anderson's fortunes soared again in a return to historical drama, *Joan of Lorraine* (1946), one of his few experiments in technique. Here the device of a play in rehearsal is used to dramatize two conflicting interpretations of Joan's character: one view, held by the actress, is that Joan is uncompromising and mystically inspired; the director believes that she is temporizing and opportunistic. The playwright's sympathy lies with the former. Another historical play, *Anne of the Thousand Days* (1948), which presents Henry VIII in a more favorable light than most previous interpretations, was well received. *Lost in the Stars* (1949) was an effective dramatization of Alan Paton's *Cry the Beloved Country* (1948), with a musical score by Weill. Next came a play on Socrates, *Barefoot in Athens* (1951). Anderson's last play, *The Bad Seed* (1955), based on a novel by William March, is a tensely psychological study of evil in the character of a child.

Anderson was one of the few modern playwrights to enunciate a systematic theory of drama. His ideas, set forth in *The Essence of Tragedy* (1935) and other writings, may be summarized as follows: (1) the play must deal with the inner life; (2) the story must be a conflict between good and evil within a single person; (3) the protagonist must represent the forces of good and must win; (4) the protagonist cannot be perfect, for he must emerge a better man at the end of the play than he was at the beginning; (5) the protagonist must be an exceptional person, or he must epitomize exceptional qualities; (6) excellence on the stage is always moral excellence; (7) the moral atmosphere must be healthy; and (8) there are certain qualities which an audience admires: positive character and strength of conviction in a man, fidelity and passionate faith in a woman; and there are other qualities an audience dislikes: in a man, cowardice and refusal to fight for a belief; in a woman, self-pity, lack of pity for others, infidelity.

Anderson published one volume of lyric poems, *You Who Have Dreams* (1925). In 1940 he gathered *Eleven Verse Plays*.

ALLAN G. HALLINE

Anderson, Patrick (b. England, 1915—   ), poet, editor. Educated at Oxford, Anderson became a resident of Montreal and has for many years been identified with Canadian letters. Active on the editorial boards of several Canadian magazines, among them *Preview*, *En Masse*, and *Northern Review*, he attracted critical attention with his first books of poetry, *A Tent for April* (1945) and *The White Center* (1946). *Poem on Canada* in the latter volume treats the country in terms of human relations and a national illusion, using epigram and symbolism. Later he published *Colour as Naked* (1953); *Snake Wine; A Singapore Episode* (1955); *First Steps in Greece* (1958). *Search Me* (1957) is autobiographical.

Anderson, Quentin (b. Minnewaukan, N.D., July 21, 1912—   ), teacher, critic. Anderson, the son of playwright MAXWELL ANDERSON, received a doctoral degree in 1953 from Columbia University, where he has taught since 1939. A specialist in 19th-century American literature, he analyzed the moral roots of HENRY JAMES' later novels in *The American Henry James* (1957), which the *Saturday Review* described as "the work of a mind large enough to confront the hardest questions raised by the fate of a very great American writer." Anderson has also edited a volume of James' stories, *Selected Short Stories* (1950).

Anderson, Robert W[oodruff] (b. New York City, April 28, 1917—   ), playwright, teacher. Anderson received his A.B. in 1939 and his M.A. in 1940 from Harvard University. From 1942 to 1946 he served in the Navy, and from 1946 to 1953 he taught writing for radio and television and for the stage. He became famous with the play *Tea and Sympathy*, produced in 1953. Widely acclaimed by the critics, it presents the problem confronting a lonely youth accused of homosexuality. Then followed *All Summer Long* (1959) and *Silent Night, Lonely Night* (1959). Anderson also wrote movie scripts from his play *Tea and Sympathy* and from Kathryn Cavarly Hulme's *The Nun's Story* (1959).

Anderson, Sherwood (b. Camden, Ohio, Sept. 13, 1876—d. March 8, 1941), short-story writer, novelist, newspaperman, poet. Anderson's childhood was spent in Clyde, Ohio, where his family was somewhat better off than he himself liked to pretend in his later autobiographical writings. His education was irregular, however, and in 1896 he went to Chicago,

where he worked as a laborer. During the Spanish American War he served briefly in the army, then returned to Chicago and entered the advertising business, working as a copywriter for several years. For a time he conducted a paint

UPI

manufacturing business in Elyria, Ohio, but when it failed he again returned to Chicago and his old job in advertising.

Meanwhile he had become interested in the literary renaissance of the middle western naturalists and in Chicago had met such writers as Carl Sandburg, Floyd Dell, George Cram Cook, Robert Morss Lovett, and Theodore Dreiser. He wrote and published two novels which attracted little attention, then in 1919 published WINESBURG, OHIO, which immediately brought him fame. A collection of related stories about life in a small town, the book develops the theme of youth in revolt against respectability and the conventions of commercial society, and it became exceedingly popular among young people throughout the country. Its style, a mixture of simplicity and soft rhetoric which later critics deprecated for its sentimentality, was influenced by the early work of GERTRUDE STEIN and in turn influenced such writers as Ernest Hemingway, Thomas Wolfe, William Saroyan, Erskine Caldwell, and John Steinbeck. Anderson never again equaled *Winesburg*, though he remained in vogue for a number of years and published one book, DARK LAUGHTER, which became a best seller. He visited Paris in 1921, later lived in various parts of the United States, and in 1926 settled on a farm near Troutdale, Virginia. He bought two weekly newspapers in nearby Marion, continued his writing, and tried, as he said, "to have some real part in the community life."

After 1926 Anderson's career as a writer was anticlimactic. In the early 1920's, the era of the *Seven Arts* and the *Dial*, of Scott Fitzgerald and Floyd Dell, his stories appealed to many young people who, when they reread him several years later, found him embarrassingly adolescent and quite outmoded. Still in spite of his sentimentalisms, cruelly exposed by Hemingway in THE TORRENTS OF SPRING (1926), he had helped a generation to grow up. His ideas about the importance of love and the need for a more humane industrialism are still valid. The best of his short stories, *Hands, I'm a Fool, Death in the Woods,* and *I Want to Know Why,* retain as much vitality as anything by Sinclair Lewis or Dreiser, his contemporaries in the naturalistic movement, and he did as much as anyone to create a public for modern American fiction. (See NATURALISM.)

Anderson died of peritonitis at Cristobal, Canal Zone, where illness had forced him to interrupt a South American cruise. He was married four times.

Anderson published: *Windy McPherson's Son* (1916); *Marching Men* (1917); *Mid-American Chants* (poems, 1918); *Winesburg, Ohio* (1919); *Poor White* (1920); THE TRIUMPH OF THE EGG (1921); *Many Marriages* (1922–23); HORSES AND MEN (1923); *A Story Teller's Story* (autobiographical, 1924); *The Modern Writer* (1925); *Dark Laughter* (1925); *Sherwood Anderson's Notebook* (1926); TAR: A MIDWEST CHILDHOOD (autobiographical, 1926); *A New Testament* (1927); *Alice and the Lost Novel* (1929); *Hello Towns!* (1929); *Nearer the Grass Roots* (1929); *The American County Fair* (1930); *Perhaps Women* (an essay against machines, 1931); *Beyond Desire* (1932); *No Swank* (1934); *Puzzled America* (1935); *Kit Brandon* (1936); *Winesburg, Ohio, and Other Plays* (1937); *Home Town* (1940). Posthumously published were *Memoirs* (1942); *Letters* (1953). His plays were produced in New York City, by the PROVINCETOWN PLAYERS.

Biographical and critical studies include Cleveland Chase, *Sherwood Anderson* (1927); James Schevill, *Sherwood Anderson: His Life and Work* (1951); Irving Howe, *Sherwood Anderson* (1951). Paul Rosenfeld compiled *The Sherwood Anderson Reader* (1947), Horace Gregory *The Portable Sherwood Anderson* (1951). Anderson is thought to have been the model for Fairchild in William Faulkner's novel *Mosquitoes* (1927).

GEORGE KUMMER

Anderson Award, Maxwell. An award of $100 for verse drama which was established at Stanford University in 1936 in honor of MAXWELL ANDERSON, formerly an instructor at the university. The contest is open to all persons interested in dramatic composition, without restrictions as to theme, length, or verse form; one-act plays are eligible.

Andersonville (1955), a novel by MAC-KINLAY KANTOR. This best seller, which won a Pulitzer Prize, depicts with grim realism the horrors of the infamous military prison during the Civil War.

Andrews, Jane (b. Mass., 1833—d. 1887?), writer of juvenile stories. Miss Andrews became a teacher in Newburyport. Among her books were *The Seven Little Sisters Who Live on the Round Ball That Floats in the Air* (1861); *Ten Boys Who Lived on the Road from Long Ago to Now* (1886); *Stories Mother Nature Told Her Children* (1889).

Andrews, Mary Raymond Shipman (b. Mobile, Ala., 1865?—d. Aug. 2, 1936), novelist, short-story writer. Mrs. Andrews' fictional description of the circumstances of Lincoln's Gettysburg address, THE PERFECT TRIBUTE (1906), sold many hundreds of thousands of copies through the years. It is a good story, sentimental within reason. Among Mrs. Andrews' other books were two collections of short stories, *The Eternal Masculine* (1913) and *The Eternal Feminine* (1916), and *A Lost Commander: Florence Nightingale* (1929).

Andrews, Roy Chapman (b. Beloit, Wis., Jan. 26, 1884—d. March 11, 1960), zoologist, explorer, author, radio commentator. Dr. Andrews' voyages were in both space and time. He first hunted whales in the East Indies and near Alaska. He then explored remote regions in Tibet, China, and Burma; his discoveries in the Gobi Desert and elsewhere threw important light on prehistoric man and extinct mammalia. He was director of the Museum of Natural History from 1935 to 1941. His experiences supplied material for many books of lively interest, among them *Whale Hunting with Gun and Camera* (1916); *Camps and Trails in China* (1918); *Across Mongolian Plains* (1921); *On the Trail of Ancient Man* (1926); *The New Conquest of Central Asia* (1932); *This Business of Exploring* (1935); *Meet Your Ancestors* (1945). *Under a Lucky Star* (1943) and *An Explorer Comes Home* (1947) comprise an entertaining autobiography.

Andrews, Stephen Pearl (b. Templeton, Mass., March 22, 1812—d. May 21, 1886), abolitionist, lawyer, economist, advocate of shorthand, linguist. This typical Yankee was an intellectual jack-of-all-trades. His first business was the law, his first great interest abolition of slavery. He went to England to gather money for his manumission views, and a casual meeting with Isaac Pitman infected him with his next great enthusiasm—shorthand, a subject on which he wrote two books. He advocated his views in New York City and in Boston, and established a school in the latter city. He knew thirty-two languages and invented a forerunner of Esperanto which he called Alwato, publishing a *Primary Synopsis* in 1871. In later years he became increasingly interested in social organization, outlined a perfect state called "Pantarchy," which was close to philosophical anarchism. He was an avowed freethinker and a contributor to the rationalist magazine *The Truth Seeker*.

Androboros (1714), a satirical farce by Robert

Hunter (?–1734) and Lewis Morris (1671–1746). The first American play of which a copy exists. It attacks an English administrator, Sir Francis Nicholson (1655–1728). (See DRAMA IN THE UNITED STATES.)

Angle, Paul M[cClelland] (b. Mansfield, Ohio, Dec. 25, 1900—   ), historian, authority on Lincoln. Among his writings and editions are: *New Letters and Papers of Lincoln* (1930); *Mary Lincoln, Wife and Widow* (with Carl Sandburg, 1932); *Lincoln—1854–1861* (1933); *"Here I Have Lived": A History of Lincoln's Springfield* (1935; rev. ed., 1950); *A Shelf of Lincoln Books* (1946); *The Lincoln Reader* (1947); *Living Lincoln* (with Earl S. Miers, 1955); *Created Equal? The Complete Lincoln-Douglas Debates of 1858* (1958).

Angoff, Charles (b. Russia, April 22, 1902—   ), journalist, biographer, novelist. Shortly after his graduation from Harvard in 1923, Angoff worked for a few months on the Revere (Massachusetts) *Budget,* then began writing feature articles for the *Post, Transcript* and *Globe,* all Boston newspapers, and occasionally sold reviews to *Forum* and *Century* magazines.

As the result of a letter-writing campaign in 1924, Angoff was hired by H. L. Mencken as an assistant on the AMERICAN MERCURY and worked there for ten years (1925–35), continuing as editor after Mencken left the magazine in 1933. Following this period, Angoff worked for several other magazines, including the *Nation,* the *American Spectator, Living Age, Scribner's,* and the *North American Review.* In 1942, after the purchase of the *American Mercury* by Lawrence E. Spivak, Angoff returned to that magazine and remained there until 1953. From 1945 to 1955 he was Research Director for the radio program "Meet the Press."

Angoff's books include many titles in the fields of literary criticism, music, history, and world affairs, such as *A Literary History of the American People* (2 v., 1931); *Palestrina, Savior of Church Music* (1944); *H. L. Mencken: A Portrait from Memory* (1956), a frank and perceptive personal recollection of that famous editor. Angoff is perhaps best known for his novels dealing with Jewish-American life. (See also JEWS IN UNITED STATES LITERATURE). The series covers the years from 1890 to the present and includes the following titles: *Journey to the Dawn* (1951); *In the Morning Light* (1951); *The Sun at Noon* (1953); *Between Day and Dark* (1959); and *Bitter Spring* (1961).

Angry Decade, The (1947), by Leo Gurko (1914—   ). This survey is an informative, intelligent, and lively history of literary and social events from the stock market crash of 1929 to Pearl Harbor in 1941.

Animal Kingdom, The (1932), a play by PHILIP BARRY. Described by John Gassner as an "unconventional comedy which showed an understanding mistress to be more truly a wife to a rich idealist than the parasitic woman of his set to whom he had bound himself in the eyes of the law." Tom Collier, after years of happiness with Daisy Sage, returns to his wife, then abandons her again for his mistress.

Anisfield-Wolf Awards. These were established in 1934 by Mrs. Edith Anisfield-Wolf in honor of her father John Anisfield. Originally the award was $1,000 for the best book on racial relations, but it was doubled to provide a second prize in creative literature. The first award was made to Harold Foote Gosnell for *Negro Politicians: The Rise of Negro Politics in Chicago* (1935).

Annabel Lee (Oct. 9, 1849), a poem by EDGAR ALLAN POE. The poem appeared in the New York *Tribune* two days after Poe's death. It is usually believed to be in memory of his wife, but it is possibly merely another poem on one of Poe's favorite themes—the death of a beautiful woman. Some have found in it obscure references to Poe's affair with SARAH HELEN WHITMAN, whose "highborn kinsmen" may have been the ones that "bore her away from me."

Anna Christie (1922), a play by EUGENE O'NEILL. This is another of the innumerable literary variations on the theme of Mary Magdalene redeemed. Anna's father, a crusty old captain of a coal barge, hopes to save his daughter from "dat old davil sea." She lives on a farm, but suddenly appears on the barge, on which the captain lives with an old drab named Marthy. The latter immediately realizes that Anna is "no good," and Anna readily admits her sins. Father and daughter leave New York on the barge and pick up a boatload of shipwrecked sailors; one of them, Mat Burke, falls in love with Anna. When she tells him her past he leaves her and gets drunk. But the play closes on the possibility that Anna may still be saved. The play is a "slice of life," but has overtones of mysticism and symbolism. O'Neill had earlier written, and unsuccessfully produced, *Chris Christopherson* (1920), from which considerable portions of the later play were taken.

Annandale. See BOOK OF ANNANDALE.

Anne of Green Gables (1908), a novel by L[UCY] M[AUD] MONTGOMERY. This perennial best seller is one of the few books written specifically for girls that have attracted a male audience too. Miss Montgomery based her plot on a simple suggestion she found in her notes: "Elderly couple apply to an orphan asylum for a boy. By mistake a girl is sent to them."

Annie Kilburn (1888), a novel by WILLIAM DEAN HOWELLS. This sociological novel calls for justice, not alms, for the poor. In it a New England lady goes crusading somewhat indiscriminately, but learns discretion as she gains experience. Howells also depicts the disintegrating effects of the new industrial order upon the simple and narrow-minded inhabitants of a New England community.

annuals and gift-books. The American annuals and gift-books were patterned on the European literary almanac, a cross between the practical almanac (an annual repository of useful information) and the literary anthology (a retrospective collection of belles-lettres). The first had appeared in France in 1765, *L'Almanach des Muses, contenant unchoix des meilleures Pièces de Poësies fugitives, qui ont paru en 1764.* The species spread successively to Germany, England, and the United States. The earliest American example was *Le Souvenir, or Picturesque Pocket Diary; containing an Almanac, Ruled Pages for Memoranda, Literary Selections, and a Variety of Useful Information for 1825,* which was published late in 1824 at Philadelphia. A year later there appeared in the same city a second volume with a similar title and also a competing publication, *The Philadelphia Souvenir; A Collection of Fugitive Pieces from the Philadelphia Press, With Biographical and Explanatory Notes, By J. E. Hall.* Both of these were more in the nature of anthologies than of original annuals. The first legitimate literary almanac to appear in the United States was *The Atlantic Souvenir,* published annually at Philadelphia for the years 1826 to 1832, and thereafter transplanted to Boston and combined with a competitor as *The Token and Atlantic*

Souvenir (for 1833 to 1842). *The Token* itself had first been published for 1828. The first literary almanac in New York, THE TALISMAN, was published in three annual volumes (for 1828 to 1830) and then reissued in 1833 as *Miscellanies First Published under the Name of The Talisman, by G. E. Verplanck, W. C. Bryant, and Robert C. Sands.*

Annuals and gift-books flourished throughout the eastern seaboard, and they appeared sporadically even in the West and South, *e.g., The Western Souvenir, A Christmas and New Year's Gift for 1829* (Cincinnati), *The Souvenir of the Lakes for 1831* (Detroit), *The Charleston Book* of 1845, and *The New-Orleans Book* of 1851. Although Philadelphia retained pre-eminence in the field, most other eastern cities produced specimens of their own, many of which signalized the name of the city in the title. More than a thousand American representatives of the species, including entire series as well as single publications, are estimated to have appeared, with the annual harvest increasing gradually down to the mid-forties. The number soared to an average of sixty each for the years 1846 to 1852. The size of editions of individual volumes ran as high as 10,000 copies. Most annuals were quartos, but miniature 24mos and 32mos were also issued. Many were embellished with leather bindings, tooled or embossed, and some even sported bindings of varnished papier-maché, mounted with medallions and inlaid with mother-of-pearl. The gift-books were, in fact, characteristic table decorations of the ormolu age, bought as much for their bindings and their richly engraved illustrations as for their contents.

Contributors to the annuals and gift-books ranged from the lesser literary lights to the great luminaries of the period. Some of the favorites were N. P. Willis, William Leete Stone, William Gilmore Simms, Willis Gaylord Clark, Charles West Thomson, Lydia Sigourney, Hannah Flagg Gould, Sarah Josepha Hale, Harriet Beecher Stowe. The general level of achievement was low. Nevertheless, the most eminent authors of the day welcomed the opportunities offered by the gift-books. Ralph Waldo Emerson had contributed his first published writings, anonymously, to *The Offering, for 1829,* and later he acknowledged others in *The Gift* and *The Diadem.* Also in *The Gift* were published five of Poe's tales, four of them for the first time. In *The Token* appeared at least twenty-seven of Nathaniel Hawthorne's stories, some of which upon reprinting were appropriately entitled TWICE-TOLD TALES. Longfellow, Lowell, Holmes, together with Irving, Bryant, Whittier, and many other writers of reputation contributed to the annuals. Indeed, of all major American writers who reached maturity by 1845, probably only Melville, Thoreau, and Whitman did not appear in the annuals and gift-books.

The annuals performed a valuable service to American letters. At a time when the writings of established English authors, unprotected by copyright, were pirated and reprinted without cost in current American publications, the annuals and gift-books published and paid for contributions by native authors. Thus they fostered the native literature at a time when professionalism in American arts was scarcely possible. They performed other services also. They assisted in the dissemination of foreign literature by printing translations from German, French, Spanish,

Russian, and Scandinavian authors. They supported social progress and reform, notably the abolitionist and temperance movements, and they fostered fraternal and religious life. Among those devoted to religion may be mentioned *The Religious Souvenir* for the years 1833 to 1839, *The Christian Keepsake and Missionary Annual* for the years 1838 to 1840 and 1847 to 1849, *The Opal: A Pure Gift for the Holy Days* of 1844 to 1849, and, the longest-lived of all the annuals, *The Rose of Sharon: A Religious Souvenir* for the years 1840 to 1857. Fraternal publications included *The Odd-Fellows' Offering for 1843* and for the following years to 1854. Reform was represented by, among others, *The Fountain: A Temperance Gift* of 1847 and *The Temperance Offering for 1853,* both of which were reissued a number of times, even under different titles. Abolition was the subject of several volumes and series, chief among which was *The Liberty Bell, By Friends of Freedom,* issued annually sponsored by Mana Weston Chapman, with four exceptions, from 1839 to 1857. It contained contributions by many prominent supporters of abolition, both American and European, among them Lowell, Emerson, Wendell Phillips, Harriet Beecher Stowe, Elizabeth Barrett Browning, Harriet Martineau, Giuseppi Mazzini, Nicholas Turgenev, and Fredrika Bremer. See ALMANACS; COMIC ALMANACS.

PHILIP ALLISON SHELLEY

Ann Vickers (1933), a novel by SINCLAIR LEWIS. The story, modeled after H. G. Wells' *Ann Veronica,* traces the career of a neurotic woman who starts as a social worker and ends as the mistress of a politician. The portrait of Barney Dolphin, a Tammany judge convicted for corruption, is the most vivid in the book. The novel has been called morbid, also "evasively sentimental." It largely lacks the humor usually found in Lewis.

Anspacher, Louis [Kaufman] (b. Cincinnati, Ohio, March 1, 1878—d. May 10, 1947), dramatist, lecturer. Anspacher studied in Vienna to be a singer and occasionally appeared on the stage, usually under an assumed name. His plays include *The Unchastened Woman* (1915); *That Day* (1917); *All the King's Horses* (1920); *Dagmar* (1923); *The Jazz Clown* (1933). He was a favorite lecturer and eager debater; among his topics were the necessity for raising the status of women, conditions in the theater, the evils of dictatorship, and the dangers of the atomic age. Posthumously published was *Challenge of the Unknown: Exploring the Psychic World* (1947).

Antheil, George (b. Trenton, N.J., July 8, 1900—d. Feb. 12, 1959), composer, author. Antheil, a concert pianist, began directing his own compositions in 1928. He had a successful musical career abroad and after his return to the United States in 1933 he became active in Hollywood. His Carnegie Hall production of his *Ballet Mécanique,* which makes use of sound-producing instruments not generally considered musical, won him a reputation for eccentricity

and a press agentry he found it hard to throw off. Antheil wrote an amusing account of his career in *Bad Boy of Music* (1945). His musical compositions are many, including operas, chamber works, and several movie scores.

Anthology Club or **Society.** This informal organization of "gentlemen of literary interests" was founded in Boston on Oct. 3, 1805, and was dissolved on July 2, 1811. Two years before the founding of the club there had been started a magazine called *Monthly Anthology, or Magazine of Polite Literature,* and one purpose of the group was to finance this magazine and supply it with material. Bryant, Daniel Webster, and Joseph Story were among those attracted to the group. Four years after both magazine and club died, the same group promoted the publication of the NORTH AMERICAN REVIEW. The Anthology Club also founded a library in Boston, known as the Anthology Reading Room but incorporated in 1807 as the BOSTON ATHENAEUM.

Anthony, Edward (b. New York City, Aug. 4, 1895—   ), newspaperman, author, publisher. Anthony worked on the Bridgeport (Conn.) *Herald* and the New York *Herald,* served on the staffs of various magazines, and became publisher of the WOMAN'S HOME COMPANION in 1943, of COLLIER'S in 1949. He was publicity director in Herbert Hoover's 1928 Presidential campaign. Among the early contributors to Franklin P. Adams' "CONNING TOWER," he has written much humorous verse of high quality, some of it collected in *Merry-Go-Roundelays* (1921). A fanciful book for children, *The Pussycat Princess* (1922), became the basis for a popular series of comic strips. His other writings include *Razzberry* (1924); *How to Get Rid of a Woman* (1928); *Every Dog Has His Say* (1947); *Oddity Land* (1957); and he collaborated with FRANK BUCK on BRING 'EM BACK ALIVE (1930), with Clyde Beatty on *The Big Cage* (1933) and its screen version.

Antigonish (composed, 1899; published, 1922), a famous quatrain by HUGHES MEARNS about a "little man who wasn't there." Originally it was an untitled verse in a play called *The Psyco-Ed,* written by Mearns for an undergraduate course in English at Harvard. In 1910 he put on the play with a group of college students, and it "made gay headway for months." Finally, in 1922, Franklin P. Adams printed the quatrain in his "CONNING TOWER." The title, Mearns explained, was chosen because at the moment the papers were carrying daily stories of a haunted house in a village called Antigona or Antigonia, but the ghost was always away when reporters called. The quatrain, which provoked many imitations—Mearns himself writing several sequels—goes as follows:

> I met a man upon the stair,
> The little man who wasn't there.
> He wasn't there again today,
> Oh, how I wish he'd go away.

Antin, Mary (b. Russia, June, 1881—d. May 15, 1949), autobiographer, sociologist. Miss

Antin came to the United States at the age of thirteen, and was educated in the schools of Boston and at Columbia University. Her books were based on her own experiences as an immigrant, and maintained two main theses—that the immigrants throughout the centuries have furnished the sinew and bone of the nation, and that natives of the United States are insufficiently aware of the wonderful nature and deep influence of American institutions and customs. Most widely read of her books was THE PROMISED LAND (1912), based in part on an earlier book written in Yiddish, *From Polotzk to Boston* (translated into English by Miss Antin, 1899). *They Who Knock at Our Gates* was published in 1914.

Anti-Rent Laws. The Dutch PATROONS from 1839 to 1846 experienced difficulties in collecting rent from their New York tenants. Soon a revolt broke out against the entire patroon system, a revolt which Governor William H. Seward used the militia to suppress. But as a consequence of the disorder "anti-rent laws" were passed in the New York legislature, of a kind to prevent some serious hardships of tenants. The revolt and its causes were used by James Fenimore Cooper as the background of his novels, SATANSTOE (1845), THE CHAINBEARER (1846), and THE REDSKINS (1846)—a trilogy called the *Littlepage Manuscripts.*

Anza, Juan Bautista de (1735–1788), Spanish-American official. Himself born in Mexico, he founded (1776) the mission and presidio of San Francisco, later served as governor of New Mexico (1777–88). He wrote extensively on his experiences. H. E. Bolton edited Anza's *California Expeditions* (5 v., 1930).

Apache Indians. Nomad tribes found in the arid deserts of the Southwest, but allied to the Athabascan peoples otherwise localized in northern sections of the continent. Like the NAVAJOS, the Apaches were for centuries the dreaded foes of the more peaceful village Indians of this section. They were also sworn enemies of the white man, and the last of our Indian "wars" was waged against these fierce nomads, whose name became a synonym for the red man at his most bloodthirsty and vindictive. Yet these deadly fighters were also expert weavers and basket-makers, and developed complex religious ceremonies and dances. The most famous of their chieftains was GERONIMO, who led bloody attacks on the whites but was finally defeated by General George Crook in 1885–86. Arizona, sometimes called the "Apache State," contains the present reservations of this tribe. They are today hard-working ranchers and farmers. The Apaches appear in several novels, including PAUL WELLMAN's *Broncho Apache* (1932); Elliott Arnold's *Blood Brother* (1947); Ed Newsom's *Wagons to Tucson* (1954) and *Ride to High Places* (1955).

Apel, Will. See HARVARD DICTIONARY OF MUSIC.

Apes, William (b. Colrain, Mass., Jan. 31, 1798—d. [?]), author. A PEQUOT INDIAN of partial white ancestry, Apes fought for the Americans in the War of 1812. In 1829 he became a Methodist missionary, and became active in seeking to correct abuses from which the Indians of Massachusetts suffered. He was a descendant of the famous Indian leader about whom he wrote his *Eulogy of King Philip* (1836). He related his own story in *A Son of the Forest* (1829); he also wrote *The Experiences of Five Christian Indians* (1833).

Apley, George. See THE LATE GEORGE APLEY.

Apostle, The (1943), a novel by SHOLEM ASCH. This continues Asch's account of the first century of the Christian era. It follows the missionary journeys of the Apostle Paul, giving vivid pictures of ancient Rome, Jerusalem, Athens, and Corinth.

Apostle to the Indians. See JOHN ELIOT.

Appeal to Reason, The (1897–1922), a radical weekly founded by Julius A. Wayland. After the Spanish American War it was taken over by Fred Warren; it ascribed all evil to the capitalistic system. The circulation grew to a total of 3,500,000. In 1918 E. HALDEMAN-JULIUS purchased a controlling interest, and it ceased publication in 1922. Stewart H. Holbrook, in LOST MEN OF AMERICAN HISTORY (1946), believes the weekly had an enormous influence in its own time and later. Its techniques were adapted by later muckrakers, although they were much more careful about their facts.

Appleseed, Johnny. His real name was either John or Jonathan Chapman. He was born in Springfield, Mass., in 1774 or 1775. As a young man he wandered westward, first to Pittsburgh, later to Marietta, Ohio, where he became an orchardist and likewise a Swedenborgian. It was presumably because of a disappointment in love that he began a nomadic existence, preaching to all he met for fifty years and distributing apple seeds everywhere. According to legend, it was to these seeds that the apple orchards of Pennsylvania, Ohio, Illinois, and Indiana owe their origin. He died in Fort Wayne, Ind., in 1847. A carefully documented biography is Robert Price's *Johnny Appleseed: Man and Myth* (1954).

Johnny Appleseed has become a folk hero, and has been celebrated in many stories and poems. He was a particular favorite of VACHEL LINDSAY, who mentioned him often and devoted to him a long poem, *In Praise of Johnny Appleseed* (1923). Monuments to him have been erected in Indiana and Ohio, and two leading brands of apple are the "Jonathan" and the "Chapman."

Appleton, Thomas Gold (b. Boston, March 31, 1812—d. April 17, 1884), poet, essayist, artist, epigrammatist. Appleton to some extent represented Boston and Puritanism in revolt. He cherished artists, and had he not been born rich he might have been an artist himself. As it was, he painted on pebblestones, which he gave to his friends as paperweights. Living in the best literary circles of Boston (his sister became Longfellow's second wife), Appleton was obliged to write, but he produced nothing notable. His *Nile Journal* (1876) has charm, but his collection of verses, *Faded Leaves* (1872), seems just that. Some of his essays, collected in *Windfalls* (1878), are pleasant but hardly memorable. Yet as a conversationalist Appleton seems to have been supreme in his day, and he is chiefly remembered for his epigrams. To him is attributed the saying, "Good Americans, when they die, go to Paris."

Apple-Tree Table, The, and Other Sketches (first collected in 1922), by HERMAN MELVILLE. This gathering, edited by Henry Chapin, includes ten prose pieces originally published in periodicals between 1850 and 1856.

Archer, Isabel. See PORTRAIT OF A LADY.

archy and mehitabel. archy is the cockroach and mehitabel is the cat in what some regard as DON MARQUIS' most original and amusing works. The two appeared frequently in the columns that Marquis conducted after 1916 in the New York *Sun* and later in the *Herald Tribune*. The sketches were collected in *archy and mehitabel* (1927); *archy does his part* (1935); *the life and times of archy and mehitabel* (1940). archy, who suffered from literary ambitions but was unable to work the shift key on the typewriter, of necessity wrote without capital letters when he did his writing in the newspaper office after the less literary denizens had gone home. mehitabel, about whom archy writes with gentle deprecation, took as her motto "toujours gai." Between them they afforded Marquis many opportunities for satirizing American life between the two World Wars. *archy and mehitabel*, a short jazz opera by George Kleinsinger and Joe Darion, was produced on Dec. 6, 1954.

Archy Moore (1836), a novel by RICHARD HILDRETH. See THE SLAVE.

Are You a Bromide? (1907), a satire by GELETT BURGESS. It appeared originally in the *Smart Set* (April, 1906). The subtitle is: "Or, the Theory of Sulphitism." Burgess divides the human race into those who originate ideas (the sulphitic) and those who follow slavishly, taking their ideas and language from others (the bromidic). The clichés which the latter repeat, and the persons themselves, Burgess calls *bromides*—*e.g.*, "If you saw that sunset in a picture you wouldn't believe it was true" or "I don't know what art is, but I know what I like." In its day the book had a salutary effect on the pompous enunciation of platitudes, but it is no longer very well known. The word *bromide*, still under the heading of "slang," is defined by Webster's *New International Dictionary* as follows: "a. A conventional and commonplace or tiresome person;—with reference to the sedative effect of medicinal bromides. b. A flat, commonplace statement or notion."

Ark, Henry. See THE RED ROVER.

Arkansas Traveler, The. One of the most famous tunes and tales of American folklore. The tune and the accompanying dialogue have been ascribed to José Tasso, a renowned fiddler in the Ohio Valley region; the dialogue is attributed by others to Col. Sandford Faulkner. Variants of the tale have been found in Maine and Pennsylvania.

Armour, Richard [Willard] (b. San Pedro, Cal., July 15, 1906—   ), teacher, critic, poet, humorist. Armour has taught English at several universities while keeping up an active career as a writer. His first book was a biography of Bryan Waller Procter (1935). He is best known, however, for his light verse, which has been published widely in American magazines. Among his collections are *Yours for the Asking* (1942); *Golf Bawls* (1946); *Leading with My Left* (1946); *Light Armour* (1954); *Nights with Armour* (1958). His punfully misleading prose accounts of history and literature include: *It All Started with Columbus* (1953); *It All Started with Europa* (1955); *Twisted Tales From Shakespeare* (1957); *The Classics Reclassified* (1960).

Arms, George Warren (b. La Grande, Ore., Feb. 1, 1912—   ), professor, critic. Arms taught at various preparatory schools and colleges before becoming a professor of English at the University of New Mexico in 1945. He compiled *A Bibliography of William Dean Howells* (with W. M. Gibson, 1948), and subsequently edited a number of Howells' works. *The Fields Were Green* (1953) is a study of 19th-century American poets. Other works include *Readings for Liberal Education* (1948) and, with J. M. Kuntz, *Poetry Explication: A Checklist of Interpretation Since 1925* (1950).

Armstrong, Paul (b. Kidder, Mo., April 25, 1869—d. Aug. 30, 1915), newspaperman, playwright. Armstrong at twenty-one was licensed as a master of steam vessels. But he turned to newspaper work and, a little later, to the theater, where he won a great success with *The Heir to the Hoorah* (1905). Thereafter he produced a quick succession of plays and vaudeville skits, and in 1909 made his greatest hit with ALIAS JIMMY VALENTINE, based on O. Henry's story A RETRIEVED REFORMATION. It has been the father of innumerable "crook" plays. His last play was *Mr. Lorelei* (1916).

Arnold, Benedict (b. Jan. 14, 1741—d. June 14, 1801), army officer, traitor. Arnold became one of Washington's most important aides and was entrusted with the fate of the American army, winning a decisive victory at Saratoga (1777). His career, especially his betrayal of his trust at West Point, has been portrayed in many dramas and novels. Among the former are plays by Hugh Henry Brackenridge, Delia Bacon, Samuel Woodworth, Clyde Fitch, John Jay Chapman, and others. Arnold in his earlier, better days is magnificently shown in Kenneth Roberts' novel ARUNDEL (1930). Earlier novels in which he figures include DANIEL PIERCE THOMPSON's *The Green Mountain Boys* (1839) and HAROLD SINCLAIR's *Westward the Tide* (1840).

Arnold, George (b. New York City, June 24, 1834—d. Nov. 9, 1865), newspaperman, humorist, poet. Arnold became a member of the famous group that gathered at PFAFF'S BEER CELLAR. He adopted several pen names—Mc-

Arone, Graham Allen, Pierrot. The McARONE
PAPERS began in *Vanity Fair* (Nov. 24, 1860),
continued in the *Leader,* and reached their close
in the *Weekly Review* (Oct. 14, 1865). After
Arnold's death his poems were edited by WIL-
LIAM WINTER to make two collections, *Drift*
(1866) and *Poems Grave and Gay* (1867);
these were combined in one volume in 1870.

Arnold, Matthew (b. Dec. 24, 1822—d. Jan.
15, 1888), British poet, essayist. Arnold crossed
the Atlantic in 1883 to see what the United
States was like and to deliver lectures here, and
again in 1886 to visit his daughter, who had
married an American. His impressions of this
country, conveyed in DISCOURSES IN AMERICA
(1885) and *Civilization in the United States*
(1888), are on the whole unfavorable but well
spiced with detail. Howard Mumford Jones finds
Arnold's tour a "curious fusion of racism, cultural snobbery, wealth, and honest concern for
'culture.' "

Arnold, Thurman W[esley] (b. Laramie,
Wyo., June 2, 1891—   ), jurist, author. Arnold began to practice law in 1914, taught in
law schools, was for a time mayor of Laramie,
served in the attorney general's office at Washington, became an associate justice of the U.S.
Court of Appeals. He is known to the public,
however, chiefly for his *Folklore of Capitalism*
(1937), a searching analysis of common misconceptions. Later books include *The Bottle-
necks of Business* (1940) and *Democracy and
Free Enterprise* (1942). He was co-author of
The Future of Democratic Capitalism (1950).

Arp, Bill. A pseudonym for CHARLES H.
SMITH.

Arrington, Alfred W. (b. Iredell Co., N.C.,
Sept. 17, 1810—d. Dec. 31, 1867), lawyer,
writer. Arrington spent most of his life on the
western frontier. Under the pseudonym Charles
Summerfield he wrote *The Desperadoes of the
Southwest* (1847) and *The Rangers and Regulators of the Tanaha* (1856). His *Poems* appeared
in 1869.

Arrow and the Song, The. A poem by
HENRY WADSWORTH LONGFELLOW which appeared originally in THE BELFRY OF BRUGES AND
OTHER POEMS (1845). Longfellow called it
"literally an improvisation," but attention has
been called to the resemblance of the poem to a
quatrain in Goethe's *Sprueche in Reimen.*

Arrow Maker, The (1910), a play by MARY
AUSTIN, produced in 1911. The theme is the
revolt of a medicine woman of the Paiute tribe
against the sanctity which keeps her remote
from human love.

Arrowsmith (1925), a novel by SINCLAIR
LEWIS. This satiric picture of the scientist in
the midst of industrialists, newspapermen, and
rich women stirred up a great controversy. Lewis
follows the career of Dr. Martin Arrowsmith
from a small-town practice, through the health
department of a small city, an "institute" sponsored by a rich man and his wife, to an isolated
West Indian island and an equally isolated
Vermont farm. Arrowsmith encounters meanness, corruption, misunderstanding, willful ob-

struction, jealousy, sensationalism, race prejudice, also a modicum of nobility and idealism.
Arrowsmith's quest is in a measure a religious
one—the truth of pure science. He is often
frustrated, and his greatest failure comes when
he himself refuses to carry to the logical extreme
his test of a new serum because it means some
people will die whom he might otherwise have
saved. But there is frequent satire, too, as good
as in BABBITT. By general agreement, moreover,
Leora, Arrowsmith's first wife, is the only likable woman character Lewis created.

Some of the medical lore for *Arrowsmith* came
from Lewis' observation of his own father, a
physician, and perhaps from his mother, the
daughter of a physician. But he depended for
many of the technical details on PAUL DE KRUIF,
whose MICROBE HUNTERS appeared the year
after *Arrowsmith* was published. JACQUES LOEB,
the famous biologist, obviously suggested the
character of MAX GOTTLIEB.

Arsenal at Springfield, The (1845), a poem by
HENRY WADSWORTH LONGFELLOW. The open-
ing lines—"This is the Arsenal. From floor to
ceiling,/ Like a huge organ, rise the burnished
arms"—were suggested to the poet by his wife
when they were on their wedding journey and
visited the Springfield Arsenal. In a letter she
said, "We grow quite warlike against war, and
I urged H. to write a peace poem." He wrote it
several months later.

Arsenic and Old Lace (1941), a comedy by
Joseph Kesselring (1902–1967). It concerns
two apparently gentle old ladies who, inspired
by the purest motives, poison derelicts for their
own good.

Arthur, Chester A[lan] (b. Fairfield, Vt., Oct.
5, 1830—d. Nov. 18, 1886), twenty-first President. Arthur was a lawyer in New York City,
became Collector of the Port, then was elected
Vice-President. He was obviously a "machine
politician," but after taking office upon the assassination of President Garfield (1881–85), he
proved an able and conscientious administrator
who supported civil service reforms. He failed
to gain a renomination; the "Stalwart Republicans" turned to JAMES G. BLAINE and lost the
election to Grover Cleveland. Arthur retired to
private life in New York City. George F. Howe
wrote his biography (1934; rev., 1957).

Arthur, Timothy Shay (b. Orange Co., N.Y.,
June 6, 1809—d. March 6, 1885), editor, author,
reformer. Arthur began as a watchmaker but
gradually drifted into writing. He contributed to
GODEY'S LADY'S BOOK and then founded several
imitations, one of which, ultimately called *Arthur's Home Magazine* (1853), had a considerable circulation; he was still editing it at his death.
He also edited the Baltimore SATURDAY VISITER
for a while and contributed to other magazines.
Meanwhile he was writing novels—against gambling, about domestic virtues, in favor of temperance. He was himself neither a teetotaler nor a
prohibitionist. Finally one of his stories gained a
vogue that made it what someone has called "a
subclassic of American literature"—TEN NIGHTS
IN A BARROOM AND WHAT I SAW THERE

(1854), the tale of a drunkard who ruins his family. It was made into a play, produced seriously at first, then as a burlesque.

Arthur Bonnicastle (1873), a novel by JOSIAH GILBERT HOLLAND. Holland pleasingly relates experiences in a private school, at Yale, and in New York; the book is probably in part autobiographical.

Arthur Mervyn (Part I, 1799; Part II, 1800), a novel by CHARLES BROCKDEN BROWN. It is a strange mixture of violent deeds and emotions, showing the strong influence of William Godwin's *Caleb Williams*. Arthur is a young man who becomes entangled with a criminal named Welbeck and is accused of being his accomplice. He clears himself and finds friends. The most vivid portion of the novel is the first-hand description of the yellow fever epidemic in Philadelphia in 1793. The book indicates Brown's great interest in abnormal psychology, but it is a confused work, impressive only in spots.

Articles of Confederation and Perpetual Union. The first attempt to form a United States was debated by Congress from 1776 to 1778 and submitted in the latter year for ratification by the states. In March, 1781, the Articles went into effect. They established "the United States of America," but the organization set up by the Articles was clumsy and impractical. Thus the delegates from each of the thirteen states voted as a unit, and nine votes constituted a majority. Congress had no power to levy taxes and had to beg the states for money. The problem of the western lands was left unsolved. There was no effective executive officer. The difficulties created by these defects ultimately led to the calling of the Constitutional Convention in May, 1787, and in 1789 the Constitution was ratified. But the Articles of Confederation served as a useful laboratory experiment.

Artie Greengroin (1945), humorous sketches by HARRY BROWN. They had appeared originally in the World War II army weekly, *Yank*.

Arundel (1930), a historical novel by KENNETH ROBERTS. Arundel was the original name of Kennebunk, Maine. It was Roberts' intention to write a series of novels that would give the history of Maine in a chronicle of a family through the generations, but he gave up the idea as the series expanded, and as he became more and more interested in the history of the country as a whole. In *Arundel*, perhaps his best novel, he deals with the expedition against Quebec and BENEDICT ARNOLD's role in it.

As a Man Thinks (1911), a play by AUGUSTUS THOMAS. "Mental healing" is the theme of this play, with the additional theme that a man's trust in his wife's fidelity is the basic fact of our civilization. The central character is a wise and humane Jewish physician, Dr. Seelig, who cures a jealous and brooding husband in the course of a plot that avoids sentimentality but allows the free expression of emotion.

Asbury, Francis (b. England, Aug. 20 or 21, 1745—d. March 31, 1816), clergyman. Asbury reached America in 1771 and in 1772 was made John Wesley's superintendent in this country. Friction with other religious leaders led to his recall (1775), but he refused to return and became an American citizen, aligning himself with the movement for separation from England. He became prominent in the organization of the Methodist Episcopal Church, was consecrated as superintendent, assumed the title of bishop (1785), and ruled the church till his death. His *Journals* (3 v.) were published in 1852. Two biographies of Asbury have appeared: E. S. Tipple's *Francis Asbury, The Prophet of the Long Road* (1916) and HERBERT ASBURY's *Methodist Saint* (1927).

Asbury, Herbert (b. Farmington, Me., Sept. 1, 1891—d. Feb. 24, 1963), newspaperman, historian. A descendant of FRANCIS ASBURY, first Methodist bishop to be ordained in America, and brought up in a strictly puritanical environment, Asbury early revolted against this environment, although one of his books is *A Methodist Saint* (1927), a life of his grandfather. His first book, however, was *Up from Methodism* (1926). His special field of writing has been the portrayal of the shadier side of the past of great American cities. He first gained fame with a story called HATRACK, which appeared in the AMERICAN MERCURY, and drew the wrath of the censors. Among his books: *The Gangs of New York* (1928); *Life of Carry Nation* (1929); *The Barbary Coast* (1933); *The French Quarter* (1936); *Sucker's Progress* (1938); *The Great Illusion: an Informal History of Prohibition* (1950).

Asch, Nathan (b. Poland, July 10, 1902—d. Dec. 23, 1964), novelist. Asch came to the U.S. at the age of thirteen; his father is the novelist SHOLEM ASCH. His book *The Road* (1937) is a "search for America," a report on the way Americans think and feel. His fiction is marked by realism, sometimes extreme—so extreme in the case of *Pay Day* (1930) that the book was suppressed. He also wrote *The Office* (1925) and *The Valley* (1935), as well as scripts for Hollywood.

Asch, Sholem (b. Poland, Nov. 1, 1880—d. July 10, 1957), novelist, dramatist. Asch is the chief Yiddish novelist of the first half of the 20th century. He lived in various European countries until 1910, then came to America and was naturalized in 1920. By 1924 his short stories, novelettes, novels, plays, and poems had become so numerous that they were published in a collected edition of eighteen volumes in Warsaw, all in Yiddish. Several of his books appeared in English between 1917 and 1933; in the latter year his *Three Cities* (Petersburg, Warsaw, Moscow) became a best seller. More sensational still was the success of *The Nazarene* (1939), a faithful, friendly portrayal of Jesus, followed by THE APOSTLE (1943) and *Mary* (1949). *East River* (1946), a novel laid in New York City, presents a part of the metropolis where men and women of many races and creeds struggle, love, hate, merge to some degree to form the complex character that we call American. Asch's later writings tend toward a mingling of the realistic and the sentimental. A more sordid realism was found in his play *The God of Vengeance,* produced by Max Reinhardt in Berlin in 1910 and closed by the police in New York in 1922. Asch's later works include *Moses* (1951); *A Passage in the Night* (1953); *The Prophet* (1955).

Ashburton, Mary. Heroine of Longfellow's HYPERION (1839), a novel of an American's wanderings in Europe. She is a young English-woman whom Paul Fleming, an American, de-sires to marry. At first she rejects him, then con-sents to become his wife. The story was written by Longfellow after he had met Fanny Appleton of Boston on a tour in Switzerland; he intended the novel to be an instrument of his courtship. At first, however, *Hyperion* greatly displeased Miss Appleton, and only some years later did she consent to marry the poet.

Ashe, Thomas (1770—[?]), British adven-turer, novelist, writer of travel books. Born in Ireland, Ashe was for a time a soldier, for a time in business, later a tutor, still later in the com-missariat of the British army. Irregularities in his accounts forced him to flee to America, where he traveled, he asserted, at least as far as the Mississippi. He was employed for a while in the government service under Jefferson. His *Travels in America, Performed in 1806, for the Purpose of Exploring the Rivers Allegheny, Mononga-hela, Ohio, and Mississippi* was published in both London and Newburyport, Mass., in 1808. The book became famous, Allan Nevins states, for its "Munchausen-like exaggerations." Ashe's account of the United States was in general un-favorable.

Ashley, Lady Brett. The captivating, neu-rotic heroine of THE SUN ALSO RISES (1926), a novel by Ernest Hemingway.

Ash-Wednesday (1930), a poem by T. S. ELIOT. The first three sections of the poem appeared separately in periodicals, indicating that the six sections which make up the *Ash Wednesday* should perhaps be considered as individual poems on the same theme rather than as one long poem. The sections are meditative, associative, and circular rather than logical, and deal with a state of mind which is only sug-gested and never clearly delineated. The domi-nant imagery is religious, and in several places the style approaches that of a litany As the title suggests, the major theme is penitence, the difficulty of the spiritual life, and the need for renunciation of both despair and hope; although some readers have difficulty with its theology, *Ash Wednesday* remains one of Eliot's most finely structured and melodic poems.

As I Lay Dying (1930), a novel by WILLIAM FAULKNER. Written in only six weeks, *As I Lay Dying* is Faulkner's favorite and certainly one of his finest novels. The story unfolds in some sixty short sections, each labeled with the name of the character who narrates his thoughts and perceptions; as in THE SOUND AND THE FURY, Faulkner uses the stream-of-consciousness tech-nique.

As the story opens Addie Bundren, a Missis-sippi farm woman, is dying; each of the mem-bers of her family—her husband, Anse; four sons, Cash, Darl, Jewel, and Vardaman, and a daughter, Dewey Dell—as well as some of her neighbors, reveals his relationship to her in words and actions. She has made Anse promise to take her to Jefferson to be buried, and the major part of the book concerns the Bundrens' journey with the coffin to the burying ground. A series of mishaps besets the family en route: in crossing a flooding river, the mules are drowned, Cash's leg is broken, and the coffin is upset and rescued by Jewel at the risk of his life. On the other side the family rests at a farmhouse, where Darl sets fire to the barn in an attempt to destroy the now-putrescent corpse; again the coffin is rescued by Jewel, who is badly burned. The family finally reaches Jefferson, where Addie is buried, Darl is taken without warning to the in-sane asylum, and Anse acquires a new wife, "duck-shaped" and pop-eyed.

In the course of the narrative it is revealed that Jewel was born of Addie's affair with Whit-field, a local preacher. Her relationship to Anse had been spiritually and emotionally barren, based on words that were just "shape[s] to fill a lack." Jewel, the child of Addie's relationship in which no words were necessary, is signifi-cantly silent; a passionate, active man, he lives intuitively and impulsively. Darl, the extreme opposite of Jewel, is extraordinarily sensitive and perceptive, but lives in the private world of his mind, several removes from reality and from human contact. Each is concerned with balance —both in terms of his trade as a carpenter and in his growing ability to balance thought and ac-tion, word and fact.

As I Like It. A department conducted by WILLIAM LYON PHELPS in *Scribner's Magazine* from 1922 to 1936. Phelps wrote about books, plays, and people in a way that won him a large audience; very frequently his judgment of a book or play secured its success. Selections from these essays appeared under the same title in three books (1923, 1924, 1926).

Asimov, Isaac (b. Russia, Jan. 2, 1920—), teacher, science writer. Asimov was educated at Columbia University, where he re-ceived his Ph.D. in 1948. While associate pro-fessor of biochemistry at the Boston University School of Medicine, he published more than forty books, both for adults and for young readers. He wrote science fiction for teen-agers under the pseudonym Paul French; in some of this he combined science fiction and detective story very successfully. In 1957 Asimov won the Thomas Alva Edison Foundation award for *Building Blocks of the Universe,* and in 1960 the Howard W. Blakeslee award from the American Heart Association for *The Living River* (1959), in which he analyzed the chemical composition of the blood and related it to other manifesta-tions in our universe. His books include: *Lucky Stars and the Pirates of the Asteroids* (1953); *The Kingdom of the Sun* (1960); *Realm of Measure* (1960). *The Intelligent Man's Guide to Science* (2 v., 1960) is an encyclopedic work covering in brief essay form all of science for the layman.

Aspern Papers, The (1888), a novelette by HENRY JAMES. According to passages in his notebook, James based *The Aspern Papers* on a story he had heard concerning the mistress of Byron, then living, who was in possession of several unpublished papers and letters of both Byron and Shelley. The narrator of *The Aspern Papers* learns that the former mistress of the romantic poet Jeffrey Aspern is still living in Italy and has in her possession a collection of the poet's papers which she will not permit to be published. In hope of somehow gaining access to the papers, the narrator rents a room from the old lady and her middle-aged niece, but his plans are frustrated when, at the old lady's death, the niece demands marriage as the price of the papers.

Assignation, The (*Godey's Lady's Book*, 1834; TALES OF THE GROTESQUE AND THE ARABESQUE, 1840), a story by EDGAR ALLAN POE. A wealthy young man rescues the young child of the Marchesa Aphrodite from drowning while her aged husband looks on indifferently. She makes an assignation with the young man for one hour after sunrise. The narrator accompanies the hero to his magnificent home. At the hour set a messenger arrives with word that the marchesa is dead; and the narrator discovers that his host, apparently asleep after taking a glass of wine, is dead too. Both had taken the same poison; the assignation had been kept. W. C. Bronson remarks that the story "surrounds death with all the luxury of Old World wealth and beauty and with the glamor of intellect, genius, and proud, calm will."

Assistant, The (1957), a novel by BERNARD MALAMUD. Set in a poor neighborhood in New York, the novel deals with Morris Bober, his wife, Ida, and his daughter, Helen, who own a grocery store. It is held up by a thug and his crony, Frank Alpine. After the robbery Alpine is drawn back inexplicably to the store, lives in the basement, and finally tries to help Morris. The book is the story of Frank's gradual implication in Morris' problems and his final understanding of that implication. Though oppressed with guilt for the robbery, he continues to steal money from Morris and is fired. Later he reveals his love for Helen and is rebuffed. When all fails in the store, Morris makes an abortive attempt at suicide; Frank saves him and runs the store during Morris' recovery. Frank finally confesses that he was one of the thieves. His changing attitude toward himself and his crimes is mirrored in his attitude toward the Jews. Finally, he himself becomes a Jew.

Malamud's style is carefully fashioned and rich, and he has a gift for revealing character through dialogue. His writing at best has a rare clarity and power.

Aston, Anthony ([?]—[?]), English actor. He arrived in Charleston, S.C., in 1703 or thereabouts and became the first professional actor, so far as is known, in American history. He also wrote plays, of which only one, *The Fool's Opera*

(*c.* 1730), survives. It is a parody of John Gay's *The Beggar's Opera.*

Astor, John Jacob (b. Germany, July 17, 1763—d. March 29, 1848), merchant. Astor arrived in the United States in 1784, opened a fur store in New York, organized trading posts in the West, bought real estate, and became a national and international power. He encouraged WASHINGTON IRVING in his interest in the West and in his writing of ASTORIA (1836), an account of Astor's fur trade in the Northwest. Money from the Astor fortune went to the great Astor Library, which, together with the Lenox Foundation, eventually formed the New York Public Library. John Jennings' novel, *River to the West* (1948), describes Astor and his great fur ventures.

Astoria, or, Anecdotes of an Enterprise Beyond the Rocky Mountains (1836; many rev. eds.), a descriptive and historical work by WASHINGTON IRVING. Caught by the speculative spirit of the age, Irving became involved in financial difficulties; for a while his writings, including *Astoria,* were frankly hack work. This is a glorification of JOHN JACOB ASTOR and the outposts of trade that he established. Much of the research was done in Astor's home. Astoria itself, once called Fort Clatsop, was a town in Oregon near the mouth of the Columbia River. In 1811 Astor established a fur trading post at this point, but sold his interest in it to British traders during the War of 1812; later Astoria was returned to the United States by the Treaty of Ghent (1814).

Asylum, The, or, Alonzo and Melissa (1811), a novel, probably written by Isaac Mitchell, a New York newspaper editor. A plagiarism, ascribed to Daniel Jackson, appeared the same year under the title, *Alonzo and Melissa, or, The Unfeeling Father.* Laid in the era of Revolution, *The Asylum* is a story in the artificial Gothic manner in which the father of Melissa parts her from Alonzo because he is poor; she escapes to Charleston, whence comes a false report of her death, while Alonzo enlists in the navy and is captured by the British. But Benjamin Franklin aids him to escape, he comes to Charleston and meets a mysterious lady who turns out to be Melissa. There is also a castle haunted by ghosts who are really smugglers working for the British. Carl Van Doren calls it "an absurd romance," but it was popular.

Atala (1801; American translation, 1802), a novel by FRANÇOIS RENÉ CHATEAUBRIAND. Later incorporated in his *Génie du Christianisme,* this romance was originally intended to form part of a trilogy with LES NATCHEZ and *René.* All three stories were suggested by a visit that Chateaubriand paid to America in 1791; he spent part of the time residing with an Indian tribe. Deeply under the influence of Rousseau, Chateaubriand paints, for most part, the noble savage, although the number of homicides, suicides, and massacres in the tale does not support his thesis materially. The characters have only a remote resemblance to real Indians.

Atall, Peter. See ROBERT WALN.

Athenaeum. See Boston Athenaeum.

Atherton, Gertrude [Franklin] (b. San Francisco, Oct. 30, 1857—d. June 14, 1948), novelist, biographer, historian. Mrs. Atherton began writing very early, but did not really start on a literary career until the late 1880's—and con-

tinued producing books of all kinds until her own late eighties. *My San Francisco*, a book of mingled history and reminiscence, appeared in her 90th year. When a reviewer in the *Saturday Review of Literature* (Feb. 12, 1947) began with a reference to Mrs. Atherton's "long and spectacular career in light fiction stretching beyond the memory of most of us," Mrs. Atherton replied vigorously (May 17) that many of her novels were based on serious and detailed historical study. Her work, which was uneven in quality but rich in variety of theme and background, included *The Californians* (1898); *Senator North* (1900); *The Conqueror* (1902); *Rezánov* (1906); *California: An Intimate History* (1914); *Black Oxen* (1923); *The Immortal Marriage* (1927); and *Adventures of a Novelist* (1932). Her most enduring book is The Conqueror, a fictional biography of Alexander Hamilton, and she edited *A Few of Hamilton's Letters* (1903). Black Oxen, with rejuvenation as its theme, joined Jurgen, The Sun Also Rises, and similar books in defying the raised eyebrows of Puritans. In the 1920's Tauchnitz, the German firm which published cheap paperback editions of American books on the Continent, reported her the most popular contemporary American writer. See The Erotic School.

Atkinson, [Justin] Brooks (b. Melrose, Mass., Nov. 28, 1894—   ), newspaperman, drama critic, writer. Atkinson began as a reporter on Springfield, Mass. and Boston papers, in 1922 joined the New York *Times* staff as editor of the book review section, then in 1925 turned drama critic, a position he held until his retirement after the 1959–60 season. From 1942 to 1946 he was a war correspondent for the *Times* in China and Russia, then returned to reviewing plays. The vivid dispatches he wrote from China won a Pulitzer Prize. The variety of Atkinson's interests is shown in his books: *Henry Thoreau, The Cosmic Yankee* (1927); *East of the Hudson* (rural wanderings, 1931); *The Cingalese Prince* (an account of a round-the-world trip on a freighter, 1934); *Broadway Scrapbook* (1947); *Once Around the Sun* (essays, 1951). Retiring as drama critic, Atkinson continued to write for the *Times* on general subjects in an irregularly appearing column called *Critic At Large*. His wife, **Oriana**, wrote *Over at Uncle Joe's: Moscow and Me* (1947); *Manhattan and Me* (1954); *The South and West of It: Ireland and Me* (1956), and several books of fiction.

Atlantic Charter. This important document was prepared by F. D. Roosevelt and Winston Churchill after an extended conference on shipboard. It was signed in August, 1941, as binding on the United States and Great Britain, for whom it affirmed altruistic aims such as Woodrow Wilson had listed in his famous Fourteen Points. Other nations signed the document as the war progressed, and it became the fundamental code of the United Nations.

Atlantic Monthly, The. Founded in Boston in November, 1857, by Moses Dresser Phillips of the publishing firm of Phillips, Sampson & Company, the *Atlantic Monthly* was purchased two years later by Ticknor & Fields for $10,000. H. O. Houghton (later Houghton, Mifflin & Company) bought it in 1874, and the Atlantic Monthly Company, a stock concern, has owned it since 1908. The magazine has enjoyed the editorship of a distinguished series of men of letters: James Russell Lowell (1857–1861), James T. Fields (1861–1871), William Dean Howells (1871–1881), Thomas Bailey Aldrich (1881–1890), Horace E. Scudder (1890–1898), Walter Hines Page (1898–1899), Bliss Perry (1899–1909), Ellery Sedgwick (1909–1938), and Edward A. Weeks (1938–   ). It was for many years regarded as the pre-eminent literary magazine of the country; in the 1960's, though points of emphasis have shifted, the *Atlantic* and *Harper's* are the sole survivors of the traditional "quality magazine" of the 19th century.

Through its first 15 years, the *Atlantic* relied mainly on New England writers, and the volumes of those early years, filled with the work of Emerson, Longfellow, Whittier, Lowell, Holmes, Hawthorne, and Harriet Beecher Stowe, set a high literary standard. A change came over the magazine with Howells' editorship, when it came to recognize Southern, Midwestern, and Far-Western writers, publishing the work of Mark Twain, Bret Harte, Mary N. Murfree, John Hay, Maurice Thompson, and Paul Hamilton Hayne. Another break came with the advent of Ellery Sedgwick, who introduced lively articles on the economic, political, social, and scientific changes in the American scene. Circulation passed 100,000 in 1921 and increased to over 260,000 by 1961. The Weeks editorship was notable for a greater breadth of international outlook and increased interest in current problems. Among leading authors published in this latter period were Stephen Vincent Benét, Robert Frost, Howard Mumford Jones, Van Wyck Brooks, Bernard De Voto, Gertrude Stein, Rebecca West, and Virginia Woolf. Ellery Sedgwick included selections from forty-six authors in *Atlantic Harvest* (1947). Helen McMahon wrote *Criticism of Fiction: A Study of Trends in the Atlantic Monthly, 1857–98* (1952). Edward Weeks and Emily Flint edited a selection from the *Atlantic's* first hundred years in *Jubilee* (1957). Mark Anthony DeWolfe Howe described *The Atlantic Monthly and its Makers* (1919).

Atlantis: The Antediluvian World (1882), a treatise by IGNATIUS DONNELLY. Donnelly took his title from Plato's story of a lost continent, but wove into his account (which is not a novel) the Bible legend of a lost paradise. The original Garden of Eden, he argued, was this same Atlantis, from which civilization spread to the rest of the earth; and then Atlantis sank into the sea. The book made a sensation, and gave many readers their first introduction to archeology.

Attaché, The, or, Sam Slick in England (4 v., 1843–44), by T. C. HALIBURTON. In these sketches Haliburton continued to write with sardonic humor observations supposedly made by the Yankee clockmaker whom he had made famous. But Haliburton, a Canadian, here chose to make fun of some of his own countrymen. The book was popular in Canada and England.

Aubert de Gaspé, Phillippe (b. Quebec, Oct. 30, 1786—d. Jan. 29, 1871), lawyer, novelist, historian. Aubert de Gaspé studied law at the Quebec seminary and was high sheriff of the district of Quebec for many years until forced to withdraw from public life because of business difficulties and debts. At the age of seventy-six, he brought out his first book, *Les anciens canadiens* (1863). This historical romance, thought to be a classic of French-Canadian literature, has been translated into English twice as *The Canadians of Old* (1864, Georgiana M. Penee; 1890, Charles G. D. Roberts). His *Mémoires* (1886) is a collection of notes and hints for historians. A son, Alfred Aubert de Gaspé, published a posthumous collection of essays and sketches, *Divers* (1893).

Auchincloss, Louis Stanton ["Andrew Lee"] (b. Lawrence, N.Y., Sept. 27, 1917—   ), lawyer, novelist, short-story writer. Auchincloss graduated from Yale and the University of Virginia, was admitted to the New York bar in 1941 and has been a member of several New York law firms. His novels deal with the upper circles of New York society and he occasionally draws on his own experience as a lawyer for background, as in *The Great World and Timothy Colt* (1956). *The Romantic Egoists* (1954), a book of short stories with a unifying theme, won a good deal of critical approval. Commenting on the book, Angus Wilson found Auchincloss a "clever and subtle student of human social be-

haviour." Auchincloss has also written *The Indifferent Children* (1947); *The Injustice Collectors* (1950); *Venus in Sparta* (1958); *Pursuit of the Prodigal* (1959); *The House of Five Talents* (1960).

Auden, W[ystan] H[ugh] (b. England, Feb. 21, 1907—   ), poet. Shortly after leaving Christ Church College, Oxford, Auden became identified with a group of left-wing poets in London, including Stephen Spender, Louis Mac-

George Cserna

Neice, and C. Day Lewis, who were the most promising young writers of the Thirties. Auden, the most talented of the group, was influenced particularly by T. S. ELIOT and Yeats, and is, with Eliot, one of the most influential of modern poets. Like Eliot, Auden experimented a great deal with earlier poetic styles and techniques, particularly that of the metaphysicals; his use of alliteration, assonance, and internal rhyme shows the influence of Old English. The development of Auden's technique and subject matter led from a cerebral, elliptic style, highly compact and complex, to the technical excellence of such later poems as SHIELD OF ACHILLES (1955), and from a Marxist orientation toward an essentially religious position based largely on Pascal and Kierkegaard.

At his very simplest level Auden might be considered as a social commentator; from the beginning his work has been concerned with the disintegration of modern life and with the ills of society that, in turn, have their roots in the ills of the individual. His strong feeling for the necessity of social commitment drew him toward Marxism, which he admired for the strict intellectual discipline it required; he could not, however, accept the absolute authority of the State or the negation of freedom and individuality present in "Collective Man." Auden is, however, by no means merely a social commentator and is even less a propagandist, in spite of some of his early satirical leftist poems, such as *The Orators* (1932) or *The Dance of Death* (1933). He is primarily concerned with the problem of finding adequate symbolic patterns to embody the major problems of the day—particularly that of the isolated individual (the "lonelies"), the inevitable fallibility of human love, and the search for some kind of personal integration or salvation.

From the mid-thirties on his poetry has tended to become conversational and discursive; like Yeats, he often uses short, irregular line-lengths and is concerned with embodying abstract ideas in concrete terms. His use of landscape imagery, for instance, is almost always directed toward objectifying some aspect of human nature, and the characters of his verse plays are projections of abstract qualities rather than dramatic personalities in their own right. Among his early works: *Poems* (1930); *Look, Stranger* (1936); *Spain* (1937); three plays in collaboration with CHRISTOPHER ISHERWOOD, *The Dog Beneath the Skin* (1935); *The Ascent of F.6* (1936); *On the Frontier* (1938); and *Letters from Iceland* (with Louis MacNeice, 1937).

Auden's work falls into two fairly distinct categories, that of primarily social and satirical poetry written during the Thirties, and that written after his emigration to America in 1939, which is almost without exception concerned with religious belief. It would appear that Auden, feeling as he does the poet's need for a "necessary impersonality," found in New York the anonymity and lack of tradition requisite for a detached, objective viewpoint. Both the *New Year Letter* (1941) and *The Sea and the Mirror* (1944) deal with the nature of the artistic process and its relationship to life, and, by extension, with the concept of life as a kind of Pilgrim's Progress, a quest whose aim is salvation. Auden developed this idea in an essay, *K's Quest,* in which he discusses various types of quest from the pursuit of the Golden Fleece to Joseph K's quest in Kafka's *The Trial*—all of which amount to a search for the Way. In *The Quest: A Sonnet Sequence* Auden somewhat satirically analyses the various pitfalls encountered by the modern man in his search for salvation. *For the Time Being: A Christmas Oratorio* (1944), which contains some of Auden's finest poetry, is an account of the birth of Jesus with pertinent parallels for modern times, as well as a statement of Auden's religious faith, based largely on Kierkegaard. *The Age of Anxiety* (1947) deals with four "lonelies" who meet during wartime in a New York bar, and their subsequent failure to achieve more than a flash of "negative knowledge," who return to duty, "reclaimed by the actual world where time is real and in which, therefore, poetry can take no interest." Also among Auden's later works: *Nones* (1951); *Selected Poetry* (1959); HOMAGE TO CLIO (1960). He has edited *The Living*

Thoughts of Kierkegaard (1952). With Chester Kallman he wrote the libretto for Stravinsky's opera, *The Rake's Progress*, and made a new translation of Mozart's *The Magic Flute* (1956).

Audrey (1902), a novel by MARY JOHNSTON. As in the same author's To HAVE AND TO HOLD, the scene is colonial Virginia. Audrey, whose parents have been killed by the Indians, becomes the ward of a wealthy young man who places her in charge of a minister and his wife. The girl grows into a beautiful young woman, and her guardian falls in love with her. But his hesitancy in declaring his love brings on a series of complications. Audrey rejects him, becomes an actress at Williamsburg, dies at last in frustrating an attempt to assassinate her guardian. Eleanor Robson played Audrey in a dramatization of the novel.

Audubon, John James (b. Santo Domingo, April 26, 1785—d. January 27, 1851), naturalist, author, artist. The son of a French naval captain, Audubon lived in Louisiana and Pennsylvania, with many trips to France. Supposedly

he was studying to be an artist, but when his father went bankrupt Audubon really had no occupation. With a partner he opened a general store in Louisville, Kentucky, but he was more interested in birds than in business. He found a loyal, self-sacrificing wife in Lucy Bakewell, who supported Audubon and their two sons for many years by acting as a governess. Constantly journeying all over the country and becoming acquainted with it in its most primitive conditions, Audubon wrote about his experiences in ingratiating bright-colored narratives and produced a series of bird paintings that are splendid as works of art, even if not always scientifically accurate. He became involved in controversy with the Scots immigrant schoolmaster ALEXANDER WILSON, who was somewhat more accurate and almost as good a writer. Like his father, Audubon was driven into bankruptcy and for a time was imprisoned. In later life, however, his genius was generally recognized. His two sons assisted him in his work; one of them, John Woodhouse Audubon, made a roundabout journey in 1849–50 to California which he described in a *Western Journal* (1906).

Audubon himself published a huge folio in parts, THE BIRDS OF NORTH AMERICA (1827–38; octavo form, 1840–44). The accompanying text, written in collaboration with William Mac-Gillivray, was separately published as *Ornithological Biography* (1831–39). The plates of *The Viviparous Quadrupeds of North America* (1842–45) were followed by a text (1846–54); in these volumes Audubon was assisted by his sons and John Bachman. In recent years much material has been culled from Audubon's journals to make various books; in particular, *Delineations of American Scenery and Character* (1926), edited by Francis Hobart Herrick, who also prepared *Audubon the Naturalist: A History of His Life and Times* (1917). Howard Corning's edition of the *Journal of John James Audubon, made during his trip to New Orleans in 1820–21* (1929) provides an entirely unchanged journal. Strong emphasis is laid on Audubon the writer in the passages selected by DONALD CULROSS PEATTIE for *Audubon's America* (1940). Peattie brings him forward "less as the naturalist than as one who knew river captains and roustabouts, pioneers and men of letters, Indians and scientists" and as one who had "a genius for the art of living." *A Mirror for the Sky* (1948) is a musical drama by Jessamyn West and Raoul Pène duBois that portrayed the life of Audubon. J. F. McDermott has edited Edward Harris' *Up the Missouri with Audubon* (1952), a journal.

Augie March, The Adventures of, a novel by SAUL BELLOW (1953). This modern picaresque novel about a youth who grows up in Chicago during the depression catapulted its author into national recognition. The book was a best seller and recipient of the National Book Award. Because he will not accept any defining role in life, Augie finds himself being swept along in a current of alternately hilarious and tragic events. Unlike his brother Simon, who marries the daughter of a wealthy Chicago coal dealer in order to rise from his lower class Jewish slum environment, Augie refuses every opportunity for a settled existence that comes his way. He suffers some hard knocks, but as he says, there is an *"animal ridens* in me, the laughing creature, forever rising up." His ability to laugh at himself as he tells his story makes Augie a memorable hero. In sharp contrast to the economy of style popular in American writing since Hemingway, Augie's prose is endlessly rich, varied, and complex. Through him the author speaks at once in the pithy language of the streets and the inversions of a Chicago University intellectual.

Aunt Polly. A character in MARK TWAIN'S TOM SAWYER and its sequels. She is Tom's aunt and guardian, and was drawn from Twain's mother.

Aurora Dawn (1947), a novel by HERMAN WOUK. It attacks radio and its tycoons in a strange style, an imitation of meandering, allusive 18th-century prose.

Auslander, Joseph (b. Philadelphia, Oct. 11, 1897—d. June 22, 1965), poet, literary historian. Popular without displaying undue sentimentality, Auslander employed conventional forms with varied themes and appeals. Among his collections: *Sunrise Trumpets* (1924); *Cyclops' Eye* (1926); *Letters to Women* (1930); *Riders at the Gate* (1938); *The Unconquerables* (1943). In collaboration with FRANK ERNEST HILL, Auslander prepared a history of poetry for young people, *The Winged Horse* (1927), followed by *The Winged Horse Anthology* (1928). He made successful published translations of La Fontaine (1930) and Petrarch (1931). Auslander and his wife, AUDREY WURDEMANN, collaborated on *My Uncle Jan* (1948), reminiscences in the form of a novel, and *Islanders* (1951), which Philip Wylie praised for "its beautiful display of meanings in mankind."

Austin, Jane Goodwin (b. Worcester, Mass., Feb. 25, 1831—d. March 30, 1894), writer of stories for girls. Mrs. Austin wrote mainly of life in New England, especially of the Pilgrim past. The best known of these tales were *Standish of Standish* (1889) and BETTY ALDEN (1891).

Austin, Mary [Hunter] (b. Carlinville, Ill., Sept. 9, 1868—d. Aug. 13, 1934), poet, critic, novelist, playwright. Mary Hunter, one of six children of George Hunter, talked to God under a walnut tree when she was five years old and never thereafter relinquished the conviction that she had special intuitive powers. In 1888 the Hunters moved to California, first as homesteaders, later as storekeepers; Mary learned much of western lore and became attached to Spanish California. In 1891 she married Stafford W. Austin, a homesteader in the Panamint district. Failing as winegrowers, the Austins moved to San Francisco, where Mrs. Austin sold her first story to the OVERLAND MONTHLY, and later to various locations in the Owens River valley, where she had her first close acquaintance with Indian life and the ways of the desert.

Mrs. Austin's life during this period was lonely and frustrated; her marriage was not a success and her only child, a daughter, suffered from mental illness. In 1905 she and her husband separated permanently. She went to live in Carmel and there met JACK LONDON, GEORGE STERLING, and other literary figures of the Coast. Her novel *Outland* (1910) is probably an account of Sterling's unhappy marriage. A few years later, believing herself ill with cancer, she journeyed to Italy, where she studied mystical exercises. When her health improved she stayed in Paris and London. Her Italian experiences confirmed her mystical mode of thought. She returned to New York in 1910 to assist in the production of THE ARROW MAKER, her most popular play.

From 1910 to 1924 Mrs. Austin's life shifted between New York and Carmel; she lectured widely, wrote many books and essays. She was active in the feminist movement, alert to social and political affairs, interested in all signs of artistic awakening in the United States. She liked the role of *chisera* (Indian prophetess), and her pronouncements were frequently based on what she chose to call her insight into aboriginal life. In 1924 she took up residence in Santa Fe, N.M., where her attention was concentrated more and more on regionalism and the folk arts. She plunged into a campaign for the preservation of Indian and Spanish handicrafts; she became an amateur folklorist; she represented New Mexico at the Boulder Dam Conference in 1927, fighting for the regional autonomy of the mountain and desert states. Her adobe house in Santa Fe, named Casa Querida ("Beloved House"), became a stopping-off place for literary friends and a center of local cultural activities. As self-appointed champion of the Indians and Spanish-Americans she was supreme.

Mrs. Austin produced thirty-two books and more than two hundred essays, as well as poems, reviews, introductions, etc. Some of her themes are virtually obsessive. The difficulties of marriage, considered from a feminist point of view, run through much of her work: *Santa Lucia, A Common Story* (1908), a novel; *Lost Borders* (1909), a collection of desert stories; *The Arrow Maker* (1911); *Love and the Soul Maker* (1914), a treatise; *No. 26 Jayne Street* (1920), a novel. In some of her work social problems become dominant, as in *The Ford* (1917), a novel about the struggle of California farmers against inevitable urban growth. Her mystical experiences afforded the background for other works: *Christ in Italy* (1912); *The Man Jesus* (1915; reissued as *A Small Town Man*, 1925); *Everyman's Genius* (1925); *Experiences Facing Death* (1931); *Can Prayer Be Answered?* (1934). But her most enduring work was as an amateur naturalist; her nature writing is strongly evocative, done in the Transcendental manner and manifesting a sometimes pantheistic ecstasy. Indeed, Mrs. Austin boasted that she had done for the desert what Thoreau had done for New England—and with a much more difficult subject. She wrote THE LAND OF LITTLE RAIN (1903); *The Flock* (1906); *California: The Land of the Sun* (1914); *The Land of Journey's Ending* (1924). Her novel *Starry Adventure* (1931) is notable for the way in which the New Mexican landscape is made to serve as, so to speak, the chief "character" of the story. *The American Rhythm* (1923) is, however, probably Mrs. Austin's most widely read work today. A treatise on poetry containing her own "re-expressions" of Indian verse, it is a strong plea for freedom of form and language as the proper techniques for an indigenous American lyricism. She noted that the Indians, working in a wholly American culture, had discovered "free verse" as their natural mode. In *One-Smoke Stories* (1934) she attempted to extend her folk theories into the practice of fiction. Her autobiography, *Earth Horizon* (1932), throws much light on her work and reveals her as in some respects a rather pathetic and frustrated woman who nevertheless sought for herself a genuinely independent philosophy in the spirit of her illustrious New England predecessors.

DUDLEY WYNN

Austin, Stephen Fuller (b. Wythe Co., Va., Nov. 3, 1793—d. Dec. 27, 1836), colonizer, official. Austin brought settlers to Texas, served as an official under the Mexicans, was imprisoned through a misunderstanding, was active in the independence movement, and served for a while with Sam Houston in setting up a Republic of Texas. E. C. Barker collected his *Papers* (4 v., 1924–28), also wrote his biography (1926).

Austin, William (b. Lunenberg, Mass., March 2, 1778—d. June 27, 1841), lawyer, legislator, short-story writer. Austin was identified with Boston and its environs throughout his life, aside from a period spent in London studying law. This residence abroad led to Austin's *Letters from London* (1804), which American lawyers enjoyed for its bright pictures of London legal lights and statesmen. It had been preceded by *Strictures on Harvard University* (1798), in which Austin applied the ideas and standards of Rousseau to his *alma mater*. Austin became a very successful lawyer, also served in the General Court and the Senate of Massachusetts. His own artistic strivings found expression in a few stories, only one of which continues to be read—PETER RUGG, THE MISSING MAN, which appeared in the *New England Galaxy* Sept. 10, 1824. Austin in this and other stories anticipated the techniques and atmosphere of Hawthorne's tales. Hawthorne mildly repaid his debt to Austin by making Peter Rugg the doorkeeper in the museum that houses *A Virtuoso's Collection* (*Mosses from an Old Manse*, 1846).

Authors' League of America. Founded in 1911 to safeguard the rights of authors. It includes the Authors' Guild and the Dramatists' Guild. A similar group, the Writers' Guild of America, serves the Screen Writers' Guild, the Radio Writers' Guild, and the Television Group.

Autobiography of Alice B. Toklas, The (1933), by GERTRUDE STEIN. The book is really Miss Stein's autobiography, written as though by her secretary, Miss Toklas. The book provoked a rejoinder from various Parisian artists and writers, *Testimony Against Gertrude Stein* (1935). In it Georges Braque wrote: "For one who poses as an authority on the epoch it is safe to say she never went beyond the stage of the tourist." For the average reader, however, Miss Stein's book possesses much fascination in its views of Parisian life and personalities, and the whole is offered in a genuinely witty style.

Autobiography of Methuselah, The (1909), a burlesque by JOHN KENDRICK BANGS. The author amuses his readers by describing the reactions of the patriarch and his contemporaries to Noah's building of the Ark.

Autocrat of the Breakfast Table, The (*Atlantic Monthly*, beginning November, 1857; in book form, 1858), a prose work by OLIVER WENDELL HOLMES. A great conversationalist, Holmes found in this series of dialogues a congenial and inspiring medium. The conversations take place at a boardinghouse breakfast table, and a variety of characters participate; the "autocrat" does not always get the best of it. Interspersed are a number of Holmes' most famous poems, among them THE DEACON'S MASTERPIECE and THE CHAMBERED NAUTILUS. The book has kept its freshness, despite its now obscure contemporary allusions. The brilliant and witty talk ranges over many topics, including science, theology, and the nature of American society. Striking, too, are many of Holmes's epigrams: "Put not your trust in money, but put your money in trust." "Sin has many tools, but a lie is the handle which fits them all." Holmes continued the series in *The Professor at the Breakfast Table* (1859), *The Poet at the Breakfast Table* (1872), and *Over the Tea Cups* (1890). In these the story element is more pronounced than in the *Autocrat*. See BREAKFAST TABLE SERIES.

Avon's Harvest (1921), a narrative in verse by EDWIN ARLINGTON ROBINSON. Avon is a New York lawyer, a fear-haunted man, who encounters again and again the same enemy. He learns of his foe's death, but is not relieved of his psychosis, and dies of what the doctor calls an "aneurism" but admits may have been "the devil." In writing this poem Robinson turned from medieval to modern themes, and joined the school of HENRY JAMES. He was interested less in the story than in the analysis of subtle states of mind.

Awake and Sing! (1935), a play by CLIFFORD ODETS. Regarded as Odets' best play, *Awake and Sing!* tells of a poverty-stricken Jewish family in the Bronx—mingled idealists and "practical" persons. Among the latter is the mother, who—with the best intentions—browbeats her husband, forces her daughter to marry a man she doesn't love, and opposes her son's romance with a poor orphan. The results are disastrous, but lead the idealistic son to devote his life to the betterment of humanity. The action is often melodramatic, but the dialogue is richly human and the characters are viewed with compassionate humor.

Awakening of Helena Richie, The (1906), a novel by MARGARET DELAND. Laid in the author's favorite Old Chester, the story tells about a woman of mystery who adopts a small boy named David and in the end is compelled to choose between him and her lover. Her moral awakening and the happiness that results are engagingly depicted. Dr. Lavendar, who appeared in earlier Old Chester tales, is again a leading character in this novel.

Awkward Age, The (1899), a novel by HENRY JAMES. James tells, with endless subtlety, the story of a girl's emergence out of "the awkward age" into modernity and understanding. Nanda and her mother are in love with the same man; the mother wants her to marry Mitchett, but the Duchess, her friend, wants Mitchett to marry her niece, Aggie. Hence a social battle, complicated by the appearance of the wealthy Mr. Longdon, who sees in Nanda a close resemblance to her grandmother, with whom he had once been in love. However, Nanda is at last freed from any subservience to social conventions she does not like.

Axe-Helve, The (in *New Hampshire*, 1923), a blank verse narrative by ROBERT FROST. The poem tells of a conversation between Frost and a neighbor and then describes the poet's visit to the neighbor's home. Insistence is laid on the joy of a workman who loves his work and who despises the inferior products of a machine age. The poem appeared first in the *Atlantic Monthly* (September, 1917).

Axel's Castle (1931), a volume of critical essays by EDMUND WILSON. These deal largely with symbolism as it appears in the works of various French, Irish, and American writers. The title refers to a poetic drama, *Axel* (1890; English translation, 1925), by Villiers de l'Isle Adam. Other authors of whom Wilson writes are Yeats, T. S. Eliot, Gertrude Stein, Rimbaud, Joyce, and Proust.

Aztec Indians. These inhabitants of Mexico at the time of the conquest by CORTEZ (1519–21) had reached an extraordinarily high stage of civilization. Their society embodied advanced artistic and commercial practices, together with an excellent system of laws and courts. Their religion, however, remained barbaric though complex. The Spaniards suppressed the Aztecs brutally, though Aztec stock remains strong in Mexico to the present day. The Aztecs are believed to have come from the North, and their language is related to that of tribes in Arizona and other parts of the United States. Two recent novels dealing with the Aztecs are Dexter Allen's *Jaguar and the Golden Stag* (1954) and *Coil of the Serpent* (1955). See QUETZALCOATL.

Aztec Treasure-House, The (1890), a novel by THOMAS A. JANVIER. It relates how Professor Thomas Palgrave, an archaeologist, went to Mexico seeking remains of the ancient Aztec civilization, particularly a treasure-house. He is accompanied in his search by a Franciscan friar, an Indian boy, and two Americans, and their numerous adventures are amusing.

B

Babbitt (1922), satirical novel by SINCLAIR LEWIS. In Zenith, the Zip City, George Babbitt—realtor, booster, joiner, self-styled "typical American"—holds forth. Middle-aged and hopelessly middle-class, he ultimately realizes that being a prosperous family man and all-round good fellow is not enough. He tries to revolt, seeks a woman who will "understand him," but finds he cannot escape. When his son elopes, however, he has the courage to turn against the conventional clichés of his own life, and tells him: "I've never done a single thing I've wanted to. . . . Don't be scared of the family. No, nor all of Zenith. Nor of yourself, the way I've been."

The novel, perhaps Lewis' best, made a tremendous sensation when it appeared. Although businessmen and boosters' clubs denounced it bitterly, it undoubtedly helped to turn some of the latters' meetings away from silly antics and toward something more adult. Lewis' observation of details in the American social landscape is superb, his dialogue and descriptions magnificently satiric. The name of the book identified an American type and gave a new word to the language.

Babbitt, Irving (b. Dayton, Ohio, Aug. 2, 1865—d. July 15, 1933), teacher, critic, essayist. Educated at Harvard and later in Paris, Babbitt ultimately became a professor of Romance languages, first at Williams (1893), then at Harvard (from 1894 to his death). His first book, *Literature and the American College*, appeared in 1908; thereafter followed *The New Laokoön* (1910), *Masters of Modern French Criticism* (1912), ROUSSEAU AND ROMANTICISM (1919), *Democracy and Leadership* (1924), and *On Being Creative* (1932). *Spanish Character* (1940) appeared posthumously.

Along with PAUL ELMER MORE, NORMAN FOERSTER, and T. S. ELIOT, Babbitt expounded the New Humanism. (See HUMANISM.) No one quite defined the term. To More it was "a moral law of character." To Babbitt it was "a standard set above temperament." To Eliot it meant, ultimately, Anglo-Catholicism. Merriam-Webster defined it as "a contemporary cult or belief calling itself religious but substituting faith in man for faith in God." Mencken and democracy, a strange combination, were made one of the chief targets of the humanists' attack. See Norman Foerster: *Humanism and America* (1930) and C. H. GRATTAN'S: *Critique of a Humanism* (1930).

Bacchus (written in 1846, published in *Poems*, 1847), one of RALPH WALDO EMERSON's most magnificent lyrics. Emerson calls for wine, but "wine which never grew in the belly of the grape," rather ideas, thoughts, images, rhythms which will interpret the world of nature and of man to him. Commentators claim that the poem shows the influence of the Persian poet Hafiz and of the Neo-Platonists, always favorites of Emerson.

Bacheller, Irving [Addison] (b. Pierpont, N.Y., Sept. 26, 1859—d. Feb. 24, 1950), newspaperman, novelist. Bacheller entered newspaper work in his early twenties, becoming in time a member of the staff of *The New York World*. In 1896 he began devoting himself to fiction—he had already published two novels, *The Master of Silence* (1890) and *The Still House of O'Darrow* (1894). EBEN HOLDEN (1900) was a great success, especially in its depiction of the northern New York types with whom Bacheller was familiar; more than a million copies were sold. Other novels included D'RI AND I (1901), *Keeping Up with Lizzie* (1911), *A Man for the Ages* (1919), and *A Candle in the Wilderness* (1930). He wrote autobiographical reminiscences in *Coming Up the Road* (1928) and *From Stores of Memory* (1938).

Back Bay. An old and for many years a very genteel section of Boston, on the south bank of the Charles River. Its name became a symbol for the social élite of Boston; it is the scene of many novels laid in that city, including William Dean Howells' THE RISE OF SILAS LAPHAM (1885).

Backlog Studies (1873), pleasant essays by CHARLES DUDLEY WARNER. Many of them had appeared in a department conducted by Warner in SCRIBNER'S MAGAZINE.

Backward Glance o'er Travel'd Roads, A (1888), a prose piece by WALT WHITMAN. The preface and perhaps the most significant piece in NOVEMBER BOUGHS, a miscellaneous collection of prose and poetry, it was included in LEAVES OF GRASS (1889), of which it is both an explanation and a defense. He remarks, "I abandon'd the conventional themes, none of which appear in it," although he adds that "I have put on record elsewhere my reverence and eulogy for those never-to-be-excell'd poetic bequests" from the Old World.

Backwoodsman, The (1818), an idyllic tale in verse by JAMES KIRKE PAULDING. It tells of the pioneer West and its freedom from convention.

Bacon, Delia [Salter] (b. Tallmadge, Ohio, Feb. 2, 1811—d. Sept. 2, 1859), critic, novelist, dramatist, upholder of "the Baconian theory." Born in a log cabin, Miss Bacon was the daughter of a missionary; and missionary zeal, rather than scholarship, inspired the great "cause" to which she devoted the later years of her unhappy life. At first a teacher, but an unsuccessful one because of poor health, she became a lecturer on literature and history. Then she wrote, unsuccessfully, *Tales of the Puritans* (1831) and a play. In 1852, led to the notion perhaps by the similarity of names, she became "the first Baconian." She was convinced that a group of Elizabethans, all the great men of that age, had gathered around Sir Walter Raleigh to compose the plays that went under Shakespeare's name. Principal among them was Sir Francis Bacon; Edmund Spenser, too, helped. Moreover, the plays were more than plays, she argued. Within them a system of ciphers concealed a great system of thought, wisdom the world was waiting for. She contended, in addition, that opening Shakespeare's grave would reveal the whole grim story; and she went to England, hovered around the famous tomb, but lost courage. Emerson for a while encouraged her; Carlyle listened to her but demanded proofs; and Hawthorne, then consul at Liverpool, befriended "the poor, shy, proud Delia Bacon, a Hawthorne figure in real life" (as Van Wyck Brooks describes her), and even wrote an introduction for her book, *The Philosophy of the Plays of Shakespeare Unfolded* (1857), although he did not accept her theory. But by the time the book appeared the poor woman had become definitely insane, and she died while its incoherence and diffuseness were exciting derision everywhere.

Among the most famous followers of Miss Bacon was IGNATIUS DONNELLY, with *The Great Cryptogram* (1888) and *The Cipher in the Plays and on the Tombstone* (1899). The British scholar Dr. Caroline F. E. Spurgeon made a thorough analysis of the imagery of Shakespeare and Bacon (*Shakespeare's Imagery*, 1935), and showed conclusively how basically disparate the two men's minds were.

Bacon, Frank (b. Marysville, Calif., Jan. 16, 1864—d. Nov. 19, 1922), actor, playwright. One of the best-loved American actors, his greatest role was the amusing inveterate liar Lightnin' Bill Jones, in LIGHTNIN', written in collaboration with WINCHELL SMITH. It began its run on August 26, 1918, and continued for 1,291 performances.

Bacon, Josephine Dodge [Daskam] (b. Stamford, Conn., Feb. 17, 1876—d. July 29, 1961), novelist. Miss Daskam (as she was then) made her first hit with *Smith College Stories* (1900), published two years after her graduation from Smith; the book is still good reading and is regarded as a classic at Northampton, Mass. Best known of her amusing satires on Americans, especially young Americans, are *The Madness of Philip* (1902), *Memoirs of a Baby* (1904), *Square Peggy* (1919), *Luck of Lowry* (1934), *The Root and the Flower* (1939).

Bacon, Leonard (b. Solvay, N.Y., May 26, 1887—d. Jan. 1, 1954), teacher, poet, critic. Bacon (Delia Bacon was his great-aunt) began teaching English at the University of California in 1910 and became an assistant professor, but resigned in 1923 to devote full time to writing. He made his reputation with many volumes of verse as one of the most intellectual, satiric, adroit, and melodious poets of the day, winning the Pulitzer Prize for poetry with his *Sunderland Capture* (1940). He was elected to the National Institute of Arts and Letters, later to the American Academy of Arts and Sciences. Among his other volumes of verse are *Ulug Beg* (1923), *Animula Vagula* (1926), *The Legend of Quincibald* (1928), *The Furioso* (1932), *The Goose on the Capital* (1936), *Rhyme and Punishment* (1936), *Day of Fire* (1944). Autobiography: *Semi-Centennial* (1939).

Bacon, Nathaniel (1647–1676), rebel. Born in England, educated at Cambridge, and fashionably married, Bacon emigrated to Virginia in 1673 and built himself a gloomy Tudor mansion on the James River. At that time Sir William Berkeley (1606–1677) was governor of the colony. He made Bacon a member of his council, but Bacon was disgusted by conditions in the colony, and remarked, "The poverty of the country is such that all the power and sway is got into the hands of the rich, who by extortious advantages, having the common people in their debt, have always curbed and oppressed them in all manner of ways." When Berkeley, in addition to his other negligences, also refused to help the settlers in their conflicts with the Indians, Bacon organized a troop of frontiersmen. Berkeley ordered him arrested as a rebel, whereupon Bacon marched his followers on Jamestown, burned the town to the ground (1676), and required citizens to take an oath of allegiance to himself. His policy was conciliatory, but before he could do much to carry it out, he died. Berkeley, enraged, took terrible vengeance on his foes, hanging twenty of them. It is said that King Charles II exclaimed: "That old fool has put to death more people in that naked country than I did here for the murder of my father." He recalled him to London, and the English for a time paid more attention to the complaints of the colonists.

An account of the rebellion was put together in a manuscript which, after the American Revolution, was found among the papers of Captain Nathaniel Burwell of Virginia. It is believed that either JOHN COTTON or his wife ANNE "of Acquia Creek," contemporaries of Bacon, was the author of the manuscript, which also includes two poems, *Bacon's Epitaph, Made by His Man* and *Upon the Death of G. B.* [General Bacon]. The former, a brief elegy, has been called worthy of Ben Jonson himself, and is written in that great elegist's direct and manly style.

Many novelists have been fascinated by the strange figure of Bacon, who appears in W. A. Carruther's *The Cavaliers of Virginia* (1835), George Tucker's *Hansford* (1857), Maude Wilder Goodwin's *White Aprons* (1896), Clifford Sublette's *Bright Face of Danger* (1926), Nathan Schachner's *The King's Passenger* (1942), P. L. Scruggs' *Man Cannot Tell* (1942), Roy Flanagan's *The Forest Cavalier* (1952), Charles B. Judah's *Christopher Humble* (1956); also in Aphra Behn's play, *The Widow Ranter* (produced in 1690) and in Ebenezer Cooke's burlesque poem, *The History of Colonel Nathaniel Bacon's Rebellion* (in *The Maryland Muse*, 1731). W. E. Washburn's *The Governor and the Rebel* (1958) debunks Bacon's heroic role.

Bacon, Peggy [Mrs. Alexander Brook] (b. Ridgefield, Conn., May 2, 1895—   ), caricaturist, illustrator, writer. She wrote and illustrated many children's books, including *The Lion-Hearted Kitten* (1927) and *Mercy and the Mouse* (1928). Among her collections of caricatures: *Off with Their Heads* (1934), *Cat-Calls* (1935), *Starting from Scratch* (1945). *The Inward Eye* (1952) is a mystery novel. In 1957 she published *The Good American Witch*.

Bacon's Rebellion. See NATHANIEL BACON.

Bad Boy, The Story of a. See STORY OF A BAD BOY, THE.

Bad Lands. Severely eroded surfaces in various sections of the American West, especially those in western South Dakota, east of the Black Hills, which include fantastic remnants of a prehistoric salt sea. Ramon F. Adams, in *Western Words* (1944), defines the term as meaning "a section of country with little vegetation, composed principally of buttes, peaks, and other badly eroded soil; also the cowboy's name for a red-light district." The term was originally a translation of the French *mauvaises terres*. H. L. Mencken notes the curious pronunciation and spelling *movey-star*.

Baer, Arthur ["Bugs"] (b. Philadelphia, 1886 —   ), sports writer, cartoonist, columnist. Baer was once a lace-designer, but at twenty-one went into a Philadelphia newspaper office as an office boy, and later became a sports writer; still later he worked on a Washington paper. He became a staff writer for King Features in New York (1930), and since then has contributed sports cartoons and columns of zany humor to papers served by that syndicate. From Baer's typewriter or lips have come many sayings, liberally appropriated by gag-stealing comics: *e.g.*, "He was born with two strikes on him"; "She used to go with the landlord, but now she goes with the lease"; "She was a good girl and wouldn't go any place without her mother, but her mother would go any place"; "They had to burn down the schoolhouse to get me out of the second grade"; "There's no such thing as a little garlic"; "Somebody told Aunt Ella she had a beautiful profile and she went through the rest of her life sideways."

Bagdad-on-the-Subway. O. HENRY's synonym for Manhattan.

Bagley, William C[handler] (b. Detroit, March 15, 1874—d. July 1, 1946), teacher, author, editor. Bagley began to teach in 1895, coming to Teachers College, Columbia University, in 1917 and retiring in 1940. He edited educational magazines and wrote important books on education, among them *Classroom Management* (1907), *Craftsmanship in Teaching* (1911), *School Discipline* (1914), *Determinism in Education* (1926), *Education, Crime and Social Progress* (1931), and *A Century of the Universal School* (1937). He also collaborated with other authors in the production of texts in spelling and American history, particularly with CHARLES A. BEARD. Bagley became a frequent critic of "progressive" education, and an exponent of "essentialism," with emphasis on the

mastery of simple fundamentals as a preliminary to further education.

Bailey, Francis (b. Lancaster Co., Pa., *c.* 1735—d. 1815), publisher, almanac maker. Bailey founded *The United States Magazine* in 1779, *The Freeman's Journal, or, North American Intelligencer* in 1781. Appealing to the large German-speaking population in his native state, he issued a *Nord Americanische Kalender* (1779) at Lancaster. In this appears for the first time in print, so far as is known, a designation of Washington as "Father of His Country" —in a caption, "Des Landes Vater," under his portrait. The first appearance in English of the phrase seems to have occurred in an editorial in *The Pennsylvania Packet*, July 9, 1789; the same periodical had used the phrase, "the Father of His People" on April 21, 1789. Juvenal had employed the phrase, *pater patriae*, to designate Cicero, and it has been given to others in the course of European history. Bailey was official printer to the Continental Congress.

Bailey, James M[ontgomery] (b. Albany, N.Y., Sept. 25, 1841—d. March 4, 1894), newsman, humorist. At the end of the Civil War Bailey and a fellow-veteran bought the Danbury (Conn.) *Times*, which in 1870 was consolidated with *The Jeffersonian* to form the Danbury *News;* in 1878 he became sole owner and turned the paper from a weekly to a daily. Bailey became widely known as "the Danbury News Man" for his humorous column of domestic and public sketches. He is sometimes regarded as the first true newspaper columnist, especially in the field of humor. In nine months he brought the circulation of the *News* from 1,920 to 30,-000; the weekly had a circulation even beyond the bounds of the United States. His books were equally popular: *Life in Danbury* (1870), *They All Do It* (1877), *England from a Back Window* (1878), *Mr. Phillips' Goneness* (1879), and *The Danbury Boom* (1880). He was in demand, too, as a lecturer, despite his deeply melancholy appearance and his insistence on never wearing a necktie.

Bailey, [Irene] Temple (b. Petersburg, Va., in early 1870's—d. July 6, 1953), novelist. Miss Bailey, a steady favorite with the reading public, found wide audiences, particularly for *Contrary Mary* (1915), *The Tin Soldier* (1919), *The Trumpeter Swan* (1920), *The Gay Cockade* (1921), *Peacock Feathers* (1924), *Silver Slippers* (1928), *Enchanted Ground* (1933), *Fair as the Moon* (1935), *The Blue Cloak* (1941), *Red Fruit* (1945). She began her literary career with a book for girls, *Judy* (1907), and frankly wrote for girls and women. In 1953 it was estimated that three million copies of her books had been sold.

Baines, Scattergood. See CLARENCE BUDINGTON KELLAND.

Bakeless, John (b. Carlisle Barracks, Pa., Dec. 30, 1894—   ), newspaperman, biographer, critic, literary and military historian. Col. Bakeless began his writing career on the *Morning Press* at Bloomsburg, Pa. At various times he was managing editor of *The Forum*, literary editor of *The Literary Digest*, and correspondent for the *Manchester Guardian*. He obtained his M.A. in 1920 and his Ph.D. in 1936 from Harvard University and has taught both at Harvard and at New York University. During his years of active war duty—from 1940 to 1945 —he was promoted through the ranks to Colonel, General Staff (Infantry), and was in Russia, Turkey, and Bulgaria; he resumed reserve status in 1946. His books include: *Economic Causes of Modern War* (1921); *Christopher Marlowe, the Man in His Time* (1937); *Fighting Frontiersman* (1948); *Eyes of Discovery* (1950); *Background to Glory* (1956); *They Saw America First* (1957), in collaboration with his wife, Katherine Bakeless; *Turncoats, Traitors and Heroes* (1959); *The Adventures of Lewis and Clark* (1961).

Baker, Carlos (b. Biddeford, Me., May 5, 1909—   ), poet, writer, teacher, critic. As a teacher of literature at Princeton University, Baker made a large contribution to critical literature with *Shelley's Major Poetry* (1948) and *Hemingway: The Writer as Artist* (1952, enlarged ed., 1956). The latter is considered one of the finest full-scale critical studies of Hemingway; it is inspired by sincere admiration, but never allows the spirit of partisanship to interfere with honest and scholarly analysis. Other books include: *A Friend in Power*, a novel (1958); *The Land of Rumbelow*, a novel (1961). Baker's verse is included in *Best Poetry of 1956* and *Best Poetry of 1957*. He was co-editor with C. D. Thorpe and Bennett Weaver of *The Major English Romantic Poets* (1957), and with Willard Thorp and James Folsom of *The American Literary Record* (1961).

Baker, George Pierce (b. Providence, R.I., Aug. 4, 1866—d. Jan. 8, 1935), teacher, editor, author. Baker was one of the most successful and creative of modern teachers. Graduating from Harvard in 1887, he stayed on to teach English and forensic; in 1895 he published a textbook called *The Principles of Argumentation*. A full professor in 1905, he published *The Development of Shakespeare as a Dramatist* (1907).

But Baker's interest turned more and more to the living theater, and in 1905 he opened his celebrated "47 Workshop," in which aspiring students were taught the art of playwriting and given the opportunity of seeing their plays performed, at first by their fellow students in the theater at Agassiz House. Edward Sheldon's SALVATION NELL (1908), later made popular by Minnie Maddern Fiske, was an actual product of the Workshop. Baker's successful alumni included Eugene O'Neill, Philip Barry, S. N. Behrman, Sidney Howard, Robert Edmond Jones, John Dos Passos, John Mason Brown, John V. A. Weaver, Rachel Field, and Thomas Wolfe, the last of whom portrayed Baker as Professor Hatcher in *Of Time and the River* (1935). Since Harvard of that day did not particularly relish Baker's activities, in 1925 he moved to Yale, where every facility was provided for him, including a theater donated by Edward

S. Harkness. The Workshop here developed into the Yale graduate school of drama, and Baker continued to give courses in playwriting, stage designing, costuming, lighting, dramatic criticism. He edited *Plays of the 47 Workshop, I–IV* (1918–25) and *Yale One-Act Plays* (1930). W. P. Kinne wrote a discriminating account of *G. P. Baker and the American Theater* (1954) with an introduction by John Mason Brown. See LITTLE THEATER IN THE U.S.

Baker, Louise. See OUT ON A LIMB.

Baker, Ray Stannard ["David Grayson"] (b. Lansing, Mich., April 17, 1870—d. July 12, 1946), essayist, biographer, editor. Baker began his writing career as a reporter on the Chicago *Record* (1892–97). His short stories in the *Century Magazine* and *Youth's Companion* brought him an offer from *McClure's Magazine* and the McClure Syndicate in New York; he remained with this group from 1897 to 1905. In 1906 he became an editor of the *American Magazine* and served until 1915. This was the muck-raking period of American journalism, and Baker did his share, but in moderate tones. Out of his work stemmed an early book, *Following the Color Line* (1908). Meanwhile Baker began a secret literary life with a series of essays published in *The American* under the pen name David Grayson, whose identity remained a deep mystery until Baker was revealed as Grayson in the March, 1916, issue of *The Bookman*. The essays, collected in book form as ADVENTURES IN CONTENTMENT (1907), *Adventures in Friendship* (1910), *Adventures in Understanding* (1925), *Under My Elm* (1942), and other titles won wide popularity for the kindly philosophy they preached. In 1910 Baker met WOODROW WILSON, and thereafter devoted most of his energies to the cause of Wilson and his ideals, so much so that Wilson named him press director at Paris in 1919 and designated him as the posthumous editor of his papers. Baker (along with Professor W. E. DODD) edited *The Public Papers of Woodrow Wilson* (6 v., 1925–26), then wrote an authorized biography, *Woodrow Wilson—Life and Letters* (8 v., 1927–39), which received the 1940 Pulitzer Prize for biography. Baker closed his literary career with *Native American* (1941), dealing with his youth in a frontier region, and *American Chronicle* (1945), the story of his later life and friendships.

Baker's Blue-Jay Yarn. In A TRAMP ABROAD (1880), by Mark Twain. After a fracas with the San Francisco police in 1865, Twain took refuge with the Nevada miner Jim Gillis in his cabin on Jackass Hill. A "finished artist in the realm of extemporized tall stories," as Delancey Ferguson describes him in his life of Clemens (1943), Jim related, among others, the blue-jay yarn, which Ferguson calls ". . . from all Mark Twain's works the most perfect example of the genuine Western tall story, patiently and skillfully built up from a matter-of-fact prelude to a sustained climax."

Baker Street Irregulars. A literary club, founded in New York City, 1934, by devotees of Sherlock Holmes, including CHRISTOPHER

MORLEY, ELMER DAVIS, and VINCENT STARRETT. Their zeal and erudition culminated in a volume called *221B: Studies in Sherlock Holmes* (1940), edited by Starrett. The title refers, of course, to the sleuth's Baker Street address; the sixteen memoirs and studies, witty but astonishingly factual, throw much light on the life, work, and secrets of The Master. The Irregulars also publish the *Baker Street Journal*. Branches of the club, all named for titles of the stories by Sir Arthur Conan Doyle, include the following: Musgrave Ritualists (New York City), Diogenes Club (Brooklyn), Speckled Band (Boston), Sons of the Copper Beeches (Philadelphia), Hounds of the Baskerville (*sic*) (Chicago), Creeping Men (Cleveland), Scandalous Bohemians (Akron), Trained Cormorants (Los Angeles), Canadian Baskervilles (Quebec), and The Solitary Cyclist (Washington, D.C.—one member).

Baldwin, Faith C[uthrell] (b. New Rochelle, N.Y., Oct. 1, 1893—   ), novelist. Miss Baldwin published her first story, *Mavis of Green Hill*, in 1921, and continued for many years to write a steady stream of competent, not-too-sentimental novels—with, occasionally, one of greater merit. *The New York Times* called her "a spinner de luxe of streamlined Cinderella stories for grown-up girls." The sale of her books reached well over ten million copies; among them may be mentioned *Those Difficult Years* (1925), *Three Women* (1926), *Office Wife* (1930), *American Family* (1935), *Station Wagon* (1939), *Medical Center* (1940), *Woman on Her Way* (1946), *Widow's Walk* (1954, poems), *Many Windows* (1958), *Blaze of Sunlight* (1959), *Testament of Trust* (1960).

Baldwin, Hanson W. (b. Baltimore, Md., March 22, 1903—   ), military analyst, journalist, writer. Baldwin graduated from the United States Naval Academy in 1924. Military editor of the New York *Times* for many years, his accurate military estimates and his analyses of the possibilities of global warfare established his reputation in this field. His writing was realistic but not pessimistic. He received the Pulitzer Prize (1942) and the Navy League Award for excellence in military reporting (1959). His books include: *The Caissons Roll* (1938); *Admiral Death* (1939); *United We Stand!* (1941); *Strategy for Victory* (1942); *The Price of Power* (1948); *Sea Fights and Shipwrecks* (1955); and *The Great Arms Race* (1958).

Baldwin, James [1] (b. Hamilton Co., Ind., Dec. 15, 1841—d. Aug. 30, 1925), editor and historian. Baldwin wrote mainly for young people, editing readers and "school speakers," preparing historical and biographical narratives, and rewriting old myths and legends. *In the Days of My Youth* (1923), his account of Quaker life in old-time Indiana, was written under the pen name Robert Dudley.

Baldwin, James [2] (b. New York City, Aug. 2, 1924—   ), writer of fiction and essayist. James Baldwin's published works include *Go Tell It on the Mountain* (1953), a story of religious experience among Harlem Negroes.

J. S. Redding in the New York *Herald Tribune* wrote of this: "Even the most insensitive of readers will put the book down with a troubled feeling of having 'looked on beauty bare.'" With this book Baldwin established his reputation as a writer of deep insight. *Notes of a Native Son* came out in 1955, and *Giovanni's Room* in 1956. Baldwin lived for many years in Paris, where the latter novel is set. In 1961 he brought out two more books: *Another Country*, a novel, and *Nobody Knows My Name: More Notes of a Native Son*, which records his last months of self-exile, his return to America and visits to Harlem and to the South during the early days of the integration upheaval.

Baldwin, Joseph Glover (b. January, 1815—d. Sept. 30, 1864), lawyer, jurist, humorist. Largely self-educated, Baldwin prepared himself to practice law in Virginia, then decided to try the fresh fields of Mississippi and Alabama, where there was less competition. Riding the circuit in these sparsely inhabited regions, he kept notes; and later he moved on to California (he was made an associate judge of the Supreme Court there), first publishing, however, his masterpiece, THE FLUSH TIMES OF ALABAMA AND MISSISSIPPI (1853). He later wrote *Party Leaders* (1855)—sober portraits of contemporary political figures like Henry Clay, Thomas Jefferson, and Andrew Jackson.

Balestier, [Charles] Wolcott (b. Rochester, N.Y., Dec. 13, 1861—d. Dec. 6, 1891), novelist, publisher. Balestier became a reporter on the Rochester *Post-Express* while still attending school, later contributed to *The Atlantic Monthly*, then began writing novels, the first of which, *A Potent Philtre* (1884), first appeared in the New York *Tribune*. But his fame is chiefly due to the fact that he collaborated on a novel, *The Naulahka* (1892), with his brother-in-law Rudyard Kipling. Kipling esteemed him highly and dedicated *Barrack-Room Ballads* (1892) to him on his untimely death; he spoke of him as one who had always walked "In simpleness and gentleness and honour and clean mirth."

Balisand (1924), a novel by JOSEPH HERGESHEIMER. The story of a Federalist in tidewater Virginia in the days of the Revolution and afterward, *Balisand* pictures the conflict between the ideals of aristocracy and Jefferson's oncoming democracy.

Ballad of the Oysterman, The (published in *The Amateur*, July 17, 1830), a satiric poem by OLIVER WENDELL HOLMES. It makes gentle fun of the romantic and sentimental ballads of the day, particularly those of Thomas Campbell, Longfellow, and Whittier.

Ballad of the Tempest, The (1849), a poem by JAMES T. FIELDS. Otherwise undistinguished, this bit of verse contains the frequently quoted lines, "'We are lost!' the captain shouted,/As he staggered down the stairs.'"

Ballad of Trees and the Master, A (1880), a poem by SIDNEY LANIER. This most famous of Lanier's lyrics was intended originally as an interlude in SUNRISE, and is to be understood, H. H. Hayden has pointed out, in connection with the pantheistic thought of that poem; it shows the healing effects of nature on a troubled spirit. The poem is free from the involutions and luxuriance that often mar Lanier's writing, and makes skillful use of triple rhymes.

ballads and balladry in the U.S. Balladry in America is as old as the earliest colonists, who brought their folk songs, along with their household goods and their Bible, to the New World; and hence ballads of English origin have had the widest circulation and exerted the greatest influence here. Firmly rooted along the entire Atlantic seaboard, some of these ballads have moved across the country with the moving frontier. *Barbara Allen* has been sung to many tunes and variants, and the story has undergone many local changes. In the cowpunching country, for example, "Bobby" is carried on a buckskin pony to a grave in the desert. Particularly rich sources of ancient balladry have been found in the Appalachian mountain regions. Cecil Sharp, the famous English folklorist, recorded many of his finds in his *English Folk Songs from the Southern Appalachians.* The practice of ballad-singing and ballad-making as it is still carried on in those regions is described by Jean Thomas in *Devil's Ditties* (1931) and *Ballad Makin' in the Mountains of Kentucky* (1939).

American life has been an inexhaustible source of ballad-making. *The Ballit of the Boll Weevil,* a characteristically touching mixture of sadness and humor, is as much a part of the cotton belt as is the hardy pest it ruefully celebrates. The experiences and feelings of real people produced *Springfield Mountain,* THE ERIE CANAL, CASEY JONES, *Sweet Betsy from Pike, The Little Mohee,* JOHN HENRY, JESSE JAMES, *Cumberland Gap, The Old Chisholm Trail,* and *The Jam on Gerry's Rocks.* "The cowboy, the miner, the tramp, the lumberjack, the Forty-niner, the soldier, the sailor, the plantation Negro (as also his sophisticated city cousin), the sailor on the Great Lakes, and even the boatmen in the early days of the Erie Canal, all have 'made up' songs," folklorist JOHN A. LOMAX wrote.

A discerning analysis of the interrelationships of poetry and music in the ballad and other song forms was made by V. C. Clinton-Baddeley in *Words for Music* (1941), and a short study of musical aspects of the ballad is found in Philip Gordon's "The Music of the Ballads," *Southern Folklore Quarterly,* September, 1942. Fortunately, the study of American balladry has consistently concerned itself with music as well as text. Many striking diversities and contrasts have been revealed. Side by side with beautiful modal melodies may be found harmonic banalities of the cheapest kind. The American custom of accompanying ballads on the guitar or dulcimer has sometimes forced a tune to adapt itself to an ordinary, almost crude chordal foundation, with results detrimental to melodic beauty and expressiveness. On the whole, however, ballad airs in this country have maintained a high level of intrinsic musical quality.

A great variety of influences can be discovered in American ballad music. Sometimes an occupa-

tional rhythm plays a strong part, even overshadowing the melody, as in *The Chisholm Trail.* The Scottish "snap" and the distinctive idiom of Irish dance tunes often make themselves felt. The folk music that people brought from the old country became the natural vehicle for their work and play songs in the new country.

The facets of American balladry are so numerous that our knowledge is still far from complete. The genesis of American Negro folk music, for example, has not yet been adequately probed. Nevertheless, the study of American balladry has been continuing for a long time. *The Journal of American Folk-Lore* of the AMERICAN FOLK-LORE SOCIETY was begun in 1888. The remarkable investigation of *Slave Songs of the South* by William F. Allen, Charles P. Ware, and Lucy M. Garrison was published as early as 1867. Probably the most important of later investigators was John A. Lomax.

Some more recent studies of American balladry include: A. O. Andrews, *The Gift to be Simple: Songs, Dances and Rituals of the American Shakers* (1940); Phillips Barry, Fanny Hardy Eckstorm, and Mary Winslow Smyth, *British Ballads from Maine* (1929); Earl Clifton Beck, *Songs of the Michigan Lumberjacks* (1941); Arthur Kyle Davis, Jr., *Traditional Ballads of Virginia* (1929); Helen Harkness Flanders and George Brown, *Vermont Folk-Songs and Ballads* (1931), also Mrs. Flanders and Marguerite Olney, *Ballads Migrant in New England* (1953); George Pullen Jackson, *White Spirituals in the Southern Uplands* (1933); George Korson, *Songs and Ballads of the Anthracite Miner* (1927); G. Malcolm Laws, Jr., *Native American Balladry* (1950); John A. and ALAN LOMAX, *American Ballads and Folk-Songs* (1934); Louise Pound, *Poetic Origins and the Ballad* (1921); Evelyn Kendrick Wells, *The Ballad Tree* (1950). Among musical collections are Helen H. Flanders, *The New Green Mountain Songster* (1939); Olin Downes and Elie Siegmeister, *A Treasury of American Song* (2nd ed., 1943); Ruth Crawford Seeger, *American Folk Songs for Children* (1948); Reed Smith and Hilton Rufty, *American Anthology of Old World Ballads* (1937).

Many examples of American balladry are obtainable in recorded form. The Archive of American Folk Song in the Library of Congress preserves thousands of recordings, made in the field, of American adaptations of English ballads and of indigenous ballads. Several selected albums of this material are available to the public. The catalogues of commercial recording manufacturers list a variety of ballad discs made by prominent native ballad singers. A selection of eight recorded ballads from the Flanders Ballad Collection of Middlebury College is available in connection with Flanders and Olney's *Ballads Migrant in New England.* A ballad discography is provided in *Folksongs on Records, Issue Three,* edited by Ben Gray Lumpkin (1950).

Although balladry is fundamentally a folk art transmitted by oral tradition, it has always attracted professional entertainers. Ballads were woven into plays by Shakespeare and his contemporaries; the early 18th century ballad operas gave Handel stiff competition in London. Topical ballads to popular tunes were widely sung here in Revolutionary times and after. In the music halls of the 19th century Sam Cowell convulsed audiences on both sides of the Atlantic with his *Lord Lovel*. In more recent times the solo singing of traditional ballads with dulcimer accompaniment has introduced a tone of nostalgic sentimentality into night-club atmospheres.

During the 19th century, composers and poets explored the artistic possibilities of the ballad for the creation of a new form. The classic example of a composed ballad probably is Schubert's famous setting of Goethe's *Erlkoenig*. In the 20th century serious composers have showed little interest in composing ballads, but many American composers have adapted traditional tunes to larger forms. See especially works by Aaron Copland, Roy Harris, Elie Siegmeister, Virgil Thomson, and Kurt Weill. In literature the ballad has recently been neglected, but an outstanding example to the contrary is found in the works of STEPHEN VINCENT BENÉT.

PHILIP GORDON

Ballads and Other Poems (1842), a collection of poems by HENRY WADSWORTH LONGFELLOW. Two of the most popular poems included in the book are THE WRECK OF THE HESPERUS, based on an actual shipwreck, and THE SKELETON IN ARMOR, on the legend of a Viking skeleton supposedly found on the New England coast. These are readable and charming, but offer little profundity or insight. The collection also contains the platitudinous "Rainy Day," the sentimental THE VILLAGE BLACKSMITH, and the often quoted EXCELSIOR. All the poems have a moral, and, like much of Longfellow's verse, are didactic and sentimental.

Balloon Hoax, The (New York *Sun*, April 13, 1844), a story by EDGAR ALLAN POE, based on an actual flight made in 1836 by Monck Mason and others. Poe proved that a hoax can be printed twice in the same paper. On April 13, 1834, the *Sun* had perpetrated the famous "Moon Hoax" and had thereby increased its circulation to the largest in the world (19,360, the editor proudly announced). The hoax consisted in reprinting a series of articles from a nonexistent Edinburgh *Journal of Science,* in which were described the marvelous bat-men (along with other wonders) that Sir John Herschel had discovered on the moon through his new telescope. The articles were written by a *Sun* reporter, Richard Adams Locke—or, possibly, by a French scientist, Joseph Nicholas Nicollet, then in the United States. In 1844 Poe, who had followed the *Sun* articles with interest, tried it again. He told how a Mr. Monck Mason and eight passengers, starting from Wales, had crossed the Atlantic in a balloon inflated with coal gas, making the trip in 75 hours and landing at Sullivan's Island, Charleston. There was

excitement for several days, and the *Sun* and Poe were greatly pleased.

Ballou, Adin (b. Cumberland, R.I., April 23, 1803—d. Aug. 5, 1890), clergyman, Christian communist, author. In January, 1841, Ballou helped form the famous Hopedale Community in Milford, Mass., the avowed object of which was to practice "brotherly love and the Gospel of Jesus Christ," and which carried on numerous economic and community enterprises, including farming, building, and publishing. Ballou was for a time president of the community, which after 1856 disintegrated into a commercial organization that turned the town into a manufacturing center. Ballou published *The Independent Messenger* from 1831 to 1839 at a time when he was preaching Unitarian and Universalist doctrines. At Hopedale he edited *The Practical Christian* as an organ of the community and wrote *Practical Christian Socialism* (1854), in which he outlined plans for a "Practical Christian Republic." Later he wrote on *Primitive Christianity and Its Corruptions* (1870). His *Autobiography* appeared in 1896. To Ballou has sometimes been attributed an influence on Tolstoy, who mentions in *The Kingdom of God Is Within You* Ballou's doctrines of non-resistance, and on Mohandas K. Gandhi, who read Tolstoy's book and put the doctrines momentously into practice.

ballyhoo. A term of unknown origin, sometimes said to be connected with Ballyholly, a village in County Cork, Ireland; explained by circus men as a blend of *ballet* and *whoop*, and defined by Webster as a noisy demonstration to attract attention. P. T. BARNUM first expounded and applied the formulas of ballyhoo; the term is applied to the shouts of a circus barker, and by extension to any loud or sensational publicity. A magazine by this name was founded in 1931 satirizing advertising and the political scene.

Balmer, Edwin (b. Chicago, July 26, 1883—d. March 21, 1959), editor, novelist. Balmer's adventure stories include *Waylaid by Wireless* (1909), *A Wild Goose Chase* (1915), *Flying Death* (1927), *The Torn Letter* (1941). He has also collaborated on stories with William MacHarg and PHILIP WYLIE. He was editor of *Redbook* from 1927 to 1949.

Baltimore, Lord (c. 1580–1632). George Calvert was born in Kipling, Yorkshire, attended Oxford, became a Member of Parliament, was knighted in 1607, and then attained various high offices under the Stuarts. He became a convert to Catholicism in 1625, was made Baron Baltimore the same year in the Irish peerage. Charles I assigned him a large tract of land in Newfoundland, but he objected on account of the climate, and was given present-day Maryland (with parts of Pennsylvania and Delaware) instead. He died before he was able to colonize it, and his oldest son, Cecilius or Cecil (1605–1675) succeeded to the barony, signed the first patent or charter (June 20, 1632); his brother Leonard (1606–1647) became governor of the province (1634–1647). It was named Maryland in honor of the English queen, Henrietta

Maria. Despite the grant from the king, Governor Calvert felt it proper to purchase the land from the Indians—with cloth, axes, hatchets, knives, and hose. From the very beginning religious tolerance became the rule in the province; in 1649 Maryland passed the first Act of Toleration on American soil. In succeeding years the fortunes of the colony and the Calverts varied with governmental changes in England. In 1688 James II lost the throne and the Calverts their colony; but the fourth Lord Baltimore became a Protestant, regained his family rights, and established the Church of England as the state faith. All Calvert rights lapsed with the American Revolution.

Bancroft, George (b. Worcester, Mass., Oct. 3, 1800—d. Jan. 17, 1891), poet, diplomat, historian. An infant prodigy, Bancroft was well educated at home and abroad. He developed such a love for Germany, its *Tuechtigkeit*

and *Gemuetlichkeit* and Hegelianism, that when he was minister from the United States during the Franco-Prussian War, France complained that he was exceeding the bounds of neutrality. On his return he went to Northampton and founded what may well have been the first "progressive" school; among its principles were the elimination of classroom discipline and the adaptation of classes to "individual variability." Bancroft was a poor teacher, or the principles were not workable; at any rate, he retired from teaching.

Bancroft the politician adhered to what was for Massachusetts of that day the unpopular popular side; he became a Jeffersonian, a Jacksonian, in later days a follower of Lincoln. It was both an idealistic and a shrewd move. He believed not merely sincerely but even flamboyantly in "the common mind," an entity surrounded in his conception with transcendental vapors. As almost the only Democrat of prominence in Massachusetts, it was inevitable that as the Jacksonians

gained power, Bancroft should rise with them —as he did, to become collector of the Port of Boston (practically the "state boss"), then Polk's secretary of the navy and later minister to England and Germany.

But Bancroft did not neglect his writing. Aside from orations and essays, and a collection of *Poems* (1823), he began in the 1830s a gigantic task—the writing of a *History of the United States,* really of the people of the United States, that would present democratic rather than Federalist ideas and ideals. The first volume appeared in 1834 and won tremendous applause, both in this country and abroad. As he went on to the remaining nine volumes (the last was published in 1874), it became more and more obvious that, as contemporaries said, "every line in the *History* is a vote for Jackson." Bancroft collected facts indefatigably, he carried on a vast correspondence, he worked endless hours every day, his notes were spread on the pages with scholarly prodigality, but his purpose remained. He saw America on a great scale as humanity's noblest experiment. He loved and extolled the energy of the American people in their westward course and in their establishment of a great republic; his volumes were a gigantic Fourth-of-July oration.

Bancroft did not, however, fail to listen to criticism, and he made efforts to improve his style as well as to tighten up the facts. He cut down the ten volumes to six in 1876. He added two volumes on the *History of the Formation of the Constitution* (1882), an important pioneer work. There was a final revision to six volumes (1883–85). He endeavored to "slaughter the adjectives," to such an extent, says Van Wyck Brooks, that "he gave an effect of truncation and bareness." John Spencer Bassett notes that Bancroft tried ardently to write a history that would not at all resemble the didactic productions of his Federalist predecessors: "There was a lofty and sonorous sense of detachment in his sentences. To the present age they seem sheer affectation, but to the men who had been reading the bald statements of fact hitherto offered as history, they seemed admirable."

Bancroft, Hubert Howe (b. Granville, Ohio, May 5, 1832—d. Mar. 2, 1918), publisher, historian, essayist, editor. Bancroft, who has been called a "history factory" rather than an author, decided to write a detailed history of "one-twelfth of the land surface of the earth," and actually did so, with the help of a dozen or so "key writers" and about 600 assistants, compiling a many-volumed series which he sold at subscription rates to his own great profit, but with little profit or credit to his literary aides. In 1893 Ambrose Bierce charged that the names of most of Bancroft's assistants were "now adorning little headboards out in the cemeteries—a result of Mr. Bancroft's scale of wages." Opinions vary as to the amount of writing that Bancroft himself did for his series; the range of credit is from four volumes out of the forty to one-third of the whole. There is almost an equal range in the warmth of approval or disapproval of the actual results, but the general judgment seems to be that Bancroft, although a "practical" man who saw to it that his accounts did not become debits, was deeply interested in writing and in his project, and that he performed a much needed task with efficiency. Even his autobiography, *Literary Industries* (1890), was in part the work of others.

Bancroft's historical surveys include *Native Races of the Pacific States* (5 v., 1874), histories of individual states and sections (Central America, Mexico, Texas, Arizona, California, Nevada, Utah, etc., published from 1883 to 1886), collections of historical essays (*California Pastorals*, 1888, and *Essays and Miscellany*, 1890, among them), and some autobiographical and miscellaneous volumes (*In These Latter Days*, 1917, and *The New Pacific*, 1900). John W. Caughey wrote his life in 1946.

Bandelier, Adolph Francis Alphonse (b. Switzerland, Aug. 6, 1840—d. March 18, 1914), archaeologist, author.   One of the earliest American archaeologists, Bandelier came to the United States as a boy, later explored various parts of the American hemisphere. His most fruitful researches were among the Pueblo Indians of New Mexico, whom he treated in a novel, THE DELIGHT MAKERS (1890), a vivid account of prehistoric Indian life in the Southwest. A later book was *The Gilded Man* (1893), which, as its title indicates, concerns the legend of EL DORADO. Bandelier became in 1903 a member of the staff of the American Museum of Natural History in New York. He published many learned works, among them one on the art of war in ancient Mexico.

Bangs, John Kendrick (b. Yonkers, N.Y., May 27, 1862—d. Jan. 21, 1922), editor, humorist, lecturer.   Bangs spent most of his placid life in Yonkers, when he wasn't away from home drawing pleasant sums for delivering lectures or down in New York for the day being funny in his PUCK office. In A HOUSEBOAT ON THE STYX (1895) Bangs assembles some of the celebrated characters of history—from Diogenes down to Sam Johnson, Napoleon, and George Washington—on his houseboat; and the results are amusing, even if, as Stephen Leacock points out, he "never got quite clear as to whether his characters were historical satires or just mediums for making fun of things today." There was a sequel, *The Pursuit of the Houseboat* (1897), which keeps up the fun. Bangs wrote other books (among the forty or so he published) almost as good, among them *Methuselah* (1888), *Coffee and Repartee* (1893), *Mr. Bonaparte of Corsica* (1895), *The Idiot* (1895), *The Enchanted Typewriter* (1899), AUTOBIOGRAPHY OF METHUSELAH (1909), and *Half Hours with the Idiot* (1917). He was on the staff of *Harper's Monthly* from 1888 to 1899, later on other Harper periodicals. Before joining Harper's he was with *Life* for four years, later served on *Puck*.

Banker's Daughter, The (1878), a play by BRONSON HOWARD.   One of the first plays to appeal to an American audience as "an American comedy"; a rewriting of an earlier play, *Lillian's Last Love* (1873). Howard described the revision in *Autobiography of a Play* (delivered as a lecture at Harvard, 1886; published, 1910).

Banning, Margaret C[ulkin] (b. Buffalo, Minn., March 18, 1891—   ), novelist, political writer.   Margaret Banning received her A.B. from Vassar in 1912 and the following year obtained a certificate from the Chicago School of Civics and Philanthropy. Though she was sometimes called "a woman writer for women readers," her novels are above average for their genre. They reflect her extensive travels and her civic interests. She was elected a member of the Commission on Education of Women of the American Council on Education. Her articles, essays on phases of American life, and stories have appeared in most of the major magazines, including the *Saturday Review*. But she gained her reputation chiefly with her more than thirty novels, among them: *Half Loaves* (1921), *Money of Her Own* (1928), *Letters to Susan* (1936), *Out in Society* (1940), *The Clever Sister* (1947), *Give Us Our Years* (1950), *Fallen Away* (1951), *The Dowry* (1955), *The Convert* (1957), *Echo Answers* (1960).

Bannister, Nathaniel Harrington (b. Jan. 13, 1813—d. Nov. 2, 1847), actor, playwright.   The place of Bannister's birth is not known, but it was either in Delaware or Maryland. A popular actor, especially in the South, he was among the pioneer dramatists in choosing American themes. His best known drama is *Putnam: The Iron Son of '76* (1859).

Bantam Books.   A firm of paperback book publishers established in New York City in January, 1946. At that time it began to release four books monthly. Ten years later, after selling three hundred million books, it was releasing fourteen books monthly.

Barbara Frietchie (1863), a poem by JOHN GREENLEAF WHITTIER.   On Sept. 6, 1862, when Frederick, Md., was occupied by Confederate troops under the leadership of "Stonewall" Jackson, Mrs. Frietchie is said to have flaunted the American flag in the face of the soldiers marching by; and General Jackson forbade any interference with her. (See THOMAS JONATHAN JACKSON.) Whittier later heard of the incident from the novelist Mrs. E. D. E. N. SOUTHWORTH, but he later admitted that it was not the 96-year-old Mrs. Frietchie but the comparatively young Mrs. Mary A. Quantrell who had raised a Union flag on her house as the troops passed. She was not molested, and some of the Confederate officers raised their hats as they went by, "To you, madam, and not to your flag!" Six days later, when Federal troops under Burnside passed through the town, Mrs. Frietchie followed Mrs. Quantrell's example.

Later CLYDE FITCH juggled still further with the facts by writing a play, *Barbara Frietchie* (1899), in which Barbara (played by JULIA MARLOWE) becomes a young girl in love with a Union officer. Fitch well reproduced the southern atmosphere, and the play was theatrically effective. However, the change in Barbara's age (supposedly ninety-six) offended many; and Mark Van Doren speaks of the "hollow rhetoric" of the play. Sigmund Romberg and Dorothy Donnelly based a musical, *My Maryland* (1927), on the poem.

Barbary Wars, also called **Tripolitan War.** From the 15th to the early 19th centuries Barbary corsairs infested the Mediterranean, inflicting great damage on commerce and taking many Christians as slaves. England, France, later the United States, and other nations bore these attacks without more than sporadic attempts to resist, even paid the pirates annual tributes. But at the close of the War of 1812 American naval units under Commodores Stephen Decatur and Bainbridge, on presidential order attacked the marauders in their home ports, captured their warships, and exacted submission from the dey of Algiers, the bey of Tunis, and the bashaw of Tripoli. The Americans thereby put an end to the piratical raids on American commerce. England and France took similar action; and in 1830 France occupied and annexed Algeria. The Barbary Wars were treated in Royall Tyler's ALGERINE CAPTIVE (1797) and James Fenimore Cooper's HOMEWARD BOUND (1838). Kenneth Roberts made use of the setting in LYDIA BAILEY (1946), as did H. L. Davis in *Harp of a Thousand Strings* (1947). Other novels set in this period include John Jennings' *The Salem Frigate* (1946); Elisabeth Meg's *Plenty of Pirates* (1953); Edison Marshall's *American Captain* (1954); Alexander Laing's *Jonathan Eagle* (1955); John Jennings' *The Wind in His Fists* (1956). See JOEL BARLOW.

Barbour, Ralph Henry (b. Cambridge, Mass., Nov. 13, 1870—d. Feb. 19, 1944), novelist. Barbour's *The Half-Back* (1899) was the first of more than a hundred books, most of them vigorous, healthy-minded books for boys, that he wrote during the course of his career. They were read widely as they were published and have continued to be favorites—despite changes in the rules of football and other games that Barbour used as backgrounds. Among his other titles: *For the Honor of the School* (1900); *Behind the Line* (1902); *The Crimson Sweater* (1906).

Barbour, Thomas (b. Martha's Vineyard, Mass., Aug. 19, 1884—d. Jan. 8, 1946), naturalist, author. He conducted zoological explorations in many parts of the world, served as director of the Harvard University Museum and the Museum of Comparative Zoology, as professor of zoology, and as custodian of the Harvard Biological Station and Botanical Garden in Soledad, Cuba. His most interesting books are *Naturalist at Large* (1943), *That Vanishing Eden: A Naturalist's Florida* (1944), *A Naturalist in Cuba* (1945).

Barclay of Ury (1847), a ballad by JOHN GREENLEAF WHITTIER. The poet pays tribute to a man of his own Quaker faith—one who in his youth and majority had won laurels as a distinguished soldier while fighting under Gustavus

Adolphus in Germany. Then he became a Friend, and suffered persecution at the hands of the people of Aberdeen, who had sought his favor while he wore a uniform but now denounced him as a "Quaker coward." Barclay bore their jeers with calm and confidence, refusing to anwer wrong with wrong.

Barefoot Boy, The (originally published in the juvenile magazine *The Little Pilgrim,* January, 1855; later collected in *The Panorama,* 1856), a tribute to the joys of childhood in the country, by JOHN GREENLEAF WHITTIER.

Bare Souls (1924), a collection of "psychographs" by GAMALIEL BRADFORD. Among his subjects are Keats, Lamb, Horace Walpole, Voltaire, and other writers.

Bargain Lost, The (1832), a story by EDGAR ALLAN POE. This is an earlier version of BON-BON (1835).

Barker, James Nelson (b. Philadelphia, June 17, 1784—d. March 9, 1858), politician, dramatist, essayist, biographer. Barker served as an assistant adjutant-general during the War of 1812, then as an alderman in Philadelphia, and in 1819 as mayor. A Jacksonian in politics, he was appointed Collector of the Port of Philadelphia, then Comptroller of the Treasury, but resigned from the latter to become a clerk in the Treasury Department until his death. Meanwhile he wrote steadily, and his plays reflect his ardent Americanism and interest in politics. *Tears and Smiles* (1807) studied Philadelphia manners. THE INDIAN PRINCESS (1808) was the first play on an Indian subject, also the first American play, produced in America, to be performed in England. MARMION (1812) was a version of Scott's poem. The theme of SUPERSTITION (1824) was principally the witchcraft madness in Salem. *The Court of Love* (produced, 1836; written in 1817 as *How to Try a Lover*) was based on a French novel. Of all these plays, *Superstition* (written in blank verse) is reckoned the best. P. H. Musser wrote a life of Barker (1929).

Barker, The (1927), a play by KENYON NICHOLSON. A circus barker's son, against his father's wishes, marries a snake charmer. His father wants him to abandon the world of the circus and become a lawyer; in the end he yields to his father's wishes.

Barlow, Joel (b. Redding, Conn., March 14, 1754—d. Dec. 24, 1812), teacher, lawyer, diplomat, poet, humorist. Educated at Yale, Barlow served in the Revolutionary Army. Later, after teaching school and becoming a lawyer, he went abroad as an agent for one or two rather dubious land companies to encourage emigration to America. In England he became friendly with THOMAS PAINE. William Godwin, and Joseph Priestley, in France was active on the side of the French Revolutionaries. At the same time he invested shrewdly in French consols, returning to America a man of wealth and reputation. In 1795, as consul to Algiers, he secured an excellent treaty with the Barbary states. Sent to negotiate a treaty with Napoleon in 1811, he was caught in the retreat from Moscow and suffered hardships so severe that he died from the effects and was buried in Poland.

V. L. Parrington says well that Barlow's "admirable prose writings have been forgotten, and THE COLUMBIAD (1807) returns always to

plague him." Ambitiously conceived as "the great American epic," it is a dull and lengthy imitation of Alexander Pope, with a strong humanitarian element which lifts infrequent passages above the general level. The poem was severely criticized in England for its many Americanisms, such words as *utilize, millennial,* and *crass* striking reviewers "as utterly foreign as if they had been adopted from the Hebrew or Chinese." As a poet Barlow survives best in THE HASTY PUDDING (1796), a mock pastoral written in praise of his native corn-meal while abroad. Among his prose works are *A Letter to The National Convention Of France On The Defects Of The Constitution of 1791* (1792) and *Advice To The Priviledged Orders* (1792). The former won him honorary citizenship in France, while the latter was suppressed in England by Pitt. He also edited *The American Mercury* with Elisha Babcock (1784–1785) and contributed to the ANARCHIAD (1786–1787), a publication of the Hartford Wits. He is the subject of *A Yankee's Odyssey* (1958), a biography by James Woodress. See HARTFORD WITS.

Barnard, George Grey (b. Bellefonte, Pa., May 24, 1863—d. April 24, 1938), sculptor. Recognized as one of the leading sculptors of his day, Barnard received training at the Chicago Art Institute and in Paris, where, in early exhibitions, he achieved a degree of success which was never completely forgiven by his colleagues in this country. One of the few Americans of his time to carve directly in stone, his work and his general philosophy of art differed sharply from that of most of his contemporaries. Among his most celebrated works are his two pediment groups for the New York Public Library; two colossal groups of figures for the State Capitol at Harrisburg, Pa.; the Lincoln statue at Lytle Park, Cincinnati; and three pieces on the Rockefeller estate at Pocantico Hills, N.Y.: *The Hewer, Woman,* and *Adam and Eve.* He is also notable as a collector of Gothic and Romanesque sculpture and architectural fragments, part of his collection forming the nucleus of *The Cloisters* in New York.

Barnes, Djuna (b. Cornwall, N.Y., June 12, 1892), newspaperwoman, playwright, poet. Miss Barnes began in newspaper work, became associated with avant-garde groups as a sponsor of the Theatre Guild, contributor to *The Little Review,* and author of three experimental plays (*Three from the Earth, An Irish Triangle, Kurzy from the Sea*) produced in 1919–20 by the Provincetown Players. In 1923 she published *A Book,* which contains stories, plays, and verses; in 1928 she published *Ryder,* which was expurgated for the American edition. In 1936 appeared *Nightwood,* with an introduction by T. S. Eliot; it is a novel dealing with life in the Parisian artistic underground and has been one of the most highly regarded modern novels among avant-garde critics and writers. She has also written *The Antiphon* (1958), a surrealistic play in blank verse.

Barnes, Harry Elmer (b. Auburn, N.Y., June 15, 1889—d. Aug. 25, 1968), historian, sociologist. After receiving his A.B. from Syracuse University with honors in 1913, and his Ph.D. from Columbia University in 1918, Barnes taught at many universities and wrote many books both for his fellow historians and for the general public. Among them are: *Sociology Before Comte* (1917); *The Genesis of the World War* (1926); *The Twilight of Christianity* (1929); *The Story of Punishment* (1930); *Can Man Be Civilized?* (1932); *History of Western Civilization* (1935), which he considered his most important historical book; *New Horizons in Criminology* (1943), in collaboration with N. K. Teeters; *Perpetual War for Perpetual Peace* (1953). His *History of Historical Writing* (1937) was revised several times.

Barnes, Margaret [Ayer] (b. Chicago, April 8, 1886—d. Oct. 25, 1967), novelist. Mrs. Barnes was a good storyteller, observing details faithfully and expressing a definite conservative creed. *Years of Grace* (1930), a vivacious family novel beginning in Chicago in the late 1880's, won the Pulitzer Prize. Other popular novels of hers were *Westward Passage* (1931), *Edna His Wife* (1935), *Wisdom's Gate* (1938). A play written with EDWARD SHELDON, *Dishonored Lady* (1930), was based on the Madeleine Smith murder case. She also dramatized Edith Wharton's AGE OF INNOCENCE (1928).

Barnes, Walter (b. Barnesville, Ohio, July 29, 1880—   ), teacher, writer. Barnes has taught at several universities and was chairman of the English Department at the School of Education, New York University. His books show a constant awareness of the changing conditions of life today, and have helped give English teachers a sense of the need for adjustment. Among them: *English in the Country School* (1913), *New Democracy in the Teaching of English* (1923), *The Photoplay as Literary Art* (1936), *The Teacher Speaks and Other Poems* (1949).

Barnum, P[hineas] T[aylor] (b. Bethel, Conn., July 5, 1810—d. April 7, 1891), circus man, impresario, author. Barnum began his career by exhibiting freaks, some fake, some genuine; also brought Jenny Lind to America. He joined forces with James A. Bailey to make the great show known for years as Barnum & Bailey, absorbed after Bailey's death in 1906 by the Ringling Brothers. He wrote a book called *The Humbugs of the World* (1866) and—possibly—the *Life of P. T. Barnum, Written by Himself* (1855, frequently revised). I. Wallace wrote a biography, *Fabulous Showman*, in 1959.

Barr, Amelia E[dith] (b. England, March 29, 1831—d. March 10, 1919), novelist. Sentimental in tone but strictly "pure," Mrs. Barr's novels were widely read for her gift of storytelling and their historical material. Especially popular were *Jan Vedder's Wife* (1885), THE BOW OF ORANGE RIBBON (1886), *Remember the Alamo* (1888), *The House on Cherry Street* (1909). In addition, Mrs. Barr wrote much verse, from which, she said, she made more than a thousand dollars annually for many years.

Barr, Stringfellow (b. Suffolk, Va., Jan. 15, 1897—   ), teacher, writer. Barr called himself: "A teacher who sometimes writes." The quality of his work, however, placed him in the forefront of America's thoughtful writers. In the field of biography, his *Mazzini: Portrait of An Exile* (1935) was acclaimed the soundest and most notable study of the Italian patriot. Another outstanding contribution to American literature was his *Pilgrimage of Western Man* (1949). Barr's universal sympathies were made keener by many travels, and he expresses with understanding the needs and contributions of people of other lands. Among his books: *Three Fables* (1932); *Let's Join the Human Race* (1950); *Copydog in India* (1955); *Purely Academic* (1958); *The Will of Zeus* (1961).

Barras, Charles M. (b. 1826—d. 1873), playwright. See THE BLACK CROOK.

Barrell, Sarah Sayward. See WOOD, SARAH SAYWARD [BARRELL] KEATING.

Barren Ground (1925), a novel by ELLEN GLASGOW. It is a work of ingenious incidents and rich characterization in which Miss Glasgow touches successfully on many themes. Dorinda Oakley, disappointed in love, takes hold of the barren acres of her father and turns them into a successful farm. A member of the "poor white" group, she proves that with determination they, too, can become wealthy. But in her relations with men she is less successful—loving one, almost marrying another, rejecting a young doctor in New York, in the end marrying the man who

had rejected her, taking care of the man she had loved when he becomes a penniless drunkard. The book is the very antithesis of the conventional romance of the South; in advertising it, Miss Glasgow's publisher used the slogan, "Realism crosses the Potomac."

Barrett, William (b. New York City, Dec. 30, 1915—   ), writer, teacher, philosopher, journalist. Although Barrett's main field of interest has been college teaching and the writing of philosophical essays and literary criticism, he has had a variety of other occupations, including ghost writing, social work, and some time as a State Department diplomat. In 1958 he published *Irrational Man,* which, as a study in existential philosophy, drew an enthusiastic response from the critics. The New York *Times* called it "the most thorough account yet written for the American layman of the philosophy that has attracted so much attention in Europe since World War II—Existentialism." Other books by Mr. Barrett include *Aristotle's Theory of Change* (1938); *What Is Existentialism?* (1947); *Zen Buddhism* (ed., 1956); *Philosophy in the Twentieth Century* (1961).

Barrett, William Edmund (b. New York City, Nov. 16, 1900—   ), popular novelist, short-story writer. At the age of twenty-nine, Mr. Barrett abandoned a successful advertising career (he was Southwestern Advertising Manager for Westinghouse Electric) in order to devote his full time to writing. After his first published work, a biography, *Woman on Horseback,* 1938, he concentrated almost exclusively on fiction: *Flight from Youth,* 1939; *To the Last Man,* 1948; *The Evil Heart,* 1946; *The Number of My Days,* 1946; *The Left Hand of God,* 1951 (made into a motion picture in 1955); *The Shadows of the Images,* 1953; *The Sudden Strangers,* 1956; *The Empty Shrine,* 1958; *The Edge of Things,* 1960. He has also published a work of historical nonfiction, *The First War Planes,* 1960. He began to demonstrate a religious preoccupation in his later works, notably *The Left Hand of God* and *The Empty Shrine,* both novels dealing with the search for faith.

Barry, Philip (b. Rochester, N.Y., June 18, 1896—d. Dec. 3, 1949), playwright. Barry attended first Yale, where a one-act play of his was produced by the Yale Dramatic Club in 1919, then Harvard, where his work with GEORGE PIERCE BAKER in the 47 Workshop led to writing of a prize play, *You and I,* produced in New York in 1922. For the most part Barry wrote comedies, occasionally with a serious note or a mystical turn; and for the most part, too, these comedies dealt with people of wealth and social standing, to whom Barry preached not too stern sermons. Notable among his plays are *Paris Bound* (1927), HOLIDAY (1929), HOTEL UNIVERSE (1930), THE ANIMAL KINGDOM (1932), *Here Come the Clowns* (1938), THE PHILADELPHIA STORY (1939).

Barrymores, The. A family of famous American actors, beginning with Maurice Barrymore and his wife. Barrymore's real name was Herbert Blythe (1847–1905) and he was born in India,

His wife was Georgiana Drew (1856–1893); she was the daughter of the famous actor John Drew (1827–1862). Their children were Lionel (1878–1954), Ethel (1879–1959), and John (1882–1942); and they scored many great stage and motion-picture successes. *The Royal Family* (1927), by GEORGE S. KAUFMAN and EDNA FERBER, satirizes the foibles of a family of actors not dissimilar to the Barrymores. Gene Fowler's GOOD NIGHT, SWEET PRINCE (1943) is mainly about John Barrymore, but tells much about the others. So do Lionel's own (ghosted) book, *We Barrymores* (1951) and Ethel's *Memories* (1955).

Bart, Lily. Chief character in Edith Wharton's THE HOUSE OF MIRTH (1905). Lily is a beautiful orphan, of good social connections but little money, whose fortunes sink from bad to worse and who finally commits suicide.

Bartleby the Scrivener (1853), a long short story by HERMAN MELVILLE. Immediately successful in *Putnam's Magazine*, *Bartleby* has since been recognized as one of the great American short stories. The narrator, who operates a law office on Wall Street, employs a young scrivener named Bartleby, who, like the two other employees, is told to copy and proofread legal documents. He eventually rejects these menial chores; his eyes glazed, he prefers to stare endlessly at a stone wall, rejecting all entreaties to work with, "I should prefer not to." Unable to persuade Bartleby either to work or to leave the office in which he seems to have taken up permanent residence, the narrator moves his business elsewhere. Bartleby is finally taken to prison, and the narrator, feeling vaguely responsible for him, visits him and arranges for him to receive special privileges. But Bartleby refuses the privileges, refuses to eat, and finally dies. Bartleby is something of a comic hero, but his fate is haunting rather than amusing. This haunted and haunting quality is, perhaps, the major effect of the tale, and emerges chiefly from the pervasive surrealistic atmosphere in which the characters are enveloped.

Bartlett, John (b. Plymouth, Mass., June 14, 1820—d. Dec. 3, 1905), bookseller, editor, publisher. Bartlett was strongly attracted to books and became a clerk in the University Book Store in Cambridge, Mass. There his self-acquired learning won him the esteem of professors and students. After a service of two years in the navy during the Civil War, Bartlett was employed by the firm of Little, Brown & Co., becoming in time a partner (1865), a senior partner (1878); he retired in 1889. His most famous book was the collection of *Familiar Quotations* (1855), which ran through nine editions in his lifetime, was revised for a 10th edition in 1914 by Nathan Haskell Dole, for an 11th edition in 1937 by Christopher Morley and Louella D. Everett (revised, 1953), and for a 13th Centennial Edition by editors unnamed in 1955. Bartlett also published *A New Method of Chess Notation* (1857); *A Shakespeare Phrase Book* (1882); and *A New and Complete Concordance to Shakespeare* (1894).

Barton, Benjamin Smith (b. Lancaster, Pa., Feb. 10, 1766—d. Dec. 19, 1815), physician, naturalist. Barton wrote *Elements of Botany* (1803), the first work of its kind to be written by an American. He taught for many years at the University of Pennsylvania and became an authority on American *materia medica*. His friend JOHN BARTRAM did drawings for his *Elements*.

Barton, Clara [Harlowe] (b. Oxford, Mass., Dec. 25, 1821—d. April 12, 1912), philanthropist, author. Miss Barton was first a teacher, then showed executive ability as a clerk in the Patent Office. At the outset of the Civil War she volunteered for hospital service, won the confidence of Lincoln, became an organizer of aid to war casualties. After the war Miss Barton induced the United States to become a member of the Red Cross and headed the American branch. Hers was the innovation by which the Red Cross gives help in any time of distress, during peace and war. She wrote *An Official History of the Red Cross* (1882) and *The Story of My Childhood* (1907). Ishbel Ross described her achievements in *Angel of the Battlefield* (1956).

Barton, William E[leazar] (b. Sublette, Ill., June 28, 1861—d. Dec. 7, 1930), clergyman, author, father of Bruce Barton. Barton wrote first *A Tale of the Cumberland Mountains* (1887), republished in 1890, with additions as *Life in the Hills of Kentucky*. Later Barton made himself an authority on the life of Lincoln, wrote *The Paternity of Abraham Lincoln, The Soul of Abraham Lincoln* (both 1920), *The Life of Abraham Lincoln* (1925), *The Lineage of Lincoln* (1929), and *Lincoln at Gettysburg* (1930). Barton is often discursive, sometimes determinedly "inspirational," but in general Lincoln scholars approved his accuracy and honesty. In 1932 appeared his *Autobiography*.

Bartram, John (b. near Darby, Pa., March 23, 1699—d. Sept. 22, 1777) and **Bartram, William** (b. Philadelphia, Feb. 9, 1739—d. July 22, 1823), botanists, explorers, authors. It is difficult to separate the achievements and writings of these two eminent scientists, father and son, the first American botanists. The father was a man of great strength and originality of mind, who theorized convincingly on the nature of fossils, advocated deep-sea soundings, and in private life freed his slaves and had them eat at the table with him. He published *Observations*, a book of his travels "from Pennsylvania to Onondaga, Oswego, and Lake Ontario," in 1751. In 1769 appeared his *Description of East Florida*—"a journal kept by John Bartram, Botanist to His Majesty the King."

It may have been to this book that Samuel Taylor Coleridge referred when he said in *Table-Talk* (1835): "The latest book of travels I know, written in the spirit of the old travelers, is Bartram's account of his tour in the Floridas. It is a work of high merit every way." But Coleridge may perhaps have been thinking of the younger Bartram's *Travels Through North and South Carolina, Georgia, East and West Florida* (1791). For William Bartram's interests extended beyond mere scientific investigations of plant life to nature itself and to human beings, especially the Indians whom he encountered in his travels. He loved the beauty of the wilderness, and awakens the reader to his own cheerful delight in it. The book with its romantic views

WILLIAM BARTRAM

of nature was read by Chateaubriand, and traces of its imagery have been found in Wordsworth's *Ruth* (1800) and others of his poems and in Coleridge's *Kubla Khan* (1816).

Baruch, Bernard [Mannes] (b. Camden, S.C., Aug. 19, 1870—d. June 20, 1965), economist. Baruch graduated from City College (N.Y.C.) and has received honorary degrees from several universities. He was a member of the Advisory Commission of the Council of National Defense, chairman of the Commission of Raw Materials, Minerals and Metals, and a member of the commission in charge of all purchases for the Allies during World War I. He became advisor to James F. Byrnes, war mobilization director, in 1943, and was made U.S. Representative to the United Nations Atomic Energy Commission in 1946. He wrote *American Industry in the War* (1941); *A Philosophy for our Time* (1954); *Baruch: My Own Story* (1957); and *Baruch, the Public Years* (1960). He is the subject of a distinguished biography, *Mr. Baruch: the Man, the Myth, the Eighty Years,* by Margaret Coit (1957). For many years a valued, if unofficial, advisor to presidents—his office a park bench in Jackson Square, opposite the White House— he has been long known as America's "elder statesman."

Barzun, Jacques [Martin] (b. France, Nov. 30, 1907—   ), teacher, critic, historian. Born in Paris, Barzun came to the United States in 1919 and became a naturalized citizen in 1933; he joined the Department of History at Columbia University in 1927, became a professor in 1945, a dean in 1955, and in 1958 was appointed provost. A frequent contributor to magazines, Barzun is notable for the philosophical and scholarly point of view he brings to the discussion of contemporary problems and personalities. His style is both subtle and lively, often polemical in tone, never pedantic. Among his books are *The French Race* (1932); *Race: A Study in Modern Superstition* (1937); *Romanticism and the Modern Ego* (1943); *Teacher in America* (1945); *Berlioz and the Romantic Century* (2 v., 1950); *God's Country and Mine* (1954); *The House of Intellect* (1959). The last, written with Barzun's customary wit and grace, aroused some lively conflicts of opinion. It is an attack on the pseudointellectual world of modern society, which the author regards as having usurped the place of true intellect within the spheres of art, science, and philanthropy. The *Saturday Review* said of it: "Barzun makes his case by citing the absurdities practiced in the name of these great enterprises rather than through criticism of art, science, or the philosophy of generosity. Yet this book creates the danger of confusion, owing, at least in part, to a mixture of motives in the author." In 1961, Barzun was named an Extraordinary Fellow at Churchill College of Cambridge University in England.

Basler, Roy P[rentice] (b. St. Louis, Mo., Nov. 19, 1906—   ), teacher, editor, critic. Basler taught at several universities, particularly the University of Arkansas and George Peabody College. His interests turned toward the critical study of Lincoln documents, and his book *The Lincoln Legend* (1935) established his authority as a scholar in this field. In *Abraham Lincoln: His Speeches and Writings* (1946) he made an excellent one-volume collection of speeches, state papers, letters, and miscellanea, correcting many errors found in earlier editions and offering a lengthy introduction studying Lincoln as a writer. He has edited the *Collected Works* of Lincoln (8 v., 1953). His latest study, with others, is *Enduring Lincoln* (1959).

Bassett, John Spencer (b. Raboro, N.C., Sept. 10, 1867—d. Jan. 27, 1928), historian, biographer, editor. Bassett taught history at Trinity College (now Duke University); he nearly lost his position when he spoke out boldly on the Negro question in the October, 1903, issue of the *South Atlantic Quarterly,* which he had founded in 1902. From 1906 on he taught at Smith College and inaugurated the *Smith College Studies in History.* Among his more important writings: *Anti-Slavery Leaders of North Carolina* (1898); *The Life of Andrew Jackson* (1911); *A Short History of the United States* (1913); *Expansion and Reform* (1926).

Bassett, Sara Ware (b. Newton, Mass., Oct. 22, 1872—   ), novelist. She has taught and has written books on various industries, beginning with *The Story of Lumber* (1912). She is best known for her agreeable, engrossing novels—*The Harbor Road* (1919), *The Green Dolphin* (1926), *Turning Tide* (1934), *The*

White Sail (1949), and *Echoes of the Tide* (1951).

Basso, [Joseph] Hamilton (b. New Orleans, Sept. 5, 1904—d. May 13, 1964), novelist, critic. Basso's journalistic experience began with the New Orleans *Item* and the New Orleans *Times-Picayune*. He was a frequent contributor to *The New Yorker* from 1944. *Beauregard: The Great Creole* (1933) was followed by several novels, including *Courthouse Square* (1936); *Days Before Lent* (1939); *Sun in Capricorn* (1942), a savage attack on a character resembling Huey Long; and *The View from Pompey's Head* (1954), which was filmed. *The Light Infantry Ball* was published in 1959, and *A Quota of Seaweed* in 1960.

Bat, The (1920), a mystery play by MARY ROBERTS RINEHART and AVERY HOPWOOD. This very successful play, which ran on Broadway for 867 performances, was based on Mrs. Rinehart's equally successful novel, THE CIRCULAR STAIRCASE (1908).

Bateman, Sidney Frances [Cowell] (b. New Jersey, March 29, 1823—d. Jan. 13, 1881), actress, playwright. Miss Cowell appeared on the stage at New Orleans in 1837, in 1839 married Hezekiah Linthicum Bateman, a theatrical manager. At the latter's St. Louis theater she produced a satirical play *Self* (1856) and in New York City *Geraldine, or Love's Victory* (1859). In 1860 she dramatized Longfellow's EVANGELINE, with her daughter Kate (1843–1917) in the leading role. Kate toured England with such success that her family followed her, and Mrs. Bateman became a prosperous manager of several London theaters. In 1880 she produced JOAQUIN MILLER's *The Danites,* the first all-American company in an American play given in London.

Bates, Arlo (b. East Machias, Me., Dec. 16, 1850—d. Aug. 24, 1918), poet, teacher, editor, novelist, author of textbooks. Bates wrote poetry, the best of which is found in *Sonnets in Shadow* (1887); several novels, among them *The Philistines* (1889), directed against smug "high society" in Boston, and *The Intoxicated Ghost* (1908); and a number of textbooks. Particularly good are *Talks on the Study of Literature* (1895) and *Talks on Writing English* (1896; second series, 1901).

Bates, Ernest Sutherland (b. Gambier, Ohio, Oct. 14, 1879—d. Dec. 4, 1939), teacher, author. Bates' best known book is *The Bible Designed to Be Read as Living Literature* (1936), a skillful and reverent rearrangement of the King James Version. He likewise dealt with the Bible in *The Friend of Jesus* (1928), an account of Judas Iscariot, and wrote *A Biography of the Bible* (1937). Bates became intensely interested in America, its creed and its great figures; his last book, published posthumously, was *The American Faith*. See BIBLE IN THE UNITED STATES.

Bates, Katharine Lee (b. Falmouth, Mass., Aug. 12, 1850—d. March 28, 1929), teacher, poet, editor. Miss Bates spent the greater part of her adult life as a professor of English at Wellesley, and much of her activity was given to editing (for example, *English Religious Drama,* 1893) and to lecturing. She wrote short stories and books for children, published several collections of poetry. But she is essentially a one-poem author; her fame rests on the widespread acceptance of AMERICA THE BEAUTIFUL (1895). Dorothy Burgess' *Dream and Deed* (1952) is the story of Miss Bates' life.

Bathtub Hoax, The. This incident represents H. L. MENCKEN's fulfillment of the notion that you can fool all of the people some of the time. On Dec. 28, 1917, Mencken published in the New York *Evening Mail* an article entitled "A Neglected Anniversary." It presented a series of preposterous statements regarding the origin of bathtub bathing in the United States in the 1840's, all of them invented by the Baltimore humorist. But his "facts" were promptly accepted as gospel and found their way into innumerable newspaper and magazine articles, lectures by "authorities," and even government publications and history texts. Mencken tried to catch up with the fraud later, but repercussions are still continuing. Curtis D. MacDougall, in his book on *Hoaxes* (1940), winds up with Mencken's masterpiece as a "grand finale." Robert McHugh edited *The Bathtub Hoax, and Other Blasts and Bravos; from the Chicago Tribune* (1958).

Battle Hymn of the Republic, The (published in the *Atlantic Monthly,* Feb. 1862, and in *Later Lyrics,* 1866), a poem by JULIA WARD HOWE. Late in 1861 Mrs. Howe and her husband Samuel Gridley Howe, both of them deeply interested in philanthropic causes and the success of the Union, visited Washington. It was after Bull Run, and the capital was a gloomy place. On their way back they sang a song popular with the soldiers of the Northern Army —*John Brown's Body.* A member of the party named J. F. Clarke urged Mrs. Howe, who had already published two volumes of verse, to write words to the music of this song—"good words for a stirring tune." That night, toward the dawn, Mrs. Howe awakened and found the words of a poem in her head, ready to march with the tune. With a sudden effort, she relates, she sprang out of bed, and in order not to awaken a baby who slept near her, she wrote, without a light, *The Battle Hymn.*

Battle of Bunkers Hill, The (1776), a poem in blank verse by HUGH HENRY BRACKENRIDGE in the form of a dialogue. American and British officers discuss successively the question of American courage.

Battle of Lovell's Pond, The (1820), a poem by HENRY WADSWORTH LONGFELLOW. This is believed to be Longfellow's first poem. The subject is the battle with the Indians near Fryeburg in Maine, May 8, 1725.

Battle of the Kegs, The (1778), a satirical poem by FRANCIS HOPKINSON. This ballad tells the story of an actual incident. Kegs charged with gunpowder were sent in January, 1778, down the Delaware River from Bordentown, in a manner designed to harass the British fleet anchored at Philadelphia. Only one of the kegs exploded, killing four men and creating a panic among the British. These mechanical kegs had been built in the cooperage of Col. Joseph Borden, Hopkinson's father-in-law. Hopkinson's verses spread rapidly through the colonies, and annoyed the British deeply. Angered as much by the poem as by the kegs themselves, they razed the home and store of Col. Borden. The poem is still amusing. It is sung to the tune of *Yankee Doodle*. See SIR WILLIAM HOWE.

Battle-Pieces and Aspects of the War (1866), a book of poems by HERMAN MELVILLE. Comprising seventy-two poems, this collection of verses on the Civil War is commemorative rather than celebratory. Melville saw the wrack of his country as something to be mourned and pitied, and, like Lincoln, his voice was raised in compassion, not revenge. In *Battle-Pieces* there is a sense of the tragedy of early death, and a renewed passion for human suffering; the best poems reflect not a condemnation of evil but a deeply elegiac temper.

Baum, L[yman] Frank (b. Chittenango, N.Y., May 15, 1856—d. May 6, 1919), newspaperman, editor, dramatist, writer for juveniles. Baum began writing children's books in 1899, and won popular success with *Father Goose* (1899). A year later his reputation was firmly established with THE WONDERFUL WIZARD OF OZ. Baum continued to the end of his life to write about misadventures in Oz, fourteen books in all. It was a land of great happiness and strange creatures—the Tin Woodman, the Cowardly Lion, the Wizard, the Scarecrow. In 1901 a musical extravaganza called *The Wizard of Oz,* starring Montgomery and Stone, packed the theaters; in 1939 a motion picture of the same name, starring Judy Garland, was equally successful. Baum also wrote books for boys under the pen names Captain Hugh Fitzgerald and Floyd Akers; for girls under the pen name Mrs. Edith Van Dyne. Three adventure tales were signed Schuyler Stanton.

Bayliss, Marguerite. See BOLINVAR.

Bayou Folk (1894), a collection of twenty-three stories by KATE CHOPIN. They are varied tales of the Creoles and Acadians of the Louisiana bayous—delicate, humorous, tragic, sympathetic.

Bay Psalm Book, The (1640). The full title is: *The Whole Booke of Psalms Faithfully Translated into English Metre.* The translators were RICHARD MATHER, THOMAS WELDE, and JOHN ELIOT, along with twenty-seven other ministers; and they used the King James Version as the basis for their translations. The book—the first bound book printed in the colonies—was published in Cambridge in an edition of 1,700 copies by Stephen Daye, a locksmith who had come to Massachusetts two years before. It sold for one shilling eightpence a copy. In time copies became extremely scarce, and on Jan. 28, 1947, one went under the hammer for $151,000 to Dr. A. S. W. Rosenbach. Only ten other copies are known to exist. See BIBLE IN THE UNITED STATES.

Beach, Rex [Ellingwood] (b. Atwood, Mich., Sept. 1, 1877—d. Dec. 7, 1949), novelist. Beach is remembered chiefly for his stories of Alaska. First of these were *Pardners* (1905) and *The Spoilers* (1906); latest, *The World in His Arms* (1945). Back of Beach's stories lay a genuine knowledge of the scenes he depicted, a real love of outdoor life, and sincere admiration of manly qualities.

Beach, Sylvia (b. New Jersey, 1887—d. Oct. 6, 1962), bookseller. An expatriate who kept a famous bookshop at No. 12 Rue de l'Odéon, Paris, commercially known as Shakespeare & Co., Miss Beach did much to encourage new and young writers of all nationalities during the late 1920's. She told the story of this venture in *Shakespeare & Co.* (1959). She published James Joyce's *Ulysses* (1922) in France, using French typesetters, and shared with him the literary and legal assaults that the book provoked. In 1950 she received the Clairovin Memorial Award for her translation of Henri Michaux' *A Barbarian in Asia*.

Beacon Hill. An elevation north of Boston Common. Named for the beacon placed there in 1635 to warn of Indian attacks, it became the fashionable residential section of Boston in the early 19th century. The great architect CHARLES BULFINCH designed several houses there and planned (1795–98) the famous Boston State House at the apex of the Hill. The whole region, with Beacon Street skirting the hill alongside the Boston Common, is known for its literary associations and old traditions.

Beadle, Erastus F[lavel] (b. Pierstown, N.Y., Sept. 11, 1821—d. Dec. 18, 1894), editor, author, publisher. In 1858 Beadle formed, with his brother Irwin P. Beadle and with Robert Adams, the New York City firm of Beadle and Adams. Orville J. Victor became their editor, and during the next thirty years he selected for the firm the thousands of tales that they published. The firm's slogan was "a dollar book for a dime," and they enormously increased the reading public of the day. They began with song books and joke books. In 1860 the first dime novel was issued. One of their great successes was Edward S. Ellis' SETH JONES, OR THE CAPTIVE OF THE FRONTIER (1860), of which 600,000 copies were sold in half a dozen languages. Others who wrote for the firm were Captain Mayne Reid, Ned Buntline, Edward L. Wheeler and Colonel Prentiss Ingraham. See THE DIME NOVEL; ORVILLE JAMES VICTOR.

Beals, Carleton (b. Medicine Lodge, Kans., Nov. 13, 1893—   ), writer on political and social conditions. His books, mainly on Latin America, include: *Mexico—An Interpretation* (1923); *Brimstone and Chili* (1927); *The Crime of Cuba* (1934); *Dawn Over the Amazon* (1943), a Literary Guild Selection; *Lands of the Dawning Morrow* (1948); *Stephen E. Austin, Father of Texas* (1953); *Further Adventures in Freelancing* (1940), the third of his biographical books; *American Earth* (1939); *Rome or Death* (1923); *Taste of Glory* (1956); *Invited Guest, President Oswaldo Dorticós of Cuba*

(1960). In all of Beals' writing the elements of thrill and adventure are balanced by a thorough knowledge of the people he writes about.

Beard, Charles A[ustin] (b. near Knightstown, Ind., Nov. 27, 1874—d. Sept. 1, 1948), historian. Educated in universities in the United States and England, Beard began teaching at Columbia University in 1904. In a protest against denial of academic freedom to his fellow-professors J. McKeen Cattell and H. W. L. Dana, he resigned from Columbia in 1917. By that time he had published his most famous book, AN ECONOMIC INTERPRETATION OF THE CONSTITUTION (1913), supplemented by *Economic Origins of Jeffersonian Democracy* (1915). V. L. Parrington points out that unsympathetic readers immediately inferred the influence of Karl Marx on the earlier book, but that Beard's concept of the political state as determined in its forms and activities by economic groups was not a modern Marxian variety of political theory. Its origins were in Aristotle, and Beard's books in addition reveal the influence of Locke and Harrington. Some of his ideas may also be found in Madison, Hamilton, and John Adams and in the discussions of the Constitutional Convention, also in the legislative debates of Webster and Calhoun. The Constitution is thus seen as English rather than French, the judicious expression of an 18th-century realism that accepted a property basis for political action.

Beard wrote many other books, mainly in the field of American history, some in collaboration with his able wife MARY R. BEARD; some were highly profitable textbooks. Among them: *The Economic Basis of Politics* (1922); *The Republic* (1943); *A Basic History of the U.S.* (1944); *American Foreign Policies in the Making, 1932–40* (1946); *President Roosevelt and the Coming of War, 1941* (1948). Beard, deeply opposed to any form of American imperialism, became more and more property-conscious and a confirmed and bitter foe of F. D. Roosevelt's ideas. Basil Rauch, in *Roosevelt from Munich to Pearl Harbor* (1950), claims that Beard distorted facts in his rage against Roosevelt. See WILLIAM C. BAGLEY; RISE OF AMERICAN CIVILIZATION.

Beard, Daniel C[arter] (b. Cincinnati, Ohio, June 21, 1850—d. June 11, 1941), naturalist, author, artist, Boy Scout leader. Beard became a founder of the Boy Scout movement in the United States and its constant mentor in woodcraft and nature lore. Among his books: *American Boys' Handy Book* (1882); *Boy Pioneers and Sons of Daniel Boone* (1909); *Do It Yourself* (1925); *The Wisdom of the Woods* (1927); and his autobiography, *Hardly a Man Is Now Alive* (1939).

Beard, Mary R[itter] (b. Indianapolis, Ind., Aug. 5, 1876—d. Aug. 14, 1958), author. Mary Ritter married CHARLES A. BEARD in 1900, and collaborated with him in several books, including *American Citizenship* (1913), *History of the United States* (1921), and *America in Mid-Passage* (1939). Entirely her own were *A Short History of the American Labor Movement* (1920; revised, 1925), *America through*

Women's Eyes (1934), and *Woman as a Force in History* (1946). With Martha Bensley Bruère she edited an anthology, *Laughing Their Way: Women's Humor in America* (1934).

Beare and Ye Club [or Cubb], Ye (1665), a play, the first in English known to have been performed in the colonies. The authors, all Virginians, were Cornelius Watkinson, Philip Howard, and William Darby. The play was accused of licentiousness, but the playwrights were acquitted upon its performance in court. The text has disappeared.

Beath, Paul R. See FEBOLD FEBOLDSON.

Beat writing. The Beat movement emerged into public attention in 1956 with the publication of Allen Ginsberg's HOWL AND OTHER POEMS and Jack Kerouac's ON THE ROAD. The movement, however, was not purely literary but expressed a state of mind embodied in the Bohemian atmosphere of New York City's Greenwich Village and San Francisco's North Beach. It later spread to Venice West, where Lawrence Lipton memorialized it in *The Holy Barbarians* (1959). The social atmosphere of the Beat movement produced a rebellious tone of disaffiliation from society and a devotion to the concept of voluntary poverty. Socially speaking, the main tone was negative, and the movement was primarily an evasion rather than an attempt to improve the conditions it protested against. An anarchic individualism was the primary motivating force—although a remarkable sameness of dress, a ritual use of "hip" language and jazz argot, and a tendency to cluster together in espresso bars and party "pads" created the image of a community with a relaxed tone and common rites.

Many of the patterns of this community were agreeable to the Beat writers, who found in its milieu an audience and an atmosphere for their work. In the term "beat" they retained the common meaning of worn-out, tired, pooped, but they saw in this depressed condition a possible way to escape the strictures and false values of conventional society. Hence *beat* took on the connotations of blessedness: beatific, beatitude, beatified. To the Beat writers, the way down was the way out, and through voluntary poverty, conscientious disaffiliation from the blandishments of an adjusted life, and complete annihilation of the motives of an acquisitive society they sought illumination and joy. The concept of illumination was central to their view of life. It might result from simple surrender to the process of experience, from sexual ecstasy, from drunkenness and abandon, from such hallucinogenic drugs as peyote and lysergic acid, from the disciplines of Buddhism, from anything that increased the illusion of receptivity to life. Their main aim was release—from the confines of social and moral judgment and from the conventions of literature.

Among the chief writers are ALLEN GINSBERG, JACK KEROUAC, GREGORY CORSO, WILLIAM BURROUGHS, LAWRENCE FERLINGHETTI, Michael McClure, Gary Snyder, and Phil Whalen. Numerous other writers shared their preoccupations in one way or another, and certain older and more established writers supported them, notably Norman Mailer, Henry Miller, Kenneth Rexroth (briefly), and William Carlos Williams. With the exceptions of Kerouac and Burroughs, the Beat writers are best known as poets; their work is often symbolized by Allen Ginsberg's *Howl*, a prophetic poem, a form of Jeremiad, written in a long line derived from the Bible, Whitman, Blake, and Christopher Smart. The poem treats a world in which all values have become dehumanized; it is a diatribe against a military and commercial society. The first section of the poem describes the fate of "the best minds of my generation." Their lives are disorderly, self-destructive, criminal, and insane. Their experience is chaotic and their suffering unredeemed. Life offers neither security nor stability, and the measures of society create a false and vulnerable order. These judgments are presented in a blend of jazz argot, surrealist imagery, and violent action. The second section of the poem ascribes to "Moloch" the immediate cause of these conditions. This generation ". . . broke their backs lifting Moloch to heaven!" The veneration of false values is the betrayal of the American dream, and the sensitive and percipient person is driven into outlawry. The third section addresses Carl Solomon (to whom the poem is dedicated) with the refrain "I am with you in Rockland" (a mental hospital), to express the author's identification with suffering human life. The footnote to *Howl*, which is a coda to the poem, declares the absolute holiness of all existence, however stultified and depraved.

Between *Howl and Other Poems* (1956) and *Kaddish* (1961), Ginsberg published various poems in magazines and attained a certain notoriety in the mass media. He traveled widely in Europe and in the United States and read his poems at various colleges, as did Gregory Corso and other Beat writers. His work remained concerned with the same basic subjects. *Kaddish* is another long prophetic poem, more overtly personal and focused on the life and death of his mother. It is permeated with a tone of deep sadness, is less hortatory and satiric than *Howl*, and suggests a greater variety and range. Ginsberg's work displays many of the interests of the Beats: drugs, hallucinogenic and addictive; sexual disorder; voluntary poverty; rejection of the society; quest for illumination; jazz rhythms and hip language; rootless wandering.

In his Beat novels (especially *On the Road*, *The Subterraneans*, and *The Dharma Bums*) Jack Kerouac presents a quasi-fictional view of the Beat milieu. The Beat novels form only a relatively small part of Kerouac's total work. His aim as a writer is to create a comprehensive image of his experience from his childhood in Lowell, Massachusetts, to the present. In this respect his work resembles that of Thomas Wolfe and Henry Miller, and like them he is extremely uneven. His obsession with the details of his own life often overloads his stories with irrelevancies, and he has no clear sense of fictional form. His works tend to be either prolonged portraits of individuals who have a special importance to him or picaresque delineations of casual events, or of experience as one thing after another.

On the Road is picaresque in structure and episodic. Its characteristic action is either hitch-hiking across country for no purpose or driving cars at outrageous speeds from New Orleans to New York to Denver to San Francisco with no particular aim in mind. The book reflects an existence that has no coherent structure. There is no reason for the actions of the novel, and the total effect is to suggest a group of people in constant flux, with no enduring loyalties to place or person. The characters seek sensation, and their few efforts to reach some condition that gives sensation context and meaning are fumbling and doomed. *The Subterraneans* is less episodic and more concentrated largely because it centers on an attempt between a man and woman to establish a valid sexual relation. The milieu is also more tightly fixed, in San Francisco's North Beach, and the result is a sharpening of effect. *The Dharma Bums* treats the same basic milieu, with extensive side trips into the mountains of California and the Pacific Northwest. The character of Japhy in this book is, like most of Kerouac's figures, modeled on a particular figure who attracts his prolonged interest. The original of the highly distorted portrait, Gary Snyder, is one of the most highly regarded Beat poets.

Of the Beat writers, Gary Snyder (b. 1930) has the most extensive genuine knowledge of Buddhism. He has a scholar's knowledge of Chinese and Japanese and has spent a great deal of time in the Orient. Snyder's poetry reflects his childhood experience in the great forests of the Pacific Northwest, his intensive studies of Amerindian legend, his studies in Oriental philosophy and religion, and his travels as a logger in the United States and as a seaman on the various oceans of the world. His first book, *Riprap* (1959), is essentially a selection from early poems that grew out of his experience working in various areas. His early work sounds a great deal like the nature poems of Kenneth Rexroth, from whom Snyder takes much of his poetic discipline. His second book, *Myths and Texts* (1960), is a highly organized presentation of life on the Pacific Coast, divided into three sections. Section 1, "Logging," shows the destruction of the natural landscape in the interests of commerce. Section 2, "Hunting," shows the destruction of the fauna. Section 3, "Fire," treats the irrational desires of men and thus clarifies the motives that led to the actions of the first two sections. He uses Amerindian legends and Buddhist myths to frame the several actions of the book, and he employs many of the verse techniques of Ezra Pound's cantos. Like Pound and Rexroth, Snyder also translates from Chinese and Japanese poetry, and he writes extremely observant and percipient prose.

Phil Whalen (b. 1923) has been associated with Snyder since their years together at Reed

College. He is also a student of Buddhism. He is an extremely beguiling writer, and of the Beat poets the most consistently humorous. Some of his most amusing poems treat his plight as an "uninspired" poet. His observation of the natural world shows his affinity with Rexroth and William Carlos Williams. *Like I Say* (1960) is a collection of his early poems. *Memoirs of an Interglacial Age* (1960) shows his development toward a more fluent and introspective verse.

Michael McClure (b. 1932), who accompanied Whalen on his first reading tour of American colleges, has been associated with the Beat writers from their first emergence. His *Hymns to Saint Geryon* contains many finely shaped poems, including a long analysis of his state of mind during an experiment with peyote. His most recent book, *Dark Brown* (1961), is an exploration of the concept of complete physical abandon. His work is very tightly conceived and ordered, with an extremely physical sense of the weight and impact of the poetic line.

Lawrence Ferlinghetti (b. 1919), in addition to being the most popular of the beat poets, is also a publisher (City Lights Books). He has provided an outlet for Ginsberg and Corso, and has printed some of his own work and the work of writers not necessarily associated with the Beat movement. His poetry is very similar to that of Jacques Prévert, whose work he has translated. His *Pictures of the Gone World* (1955) shows the influence not only of Prévert, but also of Apollinaire and Cummings. A *Coney Island of the Mind* (1958) includes some poems from the earlier book and many new poems. He is an extremely gifted public reader; he has read some of his poems to jazz accompaniment, as have Whalen and Kerouac. His work is good tempered and witty, but it has considerable bite. Unlike most of the Beat writers, he is seriously concerned with political issues, and his popularity is at least partly due to his sense of the public relevance of poetry. He has written one novel, *Her* (1960).

Gregory Corso (b. c. 1930), like Ferlinghetti, has a very winning impudence and ready wit. His first book, *The Vestal Lady of Brattle* (1955), shows his natural irreverence, but his best work appears in *Gasoline* (1958) and *The Happy Birthday of Death* (1960). His chief poetic method seems to be to allow one image to suggest another, until the highest level of logical irrelevancy is attained. He intends to be provocative and annoying; one of his favorite devices is to choose a word—*bomb, power, army, marriage*—and play variations of the several themes suggested by it. In his effort to be impudent he is sometimes dangerously frivolous, as in "Bomb," but when he controls and plays with his subject to establish a fitting tone, he can be remarkably effective, as in "Marriage." Even when he is most frivolous, there is a deep undercurrent of sadness in his work, and an abiding seriousness.

W. S. Burroughs stands apart from the other Beat writers because of the relative isolation of his life and the savagery of his work. He enjoyed a considerable subterranean reputation before *The Naked Lunch* (Paris, 1959) appeared as a whole. The typescript had been circulating for some years, and parts of the book had appeared in magazines of limited circulation. It is a long, nightmarish book, designed as the expression and revelation of a sick mind in a sick world. In it depravity reaches levels normally reserved to the wildest dreams of the criminally insane. No limit is prescribed to the imagination, and physiological processes are described with callous iteration of detail. By Burroughs' own testimony, he intends to shock the mind past complacency to a full understanding of the horror of existence. He represents a world toward which other Beat writers move only tentatively, the world of absolute need and absolute moral emptiness that his characters experience and that he symbolizes in the helpless condition of the dope addict. When moral emptiness is attained, depravity rushes to fill the void, so that in the later sections of *The Naked Lunch* a hideous inversion of morality becomes the norm. Burroughs, in spite of his avowed intentions, is the only true nihilist among the Beat writers.

The Beat movement had two separable elements. The first was a social group, the Beatniks, as they were derisively dubbed. After a period of faddish notoriety that lasted until c. 1960, the Beatniks left public attention and, in effect, ceased to exist as a coherent group. In this social sense, the Beat movement hardly represented a "generation." American Bohemia had merely taken a special and relatively transitory form that was symptomatic and clarifying but had no enduring power as a social force. In literary terms, however, the Beat movement brought to public attention the works of several writers who have remained productive and who have developed toward increasing maturity of perception.

The emergence of the Beat writers called attention to other experimental writers—notably of the San Francisco and Black Mountain groups —who had until that time been relatively ignored; the example of Kerouac and Ginsberg had some influence on other writers of prose and verse. The accomplishments of Beat writers to date are largely the introduction of special tones and personal qualities. Ginsberg's work has tone—personality—and is very carefully structured and designed. It opens out on the international tradition of literature that stems in large part from Whitman, and it brings vividly into English many of the designs of Apollinaire, Cendrars, Desnos, Breton, and other Europeans. Snyder's translations from Oriental languages are widely admired by competent Orientalists, and his original poetry has the density and force that suggest the possibility of a very distinguished career. Kerouac's novels, conceding their unevenness in texture and flaws of structure, have intermittent scenes of brilliance and persuasiveness. Numerous individual poems by Corso, Ferlinghetti, McClure, and Whalen are also considered compelling and successful.

A Casebook on the Beat (1961), edited by Thomas Parkinson, contains selections from various Beat writers, including their own explanations of their motives as writers, commentary by various critics pro and con, and an extensive bibliography. *The New American Poetry* (1960), edited by Donald M. Allen, includes Beat and other experimental poets, with extensive bibliography. Other books on the Beats are: *The Beat Generation and the Angry Young Men* (1958), G. Feldman and M. Gartenberg, eds.; *The Beats* (1960), Seymour Krim, ed.; *The Beat Scene* (1960), Elias Wilentz, ed. Francis Rigney's *The Real Bohemia* (1961) makes a sociological study of the Beatniks of San Francisco's North Beach. Lawrence Lipton's *The Holy Barbarians* (1959) uses the Venice West colony for comment on the social importance of the Beat movement.

THOMAS PARKINSON

Beau Brummell (1890), a play by CLYDE FITCH. A picturesque characterization of the famous English dandy of the early 19th century, it was RICHARD MANSFIELD's first acting triumph.

Beauchamp, Lucas, a character created by William Faulkner. Lucas, the part-Negro grandson of Carothers McCaslin, the founder of the McCaslin family, is a dignified and independent man who lives on the borderline between the white and black worlds, thus causing a great deal of consternation to those white people who consider him arrogant and disrespectful. He is a main character in INTRUDER IN THE DUST and in "The Fire and the Hearth," a short story in GO DOWN, MOSES.

Beauchampe, or, The Kentucky Tragedy (1842), a novel by WILLIAM GILMORE SIMMS. Simms used as the basis of his novel an astonishing crime that had won nationwide attention. Anna Cook, a Kentucky girl who had been seduced by Col. Solomon P. Sharp, married an attorney, Jeroboam O. Beauchamp, in 1825 and made him take an oath to kill her seducer. He tried several times, finally succeeded in stabbing Sharp to death (Nov. 5, 1825) in Frankfort. Put on trial, Beauchamp denied his guilt, was nevertheless convicted. The evening before the execution, Anna joined him, and both took an overdose of laudanum. Anna died, but Beauchamp survived to be hanged the next day. Beauchamp's own *Confession* (1826) was widely circulated; it included some verse by his wife. Thomas Holley Chivers treated the theme in his verse drama *Conrad and Eudora* (1834), Edgar Allan Poe in the tragedy POLITIAN (parts published, 1835–36; complete text, 1923). Charlotte Mary Barnes employed the plot in the blank-verse tragedy *Octavia Bragaldi, or, The Confession* (1837); Mary E. MacMichael in *The Kentucky Tragedy* (1838); Charles Fenno Hoffman in the romance GREYSLAER (1849), dramatized by some anonymous author the same year. Simms then wrote *Beauchampe, or, The Kentucky Tragedy, A Tale of Passion* (1842); and

in 1856 he expanded the first part of the book into a new novel, CHARLEMONT, OR, THE PRIDE OF THE VILLAGE, A TALE OF KENTUCKY. *Beauchampe* was revised to make the second part. After more than a century of obscurity, the plot came to life again in Robert Penn Warren's "romantic novel," WORLD ENOUGH AND TIME (1950), and in Joseph Shearing's *To Bed at Noon* (1951). See BORDER ROMANCES.

Beauties of Poetry, British and American, The (1791), a publication of MATHEW CAREY in Philadelphia believed to be the first anthology in book form published in this country.

Beauties of Santa Cruz, The (1776, published 1786), a poem by PHILIP FRENEAU. Freneau resided on Santa Cruz or St. Croix, in the Virgin Islands, for more than two years, apparently in an escape from the revolutionary troubles at home; he felt, on his return to the mainland, "as Adam did after he was banished from the bowers of Eden." The poem is too little known; it reveals Freneau as a poetical pioneer, in this instance as an anticipator of John Keats and the Romantic School.

Beautiful and Damned, The (1922), a novel by F. SCOTT FITZGERALD satirizing the younger generation. In the novel Fitzgerald defines the pervading goal of his day as "the final polish of the shoe, the ultimate dab of the clothes-brush, a sort of intellectual There!"

Beautiful Snow (*Harper's Weekly*, Nov. 27, 1858), an anonymously published poem that quickly became a folk classic. Now attributed to John Whitaker Watson (1824–1890), who reprinted it in a collection called *Beautiful Snow and Other Poems* (1869).

Beaver, Tony. A "comic god" of the West Virginia lumberjacks. His exploits took place in the Cumberland Mountains and have been related by Margaret Prescott Montague in *Up Eel River* (1928). Among other deeds, Tony invented peanut brittle when he threw surplus molasses and peanuts into the river to stop a dangerous flood.

Bechdolt, Frederick R[itchie] (b. Mercersburg, Pa., July 27, 1874—   ), newspaperman, author. Bechdolt has mainly chronicled legends of the old West, as in: *When the West was Young* (1921); *Tales of the Old Timers* (1922); *Giants of the Old West* (1930); *Riders out of Santa Fé* (1940); *Hill Racketeers* (1948).

Beck, Warren (b. Richmond, Ind., [?]—   ), teacher, short-story writer, novelist, critic. Beck has taught at several universities, and is Professor of English at Lawrence College, where he has been since 1926. His novel *Final Score* (1944) was awarded the Friends of American Writers prize, and many of his short stories have been reprinted in *Best American Short Stories;* he has collected his short stories in *The Blue Sash* (1941); *The First Fish* (1947); *The Far Whistle* (1951). He has written two other novels, *Pause Under the Sky* (1947) and *Into Thin Air* (1951). He has written numerous critical essays on Faulkner, Hemingway, Virginia Woolf, Sinclair Lewis, Mark Twain, and others. *Man in Motion; Faulkner's Trilogy* (1961) is a book-length study of *The Hamlet, The Town, The Mansion.*

Becker, Carl [Lotus] (b. Lincoln township, Iowa, Sept. 7, 1873—d. April 10, 1945), teacher, historian. Becker became a disciple of FREDERICK JACKSON TURNER at the University of Wisconsin; he spent the major part of his academic career at Cornell. There graduate students found him a man of wide scholarship, quiet wit, and polished phrases. Among his most important books, aside from textbooks, were *The Declaration of Independence; A Study in the History of Political Ideas* (1922), *The Heavenly City of the 18th-Century Philosophers* (1932), and *How New Will the Better World Be?* (1944). Charlotte Smith wrote *Carl Becker: On History and the Climate of Opinion* (1956).

Becker, May Lamberton (b. New York City, Aug. 26, 1873—d. Apr. 27, 1958), critic, anthologist, author. Mrs. Becker performed a magnificent service in spreading a love of reading and an exact knowledge of books among Americans, through her writing and lecturing. Among her books: *A Reader's Guide Book* (1923); *Adventures in Reading* (1927); *Choosing Books for Children* (1937); many anthologies, such as *Golden Tales of Our America* (1929); *Introducing Charles Dickens* (1940, with her daughter Beatrice Warde); and *The Home Book of Laughter* (1948).

Becknell, William (b. Ky., 1790?—d. 1832?), explorer, author. He traced the Santa Fe Trail in 1822; his *Journal* was published in the *Collections* (July, 1906) of the Missouri Historical Society.

Beckwourth, James P. (b. Va., April 26, 1798—d. 1867?), hunter, explorer. Beckwourth wandered over many parts of the West, and became well acquainted with Indian life. In his autobiography, *The Life and Adventures of James P. Beckwourth* (1856; re-edited by Charles G. Leland, 1892), taken down by T. D. Bonner, he relates how he became a chief of the Crow Indians and adopted their habits, their dress, and an Indian wife. His tall tales became famous; he was one of the best-known scouts of the era.

Bedott, Widow. See FRANCES M. WHITCHER.

Bedouin Song (1855), a lyric by BAYARD TAYLOR. Regarded by his age as a great writer, Taylor is known today chiefly for this poem, which achieved popularity in a musical setting as the *Bedouin Love Song.*

bedtime story. An expression probably first used on Jan. 31, 1910, by HOWARD R. GARIS in the Newark (N.J.) *Evening News.* On this date appeared a story under the heading "Sammie Littletail in a Trap." It marked the first appearance of Uncle Wiggily Longears and inaugurated a series that ultimately stretched into the thousands. These stories were widely syndicated, and many of them were later gathered into book form, delighting several generations of subteeners. In February, 1912, THORNTON W. BURGESS started syndicating his *Little Stories for Bedtime;* he had previously published two collections of stories for children. A collection of the *Little Stories* was issued in 1913 as *The Adventures of Reddy Fox.* This was the first of the *Bedtime Story Books,* of which more than twenty were published.

Beebe, Lucius [Morris] (b. Wakefield, Mass., Dec. 9, 1902—), journalist. Beebe chooses in biographical sketches to describe himself simply as a newspaperman. An early venture of his was, however, a collection of verse, *Corydon and Other Poems* (1924); and later he wrote a life of François Villon (1925) and three books (one in collaboration) on Edwin Arlington Robinson. In 1925, moreover, he collaborated with CHARLES TOWNSEND COPELAND on *The Copeland Reader.* But he became best known in somewhat more trivial fields—as an entertaining authority on nightclubs and cuisine, on the Boston legend and antique railroads. In 1952 he and Charles Clegg took over the TERRITORIAL ENTERPRISE, a famous weekly newspaper begun in Virginia City, Nev., in 1858 and suspended in 1916. Under Beebe's and Clegg's aegis, the *Territorial Enterprise* has become a popular and modern voice of the old mining town. The colorful history, past and present, of the paper is recounted in *Comstock Commotion, the Story of the Territorial Enterprise* (1954). Among his other books: *People on Parade* (1934, in collaboration with the photographer, Jerome Zerbe, Jr.); *High Iron: A Book of Trains* (1938); *Snoot If You Must* (1943); *The Stork Club Bar Book* (1946); *Mixed Train Daily* (with C. M. Clegg, 1947); *Dreadful California* (with C. M. Clegg, 1947); *American West* (with C. M. Clegg, 1955); *Hear the Train Blow* (with C. M. Clegg, 1958); *San Francisco's Golden Era* (with C. M. Clegg, 1960); *Mr. Pullman's Elegant Palace Car* (1961).

Beebe, [Charles] William (b. Brooklyn, N.Y., July 29, 1877—d. June 4, 1962), naturalist, author. Beebe early found his vocation as a worker in science, and gained world-wide renown in 1934 with a record-breaking descent into the ocean depths near Bermuda in a bathysphere. He made numerous field expeditions and recorded his observations and experiences in scientific papers and in books for the general public. Among them: *Jungle Peace* (1918); *Galapagos, World's End* (1923); *Jungle Days* (1925); *Beneath Tropic Seas* (1928); *Nonsuch, Land of Water* (1932); *Half Mile Down* (1934); *Book of Naturalists* (1944); *High Jungle* (1949); *Adventuring with Beebe* (selections from his writings, 1955).

Beecher, Catherine E[sther] (b. East Hampton, L.I., Sept. 6, 1800—d. May 12, 1878), teacher, reformer, author. Miss Beecher was the daughter of the Rev. LYMAN BEECHER; two of her brothers—EDWARD and HENRY WARD—and a sister—HARRIET BEECHER STOWE—became famous. She was among the first who sought to provide proper education for young women and helped to organize schools and colleges for them in Hartford, Cincinnati, Milwaukee, and elsewhere. Her writings deal mainly with social and political problems: slavery, wrongs suffered by women and children, evils in education, woman suffrage. Among her books are *A Treatise on Domestic Economy for the Use of Young Ladies at Home and at School* (1841) and *Physiology and Calisthenics for Schools and Families* (1856).

Beecher, Edward (b. East Hampton, L.I., Aug. 27, 1803—d. July 28, 1895), clergyman, editor, author. Another of LYMAN BEECHER's distinguished children; co-founder of *The Congregationalist* and editor-in-chief (1849–53). He published *The Conflict of Ages* (1853) and *The Concord of Ages* (1860).

Beecher, Henry Ward (b. Litchfield, Conn., June 24, 1813—d. March 8, 1887), clergyman, editor, author, lecturer. Beecher was brought up by his father, LYMAN BEECHER, "to put my hand to anything"; and he was indeed adept at

"anything" in the preaching, lecturing, and writing line. He was the only boy in the school for children conducted by his sister CATHERINE, was graduated from Amherst (1834) and the Lane Theological Seminary in Cincinnati; he was licensed to preach in 1837. He had various charges in western cities, was invited to a Boston church, finally at his wife's insistence accepted a call (1847) to Plymouth Church in Brooklyn.

Here he achieved his fame. He liked to illustrate his sermons with parables from everyday life, and displayed in many of them a sense of humor that might have made him an equally famous newspaper columnist; there were few references in his preaching to lakes of boiling pitch and eternal damnation or to the foreordination and election his father had preached. His philosophical trend, though somewhat vague, was taken from Emerson. He discarded reason as a guide and preferred the "secret chords of feeling." Parrington calls him "the high priest of emotional liberalism," who "swept his thou-

sands of idolizing followers along the path of Utopian emotionalism." He praised liberty and love, man and a manlike God, with lyric enthusiasm; and Thoreau saw him as a "magnificent pagan." He preached extemporaneously, but his sermons were taken down, printed, and widely circulated. He declared against slavery and in favor of woman suffrage. He was not friendly to Lincoln and received a cold reception when he toured in some English cities mainly because of this fact. In 1874 THEODORE TILTON charged him with adultery with Mrs. Tilton. In a trial the following year the jury disagreed, and Beecher, whom Plymouth Church had supported loyally, was given an ovation by the crowded and enthusiastic congregation. His reputation never recovered, but it is said that 40,000 persons attended his funeral.

Beecher edited THE INDEPENDENT from 1861 to 1864, *The Christian Union* from 1870 to 1881. Samuel Lee Wolff notes that in his books, from *Seven Lectures to Young Men* (1844) to *Evolution and Religion* (1885) Beecher "came a long way." The *Lectures* were addressed to clerks, mechanics, and salesmen, and have a flavor of Poor Richard; they were his most popular work. The later book came after long and apparently prayerful study of Darwin, leading Beecher finally to an acceptance of the new science as a kind of religion. Between the two books Beecher wrote lively, sensible essays on many topics, including *Plain and Pleasant Talk about Fruits, Flowers, and Farming* (1859); also a novel, NORWOOD, *or, Village Life in New England* (1868), of no merit as such but containing some good descriptions of New England landscape. His style in general was homely and racy, his details concrete; he was definitely an orator, even in print.

A statue by John Quincy Adams Ward was erected to Beecher in Brooklyn. It shows him with a kneeling Negro girl at his feet, to commemorate his labors in behalf of the slave. Robert Shaplen wrote about him in *Free Love and Heavenly Sinners* (1954).

Beecher, Lyman (b. New Haven, Conn., Oct. 12, 1775—d. Jan. 10, 1863), preacher, author. Beecher became one of the notable preachers of the day and the father of a large family, four of whom—CATHERINE, EDWARD, HENRY WARD, and HARRIET BEECHER STOWE—became famous. Beecher held pastorates at Easthampton, L.I., Litchfield, Conn., Boston, and Cincinnati; he was president of the Lane Theological Seminary in Cincinnati (1832–52). He had studied theology under TIMOTHY DWIGHT at Yale, and he strongly supported traditional Calvinism and fought what he called the "icy system" of Unitarianism. His household agonized and wept over the salvation of their souls, and regarded God as a stern detective watching children from above. So drastic was the domestic discipline that Henry Ward Beecher revolted from it toward his liberal views of religion. Nevertheless, Lyman Beecher was accused of heresy by even more conservative groups; he was acquitted by the synod. Paxton Hibben describes him going up and down the country "rallying the forces against toleration, against innovation and democracy, against the separation of church and state." He denounced the use of liquor and was strongly anti-Catholic. The Beecher household probably provided the details for Harriet Beecher Stowe's OLDTOWN FOLKS (1869). Lyman Beecher's sermons and articles were gathered in his *Works* (1852); his *Autobiography* appeared in 1864.

Beef Steak Club. A Philadelphia club of writers and artists who in the 1820's met in the studio of the engraver WILLIAM KNEASS (1780–1840).

Beer, Thomas (b. Council Bluffs, Iowa, Nov. 22, 1889—d. April 18, 1940), novelist, short-story writer, biographer, historian. Beer wrote three novels—*The Fair Rewards* (1922), *Sandoval* (1924), and *The Road to Heaven* (1928), also short stories, some collected as *Mrs. Egg and Other Barbarians* (1933, reprinted with additional stories in 1947). His *Stephen Crane* (1923) did much to revive the reputation of a long-neglected literary pioneer, although it left many gaps, only partially filled since. Later Beer wrote THE MAUVE DECADE (1926; reprinted, 1941) and *Hanna* (1929), both dealing with Crane's 1890's. He was undoubtedly influenced by Lytton Strachey, but was even more ironic; one hears an odd note of nostalgia in some of his pieces.

Beers, Clifford [Whittingham] (b. New Haven, Conn., March 30, 1876—d. July 9, 1943), humanitarian. Although Clifford Beers wrote only one book, its importance in the literature of America cannot be overestimated. In *A Mind That Found Itself* (1908), Beers, who had been taken ill three years after his graduation from Yale, told of his experiences in various mental institutions and his final recovery in the home of a kindly hospital attendant. His report of maltreatment and neglect, his vivid account of his suffering, brought light where light was needed and made America aware that basic reforms were required if adequate care was to be given to its mentally ill. He established the National Commission for Mental Hygiene (1909) and was the founder of the International Foundation for Mental Hygiene (1931). Together with a number of assistants he published a quarterly, *Mental Hygiene*, and put out numerous pamphlets to combat the general lethargy on this subject. His was the revolutionary spirit responsible for great social changes and he was fortunate in seeing some of them in his lifetime.

Beers, Ethel Lynn [pen name of Ethelinda Eliot Beers] (b. Goshen, N.Y., Jan. 13, 1827—d. Oct. 11, 1879), poet and short-story writer. Mrs. Beers became famous chiefly for her poem, *The Picket Guard* (later called ALL QUIET ALONG THE POTOMAC), published in *Harper's Weekly* in 1861. In 1879 appeared *All Quiet Along the Potomac and Other Poems*.

Beers, Henry A[ugustin] (b. Buffalo, N.Y., Jan. 2, 1847—d. Sept. 7, 1926), Yale professor, historian, biographer, poet. Beers' *History of English Romanticism* (1899, 1901) became a

standard work, read as much for its engaging style as for its obvious learning. He also wrote *A Century of American Literature* (1878), *Nathaniel Parker Willis* (1885), *The Connecticut Wits and Other Essays* (1920), and other books of literary history, and published two collections of poems. Lucius Beebe wrote an enthusiastic eulogy of Beers in the *Yale Alumni Magazine* (June, 1952).

Before Adam (1906), a novel by JACK LONDON. In the course of the story the experiences of mankind in the far distant past are described, with data supposedly taken from the narrator's dreams, in which he lives again the life of Big Tooth, a primitive ancestor. The dream technique somewhat resembles that employed by London later in THE STAR ROVER (1914).

Beggar on Horseback (1924), a fantastic comedy by GEORGE S. KAUFMAN and MARC CONNELLY, with music by DEEMS TAYLOR. This remarkably agile satire on big business and its ways with the artist takes its title from the proverbial phrase, and the idea of using a dream to express satire from a German play, Paul Apel's *Hans Sonnenstoessers Hoellenfahrt*. A poverty-stricken composer, Neil McRae, is persuaded into proposing to Gladys Cady, a rich girl. In a dream he learns the horrid consequences, as he is set to work in the Cady factory (which manufactures "widgets"), and sees the stupidity of so-called business efficiency. In desperation he murders the Cady family and is put on trial; he is sentenced to a prison cell where he manufactures endless inane lyrics. He finally finds release from prison and, on awakening, from his engagement. A movie based on the play was directed by James Cruze in 1925.

Beggars of Life (1924), an autobiography by JIM TULLY. The book won Tully his first great fame. MAXWELL ANDERSON turned the book into a play, *Outside Looking In* (1925), in which, says Arthur Hobson Quinn, "the codes and standards of tramps were revealed in an entertaining if episodic manner." James Cagney was one of the principals in it.

Behaviorism (1925), by JOHN B. WATSON. The best-known discussion of a psychological hypothesis chiefly expounded by Dr. Watson, Johns Hopkins professor, and the English psychologist, William McDougall. Behaviorism rejects introspective psychology and stresses experiment and objectivity; feeling and thinking are regarded as nonexistent except as related to behavior. Two "lectures" in the book deal, for example, with talking and thinking, and present the thesis that the whole body is implicated in mental processes.

Behrman, S[amuel] N[athaniel] (b. Worcester, Mass., June 9, 1893—   ), playwright, writer of articles and short stories, screenwriter. As a student, Behrman came under the influence of G. STANLEY HALL at Clark University, GEORGE PIERCE BAKER at Harvard, and BRANDER MATTHEWS and JOHN ERSKINE at Columbia. After many years of trying, his first play, *The Second Man* (1927), was produced and was an immediate success. This play was a contribution to the comedy of ideas, in which field Behrman continued to work. Among his other plays: *Serena Blandish* (1928), a dramatization of a novel by the English novelist, Enid Bagnold (1925); *Meteor* (1929); *Brief Moment* (1931);

Biography (1932), about a woman portrait painter and a journalist; *Rain from Heaven* (1934), one of the earliest anti-Nazi plays; END OF SUMMER (1936), a comedy on the use of wealth; *Amphitryon 38* (1937), an adaptation from the French and, ultimately, from the ancients; *Wine of Choice* (1938), on liberalism and its difficulties; NO TIME FOR COMEDY (1939), with a dramatist as protagonist; *The Talley Method* (1941); *The Pirate* (1942); *I Know My Love* (1949). A book, *The Worcester Account* (1954), autobiographical in content, was dramatized as *The Cold Wind and the Warm* (1958). Behrman turned to biography with two books, *Duveen* (1952), a work on the career of the famous art dealer, and *Portrait of Max* (1960), a brilliant profile of Max Beerbohm, fin de siècle satirist. Both biographies were considered vastly entertaining by critics.

Behrman also wrote film scripts in Hollywood, including *Queen Christina* (1933) for Greta Garbo. Brooks Atkinson notes that Behrman's "characters have a worldly air; his dialogue is lightly humorous; his plots are usually insubstantial. . . . What he writes might be dismissed as drawing-room comedy if Behrman were not interested in serious themes like politics, ethics, and cross-currents of thought."

Being a Boy (1865), reminiscences of his New England boyhood by CHARLES DUDLEY WARNER.

Belasco, David (b. San Francisco, July 25, 1859—d. May 14, 1931), actor, theatrical producer, playwright. Belasco followed a theatrical career that included many years on Broadway as a successful manager, producer, and playwright. He developed the talents of Mrs. Leslie Carter, David Warfield, Minnie Maddern Fiske, Blanche Bates, Lenore Ulric, Ina Claire,

Helen Gahagan, Lionel Atwill, Fanny Brice, and others. As a writer Belasco won great success with THE HEART OF MARYLAND (1895), ZAZA (1898), *DuBarry* (1901), THE GIRL OF THE GOLDEN WEST (1905), THE RETURN OF PETER GRIMM (1911), and *Van Der Decken* (1915). In collaboration with other playwrights he wrote HEARTS OF OAK (with JAMES A. HERNE, 1879), *The Charity Ball* (with Henry C. De Mille, 1889), THE GIRL I LEFT BEHIND ME (with FRANKLIN FYLES, 1893), MADAME BUTTERFLY (with JOHN LUTHER LONG, 1900), THE DARLING OF THE GODS (with Long, 1902), ADREA (with Long, 1904).

Belasco took over the Stuyvesant Theater on West 44th St., New York City, and renamed it the Belasco; it was associated with some of his most notable hits. He produced nearly four hundred plays, many of them by native dramatists. Without doubt he greatly influenced the American theater in the direction of greater emotionalism and more realistic stage properties and in developing the "star" system.

Beleaguered City, The (1839), a poem by HENRY WADSWORTH LONGFELLOW. This poem expresses melodiously, but not very forcefully, the doctrine of the struggle between good and evil in the heart of man. Edgar Allan Poe charged that Longfellow had plagiarized his lyric, THE HAUNTED PALACE, but there seems very little resemblance between the two poems, of which Poe's is infinitely the superior. It is now believed that Longfellow took the suggestion for the poem from a footnote in Sir Walter Scott's *Border Minstrelsy*.

Belfry of Bruges and Other Poems, The (1845), a collection of poems by HENRY WADSWORTH LONGFELLOW. The title poem recounts the glory of the ancient city of Bruges, but is of little merit. However, "The Arsenal at Springfield" is an effective portrayal of the horrors of war, even though it is weakened somewhat by the prophecy of peace to come. The book also contains the popular THE BRIDGE, as well as the excellent sonnet MEZZO CAMMIN, in which the poet looks back over his life. See I SHOT AN ARROW INTO THE AIR.

Belknap, Jeremy (b. Boston, June 4, 1744—d. June 20, 1798), clergyman, historian. Belknap wrote a *History of New Hampshire* (published in parts, 1784–1791–1792), of which William Cullen Bryant said that it was the first historical work "to make American history attractive." He wrote a satirical allegory, *The Foresters* (1792), and began a pioneer work, *American Biography* (1794–1798) on early explorers and leaders. With others Belknap founded the Massachusetts Historical Society.

Bell, Alexander Graham (b. Scotland, March 3, 1847—d. Aug. 2, 1922), and **Bell, Alexander Melville** (b. 1819—d. 1905), speech experts, inventors. The elder Bell, a teacher of the science of correct speech, wrote *Visible Speech* (1867) to demonstrate an alphabet visually showing the articulating position of the vocal organs for each sound. He also wrote books on elocution. His son developed a system for teaching speech to the deaf, but is principally known as the inventor of mechanical devices, above all the telephone (1876, 1877). Catherine Mackenzie wrote a life of the elder Bell (1928).

Bell, Eric Temple ["John Taine"] (b. Scotland, Feb. 7, 1883—d. Dec. 20, 1960), teacher, science-fiction writer. Bell joined the faculty of the California Institute of Technology in 1926 as a professor of mathematics. His numerous technical and popular books include: *Sixes and Sevens* (1945); *The Magic of Numbers* (1947); *Mathematics, Queen and Servant of Science* (1950). Under the pen name John Taine he has published many books of science fantasy; among them, *The Purple Sapphire* (1924) and *Seeds of Life* (1951). His latest book is *Last Problem* (1961).

Bell, Thomas (b. Braddock, Pa., March 7, 1903—d. Jan. 17, 1961), novelist, short-story writer. Bell had an extremely varied background before he turned writer, holding jobs that ranged from electrician to merchant seaman. He wrote *All Brides Are Beautiful* (1936), a novel; *Till I Come Back to You* (1953), a play; and *In the Midst of Life* (1961), a poignant journal of the twenty months preceding his death from cancer.

Bellah, James Warner (b. New York City, Sept. 14, 1899—   ), novelist, short-story writer, author of articles on military training. He was graduated from Columbia University in 1923 and taught English there for several years. From 1927 to 1928 he was special correspondent in China toward the end of the Chang Tso-lin campaigns. In 1929 he was commissioned as a special reporter by the *Saturday Evening Post* on all initial flights by Pan American Airways through the West Indies and Central America. Among his novels: *Frantic Years* (1927); *Dancing Lady* (1932); *South by East a Half East* (1936); *Ward 20* (1945); *Irregular Gentleman* (1948), which is autobiographical; *The Apache* (1951); *The Valiant Virginians* (1955).

Bellamann, Henry (b. Fulton, Mo., April 28, 1882—d. June 16, 1945), musician, author. Bellamann at first devoted himself exclusively to music, but in 1926 he turned novelist with *Petenera's Daughter*, went on to a great success with *Kings Row* (1940), *Victoria Grandolet* (1943), and *Doctor Mitchell of Kings Row* (1945). After his death his widow, Katherine Bellamann, completed an unfinished novel, *Parris Mitchell of Kings Row* (1948).

Bellamy, Edward (b. Chicopee Falls, Mass., March 26, 1850—d. May 22, 1898), novelist, reformer. Bellamy came from a long line of New England ministers, and although he espoused no particular creed, his essentially religious nature continually expressed itself in his ethical, antimaterialistic bent. His text was: "If we love one another, God dwelleth in us"; and his love for his fellow man turned him into an impassioned and beloved social reformer. He was educated at Union College and in Germany, returned to the United States to study law, but never practiced. Turning to journalism, he first joined the staff of the New York *Evening Post*,

then edited the Springfield (Mass.) *Union*, and founded the Springfield *Daily News* (1880). Meantime he was writing fiction of originality and stylistic distinction. *The Duke of Stockbridge*, a novel about SHAYS' REBELLION, was

published serially in 1879 (it was completed and published in book form by a cousin in 1900). *Six to One: A Nantucket Idyl* (1878) reflects his voyage to Hawaii in the previous year. *Dr. Heidenhoff's Process* (1880) and *Miss Ludington's Sister* (1884) are powerful psychological studies reminiscent of Hawthorne. His exquisitely imaginative short stories were published in *"The Blind Man's World" and Other Stories* (1898).

Fame came with the publication of LOOKING BACKWARD: 2000–1887 (1888). This "Utopia of collectivism," advocating state capitalism as a step to state socialism through nonviolent means, was immensely popular and influential. It sold nearly a million copies in ten years; it was imitated by a host of lesser utopian novels; and it led to the founding of a Nationalist Party advocating Bellamy's principles. Although familiar with Marx's work, taking over what he liked about it, Bellamy advocated techniques for achieving a new world which were quite different; Heywood Broun, in his introduction to the 1917 edition of *Looking Backward*, says of him: "When he preaches the necessity of the co-operative commonwealth, he does it with a Yankee twang." He turned an idealistic deaf ear to many opportunities to capitalize on his success, entering instead a ten-year period of controversy and campaigning. He founded the *New*

Nation in 1891. *Equality* (1897), a sequel to *Looking Backward*, was less popular, being more of a theoretical tract; but it exhibits bolder economic criticism in its attack on the profit system and its preaching of economic equality as "the corner-stone of our state." Bellamy's health broke while writing *Equality*, and he died shortly of tuberculosis. His theory of state capitalism has been influential in subsequent American economic thinking; many technical prophecies in *Looking Backward* have already been realized. See *Edward Bellamy* (1944) by AR-THUR E. MORGAN.

Bellow, Saul (b. Quebec, Canada, July 10, 1915), novelist. Bellow's work, though it has been widely discussed, does not lend itself readily to critical analysis. Bellow himself, though he has lectured and taught at colleges, does his

best to discourage formal criticism of his work, demanding in an article in *The New York Times Book Review* that it be regarded as "entertainment." His first two novels, *Dangling Man* (1944), and *The Victim* (1947), were carefully constructed, highly introspective works. The first is the journal of a young man waiting to be inducted into the Army in 1943. He has quit his job after receiving his draft notice only to be left "dangling" for nearly a year until he is finally called up. The second seems to be an allegory of anti-Semitism. Asa Leventhal, a Jew, is accused by Albee, a Gentile, of having ruined Albee's career. Though Leventhal understands that his accuser is simply a scoundrel, he is seized with a generalized typically Jewish guilt.

The reader is left to decide who finally is "the victim." Beginning with THE ADVENTURES OF AUGIE MARCH (1953), Bellow's style, always rich, became flamboyantly and rhetorically comic. Writing on "The Distractions of a Fiction Writer" in *New World Writing*, Bellow declared, perhaps with his own early work in mind, that writers "are prone to exaggerate the human personality." To correct this imbalance he turned to the external world of adventure and imagination. His characters came to life through their rich speech, or through descriptions of their physical make-up. The hero of *Henderson the Rain King* (1959) is a giant of a man with aspirations that match his bulk. Henderson responds to a voice within him that says, "I want, I want!" and goes to Africa in search of adventure. The book departs from a realistically described New Jersey–New York milieu to a fantasy world where Henderson finds his destiny in a series of comic adventures culminating in his becoming the Rainmaker for a savage tribe. *Herzog* (1961), a novel about a college teacher, is the most nearly autobiographical fiction Bellow has yet produced—though *The Adventures of Augie March* drew on his experience of the Chicago in which he was brought up from the age of nine. Bellow was one of the founding editors of a little magazine in book form, *The Noble Savage*. Readers who have admired Bellow's fiction have had to take him on his own terms: "There are critics who assume that you must begin with order if you are to end with it. Not so. A novelist begins with disorder and disharmony, and he goes toward order by an unknown process of the imagination." Whatever that process may be, Bellow has demonstrated his mastery of it. He also wrote *Seize the Day* (1956), a little-noticed yet excellent volume containing a long title story, a play, and the short story, *Looking for Mr. Green.*

Bells, The (1849), a poem by EDGAR ALLAN POE. This is probably the most sustained exercise in onomatopoeia in poetry. Poe was visiting a friend, Mrs. Marie Louise Shew, at 47 Bond St. in New York, late in the spring of 1848. Mentally and emotionally exhausted, he was, says Mrs. Shew, very much annoyed by church bells, of which there were several nearby, including the famous "silver bell" of the old Middle Dutch Church. At the same time he said that he had to write a poem for immediate publication—"I have no feeling, no sentiment, no inspiration." Then, after tea in the conservatory, Mrs. Shew took a piece of paper, wrote at the top "The Bells, by E. A. Poe," and gave him a further hint by adding the words, "the little silver bells." Poe began to write, soon stopped. Then Mrs. Shew gave him another inspirational shove: she wrote the words, "The heavy iron bells." Poe resumed but composed only seventeen lines. The manuscript survives. At first Poe called it "Mrs. Shew's poem," but soon took it over. He revised it three times; the second and last appeared in Sartain's UNION MAGAZINE, edited by John Sartain, in 1849. The poem has been called a jingle, but it follows an exact pattern in its succession of silver, golden, brass, and iron sounds, suggesting the cycle of life. Sound echoes sense in a technical tour de force. Arthur Hobson Quinn points out that the effects are secured largely by skillful contrast of close vowel sounds ("tinkle, tinkle, tinkle") with open vowels ("Hear the mellow wedding bells, golden bells").

Bells, A Collection of Chimes, The (1855), THOMAS BAILEY ALDRICH's first gathering of his verses, made when he was nineteen years old.

Bemelmans, Ludwig (b. Austria, April 27, 1898—d. Oct. 1, 1962), painter, writer. Bemelmans came to the U.S. in 1914, was naturalized in 1918. His early years here were spent working in a hotel—an experience which greatly influenced his writings. At one time he ran a restaurant of his own. He wrote and illustrated children's books, he did settings for a Broadway play, he worked in Hollywood (uncomplimentary result: his novel, *Dirty Eddie*, 1947), he contributed to *The New Yorker, Vogue, Town and Country,* and *Stage* articles and stories highly individual in style and content. He seemed naïve, but it is a highly educated, complex, and sophisticated naïveté. Among his books: *Hansi* (1934); *Golden Basket* (1936); *Castle Number Nine* (1937); *Quito Express* (1938); *My War with the United States* (an account of his experiences in the Army, 1937); *Hotel Splendide* (1941); *Small Beer* (1940); *I Love You, I Love You, I Love You* (1942); *Now I Lay Me Down to Sleep* (1944, made into a successful play in 1950); *The Blue Danube* (1945); *The Eye of God* (1949); *Father, Dear Father* (1953); an omnibus collection, *The World of Bemelmans* (1955); *The Woman of My Life* (1957); *My Life in Art* (1958); *Are You Hungry Are You Cold* (1960); *Bemelmans' Italian Holiday,* a collection of articles (1961).

Bemis, Samuel Flagg (b. Worcester, Mass., Oct. 20, 1891—   ), historian. Bemis is probably the foremost authority on the history of American foreign policy. He is Sterling Professor of Diplomatic History and Inter-American Relations at Yale University where he has taught since 1935. He has twice received the Pulitzer Prize: in 1926 for *Pinckney's Treaty, A Study of America's Advantage from Europe's Distress;* and in 1950 for *John Quincy Adams and the Foundations of American Foreign Policy.* His *Diplomatic History* (1955) was revised to give greater emphasis to twentieth century problems and was retitled *A Short History of American Foreign Policy and Diplomacy* (1959). This text is indexed, footnoted, and amplified by maps, charts, tables, and bibliographies. Bemis is coauthor of *Guide to the Diplomatic History of the United States, 1776–1921* (1935); he was editor and part author of *The American Secretaries of State and Their Diplomacy,* 10 volumes, (1927–29).

Ben Bolt (published in *The New Mirror,* Sept. 2, 1843), a sentimental ballad by THOMAS DUNN ENGLISH. Set to saccharine music, it was widely popular in its own day, then was revived when George du Maurier used it effectively in *Trilby* (1894).

Benchley, Robert [Charles] (b. Worcester, Mass., Sept. 15, 1889—d. Nov. 21, 1945), sports writer, dramatic critic, essayist, humorist, actor, screenwriter. Educated at Harvard, Benchley began by writing advertising copy for the Curtis Publishing Company, went on to editorial work in New York, wrote for the *New York World, Life* in its pre-Luce stage, *The Bookman,* and *The New Yorker.* He made movie shorts in Hollywood, appeared in several motion pictures there and later in radio programs, and came back to Scarsdale, N.Y., to live.

Benchley was primarily a writer; it was not a secret that his later appearances in the movies and on the radio bored and depressed him. Yet he won great success on the air and in some of his absurdly funny shorts such as *How to Sleep* (which won the Motion Picture Academy Award for 1935), and he continued to win applause with repetitions of his famous sketch, *The Treasurer's Report.* In his essays Benchley portrayed his whole life as a series of humiliations and frustrations. J. Bryan III said of him that he saw himself "not as the master of high comedy, but the victim of low comedy. King Lear loses a throne; Benchley loses a filling." MY TEN YEARS IN A QUANDARY (1936) reveals him at his most frustrated. He wrote, among other books: *Of All Things* (1921); *Love Conquers All* (1922); *Pluck and Luck* (1925); *20,000 Leagues Under the Sea, or, David Copperfield* (1928); *The Treasurer's Report* (1930); *From Bed to Worse* (1934); *Inside Benchley* (1942); *Benchley Beside Himself* (1943). Posthumously published was a collection called *Chips Off the Old Benchley* (1949); also *The "Reel" Benchley* (1950), a collection of six scripts of the movie shorts which he wrote and produced, and in which he hilariously appeared. His son Nathaniel wrote an appealing biography of Benchley (1955). Benchley had the ideal illustrator in GLUYAS WILLIAMS.

Bender, Harold H[erman] (b. Martinsburg, W. Va., April 20, 1882—d. Aug. 16, 1951), philologist. Bender has been recognized as perhaps the leading etymologist of this century. When the great second edition (1934) of *Webster's New International Dictionary* was in preparation, Bender with a picked staff recast and rewrote the etymologies for some 550,000 words, many never before explained. This huge undertaking required eight years of continuous research. Bender made himself an authority on Lithuanian, and in *The Home of the Indo-Europeans* (1922) presented a strong case for finding the genesis of the Indo-European languages on the plains of eastern central Europe.

Benedict, Leopold. See MORRIS WINCHEVSKY.

Benedict, Ruth F[ulton] (b. New York City, June 5, 1887—d. Sept. 17, 1948), anthropologist, poet, teacher. Dr. Benedict early won a reputation as one of the world's leading anthropologists with her studies of various Indian tribes of the West and Southwest. From 1923 until her death she taught at Columbia University. For general readers she wrote two notable books, *Patterns of Culture* (1934) and *Race, Science, and Politics* (1940). Her last book, *The Chrysanthemum and the Sword* (1946), deals with Japan. Early in her career Dr. Benedict wrote verse under the name Anne Singleton; her poems appeared in *Poetry,* the *Nation,* and other magazines.

Benefield, [John] Barry (b. Jefferson, Tex., 1877—   ), newspaperman, editor, short-story writer, novelist. Benefield served first on the Dallas *Morning News,* later on the New York *Times.* Some of his short stories appeared in the collection *Short Turns* (1926). Among his novels: *The Chicken-Wagon Family* (1925); *A Little Clown Lost* (1928); *Valiant Is the Word for Carrie* (1935); *April Was When It Began* (1939); *Eddie and the Archangel Mike* (1943); *Texas, Brooklyn and Heaven* (1948).

Benét, Laura (b. Fort Hamilton, N.Y., June 13, 1884?—   ), poet, biographer. Miss Benét was trained as a social settlement worker, but soon, like her brothers WILLIAM ROSE and STEPHEN VINCENT BENÉT, turned to writing. She published several collections of verse (*Fairy Bread,* 1921; *Basket for a Fair,* 1934; *Is Morning Sure?,* 1947), and a series of biographies for young people (*Young Edgar Allan Poe,* 1941; *Thackeray,* 1947). Among her later books are *Coleridge, Poet of Wild Enchantment* (1952); *Famous American Humorists* (1959); *In Love With Time* (1959).

Benét, Stephen Vincent (b. Bethlehem, Pa., July 22, 1898—d. March 13, 1943), poet, short-story writer, radio writer, dramatist. Benét began his career with several modestly successful collections of verse: *Five Men and Pompey*

(1915); *Young Adventure* (1918); *Heavens and Earth* (1920); *The Ballad of William Sycamore* (1923); *Tiger Joy* (1925). Then, on a Guggenheim fellowship, he went to Paris in order to

complete an epic, JOHN BROWN'S BODY (1928), which won a Pulitzer Prize and gave him lasting fame. It has become a classic of American literature for its realistic, profoundly sympathetic picture of the Civil War. Charles Laughton dramatized it and it opened in New York City in 1953. There is hardly a season when it is not being played in some part of the United States. A collection of his *Ballads and Poems* (1931) was followed by *Nightmare at Noon* (1940) and *Western Star* (1943). The last book is the first part of another epic of America left incomplete at Benét's death. In 1933 he had written for young people *A Book of Americans* with his wife Rosemary Benét.

Meanwhile Benét had turned to the writing of prose fiction. Among his short-story collections are: *Thirteen O'Clock* (1937); *Tales Before Midnight* (1939); and *The Last Circle* (posthumously published, 1946). The last also includes a number of verses. But his greatest triumph in this field is THE DEVIL AND DANIEL WEBSTER (1937), recognized immediately as one of the great stories of American literature. It was later made into an opera with music by Douglas Moore, and into a movie, *All That Money Can Buy.* Benét also wrote novels, but with less success: *Spanish Bayonet* (1926); *James Shore's Daughter* (1934). More successful were his ventures into radio, especially *They Burned the Books* (1942). Benét's early death probably resulted from overwork on war propaganda. *Stephen Vincent Benét* (1958), by Charles A. Fenton, is an authorized biography. See SOBBIN' WOMEN; A CHILD IS BORN; LITANY FOR DICTATORSHIPS; KING DAVID.

Benét, William Rose (b. Fort Hamilton, N.Y., Feb. 2, 1886—d. May 4, 1950), poet, editor, novelist, playwright. Benét engaged in magazine work and writing from the time he was twenty-one. He was the elder brother of STEPHEN VINCENT BENÉT, and ELINOR WYLIE was his second wife. A long line of distinguished collections of verse made him widely known: *Merchants from Cathay* (1913); *The Falconer of God* (1914); *The Burglar of the Zodiac* (1918); *Moons of Grandeur* (1920); *Man Possessed* (1927); *Rip Tide* (1932); *Starry Harness* (1933); *Golden Fleece* (1935); *Day of Deliverance* (1944); *The Stairway of Surprise* (1947); *The Spirit of the Scene* (1951). In *The Dust Which Is God* (1941) Benét wrote his autobiography in verse. See POETRY PACKAGE.

Benét managed to convey events both trivial and important with smoothness, excitement, and imagination. His success won a Pulitzer Prize in 1942. He wrote a play for children, *Day's End* (1939), produced by the Dock Street Theater in Charleston, S.C., and several stories for young readers. He edited a column of literary miscellany called "The Phoenix Nest" for the *Saturday Review of Literature* for many years. Not long before his death appeared an excellent and valuable compilation, THE READER'S ENCYCLOPEDIA (1948), covering world literature.

Ben Hur: A Tale of the Christ (1880), a

novel by LEW WALLACE. General Wallace, soldier, lawyer, and writer, had intended to follow up his successful novel, THE FAIR GOD (1873), with a tale of the Three Wise Men at Bethlehem. By accident he met the free-thinker ROBERT G. INGERSOLL in a railroad car, and became involved in an argument with him on the divinity of Christ. Wallace decided to study the story of Jesus and compose a novel about His times. The result, *Ben Hur,* is the story of an aristocratic young Jew, Judah Ben Hur, who is falsely accused by a friend of seeking to murder the Roman governor of Palestine and is sent to the galleys. He escapes, becomes a Roman officer, engages in a magnificent chariot race with his false friend Messala as his rival, and eventually is converted, with his mother and sister, to a belief in Christ. The book was an immense success.

William Young's dramatization (1889) enjoyed great popularity; the production in turn further stimulated book sales. Frank Luther Mott calculates that in the United States alone more than 2,500,000 copies of *Ben Hur* have been sold; to this must be added many pirated editions in England, as well as translations into European and Oriental languages. In 1926 a screen version was produced, at an alleged cost of $4 million, which was spent in part on what Robert E. Sherwood called "the most terrific chariot race in history." But the chariot race in a new version, produced in 1959, was even more spectacular.

Benito Cereno, a story by HERMAN MELVILLE. See PIAZZA TALES, THE.

Benjamin Franklin, The Autobiography of (first published in Paris as *Mémoires de la Vie Privé de Benjamin Franklin,* 1791; editions appeared in England and Germany before the American version of 1818; Franklin's grandson, William Temple Franklin, edited and altered the manuscript for publication; the first complete American edition was published by John Bigelow, 1868), BENJAMIN FRANKLIN's narrative of his life up to 1757. It gives an unsurpassed self-portrait of the Yankee turned scientist, philosopher, statesman, inventor. Woodrow Wilson, editing an edition of the book in 1901, summed it up as "letters in business garb, literature with its apron on." The book reveals Franklin, in Charles Eliot Norton's words, as "the man who, even more than Lincoln, might be called the first American." Careful studies of the original texts were made by Max Farrand and the results embodied in *Benjamin Franklin's Memoirs* and *The Autobiography of Benjamin Franklin* (both 1949).

Ben Jonson Entertains a Man from Stratford (1916), a poem by EDWIN ARLINGTON ROBINSON. A blank-verse dramatic monologue, in which Ben Jonson talks to a visitor from Stratford and analyzes their common friend Shakespeare with shrewd, mellow insight. Jonson ruminates on the puzzle presented by "this mad, careful, proud, indifferent Shakespeare." He promises that some day he and others of his boon companions will ride down to see him, "and his wife won't like us"; one remembers the legend that Shakespeare died as the result of a drinking bout in his home with Jonson.

Bennett, Emerson (b. Monson, Mass., March 16, 1822—d. May 11, 1905), novelist, poet, editor. Bennett brought out some poems, *The Brigand* (1842), at twenty, and wrote a novelette, *The Unknown Countess,* the following year. His books on life in pioneer days and in the West include *The League of the Miami* (1845); *The Bandits of the Osage* (1847); MIKE FINK (1848). *The Prairie Flower* and *Leni-Lioti* (both 1849) are his best known novels.

Bennett, James Gordon (b. Sept. 1, 1795—d. June 1, 1872), newspaper editor. Born in Scotland, Bennett came to America in 1819 and settled finally in New York City. He served on the staff of two New York newspapers, *The Enquirer* and *The Courier;* on May 6, 1835, he founded the *New York Herald* and remained its editor until his retirement in 1867. It was an aggressive, widely read paper which often attacked and was attacked. His ostensible aim was the exposure of fraud and hypocrisy, but he seemed to revel in the details. According to Gerald W. Johnson, Bennett "filled his paper with vulgarity, vituperation, and scandal, but he got the news." His son, James Gordon Bennett (1841–1918) succeeded him as editor in 1867. The younger Bennett sent Stanley to Africa to find Livingstone and supported other expeditions to Africa and the Arctic. He was the founder of the Paris edition of the *Herald* (1887). See PROFILE.

Bennett, John (b. Chillicothe, Ohio, May 17, 1865—d. Dec. 28, 1956), illustrator, writer of children's books. Bennett is remembered chiefly for two excellent books: MASTER SKYLARK (1897), laid in Shakespeare's time; and *Barnaby Lee* (1902).

Benson, Sally (b. St. Louis, Mo., Sept. 3, 1900—   ), short-story writer. Mrs. Benson's best-known book, *Junior Miss* (1941), became a successful play (1941), an equally popular movie and a radio series. *People are Fascinating* (1936) preceded this; *Meet Me in St. Louis* (1942) and *Women and Children First* (1944) followed.

Bent, Silas (b. Millersberg, Ky., May 9, 1882—d. July 30, 1945), newspaperman, public relations counsel, author. Bent worked on newspapers in St. Louis, New York, and elsewhere and served as public relations counsel for the Democratic National Committee, but was primarily a free-lance author. Among his books: *Ballyhoo—The Voice of the Press* (1927); *Justice Oliver Wendell Holmes* (1932); *Newspaper Crusaders* (1939); *Old Rough and Ready: The Life and Times of Zachary Taylor* (with S. B. McKinley, 1945).

Bentley, Eric (b. England, Sept. 14, 1916—   ), dramatic critic, teacher, editor. Brander Matthews Professor of Dramatic Literature at Columbia University since 1954, Bentley's career has included practical experience in the theater as well as scholarship. He brings to his criticism a background at Oxford and Yale along with acting and directing experience which includes work with the German poet and dramatist Bertold Brecht. Bentley's translations and stage productions of Brecht helped bring the German playwright to the attention of the American public. Bentley introduced other leading modern European playwrights through his editing of anthologies and his critical books. He writes for the *New Republic* and *Harper's*. His works include *A Century of Hero-Worship* (1944), a study of the cult of hero-worship in modern literature; *The Playwright as Thinker* (1946); *Bernard Shaw* (1947); *In Search of Theatre* (1953); and *What is Theatre?* (1956). He has edited *The Importance of Scrutiny* (1948); *From the Modern Repertoire*, 3 series (1949, 1952, 1956); *The Modern Theatre* (6 v., 1955–1960); *The Classic Theatre* (4 v., 1958–1961).

Benton, Thomas Hart [1] (b. Hillsboro, N.C., March 14, 1782—d. April 10, 1858), statesman, orator, author. Benton was senator from Missouri from 1821 to 1851. He strongly represented the interests of the West in the Senate, was a vigorous supporter of President Jackson, and was finally defeated for re-election because he supported the Union against the South. He wrote his autobiography in THIRTY YEARS' VIEW (2 v., 1854, 1856) and edited *An Abridgment of the Debates of Congress* (15 v., 1857–61). Benton appears vividly in Irving Stone's biographical novel, *Immortal Wife* (1944); his biography, *Old Bullion Benton* (1956), has been written by W. N. Chamberlain.

Benton, Thomas Hart [2] (b. Neosho, Mo., April 15, 1889—   ), painter, lithographer, memoirist. One of the leaders in the artistic battle for regionalism in painting, Benton's best-known murals are found at the New School for Social Research, the library of the Whitney Museum of American Art, the state capitol at Jefferson City, Mo. His autobiography, *An Artist in America* (1937, revised 1951), includes reproductions of many of his paintings. He worked on a mural in the Truman Library (Independence, Mo.) in 1960.

Bercovici, Konrad (b. Rumania, June 22, 1882—d. Dec. 27, 1961), author. Bercovici came to the U.S. in 1916, began writing for newspapers in 1917; in that year he published his first book, *Crimes of Charity*. His books exhibit a wide range—sociological and historical studies, novels, short stories, plays. Among them: *Dust of New York* (1918); *Ghitza and Other Romances of Gypsy Blood* (1919); *Around the World in New York* (1924); *The Story of the Gypsies* (1928); *Alexander: A Romantic Biography* (1929); *The Incredible Balkans* (1933); *It's the Gypsy in Me* (1941); *Savage Prodigal* (1948). *This Is Only the Beginning* (1941) is autobiographical.

Berenice (*Southern Literary Messenger*, 1835; in TALES OF THE GROTESQUE AND ARABESQUE, 1840), a story by EDGAR ALLAN POE. Imitating the style of the "Gothic" writers, Poe wrote this morbid tale of Egaeus in love with his cousin

Berenice. She is an epileptic whose white teeth fascinate him; while she is in a fit and apparently dead, he draws her teeth; then she comes to life again. Poe excused himself from the charge of excessive horror by saying that it was what the public wanted.

Berenson, Bernard [**Bernhard**, in later years] (b. Lithuania, June 26, 1865—d. Oct. 6, 1959), art critic. Berenson, who was brought to the United States as a boy, was educated at Harvard, later took up his residence in England, and from 1900 until his death lived in Italy. He made himself the acknowledged leader among critics of Italian Renaissance painting, and was known particularly for his painstaking studies of style and his skill in resolving doubtful attributions. Van Wyck Brooks has said that Berenson reconstructs unknown artists from their paintings as paleontologists reconstruct unknown animals from their bones. Berenson published many important works, among them *Venetian Painters of the Renaissance* (1894), *Florentine Painters of the Renaissance* (1896), *The Drawings of the Florentine Painters* (1903, revised 1938), *Three Essays in Method* (1937). His writing is known for its clarity and unhurried elegance. Among his later writings: *Seeing and Knowing* (1954); *Essays in Appreciation* (1959); *Passionate Sightseer* (1960); and *One Year's Reading For Fun* (selections from a 1942 diary, 1960).

Berkeley, Sir William (b. 1606—d. 1677), colonial governor. See NATHANIEL BACON.

Berlin, Irving (b. May 11, 1888—   ), song-writer. Born in Russia as Israel Baline, Berlin came to the United States in 1893. His first great hit was *Alexander's Ragtime Band* (1911). This was followed by such great successes as *Everybody's Doin' It, Oh, How I Hate to Get Up in the Morning* (written for *Yip, Yip, Yaphank*, a World War I Army show), *God Bless America, All Alone, Remember, Always, Easter Parade, White Christmas, Cheek to Cheek, This Is the Army, Mr. Jones, You Can't Get a Man with a Gun*. Some formed part of the popular *Music Box Revues* (1921, 1922, 1923, 1925) and other musical shows and movies with which Berlin was connected. The revue *This Is the Army* (1942), to which he devoted three and a half years of his time without compensation, earned $9,553,000 for the Army Relief Fund. By 1952 he was said to have published 850 songs. Alexander Woollcott wrote an enthusiastic biography of Berlin (1925).

Bernard, John (b. England, 1756—d. 1828), actor, autobiographer. One of the first touring stars, Bernard acted in New York, Philadelphia, and Boston from 1797 to 1819. A portion of his lively autobiography, *Retrospections of America, 1797–1811*, was published in 1887.

Bernard, William Bayle (b. Boston, Nov. 27, 1807—d. Aug. 5, 1875), dramatist, biographer. The son of an actor, Bernard appeared for a while on the stage, then turned to writing plays. His dramas of rural American and allegedly western characters were among the earliest of their kind; both Easterners and the English obtained their main impressions of life in America from such plays as *The Kentuckian* (1833). Bernard also dramatized RIP VAN WINKLE (1832), among the first of numerous versions. He edited his father's papers, *Retrospections of the Stage* (1830).

Bernays, Edward L. (b. Austria, Nov. 22, 1891—   ), newspaperman, public relations counsel. Called during World War I to assist GEORGE CREEL's Committee on Public Information, Bernays became interested in what may be called the psychological bases of the business of influencing the public (his mother was a sister of Sigmund Freud). He devised the term "public relations counsel." Among his books: *Crystallizing Public Opinion* (1924); *Propaganda* (1928); *Public Relations, a Growing Profession* (1945); *Public Relations* (1952). The central idea in his technique is to induce people to accept an idea or a product without their being conscious of the fact that inducement is taking place.

Bernstein, Leonard (b. Lawrence, Mass., Aug. 25, 1918—   ), conductor, composer, pianist, lecturer. Bernstein's extraordinarily varied career includes the following jobs: Assistant to Serge Koussevitzky at Berkshire Music Center in 1942; conductor of the New York City Symphony, 1945–1948; musical adviser to the Israel Philharmonic Orchestra, 1948–1949 season; head of conducting department of the Berkshire Music Center, 1951 to 1956; professor of music at Brandeis University, 1951–1956; assistant conductor New York Philharmonic during the 1943–1944 season, and again for the Philharmonic, co conductor and then conductor since 1957–58. His book, *The Joy of Music* (1959) contains essays and scripts from seven of his extraordinarily popular "Omnibus" lectures on TV. His musical compositions range through a wide variety. They include: *Symphony No. One, "Jeremiah"* (1942); *Hashkivenu* (a setting of part of text from Friday evening Synagogue Service, 1945); *Trouble in Tahiti* (1952), a one-act opera; and the scores for the Broadway musicals, *On the Town* (1944); *Wonderful Town* (1953); and *West Side Story* (1957); the score for the film, *On the Waterfront* (1954); and incidental music for Christopher Fry's play, *The Lark* (1957).

Berry, Frances Miriam. See FRANCES MIRIAM WHITCHER.

Berry, John (b. New York City, April 25, 1915—   ), poet, fiction writer. Berry's small body of writing draws on a background of studies and travel probably as diverse as that of any contemporary writer. *Krishna Fluting* (1959), his first novel, combines a highly controlled, symbolic style with a setting in India (where Berry had attended Viswa Bharati University). Some of his more exotic stories appear in *Fantasy and Science Fiction*. *Jawaharlal and the Three Cadavers* (1958) was reprinted in *The Best American Short Stories* (1959); a later story, *The Listener*, which first appeared in *New World Writing* #16, was later reprinted both in *The Best American Short Stories* (1961), and in *Fantasy and Science Fiction* (American and British editions). His *Notes of a Novelist* in the

Nation (1959) trace the process by which an artist who is careful of his effects goes about creating a novel. *Flight of White Crows: Stories, Tales and Paradoxes* (1961) is set in India.

Berryman, John (b. McAlester, Okla., Oct. 25, 1914—   ), poet, writer, critic. Berryman graduated from Columbia College and Cambridge University and has taught at Harvard, Princeton, the University of Washington, and the University of Cincinnati. His first poems appeared in magazines during the thirties; in 1940 twenty of his poems were published by New Directions in *Five Young American Poets*. His *Poems* appeared in 1942, *The Dispossessed* in 1948; HOMAGE TO MISTRESS BRADSTREET (1956), a long poem dramatizing Anne Bradstreet's spirit, her physical and religious suffering, was called by one reviewer a "sort of miniature WASTE LAND." Berryman has also written short stories (*The Imaginary Jew* has been widely reprinted) and a biography of Stephen Crane (1950), which was praised as the first comprehensive critical and biographical work on Crane.

Best American Short Stories, The. A series of annual anthologies begun in 1915 by EDWARD J. O'BRIEN and continued by him until his death in 1941; thereafter edited by MARTHA FOLEY. The emphasis under both editorships has been on psychology rather than plot. Small-circulation and "little" magazines frequently furnish the bulk of the material.

Beston, Henry [Sheahan] (b. Quincy, Mass., June 1, 1888—d. April 15, 1968), writer. Beston's parents were a New England physician and a Frenchwoman. After studying at Harvard in 1911, he taught for a year at the University of Lyons, France. Later he taught at Harvard, edited *Living Age* for several years, and was on the editorial board of *The Atlantic*. In 1930 he married ELIZABETH COATSWORTH, the poetess. His best-known book, *The Outermost House* (1928), is a journal of his year's residence of Thoreau-like solitude in a house he had constructed on the outer dunes of Cape Cod. It is regarded as a classic of its kind. His quiet life on a northern New England farm and his extensive travels in Europe both found their way into his work. His books include: *Full Speed Ahead* (1919); *The Book of Gallant Vagabonds* (1924); *Herbs and the Earth* (1935); *American Memory* (1937); *The St. Lawrence River* (in THE RIVERS OF AMERICA SERIES, 1942); *Northern Farm* (1948); *White Pine and Blue Water* (1950, a regional reader of the state of Maine); and *Henry Beston's Fairy Tales* (1952).

best sellers. When THE BOOKMAN was started, in February, 1895, the editor, HARRY THURSTON PECK, began publishing a list of "Books in Demand" in the bookstores of various selected cities, changing the heading to "The Six Best Sellers" in 1903. The term was soon adopted by other publications, and such lists are now a standard feature of many literary magazines and newspaper book sections. After World War II, and with the advent of paperback books, sales of books increased greatly, and the long-standing best sellers (exclusive of the Bible)—Shakespeare's *Plays, Ivanhoe,* UNCLE TOM'S CABIN, BEN HUR—were outdistanced in number of sales by more recent works. By the mid-1950's Charles Monroe Sheldon's IN HIS STEPS (1897) was estimated to have sold approximately eight million copies since its publication; following close behind was Benjamin Spock's *The Common Sense Book of Baby and Child Care* (1946) with 7,850,000 copies; Erskine Caldwell's GOD'S LITTLE ACRE (1933), nearly 6,600,000; *Better Homes and Gardens Cook Book* (1930), about 5,800,000; Margaret Mitchell's GONE WITH THE WIND (1937), 5,000,000; Dale Carnegie's How TO WIN FRIENDS AND INFLUENCE PEOPLE (1937), almost 4,900,000; Mickey Spillane's *I, the Jury* (1947), nearly 4,450,000. The three most enduring themes among best sellers are religion, self-help, and romantic adventure, with controversial issues, sexual sensationalism, and murder and its solution running close behind. One trade magazine predicted that a certain novel was sure to be a best seller: "It has everything—horror, sex, madness, and depravity, all handled with dignity and restraint." Robert Ruark's GRENADINE ETCHING (1947) was a burlesque on this type of book. Frank Luther Mott's GOLDEN MULTITUDES (1947) is a study of best sellers in the United States; so are James D. Hart's THE POPULAR BOOK (1950) and Alice Hackett's *Sixty Years of Best Sellers* (1956).

Betsy, Understood. See UNDERSTOOD BETSY.

Bett, Miss Lulu. See MISS LULU BETT.

Betty Alden (1891), a novel by JANE G. AUSTIN. It deals chiefly with the daughter of John and Priscilla Alden and her fortunes.

Beveridge, Albert J[eremiah] (b. Highland Co., Ohio, Oct. 6, 1862—d. April 27, 1927), statesman, orator, historian. Beveridge studied law, practiced in Indianapolis, was elected senator in 1899, and was defeated in 1911 when the Old Guard Republicans refused to support him. He joined Theodore Roosevelt's Progressive Party, but when he failed to win office turned to writing biographies. His *Life of John Marshall* (2 v., 1916, 1919) won praise from critics and was awarded the Pulitzer Prize. Beveridge was working on an elaborate biography of Lincoln when he died; only two volumes were published (1928). Handsome and ardent, Beveridge was one of the great speakers of his day. Mr. Dooley once said of his oratory: "Ye could waltz to it." C. G. Bowers' *Beveridge and the Progressive Era* (1932) is a biography.

Beverley, Robert (b. Middlesex Co., Va., *c.* 1673—d. 1722), traveler, historian. Beverley's family came from Yorkshire to Virginia, where Robert was born on his father's plantation. He served in the General Court, the Council, the General Assembly. A man of curious mind and shrewd insight, he gathered his observations of the world around him into an account of THE HISTORY AND PRESENT STATE OF VIRGINIA (1705; edited by Louis B. Wright, 1947).

Beyond the Horizon (1920), a play by EU-GENE O'NEILL. Two brothers on the Mayo farm love the same girl; she marries one, the other goes to sea. Then the girl thinks she is in love with the one she didn't marry, but on his return is disillusioned. He leaves once more to go to the Argentine, where he makes and loses a fortune in grain. Returning, he finds that matters have gone from bad to worse on the farm. His brother tells him they have all been failures. As he dies he is, however, happy at last, "with the right of release—beyond the horizon." An immature work, the play nevertheless won a Pulitzer Prize.

Bibelot, The. A magazine of reprints published by Thomas B. Mosher at Portland, Me., 1895–1915. Mosher was a lover of fine literature and a creator of beautiful books; his famous little magazine was an example of both his enthusiasms. It contained chiefly poetry and short stories reprinted from European authors; it is a collector's item today.

Bible, The, in the United States. When the original settlers first came to America, the Bible accompanied them, often as their sole library. First it came in the magnificent English of the King James Version (1611), later in the Douay Version of the Catholics, with its sonorous Latinisms (New Testament, 1582; Old Testament, 1609). In later generations the Bible reached these shores in all the innumerable tongues of the immigrants. To these Old World versions America soon added others. THE BAY PSALM BOOK, advertised as "the whole Book of Psalms, faithfully translated into English meter," appeared in 1640; and in 1661 the New Testament, in 1663 the complete Bible, were published as translated into the language of the Algonquin Indians by JOHN ELIOT.

In 1871 an English committee was formed to prepare a revision of the King James Version with the cooperation of American Protestant scholars. In 1894 the English version had been completed; in 1901 the American revisers published a separate translation, the edition since circulated by the Society of the Gideons. Another massive revision by Protestant scholars began in 1938, was completed in 1948; and still more recently (1961), a completely new translation of the Bible into modern English was prepared by British scholars, attracting a great deal of interest in America. The first American Catholic version of the Bible was printed in Philadelphia in 1790. It was a reprint of the Rheims-Douay Version and was the first American quarto Bible. In 1941 appeared a new Catholic version of the New Testament, followed (1948) by translations of the Old Testament books. To meet the needs of adherents of Judaism, Isaac Leeser (1806–1868) issued in 1853 a complete version of the Hebrew Scriptures in English. In 1892 plans were laid by the Jewish Publication Society to prepare an entirely new rendering, with Dr. MAX L. MARGOLIS (1866–1932) as editor-in-chief. In 1917 this work was published as *The Holy Scriptures According to the Masoretic Text.*

Another important version of the Bible is *The*

Bible: An American Translation (1931), prepared by Edgar J. Goodspeed, J. M. Powis, and others. This version is deliberately written "in the familiar language of today" and avoids all archaisms. Professor CHARLES CUTLER TORREY of Yale undertook to render the Gospels into Aramaic as an approximation of the originals, then made a translation into English, publishing the results as *The Four Gospels: A New Translation* (1933). Professor RICHARD GREEN MOULTON of the University of Chicago did much to help modern readers see the Bible as literature by rearranging the books of the Bible in a modern format to distinguish verse from prose, drama from straight narration, single sentences from paragraphs. He began in 1895 to publish books of the Bible separately in such a format, and collected all the books in a single volume in 1907. Another volume stressing literary values was ERNEST SUTHERLAND BATES' *The Bible Designed to Be Read as Living Literature* (1936), followed by an interpretive volume, *Biography of the Bible* (1937). W. W. Sloan wrote *A Survey of the New Testament* (1961).

Dr. Frank Luther Mott, in his GOLDEN MULTITUDES (1947), claims that "it is probable that there never was a year in American history in which the Bible did not exceed the next-best seller." His conservative estimate of the number of whole Bibles distributed in the United States up to the end of 1945 comes to over 200,000,-000. To this must be added such separate publications as the two Testaments by themselves, books of Psalms, other single books of the Bible. The American Bible Society alone, from its founding in 1816 to May, 1951, distributed 38,552,554 copies of the complete Bible and 367,869,450 New Testaments and portions of the Bible. Even books on the Great Book sell in huge quantities. By 1952, for example, J. L. Hurlbut's *Story of the Bible* (1904) had sold 3,000,000 copies. A warm welcome also awaited such well-written volumes as Mary Ellen Chase's *Life and Language in the Old Testament* (1955) and Edmund Wilson's *The Dead Sea Scrolls* (1955).

In American poetry there is much celebration of individual Biblical figures: Anne Hempstead Branch's Nimrod, Don Marquis' young Moses, Stephen Vincent Benét's King David, Edgar Lee Masters' Peter, Robinson Jeffers' Judas. From the Bible, too, the poets bring back modern applications of ancient themes, as Countee Cullen did in *Black Magdalens* (1925), and Edwin McNeill Poteat in *The Jericho Road* (1945). The psalm or hymn has attracted poets, as in Longfellow's THE PSALM OF LIFE (1839), Julia Ward Howe's BATTLE HYMN OF THE REPUBLIC (1861), and James Oppenheim's *Songs for the New Age* (1914). Poets have endeavored to paint new portraits of Jesus, as Whittier did in *Over-Heart* (1859), Lanier in A BALLAD OF TREES AND THE MASTER (1880), Edwin Arlington Robinson in *Calvary* (1897), Ezra Pound in *The Ballad of the Goodly Fere* (1907), and Joseph Auslander in *Encyclical* (1938). The Christmas story, in particular, has inspired numerous poems, including Joyce Kilmer's *Gates and Doors* (1917), Louis Untermeyer's *The Pilgrimage* (1923), Robinson's *Christmas Sonnet for One in Doubt* (1925), and Dorothy Parker's *The Maid-Servant at the Inn* (1928).

Two of the most popular American novels ever published retell the story of Jesus: General Lew Wallace's BEN HUR (1880) and Lloyd C. Douglas' THE ROBE (1942). In addition there have been numerous novels about other biblical figures, such as Robert Nathan's *Jonah* (1925), Elmer Davis' GIANT-KILLER (1928), Louis Untermeyer's *Moses* (1928), Gladys Schmitt's *David the King* (1946), Howard Fast's *Moses, Prince of Egypt* (1958), and in view of their American residence, Sholem Asch's trilogy, *The Nazarene* (1939), *The Apostle* (1943), and *Mary* (1949), and Thomas Mann's magnificent series of novels on Joseph and his brethren, begun in 1933. Three outstanding short stories about Christmas may be mentioned: Henry van Dyke's *The Other Wise Man* (1895), O. Henry's THE GIFT OF THE MAGI (published in *The Four Million*, 1906), and H. L. Mencken's ironic masterpiece, CHRISTMAS STORY (1946).

Among plays suggested by the Bible these may be recalled: Longfellow's *The Divine Tragedy* (1871); Don Marquis' *The Dark Hours* (1924); O'Neill's LAZARUS LAUGHED (1927); Philip Barry's *John* (1927); Marc Connelly's THE GREEN PASTURES (1930); Maxwell Anderson's *Journey to Jerusalem* (1940); Robinson Jeffers' DEAR JUDAS (produced as a play, 1947). In the series of radio programs called *The Eternal Light* (NBC, the middle 1940's) Bible stories were brilliantly used. *The Ten Commandments*, a motion picture produced by Cecil De Mille, was an outstanding success. See also RELIGION IN THE U.S.

Bickerstaff, Isaac. Pen name of BENJAMIN WEST.

Bierce, Ambrose [Gwinett] (b. Meigs Co., Ohio, June 24, 1842—d. 1914?), newspaperman, short-story writer, poet, satirist. Bierce at times deliberately obscured facts about his family and upbringing; he was frankly ashamed of his sternly religious parents, and kept on good terms with only one brother out of nine children. The only formal education he had was a year at military academy. When the Civil War broke out, he enlisted, fought bravely in several battles, and completed his service with the brevet title of major. He was no pacifist, but he came to doubt the justice of the cause for which he had fought. When the government offered him a large sum in accumulated back pay, he declined it, saying, "When I hired out as an assassin for my country, that wasn't part of the contract."

Bierce settled in San Francisco—first as night watchman at the Mint, then as a columnist, finally as literary dictator; his gibes could determine the fate of books and authors, at least on the Coast. He wrote political squibs for *The News Letter*, later ran its "Town Crier" column, and in 1868 became editor. His first story, *The*

Haunted Valley, was published in *The Over-land Monthly* in 1871. Among his friends were Mark Twain, Bret Harte, and Joaquin Miller; it was the moment of literary flowering in San Francisco.

When Bierce married, his father-in-law, Captain H. H. Day, a wealthy Nevada miner, presented the young couple with a wedding gift of $10,000. They set out for England, and there Bierce remained from 1872 to 1876. Carey Mc-Williams, in his 1929 biography, wrote: "Bierce went to England a rough, uncouth Western humorist, and came back a wit who wrote with great finish and elegance." Bierce contributed to English humorous periodicals and became intimate with literary men. In London he published three books, all gatherings of his vitriolic sketches and epigrams: *The Fiend's Delight* (1872); *Nuggets and Dust Panned Out in California* (1872); and COBWEBS FROM AN EMPTY SKULL (1874). Then, because of the failure of his health, he returned to San Francisco.

There he began his famous "PRATTLER" column for *The Argonaut.* It ran for two years (1877–79) before Bierce gave it up for a hairbrained mining expedition to the Black Hills. He returned in 1881, and the column then ran in THE WASP until 1886 when the weekly died. In that year young WILLIAM RANDOLPH HEARST took over the San Francisco *Examiner* from his father and hired Bierce to write his "Prattler" column for that paper. It continued for ten years more. It was a mixture of many things, literary criticism, gossip, occasional aphorisms, and some of Bierce's best short stories.

In 1896 Bierce went to Washington for Hearst and remained until 1909 when he resigned. Meanwhile he had begun a department in THE COSMOPOLITAN, not then owned by Hearst; he also spent much time on the preparation of his *Collected Works* (12 v., 1909–12). After much domestic unhappiness his wife divorced him in

1904. In 1913, tired of existence, he went southward and disappeared into Mexico. According to one story, he was killed in the war between Villa and Carranza; but nothing authentic has ever been printed.

Bierce (inevitably called "Bitter Bierce," the title of Hartley Grattan's biography of him, 1929) was a difficult genius who never attained full stature. At his best, Bierce is a brilliant epigrammatist and a notable forerunner of such American realists as Stephen Crane, but in spite of his voluminous writings, his fame rests largely on one book of short stories, IN THE MIDST OF LIFE (published as *Tales of Soldiers And Civilians,* 1891; retitled 1898); a book of epigrams, THE DEVIL'S DICTIONARY (1911; called *The Cynic's Word Book* in 1906 and based on Bierce's newspaper contributions); and on many anecdotes and sayings that gave him a reputation for cruel and original wit. The characters in his stories are generally abstractions, nameless types of tragic humanity. Even in his best work their individuality is subordinate to their fate, to the mood of horror and impending calamity established by suggestive realistic detail. In addition, there is a strong element of sardonic humor in Bierce's fiction, exemplified in the opening of one of his stories: "Early one June morning in 1872 I murdered my father—an act which made a deep impression on me at the time." This side of Bierce's nature is revealed most memorably in *The Devil's Dictionary:* mainly epigrammatic nuggets of cynicism and pessimism. Bierce it was who said that "woman would be more charming if one could fall into her arms without falling into her hands." Occasionally, however, his aphorisms are marred by their strained and gratuitous venom.

Among other writings of Bierce are: *Black Beetles in Amber* (1892), epigrams in verse; CAN SUCH THINGS BE? (1893), gruesome short stories; *Fantastic Fables* (1899), imitations of Aesop; *Shapes of Clay* (1903), satirical verse; and *Write it Right* (1909), an unfortunate treatise on usage in which Bierce gives a dogmatic and unscholarly list of "Don'ts" for writers. Biographies of Bierce range from Vincent Starrett's in 1920 to Paul Fatout's *Ambrose Bierce: The Devil's Lexicographer* in 1951. There is a Bierce collection at Stanford University. See also OVERLAND MONTHLY.

Big Clock, The (1946), a novel by KENNETH FEARING. An ingenious tale of a man-hunt in which the quarry must track himself down, it was made into a movie (1948) by Jonathan Latimer.

Bigelow, John (b. Malden, N.Y., Nov. 25, 1817—d. Dec. 19, 1911), editor, author, diplomat. Bigelow traveled extensively and wrote entertainingly about his experiences, served as American consul-general at Paris and later as minister to France, worked with WILLIAM CULLEN BRYANT on the New York *Evening Post,* was secretary of state to Samuel J. Tilden during the latter's service as governor of New York. Out of his experiences grew two biographies, *William Cullen Bryant* (1893) and *Samuel J.*

Tilden (1895), also an autobiography called *Retrospections of an Active Life* (5 v., 1909–13). In addition he wrote many historical works on Franklin, Frémont, Beaumarchais, and others. Margaret Clapp wrote a fine biography, *Forgotten First Citizen, John Bigelow* (1947).

Big-Foot Wallace, The Adventures of (1870), by John C. Duval (1816–1897). The story of W. A. A. WALLACE (1817–1899). Wallace was a Virginian ranger and hunter who became embroiled in the troubles between the Texans and the Mexicans in the 1830's and acquired his nickname because of unusual difficulty in finding shoes to fit him while he was a prisoner in Mexico. His adventures are related autobiographically with old-style graphic American humor. Walter Stanley Campbell wrote a biography, *Big-Foot Wallace* (1942), in which he attempted to separate fact from legend.

Biggers, Earl Derr (b. Warren, Ohio, Aug. 26, 1884—d. April 5, 1933), playwright, novelist. His first production, *If You're Only Human* (1912) was a failure; his successful mystery novel, SEVEN KEYS TO BALDPATE (1913), was made into a play by GEORGE M. COHAN and was also filmed. He wrote other novels, but is chiefly known for his series about the Chinese detective, CHARLIE CHAN. These include: *The House Without a Key* (1925); *The Chinese Parrot* (1926); *Behind That Curtain* (1928); *The Black Camel* (1929); *Charlie Chan Carries On* (1930); *Keeper of the Keys* (1932).

Biglow Papers, The. Poems and prose sketches by JAMES RUSSELL LOWELL. The first poem appeared in the Boston *Courier*, June 17, 1846, and was followed by eight others. These, together with four published in the NATIONAL ANTI-SLAVERY STANDARD, were collected in *The Biglow Papers*, 1848. A second series ran during the Civil War in *The Atlantic Monthly* and was collected in 1867. Together they made two series of satiric poems, prose sketches, and critical miscellanea.

The Biglow Papers marked Lowell's true start as a poet, as a widely known publicist of anti-slavery causes, and as an ardent defender of things American. They helped win acceptance for American speechways in the best literary circles. The first series centered upon the war with Mexico, the second upon the slavery issue. The verses were written in Yankee dialect, while the accompanying prose was mostly straight English. There were three chief characters: Hosea Biglow, a forthright commentator on current issues; his friend Birdofredom Sawin, something of a scoundrel; and the Rev. Homer Wilbur, used as a foil. With bludgeonlike blows Lowell satirized the politicians of his day and the doctrines they preached, the way in which war was made, the cowardice of editors, the folly of men of wealth and alleged statesmen North and South. One important poem avoids political issues—THE COURTIN', reckoned among Lowell's masterpieces. It inspired a best-selling novel, *Quincy Adams Sawyer* (1900), by Charles Felton Pidgin.

Even more significant is Lowell's use of Americanisms, especially Yankeeisms. For many American readers through several generations it provided the first literary introduction to "the American language." Mencken feels that in the critical material which accompanied *The Biglow Papers* Lowell "did a great service to the common tongue of the country, and must be numbered among its true friends." See YANKEE IN AMERICAN LANGUAGE AND LITERATURE.

Big Money, The (1936), a novel by JOHN DOS PASSOS. Life in the United States during the 1920's, when the cult of "big money" for everybody ended in 1929 in the stock market crash and the Big Depression, is the theme of this story. Helen E. Haines notes that Dos Passos here "mingled the expressionistic method with solid realistic narrative."

Big Road, The (1946), a poem by NORMAN ROSTEN. The poem deals in the main with the Alaska-Canada (Alcan) Highway. But sections are devoted to earlier roads. Rosten describes his work as a road-legend in which he "attempted to celebrate man through the saga of exploration and construction, using the road both as myth and history."

Big Sky, The (1947), a novel by A. B. GUTHRIE, JR. A carefully researched novel about pioneer life, it is a realistic and persuasive story of the "mountain men," living and fighting and loving with the Indians. Like the Indians, these men are vengeful, sensual, cruel.

Billboard, The. A weekly theatrical journal, founded in 1893 by W. H. Donaldson, which covered many fields of entertainment, from the theater to circus and carnival shows. At one time it provided a mailing service for show business people without permanent addresses. In January, 1961, the newspaper's circus and carnival coverage was incorporated into a magazine, *Amusement Business Week*, and *The Billboard* became *Billboard Music Week*, devoted exclusively to the various phases of the music and recording business.

Billings, Josh [pen name of **Henry Wheeler Shaw (Uncle Esek)**] (b. Lanesboro, Mass., April 21, 1818—d. Oct. 14, 1885), auctioneer, real-estate agent, humorist. Shaw, as his pen name shows, was professedly a Yankee, who in his essays and lectures created for his Josh Billings an amusing family of Yankee characters. He went to college, but as he himself testified: "Hamilton College has turned out a good many fine men—it turned me out." He became an explorer, a coal operator, a farmer, a steamboat captain, finally an auctioneer and real-estate dealer. Then he took to writing humorous essays as an avocation. He noticed that they attracted no attention, finally discovered the contemporaneous key to success by studying ARTEMUS WARD and adopting misspelling as the cap-and-bells to his wit and wisdom. He was widely quoted and misquoted, and his fame led him on to lecturing, in which he also was highly successful. He published volumes of *Sayings* (1865, 1866) and a series of *Allminax* (1869–79) in one volume (1902). Among his other publications were *Josh Billings on Ice and Other Things*

(1868); *Everybody's Friend, or Josh Billings' Encyclopedia and Proverbial Philosophy of Wit and Humor* (1876); *Complete Comical Writings of Josh Billings* (1876, 1877); *Josh Billings' Struggling with Things* (1881); *Josh Billings' Spice Box* (1881, 1882); *Josh Billings, His Works Complete* (4 v., 1888).

Some literary historians ignore Shaw or mention him slightingly; others express great admiration. Charles H. Smith, creator of Bill Arp, held that Shaw was "Aesop and Ben Franklin, condensed and abridged." Max Eastman startlingly calls Shaw "the father of imagism"; he feels there was little in New England poetry up to Shaw's date as graphic as some of the latter's metaphors—"nothing quite comparable to his statement that goats 'know the way up a rock as natural as woodbine,' which is Homeric." Brander Matthews strips one of Shaw's statements of its misspelling to make this maxim, worthy in his judgment of La Bruyère: "When a fellow gets going down hill, it does seem as though everything had been greased for the occasion." Here are some others: "I never bet—not so much because I am afraid to lose but because I am afraid I will win." "If a man is right, he can't be too radical; if he is wrong, he can't be too conservative." "It's better to know nothing than to know what ain't so." "The Muel is haf hoss and haf Jackass, and then kums to a full stop, natur diskovering her mistake." "There ain't much fun in medicine, but there's a good deal of medicine in fun."

An excellent Shaw anthology was prepared by Donald Day: *Uncle Sam's Uncle Josh* (1953). Other books on Shaw: Francis S. Smith's *Life and Adventures of Josh Billings* (1883); H. Montague's *Wit and Humor of Josh Billings* (1913); Cyril Clemens' *Josh Billings, Yankee Humorist* (1932).

Billy Budd, Foretopman (posthumously published, 1924), a novel by HERMAN MELVILLE. Like much of the poetry and prose written in the last decade of Melville's life, *Billy Budd* offers final, if finite, statements on issues Melville had pondered for a lifetime. He had dealt with the problem of the collision of good and evil as early as REDBURN (1849), developed the theme in most of the subsequent novels, and had given it poetic resolution in CLAREL (1876). In *Billy Budd* it is presented in its starkest form, with Billy and Claggart, the villainous master-at-arms, representing almost allegorically abstract opposites. Their interaction admits of no ambiguity: innocence and its obverse are inadequate for survival; the man of extreme polarity inevitably destroys himself or is destroyed, whereas the men who reconcile the opposites—Ishmael of MOBY DICK and Jack Chase of WHITE JACKET—survive.

Billy Budd is the last flowering of Melville the symbolist. Captain Vere's decision to hang Billy for the slaying of the evil Claggart represents the triumph of law. Vere, allegorically the just God of the Old Testament, realizes his first obligation is to preserve society, not self; therefore he must condemn Billy to death, despite his paternalistic feelings for him. And Billy, the representative of the New Dispensation, willingly accepts martyrdom, crying at the end, "God bless Captain Vere!" As the Christ-like Billy mounts the yardarm, the golden sun penetrates the fleecy clouds, signifying the hero's resurrection into eternal life.

Billy the Kid (b. New York City, June 23, 1859—d. July 15, 1881), sobriquet of William H. Bonney, frontier outlaw. Bonney was brought to Kansas City at the age of three, at twelve killed his first man in Silver City, N.M., for insulting his mother. After many crimes in various parts of the Southwest he joined a gang in a frontier war, and while visiting his sweetheart at Fort Sumner, N.M., was killed by a former friend, Sheriff Pat Garrett. Old-timers, journalists, dime-novelists, and balladists have built him into a folk hero. His life has been a favorite subject for biographers and novelists. C. Dykes compiled (1953) *Billy the Kid: The Bibliography of a Legend*. Patrick Floyd Garrett wrote *The Authentic Life of Billy the Kid* (1954); and Frazier Hunt's *The Tragic Days of Billy the Kid* was published in 1956.

Bingham, Caleb (b. Salisbury, Conn., April 15, 1757—d. April 6, 1817), textbook author. Bingham was one of the first to provide schoolbooks for Americans. His books include: *The Young Lady's Accidence, or, A Short and Easy Introduction to English Grammar* (1785); *The Child's Companion* (1792); *The American Preceptor* (1794); *The Columbian Orator* (1797). He translated Chateaubriand's *Atala* (1802).

Bingham, Hiram (b. Bennington, Vt., Oct. 30, 1789—d. Nov. 11, 1869); **Bingham, Hiram** (b. Honolulu, Aug. 16, 1831—d. Oct. 25, 1908); **Bingham, Hiram** (b. Honolulu, Nov. 19, 1875—d. June 6, 1956). The first Hiram Bingham was a clergyman who with his wife Sybil Mose-ley became a missionary to Hawaii, prepared textbooks in Hawaiian, and by 1839 had completed a version of the Bible in that language. His son was educated in Hawaii and in the States, taught school for a while, but also became a missionary, settling with his wife, Minerva Clarissa Brewster, in the Gilbert Islands in 1857. He translated the Bible into Gilbertese, publishing the New Testament in 1873, the whole Bible in 1890. His son was a history professor at Yale, specializing in Latin-American history. He began explorations in Latin America in 1906 and made many important historical and archaeological discoveries, including the remains of an ancient Inca city. He was a Presidential elector (1916), governor of Connecticut (1923), and U.S. Senator (1924–33). Among his books: *Journal of an Expedition across Venezuela and Colombia* (1909); *Across South America* (1911); *In the Wonderland of Peru* (1913); *The Monroe Doctrine, An Obsolete Shibboleth* (1913); *Inca Land* (1922); *Elihu Yale—The American Nabob of Queen Square* (1939); *Lost City of the Incas* (1948).

Binns, Archie (b. Port Ludlow, Wash., July 30, 1899—　　), novelist, biographer. His excellent novels of the sea and of the Northwest include *Lightship* (1934), *The Laurels Are Cut Down* (1937), *The Land Is Bright* (1939), *The Timber Beast* (1944), *Yon Rolling River* (1947). *Mrs. Fiske and the American Theatre* (1955) is a biography of Minnie Maddern Fiske. He has also written *Enchanted Islands* (a juvenile, 1956) and *Headwaters* (1957).

Birches (1916), a poem by ROBERT FROST. One of Frost's best-known poems, *Birches* describes the trees bent to the ground by ice storms; the poet imagines that they had been bent by a boy swinging on them, and wishes, when he himself is "weary of considerations," to climb toward heaven in a birch tree "till the tree could bear no more,/ But dipped its top and set me down again."

Bird, Robert Montgomery (b. Newcastle Co., Del., Feb. 5, 1806—d. Jan. 23, 1854), physician, dramatist, novelist. He received an M.D. from the University of Pennsylvania in 1827 but soon gave up his practice because of his reluctance to collect fees. His supposed friend, EDWIN FORREST, helped him out by buying several of his plays: *Pelopidas* (1830); THE GLADIATOR (1831); ORALLOOSA (1832); THE BROKER OF BOGOTA (1834). For these Bird received a tiny fraction of the profits and Forrest refused to let Bird publish them. The American copyright laws did not adequately protect the playwright at that time so Dr. Bird decided to try his hand at novel writing.

Bird's novels proved considerably more profitable for the author than his plays had been. His dramatic talent and experience infused his novels with excitement and suspense. His characters are carefully molded of conflicting passions, which in NICK OF THE WOODS (1837) produce a hero with a split personality. *Sheppard Lee* (1836), published anonymously, is a colorful satire in which the hero, a New Jersey farmer,

indulges in metempsychosis to explore the follies of contemporary life at all social levels. Bird's other books include: CALAVAR (1834); THE INFIDEL (1835); THE HAWKS OF HAWK HOLLOW (1835); *Peter Pilgrim* (1838); *The Adventures*

of Robin Day (1839). *The Broker of Bogota* was finally published in *Representative American Plays* by A. H. Quinn in 1917, and the remaining plays (except for several still in manuscript) are in Clement E. Foust's *Life and Dramatic Works of Robert Montgomery Bird* (1919).

Birdofredum Sawin. See BIGLOW PAPERS.

Birds and Men: American Birds in Science, Art, Literature, and Conservation, 1800–1900 (1955), a historical analysis by Robert Henry Welker. Columbus, Audubon, Thoreau, Burroughs, and many others contribute their observations on birds to this thorough study.

Birds' Christmas Carol, The (1887), a story by KATE DOUGLAS WIGGIN. A somewhat saccharine best seller which tells of the Bird Family, and particularly of Carol. But its main charm comes from the picture of a poor neighboring family.

Birds of Killingsworth, The (1863), a narrative poem by Henry Wadsworth Longfellow, included in TALES OF A WAYSIDE INN. Some Connecticut farmers kill the birds, whom they blame for destroying their crops. But when the birds are gone a horde of caterpillars does even more damage.

Birds of North America, The (1827–38), a treatise by JOHN JAMES AUDUBON. The volume contains more than a thousand illustrations in color, and identifies more than five hundred species of birds. First printed in England, these huge folios have become rare and expensive collectors' items. William MacGillivray assisted Audubon considerably in the preparation of the text.

Birkbeck, Morris (b. England, 1764–1825), traveler, farmer, founder of Wanborough and Albion, Ill. He was the center of a controversy in England on the advisability of British farmers settling in this country. He was a successful farmer on his own account when he came to America in 1817 to look into the arguments for emigrating. His *Notes on a Journey in America from the Coast of Virginia to the Territory of Illinois* (1818) and *Letters from Illinois* (1818) stated that Americans on the frontier were lazy and unenterprising, but that opportunities for more industrious settlers were great. With Robert Flower and the latter's brother, he purchased land and started a settlement that eventually attracted four hundred other British and seven hundred American settlers.

Birnbaum, Martin (b. Hungary, May 10, 1878–   ), art dealer, art critic. Martin Birnbaum studied at City College of New York and Columbia University where he obtained his M.A. degree in 1898 and his LL.B. degree in 1901. He also studied at the National Conservatory of Music from 1890 to 1893. All this was an indirect approach to his future work. He was associated for many years with the firm of Scott & Fowles which combined with the Wildenstein Galleries in 1953, and his outstanding work was gathering together the extraordinary collection of Grenville Lindall Winthrop, a direct descendant of the first governor of Massachusetts and a distinguished Harvard alumnus. Birnbaum has introduced many important artists to the American public and has written a number of books; among them: *Painters, Sculptors, and Graphic Artists* (1919); *Fragments of Memories* (1920); *John Singer Sargent: A Conversation Piece* (1940); *Wanderings in the Tropics* (1941); *Angkor and the Mandarin Road* (1952); *The Last Romantic* (1960, autobiography).

Birney, Earle (b. Calgary, Alb., May 13, 1904–   ), professor, poet. A member of one of the original pioneer families of Alberta, Birney began his career as a teaching fellow at the University of California from 1927 to 1930, and later taught at the University of Utah and Toronto University. In addition to his work as an educator, Birney served as literary editor for the *Canadian Forum* (1936–1940) and the *Canadian Poetry Magazine* (1946–1948). Awarded the Governor General's Award in Poetry in 1942 and 1945, Birney's poetical works include *David and Other Poems* (1942) and *Now Is The Time* (1945). He also edited *Twentieth Century Canadian Poetry* (1953). Among Birney's prose works are *Turvey* (1949), a novel in the picaresque vein; *Trial of a City* (1952); and *Down the Long Table* (1955).

Birth (1918), a novel by ZONA GALE. Family and associates look upon Marshall Pitt as a bore and a nonentity. His wife leaves him, he fails in all his ventures, and finally dies trying to rescue a pet dog. His son recognizes his goodness and courage too late. Miss Gale dramatized the novel as *Mr. Pitt* (1924).

Birthmark, The (1846), a story by NATHANIEL HAWTHORNE published in MOSSES FROM AN OLD MANSE. One of Hawthorne's best tales, it relates how a scientist, married to a beautiful woman with a birthmark on her cheek, seeks to remove the blemish. He succeeds, but she dies.

Bishop, Elizabeth (b. Worcester, Mass., Feb. 8, 1911–   ), poet. Her collection of verse,

North and South (1946), won the Houghton Mifflin Poetry Prize Fellowship and was highly praised for its wit and perception. The volume was reissued with 18 new poems as *North and South—A Cold Spring* in 1955. Although her

J. L. Castel

body of work is small, Miss Bishop is considered one of the finer contemporary poets.

Bishop, Jim [James Alonzo] (b. Jersey City, N.J., Nov. 21, 1907–   ), writer, editor, newspaperman. Bishop worked for a while on the New York *Daily Mirror*, has been associate editor of *Collier's* magazine, founding editor of Gold Medal Books, and executive editor of the *Catholic Digest*. He is perhaps best known as the author of *The Day Lincoln Was Shot* (1955), a minutely detailed reconstruction of the activities of Lincoln and John Wilkes Booth during the 24-hour period that preceded Lincoln's death. Among his other books: *The Glass Crutch* (1945); *The Golden Ham* (1956); *The Day Christ Died* (1957); *Go With God* (1958); *The Day Christ Was Born* (1960).

Bishop, John Peale (b. Charles Town, W. Va., May 21, 1892—d. April 4, 1944), poet, fiction writer, essayist. After World War I Bishop Became managing editor of *Vanity Fair*, in 1922 joined a group of expatriates in Paris, among them Fitzgerald, Hemingway, and MacLeish. His books include: *Green Fruit* (poems, 1917); THE UNDERTAKER'S GARLAND (poems in collaboration with EDMUND WILSON, 1922); *Many Thousands Gone* (short stories, 1931); *Now with His Love* (poems, 1933); *Act of Darkness* (novel, 1935); *Minute Particulars* (poems, 1936); *Selected Poems* (1941); *Collected Essays* (1948); *Collected Poems* (1948). In 1943 he was made consultant in comparative literature at the Library of Congress. After his death a John Peale Bishop Memorial Literary Prize Contest was conducted in 1945 by *The Sewanee Review* and Prentice-Hall. The resultant prize essays, stories, and poems were collected in *A Southern Vanguard* (1947), edited by Allan Tate, who notes Bishop's awareness of the tensions between the South today and the outside world. He has been compared to Keats, but also owes a debt to the 17th-century metaphysical poets.

Bishop, Morris [Gilbert] (b. Willard, N.Y., April 15, 1893—   ), teacher, versifier, translator, biographer. Bishop, a teacher at Cornell University since 1921, is known particularly for his excellent light verse. He has written: *A Gallery of Eccentrics* (1928); *Paramount Poems* (1929); *Love Rimes of Petrarch* (1931); *Ronsard, Prince of Poets* (1940); *Spilt Milk* (1942); *A Treasury of British Humor* (1942); *The Life and Adventures of La Rochefoucauld* (1951); *A Bowl of Bishop* (1954). His *Limericks Long After Lear* have appeared in the *New Yorker*. He wrote *The Widening Stain* (1942), a mystery novel, under the pseudonym W. Bolingbroke Johnson.

Bishop, Thomas Brigham (b. Portland, Me., 1835—d. 1905), song composer. Bishop wrote songs for Negro minstrel shows. To him are attributed, with very little certainty, WHEN JOHNNY COMES MARCHING HOME; SHOO, FLY, DON'T BODDER ME; and the original JOHN BROWN'S BODY.

Bissell, Richard (b. Dubuque, Iowa, June 27, 1913—   ), novelist, playwright. Bissell contributed to such outstanding Broadway hits as *The Pajama Game*, in collaboration with George Abbott (1954), and *Say Darling* (1959), in collaboration with his wife Marian Bissell and with Abe Burrows. The first was adapted from his novel *7½ Cents* (1952), and *Say Darling* is about an author making a musical from a novel. His short stories appeared in *Collier's, Esquire*, and *Holiday*. His books include: *A Stretch on the River* (1950); *The Monongahela* (1951); *High Water* (1955); and *Good Bye Ava* (1960). Much of his writing reflects his background and acquaintance with the great rivers of the Middle West.

Bitter Bierce. A nickname given to AMBROSE BIERCE.

Bitter-Sweet (1858), a poem by J. G. HOLLAND. Laid in a New England homestead, this melodramatic poem seeks to prove that there is nothing inconsistent in the simultaneous existence of good and evil. It was immensely popular in its day.

Bixby letter, The. Lincoln's famous letter of condolence, sent to Mrs. Lydia Bixby of Boston on November 21, 1864, when Lincoln was informed that she had lost five sons in battle. A strikingly beautiful work, it nevertheless roused controversy among later scholars. The holograph does not exist, though several forgeries have been put forward. Mrs. Bixby, as it turned out, had not lost five sons but only two, as F. Lauristan Bullard showed in his *Abraham Lincoln*

and the Widow Bixby (1946), but he adds that both Lincoln and the widow believed sincerely at the time that all five had been killed in action. Moreover, Lincoln's authorship of the letter has been denied, mainly by NICHOLAS MURRAY BUTLER, on oral evidence that it was JOHN HAY, Lincoln's young secretary, who "wrote" the letter. Hay himself, however, said in 1904 that the letter was genuine, and today it is generally believed that Hay merely "wrote," or transcribed, the letter in his secretarial capacity from a dictated or written draft by Lincoln. No other writing by Hay evinces an ability to compose work equal to the letter's undoubted quality.

Bixby's Hotel. This 19th century hostelry was located at the southwest corner of Broadway and Park Place in New York City and was conducted by Daniel Bixby, at one time a bookseller in Lowell, Mass. He welcomed authors and publishers to his hotel. It was the first New York home of Alice and Phoebe Cary, and James Fenimore Cooper and Washington Irving often lodged there in their later years. Others frequently seen in the hotel were Fitz-Greene Halleck, N. P. Willis, Nathaniel Hawthorne, Oliver Wendell Holmes, Bayard Taylor, and Ralph Waldo Emerson.

Black, Alexander (b. New York City, Feb. 7, 1859—d. May 8, 1940), novelist, editor, photographer. The first to experiment with a combination of stereopticon slides and spoken dialogue. His novels include *Miss Jerry* (1891), *The Seventh Angel* (1921), *Jo Ellen* (1923). He wrote an autobiography, *Time and Chance* (1937).

Black April (1927), a novel by JULIA PETERKIN. Its powerful, realistic depiction of life on an isolated South Carolina plantation excited both admiration and disapproval on its publication. The plot centers around Black April and his complete domination of all the Negroes on the plantation: no white character appears in the book.

Blackbeard. See TEACH, EDWARD.

Black Cat, The (published in [Phila.] *U.S. Saturday Post*, Aug. 19, 1843; in *Tales*, 1845), a story by EDGAR ALLAN POE, one of his greatest horror tales. The manuscript was peculiar: the story was written on half-sheets of note paper, pasted together at the ends and making one continuous piece, which Poe rolled up tightly, in a fashion that probably would have caused its instant rejection in most modern magazine offices. In the story a murderer places the dead body of his wife in a cellar vault that he conceals with cement. By a singular bit of absentmindedness, he immures in the vault at the same time a cat that he hates; its cries bring his crime to light.

Black Crook, The (1866), a play by CHARLES M. BARRAS, with music and ballet. The original play took five hours to perform; it was revived by CHRISTOPHER MORLEY in burlesque style in Hoboken (1929). It has been called the first American musical.

Blackfeet or **Blackfoot Indians.** Two groups, one of Algonquian stock who ranged from the headwaters of the Missouri north to the Saskatchewan River, the other Teton Sioux who lived chiefly in the Dakotas. The former group appears frequently in Irving's accounts of his experiences in the West and his stories of other travelers: A TOUR ON THE PRAIRIES (1835); ASTORIA (1836); THE ADVENTURES OF CAPTAIN BONNEVILLE (1837).

Black Hills. A group of mountains in western South Dakota and northeastern Wyoming, occupying an area of about 6,000 sq. miles. Aside from such attractions as an astonishing petrified forest and many caves, the Black Hills draw thousands of tourists each year to view the tremendous sculptures of GUTZON BORGLUM on Mount Rushmore—a peak 6,040 feet high, on the face of which Borglum carved (1927–41) the faces of Washington, Jefferson, Lincoln, and Theodore Roosevelt. Washington's stone nose is longer than the whole face of Egypt's Great Sphinx, and Lincoln's face is about sixty feet from chin to forehead. Albert Williams described the *Black Hills* (1953), and Paul Fatout wrote *Ambrose Bierce and the Black Hills* (1956). Hoffman Birney's novel, *The Dice of God*, has its setting in the Black Hills.

Black Horse Tavern, Hartford, Conn. Meeting place of the HARTFORD WITS in the late 18th century.

Black Mask. A monthly magazine, founded in 1919 and edited by Joseph T. Shaw. The stories Shaw published showed crime unsentimentally, and many of his authors became famous, notably DASHIELL HAMMETT. Shaw edited *The Hard-Boiled Omnibus: Early Stories from Black Mask* (1946). In 1953 *Black Mask* was taken over by the *Ellery Queen Mystery Magazine* and made a "tough 'tec" department of that magazine. It features "the detective hero of the rough-tough, guts-gore-and-gals school." See HARD-BOILED FICTION.

Blackmur, Richard [Palmer] (b. Springfield, Mass., Jan. 21, 1904—d. Feb. 2, 1965), poet, critic. Though Blackmur had no academic background, early in life he became editor of the *Hound and Horn*, a periodical on arts and letters published in Cambridge, Mass. He was awarded an honorary Litt. D. by Rutgers University and became known as a leading American critic. His criticism, though not prolific, has enduring qualities; it is tough, vigorous, and honest. Perhaps because of its quiet tone it is, however, less widely known than that of other literary critics whose stature does not match Blackmur's. He was given a Guggenheim Fellowship (1936–38), and is a member of the National Institute of Arts and Letters. Among his books: DOUBLE AGENT (1935), *The Expense of Greatness* (1940), *The Second World* (1942), *Language and Gesture* (1952), *The Lion and the Honeycomb* (1955), *Anni Mirabiles, 1921–25* (1956), *Valve in Modern Poetry* (1957).

Black Oxen (1923), a novel by GERTRUDE ATHERTON. The novelist chose a theme, then very popular, of glandular rejuvenation for this story. The Countess Zattiany, a former American belle, returns from Hungary looking twenty-eight, although actually fifty-eight, as a result of a glandular operation. Mrs. Atherton skillfully weaves in, as well, the theme of a Jekyll-Hyde double personality.

Black Riders and Other Lines, The (1895), a collection of poems by STEPHEN CRANE. The enigmatic title of this work found its genesis in a boyhood experience of Crane's. After watching the waves beat against the shore at Ocean Grove, N.J., he dreamed of black riders on black horses riding out of the surf. The dream was frightening, and the somber image remained with him.

Inspired by Emily Dickinson's poetry but not modeled upon it, *The Black Riders* and other poems of Crane derive their cadence and sometimes their framework from the Bible, as Amy Lowell was first to observe. Hamlin Garland saw another source in Olive Schreiner's *Dreams.* Crane's poems are similar, in many respects, to the free verse of W. E. Henley, Emily Dickinson, and Walt Whitman. Crane was regarded as a second Whitman. The *Nation* spoke of the poems as "at once Whitman condensed and Dickinson expanded. . . ." In substance and in structural pattern, as Professor James M. Cox has pointed out, Crane's poems frequently parallel Bunyan's *The Pilgrim's Progress.*

One half of the *Black Riders* poems are epigrammatic parables, bearing a close resemblance to the parable-poems of Ambrose Bierce. Crane's epigrammatic poems provide a bridge from Bierce to the first imagist anthologies and the early epigrammatic verse of Ezra Pound. Amy Lowell said that Crane was no poet; nevertheless it was he who anticipated the very program she took over from Pound and T. E. Hulme. Crane heralded and to some degree influenced the poetic renaissance of 1912.

The Black Riders (reissued in London in 1896) was dedicated to Hamlin Garland.

Blacksmith, The Learned. See ELIHU BURRITT.

Black Thunder (1935), a novel by ARNA BONTEMPS. The hero, Gabriel Prosser, is a slave in the days of the French Revolution who participates in several rebellions.

Blaine, James G[illespie] (b. W. Brownsville, Pa., Jan. 31, 1830—d. Jan. 27, 1893), politician, author. Blaine founded the Republican party in Maine, served as congressman, senator, and secretary of state, and was nominated for the Presidency by ROBERT G. INGERSOLL in a speech (June 15, 1876) that called him "a plumed knight." This phrase became a campaign slogan in 1876 and when he ran against Cleveland in 1884. But his opponents called him "the Tattooed Man," with reference to a famous cartoon by Bernard Gillam in *Puck* (April 16, 1884); in this he was depicted in a robe inscribed with the many scandals associated with his name. In the 1884 campaign he was defeated by another slogan, "Rum, Romanism, and Rebellion." He appears as Senator Ratcliffe in HENRY ADAMS' *Democracy* (1880). His autobiography is *20 Years in Congress* (1884–86).

Blair, James (b. Scotland, [?], 1655—d. April

18, 1743), clergyman, university president, author. Blair, a deputy to the Bishop of London, in whose diocese Virginia was included, founded the College of William and Mary and was named its president "during his natural life." He delivered many sermons which in published form brought him wide praise; in particular his 117 discourses on *Our Saviour's Divine Sermon on the Mount* (5 vols., 1722).

Blair, Walter (b. Spokane, Wash., April 21, 1900—   ), professor, author, editor. Blair, who has been a member of the faculty at the University of Chicago since 1929, has written widely on American literature, particularly American humor and folk themes: *Two Phases of American Humor* (1931); *Mike Fink, King of Mississippi Keelboatmen* (with F. J. MEINE, 1933), the first of their two books about this folk hero's exploits; NATIVE AMERICAN HUMOR, *1800–1900* (1937; revised, 1960); HORSE SENSE IN AMERICAN HUMOR (1942); *Tall Tale America: a Legendary History of our Humorous Heroes* (1944); *Davy Crockett: Truth and Legend* (1955); *Half Horse, Half Alligator: The Growth of the Mike Fink Legend* (with F. J. Meine, 1956); *Mark Twain and "Huck Finn"* (1960).

Blake, Harrison Gray Otis (b. Worcester, Mass., April 10, 1816—d. [?], 1898), letter writer, editor. Blake's fame rests on his friendship with Henry David Thoreau. After Thoreau's death, he took the thirty-nine blank-books of Thoreau's journal and made selections from them in four volumes (1881–92); Bradford Torrey edited the complete *Journals* in fourteen volumes in 1906.

Bland, James A. (b. Flushing, N.Y., Oct. 22, 1854—d. May 5, 1911), minstrel, song writer. Bland wrote Virginia's state song, *Carry Me Back to Old Virginny* (1875), and about seven hundred other ditties, including *O Dem Golden Slippers* and IN THE EVENING BY THE MOONLIGHT. J. J. Daly wrote his biography, *A Song in His Heart* (1951).

Blanshard, Brand (b. Fredericksburg, Ohio, Aug. 27, 1892—   ), teacher, writer. Blanshard studied at the University of Michigan, Columbia, and Harvard. He taught in many universities, and was Chairman of the Department of Philosophy at Yale. He was the author of *The Nature of Thought* (2 v., 1940), and co-author of *Philosophy in American Education* (1945) and *Preface to Philosophy* (1946). He edited *Education in the Age of Science* (1959). *Reason and Analysis* is in preparation.

Blazed Trail, The (1902), a novel by STEWART EDWARD WHITE. Carl Van Doren described this as an escape from civilization to the thrilling rigors of Michigan lumber camps. The book, written from personal experience, brought White favorable notice.

Bleecker, Ann Eliza (b. New York City, Oct., 1752—d. Nov. 23, 1783), poet, novelist. Mrs. Bleecker's hardships during the Revolutionary War were reflected in her melancholic poems, collected in *The Posthumous Works of Ann Eliza Bleecker* (1793). She also composed a novel in letter form, THE HISTORY OF MARIA KITTLE (1797), about an American woman captured by Indians during the French and Indian War.

Blennerhassett, Harman (b. England, Oct. 8, 1765—d. Feb. 2, 1831), associate of Aaron Burr in his alleged conspiracy to invade Mexico. Blennerhassett left England because he had married his niece, then against British law. In 1805 he became Burr's associate, was arrested, and was released without trial; he returned to England financially ruined. *The Blennerhassett Papers* were edited by William H. Safford in 1864. Blennerhassett appears prominently in Charles Felton Pidgin's novel, *Blennerhassett, or, The Decrees of Fate* (1901).

Blind Bow-Boy, The (1923), a novel by CARL VAN VECHTEN. This novel about homosexuality is called by Irene and Allen Cleaton, in *Books and Battles* (1937), "the most fantastic example of the shock brigade" of books which marked the troubled and sensational 1920's.

Blind Raftery (1924), a novel by DONN BYRNE. The story of the Gaelic poet, Anthony Raftery (1784?–1835), who taught that "certain things one believes to be good are but vulgar selfish things. . . . And we learn to be kind."

Blithedale Romance, The (1852), a novel by NATHANIEL HAWTHORNE. Brook Farm, the transcendentalist experiment in communal living in which Hawthorne took part, formed the basis for *The Blithedale Romance*, and provided the atmosphere and mood to create a world "essentially a day-dream" between fiction and reality. Some facets of the personality of MARGARET FULLER, an occasional visitor to the farm, and of FANNY KEMBLE are evident in the character of Zenobia.

The narrator, Miles Coverdale, often considered a persona for Hawthorne himself, is the central dramatic character; and the world of Blithedale is seen through his eyes. His inability to become part of the life around him, even to his being separated physically by his illness, emphasizes the isolation which is the central theme of the book. Coverdale sees important scenes from windows, or while hiding in a tree. He intellectualizes everything, and is incapable of taking life as it comes. The book concludes with his realizing his love for Priscilla when she is no longer attainable.

Around Miles revolve the other characters. Zenobia, the exotic, dark, queenly woman often seen in Hawthorne's books (HESTER PRYNNE in THE SCARLET LETTER and Miriam in THE MARBLE FAUN) has romantic conceptions of life and her place in it which cause her to commit suicide when reality intrudes. Set off against Zenobia is her half-sister, Priscilla, blonde, innocent, and under the influence of the one truly malignant character in the book, Westervelt, the mesmerist.

Hollingsworth, the ex-blacksmith with schemes for prison reform, often occupies the center of the action because he most obviously illustrates the theme of isolation. Hollingsworth finally alienates his friend Coverdale, and, ironically, is only saved when he abandons his dreams and accepts an earthbound marriage with Priscilla.

The romance is a meaningful blend of reality and the world of the characters' imaginations—a complex unfolding of characters who, in turn, reveal the narrator and themselves.

Blitzstein, Marc (b. Philadelphia, March 2, 1905—d. Jan. 22, 1964), playwright, composer, pianist. As musician and writer Blitzstein has experimented widely with formal techniques and has frequently dealt with proletarian themes. His works include: *I've Got the Tune* (radio songplay, 1937); parts of THE CRADLE WILL ROCK (opera, 1937); *No for an Answer* (opera, 1941); an adaptation of Kurt Weill's *Threepenny Opera* (1952).

Blix (1899), a novel by FRANK NORRIS. An autobiographical work, *Blix* is the love story of Condé ("Condy") Rivers, a struggling newspaperman, and "Blix" Bessemer, a rich girl. Their marriage becomes possible only when Condy is offered a job with an eastern magazine (actually *McClure's*).

Blockade, The (performed 1775), a play by SIR JOHN BURGOYNE. Burgoyne wrote the play to amuse his fellow-Britishers in Boston. He made fun of the rebels, played down the British peril. A performance on Jan. 8, 1776, was broken up by sudden word that the Americans were attacking at Bunker's Hill. Later, an anonymous playwright (not MERCY OTIS WARREN, to whom it was once attributed) retorted with another farce, *The Blockheads* (1776), satirizing Sir William Howe's unsuccessful attempt to take Dorchester Heights. See AMERICAN REVOLUTION.

Blood, Benjamin Paul (b. Amsterdam, N.Y., Nov. 21, 1832—d. Jan. 15, 1919), poet, philosopher. Blood early began composing long philosophical poems. A mystical experience resulting from inhaling nitrous oxide (laughing gas) in a dentist's chair started him on strange lines of thought which led him to repudiate monism and adopt pluralism. WILLIAM JAMES called Blood's book *The Anaesthetic Revelation and the Gist of Philosophy* (1874) one of the "stepping-stones" of his own thinking, and wrote *A Pluralistic Mystic* in his praise. Blood's *Pluriverse* was published posthumously (1920). See PLURALISM.

Blood for a Stranger (1942), a volume of poems by RANDALL JARRELL. Jarrell's first collection of poetry shows his indebtedness to the English metaphysicals and the contemporary poet W. H. AUDEN. His poems tend to be cerebral rather than emotional, and deal largely with a kind of brave defeatism and negation. Many critics found his poetry sensitive and promising.

Bloomer, Amelia [Jenks] (b. Homer, N.Y., May 27, 1818—d. Dec. 30, 1894), reformer, editor. Mrs. Bloomer wrote articles advocating reforms in education, marriage laws, suffrage, and dress. She herself wore loose trousers which came to be called "bloomers." She founded *The Lily*, a feminist temperance magazine (1849–56).

Bloomsgrove Family, Memoirs of the (1790), a novel by ENOS HITCHCOCK. The second American novel published in book form, it has a meager plot told in a series of letters. Hitchcock's main aim was to set up a model for domestic education and promote "the dignity and importance of the female character."

Bloudy Tene[n]t of Persecution, The (1644), a tract by ROGER WILLIAMS. In this Williams attacked the ideas of JOHN COTTON, who replied in *The Bloudy Tene[n]t Washed and Made White in the Bloud of the Lamb* (1647); Williams counter-attacked in *The Bloudy Tene[n]t Yet More Bloudy* (1652). Williams carries the argument for religious freedom far beyond Locke's doctrines. He urges that just as magistrates have no right to interfere in church government, so the clergy have no call to meddle with the magistracy.

B.L.T. Initials signed to BERT LESTON TAYLOR's famous column in the Chicago *Tribune*.

Blue and the Gray, The (*Atlantic Monthly*, Sept., 1867), a poem by FRANCIS MILES FINCH. These sentimental verses immortalizing the Civil War uniforms were presumably occasioned when women of Columbus, Miss., strewed flowers over the graves of both Union and Confederate dead. A play of the same title was written for Harrigan (see EDWARD HARRIGAN) and Hart (1875); it was also the title of a song by PAUL DRESSER.

Blue-Backed Speller, Webster's. See NOAH WEBSTER.

Blue Hotel, The (1899), a short story by STEPHEN CRANE. A Swede comes to a Nebraska hotel, expects to meet wild life in the West, himself creates a brawl, and is killed. Who is to blame, the Swede himself or the men he quarreled with? One of the characters remarks, "Every sin is the result of a collaboration." H. L. Mencken compares this story to the best of Kipling and Conrad in its "austere economy . . . brilliant dramatic effect . . . profound dignity." This story appears in the collection THE MONSTER AND OTHER STORIES.

Blues: A Magazine of New Rhythms, a monthly, was published from February, 1929 to the fall of 1930 at Columbus, Miss. It was edited by Charles Henri Ford, who was only sixteen years old at the time. *Blues* published the first magazine work of James T. Farrell, Erskine Caldwell, Kay Boyle, and others.

blues, the. See JAZZ.

Blue Voyage, The (1927), a novel by CONRAD AIKEN. It effectively describes the people and incidents of a transatlantic voyage, largely in the stream-of-consciousness technique.

Bly, Nellie. A pseudonym of ELIZABETH C. SEAMAN.

Blythe, Samuel G[eorge] (b. Geneseo, N.Y., May 19, 1868—d. July 17, 1947), newspaperman, memoirist. The best known of his articles was a series for *The Saturday Evening Post*, "Who's Who—and Why," which set a model for later "profiles" of prominent personalities. Among his books: *The Making of a Newspaperman* (1912); *We Have with Us Tonight* (1918); *A Calm Review of a Calm Man*, about Warren G. Harding (1923); *Reformers, Ltd.* (1928).

Boas, Franz (b. Germany, July 9, 1858—d.

Dec. 21, 1942), anthropologist. One of the world's greatest authorities in anthropology, anthropometry, and linguistics, Boas received many honorary degrees, served as official of numerous organizations. *Changes in Bodily Form of Descendants of Immigrants* (1912), in which he showed the influence of environment on so-called racial traits, was one of his most influential special studies. *The Mind of Primitive Man* (1911) changed common conceptions regarding the mentality of primitive peoples, whom Boas had studied intensively. One of his final studies was *Anthropology and Modern Life* (1928; rev., 1932). His life and influence are described in M. E. Herskovits' *Franz Boas* (1953).

Bobbsey Twins, The. The two leading characters in a series of sentimental but once highly popular books for children by Laura Lee Hope.

Bodenheim, Maxwell (b. Hermanville, Miss., May 26, 1893—d. Feb. 6, 1954), poet, novelist, playwright. Bodenheim came to New York City in his early twenties and lived in or near there for most of his life. He came to a tragic end: he and his third wife were found murdered in a dingy, heatless room. He began as a poet, wrote plays and essays, then published a series of novels, at least one of which (*Replenishing Jessica*) was suppressed for salacity. Alfred Kreymborg comments: "An artist wrote the poems, plays, and essays; an economic opportunist wrote the novels." His poetry falls into stages. At the beginning he followed the imagists, the romanticists, the naturalists; later he was ridden by social causes. In between he wrote his best poems, mature in technique and not too strident or aggressive. This "Mississippi Hamlet" (as Kreymborg called him) was always an ardent and implacable hater; he spoke his mind freely, sometimes too freely, on persons, ideas, and objects, including Ben Hecht (once an intimate friend), Harriet Monroe (who gave him his first hearing, and from whose magazine *Poetry* he received a prize in 1939), and Babette Deutsch (a fellow poet). It is said that he appeared as a character in Hecht's *Count Bruga* (1926), and took quick revenge in *Ninth Avenue* (1926). (Hecht had the last word, a not unkindly one, in his *drame à clef, Winkelberg,* 1958, written after Bodenheim's death.) The poet's main collections were *Advice* (1920), *Introducing Irony* (1922), *The Sardonic Arm* (1923), *Against This Age* (1929), *Bringing Jazz* (1930), and *Selected Poems, 1914–1944* (1946).

Body of Liberties. Code of laws drawn up by NATHANIEL WARD and adopted by the General Court of Massachusetts in December, 1641, as the first written laws of the colony.

Bogan, Louise (b. Livermore Falls, Me., Aug. 11, 1897—d. Feb. 4, 1970), poet, critic. Influenced by the English metaphysical poets, Miss Bogan's poetry is subtle, restrained, intellectual. She received two prizes from *Poetry,* and many critics have praised her warmly. She has published several collections: *Body of This Death* (1923); *Dark Summer* (1929); *The Sleeping Fury* (1937); *Poems and New Poems*

(1941); and *Collected Poems* (a co-winner of the Bollingen Prize, 1954). She has also written much criticism of a high order, especially her poetry reviews for *The New Yorker*. Her historical review of *Achievement in American Poetry, 1900–1950* appeared in 1951, and *Selected Criticism: Poetry and Prose* in 1955.

Bojer, Johan. Author of THE EMIGRANTS [1].

Bok, Edward W[illiam] (b. the Netherlands, Oct. 9, 1863—d. Jan. 9, 1930), editor, essayist, autobiographer. Bok was brought to the United States at the age of six, and began working for the Brooklyn *Eagle* when he was thirteen. Experience in the magazine field and with a syndicate service he founded brought him an offer in 1889 to edit THE LADIES' HOME JOURNAL. He married the publisher's daughter, Mary Louise Curtis, became one of the most successful magazine editors in the world, and retired in 1919.

Bok was a man of the most sublime self-confidence and egotism. He was his own hero, said his fellow editor Ellery Sedgwick; "and he habitually wrote of himself in the third person: 'Bok,' just that." He composed his autobiography, *The Americanization of Edward Bok* (1920), in that style. Yet as editor of *The Ladies' Home Journal* Bok practically revolutionized the American home. He offered a huge variety of services to his readers, particularly in connection with the care of babies and the appearance of houses. His suggested architectural plans were so extensively used that the architect Stanford White proclaimed Bok the greatest single influence for good in the architectural profession. He was also deeply interested in music and in movements for world peace, tried to communicate these interests to his readers, and provided liberal endowments for both causes. He did not like the women's clubs of his day, and ultimately persuaded clubwomen to devote more time to cultural interests and civic affairs. He campaigned against venereal disease, billboards, and the common drinking cup. Bok also published volumes of "inspirational" and platitudinous essays such as *Successward* (1890) and *Dollars Only* (1926).

Boker, George Henry (b. Philadelphia, Oct. 6, 1823—d. Jan. 2, 1890), poet, playwright. Boker wrote many plays in verse, but only FRANCESCA DA RIMINI (produced, 1855; published, 1856) won much critical success. He also wrote excellent sonnets and other lyrics. He showed great ability as minister to Turkey (1871–75) and Russia (1875–79). In Philadelphia he helped to edit LIPPINCOTT'S MAGAZINE, and did much to encourage young writers and to restore the city to literary eminence.

Bolinvar (1937; reissued, 1944), a novel by Marguerite Bayliss. A readable story of two cousins, laid in the early 19th century. One cousin comes into possession of a deadly secret affecting his kinsman, but refuses to use it to his own selfish advantage. The story culminates in a tremendous fox hunt, which starts in the Old Dominion and continues for forty-five hours across Pennsylvania and into New Jersey for well over two hundred miles; some hardy hunters, to verify Miss Bayliss' story, once rode the same long trail.

Bollingen Prize. Beginning in 1949 the Library of Congress instituted an annual series of awards in the arts with money provided by the Bollingen Foundation, a philanthropic trust created by Paul Mellon, Yale Class of 1929. A distinguished panel of "Fellows in American Letters of the Library of Congress" awarded the prize to EZRA POUND, "the author of the book of verse which, in the opinion of the jury of selection, represents the highest achievement of American poetry in the year for which the award is made" (in this case 1948) for *The Pisan Cantos*, Cantos 74–84 of his long work. The jury consisted of Conrad Aiken, W. H. Auden, Louise Bogan, Katherine Garrison Chapin, T. S. Eliot, Paul Green, Robert Lowell, Katherine Anne Porter, Karl Shapiro, Allen Tate, Willard Thorp, Robert Penn Warren, Leonie Adams, and Theodore Spencer. The poems had been written after the war in Pisa, Italy, where Pound was incarcerated before being transported to the United States to stand trial for treason. (He had been indicted on July 26, 1943, as a result of his propaganda broadcasts for Mussolini.) A controversy ensued over the advisability of honoring Pound with an award. As a result the Bollingen Foundation canceled further prizes in any field of the arts. Debate raged in the newspapers, magazines big and little, and throughout the world of letters. The strongest attack on the award and on Pound was an article by Robert Hillyer in the *Saturday Review of Literature*. This was answered by *The Case Against the SRL*, published by *Poetry* magazine. The debate may be followed in *A Casebook on Ezra Pound* (1959) which contains articles, newspaper reports, selections from the poems, and an extensive bibliography of the case. No final verdict was reached; the literary community remained divided and, in some cases, embittered. Archibald MacLeish saw the debate as part of the effort of each literary age to define the function of poetry; in *Poetry and Opinion* (1950) he expressed his thoughts in the context of a dialogue, in an effort to salvage something positive from the bitter controversy. In 1950 it was announced that the annual Bollingen Prize for Poetry would be awarded by Yale University Library. The recipients of the $1,000 prize have included America's most distinguished living poets: Wallace Stevens, John Crowe Ransom, Marianne Moore, Archibald MacLeish and William Carlos Williams, W. H. Auden, Leonie Adams and Louise Bogan, Conrad Aiken, Allen Tate, E. E. Cummings, Theodore Roethke, Delmore Schwartz, and Yvor Winters. In 1961, the Bollingen Foundation established a translation prize. It was awarded for the first time to Robert Fitzgerald, poet and translator, for his rendering of Homer's *Odyssey*.

Bolton, Isobel [pen name of **Mary Britton Miller**] (b. New London, Conn., August, 1883—   ), poet, novelist. A review by Edmund Wilson of *Do I Wake or Sleep* brought Isobel Bolton into the literary limelight. He wrote in the *New Yorker:* "She has learned from the school of Henry James . . . the device of the sensitive observer who stands at the center of the action and through the filter of whose consciousness alone the happenings of the story reach us." Critics spoke of her prose as having the poetic impressionism of Virginia Woolf: ". . . of being precise, packed with feeling, faultlessly accented in its elaborate rhythms." Her chief works: *Songs of Infancy* (1928); *Menagerie* (1928); *Without Sanctuary* (1932); *Intrepid Bird* (1934); *In the Days of Thy Youth*, an autobiographical novel (1943); *The Crucifixions* (1944); *Do I Wake or Sleep* (1946); *The Christmas Tree* (1949); *Many Mansions* (1952); *Give a Guess* (1957); *All Aboard* (1958); *A Handful of Flowers* (1958); *Jungle Journey* (1959).

Bon-Bon (1835), a story by EDGAR ALLAN POE. An earlier version of this story of a contest between a man and the devil was called *The Bargain Lost* (1832). At the climax of the story the devil, to prove a point, shows the hero a receipt for the soul of Voltaire.

Bond, Carrie Jacobs (b. Janesville, Wis., Aug. 11, 1862—d. Dec. 28, 1946), story writer, essayist, poet, song writer. Mrs. Bond published numerous collections, among them *Path o' Life* (1909), *Tales of Little Cats* (1918), *Tales of Little Dogs* (1921), *Little Monkey with a Sad Face* (1930), *The End of the Road* (1941). She compiled *Old Melodies of the South* (1918) and wrote her autobiography in *Roads of Melody* (1927). She contributed syndicated articles to newspapers, under the heading "Friendly Preachments." But Mrs. Bond became most famous for her songs set to her own music, particularly *A Perfect Day* and I LOVE YOU TRULY.

Bonifacius (1910), an essay by COTTON MATHER, later known as *Essays to Do Good*. Benjamin Franklin wrote to Cotton Mather's son Samuel that his father's essay "gave me such a turn of thinking as to have an influence on my conduct through life." Herbert W. Schneider, in *A History of American Philosophy* (1946), calls Mather "a pompous old theocrat who . . . went about from house to house 'doing good' wherever he suspected the presence of vice." He claims that Franklin's letter was a joke, and that Franklin ridiculed Mather under the pen name Mrs. Silence Dogood (1722) and later in the BUSYBODY PAPERS (1729).

Bonner, Sherwood. The pen name of KATHERINE MACDOWELL.

Bonney, William H. See BILLY THE KID.

Bonsal, Stephen (b. Baltimore, Md., March 29, 1865—d. June 8, 1950), newspaperman, diplomat, author. Bonsal served the New York *Herald* as war correspondent (1885–1907), and watched the Madero revolution in Mexico in 1910–11 for the New York *Times*. He was in the United States diplomatic service and on special missions from 1893 to 1919, in particular with the American mission to the Versailles Peace Conference. His important contributions to the analysis of international affairs include: *The Real Condition of Cuba* (1897); *The American Mediterranean* (1912); *Unfinished Busi-*

ness, Paris-Versailles 1919 (1944, awarded a Pulitzer Prize); *Suitors and Suppliants* (1946).

Bontemps, Arna [Wendell] (b. Alexandria, La., Oct. 13, 1902—   ), teacher, editor, writer. His writing has identified him with a movement often called the "Negro Renaissance." Among his books: *God Sends Sunday* (1931); BLACK THUNDER (1935); *Drums at Dusk* (1939); *Story of the Negro* (1948); *One Hundred Years of Negro Freedom* (1961). In collaboration with COUNTEE CULLEN he dramatized *God Sends Sunday* as a musical called *St. Louis Woman* (1946), which was produced in New York. He edited *Golden Slippers: An Anthology* (1941), and *Father of the Blues* (W. C. Handy's compositions, 1941). In collaboration with Langston Hughes he wrote *The Poetry of the Negro* (1949) and *The Book of Negro Folklore* (1958).

Bookbinder, Herbie. See THE CITY BOY.

book clubs. Book clubs had already existed in Germany when Harry Scherman hit on the idea of the Book-of-the-Month club in 1926. Those in Germany, however, sold their own low-priced reprints of the classics. Scherman's venture, organized for distribution only, was to be a clearing house between publisher and reader. Since it was selected by a distinguished board of literary judges, the book of the month was bound to be one of the most worthwhile, recent publications. The club was and has continued to be highly successful. It has found many imitators.

At first, book clubs were often charged by American booksellers with unfair competition. The clubs answered this charge with the claim that selling books to thousands by mail stimulated a market for books in areas where there was a limited number of retail booksellers. It has been estimated that by mid-20th century book clubs accounted for 30% of the total book sales in the United States. Because of their widespread memberships, they are considered a dominant influence in the making of a best seller.

Aside from book clubs that fall into the category of mass distributors, there are many small, select clubs catering to the interests of special groups, such as farmers, yachtsmen, and religious denominations.

Among the best-known mass distributors, following along the lines of the Book-of-the-Month club are the Literary Guild, the Junior Literary Guild, the Book Find Club, the Atlantic Monthly Book Club, the Catholic Children's Book Club, the Negro Book Club, the Teen Age Book Club, the Family Reading Club, the Heritage Club, and the Mid-Century Book Society.

book fairs. The first book fair in this country, so far as is known, was put on in the 1920's by Marshall Field & Co. in Chicago. It was a great success, with a hundred thousand visitors flocking to view the manuscripts of Daisy Ashford, Tennyson, Kipling, and Mark Twain, a $3,500 jewel-encrusted edition of Keats, and other treasures of bibliophiles. The biggest hit was EDGAR A. GUEST, who autographed until

his arm was lame. Since then book fairs, authors' luncheons, forums of literary persons, and similar events have been sponsored by the book trade to stimulate sales.

Bookman, The. A magazine of which the first issue was published in February, 1895, with Professor HARRY THURSTON PECK of Columbia University as editor; it ceased publication in 1933, after Seward Collins had made it an organ for the so-called NEW HUMANISM. Among other editors of *The Bookman* were ROBERT CORTES HOLLIDAY, JOHN FARRAR, and BURTON RASCOE. Some lively controversies were conducted in its columns, as when Hugh Walpole replied vigorously to H. L. Mencken's charge that American books were not sufficiently appreciated in England, and when Heywood Broun debated censorship with John S. Sumner, secretary of the New York Society for the Suppression of Vice. In the days of Farrar, Broun was a frequent reviewer for the magazine, and among other contributors were Robert Benchley, Sidney Howard, Laurence Stallings, Donald Ogden Stewart, Corey Ford, and Herschel Brickell. See R. S. BAKER, BEST SELLER.

Book of Annandale, The (1902), a story in blank verse by EDWIN ARLINGTON ROBINSON, part of the collection called CAPTAIN CRAIG. A man has promised his dying wife never to marry again; a wife has given the same assurance to her dying husband. The two survivors fight a spiritual battle with their consciences, but life wins out. Robinson also wrote a sonnet, HOW ANNANDALE WENT OUT (1910), which tells how a physician, tending a friend and finding him "a wreck, with hell between him and the end," makes use of "a slight kind of machine," apparently a hypodermic, and puts him out of his misery.

Book-of-the-Month Club. Launched in 1926 this, the most famous of all American book clubs, was organized by Harry Scherman, who has directed it ever since, and who is presently the chairman of the board of directors. The first book selection, distributed to 4,750 members in April, 1926, was *Lolly Willowes* by Sylvia Townsend Warner. By the end of the year, membership had grown to 40,000; two years later, in April, 1928, membership stood at 100,000; it reached a peak of 918,000 members in 1946. By 1949 the organization had distributed more than 100 million books. Selections have been of a remarkably high level: they have included several books by Pulitzer Prize winners, among them Stephen Vincent Benét's *John Brown's Body*, Pearl Buck's *The Good Earth*, Margaret Mitchell's *Gone with the Wind*, Robert Frost's *A Further Range*, Carl Van Doren's *Benjamin Franklin*, Carl Sandburg's *Abraham Lincoln*, Arthur Miller's *Death of a Salesman*, A. B. Guthrie, Jr.'s *The Way West*, and others by such Nobel Prize winners as John Galsworthy, Sigrid Undset, Sinclair Lewis, Thomas Mann, Eugene O'Neill, Winston Churchill, William Faulkner, Ernest Hemingway. The Book-of-the-Month Club distinguished itself from its German forerunners by setting up a board of judges to choose its book selections. These judges have always been eminent literary men: the first were Henry Seidel Canby, William Allen White, Dorothy Canfield Fisher, Heywood Broun, and Christopher Morley. At present, they are John Mason Brown, Basil Davenport, Clifton Fadiman, and Gilbert Highet. In the beginning, the twelve books selected each year had to be accepted by subscribers; later, choices were permitted from a constantly increasing list. In time, too, "dividend books" were sent to subscribers, giving them, in effect, a further reduction in prices. Without question, the Book-of-the-Month Club has promoted in the United States the sale and reading of an astounding number of books. It has never claimed to select consistently the "best" books; many outstanding books are of too special an interest for the club's large membership. These books, however, have regularly been listed in the *News*, the club's publication which was first issued in April, 1926. In it are discussed not only the club's chief selection, but also many other books recommended for excellence by the board of judges. Charles Lee has written *The Hidden Public, The Story of the Book-of-the-Month Club* (1958). See BOOK CLUBS.

book publishing in the United States. Stephen Daye printed the first book in British North America, the BAY PSALM BOOK at Cambridge (1640). In the 1760's Philadelphia eclipsed Boston as a publishing center, but the latter forged ahead again in the 1840's and helped primacy until well on in the 19th century, when New York City took and maintained the lead. Meanwhile religious books began to be superseded by books on politics, travel, philosophy, and practical matters, as well as by poetry and fiction.

For at least three centuries North American publications were inevitably British, either by importation or by imitation. Usually, when English books were reprinted in America, they were pirated editions from which the author derived no monetary profit. American authors were similarly pirated in England; no copyright protection existed until 1891. One effect of the copyright law has been, in general, favorable to American writers, since there no longer exists the temptation to publish foreign books for which no royalties need be paid. One other effect has been to encourage the establishment in this country of branches of English publishing firms.

The first publishers were printers who issued a book, probably always at the author's expense, with no particular pride. Daniel Appleton in 1825 was a dry-goods merchant who first carried books as a sideline, later became an important influence on American culture. Book publishing today is an immensely competitive business. With the decades many firms have disappeared or have merged with other firms. Some publishers put out annual lists of new books running into the hundreds; others are content with more modest and perhaps more rigidly selected offerings. Book clubs and reprint houses have materially increased the possibilities of

wide sales. A good list, carefully established over the years, has often furnished a backlog of steady sales very useful in dull times. Despite the tremendous competition from movies, television, and sports, book reading has gone up steadily as leisure time has increased in recent years.

Publishing in the United States follows some definite patterns. "Trade books" are those for general reading. There are also textbooks, reference works, technical and vocational volumes, juvenile books, religious publications, medical books, reprints, and other specialties. Occasionally a publishing firm may combine one or more of these and may also publish magazines. Some firms specialize in what are called "vanity publications," that is, books published at the author's expense. Many universities now sponsor presses which issue scholarly works that sometimes reach a circulation large enough to pay for the expenses of publication.

A calculation made by Savoie Lottinville at the University of Oklahoma in 1947 shows a total of 819 publishing agencies in the United States that had issued at least one book. Of these 266 represented 88 per cent of all titles. New York City was the location of 377, including most of the major publishers; Chicago claimed 66; the Boston-Cambridge area, 49; Los Angeles and its area, 31; Philadelphia, 30; Washington, D.C., 27. In 1949 a Book Industry Committee of the Book Manufacturers' Institute stated that in 1945 438,000,000 books had been produced in the United States.

In 1949 PUBLISHERS' WEEKLY noted some significant changes in the book trade over half a century. Trade organizations were firmly established, modern business techniques were increasingly employed, the book club idea had secured a firm grip on the industry, subsidiary markets (film, radio, television, reprint rights) had assumed increasing importance, book advertising had become more colorful and expert, world markets for American books had increased, the government made more and more use of books in war and peace, libraries had multiplied the demand for trade and technical books, children's book publishing had expanded, university presses had grown, censorship had been fought with considerable success on many fronts, fair trade practices had improved stability in the trade, book production had undergone enormous improvements in technology and design. A number of universities now offer courses in publishing and editing procedures.

The publisher and his flock of authors have in the meantime become figures of curiosity for the general public. The authors themselves are placed on exhibit, as a matter of business promotion, at book fairs, autographing sessions in book stores, and cocktail parties for critics and others of supposed influence. Some sensational novels have been written about writers in their business relations with publishers, literary agents, and publicity men, including Barry Benefield's *April Was When It Began* (1939); Mary Roberts Rinehart's *A Light in the Window*

(1948); Cleveland Amory's *Home Town* (1950); William Murray's *Best Seller* (1956); Hallie Burnett's *The Brain Pickers* (1957). Two earlier books depicting an almost idyllic age were Christopher Morley's classic tales PARNASSUS ON WHEELS (1917) and *The Haunted Bookshop* (1919). Other useful books on publishing include George H. Doran's *Chronicle of Barabbas* (1935, 1953); *The Bookman's Glossary* (1951); Hellmut Lehmann-Haupt's *The Book in America* (with others, 1952); Madeleine Stern's *Imprints on History* (1956); Chandler B. Grannis' symposium, *What Happens in Book Publishing* (1957).

Boomerang, The. A daily newspaper founded by EDGAR WILSON NYE at Laramie, Wyoming. Many of Nye's pieces (signed "Bill Nye") first appeared in *The Boomerang* and established his reputation as a humorist. His first book was called *Bill Nye and Boomerang* (1881).

Boone, Daniel (b. near Reading, Pa., Nov. 2, 1734—d. Sept. 26, 1820), frontiersman. Boone's father moved to the Yadkin River in North Carolina, where his son learned to love hunting and exploring and became an expert marksman. In 1760 he made his way through the wilderness to what later became Tennessee. He heard glowing talk of "the dark and bloody wilderness" soon to be called Kentucky, and with five companions explored that country for two years. Returning home, he persuaded his family to move to Kentucky, and a party set out to make a settlement. Some were killed, but the others reached their destination and founded Boonesborough on the magnificent Kentucky River. During the Revolutionary War Boone helped the colonists, and at one time was captured by the British and carried to their post at Detroit, from which he escaped to help his people when he heard that an Indian attack on Kentucky was imminent. Like the old Puritans and many of the frontiersmen Boone despised lawyers and the law, and as a consequence twice forfeited great land possessions, once by failing to register his holdings in Kentucky and so losing them all. In disgust he moved to Spanish territory near St. Louis; and later was again evicted from his holdings. But this time they were restored to him by Congress (1814), in view of his great services in opening up the wilderness. There in Missouri he died, surrounded by his descendants to the fifth generation.

Boone, the mild-mannered, courageous pioneer, became legendary even in his lifetime. He seems to have dictated an account of his exploits to John Filson, who inserted it in his *Discovery, Settlement, and Present State of Kentucky* (1784). Soon after his death Byron celebrated him in *Don Juan* (1823) as a kindly child of nature, loving the wilderness and fleeing civilization. Boone has been a favorite of novelists and biographers ever since. Cooper found in him the prototype of his NATTY BUMPPO, and he has appeared in many stories, notably Winston Churchill's THE CROSSING

(1904) and Stewart Edward White's *The Long Rifle* (1932).

Booster, The. A magazine, in French and English, originally published in Paris under the supervision of the American Country Club as an aid to tourists; a good part of the magazine consisted of travel advertisements. In September, 1937, HENRY MILLER and a group of his friends took over the magazine and made it a vehicle for their advanced literary, social, and biological views. Protests from the former owners brought about a hasty withdrawal of advertising. In April, 1938, the name was changed to *Delta;* with the Christmas issue the magazine expired.

Booth, Edwin [Thomas] (b. Bel Air, Md., Nov. 13, 1833—d. June 7, 1893), actor, son of JUNIUS BRUTUS BOOTH. He was acclaimed as an actor in the United States and abroad. His frequent playing of tragic roles was matched by the tragedy of his own career, particularly his brother's killing of President Lincoln. Eleanor Ruggles wrote an excellent biography of him called *Prince of Players* (1953); the Players Club in New York is rich in memorials of him as he made his home there in his last years.

Booth, General William, Enters Heaven. See GENERAL WILLIAM BOOTH ENTERS HEAVEN.

Booth, John Wilkes (b. Bel Air, Md., Aug. 26, 1838—d. April 26, 1865), actor, son of JUNIUS BRUTUS BOOTH and brother of EDWIN BOOTH. He had been successful in Shakespearian roles when he conceived his insane intention to assassinate President Lincoln; he was either killed, or committed suicide.

Booth, Junius Brutus (b. London, 1769—d. 1852), one of the famous family of American actors. He came to the United States in 1821 and made many tours of the country, usually in romantic dramas of violence and bloodshed.

Boothe, [Ann] Clare. See CLARE BOOTHE LUCE.

Boots and Saddles, or, Life in Dakota with General Custer (1885), by ELIZABETH B. CUSTER. This book is a vivid account of life with the noted cavalry leader, related by his wife.

Borden, Lizzie (b. Fall River, Mass., July 19, 1860—d. June 1, 1927), indicted as a murderess. She was charged with the axe-murder (Aug. 4, 1892) of her father and stepmother in Fall River, Mass., and her trial was followed with eager interest all over the country. She was acquitted, but the murder became the theme of several ballads and poems that failed to accept the verdict, also of an anonymous but widely quoted quatrain: "Lizzie Borden took an axe/ And gave her mother forty whacks;/ When she saw what she had done,/ She gave her father forty-one." Three full-length plays—Donald Blackwell's *Lizzie* (1930); John Colton's *Nine Pine Street* (1933); Reginald Lawrence's *The Legend of Lizzie* (1959)—as well as a one-act play (*Goodbye, Miss Lizzie Borden*, 1947, by Lillian de la Torre), were based on the case; also two novels, Mark E. Wilkins Freeman's *The Long Arm* (1895) and Lily Dougall's *The Summit House Mystery* (1905). Charles and Louise Samuels' *The Girl in the House of Hate*

(1953) and Edward D. Radin's *Lizzie Borden: The Untold Story* (1961) are nonfiction. *Fall River Legend* (1948), is a ballet by Agnes de Mille.

Border Romances. Novels by WILLIAM GILMORE SIMMS, giving a sensational, mainly unrealistic picture of life on the southern border. Among them were: GUY RIVERS (1834), a successful story of a fiendish Georgia bandit; *Richard Hurdis* (1838) and its sequel, *Border Beagles* (1840); BEAUCHAMPE, OR, THE KENTUCKY TRAGEDY (1842); the highly sensational *Charlemano* (1856).

Borglum, [John] Gutzon [De La Mothe] (b. near Bear Lake, Ida., March 25, 1870—d. March 6, 1941), sculptor. Borglum studied art in San Francisco and Paris. In 1904 he won a gold medal at the Louisiana Purchase Exposition with a bronze group, *The Mares of Diomedes*, now in the Metropolitan Museum, N.Y. His sculptures are found in such places as the Capitol in Washington and the Cathedral of St. John the Divine in New York City, but he is chiefly famous for his massive group of four great American leaders on Mount Rushmore, S.D. (See BLACK HILLS.) Woodrow Wilson appointed him in World War I to make an official investigation of our aircraft production, and he designed a sea wall and bridge for Corpus Christi, Tex. Robert J. Casey and Mary Borglum wrote *Give the Man Room: The Story of Gutzon Borglum* (1952).

Borland, Hal [Harold Glen] (b. Sterling, Neb., May 14, 1900—   ), newspaperman, author. Borland's youth was spent on a Colorado ranch. His brief editorials in the *New York Times* on rural life attracted wide attention. Some were republished in *Life;* a larger group were published, with illustrations by noted artists, as *The American Year* (1946). *High, Wide and Lonesome* (1956) is his own story of his boyhood. *Amulet* (1957) is a love story woven into a Civil War western, but well above the average of this genre. Other books: *This Hill, This Valley* (1957); *The Enduring Pattern* (1959); *The Seventh Winter* (1960); and *The Dog Who Came to Stay* (1961). Borland has also written under the pseudonym of Ward West.

Boss, The [1] (1903), a novel by ALFRED H. LEWIS based on the practices of corrupt big-town politicians.

Boss, The [2] (produced 1911, published 1917), a play by EDWARD SHELDON. Sheldon mingles the story of Michael Regan, a corrupt contractor and politician, with what ultimately turns out to be a love affair between Regan and the daughter of a fine family; she eventually marries him to save her father. Regan was based on James ("Fingy") Connors of Buffalo, N.Y.

Boston (1928), a novel by UPTON SINCLAIR. An elderly woman, one of the Boston BRAHMINS, suffers pangs of social conscience and goes to work in a factory, where she becomes acquainted with Sacco and Vanzetti. (See SACCO-VANZETTI CASE.) As the battle between industry and labor increases in intensity, she observes at close range the world-shaking events following the arrest of the two men for murder and their trial, appeal,

and execution. The book seethes with indignation; it partly follows the transcript of the trial record.

Boston Adventure (1944), novel by JEAN STAFFORD. In this admirable first novel Miss Stafford paints the Boston scene as perceived by Sonia, daughter of immigrants. Into a confused milieu, the old-time Puritan city, modified by degeneration of the old stock and the influx of newcomers whom the old-timers find socially and economically unacceptable, Sonia, a girl of strange moods, injects an exciting element. The witty dialogue searches out many weaknesses of the American as well as the Boston scene.

Boston Athenaeum. Founded 1805 as a reading room by the ANTHOLOGY CLUB, the Athenaeum has become a Boston institution. The building (constructed 1845) houses a large and excellent library, available to scholars and others.

Boston Cooking-School Cook Book (1896), by Fannie Merritt Farmer. The author suffered a paralytic stroke while in high school and had to give up college. On her graduation from the Boston Cooking-School in 1889, she was given the post of assistant to the principal, went on to become head of the school, and in 1902 founded her own school. She was constantly active in originating and improving recipes, and established an indispensable element in directions: the principle of level measurements. Her book has been frequently revised (1930, 1936, 1941, 1946); by 1946 2,531,000 copies had been published. The first edition made no mention of vitamins or calories and provided for twelve-course dinners. More recent editions include details from the science of nutrition, many simple meals, charts and illustrations, directions on freezing foods.

Boston Gazette, The. Two newspapers by this name appeared during the 18th century in New England. The first ran from 1719 to 1741, and was either the second or third newspaper to appear in the English colonies; the second was published from 1755 to 1798. The earlier *Gazette* was printed by JAMES FRANKLIN, but he lost the contract in 1721 and founded THE NEW ENGLAND COURANT, as radical and outspoken as the *Gazette* was conservative and reserved. The later *Gazette* was an organ of the Revolutionary party. To it JOHN ADAMS [2] contributed in 1775 some of his most notable papers.

Boston Hymn (1863), a poem by RALPH WALDO EMERSON. The poem celebrates freedom, exalts labor, denounces kings and aristocrats; it is one of Emerson's most fervid, most American utterances.

Bostonians, The (1886), a novel by HENRY JAMES. Satirically, James portrays a strong-minded Boston woman, Olive Chancellor, representing a new generation of "do-gooders," who takes life hard and is interested above all in the emancipation of women. She finds or thinks she finds a kindred soul in a beautiful and impressionable girl, Verena Tarrant, and the plot turns on the domination of one woman by the other. The theme was suggested by Alphonse Daudet's *Evangeliste* (1883), but James intended it to be at the same time "a tale very characteristic of our social conditions." Bostonians attacked the novel angrily as a false portrayal of their city, and American critics in general (William Dean Howells was a notable exception) censured James for his lack of local feeling. It was in fact one of the first American novels to deal more or less explicitly with Lesbianism. James omitted it from the definitive New York edition of his novels.

Boston Miscellany of Literature and Fashion (1842–1843). Founded apparently as an off-shoot of *Arcturus,* a critical magazine, the *Miscellany*'s contributors included Poe and Lowell.

Boston News-Letter. JOHN CAMPBELL, Boston postmaster, was actively interested in conservative politics. On April 24, 1704, he founded a newssheet, at first handwritten, called *Boston News-Letter,* credited with being the first newspaper in America. JOHN DRAPER became its editor and publisher in 1733, his son Richard its publisher in 1762. News of events abroad was garnered somewhat belatedly from English newspapers as they arrived in Boston. Young Draper changed the name first to *Boston Weekly News-Letter,* later to *The Massachusetts Gazette and Boston News-Letter.* Two years after Draper's death the newspaper ceased publication (Feb. 22, 1776); it had been for a time the only paper published during the British occupation of Boston, having espoused the Tory side.

Boston Public Latin School. Founded April 13, 1635, the first public school in America and a pioneer in the United States public school system.

Boston Quarterly Review (1838–42). A personal organ for ORESTES BROWNSON, who filled its pages mainly with his own writings. It reflected his chameleon changes of opinion in religion and politics. In 1842 he merged the magazine with the *Democratic Review.* In 1844, when this magazine declined to print any more of his contributions, he founded *Brownson's Quarterly Review,* which he edited until 1875.

Both Your Houses (1933), a play by MAXWELL ANDERSON. An exposé of corruption among congressmen, as revealed in an attempt to pass a large appropriations bill laden with graft. An idealistic young congressman gets evidence to make the corruption clear, but finds that the father of the young woman he is in love with is among the congressmen involved, even if unintentionally. The play won a Pulitzer Prize.

Botkin, B[enjamin] A[lbert] (b. Boston, Feb. 7, 1901—   ), teacher, editor. Botkin, a writer in the field of American folklore, has said: "I like to think of myself as a Bostonian by birth, an Oklahoman by adoption, and a New Yorker by preference; a teacher and researcher by temperament, and a popularizer by persuasion." He has published these works: *The Southwest Scene* (1931); A TREASURY OF AMERICAN FOLKLORE (1940); *A Treasury of New England Folklore* (1947); *A Treasury of Southern Folklore* (1949); *A Treasury of American Anecdotes* (1957); *The Illustrated Book of American Folklore* (with Carl Withers, 1958); *A Civil War Treasury of Tales, Legends and Folklore* (1960). See also FOLK-SAY; A REGIONAL MISCELLANY.

Bouchards, the. A family engaged in munitions manufacturing who play a prominent role in TAYLOR CALDWELL's *Dynasty of Death* (1938) and several later novels. The narrative begins in 1837, closes during World War II.

Boucher, Jonathan (b. England, March 12, 1738—d. April 27, 1804), clergyman, lexicographer. Boucher came to Virginia as rector of a parish and to conduct a private school. As rector at Annapolis he founded the Homony Club, a genteel literary organization. He was frank to express his loyalist sentiments in sermons as well as in conversation. In 1775 he returned to England, and there published thirteen sermons as *A View of the Causes and Consequences of the American Revolution;* he held that a good Christian would necessarily be a good subject of the British monarch. The book was dedicated to his old neighbor, General Washington.

After Boucher's death his friends published (1807) *A Glossary of Archaic and Provincial Words,* intended to supplement Samuel Johnson's *Dictionary;* he had worked on this book for thirty years. This covered part of "A"; in 1832 material up to "Bl" was published, and then the work stopped. In the latter volume is a list of thirty-eight Americanisms gathered by Boucher, also a pastoral, *Absence.* Boucher predicted that Americans would break away in speech as in government from England.

Boucicault, Dion (b. Ireland, Dec. 26, 1820—d. Sept. 18, 1890), actor, playwright. Boucicault (originally Dionysius Lardner Boursiquot) had already established his reputation in England as a skillful playwright when he came to

the United States in 1853. His first play, *London Assurance,* was produced when he was only nineteen and was a great success. His first important production in this country was *Grimaldi,* or, *The Life of an Actress* (New Orleans, 1855), in which he and his wife, as did later E. A. Sothern and Julia Marlowe, appeared. He dramatized French stories and two stories by Dickens, based another play, THE OCTOROON (1859), on Mayne Reid's novel, *The Quadroon* (1856), collaborated with JOSEPH JEFFERSON on RIP VAN WINKLE (1865). But his specialty in time became plays with Irish settings: *The Colleen Bawn* (1860); *Arrah-na-Pogue* (1864); *The Shaughraun* (1874); and others. In *Arrah-na-Pogue* Boucicault took an old tune, *The Wearing of the Green,* and wrote new words to it; this led to the universal use in Ireland of a sprig of shamrock as a symbol of love of Erin. In 1860 Boucicault inaugurated the first touring company to appear on the road in a single play. W. F. Taylor calls him "a director-playwright with a genius for theatrical effect." *The Octoroon* was successfully revived in 1960.

Boudinot, Elias [1] (b. Philadelphia, May 2, 1740—d. Oct. 24, 1821), public official, author. Boudinot became active in New Jersey politics, served in the Continental Congress, was elected its president in 1782, proclaimed a Day of Thanksgiving (1783), became a representative in Congress (1789–1805), was Director of the Mint (1805–1821). He founded the American Bible Society (1816) and was active in the education of Indians and deaf-mutes. (See next entry.) He wrote several books on religion, including *The Age of Revelation* (1801), a refutation of Tom Paine's THE AGE OF REASON (1794). George Adams Boyd wrote *Elias Boudinot, Patriot and Statesman* (1952).

Boudinot, Elias [2] (b. Georgia, 1803?—d. June 22, 1839), editor. A Cherokee, called Galagina ("Buck Deer") in his own tongue. Boudinot was educated at a mission school in Cornwall, Conn.; he adopted the name of Elias Boudinot as an act of gratitude to the school's patron. In 1823 he helped translate the New Testament into Cherokee, in 1828 became editor of *The Cherokee Phoenix,* first newspaper printed for an Indian tribe (suppressed in 1835 because it criticized the official Washington attitude toward the Cherokees), in 1833 published a novel, *Poor Sarah, or, The Indian Woman.* Meanwhile the Cherokees continued to suffer one grave injustice after another from the federal government and from the state of Georgia, and in 1838 were driven off their lands, on which gold had been discovered. Boudinot, under unfortunate influence, signed a treaty which agreed to this removal, and was assassinated soon after his arrival in Indian Territory, now Oklahoma.

Bought and Paid For (1911), a play by GEORGE BROADHURST. A frank discussion of marriage and its problems, the play's most effective character is an amusing boaster who brings about the reconciliation of a husband and wife.

Bound East for Cardiff (1916), one-act play by EUGENE O'NEILL. This play, presented by the PROVINCETOWN (Mass.) PLAYERS at Wharf Theater, was the first production of O'Neill's to reach the stage. It gives the last moments in the life of the seaman Yank, who is dying from a fall on the British tramp steamer *Glencairn.* John Gassner calls it "a lyric picture of death."

Bourinot, Arthur S[tanley] (b. Ottawa, Ont., Oct. 3, 1893—), poet. Called "the poet laureate of the Laurentians," Bourinot's verse exhibits a pleasing variety, from short odes to historical epics. His *Collected Poems* (1947) includes poetry written from 1914 to 1946.

Bourjaily, Vance [Nye] (b. Cleveland, Ohio, Sept. 17, 1922—), novelist, editor. Until his rather bawdy, semi-autobiographical *Confessions of a Spent Youth* (1960), Bourjaily was known only to a small audience. He had been editor of the influential magazine DISCOVERY, and had attracted some attention with his long novel *The Violated* (1958). In 1959 he lectured in South America on contemporary United States literature for the State Department. His first novel, *The End of My Life* (1947), the story of a young man's moral and mental disintegration during the war, deserves more attention than it received. *The House of Earth* appeared in 1953.

Bourke-White, Margaret (b. New York City, June 14, 1906—), photographer, editor. Since 1927 she has done industrial and news photography in thirty-four countries, winning the American Woman of Achievement Award in 1951. She is famous for the books done in collaboration with writer ERSKINE CALDWELL, her former husband: *You Have Seen Their Faces* (1937), one of the first books successfully to combine the techniques of journalism and photography; *North of the Danube* (1939); and *Say! Is This the U.S.A.?* (1941). Her own work (text as well as pictures) includes *Eyes on Russia* (1931); *U.S.S.R.: A Portfolio of Photographs* (1934); *Shooting the Russian War* (1942); and *Halfway to Freedom, A Study of the New India* (1949). She has been associated with FORTUNE and LIFE magazines as editor and war correspondent.

Bourne, Randolph [Silliman] (b. Bloomfield, N.J., May 30, 1886—d. Dec. 22, 1918), essayist. An early accident made Bourne a helpless cripple with a twisted face for the rest of his life. After an unhappy childhood he entered Columbia University on a scholarship and later, on another scholarship, traveled and studied in Europe. He became a radical in education and politics, hating war and detesting the society around him. For a time he wrote for *The New Republic,* but his articles expressed his views so acidly that his services were dispensed with; thereafter Bourne found it difficult to earn a living. His conversation was even more striking and impressive than his writings. His early death cut short a promising career that would have been devoted to the uncompromising preaching of liberty and human welfare. Among his books: *Youth and Life* (1913); *The Gary Schools* (1916); *Education and Living* (1917); and *Untimely Papers* (1919). Van Wyck Brooks, an intimate of Bourne's, edited *The History of a Literary Radical* (1920, reprinted 1956). Carl and Mark Van Doren said of him that "he saw human existence as a sort of drama in which hopeful youth is pitted against cynical age." In memory of him James Oppenheim wrote a fine elegy, *For Randolph Bourne* (1919).

Bowditch, Nathaniel (b. Salem, Mass., March 26, 1773—d. March 17, 1838), mathematician, authority on navigation. Self-educated, Bowditch discovered an error in Newton's *Principia Mathematica* (1686, 1687) and translated the first four volumes of Laplace's *Traité de Mécanique Céleste* (1799–1825). He made five sea voyages; setting out to revise J. Hamilton Moore's *Practical Navigator*, he wrote *The New American Practical Navigator* (1802, frequently revised). This book, which Van Wyck Brooks says "saved countless lives and made American ships the swiftest that ever sailed," helped make possible the astounding achievements of the Yankee clippers, and is still in use.

Bowen, Catherine [Shober] Drinker (b. Haverford, Pa., Jan. 1, 1897—   ), writer. Mrs. Bowen wrote first about music, later a history of Lehigh University (1924), finally a series of fictionalized biographies: of Tchaikovsky (*Beloved Friend*, 1937); of Anton Rubinstein (*Free Artist*, 1939); of Justice Oliver Wendell Holmes (YANKEE FROM OLYMPUS, 1944). The last was a great popular success, but was somewhat less well received by critics. *John Adams and the American Revolution* (1950) appeared to some critics too close to fiction in technique. *The Lion and the Throne* (1957) is a biography of Sir Edward Coke. She has also written *Adventures of a Biographer* (1959).

Bower, B[ertha] M[uzzy] (b. Cleveland, Minn., Nov. 15, 1871—d. July 23, 1940), writer of western stories. Writing merely under initials, Mrs. Bower managed to lure countless male readers into believing her a man, probably a literary cowboy. Her first book, *Chip of the Flying U* (1904), was one of her best. She continued to publish two books a year for many years, including *The Lonesome Trail* (1909), *Casey Ryan* (1921), and *The Flying U Strikes* (1934).

Bowers, Claude [Gernade] (b. Hamilton Co., Ind., Nov. 20, 1878—d. Jan. 21, 1958), ambassador, historian. Bowers, always deeply interested in American politics, frankly espoused the Democratic party in many of his activities. Among his best-known books: *The Party Battles of the Jackson Period* (1922); *Jefferson and Hamilton* (1925); *The Tragic Era: The Revolution after Lincoln* (1929); *Jefferson in Power: The Death Struggle of the Federalists* (1936); *The Young Jefferson* (1945); *My Mission to Spain* (1954); *Chile Through Embassy Windows* (published posthumously, 1958).

Bowery, The. An old and wide street in New York City, extending northward from Chatham Square to the junction of Third and Fourth Avenues at Cooper Union. It ran originally through part of Peter Stuyvesant's farm (the Dutch *bouwerij*, "farmstead," is from *bouwer*, "farmer"). During the 19th century it became a street of dance halls, beer gardens, dives, and cheap theaters. The inhabitants of the Bowery were believed to be impudent rascals of the lower classes with a remarkable dialect of their own. Aside from an early play, *A Glance at New York* (1848), which depicted Bowery characters, the street first became literature in Stephen Crane's MAGGIE, A GIRL OF THE STREETS (1893) and in his novelette, GEORGE'S MOTHER (1893). In 1900 they were published as *Bowery Tales*. A little later Edward W. Townsend, a friend of Crane, gave a more popular and less literary picture of the district in a series of stories that began with *Chimmie Fadden, Major Major Max, and Other Stories* (1895). See FADDEN, CHIMMIE. Charles Hoyt's A TRIP TO CHINATOWN (produced, 1891) made the Bowery famous, both as a street and as a song. The song tells of the various scrapes a yokel gets into when he hits the Bowery and includes the famous line, "The Bowery! the Bowery! I'll never go there any more!" The area has become New York City's skid row. When in 1947 owners of property along the street were given a chance to change its name, they rejected the proposal—by a narrow margin.

Bowles, Chester [Bliss] (b. Springfield, Mass., April 5, 1901—   ), advertising executive, diplomat, writer. Bowles left his highly successful advertising agency and entered political life in 1948 when he was elected governor of Connecticut. Later, as U.S. Ambassador to India, he did much to promote good will between the two countries. In 1960 he was appointed Under Secretary of State. Among his books: *Tomorrow Without Fear* (1946); *Ambassador's Report* (1954); *Waging the Peace* (1955); *New Dimensions of Peace* (1955); *Africa's Challenge to America* (1957); *Ideas, People, and Peace* (1958); and *The Coming Political Breakthrough* (1959). His daughter Cynthia wrote an engaging and friendly book, *At Home in India* (1956), when she was fifteen.

Bowles, Paul (b. New York City, Dec. 30, 1910—   ), composer, novelist. His early interest was music and for a brief time he studied with Aaron Copland. He has written both orchestral and ballet music; his opera, *The Wind Remains,* for which García Lorca wrote the libretto, was presented in 1943 at the Museum of Modern Art in New York City. At one time Gertrude Stein discouraged him from writing, but later she changed her mind about him. By this time he had already embarked on a literary career. His writing was allied to that of other spokesmen for an ever-renewing "lost generation." Much of his work is set in Morocco, where he lived for many years. Among his books: *The Sheltering Sky* (1949), *The Delicate Prey* (1950), *Let It Come Down* (1952), *The Spider's House* (1955), *Yallah* (1956), *The Hours After Noon* (1959—London). His wife, Jane Bowles, wrote a play, *The Summer House,* which was produced in New York City in 1954 and starred Judith Anderson.

Bowles, Samuel (b. Hartford, Conn., June 8, 1797—d. Sept. 8, 1851) and **Bowles, Samuel** (b. Springfield, Mass., Feb. 9, 1826—d. Jan. 16, 1878), newspaper editors. The elder Bowles founded the influential Springfield *Republican,* still edited by one of his descendants. His son published several travel books based on letters printed in The *Republican,* among them *Across the Continent* (1865) and *The Switzerland of America* (1869), later combined as *Our New West* (1869).

Bow of Orange Ribbon, The (1886), a novel of New York when it was still New Amsterdam, by AMELIA E. BARR.

Boyd, Ernest [Augustus] (b. Ireland, June 28, 1887—d. Dec. 30, 1946), critic. Boyd's international ancestry and background, his strong enthusiasms and prejudices, are reflected in his books, including: *Ireland's Literary Renaissance* (1922); *Studies in Ten Literatures* (1925); *H. L. Mencken* (1925); *Literary Blasphemies* (1927); *The Pretty Lady* (1934). His wife, Madeleine Boyd, wrote a novel about him, *Life Makes Advances* (1939).

Boyd, James (b. Dauphin Co., Pa., July 2, 1888—d. Feb. 25, 1944), novelist. His spirited and authentic novels of American history include DRUMS (1925); MARCHING ON (1927); LONG HUNT (1930); *Roll River* (1935); *Bitter Creek* (1939). He also wrote *Eighteen Poems* (1944) and the posthumously published *Old Pines and Other Stories* (1952).

Boyd, Julian [Parks] (b. Converse, S.C., Nov. 3, 1903—   ), teacher, historian, librarian. Boyd taught at the University of Pennsylvania, was head of several historical societies, and was made librarian of Princeton but resigned (1952) to teach history. He has edited (1938) Indian treaties originally printed by Benjamin Franklin and made a study of the Declaration of Independence. The latter was in preparation for a sixty-volume edition of the *Papers of Thomas Jefferson,* edited by Boyd, which Princeton University began to publish in 1950.

Boyd, Nancy. A pseudonym of EDNA ST. VINCENT MILLAY, used on the title page of a series of sketches, *Distressing Dialogues* (1924).

Boyd, Thomas Alexander (b. Defiance, Ohio, July 3, 1898—d. Jan. 27, 1935), newspaperman, novelist, biographer. Boyd fought as a marine in World War I and chronicled his experiences in a novel, *Through the Wheat* (1923). *In Time of Peace* (1928) depicted an ex-sergeant after the war as a hard-drinking newspaper reporter. He also wrote biographies of the renegade SIMON GIRTY, ANTHONY WAYNE, and LIGHT-HORSE HARRY LEE.

Boy Emigrants, The (1876), a story for younger readers by NOAH BROOKS. It describes incidents on an overland journey from New England to the Pacific coast.

Boyesen, Hjalmar Hjorth (b. in Norway, Sept. 23, 1848—d. Oct. 4, 1895), teacher, philologist, novelist. Boyesen came on a visit to the United States in 1869, intending to stay only a little while, but the interest William Dean Howells showed in a story about Norwegian life, GUNNAR, that he had written and then its serial publication in the *Atlantic Monthly* (published in book form, 1874) caused him to take up permanent residence in this country. He taught at Urbana University, Cornell, and Co-

lumbia. He published several scholarly books, among them *Essays on Scandinavian Literature* (1895). His books for young people were widely read and are still readable, particularly *Boyhood in Norway* (1892). Toward the end of his life

he turned to realistic fiction: *The Mammon of Unrighteousness* (1891); *The Golden Calf* (1892); and *The Social Strugglers* (1893).

Boyle, Kay (b. St. Paul, Minn., Feb. 19, 1903—   ), novelist, short-story writer, poet. Miss Boyle contributed first to the "little magazines," particularly *Broom* and *transition.* Her poetry is excellent and her novels often have a pleasant poetic tinge. Her earlier fiction tends to be psychological, under the Jamesian influence; some of her later works pay more attention to plot. Among her books: *Wedding Day* (1931); *The White Horses of Vienna and Other Stories* (1936); *Avalanche* (1944); *American Citizen* (a poem, 1944); *1939* (1948); *His Human Majesty* (1949); *The Seagull on the Step* (1955); *Generation without Farewell* (1959).

Boy Life on the Prairie (1899), a semi-fictional idyl by HAMLIN GARLAND. Much of the book later formed part of A SON OF THE MIDDLE BORDER (1914, 1917).

Boy Meets Girl (produced, 1935; published, 1936), a satire on Hollywood screen-writers by BELLA and SAMUEL SPEWACK. According to Brooks Atkinson, "The two scribbling pranksters who turn comic handsprings through the play were suggested by the fantastic Hollywood behavior of Ben Hecht and Charles MacArthur. . . . Mr. Hecht and Mr. MacArthur are not easily impressed by big industry, and they do not take Hollywood seriously. . . ."

Boynton, Henry W[alcott] (b. Guilford, Conn., April 22, 1869—d. May 11, 1947), teacher, critic, editor. Boynton ably edited many classics for use in schools, and in collaboration with THOMAS WENTWORTH HIGGINSON prepared *A Reader's History of American Literature* (1903). He published *Literature and Journalism, and Other Essays* (1904) and *Annals of American Book-Selling* (1932).

Boynton, Percy H[olmes] (b. Newark, N.J., Oct. 30, 1875—d. July 8, 1946), teacher, critic. Long associated with the University of Chicago (1903–1941); his books include *Some Contemporary Americans* (1924), *More Contemporary Americans* (1927), *The Rediscovery of the Frontier* (1931), *Literature and American Life* (1936), *The American Scene in Contemporary Fiction* (1940).

Boys, The (published in *The Atlantic Monthly*, February, 1859), an anniversary poem by OLIVER WENDELL HOLMES celebrating a reunion of his 1829 class at Harvard.

Boys from Syracuse, The (1938), a farce by LORENZ HART, with music by Richard Rodgers. Supposedly based on Shakespeare's *Comedy of Errors*, it was nevertheless as American and modern as possible.

Boy's Will, A (1913), poems by ROBERT FROST. This was Frost's first book, first published in England (an American edition appeared in 1915). The collection established the poet's reputation immediately. The title comes from Longfellow's line in *My Lost Youth:* "A boy's will is the wind's will."

Brace, Gerald Warner (b. Islip, L.I., N.Y., Sept. 20, 1901—   ), novelist, teacher. Gerald Brace studied architecture but turned to writing and teaching English at various colleges —Williams, Dartmouth, Harvard, and Boston University, among others. Although he has written only of New England, he cannot be called simply a regional writer; his scope is broader. He has written: *The Islands* (1936); *The Wayward Pilgrims* (1938); *Light on a Mountain* (1941); THE GARRETSON CHRONICLE (1947), which some critics acclaimed as the best novel of that year; *A Summer's Tale* (1949); *The Spire* (1952); *The World of Carrick's Cove* (1957); *Winter Solstice* (1960).

Bracebridge Hall, or, The Humorists (1822), forty-nine tales and sketches by WASHINGTON IRVING. The book is a continuation of THE SKETCH BOOK, with more gently romantic or Gothically melancholic narratives. Their background is sometimes American, sometimes French or Spanish, frequently English. Irving gives a pleasing but highly idealized picture of English rural scenes and rural existence. *Bracebridge Hall* greatly enhanced his reputation abroad.

Brackenridge, Hugh Henry (b. Scotland, 1748—d. June 25, 1816), clergyman, lawyer, editor, writer. Brackenridge was five when his family emigrated to America. At Princeton he met JAMES MADISON, collaborated with PHILIP FRENEAU on a commencement poem, *The Rising Glory of America* (1772). During the war he was a chaplain and an ardent advocate of the revolutionary cause. After the war religious doubts caused him to abandon the ministry and become a lawyer. In the frontier town of Pittsburgh he helped to found *The Pittsburgh Gazette* (1786), the first newspaper in that community; he also established its first bookstore and its first school. He spoke ardently for the adoption of the Constitution and favored the

rebels in the Whiskey Rebellion of 1793. He became a leader in the Republican (later Democratic) Party, and during his last years was a justice of the Pennsylvania Supreme Court. His most famous work is a remarkable comic novel, MODERN CHIVALRY (1792–1815). In this, as in his political and legal activities, he shows himself a believer in balance, against aristocratic pretensions and democratic shams alike.

Brackenridge's son, **Henry Marie** (May 11, 1786—Jan. 18, 1871), editor and writer of travel books, was a pioneer in the discussion of United States–South American relations. His views in *South America* (1817) helped to mold the Monroe Doctrine. A lawyer by vocation, he practiced as far west as St. Louis, keeping a journal that helped Irving when he wrote ASTORIA (1836). Byron first heard of Daniel Boone when he read Brackenridge's *Views of Louisiana* (1814). See BATTLE OF BUNKERS HILL.

Brackett, Charles (b. Saratoga Springs, N.Y., Nov. 26, 1892—d. March 9, 1969), screenwriter, director, producer. Much of Brackett's successful Hollywood career was carried out in collaboration with Billy Wilder. Often they directed and produced, as well as wrote, their screenplays, which include *Bluebeard's Eighth Wife* (1938), *Ninotchka* (1939), *Ball of Fire* (1942), *The Major and the Minor* (1942); *Five Graves to Cairo* (1943); *The Lost Weekend* (1945), for which he and Wilder received awards for the best screenplay of the year from the Motion Picture Academy; *A Foreign Affair* (1948); *Sunset Boulevard* (1950), adjudged Best Story and Screenplay for 1950; *Titanic* (1953), for which they again shared a similar award; *Journey to the Center of the Earth* (1959). Brackett was drama critic of *The New Yorker* for three years and also wrote a number of novels, among them: *The Counsel of the Ungodly* (1920); *Week-End* (1925); *Entirely Sur-*

rounded (1934), a *roman à clef* about Alexander Woollcott and his island colony on Lake Bomoseen, Vt.

Bradbury, Ray [Douglas] (b. Waukegan, Ill., Aug. 22, 1920—   ), fiction writer. Bradbury specializes in unearthly, fantastic tales, classified as science-fiction, which have made their way into the "best short story" collections of the day. *Punch*, reviewing an English edition of *The Illustrated Man* (1951), said that the tales "raise Bradbury to a secure place among the imaginative writers of today." Among his other books: *Dark Carnival* (1947); *The Martian Chronicles* (1950); *The Golden Apples of the Sun* (1953); *Fahrenheit 451* (1953); *The October Country* (1955); *Switch on the Night* (1955); *Dandelion Wine* (1957); *A Medicine for Melancholy* (1959). Bradbury has also written plays and movie and radio scripts, including the screenplay of John Huston's film version of *Moby Dick*.

Bradford, Gamaliel (b. Boston, Oct. 9, 1863— d. April 11, 1932), biographer, poet, dramatist. A descendant of Governor William Bradford, Gamaliel inherited frailty of health and financial competence from his mother. He composed about two thousand poems (some gathered in three volumes), wrote fifteen plays (only one printed and none produced), kept a journal running to 1,400,000 words, one-seventh of which appeared after his death as *The Journal of Gamaliel Bradford* (edited by Van Wyck Brooks, 1933). To these should be added his "spiritual autobiography," *Life and I* (1928) and a selection from his thousands of letters, *Letters, 1918–1931* (1934).

In a score of volumes he collected 114 character sketches that he called "psychographs"— his major works. This term had been used by H. A. Taine (1828–1893) to describe the verbal portraits of the great French critic, Sainte-Beuve (1804–1869). Bradford adopted the word to describe what may be called a motion picture in words, for he sought to give not a static moment of a subject's life but as many moments as possible. These books include: *Types of American Character* (1895); *Lee the American* (1912); *Confederate Portraits* (1914); *Union Portraits* (1916); *Portraits of Women* (1916); *A Naturalist of Souls* (1919); AMERICAN PORTRAITS (1922); *Damaged Souls* (his most popular work, 1923); BARE SOULS (1924); *Soul of Samuel Pepys* (1924); *Wives* (1925); *The Quick and the Dead* (1931); *Elizabethan Women* (1936).

Bradford, Roark ["Whitney Wickliffe"] (b. Lauderdale Co., Tenn., Aug. 21, 1896—d. Nov. 13, 1948), newspaperman, short-story writer, playwright. Bradford served in World War I, then became a newspaperman in Atlanta and New Orleans. A series of stories about Negroes provided material for his first book, OL' MAN ADAM AN' HIS CHILLUN (1928), which was the basis of a very successful play, THE GREEN PASTURES (prepared for the stage by MARC CONNELLY, 1930). *John Henry* (1931), which dealt with the Negro Paul Bunyan, was drama-

tized in 1940 with music by Jacques Wolfe. Other books by Bradford include *Ol' King David an' the Philistine Boys* (1930), *The Three-Headed Angel* (1937), *The Green Roller* (1949).

Bradford, William [1] (b. England, 1590?— d. May 9 [May 19, new style], 1657), governor of Plymouth Colony, historian. Bradford was elected governor of Plymouth Colony in 1621 and was re-elected thirty times, skipping five years when "by importunity I gat off." For his numerous descendants he wrote a HISTORY OF PLIMOUTH PLANTATION, not published until 1856 (by the Massachusetts Historical Society). It has come to be regarded as one of the most important of early American historical works. It was re-edited in 1952 by S. E. Morison, who modernized spelling and punctuation. The first book on the American frontier and on the conquest of the wilderness, it brings the record up to 1646. Other writings of Bradford have been rescued from manuscript form, including some of his letters, a poem, and a *Dialogue Between Some Young Men Born in New England and Sundry Ancient Men That Came out of Holland* (1855). One of his descendants, Bradford Smith, wrote an admirable biography, *Bradford of Plymouth* (1951). See EDWARD WINSLOW; GEORGE MORTON.

Bradford, William [2] (b. England, May 20, 1663—d. May 23, 1752), printer, editor, and publisher for the New Jersey and New York colonies.

Bradford, William [3] (b. New York City, Jan. 19, 1722—d. Sept. 25, 1791), grandson of WILLIAM BRADFORD [2] and "patriot printer" in Philadelphia during the Revolution.

Bradstreet, Anne (b. England, 1612?—d. Sept. 16, 1672), poet. To Mrs. Bradstreet may perhaps be traced the beginnings of the Brahmin tradition of "highbrowism" and of feminine influence in New England and the United States. Brought up in cultured surroundings, she married Simon Bradstreet, and with him and her father, Thomas Dudley, emigrated to the Massachusetts Bay Colony. There both her father and her husband became governors of the colony. She lived at first, rather unhappily, in primitive conditions; later she was able to establish something of a literary circle. Her eight children and the high position of her family kept her very busy, but she managed nevertheless to compose thousands of lines of verse. Without her knowledge her brother-in-law took many of her manuscripts to England and there in 1650 published a volume entitled, in the pretentious fashion of the times, THE TENTH MUSE *Lately sprung up in America. Several Poems, compiled with great variety of Wit and Learning, full of delight . . . By a Gentlewoman in those parts* [namely, New England]. The verses are mostly feeble imitations of the English metaphysical poets, of Edmund Spenser, and of the French Protestant poet, Guillaume de Salluste du Bartas (1544–1590). CONTEMPLATIONS (which appeared in a later edition of *The Tenth Muse*) is generally regarded as the best poem she wrote.

Her poems show a sensitivity to beauty not usually associated with the Puritans. John Berryman wrote a remarkable poem, HOMAGE TO MISTRESS BRADSTREET (1956). See POETRY IN THE U.S.

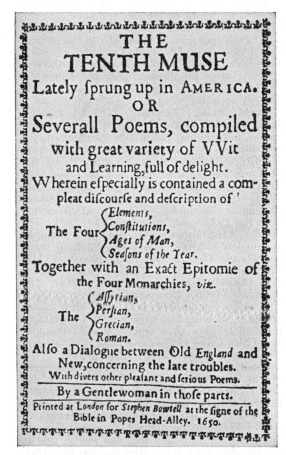

THE
TENTH MUSE
Lately sprung up in AMERICA.
OR
Severall Poems, compiled with great variety of VVit and Learning, full of delight. Wherein especially is contained a compleat discourse and description of
The Four { Elements, Constitutions, Ages of Man, Seasons of the Year.
Together with an Exact Epitomie of the Four Monarchies, viz.
The { Assyrian, Persian, Grecian, Roman.
Also a Dialogue between Old England and New, concerning the late troubles.
With divers other pleasant and serious Poems.
By a Gentlewoman in those parts.
Printed at London for Stephen Bowtell at the signe of the Bible in Popes Head-Alley. 1650.

Brady, Cyrus Townsend (b. Allegheny, Pa., Dec. 20, 1861—d. Jan. 24, 1920), clergyman, novelist. First a graduate of Annapolis and a navy officer, Brady resigned to become a railroad worker in the West, then a minister in various parts of the Middle West and the East. He wrote many historical novels, stories for boys, biographies, and histories. Among his books: *For Love of Country* (1898); *Stephen Decatur* (1900); *Border Fights and Fighters* (1902); *Indian Fights and Fighters* (1904); *Britton of the Seventh* (1914).

Brady, Mathew B. (b. Warren County, N.Y., 1823?—d. Jan. 15, 1896), photographic historian. He published *Gallery of Illustrious Americans* (1850) and is especially known for his *National Photographic Collection of [Civil] War Views* (1870) and his portraits of Lincoln.

Bragdon, Claude Fayette (b. Oberlin, Ohio, Aug. 1, 1866—d. Sept. 17, 1946), architect, poet, philosopher. Bragdon designed railroad stations and other public buildings, also stage sets. Deeply interested in mysticism, he helped translate and publish P. D. Ouspensky's *Tertium*

Organum (1920). His own books include *Architecture and Democracy* (1918), *Old Lamps for New* (1925), *The Eternal Poles* (1930), *More Lives Than One* (autobiography, 1938).

Brahma (1857), a poem by RALPH WALDO EMERSON. In terms of Hindu philosophy Emerson expresses pantheistic doctrine—that God is everywhere, that in seeking Him you have found Him in the very act of seeking.

Brahmins. Oliver Wendell Holmes called the Brahmin caste of New England "the harmless, inoffensive, untitled aristocracy"; the term has come to have a connotation of snobbishness. See ANNE BRADSTREET.

Brainard, John Gardiner Calkins (b. New London, Conn., Oct. 21, 1796—d. Sept. 26, 1828), editor, poet. Brainard won temporary fame with a poem called *Niagara* (1825), supposedly written in twenty minutes. Better-deserved fame comes from his careful researches into the folk legends of Connecticut and his versified accounts of these. His *Literary Remains* were posthumously published, 1832.

Brainerd, David (b. Haddam, Conn., April 20, 1718—d. Oct. 9, 1747), missionary, diarist. After a tense childhood and expulsion from Yale, Brainerd became a missionary to Indians along the Hudson Valley. He was a follower of JONATHAN EDWARDS and his doctrines and was betrothed to Edwards' daughter. In 1747 he died at Edwards' home from tuberculosis. Portions of his diary were published as *Mirabilia Dei inter Indicos* (1746), other sections in *Divine Grace Displayed* (1746). In 1749 Edwards printed additional portions, together with an account of Brainerd's life; in 1768 John Wesley published an abridgment. The diary appeared in full in 1822, again in 1884. It was long regarded as a guide for missionaries. Richard Ellsworth Day told Brainerd's strange story in *Flagellant on Horseback* (1950).

Braithwaite, William Stanley Beaumont (b. Boston, Dec. 6, 1878—d. June 8, 1962), poet. Braithwaite edited successive volumes of an *Anthology of Magazine Verse and Year Book of American Poetry* (1913–29), *A Golden Treasury of Magazine Verse* (1918), *The Book of Modern British Verse* (1919), and other discriminating anthologies. His own excellent verse is collected in *Lyrics of Life and Love* (1904), *Selected Poems* (1948); he also wrote *The House Under Arcturus: An Autobiography* (1941) and an account of the Brontës (1950).

Branch, Anna Hempstead (b. New London, Conn., March 18, 1875—d. Sept. 8, 1937), poet. Miss Branch published *The Heart of the Road, and Other Poems* (1901), *The Shoes that Danced, and Other Poems* (1905), *Rose of the Wind, Nimrod, and Other Poems* (1910), and *Sonnets from a Lock Box and Other Poems* (1929). Her poetry has been both enthusiastically praised and cursorily dismissed. (See NIMROD.) Her noble lyric gift tends to become complicated and is often subdued by moral or social preoccupations. Her best known poem is *The Monk in the Kitchen* (1905) with its famous lines:

Order is a lovely thing;
On disarray it lays its wing,
Teaching simplicity to sing.

Brand, Ethan. See ETHAN BRAND.

Brand, Max. The pseudonym of FREDERICK FAUST.

Brand, Millen (b. Jersey City, N.J., Jan. 19, 1906—   ), novelist, teacher. Brand has taught short-story writing at New York University. His widely-read novel, *The Outward Room* (1937), was dramatized by Sidney Kingsley as *The World We Make* (1939). Among his other writings: *The Heroes* (1939); *Albert Sears* (1947); *Some Love, Some Hunger* (1955).

Brandeis, Fanny. See FANNY HERSELF.

Brandeis, Louis D[embitz] (b. Louisville, Ky., Nov. 13, 1856—d. Oct. 5, 1941), lawyer, jurist, writer. Brandeis practiced law in Boston, acted as counsel without fee for many popular causes, was named for the Supreme Court by Woodrow Wilson, thereafter was a supporter of Justice Oliver Wendell Holmes in developing legal machinery to ensure preservation of traditional American ideals. An old-style liberal, he sometimes upheld the rights of trade unions, sometimes supported industrialists, so that he was often accused of inconsistency and was in turn both despised and loved. He wrote *Other People's Money* (1914), *Business, A Profession* (1914), *The Curse of Bigness* (1934). Solomon Goldman compiled *The Words of Justice Brandeis* (1953) and Alpheus T. Mason wrote *Brandeis, A Free Man's Life* (1946, 1956). Brandeis University, founded in Waltham, Mass., in 1948, was named in his honor.

Branley, Franklyn M[ansfield] (b. New York City, June 5, 1915—   ), educator, writer. His books for younger readers present scientific facts simply and clearly, while helping to keep a sense of wonder alive. With Nelson F. Beeler, Branley has written: *Experiments With Electricity* (1949); *Experiments With Airplane Instruments* (1953); *Experiments With Atomics* (1954). He has also written *Exploring by Satellite* (1957); *The Nine Planets* (1958). *Experiments in Sky Watching* (1959) received the Edison Award for the best children's science book. *The Moon, Earth's Natural Satellite* was published in 1960.

Brann, William Cowper (b. Humboldt, Ill., Jan. 4, 1855—d. April 2, 1898), newspaperman. After following a varied career, Brann turned to newspaper work, first on the St. Louis *Globe-Democrat*, later in Texas. His vituperative editorials resulted in his losing a position with the Houston *Post*, and in July, 1891, he founded a monthly, THE ICONOCLAST, at Austin: he became widely known as "Brann the Iconoclast." The magazine was sold in 1894, together with a printing press, to W. S. Porter (O. HENRY), who changed the name to THE ROLLING STONE. For a while Brann wrote articles for newspapers, then bought back his press and started *The Iconoclast* again, this time at Waco. There he engaged in a bitter controversy with a newspaper editor and with Baylor University. When the newspaper editor and his brother were killed in a pistol battle, Brann was blamed; and on April 1, 1898, a Capt. T. E. Davis opened fire on him; Brann retaliated and both men were fatally wounded.

Brann constantly attacked what he considered frauds and humbugs. He was without doubt the most vociferous and violent defamer in American newspaper annals. In his lifetime were published his *Speeches and Lectures* (1895?), *Potiphar's Wife* (1897), *Brann's Scrap-Book* (1898); after his death *Brann, the Iconoclast* (2 v., 1898–1903) and his *Complete Works* (1919) appeared.

Brant, Irving [Newton] (b. Linn County, Iowa, Jan. 17, 1885—   ), writer on conservation, history, and politics, biographer. Brant was trained as a newspaperman in Iowa from 1909 to 1918; later he wrote editorials for the St. Louis *Star* (1918–1923), the St. Louis *Star-Times* (1930–1938), and the Chicago *Sun* (1941–1943). He is best known for his massive six-volume biography of James Madison begun in 1937 and completed in 1961. His articles often appeared in the *New Republic* and in law journals. The James Madison series consists of: *The Virginia Revolutionist* (1941), *The Nationalist* (1948), *Father of the Constitution* (1950), *Secretary of State* (1953), *The President* (1956), *Commander-in-Chief* (1961). The series has revised historians' ideas about Madison, showing him to be a more forceful and influential figure than was previously thought. Brant also wrote *Dollars and Sense* (1933), and *The Road to Peace and Freedom* (1943).

Brant, Joseph [Indian name: **Thayendanegea**] (b. in what is now Ohio, 1742—d. Nov. 24, 1807), Mohawk Indian chief. Brant attended Eleazar Wheelock's school in Lebanon, Conn., and left as an interpreter for a missionary. Always friendly to the whites, he joined them in many engagements and took the British side in the Revolutionary War. After the war he settled in Canada, and rendered several religious documents into the Mohawk language. It is recorded that when Brant visited England in 1775 and again in 1785 he was eagerly sought after by James Boswell, was painted by George Romney, and dined with the Prince of Wales. He appears in D. W. Griffith's Revolutionary War motion picture, *America* (1924).

Brass Check, The (1919), a treatise by UPTON SINCLAIR. Much of this study of American journalism is autobiographical and relates Sinclair's experiences, usually unfavorable at that date, with newspapers.

Brattle, Thomas (b. Boston, June 20, 1658—d. May 18, 1713), New England merchant. He organized the Brattle Street Church in Cambridge and was treasurer of Harvard from 1693 to 1713. He was a foe of the Mathers, condemned the Salem witchcraft trials, and wrote *A Full and Candid Account of the Delusion Called Witchcraft* (published, 1798). He was an early and able liberal.

Bravo, The (1831), a novel by JAMES FENIMORE COOPER. An Italian in the period of the

Renaissance attempts to fight the Venetian Senate. He pretends to be a bravo, or hired assassin, and accomplishes some good, but in the end is falsely accused of murder and executed. One of Cooper's lesser novels, *The Bravo* seeks to show the superiority of democracy to aristocracy. See THE HEADSMAN; HEIDENMAUER.

Brawley, Benjamin [Griffith] (b. Columbia, S.C., April 22, 1882—d. Feb. 1, 1939), clergyman, teacher, historian. Brawley taught English at several universities, particularly Howard. He wrote on literature, especially on the contributions of the Negro, as in *The Negro in Literature and Art in the U.S.* (1918), *A Social History of the American Negro* (1921), *Paul Laurence Dunbar* (1936), *The Negro Genius* (1937). He edited *Early Negro American Writers* (1935).

Bread and Cheese Club. A club founded in 1822 (possibly a year or two later) by JAMES FENIMORE COOPER. It was limited to thirty-five members, met at first in Washington Hall, New York City (north of City Hall on Broadway), at times in the City Hotel (at Broadway and Thames Street). Among its other members were Chancellor James Kent, Bryant, Halleck, G. C. Verplanck, and S. F. B. Morse. In 1827 some of the members seceded and formed the Sketch Club, later (1847) the CENTURY ASSOCIATION.

Bread Loaf Writers' School and Conference. Under the sponsorship of Middlebury College, in Middlebury, Vt., the school for writers was founded in 1920, the annual conference established in 1925. The conference has been outstandingly successful. From the beginning ROBERT FROST took a warm interest in the conference and helped to make it both friendly and practical. Numerous authors of note have appeared at the meetings to give counsel to tyros and, occasionally, to read their own most recent productions. While mainly intended for professionals who wish criticism of their manuscripts, the conference also welcomes listeners and participants who have no manuscripts to submit. No degrees or credits are given, and the staff "does not take the view that a practicing writer can be produced by education, formal training, or criticism; certainly not in two weeks."

Bread-winners, The (published as a serial in *The Century Magazine,* August 1883—January 1884, as a novel, 1884; both times anonymously), by JOHN HAY, whose authorship was first acknowledged after Hay's death in an edition issued in 1915. The book defended the economic *status quo* against the increasing demands of labor, largely by portraying capitalists as virtuous men, labor leaders as villains. Its publication created a great sensation, and it provoked fictional replies by other writers. Best remembered of these is H. F. Keenan's *The Money-Makers* (1885), which depicts the economic struggle as one between greedy plutocrats and humanity-saving liberals.

Breakfast Table Series, by OLIVER WENDELL HOLMES. A series of volumes in which Holmes gave free play to his wit, learning, and experience of life, and sometimes told a story. The framework is a conversation, usually dominated by one person—frequently Holmes himself in easily penetrated disguise. The atmosphere is natural, and the discussion shifts readily from one topic to another. Always the group of personalities includes someone who blurts the rude truth; generally among those present is a pleasant feminine figure; often the ideas expressed are much more startling than one would expect from a Brahmin of BRAHMINS. The series began in germ with two papers that Holmes published in *The New England Magazine* for November, 1831, and February, 1832. Then, in the opening issue of *The Atlantic Monthly*, November, 1857, began THE AUTOCRAT OF THE BREAKFAST-TABLE, which was published in book form the following year. Later volumes in the series, in which there was increasing stress on the story element, were *The Professor at the Breakfast Table* (1860), THE POET AT THE BREAKFAST-TABLE (1872), and *Over the Teacups* (1891).

Break the News to Mother (1897), a song by CHARLES K. HARRIS. Harris, one of the most successful song writers in American musical history, was attending a performance of William Gillette's SECRET SERVICE (produced, 1896) when a wounded drummer boy spoke the line, "Break the news to mother." He says that he wrote the line down on his cuff the moment he heard it. The song refers to "the boys in blue," but it was the Spanish-American War, fought in khaki, that gave the song its tremendous vogue. It undoubtedly helped in stimulating the sentiment, or sentimentality, that led to Mother's Day. An earlier song (1878) by Allie E. Wardwell was called *Break the News Gently to Mother*.

Breasted, James Henry (b. Rockford, Ill., Aug. 27, 1865—d. Dec. 2, 1935), historian, archaeologist. His research and expeditions led to his writing many books on ancient Egyptian history. His *Ancient Times: A History of the Early World* (1916) was reissued as *The Conquest of Civilization* (1926). With James Harvey Robinson he wrote *A History of Europe, Ancient and Medieval,* and other textbooks.

Breitmann, Hans. The hero of a series of ballads written in GERMAN-AMERICAN DIALECT and pen name of the author, Charles Godfrey Leland. They began with what became the most famous of them: *Hans Breitmann's Party*, published May, 1857, in *Graham's Magazine*, of which Leland was then editor. He had experimented earlier with German dialect in *Meister Karl's Sketch-Book* (1855). The verses he wrote about Breitmann were very popular, and a collection of them was published as *The Breitmann Ballads* (1871). Later came *Hans Breitmann in Tyrol* (1894), and a posthumous collection, *Hans Breitmann's Ballads* (1914).

Bremer, Fredrika (b. Finland, 1801—d. 1865), Swedish novelist, poet. Her best work was called *Sketches of Everyday Life* (1828); her nonfiction works include *The Homes of the New World* (1853) and *America of the Fifties* (1924).

Brentano, Lowell (b. New York City, April 18, 1895—d. July 8, 1950), dramatist, novelist, editor. Brentano wrote successful plays: *The Spider* (in collaboration with FULTON OURSLER, 1926) and *Great Lady* (1937); novels: *The Melody Lingers On* (1934) and *Bride of a Thousand Cedars* (with Bruce Lancaster, 1939). He edited magazines, anthologies, and (with Ralph Hancock) a series of books, *Invitation to Travel* (1947 and later), describing countries in this hemisphere. He assisted his wife, Frances Isabella Brentano, in compiling an impressive anthology, THE QUESTING SPIRIT (1947), in the field of religious literature.

Brereton, John. See JOHN BRIERTON.

Breuer, Bessie [Elizabeth] (b. Cleveland, Ohio, Oct. 19, 1893—   ), newspaperwoman, novelist, short-story writer. Miss Breuer's fiction has impressed critics by its truthfulness and thoughtfulness, although she has been criticized for her experimental style. Her short stories have won places in numerous anthologies. Among her books: *Memory of Love* (1934), called by one reviewer "The American *Anna Karenina*"; *The Daughter* (1938); *The Bracelet of Wavia Lea and Other Stories* (1947); *The Actress* (1957); and *Take Care of My Roses* (1961), a tale of witchery.

Brewster's Millions (1902), a novel by GEORGE BARR MCCUTCHEON. A farcical account of what Brewster did with an unexpectedly inherited fortune, it was capably dramatized by WINCHELL SMITH and Byron Ongley in 1906; stock companies found it a sure-fire hit for many years.

Bricks Without Straw (1880), a novel by A. W. TOURGÉE. One of the earliest works to deal with racial problems in the South in the post-Civil War period, this novel has as its protagonist a New England schoolteacher in the South who sympathizes with the Negroes.

Bride Comes to Yellow Sky, The. See STEPHEN CRANE and OPEN BOAT AND OTHER TALES OF ADVENTURE.

Bridge, The [1] (1845), poem by HENRY WADSWORTH LONGFELLOW. According to Harry Hayden Clark, the poem "records Longfellow's retrospect of his sorrow following the death of his first wife, considered now from the vantage point of his present happiness with his second wife." The bridge was that over the Charles River. Longfellow was much attached to the bridge and the view offered from it, especially by night.

Bridge, The [2] (1930), poem by HART CRANE. This work is an endeavor to see America and American history mystically and symbolically. The chief symbol is "The Bridge," here Brooklyn Bridge. Crane did not intend a nationalistic panegyric or a glorification of 20th century development; on the contrary, he valued the ideals that industrialism was suppressing. Difficulties in writing included economic ones, partially solved by financial aid from Otto H. Kahn, a leading industrialist. Crane allowed himself to be constantly distracted, and suffered agonizing mental turmoil and depression over the poem and his own existence as a poet. Yet he continued writing, published some portions in mag-

azines, and *The Bridge* was published in the fall of 1930. In the poem appear Columbus, Pizarro, Priscilla, Walt Whitman, and other figures, all regarded as "bridges." Columbus, for example, is a bridge between the Old World and the New. Crane felt that he was "really building a bridge between the so-called classic experience and many divergent realities of our seething confused chaos of today." Often he shows his love of America and the American soil, even when displaying American degeneration, as in the section called "Quaker Hill." Henry W. Wells feels that "the American public has as yet scarcely appreciated the contribution of *The Bridge* to a distinctively national literature." Brom Weber calls the poem "altogether superb in its music, imagery, and most of its structure." See THE CITY IN THE SEA.

Bridge of San Luis Rey, The (1927), a novel by THORNTON WILDER. "On Friday noon, July the twentieth, 1714, the finest bridge in all Peru broke and precipitated five travelers into the gulf below." So begins Wilder's best-known novel, a brilliantly written fable that became a best seller, won the Pulitzer Prize, and was made into a movie. Brother Juniper, a Franciscan friar and Wilder's mouthpiece, witnesses the accident and wonders whether it really was an accident or a deliberate plan of the Almighty. His investigation of the victims' lives, to prove that their sudden deaths were justified, forms the core of the book. The five characters are the Marquesa de Montemayor (based on Mme. de Sévigné); the little girl Pepita, dominated by the Marquesa; Esteban, rival of his twin brother Manuel for the favors of the actress Camilla Périchole (heroine of the Offenbach operetta); Uncle Pio, a lovable adventurer; and Camilla's young son Jaimé.

Bridger, James (b. Richmond, Va., Mar. 17, 1804—d. July 17, 1881), fur trader, scout, frontiersman, the first white man to see the Great Salt Lake. Every noted figure of the Westward drive has recorded his indebtedness to Bridger for information about the Rocky Mountain area, a region he knew better than any other man of his time.

Brierton [sometimes **Brereton**], **John** (b. England, 1572?—d. 1619?), clergyman, explorer. He accompanied the expedition along the New England coast led by Bartholomew Gosnold in 1602. In that year he published *A Briefe and True Relation of the Discoverie of the North Part of Virginia*.

Brigadoon (1947), a musical fantasy by ALAN JAY LERNER with music by FREDERICK LOEWE. Its plot, centered in a vanished and occasionally reappearing Scotch village, is similar to that of a German classic, *Germelshausen*, by Friedrich Wilhelm Gerstaecker, though Lerner avowed mere coincidence.

Briggs, Charles Frederick (b. Nantucket, Mass., Dec. 30, 1804—d. June 20, 1877), editor, novelist. Briggs in 1839 published a novel, THE ADVENTURES OF HARRY FRANCO, based on his experiences at sea. In 1845 he founded the *Broadway Journal*, to which Poe contributed and of which he became editor and owner. Briggs, who found himself unable to get along with the poet (he sided with Longfellow and Lowell in Poe's controversy with them), went on to editorial work for *Putnam's Magazine,* the New York *Times,* and the Brooklyn *Union,* and he also wrote other autobiographical novels under the name of Harry Franco.

Briggs, Le Baron Russell (b. Salem, Mass., Dec. 11, 1855—d. April 24, 1934), teacher, author. Briggs taught creative writing at Harvard, where he had many students, including John Dos Passos, E. E. Cummings, and Conrad Aiken. Later he became dean of the faculty (1902–25) and president of Radcliffe College (1903–23). Among his books: *School, College, and Character* (1901) and *Men, Women, and Colleges* (1925).

Briggs, Thomas H[enry] (b. Raleigh, N.C., Jan. 25, 1877—   ), teacher, author. As professor at Teachers College, Columbia University, Briggs exerted a great influence on educational movements throughout the country by his gift of analysis and his sometimes caustic common sense. Among his writings: *The Junior High School* (1920); *The Great Investment* (1930); *Secondary Education* (1933); *Improving Instruction* (1938); *Poetry and Its Enjoyment* (1957); *Opera and Its Enjoyment* (1960); also anthologies in the field of English literature.

Bright Feather (1948), a novel by Robert Wilder (1901—   ). Clayfield Hammond, a plantation owner in Florida, takes a dim view of his grandson's attempts to befriend the Indians. The novel is a study in racial conflict, presenting in historical terms the perennial problem of the South.

Bright Shawl, The (1922), a novel by Joseph Hergesheimer. A late 19th-century American romanticist goes to Cuba for his health just before the war with Spain, gets mixed up in the Cuban rebellion, falls in love with a dancer, and when she is killed barely escapes with his own life—he cannot even keep the bright red shawl that was to have been a memory of their relationship.

Brill, A[braham] A[rden] (b. Austria, Oct. 12, 1874—d. March 2, 1948), psychiatrist, author. Dr. Brill became internationally famous as an authority on psychiatry, especially the doctrines of Sigmund Freud and Carl Jung. He familiarized Americans with Freudian terminology and interpreted Freudian doctrine. Among his writings, aside from direct translations from Freud and Jung: *Psychoanalysis, Its Theories and Practical Application* (1912); *Freud's Contribution to Psychiatry* (1944); *Lectures on Psychoanalytic Psychiatry* (1946); *Basic Principles of Psychoanalysis* (1949).

Brimming Cup, The (1921), a novel by Dorothy Canfield Fisher. In this story set in Vermont, Mrs. Fisher tells how a man of the world, mature and selfish, seeks to win Marise Crittendon from her husband Neale. The latter is too honorable to seek to hold her, but events convince her that she needs his integrity more than Vincent Marsh's passion. *Rough-Hewn*

(1922) tells of Neale and Marise earlier in their lives.

Bring 'Em Back Alive (1930), an account of Frank Buck's adventures in capturing wild animals, told in collaboration with Edward Anthony. *Wild Cargo* (1932) is a sequel by the same authors.

Brinig, Myron (b. Minneapolis, Minn., Dec. 22, 1900—   ), novelist. Some of his novels, such as *Madonna Without Child* (1929), deal with Freudian concepts. *Singermann* (1929), *This Man Is My Brother* (1932), *Sun Sets in the West* (1935), and *The Sisters* (1937) are set in Montana. He has also written *Ann Minton's Life* (1935); *You and I* (1945); *Footsteps on the Stair* (1950); *The Street of the Three Friends* (1953).

Brink, Carol [Ryrie] (b. Moscow, Ida., Dec. 28, 1895—   ), editor, writer. Her first book for children, *Anything Can Happen on the River!* (1934), is a story of France; Caddie Woodlawn won the John Newbery Medal for 1935, and Mrs. Brink dramatized it in 1945. Later juveniles include *Mademoiselle Misfortune* (1936), *Lad with a Whistle* (1941), *Buffalo Coat* (1944), and *Family Grandstand* (1952). She also wrote a biography about the singing Hutchinson family, *Harps in the Wind* (1947). More recently she has written *Family Sabbatical* (1956); and *The Pink Motel* (1959).

Brinnin, John Malcolm (b. Halifax, N. Scot., 1916—   ), poet, editor, teacher. Rebelling against his strict Catholic upbringing, Brinnin embarked upon a program of self-education, simultaneously editing various *avant-garde* periodicals. Later, he entered the University of Michigan as a regular student and supported himself by opening a bookshop, The Book Room. His volumes of poetry include: *The Garden Is Political* (1942), which deals with the atmosphere of World War II; *The Lincoln Lyrics* (1942); *No Arch, No Triumph* (1945); *The Sorrows of Cold Stone* (1951). With K. Friar he also edited *Modern Poetry: American and British* (1951).

As director of the Poetry Center at the YMHA in New York, he invited the Welsh poet Dylan Thomas to give readings in the United States. This visit provided Brinnin with much of the material for his controversial but generally sympathetic portrait, *Dylan Thomas in America* (1955). Besides teaching and lecturing at various universities, he is author of *The Third Rose; Gertrude Stein and Her World* (1959) and editor of *A Casebook on Dylan Thomas* (1960).

Brinton, [Clarence] Crane (b. Winsted, Conn., Feb. 2, 1898—   ), teacher, historian, biographer. A teacher at Harvard since 1923, Brinton writes with sound scholarship, combined with a rare vivacity and gift of phrase. Among his books: *The Political Ideas of the English Romanticists* (1926); *The Jacobins* (1930); *English Political Thought in the 19th Century* (1933); *The Lives of Talleyrand* (1936); *The Anatomy of Revolution* (1938); *Nietzsche* (1941); *Ideas and Men: The Story of Western Thought* (1950); *The Shaping of the Modern*

Mind (1953); *A History of Western Morals* (1959). He also edited the *Portable Age of Reason Reader* (1956), and *Society of Fellows* (1960).

Brinton, Howard H[aines] (b. West Chester, Pa., July 24, 1884—   ), educator, writer. Brinton, a prominent Quaker, taught mathematics and physics in several colleges, then turned to the teaching of religion. He worked for the American Friends Service Committee, and in 1936 he became Director of the Pendle Hill Graduate School for Religious and Social Study in Wallingford, Pa., a Quaker institution that offers a balanced program of worship, education, and physical work. He has published many religious works, particularly on Quakerism, including *The Mystic Will* (a study of Jacob Boehme, 1930), *Quaker Education in Theory and Practice* (1940), *The Pendle Hill Idea* (1950), *Friends for 300 Years* (1952); and he has edited *Children of Light* (essays on Quakerism, 1938).

Brisbane, Albert (b. Batavia, New York, Aug. 22, 1809—d. May 1, 1890), a social crusader. Early in life Brisbane was seized with a messianic compulsion to eliminate squalor from the world. He discovered his method in the doctrines of Charles Fourier (1772–1837), whose *Traité de l'association domestique et agricole* (1822) advocated a cooperative organization of society into phalansteries or phalanxes. In 1834 Brisbane began to form Fourierist groups in New York and Philadelphia, and in 1840 published *The Social Destiny of Man*, a mixture of passages from Fourier with his own interpretations and additions. The book made a deep impression, won an eminent convert in HORACE GREELEY, and led about 8,000 Americans to invest their goods and their future in phalanxes from Massachusetts to Green Bay, Wisconsin. Among the phalanxes was the celebrated experiment at BROOK FARM, described in Hawthorne's THE BLITHEDALE ROMANCE (1852), in which Brisbane was the model for one of the least complimentary portraits. In these phalanxes the family was regarded as an outmoded institution and even the very young were trained in masses for productive labor. (Brisbane himself married twice and had a large family, brought up capably by his wives.) All the phalanxes failed, and only that at Green Bay showed a profit; its land rose in value through no effort of its own. See also ALEXANDER WOOLLCOTT; NORTH AMERICAN PHALANX.

Brisbane himself, after the Fourierist movement died off, lived for many years in obscurity, a mild-mannered, modest dreamer, no man of action. In 1876 he published a *General Introduction to Social Sciences*, a recapitulation of the theories of association.

Brisbane, Arthur (b. Buffalo, N.Y., Dec. 12, 1864—d. Dec. 25, 1936), newspaperman, editor. Brisbane deeply revered his father, ALBERT BRISBANE, in his early years espoused good causes, yet mostly worked in direct opposition to his father's ideas and told Emile Gauvreau

once that "martyrs are the troublemakers of this world." He began his career in 1883 as a newspaperman on the New York *Sun* in the days of Charles A. Dana. From 1890 to 1897 he was managing editor of Joseph Pulitzer's New York *World*. In 1897 WILLIAM RANDOLPH HEARST lured him over to the New York *Evening Journal;* he remained in close association with Hearst for the rest of his life. In his last years he edited Hearst's New York tabloid, the *Mirror*. In addition he dealt in United States and Mexican real estate, and probably made most of his fortune that way—contrary to the doctrines of HENRY GEORGE, whom he had supported when the latter ran for mayor of New York in 1897. Brisbane is supposedly the main character in Samuel Hopkins Adams' novel *Success* (1921).

Bristow, Gwen (b. Marion, S.C., Sept. 16, 1903—   ), newspaperwoman, novelist. Miss Bristow began her career as a reporter on the staff of the New Orleans *Times-Picayune* in 1925. *The Invisible Host*, a mystery written in collaboration with her husband, Bruce Manning, was dramatized and presented in New York in 1930 under the title of *The Ninth Guest*. *Deep Summer* (1937), *The Handsome Road* (1938), and *This Side of Glory* (1940) comprise her "Louisiana trilogy," which was well received by the press. Among her other books: *Tomorrow Is Forever* (1943), *Jubilee Trail* (1950), *Celia Garth* (1959).

British Prison Ship, The (1781), a poem by PHILIP FRENEAU. On his way to the West Indies in 1780, Freneau was captured by the British and confined for six weeks, first on a prison ship, later on a hospital ship. On his release Freneau described the horror of his experiences with vivid bitterness in his poem.

British Spy, Letters of the (1803), by WILLIAM WIRT. See LETTERS OF THE BRITISH SPY.

Brittle Heaven (1935, originally called *Stardust and Thistledown*), a play about EMILY DICKINSON by Vincent York and Frederick J. Pohl.

Broadhurst, George H[owells] (b. England, June 3, 1866—d. Jan. 31, 1952), newspaperman, playwright. His greatest Broadway hits were THE MAN OF THE HOUR (1907), which dealt with political corruption, and BOUGHT AND PAID FOR (1913), later a popular movie. He made a considerable fortune from his plays, returned to England to live, but died in Santa Barbara, Calif.

Broadway. One of the world's most famous streets. It starts at Bowling Green, near the Battery, in New York City and runs northward to 242nd St., where it becomes part of the Albany Post Road. At its southern tip it still derives a maritime character from the shipping district nearby. Shortly it becomes the country's chief financial district, with Wall St. as its main tributary. Passing City Hall and Park Row, once the heart of newspaper publication in the city, Broadway becomes a mercantile district. Then it heads into a region of theaters and restaurants, centered at Times Square and the Times Building, the real Gay White Way of New York. Continuing north, it skirts Central Park, runs between rows of hotels and apartment houses, crosses the grounds of Columbia University, and moves staidly to the city line.

The term "Gay (or Great) White Way" supposedly comes from the play, *The Great White Way* (1901), by ALBERT BIGELOW PAINE. The "bright lights" of Broadway with their spectacular (and sometimes animated) advertising signs have always attracted much attention. G. K. Chesterton, seeing them for the first time, remarked, "How beautiful it would be for someone who couldn't read!" The "characters" who regard Broadway as their spiritual home speak, according to George Frazier, "an argot compounded of argots." DAMON RUNYON, laureate of Broadway in the 1930's and 1940's, reproduced its language as faithfully as he could and denied that he had originated any of the expressions. H. L. MENCKEN, however, believed that a large part of Broadway slang was "invented by gag-writers, newspaper columnists, and press agents, and the rest borrowed from the vocabularies of criminals, prostitutes, and the lower orders of showfolk."

One of the most famous of American popular songs was George M. Cohan's *Give My Regards to Broadway*. Mel Heimer wrote Broadway's story in *The Big Drag* (1947). See BIXBY'S HOTEL; BREAD AND CHEESE CLUB.

Broadway (1926), a play by PHILIP DUNNING and GEORGE ABBOTT. Cabaret performers and bootleggers are the chief characters in this melodramatic comedy of the prohibition era. Arthur Hobson Quinn praised its picture of a New York night club as having "photographic reality."

Broadway Jones (1912), a play by GEORGE M. COHAN. A young spendthrift discovers his responsibilities for the business he has inherited—responsibilities he cannot evade merely by selling it. Cohan also made it into a musical, *Billie* (1929).

Broker of Bogota, The (1834), a play by R. M. BIRD. It is a turgid melodrama noted for being one of the earliest of American writings set in a Latin-American country.

Brom Bones. The character in Washington Irving's LEGEND OF SLEEPY HOLLOW who frightens ICHABOD CRANE into flight by pretending to be the "Headless Horseman."

Bromfield, Louis (b. Mansfield, Ohio, Dec. 27, 1896—d. March 18, 1956), novelist, playwright, essayist, farmer. Bromfield's early novels—THE GREEN BAY TREE (1924); *Possession* (1925); EARLY AUTUMN (1926), which won the Pulitzer Prize; and *A Good Woman* (1927)—evinced perception, skill, and a fine feeling for description. Bromfield lived for many years in France with his wife and three daughters; his home became a Mecca for artists and writers. Although much drawn to the land and people of France, Bromfield returned with his family before the Second World War, bought a thousand-acre farm (which he called Malabar) near his birthplace, and settled down to a farmer's

life, as his forebears had done for generations. Although his restless nature compelled him to engage in varied interests which often took him away from home, he made a tremendous success of his farming venture; today Malabar is one of the country's agricultural showplaces. He seemed unable to sustain his early excellence as a novelist except in *The Rains Came* (1937), set in Malabar, one of India's coastal regions, after which the Ohio farm had been named. However, he touched new literary heights in his factual accounts of his life at Malabar. Five of these books of description and discussion are: *Pleasant Valley* (1945); *A Few Brass Tacks* (1946); *Malabar Farm* (1948); *Out of the Earth* (1950); *From My Experience* (1955). The New York *Times* compared Bromfield's later nonfiction books with Jefferson's notes on Virginia. Morrison Brown wrote *Louis Bromfield and His Books* (1956).

Brooke, Frances [Moore] (b. England, 1724 —d. Jan. 23, 1789), novelist, dramatist. The wife of a clergyman, Mrs. Brooke followed her husband to Canada, where he was chaplain to the garrison at Quebec. Her four-volume *History of Emily Montague* (1769) had a Canadian setting and is often considered the first Canadian novel. However, Mrs. Brooke's work was based on English models and had no perceptible effect on Canadian literature, though it does give a vivid picture of social life in and around Quebec in the mid-18th century.

Brooke, Tucker (b. Morgantown, W. Va., 1883—d. June 22, 1946), teacher, editor. Long a member of the Yale University faculty, Brooke became editor of *The Yale Shakespeare*. Other publications he edited are: *The Shakespeare Apocrypha* (1908), *The Works of Christopher Marlowe* (1910), *The Tudor Drama* (1911), *Shakespeare's Sonnets* (1936), and *Essays on Shakespeare and Other Elizabethans* (1948).

Brook Farm. The official name of this famous experiment in transcendentalism, communism, and "association" was the "Brook Farm Institute of Agriculture and Education." It was established on a 200-acre farm at West Roxbury, Mass., on April 1, 1841; it collapsed in 1846. GEORGE RIPLEY was a leader in the founding of the community, and numerous persons of note were from time to time associated with it— Theodore Parker, William Henry Channing, NATHANIEL HAWTHORNE, MARGARET FULLER, Charles A. Dana, G. W. Curtis (as a pupil in the school), ALBERT BRISBANE, who brought to the community the influence of Fourierism. When this doctrine was accepted the name of the farm was changed to Brook Farm Phalanx; and the end came when the uninsured "Central Phalanstery" burned down. Channing has referred to it as a "great college of social students." Emerson apparently felt that to live in Brook Farm would merely mean exchanging one prison for another, and he held shrewdly that "in the arrangements at Brook Farm, as out of them, it is the person, not the communist, that avails." It was he who called Brook Farm "the Age of

Reason in a patty-pan." Hawthorne made use of his experiences on the farm in his BLITHEDALE ROMANCE (1852). Truman Nelson saw the experiment more humorously in his novel, *The Passion by the Brook* (1953).

Brooklyn Eagle, The. Founded in 1841 by Edward C. Murphy, this daily newspaper had a distinguished career. Among noted writers who served on its staff are Walt Whitman, Edward W. Bok, H. V. Kaltenborn. The *Eagle* suspended publication on March 16, 1955.

Brooks, Cleanth (b. Murray, Ky., Oct. 16, 1906—   ), educator, critic. After receiving degrees from Vanderbilt and Tulane Universities, and from Oxford University as a Rhodes Scholar, Brooks taught English at Louisiana State University from 1932 to 1947. During this time he became associated with the so-called NEW CRITICISM. He co-edited the journal SOUTHERN REVIEW with ROBERT PENN WARREN (1935–42); he produced the college textbooks *Understanding Poetry* (1938); *Understanding Fiction* (1943) in collaboration with Warren; and *Understanding Drama* (with Robert Heilman, 1945). These texts, along with his own books *Modern Poetry and the Tradition* (1939) and *The Well-Wrought Urn* (1947), were a major influence on contemporary methods of teaching literature, emphasizing close reading and structural analysis, and urging treatment of the poem as poem apart from its place in the author's life or literary history. Brooks tends to look for and favor in poetry the qualities of wit, irony, paradox, symbolism, ambiguity, and dramatic structure, drawing the objection of other critics such as Ronald S. Crane that his approach is too narrow, although he has unquestionably enriched the appreciation of poetry.

Since 1947 he has taught English at Yale University, and has written *Modern Rhetoric* (1949) with Warren and, with W. K. Wimsatt, Jr., *Literary Criticism: A Short History* (1957). He is a member of the advisory committee on the Boswell papers; general editor, with David N. Smith, of the projected ten volumes of letters of Thomas Percy; and has contributed numerous articles to literary magazines and journals.

Brooks, Elbridge S[treeter] (b. Lowell, Mass., April 14, 1846—d. Jan. 7, 1902), newspaperman, editor, author of juveniles. Among his many books for young people are *Historic Boys* (1875), *Historic Girls* (1877), *The Century Book for Young Americans* (1894), *A Boy of the First Empire* (1895), *Chivalric Days* (1898). His books were wholesome and widely read.

Brooks, Gwendolyn E[lizabeth] (b. Topeka, Kans., June 7, 1917—   ), poet, novelist. When Miss Brooks was only thirteen her poem *Eventide* was accepted by a then popular magazine, *American Childhood*. At seventeen she became a frequent contributor of poetry to the magazine *Defender*. In 1945 *A Street in Bronzeville*, her first book of poetry, was published; and in March of the following year she received an award of $1,000 from the American Academy of Arts and Letters. *Annie Allen*, also a book of

poetry, was published in 1949 and received the Pulitzer Prize. Her first novel was *Maud Martha* (1953); a third book of poetry, *The Bean Eaters*, appeared in 1960. A bold innovator, Miss Brooks leaned in these books upon her own experience and background to delineate points of contact and contrast between the Negro and white races. In private life she is Mrs. Henry Blakely.

Brooks, Maria [Gowen] (b. Medford, Mass., 1794?—d. Nov. 11, 1845), poet, novelist. Mrs. Brooks was extravagantly praised by the English Lake School of poets; she lived for a year near Grasmere and virtually became a member of the "school." Charles Lamb said of her *Zophiël* (1833) that she couldn't possibly have composed it—"as if there ever had been a woman capable of anything so great!" Mrs. Brooks married her elderly brother-in-law when her sister died; she later became estranged from him and fell in love with a young Canadian officer. In 1823 her husband died, but her match with the officer did not come off. She attempted suicide twice and used the affair to write an autobiographical novel, *Idomen, or, The Vale of Yumuri* (1843). Living intermittently on an inherited Cuban estate, Mrs. Brooks and both her stepsons died there of fever. Her passionate and melodramatic poetry was received without favor in Boston.

Brooks, Noah (b. Castine, Me., Oct. 24, 1830—d. Aug. 16, 1903), newspaperman, government official, author. "Uncle Noah," a man of attractive personality and storytelling ability, knew Lincoln and wrote some careful historical works, *e.g.*, *Abraham Lincoln and the Downfall of American Slavery* (1894) and *Short Studies in American Party Politics* (1896). But his books for boys have survived his more "important" writings. Among them are: THE BOY EMIGRANTS (1876); *The Fairport Nine* (1880); *The Boy Settlers* (1891).

Brooks, Phillips (b. Boston, Dec. 13, 1835—d. Jan. 23, 1893), clergyman, orator, author. A bishop in the Protestant Episcopal Church, Brooks became a chief representative of the new thought and the new criticism that were remolding Protestantism. He wrote *Yale Lectures on Preaching* (1877), *Essays and Addresses* (1892), also the famous hymn, *O Little Town of Bethlehem*. He appears as a character in Arlo Bates' novel, *The Puritans* (1898).

Brooks, Van Wyck (b. Plainfield, N.J., Feb. 16, 1886—d. May 2, 1963), critic, biographer. Harvard-educated, Brooks was for a time a journalist and traveled in Europe, where his first book, *The Wine of the Puritans* (London, 1908; New York, 1909), was published. The first of many of his books to criticize the shortcomings of the Puritan heritage, *The Wine of the Puritans* approached contemporary American culture from both historical and psychological points of view, and although sometimes not entirely justified by facts, contained enough truth to make itself uncomfortably felt. In AMERICA'S COMING OF AGE (1915) Brooks continued his analysis of the American literary past, finding that the Puritan duality of isolated idealism and practical materialism resulted in a literature that had become artificially separated from life and identified with the "thin moral earnestness" of the New England highbrow. Seeking a valid tradition for American literature in which life

Robert Gumpper

and art were not divorced, he found in Walt Whitman a synthesis of literature and the vital aspects of life.

Brooks then turned to critical biography liberally supplied with psychological interpretations to illustrate the crippling effect of the Puritan dualism on the American writer; *The Ordeal of Mark Twain* (1920; rev. ed. 1933) found Twain's Calvinistic background and his provincial Missouri home responsible for his failure to fulfill his genius. Although the book provoked bitter criticism, it has proved a work that later critics of Twain and of American culture could not afford to ignore. In the same vein Brooks analyzed another American "failure": Henry James, who, rather than face the conflicting demands of life and art in America, fled to Europe. After *The Pilgrimage of Henry James* (1925) came *The Life of Emerson* (1932), completing the biographical trilogy with a story of success.

Having exposed the cultural duality of the 19th century, its resultant aesthetic sterility, and the failure of unattached idealism, Brooks turned to the creative task of hewing a valid tradition out of America's literary history. In the five volumes comprising the "Finders and Makers" series that followed, Brooks used his

earlier technique of critical biography to establish the relationship between the writer and his society, between the work and the cultural milieu out of which it emerged. Thus Brooks created the first composite picture of American cultural and literary development. THE FLOWERING OF NEW ENGLAND, *1815–1865* (1936), the first in order of publication but second in the series, was a best seller for more than a year, and was awarded the Pulitzer Prize; the other volumes (in order of the series) are *The World of Washington Irving* (1944), *The Times of Melville and Whitman* (1947), NEW ENGLAND: INDIAN SUMMER, *1865–1915* (1940), and *The Confident Years: 1885–1915* (1952). In 1956 Brooks and Otto L. Bettman made an abridgment of the series which was published as *Our Literary Heritage*, a pictorial history of the writer in America from 1800 to 1915.

Brooks has also written *Letters and Leadership* (1918); *The Literary Life in America* (1921); *Opinions of Oliver Allston* (1941); *The Writer in America* (1953); the autobiographical *Scenes and Portraits* (1954); *Helen Keller: Sketch for a Portrait* (1955); *John Sloan: A Painter's Life* (1955); *Days of the Phoenix: The 1920's I Remember* (1957); *The Dream of Arcadia: American Writers and Artists in Italy, 1760–1915* (1958); *From a Writer's Notebook* (1958); *Howells: His Life and World* (1959); *From the Shadow of the Mountain* (1961); *Fenollosa and His Circle* (1962).

Broom (November, 1921—January, 1924), one of the best-known LITTLE MAGAZINES. Originally edited by Harold A. Loeb and ALFRED KREYMBORG, it gave room to both European and American writers, and according to F. J. Hoffman and Charles Allen, "helped win the fight against the sentimentalities of the genteel tradition."

Brother Jonathan. Early in Yankee folk tradition the name Jonathan became a typical name for any Yankee, especially the country bumpkin who is smarter than he seems to be. Richard M. Dorson, in JONATHAN DRAWS THE LONG BOW (1946), his book on New England popular tales and legends, relates a number of stories in which Jonathan appears as a character. The name was early given to a personification of the United States, and was explained, by a sort of folk etymology, as due to the fact that General Washington greatly relied on the advice of his aide, Jonathan Trumbull, and sometimes said, "We must consult Brother Jonathan." A weekly called *Brother Jonathan* was founded by Park Benjamin, 1839–43. One of its editors, JOHN NEAL, wrote a novel called *Brother Jonathan* (1825), of which Carl Van Doren says that its realism soon ran "amuck into raving melodrama." Oliver Wendell Holmes used the name "Brother Jonathan" to designate the Union or the North in his poem, *Brother Jonathan's Lament for Sister Caroline*, written after South Carolina's secession, 1861.

Brother Rat (1936), a farce by John Monks, Jr. (1910—   ), and Fred F. Finklehoffe

(1910——   ). It deals, not too realistically but amusingly, with student life, mainly extra-curricular, at the famous Virginia Military Institute.

Brougham, John (b. Ireland, May 9, 1810—d. June 7, 1880), actor, playwright. Brougham came to the United States as a successful comedian, but was best known as the author of several burlesques, including two with Indian characters, *Metamora, Or, The Last of the Polly-woags* (1847) and *Po-ca-hon-tas!* (1855). He adapted novels by Dickens and Harriet Beecher Stowe for the stage, presented a *Dramatic Review for 1868* that anticipated the annual revues of a later day. In the 1860's he and DION BOUCICAULT were the most popular dramatists in America.

Broun, Heywood [Campbell] (b. New York City, Dec. 7, 1888—d. Dec. 18, 1939), newspaperman, novelist, crusader. Broun began as a sports writer for the New York *Morning Telegraph*, went on to baseball stories and literary and dramatic criticism for the *Tribune*. "It Seems to Me," his column for the old *World*, became widely known in syndicate form. In 1927 he quarreled with his editors over the SACCO-VANZETTI case, and left the paper the following year. He went to the *Telegram*, a Scripps-Howard paper (which bought the *World* in 1931), but his increasingly radical views embroiled him in frequent controversies with the Scripps-Howard management. Still another form of conversion led him into the Catholic church. In the 1930's he wrote for various periodicals, including one of his own, *Broun's Nutmeg*, published from his home in Stamford, Conn.

Broun wrote many millions of words, yet it is doubtful whether he will be remembered as more than a name and as the author of a few entertaining essays and some amusing epigrams. His fame somewhat parallels that of Dr. Johnson, whom he resembled in more ways than one: someone once called him a "one-man slum," and a fellow worker dubbed him "Six Characters in Search of a Laundry." These epithets were more affectionate than slanderous, since everybody liked the huge, kindly, untidy, unpunctual good fellow, who was compared to "a strolling friar" intent on saving the world. He had a profound hatred for all injustice; his words blazed as he denounced the Nazis and his wit sparkled on less serious occasions. Of his fellow columnist, Dorothy Thompson, he once wrote: "Miss Thompson is greater than Eliza, because not only does she cross the ice but she breaks it as she goes. Moreover, she is her own bloodhound." And on censorship: "Obscenity is such a tiny kingdom that a single tour covers it completely." Dale Kramer wrote a life of Broun (1949). The Newspaper Guild, which Broun helped to found, has established an annual award for newspaper reportage done "in the spirit of Broun."

Brown, Alice (b. Hampton Falls, N.H., Dec. 5, 1857—d. June 21, 1948), novelist, short-story writer, dramatist, poet. Miss Brown followed in SARAH ORNE JEWETT's literary foot-steps. She wrote *Meadow-Grass* (1895), *Tiverton Tales* (1899), *Country Neighbors* (1910), *Vanishing Points* (1913), and other works. Her play, *Children of Earth* (1915), won a $10,000 prize, but despite its sincere depiction of New England life was unsuccessful when produced.

Brown, Audrey Alexandra (b. Nanaimo, B.C., Oct. 29, 1904——   ), poet, memoirist. Disabled by a rheumatic illness, Miss Brown persisted in a literary career. Her journal of her illness, *The Log of a Lame Duck* (1938), is free from any trace of self-pity. Her first volume of verse, *A Dryad in Nanaimo* (1931; second edition, 1934), shows the influence of Spenser, Keats, and Christina Rossetti. Other works are *The Tree of Resurrection* (1937), *Challenge to Time and Death* (1943), *V-E Day* (1946), and *All Fools' Day* (1948).

Brown, Charles Brockden (b. Philadelphia, Jan. 17, 1771—d. Feb. 22, 1810), editor, novelist. Brown was the first American who adopted letters as his sole profession and for a time actually made a go of it; he was the first to in-

troduce the Indian into fiction; he was one of the first Americans to win a hearing abroad; he anticipated the later deep interest in psychotic characters and the explanation of their mental difficulties in the form of fiction; he likewise anticipated in his treatment of horror and his suggestion of poetic gloom the writings of Hawthorne and Poe. A follower of the Gothic school of romance, he wrote books that are at least the equal of their parallels in contemporary English literature—Walpole's *The Castle of Otranto* (1764) and Mrs. Radcliffe's *The Mysteries of Udolpho* (1794).

Brown's fame rests on six novels: WIELAND (1798); ORMOND (1799); ARTHUR MERVYN (1799–1800); EDGAR HUNTLY (1799); *Clara*

Howard (1801); *Jane Talbot* (1801). In *Wieland* Theodore hears the forceful voice of God commanding him to kill his family. In *Ormond* the heroine is pursued by a sex maniac and kills him. In *Arthur Mervyn* murder, seduction, and the horrors of disease are depicted. In *Edgar Huntly* Indians are introduced, but the main plot is a study in sleepwalking and madness. *Clara Howard* and *Jane Talbot* are studies in frustrated marriages.

Shelley was especially fond of Brown's novels; he named one of his poems after Constantia, heroine of *Ormond.* Scott took from Brown the names of two characters in *Guy Mannering;* Keats, Cooper, Hawthorne, and Poe admired Brown. Van Wyck Brooks calls him a precursor of Melville and Henry James. A deliberate rationalist, Brown said he carefully avoided "puerile superstitions, Gothic castles, and chimeras," and made use of American materials to produce his effects. D. L. Clark wrote *Charles Brockden Brown: Pioneer Voice of America* (1952). See ALCUIN.

Brown, Gold (b. Providence, R.I., March 7, 1791—d. March 31, 1857), grammarian. His *Institutes of English Grammar* (1823) and the gigantic *Grammar of English Grammars* (1851) mark the apotheosis of a certain type of linguist who once flourished unchecked. Brown held that usage is not a safe guide, but that to speak and write a language correctly the rules of a master grammarian must be committed to memory and relied on absolutely ever afterwards. Language, he maintained, has no change or growth, except towards impurity; the grammarian must be a bulwark against these alterations. In his *Grammar of Grammars,* long the Bible of fearsome schoolmarms and schoolmasters, he provided endless rules, exercises, and quotations from authors who had violated these rules and whose diction was therefore to be "corrected."

Brown, Harry [Peter McNab, Jr.] (b. Portland, Me., April 30, 1917—   ), poet, novelist, humorist, playwright, screenwriter.   Before World War II Brown worked for *Time* and *The New Yorker;* in the army he was on the staff of YANK, and wrote the ARTIE GREENGROIN sketches, collected in a book in 1945. Artie, a Brooklynite talking Brooklynese in England, makes shrewd and unconventional comments on English and American life. Brown had previously written a fine novel, *A Walk in the Sun* (1944), and went on to a play, *A Sound of Hunting* (1946). He has also written successful screenplays and the novels *Wake of the Red Witch* (1949), *Thunder on the Mountain* (1954), and *Stars in their Courses* (1960). He has won major attention through his verse collections, *The End of a Decade* (1941), *The Violent* (1943), *The Beast in His Hunger* (1949), all rich in style, sonorous in rhythm, and striking in theme.

Brown, John (b. Torrington, Conn., May 9, 1800—d. Dec. 2, 1859), crusader against slavery. So fanatic was Brown in his attitude toward slavery that when he moved with his five sons to Osawatomie, Kans., and discovered that some of his neighbors took the Southern point of view,

he murdered five of them—taking the view that he was an instrument of God. He also operated an underground railroad from his home. He had long planned an invasion of the Southland to free slaves from their owners; finally he invaded Harper's Ferry, Va., with twenty-one men, and by daybreak was in complete control of the federal arsenal and the town. Soldiers under the command of Col. Robert E. Lee crushed the venture ruthlessly, and Brown and the other survivors were arrested. Brown was tried, and conducted himself with great dignity and eloquence. He was condemned to die and was hanged.

The invasion, its tragic outcome, the speeches and letters of Brown brought about something of a reaction in his favor. His activities dramatized the coming conflict, probably made it more difficult to settle peaceably. Brown has become a favorite theme in song, story, and biography. His name was immortalized in the Union marching song, JOHN BROWN'S BODY LIES A-MOULDERING IN THE GRAVE. Thoreau, Bronson Alcott, and others mourned his passing and proclaimed his greatness. Laudatory biographies were written by W. E. B. Du Bois (1909), Oswald G. Villard (1910), Robert Penn Warren (JOHN BROWN: THE MAKING OF A MARTYR, 1929), James C. Malin (1942); Laurence Greene wrote an account of Brown in *The Raid* (1953) from the point of view of the villagers of Harper's Ferry. Leonard Ehrlich made him the hero of his novel, *God's Angry Man* (1932). Many poets have written about Brown; greatest of all is the epic poem, JOHN BROWN'S BODY (1928), by Stephen Vincent Benét. Joy K. Talbot analyzed *John Brown in American Literature* (1941).

Brown, John Mason (b. Louisville, Ky., July 3, 1900—d. March 16, 1969), drama critic, journalist, essayist, lecturer.   Brown, a graduate of Harvard, began as a reporter for the Louisville *Courier-Journal,* and taught history of drama at the University of Montana. In 1924 he joined the staff of *Theatre Arts Monthly,* remaining there until 1928. He then went to the New York *Post* and later worked for the New York *World-Telegram* and the *Saturday Review.* During World War II he served in the navy and participated in the invasions of Sicily and Normandy; his tense running accounts of what was happening, broadcast to the crews of the invading fleet, were collected in *To All Hands* (1943) and *Many a Watchful Night* (1944). Among his collected essays in criticism are *The Modern Theater in Revolt* (1929); *Two on the Aisle* (1938); *Broadway in Review* (1940); *Seeing Things* (1946); *Seeing More Things* (1948); and *As They Appear* (1952). Brown, a man of letters and a serious drama critic, as well as a highly popular lecturer, delivered facts and opinions with speed and epigrammatic verve. He also wrote *Morning Faces* (1949), a charming book about his two boys; *Through These Men* (1956), a brilliant gallery of biographical sketches; and *Daniel Boone* (1952), a biography for young people.

Brown, Margaret Wise (b. New York City,

May 23, 1910—d. Nov. 13, 1952), writer of children's books. Miss Brown has employed several pseudonyms, including Golden MacDonald, Timothy Hay, and Juniper Sage in writing *Little Lost Lamb* (1945); *The Little Island* (1946); *Horses* (1944); *The Man in the Manhole and the Fix-It Men* (1946), with Edith Thacher Hurd. Books under her own name include *The Streamlined Pig; Bumble-Bugs and Elephants; The Little Fireman* (all 1938). In ten years she wrote fifty-three books; her sales record in that period approached a million copies.

Brown, Solyman (b. Litchfield, Conn., Nov. 17, 1790—d. Feb. 13, 1876), clergyman, dentist, poet. In his extraordinarily varied career, Brown preached in Congregational and Swedenborgian churches, taught in New York private schools, became a dentist and published a magazine for dentists, *The Dental Expositor*. His poem *Dentalogia* (1833) earned him the somewhat dubious honor of "Poet Laureate of the Dental Profession." As far back as 1841 he published *The Importance of Regulating the Teeth of Children*.

Brown, Sterling A[llen] (b. Washington, D.C., May 1, 1901—   ), teacher, poet. A member of the English Department of Howard University, Brown wrote *Southern Road* (1932), *A Negro Looks at the South* (1943). He is a noted authority on Negro literary history and has edited some impressive anthologies.

Brown, Theophilus (b. Seekonk, Mass., Sept. 15, 1811—d. 1879?), tailor, poet, wit. Brown spent most of his life as a tailor in Worcester where his shop became the rendezvous of minor literati, and he made occasional excursions to the greater world of Emerson and Thoreau. He was a confirmed and cheery optimist. Hurrying once to a meeting at which Emerson was to speak, he said to a companion who feared they might be late, "If we *are* late, it is better to *miss* hearing Emerson than to *hear* anyone else." He was one of the earliest to arrange for adult education by courses of lectures he provided in Worcester. His letters were collected in 1879.

Brown, William Hill (b. Boston, 1765—d. Sept., 1793), poet, dramatist, novelist. In 1789 appeared in Boston a novel, THE POWER OF SYMPATHY, which capitalized on a scandal of the time—the supposed seduction of a young woman by her brother-in-law and her subsequent suicide—under a thin veil of fiction. The actual incident occurred in the family of the poet SARAH WENTWORTH MORTON, whose husband was the alleged seducer; strangely enough, the novel—sometimes described as "the first American novel"—was ascribed to her. The Mortons bought up all copies they could lay hands on and destroyed them, but a few survived. In 1895 the novel was reprinted serially in *The Bostonian Magazine*, and the more plausible theory was aired that Brown, a neighbor of the Mortons, was the author. He also wrote dramas, including a tragedy about Major André, *West Point Preserved* (1797); essays, verses, and a

short novel, *Ira and Isabella* (1807), a variation on *The Power of Sympathy*.

Brown, William Wells (1816–1884), Negro novelist, playwright, storyteller. See NEGRO IN AMERICAN LITERATURE.

Browne, Charles Farrar. See ARTEMUS WARD.

Browne, J[ohn] Ross (b. Ireland, Feb. 11, 1821—d. Dec. 8, 1875), traveler, newspaperman, diplomat. Browne has been held to anticipate Mark Twain in some of his writings and to foreshadow Melville's MOBY DICK in his first book, *Etchings of a Whaling Cruise* (1846). Among his other books: *Yusef, or, A Journey of the Frangi: A Crusade in the East* (1853); *Crusoe's Island, with Sketches of Adventure in California and Washoe* (1864); *An American Family in Germany* (1866). Later in life Browne was in government service, for a time U.S. Minister to China.

Browne, Lewis (b. England, June 24, 1897—d. Jan. 3, 1949), clergyman, historian, biographer, novelist, artist, lecturer. For a time associated with the Free Synagogue in Newark, New Jersey, Browne later gave up the ministry for writing and lecturing. Among his books: *Stranger Than Fiction* (1925); *This Believing World* (1926); *That Man Heine* (with Elsa Weihl, 1927); *Blessed Spinoza* (1932); *How Odd of God* (1934); *See What I Mean?* (1943). He also edited *The Graphic Bible* (1928) and *The Wisdom of Israel* (1945).

Browne, Lewis Allen (b. North Sandwich, N.H., Jan. 18, 1876—d. May 24, 1937), newspaperman, editor, writer of books for young people and of short stories. From Boston newspapers Browne came to New York to work for syndicates and on various Hearst journals. He wrote *Indian Fairy Tales* (1912). For *The Daily Mirror* he produced innumerable and varied tales day by day.

Brownell, Henry Howard (b. Providence, R.I., Feb. 6, 1820—d. Oct. 31, 1872), lawyer, historian, poet. Brownell, long an obscure writer of verse for Connecticut newspapers, won fame during the Civil War as the North's "battle laureate." One of his poems attracted Admiral David Farragut, who persuaded Brownell to join the navy and made him his personal secretary. Brownell's poems, composed while he was in action, were far superior to the mediocre verse of his early career. His *War Lyrics and Other Poems* (1866) won wide praise. See THE EAGLE OF CORINTH.

Brownell, W[illiam] C[rary] (b. New York City, Aug. 3, 1851—d. July 22, 1928), editor, critic. For many years Brownell was an editor for Charles Scribner's Sons. He issued volumes of notable criticism, including *French Traits* (1889), *Victorian Prose Masters* (1901), AMERICAN PROSE MASTERS (1909), *Criticism* (1914), *Standards* (1917), *Democratic Distinction in America* (1927). Gertrude Hall Brownell prepared in 1933 an anthology of his writings. He has been unduly neglected since his death, probably because of his emphasis on such moral qualities in literature as discipline. In *William Crary Brownell: Literary Adviser*, Me Tsung Kaung Tang sought to rehabilitate his reputation. See HUMANISM.

Brownson, Orestes Augustus (b. Stockbridge, Vt., Sept. 16, 1803—d. April 17, 1876), editor, writer on philosophy and theology, novelist. Brownson was a New Englander so thoroughly individualistic that he could not agree long with

anybody—even with himself. He was brought up as a strict Puritan, in 1822 formally joined the Presbyterian church, became a Universalist in 1824 and was later ordained a Universalist minister, was rejected because of his too-liberal views by the Universalists, came under WILLIAM ELLERY CHANNING's [1] influence, became a Unitarian minister, in 1836 founded his own church, in 1844 was converted to Roman Catholicism, but was branded as a heretic and was severely condemned when he tried to found an American form of Catholicism. Similarly in political belief he was at first a Socialist, in league with Robert Owen; he helped to organize a Workingmen's Party; he sent his son to BROOK FARM; he established an organ of the Democratic party; then he renounced democracy and rule of the people and became an advocate of a form of republicanism that showed his loss of faith in the intelligence and integrity of the common people. He cherished the conviction that there was a Divine Order, with leaders who would pursue the general welfare *of* the people but would have little or nothing done *by* the people. To spread his views Brownson established the BOSTON QUARTERLY REVIEW (January, 1838), which in 1842 was merged with the *United States Democratic Review*, in 1844 became

Brownson's Quarterly Review, continued till January, 1865, was revived in 1872, and died in 1875. Among his writings: *New Views of Christianity, Society, and the Church* (1836); *The Infidel Converted* (1840); *The Convert, Or, Leaves from My Experience* (1857); *The American Republic* (1865); *Conversation on Liberalism and the Church* (1870). The *Brownson Reader* (ed. by A. S. Ryan, 1955) follows his changes of thought.

Bruce, Charles (b. Nova Scotia, May 11, 1906 —), newspaperman, poet. After varied experience on Canadian newspapers and as a war correspondent during World War II, Bruce became superintendent of the Canadian Press. His poems appeared in many Canadian and American magazines. His books include *Wild Apples* (1927), *Tomorrow's Tide* (1932), *Personal Note* (1941), *Grey Ship Moving* (1945), *The Flowing Summer* (1947), *The Mulgrave Road* (1951) and *The Channel Shore* (1954).

Bruce, W[illiam] Cabell (b. Staunton Hill, Va., Mar. 12, 1860—d. May 9, 1946), lawyer, biographer, U.S. Senator. Bruce's legal career was spent in Baltimore, and it was from Maryland that he went to the Senate. His first book, *Benjamin Franklin, Self-Revealed* (1917), won the Pulitzer Prize in biography. Later he wrote *John Randolph of Roanoke* (1923), *Imaginary Conversations with Franklin* (1933), and several collections of essays. He was noted for his independence of viewpoint. He opposed prohibition, the Ku Klux Klan, and the New Deal vigorously.

Bruising Bill (1845), a novel by JOSEPH HOLT INGRAHAM. This is one of two tales that appeared in a single paperbound book; the other was called *Alice May. Bruising Bill* is one of the earliest works of fiction about Harvard. The incidents—a row between Town and Gown—may have been based on some actual occurrences in 1840. Harvard is called Cambridge College; the two leading characters are Edward Cassidy, the son of wealthy parents and a person of great benevolence, and William Martin ("Bruising Bill"), a product of the slums but by nature warm-hearted.

Bruno, Guido (b. Bohemia, Oct. 15, 1884—), editor, literary crusader. Frederick J. Hoffman and Charles Allen remark in *The Little Magazine* (1946): "One approaches the figure of Bruno with no little skepticism and amusement. No other man has ever actually begun and edited so many little magazines." Best known of these were *Bruno's Chap Books*, which began publication in 1915 and died the next year. Concurrently appeared *Bruno's Weekly* (July, 1915–September, 1916). This weekly absorbed another of Bruno's short-lived magazines, *Greenwich Village*, in December, 1915. *Bruno's*, a weekly, ran from January to April of 1917; *Bruno's Bohemia*, a monthly, from March to April, 1918; *Bruno's Review of Life, Love, and Letters* appeared once, apparently, in April, 1919; *Bruno's Review of Two Worlds*, a monthly, ran from November, 1920, through November,

1922. Bruno attacked censorship, analyzed and praised bohemianism, and demanded a free and secure life for the artist.

Brush, Katharine [Ingham] (b. Middletown, Conn., Aug. 15, 1902—d. June 10, 1952), novelist, short-story writer, columnist. Mrs. Brush's first fiction was contributed to *College Humor*, later she became a favorite in many magazines, particularly *Cosmopolitan*, *Good Housekeeping*, and *The American Magazine*. She was a frank, sometimes acidulous annalist of the "jazz age." Among her books were *Glitter* (1926), *Young Man of Manhattan* (1930), *The Red-Headed Woman* (1931), *Don't Ever Leave Me* (1935). One collection of her short stories, *Night Club* (1929), contains some of her best work; another gathering is entitled *Other Women* (1932). She collected sprightly contributions from her syndicated column, "Out of My Mind," in a book by that title (1943). In her autobiography, *This Is on Me* (1940), she discusses her problems as an author candidly. She also wrote numerous motion-picture scripts.

Brutus, or, The Fall of Tarquin (London, 1818; New York, 1819), a tragedy in verse by JOHN HOWARD PAYNE. When this play, based on the old Roman story that told how Brutus condemned his own son to death for treason, was produced in London, it brought back Edmund Kean to popular favor and made Payne famous. Junius Brutus Booth toured the wild West with the play in the 1820's and made the theme of hatred of tyrants a familiar one among the pioneers west of the Mississippi.

Bryan, Joseph, III (b. Richmond, Va., April 30, 1904—   ), newspaperman, editor, biographer. Bryan, at various times with *Town and Country* and the *Saturday Evening Post*, prefers free-lancing, and he has contributed articles, mainly profiles, to several magazines— *Life*, the *Post*, *Collier's*, *Reader's Digest*, and others. During the war he became well acquainted with the achievements and personality of Fleet Admiral William F. Halsey, and wrote with him *Admiral Halsey's Story* (1947), a particularly skillful collaboration. He also wrote *Aircraft Carrier* (1954); *The World's Greatest Showman* (1956).

Bryan, William Jennings (b. Salem, Ill., March 19, 1860—d. July 26, 1925), political orator, editor. "Crusading is my business," the "Great Commoner" once said; "early in life God revealed to me my power over men." In 1890 he went to Congress from a Nebraska district and in 1892 was re-elected. In 1896 he electrified the Democratic Presidential Convention with the famous speech that ended, "You shall not press down upon the brow of labor this crown of thorns, you shall not crucify mankind upon a cross of gold," and was nominated for President on a platform demanding that gold's value as against silver be reduced to a ratio of sixteen to one. After a hectic campaign that thoroughly terrified the gold-standard East, he was defeated. He was nominated again in 1900 and 1908, and again defeated. When WOODROW

WILSON became President in 1913, he made Bryan his Secretary of State. In 1915 Bryan resigned on the peace-and-war issue. In 1925 he sided with the backward-looking legislators who sought to prevent the teaching of evolution in American schools. The issue was joined when a Tennessee instructor in biology, John T. Scopes (1901–   ), was brought to trial at Dayton, Tenn. (July, 1925). The great lawyer CLARENCE DARROW undertook to defend him; Bryan led the opposition; the press of the United States, Canada, and England assembled in unprecedented numbers to report a remarkable legal proceeding. The trial came to be called the "monkey trial," and Bryan, who took the stand and whom Darrow mercilessly cross-examined, was more like a defendant than a prosecutor. Scopes was convicted and paid a fine, but by his courage made clear, as he had intended, the stupidity of the whole proceeding. Bryan died five days after the trial closed. (See SCOPES TRIAL.) In 1955 a play, *Inherit the Wind*, by Jerome Lawrence and Robert E. Lee, presented a vivid portrayal of the trial.

Bryan played a considerable role in the great CHAUTAUQUA movement, and earned what Victoria and Robert Ormond Case describe in their book on Chautauqua as "incredible popularity." Best loved of all his talks was one on "The Prince of Peace," repeated innumerable times in every state of the union until 1924. To the Cases, Bryan seems an ordinary man who was lifted into a prominence which was beyond his ability to sustain. His "sole gift was his voice. . . . He was perfect as he was. The same phrases he used in 1904 mesmerized his audiences in 1924." His *Speeches* (2 v.) were collected in 1909. His *Memoirs* appeared in 1925. He edited a weekly called *The Commoner* at Lincoln, Neb., from 1901 to 1923; it had for a while a wide circulation. Vachel Lindsay paid tribute to him in his poem, *Bryan, Bryan, Bryan, Bryan: The Campaign of 1896, as Viewed at the Time by a 16-Year-Old* (1919). But it is likely that Bryan will be longer remembered through Mencken's *In Memoriam: W.J.B.* (*Prejudices*, 5th Series, 1926), which Oscar Cargill calls "the greatest piece of journalistic vituperation produced in America." M. R. Werner wrote *Bryan*, a biography (1929).

Bryant, William Cullen (b. Cummington, Mass., Nov. 3, 1794—d. June 12, 1878), poet, lawyer, editor, critic. Bryant was the child of a strict Puritan household in which, however, there was a sincere cultivation of intellectual life. His early religious views were narrow and his early political opinions were those of a bigoted Federalist. The literary influences exerted upon him came from the classics, the Bible, and 18th-century English literature; his earliest desire was to be a poet and he put that desire into his prayers. He wrote beautiful, sincere, and sometimes great poetry in his early youth, and left it negligently in a drawer for his father to find years later and publish. He went to Williams College, but had to leave for financial reasons. He studied law, practiced for a while, learned to loathe it and its litigants. Then, with the publication of his first poems in 1817, he won enduring fame. He began writing for magazines, reading his poetry to distinguished audiences, seeking to make a living in other ways than in a law office.

In 1825 he went to New York, edited a magazine unsuccessfully, entered a period of deep gloom, and was almost on the point of returning to Boston when he was offered employment on the New York *Evening Post* (1826). He rose steadily to the top, became editor and part owner, wrote numerous articles, critiques, and editorials. In time he became famous as New York's leading citizen, who espoused liberal causes with courage and devotion, turning from his early Federalism toward democracy. He supported Lincoln, favored free trade, defended some poor tailors who had been arrested for trying to form a labor union, raised his voice to assist the cause of freedom in many lands. In the meantime his religious beliefs, too, had changed; in general he accepted the Unitarian creed, with overtones of pagan stoicism. His appearance and manner also changed. In boyhood frail, he grew into a handsome, athletic youth with some love of the convivial and more sense of humor than he revealed to a later generation. In old age he looked the Biblical prophet: William Ellery Leonard sketched "that Mosaic massive head, those deep, peering, brooding eyes, those white shaggy brows, and the great beard that, in the engraving after Sarony's photograph, has been now for a generation familiar in so many homes of our land."

There is general agreement that Bryant's earliest poems were his best, although nowhere in his long career did he fail to maintain high standards. The first draft of THANATOPSIS was

written in 1811 under the strong influence of the so-called Graveyard School of England: Thomas Gray, Edward Young, and others. It was published in *The North American Review* in 1817, and in revised and much improved form in the collected *Poems* of 1821. As a poem it far surpasses all its English models except Gray's *Elegy*. Other early and some later poems of great merit are INSCRIPTION FOR THE ENTRANCE TO A WOOD (1815), TO A WATERFOWL (1818), THE AGES (1821), A FOREST HYMN (1860), *The Death of the Flowers* (1825), *To the Fringed Gentian* (1832), SONG OF MARION'S MEN (1831), *The Battle-Field* (1839), "Oh Mother of a Mighty Race" (1847), THE FLOOD OF YEARS (1876). In these one finds Bryant's melancholic but sometimes joyous brooding on nature, his frequent thought of death, his intense patriotism, his devotion to freedom, and his inveterate tendency toward a "moral" at the close of the poem. His separate volumes of poetry include: *The Embargo* (anti-Jeffersonian satires, 1808); *Poems* (eighty-nine pieces, 1832); THE FOUNTAIN (1842); *The White-Footed Deer* (1844); *A Forest Hymn* (1860); *Thirty Poems* (1864); *Hymns* (1869); *The Little People of the Snow* (1873); *Among the Trees* (1874); *The Flood of Years* (1877). In prose he published *Letters of a Traveller* (1850; 2nd series, 1859), which includes discourses on Cooper, Irving, and others; his *Orations and Addresses* were collected later. See also THE AGES; EARTH; HYMN TO DEATH; THE INDIAN GIRL'S LAMENT; ROBERT OF LINCOLN; THE TALISMAN.

Tremaine McDowell has summed up Bryant's steady evolution as one from Federalism, Calvinism, and Classicism to Democracy, Unitarianism, and Romanticism. He feels that Bryant attained a "final mediation" between these two sets of factors. For example, he may have abandoned the extreme severities of Puritanism, but in his life and in his poetry he revealed Puritanism at its best and highest—in his nobility of thought, his devotion to duty, his care for the state as a citizen. Nor, as a romantic who at times preferred the Spenserian stanza to blank verse and couplets, did he give up his love of the classical. After his wife's death in 1866 he found consolation in translating Homer into blank verse (*The Iliad*, 1870; *The Odyssey*, 1871), renderings that lack the pre-classical strength of Homer but are good poetry in Bryant's best manner. His insistence upon purity of diction led to his drawing up an *Index Expurgatorius* for the guidance of immature staff writers on the *Post*. Its prohibitions include inflated words like *inaugurate* for *begin*, misemployed words like *mutual* for *common*, and some personal verbal prejudices against, for instance, *debut, rowdies, standpoint*.

Parke Godwin edited his *Poetical Works* (1883) and his *Complete Prose Writings* (1884), and also wrote a life with selected letters (1883). H. H. Peckham wrote an enlightening biography, *Gotham Yankee* (1950).

Bryce, James. See THE AMERICAN COMMONWEALTH.

Bryson, Lyman [Lloyd] (b. Valentine, Neb., July 12, 1888—d. Nov. 24, 1959), newspaperman, teacher, writer. Bryson worked at first for Omaha and Detroit newspapers, and later went into teaching; he taught at Michigan, the University of California, and finally at Teachers College, Columbia University, where he became professor of education in 1935. He became a specialist in adult education and was made director of the Department of Education for the Columbia Broadcasting System. In 1940 he began to conduct a popular radio program, *Invitation to Learning*, in which a host of distinguished men and women participated in cultural discussions. Dr. Bryson wrote a collection of verse, *Smoky Roses* (1916); a play, *The Grasshopper* (produced, 1917); and occasional short stories. His discussions of educational and social issues include: *Adult Education* (1936); *Which Way America?* (1939); *Science and Freedom* (1947); *Working for Democracy* (with George Kerry Smith, 1948); *Time for Reason About Radio* (1948); *The Next America: Prophecy and Faith* (1952); *The Drive Toward Reason* (1954). He edited a number of books, among them *Goals for American Education* (1950); *Freedom and Authority in Our Time* (1953); *Aspects of Human Equality* (1957).

Buchanan, James (b. near Mercersburg, Pa., April 23, 1791—d. June 1, 1868), fifteenth President, elected 1856. In his administration came the DRED SCOTT DECISION and the laying of the first Atlantic cable (both 1857); John Brown's raid on HARPER'S FERRY (1859); the admission of Minnesota, Oregon, and Kansas as states; the secession of South Carolina and six other Southern states (1860–61).

Buck, Frank (b. Gainesville, Tex., March 17, 1884—d. March 25, 1950), explorer, motion-picture producer, writer. From his boyhood Buck was interested in animals. His first expedition to study them was made to South America; later he traveled all over the world collecting animals for zoos and circuses. He was fortunate in finding a good collaborator, EDWARD ANTHONY, who wrote with him, in good salty American style, BRING 'EM BACK ALIVE (1930) and *Wild Cargo* (1932). Two of Buck's less well-known books are *Fang and Claw* (with Carol Weld, 1935) and *Animals Are Like That* (1939). His autobiography, *All in a Lifetime*, appeared in 1941. Among his motion-picture productions were versions of several of his books.

Buck, Gene [Edward Eugene] (b. Detroit, Aug. 8, 1885—d. Feb. 24, 1957), illustrator, song writer, librettist, producer, official in ASCAP. Buck wrote *Daddy Has a Sweetheart and Mother Is Her Name; Hello Frisco; Tulip Time; Lovely Little Melody; Someone, Someday, Somewhere*, etc. He became a charter member of ASCAP (1914), its president in 1924; he was frequently re-elected.

Buck, Pearl [Sydenstricker] [Mrs. Richard Walsh] (b. Hillsboro, W. Va., June 26, 1892—   ), novelist, short-story writer, translator. Mrs. Buck's missionary parents took her to China when she was five months old, and she spent many years in that country, although she returned home to attend Randolph Macon College. As a result, many of her books have a Chinese background. The best of those not directly or entirely laid in China—*Fighting Angel* (1936) and *The Exile* (1936), brought together as *The Spirit and the Flesh*—are portraits of her mother and father. She taught in Nanking from 1921 to 1931. In later years she became active in the East and West Association (its president since 1941) and in world peace movements. She was awarded a Pulitzer Prize in 1932, the William Dean Howells medal in 1935, the Nobel Prize in literature in 1938. She joined the editorial staff of the John Day Company and married its president, after her divorce from John L. Buck.

Among Mrs. Buck's books are: *East Wind— West Wind* (1930); *The Young Revolutionist* (1931); THE GOOD EARTH (1931); *Sons* (1932); *The First Wife and Other Stories* (1933); *The Mother* (1934); *The Patriot* (1939); DRAGON SEED (1942); *What America Means to Me* (1943); PAVILION OF WOMEN (1946); *Far and Near* (stories, 1947); PEONY (1948); *Kinfolk* (1949); *The Child Who Never Grew* (1950); *Come, My Beloved* (1953); *My Several Worlds: A Personal Record* (1954); *Letter from Peking* (1957); *American Triptych* (1958); *Command the Morning* (1959); *Christmas Ghost* (1960); *A Bridge for Passing* (1962). She translated a Chinese classic under the title *All Men Are Brothers* (1933). *Imperial Woman* (1956) is a fictional biography of China's last empress. She wrote other novels under the pseudonym John Sedges. Her play *Desert Incident* was produced on Broadway in 1960.

Mrs. Buck's style tends toward the Biblical, perhaps because of her missionary background. She early adopted the technique of the saga, a form popular in the United States ever since the publication of Ruth Suckow's COUNTRY PEOPLE (1924). As Leo Gurko remarks, "*The Good Earth* was almost the first book to unlock for the West the interior of China (there had been plenty of melodramatic novels about Shanghai)." Phyllis Bentley feels that Mrs. Buck's main theme is not the presentation of China to the West, but rather "the continuity of life."

Bucke, Richard Maurice (b. Eng., March 18, 1837—d. Feb. 19, 1902), physician, author. Bucke came to Canada in 1838 to study and practice medicine, and later specialized in care of the insane. His main connection with literature was through his friendship with WALT WHITMAN, out of which grew the two studies *Walt Whitman, a Contemporary Study* (1883) and *Walt Whitman, Man and Poet* (1897), as well as two works based on the poet's pantheistic philosophy, *Man's Moral Nature* (1879) and *Cosmic Consciousness* (1901). He was one of Whitman's literary executors and edited many of his letters and papers.

Buckminster, Joseph Stevens (b. Portsmouth, N.H., May 26, 1784—d. June 9, 1812), clergyman. Buckminster was a leader of the "liberal Christians" who in the first decade of the 19th century were to move toward Unitarianism. In 1805 he became minister of the fashionable Brattle Street Church, and there delivered cultured, highly intelligent addresses, collected after his death in *Sermons* (1839). He organized the ANTHOLOGY CLUB, and helped produce the *Monthly Anthology*, one of the earliest of American literary magazines. In 1806 he traveled for a year in Europe and brought back a collection of 3,000 volumes, which became the nucleus of the Athenaeum Library. Perry Miller speaks of him as "the most accomplished and cosmopolitan figure of his age."

Budd, Lanny. Hero of a long series of novels by UPTON SINCLAIR, beginning with *World's End* (1940). The illegitimate son of a Connecticut munitions millionaire, Budd becomes a latter-day "questing spirit" who, in the course of the novels, becomes intimate with many of the world's most prominent figures and witnesses many of modern history's most important events. Through Budd, Sinclair voices his convictions concerning modern political and social developments, beginning with World War I.

Budd, Thomas (b. England, [?]—d. 1698), historian. Budd came to New Jersey in 1678 and settled there long enough to have a town—Buddtown—named after him. On his return to England he published *Good Order Established in Pennsylvania and New Jersey* (1685). When a young woman slave ran away, according to legend, Budd posted notices offering a reward for her return. All closed with the appeal, "Stop the jade!" Near Buddtown is a stream called "Stop-the-Jade Run," said to have been named from this incident.

Buffalo Bill. See WILLIAM F. CODY.

Builders, The (composed, 1846; published, 1849), a poem by HENRY WADSWORTH LONGFELLOW. A strongly didactic composition, expressed in somewhat jingly rhymes. Longfellow urges us all to do our best, each in his sphere.

Building of the Ship, The (1849), a poem by HENRY WADSWORTH LONGFELLOW. In the opinion of his northern contemporaries, Longfellow attained his poetic peak in the concluding lines of this poem, beginning "Thou, too, sail on, O Ship of State!" Longfellow describes the building of a ship, interweaving the details with those of an approaching marriage between the builder's daughter and the owner's son; and with a constant symbolism, in which the ship is life itself and becomes, at the close, a metaphor of the Union. It was Longfellow's most powerful contribution to Union sentiment; Dorothy Werner calls it "the most influential poem of the period." In the hard days of World War II Longfellow's magnificent peroration played a part in an exchange of encouraging letters between Franklin D. Roosevelt and Winston Churchill. The former quoted Arthur Hugh Clough's *Say Not the Struggle Naught Availeth* to the British Prime Minister; Churchill replied with Longfellow's "Thou, too, sail on!"

The poem resembles Friedrich von Schiller's *Das Lied von der Glocke* (1799), with which Longfellow was undoubtedly familiar. Gay Willson Allen calls it Longfellow's "best and probably most famous ode," and he points out its skillful use of varying metrical devices (in *American Prosody*, 1935). One of the finest passages is surprisingly irregular in accentuation and length of line, that in which the poet describes the lordly pines "in the deer-haunted forests of Maine" before they fell. This passage anticipates the IMPRESSIONISM and FREE VERSE of a later day.

Bulfinch, Charles (b. Boston, Aug. 8, 1763—d. April 4, 1844), architect, public official. A Harvard graduate (1781), with an early interest in architecture, Bulfinch was further stimulated by a tour of Europe (1785–87) following a route suggested by Jefferson. He designed many public edifices, including the State Houses at Hartford (1792) and Boston (1795). The latter, his most famous work, set a pattern for governmental buildings. In domestic design he introduced the Adam style to New England and planned for the first time in America a row of houses of coherent design. In 1817 he was called to Washington to help in the completion of the National Capitol. Married in 1788 to Hannah Apthorp, he had eleven children, one of whom, THOMAS BULFINCH, was to become a well-known author.

Bulfinch, Thomas (b. Newton, Mass., July 15, 1796—d. May 27, 1867), clerk, teacher, writer. A son of the famous architect CHARLES BULFINCH (1763–1844), Thomas spent his life in a humble business post and devoted his leisure to writing. His *Age of Fable* (1855) is still used in some American schools as an introduction to Greek, Roman, Scandinavian, and Celtic mythology; new illustrated editions appear regularly. Less popular but still consulted is *The Age of Chivalry* (1858). These straightforward and expurgated versions of ancient myths have awakened in many young readers a love of the great tales and have served as a guide to mythological references in literature.

Bull, Ole [Borneman] (b. Norway, 1810—d. 1880), violinist. He toured the United States five times, taking the country by storm. In Cambridge, Mass., during the last years of his life, he was a familiar figure in literary and artistic circles. Longfellow introduced him as the musician in TALES OF A WAYSIDE INN. He may have been the original of Ibsen's *Peer Gynt*.

Bullard, F[rederic] Lauriston (b. Wauseon, Ohio, May 13, 1866—d. Aug. 3, 1952), clergyman, newspaperman, historian. Bullard wrote *Famous War Correspondents* (1914) and several books on Lincoln, winning a diploma of honor from the Lincoln Memorial University for his work in this field.

Bullitt, William C[hristian] (b. Philadelphia, Jan. 25, 1891—   ), diplomat, foreign correspondent. Bullitt served in the army during World War I, thereafter helped prepare the treaties of peace at Versailles. He served in important ambassadorial posts, to Russia (1933–36), to France (1936–41), and as ambassador-at-large (1941–42). Among his books: a novel, *It's Not Done* (1926); *Report to the American*

People (1940); *The Great Globe Itself* (1946). At first friendly to Russian aspirations, Bullitt in later writings urgently warned the world against the dangers of Soviet aggressiveness.

Bumppo, Natty. A character in James Fenimore Cooper's LEATHER-STOCKING TALES (1823–1841). He is called Bumppo or Deerslayer in THE DEERSLAYER, Hawkeye in THE LAST OF THE MOHICANS, Pathfinder in THE PATHFINDER, Natty Bumppo or Leatherstocking in THE PIONEERS, the trapper in THE PRAIRIE. Cooper found suggestions for Bumppo in a leatherstockinged hunter named Shipman whom he knew when he was a boy; also Daniel Boone (that "grave and noble woodsman," as Van Wyck Brooks calls him) contributed elements. The sequence of publication of the five novels was not the same as the chronology of Bumppo's career, and Cooper's treatment of him varies somewhat bewilderingly. Sometimes he sees Bumppo realistically, sometimes romantically; sometimes Bumppo talks an illiterate vernacular, sometimes he speaks with impressive poetic fervor. At Cooperstown there stands a shaft of Italian marble topped by a figure of Bumppo, with his faithful hound Hector at his feet.

Bunce, Oliver Bell (b. New York City, Feb. 8, 1828—d. May 15, 1890), publisher, playwright, editor. Bunce began life as a playwright, went on to the establishment of a publishing firm, later joined Harper's and finally Appleton as an editor. Among his plays: MARCO BOZZARIS (1850); *Fate* (1856); and *Love in '76* (1857). He helped William Cullen Bryant edit a successful series of travel books: *Picturesque America* (1872–74); *Picturesque Europe* (1875–79); and *Picturesque Palestine* (1881–84). His *Opinions and Disputations of Bachelor Bluff* (1881) was widely read.

Bunche, Ralph J[ohnson] (b. Detroit, Aug. 7, 1904——), educator. Bunche received his education at the University of California (B.A., 1927) and Harvard (M.A., 1928; Ph.D., 1934). He became head of the political science department at Howard University in 1929. Since then he has frequently served the federal government and the United Nations. His work as U.N. Mediator in Palestine (1948–49) made him internationally known, and he was awarded the Spingarn medal by the National Association for the Advancement of Colored People (1949) and the Nobel Peace Prize (1950). In 1958 he was under secretary for special political affairs to the U.N. Among his writings are *A World View of Race* (1936) and *Peace and the United Nations* (1952).

Bunker Hill. [More properly, **Bunker's Hill.**] The famous "Battle of Bunker Hill" was really fought for the most part at nearby Breed's Hill, where a group of American soldiers on the night of June 16, 1775, erected fortifications. The battle between them and the British, whom the Americans had been holding within Boston, began the following day. General Putnam gave the famous command, "Don't fire until you can see the whites of their eyes," as the British troops

advanced. The British charged again and again, finally driving the Americans toward Bunker Hill, but with heavier losses, and General Greene said, "I wish we could sell them another hill at the same price." General Joseph Warren was killed in the battle, and John Pierpont commemorated his heroism in *Warren's Address to the American Soldiers*. In 1825 the cornerstone of a monument at Bunker Hill was laid by Lafayette, and Daniel Webster delivered an oration on the occasion; in 1843 the monument was completed, and again Webster delivered an oration. Bunker Hill plays a part in James Fenimore Cooper's LIONEL LINCOLN (1825), and in H. H. Brackenridge's verse drama, THE BATTLE OF BUNKERS HILL (1776).

Bunner, H[enry] C[uyler] (b. Oswego, N.Y., Aug. 3, 1855—d. May 11, 1896), poet, short-story writer, novelist, editor. Bunner turned early to a literary career and for the greater part of his regrettably short life his course was fixed:

he became editor of PUCK within a year of its foundation in 1877, remained with it till his death, and wrote mainly for its columns. Moreover, the character of his writing was to some extent determined by the nature of *Puck*, which demanded material not merely humorous but brief. Although Bunner wrote novels (*The Midge*, 1886, the story of a bachelor and his orphan ward, is the best), he was above all a writer of short short stories, tailored to fit the pages of a magazine determined not to be boring. As such he practically founded a new genre in the United States, the anecdotal tale. Most famous of his books is SHORT SIXES: STORIES TO BE READ WHILE THE CANDLE BURNS (1891), which contains such classics as *The Love Letters of Smith*, *The Nine Cent-Girls*, and *Zenobia's Infidelity*. Later came MADE IN FRANCE: FRENCH TALES WITH A UNITED STATES TWIST (1893), ten tales transmuted rather than translated into American idiom and folkways—including one story by Bunner himself hidden away among the rest and undetected by contemporary critics. He also published *More Short Sixes* (1894) and *Love in Old Cloathes* (1896).

Bunner won distinction, moreover, as a writer of *vers de société*, under the strong influence of Robert Herrick, Heinrich Heine, and Austin Dobson. Fred Lewis Pattee regards him as "our chief writer" in this difficult if not very profound genre, of which his most famous example is "She was a beauty in the days/ When Madison was President." He was, too, an expert parodist, particularly in his multiple parodies of HOME, SWEET HOME. The best of his poems appeared in AIRS FROM ARCADY AND ELSEWHERE (1884), later in a collected edition of his poems (1896). Gerard E. Jensen presents an intimate view of Bunner in *Life and Letters of Henry Cuyler Bunner* (1940).

Buntline, Ned. The pen name of E. Z. C. JUDSON.

Bunyan, Paul. The mighty lumberjack of the American forests recalls Heracles, Thor, and Samson in his tremendous strength and his preternatural exploits, but he especially resembles Baron Münchausen. Unlike the mythological figures of Greece and Rome, Paul is a comic folk hero. Around him have gathered a host of other fabulous characters: TONY BEAVER, KEMP MORGAN, FEBOLD FEBOLDSON, JOHN HENRY, and others. The stories told about him and his friends are "TALL TALES," narratives in which the storyteller tries to surpass other storytellers. Legends of Paul Bunyan have circulated for decades. He may have appeared first in Quebec or northern Ontario, or in Maine, or farther west. James Stevens traced him to a French-Canadian logger named Paul Bunyon, who won a reputation as a prodigious fighter in the Papineau Rebellion against England in 1837 and later became famous as the boss of a logging camp. There is a French-Canadian tang in Paul's talk and ways.

He first appeared in print, so far as can be discovered, in an advertising pamphlet, *Paul Bunyan and His Big Blue Ox*, published in 1914 by the Red River Lumber Company, originally located in Minnesota. The booklet became popular immediately and was issued in larger and larger editions. Both the text and the amusing illustrations were done by W. B. Laughead, who stated: "The student of folklore will easily distinguish the material derived from original sources from that written for the purposes of this book. It should be stated that the names of the supporting characters, including the animals, are inventions by the writer of this version. The oral chroniclers did not, in his hearing, which goes back to 1900, call any of the characters by name except Paul Bunyan himself." In 1914 Douglas Malloch wrote a poem about Paul, *The Round River Drive*, which appeared in *The American Lumberman* (April 25, 1914). Later Carl Sandburg included a patterned narrative, *Who Made Paul Bunyan?*, in THE PEOPLE, YES (1936). Historians (K. Bernice Stewart, Homer A. Watt, Louise Pound) have examined sources since 1919, and many storytellers have retold the Bunyan stories—among them Virginia Tunvey, Esther Shepard, James Stevens, Glen Rounds, Dell J. McCormick, and Acel Garland. D. G.

Hoffman made a critical study of the legend in *Paul Bunyan: Last of the Frontier Demigods* (1952). See LUMBERJACKS IN AMERICAN LITERATURE.

Burdette, Robert J[ones] (b. Greensboro, Pa., July 30, 1844—d. Nov. 19, 1914), newspaperman, columnist, clergyman, lecturer. One of the earliest professional columnists, Burdette also became a professional humorist who enlarged his income greatly by lecturing. His most popular piece, "The Rise and Fall of the Moustache," was delivered, it is said, more than 5,000 times; it appeared in book form in 1877. His famous column was called "Hawkeyetems of Roaming Robert," and appeared in the Burlington (Iowa) *Daily Hawk Eye*. His books include *Hawkeyes* (1879) and *Chimes from a Jester's Bells* (1897).

Burgess, [Frank] Gelett (b. Boston, Jan. 30, 1866—d. Sept. 18, 1951), humorist, writer, neologist. Early in his career Burgess was drawn into literary activity, joining a lively group that in the 1890's published "little magazines" and sought to make San Francisco a literary and artistic center. He was editor of a magazine called *The Lark*, which ran for twenty-five issues. A quatrain of his commencing "I've never seen a purple cow," in the first issue (May, 1895), won him national fame; the verse was repeated and parodied *ad nauseam*. Later Burgess went to New York and began writing an extraordinary variety of books. One of them won him additional fame: ARE YOU A BROMIDE? in, THE SULPHITIC THEORY (1907). *Bromide*, meaning a person who utters platitudes with the air of having just invented them, has taken its place in the language; the *New English Dictionary* cites an Oxford professor who used it in 1909. Burgess became a word inventor. His two other most famous coinages are *blurb* and *goop*. The former denotes the publisher's description of a book, found on its jacket. The latter was a member of a strange and ill-behaved race of children who appeared as horrible examples in GOOPS AND HOW TO BE THEM (1900). Burgess contrived many other words; some of his amusing and often ingeniously appropriate coinages appear in *Burgess Unabridged* (1914). He also wrote novels and plays, none of which attained any great success. Two collections of sharply worded and witty epigrams are *The Maxims of Methuselah* (1907) and *The Maxims of Noah* (1913). Out of a ripe experience in being cheerful and in getting the most out of life as he advanced in years, Burgess wrote a volume of exhortations to mental and physical health, *Look Eleven Years Younger* (1937).

Burgess, Thornton W[aldo] ["W. B. Thornton"] (b. Sandwich, Mass., Jan. 14, 1874—d. June 5, 1965), editor, author. As an editor Burgess' chief connections have been with the Phelps Publishing Co. and the Orange Judd Co. in Springfield, Mass. (1895–1911); for a time he helped edit *Good Housekeeping*, then a property of the Orange Judd Co. Always a lover of the outdoors, Burgess (under the pen name of W. B. Thornton) contributed numerous articles during this period to *Country Life in America*. In 1910 he began his extraordinary career as a writer of children's books. He became the author of a syndicated column, "Burgess Bedtime Stories," that has now published more than 10,000 stories. His first book, *Mother West Wind's Children* (1910), contained sixteen animal stories, most of which had previously appeared in *Good Housekeeping*. It was the first of a series that reached eight volumes in 1918. When *Good Housekeeping* was sold in 1911, Burgess was out of a job. In February, 1912, he started syndicating what he then called "Little Stories for Bedtime." These resembled the tales he had published in the *West Wind* books, but they were shorter. A collection was published in 1913 as *The Adventures of Reddy Fox*, the first of the *Bedtime Story Series*, in which twenty volumes were published (1913–1919). Among his other books and series: the *Boy Scouts* series (1912–1915); *Green Meadows* series (1918–1920); *Burgess Bird Book for Children* (1919); *Tales from the Story-Teller's House* (1937); *The Old Briar Patch* (1947); and many others. In all of them Burgess has faithfully and pleasingly taught nature lore and preached love of "the lesser folk in fur and feathers."

Burgoyne, Sir John (b. England, 1722–1792), general, dramatist. Called "Gentleman Johnny," he was sent to Canada as commander-in-chief of the northern British army during the American Revolution. His advance was stopped at Saratoga, and he surrendered Oct. 17, 1777. This engagement may have been the turning point of the Revolutionary War, but the defeat was probably due to the ineptitude of other British generals. Back in England, Burgoyne wrote *The Maid of the Oaks* (1774) and THE HEIRESS (1786), both clever comedies. He figures prominently in Bernard Shaw's *The Devil's Disciple* (1900) and in Kenneth Roberts' A RABBLE IN ARMS (1933).

Burk, John Daly (b. Ireland, 1775?—d. April 11, 1808), editor, dramatist, historian. A political refugee from his native land, Burk reached the United States in 1796. He was a man of warm temper and a deep love of freedom. His most famous production was *Bunker Hill, or, The Death of General Warren* (performed in 1797). He also wrote a play called *Female Patriotism, or, The Death of Joan d'Arc* (performed in 1798). He founded a paper called *The Polar Star and Boston Daily Advertiser* (Oct. 6, 1796), which expired after six months; he started another paper, *The Time Piece*, that likewise failed.

Burke, Kenneth [Duva] (b. Pittsburgh, Pa., May 5, 1897—   ), critic, philosopher, translator. Burke's translations have done much to make such noted German authors as Thomas Mann, Emil Ludwig, Oswald Spengler, and Hugo von Hofmannsthal better known to the American public. In his earlier years he was active on some of the "LITTLE MAGAZINES," particularly BROOM and *Secession*.

Two of Burke's writings are particularly significant. His *Philosophy of Literary Form—*

Studies in Symbolic Action (1941) was described by Hoffman and Allen as "a masterful study of the philosophical ingredients of poetic imagination." *A Grammar of Motives*, one of two "works on human relations," was begun in 1945. The first volume deals with the nature of verbal statement, the second (*Rhetoric of Motives*, 1950), with the formation of attitudes that would lead to practical acts. His work has impressed many critics, but his language and vocabulary are difficult and have limited his audiences. Other books by Kenneth Burke: *Book of Moments: Poems, 1915–54* (1955); *The Rhetoric of Religion* (1961).

Burleycue (1931), a history of burlesque by Bernard Sobel (1888—1964), supplemented (1956) by Sobel's *Pictorial History of Burlesque*, an account that ranges from Aristophanes to Minsky.

Burlin, Natalie Curtis (b. New York City, April 26, 1875—d. Oct. 25, 1921), a collector of Indian and Negro folk songs and music, among the first to bring this material to popular attention. Among her books are *The Indians' Book* (1907) and *Hampton Series of Negro Folk Songs* (4 v., 1918–19).

Burlingame, [William] Roger (b. New York City, May 7, 1889—d. March 19, 1967), editor, writer. Burlingame worked for Charles Scribner's Sons, 1914–1926, then turned to writing verse, stories, and magazine articles. His novel *You Too* (1924) satirized advertising; among his other novels are *High Thursday* (1928), *Three Bags Full* (1936). Interested in the history of technology in the United States, Burlingame wrote *March of the Iron Men* (1938), *Engines of Democracy* (1940), *Whittling Boy* (a biography of Eli Whitney, 1941); *Of Making Many Books* (1946), a history of the first hundred years of Charles Scribner's and considered one of Burlingame's finest source books; *Inventors Behind the Inventor* (1947); *Machines that Built America* (1953); *Henry Ford* (1955); *The American Conscience* (1957), a history of moral attitudes through three centuries, 1600 to 1900 (Burlingame considered this his best book); *Scientists Behind the Inventors* (1960). Burlingame, a veteran of the first World War, was a correspondent in the second. He lived for several years in Italy and in France.

Burman, Ben Lucien (b. Covington, Ky., Dec. 12, 1896—   ), war correspondent, novelist. During World War II Ben Lucien Burman was the first to reach the Free French in North Africa after the collapse of the French government. A veteran of World War I, Burman was on the scene as a reporter this time, and it was his reporting which won him the French Legion of Honor. *Miracle on the Congo* (1942), and *Rooster Crows for Day* (1945) describe his wartime experiences in Africa. The latter won him the Thomas Jefferson Memorial Prize in 1945. These years of wartime activity interrupted Burman's series of novels on the Mississippi region which began with *Mississippi* (1929); *Steamboat Round the Bend* (1933, filmed in 1935 with Will Rogers); *Blow for a Landing* (1938); *Big River to Cross* (1940). After the war came

Everywhere I Roam (1949); *Seven Stars for Catfish Bend* (1956); *The Street of the Laughing Camel* (1959); *It's a Big Continent* (1961).

Burnett, Frances [Eliza] Hodgson (b. England, Nov. 24, 1849—d. Oct. 29, 1924), novelist, writer of children's stories, playwright. Mrs. Burnett, who settled in the United States in 1865, once boasted that she had never written a story that wasn't accepted. She will be remembered, however, principally for LITTLE LORD FAUNTLEROY (1886). The chief character was modeled on her son Vivian. He is depicted as an American-born boy who inherits an English estate, and who is a frank, affectionate lad with a gift for naïve and amusing phrases. When the book was done, a photograph of Vivian in curls and a velvet suit with lace collar, cuffs, and a sash was sent along; and this was faithfully copied by Reginald Birch, who did the illustrations. Published first as a serial in *St. Nicholas*, later as a book, *Little Lord Fauntleroy* attained a popularity that was catastrophic in its effects on the little boys of the day; their mothers promptly dressed them just like Vivian Burnett, curls and all. Mrs. Burnett's first book was *That Lass o' Lowrie's* (1877), an adult novel. However, she is better known today for *Esmeralda* (1881); *Editha's Burglar* (1888); *A Lady of Quality* (1896); and *The Secret Garden* (1911), still popular among children. Her stories are oversentimental and obviously laid in a dream world, but a very large public enjoyed them. She dramatized *Little Lord Fauntleroy* (produced, 1888). An English dramatist attempted to produce an unauthorized version of the same story, but a lawsuit confirmed Mrs. Burnett's rights, establishing for the first time in that country an author's control over his own novels. The writers of England gave Mrs. Burnett a diamond bracelet in gratitude for her success in setting up a valuable precedent. In 1927 Vivian Burnett wrote a biography of his mother called *The Romantick Lady*. See also Elizabeth Jordan's autobiography, *Three Rousing Cheers* (1938).

Burnett, Whit (b. Salt Lake City, Aug. 14, 1899—   ), newspaperman, editor, short-story writer. With his wife MARTHA FOLEY (since divorced), Burnett founded the magazine STORY, published first in Vienna in 1931, later in Palma, Majorca, finally in the United States in 1933. His name has been associated with this famous magazine for years. Burnett collected a book of his own stories in *The Maker of Signs* (1934) and wrote *The Literary Life and the Hell with It* (1939). He edited anthologies of short stories, also *The World's Best* (1950), a collection of writings by authors still living, who selected the pieces they wished included.

Burnett, W[illiam] R[iley] (b. Springfield, Ohio, Nov. 25, 1899—   ), novelist, short-story writer, screen writer. Burnett is one of the leading exponents of HARD-BOILED FICTION, usually laid in the world of gangsters. For eight years he wrote constantly—novels, stories, plays —without a single acceptance. Then came LITTLE CAESAR (1929), and his fortune was made. The book became an immediate best seller and

everywhere was accepted as a veracious picture of life in this country. It was turned into a movie, made Edward G. Robinson a star, and confirmed a tendency in Hollywood to produce tough underworld films. In his later stories, *Iron Man*, 1930; *Dark Hazard*, 1933; *Goodbye to the Past*, 1934; *Nobody Lives Forever*, 1944; *The Asphalt Jungle*, 1949; *Captain Lightfoot* (1954); *Pale Moon* (1956); *Underdog* (1957); and others, Burnett sometimes avoids the gangster milieu. He has also written movie scripts, notably *Wake Island* (1942).

Burns, John Horne (b. Andover, Mass., Oct. 7, 1916—d. Aug. 10, 1953), novelist. Burns' death at the age of thirty-six extinguished a talent that had not yet fully realized itself. His gift for colorful and forceful expression found a suitable form in only one book, THE GALLERY (1947), a series of intensely rendered sketches of G.I.'s in Naples during the war. *Lucifer with a Book* (1949) and *A Cry of Children* (1952) were less successful.

Burnshaw, Stanley (b. New York City, June 20, 1906—   ), poet, editor. Stanley Burnshaw was educated at the University of Pittsburgh and Cornell. Soon after leaving the latter institution he entered the publishing business, becoming an editor of Henry Holt & Co. in 1958. His collections of verse, *The Iron Land* (1936), *The Bridge* (1945), *The Revolt of the Cats in Paradise* (1945), and *Early and Late Testament* (1952) reveal him as a thoughtful and craftsmanlike poet.

Burr, Aaron (b. Newark, N.J., Feb. 6, 1756— d. Sept. 14, 1836), lawyer, diarist, third Vice-President of the United States. A graduate of Princeton, Burr studied law, fought well in the Revolutionary War. After the war he gained success in law and politics, organizing Tammany Hall into a strong political machine in New York. He became Vice-President under Jefferson (1801–05). His long-standing enmity with ALEXANDER HAMILTON reached a climax in a duel in which Hamilton was killed (July 11, 1804). The duel ruined Burr personally and politically, made a martyr of Hamilton. Burr wandered to the West and South (see HARMAN BLENNERHASSETT), was tried and acquitted for treason, lived abroad, again practiced law in New York, unsuccessfully married "that elegant strumpet" Madame Jumel, died on Staten Island. Burr as a writer appears chiefly in a two-volume work, *The Private Journal of Aaron Burr* (1838 and 1903), consisting of nearly a thousand pages of Burr's intimate diary entries for the years 1808– 12; and in his correspondence with his daughter Theodosia, edited by Mark Van Doren (1929). Few American historical figures have appeared so frequently in novels, for example (to name only a few), Harriet Beecher Stowe's THE MINISTER'S WOOING (1859); Gertrude Atherton's THE CONQUEROR (1902); Kenneth Roberts' ARUNDEL (1930); Elizabeth Page's *The Tree of Liberty* (1939); Anya Seton's *My Theodosia* (1941). T. P. Abernethy wrote a full account of *The Burr Conspiracy* (1954).

Burritt, Elihu (b. New Britain, Conn., Dec. 8,

1810—d. March 6, 1879), "the Learned Black-smith." The son of a cobbler, Burritt himself became a blacksmith, but had an insatiable passion for learning and for helping humanity. He was an astounding linguist who mastered more than forty languages and published a Sanskrit handbook and grammars of Arabic, Persian, Hindustani, and Turkish. Later in life Burritt became deeply devoted to the cause of pacifism, issuing a weekly newspaper, *The Christian Citizen* (1844–51), in which this cause was advocated; he also lectured widely on the same theme. He published *Sparks from the Anvil* (1846) and *Lectures and Speeches* (1866).

Burroughs, Edgar Rice (b. Chicago, Sept. 1, 1875—d. March 19, 1950), novelist. After a varied and picturesque career as soldier, policeman, cowboy, manager of a department in Sears, Roebuck & Co., gold miner, and storekeeper, Burroughs began to write. His first stories dealt with life on Mars; his first book was *Tarzan of the Apes* (1914). Thereafter he kept on writing about life elsewhere than on earth and adventures among creatures less than human; many of his tales were set in Africa, which he never visited. Tarzan became a grandfather, and still was going strong at Burroughs' death—in books, comic strips, on the air, in the movies, in many languages. One theater in India showed Tarzan pictures for two years straight. Burroughs incorporated himself; two towns (in California and Texas) were named after him; he earned millions of dollars. See TARZAN.

Burroughs, John (b. in Delaware Co., near Roxbury, N.Y., April 13, 1837—d. March 29, 1921), naturalist, essayist, critic, poet. Burroughs was affectionately called "UNCLE JOHN OF WOODCHUCK" and "The Sage of Slabsides" ("Slabsides" was a rustic cabin he built for himself on his farm at Riverby on the Hudson River). It was not Thoreau but RALPH WALDO EMERSON who most deeply influenced Burroughs. His first published contribution in *The Atlantic Monthly* in 1860 was mistaken by Lowell himself for a piece by Emerson and was so listed later in Poole's *Index to Periodical Literature*. In addition to Emerson, Walt Whitman greatly impressed him; in later years Henri Bergson was a potent influence.

Burroughs was a farm boy who deeply loved nature, though not the wild life of the forest. Birds were his special love, and his first view of Audubon's pictures made him resolve to become a naturalist. He followed diverse occupations. For a time he was a clerk in the Treasury at Washington; there he became acquainted with WALT WHITMAN. Later he was a bank examiner (1873–84). Finally he settled down at Riverby, and the fame he acquired by his numerous essays on nature and his natural history collections attracted many visitors. He became a national figure, with his snowy white beard and his broad forehead and benign expression. Universities gave him honorary degrees, he received a gold medal from the National Academy of Arts and Letters (1916), and famous men sought him out—he was a particular friend of Theodore

Roosevelt. In his honor was established the John Burroughs Medal, given to books in the field of natural history.

Most intimate of his friends was Whitman. They had met casually on a Washington street;

later Whitman became a frequent visitor to his home. Burroughs made the first biographical study of Whitman, *Notes on Walt Whitman as Poet and Person* (1867), a considerable portion of which was written by Whitman himself. Later the book was expanded into *Walt Whitman: A Study* (1896). Sometimes Whitman's influence on Burroughs seems to have been almost unconscious or automatic, as when the former said in the *Song of Myself* (1855): "Whether I come to my own today or in ten thousand or ten million years,/ I can cheerfully take it now, or with equal cheerfulness I can wait"; and Burroughs wrote, in *Waiting* (1862), his most famous poem:

> Nor time, nor space, nor deep, nor high
> Can keep my own away from me.

Yet the influence was reciprocal, and Burroughs taught Whitman to look more closely at nature and to observe accurately.

Reading Burroughs is for many people almost like actually seeing what he describes, so vivid, concrete, and pleasant is Burroughs' writing. In *Wake-Robin* (1871), *Winter Sunshine* (1875), *Pepacton* (1881), *Riverby* (1894), *Ways of Nature* (1905), *Leaf and Tendril* (1908), *Under the Maples* (1921), and other collections he wrote memorably and happily. As he expressed it in *The Summit of the Years* (1915), "I go to books and nature as a bee goes to a flower, for a nectar that I can make into my own honey." An excellent selection was made from his writings in *John Burroughs' America* (1951).

Burroughs, William S. ["William Lee"] (b. St. Louis, Mo., 1914—   ), novelist. A drug addict for fifteen years of his life, Burroughs experienced to its fullest the emptiness, degradation, and horror that come from what he calls "the junk sickness." Under the pseudonym "William Lee" he wrote *Junky* (1953), an account of his experiences with various kinds of drugs in different parts of the world. In *The Naked Lunch* (1959, Paris; although some sections of it have been printed in the *Chicago Review, Big Table,* and *Evergreen Review*), he explored drug addiction from another point of view. The book consists of a series of "episodes" which describe the author's hallucinations under the influence of drugs. His visions are horrific extensions of evils Burroughs sees around him: capital punishment, medical and academic hypocrisy, drug addiction itself. In contrast to *Junky,* Burroughs' second book is written in a complex prose ranging in style from the lowest to the highest; often obscure, it sometimes beautifully conveys the vision of a man who has experienced unimaginable horrors and has returned from the depths to tell about it. After World War II, Burroughs was one of the early mentors of the beat writers ALLEN GINSBERG and JACK KEROUAC; his works are regarded by many as "beat novels." See BEAT WRITING.

Burt, Katharine Newlin (b. Fishkill, N.Y., Sept. 6, 1882—   ), novelist. Along with her husband STRUTHERS BURT, Mrs. Burt operated a "dude ranch" in Wyoming and became familiar with pioneering conditions in the West. She wrote several superior Western novels: *The Branding Iron* (1919); *Hidden Creek* (1920); *A Man's Own Country* (1931); *Close Pursuit* (an excellent historical novel of pre-Revolutionary times, 1947); *Still Water* (1948); and *Escape from Paradise* (1952).

Burt, [Maxwell] Struthers (b. Baltimore, Md., Oct. 18, 1882—d. Aug. 28, 1954), newspaperman, teacher, rancher, writer. Burt, a "dyed-in-the-wool Philadelphian" who was born by accident in Baltimore, started out in newspaper work in Philadelphia. He went West and served as president of the company running the Bar B.C. Ranch in Wyoming. Later he and his wife lived on a smaller ranch in the same state. He began his formal writing career with the publication of a collection of verse, *In the High Hills* (1914). He went on to the publication of short stories and novels: *John O'May and Other Stories* (1918); *The Interpreter's House* (1924); *The Delectable Mountains* (1927); *Festival* (1931). *The Delectable Mountains* makes good use of the author's special knowledge of Philadelphia society and Wyoming ranches. He continued to publish verse: *Songs and Portraits* (1920); *War Songs* (1942). He wrote a lively account of Wyoming's *Powder River* (1938) and two slightly irreverent accounts of Philadelphia, *Along These Streets* (1942) and *Philadelphia: Holy Experiment* (1945).

Burton, Richard [Eugene] (b. Hartford, Conn., March 14, 1861—d. April 8, 1940), teacher, poet, critic, lecturer. For most of his life Burton taught at the University of Minnesota. In 1925 he came to New Jersey, where he became a popular lecturer and critic. He published many books: collections of poems, from *Dumb in June* (1895; 10th ed., 1927) to *Collected Poems* (1931); biographies; discussions of plays and novels; essays.

Burton, William Evans (b. England, Sept. 24, 1804—d. Feb. 10, 1860), actor, editor, dramatist, humorous essayist. A comic actor of considerable ability, Burton came to the United States in 1834 and remained here for the rest of his life. He wrote a play, *Ellen Wareham* (1833), short stories and sketches collected as *Waggeries and Vagaries* (1848), and edited *Burton's Comic Songster* (1837) and *The Cyclopaedia of Wit and Humor* (1858). He published *The Gentleman's Magazine,* 1837–40, giving EDGAR ALLAN POE a position as his assistant. Poe's moodiness and critical severity eventually led to a break; meanwhile he contributed many reviews and essays to the magazine, reprinted several of his poems in its pages, and gave it one of his greatest stories, THE FALL OF THE HOUSE OF USHER (September, 1839).

Burton's Gentleman's Magazine. See GRAHAM'S MAGAZINE.

Burwell Papers, The. A collection of papers in the custody of Nathaniel Burwell of Virginia, written around 1676 and now usually attributed to JOHN COTTON or his wife ANN. They contain the famous epitaph on Nathaniel Bacon:

None shall dare his obsequies to sing
In deserved measures, until time shall bring
Truth crown'd with freedom, and from danger
    free
To sound his praise to all posterity.

The papers were first published in the Massachusetts Historical Society *Collections* (1814); then reprinted in these with greater care in 1866.

Bury the Dead (1936), a one-act play by IRWIN SHAW. In this powerful pacifist fantasy six men, killed in World War I, refuse to be buried and at last persuade their fellow soldiers to join them in a revolt against war. John Gassner calls the play "expressionistic and macabre."

Busch, Niven (b. New York City, April 26, 1903—   ), novelist, short-story writer, screenwriter. Beginning as a newspaperman and editor—he was simultaneously a staff-writer for *The New Yorker* and a senior editor of *Time* while still in his twenties—Busch is best known as a writer of popular fiction. The backgrounds of his novels range from the Old West to twentieth century Europe and California and vary in type from fairly straightforward romantic-adventure stories to psychological studies of such representative contemporary characters as the Hollywood star, the disturbed ex-serviceman, and the American demagogue. Almost all his books are characterized by vivid detail, eventful plots, driving colloquial prose, and a predilection for turbulent characters. His books, many of which have been best sellers, include *The Carrington Incident* (1941), *Duel in the Sun* (1944), *They Dream of Home* (1944), *Day of the Conquerors* (1946), *The Furies* (1948), *The Hate Merchant* (1953), *The Actor* (1955), and *California Street* (1959). Busch's stories and articles have appeared in many magazines and there is a collection of some of his early *New Yorker* pieces, *Twenty-One Americans* (1930).

Bush, Vannevar (b. Everett, Mass., March 11, 1890—   ), electrical engineer, author, administrator, public official, inventor. Vannevar Bush was graduated from Tufts College with the degrees of B.S. and M.S. in 1913 and later took graduate work at Harvard and M.I.T., both of which awarded him the D. Eng. degree in 1916. During World War I he carried on research in connection with submarine detection for a special board of the U.S. Navy. He returned to M.I.T. in 1919 and became associate professor of electrical power transmission, and in 1932 was made vice president of the Institute and Dean of its engineering school. From 1939 to 1955, when he retired, he was president of the Carnegie Institution of Washington, D.C.

Bush's distinguished career reached a climax during World War II when he became director of the Office of Scientific Research and Development (OSRD), which guarded more vital secrets than any other organization in Washington in the war years. He was one of the foremost advisers to the administration and sought to coordinate the genius and efforts of 30,000 American scientists in a time of great peril. In his book *Modern Arms and Free Men* (1949) Bush relates science to democracy and social development, touching upon a great variety of vexing problems that claim public attention. Other books by Bush are *Operational Circuit Analysis* (1929); and *Endless Horizons* (1946), a collection of his papers and addresses covering a broad range of topics, from war on disease to the control of atomic energy. His *Principles of Electrical Engineering,* written with William H. Timbie, was first published in 1922, and went into its fourth edition in 1951.

Busy-Body Papers. "Busy-Body" was a pseudonym adopted by the author of thirty-two papers contributed in 1729 to Andrew Bradford's Philadelphia magazine, *The American Weekly Mercury.* They were written in imitation of Addison and were intended to tease Bradford's and BENJAMIN FRANKLIN's business rival, SAMUEL KEIMER. The Busy-Body, says Carl Van Doren, "was easy and humorous reading, praising virtue and good temper." It is probable that some of Franklin's friends contributed a few of the papers, among them Joseph Breintnal.

Butcher, Harry C. (b. Springville, Iowa, Nov. 15, 1901—   ), editor, radio executive, author. During World War II Butcher was assigned with the rank of captain as an aide to General Dwight D. Eisenhower. In 1946 he published *My Three Years with Eisenhower,* which John P. Marquand calls "a unique docu-

ment . . . of the war's most secret moments."

Butler, Ellis Parker (b. Muscatine, Iowa, Dec. 5, 1869—d. Sept. 13, 1937), humorist, editor. Butler often maintained that despite his enormous mass of writing, his fame was confined entirely to one story—*Pigs is Pigs,* written at the suggestion of Ellery Sedgwick, then editor of *The American Magazine,* and published in that magazine in 1905. It swept the country, went into innumerable editions, and is still funny. It tells of an express agent to whom is brought a consignment of guinea pigs. He contends that "pigs is pigs" and hence livestock and not pets, and a long dispute ensues. But while the argument is going on the guinea pigs increase so rapidly that they overrun the entire express company office.

Butler, Frances ["Fanny"] Anne. See FRANCES KEMBLE.

Butler, Nicholas Murray (b. Elizabeth, N.J., April 2, 1862—d. Dec. 7, 1947), teacher, university president, political figure, lecturer, author. He was connected with Columbia University, in one capacity or another, for sixty-seven years—at twenty-eight he became professor of philosophy, at thirty-nine president of the university, two years before his death president emeritus. His policies and the benefactions he secured for the university greatly transformed it—in its physical appearance, the policies which governed the faculty and students, the influence it wielded, and the size of its enrollment which rose from 4,000 to over 30,000. Although Butler's scholarship was perhaps underrated, he was preeminently a fund raiser and a public relations man. He lectured in an august and impressive manner, wrote many books (in some of which he was inclined to say undisputed things in a very solemn way), attracted attention all over the world, knew everyone of prominence, ran as Vice-Presidential candidate with Taft in the 1912 election, kept nine secretaries busy with his thousands of articles, speeches, and books. Among his works: *The Meaning of Education* (1898, revised 1915); *A World in Ferment* (1918); *The Faith of a Liberal* (1924); *Across the Busy Years* (autobiography, 1939); *The World Today* (1946).

Butler, William Allen (b. Albany, N.Y., Feb. 20, 1825—d. Sept. 9, 1902), lawyer, poet, humorist. Butler was active in political and social causes and became a well-known speaker. He wrote a biography of Martin Van Buren (1862), but his fame rests chiefly upon a satirical poem, NOTHING TO WEAR (published anonymously in *Harper's Weekly,* 1857, and in book form the same year without the author's consent). It tells the story of Miss Flora M'Flimsey, who spent six weeks in Paris shopping and yet was in utter despair because she had nothing to wear. Butler attacks the "spoiled children of fashion" for overlooking the plight of the wretched and the starving. The poem was widely read and imitated.

Butterfield, Roger (b. Lyndonville, N.Y., July 29, 1907—   ), newspaperman, editor, historian. Butterfield began his newspaper work in Philadelphia on the *Bulletin* and the *Evening Ledger*, joining the staff of *Time* in 1937, and later also working for *Life*. His *The American Past* (1947) is a history of the United States in text and pictures, with more than a thousand reproductions of photographs, paintings, cartoons, engravings, and drawings. He also edited *The Saturday Evening Post Treasury* (1954).

By Blue Ontario's Shores (1856), a poem by WALT WHITMAN. The form and the title of this lengthy poem underwent many changes. Originally the thought of the poem appeared in the prose preface of the 1855 edition of *Leaves of Grass*. It was called *Poems of Many in One* in the 1856 edition; in 1860 it was included in *Chants Democratic*, appeared again in 1867 under the title *As I Sat Alone by Blue Ontario's Shores*, and finally was given its present title in 1881. It is a poem of striking, deliberately extravagant individualism, in behalf of the United States and of the poet as one of its citizens: "It is I who am great or to be great, it is You up there, or any one." He says, too, "I am willing to wait to be understood by the growth of the taste of myself." See PREFACE TO LEAVES OF GRASS.

Byles, Mather (b. Boston, March 15, 1707—d. July 5, 1788), clergyman, poet, humorist. As his name indicates, Byles was of the famous Puritan family; he inherited COTTON MATHER'S great library. Byles was strongly pro-British in his sympathies during the Revolutionary War; he was dismissed by his congregation in Boston and spent his last years in retirement. For a time he was under military guard. An inveterate punster, he described his anomalous situation during the war as follows: "I have been guarded, reguarded, and now, disguarded." It is said the old wag finally marched up and down the street, guarding himself. Byles once secured Dr. Thomas Prince to preach for him, but Prince failed to appear. Not at all disconcerted, Byles reached *extempore* from the text, "Put not your trust in princes." He had his study painted brown so that people visiting him could find him "in a brown study." He imitated and corresponded with Alexander Pope, and wrote in the style of Isaac Watts; to some extent he substituted aesthetic for purely moralistic standards in poetry, but he is a very poor, dull poet. He appears briefly in Hawthorne's *Howe's Masquerade* (in *Twice-Told Tales*, 1842).

Bynner, Edwin Lassetter (b. Brooklyn, N.Y., 1842—d. Sept. 4, 1893), a novelist who wrote mainly historical romances, including *Agnes Surriage* (1886), *The Begum's Daughter* (1890), and *Zachary Phips* (1892).

Bynner, [Harold] Witter (b. Brooklyn, N.Y., Aug. 10, 1881—d. June 1, 1968), poet, playwright, translator. EDWIN LASSETTER BYNNER was his uncle. Over a long career Bynner maintained a high level of excellence in his many collections of verse, beginning with *An Ode to Harvard* (1907), later changed to *Young Harvard* (1925). After his graduation from Harvard, Bynner went on to editoral work with *McClure's* Magazine, but having had a first taste of success

with his 1907 publication, took up residence at Cornish, New Hampshire, and spent the next ten years almost entirely absorbed in the writing of poetry. During these years he wrote three one-act plays later published in *A Book of Plays* (1922). In the second decade of the twentieth century he, Arthur Davison Ficke, and Edna St. Vincent Millay were part of a group of leading young American poets who sometimes congregated at meetings of the newly founded Poetry Society of America. It was in 1916 that Bynner and ARTHUR DAVISON FICKE, who had been his classmate at Harvard, brought out SPECTRA, a slim volume of poetry supposedly embodying the aim of the Spectrist school, which was to put into words the unseen nimbus that surrounds all things. This literary hoax was perpetrated by the young poets with devilish glee, Bynner taking the name of Emanuel Morgan and Ficke signing himself Anne Knish. Intended as a spoof on much of the gibberish that went by the names of Imagist and Futurist poetry, the publication was acclaimed by eminent poets. It was two years before the truth came out. In 1961, after forty-five years, *The Spectra Hoax* was published by William Jay Smith. It gives a complete account of the affair.

Bynner was subtly influenced by the art and literature of both China and India, and traveled extensively in the Orient. *The Jade Mountain* (1929, 5th ed. 1939) is the English translation (in collaboration with Dr. Kiang Kang-hu) of *Three Hundred Pearls of the T'ung Dynasty*. Other books by Bynner are: *Indian Earth* (1929, verse); *Eden Tree* (1931, verse); *Selected Poems* (1936); *The Way of Life According to Laotzu* (1944); *Take Away the Darkness* (1947); *Journey With Genius* (1951), an account of the time he spent with D. H. Lawrence and his wife in New Mexico in 1922 and 1923. During the latter part of the 1950's and the beginning of the 1960's, despite failing sight, Bynner brought out *New Poems* (1960) and appeared in a new creative phase. Neither experimental nor avant garde, these poems express some qualities of both these attitudes, with lines of rapid insight and immediate brightness. Among his other books: *Greenstone Poems* (1917); *A Book of Plays* (1922); *Book of Lyrics* (1955). He is said to appear as a character in D. H. Lawrence's *The Plumed Serpent* (1926) (cf. *American Literature*, January, 1952).

Byrd, Richard E[velyn] (b. Winchester, Va., Oct. 25, 1888—d. March 11, 1957), naval officer, explorer, author. Byrd, a descendant of WILLIAM BYRD, engaged in numerous remarkable explorations, many of them by plane. He flew over both the North and the South Poles (1926, 1929), and took part in three important expeditions to Antarctica (1928–30, 1933–35, 1939). He wrote accounts of his flights and expeditions in *Skyward* (1928), *Little America* (1930), *Discovery* (1935), *Alone* (1938).

Byrd, William (b. Westover, on James River, Va., March 28, 1674—d. Aug. 26, 1744), planter, lawyer, public official, writer. One of

Virginia's great gentlemen, Byrd was a writer just as he was a scientist, merely as a hobby. His writings were not published until nearly a

century after his death, in *The Westover Manuscripts* (1841); *The Writings of "Colonel William Byrd"* (1901) is a standard text. Herein may be found A HISTORY OF THE DIVIDING LINE RUN IN THE YEAR 1728 [between Virginia and North Carolina], A JOURNEY TO THE LAND OF EDEN, A.D. 1733 ("Eden" was ironically Carolina), and A PROGRESS TO THE MINES, IN THE YEAR 1732. In addition, there are now available volumes of extracts from Byrd's diaries (1941, 1942). These throw considerable illumination on the social history of the day and occasionally reveal some mean and degrading aspects of Byrd's character. Byrd was also the author of a tract published anonymously in London in 1721—*A Discourse Concerning the Plague, with Preservatives Against It. By a Lover of Mankind* (republished as *Another Secret Diary by William Byrd,* 1942). The tract is a clever piece of propaganda in favor of tobacco as a deterrent of the plague. So engaging is Byrd's style and so effective his satire that he has justifiably been claimed as one of our first humorists. An aristocrat of aristocrats, he observed with disdain the inhabitants of "Lubberland," or Carolina, when he visited there; the independence and lawlessness of the people seemed to him dangerous. About his own sometimes difficult and risky experiences he wrote with unfailing good humor. Louis B. Wright and Marion Tinling have edited two volumes of excerpts from Byrd's shorthand diaries (1941, 1958).

Byrne, Donn. See BRIAN OSWALD DONN-BYRNE.

C

Cabbages and Kings (1904), a novel by O. HENRY (William Sydney Porter). In 1896 Porter was indicted for embezzlement and fled to Central and South America for a year before being sentenced to the penitentiary. Out of his adventures and misadventures during that year, he built the episodes of *Cabbages and Kings*, which can only loosely be described as a novel. The title, from the ballad on the Walrus and the Carpenter in Lewis Carroll's *Alice in Wonderland*, announces his intention "to talk of many things." All nineteen narratives are laid in a country called Coralio in Central America, and the same characters frequently reappear. The picture of life in a Latin American land as O. Henry presents it is one of mingled romance and realism. Whether he was guilty of a crime or merely of a fiscal irregularity, his difficulties with the law seem to have given him a tolerant eye for the not too morally robust characters he met in his fictional Coralio.

Cabell, James Branch (b. Richmond, Va., April 14, 1879—d. May 5, 1958), novelist, essayist, poet, historian. Cabell belonged by birth and training to the First Families of Virginia. Some of his most laborious writings are

concerned with the genealogy of his own and other Virginia families, and he held offices in several genealogical societies. His first book, *The*

Eagle's Shadow, appeared in 1904. The following year, while writing *Gallantry* (1907), Cabell was irritated by problems of local geography raised by the fact that the scene was laid in Tunbridge Wells, which he had never visited. He made up his mind that thereafter his stories would be laid in a land of his own, the history, scenery, customs, and morals of which he would himself contrive. Thus was born the medieval French province of Poictesme (probably compounded from Poitiers and Angoulême). Poictesme became a real country to Cabell and his readers. Its history from 1234 to 1750 was carefully described; its laws and legends were wrought into the fabric of Cabell's stories. The diction of the country was an odd mixture of irony and circumlocution. Its manners were courtly, its sexual morality free-and-easy. Cabell's escapism was curious, since it led to an existence that seemed romantic enough but was really futile, disillusioned, bitter. The trappings were splendid, the result boredom. In philosophy Cabell was a skeptic, a sort of American Anatole France. His heroes make love with endless women and contribute a potent ancestry to most of the European dynasties, but the women turn out to be singularly alike, and in the end all is vanity.

The books had more success with the critics than with the public, at least until the appearance of JURGEN (1919). The attempt to suppress *Jurgen* on the ground of immorality naturally led to a large increase in Cabell's income. He continued meanwhile to live a life of orthodox sobriety in Richmond. He brought together the huge epic of POICTESME in the *Storisende Edition* (18 v., 1927–30); in this edition appear all the novels dealing with Dom Manuel and his descendants, arranged in genealogical order rather than in the order in which they were published. The books form a complicated concatenated narrative—*Beyond Life* (1919); *Domnei* (1920—originally *The Soul of Melicent*, 1913); *Chivalry* (1909); *Jurgen* (1919); *The Line of Love* (1905); *Gallantry* (1907); *The Certain Hour* (1916); *The Cords of Vanity* (1909); *The Rivet in Grandfather's Neck* (1915); *The Eagle's Shadow* (1904); THE CREAM OF THE JEST (1917); *Figures of Earth* (1921); *The High Place* (1923); *The Silver Stallion* (1926); *Something about Eve* (1927); and others. The series has been described as "the most ambitiously planned literary work which has ever come out of America." Later Cabell wrote a group of three stories, *Smirt* (1934), *Smith* (1935), and *Smire* (1937), which failed to create any excitement; also *There Were Two Pirates* (1946), *Let Me Lie* (essays on Virginia, 1947), and *The Devil's Own Dear Son* (1949). *Quiet, Please* (1952) is mainly autobiographical and somewhat querulous; *I*

Remember It (1955) is subtitled "Some Epilogues in Recollection."

Cabell had something to say and said it beautifully, but too often and with too conscious art or artifice. Moreover, he made the grave error of diluting his creed with gibes on the subject of sex, and as soon as American sexual folkways changed after World War I, Cabell's popularity collapsed. Yet at the height of his fame he was praised almost ecstatically by many leading critics, including H. L. Mencken. Edward Wagenknecht in his essay, *Cabell: A Reconsideration* (1948), points out that Cabell is "above all, the novelist of acquiescence: 'to submit is the great lesson' "; Cabell's favorite theme is compromise and adjustment. Wagenknecht praises some "superbly imaginative" passages in the novels, but he quotes the artist Howard Pyle, who refused to illustrate any more of Cabell's stories for *Harper's Magazine* on the ground that they were "neither exactly true to history nor exactly fanciful."

On the question of pronouncing his own name, Cabell rhymed, "Tell the rabble my name is Cabell."

Cable, George Washington (b. New Orleans, Oct. 12, 1844—d. Jan. 31, 1925), short-story writer, novelist, historian. The death of his father and the failure of the family business obliged Cable to leave school at the age of four-

teen and go to work to support his mother and sisters. He joined the Confederate army in the spring of 1862 and served until the end of the war, recounting his experiences during this period in *The Cavalier* (1901). After the war he worked for a cotton wholesaler and tried his hand at surveying with an engineering expedition, but contracted malaria and was unable to work for almost two years. During his illness he contributed a weekly column of humorous sketches and poems to the New Orleans *Picayune*, using the pseudonym "Drop Shot." The column became popular and was soon appearing daily, and Cable was offered a position as a reporter. However, as a Calvinist, he refused to write theatrical criticism, and was dropped from the paper. He became an accountant for a firm of cotton factors, married, and pursued a rigorous course of self-education. He learned French and studied the New Orleans archives, fascinated by the city's colorful history.

Cable's first literary success was OLD CREOLE DAYS (1879), a collection of seven stories previously published in *Scribner's Monthly*. These included four of Cable's best short works: "Jean Ah Poquelin," a weird tale of a former slave trader; " 'Tite Poulette," a story dealing with miscegenation; "Café des Exilés," a story of a smuggling plot, and "Belles Demoiselles," a pathetic story of a proud father's loss. THE GRANDISSIMES, Cable's first novel, appeared in 1880; it was a study of the Louisiana Creoles, descendants of original French and Spanish settlers in the South and in Latin America. The novel deals with a feud between two aristocratic Creole families, the Grandissimes and the De Grapions. Like much of Cable's other work, it is chiefly valuable for its descriptions of locale and treatment of Creole and slave dialects.

His next book, MADAME DELPHINE (1881), which was included in later editions of *Old Creole Days*, is a long short story dealing with the unhappy place of the quadroon in New Orleans society. *The Creoles of Louisiana* (1884), a historical work, angered the Creoles because of Cable's version of their ancestry; he claimed that they were descendants of men who had come to America for commercial reasons and had married Indian and African women, "and the inmates of French houses of correction."

Cable, always an enemy of slavery, became a zealous reformer and began to write articles, later collected in *The Silent South* (1885), arguing for prison reform, the abolition of contract labor, and better treatment of the Negroes. His writings found small favor in the South as a whole, and the Creoles particularly resented his stories about them, charging that his characters from the uneducated lower-class Creoles did not represent the group as a whole. Partially as a result of his southern unpopularity, Cable moved to Massachusetts, where he was active as a reformer and philanthropist and continued to write on social problems, as in *The Negro Question* (1888) and *The Southern Struggle for Pure Government* (1890).

About the turn of the century he again turned to fiction, but this work was without his early richness and color. He is chiefly remembered as an important figure in the beginning of the local-color movement who depicted New Orleans society with exotic brilliance and charm.

In his treatment of race relations and violence he foreshadowed such modern writers as ROBERT PENN WARREN and WILLIAM FAULKNER.

Other books by Cable include: DR. SEVIER (1884); *Bonaventure* (1888); *Strange True Stories of Louisiana* (1889); *John March, Southerner* (1894); *Strong Hearts* (1899); *Bylow Hill* (1902); *Kincaid's Battery* (1908); "*Posson Jone'*" *and Père Raphaël* (1909); *Gideon's Band* (1914); *The Amateur Garden* (1914); *The Flower of the Chapdelaines* (1918); *Lovers of Louisiana* (1918).

Cabot, John [Caboto, Giovanni] (1450–1498), Italian explorer. He emigrated to England around 1484; under patent from Henry VII he sailed in 1497 in search of a route to Asia and landed after fifty-two days (June 24, 1497) on Cape Breton Island. In a second voyage (1498) he explored other portions of North America, as basis for England's claim to the continent. His son Sebastian (1476?–1557), likewise an explorer in many parts of the Old and New World, reached the La Plata (1526). His journey to North America was described by Peter Martyr in Latin (1516), by Richard Eden in English (1555).

Cadillac, Antoine de la Mothe (b. France, 1658—1730), soldier and administrator. He established a post at Detroit (1701) and served there for eleven years, then was transferred to Louisiana as governor (1713–16), retired to Gascony (1717).

Cadman, Charles Wakefield (b. Johnstown, Pa., Dec. 24, 1881—d. Dec. 31, 1946), composer, critic, lecturer, editor. Cadman was among the first American composers to become interested in Indian songs and customs. His works range from songs (*From the Land of the Sky-Blue Water*) to symphonic and operatic creations. Two of his operas, *The Garden of Mystery* (1925) and *The Witch of Salem* (1926), were laid in New England; the former was based on Hawthorne's short story, RAPPACINI'S DAUGHTER (*Mosses from an Old Manse*, 1846). *Shanewis* (1918) was an opera with an Indian story (libretto by Nelle Richmond Eberhardt). *The Willow Tree* was the first radio opera (produced by NBC, Oct. 4, 1932).

Caesar, Irving (b. New York City, July 4, 1895—   ), song writer. Caesar wrote several hit musicals, including *No, No, Nanette* (1924). Among his widely sung lyrics are *Sometimes I'm Happy* and *Tea for Two*.

Cahan, Abraham (b. Russia, July 7, 1860—d. Aug. 31, 1951), newspaperman, editor, novelist. Cahan came to the United States in 1882. He joined the staff of Yiddish journals published in New York City, finally becoming (1897) the first editor of the Socialist daily *Vorwaerts* ("*Forward*"). It attained under his guidance a wide circulation (up to 245,000 a day), put up its own building in New York and a printing plant in Chicago, acquired a radio station. After the rise of the Soviet government Cahan took a strong stand, maintaining that "communism is despotism without any rights for anyone at all." He also wrote fiction: *The Imported Bridegroom*

and Other Stories of the New York Ghetto (1898), *Yekl, a Tale of the New York Ghetto* (1896), and THE RISE OF DAVID LEVINSKY (1917), besides much in Yiddish that has not been translated. William Dean Howells was one of the first critics to review Cahan's fiction favorably. See JEWS IN UNITED STATES LITERATURE.

Cain, James M[allahan] (b. Annapolis, Md., July 1, 1892—   ), newspaperman, novelist, playwright. Cain began as a reporter on the Baltimore *American*, then worked on the Baltimore *Sun*, taught journalism at St. John's College in Annapolis, became an editorial writer on the New York *World*. After that he did magazine, syndicate, and motion-picture work, publishing his first novel, THE POSTMAN ALWAYS RINGS TWICE, in 1934. Other novels of his: *Serenade* (1937); *Mildred Pierce* (1941); *Past All Dishonor* (1946); *The Butterfly* (1947); *The Moth* (1948); *This Man and This Woman* (1951); *Mignon* (1955). His first novel made him the chief exemplar of the "hard-boiled" school of writers; the influence of Ernest Hemingway was obvious (see HARD-BOILED FICTION). It tells what happens when a young hobo saunters into a roadside sandwich stand run by a Greek and his American wife; the hobo takes one look at the wife and decides to settle down to work at the stand. The violence and passion that ensue move at breathless speed. The novel was filmed.

Caine Mutiny, The (1951), a novel by HERMAN WOUK. A college boy begins his service in World War II on the mine sweeper *Caine*. He takes part in a desperate mutiny of the officers against their inefficient and cowardly commander; the episode turns the boy into a real fighter. The novel is one of remarkable and sustained narrative power, one of humor as well as of grim suspense and terror. It became an immediate best seller; later, a successful play and an impressive movie.

Cajun. The word is a corruption of the word *Acadian*, and refers to the French settlers deported by the British from Acadia (now Nova Scotia) in 1755. Henry Wadsworth Longfellow used the episode in his narrative poem, EVANGELINE (1847). A number of the exiles settled in French speaking Louisiana in the bayou regions, where they have maintained their unity to this day and have continued to speak their own kind of French.

Calamity Jane [nickname of **Martha Jane** (**Canary**) **Burke**] (b. probably Princeton, Mo., 1852?—d. Aug. 1, 1903). Reared in a Montana mining community, Calamity Jane learned to ride and shoot, and gained a reputation for marksmanship. She was probably a scout with General George Custer and a circuit rider on the pony express. At her death she asked to be buried next to her friend JAMES B. [WILD BILL] HICKOK. She was the heroine of *Deadwood Dick on Deck, or Calamity Jane the Heroine of Whoop Up,* one of a series of dime novels by EDWARD L. WHEELER that began in 1884.

Calamus [1] (1860), a section of poems in

WALT WHITMAN'S LEAVES OF GRASS, was included in the third edition and intended as a complementary section to CHILDREN OF ADAM. There are thirty-nine poems in the group, among them such striking and impressive pieces as *Whoever You Are Holding Me Now in Hand*, *The Base of All Metaphysics*, *I Saw in Louisiana a Live-Oak Growing*, I HEAR IT WAS CHARGED AGAINST ME, and *Full of Life Now*. In general, the poems celebrate "the manly love of comrades," and have been cited as evidence that Whitman was a homosexual. The name *Calamus* is derived from that of a plant (sometimes called "sweet flag") which "symbolizes with its close-knit leaves the mutual support gained from comradeship." See CALAMUS [2].

Calamus [2] (1897), a series of letters from WALT WHITMAN to Peter Doyle, 1868–1880. Doyle was an unschooled Confederate soldier who became a streetcar conductor in Washington, D.C., during the period of Whitman's residence there. These letters were published after the poet's death with the appropriate title taken from *Leaves of Grass*. See CALAMUS [1].

Calavar (1834), a novel by ROBERT MONTGOMERY BIRD. Bird, a follower of James Fenimore Cooper, found in the early history of Mexico material for this historical romance. The exploits of Cortez are described in detail. A sequel, THE INFIDEL, appeared in 1835.

Calaveras County, Celebrated Jumping Frog of. See CELEBRATED JUMPING FROG.

Caldecott Medal. An award, first made in 1938, given to the illustrator of the most distinguished picture book for children published during the preceding year. The recipient is named by the same committee that awards the Newbery Medal. It was established by FREDERIC G. MELCHER, editor of *Publishers' Weekly*, in honor of the distinguished British artist, Randolph Caldecott (1846–1886), best remembered for his illustrations for children's books.

Caldwell, Erskine [Preston] (b. Coweta Co., Ga., Dec. 17, 1903—   ), newspaperman, short-story writer, novelist, screenwriter. GEORGE W. CABLE's last novel was published in 1918; Caldwell's first novel, *The Bastard*, appeared eleven years later. Yet much more than a decade, in the social, spiritual, and literary senses, really intervened between the two books. The South attacked Cable for what today would seem mere peccadilloes; Caldwell really spoke out. In addition to the heated quarrels aroused by his vivid pictures of the "po' whites" and Negroes in the South, he was also accused of indecency; but he emerged triumphant from the legal encounters that resulted. Caldwell has shown a keen sense of social justice in his writings, and there can be no question but that his appallingly vivid depiction of degeneration and cruelty helped to awaken the conscience of the South. The *Atlanta Journal*, reviewing *This Very Earth* (1948), called him an artist whose "appeal is to humanity, to fairness and decency."

Caldwell is best remembered for TOBACCO ROAD (1932), the story of the repellent and unforgettable Jeeter Lester family on a back road

of Georgia. The Lesters and their neighbors could have provided a corps of psychiatrists with enough material for a lifetime of study. Though *Tobacco Road* is essentially a comedy, Oscar Cargill writes that "Jeeter Lester, symbolic of countless impoverished farmers in the South, though they all may not be as ignorant as he, is a pitiable figure whom all the riotous laughter of the book or the play does not help us to forget." In 1934 the novel was dramatized by Jack Kirkland and became one of the most successful plays ever produced in the American theater.

Caldwell began his writing with some powerful short stories: *Country Full of Swedes*, which won the *Yale Review* $1,000 Award for Fiction in 1933; *Saturday Afternoon*, described by Leo Gurko as "perhaps the best story of a lynching in American literature"; *Kneel to the Rising Sun* (a story collection, 1935). Some of the earlier tales were collected in *We Are the Living* (1933).

He collaborated with his former wife Margaret Bourke-White on three picture-and-comment documentaries: *You Have Seen Their Faces* (1937), *North of the Danube* (1939), and *Say! Is This the U.S.A.?* (1941). During World War II they were in Russia as war correspondents, an experience which produced his *All Out on the Road to Smolensk, Moscow Under Fire*, and *All Night Long* (all 1942). Other works are GOD'S LITTLE ACRE (1933); *Journeyman* (1935); *Trouble in July* (1940); *Stories* (1944); *A House in the Uplands* (1946); *The Sure Hand of God* (1947); *Jackpot* (stories, 1940); *A Place Called Estherville* (1949); *The Humorous Side* (stories, 1951); *The Courting of Susie Brown* (stories, 1952); *A Lamp for Nightfall* (1952); *Love and Money* (1954); *The Sacrilege of Alan Kent* (1936); *Claudelle Inglish* (1959). Caldwell wrote his literary autobiography in *Call It Experience: The Years of Learning How to Write* (1951). By 1962 he had written thirty-eight books, the sales of which approach 25,000,000.

Caldwell, [Janet Miriam] Taylor (b. England, Sept. 7, 1900—   ), novelist. Miss Caldwell came to this country at the age of seven; she served as a yeoman in the United States navy during World War I. Her literary career, an extraordinary succession of best sellers, began with *Dynasty of Death* (1938), a story of two great families in control of a huge munitions trust; this story was continued in *The Eagles Gather* (1940) and *The Final Hour* (1944). *The Earth is the Lord's* (1941) is a romance about Genghis Khan. *The Turnbulls* (1943) describes the private life and destiny of a cotton industrialist in England. *The Wide House* (1945) lays emphasis on the racial and religious storms preceding the Civil War. *This Side of Innocence* (1946) is laid in New York in the decades after the Civil War, the plot again concerning families of wealth and power, internecine battling among relatives, details of high finance and industrial backgrounds, careful historical data. Later books include *There Was a Time* (1947); *Melissa* (1948); *The Devil's Advocate* (1952); *Never Victorious, Never De-*

feated (1954); *The Sound of Thunder* (1957); *Dear and Glorious Physician* (1959); *The Listener* (1960); *Your Sins and Mine* (1961). She signs her work Taylor Caldwell, but has also used the pseudonym Max Reiner.

Calef, Robert (b. England, 1648—d. April 13, 1719), merchant, writer. Calef came to Boston in 1688 and became a citizen of note. He was a Puritan who didn't like the Salem witchcraft trials (1692), and who spoke his mind plainly about them. In 1693 COTTON MATHER published WONDERS OF THE INVISIBLE WORLD, a narrative of some of the trials, with numerous observations on devils and their activities in Salem and nearby points. Calef commented freely on the book, on Mather and his father Increase Mather, and, apparently, on their selfish reasons for fomenting the witchcraft disturbances. Cotton Mather thereupon brought a suit for slander against Calef, but the case was dropped. Then Calef wrote a book on the trials, MORE WONDERS OF THE INVISIBLE WORLD. But no Boston printer would take it, and Calef sent it off to London to be published. It appeared in 1700 and made a great stir in the colony. According to one story, INCREASE MATHER caused the book to be burned in Harvard Yard; he was then president of the college. Cotton Mather called Calef "a very wicked sort of Sadducee."

Calhoun, John C[aldwell] (b. near Abbeville, S.C., March 18, 1782—d. March 31, 1850), lawyer, statesman, orator, Vice-President of the United States. Calhoun was elected to the state legislature in 1808, to Congress in

1811. Under various administrations he was Secretary of War, Secretary of State, Vice-President, and a senator. He was known as a champion of states' rights. His speeches and miscellaneous writings were gathered in *Works* (6 v., 1853–55). MARGARET L. COIT wrote *John C. Calhoun: American Portrait* (1950), and

Charles M. Wiltse wrote a three-volume biography (1944–52).

Caliban by the Yellow Sands (1916), a masque by PERCY MACKAYE. It was composed and performed in honor of the tercentenary of Shakespeare's death, May 25 to June 5, 1916, in the stadium of the College of the City of New York. MacKaye saw Caliban as "that passionate child-curious part of us all" and showed his regeneration through Prospero's wisdom and his love for Miranda. Scenes from other Shakespearean plays form part of the action.

California and Oregon Trail, The (1849), a narrative of travel by FRANCIS PARKMAN. See OREGON TRAIL.

California Pelican, The. A comic monthly published at Berkeley for University of California students.

Calkins, Earnest Elmo (b. Geneseo, Ill., March 25, 1868—   ), advertising man, writer. Calkins founded "Calkins & Holden, first modern advertising agency, introduced new methods now standard" (*Who's Who in America*). He was deaf from his sixth year, but found this ailment a stimulus rather than an affliction. Two of his books make reference to this fact: *Louder, Please* (1924) and *And Hearing Not: Annals of an Adman* (1946), both memoirs of his busy and successful life. Among his other books: *The Business of Advertising* (1915); *The Advertising Man* (1922); *Business the Civilizer* (1927); *On the Care and Feeding of Hobby Horses* (1934).

Callaghan, Morley [Edward] (b. Toronto, Ont., 1903—   ), Canadian newspaperman, lawyer, short-story writer, novelist. Callaghan, while working on the Toronto *Star*, met Ernest Hemingway, who encouraged him to write fiction, later introduced him to the American expatriates in Paris and secured him an opportunity to contribute to *This Quarter, transition,* and other similar periodicals. Callaghan became a member of the "hard-boiled" school of writers (see HARD-BOILED FICTION), but with reservations, due perhaps to his firm religious beliefs. His work appears in many of the O'Brien "best short story" collections, also in book form. Among the latter: *Strange Fugitive* (1928); *It's Never Over* (1930); *Broken Journey* (1932); *They Shall Inherit the Earth* (1935); *More Joy in Heaven* (1937); *The Loved and the Lost* (1951); besides several story collections. His stories center around bootleggers, a man hanged for murdering a policeman, people suffering in the depression of 1929–32, a criminal who tries to make good, the failure of men's faith. *The Varsity Story* (1948) is a fictional account of the University of Toronto. Recent work is *The Many Colored Coat* (1960).

Call of the Wild, The (1903), a novel by JACK LONDON. It is believed that London was influenced in writing this famous story of a dog who goes native and joins a wolf pack, by reading E. R. Young's *My Dogs in the Northland.* The background is a cruel Alaska winter; among the human characters are Buck's master, grief at whose death makes the dog take to the wilds, and other prospectors in the KLONDIKE GOLD RUSH. London works out in the course of the story his ideas on the need for adaptation to survive and on the influence of heredity. The book is at once sentimental and poetic.

Calumet "K" (1901), a novel by SAMUEL MERWIN and HENRY KITCHELL WEBSTER. A story of business conflicts and business efficiency, written briskly and with a certain narrative skill, the book was popular for many years.

Calvert, Clay. The chief character in HAROLD L. DAVIS' HONEY IN THE HORN (1935).

Calvert, George Henry (b. near Bladensburg, Md., June 2, 1803—d. May 24, 1889), poet, dramatist, novelist, essayist. Calvert came, as his name indicates, of good Maryland stock, was educated at Harvard and in Germany, lived after 1840 in Newport, R.I. He wrote intelligently and gracefully, but with no great merit. He made Benedict Arnold and Major André the subjects of a tragedy in 1864, published *Poems* (1847) and *Comedies* (1852), discussed *Goethe: His Life and Works* (1872), issued a final collection, *Threescore and Other Poems* (1883).

Calvert, Maryland. Leading woman character in David Belasco's THE HEART OF MARYLAND (1895), a Civil War play. She is a southern sympathizer, but the play turns on her dramatic rescue of her northern lover from death.

Calvert family of Maryland. See under BALTIMORE, LORD.

Calverton, V[ictor] F[rancis] [formerly George Goetz] (b. Baltimore, Md., June 25, 1900 —d. Nov. 20, 1940), critic and editor. While working as a timekeeper for Bethlehem Steel, Calverton saved enough money to enter Johns Hopkins University. At the age of twenty-three he founded the *Modern Quarterly* (after 1933 the *Modern Monthly,* reverting to a quarterly in 1938), a literary magazine which published the work of left-wing liberals and radicals. Calverton himself was a Marxist, but generally in opposition to the Stalinist Communists. He was the author of a number of books which interpreted American literature, history, and culture from a Marxist and sociological point of view. Among these were *The Newer Spirit* (1925); *Sex Expression in Literature* (1926); *The Bankruptcy of Marriage* (1928); *The New Grounds of Criticism* (1930); *American Literature at the Crossroads* (1931); *For Revolution* (1932); *The Passing of the Gods* (1934); *The Making of America* (1938); and *The Awakening of America* (1939). He was also the author of a history of early utopian experiments in America, *Where Angels Dared to Tread* (1941); a collection of short stories, *Three Strange Lovers* (1929); and a novel, *The Man Inside* (1935).

calypso songs. A *calypso* is a style of music, usually with words, which originated in Trinidad as a folk art; in its pure form, the lyrics are improvised. Calypso has gained popularity in the United States, in radio, recordings, and night clubs. Typical calypso ballads are *Jeremiah, Rum and Coca-Cola, Roosevelt in Trinidad.*

Cambridge History of American Literature, The (4 v., 1917, 1918, 1921), edited by WILLIAM PETERFIELD TRENT, JOHN ERSKINE, STUART P. SHERMAN, and CARL VAN DOREN. This scholarly account of the progress of American literature in all its ages and ramifications is on a larger scale than any previous history, is the first composed with the collaboration of scholars from all parts of the United States and Canada, provides an extensive bibliography, and aims to furnish "a survey of the life of the American people as expressed in their writings rather than a history of *belles-lettres* alone."

Cambridge Press, The. This earliest press in the English colonies was conducted from 1638 to 1692, and it printed the BAY PSALM BOOK and the Eliot Indian Bible (see JOHN ELIOT), as well as other contemporary books. When the press and a supply of type arrived in this country, they were set up in the house of President Dunster of Harvard. Its printers ranged from Stephen Daye to Samuel Green, Jr. It became a focal point for the intellectual and theological life of the period; many controversies of the time occasioned books from the Cambridge Press.

Cameron, George Frederick (b. New Glasgow, Nova Scotia, Sept. 24, 1854—d. Sept. 17, 1885), Canadian poet, editor. According to Archibald Lampman, Cameron was "most certainly the poet of most genuine and fervid poetic energy that this country [Canada] has yet produced." Charles J. Cameron, his brother, made a selection of his poems, *Lyrics on Freedom, Love, and Death* (1887).

Camp, Walter [Chauncey] (b. New Britain, Conn., April 7, 1859—d. March 14, 1925), athletic director, writer. Camp served on the national rules committee for football, which brought about several important innovations in the game. He became a successful businessman, also coached at Yale. He became the country's foremost football authority, established football as a major college sport, wrote football stories for boys. He originated the famous "Daily Dozen" physical exercises, with instructions in articles, books, and phonograph records. He wrote *Football Without a Coach* (1920), *Book of Sports and Games* (rev. ed., 1923); also stories, *The Substitute* (1908) and *Jack Hale at Yale* (1909).

campaign biography. A distinct genre of American writing, campaign biographies are an invariable accompaniment of Presidential elections. Probably the first example was the biography done by NATHANIEL HAWTHORNE of his old friend FRANKLIN PIERCE. It was a small volume which appeared in 1852. Whether or not it helped Pierce is not clear, but the new President rewarded Hawthorne with a consulship at Liverpool. Some of the early lives of Lincoln were in the nature of political propaganda, among them a biography by WILLIAM DEAN HOWELLS for which he received $160 (1860). In 1876 Howells prepared a campaign biography of Rutherford B. Hayes, and WILLIAM T. ADAMS (Oliver Optic) wrote one of Grant. General LEW WALLACE did a life of Benjamin Harrison, WOL-

COTT BALESTIER one of James G. Blaine. Twentieth-century candidates take campaign biographies as a matter of course; RUPERT HUGHES did one of Governor Thomas E. Dewey in 1944, IRVING STONE one of Governor Earl Warren in 1948, Noel F. Busch one of Adlai E. Stevenson in 1952. JAMES D. HART has assembled a collection of campaign biographies at the University of California.

Campanius, John (b. Sweden, Aug. 15, 1601—d. Sept. 17, 1683), Swedish missionary, translator. Campanius was a minister from 1643 to 1648 in New Sweden, later a part of New Jersey, Delaware, and Pennsylvania. There he became interested in the Delaware Indians, and in their behalf translated Luther's *Small Catechism* into what he called the American-Virginian language. Campanius was probably the first Protestant missionary in America, and Luther's book was apparently the first Protestant manual translated into any Indian language. It did not appear in print until 1696; a facsimile reprint appeared in 1937 in connection with the New Sweden Tercentenary Celebration. Campanius lacked a complete knowledge of the syntax of the language of the Indians, and he had no models to go by; it has been conjectured that some of his errors were owing to the fact that he knew only the trade jargon which the Indians and the Swedes employed in their intercourse.

Campbell, Anne (b. Lynn, Mich., June 19, 1888—   ), "writer of verse" (Miss Campbell's own description). Frankly an imitator of EDGAR A. GUEST, Miss Campbell (Mrs. George W. Stark) began producing verses in 1922 for the Detroit *News* (Guest was writing for the Detroit *Free Press*), and her verse soon reached syndication. It appeared, usually six days a week, in newspapers all over the United States, Canada, England, and Ireland.

Campbell, Bartley (b. Pittsburgh, Pa., Aug. 12, 1843—d. July 30, 1888), newspaperman, editor, playwright, producer. As a drama critic Campbell was attracted to writing for the stage. In 1871 his *Through Fire* was produced, the first of a series of melodramas and social dramas, some highly successful but none ever published. *My Partner* (1879), a study of frontier life, is regarded as his best. In *The White Slave* (1882), based on Dion Boucicault's THE OCTOROON, occurs a classic melodramatic line. The brutal owner of Liza threatens to send her to the fields, clad in rags. She replies: "Rags are royal raiment when worn for virtue's sake." Other Campbell plays are *Peril, or, Love at Long Branch* (1872), *Bulls and Bears* (1875), *Paquita* (1885). In 1869 Campbell founded the *Southern Literary Monthly* in New Orleans.

Campbell, John (b. Scotland, 1653—d. 1728), newspaperman. An emigrant to Massachusetts in about 1695, Campbell became a writer for newspapers in Boston and in 1702 was appointed postmaster. See BOSTON NEWS-LETTER.

Campbell, John Charles (b. La Porte, Ind., Sept. 14, 1867—d. May 2, 1919), educator. Campbell taught in Southern mountain schools for many years, and wrote *The Southern Highlander and his Homeland* (1921). His wife, Olive (Dame Campbell) (1822—   ), with Margaret Butler, founded the John C. Campbell Folk School in Brasstown, N.C., modeled after the Danish Folk Schools, to supplement the public education of young adults with a "community living" curriculum which includes recreational, cultural, economic, and educational features. With Cecil Sharp, she compiled *English Folk Songs from the Southern Appalachians* (1928).

Campbell, Joseph (b. New Rochelle, N.Y., Mar. 26, 1904—   ), mythologist. Campbell has made extensive studies in Europe and America in literature, mythology, philology, and art history. He became a member of the literature department of Sarah Lawrence College in 1934, teaching a course in comparative mythology. Campbell did not begin publishing until *Where the Two Came to Their Father: A Navaho War Ceremonial* (1943, with J. King and M. Oakes). This was the first book in the Bollingen series. The next year saw the appearance of *A Skeleton Key to Finnegans Wake*, written with Henry Morton Robinson. The book remains an indispensable adjunct to Joyce's cryptic masterpiece. Throughout his studies, his books, and his several editions of foreign works, Campbell consistently found the same mythological archetypes. In *The Hero With A Thousand Faces* (1949) he describes a single story, or monomyth, which he believes all myths recapitulate in whole or part. Using Freudian and Jungian concepts along with his own erudition, Campbell retells myths of many times from many parts of the world—Indian, Greek, Christian, Eskimo, Tibetan, Chinese, Japanese, Australian—and shows that each contains the story of a hero's departure, initiation, and return. The book has importance in anthropology, mythology, and literary criticism. Campbell married Jean Erdman, modern dancer, in 1938. Among his books: *Grimm's Fairy Tales: Folkloristic Commentary* (1944); *The Portable Arabian Nights* (1952); *Masks of God: V. I, Primitive Mythology* (1959); *V. II, Oriental Mythology* (1962).

Campbell, Thomas. Author of GERTRUDE OF WYOMING.

Campbell, Walter Stanley ["Stanley Vestal"] (b. Severy, Kans., Aug. 15, 1887—d. 1957), teacher, biographer, historian, poet. Under his pen name Campbell has written many books dealing with the Old West and with the art of writing; among them, *Fandango, Ballads of the Old West* (1927); *Kit Carson* (1928); *Sitting Bull* (1932); *Mountain Men* (1937); *Professional Writing* (1938); *Big-Foot Wallace* (1942); *The Missouri* (1945); *Jim Bridger* (1946); *War Path and Council Fire* (1948); *Dodge City* (1952); *Joe Meek* (1952). Under his own name he has edited documents and books relating to Indians and explorations. He compiled *The Book Lover's Southwest: A Guide to Good Reading* (1955).

Campbell, [William] Wilfred (b. Berlin, Ont., June 1, 1861—d. Jan 1, 1918), poet, novelist. Like his father before him, Campbell decided early to become an Episcopal priest. He attended Wycliffe College and the University of Toronto, and continued his studies at the Episcopal Divinity School at Cambridge, Mass. During his residence there he was encouraged in his poetical career by Oliver Wendell Holmes. He was ordained in 1885 and assigned the parish of West Claremont, Mass., but resigned from his church offices in 1891, feeling that their formality and dogmas restricted him. Campbell was elected Fellow of The Royal Society of Canada in 1894 and received an LL.D. from the University of Aberdeen in the four hundredth year of its founding.

A dweller in Canada's "Lake District," Campbell is associated with a school of poets known as "The Group of the Sixties," so called because the birth dates of each of the poets fell close to the year 1860. Among others of this group were Archibald Lampman, Dr. Duncan Campbell Scott, Archdeacon Frederick George Scott, and Bliss Carman. Campbell's poetry began to receive attention during the 1880's. In addition to contributions to periodicals, he wrote the following books of poems: *Snowflakes and Sunbeams* (1888); *Lake Lyrics* (1889); *The Dread Voyage and Other Poems* (1893); *Mordred and Hildebrand* (1895); *Beyond the Hills of Dream* (1899). Collections of Campbell's poems include: *Poems of Wilfred Campbell* (1905); *Poetical Tragedies* (1908); *Sagas of Vaster Britain* (1914); *Poetical Works of Wilfred Campbell* (1922). He also edited two anthologies: *Poems of Loyalty* (1913) and *The Oxford Book of Canadian Verse* (1914).

Campbell is noted for his historical novels as well, especially *Ian of the Orcades* (1906), a Scottish romance, and *A Beautiful Rebel* (1909), a novel of the War of 1812. His historical and descriptive sketches of Canada include: *The Beauty, History, Romance and Mystery of the Canadian Lake Region* (1910), and the first volume of *The Scotsman in Canada* (1912). Carl Frederick Klinck wrote a comprehensive study of Campbell in 1942.

Campbell, William Edward March. See WILLIAM MARCH.

Canadian literature in English. The existence of a flourishing Canadian literature in the English language is readily apparent, but its historical development cannot be understood without some definition. The name "Canada" originally signified the French colony along the St. Lawrence River; after General Wolfe took Quebec for the British in 1759, it stood for the same area and people, but under British rule. In 1791 Upper Canada (now Ontario) was separated from Lower Canada (now Quebec). In 1867 the British North America Act established Canada as a confederation of four provinces north of the United States border; later these were joined by six others, so that the new nation stretched from sea to sea. *Canadian* as a historical term may thus include restrospectively a province like Nova Scotia, which had a proud and independent existence as a British colony early in the 18th century, and Newfoundland,

which dates from the very beginning of Britain's colonial expansion. As a term applied to literary history of all periods, *Canadian* should include *la littérature canadienne*—CANADIAN LITERATURE IN FRENCH. This article, however, will be limited to what has been written in English.

Canada, therefore, is an environment for literary works produced by *sojourners* from the time of Jacques Cartier (about 1534) to the present day; by *settlers* mainly since the introduction of printing at Halifax in 1752, Quebec City in 1764, Montreal in 1776, and Niagara in 1792; and by the *native-born* since about 1800. Major writings of intellectual or artistic quality by the settlers or by the native-born are claimed for this country's literature, as are also those books by sojourners which have their principal reference here. In practice this formula arouses very little controversy regarding claims for works written in early or in recent years, from the *Jesuit Relations* of the 17th century to the posthumous *Hear Us O Lord From Heaven Thy Dwelling Place* (1961) by MALCOLM LOWRY. It registers properly the depth and breadth of the Canadian cultural heritage—including the background of literature in the British Isles and France, the fruitful interaction of English and French literatures upon one another (on the other side of the Atlantic and in Quebec), and the contribution made by the United States in colonial and recent times.

The English, for example, ultimately appropriated the results of French exploration and discovery, but they had even earlier shared the French narratives, in the original or in translation, concerning voyagers and travelers like Jacques Cartier, Samuel de Champlain, Father Louis Hennepin, Baron de Lahontan, and the Jesuit P. F. X. Charlevoix. Knowledge about settlement in the American colonies and the associated Canadian areas was circulated abroad, in the works of the New England Puritans (some of whose "Loyalist" descendants came to Nova Scotia and New Brunswick), and in historical-descriptive books like *The History of the Five Indian Nations of Canada* (London, 1750) by CADWALLADER COLDEN, a resident of New York State, the home of other Loyalists who fled to Upper Canada after the American War of Independence.

The dates given for the introduction of printing apply also to the beginnings of journalism—to the official gazettes of the various colonies; newspapers developed from these toward the end of the 18th century. Canadian-printed books lagged behind, appearing a generation or two later. But one important literary work, published in England, came out of the former French colony in the interval between Wolfe's conquest and the arrival of the Loyalists. This was *The History of Emily Montague* (1769) by Mrs. FRANCES BROOKE (1724–1789), who lived in Quebec City with her husband, the chaplain of the garrison, in the mid-1760's. Her novel, in the epistolary fashion of Samuel Richardson (whom she had known in England), was devoted to a lively analysis of love as an "intellectual pleasure." It is notable for wit, elegance, common sense, and a reflection of contemporary society, all nicely fitted into the romantic scenery and New World conditions of Quebec. The early date (1769) leaves only Mrs. Charlotte Lennox as a rival of Mrs. Brooke for the title of first North American novelist.

The Loyalists—known below the United States line as Tories—came in the 1780's to the Maritime Provinces and to the areas now known as Quebec and Ontario. They brought with them ready-made American culture on various social levels, the literary stratum in Nova Scotia and New Brunswick being represented chiefly by Tory satire, and in Upper Canada, by gazettes and newspapers reflecting internal politics. In the city of Quebec, where the Loyalist migration was not keenly felt, the *Gazette* (established 1764) kept on recording events for the official and military capital of British North America. Montreal, possessed of its own *Gazette* (established in 1778), was the center for the fur trade and other business with the West and the South (*i.e.* the United States). Canada's first distinctive "North American" period lasted until after the War of 1812–14 against the United States, when greatly increased British immigration (especially after 1830) gave rise to a new era.

The pattern of early publications may be discovered in the following representative facts. In John Lambert's *Travels Through Lower Canada, and The United States* (1810), half the space was given to Quebec City; histories of Canada were published by George Heriot (in England, 1804) and by the Loyalist William Smith (in Quebec, 1815); the Earl of Dalhousie sponsored a Literary and Historical Society founded in 1824. More appropriate to Montreal were remarkable accounts of the fur trade, SIR ALEXANDER MACKENZIE's *Voyages from Montreal* (London and Edinburgh, 1801) and Alexander Henry, the Elder's *Travels and Adventures* (New York, 1809). A former employee of the North West Company in Montreal founded and edited a literary journal, *The Scribbler* (1821–27), soon to be followed by *The Canadian Magazine* (1823–25) and *The Canadian Review* (1824–26), edited by two Scots, David Chisholme and Dr. A. J. Christie. Poetical works were published by Margaret Blennerhasset, wife of the expatriate Irish-American HARMAN BLENNERHASSET (*The Widow of the Rock*, Montreal, 1824) and by the Canadian-born Levi Adams (*Jean Baptiste*, Montreal, 1825, and *Tales of Chivalry and Romance*, Edinburgh, 1826). Adam Hood Burwell of Colonel Thomas Talbot's settlement in Upper Canada published poems in the Montreal *Scribbler* in the early 1820's. British-born firebrands Robert Gourlay (1778–1863) and William Lyon Mackenzie (1795–1861) rocked Upper Canada by their political journalism after they arrived in 1817 and 1820 respectively.

With certain local differences, the pattern of literary activity was similar in the Maritime Provinces. In Halifax John Howe edited a *Nova*

Scotia Magazine as early as 1789–91, a parallel to the *Quebec Magazine*, in English and French (1792–94). John Howe's son, the famous JOSEPH HOWE, later a Canadian statesman, conducted the *Nova Scotian* after 1828; in this newspaper literary influences of Washington Irving and *Blackwood's Magazine* were discernible as a series of papers called "The Club" led to THE CLOCKMAKER (1836) of THOMAS CHANDLER HALIBURTON (1796–1865). When they were published in a series of books, these humorous essays about Sam Slick and the Squire made Haliburton internationally famous and gave him a secure place in the development of American humor. Thomas McCulloch (1776–1843) deserves mention beside his more famous compatriot; the author of *Letters of Mephibosheth Stepsure* (1821–23) is now being hailed as "the founder of genuine Canadian humor." A New World poet named Oliver Goldsmith (1787–1861) published *The Rising Village* in London in 1825.

Howe, Haliburton, and Goldsmith were born in Nova Scotia; their emergence in literature coincides with that of a native-born Upper Canadian, Major JOHN RICHARDSON (1796–1852), whose *War of 1812* is the principal record of that American-British-Canadian-Indian struggle along the borders of the yet undeveloped West. Richardson's knowledge of this campaign was personal; he had fought beside Tecumseh, and had been on the field of Moraviantown when the celebrated Shawnee died. His best novel, *Wacousta* (1832), was based on family lore concerning Pontiac, dating back to the days of Major ROBERT ROGERS, known to Americans as the author of PONTEACH. Richardson ended a career which included residence in London, Paris, Spain, and the West Indies as an author of paperback novels in New York (1852).

In the 1820's, partly because Upper Canada was "discovered" by the British through publicity given to the American War of 1812–14, a wave of immigration began, chiefly from England, Ireland, and Scotland, and reached flood level after 1830. The percentage of Americans in the population dropped considerably as thousands of half-pay British officers, adventurous gentlemen, journalists, tradesmen, and simply poor people took up land near lakes Ontario, Erie, and Huron. Travel literature of the period was written by John Howison, E. A. Talbot, John Mactaggart, Sir George Head, Francis Hall, John McGregor, Thomas Magrath, Patrick Shirreff, Francis Marryat, Samuel Strickland, William Kingston, and others.

John Galt (1779–1839), the famous Scottish novelist, acted as a superintendent of the Canada Company (a colonization project), and published two books of Canadian fiction, *Lawrie Todd* (1830) and *Bogle Corbet* (1831). His friend Dr. William "Tiger" Dunlop (1792–1848), a veteran of *Blackwood's* literary revels, came out to settle and to write amusing variations on the themes of American campaigns and emigrant handbooks. Two sisters of Agnes Strickland (the biographer of queens of England), namely Mrs. CATHERINE PARR TRAILL (1802–1899) and Mrs. SUSANNA MOODIE (1803–1885), refined travel and emigrant literature in *The Backwoods of Canada* (1836) and *Roughing It In The Bush* (1852), respectively. The gentility of these ladies, fostered in an English home, matched American gentility (probably also English in inspiration), to be found in the mid-century ladies' magazines published in the United States. Their writings helped to sustain the reputation of *The Literary Garland* (1838–51), a Montreal journal, edited at first by John Gibson and later by Mrs. E. L. Cushing and Mrs. Harriet V. Cheney. The latter were both daughters of Mrs. Hannah Foster, author of one of the earliest novels in the United States, THE CO- QUETTE (1797). The lyrics of CHARLES SANG- STER (1822–1893), published in 1856 and 1860, and an anthology, *Selections from Canadian Poets*, edited by Edward Hartley Dewart in 1864, stand as examples of the verse of a period when the feminine and social aspects of colonialism appeared to prevail.

Charles Heavysege (1816–1876), a Montreal cabinetmaker who produced belated Shakespearean poetic dramas, and Alexander Mc- Lachlan (1820–1896), a voice from the farm, ignored or scorned the "cultural" movement. Canadian interest in the country's history remained strong. The journalists were only half bookish; domestic politics was their chief concern, both before and after the rebellion of 1837–38 in the Canadas. Systematic exploration, farther and farther west, yielded scientific papers by men such as Sir John William Dawson (a Nova Scotian), Sir William Logan, and Henry Youle Hind, all of whom were geologists. The influence of Britain upon its emigrant sons and daughters was generally beneficent and nourishing while it was tempered by distance, as the American influence was also tempered by a very great Canadian distrust of the political intentions of the United States. In spite of this, Canadians kept on borrowing from American culture, but all, even those of non-British origin, borrowed like Britons. Such was the "spirit of Canada" as it was exhibited by THOMAS D'ARCY McGEE (1825–1868), an exile from Erin who became a "Father" of Canadian Confederation, teaching Canadians what he had learned in the "Young Ireland" movement of the 1840's—how to employ ballads, orations, and histories in the making of a nation.

After four provinces joined in a Dominion in 1867, the Canadian spirit was exhibited chiefly in a vigorous thrust westward, described, for example, in the works of CHARLES MAIR (1838–1927), and symbolized by the Riel uprisings of 1870 and 1885, as well as by the completion of the first Canadian transcontinental railway, the Canadian Pacific, in 1885. Isabella Valancy Crawford (1850–1887) wrote strong, imaginative poems about pioneers, city folk, and cowboys. Pauline Johnson (1861–1913), an Ontario Indian girl who recited her poems everywhere, eventually resided on the Pacific Coast. ROBERT

W. SERVICE (1876–1958), author of *Songs of a Sourdough* (1907), went far north to create world-famous images of the Yukon, where there was gold before the old Canadian dream of a Northwest Passage was realized. Sir GILBERT PARKER (1862–1932), whose novels ranged over the Empire, conceived his Canadian prose tales —*Pierre and His People* (1892), for example— with all the poetry that was in him. Fiction of the West seemed romantic even when it was close to accurate reporting. CHARLES W. GORDON (better known as "Ralph Connor") (1860–1937) moved from nostalgia for Glengarry, a county in Ontario, to excitement about the Great West and his hopes for strong religious adventure. Millions of people read his books, as they did those of his American contemporary, James Oliver Curwood.

Such literature was not calculated to give the reading world a proper impression of growing villages, towns, cities, and industrial centers in the East. Until the First World War, indeed, the agricultural nature of the home bases for expansion is apparent. Small-town piety provided material for much popular fiction and verse, until the acme was reached in the gentle burlesque of *Sunshine Sketches of a Little Town* (1912), by STEPHEN LEACOCK (1869–1944). This brilliant economics professor from McGill spent his writing career in a vast number of similar efforts to entertain by sane displays of incongruity— the typically Canadian substitute for, and equivalent of, a "muckraking" school (see MUCKRAK- ING LITERATURE). The rural life of Quebec was sentimentally and amusingly interpreted in the verses of WILLIAM HENRY DRUMMOND (1854–1907), the "habitant poet" (see HABITANT). Domestic fiction of high quality was provided for the young in two notable and popular works: *Beautiful Joe. The Autobiography of a Dog* (1894), by Marshall Saunders (1861–1947), a native of Nova Scotia, and ANNE OF GREEN GABLES (1908), by L. M. MONTGOMERY (1877–1942), who was born in Prince Edward Island. The perennial interest in history of the Old Regime in Quebec brought forth THE GOLDEN DOG (1877), by WILLIAM KIRBY (1817–1906) of Niagara, a book long regarded as Canada's principal contribution to historical romance.

Recalling the small town can also serve to explain why regionalism was strong in the East, and also why it was not stronger—that is to say, why some writers cultivated literature close to home and others simply had to seek opportunities elsewhere. A young woman from Brantford, Ontario, could become a journalist, travel around the world, and pay her way by writing articles, not to speak of being married to an Englishman in India; this was true of Sara Jeannette Duncan (Mrs. Everard Cotes, 1862–1922), author of *The Imperialist* (1904) and many other novels. The United States also, in the 1890's, provided richer financial returns for periodical verse and prose than Canadians had known before or have known since. CHARLES (later Sir Charles) G. D. ROBERTS (1860–1943), a native of New Brunswick, gave up school and college teaching to do free-lance writing in the United States and Britain, certainly outside of Canada, from 1896 to 1925. Although he was sensitive to many fashions in these years, he wrote his most memorable poems on themes suggested by his New Brunswick home and the Nova Scotian land of Evangeline. His meticulously accurate, poetic short stories of animal life are noteworthy literary adaptations of popular ideas about evolution. BLISS CARMAN (1861–1929), his cousin, lived in the United States from 1890 to 1929; his sensitivity made him an unusually interesting poet of the post-Emersonian-Victorian period which led not so much to "the Georgians" as to the Montreal School of the late 1920's and thereafter. He was most popular for *Low Tide on Grand Pré* (1893) and for *Songs from Vagabondia* (published jointly with Richard Hovey, 1894), written while his mythology of Mother Earth was taking a distinctively Canadian turn.

In this respect he was joined by one of the stay-at-home poets, WILFRED CAMPBELL (1861–1918), whose imperialist "Laureate poems" fade badly in comparison with his works built upon primitive religion, nature myths, and the spell of the Lake Huron–Georgian Bay region. Campbell was soon drawn to a position in the civil service at Ottawa, the capital of the Dominion, which offered literary companionship with ARCHIBALD LAMPMAN (1861–1899) and DUNCAN CAMPBELL SCOTT (1862–1947). Lampman displayed the rarest genius for nature poetry while he was content with the woods and fields of Ontario. Scott, distinguished for artistic taste and controlled emotion, won from the wilderness and the Indian people a poetic imagery happily blending man and nature. These men were aware of the encouraging American market for periodical poetry and of the opportunities which Roberts and Carman could open up for them, but they stayed at home and developed their individual talents. They do not, however, deserve the labels of escapists and cultural laggards. They attempted quietly to deal with current fashions and trends—not by imitating foreign methods, but rather by treating the spiritual necessities which generated those fashions, without argument, by means occult rather than naïve. They belonged in their own way to the generation in which RICHARD MAURICE BUCKE (1837–1902) of London, Ontario, could detect the prophet in Walt Whitman and make a religion of "cosmic consciousness."

MARJORIE PICKTHALL (1883–1922), English-Canadian in origin but "Celtic" in imagination and craftsmanship, won admirers during and after the First World War for her devotion to "beauty" in its richest aspects. WILSON MAC-DONALD (1880–   ), displayed a gift for the "lyric cry" and offered "flagons of beauty" more often than the cups of satire which his contemporaries, facing a bitter postwar era, thought him capable of providing. JOHN McCRAE (1872–1918), a Canadian doctor, wrote "In Flanders' Fields," the most famous poem about the War of 1914–18, in which he perished. New poetic needs soon made themselves felt, although innovations in critical opinion were inhibited by the presence of Charles G. D. Roberts in Toronto from 1925 to 1943. E. J. PRATT (1883–   ), a rugged and amiable Newfoundlander, was not deterred from going his own way in the very college at Toronto—Victoria College—where Marjorie Pickthall had found critical encouragement. With a fine sweeping style, a great love of words, a delight in people and things, and a command of allegory, Pratt used the powers of sea and majestic land to acknowledge the savagery and honor the compassion of men. His most characteristic narratives are *The Witches' Brew* (1925), *The Roosevelt and the Antinoe* (1930), *The Titanic* (1935), *Brébeuf and His Brethren* (1940), and *Towards the Last Spike* (1952), concerned, respectively, with alcoholic prohibition, a rescue at sea, the shipwreck of a great liner, the Jesuit martyrs of Fort Ste. Marie, and the construction of Canada's first transcontinental railway. A national poet in many other ways, Pratt is so in general acceptance by both French and English readers. With him poetry in Canada turned academic, but he did not lose the common touch.

Some poems by Pratt appeared in *New Provinces*, edited by FRANK R. SCOTT in 1936, an anthology representing a group to which Pratt remotely belonged because of a scholarly and creative interest in experimental poetics and a concern about social welfare. Scott, A. J. M. SMITH, and soon A. M. KLEIN, were more explicit than Pratt in their attack upon problems of economic depression and European fascism; and they were ready in the 1920's to go along with their young contemporaries in England and America who were beneficiaries of the symbolists, the imagists, Frazer's *Golden Bough*, Donne, Yeats, Edith Sitwell, and T. S. Eliot. These McGill writers brought Canadian poetry into an academic and cosmopolitan phase, nourished by literary criticism in the universities and by international movements. Scott was the most persistent advocate of social reform, but he wrote with a mature sense of humor and a desire to retain the best things, like art, in the planned amelioration of all men's lives. DOROTHY LIVESAY swung far to the left before she mingled her hopes for social reconstruction with more personal views of human needs. A. M. Klein, trained in Jewish lore, was absorbed in anger about Nazi anti-Semitic horrors and in zeal for the building of a new Israel. His studies of Joyce and his experimentation with striking language mark his Montreal poems as well as the modern pentateuch and the psalms for the Jewish people which are to be found in his highly original book *The Second Scroll* (1951). A. J. M. Smith, the leader of the group in the early years, was always more moderate with regard to special causes, except the cause of pure poetry; in *News of the Phoenix* (1943) and *A Sort of Ecstasy* (1954) his purpose is plainly spiritual, and his meanings reside in subtly contrived forms.

The response of the intellectuals to the depression years of the 1930's is clear enough in these poems of the *New Provinces* group; and supplementary evidence exists in the files of *The Canadian Forum*, in Earle Birney's *Down the Long Table* (1955), and in HUGH MACLEN-NAN'S *The Watch That Ends The Night* (1959). FREDERICK PHILIP GROVE (1871–1948) recorded the plight of the prairie farmers and his own struggle for adjustment. The titles of his novels are unusually revealing: *A Search for America* (1927), *Our Daily Bread* (1928), *Fruits of the Earth* (1933), and *In Search of Myself* (1946), his autobiography. Grove always wrote in a mood of high seriousness and with a desire to transcend naturalism; his work is uneven, and his narratives fall short of his excellent essays in *Over Prairie Trails* (1922) and *The Turn of the Year* (1923). This Swedish-Canadian can best be understood in terms of acquaintance with midwestern American fiction; and he had a Scandinavian sense of Ultima Thule. The troubles of industry in Ontario, where he later made his home, moved him to write an ambitious but unwieldy novel, *The Master of the Mill* (1944). Grove himself appears to stand aloof; he sees much, thinks hard, and communicates with difficulty.

Any feeling of remoteness in JALNA (1927) by MAZO DE LA ROCHE (1885–1961) is delightfully different. The author shows passionate concern for her characters, although the setting seems to most Canadians a kind of inspired contrivance. Her Jalna world could exist and has indeed existed near Toronto and Hamilton, unknown to all except a special class of gentlemen farmers; yet it justifies itself chiefly because she has given it permanence. All readers of Miss de la Roche's series of Jalna novels, year after year, in English and in translation, have an intimate knowledge of the home of the exciting Whiteoak family. What Stephen Leacock had done for the evangelical novel of small-town piety, Mazo de la Roche did for more purely domestic fiction; and in both cases the development to mastery was indigenous.

The historical romance proceeded along lines laid down by Kirby and his contemporaries, but with evidences of improving craftsmanship and stronger realism. *The Viking Heart* (1923) of Laura Goodman Salverson (1890–) and the prairie novels of Frederick Niven (1878–1944) are examples from the West, as *His Majesty's Yankees* (1942) and *Pride's Fancy* (1946) by Thomas H. Raddall (1903–) are from the East. THOMAS B. COSTAIN (1885–1965), a United States author, has devoted himself to historical works, such as *High Towers* (1949) and *Son of a Hundred Kings* (1957), set in Canada, the land of his birth. But novels more strictly realistic in purpose, especially those of MORLEY CALLAGHAN (1903–) and Hugh MacLennan (1907–), have won a popular as well as a critical audience. After meeting Hemingway in Toronto in the early 1920's, Callaghan went abroad to become acquainted with brilliant expatriate American writers in Paris and to bring home an understanding of the aims and techniques of REALISM, or naturalism, as it was between the wars (especially perhaps in the works

of Sherwood Anderson). Callaghan's individuality in tone and style won recognition in the United States and, more than once, a reputation for dullness among the uncritical in Canada. His short stories were collected, at their best, in *Now That April's Here* (1936) and *Stories* (1959); his many novels began with *Strange Fugitive* (1928) and included *Such Is My Beloved* (1934), *The Loved and the Lost* (1951), and *The Many Colored Coat* (1960). Callaghan shuns the spectacular as well as the doctrinaire in social theory; he does not reveal character as a kind of extension of environment. He plays upon personal relationships which become symbolic by unemphatic suggestion, and ironical because irony is built into human affairs.

MacLennan tries to cope with life in a broader way; a Cape Breton man with a strong conscience, he has an affinity for the problem novel. *Barometer Rising* (1941), set in Halifax at the time of the great 1917 explosion, shows him at his best in style and structure. He portrayed in *Two Solitudes* (1945) the social and personal dilemmas of French and English in Quebec. *The Precipice* (1948) and *Each Man's Son* (1951) were followed by a great popular success, *The Watch That Ends The Night* (1959), the story of three people who come through depression and war, still face to face with life and death. MacLennan writes competently, and at times eloquently, with genuine narrative skill, while he falters before self-imposed lines of inquiry which seem to call for indirection of expression. In *The Village of Souls* (1933), *God's Sparrows* (1937), *Day of Wrath* (1945), and *Mr. Ames Against Time* (1949), Philip Child (1898–) shows an inclination to employ parable and psychological study but, no less than MacLennan, a conscious desire to regulate the reader's ideas about good and evil.

Both of these authors may have helped to prepare the way for the recent immigrant and "racial" novels which concentrate upon the new Canadians who have poured into Canada since Hitler began to shake Europe. Some examples are: *The Rich Man* (1948), by Henry Kreisel (1922–); *The Sacrifice* (1956), by Adele Wiseman (1928–); *Under the Ribs of Death* (1957), by John Marlyn (1912–); and, among other novels by MORDECAI RICHLER (1931–), *Son of a Smaller Hero* (1955) and *The Apprenticeship of Duddy Kravitz* (1959). An immigrant in the Irish tradition is the central figure in *The Luck of Ginger Coffey* (1960) by BRIAN MOORE (1921–), himself a newcomer from Ireland who had previously published *Judith Hearne* (1955) and *The Feast of Lupercal* (1957). Any resemblance to MacLennan is accidental if one moves from Moore's problem novels into those of the "apprenticeship" kind. DAVID WALKER (1911–), a former army officer who now lives in New Brunswick, will be mentioned in this connection chiefly because he may represent the talented newcomers from Britain; he is widely known for a half-dozen novels, especially for the Highland story, *Geordie* (1950), and *Where the High*

Winds Blow (1960), set in the Canadian north.

Realism of an intense psychological kind is successfully handled in *As For Me and My House* (1941), by Sinclair Ross (1908—   ), in his study of a man and wife in a prairie setting which shatters both of them. There is also realism of the all-seeing eye. ROBERTSON DAVIES (1914—   ), essayist, dramatist, and novelist, is one of the chief exponents. His *Diary of Samuel Marchbanks* (1947) and other books of essays urbanely expose to ridicule a wide range of his neighbors' cultural pretensions. Davies shows no desire to be a spiritual guide; he enjoys exploding firecrackers. The fun continues in his Salterton novels, *Tempest Tost* (1951) and *Leaven of Malice* (1953). Many of the plays which make him a leading dramatist carry on this salutary battle of sophistication with provincialism. ETHEL WILSON (1890—   ) of Vancouver wrote a book entitled *The Innocent Traveller* (1949), but it is generally conceded that her own innocence is related to deep experience. When she recently described herself as a "country cat among my friends the falcons," she was rejoicing in isolation and independence which enabled her to observe, analyze, and describe types like Miss Tritt, the nobody in *The Equations of Love* (1952). RODERICK HAIG-BROWN (1908—   ), a nature essayist of the West Coast, also enjoys isolation in which to compose his masterpieces of sporting literature. And along the same coast, among the Queen Charlotte Islands, EMILY CARR (1891–1945), the strongest individualist among Canadian painters, repeated her totem-pole art in the superb prose sketches of *Klee Wyck* (1941) and *The Book of Small* (1942).

Not far from these authors, in a suburb of Vancouver, MALCOLM LOWRY (1909–1957), author of *Under the Volcano* (1947), lived from 1939 until 1954. The English-speaking world has recently been made aware that he thus adopted a small bit of Canada for his home during his most productive period; considerable proof is in the poems now being published and in the book of short stories, *Hear Us O Lord From Heaven Thy Dwelling Place* (1961). *Under The Volcano*, a major novel of modern times, employs symbols derived from Mexico to describe the last days of an alcoholic. It would be useless to look for anything like Lowry's linguistic brilliance in any other Canadian novelist, but *The Mountain and the Valley* (1952) by Ernest Buckler (1908—   ) displays considerable power over symbols and imagery. And there is a strange richness of suggestion pervading *The Double Hook* (1959), by Sheila Watson. Buckler is a Nova Scotian, and Mrs. Watson, an Albertan.

The contemporary poets and critics are to be found chiefly in the cities, near or in the universities. In Vancouver are Roy Daniells (1902—   ), author of *Deeper Into The Forest,* a book of poems (1948); George Woodcock (1912—   ), travel writer, critic, and editor of the journal *Canadian Literature* (1959—   ); and EARLE BIRNEY (1904—   ), who is widely known as the poet of *David*

and Other Poems (1942), *Now Is Time* (1945), and *The Strait of Anian* (1948). Birney's desire to experiment is evident in his unusual poetic diction, in his tour de force of good-natured satire about Vancouver (*Trial of a City,* 1952); and in two novels, one of which is a picaresque war story entitled *Turvey* (1949). The most-admired of his works is "David," a parable of learning, decision, and sacrifice involving mountain climbers in the Rockies. In Edmonton are Wilfred Watson (1911—   ), who has one book of verse, *Friday's Child* (1955), and Eli Mandel (1922—   ), whose *Fuseli Poems* appeared in 1960. London, Ontario, also has two poets (both in the University of Western Ontario), JAMES REANEY (1926—   ), whose *The Red Heart* (1949) and *A Suit of Nettles* (1958) established him as a leading myth-maker, and Ronald Bates (1924—   ), author of *The Wandering World* (1959). The group to which Reaney, Watson, Mandel, and Bates belong has grown out of critical movements in the University of Toronto, particularly at Victoria College, where Northrop Frye (1912—   ), the distinguished author of *Fearful Symmetry* (1947), a study of Blake, and *Anatomy of Criticism* (1957), has exerted a profound influence upon Canadian intellectuals. Others who have displayed a similar interest in myth, fantasy, surprise, and song are Jay Macpherson (1932—   ), poet of *The Boatman* (1957); the late Anne Wilkinson (1910–1961); Margaret Avison (1918—   ), who recently published *Winter Sun* (1960); Phyllis Webb (1927—   ), and Daryl Hine (1936—   ) of Montreal.

Apart from this group is Robert Finch (1900—   ), who was represented in *New Provinces* (1936) and who recently published *Acis in Oxford* (1961). CHARLES BRUCE (1906—   ) is generally identified with his former home in the Maritime Provinces. Raymond Souster (1921—   ), also of Toronto, has several books, including *Go To Sleep World* (1947), and is editor of Contact Press. With him and Ronald Hambleton (1917—   ) one comes to a very different set of poets who appear to be centered in Montreal. They are heirs but not followers of the McGill men of the 1920's, Smith, Scott, and Klein. Each generation has seen a new burst of song. In the 1940's Patrick Anderson (1915—   ) led the short-lived *Preview* (1942) movement which brought into prominence PATRICIA K. PAGE (1916—   ); her ironic social studies in vivid psychological imagery were to be found in *As Ten, As Twenty* (1946) and *The Metal and the Flower* (1954). After her came Kay Smith (1911—   ), Miriam Waddington (1917—   ), and Louis Dudek (1918—   ). The latter has been very active as a teacher, critic, anthologist, and author of *East of the City* (1946), *The Searching Image* (1952), *Europe* (1955), and *Laughing Stalks* (1958). The youngest of this new group is Leonard Cohen (1933—   ), and the acknowledged leader is now IRVING LAYTON (1912—   ), whose many volumes include *The Bull Calf and Other Poems* (1956), *Red*

Carpet for the Sun (1959), and *The Swinging Flesh* (1961). Layton boasts about his lust for life, which indeed he possesses; the learning and skill with which he can release and control this zest confounds his critics and makes him a major Canadian poet.

This review of the poets has omitted Anne Marriott (1913—), author of *The Wind Our Enemy* (1939), an expression of prairie lands and people in time of drought; and (in the East, between Toronto and Montreal), at Queen's University in Kingston, George Whalley (1915—), who published *No Man An Island* in 1948, and Douglas Le Pan (1914—), who dealt with the war in Italy in *The Wounded Prince* (1949) and *The Net and the Sword* (1953). In Ottawa, at Carleton University, is George Johnston (1915—), author of the casual, witty poems of *The Cruising Auk* (1959). Associated with Ottawa and the diplomatic service is R. A. D. Ford (1915—), whose *A Window on the North* (1956) deals with Canadian and Russian scenes. Ralph Gustafson (1909—), formerly of Bishop's College, Lennoxville, now lives in New York but writes for Canadians. A New Brunswick group marked by "straightforwardness" has been recognized by Professor Desmond Pacey, author of *Creative Writing in Canada* (1961); it includes Fred Cogswell (1917—), editor of the successful poetry magazine entitled *The Fiddlehead*, Elizabeth Brewster (1922—), and Alden Nowlan (1933—).

There is no room in this article to do justice to many other topics relevant to Canadian literature. A few headings are all that can be given, but they must include reference to the vast subject of French-Canadian literature; the writings of a long line of noted historians, natural scientists, social scientists, and humanists; the contribution of devoted publishers, especially the late Dr. Lorne Pierce (1890–1961); the influence of the churches, schools, and universities; the literature of "foreign language" and "racial" groups; the "national" and the "little" magazines; dramatic literature, especially the plays of Robertson Davies; the rich, but brief, period of radio drama, under Andrew Allan of the Canadian Broadcasting Corporation, which brought out radio playwrights like Lister Sinclair (1921—), Len Petersen (1917—), and Joseph Schull (1910—); the development of TV drama and the current success of Arthur Hailey; the world-famous Stratford (Ontario) Shakespeare Festival; the new exchange of scholars and creative artists, especially with the United Kingdom, supported by the Canada Council; and the continuous pressure of American culture through books, magazines, films, and television.

Sources of further information on Canadian literature include: Ray Palmer Baker, *A History of English-Canadian Literature to the Confederation* (1920); Clara Thomas, *Canadian Novelists, 1920–1945* (1946); Walter P. Percival, ed., *Leading Canadian Poets* (1948); Edward A. McCourt, *The Canadian West in Fiction* (1949);

Julian Park, ed., *The Culture of Contemporary Canada* (1957); A. J. M. Smith, ed., *The Book of Canadian Poetry* (1957); Ralph Gustafson, ed., *The Penguin Book of Canadian Verse* (1958); Desmond Pacey, *Ten Canadian Poets* (1958) and *Creative Writing in Canada, A Short History of English-Canadian Literature* (1961); Malcolm Ross, ed., *The Arts in Canada* (1958); C. F. Klinck and R. E. Watters, eds., *Canadian Anthology* (1959), containing a bibliography; R. E. Watters, *A Check List of Canadian Literature and Background Materials 1628–1950* (1959).

Three important quarterlies are: *The Dalhousie Review* (1921—), of Halifax, N. Scot.; *Queen's Quarterly* (1893—), of Kingston, Ont.; and *The Tamarack Review* (1956—), of Toronto. *Canadian Literature* (1959—), a quarterly of The University of British Columbia, Vancouver, publishes an annual bibliography. *The University of Toronto Quarterly* (1930—) contains an annual review of "Letters in Canada."

Carl F. Klinck

Canadian literature in French. French-Canadian literature dates back to the middle of the 19th century. The first major literary achievement by a French-Canadian author was François-Xavier Garneau's *Histoire du Canada,* a four-volume survey of the first three hundred years of Canada's history. The first volume came out in 1845 and the series was completed in 1852. In 1848 the first Canadian government responsible to the elected assembly was established. Both events, the literary and the political, were the culmination of a long and continuous development from colonial dependency to nationhood; both marked the end of an era and the beginning of a new age. Garneau's work was hailed as the "national Bible" of the French Canadians, and its influence, both literary and political, was considerable and lasting.

There had been some writing done in New France, but these pioneer authors were all Frenchmen born and educated in France, and their works' significance was more historical than literary. These early chronicles are among the main sources of Canada's early history, and they are an important part of the nation's cultural heritage. They do not constitute a national literature, however; this started to develop only in the second half of the 19th century. The most important of these early documents are the memoirs of Cartier and Champlain; the historical narratives of Lescarbot, Sagard, Leclercq, La Potherie, Hennepin, Charlevoix, and Lahontan; the correspondence and spiritual writings of Marie de l'Incarnation; and the *Relations des Jésuites.* There was also published in Paris in 1664 the *Histoire naturelle et véritable des mœurs et productions de la Nouvelle-France* by Pierre Boucher; the first work by a Canadian-born author was the *Annales de l'Hôtel-Dieu de Montréal* by the nun Marie Morin (1649–1717). Many other diaries, memoirs, and chronicles are known to us today, as well as songs, poems, and tales, but none of them deserves much consideration. When New France fell under the British rule in 1763, there was no French-Canadian literature worthy of the name.

Nor was it produced in the first seventy-five years that followed the British conquest. The introduction of printing in 1764 led to the publication of newspapers, magazines, pamphlets, and a few books, but most of this early production could boast little, if any, literary merit. The most influential literary and political newspaper of the early 19th century was *Le Canadien*, the organ of the French-Canadian patriots who were fighting for the survival of the French-speaking majority that was ruled and exploited by a small group of British colonists.

The first book of verse came out in 1830, *Épîtres, satires, chansons et autres pièces de vers* by Michel Bibaud. The first novel was *L'Influence d'un livre* by Philippe Aubert de Gaspé, Jr., published in 1837, and the first play was Antoine Gérin-Lajoie's *Le Jeune Latour* (1844). Among the books published at that time were also novels such as *Les Fiancés de 1812* by Joseph Doutre, and *Charles Guérin* by Pierre Chauveau; historical books such as Michel Bibaud's *Histoire du Canada* in three volumes, as well as books of law, agriculture, medicine, and religion.

Most of the best prose and verse published in newspapers and magazines in the first half of the 19th century was collected by James Huston in a four-volume anthology entitled *Répertoire national* (1848–1850). All this is of limited literary value. When Lord Durham wrote, in a famous report, that the French Canadians had "no literature and no history," he was right as far as literature went, but wrong with respect to history—as Garneau immediately set out to demonstrate. In revealing the basic characters and aspirations of the French-Canadian people as he recorded their past history, Garneau provided his contemporaries with a major reference book from which writers could draw their subjects and inspiration.

The development of a native literature reflected the growth of the French-Canadian community. The foundation of colleges, libraries, literary clubs, bookstores, and magazines contributed to the improvement in the literary quality of the production, and the first books still readable today appeared between 1845 and 1866. Most writers of the first generation were quite naturally men of action, militant writers rather than artists. Most of the literature of the time was historical, sociological, political, and religious, and it was provincial in scope, light in substance, and deficient in technique. Of local interest were the works of those who wrote mainly to assist the French Canadians in their struggle for survival. Such are the recorded speeches of public men like Papineau, La Fontaine, Morin, and Cartier; the writings of religious leaders such as Jean Holmes, Antoine Racine, and Louis-François Laflèche, as well as

of the better journalists, Jacques Labrie, Jean-Charles Taché, and Étienne Parent.

Quebec City was then the metropolis of Lower Canada, and most writers of the first generation lived and worked in this capital city of the colony. There was established in 1852 the first Canadian university in which French was the language of tuition; there were established the first newspapers, magazines, and bookstores; there Garneau wrote his *Histoire du Canada;* and there lived most of the other historical writers of the time: Jean-Baptiste Antoine Ferland, whose *Cours d'histoire du Canada* remains a basic reference book for the history of New France; Henri-Raymond Casgrain, the author of many monographs, including biographies of Marie de l'Incarnation, Montcalm, and Lévis; Louis-Philippe Turcotte; Alexandre Taché; Charles-Honoré Laverdière; and others.

The works of many versifiers are included in Huston's *Répertoire national,* such as those of the historian Garneau, of Joseph Lenoir, and of Louis-Joseph Fiset, but the first poet worthy of the name was Octave Crémazie, whose inspiration was mainly historical and patriotic and whose influence was much greater than his literary talent justified. Poetry remained mainly historical in inspiration and romantic in style for some forty years. The major poet of the time was LOUIS-HONORÉ FRÉCHETTE and his most important piece of work was his *Légende d'un peuple,* a series of epics inspired by the leading men and main events of French Canada's history. Other poets of the first generation were Pamphyle Lemay, the poet of rural life; William Chapman, Fréchette's rival in oratorical developments; and Alfred Garneau, who opened a new era in turning his back on historical subjects to express the intimate feelings of his soul.

Similarly, most early Canadian novels were historical. The best work of fiction of that period was *Les Anciens Canadiens* by PHILIPPE AUBERT DE GASPÉ, a chronicle of the life of the *seigneur* and *habitant* under the old regime. Gaspé also wrote very interesting *Mémoires;* he is, with Garneau, the best prose writer of his generation. The most popular historical novels of the time were *Une de perdue, deux de trouvées* by Georges Boucher de Boucherville; *Jacques et Marie* by Napoléon Bourassa; and those of Joseph Marmette and Laure Conan. *Angeline de Montbrun* by Laure Conan was the first psychological novel to be published in Canada. Short stories, tales, and legends were also written at the time, and the best collections of such works of fiction were *Forestiers et voyageurs* by Joseph-Charles Taché, and those of Casgrain, Faucher de Saint-Maurice, Louis Fréchette, and Hubert LaRue.

Worthy of mention also are journalists such as Hector Fabre, Napoléon Legendre, and, foremost, Arthur Buies; orators such as Wilfrid Laurier, Adolphe Chapleau, and Honoré Mercier. By the end of the 19th century, there had appeared a few books of verse, three or four novels, and as many collections of short stories, which marked the beginning of creative writing in French in Canada, but most of the writing was still militant literature dedicated to the religious and ethnic survival of a small community separated from the rest of the continent by the language barrier.

At the turn of the century, new trends developed in French-Canadian letters. Without completely turning their backs on historical subjects, most writers began to look at the contemporary scene and to pay more attention to the inner life. Montreal became a more active literary center than Quebec City, and smaller centers started to contribute authors to the nation. The leading writers were poets, historians, or journalists; strangely enough, few novels were published during that period, and none of them is remarkable. The better works of fiction were then collections of folksy tales and sketches such as Adjutor Rivard's *Chez nous,* Marie-Victorin's *Croquis laurentiens,* and Lionel Groulx's *Rapaillages.*

Poetry, on the other hand, flourished throughout that period. Fréchette, Lemay, and Chapman were still writing at the turn of the century; historical subjects were still in fashion and the regional school grouped many poets, such as Blanche Lamontagne, the poetess of Gaspé; rustic poets such as Jules Tremblay, Adolphe Poisson, Louis-Joseph Doucet, and Gonzalve Desaulniers. Nérée Beauchemin was the outstanding poet of the group, as demonstrated in his *Floraisons matutinales* and *Patrie intime;* Albert Ferland, the poet of the Canadian forests, was the most original of the group. Traditions of the 19th century were thus maintained well into the 20th century, and the romantic school still had several adepts.

New trends, new themes, and new techniques were introduced, however, mainly by poets of the École littéraire de Montréal and by a few independent poets. Baudelaire's influence superseded that of Hugo, and Verlaine, Rollinat, Rodenbach, Régnier, and other French poets had their Canadian disciples too. Poetry became more personal than historical, more lyrical than narrative; the general evolution was from the outer world to the inner life. Romanticism still prevailed in the works of a few members of the École littéraire, such as in Charles Gill's epic *Le Cap Éternité* or in the sentimental poems of Albert Lozeau. Other poets, such as Jean Charbonneau and Alphonse Beauregard, were more attracted to philosophical themes in the manner of Sully-Prudhomme, while Louis Dantin and Lucien Rainier were, in the main, religious poets. There was also the exotic Arthur de Bussières, and Albert Dreux introduced the *vers libre* in Canada. The most accomplished artists of that generation were, however, Guy Delahaye with his *Phases,* and ÉMILE NELLIGAN, who produced some of the best poems ever written in Canada before going out of his mind in his early twenties. Thanks to him and to Beauchemin, Lozeau, and Delahaye, by the time of World War I French-Canadian poetry had attained a standard never reached in the 19th century; it was more diversified in inspiration

and more accomplished in craftmanship than ever before.

The best prose throughout that period was written by men of action or by scholars. Journalists of the nationalist school had a deep influence on many intellectuals, and they produced some gifted writers. The leader of the nationalist movement was Henri Bourassa, a sharp journalist and a great debater; he was supported by men like Olivar Asselin, Jules Fournier, and Paul-Émile Lamarche. Economists like Errol Bouchette and Edmond de Nevers are worthy of mention here, and one of the best prose writers of the time was Léon Gérin, whose essays on sociology were collected in *Le Type économique et social du Canadien* and in *Aux Sources de notre histoire.*

Many historical works appeared during that period, mainly in the field of biography. Narcisse-Eutrope Dionne, Alfred De Celles, Ernest Gagnon, Auguste Gosselin, and Laurent-Olivier David popularized important figures of the past and present. The two leading historians of the time, however, were Thomas Chapais and Joseph-Edmond Roy. The latter wrote many monographs and two larger works, *Histoire du notariat* and *Histoire de la seigneurie de Lauzon,* which throw much light on the daily life and customs of Canadians of the past. Chapais, for his part, in addition to writing biographies of Talon and Montcalm, completed Garneau's survey by writing a general history of Canada covering the period 1763–1867; his *Cours d'histoire du Canada* is a detailed study of British colonial policy in Canada and of the constitutional development of the colony into an independent nation.

Finally, during that period, Adjutor Rivard, Camille Roy, Henri d'Arles, Louis Dantin, and others contributed to make French-Canadian letters better known by reviewing the better books as they came out.

Definite progress was achieved in most fields of literary activity between the two World Wars. Louis Hémon's *Maria Chapdelaine* clearly showed that, with a Canadian theme, a gifted writer could achieve a book of universal appeal. It was an achievement which local authors could endeavor to emulate. Then, the First World War made rural Quebec a highly industrialized province, and the resulting social transformations were soon reflected in the local literature, mainly in the novels of the '20's and '30's. Traditional, folksy subjects still attracted some novelists, such as Damase Potvin (*La Robe noire*), as did historical subjects, as may be seen with Lionel Groulx (*Au Cap Blomidon*), Robert de Roquebrune (*Les Habits rouges* and *La Seigneuresse*), and Léo-Paul Desrosiers, Canada's best historical novelist (*Les Engagés du grand portage, Les Opiniâtres*).

Other novelists, however, showed their concern for economic, social, and religious problems resulting from the deep changes then going on in the traditionally rural French Canada. Most significant among those are *Marcel Faure* and *Les demi-civilisés* by Jean-Charles Harvey;

André Laurence by Pierre Dupuy; *La Chesnaie* by Rex Desmarchais. Problems of the married couple were explored by Jovette Bernier in *La Chair décevante* and by Harry Bernard in *Juana, mon aimée* and other novels. The best novels of the '30's, however, were portrayals of rural manners and customs, such as *Un Homme et son péché* by Claude-Henri Grignon, *La Pension Leblanc* by Robert Choquette, and, above all, *30 arpents* by Ringuet (Philippe Panneton). Remarkable also was the poetical epic by Félix-Antoine Savard, *Menaud, maître-draveur.* All these authors showed more skill in the art of writing and a deeper insight into the human soul and into social problems than had their predecessors. French-Canadian fiction was forging ahead.

So was poetry. The romantic trend was still alive, thanks to ROBERT CHOQUETTE and to a group of poetesses that included Simone Routier, Medjé Vézina, Eva Sénécal, and Jovette Bernier. More influenced by the French *Parnasse* were PAUL MORIN, whose *Paon d'émail* is one of the most polished books of verse published in Canada, and Alfred Desrochers, the poet of *À l'Ombre de l'Orford.* Other poets of that generation were René Chopin, Rosaire Dion-Lévesque, Gustave Lamarche, Georges Bugnet, and Clément Marchand. In 1937, there appeared *Regards et jeux dans l'espace* by Saint-Denys-Garneau, a small book that influenced many younger poets and is now considered a turning point in the recent history of Canadian poetry.

More literary essays and book reviews were collected in book form between the two wars than before or after. The best critics of the time were Albert Pelletier, Marcel Dugas, Louis Dantin, Claude-Henri Grignon, Maurice Hébert, Victor Barbeau, and Séraphin Marion. History remained the favored field of literary activity during that period. The most active historians were Pierre-Georges Roy, Olivier Maurault, Marie-Claire Daveluy, Aegidius Fauteux, Gustave Lanctôt, and Jean Bruchési. The leading historian of the period was Lionel Groulx, whose nationalistic interpretation of Canada's historical development was much discussed. A philosopher like Louis Lachance, an economist like Edouard Montpetit, and journalists such as Victor Barbeau, Georges Pelletier, and Louis Francoeur have contributed some of the good prose of the period. When World War II broke in 1939, French-Canadian literature had reached a standard never attained before. It was soon to reach still higher levels.

The recent growth of French-Canadian letters is naturally accompanied by an inner crisis. By the time of World War II, several authors had already broken away from the provincial traditions of the past generations and grappled with more universal themes, as they had experimented with new techniques. Their example was to be followed by most of the younger writers, and French-Canadian literature is now more cosmopolitan, more individualistic, and more diversified than it ever was before.

The novel reached new peaks with GABRIELLE ROY, Germaine Guèvremont, Roger Lemelin, Yves Thériault, and André Langevin. Gabrielle Roy is the dominant figure here with *Bonheur d'occasion,* which portrays a poverty-stricken family during the depression of the '30's; *La Petite poule d'eau,* two poetical narrations of her youth in her native Manitoba; the portrait of a common man, *Alexandre Chenevert;* and the largely autobiographical stories of *Rue Deschambault.* Germaine Guèvremont's *Le Survenant* is a highly poetical novel of a rural family, while Roger Lemelin's novels are fine satires of parochial customs in Quebec City, such as *Au Pied de la pente douce* and *Les Plouffe.* The prolific Yves Thériault has achieved at least two very good novels, one about Eskimo life, *Agaguk,* the other about Indian life, *Ashini.* André Langevin seems to be the most promising of the younger novelists; *Poussière sur la ville* is his best novel so far.

Other novelists of distinction are Robert Charbonneau (*Ils Posséderont la terre*), Robert Elie (*La Fin des songes*), André Giroux (*Le Gouffre a toujours soif*), all writers of psychological novels. Short-story writers are not very many, but a few are successful, such as Anne Hébert (*Le Torrent*), Claire Martin (*Avec ou sans Amour*), and Jacques Ferron, whose best short stories have not yet been collected in book form.

The few authors who write successfully for the stage all belong to the present generation: they are Gratien Gélinas (*Tit-Coq* and *Bousille et les justes*); Marcel Dubé (*Zone, Florence,* and *Un Simple soldat*); Jacques Languirand (*Le Gibet* and *Les Insolites*); Paul Toupin (*Brutus* and *Le Mensonge*).

Traditional poetry is maintained by poets such as Clément Marchand (*Les Soirs rouges*), Jeannine Bélanger (*Stances à l'éternel absent*), Éloi de Grandmont (*Premiers secrets*), and Sylvain Garneau (*Objèts trouvés*). Most of the recent poetry is, however, rather esoteric and shows the dominant influence of the French surrealists. Alain Grandbois is the leading French-Canadian poet today (*Les Îles de la nuit, Rivages de l'homme*), and his influence on the young generation is deep and extensive. The better poets of the day are Anne Hébert (*Poèmes*), Rina Lasnier (*Le Chant de la montée, Présence de l'absence*), and Pierre Trottier (*Le Combat contre Tristan*). Many young poets show much promise, especially Jean-Guy Pilon, Roland Giguère, Paul-Marie Lapointe, Fernand Ouellette, Gilles Hénault, and Francis Dumont.

The best essays are by Jean Le Moyne (*Convergences*), Jacques Lavigne (*L'inquiétude humaine*), Roger Duhamel, René Garneau, François Hertel, Jean-Charles Falardeau, Jean-Louis Gagnon, and Marcel Raymond. Historical works are still many, and the best ones are by Guy Frégault (*Iberville le conquérant, La Civilisation de la Nouvelle-France, Bigot,* etc.), Marcel Trudel, Michel Brunet, and Jean Bruchési.

French-Canadian literature has recently been accorded more attention abroad than ever before and it is now taking its place among the national literatures of the Western hemisphere.

Historical and bibliographical works on French-Canadian literature include the following: Auguste Viatte, *Histoire littéraire de l'Amérique française;* Gerard Tougas, *Histoire de la littérature canadienne-française;* Guy Sylvestre, *Anthologie de la poésie canadienne-française;* Gérard Martin, *Bibliographie sommaire du Canada français;* I. F. Fraser, *The Spirit of French Canada.*

GUY SYLVESTRE, F.R.S.C.

Canal Town (1944), a novel by SAMUEL HOPKINS ADAMS. One of the later stories of an always reliable spinner of yarns, the book has a double interest. It tells about the frontier of 1820—at that time no farther west than Palmyra, N.Y.—which thrilled with expectancy as "Clinton's ditch," the new Erie Canal, inched ahead. With this is combined a doctor's battle against old superstitions and ingrained folkways.

Canby, Henry Seidel (b. Wilmington, Del., Sept. 6, 1878—d. April 5, 1961), teacher, editor, literary critic, biographer. A graduate of Yale University, Canby taught there for more than two decades. For some years following World War I, he served as literary editor of the *New York Post.* In 1924 he helped to found and became the first editor of the SATURDAY REVIEW OF LITERATURE, now the *Saturday Review.* In 1926, Canby was named chairman of the editorial board of the newly formed BOOK-OF-THE-MONTH CLUB and served in this capacity for twenty-eight years.

During the long period of his prominence in literary criticism Mr. Canby opposed all forms of censorship. Allan Nevins called him "the most constructive single figure on the literary scene." Canby, however, always considered himself primarily a teacher. H. L. Mencken, never inclined to be kind to teachers, called Mr. Canby "an idealist, but the type which remembers that there is such a thing as reality." Of Canby's writing, Mencken commented that, "there is never any strain, never any sacrifice of simplicity or effect, but all the same it shows hard and honest effort."

Among Canby's many books are: *The Short Story* (1902), a standard text for many years; *Walt Whitman: An American* (1943); *Turn West, Turn East: Mark Twain and Henry James* (1951). In the middle 1930's he began writing a series of volumes in which his autobiography is skillfully interwoven with reflections on American education, literature, and culture: *The Age of Confidence* (1934); *Alma Mater: The Gothic Age of the American College* (1936); and AMERICAN MEMOIR (1947). His favorite subject was the study of Thoreau. His wife, Marion Ponsonby Gause, was a poet.

Candidates, The (1770), a play by ROBERT MUNFORD. Local elections are satirized in this play, which introduced a Negro on the stage for the first time.

Cane, Melville [Henry] (b. Plattsburg, N.Y., April 15, 1879—), lawyer, poet. Cane began contributing verse to magazines in the early 1900's, published *January Gardens* (1926), *Behind Dark Spaces* (1930), and *Poems, New and Selected* (1938). *And Pastures New* (1956) contains, in addition to new poems, old work Cane wanted to preserve. *Bullet-Hunting* appeared in 1960. He helped edit *The Man From Main Street: A Sinclair Lewis Reader* (1952) and wrote a prose work, *Making a Poem* (1953).

Canfield, Dorothy. See DOROTHY CANFIELD FISHER.

Caniff, Milton A[rthur] (b. Hillsboro, Ohio, Feb. 28, 1907—), cartoonist. Beginning in 1921, Caniff did cartoons for various newspapers, soon became one of the most widely syndicated comic-strip artists in the country, with his adventure story *Terry and the Pirates,* *Male Call* (a World War II feature that ran in *Stars and Stripes* and more than two thousand camp newspapers), and *Steve Canyon.* In a contribution to the symposium, *While You Were Gone* (ed. by Jack Goodman, 1946), Caniff discusses the comics with shrewdness and wit.

Cannery Row (1945), a novel by JOHN STEINBECK. In this episodic work Steinbeck returned to the manner of TORTILLA FLAT (1935) and produced a rambling account of the adventures and misadventures of workers in a California cannery and their friends. One character, Doc, was reportedly modeled on the marine biologist, EDWARD F. RICKETTS (1896–1948), with whom Steinbeck collaborated on *The Sea of Cortez* (1941), a study of the fauna of the Gulf of California as observed on a boat trip.

Cannon, Charles James (b. New York City, Nov. 4, 1800—d. Nov. 9, 1860), poet, story writer, playwright, customhouse clerk. Cannon began as a miscellaneous writer with a collection called *Facts, Feelings, and Fancies* (1835), won his greatest success with a tragedy set in Ireland, *The Oath of Office* (produced 1850), went on to several publications, some of Roman Catholic content. In 1851 he collected his *Poems: Dramatic and Miscellaneous.*

Cannon, Jimmy (b. New York City, April 10, 1909—), newspaperman, columnist. In 1946 Cannon became a sports columnist for the New York *Post,* but his syndicated column appears elsewhere as well. He is an outspoken, blunt, and clever writer. His first book was called *The Sgt. Says* (1942). Then came two collections of sport pieces, *Nobody Asked Me* (1950) and *Who Struck John?* (1956).

Cannon, Legrand, Jr. (b. New Haven, Conn., Dec. 1, 1899—), novelist. Cannon began as a businessman, later wrote three novels about New Hampshire, *A Mighty Fortress* (1937), *The Kents* (1938), and his most successful work, *Look to the Mountain* (1942).

Can Such Things Be? (1893), twenty-four stories by AMBROSE BIERCE. These tales in the

Gothic tradition, are short, mercilessly logical, cold, and unemotional. As always with Bierce, the plots are ingenious, often cruel and cynical in their outlook. Almost invariably the stories end in the death of the chief character, but the death is not likely to strike the reader as pathetic or tragic; it is like the final move in a chess game. The humor is macabre, born in the brain and not the heart. The episodes are for the most part laid in California during the Civil War era.

Canterbury Pilgrims, The (1903), a comedy by PERCY MACKAYE. One of the most popular of MacKaye's plays, in 1917 it became the libretto of an opera with music by REGINALD DE KOVEN. In the play Chaucer travels with his characters and is pursued by the Wife of Bath. After tricks and countertricks, King Richard marries her to the waiting Miller.

Cantos I–XVI (1926), the first installment of EZRA POUND's longer Cantos.

Cantwell, Robert E[mmett] (b. Little Falls [now known as Vader], Wash., Jan. 31, 1908—   ), journalist, novelist, biographer. After his first story in the AMERICAN CARAVAN, Robert Cantwell went to New York and succeeded in getting a contract to write a novel, which was published in 1931 under the title *Laugh and Lie Down.* He contributed to various magazines, among them the *New Republic* and the *Nation.* He was an associate editor of *Time* from 1935 to 1945, then literary editor of *Newsweek.* In 1948 he published the biography *Nathaniel Hawthorne; the American Years.* It received good reviews, although the critics deplored the excessive detail which Cantwell used in an attempt to dispel the idea of Hawthorne as a recluse. He wrote on American naturalists for *Sports Illustrated Magazine;* his biography of Alexander Wilson, the ornithologist, was published in 1961. Among his other books: *The Land of Plenty* (1934), *Famous American Men of Letters* (1956), a collection of short biographies for children.

Canty. The young beggar in Mark Twain's THE PRINCE AND THE PAUPER (1881) who is the physical double of Edward, Prince of Wales, and who changes places with him.

Cape Cod (chapters appeared in *Putnam's Magazine,* 1855, and the *Atlantic Monthly,* 1864; the whole was published posthumously, 1865), sketches by HENRY DAVID THOREAU. Thoreau visited the Cape and nearby Nantucket in 1849, 1850, and 1855, and wrote about the region with a mixture of scientific observation and poetic insight. According to some, it was this book which made the Cape widely known and brought it many visitors.

Caponsacchi (1926), a play by ARTHUR GOODRICH based on Robert Browning's *The Ring and the Book* (1872). Its three acts are a faithful reproduction of Browning's masterpiece, but in skillful dramatic form; it was successfully produced with Walter Hampden in the leading role.

Capote, Truman (b. New Orleans, La., Sept. 30, 1924—   ), novelist, short-story writer. Although born and raised in the South, Capote does not consider himself primarily a Southern writer, nor is he in the sense that Faulkner or Warren, with their emphasis on the land and its traditions, are Southern writers. Capote's concern with Gothic romance, with the gradual

removal of distinctions between dream and reality which, according to Freud, create a sense of the uncanny, is his main tie to the Southern literary tradition. Capote's first novel, OTHER VOICES, OTHER ROOMS (1948), is steeped in a nightmarish and other-worldly atmosphere that becomes more pronounced as its hero, Joel Knox, journeys from his childhood home to Noon City and to his father's dilapidated mansion at Skully's Landing, and finally to the mysterious Cloud Hotel, the place of his final revelation. THE GRASS HARP (1951; dramatized 1952), lighter and less Gothic in tone than *Other Voices, Other Rooms,* is also a novel of initiation, but depends for its effect on humor and to a degree on the uncanny. *Breakfast at Tiffany's* (1958), different in tone and setting from both the preceding novels, centers on Holly Golightly, whose strange combination of honesty, vivacity, and zaniness leads her to "camp out" in New York, befriending stray cats and crooks in her search for identity, which, Capote implies, must precede the ability to love, as loving, in turn, precedes freedom. Capote's other works include *Local Color* (1950), a book of photographs and essays; *A Tree of Night* (1956), a collection of short stories; *The Muses Are Heard* (1956), an account of the State Department tour of *Porgy and Bess* through Russia; *Observations* (with Richard Avedon, 1959), a volume of photographs and prose sketches of a number of celebrities. Capote also wrote the book for the Broadway musical comedy *House of Flowers* (1954) and the scripts for several movies.

Capp, Al[fred Gerald] (b. New Haven, Conn., Sept. 28, 1909—   ), cartoonist, essayist. Originally Capp intended to become a serious artist, but his great creation is *Li'l Abner*, a comic strip which began its enormously successful career on August 12, 1934. It was made into a movie by Capp in 1940, and became a musical comedy in 1956. In an article written for the *Encyclopaedia Britannica Supplement* (1946), Capp points out that "the comic strip during the decade 1937–46 became, in terms of the constancy of its followers, the most popular United States entertainment, surpassing radio and the motion picture."

Cappy Ricks (1916), a novel by PETER B. KYNE. The amusing and shrewd Cappy Ricks is a shorebound old millionaire who manages a fleet of sailing and steam vessels to excellent advantage and takes good care of his good-looking motherless daughter, Florrie. He appears also in other books by Kyne.

Capra, Frank (b. Italy, May 18, 1897—   ), motion-picture director and producer. Capra came to the United States at the age of six and studied at the California Institute of Technology. He entered the motion-picture business in 1921 and distinguished himself by directing or producing many notable pictures, including *Platinum Blonde* (1931); *It Happened One Night* (1934); *Mr. Deeds Goes to Town* (1936); *Lost Horizon* (1937); You CAN'T TAKE IT WITH YOU (1938); STATE OF THE UNION (1948). He has received three Academy Awards for direction, two for his productions. Lewis Jacobs notes that "Capra's best pictures are marked by a sense of humor, an awareness of American life, and a shrewd use of topical events, all these being traits developed from his early association with screen-comedy specialists."

Captain Blood (1922), a novel by Rafael Sabatini (1875–1950). An exciting story of the Spanish Main, it tells of an English gentleman who turns pirate because he is outraged by the way people are treated; there is more than a touch of Jonathan Swift in his misanthropy. The novel was very successful and was followed by two sequels, *Captain Blood Returns* (1931) and *The Fortunes of Captain Blood* (1936).

Captain Bonneville, The Adventures of (1837), a narrative prepared by WASHINGTON IRVING from the documents of Captain Benjamin Louis Eulalie de Bonneville (1796–1878). Bonneville graduated from West Point, explored northwestern sections of the United States in 1832–35, served in the Mexican and Civil Wars. While engaged upon ASTORIA (1836), Irving met this soldier-explorer at the home of John Jacob Astor. Irving bought his maps and papers and rewrote his story, which forms a sequel to *Astoria*. As before, Irving shows himself friendly to the red men, and condemns the perfidy and cruelty of the white trappers. This work was reissued in 1961.

Captain Craig (1902), a narrative poem by EDWIN ARLINGTON ROBINSON. One of Robinson's longest and most characteristic poems, it describes a picturesque and talkative old vagabond. Captain Craig preaches the doctrine that "God's humor is the music of the spheres" and that one must "laugh with God." Yet, as Louis Untermeyer points out, "for all its technical sprightliness and dialectic repartee, there is something a bit owlish in its unblinking seriousness, even in its irony. Captain Craig himself seems less a character-study than a peg on which to hang a great quantity of brilliant, sometimes beautiful, but finally tiresome talk." See BOOK OF ANNANDALE.

Captain from Castile (1945), a novel by SAMUEL SHELLABARGER. A romantic novel about the conquest of Mexico by Cortez, with plenty of love-making, fighting, and perils of various kinds. It became a best seller and was made into a movie (1948).

Captain from Connecticut, The (1941), a novel by C. S. FORESTER. The only story with an American setting by the creator of the famous Captain Hornblower, this novel chronicles the adventures of Captain Josiah Peabody of the frigate *Delaware* during the War of 1812. Off Haiti he breaks up a British convoy, later pillages his way through the rich British islands of the Antilles, and finally is cornered in French Martinique. There his adventures end when he marries the daughter of the French governor.

Captain Jinks of the Horse Marines (1901, revived 1925), a comedy by CLYDE FITCH. An American-born opera singer who has assumed an Italian name ("Mme. Trentini") and made a fortune abroad comes back to New York. She is met at the dock by three men who have made an arrangement among themselves that each of them will try to win her and that whoever succeeds will share her fortune with the remaining two. Jinks is successful, but the others betray him and the opera singer indignantly throws him over. He makes his peace with her, however, and all is well. Ethel Barrymore made her stage debut in this play.

Captain of the Gray-Horse Troop, The (1902), a novel by HAMLIN GARLAND. Garland writes about the Sioux Indians, exploited by unscrupulous cattlemen and frontiersmen; beneath the romantic plot is a serious social message.

Captain Sam Grant (1950), a biography by LLOYD LEWIS. In 1945 Lewis, a Chicago newspaperman, decided to do a life of ULYSSES S. GRANT based as far as possible on original data. With great enthusiasm, as he chronicles in letters to D. Angus Cameron, he set out on his task; the letters he wrote, lively reading in themselves, were later collected as *Letters from Lloyd Lewis* (1950). The first volume was the only one to appear; Lewis died of a heart attack before it was published. Lewis makes Grant a likable human being again. He dispels the familiar legend about his heavy drinking, shows that Grant, later called "the Butcher," detested bloodshed and refused even to hunt animals.

Captain Stormfield's Visit to Heaven (1909), MARK TWAIN'S satire on conventional notions of heaven and religion. Inspired by a popular sentimental novel, THE GATES AJAR, it was written in 1868, but held back from publication because Twain thought it would shock the public. When it was published in 1909, "it created," says DeLancey Ferguson, "a mild ripple of amusement and that was all." See also REPORT FROM PARADISE.

Captivity and Restauration of Mrs. Mary Rowlandson, Narrative of the (1682). This was the first and, in the opinion of Albert Keiser, "probably the best of the many so-called 'Indian captivities.'" (See INDIAN CAPTIVITY NARRATIVES.) Its full title was *The Soveraignty and Goodness of God: Together with the Faithfulness of His Promises Displayed; Being a Narrative of the Captivity and Restauration of Mrs. Mary Rowlandson*. It became immensely popular, was probably the first American best seller written by a woman, and appeared in at least thirty reprints, including C. H. Lincoln's edition of *Narratives of the Indian Wars, 1675–1699* (1913). Mary White Rowlandson (c. 1635–c. 1678), the wife of a minister at Lancaster, Mass., was taken captive with her young daughter Sarah on Feb. 10, 1675, during King Philip's War. She was held for seven weeks and five days, and was transported to twenty different Indian camps; her child died in her arms during the ordeal. Mrs. Rowlandson was released after a ransom had been paid, and she retained enough self-possession to write her narrative of the Indian attack and her subsequent tribulations with realism, dignity, and cheerfulness. She made accurate observations on the habits of her captors and commented shrewdly on their characters, though the only positive merit she could ascribe to her abductors was that "not one of them ever offered the least abuse of chastity to me, in word or action."

Carberry, Letitia. See TISH.

Cardiff Giant. In 1869 there was "discovered" at Cardiff, N.Y., a ten-and-a-half-foot high statue of a man carved in gypsum. The discovery aroused immense interest, and great crowds paid admission fees to see the "petrified" man, allegedly an American aborigine. The statue had undoubtedly been buried so that it might be disinterred; the stone actually came from Iowa. Concerned in the hoax were David Hannum and E. N. Westcott's father; Hannum later served as the model for Westcott's DAVID HARUM. The giant now resides in the Farmers' Museum, Cooperstown, N.Y.

Cardigan (1901), a novel by ROBERT W. CHAMBERS. It is a story of the American Revolution that begins in May, 1774, and ends with the Battles of Lexington and Concord the following year. The hero, young Michael Cardigan, is a nephew of Sir William Johnson. The latter trusts Cardigan more than he does his own sons; but Cardigan turns to the patriots, experiences numerous dangers among the Indians and others, and meets important Revolutionary characters.

Cardinal, The (1950), a novel by HENRY MORTON ROBINSON. The story tells of Stephen Fermoyle, born in a Boston suburb of poor but devout parents, who becomes a priest, ends up as a cardinal, and may be destined to be the first American pope. Robinson tells the story in full detail, with sentiment but little sentimentality, and draws an honest picture of a priest in the world today, beset with its special difficulties, problems, and temptations.

Cardinal's Snuff-Box, The (1900), a novel by HENRY HARLAND. An English novelist falls in love with an Italian duchess; his romance is assisted by his uncle, a cardinal. The scene is an Italian villa. The style is polished—far beyond the intrinsic merits of the novel.

Cardozo, Benjamin Nathan (b. New York City, May 24, 1870—d. July 9, 1938), lawyer, associate justice of the Supreme Court, writer on legal topics. Cardozo wrote five important books on law: *The Nature of the Judicial Process* (1921); *The Growth of the Law* (1924); *The Paradoxes of Legal Science* (1928); *Law and Literature* (1931); and *Law Is Justice* (1938). These books and some of his addresses and essays were reprinted in his *Selected Writings* (1947), edited by Margaret E. Hall. Cardozo's legal opinions were regarded as classics both of the law and of style. A liberal in his thinking, he argued that social justice and social change took precedence over the niceties of legal precedent. He was a shy, kindly person, always patient and courteous. When he resigned from the New York bench to go to Washington, Franklin D. Roosevelt, then governor of the state, began his letter of farewell, "Beloved Chief Justice."

Carey, Henry Charles (b. Philadelphia, Dec. 15, 1793—d. Oct. 13, 1879), publisher, writer on political economy. The son of MATHEW CAREY, he wrote an *Essay on the Rate of Wages* (1835), *Principles of Political Economy* (3 v., 1837–40), *Principles of Social Science* (3 v., 1858–59), *The Unity of Law* (1872). At first a free trader, Carey became in time an ardent high-tariff advocate, an intense nationalist, and an Anglophobe. V. L. Parrington calls Carey "our first professional economist," and says his eighty-six years were filled with "enormous labors in the twin fields of economics and sociology."

Carey, Mathew (b. Ireland, Jan. 28, 1760—d. Sept. 16, 1839), publisher, editor, essayist, poet, economist. Forced to flee from Ireland because of his violent attacks on English rule, Carey came to America in 1784 and began a long journalistic and publishing career. He edited many magazines, in particular *The American Museum* (1787–92), which he founded; V. L. Parrington called it "one of the ablest 18th-century American magazines." Anticipating his son Henry (see above), Mathew wrote mainly on economic problems, for example, *Essays on Banking* (1816) and *An Appeal to the Wealthy of the Land* (1836). He attacked William Cobbett in *The Porcupiniad* (1796). See BEAUTIES OF POETRY; COLUMBIAN MAGAZINE.

Cargill, Oscar (b. Livermore Falls, Me., March 19, 1898—   ), teacher, editor, literary critic, historian. Cargill began teaching at New York University in 1925, became professor of English there in 1945, and chairman of the department of English in 1956. He became a member of the board of directors of New York University Press, Inc. in 1957. Among his books: *Drama and Liturgy* (1930); *Intellectual America* (1942); *New Highways in College Composition* (with collaborators, 1942); *Thomas Wolfe at Washington Square* (with T. C. Pollock, 1954); *The Novels of Henry James* (1961). He has edited, among other books: Walt Whitman's *The Wound Dresser* (1949); Walt Whitman's *Leaves of Grass* (1950); Henry James' *Daisy Miller* and *Washington Square* (1956).

Caribbean Sea, the ("the Spanish Main"). Part of the Atlantic Ocean, bounded by South and Central America and by the Greater and Lesser Antilles. It was named for the CARIB INDIANS, the word *carib* signifying "strong" or "wild." Its surface is broken by many islands, from Cuba (42,000 sq. miles) to minute cays or keys. It has been a focal point of American history since Columbus and other explorers first sailed into its waters. Pirates infested it for centuries; slave traders from Africa set up their marts in the ports. Here the great Negro liberator Toussaint l'Ouverture (1743–1803) was born. Today its islands are the playground of the Western world and have offered settings for novels and plays, perhaps the greatest of which is Eugene O'Neill's play, THE EMPEROR JONES (1921). Valuable insights are furnished in a collection of papers delivered at the 1951 and later conferences on the Caribbean under the auspices of the University of Florida, *The Caribbean: Peoples, Problems, and Prospects* (1952), edited by A. Curtis Wilgus. Paul Blanshard wrote *Democracy and Empire in the Caribbean* (1947).

Carib Indians. A tribe formerly living in and around Central America. Their origins are unknown: they may have been a nomadic offshoot from the Appalachian tribes of Florida; possibly they came from the Amazon region. The Caribs, almost uniquely, had one language for their men, another for their women. It is believed that the former was a survival of their original Appalachian tongue, the latter the Arawak tongue spoken by the natives of the islands which were conquered by the Caribs, who kept the native women for wives. The Arawakan language, described by the Spaniards as "soft and not less liquid than Latin," contributed to English the word *hurricane,* also perhaps *hammock;* the former was originally the name of a god. The Carib tongue gave us *cannibal, canoe, guava,* and *tobacco.* Father JEAN BAPTISTE LABAT gives a vivid account of the Caribs in his *Nouveau voyage aux isles de l'Amérique* (8 v., 1724–42).

Carleton, Henry Guy (b. Fort Union, N.M., June 21, 1856—d. Dec. 10, 1910), engineer, playwright, editor, humorist. Carleton wrote and produced numerous plays, including *Memnon* (1881), *The Gilded Fool* (1892), *The Butterflies* (1893), and *Ambition* (1894). None were good, though *The Butterflies,* written for John Drew and MAUDE ADAMS, established Miss Adams' reputation. Carleton also contributed

humorous material to LIFE, of which he became managing editor in 1893. His best-known sketches dealt with a card-playing group of colored folks, collected as *The Thompson Street Poker Club* (1884) and *Lectures Before the Thompson Street Poker Club* (1889), in which the free-spoken protagonists bore such names as the Rev. Thankful Smith and Cyanide Whiffles.

Carleton, Will[iam McKendree] (b. near Hudson, Mich., Oct. 21, 1845—d. Dec. 18, 1912), poet, newspaperman, short-story writer, lecturer. Carleton, born on a farm, knew rural America well, wrote about the joys and problems of

farmers in his smoothly written, sentimental ballads, and won wide popularity in farming districts as well as among city dwellers afflicted with nostalgia. FARM BALLADS (1873) includes his famous poem, OVER THE HILL TO THE POOR HOUSE. Other collections of Carleton's verse are: *City Ballads* (1885); *City Legends* (1889); *City Festivals* (1892). He became a popular lecturer and recited his own verses widely.

Carlson, Natalie S[avage] (b. Winchester, Va., Oct. 3, 1906—   ), writer. After one semester at the University of California, Miss Carlson turned to reporting, and from this to writing juveniles. These have enchanted both the young and the lately-young. *The Talking Cat* won the New York Herald Tribune Book Festival Award in 1952, *Alphonse, That Bearded One,* the same award in 1954. Other books by Natalie Carlson are: *Wings Against the Wind* (1955); *Sashes Red and Blue* (1956); *Hortense, the Cow for a Queen* (1957); *The Happy Orpheline* (1957); *The Family Under the Bridge* (1959);

Evangeline, Pigeon of Paris (1960); *The Song of the Lop-Eared Mule* (1961).

Carman, [William] Bliss (b. Fredericton, N.B., April 15, 1861—d. June 8, 1929), poet, essayist, lecturer. He taught, dabbled in real estate, acted as chairman on a railroad survey, finally went to Harvard for further education. There he met the picturesque RICHARD HOVEY, and the two cheerfully made up their minds that they would be poets, come what may. Carman's most notable work came from this friendship. He and Hovey collaborated on SONGS FROM VAGABONDIA (1894), *More Songs from Vagabondia* (1896), and *Last Songs from Vagabondia* (1901). These are singable (many have been set to music), readable, and present a mood true to the title. Critics suspicious of the facile melody of the two poets regarded the three volumes as expressing artificial moods—a form of hobohemia.

Carman finally settled down as a member of the editorial staff of THE INDEPENDENT and other magazines, but continued to write poetry profusely and published many volumes: *Low Tide on Grand Pré* (1893); *Behind the Arras* (1895); *Pipes of Pan* (5 v., 1902–05); *The Rough Rider and Other Poems* (1909); *April Airs* (1916). He lived in the United States but continued to make frequent visits to Canada, where he was regarded as the country's greatest poet. In 1928 he was made Poet Laureate. Odell Shepard wrote his biography (1924).

Carmer, Carl [Lamson] (b. Cortland, N.Y., Oct. 18, 1893—   ), teacher, writer, editor, broadcaster. Carmer spent several years teaching composition and literature at Syracuse, Rochester, Hamilton (his Alma Mater), and Alabama. In 1927 he went as a columnist to the New Orleans *Morning Tribune*, later became assistant editor of *Vanity Fair* and of *Theatre Arts Monthly*. In 1928 he printed privately a collection of verse, *Frenchtown;* another verse gathering, *Deep South,* appeared in 1930. While in Alabama Carmer had gone up and down the state studying its folklore and legends, observing the ways of the people, listening to their casual talk. His collection of material took shape in a remarkable book, STARS FELL ON ALABAMA (1934), a best seller. It gives a picture of a people—objective, humorous, poetic—and it tells many stories with skill. Carmer wrote a similar book about his native state, *Listen for a Lonesome Drum* (1936), then a book of folk tales for younger readers, *The Hurricane's Children* (1937), and a book on *The Hudson* (1939) in "The Rivers of America" series; later he became editor of the series. He also undertook a radio program, "Your Neck o' the Woods," in which the treasures of folk tale and folk song were explored on the air. With Carl Van Doren he prepared *The American Scriptures* (1946). Among his books: *Windfall Fiddle* (1950), which won the Herald Tribune Childrens Book Award; *The Susquehanna* (1955); *The Screaming Ghost* (1955); *Pets at the White House* (1959).

Carnegie, Andrew (b. Scotland, Nov. 25, 1835—d. Aug. 11, 1919), industrialist, philanthropist, writer on economic topics. The descendant of a family of weavers, Carnegie came to the United States in 1848 and by his remarkable ability worked his way up to a commanding position in the steel industry. In 1901 he retired and devoted the rest of his life to planning the disposal of his fortune. He provided the funds for numerous Carnegie Library buildings all over the country, for public education, and for international peace. He endowed the Carnegie Corporation of America with $125,000,000 to continue his donations after his death. He wrote *Triumphant Democracy* (1886), a sincere and impressive panegyric of the United States; THE GOSPEL OF WEALTH AND OTHER TIMELY ESSAYS (1900); an *Autobiography* (1920); *The Empire of Business* (1933). He was, in his books, a disciple of Herbert Spencer. See LIBRARIES IN THE U.S.

Carnegie, Dale (b. Maryville, Mo., Nov. 24, 1888—d. Nov. 1, 1955), lecturer, author, broadcaster, teacher of public speaking. Carnegie taught thousands of people to speak in public with greater confidence; and in his books he gave millions of insecure readers suggestions for attaining greater poise and even aggressiveness. HOW TO WIN FRIENDS AND INFLUENCE PEOPLE (1936), translated into thirty-one languages, has sold more than five million copies. His other books include *Public Speaking and Influencing Men in Business* (1926), *Lincoln the Unknown* (1932), *How to Stop Worrying and Start Living* (1948).

Carolina Folk Plays. On March 14, 1919, under the inspiration of Frederick H. Koch, at that time a member of the faculty of the University of North Carolina, a group called "the Carolina Playmakers" began to produce short plays in a theater improvised in Gerrard Hall. "The little homespun plays found an eager and lusty welcome," records Koch. According to Koch, the phrase "folk play" was used for the first time in the Carolina project, although he had earlier experimented with such drama in the University of North Dakota. The playwrights and the performers were interested not merely in drama, but in the life around them. The plays were taken on tour and revived interest in the theater in a region that had seemed barren soil indeed. Beginning in March, 1928, Koch edited and published *The Carolina Play-Book*, an illustrated quarterly of native plays and articles. In 1922 he issued the first of a series of *Carolina Folk-Plays;* others followed in 1924 and 1928 and were collected in a single volume (1941). Here may be found plays by authors who later went on to national fame, especially PAUL GREEN and THOMAS WOLFE; others who made important contributions include Elizabeth A. Lay, Erma Green, and Wilbur Stout.

Carolina Israelite, The. See HARRY GOLDEN.

Carpenter, Edward Childs (b. Philadelphia, Dec. 13, 1872—d. Oct. 7, 1950), newspaperman, playwright, novelist. Carpenter became financial editor of the Philadelphia *Inquirer* (1905–16), but while serving in that position wrote several successful novels—among them, *Captain Courtesy* (1906), *The Code of Victor Jallot* (1907), and *The Easy Mark* (1912). He had even more success with his plays: *The Challenge* (1911), *The Cinderella Man* (1916), *The Pipes of Pan* (1917), *The Bachelor Father* (1928), *Order, Please* (1934), and others. Arthur Hobson Quinn calls Carpenter "the most consistent exponent of a sincere attempt to treat the romance that can be drawn out of familiar life," and regards *The Pipes of Pan* as his best play.

Carpet-Bag, The. A humorous weekly published in Boston (March 29, 1851—March 26, 1853), under the editorship of BENJAMIN PENHALLOW SHILLABER, whose sketches of MRS. PARTINGTON appeared in the magazine. Other well-known contributors were Charles F. Browne (Artemus Ward), G. H. Derby (John Phoenix), John T. Trowbridge, Sylvanus Cobb, and Elizabeth Akers. Most prominent was Samuel L. Clemens, whose first published piece, *The Yankee Frightening the Squatter*, appeared in *The Carpet-Bag* anonymously, May 1, 1852. Clemens obviously read with care and enjoyment the "Mrs. Partington" sketches, and Aunt Polly in *Tom Sawyer* (1876) is strikingly similar to Mrs. Partington. Shillaber's picture of her mischievous boy Ike gave Clemens hints for Tom Sawyer.

Carr, Emily (b. Victoria, Br. Col., Dec. 13, 1871—d. March 2, 1945), artist, essayist. Miss Carr studied art in San Francisco, England, and France, then returned to Vancouver Island where she devoted her life to studying and painting the native Indians and their environment. Her style of painting is original and she paints almost as well with words as with colors. Her literary works (illustrated) comprise: *Klee Wyck* (1941); *The Book of Small* (1942); *The House of All Sorts* (1944); *Growing Pains: The Autobiography of Emily Carr* (1946); *The Heart of a Peacock* (1953); *Pause—A Sketch Book* (1953). C. Pearson wrote her biography, *Emily Carr as I Knew Her* (1954).

Carr, Gene (b. New York City, Jan. 7, 1881—d. Dec. 9, 1959), cartoonist, comic-strip artist. For New York newspapers he created popular cartoon and comic-strip characters—Lady Bountiful, Little Nell, Flirting Flora, Father (*Nobody Works Like Father*), and others; also two striking series, *Just Humans* and *Metropolitan Movies*. Thomas Craven notes that "Gene Carr's children, and he has been drawing them since the publication of 'Kid Cartoons' in 1922, are neither tough nor worldly wise, but oldstyle youngsters of pathetic tenderness and whimsical humor."

Carr, John Dickson ["Carr Dickson," "Carter Dickson"] (b. Uniontown, Pa., 1906—   ), mystery writer. A popular writer of mystery stories in the literate English tradition, often with overtones of the macabre, Carr's books reflect his enthusiasm for Sir Arthur Conan Doyle's Sherlock Holmes and his long residence in England (1931–1948). While in England he worked for the B.B.C. and collaborated with Adrian Conan Doyle on *The Life of Sir Arthur Conan Doyle* (1949). His books, which stress the intellectual or puzzle element in the solution of crimes and frequently have a historical setting, include *The Bride of Newgate* (1950); *Behind the Crimson Blind* (1952); *Poison in Jest* (1952); *Eight of Swords* (1953); *Cut-Throat* (1955); and *The Dead Man's Knock* (1958).

carriers' addresses. In the early 18th century, shortly before New Year's Day, it was the custom for local newspapers to print an extra sheet headed *Carrier's Address*, sometimes *New Year Verses*. Sometimes authors of note provided the verses. Three written by AQUILA ROSE (1695?–1723) are among the earliest known examples; they appeared in the *American Weekly Mercury* of Philadelphia for 1720, 1721, 1722. Presumably a greeting from the newsboy, these verses are not only the oldest of their kind in America, but none of an earlier date have been discovered in England where such addresses were likewise common. The earliest actual American broadside discovered by Clarence Brigham in his investigations for *Journals and Journeymen* (1950) was done for the *American Weekly Mercury* in 1735. BENJAMIN FRANKLIN issued such yearly verses for the *Pennsylvania Gazette*. Other eminent writers of carriers' addresses were JOEL BARLOW, PHILIP FRENEAU, JOHN GREENLEAF WHITTIER, and even NATHANIEL HAWTHORNE. It was not until 1870 that the larger newspapers began to regard the custom as undignified and started issuing almanacs instead. When this happened some printing firms issued addresses unmarked with the name of any particular newspaper and brought by the carriers to help them in their quest for gratuities. The last genuine carriers' address Brigham was able to find was dated 1904. The contents of the verses varied from a summary of the year's news to a political appeal and often emphasized the carriers' hardships. According to Brigham, the largest collections of carriers' addresses are in the Brown University Library and in that of the American Antiquarian Society at Worcester, Mass.

Carroll, Gladys Hasty (b. Rochester, N.H., June 26, 1904—   ), novelist, short-story writer, author of books for children. Mrs. Carroll's books have presented the people of New England, especially Maine, as members of a still living and growing community. Carrying on the work of earlier novelists like SARAH ORNE JEWETT and MARY E. WILKINS FREEMAN, she wrote *As the Earth Turns* (1933); *A Few Foolish Ones* (1935); *Neighbor to the Sky* (1937); and a short-story collection, *Head of the Line* (1942). *Dunnybrook* (1944) is a fictional narrative based on fact, the study of a Maine community and of one of its families through several generations. Among her later novels: *While the Angels Sing* (1947); *West of the Hill* (1949); *Christmas Without Johnny* (1950); *One White Star* (1954); *Sing Out the Glory* (1957). *As the Earth Turns* was translated into fifteen languages. A play based on it has become an annual event in Berwick, Maine, where Mrs. Carroll lives. Each year it is produced at the foot of Hasty field, property of her grandparents. The proceeds go into a community fund.

Carruth, [Fred] Hayden (b. near Lake City, Minn., Oct. 31, 1862—d. Jan. 3, 1932), author, editor. Carruth was perhaps best known in his later years as writer of "The Postscript," an extremely popular page in THE WOMAN'S HOME COMPANION. He was on the staff of the *Companion* from 1905 until his death. Carruth became generally known through his newspaper, the *Estelline Bell* [Dak.] (1883–86). His humorous writings in that paper were widely reprinted. He became an editorial writer on the New York *Tribune* (1888–92), and he edited the "Editor's Drawer" of *Harper's Magazine* (1900–02). From about 1892 to 1905 he contributed regularly to many magazines, mostly short humorous stories; some verse, sketches, and adventure serials for older children. His books include *The Adventures of Jones* (1895); *The Voyage of the Rattletrap* (1897); *Mr. Milo Bush and Other Worthies, Their Recollections* (1899); and, above all, *Track's End* (1911), ranked among the best American stories for boys.

Carruth, Hayden (b. Waterbury, Conn., Aug. 3, 1921—   ), poet, critic, editor, fiction writer, and grandson of [FRED] HAYDEN CARRUTH. After having published verse for a number of years in such magazines as *The New Yorker, The Nation, Partisan Review, Saturday Review, Encounter, Botteghe Oscure,* and *Poetry* (where he was also editor-in-chief 1949–50), Carruth brought out his first collection, *The Crow and The Heart* in 1959. Using the traditional verse forms to convey a wide range of feelings and content, he is always intelligent, always absorbed in his craft. The opening stanza of *Night in the Garden* illustrates his ability to sound a familiar note without being imitative; it is deceptively prosaic in the manner of Yeats: "Beauty is in the blood./ Blush not, nor bloom too early./ Tighten the vein's bud./ Be ugly nearly."

Carruth's willingness to "Be ugly nearly" gives his verse great emotional force, something he calls his "bedrockism." His second book of verse, *Journey to a Known Place*, appeared in 1961.

Carryl, Charles Edward (b. New York City, Dec. 30, 1841—d. July 3, 1920), stockbroker, writer of books for children. Carryl began his literary career by issuing a *Stock Exchange Primer* (1882), but this was followed by books of a totally different character—the classic *Davy and the Goblin* (1885); *The Admiral's Caravan* (1892); *The River Syndicate and Other Stories* (1899, for older readers); *Charades by an Idle Man* (1911). These children's books, written in a style reminiscent of Lewis Carroll, contain some brilliant nonsense verse.

Carryl, Guy Wetmore (b. New York City, March 4, 1873—d. April 1, 1904), poet, novelist, humorist, writer for children. Guy Wetmore was the son of CHARLES CARRYL; his promising career closed when a bungalow in which he was

living caught fire and he died as the result of exposure following the accident. The father had a gift for rollicking ballads, but his son, in his parodies of Aesop, Mother Goose, and the Grimm fairy stories, far surpassed the elder Carryl and other verse writers in the same field. Carryl called his books *Fables for the Frivolous* (1898); *Mother Goose for Grown-Ups* (1900); *Grimm Tales Made Gay* (1902). Louis Untermeyer calls him "an extraordinary versifier—with the exception of Ogden Nash, perhaps the most brilliant American writer of light verse."

Carson, Kit [Christopher] (b. Madison County, Ky., Dec. 24, 1809—d. May 23, 1868). American trapper and guide. Carson crossed the Mohave desert in 1830 and served as a guide to Frémont's first expedition in 1842. As an Indian fighter and later as a lieutenant-colonel in the Civil War, he became the hero of numerous dime novels. He dictated a brief autobiography to an army surgeon, De Witt Peters, which appeared as *The Life and Adventures of Kit Carson, The Nestor of the Rocky Mts.* (1858). Joaquin Miller's poem, KIT CARSON'S RIDE, describes the scout's wedding day and his frenzied gallop with his bride through a prairie fire. An impressionistic biography is Stanley Vestal, *Kit Carson, The Happy Warrior of the Old West* (1928).

Carter, John F[ranklin] ["Jay Franklin"] (b. Fall River, Mass., April 27, 1897—   ), journalist, diplomat, writer. Carter was one of the organizers of TIME and represented newspapers in Europe. During Franklin D. Roosevelt's administration he ran a syndicated newspaper column, *We the People*, which was pre-eminently a voice for the New Deal. At about this time he wrote entertaining and unusual detective stories under the pseudonym "Diplomat." His amateur sleuth, Denis Tyler, appeared against colorful backgrounds of diplomatic intrigue that afforded Carter the opportunity to satirize the world of politics and diplomacy in which he lived. In later years his sympathies were drawn to the Republican camp. His syndicated column continued to come from his Washington, D.C., headquarters. *Republicans on the Potomac* (1953) was adjudged not up to his standard, but shows the change in his political affiliations. The books here listed are the best of some thirty which he has published during thirty-five years of writing: *Man is War* (1926); *The New Dealers* (1934); *The Rectory Family* (1937); *Remaking America* (1941); *The Catoctin Conversation* (1947); *The Rat Race* (1948); *Champagne Charlie* (1950); *Power and Persuasion* (1960).

Carter, Nick. There never was a real detective by this name, but millions of readers, from about 1870 on, fervently believed that there was —and credited him with achievements surpassing those of ALLAN PINKERTON (1819–1884), who may have provided Nick's creator with hints as to methods and cases. Apparently Nick was invented by JOHN R. CORYELL (1848–1924), who wrote popular fiction profusely under an amazing number of pseudonyms. He seems to have worked in a writing team with THOMAS CHALMERS HARBAUGH (1849–1924) and Frederick Van Rensselaer Dey (1861?–1922), who wrote numerous Nick Carter stories. Apparently Nick made his first appearance in *The Old Detective's Pupil* (1886). Among others who made use of Nick Carter in their stories were Frederick William Davis, GEORGE CHARLES JENKS, and Eugene Taylor Sawyer. Altogether more than a thousand "Nick Carter" stories were written. The character also was used in the movies and for radio mystery plays.

Cartier, Jacques (1494?–1557?), French explorer. He made three voyages to Canada, exploring the Gulf of St. Lawrence (1534), and again went up the same river to where Montreal now stands (1535), making an attempt to colonize it (1541–42). French claims to the region were based on his voyages.

Cartoon Cavalcade (1943), edited by THOMAS CRAVEN assisted by Florence and Sydney Weiss. The volume gives a history of American civilization and its characteristic humor for approximately five decades.

Cartwright, Peter (b. Amherst Co., Va., Sept. 1, 1785—d. Sept. 25, 1872), clergyman, memoirist. An itinerant Methodist preacher in Kentucky and Illinois, Cartwright is remembered as the unsuccessful opposition candidate to Lincoln when he ran for Congress. Cartwright wrote about his experiences in his *Autobiography of Peter Cartwright, The Backwoods Preacher* (1856), and *Fifty Years as a Presiding Elder* (1871).

Carus, Paul (b. Germany, July 18, 1852—d. Feb. 11, 1919), philosopher, editor. In 1884 Carus was compelled to leave Germany because of his liberal views. He settled in Chicago, and in 1887 became editor of *The Open Court*, later also of *The Monist* (from 1890), and established the Open Court Publishing Company for philosophical and scientific treatises. He wrote *Monism and Meliorism* (1885), *Monism: Its Scope and Import* (1891), *The Religion of Science* (1893), *God* (1908), and other books. A guide to his own thought is *Philosophy as a Science: A Synopsis of the Writings of Paul Carus* (1909). In 1927 appeared *The Point of View: An Anthology of Religion and Philosophy Selected from the Works of Paul Carus*. According to HERBERT W. SCHNEIDER (*History of American Philosophy*, 1946), "Carus preached his faith in cosmic order as the very heart of all religion, at the same time cultivated a respect for other philosophies; his personal catholicity and his liberal editorial policies were an influential factor in awakening an ignorant American public to the basic problems and traditions, both Western and Eastern, of free and critical speculation on the import of natural knowledge."

Caruthers, William Alexander (b. Virginia c.1800—d. Aug. 29, 1846), novelist. Very little is known about Caruthers. It is conjectured that he attended Washington (later Washington and Lee) College, and we know that he studied to be a physician, since he practiced in Savannah. His first publication was a delight-

ful article on the Natural Bridge in Virginia that appeared in the *Knickerbocker Magazine* in 1820. Later he published three novels: *The Kentuckian in New York, or, The Adventures of Three Southerners* (1834); *The Cavaliers of Virginia* (1835), a story of Bacon's Rebellion; and *The Knights of the Horseshoe, A Traditionary Tale of the Cocked Hat Gentry in the Old Dominion* (1845). V. L. Parrington sees the Virginia novelist as an early liberal who pleaded for better understanding between South and North, who foresaw that "mortification" would attack the country if the issue of slavery was not settled, and who looked with grave foreboding on the emergence of the "poor whites" in South Carolina. Parrington also stresses Caruthers' exuberant humor. Other critics find him dull. C. C. Davis in his *Chronicler of the Cavaliers: A Life of Dr. W. A. Caruthers* (1953) finds him a noteworthy mirror of his age.

Carvel, Richard. See RICHARD CARVEL.

Carver, Jonathan (b. New York City, April 13, 1710—d. Jan. 31, 1780), explorer, diarist. Although Carver married in 1746, he later contracted a bigamous marriage in England. In his chief book he borrowed freely without credit. It is uncertain how far his *Three Years' Travels Through the Interior Parts of North America* (1778) really extended. Possibly he journeyed seven thousand miles, reaching the Great Lakes and the Mississippi Valley. His book became very popular, was greatly admired by such writers as Wordsworth, Coleridge, Chateaubriand, and Schiller. It gives spirited, perhaps imaginary accounts of Middle Western fauna and flora, the forests and settlements of the Great Lakes region, various engagements of the French and Indian War, the manners and customs of the Indians.

Carver Memorial Award, George Washington. This was established in 1943 in memory of the great Negro educator and scientist, George Washington Carver (c.1864–1943). Born of slave parents in Missouri, he received degrees at Iowa State College, taught at Tuskegee Institute in 1896, and became internationally famous for his work in agricultural research, especially in the industrial uses of the peanut. The award is given to "any work of fiction, nonfiction, or poetry which seems to the judges [the editors of Doubleday & Company] to make an effective contribution to the Negro's place in American life." The prize is $2,500 ($1,500 outright and $1,000 as an advance on royalties). The award was given in 1945 for the first time to Fannie Cook's *Mr. Palmer's Honey*.

Cary, Alice (b. near Cincinnati, Ohio, April 26, 1820—d. Feb. 12, 1871) and **Cary, Phoebe** (b. near Cincinnati, Sept. 4, 1824—d. July 31, 1871), poets. Their first volume, *Poems* (about one-third by Phoebe), appeared in 1849, bringing in sufficient royalties to enable them to live modestly in New York City. They wrote pious moralisms in too-careful verse that was diffuse and often melancholic; yet their poetry often showed a love of nature and a desire to help mankind. Alice, reckoned the better of the two, wrote *Lyra and Other Poems* (1852); Phoebe, strangely enough an able parodist when she chose, published *Poems and Parodies* (1854).

Casamassima, Princess. See THE PRINCESS CASAMASSIMA.

Case, Frank (b. Buffalo, N.Y., 1870—d. June 7, 1946), hotel manager, memoirist. Case's fame was joined almost entirely with that of the Algonquin Hotel, West 44th St., New York City, which in time he came to manage and own and where the literati of the city gathered under his kindly guidance. Many theatrical folk regarded the Algonquin as the nearest place to home they could find. In its lobby and rooms could frequently be found the Barrymores, John Drew, H. L. Mencken, Joseph Hergesheimer, George S. Kaufman, Marc Connelly, Robert Benchley, Heywood Broun, Alexander Woollcott, Dorothy Parker, Robert Sherwood, Franklin P. Adams, and many another literary or histrionic figure of note. The Algonquin was particularly known as the meeting place of an informal luncheon group called "The Round Table," a sort of witty, would-be literary dictatorship. Case's daughter, Margaret Case Harriman, describes this group in *The Vicious Circle* (1951). Case himself set down his memories in two entertaining books, *Tales of a Wayward Inn* (1938) and *Do Not Disturb* (1940). He also wrote a cookbook, *Feeding the Lions* (1942).

Casey, Robert J[oseph] (b. Beresford, S.D., Mar. 14, 1890—d. Dec. 4, 1962), editor, writer. Casey worked on the Des Moines *Register and Leader*, the Houston *Post*, and the Chicago *Daily News*. While on home grounds he managed to see almost everything and know almost everybody; during World War II he somehow got to all the war fronts. He has a great ability to observe accurately and quickly, and then to tell the story with efficiency and warmth. Casey held various editorial positions for about ten years, then went back to writing stories. Among his books: *The Land of Haunted Castles* (1921); *The Cannoneers Have Hairy Ears* (1927); *Baghdad and Points East* (1928); *Cambodian Quest* (1931); *I Can't Forget* (1941); *Torpedo Junction* (1942); *Such Interesting People* (1943); *This is Where I Came In* (1945); *Battle Below: The War of the Submarines* (1945); *More Interesting People* (1947); *The Black Hills and Their Incredible Characters* (1949); *The Texas Border and Some Borderliners* (1950); *Chicago Medium Rare* (1952); *Give the Man Room* (a life of Gutzon Borglum, 1952, with Mary Borglum).

Casey at the Bat (published under the pseudonym "Phin" in the San Francisco *Examiner*, June 3, 1888), a humorous poem by Ernest Lawrence Thayer (b. Aug. 14, 1863—d. Aug. 21, 1940). The verses relate how the mighty Casey, hero of the Mudville baseball team, strikes out and loses the game. The poem became famous when DeWolf Hopper, a well-known entertainer, made it part of his between-the-acts repertoire. Other versifiers tried to steal the credit from Thayer, even claiming royalties

from Hopper. The poem has become, says Louis Untermeyer, "the acknowledged classic of baseball, its anthem and theme song." Jeremy Gury wrote the libretto and William Schuman the music for an operetta, *The Mighty Casey* (1953).

Casey Jones, a ballad. Jones was the engineer on Locomotive No. 638, supposedly on the Illinois Central Railroad. He was late, as engineers sometimes are, and the result, as he sped his train beyond the limits of safety, was a collision in which Jones and others were killed. In 1909 two other railroad men (the authorship has been disputed) wrote a ballad about Jones that has become the greatest of all railroad songs. It breaths, says Sigmund Spaeth, "the nonchalant recklessness of the old-time engineer. . . . It runs for the most part in true ballad style, and it is only the unexpected close that puts it in the comedy class"—the lines in which Mrs. Jones suggests that her children already have "another Papa on the Salt Lake Line." Presumably the poem's real-life hero was John Luther Jones, who was born in or near Cayce, Ky.; in July, 1948, his widow, described as "Mrs. Casey Jones," was grand marshal at a Railroad Fair in Chicago. (She died in 1958, aged 92.) The ballad hero is the subject of a play (1938) by Robert Ardrey and a narrative for young readers (1944) by Irwin Shapiro.

Casket, The. See GRAHAM'S MAGAZINE.

Cask of Amontillado, The (published November, 1846 in *Godey's Lady's Book*), a tale of gruesome revenge by EDGAR ALLAN POE. Montresor relentlessly leads a man to his death, luring him on with a tale of a choice amontillado wine stored in an underground vault. As Montresor walls his victim in the vault that is to be his tomb, the last sound heard is the faint jingle of bells on the unfortunate man's carnival costume. "There is not one word to spare" in the tale, says Arthur Hobson Quinn. Joseph Wood Krutch characteristically sees the story as another example of Poe's profound interest in the morbid and neurotic, in this instance a case of "simple sadism." Bernardine Kielty finds the story "reminiscent of Balzac's *La Grande Bretèche*."

Caspary, Vera (b. Chicago, Ill., 1904—   ), novelist, screenwriter. Miss Caspary first came into prominence as a writer of good, tight mystery fiction with the publication of *Laura* (1942). One of her earliest novels was *The White Girl* (1929). Unpublished works include many screen "originals"; also adaptations and screenplays. She received the Screen Writers Guild awards for the adaptation of *Letter to Three Wives*, and for the "original" story entitled *Les Girls*. Her work includes: *Thicker than Water* (1932); *Bedelia* (1945); *The Weeping and the Laughter* (1950); *The Husband* (1957). *Evvie*, published in 1960, shows her increasing interest in psychological interpretation and character development.

Cassandra Southwick (1843), a poem by JOHN GREENLEAF WHITTIER. Lawrence Southwick of Salem received Quakers as guests in his home, and his young son and daughter refused to attend church services. The Southwicks were fined, and were unable or unwilling to pay; the children were condemned by John Endicott (1589?–1665), governor of the colony, to be sold as slaves in Virginia or the Barbadoes. But no sea captain could be found who was willing to convey them to the slave market, and they were freed. Whittier's stirring ballad about this incident is put into the mouth of Cassandra Southwick. The poem is an attack on the harsher manifestations of Puritanism, and it contains a powerful denunciation of slavery. It has also been conjectured that Whittier was thinking of himself when he made Cassandra bemoan her isolation from the community and the sacrifices she was making.

Cassidy, Hopalong. A character who first appeared in *Bar 20* (1907), a western novel by CLARENCE E. MULFORD. This book was followed by many others; seventeen years after its appearance Mulford took his first trip West to see the wild and woolly places he had written about. In 1934 Paramount Pictures began filming Mulford's stories, with Bill Boyd playing Hopalong Cassidy. Mulford had written only twenty-eight Hopalong stories, but the movie producers put out many more, giving Mulford his royalties just the same. On television Boyd became a national hero; imitating him became a nation-wide juvenile craze.

Cassill, R[onald] V[erlin] (b. Cedar Falls, Iowa, May 17, 1919–   ), fiction writer, critic, teacher. Cassill often writes about bohemian characters and as a result has been sometimes labeled a beat writer; actually he is a conservative. His novel *Eagle on the Coin* (1950) was well received; since then about forty short stories have appeared in magazines and anthologies. Some of the best of these were in *Fifteen by Three* (1957), which included stories by HERBERT GOLD and James B. Hall. Cassill won an *Atlantic* "First" award for a short story in 1947. *Clem Anderson* (1961), the story of the rise and fall of a writer, followed a spate of about a dozen paperback potboilers since *Eagle on the Coin*. It was greeted with mixed reviews.

Cassique of Kiawah (1859), a novel of colonial life in Charleston by WILLIAM GILMORE SIMMS.

Cass Timberlane (1945), a novel by SINCLAIR LEWIS. This story of a Middlewestern lawyer and judge who has trouble with his young wife who runs away and comes back, was called a "shiny-paper romance" by the New York *Times* and did not seem to critics up to the standard of Lewis' best books. It was turned into a movie in 1947 and still failed to please. *Time* said that "out of a disastrous awe for the author of several better books, the film has accentuated the banality with loving care."

Castañeda, Carlos Eduardo (b. Mexico, Nov. 11, 1896—April 4, 1958), historian. Castañeda came to the U.S. in 1908 and studied at the University of Texas; he also studied at the Universities of Mexico and Havana and at William and Mary College. He taught Spanish at

the last-named institution, then joined the staff of the University of Texas to teach history in 1927. His specialty became the history of Texas from the Mexican point of view. Among his books: *The Mexican Side of the Texan Revolution* (1928); *The Finding of Texas* (1936); *The Winning of Texas* (1936); *End of the Spanish Régime in Texas* (1942).

Castilian Days (1871), a book of travel observations by JOHN HAY. In its seventeen sketches Hay discusses and describes Spanish history, pastimes, holidays, and customs, laying particular stress on the constant and intimate connection of Spain and the church. The book was in general well received, but then and later was attacked by some because of its attitude toward Catholicism.

Casting Away of Mrs. Lecks and Mrs. Aleshine, The (1886), a comic novel by FRANK R. STOCKTON. Asa Don Dickinson well describes this very entertaining novel as one in which Stockton applies "a Robinson Crusoe story to the unbreakable domestic habits of two middle-aged women." The two women, both widows, decide to leave their little New England village and "see the world." On their voyage across the Pacific they are shipwrecked. The women, together with a Mr. Craig, make their way to a desert island where they find a deserted but comfortable house to live in; each week they conscientiously deposit a sum in a ginger-jar for board. Soon they are joined by a missionary, his daughter, and others; Craig marries the daughter. Rescued, they make their way back to the United States, are caught in a blizzard, finally land in Pennsylvania where there is more marrying. The more improbable the tale grows, the more realistic Stockton makes the details. There was a sequel, *The Dusantes* (1888).

Castlemon, Harry. Pen name of C. A. FOSDICK.

Cat and the Canary, The (1922), a mystery play by John Willard (1888–   ). Annabelle West is to be heiress of a large fortune and the eerie house that goes with it—provided that she can prove she is of sound mind. Naturally all the other heirs try to drive her crazy so she cannot be the heiress. The play was almost enough to drive the audience crazy, however, as John Chapman pointed out, what with its sliding panels and clutching claws, its disappearing corpse, its colored woman with her voodoo activities.

Catcher in the Rye, The (1951), a novel by J. D. SALINGER. This short work captured the imagination of a whole generation of young people. The narrator, Holden Caulfield, an adolescent boy who has run away from prep school, speaks a colloquial prose which uniquely conveys contemporary youth's dissatisfaction with adult society. The book is an extended 277-page monologue by Holden that begins:

If you really want to hear about it, the first thing you'll probably want to know is where I was born, and what my lousy childhood was like, and how my parents were occupied and all before they had me, and all that David Copperfield kind of crap, but I don't feel like going into it, if you want to know the truth.

That there is a great deal of craftsmanship in this seemingly artless approach may be demonstrated by the plethora of literary studies that have appeared in the literary quarterlies, in large circulation magazines, and in student papers in the many schools and colleges where the book is required reading. Ten years after publication, the book had sold over 1,500,000 copies in American editions, and had been translated into a dozen foreign languages. The novel is based in part on two short stories, *I'm Crazy*, published in *Collier's* in 1945, and *Slight Rebellion off Madison*, published in the *New Yorker* in 1946. The book has been criticized as an overextended short story and called a mere *tour de force*. On the other hand, it has been favorably compared to *Huckleberry Finn*. The image of Holden standing in his imaginary field of rye where "I have to catch everybody if they start to go over the cliff" has probably been indelibly imprinted on the minds of millions of readers.

Catesby, Mark (b. England, 1679?—d. Dec. 23, 1749), English naturalist, explorer, author. Although Catesby was thoroughly familiar with nature in his native land, his reports deal mainly with American scenes. *The Natural History of Carolina, Florida, and the Bahama Islands* (1731, 1743) was illustrated with the author's own paintings. Another, more technical book was *Hortus Britanno-Americanus, or a Collection of 85 Curious Trees and Shrubs, the Production of North America Adapted to the Climate and Soil of Great Britain* (1737).

Cathedral, The (1869), a poem by JAMES RUSSELL LOWELL. Of the 812 blank verse lines of this poem, Lowell wrote to William Dean Howells, the editor of *The Atlantic* (which published the poem in its January, 1870 issue): "You won't have room in your menagerie for such a displeaseyousaurus." The poem was originally called "A Day at Chartres," and is a description of a day at the French city and in the cathedral. It is written in a mixture of the conversational and the poetio, goes back to the past and considers the present. It deals primarily with the conflicting values of science and religion and the troubles which that conflict has brought to souls in search of God. It is, at the same time, an attempt to reconcile the present of America with the past of Europe, the Yankee with the classicist. The locale recalls a later work, Henry Adams' famous MONT SAINT-MICHEL AND CHARTRES (1905).

Cather, Willa [Sibert] (b. near Winchester, Va., Dec. 7, 1876—d. April 24, 1947), newspaperwoman, teacher, editor, novelist, short-story writer, poet. Miss Cather was a southerner by birth, a Nebraskan by early residence and schooling, a member of the staff of a Pittsburgh paper, then a teacher in the Allegheny, Pa., High School. Later she served on the staff of *McClure's Magazine* in New York, finally becoming a free-lance writer who traveled widely abroad.

She thought for a while of settling in France, but instead became a lover of the Southwest. She spent her last years quietly in New York City, where she shunned publicity and turned rather crotchety, and where she died.

Bettmann Archive

Miss Cather began her career with a well-written but not important volume of verse, *April Twilights* (1903). Her first novel, ALEXANDER'S BRIDGE (1912), was followed by three excellent novels dealing with immigrants to the United States. O PIONEERS! (1913) depicts Alexandra, doomed to spiritual solitude among her own people. The heroine of THE SONG OF THE LARK (1915), Thea Kronborg, was drawn from Olive Fremstad, the opera singer. MY ÁNTONIA (1918) is a portrait of a pioneer woman, it is regarded as her best novel. Her next few novels give Miss Cather's interpretation of various aspects of this country. ONE OF OURS (1922) won a Pulitzer Prize, but William Lyon Phelps, presenting Miss Cather in 1929 at Yale for the honorary degree of Doctor of Letters, said (among other eulogies of her work): "Her worst novel, *One of Ours*, received the Pulitzer Prize because in that year her worst novel was better than everybody else's masterpiece." Better than this, certainly, were *A Lost Lady* (1923), THE PROFESSOR'S HOUSE (1925), and *My Mortal Enemy* (1926). DEATH COMES FOR THE ARCHBISHOP (1927) and SHADOWS ON THE ROCK (1931) show Miss Cather's interest in Catholicism. They turn, as Percy H. Boynton phrases it, "from the Anglo-Saxon, Protestant American scene to the early days of

Spanish-American and French colonial culture and find security in the most substantially enduring tradition in the modern Occident—the authority of the Church of Rome." *Lucy Gayheart* (1935) and SAPPHIRA AND THE SLAVE GIRL (1940) received relatively little attention. In addition Miss Cather published several collections of short stories or novelettes: *The Troll Garden* (1905); YOUTH AND THE BRIGHT MEDUSA (1920); *Obscure Destinies* (1932); and *The Old Beauty and Others* (published posthumously, 1948). Many of these stories are about artists, and several rank with her best work. She also issued a collection of essays, *Not Under Forty* (1936).

Maxwell Geismar, who calls Miss Cather "Lady in the Wilderness," notes that she followed a strange spiritual evolution. There was a long search which pushed its way back from the epoch of the American pioneers and tycoons to the New Mexico of the 1850's and the Quebec of the early 1700's. T. K. Whipple once described her literary development as "the victory of mind over Nebraska." In time she came to hate the modern scene and modern ways. She refused to permit any of her books to be used in classrooms, and after the failure of A LOST LADY as a movie she would not allow any more of her books to be filmed. Geismar sums her up as "an aristocrat in an equalitarian order, an agrarian writer in an industrial order, a defender of the spiritual graces in the midst of an increasingly materialistic culture." Lloyd Morris regards her as one in whose books "skepticism about the American present took the form of an elegy on the American past. . . . In her work America contemplated the victory of industrial civilization and material prosperity, and the defeat of a dream."

Many critics have complained about the restraint of Miss Cather's prose style, calling it the result of a spinsterish fear of coming to terms with life. It may be closer to the truth, however, to say that her early study of the classics gave her an ingrained distaste for romantic bombast; certainly her portrayals of the moral victories of the pioneers, the calm certitude that follows a hard struggle, are well served by her quiet manner. Miss Cather had this to say about her writing: "If the novel is a form of imaginative art, it cannot be at the same time a vivid and brilliant form of journalism. . . . Whatever is felt upon the page without being specifically named there —that, one might say, is created. It is the inexplicable presence of the thing not named, of the overtone divined by the ear but not heard by it, the verbal mood, the emotional aura of fact or the thing or the deed, that gives high quality to the novel or the drama, as well as to poetry itself."

Miss Cather's will directed that her letters were never to be published. Mildred R. Bennett's *The World of Willa Cather* (1951) gives much incidental information, including the characters in real life who suggested some of her fictional characters. David Daiches in *Willa Cather: A Critical Introduction* (1951) feels that Miss

Cather was "moving toward a new kind of art." The late E. K. Brown wrote *Willa Cather: A Critical Biography* (1953; the book was completed by Leon Edel); Edith Lewis pictured *Willa Cather 'Living'* (1953); Elizabeth Sergeant composed *Willa Cather: A Memoir* (1953).

Catherwood, Mary [Hartwell] (b. Luray, Ohio, Dec. 16, 1847—d. Dec. 26, 1902), teacher, novelist. Mrs. Catherwood made a specialty of life in old-time French America and the Old West and won the commendation of FRANCIS PARKMAN for her fidelity to history. The first of her novels to win wide popular success was THE ROMANCE OF DOLLARD (1889); others were *The Story of Tonty* (1890); *The Lady of Fort St. John* (1891); and *Lazarre* (1901), a romance of the lost Dauphin.

Catholic Authors: Contemporary Biographical Sketches, 1930–47 (1948), edited by MATTHEW HOEHN, O.S.B. In this valuable compilation sketches of 620 authors, both American and foreign, appear. The material avoids a mere marshaling of facts, and the articles are often very readable. A second volume was published in 1952, including 374 additional biographies.

Catholic Book Club, Inc. Founded in 1928, this club includes in its selections fiction and non-fiction, in translation as well as by American and English writers.

Catholic Encyclopedia. A reference work in seventeen volumes which appeared in 1907–27 under the editorship of Charles G. Herberman, Edward A. Pace, and others.

Catholic Poetry Society of America. Founded in 1931 by the editors of several Catholic magazines, this society publishes a magazine, *Spirit*, in which some notable poetry has appeared.

Catlin, George (b. Wilkes-Barre, Pa., July 26, 1796—d. Dec. 23, 1872), explorer, artist, writer. Although Catlin's mother had as a child been captured by Indians in the Wyoming Massacre, Catlin felt no strong resentment toward the red men; he ultimately resolved to devote his life to making a pictorial and verbal record of Indian customs. He went to live among Indians in Florida and the West, studied their languages, painted them, exhibited his pictures, and wrote books about his observations and experiences. Late in life he also undertook explorations of South America. Sometimes his statements were doubted, but today he is recognized as a sincere and intelligent observer. Many of his paintings are now in the Smithsonian Institution. Among his books are: *Letters and Notes on the Manners, Customs, and Conditions of the North American Indians* (1841); *North American Indian Portfolio* (1844); *Life Among the Indians* (1867); *Okeepa, A Religious Ceremony, and Other Customs of the Mandans* (1867); *Last Rambles Amongst the Indians of the Rocky Mountains and the Andes* (1868). Loyd Haberly wrote a eulogistic life of Catlin, *Pursuit of the Horizon* (1948).

Cat on a Hot Tin Roof (1955), a play by TENNESSEE WILLIAMS. Set on a plantation in the Mississippi Delta country, the play centers on the wealthy Pollitt family, and opens just after the other members of the family have discovered that "Big Daddy" Pollitt is suffering from incurable cancer. Gooper, the oldest son, and his wife Mae plot to insure that Big Daddy's money and property goes to them and their brood of children rather than to the younger son Brick, an alcoholic ex-football star. Brick's wife Maggie ("the cat") is childless and is growing bitter and frustrated because Brick blames her for driving his friend, Skipper, to his death by convincing him that the friendship between the two men was latently homosexual. In a scene with Big Daddy, Brick accuses the world in general and the family in particular of "mendacity," although Brick himself is living a lie in his inability to face the implications of his relationship with Skipper, his rejection of Maggie, and his escape into alcohol. Forced into an admission of his failings by Big Daddy, Brick strikes back by telling Big Daddy that he is dying of cancer. Finally, knowing that Big Daddy favors Brick and would like Brick to have a child, Maggie announces, to the consternation of all, that she is pregnant; Brick, although he knows she lies, does not contradict her, and the play ends with a hope of reconciliation between them.

Catton, Bruce (b. Petoskey, Mich., Oct. 9, 1899–   ), newspaperman, government official, historian. Catton worked for various papers in Cleveland, Boston, and Washington, then entered government service in 1942. He was Director of Information for the War Production Board, and later was with departments of Commerce and Interior. *The War Lords of Washington* (1948) grew out of the WPB experience. His Washington column and book reviews appeared in the NATION for a number of years. He became deeply interested in the Civil War, but it was not until 1952 that he began devoting full time to writing Civil War history. *Mr. Lincoln's Army* (1951) deals with the early years of the conflict, and *Glory Road* (1952) relates the campaigns of 1862–63. His editorship of *American Heritage* magazine ran from 1954 to 1959. Following this date he was made Senior Editor. *A Stillness at Appomattox* (1953), third in the trilogy of the Union Army of the Potomac, won the Pulitzer prize for history in 1954. Other books by Bruce Catton are: *Banners at Shenandoah* (1955); *The Hallowed Ground* (1956); *America Goes to War* (1958); *Grant Moves South* (1959).

Cavender's House (1929), a narrative poem by EDWIN ARLINGTON ROBINSON. It tells how Cavender, who had pushed his wife off a cliff because he suspected her of infidelity, is still uncertain twelve years later; and describes the thoughts that torment him as he wanders to the edge of the cliff again.

Cawdor (in *Cawdor and Other Poems*, 1928), a narrative poem by ROBINSON JEFFERS. Based on the story of Phaedra and Hippolytus, *Cawdor* deals with the desire of Fera Cawdor for her stepson, Hood, who rejects her advances. Caw-

dor, suspecting the boy has seduced Fera, kills him. Later Cawdor learns that Hood was innocent, but suffers from his inability to expiate his guilt, knowing there is no future life and no punishment on earth to cleanse him.

Cawein, Madison [Julius] (b. Louisville, Ky., March 23, 1865—d. Dec. 8, 1914), poet, called "the Keats of Kentucky." Cawein wrote too easily, was imitative, and repeated himself; yet some of his poems reveal a genuine richness of imagery and sweetness of melody. He wrote between thirty and forty books, beginning with *Blooms of the Berry* (1887) and closing with *The Cup of Comus* (1915). His poems were collected in five volumes in 1907, and in 1902 a selection made by Edmund Gosse was issued in England as KENTUCKY POEMS.

Celebrated Jumping Frog of Calaveras County, The (1865), a tall tale by MARK TWAIN. In Twain's first famous story, the miner Jim Smiley makes a bet that his frog Dan'l Webster can jump farther than the frog casually selected by a stranger. While Jim's attention is distracted, the stranger loads Dan'l down with quail shot—a fact Jim doesn't discover until the stranger departs. Mark Twain did not invent the story. It was a folk tale current in mining camps during the earlier years of the gold rush era, and versions have been found in print in the Sonora *Herald* of June 11, 1853, and the San Andreas *Independent* of Dec. 11, 1858. Twain's version first appeared in *The Saturday Press* of New York on Nov. 18, 1865, under the title *Jim Smiley and His Jumping Frog*. It was reprinted in Beadle's *Dime Book of Fun* in 1866. Then it appeared, with other sketches, as Twain's first book, *The Celebrated Jumping Frog* (1867). Twain chose to embroider the tale considerably with the elaborate detail that he loved. On its first appearance it was greeted with national acclaim and established Twain's fame. James Russell Lowell praised it as the finest piece of American humor, William Dean Howells called it Twain's most stupendous invention. An annual Frog-Jumping Tournament is now held in Angels Camp, Calif. An opera based on the story was produced by the composer Lukas Foss at Tanglewood (1950).

Celestial Railroad, The (1843), a short story by NATHANIEL HAWTHORNE, later included in MOSSES FROM AN OLD MANSE. It is a modern treatment of *Pilgrim's Progress*, in which the traveler uses up-to-date facilities for his journey but finds himself beset by age-old pitfalls.

censorship of literature. The history of censorship in the United States goes back to colonial times. The Massachusetts Bay Colony had by far the most stringent regulations on what matter could be published. No formal censorship law was passed, but the theocracy practiced censorship at will. In 1650 William Pynchon's *The Meritorious Prince of Our Redemption*, which attacked the orthodox view of the atonement, was condemned as heretical by the Massachusetts General Court and burned in the Boston market place. In 1654 the General Court ordered the colonists to turn books on the beliefs of the

Quakers over to the authorities to be burned, and in 1669 Thomas a Kempis' *Imitation of Christ* was revised to suit the beliefs of the General Court before it could be reprinted.

Forty years before the Revolution, the political climate of New York led to the trial of JOHN PETER ZENGER, the publisher of the New York *Weekly Journal,* for seditious libel. His acquittal was the first great victory in the fight for freedom of the press in the United States. After the Revolution the Sedition Act of 1798 impinged upon the freedoms of citizens and aliens alike, and remained in effect until the presidency of Jefferson. Political censorship did not recur until the first World War, but literary censorship began to be more frequent.

In 1815 the first prosecution of books on the charge of obscenity occurred in Pennsylvania. In 1842 and 1865 Congress prohibited the importation and mailing of obscene matter, but the first comprehensive obscenity law, dealing with the circulation of obscene materials in the mails, was not passed until 1873. Anthony Comstock, who was largely responsible for securing the passage of the law, became the secretary of the New York Society for the Suppression of Vice shortly after its founding in 1873, inspired the founding of the Boston Watch and Ward Society, and was perhaps the most important single figure in the history of American censorship. The New York and Boston societies set the pattern for many private censorship groups that by putting pressure on local postmasters, customs inspectors, book distributors, and booksellers could often effectively ban a book without taking legal action.

In the early decades of the present century, opponents of obscenity and radicalism prosecuted and banned, under the existing laws, Theodore Dreiser's THE GENIUS, Sherwood Anderson's DARK LAUGHTER, Upton Sinclair's OIL!, the works of Trotsky, Bertrand Russell's *What I Believe,* and Lenin's *State and Revolution.* The federal government prohibited the importation of many of the works of Boccaccio, Voltaire, and Rabelais, but because of the lack of co-ordination between Customs and the Post Office Department, many books which could not be imported could be circulated in the mails, and vice versa. However, more strict interpretation and application of the laws by the courts soon began to limit capricious banning of books by private individuals and groups. In 1930, after Dreiser's AN AMERICAN TRAGEDY had been banned in Boston, the Massachusetts state law was changed so that a book could not be banned merely because it contained obscene or indecent language; the book had to be considered as a whole and could be banned only if its total effect were obscene.

The Hicklin rule, which had been adopted by U.S. courts in 1868, gave as the standard definition of obscenity that which tends to "deprave or corrupt those whose minds are open to such immoral influences." In 1913 Judge Learned Hand rejected the Hicklin rule on the grounds that literary expression is too valuable to society to be so circumscribed that it is harmless to children and innocuous to the most corruptible of adults. Judge Hand's opinion was crystallized in 1933 by Judge John M. Woolsey's precedent-setting decision on obscenity in the case of James Joyce's *Ulysses.* Judge Woolsey ruled that a book may be banned as obscene if it tends to excite the sexual impulses or lead to sexually impure thoughts in a normal adult, stating that "it is with the normal person that the law is concerned." He admitted the opinion of recognized literary critics as relevant to the appraisal of the book, and judged that *Ulysses* was, if anything, "emetic" rather than "aphrodisiac." Judge Woolsey's decision on what constitutes obscenity was adopted in most state and federal courts. In 1957 the United States Supreme Court confirmed the rejection of the Hicklin rule and stated the test of obscenity to be "whether to the average person, applying contemporary community standards, the dominant theme of the material taken as a whole appeals to prurient interest."

WALTER KERR has eloquently argued the case against censorship in *Criticism and Censorship* (1956), pointing out that censorship invariably encourages mediocre and inferior art. *The Censorship of Books* (1954), edited by W. M. Daniels, ranges over the entire literature of censorship, from John Locke and the First Amendment down to present times, with more than fifty selections of argument pro and con. Paul Blanshard's *The Right to Read: the Battle Against Censorship* (1955) makes the case against indirect pressure by private groups. *The Freedom Reader* (1955), edited by E. S. Newman, is an anthology of documents and opinions. Other books on the subject include: *The Blessings of Liberty* (1956), by Zachariah Chafee; *Censorship of Books* (1957), by David Fellman; *First Freedom* (1960), edited by R. B. Downs; *Book Selection and Censorship* (1960), edited by M. Fiske; and *Literary Censorship: Principles, Cases, Problems* (1961), edited by K. Widmer.

centonism. The art or practice of composing a *cento, i.e.,* a literary composition, especially a poem, formed by combining separate verses of existing works in a patchwork or pastiche. A certain amount of centonism may be found in the work of modern poets, particularly T. S. ELIOT and EZRA POUND.

Century Association, The ["The Century Club"], New York City. An association composed of "authors, artists, and amateurs of letters and the fine arts," founded in 1846. Among its presidents have been GEORGE BANCROFT, WILLIAM CULLEN BRYANT, ELIHU ROOT.

Century Cyclopedia of Names. See NEW CENTURY CYCLOPEDIA OF NAMES.

Century Dictionary and Cyclopedia (1871), a reference work published by the Century Co. under the editorship of WILLIAM WRIGHT WHITNEY.

Century Illustrated Monthly Magazine, The. *Scribner's Monthly*, subtitled "An Illustrated Magazine for the People," was founded by Roswell Smith, who conceived the original idea, Dr. JOSIAH G. HOLLAND, popular essayist and poet, and Charles Scribner, of the famous book publishing house. Holland became editor, Smith business manager and later president of the company that took it over and renamed it the *Century*. It entered the field as a strong competitor of *Harper's New Monthly* in November, 1870. It was copiously illustrated with fine-line woodcuts by Timothy Cole, George Kruell, Francis G. Attwood, and others; and it was unusually well printed (1874–1914) by Theodore Low DeVinne.

Though *Scribner's* began by using some serials by foreign writers, as *Harper's* was doing, it soon was filling its fiction pages with the work of Holland, Rebecca Harding Davis, H. H. Boyesen, Frances Hodgson Burnett, Bret Harte, George W. Cable, Henry James, Frank R. Stockton and "Saxe Holm" (Helen Hunt). Greatest of the non-fiction serials was Edward King's copiously illustrated *The Great South*. This was followed by a number of short stories and serials depicting Southern life by Cable, Joel Chandler Harris, Thomas Nelson Page, James Lane Allen, and others. Departments of comment and miscellany conducted by RICHARD WATSON GILDER and Richard Henry Stoddard were important in the magazine, as were Charles Dudley Warner's *Back-Log Studies* (1871–1872), nature essays by John Burroughs and John Muir, and art criticism by W. C. Brownell and Clarence Cook.

Management differences caused a split in the Scribner house in 1881, and the magazine's name was changed to *Century Illustrated Monthly Magazine* by the new ownership. Gilder was the new editor. The magazine's policy changed but little, except for increased emphasis on public affairs. In the 1880's the magazine featured a series on the Civil War, including the recollections of Generals Grant, McClellan, Eads, Johnston, Hill, Longstreet, Beauregard, and many others. Even unmilitary Mark Twain told of his war experiences. Other important non fiction serials were George Kennan's *Russia and the Exile System* (an international sensation) and an 1890 feature on the California gold hunters.

Important fiction serials came from W. D. Howells, Mrs. Humphry Ward, Jack London, and Mark Twain (with a slightly bowdlerized version of *Huckleberry Finn*). The *Century* exploited the new craze for historical fiction with S. Weir Mitchell's *Hugh Wynne* and F. Marion Crawford's *Via Crucis*.

The magazine's highest circulation of 200,000 was reached shortly before 1890. Roswell Smith died in 1892; Gilder carried on as editor until 1909, when ROBERT UNDERWOOD JOHNSON, long an associate editor, took over for a few years.

But the *Century* was losing its audience. After 1913 it had a journalistic emphasis; under Glenn Frank's editorship (1921–1925) it was again more literary, with many distinguished contributors; but it expired with three quarterly numbers in 1929–1930.

Century of Dishonor, A (1881), an account by HELEN HUNT JACKSON of governmental mistreatment of the Indians. The book was based on careful investigation, and was followed by the widely read romance, RAMONA (1884), on the same theme. See MISSION INDIANS.

Cerf, Bennett [Alfred] (b. New York City, May 25, 1898——), book publisher, editor. Founder (in 1927), part-owner, and president of Random House, Cerf is one of America's best-known publishers. He is hardly less well-known as a purveyor of puns and other forms of humor to the reading public through the medium of humorous magazine columns and collections. His infatuation with humor began when he edited the Columbia *Jester* before his graduation in 1919. He worked for Boni and Liveright, publishers of the original Modern Library series of inexpensive reprints of the classics. In 1925 he purchased the series and within a few years made it an astonishing success. As president of Random House, Cerf has published the works of many distinguished authors.

Certain Rich Man, A (1909), a novel by WILLIAM ALLEN WHITE. The story of John Barclay, a member of the *nouveau riche* in the period following the Civil War, of his evil ways and his regeneration.

Chafee, Zechariah, Jr. (b. Providence, R.I., Dec. 7, 1885—d. Feb. 8, 1958), lawyer, teacher, publicist, writer. After graduating from Brown University, Chafee had a brief business career, then began studying at the Harvard Law School (1910). He graduated in 1913, practiced for three years, then returned to teaching at Harvard University and became professor there in 1919. He was a member of many commissions, including that on Freedom of the Press and the U.N. Subcommission on Freedom of Information and the Press. He drafted the important Federal Interpleader Act of 1936. Among his writings: *Freedom of Speech* (1920); *The Inquiring Mind* (1928); *America Now* (1938); *Cases on Equitable Remedies* (1939); *Free Speech in the United States* (1941); *Government and Mass Communication* (1947); *Freedom of Speech and the Press* (1955); *The Blessings of Liberty* (1956).

Chainbearer, The (1845), a novel by JAMES FENIMORE COOPER. The second in the trilogy of *The Littlepage Manuscripts*, it expresses Cooper's detestation of frontier "leveling" and of self-government carried to extremes. Mordaunt Littlepage seeks to improve the family "patent" and comes into conflict with squatters. See ANTI-RENT LAWS; REDSKINS; SATANSTOE.

Chalkley, Thomas (b. England, 1675—d. 1741), sea captain, preacher, author. Chalkley, a Quaker, preached in England and at times in the colonies. He is remembered because of a passage in Whittier's SNOW-BOUND (1866), in which Whittier calls him "gentlest of skippers, rare sea-saint," and retells an exciting episode from his *Journal* (1747).

Chambered Nautilus, The (1858), a poem by OLIVER WENDELL HOLMES. This poem first appeared in *The Atlantic Monthly* (February, 1858), afterwards in collections of Holmes' poems. The nautilus, a sea creature that enlarges its shell as it grows, is a possible symbol for the soul which can build itself more and more stately mansions as the swift seasons roll, leaving its "low-vaulted past." Harry Hayden Clark has found numerous sentences in Emerson that prefigure or parallel the thought of Holmes; and Nelson F. Adkins has studied the scientific and poetic backgrounds of the poem. Holmes was especially proud of its verse pattern, and said he had written it in "the highest state of mental exaltation and crystalline clairvoyance" that had ever been granted to him.

Chamberlain, George Agnew (b. Brazil, March 15, 1879—   ), novelist, diplomat. Chamberlain was educated at Princeton University, became a consular official in various parts of Latin America, acquired a reputation as the author of well-told and spirited romances, and in later years resided in New Jersey. Among his books: *Through Stained Glass* (1915); *John Bogardus* (1916); *The Lantern on the Plow* (1924); *In Defense of Mrs. Maxon* (1938); *Knoll Island* (1943); *Scudda-Hoo! Scudda-Hay!* (1946; movie version, 1948); *Lord Buff and the Silver Star* (1955).

Chamberlain, John [Rensselaer] (b. New Haven, Conn., Oct. 28, 1903—   ), critic. Chamberlain became assistant editor of the New York *Times Book Review*, later conductor of a daily book column. In 1936 he became an editor of *Fortune;* he has also contributed literary articles to *Life*. His *Farewell to Reform* (1932) deals with matters economic and political; he also wrote *Challenge to the New Deal* (1934); *The American Stakes* (1940); *MacArthur, 1941–51* (1954).

Chamberlin, William Henry (b. Brooklyn, N.Y., Feb. 17, 1897—   ), newspaperman, lecturer, editor, authority on world affairs. Chamberlin went to Russia in 1922 as correspondent for *The Christian Science Monitor;* he stayed in Russia until 1934 and also became familiar with other European countries. He has lectured and written extensively on Russia and factors leading to World War II. His attitude toward the Soviet Union was at first friendly and sympathetic, later disillusioned. Among his books: *Soviet Russia* (1930); *Russia's Iron Age* (1934); *Collectivism—A False Utopia* (1937); *Japan Over Asia* (1937; rev. ed., 1939); *The Russian Enigma: An Interpretation* (1943); *The European Cockpit* (1947); *Beyond Containment* (1953); *Evolution of a Conservative* (1959).

Chambers, Robert W[illiam] (b. Brooklyn, N.Y., May 26, 1865—d. Dec. 16, 1933), painter, novelist, short-story writer, poet. Chambers, a painter and an illustrator, began writing with *In the Quarter* (1894) and a collection of short stories, *The King in Yellow* (1895; reprinted 1938). His horror stories helped to mold the science-fiction school of writing. Then Chambers turned successfully to writing historical romances, beginning with four about the Franco-Prussian War (of which *The Red Republic*, 1894, was perhaps the best). CARDIGAN (1901), a novel of the American Revolution, finally made him well-known; thereafter his novels, many of them ephemeral, were steady best sellers. *Iole* (1905), later turned into a play, delighted ELBERT HUBBARD; he thought Chambers was caricaturing him in the leading character. But Chambers really had in mind a French poet, Aristide Bruant, who declaimed his verses from the tops of café tables in Paris. His *Tracer of Lost Persons* (1906) has as its sleuth one Mr. Keen, somewhat erroneously described as the "most famous of all detectives." There is a Robert W. Chambers collection at the University of Texas.

Champlain, Samuel de (1567?—1635), French explorer. He first made himself familiar with the lands of the Caribbean Sea, later accompanied fur-trading expeditions to the Gulf of St. Lawrence and ascended the St. Lawrence River to the Lachine Rapids (1603). He also explored portions of Nova Scotia, founded Quebec (1608), went down the New York lake that bears his name (1609), and visited the Great Lakes (1615). The British captured Quebec and took him to England as a prisoner. Subsequently he became governor of the French colony (1633–35). He wrote several books recording his journeys and observations, summing them up in his *Voyages de la Nouvelle France* (1632). Morris Bishop wrote an admiring biography of him (1948). A collected edition of his *Works* was published in Toronto in 1922–27.

Chan, Charlie. The pudgy, wise, and smiling Chinese detective residing in Hawaii who appears in a number of stories by EARL DERR BIGGERS. He has a large and constantly growing family (one of whom in the latter tales begins to learn the sleuthing business from his father), and he is given to philosophical reflections, many of them supposedly culled from Chinese sages. Howard Haycraft says that Charlie "has probably inspired more genuine personal affection than any other sleuth in recent years." Biggers himself once said, "If I understand Charlie Chan correctly, he has an idea that if you understand a man's character you can nearly predict what he is apt to do in any set of circumstances." Chan first appeared in *The House Without a Key* (1925), later in other novels, in the movies (where Warner Oland became identified with him), and in many radio sketches. He undoubtedly influenced John P. Marquand's conception of the Japanese sleuth, MR. MOTO.

Chance Acquaintance, A (1873), a novel by WILLIAM DEAN HOWELLS. A New York girl, Kitty Ellison, while on a trip along the St. Lawrence and into Quebec, falls in love with a proper Bostonian, Miles Arbuton; and they become engaged. But Miles, meeting some fashionable and snobbish acquaintances, ignores Kitty and she breaks the engagement, knowing she can never be happy with a member of the

Brahmin caste. The plot forms a complement to the honeymoon trip in the same region that Howells had described in THEIR WEDDING JOURNEY (1871). The novel has been called "the American *Pride and Prejudice.*"

Chancellorsville, Battle of (May 2–4, 1863), the culmination of a campaign, under the leadership of General Joseph Hooker, in which the Northern army attempted to flank General Lee's position around Fredericksburg and cut his communication with Richmond. Lee didn't wait, and Hooker, because of his vacillation in meeting a surprise attack, was defeated and forced to withdraw over the river. According to family tradition, STEPHEN CRANE heard much about the Battle of Chancellorsville from his uncle Edmund Crane, who had taken part in it, and this information provided the background for the battle described in THE RED BADGE OF COURAGE (1895).

Chandler, Raymond (b. Chicago, July 23, 1888—d. Mar. 26, 1959), mystery writer, scriptwriter. Educated abroad, Chandler at first wrote verse, essays, book reviews, and special articles for British daily and weekly papers. After World War I, in which he served in the Canadian and British forces, he returned to the U.S., entered business, and became an officer in various independent oil corporations. In the early 1930's he began to write for the pulps, and in 1933 *Black Mask* bought a story of his called *Blackmailers Don't Shoot.* Thereafter his success was steady. In 1939 appeared *The Big Sleep,* followed by *Farewell, My Lovely* (1940); *The High Window* (1942); *The Lady in the Lake* (1943); *Red Wind* (1946); *Spanish Blood* (1946); THE LITTLE SISTER (1949); *The Long Goodbye* (1954); *Playback* (1958). He also published a collection of short stories, *Five Sinister Characters* (1945). *The Simple Art of Murder* (1950) collected twelve novelettes and stories, with a highly literate commentary by the author. His novels depict a world in which bigtime racketeers deal dangerously with corrupt policemen and politicians.

Channing, Edward Tyrrell (b. Newport, R.I., Dec. 12, 1790—d. Feb. 8, 1856), editor, teacher. A younger brother of WILLIAM ELLERY CHANNING [1], EDWARD CHANNING practiced law, helped to found and edit THE NORTH AMERICAN REVIEW, finally was appointed Boylston Professor of Rhetoric at Harvard. He had a strong influence on literature but published nothing. Many important writers of the day came under his guidance, including Emerson, Thoreau, Holmes, Lowell, Edward Everett Hale, R. H. Dana, Jr. Dana edited Channing's *Lectures* (1856). These, according to Samuel Lee Wolff, show a strong indebtedness to the *Lectures on Rhetoric and Oratory* (1810) of one of his predecessors in the Boylston chair, JOHN QUINCY ADAMS. Channing made extensive use of personal conferences in his teaching and encouraged his students to develop a workable, unornate style.

Channing, William Ellery [1] (b. Newport, R.I., April 7, 1780—d. Oct. 2, 1842), clergyman, propagandist. At first a teacher, Chan-

ning was ordained as Congregational minister in 1803 and became pastor of the Federal Street Church in Boston, remaining there until his death. Two great causes engaged him all his life —Unitarianism and abolitionism—although by temperament he hated controversy. He early became convinced that Calvinism was not for him, and at the ordination of JARED SPARKS in 1819 preached a sermon that resulted in the establishment of Unitarianism. In 1821 he helped to found and edit a magazine, *The Christian Register,* that advocated Unitarian doctrines, and in 1825 he founded the American Unitarian Association. In the interests of the movement to abolish slavery, he wrote *Slavery* (1835), *The Abolitionist* (1836), *Emancipation* (1840), and *The Duty of the Free States* (1842). His essay *On National Literature* (1830) insisted that American writing and writers deserved more encouragement.

In writing *Introductory Remarks* for a collected edition (1841) of his own works, Channing said the master passions of his life were two: respect for human nature and reverence for human liberty. Herbert Schneider analyzed his creed: "Slavery, bigotry, and worldliness are the three enemies, respectively, of republicanism, rationalism, and pietism; and it was to the struggle against these enemies that Channing's humanitarianism was wholeheartedly devoted." Robert L. Patterson has written *The Philosophy of W. E. Channing* (1952).

Channing, William Ellery [2] (b. Boston, Nov. 29, 1818—d. Dec. 23, 1901), poet, essayist. Channing was the nephew of WILLIAM ELLERY CHANNING [1]. He studied at Harvard for three months, tried farming in northern Illinois, and practiced journalism in Cincinnati, where he married Ellen Fuller, the younger sister of MARGARET FULLER. He settled in Concord, Mass., in 1842, near Ralph Waldo Emerson, who published his verses and essays in The Dial. He wrote for Horace Greeley's New York Tribune and edited New Bedford Mercury (1856–59). He published nine volumes of poetry and prose, besides countless contributions to newspapers and magazines. Most significant are: The Spider, a sprightly verse which appeared in the New England Magazine (1835) and probably suggested Emerson's THE HUMBLEBEE; Poems (1843), and Poems, Second Series (1847), the 1843 volume provoking one of Poe's most scathing reviews; and Thoreau, the Poet-Naturalist (1873), the first biography of his closest friend. F. B. SANBORN republished this work (1902) with some additions and in the same year edited what he considered the best of Channing's verses, Poems of Sixty-Five Years.

Channing wrote some charming lyrics, but his work is remarkably uneven; Thoreau called his style "sublimo-slipshod." His prose, except in his unpublished notebooks, is artificial and pretentious, but his life of Thoreau has been an important source book for later biographers. His chief significance, however, lies in his contribution to the life and work of the Concord writers, all good friends of his; he was the most constant of Thoreau's walking companions and encouraged his nonconformity. See TRANSCENDENTALISM.

Channing, William Henry (b. Boston, May 25, 1810—d. Dec. 23, 1884), clergyman, propagandist, editor. A nephew of WILLIAM ELLERY CHANNING [1], cousin of WILLIAM ELLERY CHANNING [2], Channing was interested in helping humanity, took part in the BROOK FARM and in the Fourierist movement. He was a Unitarian leader, with doubts. Channing wrote The Gospel of Today (1847), The Civil War in America (1861), and a biography of his celebrated uncle (1848). See ODE INSCRIBED TO W. H. CHANNING.

Chanteys. See SAILORS' SONGS.

Chanting the Square Deific (1865), a poem by WALT WHITMAN in which he sums up his religious ideas. He names as four sides of the square Jehovah, representing inexorable natural law; Christ, representing consolation and love; Satan, representing the individual will; and Santa [sic] Spirita, a feminine soul including everything—all life on earth, God, Saviour, Satan.

Chaparral. A humorous monthly at Stanford University, founded 1899.

Chap-Book, The. A semi-monthly magazine, founded at Cambridge (1893), which removed to Chicago in 1894 along with the publishing firm of Stone & Kimball. It earned a high reputation because of the rigid literary standard it set. Both American and foreign authors contributed freely to its pages, including Henry James, Eugene Field, Max Beerbohm, William Ernest Henley, Bliss Carmen, and H. G. Wells. In its design it imitated the English periodical The Yellow Book; it was itself imitated by The Lark

and other American "little magazines." In 1898 it merged with The Dial.

chapbooks. During the early part of the 19th century the reading of all kinds of literature, good, bad, and indifferent, was greatly encouraged by the wide sale of what were called chapbooks—small books sold at a low price: the word chap is a cognate of cheap. Their vogue recalls that of the paperback books of the present day. These small books were usually sold by peddlers (chapmen) on foot or on horseback. ISAIAH THOMAS, Worcester, Mass., printer, was the best-known publisher of chapbooks. His publications contained stories, orations, collections of jests, moral tales, ballads, biographical sketches, fables, reproductions of well-known writings.

Chaplin, Charlie [Charles Spencer] (b. England, April 16, 1889—   ), actor, producer. This extraordinary pantomimist made his screen debut in the United States with the Keystone Film Co., and became famous all over the world for his creation of a particular kind of clown— the little tramp with a derby, diminutive mustache, baggy trousers, oversize shoes, and cane. His movies made since 1915, such as The Tramp, The Vagabond, Shoulder Arms, The Kid, The Gold Rush, City Lights, and Modern Times, show his unique mixture of satire, pathos, and fantasy. Later he appeared in a powerful attack on the pre-World War II totalitarian madness, THE GREAT DICTATOR (1940); in a tragicomic psychological study, Monsieur Verdoux (1947); in Limelight (1952); and in a great satire on American society, King of New York (1958). He always took an active part in preparing his scripts and, frequently, his background music; some later scripts, like Monsieur Verdoux, he wrote himself. He never became a citizen; in 1952 he was refused re-entry to the United States because of his alleged Communist sympathies; resides in Switzerland. Robert Payne writes understandingly of Chaplin in The Great God Pan (1952); Hart Crane used his early screen character as a symbol in Chaplinesque (1921).

Chapman, Frank M[ichler] (b. Englewood, N.J., June 12, 1864—d. Nov. 15, 1945), ornithologist, editor. Chapman began as an ardent amateur, became Curator of Ornithology at the American Museum of Natural History and a worldwide authority on birds. He founded and edited Bird-Lore, greatly improved museum techniques of displaying birds and bird life, and wrote important manuals, principally the Handbook of Birds of Eastern North America (1895), still regarded as a standard work in its field.

Chapman, John or **Jonathan.** See JOHNNY APPLESEED.

Chapman, John Jay (b. New York City, March 2, 1862—d. Nov. 4, 1933), critic, essayist, poet, playwright. Chapman, educated at Harvard and thoroughly saturated with Boston traditions, practiced law unwillingly for ten years, then turned to writing as a means of expressing his intense, often crotchety and wrongheaded, but always vigorously worded views on literature, politics, and religion. At least twice he suffered nervous breakdowns. Yet he was one of the most remarkable men of his time, who sometimes expressed himself with extraordinary felicity and force. One of his most understanding interpreters, Edmund Wilson, says "his career was a curious one. He was a moralist, a literary critic, a poet, and a politician; and his character was passionate, erratic, intransigent, and self-willed. There is in him something of a more limited Tolstoy and something of the traditional American crank. . . . His prose is among the best of his period." Among his books: *Emerson and Other Essays* (1898); *Causes and Consequences* (1898); *William Lloyd Garrison* (1913); *Memories and Milestones* (1915); *Letters and Religion* (1924).

Chapman, Maristan. Pen name of J. Stanton H. Chapman and Mary H. I. Chapman. See HAPPY MOUNTAIN.

Chappell, George S[hepard]. See WALTER E. TRAPROCK.

Character and Opinion in the United States (1920), essays by GEORGE SANTAYANA. Here Santayana discusses the nature of American civilization and the traits of Americans. He includes memories of his fellow professors at Harvard, WILLIAM JAMES and JOSIAH ROYCE. The essays were written some years after Santayana had gone to live abroad.

Charlemont, or, The Pride of the Village (1846), a novel by WILLIAM GILMORE SIMMS. In 1842 Simms had published BEAUCHAMPE, his account of the so-called "Kentucky Tragedy" that attracted such widespread attention in his day. In *Charlemont* he expanded the first part of the story, which describes the seduction and desertion of Margaret Cooper.

Charlotte, a Tale of Truth [usually called **Charlotte Temple**] (published in England, 1791; in the United States, 1794), a novel by SUSANNA HASWELL ROWSON. One of the best sellers of all time, this is the supposedly true story of the seduction of a young English girl by a British officer whom she follows to New York. There he abandons her and she dies in childbirth; he repents bitterly and in a duel kills a man who had sought to lead her further astray. This novel, stemming, as Alexander Cowie phrased it, "from the Richardsonian tradition of the harassed female," had an extraordinary sale, long continued. A sequel, *Charlotte's Daughter* (1828), published posthumously, plays on the incest motive, not too successfully. A copy of the first edition of *Charlotte* was sold in 1955 for $5,000.

Charnwood, Lord Godfrey Rathbone Benson (b. England, Nov. 6, 1864—d. Feb. 3, 1945), English statesman, biographer. His *Abraham Lincoln* (1916) has become a classic; he also wrote *Theodore Roosevelt* (1923). Charnwood saw Lincoln as a much more complex character than was generally believed, and analyzed his traits and achievements with great literary skill.

Charteris, Leslie (b. Malaya, May 12, 1907—), writer of adventure fiction. His Simon Templar stories under the title of *The Saint* had such immediate and widespread popularity that they spilled over into movies, radio, TV, and comic strips. Charteris was born Leslie Charles Bower Yin, the son of an Englishwoman and of a Chinese surgeon who was a lineal descendant of the Yins, emperors of China from 1760 to 1120 B.C. He legally took the name of Charteris in England in 1928. An early book was *Meet the Tiger* (1928). *Enter the Saint* (1930) brought Simon Templar on the scene, and some thirty books later "the Saint" was still confounding and entertaining readers in *The Saint on the Spanish Main* (1959).

Chase, Edna Woolman. See ILKA CHASE, also VOGUE.

Chase, Ilka (b. New York City, April 8, 1905—), actress, novelist, autobiographer. Miss Chase's mother was Edna Woolman Chase (b. Asbury Park, N.J., March 14, 1877—d. March 20, 1957), who was editor-in-chief of VOGUE. Ilka was introduced to "society" at an early age, and from her childhood regarded celebrities of all kinds as common fry. She went on the stage at eighteen, appeared in numerous plays, movies, and radio programs. She early acquired a reputation for smart and biting remarks, as when she found she had on hand a quantity of beautifully printed calling cards left over from her first marriage. It seemed a pity, she said, to waste them, and she promptly sent them to the second wife of her ex-husband, with a kind note: "Dear Julia, I hope these reach you in time." Her first autobiographical volume, *Past Imperfect* (1942), had a great success for its frankness and wit. Its successor, *Free Admission* (1948), did not do so well. She also wrote fiction: *In Bed We Cry* (1944); *I Love Miss Tilli Bean* (1946); and *New York 22* (1951), but with only moderate acclaim. Miss Chase's background is brightly depicted in her mother's self-portrait, *Always in Vogue* (1954).

Chase, Mary Coyle (b. Denver, Colo., February 25, 1907—), playwright, author. *Now You've Done It* (1937) and her other early plays achieved little theatrical success, but in 1944 her play HARVEY was produced on Broadway by Brock Pemberton. An immediate success, it won her the Pulitzer Prize in 1944-45. *Harvey's* success lay in its highly imaginative "escapist" plot involving a six-foot invisible rabbit. Her next two plays, *Mrs. McThing* (1952) and *Bernadine* (1952), were also well received on Broadway. *Midgie Purvis* opened on Broadway in 1961 to considerably less enthusiasm. Mrs. Chase also wrote a children's book, *Loretta Mason Potts* (1958).

Chase, Mary Ellen (b. Blue Hill, Me., Feb. 24, 1887—), teacher, novelist, essayist. Brought up in Maine with a classical education, Miss Chase taught first in country schools and in several private schools. She taught English at the University of Minnesota, and from 1926 on at Smith College. She began writing at an early age; her first sale was a football story to the *American Boy*. Aside from fiction she wrote *Constructive Theme Writing* (1929) and *The Golden Asse; and Other Essays* (1929). Her frequent summers in England resulted in a book of humorous essays, *This England* (1936). Her autobiography, *A Goodly Heritage* (1932), is among her best works and deals mainly with her teaching experiences; its sequel is *A Goodly Fellowship* (1939). A later autobiographical work, *The White Gate* (1954), is subtitled "Adventures in the Imagination of a Child." She also wrote two interpretations of the Bible, *The Bible and the Common Reader* (1944) and *Life and Language in the Old Testament* (1955); and two biographies, *Jonathan Fisher: Maine Parson, 1768–1847* (1948) and *Abby Aldrich Rockefeller* (1950).

Miss Chase has been one of the leading regional writers of the times, interpreting Maine, past and present, at its best and most characteristic. Her vigorous, clean-cut prose and her subtle portrayals, especially of her feminine characters, give her novels a depth and solidity, as well as a universality, lacking in most writers who limit themselves to one particular section of the country. She wrote first several stories for young people, including the popular *Mary Christmas* (1926), followed by *Uplands* (1927) and *Gay Highway* (1933). *Mary Peters* (1934) and *Silas Crockett* (1935, see THE CROCKETTS), two chronicle novels, are probably her most enduring works. *Dawn in Lyonesse* (1938), for once not set in Maine, is an interesting modern parallel of the Tristan and Isolde story. Later novels are *Windswept* (1941); *The Plum Tree* (1949); *The Edge of Darkness* (1957); *Sailing the Seven Seas* (1958); and *Lovely Ambition* (1960).

Chase, Richard V[olney], Jr. (b. Lakeport, N.H., Oct. 12, 1914—d. Aug. 28, 1962), critic. During the nineteen-fifties, Chase emerged as one of the leading critics of American literature. *The American Novel and Its Tradition* (1957) was quickly recognized as a definitive work. Chase, a professor of literature at Columbia University, has moved easily through the jungle of modern criticism, refusing to accept any label, even that of "highbrow." He views the American novel as descendant of the European, but differing from it in its characteristic employment of "romance" rather than "REALISM." Through the form of "romance," which deals less with character than with action and is not bound to realistic detail, the great American novels have embraced the violent contrarieties of our native culture. Chase's description of a native American tradition has been especially instructive for and influential with English and European readers. Perhaps the most impressive thing about this critic is that his definitions do not restrict new writers, but encourage experiment, originality, and even modification of his thesis. His other books: *Emily Dickinson* (1953), and *Walt Whitman Reconsidered* (1955), both in the AMERICAN MEN OF LETTERS SERIES; *Quest For Myth* (1949); *Herman Melville* (1949); and *The Democratic Vista* (1959), a book of conversations about American culture dramatized like Platonic dialogues. Chase's articles appear frequently in such magazines as *Partisan Review*, *Kenyon Review*, *Commentary*, and the *Nation*.

Chase, Stuart (b. Somersworth, N.H., March 8, 1888—   ), economist, semanticist. Under the influence of HENRY GEORGE, Chase became deeply interested in social problems, especially those relating to conservation, consumer education, semantics, and labor problems. Among his books: *The Tragedy of Waste* (1925); *Your Money's Worth* (in collaboration with F. L. Schlink, 1927); *A New Deal* (1932—before the New Deal was launched by President Roosevelt); *The Economy of Abundance* (1934); *The Tyranny of Words* (1938); *A Primer of Economics* (1941); *The Proper Study of Mankind* (1948; rev. 1956); *Power of Words* (1954); *Some Things Worth Knowing: A Generalizer's Guide to Useful Knowledge* (1958); and *Live and Let Live* (1960). Chase has great powers of exposition, and his ideas have exerted a wide influence, particularly in directing attention to the effects, good and bad, of technological change.

Chastellux, Marquis François Jean de (1734–1788), French soldier. This major-general in Rochambeau's army served from 1780 to 1782. Several years later he published an account of his observations, *Travels in North America, in the Years 1780, 1781, and 1782* (2 v., 1786). An English translation appeared in London the following year.

Chateaubriand, Vicomte François René de (1768–1848), French author. Chateaubriand spent five months in America in 1791, and drew upon his recollections of the United States in his novels *Atala* (1801), *René* (1802), and *Les Natchez* (1826). The resulting cult of the "noble savage" had a wide influence in the Romantic movement; one American author, Timothy Flint, wrote a novel, *Francis Berrian, or, The Mexican Patriot* (1826), in obvious imitation of the French writer.

Chauncy, Charles (b. Boston, Jan. 1, 1705—d. Feb. 10, 1787), clergyman, controversialist. Chauncy's great-grandfather, Charles Chauncy (1592–1672), also a clergyman, had been the second president of Harvard where the younger Chauncy was graduated in 1724. In 1727 he became pastor of the First Church (Congregational) of Boston, and remained there for the rest of his life. It was his great mission to overthrow the harsher doctrines of Calvinism. He began by opposing the revivals of "the GREAT AWAKENING" which had become a feature of religion in New England under the leadership of JONATHAN EDWARDS (1703–1758), George Whitefield (1714–1770), and the "men of feeling." Chauncy fought the battle of rationality and optimism; and furthermore, after pondering in secret for many years on the theme, he came to believe that God would ultimately save all sinners from damnation. In 1782 he published anonymously a book that created a sensation and marked the beginning of Universalism in New England—*The Salvation of All Men: The Grand Thing Aimed at in the Scheme of God.* Earlier he had published a *Sermon on Enthusiasm* (1742) and *Letters to Whitefield* (1744, 1745). Later he issued *The Benevolence of the Deity* (1784). He fought the British attempt to force bishops on the American church, and as an ardent patriot before and during the Revolution wrote a number of political tracts.

Chautauqua. An adult education movement, combined with a book club and summer school activities. The movement grew out of an intelligent young minister's desire for better-trained Sunday School teachers. John H. Vincent (1832–1920) undertook to train teachers by gathering them in groups each summer for all-day study. Then he decided to start a summer school on a more ambitious scale, took over a defunct camp site at Lake Chautauqua, N.Y., and named the institution "the Sunday-School Teachers' Assembly." Forty young people attended in the summer of 1874, and Chautauqua was born. The idea eventually spread to all parts of the world; millions of people attended Chautauqua lectures and enjoyed "planned recreation" in great brown tents all over the United States. In 1878 Chautauqua started a Literary and Scientific Circle that was the first American book club. The list of contributors to Chautauqua lecture platforms and book publications was virtually a Who's Who of the times.

By 1924 the movement was beginning to decline, although it has continued in a restricted area and with many changes. At its height it was an immensely powerful cultural force and gave the public reliable information on such subjects as equal suffrage, soil conservation, child welfare, and the humanities. It helped make rural areas part of the nation. Sinclair Lewis jeered at Chautauqua in MAIN STREET (1920), and Herbert Asbury has called it "a sort of intellectual soothing syrup especially prepared for the Bible Belt." But Victoria and Robert Ormond Case have given it fairer treatment in *We Called It Culture: The Story of Chautauqua* (1948), as did Harry P. Harrison in *Culture Under Canvas; the Story of Tent Chautauqua* (1957). In reality Chautauqua did more to change Main Street than did Lewis' satiric work. THOMAS W. DUNCAN's *O Chautauqua!* (1935) is a novel based on the author's own experiences. See LYCEUMS.

Chayefsky, Paddy (b. New York City, Jan. 29, 1923–), playwright, producer. Chayefsky began his dramatic writing on television depicting the ordinary lives of some of the ordinary people he had known while growing up in New York during the depression. *Marty* (1953) told sympathetically the love story of a plain Bronx butcher and a plain old-maid schoolteacher with humor and realism. The movie version (1955) won an Academy Award. Two other television plays, *The Bachelor Party* (1954) and *The Catered Affair* (1955), were made into movies, as was the stage play *The Middle of the Night* (1959), with which Chayefsky turned from television to the theater.

Both praised and censured for his adherence to naturalistic dialogue in the "tape-recording school" of dramatic style, Chayefsky began to feel while working with the two inarticulate protagonists of *The Middle of the Night* that realism is "confining" and "unimportant." In his play *The Tenth Man* (prod. 1959, pub. 1960) he combined a shabby "realistic" setting with a fantastic East European legend, and made strong comments on the events. In 1960 he went to Israel for research and turning to the Bible for his story, to stylization for his method, and occasionally to poetry for his language, he wrote *Gideon* (1961), an ironic story of man's refusal to accept God's assurance even after a series of miracles. The play was produced on Broadway.

Chayefsky has also published *Television Plays* (1955); *The Goddess*, an original movie script, was filmed in 1958. See TELEVISION WRITING.

Cheaper by the Dozen (1948), a family saga by Frank B. Gilbreth, Jr., and Ernestine Gilbreth Carey. Next to Clarence Day, Jr.'s, *Life with Father*, this has probably been the most widely read of the many sprightly accounts of life in an American home. The book was turned into an amusing movie in 1950.

Cheetham, James (b. England, 1772—d. Sept. 19, 1810), newspaper editor, biographer. Cheetham's connection with liberal movements in England forced him to leave that country for the United States in 1798. He joined DE WITT CLINTON in buying an interest in the New York *Argus*, changed the name to *American Citizen*, and became a spokesman of the Republicans (later called Democrats). He wrote a savage attack on Aaron Burr for his methods in seeking to win the Presidency in 1800; in 1809 he published a vindictive biography of Thomas Paine, who was a difficult and unpleasant old man when Cheetham made his acquaintance.

Cheever, Ezekiel (b. England, Jan. 25, 1615?—d. Aug. 21, 1708), educator. Cheever came to America in 1637 and immediately began a distinguished career as a schoolmaster, ultimately becoming headmaster of the Boston Latin School. During his life he was known as a rigid disciplinarian and outstanding scholar, but his chief fame came to him posthumously for his textbook called *Accidence, A Short Introduction to the Latin Tongue* (probably 1750). One of the earliest American schoolbooks, it went into more than twenty editions and was used for more than a century after its first appearance.

Cheever, John (b. Quincy, Mass., May 27, 1912–), fiction writer. His short pieces appeared in a number of magazines, including *The New Yorker*. Among his books: *The Way Some People Live* (1943); *The Enormous Radio and Other Stories* (1953); *The Wapshot Chronicle* (1957), a best seller that received generous critical acclaim; *The Housebreaker of Shady Hill and Other Stories* (1958); *Some People, Places and Things That Will Not Appear in My Next Novel* (1961). Mr. Cheever received two Guggenheim fellowships.

Chenery, William L[udlow] (b. June 26, 1884–). See COLLIER'S.

Cheney, John Vance (b. Groveland, N.Y., Dec. 29, 1848—d. May 1, 1922), librarian, poet, essayist. Cheney, an associate of Edwin Markham, Joaquin Miller, and other literary lights of California, won a moderate reputation with his collections of lyrics, including *Thistle-Drift* (1887) and *Poems* (1905).

Cheney, Sheldon [Warren] (b. Berkeley, Cal., June 29, 1886—), writer, lecturer on art and theatre. Cheney's idea of a "living, creative vision" in art made him a champion of modern art and an uncompromising modernist in the field of the theatre. One of his earliest books on the theatre was *The Theatre: 3,000 Years of Drama, Acting and Stagecraft*, published in 1929 and considered a standard history of the theatre. *A Primer of Modern Art* (1923) also remains a perennial favorite. In 1936 he wrote *Art and the Machine* in collaboration with his second wife, Martha Candler Cheney. In 1945 he brought out a history of mysticism through the ages in the form of biographies of well-known saints and seers: *Men Who Have Walked With God*. The critical reception was mixed, but the reading public welcomed it, and there were four reprints in three months. His most recent work was the *New World History of Art* (1956). In 1916 he founded THEATRE ARTS MAGAZINE.

Cherokee Indians. The Cherokees occupied the Piedmont and Appalachian regions in what is now North and South Carolina, Georgia, and Tennessee. Because the British had helped them resist the borderers who tried to seize their lands, the Cherokees became their allies in the Revolutionary War. In 1794 they made a treaty with the new nation, which they consistently and honorably kept. Unquestionably the most advanced of all Indian tribes, the Cherokees realized that they must adjust to new conditions and passed efficiently from a hunting to an agricultural society. The Cherokee chieftain SEQUOYA performed the prodigious feat of creating an alphabet; the Cherokees quickly became literate, published books and newspapers (*The Cherokee Phoenix*, founded in 1828; *The Cherokee Advocate*, founded in 1844), adopted a constitution on the model of the United States'. Nevertheless, they were treated with the utmost barbarity. Their lands were taken away in complete violation of their treaty rights. During Van Buren's Presidency (1837–1841) the infamous "March of Tears" took place. The Cherokees were forcibly removed from their lands to what were in effect concentration camps; more than 4,000 died on the way. Ultimately they reached what is presently Oklahoma. Now full American citizens, they have produced many men of prominence.

The Indians in the novels of WILLIAM GILMORE SIMMS were based on his knowledge of the Cherokees; more recent novels dealing with them are Caroline Gordon's *Green Centuries* (1941), Dale Van Every's *The Captive Witch* (1951), and Don Tracy's *Cherokee* (1956). Lynn Riggs wrote a play, *The Cherokee Night* (1936). Marion Starkey described *The Cherokee Nation* (1946).

Chesnut, Mary Boykin (b. [?], 1823—d. [?], 1886), diarist. Mrs. Chesnut, wife of an ardent secessionist, had a ringside seat at the events leading to the Civil War, and recorded her observations with humor and understanding in a diary running to some 400,000 words. It was published in 1904, but with some of the best passages prudishly omitted; Ben Ames Williams reissued it as A DIARY FROM DIXIE (1949).

Chesnutt, Charles W[addell] (b. Cleveland, Ohio, June 20, 1858—d. Nov. 15, 1932), novelist. Chesnutt is sometimes called "the first Negro novelist." He was a teacher, a newspaperman, and a lawyer; in August, 1887, his first story, *The Goophered Grapevine*, was published in the *Atlantic;* a series of such stories made up his first book, *The Conjure Woman* (1899), centered around Uncle Julius McAdoo, not too unlike Uncle Remus. Chesnutt's later books frankly considered race prejudice: *The Wife of His Youth and Other Stories of the Color Line* (1899); *The House Behind the Cedars* (1900); *The Colonel's Dream* (1905). In 1928 he received the Spingarn gold medal award for "pioneer work as a literary artist depicting the life and struggle of Americans of Negro descent." Helen N. Chesnutt's *Charles W. Chesnutt, Pioneer of the Color Line* (1952) describes him as "a pioneer Negro author, the first to exploit in fiction the complex lives of men and women of mixed blood."

Chester, George Randolph (b. Ohio, 1869—d. Feb. 26, 1924), novelist, short story writer, critic. Chester wrote stories that won great popularity, particularly in *The Saturday Evening Post*. The best known told of a character named GET-RICH-QUICK WALLINGFORD, who managed to make money by means that were just barely legal but generally amusing. A play by GEORGE M. COHAN was based on the stories (1910).

Chevigny, Hector (b. Missoula, Mont., June 28, 1904—d. Apr. 20, 1965), writer, historian, radio writer, autobiographer. Chevigny first published two books on Russia's exploration of Alaska and the northeast coast in the early 19th century, *Lost Empire* (1939) and *Lord of Alaska* (1942). In 1943 he became blind, but his literary output thereafter has been phenomenal, including short stories, magazine articles, and more than a hundred radio scripts. His book *My Eyes Have a Cold Nose* (1946) made a deep impression. It tells the story of Chevigny's sudden affliction and the way he trained himself to go on living and working with the help of his boxer, Wizard, trained in the Seeing Eye School at Whippany, N.J. *Woman of the Rock* (1949) is a novel about a woman evangelist, apparently suggested by the career of Aimee Semple McPherson.

Cheyenne Indians. An Algonquian Indian tribe that lived originally in the South, later removed to Oklahoma, and finally settled in Montana and nearby. They were severely defeated by Custer in 1868, and took revenge on him by joining Sitting Bull and the SIOUX INDIANS in the Battle of Little Big Horn (1876). HAMLIN GARLIN knew this tribe well and often wrote of them, especially in the prose poem *The Silent Eaters* (in *The Book of the American Indian*, 1923) and THE CAPTAIN OF THE GRAY-HORSE TROOP (1902). George Bird Grinnell wrote *The Fighting Cheyennes* (1915; reprinted, 1956). They also appear in Howard Fast's *The Last Frontier* (1941) and Jack Schaefer's *The Canyon* (1953). Cheyenne, Wyoming, is named for the tribe.

Chicago (1913), a poem, and **Chicago Poems** (1916), a collection, by CARL SANDBURG.

Chidsey, Donald B[arr] (b. Elizabeth, N.J., May 14, 1902—　　), novelist, biographer. Chidsey became well-known as a writer of adventure, romance, and mystery. His stories enlivened the pages of such magazines as *The Saturday Evening Post, Collier's, Red Book,* and *Cosmopolitan.* His early life contained many of the elements and situations that he wrote about. His travels took him from the Far East to Australia and the South Pacific. In Tahiti he managed a copra plantation, in Honolulu a gambling speakeasy. Besides several hundred detective or adventure stories and travel articles, he wrote numerous historical novels and biographies. Among the latter are *Bonnie Prince Charlie* (1928), and *John the Great: the Times and Life of John L. Sullivan* (1942). Three of his histories are: *July 4, 1776* (1958), *Valley Forge* (1959), and *The Battle of New Orleans* (1961).

Child, Francis J[ames] (b. Boston, Feb. 1, 1825—d. Sept. 11, 1896), teacher, philologist, ballad collector. Having graduated from Harvard in 1846, Child taught mathematics there until 1848, then political economy and history for a year. But his bent was toward comparative philology, and after further study in Germany he went back to teach at Harvard, first rhetoric and composition, later in his special field of Middle English. He became an authority on Chaucer and his contemporaries, but for many years occupied himself with the collection in eight volumes of ENGLISH AND SCOTTISH POPULAR BALLADS (1857–58), which appeared in revised form in 1883–98 (10 v.) The work immediately became the most authoritative publication on the subject and has not been superseded. It printed 305 distinct English and Scottish ballads, as many as possible from manuscript sources, usually with all the known versions of each, in addition to an exhaustive critical apparatus and notes on distribution. Few important additions have been made to the collection. Child has numerous disciples. His teaching and his great collection gave stimulus to the gathering of other ballads in the United States and elsewhere. See DIALECT SOCIETY.

Child, Lydia Maria [Francis] (b. Medford, Mass., Feb. 11, 1802—d. Oct. 20, 1880), novelist, crusader. Mrs. Child established the *Juvenile Miscellany* (1826), the first monthly for children in the United States; she wrote the first antislavery book, *Appeal in Favor of That Class of Americans Called Africans* (1833); she was among the first to compose books helping women in their household problems, *The Frugal Housewife* (1829) and *The Mother's Book*

(1831); she was a pioneer in advocating women's suffrage and sex education, and wrote *A History of the Condition of Women in Various Ages and Nations* (1835). She also wrote fiction, of little importance, although occasionally displaying her originality of concept: HOBOMOK (1824), in which an Indian marries a white girl; *The Rebels* (1825), picturing Boston before the Revolution; *Philothea* (1836), set in ancient Greece; and *A Romance of The Republic* (1867), which deals with abolitionism. Probably the only writing of Mrs. Child's that is actively remembered is a poem she wrote on *Thanksgiving Day* (1857), one stanza of which begins:

> Over the river and through the wood,
> To grandfather's house we'll go.

H. W. Sewall collected some of her correspondence in a volume of *Letters* (1883). See KNICKERBOCKER SCHOOL.

Childers, James Saxon (b. Birmingham, Ala., April 19, 1899—　　), novelist, critic, author, publisher, teacher. Childers served in the army in both World Wars, was at one time literary editor of the Birmingham *News* and a teacher at Birmingham Southern College. Among his books: *The Uneducated Poets* (1925); *The Bookshop Mystery* (1929); *From Siam to Suez* (1931); *Sailing South American Skies* (1936); *Mumbo Jumbo Esquire* (1941); *War Eagles* (1943); *Tomorrow We Reap* (with James Street, 1949); *The Nation on the Flying Trapeze* (1960). He is president of Tupper and Love, Inc., a book publishing house.

Child Is Born, A (1942), a radio play by STEPHEN VINCENT BENÉT. One of the many plays in which Benét demonstrates that radio is a natural medium for verse and narrative. He retells, with beauty and impressiveness, the ancient story of the birth of Jesus. Alfred Lunt and Lynn Fontanne were the chief performers in the original production, which has often been repeated as a Christmastide favorite.

children, rhymes for. See NURSERY RHYMES.

Children of Adam. A group of poems in WALT WHITMAN's LEAVES OF GRASS. *Children of Adam* first appeared in the 1860 edition of *Leaves of Grass* as fifteen poems entitled *Enfans d'Adam;* Whitman deleted one poem, added two others, and translated the title into English in the edition of 1867. The section created a great deal of controversy because of its forthright praise of physical love, procreation, and the beauty of the human body. Whitman intended *Children of Adam* to be a companion section to CALAMUS [1] (1860), in which he celebrated the love of comrades.

Children of the Night, The (1897, reprinted 1905), a collection of poems by EDWIN ARLINGTON ROBINSON. In it are included some poems from Robinson's earlier collection, *The Torrent and the Night Before* (privately printed, 1896). President Theodore Roosevelt read and liked the volume, and made Robinson a clerk in the New York Custom House, a sinecure. The book includes such admired pieces as *Luke Havergal,*

RICHARD CORY, and *Two Men*, and reveals Robinson's mastery of psychological portraiture.

children's books. In following the course of children's literature from the Puritan beginnings in New England to the present heyday of our child-centered culture, a panorama of social history, religious and educational theories, fashions, and behavior unfolds before us. The story begins in New England, with the coming of the *Mayflower*. The Puritans brought with them a portion of the English heritage, but it was a heritage confined and intensified by the fervor of their religious beliefs; to the austerity and rigor of an alien coast they brought an obsession with the soul's salvation. The books addressed to children were shaped to this theme. Most of them had made their initial appearance in England, and were expected to suit the New World as admirably as they had served their purpose in the Old. Among the earliest children's books printed in America was a text on Puritan behavior entitled *The Rule of the New Creature to be practiced every Day, in all the Particulars of it which are Ten.*

The influence of JOHN COTTON, the great preacher of the day, was all-pervading. His *Spiritual Milk for Boston Babes drawn from the Breasts of Both Testaments for their Soul's Nourishment* was first published in England in 1646. It survived more than a hundred years; much of it was later incorporated in *The New England Primer.* James Janeway's well-known *Token for Children, Being an Exact Account of the Conversion, Holy and Exemplary Lives and Joyous Deaths of Several Young Children,* was made available to colonial children in 1700. To the original English text, COTTON MATHER, the grandson of John Cotton, gave evidence of some pride of place. He added *A Token for the Children of New England of some Examples of Children in whom The Fear of God was remarkable budding before they died in several parts of New England. Preserved and published for the Encouragement of Piety in other Children.*

BENJAMIN HARRIS of Boston, printer and proprietor of The London Coffee House, was a refugee from religious persecution in England, where he had suffered the pillory because of his publications in behalf of the Puritan faith. It was he who printed the *New England Primer* (earliest extant edition 1727), which was to become the chief instrument of education, piety, and diversion for a period of one hundred and fifty years. It contained the Westminster Catechism and a rhymed alphabet that must have been a source of joy to children unaccustomed to the pleasure of meter and assonance, and it was illustrated with crude woodcuts to entice and capture the imagination. The shadow of political change and unrest can be traced in the various editions of the *Primer*, in which religious concerns were gradually overshadowed by politics and the course of history.

Whales in the Sea
God's Voice Obey.

reads the couplet for the letter *W* in an early version.

By Washington
Great deeds were done.

illustrates the letter at a later date.

Two great books of the Puritan heritage must be considered, though neither was intended for children. The Bible itself must have been drama and poetry to the children who lived with it in daily association, and John Bunyan's *Pilgrim's Progress*, with its adventures, gave relief from solemnity and dire prophecy. The poems of Isaac Watts, *Divine and Moral Songs*, though the work of a dedicated Puritan, had its moments of music and felicity, and this too leavened the austerity of the reading of colonial children.

A Bible for children was published in 1763 by Andrew Stewart of Philadelphia. There followed various "Thumb Bibles" and metrical versions, one of the most popular being *The History of the Holy Jesus.*

The wisemen from the East do come,
Led by a shining Star,
And offer to the new-born King,
Frankincense, gold and myrrh.

The Puritan influence waned with the growth of the country. Philadelphia, New York, Worcester, Hartford, and New Haven became centers of printing and publishing, as well as Boston. The turmoil of the Revolution placed emphasis on temporal affairs. The chapbooks of England and the spirited and gay publications of JOHN NEWBERY found their way to America, largely through the efforts of Isaiah Thomas, American patriot and printer, who imported the Newbery books, gave them his own imprint, and with patriotic zeal hastily but inconsistently changed "kings" to "commoners" and "London" to "Boston" in an early effort to give children a sense of pride of place and heritage.

The best of Newbery's titles thus infiltrated the Colonies: *The History of Giles Gingerbread, a little boy who lived upon Learning; Nurse Truelove's New Year's Gift; Mother Goose's Melody;* and his most famous, *Little Goody Two Shoes.* The woodcuts of Thomas Bewick also came to be known in the colonies and were responsible for influencing the fine American artist, Alexander Anderson (1775–1870), who abandoned engraving on copper plates to develop his own great gift as a maker of block prints.

The Revolution established America's political independence, but the intellectual ties held strong and firm, and the opinions held in England were also cherished in the minds of the Americans. The sprightliness of Newbery was lost in the rise of the didactic school in England. Thomas Day's *Sandford and Merton*, Maria Edgeworth's stories, the works of Mrs. Barbauld and Mrs. Trimmer, and all the dreary disciples of Rousseau's theory of education, with their stories drenched in a practical morality, tempered by a dash of rules of etiquette, furnished the reading material of American children. One American, a man with a genuine passion for New England sights and sounds, embarked upon a work that had the taste of native air in it. He was SAMUEL GOODRICH (1793–1860) of Con-

A LITTLE PRETTY
POCKET-BOOK,
INTENDED FOR THE
INSTRUCTION and AMUSEMENT
OF
LITTLE MASTER TOMMY,
AND
PRETTY MISS POLLY.
With Two LETTERS from
JACK the GIANT-KILLER;
AS ALSO
A BALL and PINCUSHION;
The Use of which will infallibly make TOMMY a good Boy, and POLLY a good Girl.
To which is added,
A LITTLE SONG-BOOK,
BEING
A New ATTEMPT to teach CHILDREN the Use of the English Alphabet, by Way of Diversion.

THE FIRST WORCESTER EDITION.

PRINTED at WORCESTER, Massachusetts.
By ISAIAH THOMAS,
And SOLD, Wholesale and Retail, at his Book-Store. MDCCLXXXVII.

necticut, who, as Peter Parley, wrote *Tales of Peter Parley About America* (1827). He soon abandoned his native theme in favor of the countries of the world and all manner of books of fact and moral precept. As a boy he had been greatly stirred by the writing of Hannah Moore, one of the English writers who deplored any reference to giants and other imaginary creatures. Her *Shepherd of Salisbury Plain*, a story of virtue rewarded, was so admired by him that he attempted to write in her image.

JACOB ABBOTT (1803–1879), a teacher, preacher, and professor at Amherst, invented the first American boy who captured the interests of readers. Dedicated to the idea that young Americans should be filled with information, preferably about Europe, he began his series of Rollo books in 1834 with *Rollo Learning to Talk* and *Rollo Learning to Read,* and followed Rollo, volume upon volume, as he grew in learning and traveled through the capitals of Europe. But in another series of stories, the Franconia tales, Abbott wrote with release of spirit, creating a lively picture of New England with characters of singularity and charm. These tales, based on

memories of his own boyhood in Maine, foreshadowed the dimensions of the future.

Certain folk concepts of American life began to emerge. HORATIO ALGER (1834–1899), and WILLIAM TAYLOR ADAMS ("Oliver Optic") (1822–1897), wrote books of no literary value, but held true to the belief in "Luck and Pluck," and played variations upon the themes of the poor boy who becomes famous and the boy hero on battlefield and on shipboard.

A distinctive book of American life came into being in 1870 with the publication of Thomas Bailey Aldrich's STORY OF A BAD BOY, which holds appeal for the child of today. Here was a good tale told by a distinguished writer who had no motive other than recounting his own boyhood pranks and pleasures.

Meanwhile, a golden era was being ushered in through the medium of magazines for children. THE YOUTH'S COMPANION, an offshoot of the church paper and Sunday-school literature, introduced boys and girls to Wilkie Collins and Rudyard Kipling. In 1867 Horace Scudder, writer and literary adviser to Houghton, Mifflin of Boston, began to edit *The Riverside Magazine;* he opened its pages to the best writers and artists of the day, notably FRANK STOCKTON (1834–1902) with his *Ting-Aling Tales,* and Hans Christian Andersen, whose stories appeared there before their publication in Europe. *Our Young Folks* appeared in the 1870's, edited by JOHN TROWBRIDGE, the author of the Jack Hazard series of adventure stories for boys. Harriet Beecher Stowe was a contributor, and Lucy Larcom served on the editorial board. In 1873 it was merged with the ST. NICHOLAS, the most famous of all children's magazines; its editor was Mary Mapes Dodge, whose HANS BRINKER OR THE SILVER SKATES (1865) solidly endures as a classic.

With the printing of *St. Nicholas* by Scribner's in New York, the publishing center shifted from Boston to the greater metropolis. Under the leadership of Mrs. Dodge, a woman of broad interests and imagination, the magazine became the proving ground, in both text and pictures, for a galaxy of writers and artists. Its contributors included Sarah Orne Jewett, LUCRETIA HALE, with her PETERKIN PAPERS, Laura Richards, LOUISA MAY ALCOTT, and, above all, HOWARD PYLE, writer, teacher, artist, and the towering influence on the making of children's books at the turn of the century.

Meanwhile, two children's books came into being which described the American scene and the American way of life in such a way that they captured the imagination of the whole world. One was LITTLE WOMEN, written in 1867 by Miss Alcott, based on the experiences of her own girlhood and growing up. The other was Mark Twain's THE ADVENTURES OF TOM SAWYER (1871), followed by THE ADVENTURES OF HUCKLEBERRY FINN (1884). Mark Twain's boy on the Mississippi was a far cry from Rollo, and even from Thomas Bailey Aldrich's Bad Boy, who was well endowed and aristocratic. *The Adven-*

tures of Tom Sawyer signaled the high point of children's literature in America, and won recognition in the children's literature of the world.

In the first decade of the 20th century certain social forces influenced the production of books for children: the rise of departments for children in public libraries, and their demands for better books for children; the pressure of the budding progressive-education movement, and its emphasis on the use of many books in the classroom instead of a single text; and an aroused adult opinion which struck out against the cheap serials of the day. A new concept of internationalism and a new idealism swept the country after World War I. Authentic and excellent books depicting life in the countries of the world were considered proper preparation for the One World concept. American children had always been interested in children in other parts of the world, but the available books had often been superficial. There now appeared books written by people who had lived and worked in foreign countries; fine stories of native men and women; and stories that not only depicted life in foreign lands, but the habits of thought of their peoples as well. Kate Seredy's *The Good Master* belongs to this period, as do the stories of India from the pen of Dhan Gopal Mukerji, *Gay-Neck the Pigeon* and *Ghond the Hunter.*

The market grew with the demand, and for the first time publishers created special departments for children's books under the editorship of teachers, librarians, and other people drawn to the cause of children. A body of criticism developed; *The Horn Book Magazine,* begun in 1924, is a journal devoted to the consideration of books for children. The *New York Times* and the New York *Herald Tribune* allotted pages of space to reviews and criticism. The Newbery Medal, established to encourage writers of children's books, was first awarded to the noted historian Hendrik Willem Van Loon in 1922 for his STORY OF MANKIND. Carl Sandburg's ROOTABAGA STORIES (1922) created in fantasy the gusto and color of America—its zigzag railroads, zanies, beggars, and romance of the Midwest and beyond. To the fairy tales and folklore of the brothers Grimm, Hans Christian Andersen, and JOEL CHANDLER HARRIS were added tales from Czechoslovakia, Albania, Finland, Russia, and more distant and exotic cultures.

Picture books, which had formerly been considered the province of European publishers, found a breathless public in America beginning with C. B. Falls' *A.B.C. Book* (1923), and continuing through the *Poppy Seed Cakes* (1924) of MAUDE and MISKA PETERSHAM to WANDA GÁG's classic *Millions of Cats* (1928) and Edgar and Ingri d'Aulaire's *Ola* and *Children of the North Lights,* which were executed in brilliant color and the old technique of lithographic printing from stone. LUDWIG BEMELMANS, with his incomparable *Madeline* (1939), and Theodore Geisel (DR. SEUSS) in his galloping line and strong color became the founders of a picture-book technique which, though foreign in background and fantastic in inspiration, became a cornerstone of an American tradition.

Novelists of note and other writers for adults addressed themselves to children: RACHEL FIELD with her full-bodied *Hitty;* Esther Forbes in *Johnny Tremaine;* Walter Edmunds in his fine historical stories such as *The Matchlock Gun* and *Tom Whipple.* E. B. WHITE is the author of the delightful *Charlotte's Web* (1952). The period was rich indeed, and American publishers were acclaimed in the world markets for the quality of book illustration, the variety and vigor of the men and women who wrote for children, the excellence of book design, and the standards of choice that governed the publishing of books for children.

The pressures that came to bear on books for children after World War II were once more born of a desire to remake the world. Many books of propaganda, directed to wiping out the Nazi and fascist ideas of race hatred, strained credulity and failed. But from this conscious effort to weed out prejudice there came a fine literature for Negro children that placed them naturally in their own world and gave new understanding to those children who had perhaps been blind to compassion. Such books as *Shuttered Windows* by Florence Crannell Means and Ann Petry's *Harriet Tubman* marked a great advance in the reading interests of children. The stories of the war are just beginning to come with any sense of proportion and genuine creation of character. Dola de Jong's *The Level Land* reaches a high point of compassion and judgment without softening brutal truths.

Science and space are the characteristic interests of the immediate scene, much of the interest arising from the natural curiosity of children, some of it urged upon them by a country which feels that the salvation of the political future lies mainly in a citizenry dedicated to science. Curiously enough, there is also a resurgence of interest in poetry. Perhaps the key book of this decade is the beautiful and satisfying book which combines these two interests: *Imagination's Other Place,* an anthology of poems of science and mathematics compiled by Helen Plotz.

FRANCES CLARKE SAYERS

Children's Hour, The [1] (1860), poem by HENRY WADSWORTH LONGFELLOW. It is one of Longfellow's most charming pieces, devoted to those "blue-eyed banditti," his three daughters —"grave Alice and laughing Allegra and Edith with golden hair." They come down "between the dark and the daylight" and overwhelm him with their kisses. The three girls described were children of his second marriage to Frances Appleton.

Children's Hour, The [2] (1934), play by LILLIAN HELLMAN, based on an actual case in Edinburgh. A child at a boarding school maliciously starts a rumor that the two heads of the school are Lesbians, with tragic results. An attempt was made to suppress the play. It was filmed successfully in 1936 without the Lesbian theme; in 1962, less well, with it. Hellman acknowledged her debt to the late William Roughead's essay, "Closed Doors, or the Great Drumsheugh Case" in his book, *Bad Companions* (1931).

Childs, Marquis W[illiam] (b. Clinton, Iowa, March 17, 1903—), columnist, writer of books on political and economic topics. Childs worked for the St. Louis *Post-Dispatch* from 1926 to 1944, in the latter year became a columnist with the United Features Syndicate. He has gathered his studies and impressions in numerous books, including *Sweden—The Middle Way* (1936); *Washington Calling* (1937); *This Is Your War* (1942); *The Cabin* (a novel, 1944); *The Farmer Takes a Hand* (1952); *Eisenhower, Captive Hero* (1958); with JAMES RESTON, he edited *Walter Lippmann and his Times* (1959).

Chillingworth, Roger. A character in Hawthorne's THE SCARLET LETTER, vengeful husband of HESTER PRYNNE.

Chimes (1926), a novel by ROBERT HERRICK. In it he attacked the big-business methods prevalent at the University of Chicago, of whose faculty he was then a member. His friend ROBERT MORSS LOVETT, who had suggested the writing of a college novel, urged Herrick to avoid a picture of their own university; and he says that he and others "resented especially Herrick's treatment of the first two presidents of the university, who had been generous in granting him freedom and support for his career and defending him when some of the trustees were scandalized at his realism." The title refers to the famous chapel chimes.

Chimmie Fadden. See FADDEN, CHIMMIE.

Chinese Nightingale, The (1915), a poem by VACHEL LINDSAY. Lindsay called this "A song in Chinese tapestries" in a subtitle. He contrasts the sordid slum surroundings of Chang, the Chinese laundryman in San Francisco, with something very romantic and beautiful that might have happened to Chang in ages long ago. "Nearly everyone, including Lindsay," says Harry Hayden Clark, "has agreed that this is by all odds his most coherently constructed and most hauntingly and delicately beautiful poem."

Chingachgook. An Indian chieftain in Cooper's LEATHERSTOCKING TALES (1823–1841), who is seen at his best in THE LAST OF THE MOHICANS (1826). Cooper may have had a real Indian in mind as he first presented Chingachgook in THE PIONEERS, but gradually the figure of the Indian, intimate friend of NATTY BUMPPO, was more and more idealized. He is grave, silent, courageous, self-sacrificing, wise—the real "noble savage."

Chinook language. The Chinooks were an Indian tribe who lived along the Columbia River along the coast. Their language was the principal element in an amalgam formed in the late 18th century with various other Indian languages, with contributions from French, English, and probably Russian. This language was widely used all over the Northwest, from the Cascade Mountains to the coast, and was a means of communication—a lingua franca—between traders and Indians. The vocabulary was very limited, but it seems to have contributed a few words to American English, as recorded by H. L. Mencken: *skookum, siwash, potlach*, possibly *cayuse* and *hooch*. A fifteenth edition of Gill's *Dictionary of the Chinook Jargon* appeared in Portland, Oregon, as late as 1909. FRANZ BOAS collected *Chinook Songs* (1888).

Chisholm Trail, The Old. A widely sung cowboy ballad. The trail ran from eastern Texas to southern Kansas and gave Texan cattlemen an opportunity to drive their cattle to market. It was named for a halfbreed Indian trader, Jesse Chisholm. Wayne Gard wrote *The Chisholm Trail* (1954).

Chita: A Memory of Last Island (1889), LAFCADIO HEARN's beautifully written story of the destruction of an island in the Gulf of Mexico off the Louisiana coast by a tidal wave in 1856.

Chivers, Thomas Holley (b. Washington, Ga., Oct. 18, 1809—d. Dec. 18, 1858), physician, poet. The son of a wealthy plantation owner, Chivers never practiced medicine systematically. He was an enthusiast and a dreamer, joining all the cults and sects of his day, apparently simultaneously; he was a Swedenborgian, a transcendentalist, a spiritualist, a Fourierist. According to Edd Winfield Parks, all that he wrote was autobiographical, "a cathartic." He had an extraordinary gift for bringing words together in what was sometimes exquisite melody and occasionally sheer nonsense. He published *The Lost Pleiad and Other Poems* (1845), *Eonchs of Ruby, A Gift of Love* (1851), *Memoralia* (1853), *Virginalia* (1853).

After EDGAR ALLAN POE's death Chivers claimed that Poe had plagiarized from him; the retort was that he had plagiarized from Poe. Both charges were apparently true, but whereas Poe turned his slight borrowings into masterpieces, Chivers had created only a pale imitation of Poe. He wrote a *Rosalie Lee* which Poe was alleged to have stolen in his ANNABEL LEE. Chivers' poem begins with the lines:

Many mellow Cydonian suckets
 Sweet apples, anthosmial, divine,
From the ruby-rimmed berylline buckets,
 Star-gemmed, lily-shaped, hyaline.

Poe seems to have liked the generous physician who offered his rival poet a haven for life on his estate, and he published some of Chivers' poems in the *Southern Literary Messenger*. Chivers' influence has been traced in the work of such poets as Swinburne and Rossetti. He wrote a life of Poe, first published in 1952 with Richard Beale Davis as editor. See BEAUCHAMPE.

Choate, Rufus (b. Essex, Mass., Oct. 1, 1799—d. July 13, 1859) and **Choate, Joseph H[odges]** (b. Salem, Mass., Jan. 24, 1832—d. May 14, 1917), lawyers, orators, publicists— uncle and nephew. These brilliant and famous men carried on a tradition of legal competency and oratorical ability for almost a century. The older Choate practiced mainly in Boston, the younger in New York. Rufus Choate succeeded Daniel Webster in the Senate (1841), served as attorney-general in Massachusetts for a short term. Joseph helped with the prosecution of the Tammany Tweed Ring and took part in numerous cases involving large corporations, generally as their counsel. He was made ambassador to England (1899–1905) and head of the American delegation to the International Peace Conference at the Hague (1907).

Both were great speakers, the elder more fiery and rhetorical. It was Rufus Choate, representing an antidemocratic tradition never absent from American life, who in 1856 said of the Declaration of Independence that its statements on natural rights were only "glittering and sounding generalities." Emerson replied, "Glittering generalities! He means blazing ubiquities!" Choate did not care much for the transcendentalists and denounced "the trashy sentimentalism of our lute-string enthusiasts." He worked on a history of Greece that he never completed or published, and said that he never chose a word until he had thought of at least six synonyms. His daughter, Helen Choate Bell, carried on his reputation for wit in Boston.

Rufus Choate's speeches and miscellaneous writings are preserved in his *Works* (2 v., 1862) and *Addresses and Orations* (1878). Joseph Choate published *American Addresses* (1911) and *The Boyhood and Youth of Joseph Hodges Choate* (1917). *Arguments and Addresses* appeared posthumously (1926). C. M. Fuess wrote a life of Rufus Choate (1928); E. S. Martin, one of J. H. Choate (2 v., 1920).

Chodorov, Edward (b. New York City, April 17, 1904—), playwright, scenarist. Deeply interested in the theater from childhood, Chodorov was made stage manager for the production of *Abie's Irish Rose* at the incredibly early age of twenty. After further experience on the stage and in movie productions, Chodorov, in collaboration with Arthur Barton, produced a satire on the movie capital, *Wonder Boy* (1931). He returned to Hollywood and prepared numerous scripts there, later came back to Broadway with *Kind Lady* (1935), a crook play with psychological slants which one reviewer found "a nerve-racking tour de force." Other Chodorov plays to appear on Broadway were *Those Endearing Young Charms* (1943) and *Decision* (1944).

Chodorov, Jerome (b. New York City, Aug. 10, 1911—), playwright, director. In collaboration with Joseph Fields, Chodorov wrote several successful and entertaining plays and musicals for Broadway. Among those adapted from short stories that originally appeared in the *New Yorker* were: *Junior Miss* (1942), from Sally Benson's stories of a thirteen-year-old problem child; and *My Sister Eileen* (1940), chronicling the trials and delights of two sisters from Ohio living in the razzle-dazzle, soot, and incongruity of Greenwich Village. *Wonderful Town* was a musical version of the latter play,

which was based on the stories by RUTH McKENNEY. In 1953 it received the Drama Critics' Circle Award for the best book for a musical. Chodorov and Fields also collaborated on *The Ponder Heart* (1954), taken from a long short story by EUDORA WELTY.

Choir Invisible, The (1893, under the title *John Gray;* 1897, under present title, in expanded version), a novel by JAMES LANE ALLEN. This historical romance of pioneer Kentucky tells of John Gray's love for a married woman. It became a best seller.

Chopin, Kate [O'Flaherty] (b. St. Louis, Mo., Feb. 8, 1851—d. Aug. 22, 1904), novelist, short-story writer, critic. On her mother's side Mrs. Chopin was of French descent; when she married Oscar Chopin and moved to Louisiana she

took a deep interest in the picturesque life of the CREOLES and CAJUNS. She returned to St. Louis after her husband's death, wrote for local papers and several children's magazines and finally won acceptance for her stories in *Harper's* and the *Century.* She also turned to novel writing, not with great success. *The Awakening* (1899), which treated the themes of extramarital love and miscegenation, aroused a storm of criticism that practically silenced her for the rest of her life. In her short stories—twenty-three in BAYOU FOLK (1894) and twenty-one in *A Night in Acadie* (1897)—she produced several narratives that Fred Lewis Pattee describes as "among the few unquestioned masterpieces of American short-story art."

Choquette, Robert (b. Manchester, N.H., April 22, 1905—), poet. Choquette moved to Montreal at the age of ten, and has since lived in Canada. Early in his career he traveled abroad for *The Gazette* and was later editor of *La Revue Moderne*, in which magazine he helped the best French-Canadian writers of his generation find a voice. Professionally honored by L'École des Beaux Arts à Montreal and the Association of French-Canadian writers, he has also won many prizes for his poetry and has given a series of radio speeches and readings of Canadian authors.

Choquette wrote a long radio series, *Métropole*, the film *Curé de Village* (1936), and some rural novels. However, his greatest achievement is his poetry. His first book of poems, *À Travers les Vents* (1925), was published when he was twenty years old. In this volume he showed a passionate, though perhaps naïve, feeling for the north country, more lyrical and less morbid than much Canadian writing about that region. His usual theme was the opposition of the new country and the old religion, though he was not a truly philosophical poet.

His early poetry shows an affirmation of life in new rhythms; the chief weakness seized upon by his critics is his tendency to absorb, rather than to reflect, experience. His poetry is a spontaneous view of things. His second book of poems, *Metropolitan Museum* (1931), has been called "the credo of a modern man." In it his mastery of material is more precise and his thought more refined. The series of poems contrasts the serene art in the museum with the frantic life of the city around it. He sees New York as the visible manifestation of the ability of the forces of nature to conquer mankind.

Among his other works are *Poésies Nouvelles* (1933) and *Suite Marine* (1953). The latter volume presents a culmination of his thought, and is a hymn to abstract beauty and nature.

Chrisman, Arthur Bowie (b. near White Post, Va., July 16, 1889—d. Feb. 24, 1953), teacher, farmer, lecturer, writer. While he was working on a story that involved a Chinese character, Chrisman turned to a study of China and produced a book for children, *Shen of the Sea* (1925), that won the Newbery Medal. Later came *The Wind That Wouldn't Blow* (1927) and *Treasures Long Hidden* (1941).

Christian Disciple, The. See THE CHRISTIAN EXAMINER.

Christian Examiner, The. A bimonthly Unitarian magazine founded in January, 1824. It was originally called *The Christian Disciple*, founded in 1813 by WILLIAM ELLERY CHANNING [1] and others. It published articles of distinction and was highly regarded. It ceased publication in 1869.

Christian Herald, The. A Protestant magazine, originally founded in 1878 as a New York edition of a London magazine of the same name. T. DE WITT TALMAGE was one of its early editors; Daniel A. Poling was later its editor for many years. An anniversary anthology was published to mark its 75th year of publication: *Golden Moments of Religious Inspiration: A Treasury of Faith from the Christian Herald.*

The magazine is the most widely circulated nondenominational Protestant magazine in the U.S.

Christian Philosopher, The (1721), essays by COTTON MATHER. In this early attempt to reconcile science and religion, Mather wrote: "The essays now before us will demonstrate that [natural] philosophy is no enemy, but a mighty and wondrous incentive to religion. . . . The works of the glorious God in the creation of the world are what I now propose to exhibit. . . . Glorious God, I give thanks to thee for the benefits and improvements of the sciences, granted by Thee unto these our later ages." Yet Herbert Schneider, in *History of American Philosophy* (1946), after pointing out that some Puritans "imagined" that "God himself is interested not so much in his own glory as in the happiness of his creatures," held that Mather's *Christian Philosopher* is "one of the earliest American exhibitions of this conceit, based on the argument from fitness and design in nature." Mather gives an outline of recent developments in science and concludes that God can interfere in man's affairs.

Christian Science Monitor, The, a daily newspaper published by the Christian Science Publishing Society. MARY BAKER EDDY instructed Archibald McLellan to direct the paper's first issue (1908) and assume its editorship. Since that time it has gradually increased its circulation and is now read in over a hundred countries. Its largest public is probably in the Midwest and Pacific regions in the United States.

Since its founding, the *Monitor* has maintained a primary purpose: to disseminate significant news. It led the fight against "Yellow Journalism" in the early part of this century. Since it is economically self-sufficient it is not bound by any political or financial ties. Its commitment to Christian Science occasionally dictates the selection of material (*e.g.,* liquor or cigarettes are never mentioned and death is referred to as "passing on"), but the reporting of news is usually accurate and complete.

Each issue contains a page titled "The Home Forum" which includes reproductions of famous paintings, literary excerpts and essays, poetry, and a religious article (usually in a foreign language).

Erwin Canham, an editor of the *Monitor*, has discussed the paper's history in *Commitment to Freedom* (1958).

Christie, Anna. See ANNA CHRISTIE.

Christmas, Joe, the protagonist of LIGHT IN AUGUST, by William Faulkner. The illegitimate child of Milly Hines and a man supposed to be Mexican, Joe is placed in an orphanage by his fanatically religious grandfather, who believes him to be part Negro. He is adopted by a strict Calvinist couple, who know nothing of his origins; although Joe himself occasionally claims that he is a "nigger." After wandering over the Southwest for several years, Joe arrives in Jefferson, Mississippi, where he has an affair with a white woman, kills her, and becomes the object of a manhunt.

Christmas Night in the Quarters (published in *Scribner's Monthly*, January, 1878), a poem by IRWIN RUSSELL. One of the earliest Negro dialect poems, Russell's production takes the form of an operetta presenting some vivid pictures of plantation life.

Christmas Story (published in *The New Yorker*, 1944; in book form, 1946), a short story by H. L. MENCKEN. It tells how a benevolent Baltimorean tries to see that for at least one year the turkey dinner furnished free to derelicts will not be accompanied by hymns, speeches, and exhortations. He fails, rather sensationally.

Christowe, Stoyan (b. Greece, Sept. 1, 1898—   ), newspaperman, memoirist, writer. As he relates in his autobiography, *My American Pilgrimage*, Christowe was born in Macedonia and came to the United States with his father early in the 20th century. Industrial conditions were bad, the boy lived in a community completely shut off from contact with other groups. From the beginning Christowe rebelled against this way of life. Even in days of greatest hardship he found life in America good. To see more of the country he became a section hand on the Great Northern Railroad, then laying tracks across Montana. When his father died Christowe went to Chicago to seek further education. He became an American citizen in 1924, then reporter for various newspapers including the *Chicago Daily News* and the North American Newspaper Alliance. He has written many fictional and nonfictional articles for magazines as well as several books about the Balkans and the United States: *Heroes and Assassins* (1935); *Mara* (1937); *This Is My Country* (1938); *The Lion of Yanina* (1941); *My American Pilgrimage* (1947).

Christus, A Mystery (1872, a single volume containing THE GOLDEN LEGEND, 1851; THE NEW ENGLAND TRAGEDIES, 1868; *The Divine Tragedy*, 1871), a trilogy of dramatic poems by HENRY WADSWORTH LONGFELLOW. The poet regarded *Christus* as his greatest work, but critics and posterity have failed to uphold his judgment.

Christy, Edwin P. (b. Philadelphia, 1815—d. 1862), actor, singer. Christy was the founder and leader of the famous troupe called Christy's Minstrels and is generally regarded today as the originator of "Negro minstrelsy." He was the first to seat his men, all in blackface, in a semicircle on the stage, with an "interlocutor" in the middle and comic "end men." He was so successful that in time all pseudo-Negro entertainers came to be known as "Christy Minstrels." When he retired in 1854, his successor, George Harrington, changed his name to George Christy. (See NEGRO MINSTRELS.)

Chronicle of the Conquest of Granada, A (1829; revised, 1850), a semifictional account of the winning of Granada from the Moors by WASHINGTON IRVING. Irving's sympathies are on the side of the civilized, intelligent Moors, as against the arrogant monkish zealots of the 15th century. The work was based on careful research carried on during Irving's residence in Spain,

but is presented in the form of tales (often humorous) based on an alleged writing of the mythical Fray Antonio Agapida. Irving himself considered the book to be one of his chief works, and Coleridge praised it warmly.

Chronicles of America, The. This invaluable series, begun in 1918, reached fifty volumes by 1924, was augmented in the early 1950's by six additional volumes. It was edited first by ALLEN JOHNSON, later by ALLAN NEVINS. The volumes are arranged under nine headings: "The Morning of America," "The Winning of Independence," "The Vision of the West," "The Storm of Secession," "The Intellectual Life," "The Epic of Commerce and Industry," "Reconstruction and World Politics," "The Era of World Power," and "Our Neighbors." Other books continued the history through the New Deal. The authors include some of the most eminent historians of the day.

Chubb, Thomas Caldecot (b. East Orange, N.J., Nov. 1, 1899—   ), poet, biographer, and a writer of graceful, melodious verse. His verse is collected in *The White God and Other Poems* (1920), *Ships and Lovers* (1933), *Cliff Pace and Other Poems* (1936), *A Time to Speak* (1943), and *Cornucopia* (1953). He has written biographies of Boccaccio (1930) and of the satirist Aretino (1940). Among his recent works are *The Byzantines* (1959) and *The Months of the Year*, translations of Italian poems (1960).

Church, Benjamin (b. Duxbury, Mass., Mar., 1639—d. Jan. 17, 1718), and **Church, Thomas** (b. 1673—d. 1748). The father took a leading part in King Philip's War (1675–76) and wrote *The History of King Philip's War*, published in 1865 in an edition prepared by Henry Martyn Dexter. J. B. Larned calls it "one of the most interesting and realistic narratives of Indian warfare which has come down to us." His son published *Entertaining Passages Relating to King Philip's War* (1716) from his father's notes.

Church, Benjamin III (b. Newport, R.I., Aug. 24, 1734—d. 1776?), physician, poet, pamphleteer. Grandson of Benjamin Church the Indian fighter, the later Church was a fifth columnist, pretending loyalty to the Revolutionary cause while serving British interests. It is said that he carried his literary duplicity even further, writing essays defending the patriots and preparing the Tory responses to his own arguments. In October, 1775, he was tried by court martial, found guilty, and imprisoned for a time. On parole, he was allowed to sail from Boston in May, 1776; his ship was apparently lost at sea. His verse closely imitates British models, as in *The Choice: A Poem After the Manner of Pomfret* (1802).

Churches Quarrel Espoused, The (1710), by JOHN WISE. The fearless pastor of the Second Church of Ipswich, Mass., replied in this work to *Questions and Proposals* (1705), put forth by INCREASE and COTTON MATHER. The Mathers had proposed a central organization of churches that would have put an end to the free activities of independent churches. Wise was held in high regard by the patriots preceding the Revolution, and his book was reprinted in 1772 and again in 1860.

Churchill, Winston (b. St. Louis, Mo., Nov. 10, 1871—d. March 12, 1947), novelist. Churchill was a graduate of Annapolis but never served in the navy. After writing a moderately successful novel, *The Celebrity* (1898), supposedly a satire on RICHARD HARDING DAVIS, he went on to bestsellerdom with RICHARD CARVEL (1899), a story of the American Revolution, and the novels that succeeded it. At first, Churchill composed mainly historical romances: THE CRISIS (1901), a vivid novel of the Civil War; THE CROSSING (1904), a romance of the settlement of the Inland Empire; CONISTON (1906), a study of a political boss in New Hampshire; MR. CREWE'S CAREER (1908), a story about state politics controlled by a railroad. Becoming interested in contemporary social conditions and in religion, he also wrote THE INSIDE OF THE CUP (1913), dealing with the relations of religion and modern society; *A Far Country* (1915), a story of a modern prodigal son; *The Dwelling Place of Light* (1917), in which the restless modern world is contrasted with eternal truths. In 1913 Churchill ran for governor of New Hampshire on the Progressive Party (Theodore Roosevelt) ticket. Among his last writings was *The Uncharted Way: The Psychology of the Gospel Doctrine* (1940).

Churchill built his stories on a solid substructure of fact and voluminous research. He rewrote *Richard Carvel* five times. Possibly his learning somewhat hampered the free flow of his imagination; Harold Williams says of him, "He is plainly not an easy or facile writer, and intellectual considerations weigh more heavily with him than the more unconscious aims of the artist." V. L. Parrington calls him "a conscientious middle-class romantic." Churchill himself admitted that his novels were mid-Victorian in tone. Charles C. Walcutt discusses *The Romantic Compromise in the Novels of Winston Churchill* (1951).

Chute, Marchette G[aylord] (b. Wayzata, Minn., 1909—   ), literary historian, biographer. Vivid local color enlivens all Miss Chute's biographies, so that even in *Geoffrey Chaucer of England* (1946), where relatively few facts are on record, the man comes alive and the whole is eminently readable. Other biographies by Miss Chute are *Shakespeare of London* (1951); *Ben Jonson of Westminster* (1953); a book for young readers, *The Wonderful Winter* (1954); *Stories from Shakespeare* (1956); *Two Gentle Men: The Lives of George Herbert and Robert Herrick* (1959); and *Jesus of Nazareth* (1961). Her earliest published work was a set of verses for children, *Rhymes About Ourselves* (1932). *The Search for God* (1941), and a sequel, *The End of the Search* (1947), are Bible studies that attempt to remain uninfluenced by later commentaries while absorbing the early meaning of the Scriptures.

Ciardi, John (b. Boston, June 24, 1916—   ), teacher, poet. John Ciardi was instruc-tor of English from 1940 to 1942 and in 1946 at the University of Kansas City; instructor at Harvard from 1946 to 1948; Briggs Copeland Assistant Professor from 1948 to 1953. After that some of his varied activities included being English Professor at Rutgers University, Director of the Bread Loaf Writers Conference, and Poetry Editor of the *Saturday Review*. His poetry is contemporary, filled with a genuine sense of humor, homely wit, and an abiding love of humanity. He was undoubtedly influenced by T. S. Eliot and Jules Laforgue, but not excessively. His earliest collection, *Homeward to America* (1940), contains many felicitous lyrics. Then came war service, followed by *Other Skies* (1947), in which the mood was deeper and more mature. The humor and felicity continued, however, as in his *Elegy Just in Case:*

> Here lie Ciardi's pearly bones
> In their ripe organic mess.
> Jungle blown, his chromosomes
> Breed to a new address.

Among his books: *From Time to Time* (1951); *Dante's Inferno* (1954, translation), in idiomatic English to recall Dante's use of the vernacular; *As If* (1955); *I Marry You* (1958); *How Does A Poem Mean* (1959); *39 Poems* (1959); *The Reason for the Pelican* (1959, children's poems); *In the Stoneworks* (1961); and *Dante's Purgatorio* (1961, a translation).

Cíbola, The Seven Cities of. The land of the Zuñis, who in the 16th century occupied seven pueblos in what is now western New Mexico. The Spaniards believed that these pueblos concealed fabulous wealth, supposedly collected by a kinsman of Montezuma who had fled from Mexico and established a kingdom of his own. There, the Spaniards said, ships from China came and landed their rich cargoes. On the plains nearby wandered huge herds of cattle, of deformed shape and frightening aspect—the white men later called them buffaloes. Gold and silver were so abundant that everyone used them for tableware. The Spanish explorer Cabeza de Vaca (1490?—1557) first started the legend. Then FRANCISCO VÁSQUEZ CORONADO (1510—1554) sought to verify the stories by sending a Franciscan friar, Fray Marcos, out to visit the region; he brought back a report of so many marvels that Coronado went to see for himself. The reality disgusted him, and he wrote to the viceroy in Mexico: "I can assure your honor that the friar told the truth in nothing that he reported."

Cimarron (1930) a novel by EDNA FERBER. It deals with the spectacular land rush of 1889 in Oklahoma, beginning when the country was still Indian Territory, continuing through the oil boom and thereafter. The book depicts the degeneration of Yancey Cravat, brilliant editor, lawyer, and wanderer, and the accompanying evolution of his wife Sabra into a practical and tenacious businesswoman, ultimately a congresswoman. Filmed in 1960.

Circuit Rider, The (1874), a novel by ED-

WARD EGGLESTON. Here Eggleston makes a study of the frontier and its crudities, at the same time describing the impact of Methodism on the frontier. (Eggleston was himself a Methodist minister.) Its hero is Morton Goodwin, a young Methodist preacher who suffers from a rejection in love but finally rescues himself through religion, becomes a circuit rider, and learns what joys and perils accompany preaching in the wilderness. Eggleston presents both sides, shows the contrast between the refined Methodism of the eastern cities and the nerve-racking ecstasies of the frontier. Other treatments of these frontier preachers include John L. Dyer's *The Snow-Shoe Itinerant* (1889), Corra Harris' *A Circuit Rider's Wife* (1910), and Sidney and Marjorie Greenbie's *Hoof-Beats to Heaven* (1955), a biography of PETER CARTWRIGHT.

Circular Staircase, The (1908), a mystery story by MARY ROBERTS RINEHART. Its publication established her reputation as a writer of crime stories which display a sense of humor as well as ingenuity. The story became a play called THE BAT, in which the plot (as altered by the author and Avery Hopwood) made the supposed official detective the criminal—a device that has become a favorite with detective-story writers.

circus, the. The circus plays a large part in American fiction, especially for boys. The circus has a chief role in that fine old-time juvenile, James Otis' *Toby Tyler, or, Ten Weeks with a Circus* (1881). COURTNEY RYLEY COOPER developed a passion for the circus, wrote *Memories of Buffalo Bill* (1920), *Under the Big Top* (1923), *Annie Oakley* (1927), and *Circus Day* (1931). Two good circus stories are JIM TULLY's *Circus Parade* (1927) and Walter D. Edmonds' *Chad Hanna* (1940); three circus plays are Margaret Mayo's *Polly of the Circus* (1907), Kenyon Nicholson's *The Barker* (1927), and Halstead Welles's *A Temporary Island* (1948). Other interesting books on the circus include Emmett Kelly's *My Life in Tatters and Smiles* (1954), Marian Murray's *Circus! from Rome to Ringling* (1956), and EDWARD HOAGLAND's *Cat Man* (1956).

Circus in the Attic, The (1948), a collection of two novelettes and twelve short stories by ROBERT PENN WARREN. The stories have rural and small-town settings, and were described by *Time* as having only "a notebook quality of careful, detailed observation"—not of finished fiction.

City Boy, The (1948), a novel by HERMAN WOUK. Herbie Bookbinder, an eleven-year-old who lives in the Bronx, spends a summer at camp and encounters many new experiences. The book is considered a particularly poignant evocation of a boy's mind.

City in the Sea, The (earliest version, 1831, in *Poems*, under the title *The Doomed City*; printed as *The City of Sin* in the *Southern Literary Messenger*, August, 1836; called *The City in the Sea* in *The Raven and Other Poems*, 1845), a poem by EDGAR ALLAN POE. It is one of his most melodious. Especially famous are the lines about the "marvelous shrine"

Whose wreathèd friezes intertwine
The viol, the violet, and the vine.

Gay Wilson Allen has noted that there is free stress in the opening lines, but as the poem progresses it becomes more regular in rhythm, partly as the result of the reiteration and alliteration. The powerful lines,

While from a proud tower in the town
Death looks gigantically down . . .

were echoed by Hart Crane in the section of THE BRIDGE [1] (1930) called "The Tunnel," a description of a subway ride under the East River from Manhattan to Brooklyn. There Crane has a vision of Poe, and he asks:

And did their riding eyes right through your side,
And did their eyes like unwashed platters ride?
And Death, aloft,—gigantically down
Probing through you—toward me, O evermore!

City Novel, The American (1954), an analysis by Blanche Housman Gelfant. Mrs. Gelfant traces the development of a definite literary subgenre from THEODORE DREISER to the writers of the 1943–53 decade. Among those examined are Thomas Wolfe, Sherwood Anderson, Edith Wharton, John Dos Passos, James T. Farrell, Nelson Algren, Betty Smith, Leonard Bishop, and Willard Motley. Writers like these have conceived that life in a city is a distinct form of living; in some of the novels she discusses, the city itself becomes a character—as in Dos Passos' writings. She finds that in recent years the stress has fallen increasingly on either violence or sentiment as factors in urban existence. Algren's THE MAN WITH THE GOLDEN ARM (1950) illustrates the former; Betty Smith's A TREE GROWS IN BROOKLYN (1943) the latter. Mrs. Gelfant supplies a useful bibliography.

City That Was, The (1906), a newspaper story by WILL IRWIN that was published in the New York *Sun* on the day following the great San Francisco earthquake (April 18, 1906). It narrated the epic of a city that had been blasted out of existence. Overnight it made Irwin a spectacular figure in the American newspaper world, and not long afterwards he was called to the managing editorship of *McClure's Magazine*.

Civil Disobedience (1849), an essay by HENRY DAVID THOREAU. This was a lecture, printed for the first time in Elizabeth Preston Peabody's *Aesthetic Papers*. Then called *Resistance to Civil Government*, it later took the present title when Thoreau included it in collections of his essays. It was written in 1848, as a commentary on his experiences and reflections during his night in jail in July, 1848. He had refused to pay his poll tax for six years, but was outspoken about the non-payment when the country was in the midst of the iniquitous Mexican War. The essay had far-reaching consequences, influencing Mahatma Gandhi in his doctrines of passive resistance. Thoreau was a student of Hindu philosophy; consequently, his doctrines were only returning home when they reached the Indian leader. The essay preaches doctrines of philosophical anarchism not very different from those set forth in William Godwin's *Political Justice* (1793) which had gained a wide hearing in the United States. Thoreau wrote, "I accept the motto,—'That government is best which governs least;' and I should like to see it acted up to more rapidly and systematically." He held, "We must be men first and subjects afterwards. . . . I was not born to be forced. I will breathe after my own fashion. . . . If a plant cannot live according to its nature, it dies; and so does a man." Having made his dramatic gesture, he paid his tax thereafter.

In the judgment of Arthur M. Schlesinger Jr., Thoreau, by his actions and his writings, set himself apart from the other transcendentalists. He holds that "of all the New England group who shunned political choice, Thoreau alone lived at a degree of moral tension which imposed responsibilities equivalent to those borne by men who sought to govern. The writings and life of Thoreau presented democracy with a profound moral challenge."

Civil War in literature, the. War between the North and South seemed imminent when South Carolina and other slaveholding states seceded from the Union shortly after the election of ABRAHAM LINCOLN to the Presidency in 1860. With the Confederate attack on the Federal arsenal at Fort Sumter, S.C., April 12, 1861, the Civil War began.

To the North, the primary objective of the war was the restoration of the Union; after 1862, freeing of the slaves became a secondary aim. Though the northern states had several advantages—superior numbers, a balanced economy, and naval supremacy—the secessionists were confident of victory. They doubted northern willingness to fight for preservation of the Union, and were confident that England and France, dependent on southern cotton, would recognize the independence of the Confederacy and give material aid as well. Lincoln maintained that the secessionists were merely rebels defying their government, but by proclaiming a blockade of southern ports and by banning trade with the seceded states he in fact recognized the existence of a state of war.

The Union rout at Bull Run (July 21, 1861) led Lincoln to name GEORGE B. McCLELLAN as commander in chief of the northern forces. Dismissed after the Seven Days' Battle (June 26–July 2, 1862), McClellan was reinstated and repulsed the Confederate troops under ROBERT E. LEE at Antietam, Maryland (Sept. 17, 1862), in what was the bloodiest day of the war. Though McClellan was again removed for failing to pursue the Southerners, the technical victory at Antietam enabled Lincoln to issue a preliminary Emancipation Proclamation (Sept. 22, 1862), which stated that the slaves would be freed if the South did not surrender before January 1, 1863, the date on which the final Proclamation was made.

Defeated at Vicksburg (July 4, 1863) after a long and costly campaign led by ULYSSES S. GRANT, and at Gettysburg (July 1–3, 1863) by George B. Meade, the Confederates found themselves surrounded on the west and north by Union soldiers and on the east and south by the Union navy. In March, 1864, Grant was made supreme commander of the Union forces and turned to an assault on Richmond, the Confederate capital. In May his successor in the western theater, WILLIAM T. SHERMAN, began his famous march through Georgia, while PHILIP SHERIDAN devastated the Shenandoah Valley. After a gallant defense, Lee was forced to evacuate Richmond (April 2, 1865), and was prevented by Sheridan's forces from escaping with his battered army. On April 9, 1865, Lee surrendered to Grant at Appomattox, Virginia.

With the possible exception of the Napoleonic Wars, no other conflict has produced more books. It has been estimated that more than a hundred thousand volumes have been written on the Civil War. CARL SANDBURG's *Lincoln* and Margaret Mitchell's GONE WITH THE WIND started the more recent flood. A Civil War Book Club was established in October, 1955.

Civil War writing falls under several headings:

1. *Oratory and polemics.* Never was formal oratory so noble and effective as in the decades preceding the attack on Fort Sumter. Webster, Clay, Calhoun, Hahne, Everett, Douglas, and Lincoln spoke well on the issues of slavery, states' rights, and compromise. The spirit of polemic was also carried into print. Most writers of the time contributed to the heated discussion of the problems that led to the war. During the conflict itself Lincoln rose to the heights. His addresses, state papers, and letters are among the best examples of American prose.

2. *Biography, history, and memoirs.* The War Between the States produced memoirs in profusion. Grant, Sherman, Sheridan, and McClellan all published important recollections of the war. A prodigious literature has gathered around Lincoln, becoming year by year the largest devoted to any man in history. His apparent simplicity contrasted with the real complexities of his character has provoked commentator after commentator to write at length about him and his times. Carl Sandburg and Lord Charnwood are particularly memorable in this endeavor (See BIOGRAPHIES OF ABRAHAM LINCOLN). History, biography, poetry, drama, motion pictures, and radio and television plays have all contributed to the immortalization of Lincoln. Historians, notably JAMES FORD RHODES and James Garfield Randall, have written at great length about the war. The atmosphere of the capital city is vividly conveyed in MARGARET LEECH's Pulitzer Prize book, *Reveille in Washington, 1860–65* (1941). Another Pulitzer Prize winner is DOUGLAS S. FREEMAN's *Robert E. Lee* (4 v., 1942–44). Other significant books include: Kenneth P. Williams, *Lincoln Finds a General* (1952); ALLAN NEVINS, *Statesmanship of the Civil War* (1953); CLIFFORD DOWDEY, *The Land They Fought For* (1955); FLETCHER PRATT, *Civil War in Pictures* (1955); Ned Bradford,

Battles and Leaders of the Civil War (1956); JEFFERSON DAVIS, *The Rise and Fall of the Confederate Government* (1958); Earl Schenck Miers, *The Great Rebellion: the Emergence of the American Conscience* (1958); Richard Ernest Dupuy, *The Compact History of the Civil War* (1960); Otto Eisenschiml, *The Hidden Face of the Civil War* (1961); Archer Jones, *Confederate Strategy from Shiloh to Vicksburg* (1961); and Edwin Charles Rozwenc, *The Causes of the American Civil War* (1961). BRUCE CATTON has become a leading authority on the Civil War with such books as *Mr. Lincoln's Army* (1951); *Glory Road* (1952); *A Stillness at Appomattox* (1953); and *This Hallowed Ground* (1956). In the area of biography two recent works are of considerable use: John F. C. Fuller's *Grant and Lee: a Study in Personality and Generalship* (1957) and Ezra J. Warner's *Generals in Gray: Lives of the Confederate Commanders* (1959). Particularly valuable as an anthology is HENRY S. COMMAGER's *The Blue and the Gray* (1950).

3. *Poetry*. Events of the Civil War provided occasional poets on both sides of the conflict with much material. The history of John Brown's raids gave rise to: E. C. Stedman's "How Old Brown Took Harper's Ferry"; Henry Howard Brownell's "The Battle of Charleston"; John Greenleaf Whittier's "Brown of Osawatomie"; and in the 20th century, to Stephen Vincent Benét's epic poem, JOHN BROWN'S BODY [2]. Bayard Taylor, A. J. H. Duganne, Thomas William Parsons, T. B. Read, and Thomas Dunn English treated such topics as the battle of the *Merrimac* and the *Cumberland*, Emancipation, and Sherman's March to the Sea. Of course, Lincoln's death stimulated the greatest poetical reaction of the era. R. H. Stoddard's "Abraham Lincoln"; James Russell Lowell's "Ode Recited at the Harvard Commemoration"; and Walt Whitman's "When Lilacs Last in the Dooryard Bloom'd" and "O Captain! My Captain!" all mourn the great leader. Edwin Markham later eulogized Lincoln in "Lincoln, the Man of the People." Any list of Civil War poems should also include William Cullen Bryant's "The Past" and "The Death of Slavery"; Lowell's "The Biglow Papers"; Whittier's "Ichabod" and "Barbara Frietchie"; and Oliver Wendell Holmes' "Brother Jonathan's Lament for Sister Caroline."

Poets who published books of their own Civil War poems include: HENRY HOWARD BROWNELL, *Lyrics of a Day* (1864) and *War Lyrics* (1866); George Henry Baker, *Poems of the War* (1864); Walt Whitman, DRUM TAPS (1865); and Herman Melville, BATTLE-PIECES AND ASPECTS OF THE WAR (1866). From the South came the work of Henry Timrod, PAUL HAMILTON HAYNE, and ABRAM JOSEPH RYAN. Two songs rallied the North and South respectively: Julia Ward Howe's "Battle Hymn of the Republic" and Dan Emmett's "Dixie."

Collections were made, North and South, of some of the poems connected with the war. They include: Frank Moore, ed., *Rebel Rhymes and Rhapsodies* (1864); Richard Grant White, ed.,

Poetry, Lyrical, Narrative, and Satirical of the Civil War (1866), WILLIAM GILMORE SIMMS, ed., *War Poetry of the South* (1866); William Gordon McCabe, ed., *Ballads of Battles and Bravery* (1879); Francis F. Browne, ed., *Bugle Echoes, Northern and Southern* (1886); H. M. Wharton, ed., *War Songs and Poems of the Southern Confederacy* (1904). A recent anthology is *A Civil War Treasury of Tales, Legends, and Folklore* (1960).

4. *Fiction*. More novelists have written about the Civil War than any other single national event. Mainly, they have depended on such staple themes as the struggle between brothers, the personality of Lincoln, the maturation of young men at war, and the nostalgic dream of the antebellum South. Among the earliest novels concerned with the war were Henry Morford, *Shoulder Straps* (1863), *The Coward* (1863), and *In the Days of Shoddy* (1864); John Esten Cooke, *Surry of Eagle's Nest* (1866); Jeremiah Clemens, *Tobias Wilson: A Tale of the Great Rebellion* (1867); Sidney Lanier, TIGER LILIES (1867); John W. De Forest, MISS RAVENEL'S CONVERSION (1867); Edward P. Roe, *His Sombre Rivals* (1883); S. Weir Mitchell, *Roger Blake* (1886); and Thomas Nelson Page, TWO LITTLE CONFEDERATES (1888) and RED ROCK (1898). Edward Eggleston, in THE GRAYSONS (1888), was one of the first to introduce Lincoln as a character in a fictional work. The most faithfully remembered and intensely studied book of the war is Stephen Crane's fine psychological study, THE RED BADGE OF COURAGE (1895). It marked the turning point toward realism in American fiction. Other noteworthy novels on diverse aspects of the war are: Irving Bacheller, EBEN HOLDEN (1900); Winston Churchill, THE CRISIS (1901); Ellen Glasgow, *The Battleground* (1902); Mary Raymond Shipman Andrews, THE PERFECT TRIBUTE (1906); Mary Johnston, THE LONG ROLL (1911) and *Cease Firing* (1912); Upton Sinclair, *Manassas, A Novel of the War* (1923); and James Boyd, MARCHING ON (1927).

With the 1930's came a change in Civil War fiction. It became increasingly serious and attempted to throw light on present-day parallels. The analogies were tailor-made. The problems of southern reconstruction paralleled those of the Great Depression; Lincoln became a symbol of the strong, honest leader that the country so desperately needed; and the plight of the plantation slave made an ironic juxtaposition with the continuing problems of the 20th-century Negro in America. In the South historical authenticity was carefully maintained, but realistic substance was often beclouded by a romantic loyalty to a lost cause. Among the important novels of this period are: Joseph Hergesheimer, *The Limestone Tree* (1931); John Peale Bishop, *Many Thousands Gone* (1931); DuBose Heyward, *Peter Ashley* (1932); Stark Young, *So Red the Rose* (1934); MacKinlay Kantor, *Long Remember* (1934), *Arouse and Beware* (1936), and ANDERSONVILLE (1955); Margaret Mitchell, *Gone with the Wind* (1936); Caroline Gordon,

None Shall Look Back (1937); Edgar Lee Masters, *The Tide of Time* (1937); Hervey Allen, *Action at Aquila* (1938); William James Blech, *The Copperheads* (1941); Louis Bromfield, *Wild Is the River* (1941); James Street, *Tap Roots* (1942); Joseph S. Pennell, THE HISTORY OF ROME HANKS (1944); Ben Ames Williams, HOUSE DIVIDED (1947) and *The Unconquered* (1953); ROSS LOCKRIDGE, *Raintree County* (1948); Bruce Lancaster, *No Bugles Tonight* (1948) and *Roll Shenandoah* (1956); Jere Wheelright, *The Gray Captain* (1954); Ambrose Bierce, *Ambrose Bierce's Civil War* (1956); John Brick, *Jubilee* (1956); Harold Sinclair, *The Horse Soldiers* (1956); Upton Sinclair, *Theirs Be the Guilt* (1959); and Henry Allen, *Journey to Shiloh* (1960).

Rebecca W. Smith covered part of the fictional output in *The Civil War and Its Aftermath in American Fiction, 1861–99* (1932). Robert A. Lively wrote *Fiction Fights the Civil War* (1956), a survey of over five hundred Civil War novels with an extensive bibliography.

5. *Drama.* Both fiction and drama of the Civil War began their course with the publication of Harriet Beecher Stowe's UNCLE TOM'S CABIN (1852) and its prompt dramatization nearly eight years before the outbreak of war. But the speed with which the theater made use of contemporary materials during the war was extraordinary. As early as Jan. 16, 1861, an anonymous play, *Our Union Saved*, was produced in New York. The following month George H. Miles inserted a patriotic tableau into a spectacle called *The Seven Sisters,* and drew audiences for 177 nights. Bull Run was fought on July 21, 1861, and on August 15 *Bull Run*, a play by Charles Gayler, was on the boards. Occurrences such as this were numerous, but the plays so hastily put together have little artistic value. In the 1870's Dion Boucicault dominated the theatrical scene. Although several of his plays and adaptations are concerned with the South, only one—*Belle Lamar* (1874)—is directly concerned with the Civil War. J. Culver wrote an action-packed melodrama, *Loyal Mountaineers: or The Guerrilla's Doom* (1889) after Cyrenus Osborne Ward had earlier offered the ambitious five-act play *The Great Rebellion: Reminiscences of the Struggle that Cost a Million Lives* (1881). More recent dramas dealing with the Civil War are Sinclair Lewis, *Jayhawker* (1935); MacKinlay Kantor, *Andersonville* (1955); Paul Green, *Wilderness Road* (1956); and Robert D. Hock, *Borak* (1961).

Clapp, Margaret Antoinette (b. East Orange, N.J., April 11, 1910—   ), educator, author. In 1947, Miss Clapp's biography, *Forgotten First Citizen: John Bigelow* was awarded the Pulitzer Prize for biography. BIGELOW (1817–1911) was a New York author, journalist, politician, and diplomat. The book was praised for its scholarly account of the life of a neglected figure in American history and for its copious background on life and politics in New York around the turn of the century. In 1949, after a distinguished career as a teacher, Miss Clapp became president of Wellesley College.

Clare, Ada. See MCELHENEY, JANE.

Clarel (1876), a long poem by HERMAN MELVILLE. Set in and around Jerusalem and based on Melville's own trip to the Holy Land in the late 1850's, *Clarel* is both a guided tour to sacred spots and a symposium on the major philosophical problems of the day. The central figure of the poem, the questor, is Clarel, a young and relatively innocent theological student who is oscillating between faith and doubt. In Jerusalem he falls in love with Ruth, a young Jewish girl, and leaves her to join a heterogeneous group of pilgrims journeying from Jerusalem to Gethsemane, to the Dead Sea, to Bethlehem, and back to Jerusalem. The pilgrims talk constantly, and most of the talk is directed to Clarel, a willing listener. Taken collectively, the pilgrims represent virtually every religious and social persuasion possible: Nehemiah, a saintly old man who knows the time of the Second Coming but not the time of day; Vine, the seclusive aesthete, who resembles Melville's old friend NATHANIEL HAWTHORNE; Derwent, an Emersonian apostle of an optimistic Christianity; Mortmain and Ungar, bitter and cynical pessimists; Margoth, a geologist and materialist, who is held in general contempt; the Dominican friar who defends Roman Catholicism; and others in profusion—prodigals, revolutionaries, Arabian guides, monks—the full panorama of desert society. Ruth dies just as Clarel returns to Jerusalem, and at the end of the poem Clarel is alone to face a new reality with a new wisdom.

Clarel is not a poem of sentiment but a poem of ideas, and the final question it raises is broadly cultural: Is Western civilization, having lost its traditional faith through the incursions of science, doomed to an ultimate sterility? Technically, the poem suffers from constant inversions, ellipses, lack of action and narrative flow; at best, however, it is a masterly presentation of place in verse full of a hard intellectual resonance.

Clarion, The (1914), a novel by SAMUEL HOPKINS ADAMS. An attack on quackery and dishonest journalism, the novel relates the story of Hal Surtaine, a young man of high principles who purchases a newspaper with money his father has made from a patent medicine concern; Hal must decide whether or not to publish the truth about the concoction to which he owes his fortune.

Clark, Barrett H[arper] (b. Toronto, Ont., Aug. 26, 1890—d. Aug. 5, 1953), literary historian, drama critic, and editor. Early in his career, Clark became a prominent authority on the drama. He edited many collections of plays, translated dramas from the French, wrote a biography of Eugene O'Neill (1926, 1947), served as a play reader for Samuel French, became director of the Dramatists' Play Service, lectured, was drama editor of *Drama Magazine*. He performed an important service in recovering what he called "AMERICA'S LOST PLAYS" and editing them for students today (beginning in 1940). Among his anthologies are *One-Act*

Plays (1929) and *Favorite American Plays of the 19th Century* (1943). Other books: *A Study of the Modern Drama* (1925); *Oedipus or Pollyanna* (1927); *An Hour of American Drama* (1930); *Intimate Portraits* (1951).

Clark, Charles Badger (b. Albia, Iowa, Jan. 1, 1883—   ), poet. Clark has specialized in cowboy life and western lore. One of his poems, THE GLORY TRAIL (in his collection *Sun and Saddle Leather*, 1915), is frequently sung by cowboys under the title *High Chin Bob*. His poems are also collected in *Grass-Grown Trails* (1917) and *Sky Lines and Wood Smoke* (1935). *Spike* (1923) is a collection of short stories.

Clark, Charles Heber ["Max Adeler"] (b. Berlin, Md., July 11, 1847—d. Aug. 10, 1915), newspaperman, humorist. Heber was a humorist who later in his life winced at the reputation he had made. As Max Adeler he had indulged in wild, fantastic humor, particularly in a book of suburbanite sketches called OUT OF THE HURLY-BURLY, OR LIFE IN AN ODD CORNER (1874), very popular in its day. His high-tariff views led him to the editorship of trade magazines and into the company of financiers.

Clark, Eleanor [Mrs. Eleanor C. Warren] (b. Los Angeles, Calif., July 6, 1913—   ), novelist, essayist. Miss Clark attended Vassar College. Her first novel, *The Bitter Box* (1946), was well received. *Rome and a Villa* (1952) is a series of impressionistic essays on the Eternal City. Other books by Miss Clark include: *The Song of Roland* (1960), and a translation of Ramón Sender's *Dark Wedding* (1945). In 1952 she married ROBERT PENN WARREN.

Clark, George Rogers (b. near Charlottesville, Va., Nov. 19, 1752—d. Feb. 13, 1818), surveyor, Indian fighter, soldier. Clark's observations in the wilderness of the "Old Northwest" led him to conclude that the British were instigating the Indian raids that harassed American settlers in Kentucky. He obtained authority from Patrick Henry, governor of Virginia, to raise a force for the conquest of the Northwest. With only 150 riflemen, he took town after town as far as the Mississippi, and although the British recaptured Vincennes, the chief posts were all in the hands of Clark at the time of the Revolution. This fact resulted in the cession of the region to the United States. Clark's story is told by himself in M. M. Quaife's novel *The Capture of Old Vincennes* (1927); John Bakeless' *Background to Glory* (1956) is a biography of Clark. He and his Rangers appear in much fiction, including R. M. Bird's *Nick of the Woods* (1837); Daniel Pierce Thompson's *The Rangers* (1851); Maurice Thompson's ALICE OF OLD VINCENNES (1900); Winston Churchill's THE CROSSING (1904); Louis Zara's THIS LAND OF OURS (1940); Harold Sinclair's *Westward the Tide* (1940). Clark's brother WILLIAM participated in the Lewis and Clark Expedition.

Clark, Lewis Gaylord (b. Otisco, N.Y., Oct. 5, 1808—d. Nov. 3, 1873) and **Clark, Willis Gaylord** (his twin brother, d. June 12, 1841), editors, humorists. The Clarks together edited the KNICKERBOCKER MAGAZINE and made it the leading periodical of the antebellum period. Both had a gift for humorous and fanciful writing; Willis in addition wrote religious verse, which was praised by Poe. His death from tuberculosis cut short a promising literary career. He published a volume of verse, *The Spirit of Life* (1833), and his brother edited his *Literary Remains* (1844). Lewis Clark also wrote a volume of memoirs, *Knick-Knacks from an Editor's Table* (1852). See KNICKERBOCKER SCHOOL.

Clark, Walter van Tilburg (b. East Orland, Me., Aug. 3, 1909—   ), teacher, poet, short-story writer, novelist. Clark first wrote verse, then short stories; he was represented in O. Henry Prize Memorial collections for several years in succession. The novel, THE OX-BOW INCIDENT (1940), was made into an unusually powerful and thoughtful movie in 1942 by Lamar Trotti. *The City of Trembling Leaves* (1945) Clark described as "a token biography of Reno, a city of adolescence." *The Track of the Cat* (1949) features a sinister and symbolic black panther. It was produced as a movie in 1954. *The Watchful Gods* (1950) is a collection of short stories. In 1945 Clark won the O. Henry Short Story Award for *The Wind and the Snow of Winter*. He is a frequent contributor to the *Yale Review*, the *New Yorker*, *Atlantic Monthly*, and others; was made a Fellow of Wesleyan University Center for Advanced Studies, 1960–61; and teaches Creative Writing at San Francisco State College.

Clark, William (b. Caroline Co., Va., Aug. 1, 1770—d. Sept. 1, 1838), soldier, explorer. Like his brother, GEORGE ROGERS CLARK, William penetrated the wilderness in action against the Indians. He was invited in 1803 by his friend Captain MERIWETHER LEWIS to join him in an expedition sponsored by Jefferson: the purpose was to find a route to the Pacific Ocean. This resulted in the epoch-making Lewis and Clark Expedition (1804–06). Clark was made governor of the Missouri Territory, remained so until 1821, then became Superintendent of Indian Affairs for the rest of his life. His and Lewis' diary appeared in 1814.

Clarke, George Herbert (b. England, 1873—d. Mar. 27, 1953), Canadian poet. Clarke came to Canada as a boy, taught in U.S. colleges for a while (he edited THE SEWANEE REVIEW at the University of the South, 1920–25), was head of the Department of English in Queen's University, 1925–1943. In that year he was awarded the Lorne Pierce Medal of the Royal Society of Canada for distinction in Canadian literature. Three collections of his verses appeared, *At the Shrine and Other Poems* (1914), *The Hasting Day* (1930), and *Parley and Other Poems* (1934). He wrote numerous patriotic odes, and described natural backgrounds with skill and insight.

Clarke, James Freeman (b. Hanover, N.H., April 4, 1810—d. June 8, 1888), preacher, editor, biographer, historian. A graduate of Harvard Divinity School, Clarke joined a number of other Harvard men in a movement to the

West. In 1835 they established a Unitarian magazine, WESTERN MESSENGER, in Cincinnati, of which Clarke was an editor until 1839. In 1841 he returned to Boston to establish the Church of the Disciples, and became a militant leader in the TRANSCENDENTALIST movement. He published numerous books, among them *Ten Great Religions* (two parts, 1871, 1883); *Memorial and Biographical Sketches* (1878); *Self-Culture* (1880); *Autobiography* (1891). In a collection called *The Disciples' Hymn Book* (1844) he included some original pieces of his own. A. S. Bolster, Jr., wrote *James Freeman Clarke: Disciple to Advancing Truth* (1954). He was an apostle of German culture in the United States, and John Wesley Thomas wrote a book (1949) on that aspect of his career.

Clarke, John (b. England, 1609–d. 1676), clergyman. A Baptist, Clarke along with Obadiah Holmes and John Crandall came from Newport, R.I., to Lynn, Mass., in 1651 and there raised publicly certain theological questions that infuriated the other ministers and their followers; in addition they kept their hats on in the meetinghouse until these were removed from their heads by force. The three men were tried and fined. Clarke eventually returned to Rhode Island, where he had been one of the founders of Newport, serving as both physician and minister. He wrote *Ill News from New England* (1652), an attack on the intolerance of the Massachusetts ministers.

Clarke, MacDonald (b. Bath, Me., June 18, 1798–d. March 5, 1842), poet. A member of the bohemian set of his day, Clarke was called "the mad poet of Broadway" and actually died in the asylum for the insane on Blackwell's Island, New York City. In his own lifetime a collection was published called *Elixir of Moonshine by the Mad Poet* (1822); his *Poems* were collected in 1836. In an *Epigram* he wrote:

Tis vain for present fame to wish—
Our persons first must be forgotten;
For poets are like stinking fish—
They never shine until they're rotten.

classical influence. See GREEK AND ROMAN INFLUENCE.

Clavers, Mary. Pen name of CAROLINE KIRKLAND.

Clay, Bertha M. [pen name of an English novelist, Charlotte Monica Braeme] (1836–1884). The name was appropriated by some American publishers for imitative tales of the sentimental-melodramatic kind that Miss Braeme wrote. Among writers believed to have employed this pseudonym were JOHN R. CORYELL, THOMAS CHALMERS HARBAUGH, and Frederick Van Rensselaer Dey.

Clay, Henry (b. Hanover Co., Va., April 12, 1777–d. June 29, 1852), statesman, orator. Often called "The Great Pacificator," Clay is one of the most likable and fascinating figures in American history. He was almost constantly in public service. He became a member of the

Virginia state legislature in 1803, reached the United States Senate in 1806, was Speaker of the House or Senator almost continuously during his later lifetime, served as John Quincy Adams' secretary of state. He was a perpetual candidate for the Presidency, but knowingly jeopardized his chances several times by voting for measures unpopular in the North (he said in a speech in 1850, "I would rather be right than President"). He was undoubtedly sincere, even though he changed his opinions frequently and shifted from ardent Jeffersonianism in his youth to an equally ardent Hamiltonianism in his later years. He was not a man of great intellect, but he served the country well in his absolute devotion to the unity of the nation. He did everything possible, along with his great colleagues Webster and Calhoun, to prevent a split that would lead to war; and his name is closely connected with the COMPROMISE OF 1850.

Clay lives but dimly in literature. He was preeminently a speaker, not a thinker. The substance is thin, and Clay cannot justly be compared with Webster and Calhoun. "But," says A. C. McLaughlin, "if Clay's words do not now move us deeply, they did move and captivate the men to whom he spoke, and that is the aim of oratory." He is believed to have been the model for the satiric portrait of a politician in J. K. Paulding's novel, KONINGSMARKE (1823). He appears in Mary Dillon's romance, *The Patience of John Morland* (1909), and in Alfred Leland Crabb's *Home to Kentucky* (1953).

Cleghorn, Sarah N[orthcliffe] (b. Norfolk, Va., Feb. 4, 1876—d. April 4, 1959), poet, novelist. Miss Cleghorn, a New England individualist by ancestry, residence (Arlington, Vt.), and inclination, was devoted to social causes not always popular with editors. She arranged her poems in three groups: "sunbonnet poems" about New England; mystical poems; and "burning poems" on social subjects. She wrote one famous quatrain, a fierce protest against child labor:

The golf links lie so near the mill
That almost every day
The laboring children can look out
And see the men at play.

Her poems were collected in *Portraits and Protests* (1917). She wrote her autobiography in *Threescore* (1936) and published two novels, *The Turnpike Lady* (1907) and *The Spinster* (1916).

Clemens, Cyril (b. St. Louis, Mo., July 14, 1902—   ), biographer, historian. A kinsman of Mark Twain, Clemens wrote several books about him, also wrote books dealing with Josh Billings, "Petroleum" V. Nasby, Lytton Strachey, Dan Beard, and President Harry Truman. In 1936 he began editing *The Mark Twain Quarterly*. He founded the Mark Twain Association and the *Mark Twain Journal* (1936).

Clemens, Jeremiah (b. Huntsville, Ala., Dec. 28, 1814—d. May 21, 1865), lawyer, soldier, statesman, novelist. Clemens had a distinguished political career in Alabama and was elected to the Senate in 1849. But his support of Fillmore for President alienated his constituents, and he retired from political activity to write novels. *The Rivals* (1860), a story of Burr and Hamilton, was his best effort.

Clemens, Samuel Langhorne. See MARK TWAIN.

Clements, Colin [Campbell] (b. Omaha, Neb,. Feb. 25, 1894—d. Jan. 29, 1948), playwright, novelist. Clements often wrote in collaboration with his wife, Florence Ryerson. They worked together on many plays, stories for children, and mystery novels. Much of the actual writing was done by Miss Ryerson after a complete discussion of plot, characters, and dialogue. Their most popular play was *Harriet* (1943), starring Helen Hayes in the role of Harriet Beecher Stowe. Another was *Strange Bedfellows* (1948), a drama of woman suffrage.

Clemm, Virginia (b. Aug. 15, 1822—d. Jan. 30, 1847), EDGAR ALLAN POE's "child wife," whose tragic death from consumption inspired ANNABEL LEE (1849). He married her on May 16, 1836; the marriage bond certified falsely that she was "of the full age of 21 years." Rumors of an earlier marriage are not accepted today by the best Poe authorities. In 1846 a visitor described her "unearthly look." Sarah Helen Whitman spoke of her as "always animated and vivacious" and paid tribute to Poe's unfaltering devotion to his wife. In ULALUME (1847), according to Quinn, Poe "depicts a struggle in the mind of a man between the human passion for one woman and the spiritual love he still cherished for the memory of his 'lost Ulalume.' "

Cleveland, [Stephen] Grover (b. Caldwell, N.J., March 18, 1837—d. June 24, 1908), the twenty-second President of the United States. Cleveland practiced law until 1870, was elected sheriff of Erie County, mayor of Buffalo, and governor of New York. In 1884 he ran for President on the Democratic ticket against JAMES G. BLAINE and won by a comfortable majority. During his administration a Presidential Succession act was passed, an anarchist riot took place in HAYMARKET SQUARE in Chicago, and the Interstate Commerce Act was passed. In the second year of his administration Cleveland married Frances Folsom in the first Presidential wedding held in the White House. In the 1888 election he was defeated by BENJAMIN HARRISON, but in 1892 he ran against Harrison again, defeating him by a large majority and thus succeeding his successor. During his second term he faced crucial difficulties, national and international. An economic panic took place in 1893 which he mitigated in part by securing the repeal of the Silver Purchase Act passed in Harrison's administration.

Cleveland was probably the best example and the most sincere preacher of rugged individualism who ever occupied the White House. Allan Nevins called his 1933 Pulitzer Prize biography of Cleveland "a study in courage," and said of

him that he was "John Bunyan's Valiant-for-Truth transferred to the 19th century." Cleveland's *Writings and Speeches* were collected in 1892, his *Letters* in 1933.

Cliff Dwellers, The (1893), a novel by HENRY B. FULLER. Fuller, a pioneer in the depiction of life in the overgrown and monstrous cities of today, perhaps originated the term "cliff dwellers" to describe the denizens of huge urban apartment houses and skyscrapers. In his story a Chicago skyscraper is the central locale of the book, and he satirically depicts the effects of wealth and of the quest for wealth on a large number of characters.

Clinton, De Witt (b. Little Britain, N.Y., March 2, 1769—d. Feb. 11, 1828), statesman. Clinton, a nephew of GEORGE CLINTON, was at various times in his career an assemblyman, a member of the New York Senate, a United States Senator, mayor of New York City, and governor of New York State at the time the Erie Canal was constructed (opened Oct. 26, 1825). He was a progressive administrator, and while he was canal commissioner was the Canal's chief supporter. Fitz-Greene Halleck, who thought Clinton pompous and long-winded, attacked him satirically in *Governor Clinton's Speech* (1827). Clinton's interest in fostering American literature was shown in a *Discourse* delivered in 1815 before the Literary and Philosophical Society of New York.

Clinton, George (b. Little Britain, N.Y., July 26, 1739—d. April 20, 1812), first governor of New York. In his opposition to the adoption of the Constitution he carried on a controversy with ALEXANDER HAMILTON in the columns of the New York *Journal*, where Clinton published seven letters under the pen name "Cato" with replies in the *Daily Advertiser* by Hamilton under the name "Caesar." Clinton became Vice-President in 1804, later unsuccessfully sought to be President. His *Public Papers* were gathered in ten volumes, 1889–1911.

Clinton, Sir Henry (b. 1738?–d. 1795), British commander during the Revolutionary War. He succeeded Howe in 1778, participated in the Battles of BUNKER(s) HILL, Long Island, and Monmouth, as well as the siege and capture of Charleston. He wrote an account of his experiences in a *Narrative* (1783).

clipper ships. A type of vessel developed about 1840–55 by American shipbuilders. Clippers dominated the seas until the Civil War because of their speed. They were full-rigged vessels, carrying a large sailing area on their tall, raking masts, and had fine, bold lines and an overhanging bow. They sailed to China, to Europe, and during the Gold Rush era to California, often maintaining an average speed of fifteen miles per hour. Three American women writers have published excellent stories of clipper ships: Agnes D. Hewes' *Glory of the Seas* (1933); Isabel Hopestill Carter's *Shipmates: A Tale of the Seafaring Women of New England* (1934); and Mary Ellen Chase's *Silas Crockett* (1935). S. E. Morison, in his collection of papers, *By Land and By Sea* (1953), includes an account of "The Clipper Ships of Massachusetts."

Clockmaker, or, The Sayings and Doings of Samuel Slick, of Slickville, The (in three series, 1837, 1838, 1840), humorous sketches by T. C. HALIBURTON. Slick is an itinerant Yankee clockmaker, slangy, ill-bred, energetic, shrewd —and funny. The Canadian humorist's account of Slick's adventures and remarks won wide popularity in Canada, the United States, and England, and exerted a great influence on the development of humor in the United States. The purpose of the book was less to satirize New Englanders than to hold them up to Nova Scotians (Haliburton was a judge in Nova Scotia) as models of quick-thinking and practical efficiency.

close-up. A literary term derived from photographic technique. In writing, it signifies a study of the subject's intimate details; it is, in effect, a synonym for *The New Yorker* type of profile. It is appropriately used by *Life* for articles accompanied by numerous photographs.

Clune, Henry W[illiam] (b. Rochester, N.Y., Feb. 8, 1890—   ), newspaperman, columnist. Clune worked for the Rochester *Democrat and Chronicle*, and later conducted a popular column, *Seen and Heard*. Clune has written two novels, *The Good Die Poor* (1937) and *The Big Fella* (1956), an amusing, candid book about his newspaper career, *Main Street Beat* (1947); and a fictional life of George Eastman, *By His Own Hand* (1952).

Clurman, Harold (b. New York City, Sept. 18, 1901—   ), critic, stage director, author. In more than thirty years in the theatre, Clurman directed over fifty plays. His *The Fervent Years* (1945) is the story of the Group Theatre. In the 1920's Clurman returned from France enthusiastic over Jacques Copeau's community theatre. He was joined by another young man, Lee Strasberg, who had become imbued with the theories of Stanislavsky. Together they founded the Group Theatre in the midst of the great depression. This famous experimental theatre developed the talents of CLIFFORD ODETS, WILLIAM SAROYAN, ELIA KAZAN, Robert Lewis, Franchot Tone, John Garfield, and Morris Carnovsky. Strasberg went on to fame as director of the controversial Actors Studio, Clurman to prominence as a Broadway director. A highly literate theater man who never lost his faith in the importance of social criticism in the drama, Clurman said this was his motto: "He knows no theater who only theater knows." He also wrote *Lies Like Truth* in 1959, a collection of theatre criticism.

Coal Dust on the Fiddle (1943), songs and stories of the bituminous coal industry, collected by George Korson. This is an expansion of an earlier volume by Korson, *Minstrels of the Mine Patch* (1938), which dealt with one section of Pennsylvania only. In the later collection Korson describes new surveys made in Ohio, Illinois, Indiana, West Virginia, Virginia, Kentucky, Ten-

nessee, and Alabama, also Nova Scotia. He has collected songs, ballads, stories, legends, folk remedies, sayings, and unwritten history; and his book pictures informally the social aspects of the bituminous industry.

Coates, Robert M[yron] (b. New Haven, Conn., April 6, 1897—   ), novelist, short-story writer, art critic. After World War I Coates began writing for the "LITTLE MAGAZINES," later turned to art criticism for *The New Yorker* and to the writing of short stories and novels. Coates' novel *The Eater of Darkness* was first published in 1929, and again in 1960. Coates followed this novel by: *Yesterday's Burdens* (1933); *The Bitter Season* (1933); *Wisteria Cottage* (1948), based on an actual murder case; *The Farther Shore* (1957), another study in criminal psychology. He collected his short stories in *All the Year Round* (1943); *The Further Shore* (1955); *The View from Here* (1960).

Coatsworth, Elizabeth [Jane] (b. Buffalo, N.Y., May 31, 1893—   ), poet, novelist, children's writer. An energetic traveler and long a resident in Massachusetts and in Maine, Miss Coatsworth has brought a variety of scenes into her writing. Her verses are collected in *Fox Footprints* (1923); *Compass Rose* (1929); *Country Poems* (1942); and *The Creaking Stair* (1949). Her setting in these is most frequently the farm or the sea. Her phrasing is felicitous and musical, her observation imaginative and accurate. She has written over forty books for children. *The Cat Who Went to Heaven* (1930) won the Newbery Award. Her novels were less successful, including *Here I Stay* (1938); *The Trunk* (1941); and *Silky* (1953). Two books about Maine, *Country Neighborhood* (1944), and *Maine Ways* (1947), won much praise. In 1958 she had three publications: *The White Room*, a novel; *Poems*, a collection; *The Cave*, a juvenile. *Pika and the Roses*, a juvenile, and *Peaceable Kingdom*, a collection of poems, came out in 1959.

Cobb, Irvin S[hrewsbury] (b. Paducah, Ky., June 23, 1876—d. March 10, 1944), humorist, writer, actor. Cobb was the descendant of a Vermont governor and of a Virginia governor; and although the southern drawl is present almost everywhere in his writings, there is now and then a sharp saying that has a Yankee twang. He was a representative of American humor at its most characteristic, a direct follower of BILL NYE, ARTEMUS WARD, and MARK TWAIN.

Reverses in family fortunes made it impossible for Cobb to continue his education and study law. He began working for the Paducah *News*, went on to the Cincinnati *Post*, the Louisville *Evening Post*, and the Paducah *Daily Democrat*. In 1904 he came to New York and landed on the *Evening Sun;* his reputation as a first-rate newspaperman was made almost immediately. For several years he was a rewrite man, a reporter, and a columnist for the *Evening World*. In 1911 he joined the staff of *The Saturday Evening Post*. His popularity as a writer also won him many engagements as a lecturer; he was one of the most agile and entertaining public speakers of the day. From 1922 to 1932 he wrote for the *Cosmopolitan*.

Cobb's first book, *Back Home* (1912), was followed by a long series of volumes, many of them collections of material which had appeared earlier in magazines. Most popular were the Judge Priest stories, laid in the southern background so familiar to Cobb: OLD JUDGE PRIEST (1915); *Judge Priest Turns Detective* (1937); and Cobb's first novel, *J. Poindexter, Colored* (1922), about the judge's servant Jeff. Other stories are collected in *The Escape of Mr. Trimm* (1913) and other volumes. One of his most popular pieces was *Speaking of Operations* (1916), an account of a personal experience. He wrote lively travel books, such as *Europe Revised* (1914), and many humorous skits. The total of Cobb's writing was immense. He wrote several dozen books, more than three hundred stories, and, according to his own estimate, "anywhere from two thousand to five thousand feature articles, and I don't know how much alleged humor." He estimated that as a newspaper reporter covering the Thaw trial, he transmitted 500,000 words in longhand from the courtroom.

In 1932, when the movies began to film the Judge Priest stories, Cobb settled in Hollywood as a script writer. He made his acting debut in 1934 as a river captain along with Will Rogers in the movie based on Burman's *Steamboat Round the Bend*, and played successfully in other pictures.

Cobb's autobiography, *Exit Laughing* (1941), is in his best style of kindly humor, with himself as a frequent victim. His daughter's life of him, *My Wayward Parent* (1945), reveals him as an endlessly energetic person, unconventional, careless, and lovable.

Cobb, Joseph B[eckham] (b. Lexington, Ga., April 11, 1819—d. Sept. 15, 1858), essayist, critic, novelist. Cobb wrote a romance, *The Creole* (1850), in which the pirate Lafitte appears; also sketches called *Mississippi Scenes* (1851). His essays, *Leisure Labors* (1858), contain frank criticisms of contemporary writers.

Cobb, Sylvanus, Jr. (b. Waterville, Me., June 5, 1821—d. July 20, 1887), novelist. Cobb was a favorite and voluminous storyteller for the New York weekly *Ledger*. Some of his tales were later printed in book form; among them *The Golden Eagle* (1850); *The Privateer of the Delaware* (1855); *The Patriot Cruiser* (1863); and THE GUNMAKER OF MOSCOW (1888). See THE NEW YORK LEDGER.

Coblentz, Stanton A[rthur] (b. San Francisco, Aug. 24, 1896—   ), reviewer, poet, editor. His verse maintains a high level of merit and often produces striking effects. Among his collections: *The Thinker and Other Poems* (1922); *The Lone Adventurer* (1927); *The Answer of the Ages* (1931); *The Merry Hunt and Other Poems* (1934); *The Pageant of Man* (1936); *Winds of Chaos* (1942); *An Editor Looks at Poetry* (1947); *Garnered Sheaves: Selected Poems* (1949). His prose works include *From Arrow to Atom Bomb* (1953); *The Long Road to Humanity* (1959); *The Swallowing Wilderness* (1961).

Cobwebs from an Empty Skull (1874), short and pointed fables published by AMBROSE BIERCE under the pseudonym "Dod Grile." Fred Lewis Pattee calls these satirical pieces "his most original and typical work."

Cockloft Hall. The name given by WASHINGTON IRVING in his SALMAGUNDI PAPERS (1807) to the Gouverneur Kemble mansion on the Passaic River in New Jersey. Irving and others came there frequently, and Irving pictures it as "a place as full of whims and oddities as its tenants."

Cocktail Party, The (1949, pub. 1950), a play in verse by T. S. ELIOT. This often witty and sometimes powerful play begins and ends at a cocktail party, the representative modern gathering. Its principal characters suffer from radical loneliness and a lack of self-knowledge. Through the mediation of an uninvited guest who is ostensibly a psychoanalyst, but partly a sort of mysterious father-confessor, three of them attain "salvation." A married couple achieve a modest degree of enlightenment which enables them to save their marriage; a young woman becomes a nursing sister and is martyred in Africa. The verse of the play is generally colloquial and unobtrusive, preserving the cadences and vocabulary of ordinary cultured speech, but has moments of intensity and eloquence.

Cody, William Frederick ["Buffalo Bill"] (b. Scott County, Iowa, Feb. 26, 1846—d. Jan. 10, 1917), scout, showman, folk hero. A man of limited formal education, Cody early acquired all the tricks of horsemanship and marksmanship. He became a gold prospector, a rider for the PONY EXPRESS, a hunter of horse thieves and hostile Indians, a member of Kansas guerrilla bands, a soldier in the Union army, and a hunter of bison. E. Z. C. Judson, who as "Ned Buntline" became the father of the dime novel, asserted that he gave Cody the name "Buffalo Bill," based on the hunter's skill in killing bison (Cody said he killed 4,861 of the animals in a single season). Judson wrote a series of novels about Cody's career, also produced a play, *The Scout of the Plains* (1872), in which Buffalo Bill appeared personally. After this, love of the limelight completely conquered the famous scout. In 1883 he organized a group of hunters and rough-riders who appeared at the Omaha fair grounds and made a great hit. Later, Cody found an astute manager, Nate Salsbury, who really created *Buffalo Bill's Wild West Show*, which toured for twenty years. In time they acquired for the show ANNIE OAKLEY, whose fame soon equaled Buffalo Bill's. A great success, the show went east and, finally, abroad. After the death of Salsbury, Cody's recklessness with money caused him to lose control of his show and end his life in poverty.

Being a hero became Cody's prime vocation. For almost fifty years, in more than a thousand novels, in melodramas, and in his own shows

Cody remained "the finest figure of a man that ever sat on a steed." Wyoming even named a town after him and keeps his birthday as a holiday. Colonel Prentiss Ingraham, who constituted himself Cody's official biographer, made him the hero of more than two hundred dime novels. More recently, Henry Blackman Sell and Victor Weybright prepared a striking pictorial biography of Cody, *Buffalo Bill and the Wild West* (1955). Cody himself is the author of *The Life of Hon. William F. Cody* (1879), *The Story of the Wild West and Campfire Chats* (1888), and *True Tales of the Plains* (1908).

Coe, Charles Francis (b. Buffalo, N.Y., Nov. 25, 1890—   ), lawyer, penologist, writer of articles on crime, novelist. An eminent lawyer, Coe has also gone into many other fields. His autobiography, *Never a Dull Moment* (1944), shows that he enjoyed experimenting with various ways of making a living—sometimes a not very fat living. He became acquainted with many kinds of people; he was particularly interested in prize fighters. Among his books: *Me . . . Gangster* (1927); *The River Pirate* (1927); *Hooch* (1928); *Show Down* (1940). He collaborated with Jack Dempsey on *In This Corner* (1935).

Coffin, Charles Carleton (b. Boscawen, N.H., July 26, 1823—d. March 2, 1896), civil engineer, writer, lecturer. Coffin began as a self-taught civil engineer and surveyor, went on to reporting the battles of the Civil War for a Boston paper. After the war he began writing vigorous, manly stories for boys that would help make them better citizens: *The Boys of '61* (1881; published originally as *Four Years of Fighting*, 1866); *The Boys of '76* (1876); *The Story of Liberty* (1879); *Life of Lincoln* (1892); and others. In his last years he lectured widely and often, served in the state legislature.

Coffin, Long Tom. A character in James Fenimore Cooper's sea story, THE PILOT (1823). Cooper knew the sea and sailors better than he did Indians, and Coffin may be regarded as an even better character study than Leatherstocking. Perhaps Long Tom may be called a Leatherstocking with a harpoon instead of a rifle, a peajacket instead of a hunting shirt. During the Revolutionary War he takes part in some daring actions in the course of which American vessels, under the guidance of the mysterious "Pilot," raid the British coast and do a little kidnaping as a way of stopping the annoying British habit of impressing sailors.

Coffin, Robert P[eter] Tristram (b. Brunswick, Me., March 18, 1892—d. Jan. 20, 1955), poet, teacher, essayist, editor. Coffin grew up on a Maine salt-water farm, went to a rural schoolhouse, then to Bowdoin, Princeton, and Oxford. He taught at Wells College, then at Bowdoin. He lectured all over the country on many topics, but chiefly on his own poetry; he made recordings of fifty of his poems for the Library of Congress. He managed, in the midst of all his other activities, to run two farms and frequently to make drawings for his books. His books of verse are: *Golden Falcon* (1929); *Ballads of*

Square-Toed Americans (1933); *Strange Holiness* (1936, Pulitzer Prize); *Saltwater Farm* (1937); *Maine Ballads* (1938); *Primer for America* (1943); *Poems for a Son with Wings* (1945); *People Are Like Ballads* (1946); *Col-*

The Macmillan Company

lected Poems (1948); *Selected Poems* (1955). In prose he wrote *The Kennebec* (in RIVERS OF AMERICA SERIES, 1937); *Book of Uncles* (1942); *Mainstays of Maine* (1944); *One-Horse Farm* (1949); *Coast Calendar* (1949); *Maine Doings* (1950).

If there had been such an office as "Poet Laureate of Maine," Coffin would have had no rival for the position. In his verse and prose he lovingly describes and praises his native state and his place of residence for the greater part of his life. Possibly because the United States contains Maine, Coffin shows himself very fond of America too. For instance, in *Primer for America* he talks about the country at large with magnificent directness, making universals out of such particulars as the invention of the telephone, Coffin's old grandmother, tall barns ("our American cathedrals"), New England piecrust, country doctors, Grand Banks fishermen, Civil War soldiers, grocery-store loiterers, the Wright brothers, baseball players. America, he says, "is promises—promises kept." Coffin's poetry is marked by freshness of detail, by a vigilant sensitivity, by a purposive irregularity of rhythm, and by a frank colloquialism. The results are often startlingly good. The same qualities appear in his prose. John Holmes feels that Coffin's poetry is "full of tang and muscular exertion, of pride in life and joy in mankind." William Lyon Phelps calls *Strange Holiness* "a revelation of simple and familiar sights and sounds."

Cohan, George M[ichael] (b. Providence, R.I., July 3, 1878 [changed by Cohan to July 4, for dramatic effect]—d. Nov. 5, 1942), actor, song writer, playwright, director, producer. One of the most beloved figures on the American stage, Cohan began acting while still a child, became a member of a theatrical troupe, "The Four Cohans," starring his parents, his sister Josephine, and himself. Before he was 21 Cohan had written 150 vaudeville sketches, most of them for other performers. His first legitimate stage production was *The Governor's Son* (1901), then came an expanded vaudeville sketch, *Running for Office* (1903). In 1904 he produced *Little Johnny Jones,* in which he played a role always thereafter associated with him, "the Yankee Doodle Boy." He wrote more than forty dramas and musical comedies, appearing in many of them himself; among them *Forty-Five Minutes from Broadway* (1906); GET-RICH-QUICK WALLINGFORD (1910); BROADWAY JONES (1912); SEVEN KEYS TO BALDPATE (1913); *The Miracle Man* (1914); *The Song and Dance Man* (1923); *Gambling* (1929). His OVER THERE became the theme song of World War I; for writing it he was awarded a Congressional Medal two decades later. *Give My Regards to Broadway* was similarly the theme song of New York's Great White Way, but in later years Cohan disliked and avoided Broadway. Among other songs of his that attained a wide popularity were *I'm a Yankee Doodle Dandy, Grand Old Flag,* and *Mary Is a Grand Old Name.* Billy Rose once wrote: "I can remember when almost everyone on Broadway walked and talked like its favorite song-and-dance man. They imitated his bantam-rooster strut, the funny way he cocked his head, his manner of cracking wise out of the side of his mouth." In 1937 Cohan came out of retirement to play Franklin D. Roosevelt in *I'd Rather be Right,* a satire by George S. Kaufman and Moss Hart.

Cohen, Morris R[aphael] (b. Russia, July 25, 1880—d. Jan. 29, 1947), philosopher, teacher. Cohen came to the United States at the age of twelve, graduated from the College of the City of New York and from Harvard, taught at the former institution from 1906 until 1942. He was widely known in the universities of the country, and his teachings exerted considerable influence. He was especially interested in the philosophy of law. Harold Laski once termed him "the most penetrating and creative United States philosopher since William James"; and it was also said that he had made a deep impression on the interpretation of law. Reviewing his *Faith of a Liberal* (1946), George N. Shuster concludes that Cohen was "one of the most astute, fearless, and helpful critics this country has ever had." Cohen also wrote *Reason and Nature* (1931); *Law and the Social Order* (1933); *Introduction to Logic and Scientific Method* (with E. Nagel, 1934); *Preface to Logic* (1944); *A Dreamer's Journey* (1949).

Cohen, Octavus Roy (b. Charleston, S.C., June 26, 1891—d. Jan. 6, 1959), newspaperman, short-story writer, novelist. Cohen wrote for various newspapers in the South, then for *The*

Saturday Evening Post and other magazines. His stories dealt with a group of Negroes in Birmingham, Ala., whose antics in love and gambling were humorously portrayed. Later he wrote mystery stories with much ingenuity of plot and action. Among his books: *Polished Ebony* (1919); *Highly Colored* (1921); *Assorted Chocolates* (1922); *Florian Slappey Goes Abroad* (1928); *Epic Peters, Pullman Porter* (1930); *Florian Slappey* (1938); *Kid Tinsel* (1941); *Dangerous Lady* (1946); *More Beautiful Than Murder* (1948); *Love Can Be Dangerous* (1955).

Cohn, David L. (b. Greenville, Miss., Sept. 20, 1897—d. Sept. 12, 1961), social historian, memoirist. Cohn went into business in New Orleans and New York, but writing lured him, and he found himself studying the past in a series of books written with an unusual mixture of learning and liveliness, as when he surveyed America as seen through fifty years of Sears-Roebuck mail-order catalogues. *Love in America* (1943), a bachelor's analysis of love and marriage, is as amusing as it is accurate; *Combustion on Wheels* (1944) provides a ride through history in automobiles; *This Is the Story* (1947) is an account of Cohn's experiences on an army inspection tour in Western Europe, the Mediterranean, and different parts of Asia. In 1935 Cohn published *God Shakes Creation,* a description of the Delta region of Mississippi in which he was born, and an analysis of race relations there. In 1948 it was reissued with additions as *Where I Was Born and Raised.* In 1956 he wrote *The Fabulous Democrats.*

Coit, Margaret L. (b. Norwich, Conn., May 30, 1922—   ), biographer, author. Miss Coit's first book, *John C. Calhoun: American Portrait* (1950), received praise from the press, and was awarded the Pulitzer Prize in 1951. It is closer to a living portrait of the man and his times than any other biography. Seven years later she published another biography of equal excellence, *Mr. Baruch: The Man, the Myth, the Eighty Years* (1957). Her writing is distinguished by a scholar's passion for accuracy and a sense of drama. The Baruch story combines biography with a chronicle of the social and the political events through which Mr. Baruch lived; a fortunate treatment, since his involvement in some of the events was a minor one, but the interest is sustained by the broader view of an American era of great vividness. The *Fight for Union* came out in 1961.

Colby, Frank M[oore] (b. Washington, D.C., Feb. 10, 1865—d. March 3, 1925), teacher, editor, essayist, humorist. A good deal of Colby's life was spent in the useful drudgery of editing the NEW INTERNATIONAL ENCYCLOPEDIA. By way of relief he wrote numerous essays and reviews in which he displayed a caustic common sense, clothed in emphatic epigrams. Some of these were collected in book form: *Imaginary Obligations* (1904); *Constrained Attitudes* (1910); *The Margin of Hesitation* (1921). He had a small but enthusiastic following, among whom was Clarence Day, Jr. After Colby's death Day edited *The Colby Essays* (1926). A decade or two later anthologists began to rediscover Colby, and he became a more customary inclusion in collections of humor than a great many better-known wits.

Colcord, Lincoln [Ross] (b. at sea off Cape Horn, Aug. 14, 1883—d. Nov. 16, 1947), nautical authority, poet, novelist. A descendant of five generations of seafarers, Colcord had his roots in Maine. He spent many months at sea, in between studies at the University of Maine. At first a civil engineer, Colcord soon began writing for newspapers and magazines. In 1936 he became secretary of the Penobscot Marine Museum, in 1941 was associate editor of *The American Neptune* (published at Salem, Mass.). His publications include *Vision of War* (1915), a book-length poem; *The Game of Life and Death* (1914), his best known book of fiction about the sea; and *An Instrument of the Gods* (1922), likewise fiction. In 1929 Colcord exposed a book of alleged sea experiences entitled *The Cradle of the Deep,* written by an actress who called herself Joan Lowell. The Book-of-the-Month Club had made the book its selection for the month; when Colcord showed it was merely romantic fiction, the club offered refunds on it. A year later, Miss Lowell published *Kicked Out of the Cradle.* His sister, Joanna Colcord (1882–1953), was a prominent social worker and author of *Songs of the American Sailormen* (1938) and *Sea Language Comes Ashore* (1945).

Colden, Cadwallader (b. Ireland, of Scots parentage, Feb. 7, 1688—d. Sept. 28, 1776), historian, physician, scientist. Colden, a man of many abilities, emigrated to America from Scotland in 1708 or 1710, and settled in Philadelphia, later in New York. He immediately attracted attention for his learning and was given many important official positions, becoming lieutenant-governor in 1761. He knew Franklin well and corresponded with Dr. Samuel Johnson and with the great Swedish botanist Linnaeus, whose system he introduced into American botany. He was an ardent loyalist, and as feeling against England increased he became unpopular; because he defended the Stamp Act he was burned in effigy. He was very much interested in the Indians, and produced a book, *The History of the Five Indian Nations of Canada* (1727; reprinted, 1866, 1902), which is still, says George Parker Winship, "a mine of facts, although the research of later times has rendered many of its statements unsatisfactory." His *Letters and Papers* were collected by the New York Historical Society (1918–37).

Coliseum, The (1833), a poem by EDGAR ALLAN POE. It was later incorporated in the text of his blank-verse drama *Politian,* published in part in the *Southern Literary Messenger* (1835–36).

College English. In 1928 Wilbur W. Hatfield, at that time owner, publisher, and editor of *The English Journal,* official organ of the National Council of Teachers of English, began publishing a *College Edition* of this magazine. It gradually assumed the proportions of a separate magazine. In October, 1939, it assumed its present name.

College Humor. A monthly founded in 1920 by a young editor, H. N. Swanson, later a film director and literary agent in Hollywood. At first the magazine merely reprinted jokes, verses, stories, and cartoons from the innumerable college humor periodicals all over the country. For a piece to be printed in *College Humor* was a mark of distinction and editors of other magazines carefully read the productions of these college writers in the hope of discovering new and fresh talent. Later, original material was printed in the magazine. One of its discoveries was KATHARINE BRUSH. The magazine ceased publication in 1943.

College Widow, The (1904), a comedy by GEORGE ADE. Ade managed to bring into this amusing and effective comedy all the conventionally humorous characters and traits of the college scene, in this case supposedly a midwestern educational institution. All the types, says A. H. Quinn, "were exaggerated, from the president down to the waiters. . . . There is some shrewd comment on modern athletics implicit in the conversation of the characters." The "college widow" of the play is the daughter of the president; she is asked to use her fascination to make a certain halfback play on the Atwater rather than the Bingham team; the third act presents a thrilling football game. The play, one of the earliest to deal humorously with college life, made a big hit. As in all his writings, Ade avoided smut and double meanings; one reviewer noticed that there wasn't a cocktail or barroom joke in the play. It made two million dollars for Ade. It continues to be played, and has been called "one of the theater's indestructibles."

Collier, John [1] (b. Atlanta, Ga., May 4, 1884—d. May 8, 1968), social worker, authority on Indians. Collier's first publication was a book of verses, *The Indwelling Splendor* (1911). He founded the National Board of Review for Motion Pictures in 1910 and acted as its secretary until 1914; edited *American Indian Life* from 1926 to 1933; became U.S. Commissioner of Indian Affairs and served till 1945; thereafter served as president of the National Indian Institute. He wrote *The Indians of the Americas* (1947), an account of our often dishonorable dealings with the Indians and a tribute to the way in which the Indians have helped the United States, especially in recent wars.

Collier, John [2] (b. England, May 3, 1901—), novelist, short-story writer. He began his literary career as a poet—his early work is collected in *Gemini* (1931)—and for several years he was poetry editor of *Time and Tide,* the British literary magazine. His first published book, however, was *His Monkey Wife: Or Married to a Chimp* (1931), a novel in his typical fantastic vein. Since that time he has won a wide reputation as a fantasist and satirist, whose tales of supernatural and psychological grotesquerie are related with great ingenuity, wit, and style. Among his novels are *Epistle to a Friend* (1931), *Full Circle* (1933), and *Defy the Foul Fiend* (1934, reprinted 1958), and he is the author of numerous collections of short stories, including *No Traveller Returns* (1931), *Green Thoughts* (1932), *The Devil and All* (1934), *Variations on a Theme* (1935), *A Touch of Nutmeg* (1943), and *Fancies and Goodnights* (1951). Collier has lived in the United States since 1942—in Virginia and California—and a large proportion of his later stories have had American settings and have first appeared in American magazines.

Collier's. A now-defunct weekly magazine which attained a circulation of several million, published by the Crowell-Collier Publishing Co. The name comes from Peter Fenelon Collier (1849–1909), who established a publishing firm around 1875, largely for the issuance of classics and encyclopedias. In 1888 he founded a magazine called *Once a Week*, which in 1898 became *Collier's*. It had, at the turn of the century, two famous editors—NORMAN HAPGOOD (1902–13) and MARK SULLIVAN (1914–17), who made it a liberal, crusading publication. Later FINLEY PETER DUNNE took over as editor (1917–19) and turned the magazine toward lighter material. William L. Chenery (1925–43) brought many famous names to its pages. The last of its great editors was EDWARD ANTHONY, who maintained its reputation for unusual feature stories and good fiction until January, 1956, when the magazine ceased publication. The literary quality of some of its material was high, as is evidenced in the collection *Collier's Best* (1951), edited by Knox Burger.

Colman, Benjamin (b. England, 1673—d. 1747), clergyman, writer on theology, literary critic, poet. When an anti-COTTON MATHER group set up the Brattle Street Church and invited a young man, who had received Presbyterian ordination in England, to become their pastor, Mather in his diary prayed that God would make him an instrument to defeat the "designs that Satan may have in the enterprise." Yet in 1721, when Mather was in danger of his life from an angry mob because he had advocated inoculation against smallpox, Colman was one of those who came to his defense in a pamphlet. Colman was definitely a liberal, opposed alike to the fanaticism and to the bad manners of the Mathers. Ebenezer Turell, his son-in-law, said in the quaint but affecting biography he wrote of Colman (1749) that "he was a good master of address and carried all the politeness of a court about him." In fact, it seems to have been part of his intellectual and spiritual mission to mend communications with England. Colman visited his parishioners faithfully, giving the wealthy ones copies of his sermons; in the case of the needy "he ordinarily inquired of their bodily wants, which were soon supplied either by himself or charitable friends to whom he instantly applied on their behalf."

Among his ninety publications perhaps the most striking is that called *The Government and*

Improvement of Mirth (1707). Thomas H. Johnson says that in this volume "Colman's conception of mirth and its government is that of traditional Puritanism, but the spirit informing it is that of the 18th-century English nonconformist and Low-Church piety." Colman says, "We daily need some respite and diversion, without which we dull our powers; a little intermission sharpens 'em again." But he says, too, "Above all kinds of vain mirth deliver me from the Drunken Club, who belch out noisy ribaldry, rank of the foul lees within." See GUSTAVUS VASA.

Colman was Jonathan Edwards' "Correspondent" in NARRATIVE OF SURPRISING CONVERSIONS.

Colon and Spondee. One of the earliest columns in American literature, conducted in collaboration by ROYALL TYLER (Spondee) and JOSEPH DENNIE (Colon) in *The Farmers' Museum* and other periodicals during 1794 and later years. Tyler wrote the verse, Dennie the prose.

Colonel Carter of Cartersville (1891), a novel by F. HOPKINSON SMITH. In this story of the misadventures of a Virginian stranded in New York City, Smith gives a sympathetic picture of the southerner of fiction, if not always of fact. Carter has no money, but lives on loans; he has a wild scheme for building a railroad; he is kindly, chivalrous, and likable even at his most comic. Augustus Thomas dramatized the story in a play with the same title (1892). *Colonel Carter's Christmas* (1903) was a sequel.

Colonel Crockett's Tour to the North and Down East, An Account of (1835). See DAVY CROCKETT.

Colonel Sellers. See SELLERS, COLONEL BERIAH.

Colonial Mind, The (1927), a study of American history and thought by VERNON LOUIS PARRINGTON. Parrington begins his analysis with Puritan ideas and closes with the triumph of Jefferson and back-country agrarianism. He shows how the Puritans made it their mission to challenge the traditional social solidarity of English life. The role of the Puritan theocrats and of such independents as Roger Williams and Thomas Hooker is studied. The importance of the Scotch-Irish immigration is stressed, as is of course that of the frontier. In the foreword Parrington wrote that his point of view was "liberal rather than conservative, Jeffersonian rather than Federalistic"—an understatement. Already apparent is Parrington's conception of American history as a great struggle between equalitarianism and plutocracy, a struggle that determined not merely political fortunes but also the nature of American literature.

Colton, John (b. 1889?—d. Dec. 28, 1946), dramatist. Colton was a clever playwright, one who knew how to squeeze the final drop of emotion and sensation out of theatrical effects. He had great success with *Rain* (in collaboration with Clemence Randolph, 1922), based on W. Somerset Maugham's short story *Miss Thompson;* and *The Shanghai Gesture* (1926), in which Mother Goddam, the keeper of a Shanghai brothel, takes a fiendish revenge on an English-man who had deserted her twenty years earlier. Less important were *Nine Pine Street* (1933), based on the Lizzie Borden case, and *Saint Wrench* (1933).

Colton, Walter (b. Rutland, Vt., May 9, 1797—d. Jan. 22, 1851), naval chaplain, news-paperman, historian. Colton described a num-ber of his sea journeys in books, his best remem-bered being *Deck and Port* (1850), the story of a voyage to California. He remained in that state, along with Robert Semple founded its first newspaper, *The Californian* (1846), and wrote an important historical work, *Three Years in California* (1850).

Colum, Mary [Gunning Maguire] (b. Ireland, 188-?—d. Oct. 22, 1957) and **Colum, Padraic** (b. Ireland, Dec. 8, 1881—   ), Irish-born American citizens, writers. Mr. and Mrs. Colum, married in 1912, came to the United States in 1914. Mrs. Colum set forth some of her ideas on literature in *From These Roots* (1937) and told of her life and her many friendships in *Life and the Dream* (1947). Padraic Colum at an early age became a part of the Irish literary revival. He wrote a peasant drama, *Broken Soil*, at the age of twenty; it was later rewritten and then published as *The Fiddler's House*. Many collections of excellent poetry, many books for children, books of personal reminiscence, and other volumes have come from his pen. Among them are *A Boy in Eirinn* (1913), *Dramatic Legends* (1922); *The Voyagers* (1925); *Poems* (1932); *A Half-Day's Ride* (1932); *The Fren-zied Prince* (1947); *Collected Poems* (1953); *The Flying Swan* (1956); *Our Friend James Joyce* (with Mary Colum, 1958); *Ten Poems* (1958); *Ourselves Alone!* (1959).

Columbia (1777), a patriotic song by TIMOTHY DWIGHT. This was composed while Dwight was serving as chaplain to the American army in the campaign against Burgoyne. The refrain became famous:

Columbia, Columbia, to glory arise—
The queen of the world and the child of the skies.

Columbia, the Gem of the Ocean (1843?). This American patriotic song has an obscure history, and may originally have been entitled *Britannia, the Pride of the Ocean*, for British consumption. It is said that Thomas à Becket, a young English actor, wrote it while playing at a Philadelphia theater for another English actor named David Taylor Shaw, to be sung at a benefit performance for the latter. Then Shaw published it as "written, composed, and sung by David T. Shaw, and arranged by Thomas à Becket, Esq." Later Becket published it as "writ-ten and composed by T. à Becket, and sung by D. T. Shaw." According to other accounts, the poem was written by Stephen Joseph Meany in England in 1842, with music by Thomas F. Williams—with the British title. Or it may have been taken later to London by an American actor named Edward Loomis Davenport (1815–77)

and sung there under its English title. Burton E. Stevenson makes two points regarding the song: (1) The line "the home of the brave and the free," reminiscent of *The Star-Spangled Banner*, would seem to indicate American priority. (2) The line "gem of the ocean" seems to mean Eng-land rather than the United States. At any rate, the poem is an unpoetic, rhetorical production, hardly worthy of either nation.

Columbia Dictionary of Modern European Literature (1947), edited by Horatio Smith un-der the sponsorship of the Columbia University Press. Assisted by 239 contributors from American and Canadian universities, Smith gathered 1,167 articles on the authors of con-tinental Europe "in the 20th century and the immediately preceding and closely related dec-ades." No hard-and-fast dates were set; thus Victor Hugo, who died in 1885, is omitted, but Baudelaire, who died in 1867, is included, sig-nifying his close relationship to modern litera-ture. Thirty-one literatures are represented. French authors are the most numerous, then German, Russian, Italian, Spanish, Polish, and Czech, in that order. Most of the articles were written directly in English by the specialists who prepared them. Articles of a general nature as well as on particular authors are included, on Albanian, Portuguese, and Russian literature, for example, and on the literature of the Faroe Islands; also on surrealism, French naturalism, etc. An invaluable reference work, the *Dic-tionary* has the additional merit of being fre-quently, eminently readable.

Columbia Encyclopedia, The (1935, rev. 1950). This one-volume encyclopedia was pre-pared under the sponsorship of the Columbia University Press. With remarkable compactness (it runs to 6 million words) it manages to give approximately the same amount of information obtainable in reference works of many volumes. The size of the page, the type used in printing, the compactness of the information, the char-acter of the inclusions, and the intelligence of the editing represent a most successful experi-ment in reference books.

Columbiad, The (1807), a poem by JOEL BARLOW. Barlow was an exceedingly able man who, in this instance, wrote an exceedingly bad and dull poem. It is an expansion of his poem *The Vision of Columbus,* published twenty years earlier; this had been very popular and Barlow thought he could do even better if he worked on a grander scale and in a grander style. But it turned out that the poem was grandiose rather than grand. A radiant seraph named Hesper re-veals the future of America to Columbus in his old age; included is a vision of United Nations, assembled on American soil. V. L. Parrington believes that Barlow, in the light of his Eu-ropean experience, sought to lace the narrative with political ideas, making an epic that glori-fied the great republican experiment. The senti-ments, says Parrington, were "those of an enlightened and generous man," but he feels that even if Barlow had pulled himself "out of the bog of many a Connecticut provincialism," he "stuck fast in the bog of provincial poetry." Barlow denounced slavery, and his lines on "Soul-searching Freedom," even if rhetorical and abstract, have an emotional impact that may still be felt.

Columbian Lady's and Gentleman's Magazine, The. Founded in New York, 1844; expired, 1849. John Inman was the editor, and he secured as contributors some of the important writers of the day, including Poe and J. K. Paulding. But the magazine proved unsuccessful as a rival to GRAHAM'S. It made a feature of engravings and colored fashion plates.

Columbian Magazine, The. Founded by MATHEW CAREY in Philadelphia, September, 1786; expired, 1792. As the name indicates, the general purpose was patriotic; it intended to show that America, too, had good writers. FRANCIS HOPKINSON and C. B. BROWN were among the contributors. The magazine was interested in general knowledge and especially scientific developments as well as in literature; and when it was merged in 1790 with the *Philadelphia Magazine and General Asylum* (the two were then called *University Asylum and Columbian Magazine*), Dr. BENJAMIN RUSH became the chief contributor. In the *Columbian* appeared much of the work of JEREMY BELKNAP, particularly a series of satirical letters on the early history of New England, later collected as *The Foresters* (1792).

Columbus (composed, 1844; published, 1847), a poem by JAMES RUSSELL LOWELL. Cast into the form of a monologue in blank verse, this impressive poem makes Columbus a more thoughtful, more widely cultured, more imaginative person than he is usually supposed to be. Lowell puts into his mouth his own sentiments, at that stage in his growth, regarding Europe, which he conceives as an "effete" world that "reels on to judgment." In the New World, on the contrary, "a whole ideal man" may be born and thrive.

Columbus, Christopher [Italian—original form of name probably **Cristoforo Colombo;** Spanish form, **Cristóbal Colón**] (b. at or near Genoa, Italy, 1451—d. May 20 or 21, 1506), discoverer of America. Convinced that the earth was round and that an open sea lay between the western shore of Europe and the Indies, Columbus obtained a subsidy from the Spanish monarchs Ferdinand and Isabella, set sail from Palos, Spain, on August 3, 1492, and landed on an island in the Caribbean Sea, October 12. He believed that he had attained his goal, and called the natives "Indians." He named his landing place "San Salvador"; it is not known precisely which island this actually was.

Columbus went on to other voyages and discoveries; he never, however, touched the shore of North America. Despite the grandeur and importance of his discovery, his life became a tragic one. He was accused of harsh treatment of the natives and had difficulties with fellow Spaniards. In 1500 he was brought back to Spain in chains, and made his fourth and last voyage in 1502–04, returning to Spain in the vain hope of obtaining reinstatement in his honors. He died in poverty and neglect, still believing he had discovered the coast of Asia. There is much dispute on which tomb erected to him actually contains his bones, but it is likely that the one in the Dominican Republic has that honor.

Although the New World Columbus had discovered was not named in his honor, many important memorials preserve his fame; also the names of a dozen American towns and the Republic of Colombia. Historians have devoted much attention to Columbus. The best-known biography is Washington Irving's THE LIFE AND VOYAGES OF CHRISTOPHER COLUMBUS (3 v., 1828); also important is Justin Winsor's *Christopher Columbus* (1892). Superseding all previous works, Samuel Eliot Morison's *Admiral of the Ocean Sea* (Pulitzer Prize winner, 1942) and *Christopher Columbus, Mariner* (1955) bring together the best results of scholarship to the date of their publication. Alice Bache Gould has devoted more than forty years to study of the archives on Columbus' voyages. His discoveries have stirred poets, philosophers, and storytellers, but no first-rate novel or play or poem has thus far been written about him. Possibly the best poem is Walt Whitman's *The Prayer of Columbus* (1874), and the most widely read, Joaquin Miller's rhetorical *Columbus* (1896).

Columbus, The Life and Voyages of (3 v., 1828), a biography by WASHINGTON IRVING. While an attaché in the American Legation at Madrid, Irving gathered materials for this massive work. He had access to many treasures of source material, including some made available to him by the Duke of Veraguas, a descendant of Columbus. His view of the discoverer is an exalted one and has since his time been questioned, but he produced a clear, well-written biography. Later he added an account of *The Companions of Columbus* (1831).

Columbus, The Vision of (1787), a poem by Joel Barlow. See COLUMBIAD.

columnists. Newspapermen who write byline articles published periodically containing news, gossip, or editorial interpretation. Many such columns are syndicated, and they may appear daily or at regular intervals in several hundred newspapers.

The first American columnists may have been ROYALL TYLER and JOSEPH DENNIE who contributed jocular and serious items to various newspapers and magazines under the pseudonyms "COLON" and "SPONDEE" in the final decade of the eighteenth century. Other colonial and early national papers carried columns; some of BENJAMIN FRANKLIN'S, WASHINGTON IRVING'S, and JAMES KIRKE PAULDING'S writings anticipate modern columns.

It was not, however, until the 1880's that the column became a literary genre in the contemporary sense. Pioneers in making it so were three great newspapermen—AMBROSE BIERCE, EUGENE FIELD, and BERT LESTON TAYLOR. Bierce's San Francisco "Prattle" is described by Gertrude

Atherton as "brilliant, scarifying, witty, bitter, humorous, and utterly fearless." Field was a graceful writer of light and sentimental verse who had a love of books, and he communicated his love to a host of readers. Taylor made his initials B.L.T. famous; he was perhaps the first to urge readers of a literary bent to contribute items to his column. One of Taylor's contributors was FRANKLIN PIERCE ADAMS. Later Adams started a column of his own for a Chicago paper, but in 1904 moved on to New York where he made the initials F.P.A. even better known than B.L.T. He combined the techniques of Field and Taylor, writing excellent light verse and winning a large following of "contribs," among them some of the coming authors of the new literary generation.

Then came the heyday of the purely literary column in New York, with such men as HEYWOOD BROUN, DON MARQUIS, and CHRISTOPHER MORLEY offering an amazing variety of humor and fantasy, good verse and excellent prose. Among other noted columnists of that day two or three may be mentioned: O. O. MCINTYRE, supposedly a small-townsman in New York; WILL ROGERS, latest of the cracker-barrel philosophers; and by way of variety, "Uncle Henry" Wallace, who conducted in *Wallace's Farmer* a famous column, read all over the country, called "Uncle Henry's Sabbath School Lesson." When Wallace died in 1916 it was found that he had completely vanquished that great foe of the columnist, the deadline. He had left a twenty-two-year advance supply of his column, and his magazine continued to publish this feature until 1938.

Among later columnists only a few can be mentioned among the six or seven hundred who perform their literary stints in newspapers. Many of them are capably analyzed in the work of one of them, Charles Fisher's *The Columnists: A Surgical Survey* (1944). He writes caustically about WALTER LIPPMANN, WESTBROOK PEGLER, WALTER WINCHELL, DOROTHY THOMPSON, Raymond Clapper, Fletcher Pratt, Frank Kent, DREW PEARSON, DAVID LAWRENCE, Marquis Childs, and others. Fisher concludes that the columnist is the "autocrat of the most prodigious breakfast table ever known. He is the voice beside the cracker barrel amplified to transcontinental dimensions." Olin Hinkle and John Henry told *How to Write Columns* (1952).

Come up from the Fields, Father (1865), a poem by WALT WHITMAN. An affecting picture of the arrival of bad news at a home in Ohio, from which a boy had gone to join the Union army. Perhaps the lines represent Whitman's imaginative reconstruction of a scene that must many times have resulted from the hundreds of letters that he himself wrote for soldiers when he worked as a volunteer in the hospitals at Washington. It is one of his few poems that attempt something in the nature of drama and character portrayal.

Comfort, Will Levington (b. Kalamazoo, Mich., Jan. 17, 1878—d. Nov. 2, 1932), newspaperman, fiction writer. After working on newspapers in Detroit, Cincinnati, and Pittsburgh, Comfort turned to fiction. Most of his writing was hack work and decidedly melodramatic, but he reached a higher level in his novel *Routledge Rides Alone* (1910), based on his own experience in the Russo-Japanese War, an account of war so lurid that peace societies circulated it as propaganda. Comfort told the story of his life with more than customary candor in *Midstream* (1914).

comic almanacs. From the beginning the almanacs so popular with colonial readers and their successors emphasized humor. The Yankee was a constant figure in the almanacs, and in Franklin's famous portrait of Poor Richard a wry smile may be perceived. Often the compiler of early almanacs did no more than perform that feat which modern comedians call a "switch"; that is, they took an old joke and gave it contemporaneous details and coloring. In time, some almanacs became deliberately and primarily comic, at least in intent. Apparently there was a growing public for such publications free from the agricultural, meteorological, and statistical data and the moralizing that formed the staple of earlier almanacs. The first of this special type is believed to have been *The American Comic Almanac*, published at Boston by Charles Ellms in 1831; it contained crude jokes and crude pictures. It caught the popular fancy and had many imitators: *Comic Token* and *Broad Grins* (both 1832); *American Comic Annual* (1833); Elton's *Comic All-My-Neck* (1834); Finn's *Comic Almanac* (1835).

Most famous of the comic almanacs was Davy Crockett's *Almanac of Wild Sports of the West and Life in the Backwoods* (1835). Crockett died the next year, but his heirs continued to publish Crockett almanacs. Later one Ben Hardin or Harding (possibly mythical) took them over. In 1839 the firm of Turner & Fisher of New York began to publish the Crockett almanacs, and continued to do so until 1856. The anecdotes and tall tales were in Yankee dialect; the text was accompanied by crude woodcuts. Other comic almanacs appeared up to the outbreak of the Civil War: *The Rip Snorter; Whim Whams; The Merry Elephant; The Devil's Comical Texas Oldmanick*. William Murrell, writing *The History of American Graphic Humor* (vol. 1, 1934; vol. 2, 1938), found "the illustrations in many instances much more humorous than the texts." See ALMANACS; ANNUALS.

comics, the. A popular term for "newspaper cartoon strip features," or "comic strips." In their beginnings, the comics were tough, dealt with bums and thugs. The first comic strip appeared on February 16, 1896, in Joseph Pulitzer's New York *Sunday World*. It was a three-quarter-page colored panel entitled "The Great Dog Show in M'Googan's Avenue," and was peopled with alley cats, stray dogs, and drunks. In the center was a child in a bright yellow nightgown, a malicious, nasty creature called "the Yellow Kid." He became popular immediately, and the artist, RICHARD OUTCAULT, was soon lured from the *World* to the New York

Journal. Pulitzer hired another artist, GEORGE LUKS, to do a Yellow Kid feature for him; and the resultant war between the two papers is believed to have given rise to the phrase "yellow journalism."

With the progress of time, newspaper publishers discovered the circulation-building effects of the comics, particularly in winning children as readers. The comics were somewhat purified, for a while, with such characters as Buster Brown and Little Nemo. The KATZENJAMMER KIDS were on the whole an improvement over the Yellow Kid. Syndication came in 1915, and then arrived such nationally known figures as Mutt and Jeff, Barney Google, Jiggs, Krazy Kat (perhaps the greatest of them all, see GEORGE HERRIMAN), the Gumps, Orphan Annie, Terry, Blondie and Dagwood, Joe Palooka, Tarzan, Buck Rogers, Superman, DICK TRACY, Felix the Cat, the Pussycat Princess, Li'l Abner, Skippy, Barnaby, Pogo, Peanuts, and many others that now form part of our American mythology and folklore.

The "comics" are, in the main, not at all comic and are not intended to be. This is especially true of the more recent development, comics in book form, sold in vast quantities to an audience adolescent not only in years. B. W. Huebsch points out that the comics, along with the movies and radio, provide "package thrills for the millions," and that they "can be enjoyed without the effort of thinking which reading implies." Comics have been charged with the destruction of reading as a habit, despite the fact that there seems to be an ever increasing circulation of books and certainly a tremendous increase in periodicals in this country. They are charged, too, with sensationalism, with the formation of bad habits in morals and manners, with fantastic exaggerations that are destructive of intelligent thinking, with bad taste and bad grammar, with a tendency toward the formation of aggressiveness, sadism, eroticism, and other mental dangers.

It was not until the 1940's that the comics really took a firm grip on the mentality of the country. By 1946 the claim was made that comic books had a monthly sale of 49,596,000 copies. By 1948 articles, radio broadcasts, and speeches were appearing, vehemently arguing the pros and cons of the comic book question. *Collier's* joined the fray with an article by Judith Crist, "Horror in the Nursery" (March 27, 1948). This was mainly a report of an interview with Dr. FREDERIC WERTHAM, senior psychiatrist of the New York City Department of Hospitals. In one story that he analyzed he found thirty-seven killings and corpses and fifteen pools of blood; and he warned that these murderous sensations were particularly dangerous because "the sex desires are mixed with violence." After further study Dr. Wertham published *The Seduction of the Innocents* (1954), a drastic attack that provoked a widespread controversy. For the defense, King Features put forth in the *Public Relations Journal* (November, 1951) a statement by its art director, Joseph W. Musial, on *Comic Books and Public Relations* that answers sensibly eleven common questions about the comics. The National Council of Teachers of English issued Constance Carr's pamphlet suggesting *Substitutes for the Comic Books* (April, 1951). Meanwhile New York University's School of Education provided a graduate course in writing comic books, and committees of New York City teachers began to look into them as a possible "educational device for slow learners." Coulton Waugh's *The Comics* (1947) and Stephen Becker's *Comic Art in America* (1960) are full-length accounts of the comic strip and its rapid progress to fame and fortune. Beginning with WALT KELLY's "Pogo," the comic strips began to take on a new sophistication and venture upon social criticism and satire. This trend has been continued by Charles Schultz in "Peanuts," Jules Feiffer in a series about neurotic misfits, and, more broadly, William Gaines in *Mad* magazine.

Coming of Age in Samoa (1928), by MARGARET MEAD. The celebrated anthropologist describes her book in a subtitle as "a psychological study of primitive youth for Western civilization." She sets out to answer the question: Are the disturbances which vex our adolescents due to the nature of adolescence itself or to the civilization in which they live? The chief lesson she learned from her examination of Samoan culture was this: "Adolescence is not necessarily a time of stress and strain, but cultural conditions make it so." In Samoa the young girls pass through the same physical changes as in western lands, but these changes are calmly taken for granted, little attention is paid to them, and there is no emotional tension. Accompanying this placidity is, however, a degree of freedom in sex relations before marriage foreign to western notions. In a foreword FRANZ BOAS says of her book that it "confirms the suspicion long held by anthropologists, that much of what we ascribe to human nature is no more than a reaction to the restraints put upon us by our civilization."

Commager, Henry Steele (b. Pittsburgh, Pa., Oct. 25, 1902—   ), teacher, historian. Commager, a specialist in American history, became professor of history at Columbia University in 1939. His writings are popular among both scholars and the general public. Among his books: *The Growth of the American Republic* (with S. E. MORISON, 1931, 1942); *Theodore Parker* (1936); *The Heritage of America* (with ALLAN NEVINS, 1939); *Majority Rule and Minority Rights* (1943); *The American Mind* (1950). He has edited some excellent anthologies: *Documents of American History* (1934), which he considers one of his most significant contributions to history; *The St. Nicholas Anthology* (2 v., 1948, 1950), and *The Blue and the Gray* (2 v., 1950). Other books: *Freedom, Loyalty, Dissent* (1954); *Atlas of the Civil War* (1958). A forty-volume encyclopedia of American history, *The Rise of the American Nation*, has been in process for some time.

Command Decision (1947), a novel by WILLIAM WISTER HAINES, produced as a play in

1948. Out of his own experience, Haines wrote a powerful story of an Allied bomber center in Europe during World War II.

Commemoration Ode (July 21, 1865), by JAMES RUSSELL LOWELL. This is more exactly entitled *Ode Recited at the Harvard Commemoration,* but Lowell himself, like everyone else, familiarly called it *Commemoration Ode.* Not long after Lee's surrender at Appomattox the President and Fellows of Harvard asked Lowell to prepare an ode for a day of commemoration for the Harvard students who had died in the war. Although dubious of his own ability to write lofty poetry, Lowell consented, deciding on a form featuring lines of irregular length but provided with a pattern of rhyme. He wrote the poem a night or two before its delivery, working from ten o'clock at night till four in the morning. He was discouraged by its reception and his own rereading of it. Preparing the poem for publication in a private printing in 1865, he added sixty-six lines—the magnificent sixth strophe that begins, "Such was he, our Martyr-Chief." In 1877 the poem was included in the collection called THE CATHEDRAL.

Commentaries on American Law (4 v., 1826–30), by JAMES KENT. A famous lawyer, jurist, and legal scholar, Kent, after his retirement from the bench in 1823 and his resumption of teaching at Columbia University, delivered lectures that became the basis of his influential *Commentaries.* Writing from a Federalist point of view, he discussed international law, the Constitution, our form of government, state laws, the rights of persons and of property. Closely associated with the literary men of the day and himself possessing considerable gifts of style, especially in exposition, Kent soon took a place in American teaching alongside Blackstone.

commentator. A term frequently employed in the United States to designate a radio speaker who interprets the news, but employed by Bernard Sobel to describe the commentator in drama—a role as old as the chorus in Greek drama and as recent as the "master of ceremonies" in music reviews, in night clubs, and on the air. During the Middle Ages the Fool or Vice often played the role of satiric commentator, as did the Harlequin in the Italian *commedia dell'arte.* In the United States the role was assumed by the interlocutor in blackface minstrel shows, by the company managers of traveling repertory troupes, sometimes by actors in the show itself. A revival of the Greek chorus is found in Thornton Wilder's *Our Town,* where the stage manager introduces the characters and talks about them.

Committee on Public Information. Aware of the importance of "communication" with the public, so that it might be kept properly informed of war issues and events, Congress in April, 1917, established a Committee on Public Information, of which GEORGE CREEL was appointed chairman. In World War II the Office of War Information undertook similar measures of propaganda on an even larger scale.

Committees of Correspondence. When it became evident in the early 1770's that activities against British measures were largely futile if taken by the colonies singly, SAMUEL ADAMS undertook to set up an intercolonial organization to provide for joint action among the colonies. He established the first Committee of Correspondence in Boston in 1772; other towns in Massachusetts established similar committees. The movement spread to most of the other colonies; in Virginia PATRICK HENRY and THOMAS JEFFERSON were especially active in advocating such committees. Adams prepared several papers for circulation.

Commoner, The Great. A title admiringly applied to a succession of statesmen—to William Pitt the Elder in England and to HENRY CLAY and WILLIAM JENNINGS BRYAN in the United States. Edmund Vance Cooke addressed a poem to Lincoln as "the Uncommon Commoner." See WILLIS J. ABBOT. Bryan edited a weekly magazine called *The Commoner* (1901–23).

Common Glory, The (1947), a "symphonic drama" by PAUL GREEN. Intended as a companion piece to *The Lost Colony* (1937, see under RALEGH), this play glorifies America, especially the role played by Thomas Jefferson in establishing democracy. It was first performed at Williamsburg by young people of Virginia (including groups from the College of William and Mary) in a lakeside theater in a lovely natural setting. Opening with a scene in George III's palace in London in 1775, it follows the course of the American Revolution, with Jefferson and Virginia in central roles. Its literary style "is never far from music," said Brooks Atkinson in reviewing the first performance.

Common Lot, The (1904), a novel by ROBERT HERRICK. It depicts the fashion in which a young Chicago architect succumbs to commercialism and builds houses that later are destroyed in a fire with loss of life. His wife helps to regenerate and save him.

Common Sense (published Jan. 10, 1776), a pamphlet by THOMAS PAINE. This is possibly the most influential writing of its kind ever published. Paine landed in America in November, 1774, managed to obtain some small literary jobs, became deeply interested in the cause of American independence. Dr. BENJAMIN RUSH met Paine in a Philadelphia bookshop in February, 1775, and suggested that he write an appeal for independence, also suggested the title. After some difficulty in finding a publisher, the pamphlet was issued, and sold 100,000 copies in three months. It boldly cast aside all theoretical considerations and based its appeal on the economic advantages that would come if the colonists cut their ties with England. It attacked the monarchical principle and the Tory assumption that the English constitution was divine. Americans were won over; Paine's appeal was worth an army. The pamphlet contains a famous statement: "Government, even in its best state, is but a necessary evil; in its worst state, an intolerable one." *Common Sense* appeared while Paine was serving with the Continental Army. He was rewarded with a position in the government, but lost it, and then was voted the thanks of Congress, the sum of $3,000, and an estate at New Rochelle, N.Y. Richard Gimbel prepared a valuable *Bibliographical Check List of Thomas Paine's "Common Sense"* (1956), listing all the known variants of the more than 150 editions of Paine's pamphlet. The data came in part from the Gimbel's Paine Collection, begun in 1937.

Commonweal, The. A magazine published in New York City by Roman Catholic laymen. It is of high literary excellence. It was founded on Nov. 12, 1924, and throughout its course it has followed an independent line, one sometimes disapproved by the local hierarchy. An anthology, *The Commonweal Reader* (1949), was edited by Edward S. Skillin.

Compensation (1841), an essay by RALPH WALDO EMERSON, first published in his *Essays* (1841). It is possibly the most famous and influential of Emerson's writings, rich in his characteristic paradoxes and offering his combination of Platonic wisdom and Yankee horse sense. The central thought is repeated under various guises and in brilliant epigrams. Perhaps it is most simply stated in the often quoted sentence that "every sweet hath its sour; every evil its good." Again he says, "Every act rewards itself" and, "For everything you have missed you have gained something else; and for everything you gain, you lose something." It follows, says Emerson, that "it is as impossible for a man to be cheated by anyone but himself, as for a thing to be and not to be at the same time." In other words, there is no need to look toward a future world for reward and punishment.

Composers, Biographical Dictionary of (1953), edited by Percy M. Young. Biographies of more than five hundred composers, including many American names. Among the latter are Gershwin, Foster, Copland, Roy Harris, and William Billings. Emphasis is laid on works especially suitable for performance.

Compromise of 1850. At the close of the Mexican War (1846–48), violent debate broke out in Congress on whether the newly annexed territories would be slave or free. HENRY CLAY and DANIEL WEBSTER, who wished to see the Union preserved at all costs, supported compromise measures as against the pro-slavery measures advocated by JOHN C. CALHOUN in his address of March 4, 1850. Webster replied to Calhoun in his famous *Seventh of March Speech.* JOHN GREENLEAF WHITTIER subsequently composed his greatest poem, ICHABOD (1850), with its magnificent invective directed against Webster for having supported the compromise. The bill nevertheless passed. In later years Whittier somewhat regretted the lashing he had given Webster, and in THE LOST OCCASION (1881) paid tribute to the greatness of his character and his oratory.

Compson family, the. A group of characters in THE SOUND AND THE FURY and other works by WILLIAM FAULKNER. One of the old, aristocratic families of YOKNAPATAWPHA COUNTY, the Compsons trace their American ancestry back to the early 18th century, but by the early 20th century the family is decaying. In the 1930's the family property is sold and the last male Compson is a childless bachelor. Members of the family (see page 199) are the following:

Benjamin Compson. Christened Maury, after his mother's only brother, and renamed when it is apparent that he is an idiot, Benjy narrates the opening section of *The Sound and the Fury.*

Candace Compson [Caddy]. After having been seduced by Dalton Ames, Caddy is hastily married to Sydney Herbert Head, a northern banker. Ames is the father of Quentin, whom Caddy brings back to Jefferson to be raised by her family. Caddy disappears, divorces Head, marries a "minor moving picture magnate" in Hollywood, divorces him, and is last heard of in Paris during the German occupation. She appears as a child in "That Evening Sun."

Jason Lycurgus Compson I. The first Compson to settle in Mississippi, Jason bought Compson's Mile from Ikkemotubbe, a Chickasaw chief, and built the Compson house with the help of the French architect who built Thomas Sutpen's mansion (see THE SUTPEN FAMILY).

Jason Lycurgus Compson II. A brigadier general during the Civil War, Jason II was the only friend of Thomas Sutpen, to whom Sutpen tells part of the story of his life, as related in ABSALOM, ABSALOM!

Jason Compson III. Originally a lawyer, Jason III drifts toward dipsomania and spends his time reading and writing satiric Latin verses. He sells part of the family property to pay for Caddy's wedding and for Quentin III's education at Harvard.

Jason Compson IV. A shrewd, practical, selfish man, Jason IV becomes a storekeeper. After the other members of the family have died or disappeared, Jason sells what is left of the property and goes to live in town. Since he does not marry, the Compson name ends with him. He appears as a child in "That Evening Sun."

Quentin Compson. The daughter of Caddy and Dalton Ames, Quentin is named before her birth after her uncle Quentin III. At seventeen she steals money sent to her uncle Jason for her support, but hidden by him, runs away with a carnival pitchman, and is never heard of again.

Quentin MacLachan Compson III. A hypersensitive, introspective young man, Quentin narrates the second part of *The Sound and the Fury* and the short story "That Evening Sun," and is one of the narrators of *Absalom, Absalom!* Because of his inability to reconcile his conception of honor with the realities of the world in which he lives, he commits suicide while at Harvard in 1910.

Compton, Arthur H[olly] (b. Wooster, Ohio, Sept. 10, 1892—d. March 15, 1962), physicist. An outstanding American scientist, Compton taught physics at several universities and joined the faculty of Washington University, St. Louis,

COMPSON GENEALOGY

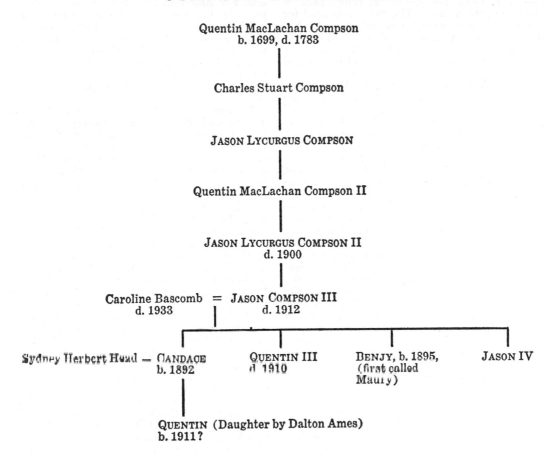

Quentin MacLachan Compson
b. 1699, d. 1783

Charles Stuart Compson

JASON LYCURGUS COMPSON

Quentin MacLachan Compson II

JASON LYCURGUS COMPSON II
d. 1900

Caroline Bascomb = JASON COMPSON III
d. 1933   d. 1912

Sydney Herbert Head — CANDACE   QUENTIN III   BENJY, b. 1895,   JASON IV
b. 1892   d. 1910   (first called
Maury)

QUENTIN (Daughter by Dalton Ames)
b. 1911?

in 1945. He produced a number of books, among them important studies of X-rays. He also wrote *The Freedom of Man* (1935); *The Human Meaning of Science* (1940); *Atomic Quest: A Personal Narrative* (1956). He was awarded the Nobel Prize for Physics in 1927. His older brother, **Karl Taylor Compton** (b. Wooster, Ohio, Sept. 14, 1887— d. June 22, 1954), also a physicist, teacher, administrator, and writer, taught at Princeton University, was president of the Massachusetts Institute of Technology from 1930 to 1948, performed important government services, and wrote many scientific papers.

Compton, Francis Snow. A pen name used by HENRY ADAMS on the title page of his novel *Esther* (1884).

Compton, Wilson M[artindale] (b. Wooster, Ohio, Oct. 15, 1890—   ), economist, teacher, administrator. Wilson Compton has written several authoritative books on conservation education, including: *The Organization of the Lumber Industry* (1916); *Trade Associations and the Law* (1930); *Looking Ahead from Behind at American Forestry* (1960).

Compton's Pictured Encyclopedia. An excel-

lent reference work, originally edited by Guy Stanton Ford and published in ten volumes (1922–28); it is frequently revised and reprinted. Intended particularly for children, it is often consulted by their elders.

Comstock, Anthony (b. New Canaan, Conn., March 7, 1844—d. Sept. 21, 1915), censor of literature and art. He founded the Society for the Suppression of Vice and became its secretary for life. He conducted relentless campaigns against what he regarded as obscenity, secured the passage of an act (1873) excluding "immoral" matter from the mails, caused the conviction of countless persons, and destroyed 160 tons of obscene literature and nearly 4 million pictures. Supposedly Comstock had read all this literature and had seen all the pictures, but with no effect upon his rugged moral nature. His life, works, and influence were ably discussed in a biography, *Anthony Comstock, Roundsman of the Lord* (1927), by Heywood Broun and Margaret Leech.

Comstock Bonanza (1950), writings by MARK TWAIN and others, collected and edited by Duncan Emrich. Among those included, besides Clemens, are BRET HARTE, Fred Hart, Joseph T. Goddman, James W. Gally, Dan de Quille, and Sam Davis. The items appeared for the most part in newspapers reflecting the Nevada background. They reveal one or two of the writers, particularly Gally, De Quille, and Davis, as undeservedly forgotten masters of humor and local color.

Comstock Lode. In the early 1850's prospectors had searched through the valleys on the eastern side of the Sierras and had found small quantities of placer gold. Not till 1859, however, were the surface outcroppings of the Comstock Lode discovered in Nevada—one of the most famous of the world's mineral treasure stores which at its best yielded $20,000,000 worth of mingled gold and silver annually, and in time produced a total of $400,000,000 worth of precious ore. The shaft ultimately went down 2,300 feet, but the generation of stifling gases at this depth prevented further penetration of the mine, which ceased to be worked after the middle 1870's. The discovery produced a great influx of prospectors. MARK TWAIN, who had accompanied his brother Orion to Nevada when the latter was appointed Acting Governor of the territory in 1861, soon drifted to Virginia City at the site of the Comstock Lode. He staked claims without much success, acquired the experience that proved better than a Comstock Lode, the material for ROUGHING IT (1872). He also wrote letters (some of them reprinted in *Mark Twain of the Enterprise*, ed. by Henry Nash Smith, 1957) to the *Territorial Enterprise* of Virginia City, then in 1862 joined the paper's staff. It was then that he adopted "Mark Twain" as his pseudonym; it had been used earlier by Capt. ISAIAH SELLERS, who was still alive when Clemens took over the name.

Conant, James Bryant (b. Dorchester, Mass., March 26, 1893—   ), chemist, teacher, administrator, writer, ambassador. Trained in science, Conant began teaching at Harvard in 1916, became Chairman of the Chemistry Department in 1931, was President of Harvard University from 1933 to 1953. During World War II he was associated with the Manhattan Project for development of the atomic bomb. He was U.S. High Commissioner for Germany from 1953 to 1955 and Ambassador to that country from 1955 to 1957. Subsequently he devoted himself to studying American secondary education.

Conant wrote *Our Fighting Faith* (1952) and *Education in a Divided World* (1948); and various works in the field of science such as *Science and Common Sense* (1951) and *Modern Science and Modern Man* (1952). He aided in the preparation of two famous reports—Henry DeWolf Smyth's *Atomic Energy for Military Purposes* (1945) and the Harvard University report on education, *General Education in a Free Society* (1945). His *Germany and Freedom* appeared in 1958 and *The Child, the Parent and the State* in 1959. A grant from the Carnegie Corporation made possible Conant's two-year evaluation of American high school education. *The American High School Today* (1959), presents his views on needed reforms and supports these views with a battery of facts. *Education in the Junior High School Years* was published in 1960; in *Slums and Suburbs* (1961), he emphasizes the need for immediate reforms in our cities, as well as schools and values, and underscores their present state of decay.

Concord, Massachusetts. A town of about 9,000 population, famous in history and literature. Concord—seventeen miles northwest of Boston—was settled in 1635. It was a center of patriotic feeling during the pre-Revolutionary period. Here the first Provincial Congress met in 1774, with JOHN HANCOCK presiding, and here the minute men were organized and supplies stored. Early on April 19, 1775, the British sent a force of eight hundred men to seize these supplies, but the Americans had been warned in time by PAUL REVERE and his helpers. The Battle of Concord was fought over a bridge that spanned the Concord River; the battle was celebrated in Emerson's poem the *Concord Hymn* (1837), with its line about the embattled farmers who "fired the shot heard round the world." Among famous residents of the town were Emerson, Hawthorne, Thoreau, the Alcotts, William Ellery Channing, and F. B. Sanburn. BRONSON ALCOTT established here a Concord School of Philosophy (1879), which became a center of transcendental thought. There are many spots of interest in the town—the homes of the Alcotts, Emerson, and Hawthorne; Antiquarian House; the Minute Man Statue at the Bridge; the Sleepy Hollow Cemetery. In 1915 Charles Ives composed a sonata called *Concord, Mass., 1846–1860,* in four sections: "Emerson," "Hawthorne," "The Alcotts," "Thoreau." See CONCORD SCHOOL.

Concord School. A name sometimes given to the group of writers who resided in Concord, Mass., during the mid-19th century and who are also called the "Transcendental School." William Phillips held that "the Concord School may be said to mark the first appearance, in full intellectual dress, of an American intelligentsia. Revolting against the all-absorbing commercialism of the day and against the bleakness of the Puritan heritage, they set out quite consciously to form, as Emerson put it, 'a learned class.'" Noted members of the "school" were RALPH WALDO EMERSON, HENRY DAVID THOREAU, NATHANIEL HAWTHORNE, the ALCOTTS, and WILLIAM ELLERY CHANNING [2]. Noted member of the group, Bronson Alcott, founded various educational institutions. The last of these was one over which he presided as dean at the age of eighty—the Concord School of Philosophy, founded by him and WILLIAM T. HARRIS in 1879 to bring together New England transcendentalism and western democratic idealism. It ceased its sessions in 1887, the year before Alcott died. See TRANSCENDENTALISM.

Condensed Novels and Other Papers (1867),

parodies and imitations by BRET HARTE. The pieces in this first prose book of Harte's fall into three groups: fourteen "Condensed Novels," twelve "Civic Sketches," seven "Legends and Tales." It is a mistake to regard these pieces as merely parodies, although some are definitely of that nature, such as *Muck a Muck, An Indian Novel, after Cooper;* or *Mary McGillup, a Southern Novel.* Others may rather be characterized as ironic imitations, still others as attempts on Harte's part to come sincerely as close as he could to a great writer's way of writing. This is particularly true of the imitation of Dickens, *The Haunted Man,* of which Fred Lewis Pattee writes: "No travesty here: it is interpretation, it is appreciation, it is admiration undisguised. . . . Other writers schooled Harte: Dickens molded and made him." Harte had the ability to place himself within the skin of other writers, to see and understand the mechanism of their tricks and mannerisms, and then to reproduce them in brief. Thus one finds almost pure Hawthorne, Irving, N. P. Willis, Victor Hugo among these sketches and stories. Out of his analysis of his predecessors and contemporaries, Harte was able to attain an artistry that deeply influenced the development of the short story in the United States.

Conduct of Life, The (a series of lectures given first at Pittsburgh, 1851; later in Boston; published, 1860), by RALPH WALDO EMERSON. In these nine lectures Emerson brilliantly restates some of his favorite doctrines on fate, power, wealth, culture, behavior, worship, "considerations by the way," beauty, illusions. They are sometimes transcendental in tone, sometimes shrewdly practical. Among his epigrams and sayings are these: "Coal is a portable climate." "Solitude, the safeguard of mediocrity, is to genius the stern friend." "One of the benefits of a college education is to show the boy its little avail." "Shallow men believe in luck."

Confederacy. The group of southern states that seceded from the Union at various times in 1861—Virginia, North and South Carolina, Georgia, Alabama, Tennessee, Louisiana, Arkansas, Mississippi, Florida, and Texas—and formed a separate government. JEFFERSON DAVIS became President of the Confederacy, ROBERT E. LEE its most eminent leader. Montgomery, Ala., was at first its seat of government, then Richmond (May 21, 1861). In the Constitution adopted by the seceding states, the official title of their government was "Confederate States." The best *Story of the Confederacy* is that of R. S. Henry (1931, 1948). More recent is Clement Eaton's *History of the Southern Confederacy* (1954). R. B. Harwell compiled *Confederate Belles-Lettres: A Bibliography* (1941). See CIVIL WAR.

Confederation, The. The union of the colonists (1777–89) under the ARTICLES OF CONFEDERATION. See NEW NATION.

confession magazines and confession stories. Magazines that publish "true" stories, in many cases allegedly written by those who actually experienced the events related (usually of a sordid or sensational character). A number of magazines publishing tales of this kind have an enormous circulation. Most confession-writers aim at a degree of realism in their narratives that will make readers feel that their stories are true rather than fiction. An allied group of magazines provide the life stories of movie stars. The writing of these "true" stories is a fairly profitable specialty of a considerable number of professional authors.

Confidence-Man, The: His Masquerade (1857), a novel by HERMAN MELVILLE. The novel is set aboard a Mississippi riverboat on April Fool's Day. It is a satire, but unfortunately almost completely lacking in plot, and filled with dialogues in which the characters are not clearly defined or even, at times, distinguishable. The Confidence Man, whose disguise changes as the book proceeds, is a smiling, intelligent hypocrite whose single pleasure in life is in the exercise of his evil spells. If he succeeds, it is because he knows what men want and fear most; he knows that among the desperate there is always a market for false hope, and among the unwary, a market for false pity. He sells patent medicine for incurable diseases and solicits funds for nonexistent charities, capitalizing on mankind's gullibility. The "gimlet-eyed" realist who tries ineffectually to expose the Confidence Man fails because in a world without principle the Confidence Man is king and evil generally triumphs.

Congo, The: A Study of the Negro Race (1914), a poem by VACHEL LINDSAY. It falls into three sections: "Their Basic Savagery," "Their Irrepressible High Spirits," "The Hope of Their Religion"; and it is written with extraordinarily emphatic rhythm and skillful use of refrains. Lindsay recited it effectively, and it has been a favorite piece for choric recitations. Lindsay called it a "roaring, epic, rag-time tune."

Congregationalist. See EDWARD BEECHER.

Congressional Government (1885), a treatise by WOODROW WILSON. It was his doctoral thesis at Johns Hopkins, and was greatly influenced by the political experiences of the country during the Reconstruction period and by British parliamentary ideas and procedures. Wilson was an enthusiastic reader of Walter Bagehot and accepted his concept of a cabinet that would have centralized responsibility and sensitivity to the wishes of the electorate.

Congressional Library. See LIBRARY OF CONGRESS.

Congressional Record, The. Records of the proceedings of the nation's legislative body were kept from the beginning. But the *Journals of the Continental Congress* were not collected till the twentieth century (in 34 volumes, 1904–37). The *Annals of Congress* (1789–1824) began with the first meeting of the Congress of the United States. The name was changed to *Register of Debates* (1824–37), then *Congressional Globe* (1837–72), finally *Congressional Record* (1872–   ). This is printed daily during sessions of the Congress; the printer must have a copy ready for every congressman on the morning after the session—with such deletions, extensions, corrections, and modifications as the congressman desires. Sometimes the daily *Record* runs to only four pages; once it reached an all-time high of 437 pages. Ten copies go to the President; one hundred to each senator; sixty-eight to each representative. The public may subscribe.

Coniston (1906), a novel by WINSTON CHURCHILL. Churchill became interested in the politics of his own New Hampshire, and to some extent embodied his observations and conclusions in this story, laid in the years between President Jackson and President Grant. His chief character is Jethro Bass, an able but corrupt Vermont politician whose quest for power leads him to break with the woman he loves. Bass was modeled on Ruel Durkee, a New Hampshire political boss.

Conkling, Grace [Walcott] Hazard (b. New York City, Feb. 7, 1878—d. Nov. 15, 1958), poet, teacher, lecturer. Mrs. Conkling became a member of the faculty of Smith College in 1914. Her published collections of verse include *Afternoons of April* (1915); *Wilderness Songs* (1920); *Flying Fish* (1926); *Witch and Other Poems* (1929). She was a member of the group of poets who in the 1920's practiced the imagist technique (see IMAGISM), and some of her work is graceful and picturesque.

Conkling, Hilda (b. Catskill-on-the-Hudson, N.Y., Oct. 8, 1910—   ), poet. The daughter of GRACE HAZARD CONKLING began "talking" verse, primarily in the Imagist manner, at the age of four and continued facilely thereafter; her mother wrote down the results, which were published in two collections, *Poems by a Little Girl* (1920) and *Shoes of the Wind* (1922). Alfred Kreymborg regards the poems as "the normal fancies of an outdoor child. Hilda's poems take a natural, not a sentimental place in our affection."

Conkling, Roscoe (b. Albany, N.Y., Oct. 30, 1829—d. April 18, 1888), lawyer, orator, politician. Active in the intrigues of the Republican party after the Civil War, Conkling is described by William Harlan Hale as "the debonair and cynical young oracle of vengeance, whose object of special solicitude was the class of big holders of government securities." Because of his opposition to an appointment of Garfield's, he resigned his Senate seat, but failed to win vindication by re-election. He was an effective orator, who coined many striking but sometimes grandiose phrases. In his speech nominating Grant he assured the voters that he would "hew to the line of right, let the chips fall where they may."

Connecticut Wits. See HARTFORD WITS.

Connecticut Yankee in King Arthur's Court, A (1889), a novel by MARK TWAIN. A blow received on the head during a quarrel conveys the superintendent of a Hartford arms factory back to the days of King Arthur, with all his

Yankee ingenuity and know-how intact. His encounters with the world of chivalry make amusing reading; Mark Twain uses the opportunity to satirize the Old World, medieval "chivalry," kings, and the church. Many of the characters made famous in various renderings of the Arthurian saga appear, but seen with the Yankee's practical, unimpressed eye. He introduces some modern inventions, and knows some things not discovered until centuries later (he has foreknowledge of an eclipse, for example), so that he can ludicrously surprise King Arthur and his court. In one scene he transfers five hundred knights from horseback to bicycles. He marries a young girl whose speech resembles the long-winded sentences of the Germans, and they have a daughter called Hello-Central.

To his own surprise Mark Twain was "prodigiously pleased" with the story when he reread it some years later. His friend William Dean Howells regarded it as "a masterpiece of humor beside the great work of Cervantes," and Alexander Cowie praises Twain's social criticism.

In 1927 Herbert Fields wrote and produced a musical play in two acts and a prologue called *A Connecticut Yankee*, based on the book, with lyrics by Lorenz Hart and music by Richard Rodgers. The production was very successful and the play has frequently been revived. Movie versions were made in 1921, 1931 (with Will Rogers as the Yankee), and 1949. It has often been dramatized on television.

Connell, Evan S[helby], Jr. (b. Kansas City, Mo., August 17, 1924—   ), writer of fiction. Connell was a winner of several awards for short-story writing and a Eugene Saxton Grant in 1952. Plotting is incidental in all of Connell's work and shock technique entirely absent. Among his published works: *The Anatomy Lesson and Other Stories* (1957); *Mrs. Bridge* (1959); *The Patriot* (1960). Connell's writing has appeared in various anthologies and in magazines.

Connell, Richard [Edward] (b. Poughkeepsie, N.Y., Oct. 17, 1893—d. Nov. 22, 1949), novelist, short-story writer. Connell first worked on newspapers and in the advertising business. In 1919 he began to write fiction, also occasional scripts in Hollywood. His collections of shorter fiction include *The Sin of Monsieur Petipon* (1922), *Apes and Angels* (1924), and *Ironies* (1930). Among his novels: *Mad Lover* (1927), *Playboy* (1936), *What Ho!* (1937).

Connelly, Marc[us Cook] (b. McKeesport, Pa., Dec. 13, 1890—   ), newspaperman, versifier, dramatist. After working on several Pittsburgh papers, Connelly went on to New York, where he wrote lyrics for plays and articles for newspapers, and became fascinated with the theater. A friendship with GEORGE S. KAUFMAN resulted in collaboration on several successful plays: DULCY (1921), a clever comedy taking its central character from a stupid but well-meaning young woman who had originally appeared in FRANKLIN P. ADAMS' column in the New York

Tribune; To the Ladies (1922), a study in illusions; MERTON OF THE MOVIES (1922), a dramatization of HARRY LEON WILSON's satiric novel about Hollywood in its early days; and BEGGAR ON HORSEBACK (1924), a dream play, perhaps the finest success of the collaboration. Later, by himself, Connelly wrote *The Wisdom Tooth* (1926), a clerk's futile but pleasant dream of how he defies his employer; THE GREEN PASTURES (1929), based on ROARK BRADFORD's Negro stories and considered Connelly's greatest play; *The Farmer Takes a Wife* (1934), with characters taken from WALTER D. EDMONDS' *Rome Haul* (1929); *A Story for Strangers* (1948), a parable about a talking horse. In 1947 Connelly became associate professor of playwriting at Yale's Graduate School of Fine Arts, with the hope, as he expressed it, of persuading his students to write for the world, "not just for Broadway."

Conner, Charlotte Barnes. Author of THE FOREST PRINCESS.

Conning Tower, The. A famous newspaper column conducted by FRANKLIN P. ADAMS in New York City, beginning in the *Tribune* in 1913 and closing in the *Post* in 1941. Many authors of the day found an important outlet in this column, among them Dorothy Parker, Ring Lardner, George S. Kaufman, Deems Taylor. Some noted fictional characters also first appeared in "The Conning Tower," among them Dulcy, central character of Marc Connelly's play (see above). Henry Seidel Canby described vividly the significance of F.P.A.'s column in the era of the 1920's, and showed that the noted writers, artists, and musicians of the day were made to live in the column as "a sophisticated society of week-enders, poker-players, light-verse adepts, wisecrackers, sardonic philosophers, and critics skeptical of the current 'normalcy.'"

Connolly, James B[rendan Bennet] (b. Boston, 1868?—d. Jan. 20, 1957), war correspondent, writer of sea stories. Connolly early won fame as an Olympic champion; later he reported Mexican incidents and World War I for *Collier's;* his main literary activity was writing realistic sea stories, laid mainly in Gloucester and the ocean paths that Gloucester fishermen seek. Among his books· *Out of Gloucester* (1902); *The Seiners* (1904); *Open Water* (1910); *Book of the Gloucester Fishermen* (1927); and an autobiography, *Sea-Borne: Thirty Years A-Voyaging* (1944).

Connor, Ralph. The pen name of CHARLES WILLIAM GORDON.

Conqueror, The (1902), GERTRUDE ATHERTON's "dramatized biography" of ALEXANDER HAMILTON. Based partly on oral, partly on documentary tradition, it is a highly idealized portrait of a man who was a figure of controversy in his own day and has continued so to the present. Mrs. Atherton describes brilliantly Hamilton's early life in the West Indies and his later career as a patriot and statesman, but overdramatizes the conflict with Burr. She even makes MADAME JUMEL, supposedly once deeply

in love with Hamilton, later spurned by him, a chief factor in instigating the challenge to a duel with Burr, who much later married Madame Jumel. See SIR WILLIAM JOHNSON.

Conqueror Worm, The (*Graham's Magazine*, Jan. 1843), a poem by EDGAR ALLAN POE. It was included in his collection of 1845, *The Raven and Other Poems*, and was also interwoven with the story called LIGEIA, originally published without it in 1838. It is believed that the germ of the poem was in *The Proud Ladye*, a poem by Spencer Wallis Cone which Poe reviewed in *Burton's Gentleman's Magazine* in June, 1840. The poem describes the tragedy of mankind, conquered by the Worm (or the Serpent), the spirit of evil. Though often banal and didactic, at moments it is truly tragic or horrifying.

Conquest of Canaan, The [1] (1785), epic poem by TIMOTHY DWIGHT. The poem is an allegory in which Dwight somewhat clumsily equates the conquest of Canaan, as narrated in the Old Testament, with the taking of Connecticut from the British. In eleven books and 10,000 lines, all in heroic couplets, Dwight made the first attempt, as he himself claimed, to write an epic poem of America. The incongruity of the eras depicted, and the highfalutin style, at times become ludicrous. W. C. Bronson calls the poem "an honest, respectable piece of work," but holds it is without a glimmer of genius or even high talent.

Conquest of Canaan, The [2] (1905), novel by BOOTH TARKINGTON. Canaan is a town in Indiana where intolerance and narrow-mindedness hold sway. Joe London, making his way against great obstacles, wins out against the townspeople, marries a beautiful heiress, Ariel Tabor, and becomes the town's mayor.

Conquest of Mexico, History of the (3 v., 1843), by WILLIAM H. PRESCOTT. This is the brilliantly told story of the conquest of Mexico by Cortez and a handful of Spanish soldiers who invaded the empire of Montezuma contrary to the orders of Cortez' superior officer. Prescott's painstaking research (conducted stubbornly despite constant and serious eye trouble) made the book so accurate in its account of Aztec civilization and the Spanish conquest that it is still authoritative.

Conquest of Peru, History of the (1847), a historical narrative by W. H. PRESCOTT. The great success of THE CONQUEST OF MEXICO led Prescott to go on to a similar volume on the overrunning of Peru by Pizarro and his marauders. The work falls into five sections: the civilization of the Incas, the discovery of Peru, the conquests, the civil wars among the conquerors, the settlement of the country. Prescott concludes that the socialistic system of the Incas "was the most oppressive, though the mildest, of despotisms." He is no hero-worshiper of Pizarro, although he regards him and his exploits indulgently.

Conquest of the Missouri, The (1909, reprinted 1946), by JOSEPH MILLS HANSON. An account is given in this volume of the "life and exploits of Captain Grant Marsh." Marsh (1832–1916) was a great riverman who helped to survey and conquer the upper Missouri River valley, to subdue the Sioux Indians (he was the first to report Custer's annihilation), and to open to civilization the vast territory which this tribe had occupied. His wood-burning stern-wheelers kept communications open in the wilderness from the 1860's to the 1880's, and his notes were of great military assistance to the government.

Conquistador (1932), epic poem by ARCHIBALD MACLEISH. This long narrative in modified terza rima is adapted from the account of the conquest of Mexico written by Bernal Díaz del Castillo, with scenic impressions based on MacLeish's own trip through Mexico by foot and mule-back in the winter of 1929. Seen through the eyes of this conqueror, the conquest was not made to carry out the expansion plans of the Spanish governors, mercenaries, or missionaries, but rather was done against their advice through the love of individual men for adventure, challenge, even bloodshed. When the conquest is actually completed and the civilizers follow, there is no more use for the conqueror, and he mourns that "the west is gone now." The poem won a Pulitzer Prize.

Conrad, Barnaby (b. San Francisco, March 27, 1922–   ), painter, writer. After obtaining his B.A. at Yale in 1944, Barnaby Conrad spent much of his time in and near Spanish bullrings. Like another aficionado, Tom Lea, Conrad regarded himself as a painter who could write. His work is a product of his own experience in the bullring as well as that of celebrated *toreros* whom he has known, and includes one of the best known books on bullfighting in English. *Matador* (1952) communicates much of the tension and brutality of the bullring. Conrad's books include: *The Innocent Villa* (1949); *La Fiesta Brava* (1953); *My Life as a Matador* (1954); *Gates of Fear* (1955); *The Death of Manolete* (1957); *San Francisco* (1959); *Dangerfield* (1961), the story of a famous (unspecified) novelist, probably suggested by Sinclair Lewis, who had once employed Conrad as a secretary, and two translations, *Wounds of Hunger* (1958); *The Second Life of Captain Contreras* (1960).

Conrad, Robert Taylor (b. Philadelphia, June 10, 1810—d. June 27, 1858), lawyer, newspaperman, poet, playwright. Conrad practiced law in his native city, became judge of the court of criminal sessions and mayor of Philadelphia. He loved literature and wrote constantly. In 1843 he was chairman of the committee which awarded $100 to Poe for *The Gold Bug*. He wrote several plays, including *Jack Cade* (1835), and although his own time rated him highly, he is seen today as a bombastic, stilted writer of small importance.

Considine, Bob [Robert Bernard] (b. Washington, D.C., Nov. 4, 1906—   ), newspaperman, columnist. Considine has worked on various Washington and New York City newspapers and has written a number of books, including *MacArthur the Magnificent* (1942); *Innocents at Home* (1951); *Panama Canal* (1951); *Christmas Stocking* (1958). He has collaborated on other books—with Capt. Ted W. Lason on *Thirty Seconds over Tokyo* (1943); with Gen. Jonathan M. Wainwright on *General Wainwright's Story* (1946); with Babe Ruth on *The Babe Ruth Story* (1948). He has also written movie scripts.

Conspiracy of Pontiac, A History of (1851), the first of a series of books by FRANCIS PARKMAN intended to describe the struggle between the British and the French for the rule of North America. Parkman pays constant attention to the part played by the Indians in this struggle; and his opening volume tells about the Ottawa Indian chief who led a rebellion against the English in the Ohio Valley and regions farther east (1763–65).

Conspirator, The (1850), a romance by ELIZA ANN DUPUY in which Aaron Burr is the chief character.

Constantius and Pulchera, The History of, or, Constancy Rewarded (1795), an anonymous novel. The story is laid in the period of the American Revolution, but the background is international. In the course of the hero's experiences he is seized by a British press gang, and the heroine has misadventures as a prisoner on various British vessels. Such history as the book contains is pale, says Alexander Cowie, alongside the extravagant plot. "It may, in fact, have been intended as a burlesque," he concludes.

Constitution, The. See OLD IRONSIDES.

Constitution of the United States. On May 25, 1787, a convention was organized in the Philadelphia State House to revise the Articles of Confederation. The convention continued to meet until Sept. 17, 1787, when the Constitution was formally adopted and signed; it was ratified by September 28. The original is now in the National Archives Building in Washington, in a bronze and marble shrine.

The Constitution, after a brief preamble, is divided into seven *Articles*. These deal with (1) legislative organization and powers; (2) the President and his functions; (3) judicial powers and certain legal restrictions; (4) the powers of the states and restrictions upon them; (5) the amendment of the Constitution; (6) the supremacy of the Constitution, also prohibition of religious tests for office; (7) the machinery of ratification for the Constitution. Some states refused to ratify unless there was immediately added a "Bill of Rights"; by Dec. 15, 1791, the First Congress had secured adoption of the first ten amendments. Since then thirteen other amendments have been adopted; the eighteenth, dealing with the prohibition of intoxicating liquors, was nullified by the twenty-first.

Compromise was the procedure of the Constitutional Convention. No matter what their reservations were on individual points, the delegates were convinced that a strong central government must be set up at once; and that it would be better to agree on compromises than to deadlock the Convention. The Constitution represents a compromise between centralization and local autonomy. It shows as strong a dependence on British political philosophy, particularly John Locke, as does the Declaration of Independence. Most authorities feel that its genesis is not French but English, in its acceptance of property as the basis of political action.

The Records of the Federal Convention are most usefully available in the four-volume edition (1911–37) edited by Max Farrand. The *Debates* that preceded the ratification of the Constitution were collected in five volumes (1836–45) by JONATHAN ELLIOT. The most famous of the arguments for ratification were papers called THE FEDERALIST, printed in the form of letters to newspapers in 1787–88; the authors were principally ALEXANDER HAMILTON and JAMES MADISON. An immense body of writings has gathered around the origin and making of the Constitution and around the background and philosophy of the makers. Exceedingly important has been the interpretation of the Constitution by the courts, especially the Supreme Court—as presented, for example, in *Basic Constitutional Cases* (1948), edited by C. Gordon Post and others. The many varying interpretations to which the Constitution has been subjected and the heated and sometimes dangerous debates that have arisen over the wording of its clauses provide history's most weighty contribution to the science of semantics. Nevertheless, it is true that in general the Constitution is phrased in clear and simple language; its style is on the whole much superior to most legal enactments. W. E. Gladstone once proclaimed: "The American Constitution is the most wonderful work ever struck off at any given time by the brain and purpose of man."

In his notable study, AN ECONOMIC INTERPRETATION OF THE CONSTITUTION (1913), Charles A. Beard strongly emphasizes the view that property is the master force in every society, and that the development of the United States cannot be understood until one understands the role property interests played in shaping the fundamental law. An elaborate treatment is *The American Constitution, Its Origins and Development* (1948), by Alfred H. Kelly and Winifred A. Harbison. Other important volumes are Carl Swisher's *American Constitutional Development* (1943, 1954), W. W. Crosskey's *Politics and the Constitution in the History of the United States* (2 v., 1953), B. A. Findlay's *Guaranteed for Life: Your Rights Under the Constitution* (1955), and T. R. Powell's *Vagaries and Varieties in Constitutional Interpretation* (1956).

Constitutional Courant, The. A single issue of this paper appeared on Sept. 21, 1765. It attacked the Stamp Act and reproduced a *Pennsylvania Gazette* cartoon representing a snake in eight sections which symbolized the colonies and bore the motto, "Join or Die." The editor was James Parker, who from 1758 to 1760 had printed THE AMERICAN MAGAZINE at Woodbridge, N.J. The editor's name is sometimes given as William Goddard.

Contemplations (1678), a poem by ANNE BRADSTREET, published in the second edition of her TENTH MUSE (1650). The poem is a meditative and descriptive poem obviously written under the influence of Edmund Spenser and Giles Fletcher.

Continental Army, The. A term applied to the soldiers raised in the thirteen colonies to wage war against England. The Continental Army did not include the militia and the guerrilla forces. It was a term first used by Congress in June, 1775, when it appropriated $6,000 for the support of a "Continental Army" and made Washington commander-in-chief. But thereafter Congress did little to help maintain the morale and the supplies of the army. The most vivid and full account of this astonishing group is given in Lynn Montross' *Rag, Tag, and Bobtail: The Story of the Continental Army, 1775–1783* (1952).

Continental Congress, The. In 1774 the Continental Congress met in Philadelphia with delegates from all the colonies except Georgia, its chief purpose being that of offering more determined resistance to British measures. It governed the country, with varying degrees of efficiency, until the establishment of the Union in 1789. The first Congress addressed the British king in a statement of grievances, later its members adopted the DECLARATION OF INDEPENDENCE. They appointed Washington commander-in-chief, sent representatives abroad, set up the ARTICLES OF CONFEDERATION (which gave them written powers as the Congress of the Confederation), and prepared the way for the CONSTITUTION. Lynn Montross tells the story of the fifteen years of the Congress in *The Reluctant Rebels* (1950). *The Journals of the Continental Congress* were collected in thirty-four volumes (1904–37).

Continental currency. The Continental Congress, lacking real authority to tax the people, used the worst possible substitute: it issued paper money lavishly, to which its own name was attached. Its value depreciated rapidly; a pound of sugar cost $10. Hence the expressions, "not worth a continental" and "I don't give a continental."

Contrast, The (1787), a play by ROYALL TYLER. *The Contrast* marks the true beginning of American drama. Tyler, a Bostonian of good family who was active as a patriot during the Revolutionary War, had considerable literary abilities, particularly as a comic writer. Serving as a major in the Army in the course of Shays' Rebellion (1786–87), he was sent as an observer to New York City in March, 1787. There he visited the theater and became acquainted with Thomas Wignell, the leading American comedian of the day. Tyler must have carried the manuscript of his play in his baggage, since hardly a month later, on April 16, *The Contrast* was given at the JOHN STREET THEATER, the first native comedy to be produced by a company of professional actors. Wignell himself played the role of Jonathan, first of the innumerable stage Yankees of American and foreign drama. Tyler presented Wignell with the copyright; the latter published the play in 1790 by subscription.

The plot involves a complicated series of courtships and philanderings, centering mostly around Billy Dimple, a wealthy Anglophile who is affianced to the clever Maria but pays attention carelessly to other women. He finally loses his wealth and also Maria, who marries the staid but attractive Colonel Manly, a Revolutionary officer. Dimple has a manservant, Jessamy, who tries to educate Jonathan, Manly's attendant, in the ways of the world, but Jonathan remains truly rural.

It is because of Jonathan that the play has retained so vigorous a life. He is presented in decided contrast to Jessamy, who is proud to be the servitor of wealthy and fashionable men. He expects to marry Tabitha Wyman, the deacon's daughter, and later when he fails to make any headway with a fashionable maid he exclaims, "If this is the way with your city ladies, give me the twenty acres of rock, the Bible, the cow, and Tabitha, and a little peaceable bundling." This stage Yankee had an immense influence and became a symbol of American defiance to British criticism of America. Within a few years many imitations of Jonathan held the stage, in William Dunlap's *The Modest Soldier* (1787) and THE FATHER (1788), Samuel Low's *The Politician Outwitted* (1788), the anonymous *The Better Sort* (1789), SUSANNA ROWSON's *Americans in England* (1796), and the anonymous *The Traveler Returned* (1798).

Convention and Revolt in Poetry (1919), by JOHN LIVINGSTON LOWES. This is a survey of the history of poetry, especially English and American. The author shows that the historical development of poetry has been an alternation between convention and revolt. Harry Hayden Clark calls it a "learned and stimulating book."

Conversation at Midnight (1937), a poetic mélange by EDNA ST. VINCENT MILLAY. Eight men, assembled after dinner in a Washington Square house, discuss—poetically and satirically—everything from modern plumbing to the Supreme Court.

Converse, Frederick S[hepherd] (b. Newton, Mass., Jan. 5, 1871—d. June 8, 1940), musician, composer, teacher. Converse was the first American composer to write an opera that received its first production in the United States; his *The Pipe of Desire*, a one-act piece laid in fairyland, based on the book by George Edwards Barton, was presented at the Metropolitan Opera House in New York City in 1910. Later he wrote both music and book for *The Sacrifice,* produced in Boston in 1911. Converse also composed THE MYSTIC TRUMPETER (1905), a musical composition based on Walt Whitman's poem of the same name (1872), and a tone poem called *California* (1927).

Conway, Moncure D[aniel] (b. near Falmouth, Va., Mar. 17, 1832—d. Nov. 15, 1907), clergyman, editor, reformer, biographer. Conway's life was one of constant evolution. A descendant of slaveholding southerners, he became an ardent abolitionist. His parents followed Methodism with fanatical zeal, but Conway turned to Unitarianism, finally became president of the New York Freethinkers' Society. In later years he wrote books about Carlyle (1881), Emerson (1882), and Hawthorne (1890), all of them very popular. His most celebrated work is his life of Thomas Paine (1892) and his edition of Paine's writings (1894–96). He also wrote a novel about the Civil War, *Pine and Palm* (1887), and an *Autobiography* (1904).

Conway Cabal (1777). A conspiracy among several of Washington's generals to deprive him of power. General Thomas Conway was only a minor conspirator, but his name was attached to the group. Others who were possibly implicated were Generals HORATIO GATES, Charles E. Lee, JAMES WILKINSON, Thomas Mifflin, and also probably a few congressmen. Some of these conspirators appear in Maxwell Anderson's VALLEY FORGE (1934) in the act of intrigue.

Conwell, Russell H[erman] (b. S. Worthington, Me., Feb. 15, 1843—d. Dec. 6, 1925), clergyman, lecturer, author. Conwell followed many pursuits before he became minister of a church in Lexington, Mass., and then one of the most celebrated lecturers in the country, first on the Redpath, later on the Chautauqua circuit. Most famous of his lectures was ACRES OF DIAMONDS, delivered more than 6,000 times with all his original enthusiasm. It was Chautauqua's most reliable stand-by, and he deeply influenced millions of listeners with his doctrine that wealth and power lay within the grasp of everyone, that no one had the "right to be poor," and that "love is the grandest thing on God's earth, but fortunate is the lover who has plenty of money." Conwell amassed a large fortune, used it mainly in helping poor youths to get an education, then founded Temple University, his greatest monument.

Cook, Ebenezer (b. England, c. 1672—d. 1732), poet, satirist. According to one of his poems, THE SOT-WEED FACTOR; OR, A VOYAGE TO MARYLAND (London, 1708), Cook was an Englishman who visited America and on his return gave his unfavorable and contemptuous observations of colonial life in verse that imitated Butler's *Hudibras*. He may actually have been an American who was given the title "Laureate" by Lord Baltimore. He may also have been the author of several elegies and may have written *Sotweed Redivivus* (1730), a serious treatise in verse on tobacco and its overproduction. He may likewise have composed a burlesque poem on the rebellion of NATHANIEL BACON. Whoever he was, he became the hero of a satirical novel, *The Sot-Weed Factor* (1960) by John Barth.

Cook, Fannie (b. St. Charles, Mo., Oct. 4, 1893—d. Aug. 25, 1949), teacher, civic worker, lecturer, novelist. Mrs. Cook won various awards for her work among sharecroppers and for her contributions to interracial welfare. Her novel,

Mrs. Palmer's Money, won in 1946 the first George Washington Carver Memorial Award of $2,500 for making, among the year's publications, "the most effective literary contribution to the Negro's place in American life." She also wrote *The Hill Grows Steeper* (1938), *Boot-Heel Doctor* (1941), and *Storm Against the Wall* (1948).

Cook, George Cram (b. Davenport, Ia., Oct. 7, 1873—d. Jan. 14, 1924), teacher, novelist, playwright, actor, poet. An ardent reader and a dreamer, Cook was a key figure in the American LITTLE THEATER. In 1903 he published *Roderick Taliaferro,* a story of Montezuma's empire, in 1911 *The Chasm,* a socialist novel.

In 1913 Cook married SUSAN GLASPELL—his third marriage—and his career took a new turn. They went to Provincetown, Mass., and there in 1915 organized the PROVINCETOWN PLAYERS. The theater was an old fish-house on a wharf owned by Mary Heaton Vorse; it had been used by Mrs. Wilbur Daniel Steele as a studio. Here were produced the first plays of EUGENE O'NEILL, often in outdoor settings that repeated the scenes of the plays; "Jig" Cook himself took the role of Yank in the first production of BOUND EAST FOR CARDIFF. A one-act comedy on a Freudian theme, SUPPRESSED DESIRES (1915), by Cook and his wife, actually inspired the undertaking; this was first given in a private home at Provincetown. The success of the venture encouraged the group to undertake theater operations in New York (1916–29). Various locations were employed, two on Macdougal Street in Greenwich Village. In 1920 the Players produced O'Neill's THE EMPEROR JONES; so great was its success that it had to be moved to an uptown theater. They also gave Cook's *The Spring* (1921), Glaspell's *The Verge* (1922), and O'Neill's *Diff'rent* (1921) and *The Hairy Ape* (1922).

Having fulfilled his purpose of giving new impetus to American drama and not wishing to compete with the commercial theater, Cook lost interest in the project, and in 1921 sailed for Greece where he settled down, grew a prophet's beard, fraternized with the peasants and local poets, and won general esteem. On his death his grave was marked by a stone taken from the ruins of Apollo's temple at Delphi. His widow wrote an affectionate account of him in *The Road to the Temple* (1926).

Cook, James (1728–1779), English naval officer, explorer. From 1759 to 1767, Cook explored the St. Lawrence River and the coasts of Labrador and Newfoundland. His accuracy brought him an assignment to explore the South Pacific Ocean. In 1776 he was ordered to find a direct passage from the Pacific Ocean across the American continent to the Atlantic. He made extensive surveys of the northwest coast of North America and rediscovered the Sandwich (Hawaiian) Islands. He was killed by natives there in 1779. John W. Vandercook's *The Great Sailor* (1951) is a biography of Cook. He was the subject of numerous 19th century English biographies and recently of some American pub-

lications: *The Great Sailor* (1951) by John Vandercook; *Captain Cook and the South Pacific* (1955) by John Gwyther. *Within the Sound of the Waves* (1941), by William Chickering, *Lost Eden* (1947), by Paul McGinnis, and *Return of Lono* (1956), by Oswald Bushnell, are all novels based on Captain Cook's adventures in Hawaii. John Beaglehole edited his *Journals on His Voyages of Discovery* (4 v., 1955–58).

cookbooks, American. The first cookbooks printed in America appeared in the middle of the 18th century and were merely reprints of English cookbooks. The first cookbook written by an American woman was Amelia Simmons' *American Cookery* (1796), with more than 170 recipes. Other books followed: *The Family Receipt Book* (1819); the novelist Eliza Leslie's *Seventy-Five Receipts for Pastry, Cakes, and Sweetmeats* (1828); the antislavery leader Lydia Maria Child's *The Frugal Housewife* (1829), which went through twenty-six editions in twenty-one years. Sarah Josepha Hale, editor of *Godey's Lady's Book,* turned out a *Receipt Book* (1846) that was in great demand. Mary Virginia Hawes Terhune, who wrote stories under the pen name Marion Harland and whose son was ALBERT PAYSON TERHUNE, compiled a popular volume called *Common Sense in the Household* (1871). Cooking schools produced their own cookbooks. Accurate measurements came in with Fannie Farmer's fabulously popular BOSTON COOKING-SCHOOL COOKBOOK (1896), still widely sold today. Cookbooks frequently sell in the hundreds of thousands. Many specialize—in the foods of certain national or racial groups, in chicken or salads, in recipes for two people or for a person living alone, in recipes garnered from noted restaurants, in low-calorie foods.

Cooke, [Alfred] Alistair (b. England, Nov. 20, 1908—   ), journalist, broadcaster, author. Cooke attained celebrity in this country and England as a versatile and sympathetic commentator on current affairs and popular culture in the United States. In 1934, after a two-year stay in the United States as a Commonwealth Fellow at Yale and Harvard, he became film critic for the British Broadcasting Company (1934–37) and his interest in this field ultimately expressed itself in two books: *Garbo and the Night Watchmen* (1937) and *Douglas Fairbanks* (1940). He was the London correspondent of the National Broadcasting Company in 1936–37, a commentator on American affairs for the British Broadcasting Company from 1938, and a reporter on American affairs for the *London Times* (1938–42), the *London Daily Herald* (1941–43), and, finally, the *Manchester Guardian* (1945–   ). He became the latter's chief American correspondent in 1948. In 1952, Cooke became the host of the award-winning television series, *Omnibus.* His books since 1950 include *A Generation On Trial* (1950), an account of the Alger Hiss trials which Arthur Schlesinger, Jr., described as "a superb piece of writing, lively, perceptive, ironic, and compassionate"; *One Man's America* (1952), a collection of informal essays on life and manners in America originally designed for the British radio audience; *Christmas Eve* (1952); *A Commencement Address* (1954). He edited *The Vintage Mencken* (1954).

Cooke, John Esten (b. near Winchester, Va., Nov. 3, 1830—d. Sept. 27, 1886), novelist, biographer, historian. Cooke was of the First Families of Virginia, by birth and in spirit. His older brother, PHILIP PENDLETON COOKE, and a

cousin, JOHN PENDLETON KENNEDY, were likewise authors. General J. E. B. STUART was his nephew by marriage. Cooke wrote historical novels, with JAMES FENIMORE COOPER as a literary model. After serving in the Confederate ranks, he wrote other novels with the Civil War as a background. The three generally reckoned his best are THE VIRGINIA COMEDIANS (1854), a romantic account of the love affairs of a Virginia gentleman; its sequel, HENRY ST. JOHN, GENTLEMAN (1859), laid in the period preceding the Revolution; and *Surry of Eagle's-Nest* (1866), in which the life of the hero parallels the career of Stonewall Jackson. Cooke also wrote biographies of Jefferson (1854), Stonewall Jackson (1863), Lee (1871), and Samuel J. Tilden (1876). One of his best books is *Virginia: A History of the People* (1883). Carl Van Doren notes that Cooke was "one of the first who contributed to the poetic idealization of the antebellum South which has been one of the most prominent aspects of American fiction since 1865." See also LEATHER STOCKING AND SILK, OR, HUNTER JOHN MYERS AND HIS TIMES; MY LADY POCAHONTAS.

Cooke, Philip Pendleton (b. near Martinsburg, Va. [now W. Va.], Oct. 26, 1816—d. Jan. 20, 1850), lawyer, author. This older brother of JOHN ESTEN COOKE died in his early thirties of tuberculosis. His literary career was that of a fine gentleman rather than a professional writer. He published only one volume— *Froissart Ballads and Other Poems* (1847). His most famous piece was FLORENCE VANE, published in *Burton's Magazine* in 1840.

Cooke, Rose Terry (b. West Hartford, Conn., Feb. 17, 1827—d. July 18, 1892), teacher, poet, story writer. Miss Cooke has become a writer more highly esteemed by critics and literary historians than by the reading public. Pre-eminently a social historian of a New England already fading in her time, she began her career by writing a novel about the Mormons in Utah, about whom she knew nothing by direct observation. Moreover, all through her life she felt that she was really fulfilling her literary vocation by writing poetry, and that her fiction was secondary. Yet some of the best accounts of the people of New England are found in her stories and sketches: *Somebody's Neighbors* (1881); *Root-Bound and Other Sketches* (1885); *The Sphinx's Children and Other People's* (1886); *Huckleberries Gathered from New England Hills* (1891). She wrote simply and sympathetically and with unfailing humor. Her poems were gathered in a single volume in 1860 and again in 1888.

Coolbrith, Ina Donna (b. near Springfield, Ill., March 10, 1842—d. Feb. 29, 1928), teacher, librarian, poet. Miss Coolbrith went to California as a child in 1852 in a prairie schooner, and thereafter she was closely identified with the literary history of that state. She was a co-editor of the OVERLAND MONTHLY, and with BRET HARTE and CHARLES WARREN STODDARD formed the "Golden Gate Trinity," the nucleus of San Francisco's flourishing literary colony. She became the librarian of the Bohemian Club, the only woman in its precincts, and at the Panama-Pacific Exposition in 1915 organized a World Congress of Authors. She was made Poet Laureate of California by the legislature. Her poetry is pleasant but not important. Her final collection is *Songs from the Golden Gate* (1895).

Coolidge, [John] Calvin (b. Plymouth Corners, Vt., July 4, 1872—d. Jan. 5, 1933), thirtieth President of the United States. After graduation from Amherst, Coolidge studied law and practiced in Northampton, Mass. He became successively city councilman, city solicitor, mayor, state representative, state senator, court clerk, lieutenant governor, governor, and Vice-President. His political creed was uncompromisingly Republican. He became President on Harding's death, Aug. 2, 1923, was nominated and elected for a new term in 1924. At a time of overwhelming national prosperity (before the 1929 depression), he constantly praised and practiced frugality, both public and private. After Hoover's election he retired and began writing a daily syndicated article of two hundred words, no more, no less. He also composed an *Autobiography* (1929).

Coolidge's reputation for grim taciturnity has been somewhat exaggerated. His style was generally spare, but sometimes long-winded and hackneyed. Some 82,000 pieces of Coolidge correspondence were presented to the Library of Congress (1929, 1954). In 1950 enough material to make eleven bound volumes of transcripts recording Coolidge's press conferences was unearthed in the Forbes Library at Northampton. The most expressive book about Coolidge is William Allen White's biography, A PURITAN IN BABYLON (1938).

Coolidge, Susan. Pen name of SARAH CHAUNCEY WOOLSEY.

Cool Tombs (1915; published in CORNHUSKERS, 1918), a poem on death by CARL SANDBURG. It is written in free verse, and makes effective use of the phrase "in the dust, in the cool tombs" to establish a pattern.

Cooper, Courtney Ryley (b. Kansas City, Mo., Oct. 31, 1886—d. Sept. 29, 1940), press agent, newspaperman, novelist, feature writer. Cooper began with the circus, and some of his best books are about life under the big tent. He wrote *Memories of Buffalo Bill* (with L. F. Cody, 1918); *Under the Big Top* (1923); *Lions 'n' Tigers 'n' Everything* (1924); *Annie Oakley* (1927); *Circus Day* (1931). Cooper led a sensational career with theatrical people, on the battlefront in World War I, and in association with Secret Service men (*The Eagle's Eye*, in collaboration with W. J. Flynn, 1918, told of the latter). He went to Hollywood to write and direct several crime pictures, spent his last days investigating fifth-column activities in Mexico. See GORDON W. LILLIE.

Cooper, Frank. Pen name of W. G. SIMMS.

Cooper, James Fenimore (b. Burlington, N.J., Sept. 15, 1789—d. Sept. 14, 1851), novelist. Christened simply James Cooper, the author added his mother's family name, Fenimore, in 1826. In 1790 the Cooper family moved from

New Jersey to a huge tract in central New York, a colonial grant purchased by Cooper's father, who established Cooperstown and built a pretentious manor estate on Otsego Lake. Here Cooper spent his boyhood, learning much about frontier and wilderness life from the rude inhabitants of the place—lore which he put to

good use in his later writings. He was educated in Albany and at Yale; later he shipped as a merchant seaman and served for three years as a midshipman in the navy, chiefly on the Great Lakes. For a time afterwards he lived in New York City, later in Paris, then in 1833 he returned to the family estate in Cooperstown, where he died in 1851.

Cooper published his first novel in 1820, but THE SPY, published the following year, was his first work to attract attention. It created such a furore that the author decided to devote himself entirely to a literary career. In 1823 he published THE PIONEERS, the first in order of writing, but not of narrative, of the LEATHER-STOCKING TALES, Cooper's most popular works. THE LAST OF THE MOHICANS is generally regarded as the best of the series and his best book. Others in the series are THE DEERSLAYER, THE PATHFINDER, and THE PRAIRIE. Interspersed and following were other novels. THE PILOT, which became immensely popular in its own time, was written to show that, unlike Scott's *The Pirate* (1822), a sea story should contain authentic details of seamanship. Cooper's interest in the sea also produced a *History of the Navy of the United States.* Later he turned to the Anti-Rent War of Dutch colonial times in New York for a trilogy, *The Littlepage Chronicles.* Cooper's last novels became more and more spiritless and testy, and today they have only an academic interest.

In his personality Cooper was a man of paradoxes. At heart a deeply patriotic American, he nevertheless managed to offend large numbers of his countrymen through his criticism of American customs, political license, and what he chose to regard as the boorishness of the frontier traders and farmers. On the one hand he praised the "natural man," the Indian or white scout who lived at one with the wilderness; on the other he acclaimed the cultured values of the European landed gentry. He did not fail to fill his novels with social criticism nor to people them with vicious characters, some drawn from life. He wrote tracts and pamphlets to defend himself, and he spent much of his energy and income in pursuing libel litigations through the courts, often conducting his own case. He was widely attacked in American newspapers, yet he was the first American author to win international fame, and many of the most eminent persons of his time, at home and abroad, regarded him highly. As a literary artist Cooper lacked the facility of style and characterization possessed by his British contemporary, Sir Walter Scott. His characters, especially his women, were often stereotypes. His prose was inclined to be awkward, ranging from the flatly pedantic to the lushly ornate. Yet in some of his characters, especially NATTY BUMPPO and other men of the woods, Cooper achieved memorable portraits; and in his descriptive writing, the first attempt at large-scale interpretation of nature in America, he occasionally rose to heights of genuine eloquence. Moreover, he wrote with a brisk narrative style and constructed lively plots. Many of his novels still retain their popularity, especially among young readers who relish good adventure stories. This fate would have much displeased their author, who intended his novels as serious criticisms of American life, but he failed to organize his beliefs into a fully consistent social philosophy which might have attracted succeeding generations of mature readers.

Cooper's works include: PRECAUTION (1820); *The Spy* (1821); *The Pioneers* (1823); *The Pilot* (1823); *The Last of the Mohicans* (1826); *The Prairie* (1827); THE RED ROVER (1827); NOTIONS OF THE AMERICANS (1828); *History of the Navy of the United States* (1834); HOMEWARD BOUND (1838); *Home As Found* (1838); *The Pathfinder* (1840); *The Deerslayer* (1841); WING-AND-WING (1842); AFLOAT AND ASHORE (1844); MILES WALLINGFORD (1844); SATANSTOE (1845); THE CHAINBEARER (1845); THE REDSKINS (1846). *The Works of J. Fenimore Cooper* (12 v., 1849–51) was edited by Cooper himself. An edition of his *Works* containing all his novels except NED MYERS (1843) and his short tales and nonfiction prose was published in 1859–61 (32 v.). See THE AMERICAN DEMOCRAT (1838). The Household Edition of his *Works* (32 v., 1876–84) had introductions to many of the writings by his daughter SUSAN FENIMORE COOPER. His *Works* also appeared in 1895–1900 (33 v.). His *Correspondence* was edited (2 v., 1922) by his grandson James F. Cooper. Lives of Cooper have been written by T. R. Lounsbury (1882), W. B. S. Clymer (1900), Henry W. Boynton (1931), and James Grossman (1949). Arvid Shulenberger has analyzed *Cooper's Theory of Fiction* (1955). Cooper appears as a character in Bellamy Partridge's novel, *Big Freeze* (1948), and he figures prominently in James Russell Lowell's A FABLE FOR CRITICS (1848). Cooper's birthplace in Burlington, N.J., is now a Cooper museum, and there is an impressive monument to him at Cooperstown. See COOPERSTOWN; WILLIAM COOPER, THE BRAVO; THE CRATER; THE MANIKINS; LIONEL LINCOLN; THE HEADSMAN; THE HEIDENMAUER; THE SEA LIONS; THE TWO ADMIRALS; THE WATER WITCH; THE WEPT OF WISH-TON-WISH; WYANDOTTE.

EDWIN S. FULCOMER

Cooper, Lane (b. New Brunswick, N.J., Dec. 14, 1875—d. Nov. 27, 1959), teacher, biographer, historian, editor. Cooper began teaching at Cornell in 1902, became a professor of English in 1915, and continued as such till his retirement in 1943. He has edited and written many books, particularly on Greek literature, including *The Greek Genius and Its Influence* (1917); *An Aristotelian Theory of Comedy* (1922); and *Experiments in Education* (1943).

Cooper, Louise Field (b. Hartford, Conn., March 8, 1905—   ), newspaperwoman, short-story writer. Mrs. Cooper for many years contributed what the *Saturday Review of Literature* called "gently-bred, double-take vignettes" to

The New Yorker. These were mostly inspired by peaceful, suburban Woodbridge, Conn., where she and her family resided. Among her books: *The Lighted Box* (1942); *The Deer on the Stairs* (1947); *Summer Stranger* (1947).

Cooper, Myles (b. England, 1735–1785), clergyman, educational administrator, loyalist. Cooper served as the second president of King's [Columbia] College, from 1763 to 1775, then fled to England. There he wrote *National Humiliation and Repentance Recommended* (1777). A biography of him was written by Clarence H. Vance (1930).

Cooper, Peter (b. New York City, Feb. 12, 1791—d. April 4, 1883), inventor, industrialist, philanthropist, author. Cooper made many important inventions, built several large factories, founded Cooper Union, and attacked some of the evils of the day in his *Autobiography* (1877) and his *Ideas for a Science of Good Government* (1883). He was a picturesque figure, sharing with Bryant the distinction of being "the patriarch of Broadway." Edward C. Mack wrote admiringly of him in *Peter Cooper: Citizen of New York* (1949).

Cooper, Susan Fenimore (b. Scarsdale, N.Y., April 17, 1813—d. Dec. 31, 1894), writer, editor, biographer. Miss Cooper, who never married, devoted herself to the study of nature and to writing about it, also to the preparation of material about her famous father, JAMES FENIMORE COOPER. Her best-known work was called *Rural Hours* (1850). *Pages and Pictures* (1861) contains selections from her father's books along with comments on them; she also wrote prefaces for the volumes of an edition (1876–84) of his writings.

Cooper, Thomas (b. England, Oct. 22, 1759—d. May 12, 1839), scientist, writer. An English liberal who favored the cause of the French Revolution, Cooper sought a more sympathetic environment in the United States. He joined the Jeffersonians and began writing political pamphlets attacking the Federalists; these were collected later in *Political Essays* (1799). In *Some Information Respecting America* (1795) Cooper for the first time used a famous phrase: "The government is a government *of* the people and *for* the people." He became an American citizen, was appointed to the faculty of Dickinson College, later became professor of chemistry at South Carolina College and eventually its president. He was a pioneer in applying the results of scientific research to the Bible, and on frequent occasions showed himself a bold reformer. An English geologist said he was "a most remarkable man, some of whose screws were uncommonly loose." Dumas Malone wrote a life of him (1926).

Cooper, William (1754–1809), author, father of JAMES FENIMORE COOPER. Originally a resident of Burlington, N.J., Cooper (usually called "Judge Cooper") removed to a large estate at Cooperstown, N.Y., and there lived the life of a "lord of the marches," with land holdings that at one time amounted to 750,000 acres, mostly unexplored. He was described as "a testy and choleric gentleman easily wrought into passion," who supported Federalism vigorously. Alexander Cowie depicts him as "an energetic man possessed of many talents, including the gift for vigorous narrative." He published at Dublin *A Guide to the Wilderness* (1810), a book on the settlements in western New York. He appears as Judge Temple in his son's *The Pioneers* (1823).

Cooperstown, N.Y. When JAMES FENIMORE COOPER was about a year old his father moved the family into the wilderness at the outlet of Lake Otsego, where in 1788 he had founded Cooperstown. Here young Cooper spent his boyhood, and here he spent his last years. In 1838 he published *Chronicles of Cooperstown*. Many of his novels describe wilderness conditions in this village, although Indians were already few in number in the vicinity. THE DEERSLAYER (1841) takes place on Otsego Lake (the "Glimmerglass" of Cooper's stories) and along its borders. Otsego Hall, built by WILLIAM COOPER, is made the residence of Marmaduke Temple in THE PIONEERS (1823), and Judge Temple in the same book is the novelist's father. NATTY BUMPPO's original was possibly an old hunter named Shipman, who used to offer his game at Judge Cooper's door. Since 1940 Cooperstown has undergone a restoration that recalls Williamsburg, Va., and numerous mementoes of Cooper and his family can be found there. It also contains the National Baseball Museum and Hall of Fame, in honor of Abner Doubleday, who lived there when, it was said, he invented the game in 1839.

Cooper Union (also called **Cooper Institute**), New York City. It was founded by PETER COOPER in 1857–59 for the "advancement of science and art," since then giving free courses in science, chemistry, engineering, and art. Here Lincoln delivered on Feb. 27, 1860, his famous *Cooper Institute Address*, which helped him win the Republican nomination.

Copeland, Charles T[ownsend] (b. Calais, Me., April 27, 1860—d. July 24, 1952), teacher, editor, lecturer. Copeland joined the faculty of Harvard in 1893, became a professor in 1925, retired in 1928. He was a Harvard legend from his early days at the university. Affectionately called "Copey"—behind his back—by his students, he drew large numbers to his classes through his skill in lecturing and reciting poetry. He edited some of his favorite selections in *The Copeland Reader* (1926). Fleetwood, the English instructor in Charles M. Flandrau's *Diary of a Freshman* (1901), is said to have been drawn from Copeland. Alexander Woollcott wrote appreciatively of him in *Enchanted Aisles* (1924) and James Donald Adams constructed a biography *Copey of Harvard* (1959) from the reminiscences of his former students.

Copland, Aaron (b. Brooklyn, N.Y., Nov. 14, 1900—   ), composer, author. One of America's most illustrious and popular contemporary composers, Copland has agitated vigorously on behalf of 20th century music, has taught and lectured extensively, at Harvard and elsewhere.

Among his many musical productions are *El Salón México* (1934), *Billy the Kid* (a ballet, 1938), *Lincoln Portrait* (1942), *Rodeo* (a ballet, 1942), *Appalachian Spring* (a ballet, 1944), *The Tender Land* (1954). He has also composed film scores, including that for *Our Town* (1940). His writings include *Our New Music* (1941), *Music and Imagination* (1952), *What to Listen for in Music* (1939; revised, 1957), and *Copland on Music* (1960).

Copperheads. Northerners (mainly Democrats) who during the Civil War favored the cause of the South and advocated a negotiated peace. They were made the subject of Bret Harte's poem, *The Copperhead* (1868), of Harold Frederic's novel, *The Copperhead* (1893), and of Augustus Thomas' play, *The Copperhead* (1918).

Copway, George. See KAH-GE-GA-GAH-BOWH.

copyright. The framers of the Constitution sought to protect authors by stating that the Congress "shall have power to promote the progress of science and the useful arts by securing for limited times to authors and inventors the exclusive right to their respective writings and discoveries." This merely extended to this country common-law and statutory rights already prevalent in England. In 1790 the first Copyright Law was passed. It failed to protect foreign authors, however, and pirating of foreign books became prevalent to an extent that kept American authors poor until the end of the 19th century. In 1909 our present law, with modifications introduced from time to time, was passed. Since 1955 it has extended copyright to authors in foreign countries that, like the United States, have ratified the Universal Copyright Convention, if their books have a copyright notice. Copyright runs for twenty-eight years, may be renewed for an equal period. A good concise summary of copyright law is *A Copyright Guide* by Harriet F. Pilpel and Morton David Goldberg (1960).

Coquette (1928), a play by GEORGE ABBOTT and Ann Preston Bridgers. It is a melodrama in which a father shoots the juvenile lead in order to protect the good name of his daughter, and the daughter commits suicide to save her father. The play is laid in the South, and, according to E. M. Gagey (*Revolution in American Drama*, 1947), "well represents the foolish persistence of an outmoded chivalric code," in that section of the country. Its star was Helen Hayes.

Coquette, The (1797), a novel by Hannah Webster Foster, published anonymously. In the form of letters it purported to give an account of the seduction of the author's cousin, Elizabeth Whitman, supposedly by Pierpont Edwards, son of Jonathan Edwards, and of her death in childbirth. (Another contemporary account makes the seducer Aaron Burr.) H. R. Brown, in his introduction to a reprint of the novel (1939), remarks that the book, which became very popular, was "the most striking example in early American fiction of the pervasive influence of Samuel Richardson."

Corbett, Elizabeth Frances (b. Aurora, Ill., Sept. 30, 1887—   ), novelist, biographer. More than forty-five pleasant books have flowed from the pen of this popular author of unaffectedly homey, familiar, "sincere and tactful" escapist fiction. Her family audience has especially delighted in "the Graper girls" and "Mrs. Meigs" series. She has also been published widely in magazines. Among her works: *Cecily and the Wide World* (1916); *Mr. and Mrs. Meigs* (1940); *Out at the Soldiers' Home* (semi-autobiographical, 1941); and *Hidden Island* (1961).

Corbin, Alice. See ALICE HENDERSON.

Corey, Giles. One of the victims of the SALEM WITCHCRAFT TRIALS, Corey became an admired figure in New England legend and poetry. A man of eighty, he died unflinchingly pressed under heavy weights in 1692; his wife was hanged at the same time. It was part of the legend that sprang up after his death that his ghost reappeared in Salem before times of disaster for that city. An account of his martyrdom appeared in Robert Calef's MORE WONDERS OF THE INVISIBLE WORLD (1700), a contemporary ballad was written about him, Longfellow made him the subject of the second of his NEW ENGLAND TRAGEDIES (*Giles Corey of the Salem Farms*, 1868), Mary E. Wilkins Freeman wrote a six-act play about him (*Giles Corey, Yeoman,* 1893), and he appears in Arthur Miller's play *The Crucible* (1953).

Corey, Paul [Frederick] (b. Shelby Co., Iowa, July 8, 1903—   ), editor, novelist, writer on economic and political affairs. A graduate of the University of Iowa, Corey worked for several years on *The Economist* and the staff of the *Encyclopaedia Britannica,* traveled abroad, devoted himself more and more to the study of farm conditions in the United States. *Buy an Acre* (1944) was his most popular nonfiction publication; he also has written *Homemade Homes* (1950). Among his novels are a trilogy with a middle western setting: *Three Miles Square* (1939), *The Road Returns* (1940), and *County Seat* (1941); and *Acres of Antaeus* (1946); *Milk Flood* (1956).

Corle, Edwin (b. Wildwood, N.J., May 7, 1906—   ), novelist, writer on the West and Southwest. Corle has written *Mojave* (1934); *Fig Tree John* (1935); *People on the Earth* (1938); *Listen, Bright Angel* (1946); *Billy the Kid* (1953). His *Desert Country* (1941) and *The Gila: River of the Southwest* (1951) are animated and authoritative nonfiction descriptions.

Corn (written, 1874; published, 1875), a 200-line poem by SIDNEY LANIER. Its rejection by William Dean Howells, editor of the *Atlantic Monthly,* brought on an emotional crisis for Lanier, though he eventually emerged from it with the conviction that "my business in life was to make poems." Corn, in the poem, is the image of "the poet soul-sublime," and the theme proceeds from aesthetic analysis to an attack on the cotton trade. In short, the poem, which appeared finally in *Lippincott's Magazine,* is a somewhat confusing mixture of poetic and agrarian theory.

Cornhuskers (1918), a collection of poems by CARL SANDBURG. This volume received a special Pulitzer award in 1919. The opening poem, PRAIRIE, "is composed of glorious patches and irreconcilable journalese," Alfred Kreymborg holds. Among other noteworthy poems included in this gathering were *Caboose Thoughts, Wilderness, Chicago Poet, Testament, Haunts.* Louis Untermeyer praises the "fresh blend of proper names and slang" in this collection as "Sandburg's most characteristic idiom." See COOL TOMBS.

Cornwallis, Lord Charles (b. England, Dec. 31, 1738—d. Oct. 5, 1805), English soldier, public official. Cornwallis was made a major general in the British army in 1775, and the following year was sent with seven regiments to reinforce Sir William Howe in America. He won some important victories, but when he appeared in the South he was forced into Yorktown and there surrendered to Washington (Oct. 19, 1781). He subsequently served as governor general of India, helped suppress a rebellion in Ireland, and negotiated a treaty with Napoleon (1802).

Coronado, Francisco Vásquez de (b. Spain, 1510–54), explorer. In search of Quivira, a city supposedly of fabulous wealth, he set out in 1540 from Mexico, ascended the Colorado River, discovered the Grand Canyon, explored California, and extended his journeys as far as eastern Kansas. Failing to discover Quivira, he returned in 1542, and died in disgrace. J. Frank Dobie wrote a novel called *Coronado's Children* (1931). Herbert E. Bolton's *Coronado, Knight of Pueblos and Plains* (1949), did much to rehabilitate his fame as one of the greatest explorers. See CIBOLA.

Corso, Gregory (b. New York City, March 26, 1930—   ), beat poet. Emerging from the background of a Lower East Side slum and a jail sentence at the age of sixteen, Corso educated himself, met ALLEN GINSBERG, and began to write poetry. His native power with words led many to think of him as a kind of noble savage or naïf. He always speaks cryptically in public as well as in his verse. Like many of the "beat," he enjoys poking fun at society and its conventions. Corso's books of poetry include *The Vestal Lady of Brattle* (1955); *Gasoline* (1958); *Bomb* (1958); *The Happy Birthday of Death and Other Poems* (1960). See BEAT WRITING.

Corson, Hiram (b. Philadelphia, Nov. 6, 1828—d. June 15, 1911), teacher, critic. Corson served as professor of English at Cornell from 1870 to 1903. He was a popular lecturer, both within the college and to clubs. His deep interest in Robert Browning (he published an *Introduction* to the study of the poet in 1886) led him to foster the formation of Browning study groups. He wrote a similar introductory book on Shakespeare (1889), *A Primer of English* (1892), and *Aims of Literary Study* (1895).

Cortez [or Cortes], Hernando (b. Spain,

1485–d. 1547), Spanish conqueror of Mexico. He sailed from Cuba in 1518, coasted along Yucatan and Mexico, landed and founded Vera Cruz and then destroyed his fleet so his men would have no thoughts of returning. He conquered the AZTEC armies as he marched inland, and entered Mexico City on Nov. 8, 1519. He took Montezuma as a hostage, but Montezuma later died of wounds received while he was addressing an Aztec army in revolt against the Spaniards. Cortez for a time was driven back, but finally made himself master of Mexico. He was deposed (1526), then recalled to Spain and received with honors (1528); in a return to Mexico he discovered Lower California (1536). He returned to Spain to die on his estate at Seville.

Some letters of his on the conquest of Mexico have been preserved, but the details of the expedition were best given in Bernal Díaz' *True History of the Conquest of Mexico* (3 v., 1632). W. H. Prescott wrote a picturesque HISTORY OF THE CONQUEST OF MEXICO (3 v., 1843), Archibald MacLeish used Díaz' account as the basis of his powerful poem *Conquistador* (1932). Fernando Benitez told his story in a historical volume, *In the Footsteps of Cortes* (1952). Three novels laid in this period are Lew Wallace's THE FAIR GOD (1873), Samuel Shellabarger's CAPTAIN FROM CASTILE (1945), and Alexander Baron's *The Golden Princess* (1955).

Corwin, Norman [Lewis] (b. Boston, May 3, 1910–   ), radio writer, producer, director. Corwin joined the Columbia Broadcasting System in 1938, and from the start was given a free hand in working out programs. His scripts were collected in a series of volumes: *The Plot to Overthrow Christmas* (1940); *Thirteen by Corwin* (1942); *More by Corwin* (1944); ON A NOTE OF TRIUMPH (1945); *Untitled and Other Works* (1947). His prize-winning opera, *The Warrior*, was produced at the Metropolitan Opera House (1947). *Dog in the Sky* (1952) is a reworking in prose narrative of his radio play, *The Odyssey of Runyon Jones*. His satirical drama, *Seems Radio Is Here to Stay*, was selected by Max Wylie as "the best verse experiment" of the year and was reprinted in Wylie's collection, *Best Broadcasts of 1938–39* (1939). Corwin has shown from the beginning of his career a mingling of humor and sentiment, fertility in invention, and skill in employing new techniques. In addition to his own scripts, Corwin helped produce many others of merit. In 1947 he received the Wendell Willkie One World Award, and was sent on a journey around the world, from which he brought back recordings that became part of thirteen *One World Flight* broadcasts. See also MY CLIENT CURLEY.

Coryell, John Russell (b. 1848?[–52?]—d. July 15, 1924), a dime novelist who wrote under many pen names, particularly NICK CARTER. He formed one of a group of hack-writers who wrote on demand sensational, romantic, and sentimental fiction of all kinds, including such titles as *The American Marquis, The Old Detective's Pupil, Among the Nihilists, Nick Carter*

Down East, and *Wife or Stenographer—Which?*

Cosmopolitan, The. A magazine founded in Rochester, N.Y., in 1886 by Joseph N. Hallock. In 1887 its editorial offices were moved to New York; when John Brisben Walker became the owner and editor in 1889, it became one of the most popular magazines of the day. Walker sold the magazine to WILLIAM RANDOLPH HEARST in 1905; in 1925 Hearst merged it with *Hearst's International*, but kept the name and the volume numbering of *The Cosmopolitan*. It has numbered some of the most distinguished writers of several generations among its contributors, especially in the realm of fiction, and at one time also published books.

Costain, Thomas [Bertram] (b. Brantford, Ont., May 8, 1885—d. Oct. 8, 1965), editor, novelist. Costain came to America in 1920, after editing *Maclean's*, a Canadian magazine, and became a naturalized citizen. He was fiction editor of THE SATURDAY EVENING POST and worked for Doubleday & Co., Twentieth Century-Fox Film Corp., and elsewhere. Though he is best known for his numerous historical novels, Costain, commenting on his editorial days, wrote: "The fourteen years I spent with the *Saturday Evening Post*, during most of which time I was chief associate editor to GEORGE HORACE LORIMER and part of my work was to act as scout for material, was a very interesting and exciting span. Since I climbed over the fence there has been a tendency to forget all about that period. If I have the time I plan to write some autobiographical material and will deal rather fully with the work of a literary scout." One of his best books is a biography of the Biblical military leader *Joshua* (1943), done with Roger MacVeagh. His historical novels combine factual accuracy with rapid movement and plenty of sex; they include *Ride with Me* (1944); *The Black Rose* (1945); *The Moneyman* (1947); *Son of a Hundred Kings* (1950), a book about his boyhood; *The Silver Chalice* (1952); *The Tontine* (1955); *Below the Salt* (1957); *The Darkness and the Dawn* (1959). His daughter Molly (Mrs. Howard Haycraft) has written biographies of Queen Victoria, Sarah Siddons, and Arabella Stuart for girls.

Cotton, Ann and **John**. Dim figures in early Virginian history (see NATHANIEL BACON). It is generally held by historians that John Cotton wrote THE BURWELL PAPERS, and that Ann made a condensation of these documents. Mrs. Cotton addressed her narrative to "C.H.," who has been identified as Christopher Harris, an Englishman who had lived in Virginia. Howard Mumford Jones insisted that "Virginia never saw a gifted literary woman named 'Mrs. Ann Cotton,'" and attributes the version to "some literary hack." Moses Coit Tyler, Jay B. Hubbell, Francis Burton Harrison, and C. E. Schorer offer evidence for a contrary view.

Cotton, John (b. England, Dec. 4, 1584—d. Dec. 23, 1652), clergyman, writer. Dissatisfied with conditions in the Anglican Church, Cotton emigrated to Boston in 1633 and, already famous, was received by the townspeople with a season of prayers and fasting. He became one of the most important spiritual leaders of the new colony, along with THOMAS HOOKER, with whom he wrote a *Survey of the Sum of Church Discipline* (1648). He would study twelve hours

a day, his grandson COTTON MATHER reported, "and would call that a scholar's day." Frankly aristocratic, he sought to build a Christian theocracy in which the priest would be set above the magistrate. His preaching was excellent; a contemporary poet, Nathaniel Morton, wrote of him:

A man of might at heavenly eloquence,
To fix the ear and charm the conscience.

He engaged in a controversy with ROGER WILLIAMS (see BLOUDY TENE[N]T OF PERSECUTION); and he once denounced democracy as "the meanest and worst of all forms of government." Among his writings: *God's Promise to His Plantation* (1630); *The Keys of the Kingdom of Heaven* (1644); MILK FOR BABES (1646); *The Bloudy Tene[n]t* (1647). The first biography ever written about an American was JOHN NORTON's life of Cotton, *Abel Being Dead Yet Speaketh* (1658; reprinted, 1834). Cotton collections are found in the Boston Public Library and at Bowdoin College.

Counsellor-at-Law (1931), a play by ELMER RICE. George Simon, a ruthless lawyer, fights off an attempt to disbar him. The drama was exceedingly popular and has been revived often; much of the popularity is perhaps owing to the subordinate characters in the play, an entertaining group of rogues.

Country Lovers, The (1804), a humorous poem by THOMAS GREEN FESSENDEN. The poem's Yankee dialect and stanza pattern antici-

pate Lowell's THE COURTIN' (1867). The poem is sometimes called *Jonathan's Courtship*.

country newspaper, the. A characteristic product of American journalism, in which news at its simplest may be found. Members of the small community that a country newspaper serves enjoy the pleasure of frequently seeing their names in print. Such a paper is usually a one-man business enterprise; the owner is also editor, reporter, circulation and advertising manager, and, sometimes, printer of the paper. Its editorials often equal in merit those appearing in the best urban papers. Writing of *The Southern Country Editor* (1948), Thomas D. Clark concludes that he was a philosopher, often a brave man. Murder, he reports, was an occupational risk. In recent years some of these newspapers have tended to degenerate by accepting syndicated columnists and syndicated articles, instead of depending on local products. Perhaps the most famous small-town paper of recent years was the EMPORIA (Kans.) GAZETTE, edited by WILLIAM ALLEN WHITE. It attained a wide circulation, far beyond the boundaries of Emporia. Earl V. Chapin gives an amusing account in *Long Wednesdays* (1953) of his experiences as a country editor in Tamarack, Minn. HARRY GOLDEN has become famous for the witty essays he wrote for his newspaper *The Carolina Israelite*.

Country of the Pointed Firs, The (1896), sketches by SARAH ORNE JEWETT. Thinly bound together by a faint thread of plot, these sketches describe a Maine community, an isolated seaport town. Local color is deftly applied, and humor mingles with sentiment in descriptions of characters who are resolutely themselves. Willa Cather thought so well of the book that she placed it alongside *Huckleberry Finn* and *The Scarlet Letter*.

Country People (1924), a novel by RUTH SUCKOW. This realistic family saga, covering three generations of a German-American family in Iowa, from the mid-19th century to the early 20th, established the author's reputation as one of the significant novelists of her time.

County Chairman, The (1903), a play by GEORGE ADE. Tilford Wheeler, the chairman, is the leading character of this play directed against political corruption.

Cournos, John (b. Russia, March 6, 1881—), novelist, critic, poet, translator. Cournos was brought to the United States in 1891; he held many jobs before turning to newspaper work and writing. His first three stories—*The Mask* (1919), *The Wall* (1921), *Babel* (1922) —formed a trilogy based largely on his own experiences. *The New Candide* (1924) satirizes certain American customs, but without bitterness. A sentence in *The Wall* was quoted by Charles C. Baldwin as summing up Cournos' creed: "The good healer, Time, wears pain down to beauty." His later books are primarily biographical and historical studies for young people; among them: *Famous Modern American Novelists* (1952), and lives of Roger Williams (1953) and John Adams (1954).

Courtin', The (1867), a poem in Yankee dialect by JAMES RUSSELL LOWELL. Published in the *Second Series* of THE BIGLOW PAPERS, it marked a pleasant diversion from the main political and satirical trend of these poems. Lowell, in writing this story of a rural courtship, was undoubtedly influenced by Thomas Green Fessenden's THE COUNTRY LOVERS (1804) and by numerous other dialect poems in New England newspapers, often, as Harold W. Thompson points out, "in celebration of comic Yankee love." Lowell, despite his wide and deep culture, was more at home in the homely Yankee speech than in ordinary English, although no doubt he was fully aware that in *The Courtin'* he was following a pastoral tradition as old as Theocritus. The poem takes its place with the best of that tradition, and is, besides, a notable example of native American humor and sentiment.

Courtship of Miles Standish, The (1858), a long narrative poem by HENRY WADSWORTH LONGFELLOW. Like many other 19th-century American writers, Longfellow was concerned with investing the American scene with a useful native mythology, especially in his three long narrative poems—EVANGELINE (1847), HIAWATHA (1855), and *The Courtship of Miles Standish*.

The story concerns the early days of the settlement at Plymouth. The captain of the colony, Miles Standish, sends his friend and emissary, John Alden, to woo Priscilla. She prefers John to the older man, despite the honest pleas John offers on Miles' behalf. When Miles is reported killed in the war, the lovers are left free to plan marriage. Miles returns on the eve of the wedding and gives the young lovers his blessing. This poem, like most of the Longfellow canon, has been relegated to the schoolroom. Despite its early popularity, the weight of sentimentality and moralizing far overpowers any poetic values.

Cousins, Norman (b. Union, N.J., June 24, 1912—   ), writer, editor. In 1942 Cousins assumed the editorship of the SATURDAY REVIEW OF LITERATURE, which became the *Saturday Review* to indicate the much wider range of subject matter it had assumed as a result of Cousins' deep interest in political affairs and in other arts of communication than literature. During World War II he served for three years in the Office of War Information. In 1948 he received the Thomas Jefferson award for the Advancement of Democracy in Journalism. Among his books: *The Good Inheritance: The Democratic Chance* (1942); *Modern Man is Obsolete* (1945); *Who Speaks for Man?* (1952). He has also edited several anthologies.

Covarrubias, Miguel (b. Mexico, Nov. 22, 1905—d. Feb. 4, 1958), caricaturist, painter, archaeologist, anthropologist, geographer. This great Mexican artist began his career at the age of fifteen, and was successful as a caricaturist almost from the start. The Mexican government sent him on a scholarship to New York in 1923; at twenty-one he designed the sets for a Theatre Guild production of *Androcles and the Lion*, be-

gan working for newspapers and *Vanity Fair*, published the *Prince of Wales and Other Famous Americans* (1925), a book of caricatures. Then other interests, especially in the field of anthropology, began to attract him. With Mrs. Covarrubias he went to live in the East Indies and produced with her *The Island of Bali* (1937), a mixture of paintings, drawings, photographs, and prose. His *Mexico South* (1946) was the result of a similar collaboration over a period of three years. The *Saturday Review* said, on the appearance of this volume, "His maps, paintings, drawings, photographs, prose, and caricatures work together now to tell the story of how people became what they are, and why." *The Eagle, the Jaguar, and the Serpent* (1954), an illustrated history of Indian and Eskimo art in North America, was followed by *Indian Art of Mexico and Central America* (1957), also lavishly illustrated.

Covered Wagon, The (1922), a novel by EMERSON HOUGH. The book came late in Hough's career and was his greatest success. It is the story of the dangerous and difficult migration westward of a train of two hundred wagons in 1848. Throughout the narrative runs the story of the love of two men for a gentle schoolteacher. The men become bitter enemies, but the death of one solves the problem of a choice between them. Kit Carson comes with news of the discovery of gold, and only a small portion of the wagons continue on to their original goal. The novel was the result of careful research and expresses the author's love of nature and knowledge of frontier hardships. It was made by James Cruze into a successful movie (1923) described by Robert E. Sherwood as "the one great American epic that the screen has produced."

cover story. A term used by TIME magazine to describe a feature article about the person whose portrait appears on the cover of an issue.

cowboys. At the time of the Revolution the term *cowboy* was used to describe any member of a gang of ruffians attached to the British cause who spread fire and rapine through New York and Pennsylvania. These guerrillas tried the same tactics in the War of 1812, but encountered equal ruthlessness among their American opponents. Phil Stong (*Cowboys and Americans*, 1939) states that not till around 1880–1900 did America discover "the splendid creature of romance it had been overlooking, the western cowboy of song and legend." He asserts that cowboys do not ride mustangs commonly; that the great cowboy states are Montana and Wyoming; that cowboys rarely wear cowboy costumes; that they do not yell "Yippee" or "Hi-ho" because the finest breeds of beef cattle are easily alarmed; that the lasso and its uses were derived from Mexicans.

Reliable collectors have gathered many ballads from the cowboys, such as *Git Along, Little Dogie; The Cowboy's Dream;* and *The Cowboy's Lament*. Among collectors of cowboy songs are N. Howard Thorp (*Songs of the Cowboys,*

1908) and CHARLES J. FINGER. Folklore specialists have also been fascinated by the cowboy,
as in the legends of Pecos Bill and the White
Mustang. WILL ROGERS took the cowboy to the
stage, the motion-picture screen, and the printed
page in an amiable form that was probably fairly
true to life. STEWART EDWARD WHITE, OWEN
WISTER, and WILL JAMES wrote entertainingly
about cowboys. More recent books include C. L.
Sonnischen's *Cowboys and Cattle Kings* (1950);
Bruce Grant's *The Cowboy's Encyclopedia*
(1951); and J. B. Frantz and J. E. Choate, Jr.'s
The American Cowboy Myth and the Reality
(1955). See also PHILIP ASHTON ROLLINS.

Cowboy Songs and Other Frontier Ballads
(1910; rev., 1938), collected by JOHN A. LOMAX
(later edition in collaboration with Alan Lomax).
The best collection in this field. See HOME ON
THE RANGE.

Cowell, Henry [Dixon] (b. Menlo Park.,
Cal., Mar. 11, 1897—d. Dec. 10, 1965), composer. He first won his reputation for experi-
mentalism in his music, but later, as he turned
to native themes and somewhat simpler forms,
his work found wide favor among listeners. He
has been editor of the quarterly *New Music*,
and has done much to promote the cause of
American music. Among his compositions are
Old American Country Set (1937); *Tales of
Our Countryside* (1940); *American Pipers*
(1943); *To America* (1946); *O'Higgins Chile*
(an opera, 1950). He has also written a biography of Charles Ives (1954).

Cowie, Alexander (b. St. Paul, Minn., March
8, 1896—   ), teacher, critic, historian. An
authority on American fiction, Cowie has taught
at Wesleyan University since 1924, attained
professorial rank in 1949. He wrote a book on
John Trumbull in 1936. His *The Rise of the
American Novel* (1948) is a learned and entertaining work. *American Writers Today* (1956)
is his most recent book.

Cowley, Malcolm (b. near Belsano, Pa., Aug.
24, 1898—   ), poet, editor, critic, translator.
A member of the American expatriate colony
abroad in the 1920's, Cowley helped to get out
two expatriate magazines, *Secession* and *Broom*,
and made a study of expatriate psychology in
EXILE'S RETURN (1934; rev. ed., 1951). His collections of verse are *Blue Juniata* (1929) and
Dry Season (1942). His criticism, *After the
Genteel Tradition; American Writers Since 1910*
(1937; reissued in 1959) and *The Literary
Situation* (1954), has been well regarded. He
has edited a number of books, among them *The
Portable Hemingway* (1944); *The Portable
Faulkner* (1946); *The Complete Walt Whitman*
(1948); *The Portable Hawthorne* (1948); *The
Stories of F. Scott Fitzgerald* (1950). He wrote
the introduction to a valuable facsimile edition
of the 1855 version of Walt Whitman's *Leaves
of Grass* (1959).

Cowperwood, Frank. Chief character in Theodore Dreiser's trilogy—THE FINANCIER (1912),
THE TITAN (1914), and THE STOIC (1947). It
is believed that Dreiser had the financier Charles
T. Yerkes in mind when he depicted Cowper-

wood and his career. He appears also in *The
Bulwark* (posthumous, 1946).

Coxe, George Harmon (b. Olean, N.Y., April
23, 1901—   ), writer of mystery tales.
Coxe's first book was *Murder with Pictures*
(1935), and thereafter he has kept up a steady
output of fast-paced detective stories. He has
also written many short tales for magazines.
Among his books: *Four Frightened Women*
(1939); *Assignment in Guiana* (1942); *The
Jade Venus* (1945); *Eye Witness* (1950); *The
Crimson Clue* (1953).

Cozzens, Frederick S[wartwout] (b. New
York City, March 11, 1818—d. Dec. 23, 1869),
wine merchant, essayist, humorist. Cozzens followed in his father's footsteps as a wholesale
food purveyor, but was an enthusiastic amateur
in the literary field. He edited (1854–61) a
trade magazine, *The Wine Press.* He published
several collections of his writings, including
Yankee Doodle (1847) and his most popular
work, *The Sparrowgrass Papers* (1856), a
humorous and still readable account of a city
man's experiences in the country.

Cozzens, James Gould (b. Chicago, Aug. 19,
1903—   ), novelist. Cozzens has always
been a writer (he made the *Atlantic Monthly*
when he was only sixteen), and his writing has
consistently displayed finished craftsmanship
and competency. His keen interest in various
aspects of life is illustrated successively in his
novels: the sea and sailors in *S.S. San Pedro*
(1931); the medical profession in *The Last
Adam* (1933); the ministry in *Men and Brethren*
(1936); the law in *The Just and the Unjust*
(1942); the army during World War II in the
Pulitzer Prize winner *Guard of Honor* (1948).
By Love Possessed (1957), enthusiastically
praised all over the country (though a reaction
set in later), somewhat surprisingly became a
best seller. Cozzens revels in endless detail, but
his fellow novelist, John P. Marquand, testified,
"If he tried he could not be dull," and called
him "a superb fictional craftsman." Brendan
Gill finds in him an "absence of deep feeling"
and a "failure to commit himself beyond irony."
Bernard De Voto has compared him to William
Faulkner and Ernest Hemingway. Dwight Macdonald disparaged his work in an explosive
article, "By Cozzens Possessed," in *Commentary.*

cracker. Defined by Webster's *New International* as "one of the lower class of the white
population of the southern United States, especially of Georgia and Florida, inhabiting the
hills and backwoods." This group has often appeared in fiction laid in the South, particularly
in the novels of ERSKINE CALDWELL.

**cracker-barrel [or cracker-box] philosophers
and humor.** The cracker barrel or box in the
"general store," common in New England and
other American communities, was a gathering
place for those who came to enjoy a little gossip and exchange of anecdotes. Traditionally,
much rustic wit was generated in these exchanges; traditionally, too, such rustic talk was
far superior in ultimate wisdom to the sophisticated but unsound conversation of city folk.

Thus it early became a custom among American humorists to disguise their epigrams and characterizations in some form of non-standard English, such as Yankee speech. The traditional homespun philosopher was given to the deliberate manufacture of malapropisms and solecisms. Sometimes the disguise took the form of misspelling, mispronunciation, or learned word-mangling; everywhere was the homely simile, the down-to-earth metaphor. Writers of high literary standard did not hesitate to join the ranks of the rustic philosophers—James Russell Lowell, for example, in the BIGLOW PAPERS. Jeanette Tandy treated some important writers of this type in *Crackerbox Philosophers in American Humor* (1925).

Craddock, Charles Egbert. Pen name of MARY NOAILLES MURFREE.

Cradle Will Rock, The (1937), a musical drama by MARC BLITZSTEIN. Originally sponsored by the WPA Theater, the play was canceled on opening night because of its attack on capitalism. Actors and audience moved to a nearby theater and the play was put on without scenery, costumes, or properties. The author played the score and provided a running commentary on the action. This arrangement proved so successful that it was retained when ORSON WELLES produced the play on Broadway shortly after. George Jean Nathan described it as "except for a few scattered moments, the miscegenation of a Union Square soapbox and a talented jukebox," but the play was an interesting attempt to create a popular musical with the seriousness and the musical variety and continuity of opera. It was revived by Michael Meyerberg in 1947.

Crafts, William (b. Charleston, S.C., Jan. 24, 1787—d. Sept. 23, 1826), lawyer, public official, essayist, poet. His mother was a Northerner and he was Harvard-educated. He had no more than superficial talents in his various endeavors. His verses, imitative of the English romantics, appeared in local papers. He collected them in *The Raciad and Other Occasional Poems* (1810) and *Sullivan's Island and Other Poems* (1820).

Craig, Hardin (b. Owensboro, Ky., June 29, 1875—d. Oct. 13, 1968), teacher, scholar, author. Craig was educated at Centre College in Kentucky, Princeton University, the University of Jena, and Oxford. He had a distinguished career as a teacher at Princeton, the Universities of Minnesota, Iowa State, Stanford, North Carolina and Missouri. A scholar of Medieval and Renaissance English literature, especially Shakespeare, Professor Craig has written a number of outstanding textbooks and critical works, including *Shakespeare: A Historical and Critical Study* (1931, with annotated texts of twenty-one plays reprinted 1958); *The Enchanted Glass: The Elizabethan Mind in Literature* (1936, reprinted 1952); *An Interpretation of Shakespeare* (1948); *The Complete Works of Shakespeare* (1951, ed.); *The History of English Literature* (1950, ed.); *An Introduction to Shakespeare* (1950); *English Prose of the Nineteenth Century* (1953, ed. with J. M. Thomas); and *English Religious*

Drama of the Middle Ages (1955). He is also the author of *Literary Study and the Scholarly Profession* (1944); *Freedom and Renaissance* (1949, a series of lectures about problems in civilization and literature); and *Woodrow Wilson at Princeton* (1960).

Craig's Wife (produced, 1925; published, 1926), a play by GEORGE KELLY that won the Pulitzer Prize (1926). It is a study of a selfish, narrow woman, more interested in her house than in her husband, and so domineering and stupid that at last her marriage breaks down, everyone leaves her, and she is left with the house. The play became a favorite of little theaters, was used several times for motion-picture plots, and was often heard on the radio. Alexander Woollcott said that Harriet Craig was "a woman who would rather have her husband smoke in hell than in her living room."

Cram, Ralph Adams (b. Hampton Falls, N.H., Dec. 16, 1863—d. Sept. 22, 1942), architect, writer on architecture, art critic. While studying architecture in a Boston office, Cram also served as art critic for the Boston *Transcript*. He continued his studies in various countries abroad, specialized in Gothic architecture, and brought about a revival of interest in Gothic design, especially for churches. He was the architect for churches all over the country, altered the original plan of St. John the Divine in New York City to fit his ideas. Among his books: *Church Building* (1906, 1924); *The Gothic Quest* (1907); *American Church Building of Today* (1929), and *My Life in Architecture* (1936).

Cranch, Christopher Pearse (b. Alexandria, Va., March 18, 1813—d. Jan. 20, 1892), clergy-

man, essayist, poet, painter. Cranch had a talent for humor, evidenced in his two juveniles (*The Last of the Huggermuggers*, 1856, and

Kobboltozo, 1857) and in some of his drawings
and caricatures, that was somewhat suppressed
by his environment and occupation. He had
ample means, lived for many years in Rome and
Paris, was definitely a dilettante. His best-known
work was an able translation of the *Aeneid*
(1872), his best single poem *Stanzas.* His verses
were collected in *The Bird and the Bell* (1875).

Crane, Frank (b. Urbana, Ill., May 12, 1861—
d. Nov. 5, 1928), clergyman, columnist. At the
height of his career, Crane was the most widely
syndicated of American columnists. Amy Loveman characterized his essays as "a composite of
quotations, platitudes, truisms, glittering generalities, and a good deal of sound common
sense," which won him an enormous following.
Some of his writings were collected in *Adventures in Common Sense* (1916); *Four-Minute
Essays* (10 v., 1919); *The Crane Classics* (10
v., 1920).

Crane, [Harold] Hart (b. Garretsville, Ohio,
July 21, 1899—d. April 27, 1932), poet. Crane
was a poet from the age of thirteen. Little
understood by his unsympathetic father, a well-
to-do Cleveland candy manufacturer who sought
to make "a man" out of him, or by his doting
mother, who alternately indulged and denied
him, Hart Crane had his full quota of misery
in adolescence and merely compounded it in
manhood. The Cranes quarreled violently over
their son. Education stopped for him with the
public schools, but at seventeen, after six months
at his maternal grandfather's fruit ranch on the
Isle of Pines, he came to New York to write
and to prepare for college. His talents and his
precocity, however, recommended him to the
bohemian literati, and his education was permanently postponed. This may have been his
salvation as a poet, for Crane could pick up
what he wanted as he ran; his mind had none
of the trammels that the college man unconsciously acquires. A deficient substance, a want
of allusiveness, is not Crane's limitation. He
knew Donne, Marlowe, Poe, Melville, Whitman,
Dickinson, Laforgue, Rimbaud, Dostoevski,
Eliot, and Sandburg better than casually, reflecting them in his verse. Irregularly employed,
Crane forged ahead as a poet.

From *Bruno's Bohemian* he moved on to the
Little Review, Pagan, Poetry, and *The Dial.* In
1926 appeared WHITE BUILDINGS, his first volume of verse. He appealed to Otto Kahn for
financial aid, and it was through the largesse of
that modern Maecenas that THE BRIDGE [2] (a
limited edition inscribed to Kahn, 1929; general
edition, 1930) was written. A Guggenheim Fellowship carried him to Mexico and work on a
poem on Montezuma, and it was on his return
from Vera Cruz, on the steamship *Orizaba,* that
he took his life by leaping overboard.

In 1933 appeared Crane's *Collected Verse.*
Incorporated in this, the earlier *White Buildings*
signalizes at once both his debt to T. S. ELIOT
and his revolt against that Missouri Oxonian.
Crane looked upon *For the Marriage of Faustus
and Helen,* the major piece in this first volume,
as "an answer to the cultural pessimism" of

Eliot. The Fausti of the world—its poets—are
bidden to enjoy the evanescent yet perdurable
beauty of its Helens. Bathing in the "gleaming
tides" cleanses one of pessimism and makes one
newly generative, as it did Erasmus. There is
a "world dimensional for those untwisted by the
love of things irreconcilable. . . ." Passionate
perception rather than intellectual scrutiny is
the proper character for the "vision" of the poet.
This idea is central in Crane and is his meaning
when elsewhere he writes that "wine redeems
the sight." Crane's own clear vision found its
most loved object in this first volume—"that
great wink of eternity," the sea. His best pieces
all have to do with it: *Emblems of Conduct,
North Labrador, At Melville's Tomb,* and
Voyages.

Loving the sea, Hart Crane was drawn to
Arthur Rimbaud and his *Le bateau ivre* rather
than to Coleridge, for the former immerses himself whereas the latter merely floats. Rimbaud's
methods and his effects were closely studied by
the American—in technique Rimbaud was Hart
Crane's master. But this should be observed:
Crane struggled to fuse more disparate impressions than Rimbaud ever brought together; he
sought to reach the ultimate in aesthetic economy, as a letter to Harriet Monroe elucidating
one of his poems makes clear. Crane's incoherence comes from this physical effort; but so,
too, do some of his grandest effects—as when he
describes Brooklyn Bridge as "harp and altar
of the fury fused." He is at his best, however,
when from inspiration drawn from love, the
economy of expression is natural and not forced:

> The sun beats lightning on the waves,
> The waves fold thunder on the sand.

The element ever invited him: he is the Pali-
nurus of American poets.

Hart Crane has his monument in Brooklyn
Bridge, the structure that inspired his greatest
poem and a poem which, after all its faults have
been enumerated, is still one of the best of
modern times. In his letters to Otto Kahn, since
published in *Hound and Horn,* Crane makes
clear not only the symphonic structure of his
masterpiece but also states the "movements" of
the composition with considerable explicitness.
Though he altered his design to some extent and
dropped passages that were described to Kahn,
the poet's own elucidation is still the best commentary on *The Bridge.*

Yet the wrong emphasis must not be put upon
his declaration, "What I am really handling, you
see, is the Myth of America." Allen Tate, for
all his devotion to Crane, does his friend an
unwitting disservice when he asserts that, "if
we subtract from Crane's idea its periphery of
sensation, we have left only the dead abstraction, the Greatness of America. . . ." Why this
operation should ever be performed upon *The
Bridge* is a mystery; it is comparable to saying
that eliminate the music from Dvořák's *New
World Symphony* and all you have left is a dead
abstraction, the Greatness of America. The truth

is that what Tate describes as sensation—the imagery, the symbolism—is the poem itself, whereas the "Myth of America" (not quite the same thing as "the Greatness of America") is peripheral. As Crane carefully explains to Otto Kahn, one can get "the chronological historical angle" from "any history primer." He meant, and he succeeded in getting, his music and his imagery to suggest great passages out of the American Myth to a meditative mind partially narcotized by the symphonic flood. We should inquire not whether he presents a plausible legend, like Homer, but whether the total experience is plausible, whether the myth is introduced naturally or is forced.

Though Crane wrote Allen Tate that his poem is not perfectly "realized," its realization is closer than he allowed. Of all the poems by moderns that have the analogy of musical composition for their design, *The Bridge* is the most satisfactory. Crane has carried nearest to perfection the idea that teased Whitman, Lanier, Mallarmé, Pound, Eliot, and Wallace Stevens. Though a measure of his greatness, the total composition is not his chief triumph; it is the fusing of fire and water in his scintillating imagery, fire of the poet's passionate heart and water, not merely of the aqueous humor, but of the tidal depths and shallows, such as lovingly laved the Parsee, Starbuck, Ahab—and the White Whale. See under JOSEPH STELLA and SAMUEL GREENBERG.

OSCAR CARGILL

Crane, Ichabod. The gawky schoolmaster whom the burly Brom Van Brunt outwits in Washington Irving's LEGEND OF SLEEPY HOLLOW (in *The Sketch Book*, 1819). Both are suitors for the hand of Katerina Van Tassel; Brom scares the schoolmaster out of the running by pretending to be a headless horseman. Irving says that on a windy day Ichabod looked like "some scarecrow eloped from a corn-field."

Crane, Nathalia [Clara Ruth Abarbanel] (b. New York City, Aug. 11, 1913—   ), novelist, poet. Some of her poems were submitted for publication at the age of nine, appeared without reference to her age, and were accepted as adult productions. *The Janitor's Boy* (1924), her first collection, created a sensation; later collections —*The Singing Crow* (1926); *Pocahontas* (1930); *Swear by the Night* (1936)—both puzzled and pleased readers. There was much naïveté, but also an astonishing command of poetic technique, the obvious influence of EMILY DICKINSON, and philosophizing that seemed beyond Nathalia's years. She also produced two novels of no particular merit, and in later years turned to teaching.

Crane, Stephen [Townley] (b. Newark, N.J., Nov. 1, 1871—d. June 5, 1900), war correspondent, novelist, short-story writer, poet. The fourteenth child of the Reverend J. T. Crane, D.D., presiding elder of the Newark district, and Mary Helen Peck Crane, Stephen started life with printer's ink in his veins, as both his parents were writers and two of his brothers were newspaper reporters. He wrote stories when he was but eight; at sixteen he did ghost-writing for his New York *Tribune* correspondent brothers and reporting for his mother's column in that paper.

Crane grew up in full rebellion against the Methodist strain in his family tradition and engaged in the "vices" that his father—a learned divine, a manuscript preacher, and a noted wit —preached against and wrote about: baseball, which Stephen preferred to books; the theater, to which he aspired by writing plays; and novels, which he not only read but wrote. Nor would his father have approved of Stephen's having love affairs with a woman who was already betrothed (Helen Trent), with a woman who was already married and who later obtained a divorce (Lily Brandon Munroe), with an actress (Amy Leslie), and with the twice-married hostess and proprietess of a night-club brothel (Cora Howorth, also known as Cora Taylor). A woman of broad culture, Stephen's mother was the daughter of the Reverend George Peck, an eloquent Methodist minister and at one time the editor of the *Christian Advocate* (the official organ of the Methodist Episcopal Church). A niece of Bishop Jesse Peck, one of the founders of Syracuse University, she was much concerned in the cause for temperance. She died when Stephen was beginning his twenty-first year (on Dec. 7, 1891); his father had died in 1880. As for the soldier strand in Crane's heritage, the Cranes during the American Revolution (to quote Stephen Crane) "were pretty hot people. The old man Stephen served in the Continental

Congress (for New Jersey) while all four sons were in the army . . . the family is founded deep in Jersey soil (since the birth of Newark), and I am about as much of a Jerseyman as you can find."

Schooled in Asbury Park and then at the Pennington Seminary (New Jersey), Crane attended the Claverack College and Hudson River Institute (1888 to 1890). After one semester at Lafayette College, where he joined the Delta Upsilon fraternity, he spent one semester at Syracuse University (spring, 1891), and here in the Delta Upsilon house he wrote his first draft of MAGGIE: A GIRL OF THE STREETS. Knowing *then* very little about the Bowery, slum life, and prostitution, Crane invented the plot of his story about a girl turned streetwalker—trapped by her environment. His literary source was Flaubert's *Madame Bovary,* Crane's *Maggie* being *Madame Bovary* recast in Bowery style. He published *Maggie: A Girl of the Streets* at his own expense in 1893. The *Tribune* published five of his Sullivan County sketches and *Cosmopolitan* magazine published "A Tent in Agony" in 1892. In the latter part of his twenty-first year he began THE RED BADGE OF COURAGE, completing the first draft early in 1893, and in his twenty-third year he spouted off the verses comprising THE BLACK RIDERS, which was published in 1895. *The Red Badge* (1895) first appeared in a short newspaper version in the Philadelphia *Press* from Dec. 3 to Dec. 8, 1894. His third novel, GEORGE'S MOTHER, begun in 1893 and completed late in 1894, was not published until 1896, when *Maggie* was reissued in revised form and in hard covers. The London edition (1896) had the variant title *Maggie: A Child of the Streets.* This year he issued also a collection of short stories, THE LITTLE REGIMENT AND OTHER EPISODES OF THE AMERICAN CIVIL WAR, and in 1897 he published his fourth novel, THE THIRD VIOLET, which he had completed at the end of 1895. Crane described it as the story "of life among the younger and poorer artists in New York."

Crane spent the early part of his twenty-third year out in the Far West and in Mexico, traveling for the Bacheller and Johnson syndicate to gather material for sketches and short stories. The main thing he wrote out West, apart from newspaper sketches such as "Mexican Sights and Street Scenes," was a war tale, "A Mystery of Heroism." His only western tale this year (1895) was "Horses—One Dash!", which he wrote in Philadelphia while trying to hire himself out to the Philadelphia *Press* as drama critic. His best western tales were written much later. The single perfect bead on his string of western tales is "The Bride Comes to Yellow Sky," which he wrote in England in 1897. THE BLUE HOTEL was written in England in 1898.

In 1896 (he was now famous on both sides of the Atlantic as the author of *The Red Badge of Courage*) two articles about him pointed out the important fact that Crane's ancestry included several clergymen and soldiers. "It is an interesting study in heredity," said the *Monthly Illus-* *trator,* "to note the influence of these two professions in Mr. Crane's literary work, the one furnishing the basis of style, the other of incident." Crane got from his parents not only a natural bent for writing but also a marked predilection for frequently casting his ideas, incidents, and even his style in Biblical form or fashion.

Irving Bacheller sent Crane to Jacksonville, Florida, to cover a filibustering expedition to Cuba, and en route there on the *Commodore* he was shipwrecked on New Year's Day of 1897. He recreated his experiences after the *Commodore* disaster in THE OPEN BOAT, which has been called one of the finest short stories in the English language. Meanwhile he had fallen in love with Cora Taylor at her Hotel de Dream in Jacksonville. During his final three years in England she lived with him as his wife. Unable to get to Cuba, Crane went to Greece as war correspondent for the New York *Journal.* Writing under the pseudonym of "Imogene Carter," Cora was with Stephen in Greece—the "first" woman war correspondent. When the Greco-Turkish war ended, they went to London, and in July, 1897, rented a house at Oxted, Surrey. Here Stephen soon began his close friendship with Joseph Conrad. In April, 1898, Crane left England for Cuba to report on the Spanish-American War, leaving Cora behind to manage somehow for herself. In New York City he tried to enlist in the Navy, but was turned down. He accepted an offer of the New York *World* and submitted twenty dispatches from Cuba, including "Stephen Crane's Vivid Story of the Battle of San Juan" (the *World,* July 14, 1898). On being refused an advance by Pulitzer's paper, he switched to the New York *Journal* and sent it twenty dispatches between August 5 and November 9. The war was over by mid-August, but Crane stayed on in Havana to write story after story, article after article. Here he also wrote the first draft of ACTIVE SERVICE (1899), a novel of the Greek war, which he reworked when he finally returned to Cora and England nine months after his departure. He and Cora settled at Brede Place, a 14th-century manor house in Sussex, and here the pair bled themselves financially by entertaining a constant stream of guests, some of them uninvited—"Indians," Crane called them.

No sooner had he landed in England than creditors leaped at him; financial troubles and ill health plagued Crane during his stay at Brede Place, the last full year of his short life. Threatened with bankruptcy, he tried desperately to write himself out of debt, but never succeeded. He began writing three types of stories: tales of western American life similar to "Twelve O'Clock," the Whilomville tales of childhood (published posthumously as WHILOMVILLE STORIES, 1900), and more war tales, two of them short masterpieces: "Upturned Face," published in *Ainslee's Magazine* (March, 1900), and "An Episode of War," which was first printed in the posthumous collection *Last Words* (1902). After *The Open Boat and Other Tales of Adven-*

ture and *Pictures at War,* which duplicates *The Little Regiment* collection but adds to it *The Red Badge of Courage,* Crane published the next year (1899) War Is Kind, his second volume of poetry; *Active Service;* and The Monster and Other Stories, its title story having appeared in 1898 in *Harper's Magazine.* That concludes Crane's book list except for posthumous publications such as *Bowery Tales, Whilomville Stories,* and Wounds in the Rain (1900); *Great Battles of the World* (1901); *Last Words* (1902); and *The O'Ruddy* (1903), a romance left unfinished by Crane and completed by Robert Barr.

The panic of his snarled finances and of his hopeless prospects for survival are evoked in the letters Stephen and Cora wrote James B. Pinker, Crane's literary agent and financial godfather in London, particularly during Crane's last months in 1900. (See R. W. Stallman and Lillian Gilkes, eds., *Stephen Crane: Letters,* 1960.) Suffering from tuberculosis, Crane collapsed early in April, 1900, and, on the advice of medical specialists, he left Dover—Conrad, H. G. Wells, and Robert Barr seeing him off—for the Black Forest in Germany, where at Baden-weiler he died on June 5. Cora sailed on the *Bremen* from Southampton with Crane's body, and, after a service at the Metropolitan Temple in New York City, Stephen was interred in the Crane family plot at Hillside, New Jersey. Cora returned to Jacksonville, Fla., in 1902 and built a new house on the Row called the Court, which she operated until her death at forty-five in 1910. (See Lillian Gilkes, *Cora Crane: A Biography of Mrs. Stephen Crane,* 1960.)

Seeing Crane for the last time, H. G. Wells wrote in the *North American Review* (August, 1900): "If you would figure him as I saw him, you must think of him as a face of a type very typically American, long and spare, with very straight hair and straight features and long, quiet hands and hollow eyes, moving slowly, smiling and speaking slowly, with that deliberate New Jersey manner he had, and lapsing from speech again into a quiet contemplation of his ancient enemy. For it was the sea that had taken his strength, the same sea that now shone . . . warm and tranquil beneath the tranquil evening sky."

The notion that Crane died "tragically young," "a boy spiritually killed by neglect," is contradicted by the fact that no man of his generation was more admired and loved or received greater critical recognition. What killed him was not literary neglect but his own will to burn himself out, his Byronic craving to make of his body "a testing ground for all the sensations of life." Like Dylan Thomas in our own day, the *Times Literary Supplement* recently remarked (Nov. 25, 1960), "Crane appears as a notable example of that phenomenon of our time, the heroic, immensely fertile and talented author of one or two masterpieces, self-destroyer. A Dylan Thomas with, perhaps one should add, a touch about him of Mr. Graham Greene, for Crane could never keep his nose out of any war or

revolution that happened to be going on anywhere; there was a pattern in his brief life of repeated absence from home on assignments that again touches off a peculiarly contemporary chord." "I decided that the nearer a writer gets to life, the greater he becomes as an artist," said Crane, whose training as a newspaper reporter accounts in part for his theory. He subscribed to Hamlin Garland's veritism, the theory that art is founded on personal experience and copies reality, and to W. D. Howells' critical standard of "realism," which meant truth and fidelity to the facts of experience; almost everything Crane wrote was motivated by this principle. Yet his art was at its greatest when he wrote at some distance from the reality he had experienced, or when, on the other hand, he wrote out of no personal experience—as in *The Red Badge of Courage.* As artist he transcended the realities which as journalist he felt committed to know at first hand. In a frenzied search for experiences, he needlessly expended himself, exhausted his health, and thus wasted his genius.

He produced too much, he kept repeating himself, and too often the artist succumbed to the journalist, especially in *Active Service, Great Battles of the World,* and The O'Ruddy. His writings fill twelve volumes: eighty-six sketches and tales, five brief novels, two volumes of verse, and a mass of journalistic stuff. Not listed in this group are innumerable newspaper articles and uncollected sketches not included in *The Work of Stephen Crane,* edited by Wilson Follett (1925–27). Crane's sketches of New York City street life, which he thought were among his best things, are collected in *Stephen Crane: New York City Sketches,* in preparation by R. W. Stallman. Also forthcoming is *Stephen Crane: Sketches and War Dispatches,* co-edited by R. W. Stallman and E. R. Hagemann. On the other hand, it is also true that some of the pure Crane shone even at the end of his cometlike career. As Sherwood Anderson said: "Suppose he did put a pretty little patent-leather finish on some of his later tales. Take him for what he was—his importance."

Although his works were published in the 19th century, he and, particularly, Henry James mark the beginning of modern American fiction. Crane's writings look backward to Twain and forward to Hemingway, who praised *The Red Badge of Courage* as "one of the finest books of our literature . . . it is all as much of one piece as a great poem is." While Crane's influence can be documented by a formidable catalogue of specific echoes in later American fiction, it persists more significantly in less subtilized form: his naturalistic outlook is found in modern novels of slum life, and his concept of the soldier as Everyman, in modern novels of war. Maggie's brother is a forebear of Studs Lonigan, and Crane in several of his stories ("An Episode of War" is one example) foreshadows Hemingway. *A Farewell to Arms* is an inverted *Red Badge of Courage:* the one deals with disenchantment and withdrawal, the other with quest and ironic triumph. Crane in his use of dialect and in his stories of childhood is linked to Kipling and Twain; his best-known follower is Booth Tarkington. Crane's Tom Sawyer is Jimmie Trescott in "Making an Orator"; and his SULLIVAN COUNTY SKETCHES (collected by Melvin Schoberlin in 1949) and *Whilomville Stories* had their inspirational source in Twain's *Roughing It* and *Life on the Mississippi* (Crane's favorite book). More important is the kinship Twain and Crane establish in the history of American literature: they each brought new subject matter into fiction. *The Red Badge* has the same form as *Huckleberry Finn* in its repetitions of ironic episodes; both works deal with heroes in quest of selfhood.

Crane's importance is less, however, that he brought new subject matter into fiction, than that he was an innovator in technique and a unique stylist. *The Red Badge of Courage* is a literary exercise in language, in the patterning of words and the counterpointing of themes, tropes, and colors; it is far more than a war novel to be praised for its "realism." It is a symbolic construct. No work of art is what it appears to be. Crane's style is prose pointillism. It is composed of disconnected images which coalesce like the blobs of color in French impressionist paintings, every word-group having a cross-reference relationship, every seemingly disconnected detail being interrelated to the configurated whole. There is a striking analogy between Crane's use of colors and the painting method of the French impressionists; it is as though he had known about their theory of contrasts and had composed his own prose paintings by the same principle. "Impressionism was his faith," said his painter friend R. G. Vosburgh. As H. G. Wells concluded: "There is Whistler even more than there is Tolstoy in *The Red Badge of Courage*."

Like *The Red Badge*, *Maggie* and *The Open Boat* are constructed by a concatenation of striking contrasts, alternations of contradictory moods. Crane's fiction at its best probes the thought and actions of trapped or baited men fighting the destructive forces in nature, in other men, or in themselves. Crane is always dealing with the paradox of man's plight. Paradox patterns his best stories and defines their kinship (for example, "The Bride Comes to Yellow Sky" and "The Upturned Face"). Every Crane story worth mentioning is designed upon a single ironic incident, and they are all concerned with virtually the same problem: the moral problem of conduct. It is the same with the works of Joseph Conrad. Technically Crane's affinities are with Chekhov, whose stories build up to a crucial moment of impasse and collapse—nothing happens. Crane, like Chekhov, is a master of the contradictory effect. All Crane stories end in irony; *Maggie* and *George's Mother* end not with a bang, but with a whimper.

In *Maggie* Crane broke new ground. The then seemingly sordid realism of that story of the demiworld of New York City initiated the subsequent literary trend of the next generation.

Maggie anticipated the sociological realism of Frank Norris, Theodore Dreiser, and James T. Farrell (see NATURALISM). *Maggie*, however, is not a realistic photograph of slum life. Not copyistic of reality, *Maggie* is rather a tone painting like *The Red Badge* and "The Open Boat." They are all exemplars of the art-novel—a category to which all Crane's best works belong. A great stylist, Crane uses language poetically, that is, reflexively and symbolically. The works that employ this reflexive and symbolic language constitute what is permanent of Crane.

After his death Crane was completely forgotten until the poetic renaissance of 1912, a revival of vers libre stemming from Walt Whitman, Emily Dickinson, and W. E. Henley. Crane's experimental FREE VERSE heralded and somewhat influenced the imagist movement of Ezra Pound and Amy Lowell. But he did not enter the public domain until the 1920's, when Vincent Starrett's selection of Crane's short stories in *Men, Women and Boats* (1921), Thomas Beer's *Stephen Crane* (1923), and Follett's twelve-volume edition of *The Work* (1925–27) appeared. This revival of Crane was brought about mainly by Beer's impressionistic biography, an undocumented and stylized portrait. Equally important was the shock of recognition by American authors of the 1920's (*viz.* Hergesheimer, Cather, Anderson) that Crane's art had kinship with their own. In Crane, a writer's writer, they recognized a contemporary. In the 1940's Crane came to the fore again with the reprinting of the Conrad and Wells essays, Carl Van Doren's edition of *Twenty Stories* (1940), and the reissue of Beer's biography (1941). Public interest in Crane was spread by the motion picture of his *Red Badge of Courage*, produced by Gottfried Reinhardt and directed by John Huston in 1951. Until the 1950's critical scrutiny of Crane's works remained nonexistent. This second Crane revival began with John Berryman's *Stephen Crane* (1950), a biography reworking Beer in theme and style but done anew from the angle of Freudian interpretations of Crane's works as revelations of his personality. R. W. Stallman's introduction to the Modern Library edition of *The Red Badge of Courage*, his 1952 essay "Stephen Crane: A Revaluation," and his *Stephen Crane: An Omnibus* (1952), with critical notes and introductions to all Crane's works, promulgated the present-day explicatory and interpretive controversy about their structure and meaning. This controversy still rages, notably on *The Red Badge of Courage*.

Louis Zara's *Dark Rider: A Novel Based on the Life of Stephen Crane* (1961) is a brilliant recreation of scholarship recast in fictional form. The present need remains, however, for a definitive biographical and critical study, for a definitive textual edition of Crane's works, and a revised bibliography bringing up to date *Stephen Crane: A Bibliography*, by Ames W. Williams and Vincent Starrett (1948). Supplementary bibliographies are indicated in the following list of writings on Crane, a selection from a formidable mass of Crane commentaries: Daniel G. Hoffman's *The Poetry of Stephen Crane* (1957); Daniel G. Hoffman's introduction to *The Red Badge of Courage and Other Stories* (1957); Lettis', McDonnell's, and Morris's edition of *The Red Badge of Courage: Text and Criticism* (1960), a collection of essays and a check list of criticisms on *The Red Badge;* Corwin Knapp Linson's memoirs, *My Stephen Crane,* edited with an introduction by Edwin H. Cady (1958); *Literary History of the United States,* edited by Spiller and others (rev. ed. 1953), and its *Bibliography Supplement,* edited by Richard M. Ludwig (1959); *Modern Fiction Studies: Stephen Crane Special Number,* 5 (Autumn, 1959), an important collection of Crane studies; V. S. Pritchett's introduction to *The Red Badge of Courage and Other Stories* with a note on the texts of *Maggie* and *The Red Badge of Courage* by R. W. Stallman (London, 1960); R. W. Stallman's "Stephen Crane: A Revaluation," in *Critiques and Essays on Modern Fiction: 1920–51,* edited by John Aldridge (1952), containing also a checklist on Crane; R. W. Stallman's notes and introductions to *Stephen Crane: An Omnibus* (1952, 1954); R. W. Stallman's edition of *The Red Badge of Courage and Selected Stories* (1960), presenting the definitive edition of *The Red Badge* and an extensive check list of writings on Crane; R. W. Stallman's and Lillian Gilkes' edition of *Stephen Crane: Letters* (1960); R. W. Stallman's "Crane's *Maggie* in Review," in *The Houses That James Built* (1961), presenting two dozen contemporary *Maggie* reviews reproduced here for the first time; C. C. Walcutt's "Stephen Crane: Naturalist and Impressionist," in his *American Literary Naturalism: A Divided Stream* (1956); and Bernard Weisberger's "The Red Badge of Courage," in *Twelve Original Essays on Great American Novels* (1958).

R. W. STALLMAN

Crapsey, Adelaide (b. Brooklyn, Sept. 9, 1878—d. Oct. 8, 1914), poet. The daughter of a noted heterodox minister, Adelaide Crapsey was raised in Rochester, New York, in a liberal and cultivated atmosphere. She attended school at Kemper Hall, Wisconsin, and Vassar College, later studying archaeology in Rome. During most of her brief life she was a teacher of literature at private girls' schools and at Smith College. Most of her poetry was composed in her last year, when she was dying of tuberculosis at Saranac. Delicacy, firmness, and concentration are the principal characteristics of her verse, and its most typical form is the "cinquain," an innovation of Miss Crapsey's (derived from certain Japanese lyric forms, the *tonka* and *haiku*), a five-line, unrhymed stanza, with successive lines of two, four, six, eight, and two feet. A collection of poetry, *Verse* (1915), and an unfinished technical study, *Analysis of English Metrics* (1918), were published posthumously.

Crater, The, or, Vulcan's Peak (1847), a novel by JAMES FENIMORE COOPER. On an island in the Pacific is created a Utopia, happy and successful until several clergymen, a lawyer, and an editor sow seeds of dissension. At the end the island and its people sink into the sea. The book expresses Cooper's disillusionment with democratic procedures. He regarded it as "a remarkable book," which "ought to make a noise." The book in part expounds the economic views of his former publisher, HENRY C. CAREY, but Cooper shows that while these views are sound, "man's innate perversity is inescapable." Recent research by W. B. Gates shows that Cooper took much of his material from *The Voyages of Captain James Cook* (1846) and Lt. Charles Wilkes' *Narrative of the U.S. Exploring Expedition* (5 v., 1844).

Craven, Thomas (b. Salina, Kans., Jan. 6, 1889—d. Feb. 27, 1969), art critic, lecturer. An individualistic thinker on the subject of art and the world in general, Craven did not particularly please artists and art connoisseurs. But his work did much to make some of the notable painters, especially recent ones, familiar in such books as *Men of Art* (1931); *A Treasury of Art Masterpieces* (1939); *The Story of Painting* (1943). Particularly enjoyable and valuable is his CARTOON CAVALCADE (1943).

Crawford, F[rancis] Marion (b. Italy, Aug. 2, 1854—d. April 9, 1909), writer, playwright, historian. The nephew of JULIA WARD HOWE and the son of Thomas Crawford, a noted sculp-

tor, Crawford spent a good deal of his early life and his later years in Italy, which became the scene of many of his novels. He was a vigorous traveler, knew many parts of the world (especially India) well, and was an astonishing linguist, with a command of fifteen or more languages; he once kept a diary in Urdu. At one time he wanted to be an opera singer, at another a politician, but he satisfied his ambitions in the form of stories: *A Roman Singer* (1884) and *An American Politician* (1884). He established enormous popularity with the publication of Mr. Isaacs (1882), the story of a diamond merchant in India. He wrote forty-five novels, some of them historical like *Via Crucis* (1898), and *In the Palace of the King* (1900); others contemporary in their setting, among them: *Dr. Claudius* (1883); Saracinesca (1887); *A Cigarette Maker's Romance* (1890); *The White Sister* (1909). Crawford's backgrounds are skillfully and authentically drawn; he has an astonishing narrative verve. But his old-fashioned romanticism has lost its former popularity. See Francesca da Rimini.

Crawford, Isabella Valancy (b. Ireland, Dec. 25, 1850—d. Feb. 12, 1887), Canadian poet. After emigrating from Ireland, Miss Crawford spent her short life mainly in Ontario. In 1884 she published a collection of her verses, *Old Spookses' Pass*, many Canadian in setting. In 1905 a selection from her writings, *Collected Poems*, was edited by John W. Garvin.

Crawford, John Wallace [Jack] (b. Ireland, March 4, 1847—d. Feb. 28, 1917), miner, soldier, Indian fighter, Indian agent, poet, known as the "Poet Scout." Crawford was at first a miner, then a fighter in the Civil War, later chief of scouts for the Black Hill Rangers, finally a rancher on the Rio Grande. He also believed himself a poet, often recited his own verses in the entertaining lectures that he gave. He published *The Poet Scout* (1879) and other volumes in verse and prose, and helped establish the western legend.

Crawford, Mary Caroline (b. Boston, May 5, 1874—d. Nov. 15, 1932), antiquarian, historian. Among her books: *The Romance of Old New England Churches* (1904); *The Romance of the American Theater* (1913); *In the Days of the Pilgrim Fathers* (1920).

Crayon, Geoffrey. The pseudonym under which Washington Irving published *The Sketch Book* (1819). Later appeared *The Crayon Miscellany* (1835).

Crazy Horse (1849?–1877). A Sioux chieftain who, with Sitting Bull, led his tribe in an uprising (1875) against the white invasion of the Black Hills. In the course of the conflict, General Custer was killed (1876) at the Battle of the Little Big Horn. Crazy Horse plays an important role in John G. Neihardt's *Song of the Indian Wars* (1925). His Indian name was Tashunca-uitco. He was killed while resisting imprisonment.

Cream of the Jest, The (1917; rev. ed., 1920), a novel by James Branch Cabell. This "comedy of evasions" is the story of an author,

Felix Kennaston, who by means of a hieroglyphic disk escapes into a dream world where he pursues a changing yet always similar image of the loved one. She turns out to be his wife.

creative writing. A somewhat dubious pedagogical term, intended to describe a form of writing poetry, stories, and plays—encouraged in American schools in reaction against the formal rhetorical writing of the 19th century. It serves in many instances to give vent to frustrations, unsatisfied desires, adolescent longings in a way not possible with the older type of essays, "themes," etc. Progressive educators particularly favored this academic genre, but it was soon adopted in schools of all kinds; and courses in "creative writing" became a common part of the English course of study. The term is now applied to all academic courses in writing.

Creek Indians. An Indian confederacy, the members of which spoke the Muskhogen language. They originally lived in Alabama and Georgia; later removed to Oklahoma. Allies of the British, they fought Jackson. William Gilmore Simms, whose father served in Jackson's army, heard details of the fighting from his lips, and later visited the Creeks and learned to know them well. They appear in his poems, his essays, his short stories, and two of his novels. They appear also in *Yamoyden: A Tale of the Wars of King Philip* (1820), a long poem by James W. Eastburn and Robert C. Sands. In *A Tour of the Prairies* (1835) Washington Irving speaks of the gaily bedecked Creeks; and they are likewise mentioned in Chateaubriand's Indian tales.

Creekmore, Hubert (b. Water Valley, Miss., Jan. 16, 1907—d. May 23, 1966), poet, novelist, critic. Creekmore's novels reflect the depth of his feelings for the South, where his family lived since the 18th century. His is not the South of Faulkner or Caldwell; it is concerned less with the social evils of the region than with people as human beings. His writing had a powerful emotional impact in *The Chain in the Heart* (1953), the story of three generations in a Negro family, from just after the Civil War to 1930. Creekmore's poetry, sound in construction but not overly dramatic, invades his prose to its advantage. Among his books: *Personal Sun* (1940); *The Stone Ants* (1943); *The Fingers of Night* (1946); *The Long Reprieve* (1946); *Formula* (1947); *The Welcome* (1948); *No Harm to Lovers* (1950). *A Little Treasury of World Poetry* (1952) includes translations from Egyptian, Babylonian, and Chinese, as well as European and South American verse. His *Lyrics of the Middle Ages* appeared in 1959.

Creel, George (b. Lafayette Co., Mo., Dec. 1, 1876—d. Oct. 2, 1953), newspaperman, public relations counsel, writer. After service on various western papers, Creel was in 1917 appointed by President Wilson chairman of the government Committee on Public Information. Later he served on other official bodies, in the meantime writing for magazines (particularly *Collier's*) and publishing several books. Among his writings are *Quatrains of Christ* (1907); *Wilson and the Issues* (1916); *Ireland's Fight for Freedom*

(1919); *The World, the War, and Wilson* (1920); *How We Advertised America* (1924); *Sam Houston* (1928); *War Criminals* (1944); *Russia's Race for Asia* (1949). In his autobiography, *Rebel at Large* (1947) he tells entertainingly of his fifty years as a fighter for political and economic reforms.

Creeley, Robert (b. Mass., May 21, 1926—), poet. Robert Creeley was educated at the Holderness School, Plymouth, and at Harvard. He worked with the American Field Service in India and Burma and has lived in France, Mallorca, and Guatemala. Creeley occupies an important position in the advance guard of American poetry and has been editor of one of its principal forums, the *Black Mountain Review*. He was also associated with similar magazines in Germany and Japan. Creeley's poetry is characterized by extreme concentration, the perfectly articulated probing of personal pain, wit, a remarkable use of the broken rhythms, the flatness of ordinary speech. Among his collections are *The Kind of Act* (1953), *All That Is Lovely in Men* (1957), *The Whip* (1958), and *A Form of Women* (1959).

Creole. A term used in the United States to designate the descendants of French (sometimes Spanish) settlers in Louisiana (especially New Orleans) who came directly from Europe to America, and not indirectly, as did the exiled Acadians (known as Cajuns). Early Creole society was aristocratic in culture and manners, and the members of it prided themselves on the purity of their French. Later the term was adopted by a class of comparatively well-to-do French-speaking persons of mixed Negro and white ancestry who were among the chief artisans and petty tradesmen of New Orleans toward the end of the 19th century. This use of the term was at first resented by the whites, but it gradually became common. In addition, there is a variety of French spoken in Haiti which is called Creole but is not connected with the use of the term in Louisiana.

Crespi, Juan (1721–1782), a Spanish explorer and missionary who accompanied Gaspar de Portola (1723?–1784) in his thousand-mile march north from Mexico that resulted in the discovery of San Francisco bay. His diaries have survived and appear in H. E. Bolton's *Fray Juan Crespi, Missionary and Explorer* (1927).

Creston, Paul (b. New York City, Oct. 10, 1906—), violinist, composer, director of radio programs, teacher. Entirely a product of Manhattan, Creston was largely self-taught. His *First Symphony* (1940) won fame for him. He is particularly interested in the rhythmical side of music; other elements he considers secondary. He did an orchestral piece, OUT OF THE CRADLE ENDLESSLY ROCKING, based on a poem by Walt Whitman, in 1934; also three poems from Whitman for cello and piano. *Principles of Rhythm* (1961) was his most recent book. He received the Music Award from the American Academy of Arts and Letters in 1943.

Crèvecœur, Michel Guillaume Jean de ["J. Hector St. John"] (b. France, 1731—d. 1813), traveler, agriculturist, memoirist. Crèvecœur emigrated to America in 1754, settling on a farm in New York State. He returned to Europe in 1780 and came back to New York City in 1783 as French consul. His insight into the American character and his guesses as to its future development have been justified by time. His best-known book is LETTERS FROM AN AMERICAN FARMER (1782). He also wrote VOYAGE DANS LA HAUTE PENSYLVANIE ET DANS L'ÉTAT DE NEW-YORK (1801). *Sketches of 18th-Century America* was not published until 1925. Julia P. Mitchell wrote a biographical study of Crèvecœur (1916). Vernon L. Parrington analyzes him admiringly in *Main Currents in American Thought* (1927), and R. W. B. Lewis discusses him in *The American Adam* (1955).

Crichton, Kyle [Samuel] (b. Peale, Pa., Nov. 6, 1896—d. Nov. 24, 1960), author, editor. A graduate of Lehigh University, Crichton worked in coal mines and steel mills, and was an associate editor of *Scribner's Magazine* and *Collier's Weekly*. Under the pen name Robert Forsythe he wrote for the Communist *Daily Worker* and the *New Masses* the biting articles on American celebrities collected in *Redder Than the Rose* (1935) and *Reading From Left to Right* (1936). Under his own name he wrote illustrated interviews for *Collier's Weekly* and published a number of biographies, including *The Marx Brothers* (1950), and two novels: *Proud Purple* (1944), a story of a Spanish family in New Mexico; and *The History of the Adventures of George Whigham and His Friend Mr. Claney Hobson* (1951), a farce on New York society.

Cries of New York, The (1814). This was described as "printed and sold by Samuel Wood in the Juvenile Book-Store." It is perhaps the most important of the little books of "Cries" prepared toward the beginning of the 19th century as vocational guides for children who expected to engage in peddling or other occupations. Vocation advice was accompanied by short homilies encouraging the small peddlers to industry. The books often expressed indignation at the plight of chimney sweeps exposed to cold and hardship.

Crisis, The (1901), a historical novel by WINSTON CHURCHILL. The action centers in St. Louis during the controversy over free and slave states; the hero, Stephen Brice, is a Yankee, the heroine, Virginia Carvel, a southern girl. The novel shows the inevitability of war, yet stresses the fact that neither side wanted it. There is a notable portrait of Lincoln, whom Walter Barnes regarded as "the real hero" of *The Crisis*.

Critical Fable, A (1922), an imitation of J. R. Lowell's FABLE FOR CRITICS (1848) from the pen of his kinswoman, AMY LOWELL. The poem was published anonymously, and Miss Lowell herself started an enthusiastic boom for LEONARD BACON as the author—an attribution that H. S. Canby accepted in the *Saturday Review of Literature*. It became a popular literary game to find the author, but the secret was officially revealed when Miss Lowell mentioned the poem as hers in the British *Who's Who* of 1923. In the earlier *Fable* Lowell holds a conversation with Apollo; in the later version the author conducts a dialogue with the earlier Lowell. A score of poets in the 1920's are discussed, sometimes with keen insight, frequently with humor, occasionally with spitefulness. Miss Lowell complacently calls herself an electrical storm with the rainbow in tow, and refers to her "unique and surprising profusion."

Critics and Crusaders: A Century of American Protest (1947), biographical sketches of sixteen men and two women by Charles A. Madison (1895—   ). Included are individualists and anarchists, fanatics in social causes, unorthodox economists, and one Communist—JOHN REED.

Critics' Circle, New York Drama. A group of twelve New York critics, reporters on new plays for New York City newspapers and two or three New York magazines, who meet once a year to select the "best" play of the season.

Croaker Papers, The. A series of humorous verses that appeared from March 10 to July 24, 1819, in the New York *Evening Post,* under the pseudonym "Croaker & Company." Croaker was the name of a doleful character in Oliver Goldsmith's *The Good-Natured Man* (1768). In the *Post* verses "Croaker" was JOSEPH RODMAN DRAKE, "Croaker, Jr." was his intimate friend, FITZ-GREENE HALLECK; the authorship was never admitted. A pirated edition appeared in 1819; a collected edition, called *The Croakers,* in 1860. Drake and Halleck were the first to make Broadway and its environs, its people and politics, a source of literary discussion. Alfred Kreymborg calls them "the first newspaper columnists," and points out that with them "an age of entertainment had arrived, a type of amusement castigated in Puritan New England."

Crockett, Davy (b. near Rogersville, Tenn., Aug. 17, 1786—d. March 6, 1836), frontiersman, public official, soldier, autobiographer. Crockett's father was a veteran of the Revolutionary War and an Indian fighter. Crockett grew up pretty wild, but his neighbors liked him and said of him that "no one can dance longer or sing louder or get into more scrapes than Crockett's lad." He went to school for a while, married at eighteen. The Crocketts moved to a new settlement on the Mulberry Fork of the Elk River; there, says Crockett, "I began to distinguish myself as a hunter and to lay the foundation for all my future greatness." He became a tremendous killer of "b'ars," engaged in the Creek War under General Jackson and won his commendation, decided he could collect votes as easily as he killed "b'ar," and became a politician. He dispensed rough justice as a magistrate, was elected first to the Tennessee legislature and then to Congress, and became known as "the coonskin Congressman."

Long an outspoken admirer of Andrew Jackson, Crockett changed sides in January, 1829. Immediately the newspapers and pamphlets of the time reversed themselves, and he suddenly became the hero of the Whig faction, the villain of the Jacksonians. In either case Crockett's experiences became the grist for the humor of the period, and he became something of a myth during his own lifetime. Sometimes actual contact with Crockett surprised people, as when the Jacksonville *Banner* wrote that he was "an honest, independent, intelligent man, with strong and highly marked traits of originality." To set people straight, Crockett wrote his own *Narrative* (1834), possibly with the assistance of Thomas Chilton. In 1835 he published *An Account of Col. Crockett's Tour to the North and Down East.* He opposed Jackson on the issue of a national bank and, greatly to his credit, he was against the President's orders to break the treaty with the Creek Indians. Finally defeated, he made up his mind to help the Texans win their independence, and died fighting heroically at the ALAMO. He was speedily made a major demigod of American folklore, who could talk the language of animals, ride the lightning, lie with extravagant grandeur, and whip his weight in wildcats.

To the Americans of his day, Crockett was the supreme exponent of mother-wit and one of the earliest to show disdain, largely assumed, for mere "book-larnin'." Actually he took some care to become educated himself and to give his children proper schooling; one of his sons became a teacher. Constance Rourke calls his *Narrative* "a classic in our literature because it was one of the first to use the American language with fullness and assurance, and because it reveals a way of life in a distinctive style." Even before Crockett's death the almanac makers, perhaps with his approval, began to turn to him for subject matter, and from 1835 to 1856 the almanacs continued to appear. About fifty issues of *Crockett Almanacs* have been discovered. They gave the usual meteorological and astronomical data, also information on natural history, sometimes introduced Daniel Boone, Mike Fink, the sea serpent, and other figures in folklore. But, says Constance Rourke, "Crockett remained the dominating figure—the mythical, comical Crockett."

He has of course appeared in many short stories, novels, plays, ballads, and folklore collections. J. K. Paulding probably had Crockett in mind when he drew the character of Col. Nimrod Wildfire in THE LION OF THE WEST (1831). In 1933 the Carolina Playmakers produced John Philip Milhous' folkplay, *Davy Crockett, Half Horse, Half Alligator.* A "ballet ballad" called *The Eccentricities of Davy Crockett* was produced in New York in 1948. Constance Rourke's *Davy Crockett* (1934) is an important biographical study, and Richard M. Dorson wrote the authoritative *Davy Crockett, American Comic Legend* (1939). J. A. Shackford's *David Crockett: The Man and the Legend* (1955) chiefly presents the historical Crockett. The Nashville Series of the *Crockett Almanacs* was reprinted in 1955. A song, *Davy Crockett,* became immensely popular with the younger generation in the mid-1950's, occasioning a remarkable revival of Crockett's fame. For a few years no self-respecting American boy was without a Davy Crockett coonskin cap.

Crocketts, the. A Yankee family whose fortunes for four generations are chronicled in MARY ELLEN CHASE's novel *Silas Crockett* (1935). Silas himself commands a clipper, his son dies in a sea-storm, his grandson is master of a coastwise steamer, his great-grandson is forced by poverty to leave college and work in a herring-factory. The theme of the novel is the hardship worked by the introduction of steamships.

Crosby, Frances Jane ["Fanny"] (b. Putnam Co., N.Y., March 24, 1820—d. Feb. 12, 1915), hymn writer. Although blind from infancy, Miss Crosby began composing hymns in 1864, and completed some six thousand, it is believed. The most famous was *Safe in the Arms of Jesus*. She published several collections of verse, also *Fanny Crosby's Life Story, by Herself* (1903). John Hawthorne wrote her biography (1931).

Crosby, John [Campbell] (b. Milwaukee, Wis., May 18, 1912—   ), radio and television columnist. Crosby's column for the New York *Herald Tribune* has been syndicated in other papers as well, and is written with objectivity, common sense, and wit. *Out of the Blue* (1952) is a collection of his best pieces.

Cross, Wilbur L[ucius] (b. Mansfield, Conn., April 10, 1862—d. Oct. 5, 1948), teacher, biographer, editor, governor of Connecticut. In the course of an extraordinarily rich career Cross remained always the type of intellectual Yankee; toward the close of his life he reviewed his experiences under the title, *Connecticut Yankee* (1943). He was educated at Yale, became an instructor in English in 1894, rose to a professorship in 1902, was made dean of the Graduate School in 1916. Speaking at a Democratic party rally in June, 1930, he so delighted his audience with his horse sense and homely wit that he was nominated for governor that year and elected four times in succession (1931–1939). He won an enviable reputation as an authority on English fiction, with his *Development of the English Novel* (1899); *Life and Times of Laurence Sterne* (1909); rev. ed., 1925 and 1929); *History of Henry Fielding* (1918); *Modern English Novel* (1929); *Four Contemporary Novelists* (1930). His annual Thanksgiving Day Proclamations were famous for their beauty of style and depth of sentiment. He edited THE YALE REVIEW from its foundation in 1911 to 1939.

Crossing, The (1904), a novel by WINSTON CHURCHILL that depicts the settlement of the Inland Empire. It begins in North Carolina, continues to the unsettled West, closes in New Orleans. George Rogers Clark and Daniel Boone appear in the novel. V. L. Parrington holds that the story "breaks in two: the first half [is] Churchill's best work in romance, the last half his worst." See SIMON KENTON.

Crossing Brooklyn Ferry (1856 in LEAVES OF GRASS, where it was called *Sun-Down Poem;* somewhat rev. in 1881), a poem by WALT WHITMAN, mainly a dramatic monologue addressed to the reader. Whitman loved to sit in the pilothouse of the picturesque vessels that carried crowds of passengers and many horse-drawn vehicles between Manhattan and Brooklyn. The poet expresses his intense feeling of identification with "the great tides of humanity" and praises physical objects, the "dumb, beautiful ministers."

Cross of Gold speech. See W. J. BRYAN.

Crothers, Rachel (b. Bloomington, Ill., Dec. 12, 1878—d. July 5, 1958), playwright. Miss Crothers was always interested in the place of women in the modern world, and devoted many of her clever plays to this theme. Edmond M. Gagey said of her in *Revolution in American Drama* (1947), "A keen and sagacious playwright, Miss Crothers in her long and successful career showed an unerring instinct for selecting a timely subject, treating it with apparent daring, properly diluted with sentimentality, and ending with the conventional—or at least the matinee audience—viewpoint." Among her plays: *Nice People* (1921); *Mary the Third* (1923); *Let Us Be Gay* (1929); *As Husbands Go* (1931); *When Ladies Meet* (1932); SUSAN AND GOD (1937).

Crothers, Samuel McChord (b. Oswego, Ill., June 7, 1857—d. Nov. 9, 1927), clergyman, essayist. At first a Presbyterian, then a Unitarian minister, Crothers became a center of liberal faith in the Middle West. He was later a preacher in Boston and Cambridge. As an essayist of mellow wisdom and humor, Crothers first won fame with THE GENTLE READER (1903). Other books of his that attracted a wide audience are *The Pardoner's Wallet* (1905), *By the Christmas Fire* (1908), and *The Cheerful Giver* (1923).

Crouse, Russel (b. Findlay, Ohio, Feb. 20, 1893—d. Apr. 3, 1966), newspaperman, historian, playwright, producer. Crouse worked for nearly twenty years on various newspapers in the Middle West and in New York before he entered the theatre. In 1931 he did the libretto for the musical comedy *The Gang's All Here,* which was not particularly successful. He established himself as an author with two books on 19th century American life, *Mr. Currier and Mr. Ives* (1930) and *It Seems Like Yesterday* (1931). In 1934 he met HOWARD LINDSAY and began work on the book for the musical *Anything Goes;* since then their partnership has been one of the most productive and successful in American theatre. Their collaboration has produced LIFE WITH FATHER (1939), based on the books by Clarence Day, which ran for eight years; STATE OF THE UNION (1945), a satire on American politics which won the Pulitzer Prize; *Life with Mother* (1948), based on other stories by Clarence Day; *Call Me Madam* (1950); *The Great Sebastians* (1956); *Tall Story* (1959). Crouse has also written the book on which *The Sound of Music* (1960) was based. With Lindsay he produced Joseph Kesselring's ARSENIC AND OLD LACE (1940).

Crowell, Grace Noll (b. Inland, Iowa, Oct. 31, 1877—   ), poet. For many years Mrs. Crowell has been writing graceful verses, skillfully worded and rhymed, and animated with delicate sentiment. Her first collection, *White Fire* (1925), has been followed by almost a score of others, including *Silver in the Sun* (1928); *Flames in the Wind* (1930); *Songs of Hope* (1938); *Between Eternities* (1944); *Songs for Comfort* (1947); *Apples of Gold* (1950); *Bright Harvest* (1952); *Journey into Dawn* (1955); *Songs of Triumph* (1959); *Vital Possessions* (1960).

Crowninshield, Frank [**Francis Welch**] (b. France, June 24, 1872—d. Dec. 28, 1947), editor, critic, humorist. Crowninshield's father, a painter, resided abroad, and the boy was educated in several European schools. At eighteen he went to work for G. P. Putnam's Sons, soon turned to editorial work on *The Bookman*. He was for the greater part of his most active years on VANITY FAIR, which he joined in 1914; in 1935 he became editorial adviser to all the Condé Nast magazines. He was a well-known figure in literary and artistic circles, a witty man with a good heart whom Dorothy Parker called "the last of the species known as gentlemen." He was generous with his time and his money, delivered some of the most amusing after-dinner speeches on record, made *Vanity Fair* (in the language of *Time*) "a gourmet's selection of new, high-flavored literary and artistic dishes, sandwiching new writers like F. Scott Fitzgerald and Anita Loos and E. E. Cummings between the paintings of Matisse, Segonzac, Laurencin," and others. He was one of the seven founders of the Museum of Modern Art and its first secretary. Besides numerous articles, he wrote *Manners for the Metropolis* (1908) and *The Bridge Fiend* (1909).

Crowther, Samuel (b. Philadelphia, June [?], 1880—d. Oct. 27, 1947), newspaperman, historian, biographer. A newspaper writer in the field of politics and economics, Crowther won the friendship of many men of prominence and helped to explain their aims and ideals, as in his biographies of or collaborations with Thomas A. Edison, Harvey Firestone, and Henry Ford. He composed a book on *Prohibition and Prosperity* (1930) and on *America Self-Contained* (1933), also an account of *American Rowing* (1905), besides numerous other volumes.

Croy, Homer (b. near Maryville, Mo., March 11, 1883—d. May 24, 1965), newspaperman, novelist. Croy began his career by writing for country, and later city newspapers. He was the first person to travel around the world taking motion pictures. Although his novels are mainly humorous, *West of the Water Tower* (1923) is a serious, realistic story that reflects the influence of Dreiser and Hardy. An amateur historian, Croy has written many books on American folklore and frontier history, among them: *Wheels West, the Story of the Donner Party* (1955), and *Last of the Great Outlaws, the Story of Cole Younger* (1956). *Our Will Rogers* (1953) was regarded as a highly fitting biography of America's beloved humorist. Croy's other works include: *How Motion Pictures Are Made* (1918); *They Had to See Paris* (1926), which became Will Rogers' first talking picture; *Mr. Meek*

Marches On (1941); *Family Honeymoon* (1942); *Jesse James Was My Neighbor* (1949); *Lady from Colorado* (1957); *Trigger Marshall* (1958); *The Star Maker: TV Story of D. W. Griffith* (1959).

Crystal, The (1880), a poem by SIDNEY LANIER that has provoked discussion among his commentators. Lanier addresses the shades of many great poets in human history, finds them all wanting in one quality or another, and turns finally to Jesus as "man's best friend." A. H. Strong calls the poem Lanier's greatest and finds in it his "clearest confession of his faith in Christ." A. H. Starke sees Lanier merely hailing "Jesus as the perfect man."

Cudjo's Cave (1863), a novel by J. T. TROWBRIDGE. It describes conditions in Tennessee during the early years of the Civil War, particularly relations between Confederate and Union sympathizers.

Cullen, Countee (b. New York City, May 30, 1903—d. Jan. 9, 1946), poet, teacher. A Negro poet of widely acknowledged genius, Cullen became famous with his first book, *Color* (1925). Thereafter he won many awards, particularly for poems on racial themes. He wrote one novel, *One Way to Heaven* (1931), and edited *Caroling Dusk: An Anthology of Verse by Negro Poets* (1927). Later collections of his own verse are *The Ballad of the Brown Girl* (1928); *Copper Sun* (1927); *The Black Christ and Other Poems* (1929); *The Medea and Some Poems* (1935). Herbert Gorham notes that "there are times when he is the more obvious Negro poet sentimentalizing about himself and his people, but the admirable aspect is the direct evidence that he transcends this limitation time and again and becomes sheer poet." For a time Cullen edited the Negro magazine *Opportunity*. After 1934 he taught junior high school in New York, and published stories for children: *The Lost Zoo* (1940); *My Lives and How I Lost Them* (1942).

Culprit Fay, The (posthumously published 1835), a poem by JOSEPH RODMAN DRAKE. With the Hudson River as a background, Drake endeavors to transport fairy lore to America. The poem was influenced by S. T. Coleridge's *Christabel*. It is noteworthy for its descriptions of American nature—birds and flowers and insects. William Ellery Leonard compared the poem to Michael Drayton's *Nymphidia* (1627) and noted that Drake anticipated Bryant in his treatment of American scenes.

Cumberland, The. An American frigate which was sunk March 8, 1862, in an encounter with the Confederate ironclad *Virginia* (originally, when under Union control, called the *Merrimac*). Its sinking meant the end of the wooden warship era; a day later the *Virginia* was itself defeated by the *Monitor*. The sinking of the *Cumberland* inspired Thomas Buchanan Read's *The Attack*, H. W. Longfellow's *The Cumberland*, G. H. Boker's *On Board the Cumberland*, and Herman Melville's *The Cumberland*.

Cummings, E[dward] E[stlin] [his own preference until the 1930's: **e. e. cummings**] (b. Cambridge, Mass., Oct. 14, 1894—d. Sept. 3, 1962), poet, novelist, painter. Of all the post-World War I writers in the renaissance

UPI

of American literature, none possessed a greater lyrical gift or more imagination than E. E. Cummings. In prose he has written one of the half-dozen best American novels of the 20th century; in verse he has produced a large mass of work, both lyrical and dramatic, from which at least several dozen poems have achieved a durable place in the esteem of critics and readers alike. As a painter he has done work which, though far less important that his writing, is pleasing and intelligent. Cummings' superficial reputation is that of an American dadaist, a writer bent on shocking the complacency of his readers, but this should not be allowed to obscure his profounder merits. It is true that he has experimented persistently with novel forms, unconventional typographical arrangements, oddities of spelling and punctuation, in addition to his use of both technical and wildly impolite language; but the reader who turns a second or third time to Cummings' work easily discovers that, although the poet is not averse to employing shock for its own sake, most of his technical innovations possess a genuine poetic content. His strange typography and punctuation, for example, effectively reinforce or amplify not only the poem's rhythmical structure but its innermost patterns of meaning. Most of Cummings' work exhibits an unmistakably strong feeling. His many erotic verses include a few that are among the loveliest we possess, and the same may be said of his elegiac poems. His descriptive pieces,

though occasionally spoiled by mere cleverness, are usually apt and vivid. In his satires he has elevated a supreme gift for invective to the domain of formal art, without ever losing the vigor and rhythmical elegance of natural speech. Such poems as *the Cambridge ladies who live in furnished souls; here is little Effie's head; my girl's tall with hard long eyes; somewhere I have never travelled,gladly beyond; anyone lived in a pretty how town; my father moved through dooms of love;* and many others are among the most widely known works produced by the American *avant-garde*.

Cummings' first published work was a novel based on his experience as an inmate of a French prison during World War I (he was later exonerated from the offense charged against him). Called THE ENORMOUS ROOM (1922), the book is today regarded as a classic of modern literature. Cummings' many volumes of poetry include: *Tulips and Chimneys* (1923); *XLI Poems* (1925); a collection called *&* (1925); *Is 5* (1926); a book with no title at all (1930); *ViVa* (1931); *No Thanks* (1935); *1/20* (1936); *Collected Poems* (1938); *50 Poems* (1940); *1 × 1* (1944); χαιρε: *71 Poems* (1950); *Poems, 1923–1954* (1954); *95 Poems* (1958). He has also published two plays, HIM (1927) and *Santa Claus* (1946); a book of drawings and paintings called *CIOPW* (1931), containing work in charcoal, ink, oil, pencil, watercolor (hence the title); a travel diary, EIMI (1933); a satirical ballet, *Tom* (1935); and *i, Six Nonlectures* (delivered at Harvard, published 1953). Charles Norman has written his biography, *The Magic-Maker: E. E. Cummings* (1958). A collection of "fugitive pieces," *E. E. Cummings: A Miscellany* (1958), was edited by George J. Firmage. S. V. Baum edited Ε Σ ΓΙ: *eec. E. E. Cummings and the Critics* (1962), an anthology of critical essays.

Cummins, Maria Susanna (b. Salem, Mass., April 9, 1827—d. Oct. 1, 1866), novelist. Miss Cummins is remembered chiefly for THE LAMPLIGHTER (1854), a novel that was for many years a best seller. It is the story of Gerty, a paragon of virtuous self-sacrifice, and, according to Alexander Cowie, aims "to teach humble submission to suffering." The best part of the book is that which deals with the kind lamplighter, Trueman Flint.

Cuppy, Will[iam Jacob] (b. Auburn, Ind., Aug. 25, 1884—d. Sept. 19, 1949), humorist, critic. Cuppy as a humorist made a specialty of "How to" books on the burlesque side: *How to Be a Hermit* (1929); *How to Tell Your Friends from the Apes* (1931); *How to Become Extinct* (1941). His pages are usually garnished with footnotes, and he warns readers against paying attention to what he says. *The Decline and Fall of Practically Everybody* (1950), a book of unconventional history, became a best seller. A specialist in crime tales, he reported on nearly four thousand detective and western novels for the New York *Herald Tribune Weekly Book Review*. *How to Attract the Wombat* (1949) contains a miscellany of pieces. Frank Sullivan speaks of Cuppy's "wry, cool, wise, laconic humor." Burton Rascoe describes him as "riddled and raddled with education," and Charles Poore says that he always struck "while the irony was hot."

Curfew Must Not Ring Tonight! (1867), a poem by ROSE HARTWICK THORPE. It appeared in a Detroit newspaper and won immediate popularity with its sentimental tale of an English lord condemned to death for spying and saved by his sweetheart: she clings to the clapper of the bell that is supposed to announce curfew, the hour of his death. David Belasco drew on the ballad in his Civil War play, THE HEART OF MARYLAND (1895), which has a famous bell-clapper scene. Reprinted in *The New Yorker* Magazine (1939), the poem was illustrated—and demolished—by JAMES THURBER.

Curme, George Oliver (b. Richmond, Ind., Jan. 14, 1860—d. April 29, 1948), teacher, philologist. Curme taught languages, mainly German, at several American universities, and became known as one of the leading authorities on linguistics in the United States. In addition to textbooks on German and French, he wrote a number of books which greatly influenced the study of English grammar and standards of speech: *College English Grammar* (1925); *English Syntax* (1931); *Parts of Speech and Accidence* (1935); and *Principles and Practice of English Grammar* (1946). He accepted usage as the standard, defended the split infinitive, and felt that the distinction between *shall* and *will* would probably not survive.

Currier & Ives. Nathaniel Currier (b. Roxbury, Mass., Mar. 27, 1813—d. Nov. 20, 1888), lithographer. He started in business in New York City about 1834. From the beginning he specialized in vivid pictures of American scenes, customs, and events. In 1857 J[ames] Merritt Ives (1824–1895) became his partner, and the prints thereafter appeared under the firm name of Currier & Ives. The Currier & Ives prints are not great art but provide a colorful and comprehensive picture of the 19th century American scene. The originals today are considered collectors' items. They have been often reproduced, notably in *Currier & Ives' America* (1952), edited by Colin Simkin.

Curry, John Steuart (b. Dunavant, Kans., Nov. 14, 1897—d. Aug. 29, 1946), painter. Curry's best work depicts life in Kansas, especially rural life. His paintings hang in most of the principal galleries of the country, and his murals decorate many public buildings.

Curti, Merle (b. Papillion, Neb., Sept. 15, 1897—   ), historian. Frederick Jackson Turner Professor of History at the University of Wisconsin since 1947, Curti has lectured and travelled all over the United States, and in Mexico, England, and India. His outlook on American history has been as broad as his travels; his works both reflect the influence of European traditions and stress the importance of regional peculiarities. *The Growth of American Thought* (1943) revealed the scope of his interests. This was the first synthesis of American thought to

include histories of subjects like technology, natural science, philosophy and theology; it was also the first successful attempt to relate all the aspects of American thought to their social setting. Curti studied at Harvard with EDWARD CHANNING, SAMUEL ELIOT MORISON and FREDERICK JACKSON TURNER; as Chairman of the Social Science Research Council Committee on historiography he worked with CHARLES A. BEARD. Turner was undoubtedly the greatest influence on him. In *The Making of an American Community* (1959), he tested Turner's FRONTIER thesis through an exhaustive study of Trempealeau County, Wisconsin, conducted with a group of scholars. Among his other books: *The Social Ideas of American Educators* (1935), *Peace or War: The American Struggle 1636–1936* (1936), and *The American Paradox* (1956).

Curtin, Jeremiah (b. Greenfield, Wis., Sept. 6, 1840?—d. Dec. 14, 1906), philologist, student of comparative religion, historian. Curtin, living among people of various national descents, early became interested in popular tales. He was a special authority on Russian, translating Tolstoy and other Slavic authors, writing on southern Siberia, and editing the fairy tales of Eastern Europe. Among his books: *Myths and Folklore of Ireland* (1890); *Creation Myths of Primitive America* (1898); *The Mongols in Russia* (1908); *Wonder Tales from Russia* (1921).

Curtis, George Ticknor (b. Watertown, Mass., Nov. 28, 1812—d. Mar. 28, 1894), lawyer, biographer, historian, author of legal treatises. For the most part Curtis practiced in New York City, where he moved in 1862. He became an authority on patent and copyright law. He was a Whig and opposed to abolition, but during the war supported the Union cause. He published many scholarly books, including a biography of James Buchanan (1883), a constitutional history of the United States (1854–1858), and a treatise on copyright (1847).

Curtis, George William (b. Providence, R.I., Feb. 24, 1824—d. Aug. 31, 1892), essayist, editor, publicist, orator. "He was a great man of letters, he was a great orator, he was a great political journalist, he was a great citizen, he was a great philanthropist." This was the eulogy pronounced by William Dean Howells when Curtis died. Oliver Wendell Holmes, Sr., wrote: "No American writer came so near taking the place of Washington Irving in the affections of his countrymen; no one has been more generally missed and lamented than he will be." A few years later, in *Mere Literature* (1896), Woodrow Wilson declared: "Among men of letters Lowell is doubtless most typically American, though Curtis must find an eligible place in the list." Yet the man thus praised by his contemporaries is now almost unknown to the general reader.

Curtis won fame as an author mainly with three books: *Nile Notes of a Howadji* (1851), travel sketches; the POTIPHAR PAPERS (1853), satirical commentaries on upper-crust life in New York; and PRUE AND I (1856), a collection of personal essays on the theme that wealth is not a requisite of happiness. *The Howadji in Syria* and *Lotus-Eating* (both 1852) have their charm also. *Literary and Social Essays* (1894) contains his best political and critical writing. His "Easy Chair" essays for *Harper's* were mainly on topical subjects.

Curtis was a true son of New England. As a youth he lived for two years at BROOK FARM, where he fell under the influence of RALPH WALDO EMERSON and the Transcendentalists (see TRANSCENDENTALISM). All his life he exemplified Emersonian individualism, even to the extent of not going to college. He traveled for four years in Europe, North Africa, and the Middle East instead, gathering the impressions which he put into his first books. Later he turned to politics, believing that "good citizens were needed more than good romancers." An ardent antislavery man and staunch supporter of Lincoln, he became one of the ablest of the early leaders of Civil Service reform and was known for his independent spirit in a time when party loyalty was an American fetish. His orations, though not as forceful as Webster's, possessed a gentle sincerity that pleased his listeners immensely. He lectured widely; one lecture, *Political Infidelity*, was delivered more than fifty times. All in all, Curtis was one of the most widely admired and respected figures of his age. Gordon Milne has done an admirable analysis

in *George William Curtis and the Genteel Tradition* (1956).

ELDON C. HILL

Curwood, James Oliver (b. Owosso, Mich., June 12, 1878—d. Aug. 13, 1927), writer of adventure and outdoor stories. He knew the wilderness well, especially the Hudson's Bay country. Best known of his twenty-six books is *The Valley of Silent Men* (1920). *Son of the Forest* (1930) is an autobiography.

Cushing, Frank Hamilton (b. Northeast, Pa., July 22, 1857—d. Apr. 10, 1900), ethnologist, explorer. Cushing was always interested in Indian culture, and in later life, he made himself a great authority on the ZUÑIS. They became so fond of him that they adopted him as a member of their tribe and helped him with his researches. He discovered the so-called "SEVEN CITIES OF CIBOLA," and wrote treatises on *Zuñi Fetiches* (1881), *Myths of Creation* (1882), *Adventures in Zuñi* (1883), *Zuñi Folk Tales* (1901).

Cushing, Harvey (b. Cleveland, Ohio, April 8, 1869—d. Oct. 7, 1939), surgeon, writer. The Cushing family, which had produced noted physicians for three generations before Harvey, won enduring fame through his important research in the structure of the brain and his amazing operative procedures. He was as handy with the pen as with the scalpel; among his books are *The Life of Sir William Osler* (1925, awarded the Pulitzer Prize); *From a Surgeon's Journal* (1936); *The Medical Career* (1940). He delivered a satirical address (1933) on *Homo Chirurgicus* before the Boston Surgical Society. His biography has been written by Elizabeth Thomson (1950).

Cushman, Charlotte [Saunders] (b. Boston, July 23, 1816—d. Feb. 17, 1876), actress. A finished actress with a fine voice, Miss Cushman at first intended to become an opera singer. She won her first success (1837) as Nancy Sikes in *Oliver Twist*, later played many roles with great success, particularly in Shakespearean drama. She is the subject of *A Life of Charlotte Cushman* (1894), by W. T. Price.

Custer, Elizabeth Bacon (b. Monroe, Mich., April 8, 1842—d. April 4, 1933), biographer, writer on frontier life. Mrs. Custer accompanied her husband, General **George Armstrong Custer** (1839–1876), throughout his army career, until his death at the Battle of Little Big Horn. After his death she wrote BOOTS AND SADDLES, OR, LIFE IN DAKOTA WITH GENERAL CUSTER (1885); *Tenting on the Plains* (1887); *Following the Guidon* (1890); *The Boy General* (1901). Custer's own sketches, first published in *The Galaxy*, were collected in *My Life on the Plains* (1874). In 1947 two psychiatrists, Dr. Paul R. Hawley and Dr. Karl Menninger, examined Custer's character and career, and concluded that he was definitely psychotic and in frustration had ordered the attack "that was one of the worst botched jobs in the annals of Indian warfare." General and Mrs. Custer's letters were collected in *The Custer Story* (1950).

Charles Kuhlman wrote *Legend into History: The Custer Mystery* (1951); E. I. Stewart discussed *Custer's Luck* (1955); Jay Monaghan wrote *Custer* (1959). Custer appears frequently in fiction, as in Cornelia Meigs's *Railroad West* (1937), Ernest Haycox's *Bugles in the Afternoon* (1944), Will Henry's *No Survivors* (1950), Hoffman Birney's *The Dice of God* (1956).

Custis, George Washington Parke (b. Mt. Airy, Md., April 30, 1781—d. Oct. 10, 1857), playwright. Custis was the grandson of Martha Washington through her first marriage. Washington adopted him and his sister after the death of their father. He wrote several plays, including one on *Pocahontas* (1830), also *Recollections and Private Memories of Washington* (1860).

Custis, John Parke. See THE INDIAN PROPHECY.

Custom of the Country, The (1913), a novel by EDITH WHARTON. The heroine is a beautiful but ruthless social climber named Undine Spragg who, through several marriages and divorces, samples the pleasures of money and aristocratic titles. Miss Wharton's disgust with the vulgarity of midwesterners, the "customs" of the nouveau riche, tends to usurp any interest and affection she may have felt for her main characters.

Cynic's Word Book, The (1906), by AMBROSE BIERCE. See THE DEVIL'S DICTIONARY.

Cytherea (1922), a novel by JOSEPH HERGESHEIMER. One of Hergesheimer's oddest stories, this is a study in fetishism. A 47-year-old broker, Lee Randon, wearied of his aging wife, falls in love with a doll that he sees in a New York shopwindow. He calls the doll Cytherea and makes her an emblem of Venus. Later he runs off to Cuba with a married woman who seems to embody all the beauty and attractions of Cytherea. But she dies, and Randon feels that he has been tricked by life and his own fantasies. According to Earle F. Walbridge, the actress Lillian Gish was the original for the character of Mina Raff in the novel.

D

Dabney, Virginius (b. University, Va., Feb. 8, 1901—   ), newspaper editor. Dabney joined the staff of the Richmond *Times-Dispatch* in 1928, became its editor in 1936. He contributed historical articles to reference works and magazines, lectured extensively, wrote *Liberalism in the South* (1932), *Below the Potomac* (1942), *Dry Messiah: The Life of Bishop Cannon* (1949). He received a Pulitzer Award for editorial writing (1947).

Dabneys, The. A family whose story is chronicled in several novels by JAMES STREET: *Oh, Promised Land* (1940); *Tap Roots* (1942); *Tomorrow We Reap* (1949); *Mingo Dabney* (1950). The stories are set mainly in Mississippi.

dada or dadaism. A revolutionary movement in the arts begun in Switzerland in 1915 by students protesting the meaningless destruction of war; their most prominent figure was the poet Tristan Tzara. Their method consisted, to a large degree, of the reduction of sense to nonsense in poetry, drama, painting, and the dance. Its influence in Europe was short lived; in the United States it was brief indeed. In New York it was introduced by Marcel Duchamp, Francis Picabia, and Arthur Cravan (a nephew of Oscar Wilde) and by an art exhibit at Grand Central Gallery in 1917. (This exhibit was revived in part at the Museum of Modern Art in 1961.) Duchamp's contribution to the exhibit was entitled "La Fontaine"—a urinal. Though the sponsors of the exhibit managed to hide it behind a partition, it caused a sensation nonetheless, as did a speech filled with four-letter words delivered by Cravan. In 1929 Duchamp and Man Ray assembled a single number of a publication they called *New York Dada*. A few Americans in Paris momentarily were influenced by the dadaist creed: E. E. Cummings, Matthew Josephson, and especially Margaret Anderson, who published some dadaist work in the LITTLE REVIEW. *The Dada Painters and Poets*, edited by the avant-garde artist and writer Robert Motherwell, contains the writings of many dadaists.

Daddy-Long-Legs (1912), a novel by JEAN WEBSTER. A sentimental tale of an orphan who finds romance with the help of a kindly trustee; it was written for young girls but was equally popular with adults. It was made into a successful play in 1914, and in the 1950's into a musical film starring Fred Astaire.

Dahl, Francis W. (b. Wollaston, Mass., Oct. 21, 1907—   ), cartoonist. Beginning in 1930, Dahl furnished daily pictures to the Boston *Herald*. From these several collections were made —*Left-Handed Compliments* (1941); *Dahl's Cartoons* (1943); *What? More Dahl* (1944); *Dahl's Boston* (1946); *Dahl's Brave New World* (1947); *Birds, Beasts, and Bostonians* (1954). Dahl's *Boston* was done in collaboration with CHARLES W. MORTON, who wrote some cheerful verbal satire to accompany Dahl's drawings. His weekly cartoon, *The Greenwoods*, began appearing in the *Saturday Evening Post* in 1958.

Dahl, Roald (b. England, Sept. 13, 1916—   ), novelist, short-story writer. An officer in the Royal Air Force, Dahl popularized the mythical gremlins in his book *The Gremlins* (1944). In 1946 he published *Over To You*, ten stories of flying and fliers. Moving to the United States, he began publishing stories in the *New Yorker* magazine, and soon became known for his mastery of the macabre. He twice received the Edgar Allan Poe Award. His books include: *Some Time Never* (1948); *Someone Like You* (1953); *Kiss Kiss* (1960). *James and the Giant Peach* appeared in 1961.

Daisy Miller (1878), a novelette by HENRY JAMES. James takes what he regards as a typically American girl and contrasts her to the sophisticated society of Europe. The book aroused criticism when it first appeared, some reviewers taking it as a libel on American manners, but many readers felt that James had delineated a charming type of girlish innocence, even if Daisy was somewhat careless of external standards and came to a tragic end. The book became one of the most popular of James's writings.

Daly, [John] Augustin (b. Plymouth, N.C., July 20, 1838—d. June 7, 1899), drama critic, producer, playwright. Always deeply interested in the theater, Daly was at first a writer about the stage for several New York papers, in 1862

produced his first play, *Leah the Forsaken*, an adaptation from the German that was greeted with general approval. Thereafter he went on to the writing (frequently adaptation) of numerous plays, some produced under his own direction—he made his debut as a manager with the London melodrama UNDER THE GASLIGHT (1867). Thereafter he won success with plays of his own, plays by other authors, and revivals;

on the stages of the various theaters that he owned (including one in London) appeared many of the famous actors of the day. A "Daly first night" became a social event, and Daly himself was widely esteemed because of his competence in the theater and his kindliness and generosity, although in the theater he was, like most producers, an autocrat. Arthur Hobson Quinn says that "modern American drama began with Augustin Daly." Only five or six of his plays were originals, and these in published form, says Sculley Bradley, "reveal a master of theatrical technique whose works remained subliterary." HORIZON (1871), his best original play, gave a new realism of setting and atmosphere to the frontier drama; Divorce (1871) and Pique (1875) were early approaches to the social problem play. Marvin Felheim ably discusses The Theater of Augustin Daly (1956).

Daly, Elizabeth (b. New York City, Oct. 15, 1878—d. Sept. 2, 1967), poet, mystery writer. After obtaining a B.A. from Bryn Mawr and an M.A. from Columbia University, Elizabeth Daly went on to produce amateur plays and pageants. It was not until 1940 that her first book, Unexpected Night, appeared. She was then over sixty. This was not, however, her first appearance in print. At the age of sixteen she had launched into the writing of poetry with remarkable success. In those early years Life, Puck, and Scribner's had published her light verse. Following upon the creation of her urbane, bookish detective, Henry Gamadge, in Unexpected Night, Miss Daly continued to publish a number of well-plotted whodunits. Deadly Nightshade came out in 1940; Murder in Volume 2 in 1941; Wrong Way Down in 1946. The reader's credulity is somewhat stretched in the solutions Henry Gamadge presents, but the detective himself remains credible. In fact, he has inspired so much belief that Miss Daly received many letters addressed to him personally.

Daly, Maureen (b. Ireland, March 15, 1921—   ), novelist, short-story writer. While still a high school senior Miss Daly wrote a tale called Sixteen, which won first prize (1937) in a contest for students sponsored by Scholastic Magazine, and was chosen by Harry Hansen for the O. Henry Prize Award collection of 1938. Miss Daly's novel Seventeenth Summer (1942) has gone into edition after edition and has been described as "the Little Women of the 20th century." It tells, with sincerity and humor, experiences that might have occurred to Miss Daly herself. She has conducted a syndicated column for teenagers and written numerous children's books. Among them are Smarter and Smoother (1944); What's Your P.Q., Personality Quotient? (1952). Her most recent book is Moroccan Roundabout (1961).

Daly, Thomas A[ugustine] (b. Philadelphia, May 28, 1871—d. Oct. 4, 1948), newspaperman, editor, columnist, poet. Daly had a gift of mimicry, and one story his friends loved to hear him tell was an account of an Italian baseball game. As a result he wrote his famous dialect poem, Mia Carlotta, followed by others

of the same kind, which were collected in Canzoni (1906); Carmina (1909); Madrigali (1912); McAroni Ballads (1919); McAroni Medleys (1931); Selected Poems of T. A. Daly (1936); and Late Lark Singing (1946). Daly was an adept versifier who did Irish dialect poems as clever and sympathetic as those he composed in Italian dialect. He could also write excellent straight verse and he recited effectively. Poetry was Daly's avocation; he was by profession a notable newspaperman, writer of a column which appeared in the Philadelphia Evening Ledger in 1891, later in the Evening Bulletin.

Damnation of Theron Ware, The (1896), a novel by HAROLD FREDERIC. It portrays a clergyman and suggests the disintegration of religious orthodoxy. It made a great sensation in its own time and has been reprinted several times in recent years.

Damon, S[amuel] Foster (b. Newton, Mass., Feb. 22, 1893—   ), teacher, poet, critic, biographer. A teacher of literature himself, Damon mingled intimately with many noted literary figures and in particular became an authority on Amy Lowell. His verses, collected in Astrolabe (1927) and Tilted Moons (1929) are often humorous in tone. His biographies of William Blake (1924) and Thomas Holley Chivers (1930); his orchestral suite, Crazy Theater Music (1938); his Seven Songs (1951); and other works show his versatility. In 1929 Damon became curator of the great Harris Collection of American Poetry and Plays at Brown University; he became a full professor there in 1936. He has also written plays, among them Witch of Dogtown (1954) and Punch and Judy (1957).

Damrosch, Walter [Johannes] (b. Germany, Jan. 30, 1862—d. Dec. 22, 1950), conductor, composer, broadcaster. In the course of his career as a musician, Damrosch, who came to the United States when he was nine years old, often found inspiration in American themes and books, as in the opera The Scarlet Letter (1894); An Abraham Lincoln Song (1936); Death and General Putnam (based on ARTHUR GUITERMAN's ballad, 1936); THE MAN WITHOUT A COUNTRY (1937). During the 1930's his educational radio broadcasts for children formed the chief musical fare in many American schools. His father, Leopold Damrosch (1832–1885), was a noted conductor, the founder of the New York Oratorio Society (1873) and the New York Symphony Society (1878). He did much to popularize the work of Liszt, Schumann and Wagner in this country.

Dana, Charles A[nderson] (b. Hinsdale, N.H., Aug. 8, 1819—d. Oct. 17, 1897), newspaperman, reformer, editor, government official. Dana began as an ardent reformer who sought to cure the obvious ills of society with ideas put into practice in the BROOK FARM experiment. When that failed, Dana turned to newspaper work, first as editor of the Boston Daily Chronotype, then as city editor and later managing editor on the New York Tribune at $10 per week, a post he held for thirteen years. But then he disagreed with HORACE GREELEY on the policies governing the Civil War and was discharged. For a while he was connected with the War Department, finally becoming assistant Secretary under Stanton and doing much to confirm Lincoln's faith in Grant.

After the war he secured enough capital to buy the New York *Sun*, which he made the leading newspaper in the United States. He took as the motto of the paper: "If you see it in the *Sun*, it's so"; for a newspaperman (or a printer) to have worked for Dana was a cachet of honor. He gave up completely his idealistic beliefs and dedicated himself to a doctrine of *laissez-faire* and to an idolatry of capitalistic enterprise; but he violently attacked the graft that developed in Grant's administration. Cynical, scintillant, and skillful, he actually cared more for a phrase than for a fact, and he surrounded himself with some of the best newspaper writers of the day. Bourke Cockran said of him, "With a word he could smash a hypocrite, with a phrase expose a humbug." Maude Wilder Goodwin compared the *Sun* and LAWRENCE GODKIN's *Post* by asserting that Godkin made virtue unattractive in the evening while Dana made vice glamorous in the morning. The two papers denounced each other bitterly and exchanged issue-by-issue insults. Dana himself favored a paper that would steer "a middle course between the mental eccentricity of the *Tribune* and the moral eccentricity of the *Herald*"—a place the *Times* later tried to fill. H. L. Mencken said of Dana that he "produced the first newspaper on earth that was decently written." Dana wrote a book, *The Art of News-*

paper Making (1895). C. J. Rosebault wrote *When Dana Was the Sun* (1931), Candace Stone wrote *Dana and the Sun* (1938).

Dana, Henry Wadsworth Longfellow (b. Boston, Jan. 26, 1881—d. April 27, 1950), teacher, lecturer, editor, biographer. A descendant of RICHARD HENRY DANA, JR. and of Longfellow, Dana devoted several of his writings to them: *The Craigie House—The Coming of Longfellow* (1939); *The Dana Saga* (1941); *Longfellow and Dickens* (1943); an edition of *Two Years Before the Mast* (1946). Dana was also an authority on European drama, especially that of Russia, and the author of *A Handbook of Soviet Drama* (1938); *Drama In Wartime Russia* (1943); and *Seven Soviet Plays* (1948).

Dana, James Dwight (b. Utica, N.Y., Feb. 12, 1813—d. April 14, 1895), geologist, zoologist. After work with an expedition in the South Seas, Dana became professor of natural history at Yale. In 1837, when he was only twenty-four years old, he published his *System of Mineralogy*, which became a classic in its field. Dana, as he made clear in his *Manual of Geology* (1862), looked upon geology as a historical science. Other books of his are *Crustacea* (1852–54), *Corals and Coral Islands* (1872); and *Characteristics of Volcanoes* (1890). His books were standard textbooks and had millions of readers.

Dana, Richard Henry, Sr. (b. Cambridge, Mass., Nov. 15, 1787—d. Feb. 2, 1879), poet, editor, lecturer. Originally a lawyer who apparently never practiced, Dana was mainly interested in writing. His contemporaries, espe-

cially Lowell in *A Fable for Critics* (1848), attributed to him a good deal more ability than he ever manifested in his productions. At one time (1821) he conducted for six months a magazine called *The Idle Man*, and Lowell says:

That he once was *The Idle Man* none will
    deplore,
But I fear he will never be anything more.

As associate editor of the *North American Review* he accepted Bryant's *Thanatopsis* in 1817.
He contributed to numerous newspapers and magazines, gave lectures on literary subjects, published *The Buccaneer and Other Poems* (1827)
and *Poems and Prose Writings* (1833). Tremaine McDowell says that Dana was "Boston's
most severe critic of outmoded classicism and
its most extravagant champion of romanticism."

Dana, Richard Henry, Jr. (b. Cambridge,
Mass., Aug. 1, 1815—d. Jan. 6, 1882), writer,
lawyer. At Harvard he studied under EDWARD
TYRRELL CHANNING, who taught him—along
with other famous pupils like Emerson, Holmes,

Motley, and Parkman—something of the art of
writing. In later years Dana repaid his debt by
editing Channing's brilliant lectures (1856). His
sight suffered during his student days at Harvard,
and rather than take a conventional pleasure
voyage, he shipped out from Boston as a common sailor on the vessel *Pilgrim* in 1834. Gold
had not yet been discovered and the *Pilgrim* was
heading for California to purchase hides. Dana
returned home on the *Alert* in 1836, his health
much improved. Out of the notes he kept in his
journal he wrote what has become a classic of
American literature, TWO YEARS BEFORE THE
MAST (1840). His description of Cape Horn,
the storms at sea, the little-known land which is
now the state of California; his sympathetic accounts of the abuses he and his mates suffered;
all these found attentive reception, and a number
of maritime reforms came about because of
Dana's accurate chronicle under the guise of
fiction.

In the meantime Dana had re-entered Harvard (1836) and a year later was graduated at
the head of his class. For a while he taught at
Harvard, but in 1840 was admitted to the bar.
The oppression of sailors that he had witnessed
gave him a fervent interest in seamen and he
became known as the "sailors' lawyer"; his office,
it is said, smelled like a forecastle, so crowded
was it with men of the sea. He battled for them

and their rights and compiled a manual, *The
Seaman's Friend* (1841), that became an authority frequently consulted in the United States
and in England. He was also an abolitionist and
was deeply interested in international law. According to Van Wyck Brooks, he "alienated all
his paying clients" by his fervor in behalf of the
downtrodden.

Dangerfield, George (b. England, Oct. 28,
1904—   ), author. Dangerfield graduated
from Oxford in 1927 and came to America in
1930. From 1933 to 1935 he served as the literary editor of the old *Vanity Fair* magazine. In
1953 he received both the Pulitzer Prize and the
Bancroft Prize for his work in American history.
His book, *The Era of Good Feelings,* written in
1952, received enthusiastic critical notices. Some
other books: *The Strange Death of Liberal England* (1935); *Victoria's Heir* (1941); *Chancellor
Robert R. Livingston of New York 1746–1813*
(1960).

Daniels, Jonathan [Worth] (b. Raleigh, N.C.,
April 26, 1902—   ), newspaperman, writer,
public official. The son of JOSEPHUS DANIELS
naturally followed in his father's footsteps, and
after working for the Louisville *Times* became a
reporter for the Raleigh *News and Observer,*
which his father owned. In 1948, on his father's
death, he became its editor officially, though he
had held that post unofficially in his father's lifetime. From 1943 to 1945 Daniels was administrative assistant to President Franklin D. Roosevelt.
Frontier on the Potomac, which he published in
1946, describes the lively Washington scene of
these years. He began his career as an author
with a novel—*Clash of Angels* (1930)—but he
is best known for his candid depictions of conditions in North Carolina and elsewhere in the
South, and in Washington. Among his books:
A Southerner Discovers the South (1938); *A
Southerner Discovers New England* (1940); *Tar
Heels: A Portrait of North Carolina* (1941);
The Man of Independence (1950, a life of
President Truman); *The End of Innocence*
(1954), a rich store of Washington lore in the
days of Woodrow Wilson, culled from the
diaries of Daniels' father, Josephus, when he was
Secretary of the Navy and Ambassador to Mexico. *Prince of Carpetbaggers* (1958), was followed by *Stonewall Jackson* (1959), and *Robert
E. Lee* (1960).

Daniels, Josephus (b. Washington, N.C., May
18, 1862—d. Jan. 15, 1948), newspaperman,
cabinet official, ambassador. Daniels began
working on a newspaper when he was only
eighteen. He became editor of the Raleigh *News*
in 1884 and so continued for the rest of his life.
He was a great newspaperman, always fighting,
although personally a mild and friendly man. He
became secretary of the navy under Wilson and
was a capable administrator, but was widely
attacked and caricatured for his attacks on privilege in the navy and for his insistence on making the navy "dry." In 1933 Roosevelt appointed
Daniels ambassador to Mexico, and he did much
to build friendly relations and close cooperation
with that nation. He wrote a series of auto-

biographical volumes of great historical value: *Editor: In Politics* (1940); *The Wilson Era* (2 v., 1944, 1945); *Shirt Sleeve Diplomat* (1947).

Danites in the Sierras, The (produced, 1877; published, 1882), a play by JOAQUIN MILLER. The plot revolves around an attempt of the Danites, a secret association of Mormons, to take revenge on Nancy Williams, a young girl who disguises herself in male costume and lives alone in a cabin in the Sierras to avoid their pursuit. The play, which shows the influence of BRET HARTE, was one of the most popular of frontier dramas and was equally popular in London when played there in 1880. The characters are conventional, but Arthur Hobson Quinn praises the "directness in the dialogue" and "the pulsing humanity" of the play.

Dannay, Frederic. See ELLERY QUEEN.

D'Arcy, Hugh Antoine. See THE FACE ON THE BARROOM FLOOR.

Dargan, Olive [Tilford] ["Fielding Burke"] (b. Grayson Co., Ky., 1869—d. Jan. 22, 1968), dramatist, novelist. Miss Dargan wrote melodious verse, also several plays in verse. Among her collections are *Semiramis and Other Plays* (1904); *Lords and Lovers and Other Dramas* (1906); *Path Flowers and Other Poems* (1914); *Lute and Furrow* (1922). As Fielding Burke she wrote two proletarian novels, *Call Home the Heart* (1932) and a sequel, *A Stone Came Rolling* (1935). Among her other books: *From My Highest Hill* (1941), *Sons of the Stranger* (1947); *Spotted Hawk* (1958).

Daring Young Man on the Flying Trapeze, The (published in *Story*, 1934, and in the same year as the title work in a collection), a short story by WILLIAM SAROYAN. A mingling of fantasy and realism, this early work did much to establish its author's reputation.

Darius Green and His Flying Machine (OUR YOUNG FOLKS, March, 1867; in the collection, *The Vagabonds and Other Poems*, 1869), a famous humorous poem by JOHN TOWNSEND TROWBRIDGE. It is about a man who believed firmly that "the air is also man's dominion."

Dark Laughter (1925), a novel by SHERWOOD ANDERSON. The chief character, John Stockton, becomes weary of the shoddy newspaper work he is doing, drifts in an open boat down the Illinois and Mississippi Rivers, under the name Bruce Dudley starts working in a factory in his native town, is involved in an affair with his employer's wife, Aline Grey, and runs away with her. The white man, Anderson seeks to show, has been corrupted by civilization; and today only the Negro, with his "dark laughter," has escaped, with scorn for the white man's moral scruples.

Darling of the Gods, The (1902), a romantic tragedy by DAVID BELASCO and JOHN LUTHER LONG. The Princess Yo-San, betrothed to a man she does not love, sets him an impossible task—the capture of a notorious outlaw, Prince Kara. Kara had once saved the life of Yo-San, but without revealing himself; now she tries to save him and does so by betraying the hiding-place of his followers. But he returns to his men and dies with honor, surrounded by the dead bodies of the samurai. Long based the play on an incident in Japanese history. The play, lavishly produced, ran for two years, and was also successfully presented in London, Berlin, and elsewhere.

Darrow, Clarence S[eward] (b. Kinsman, Ohio, April 18, 1857—d. March 13, 1938), lawyer, lecturer, reformer, writer. Darrow, with only a meager education (supplemented by books in his father's library), became perhaps the best-known lawyer and nonpolitical figure of his times. He practiced at first in a small Ohio town, later went to Chicago and rose rapidly in his profession, becoming at length a well-paid railroad lawyer. But he was irked at the type of cases he had to defend, and his sympathy often lay with the lowly persons who were suing the railroads. In the famous EUGENE DEBS case he resigned his position and won an acquittal for Debs; later he defended Nathan Loopold and Richard Loeb, murderers of young Bobby Franks in 1924, and saved them from being sentenced to death. He was the chief counsel for J. T. Scopes, who was accused of violating Tennessee law by teaching evolution in a public school; in the resulting "monkey trial" Darrow lost his case but succeeded in destroying the reputation of the aging WILLIAM JENNINGS BRYAN, who argued in court on the side of the prosecution. (See SCOPES TRIAL.) Darrow was never so happy as when defending an unpopular cause or trying to save a persecuted defendant. He himself once stood in the dock, on a charge of bribing a jury, but was acquitted. His fame as a public speaker was nation-wide.

Irving Stone, in *Clarence Darrow for the Defense* (1941), speaks of the "amazing mixture of cynicism, compassion, and incredibly brilliant intelligence that made up Darrow's character," but Oscar Cargill is inclined to stress Darrow's "befuddled human sympathy" as leading to disrespect for the law and the condonation of "antisocial acts of impulse." Darrow wrote two novels, *Farmington* (1904) and *An Eye for an Eye* (1905), reflecting his own experiences and expounding his belligerent creed. He wrote *Crime: Its Cause and Its Treatment* (1922), and with Wallace Rice edited an anthology, *Infidels and Heretics* (1929). He told *The Story of My Life* (1932), in large part a continuation and expansion of *Farmington*. Paul Muni impersonated him superbly in Jerome Lawrence and Robert E. Lee's *Inherit the Wind* (1955), a play based on the Scopes trial, later made into a movie (1960); and he also figures largely in Meyer Levin's *Compulsion* (1956, a book, a play, and a movie), based on the Loeb-Leopold case. *Attorney for the Damned* (edited by Arthur Weinberg, 1957), contains nine of Darrow's summations and four speeches made outside the courtroom.

Daughter of the Middle Border, A (1921), HAMLIN GARLIN's sequel to his autobiographical narrative, SON OF THE MIDDLE BORDER (1917). It deals with his marriage and later career, and won a Pulitzer Prize.

Davenport, Marcia (b. New York City, June 9, 1903—   ), editor, music critic, biographer, radio commentator, novelist. As the daughter of the famous singer Alma Gluck, Mrs. Davenport was born into the world of music; and her vivacious fiction frequently reflects this background. Her first book was a life of Mozart (1932, revised 1956); she followed this with many novels: *Of Lena Geyer* (1936); *The Valley of Decision* (1942); *East Side, West Side* (1947); *My Brother's Keeper* (1954); *Constant Image* (1960).

Davenport, Russell [Wheeler] (b. S. Bethlehem, Pa., July 12, 1899—d. April 19, 1954), newspaperman, editor, poet, husband of MARCIA DAVENPORT. Active in journalism (especially on *Time, Life,* and *Fortune*) and in politics, Davenport often expressed himself fervently in verse, particularly in *My Country* (1944), in which he reveals himself as a patriot deeply moved by American problems during the war. He later wrote *Dignity of Man* (1955).

David Harum (1899), a novel by EDWARD N. WESTCOTT. Published after the author's death, it met with instantaneous success in its own day and continued to sell steadily for many years; its total sale is well in the millions. In 1900 a stage version was presented, with William H. Crane as David, and later a film adaptation with Will Rogers. The subtitle is *A Story of American Life,* and John Oliver Hobbes declared that there was a David Harum in every real American family. The book tells the story of an up-state New York country banker, quaint and somewhat illiterate, shrewd but kindly, given to homely sayings. Some of these have become proverbial: "Do unto the other fellow the way he'd like to do unto you an' do it fust." "They say a reasonable number of fleas is good fer a dog—keeps him from broodin' over bein' a dog." "The' ain't nothin' truer in the Bible 'n that sayin' thet them that has, gits." There is a slight love story in the novel, in which David plays his kindly part, but it is David who is the main attraction. Particularly famous is the horse-trading scene.

Davidson, Donald [Grady] (b. Campbellsville, Tenn., Aug. 18, 1893—d. April 26, 1968), critic, poet. Davidson was a member of the "FUGITIVE group" of poets at Vanderbilt University, and one of the founders and editors of *The Fugitive* magazine. His southern conservatism exerted a strong influence on younger southern writers and intellectuals. He was a prominent member of the group that published I'LL TAKE MY STAND (1930), a collection of essays which served, in a sense, as the manifesto of recrudescent southern agrarianism. In *The Attack on Leviathan* (1938) he made a critical analysis of economic centralization in the North. His poetry has appeared in three volumes, *The Piper* (1924), *The Tall Men* (1927), and *Lee in the Mountains* (1938). He taught at Vanderbilt University for many years. *Southern Writers in the Modern World,* a group of essays, appeared in 1958.

Davidson, Jo[seph] (b. New York City, March 30, 1883—d. Jan. 2, 1952), sculptor. After giving up his premedical studies at Yale, Davidson went to New York and then to Paris to study sculpture. He first attained prominence as the sculptor of many of the important figures at the Versailles Conference in 1918: Woodrow Wilson, Marshal Foch, General Pershing, Clemenceau, etc. Later, he did busts of such literary figures as Anatole France and Walt Whitman and portrait busts of such eminent contemporaries as Franklin D. Roosevelt, Robert La Follette, Winston S. Churchill, Will Rogers, Rabindranath Tagore, and many others. Through his numerous sensitive, impressionistic studies, he consciously created a permanent sculptural record of many of the most influential men of his time. Davidson's autobiography, *Between Sittings,* was published in 1951.

Davidson, Thomas (b. Scotland, Oct. 25, 1840—d. Sept. 14, 1900), teacher, philosopher. Davidson came to Canada in 1866, shortly thereafter began teaching in the St. Louis public schools. He founded several schools at which his own doctrines were taught, many of them representing a reaction against Hegelianism and a return to Plato and Aristotle. His Fellowship of the New Life (one of his English activities) is regarded as a forerunner of the Fabian Society. But Davidson himself was greatly opposed to socialism. Another of his schools was the Breadwinner's College in New York, conducted for workers. In his biography of Davidson (1907) William Knight calls him "the wandering scholar"; William James' memorial article (1905) described him as "a knight-errant of the intellectual life." He wrote *Aristotle and Ancient Educational Ideals* (1892); *Education of the Greek People* (1894); and *The Education of the Wage-Earner* (1905). See IDEALISM.

Davies, [William] Robertson (b. Thamesville, Ont., Aug. 28, 1913—   ), critic, dramatist, novelist, editor. After receiving a degree in Shakespearean studies from Balliol College, Oxford, in 1938, Davies joined the Old Vic Company as an actor and teacher. He returned to Canada in 1940 as literary editor of *Saturday Night,* a Toronto magazine, and later became editor and publisher of the Peterborough (Ont.) *Examiner.* His column, "A Writer's Diary," appears in the Toronto *Star* and other newspapers. In his first full-length play, *Fortune My Foe* (1949), as in much of his subsequent writing, Davies revealed his preoccupation with Canadian problems and character. He has since written numerous plays, ranging in type from fantasy to satiric farce. Five of his short comedies were collected in *Eros at Breakfast and Other Plays* (1949). His most recent plays, *A Jig for the Gypsy* (1954) and *Hunting Start* (1955), were produced at Toronto's Crest Theatre.

Davies' first novel, *Tempest-Tost* (1951), described the misadventures of a group of amateurs involved in a production of *The Tempest.* Two later novels, *Leaven of Malice* (1954) and *A Mixture of Frailties* (1958), were also in a comic vein and were praised for their charm, urbanity, and wit. *Love and Libel,* Davies' dramatization of *Leaven of Malice,* had a brief

New York run in 1960. With Tyrone Guthrie and others, Davies has written three volumes on the Stratford (Ont.) Shakespearean Festival, of which he has been a governor since 1953: *Renown at Stratford* (1953), *Twice Have the Trumpets Sounded* (1954), and *Thrice the Brinded Cat Hath Mew'd* (1955). Other books by Davies are *Shakespeare's Boy Actors* (1939); *Shakespeare for Young Players* (1942); *The Diary of Samuel Marchbanks* (1947); *The Table Talk of Samuel Marchbanks* (1949); and *A Voice from the Attic* (1960), a collection of literary essays addressed to what Davies calls the "clerisy," that part of the reading public which reads "for pleasure and with some pretension to taste."

Davis, Adelle (b. Linton, Ind., Feb. 25, 1904——), writer on nutrition. Miss Davis attended Purdue from 1923 to 1925, received her B.A. from the University of California at Berkeley in 1927, and her M.A. from the University of Southern California in 1937. She was Dietician at Bellevue Hospital, 1927–28; Supervisor of Nutrition in public schools in Yonkers and New York City, 1928–30; a consulting nutritionist from 1931 to 1960, mostly in Los Angeles. Her belief that nutrition is a fascinating and personal subject is evident in her writing. She writes with simplicity and directness. Among her highly popular books are: *Vitality Through Planned Nutrition* (1942); *Let's Cook It Right* (1946); *Let's Have Healthy Children* (1010)j *Let's Eat Right to Keep Fit* (1953).

Davis, Charles Augustus (b. 1795—d. Jan. 27, 1867), merchant, newspaperman, humorist. During the great frontal attack of the humorists on Andrew Jackson's administration, the most widely read satires were those of SEBA SMITH, who in 1830 began to publish in the Portland *Courier* a series of letters, supposedly written by one Major Jack Downing and composed in homespun Down East speech. Then in June, 1833, the New York *Daily Advertiser* ran a series of letters, allegedly from the same J. Downing but really written by Davis, who knew nothing about New England and who was a hanger-on in the New York circle of literati. Davis was a staunch conservative, warmly hostile to Jackson. His J. Downing was more naïve than Jack Downing, and of course not well acquainted with Yankeeland. Nevertheless, the Davis letters became, according to Walter Blair, even more famous than those of Smith, and "many historians mention Davis and not Smith as Downing's creator." The letters were collected as *Letters of J. Downing, Major, Downingville Militia* (1834).

Davis, Clyde Brion (b. Unadilla, Neb., May 22, 1894—d. July 19, 1962), newsman, novelist. Davis worked on newspapers from coast to coast in every possible capacity. One of the best of his novels is "THE GREAT AMERICAN NOVEL" (1938), the story of a newspaperman whose roving life is spent in dreaming about the great American novel he expects to write; meanwhile his life *is* that novel. Davis' fiction is marked by insight and variety. Among

his book: *The Anointed* (1937), an ironical story of a sailor who thinks he is divinely inspired; *Nebraska Coast* (1939), an unconventional tale of pioneer life based in part on the experiences of Davis' family; *Follow the Leader* (1944), about a war hero; *The Rebellion of Leo McGuire* (1944), about a "good" burglar; *The Stars Incline* (1946), another newspaper story; *Temper the Wind* (1948), which tells of a garage mechanic who becomes a prize fighter; *Thudbury* (1952); *The Newcomer* (1954); *The Big Pink Kite* (1960). He also wrote *The Arkansas* (1940), in the "RIVERS OF AMERICA" SERIES, and some amusing memoirs, *The Age of Indiscretion* (1950).

Davis, Elmer [Holmes] (b. Aurora, Ind., Jan. 13, 1890—d. May 18, 1958), newspaperman, writer, news analyst. Davis wrote *A History of the New York Times* (1921) after ten years on the paper's staff. He joined the staff of CBS in 1939, interrupted his work there to serve as director of the Office of War Information (1942–45), then returned to radio work. Davis won an enviable reputation as an interpreter of the news, which he presented with a dry truthfulness and with neither fear nor favor. He also wrote novels and short stories, including *I'll Show You the Town* (1924); *Friends of Mr. Sweeney* (1925); *Strange Woman* (1927); and GIANT-KILLER (1928). The last-named tells the story of King David from a rationalist viewpoint, with David taking credit for great deeds performed by others. E. B. White said of Davis that he "gets up in the morning to work in defense of freedom as methodically as most of us get up and brush our teeth." A book of essays, *Not to Mention the War* (1940), was followed by *But We Were Born Free* (1954) and *Two Minutes Till Midnight* (1955). Roger Burlingame wrote a biography of Davis called *Don't Let Them Scare You* (1961).

Davis, Gussie L. Composer of IN THE BAGGAGE CAR AHEAD.

Davis, H[arold] L[enoir] (b. Douglas Co., Ore., Oct. 18, 1896—d. Oct 31, 1960), cattle herder, surveyor, sheriff, poet, novelist. Davis won a prize from *Poetry* (1919) and a Guggenheim Fellowship (1932). His HONEY IN THE HORN (1935), a story of frontier life in Oregon, took the $7,500 Harper prize and the Pulitzer award for fiction. Later he wrote *Harp of a Thousand Strings* (1947), a narrative ranging from the western prairies to the French Revolution; *Beulah Land* (1949) and *Winds of Morning* (1951), both frontier novels; *Team Bells Woke Me* (1953), a sheaf of fine short stories; *Distant Music* (1957), a family chronicle set in southeastern Oregon. His poetry deals with outdoor life.

Davis, Jefferson (b. Christian Co., Ky., June 3, 1808—d. Dec. 6, 1889), soldier, statesman, author. Educated at West Point, Davis served in the Indian wars and in the war with Mexico; later he was a member of the House of Representatives, in the Senate, and as secretary of war under President Pierce. When the Civil War broke out he was chosen as President of the

CONFEDERACY. His policies, however, aroused much controversy within Confederate ranks. He was captured and imprisoned at the end of the war; many northern leaders signed a petition for his release, and he spent his last years peacefully on his estate near Biloxi, Miss. He closed his *Rise and Fall of the Confederate Government* (2 v., 1881) with a call for an end to recrimination and held that "on the basis of fraternity and faithful regard for the rights of the states, there may be written on the arch of the Union, *Esto perpetua.*" Harnett T. Kane draws a friendly portrait of Mrs. Davis in his novel, *Bride of Fortune* (1948). Hudson Strode published *Jefferson Davis: American Patriot* (1955).

Davis, John (b. England, Aug. 6, 1774—d. April 24, 1854), bookseller, traveler, novelist. Davis said, "The United States is the country of my literary birth." Among his books with American settings are *The Farmer of New Jersey* (1800); a sequel, *The Wanderings of William* (1801); THE FIRST SETTLERS OF VIRGINIA (1805); *Walter Kennedy* (1805). Gilbert Chinard says Davis, as a disciple of Rousseau, "should take first rank among the romantic observers of America." Davis also published his *Travels in America* (1803). He says he traveled mainly on foot, and he "entered, with equal interest, the mud-hut of the Negro and the log-house of the planter." Thelma Kellogg wrote his biography: *The Life and Works of John Davis* (1924).

Davis, Owen (b. Portland, Me., Jan 29, 1874—d. Oct. 14, 1956), mining engineer, playwright, motion-picture and radio scriptwriter. A writer of great intelligence, Davis might under other circumstances have become a notable dramatist. He began with a serious verse tragedy and, discouraged by its failure to win a hearing, went on to write innumerable melodramas. His plays of this type include westerns, society plays, plays based on sexual themes; the most famous were NELLIE, THE BEAUTIFUL CLOAK MODEL (1906) and *The Nervous Wreck* (1923). More literary are *The Detour* (1921) and ICEBOUND (1923), which won a Pulitzer Prize. In his later years Davis collaborated with his son, Owen Davis, Jr. He successfully dramatized numerous novels, especially *Ethan Frome* (1936). Davis wrote his autobiography in *I'd Like to Do It Again* (1931), added to it in *My First 50 Years in the Theatre* (1950).

Davis, Rebecca [Blaine] Harding (b. Washington, Pa., June 24, 1831—d. Sept. 29, 1910), novelist. One of the earliest American realists, Mrs. Davis allowed her work to be vitiated by sentimentality and too obvious propagandizing. She won a hearing with a story published in the *Atlantic Monthly* (April, 1861) called *Life in the Iron Mills*, based largely on her own observations; she warned her readers, "I want you to hide your disgust, take no heed to your clean clothes, and come right down with me—here into the thickest of the fog and mud and effluvia." Thereafter she published several novels—MARGARET HOWTH (1862), a study of slum life; *Waiting for the Verdict* (1868), a story

about racial bias; *John Andross* (1874), a tale of political corruption—to name a few.

Davis, Richard Harding (b. Philadelphia, April 18, 1864—d. April 11, 1916), newspaperman, war correspondent, short-story writer, novelist, playwright. Called "the Beau Brummell of the Press" and confident that he was

the only New York City reporter who would look well in evening clothes, Davis gave the impression of being a fraud but was actually a person of great ability, undoubted courage, and wide information; and he was a master storyteller. The son of REBECCA HARDING DAVIS, he established himself in New York on the *Sun*, then went on to serve other papers. When during the Spanish-American War period the *Journal*, for which he was then working, colored one of his articles in a way to slur the Spaniards (whom Davis hated) untruthfully, Davis wrote a letter to a rival paper, the *World*, correcting the article (since the *Journal* would publish no retraction)—and lost his job. He "covered" assignments all over the world, reported many wars, major and minor, and talked to generals as an equal. Although forbidden by the rules of war, he took part in the Battle of San Juan Hill and was offered a commission by Theodore Roosevelt, which he declined. In World War I he was so eager to get to the battle line that he was almost shot by the Germans as a spy. When he reported the English boat races he wore a boating costume, and at the yacht-club races he was faultless as a yachtsman. He announced his engagement to the world by sending his fiancée a ring by a messenger boy who traveled eight thousand miles against all sorts of difficulties, with bulletins on his progress given daily to the press.

Davis' fiction is, naturally, laid in countries all over the world, his characters of all varieties, but all highly theatrical. His style is the rapid communication of a brilliant reporter, the plots what Davis might have imagined as occurring in his own sensational life. VAN BIBBER is a socialite who is kind to the poor and gets mixed up in amusing adventures (*Van Bibber and Others,* 1892), young GALLEGHER is in the newspaper business (*Gallegher and Other Stories,* 1891), excitement is in the blood of Captain Macklin and others like him (*Captain Macklin,* 1902; SOLDIERS OF FORTUNE, 1897), suspense and danger can be found in London (*In the Fog,* 1901) or South America (*The Exiles,* 1894; *The Dictator,* 1904). Inevitably Davis' stories found their way to the stage; he himself wrote more than twenty plays, some based on his own stories.

Despite his facility in composition, Davis was not a notable stylist; but he knew how to spin a yarn. Moreover, he well represented his age, the "mauve decade." Out of a combination of his and CHARLES DANA GIBSON's talents emerged in the literature and popular art of the period a conception of an ideal American male: tall, handsome, constantly on the go, chivalrous, good to the poor and downtrodden, courageous, a keeper of the code of good manners and noble conduct. This ideal male did not long survive the events of the early 20th century.

Davis, Robert ["Bob"] H[obart] (b. Brownsville, Neb., March 23, 1869—d. Oct. 11, 1942), newspaperman, columnist, writer. Davis became a newspaper reporter in San Francisco, ultimately drifted to New York and became Sunday editor of the *World*. Then he became associated with FRANK MUNSEY and edited the magazine to which that publisher gave his name, as well as other magazines in the Munsey chain. As an editor Davis gave generous and intelligent assistance to many young writers, including O. Henry. When Munsey died in 1925 Davis joined the *Sun* and conducted a widely syndicated column. He traveled to many parts of the world, and his essays and reminiscences were gathered in *Over My Left Shoulder* (1926); *Bob Davis Recalls* (1927); *Bob Davis Abroad* (1929); *Bob Davis at Large* (1934); *People Everywhere* (1936); and others. He wrote an often reprinted essay, "I Am the Printing Press."

Davis, William Stearns (b. Plymouth, Mass., March 3, 1822—d. Dec. 3, 1907), lawyer, historian, novelist. A greatly esteemed scholar, especially in the field of ancient history, Davis wrote excellent histories and textbooks, but also made good use of his learning in several novels. Among the former: *The Influence of Wealth in Ancient Rome* (1910), *A Day in Old Athens* (1914); *Life on a Medieval Barony* (1923); among the latter: *A Friend of Caesar* (1900), *A Victor of Salamis* (1908), *Belshazzar* (1925).

Daw, Marjorie. See MARJORIE DAW.

Dawson, Coningsby [William] (b. England, Feb. 26, 1883—d. Aug. 10, 1959), newspaper correspondent, novelist, poet. Dawson came to the United States in 1905, became a specialist in Canadian affairs for English newspapers, lived in Newark, N.J., later in California. He first won an audience with his novels, *The Garden Without Walls* (1913) and *The Raft* (1914). Among his other novels are *The Kingdom Round the Corner* (1921), *The Coast of Folly* (1924), and *The Moon Through Glass* (1934). A remarkable novelette of his, *The Unknown Soldier* (1929), is a tale of the return of Jesus to earth during World War I. He also published a collection of poems, *Florence on a Certain Night* (1914).

Day, Clarence [Shepard], Jr. (b. New York City, Nov. 18, 1874—d. Dec. 28, 1935), essayist, artist. From 1920 to 1935 Day published seven books. Six of them, all marked by unorthodox humor, attracted little attention from the general public, although from the beginning connoisseurs of style cherished Day. They were: *This Simian World* (1920), highly praised by Justice O. W. Holmes, among others; *The Crow's Nest* (1921); *Thoughts Without Words* (1928); *God and My Father* (1932); *In the Green Mountain Country* (1934), an impressive description of former President Coolidge's funeral; and *Scenes from the Mesozoic* (1935). But in 1935 also appeared LIFE WITH FATHER, followed by the posthumous *Life with Mother* (1936), and Day became a classic. The two books sold widely, and they provided the basis for two excellent plays, later made into movies; in dramatic form *Life with Father* (which opened in 1939) established a record for longevity with 3,224 performances. An invalid for the greater part of his life, Day composed his later books with great physical difficulty. His ebullient "Father" has become, said Alexander Woollcott, "a part of American lore and seems likely to remain as familiar a legendary figure as Mr. Dooley or Uncle Remus or Huckleberry Finn—Father, violent, sturdy, capable, fond, irascible, naïve, honorable, but above all violent." Day was a constant and valued contributor to *The New Yorker* magazine, whose humorous moods and modes he helped to form. H. S. Canby calls him "an unsparing realist with a kind heart."

Day, Holman [Francis] (b. Vassalboro, Me., Nov. 6, 1865—d. Feb. 19, 1935), poet, novelist, playwright. After graduation from Colby College, Day did editorial work on newspapers and magazines in Maine. It was not until 1900, when he published a collection of poems, *Up in Maine,* that he began to write books, but after that the flow of his publications was steady. Especially popular were his collections of verses, particularly *Pine Tree Ballads* (1902). His novels, too—*Squire Phin* (1905), *King Spruce* (1908), *The Ramrodders* (1910), *The Rider of the King Log* (1919)—were widely read. In his era he was Maine's chief literary interpreter. Richard M. Dorson, investigating folklore in New England, found that Day tapped native sources at first hand, and praised his kind of ballad as "straightforward rhyming that intensifies the rhythms of storytelling speech and suits

its homely folk material." Many of the tales Day told are humorous, but he also told supernatural stories and legends of witches and "haunts." There are many portraits of Yankee types.

Day Is Done, The (1844), a poem by HENRY WADSWORTH LONGFELLOW. It appeared as an introduction to a collection of minor poems, *The Waif*, edited by Longfellow. Hence Longfellow says that the poem he wishes read to him, "some simple and heartfelt lay," should be taken, not from "the grand old masters," but from "some humbler poet." The poem has been praised for the felicity of its images, the gracefulness of its rhythm, its general ease. Particularly famous is the beautiful closing stanza, beginning "And the night shall be filled with music."

Day of Doom, The (1662), a narrative in ballad style picturing the Last Judgment, by MICHAEL WIGGLESWORTH. Frank Luther Mott calls this "the first American best seller." It appeared in an edition of 1,800 copies, nearly all sold within a year, and was constantly reprinted. It was familiar to every New Englander, and its dreadful jingles and morbid sensationalism were deeply impressed on Yankee minds, since every child for decades was required to memorize the poem. James Russell Lowell wrote sardonically that it was "the solace of every fireside, the flicker of the pine knots by which it was conned perhaps adding a livelier relish to its premonitions of eternal combustion." In the poem doom breaks upon a peaceful world, Christ takes his place as an inexorable judge, the dead arise, saints (very few) are separated from sinners (uncountably numerous). Babes who died before being baptized are charitably assigned "the easiest room in hell." Then the fire is lighted, the sulphurous fumes ascend, the sinners are dragged away. "Christ pities not your cry," the poet exults. "Depart to hell, there may you yell and roar eternally." The volume that contained the poem also had some other verses by Wigglesworth, including a poem on *Vanity of Vanities* that Louis Untermeyer praises for its "gentle poetic persuasion." Wigglesworth himself announced it as a "Song of Emptiness to Fill Up the Empty Pages Following."

Day of the Locust, The (1939), a novel by NATHANAEL WEST. West's last novel, written after he went to Hollywood as a scriptwriter, is not so much a story of Hollywood as a kind of parable of the failure of the American dream. Homer Simpson, the central character, finds himself in the midst of people who have been brought up on the movies and are bored with life as they find it. He is typical of the thousands of middle-aged middle-class folk who save their money and go to California in search of sunshine and glamour, only to find monotony and tinsel, and finally to die. Other characters include Faye Greener, a stage-struck and empty-headed blonde; her father Harry, a former music-hall performer; Tod Hackett, an idealist who came to Hollywood to learn scenery design and gave up his own attempts at art; a Mexican who owns fighting cocks; a man who dresses in gaudy cowboy outfits; and a bookmaking dwarf. West's

characters are a mélange of degeneracy, failure, and boredom, grotesques inhabiting the satiric half-world West has created.

The book was to have been entitled *The Cheated*, a story of people who wanted to believe a dream and could not face disagreeable realities. The novel's underlying motif is the falsity of American values: everything in the book is phony—the language, the buildings, the actors, and finally, life itself as seen in Hollywood. If the novel is depressing in its truth, it is brilliant in its power and artistry.

Days (composed in 1852, published in *The Atlantic Monthly*, November, 1857, then in *May-Day and Other Pieces*, 1867), one of the most characteristic of RALPH WALDO EMERSON's poems. It repeats, in beautiful imagery and pleasing melody, the thought expressed in his essay *Works and Days:* "He only is rich who owns the day. . . . [The days] come and go like muffled and veiled figures, sent from a distant friendly party; but they say nothing, and if we do not use the gifts they bring, they carry them as silently away."

Days of H. L. Mencken (1947). An omnibus volume that brings together the three mellow books in which the notable Baltimorean (see H. L. MENCKEN) relates the story of his turbulent and fruitful life: *Happy Days* (1940), *Newspaper Days* (1941), *Heathen Days* (1943). It is written in what one critic described as "easy, slippered prose," and tells the story of a man who from the beginning realizes the world is going to perdition, but realizes also what fun he has had in telling the world how faulty it is and in venting his numerous and enjoyable prejudices, crotchets, and dislikes.

Dazey, Charles Turner. Author of IN OLD KENTUCKY.

Deacon's Masterpiece, The, or, The Wonderful "One-Hoss Shay" (published in *The Atlantic Monthly*, September, 1858, in an installment of THE AUTOCRAT OF THE BREAKFAST TABLE), a poem by OLIVER WENDELL HOLMES. Holmes in a subtitle describes this poem as "a logical story." It can be read as a humorous tale of a New England deacon who built a chaise that would last forever, and as such it is very amusing. But apparently Holmes meant the "shay" to be a symbol of Calvinism, and its breakdown to mean the decay and disintegration of that hard creed; he sought to show that a system built exclusively on logic cannot last. This theme he treated elsewhere in his writings, especially in his comments on Jonathan Edwards. Gay Wilson Allen notes that "the monotonous rhyme and absurd rhythm are part of the humor of this piece, but the versification is little better than doggerel."

Dead End (produced, 1935; published, 1936), a play by SIDNEY KINGSLEY. On a "dead end" street that leads to the East River in New York City, a region where luxurious apartments overlook the slums, live five children whose environment produces in them a hatred of people and of law. A young woman of the neighborhood does her best to improve conditions, but with little success; there is constant contrast between the "better classes" above and the slum people below. The play was turned into an effective movie (1937), played by the same young actors who had appeared in the stage version; they became famous as the "Dead End Kids" and went on to make several other motion pictures.

Deadwood Dick. A favorite character in the dime novels written by EDWARD L. WHEELER and his imitators; among them, *Deadwood Dick on Deck, or, Calamity Jane, the Heroine of Whoop Up; The Double Dagger, or, Deadwood Dick's Defiance; Deadwood Dick in Denver.* The original of Deadwood Dick is not known definitely. One claimant was Robert Dickey (1840–1912), who served as a scout under Gen. George Crook, and was also a trapper and fur merchant. He had many thrilling adventures. Another is Richard W. Clarke (1845–1930), who took part in Deadwood, S.D., historical celebrations.

Deal, Borden (b. Pontotoc, Miss., Oct. 12, 1922–   ), novelist, essayist. The most important influence on Borden Deal's writing was the work and thought of C. G. Jung: his theory of the collective unconscious, his theory of the archetype, his work on psychology and religion. In his novels Deal developed the idea—derived from Jung—that each man contains within himself the entire universe; so each man acts for the whole of human experience, rather than for himself alone. In this way he hoped to write about man in his true heroic stature. *Dunbar's Cove* (1957), written under a Guggenheim Fellowship, was acclaimed a novel of great power. It is the story of a Tennessee farm family and the Big Dam. None of Deal's later books achieved the immense success of his first major novel. *Dunbar's Cove* was published in ten languages. Twentieth Century Fox made it into a motion picture entitled *Wild River* in 1960. Among Deal's other books: *Walk Through the Valley* (1956); *Search for Surrender* (1957); *Killer in the House* (1957); *The Insolent Breed* (1959). He also wrote paperback books under the pseudonym of Lee Borden.

Dean, Vera Micheles (b. Russia, March 29, 1903–   ), editor, author, lecturer. Mrs. Dean received her master's degree from Yale in 1925, her Ph.D. from Radcliffe in 1928. She joined the Foreign Policy Association in 1928 and became research director in 1938. Her books, which are energetic efforts to bridge the gulfs between nations, have won for her the French Legion of Honor and the Radcliffe College Alumnae Medal. Speaking of *Europe and the United States* (1950) the New York *Herald Tribune* made a comment that could refer as well to her other books: "It is tolerant and humane in the best sense, a book to be studied and savored." Her more recent works: *Foreign Policy Without Fear* (1953); *New Patterns of Democracy in India* (1959); *Builders of Emerging Nations* (1961).

Dear Judas and Other Poems (1929), by ROBINSON JEFFERS. One of the numerous literary attempts to rehabilitate the reputation of Judas is made in the title poem of this collection. It portrays a Judas who loves Jesus but finds him grown too fond of power. Consequently he betrays him in the belief that he will be jailed for a few days and then released, and so may be saved from execution as a rebel. This dramatic poem was staged in 1947 in New York with a cast of forty, music of J. S. Bach, costumes, masks, and dancing mutes.

Death Comes for the Archbishop (1927), a novel by WILLA CATHER. Often regarded as Miss Cather's masterpiece, this narrative is so closely based on the lives of two eminent French clerics, Bishop Jean Baptiste Lamy (1814–1888) and his vicar-general, Father Joseph Machebeuf, that the story resembles closely the *vita* of a saint—a *vita* done with genius. In the book the men are called Fathers Latour and Vaillant; Henry Seidel Canby calls them "Peter and Paul of the desert." The vineyard they work in is a strange one—"blazing sand, adobe town, red mountains, Indian ceremonials, hieratic mystery, violent colors, fire and ice," as one critic describes it. They brave all adversities to attain their end, finally build a cathedral in the wilderness. The story is told as the archbishop waits for death; an old man, he looks back on a lifetime of hardship and accomplishment. Although the novel was highly esteemed and has retained a steady audience, some critics see in it the failing of Miss Cather's creative imagination and an increasing reliance on history as the subject matter of her stories. (See also ARCHBISHOP LATOUR.)

Death in the Afternoon (1932), a book of miscellaneous prose pieces by ERNEST HEMINGWAY. It is mainly concerned with bullfighting in Spain and the philosophic thoughts that this sport aroused in Hemingway. Alfred Kazin saw in this book a change for the worse in Hemingway. "The sense of shock, the stricken malaise of his first stories, were now transformed," he commented, "into a loud and cynical rhetoric. 'Madame, all our words from loose using have lost their edge,' Hemingway tells the Old Lady; and proves it by his own example."

Death in the Deep South (1936), a powerful novel by WARD GREENE based on the trial and lynching of Leo Frank in 1915. It was filmed as *They Won't Forget* (1937).

Death in the Schoolroom, a fictional sketch by WALT WHITMAN. It was based on an incident that occurred while Whitman was teaching in Babylon, L.I. It was the first of his rare attempts at writing fiction.

Death of a Salesman (1949), a play by ARTHUR MILLER. The play is felt by most critics to be a bitter indictment of American values. Willy Loman, a traveling salesman, experiences a profound sense of failure as he discovers signs of aging in himself and takes stock of his accomplishments. The play ends in his suicide. This was Miller's first success on the stage, and it won him the acclaim of critics and audiences alike.

Death of the Hired Man, The (1914), a narrative poem by ROBERT FROST. One of Frost's most famous pieces—deft in character revelation, well done as poetry, dramatic; it has been successfully performed as a one-act play. Two characters appear, a farmer and his wife; another character is discussed, the hired man, once proud and respected, lately broken in health and spirit. He has been in the habit of going off and leaving them for other employment, then coming back in time of need; and now he has returned again. The farmer does not want to keep him; the wife pleads for him. When the farmer seeks him out, he is dead. The story "unfolds itself in undertones," remarks Louis Untermeyer. Famous lines are those in which the husband and wife exchange definitions of home. Home, says the former, "is the place where, when you have to go there, they have to take you in." Home, says the wife, is "something you, somehow, haven't to deserve."

Deathsong of a Cherokee Indian, The. See next entry.

death songs, Indian. How widespread the custom was has not yet been determined, but certainly Indians in many parts of America were practitioners of the death song—sung when the end was near, sometimes given the form of a dream. Margot Astrov calls it "a noble custom," and states that sometimes the song gave "the essence of a world view, grim but serene." These songs greatly impressed white men and came to constitute a poetic genre; it has been studied by Frank E. Farley in *The Dying Indian* (*Kittredge Anniversary Papers*, 1913). One such song appeared in Sarah W. A. Morton's *Ouabi, or, The Virtues of Nature* (1790), but the best-known is *The Deathsong of a Cherokee Indian*, attributed variously to PHILIP FRENEAU, a Mrs. John Hunter, and ROYALL TYLER (in whose play, THE CONTRAST, it was sung). One version of the poem may be found in Joseph Ritson's *Origin and Progress of Natural Song* (1783), another in Mathew Carey's *American Museum* (Jan. 1, 1787), where it was assigned to Freneau; but it does not appear in Freneau's collected works. Definitely Freneau's are two other death songs, THE DYING INDIAN and *The Prophecy of King Tammany*.

Debs, Eugene V[ictor] (b. Terre Haute, Ind., Nov. 5, 1855—d. Oct. 20, 1926), American socialist leader, orator. Founder of the Social Democratic Party and its leader during the period of its greatest influence (1897–1916), Debs was five times a candidate for the presidency and was renowned for his campaign oratory: "While there is a soul in prison, I am not free," he said. He had first come to prominence as a leader of the famous Pullman strike in Chicago in 1894, as a result of which he went to prison. Although he never achieved his goal in the Presidency, Debs was for a time a powerful figure in American politics who always insisted on the primacy of democratic procedures; he made a deep impression on many American writers and public men. His life was fictionalized in Irving Stone's *Adversary in the House* (1947), and his *Writings and Speeches* were collected (1948) by Arthur M. Schlesinger, Jr.

De Casseres, Benjamin (b. Philadelphia, 1873—d. Dec. 6, 1945), newspaperman, drama critic, poet, biographer. De Casseres regarded himself as a startling innovator, and wrote flamboyant essays for some of the New York papers. His style tended, however, toward the hifalutin, as when he said of Emerson, "His thought rounded the spheres, his dreams topped the Cosmos. He walks in ether and is part of the barred and crimson sunset." Among his books: *The Shadow-Eater* (1915); *Mirrors of New York* (1925); *Black Suns* (1936); *Don Marquis* (1938).

Decatur, Stephen (1779–1820), American naval officer. See BARBARY WARS.

Declaration of Independence, The. One of the most potent and influential political documents in the history of mankind, the Declaration of Independence was mainly the work of THOMAS JEFFERSON. On June 7, 1776, RICHARD HENRY LEE of Virginia laid before the Continental Congress, in session at Philadelphia, a resolution that "these United Colonies are, and of right ought to be, free and independent states," bringing the issue of freedom from Great Britain to the point of action. On June 10 a committee was appointed to draft a Declaration: THOMAS JEFFERSON, JOHN ADAMS [2], BENJAMIN FRANKLIN, Roger Sherman, and Robert R. Livingston. The committee itself chose Jefferson as chairman and authorized him to write the draft of the Declaration. With a few changes by Adams and Franklin, this draft was presented by the Committee of Five to Congress on June 28. Jefferson's so-called "Rough Draft" is not the document as it read when first submitted to Franklin. It is Jefferson's original paper, together with all the corrections, additions, and erasures made between the day submitted to Franklin and July 4, 1776.

The purpose of the Declaration is set forth in the Preamble: "When in the course of human events, it becomes necessary for one people to dissolve the political bands which have connected them with another . . . they should declare the causes which impel them to the separation." The Declaration was not designed to declare independence, but rather to explain to the world the colonists' reasons for declaring independence. In the second main part of the Declaration, Jefferson formulated a political philosophy affirming the right of a people to establish and to overthrow its own government: ". . . that to secure these rights, Governments are instituted among Men, deriving their just powers from the consent of the governed,—that whenever any Form of Government becomes destructive of these ends, it is the Right of the People to alter or to abolish it . . ."

Jefferson goes on to state that those certain conditions which will justify revolution prevail in the colonies, and that the people have submitted to them as long as it is possible: "Prudence, indeed, will dictate, that governments long established should not be changed for light and transient causes. . . . But when a long train of abuses and usurpations . . . evinces a design to reduce them under absolute despotism, it is their right . . . to throw off such government . . ." Jefferson then lists the oppressive measures of the King. The Declaration asserts that the prevalence of these conditions is due to the tyranny of the King and not to any act the colonists have committed or left undone: "In every stage of these oppressions we have petitioned for redress . . ." The colonists must therefore either throw off the yoke or submit to be slaves. The conclusion of the Declaration asserts their choice of freedom over slavery.

Jefferson's formulation of a political philosophy justifying revolution attests the continuing influence of Locke, and the theories of natural law and right, social compact, sovereignty of the people, and derivative authority of government. Locke had argued that, in his original state of nature, man was governed by the law of nature; then, in the interest of survival, he joined in society with others. By means of the social compact, a government was established. But the granting of powers to the government did not divest individuals of all their "natural rights." The government had agreed to protect these, and its violation of them entitled men to revolt.

On July 1, Congress sat as a committee to debate the Lee resolution for independence. On July 2, Congress, sitting in formal session, took the final, unanimous vote for independence. Adams thought that the adoption of this resolution should be celebrated "from one end of this continent to the other, from this time forward, forevermore."

Congress next debated the form and content of the Declaration prepared by Jefferson, making several changes. On July 4, the amended Declaration of Independence was approved and its publication authorized. The Committee of Five was ordered to "superintend and correct the press." All through the night the printers worked. On July 19, Congress ordered the Declaration engrossed on parchment, with the title changed to "The Unanimous Declaration of the 13 United States of America." On August 2 it was signed by the members of Congress then present.

It is sometimes alleged that the Declaration contained no novel ideas, but this charge involves a complete misunderstanding of the document. As Julian P. Boyd puts it, Jefferson, when he wrote the Declaration, was "the inspired amanuensis of the people." He was expressing the frequently uttered thoughts of the members of Congress and the people who elected them. It was his not because of the ideas expressed, but for its style. Yet when Jefferson spoke of the ideas as deriving from "the American mind," he must have conceived of that mind as richly eclectic. The concepts of equality, of the right to revolt, of the functions of government expressed in the Declaration were the final fruitage of a growth of centuries. Jefferson was particularly indebted to John Locke, whose *Two Treatises of Civil Government* (1690) and *Letters Concerning Toleration* (1689, 1690, 1692) deeply influenced American thought and made him "America's philosopher." In his list of

human rights Locke included "property," for which Jefferson substituted "the pursuit of happiness"; but as far back as 1651 John Hall, a friend of Thomas Hobbes, had urged that the liberty to make one's life "happy and advantageous" was a "privilege stemming from God and nature." The statement has often been made, too, that Jefferson owed much of his thought and language to George Mason's magnificent Virginian Declaration of Rights (June 12, 1776). Boyd, after a painstaking examination of the evidence, states that Jefferson undoubtedly copied words from his own proposed constitution for Virginia (a part of which was adopted June 29, 1776), but that it "must in all probability remain a matter of opinion" that he was directly influenced by the Mason Declaration.

The most warmly discussed phrase in the Declaration has, of course, been that which reads, "All men are created equal." Obviously the rest of the thought is that men are equal in certain "unalienable rights"; among them, "life, liberty, and the pursuit of happiness." Lincoln said that nobody ever misunderstood Jefferson's statement on equality "except a fool or a knave."

Important studies of Jefferson's sources and versions were made by John H. Hazelton in *The Declaration of Independence: Its History* (1906), Carl Becker in *The Declaration of Independence: A Study in the History of Political Ideas* (1942), Julian P. Boyd in *The Declaration of Independence: The Evolution of the Text* (1945), Edward Dumbauld in *The Declaration of Independence and What It Means Today* (1950), Dumas Malone in *The Story of the Declaration of Independence* (1954). The famous document is today housed in a shrine in the National Archives Building, Washington, D.C.

Declaration of Independence of American Literature, The. A phrase sometimes applied to Emerson's The American Scholar (1837), and occasionally to Walt Whitman's Democratic Vistas (1871) and Van Wyck Brooks's America's Coming of Age (1915).

Deephaven (1877), sketches of a New England town woven into a story by Sarah Orne Jewett. Two young women pass a summer in a deserted seaport and meet many of the kindhearted, eccentric, lively, or forlorn characters of the place, all of them well described. The book was one of the earliest works of regional American fiction. The town itself—said to be South Berwick, Me.—is as real as any character in the book.

Deerslayer, The (1841), a novel by James Fenimore Cooper. In the series of Leather-Stocking Tales, this is the first in the fictitious chronology of Natty Bumppo's life, the last in actual order of publication. The action occurs on, in, and near Lake Otsego, called "Glimmerglass" in the story. Nat is shown as a young hunter living among the Delaware Indians and joining with them in fighting the Hurons, who are at last driven off with the help of the British. Judith Hutter, a soiled enchantress whose family Deerslayer helps to defend, falls in love with him, but he resists her advances because she has too much of the settlement about her. The Delaware chieftain Chingachgook is an important personage in the book, which Albert Keiser calls "one of the best, if not the best, of Cooper's Indian tales." But Mark Twain called it "simply a literary *delirium tremens*." See WILLIAM KIDD.

   de Ford, Miriam A[llen] [Mrs. Maynard Shipley in private life] (b. Philadelphia, Aug. 21, 1888–   ), poet, writer, associate editor of *The Humanist*. After receiving her A.B. from Wellesley College in 1911, Miriam de Ford devoted herself to poetry, biography, literary history, true crime, science fiction, and fantasy as well as to Latin translations and sociology. Her poetry and stories have received numerous awards, and are represented in many anthologies. A director of Mystery Writers of America, Inc., she won three consecutive prizes in the annual contest of *Ellery Queen's Mystery Magazine*. *Last Generation*, a short story on the possible destruction of the world in 1988, appeared in *Harper's* magazine in 1946 and has been translated into English, French, Italian, and Dutch. Her books include: *Love Children: A Book of Illustrious Illegitimates* (1931); *Who Was When? A Dictionary of Contemporaries* (1939), which was revised in 1949; *Psychologist Unretired: the Life-Pattern of Lillian J. Martin* (1948); *Up-Hill All the Way; the Life of Maynard Shipley* (1956); *The Overbury Affair: The Murder Trial that Rocked the Court of King James I* (1960).

   De Forest, John W[illiam] (b. Seymour, Conn., May 31, 1826–d. July 17, 1906), novelist, memoirist, author of travel books. De Forest traveled widely, knew several languages. At the outbreak of the Civil War he entered the Union army and served for three years, after the war was head of the Freedmen's Bureau in South Carolina. His fame is chiefly dependent on the novel called MISS RAVENEL'S CONVERSION FROM SECESSION TO LOYALTY (1867), based largely on his own experiences and observations and notable for a realistic treatment of war that anticipated STEPHEN CRANE. De Forest also wrote a historical novel, *Witching Times* (1856); a novel of social conflict, *Seacliff* (1859); a novel of Western adventure, *Overland* (1871); a satire on political corruption, HONEST JOHN VANE (1875). *A Volunteer's Adventures*, memoirs of the war, was posthumously published in 1946. Later came a sequel, *A Union Officer in the Reconstruction* (1948). De Forest influenced and was praised by W. D. HOWELLS. Alexander Cowie considers him a man born out of his time; with his will to be a full-blown realist, "he should have been born earlier or much later." See KATE BEAUMONT.

   deism. A system of religious thought which postulates a Supreme Being that created the world, runs it by established laws, and judges man, but which does not accept the divinity of Jesus or the divine inspiration and miracles of the Bible. Deism has been called "natural" religion; it is based on "reason" and hence opposed to "revealed" religion. Deism sprang up with the spread of scientific knowledge during the Renaissance period and reached its height during the 18th century. In England its followers included Lord Herbert of Cherbury (1583–1648), the third Earl of Shaftsbury (1671–1713), and Lord Bolingbroke (1678–1751); in France, Voltaire (1694–1778) and the Encyclopedists. Their ideas affected literature—for example, Pope's *Essay on Man* (1733–34) and the views of nature entertained by Wordsworth, Shelley, and others—and these in turn influenced American writers such as JOEL BARLOW and THOMAS PAINE. In THE AGE OF REASON (1794–96), the latter wrote: "I do not believe in the creed professed by the Jewish church, by the Roman church, by the Greek church, nor by any church that I know of. My mind is my own church." Leading American writers and statesmen were avowed deists, among them Franklin, Washington, and Jefferson; a belligerent deist was ETHAN ALLEN (REASON THE ONLY ORACLE OF MAN, 1784). Herbert W. Schneider (*History of American Philosophy*, 1946) holds that "the transition from Puritanic Platonism to deism and natural religion was easy, gradual, and largely unconscious. For the Puritans were obviously not so dependent on the Biblical revelation of law and covenant as they pretended to be." See ENLIGHTENMENT.

   De Jong, David Cornel ["Tjalmar Breola"] (b. the Netherlands, June 9, 1905–d. Sept. 5, 1967), short-story writer, novelist. De Jong came to the United States when he was thirteen. He wrote novels of both his native and his adopted land. *Belly Fulla Straw* (1934) tells the story of a Dutch immigrant family. It was followed by many other books, among them: *Old Haven* (1938); *Day of the Trumpet* (1941); *Domination of June* (1944), a volume of poetry; *With a Dutch Accent* (1945), which describes his own experiences; *Somewhat Angels* (1945); *Snow-on-the-Mountain* (1946) contains some of his numerous short stories; *The Desperate Children* (1949); *Two Sofas in the Parlor* (1952); *Outside of Four Walls* (1961).

   DeKoven, [Henry Louis] Reginald (b. Middleton, Conn., April 3, 1859–d. Jan. 16, 1920), composer, music critic. Educated in Europe, DeKoven became a music critic for Chicago and New York City newspapers, went on to compose music of many kinds: grand operas, orchestral suites, songs, sonatas. Among the operas are *Robin Hood* (1890), *Rob Roy* (1894), THE CANTERBURY PILGRIMS (1917, a grand opera with a libretto by PERCY MACKAYE), RIP VAN WINKLE (1920). He will probably be longest remembered for his song, O PROMISE ME, originally sung in *Robin Hood*.

   de Kruif, Paul (b. Zeeland, Mich., March 2, 1890–d. Feb. 28, 1971), popular writer on science and medicine. De Kruif (whose name is pronounced to rhyme with *knife*) studied bacteriology at the University of Michigan and the Rockefeller Institute. He supplied Sinclair Lewis with much of the technical background for ARROWSMITH (1925). De Kruif wrote: *Our Medicine Men* (1922); MICROBE

HUNTERS (1926); *Hunger Fighters* (1928); *Men Against Death* (1932); *Yellow Jack* (1934, a play with Sidney Howard); *Health Is Wealth* (1940); *Life Among the Doctors* (1949); *A Man Against Insanity* (1957). His books are widely read for their liveliness of style in describing the achievements of men of science. *Time* reported (July 29, 1946) that de Kruif had been attacked in the American Medical Association *Journal* for attempts to popularize the use of several drugs before they had been thoroughly tested and approved by medical men.

de la Guard, Theodore. Pen name of NATHANIEL WARD.

Deland, Margaret[ta Wade Campbell] (b. Allegheny, Pa., Feb. 23, 1857—d. Jan. 13, 1945), novelist, short-story writer. Brought up near Pittsburgh in a small town called Manchester (the "Old Chester" of her stories), she learned to delight in the out-of-doors, an enthusiasm she retained throughout her life and often imparted to her novels.

John Ward, Preacher (1888) is Mrs. Deland's best-known novel. Its scene is Ashurst, a town which "rather prided itself on being half asleep." Ward, a Calvinist, marries Helen Jeffrey, a woman with freethinking tendencies. He suffers keenly as a result of the conflict between his love for his wife and his strict faith. His public prayer for her salvation causes a furor in the community, but in the end he dies without getting his wish to hear her confess that she has "seen the light." The novel was considered rather shocking when it appeared, but today seems heavy reading.

THE AWAKING OF HELENA RICHIE (1906) and its sequel, *The Iron Woman* (1911), portray a selfish and forceful woman who gradually rises to an understanding of her shortcomings. *The Rising Tide* (1916) is a sociological novel dealing with the woman suffrage movement. *The Vehement Flame* (1922) is the story of a romance between a youth and an older woman. *The Kays* (1926) and *Captain Archer's Daughter* (1932) are novels of New England life. OLD CHESTER TALES (1898) is probably her most enduring collection of short stories, although *Doctor Lavendar's People* (1903) is well regarded. Other books derived from early memory are *Around Old Chester* (1915), *New Friends in Old Chester* (1924), *Old Chester Days* (1935), *If This Be I (As I Suppose It Be)* (1935) and *Golden Yesterdays* (1941).

Mrs. Deland's greatest gift was for characterization, and her portraits are realistic and lively.

ELDON C. HILL

Delano, Alonzo (b. Aurora, N.Y., July 2, 1802?—d. Sept. 9, 1874), humorist, historian. Delano was an early practitioner of the type of comic writing associated with pioneering days in California. He set out for California on April 19, 1849, arrived there by mid-September after suffering considerable hardship on the way. He earned more money by his pen than as a merchant or miner, and his sketches (signed "The Old Block") were published in various newspapers. Many of them were collected in *Pen-Knife Sketches* (1853) and *Old Block's Sketch-Book* (1856). His *Life on the Plains and Among the Diggings* (1854) has historical value and was reprinted in 1936.

Delano, Amasa (b. Duxbury, Mass., Feb. 21, 1763—d. April 21, 1823), sea captain, memoirist. Delano's *Narrative of Voyages and Travels: Comprising Three Voyages Round the World* (1817) furnished material for Herman Melville's *Benito Cereno* (1856). The book also contains a long account of the mutiny on the *Bounty* and the colony of mutineers on Pitcairn's Island.

De La Roche, Mazo (b. Newmarket, Ont., Jan. 15, 1879—d. July 12, 1961), Canadian novelist, playwright. Jalna, the title of her first novel, was the seat of the Whiteoak family whose history she has explored in many other books. JALNA won the $10,000 *Atlantic Monthly* prize in 1927. She later turned it into a play which starred Ethel Barrymore in the leading role. Other novels in the series are: *Whiteoaks of Jalna* (1929); *Finch's Fortune* (1931); *The Master of Jalna* (1933); *Young Renny* (1935); *Whiteoak Harvest* (1936); *Whiteoak Heritage* (1940); *Wakefield's Course* (1942); *The Building of Jalna* (1944); *Return to Jalna* (1946); *Mary Wakefield* (1949); *Renny's Daughter* (1951); *The Whiteoak Brothers* (1953); *Variable Winds at Jalna* (1954); *Centenary at Jalna* (1958); *Morning at Jalna* (1960). Altogether more than 2 million copies of the Jalna saga have been sold, and they present an entertaining, authentic picture of English provincials on an estate in southern Ontario. Miss De La Roche's *Ringing the Changes* (1957) is her autobiography.

de la Torre, Lillian (b. New York City, March 15, 1902—   ), mystery and true crime writer. Beginning at the age of forty, this popular writer produced a series of stories about Samuel Johnson and James Boswell as a detective team. The stories, modeled on the Sherlock Holmes series, appear in *Ellery Queen's Mystery Magazine* and are available in collections like *The Detections of Dr. Sam: Johnson* (1960). *Elizabeth Is Missing* (1945) is an example of Miss de la Torre's ability to solve real historical mysteries. She also wrote *The 60 Minute Chef* (cookbook, with Carol Truax, 1947), and edited *Villainy Detected* (1947), an anthology, in addition to many other books, stories and crime plays.

Delaware Indians. A name given by white men to the tribes that inhabited the Delaware River Valley. They were of Algonquin stock, and in Delaware and neighboring states called themselves the Leni-Lenape ("the men of our nation" or "the original people"). They were a friendly people with whom the white settlers had few difficulties. They frequently made treaties, like that with Penn in 1682, and were particularly friendly with the Swedish settlers. They lived by agriculture, hunting, and fishing, and were comparatively few in number. The Rev. JOHN

HECKEWELDER (1743–1824) gave an authentic and copious account of them in his *History, Manners, and Customs of the Indian Nations Who Once Inhabited Pennsylvania and the Neighboring States* (1819). JAMES FENIMORE COOPER, when he came to describe these Indians in the LEATHER-STOCKING TALES, made good use of the material in the Heckewelder book, which saw the Indian as a noble savage. An early picture of them is also found in James Kirke Paulding's novel KONINGSMARKE (1823); Paulding lays his scene among the Swedish settlers of Delaware and the Indians of Pennsylvania. The Delaware Indians after 1720 moved into Ohio, where they sided with the French against the English and with the English against the Americans. An attack on one of their settlements in 1782 led some of them to flee to Ontario; others migrated to Oklahoma, where two groups now live. One of their chieftains, Tamend, who appears in LAST OF THE MOHICANS, gave rise to the name *Tammany*. See also WALAM OLUM.

De La Warr, Thomas West, Baron (1577–1618), a British administrator. He became Governor and Captain General of the colony of Virginia (1610) and managed to prevent the disruption of the colony. He returned to England for aid (1611), died on a second voyage to Virginia (1618). Delaware was named for him. He wrote a *Relation of the Colony of Virginia* (1611).

De Leon, Thomas Cooper (b. Columbia, S.C., May 21, 1839—d. March 19, 1914), novelist, playwright, memoirist. In addition to two novels (*Creole and Puritan*, 1889, and *Crag-Nest*, 1897), De Leon wrote memoirs of life under the Confederacy (*Four Years in Rebel Capitals*, 1890) and of the South after the war (*Belles, Beaux, and Brains of the '60s*, 1907). But he was chiefly renowned for a burlesque, *Hamlet Ye Dismal Prince* (1870), which struck contemporary critics as very funny when it was produced the same night as Edwin Booth's performance of *Hamlet*.

Delight Makers, The (1890), a novel by ADOLF F. BANDELIER. The author, who had spent eight years in explorations among the Pueblo Indians of New Mexico, tells in his story about the cliff-dwellers in the Southwest long before the advent of the white man. Alfred Keiser says that Bandelier "succeeded remarkably well in recreating a civilization that flourished so long ago. Bandelier's work takes high rank as an accurate portrayal of Indian life."

Delilah (1941), a novel by MARCUS GOODRICH. The story of a United States destroyer in the days preceding American participation in World War I. The details are very well done, and the ship itself is given a personality and a symbolism in a way that recalled to some critics Melville's *Moby Dick*.

Delineator, The. A magazine famous for being edited for a time by THEODORE DREISER (1907–10). Founded in 1873 by Ebenezer Butterick, a tailor of Fitchburg, Mass., as a magazine for women containing tissue-paper dress patterns and fashion plates, it moved to New York and in 1894 began publishing fiction of a type likely to appeal to women. It attained in time a circulation of over two million. In May, 1937, it merged with the *Pictorial Review*. Another editor of note was HONORÉ WILLSIE MORROW (1914–1920).

Dell, Floyd (b. Barry, Ill., June 28, 1887—d. July 23, 1969), journalist, novelist, playwright. After a brief apprenticeship on a Davenport, Iowa, newspaper in 1905, Dell came to Chicago where he worked on various newspapers and became associated with the new group of young Midwestern writers known as the "Chicago School." In 1914 he moved to New York and became an associate editor of the leftist periodicals MASSES and its successor the LIBERATOR. During this period he began to write plays, and with the publication of his novels MOON-CALF (1920), its sequel *The Briary-Bush* (1921), *Janet March* (1923), and others, became known as a spokesman for the jazz age and life and love in Greenwich Village. His most successful play was the comedy *Little Accident* (1928), based on his novel *The Unmarried Father* (1927). With PAUL JORDAN SMITH he prepared an excellent edition of Burton's *Anatomy of Melancholy* (1927). He has also written *Love in the Machine Age* (1930), a reasoned statement of his attitudes toward sex and a contribution to the change in American sexual mores after World War I. His autobiography *Homecoming* appeared in 1933, and indicates that much of the material in his first two novels was a sifting of his own experience.

Della Cruscanism. An English school of poetry, started by some young Englishmen at Florence, Italy, among them Robert Merry (1755–98). "Della Crusca" means literally "of chaff"; the group adopted its name from the Academy della Crusca which was founded in 1582, its purpose being to winnow the "chaff" from the Italian language. Their style was silly, sentimental, and pretentious, but very popular for a time. They were attacked scathingly by William Gifford in the satirical poems *Baeviad* (1794) and *Maeviad* (1795). Their affected style seems to have been anticipated by the American versifier Joseph Brown Ladd (1764–86). His *Poems of Arouet* (1786) appeared almost simultaneously with the rise of the English school in Florence. A few years later the movement had gained a great hold in this country, chiefly in the writings of SARAH WENTWORTH MORTON, who was called "the American Sappho" by her admirers and who eulogized the Della Cruscan manner in an address prefixed to her narrative poem, *Ouabi, or The Virtues of Nature* (1790). The style also appeared in the verses of ROBERT TREAT PAINE, JR., whose efforts to combine Della Crusca with Pope "would have crushed a more genuine talent," says Samuel Marion Tucker. Royall Tyler was one of those who satirized the movement.

Delmar, Viña [Croter] (b. New York City, Jan. 29, 1905—   ), novelist, playwright, short-story writer. Miss Delmar's first novel, *Bad Girl*, a realistic narrative about the loves of a young typist, was a best seller in 1928. Its success was followed up with *Loose Ladies* (1929), *Kept Woman* (1929), *Women Live Too Long* (1932), and *The Marriage Racket* (1933)— books which were considered rather sensational and even censorable in their time. Then, for almost two decades, aside from occasional short stories in popular magazines, she published no new work. In 1950, however, *About Mrs. Leslie* appeared, then *The Marcaboth Women* (1951), *The Laughing Stranger* (1953), *Beloved* (1956), and *Breeze From Camelot* (1959). While Miss Delmar's later books have commanded a wide audience, they have seldom achieved the success or the moderate critical approval of her first novel. She is also the author of two plays produced in New York, *The Rich Full Life* (1945) and *Midsummer* (1953).

Delphian Club. A Baltimore literary association, founded Aug. 31, 1816. Its members included John Pierpont, H. M. Brackenridge, Francis Scott Key, William Wirt, John Howard Paine, Rembrandt Peale, John Neal, Samuel Woodworth, and John P. Kennedy. Under Neal's editorship they issued a periodical, *The Portico*, from 1816 to 1818 when the club expired. The magazine, like the members, expressed a strongly nationalistic and antiforeign viewpoint. JOHN NEAL told about the club in his *Wandering Recollections* (1869), John E. Uhler described it in the *Maryland Historical Magazine* (December, 1925).

De Mille, Agnes (1905–   ), dancer, choreographer, author. Miss De Mille is particularly well known for choreographic productions in such musical plays as OKLAHOMA!, *Carousel*, and *Brigadoon*. She has written her autobiography in two books: *Dance to the Piper* (1952) and *And Promenade Home* (1958).

De Mille, Cecil B[lount] (b. Ashfield, Mass., Aug. 12, 1881—d. Jan. 21, 1959), playwright, movie director. With his brother William, De Mille wrote and produced two plays, *The Genius* (1906) and *The Royal Mounted* (1908), and is credited with help on David Belasco's THE RETURN OF PETER GRIMM (1911). When he went to Hollywood in 1913 his real career began; and he left a deep impress on motion-picture production and the viewpoints of the industry. He developed the use of crowd scenes and "spectacle" movies; *Time* credits him with doing "more than any other man, with his extravagant bathing scenes, to turn the U.S. bathroom into a national pride." *Time* adds: "He was the first Hollywoodian to risk a movie on an all-out religious theme (*The Ten Commandments*, 1923). He was among the first to use 'effect lighting.' He was among the first to use color in a feature. . . . For three decades De Mille's name has been loosely used as shorthand for fustian and splendiferous vulgarity. Because he is an artist in ham, his artistry has sometimes not been widely enough appreciated." Among his major works: THE SQUAW MAN (1913 and 1918); *The King of Kings* (1927); *The Sign of the Cross* (1931); *Reap the Wild Wind* (1942); *The Unconquered* (1947); *Samson and Delilah* (1949);

The Ten Commandments (1957). He also collaborated with his brother, **William Churchill De Mille** (b. Washington, D.C., July 25, 1878—d. March 5, 1955), on a number of stage productions. William De Mille, who in his later years taught drama at the University of Southern California, was also a playwright and lecturer. His best-known play was *Strongheart* (1905).

Deming, Philander (b. Carlisle, N.Y., Feb. 6, 1829—d. Feb. 9, 1915), lawyer, writer of fictional sketches. Deming knew the Adirondacks well and wrote about them realistically in *Adirondack Stories* (1880) and *Tompkins and Other Folks* (1885).

democracy. Our most disputed ideological term. A paradox, it needs to be defined paradoxically. So far as American political doctrine is concerned, it does not mean that all men are equal, except in questions of "life, liberty, and the pursuit of happiness," but the whole course of American history has tended toward the establishment of equalitarianism in politics, economics, and society. JAMES MADISON attempted a distinction in THE FEDERALIST (1788): "In a democracy the people meet and exercise the government in person; in a republic, they assemble and administer it by their representatives and agents." Our American doctrines of democracy stem politically from the Greeks, ethically from the Bible, philosophically from John Locke. The fundamental American document of democracy is the DECLARATION OF INDEPENDENCE, its leading Presidential exponents Jefferson, Jackson, Lincoln, Wilson, and Franklin Delano Roosevelt.

Democracy (1880), a novel by HENRY ADAMS. It was published anonymously and can only loosely be described as a novel, but it gives an effective satirical picture of social and political Washington in its day as seen by a disillusioned man. Among those pictured are President Hayes (see RUTHERFORD B. HAYES) and James G. Blaine. Another character, Representative Gore, may be Adams himself. The story is told in terms of a young New York widow who had gone to the capital city in search of power. Parrington comments that "the economic sources of political corruption are ignored, and the evil is traced to the principle of democracy." President Theodore Roosevelt in 1905 characterized it as a book which had created a furor "among the educated incompetents" and as "mean and base." It was reprinted in 1952. See SENATOR RATCLIFFE.

Democratic Vistas, a philosophical tract by WALT WHITMAN, written in 1867–68 and published as a book in 1871. Whitman started out to reply to Carlyle's dour view of democracy in "Shooting Niagara: And After?" but as he worked on his reply he reluctantly came to agree with much of Carlyle's indictment. He admitted the "depravity of the business classes of our country," and that "Society, in these States, is canker'd, crude, superstitious, and rotten . . ." But he held on to his belief in the innate honesty and perfectibility of the common people, and argued that "Political democracy . . . with all its threatened evils, supplies a training-school for making first-class men." This pragmatic approach to social philosophy anticipated the "PRAGMATISM" of William James and John Dewey. Despite the extremely awkward style and diction, this essay is an important contribution to American social thought.

G.W.A.

Demon of the Absolute, The (1928), a book of literary criticism by PAUL ELMER MORE. Considered by some critics to be the best statement of More's critical method, *The Demon of the Absolute* presents an argument against "rationalism, or reason run amuck" which sets up its own absolutes in nature; More finds that "certain standards of taste exist, which approximate, more or less, to universality," and upholds these tastes as standards of value for literary critics. Like IRVING BABBITT, the humanist critic with whom he is often associated, More holds Rousseau responsible for romanticism, sentimental humanitarianism, illusions of progress, and a belief in the innate goodness of man, which More considers to be fallacious because of man's dual nature. *The Demon of the Absolute* advocates standards of taste based on tradition, classicism as opposed to romanticism, and the application of ethical criteria to the examination and evaluation of literature.

Demos and Dionysus (published in 1925 in the collection DIONYSUS IN DOUBT), a dialogue in verse by EDWIN ARLINGTON ROBINSON. In this lively and forceful poem Robinson expresses his more than passing doubts about democracy. The poem becomes a violent attack on the extent to which democracy suppresses the individual and reduces mankind to a mediocre level. Humanitarian efforts, however well-meaning, may help to bring about this sad result, although "the few" must save the many or the many will fall —a personal extension of the Calvinistic doctrine familiar to Robinson as part of his heredity and environment. In the poem Dionysus calls democracy a "faith in something somewhere out of nothing," and he denies that reason can save the world—it will only make "a dislocated and unlovely mess for undertakers." He identifies equality with uniformity and monotony. Much of the doctrine of the poem seems to have come from the writings of Emerson, who similarly feared the masses as "rude, lame, unmade, pernicious in their demands and influence."

Dempsey, David K[napp] (b. Perkin, Ill., June 9, 1914—   ), newspaperman, writer, novelist. Mr. Dempsey received an A.B. degree in 1937 from Antioch College, did postgraduate work at Yale (1937–38) and at Columbia University (1939–40). His writings include magazine articles, short stories, criticism, book reviews, and collaboration on two books of reportage: *Uncommon Valor* (1946) and *U.S. Marines on Iwo Jima* (1945). Mr. Dempsey brought his experience as a veteran war correspondent and *New York Times* reporter to

much of his literary work. *Flood* (1956) is a vivid documentary of the awesome catastrophe which raged on the night of August 19, 1955, between the headwaters of the Delaware and Connecticut Rivers. A novel, *All That Was Mortal*, was published in 1958.

Dennett, Tyler (b. Spencer, Wis., June 13, 1883—d. Dec. 29, 1949), teacher, historian, biographer, public official. Dennett lectured on history at Johns Hopkins and at Columbia, served in various capacities in the State Department under Charles Evans Hughes, was appointed professor of international relations at Princeton in the School of Public and International Affairs. He became president of Williams in 1934, resigning three years later to devote himself to writing. Among his books: *The Democratic Movement in Asia* (1918); *Americans in Eastern Asia* (1922); *Roosevelt and the Russo-Japanese War* (1924); and a life of John Hay (1934) which won a Pulitzer award.

Dennie, Joseph (b. Boston, Aug. 30, 1768—d. Jan. 7, 1812), lawyer, editor, essayist. Now fallen into complete oblivion, Dennie in his own time was regarded as perhaps our chief writer, an "American Addison." As an editor he was something of a genius, and attracted to his periodicals many notable English and American writers—among the former Thomas Moore (an intimate friend), Leigh Hunt, Thomas Campbell, and "Monk" Lewis. At the beginning of his career he formed an alliance with ROYALL TYLER; together they published satirical pieces under the pseudonym of COLON (Dennie) AND SPONDEE (Tyler). At this stage Dennie acquired the wild bohemian habits that distinguished him for the rest of his short life. His greatest success was obtained, nevertheless, under the pseudonym of "The Lay Preacher," his by-line for inspirational essays, practically sermons, that made him one of the most widely read authors of his day. At another time he employed the pen name "Oliver Oldschool, Esq." for essays that for a time influenced Washington Irving. He was an embittered Federalist who often regretted that he had not been born in England and hated things characteristically American, like Noah Webster's Dictionary. Among the magazines he edited were *The Tablet* (1795), *The Farmer's Weekly Museum* (1796–99), and THE PORT FOLIO (1801–27). From these some of his essays were collected in book form—particularly *The Lay Preacher, or, Short Sermons for Idle Readers* (1796, 1817); this was reprinted in 1943. Milton Ellis wrote on *Joseph Dennie and His Circle* (1915). See THE EAGLE.

Densmore, Frances (b. Red Wing, Minn., May 21, 1867—d. June 5, 1957), ethnomusicologist, consultant of Bureau of American Ethnology. Miss Densmore, the greatest American authority on the songs and music of Indian tribes, began her career as a piano teacher and lecturer on Wagnerian music. She was attracted by Alice Cunningham Fletcher's pioneer work on the music of the Omahas (1911), and her *Chippewa Music* (1910–13) was the first of a long series of studies on Indian music and tribal customs. An epitome of her writings was made in *The American Indians and Their Music* (1926). She gave in her works a new conception of the so-called "savage" red man. More than any other person she helped preserve the music and poetry of the American Indian; she made detailed analyses of the music and the circumstances under which it was created and sung, while providing at the same time graceful English translations. Although she never claimed the title of poet, Miss Densmore was in fact a splendid poet. Among the achievements of her later years was work on the Smithsonian-Densmore Collection of sound recordings of American Indian music. In 1940 she received an award from the National Association of American Composers and Conductors for services to American music. She died in her ninetieth year and remained active until well into the 1950's, publishing in 1953 *The Belief of the Indian in a Connection Between Song and the Supernatural.* See IMAGISM and DREAM SONGS, INDIAN.

Depew, Chauncey M[itchell] (b. Peekskill, N.Y., April 23, 1834—d. April 5, 1928), lawyer, U.S. Senator from New York (1899–1911), memoirist. So highly regarded was Depew that his *Orations, Addresses, and Speeches* were collected in eight volumes (1910); his sprightly autobiography, *My Memories of Eighty Years,* appeared in 1922. Depew was a famous after-dinner speaker and often displayed a truly Gallic wit; his private conversation was sometimes caustic, sometimes ribald. He once compared Henry Cabot Lodge to Lodge's own New England landscape—"naturally barren, but highly cultivated." Shortly before his death at ninety-four, he said his only exercise was acting as pallbearer for friends who took exercise. Depew was regarded as the ablest of the legal and political apologists for the great corporations of the day and for the group of magnates centered in the New York Central Railroad.

Derby, George Horatio ["Squibob," "John Phoenix"] (b. Dedham, Mass., April 3, 1823—d. May 15, 1861), engineer, humorist. Derby deserves to be celebrated as the great-grandfather of American humor, for—despite the fact that his writings are little read today—he influenced writers through at least three generations. Derby was a cultivated, well-informed person, who graduated high in his class at West Point, and a capable explorer and engineer, whom the government sent to the West Coast to make some important surveys. He began contributing to newspapers under pseudonyms, indulging his natural love of fun. His writings show the influence of the "tall tale" type of humor; he was a master of the anecdote that tells an impossible incident with the most solemn of faces. Both MARK TWAIN and BRET HARTE owed much to his technique. His irreverence was likewise one of his most characteristic traits, and was similarly imitated by the western school of humorists. He extracted humor from weird figures of speech, big words, and high-sounding expressions, but often delivered himself of shrewd aphorisms, and in this respect was again a model for Mark Twain.

His contributions appeared in various newspapers from 1849 to 1856. He wrote the first PIKE COUNTY BALLAD, in the *Vallectos Sentinal* (June 31, 1854). A collection called *Phoenixiana, or, Sketches and Burlesques* (1856) went into edition after edition and gave him a nation-wide reputation. This was followed by THE SQUIBOB PAPERS (1865). "Phoenix" is still surprisingly readable—for example, his famous account of how the editor of the San Diego *Herald* left him in charge of the paper while he went on a trip, and how Derby changed the politics of the paper from Democratic to Whig; also Derby's scheme for avoiding the use of adjectives by substituting a numbering system. George R. Stewart wrote a life of Derby entitled *John Phoenix, Esq.* (1937).

Derleth, August [William] (b. Sauk City, Wis., Feb. 24, 1909—d. July 4, 1971), writer. Derleth's fiction derives mainly from his native region; he has made it the locale of his SAC PRAIRIE SAGA, a series of novels depicting life in a Middle Western community from the early 1800's until the present. A smaller group of novels, his *Wisconsin Saga,* includes *Bright Journey* (1940) and *The Hills Stand Watch* (1960). Sinclair Lewis wrote of Derleth, "He is a champion and a justification of 'regionalism.'" Among his novels: *Still Is The Summer Night* (1937); *Wind Over Wisconsin* (1938); *Restless Is the River* (1939); *The Shield of the Valiant* (1945). *Sac Prairie People* (1948) and *Wisconsin Earth* (1948) are collections of stories. His *Village Year* (1941) and *Village Daybook* (1947) give passages from his *Journal*—descriptions, anecdotes, reflections. Derleth has also written detective stories (his detective is Solar Pons, an echo of Sherlock Holmes; he also has a "Judge Peck" series); *Still Small Voice* (1940), a biography of Zona Gale; several volumes of verse. He has edited numerous anthologies, among them a science-fiction collection, *Worlds of Tomorrow* (1953). His *Selected Poems* (1944) are introduced by EDGAR LEE MASTERS. An immensely facile and productive writer, he shows in his fiction a tendency to be both realistic and sentimental.

Descent into the Maelstrom, A, a story by EDGAR ALLAN POE, possibly submitted to the Baltimore *Saturday Visiter* contest in 1833, more probably written for publication in *Graham's Magazine,* 1841; included in *Tales,* 1845. Poe tells how two Norwegian fishermen are drawn during a storm into a maelstrom. The men are brothers; one goes insane, the other lashes himself to a cask and comes to the surface with his hair whitened from fear and his expression altered. The survivor tells the story; his language has been criticized by some as too erudite. The tale is garnished with the sort of scientific lore with which Poe liked to mesmerize his readers, including a passage cribbed from the *Encyclopaedia Britannica.* George Edward Woodberry points out that in a later edition of the *Encyclopaedia* the author of the article on "Whirlpools" credited Poe with learning copied from the earlier edition and went on to quote "facts" which Poe had invented. Poe thought this story one of his best.

Desire Under the Elms (1924), a tragedy by EUGENE O'NEILL. Set in New England, the play deals with an elderly farmer and his three sons. The two elder brothers decide to leave home for California just as Ephraim, the father, returns home with Abbie, a woman of 35, his new wife. Abbie seduces Eben, the youngest son, hoping she can bear a son by him and claim that the child is Ephraim's. When it appears to Eben that Abbie has used him only for her own ends, he threatens to expose her infidelity, and to prove her love for him she smothers the child. The play exemplifies O'Neill's deep interest in Freudian psychology, and is considered one of his best works.

De Smet, Pierre-Jean. See SMET, PIERRE-JEAN DE.

De Soto, Hernando [also, **Fernando da Soto**] (1500?–1542), Spanish explorer. De Soto visited regions in Central America and Peru and then led an expedition to conquer Florida (1539–42). His expedition went far beyond the boundaries of present-day Florida: he ventured as far as the west bank of the Mississippi River (1541); he was often in conflict with hostile Indians. Unable to find the gold he was seeking, De Soto started to turn back, died on the banks of the great river he had discovered, and was buried in its waters by his followers. George H. Miles wrote a play *Hernando de Soto* (1852); Walter Malone an epic with the same title (1914). A translation of Garcilaso de la Vega's story of his expedition was published in 1951.

detective story. Also **shocker, police novel, mystery story, whodunit,** etc. A form of narrative fiction in which the pattern of events is generally as follows: the commission of a crime (usually murder), the gathering of clues and their interpretation (generally by a police officer, a private detective, or a gifted amateur), the detection of the evildoer and his exposure in a climactic scene (sometimes a court trial, more frequently a private confrontation). An early example was William Godwin's *Adventures of Caleb Williams* (1794), which was immensely popular in England and the United States. When Cooper began to tell about his noble red men in the LEATHER-STOCKING TALES (1823–41), he laid emphasis on their power to read clues and on Natty Bumppo's cleverness in imitating them.

In the 19th century, a number of circumstances helped to create the modern police novel. In 1829 Sir Robert Peel created the first police force in London. They had their headquarters in Scotland Yard, which was to become indispensable in thousands of detective stories, and were subject to call for help in solving crimes committed in any part of Great Britain. Then, in France, was enacted the strange career of François Eugène Vidocq (1775–1857), a police officer who from 1809 to 1827 was head of a small, specialized police force in Paris, and who in 1829 published his highly romanticized *Mémoires* in four volumes. He inspired Dumas, Victor

Hugo, and Dickens, furnished material for the detective novels of Émile Gaboriau (1835–73), and was familiar to Poe.

Finally there was Edgar Allan Poe in the United States. In 1841 Poe created the genre of the detective story when in *Graham's Magazine* (April, 1841) there appeared his story, THE MURDERS IN THE RUE MORGUE. Poe strongly stressed intellectual analysis as a means of solving crime; he created the eccentric fictional detective and provided him with a highly convenient Boswell; he made his detective display marvelous powers of deduction, but when his feats were explained they seemed absurdly simple. In *Murder for Pleasure: The Life and Times of the Detective Story* (1941) Howard Haycraft remarks: "A hundred years of imitation have rendered [Poe's story] so much formula: the preliminary account of the crime, the visit to the scene, Dupin's satisfaction with what he finds, his companion's blank mystification, the methodical stupidity of the official police, the dénouement, arranged by the detective; the inevitable explanation." Haycraft calls this story an example of the physical type; Poe's second tale, THE MYSTERY OF MARIE ROGÊT (three installments, 1842–43), the mental type; his last story of this kind, THE PURLOINED LETTER (1845), the balanced type.

Since Poe, crime has played a larger and larger role in fiction. In Frank Luther Mott's calculations of best sellers, he found that eighteen murder mysteries were among the books that had attained wide popularity during the period he covered (colonial times to 1945), even though he omitted from his list many cheap reprints of Gaboriau's police novels as well as all the dime novels featuring detectives, such as "Old Cap Collier," "Old Sleuth," and "Nick Carter." These antedated Sherlock Holmes, whose vogue in the United States was tremendous. One of the earliest American detective-story writers was ANNA KATHARINE GREEN. The list of detective-story writers in recent decades is amazingly long; among the better-known and most successful have been EARL DERR BIGGERS, CAROLYN WELLS, MARY ROBERTS RINEHART, MELVILLE DAVISSON POST, DASHIELL HAMMETT, ELLIOT PAUL, ERLE STANLEY GARDNER, RAYMOND CHANDLER, ELLERY QUEEN, REX STOUT, LESLIE CHARTERIS, Leslie Ford, MIGNON EBERHART, FRANCES and RICHARD LOCKRIDGE, JOHN DICKSON CARR, and Mickey Spillane. Some of these are pen names, of which some detective-story writers (like Carr) find it necessary to take two or three in order to disguise their embarrassing fecundity in devising crime puzzles.

There have been dissenters, of course, as when Edward A. McCourt put in a plea for westerns as against detective stories (*Home on the Range*, in the *Saturday Review of Literature*, Nov. 2, 1946). He held that "the exaltation of the detective story from the merely entertaining to the 'significant' is the outcome of a colossal, possibly unintentional conspiracy on the part of the intelligentsia to justify its small-boy craving for the sensational." In the 1950's the critic Edmund Wilson carried on an extended polemic against detective stories.

In 1937 crime-story authors formed the MYSTERY WRITERS OF AMERICA, an association which awards annual "Edgars" in several categories, publishes anthologies, and negotiates advantageous contracts for its members. *The Third Degree* is its official publication.

De Tocqueville, Alexis. See TOCQUEVILLE.

Deutsch, Babette (b. New York City, Sept. 22, 1895—   ), poet, critic. Miss Deutsch has not only written much excellent poetry but has been noted for her sensitive and acute criticism. She is also a translator of Russian and German verse, usually in collaboration with her husband, Avrahm Yarmolinsky. Her poems, marked by acute observation and novel imagery, explore the contemporary scene, often in terms of its social implications. Her collections of verse include *Banners* (1919); *Honey out of the Rock* (1925); *Fire for the Night* (1930); *Epistle to Prometheus* (1931); *One Part Love* (1939); *Take Them, Stranger* (1944); *Animal, Vegetable, Mineral* (1954); and *Coming of Age: New and Selected Poems* (1959). Her criticism includes *Potable Gold* (1929); *This Modern Poetry* (1935 and enlarged as *Poetry in Our Time*, 1952, 1956, 1962). Prose works by Miss Deutsch include: *Heroes of the Kalevala, Finland's Saga* (1940); *Walt Whitman, Builder for America* (1941); *The Reader's Shakespeare* (1946); and *Poetry Handbook* (1957, rev. and enlarged, 1961).

Devil and Daniel Webster, The (1937), a story by STEPHEN VINCENT BENÉT. This tale became a classic of American literature as soon as it was published in the *Saturday Evening Post*. It tells the story of Jabez Stone, a New Hampshire farmer, who sells his soul to the devil and then, when "Mr. Scratch" comes to collect, retains the great lawyer and orator to save him. By his eloquence before a jury of remarkably depraved characters, Webster manages to secure Stone's acquittal. Benét made a superb adaptation of an ancient folklore theme to American folkways. Douglas Stuart Moore based an opera on the story (1938). A movie version was called *All That Money Can Buy*.

Devil and Tom Walker, The (1824), a story by WASHINGTON IRVING. This appeared in Irving's TALES OF A TRAVELER and describes a typical Yankee contest—between the devil, who expects his usual contract to be fulfilled, and Tom, who tries to get out of an awkward bargain. The devil wins in the end; Maximilian Rudwin, commenting on the story, says that "Irving must be put down as a realist." John B. Hymer wrote a "fantastic musical travesty" (1908) based on Irving's story and employing his title.

Devil in American literature, The. The devil came to America, one may assume, along with the voyagers on the *Mayflower*, and was a resident in good standing with the Puritans and later in the other colonies. Cotton Mather, writing his *Discourse on the Wonders of the Invisible World* (1682) declared firmly, "That

there is a Devil is a thing doubted by none but such as are under the influences of the Devil. For any to deny the being of a Devil must be from an ignorance or profaneness worse than diabolical." He feared that "the Devil has made a dreadful knot of witches in the country." Satan ("Old Scratch," "Old Nick," "the dickens") was a perennial theme for denunciation at prayer meetings; and as late as 1876 J. G. Holland was able to state, "One of the principal objects of American reverence is the Devil. There are multitudes who are shocked to hear his name mentioned lightly, and who esteem such mention profanity." Emerson, however, spoke of "the dear old devil," and a Unitarian minister was unfrocked for wishing to extend the doctrine of universal salvation to Satan.

American writers have occasionally made the devil an important character in their stories. Among the more striking tales may be mentioned Irving's THE DEVIL AND TOM WALKER (1824); Poe's *The Bargain Lost* (1832), which became his BON-BON (1835); also his DUC DE L'OMELETTE (1832) and DEVIL IN THE BELFRY (1839); Hawthorne's THE DEVIL IN MANUSCRIPT (1851); Frederick Beecher Perkins' DEVIL-PUZZLERS (1871); Mark Twain's THE MYSTERIOUS STRANGER (1916); Stephen Vincent Benét's THE DEVIL AND DANIEL WEBSTER (1937); and Shirley Barker's *Peace, My Daughters* (1949). An amusing novel, Douglas Wallop's *The Year the Yankees Lost the Pennant* (1954), made the devil a leading character; this became a Broadway hit called *Damn Yankees* (1955) and later a moving picture. W. B. Stein has written *Hawthorne's Faust: A Study in the Devil Archetype* (1953). Basil Davenport has edited an anthology, *Deals with the Devil* (1958).

Devil in Manuscript, The (1851), a story by NATHANIEL HAWTHORNE. Part of the collection called THE SNOW IMAGE AND OTHER TWICE-TOLD TALES, this story tells of a visit to a lawyer who is trying to turn novelist and is writing the narrative of "a fiend as represented in our traditions and the written records of witchcraft." But a devil is in the papers; moreover, no less than seventeen publishers have already turned down his book. He throws his manuscript into the fire, and the fiend leaps up in one bright blaze—and sets the town on fire!

Devil in the Belfry, The (1839), a story by EDGAR ALLAN POE. It was called by G. E. Woodberry "a grotesque sketch" and by Hervey Allen "a satire on the credulity of the mob." The devil here is "a finicky little personage." F. O. Matthiessen says that for this story Poe "took a hint from Irving's old Dutch material for a farce about the clock that struck thirteen in the borough of Vondervotteimittiss."

Devil-Puzzlers (1871), a story by FREDERICK BEECHER PERKINS. The hero of this tale of a frustrated devil has the cleverness to insert an escape clause in the contract he makes with his Infernal Majesty. He stipulates that, at the expiration of the period mentioned in the contract, he will be left unharmed in body and soul, provided that the devil proves unable to answer three questions. Satan manages to reply to the first question, on predestination and free will, and even to the second, on the immortality of the soul in the light of modern science. At this moment the hero's wife comes in, and she puts the third question: Which is the front end of *this?*—and she hands him her bonnet. He is unable to reply and angrily makes his exit by the window in a blast of thunder. Brander Matthews called this story "diabolically philosophical."

Devil's Dictionary, The (called *The Cynic's Word Book,* 1906; retitled, 1911), a collection of about two thousand original epigrams and brief essays by AMBROSE BIERCE. According to Bierce, he began writing the definitions for a weekly paper, probably THE WASP of San Francisco. He addresses his definitions to those "who prefer dry wines to sweet, sense to sentiment, wit to humor, and clean English to slang." In the definitions he expresses caustically his aversion to democracy, socialism, communism, and labor unions, but also to people with money, writers of the day as such, the human mind, and human beings. He describes *plan* as a way of bothering "about the best method of accomplishing an accidental result," *wit* as "the salt with which the American humorist spoils his intellectual cookery by leaving it out," *alone* as "in bad company," *impunity* as "wealth," *once* as "enough," *adage* as "boned wisdom for weak teeth." Harry Levin calls the *Dictionary* "no more than an alphabetical compendium of Bierce's deadliest witticisms and most philosophical epigrams."

De Vinne, Theodore L[ow] (b. Stamford, Conn., Dec. 25, 1828—d. Feb. 16, 1914), master printer, historian. He founded and managed Theo. L. De Vinne & Co., later the De Vinne Press, and became widely known for the excellence and artistry of his printing and engravings. He printed such noted Magazines as *St. Nicholas, Scribner's, The Century,* and also the earlier books of the GROLIER CLUB, of which he was a founder and the sixth president. Among his books: *The Invention of Printing* (1876); *Historic Printing Types* (1886); *The Practice of Typography* (4 v., 1900–04).

De Voto, Bernard A[ugustine] (b. Ogden, Utah, Jan. 11, 1897—d. Nov. 13, 1955), teacher, editor, author. De Voto was a voluminous writer with widely varying interests. His writings appeared in many kinds of periodicals, from the journals of learned societies to *College Humor.* He edited the SATURDAY REVIEW OF LITERATURE from 1936 to 1938, became the third occupant of *The Editor's Chair* in HARPER'S MAGAZINE (1935–1955).

His books fall into at least four categories. He first won fame when he replied vigorously, in MARK TWAIN'S AMERICA (1932), to *The Ordeal of Mark Twain,* VAN WYCK BROOKS's disparaging book on Clemens; this was followed by *Mark Twain at Work* (1942); he also edited Selections from Clemens' *Autobiography,* calling it *Mark Twain in Eruption* (1940). He wrote many controversial essays on literature, education, and

social history, some of them collected in *Forays and Rebuttals* (1936), *Minority Report* (1940), *The Literary Fallacy* (1944), *The World of Fiction* (1950), and *The Easy Chair* (1955). The work that he himself regarded as his most

Blackstone

important was his historical writing, principally *The Year of Decision* (1943), ACROSS THE WIDE MISSOURI (1947), which won a Pulitzer Prize, and *The Course of Empire* (1952). He edited *The Journals of Lewis and Clark* (1953). Finally his novels and short stories must be mentioned: *The Crooked Mile* (1924), *Mountain Time* (1947), and others; also several written under the pen name John August.

De Voto was the center of many controversies, in some of which he became involved because of his anger at American authors who knew little of American history or American life in the large and who neglected American themes. He thought of himself as a hard-boiled realist; his books reveal him as a great scholar who energetically blows the dust off books. In *The Hour* (1951) he celebrates with lyric delight that social invention, the cocktail hour plus the dry martini. No writer in our history has had a more comprehensive knowledge of the realities of American life in all its stages, from the westward rolling of civilization to our own age of mechanisms and gadgets. His own intense and sometimes belligerent interest in whatever subject he happened to be writing about was infectious; and his frankly admitted prejudices were maintained with unflagging gusto.

De Vries, Peter (b. Chicago, Ill., Feb. 27, 1910—   ), novelist, editor. Appropriately enough, De Vries' first published novel, *But Who Wakes the Bugler?* (1940), was accompanied by illustrations from the brush of Charles Addams, the *New Yorker* cartoonist of the drolly monstrous. Though the book was hailed as "first class fun" by the *New York Times* reviewer, the same critic also noted that De Vries' humor was more "lunatic than laughable." He has consistently been preoccupied, always with his tongue boring sharply into his cheek, with the individual's capacity for the insane and society's tendency toward the absurd. His later novels, such as *Tunnel of Love* (1954), *Comfort Me with Apples* (1956), and *The Tents of Wickedness* (1959), delineate the grotesqueries of suburban life and are euphemistically set in Decency, Connecticut (De Vries has been a long-time resident of Westport, Connecticut). His other works include: *The Handsome Heart* (1943); *Angels Can't Do Better* (1944); *No, But I Saw the Movie* (1952, a collection of short stories garnered from the pages of the *New Yorker*); *The Mackerel Plaza* (1958); and *Through the Fields of Clover* (1961). De Vries received his B.A. at Calvin College in Michigan in 1931, and also studied at Northwestern University. He was associate editor of *Poetry* magazine in 1938, and in 1942 he became co-editor. Since 1944, he has been on the editorial staff of the *New Yorker*.

Dewey, John (b. Burlington, Vt., Oct. 20, 1859—d. June 1, 1952), teacher, philosopher, educational reformer. A shy, sweet-tempered, absent-minded man, Dewey was in many ways the chief educational and philosophical force of the first half of the 20th century. In philosophy he was a follower of WILLIAM JAMES and a pragmatist. In education he was the founder of the so-called progressive movement, which to him meant "learning by doing," but his Yankee common sense prevented him from sharing the fallacies and committing the excesses of some of his later disciples. He was a fearless leader, ready to risk his academic skin and his jobs at the Universities of Chicago and at Columbia in the cause of freedom of speech and thought.

As a writer he lacks clarity and smoothness, and sometimes his sentences may be given dubious interpretations. Many philosophers admire him warmly, even if they disagree with him. Brand Blanshard, contrasting him with Santayana, calls him "a plebeian, both in his temperament—or absence of it—and in his writing. His philosophy was a philosophy of action rather than of contemplation." Dewey himself said: "Philosophy is of account only if it affords guidance to action."

Dewey wrote indefatigably during his long lifetime. He began with a *Psychology* (1886). Among his other books (aside from a long array of important articles for learned magazines) were: *Outline of a Critical Theory of Ethics* (1891); *The School and Society* (1900; rev., 1908, 1932); *Studies in Logical Theory* (with others, 1903); *The Influence of Darwin on Philosophy and Other Essays* (1910); *How We Think* (1910); *Interest and Effort in Education* (1913); *Schools of Tomorrow* (with his daughter Evelyn, 1915); *Democracy and Education*

(1916); *Essays in Experimental Logic* (1916); *Human Nature and Conduct* (1922); *Experience and Nature* (1925); *The Quest for Certainty* (1929); *Art as Experience* (1934); *The Theory of Inquiry* (1938); *Freedom and Culture* (1939); *Problems of Man* (1946); *Knowing and the Known* (with A. F. Bentley, 1949). A. H. Johnson edited *The Wit and Wisdom of John Dewey* (1949). Discussions of Dewey have been endless. Two books may be noted: Irwin Edman's *John Dewey* (1954) and M. C. Baker's *Foundations of Dewey's Educational Theory* (1955). See PRAGMATISM.

Dewey, Melvil (b. Adams Center, N.Y., Dec. 10, 1851—d. Dec. 26, 1931), librarian. Dewey became famous as the inventor of the "Dewey Decimal System," now extensively used as a readily remembered way of classifying books (though large libraries more often use the Library of Congress classification). Dewey devised his system while a student librarian at Amherst College (1874–76), later became librarian at Columbia University, where he founded the first library school (1887). He was also an advocate of simplified spelling. See THE LIBRARY JOURNAL.

Dexter, Timothy (b. Malden, Mass., Jan. 22, 1747—d. Oct. 23, 1806), merchant, philosopher, wit. Dexter, who described himself as "First in the East, First in the West, and Greatest Philosopher of All the Known World," also took the title "Lord Timothy Dexter." His whole life was filled with profitable blunders, which no one enjoyed more than he himself. He picked up Continental currency when it wasn't worth the paper it was printed on, reaped a fortune when the government began to redeem it. He sent 42,000 warming pans to the West Indies (anticipating the salesman who sold refrigerators to the Eskimos); the pans were bought by eager plantation owners who used them to ladle molasses. Whalebone bought by an "error" to "stay" ship rigging turned out to be very valuable when corsets suddenly came into fashion again. He built himself a great mansion in Newburyport, appointed a poet laureate, and held a mock funeral for himself. Later he beat his wife, it is said, because she did not shed enough tears at the funeral oration.

Most of these exploits Dexter himself put into a book, telling them generally at his own expense, as if he had been a great fool whom the wiseacres of his time and town deceived with a leer—and yet somehow Dexter always came out on top. His account was called *A Pickle for the Knowing Ones, or Plain Truths in a Homespun Dress* (1802). Dexter had before this written freely for the newspapers, in a style of spelling that was all his own and with complete disregard for punctuation; generally the editors had amended his copy. In his book he was on his own: the spelling was unique, and there was no punctuation. Dexter describes his love affairs, gives his interpretation of original sin, sets forth his ideas on bridges, suggests an international peace congress, and advocates adding another day to the week—a working day. In a second edition (1805) he includes a page of "stops"—all periods, commas, etc.—for those who love punctuation and tells them to "peper and solt as they plese." It is said that his book went into ten editions. He left a charity bequest to Newburyport which is still active. John P. Marquand, a connoisseur of eccentrics, wrote a life of Dexter (1925) and revised it in 1960.

Dial, The. Four magazines with this name have appeared since 1840. The first was an organ of the Transcendentalist movement and was founded by THEODORE PARKER, BRONSON ALCOTT, ORESTES BROWNSON, MARGARET FULLER, JAMES FREEMAN CLARKE, and RALPH WALDO EMERSON. Miss Fuller was the editor for the first two years; Emerson took over until 1844, when the magazine died. In its short life it exerted great influence and gave an audience to Thoreau, the two Channings, Jones Very, and other Transcendentalist writers. The second *Dial* was founded by MONCURE CONWAY in Cincinnati in 1860. Conway, a young Congregationalist minister who had defended Tom Paine's writings, abolition, and other unorthodox creeds, envisioned it as "a legitimation of the Spirit of the Age, which aspires to be free in thought, doubt, utterance, love and knowledge." Among other contributions during its first—and last—year of existence, the magazine published poems by Emerson and the young W. D. Howells, and O. B. Frothingham's book *The Christianity of Christ*, a series which aimed to rescue the basic teachings of Christ from the distortions of dogma. In 1880 Francis F. Browne founded the third *Dial* in Chicago as a conservative literary journal. In 1898 the CHAPBOOK was incorporated into *The Dial*. Later editors were RICHARD HENRY STODDARD and William Henry Smith. In its conservative Chicago days it acclaimed ELSIE VENNER but condemned THE RED BADGE OF COURAGE, LEAVES OF GRASS, and the dramas of Ibsen. In 1916 *The Dial* moved to New York. There, under the editorship of C. J. Masseck, it began to publish the works of new writers. During this period CONRAD AIKEN, John Massey, PADRAIC COLUM, RANDOLPH BOURNE, and VAN WYCK BROOKS were listed as editors. Scofield Thayer became editor in 1919 and *The Dial* began to publish works of famous authors the world over: T. S. Eliot, Thomas Mann, Anatole France, George Santayana, D. H. Lawrence, Sherwood Anderson, Jules Romains, Edna St. Vincent Millay, William Butler Yeats, Edward Arlington Robinson, Ezra Pound, E. E. Cummings, and Gertrude Stein. MARIANNE MOORE became editor in 1925. The magazine ceased publication in 1929. In October 1959 a new *Dial* magazine appeared under the editorship of James Silberman. A literary quarterly, it has printed the work of Bernard Wolfe, Herbert Gold, R. V. Cassill, and the Indian writer Budhaeva Bose.

dialect in American literature. Naturally enough, it is in humorous writing that dialect plays its major role. The pioneers of American humor introduced it early in the 19th century and it soon became a stock element in the stuff of comedy. Our own period has seen the older types challenged, or indeed superseded, by the cult of informality and slang. Historically it was the *Waverley* novels of Sir Walter Scott, very popular in America, that influenced the employment of dialect. Along with the localization of characters and the suggestion of their backgrounds, the portrayal of peculiarities of their speech seemed essential too.

The term *dialect* usually refers to substandard language, primarily to local or regional peculiarities that diverge from the accepted usage of the educated. The peculiarities may be of vocabulary, grammar, pronunciation, spelling, or syntax. Slang hardly deserves classification as dialect, though it is sometimes hard to draw a line of demarcation. Dialect is relatively static, slang is transient; but slang terms sometimes are stabilized into dialect and sometimes, when there is liking for them or they fill a need, they may make their way into the standard language. In this discussion an endeavor is made to indicate in broad lines the types of dialect appearing as our national literature has developed.

In colonial writing, dialect plays a negligible part, if any. The pioneer dialect-speaking character of significance was the Down East Yankee, Jonathan, of Royall Tyler's play THE CONTRAST (1787). Jonathan speaks colloquially, not the usual book English of the other characters, and he knows some of the slang of the day ("I'll swamp it," "I vow"). Following Tyler's hit, Yankee plays began to appear all over the country. During the 1830's they were the most popular type of drama. Of importance, too, in the wake of Benjamin Franklin's POOR RICHARD were the almanacs, which enlivened themselves by using the New England vernacular. It began to appear in jest books and newspapers and travel books. Various other characters alongside the Yankee rustic and the Yankee peddler (originated in T. C. HALIBURTON's *Sam Slick* of 1836) speak it. It became pretty stock, with its serving up of such expressions as "do tell," "I want to know," "tarnal," and its devotion to illiterate spellings. In the 1840's and 1850's there was wide contribution to newspapers of letters composed in rural dialect. The utilization of Down East talk to make characters more lifelike, vivid, and folksy flourished from about 1825 onward and reached its heyday about 1830–70. The popular humorists of the midcentury, such as Benjamin Shillaber (1814–1890), who created MRS. PARTINGTON, and FRANCES WHITCHER (1811–1852) of GODEY'S LADY'S BOOK, who created the Widow Bedott, belong to the Down East dialect writers.

On the whole the dialect of the New England region appears at its best in Lowell's BIGLOW PAPERS (1848, 1861–62). In the later *Papers* Lowell strove confessedly for scientific accuracy in presenting the rural speech he knew. His language, marked as it was by amusing turns of speech, peculiar vocabulary, homely metaphors and similes, and unlettered spellings, appealed to his readers no less than did his political and social satire and entertaining sayings. It was

Lowell who inaugurated the popularity in verse of rustic speech. Among his ultimate followers were WILL CARLETON (1845–1912), JAMES WHITCOMB RILEY (1849–1916), EUGENE FIELD (1850–1895), SAM WALTER FOSS (1858–1911), and other interpreters of their widely scattered regions.

Contemporary with the Down Eastern rustic and running parallel with him for a time was the Kentuckian. Other frontier characters, huntsmen, boatmen, and local figures followed. Their habitat was the old Southwest, Tennessee, Georgia, Louisiana, Mississippi, and Arkansas. They were celebrated in a rollicking literature chronicling their boasting and tall tales. The "ring-tailed roarer, half horse and half alligator" was one of their products. This era may be dated from SEBA SMITH's *Jack Downing Letters* of 1830 and it extended beyond the Civil War. Conspicuous figures, played up in the almanacs and other publications, were the historical DAVY CROCKETT, who gained legendary stature, and MIKE FINK, "last of the Keelboatmen." George W. Harris' yarn-telling hero in SUT LOVINGOOD (1867), whose spicy American vernacular was far from that of the Yankee, was especially influential. In this region the tall tale, told with gusto and exuberance, flourished vigorously. Strange words appeared and were given diffusion (*absquatulate, cahoots, cattawampus, flabbergasted, rambunctious, sockdolager*). Newspaper hoaxes and contributions from illiterate letter-writers retained popularity. Accounts of local manners, customs, and amusements are given with the boisterous humor supposed to appertain to the Southwest. The contrast is strong with the highly mannered narration and talk prevailing in contemporary fiction and short stories. On the whole, Seba Smith (1792–1868) is the best writer of dialect for backwoods and frontier portrayals, as Lowell was for the Down Eastern.

In any chronological survey of dialect in American literature, a group of newspaper humorists of the Civil War period looms large. These preceded and influenced MARK TWAIN. Chief among them were Charles Farrar Browne (1834–1867), who called himself ARTEMUS WARD, David Ross Locke (1833–1888), who assumed the name of PETROLEUM VESUVIUS NASBY, ROBERT H. NEWELL (1836–1901), who wrote as Orpheus C. Kerr, and Henry Wheeler Shaw (1818–1885), whose pseudonym was JOSH BILLINGS. A younger group of these newspaper humorists included MELVIN B. LANDON (1839–1910), who called himself Eli Perkins, ROBERT BURDETTE (1844–1914), and EDGAR WILSON (Bill) NYE (1850–1896). FINLEY PETER DUNNE (1867–1936) launched his popular Irish commentator, Mr. Dooley, in 1898. These men wanted new methods and unlocalized comedy. They sought and achieved nationwide appeal. Their humor lay chiefly in verbal expression, and it was not that of one region. Mainly they relied more and more on eccentricities of language, on the handling of sentences, grammar, quotations, and metaphors and similes, than on

creating characters and background. Sometimes, too, their devices in verbal form were pretty crude. One of Artemus Ward's specialties was deliberately unlettered spellings ("enahow," "snaik," "goaks," "yooth," "Sylvanus Kobb's last tail"). And there was liking among the group for pseudo-Shakespearean and romantic archaisms of the "Dost thou?" "I dost" type. Sometimes the humor lay in the verb forms, "I asked her if we could glide in the merry dance . . . and we glode." Culmination came with Mark Twain, whose HUCKLEBERRY FINN appeared in 1884. Twain did not limit himself to a single locality or to one type of device but exhibited all the linguistic whimsicalities of his predecessors, *i.e.*, malapropisms, puns, misquotations, understatement, exaggeration, incongruities, illiteracies, absurd spellings. The humor, the poetry too, of all types of folk speech became grist for his mill.

In fiction dialect reaches major importance with the arrival of the local color school. Earlier novelists had made some use of it. H. H. BRACKENRIDGE'S MODERN CHIVALRY (1792) had an Irish clown, Teague O'Regan, but he was a transplantation from the English stage. WASHINGTON IRVING had Yankees in his *Knickerbocker History* and his ICHABOD CRANE is a Yankee, but they talk little and that little lacks the flavor of America. Cooper's LEATHERSTOCKING speaks a quaint language sprinkled with archaisms of vocabulary and pronunciation and lapsing into poetical rhapsody when his topic is nature. Cooper's David Gamut is also a Yankee and some of his characters from other lands, in his various books, speak brands of English colored by their mother tongues. J. P. KENNEDY and WILLIAM GILMORE SIMMS also try dialect at times. Hawthorne did not. Even his children speak pure English, though his skilled handling makes their talk seem natural. On the whole the advent of the local color school in the last half of the century marks a new period. These writers continue the tradition of regional portrayal, with attention to realistic detail. The Yankee reappears in the group of New England novels of Mrs. H. B. STOWE, *Oldtown Folks* (1869) in particular. Edward Eggleston's THE HOOSIER SCHOOLMASTER (1871) sets forth the speech of the country folk of Indiana. BRET HARTE from 1868 onward depicted California, MARY N. MURFREE reproduced the dialect of the Tennessee mountains, 1884–97, G. W. CABLE wrote of New Orleans and Louisiana in the 1870's, notably in OLD CREOLE DAYS (1879), and JOEL CHANDLER HARRIS' Uncle Remus (1880–1910) told his animal tales in the folk speech of the Georgia Negroes of his region. The high tide of local dialect lasted till the end of the century. The New York novel DAVID HARUM (1898) is a salient example, some say, of the "B'Gosh School" of fiction.

WALT WHITMAN is hardly to be described as a dialect writer but he cannot be excluded from a discussion of the American vernacular. He was a rebel against literary English. He championed the vigor of colloquialisms, even of vulgarisms and slang. He was ready to accept such terms as *skedaddle, shebang, yap, out with the bhoys, souse, yawp* in his prose and at times in his verse, and he did not mind manipulating standard words in his verse (*civilizee, imperturbe, philosoph*). He did much to influence oncoming writers toward the freer and more colloquial, more uncouth if you will, use of language.

Negro dialect in our literature has been an artificial product having little relation to real Negro speech. Its popularity followed the success of DAN EMMETT's "Jim Crow" melodies and dances (1830 or 1831), and of the succeeding Negro minstrelsy. A traditional Negro dialect became established ("debbil," "trabble," "gwine," "massa," "honey," "de Lawd"). Really there is as much regional and individual divergence among Negroes as among whites. Addison Hubbard in *American Speech* (I, 1926) brought together, transcribed by competent persons, a passage from Aesop's *Fables* as it might be spoken by Negroes from Harlem, East North Carolina, South Carolina, Georgia, Mississippi, and Louisiana. The dialect in these and in O'Neill's EMPEROR JONES and DuBose Heyward's PORGY is a far cry from the slapstick Negro minstrelsy type or the strange Gullahesque bits in Poe's THE GOLD BUG.

The comedy German was also handed a stock dialect stemming from the popular *Hans Breitmann Ballads* (see under BREITMANN) of the 1860's and 1870's by Charles Godfrey Leland ("Dey vented to dis berson's house/ To see some furnidure"). For a time the Irishman with his *begorry, bhoys, mavourneen,* and *shillelagh* had a place in journalism and song, culminating in the philosophical MR. DOOLEY (1898–1910). The Dooley dialect is marked by strong *r's,* aspirated *d's* and *t's,* and archaic vowels ("wurruld," "ye could niver be a rale pathrite"). Pennsylvania German, often called Pennsylvania Dutch, entered dialect writing, and we have had served up to us in our time the broken English of Italians, of Mexicans in the Southwest, and of Scandinavians from Minnesota and the Dakotas. WALLACE IRWIN's Schoolboy (*Letters from a Japanese Schoolboy,* 1909) had a picturesque dialect of English, and New York City Yiddish has had many popular successes, such as Montague Glass' POTASH AND PERLMUTTER stories (1910) and MILT GROSS' *Nize Bebe* (1925). An Indian brand of English has been little heard from. Monosyllables, truncated sentences, and grunts ("Ugh!") mostly make it up. Or, educated in schools, Indian characters speak standard English.

Efforts are now directed more and more, in plays, novels, and short stories, toward "giving talk as it is talked." SINCLAIR LEWIS, for instance, had a sensitive ear for various types of American speech. The hardboiled school of fiction (DAMON RUNYON was influential here) strives to reproduce the language of the underworld and of the criminal classes, a sort of tough-guy-ese. (See HARD-BOILED FICTION.) RING LARDNER brilliantly captured the speech of athletes and other semi-educated persons.

Some ultrarealists use words hitherto taboo, often seemingly to arrest attention or perhaps to shock. Rural mispronunciations and unlettered spelling still appear. But with the coming of interest in phonetic analysis closer representation of consecutive utterance is sought. Sentence fragments such as "How come?", "You been away?", amalgams such as *gotta, dincha, attaboy,* mutilations such as *ittybitty,* and wordplays of many types are frequent. The clever ventures of O. Henry ("Broadway is New York's Yappian Way," "The Statue of the Dinkus Thrower in the Vatican") which perhaps deserve literary recognition, have been succeeded by the violent perpetrations of *Billboard* and *Variety,* from which derive the verbal acrobatics of certain columnists. The ingenious concoctions of *Time* (*intelligentsiacs, ballyhooligans*) are now volunteered less frequently. If for rural dialect the lid was off in much of the last century, the lid is off now, for better or worse, in other areas also. Witness the grotesqueries of the advertisements of films and other publicity (*colossapendous, stupeficient*), or the uninhibited coinages of trade names (*Quink, Socony, Vegamato*). But these ventures are outside the literary field. Harold Wentworth compiled the *American Dialect Dictionary* (1944). See HUMOR IN THE U.S.

LOUISE POUND

Dialect Society, American. A notable organization, founded by FRANCIS JAMES CHILD (1889). *Dialect Notes* has appeared from time to time since 1904 and offers useful material to scholars. The first of a series of *Publications* appeared in 1944.

Dialogues in Limbo (1925), ten Platonic discourses by GEORGE SANTAYANA. Six shades— five of them ancient Greeks—discourse with "the spirit of a stranger still living on earth" on the world and experience, ethics, reason, the life of the mind, self-government. In an edition published in 1948 three more dialogues were added.

Diamond, David (b. Rochester, N.Y., July 9, 1915—   ), composer. Diamond's *Sinfonietta* won a $2,500 award offered by Paul Whiteman in 1935 for "the best orchestral work written by an American and reflecting the American spirit." The work was based on a poem by Carl Sandburg, and Diamond often turned to American authors, including Melville and E. E. Cummings, for the themes of his later works. His ballet, *The Dream of Audubon,* was produced in 1941, and in 1951 he composed the incidental music for Tennessee Williams' *The Rose Tattoo.* He has contributed to *Modern Music, Decision,* the *New York Herald Tribune* and the *Musical Quarterly.*

Diamond Dick. A favorite character in dime novels. He was a creation of GEORGE CHARLES JENKS (1850–1929), who wrote under the pen name W. B. Lawson.

Diamond Lens, The (*Atlantic Monthly,* January, 1858), a tale by FITZ-JAMES O'BRIEN. One of the most famous stories of the mid-19th century, this tale relates how the inventor of a new microscope was suddenly able to see a charming sylph in a drop of water; when she died he went insane. Of this story and O'Brien's *The Wondersmith* (likewise published in *The Atlantic*, October, 1859) William Winter said that they "electrified magazine literature," and set a model of excellence for short-story writing in this country.

Diamond Lil (1928), a play by Mae West (1892—   ), who took the main role. The heroine is the mistress of Gus Jordan, a Bowery saloonkeeper who is also a white slaver. Diamond Lil is so called because of the large amount of "ice" Gus has lavished on her; she is generous with her favors. The resulting complications include a murder, several shootings and arrests. At the close of what Wolcott Gibbs calls "this lively, if somewhat untidy drama," Lil chooses as her favorite an alleged Salvation Army captain, in reality a prominent member of the Vice Squad. The play made Mae West famous because of (1) her peculiar walk or writhe, "certainly one of the most hilarious performances in the theater," said Gibbs; and (2) her husky-voiced pronouncement of the line, "Come up and see me some time." Bernard Sobel remarks that the play, although "hokum melodrama," presents "one of the few authentic pictures of Tenderloin night life" in the alleged Gay Nineties. It was successfully revived in 1949.

Diaries, American (1945), an annotated bibliography compiled by William Matthews and Roy Harvey Pearce. This list covers diaries written before 1861.

Diary from Dixie, A (pub. 1904, 1942, 1949), by MARY BOYKIN CHESNUT. A famous diary (from Feb. 12, 1861, to Aug. 2, 1865) of a woman in the South during the days of the Civil War; it was published piecemeal, with expurgations when Mrs. Chesnut was being too frank. It finally appeared in practically complete form under the editorship of Ben Ames Williams. Mrs. Chesnut herself was the wife of James Chesnut, Jr., a dignified gentleman of great integrity. He was the first Southerner who resigned from the U.S. Senate, the man sent to demand the surrender of Fort Sumter, a general in the Confederate Army, a member of the Confederate Senate. Mrs. Chesnut followed him everywhere in his missions, heard about everything, knew everyone, and in her diary expressed herself freely. She did not fail to understand the tragedy of her times but preferred laughter to melancholy. She was, moreover, antislavery and spoke vigorously on the subject without being pro-Northern. Her quick portrait of someone named Brewster: "Brewster is the most careless creature. He may have godliness but he has not the next thing to it."

Diary of a Public Man, The (*North American Review*, August–November, 1879; 1946 in book form). When this alleged diary first appeared, it created a sensation by its vivid description of events preceding the election of Lincoln, his inauguration, and the fateful days that followed. The diary gave the first account of how Stephen A. Douglas held Lincoln's hat during the inaugu-

ration exercises—an incident now part of the Lincoln legend. The anonymous diarist reported talking to Lincoln as President-elect twice and as President once. Yet no one knew who he was; and one historian after another has tried to solve the mystery. The great Lincoln scholar James G. Randall, "after an elaborate elimination and checking," was unable to find an author for the diary, and held, moreover, that its authenticity cannot be "proved beyond the possibility of a reasonable doubt." It seems to be a general view that the author, whoever he was, had portions of a genuine diary to work on, but embellished them with the skill of a good novelist.

Diary of George Templeton Strong, The (4 v., 1952). This remarkable journal was the production of an able and independent-minded New York City citizen, trained at Columbia University and one of its trustees, a Trinity Church vestryman, one of the founders of the Philharmonic Society and of the School of Mines at Columbia, a lawyer of note, and a good businessman. He knew all the notable men of the city and the nation, and spoke about them with such frankness in his diary that it was judged advisable not to publish it while it still could hurt people's feelings. He made his first entry on Oct. 5, 1835, and continued the diary for forty years; it contains about 5 million words, from which Allan Nevins made a selection for publication. Strong liked men who worked for themselves and distrusted both southern slave owners and northern capitalists; neither, he thought, could be quite gentlemen. He was prejudiced against all the races and creeds with which New York City began to fill up in his day, and he sneered at the "unwashed democracy." But he had a mind for the graphic and described vividly famous crimes, P. T. Barnum's publicity stunts, the laying of the Atlantic cable, the ravages of cholera, the fire at the Academy of Music. He saw Thackeray and Fernando Wood, and as an official of the Sanitary Commission talked with Lincoln.

Dickinson, Asa Don (b. Detroit, Mich., May 15, 1876—d. Nov. 14, 1960), librarian, editor, critic. Dickinson was librarian in several cities and at several colleges. He served at Brooklyn College (1931–44), where he planned that institution's new library building. A useful series prepared by him includes *One Thousand Best Books* (1924), *Best Books of Our Time, 1901–25* (1928), *Best Books of the Decade 1926–35* (1937), *Best Books of the Decade 1936–45* (1948), *The World's Best Books: Homer to Hemingway* (1953). In addition he edited several anthologies for children.

Dickinson, C. Roy (b. Newark, N.J., March 14, 1888—d. 1949), editor, short-story writer. Dickinson was with *Cosmopolitan Magazine* (1910–15) and *Puck* (1915–16) before joining *Printers' Ink* (1919–42), becoming president of the Printers' Ink Publishing Co. in 1933. One story of his, with amusing philosophical implications, was *The Ultimate Frog* (1939). He also wrote *Wages and Wealth* (1931) and *The Cowards Never Stirred* (1933).

Dickinson, Emily [Elizabeth] (b. Amherst, Mass., Dec. 10, 1830—d. May 15, 1886), poet. The most remarkable fact about Emily Dickinson's life is that, although she lived in one town, in one house, all her life, little is known about

her. The facts of her existence are straightforward, but reveal none of the sources of the knowledge of ecstasy and despair that infuses her poetry. One of three children of lawyer Edward Dickinson, who was also treasurer of Amherst College, she shared with her brother Austin and her sister Lavinia a cultivated Calvinist home in Amherst, Mass. She stayed close to the house even early in her life, and after 1862 rarely even went out of doors. After a normal education at Mount Holyoke Female Seminary and Amherst Institute she retired from the community, rarely coming down from her room even to meet her guests. She always dressed in white and in the eyes of her neighbors became something of a town character.

The details of Miss Dickinson's external life thus seem as deceptively simple as they are impossible to know—but she also recorded a complex spiritual existence in superb poetry. In her own words she summed up something of her actual experience [in a letter to T. W. HIGGINSON, April 25, 1862]:

I went to school, but in your manner of the phrase had no education. When a little girl, I had a friend who taught me Immortality; but venturing too near, himself, he never re-

turned. Soon after, my tutor died, and for several years my lexicon was my only companion. Then I found one more, but he was not contented I be his scholar, so he left the land.

One of the great mysteries and games of Dickinson scholarship is identifying the men in her life. Several men had a great meaning to her and to one of them she wrote, but never mailed, a series of letters addressing him as "master." The two possible intended recipients were the Reverend Charles Wadsworth, an older, married man, whose trip to a California pastorate and subsequent return may have been cryptically referred to by Miss Dickinson; and SAMUEL BOWLES, editor of the Springfield Daily Republican and publisher of one of her early poems. Other important personal influences on her were her father, who remained a pervasive force all her life; Benjamin F. Newton, a short-lived young lawyer who guided her early study and introduced her to the works of Emerson; Thomas Wentworth Higginson, a colonel in the Civil War, liberal visionary, and man of letters; and Judge Otis P. Lord, a politician and friend of the family, with whom she shared some sort of love in the late 1870's.

Though Miss Dickinson wrote poetry throughout her life, only seven poems of the almost two thousand she wrote were published in her lifetime. The poems are uniformly short, consisting usually of four-line stanzas with very weak rhymes, but no factual description can convey their power. Her diction is taken from the homespun traditions of New England and its Calvinist backgrounds and, probably because of her lack of professional acquaintances, it retains its rude, tough shape. It has been said, with too much leniency, that the "awkwardness of her poetry became a metaphor of life itself." Nevertheless, the fact is that the power and flashes of illumination, the curious exactness of her best poems indicate a poetic genius of first rank, despite its uneven manifestation.

Her poetry deals in a terse, aphoristic style with that central problem of romantic art: the relationship between the natural and the spiritual orders of being—in terms of her verse, between the concrete New England world and the divine prototype. This tension is manifest in most of her poems and relates her directly to that tradition of American letters, stated by Emerson and simultaneously revealed by Dickinson and Walt Whitman, which finds current voice in Robert Frost. The modernity of Miss Dickinson's expression is seen in her love of word and image. On the surface such poets seem to be simply realists examining the world, lovers of nature's objects, though not naturalists; but finally the meaning of their poetry is in the spiritual truth it reveals through the natural fact.

Miss Dickinson's poetry is not divorced from the tradition of Calvinism despite her personal rejection of its tenets, and in this respect her resemblance to Hawthorne is obvious. Their common literary and philosophical ancestor was

JONATHAN EDWARDS, who saw that the purpose of existence is to strive for the kind of freedom gained only through work and agony, and that this freedom is an individual achievement and comes through the self. Thus, in her poetic vision of individual realization and her poetic expression of the nature-spirit dualism, Miss Dickinson was true to her heritage. Isolated physically, unaware of the power of the country that spurred Emerson's and Whitman's spirits, she forged significance and triumph from private anguish and recorded it with exceptional poetic skill.

Sometime during the year 1858 Miss Dickinson began putting her poems into packets—five or six sheets written in ink and sewn together. Two-thirds of her poems were found in this state. The bulk of her verse—for only a few childish verses exist from before 1858—was written between 1859 and 1865 though she wrote until the end of her life. Most of her poems were written in three stages of drafts and were included in letters to her friends for their opinions. This method of composition in part accounts for the confusion in the texts that existed until recently.

Because of this confusion some note ought to be made of the various editions of Emily Dickinson's poetry. The first series of her poems was issued by Mrs. David Peck Todd and Col. Higginson at Lavinia's instigation. They rewrote, polished, and completed the poems in accordance with the standards of poetry of the day. In 1914, eighteen years after the three volumes of altered poetry appeared, Martha Dickinson Bianchi edited a volume of the poems called THE SINGLE HOUND with an accurate text, but later editions by Mrs. Bianchi revert to the altered texts until her edition of *Unpublished Poems* (1935), her last edition. In 1945, MABEL LOOMIS TODD and Millicent Todd Bingham published *Bolts of Melody* with fairly accurate texts, but the definitive edition of Emily Dickinson's poems, in their original state, had to await until 1958, with the three-volume *Poems of Emily Dickinson* (edited by Thomas H. Johnson). Emily Dickinson has inspired an immense amount of scholarly and critical activity, but also some purely creative efforts. A number of plays have been based on her life, including Susan Glaspell's Pulitzer Prize winner, ALISON'S HOUSE (1930), and Dorothy Gardner's EASTWARD IN EDEN (1947). Laura Benét's *Come Slowly Eden* (1942) is a biographical novel. See POETRY; BRITTLE HEAVEN.

RICHARD C. ROBEY

Dickinson, John ["Fabius"] (b. Talbot Co., Maryland, Nov. 8, 1732—d. Feb. 14, 1808), lawyer, merchant, landowner, pamphleteer. As a man of wealth who was trained in law in England, Dickinson might have been expected to join the ranks of the Tories during the revolutionary period. But he became instead, as V. L. Parrington phrases it, "the spokesman of the American Whigs." Moses Tyler gave him a broader title, "the penman of the Revolution." Dickinson was, that is, a rich man and a conservative who believed that a sound government should be founded on moderation, justice, and fair dealing together with respect for property

rights. He never wanted to see the colonies severed from England, but his numerous pamphlets on taxation and other problems and his LETTERS FROM A FARMER IN PENNSYLVANIA TO THE INHABITANTS OF THE BRITISH COLONIES (Dec. 2, 1767—Feb. 15, 1768) increased in intensity of tone and exerted a profound influence both in the colonies and abroad. Dickinson refused to sign the Declaration of Independence; he hoped that conciliation would still win the day. He wrote many of the state papers of the Continental Congress, participated in the Constitutional Convention, and wrote his *Letters of Fabius* (1788) urging ratification, and (strangest act of all) composed in 1797 a second series of *Letters of Fabius* eloquently recommending the French cause. Dickinson wrote a song that became famous, A Song for American Freedom, called the LIBERTY SONG (Boston *Gazette*, 1768). He was one of the founders of Dickinson College, which is named for him.

Dickinson, Jonathan. A Quaker merchant known only for his diary, GOD'S PROTECTING PROVIDENCE.

Dickinson, Thomas H. (b. Charlotte County, Va., Nov. 9, 1877—   ), teacher, writer. After serving with the army in the Spanish-American War, Dickinson was graduated from Ohio State University in 1899. He received his Ph.D. from the University of Wisconsin in 1906. He was a professor of English at Ohio State,

Baylor, and Wisconsin Universities from 1906 to 1913. The years 1918–1922 were spent with the American Relief Administration in Europe. He also served with the United Nations Relief and Rehabilitation Administration, 1945–1946. In his writings Dickinson concerned himself primarily with contemporary drama and wrote a number of plays himself. His works reflect his inclination "to treat literary and art activities as agents of an enlarging social process." Dickinson's books: *The Case of American Drama* (1915); *Contemporary Drama of England* (1917); *The Insurgent Theatre* (1917); *Russia in the Red Shadow* (1922); *The United States and the League* (1923); *The New-Old World* (1923); *Playwrights of the New American Theatre* (1925); *An Outline of Contemporary Drama* (1927); *The Making of American Literature* (1932); *The Theatre in a Changing Europe* (1937); *American Democracy and World Order* (1955). He edited: *The Plays of Oliver Goldsmith* (1908); *The Plays of Robert Greene* (1909); *Chief Contemporary Dramatists* (1915; 2nd Series, 1921; 3rd Series, 1930); *Types of Contemporary Drama* (2 v., 1935); *Contemporary Plays* (co-editor, 1925). His plays: *The Unbroken Road* (1909); *In Hospital* (1909); *The Portrait of a Man as Governor* (1928); *Winter Bound* (1929).

dictionaries. Dictionaries have always been popular in the United States and reflect the deep interest of Americans in words and their use. The total sale of dictionaries in this country rivals that of Bibles. Dr. Samuel Johnson's was the one most popular in early days, and for seventy-five years, according to the reckoning of Frank Luther Mott, had a good sale. Webster's has of course sold the largest number steadily for the longest period of time, since the first edition of his major work appeared in 1828; his name became a synonym for *dictionary*, especially as G. and C. Merriam took over the enterprise. Worcester's was a bitter competitor for many decades after its first appearance in 1830. Other dictionaries that have had large sales are those of Funk & Wagnalls, the John C. Winston Co., the World Publishing Co., Random House (the *American College Dictionary*). With these should be reckoned the various editions of Roget's *Thesaurus*, dictionaries of synonyms, dictionaries of Americanisms and of slang, of American English, of Western words, etc. See below and also NOAH WEBSTER. Stewart A. Steger prepared a history, *American Dictionaries* (1913), with a bibliography; and J. R. Hulbert wrote on *Dictionaries British and American* (1955).

Dictionary of American Biography, The (21 v., 1928–36), published under the auspices of the American Council of Learned Societies and edited first by ALLEN JOHNSON, then by DUMAS MALONE. Supplements were issued in 1944 and 1958. In 1946 a Centenary Edition appeared; it included 14,285 sketches, varying in length from 100 to 15,000 words and prepared by 2,601 contributing scholars. The *D.A.B.* presents a vast panorama of the men and women who made America in all its varying eras. Living persons are excluded. See JOHN FRANKLIN JAMESON.

Dictionary of American English, A (4 v., 1938–44), edited by Sir William A. Craigie and James R. Hulbert, with a large staff of contributing specialists. It was twenty-five years in the making. The end of the 19th century was selected as a suitable stopping place, leaving of course for later collection an immense body of words produced during the years since 1900.

Dictionary of American History, The (6 v., 1940), edited by JAMES TRUSLOW ADAMS. A valuable compilation of 6,425 articles prepared by more than a thousand scholars.

Dictionary of Americanisms, A (1848), edited by John R. Bartlett. This work went through four editions by 1877, and was reprinted in 1896. Described as a "Glossary of Words and Phrases Regarded as Peculiar to the United States," it contains about 3,725 terms, arranged in six, then (in the 1859 ed.) in nine categories.

Dictionary of Modern European Literature, Columbia (1947), edited by Horatio Smith. See COLUMBIA DICTIONARY OF MODERN EUROPEAN LITERATURE.

Di Donato, Pietro (b. West Hoboken, N.J., April 13, 1911—   ), writer, biographer. *Esquire* first published Di Donato's story, *Christ in Concrete;* almost entirely autobiographical, it told the story of a family of Italian immigrants, including the memorable scene of the father's death in the collapse of a building when the boy was twelve years of age. From this story Di Donato developed his full-length novel of the same name. For nearly twenty years thereafter, he published little significant writing. *Three Circles of Light* (1960) again deals with his family. His other books include *This Woman* (1958); and *Immigrant Saint: The Life of Mother Cabrini* (1960).

Dietz, David H[enry] (b. Cleveland, Ohio, Oct. 6, 1897—   ), journalist, writer, lecturer. David Dietz became a member of the editorial staff of the Cleveland *Press* in 1915, and science editor of the Scripps-Howard newspapers in 1921. In 1926 he became a lecturer in general science at Western Reserve University. His popular science books for young people include: *The Story of Science* (1931); *Medical Magic* (1937); *Atomic Energy in the Coming Era* (1945), a work translated into thirteen languages; *All About Satellites and Space Ships* (1958); and *All About Great Medical Discoveries* (1960).

Dietz, Howard (b. New York City, Sept. 8, 1896—   ), press agent, librettist, writer of lyrics. Some of the most popular stage and movie hits of the day were the work of Dietz, often in collaboration with noted composers or with other librettists. Among them were *Dear Sir* (with JEROME KERN, 1924); *Merry-Go-Round* (with Morrie Ryskind, 1927); *The Little Show* (1929); *Second Little Show* (1930); *Revenge with Music* (1934); *Jackpot* (1944); *Inside U.S.A.* (1948). Among song hits for which Dietz supplied the words are *Moanin'*

*Low, Something to Remember You By, Dancing
in the Dark, You and the Night and the Music.*
In 1950 he adapted *Fledermaus* into English
for the Metropolitan Opera Company; he has
also made an adaptation of Puccini's *La Bohème.*

digest magazines. A type of magazine that
attained a tremendous success with the birth and
development of THE READER'S DIGEST (1921).
Immediately a host of imitators sprang up, some
to last only briefly, others to establish a solid
circulation. These other digests were either direct
imitators of *The Reader's Digest* in its general
appeal, or specialized in the fields of education,
science, the Negro, one or another religious sect,
sports, etc. Intellectuals are prone to look down
on these magazines, which are described as
affording "hit-and-run reading." Roger Butterfield, in a survey of twenty-one such periodicals,
finds that sex is an outstanding interest of their
readers, but that the "success story" is very
popular, as are articles about science (not always very accurate), especially in its industrial
applications. The interest in people is peculiar,
for articles about "contemporary nonentities" are
twice as numerous as those about "contemporary
celebrities." Nevertheless, the readers of these
magazines have an abiding interest in current
social problems, especially in the world at large.

Digges, Thomas Atwood (b. Maryland,
1741?–d. 1821?), an American patriot friendly
with many leaders of the revolutionary cause,
who was in Portugal during the Revolution. To
Digges has been attributed a novel entitled *The
Adventures of Alonso, Containing Some Striking Anecdotes of the Present Prime Minister of
Portugal.* It was published in London anonymously in 1775 and was described as being "by
a native of Maryland, some years resident in
Lisbon." It tells of the adventures of a young
merchant, has some passages in consonance with
Digges' known ideas of government. It may be
called the first American novel.

Dillon, George (b. Jacksonville, Fla., Nov.
12, 1906—d. May 12, 1968), poet, editor. Dillon won a Guggenheim Fellowship in 1932–33.
He published *Boy in the Wind* (1927); *The
Flowering Stone* (1931), which was awarded
a Pulitzer Prize; and, in collaboration with EDNA
ST. VINCENT MILLAY, a translation of Baudelaire's *Les Fleurs du Mal* (1935). He was the
editor of POETRY from 1937 until 1950. Alfred
Kreymborg notes that didactic and scientific
notes are heard in Dillon's poetry, but turned
into distinctive lyrics.

dime novel, the. A literary genre that owed
its origin to ERASTUS F. BEADLE (1821–1894),
who attained an amazing success when he published a *Dime Song Book* in Buffalo. In 1858 he
moved to New York City, and together with his
brother Irwin—and, later on, Robert Adams—
started a revolutionary publishing experiment.
After trying joke books and other collections, he
began the publication of yellow-backed "dime"
novels, dealing chiefly with pioneer life, the
Revolution, Indian fighting, and similar episodes
in early American history. The Civil War helped
Beadle & Adams to attain a huge success, since

easy and inexpensive reading matter in dime
novels was exactly what the soldiers wanted. By
the middle of 1865 the firm had sold more than
4 million dime novels, some items selling as
many as 80,000 copies. The two best sellers

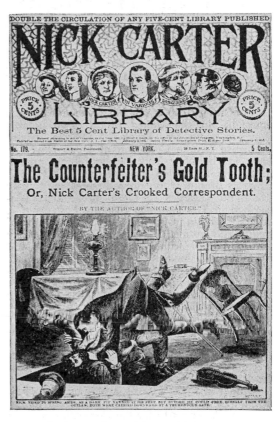

were an Indian story, MALAESKA (1860), by
Mrs. Ann S. Stephens (1813–1886), and SETH
JONES, OR THE CAPTIVE OF THE FRONTIER
(1860). Beadle & Adams ran many series of
"dime novels" simultaneously, exploiting the
market as much as possible; and of course other
firms soon offered strong competition. NICK
CARTER was one favorite character, not yet deceased; "Old Cap Collier" another. The more
sensational dime novels were close relatives of
the "penny dreadfuls" popular in England during this same period.

At the beginning only original stories were
printed, but the idea soon occurred to publishers
that they might also put out cheap reprints of
full-length novels, especially British novels unprotected by copyright. Even old-line houses
entered into the ensuing fray, usually at prices
above a dime. These cheap reprints died out
when a more durable type of book became available at fifty cents a copy.

An immediate predecessor of Beadle's shockers
was the fiction of EDWARD Z. C. JUDSON (1820–
86), who wrote western stories and plays, also
sea stories, under the pen name "Ned Buntline."
One of the earliest of his tales was *Magdalena,
the Beautiful Mexican Maid* (1847). Many

others, some of them authors either then or later of good literary reputation, wrote dime novels, often under one or more pen names, as is shown in Edmund Lester Pearson's chronicle, *Dime Novel* (1929). Irvin S. Cobb, remembering his boyhood, made *A Plea for Old Cap Collier* (1921). At the height of their vogue, the dime novels aroused moral outcries somewhat similar to those the comics evoked later. As F. L. Pattee points out: "That they were a moral menace is doubtful. Never did they condone wickedness. On the contrary, they were melodramatic in their contention that crime and villainy always are punished."

Collecting dime novels has become a popular specialty in the United States. Two notable fanciers were Dr. Frank P. O'Brien, whose immense Beadle Collection of Dime Novels is now in the New York Public Library and is described in one of its Bulletins (1922), and Charles Bragin, who gathered more than twenty thousand varieties of these publications (described in *The Saturday Evening Post*, Aug. 3, 1946). Bragin says that most "dime novels" really sold for a nickel. The authors occasionally received considerable sums for their pieces, but were usually paid $75 a story, he reported. Bragin founded a Dime Novel Club, which issued numerous facsimile reprints of old thrillers. Albert Johannsen wrote *The House of Beadle and Adams* (2 v., 1950), Arthur Guiterman *A Ballade of Dime Novels*.

Dimmesdale, Arthur. The minister in Nathaniel Hawthorne's THE SCARLET LETTER (1850) who is the unrevealed father of Hester Prynne's illegitimate child. His sense of guilt leads to his confession and death in public.

Dinner at Eight (1932), a play by GEORGE S. KAUFMAN and EDNA FERBER. Millicent Jordan plans a dinner party for the Ferncliffes, socially prominent Britishers visiting the United States. Each guest faces a crisis in the interval between the invitation and the dinner; their lives for the time being are entangled. The guests of honor are unable to come, but the dinner proceeds with a substitute couple. Edmund Gagey holds that the authors "took delight in presenting the sordid, undercover background of a fashionable dinner party to which are invited a remarkably unpleasant set of guests."

Dinsmore, Elsie. A character in twenty-eight novels by MARTHA FINLEY (1828–1909). She began publishing the Elsie stories in 1867, continued until 1905. They were the most popular children's books of their day. In the course of the series Elsie grows up, marries her father's friend, and finally becomes a grandmother—shedding an incredible quantity of tears on the way. To present-day adults Elsie seems "a nauseous little prig"; children suddenly stopped reading her around 1900.

Dionysus in Doubt (1925), title poem of a collection by EDWIN ARLINGTON ROBINSON, which also includes DEMOS AND DIONYSUS. The poem is another expression of the poet's fear and doubt of modern political developments, as set forth in a conversation with the Greek god.

He denounces the hope of an "ultimate uniformity," which some will call "freedom and efficiency," whereas others will "rather call it hell."

Diplomat in Carpet Slippers (1945), by JAY MONAGHAN. The theme of this lively volume is Lincoln's handling of foreign affairs, with treatment of some episodes not generally known. The personalities are dramatically sketched, and more credit than usual is given to Lincoln's acumen in international dealings.

Disappointment, The, or, The Force of Credulity (1767), a play by Col. Thomas Forrest ("Andrew Barton"). This satire came close to being the first play produced professionally in an American theater. It satirized the contemporary mania for seeking pirate treasure and made personal references to some residents of Philadelphia. As a result it was withdrawn from production, and *The Prince of Parthia* was played instead (April 24, 1767).

Discourses in America. Three lectures delivered by MATTHEW ARNOLD on his tour of the United States in 1883 and published in 1885.

discovery. A magazine in paperback form that appeared in 1953 after the success of NEW WORLD WRITING had demonstrated the feasibility of publishing a paperback literary periodical aimed at a large audience. The magazine concentrated on American writing, mostly fiction and poetry, with a few essays. The first number, edited by John W. Aldrich and Vance Bourjaily, contained work by Hortense Calisher, Chandler Brossard, Kenneth Fearing, William Styron, Norman Mailer, and Herbert Gold, in addition to fiction and poetry by previously unknown writers. The quality of the writing was high, but never obscure or tortured. William Styron's novella, *The Long March*, printed in the first issue, has since come to be regarded as a small classic. Unfortunately only six issues in all were to appear—the last in July 1955. Originally intended as a literary magazine, *discovery* became "a sort of continuing anthology of new writing." Though not a financial success, the magazine had a steady readership of 150,000, and could boast of having published some of the best young American authors of the fifties. The second issue contained a manifesto by Bourjaily (by then the sole editor) called "No More Apologies—A Critical Note." He contrasted the work of his contemporaries with that being produced by the older giants of American writing: Dos Passos, Hemingway, Faulkner. He named the new writers who, though they had not "yet produced as fine an individual work as the very best of what the older men have done . . . yet . . . the promise of masterpieces may be seen in them." These were Norman Mailer, J. D. Salinger, John Horne Burns, Carson McCullers, William Styron, Hortense Calisher, Nelson Algren, and Calder Willingham—he might have added himself.

Discovery of Europe: The Story of American Experience in the Old World (1947), an anthology edited by PHILIP RAHV. Rahv ranges from 1772 to 1939 in this discriminating gathering of significant passages. Included are Franklin, John and Abigail Adams, Jefferson, Ticknor, Irving, Cooper, Melville, Emerson, Hawthorne, Howells, Mark Twain, Henry James, Walter Hines Page, Lincoln Steffens, Gertrude Stein, Edmund Wilson, Henry Miller, and others.

Disenchanted, The (1950), a novel by BUDD SCHULBERG. The central character is Manley Halliday, a famous novelist of the 1920's, who is obviously intended as a portrait of F. SCOTT FITZGERALD. In the early 1930's Schulberg had met Fitzgerald in Hollywood; at another time he and Fitzgerald had spent a weekend at Dartmouth to gather data for a college story that the novelist was writing for the movies. Schulberg himself feels that at least fifty per cent of *The Disenchanted* is true. It is melodrama close to tragedy, like Fitzgerald's own life. The book was dramatized in 1958, and the role of Halliday was played by Jason Robards, Jr.

Disinherited, The. A historical novel in four sections by HERVEY ALLEN. It describes pre-Revolutionary days in a varied series of episodes and with a cast of many characters. The parts of the novel include *The Forest and the Fort* (1943), *Bedford Forest* (1944), *Toward the Morning* (1948). These, along with an unfinished sequel, were published as an omnibus volume, *The City in the Dawn* (1950), after Allen's death. John K. Hutchens speaks of the third section as "a quasi-novel that could be subtitled 'Scenes from Pre-Revolutionary War Life in Pennsylvania.' What people ate and drank, how they brushed their teeth and traveled. The lurking terror of Indian attack. Allen does this kind of thing extremely well."

Dismal Swamp, The. A marsh approximately thirty by ten miles, extending from Norfolk, Va., south into North Carolina. It is now partially reclaimed. Here DRED, the runaway slave who is the chief character in Harriet Beecher Stowe's novel by that name (1856), lived. Longfellow wrote *The Slave in the Dismal Swamp* (1842).

Disney, Walt[er Elias] (b. Chicago, Dec. 5, 1901—   ), cartoonist, producer of animated sound cartoons, pictures combining cartoons and live actors, and natural history films. Disney's extraordinary career began with his production of the *Alice Comedies* (a mingling of a live girl with animated cartoons) in 1923-26. Then he went on to *Oswald, the Rabbit* (1926-28), finally to the continuous and immensely popular MICKEY MOUSE and *Silly Symphony* series (since 1928). Mickey Mouse and Donald Duck (who made his first appearance in 1934) have become characters known all over the world. Two of Disney's most famous short cartoons are *The Three Little Pigs* (1933) and *Ferdinand the Bull* (1939). In 1938 he dared to produce the first feature-length cartoon, *Snow White and the Seven Dwarfs,* despite skeptical warnings of failure; it promptly broke attendance records throughout the country. Other full-length cartoons include *Pinocchio* (1940); *Fantasia* (with Deems Taylor, a cartoon interpretation of classical music, 1940); *Bambi* (1942); *Dumbo* (1941); *Alice in Wonderland* (1951); *The Lady and the Tramp* (1955); *The Sleeping Beauty*

(1959). Disney has also produced live film versions of classic children's books, such as *Treasure Island* (1950) and *Swiss Family Robinson* (1961). One of his most interesting experiments has been the production of full-length color films of animal life in various parts of the world: *Beaver Valley* (1950); *Water Birds* (1952); *The Living Desert* (1953); *The Vanishing Prairie* (1954); and others. Thomas Craven has eulogized Disney as a skilled craftsman who "developed by infinite trial and error the universal medium for the creation of humor." Much Disney material is available in books for children.

Dissertation on the Canon and Feudal Law, A (published anonymously and without title in the Boston *Gazette*, August, 1765; reprinted in the London *Chronicle*, then in revised form as a pamphlet, 1768), four essays by JOHN ADAMS [2]. The title seems to be a purposely misleading one; the essays deal mainly with the historical struggle between corporate aggression and individual liberty, with the Stamp Act as an illustration. Though his discussion of "the inherent rights of mankind" is philosophical as well as political, the essays were instrumental in bringing about the repeal of the Stamp Act and establishing Adams' reputation as a patriot.

dissertations, doctoral. Thousands of dissertations are produced annually at American universities, written "in partial fulfillment of the requirements for the doctor's degree." Some reach book form, others are abstracted in several printed pages, with typed or microfilmed copies of the complete dissertation placed in the university library and elsewhere. They are generally formal expositions and arguments intended to solve some specific problem of research, usually minute. Often dissertations treat the obvious with elaborate pedantry; Abraham Flexner brings this up in his *Universities: American, English, German* (1930). Some dissertations, however, offer valuable assistance to the understanding of the topic treated, and a number (*e.g.,* Lionel Trilling's *Matthew Arnold,* 1939) have proved definitive in their fields. As an aid to research, the Library of Congress published a *List of Doctoral Dissertations* (1915 and later); universities have lists of their own students' dissertations. The H. W. Wilson Co. also issued compilations of *Doctoral Dissertations Accepted by American Universities*—in recent years the titles have numbered several thousand annually. Those of special interest to students of American literature appear in annual lists compiled by Professor Lewis Leary and others for *American Literature. Dissertation Abstracts* (originally *Microfilm Abstracts*) is published at Ann Arbor, Mich. Beginning on a small scale in 1938, it now appears in monthly issues which, bound, make three thick volumes annually.

Ditmars, Raymond L[ee] (b. Newark, N.J., June 20, 1876—d. May 12, 1942), naturalist, author. An eminent zoologist who became Curator of Reptiles for the New York Zoological Society in 1899 and was placed in charge of the Departments of Mammals in 1910, Ditmars was also a lively writer on subjects connected with his specialties. Among his books: *The Reptile Book* (1907); *Strange Animals I Have Known* (1931); *Confessions of a Scientist* (1934); *The Fight to Live* (1938).

Diverting History of John Bull and Brother Jonathan, The (1812), a satire by "Hector Bullus" (JAMES KIRKE PAULDING). An attack on England and the British. Bullock island represents England and Jonathan's thirteen farms represent the American colonies. The story tells of the settling of the farms and of the revolt against England. The book is violently anti-British in tone; Paulding, whose family had been forced to leave their home by Tory threats, hated the British vehemently and resented their slurs on the new nation. This was one of several books expressing his Anglophobia.

Divine Tragedy, The (1871), a play by HENRY WADSWORTH LONGFELLOW. See BIBLE IN THE UNITED STATES; CHRISTUS.

Divinity School Address, The (July 15, 1838), a lecture by RALPH WALDO EMERSON. It was delivered before the graduates of Divinity College, Cambridge, and resulted in a widespread controversy. Emerson himself called the controversy "a storm in our washbowl," H. S. Commager described it as "a tempest in a Boston tea-cup," while to V. L. Parrington the address seemed to be "the bible of transcendental religion." Historical Christianity was condemned because "it is not the doctrine of the soul, but an exaggeration of the personal, the positive, the ritual." As Paul Elmer More expressed it, Emerson "suavely displaced" the person of Jesus for "the chorus of thoughts and hopes" in any human soul. Emerson said, "If a man is at heart just, then in so far is he God."

Dix, Beulah Marie (b. Kingston, Mass., Dec. 25, 1876—   ), novelist, playwright, author of juveniles, screenwriter. A prolific and expert writer, Miss Dix was best known for her stories *Hugh Gwyeth* (1899); *Soldier Rigdale* (1899); *A Little Captive Lad* (1902); *Merrylips* (1906); *Alison's Lad* (1910); *Fighting Blade* (1912); *Pity of God* (1932).

Dix, Dorothy. See ELIZABETH MERIWETHER GILMER.

Dixie. A song, originally titled "I Wish I Was in Dixie's Land." Composed in 1859 by minstrel DANIEL DECATUR EMMETT (1815–1904), it was sung that year in Bryant's Minstrel Show and published the following year; it became an immediate hit, especially in the South. The lines have been somewhat modified from the original version; the last line, for example, "In Dixie's land we'll took our stand," has become, "In Dixie land I'll take my stand." Confederate soldiers sang the words with enthusiasm, but Fanny Crosby wrote a Northern version of the text in 1861, "Dixie for the Union." The Southern version was used against Lincoln in the 1860 campaign, but when he was serenaded at the White House a few days before his assassination, he closed his speech to the serenaders by saying, "I see you have a band with you. I should like to hear it play 'Dixie.' I

have consulted the Attorney General, who is here by my side, and he is of the opinion that 'Dixie' belongs to us. Now play it."

The origin of the word *Dixie* is obscure. It has been suggested that it has some connection with the Mason and Dixon Line. Others claim that a Louisiana bank, printing its pre-Civil War bills in French with a big "DIX" (ten) in the middle of the ten dollar notes, made the South the land of the "dixies." Yet another derivation is from the name of a slaveholder on Manhattan Island in the late eighteenth century; so benevolent was he that when his slaves were moved down south, they pined for "Dixie's land" up north, which became the name for a nostalgic paradise of the good life. Then, after fifty years of referring to the North, this paradise took up residence in the South along with the slaves.

Dixon, Thomas (b. Shelby, N.C., Jan. 11, 1864—d. April 3, 1946), Baptist clergyman, lawyer, legislator, novelist, dramatist. An unreconstructed southerner, Dixon in *The Clansman* (1905) wrote a novel which became the first million-dollar movie, *The Birth of a Nation* (1914), and which is said to have led to the revival, in a degenerate form, of the KU KLUX KLAN. Dixon himself was devoted to upholding "racial purity." He wrote other novels, some exceedingly popular, and also several plays and motion pictures. Calling himself a "reactionary individualist," Dixon strongly opposed Communism, and also the New Deal, although he was a Democrat. See THE LEOPARD'S SPOTS.

Doane, George Washington (b. Trenton, N.J., May 27, 1799—d. April 27, 1859), Episcopal bishop, hymn writer. Among Bishop Doane's best hymns were *Thou Art the Way, to Thee Alone* and *Softly Now the Light of Day*. William C. Doane prepared *The Life and Writings of G. W. Doane* (4 v., 1860–61).

Dobie, Charles Caldwell (b. San Francisco, March 15, 1881—d. Jan. 13, 1943), novelist, short-story writer, playwright. Dobie was an inveterate lover of his native city, which is the scene of many of his books, whether fact or fiction. Among them: *San Francisco: A Pageant* (1933); *San Francisco Tales* (1935); *San Francisco's Chinatown* (1936); *San Francisco Adventures* (1937).

Dobie, J[ames] Frank (b. Live Oak Co., Texas, Sept. 26, 1888—d. Sept. 18, 1964), historian, folklorist. After managing a 200,000-acre ranch (1920–21), Dobie taught in various universities, mainly the University of Texas. An editorial in the New York *Herald Tribune* (1944) described Dobie as "hardly the conventional type of teacher. He has a very slow drawl, he usually wears a big hat, he has no 'side,' and he seems to find more spiritual satisfaction in talking with an old Mexican in the Sierra Madres or a busted cowpuncher in Wyoming than in passing the time of day with the brainiest academician." Cambridge University gave him an honorary M.A. degree, with this citation, "De bobus longicornibus quod ille non cognovit, inutile est aliis cognoscere," rendered by the *Herald Tribune* thus: "What the gentleman doesn't know about longhorn cattle isn't worth knowing." A visiting professor at the English university, Dobie reported his observations genially and acutely in *A Texan in England* (1945). *Time* calls him "the Southwest's most raucously successful cultural historian." Among his books: *Coronado's Children* (1931); *Tales of the Mustangs* (1936); *The Flavor of Texas* (1936); *Apache Gold and Yaqui Silver* (1939); *Guide to Life and Literature in the Southwest* (1943, rev. and enlarged, 1952); *The Voice of the Coyote* (1949); *The Mustangs* (1952); *Tales of Old-Time Texas* (1955); *I'll Tell You a Tale* (1960).

doctoral dissertations. See DISSERTATIONS.

Doctor Grimshawe's Secret (1882), a novel by NATHANIEL HAWTHORNE. It was left unfinished at his death and edited by his son Julian. It is called by Willard Thorp "an abortive romance" and joined with *The Ancestral Footstep* as two attempts by Hawthorne to express the feelings of an American returning to his homeland. The treatment was suggested by his own experiences while serving as consul at Liverpool (1853–57). *Doctor Grimshawe's Secret* tells of an American and his sister who, separated for years, find themselves at their ancestral home, which had been abandoned by their forefather in the days of Cromwell and to which the American is still the heir. The tale is obviously meant to be symbolic.

Doctor Heidegger's Experiment (*Salem Gazette*, March, 1837; in *Twice-Told Tales*, 1837), a story by NATHANIEL HAWTHORNE. The story is a version of the "fountain of youth" theme, perhaps with echoes from Jonathan Swift. Three elderly men and an aged widow agree to drink a magic potion that a medical friend of theirs has prepared. They are restored to youth, and the three men, in wooing the widow whose beauty has been regained, display all the foolishness they had shown when young. Then their youth fades again, but they have learned nothing from the experiment and resolve to go to Florida to look for the Fountain of Youth.

Doctor Sevier (1882), a novel by GEORGE W. CABLE. This is one of Cable's New Orleans stories. It is less about Dr. Sevier, a kindly and laconic physician, than about his young protégé, John Richling, and the development of his character. The corruption of New Orleans in the era before the Civil War is attacked. Alexander Cowie calls *Doctor Sevier* "probably Cable's best novel after THE GRANDISSIMES. . . . The novel as a whole is untidy, but it contains vast stores of social commentary—on life and letters, politics, and commerce."

documentary. A dramatic presentation, on the air or on a screen, of factual material. Documentaries present such subjects as the impoverishment of lands by drought and flood, city planning, social hygiene, a sculptor at work, the plight of an Indian tribe. Robert Flaherty (1884–1951) is credited with being "the father of the documentary," although the word was only later attached to his superb film *Nanook of the North* (1920), which led the way toward this new type of production. Such documentaries do not depend on plot in any highly dramatic sense; their reliance is rather on first-rate photography directed with intelligence and honesty and with insight into some vital problem or great event of history or into the character of a great personality. Flaherty's influence was greater in Europe than in the United States, but he gave a great impetus to American noncommercial films and also affected the procedures in some commercial productions—*Trader Horn* (1931) and *The Citadel* (1938), for example. The greatest of Flaherty's followers was PARE LORENTZ (1905–   ), with his *Plough That Broke the Plains* (1936) and *The River* (1938). A long-lived and impressive series of documentaries appeared month by month as *The March of Time* (beginning 1934). Iris Barry discussed *The Documentary Film, 1922–45* (Museum of Modern Art publication, 1945), listing films from *In Seville*, produced by Pathé Frères in 1909, to *To the Shores of Iwo Jima*, produced for the government by Warner Brothers. Raymond Spottiswoode wrote *Film and Its Techniques* (1951) about documentaries.

Dodd, William E[dward] (b. Clayton, N.C., Oct. 21, 1869—d. Feb. 9, 1940), teacher, historian, editor, ambassador. Dodd, a specialist in American history, wrote important volumes in that field: *Jefferson Davis* (1907); *Statesmen of the Old South* (1911); *Expansion and Conflict* (1915); *Lincoln or Lee* (1928); *The Old South* (1937). He turned to contemporary issues in *Woodrow Wilson and His Work* (1920); and he was appointed by President F. D. Roosevelt as Ambassador to Germany (1933–37). He wrote about his experiences, especially his reaction to Nazism, in his journals published as *Ambassador Dodd's Diary 1933–38* (1941).

Dodge, Mary [Elizabeth] Mapes (b. New York City, Jan. 26, 1831—d. Aug. 21, 1905), editor, author of children's books. Mrs. Dodge's fame rests on two achievements: a perennially popular children's classic, HANS BRINKER, OR, THE SILVER SKATES (1865); and her editorship of the children's magazine ST. NICHOLAS (1873–1905). The story was translated into many languages and was honored by the French Academy. To the magazine she attracted most of the noted writers of the day (including Kipling and Mark Twain), and made her name and the magazine's name household words. She wrote other books besides *Hans Brinker*, such as *Donald and Dorothy* (1883), but none attained the great fame of that story.

Dodsworth (1929), a novel by SINCLAIR LEWIS. Dodsworth, a "captain of industry" from Babbitt's metropolis of Zenith, is persuaded by his frivolous wife Fran to make a tour of Europe. She has several love affairs, and at last breaks off with Dodsworth. He in turn, after months of loneliness, falls in love with the widowed Mrs. Cortright, who persuades him to take a more social view of industry and inspires him with plans to build a truly American suburb in Zenith. Fran is cast off by her lover's family, and she induces Dodsworth to take her back home. But their reconciliation comes too late. There is a decided difference between Babbitt and Dodsworth, but the book, as Leo Gurko points out, "did little to disturb the faith of most Americans in things as they were, and served to introduce the Lewis who in the 30's, was to descend fretfully into weak apologetics for the very Main Streets he had once so aggressively denounced." Yet Lewis' contrasting pictures of American and European civilization exhibit him, as Philip Rahv points out, as "making full use of his gift for reproducing national patterns of behavior with wonderful accuracy and efficiency." The playwright Sidney Howard made a strong play out of the novel (1934), and the play was successfully transferred to the screen (1936).

Doesticks, Q. K. See MORTIMER THOMSON.

Doesticks, What He Says (1855), comic sketches of New York society by MORTIMER THOMSON. They appeared in the New York *Tribune* and were marked, says James R. Aswell, by "a sprightly debunking impudence."

Dogood Papers, The (*New England Courant*, April–Oct., 1722), essays by BENJAMIN FRANKLIN. Franklin was only sixteen when he began contributing these essays (signed "Silence Dogood") to his brother James' newspaper. He was under two strong influences: COTTON MATHER (who had written *Essays to Do Good*, 1710) and Addison and Steele's *Spectator Papers* (1711–12). It was not until 1864 that James Parton, in his biography of Franklin, revealed that the papers had been written by him. His chief character is a woman with cheerful common sense who expresses the views of the poor and lowly, is not always elegant in her speech, and is fond of homely sayings and proverbs. Already one may catch the atmosphere of the coming Revolution, as when Franklin writes: "Without freedom of thought there can be no such thing as wisdom; and no such thing as liberty without freedom of speech."

Dole, Nathan Haskell (b. Chelsea, Mass., Aug. 31, 1852—d. May 9, 1935), teacher, newspaperman, novelist, translator, critic, editor. Dole taught school in Massachusetts, worked on newspapers in several parts of the country, was an editor at the Thomas Y. Crowell Company, admired Omar Kháyyám and wrote a novel about him, *Omar the Tent-Maker* (1899). He edited anthologies and the 10th edition of Bartlett's *Familiar Quotations*, and translated competently from Russian, Spanish, Italian, and French texts.

Dolittle, Doctor. In 1920 Hugh Lofting, Anglo-American writer, published *The Story of Dr. Dolittle*, and thereafter his juvenile admirers kept him busy writing further accounts of the eccentric country doctor whose love for animals leads him to learn their languages and devote himself to taking care of them rather than human beings. Originally the story was sent home from the front in World War I in letters to Lofting's children, with illustrations; it was Mrs. Lofting who suggested putting them into book form. Among the sequels: *The Voyages of Dr. Dolittle* (1922, awarded Newbery Prize); *Dr.*

Dolittle's Garden (1927); *Dr. Dolittle's Return* (1933).

Dolliver Romance, The, a fragment by NATHANIEL HAWTHORNE. This romance was originally scheduled to be published in serial form, starting with the January, 1864, issue of *The Atlantic Monthly*. It was the first time that Hawthorne attempted serial publication; but, due to his increasing illness, the scheme was never carried out. Two chapters of the three-chapter manuscript were finally published posthumously in the magazine, and the entire manuscript appeared in 1876.

The theme of the fragment is the elixir of life and its promise of immortality. What exists of the plot concerns the attempts of Dr. Dolliver to create an elixir of life, not for selfish reasons, but that he might live to take care of his granddaughter Pansie. What little appears of Pansie in the fragment indicates the development of another of the author's fascinating young girls, such as Pearl in THE SCARLET LETTER, and Phoebe in THE HOUSE OF THE SEVEN GABLES.

The story develops the contrast between Dr. Dolliver's selflessness and Colonel Dabney's demands for the elixir; Dabney dies of an overdose, and Hawthorne is ambiguous as to whether the Colonel did restore his youth before he died.

What exists of the manuscript can only hint at what Hawthorne might have made of it. The romance exhibits no new themes, but contains the sketches of characters who might have become fully realized in Hawthorne's imagination.

Domain of Arnheim, The (published in the *Columbian Magazine*, March, 1847), a story by EDGAR ALLAN POE. This was an expansion of *The Landscape Garden* (*Ladies' Companion*, October, 1842), and is allied in theme to LANDOR'S COTTAGE (*Flag of Our Union*, June 9, 1849). Poe describes how Ellison, who has become fabulously wealthy, is able to indulge his ideas of landscape gardening and architecture on a vast scale. *Landscape Garden* gave Ellison's plans; *The Domain of Arnheim* tells how he carried them out. In a letter to Sarah Helen Whitman, Oct. 18, 1848, Poe said that *The Domain of Arnheim* "expresses *much of my soul.*"

Domestic Manners of the Americans, The (1832). See FRANCES TROLLOPE.

Donatello, Count. A character in Hawthorne's THE MARBLE FAUN (1860). He is the Italian admirer of Miriam, and he bears a resemblance to the Faun of Praxiteles; Hawthorne leaves unsettled whether his ears, if his concealing locks should be lifted, would be revealed human or animal. He is depicted as amoral, a human being corresponding to Adam before the fall, not knowing sin or suffering.

Donn-Byrne, Brian Oswald (b. Brooklyn, N.Y., Nov. 20, 1889—d. June 18, 1928), novelist, short-story writer, poet. Donn-Byrne went to Ireland, his parents' native land, at an early age; returned to New York City in 1911 to marry, make a living as an editor, and begin his literary career under the name Donn Byrne; then went back to Ireland to live. He despised the United States and did his best to conceal the fact that he had been born in Brooklyn and not Ireland; some critics regarded him as a synthetic Irishman. As a newspaperman he had the dubious distinction of being discharged from the New York *Sun* for writing "poor English." Obviously his elegant style, as it developed in his masterpiece, MESSER MARCO POLO (1921) and later books, was not such as a city editor would welcome. Among the best of his books, aside from *Messer Marco Polo*, was BLIND RAFTERY (1924); he also wrote many short stories of distinction, collected in *The Changeling* (1923); *Rivers of Damascus* (1931); *The Woman of the Shee* (1932). Throughout his writings he expressed a creed of romantic search for beauty and devotion to chivalric ideals. Winthrop Wetherbee, Jr., prepared *Donn-Byrne: A Bibliography* (1950).

Donnelly, Ignatius (b. Philadelphia, Nov. 3, 1831—d. Jan. 1, 1901), orator, public official, editor, novelist, historian. Donnelly (called "The Great Apostle of Protest") first became a lawyer, then migrated West to found an "ideal community" called Nininger City in Minnesota. To help build the town, Donnelly began to publish *The Emigrant Aid Journal*, "unquestionably the most intellectual periodical ever issued in the interests of real-estate promotion," says Stewart H. Holbrook. Literary and musical societies were formed, and all seemed to be going well, when the panic of 1857 hit the country and Nininger City collapsed. Donnelly blamed "the bankers," and ever afterward inveighed furiously against them. He was elected to some state offices and to the House of Representatives where he became says Holbrook, "perhaps the most erudite man ever to sit in Congress." He was a great orator and used his powers as a speaker in debates over the conduct of the Civil War.

In 1882 appeared his most popular book: ATLANTIS: THE ANTEDILUVIAN WORLD (reprinted, in an edition prepared by Egerton Sykes, 1949), a serious attempt to prove that the world's original civilization had been developed on the lost continent that Plato had first mentioned. *Ragnarok* (1883) explains certain geological facts as due to the earth's contact with a great comet ages ago. The novel *Caesar's Column* (1891) resembles Bellamy's *Looking Backward* (1888); it foretells many political changes, also inventions made actual since his time. In the meantime Donnelly helped form the National People's Party (the "Populists"), which by 1892 had become a great force in the country. Its ideas for reforming political, economic, and social conditions were mainly Donnelly's, and in 1900 he was the Vice-Presidential candidate of his party.

Donnelly later became a fanatic devotee of DELIA BACON's theory that Francis Bacon had written the plays of Shakespeare. In a tome called *The Great Cryptogram* (1888) and again in *The Cypher in the Plays and on the Tombstone* (1899) Donnelly sought to establish the truth of this theory by unraveling a cypher, supposedly devised by Bacon, to be found in the plays and elsewhere. Never a man to do anything by halves, Donnelly gave "proof" that Bacon had likewise written Marlowe's plays, Montaigne's essays, and Burton's *Anatomy of Melancholy*.

Donner Party, The. A group of immigrants, including the Donner family from Sangamon Co., Ill., camped at a lake in the Sierra Nevada Mountains while on their way to California in October, 1846. Then early and heavy snow blocked the passes, and they were obliged to remain where they were all winter. Of eighty-seven persons caught in the winter trap, only forty-seven survived—partly by practicing cannibalism. They were finally rescued by settlers from California. George Stewart in *Ordeal by Hunger* (1936) and Homer Croy in *Wheels West* (1955) have told the story of the Donner party. The episode is part of the plot in Bret Harte's GABRIEL CONROY (1876) and in Norah Lofts' *Winter Harvest* (1955).

Dooley, Mr. The hero of FINLEY PETER DUNNE's famous sketches. He is described as "the traveler, archaeologist, historian, social observer, saloonkeeper, economist, and philosopher, who has not been out of the ward for 25 years but twice." See HENNESSY.

Doolittle, Hilda ["H. D."] (b. Bethlehem, Pa., Sept. 10, 1886—d. Sept. 27, 1961), poet, translator, novelist. Educated in the United States, Miss Doolittle went to Europe in 1911 and became acquainted with poets associated with IMAGISM. In 1913 she married the English poet Richard Aldington and thereafter lived abroad. Her earliest volume, *Sea Garden* (1916), was followed by *Hymen* (1921); *Heliodora and Other Poems* (1924); *Collected Poems* (1925 and 1940); *Hippolytus Temporizes* (1927), a verse tragedy; and *The Flowering of the Rod* (1946). Much of her early verse was published in *Poetry*, where she was one of the leaders of the Imagist school. Of all the Imagists she carried forward the method most fruitfully in her later work, combining the sharpness and clarity of Imagist technique with a profound symbolism often modeled on themes from classical antiquity. She translated the *Ion* of Euripides (1937). *By Avon River* (1949) was an essay on Shakespeare and other Elizabethans. In her fiction she dealt usually with historical themes, writing with great precision and delicacy, as in *Palimpsest* (1926); *Hedylus* (1928); and *Bid Me to Live* (1960), set during World War I, sketching many leading literary figures of the day. A book-length poem, *Helen in Egypt*, appeared posthumously in 1961, with an introduction by Horace Gregory.

Dorsey, George A[mos] (b. Hebron, Ohio, Feb. 6, 1868—d. March 29, 1931), teacher, museum curator, anthropologist. Dorsey wrote books on the American Indian—*Traditions of* the Arikara (1904), *The Mythology of the Wichita* (1904), and *Pawnee Mythology* (1906) —that gave him a solid reputation among scholars. For popular consumption he wrote *Why We Behave Like Human Beings* (1925), which became a best seller, also *Man's Own Show: Civilization* (1931).

Dorson, Richard M. See JONATHAN DRAWS THE LONG BOW.

Dos Passos, John [Roderigo] (b. Chicago, Jan. 14, 1896—d. Sept. 28, 1970), novelist, poet, playwright, essayist. The grandson of a Portuguese immigrant, Dos Passos went to Choate and to Harvard, and when World War I

Sylvia Salmi

broke out graduated, as Alfred Kazin phrases it "into the most distinguished of all the lost generation's finishing schools, the Norton-Harjes Ambulance Service subsidized by a Morgan partner." The whole of his busy life as a writer reveals him as torn bitterly and tragically between two extremes: a deep individual fastidiousness and a highly sensitive, exacerbated social conscience. Kazin remarks that, like Emerson, "he likes Man, not men." Profoundly attached to liberty as the founders of America conceived it, he hates the mechanistic age that swallows up liberty and the men who are the tools of their own technology.

Dos Passos began with novels of World War I, particularly THREE SOLDIERS (1921), which, like much of his later work, evoked extreme praise and extreme blame. For a time he was a newspaper correspondent and magazine free-lance writer in Spain, Mexico, and the Near East; he was always an ardent traveler, in his own land and abroad. In 1922 he published *A Pushcart at the Curb* (verse). He came to maturity as a novelist with MANHATTAN TRANSFER (1925), called by John Chamberlain "a collective portrait of the huge sprawling organism of New York

City." In its technique it anticipates his later work, since here he seeks to give a picture of the whole by producing a long procession of merging human lives that represent the mass scene. Thereafter Dos Passos became more and more interested in the "little man," especially when he became involved in the SACCO-VANZETTI case. His plays were noted for their "movie" technique: THE GARBAGE MAN (produced as *The Moon is a Gong* (1926); AIRWAYS, INC. (1928); *Fortune Heights* (1933). They were collected in *Three Plays* (1934).

Then came the trilogy called *U.S.A.* (1938), comprising: THE 42ND PARALLEL (1930; see under THE FORTY-SECOND PARALLEL); *1919* (1932; see under NINETEEN-NINETEEN), and THE BIG MONEY (1936). *U.S.A.* was regarded by many critics as a massive achievement. It exemplifies the special technique that Dos Passos has often used to tell a story; a combination of narrative proper, the "Camera Eye," the "Biographies," and the "Newsreel." The story is not easy to follow. The huge diversity and dynamism of the details make an impression as bewildering as life itself. Often the passages turn into prose poems, usually expressive of the author's despair. A new series of novels in sequence began with *Adventures of a Young Man* (1939), the story of the disillusionment of a young American Communist in Spain, and continued with NUMBER ONE (1943), a mordant study of a southern politician believed to be Huey Long, and *The Grand Design* (1949), an unfavorable picture of the Roosevelt era. This trilogy later became a single volume *District of Columbia* (1952). THE GROUND WE STAND ON (1941) expresses Dos Passos' conception of American history. Two books of personal observation are *State of the Nation* (1944) and *Tour of Duty* (1946). Later books are: *The Prospect Before Us* (1950); *Chosen Country* (1951); *The Theme Is Freedom* (1956); *The Great Days* (1958); *Prospects of a Golden Age* (1959); *Midcentury* (1961).

Estimates of the work of Dos Passos vary widely. Joseph Warren Beach called him "an artist of bold originality, ingenuity, and dash." Alfred Kazin called him "first of the new naturalists." George Snell saw him producing "the first and still more artistic, long fiction based on broad social issues."

Double Agent, The (1935), a collection of twelve articles and reviews by RICHARD P. BLACKMUR. After defining the function of criticism as "to promote intimacy with particulars" and to evaluate achievement, Blackmur turns to a close reading of some difficult modern poets: Hart Crane, Wallace Stevens, Ezra Pound, Marianne Moore, and T. S. Eliot. From their poems, studied apart from biographical and social backgrounds, Blackmur derives general principles of poetic technique. At the same time he elucidates the principles of literary criticism itself. A poem is a "double agent," a content plus a form. The content and the form *together* comprise the poem's meaning.

Douglas, Lloyd C[assel] (b. Columbia City, Ind., Aug. 27, 1877—d. Feb. 13, 1951), Lutheran, later Congregational clergyman, novelist. After serving as a pastor for more than a quarter of a century, chiefly in university centers, Douglas turned to novel-writing and published his first story, *The Magnificent Obsession* (1929), when he was over fifty. It was a great success, and he went on to writing other novels, including *Precious Jeopardy* (1933); *Green Light* (1935); *White Banners* (1936); *Disputed Passage* (1939); THE ROBE (1942); and *The Big Fisherman* (1948). These made him one of the most widely read authors of all time. His tone is religious, but the preaching is generally not overly obtrusive; and Douglas does not neglect feminine interest. Ernest Sutherland Bates said: "Always there are the impossible characters and overnight conversions, the lucky accidents, and the endings of health, wealth, and happiness." One reviewer in THE ATLANTIC MONTHLY commented on the "flavor of spiritual fascism" in Douglas. But Leo Gurko traces Douglas' ancestry straight back to HAROLD BELL WRIGHT. His autobiography, *Time to Remember* (1951), was continued by his daughters, Betty Douglas Wilson and Virginia Douglas Dawson, in *The Shape of Sunday* (1952). In 1955 a collection of his sermons, *The Living Faith*, was published.

Douglas, Stephen A[rnold] (b. Brandon, Vt., April 23, 1813— d. June 3, 1861), lawyer, statesman, orator, public official. Douglas, one of the ablest men to enter American public life, served as judge, congressman, senator. His fame rests chiefly upon his famous debates with Lincoln (1858) in a senatorial contest, resulting in his re-election to the Senate; but Lincoln became a national figure and in 1860 defeated him for the Presidency. Douglas was as short as Lincoln was tall, and was admiringly called "the little Giant." When the call to arms came, he declared firmly for the Union, offered Lincoln his complete support, and shattered southern hopes of a divided North. Roger Butterfield says that Douglas "spoke for 'Go Ahead' Americans who wanted to forget about the slavery problem and continue expanding all over the western hemisphere."

Douglas, William O[rville] (b. Maine, Minn., Oct. 16, 1898—   ), teacher, lawyer, Supreme Court justice, author. Douglas began his distinguished career as a high-school teacher in Yakima, Wash. He then turned to law, was admitted to the bar in New York, practiced in New York City, and taught law at Columbia and Yale Universities. He went into government service in 1929, was named to the Supreme Court ten years later by President Roosevelt. Always an outdoor man and a lover of nature, he began exploring foreign regions, and on his return from several trips wrote three books that were both expert reports on political conditions abroad and vivid and accurate depictions of foreign scenes. He began with *Strange Lands and Friendly People* (1951), about the Middle East and India, and went on to *Beyond the High Himalayas* (1952) and *North from Malaya* (1953). He compiled *An Almanac of Liberty* (1954). Other books by Judge Douglas are: *Democracy and Finance* (1940), *Of Men and Mountains* (1950), *My Wilderness* (1960), *A Living Bill of Rights* (1961).

Douglass, Frederick (b. Tuckahoe, Md., Feb. [?], 1817—d. Feb. 20, 1895), newspaperman, orator, memoirist. Douglass, one of the most celebrated members of his race to appear in the United States, was the son of a Negro slave and a white father. As he grew up he had several masters but managed to escape to the North. His career began unexpectedly on Aug. 11, 1841, when he was invited to speak at an antislavery convention in Nantucket. His address made such an impression that he was soon in great demand at meetings and won national renown as an orator. Because of his views he was mobbed and beaten and then wrote an account of his experiences, *Narrative of the Life of Frederick Douglass* (1845), which had supporting documents from WILLIAM LLOYD GARRISON and WENDELL PHILLIPS. With the help of fees received from lectures in Great Britain he established at Rochester, N.Y., in 1847 a newspaper, *The North Star*, which was published for seventeen years. In 1855 he published a revised edition of his autobiography. He advocated in his newspaper industrial education for Negroes, women's suffrage, and the use of Negro troops in the Civil War. He held various public offices after the war. Two excellent fictionalized biographies deal with Douglass, Edmund Fuller's *A Star Pointed North* (1946) and Shirley Graham's *There Was Once a Slave* (1947).

Douglass, William (b. Scotland, 1691—d. 1752), physician, historian. Douglass studied medicine at Edinburgh, Leyden, and Paris, toured the West Indies, and then settled (1718) in Boston. He was a man of skeptical and experimental mind, with a turn for the literary; he loved to argue and attack. He composed a series of historical papers mingling his interests in medicine, economics, politics, and humanity in general. All these papers he combined in a two-volume work, *Summary, Historical and Political, of the British Settlements in America* (published in London, 1735). Part of the work was general in character, the rest was an analysis of the separate colonies. His specific purpose was the education of English officials on American affairs. He laid it down as a fundamental principle that since America had been settled by malcontents, fraudulent debtors, and convicts, it was essential to have strong royal control over popular legislatures.

Dowdey, Clifford [Shirley], Jr. (b. Richmond, Va., Jan. 23, 1904—   ), newspaperman, editor, novelist, historian. Dowdey wrote mainly historical novels when, after 1935, he gave up newspaper and editorial work. Among his notable performances are *Bugles Blow No More* (1937); *Gamble's Hundred* (1939); *Tidewater* (1943); *Where My Love Sleeps* (1945); *Weep for My Brother* (1950); *The Proud Retreat* (1953); *The Land They Fought For* (1955); *The Great Plantation* (1957); *Lee's Last Campaign* (1960). In *Experiment in Rebellion*

(1946) he turned to straight history, a human and lively account of the Civil War as localized in Richmond. The book pioneered a trend of narrative interpretive history.

down east. New England, especially Maine (and also Nova Scotia), is often described as "down east." The natives of "down east" are Yankees, and they made their way into literature at an early date, especially into American humor. Generally the "down-easter" was portrayed as a stupid and awkward character, speaking a nasal dialect all his own. See YANKEE IN AMERICAN LANGUAGE AND LITERATURE.

Down Easters, The (1833), a novel by JOHN NEAL. A melodramatic story in which two men are rivals for the hand of a widow. She elopes with one of them, but soon dies; her husband is revealed as having already been involved with another woman, who commits suicide. Tremaine McDowell comments that "in the opening pages Neal etched a striking series of Yankee portraits, then degenerated into bombast."

Downey, Fairfax [Davis] (b. Salt Lake City, Utah, Nov. 28, 1893—   ), newspaperman, editor, historian. Downey began his long series of amusing, well-informed accounts of the past with *A Comic History of Yale* (1924), went on to *When We Were Rather Older* (1926); *Richard Harding Davis—His Day* (1933); *Portrait of an Era, As Drawn by C. D. Gibson* (1936); an anthology, *Laughing Verse* (1946); *Our Lusty Forefathers* (1947); *Horses of Destiny* (1949); *The Shining Filly* (1954); *Sound of the Guns* (1956); *General Crook, Indian Fighter* (1957); *Clash of Cavalry* (1959); *Storming of the Gate* (1960).

Downing, Jack. Supposed author of satirical papers which began to appear in the Portland (Me.) *Courier* in 1830 and which turned in time to a criticism of Andrew Jackson and his policies. The original papers were composed by SEBA SMITH, but many imitators sprang up in various parts of the country who shamelessly used Jack Downing as a pen name. The best of them was CHARLES A. DAVIS. Smith always signed the papers "Major (or Captain) Jack Downing"; Davis signed his "J. Downing, Major."

Dragon Seed (1942), a novel by PEARL BUCK. An impressive tale of how the wisdom of the old is acquired through experience by the young. Old Ling Tan knows that as long as some have too much land and others too little, wars will continue. But his children have to learn this for themselves. They realize in the end that the great wisdom is to live out their lives on the land and hold it till the enemy has gone.

Drake, Daniel (b. near Plainfield, N.J., Oct. 20, 1785—d. Nov. 6, 1852), physician, teacher, scientist. At an early age Drake was taken by his family to the region that ultimately became Kentucky; in his professional life he was active both there and in Ohio, where he founded a medical college (1819). He also helped establish other educational institutions. His chief scientific writing was *Treatise on the Principal Diseases of the Interior Valley of North America*

(2 v., 1850–54). His entertaining letters were collected in a volume entitled *Pioneer Life in Kentucky* (1870), edited by his son (re-issued from the manuscript text, 1948, by E. F. Horine). He was called "the Benjamin Franklin of the West," and in his writings shows a deep interest in humanity (especially slaves) as well as in scientific matters.

Drake, Sir Francis (b. England c. 1540—d. Jan. 28, 1596?), explorer. Many of his exploits were connected with America. In 1567 he took part in an expedition to the Gulf of Mexico. Commissioned as a privateer in 1570, he made three expeditions (1570–72) to the West Indies, where he plundered Spanish ships and settlements and was the first Englishman to see the Pacific (1573). In 1577 he set sail to explore the Straits of Magellan, turned north along the coast of Chile and Peru, and reached the coast of California, which he named New Albion. Unable to return to the Atlantic, he circumnavigated the globe, the first Englishman to do so, returning to Plymouth in 1580. Later he again sailed to the West Indies and captured several important towns: on his return voyage he stopped at Jamestown and carried back the first colonists to England, also potatoes and tobacco. In 1585 he joined Sir John Hawkins in an unsuccessful expedition to the West Indies, in the course of which he died on board his ship at Portobello. His role in the defeat of the Spanish Armada (1588) was felt in America through the diminished strength of the Spanish Empire. His career is spiritedly set forth in Alfred Noyes' epic poem *Drake* (1908). He appears also in Charles Kingsley's *Westward Ho!* (1855), in Van Wyck Mason's *The Golden Admiral* (1953), and in C. V. Terry's *Buccaneer Surgeon* (1954). Drake's own accounts of his explorations are an important historical source, especially his *The World Encompassed by Sir Francis Drake* (London, 1628), which gives the first English account of California. Drake's role in the early development of the Pacific Coast is analyzed by Robert F. Heizer in *Francis Drake and the California Indians, 1579* (1947).

Drake, Joseph Rodman (b. New York City, Aug. 17, 1795—d. Sept. 21, 1820), poet, satirist. Drake's early death from tuberculosis prevented the full development of his powers as a poet, but his verses reveal his technical skill, his graceful fancy, and his genuine interest in the American scene. Like Keats, to whom he has often been compared, he studied medicine, but after obtaining a degree preferred to conduct a pharmacy, on Park Row, New York City. With his friend FITZ-GREENE HALLECK he composed the CROAKER PAPERS, clever skits on men and manners contributed (1819) to the New York *Evening Post*. THE CULPRIT FAY (posthumously published, 1835) was a story of a "fay" who loved a mortal maiden. The scene was the banks of the Hudson. Elsewhere he spoke of "my own romantic Bronx." His most famous poem is the sincere eulogy, THE AMERICAN FLAG. Halleck wrote a beautiful tribute *On the Death of Joseph Rodman Drake*, and a New York City park, where he lies buried, was named in his honor. See KNICKERBOCKER SCHOOL.

Drake, Temple, a character in SANCTUARY and REQUIEM FOR A NUN, by William Faulkner. A seventeen-year-old college student in SANCTUARY, Temple is a provocative and irresponsible girl who invites by her actions the rape she half fears and half desires. Playing the part of the victim, she subsequently allows herself to be kept at a brothel by POPEYE, and perjures herself at the murder trial of an innocent man, less out of malice toward the accused than out of indifference. In *Requiem for a Nun* she persists in her former attitudes by refusing, until the very end, to see herself as anything but the victim, a respectable woman wronged by circumstance.

drama in the U.S. American drama started with numerous disadvantages, the greatest being the unfavorable view of the stage held in the colonies north of Virginia. Although the Pilgrims landed in New England in 1620, more than a century passed before the English colonist started writing plays of even minor consequence. The theater, it is true, found some amateur support in the colleges, at Harvard, Yale, and William and Mary. At Harvard in 1690 there was apparently even a production of a historical play, GUSTAVUS VASA, by a young clergyman, the Reverend Benjamin Colman. In September, 1736, the students of William and Mary College presented a succession of British plays, including Joseph Addison's stilted "classic" tragedy *Cato* and George Farquhar's *The Recruiting Officer* and *The Beaux' Stratagem*. But the impetus to write drama of some length and substance depended upon the growth of interest in professional theater, first observable in Virginia and the Carolinas as a result of the arrival of the Hallams, a British acting company. At Williamsburg in September of 1752 they presented *The Merchant of Venice* and Jonson's *The Alchemist.* Leaving Virginia the following year, the company went to New York; they also performed later in Philadelphia and in Charleston, S.C. In 1763 the players, who by then were calling themselves the American Company, presented *The Prince of Parthia,* the first American play to receive a professional stage production.

The Prince of Parthia was written by THOMAS GODFREY (1736–1763), who had probably seen the American Company perform in Philadelphia. It was posthumously published by a friend in 1765, and was produced at the Southwark Theatre in Philadelphia on April 24, 1767; there appears to have been only one performance. A revival of this early work evidently did not take place until March of 1915, when it was staged at the University of Pennsylvania. As was likely to be the case with an 18th-century tragedy, it was written in blank verse, used soliloquies, and was made up of familiar romantic ingredients. A villainous Parthian prince misrepresents his elder brother to their royal father, whom he then proceeds to murder. After the unfilial son usurps the throne, he is overthrown by the virtuous elder brother, who

leads an army against him. But the victorious hero kills himself upon discovering that the maiden he loved (who was also desired by both his father and his brother . . .) poisoned herself on being led to believe that he had been slain in battle.

Although this first play produced in the colonies looked to the Old World for both style and theme, only three years later an American turned to a thoroughly American subject: Indian warfare. PONTEACH, OR THE SAVAGES OF AMERICA, was written by Major ROBERT ROGERS, an adventurer who had himself fought both Pontiac and the Cherokee. An undistinguished play in the blank verse then regarded as fitting for serious drama, it was published in London in 1766, but never performed.

The privately performed ANDROBOROS, written in 1714 by Robert Hunter, the governor of New York, is believed to be the first play written and printed in America. It was a political satire aimed at the governor's political opponents, including the leaders of Trinity Church in New York City. During the Revolutionary War both sides wrote satires against each other. Noteworthy was the satire on the royalists (called "a swarm of court sycophants, hungry harpies, and unprincipled danglers") in THE GROUP (1775), a burlesque written by General Warren's sharp-tongued wife, Mrs. Mercy Otis Warren, and printed a day before the Battle of Lexington. Mrs. Warren also badgered the British shortly after Bunker Hill with a dramatic exercise called *The Blockheads, or The Affrighted Officers.*

Comedy had been in vogue throughout the century, but it was not until the appearance of THE CONTRAST that American theater produced its first genuine comedy of manners. The second play by an American to receive professional production, *The Contrast* was a lively affair spiced, in the 18th-century manner, with some witty dialogue, vivid character sketches, and neat turns of plot. It opened at the famous John Street Theatre in New York on April 16, 1787. It was written by ROYALL TYLER (1757–1826), a Harvard College graduate who became aide-de-camp to General Benjamin Lincoln during the Revolutionary War and later attained distinction in the legal profession. In spite of some resemblance to Sheridan's *The School for Scandal,* Tyler's play is essentially American in spirit, owing to its author's partiality for the native virtues of honest dealing and unaffected conduct. Tyler also wrote a farce, *May Day in Town,* which was produced about a month after *The Contrast;* a third play, dealing with land speculation, *A Georgia Spec, or Land in the Moon,* was shown both in Boston and New York in 1797. Although Tyler wrote genial comedy in *The Contrast,* he included considerable social satire in his portrait of an Anglophile dandy, Dimple, who courts two coquettes simultaneously. Opposed to the foppish Dimple is the bluff and honest Colonel Manly, who is rewarded with the hand of the fair heroine Maria.

Manly's servant, Jonathan, is another home-spun character; his plain practicality made him the prototype of the popular country figure known as the "stage Yankee." (See YANKEE IN AMERICAN LANGUAGE AND LITERATURE.) An entire species of "Yankee" comedy came into vogue, with rustic characters bearing such names as Nathan Yank, in James Nelson Barker's comedy of manners *Tears and Smiles* (1807), a play that was suggested by *The Contrast*, and Jonathan Ploughboy in the otherwise conventional operatic play, THE FOREST ROSE, OR AMERICAN FARMERS, by Samuel Woodworth, first produced in New York in 1825. Similar Yankee characters, Lot Sap Sago and Deuteronomy Dutiful, appeared in C. A. Logan's *Yankee Land* (1834) and *The Vermont Wool Dealer* respectively, and Jebedia Homebred and SOLON SHINGLE in Joseph S. Jones' *The Green Mountain Boy* (1833) and *The People's Lawyer* (1839) respectively. The early American plays, however, were as undistinguished as they were imitative.

A rash of "Indian" plays glorifying "the noble savage," romantic in sentiment despite the native characters, did not materially alter the conventional course of playwriting. One Indian play, METAMORA, OR THE LAST OF THE WAMPANOAGS, by John Augustus Stone, did make an impression, and won a prize offered by the popular American actor EDWIN FORREST for the best play dealing with an American subject. Forrest played the noble chieftain betrayed by unscrupulous English colonists and toured in the play for years. A reaction against this type of drama began in 1846, but long before then numerous "Indian" plays, including a *Pocahontas* (1830) and a *Last of the Mohicans* (1831), had already demonstrated that no great advance toward *American* theater could be registered so long as the sentiment in the plays with native themes remained conventionally romantic.

A national style of theater, except for frontier theatricals, minstrel shows, and other nonliterary ventures, was simply not in accord with the strivings of a nation that looked abroad for cultivated art and literature. The young Walt Whitman could dream of a truly democratic American drama, but the plays written by Americans were steeped in a theater that was indeed "popular" but not significantly democratic. It reflected the main trends of the English and Continental European stage, the vogue of Shakespeare (sustained by star actors, native or British, who toured extensively), the popularity of historical drama, and the growth of melodrama. These tendencies, along with a diminishing taste for high comedy and a growing taste for farce, account for the character of the native plays. Even those that carried a social message or reflected American problems, such as Dion Boucicault's play about the Negro race problem, *The Octoroon* (1859), assumed the shape of melodrama.

American's first professional playwright, WILLIAM DUNLAP (1766–1839), became one of the most prolific adapters of German and French types of romantic comedy, drama, and melodrama, especially as developed by the popular German playwright Kotzebue. Dunlap adapted more than a dozen of the latter's plays, starting with *The Stranger,* produced in 1798. The Shakespearean influence appeared in Dunlap's Elizabethan domestic tragedy *Leicester* (1807), previously produced, in 1794, under the title of *The Fatal Deception*. His *André* (1774, revived in 1803 under the title of *The Glory of Columbia*), dealing with the ill-fated British spy Major André, was a historical play in turgid blank verse. Dunlap also wrote several lengthy volumes, including a famous *History of the American Theatre* (1832), the first American chronicle of the stage.

Among other early historical dramas SUPERSTITION, produced in Philadelphia in 1824, is worth noting for its attack on religious fanaticism and witch-hunting in New England. This otherwise undistinguished work, marred by stilted blank verse, antedated Hawthorne's famous story *The Gray Champion* by nearly a dozen years and dimly foreshadowed Arthur Miller's Salem witch-hunt tragedy, *The Crucible* (1953). The author of this period play was JAMES NELSON BARKER (1784–1858), mayor of Philadelphia in 1819 and comptroller of the United States Treasury during the last twenty years of his life. *Superstition* was the climax of his career as a writer for the stage, which began with his comedy of manners *Tears and Smiles,* performed in Philadelphia in 1807. Barker also wrote an opera, the first dramatic treatment of the Pocahontas story, entitled THE INDIAN PRINCESS, OR LA BELLE SAUVAGE, produced in Philadelphia in 1808. He turned Sir Walter Scott's famous narrative poem *Marmion* into a play in 1812.

ROBERT MONTGOMERY BIRD (1806–54) made a strong impression in the theater with THE GLADIATOR, a tragedy in verse about the revolt of the Roman gladiators led by Spartacus; Edwin Forrest produced the play in New York and Philadelphia in 1831. Another tragedy, ORALLOOSA, dealing with the conquest of Peru by the Spaniards, was successfully produced in 1832. Two years later he won even greater success with THE BROKER OF BOGOTA, first produced in New York in 1832 by Forrest, who appeared in the play from time to time for some thirty years. The play was a domestic tragedy noteworthy because Bird made the action revolve around middle-class characters.

Most successful among the early dramatists was JOHN HOWARD PAYNE (1791–1852), who had his first play, *Julia, or the Wanderer,* produced in 1806 at the Park Theatre, New York, when he was not quite fifteen years old. Payne was a versatile playwright, author of some sixty plays, many of them adapted from the English and French drama of his time. He succeeded with historical tragedy, such as BRUTUS (by his own admission compounded of seven earlier treatments of the subject), with historical comedy, such as *Charles the Second, or The Merry Mon-*

arch (both produced first in London, in 1818 and 1824 respectively), and especially with melodramas, such as *Therese, the Orphan of Geneva*. His *Clari, or the Maid of Milan*, first presented in 1823, brought him great popularity when its heroine's sentimental song, HOME, SWEET HOME, swept the country. Clari's song, set to a Sicilian air by Sir Henry Rowley Bishop, expressed longings for her rustic home which made her leave the Duke who was keeping her as his mistress. Payne had another great success with his domestic tragedy *Richelieu*, in which the famous French statesman seduced a merchant's wife; the play was first produced in London in 1829 under the title of *The French Libertine*. Although Payne's plays had little intrinsic merit, they made him a public figure on both sides of the Atlantic. He was in love with Shelley's wife, Mary Wollstonecraft, collaborated with Washington Irving on two plays (one of these was *Richelieu*), and counted among his English friends Coleridge, Charles Lamb, and the famous actor-manager Charles Kemble.

Romantic comedy, of which Payne's *Charles II* was representative, continued to be in favor with American playwrights during the first half of the 19th century. A popular work in this vein was TORTESA, THE USURER, a verse play by NATHANIEL PARKER WILLIS (1806–1867), who is best remembered as an editor who gave encouragement to Edgar Allan Poe and other American writers. In *Tortesa, the Usurer* Willis actually used a Florentine source, but there are echoes of *Romeo and Juliet* in this romantic play about a young woman who, after being married to a man she did not love, apparently died and was buried, but revived during the night and escaped with her lover.

Romantic tragedy attained some literary and dramatic distinction in FRANCESCA DA RIMINI, a play by GEORGE HENRY BOKER (1823–1890) based on the familiar medieval tragedy of love Dante recounted in the *Inferno*. Written in sturdy blank verse and possessing appealing characters, *Francesca da Rimini* is the outstanding example of literary drama in the 19th-century American theater. It was first presented at the Broadway Theatre, New York, on September 26, 1855, and revived twice with much success—once in Philadelphia in 1882 with the young OTIS SKINNER in the role of the ill-fated Paolo, who loves his brother's wife, and again during the winter season of 1901–02 at the Grand Opera House in Chicago, with Skinner this time playing the heroine's husband. *Francesca da Rimini* was the high point of Boker's literary career, which included *Calaynos*, a verse play about the conflict between Christians and Moors in Spain, successfully presented in London in 1849; *The Betrothal*, a comedy in verse that had flourishing productions both in New York and London in 1850 and 1853; and *Leonor de Guzman*, a romantic tragedy drawn from Spanish history, popular both in New York and Philadelphia in 1854.

Francesca da Rimini must be regarded as a terminal point in the development of one type of American drama, for there was no future for romantic tragedy in the American theater until some three-quarters of a century later, when Maxwell Anderson started writing successful verse plays with ELIZABETH THE QUEEN (1930). A richer prospect remained open for comedy of manners, successfully represented in 1845 with Mrs. Anna Cora Mowatt's FASHION, OR LIFE IN NEW YORK, which moved toward its conventional conclusion with satiric vivacity. Both Mrs. Tiffany, a newly rich society woman, and her daughter Seraphina become infatuated with a fortune-hunting impostor, Count Jolimaitre, who is ultimately exposed as a fraud. Seraphina is saved from an ill-advised elopement and her father is freed from blackmail by the latter's homespun friend Adam Trueman, who scorns pretense and is unimpressed by titled foreigners. Mrs. Mowatt (1819–1870) also had a successful career as an actress. Her experiences with the theater gave her the material for her famous *Autobiography of an Actress* (1854), as well as two works of fiction, *Mimetic Life* (1856) and *Twin Roses* (1857).

It was to be some time, however, before *Fashion* was to be equaled in quality or success by another American comedy. Melodrama ruled the theatrical world, although by 1850 its range began to widen to include problem plays, dramas of social tension, and, in time, even some rudimentary treatments of psychological conflict. A prolific and very successful playwright was the Irish-born dramatist and actor-manager DION BOUCICAULT (1820–1890), who came to the United States in 1853 and ground out a variety of plays, among which were adaptations from the French, dramatizations of novels by Dickens and Sir Walter Scott, comedies of Irish life (the most famous was *The Colleen Bawn* in 1860), and melodramas. He also contrived an extremely popular dramatization of Washington Irving's story RIP VAN WINKLE (1865), on which he collaborated with the popular stage star JOSEPH JEFFERSON, and one famous problem play, THE OCTOROON, OR LIFE IN LOUISIANA. Based on Mayne Reid's novel *The Quadroon* (1856), this suspense-laden melodrama created a sensation when it opened in New York at the Winter Garden on December 5, 1859; but for a play written shortly before the outbreak of the Civil War, *The Octoroon* was a singularly pacifying drama which placated the South with sympathetic portraits of the Southern gentry. It differed in this respect from another melodrama devoted to the race problem, UNCLE TOM'S CABIN (1853), George L. Aiken's dramatization of the Harriet Beecher Stowe novel which had been published serially in 1851–52. Designed to expose the evils of slavery, this play helped to whip up antislavery sentiment.

Melodrama in the United States, however, suffered a long decline in substance. It degenerated into undistinguished ten-twent'-thirt' thrillers even in the hands of such an efficient practitioner as OWEN DAVIS, who wrote some three hundred plays after his entry into the theater with *Through the Breakers* in 1898. In the latter half of the 19th century it seemed as if plays were more and more designed for spectacular stage effects, such as the scene in AUGUSTIN DALY's UNDER THE GASLIGHT (1867), the high point of which was the rescue of its unfortunate heroine from an oncoming locomotive. Daly (1838–1899), an important stage producer in New York, became known as a prolific adapter and playwright to whom over ninety plays were credited.

The succession of "melodramatists" whose sole object was to provide thrills and entertainment extended well into the 20th century and had some able practitioners indeed. Among these we may single out the popular actor, playwright, and producer GEORGE M. COHAN (1878–1942) for his *Seven Keys to Baldpate* (1913), in which a writer in search of solitude in a friend's house discovers that it has become a rendezvous for criminals, and BAYARD VEILLER (1871–1943), best known for his three melodramas, WITHIN THE LAW (1912), THE THIRTEENTH CHAIR (1917), and *The Trial of Mary Dugan* (1928). The last was an ingenious courtroom play in which a Follies girl accused of murdering a financier narrowly escapes the electric chair. Elmer Rice, who later became better known as a writer of social drama, started his stage career by introducing motion-picture flashback technique into his melodrama ON TRIAL (1914). A variant form of murder mystery also gained popularity, the most popular being William Gillette's *Sherlock Holmes* (1899), which this effective actor played constantly until 1932, and THE BAT (1920), by Mary Roberts Rinehart and Avery Hopwood.

A "psychological" variant of melodrama which won considerable popularity was THE WITCHING HOUR (1908), by Augustus Thomas (1859–1934). In this play a character employs mental telepathy in order to clear a friend condemned to the electric chair for a crime actually committed by the district attorney. New dimensions of "social" or "problem play" playwriting also appeared in the theater. "Social drama," indeed, began to be written rather frequently after 1880 in response to growing industrialization, financial speculation, monopolistic business, and friction between capital and labor. BRONSON HOWARD (1842–1908), who started out as a newspaper reporter and won attention as a serious playwright in 1870, is especially remembered for *Baron Randolph* (1881), his drama of class conflict, and *The Henrietta* (1887), his satire on Wall Street speculation. STEELE MACKAYE (1824–1894), best known for developing stage machinery and overhead lighting, contributed a provocative labor play, *Paul Kauvar, or Anarchy*, in 1887. CHARLES KLEIN (1867–1915), who won success with his sentimental dramas *The Auctioneer* (1901) and *The Music Master* (1904), in which the popular actor DAVID WARFIELD played leading roles, made exciting melodrama out of the struggle of a young man against a "malefactor of great wealth" in *The Lion and the Mouse* (1905), and paid tribute to the working-class girl in *Maggie Pepper* (1911). EDWARD SHELDON (1886–1946) advanced somewhat beyond these simple plays—though without foregoing melodramatic contrivance—with his racial problem play THE NIGGER (1910), in which a politically ambitious Southerner discovers that he is partly Negro in his origins, and with THE BOSS (1911), the story of an unscrupulous politician. Theodore Roosevelt's clashes with big business and the excitement of "muckraking" journalism, which exposed scandals in city government, proved so contagious that even the urbane CLYDE FITCH (1865–1909), whose reputation rested on light comedies such as *The Climbers* (1901) and CAPTAIN JINKS OF THE HORSE MARINES (1902), started firing away at political corruption in his last play, *The City* (1909).

The main limitation of these and other treatments of the social scene was the artificiality of the characters and the plot. The dialogue reflected these faults and added to them the banalities of sentimentality and moral reformation then current in popular literature. Whatever realism the plays possessed lay on the surface. No matter how much later they reached the stage than Ibsen's *Ghosts* and *An Enemy of the People*, the plays were pre-Ibsenite or pseudo-Ibsenite in sentiment and opinion. The "realism" of the type of American playwriting that remained in vogue until 1920 was, with few exceptions, on a par with the so-called naturalism of DAVID BELASCO (1859–1931), which was little more than a passion for putting the actual thing on the stage. Belasco duplicated a Childs' Restaurant on stage in 1912, but he could not bring himself to renounce the plot contrivances and sentimentalities that proved so profitable in the plays he produced and often partially wrote. His showman's taste led him to the romanticized Orient with *Madame Butterfly* (1900) and to the occult with THE RETURN OF PETER GRIMM (1912). Even when he produced a relatively realistic character study, *The Easiest Way* (1909), he evidently considered that the essence of realism was the theatrical boardinghouse he reproduced as the set.

Mechanical means such as Belasco employed could make the theater spectacular, but they could not make it genuinely realistic; mere pictorialism could only prove a deception to those who equated realism, however superficial, with progress. A new outlook, ensuring penetration into individual character and social reality, was needed. Realism had to be developed in depth, as it were, and this required, above all else, an unconventional spirit and a keen intellect. The alternative to genuine realism was genuine imagination, which entailed inventiveness rather than literalness, and creative selectivity rather than imitation, no matter how spectacular; and effective inventiveness and selectivity also required a penetrating mind and lively intelligence. New ideals and principles of theater were needed, and these came from many quarters—from influential literary figures, such as Zola in Europe and William Dean Howells in America, from theoreticians and visionaries of the theater, from the experiments of European stage directors, such as Reinhardt and Stanislavsky, but, above all, from the strivings of European and American playwrights themselves. It is not extravagant to say, indeed, that progress came, in large part, from a transfer of power and influence from actor-managers to playwrights; an actor's theater became a playwright's theater.

While the American drama was a feeble commodity throughout the 19th century and the first two decades of the 20th, the theater itself had been a thriving, if not indeed an exciting, institution due to the talent of star actors who played in New York and toured the country extensively, bringing their own companies with them or drawing upon resident stock companies in numerous cities for a supporting cast. Their personalities awed or entranced the public, and their names carried a prestige that relatively few performers possessed after 1920.

The roster of stars available, at one time or another, to the American stage before World War I included such attractive names as Edmund Kean, JUNIUS BRUTUS BOOTH, William Charles Macready, FANNY KEMBLE, Sarah Bernhardt, Sir Henry Irving, Edward A. Sothern, Tommaso Salvini, HELENA MODJESKA, and Eleonora Duse, in the foreign contingent, and EDWIN FORREST, Joseph Jefferson, Anna Cora Mowatt, JAMES H. HACKETT, CHARLOTTE CUSHMAN, JULIA MARLOWE, EDWIN BOOTH, RICHARD MANSFIELD, Ada Rehan, Lillian Russell, John Drew, MAUDE ADAMS, and Mrs. Fiske among the natives. None of the American playwrights contemporary with these actors achieved comparable reputations. The situation changed radically only after 1920, when progressive theater groups and critics aimed at ensemble performance and set themselves sternly against the star system. Although there were many excellent actors on the American stage after 1920, none of them (not even Katharine Cornell, Helen Hayes, and the Lunts) overshadowed Eugene O'Neill and Tennessee Williams or, for brief periods, Philip Barry, Maxwell Anderson, Clifford Odets, Arthur Miller, Rodgers and Hammerstein, and perhaps a few other playwrights. After 1914 the theater became increasingly dependent upon the talents of the playwrights, a situation which remained unchanged until the writers began to lose their influence by default in the 1950's, when, with the rise of such powerful personalities as Joshua Logan and ELIA KAZAN, it seemed as if a so-called director's, rather than playwright's, theater had come into being.

Progress in the drama, however, could not come from playwrights without the support of forward-looking individual managers such as ARTHUR HOPKINS (1878–1950) and aggressive "art-theater" or little-theater groups. These sprang up in considerable profusion throughout the country after 1914, giving rise to a folk-theater movement and to many so-called regional plays produced locally. The best-known examples of American regional drama (see LITTLE THEATER) are inevitably those plays that reached Broadway or were actually written with an eye to Broadway though based on folk material—notably PORGY (1927), by DUBOSE and DOROTHY HEYWARD, which became the memorable GEORGE GERSHWIN folk-opera *Porgy and Bess* in 1935, and GREEN GROW THE LILACS (1930), by Lynn Riggs, which Oscar Hammerstein II and Richard Rodgers turned into the celebrated musical comedy OKLAHOMA! in 1943.

Especially important was the little-theater movement that gained momentum in New York City, the center of the professional theater. Here the two most influential groups were the PROVINCETOWN PLAYERS, founded in 1915, from which Eugene O'Neill emerged as the leading American playwright, and the Washington Square Players, established at about the same time. The latter became the parent organization of the THEATRE GUILD, which rapidly became the leading American theatrical company after 1919. A dozen years later, a Guild splinter group, led by HAROLD CLURMAN and Lee Strasberg, became the Group Theatre (see THE GROUP), which first produced the plays of CLIFFORD ODETS, Sidney Kingsley, and William Saroyan. These progressive groups and a few courageous individual producers ensured the rise of modern drama in America. They gave equal support to the two main streams of modern American playwriting—the genuinely realistic, predominantly social or psychological drama, and the imaginatively stylized, poetic or expressionistic drama. (See EXPRESSIONISM.) O'Neill, especially, followed both streams in the 1920's, with work as disparate as his naturalistic *Beyond the Horizon* and *Desire under the Elms,* on the one hand, and his expressionistic *Emperor Jones* and *The Hairy Ape* on the other. Other playwrights followed O'Neill's example. Thus ELMER RICE distinguished himself alternately with his expressionistic ADDING MACHINE (1923) and his realistic STREET SCENE (1929); and MAXWELL ANDERSON succeeded on Broadway as a realistic playwright in the 1920's with *What Price Glory?* and *Saturday's Children,* and as a poetic playwright in the 1930's with such verse plays as *Elizabeth the Queen* and *Winterset.*

Undoubtedly strong European influences were operative in the development of the American drama in the main modern directions. The example of Ibsen, Hauptmann, Chekhov, Gorki, Galsworthy, and Shaw helped to move the American theater toward a realistic orientation in the choice and treatment of subject matter. The example of Strindberg (for whose post-realistic plays O'Neill entertained great admiration), Maeterlinck, Molnar, Pirandello, Andreyev, Brecht, and the sociological German expressionists Kaiser and Toller inspired opposite leanings toward imaginative and "theatricalist" theater. But there were also some early stirrings of modern theater on the American scene itself.

The most important as well as the earliest of the new realists was the actor, manager, and playwright JAMES A. HERNE (1839–1901). After adapting as well as helping to stage many run-of-the-mill plays, he wrote MARGARET FLEMING, which had three tryout performances, beginning on July 4, 1890. It was the first truly realistic play of American life, and it contained an unconventional treatment of a moral problem in closing with a woman's willingness to care for her husband's illegitimate child and to be reconciled with her wayward mate. The puritanical opposition of the theater-owning managements in Boston forced Herne to present the play privately in 1891 in a small Boston playhouse, where it had a critical success (Hamlin Garland and Thomas Bailey Aldrich were among the eminent authors of the time who praised it), and Herne sank his own money, earned with an earlier conventional melodrama, into the production. The play was presented in New York on December 9, 1891, at Palmer's Theatre; in Chicago in 1892; in New York again in 1894; and in Chicago again with Herne's daughters Chrystal and Julie Herne playing the title role in 1907 and 1915 respectively. Herne wavered considerably between realism and popular Victorian playwriting, but tried to adhere to the principles he propounded in his essay "Art for Truth's Sake in the Drama" (Arena, February, 1897). Herne wrote a second realistic drama, SHORE ACRES, in 1892, a vivid picture of life in New England which became extremely popular. But it is Margaret Fleming that made him a precursor of modern American realists in the theater, a position already granted him in the 1890's by WILLIAM DEAN HOWELLS, the leading realistic novelist in America at that time.

Some advance was also achieved by the scholar and poet WILLIAM VAUGHN MOODY (1869–1910), who, after writing philosophical verse dramas, developed a realistic conflict between a puritanical young woman and a rough individualist in a play first entitled A Sabine Woman (1906) and then THE GREAT DIVIDE when produced in 1909. This work was a widely recognized contribution to the rising tide of critical realism in the American theater; it was played successfully in New York and then toured by Henry Miller and Margaret Anglin in 1906. Perhaps the most remarkable feature of The Great Divide, in which Moody predicated a "great divide" between conscience-burdened New England and the free American frontier, was the idea that the heroine of the play could fall in love with a man who had virtually violated her in the Wild West. Realism was also sustained, although less successfully, by Moody's next prose play, The Faith Healer (1909), which deals with the psychological crisis of a man who possesses occult powers but whose power to heal vanishes when he loses self-confidence in an unbelieving world. Another thrust in the modern direction was made by EUGENE WALTER (1874–1941) with one of his melodramatic plays, THE EASIEST WAY

(1908), in which a wealthy man's mistress makes an effort to leave him but is unable to reconcile herself to a life of poverty after having enjoyed leisure and luxury.

Even "society" comedy began to reflect a trend toward keener realism, which was particularly observable in Langdon Mitchell's comedy of divorce in fashionable circles, The New York Idea, presented in 1906 by the progressive actress-manager "Mrs. Fiske," Minnie Maddern Fiske (1865–1932). More frequently the playwrights turned out farce-comedies such as Winchell Smith and Frank Bacon's folksy play LIGHTNIN' (1918), and, after 1920, briskly urban and broadly satirical, so-called wisecracking, plays. Most successful were the farces and comedies of GEORGE S. KAUFMAN (1889–1961) and BEN HECHT (1894—   ). These playwrights and their collaborators accounted for such deflationary entertainments as MERTON OF THE MOVIES (1922), June Moon (1929), and THE MAN WHO CAME TO DINNER (1939); THE FRONT PAGE (1928) and Twentieth Century (1932) respectively. Noteworthy among other American authors who made satire their province was GEORGE KELLY, a glum satirist who won success with THE SHOW-OFF (1924) and with CRAIG'S WIFE (1925), his bleak indictment of self-centered middle-class American women. Deflationary tactics became so prevalent in the New York theater that they even infiltrated the world of musical comedy, especially in the case of PAL JOEY, a relentless exposé of egotism compounded by John O'Hara, Richard Rodgers, and Lorenz Hart in 1940.

A neoromantic movement started off at the turn of the century with relatively meager results. There was little advance in poetic drama except for Percy MacKaye's THE SCARECROW (1908), a tragic fantasy in prose based on Hawthorne's tale FEATHERTOP. MacKaye had a strong vein of poetry in his many plays, masques, and operas, but he never again achieved the dramatic power of The Scarecrow. Other playwrights made little impression with their poetic plays on the Broadway stage until the successful production of Maxwell Anderson's blank-verse tragedy Elizabeth the Queen in 1930. A poetic renaissance was promised for a time by the popular success of other historical plays by Anderson, especially Mary of Scotland (1933) and Anne of the Thousand Days (1948), as well as his two verse plays that dealt with contemporary life, Winterset (1935) and HIGH TOR (1936). But verse drama remained a relatively exotic genre in the American theater, despite the success of these plays and of T. S. Eliot's THE COCKTAIL PARTY (1949) and Christopher Fry's The Lady's Not for Burning (1948), both imported to Broadway from the British stage. Among American playwrights of the 1950's only Archibald MacLeish won popular success with poetry when his drama J.B. (q.v.) reached Broadway in the 1959–60 season after production at Yale University by F. Curtis Canfield.

However, even prose dramas were apt to

convey poetic atmosphere and feeling. This was especially the case in the work of O'Neill, Paul Green, LYNN RIGGS, Odets, Saroyan, and Tennessee Williams; several of the playwrights wrote flavorsome dialect and evinced a poetic feeling for nature and local color, especially in regional folk pieces and in one noteworthy folk fantasy, Marc Connelly's THE GREEN PASTURES (1930). Several writers also resorted to imaginative formal devices, as evidenced by O'Neill's reliance on masks to delineate character in *The Great God Brown* (1926), and Williams' use of a "memory play" framework in THE GLASS MENAGERIE (1945). So-called dream technique or fantastic distortion combined with abrupt telegraphic dialogue produced eerie effects of expressionism in plays by O'Neill (*The Emperor Jones* and *The Hairy Ape*), Elmer Rice (*The Adding Machine*), and John Howard Lawson (*Roger Bloomer* and PROCESSIONAL), and others after 1920. Expressionist extravaganza even found its way into comedy, as in Kaufman and Connelly's anticonformist satire BEGGAR ON HORSEBACK (1924), and into musical comedy, as in Moss HART's *Lady in the Dark* (1941). In the depression of the 1930's various efforts were made to blend drama with social criticism, as in the leftist protest plays *Waiting for Lefty* (1935) by Clifford Odets, BURY THE DEAD (1936) by Irwin Shaw, and THE CRADLE WILL ROCK (1937) by Marc Blitzstein. Imaginative theater also appeared in the documentary dramas, on topical matters such as the TVA and slum clearance (*Power* and *One-third of a Nation*), produced during the same period (1935–39) by the Works Progress Administration's FEDERAL THEATER PROJECT. These so-called Living Newspapers arrestingly combined social fact with inventive theatricality, direct address to the audience, vaudeville skits, and symbolism; in *Power*, for example, the justices of the United States Supreme Court were represented by nine masks placed on a table.

There can be no doubt that despite strong leanings toward realism, the American theater was anything but indifferent toward imaginative drama. Even specialists in social realism, urbane comedy, and lusty farce were likely to attempt fantasy or to employ nonrealistic techniques from time to time. Thus PHILIP BARRY (1896–1949), the suave author of many a society comedy of the caliber of HOLIDAY (1928) and THE PHILADELPHIA STORY (1939), made several attempts to write morality plays for the times, such as HOTEL UNIVERSE (1930), a cross-section of modern life abounding in symbolism, and *Here Come the Clowns* (1938), an allegory of good and evil. Barry considered his only half-successful forays into symbolic drama decidedly more important than his successful drawing-room comedies. The same partiality for departures from realistic style and technique was shown by O'Neill, Williams, Arthur Miller, and THORNTON WILDER, all of whom also manifested considerable talent for observing everyday reality.

Wilder, distinguished both as a playwright and novelist, was especially adept as well as consistent in his endeavor to achieve stylization and a high degree of theatricality, as his full-length plays OUR TOWN (1938), THE SKIN OF OUR TEETH (1942), *The Matchmaker* (1956), and many fugitive one-act pieces amply demonstrate. *Our Town*, in which Wilder blended Chinese theatricalist stylization with simple realism, proved to be an exceptionally appealing feat of creative sympathy and imagination. It became one of the most successful American plays in the United States and abroad. In employing the conventions of the Chinese theater (that is, symbolic properties and a narrator, who also serves as the ubiquitous property man in full sight of the audience), Wilder was refreshingly original even if he was not the first American playwright to resort to Oriental stylization. An early experiment in this vein, *The Yellow Jacket*, by George C. Hazelton and J. H. Benrimo, had proved popular in 1913. But this was an arch and artificial imitation of Chinese theater, whereas *Our Town* is most affectionately regarded for its simple humanity. Proceeding more self-consciously in *The Skin of Our Teeth*, Wilder nevertheless rooted this play, too, in human reality—in the splendors and miseries of the human race; specifically, in the anguish and endurance of humanity, once more facing a world crisis in the early 1940's from which escape even "by the skin of our teeth" seemed dubious.

The attractions of imaginative drama affected even so determined a social realist as ARTHUR MILLER after his Ibsenist problem play *All My Sons* (1947). He employed expressionistic play-structure in DEATH OF A SALESMAN (1949), in which the salesman-hero's memories and fantasies developed Miller's theme of the failure of materialism and success-worship. Miller also sought to achieve imaginative form and tone in *The Crucible* (1953), a historical tragedy dealing with the Salem witchcraft trials, and in *A View from the Bridge* (1955), a drama of passion and lost honor set on the New York waterfront and distinctly patterned after Greek tragedy.

The career of EUGENE O'NEILL (1888–1953) is virtually a summary of all but one of the most important aspects of the modern drama, the exception being "social drama," or the direct treatment of contemporary political, social, and economic conflicts. O'Neill combined vigor with imagination, toughness with sensitivity, and realistic detail with atmospherics or symbols. He dealt with authentic American types and backgrounds, but often shifted his emphasis from commonplace reality to religious questionings, cosmic longings, and spiritual struggles. He also conducted numerous experiments in modern dramatic styles, ranging from realism to expressionism, and from the one-act play form, of which he achieved mastery with half a dozen sea pieces early in his career (1914–18), to oversized plays, running to as many as nine acts in the case of STRANGE INTERLUDE (1928), and constituting a trilogy in the case of MOURN-ING BECOMES ELECTRA (1931). O'Neill's partly naturalistic one-act plays, especially those dealing with the sea, were suffused with ironic circumstances, oppressive moods, and symbolic atmosphere suggestive of the lostness of humanity and the malignity of fate. The same qualities distinguished his early, more or less naturalistic, full-length dramas BEYOND THE HORIZON (1920), ANNA CHRISTIE (1921), and DESIRE UNDER THE ELMS (1924), in all of which family relationships and the duel of the sexes produced intense conflicts and attained symbolic significance.

At the same time, feeling drawn to the dramatic techniques favorable to subjective and philosophical drama, he turned to expressionism under the avowed influence of Strindberg's experiments, one of which, *The Spook Sonata*, O'Neill helped to produce in Greenwich Village as a member of the Provincetown Players. O'Neill's early experiments in subjective dramaturgy, *The Emperor Jones* (1920) and *The Hairy Ape* (1922), were impressive. THE EMPEROR JONES, in which a fleeing Negro dictator is overwhelmed by ancestral memories and atavistic fears while losing his way in a Caribbean jungle, was completely successful; and THE HAIRY APE, dealing with the symbolic search of a burly stoker for a place in the world as a human, rather than as a subhuman, being constituted provocative and powerful drama despite a somewhat confusing shift of focus. In ALL GOD'S CHILLUN GOT WINGS (1924) O'Neill treated racial tension in a largely metaphysical vein with the aid of expressionistic stylization. He also conveyed the alienation of the artist and the spiritual bankruptcy of the seemingly "adjusted" philistine in American society by means of the interchangeable masks of THE GREAT GOD BROWN (1926). His concern with the divided nature of modern men and women in *Strange Interlude* (1928) produced a multi-leveled account of an emotionally shattered woman's life with the help of the Joycean "interior monologue." In this intentionally novelistic work he endeavored to sustain psychological drama with extravagant recourse to the Elizabethan convention of the aside, in which a character expresses his secret thoughts without being overheard by any of the characters who share the stage with him.

In his next major effort, *Mourning Becomes Electra* (1931), O'Neill domesticated Greek tragedy by stating the Orestean theme in Freudian terms and giving the action a New England setting. O'Neill returned to primarily realistic dramaturgy in this work, but also used symbolic elements and masklike effects. A renewed reliance on realism appeared especially in his genial comedy of turn-of-the-century American life, *Ah, Wilderness!* (1933), and in the plays he wrote during his long retirement: THE ICEMAN COMETH (1946), *A Moon for the Misbegotten* (1947), the autobiographical LONG DAY'S JOURNEY INTO NIGHT (1956), and A

Touch of the Poet (1958). Recurrent themes in these latter-day works, as well as in the long one-act play *Hughie*, were man's lostness and dependence on sustaining illusions. O'Neill's pessimism, temporarily in abeyance when he wrote *Ah, Wilderness!*, returned in full force in his last plays. O'Neill's career had two great periods, an early and a late one, separated by a hiatus of a dozen years, but his viewpoint was consistent and was given urgency by his dramatic talent whether he favored its realistic or expressionistic aspect. In favoring the former in the late plays, moreover, he was able to write with renewed power and enriched sympathy, strengthening his position as the playwright to whom the American theater owed a large measure of its claim to international importance. This was especially evident when O'Neill received the Nobel Prize for literature in 1936. He became an international figure in the 1920's, and he remained one after his death, chiefly as a result of posthumous productions in Sweden, where several of his late plays first appeared on the stage.

In the first decade after World War I several of O'Neill's contemporaries, notably Elmer Rice and SIDNEY HOWARD (1891–1939), acquired impressive reputations, the former with *Street Scene* (1929) and COUNSELLOR-AT-LAW (1931), the latter with his folk comedy THEY KNEW WHAT THEY WANTED (1924), the medical drama *Yellow Jack* (1934), and numerous competent dramatizations of novels (especially *Dodsworth*, 1934) and adaptations from the French (especially *The Late Christopher Bean*, 1934). In the second decade Maxwell Anderson was sometimes considered O'Neill's rival on the strength of his poetic plays, from *Elizabeth the Queen* to *Winterset*, although his versification was usually flabby and his tragic sense largely derivative. Clifford Odets was acclaimed as the new hope of the theater on the basis of his vitality as a social dramatist in WAITING FOR LEFTY (1935), AWAKE AND SING (1935), and GOLDEN BOY (1937). During the 1940's Tennessee Williams and Arthur Miller arrived on Broadway with *The Glass Menagerie* and *All My Sons* respectively, then acquired world-wide reputations with the psychological and social dramas A STREETCAR NAMED DESIRE (1947) and *Death of a Salesman* (1949), and strengthened their position with later plays, such as Williams' *Cat on a Hot Tin Roof* (1955) and Miller's *The Crucible*.

It was evident indeed before 1960 that the American drama, regardless of its limitations and in spite of the increasingly unfavorable conditions of theatrical production, had achieved an impressive record and was highly regarded abroad, especially in England, Central Europe, and Scandinavia. No other American playwright actually came within hailing distance of O'Neill, but the aforementioned authors accounted for a good deal of the vitality and vigor of the American stage after 1920; their labors were supplemented by the work of Paul Green, Lillian Hellman, Robert Sherwood, S. N. Behrman, Sidney Kingsley, William Saroyan, William Inge, and others.

Author of the moving Negro chronicle IN ABRAHAM'S BOSOM (1927), the Southern family drama THE HOUSE OF CONNELLY (1932), and the antiwar satire *Johnny Johnson* (1937), among other works, PAUL GREEN brought deep sympathies, a fine sense of justice, rich regional flavor, and technical innovation to his plays. He also worked with fervor and skill in the special art of pageant writing, most notably in his first "symphonic drama," *The Last Colony* (1937). He gained undisputed mastery of the one-act play genre with such powerful pieces as *White Dresses* (1928) and *Hymn to the Rising Sun* (1936). Thornton Wilder cultivated a rich vein of fantasy and Yankee shrewdness in a manner that was at once philosophical and theatrical in *Our Town, The Skin of Our Teeth,* and even in so lighthearted a farce as *The Matchmaker.*

LILLIAN HELLMAN revealed a strong talent for blending social realities, moral judgment, and realistic portraiture in hard-driving and penetrating plays, such as her psychological drama THE CHILDREN'S HOUR (1934), her social satire THE LITTLE FOXES (1939), her challenging wartime play WATCH ON THE RHINE (1941), and her Chekhovian cross-section of failure in American life, *The Autumn Garden* (1951).

ROBERT SHERWOOD'S talent for showmanship was abundantly evident in his urbane romantic comedies THE ROAD TO ROME (1926) and REUNION IN VIENNA (1931). His concern with the state of the world deepening, he dramatized failure of nerve among intellectuals in his Western melodrama THE PETRIFIED FOREST (1935) and a recovery of nerve in THERE SHALL BE NO NIGHT (1940). He also produced a brilliantly theatrical antiwar protest in IDIOT'S DELIGHT (1936), and turned his political idealism into a moving tribute to human greatness in ABE LINCOLN IN ILLINOIS (1938).

S. N. BEHRMAN developed an individual style of thoughtful comedy with *The Second Man* (1927), *Biography* (1932), END OF SUMMER (1936), and NO TIME FOR COMEDY (1939), in which he expressed a growing concern with the state of the world. Sidney Kingsley specialized successfully in social realism with the hospital-drama MEN IN WHITE (1933), the naturalistic study of slum life DEAD END (1935), and the moral analysis of *Detective Story* (1949), a warning against inflexible righteousness. He also enriched political drama with his historical play *The Patriots* (1943), deriving a lesson in national unity from the early years of the American republic, and with his antitotalitarian *Darkness at Noon,* a deft dramatization of Arthur Koestler's famous novel.

WILLIAM SAROYAN delighted playgoers with his improvisatory playwriting in such half-fanciful plays as *My Heart's in the Highlands* and THE TIME OF YOUR LIFE (both 1939).

WILLIAM INGE attained a rueful type of small-town realism, at once penetrative and compassionate, in *Come Back, Little Sheba* (1950), *Picnic* (1953), *Bus Stop* (1955), and *Dark at the Top of the Stairs* (1957).

With additional contributions after 1920 from numerous reliable writers such as Paul Osborn, ZOË AKINS, RACHEL CROTHERS, Philip Barry, George Kelly, SAM and BELLA SPEWACK, JOHN VAN DRUTEN, Robert Anderson, HOWARD LINDSAY and RUSSELL CROUSE, and from mavericks such as Edwin Justus Mayer, John Balderston (*Berkeley Square*), John Howard Lawson, Lynn Riggs, the poet ROBINSON JEFFERS, DAN TOTHEROH, and Edward Albee, American dramatic output of the 1920–60 period looked like a bumper harvest.

In the creation of realistic drama American playwrights were unexcelled after World War I, and in the writing of social drama Rice, Lawson, Kingsley, Odets, Hellman, and Miller were excelled only by the German playwright Bertolt Brecht (1898–1956). In the art of cultivated "high" comedy or "comedy of manners" American playwrights fell below British and French standards, but exceptions may be noted in the case of Barry, Behrman, and the London-born John Van Druten (1901–1957), who first established himself as a playwright in England. In "low comedy" and farce American writers, led by George S. Kaufman, cut a wide swathe with their gusto and lively irreverence. Only in the areas of distinctly fanciful playwriting did American playwrights of the 1920–60 period reap a meager harvest, but exceptions could be noted in the development of folk drama by Paul Green and Lynn Riggs, in the creation of "music drama" by George Gershwin and Gian-Carlo Menotti, and of MUSICAL COMEDY, where American supremacy was established by Jerome Kern, Irving Berlin, Oscar Hammerstein II, Moss Hart, and Richard Rodgers, Frank Loesser, Alan Jay Lerner and Frederic Loewe, Abe Burrows, and others with such productions as *Porgy and Bess, Oklahoma! South Pacific, Guys and Dolls, West Side Story,* and *My Fair Lady.*

It would be misleading, however, to conclude a review of the American drama after World War I on an optimistic note without also observing signs of deterioration and distress. Granting the obvious superiority of the plays and the productions to most prewar achievements in the American theater, it must be noted that the improvement in quality was accompanied by a continual decrease in quantity. By 1960 the professional American theater had shrunk to a fraction of its former size, and it had become an unprofitable enterprise on the whole except in the specialized area of popular musical entertainment. The compensating developments were the impressive growth of amateur production on numerous campuses and in relatively small communities, and the rise in New York of so-called off-Broadway enterprise, consisting of more or less experimental productions in out-of-the-way little theaters on some sort of stock-company basis. This last-mentioned venture, in addition to producing provocative European plays and reviving prominent foreign and native works, introduced such avant-garde American writers in the late 1950's and the 1960's as EDWARD ALBEE (*The Zoo Story* and *The American Dream*), JACK GELBER (*The Connection*), and JACK RICHARDSON (*The Prodigal* and *Gallows' Humor*). But by 1960 the off-Broadway theater was also threatened by inflationary production costs. It was evident, moreover, that a diminution in the resources of playwriting and a narrowing of interests—in the case of the new avant-garde, to a veritable cult of nihilism and abstraction—had taken place. A general decline in creative energy was apparent. It had begun, in fact, by the end of the 1930's, and it was halted, from time to time, only by the fortunate emergence of some talented playwright, such as Williams, Miller, or Inge.

In the 1920's the theater's resources were greatly enriched by the rise of sophistication, skepticism, and candor, and by the growth of social criticism and psychological analysis. Assimilating European advances in realism and expressionism, adopting an open mind toward sex, and conducting a vigorous campaign against puritanism and philistinism, the young dramatists of the 1920's devoted themselves to artistic experiment and social rebellion. The results were most apparent in the early work of O'Neill and in the breezily skeptical Kaufman farce-comedies, but they could be seen invigorating a great variety of dramatic effort, ranging from the folksy comedy of Sidney Howard's *They Knew What They Wanted* to the fashionable high comedy of Philip Barry's *Holiday* and Behrman's *The Second Man;* and from the vivacious expressionistic satire of Kaufman and Connelly's *Beggar on Horseback* (1924) and Lawson's *Processional* (1925) to sultry protests against materialism and arid existence devoid of beauty or romance, such as Lawson's expressionistic drama of disoriented youth *Roger Bloomer* (1923), and Sophie Treadwell's expressionistic murder melodrama *Machinal* (1928). The American theater of the twenties was alive with intelligence, scorn, and protest, and it was bent on making provocative discoveries in dramatic style that would serve its interests. Long after the conditions favorable to theater of the period had vanished, one could still find its spirit playfully alive in the work of the playwrights who had survived from the period: Barry's *Philadelphia Story;* Kaufman and Hart's *The Man Who Came to Dinner;* Thurber and Nugent's *The Male Animal;* Rice's *The Dream Girl;* and Wilder's *The Matchmaker,* not to mention the heavy psychological artillery that continued to rumble in O'Neill's work.

The depression decade of the 1930's manifested noteworthy vitality despite the domestic tensions and international upheavals of the period, the threat of fascism, and the coming of a second world war. The creative energy of the twenties spilled over into the next decade, bringing with it such weighty work as O'Neill's *Mourning Becomes Electra* and Max-

well Anderson's verse tragedies. Augmented or transformed vitality appeared in the work of other established writers, such as Sherwood (*The Petrified Forest, Idiot's Delight,* and *Abe Lincoln in Illinois*), and Paul Green (*Johnny Johnson*), who responded as far as temperament and talent would allow to the challenge of the decade. Moreover, fresh creative energies appeared in a new generation which included Odets, Hellman, Kingsley, JOHN WEXLEY, Robert Ardrey, E. P. Conkle, Irwin Shaw, John Steinbeck, and Saroyan. Masterpieces were few in that period, but energy was abundant. American social drama was at its peak in the 1930's, and its influence was felt by the generation that entered the theater at the conclusion of World War II; it is well to remember that both Williams and Miller had been depression-period writers in their youth.

The first half of the 1940's was a relatively sterile period in the American theater. Its playwrights were, in the main, incapable of rising to the occasion of World War II sufficiently to write heroic drama, and at the same time they maintained a self-imposed moratorium on the sophistication that had flourished in the twenties and on the social criticism that had sparked the theater of the thirties. With the end of the war in 1945 a new burst of creativity appeared in the theater. The theater of the second half of the decade was galvanized into some semblance of life by Williams, Inge, and Miller, ARTHUR LAURENTS (*Home of the Brave*), John Patrick (*The Hasty Heart*), Mary Chase (*Harvey*), GARSON KANIN (*Born Yesterday*), and Lindsay and Crouse (*State of the Union*).

But the promised renascence of the American drama failed to materialize after 1950. A combination of social and political circumstances, including cold war jitters and McCARTHYISM, resulting in a reduction of intellectual ferment and a diminution of idealistic fervor, left the new decade of the fifties limp and diffident except for an occasional explosion of protest, such as Arthur Miller's *The Crucible* and Williams' symbolist *Camino Real.* Among the new writers who appeared on Broadway only ROBERT ANDERSON (*Tea and Sympathy*) rose distinctly above the average. Some new plays of the fifties, many of them adaptations (adaptations multiplied as playwriting lost personal passion), achieved various degrees of distinction—Hellman's *Toys in the Attic,* Patrick's *Teahouse of the August Moon,* Van Druten's *I Am a Camera,* PADDY CHAYEFSKY's *The Tenth Man,* MacLeish's verse drama *J.B.,* William Gibson's *Two for the Seesaw* and *The Miracle Worker,* Lorraine Hansberry's drama of urban Negro life *Raisin in the Sun,* and KETTI FRINGS' dramatization of Thomas Wolfe's novel LOOK HOMEWARD ANGEL. In addition to introducing Gelber, Richardson, and Albee, off-Broadway enterprise also gave a new lease on life to previously unsuccessful plays, such as Williams' chronicle of frustration *Summer and Smoke,* O'Neill's powerful drama *The Iceman Cometh,* Paul Osborn's homespun comedy *Morning's at Seven,* and Edwin Justus

Mayer's tartly romantic *Children of Darkness*.

The harvest of original new drama was, however, plainly meager for a period of some dozen years. Not the least disturbing, moreover, was the absence of proof that the promising playwrights of the previous decade, including Williams, Miller, and Inge, were moving toward enriched artistry and augmented significance. There was more evidence of stalemate than of progress in the drama after the American theater had rounded out its fourth post-Victorian or "modern" decade. Perhaps a new dispensation would reach the stage before long, but in 1962 it was not at all clear what this dispensation would be, where it would originate, and what course it would follow. It was apparent only that the economic foundations of the theater would have to be strengthened, possibly with the aid of federal as well as local subsidy, and that the condition of the stage would depend, to a considerable degree, on the condition of American society and the increasingly precarious state of the world.

Important historical and critical works on American drama include T. Allston Brown, *History of the American Stage* (3 v., 1903); Arthur Hornblow, *A History of the Theatre in America* (2 v., 1919); Helen Deutsch and Stella Hanau, *The Provincetown* (1931); Eleanor Flexner, *American Playwrights: 1918–1938* (1938); Burns Mantle, *Contemporary American Playwrights* (1938); Arthur Hobson Quinn, *A History of the American Drama* (2 v., 1945); Glenn Hughes, *A History of the American Theatre, 1700–1950* (1951); John Gassner, *The Theatre in Our Times* (1954); Eric Bentley, *The Dramatic Event: An American Chronicle* (1954); Alan Downer, *Fifty Years of American Drama, 1900–1950* (1957); Joseph Wood Krutch, *The American Drama Since 1918* (rev. ed. 1957); Barnard Hewitt, *Theatre, U.S.A., 1668–1957* (1959); Elmer Rice, *The Living Theatre* (1959); John Gassner, *Theatre at the Crossroads* (1960); Alan Downer, *Recent American Drama* (1961).

Important collections of plays include: Burns Mantle and Garrison P. Sherwood, eds., *The Best Plays of 1919–1920 to 1923–1924* (annual volumes, 1920–24); *The Best Plays of 1924–25 to 1958* (annual volumes since 1924); *The Best Plays of 1909–1919* (1933); *The Best Plays of 1899–1909* (1944); Barrett H. Clark and Kenyon Nicholson, eds., *The American Scene* (1930), which contains thirty-four one-act plays; Margaret Mayorga, ed., *One-Act Plays by American Authors* (1937); Pierre De Rohan, ed., *Federal Theatre Plays* (2 v., 1938); Eugene O'Neill, *The Plays of Eugene O'Neill* (3 v., 1948); John Gassner, ed., *A Treasury of the Theatre*, v. 2 (1951) and *Library of Best American Plays* (6 v., 1939–1961); Arthur Hobson Quinn, ed., *Representative American Plays. From 1767 to the Present Day* (7th ed., 1953); Jack Gaver, ed., *Critics' Choice: New York Drama Critics' Circle Prize Plays, 1933–1955* (1955).

JOHN GASSNER

dramatic criticism. Although dramatic criticism did not become an accepted department of American journalism until the end of the Civil War, criticism of colonial productions appeared as early as 1787 in *The Daily Advertiser, The Gazette of the United States,* and *The Commercial Advertiser.*

Some of America's early dramatic criticism was penned by men who made their names in other literary fields. WASHINGTON IRVING, a frequent critic in his brother's *Morning Chronicle,* challenged the presumptuous New York critics in 1801 by writing, "Have they ever been to Europe? Have they ever seen a Garrick, a Kemble, or a Siddons? If they have not I can assure you they have no right to the title of critics."

WALT WHITMAN criticized the star system, exaggerated styles of acting, and the lack of American plays in "Why Can't We Have Something Worth the Name of American Drama?" and other articles in the *Brooklyn Eagle.* HENRY JAMES and EDGAR ALLAN POE reviewed in the *Nation, Atlantic Monthly* and *Century Magazine.*

Because the critics as well as the audiences seldom saw a play they hadn't seen many times before, criticism was concerned mainly with acting, which was judged in great detail and compared with interpretations of other performers seen in the same role. Little attention was paid to the costumes, scenery, or the play itself.

Modern dramatic criticism began in 1865 with the appointment of WILLIAM WINTER (1836–1917) as drama critic of the New York *Tribune.* Until his retirement in 1909, Winter was the most influential critic in American theater. His perceptive discussions of acting and his penetrating analyses of European playwriting styles were a powerful force in shaping American drama of the twentieth century.

JAMES GIBBONS HUNEKER (1860–1921), critic of the *New York Times* and a sophisticated stylist with a comprehensive knowledge of the European stage, also helped broaden the horizon of American theater. WILLIAM LEGGETT, FITZ-JAMES O'BRIEN, and J. Ranken Towse were other critics of stature in an era when the drama critic also reviewed concerts, ballets, burlesques, spectacles, and variety shows.

As the quality of American theater improved so did dramatic criticism. The American critic no longer had to travel to England as Washington Irving suggested. New standards of excellence were demanded in acting, playwriting, production, and design. With the appearance of new plays by American playwrights, critics devoted most of their review to the play itself and comments on the acting were relegated to the final paragraphs.

GEORGE JEAN NATHAN (1882–1960) emerged as the most important critic of the early 1900's and continued to dominate the field for forty years. In the beginning of his career Nathan strongly advocated the works of Ibsen and Strindberg and protested against the lack of taste and intelligence in American theater. He urged both critics and the public to insist that playwrights raise their standards, and was one of the first critics to praise the plays of O'Neill. A voluminous writer with a sophisticated and cynical style, Nathan incessantly pointed out the insincerity and artificiality of current plays in reviews for *Harper's Weekly, Smart Set, The Saturday Review of Literature, Esquire,* and *Scribner's.* His books include: *Mr. George Jean Nathan Presents* (1917); *The Popular Theatre* (1918); *The Critic and the Drama* (1922); *Materia Critica* (1924); *The House of Satan* (1926); *Art of the Night* (1928); *The Testament of a Critic* (1931); *Since Ibsen* (1933); *Passing Judgments* (1935); *The Theatre of the Moment* (1936); *The Morning After the First Night* (1939); *Theatre In the Fifties* (1953); and *The Magic Mirror* (1960).

JOHN MASON BROWN (1900–   ) raised another vigorous voice in reviews for *The Saturday Review of Literature* and in his books, which include *Upstage: the American Theatre in Performance* (1930); *The Art of Playgoing* (1936); *Two on the Aisle* (1938); *Broadway In Review* (1940); *Seeing Things* (1946); *Seeing More Things* (1948); *Still Seeing Things* (1950); and *As They Appear* (1952).

Stark Young, critic of the *New Republic,* HEYWOOD BROUN (*Seeing Things At Night,* 1921), and ALEXANDER WOOLLCOTT (*Enchanted Aisles,* 1924) are also remembered as perceptive critics and distinctive stylists.

In recent years the power of the New York critics increased to the extent that producers claim the reviewers of two or three daily newspapers determine the life of a play. BROOKS ATKINSON (1894–   ), drama critic of the *New York Times* from 1926 until 1960, has been acknowledged as the most powerful critic in America. Atkinson's lucid and knowledgeable reviews set an increasingly high standard for American theater. He was critical of commercial drama and did much to encourage the off-Broadway movement of the Fifties and the growth of theater outside New York.

WALTER KERR, drama critic of the New York *Herald Tribune* and author of *How Not To Write A Play* (1955) and *Critics and Censorship* (1957), Robert Brustein, of the *New Republic,* and HAROLD CLURMAN, of the *Nation,* are well versed critics who work in the theater as well as report it.

Analyses of the theater in general have been as influential as reviews of actual current productions. FRANCIS FERGUSSON and ERIC BENTLEY have made important contributions in the theoretical area of dramatic criticism. Fergusson, in his *Idea of a Theatre* (1949) and *The Human Image in Dramatic Literature* (1957), made profound and searching explorations into the fundamentals of drama. Bentley's works include: *Playwright As A Thinker* (1946), *In Search of Theatre* (1953); *The Dramatic Event, an American Chronicle* (1954); and *What Is Theatre?* (1956).

Dramatists' Guild (originally, Association of Dramatists). An association formed 1926 by 131 playwrights in New York City, under the leadership of GEORGE MIDDLETON, for their protection in making contracts with producers and now generally accepted by the latter. It is part of the Authors' League of America. A subsidiary organization is the Dramatists' Play Service, founded by BARRETT H. CLARK, which provides plays and makes royalty arrangements with amateur players.

Draper, John W[illiam] (b. England, May 5, 1811—d. Jan. 4, 1882), teacher, scientist, historian. After the death of Draper's father in 1832, the family migrated to the United States. Draper won renown in the field of science, occupied important posts in various universities, organized a medical school in New York. His most important writings are *A History of the Intellectual Development of Europe* (1863) and *A History of the Conflict Between Religion and Science* (1874), both under deist and Spencerian influence. Donald Fleming analyzed *John W. Draper and the Religion of Science* (1954).

Draper, Ruth (b. New York City, Dec. 2, 1884—d. Dec. 30, 1956), actress. This granddaughter of CHARLES A. DANA won a worldwide reputation as a satiric monologist. She wrote her own sketches, among the most famous of which were *Opening a Bazaar* and *Three Women and Mr. Clifford.*

dream songs, Indian. This type of Indian music has been most fully treated in FRANCES DENSMORE's paper, *The Belief of the Indian in a Connection between Song and the Supernatural* (Bureau of American Ethnology, *Bulletin* 151). The "dream song" may come to an Indian in natural sleep, but the first important song of this kind is likely to come during a fasting vigil or as a result of taking jimson weed, a drug. "The silence becomes vibrant, it becomes rhythmic, and a melody comes to his mind." It is a highly individual song, which no one sings except the warrior to whom it has come, although the dream songs of the warriors of former days are sometimes sung in the war dances as an honor to their memory. Generally some bird or other animal may then become part of his name, as in the case of Brave Buffalo, a Sioux who had his first dream, about a buffalo, when he was ten years old. Or the warrior may wear some symbol that recalls the dream. Through his dream song the Indian maintains contacts with supernal powers, who can give him aid in every undertaking. One Pawnee heard thunder in his dream, learned the song that recorded the fact, and sang it when he went to war: "Beloved, it is good./ He, the thunder is saying quietly,/ It is good." Margot Astrov gives several examples of dream song in her anthology, *The Winged Serpent* (1946).

Dred: A Tale of the Great Dismal Swamp (1856), novel by HARRIET BEECHER STOWE. In this novel she continued the description of slavery begun in *Uncle Tom's Cabin* (1852). Dred is a runaway slave living in the Dismal Swamp; the story reveals the deteriorating influence of slavery on white masters and suggests that the solution is a system of paternalistic emancipation. In the story itself, however, the problem is resolved by removing the fugitives to Canada. The book was popular in England and helped in the emancipation of British labor.

Dred Scott Decision. See SCOTT, DRED.

Dreiser, Theodore [Herman Albert] (b. Terre Haute, Ind., Aug. 27, 1871—d. Dec. 27, 1945), novelist. The son of a crippled mill superintendent who was employed only intermittently and a doting mother who did her best to en-

UPI

courage her boy's yearning for knowledge, Dreiser learned the facts of poverty at an early age; all his life he remained exceedingly sensitive to manifestations of hardship and oppression. When he was fifteen a priest who heard his confession one day told him that he must not read science and philosophy on threat of being forbidden to attend Communion. He chose to continue his reading, but he did not abandon the Church without a struggle; in the end he became extremely bitter toward organized religion. With his mother's help he finished high school, then at seventeen worked as a janitor in Chicago until his old high-school teacher, Mildred Fielding, insisted on paying his expenses for a year at the University of Indiana.

Dreiser became a newspaperman, worked in St. Louis, Chicago, Pittsburgh, and New York. He was encouraged in his attempts to write fiction by his editors and fellow workers and especially by his brother Paul, a successful songwriter, who lent him money, invented jobs for him, and helped him through the devastating spells of depression that attacked him. In *Twelve Men* (1919) Dreiser did a portrait of his brother that reveals the deep affection between the two. (See PAUL DRESSER.)

Dreiser finished SISTER CARRIE, his first novel, in 1900 and sent it to Doubleday, Page & Co., where FRANK NORRIS read it and accepted it with enthusiasm. A contract was signed during the absence of Doubleday, the head of the firm, who returned from Europe and he was horrified when he read the manuscript. He called a conference with Dreiser to discuss cancellation of the contract, but Dreiser, upon the advice of Norris, refused to release the publishers. Doubleday fulfilled the letter of the contract: a thousand cheap copies of *Sister Carrie* were printed, but they were not advertised, displayed, or distributed. Norris sent out many review copies, but the press echoed the publisher's disgust. Despondent and embittered, Dreiser contemplated suicide until he was again rescued by his brother Paul, who got him a job with the Butterick Publications. (See THE DELINEATOR.) Here Dreiser succeeded so well that in a few years he was head of the firm, with what was then the enormous salary of $25,000.

Encouraged by Paul and a few discriminating critics, Dreiser published JENNIE GERHARDT in 1911. Though it, like *Sister Carrie*, is a sympathetic portrait of a sinful woman, it met with a better reception and Dreiser began to acquire the recognition he deserved. In 1912 came THE FINANCIER, the first of his "Trilogy of Desire" concerning the life of FRANK COWPERWOOD; the second in the trilogy was THE TITAN (1914). Cowperwood, a superman, struggled and clawed his way upward from poverty to a position of wealth and power, experiencing many erotic adventures on the way. The stories, based on the career of Charles T. Yerkes, traction magnate of Philadelphia and Chicago, were thoroughly documented by Dreiser in the best tradition of literary NATURALISM. In the light of Dreiser's later belief in socialism, it is a temptation to read the Cowperwood novels as satires, but this was almost certainly not Dreiser's intention at the time. Cowperwood is presented as the hero, a Nietzschean figure whose struggle for success somehow promotes the evolutionary aspirations of all mankind.

THE "GENIUS" (1915) concerns another superman, this time an artist, Eugene Witla, who was modeled on the painter Everett Shinn, who fascinated Dreiser, on a young art editor of the Butterick Publications who committed suicide, and on Dreiser himself. It is by far the most personal of Dreiser's novels, and Witla's complex and turbulent love life was close to Dreiser's own: the author had been divorced from his first wife, was now living with the actress Helen Patges, whom he later married, and at the same time was engaged in several other affairs. Dreiser told Helen later that he liked to carry on two or more affairs simultaneously; it stimulated him to be caught in the tension between women competing for his love, and he wrote the better for it.

From 1921 to 1924 Dreiser lived in California in the midst of the movie colony, but then went to upper New York State to collect material for AN AMERICAN TRAGEDY, a novel based on the celebrated Chester Gillette–Grace Brown murder case of 1906. The book, packed with meticulous documentation which constituted an overwhelming indictment of American social and business values, appeared in two volumes in 1925. Not Clyde Griffiths, the weak hero who is convicted for the murder of his pregnant sweetheart, but society is made responsible for the tragedy, a society which has fascinated the youth with its glitter while failing to provide him with moral restraint. Nevertheless, the novel seems more hopeful and positive than Dreiser's earlier works and furnishes in the idea of social reform a change from the sense of purposelessness of the earlier novels.

Dreiser's popularity in Europe, particularly in Russia, increased rapidly during the 1920's; in October, 1927, he was invited by the Soviet government to visit Russia as its guest. By-products of this trip were *Dreiser Looks at Russia* (1928) and *Tragic America* (1931), expressing his faith in socialism as opposed to his former groping, despairing fatalism. Returning to the United States, he became active in left-wing organizations; in 1931, with Dos Passos and others, he formed the Dreiser Committee to investigate the conditions of the coal miners in Bell and Harlan Counties in Kentucky. Feeling ran so high that the Bell County grand jury indicted the committee for criminal syndicalism, but after wide publicity and national indignation the charges against the committee were dropped.

The Stoic, last of the Cowperwood trilogy, was published posthumously in 1947, although Dreiser had written most of it many years before. It is not a good novel; by the time he came to write it he had outgrown the attitudes which prevailed in the earlier Cowperwood stories. Nevertheless, it is interesting to the student for its discussion of Hinduism, to which the book's heroine turns in her final despair. Rather surprisingly, Dreiser apparently also turned to Oriental mysticism; at least he studied it seriously, and he seems to have found in the leap to pure Spirit a usable antidote to his purposeless wandering in the materialistic flux. Nor is Brahminism so far, perhaps, from the concept of life's aimlessness that dominated Dreiser's early gropings. At any rate he found in it an expression of his love for man, an ideal expression far superior to anything he could find in institutionalized society.

The Bulwark (1946) was begun as early as 1910, an awkward story that seemed quite unsatisfactory when it was published. Dreiser's great contribution to naturalism had been completed in his small group of major novels. Indeed, he often expressed his naturalistic theories and his philosophy of life more directly in his autobiographical works, *A Traveler at Forty* (1913), *A Hoosier Holiday* (1916), *A Book About Myself* (1922; later republished as *Newspaper Days,* the title Dreiser originally gave it), and particularly *Hey-Rub-a-Dub-Dub: A Book of the Mystery and Terror and Wonder of Life* (1919). By the time he died the tide of naturalism had turned and a new conservatism was on the way. The crusading novelists were dead or silent,

with perhaps the exception of JAMES T. FARRELL, to whom Dreiser in his old age turned for criticism and encouragement.

The most formidable obstacle to an appreciation of Dreiser's work has been his style—so frequently described as "elephantine" as to have won a certain proprietary right to the adjective. While there are many passages of forceful and passionate writing in his novels, his style is often dull, awkward, and banal. Nevertheless, with all his faults, Dreiser created an image of American life which has had a wide and enduring relevance. He indicated the tragic possibilities inherent in the conflict between the individual driven by a desire for self-realization and a society characterized by repressive and narrow moral and social conventions, on the one hand, and the glorification of material success, on the other. There is in his work an integrity, a compassion, a dedication to the task of finally making moral and metaphysical sense out of his vast apparatus of realistic detail, which places it among the best of modern American fiction.

No collected edition of Dreiser's works exists. Full-length studies are: *Forgotten Frontiers: Dreiser and the Land of the Free* (1932; reprinted, 1946, as *Dreiser and the Land of the Free*), by Dorothy Dudley, a fictionalized biography; *Theodore Dreiser: Apostle of Nature* (1949), by Robert H. Elias; *My Life with Dreiser* (1951), by Helen Dreiser. Critical works include *Theodore Dreiser* (1951), by F. O. Matthiessen, and *The Stature of Theodore Dreiser* (1955), a collection of biographical and critical essays edited by Alfred Kazin and Charles Shapiro. His *Letters* (3 v., 1959) were edited by Robert H. Elias.

CHARLES CHILD WALCUTT

Dresbach, Glenn [Ward] (b. Lanark, Ill., Sept. 9, 1889—   ), poet. Dresbach received many awards and prizes for his graceful poetry, much of it vividly descriptive of Southern and Southwestern scenes. Among his collections: *The Road to Everywhere* (1916); *In Colors of the West* (1922); *Cliff Dwellings and Other Poems* (1926); *Star-Dust and Stone* (1928); *The Wind in the Cedars* (1930); *Selected Poems* (1931); *Collected Poems* (1948; enlarged ed., 1950).

Dresser, Paul (b. Terre Haute, Ind., April 21, 1857—d. Jan. 30, 1906), song writer. Dresser's name was originally Dreiser; he was the brother of THEODORE DREISER. Sigmund Spaeth says: "Dresser is widely remembered as one of the most lovable characters in the history of Tin Pan Alley. A huge mountain of a man, with a heart as big as his body, his generosity was notorious." Spaeth is convinced that Dresser believed in the sentimentalities he put into such widely popular songs as *I'm Still Your Mother, Dear* (1897); ON THE BANKS OF THE WABASH, FAR AWAY (1899); *The Blue and the Gray, or, A Mother's Gift to Her Country* (1900); *My Gal Sal* (1905). The Wabash song (Theodore Dreiser said he had helped compose it) became Indiana's official

State Song and deserves, says Spaeth, "a place among the best of the folk and folk-like music of America."

D'ri and I (1901), a novel of the War of 1812 by IRVING BACHELLER. The leading character is Darius Olen, a stalwart woodsman, who watches over the son of his employer in many stirring adventures.

Driscoll, Charles B[enedict] (b. Wichita, Kans., Oct. 19, 1885—d. Jan. 15, 1951), newspaperman, editor, columnist, memoirist. After working on various Middle-Western papers, Driscoll became an editor with the McNaught Syndicate. Much of his own writing appeared as syndicated material in many newspapers. When O. O. MCINTYRE died in 1938 Driscoll took over his popular column, "New York Day by Day"; he also published a biography of his predecessor. He began telling the candid story of his own life in *Kansas Irish* (1943) and *Country Jake* (1946). He was held to be the world's greatest authority on pirates and their lost treasure, having visited many places where loot had been buried or sunk in the sea; he wrote *Doubloons, The Story of Buried Treasure* (1930); *Driscoll's Book of Pirates* (1934), and *Pirates Ahoy!* (a series of syndicated stories, 1927–28; published as a book, 1941).

Drummond, William Henry (b. Ireland, April 13, 1854—d. April 6, 1907), Canadian poet, physician, teacher, storyteller. Drummond's busy life as medical man, teacher of medical jurisprudence, and (in his later years) operator of a silver mine was refreshed at regular intervals by his composition of poems in the dialect of French Canada. These poems are a mingling of humor and sentiment, at times slightly satirical. His nondialect verse failed to attract attention only because the other had more novelty. The *habitant* on his little farm, the *voyageur* journeying on dangerous rivers, the woodsman, are all immortalized in their humor, pathos, and picturesqueness. Drummond's recitation of his own poems was very effective. He published several collections: *The Habitant and Other French-Canadian Poems* (1905); *Johnnie Courteau and Other Poems* (1901); *The Voyageur and Other Poems* (1905). A collected edition of his verse and other writings appeared in 1912.

Drums (1925), a historical novel by JAMES BOYD. Boyd writes realistically of his hero Johnny Fraser's service in the Revolutionary War with Paul Jones and General Morgan. See JOHN BEAUCHAMP JONES.

Drums Along the Mohawk (1936), a historical novel by WALTER D. EDMONDS. The bitter struggle in the Mohawk Valley between the rebels of the Revolution and their British foes is vividly portrayed. Stress is laid on the destructiveness of the Tories and their Indian allies. The novel was based on careful research; Edmonds, himself a native of the valley, had long been interested in doing a novel on this phase of the Revolutionary War. He described his research processes in *How You Begin a Novel* (*Atlantic Monthly*, Aug., 1936).

Drum-Taps (1865), poems by WALT WHITMAN. To this was added in 1866 a *Sequel to Drum-Taps* which contains some of Whitman's most famous poems, including O CAPTAIN! MY CAPTAIN! and WHEN LILACS LAST IN THE DOORYARD BLOOM'D. The collection was gathered into a new edition of LEAVES OF GRASS in 1867.

Drunkard, The, or, The Fallen Saved (1844), a play by William H[enry] Smith (1806–72). This was a sentimental and melodramatic plea for temperance, and was occasionally revived for purposes of burlesque in the early 20th century. The most extraordinary revival was in Hollywood, where the play opened on July 6, 1923, at the Theatre Mart and closed on October 10, 1959, having run twenty-six years consecutively. Originally it was booked at the Mart for three weeks and on opening night it had exactly five paid admissions in the house. On closing date it was estimated that over three million people had seen the play since it opened. W. C. Fields, notoriously antitemperance, saw it thirty times. Beer was served at the performances.

Drury, Allen [Stuart] (b. Houston, Tex., Sept. 2, 1918—   ), novelist, journalist. Drury's assignments in Washington for various newspapers and magazines supplied him with material for his novel *Advise and Consent* (1959), a sprawling, improbable chronicle of a battle for Senate confirmation of a Secretary of State. It won a Pulitzer Prize in 1960, and was dramatized for the stage (1960) and motion pictures (1962).

Du Bois, William E[dward] B[urghardt] (b. Great Barrington, Mass., Feb. 23, 1868—d. Aug. 27, 1963), educator, author. The Negro race in the United States has produced no better writer of English prose than Du Bois; his THE SOULS OF BLACK FOLK (1903) is a fine example of English prose as well as a plea for greater understanding of Negroes. The descendant of a French Huguenot and an African slave, Du Bois is a scholar in Greek and Latin, as well as a trained sociologist. He has taught at numerous universities in the United States. Among his books: *The Suppression of the Slave Trade* (1896); *The Philadelphia Negro* (1899); *John Brown* (1909); *The Negro* (1915); *Dark Princess* (a novel, 1928); *Black Folk: Then and Now* (1939); *Color and Democracy* (1945); *The World and Africa* (1947); *In Battle for Peace* (1952); *The Black Flame: A Trilogy*, which consists of *The Ordeal of Mansart* (1957), *Mansart Builds a School* (1959), *Worlds of Color* (1961). Du Bois edited *The Crisis* from 1919 to 1932, he was editor-in-chief of the *Encyclopedia of the Negro* (1933–46), and became vice-chairman of the Council of African Affairs (1949). He is a member of the National Institute of Arts and Letters. In *Dusk of Dawn* (1940) he tells something of his own life, and subtitles it: *An Autobiography of a Race Concept*.

Duc de L'Omelette (Philadelphia *Saturday Courier*, March 3, 1832), a story by EDGAR ALLAN POE. In it the devil poses as a gambler who can lose. Possibly the tale was intended as a burlesque on popular fiction of the day.

Du Chaillu, Paul B[elloni] (b. France, July 31, 1835—d. April 30, 1903), explorer, writer of travel books. Du Chaillu's earlier years seem to have been spent on the African coast, where his father was a trader. He came to the United States probably in 1852, and managed in 1856 to secure funds for exploring Africa under the sponsorship of the Philadelphia Academy of Natural Sciences. After four years he returned with what sounded like wild tales of chimpanzees and gorillas (*Explorations and Adventures in Equatorial Africa,* 1861) and was attacked as a fabricator. He was in Africa again from 1863 to 1865 and emerged with material for several additional books, among them *Wild Life Under the Equator* (1869), *Lost in the Jungle* (1869), *My Apingi Kingdom* (1870), and *The Country of the Dwarfs* (1871). Again he was violently attacked, this time particularly for his stories of African pygmies. Yet later explorers largely confirmed Du Chaillu's observations; his chief fault was that he told his yarns so well that they sounded like fiction. In later years Du Chaillu visited Scandinavia and wrote two books on his travels; he died in Russia while gathering material for still another volume.

Duffus, R[obert] L[uther] (b. Waterbury, Vt., July 10, 1888—   ), newspaperman, commentator on economic and social developments, novelist. Two of Duffus' most important publications are *Books: Their Place in a Democracy* (1930) and *Our Starving Libraries* (1933). In collaboration with Frederick P. Keppel he wrote of *The Arts in American Life* (1933). In 1937 he joined the staff of *The New York Times,* writing frequently for its Sunday sections. His first volume of reminiscences, *The Innocents at Cedro* (1944), is particularly good in its memories of Thorstein Veblen, portrayed as a gentler, milder person than he ordinarily appears. A novel, *Non-Scheduled Flight* (1950), portrays vividly happenings on a flight from New Orleans to Guatemala. *Williamstown Branch* (1958) describes his boyhood.

Dugan, Alan (b. New York City, Feb. 12, 1923—   ), poet. He won his first poetry prize in 1943 while he was attending Queens College. In 1946 *Poetry Magazine* awarded him a prize and in 1960 his work was chosen to be included in the Yale Series of Younger Poets. His *Poems* (1961), which won the National Book Award and the Pulitzer Prize in 1962, reveal strong feeling and an original point of view.

Duganne, Augustine Joseph Hickey (b. Boston, 1823?—d. Oct. 20, 1884), soldier, author. Duganne tried desperately to establish himself as an important literary figure, but without success. He produced a play, *The Lydian Queen* (1848), and published paperbacked novels. When the Civil War broke out he joined the Union army as lieutenant colonel. His experiences in southern prison camps resulted in his most important book, *Camps and Prisons* (1865). His *Poetical Works* appeared in 1855.

du Jardin, Rosamond Neal (b. Fairland, Ill., July 22, 1902—   ), novelist, poet, short-story writer. Between 1930 and 1962 Mrs. du Jardin

had written more than a hundred short stories, many receiving publication in magazines like *Cosmopolitan, Red Book,* and *Good Housekeeping.* Her very active writing career includes adult novels, and of more recent interest, novels for teen-agers. The latter, she feels, "helps to supply a bridge between juvenile and adult reading." Of her writing purposes, she has said: "I stress a wholesome family relationship and try to emphasize the importance of thinking for oneself, of being an individual." Adult novels: *All Is Not Gold* (1935); *Only Love Lasts* (1937); *Tomorrow will be Fair* (1946). Novels for teenagers: *Practically Seventeen* (1949); *Double Date* (1951); *Boy Trouble* (1953); *A Man for Marcy* (1954); *Senior Prom* (1957); *Wedding in the Family* (1958); *Double Wedding* (1959).

Dukesborough Tales (1871), short stories by RICHARD MALCOLM JOHNSTON. These were revisions of stories originally published as *Georgia Sketches* (1864). The scene of the stories, the imaginary Dukesborough, was Powelton, near which stood Johnston's plantation birthplace "Oak Grove." He wrote about school life, family feuds, red-letter days in the village, always sympathetically and humorously, and showed himself, says Carlos Baker, "a gifted raconteur in the leisurely manner."

Dulcy (1921), a comedy by GEORGE S. KAUFMAN and MARC CONNELLY. The leading character, a perpetrator of bromides and platitudes, was transferred from a column by Franklin P. Adams. In the play she is, in addition, a blunderer who almost ruins a business deal for her husband. But her efforts unexpectedly turn out all right.

Dunbar, Paul Laurence (b. Dayton, Ohio, June 27, 1872—d. Feb. 9, 1906), poet, novelist. The famous Negro poet's predecessors in the

use of Negro dialect were white writers like Irwin Russell, Stephen Collins Foster, Joel

Chandler Harris, and Thomas Nelson Page, but none of them was able to portray Negro life with the sincerity and knowledge that Dunbar displayed. He lived in an era when literary regionalism and the use of dialect were the vogue; he was especially under Page's influence, and as an admirer of Robert Burns and James Whitcomb Riley wrote poetry in the sentimental school. He was, too, under the sway of the plantation and its traditions; and the master is shown as "smilin' on de darkies from de hall." As an Ohioan he did not know the Deep South, and the somewhat bitter portrayal of Negro life in a white culture was still to come. His mother had been a slave, and he listened to her stories; and he knew many small Negro communities in various parts of the country. He regretted the neglect of his poems not in dialect; he was unquestionably skillful in both media. His early verse collections, *Oak and Ivy* (1893) and *Majors and Minors* (1895), were brought together in the famous *Lyrics of Lowly Life* (1896). Later came *Lyrics of the Hearthside* (1899), *Lyrics of Love and Laughter* (1903), and *Lyrics of Sunshine and Shadow* (1905). His novels (including *The Uncalled*, 1898, and *The Sport of the Gods*, 1902) have been called "inept," "conventional," "weak." L. K. Wiggins prepared *The Life and Works of P. L. Dunbar* (1907); B. G. Brawley wrote his biography in 1936.

Duncan, Isadora (b. San Francisco, May 27, 1878—d. Sept. 14, 1927), dancer, writer. One of the first exponents of the "modern dance," Miss Duncan created a sensation in Europe with her interpretive programs on naturalistic and classical Greek themes. She established dance schools in several European capitals with considerable success, and also one in the United States, but her popularity in this country never equaled her reputation abroad. She was, nevertheless, widely acclaimed by the young American expatriate writers of the early 1920's, who much admired her break with the conventions of her art and with conventions in general. She married the celebrated Russian lyric poet Sergei Esenin in 1922. Miss Duncan wrote *The Art of the Dance* (1928), and spoke in frank terms of her own career in *My Life* (1927). She died in an automobile accident.

Duncan, Norman (b. Canada, July 2, 1871—d. Oct. 18, 1916), newspaperman, storyteller, teacher. By chance Duncan went to Newfoundland to gather material for a volume of sea stories, his first trip of any kind at sea or in a sailing vessel. From then on, he was deeply attracted to sea life, and his best books had the ocean as their background: *Doctor Luke of the Labrador* (1904); *The Adventures of Billy Topsail* (1906); *The Cruise of the Shining Light* (1907); *Australian Byways* (1915).

Duncan, Robert (b. Oakland, Calif., Jan. 7, 1919—), poet. An original and highly distinctive poet, Duncan occupies an important place in the new American poetry as a practicing artist, theorist, and spokesman. His collections of verse, which include *Caesar's Gate* (1955), *Letters* (1958), and *Selected Poems* (1959),

are characterized by intensity, disciplined irony, precise and personal music.

Duncan, Thomas W[illiam] (b. Casey, Iowa, Aug. 15, 1905—), newspaperman, teacher, actor, writer. After working for Des Moines papers, Duncan taught English and journalism at the Des Moines College of Pharmacy and at Grinnell College (1934–44). He was active in the Iowa literary revival of the 1930's, and began publishing verse: *Hours from a Life* (1927); *Elephants at War* (1935); and novels: *O, Chautauqua* (1935); *We Pluck This Flower* (1937); *Ring Horse* (1940); *Gus the Great* (1947); *Big River, Big Man* (1959); and *Virgo Descending* (1961).

Dunham, Katherine (b. Chicago, 1914—), dancer, choreographer, anthropologist, writer. After obtaining her degree at the University of Chicago, Miss Dunham did research work in the West Indies, especially in Jamaica. Her first major dancing performance was given in Chicago in 1934; she appeared thereafter in *Cabin in the Sky* (1941) and in various other plays and movies, also with several symphony orchestras. *Journey to Accompang* (1946), in its description of a small mountain village in Jamaica, is a strange mixture of anthropology and mysticism, expert discussion of dancing technique and sheer love of adventure. She has written numerous magazine articles on the dance and the theater; in *Esquire* she has used the pen name "K. Dunn." *Touch of Innocence* appeared in 1959.

Dunlap, William (b. Perth Amboy, N.J., Feb. 19, 1766—d. Sept. 28, 1839), artist, dramatist,

theatrical manager, historian. Sent to England to study under Benjamin West, Dunlap deserted his early love for painting, haunted the theaters for three years, came back determined to make the drama his vocation. He was never a great dramatist, but he wrote effectively and composed sixty-five plays, including adaptations of foreign dramas. Not long after 1787 he wrote a comedy, *The Modest Soldier, or, Love in New York,* which has not survived. It contained, said Dunlap, "a Yankee servant," and was obviously based on THE CONTRAST, by Royall Tyler. His first play to be produced was THE FATHER (1789). Dunlap himself thought THE ITALIAN FATHER (1799) his best play, though critics have usually preferred his blank-verse tragedy, *André* (1798).

Dunlap ran a theater and company of his own until he went bankrupt. He was an intelligent producer, designed sets himself, wrote a *History of the American Theater* (1832) and a *History of the Rise and Progress of the Arts of Design in the U.S.* (1834). In later years he returned to his interest in painting. The Dunlap Society has issued some of his writings. Dorothy C. Barck edited *The Diary of William Dunlap* (3 v., 1930), using material selected from eleven of Dunlap's thirty or more manuscript diaries. Oral S. Coad wrote *William Dunlap: A Study of His Life and Works* (1917). There are collections of Dunlap manuscripts in the New York Historical Library and at Yale.

Dunne, Finley Peter (b. Chicago, July 10, 1867—d. April 24, 1936), newspaperman, editor, humorist. Dunne began his career on several Chicago newspapers, creating his "Mr. Dooley" for the Chicago *Post.* Later he was on the staff of the New York *Morning Telegraph.* Leaving newspaper work, he became part owner of the AMERICAN MAGAZINE, to which he contributed a pungent department entitled "The Interpreter's House," and later was made editor of COLLIER'S. He retired several years before his death. He was a genial, generous, witty man who hated to write. Thomas A. Daly described him as "a kind of leprechaun."

Dunne's fame rests entirely and solidly on his creation of MR. DOOLEY. Martin Dooley is a Chicago Irishman of undiminished brogue who presides over a small saloon on Archey Road. Dooley was modeled, Dunne said, on a saloonkeeper named James McGarry. In his earlier pieces Dunne called his philosophic barkeeper Col. McNeery, but when McGarry objected to the too ready identification, Dunne changed the name to Dooley.

From behind his particular bar of justice, Mr. Dooley reviews the events of the world with a wit and wisdom his era found irresistible. He makes his remarks to his own Boswell, his friend Malachi Hennessey, whom Dooley describes as "a post to hitch ye'er silences to." Many other characters come in from time to time and play their roles in Dunne's symposia. As Lloyd Morris points out, Dooley's remarks were followed by all men in public life, who with good reason dreaded the puncturing barb of Dooley's scorn. Dooley's appeal, says Morris, "was like a social plumb line. It not only struck the plain people at the bottom but reached to the intellectuals at the top. He was a favorite of such improbable readers as Henry Adams and Henry James." Possibly Mr. Dooley's most famous utterance was this: "Whether th' Constitution follows th' flag or not, th' Supreme Court follows th' illiction returns." "There's only one thing," said Dooley elsewhere, "that would make me allow mesilf to be a hero to the American people, and that is it don't last long."

Dunne wrote more than seven hundred essays about Mr. Dooley, only about a third of which were collected in book form. *Mr. Dooley in Peace and War* (1898) was followed by *Mr. Dooley in the Hearts of His Countrymen* (1898); *What Mr. Dooley Says* (1899); *Mr. Dooley's Philosophy* (1900); *Mr. Dooley's Opinions* (1901); and several other collections down to 1919, when Dooley at last fell silent. A collection called *Mr. Dooley at His Best* (1938), edited by Elmer Ellis, has an introduction by Dunne. Thomas L. Masson once remarked that "if all the newspaper files and histories were destroyed between the years 1898 and 1910, and nothing remained but Mr. Dooley's observations, they would be enough" to reconstruct the life of those years.

Dunning, Philip [Hart] (b. Meriden, Conn., Dec. 11, 1890—d. Feb. 10, 1957), playwright, producer. John Chapman described Dunning in 1926 as a young man "who had done song-and-dance acts, played summer stock, and written some plays." His BROADWAY (1926), with GEORGE ABBOTT, was picked as one of the ten best plays of the season, and was printed in Van H. Cartmell and Bennett Cerf's *Famous Plays of Crime and Detection* (1946). Dunning wrote other successful plays, often in collaboration. Among them: *The Understudy* (1927); *Lilly Turner* (1932); *Kill That Story* (1934); *Page Miss Glory* (1934); *Remember the Day* (1935) —all exploiting, as Bernard Sobel says, "the same vein of hearty comedy."

Dunton, John (1659–1733), an English bookseller who traveled in New England for several months in 1686 and published impressions of his visit in *The Life and Errors of John Dunton* (1705). His fictional *Letters from New England* were not printed until 1867.

Dupin, C. Auguste. An amateur detective introduced into three stories of Edgar Allan Poe, THE MURDERS IN THE RUE MORGUE (1841), THE MYSTERY OF MARIE ROGÊT (three parts, 1842–43), and THE PURLOINED LETTER (1845). His personality, his unofficial status, his bewildered friend and admirer who narrates the stories, his use of clues, his dextrous employment of unjust suspicions, his logic in unveiling the criminal—all these traits have become characteristic of later fictional detectives; with Dupin the true detective story begins its strange and multifarious career. A letter published in the New York *World* (1879) claimed that Poe took the name from one C. Auguste Dupont, a man of great analytical powers who frequently helped the police of Paris; a friend, who wrote the letter and signed the initials F.D.C., claimed that he had told Poe about him. Dupin was not modeled on the famous French police officer Vidocq, says Howard Haycraft, since Poe was specifically trying to show the superiority of the gifted amateur to the professional.

Du Ponceau, Pierre [Peter] Étienne [Stephen] (b. France, June 3, 1760—d. April 1, 1844), historian, philologist, lawyer. Educated in France, Du Ponceau came to America as Baron Steuben's secretary and served him as aide-de-camp, with the rank of captain. Forced to leave because of illness, he became an American citizen in 1781, was admitted to the bar in 1785, and became an authority on international law. He was elected president of the American Philosophical Society in 1828. In addition to writings on law and philology (including dissertations on the Chinese system of writing and on the grammar of some of the Indian tribes), he wrote *A Discourse on the Necessity and the Means of Making Our National Literature Independent of That of Great Britain* (1834), a pioneer work in its field.

Dupuy, Eliza Ann (b. Petersburg, Va., 1814—d. Jan. 15, 1881), novelist. In addition to numerous short stories written for the New York *Ledger* under the pen name Annie Young, Miss Dupuy wrote several historical novels, the best-known of which were *The Conspirator* (1850), with AARON BURR as the central figure, and *The Huguenot Exiles* (1856), based in part on her own family history.

Durant, Will[iam James] (b. N. Adams, Mass., Nov. 5, 1885—   ), teacher, philosopher, historian. Durant, perhaps the greatest popularizer of philosophic ideas in American publishing history, wrote *The Story of Philosophy* first as a lecture series, then as a series for THE LITTLE BLUE BOOKS of Haldeman-Julius. When the lectures were printed as a book in 1926, they attained a phenomenal success. The grand total of copies sold soon passed the million mark, and the book was translated into a dozen languages. Aside from a novel, *Transition* (1927), largely autobiographical, Durant devoted himself thereafter to writing *The Story of Civilization* on a grand scale: *Our Oriental Heritage* (1935); *The Life of Greece* (1939); *Caesar and Christ* (1944); *The Age of Faith* (1950); *The Renaissance* (1953); *The Reformation* (1957); *The Age of Reason Begins* (1961), in collaboration with Ariel Durant. Durant sees little use in history unless it illuminates the present, and his own accounts are intended to interpret the 20th century in terms of the past and the past in terms of the 20th century.

Duranty, Walter (b. England, May 25, 1884—d. Oct. 3, 1957), journalist, novelist. Educated at Harrow and Cambridge, Duranty wandered for several years through England, France, and America, earning a scant living as a tutor and free-lance writer. In 1913 he joined the Paris bureau of the *New York Times*, serving one year in World War I as a correspondent with the French Army. In 1921 he was sent to Russia, and his objective and factual reporting from that country won him the reputation of being one of the ablest of foreign correspondents. In 1932 he was awarded the Pulitzer Prize for reporting. Although his fiction—*One Life, One Kopeck* (1937), *The Gold Train* (1938), *Return to the Vineyard* (1945, with Mary Loos)—was not favorably received, a number of his books on Russia have been praised as highly informed, unbiased, and skillfully written. Among the latter are *Moscow Trials* (1929); *Duranty Reports Russia* (1934); *I Write as I Please* (1935); *The Kremlin and the People* (1941); *USSR* (1944); and *Stalin & Co.: The Politburo—the Men Who Run Russia* (1949).

Dutchman's Fireside, The (1831), a novel by JAMES KIRKE PAULDING. The story tells how Sybrandt Nestbrook, a rural lad in the period of the French and Indian Wars, woos a fashionable girl whose hand is sought by many suitors. The hero undergoes adventures on the frontier, is reported killed, but returns in time to win the hand of his Catalina Vancour. Westbrook seems to have been modeled in part on Paulding himself. Alexander Cowie calls this Paulding's best novel, and praises the faithfulness with which it depicts old Dutch life. See SIR WILLIAM JOHNSON.

Duval, John C. See THE ADVENTURES OF BIG-FOOT WALLACE.

Duyckinck, Evert Augustus (b. New York City, Nov. 23, 1816—d. Aug. 13, 1878), and **Duyckinck, George Long** (b. New York City, Oct. 17, 1823—d. March 30, 1863), editors, literary historians, biographers, encyclopedists. These brothers were active in the literary life of New York City and the nation during the middle years of the 19th century and exerted a beneficent influence in helping new and young authors and in spreading sound literary information and criticism. They often worked together; for example, in editing the New York LITERARY WORLD [1] (1847–53) and in compiling their monumental and still valuable two-volume *Cyclopaedia of American Literature* (1855). In the latter work they discussed all the important authors up to and including their own times, and made a point of providing liberal selections from these authors' writings, so that the book was also an anthology. It ran to 1,470 pages. In 1866 Evert Duyckinck prepared a *Supplement* of 160 pages. In 1875 Michael Laird Simons brought the book down to 1873, with the two volumes running to 2,080 pages. The elder Duyckinck edited *Arcturus* (1840–42). His extensive library was bequeathed to the New York Public Library, together with his correspondence and notebooks. The younger brother wrote biographies of George Herbert (1858), Jeremy Taylor (1860), and others.

Lowell gave Evert Duyckinck a place in *A Fable for Critics* (1848), calling him a ripe scholar and a neat critic, "who through Grub Street the soul of a gentleman carries." His house was a rendezvous for men of letters in his day; he encouraged Melville at a time when he particularly needed help, and Hawthorne, Bryant, Irving, Lowell, Simms, and many others were his intimate friends. Robert E. Spiller says that the contributors to the *Literary World* made it "as brilliant a literary journal as this country has known."

Dvořák, Anton (1841–1904), Czech composer and music director. In a prolonged visit to the United States, this great musician directed the National Conservatory of Music in New York (1892–95) and was deeply impressed with the musical possibilities of American, Negro, and Indian folksongs. His *New World Symphony* (1893) includes fragments and echoes of some of these folksongs; for example *Swing Low, Sweet Chariot;* YANKEE DOODLE; and *Peter Gray.* According to Sigmund Spaeth (*A History of Popular Music in America,* 1948), William Arms Fisher turned the "Largo" of the symphony into a song called *Goin' Home* (1922), "now widely accepted as an authentic Negro spiritual, even though entirely the work of two white men." Then in 1934, Billy Hill and Peter De Rose built a song hit, *Wagon Wheels,* on *Goin' Home* and *Swing Low.* Dvořák's popular HUMORESQUE, written for the violin, gave its title to Fannie Hurst's short story by that name (1919), made later into a motion picture (1920).

Dwiggins, W[illiam] A[ddison] (b. Martinsville, Ohio, June 19, 1880—d. Dec. 25, 1956), illustrator, book designer, writer. As an associate of several presses and publishers, Dwiggins had a marked and beneficial influence on page design and book format. He urged a reform of paper currency design and in 1945 published a strange but impressive play, *Millennium 1* which presented the not unfamiliar idea of machines taking over the rule of the earth. In the play characters like 00, Action 5, .33+, and N77 run affairs. But man—known as homogrub—still exists, and seeks to regain control.

Dwight, John S[ullivan] (b. Boston, May 13, 1813—d. Sept. 5, 1893), clergyman, music critic, editor. One of the earliest and most influential of the transcendentalists, Dwight was active at BROOK FARM, wrote for THE DIAL, and became music editor of a Brook Farm periodical called *The Harbinger* (1845–49), which continued to be published after the colony passed out of existence. In 1852 he founded the important *Dwight's Journal of Music,* organized music groups in Boston and nearby, and became a leading authority in the field. He was much attracted to German romanticism and was influential in introducing German philosophical ideas in America. His sister, **Marianne Dwight Orvis** (1816–1901), was likewise a transcendentalist and wrote the *Letters from Brook Farm, 1844–47* (1928). See TRANSCENDENTALISM.

Dwight, Theodore (b. Northampton, Mass., Dec. 15, 1764—d. June 12, 1846), lawyer, editor, poet. Like his brother Timothy, Dwight was one of the Connecticut Wits, and in THE ECHO and THE POLITICAL GREENHOUSE wrote passable verse. He was a staunch Federalist, attacking the anti-Federalists in his *History of the Hartford Convention* (1833) and in *The Character of Thomas Jefferson* (1839). His son, **Theodore Dwight, Jr.** (b. Hartford, Conn.,

March 3, 1796—d. Oct. 16, 1866), was an editor (*Dwight's American Magazine,* 1845–52) and the author of travel books and biographies. He wrote a quaint volume, in some respects well ahead of his generation: *The Father's Book, or, Suggestions for the Government and Instruction of Young Children* (1834). In it he advocated that "children should be made as comfortable as possible at church," and he hoped the time would come when "good men would give due attention" to the improvement of toys and games for children. See HARTFORD WITS; THE ECHO.

Dwight, Timothy [1] (b. Northampton, Mass., May 14, 1752—d. Jan. 11, 1817), clergyman, teacher, poet. Ready for college at eight, and entering Yale at thirteen, Dwight graduated with full honors and, after an active career as teacher, chaplain in the Continental army,

TIMOTHY DWIGHT (1752–1817)

minister, and literary man, came back to Yale as president in 1795 and as professor of theology; he held both positions until his death. About seventy years later his grandson and namesake, **Timothy Dwight [2]** (b. Norwich, Conn., Nov. 16, 1828—d. May 26, 1916), likewise served as president of Yale (1886–98).

Few men have led such varied lives as the elder Dwight, or spoken authoritatively on so many matters with such supreme self-confidence. He was a great preacher, a theologian who was the grandson and successor of JONATHAN EDWARDS, a capable administrator, a man ready to give his judgments on law, politics, finance, agriculture, or literature. V. L. Parrington, who decidedly disliked Dwight's politics and theology, said: "The great Timothy seems to a later generation to have been little more than a walking depository of the venerable Connecticut *status quo."* Probably his fame rests most securely on his literary productions as a member of the "Connecticut Wits." He wrote, in what he believed was "the grand style," a Biblical epic, THE CONQUEST OF CANAAN [1]. One English reader defied anyone to read the poem "without yawning an hundred times"; and Alexander Cowie remarks that Dwight and his fellow "Wit," JOEL BARLOW, each with a burning desire to win fame for their nation in epic poems, were "lured to their ultimate ruin in morasses of heroic couplets." His best piece was the bucolic poem, GREENFIELD HILL (1794), describing the charming Connecticut village in which he lived for years. His stanch Federalism appeared in such works as *The Duty of Americans at the Present Crisis* (1798). He attacked the theater in *Essay on the Stage* (1824); his popular sermons were collected in *Theology, Explained and Defended* (1818–19). See HARTFORD WITS; COLUMBIA.

Dying Cowboy, The. An American folk song, also known as *The Cowboy's Lament*. Louise Pound holds it to be "a plainsman's adaptation of *An Unfortunate Rake,* current in Ireland as early as 1790."

Dying Indian, The (1784), a poem by PHILIP FRENEAU. One of the finest of Freneau's poems and one of the earliest of American writings to set forth a picture of "the noble red man," as a complement to the more popular notion of "the ferocious savage." Elsewhere, as Harry Hayden Clark points out, Freneau viewed the Indian "not through primitivistic but through realistic eyes as barbarous and cruel." In his short poem *The Indian Convert,* for example, he portrays the native in an unfavorable light. See DEATHSONGS.

E

Each and All (*Western Messenger*, February, 1839), a poem by RALPH WALDO EMERSON. It was included in the *Poems* of 1847. An expression of Emerson's intense faith in the oneness of the universe, the poem praises "the perfect whole" in which all parts depend on one another: "Nothing is fair or good alone." The poem was inspired by a walk along the seashore, described in the poet's *Journals*. H. H. Clark points out that Emerson was influenced by neo-Platonic concepts and by an essay in Coleridge's *The Friend*.

Each in His Own Tongue (1906; in a collection by the same title, 1909), verses by William Herbert Carruth (1859–1924). Extremely popular and reprinted several times since its original publication the poem was sometimes called *Evolution*, from its most famous line, "Some call it Evolution, others call it God."

Eagle, The. A newspaper, also called *The Dartmouth Centinel*, published from 1793 to 1799 in New Hampshire. It was especially notable for the contributions of JOSEPH DENNIE and ROYALL TYLER.

Eagle and the Mole, The (published in *Nets to Catch the Wind*, 1921), a poem by ELINOR WYLIE. In it she bids the reader avoid "the reeking herd" and "the polluted flock," and live like the stoic eagle. The poem, along with others in the collection, is an expression, says Alfred Kreymborg, of the poet's "aristocratic scorn" and her "adoration of symbolic animals."

Eagle of Corinth, The (1862), a poem by HENRY HOWARD BROWNELL. On Oct. 3–4, 1862, Corinth, in northeastern Mississippi, was the scene of a battle in which General W. S. Rosecrans defeated the Confederate forces. During the Confederate attempt to recapture the city, a live eagle was carried by the Eighth Wisconsin instead of a flag. It circled over the battlefield during the engagement and suggested the poem to Brownell.

Eagle That Is Forgotten, The (published in *General William Booth Enters into Heaven and Other Poems*, 1913), a poem by VACHEL LINDSAY. It is an elegy dedicated to the memory of the liberal and courageous governor of Illinois, JOHN PETER ALTGELD (1847–1902).

Eakins, Thomas (b. Philadelphia, July 25, 1844—d. June 25, 1916), painter, sculptor, teacher. Eakins first attended the Pennsylvania Academy of Fine Arts, then studied in Paris. On his return to Philadelphia he took up the study of anatomy at Jefferson Medical College as an aid in his work; some of his paintings present medical clinics. He stressed realism, particularly in his depiction of the human body. In 1873 he joined the staff of the Pennsylvania Academy, and later was appointed its dean. Famous paintings of his include *The Clinic of Dr. Gross, The Clinic of Dr. Agnew, The Writing Master, Chess Players, Max Schmitt in a Single Scull,* and *The Thinker*.

Eames, Wilberforce (b. Newark, N.J., Oct. 12, 1855—d. Dec. 6, 1937), librarian, bibliographer. Eames joined the staff of the Lenox Library in 1885 and in 1895 became chief bibliographer of the New York Public Library. His specialty was Americana; he continued Sabin's *Dictionary of Books Relating to America* (1885–92). Among his books: *John Eliot and the Indians* (1915) and *The First Year of Printing in New York* (1928).

Earle, Alice Morse (b. Worcester, Mass., April 27, 1853—d. Feb. 16, 1911), historian. Mrs. Earle's specialty was colonial history, and her books in this field are both accurate and lively. Among them are *The Sabbath in Puritan New England* (1891); *Customs and Fashions in Old New England* (1893); *Colonial Dames and Goodwives* (1895); *Child Life in Colonial Days* (1899); *Stage-Coach and Tavern Days* (1900); *Two Centuries of Costume in America* (1903).

Earl of Pawtucket, The (1903), a comedy by AUGUSTUS THOMAS. The star of the original production was Lawrence d'Orsay; the play made a great hit and ran for 191 performances. Against the background of the old Waldorf-Astoria Hotel in New York City a British nobleman pretends to be an American named Montgomery Putnam in order to win the hand of an American girl. She turns out to be the divorced wife of the man whose name he has taken. He blunders blandly on to a happy ending.

Early Autumn: A Story of a Lady (1926), a novel by LOUIS BROMFIELD. A bleak story of the effect of Puritanic views on a woman who seeks in vain to escape. Her marriage to a wealthy New Englander puts her in a prison of tradition with unhappy people all around her. She is ready to get away when she is trapped into staying—knowing what a drab existence will be hers in the future. Bromfield was one of the first to portray a typical New England figure —Michael O'Hara, self-made man and politician, who is denied entrance into the "high society" circles of the town. The novel won a Pulitzer Prize.

Early Western Travels, 1748–1846 (32 v., 1904–07), edited by REUBEN GOLD THWAITES. Annotated reprints of narratives describing early explorations of the West.

Earth (1835), a poem by WILLIAM CULLEN BRYANT. Inspired by Italian scenery as he observed it in 1834, Bryant wrote this poem, some passages of which, W. A. Bradley states, are "perhaps more impressive than anything he had written since *Thanatopsis*." Bradley stresses particularly Bryant's power to give "an imaginative sense of immensity."

Easiest Way, The (1909), a play by EUGENE WALTER. Laura Murdock is the mistress of a wealthy man, but falls in love with John Madison, a newspaper reporter. She tries to reform, but in destitution returns to her rich lover. John repudiates her when he returns with the money to marry her and finds out. A. H. Quinn concludes that the play is merely "a skillfully contrived melodrama, in which Walter had the courage to run the motive through to an unhappy ending."

Eastburn, James W[allis] (b. England, Sept. 26, 1797—d. Dec. 2, 1819), clergyman, hymn writer, poet. Eastburn came to New York when he was six, and became an Episcopal clergyman in Virginia. He was one of the first American writers to depict the Indian in a friendly light. In collaboration with ROBERT C. SANDS, a New York editor (1799–1832), he wrote an epic in six cantos entitled *Yamoyden: A Tale of the Wars of King Philip* (1820). He and his friend divided the material, some of which came from hasty reading of William Hubbard's NARRATIVE OF THE TROUBLES WITH THE INDIANS IN NEW ENGLAND (1677). Before the book was published Eastburn died at sea on a voyage undertaken for his health. Throughout the poem the Indians are represented as entirely in the right, the Puritans as altogether in the wrong. In the fourth canto felicitous use is made of the customs, rites, and superstitions of the Indians. A review of the poem by J. C. Palfrey appeared in the *North American Review* (April, 1821), in which the authors were praised for making such good use of early American history. Several writers were inspired to imitate the poem.

Eastlake, William (b. New York City, July 14, 1917—   ), novelist, short story writer. Eastlake attended the Alliance Française, Paris. After his return to the United States he moved to a cattle ranch in northern New Mexico, the country that serves as a background for his novels: *Go in Beauty* (1956); *Bronc People* (1958); and *Pilgrims to the Wake* (1961). His short stories have appeared in *Collier's, Saturday Evening Post, Hudson Review, Evergreen Review, Harper's, Kenyon Review,* and others. He is represented in Martha Foley's *Best Short Stories of 1955, 1956, 1957;* in the *O. Henry Prize Stories of 1959;* and in *Fiction of the Fifties* (1959).

East Lynne (1861), a novel by Mrs. Henry Wood. This English novel of intrigue among characters of high social rank was a best seller in the United States and was equally popular as a play. Lady Isabel Vane mistakenly accuses her husband of infidelity and runs off with another man. Later, disguised as a nurse, she is hired by her remarried husband to care for her own children. Disclosure of the pretense and their reconciliation occur at her deathbed. It is said that Miss Lucille Western, an emotional actress of the time, paid Clifton W. Tayleure, an actor who occasionally wrote plays, $100 to dramatize *East Lynne* and then, in a single season, performed the tear-jerker more than nine hundred times.

Eastman, Charles A[lexander] [Indian name: Ohiyesa] (b. Redwood Falls, Minn., 1858—d. Jan. 8, 1939), physician, historian, autobiographer. Of Indian (Sioux) descent, Eastman devoted his writings to accounts of his own life and to the history and glorification of the red man. Among his books: *An Indian Boyhood* (1902); *Red Hunters and the Animal People* (1904); *Old Indian Days* (1907); *Wigwam Evenings* (with his wife Elaine Goodale Eastman, 1909); *The Soul of the Indian* (1911); *From the Deep Woods to Civilization* (1916); *Indian Heroes and Great Chieftains* (1918).

Eastman, Charles Gamage (b. Fryeburg, Me., June 1, 1816—d. Sept. 16, 1860), newspaperman, poet. His verses, collected in *Poems* (1848), won him a wide popular reputation. He was called "the Burns of New England." He established two periodicals, *Spirit of the Age* (1840) and *Vermont Patriot* (1846).

Eastman, Mary H[enderson] (b. Warrenton, Va., 1818—d. 1880), historian, writer on Indian legends, storyteller. It is believed that Mrs. Eastman's *Dahcotah, or, Life and Legends of the Sioux Around Fort Snelling* (1849) inspired Longfellow to write HIAWATHA (1855). She also compiled *The American Aboriginal Portfolio* (1853). Her *Aunt Phillis's Cabin; or, Southern Life As It Is* (1852) was a rejoinder to H. B. Stowe's *Uncle Tom's Cabin* (1852). Her husband, **Seth Eastman** (b. Brunswick, Me., Jan. 24, 1808—d. Aug. 31, 1875), an artist and an army officer, became familiar with Indian tribes in the course of his service and was called upon to illustrate several books dealing with them. Among them were Henry R. Schoolcraft's *Information Concerning the History, Condition, and Prospects of the Indian Tribes of the U.S.* (published by order of Congress, 1851–57) and some books by his wife, among them *Dahcotah*.

Eastman, Max [Forrester] (b. Canandaigua, N.Y., Jan. 4, 1883—d. March 25, 1969), poet, critic, teacher, essayist, historian, editor. Eastman, whose father and mother were both Congregational ministers, began his career as a teacher of philosophy and psychology at Columbia University. He was then primarily interested in aesthetics; some of his best books were in this field, particularly *The Enjoyment of Poetry* (1913) and THE ENJOYMENT OF LAUGHTER (1936). But the First World War drew him into the vortex of political and economic controversy; he became a Marxist, but was subsequently a bitter opponent of the Stalinist development of Marxism. He edited Karl Marx and translated some of Pushkin and Trotsky. He helped found and edit two important magazines, THE MASSES (1911) and THE LIBERATOR (1917) and was tried for sedition when the former was suppressed for antiwar writings in 1917. His first book, *The Enjoyment of Poetry*, went into over twenty editions. It is a study of the psychology of literature and its popularity continues. Other books by Eastman are: *Marxism: Is It Science?* (1940); *Heroes I Have Known* (1942); *Lot's Wife,* (narrative poem) (1942); *Enjoyment of Living* (1948); *Poems of Five Decades* (1954);

Reflections on the Failure of Socialism (1955); *Great Companions—Critical Memoirs of Some Famous Friends* (1959).

Eastman, Seth. See MARY H. EASTMAN.

East of Eden (1952), a novel by JOHN STEINBECK. The most ambitious of Steinbeck's novels, *East of Eden* is based on a reconstruction of the Biblical story of Cain and Abel and centers around the lives of Adam Trask and his two sons, Cal and Aron. Both the "Adam" and the "Abel" of the story, Adam Trask fights with his brother Charles for the love of their father, then sets out from their New England farm on a series of journeys that finally bring him and his new wife, Cathy, to the Salinas valley in California. Cathy, an incarnation of pure evil, bears Adam twin sons and then deserts him to become a prostitute, leaving Adam emotionally crippled. Thanks to the intervention of Lee, the Chinese servant, and the fatherly wisdom of Sam Hamilton, Adam partially recovers and is able to raise the children, but as the boys grow older it is apparent that they are reenacting the Cain and Abel drama in themselves. Adam favors Aron at the expense of Cal, and is unable to forgive Cal when he drives Aron to his death by telling him that their mother is a prostitute. The moral and philosophical import of the book lies in its long center section in which Lee and Adam discuss God's admonition to Adam after the Fall, and the implications of the Hebrew word "timshel," which Steinbeck interprets to mean "thou mayest" (rather than "thou shalt") conquer over sin. Given a choice, man is free and can decide for himself; Adam's final realization of this enables him to forgive Cal at the close of the book.

Eastward in Eden (1947, pub. 1949), a play by Dorothy Gardner based on the life of Emily Dickinson. Miss Gardner accepted the theory that it was Emily's unrequited love for Charles Wadsworth, a married Philadelphia clergyman, that turned her into a recluse. Brooks Atkinson thought the play came closest of any thus far to recapturing Emily's elusive character.

Eaton, Evelyn Sybil Mary (b. Switzerland, Dec. 22, 1902—   ), Canadian-American writer. An American citizen since 1944, Miss Eaton began teaching creative writing at Sweet Briar College in 1950. She has written many sensitive novels with historic settings, including: *Desire-Spanish Version* (1932); *Quietly My Captain Waits* (1940); *In What Torn Ship* (1944); *Every Month Was May* (1947); *Give Me Your Golden Hand* (1951); *Flight* (1954); *I Saw My Mortal Sight* (1959). Her poetry includes: *Stolen Hours* (1923); *Birds Before Dawn* (1943); *Small Hour* (1955). *Every Month Was May* (1947) and *The North Star is Nearer* (1949) have autobiographical sketches of her childhood and youth in Canada, England, and France.

Eaton, Walter Prichard (b. Malden, Mass., Aug. 24, 1878—d. Feb. 27, 1957), teacher, critic, author of books for boys. Eaton worked on Boston and New York newspapers, became professor of playwriting at Yale (1933–47), and wrote extensively on the theater. Among his books:

The American Stage of Today (1908); *The Idyl of Twin Fires* (1915), a novel; *The Actor's Heritage* (1924); *The Theater Guild* (1929); *New England Vista* (1930).

Eben Holden (1900), a novel by IRVING BACHELLER. Laid in the middle years of the 19th century, it tells about an orphan lad who is befriended by a hired man, later gets a job on the New York *Tribune* with Horace Greeley, and fights for the North in the Civil War. Eben, noted for his homely sayings, watches over him paternally throughout. It was one of the most popular books of the day.

Eberhart, Mignon [Good] (b. Lincoln, Neb., July 6, 1899—   ), writer of detective fiction. In many of Mrs. Eberhart's stories the sleuth is a nurse, particularly the popular Sarah Keate. Her first book was *The Patient in Room 18* (1929). Most widely read were *While the Patient Slept* (1930) and *From This Dark Stairway* (1931). Others include *The Dark Garden* (1933); *The Glass Slipper* (1938); *The Sisters* (1944); *Five Passengers from Lisbon* (1946); *Never Look Back* (1951); *Unknown Quantity* (1953); *Man Missing* (1954); *Melora* (1959); *Jury of One* (1960). Howard Haycraft says that her stories blend "the conventional American-feminine method" with the psychological method found in Mrs. Belloc Lowndes' stories.

Eberhart, Nelle Richmond (b. Detroit, Mich., Aug. 28, 1871—d. Nov. 5, 1944), teacher, poet, librettist. Mrs. Eberhart collaborated frequently with the noted composer Charles Wakefield Cadman; for him she wrote the lyrics of two famous songs, *At Dawning* (1906) and *From the Land of the Sky-Blue Water* (1909). She supplied Cadman with lyrics for other Indian songs and with him wrote an opera, *A Witch of Salem* (1920), also the first radio opera, *The Willow Tree* (produced by NBC, Oct. 4, 1932).

Eberhart, Richard (b. Austin, Minn., April 5, 1904—   ), teacher, poet, lecturer, business-

man. Eberhart's experiences have been varied, ranging from teaching all over the United States to tutoring the son of King Prajadhipok of Siam, and acting as vice-president of a wax company. During World War II he served in the United States Naval Reserve and was discharged in 1946 with the rank of lt. commander. His first book was *A Bravery of Earth* (1930), followed by many others, mainly verse, as: *Poems, New and Selected* (1944); *Selected Poems* (1951); *Great Praises* (1957); *Collected Poems, 1930–1960* (1960). In 1959 President Eisenhower appointed him to the Advisory Committee on the Arts for the National Cultural Center in Washington. In 1960 he was elected to the National Institute of Arts and Letters. He served as Consultant in Poetry at the Library of Congress (1959–1961). In 1962, he was co-winner with John Hall Wheelock of the Bollingen Prize in Poetry.

Echo, The. A composite work of several of the "Connecticut Wits," but mainly the production of THEODORE DWIGHT and RICHARD ALSOP. A verse satire, it appeared in twenty sections in the *American Mercury* (1791–1805) and then as a collection (1807). The poem is vehemently and dogmatically Federalist in tone; Jefferson and others who revealed democratic tendencies were particular victims of the often effective ridicule. Samuel Marion Tucker called it "the one really clever and original literary satire of its time in America." See HARTFORD WITS.

Economic Interpretation of the Constitution, An (1913), a treatise by CHARLES A. BEARD. A famous book, in which Beard coolly examines the motives of the makers of the Constitution and claims that as men of property they were chiefly interested in constructing a charter to protect their wealth. Beard later complained that many of his followers stuck too literally to the theory of economic determinism. He said, "The economic interpretation is *one* key to history, not *the* key."

Eddy, Mary [Morse] Baker [Glover Patterson] (b. Bow, N.H., July 16, 1821—d. Dec. 3, 1910), religious leader, editor, author. The founder of the new belief usually called Christian Science, Mrs. Eddy published SCIENCE AND HEALTH (1875) as an exposition of her ideas and as the official statement of the organization she headed. The sales of this book have been very large. In this book and others of her *Miscellaneous Writings* (1896) she taught that pain, disease, old age, and death were "errors." She founded the Church of Christ, Scientist, in Boston (1879) and THE CHRISTIAN SCIENCE MONITOR. She wrote under the influence of Phineas P. Quimby (1802–1866) and the Transcendentalists, particularly Emerson, who had once said, "Never name sickness." Toward the end of her remarkable career she was subjected to attacks by the New York *World*, *McClure's Magazine*, and Mark Twain, who wrote a book on *Christian Science* (1907) ridiculing her doctrines. These doctrines were summarized in the first sentence of *Science and Health:* "The Prayer that reforms the sinner and heals the sick is an absolute faith that all things are possible to God." Stewart H. Holbrook speaks of Mrs. Eddy as "by all means the most dynamic American of her sex down to the present." E. F. Dakin's *Mrs. Eddy* (1929) includes a bibliography of her writings and the controversial literature her work provoked.

Eddy, Sherwood (b. Leavenworth, Kan., Jan. 19, 1871—d. March 4, 1963), social worker. As a Y.M.C.A. executive much of Eddy's work was done in various Asian countries, and he wrote books to help Americans understand these lands. Among them were: *India Awakening* (1911); *The New Era in Asia* (1913); *The Students of Asia* (1915); *The Challenge of Russia* (1930). He also wrote *God in History* (1947) and told the story of his life in *Eighty Adventurous Years* (1955) and *Why I Believe* (1957).

Edel, J[oseph] Leon (b. Pittsburgh, Pa., Sept. 9, 1907—   ), biographer, literary critic. Leon Edel attended McGill University, Montreal, in 1927 and 1928, and obtained a Doctor of Letters degree from the University of Paris, France, in 1932. He has been both a newspaperman and a teacher. His books include: *James Joyce: the Last Journey* (1947); *Henry James: the Untried Years* (1953); *Willa Cather* (1953), in collaboration with E. K. Brown; *The Psychological Novel* (1955); and *Literary Biography* (1957).

Edgar Huntly; or, Memoirs of a Sleep-Walker (1799), a novel by CHARLES BROCKDEN BROWN. The plot involves a supposed murder, an attempted murder, and a real murder. Clithero Edny kills his benefactress' brother to protect her and later attempts to kill her. Mary Waldegrave's brother is actually murdered, and Clithero is a suspect. But it turns out that Indians committed the crime. Alexander Cowie calls the novel "a fine detective story," and points out the influence of the pit scene in the story on Poe's *The Pit and the Pendulum*. The Indian characters are not idealized; Cowie notes that Cooper first attacked Brown, then imitated him.

Edgars. Imitating the "Oscars" awarded for distinguished work in the field of motion pictures, the Mystery Writers of America began in 1946 the award of "Edgars," named in honor of Edgar Allan Poe. The award at first consisted of a special limited edition of the Viking Press's *Portable Library Poe*. A bust of Poe is now awarded. The awards are given in several categories: the best mystery novel, movie, short story, radio program, mystery story criticism, factual crime story. Julius Fast's novel, *Watchful by Night*, was the winner of the first award.

Edict by the King of Prussia (Philadelphia *Public Advertiser*, September, 1773), a hoax by BENJAMIN FRANKLIN that was reprinted in Vol. VI of his *Writings*. The piece, which was read by Franklin in England to a group of English friends, was a circumstantial account of a claim to English territory supposedly presented by Frederick the Great. He based his claim on the fact that England itself had been settled by colonists from Germany, had never been emancipated, and had hitherto rendered little revenue to "our august house." It went on with straight-faced logic to strengthen this case with numerous details, set forth in addition what Englishmen would be permitted to do in the future in the way of manufacturing goods, and noted that thereafter he intended to send all German criminals to settle in England. The English sense of humor prevailed, once the nature of the hoax was perceived, and the *Edict* was widely reprinted. Carl Van Doren points out (in his life of Franklin, 1938) that Jefferson the following year stated there was no more reason why Britain should rule the English colonists in America than that Saxony should claim that right over the Saxon peoples in Britain.

Edison, Thomas A[lva] (b. Milan, Ohio, Feb. 11, 1847—d. Oct. 18, 1931), inventor, industrialist. Indirectly Edison greatly influenced the craft of writing by his inventions in various fields: the typewriter, the motion-picture camera, the phonograph. In his laboratories at Newark, Menlo Park, and West Orange, N.J., were perfected the contrivances for which patents were issued. *The Diary and Sundry Observations of Thomas Alva Edison* (edited by Dagobert D. Runes, 1948) showed him as a whimsical person with something of a poet's imagination. He is credited with the definition of *genius* as 2% inspiration and 98% perspiration.

editorial. The journalistic essay in which a newspaper expresses its opinion, as opposed to the news stories in which (theoretically) events are reported without bias. Editorials in most newspapers are usually reserved for the "editorial page"; occasionally important editorials may be printed on the front page, in which case it is customary to differentiate them from the news columns by typographical treatment, heading, or the like. The content of editorials may range from analysis of important political or international events to the expression of the publisher's sentiments on the first day of spring.

Editor's Drawer, The, and **The Editor's Easy Chair.** Two departments in HARPER'S MAGAZINE. The former was started in 1852, the latter in 1851. The "Drawer" had many humorous contributions, and its editors included Charles Dudley Warner and John Kendrick Bangs. The "Chair" was more definitely associated with particular persons who spoke their views on many matters, significant or whimsical. Its successive occupants were D. G. Mitchell, George William Curtis, William Dean Howells, E. S. Martin, Bernard De Voto, John Fischer.

Edman, Irwin (b. New York City, Nov. 28, 1896—d. Sept. 4, 1954), teacher, philosopher, essayist, poet. Edman was a graduate of Columbia University, rose to a professorship there. In his easy, attractive style he popularized many philosophical notions, without making any notable contributions of his own. Taking the position of the "questing philosopher," he was a Pragmatist tempered by Platonism and an easy-going worldliness. He was described by Houston Peterson as one who might, even in his 50's, "be taken at a distance for a slightly disheveled, absent-minded freshman looking for a nonexistent class-room. But there was nothing absent-minded about this little man with the incredible memory and strange voice when he lectured to large classes on the philosophy of art or conducted seminars on idealism, mysticism, or contemporary thought." Among his books: *Poems* (1925); *Four Ways of Philosophy* (1937); *Philosopher's Holiday* (1938); *Arts and the Man* (1939); *Philosopher's Quest* (1947); *Under Whatever Sky* (1951).

Edmonds, Walter D[umaux] (b. Boonville, N.Y., July 15, 1903—   ), novelist. Edmonds made his native region of northern New York as much his own literary property as it is possible for an author to do. Practically all his life he lived in the attractive village in which he was born, with its many historic memories; and the Black River, the Black River Canal, and the Erie Canal dominated his imagination. His stories are historical in setting, lively in manner. Among them: *Rome Haul* (1929); *Erie Water* (1933); DRUMS ALONG THE MOHAWK (1936); *Chad Hanna* (1940); *In the Hands of the Senecas* (1947); *The Wedding Journey* (1947). He has also written a number of juveniles, including *Tom Whipple* (1942), and *Uncle Ben's Whale* (1955); and two books of history: *The First Hundred Years* (1948), and *They Fought With What They Had* (1951).

Education for Ladies (1947), a historical account of ideas on female education in magazines for women, by Eleanor Wolf Thompson. Miss Thompson studied the period from 1830 to 1860, when the air was filled with all sorts of ideas for social reforms. Women began to assume a more important place; and, to reflect their new outlook, a number of small magazines sprang up. These were often sentimental and mawkish in tone, as their titles indicate—*Ladies' Garland, Ladies' Pearl, The Friend of Virtue, The Southern Rosebud, The Lily, The Magnolia.* They wanted young women to have more than "accomplishments," such as the ability to sing a sentimental song languishingly. Gradually more advanced schools were opened to them, including medical schools.

Education of Henry Adams, The (privately printed, 1907; posthumously published, 1918). This autobiography of a man who was the grandson of one President and the great-grandson of another is one of the most brilliant works in American literature. Written in the third person, it might be an account of the experiences of any sensitive man of his times, for its concerns are universal more than individual. It deals with a generation caught in a world whose values had been shaken by the discoveries of modern science, and shows Adams' attempt to find coherence in the new world. Henry Adams considered his "education" a failure. The book is sometimes factually inaccurate, and does not include the thirteen years of Adams' married life nor the seven years following his wife's suicide. Nevertheless, *The Education* is a modern restatement of a problem as old as the Greeks—man's need for unity in a complex world. Originally subtitled *A Study of Twentieth-Century*

Multiplicity, the *Education* was conceived as a companion volume to Mont-Saint-Michel and Chartres: A Study in Thirteenth Century Unity (privately printed, 1904; published, 1913). The two periods were symbolized respectively by the dynamo and the Virgin. In *The Education* the dynamo, representing modern mechanistic force, acts upon passive man who has lost his position as the center of the universe. Feeling himself an eighteenth century man out of place and dissatisfied with the modern world, Adams criticized his age for its inverted values in which, he said, "men become every year more and more creatures of force, massed about central power-houses. The conflict is no longer between the men, but between the motors that drive the men."

Education of H°y°m°a°n K°a°p°l°a°n, The (1937), a collection of humorous sketches by Leonard Ross (pen name of Leo Calvin Rosten). Mr. Parkhill, who conducts the beginners' grade in the American Night Preparatory School for Adults, regards the school as not merely a place where foreigners may learn the English language—"It [is] an incubator of Americans, a kind of intellectual Ellis Island." Ross' account of what takes place (published originally in *The New Yorker*) makes hilarious reading. A sequel, *The Return of H°y°m°a°n K°a°p°l°a°n* appeared in 1959.

Edwards, Gus (b. Germany, Aug. 18, 1879 —d. Nov. 7, 1945), singer, actor, producer, song writer. Edwards went on the stage at an early age, won renown as a singer, wrote popular songs of his own. His earliest hit was *I Couldn't Stand to See My Baby Lose* (1899). The best known of his songs are *Tammany* (1905); School Days (1907), which made him famous and led him to establish a music publishing firm; and *By the Light of the Silvery Moon* (1909). He made a specialty of encouraging new talent, including Eddie Cantor, Joe Cook, Jr., Groucho Marx, Lila Lee, Mae Murray, Helen Menken, and others. A motion picture, *The Star Maker* (1939), presented some of the more startling incidents of his career and revived some of his famous songs.

Edwards, Harry Stillwell (b. Macon, Ga., April 23, 1855—d. Oct. 22, 1938), lawyer, editor, public official, storyteller. Edwards had won a $10,000 prize for his novel *Sons and Fathers* (1896), and had published other volumes, but it was not until he was sixty-four that this distinguished Southerner wrote the little book that made his name—*Eneas Africanus* (1919). It is the story of a colored man who in 1865 becomes separated from his master and then for eight years wanders through the South —a humorous pilgrimage in a wilderness. His former master tries to find him; they are finally reunited. Edwards also wrote *Eneas Africanus, Defendant* (1921).

Edwards, Jonathan (b. East Windsor, Conn., Oct. 5, 1703—d. March 22, 1758), theologian, philosopher. One of the most extraordinary men produced on the American continent, Edwards was a precocious child with a deep interest in nature, science, philosophy, and theology. He entered Yale College at thirteen, and at seventeen experienced a mystic conversion which he described twenty years after in his "Personal Narrative." The pattern of Edwards' philosophi-

cal thought had begun to take shape while he was still a student at Yale, during which time he wrote his "Notes on Natural Science" and "Notes on the Mind." He lived in an age of scientific discovery; the works of Newton and Locke, just published at the end of the previous century, stimulated him to see the world, like Locke, in terms of sense impressions from which ideas are derived, and in terms of natural and immutable laws which reflect the perfection and absolute sovereignty of the Creator. Thus Edwards came to a philosophically idealistic and mystic view that all natural manifestations are shadows of a divine reality, and that, as ideas are a result of sense impressions, so moral grace is acquired through the senses, not through will or reason.

In the "Treatise on Grace" (published posthumously in 1865) Edwards differentiates between "common grace" and the regenerative "supernatural grace," which accompanies conversion and which grants the individual a new sense of spiritual awareness. This doctrine contained two concepts radically new in Puritan thought: conversion was an unmistakable occurrence, and involved the emotions even more than the reason. The Puritan church in the latter part of the seventeenth century had admitted all who wished to join to church membership and to communion, in the belief that communion might be a means of grace for the unregenerate. Edwards insisted that communion was a sacrament only for those who had already experienced conversion. This seemed intolerable to his parish, used to more lax standards, and it was primarily for this reason that he was asked to resign his leadership of the Church at Northampton in 1750. His beliefs on the place of the emotions in religious experience led him to champion the "GREAT AWAKENING" (c.1734–40) in which he saw dramatic conversions to be evidence of the "peculiar and immediate" manifestation of God.

Edwards' theology was more basically Calvinistic than that of the earlier Puritan divines, who emphasized the covenantal relation between man and God, rather than the absolute supremacy of a God bound by no contract. Edwards also followed Calvinistic thought in his assertions on the reality of sin; he felt sin to be a "property of the species" which both justified God's punishment of man and made possible mercy and redemption. His sermon on SINNERS IN THE HANDS OF AN ANGRY GOD (1741), so horrifying to later readers, was in fact an exhortation on the necessity of salvation as well as a reminder of the torments that awaited the unregenerate. He believed "that the essence of all religion lies in holy love," that all virtue is disinterested benevolence that springs from "love to Being" and finally from God as the summation of Being, and all sin from a defect or distortion of that love.

The last eight years of Edwards' life were spent in the frontier settlement of Stockbridge, where he was a missionary to the Indians and composed his most important writings. Upon the death of his son-in-law, Aaron Burr, Sr., who had been president of the College of New Jersey (later Princeton), Edwards was asked to assume the presidency of the college; he died almost immediately after taking office. His most important works include: *God Glorified in the Work of Redemption* (1731); *A Devine and Supernatural Light* (1734); *A Faithful Narrative of the Surprising Work of God in the Conversion of Many Hundred Souls* (1737; see NARRATIVE OF SURPRISING CONVERSIONS); *Some Thoughts Concerning the Present Revival of Religion in New England* (1742); *A Treatise Concerning Religious Affections* (1746); *A Farewell Sermon* (1751); *Charity and Its Fruits* (1851); *A Careful and Strict Enquiry into . . . Freedom of Will* (1754; see FREEDOM OF THE WILL). Other, posthumous writings are: *The Great Christian Doctrine of Original Sin Defended* (1758); *IMAGES OR SHADOWS OF DIVINE THINGS* (1948, taken from Edwards' notebooks now in the Yale University Library); *The Nature of True Virtue* (1765); *Concerning the End for Which God Created the World* (1765).

Edwards has deeply influenced American literature; Emerson's TRANSCENDENTALISM owes much to Edwards' theology, as do the works of Hawthorne, Melville, and Whitman, who wrestled with many of the same problems of good and evil in fiction and poetry as Edwards did in his sermons and essays.

Egg and I, The (1945), an autobiographical narrative by BETTY MACDONALD. "From the unconventional account of an unconventional birth to the story of a fire, it is all written with a gusto and verve—and often hilarity—hard to match," said Frank Luther Mott, discussing books that have sold more than a million copies. Mrs. MacDonald raised chickens—hence the title.

Eggleston, Edward (b. Vevay, Ind., Dec. 10, 1837—d. Sept. 2, 1902), clergyman, novelist, editor, historian. Eggleston was a restless, colorful, complex man who engaged in a great variety of occupations. "He tried for too many prizes

and always fell short of winning the highest," says W. P. Randel in his life of Eggleston (1946). His novels, still eminently readable, form a milestone in the development of regional fiction. He was an ardent reformer, campaigned against religious denominationalism, advocated kindergartens for young children, vigorously advocated copyright reform. Most famous of his novels are THE HOOSIER SCHOOLMASTER (1871); *The End of the World* (1872); THE CIRCUIT RIDER (1874); ROXY (1878); THE HOOSIER SCHOOLBOY (1883); and THE GRAYSONS (1888).

Eggleston, George Cary (b. Vevay, Ind., Nov. 26, 1839—d. April 14, 1911), teacher, newspaperman, author of books for boys, historian. The younger brother of EDWARD EGGLESTON, he began teaching in a small country school at the age of sixteen, and his experiences helped provide his brother with data for THE HOOSIER SCHOOLMASTER. Later he studied law, fought during the Civil War in the Confederate army, became a newspaperman in New York. He was literary editor of the New York *Evening Post* during Bryant's régime, then, for eleven years, an editorial writer for Pulitzer on the *World.* Perhaps his best book is his memoir, *A Rebel's Recollections* (1874). He also wrote *Strange Stories from History* (1886) and the romantic novels, *Dorothy South* (1902) and *Evelyn Byrd* (1904).

Eighth of January, The (produced Jan. 8, 1829), a play by RICHARD PENN SMITH. This play celebrated the victory of Andrew Jackson in the Battle of New Orleans in 1815, but its real purpose was to celebrate his triumph in becoming President; also, the triumph of democracy over the so-called "Adams dynasty."

Eimi (1933; reprinted, 1948), a narrative of travel in Russia by E. E. CUMMINGS. This book is written in a stream-of-consciousness style, including puns, parodies, and typographical innovations common enough in Cummings' other writings but less acceptable to the public in a travel book than in a poem. At its later appearance readers had become somewhat more accustomed to such cryptograms and better able to decipher them. The title (pronounced to rhyme with "Mamie") is Greek and means "I am." Cummings told what he himself had seen, heard, and felt. He described a theater audience: "everywhere a mysterious sense of behaving, of housebrokenness, of watch-your-stepism." *Time* said of the book: "It is certainly the wittiest, and just possibly the most reliable, of all the Moscow travel accounts."

Einstein, Albert (b. Germany, Mar. 14, 1879 —d. April 18, 1955), "theoretical physicist" (his own description in *Who's Who in America*). The famous German, who expounded the theory of relativity and developed the equation $(E = mc^2)$ that made possible the manufacture of the atomic bomb, taught in various German, Czech, and Swiss universities, and announced in 1905 his *Special* and in 1915 his *General Theory of Relativity* (English translation entitled *Relativity; the Special and the General Theory,* 1920). In 1933 he was teaching in Germany when the Nazis came to power; he left for the United States and became an American citizen in 1940. In 1933 he became a life member of the Institute for Advanced Study at Princeton. A shy, kindly little man whose favorite pastimes were sailing and playing the violin, he was a beloved member of the community until his death. He was exceptionally modest: at a Hollywood reception where he was greeted with fantastically eulogistic speeches he replied, "Thank you, but I'd be crazy to believe what you say about me." He is rumored to have said, "I can't explain my equation to you, but I'll gladly play it on the fiddle"; also, "I never believed an axiom."

Endeavors to explain Einstein's theory are likely to lose something of "the sublime poetry of the mathematical original." In the general conception, Einstein has been considered to have abolished the meaning of absolute time and absolute space: time becomes a dimension similar to length, breadth, and thickness. Among Einstein's books are *Meaning of Relativity*

(1923; revised, 1945); *Investigations on the Theory of the Brownian Movement* (1926); *About Zionism* (1931); *On the Method of Theoretical Physics* (1933); *The World as I See It* (1934); *The Evolution of Physics* (with Leopold Infeld, 1938). He won the Nobel Prize for Physics in 1921. In 1939 he signed a historic letter to President Roosevelt explaining the potentialities of atomic energy. Some of his best miscellaneous essays are collected in *Out of My Later Years* (1950). Lincoln Barnett wrote a helpful explanation of Einstein's theories for the layman in *The Universe and Dr. Einstein* (1948). Antonina Vallentin wrote *The Drama of Albert Einstein* (1954).

Eiseley, Loren [Corey] (b. Lincoln, Neb., Sept. 3, 1907—　　　　), poet, essayist, teacher. Eiseley, Professor of Anthropology and Provost of the University of Pennsylvania, is the author of *The Immense Journey* (1957), a work on physical anthropology and archeology. It combines sound scientific knowledge with high literary quality, and has been compared with Rachel Carson's *The Sea Around Us.* Professor Eiseley has also written *Darwin's Century* (1958) and *The Firmament of Time* (1960).

Eisenhower, Dwight D[avid] (b. Denison, Tex., Oct. 14, 1890—d. March 28, 1969), soldier, university administrator, 34th President of the United States. In 1915 Eisenhower graduated from the U.S. Military Academy; he served in the army and won steady promotion. In 1942 he was made commander of the Allied forces landing in North Africa, became a full general in February, 1943; he was appointed Supreme Commander of the Allied Expeditionary Forces in Europe, led the Normandy invasion, and directed the overthrow of the Nazis in 1944–45. For a time he continued to command the U.S. Occupation Forces in Germany, then returned to become Chief of Staff in Washington. Eisenhower told his own story in *Crusade in Europe* (1948). He was president of Columbia University from 1948 to 1952. On Dec. 16, 1950, he took leave of absence to serve as Supreme Allied Commander in Europe and to set up the forces of the North Atlantic Treaty Organization.

In July, 1952, Eisenhower resigned from the army. He had been eyed for nomination as President by both Republican and Democratic leaders. He accepted the Republican bid and defeated Adlai E. Stevenson, the Democratic candidate. Eisenhower took a middle road in his policies, his announced creed being one of "dynamic conservatism," and generally veered somewhat to the right; however, he advocated the repeal of none of the New Deal and Fair Deal enactments. He sought to balance the budget, favored private enterprise as opposed to government control and operation, and continued foreign aid. Despite serious illnesses, he ran for a second term and was re-elected in 1956.

Many books have been written about Eisenhower's picturesque and extraordinary career. Among these are H. C. Butcher's *My Three Years with Eisenhower* (1946); Kevin McCann's *The Man from Abilene* (1952); R. J. Donovan's

Eisenhower: The Inside Story (1956); Richard Rovere's *Affairs of State: The Eisenhower Years* (1956); General Walter Bedell Smith's *Eisenhower's Six Great Decisions: [Europe 1944–45]* (1956); Marquis Childs' *Eisenhower: Captive Hero* (1958). Eisenhower himself wrote *Eisenhower's Own Story of the War* (1946).

Crusade in Europe (1948) turned out to be a significant book from the legal standpoint. General Eisenhower and Doubleday entered into a contract whereby the publisher bought the whole property from the author for a lump sum rather than paying him royalties as earned. Under the tax law as it then existed, the proceeds were construed as capital gain rather than ordinary income, on the ground that in this case the author was not a professional writer and did not customarily receive income from that source. That construction was permitted by the Internal Revenue Code in that case as well as in other earlier cases. The widespread publicity occasioned by the tax treatment of *Crusade in Europe* led Congress subsequently to enact the so-called Eisenhower Amendment to the Internal Revenue Code, which deprived subsequent nonprofessional authors of this opportunity to pay tax on their literary earnings at capital gains rates rather than at ordinary income rates.

El Dorado. Literally, the Spanish term means "The Gilded Man." A tribe of Indians near what is now Bogotá, Colombia, used to inaugurate new chieftains in an elaborate ceremony which included daubing them with oil and sprinkling gold dust all over their bodies. In time the Indians of this region were conquered by another tribe and the ceremony ceased. But the legend persisted and met the Spaniards on their conquest of South America. Everywhere they heard of El Dorado, the King of Manoa; and they dreamed of a land where everything was made of gold and jewels. Many expeditions set out in search of El Dorado. These adventurers discovered and crossed the passes of the Andes, they discovered the Amazon River, they encountered innumerable dangers and discomforts. The most famous quest was made by an Englishman, Sir Walter Raleigh, who made two attempts to find Manoa in 1595 and in 1616. He told the story himself in *The Discovery of the Large, Rich, and Beautiful Empyre of Guiana, with a Relation of the Great and Golden City of Manoa, Which the Spaniards Call El Dorado* (1596).

Both Milton (in *Paradise Lost*) and Voltaire (in *Candide*) mention El Dorado. In 1849 the name was attached to California during the Gold Rush, and BAYARD TAYLOR wrote *Eldorado* (1850) to describe a visit to this land of gold. But Edgar Allan Poe wrote his poem of the same name (printed in *Flag of Our Union*, April 21, 1849) to describe a quest for supernal beauty rather than a quest for gold.

Eldridge, Paul (b. Philadelphia, May 5, 1888–   ), teacher, poet, novelist. Long a teacher of romance languages in the high schools of New York (1914–46), Eldridge began writing books early in the 1920's and continued to do so after his retirement from teaching. His style and choice of subject tends to be somewhat sensational and the influence of French writers like de Maupassant is evident in his writings such as: *My First Two Thousand Years* (1928, novel, written with GEORGE SYLVESTER VIERECK); *Cobwebs and Cosmos* (1930, verse); *One Man Show* (1933, stories); *Madonna with the Cat* (1942, novel); *Crown of Empire* (1957, history); *Tales of the Fortunate Isles* (1959, stories); *The Second Life of John Stevens* (1960, novel); *The Tree of Ignorance* (1961).

Eleonora (published in *The Gift*, 1842), a story by EDGAR ALLAN POE. As much a prose poem as a story, *Eleonora* tells of a youth who weds his beautiful cousin and resides in the Valley of the Many-Colored Grass. She dies; he lives for a while with her mother, then remarries—but learns in a dream that he has not been untrue to the memory of Eleonora. This "pictorial myth," as George Woodberry calls it, is obviously a story of Poe and Virginia Clemm and Mrs. Clemm.

Eliot, Charles W[illiam] (b. Boston, March 20, 1834—d. Aug. 22, 1926), teacher, educational administrator, chemist. After teaching chemistry at Harvard and the Massachusetts Institute of Technology, Eliot was elected president of Harvard, though the classicists objected to him as a prejudiced scientist and the scientists objected to him as an educational theorist. He remained president of Harvard from 1869 to 1909 and helped make the university one of the greatest and best known in the world. He also helped establish Radcliffe College (1894). He introduced an "elective system" that had a profound influence at Harvard and on college and secondary education everywhere in the United States. He improved the graduate and professional schools, attracted many great scholars to the faculty, interested himself in civic causes, particularly civil service reform and international peace.

Eliot once made a chance remark, in protest against the idea that education needs elaborate physical equipment: "All the books needed for a real education could be set on a shelf five feet long!" An important publisher of books bought on subscription, P. F. Collier & Son, took him up on his remark and induced him to edit the famous "Harvard Classics" (1909–10), a fifty-volume set occupying five feet of shelf space. He wrote *The Happy Life* (1896), *Educational Reform* (1898), *The Durable Satisfactions of Life* (1910), *A Late Harvest* (1924), and other books. Henry James wrote a biography of Eliot (2 v., 1930) that won a Pulitzer Prize. W. A. Neilson wrote an earlier life (1926).

Eliot, George Fielding (b. Brooklyn, N.Y., June 22, 1894—   ), army officer, military critic. In the years preceding World War II Eliot acquired a reputation as a military expert. He wrote voluminously for newspapers and magazines, and his books had a wide circulation. Among them: *Eagles of Death* (1930); *If War Comes* (1937); *The Ramparts We Watch* (1938); *Bombs Bursting in Air* (1939); *Hour* *of Triumph* (1944); *If Russia Strikes—* (1949); *Victory Without War* (1958).

Eliot, John (b. [Aug. ?] 1604—d. May 21, 1690), teacher, missionary, linguist. Eliot, well educated at Cambridge, taught for a while in England, then emigrated in 1631 with the Winthrop family to New England. He settled finally at Roxbury and became a teacher and later pastor in the church there; he also helped to found the famous Roxbury Latin School. His chief interest became the conversion of the Indians to Christianity, to teach them, he said, "original sin and the damned state of man." He published a translation of the New Testament into the dialect of the Naticks, a Massachusetts branch of the Algonquins (1661), and a version of the entire Bible two years later. In 1903 a study of Eliot's Bible by James Hammond Trumbull resulted in the *Natick Dictionary*. Eliot popularized one Indian word—MUGWUMP (originally spelled *mugquomp*), a term for *chief* that he used in place of *duke* as it appears in the Authorized Version of Genesis, xxxvi. Eliot was zealous in his labors for the Indians, usually regarded by other Puritans as convenient slaves; he helped them set up independent communities, schools, and seminaries for ministers, but all these were swept away in King Philip's War (1675–76).

He had long meditated the outlines of a "Christian Utopia," founded strictly on the Bible. In 1659 he published *The Christian Commonwealth*. In this he rejected all ideas of "natural rights," insisted that there were only duties, in complete obedience to the Scriptures. Society was to be organized in a hierarchy of magistrates; the rebel would be a social outcast to be silenced at all costs. Earlier in his own career Eliot had voted to banish ANNE HUTCHINSON, accused of heresy. Now Eliot was condemned. In a session of the General Court, held at Boston on May 22, 1661, the book was ordered suppressed for fear of angering the restored monarchy in England. Eliot had to make a public retraction. See BAY PSALM BOOK.

He wrote several books in Indian language as well as English: *Up-Bookum Psalmes* (1663); *Communion of Churches* (1665); *The Indian Primer* (1669); *The Harmony of the Gospels* (1678).

Eliot, T[homas] S[tearns] (b. St. Louis, Mo., Sept. 26, 1888—d. Jan. 4, 1965), poet, critic, editor. Eliot studied at Smith Academy and Milton Academy, and in 1906 entered Harvard, where his attendance in the classes of IRVING BABBITT, the New Humanist critic of Romanticism, became an important factor in determining his development as a poet and critic. (See HUMANISM.) Upon completing his undergraduate courses, he attended the Sorbonne for a year, then returned to Harvard; his program for the doctorate included Sanskrit and Pali and a dissertation on the philosophy of F. H. Bradley. In 1913, however, he went abroad on a Sheldon traveling fellowship, studying at Oxford and in Germany, and the outbreak of World War I prevented his return to Harvard for his final doc-

toral examinations. In England Eliot taught school and worked for Lloyd's bank, dealing in prewar enemy debts and foreign exchanges. When the United States entered the war, he was rejected for naval service. In 1917 he became an

UPI

assistant editor of *The Egoist,* and in 1922 he founded and edited *The Criterion,* a quarterly review which continued until 1939. In 1935 he joined Faber & Faber, the British publishing firm, having become a British subject in 1927. He married two times, first in 1915 to Vivien Haigh-Wood, who died in 1947, and secondly in 1957 to Esmé Valerie Fletcher.

As a boy Eliot had published both verse and prose sketches in school publications, notably a comic poem in the manner of Byron, and at Harvard he became an editor of the *Advocate,* to which he contributed a number of poems revealing an early acquaintance with modern verse techniques and a growing disaffection with certain aspects of American culture. An important early influence was the poety of Jules Laforgue, which Eliot had encountered by way of Arthur Symons' essays on the French *Symbolistes*. It is said that the first drafts of some of Eliot's famous later poems were composed while he was still at Harvard. In London he made the acquaintance of EZRA POUND, who arranged for the publication of his first mature work (including THE LOVE SONG OF J. ALFRED PRUFROCK) in *Poetry* (June, 1915) and who wrote enthusiastically, both in America and in England, about Eliot's accomplishments. To what extent Pound influenced Eliot and to what extent the two came to similar points of view by independent routes, cannot be determined now with much certainty, but at least Pound's enterprise and stubborn insistence on a thoroughly professional discipline must have furnished an important example to the younger poet. In fact, Eliot's first separately published critical work was *Ezra Pound, His Metric and Poetry* (1917), and elsewhere he has recorded his debt to Pound for the latter's assistance in revising and shortening the final draft of *The Waste Land.*

Eliot's first book of poems, *Prufrock and Other Observations,* was published in London in 1917. It was followed by *Poems* (1920); THE WASTE LAND (1922); THE HOLLOW MEN (1925); *Poems, 1909–1925* (1925); ASH WEDNESDAY (1930); *Sweeney Agonistes; Fragments of an Aristophanic Melodrama* (1932, see SWEENEY); *The Rock* (1934); *Collected Poems* (1936); *East Coker* (1940); *Burnt Norton* (1941); *The Dry Salvages* (1941); the latter three, with *Little Gidding,* were collected in FOUR QUARTETS (1943). (See GERONTION.) The importance of Eliot's poetry in shaping the development of 20th-century Anglo-American literature can scarcely be exaggerated, especially that of *The Waste Land,* which is thought by many critics to be his best poem. His influence spread quickly in the 1920's and has not diminished; his poems have been the chief instruments in popularizing among writers the techniques of symbolism, the desiderata of control and precision in the use of language, the notion of poetic form as a dynamically mobile structure; even Eliot's personal style—a concise diction, a dry irony, the use of descending cadences—has been widely imitated and occasionally parodied. The early poems, including *The Waste Land* and *The Hollow Men,* may be broadly characterized as negative, *i.e.,* deriving their chief motifs from a critical and sharply ironic appraisal of the positivistic elements in modern western culture, although this is countered by a steadily deepening emphasis on the values to be sought in tradition, spiritual awareness, conservatism, and responsibility to history. Beginning with *Ash Wednesday* Eliot's poetry has been more pointedly affirmative and appears to have been intended as a conscious contribution to the Anglo-Catholic literature of faith. Throughout all the poetry certain recurrent symbolic themes are apparent: sexuality, childhood, the rose and other tokens of Christianity, and—rather surprisingly in a poetry whose total impression is of an almost exclusive urbanity—images of nature, especially birds. One other book of verse should be noted, *Old Possum's Book of Practical Cats* (1939), a collection of light verse; "Possum" is a nickname acknowledged by Eliot (possibly in part as a euphemism for "Parson," a name applied half maliciously by some of his critics) and it appears in a number of Ezra Pound's *Cantos.*

Eliot's criticism is an indispensable adjunct to his poetry, and neither can be fully appreciated without the other. From the literary point of view, his most valuable essays have been those in which he calls attention to the merits and techniques of the minor Elizabethan dramatists and the 17th-century metaphysical poets, as well as a small group of essays in which he discusses his own methods of composition and literary analysis. Among the latter the essay called *Tradition and the Individual Talent* has acquired particular prominence, is widely quoted, praised, and attacked, and is standard fare in many university courses. But Eliot has also written important essays on classical literature, on Dante, on the symbolist poetry of France, and on 20th-century literature. In his historical, philosophical, and religious essays he has argued brilliantly for the conservative tradition and for the restoration of the unified religio-aesthetic society which he believes to have existed in Europe before the advent of the rationalistic delusions. Eliot's first important volume of criticism was THE SACRED WOOD (1920); others have been: *Homage to John Dryden* (1924); *Shakespeare and the Stoicism of Seneca* (1928); *For Lancelot Andrewes* (1928); *Dante* (1929); *Thoughts After Lambeth* (1931); *Selected Essays* (1932); *The Use of Poetry and the Use of Criticism* (1933); *After Strange Gods* (1934); *Elizabethan Essays* (1934); *Essays Ancient and Modern* (1936); *The Idea of a Christian Society* (1939); *Poetry and Drama* (1951); *The Three Voices of Poetry* (1954); *On Poetry and Poets* (1957); *The Elder Statesman* (1959).

Eliot's interest in the theater has been active and lifelong, and has proceeded chiefly in the direction of restoring the verse drama to a place of practical esteem in the modern stage repertoire. His early efforts were the fragmentary *Sweeney Agonistes* and *The Rock,* never successfully performed. MURDER IN THE CATHEDRAL (1935), however, achieved a great success and has been very frequently performed in England and America since its first production by the Friends of Canterbury Cathedral. Based on the martyrdom of Thomas à Becket, the drama is a work of symbolism written in alternating lyrical and prosaic passages and employing devices common to classical and medieval drama—for example, a verse chorus. Eliot has said, however, that he believes the chief problem of the verse drama today is the proper adaptation of verse technique to the modern naturalistic stage: verse drama must acquire the same "realism" as prose drama in the presentation of scenes from ordinary life. His later plays have moved progressively in this direction, retaining a loosely metrical verse pattern but venturing into essentially Ibsenian modes of dealing with contemporary society. Eliot's other plays are: THE FAMILY REUNION (1939); THE COCKTAIL PARTY (1950); *The Confidential Clerk* (1954). *The Complete Poems and Plays* of Eliot appeared in 1952.

Although Eliot's poems and critical theories were among the foremost instruments in discrediting the shallow gentility of post-Victorianism, Eliot himself, in both his writing and his public character, has affected an older and perhaps in some respects sterner gentility which has deeply colored intellectual life in the 20th century. In his public appearances Eliot often presents himself as a mildly clerical English man of leisure, devoted to punctilious and circumscribed entertainments and to a rather exacting decorum. That this is a pose, at least in part consciously assumed, has been shown by Eliot himself in his occasional recourse to an equally calculated comic vulgarity—like other leaders of the poetic revolution he knows the value of shock—but of course his genuine artistic seriousness, when dealing with matters of importance, belies any ultimate frivolity. Nevertheless, this aspect of Eliot's artistic personality, prissiness not devoid of mock-humility and dogmatism, has sometimes aroused his antagonists to a pitch far exceeding polite controversy. Actually, although in general Eliot has been the most admired Anglo-American writer of the 20th century, from the beginning he has provoked strong opposition, and historians may eventually conclude that the most important responses to his work have been the counteractions—not only of the men of his own generation (e.g., WILLIAM CARLOS WILLIAMS) who have chosen different paths, but of leading poets in succeeding generations who have sought, usually in a friendly way, to reverse the force of his influence: the names of W. H. AUDEN and Dylan Thomas come prominently to mind. Eliot remains the undisputed dean of English letters, however, and possesses extraordinary power in the literary world. He has used his power wisely on the whole, has written many reviews and introductions to help worthy young authors and to right imbalances in the reputations of the past. He himself has been given degrees by scores of European and American universities, and was awarded the Nobel Prize for literature in 1948. Since 1952 he has been president of the London Library.

Finally, readers should note that Eliot's public character is by no means entirely superficial or unmeaningful. His career has been a programmatic search for sources, a backtracking through time and distance in pursuit of origins and the tradition stemming from them. A descendant of Sir Thomas Elyot (1490?–1546, English author, diplomat, etc.), T. S. Eliot removed by stages from Missouri to his ancestral England and to a certain extent from the 20th century to the 16th, thereby seeking the specifics of cultural continuity upon which his beliefs depend, and in his poem *East Coker* he celebrates his descent. His whole work is a poetic fiction with deep historical roots, devoted to establishing a poetic character, or *persona*, of great but definable complexity—the man of spirit in an antagonistic world. Undoubtedly Eliot's public manner of comportment is an extension of this mask.

The mass of printed discussion surrounding Eliot and his work is enormous. Readers may find in the following books references to much else that has been written about him: Leonard Unger's *T. S. Eliot: A Selected Critique* (1948); Rossel Hope Robbins' *The T. S. Eliot Myth* (1951); Donald Gallup's *T. S. Eliot, A Bibliography* (1953); George Williamson's *A Reader's Guide to T. S. Eliot* (1953); Philip Wheel-

wright's *The Burning Fountain: A Study in the Language of Symbolism* (1954); Grover Smith's *T. S. Eliot's Poetry and Plays: A Study in Sources and Meaning* (1956); *T. S. Eliot: A Symposium for His Seventieth Birthday* (1958), edited by Neville Braybrooke.

HAYDEN CARRUTH

Eliza. A character in Harriet Beecher Stowe's UNCLE TOM'S CABIN (1852). She is a daughter of Cassy, once Legree's favorite, later a "wreck of beauty" who is finally reunited with her daughter; Eliza also is rejoined by her husband George Harris, who follows her by the Underground Railway after she makes her famous escape across the Ohio River on the ice, carrying her boy Harry.

Elizabeth the Queen (1930), a historical drama by MAXWELL ANDERSON. Anderson employs both blank verse and poetic prose in this account of the love story of the Earl of Essex and the Queen of England, whom "a kingdom kept apart." Essex seeks power and war; Elizabeth, setting her country above her lover, prefers peace. Essex threatens the throne, is tried and condemned. In the end Essex realizes she is right and goes off to his execution stoically.

Ellery Queen. See QUEEN, ELLERY.

Ellin, Stanley (b. New York City, Oct. 6, 1916—), mystery writer, novelist. Ellin attended Brooklyn College and was employed in a number of different jobs before turning to fiction. His first published novel was *Dreadful Summit* (1948), a suspense story which explores the psychological causes leading to vengeance. Other books by Ellin are: *The Key to Nicholas Street* (1951); *Mystery Stories* (1956), a collection of short stories; *The Eighth Circle* (1958); and *The Winter After This Summer* (1960). For ten years all Ellin's short stories were published in *Ellery Queen's Mystery Magazine.*

Elliot, Jonathan (b. England, 1784—d. March 12, 1846), editor, printer, publisher. Elliot came to the United States in 1802, fought as a volunteer under Simon Bolívar, served with American forces in the War of 1812. In December, 1813, he issued the first evening paper in Washington, the *Evening Gazette,* under his control until 1826. He handled all the government printing for many years and was strongly Federalist in his sympathies. In 1828 he began publishing an anti-Jackson newspaper called *We, the People.* His most important service to posterity was in editing and publishing *The Debates in the Several State Conventions on the Adoption of the Federal Constitution* (5 v., 1836–45; reprinted, 1937).

Elliott, Maud Howe (b. Boston, Nov. 9, 1854—d. March 19, 1948), historian, biographer, author of travel books. The youngest of Julia Ward Howe's daughters was a social and civic leader in Newport, R.I., where she resided for many years. She met the notables of several generations in her long life, became the wife of an English painter, and devoted several of her books to "minor sagas" (as *Time* called them) chronicling her times. She campaigned for women's rights and for Theodore Roosevelt. Her best-known book was a biography of her mother, *The Life and Letters of Julia Ward Howe* (2 v., 1916), written in collaboration with her sisters LAURA ELIZABETH RICHARDS and FLORENCE HOWE HALL; this received a Pulitzer Prize. Among her other books: *A Newport Aquarelle* (1883); *Laura Bridgman* (with Mrs. Hall, 1902); *Three Generations* (1923); *Uncle Sam Ward and His Circle* (1938); *This Was My Newport* (1944).

Ellis, Edward S[ylvester] (b. Geneva, Ohio, April 11, 1840—d. June 20, 1916), teacher, novelist, historian. Ellis was one of the most successful of the "dime novelists" (see DIME NOVELS). His SETH JONES (1860) sold 450,000 copies on its original publication, thereafter became a standard "number" in various dime and half-dime libraries. Later Ellis wrote a six-volume illustrated *History of the United States* (1896) that was sold by subscription all over the country. He wrote his dime novels under seven pseudonyms.

Ellis, Griffith O[gden] (b. Urbana, Ill., Nov. 19, 1869—d. Feb. 4, 1948), editor, publisher. Long on the staff of the Sprague Publishing Co. of Detroit and its president from 1908 to 1939, Ellis was active in the Boy Scout movement. When a young relative complained that all the magazines of the day were full of "girls' stories," Ellis founded THE AMERICAN BOY (1901), which took over YOUTH'S COMPANION (1929), but ceased publication in 1941.

Ellis Island. In 1892 Ellis Island replaced Castle Garden as a receiving station for immigrants. Two more islands were created in 1898 and 1905 by filling in nearby places; all three are now connected by causeways and are virtually one island. In earlier days the Dutch used the island (then called Oyster Island) as a picnic ground; later it was called Gibbet Island after the pirate Anderson was hanged there in 1765. Still later it was bought by a New Jersey merchant who gave it its present name. For many years it was the headquarters of the Immigration and Naturalization District of southern New York and northern New Jersey, through which many hundreds of thousands of emigrants from Europe passed. The federal government abandoned its offices there in 1953 and the Ellis Island ferry made its last run to the station on Nov. 29, 1954.

Ellison, Ralph [Waldo] (b. Oklahoma City, Okla., March 1, 1914—   ), writer, teacher. Ellison studied at Tuskegee Institute. He has contributed several short stories and essays to various publications, and lectured at New York, Columbia, and Fisk universities, and at Bard College. His first novel, INVISIBLE MAN (1952), was hailed as an impressive work and an outstanding novel on the Negro in America. Its hero progresses from youthful affirmation to total rejection, and learns that his search for himself entails contention with Negroes as well as whites.

Ellsberg, Edward (b. New Haven, Conn., Nov. 21, 1891—   ), engineer, naval officer, author. His numerous books of fiction and nonfiction, based in most instances on his own naval experiences, make lively reading. During his period of service with the navy from 1914 to 1926, and later during World War II, Ellsberg won fame as a salvage submarine expert. Among his books: *On the Bottom* (1929); *Pig Boats* (1930); *Ocean Gold* (1935, a juvenile); *S-54* (1932); *Hell on Ice* (1938); *Captain Paul* (1941); *Under the Red Sea* (1946); *Mid-Watch* (1954); and *The Far Shore* (1960). He has several inventions to his credit, including the underwater torch for cutting steel, and he has designed a system for salvaging submarines. Rear Admiral Ellsberg wrote of his own work: "This eternal conflict between the sea and the men who dare embark upon it is the source of as much drama in actual life as ever Homer sang of three millennia ago."

Elmer Gantry (1927), a novel by SINCLAIR LEWIS. The novel deals with a brazen ex-football player, Elmer Gantry, who enters the ministry and, through his half-plagiarized sermons, his physical attractiveness, and his unerring instinct for promotion, becomes a successful evangelist and later the leader of a large middle-western church. Before writing the novel, Lewis spent a good deal of time researching the less attractive aspects of midwestern American protestantism; his book was realistic enough to shock both the faithful and the unfaithful. Churchmen denounced Lewis; H. L. Mencken decorated him for his bravery in attacking the philistines. A film based on the book appeared in 1960.

Elsie Dinsmore. See DINSMORE, ELSIE.

Elsie Venner: A Romance of Destiny (1861), a novel by OLIVER WENDELL HOLMES. This was originally, like so much else of Holmes's work, published in *The Atlantic Monthly* as a serial (beginning December, 1859), and was then called *The Professor's Story*. Although subtitled a "romance," the story is in reality a strange but effective mixture: a series of discursive descriptions and characters, an analysis of New England traits and ideas, an allegory illustrating Holmes's views on predestination and free will, an anticipation of modern mental hygiene and psychiatry. The heroine's mother was bitten by a snake and she is consequently born with a strong serpent-complex; she is half-snake, half-woman. Whether Holmes had any confidence in this sort of superstition or not is immaterial. He posits it as a condition of his story: to what extent can Elsie overcome the "condition" into which she was born? She falls in love with Bernard Langdon, who does not care for her, even after she saves his life when he is bitten by a rattlesnake. She becomes ill when Bernard rejects her, and dies. The book is one of Holmes' attacks on Calvinism, as usual not a frontal one. But the religious press of the time saw the point immediately, and the *Northwest Christian Advocate* of Chicago even ran a series of articles warning its readers against the story. None of his contemporary critics seemed able to understand Holmes's thesis, that Elsie was a case for the doctor, not the minister. Yet modern medicine does not find in Holmes more than accidental anticipations of psychiatry. C. P. Oberndorf edited abridgments of *The Psychiatric Novels of Oliver Wendell Holmes* (1943), with illuminating introductions.

Elson, Henry W[illiam] (b. Muskingum Co., Ohio, March 29, 1857—d. Jan. 29, 1954), teacher, college administrator, historian, lecturer. In 1895 Elson left the ministry and became a lecturer, teacher, and writer, serving on various college faculties and as president of Thiel College (1916–21). He was noted as an authority on American history, many of his textbooks selling widely—one of them, *Modern Times and the Living Past* (1921), more than a million copies.

El Supremo (1916), a novel by EDWARD LUCAS WHITE. *El Supremo* tells how an American adventurer goes to Paraguay in 1815 to attempt the overthrow of Rodríguez de Francia, an early example of Latin-American dictators. The pages are filled with rich, plausible details, woven into an exciting narrative.

Elwood, Muriel (b. England, April 11, 1902—), writer of historical novels, biographer. Muriel Elwood came to the United States in 1927 and was naturalized in 1946. Among her books: *Pauline Frederick: On and Off the Stage* (1939); *So Much as Beauty Does* (1941), and a series of novels which deal mainly with the fortunes of a single family in the pioneer days of Montreal: *Heritage of the River* (1945), *Deeper the Heritage* (1946), *Toward the Sunset* (1947), *Web of Destiny* (1951). *Against the Tide* (1950) has a Los Angeles background. *The Deluge* came out in 1959, and *Bigamous Duchess* in 1960.

Ely, Richard Theodore (b. Ripley, N.Y., April 13, 1854—d. Oct. 4, 1943), teacher, economist, writer. Ely taught first at Johns Hopkins, later at the University of Wisconsin. He made it his special purpose to inform the general public about the fundamental principles and facts of economics. Among his books: *Problems of Today* (1888); *Outlines of Economics* (1893; rev., 1908); *Socialism and Social Reform* (1894); *Monopolies and Trusts* (1900); *Studies in the Evolution of Industrial Society* (1903); *Hard Times: The Way In and the Way Out* (1931).

Emancipation Proclamation, The. As early as July 22, 1862, Lincoln submitted to his cabinet the draft of a proclamation freeing the slaves as a military measure. The cabinet members all concurred in the necessity of such a measure, but Seward urged that it be withheld until the North had won some kind of victory. Then came the victory at Antietam (September 17), and on September 22 the Emancipation Proclamation appeared, announcing to the three million slaves in the country that if their masters were still in rebellion on Jan. 1, 1863, they should regard themselves as free. Slaves in the border states or parts of them that were not in rebellion were not freed by the proclamation. But as northern armies captured a region, the slaves were manumitted. The slaves in Confederate territory were not greatly affected by the proclamation; there were no rebellions and perhaps Lincoln neither contemplated nor desired any such result. The London *Spectator* commented: "The principle is not that a human being cannot justly own another, but that he cannot own him unless he is loyal to the United States." Only with the Thirteenth Amendment to the Constitution (ratified Dec. 18, 1865) were the slaves in all parts of the United States freed. See CIVIL WAR.

Embree, Edwin R[ogers] (b. Osceola, Neb., July 31, 1883—d. Feb. 21, 1950), newspaperman, college administrator, anthropologist. After graduation from Yale, Embree served on its faculty in various capacities, was an officer of the Rockefeller Foundation, became president of the Julius Rosenwald Fund; the Fund went out of existence in 1948. In the last capacity, he specialized in the study of races, particularly in relations of whites and Negroes, also studied conditions in Europe and the Far East. Among his publications: *Brown America: The Story of a New Race* (1931); *Indians of the Americas* (1939); *Thirteen Against the Odds* (1944).

Emerson, Ralph Waldo (b. Boston, May 25, 1803—d. April 27, 1882), poet, philosopher, clergyman. Emerson's father was a liberal minister at the famous First Church in Boston; his mother, Ruth Haskins, was the daughter of

a cooper and distiller. Their sons went through Boston Latin School and Harvard College. Emerson entered Harvard in 1817, working his way through; his father had died some years before and had left his mother in straitened circumstances. He studied Latin, Greek, and French but neglected mathematics. He listened to the lectures of GEORGE TICKNOR and EDWARD EVERETT. A slowly maturing, cautious, self-scrutinizing Yankee, Emerson graduated thirtieth in a class of fifty-nine. He was described by a classmate as "a Saxon blond, pale face, light hair, blue eyes." Even as an undergraduate Emerson recognized the prime requisites of his life—solitude and independence. "A room alone was the best thing in my college course," he wrote. (See also under SAMPSON REED.)

After graduation, in order to help his family and pay his debts, he taught school, but at twenty-one he had decided on the ministry: "I deliberately dedicate my life, time, and talent and hopes to the church." In 1825 he enrolled in Harvard Divinity School and in October, 1826, he was "approbated to preach." He married a delicate, consumptive girl, Ellen Tucker of Concord, N.H., and soon became pastor of the Old Second Church of Boston. But he was an unwilling minister. He repeated sermons frequently, one of them no fewer than twenty-seven times. By 1831, after a short but happy marriage, his wife died. The year following he resigned his pastorate after he had made known to his parishioners his unwillingness to continue administering the Lord's Supper. "Religion," he concluded, "is to love, it is to serve, it is to think, it is to be humble. It is my desire in the office of a Christian minister, to do nothing which I cannot do with my whole heart." Emerson early held to the idea that "every real man must be a nonconformist."

Emerson sailed for Europe and saw Walter Savage Landor in Florence, but found him an exhibitionist who was not the same in conversation as in his books. His visit to the Jardin des Plantes of Paris in July, 1833, gave him a sense of the occult relation between animals and man and the basis for his conviction of the essential unity of all things. In August he climbed High-gate Hill to see Coleridge. But his visit was a failure; Coleridge, in a cascade of words, was incomprehensible. Nevertheless, Coleridge's books helped him to build his own system of criticism and to reconcile Platonism with transcendental idealism, paving the way which his thought was to follow for many years to come. When Emerson appeared at Craigenputtock, Carlyle labeled him the "lonely wayfaring man." His friendship with Carlyle lasted the rest of his life and proved to be the most fruitful of all. Each of the two men made the other known in his own country. Both were seers and prophets who rebuked their age, both were hostile critics of the materialism of their time. However, there were differences which appeared as the friendship ripened. Emerson proved better tempered, more tender, an optimist rather than a pessimist, interested in the present and future rather than the past, true to democratic principles and an opponent of slavery as Carlyle was not. He made two more trips to England, in 1847 and 1872, but his first trip was by far the most important to his development.

In the years from 1833 to 1838 Emerson challenged the prevalent thought of New England and earned a national reputation. In 1836 his first book, NATURE, appeared, but it took thirteen years to sell the first edition of five hundred copies, and he was not popular in any sense until 1860. In 1835 he settled in Concord, and in the same year married Lydia Jackson. A legacy from his first wife augmented by lecturing gave him an adequate living, and he now became "the Sage of Concord," who entertained such fellow Transcendentalists as Margaret Fuller, the Alcotts, W. H. Channing, Hawthorne, Thoreau, and many others. It was said that "the Emerson house was a cure of souls."

Emerson was not a dreamer but a hard-working writer who wrote as a rule six hours a day. His best work was done between 1836 and 1860. This period includes his ESSAYS (First Series, 1841; Second Series, 1844); *Poems* (1847); REPRESENTATIVE MEN (1850); ENGLISH TRAITS (1856); THE CONDUCT OF LIFE (1860). His two best-known addresses were THE AMERICAN SCHOLAR (1837), called by O. W. Holmes "the intellectual Declaration of Independence," and the DIVINITY SCHOOL ADDRESS (1838), which caused a tempest in Boston's teapot owing to its challenge of orthodoxy. He was editor of THE DIAL (1842–44) and contributed to the *Atlantic Monthly*.

Emerson belonged to what William James called the "healthy-minded" mystics. Intuition was the only way to approach reality, he held. On the purely mystical side of his nature he owed more to Plotinus than to Plato. The tone of spiritual elevation in Plotinus mirrored his own spirit. From him Emerson perceived the truth that "all life is a kind of spiritual vision." He felt kinship with his stress upon intuition, upon the direct perception of mystical experience, upon the doctrine of the journey of the soul of man toward the Great Soul (which Emerson called the Over-Soul), upon the mysterious efficacy of lonely contemplation, and upon his faith that nothing that truly *is* can ever perish. Echoes of Plotinus' philosophy appear most clearly in his essay THE OVER-SOUL and in his ripest book, *The Conduct of Life*. One must not consider Emerson merely rapt in a cold meditation on the supremacy of the moral laws of the universe. He knew the writings of Boehme and Swedenborg. He was sympathetic with every genuine religious experience, though he thought theology uncertain. At forty he read eagerly in the *Vedas*, the *Bhagavad-Gita*, and the *Vishnu Purana*. "I believe," he wrote in his *Journal*, "I am more of a Quaker than anything else. I believe in the still small voice, and that voice is Christ within us."

We may easily discern three main points in Emerson's philosophy of Transcendentalism: (1) The soul is divine and identical in all men. We have the same instincts and desires; there is a spark of eternity in every man, and he possesses *within himself* the means of all knowledge. (2) Nature is only another side of God, "the gigantic shadow of God cast on our senses." Every law in nature has a counterpart in the intellect. There is a perfect parallel between the laws of nature and the laws of thought. Material elements have a close affinity with the moral elements; they simply represent action on an inferior plane: "Whenever you enumerate a physical law, I hear in it a moral rule." (3) God is the Over-Soul, and this has unobstructed access to each soul, and each soul has unobstructed access to the Over-Soul. Every man may commune with God if he wills: "I am born into the great, the universal mind—of this universal mind each man is one more incarnation—all its properties consist in him. I am part and parcel of God," he wrote.

In Emerson's prose the unit is the sentence and seldom the paragraph. Each sentence is a thought clearly and epigrammatically put, but there is often a doubtful relationship with the sentences that follow or precede it. The fact is that Emerson had an unsystematic habit of mind. He would sink into a receptive mood, let the thoughts come, jot them down without much method. He had many flashes of genuine inspiration but no logical, systematic development of ideas. The drift of his paragraphs is often obscure. His sentences are short and incisive, giving a staccato effect, but at times his brilliance palls. His diction is racy, of the soil, as witness his "Hitch your wagon to a star," a concrete expression of an abstract idea.

Emerson's own estimate of his skill as a poet was modest: "I am born a poet,—of a low class without a doubt, yet a poet. That is my nature and vocation. My singing, to be sure, is very husky, and is for the most part in prose. Still I am a poet in the sense of a perceiver and dear lover of the harmonies that are in the soul and in matter, and specially of the harmonies between these and those." His poetry is didactic and fused with an ethical element. He was discriminating, however, in the choice of the right word. He had the vision of the poet but was unable to transmute it into song; he did not have a good ear for poetry. But his poems contain the very quintessence of his teaching.

In the last ten years of his life there was a gradual failing of his mental powers. At Longfellow's grave he said, "The gentleman was a sweet beautiful soul, but I have entirely forgotten his name." He had known the poet for fifty years. In old age, not remembering he had written them, he read one of his Essays to his daughter Ellen: "Why, those things are really very good," he said.

He died in Concord and is buried there in Sleepy Hollow Cemetery.

His son, Edward Waldo Emerson, edited the standard edition entitled The Complete Works of Ralph Waldo Emerson (12 v., 1903–04). This has been supplemented by C. C. Bigelow in Uncollected Writings (1912) and C. F. Gohdes in Uncollected Lectures (1932). His Journals were edited by his son and W. E. Forbes (10 v., 1909–14). His correspondence has been gathered by RALPH L. RUSK (6 v., 1939). Rusk has also written the best biography (1949). Other biographies are by George W. Cooke (1881), Oliver W. Holmes (1885), Richard Garnett (1888), George E. Woodberry (1907), O. W. Firkins (1915), Van Wyck Brooks (1932), Townsend Scudder (1936). Cooke has also prepared a bibliography (1908); G. S. Hubbell compiled a Concordance (1932). A European view is given in Marie Dugard's Emerson: Sa Vie et Son Oeuvre (1907). Very useful is F. I. Carpenter's Emerson Handbook (1953). A special kind of biography is S. E. Whicher's Freedom and Fate: An Inner Life of R. W. Emerson (1953). Emerson's papers are assembled at the Harvard University Library. See LYCEUMS; TRANSCENDENTALISM; BACCHUS; BOSTON HYMN; BRAHMA; COMPENSATION; CONCORD SCHOOL; DAYS; EACH AND ALL; GOOD-BYE, PROUD WORLD; HUMBLE-BEE; THE INITIAL, DAEMONIC AND CELESTIAL LOVE; MERLIN; ODE INSCRIBED TO W. H. CHANNING; RHODORA; SAADI; SELF-RELIANCE; TERMINUS; THRENODY; VOLUNTARIES.

HERBERT FAULKNER WEST

Emigrants, The [1] (translated from the Norwegian, 1925), a novel by Johan Bojer (1872–1959). Bojer's story is an account of the trials and eventual triumphs of a group of Norwegian immigrants in the Dakota Territory.

Emigrants, The [2] (1951), a novel by Vilhelm Moberg (1898–   ). In this story, the Swedish novelist recounts the adventures of a group of migrants who find in America a land free of masters. It was followed by Unto a Good Land (1954).

Emigrants, The, or, The History of an Expatriated Family (1793), a novel by Captain GILBERT IMLAY. The story of an English family removed to the Pennsylvania border, this is a highly romanticized account of frontier life and a glorification of the Indian.

Emma and Eginhard (1872; published in TALES OF A WAYSIDE INN, Part Three, 1873), a narrative poem by Henry Wadsworth Longfellow. A king's daughter outwits her father's supervision—and is forgiven by him. Longfellow took the story from an old chronicle, De Factis Caroli Magni, as it was repeated in a lecture by Charles Perkins (Longfellow's Diary, May 12, 1872). Harry Hayden Clark calls Emma and Eginhard "this un-Victorian story"; it follows Chaucer rather than Tennyson as a model.

Emmett, Daniel Decatur (b. Clinton, Ohio, Oct. 29, 1815—d. June 28, 1904), minstrel, songwriter. Emmett wrote the song DIXIE (1860) and, according to Sigmund Spaeth, "not only played a leading part in creating the American minstrel show but gave perhaps the most sympathetic interpretation of the Negro in song up to the time of Stephen Foster." Emmett wrote both the words and music of the popular folksongs, Old Dan Tucker (1843) and My Old Aunt Sally (1843). Other songs generally attributed to him are Jordan Is a Hard Road to Travel (1853) and The Blue-Tail Fly (also called Jimmy Crack Corn, 1846). After working with a circus he organized the Virginia Minstrels in

1842, a new type of vaudeville that survived for many decades. (See MINSTRELS.) In 1857 he joined the Bryant Minstrels, for whom he wrote *Dixie*. After the war he again organized a troupe of his own.

Emperor Jones, The (produced, 1920; published, 1921), a play by EUGENE O'NEILL. O'Neill lays the scene of the play "on an island in the West Indies [presumably Haiti] as yet un-self-determined by white marines." On this island a former Pullman car porter, Brutus Jones, has made himself emperor. He is wanted in the States on two murder charges. But on the island he is a contemptuous monarch, looting the blacks and secure in his confidence that he can be killed only by a silver bullet. At last the natives rebel and Jones is obliged to flee to the jungle. He encounters phantoms from the past, circles the jungle, and is finally killed by his subjects—with silver bullets as he had predicted. In this, perhaps his finest artistic creation, O'Neill found himself and began to create new techniques or to revive old ones he found useful. The chief character is a twisted, warped, and lost soul; the movement of the play is a cunning and subtle interweaving of the physical and the psychological. The steady beat of tom-toms throughout the jungle scenes has as powerful an effect on the audience as it has on Emperor Jones.

According to an interview in the New York *World* (Nov. 9, 1924), O'Neill got the idea for the play from an old circus man who told him a story about a former president of Haiti who predicted no one would ever kill him with a lead bullet—he'd get himself first with a silver one. A year later he read something about a religious dance in the Congo, and the play was born. O'Neill was also influenced by Henri Christophe, the slave-born general who helped free Haiti from the French in 1811 and who called himself King Henry I. The play took New York by storm, and had to be moved from a small theater on Macdougal Street (the Provincetown Theatre) to an uptown theater. Louis Gassner says of the play that this "simple expressionist study of a man's atavistic fears" once rocked the theater, but is "now curiously regarded by literal practitioners of social criticism as reactionary because it revealed a Negro retrogressing to his 'aboriginal fears'—as if regression were a stigma applicable to no other race." The play was made into an opera (1933) by Louis Gruenberg (the libretto by Kathleen de Jaffa) and produced a sensation at the Metropolitan with Lawrence Tibbett as Jones. It became a movie in the same year, the title role played by Paul Robeson.

Emporia Gazette, The. A newspaper published and edited at Emporia, Kans., by WILLIAM ALLEN WHITE from 1895 until his death. His son, William L. White, carried on the paper thereafter.

Encantadas, The, or, The Enchanted Isles (first published serially in *Putnam's Monthly* in 1854 under the pen name Salvator R. Tarn-

moor; later included in PIAZZA TALES, 1856), ten sketches by HERMAN MELVILLE. These sketches are laid in the Galapagos Islands off Ecuador. Melville, aged twenty-one, then a first-class seaman on the whaler *Acushnet*, visited the islands in the autumn of 1841. How long he stayed is not known, but the islands remained deeply imprinted on his memory. Perhaps his use of a pseudonym was dictated by the sharp decline of his fame that came with the publication of MOBY DICK (1851) and PIERRE (1852). Of these new tales, Lewis Mumford said, "The style is again accurate, pliant, subtle, bold. There is not the fantest sign that his literary powers were falling off, or his voice sinking to a whisper." The giant tortoises on the islands fascinated him. He called them "these mystic creatures, suddenly translated by night from unutterable solitudes to our peopled deck." Seven of the sketches are descriptive, the remaining three introduce human characters; one, especially powerful, the tale of a half-breed woman, contributes to Melville's somber doctrine of good and evil.

Encyclopaedia Britannica. A famous work of reference. The first edition appeared in Edinburgh in 1768; it consisted of three volumes put out by a "society of gentlemen." Other editions, constantly increasing in size and authority, appeared in England, and American scholars were sometimes called upon for contributions, the first such being Edward Everett, president of Harvard. The *Encyclopaedia* became a popular work of reference in the United States, so much so that in 1901 it was bought by two Americans, for a time became the property of Sears, Roebuck & Co., and then was sold to the University of Chicago. The American editors still seek to maintain the *Encyclopaedia's* international scope and character.

Encyclopedia Americana. A reference work first published in 1903–04 and completely revised since then. It emphasizes American subjects, with particular attention to science, technology, and biography. It has good illustrations and maps, and is carefully cross-indexed. The articles are short, prepared and signed by authorities in their fields.

Endicott or **Endecott, John** (b. England, 1589?—d. 1665), colonial administrator. He came to America in 1628, was acting governor of the Massachusetts Bay Colony until 1630, when Governor JOHN WINTHROP arrived. Thereafter he was assistant governor from time to time, and served as governor in 1644, 1649, 1651–53, 1655–64. Though competent as an administrator, he was cruel and intolerant in character and an extremist in doctrine. Under his administration Quakers were severely persecuted and four were executed. In *Endicott and the Red Cross* (TWICE-TOLD TALES, 1837) Hawthorne tells how Endicott cut the sign of the cross from the British ensign because he regarded it as a sign of popery. The first of Longfellow's NEW ENGLAND TRAGEDIES (1868) is called *John Endicott* and tells how the governor persecuted the Quakers in Boston and condemned his own son when he attempted to aid the daughter of one of them.

End of Summer (1936), a social play laid at a summer home in Maine, by S. N. BEHRMAN. It has a brilliant portrait of a psychiatrist.

Endymion (*Atlantic Monthly*, February 1888; included in *Heartsease and Rue*, 1888), a poem by JAMES RUSSELL LOWELL. To make his poem Lowell gathered a "heap of fragments" from his notebooks and wove them together into what became, as he subtitled it, "A Mystical Comment on Titian's 'Sacred and Profane Love.' " The poem, written like Keats's *Endymion* in run-on couplets, falls into seven sections. Lowell is not sure whether he prefers the lovely goddess, inaccessible still, or a woman to be loved.

Engle, Paul [Hamilton] (b. Cedar Rapids, Iowa, Oct. 12, 1908—   ), teacher, poet, novelist. In 1941 Engle was awarded a prize of $1,000 for his collection of poems, *West of Midnight*. Prior to this he had issued *Worn Earth* (1932), *American Song* (1934), *Corn* (1939). *American Child* appeared in 1945, an enlarged edition in 1956. *Poems in Praise* appeared in 1959, and *Prairie Christmas* in 1960. All of Engle's publications have won warm approval from the critics, who saw him in his earlier writings as an able disciple of Whitman, in all his writings as an imaginative portraitist of the American scene. He has dealt with Iowa, his home, as in the novel *Always the Land* (1941). The prologue to his *American Song*, beginning "Blow, long trade winds of American speech," and the final poem in the same volume, *America Remembers*, give long and poetic vistas of American history. In his later poems Engle has turned to erotic themes, as in *The Word of Love* (1951). He has taught at the University of Iowa since 1937, and his special concern has been the development of the creative writing program there. *Midland*, a 650-page anthology of poetry and fiction by people who were students in this writing program, was published in 1961. Most of the material had been published in magazines such as *The New Yorker, Esquire, Harper's, Poetry, Botteghe Oscure* and *Sewanee Review*.

English, teaching of. See TEXTBOOKS.

English, Thomas Dunn (b. Philadelphia, June 29, 1819—d. April 1, 1902), physician, lawyer, public official, author. English practiced medicine in Newark, N.J., served in the New Jersey Assembly and then in Congress, and wrote indefatigably in every possible field. Among his writings were more than twenty plays, only one of which, *The Mormons, or, Life at Salt Lake City* (1858), won much success. Similarly only one of his several novels, *Jacob Schuyler's Millions* (1886), won more than mild applause. He wrote for newspapers, edited and published a humorous magazine, *John Donkey*, and composed *Fairy Stories and Wonder Tales* (1897).

At one time English was a friend of Poe's, but later became a bitter enemy. Poe sued the publisher of the New York *Evening Mirror* for printing a statement by English accusing him of forgery, and damages of $225 were assessed against the publisher. In addition, Poe, according to a letter he wrote Henry Beck Hirst (June 27, 1846), gave English "a flogging which he will remember to the day of his death—and, luckily, in the presence of witnesses." In an earlier letter (Sept. 8, 1844) Poe called English "a bullet-headed and malicious villain." He also ridiculed him as "Thomas Dunn Brown" in THE LITERATI OF NEW YORK CITY (1846).

The fame of English rests on a single poem, BEN BOLT, which appeared in the *Mirror* (Sept. 2, 1843), was set to music by Nelson Kneass, and was sung in a play, *The Battle of Buena Vista*. In 1894 *The Select Poems of Dr. Thomas Dunn English* appeared in a private edition issued by English's daughter, Miss Alice English. In the same year George Du Maurier revived the song *Ben Bolt* by having Trilby sing it in his novel *Trilby*; and it swept America and England again.

English and Scottish Popular Ballads (1882–98), edited by FRANCIS JAMES CHILD. A great monument of American scholarship and an early contribution to the comparative study of literature.

English Notebooks, Passages from the (2 v., 1870), by NATHANIEL HAWTHORNE. These were published posthumously by Mrs. Hawthorne, who, according to Thomas H. Johnson, "bowdlerized the manuscript text and omitted many personal allusions." An edition from manuscript sources was published by Randall Stewart (1941). A considerable portion of the material was used by Hawthorne in OUR OLD HOME (1863). The *Notebooks* tell the story of his busy life in England as an American consul, also mention literary projects he was unable to carry out, and give the germ ideas of some that did materialize. He makes keen observations on English life and writes some memorable passages of description. In general the book is cheerful and records many pleasant days of travel.

English Traits (1856), an analysis of the English people by RALPH WALDO EMERSON. After two visits to England, Emerson in 1848 delivered a series of lectures describing his impressions; these were published eight years later as *English Traits*. He tells of his visits to Coleridge, Carlyle, and Wordsworth, then discusses "Race," "Ability," "Character," "Aristocracy," "Wealth," "Religion," "The Times," and other subjects. He finds himself amused by English ceremonials and the bewigged officials, is deeply impressed by English writers (especially Carlyle), likes the English and lauds them, but with eyes open to their defects. Robert E. Spiller holds that the book "achieved critical detachment without loss of sympathy" and that it "marks in Emerson's own work the turn from a personal to a social perspective." In studying the English, he was concerned for the first time with the problem of man functioning *en masse*."

Enjoyment of Laughter, The (1936), an analysis of humor by MAX EASTMAN. It represents a complete rewriting of an older book, *The Sense of Humor* (1921); one reviewer remarked that the later book is "much louder and funnier." Up and down the ranges of humor in its many forms (including pictorial—the book is a gallery of magnificent cartoons), Eastman discusses why we laugh like human beings, the varieties of humorous experience, irony (all the way back to Plato), the humor people see in puns (he collects some of the best), exaggeration and understatement, "the ten commandments of the comic arts." From some famous comedians and wits he elicited their views of humor, including W. C. Fields' conclusion that "if it causes pain, it's funny; if it doesn't, it isn't."

Enlightenment, The Age of (sometimes called "the Age of Reason"). This important era in the history of the Western world is usually described as the period of nearly two centuries from about 1630 to the end of the 18th century. Those who followed the teachings of the writers and philosophers of this period believed that "reason" could overcome all difficulties and solve all problems—ignorance, superstitions, preconceptions, errors, bad laws, bad institutions. During this period natural science came into its own, a deep interest in the welfare of man was developed, willingness to let other people follow their own ideas and beliefs was practiced. Ethics rather than theology was stressed, but the men of the Enlightenment were not atheists (in the field of religious belief they called themselves *deists*). It was an age of decorum, wit, social graces, subdued imagination in literature and art. The novel came to flower, neo-classical poetry flourished. In politics it was an age when certain "rights" of human beings were recognized, as in the DECLARATION OF INDEPENDENCE; and monarchs lost the aura of divinity. It was, too, an age of self-revelation, and some of the most pleasant letters, diaries, journals, and confessions date from this period. In America all our great Revolutionary heroes were men of the Enlightenment; it was they who wrote the Declaration and the Constitution. Particularly to be recalled are Franklin and Jefferson. An admirable anthology is Crane Brinton's *The Portable Age of Reason Reader* (1956). See DEISM.

Enormous Room, The (1922), an autobiographical narrative by E. E. CUMMINGS. On a false charge of treason, Cummings was imprisoned in a French military camp (1917–18). Ironically following the pattern of John Bunyan's *Pilgrim's Progress,* Cummings describes his own experiences and tells how his companions in the camp reacted to their harsh treatment. The book has been compared to John Dos Passos' THREE SOLDIERS (1921) in its deglamorization of war. Cummings' prose is highly descriptive, lyrical even in its bitter attacks on man's inhumanity to man. Although not well received on its publication, the book has since come to be regarded as one of the finest examples of American writing.

Enough Rope (1926), a collection of poems by DOROTHY PARKER. The book established Mrs. Parker's fame as a poet of great technical skill and of striking content whom readers ordinarily averse to poetry greatly enjoy. As Edmund Wilson put it, "Dorothy Parker's unprecedented feat has been to raise to the dignity of poetry the 'wise-cracking' humor of New York." The book went through eleven printings by 1928, then was included in *Not So Deep as a Well* (1936). The poems obviously show the influence of A. E. Housman and Edna St. Vincent Millay. Mrs. Parker, like the latter, celebrates many "glib ladies" (as Alfred Kreymborg calls them), who frequently protest too much. The younger generation of the 1920's loved to quote her flippancies, but largely ignored the bitterness underneath, also the occasional deep-seated sentiment. Two poems in the volume continue to be quoted: *Résumé,* on suicide, and *News Item,* about girls who wear glasses.

Enters, Angna (b. New York City, April 28, 1907—   ), dancer, artist, author. Calling herself a "dance mime" (a term she originated) Miss Enters presented, from 1926 on, over one hundred Episodes and Compositions in Dance Form in the United States and abroad. Among her books: *First Person Plural* (1937); *Love Possessed Juana* (1939); *Silly Girl* (1944), personal memories, self-illustrated; *Among the Daughters* (1955); *Artist's Life* (1958), continues *Silly Girl,* and is a chronicle of self-education. Miss Enters exhibited drawings and paintings at the Metropolitan Museum of Art, the Baltimore Museum of Art, the Honolulu Museum of Art, and various other museums throughout the United States. Also a designer for the stage, she designed costumes and settings for García Lorca's *Yerma,* among others.

epitaphs. Tombstone inscriptions have since ancient times engaged the efforts of poets and prose writers of all degrees of ability, from the sublime to the ridiculous. "Nowhere," said Benjamin Jowett, "is there more true feeling and nowhere worse taste than in a churchyard." From the beginning, in the cemeteries of the United States, epitaphs were quaint, sometimes unconsciously humorous, as they had been in England; the writers of epitaphs in English somehow failed to catch the delicate poetry and the adequacy of the grave inscriptions one finds in the *Greek Anthology.* Thus Cotton Mather is said to have written on Anne Bradstreet:

In books a prodigy, they say—
A living encyclopedia.

Other women fared better—Rachel Jackson, for example, for whom her husband, the President, wrote a touching inscription; and Susy Clemens, for whose grave her father, Mark Twain, adapted a beautiful epitaph by Robert Richardson. Benjamin Franklin wrote an epitaph for himself at the age of twenty-three, which compares him to the cover of an old book; it was an adaptation of an old idea, used many times before and since.

Among early anonymous efforts is the following, found in a graveyard in Augusta, Me.: "After Life's Scarlet Fevers She Sleeps Well." The code of the Old West becomes clear in an epitaph in Cripple Creek, Colo.: "He Called Bill Smith a Liar." In Dodge City, Kans., this is said to have been found: "Played Five Aces. Now Playing the Harp." A proposed epitaph to a waiter reads:

> Bye and bye
> God caught his eye.

Elbert Hubbard liked to tell a story about a marble cutter who carved on the base of a monument the legend, "Lord, she was Thine," and accidentally left off the *e* in *Thine*. A rich gathering is C. L. Wallis' *Stories on Stone: A Book of American Epitaphs* (1954). See OBIT- UARIES.

E Pluribus Unum. A motto for the Seal of the United States, first proposed on Aug. 10, 1776 by a committee composed of Franklin, John Adams, and Jefferson; it was adopted June 20, 1782. The motto itself was used on the title page of the *Gentleman's Journal* (January 1692). It means "one from many." It appeared officially for the first time on a coin in New Jersey (1786).

Epstein, Sir Jacob (b. New York City, Nov. 10, 1880—d. Aug. 19, 1959), sculptor, mem- oirist. After studying in Paris under Rodin, Epstein made his permanent residence in Lon- don. He was knighted in 1954. He made no attempt at realism in his figures, and some re- garded his figures as unpleasantly grotesque. On the other hand, his works seem to most ob- servers impressive for power, imagination, and originality. Among his noted statues are those of *Mother and Child*, *Rima* (the bird girl of Hudson's *Green Mansions*), *Day*, *Night*, *Adam*, *Genesis*, *Ecce Homo*, *Venus*; he also did strik- ing portrait busts of Winston Churchill, Ber- nard Shaw, John Dewey, Joseph Conrad, and Lady Gregory. He wrote an autobiography, *Let There Be Sculpture* (1940).

Equilibrists, The (published in *Two Gentle- men in Bonds*, 1927), a ballad by JOHN CROWE RANSOM. The poem presents two lovers who burn hot and cold between sin and honor. Henry W. Wells sees the poem as "expressing the fail- ure of a love that hovers between platonic and physical, a frequently repeated theme in Ran- som's humorous ironies. Idealization of southern womanhood stands opposed to an irresistible frankness and *joie de vivre*."

Ericson, Leif (fl. 999–1003), Norse nav- igator and explorer. This famous sailor is believed to have landed on the shores of Amer- ica in about the year 1000. A son of Eric the Red (who colonized Greenland, 986), Leif may have been born in Iceland but seems to have been reared in Greenland. He heard from Norse mariners that they had occasionally sighted land far to the west. He bought a ship, hired a crew of thirty-five, and apparently reached the Amer- ican continent. He named three places—Hel- luland, Markland, and Vinland, sometimes identified as Labrador or Newfoundland, Nova Scotia, and New England at Cape Cod. At Vinland, where grapes grew in profusion, he is believed to have landed, but the evidence is dubious. There are also tales that two brothers of Leif made expeditions inland, and that one was killed by Indians. The information regard- ing Leif's voyages comes from the *Saga of Eric the Red* and the *Saga of Olaf Tryggvason*. Long- fellow had these old legends in mind when he wrote THE SKELETON IN ARMOR (1840). A de- tailed and well-argued attempt to establish numerous and somewhat different landing-places was made in Edward Reman's *Norse Discoveries and Explorations in America* (1949).

Erie Canal. A waterway connecting the Hudson River with Lake Erie. It extends 363 miles from Albany to Buffalo, and was often called "Clinton's Big Ditch" after Governor De Witt Clinton, under whose administration the work was carried out. Completed in 1825, the canal drastically reduced the cost of freight and opened up great markets to the merchants of New York City. A great wave of settlers from New England traveled to the Middle West via the canal. It has been the inspiration for nu- merous books, among them W. D. Edmonds' *Erie Water* (1933); S. H. Adams' *The Erie Canal* (1943, a juvenile), *Canal Town* (1944, a novel), and *Chingo Smith of the Erie Canal* (1958); and E. L. Meadowcroft's juvenile, *We Were There at the Opening of the Erie Canal* (1958). Walter D. Edmonds wrote often about the canal, as in *Mostly Canallers* (1934); his *Rome Haul* (1929) was dramatized by Marc Connelly and Frank B. Elser as *The Farmer Takes a Wife* (1934). S. H. Adams describes life along the canal in his novels CANAL TOWNS (1944) and *Banner by the Wayside* (1947).

Ernst, Morris L[eopold] (b. Uniontown, Ala., Aug. 23, 1888—   ), lawyer, writer. A grad- uate of Williams College and the New York Law School, Ernst joined the law firm of Greenbaum, Wolff and Ernst in 1915. His law career found him drafting insurance and banking legislation for New York's Governor Lehman, and serving as Special Council to the War Production Board, personal representative for President Roosevelt during the war on various missions to England, and a member of President Truman's Civil Rights Committee. As a writer he contributed pieces to law review journals and other publica- tions. His books from the first dealt with what Ernst felt were some of the more pertinent prob- lems confronting America, such as censorship, divorce, and sexual behavior. *The First Freedom* (1946) advocated less rigid censorship of radio and the press, arguing that America, having just won a long and tedious war, could scarcely afford to jeopardize the freedoms and principles she had so vigorously defended. *American Sex- ual Behavior and the Kinsey Report* (1948), written in collaboration with D. Loth, analyzed the famous *Report*, and urged redefining of sexual normalcy. *Report on the American Com- munist* (with D. Loth, 1952) was recognized as a significant, though not very detailed, analysis of Communism in America. *Utopia 1976* (1955) was Ernst's view of America in twenty years' time. It was a highly personal and optimistic vision of America's future. In 1958 he was hired by the Dominican Republic to investigate the disappearance of exiled leader Dr. Jesus de Galindez, and his report stated that there was no evidence linking the Dominican government with the disappearance. Ernst's other books: *To the Pure* (with W. Seagle, 1928); *Censored* (with Pare Lorentz, 1930); *America's Primer* (1931); *Hold Your Tongue!* (with A. Lindey, 1932); *Ultimate Power* (1937); *The Censor Marches On* (with A. Lindey, 1940); *Too Big* (1940); *The Best Is Yet* (1945); *So Far So Good* (1948); *For Better or Worse* (with D. Loth, 1952); *Touch Wood* (1960).

Erotic School, The. A name given to a group of writers *c.* 1888 by newspaper critics, who decried the extremes to which these writers, among them, Amélie Rives (see PRINCESS TROUBETZKOY), EDGAR SALTUS, GERTRUDE ATHERTON, and ELLA WHEELER WILCOX, went in rebelling against the stricter rules of Mrs. Grundy. These writers anticipated to a certain extent the revolt that came after World War I. They acted chiefly under the influence of the art-for-art's-sake movement in England.

Erskine, John (b. New York City, Oct. 5, 1879—d. June 2, 1951), teacher, novelist, editor, essayist, musician. Erskine led a rich and varied life, in the course of which he did many things well and some of them unexpectedly well, as when he pulled the Metropolitan Opera Co. out of a financial bog. He was at the beginning a scholar and teacher, specializing in Elizabethan poetry, but he took all literature as his province and made it, as one of his pupils said, "an art to be lived and loved." Then with the publication of THE PRIVATE LIFE OF HELEN OF TROY (1925), which attained an extraordinary popular success, he began a new career. The book dealt irreverently with ancient Greek figures and helped confirm the trend of the 1920's toward idol-breaking. Erskine followed up this book with others of similar character: *Galahad* (1926); ADAM AND EVE (1927); *Penelope's Man* (1928); *Tristan and Isolde* (1932); and others. But he failed to repeat the success of his first novel. He wrote in many other fields—against prohibition, on *The Influence of Women and Its Cure* (1936), on the love of books, and on other topics; he also became a popular lecturer, noted alike for his learning and his wit. Music became one of his chief interests, and in later years he began telling the story of his life—entertainingly, sometimes a little maliciously—in *The Memory of Certain Persons* (1947); *My Life as a Teacher* (1948); *My Life in Music* (1950). *My Life as a Writer* was begun but not completed.

Esenwein, J[oseph] Berg (b. Philadelphia, May 15, 1867—d. Nov. 7, 1946), editor, teacher of writing. Esenwein was editor of LIPPINCOTT'S MAGAZINE (1905–14), began editing *The Writer's Monthly* in 1915, in connection with his teaching and textbook activities. He published books on short-story writing, the art of versification, the art of public speaking, writing for magazines, writing children's books, and other kinds of writing.

Eskimos. Tribes of Mongolian origin who have been living since prehistoric times along the north coast of North America, in Labrador, and in regions nearby. The tribes of Alaska are allied to them, and they are believed to be kin to North American Indian groups. Although they inhabit a vast range of territory, they probably do not number more than 50,000 people. They have long been in contact with whites and have been friendly and hospitable to travelers among them. Their language is quite distinct from that of Indian tribes, and they have contributed only a few words to English, such as *kayak* and *igloo*. The name "Eskimo" is said to mean "eater of raw flesh." VILHJALMUR STEFANSSON and Peter Freuchen have written vivid accounts of Eskimo civilization. Cf. also Father Roger Buliard's *Inuk* (1951), Heluiz Washburne's *Children of the Blizzard* (1952), Douglas Wilkinson's *Land of the Long Day* (1956).

essay, the. This vehicle for literary discussion, formal or informal, has been as popular in the United States as in Europe and has taken as many diverse forms. Beginning with imitations of the English forms, the American essay not only carried on the tradition of Addison and Steele, Johnson, Hazlitt, and Arnold, but developed forms of its own. Its most notable contribution has been a more varied use of language: colloquialisms, homespun sayings, original coinages are commonly found in the American essay.

Memorable American essayists have often been noted for their individualism. Cotton Mather, Jonathan Edwards, Franklin, Paine, Jefferson, Hamilton, and John Adams of the Colonial and Revolutionary periods are still read. Less well-remembered writers from the early periods are Noah Webster, John Trumbull, Timothy Dwight, Philip Freneau, Benjamin Rush, and Francis Hopkinson.

In the nineteenth century the essay flourished in many forms. Washington Irving was the first great figure; Emerson soon took a place beside him. Irving's *Sketch Book* inaugurated the tradition of painting local scenes and types in essay form. Augustus Longstreet and Mark Twain are the best-known followers of Irving in this respect. (See HUMOR.) Emerson's serious themes were developed by writers such as Thoreau, Whitman, William James, and Henry Adams. Among the lesser contemporaries of Irving and Emerson were James Kirke Paulding, Hugh Henry Brackenridge, Joseph Dennie, and the contributors to the *North American Review*, among them William Ellery Channing, Richard Henry Dana, Sr., and two poets who were also serious and influential literary critics, William Cullen Bryant and James Russell Lowell. Two notable essayists not easily identified with any particular movement were Edgar Allan Poe and Oliver Wendell Holmes. Toward the end of the century numerous essays were produced in the controversy between the "idealists" and the "realists." Among the former were Richard Henry Stoddard, Bayard Taylor, Thomas Bailey Aldrich, Edmund Clarence Stedman, and Charles Dudley Warner. The names of the realists are more familiar today: William Dean Howells, Henry James, Hamlin Garland, and Frank Norris.

In the twentieth century the forms of the essay, along with most other aspects of American life, became increasingly specialized. The general essay, once the domain of literate men in any field, had fewer practitioners. A few who have carried on the tradition are Christopher Morley, Bernard De Voto, William Beebe, Henry Seidel Canby, Philip Wylie, Robert M. Coates, S. J. Perelman, James Thurber, and E. B. White. Other recent names are A. J. Liebling, Peter Viereck, James Baldwin, and Leslie Fiedler. Most other contemporary essayists, though they may occasionally venture into the field of the general essay, are usually known best for one specialty, such as scholarship, reportage, sociology, or the theater. Among serious scholars and philosophers who were notable stylists in the early part of the century were George Santayana, Josiah Royce, William James, and John Dewey. In jurisprudence Justices Oliver Wendell Holmes, Jr., Louis D. Brandeis, Felix Frankfurter, and Hugo Black are famous for the style of their written decisions. In other fields may be mentioned Thorstein Veblen, Vernon L. Parrington, Allan Nevins, Carl Becker, Ruth Benedict, and Margaret Mead. Woodrow Wilson is perhaps the only modern public figure whose essays endure. Among serious analysts of contemporary American culture who have achieved a wide audience for their essays are Stuart Chase, J. C. Furnas, George F. Kennan, David Riesman, Paul Goodman, C. Wright Mills, and Vance Packard. The stylistic problem of presenting specialized and complex material in a form palatable to a general audience has led to some criticism of the mixed style many popularizers are led to employ.

Among the literary scholars who wrote memorable essays in this century were George F. Babbitt, Paul Elmer More, F. O. Matthiessen, James Gibbons Huneker, Constance Rourke, John Erskine, Carl Van Doren, Mark Van Doren, and Richard Chase. Some of those who helped make literary criticism a separate subject with its own essay style were T. S. Eliot, John Crowe Ransom, Allen Tate, Robert Penn Warren, Cleanth Brooks, and Lionel Trilling. Other popular literary essayists have included H. L. Mencken, Randolph Bourne, Waldo Frank, Lewis Mumford, Van Wyck Brooks, Malcolm Cowley, James T. Farrell, Granville Hicks, J. Donald Adams, John Ciardi, Leslie Fiedler, and George Steiner.

The field of newspaper writing includes numerous kinds of essays: columns on sports, society, theater, and political analysis, as well as editorials. Even within such a specialized area as current events analysis, styles range from the austere, reasoned evenness of Walter Lippmann to the colloquial, epigrammatic speech of Westbrook Pegler. Among earlier newspapermen whose writing in various fields remains known are Stephen Crane, Ambrose Bierce, Joseph Pulitzer, Ring Lardner, Franklin P. Adams, Don Marquis, and Alexander Woollcott. Contemporaries with high reputations include James Reston, Richard H. Rovere, and Murray Kempton. In the entertainment and theater world memorable pieces have been written by Brander Matthews, George Jean Nathan, Wolcott Gibbs, Walter Kerr, Gilbert Seldes, and Eric Bentley.

The death of the essay has often been predicted. It is true that the general essay as exemplified by the work of E. B. White and others is practiced less and less, but specialized forms of essay-writing have proliferated during the twentieth century.

Essay for the Recording of Illustrious Providences (1684), a treatise by INCREASE MATHER, republished twice in the 19th century as *Remarkable Providences*. A collection of reports involving supernatural incidents in early New England history, the book claims to examine these cases scientifically, sometimes attacking popular superstition in order to prove and illustrate the direct intervention of God in human affairs. In spite of its pseudoscientific approach, the book contributed to the atmosphere of fanaticism which resulted in the Salem witchcraft trials. Mather, however, repudiated the extremity of the trials in his *Cases of Conscience Concerning Evil Spirits* (1693).

Essays, First and Second Series (1841, 1844), by RALPH WALDO EMERSON. In the *First Series* Emerson wrote on history, self-reliance, compensation, spiritual laws, love, friendship, prudence, heroism, the over-soul, circles, intellect, and art. In the *Second Series* he wrote on the poet, experience, character, manners, gifts, nature, politics, nominalism and realism, and New England reformers. Many of the essays were first employed as lectures; and like many of Emerson's writings they are rather a string of shining jewels more or less heaped together than gems carefully arranged in a pattern. Some of his most famous sayings come from these essays, and they often, it has been said, join "a Yankee shrewdness with an almost Oriental mysticism." Despite the lack of coherence in the essays, Robert E. Spiller finds unity in the thought animating all of them: "Description of the universe and its laws, analysis of the moral faculties in human relationships in general, and studies of more nearly particular problems of experience."

Estes, Eleanor (b. West Haven, Conn., May 9, 1906—   ), writer of juvenile fiction. The Moffat family and their pets are Miss Estes' best-known creation. In 1951 Miss Estes won the Herald Tribune Spring Book Festival Award for *Ginger Pye* (1951), and the Newbery Medal for the most distinguished contribution to American literature for children that year. Among her books: *The Moffats* (1941); *The Witch Family* (1960). LOUIS SLOBODKIN and Edward Ardizzone have been her illustrators.

Esther (1884), a novel by HENRY ADAMS published under the pseudonym Frances Snow Compton. It relates under a thin veil something of the story of Adams' own marriage; the heroine, who resembles Marian Adams, falls in love with the clergyman Stephen Hazard, but they separate because of incompatibility in their religious views. Adams in the book makes clear his own loss of religious faith. Another prominent character is the artist Wharton, recalling in many ways the sculptor AUGUSTUS ST. GAUDENS, who created the impressive memorial to Mrs. Adams in the Rock Creek Cemetery in Washington. The letters gathered in *Henry Adams and His Friends* (1947) include some to Adams' publisher, Henry Holt, which express Adams' view that the novel was merely an experiment in publishing—to see how well a novel could sell without advertising. Oscar Cargill notes parallels between the clergyman in the book and Adams himself, and advances the theory that the suggestion of suicide made to Esther in the novel may have seemed to Adams in later years not unconnected with his wife's suicide.

Ethan Brand (published in the *Dollar Magazine*, Philadelphia, May, 1851, under the title *The Unpardonable Sin*, later included in THE SNOW IMAGE, 1851), a story by NATHANIEL HAWTHORNE. Ethan, who has tended a limekiln in his native village, returns to it convinced that he has committed "the unpardonable sin"—intellectual pride. He destroys himself in the kiln; his successor finds a whitened human skeleton with a marble heart. Many critics have seen in the story a depiction of Hawthorne's own nature as he himself diagnosed it. Bliss Perry wrote that Hawthorne "believed in "an Unpardonable Sin; and it is by this faith in the reality of the moral life that he takes his rank as an artist." Perry likened Brand to Empedocles of old "casting himself despairingly into the crater of Mount Etna." Mark Van Doren said, "The tale is justly celebrated, though it is not perfect. . . . Yet the night scene at the kiln, the lost laughter of the hero returning to die, and the death itself—these are tremendous things, and Hawthorne nowhere else accomplished their like."

Ethan Frome (1911), a novel by EDITH WHARTON. This is usually reckoned to be Mrs. Wharton's masterpiece, though she herself did not think so. It is an ironic tragedy of love, frustration, jealousy, and sacrifice. The scene is a "typical" New England village, where Ethan barely makes a living out of a stony farm and exists at odds with his wife Zeena (short for Zenobia), a whining hypochondriac. Mattie, a cousin of Zeena's, comes to live with them, and love inevitably develops between her and Ethan. They try to end their hapless romance by steering a bobsled into a tree; but both end up cripples, tied for a long life of despair to Zeena

and the barren farm. Zeena, however, is transformed into a devoted nurse as Mattie becomes the nagging invalid. George Snell said of Zenobia, "Seldom in our fiction has the embittered, unloved, shrewish wife been better portrayed." Owen Davis and his son Donald made an excellent dramatization of the novel in 1936.

Ethnogenesis (1861), a poem by HENRY TIMROD. Filled with enthusiasm for the newborn Confederacy, Timrod prophesied its victory in war and its greatness in peace. The poem was included in his *Poems* (1873).

Ethnology, Bureau of (American). Founded in 1872 and incorporated into the Smithsonian Institute in 1879. Major JOHN WESLEY POWELL, who became its first director, employed specialists to study particular Amerindian problems. Their *Reports* have contributed to a scientific understanding of Indian tribes and their cultures. Many famous anthropologists and other specialists have worked for the Bureau, among them FRANZ BOAS and FRANCES DENSMORE.

etiquette, books on. A mirror (even if somewhat distorted) of the development of American culture may be found in the books on etiquette that have from age to age molded our manners. Religion and law at first laid down rules for American manners. Thus many of the colonies legally punished scandalmongering, cursing, lying, flirting, even making faces. Modes of dress were also governed, mainly to prevent the "lower classes" from imitating the finery of the aristocrats. Young children were taught, first of all, to pay implicit respect to their elders. Silence in the meetinghouse and at meals was enjoined upon them; they were not to go "singing, whistling, nor hollowing along the street." Girls were expected to maintain "a retiring delicacy." Idleness was severely denounced. As early as 1754 *The School of Good Manners* was published for the benefit of young people. British manuals became popular as wealth grew in the colonies; from these or native imitations Americans sought to learn what to wear, how to arrange a dinner, how to converse in company.

The birth of the Republic brought about few changes until the era of Jackson, when a new conception arose—that anybody might become a lady or gentleman by an exhibition of proper manners. The manners inculcated were sometimes strange, as when "Fanny Fern" (Mrs. James Parton) enjoined, "Always keep callers waiting, till they have had time to notice the outlay of money in your parlors." Arthur Schlesinger, in his study of American etiquette books called *Learning How to Behave* (1946), estimates that, aside from revisions and new editions, twenty-eight different manuals appeared in the 1830's, thirty-six in the 1840's, and thirty-eight more in the 1850's. Then came the Civil War and the economic boom that followed it. Profiteers and parvenus, a sham aristocracy, wanted to learn manners, especially transatlantic manners, in a hurry; and magazines and books did all they could to help them. Entertaining details are given in Dixon Wecter's *The Saga of American Society* (1937). Journalism leaped to the rescue, and EDWARD BOK relates (*The Americanization of Edward Bok*, 1922) that when he engaged Isabel A. Mallon to conduct, under the pen name of Ruth Ashmore, a department on social proprieties and problems for *The Ladies' Home Journal*, her "Side Talks with Girls" brought her 158,000 letters in sixteen years.

After World War I a new crop of millionaires appeared, rather more ruthless than the post-Civil War ones; prohibition produced strange crudities of manners, with the bootlegger as the arbiter of elegance; the younger generation concluded it was smarter to be rowdy or smart-alecky than to be gracious. A more informal spirit of fellowship developed between the sexes, and movies brought into vogue Hollywood's notion of good manners. Yet more books on etiquette were sold than ever before. Two in particular became popular and sold by the hundreds of thousands: Lillian Eichler (Mrs. T. M. Watson) published her *Book of Etiquette* in 1921, EMILY POST her *Etiquette, the Blue Book of Usage* in 1922 (tenth edition, 1960). Many other persons, sometimes socialites with the help of ghost writers, offered their advice; for example, Amy Vanderbilt in *Everyday Etiquette* (1956). These arbiters of manners faced a difficult problem. Their business depended on the assumption that there was a fixed code of etiquette, but the spirit of the age was against them. As successive editions of their books appeared, it became obvious that they preferred making concessions to losing sales.

The changes have probably been for the better. Stilted formalities are no longer emphasized: the rules of etiquette are usually the rules of reason, kindness, and good taste. There are still numerous manuals for children, among them Mrs. Post's excellent *Children Are People* (1940). One important development has been the increased emphasis on courtesy in business dealings, especially with the incursion of women into industry. Nella Braddy's *Book of Business Etiquette* (1922) and Mary A. Hopkins' *Profits from Courtesy* (1937) are two such examples. Men, too, have received separate advice, as in R. H. Loeb, Jr.'s *He-Manners: Young Man's Book of Etiquette* (1955).

Eureka (1848), an "essay on the material and spiritual universe" by EDGAR ALLAN POE. Under the strong influence of Newton and La-place, Poe presented a view of the universe as a mystic and material unity, with all parts interdependent and all equally cause and effect. In this way he sought to solve problems both major and minor: the problem of good and evil, for example, and the problem of composing a fictional story. The result is, as H. H. Clark expresses it, a "magnificent vision of a universe of ordered harmony." The piece is a contribution to scientific and philosophical thought and at the same time a prose poem. Alfred Kreymborg notes that this essay had a great influence on some French writers, particularly on Paul Valéry; the latter claimed that the essay was "the intuitive progenitor of Einstein's relativity." Poe cer-tainly saw the possibility of non-Euclidean geometry. He laid a strong emphasis on intuition, an emphasis that scientists now admit is valid, since "hunches" have often led to important scientific discoveries.

European Literature, Columbia Dictionary of. See COLUMBIA DICTIONARY.

Europeans, The (1878), a novel by HENRY JAMES. Two expatriates, the Baroness Muenster and her brother Felix Young, come to Boston to visit some relatives they have never seen. The baroness futilely tries to make a wealthy marriage; Felix becomes prosperous by painting portraits of the Bostonians he meets. A contrast is drawn between the sophistication of the pair and the strait and strict New Englanders. Felix marries one of his kinswomen, who is eager to escape from her bleak environment.

Eutaw Springs. Scene of the important battle, Sept. 8, 1781, in South Carolina at which General Nathanael Greene and his American forces finally compelled the British to withdraw northward. Military historians regard the battle as a turning point of the Revolution. Concerning the battle PHILIP FRENEAU wrote his beautiful elegy, *To the Memory of the Brave Americans* (1781), which Sir Walter Scott is said to have learned by heart. On the same theme WILLIAM IOOR wrote a play, *The Battle of Eutaw Springs* (1807; produced, 1813), and WILLIAM GILMORE SIMMS a romance, *Eutaw* (1856), a sequel to his earlier *The Forayers* (1855). Of these two novels Alexander Cowie says that despite certain deficiencies "they are still among the most readable stories of adventure in the history of the American novel."

Evangeline, A Tale of Acadie (1847), a narrative poem by HENRY WADSWORTH LONGFEL-LOW. As early as 1829 Longfellow was interested in the Acadians, and planned to write a sketch, *Down East: The Missionary of Acadie*, to be included in a series of *New England Sketches*. In 1838 an Episcopal clergyman, Horace Lorenzo Connolly, told Nathaniel Haw-thorne the story of a young couple who had been separated by the British order expelling about 6,000 inhabitants from Acadie, a region in Nova Scotia. The bride set off in search of her husband, and at last found him on his death-bed. Connolly urged Hawthorne to write a novel based on this incident, and Hawthorne considered it carefully for a long time. But in 1840, at a dinner in Longfellow's home at which Connolly was present, the story was retold in the poet's hearing. Hawthorne said, "The story is not in my vein," and Longfellow, with Haw-thorne's consent, took it over. He conducted minute researches for several years, but was held up by other tasks; he finally started to write the poem on Nov. 28, 1845, completed it Feb. 27, 1847. It appeared that year, and won an immediate success.

The poem was written in dactylic hexameters, under the influence of Goethe's *Hermann und Dorothea* (1797), Esaias Tegnér's *The Children of the Lord's Supper* (1820), and *Frithjofs Saga* (1825). It tells how the bridegroom Gabriel

Lajeunesse is carried to Louisiana, and the bride Evangeline Bellefontaine to New England. She follows him, and after years of fruitless wandering comes, an old woman, to Philadelphia, where as a Sister of Mercy she cares for the poor and sick. There, during an epidemic, she at last finds Gabriel dying in the almshouse. Her own death follows, and both are buried in the Catholic cemetery.

Longfellow's accuracy has sometimes been questioned, and it has also been said that he exaggerated the barbarity of the expulsion. His hexameters have likewise been criticized as not really suited to the genius of English and more frequently prose than verse. But the supreme skill of his narration, the strength of his character portrayal, and the sympathy awakened by his lines have more than compensated for any possible errors in history or failure in metrics. As Manning Hawthorne (great-grandson of the novelist) and Henry Wadsworth Longfellow Dana (grandson of the poet) point out in *The Origin and Development of Longfellow's "Evangeline"* (1947), an "extraordinary number" of editions, translations, and commentaries have kept the poem alive. There have been numerous dramatizations, musical settings, and film versions. Statues suggested by the poem have been erected at Grand Pré, Nova Scotia, and St. Martinville, La.

Evans, Augusta J[ane] (b. Columbus, Ga., May 8, 1835—d. May 9, 1909), novelist. In later life she wrote under her married name, Wilson. Miss Evans' sentimental tales were popular in her own day, particularly her St. Elmo (1866). Its heroine, remarks Frank Luther Mott, is "a paragon girl" who makes it her business to reform a worldly sophisticate and of course to marry him. The banality of the story is only partially concealed by a display of erudition that deeply impressed its readers. Despite the ridicule the book received from critics, children were named St. Elmo, and so were towns, streets, and hotels. Miss Evans also wrote *Beulah* (1859) and, after a long career, *Devota* (1907). W. P. Fidler wrote her biography (1951).

Evans, Donald (b. Philadelphia, July 24, 1884—d. May 26, 1921), poet. Evans, who died by his own hand, was the hero of Greenwich Village and the sophisticated set for a decade; his volumes of verse—*Discords* (1912), *Sonnets from the Patagonian* (1914), *Two Deaths in the Bronx* (1916), *Nine Poems from a Valetudinarian* (1916), and *Ironica* (1919)—contain many striking lines and influenced some of his contemporaries, including Wallace Stevens and E. E. Cummings. Evans, says Alfred Kreymborg, "had a genius for exquisite masks of cynicism. Some masks were borrowed from London and Paris; the rest he fashioned himself. He wore them all in graceful defiance of society."

Evans, George. See In the Good Old Summer Time.

Evans, Nathaniel (b. Philadelphia, June 8, 1742—d. Oct. 29, 1767), clergyman, poet.

Evans' early death prevented the development of his poetic talent, although he was highly regarded by his contemporaries. He was a member of the group headed by Francis Hopkinson, and like others of the group imitated the English poets of his day. Some of his poems were suggested by events in the French and Indian War. Elsewhere he paid tribute to Franklin as a scientist, and his most ambitious effort was his *Ode on the Prospect of Peace*. His *Poems on Several Occasions, with Some Other Compositions* was published posthumously (1772).

Evans, Warren Felt (b. Rockingham, Vt., Dec. 23, 1817—d. Sept. 4, 1889), clergyman, psychologist. Deeply under the influence of transcendental thought, Evans became a disciple of Phineas P. Quimby. Later he developed Quimby's ideas of mental healing along lines of his own, and published several books for those who could not come to the sanitarium he established (1870) at Salisbury, Mass. Among them were *The Mental Cure* (1869); *Mental Medicine* (1872); *Soul and Body* (1876); *Esoteric Christianity and Mental Therapeutics* (1886).

Evarts, Hal George (b. Topeka, Kans., Aug. 24, 1887—d. Oct. 18, 1934), trapper, guide, writer of western stories. Evarts, a lover of the outdoors, became an authority on hunting and fishing in the undeveloped West of the early 19th century, especially the old Indian Territory and Wyoming. He made no attempt at fine literary art, but wrote straightforwardly and effectively. His best-known book is *Tumbleweeds* (1923), about riders of the cattle ranges in the Cherokee Strip. Others include *The Cross Pull* (1920); *Passing of the Old West* (1921); *Spanish Acres* (1925); *Shortgrass* (1932).

Everett, Alexander Hill (b. Boston, March 19, 1790—d. June 29, 1847), diplomat, poet, essayist, editor. Perhaps Everett's greatest literary service was that, as minister to Spain, he appointed Washington Irving as an attaché to the legation at Madrid, thus shaping Irving's future career. He was himself a learned, witty man who wrote excellent books and papers on matters political and literary, translated Theocritus and Goethe, and was among the first to give attention to Oriental studies. His volumes on *Europe* (1822) and *America* (1827) were translated into German, French, and Spanish.

Everett, Edward (b. Dorchester, Mass., April 11, 1794—d. Jan. 15, 1865), clergyman, teacher, statesman, diplomat, orator, biographer. Edward was the younger brother of Alexander Everett and an even abler man. His great personal beauty and charm caused him to be called "Apollo" and "Cicero," while Emerson referred to his "precise and perfect eloquence." His career was a series of careers. He began as a Unitarian minister, went on to become a distinguished professor of Greek at Harvard, edited the North American Review (1820–24), finally began what was to be his true lifework by running for Congress, where he served for ten years (1825–35). Thereafter he was governor of Massachusetts (1836–39), minister to England (1841–45), president of Harvard (1846–

49), secretary of state (1852–53), and United States Senator (1853–54). Up to the outbreak of the Civil War he was inclined toward compromise on the slavery question, thereafter he spoke vigorously for the Union.

Posterity remembers Everett because he delivered a two-hour oration at Gettysburg, Lincoln following him with his three brief paragraphs. Lincoln himself had no thought but that Everett would overshadow him, but there is evidence that Everett realized the greatness of Lincoln's address. Everett's style was artificial and grandiose, but his addresses were immensely popular, and his *Orations and Speeches on Various Occasions* (1853–68) reached a ninth edition in 1878. It is strange to discover in Everett, however, frequent traces of comfortable humor. He was one of the first to argue that the common language was better spoken—and written—in America than in England. P. R. Frothingham wrote on *Edward Everett, Orator and Statesman* (1925).

Evergreen Review. This quarterly magazine of fiction, poetry, criticism, and articles on general subjects is both international and *avant-garde*. Since beginning publication in 1957, the editors, Barney Rosset and Donald Allen, have published a variety of writing, including work of European existentialists and American "beats." The magazine has offered a forum for certain writers in the San Francisco-Monterey areas: Kenneth Rexroth, Henry Miller, Charles Olson, William S. Burroughs, and the younger Allen Ginsberg, Jack Kerouac, Gregory Corso, Robert Creeley, Frank O'Hara, Denise Levertov, and others. (See BEAT WRITING.) With the exception of John Wain, the magazine has published little from England, but many stories and articles by French writers such as Jean Paul Sartre,

Albert Camus, Samuel Beckett (an Irishman who writes in French), Alain Robbe-Grillet, and Eugène Ionesco. A late development was the editors' effort to extend *Evergreen*'s purview to other than literary arts. The magazine now publishes reproductions and studies of art work by abstract expressionists as well as articles on jazz by such critics as Martin Williams and Nat Hentoff.

Eve's Diary (1906), the supposed diary of the first woman, by MARK TWAIN. It was a humorous skit written as a companion piece to *Extracts from Adam's Diary* (1904). Its last line, supposedly composed by Adam after Eve's death, became Olivia Clemens' epitaph: "Wheresoever she was, *there* was Eden."

Ewen, David (b. Austria, Nov. 26, 1907–), author, musicologist. Ewen's books— over forty in number—have had a wide sale. Ewen is the author of several biographies of contemporary composers and conductors, such as *The Story of Arturo Toscanini* (1951); *A Journey to Greatness: The Life and Music of George Gershwin* (1956); *Richard Rodgers* (1957); *The World of Jerome Kern* (1960); and *Leonard Bernstein* (1960). He also wrote a number of comprehensive surveys and reference books dealing with all phases of music and the history of music, among which are *From Bach to Stravinsky* (1933); *Music Comes to America* (1942); *Dictators of the Baton* (1943); *Music for the Millions* (1944, republished in 1954 as *Ewen's Masterworks*); *The Book of Modern Composers* (1953); *The Milton Cross Encyclopedia of Great Composers* (1942, in collaboration with Milton Cross); *The Complete Book of Twentieth Century Composers* (1952); *The Home Book of Musical Knowledge* (1954); *Encyclopedia of the Opera* (1955); *Panorama of American Popular Music* (1957); *The Complete Book of The American Musical Theater* (1958); *Encyclopedia of Concert Music* (1959); *The History of Popular Music in America* (1961); and *The Story of the American Musical Theater* (1961). These books, encyclopedic in character and written in an easy, non-technical style, have served as standard family reference books.

Excelsior (1841), a poem by HENRY WADSWORTH LONGFELLOW. The poem is believed to have been suggested to the poet by the motto on the New York state shield. It became immensely popular in its own day as a fervent exhortation toward the seeking of higher goals; it has been frequently parodied. See THE SONG OF THE CHATTAHOOCHEE.

Exile's Return (1934), a memoir of the "lost generation" by MALCOLM COWLEY. This is a vivid and persuasive account of what happened to the young Americans who flocked to Europe, especially Paris, in the 1920's. In it appear some of the notable figures of the time—William Faulkner, John Dos Passos, Scott Fitzgerald, Hart Crane, Ezra Pound, Ernest Hemingway, and others. Cowley himself had a large share in their literary and bohemian adventures. The book was revised and augmented in 1951.

expressionism. An artistic theory and mode of practice first developed by various European painters (mainly German) of the early 20th century. It was carried into literature by German dramatists and thence spread to the novel. Among its earliest literary exponents was James Joyce. In essence expressionism seeks to convey import through the objects of feeling. Thus reality is translated rather than described, sometimes into abstractions, but, in the early phases, more often into details of human response, as in paintings of human figures or accounts of subconscious thought. Distortion, as in a theater set, is justified as a means of realizing the affective or valuational aspects of reality. In practice the literary uses of expressionism merged with symbolism, as in Joyce, T. S. Eliot, Eugene O'Neill, and many others.

Ezekiel, Moses [Jacob] (b. Richmond, Va., Oct. 28, 1844—d. March 27, 1917), sculptor. Ezekiel was graduated from the Virginia Military Institute in 1866, after having fought with honor in the Civil War. For a time he studied medicine, later was a pupil and friend of Liszt, but found that he preferred sculpture. He studied in Berlin and won high honors with his work. Among his famous pieces are a bust of *Washington, Religious Liberty, Virginia Mourning Her Dead, The Madonna, Robert E. Lee, Thomas Jefferson, Longfellow, Poe, Industry.*

F

Fable, A (1954), a novel by WILLIAM FAULK-NER. Set in France a few months before the end of World War I, *A Fable* is both an allegory of the passion of Christ and a study of a world that has chosen submission to authority and the secular values of power and chauvinism instead of individuality and the exercise of free will. The novel centers on the fate of a young corporal, born in a cow-shed and raised by his two half-sisters, Marya and Marthe; he enlists in the French army and, with the aid of twelve companions, incites a mutiny in the trenches which results in a temporary armistice. Betrayed by a member of his own regiment, the corporal is executed for cowardice, along with two other military criminals, becoming a martyr to his principles and his belief in humanity. When the gravesite is struck by an enemy shell, his body disappears. Most of the characters in the novel are nameless personifications of abstractions, and most of the named characters—Marya, Marthe, Magda—are intended to represent the figures their names suggest. The novel suffers from largely two-dimensional characterization and lack of dramatic immediacy; the slow revealing of events, the lengthy descriptions (although often brilliant), and the symbolism and mysticism of the book make it difficult reading. It was regarded with reservations by most reviewers.

Fable for Critics, A (1848), a satire in verse by JAMES RUSSELL LOWELL. Published anonymously, it was soon recognized as Lowell's. The "fable" of the poem is negligible and confusedly handled, with the god of poetry, Apollo, and a contemporary American critic as the main characters. The chief writers of the day are described in rapid satiric profiles, written in what are often rough and uneven anapestic tetrameters that frequently close with startling rhymes. The wit and turbulent humor anticipate his great BIGLOW PAPERS. Among those he characterized in his poem are Emerson, Longfellow, Holmes, Whittier, Hawthorne, Cooper, Poe, Halleck, Griswold, Willis, Alcott, Bryant, Margaret Fuller, Theodore Parker, John Neal, Harry Franco, Lydia Maria Child, and—himself. Frequently Lowell mingled eulogies with deprecations. Many of his verdicts have been sustained by the judgment of posterity; others were unjust.

In writing the *Fable*, Lowell apparently took as models such poems as Pope's *Dunciad* (1728), Leigh Hunt's *The Feast of the Poets* (1814), and Byron's *English Bards and Scotch Reviewers* (1809). He repeated the devices of the *Fable* in *The Origin of Didactic Poetry* (1857), and his kinswoman AMY LOWELL imitated him in A CRITICAL FABLE (1922), but far less brilliantly.

Lowell is deliberately vengeful in the *Fable*. This is shown most emphatically in the passages on MARGARET FULLER, who had belittled him in her essay on *American Literature*. WILLIAM CULLEN BRYANT had once accused Lowell of plagiarism, hence the remarks on his icy coldness, which Lowell later regretted. EDGAR ALLAN POE had attacked Lowell's friend Longfellow but had been on the whole friendly to Lowell, hence the mixed praise and blame for him in the *Fable*. Poe replied by assailing Lowell's confused metrics. He also attacked Lowell for his lack of appreciation of Southern writers; he was himself the only southern writer given any space in the *Fable*. He attributed this defect to Lowell's over-ardent abolitionism. But the poem is notable for its sturdy insistence that literary America had come of age; it is in general a noteworthy and pioneering endeavor to summarize and appraise American literature up to its time.

Fables in Slang (1899), stories by GEORGE ADE. One morning, at a loss to know what to write for the Chicago *Record*, Ade decided to compose a fable in language that was modern and undignified. The result, the story of Luella and her sister Mae, appeared on Sept. 17, 1897. There was little actual slang, the Americanisms were those of Indiana. Further *Fables*, appearing first in the *Record*, later in other newspapers, made a great hit. A collection of the stories appeared in December, 1899; more than 69,000 copies were sold in 1900, and Ade became famous. Years later, when Franklin D. Roosevelt needed to make a point with his cabinet, he would read one of Ade's *Fables* to them—just as Lincoln had read Artemus Ward in similar circumstances.

Fabulous Forties, The (1924), a historical survey of the 1840's by MEADE MINNIGERODE. This decade was "a brilliant three-ring circus"; to depict it, Minnigerode gathered from newspapers and other contemporary records a mass of well-arranged material on what people ate and wore, what their favorite hotels were, how the elections were conducted, what the "ladies" of the time did to occupy themselves, what foreign visitors made tours of the country. He writes in detail about P. T. Barnum, perhaps the presiding genius of the era; and he closes with an account of the discovery of gold in California and the rush of the forty-niners to get rich quick.

Face on the Barroom Floor, The (1872 or 1887), a poem by John Henry Titus or Hugh Antoine D'Arcy. This much-recited doggerel has been the topic of a strange dispute. One version of it, inferior in rhythm and spirit, was published by Titus (1853?–1947) in the Ashtabula (Ohio) *Sentinel* (1872). Another version, called simply *The Face upon the Floor*, appeared in the New York *Dispatch* (Aug. 7, 1887), with an actor named D'Arcy credited as author. In 1934 Titus brought legal action to prevent a song publisher from using his title for the song. Titus is said to have written 1,800 poems, the only one of which to attain fame was his saloon piece. According to tradition D'Arcy took as the setting for his poem a now extinct barroom on Union Square, New York City, called "Joe's."

Fadden, Chimmie. A Bowery character in stories by Edward W. Townsend, based on one "Chuck" Connors. Many of them appeared in the New York *Sun* at the turn of the century, later in books: *Chimmie Fadden, Major Max, and Other Stories* (1895) and *Chimmie Fadden Explains* (1895). See THE BOWERY.

Fadiman, Clifton (b. New York City, May 15, 1904—   ), critic, lecturer, radio entertainer. Fadiman has contributed to many magazines and newspapers, was on the editorial staff of Simon and Schuster (1927–35), and was book editor of the *New Yorker* (1933–43). From 1938 to 1948 he was master of ceremonies of the radio program INFORMATION, PLEASE. He is one of the judges of the Book-of-the-Month Club. He has edited several anthologies and classics, collected some of his pieces in *Party of One* (1955) and *Any Number Can Play* (1957); edited with Charles Van Doren, *American Treasury, 1455–1955* (1955). *Voyages of Ulysses* (1959) and *Adventures of Hercules* (1960) are children's books; *Lifetime Reading Plan* came out in 1960.

Faint Perfume (1923), a novel by ZONA GALE. To Leda, a poor girl living with unsympathetic relatives, comes a "faint perfume" of romance with the husband of one of the relatives. But his wife refuses to divorce him, and he and Leda are obliged to part. The novel was successfully dramatized by the author in 1933.

Fairfax, Beatrice. The pen name under which **Marie Manning** (b. 1878?—d. Nov. 28, 1945) and others wrote a column of "Advice to the Lovelorn" in the New York *Journal,* beginning on July 20, 1898, which sometimes elicited 1,400 letters a day. It was syndicated by King Features. Despite the title of her column, Miss Manning avoided the vapid sentimentality of some of her competitors and counseled, "Dry your eyes, roll up your sleeves, and dig for a practical solution." She wrote stories and several books under her own name.

Fairfield, Sumner Lincoln (b. Warwick, Mass., June 25, 1803—d. March 6, 1844), poet, teacher, actor, editor. Fairfield wrote and published many poems, collected in his *Poems and Prose Writings* (1841). He is chiefly remembered for *The Last Night of Pompeii* (1832); he accused Bulwer Lytton of having plagiarized this in his novel, *The Last Days of Pompeii* (1834).

Fair God, The (1873), a historical novel by LEW WALLACE. A story of the conquest of Mexico by CORTEZ, the tale centers on Montezuma's futile efforts to resist the Spanish invader. The "fair god" is Quetzalcoatl, Aztec god of the air. Wallace began working on the story in 1843 and wove into it much careful research. The book became immediately popular, went through twenty editions in ten years.

Faithful Narrative of the Surprising Work of God, The. See NARRATIVE OF SURPRISING CONVERSIONS.

Falcon of Ser Federigo, The (1863), a narrative poem by HENRY WADSWORTH LONGFELLOW, one of the TALES OF A WAYSIDE INN (1860–63). The student tells this tale, which is taken from Boccaccio's *Decameron.* Longfellow tells the tale skillfully using run-on couplets.

Fall of British Tyranny, The, or American Liberty Triumphant (1776), a play by John (Joseph?) Leacock. This play was never produced. It portrays the course of events in the opening year of the Revolution, with the scenes laid first in England and then in America, where the Battle of Lexington and succeeding events are shown. The characters have assumed names: Lord North is Lord Catspaw, Pitt is Lord Wisdom, General Howe is Elbow Room, and General Burgoyne is Caper.

Fall of the City, The (1937), a radio drama in verse by ARCHIBALD MACLEISH. The play is a dramatic application of President Franklin Roosevelt's doctrine that "the only thing we have to fear is fear itself." The people of the city are demoralized by the enemy's propaganda and bow down before his approach. But the one man who looks upon their conqueror at close range finds inside his glittering armor no face, no substance: nothingness. "The people invent their oppressors," he declares.

Fall of the House of Usher, The (1839, in *Tales of the Grotesque and Arabesque,* 1840), a story by EDGAR ALLAN POE. A fantastic but powerful tale, practically a prose poem; it contains the poem, THE HAUNTED PALACE. A friend comes to visit Roderick Usher in his gloomy, decayed mansion. They read together, and Roderick plays curious musical pieces of his own composition. Roderick's twin sister Madeline has been placed in the family vault for dead, but he is convinced she still lives, and when she appears suddenly in her shroud to Roderick and his friend, brother and sister die simultaneously. As the friend leaves the house and looks back in the moonlight, he sees it suddenly split asunder and fall into the tarn. The story is one in which atmosphere is evoked to a superb degree, without neglect of plot or characterization. The sound effects in themselves show Poe's mastery of language. Students of psychiatry have found in Roderick a careful analysis of the schizophrenic mind, as also in Poe's WILLIAM WILSON.

Falstaff, Jake. The pen name of HERMAN FETZER.

Family Reunion, The (1939), a play by T. S. ELIOT. This is the story of Lord Monchensey, who murders his wife and returns home to his mother Amy eight years later, pursued by Furies, hoping to find peace. The play is written in cadenced verse which rises to intenser meters at moments of dramatic tension. It has been performed widely, the most recent major production in America having been at the Phoenix Theater, New York City, in 1958, where the cast included Florence Reed and Lillian Gish.

Faneuil Hall. A famous meeting place in Boston, built as the result of a donation by a Boston merchant, Peter Faneuil (1700–1743). It was designed by John Smibert in 1740, in 1806 was enlarged by CHARLES BULFINCH. During the Revolution many important meetings took place there, and in later days all the famous orators of America spoke within its walls. It has been called "the Cradle of Liberty."

Fanny (1819), a poem by FITZ-GREENE HALLECK satirizing a socialite and her father. A member of the "codfish aristocracy," the father makes a temporary splurge, subsides into poverty and obscurity. The poem has been highly praised for its Byronic humor.

Fanny Herself (1917), a novel by EDNA FERBER. It is the story of Fanny Brandeis, a woman who must choose between a successful business career and marriage. The character also appears in other stories by Miss Ferber.

Fanshawe (1828), a novel by NATHANIEL HAWTHORNE. Despite its small sale, the book was fairly well received for a first novel, but Hawthorne made every effort to recall the book and had all the copies destroyed that he could locate, even those of his sisters. After his death, his wife had no knowledge of the work's existence. The plot and many of the characters are derived from the novels of Scott, and much of the detail is adapted from the Gothic novel so popular in England at the end of the eighteenth century.

Set in "Harley College," an obvious sketch of his *alma mater,* Bowdoin, the novel concerns itself with the attempted seduction of Ellen Langdon, the ward of Dr. Melmoth, Harley's president, and her rescue by the hero, Fanshawe, a scholar whose studies have isolated him from the world. The book has little literary value, but is important in showing the development of Hawthorne's technique and treatment of character.

fantascience. See SCIENCE-FICTION.

Far Above Cayuga's Waters. The Cornell Alma Mater song, the words for which were written by C. K. Urquhart. The tune is that of *Annie Lisle* (1860, with words and music by H. S. Thompson). Other schools have used the same tune (sometimes called *Amici*), "making it perhaps the best known of all tunes in academic circles," says Sigmund Spaeth.

Farewell Address (Sept. 17, 1796), by GEORGE WASHINGTON. In this famous and influential document the first President, using *Claypoole's American Daily Advertiser* as his medium, addressed the American people and gave them his counsel on conducting the future course of the American government and on their own attitude toward public affairs. National unity and the best means of preserving it were the theme of his address, and he warned against sectional jealousy and party factions. He stressed the need of religion, morality, and education, urged that public credit be sustained, advised

that impartial good faith be practiced toward all nations, and admonished against permanent entangling alliances with foreign nations. Washington had long meditated on the contents of such an address, and had sought counsel from Alexander Hamilton and James Madison before writing it. He revised carefully all ideas and phrases submitted to him; whether he wrote it all himself or not, the *Address* is a powerful expression of his views.

Farewell to Arms, A (1929), a novel by ERNEST HEMINGWAY. A story of World War I, in which the fortunes of an American lieutenant, Frederic Henry, and an English nurse, Catherine Barkley, become inevitably and remorselessly interwoven with the fortunes of war. When the lieutenant is wounded, the nurse takes care of him at Milan. They live happily together through the summer months, but even though she is pregnant she refuses to marry him, fearing that this will lead to her being sent back to England. The American goes back to the battlefront, and witnesses the retreat of the Italian army from Caporetto—one of the great battle scenes in literature and one that because of its frank description of the attitude of the Italian soldiers led to Hemingway's being barred from Italy and the book's suppression there. The lieutenant deserts, rejoins the nurse, and is with her when her child is born at Lausanne, where both mother and child die. The theme is ancient—a love ending with the death of one of the lovers —but Hemingway treats it with imagination, gives it a setting of powerful vividness, joins it with the tragedy of mankind itself, often reaches high poetry in his style. The novel was dramatized by LAURENCE STALLINGS (1930) and film versions were made in 1932 and 1958.

Farley, Harriet (b. Claremont, N.H., Feb. 18, 1817—d. Nov. 12, 1907), editor, essayist. Miss Farley was a pioneer in the idea that workingmen and workingwomen are entitled to culture as well as better wages and living conditions. Of a well-to-do New England family (her father was a clergyman), she chose to become a mill hand rather than a teacher. The owners of the Lowell, Mass., mill where she worked encouraged the formation of self-improvement clubs. One enterprise was a magazine, *The Lowell Offering, Written and Edited by Female Operatives,* to which Miss Farley began to contribute; in time she became its editor (1842–45). It ceased publication for a while, then in 1847 began to appear again as the *New England Offering* (1847–50). The magazine attained wide fame in the United States and England. Some of Miss Farley's essays and other material from the *Offering* were collected in *Mind Among the Spindles* (1844). Hannah Josephson wrote of her in *The Golden Threads: New England's Mill Girls and Magnates* (1949).

Farm Ballads (1873), sentimental poems by WILL CARLETON. They depict farm life in Michigan with some degree of realism. The collection contains Carleton's most famous poem, OVER THE HILL TO THE POOR HOUSE.

Farmer, Fannie [Merritt] (b. Boston, March

23, 1857—d. Jan. 15, 1915). See BOSTON COOKING-SCHOOL COOK BOOK.

Farmer, Letters from an American. See LETTERS FROM AN AMERICAN FARMER.

Farmer's Almanack. See OLD FARMER'S ALMANAC.

Farrar, John [Chipman] (b. Burlington, Vt., Feb. 25, 1896—   ), publisher. After working for the New York *Sunday World,* Farrar became editor of THE BOOKMAN, later an editor with Doubleday, Doran & Co. In 1929 he formed with Stanley Rinehart the firm of Farrar & Rinehart, a notable publishing venture. He withdrew in 1944 and in 1946 established with Roger W. Straus, Jr., the firm of Farrar, Straus & Co., which became Farrar, Straus, & Cudahy shortly thereafter. Throughout his career as a book publisher Farrar has been known for his willingness to promote young, sometimes experimental authors within the context of commercial publishing. Farrar has published several volumes of his own verse, including *Songs for Parents* (1921), and a collection of plays, *Indoor and Outdoor Plays for Children* (1933). In collaboration with STEPHEN VINCENT BENÉT he wrote a play, *That Awful Mrs. Eaton* (produced in 1925), set in the era of Jackson's squabbles with the ladies of his cabinet. *For the Record* came out in 1943. Farrar is believed to be the Johnny Chipman who appears in two of Benét's novels, *The Beginning of Wisdom* (1921), and *Young People's Pride* (1922), and the Johnny Chapman of CYRIL HUME's *Wife of the Centaur* (1923).

Farrell, James T[homas] (b. Chicago, Feb. 27, 1904—   ), novelist. If a novelist needs many vocations in order to understand the quality of experience, then Farrell is eminently qualified. He has worked in a shoe store, an express office, a gasoline filling station, a cigar store, a concern selling advertising, an undertaking establishment, a newspaper office. His earliest stories, dealing with STUDS LONIGAN, began to appear in 1932; they aroused heated controversy, for Farrell practiced a frankly naturalistic mode of writing that did not hesitate to unveil the crudities of life among the people of his stories, mostly poor city people. Yet Farrell worked with obvious sincerity, eschewing any merely sensational intent. *Time* once said, "The Farrell prose is still a better cure of insomnia than almost anything else between covers." F. O. Matthiessen, while agreeing that Farrell's prose was "without variety or resilience" and that his word-sense was "very dull," praised Farrell for his honesty, his "thoroughgoing and valid" psychology, and his understanding of social change. Many critics would concur. Many of the characters in Farrell's stories are of Irish descent, as in the Studs Lonigan trilogy, the Danny O'Neill tetralogy, etc. Farrell made it his practice to write five pages every day without fail, and published many books; some of the most important are: YOUNG LONIGAN (1932); *The Young Manhood of Studs Lonigan* (1934); *Judgment Day* (1935) (these three comprise the Studs Lonigan group); *A World I Never Made* (1936); *No Star Is Lost* (1938); *Father and Son* (1940); *My Days of Anger* (1943) (these four concern Danny O'Neill); *Gas House McGinty* (1933); *Can All This Grandeur Perish* (1937); *Ellen Rogers* (1941). His *A Note on Literary Criticism* (1936) is one of the most important literary statements of the "proletarian" point of view of the 1930's. Many of his later books are collections of short stories, such as *$1000 a Week and Other Stories* (1942); *An American Dream Girl* (1950); *A Dangerous Woman and Other Short Stories* (1957).

Far West, The. The "Far West" is a relative term, the definition of which has varied greatly. When Cooper wrote of the Far West he meant parts of New York State; Mark Twain thought of Nevada and the Rockies as the Far West. In general, it was the land of the farthest pioneers. Now the Far West means for most people the three states bordering on the Pacific Ocean. It is in that sense of the term that JOSEPH HENRY JACKSON wrote an introduction to *The Far West* (1948) in the "Look at America Series." This region (with the neighboring sections of Nevada, Utah, Idaho, Montana, Colorado, and Wyoming) has attracted or produced many notable writers, from temporary residents—Twain, Harte, Bayard Taylor, R. H. Dana, Joaquin Miller, and Edward Rowland Sill—to permanent settlers and natives like Frank Norris, Mary Austin, Gertrude Atherton, Jack London, Frank Norris, Upton Sinclair, John Steinbeck, and William Saroyan. Its classics range from ASTORIA (1836) and TWO YEARS BEFORE THE MAST (1840) to H. L. Davis' HONEY IN THE HORN (1935).

Fashion, or, Life in New York (1845), a play by Anna Mowatt (1819—1870). This play has a somewhat confused plot, in the course of which a rich couple's daughter wishes to marry a fake count, but is urged by her father to wed a clerk who has discovered that the father has been indulging in forgery. A friend of the father finally saves her from both. The play, with its satiric thrusts at the mother, Mrs. Tiffany, who seeks to break into society, was a great success. It was revived in New York in 1958.

Fast, Howard (b. New York City, Nov. 11, 1914—   ), novelist, short-story writer. Fast has mostly devoted himself to writing historical novels, and some of them offer a new and convincing interpretation of American history; among them are *The Last Frontier* (1941); *The Unvanquished* (1942); *Patrick Henry and the Frigate's Keel* (short stories, 1945). From the beginning of his career, however, Fast showed a tendency to mingle propaganda with the storytelling, and such works as *Citizen Tom Paine* (1943) and *Freedom Road* (1944) avowedly grew out of his association with the Communist Party. Similarly, *The American* (1946) espoused a radical cause in its praise of Governor Peter Altgeld of Illinois. Fast later broke with Communism, though retaining his radical convictions, and described his disillusionment with the party in *The Naked God* (1957). His *Spartacus* (1958) is a sympathetic portrayal of the Roman revolutionary; it became a spectacular moving picture (1960). *Moses, Prince of Egypt* (1958) is a romantic retelling of the

Biblical story. *April Morning*, the story of a little boy in the American Revolution, appeared in 1961.

Father, The, or, American Shandyism (1789), a play by WILLIAM DUNLAP. This play, the second native American comedy, is called by Alexander Cowie "a creditable but not really distinguished work." The plot describes the rescue of two young women from an impostor, Captain Haller's servant Ranter, who pretends to be a British officer and who woos a neglected wife while he really intends to marry her wealthy young sister. The guardian of the two women appears in time to rescue them. The play, revised in 1806, was then called *The Father of an Only Child.*

Faulkner, William (b. New Albany, Miss., Sept. 25, 1897—d. July 6, 1962), short-story writer, novelist. Faulkner came from a family long settled in northern Mississippi. His great-grandfather, William C. Faulkner (who later changed the spelling of his name to *Falkner*) was a plantation owner, a colonel in the Confederate army, a railroad builder, and, significantly, a novelist. His THE WHITE ROSE OF MEMPHIS was published in 1880 and enjoyed a considerable measure of popular success. Whenever the younger Faulkner's third-grade teacher asked the children what they meant to be, the future Nobel Prize winner would answer: "I want to be a writer like my great-granddaddy."

The crowded and exciting life of Colonel William Falkner ended violently in 1889 when a former business partner and political rival shot him down on the streets of his home town, Ripley, Mississippi. This and other episodes from Colonel Falkner's life were to furnish the raw material for such novels as SARTORIS and THE UNVANQUISHED, where Colonel Falkner is obviously the prototype of COLONEL JOHN

SARTORIS. Faulkner's grandfather, John Wesley Thompson Falkner, also provided suggestions for the novels: he would seem to be the model for Bayard Sartoris ("Old Bayard"), who is the young hero of *The Unvanquished,* and who is also seen as the aging banker of *Sartoris, The Town,* and some of Faulkner's short stories.

Murry Falkner, the father of the novelist, married an Oxford girl, Maud Butler, and, though William was born at New Albany, the Falkners moved to Oxford a few years later in 1902. As the family line descended to William Faulkner there was a concomitant recession from Sartoris-like violence to the humdrum life of the small town. Murry Falkner ran a livery stable and then a hardware store before becoming business manager of the University of Mississippi, which is located at Oxford.

William Faulkner was to attend the University of Mississippi for little more than a year. He was not an eager student and cared little for formal education. He had dropped out of high school at the end of the tenth grade and had to be admitted to the university as a special student, a status which he could claim as a World War veteran. Having been turned down in his attempt to enter the American Air Force because of insufficient height, Faulkner enlisted in the Royal Canadian Air Force in 1918. But the war ended before he had received his commission or been able to see service on the western front. Indeed, he was made an honorary second lieutenant only on December 22, after he had been mustered out.

In the years that followed, Faulkner was in and out of Oxford and in and out of one job after another—housepainter, store clerk, dishwasher in a restaurant, even a rum-runner during Prohibition days—as he tried to find himself and establish himself as a writer. But Faulkner did not postpone marriage until he had established himself as a novelist. His boyhood sweetheart, Estelle Oldham, had returned to Oxford with her children, a boy and a girl, after divorcing her first husband. In 1929 Faulkner married her. Two children were born to this marriage, a boy (who died in infancy) and a girl.

Unlike many American writers who took up residence in New York or just outside it, Faulkner continued to live in his home town, close to his chosen material. Beginning in 1936, it is true, he went to Hollywood from time to time to work as a writer on various motion pictures. Later he undertook cultural missions for the State Department to France, Brazil, and Japan. But until 1957, except for occasional sojourns in New York, Oxford remained his home base. In 1957–1958, however, Faulkner was Writer in Residence at the University of Virginia. His daughter, now married, lives in Charlottesville, Virginia, and in recent years the Faulkners divided their time between Oxford and Charlottesville. Faulkner held an honorary post in the University of Virginia Library until the time of his death in 1962.

An important element in Faulkner's education and in his special preparation for a literary career came from his friendship with a fellow townsman, Phil Stone. Stone, who took his Bachelor of Arts degree and, later, a law degree, at Yale, made Faulkner's acquaintance in 1914. He suggested authors for Faulkner to read, tried to put him in touch with the literary movements of the day, and helped finance Faulkner's book of poems, *The Marble Faun,* which appeared in 1924. (When the printer of this volume spelled Faulkner's name with a *u*, Faulkner accepted the change and thus restored the mid-nineteenth century spelling of the family name.)

Faulkner accompanied Stone to New Haven in 1918 and lived there for a few months, working in the Winchester arms factory. Later on, Stone suggested that Faulkner ought to try to get to New York, in the hope that in this great center of the publishing business he might meet

Ralph Thompson

other writers and editors. In 1923 Faulkner did come to New York, and stayed with STARK YOUNG, the drama critic, who had formerly taught at the University of Mississippi. Among other jobs in New York Faulkner clerked in a book store managed by Elizabeth Prall, a friend of Young's; but soon he was back again in Oxford as university postmaster. It was scarcely a job calculated to hold the imagination of a restless young genius, and Faulkner finally retired from it with the now celebrated comment: "I won't be at the beck and call of every son-of-a-bitch who happens to have two cents." Early the next year, 1925, Faulkner went to New Orleans and there became acquainted with SHERWOOD ANDERSON, who had shortly before married Faulkner's friend, Elizabeth Prall.

It was through his association with Anderson that Faulkner produced his first novel. According to Faulkner, when Sherwood Anderson found that Faulkner had written a book, he promised to persuade his publisher to accept it

provided that he himself would not have to read it. So in 1926 Boni and Liveright published *Soldier's Pay.* It received some favorable notices, though as an experimental novel by an unknown author, it did not sell. But it inaugurated Faulkner's long and brilliant career as a writer of fiction.

In the latter part of 1925 Faulkner and a friend shipped on a freighter to Europe for a walking trip through France and Germany. The trip supplied material for later stories. Faulkner returned to New York early in 1926 in time for the publication of *Soldier's Pay,* and returned to the Mississippi gulf coast in order to write his second novel, *Mosquitoes.*

It was only with his third novel, *Sartoris* (1929), that Faulkner turned to the locale which he was to make famous. Sherwood Anderson had said to Faulkner: "You're a country boy; all you know is that little patch up there in Mississippi where you started from. But that's all right too." In *Sartoris* Faulkner began to write about this little patch of northern Mississippi. In doing so, he created YOKNAPATAWPHA COUNTY and its county seat, Jefferson, a composite of several of the Mississippi towns that he knew. (Jefferson is derived primarily from Oxford, but there are also touches of Ripley, New Albany, and Holly Springs.) He peopled his mythical county with the human beings whom he knew and, as we have already remarked, with characters drawn from his own family history.

In *Sartoris* Faulkner also began to develop the themes which run through his greatest work. True, the style of his novel is still mannered in something of the fin-de-siècle fashion of his two early novels, and its world somewhat resembles that of Eliot's THE WASTE LAND. The protagonist is a restless young man, burnt out with his experiences in the war, returning to a life emptied of meaning, and craving violence as a kind of substitute for meaning. But this particular world-weary soldier, "young Bayard," is returning to a stable community. The deracinated young southerner, in his fury and despair, is thus silhouetted against the traditional order of the old South.

In 1929 also appeared Faulkner's first great novel, THE SOUND AND THE FURY, a work still regarded by many critics as his finest. Like *Sartoris,* this novel is laid in Yoknapatawpha County, but it is centered within one household; though some episodes occur as far away as Cambridge, Mass., the focus remains almost obsessively with the family and with the relationships within the house. The Compsons, formerly one of the aristocratic families of the county, have fallen on evil days. The mother is a weak and whining hypochondriac who has poisoned the whole family relationship; the husband has taken to drink and cynicism; the daughter, Candace, has become a wanton and has finally left home. The three sons are Benjy, an idiot; Quentin, an obsessed young intellectual; and Jason, an embittered "practical" man.

Because of the audacity of its technique, the book became a kind of critical sensation. Faulkner said that he began to tell the story entirely "through the eyes of the idiot child since I felt that it would be more effective as told by someone capable only of knowing what happened, but not why. I saw that I had not told the story that time. I tried to tell it again, the same story through the eyes of another brother [Quentin]. That was still not it. I told it for the third time through the eyes of the third brother [Jason]. That was still not it. I tried to gather the pieces together and fill in the gaps by making myself the spokesman."

The Sound and the Fury is a difficult work, though the idiot's section actually causes less trouble to the attentive reader than might be supposed. It is also probably Faulkner's most lyrical book; many people feel that it is his most despairing book. But it has its positive elements: there is the Negro servant, Dilsey, with her powerful religious faith and her competence and her compassion; and there is the total perspective in which the author has placed all the events.

One year later Faulkner published his short novel As I Lay Dying. In some ways it is Faulkner's most brilliant work. Like *The Sound and the Fury*, this novel deals with a southern family, though this time a poor white family living in the hills. The story is at once comic, horrifying, and heroic, but Faulkner maintains a complete control of his tone throughout the novel and only the imperceptive reader will feel that the story is merely comic or merely horrifying or that it represents some uneasy mixture of the two.

In spite of the brilliance of *The Sound and the Fury* and of *As I Lay Dying*, it was not until 1931 that any of Faulkner's books achieved wide sales and financial success. In that year he published Sanctuary. Faulkner once wrote that he decided, after his first two novels had failed to sell, to invent "the most horrific tale I could imagine" and that he wrote it in about three weeks. This he sent in the summer of 1929 to his publisher, who wrote back to him at once that he couldn't publish it: "We'd both be in jail." Faulkner had gotten a job on the night shift at the power plant of the university and by about eleven o'clock, when most people had gone to bed and the requirements for steam went down, he had time to write. So "on these nights, between 12 and 4, I wrote *As I Lay Dying* in six weeks, without changing a word." He sent it off to his publisher and more or less forgot about *Sanctuary* until suddenly, after *As I Lay Dying* had been published, he received the galley proofs. "Then I saw that [*Sanctuary*] was so terrible that there were but two things to do: tear it up or rewrite it. . . . So I tore the galleys down and rewrote the book. It had been already set up once, so I had to pay for the privilege of rewriting it, trying to make out of it something which would not shame *The Sound and the Fury* and *As I Lay Dying* too much. . . ."

Faulkner did do a thorough revision, as the galley proofs, which have been preserved, show.

Indeed, *Sanctuary* has been too much maligned. It is bitter and terrible, but it is not merely titillating, nor is it irresponsible in its vision of evil. Whether the public sensed its deeper virtues or was merely pleasurably shocked by the nature of the plot, Faulkner's name became a drawing card and henceforward he was able to place stories in the better-paying magazines. It is significant that collections of his stories, *These Thirteen* and *Doctor Martino and Other Stories*, appeared in 1931 and 1934. Faulkner is a master of the short story; some of those printed in these collections are the finest of our time.

The succession of great novels continued in a brilliant display of power. One of the finest of them, Light in August, appeared in 1932. It is another story of Yoknapatawpha County, though the older and aristocratic families of the town hardly appear in it, nor, for that matter, do the Negroes. It is the story of white men, yeomen, and poor whites.

Light in August exhibits one of Faulkner's most crowded canvases. It is packed with interesting characters and has a plot far too complicated to be summarized. One can risk, however, one generalization: it is one of Faulkner's many books about the importance of community, and surely a basic theme is the Puritan's alienation from nature and his fear of the feminine principle. Its Puritan characters strive to hold themselves in rigid stance above the relaxed female world. Faulkner finds the spectacle—as with *As I Lay Dying*—sometimes monstrous, sometimes comic, and sometimes heroic.

Absalom, Absalom! is perhaps Faulkner's masterpiece. In it we again meet Quentin Compson, the sensitive brother who commits suicide in *The Sound and the Fury*. Just before he leaves Mississippi to enter Harvard he becomes involved in the story of Thomas Sutpen, who had come out of nowhere seventy-six years before to erect a great plantation house, intending to found a dynasty of plantation owners. The decaying mansion still remains, but Sutpen's daughter, Judith, has long been dead, and his son, Henry, has never been heard of since he killed his sister's fiancé at the very gates of Sutpen's Hundred just after the Civil War. In the novel Quentin and his Canadian roommate at Harvard sift the meager evidence in an attempt to account for the ancient events.

Absalom, Absalom! is in some sense Faulkner's most difficult novel. In reviewing the tiny sheaf of facts as interpreted by different personalities there is so much subjective interpretation, so much conjecture and speculation, that the indolent reader may give up in despair. But *Absalom, Absalom!* is much more than a virtuoso display of eerie Gothicism and much more than a somber commentary upon the Negro problem. It raises profound questions about the meaning of the past and its availability to man, and considers the loyalties that are rooted in the deeper, irrational layers of man which, though they often seem absurd when examined under the glare of pure reason, nevertheless make man human and not a mere calculating monster.

Absalom, Absalom! was followed in 1938 by the most seriously underrated of Faulkner's novels, *The Unvanquished.* This book returns us to the fortunes of the Sartorises, and ends with one of Faulkner's finest triumphs, his account of the coming to manhood of Bayard Sartoris.

In 1940 Faulkner published *The Hamlet,* the story of how the poor white Flem Snopes, who represents sheer rapacity, takes over a little farming community some miles out from Jefferson, and finally, having beaten down all opposition, marries the beautiful Eula Varner. Eula is already with child by another man and Flem is impotent, but he wants the "marriage" as a kind of badge of triumph. *The Hamlet* contains some of Faulkner's richest humor, including the famous tale of the spotted horses. Seventeen years later Faulkner brought Flem Snopes into Jefferson in *The Town* (1957). *The Mansion* (1959) completes this trilogy of novels on the SNOPES FAMILY. (See THE HAMLET for the trilogy.)

GO DOWN, MOSES AND OTHER STORIES (1942) has to do with the fortunes of the McCaslin family. It contains "The Bear," the most celebrated of all Faulkner's short stories, and perhaps his finest, though another story in this volume, "The Fire and the Hearth," is in its own way magnificent too. Lucas Beauchamp, Faulkner's great Negro character, first seen in the latter story, is saved from a lynching in INTRUDER IN THE DUST (1948), a novel that deals with the modern South. It is this South also that is portrayed in REQUIEM FOR A NUN (1951), a sequel to *Sanctuary.*

A FABLE (1954) retells the story of Christ's passion as re-enacted in the life of a corporal in the French Army in the First World War. *A Fable* is probably Faulkner's most ambitious work, but many critics have felt that his deserting Yoknapatawpha County was a mistake and have deplored the tendency of this novel to turn into a kind of allegory.

The critics of Faulkner's early work had considerable difficulty in deciding what to make of it. Perhaps the first serious consideration came in 1939 with George Marion O'Donnell's article entitled "Faulkner's Mythology." O'Donnell quite rightly saw Faulkner as a traditional writer and indeed called him a traditional moralist. In *Sanctuary,* for example, O'Donnell found no meaningless display of horrors, but a kind of allegory in which the heroine stood for "Southern Womanhood Corrupted but Undefiled," whose drunken escort could be called "Corrupted Tradition," and who, in her encounter with POPEYE, falls into "the clutches of amoral Modernism . . . which is itself impotent, but which with the aid of its strong ally Natural Lust ('Red') rapes Southern Womanhood unnaturally and then seduces her so satisfactorily that her corruption is total, and she becomes the tacit ally of Modernism." O'Donnell overemphasized the allegorical import and portioned out the symbolism almost too neatly. But his essay pointed in the right direction in its insistence that Faulkner was an artist dealing responsibly with a traditional society.

Malcolm Cowley's introduction to *The Portable Faulkner* in 1946 has exercised a powerful influence upon subsequent criticism. His essay stressed the continuity and consistency of Faulkner's work and pointed up Faulkner's concern with "the tragic fable of Southern history." Indeed, Cowley set a whole generation of reviewers and critics talking about Faulkner's work as a "myth or legend of the South." In this legend the planters established a society which lived by a single-minded code but which sanctioned slavery, something that put a curse on the land and brought about the Civil War. After the war had been lost, they freed their land from the carpetbaggers but found that they had enemies at home, "the unscrupulous tribe of Snopes." But as "a price of victory . . . the Snopeses had to serve the mechanized civilization of the North, which [is] morally impotent in itself, but which, with the aid of its Southern retainers, ended by corrupting the Southern nation."

Cowley's essay thus cut the grooves in which Faulkner criticism has tended to run ever since. The excesses of much of this later criticism come from oversimplifications of the thesis set forth briefly in Cowley's useful essay. Later writers, knowing little of the rich diversity of the southern social structure, tend to turn all poor southerners into Snopeses and all of Faulkner's gentlefolk into decadent aristocrats. Or, because of the intensity of current interest in the race problem and in civil rights, critics bear down upon certain moral issues almost independently of the fictional context: Faulkner is exposing the cruelty of the South and showing that southern society was rotten to the core (or perhaps he is scolded because he is not severe enough in so exposing it).

When Faulkner is not the victim of moralizing literary sociologists, he is frequently kidnaped by the symbol-mongers, who tirelessly improve upon hints which are indeed to be found in the fiction, hints of allegorical and symbolical meanings—but which the symbol-monger tends to abstract from the imaginative structure and to develop irresponsibly and out of context: every character who dies at thirty-three is a "Christ-figure," horses become symbols of destruction, rain comes to signify death!

Like every other great artist, Faulkner used symbols. His best work is rooted in the experience of southern history, but the significance of his use of the southern heritage must be understood. As a novelist, Faulkner dealt not only with the problems of 20th-century man, but with the universal problems of mankind. In order to write about human beings, he naturally made use of the human beings he knew best in the setting that he knew best. This setting provided him with a very important resource, for the background of a traditional society allowed the novelist to give to modern problems a special focus. Man's loss of community, his alienation and his loneliness, are common themes in 20th-century fiction, but the loneliness of Hightower and the alienation of Joe Christmas and the general break with the community made by half a dozen other characters in *Light in August* take on a special urgency and significance when seen against the background of Yoknapatawpha County, in which a living community exists—whether it be regarded as baleful in its paralyzing inertia or nourishing in its vitality.

Again, because in the South moral problems tend to be concrete, with good and bad polarized and not often shading off into a neutral gray penumbra, the whole problem of values can be put with dramatic force and conviction. Faulkner's concern with the larger issues of our time is plain in *A Fable*; but he has been more successful in dealing with these problems in the novels of Yoknapatawpha County, where they arise from a concrete context and are dramatized within that context.

Faulkner was a man of slight build, with graying hair, and fine dark eyes. He was quiet, even self-effacing. But in spite of his essential shyness and old-fashioned courtliness of manner, all kinds of legends have grown up about him, including stories about his Bohemian behavior. But the quality and the quantity of Faulkner's work make it quite clear he was a dedicated and energetic craftsman who could not often take a holiday from the world of responsible endeavor. The sheer quantity is impressive, and it is not work that was casually dashed off: Faulkner was very much the conscious artist. There is plenty of evidence (in terms of drafts and revisions) to show that he was careful to write and rewrite until his own artistic conscience had been satisfied.

Some of the more amusing Faulkner stories have to do with his Hollywood experiences, including that saga of cross purposes in which the studio that had been paying him for six months couldn't find him in Hollywood and, in response to frantic telegrams, finally discovered that he was sitting quietly at home in Mississippi. But it should be said that Faulkner had taken his movie script work seriously, though he apparently had sealed it off in a separate compartment from the work on his novels and stories. Perhaps his ability to write without embarrassment or condescension for the audience of *The Saturday Evening Post* as well as for the intellectual shows a healthy lack of self-consciousness. It is hard to think of another American writer who could do so.

Faulkner is clearly one of the greatest American novelists. The award of the Nobel Prize in 1949 was merely a special recognition of what most serious critics of fiction had already come to agree upon. Some of Faulkner's later novels were disappointing and those of the last twenty years scarcely came up to those of the great period from 1929 to 1942, but it is a measure of the vitality of Faulkner's creative urge that it never occurred to him to rest upon his laurels. He was still capable of magnificent writing in the latter part of his life: witness portions of *A Fable* and *The Mansion*.

His major works include *Soldier's Pay* (1926);

Mosquitoes (1927); *Sartoris* (1929); *The Sound and the Fury* (1929); *As I Lay Dying* (1930); *Sanctuary* (1931); THESE THIRTEEN (short stories, 1931); *Light in August* (1931); *A Green Bough* (verse, 1933); *Doctor Martino and Other Stories* (1934); *Pylon* (1935); *Absalom, Absalom!* (1936); *The Unvanquished* (1938); THE WILD PALMS (1939); *The Hamlet* (1940); *Go Down, Moses and Other Stories* (1942); *Intruder in the Dust* (1948); KNIGHT'S GAMBIT (stories, 1949); *Collected Stories of William Faulkner* (1950); *Requiem for a Nun* (1951); *A Fable* (1954); *Big Woods* (stories, 1955); *The Town* (1957); *The Mansion* (1959); *The Reivers* (1962).

The amount of criticism devoted to Faulkner is enormous. *William Faulkner: Three Decades of Criticism* (1960), edited by F. J. Hoffman and Olga W. Vickery, contains a useful, up-to-date, selective bibliography. In addition to the essays by O'Donnell and Cowley already mentioned, Robert Penn Warren's essay entitled "William Faulkner" is excellent. On Faulkner's style Conrad Aiken's "William Faulkner: The Novel as Form" and Warren Beck's "William Faulkner's Style" are very helpful. (All five of these essays are reprinted in *Three Decades of Criticism*.) Andrew Lytle, in three long review essays in *The Sewanee Review* (Winter, 1949; Winter, 1955; and Summer, 1957), has written more acutely than anyone else about Faulkner in relation to the structure of southern society and the nature of southern history.

Material on Faulkner and his family background can be found in Robert Coughlan's *The Private World of William Faulkner* (1954), in Robert Cantwell's "The Faulkners" (reprinted in *Three Decades of Criticism*) and in Cantwell's introduction to the Signet edition of *Sartoris* (1953).

Discussion by Faulkner of his own work is to be found in Jean Stein's "William Faulkner: An Interview" (reprinted in *Three Decades of Criticism*), in *Faulkner at Nagano* (1956), edited by Robert A. Jelliffe, and in *Faulkner in the University* (1959), edited by F. L. Gwynn and J. L. Blotner. This latter book is an editing of tape recordings made at the University of Virginia in which Faulkner answers questions by students about his work.

Recent book-length studies of Faulkner are Olga W. Vickery's *The Novels of William Faulkner* (1959) and Hyatt H. Waggoner's *William Faulkner from Jefferson to the World* (1959). Helpful condensed accounts of Faulkner's work are to be found in Michael Millgate's pamphlet in the "Writers and Critics" series (1961), in that by William Van O'Connor in the *University of Minnesota Pamphlets on American Writers* (1959), and in the volume by F. J. Hoffman in Twayne's "United States Authors" series (1961).

CLEANTH BROOKS

Faust, Frederick ["Max Brand"] (b. Seattle, Wash., May 29, 1892—d. about May 12, 1944), poet, story writer, motion-picture script writer.

Under his own name, Faust published two books of poems, *The Village Street and Other Poems* (1922) and *Dionysus in Hades* (1931). Under his favorite pen name and other pseudonyms he published about one hundred books. The "Max Brand" books are old-style westerns, done with astonishing storytelling power. The series begins with *The Untamed* (1918); perhaps the most famous is *Destry Rides Again* (1930). In their original printings, in Pocket Book reprints, and in editions abroad they have sold millions of copies. In addition Faust wrote the motion pictures about Dr. Kildare, and wrote books featuring the same character.

Fawcett, Edgar (b. New York City, May 26, 1847—d. May 2, 1904), novelist, poet, playwright, essayist. Fawcett devoted most of his novels to a mild ridicule of New York society. He wrote fluently but without much skill. Among his best novels are *Purple and Fine Linen* (1873), *An Ambitious Woman* (1884), and *Social Silhouettes* (1885). His plays, especially *Americans Abroad* (1881), also indulged in social satire.

Fay, Theodore [Sedgwick] (b. New York City, Feb. 10, 1807—d. March 24, 1898), writer, editor, diplomat, lawyer. Fay succeeded his father as editor of the New York *Mirror* and as the author of a column called "The Little Genius," some of his contributions to which were later collected in *Dreams and Reveries of a Quiet Man* (2 v., 1832). After 1833 he traveled abroad, supplying the *Mirror* with travel sketches. *Norman Leslie* (1835) was his first and by far his best novel. The plot was apparently based on an actual murder case: a girl disappears and a murder is suspected; Norman is tried and acquitted; later the girl reappears in Paris. Fay, says Alexander Cowie, "wrote with an easy, well-bred, rather gay and cosmopolitan air." His later novels, among them *Hoboken: A Romance of New York* (1843), did not do so well. He spent the latter part of his life in diplomatic posts. He also wrote *The Three Germanys* (2 v., 1889).

Fearing, Kenneth [Flexner] (b. Oak Park, Ill., July 28, 1902—d. June 26, 1961), editor, poet, novelist. A good deal of Fearing's writing has been done anonymously or under pseudonyms. William Abrahams, reviewing his *Stranger at Coney Island* (1949), noted that it dealt again with "the Fearing subject," namely, "an urban, mechanical society in which even the forms of belief have been lost, where the juke-box is like a 'beating human heart.'" Abrahams also felt that in Fearing's earlier poetry—the *Poems* (1935); *Dead Reckoning* (1938); *Collected Poems* (1940); *The Afternoon of a Pawnbroker and Other Poems* (1943)—there was apparent a brilliant "staccato surface" along with the "rowdy satire"; these were replaced in later poems by an "elegiac sentimentality." Fearing's first novel was *The Hospital* (1939), which called forth high praise. One of the most popular of his novels was a murder story, THE BIG CLOCK (1946), which was made into a film in 1948; a similar story is *The Loneliest Girl in*

the World (1951). *The Generous Heart* appeared in 1954, *New and Selected Poems* in 1956, and *The Crozart Story* in 1960.

Feathertop (*The International Magazine*, 1852), a story by NATHANIEL HAWTHORNE. It tells about a scarecrow who comes alive in 17th-century New England. On this story Percy MacKaye based his play, THE SCARECROW (1908), which was later turned into an impressive silent movie, *Puritan Passions*. Mark Van Doren speaks of the influence of Ludwig Tieck and of Jonathan Swift on Hawthorne's conception in this story, but concludes that it is "more like Hawthorne at his most intelligent . . . Mother Rigby is one of Hawthorne's best witch-women." The story was included in later editions of MOSSES FROM AN OLD MANSE.

Feboldson, Febold. A legendary character closely resembling PAUL BUNYAN. Chief relator of the Feboldson activities was Paul R. Beath. Beath, a native of Illinois, came to live in Gothenburg, Neb., at an early age; in 1927 or 1928 he was attracted by some stories about Feboldson that were appearing in the Gothenburg *Times* from the pen of Don Holmes. But Holmes attributed the creation of the character to Wayne T. Carroll, a local lumber dealer who wrote in the Gothenburg *Independent* tales about Feboldson under the pen name "Watt Tell." Later Carroll used Feboldson in advertising for his lumber company—an origin exactly like Bunyan's. But Feboldson could not be a lumberman on the Great Plains. He consequently became a folk hero wrestling with "the adversities of the plains," says Paul R. Beath, "tornadoes, droughts, extreme heat and cold, Indians, politicians, and disease." He owes his continued existence mainly to Beath, who in 1937 prepared for the Federal Writers' Project in Nebraska a pamphlet entitled *Legends of Febold Feboldson* and later (1948) published *Febold Feboldson: Tall Tales from the Great Plains*.

Federalist, The (1787–88). A series of eighty-five papers by ALEXANDER HAMILTON, JAMES MADISON, and JOHN JAY written to bring about ratification of the CONSTITUTION. Seventy-seven were published originally under the pen name "PUBLIUS" in several New York City newspapers. They were collected in book form in 1788, with eight additional essays. In sober, convincing style they discussed dangers from foreign influence and from dissensions among the states, union as a safeguard against domestic faction and as a means of securing economy, the defects of the Confederation, military power, taxation, republican principles, powers conferred by the Constitution, the architecture of the new government, the character of the House of Representatives and the Senate, the Executive Department and the Judiciary, and other problems raised by the Constitution. So authoritative was this treatment by men who had themselves played a principal role in framing the great document that the *Federalist* papers have been taken into account by our courts in deciding Constitutional questions. Carl Van Doren has, however, expressed doubt that the "Publius" series "had any great influence on political opinion in New York, which did not ratify the Constitution until after ten other states had done so." But it is unquestionable that these papers, which take their place with Aristotle's *Politics*, Machiavelli's *Prince*, Hobbes's *Leviathan*, and Marx and Engels' *Communist Manifesto* among the most outstanding studies in the practical application of political theory, have exerted an enormous influence in many lands. They appeared in French in 1792, later were translated into Portuguese, Spanish, German, and Italian, and were often reprinted when Latin-American revolutions occurred. Van Doren speaks of "the remarkable parallel between the arguments in favor of the United States and the arguments brought forward in favor of the United Nations." It has been a consistent best seller, and many editions have appeared. Jefferson's praise, bestowed in 1788, still is widely echoed: "The best commentary on the principles of government which ever was written."

The authorship has remained in some dispute. A copy of the two-volume edition of 1788 was specially bound by Hamilton for presentation to General Washington; in it Madison made extensive autograph annotations indicating the authorship of each paper. Yet in an 1802 edition the names of the individual writers were still a secret. In 1804, however, Hamilton, about to fight the duel with Burr that (as he seemed to have anticipated) cost him his life, set down a memorandum giving the authorships. They were not accurate, a fact that Van Doren perhaps justly attributes to his "troubled state of mind." His chief mistake was to deny Madison credit for twelve essays that he had written and

for a major part in three more; the existence of the manuscripts for some of these makes the mistake clear. Hamilton undoubtedly wrote a good majority of the essays, probably fifty-one, and had a hand in three others. Jay wrote five; the rest were probably Madison's. Paul Leicester Ford edited *The Federalist* (1898), and John S. Bassett compiled *Selections* from it (1921). Charles A. Beard edited the *Enduring Federalist* (1959). In 1960 Gottfried Dietze published *The Federalist: A Classic on Federalism and Free Government*. In 1961 new editions appeared by Jacob E. Cooke, Benjamin F. Wright, and Clinton J. Rossiter.

Federalist party, The. A party which strongly favored the adoption of the Constitution, counted Washington among its adherents, and contributed materially to the formation of a strong American government. It broke apart, but some of its principles were carried on under other party names—the Whigs, the Free Soilers, and the Republicans (after 1856) in particular. JOHN QUINCY ADAMS once said that the Federalist mind was "compounded of the following prejudices":

"1. An utter detestation of the French Revolution and of France, and a corresponding excess of attachment to Great Britain . . .

"2. A strong aversion to republics and republican government . . .

"3. A deep jealousy of the southern and western states, and a strong distrust of the slave representation in the Constitution of the U.S.

"4. A belief that Mr. Jefferson and Mr. Madison were servilely devoted to France, and under French influence."

The Federalists were in power from 1789 to 1801, and they helped to mold and to harden our governmental procedures. Opposed to them were the followers of Jefferson, then called the Republicans. The Federalists wanted efficiency at any cost; the Republicans under Jefferson were always in dread lest the power of the central government become too strong and human liberty be lost. The Federalists wished to rule for the benefit of the people, and did so honestly, capably, and faithfully, but they did not want the people themselves to have much to say about the character of the government. The Jeffersonians professed a mystic faith in the people and their ability to rule themselves. Neither group was completely consistent. Washington was staunch in upholding freedom; Jefferson, when he came to power, greatly strengthened the central government.

The Alien and Sedition Acts of 1798 brought about the overthrow of the Federalists, since these acts were regarded as an attempt to control political thought and action. An internal feud between John Adams and Alexander Hamilton over the war against Napoleon also caused a serious split; and Hamilton's devotion to the mercantile and moneyed classes occasioned a popular reaction. The Federalist party disappeared from the ballot after 1816, when Monroe secured 183 electoral votes as against 34 for Rufus King, the Federalist candidate.

Federal Theater Project. This was the most extraordinary project in the history of American drama. When the depression that began in 1929 was still being fought vigorously, one essential part of the battle was undertaken by the WORKS PROGRESS ADMINISTRATION (WPA), which sought, among other things, to provide a modest livelihood for artists of all types without hampering their creative freedom. On Aug. 27, 1935, Hallie Flanagan, a former student of GEORGE PIERCE BAKER and for ten years director of the Vassar Experimental Theater, became director of the Federal Theater Project. She organized five regional theaters: the Living Newspaper, a dramatic discussion of social and economic problems; the popular price theater, for original plays by new authors; the experimental theater; the Negro theater; and the tryout theater. These theaters were established all over the country, and in four years put on thousands of productions. These included revivals like Marlowe's *Dr. Faustus* and Elmer Rice's *Adding Machine;* new plays like the documentaries *Triple-A Plowed Under* (1936), *Injunction Granted* (1936), and (greatest of them all) Arthur Arent's *One-Third of a Nation* (1938) on the housing problem. Two series of *Federal Theater Plays* were issued in 1938.

By that year strong opposition to the Project made itself felt in Congress, as Miss Flanagan later related in *Arena: The Story of the Federal Theater* (1940). The case against it was tried behind closed doors "with no adequate presentation of the evidence," comments Edmond M. Gagey (*Revolution in American Drama*, 1947). "The highlight in this Congressional farce-tragedy came," he says, "with the question by Representative Joe Starnes as to whether 'this Marlowe—author of *Dr. Faustus* [1588]—was a Communist.'" The Project was closed by Congress on June 30, 1939.

Federal Writers' Project. Established (1934) under Henry G. Alsberg as part of the WORKS PROGRESS ADMINISTRATION (WPA), the Federal Writers' Project was most active from 1935 to 1939 when it produced its massive series of "American Guides" to the various states; the series closed in 1941. The project also produced almanacs, historical leaflets, compilations of folklore, etc. In addition to forty-eight state directors, who enlisted local sponsorship and cooperation, the project at one time included 6,600 workers in state and local branches. It came to an end because of the general opposition to the idea of supporting persons of artistic and literary ability as a special group, yet while it lasted it was a unique and in many ways excellent program of government sponsorship in the arts.

Feeley, Mrs. A beer-drinking female who, with various friends, conducts a series of comic escapades in novels by MARY LASSWELL; the first was called *Suds in Your Eye* (1942).

Feibleman, Peter S[teiman] (b. New York City, Aug. 1, 1930—   ), novelist. Feibleman attended the drama department of the Carnegie Institute of Technology and studied at Columbia University, and worked as an actor in Spanish, French, and Italian films for eight years. His first novel, *A Place Without Twilight* (1958), won a good deal of critical acclaim. Set in New Orleans, it deals with a "twilight" colored girl, not quite black yet not quite white, and with her search for self-realization. *Daughters of Necessity* (1959), also set in the South, treats symbolically the relationships between a man and the five women in his family. Although some critics find Feibleman somewhat melodramatic, his writing is imaginative and powerful. He dramatized his first novel for Broadway production in 1961.

Female American, The, or, The Adventures of Unca Eliza Winkfield (London, 1767; Newburyport, Mass., 1790), an adventure story. The book claims to present the actual experiences, often fantastic, of the person named in the title. It shows the early settlers of Virginia, the marriage of Unca's father to an Indian princess, Unca's education in England, adventures on shipboard and on a desert island, Unca's work as a missionary. The book was the first ambitious work of fiction by an American, published in America.

Female Poets of America, The. See RUFUS W. GRISWOLD.

Female Quixotism: Exhibited in the Romantic Opinions and Extravagant Adventures of Dorcasina Sheldon (1801), a novel by TABITHA TENNEY (1762–1837). Mrs. Tenney, an effective satirist, made it her purpose to check the excesses of novel reading on the part of romantically minded women like her thirty-four-year-old heroine. The novelist herself had obviously done much reading, not merely in the sentimental and Gothic romances of her day, but in Shakespeare, Richardson, Fielding, Smollett, and Sheridan. But she had particularly in mind CHARLOTTE LENNOX's widely read parody, *The Female Quixote* (1752). Mrs. Tenney's Dorcasina has a practical maid, Betty, who does her best to restrain her; and at moments of crisis her father steps in, so that she never suffers very deeply from her indiscretions as she seeks a lover. Twice she rejects offers of marriage as not sufficiently romantic, and at the end she is still unwed and turns to a quiet spinsterhood and good deeds.

Fenollosa, Ernest F[rancisco] (b. Salem, Mass., Feb. 18, 1853—d. Sept. 21, 1908), poet, art critic, Orientalist. After living in Japan and teaching for twelve years at the University of Tokyo, Fenollosa returned to the United States, where he became curator of the Boston Museum of Fine Arts and a widely received lecturer. Eventually he returned to Japan, then went to England; he died in London. His collected poems appeared as *East and West* (1893); his greatest art book was posthumous, *Epochs of Chinese and Japanese Art* (2 v., 1912). Fenollosa was one of the great Western authorities on Oriental art and literature. During a time of frantic Westernization and modernization in Japan, Fenollosa saved many ancient Japanese art treasures from mishandling and destruction.

His private collection formed the nucleus of the Fenollosa-Weld Collection in the Boston Museum.

But perhaps his most permanent contribution lies in the fact that after his death his notes and papers were turned over to the poet Ezra Pound, and Pound made of them the celebrated translations from Li Po and others which are found in his *Cathay* (1915), as well as versions of classical Japanese drama found in *Certain Noble Plays of Japan* (1916).

Ferber, Edna (b. Kalamazoo, Mich., Aug. 15, 1887—d. April 16, 1968), novelist, short-story writer, playwright. An adroit student of character, Miss Ferber began her career by studying an attractive member of a new social type, the woman in the business world, devoting to her several collections of short stories: *Roast Beef Medium* (1913); *Personality Plus* (1914); *Emma McChesney & Co.* (1915). She continued to write excellent stories based on keen observation of life in America, went on to a series of successful novels: *The Girls* (1921); the Pulitzer Prize winner So Big (1924), later made into a movie; Show Boat (1926); Cimarron (1930). These are the best of her books. Her later novels have been less successful. *Show Boat* was made into a highly successful operetta (1927), with lyrics by Oscar Hammerstein III and music by Jerome Kern. In collaboration with George S. Kaufman, Miss Ferber wrote several plays. *Minick* (1921), based on one of the best of her short stories; *The Royal Family* (1927), which exhibited the Barrymores in humorous vein; Dinner at Eight (1932); *Stage Door* (1936). *Saratoga Trunk* (1941), a novel, was presented on Broadway as *Saratoga* (1960). She recounted the story of her life in *A Peculiar Treasure* (1939). Among her later novels are *Giant* (1952) and *Ice Palace* (1958). See Fanny Herself.

Ferguson, Charles W[right] (b. Quanam, Texas, Aug. 23, 1901—   ), minister, editor, author. Charles Ferguson attended Clarendon Junior College and Southern Methodist University in Texas, Union Theological Seminary and the New School for Social Research in New York City. He was a Methodist minister from 1923 to 1925, an associate editor of the Bookman, and a religious editor of Doubleday, Doran & Co., 1926–1930. In 1934 he joined the Reader's Digest as an associate editor and in 1940 was made senior editor. In 1946 he was on loan as cultural relations officer, U.S. Embassy, London. A vivid style characterizes his diverse writings: *The Confusion of Tongues: A Review of Modern Isms* (1927); *Pigskin* (1928), a novel; *Fifty Million Brothers: a Panorama of American Lodges and Clubs* (1937); *A Little Democracy is a Dangerous Thing* (1948); *Naked to Mine Enemies: The Life of Cardinal Wolsey* (1958); *Say It With Words: Language for the Layman* (1959).

Fergusson, Francis (b. Albuquerque, N.M., Feb. 21, 1904—   ), drama critic, teacher. Fergusson began his association with the theater in 1926 when he entered the American Labora-

tory Theatre in New York where he was a student of Richard Boleslavsky and Maria Ouspenskaya of the Moscow Art Theatre, whose teaching greatly influenced Fergusson's later work. He taught and directed the College Theatre at Bennington College from 1934 to 1947, and became a member of the Institute for Advanced Study at Princeton from 1948 to 1949. During this time he wrote *The Idea of a Theater* (1949) which is often considered to be the most important work on the drama written in the United States. In a series of interconnected essays beginning with an analysis of the "tragic rhythm of action" in *Oedipus Rex*, and ending with a discussion of the work of T. S. Eliot, Fergusson develops his idea of drama as the imitation of action, with emphasis on its mythic and ritualistic bases, on its anagogical interpretation as the search of the human soul for its own essence, and on the dramatic progression from purpose to passion to perception. He elaborated this thesis in a full-length study of *The Purgatorio: Dante's Drama of the Mind* (1953). *The Human Image in Dramatic Literature* appeared in 1957.

Fergusson, Harvey (b. Albuquerque, N.M., Jan. 28, 1890—   ), editor, screenwriter, novelist. His earliest novel, *The Blood of the Conquerors* (1921), was the first of a trilogy on the development of the Southwest from the time of the Spanish landowners to the present; the later stories were called *Wolf Song* (1927) and *In Those Days* (1929). *The Life of Riley* appeared in 1937. *Home in the West* (1945) is autobiographical. *Grant of Kingdom* was published in 1950 and *The Conquest of Don Pedro* in 1954. He is Francis Fergusson's brother.

Ferlinghetti, Lawrence (b. Yonkers, New York, 1919—   ), publisher, poet. An owner of San Francisco's City Lights Bookshop and publisher of City Lights Books. Ferlinghetti was an important figure in the "San Francisco Renaissance" even before his own poetry began to appear. He encouraged young writers by giving them a place in his bookshop where they could meet and read their poetry, and by publishing their work in either his "Pocket Poets" series of small paperbacks, or in the mimeographed magazine, *Beatitude*. Among his books: *Pictures of the Gone World* (1955); *A Coney Island of the Mind* (1958); *Her* (1960), a novel; *Starting From San Francisco* (1961). See Beat Writing.

Fern, Fanny. The pen name of Sara Payson Willis.

Fernald, Chester Bailey (b. Boston, March 18, 1869—d. April 10, 1938), story writer, playwright. When he was twenty years old Fernald went to San Francisco and became an authority on that city's Chinatown, about which he wrote his two best-known books: *The Cat and the Cherub and Other Stories* (1896) and *Chinatown Stories* (1899). He traveled extensively, writing stories of the sea and the Spanish-American War, and in 1907 went to live in London, where he devoted himself chiefly to the theater.

Ferril, Thomas Hornsby ["Childe Herald"] (b. Denver, Colo., Feb. 25, 1896—   ), poet, essayist, newspaperman, columnist. Ferril is an authority on the literature of the ROCKY MOUNTAIN REGION and has himself contributed to it. Since 1939, he and his wife, Helen, have published and edited the *Rocky Mountain Herald,* a pioneer weekly. His poems were collected in *High Passage* (1926); *Trial by Time* (1944); and *New and Selected Poems* (1953 and 1960). A number of his prose contributions to the *Herald,* together with several essays contributed to *Harper's Magazine,* were collected in *I Hate Thursday* (1946). *And Perhaps Happiness,* a play in verse, appeared in 1957.

Ferris, Helen [Josephine] (b. Hastings, Neb., Nov. 19, 1890—   ), editor, author of books for children, authority on children's reading. After work with various magazines for young people, Miss Ferris became editor of the JUNIOR LITERARY GUILD in 1929 and thereafter exerted a major and favorable influence on the types of books published for children. She was the author of *Writing Books for Boys and Girls* (1952). She edited numerous anthologies for girls, including *When I Was a Girl* (1930); *Five Girls Who Dared* (1931); *Challenge* (1936); *Love's Enchantment* (1944); *Girls, Girls, Girls* (1957); *Favorite Poems Old and New* (1957); and *Brave and the Fair* (1960). She also wrote *Girls' Clubs: Their Organization and Management* (1918); *This Happened to Me* (1929); *Tommy and His Dog, Hurry* (1944); *"Watch Me," Said the Jeep* (1944). With Eleanor Roosevelt she wrote *The United Nations and Youth* (1950).

Fessenden, Thomas Green ["Dr. Caustic," "Christopher Caustic," "Peter Pepper Box"] (b. Walpole, N.H., April 22, 1771—d. Nov. 11, 1837), lawyer, inventor, agricultural editor, satirist, poet, essayist. Fessenden's unbridled and scurrilous attacks on Jefferson and other anti-Federalist leaders greatly injured his fame. His best satiric piece was written in his Dartmouth College days. In their composition classes the students wrote solemn pieces modeled slavishly on English originals. But on one occasion Fessenden turned in THE COUNTRY LOVERS, OR, MR. JON. JOLTHEAD'S COURTSHIP WITH MISS SALLY SNAPPER. Many years later Lowell echoed both the rhythm and the phrasing of this poem when he came to write THE COURTIN'. Among Fessenden's publications were, in verse, *Terrible Tractoration!!* (1803), *Original Poems* (1804), *Democracy Unveiled* (1805); in prose, *Essay on the Law of Patents* (1810), *The Ladies' Monitor* (1818). In 1822 he founded the *New England Farmer* and edited it until his death. Porter G. Perrin wrote *The Life and Works of T. G. Fessenden* (1925).

Fetzer, Herman ["Jake Falstaff"] (b. Akron, Ohio, June 24, 1899—d. Jan. 17, 1935), newspaperman, columnist. Fetzer, whose pseudonym did not belie him, once said, "From my mother's people I acquired a portly waist, a love of fine-split disputation, an ungodly temper, and a passion for story-telling and story-hearing." He wrote a column called "Pippins and Cheese" for Akron and Cleveland papers, published *The Book of Rabelais* (1928) and a col-

lection of poems, *The Bulls of Spring,* which appeared posthumously (1937). Posthumous, too, was a pleasant autobiographical volume, *Jacoby's Corners* (1940).

Few Figs from Thistles, A (1920), a collection of poems by EDNA ST. VINCENT MILLAY. This was Miss Millay's second collection and differed considerably in tone from the verses collected in RENASCENCE (1917). Where the latter was lyrical and romantic, *A Few Figs* was sophisticated, bored, cynical—but exceedingly brilliant in phrasing and rhythm. The poems had the atmosphere of Greenwich Village and were endlessly quoted by Villagers and their imitators. Among them are some of the poems most likely to preserve Miss Millay's fame, such as the *First Fig,* beginning, "My candle burns at both ends." There are also such fine lyrics as *Recuerdo* and *The Philosopher.*

Ficke, Arthur Davison (b. Davenport, Iowa, Nov. 10, 1883—d. Nov. 30, 1945), poet, critic, novelist. A man of delicate sensibilities, Ficke's interests were divided between art (especially Japanese) and poetry. In the former field he published *Twelve Japanese Painters* (1913) and *Chats on Japanese Prints* (1915). As a poet he was especially notable for his sonnets; his two interests combined in *Sonnets of a Portrait Painter* (1914). He contributed a group of poems to the first issue of *Poetry.* Along with Witter Bynner he wrote the burlesque poems called SPECTRA (1917), parodying some of the excesses of poets in his day.

Fiedler, Leslie A. (b. Newark, N.J., March 8, 1917—   ), literary critic and educator. Primarily a student of American literature and mores, Fiedler has in addition a background in Italian studies. He has been associated with the Department of English of Montana State University for several years, having been the department chairman from 1954 to 1956. He has also been a Fulbright fellow and lecturer at the Universities of Rome and Bologna from 1952 to 1954.

Fiedler's critical views on poetry take into account the relationship of literature to myth and archetype. Fiedler reacts against trends in criticism which view the poem apart from the poet and the poet's art as an "impersonal one"; he believes that the poet's personality and background are essential for a full understanding of any poem. These ideas were fully set forth in "Archetype and Signature," an essay which appeared in the *Sewanee Review* in 1952.

In his controversial but often brilliant criticism, he makes use of Freudian and Jungian concepts with frequent reference to social and political history. *An End to Innocence* (1955) included essays on Whittaker Chambers, Alger Hiss, and Senator McCarthy, in addition to current literary studies. Perhaps the best known essay in this collection is "Come Back to the Raft Again, Huck Honey!" which pointed out the homosexual themes of major American novels, especially those of Cooper, Melville, and Twain. Fiedler sees in a large portion of American literature the theme of escape from a female-dominated society. He sees it manifested in close male relationships in the wilderness and on the seas, such as those between Natty Bumppo and Chingachgook in *The Leather-Stocking Series*, Ishmael and Queequeg in *Moby Dick*, and Huck and Jim in *Huckleberry Finn*.

Fiedler expanded his Freudian and mystic interpretations in *Love and Death in the American Novel* (1959), and added essays on similar subjects in *No! In Thunder* (1960). An excellent editor, he compiled *Art of the Essay* (1959), a college text of interest to the general reader, and *Selected Poems of Walt Whitman* (with Richard Wilbur, a paperback, 1959).

Field, Eugene (b. St. Louis, Mo., Sept. 2, 1850—d. Nov. 4, 1895), newspaperman, columnist, poet, humorist, translator. Possibly one ought to add "prankster" to the list of Field's vocations, since there was nothing he enjoyed

more than playing practical jokes upon his friends, acquaintances, and perfect strangers; he seems to have had no real enemies. According to legend, his pranks led to his expulsion from the three colleges he attended. He worked on newspapers in St. Joseph, St. Louis, Kansas City, and Denver, but finally settled in Chicago in 1883 and remained there for the rest of his life on the *Daily News*. He was one of the earliest of the columnists who became a feature of American newspaperdom. Carl Van Doren says of his column "Sharps and Flats": "He poked

fun at current folly, he turned out yards of brisk, bright verses." From his newspaper writing he gathered material for his numerous books. Among them were: THE TRIBUNE PRIMER (1882); *A Little Book of Western Verse* (1889); *Echoes from the Sabine Farm* (with his brother, Roswell Field, 1891); *With Trumpet and Drum* (1892); LOVE AFFAIRS OF A BIBLIOMANIAC (1896); *Collected Works* (10 v., 1896). His favorite themes were book-collecting and Horace (he translated the latter freely), Chicago's cultural taste or lack of it, local feuds, visiting notables. He wrote some of his best poems about and for children. Gay Wilson Allen remarks that "the sentimentality of Field is so out-of-fashion today with educated Americans that his smooth, facile, and melodious versification is generally unappreciated." An excellent analysis is R. A. Day's *The Birth and Death of a Satirist* (*American Literature*, January, 1951). See LITTLE BOY BLUE.

Field, Joseph M. (b. Ireland, 1810—d. Jan. 28, 1856), actor, newspaperman, humorist. Field went to St. Louis in its early days and wrote newspaper and magazine sketches that were collected in *Three Years in Texas* (1836), *The Drama in Pokerville and Other Stories* (1847), and other volumes. He also wrote plays. In the St. Louis *Reveille* (Oct. 21, 1844; June 14, 21, 1847) he told MIKE FINK stories; Walter Blair calls these "the best early compilation of Mike Fink tales." Field's stories were based, reports Blair, "in part upon oral narratives of Charles Keemle, a former trapper; in part, according to Field, upon many tales heard in many places." Mark Twain, in such pieces as *Dandy Frightening the Squatter*, may have been specifically indebted to Field's stories and quips.

Field, Rachel [Lyman] (b. New York City, Sept. 19, 1894—d. March 15, 1942), poet, novelist. Miss Field wrote several novels with New England settings which attained wide popularity, among them being *Time Out of Mind* (1935); *All This, and Heaven Too* (1938); *And Now Tomorrow* (1942). Equally well known are some of her books for children: *Polly Patchwork* (1928); *Hitty, Her First Hundred Years* (1929); *Hepatica Hawks* (1932). *Points East* (1930) shows her skill and melody as a poet.

Field and Stream. A monthly magazine devoted to hunting and fishing. It was founded in 1896 as *Western Field and Stream*, adopted its present name in January, 1898. In 1946, to celebrate its semicentenary, *The Field and Stream Reader*, containing stories and articles taken mainly from issues of the preceding quarter-century, was published; it was followed in 1955 by the *Field and Stream Treasury*.

Fields, James T[homas] (b. Portsmouth, N.H., Dec. 31, 1817—d. Aug. 24, 1881), publisher, editor, poet, memoirist. Fields became the leading publisher of the United States, the confidant and adviser of many authors. He headed the firm of Ticknor & Fields, which was absorbed by Houghton, Mifflin & Co. in 1878 and was editor of the *Atlantic Monthly* 1861–1871. The OLD CORNER BOOKSTORE in Boston, where

Fields sat behind his green curtain, was an institution, a gathering place for famous authors. He was an active poet, and some of his verse survives in popular memory—the amusing poem called *The Owl-Critic*, for example, and the lines in the BALLAD OF THE TEMPEST, " 'We are lost!' the captain shouted, as he staggered down the stairs." He devoted two volumes to memories of Hawthorne and Dickens, but his best book is YESTERDAYS WITH AUTHORS (1872), a miscellany of recollections, conversation, letters, portraits. His wife, **Annie Adams Fields** (1834–1915), kept a journal and on it based her book *James T. Fields: Biographical Notes and Personal Sketches* (1881). She wrote several other books —collections of verse, essays and criticisms, and biographies of authors she knew well, including Mrs. Stowe, Hawthorne, C. D. Warner, and Sarah Orne Jewett. J. C. Austin has written *Fields of the Atlantic Monthly* (1954).

Fields, Lewis ["Lew"] Maurice (b. New York City, Jan. 1, 1867—d. July 20, 1941), American comedian. See JOSEPH M. WEBER.

Fierro, Martin. See MARTIN FIERRO.

Fifth Column and First Forty-Nine Stories, The (1938), a play and short stories by ERNEST HEMINGWAY. *The Fifth Column* was produced, in an adaptation by Benjamin Glazer, in 1940. It describes the interaction of Fascist and Communist intrigue in Madrid during the Spanish Civil War. In his preface Hemingway wrote: "It will take many plays and novels to present the nobility and dignity of the cause of the Spanish people." The title was apparently taken from a radio address by a Franco general, Emilio Mola, after the fall of Toledo: "We have four columns advancing upon Madrid. The fifth column [sympathizers within the city] will rise at the proper time."

Fifty-Four Forty or Fight! (1909), a novel by EMERSON HOUGH. It deals with the controversy with Great Britain over the boundary line between Oregon and Canada; the phrase was first used by William Allen in 1844, and it was adopted as a slogan in the Presidential candidacy of JAMES K. POLK that year. On his election, however, Polk effected a compromise by which the disputed territory was split in two at the 49th parallel, and war was avoided.

Fifty Grand (in MEN WITHOUT WOMEN, 1928), a short story by ERNEST HEMINGWAY. It is about a prize fighter who is bribed to allow himself to be defeated.

Fillmore, Millard (b. Locke, N.Y., Jan. 7, 1800—d. March 8, 1874), 13th President of the United States. Fillmore was first a lawyer in Buffalo, was elected to the state legislature, served several terms in Congress, and was elected Vice-President on the ticket with Zachary Taylor in 1848. In 1850 Taylor died, and Fillmore was sworn in as President on July 9. He made Daniel Webster his secretary of state, and used his influence as President to secure the passage of the COMPROMISE OF 1850; he also signed the Fugitive Slave Law. During Fillmore's administration Perry made his landing in Japan. In 1852 Fillmore was unable to secure the Whig Presidential nomination; in 1856 he was nominated by the Know-Nothings but was defeated by Buchanan. During his later years he was chancellor of the University of Buffalo. F. H. Severance collected his *Papers* (1907) for the Buffalo Historical Society; W. E. Griffis wrote *Millard Fillmore, Constructive Statesman* (1935).

Filson, John (b. East Fallowfield, Pa., 1747?— d. Oct [?], 1788), explorer, historian. Filson wrote the first history of Kentucky, *The Discovery, Settlement and Present State of Kentucke* (1784). The book is notable for an appendix giving the first account of Daniel Boone (based apparently on conversations with the famous scout) and for a map of Kentucky that was surprisingly accurate. Filson continued his explorations, and was killed by an Indian.

Financier, The (1912), a novel by THEODORE DREISER. This story was the beginning of a trilogy, and was succeeded by THE TITAN (1914) and *The Stoic* (1947). All three deal in epic detail with a typical industrial and financial magnate of the early 20th century. Dreiser frankly admitted that he based his central character, Frank Algernon Cowperwood, on the powerful figure of Charles T. Yerkes (1837–1905), who had gained control of the Chicago street-railway system. The book begins in Philadelphia (where Yerkes was born) and goes on to Chicago. It gives in immense and ruthlessly realistic detail portraits of Cowperwood, his associates and enemies (sometimes the same people), his numerous women. Alexander Cowie feels that, in Cowperwood, Dreiser "was for a time seduced into something like admiration for glamorous big-time operators."

Finch, Francis Miles (b. Ithaca, N.Y., June 9, 1827—d. July 31, 1907), jurist, poet, teacher. Finch was an associate judge of the New York Court of Appeals, then taught law at Cornell. He wrote pleasing, melodious verse; two of his patriotic poems, *Nathan Hale* (1853) and THE BLUE AND THE GRAY (1867), have been endlessly recited. His poems were collected in *The Blue and the Gray and Other Poems* (1909).

Finck, Henry Theophilus (b. Bethel, Me., Sept. 22, 1854—d. Oct. 1, 1926), music critic, gourmet. The greater part of Finck's career was spent as a music critic for the New York *Evening Post* and *The Nation*. He was particularly noted for his warm advocacy of Wagner's music, as in *Wagner and His Works* (2 v., 1893); he also wrote on Chopin, Grieg, Richard Strauss, and others. In addition Finck was an authority on food and cooking, and often reviewed books on these subjects for the *Post*.

Fineman, Irving (b. New York City, April 9, 1893—   ), engineer, teacher, author. Fineman turned to writing as a profession when his first novel, *This Pure Young Man* (1930), won a Longmans, Green prize. *Hear, Ye Sons* (1933), *Doctor Addams* (1938), and the autobiographical novel *Jacob* (1941) won wide acclaim. *Ruth* (1949) gives a modernistic interpretation to a Biblical theme. His attachment to his Hebraic heritage helps him to interpret Biblical themes with contemporary freshness. He also wrote the script for the film *Wheat* (1932). Turning to the theater, he wrote *Akiba, A Child's Play* (1950) and *Fig Tree Madonna* (1951). *Helen Herself* (1957) is a recent novel.

Finger, Charles J[oseph] (b. England, Dec. 25, 1869—d. Jan. 7, 1941), sailor, musician, railroad man, author, editor. After many adventures in Latin America Finger came to the United States and was naturalized in 1896. His *Tales from Silver Lands* (1924) won a Newbery Medal; his romance, *Courageous Companions* (1929) won a Longmans, Green juvenile fiction prize. Among his other books are *Ozark Fantasia* (1927); the autobiographical *Seven Horizons* (1930); *Footloose in the West* (1932); *Golden Tales from Far Away* (1940). For a time he helped edit *Reedy's Mirror*, which he took over and renamed ALL'S WELL, or THE MIRROR REPOLISHED (1920–1935). See THE MIRROR [2].

Fink, Mike (b. Fort Pitt, Pa., 1770?–d. 1823?), folk hero. Born on the frontier, Fink (Scotch-Irish, despite his name) was at first an Indian scout and soon became renowned for his accuracy as a marksman. But as the Indian tribes disappeared across the Mississippi, Fink and the other scouts became boatmen. He soon became known as "King of the Keelboatmen" and "The Snapping Turtle of the Ohio." In character he was, says Bernard De Voto, "Casanova, together with Paul Bunyan, merged into Thor." The battle waged by the boatmen against the river made them wild and reckless, and some of the stories told of Fink show that he had a strong sadistic strain. He was of the humorists who believe that no joke's a joke unless it's carried too far. The first recorded account of Fink was made by Morgan Neville in the *Western Souvenir* (1829), where he wrote of him as "The Last of the Boatmen." One of the *Crockett Almanacs* tells of an encounter in marksmanship between Crockett and the boatmen, in which the former is worsted. JOSEPH M. FIELD gave one of the ten or eleven versions of Fink's death in *The Drama in Pokerville* (1847). Use of the Fink legend was also made in T. B. THORPE'S *The Mysteries of the Backwoods* (1846), Emerson Bennett's *Mike Fink* (1848), JOHN G. NEIHARDT's *The River and I* (1910), and elsewhere. The legend is historically and impressively surveyed in Walter Blair and Franklin J. Meine's *Mike Fink, King of Mississippi Keelboatmen* (1933). Julian Lee Rayford wrote a robust novel, *Child of the Snapping Turtle* (1951).

Finkelhoffe, Fred L. Co-author of BROTHER RAT.

Finley, John. See HOOSIER.

Finley, Martha Farquharson (b. Chillicothe, Ohio, April 26, 1828—d. Jan. 30, 1909), teacher, novelist. Miss Finley wrote under the name Martha Farquharson. Although some of her books were meant for adults, her fame was gained as a writer of Sunday-school stories for girls, notably her "ELSIE DINSMORE" tales (1868–1905) which ran to twenty-eight volumes,

each in a blue or red cover with a pansy imprinted on it. She also wrote stories about "Mildred" (7 v., 1878–94). For a long time enormously popular, the "Elsie" books finally began to go out of print in the middle 1940's, "to the pleasure of librarians," said one commentator, "who for one reason or another always intensely disliked them." Janet E. Brown wrote *The Saga of Elsie Dinsmore: A Study in 19th-Century Sensibility* (1945).

Finn, Huckleberry. See HUCKLEBERRY FINN.

Fire-Bringer, The (1904), a play in verse by WILLIAM VAUGHN MOODY. This is the first part of a trilogy; the second in plot-order is THE MASQUE OF JUDGEMENT (1900); the third is *The Death of Eve* (1912), of which only Act I was completed.

Firestone, Clark Barnaby (b. Lisbon, Ohio, Sept. 10, 1869—d. June 3, 1957), newspaperman, poet, writer on travel and folklore, banker. Among Firestone's well-documented and entertaining volumes are *The Coasts of Illusion* (1924); *Sycamore Shores* (1936); *Bubbling Water* (1938); *Flowing South* (1941).

First Settlers of Virginia, The (1802), a novel by JOHN DAVIS. Davis, an Englishman, set this first idealistic treatment of the American Indian in Virginia and followed closely the facts and legends that had gathered around Capt. JOHN SMITH. Alexander Cowie praises the freshness of Davis' descriptions and the sympathy with which he treated the Indians.

Fischer, Louis (b. Philadelphia, Feb. 29, 1896—   ), writer. Fischer's roving assignments have carried him all over the world. His analyses of Russian, Indian, Spanish, and other political scenes and figures show wide knowledge and keen insight. Among his books: *Oil Imperialism* (1926); *The Soviets in World Affairs* (1931); *Men and Politics, an Autobiography* (1941); *Gandhi and Stalin* (1947); *The Life and Death of Stalin* (1952); *Russia Revisited* (1957). He edited *Mahatma Gandhi*, which was published in 1950. He is a Fellow of the International Institute of Arts and Letters.

Fish, Williston (b. Berlin Heights, Ohio, Jan. 15, 1858—d. Dec. 19, 1939), lawyer, poet, free-lance writer. Fish contributed many articles and poems to *Puck*, *Life*, and *Harper's Weekly*, but only one is still read. On Sept. 3, 1898, *Harper's Weekly* printed a document purporting to be the last will and testament of one Charles Lounsbury, but really composed by Fish. Among its bequests, for example, was to children, "only for the life of their childhood, all and every, the dandelions of the fields and the daisies thereof, with the right to play among them freely." The will was published as a small book in 1908.

Fisher, Dorothy Canfield [formerly **Dorothy Canfield**] (b. Lawrence, Kans., Feb. 17, 1879—d. Nov. 9, 1958), novelist, short-story writer, critic, translator. The recipient of honorary degrees and a member of the National Institute of Arts and Letters, Mrs. Fisher was a kindly but discriminating interpreter of American life, especially in New England, from the

beginning of her career. Among her most widely
read novels are THE SQUIRREL CAGE (1912);
The Bent Twig (1915); THE BRIMMING CUP
(1921); *Rough Hewn* (1922); *Her Son's Wife*
(1926); *The Deepening Stream* (1930). In
Four-Square (1949) seventeen of her short
stories were collected. The best of her nonfiction work is *Vermont Tradition; The Biography
of an Outlook on Life* (1953). Elizabeth Yates
has written her biography, *Pebble in a Pool: The
Widening Circles of Dorothy Canfield* (1958).
See UNDERSTOOD BETSY.

Fisher, [Alvero] Vardis (b. Annis, Idaho,
March 31, 1895—d. July 9, 1968), novelist.
Fisher, born in a Mormon family, taught English
at the University of Utah and at New York
University. He won his first fame with a tetralogy
of novels about an autobiographical hero, Vridar
Hunter: IN TRAGIC LIFE (1932); *Passions Spin
the Plot* (1934); *We Are Betrayed* (1935); *No
Villain Need Be* (1936). Later he wrote essays,
psychological and historical novels, and other
books. During the WPA era he directed the
federal project that prepared the *Idaho State
Guide* (1937). A novel about the early Mormons, *Children of God* (1939), won the Harper
Prize Novel award. With *Darkness and the Deep*
(1943) he began a series of stories portraying
the development of primitive man, which he
called *Testament of Man. Peace Like a River*
(1958), *My Holy Satan* (1959), and *Orphans
In Gethsemane* (1960) are part of this series.
Love and Death came out in 1960, and *Suicide
or Murder: The Strange Death of Meriwether
Lewis* was published in 1961.

Fiske, John (b. Hartford, Conn., March 30,
1842—d. July 4, 1901), philosopher, historian.
Fiske's real name was Edmund Fisk Green; in
1855 he legally adopted the name of his great-
grandfather, John Fisk, which five years later
became Fiske. As a child Fiske was noted for
his precocity, as a man for his great weight
(more than 300 pounds—he was called "the
largest author in America"). He began his career as a philosopher. His ardent espousal of the
doctrines of evolution and of Herbert Spencer's
ideas caused him to become suspect in many
academic and ecclesiastical quarters. In middle
life he turned to writing the history of America,
and won a great audience; he wrote in a pleasing, lucid style and with warm patriotism. At the
beginning of his days at Harvard the President
and Fellows of that university admonished him
for reading Comte during divine service and deprived him of the tutorship in history to which
his brilliant gifts seemed to entitle him. Seven
years later he was appointed a lecturer at
Harvard on positivist philosophy, but he was
never given a professorship; the highest rank
he attained was that of assistant librarian. Outside the university he was a popular lecturer on
evolution and the "free enterprise" ideas of
Spencer. Among Fiske's books are *The Outline
of Cosmic Philosophy* (1874); *Darwinism and
Other Essays* (1879); *The Destiny of Man
Viewed in the Light of His Origin* (1884);
The Beginnings of New England (1889); *The*

American Revolution (1891); *A Century of Science and Other Essays* (1899); *How the United
States Became a Nation* (1904). T. S. Perry
wrote *John Fiske* (1906), J. S. Clark compiled
The Life and Letters of John Fiske (2 v., 1917),

Ethel F. Fiske, *The Letters of John Fiske*
(1940).

Fitch, [William] Clyde (b. Elmira, N.Y., May
2, 1865—d. Sept. 4, 1909), playwright. Fitch
began his career by writing BEAU BRUMMELL
(1890) for the actor Richard Mansfield. Further
dramatic triumphs were *Nathan Hale* (1899);
The Cowboy and the Lady (1899); BARBARA
FRIETCHIE (1899), which was later made into
a musical comedy, *My Maryland* (1927), with
music by Sigmund Romberg; and CAPTAIN
JINKS OF THE HORSE MARINES (1901). Although Fitch's earlier plays are primarily romantic melodramas of the type that dominated
the stage during the period, they are redeemed
by his wit and by the appeal of his characters.
His later plays constitute his more important
contribution to the American stage; his mastery
of social comedy and satire is shown in such
plays as *The Climbers* (1901); THE GIRL WITH
THE GREEN EYES (1902); *The Woman in the
Case* (1905); *The Truth* (1906); *The Straight
Road* (1906); *The City* (1909).

Fitch, George (b. Galva, Ill., June 5, 1877—
d. Aug. 9, 1915), newspaperman, humorist.
Although Fitch wrote other stories, those that
centered around "old Siwash College" (believed
to be Knox College in Illinois) won him his
widest fame. They were hilarious tales of a carefree generation, and were collected in *The Big*

Strike at Siwash (1909) and *At Good Old Siwash* (1911).

Fitts, Dudley (b. Boston, Mass., April 28, 1903—d. July 10, 1968), editor, translator, teacher. Fitts established a reputation as a leading translator of the poetry and drama of the ancient Greeks and the contemporary poetry of Latin America. His own verse appeared in *Two Poems* (1932) and *Poems 1929–36* (1937). In collaboration with Robert Fitzgerald he translated Sophocles' *Oedipus Rex* (1949) and the *Alcestis* of Euripides (1936); he edited *Greek Plays in Modern Translation* (1948) and translated four plays of Aristophanes. In his *Anthology of Contemporary Latin-American Poetry* (1942), translations (by various hands) appear on pages facing the Spanish or Portuguese originals. The volume gives an impressive panorama of the many noteworthy poets of Latin America and includes important biographical and critical data supplied by Fitts. He was co-editor of *The Poem Itself*, published in 1960.

Fitzgerald, F[rancis] Scott [Key] (b. St. Paul, Minn., Sept. 24, 1896—d. Dec. 21, 1940), novelist, short-story writer, playwright. Fitzgerald was the superb laureate of "the lost generation" that World War I created; but despite

the great renown he won he could not quite save himself. He himself described his age as "a new generation grown up to find all Gods dead, all wars fought, all faiths in man shaken." It was an age so deliberately and determinedly cynical that it became naïve. It showed its resentment of the chief "moral reform" of the 1920's, Prohibition, by making vile gin in bathtubs, haunting dirty but glamorous speakeasies, and sneering at chastity. It had no interest in politics or government, regarded life as a personal matter, and insisted on being amused at all times. Fitzgerald called it the "Jazz Age"; it ran from the May Day riots of 1919 to the "big bust" of 1929. Fitzgerald's greatness lay in one singular fact:

despite all appearances to the contrary he knew that something was wrong, and this feeling is implicit everywhere in his glittering stories, especially those toward the end.

Fitzgerald, of a prosperous family which included among its ancestors the author of *The Star-Spangled Banner*, came to Princeton to study. EDMUND WILSON, in a memorable poem of *Dedication* for the posthumous volume containing *The Crack-Up* (1945) and other pieces by and about Fitzgerald, pictures him as he saw him for the first time—"the pale skin, hard green eyes, and yellow hair." He was in the army but saw no action in the war, and in fact spent most of his time writing his first novel, THIS SIDE OF PARADISE (1920). It made an instantaneous success, critical and financial. Thereafter he lived like a character in one of his own novels—commuting between the plush hotels and better speakeasies of the United States and the fashionable resorts of Europe, mingling with the wealthy, the expatriates, the sophisticates of many lands. He was familiar with the Riviera and Paris, New York, Long Island, and Washington, ultimately with Hollywood at its most pretentious. He was a prodigal son well supplied with money (which he worked desperately to earn); he was brilliant, rowdy, ultimately barren. He continued to write, and some of his books showed genius. A collection of short stories, *Flappers and Philosophers* (1920), was issued to take prompt advantage of the success his first book had won. Then came THE BEAUTIFUL AND DAMNED (1921); *Tales of the Jazz Age* (1922); *The Vegetable* (a play, 1923); THE GREAT GATSBY (1925); *All the Sad Young Men* (short stories, 1926); TENDER IS THE NIGHT (1934; rev. ed., 1951); *Taps at Reveille* (short stories, 1935); *The Last Tycoon* (incomplete, 1941). Of all these *The Great Gatsby*, the story of a bootlegger, retains the greatest popularity, although some critics believe that *The Last Tycoon*, a novel about Hollywood, is really his best.

At the age of thirty-nine Fitzgerald suddenly reached a crisis, physical and spiritual, that he himself described in his famous autobiographical essay, *The Crack-Up*, which appeared originally in three installments in *Esquire* magazine (February, March, April, 1936). Everything became bitter in his mouth, life lost its savor (he quoted St. Matthew); and he tried to think it out. He reached the conclusion that he must find out "why I had become identified *with the objects of my horror or compassion.*" His beautiful wife Zelda's mental breakdown contributed to the sense of deep personal tragedy. He made up his mind that he must be a writer only—no longer "an entire man in the Goethe-Byron-Shaw tradition." He had always realized that he was "a moralist at heart, and really want[ed] to preach at people in some acceptable form, rather than entertain them."

A collection of Fitzgerald's manuscripts may be found at Princeton University, which when it approached its bicentenary celebration published an excellent collection of *Lives of 18 from Princeton* (edited by Willard Thorp, 1946), including a sketch of Fitzgerald by Arthur Mizener. Mizener feels that Fitzgerald "had a kind of instinct for the tragic view of life." Mizener later enlarged his sketch into a full-length biography, *The Far Side of Paradise* (1951); meanwhile Budd Schulberg had written a novelized biography, THE DISENCHANTED (1950), based on personal acquaintance with Fitzgerald. Alfred Kazin edited *F. Scott Fitzgerald: The Man and His Work* (1951), a collection of articles about him over a thirty-year period. Sheilah Graham's *Beloved Infidel* (1958) is a frank account by Fitzgerald's Hollywood companion of his last years. In 1958 Arthur Mizener edited *Afternoon of an Author: A Selection of Uncollected Stories and Essays* by Fitzgerald.

Fitzgerald, Robert S[tuart] (b. Geneva, N.Y., Oct. 12, 1910——   ), poet, critic, translator. Fitzgerald studied at Trinity College, Cambridge, from 1931 to 1932 and received his A.B. degree in 1933 from Harvard. He became a reporter for the New York *Herald Tribune*, then a staff writer for *Time*. In 1946 he turned to teaching, and was on the faculties of Sarah Lawrence College and Princeton, Indiana, Notre Dame, and Washington Universities. Among his books: *A Wreath for the Sea* (1943); *In the Rose of Time* (1956). He translated *The Oedipus Cycle of Sophocles* in collaboration with Dudley Fitts (1939; reprinted in 1941 and 1949); also *Homer: The Odyssey* (1961).

Five-Foot Shelf. See CHARLES W. ELIOT.

Five Little Peppers and How They Grew (1881), a story for children by HARRIET MULFORD STONE LOTHROP, who wrote under the name of Margaret Sidney. The story appeared originally in *Wide Awake* (1880), a magazine for young readers. In book form the story was a great success; it is said that in 50 years more than 2 million copies were sold. The story was one of a struggle against poverty, and Mrs. Lothrop accompanied the plot with numerous moral lessons. There were several sequels: *The Five Little Peppers Midway; The Five Little Peppers Grown Up;* and others. However, the original story remained the most popular. Frank Ray Felder wrote a successful dramatization, *The Five Little Peppers* (1952).

Flaccus. Pen name of THOMAS WARD.

Flagg, James Montgomery (b. Pelham Manor, N.Y., June 18, 1877—d. May 27, 1960), illustrator, author. Flagg is best remembered for a World War I recruiting poster of Uncle Sam pointing a finger, with the caption, "Uncle Sam Wants You!" Among his books: *Yankee Girls Abroad* (1900); *Tomfoolery* (1904); *All in the Same Boat* (1908); *City People* (1909). *Roses and Buckshot* (1946) is an autobiography.

Flammonde (1915), a poem by EDWIN ARLINGTON ROBINSON. One of Robinson's poems of "Tilbury Town," this is a penetrating study of a character who is "the Prince of Castaways," a man who lives by borrowing. But Flammonde is remembered by the poet because he somehow manages to understand the people of the town better than others and to help them through his deep sympathy.

Flandrau, Charles Macomb (b. St. Paul, Minn., Dec. 9, 1871—d. March 28, 1938), newspaperman, writer. Flandrau's literary gift was displayed in three different directions. His memories of college days were embodied in a series of satiric stories: *Harvard Episodes* (1897); *The Diary of a Freshman* (1901); and *Sophomores Abroad* (not collected in book form till 1935). A visit south of the border resulted in a travel book, *Viva Mexico* (1908). His pleasant essays were collected in *Prejudices* (1911) and *Loquacities* (1935).

Flanner, Janet (b. Indianapolis, Ind., March 13, 1892——   ), writer. The Paris correspondent of the *New Yorker* magazine, under the name Genêt. She was one of the few women awarded the French Legion of Honor. She has written accounts of art and profiles for the *New Yorker*. She wrote *The Cubical City* (1926), a novel, and *American in Paris* (1940), and translated Colette's *Claudine À L'École* (1930) and *Chéri* and *Ma Vie Avec Maeterlinck* by Georgette Le Blanc.

Flavin, Martin (b. San Francisco, Nov. 2, 1883—d. Dec. 27, 1967), novelist and playwright. Flavin pursued a business career for two decades before he turned to writing, first to playwriting and then to fiction. Arthur Hobson Quinn praises Flavin's drama *Children of the Moon* (1923), as well as *The Criminal* (1929) and *Amaco* (1933), calling the last "a thoughtful, sincere dramatization of the rise of the machine and its effect upon the workers." Flavin's novel *Journey in the Dark* (1943) won a Pulitzer Prize as well as the Harper Novel award. Later came *The Enchanted* (1947), the story of a group of children who seek to escape from the adult world. In a travel book, *Black and White: From the Cafe to the Congo* (1950), Flavin revealed himself as an honest, searching investigator. *Cameron Hill* was published in 1957.

Fletcher, Jefferson B[utler] (b. Chicago, Nov. 13, 1865—d. Aug. 17, 1946), teacher, critic, historian, poet, translator. Fletcher taught comparative literature at Columbia University and made many scholarly contributions to a better understanding of other literatures, especially of Italian. He wrote a book on Dante (1916) and translated the *Divine Comedy* (1921). His own poetry was collected in *The Overture and Other Poems* (1911). He was regarded by some as the greatest American authority on the Italian Renaissance.

Fletcher, John Gould (b. Little Rock, Ark., Jan. 3, 1886—d. May 10, 1950), poet, critic. Glenn Hughes called Fletcher "pictorialist and mystic," and French critic Jean Catel characterized him as "the great dreamer of contemporary American poetry." But Edmond Wilson held that his work was "a great wall of hard descriptive prose mistakenly presented as poetry." Always a close student of painting, Fletcher emphasized the pictorial in his poetry, but with no loss of melody and with constant emphasis on musical variety. After much early experimentation Fletcher arrived at a creed of poetry that coincided with the activities of the Imagist school (see IMAGISM), in which Amy Lowell joined him when she met him in London in June, 1913. He never abandoned set verse forms, but felt that modern life demanded new rhythms, new patterns, and new subject matter in poetry. He liked to write his poems in the contrapuntal forms familiar in music—sometimes to their detriment. He was the least popular of the Imagists, despite the warm praise bestowed on him by many critics. Among his books: *Irradiations: Sands and Spray* (1915); *Goblins and Pagodas* (1916); *Breakers and Granite* (1921); *Paul Gauguin: His Life and Art* (1921); *The Black Rock* (1928); *John Smith—Also Pocahontas* (1928); *XXIV Elegies* (1935); *Life Is My Song* (autobiography, 1937); *Selected Poems* (1938, awarded a Pulitzer Prize); *The Burning Mountain* (1940); *Arkansas* (prose history, 1947). His widow, Charlie May Fletcher, wrote an affecting account of him, *Johnswood* (1953). See I'LL TAKE MY STAND.

Fletcher, Lucille. See MY CLIENT CURLEY.

Flexner, Abraham (b. Louisville, Ky., Nov. 13, 1886—d. Sept. 1, 1959), educator, biographer. After teaching in the Louisville high school, Flexner turned to the investigation of education and procedures for improving it. His writings were fearless, sometimes startlingly realistic as he collected instances of inefficiency, feebleness, and inadequacy in American teaching and school administration. Among his books: *The American College* (1908); *Medical Education in the United States and Canada* (1910); *A Modern School* (1916); *A Modern College* (1923); *Medical Education: A Comparative Study* (1925); *Universities—American, English, German* (1930); *I Remember: An Autobiography* (1940); also lives of Henry S. Pritchett (1943) and Daniel C. Gilman (1946).

Flexner, Anne Crawford (b. Georgetown, Ky., June 27, 1874—d. Jan. 11, 1955), playwright. The wife of Dr. ABRAHAM FLEXNER wrote several plays, among them a dramatization of MRS. WIGGS OF THE CABBAGE PATCH (1903); *A Lucky Star* (1909); *The Marriage Game* (1916); *Aged 26* (1937). The last was based on the life of John Keats.

Flint, Timothy (b. North Reading, Mass., July 11, 1780—d. Aug. 16? [18?], 1840), missionary, novelist, historian, editor. Flint began as a missionary in the Mississippi Valley. He described his experiences in *Recollections of the Last Ten Years* (1826), then went on to writing romances under the influence of Chateaubriand. These included *Francis Berrian, or, The Mexican Patriot* (1826); *Arthur Clenning* (1828); *George Mason, the Young Backwoodsman* (1829); *The Lost Child, a Romance* (1830). J. E. Kirkpatrick wrote *Timothy Flint, Pioneer, Missionary, Author, Editor* (1911).

Flood of Years, The (1876), a poem by WILLIAM CULLEN BRYANT. This is a reconsideration of the ideas on death and immortality that the poet had expressed in THANATOPSIS more than six decades earlier. The poem is a noble and ex-pressive one in the resonant blank verse that Bryant loved and wrote so well. He expresses deep sympathy with mankind and a hesitant belief in personal immortality.

Florence Vane (*Burton's Gentleman's Magazine*, March 1840), a sentimental ballad by PHILIP PENDLETON COOKE (1816–1850), which received a musical setting and became a great favorite. It was translated into many other languages.

Florida, Folksongs of (1950), collected and edited by Alton C. Morris, with musical transcriptions by Leonhard Deutsch. The 243 songs include traditional English and Scottish ballads, Negro and Bahaman songs, shanty songs, and some that seem to be Irish.

Florida of the Inca, The (1605), by Garcilaso de la Vega (1539—1616). Garcilaso was the son of a Spanish grandee and a royal princess of the deposed Inca line; he called himself "El Inca." He spent thirty-two years composing this account of De Soto's explorations in the region now called the Southeast and the Southwest of the United States. It is an intimate, accurate, well-written narrative.

Flowering of New England, The (1936), a literary history by VAN WYCK BROOKS. The book, a critical recounting of the years of literary pre-eminence in Boston and Concord, eventually took its place in Brooks' five-volume literary history of the United States. It won a Pulitzer Prize and in 1938 the award of the Limited Editions Club as being the book, of all published within a three-year period, "most likely to become a classic."

Flush Times of Alabama and Mississippi, The (1853), humorous sketches of the frontier by JOSEPH G. BALDWIN. Written in the classic prose of which Baldwin was so fond, these stories are nevertheless first-hand descriptions of the crooks, boasters, sharpers, and orators who found "flush times" awaiting their schemes among the naïve settlers. The realism of the sketches, as well as their rollicking wit, in many ways presage the Mississippi tales of Mark Twain.

Flynt, Josiah. See J. F. WILLARD.

Foerster, Norman (b. Pittsburgh, Pa., April 14, 1887—   ), teacher, critic, editor. A professor of English at the University of North Carolina (1914–30) and the University of Iowa (1930–44), Foerster became a leader in the movement known as the New Humanism and greatly influenced literary criticism in the United States. His position was somewhat less inflexible than that of IRVING BABBITT, however, and he was primarily interested, Alfred Kazin suggests, in restoring "the dignity and gentility of other days." Commenting on a phase of his work, Foerster writes: "As director of the School of Letters at the University of Iowa, I sponsored (at the very time neo-humanists were being belabored for indifference to literary creation) a program that opened the Ph.D. degree to candidates publishing a novel, a book of poems, in place of the usual academic dissertation. Helping in this work were writers like Benét, Frost, MacLeish, R. P. Warren, who came for visits and read manuscripts. The plan is still in operation at Iowa; so far as I know, nowhere else." Among his writings: *Nature in American Literature* (1923); *American Criticism* (1928); *The American Scholar* (1929); *Toward Standards* (1931); *The Humanities After the War* (1944); *The Humanities and the Common Man* (1946). See HUMANISM.

Foley, Martha (b. Boston, [?]—   ), newspaperwoman, editor, short-story writer, lecturer. Miss Foley worked for various newspapers in the United States and Europe before she and her husband WHIT BURNETT founded the magazine STORY in Vienna in 1931. She continued with the magazine when it moved to New York in 1933 and helped to make it one of the most influential organs of advanced writing in the country. At the death of Edward J. O'Brien in 1941, she took over the editorship of the annual BEST AMERICAN SHORT STORIES, which she co-edited with her son David Burnett beginning 1958. With David Burnett she compiled *The Best of the Best Short Stories, 1915 to 1950* (1952).

Folger, Henry Clay (b. New York City, June 18, 1857—d. June 11, 1930), lawyer, oil magnate, collector of Shakespeareana. For his great library of Shakespeare materials Folger erected a $2,500,000 building in Washington, D.C., the cornerstone of which was laid on May 28, 1930, two weeks before his death. It was opened to the public on April 23, 1932. He left it an endowment of $7 million and gave its management to the trustees of his alma mater, Amherst College. Many scholars and theatrical workers use the unsurpassed resources of the Folger Shakespeare Library, which is headed by Louis B. Wright, and its staff maintains correspondence with Shakespearean specialists all over the world. Much material relating to English history and literature of the 16th and 17th centuries is also available for research purposes. The library contains seventy-nine Shakespeare first folios; no other library owns more than five. Its fine replica of an Elizabethan theater was opened in 1949 with seven performances of *Julius Caesar* (and an eighth on television); the players were the Masquers of Amherst College. Annual lectures are given on April 23, Shakespeare's probable birthday. Scholarships and fellowships are awarded annually. The Folger paperbacks, edited by Louis B. Wright and Virginia La Mar, are excellent cheap editions of the plays and include about ten titles.

Folger, Peter (b. England, 1617?—d. 1690?), teacher, surveyor, missionary, interpreter, artisan, verse writer. Folger, the maternal grandfather of Benjamin Franklin, came to Massachusetts in 1635; in 1644 purchased Mary Morrell (or Morrils) who was an indentured servant, and married her; in 1659 he went to Nantucket and worked there for Tristram Coffin and his associates as a general factotum. At one time he participated in a rebellion against the proprietors and spent some time in jail. He may have published his long poem, *A Looking Glass for the Times, or, The Former Spirit of New England Revived in This Generation*, in 1676 or 1677; it

is possible, however, that it appeared after the author's death and that he incurred no risk by its publication. Samuel Marion Tucker called it "very bad verse," but it has also been called "a manly plea for tolerance in an age of intolerance."

folklore in American literature. Critics and literary historians have frequently emphasized the dependence of American literature upon European models and traditions, but the fact is that no literature can long survive without a root in native culture and from the first American authors turned progressively more often to the lore of their own people. WASHINGTON IRVING gathered much native material for his Knickerbocker comedy and his legends of the Hudson valley; however, he was deeply indebted to European concepts of gentility, and thus gave to the profession of letters in America a rather uncharacteristic direction. But before him authors like H. H. BRACKENRIDGE and ROYALL TYLER had introduced native characters, and PHILIP FRENEAU, by romanticizing the red man in his elegiac poems, prepared the way for JAMES FENIMORE COOPER. WILLIAM CULLEN BRYANT turned to folklore for some of his themes, as did EDGAR ALLAN POE, but neither made a systematic use of native materials.

Cooper was the first to use folk themes extensively, especially in his LEATHER-STOCKING TALES, where he employed the lore of the Five Tribes as he found it in Heckewelder and elsewhere. Leatherstocking was our first folk hero, enlarged from the legend of Daniel Boone and made somewhat more tractable than his prototype, but still acceptable at home and abroad. "Here," said Lowell, "was our new Adam of the wilderness, a figure as poetic as that of Achilles, as ideally representative as that of Don Quixote. . . ."

NATHANIEL HAWTHORNE's preoccupation with folklore is apparent in his *Notebooks*, which contain the germs of many of his tales: a mantle, the plague, a veil, mesmerism, plants with mystical potency, strange omens, and other folk themes that suggested to Hawthorne the symbols for his deeply moral narratives. THE GREAT STONE FACE, for example, is a genuine rural legend, as is YOUNG GOODMAN BROWN, and THE SCARLET LETTER draws on the folk tradition of Puritanism. THE HOUSE OF THE SEVEN GABLES he regarded as "a legend . . . from an epoch now gray in the distance . . . bringing with it some of its legendary mist."

Minor novelists drew heavily upon popular lore. JAMES K. PAULDING related in KONINGSMARKE the amusing story of the long Finn; in his play THE LION OF THE WEST pictured the comic backwoodsman Davy Crockett as Colonel Nimrod Wildfire; and in WESTWARD HO! burlesqued Natty Bumppo as Ambrose Bushfield. WILLIAM GILMORE SIMMS wove his fiction around the legends of Marion and the tales of Murrell and his gang. JOHN PENDLETON KENNEDY, WILLIAM ALEXANDER CARUTHERS, and JOHN ESTEN COOKE glamorized their beloved South with Cavalier myth. SYLVESTER JUDD in

MARGARET and Mrs. HARRIET BEECHER STOWE in her yarns of Sam Lawson converted their books into rich storehouses of New England custom and tradition. ROBERT M. BIRD introduced to literature in NICK OF THE WOODS that phantom of terror, the Jibbenainosay, and that curious creature of the "dark and bloody ground" of Kentucky: the ring-tailed roarer, half-horse, half-alligator.

The Transcendentalists were not much interested in folklore, but none of our writers has made more extensive use of it than HENRY WADSWORTH LONGFELLOW. His gift for folk expression displayed itself in facile ballad and metrical romance, beginning with such pieces as THE BATTLE OF LOVELL'S POND and *Lover's Rock* and continuing with THE WRECK OF THE HESPERUS, THE SKELETON IN ARMOR, EVANGELINE, THE SONG OF HIAWATHA, THE COURTSHIP OF MILES STANDISH. In TALES OF A WAYSIDE INN he used many folk themes, especially the popular tale of Paul Revere's ride and the Norse saga of King Olaf.

JOHN GREENLEAF WHITTIER shared Longfellow's love of balladry and was interested even more in New England legend. MOGG MEGONE illustrates his extended handling of Indian legend, while *The Witch of Wenham* and *The Wreck of Rivermouth* embody local superstition. Much early lore is packed in LEAVES FROM MARGARET SMITH'S JOURNAL. Among the ballads, BARBARA FRIETCHIE, MAUD MULLER, and especially SKIPPER IRESON'S RIDE are noteworthy, and the TELLING THE BEES is a touching use of ancient custom also referred to in HUCKLEBERRY FINN.

JAMES RUSSELL LOWELL, turning to the tradition of SAM SLICK and JACK DOWNING, made his great contribution to the literature of folklore in his BIGLOW PAPERS, where he recorded native speech with considerable accuracy and in the person of Birdofredom Sawin uttered much folk wisdom. THE COURTIN', in which the poet let himself go, is as "hahnsome as a girl in a gingham apron."

OLIVER WENDELL HOLMES was little interested in folklore, but HERMAN MELVILLE, like Hawthorne, sought many of his themes among the legends of the people, especially that of the huge white whale, as fabulous as the big bear of Arkansas and a great deal more significant. MOBY DICK is truly "one of the first great mythologies created in the modern world."

WALT WHITMAN came nearest to Homer in his folk attitudes. He nourished his imagination on the great myths of the Greeks, then drifted into the carefree camaraderie of the open road in America, looking on everything with the eyes of a prophet. Near the close of his career he addressed in Platte Canyon the "Spirit that Form'd this Scene" with the stirring animism that had characterized his awareness of "these States" as a whole. Into the SONG OF MYSELF he swept such folk references as the murder of the young men at Goliad, the western turkeyshoot, coon-seekers going through the regions of the Red River, woolly pates hoeing in the sugar field, the Missourian crossing the plains with his wares and cattle—these and many more. His prototypical American possessed far more than human stature. Unfortunately Whitman lacked the ear for folk rhythm and phrase, or perhaps he employed too much "false festiveness, coyness, posturing, and embracing," as Ludwig Lewisohn says, for him to be accepted by the folk. However, his art, with its incremental repetition, its parallelism, and its catalogues, is close to natural lyricism and constitutes the marshland between folklore and literature.

During the second half of the 19th century gentility gradually gave way to local color, opening the way for a more realistic use of folk materials. Ironically, however, when the self-styled realist, BRET HARTE, tried to prove that whatever the frontiersman lacked in culture he made up in innate moral virtue, he established a school of romantic hokum that has not only set the pattern for all westerns but has survived even the hard-boiled naturalism of JOHN STEINBECK. Other local-colorists were somewhat more successful. EDWARD EGGLESTON used the Cinderella motif to portray the folkways of poor whites in Indiana. MARY NOAILLES MURFREE sought out the superstitions of the Smoky Mountains but did not go to the roots of life there as have ELIZABETH MADOX ROBERTS and JESSE STUART in Kentucky. GEORGE W. CABLE used voodooism and other exotic customs in his *Creole Tales.* JOEL CHANDLER HARRIS published the animal symbolism of the Negro in the homely philosophy of Brer Rabbit. Later FINLEY P. DUNNE created in Mr. Dooley a great mythological figure of Irish-America and Charles Godfrey Leland told amusingly of German-American ways in *Hans Breitmann's Ballads.* (See HANS BREITMANN.)

When MARK TWAIN leaped to fame astride a jumping frog, he used a yarn known not only in the West but often told by Negroes along the levees of the Mississippi. ROUGHING IT contains such folk elements as the story of the buffalo hunt, a characteristic tall tale; the story of the old ram, well known in ballad lore; and the story of Dick Baker and his cat, which fits into the Uncle Remus type of bestiary. Baker's bluejay yarn belongs here by right but somehow got into A TRAMP ABROAD. As for Colonel Sellers, he may have been modeled on the rascally Simon Suggs (see SOME ADVENTURES OF SIMON SUGGS), thinks Constance Rourke, and adds, "If he was not the fabulous single figure toward which the national types had tended to merge, his stride was great; he was accepted throughout the nation as its own." In LIFE ON THE MISSISSIPPI Twain recalled the tall talk of the keelboatmen as the Child of Calamity discourses on the nutritiousness of Mississippi water or goes through the extravagant ritual of "Whooooop! bow your neck and spread, for the Pet Child of Calamity's a-coming!" And in TOM SAWYER and HUCKLEBERRY FINN the author used enough Negro superstitions and backcountry lore to make the reputation of a lesser artist. Twain's art had the garrulity of native storytellers, their incongruity and their irreverence, but he lifted the poetry of folk speech to new heights of splendor.

Later came the folk literature of capitalism —THE GILDED AGE, THE RISE OF SILAS LAPHAM, THE OCTOPUS, THE PIT, THE FINANCIER, MAIN STREET, and a host of others. Realism and bitterness marked the works of such writers as THEODORE DREISER, SINCLAIR LEWIS, JOHN DOS PASSOS, and JAMES T. FARRELL. Undoubtedly, to a certain extent these writers countered the rosy glow left by the local-colorists, but they did so by turning to new urban themes, and others had to retrieve the still-untapped resources of the country folk. More and more 20th-century writers turned to a realistic treatment of the pioneer, the mountain man, the farmer. JOHN A. LOMAX gathered cowboy songs and frontier ballads, helping to rectify the inaccuracies of OWEN WISTER's Western novels. ROARK BRADFORD gave us OL' MAN AN' HIS CHILLUN, and such works as GREEN PASTURES, PORGY, and SCARLET SISTER MARY present authentic folk materials. OLIVER LA FARGE, by indicating the adaptations of the Navahos to the necessities of the land, has put an end to considerable foolishness about the Indian. VACHEL LINDSAY has sung with compassion about the Chinese laundryman, the Negro, and the Salvation Army. WILLA CATHER treated sympathetically the folkways of Bohemians, Germans, and Scandinavians, and O. E. RÖLVAAG brought out the Viking strain in his characters in their adjustments to a new land and a new society. CARL SANDBURG has found native symbols in innumerable acts and traditions of the people.

ROBERT FROST's poetry is close to daily living, to the comedies and tragedies of hard-handed New Englanders. STEPHEN VINCENT BENÉT in THE DEVIL AND DANIEL WEBSTER transformed pseudofolklore into a modern classic and in *Johnny Pye and the Fool-Killer* treated expertly a myth that had previously fascinated O. Henry. H. L. DAVIS in HONEY IN THE HORN told a lusty folk tale of the Oregon frontier. More recently John Steinbeck has given us the lore of the *paisano* in TORTILLA FLAT and of the "Okies" in THE GRAPES OF WRATH. Many other such genre studies, written in unaffected prose, add distinctly to the veracity of literature in America.

In spite of this body of lore it cannot yet be said that we are a folk. Oral tradition is necessarily regional, and the United States contains many folk units, such as the Down-East Yankees, the Smoky Mountaineers, the Pennsylvania Germans, the Louisiana Cajuns, the Minnesota Swedes, the southern Negroes, the southwestern Indians and Latin Americans, each possessing special folkways and sayings. Occupationally, too, tales have been varied: tales about sailors, miners, lumberjacks, wheat harvesters, railroaders, cowboys, oilfield workers, and doubtless many others. Each group has developed its own jargon and superstitions, proverbs and humor. Throughout the history of American literature writers have turned to these sources, more so today than ever before, and the folk of America have been responsible for much of the characteristic color and richness of our writing.

ERNEST E. LEISY

Folk-Say: A Regional Miscellany (1925–35), edited by B. A. BOTKIN. In the volumes of this annual miscellany Botkin exhibits what he calls "the new regionalism," which differs from the early local-color school in being "retrospective rather than prophetic, with an insatiable curiosity about the past of history and tradition," and in laying a strong emphasis on folklore. The material includes poems, stories, and plays, with details and motifs taken from folklore; likewise many accounts of popular tales, ballads, and customs—for example, articles on "Indiana Log-Rolling," "Choctaw Fables," "Pioneer Medicine in New Mexico," etc.

folksongs, American. See BALLADS.

Folkways (1907), a sociological treatise by WILLIAM GRAHAM SUMNER. This was a highly influential work in which the eminent Yale professor of sociology summed up much of his thinking, which was deeply influenced by Herbert Spencer and other evolutionists. Sumner looked at the order of nature in terms of the folkways or "mores," a term to which his book gave wide currency. Merle Curti states that Sumner "lent support to an economic conservatism that found the security of the individual in the acceptance of his lot as both necessary and, in the larger scheme of things, good." Because of Sumner's emphasis on the relativity of ethical customs his book was regarded as subversive of religion; in some libraries it was kept on a restricted shelf.

Following the Equator (1897), a travel book by MARK TWAIN describing a lecture tour he made around the world. It contains lengthy passages on Australia, India, and South Africa; it tends toward the factual and is padded with quoted material. Twain was not a well man when he undertook this tour to pay off debts incurred in his business enterprises, and the book shows signs of the author's weariness. Yet it is sprinkled with striking epigrams, mainly the fruit of Twain's bitterness at this period, including some of his most quoted statements. In the book may be found, too, outbursts of social indignation. Mrs. Clemens read the manuscript carefully and improved it by suggesting that Twain restrain his love of technical minutiae. She also objected, however, to such words as *stench, offal,* and *breech-clout.*

Fontaine, Robert. Author of THE HAPPY TIME.

Fool's Errand, A (1879), a novel "by One of the Fools" (ALBION W. TOURGÉE). One of the great popular successes of its day, this anonymously published novel was hailed by some critics as "the great American novel." The "fool's errand" referred to is the attempt to remold the South in the image of the North, after the Civil War; the conclusion reached in the novel is that reconstruction has failed. Tourgée was a Northerner by birth, but had long lived in the South as a journalist. The novel often becomes autobiographical; the hero is represented as a Union colonel who moves from Michigan to a Southern plantation after peace is declared and there tries to carry out ideas for helping the South. Later Tourgée documented his story in a signed publication called *The Invisible Empire* (1883); he wrote a sequel, BRICKS WITHOUT STRAW (1880), with a Southern hero and a Northern heroine. Steele MacKaye made a veracious dramatization of *A Fool's Errand* (1881).

Foote, John Taintor (b. Leadville, Colo., March 29, 1881—d. Jan. 28, 1950), novelist, short-story writer, playwright, screen producer. Perhaps Foote will be best remembered for his stories of dogs (*e.g., Dumb-Bell of Brookfield*, 1917), horses, and other animals. He wrote about an outdoor man, *Blister Jones* (1913), who reappeared in some of his later tales, among them *A Fowl Disaster* (1941). Foote also wrote *The Look of Eagles* (1916) and *Pocono Shot* (1925).

Foote, Mary Hallock. Author of LED HORSE CLAIM.

Foote, Shelby D[ade] (b. Greenville, Miss., Nov. 17, 1916—   ), novelist. Foote attended the University of North Carolina, then served in the army and with the marines for over five years. He has written primarily about the South. His novels include *Tournament* (1949); *Follow Me Down* (1950); *Love in a Dry Season* (1951). *Shiloh* (1952) is his most popular work. *Jordan County* (1953) includes three novelettes and four short stories set in the Mississippi Delta country. The first of three projected historical volumes, *The Civil War: A Narrative*, appeared in 1958.

Forayers, The (1855), a novel by W. G. SIMMS. See EUTAW SPRINGS.

Forbes, Esther [Mrs. A. L. Hoskins] (b. Westborough, Mass., 1894?—d. Aug. 12, 1967), writer, historian. Miss Forbes' favorite setting was New England. Among her historical novels are *O Genteel Lady!* (1926); *A MIRROR FOR WITCHES* (1928); *The General's Lady* (1938); *Johnny Tremaine* (1943); *The Running of the Tide* (1948); *Rainbow on the Road* (1954). *Paul Revere and the World He Lived In* (1942) was awarded a Pulitzer Prize. She later wrote, with Lynd Ward, *America's Paul Revere* (juvenile).

Forbes, Kathryn (b. San Francisco, March 20, 1909—d. May 15, 1966), writer, novelist. Miss Forbes' true name is Mrs. Kathryn Anderson McLean; she took her pen name from her paternal grandmother. Her maternal grandmother was a Norwegian immigrant, and Miss Forbes began writing short stories about her that were collected as *Mama's Bank Account* (1943). They won wide recognition for their kindly humor and deep sympathy with an immigrant group. In 1944 a dramatization by JOHN VAN DRUTEN called *I Remember Mama* (1948) aroused enthusiasm among critics and audiences. Later the play became a television series. In

1947 Miss Forbes wrote *Transfer Point*, a story of a ten-year-old girl and a San Francisco trolley car; in 1956, *Dog Who Spoke to Santa Claus*.

Force, Peter (b. Passaic Falls, N.J., Nov. 26, 1790—d. Jan. 23, 1868), printer, publisher, archivist, historian. Force became an apprentice printer at the age of ten, at twenty-two was elected president of the New York Typographical Society. He worked as a printer and publisher in Washington, with some necessary excursions into politics. He was an alderman and in 1836–40 mayor of the capital city. He became deeply interested in preserving important historical records. In 1820–24 and 1828–36 he issued the *National Calendar and Annals of the U.S.* He also published *Historical Tracts* on early American history, from 1836 to 1846, and AMERICAN ARCHIVES between 1837 and 1853. In 1867 his great collection of books and papers was acquired by the Library of Congress.

Ford, Corey ["John Riddell"] (b. New York City, April 29, 1902—   ), humorist, freelance writer, playwright. In addition to the books and articles published under his own name, Ford wrote pungent parodies under the pen name John Riddell. Among his books: *Three Rousing Cheers for the Rollo Boys* (1925); *Salt Water Taffy* (1929); *Short Cut to Tokyo* (1943); *Cloak and Dagger* (1946, with Alastair MacBain); *How to Guess Your Age* (1950); *Office Party* (1951); *The Day Nothing Happened* (1959), and, under his pseudonym, *Meaning No Offense* (1928) and *The John Riddell Murder Case* (1930).

Ford, Ford Madox [born: Ford Madox Hueffer] (b. England, 1873–d. 1939), novelist, critic. In the course of a long and varied literary career Ford came into contact with many American authors. Though he was a successful writer, he is equally well remembered for his influence on other English and American writers. The first of these was Joseph Conrad who sought out Ford, "the foremost English stylist" of the nineties, to collaborate on three novels. Ford became friendly with STEPHEN CRANE and HENRY JAMES, and James used Ford as the model for Merton Densher in THE WINGS OF THE DOVE. In 1908 Ford founded *The English Review* and began to print the poetry of EZRA POUND, then newly arrived in London. Pound's conversations with Ford first introduced him to the principles that later became known as IMAGISM—principles that Pound employed in editing T. S. Eliot's THE WASTE LAND and that influenced a whole generation of American writers. In Pound's HUGH SELWYN MAUBERLEY, the section about the "stylist" in exile was a portrait of Ford. After the war Ford became an active figure among the American expatriates in Paris. He printed ERNEST HEMINGWAY'S work in his *transatlantic review* and soon made him his assistant editor. He also printed some of the first poems of E. E. CUMMINGS. During his last years Ford spent much time in the United States traveling and lecturing. The influence of his critical ideas on his friends, ALLEN TATE and his wife CAROLINE GORDON, the novelist, can be seen in their textbook, *The House of Fiction*.

Ford, Henry (b. near Dearborn, Mich., July 30, 1863—d. April 7, 1947), industrialist. Ford applied the principles of mass production to build automobiles at lower prices than was at the time customary. He sold immense numbers of them, placing America on four wheels and making rapidity of locomotion a national habit. He set up historical monuments, delved into politics unsuccessfully, established a newspaper. He composed several books in collaboration with SAMUEL CROWTHER, among them *My Life and Work* (1923). Upton Sinclair wrote *The Flivver King—A Story of Ford-America* (1937), and Allan Nevins and F. E. Hill wrote *Ford: The Times, the Man, the Company* (1954). The Ford Foundation, established 1936, has done much toward furthering peace, improving college salaries, protecting freedom of speech, extending knowledge. Dwight Macdonald analyzed *The Ford Foundation: The Men and the Millions* (1956).

Ford, John [original name: **Sean O'Feeney**] (b. Cape Elizabeth, Me., Feb. 1, 1895—   ), motion-picture director and producer. Ford became famous with the production of his motion picture of Irish life, *The Informer* (1935). Among his other notable pictures are *Four Sons* (1928); *Arrowsmith* (1931); *The Plough and the Stars* (1937); *Grapes of Wrath* (1940); *How Green Was My Valley* (1941). During World War II he made two powerful documentaries for the navy, *Midway* and *December 7th*. *They were Expendable* came out in 1945, and *The Fugitive* in 1947. Since then he has done numerous Westerns like *Fort Apache*, and in 1959 what might be called a Civil War Western, *The Horse Soldiers*.

Ford, Paul Leicester (b. Brooklyn, N.Y., March 23, 1865—d. May 8, 1902), novelist, bibliographer, historian. Ford was a hunchback, and was educated privately, partly in his father's extensive library. At the age of eleven Ford printed on an amateur printing press a *Webster Genealogy*—Noah Webster was his great-grandfather. Later, with his father, Gordon Lester Ford, and his brother, Worthington Ford, he issued some important bibliographies, *Winnowings in American History* (15 v., 1890–91). He wrote various historical and biographical works, among them *The True George Washington* (1896) and *The Many-Sided Franklin* (1899), still readable. But his literary fame rests chiefly on two novels: the story of a politician, THE HONORABLE PETER STIRLING AND WHAT PEOPLE THOUGHT OF HIM (1894) and JANICE MEREDITH: A STORY OF THE AMERICAN REVOLUTION (1899). The former was generally taken to be a portrait of Grover Cleveland. The latter became an immediate best seller. The book was dramatized and had a long run. While the book was at the height of its popularity, Ford's brother Malcolm, who had been disinherited by their father, shot and killed him, and then committed suicide.

Ford, Sewell (b. Levant, Me., March 7, 1868—d. Oct. 26, 1946), short-story writer, novelist. Ford was chiefly noted for the tales he wrote about two comic characters named "Torchy" and "Shorty McCabe." Among his collections: *Shorty McCabe* (1906); *Cherub Divine* (1909); *Just Horses* (1910); *Torchy* (1911); *Inez and Trilby May* (1921).

Ford Foundation Prize, Julia Ellsworth. This was established by Julia Ellsworth Ford in 1934 for the purpose of "encouraging originality and imagination in children's literature in the U.S.," and is awarded annually (usually a sum of $1,250). The award is administered through Julian Messner, Inc.

Forester, C[ecil] S[cott] (b. Egypt, Aug. 27, 1899—d. April 2, 1966), novelist. An English writer who settled in California as a member of the British Information Service in 1940, Forester is best known for his novels about Horatio Hornblower, which carry the hero from midshipman to admiral in the British navy. He wrote many swashbuckling novels with other heroes, among them: *Lord Nelson* (1929); *The African Queen* (1935); *Flying Colors* (1939); *Randall and the River of Time* (1951); *The Good Shepherd* (1955). THE CAPTAIN FROM CONNECTICUT (1941) is his only book with an American setting.

Forester, Frank. Pen name of HENRY WILLIAM HERBERT.

Forest Hymn, A (1825), a poem by WILLIAM CULLEN BRYANT. Written in resonant blank verse, it begins with the famous line, "The groves were God's first temples," and goes on to express views of the universe similar to Wordsworth's early poems. The feeling is markedly pantheistic, despite the fact that Bryant expresses a belief in a personal creator, a God of wrath as well as of love.

Forest Princess, The (produced in 1844 in England; 1848, in Philadelphia), a play by Charlotte Barnes Conner in which POCAHONTAS appears.

Forest Rose, The; or, American Farmers (1825), a play by SAMUEL WOODWORTH. The type of stage Yankee created by Royall Tyler in THE CONTRAST (produced, 1790) evoked many imitations, none more popular than Jonathan Ploughboy in Woodworth's melodrama. Arthur Hobson Quinn calls him "a type and a caricature, to be sure, but he moves among the other conventional characters with a flavor of earth that is the more appealing perhaps by their very conventionality."

Forever Amber (1944), a historical novel by KATHLEEN WINSOR. *Life* described the book as "about a beauty who went from mattress to mattress across Restoration London." Unsuccessful attempts were made in Massachusetts to have it legally suppressed. It sold more than a million copies in a year, and continued to sell well thereafter. It was also filmed.

Forlorn Demon, The (1953), a collection of essays by ALLEN TATE. Through studies of Dante, Poe, Samuel Johnson, Longinus, and Hart Crane, Tate examines the relationship between ideas and experience. His criterion for literary excellence is the degree to which ideas have been transmuted into action, thought into gesture. In three essays on Poe, Tate analyzes the split in the modern mind between experience and intellect. It was Poe himself, according to Tate, who discovered this split and gave us "our great subject, the disintegration of the modern personality. . . ."

Forrest, Edwin (b. Philadelphia, 1806—d. 1872), actor. Forrest, noted for his Shakespearean roles, first became famous when he

EDWIN FORREST IN *The Gladiator*

played Othello in New York (1826). He encouraged American writers, several of whom wrote plays for him, but sometimes quarrels resulted; and a feud with the English actor William Charles Macready led to a riot when the latter appeared in the Astor Place Theatre (May 10, 1849). He left his estate to found the Forrest Home for aged actors in Philadelphia.

Forrest, Col. Thomas. Author of THE DISAPPOINTMENT OR, THE FORCE OF CREDULITY. See ROBERT MONTGOMERY BIRD; THE GLADIATOR.

Fort, Charles [Hoy] (b. Albany, N.Y., Aug. 9, 1874—d. May 3, 1932), newspaperman. Fort gathered amazing stories of strange and apparently inexplicable happenings in an endeavor to show that science was still limited in its ability to explain certain phenomena. He wrote *The Book of the Damned* (1919); *New Lands* (1923); *Lo!* (1931); and *Wild Talents* (1932). *The Books of Charles Fort* (1941) collected these in an omnibus volume edited by Tiffany Thayer. A notable group of Fort's admirers, including Thayer, Booth Tarkington, Theodore Dreiser, and Alexander Woollcott, founded the Fortean Society (1931) and issued a magazine called *Doubt* (1937). The society was dedicated to "the frustration of science."

Fortune. A monthly magazine, founded in New York by HENRY R. LUCE in 1930. It is dedicated to the glorification of American business and industry, and publishes elaborately prepared and illustrated articles which are often of general interest. Sometimes the approach is sociological rather than economic, as in an excellent article on the summer schools of New York. The subscription price limits the magazine to prosperous readers, yet on occasion the editors have taken a stand opposed to the opinions of its readers, as when it was among the first industrial organs to assert that collective bargaining between capital and labor was desirable.

Forty-niners. A name given to those who emigrated to California during the gold rush of 1849. About a hundred thousand in number, the emigrants came by way of the sea (around Cape Horn or across Panama) or overland, usually experiencing considerable hardship on either route. Many were adventurers, misfits, or criminals, but there were also a good number of business and professional men, including some eminent journalists—BRET HARTE, for example—who found in the new life as rich a source of fame and income as others found in the mines. When the centennial year of the gold rush arrived, many narratives of the Forty-niners were published or reprinted or gathered into anthologies, among them Bayard Taylor's *Eldorado;* "Dame Shirley's" *The Shirley Letters; Gold Rush: The Journals, Drawings, and Other Papers of J. Goldsborough Bruff, 1849–51;* Evelyn Wells and H. C. Peterson's *The '49ers;* Joseph Henry Jackson's *Gold Rush Album.*

Forty-second Parallel, The (1930), a novel by JOHN DOS PASSOS. It is the first of a trilogy which was collected in 1938 as U.S.A. The individual episodes and the characterization, the setting and the commentaries, are in themselves less important than the effectiveness of the whole book and the entire trilogy. Dos Passos employs with supreme skill the expressionist techniques that were coming into fashion during the first decades of the century. There is no definite plot; the book flows in a stream of time and is designed to show the United States rather than to narrate the lives of the various—almost innumerable—individuals who figure in it. The method of narration was a bold innovation. Dos Passos uses systematically the "News-Reel," describing the social background; "Biographies," profiles of prominent personalities; "Novels," which deal with the more ordinary characters of the time; "the Camera Eye," by means of which the author himself can supply a sort of Greek choric commentary on what is happening. The result is sometimes confusing, more often a powerful presentation of a vast panorama of human nature and of history. The book and the trilogy founded a new school in American fiction. Alfred Kazin speaks of *U.S.A.* as "a national epic, the first great national epic of its kind in the modern American novel."

Forty-Seven Workshop. See G. P. BAKER.

For Whom the Bell Tolls (1940), a novel by ERNEST HEMINGWAY. Laid in the era of the Spanish Civil War (1936–39), the story follows the fortunes of Robert Jordan, an American volunteer on the side of the Loyalist forces. He is sent to join a guerrilla band in order to blow up a bridge, and the narrative tells his experiences during the three days in the course of which he decides that the enterprise is one that will do more harm than good, falls passionately in love with Maria, a girl who has been tragically wronged by the Falangists, seeks to have the order to blow the bridge countermanded, finally carries it out, but is fatally wounded as he does so. The novel introduces a host of well-drawn characters, in particular that of a dominating woman named Pilar, fanatically devoted to the Republic. The title of the book is taken from one of John Donne's *Devotions:* "No man is an island, entire of itself; every man is a piece of the continent. . . . therefore never seek to know for whom the bell tolls; it tolls for thee." In the course of the novel Hemingway shows how the communists used the Spaniards as tools for their own ends. Leo Gurko sees in the novel a continuation of Hemingway's preoccupation with death as a theme and a form of art. According to Alfred Kazin the novel is unsatisfactory "because it is a strained and involuntary application of Hemingway's essentially anarchical individualism, his brilliant half-vision of life, to a new world of war and struggle too big for his sense of scale."

Fosdick, Charles Austin ["Harry Castlemon"] (b. Randolph, N.Y., Sept. 16, 1842—d. Aug. 22, 1915), author of books for boys. Fosdick's experiences as a volunteer in the Civil War and his still earlier experiences as a boy in a small community and in Buffalo provided him with material for his fifty-eight volumes. They are straightforward narratives, teaching manliness and other virtues, and they rivaled the stories of Alger and Henty in popularity. Among them

were *The Gunboat Series* (1864–68); *The Rocky Mountain Series* (1867–71); *The Rod and Gun Series* (1883–84). The first was *Frank, the Young Naturalist* (1864), which told about Fosdick himself as a boy.

Fosdick, Harry Emerson (b. Buffalo, N.Y., May 24, 1878—   ), clergyman, author. The nephew of Charles Austin Fosdick, he was ordained a Baptist minister and won a wide reputation for his reconciliation of older theological views with the demands of modern life. He became the pastor of Riverside Church in New York City and a teacher at the nearby Union Theological Seminary. Brand Blanshard said that during the 1920's and 1930's Fosdick was "the most eloquent voice in the American pulpit." In addition to frequent radio addresses, Fosdick wrote a number of books that attained wide circulation, among them *The Manhood of the Master* (1913); *The Meaning of Prayer* (1915); *As I See Religion* (1932); *Successful Christian Living* (1937); *Living Under Tension* (1941); *On Being a Real Person* (1943); *The Man From Nazareth* (1949); *A Faith for Tough Times* (1952); *John D. Rockefeller, Jr.* (1956); *The Living of These Days* (1956, autobiography); *Jesus of Nazareth* (1957); *A Book of Public Prayers* (1959); *Dear Mr. Brown* (1961).

Foss, Sam Walter (b. Candia, N.H., June 19, 1858—d. Feb. 26, 1911), poet, editor, columnist, librarian. Foss, as proprietor of the *Saturday Union* in Lynn, Mass., found it necessary to conduct a column and discovered he had a facility in writing humorous verse. Thereafter he became a contributor to *Puck* and *Judge*, and in 1894 began writing a daily poem for a syndicate. Often he wrote in dialect; generally he expressed a creed of unshatterable and cheerful optimism. His verses were collected in *Back Country Poems* (1892); *Dreams in Homespun* (1897; this includes his most famous poem, THE HOUSE BY THE SIDE OF THE ROAD); *Songs of the Average Man* (1907; with additions, 1911); and other volumes. F. L. Pattee calls his poetry "genuine and distinctive."

Foster, Hannah Webster. See THE COQUETTE.

Foster, Stephen [Collins] (b. Lawrenceville, Pa., July 4, 1826—d. Jan. 13, 1864), song writer and composer. Although Foster's first job was as a bookkeeper for his brother, he apparently had little head for figures; later, he was frequently victimized by shrewd music publishers. He never won financial success. His short life was a combination of song with neurotic illness, alcoholism, and extreme poverty. At one point he was found nearly dead from starvation in a Bowery hotel. Among his most famous songs are OLD FOLKS AT HOME; *Jeannie with the Light Brown Hair;* OH, SUSANNA; OLD BLACK JOE; *Come Where My Love Lies Dreaming; Old Dog Tray; Camptown Races; Nelly Bly; Nelly Was a Lady;* MY OLD KENTUCKY HOME; *Beautiful Dreamer;* MASSA'S IN DE COLD, COLD GROUND. Deems Taylor said of his melodies, "A child can sing them; so can a coloratura." Although Foster seems to have had little actual contact with

Negroes, many of his songs are in Negro dialect and express a somewhat sentimentalized version of the Negro slave's view of life. Foster, Sigmund Spaeth notes, has never been matched by any other song writer for sustained popu-

larity; his songs are as much a part of the American musical consciousness as any purely folk melodies. Foster greatly admired Edgar Allan Poe, and perhaps learned some of his secrets from him. Edmund Wilson points out that the words to the songs "are very good in their several veins and have blended indissolubly with the melodies. . . . He condensed little drops of emotion that have never lost their virtue or freshness." John Tasker Howard has written *Stephen Foster, America's Troubadour* (1934, 1954).

Fountain, The (1926), a play by EUGENE O'NEILL. This drama deals with Ponce de Leon; the dramatist has him fall in love with a woman much younger than himself, then seek the FOUNTAIN OF YOUTH in Florida in order to content his mistress. He fails tragically, but dies at peace as the result of a vision of eternal life. The play, produced in 1925, had only a short run. A. H. Quinn calls it "an experiment in symbolism," in which Ponce de Leon recognizes the real meaning of the Fountain of Youth, "the Eternal Becoming which is Beauty."

Fountainhead, The (1943), a novel by AYN RAND. The hero, supposedly patterned after FRANK LLOYD WRIGHT, is an architect of enormous self-conceit who nevertheless succeeds in justifying his faith in the permanent values of honest design. The book was a best seller.

Fountain of Youth, The. The early Spanish explorers of America fervently believed and hoped that somewhere in the New World there would be found a whole bubbling fountain of the *elixir vitae* for which alchemists had been searching through the centuries. Among others, Ponce de Leon, governor of Puerto Rico, made up his mind to find the Fountain of Youth. He set out in 1513 with three ships, discovered Florida, coasted along its east and west shores, visited the Bahamas, but was unable to find the fabled Bimini. On a second expedition to Florida he engaged in a battle with hostile Indians and died from a wound by a poisoned arrow. One island which was named Bimini by the explorers later became a convenient stopping-place for buccaneers, and during the prohibition era it was a busy haunt of bootleggers. Eugene O'Neill's THE FOUNTAIN (1926) deals with Ponce de Leon and his search.

Fourier, Charles (b. France, 1772—d. 1837), sociologist whose ideas exerted a strong influence in the United States, especially on Transcendentalists and on experiments with utopian colonies. Fourier advocated the creation of "phalansteries," units of 1,600 persons of varying but complementary ability, who would live as one family together. The leading American Fourierist was PARKE GODWIN (1816–1904), of the New York *Post*, who wrote *A Popular View of the Doctrine of Charles Fourier* (1844). When ARTHUR BRISBANE became influential at Brook Farm it was turned into a phalanstery; the Fourierist organ *The Phalanx* and its successor *The Harbinger* were published there. Brisbane's *Social Destiny* (1840) was one of the earliest discussions of Fourierism. BRONSON ALCOTT's FRUITLANDS, in Massachusetts, was another well-known Fourierist colony, and others were located at Red Bank, N.J., and near Ripon, Wis. Emerson scorned the movement as unidealistic, saying in a striking passage from his *Journals:* "Fourier learned from Owen all the truth he had, and the rest of his system was imagination, and the imagination of a banker. The Owen and Fourier plans bring no *a priori* convictions. They are come at merely by counting and arithmetic . . . The Spartan broth, the hermit's cell, the lonely farmer's life are poetic; but the phalanstery, the 'self-supporting village' are culinary and mean."

Four in America (1947), essays on George Washington, U. S. Grant, Wilbur Wright, and Henry James by GERTRUDE STEIN. Miss Stein tries to imagine what would have happened had Grant become a religious leader, Wright a painter, James a general, and Washington a novelist.

Four Million, The (1906), a collection of twenty-five stories by O. HENRY. The title refers to the population of New York City at the time and is in contrast to Ward McAllister's famous remark (1888) that "there are only about four hundred people in New York society." It contains one of O. Henry's most famous stories, THE GIFT OF THE MAGI, but perhaps the best piece is *An Unfinished Story*. O. Henry's favorite characters, shop girls, tramps, the humble folk in general, people these tales in abundance and give utterance to the author's uniquely humorous sentimentality. The book became a best seller.

Four Quartets (1943), four related poems by T. S. ELIOT. Said to have been modeled on the late quartets of Beethoven, each poem is structurally analogous to the classical sonata form, progressing through five "movements" in which themes and variations are introduced, developed, and finally resolved. The *Quartets*, considered by some critics to be Eliot's finest work, are both the record of a journey from skepticism to faith and an attempt to communicate a religious experience in an age lacking traditional religious belief.

Each poem has as its primary image one of the four elements, air, earth, water, and fire, and each is located, by its title, at a specific place: "Burnt Norton" refers to a seventeenth century manor house; "East Coker" to the Somersetshire village from which Eliot's ancestor set out for the New World; "The Dry Salvages" to a group of rocks off the coast of Massachusetts, a landscape familiar to Eliot from childhood; and "Little Gidding" to the English village to which Nicholas Ferrar retired in the seventeenth century to lead a life of devotion, a place which Eliot himself visited. The progression of the poems is from abstraction and deeply personal experience to universal experience; thus the first poem is much more "obscure" and dependent upon the rest of the group for its explication than the last poem, which can be understood without reference to the preceding three. The subject of "Burnt Norton" is the unexpected and unsought moment of joy at the "still point" out of time where the pattern of life and of past, present, and future can be apprehended. "East Coker" deals with the passage of time and the cyclic nature of human life and history. "The Dry Salvages" contrasts the time of the river, which is human time, with that of the sea, which is eternity. "Little Gidding" celebrates a visit to the chapel "where prayer has been valid" for a moment of dedication that has transcended time and space and in which the themes and images of the preceding poems find their resolution.

Four Saints in Three Acts (1934), a libretto by GERTRUDE STEIN, for an opera composed by Virgil Thomson. The four Saints are St. Theresa, St. Ignatius, and the unhistorical St. Settlement and St. Chavez. Thomson added two characters to represent the laity. Largely plotless, the opera concerns imaginary incidents in 16th-century Spain. It was premiered at Hartford, Conn., in 1934.

Fowler, Gene [Eugene Devlan] (b. Denver, Colo., March 8, 1890—d. July 2, 1960), newspaperman, editor, writer. Although Fowler turned early from newspaper work and scriptwriting, he remained essentially a newspaperman. Everywhere he displays a genius for making facts as lively as fiction. In Hollywood he wrote at least twenty-five scripts, among them

Union Depot (1932), *Call of the Wild* (1935), *Jesse James* (1939). But he hit his stride writing biographies, particularly accounts of picturesque contemporaries whom he knew personally. Fowler is sympathetic but not biased; he tells the truth as he saw it, sometimes to the discomfiture of naive hero-worshipers. First of these books was *The Great Mouthpiece* (1931), about a New York lawyer of not unblemished renown. There followed *Timberline* (1933), the account of two extraordinary Denver editors; GOOD-NIGHT, SWEET PRINCE (1943), a biography of John Barrymore and undoubtedly Fowler's best book; *Beau James* (1949), which brilliantly describes the life and times of Jimmy Walker, once mayor of New York; *Schnozzola: The Story of Jimmy Durante* (1951); *Minutes of the Last Meeting* (1954), sketches of famous theatre people woven around a biography of Sadakichi Hartmann; *A Solo in Tom-Toms* (1933, in a private printing; 1946, for general circulation), and *Salute to Yesterday* (1937) deal with Fowler's earlier years. *Skyline* appeared posthumously in 1961.

Fox, Emmet (b. Ireland, July 30, 1886—d. Aug. 13, 1951), minister, writer, lecturer. Fox came to the United States from England in 1931 and became an American citizen and pastor of the Church of the Healing Christ in New York City, a New Thought center. His ministry was immensely successful. His quiet authority, conversational tone, and scholarliness were sparked by spontaneous humor; his books had, and continue to have, enormous sales. *Power Through Constructive Thinking* (1932), was his first; *The Sermon on the Mount* (1934), a basic textbook in Scientific Christianity, has been a best seller for over two decades. Other books by Emmet Fox include: *Find and Use Your Inner Power* (1941); *Make Your Life Worth While* (1946); *Stake Your Claim* (1952); *The Ten Commandments* (1953).

Fox, John [William], **Jr.** (b. Stony Point, Ky., Dec. 16, 1863—d. July 8, 1919), novelist, short-story writer. His fame rests chiefly on two novels which became best sellers: THE LITTLE SHEPHERD OF KINGDOM COME (1903) and THE TRAIL OF THE LONESOME PINE (1908). Both novels were successfully dramatized by EUGENE WALTER (1912 and 1916). Earlier there had been other stories and novels by Fox, mainly laid in Kentucky and nearby, and they were followed by *The Heart of the Hills* (1913) and a historical novel, *Erskine Dale: Pioneer* (1920). Fox's short stories and sketches were collected in *A Cumberland Vendetta* (1895); *Hell fer Sartain* (1897); *Blue Grass and Rhododendron* (1901); and *Christmas Eve on Lonesome, and Other Stories* (1904). See THE KENTUCKIANS.

Foxes of Harrow, The (1946), a novel by Frank Yerby. Stephen Fox, a gambler, becomes an important plantation owner in Louisiana, tries to establish a respectable family, is ruined by the Civil War. A popular historical romance.

Fra Elbertus. See ELBERT HUBBARD.

Francesca da Rimini (prod., 1855; published,

1856), a play by GEORGE HENRY BOKER. Often considered the best American 19th-century play, this verse drama is, at any rate, its author's masterpiece. Sculley Bradley remarks that of seven plays in four languages based on the brief episode in Dante's *Inferno*, Boker's "is the only one to conceive the pathos of the deformed husband, without sacrificing the enduring appeal of the young lovers, and to understand that callous society, not fate, was the agent of the tragedy." Another play by the same title was written by F. MARION CRAWFORD (1902), originally for production by Sarah Bernhardt. Though less meritorious than Boker's version, it commands respect for its direct and lucid characterizations.

Franck, Harry A[lverson] (b. Munger, Mich., June 29, 1881—d. April 17, 1962), teacher, lecturer, author of travel books. Franck, who began his career as a French teacher, visited many parts of the earth, often employing that best of all ways to see a country—walking. Franck has been called "the Prince of Vagabonds." He composed a host of travel books, all written with zest, frankness, and accuracy. He served two years in World War I and—though he was sixty when it began—four and a half years in World War II. He received a Purple Heart Award, and was discharged with the rank of Major. Among his most colorful awards is the Order of the Million Elephants and the White Parasol by King Sisavong Vat of Luang Prabang (Laos). Among his books: *A Vagabond Journey Around the World* (1910); *Four Months Afoot in Spain* (1911); *Roaming through the West Indies* (1920); *Roving through Southern China* (1925); *Foot-Loose in the British Isles* (1933); *Rediscovering South America* (1943). His wife, Rachel Latta Franck, wrote *I Married a Vagabond* (1939).

Franco, Harry. Pen name of CHARLES FREDERICK BRIGGS. See THE ADVENTURES OF HARRY FRANCO.

François, The Adventures of (1898), a novel by S. WEIR MITCHELL. This is a spirited historical novel laid in the period of the French Revolution and devoted to the career of a "foundling, thief, juggler, and fencing master." The story is based on careful research, and the hero was an actual historical personage. THE RED CITY (1907) was a sequel. Mitchell's son, the playwright Langdon Mitchell, dramatized the story in 1900.

Frank, Waldo [David] (b. Long Branch, N.J., Aug. 25, 1889—d. Jan. 9, 1967), editor, writer, translator. Frank's specialty was the interpretation of contemporary civilization, particularly Latin America. He did much to help attract attention to new writers such as Hart Crane. Novels of his that attracted wide attention were *The Dark Mother* (1920); *Rahab* (1922); *Holiday* (1923); *The Death and Birth of David Markand* (1934); *The Bridegroom Cometh* (1938); *Summer Never Ends* (1941); *The Invaders* (1948); *Not Heaven* (1953). His works of nonfiction include: *Virgin Spain* (1926); *Dawn in Russia* (1932); *Chart for Rough Water* (1940); *Bridgehead: The Drama*

of Israel (1957); *The Rediscovery of Man* (1958); *Cuba: Prophetic Island* (1961). W. R. Bittner's *The Novels of Waldo Frank* (1958) is a critical essay.

Franken, Rose (b. Gainsville, Texas, 1898—   ), novelist. Miss Franken's celebrity is largely based on her *Claudia* series, a group of novels dealing with the happy domestic life of her girlish heroine over the course of two decades. These light, often sentimental books were notable for their extensive reliance on the gay, idiosyncratic speech of the chief protagonists, Claudia and her husband David. Though critics often relegated the stories to the category of "women's fiction," they generally conceded them to be pleasant and smoothly written. Miss Franken's novels, a number of which were serialized before publication in book form, include *Claudia* (1929); *Claudia and David* (1940); *Another Claudia* (1943); *From Claudia To David* (1950); *The Fragile Years* (1952); *Rendezvous* (1953); *Third Person Intimate* (1955); *The Antic Years* (1958); and the *Claudia Omnibus* (1958). Miss Franken was also a playwright and several of her plays received critical commendation. Among her works for the theater are *Mr. Dooley, Jr.* (1932); *Another Language* (1934); *Claudia* (1941); and *Outrageous Fortune* (1944).

Frankenberg, Lloyd (b. Mount Vernon, N.Y., Sept. 3, 1907—   ), poet, anthologist. Frankenberg set himself the task of making poetry enjoyable to the general reader. *Pleasure Dome: On Reading Modern Poetry* (1948), essays on American and English poets, tried to establish the relationship of verse procedures and rhythms to those of prose. Frankenberg produced a recording, *Pleasure Dome: An Audible Anthology of Modern Poetry* (1948), for which T. S. Eliot, Marianne Moore, E. E. Cummings, W. H. Auden, William Carlos Williams, Ogden Nash, Dylan Thomas, and Elizabeth Bishop read from their poems. Frankenberg published *The Red Kite*, a collection of his own poems in 1939, and *A Round of Poems* (1956, recording).

Frankfurter, Felix (b. Austria, Nov. 15, 1882—d. Feb. 22, 1965), lawyer, associate justice of the U.S. Supreme Court, author of books on legal topics. After a brief career practicing law, Frankfurter taught at Harvard Law School (1914–39) and engaged in various governmental pursuits until his appointment to the Supreme Court (1939). He has written several legal textbooks, as well as *The Case of Sacco and Vanzetti* (1927); *The Public and Its Government* (1930); *Mr. Justice Holmes and the Supreme Court* (1939); and *Law and Men* (1956). *Felix Frankfurter, Scholar on the Bench*, by H. S. Thomas appeared in 1960; *Felix Frankfurter Reminisces* (1960), edited by Harlan B. Phillips, was on the best-seller list for some time.

Frankie and Johnnie. Perhaps the most famous of American folk ballads. No one knows who wrote the words or the music, or when it was first sung in the United States. It relates, with an amusing mixture of glee and gloom, the story of Frankie, who had many lovers but only one "man," who "done her wrong." Sigmund Spaeth traces its possible ancestry back to 1840, and it may be even older; innumerable versions are in existence. Plays by Mae West, John Huston, and Jack Kirkland were built around the ballad, as well as a movie, a ballet, and an animated cartoon. Carl Sandburg called it the American "classical gutter song."

Frank Leslie's Illustrated News. See FRANK LESLIE.

Franklin, Ann (b. Boston, Oct. [?], 1696—d. April 19, 1763), America's first woman printer. Her husband JAMES FRANKLIN (1696–1735) was Benjamin Franklin's older brother. At the death of James, she took over his business and conducted it until 1748, when their son James became its manager. When he died in 1762 she and a printer named Samuel Hall ran it in partnership. Ann and the younger James founded the Newbury *Mercury* in 1758.

Franklin, Benjamin (b. Boston, Jan. 17, 1706 —d. April 17, 1790), printer, philosopher, scientist, statesman, writer. Franklin sums up in his activities and ideas so much of his time that he may be considered an epitome of the 18th

century. He was the tenth and youngest son of Josiah Franklin, a tallow chandler and soapmaker. After some two years of schooling, he went to work for his father at the age of ten. Two years later he was apprenticed to his brother James, a printer who later (1721) established the NEW-ENGLAND COURANT, in which young Benjamin's first literary productions, THE DOGOOD PAPERS (1722), appeared. During this period, Franklin tells us, he began his lifelong habit of concentrated reading which made him a self-educated man.

In 1723 as a result of quarrels with his brother he left Boston for Philadelphia, where he found employment in a printing shop and attracted the attention of Governor Keith, who recommended that the young man set up in business for himself and who offered to help him financially if he would go to England for equipment. In London, finding that promised letters of credit from the governor had not arrived, Franklin again went to work as a printer, meanwhile continuing his writing. In answer to William Wollaston's *The Religion of Nature Delineated*, he wrote and printed *A Dissertation on Liberty and Necessity, Pleasure and Pain* (1725), a liberal exposition of current ideas on necessity and a pamphlet which he later pretended to disavow.

Returning to Philadelphia in 1726, Franklin worked as a clerk for a Quaker merchant, then was employed again as a printer by SAMUEL KEIMER, before establishing his own printing business in 1728. Keimer having anticipated him in the publication of a newspaper, Franklin, in collaboration with Joseph Brientnal, contributed to Andrew Bradford's *American Weekly Mercury* a series of essays called "The Busy Body" (see BUSY BODY PAPERS) (1728) in which he effectively demonstrated by contrast the dullness of Keimer's competing weekly. The result was that in 1729 the latter sold Franklin the PENNSYLVANIA GAZETTE, in the columns of which the new owner made his name and notions well-known throughout the city. As a man of business he worked hard, but made it a point to appear to work even harder than he did. He won friends with ease, inspired confidence, and soon was recognized as a leader in local affairs. In 1727 he established the Junto, a debating society for young men who met to argue moral and political questions; not long afterward he initiated projects for establishing a city police, for the improvement of city fire companies, and for the paving, better lighting, and better cleaning of city streets. In 1731 he was influential in establishing a circulating library in Philadelphia, the first of its kind in America. (See LIBRARIES IN THE U.S.) Later he helped establish the American Philosophical Society, a municipal hospital, and an academy which grew to become the University of Pennsylvania. From 1726 to 1751 he was clerk of the Pennsylvania Assembly, and from 1737 to 1753 he was deputy postmaster for Philadelphia. For a few months he conducted THE GENERAL MAGAZINE (1741), the second monthly ever projected in America.

Perhaps the best remembered of his activities during these years, however, was the annual publication from 1732 to 1757 of POOR RICHARD'S ALMANACK with its scores of proverbs which made Franklin's name a byword throughout the colonies. Other occasional writings included essays on such practical matters as Indian affairs, paper currency, and local reform, and were characterized by sagacity and homely humor. His *Advice to a Young Man on the Choice of a Mistress* (1745), *Reflections on Courtship and Marriage* (1746), and *The*

Speech of Polly Baker (1747), often reprinted, have become classics in the application of common sense to morality.

In 1748, at the age of forty-two, Franklin had acquired enough wealth to entrust his business to a partner and look forward to a life of retirement. For some time he had been interested in scientific experiments. As early as 1737 he had written a study of earthquakes and had investigated the movements of windstorms. He had invented a fireplace (cf. his *Account of the New Invented Pennsylvania Fireplace,* 1744), perfected a clock, and was drawn toward experiments in electricity. These last established his fame as a scientist. He corresponded with scientists in England, and he described his own findings in *Experiments and Observations in Electricity* (1751; reprinted with additions, 1753, 1760–62). But colonial affairs in America did not allow Franklin to remain in retirement long. In 1751 he became a member of the Pennsylvania Assembly. Two years later he was sent to represent that body at the Albany Congress, called to unite the colonists in war against the French. In the same year he was appointed deputy postmaster-general for the colonies. Finally, in 1757, he was sent by the Assembly to England to appeal directly to Parliament for settlement of a dispute with the proprietors of Pennsylvania. In England he visited with Collinson, Fothergill, Priestley, and other scientists, and corresponded with Lord Kames, David Hume, and Samuel Johnson. He was awarded an LL.D. by St. Andrews (1759) and a D.L.C. by Oxford (1762), and he published various papers on scientific and political subjects, including *An Historical Review of the Constitution and Government of Pennsylvania* (1759) and *The Interest of Great Britain Considered with Regard to Her Colonies* (1760). He returned to Philadelphia in 1762, but was almost immediately sent off to England again, this time to obtain a recall of the Pennsylvania charter. As it turned out, he did not come back to America until 1775, thirteen years later.

The events which led up to the American Revolution required Franklin to shoulder new responsibilities. His *Cool Thoughts on the Present Situation of Affairs* (1764), his forthright *Preface to the Speech of Joseph Galloway* (1764), in which he demanded that American colonials be granted the same rights as British subjects at home, his statements before the House of Commons on the Stamp Act, and his plainspoken opposition to the Townshend Act (see his EDICT BY THE KING OF PRUSSIA, 1773, and *Rules by Which a Great Empire May Be Reduced to a Small One,* 1773) increased his prestige and reputation, with the result that he was named colonial agent for Georgia (1768), New Jersey (1769), and Massachusetts (1770), and became practically an ambassador from the New World to the Old. Until the coercive acts of 1775, Franklin worked strenuously for reconciliation between England and America, only gradually growing to the conviction that separation from the mother country was inevitable. In

the spring of that year, certain now that Lord North was forcing the colonies into revolt, he returned to Philadelphia, where he was chosen a member of the second Continental Congress and became our first postmaster-general. He served on commissions to induce Canada to join the colonies in rebellion, to advise with Washington on defense, to treat with Lord Howe on proposals for peace, and to work with Jefferson in drafting the DECLARATION OF INDEPENDENCE. (See also THOMAS PAINE.) In September, 1776, he was appointed, with Silas Deane and ARTHUR LEE, to a commission to negotiate a treaty with France. Late that year he sailed again for Europe.

In France seventy-year-old Franklin was greeted by the people as a sage and a Rousseauistic philosopher, though the French government did not at once officially recognize him or his mission. His simple dress, his shrewd but benign countenance, his wit and homely wisdom made him seem a symbol of the Age of Enlightenment and of the promise of America. He lived for nine years at Passy, near Paris, in constant familiar correspondence with men of science, in more frivolous epistolary exchanges with Mme. Helvetius and Mme. Brillon, and amusing himself and his friends by running off on his private press such "bagatelles" as *The Ephemera* (1778), *The Morals of Chess* (1779), *The Whistle* (1779), and *The Dialogue Between Franklin and the Gout* (1780). Public duties were not, however, neglected. Early in 1778, when Burgoyne's defeat inspired French confidence in American success, he succeeded in securing a treaty of commerce and defensive alliance and, when later in the same year he was appointed plenipotentiary to the French court, obtained repeated loans and negotiated commercial treaties with Sweden and Prussia. In 1783, with John Jay and John Adams, he was one of the commissioners who signed the Treaty of Paris, but it was not until two years later that he was finally recalled by Congress.

Now in his eightieth year, Franklin was prepared to lay aside all public responsibilities. But soon after his arrival in Philadelphia he was chosen president of the Executive Council of Pennsylvania and served in this position for three years. In 1787 he was a member of the Constitutional Convention where, when his own ideas were not adopted, he pled for effective and democratic compromise. During the last five years of his life, Franklin lived with his daughter on Market St. in Philadelphia. There he puttered with inventions—a device for lifting books from high shelves, an easy chair completely equipped for an old man's comfort—and he enjoyed to the last his "agreeable and instructive" correspondence with friends abroad. His *Autobiography,* begun in 1771 and never completed, recounts his life until 1757, with some random remarks which carry it to 1759, and is perhaps the most lasting monument to his wisdom and to his peculiar combination of sagacious common sense and optimistic assurance that all men may better themselves. His plain style, his practicalness, and his honest pragmatism—touched now with humor, now with a hint of Shandyesque sentimentality—made him a truly representative man of his age. The *Autobiography* has been called the first American book which belongs permanently to literature.

There have been many editions of Franklin's works, including *The Complete Works of Benjamin Franklin* (10 v., 1887–88), edited by JOHN BIGELOW, and *The Writings of Benjamin Franklin* (10 v., 1905–07), by A. H. Smythe. In 1956, in connection with the celebration of the 250th anniversary of Franklin's birth, the Yale University Press announced plans for a new and definitive edition of all Franklin's writings. The best edition of the *Autobiography* is by John Bigelow (3 v., 1874). Excellent representative selections of his work are in *Benjamin Franklin* (1936), edited by F. L. Mott and C. E. Jorgensen, which contains a useful introduction and bibliography. A *Franklin Bibliography* was issued by P. L. Ford in 1889. Among biographical and analytical studies of Franklin are: James Parton, *The Life and Times of Benjamin Franklin* (1864); J. B. McMaster, *Benjamin Franklin as a Man of Letters* (1887); E. E. Hale and E. E. Hale, Jr., *Franklin in France* (1888); S. G. Fisher, *The True Benjamin Franklin* (1889); P. L. Ford, *The Many-Sided Franklin* (1899); J. C. Oswald, *Benjamin Franklin Self-Revealed* (1917); M. R. Eiselen, *Franklin's Political Theories* (1928); Bernard Faÿ, *Franklin, Apostle of Modern Times* (1929); Carl Van Doren, *Benjamin Franklin* (1938). The detailed article in the *Dictionary of American Biography* by CARL BECKER has been called the best short treatment of Franklin. See BENJAMIN FRANKLIN, THE AUTOBIOGRAPHY OF.

LEWIS LEARY

Franklin, James (b. Feb. 4, 1697—d. Feb. [?], 1735), printer, editor. The half-brother of the more famous Benjamin initiated him into the business of being a printer and an editor. He founded the NEW ENGLAND COURANT (1721) and the *Rhode Island Gazette* (1732). See BOSTON GAZETTE.

Franklin Evans (1842), a novel by WALT WHITMAN. A conventional liquor reform novel of the time, this is the story of a country boy who in New York City and elsewhere suffers many torments and degradations as a result of his addiction to alcohol, but who finally reforms and settles down to an honorable life. Four years after its publication (it seems to have sold about two thousand copies) Whitman reprinted it as a serial in the Brooklyn *Eagle*, of which he was then editor. Later he concluded that preachments of this sort were out of his sphere, and he called the book "damn rot" and, says Alexander Cowie, "implied that he wrote it (partly with the inspiration of liquor) merely for the sake of the money it might bring in."

Fraternity Village. Scene of more than a hundred stories by BEN AMES WILLIAMS. Sixteen of the stories were selected by Williams for a collection called *Fraternity Village* (1949). The stories have received high praise from critics for their humanity and humor.

Fréchette, Louis [Honoré] (b. Lévis, Que., Nov. 16, 1839—d. May 31, 1908), lawyer, poet, journalist, translator. As a young man, Fréchette was an impatient student and ran away to Ogdensburg, New York, but returned almost immediately to gain a law degree at Laval University. His first volume of poems was *Mes loisirs* (1863). He contributed articles to *Le Journal* and other newspapers. In 1867 he moved to Chicago, and worked as a foreign correspondent until 1871. There he wrote *La Voix d'un exile* (1871), an attack in verse on Canadian politicians. Upon his return to Canada he became involved with politics and was elected to the federal parliament. His poetic works include *Pêle Mêle* (1876); *Les fleurs boréales* (1879); *Les oiseaux de neige* (1880); *La légende d'un peuple* (1887); *Les feuilles volantes* (1891). In 1880 the French Academy honored *Les fleurs* and *Les oiseaux* and Fréchette became Canada's first poet laureate. His prose includes *Lettres à Basile* (1872); *Originaux et détraqués* (1892); *La nöel au Canada* (1900). He was author of several plays and translated G. W. Cable's OLD CREOLE DAYS and W. D. Howells' A CHANCE ACQUAINTANCE into French. His poetry has been highly praised; it is considered to be influenced by Victor Hugo, one of his favorite authors.

Frederic, Harold (b. Utica, N.Y., Aug. 19, 1856—d. Oct. 19, 1898), novelist, newspaperman. Frederic was a serious and skillful journalist who graduated from the rough-and-tumble

of political reporting in upper New York state to a post as London correspondent of the New

York *Times*. His observations of European political affairs were highly regarded in the United States for their astuteness and for the liveliness with which they were recorded. From his youth, however, Frederic had nourished an ambition for creative writing, and he turned to fiction. He deserves to be remembered for his contributions to the early development of fictional realism in America.

Frederic's best work was done in the evocation of the remembered scenes of his youth in the Mohawk Valley. His early training in political reporting gave him a factual bent which enabled him to describe social problems convincingly. To this he added, in THE DAMNATION OF THERON WARE (1896), his best-known novel, a dash of religious controversy. His influence in breaking down the saccharine conventions of the local-colorists, who dominated American literature in the 1880's and 1890's, was an important preparation for the work of STEPHEN CRANE, FRANK NORRIS, and THEODORE DREISER.

Frederic's novels include SETH'S BROTHER'S WIFE (1887); *The Lawton Girl* (1890); IN THE VALLEY (1890); *The Return of the O'Mahoney* (1892); *The Copperhead* (1893); *Marsena, and Other Stories* (1894); *The Damnation of Theron Ware* (1896; reprinted, 1924, with an introduction by Robert Morss Lovett); *March Hares* (1896); *Gloria Mundi* (1898); *The Market Place* (1899).

Freedom of the Will, The (1754), a theological treatise by JONATHAN EDWARDS in which he examines the psychology of desire and the interrelationship between the emotions and the will. V. L. Parrington calls the book not only Edwards' "most important contribution to theology, but the last great defense of the conservatism that was stifling the intellectual life of New England." To Thomas H. Johnson the treatise "is a courageous facing of the rigors of existence, one that avoids the cosmic optimism of thinking mere flawless regularity is enough."

Freeman, Douglas Southall (b. Lynchburg, Va., May 16, 1886—d. June 13, 1953), editor, historian, teacher, broadcaster. Freeman won the Pulitzer Prize for his exhaustive and distinguished *Robert E. Lee* (4 v., 1934), continued in *Lee's Lieutenants* (3 v., 1942–44), then went further back in American history with a six-volume life of Washington (1948–1954). (See GEORGE WASHINGTON.) He made immense researches for these biographies during a busy career as editor of the influential Richmond *News Leader* and as a daily broadcaster. Volume 7 of the life of Washington was completed by J. A. Carroll and M. W. Ashworth (1957).

Freeman, Mary E[leanor] Wilkins (b. Randolph, Mass., Oct. 31, 1852—d. March 13, 1930), novelist, short-story writer. Born and bred in New England, Mary Wilkins was prevented from attending school regularly by ill health, but as a young girl she read so widely and so seriously that she largely overcame the deficiency of formal education. In her teens she wrote verse, contributing to ST. NICHOLAS and other magazines, and her first book, *Decorative Plaques* (1883), was a volume of poems. When her family's fortunes declined, however, she found it necessary to begin writing for money, and she quickly became one of the most successful producers of periodical fiction in the country.

In the broadest sense Miss Wilkins' subject was what has been called "the decline of New England." As free land was opened in the West after the Civil War, much of the youth of the East was drained away; the less adventurous men and the women remained behind, the types whom Miss Wilkins came to know intimately. Her heroines were, to a remarkable extent, unmarried women past fifty. It was her work to chronicle what W. F. Taylor has termed "the drab-colored annals of a folk from whom much of the more vigorous stock had been exhausted." Her stories, in consequence, are close studies of character, intimate psychological portraits, set against realistic descriptions of the New England scene.

A HUMBLE ROMANCE AND OTHER STORIES (1887) and A NEW ENGLAND NUN AND OTHER STORIES (1891) probably contain her best work, though *The Wind in the Rosebush* (1903), a collection of ghost stories, also should be mentioned. Her novels have generally not been thought quite as successful. Among them are THE REVOLT OF MOTHER (1890); *Jane Field* (1893); *Pembroke* (1894); *Jerome* (1897); *The Heart's Highway* (1900); *The Portion of Labor* (1901). Of these, the last is the best, a love story woven into a study of labor relations in a New England mill. Miss Wilkins' only play, *Giles Corey, Yeoman* (1893), was not a success.

At the age of forty-nine, in 1902, Miss Wilkins married Dr. Charles M. Freeman of Metuchen, N.J. She continued to write, but none of her later works is as important as those she published as Mary Wilkins. In 1925 she received the William Dean Howells Medal from the American Academy of Arts and Letters, and in 1926 she was elected to the National Institute of Arts and Letters, one of the first women to receive this honor. But she outlived her vogue, and died almost unnoticed. The only biography is *Mary E. Wilkins Freeman* (1956) by Edward Foster.

ELDON C. HILL

free verse, free rhyme in American poetry.
Free verse (sometimes called *vers libre*) is a literary phenomenon that has attracted wide public attention, largely within the 20th century. It is regarded as being a movement typically modern and typically American, and it is believed that if it originated at all beyond our shores, the seed came first from France. In actual fact the avoidance of mathematically accurate metrics (in rhythm, line-length, and sound repetition) which is characteristic of free verse represents a dichotomy within English poetry that is as old as English poetry itself; and so-called free verse—that is, verse of deliberately irregular pattern—can be found throughout the whole course of English literature.

During the 19th century it was mainly American poets who sounded the tocsin of revolt against the old and familiar metrics. They felt intensely that these old techniques were no longer suitable for expressing the tumultuous thoughts and bewildering emotions of a new land and a new age. Foremost in establishing new patterns were RALPH WALDO EMERSON, WALT WHITMAN, EMILY DICKINSON, and STEPHEN CRANE. Emerson placed greater emphasis on images, cadenced phrases, and rhetoric than on rhymes and meter. Whitman, though one occasionally hears the rhythms of Ossian in his poetry, was most strongly affected by the parallelistic lines of the Bible—likewise Ossian's source. Henry Seidel Canby stresses his long rolling lines, his catalogues, his exhortations, his dialogues with himself, also his "extensive, sometimes tiresome use of alliteration." Only the careless reader, moreover, can fail to note Whitman's employment of assonance and internal rhyme. On the other hand, Whitman's pattern was so loose that it encouraged discursiveness and loquacity. Emily Dickinson was in general conventional enough as far as internal rhythm, line length, and stanzaic structure went, but she boldly innovated in the kind of rhymes she employed. She continued the loosening of the bonds which Emerson began, pointing toward Stephen Crane and the Imagists. Whether Crane knew Miss Dickinson's poetry and to what extent he was influenced by the French Symbolists has been argued. His poems, all short, have a sardonic irony and a disillusioned stoicism that places them in a class apart from the free verse written since his time.

Early in the 20th century the trend toward metrical freedom reached a peak in the so-called "new poetry," in the spate of verse magazines, and particularly in the Imagist movement. A few of the poets who won renown then wrote free verse—among them CARL SANDBURG and EDGAR LEE MASTERS. The Imagist movement was both American and English, and was spawned in London between 1908 and 1912. T. E. Hulme, Richard Aldington, and F. S. Flint were the English instigators; HILDA DOOLITTLE, EZRA POUND, JOHN GOULD FLETCHER, and AMY LOWELL the American members of the partnership. They wrote in what they called "unrhymed cadence," they stressed the stripped-down and clear image, they sought to use the language of common speech. Meanwhile the "little magazines" (which, in Keith Preston's satiric quatrain, "died to make verse free") proliferated and did much to encourage experimental forms. The post-war generation—such poets as T. S. ELIOT, ARCHIBALD MACLEISH, E. E. CUMMINGS, CONRAD AIKEN, WALLACE STEVENS—emphasized the need for rigor in free verse and often returned to conventional forms, giving them new force and functional validity. (See IMAGISM.)

The purpose of verse with no fettering meter or rhyme is to give an effect of directness. But the indictment by T. S. Eliot in 1917 still holds: "*Vers libre* . . . is a battlecry of freedom, and there is no freedom in art." Writing free verse, said Eliot, is like playing tennis without a net. Unresistant material is not material for an artist, and the really noteworthy writers of "free" verse have set up for themselves disciplines of sound and rhythm as severe as any under which Chaucer, Pope, or Tennyson worked.

Fremantle, Anne (b. France, June 15, 1910—), biographer, novelist, historian, journalist, teacher. Of distinguished English parentage, Anne Fremantle had a varied career in Britain before becoming an American citizen in 1947. She was successively a book reviewer for *The New Statesman* and the London *Times,* a labor candidate for Parliament, the first *Times* correspondent to Soviet Russia, an ambulance driver in wartime London, and a broadcaster in French and German for the British Broadcasting Company. Although her earliest published work was *Poems* (1931), she is best known as a biographer and historian. Among her biographies are *George Eliot* (1931); *Loyal Enemy* (1938, a biography of Marmaduke Pickthall); *Desert Calling* (1949, a biography of Charles de Foucauld); and *This Little Band of Prophets* (1959, biographies of leaders of the Fabian movement). She edited *The Wynne Diaries* (1952); *A Treasury of Early Christianity* (1953); *The Age Of Belief* (1956); and *The Papal Encyclicals* (1957). She is also the author of two novels, *James And Joan* (1948) and *By Grace Of Love* (1957), and has been an editor for COMMONWEAL and the Catholic Book Club.

Frémont, Jessie Benton. See JOHN C. FRÉMONT.

Frémont, John C[harles] (b. Savannah, Ga., Jan. 21, 1813—d. July 13, 1890), soldier, explorer, memoirist. Frémont was the natural son of a French refugee. He turned to exploration and then to writing lively, accurate accounts of what he had discovered. Much of the land he visited was beyond the Missouri and the Mississippi. His *Report of the Exploring Expedition to the Rocky Mountains and to Oregon and Northern California* (1845) was widely read for its literary skill (due in part to the help of his wife), and the practical suggestions it gave later travelers. In 1956 Allan Nevins edited Frémont's *Narratives of Exploration and Adventure.* When attempts were made to seize California from the Mexicans and also to prevent it from falling into the hands of the British, Frémont took an active role in winning California for the United States. He quarreled with General Kearney and was court-martialed. For a brief period he was Senator from California. In 1856 he became the first Presidential candidate of the Republican party. During the Civil War, he held several military commands, but Lincoln forced him to rescind a proclamation freeing slaves that he had issued as commander of the Department of the West.

Frémont was at times very wealthy, but after the war sank into poverty. His wife, Jessie Benton Frémont, managed to support him and their family by means of her writings. She helped him with his *Memoirs* (1887), and herself wrote *The Story of the Guard: A Chronicle of the War* (1863), *A Year of American Travel* (1878), *Souvenirs of My Time* (1887), *Far West Sketches* (1890), and *The Will and The Way Stories* (1891). Frémont was finally granted a pension as a major general in the retired list, but died soon after. Mrs. Frémont died in 1902. Allan Nevins wrote the best biography of "the Pathfinder of the West" (1928). Irving Stone wove the story of the Frémonts into an excellent novel, *Immortal Wife* (1944). William Brandon wrote an exciting account, *The Men and the Mountains: Frémont's Expedition* (1955). *Exploring with Frémont: The Private Diaries of Charles Preuss, Cartographer for John C. Frémont on his First, Second and Fourth Expeditions to the Far West* (1958) was translated and edited by Erwin G. and Elisabeth K. Gudde.

French, Alice ["Octave Thanet"] (b. Andover, Mass., March 19, 1850—d. Jan. 9, 1934), novelist, short-story writer. Miss French resided for years in Iowa and Arkansas. Her well-told stories are in the "local color school" (see REGIONALISM) and are laid mostly in the villages of rural Arkansas. She had a special interest in the labor problems of her day—espousing co-operatives, however, rather than labor unions. In THE MAN OF THE HOUR (1905) she told the story of John Winslow's economic education in such a way as to defend old-fashioned "individual enterprise." Other books of hers are *Knitters in the Sun* (1887); *We All* (1888); *Stories of a Western Town* (1893); *The Heart of Toil* (1898); *A Slave to Duty and Other Women* (1898); *Stories That End Well* (1911).

French, Allen (b. Boston, Nov. 28, 1870—d. Oct. 6, 1946), writer of books for boys. His *General Gage's Informers* (1932) gave data indicating that the opening shot in the American Revolution came from an American musket. Boys enjoyed his *Sir Marrok* (1902), *The Story of Rolf and the Viking's Bow* (1904), *Friend Tim* (1906), and others.

French, Daniel Chester (b. Exeter, N.H., April 20, 1850—d. Oct. 7, 1931), sculptor. In Boston French received his first lessons and tools from May Alcott (younger sister of Louisa) and some anatomy lessons from Dr. WILLIAM RIMMER. Later he spent one month in J. Q. A. Ward's studio in New York and studied for a year in Florence under THOMAS BELL. His statue "The Minute Man" (1875) was created for the town of Concord, Mass.; this and his "Lincoln" (1922) in the Lincoln Memorial are perhaps his best-known works. Among his other creations are the statue of John Harvard (1884), at Harvard University; "The Republic," exhibited at the Chicago Exposition of 1893; and groups representing "Europe," "Asia," "Africa," and "America" (1907) at the New York Custom House.

French and Indian War[s]. A series of armed conflicts on this continent, it corresponded closely with the Seven Years' War then proceeding on European territory, and demonstrated that the greater European wars in all probability would bring about wars in North America. Four such European wars caused bloody struggles between the British and the French here, with Indian tribes playing an important role, often on the side of the French. These conflicts were: King William's War (1689–97), Queen Anne's War (1701–13), King George's War (1744–48), and the French and Indian War (1754–60). They corresponded to the War of the Grand Alliance, the War of the Spanish Succession, the War of the Austrian Succession, and the Seven Years' War in Europe.

In North America these wars decided whether England or France would rule the continent. The prize was the West—especially the Ohio Valley —and Canada. In King William's War, the British captured some important territory, failed to take Quebec, and finally gave back all they had won. In Queen Anne's War the French invaded New England, but at the end ceded important Canadian territory to England, including Acadia. In King George's War the British won some new territory, but restored it to France by treaty. Finally, in the French and Indian War the fortunes of the combatants wavered to and fro; the Battle of Quebec (1759) decided the war in favor of the British. France gave up her empire in North America (1763).

FRANCIS PARKMAN was the great historian of the French-British struggle, especially in his *Montcalm and Wolfe* (1884) and *A Half-Cen-*

tury of Conflict (1892). Cooper, in THE LAST OF THE MOHICANS (1826), THE DEERSLAYER (1841), and SATANSTOE (1845), depicted incidents of these wars. Other fiction laid in this period includes Willa Cather's SHADOWS ON THE ROCK (1931); Grace Zaring Stone's *The Cold Journey* (1934); Evelyn Eaton's *Quietly My Captain Waits* (1940); Noel Gerson's *Savage Gentleman* (1950); Arthémise Goertz's *New Heaven, New Earth* (1953); Margaret Widdemer's *The Golden Wildcat* (1954).

French influence in America. The first report of the new empire that France sought to carve for herself came from the pen of Champlain, who has been compared, both as a soldier and as a writer, to Caesar. Even more important were the reports of the Jesuit missionaries, known as *The Jesuit Relations and Allied Documents: Travels and Explorations of the Jesuit Missionaries in New France, 1610–1791*, translated into English under the editorship of Reuben Gold Thwaites (73 v., 1896–1901). Some of these had appeared in France as early as 1632; and some of the writers showed a distinguished command of language. Other accounts were written by members of the Franciscan order. Best known of these was Father Louis Hennepin's *Description de la Louisiane* (1683), which ran to thirty-five editions in five languages.

From a layman, Louis-Armand de Lorn d'Arce, Baron de Lahontan, came a remarkable and influential work, *Nouveaux Voyages* (2 v., 1703), which was translated into English in the year of its publication and has been reissued in more than fifty editions in five languages. Lahontan observed the Indian and proceeded to philosophize about his nobility in a fashion that is still popular. French critics have pointed out that Montesquieu and Rousseau drew inspiration from Lahontan's "noble savage," Adario, and from the Jesuit observers. The history of the French struggle with the British has been best told in books by FRANCIS PARKMAN. He wrote of the endeavor of the Jesuits to convert the Indians and the vast contributions of French priests in the discovery and exploration of the West, the establishment of a régime in Canada, the half-century of conflict with the British.

The French lost their empire around 1763, but there remained to them in the New World, besides the small possessions of French Guiana and the French West Indies, two large areas of influence: French Canada and Louisiana. French Canada remained inveterately French. Similarly Louisiana continues to offer examples of French folkways and language survivals. The French element of the population, calling itself Creole, was welded into a self-conscious unity by the increasing incursion of Anglo-Saxons from the North. During the first half of the 19th century the most important Creole writers appeared: CHARLES ÉTIENNE ARTHUR GAYARRÉ (1805–1895), who wrote histories, among them a *Histoire de la Louisiane* (1846–47); the two brothers FRANÇOIS-DOMINIQUE ROUQUETTE

(1810–1890) and ADRIEN-EMMANUEL ROUQUETTE (1813–1887), who wrote lyrics idealizing nearby Choctaw Indians; and CHARLES TESTUT (1819?–1892?), who wrote historical novels.

There has been a constant flow of intelligent observers from France whose reports on the United States have sometimes exerted marked influence in this country. Pierre François Xavier de Charlevoix included such observations in his *Histoire de la Nouvelle France* (1744), and this section of his book appeared in an English translation (2 v., 1761) as *Journal of a Voyage to North America*. Jacques Pierre Brissot de Warville published a sympathetic account of his *Nouveau Voyage dans les États-Unis de l'Amérique* (3 v., 1791), two volumes of which were translated by Joel Barlow (1792); and Ferdinand M. Bayard wrote *Voyage dans l'Interieur des États-Unis* (1797). CHATEAUBRIAND visited the United States in 1791 and recorded his impressions in several romantic novels: *Atala* (1801); *René* (1802); *Les Natchez* (1826). Michel Chevalier published (1834) a book of his observations that were rendered into English (1839) as *Society, Manners, and Politics in the U.S.* Guillaume Tell Poussin wrote *De La Puissance Américaine* (2 v., 1843) and Louis Xavier Eyma wrote *Excentricités Américaines* (1860). Philarète Chasles published in 1851 a collection of his essays taken mainly from the *Revue des Deux Mondes—Études sur la Littérature et les Moeurs des Anglo-Américains au XIXᵉ Siècle*. To these books should be added the famous writings of the French-born St. Jean de Crèvecœur. Most important is, of course, COUNT ALEXIS DE TOCQUEVILLE's *De la Démocratie en Amérique* (2 v., 1835; 2 supplemental v., 1840); the best English translation is Phillips Bradley's (2 v., 1945). De Tocqueville showed an astonishing insight into American history and destiny; a century later, his prescience seemed unique.

Many other French writings influenced American thought, even though their authors never visited America. Montesquieu (1689–1755) unquestionably affected the thought of the American patriots; later, the ideas of Rousseau played a greater role. Subsequent French reformers who were influential in the United States include François Fourier, Étienne Cabet, and Auguste Comte.

In more distinctly literary realms, French naturalism found an echo in the writings of Stephen Crane, Hamlin Garland, Frank Norris, Theodore Dreiser, and others. In poetry the Parnassians (*e.g.*, Leconte de Lisle, Sully Prudhomme, Paul Verlaine) and a little later the Symbolists (Stephen Mallarmé, Maurice Maeterlinck, *et al.*) exerted a powerful influence in all the Americas. French culture affected Latin America from the very beginning, and the influence is still felt there. The intellectuals of Spanish and Portuguese descent have found France more of a spiritual home than the lands from which their ancestors had come. In literature, French models were followed more often than Spanish.

Americans have frequently gone to Paris to write, especially after World War I. Paris has been the scene of several American masterpieces, as Henry James's *The Ambassadors* (1903), Ernest Hemingway's *The Sun Also Rises* (1926), and Elliot Paul's *The Last Time I Saw Paris* (1942), as well as the amusing reminiscences contained in Cornelia Otis Skinner and Emily Kimbrough's *Our Hearts Were Young and Gay* (1942).

Freneau, Philip [Morin] (b. New York City, Jan. 2, 1752—d. Dec. 18, 1832), poet. Freneau was the son of Pierre Fresneau, of Huguenot ancestry, and Agnes Watson Fresneau, of a Scotch family long settled in New Jersey. His

boyhood was spent at Mount Pleasant (now Matawan), N.J., where he was educated at home and in private schools; at the age of sixteen he entered the College of New Jersey (now Princeton) as a sophomore, in the same class with JAMES MADISON and HUGH HENRY BRACKENRIDGE. The three collaborated in literary exercises, producing a collection of versified *Satires Against the Tories,* and Brackenridge joined Freneau in composing both an embryonic novel, *Father Bombo's Pilgrimage,* and a longer, more serious commencement poem, *The Rising Glory of America* (1771), published anonymously a year later. After graduating, Freneau turned briefly to schoolteaching and the study of theology. He published a volume of poems called *The American Village* (1772), which "was damn'd by all good and judicious judges," the poet said, lamenting that "my name was on the title page." He signed his name to no other writing for fourteen years.

At the outbreak of revolutionary activities,

Freneau was in New York turning out caustic satirical poems, such as *General Gage's Soliloquy* (1775) and *General Gage's Confession* (1775). Then, after involvement in a bitter exchange of versified insults, he left America in 1776 for two idyllic years in the Caribbean, chiefly on the island of St. Croix. There he wove the tropic splendors around him into a romantic, descriptive poem, THE BEAUTIES OF SANTA CRUZ (1776), while at the same time he fumbled through a funereal philosophic poem called THE HOUSE OF NIGHT (1776), which may have been an attempt to rationalize his flight from revolutionary activities. In 1778 he returned to his homeland, probably in response to the news of intense fighting there, but was captured en route by the British. He was released just in time to find his native fields devastated by the Battle of Monmouth.

Touched now by the reality of war, Freneau henceforth devoted himself wholeheartedly to the Revolution. He immediately became a militiaman, a privateer who ran supplies through the British blockade, and a writer of patriotic verse for Brackenridge's short-lived *United States Magazine* (1779). When captured again, in May, 1780, and incarcerated on the prison ships in New York harbor, his blood rose hotly at the treatment given prisoners of war. Released in July, he vowed forevermore to keep his satirical arrows flint-sharp against the British "hellhounds." He dashed off his denunciatory THE BRITISH PRISON-SHIP (1780), as vitriolic a poem of hate as was ever produced in America. He went to Philadelphia, where he worked for a while as a clerk in the post office, then became an editor of the patriotic *Freeman's Journal,* the columns of which he filled with sustained invective against the enemy, earning his sobriquet as "The Poet of the American Revolution."

When the war was over Freneau found himself increasingly involved in petty political bickering in Pennsylvania, and in 1785 he threw up his pen in disgust and turned, as he had ten years before, to the sea. For six years he was a sea captain of coastal vessels, plying between New York, Philadelphia, and Charleston, becoming increasingly popular for the lightly satirical poems he contributed to newspapers in whatever port he found himself. *The Jug of Rum, The Virtue of Tobacco, The Pilot of Hatteras* were among his best-known works of this period, reprinted in papers up and down the coast. The verse was flippant, humorous, critical, always good-humored. His most noteworthy poems, however, were works of romantic fancy that were less popular in his own time.

After his marriage in 1790 to Eleanor Forman, Freneau abandoned the sea to become editor of the New York *Daily Advertiser.* In the autumn of 1791, after and perhaps as a result of his appointment by Jefferson to a post as translator in the State Department, he established the NATIONAL GAZETTE in Philadelphia. Encouraged by Jefferson, aided by Madison and other prominent Republicans, he launched into bitter attacks on the policies of such Federalists as Alexander Hamilton and John Adams, becoming such an irritation to the administration that Washington called him "that rascal Freneau," though Jefferson loyally maintained that he had saved our constitution "when it was galloping fast into monarchy."

The yellow fever epidemic of 1793, together with the effective opposition of the Hamilton-supported GAZETTE OF THE UNITED STATES, put an end to Freneau's activities as a liberal journalist in the national capital. He returned to Monmouth to found the *Jersey Chronicle* (1795–96), in which he continued advocacy of Republican principles. That paper failing, he settled again in New York as editor of the *Time-Piece and Literary Companion* (1797–98) until the Sedition Law, in its turn, put a stop to his freely expressed attacks and forced him again to his family home in New Jersey. In retirement there, he contributed a series of essays to the Philadelphia *Aurora* over the signature of "Robert Slender" (1799–1801), a simple countryman who knew nothing of politics except what he read in his newspaper. With the election of Jefferson in 1800, Freneau apparently felt that his contribution to independence in America was completed. His advocacy of the rights of the common man had made him enemies, had interfered time and again with the progress of his literary career. Somewhat embittered, he retired to private life and rejected offers of political appointment. He discouraged a movement among his farmer neighbors who wished to send him to Congress. After 1803 he again became a sea captain, now venturing as far as Madeira and the Azores. His last years were spent on the family acres in Monmouth, under a darkening cloud of poverty. He continued to publish his verses, during the War of 1812 and again in 1822 as he hopefully gathered materials for a projected last volume. He died of exposure at the age of eighty as he made his way homeward across the fields in a snowstorm.

Freneau's accomplishment, increasingly apparent, nevertheless fell far short of his early intention. As a young man he had dreamed of triumphs in the tradition of the great literary masters on whom he had been bred. The Virgilian, Horatian, and Miltonic qualities of much of his college verse, his verbal and metrical debts to Pope, Thomson, Gray, and others, show him as an apprentice advancing along well-worn paths, but the almost Keatsian imagery of THE POWER OF FANCY (1770) and the unresolved philosophical questioning of *The House of Night* (1779; enlarged for *Poems*, 1786) have led some critics to judge him a genuine poet in the old-world manner, thwarted in his career by the events of his lifetime. Freneau early demonstrated a quick sensitivity to criticism and an irrepressible tendency to chasten and improve his critics, qualities that led him abruptly to satire and to a deep hatred of all things English. His best mature writing was done when the Revolution was over, in a simple, native idiom which sang almost self-consciously of American

men and manners or developed the natural philosophies of politics and religion that might guide rational freemen. As in his later life Freneau would wear no clothing or eat no food that was not of native origin, so in his verse he became nationalistic almost to the point of parochialism.

But for all this, and to some extent because of it, Freneau developed, not only as the outstanding poet in America who represented the transition from 18th-century traditionalism to the free-soaring romanticism of the 19th century, but also as America's first full-scale romantic poet. *The Wild Honey Suckle* (1786) and THE INDIAN BURYING GROUND (1788) break bravely from formalized poetic tradition to forecast, twelve years before Wordsworth's *Lyrical Ballads,* the renaissance of wonder which characterized the Romantic movement. As a patriotic satirist and a writer of rousing war songs, Freneau was unexcelled in his lifetime. As a commentator on the foibles of his countrymen as they struggled toward personal and corporate freedom, his newspaper verse is of major historical importance, and his prose also deserves attention, especially such essay series as *The Pilgrim* (1782–84), *Tomo Cheeki: The Creek Indian in Philadelphia* (1791–97), the letters of "Robert Slender" (1799–1801), and his occasional humorous accounts of the misadventures of "Hezekiah Salem" (1788–97), a defrocked New England deacon. As both editor and contributor, Freneau was among the first of the truly professional American journalists. See THE DYING INDIAN; THE INDIAN STUDENT.

In spite of his innovations in form and style, however, and in spite of his foreshadowing of Whitman's exuberant Americanism and his Emerson-like insistence on individualism, Freneau belonged essentially to the 18th century. His humanitarianism, his faith in the natural goodness of man, his primitivism and perfectionism, bound together by his belief that Nature, including man, was a revelation of God, were strains transplanted to America from the rich yield of the Enlightenment. His skepticism, his prejudices, his tendency to descend precipitately in argument from principle to personality, and the confused stimulation of changing standards under which he developed kept Freneau from making a synthesis which was ever satisfactory even to himself. He had few literary followers, for his lifelong quest to discover how free men could most effectively justify their right to freedom led him often to stubbornly held convictions which fitted ill with the prevailing notions of culturally ambitious and imitative early 19th-century America. He was consistent, crotchety, and contentious, even to the point of standing obstinately still while the democratic world to which he had sacrificed so much labor and talent advanced beyond him. His chief contributions as a man of letters were a dogged insistence on fundamental philosophical and political principles, an occasional lyricism which involved the use of fresh tropes and the employment of native themes, and the development of an easy colloquialism which seemed, if indeed it was not, unmistakably American. See POETRY IN THE U.S.

LEWIS LEARY

[Professor Leary's own work, *That Rascal Freneau: A Study in Literary Failure* (1941), is a standard biography of Freneau. Modern editions of Freneau's writings include *The Poems of Philip Freneau* (3 v., 1902–07), edited by Fred L. Pattee, and *The Prose of Philip Freneau* (1955), edited by Philip M. Marsh. See also Professor Leary's *The Lost Poems of Philip Freneau* (1946). An important critical work is Nelson F. Adkins' *Philip Freneau and the Cosmic Enigma* (1949).]

Frescoes for Mr. Rockefeller's City (1933), poems by ARCHIBALD MACLEISH. In these free-verse celebrations MacLeish expresses his deep but unconventional patriotism. He looks at the American landscape, considers the coming and the helpfulness of the immigrants, describes empire-building in the West by explorers and then by venal financiers, expresses his belief that Americans will cure their social ailments without doctrinaire ideology. The poems are, supposedly, panels to replace six murals that had been removed from Rockefeller Center because the artist Diego Rivera had been too outspoken in his pictorial comments on modern capitalist civilization.

Fresh the American (1881), a comedy by ARCHIBALD CLAVERING GUNTER. F. N. Fresh is an American millionaire who travels abroad and in the spirit of Mark Twain deliberately shows his defiance of European and Oriental toadyism and snobbery. His mood is mainly humorous, but he is angry when the helpless are oppressed.

Friendly Club. Two literary clubs had this name. One was founded c. 1785 in Hartford and included in its membership the writers known as the HARTFORD WITS; it went out of existence in 1807. The other was a continuation of the Philological Society of New York and took the new name in 1789. Among its members were WILLIAM DUNLAP, NOAH WEBSTER, CHARLES BROCKDEN BROWN, JAMES KENT, and RICHARD ALSOP. Dr. ELIHU HUBBARD SMITH seems to have moved in both groups.

Friendship Village (1908), stories by ZONA GALE. The narrator is a woman who goes from a large city to a small community in the Middle West (like Portage, Wis., Miss Gale's own home) and finds the people there more truly representative of America than those she had known. Often the plot problems are small social difficulties, which are treated with humor and realism. The book had several sequels.

Fries, Charles C. See AMERICAN ENGLISH GRAMMAR.

Frings, Ketti (b. Columbus, Ohio —), novelist, playwright. Ketti Frings wrote two novels, *Hold Back The Dawn* (1942) and *God's Front Porch* (1945), but she is best known as a playwright and motion-picture script writer. She composed the scenarios for *Come Back*

Little Sheba (1952); *About Mr. Leslie* (1954); *Fox Fire* (1955); and *The Shrike* (1955). Her dramatic version of Thomas Wolfe's *Look Homeward, Angel* (1957) won the Pulitzer Prize and the Drama Critics Circle Award.

Frohman, Charles (b. Sandusky, Ohio, June 17, 1860—d. May 7, 1915) and **Frohman, Daniel** (b. Sandusky, Ohio, Aug. 22, 1851—d. Dec. 26, 1940), theatrical producers. The two brothers were among the most active producers of their time, and Charles was as successful in London as in New York. Charles founded the Empire Stock Company and developed such great stage personalities as MAUDE ADAMS, JULIA MARLOWE, Elsie de Wolfe, and William Faversham. He went down with the *Luisitania*. His brother Daniel managed many New York theaters, was active in bringing ROBERT MANTELL, Henry Miller, and other actors before the public, and introduced DAVID BELASCO as a playwright.

From Here to Eternity (1951), a novel and later a movie by JAMES JONES. This long, violent book made a great sensation and became an immediate best seller. It is a story of life in the regular army before the Japanese attack at Pearl Harbor in 1941. Jones's style is vivid and fluent; some critics have compared him to Thomas Wolfe. The exceedingly salty dialogue of his soldier-characters probably accounted in part for the book's popularity. The title is from a poem by Kipling, whose *Gentlemen Rankers* are "damned from here to eternity."

Fromm, Erich (b. Germany, March 23, 1900 —), psychoanalyst, philosopher. Fromm was trained at the Universities of Heidelberg and Munich and at the Psychoanalytic Institute in Berlin. Until 1932 he worked in Frankfurt's Psychoanalytic Institute and at the Institute for Social Research at the University of Frankfurt. In 1934 he came to the United States and joined the International Institute for Social Research in New York City. He lectured at Columbia University and at Yale, and later was on the faculty of Bennington College. In 1951 he began teaching psychoanalysis at the National Autonomous University of Mexico. He has also taught psychology at Michigan State University. He has written *Escape From Freedom* (1941), an inquiry into the meaning of freedom and the social and cultural conditions which have disposed modern man to seek an escape from freedom into authoritarianism. *Man for Himself: An Inquiry into the Psychology of Ethics* (1947) is a continuation of the former work and develops the theory that man is "for himself" and must determine his own standards. His later books include *The Forgotten Language: An Introduction to the Understanding of Dreams, Fairy Tales and Myths* (1951); *The Sane Society* (1955); *The Art of Loving* (1956); *Sigmund Freud's Mission* (1959); *Zen Buddhism and Psychoanalysis* (1960); *May Man Prevail?* (1961).

From Native Roots (1949), a survey by Felix Sper. Sper examines the American regional theater, tracing it from early times to the present day. He makes an analysis of fourteen regional units and includes a bibliography of more than fifty pages. See LITTLE THEATER.

Frontenac, Comte Louis de Baude de (b. France, 1622—d. 1698), French colonial officer. Many important exploits have been ascribed to Frontenac—an expansion of French territory, conflicts with the Indians, the defense of Canada. But researches by W. J. Eccles in 1954 stripped Frontenac of his importance and showed that he was great only in the amount of his debts. An earlier account was FRANCIS PARKMAN's *Count Frontenac and New France Under Louis XIV* (1877).

frontier, the. According to Frederic L. Paxson, in his *History of the American Frontier* (1924), the American frontier "was a line, a region, or a process." The colonies along the Atlantic seaboard were the first frontier; thereafter waves of emigration spread west and southwest. The best account of these first settlers is R. V. Coleman's *The First Frontier* (1948). Thereafter, according to Ray Allen Billington and James Blaine Hedges' *Westward Expansion: A History of the American Frontier* (1949), the westward movement went ahead in two stages: trans-Appalachian, trans-Mississippian. Each stage marked a "repeated rebirth of civilization." An area of free land on the western edge of the advancing settlements tempted a stream of new settlers, attracted by the hope of economic betterment or the chance for adventure. They came as easterners, but soon had to modify their ways. Highly developed political forms gave way to simple associations of the settlers, specialized trades were found to be not so good as work accomplished by individuals and groups without much formal division of labor, complex social activities were abandoned in favor of husking bees or house raisings. Innovation, adaptability, invention, ingenuity became characteristic of frontier life. The frontier itself, in any particular place, evolved in successive stages, usually advancing from the culture of the fur trader to that of the cattleman, then perhaps to that of miners, afterward to farmers of a simple type, to be replaced perhaps by "equipped farmers" on a large scale, finally to a region with many urban dwellers. But regions differed, and often their characteristics strongly affected national as well as local politics and economy. The frontiersmen were at times romantic characters: coonskinned trappers and leather-clad "mountain men," hard-riding cowboys and bad men and vigilantes. But the true hero of the frontier, according to Billington and Hedges, "was the hardworking farmer who, ax in hand, marched ever westward until the boundaries of his nation touched the Pacific."

There have been many varying conceptions of the nature of the frontier. One judgment, spiritedly set forth by Waldo Frank in *Our America* (1919), Van Wyck Brooks in *The Ordeal of Mark Twain* (1920), and Lewis Mumford in THE GOLDEN DAY (1926), saw the frontier in its cultural and spiritual aspects as largely a product of the Puritans, and conse-

quently dour, barren, and bleak. These views were reflected in R. B. Perry's *Puritanism and Democracy* (1944), which said, "The bitterness of frontier experience has left an ineffaceable imprint on the American mind. It helps to explain that 'American malady' of joylessness to which critics such as Langdon Mitchell have referred." Against such critics Bernard De Voto vehemently inveighed in *Mark Twain's America* (1932), with its numerous sections on the rough hilarity, exuberant folk-tales, and uninhibited folk-heroes of the frontier. In particular De Voto urged that "Mark Twain was a frontier humorist. . . . From the laughter of anonymous frontier storytellers to the figure of Huckleberry Finn a clearly traced line exists, and Huckleberry Finn could have arrived along no other path." (See MARK TWAIN.) Anthologists and private collectors have found an immense literature of exploration and autobiography centered on the frontier in various ages. The distinctive humor of the frontier has been studied by such specialists as FRANKLIN J. MEINE, CONSTANCE ROURKE, WALTER BLAIR, and Moody C. Boatright. The humor of the frontier is revealed in such volumes as Thomas D. Clark's *The Rampaging Frontier* (1939) and Harold W. Thompson's *Body, Boots, and Britches* (1940).

Possibly the first great figure to write fiction about the frontier was JAMES FENIMORE COOPER, whose own early days were spent on a disappearing frontier, for which he shows a sentimental nostalgia. Several of JAMES KIRKE PAULDING's novels portray frontier life. Among other books (occasionally autobiographical) that deal with frontier life are: Timothy Flint's *George Mason, the Young Backwoodsman* (1829); Robert Montgomery Bird's NICK OF THE WOODS (1837); Emerson Bennett's *The Bandits of the Osage* (1847) and *Forest and Prairie, or, Life on the Frontier* (1860); Joseph G. Baldwin's FLUSH TIMES OF ALABAMA AND MISSISSIPPI (1853); Edward Eggleston's THE HOOSIER SCHOOLMASTER (1871); Ralph Connor's *The Sky Pilot* (1899); Winston Churchill's THE CROSSING (1904); Willa Cather's O PIONEERS (1913), MY ÁNTONIA (1918), and DEATH COMES FOR THE ARCHBISHOP (1927); Hamlin Garland's *They of the High Trails* (1916); Emerson Hough's *The Covered Wagon* (1922); Johan Bojer's *The Emigrants* (1925); Ole Edvart Rölvaag's GIANTS IN THE EARTH (1924) and PEDER VICTORIOUS (1932); ZANE GREY's *The Thundering Herd* (1925); Thomas Boyd's *Shadow of the Long Knives* (1928); Maud Hart Lovelace's *Early Candlelight* (1929); James Boyd's *The Long Hunt* (1930); Edna Ferber's *Cimarron* (1930); Elizabeth Madox Roberts' THE GREAT MEADOW (1930); Stewart Edward White's *The Long Rifle* (1932); Rose Wilder Lane's *The Hurricane* (1933); Stephen Vincent Benét's *James Shore's Daughter* (1934); Harold L. Davis' HONEY IN THE HORN (1935) and *Beulah Land* (1949); Conrad Richter's *Early Americana* (1936) and *The Fields* (1946); Felix Holt's *The Gabriel Horn* (1951); H. M. Drummond's *Hoot Owls and*

Orchids (1956). Along with these went in-numerable stories of the West and its bad men and quick-shooting sheriffs, a genre now equally popular in movies, radio, and television.

The westward movement has also been a favorite with the poets—some of them anony-mous, as in the numerous cowboy ballads. Among those who have written about the West and the frontier are HAROLD L. DAVIS, BRET HARTE, VACHEL LINDSAY, JOAQUIN MILLER, JOHN G. NEIHARDT, CARL SANDBURG, LEW SARETT, Alfred B. Street, and WALTER STANLEY CAMPBELL ("Stanley Vestal"). Perhaps the finest poetry on the pioneer and the frontier was that written by WALT WHITMAN, particularly his SONG OF THE BROAD-AXE (1856) and PIO-NEERS! O PIONEERS! (1865). The great classic of personal experience on the frontier is Mark Twain's ROUGHING IT (1872). Two good his-tories are Frederick J. Turner's *The Frontier in American History* (1920) and Lucy Lockwood Hazard's *The Frontier in American Literature* (1927). Also see CLAUDIA LARS. Recent his-torical studies include: *American Frontier* (1955) by Nelson Keyes; *Frontier America* (1959) by Thomas D. Clark.

Frontier in American History, The (1920), essays by FREDERICK JACKSON TURNER. This volume collected a number of papers that Turner had been writing from the time when he first presented his revolutionary address on "The Significance of the American Frontier" (Amer-ican Historical Society, July 12, 1893; pub-lished, 1894). Turner believed in particular that the form and spirit of American democracy were a direct product of the frontier with its free lands, its stimulation of ingenuity and resource-fulness, its dominant individualism. This "fron-tier hypothesis," as it has been called, was at once recognized as an historical idea of great importance and made Turner, then and there-after at the University of Wisconsin, a national figure. In *Frontier Folkways* (1935) James G. Leyburn challenged the Turner thesis; it has also been challenged by LOUIS B. WRIGHT in his *Culture on the Moving Frontier* (1955), in which he proves that the frontier type of society strongly followed the Anglo-Saxon tradition of English law, English literature, the English lan-guage, British religion and customs, and so established the pattern of American society. Other discussions are H. N. Smith's VIRGIN LAND (1950); Harvey Wish's *Society and Thought in Early America* (1950); W. P. WEBB's *The Great Frontier* (1952); E. S. Wallach's *The Great Reconnaissance* (1955).

Frontier Index, The. A strange "press on wheels," founded in May, 1866, at Kearney City, Neb., by Frederick Kemper Freeman (1841–1928) and operated by him and his brother Lewis. It moved westward with the steady advance of the Union Pacific Railroad, appearing triweekly in various towns in Ne-braska, Wyoming, and Utah. In Corinne, Utah, it was renamed *Freeman's Farmer* and halted its westward progress.

Front Page, The (1928), a comedy of news-paper life by BEN HECHT and CHARLES MAC-ARTHUR. Both Hecht and MacArthur were alumni of Chicago journalism and are believed to have taken Walter Howey of the Chicago City Press as the model for the play's trumpet-toned managing editor, Walter Burns. The play, Brooks Atkinson says, "bowled over the public with the excitement and sting of a callous news-paper story." Critics agree generally that the play was realistic in its profanity and many of its details, but was essentially a romantic pres-entation of the newspaper world. It was revived in 1946.

Frost, A[rthur] B[urdett] (b. Philadelphia, Jan. 17, 1851—d. June 22, 1928), illustrator, cartoonist. Frost was a favorite magazine and book illustrator. He produced several collections of his own, including *Stuff & Nonsense* (1884), *The Bull Calf and Other Tales* (1892), and *Carlo* (1913), but he was best known for his humorous contributions to *Life* and for his il-lustrations for books by Mark Twain, H. C. Bunner, John Kendrick Bangs, and, above all, Joel Chandler Harris. Henry W. Lanier wrote a life of *A. B. Frost, the American Sportsman's Artist* (1933).

Frost, Frances [Mary] (b. St. Albans, Vt., Aug. 3, 1905—d. Feb. 11, 1959), poet, nov-elist, newspaper writer, teacher. A frequent contributor to magazines and newspapers, Miss Frost won a reputation particularly for her grace-ful poems of New England scenery and life. Among her collections of verse are: *Hemlock Wall* (1929); *Blue Harvest* (1931); *These Acres* (1932); *Pool in the Meadow* (1933); *Road to America* (1937); *Christmas in the Woods* (1942); *Mid-Century* (1946); *This Star of Wonder* (1953); *This Rowdy Heart* (1954). Among her novels are *Innocent Summer* (1936) and *Uncle Snowball* (1940). She is also known for her children's books, such as the series about Windy Foot.

Frost, Robert [Lee] (b. San Francisco, March 26, 1874—d. Jan. 29, 1963), poet. It might be said of Frost that he was born first in San Fran-cisco and again in New England, where he came to live after his father's death in 1885. If a great poet can be associated with a region, Frost must be placed in New England; but the fullest mean-ing of his poetry speaks for the nation and for mankind as a whole.

Frost's early life was not marked with notable poetic success. After two beginnings at college, first Dartmouth, then Harvard, he farmed for five years (1900–05) at Derry, New Hampshire, and held a series of jobs, from bobbin boy at the mills of Lawrence, Massachusetts, to editor and schoolteacher. Through all these changes, Frost's underlying determination was to be a poet; however, from his first published poem, "My Butterfly" (1894), until 1912 he saw only fourteen poems in print.

His determination finally caused him to leave this country for England, where he could make poems "without further scandal in the family." During his three-year stay in England, Frost found professional esteem and friendship with

Rupert Brooke, Lascelles Abercrombie, Wilfrid Gibson, and the critic Edward Thomas. He found a voice and a vision of his country from this new perspective, and wrote about New England in England. His first two books, A

Boy's WILL (1913) and *North of Boston* (1914), were published there.

In 1915 Frost returned to America. That year saw the publication of an American edition of *North of Boston*. His already significant English following was to be matched and exceeded by a growing American one. Rather than identify himself with any of the popular poetic movements in America, most notably the "new" poetry, he returned to a farm in New Hampshire and continued to write about country things. Frost's regionalism is of a special variety; he finds meaning through experience in New England, but that meaning is not purely local; he speaks of the individual yet universal concerns of man's role in the world and of the spiritual and physical demands made upon him. His attitude toward the world puts him in the tradition of Ralph Waldo Emerson and Emily Dickinson; all three try to penetrate the veil of natural fact for the spiritual truth which it reflects. It is not surprising that his most frequent themes in his attempt to deal with this nature-spirit dualism are the juxtaposition of man and nature.

Frost usually treats the theme of man's position in the world of nature in such a way as to present both the human viewer and the natural object as distinct but complementary entities; thus the two pairs of lovers—man and woman, buck and doe—in "Two Look at Two" are im-

plicitly compared to one another, although separate and existing, both literally and figuratively, each pair in its own pasture. Similarly, in "Tree at My Window" the poet and the tree figuratively see each other in a reciprocal relationship that is still separated by the man's concern with inner, and the tree with outer, weather. The theme of loneliness is especially evident in "The Runaway," "Bereft," "Desert Places," and "The Sound of Trees." Often man is compelled to adjust to some permanent aspect of life, such as a mountain or even death, so that his isolation is made manifest.

The need of balance between the outer world of experience and the inner world of vision is manifest in BIRCHES, in which the poet desires both to climb toward heaven and to be swung back to earth as the birch dips with his weight. This tension between ascent and descent, inner and outer is again present in WEST-RUNNING BROOK: a contrary thing in itself in a region where brooks run east to the sea, the west-running brook becomes a symbol of man and of all natural things that have a tendency to turn backward upon themselves, throwing, like the brook, a white wave back in the direction of their source.

Frost's poetic development is seen as early as *North of Boston*, in which all the poems are on New England themes and the dramatic cast of his verse is clear. The symbolic presentation of "The Mountain" is early evidence of the tendencies discussed above. His next important book of poems was MOUNTAIN INTERVAL (1916), a book of short poems in which the speaker is usually confronted by nature and reacts with wonder. The drama of the poems is created without the help of dialogue; an object seems to pose a question, such as the bird in "The Oven Bird," and the poet knows the answer.

In 1923 Frost published NEW HAMPSHIRE, which marks the overt entry of a satiric tone into his poems. For the first time Frost is conscious of himself as a poet; this consciousness forms the subject of some of the poems, for example, "I Will Sing You One-O" and "An Empty Threat." The book includes many poems in his simpler manner, such as the popular STOPPING BY WOODS ON A SNOWY EVENING. *West-Running Brook* (1928), Frost's next book of poems, was followed by A FURTHER RANGE (1936), in which the poems are divided into poems "Taken Doubly" and poems "Taken Singly." This volume marks an obvious turn of Frost's mind to matters more abstract and philosophical.

As Frost entered old age, his concerns became more abstract and his metaphysics more obvious. The tendencies which were submerged in his earlier verse came to the surface in A MASQUE OF REASON (1945), a verse drama on Job, God, and the Devil, and A MASQUE OF MERCY (1947), again on the relationship of man and God. Frost began to ask ultimate questions in an outspoken manner; he became less the poet of nature and more the poet of mind.

Technically, Frost's poetry is built on what he calls "sentence sounds" derived from colloquial speech; the accents and tones of the sentence sounds, combined with the beat of a metric pattern, create a tension within the line that is the structural counterpart of the metaphysical tension of ideas found in his best poems. Although he is equally at home with the short lyric, much of his poetry resembles the dramatic monologue perfected by Browning, or departs from Browning's model into the dialogue of THE DEATH OF THE HIRED MAN or "The Witch of Coos."

Frost was awarded the Pulitzer Prize for *New Hampshire* (1924), *Collected Poems* (1931), *A Further Range* (1937), and *A Witness Tree* (1943). Unlike most serious poets, he has found a wide popular audience, possibly because of the rustic and simple-seeming appearance of his work. His poetry, however, like Emily Dickinson's, is full of subtle ironies, terse, immediate images, and many levels of meaning. His poetry includes *The Lovely Shall be Choosers* (1929); *The Lone Striker* (1933); *Steeple Bush* (1947); *Complete Poems* (1949); THE ROAD NOT TAKEN (1951); *Hard Not to be King* (1951); and *Aforesaid* (1954). Critical works on Frost include Reginald L. Cook's *Dimensions of Robert Frost* (1958); John F. Lynen's *Pastoral Art of Robert Frost* (1960); George W. Nitchie's *Human Values in the Poetry of Robert Frost* (1960); Elizabeth S. Sergeant's *Robert Frost: The Trial by Existence* (1960). See also THE AXE HELVE and MENDING WALL.

Fruitlands. A utopian society founded by AMOS BRONSON ALCOTT at Harvard, Mass., in 1842; it went out of existence the next year. Alcott envisaged a society in which all family life would disappear in a communal physical, mental, and spiritual development. The members were to live on a vegetarian diet, principally apples; to do all manual tasks in common; and to dwell in sweetness and light. Paul Elmer More described the Fruitlands colonists as "altruistic humbugs," and Louisa May Alcott pictured them with gentle humor in *Transcendental Wild Oats*, a fictional sketch in *Silver Pitchers* (1876). C. E. Sears wrote an account of *Bronson Alcott's Fruitlands* (1915).

Fuchs, Daniel (b. New York City, June 25, 1909—   ), novelist, short story writer, scenarist. Though he had been known for a number of years as a short-story writer for magazines such as *The New Yorker*, *Esquire*, *Collier's*, and the *Saturday Evening Post*, it was not until 1961 that Fuchs' three excellent early novels were rediscovered and republished in one volume called *Three Novels*. The titles were: *Summer in Williamsburg* (1934); *Homage to Blenholt* (1936); and *Low Company* (1937). All dealt with Jewish slum life on New York's LOWER EAST SIDE, with the result that Fuchs was compared to Nelson Algren, James T. Farrell, and Saul Bellow. Critic Robert Gorham Davis praised Fuchs' work in these novels for "its own distinct individuality and particularly its own brand of humor."

Fuess, Claude M[oore] (b. Waterville, N.Y., Jan. 12, 1885—   ), teacher, historian, biographer, editor. In addition to long service as headmaster in Phillips Academy, Andover, Mass., Fuess wrote numerous sound biographies, among them lives of *Caleb Cushing* (1923); *Rufus Choate* (1927); *Daniel Webster* (1930); *Carl Schurz* (1932); *Calvin Coolidge* (1940); *Stanley King of Amherst* (1954); also *Andover: Symbol of New England* (1959); *Creed of a Schoolmaster* (1939). He edited several school texts and an excellent anthology, *Unseen Harvests: A Treasury for Teachers* (1945). His autobiography, *Independent Schoolmaster*, was published in 1952.

Fugitives, The. A group of southern Agrarian writers, critics, and poets who published the magazine, *The Fugitive* (1922–25). See NEW CRITICISM; I'LL TAKE MY STAND.

Fuller, Henry B[lake] ["Stanton Page"] (b. Chicago, Jan. 9, 1857—d. July 28, 1929), novelist, poet, critic. He turned early to novel writing and was successful from the start with a story laid in Italy, *The Chevalier of Pensieri-Vani* (1890). His best-known book was THE CLIFF-DWELLERS (1893), a novel about Chicago, the first notable American city novel. Among others that he wrote are *The Chatelaine de la Trinité* (1892); *With the Procession* (1895); *From the Other Side* (1898); *A Sicilian Romance* (1900); *Under the Skylights* (1901); *Waldo Trench and Others* (1908); and the posthumously published *Not on the Screen* (1930). Fuller was also book critic for Chicago newspapers and was active in Chicago's literary circles, especially those engaged in making *Poetry* the most important magazine of its kind in the country. Fuller himself issued two collections of verse, *The New Flag* (1899) and *Lines Long and Short* (1917). He was one of the forerunners of naturalism in the United States, particularly in *The Cliff-Dwellers*, which portrays the greed and futility of a material civilization. Edmund Wilson pronounces Fuller "superior as a novelist of manners to W. D. Howells," and Howells himself praised him highly. Alfred Kazin considers him "a graceful and impressionistic artist who was a realist *malgré lui*."

Fuller, Iola. Author of THE LOON FEATHER.

Fuller, [Sarah] Margaret, Marchesa Ossoli (b. Cambridgeport, Mass., May 23, 1810—d. June 19, 1850), teacher, translator, poet, transcendentalist, editor, critic, writer on social questions. Educated by her intellectual father as if she were a boy (a horrifying procedure in those days), Miss Fuller surpassed in scholarship and in critical acumen most of the men of her day; and they almost unanimously disliked her intensely. She had a gift for languages and knew many well. She taught school for a while, and held forth every Saturday afternoon in "conversations" that spellbound Boston intellectuals. She translated vigorously from the German; her admiration of Goethe was infectious. With Emerson she started THE DIAL (July, 1840–April, 1844) as a medium for the transcendentalists; it was vigorous only as long as she was editor. She became a powerful critic of literature on the New York *Tribune*. Her unfavorable remarks on Lowell and Longfellow especially enraged some of the Boston Brahmins. Yet Poe praised her ability as a critic and her freedom from adulation, although he censured her grammatical

and stylistic carelessness. He satirized her in *How to Write a Blackwood Article* (1838).

In 1846 came the turning point in Miss Fuller's career: she fulfilled an ardent wish and went to Europe, where she mingled with the leading authors of the day, showed her deep interest in Italy's endeavors to win freedom, met Giovanni Angelo, Marquis Ossoli, who was ten years younger than she was, and became his mistress. They had a son, and family life was rather difficult. They were later married, although the exact date of the marriage is unknown. She became very active in the hospitals when fighting began in Italy, and began to write a book on Guiseppe Mazzini (1805–1872) and the war of liberation. In May, 1850, the family set sail for New York. Their vessel was shipwrecked off Fire Island; the body of the infant son was washed ashore. The other bodies were never recovered.

During her lifetime Miss Fuller published a perceptive travel book on the Middle West, *Summer on the Lakes* (1844); a volume attesting to her keen and constant interest in feminism, *Woman in the 19th Century* (1845); and *Papers on Literature and Art* (1846). Posthumously appeared *At Home and Abroad* (1856) and memoirs called *Life Without and Life Within* (1859). Horace Greeley published her complete works in 1869.

Lowell disliked her intensely, and gave considerable space to her in A FABLE FOR CRITICS, stressing her spitefulness and her egotism. During the BROOK FARM experiment Hawthorne knew her well, and he vented his anger against her in several places—above all in THE BLITHE-DALE ROMANCE where some of her traits seem to appear in the character of Zenobia. On the other side of the ocean Carlyle made some puzzled references to her. In his *Journal* he relates: "Yesternight there came a bevy of Americans from [introduced by] Emerson, one Margaret Fuller the chief figure of them—a strange, lilting, lean old maid, not nearly such a bore as I expected." To him is attributed a comment on Miss Fuller's sublime announcement, "I accept the universe!" Carlyle said, "By God! She'd better!" Yet Carlyle also thought her courage "high and clear" and called her "a truly heroic mind, altogether unique, so far as I know, among the writing women of this generation." Carlyle's friend Emerson both respected and feared her; and he said about her in his *Journal*: "Strange, cold-warm, attractive-repelling conversation with Margaret, whom I always admire, and sometimes love; yet whom I freeze and who freezes me to silence when we promise to come nearest." Among modern critics, V. L. Parrington said, "Her tragic life, despite its lack of solid accomplishment, was an epitome of the great revolt of the New England mind against Puritan asceticism and Yankee materialism."

Despite the comparative unimportance of her writings, much literature has gathered around Miss Fuller—naturally enough, in view of her paradoxical and dynamic personality, her intimate connection with the great of her time, and her tragic death. Nason Wade wrote on her as *Margaret Fuller: Whetstone of Genius* (1940) and edited her *Writings* (1941); Madeleine B. Stern wrote a fictional but accurate biography of her (1942), to succeed earlier lives by Julia Ward Howe (1883), T. W. Higginson (1884), Margaret Bell (1920), and Katharine Anthony (1931). There are extensive collections of Margaret Fuller manuscripts in the Boston Public Library and the Harvard College Library. See TRANSCENDENTALISM.

Fulton, Robert (b. Lancaster Co., Pa., Nov. 14, 1765—d. Feb. 24, 1815), engineer. Fulton started as a painter, devoted himself to mechanical and engineering activities after 1793. He made several important inventions, but is particularly renowned for his application of steam to navigation. He succeeded with the *Clermont,* which steamed up the Hudson to Albany and back (Aug. 17–22, 1807). Fulton thereafter designed many steamboats, also a torpedo boat; and he invented a submarine, but could interest no government in it. He had great faith in canals and wrote a *Treatise on the Improvement of Canal Navigation* (1796).

Function of the Poet, The (delivered as a lecture, 1855; published, 1929) by JAMES RUSSELL LOWELL. Lowell sees no reason "why our continent should not sing as well as the rest"; and he views American history as a great epic, "whose books are States, and which is written on this continent from Maine to California." In general the lecture urged that the American scene was sufficient inspiration for any poet.

Furlong, Charles Wellington (b. Cambridge, Mass., Dec. 13, 1874—   ), army officer, explorer, writer, art instructor. Furlong's career led him into many picturesque and heretofore inaccessible parts of the earth: he traveled by canoe up the Orinoco, made ethnological expeditions in various parts of South America; broke trail across the Andes, and hunted treasure in Bolivia. He was the first outsider to set foot inside the French Guiana penal colony; a chronicle of his visit published in *Harper's* magazine in 1911 was one of the factors which eventually contributed to the dissolution of the colony. From 1896 to 1904 he was art instructor at Cornell University. During thirty-one years of service with the United States army, he prepared a number of military handbooks. His books include: *Gateway to the Sahara* (1909); *Tripoli in Barbary* (1911); and *Let 'Er Buck* (1921).

Furnas, Joseph Chamberlain (b. Indianapolis, Ind., Nov. 24, 1905—   ), writer, magazine reporter. Furnas graduated from Harvard College in 1927, and began free-lance writing in 1931. *And Sudden Death* (1935), an article written for *Scholastic* magazine and later expanded with Ernest M. Smith for the *Reader's Digest*, attracted attention to his reportorial ability and was widely reprinted. *The Prophet's Chamber* appeared in 1935 and *Many People Prize It* in 1937. *How America Lives* (1941) was a study of sixteen typical American families written in collaboration with the editors of the *Ladies' Home Journal*. His next book, *Anatomy of Paradise* (1948), about Hawaii and the South Sea Islands, combined a popular presentation with scholarly footnotes, index, and references. It received the Anisfield-Wolf award for a nonfiction contribution to improved interracial relations. *Voyage to Windward* (1951) is a life of Robert Louis Stevenson. *Goodbye to Uncle Tom* (1956) examines *Uncle Tom's Cabin* and its deleterious influence on the popular image of the Negro. *The Road to Harper's Ferry* (1959) is a detailed account of John Brown and the "secret six" who accompanied him on his raid.

Furnas' articles have appeared in many magazines, including *The Saturday Evening Post*.

Furness, Horace Howard (b. Philadelphia, Nov. 2, 1833—d. Aug. 13, 1912), lawyer, scholar, editor. Beginning in 1866 Furness devoted himself to the preparation of the *Variorum Shakespeare*, a monumental series which opened with the publication of *Romeo and Juliet* (1871). Numerous volumes appeared until the death of Furness, and the work was then continued, but not completed, by his son, **Horace Howard Furness, Jr.** (b. Philadelphia, Jan. 24, 1865—d. April 15, 1930). The series was originally a project of the Shakespearean Society of Philadelphia (founded 1851). Furness himself is said to have been inspired by FANNY KEMBLE's Shakespearean readings. It was Furness, says Henry Seidel Canby, "whose editorial note on a lumbering comment by a German scholar was only a six-word quotation from Lawrence Sterne: '"My God!" said my Uncle Toby.'" Van Wyck Brooks calls Furness "an artist among scholars." The Horace Howard Furness Memorial Library of Shakespeareana is now a part of the library of the University of Pennsylvania.

Further Range, A (1936), a collection of poems by ROBERT FROST. The verses in this gathering include a large number of humorous and satirical pieces, also a group of epigrams called "Ten Mills." The politics of the day greatly interested the poet; the longest poem in the book, *Build Soil*, has a note by the poet saying that it was "delivered at Columbia, May 31, 1932, before the national party conventions of that year." "The desire to sermonize had grown on him," Willard Thorp commented on the book.

Fyles, Franklin (b. Troy, N.Y., [?], 1847—d. July 4, 1911), drama critic, playwright. Fyles, who covered the theater in New York for the *Sun* from 1885 to 1903, wrote a book on *The Theater and Its People* (1900), also several plays: THE GIRL I LEFT BEHIND ME (with DAVID BELASCO, 1893); *Cumberland '61* (1897); *Kit Carson* (1901).

G

Gabriel, Gilbert W[olf] (b. Brooklyn, N.Y., Jan. 18, 1890—d. Sept. 3, 1952), newspaperman, critic, lecturer, novelist. Gabriel was literary editor and then music critic of the New York *Sun*, later drama critic of various New York papers, of *The New Yorker*, and other magazines. He served in the army in both World Wars; his novel, *I Got a Country* (1945) was based on his experiences while serving in Alaska; *Love from London* on experiences in that town (1944). He collaborated on a play, *Clap Hands* (1934), and wrote several other books, including *The Seven-Branched Candlestick* (1916); *Brownstone Front* (1924); *Famous Pianists and Composers* (1928); *I, James Lewis* (1931); *Great Fortune* (1933).

Gabriel, Ralph Henry (b. Reading, N.Y., April 29, 1890—   ), teacher, historian. A graduate of Yale in 1913, Gabriel began teaching there two years later and became associated with that university. He was editor of the notable PAGEANT OF AMERICA (15 v., 1925–29) and himself wrote two of the volumes. A member of the U.S. National Commission for UNESCO, he was the U.S. Delegate to the tenth conference in 1958 and became Professor of American Civilization at the School of International Service, American University, Washington, D.C. He also wrote: *The Evolution of Long Island* (1921, reprinted 1960); *Toilers of Land and Sea* (1926); *The Lure of the Frontier* (1926); *The Course of American Democratic Thought* (1940, rev. ed. 1956); *Elias Boudinot, Cherokee, and His America* (1941); *Main Currents in American History* (1942); *Religion and Learning at Yale* (1958); *Traditional Values in American Life* (1960).

Gabriel Conroy (1876), a novel by BRET HARTE. The longest of Harte's fictional writings, it gives a vivid picture of mining conditions during the early days of the gold rush. Among the characters is Harte's famous gambler, JACK HAMLIN.

Gadsden Purchase, The. Captain James Gadsden (1788–1858), grandson of Christopher Gadsden (1724–1805) of Revolutionary War fame, was minister to Mexico in 1853–54, and in the former year negotiated the purchase by the United States from Mexico of a tract of land, about 45,000 square miles in extent, located in what is now New Mexico and Arizona. An account of the transaction and the territory is given in P. N. Garber's *The Gadsden Purchase* (1923).

Gág, Wanda (b. New Ulm, Minn., March 11, 1893—d. June 27, 1946), artist, illustrator, translator, author of books for children. Miss Gág (pronounced Gog), of Czech descent, made her way from an environment of extreme poverty into a position of leadership among the artists of this country; her work found permanent exhibition in the Metropolitan Museum of Art and in many other galleries. In 1928 she published her first book for children, *Millions of Cats*, which immediately became a classic. Making use of her own translations from Grimm, she illustrated *Tales from Grimm* (1936), *Snow White and the Seven Dwarfs* (1938), and *Three Gay Tales from Grimm* (1943). She also did pictures for *The Funny Thing* (1929), *Snippy and Snappy* (1931), *Gone Is Gone* (1935); and in *Growing Pains* (1940) she depicted in diary form her own life from the age of fifteen to twenty-four, a book described by one reviewer as "a unique record of the evolution of an artist." Lewis Gannett described her work as marked by "dedicated intensity, creative fire, wild beauty, and warm gaiety."

Gage, Frances Dana [Barker] ["Aunt Fanny"] (b. Marietta, Ohio, Oct. 12, 1808—d. Nov. 10, 1884), reformer, lecturer, editor, author of children's stories. Mrs. Gage spoke and wrote freely on slavery, women's rights, the temperance movement, and other causes, and suffered many unpleasant experiences as a result of her zeal. In her later years she began writing sketches and poems for children. Her best-known work was *Elsie Magoon, or, The Old Still-House in the Hollow* (1867). She also wrote *Gertie's Sacrifice* (1869) and *Steps Upward* (1870).

gags and gag-writers. Originally *gagging* was a slang term for an actor's extemporaneous jesting. Once in a while a gag proved so successful that it became part of the "act." Now, however, a *gag* may be, according to Merriam-Webster, "any clever or amusing remark, bit of dialogue, anecdote, or the like; also, sometimes, a comic episode." This new meaning has created a new vocation, that of the *gag-writer*. He provides the jokes, dialogue material, comic business, and wisecracks for comedians on the stage, the screen, radio, and television, night club performances, and newspaper gossip columns. This division of labor is by no means new or even unnatural. As someone remarked, when Walter Hampden appears in *Hamlet* or José Ferrer in *Othello*, we don't expect them to write their own lines. Vaudeville sketches have in the past often been furnished by professional writers, but the demand for their services was a modest one—a single sketch would last an actor or a team all their lives. It is radio and television, with their insatiable appetites, that have created the need for large crews of literary laborers. These writers not only draw heavily from past authors, but also frequently steal each other's jokes.

Making a collection of books, brochures, and magazines is the first step taken by the modern joke-writer. One of the earliest good collections in this country was that of Thomas L. Masson, editor of *Life*, 1893–1922. Ed Wynn, the ingenious comic actor, has a large collection, constantly added to. First of the great gag-writers of the radio era was David Freedman, an experienced writer of comedy who found when he began working for radio comics that he couldn't possibly get enough jokes out of his own head. He began gathering books of humor, collections of jokes, old humorous periodicals, the college humorous papers, the old masters of humor. Then he went on to the business of analyzing the jokes and filing them under appropriate headings. The number of items in his files ran to about fifty thousand. Another early collector was Harold Horne, whose New York office was known as Hal Horne, Inc. Jokes could be bought from Horne either in the raw or with a "twist" given them by Horne's organization that made them immediately usable. He took orders from public speakers, club women, publishers of almanacs and jokebooks, song writers, radio writers, radio announcers, cartoonists, and press agents. Other successful gag-writers are Harry Cohn, Eugene Conrad, Billie K. Wells, Mort Lewis, Philip Rapp, Eddie Davis, Arthur Phillips, Sam Perrin, Ralph Spence, George Balzer, Milt Josefsberg, John Tackaberry, Charles Sherman.

Gaine, Hugh (b. Ireland, 1727—d. April 25, 1807), bookseller, printer, publisher. Gaine was the founder of one of New York City's early newspapers, the weekly *Mercury*, which began publication in 1752. His bookshop, The Bible and Crown, was a center of literary activity. In 1768 he became the official printer of the Province of New York. Paul Leicester Ford edited his *Journals* (2 v., 1902).

Galbraith, John Kenneth (b. Canada, Oct. 15, 1908—   ), economist, author. One of the most influential of modern American economists, Galbraith has had a distinguished career in education and government. After attending the Universities of Toronto, California, and Cambridge, he taught at Princeton and Harvard, served in the National Defense Advisory Commission and the Office of Price Administration during World War II, and was director of the Strategical Bombing Survey (1946) and the Office of Economic Security Policy (1946). In succeeding years he resumed teaching at Harvard, was a member of the board of editors of *Fortune* magazine (1943–48), and published four books: *American Capitalism* (1951), *A Theory of Price Control* (1952), *The Great Crash* (1955), and *The Affluent Society* (1958). These books —largely critiques of the economic aspects of contemporary American social structure and aims—were notable for their polished and epigrammatic style, their tone of moderation and concern, and the thoroughness and originality of their challenge to prevailing economic assumptions. In 1961 he became United States Ambassador to India.

Gale, Zona (b. Portage, Wis., August 26, 1874—d. December 27, 1938), novelist, short-story writer, dramatist, poet. The only child of deeply religious parents, Miss Gale spent a sheltered childhood in Portage, the small midwestern city that was to dominate her life and work. After graduating from the University of Wisconsin in 1895, she worked as a reporter for several Milwaukee newspapers. In 1901 she joined the staff of the New York *World*, but resigned eighteen months later to devote her full time to free-lance writing. Undismayed by numerous rejection slips, she finally sold a short story to *Success* in 1903. Subsequently her stories began to appear in leading magazines, and her first novel, *Romance Island*, was published in 1906.

The sentimentality that characterized Miss Gale's early writing was evident in her popular series of stories about a mythical Friendship Village. But despite their one-sided view of small-town American life, the author's talent for accurate observation gave them an aura of reality. By this time Miss Gale had begun her lifelong association with humanitarian causes. She was an ardent suffragette and pacifist, and fought against racial discrimination. Dissatisfied with her life in New York, she returned to Portage, and spent the rest of her life there.

During World War I her pacifist views brought her the enmity of some of her Portage neighbors, who suspected her of being a German sympathizer. This experience greatly altered her conception of village life, which she had been unable to see as a mixture of virtues and defects. This change in attitude is reflected in BIRTH (1918), in which she depicted a small town with affection but with unwavering realism. Her short novel, MISS LULU BETT (1920), was an immediate success. Published in the same year as Sinclair Lewis' *Main Street*, it told with deft irony the bittersweet story of a middle-aged drudge, exploited by her dull, selfish relatives. Her dramatization of the novel won the Pulitzer Prize in 1921 and, as the *Nation* later said, "belongs among the very earliest of plays which broke away from theatrical convention to establish upon the stage a new American literature." In the same realistic vein were FAINT PERFUME (1923), which pitted the sensitivity of her heroine against the crassness of middle-class life, and two collections of short stories, *Yellow Gentians and Blue* (1927) and *Bridal Pond* (1930). A strain of mysticism, inherited from her parents and hinted at in earlier work, was apparent in *Preface to a Life* (1926) and in much of her subsequent writing.

Now a spectacularly successful author, Miss Gale continued to fight for civic and social betterment and became an impassioned supporter of Senator ROBERT M. LA FOLLETTE and his Progressive movement. In 1928 she married William L. Breese, a Portage businessman to whom she had been devoted since childhood. Her last years were embittered by a rupture with the La Follettes. After her return from a trip to Japan, her health declined and she died in a Chicago hospital. Her last novel, *Magna*, was published posthumously in 1939.

Similar in some respects to the work of

Dreiser, Sherwood Anderson, and Sinclair Lewis, her best books helped create a new literary attitude toward provincial America. In his biography, *Still Small Voice* (1940), August Derleth wrote: "If even the best of her work is not great in the long run, yet it remains the tangible strength of Zona Gale's certain, unwavering, still small voice."

Gales, Joseph (b. England, Feb. 4, 1761—d. Aug. 24, 1841), newspaper editor. As editor of an English newspaper in Sheffield, Gales espoused such liberal views that he was forced to flee to the Continent and then to the United States, where he founded in 1799 a Jeffersonian newspaper, the Raleigh (N.C.) *Register*. His son Joseph (1786–1860) joined him as an editor and publisher. The son in 1810 bought the *National Intelligencer* in Washington; this tri-weekly was then (in 1813) converted into a daily and made a specialty of reporting the proceedings of Congress. It has become a valuable source of material for historians. The younger Gales, along with William W. Seaton (1785–1866), also published a *Register of Debates of Congress* (14 v., 1825–37), the *Annals of Congress* (v. 3–42, 1849–56), and the *American State Papers* (38 v., 1832–61).

Gallagher, William Davis (b. Philadelphia, Aug. 21, 1808—d. June 27, 1894), poet, editor, public official. In his early years Gallagher removed to Ohio, recording his observations on the beauties of the western wilderness in conventional but effective verse—three collections called *Erato* (two published in 1835, the third in 1837), and *Miami Woods and Other Poems* (1881). In addition he issued *Selections from the Poetical Literature of the West* (1841), one of the first anthologies of regional literature. He served on the staffs of various newspapers in Louisville, Cincinnati, and elsewhere; his political activities won him an appointment from Lincoln as special collector of the customs. See THE POETS AND POETRY OF THE WEST.

Gallatin, [Abraham Alphonse] Albert (b. Switzerland, Jan. 29, 1761—d. Aug. 12, 1849), statesman, diplomat, ethnologist. Gallatin came to America in 1780, helped American troops in the war, was appointed to teach French at Harvard, in 1783 removed to Virginia. There he bought an extensive tract, became acquainted with Washington, and entered politics; in 1793 he was elected United States Senator, but held that office only two months, being disqualified because of the date of his citizenship. In later years he became a prominent financier, representing what was then called the Republican party against the Federalists. He served three terms in Congress, then was appointed Secretary of the Treasury by Jefferson and instituted many important reforms, but was blamed for the weakness of our military defenses in the War of 1812. He was one of the negotiators of the Treaty of Ghent which ended that war. He served later as minister to France and to Great Britain. He was greatly interested in America's aborigines, and his book called *Synopsis of the Indian Tribes within the United States, East of the Rocky Mountains and in the British and Russian Possessions in North America* (1836) won him a reputation as "the father of American ethnology"; he helped found an Ethnological Society. He also issued a pamphlet on *The Oregon Question* (1846). His *Writings* were edited by Henry Adams (3 v., 1879), who also published a biography (1879). The most recent biography is Raymond Walters' *Albert Gallatin: Jeffersonian, Financier, and Diplomat* (1958).

Gallegher (1891), a short story by RICHARD HARDING DAVIS. The hero is an Irish-American lad, office boy on a daily paper. A burglary involving murder takes place; Gallegher plays detective, runs down the story, and brings in copy to his newspaper, which scores a scoop. The story gave its name to a collection of tales by Davis, including some about CORTLAND VAN BIBBER.

Gallery, The (1947), a set of episodes by JOHN HORNE BURNS. Out of his own experiences, Burns wrote this powerful novel about the American occupation of Naples, Italy, in August, 1944. Charles Poore described it as "a rather unusual farewell to arms. It is a rancorously vivid portfolio of portraits of many Allied soldiers and Italian civilians." Edmund Wilson pointed out that Burns had undoubtedly been influenced in technique by John Dos Passos' *U.S.A.* (*q.v.*).

Gallico, Paul [William] (b. New York City, July 26, 1897—   ), newspaperman, sports columnist, short-story writer, novelist. Gallico, a first-rate newspaperman, wrote some of the most engaging fiction of his day, varying from realism to straight romance. He came to look at sports with a jaundiced eye, writing an excellent analysis in *Farewell to Sport* (1938). Among his other books: *Adventures of Hiram Holliday* (1939); *The Snow Goose* (1941); *Golf Is a Friendly Game* (1941); *The Lonely* (1949); *Love of Seven Dolls* (1954); *Thomasina* (1957). *Confessions of a Story Writer* (1946) tells how his stories and books came into being, and reprints many of his shorter pieces. *The Steadfast Man* (1958) is a biography of St. Patrick; *Mrs. 'Arris Goes to Paris* (1959) and *Mrs. 'Arris Goes to New York* (1960), the extracurricular adventures of a London char, are among Gallico's most delightful combinations of whimsey and sharp characterization.

Gallup, George H[orace] (b. Jefferson, Iowa, Nov. 18, 1901—   ), public opinion statistician. Trained in methods of industrial and commercial research, Gallup founded the Institute of Public Opinion (1935) and began measuring public reactions in various directions, finally began to forecast such reactions, especially in the realm of political elections. Besides numerous articles, he wrote *The Pulse of Democracy: A New Technique for Measuring Reader Interest* (1940). Like other pollsters, he suffered his most disastrous failure when he concluded that Thomas E. Dewey was certain to defeat Harry S. Truman in the 1948 election.

Game, The (1905), a novelette by JACK LONDON. A young fighter, engaged to be married, is begged by his fiancée to abandon boxing, but insists on fighting one last fight. An accidental slip on the canvas leads to a blow that causes his death. The story is one of London's best—written without undue sentimentality, carefully contrived, inevitably tragic.

Gamesters, The, or, Ruins of Innocence (1805), a novel by Caroline Matilda Warren. This sentimental, moralistic novel was intended to paint the evil consequences of gambling and to offer a characteristic example in the person of its leading character, an orphan who is corrupted by bad company and finally ends in suicide. The language is formal and dull, the plot monotonous. The book was reprinted several times.

Gamow, George (b. Russia, March 4, 1904—d. Aug. 19, 1968), scientist and writer. Gamow interested himself in a wide variety of scientific fields as a theoretician, applied scientist, teacher, and popularizer. Educated at the University of Leningrad, he later taught and did research at Leningrad, Gottingen, Copenhagen, and Cambridge before coming to the United States to accept the chair in theoretical physics at George Washington University. In 1956 he moved to the University of Colorado. The same year UNESCO awarded him the Kalinga prize for popularization of science, and it is for his numerous books for the layman that he is best known. His "Mr. Tompkins" books have introduced many readers to the fields of relativity, nuclear physics, physiology, and genetics. The amusing instructive adventures of Mr. Tompkins are typical of the lively and engaging presentation in all of Gamow's popular books, some of which he illustrated himself.

Gamow is also well known among scientists for his theoretical research in the fields of radioactivity, nuclear physics, thermonuclear physics, cosmology, the origin of the elements, and fundamental biology. In applied science he is credited, with Hans Bethe and Edward Teller, for major contributions to the successful engineering of thermonuclear reactions in the hydrogen bomb. Besides the "Mr. Tompkins" books he wrote *The Birth and Death of the Sun* (1941); *One, Two, Three . . . Infinity* (1947); and *Matter, Earth and Sky* (1958) among others.

Gannett, Frank E[rnest] (b. Bristol, N.Y., Sept. 15, 1876—d. Dec. 3, 1957), newspaperman, editor, publisher. Gannett began with the Ithaca (N.Y.) *Daily News*, became owner of a large group of papers, mainly in New York state. It was for its time the largest combine of newspapers under single control. An account of Gannett's success was given by Samuel T. Williamson in *Imprint of a Publisher: The Story of Frank Gannett and His Newspapers* (1948). Gannett himself wrote *Britain Sees It Through* (1944) and *Winging Round the World* (1947).

Gannett, Henry (b. Bath, Me., Aug. 24, 1846—d. Nov. 5, 1914), geographer, cartographer. Gannett helped found the NATIONAL GEOGRAPHIC SOCIETY in 1883, and his books on geography and cartography—*A Manual of Topographic Methods* (1893); *Physiographic*

Types (2 v., 1898, 1900); *Gazeteer of Texas* (1902); *The Origin of Certain Place Names in the U.S.* (1902; reprinted, 1947); and others —earned him the name of "father of American map-making."

Gannett, Lewis [Stiles] (b. Rochester, N.Y., Oct. 3, 1891—   ), newspaperman, war correspondent, literary critic. In 1928 Gannett became a staff member of the New York *Herald Tribune*, in 1931 began conducting "Books and Things," a column of literary criticism. It became one of the most widely read and esteemed departments of literary journalism in the country. He retired in 1956. Among his own books are *Young China* (1926); *Sweet Land* (1934); *Cream Hill: Discoveries of a Weekend Countryman* (1949). In 1953 he became editor of a new series of historical works, THE MAINSTREAM OF AMERICA.

Gant, Eugene. Gant is the name under which THOMAS WOLFE usually appears in his autobiographical novels, LOOK HOMEWARD, ANGEL (1929) and OF TIME AND THE RIVER (1935). In THE WEB AND THE ROCK (1939) and YOU CAN'T GO HOME AGAIN (1940), Gant becomes George Webber. Other characters with the same family name are likewise drawn from life—Oliver Gant, Eugene's father; Eliza Gant, his mother; Ben Gant, his older brother; and others.

Garbage Man, The (1925), a play by JOHN DOS PASSOS. The plot shows two young people misled by a visible devil called "The Garbage Man," who is also known in the play by other names. He lures them into crime until they revolt and escape to a simpler environment. The play was produced under the title *The Moon Is a Gong*, March 12, 1926, at the Cherry Lane Theatre in New York, and was published in that year.

Garcilaso de la Vega. Author of THE FLORIDA OF THE INCA.

Gard, Robert. Author of GRASSROOTS THEATRE.

Gardiner, Sir Christopher. A mysterious character who appeared in New England in the early 1630's, accompanied by an equally mysterious woman, and who turned out to be an agent of FERDINANDO GORGES in his attempts to win rulership over New England. He lived in Maine for a while, then disappeared, to turn up in England as a witness for Gorges before the Privy Council. His strange eruption into New England affairs attracted the attention of several writers. The first to make use of him was Catharine Maria Sedgwick, who introduced him under the name Sir Philip Gardiner as the villain of her novel HOPE LESLIE (1827), in which he attempted to kidnap the heroine. Then JOHN LOTHROP MOTLEY, the historian, included him as a character in his romance called *Merry-Mount* (1849). John T. Adams, author of several historical novels, made him a character in his *Knight of the Golden Melice* (1856). But he won greatest prominence when Longfellow wrote the *Rhyme of Sir Christopher Gardiner* (1873) as the last of his *Tales of a Wayside Inn*.

All these writers used their imaginations freely in their accounts of Sir Christopher.

Gardner, Erle Stanley (b. Malden, Mass., July 17, 1889—d. Mar. 11, 1970), lawyer, detective story writer. Probably the most successful writer of crime fiction in the entire history of publishing, Gardner for the most part employs two sleuths, the lawyer Perry Mason, hero of a long series—*The Case of the Velvet Claws* (1933, Gardner's first book), *The Case of the Lucky Legs* (1933), *The Case of the Perjured Parrot* (1939), *The Case of the Borrowed Brunette* (1946), etc.—and Douglas Selby, who appears in a number of other volumes with similarly standardized titles: *The D.A. Calls It Murder* (1944), *The D.A. Holds a Candle* (1945), *The D.A. Breaks an Egg* (1949), etc. In addition Gardner used several pseudonyms —A. A. Fair, Charles J. Kenny, and others. Under the pseudonym of A. A. Fair he wrote over twenty books. He writes with incredible facility. His first book was completed in three and a half days. In that same month he wrote eleven novelettes and a 27,000-word feature story.

Most of Gardner's stories are written to a formula and turn on a point of law. In the Perry Mason books, his lawyer-sleuth takes what looks like a hopeless case, discovers in it factors that involve collision with the police and the district attorney's office, seems in danger of immediate disbarment, and emerges triumphant in a clever court scene. It is, however, the details that make the stories such great successes. To date, Gardner has written more than 100 books, 110 million copies of which were sold in original publications and in reprints in the United States and Canada. Alva Johnston has written a somewhat puzzled but still admiring account of *The Case of Erle Stanley Gardner* (1947). He notes that only once was Gardner caught in a legal blunder, and claims that "the Perry Mason books have taught law to lawyers"; thus *The Case of the Curious Bride* (1934) gave a winning tip to an Arizona prosecutor. Gardner himself rarely has practiced law since he won success with his writing, though he has occasionally liked to take on a difficult defense and has been active in helping to organize assistance for persons unjustly accused of crimes.

Garfield, James A[bram] (b. Orange, Ohio, Nov. 19, 1831—d. Sept. 19, 1881), soldier, congressman, 20th President of the United States. Garfield worked his way through Western Reserve Eclectic Institute in Hiram, Ohio, and graduated from Williams College. He became president of Western Reserve at the age of twenty-six, took part in the Civil War, rose to be a major-general, and then, after being chosen as a "dark horse" candidate, was elected President in 1880. A disappointed seeker of federal office shot him on July 2, 1881. He died a few months later in a private cottage at Elberon, N.J. His writings were collected in *The Works of James A. Garfield* (2 v., 1882–83). He had a great admiration for the president of Williams when he attended that college, and he said, "Give me a log with MARK HOPKINS on one end

and me on the other, and you may have all the buildings, apparatus, and libraries without him." The career of the hero of Albion W. Tourgée's *Figs and Thistles* (1879) is based on that of Garfield. Biographies of Garfield have been done by T. C. Smith (1925) and R. G. Caldwell (1931).

Garis, Howard R[oger] (b. Binghamton, N.Y., April 25, 1873—d. Nov. 5, 1962), newspaperman, author of books for children. Garis joined the staff of the Newark (N.J.) *Evening News* in 1896 and continued with it for the rest of his career. Some stories for children about a lovable rabbit named Uncle Wiggily were first written (1910) for the *News,* and Garis used for them the term *Bedtime Stories,* apparently the first time this description was employed. He wrote for this series steadily, and the tales were widely syndicated. Some appeared in book collections, amounting in the course of the years to more than thirty-five volumes. In addition Garis wrote the *Curlytop Series* (10 v.), the *Daddy Series* (10 v.), the *Teddy Series* (7 v.), besides many others. Altogether Garis published more than three hundred volumes. It has also been calculated that about twelve thousand Uncle Wiggily stories were written by Garis.

Garland, [Hannibal] Hamlin (b. West Salem, Wis., Sept. 4, 1860—d. March 4, 1940), short-story writer, novelist. Born in a tiny village on the western edge of Wisconsin, Garland came to know intimately the life of the settlers of the

UPI

plains, a life he later portrayed in works which have been called "the chief forerunners of American realism." In 1869 Garland's family moved from Wisconsin to Iowa. Twelve years later they again moved west and homesteaded in the Dakota Territory, but Garland remained behind to seek work in Illinois, Wisconsin, and elsewhere before staking a claim in 1883 in what is now McPherson County, S.D., where he spent a lonely winter establishing his right to the land. After one year he sold his claim for $200 and went to Boston, determined to further his education.

Rejected by Harvard, Garland began an experiment in self-education in the Boston Public Library. He read the works of Darwin, Huxley, Helmholtz, and Haeckel, as well as many American authors. In 1884 he became first a student and then a teacher in the Boston School of Oratory. It was during this period that he made the acquaintance of Edward Everett Hale, Minot Savage, Oliver Wendell Holmes, Edwin Booth, and William Dean Howells. Largely through the help of his friends, he was invited to lecture before clubs in and around Boston, his subjects ranging from Michelangelo to Joaquin Miller. He also reviewed books for the Boston *Transcript*.

In 1887 Garland returned to the West to visit his kinspeople; already under the influence of the social doctrines of HENRY GEORGE and the realistic fiction of WILLIAM DEAN HOWELLS, he saw in the harsh and barren lives of the Midwestern farmers material for stories that might be both a cry for social justice and a true reflection of Midwestern life. He returned to Boston and began to write the sketches and tales that were later collected in MAIN-TRAVELLED ROADS (1891). Other stories written between 1887 and 1890 were collected and published in *Prairie Folk* (1892) and *Wayside Courtships* (1897); these two books were later combined in *Other Main Travelled Roads* (1910).

Howells praised the first book, but the public found Garland's somber picture of farm life not to its taste. Garland, however, continued in his concern with social and economic reforms, and in 1892 published three novels dealing primarily with political corruption: *A Member of the Third House; Jason Edwards;* and *A Spoil of Office.* His novelette *A Little Norsk*, a story of Dakota farm life and far better than the novels, also appeared in 1892. The following year he again went west and in Chicago founded the "Cliff Dwellers," a group of young Midwestern writers. In 1894 he published *Crumbling Idols*, a collection of essays, in which he presented a literary theory that he called "veritism"; somewhat similar to Howells' realism, it was concerned with accurate observation and representation of detail, but it went beyond Howells' theories in its emphasis not only on the surface appearance of reality but on the metaphysical and psychological implications that realism, the depiction of the unpleasant as well as the pleasant aspects of life, could convey. Although Garland himself never fully succeeded in embodying his theory in fiction, his ideas foreshadowed the work of the younger realists such as Stephen Crane, E. W. Howe, and Harold Frederic; to a

somewhat lesser degree Garland's belief that the environment was the crucial factor in shaping the lives of men anticipated the naturalist movement which flowered about the turn of the century in the writings of Crane, Frank Norris, and Theodore Dreiser.

Garland's next novel, ROSE OF DUTCHER'S COOLLY (1895), considered by some critics to be his best, is the story of a Wisconsin farm girl and her struggle to escape the drudgery and spiritual barrenness of farm life; she studies at the University of Wisconsin and then goes to Chicago in pursuit of her dream of becoming a writer. Rose emerges as a well-defined character, and the descriptions of literary life in Chicago in the early nineties are well drawn, yet the novel had little popular success. In an attempt to please his audience, or perhaps because his enthusiasm for social reform was declining, Garland spent the next dozen years writing novels about the Indians and the Far West; ironically, these relatively inferior works, filled with stock characters and romantic plots (although tempered with a shade of realism), were highly popular. THE CAPTAIN OF THE GRAY HORSE TROOP (1902), the best known of these books, contains realistic descriptions and some appeal for better treatment of the Indians, but has poor characterization and motivation. Other novels of this period include *Hesper* (1903), which deals with labor problems among miners; *Money Magic* (1907), a romantic story of a gambler and a Middle Western woman; *Cavanaugh, Forest Ranger* (1910), perhaps his best popular work, a realistic treatment of cattlemen in the Far West; and *The Forester's Daughter* (1914), a romantic story with a Colorado setting.

Already, however, Garland had conceived the first of the books that mark the last phase of his work. As early as 1898 he had begun to write an autobiographical narrative of pioneer life, which was finally published in 1917 as A SON OF THE MIDDLE BORDER. This was followed by A DAUGHTER OF THE MIDDLE BORDER (1921), *Trail-Makers of the Middle Border* (1926), and *Back-Trailers from the Middle Border* (1928). Arthur Hobson Quinn has said that these four books "form an epic of migration, of struggle and discouragement, of the conquest of unfriendly nature, and of human indifference which no historian of literature or of life may neglect."

Garland's work after 1930, when he moved from New York to California, is limited to *Roadside Meetings* (1930), *Companions on the Trail* (1931), *My Friendly Contemporaries* (1932), and *Afternoon Neighbors* (1934), all of which are literary reminiscences or what he called "literary log books," and two works on spiritualism: *Forty Years of Psychic Research* (1936) and *The Mystery of the Buried Crosses* (1939).

As a writer Garland believed in two concepts: "Truth is a higher quality than beauty" and "To extend the reign of justice should everywhere be the duty and design of the artist." Working with these principles, Garland turned out a number of books that possess power and the vigor of authenticity, but are generally lacking in polish. Yet his works are invaluable records of a vanished era, and some of them, particularly *Main-Travelled Roads* and *A Son of the Middle Border,* retain the spark of life that make them still very much worth reading.

ELDON C. HILL

Garland, Robert (b. Baltimore, Md., April 29, 1895—d. Dec. 17, 1955), newspaperman, drama critic, playwright, actor. Garland worked on several Baltimore papers, then on the New York *World-Telegram* and the New York *Journal American.* He wrote numerous short stories, scenarios, one-act plays, and the following full-length plays, among others: *The Double Miracle* (1915); *At Night All Cats Are Grey* (1933); *Calling All Men* (with Leonard Sillman, 1937); *No More Perfect Paradise* (with Cynthia White, 1941).

Garneau, François-Xavier (b. Montreal, June 15, 1809—d. Feb. 3, 1866), notary, clerk, historian, poet. Garneau's early life was spent in Montreal, where he worked as a notary and accountant. In 1828, he made a brief trip to the United States. The periodical *Le Canadien* published his first poem in 1831, and in the same year he traveled to Europe. Two years in England and France and an acquaintance with their institutions and historians inspired his monumental history of Canada. After his return to Canada in 1833, he continued his literary activities, contributing poetry to various magazines and founding two periodicals. The first volume of *Histoire du Canada* appeared in 1845 (v. 2, 1846; v. 3, 1848; v. 4, 1852), and was later translated into English by A. Bell. *Voyage en Angleterre et en France* (1855) recounts his trip abroad.

Garrard, Lewis H. (b. Cincinnati, Ohio, 1829–d. 1887), explorer, travel writer. When Garrard was still in his teens he went with a trade caravan to Bent's Fort on the Arkansas River and observed keenly the manners, language, and characters of the traders, trappers, Indians, and settlers with whom he came in contact. He recorded his experiences in *Wah-to-yah and the Taos Trail* (1850; reprinted, 1938, with introduction by Ralph B. Bieber as Vol. VI of the *Southwest Historical Series*). Henry Nash Smith notes that Garrard had "a rare natural ability to record the rich metaphors of the trapper language."

Garreau, Louis-Armand (b. New Orleans, Sept. 13, 1817—d. Mar. 28, 1865), novelist. Garreau is remembered chiefly for *Louisiana: Épisode emprunté à la Domination Française en Amérique* (1862). This is a tale of the anti-Spanish conspiracy of 1768, a favorite theme of CREOLE authors; it drew upon some of the historical narratives of Garreau's predecessor, CHARLES ÉTIENNE ARTHUR GAYARRÉ.

Garretson Chronicle, The (1947), a novel by GERALD WARNER BRACE. Brace describes with grace and charm the intricate social balances that make up New England society. The narrator of his story is a dissident Yankee who plays with the village Irish boys and otherwise upsets conservative social conventions.

Garrett, George Palmer, Jr. (b. Orlando, Fla., June 11, 1929—   ), novelist, poet. Garrett became known for writing about extraordinary events in a quietly realistic manner. His poems are conversational, yet philosophic, in the manner of Wallace Stevens. His novel, *The Finished Man* (1959), deals with politics in Florida; he is author of the picaresque novel *Which Ones Are the Enemy?* (1961). "An Evening Performance" appeared in *The Best American Short Stories of 1960.*

Garrigue, Jean (b. Evansville, Ind., Dec. 8, 1914—   ), poet. Jean Garrigue was educated at the University of Chicago and subsequently taught at the University of Iowa, Bard College, and Queens College. Her first work appeared in collection in *Five Young American Poets* (1944), followed by *The Ego and the Centaur* (1947), *The Monument Rose* (1953), and *A Water Walk by the Villa D'Este* (1959). Her poems combine lyric celebration of nature with a profound and delicate self-scrutiny. Richard Eberhart speaks glowingly of the "cool, free play and deep sincerity" of her verse, and other critics have praised her poetry for its great inventiveness and vitality of language, richness of detail, and intricate and personal music.

Garrish, Mr. A character in William Dean Howells' ANNIE KILBURN (1889) and *The Quality of Mercy* (1892). He is stubbornly conservative and protests strongly against any social or other changes.

Garrison, Theodosia (b. Newark, N.J., 1874—d. Oct. 9, 1944), poet. Among her collections of pleasing lyrical verses are *Joy o' Life and Other Poems* (1909); *Earth Cry and Other Poems* (1910); *As the Larks Rise* (1921).

Garrison, William Lloyd (b. Newburyport, Mass., Dec. 12, 1805—d. May 24, 1879), cobbler, carpenter, printer, editor, poet, abolitionist. Brought up in poverty and privation, Garrison became, as V. L. Parrington called him, "the flintiest character amongst the New England militants." When he had found what he believed to be the truth or when he saw an evil that should be corrected, he spoke with a courage that seemed to others foolhardiness and that made him one of the most hated and also one of the most respected men of his time. Slavery in particular aroused his bitter hatred, and on Jan. 1, 1831, he put forth the first issue of a little weekly newspaper, THE LIBERATOR, the "Salutatory" of which contained the defiant words, "I will be heard!" Immediately underneath the title of the weekly appeared the sentence: "Our country is the world—our countrymen are all mankind." The violent sentiments he expressed led to equally violent attacks on him; in 1835 a mob dragged him through the streets of Boston with a rope around his body.

He organized an Anti-Slavery Society, the first of its kind, and gradually gained the attention of a brilliant group of orators and writers.

Historians today are inclined to believe that other abolitionists, like James Gillespie Birney (1792–1857) and Theodore Dwight Weld (1803–1895), played a more important role than Garrison in ending slavery. In 1865, the 13th

Amendment to the Constitution became law, abolishing slavery, and *The Liberator* ceased publication that year. During the last years of his life Garrison supported other causes: woman suffrage, temperance, world peace. R. B. Nye wrote an impartial account in *Garrison and the Humanitarian Reformers* (1955).

Gassner, John W[aldhorn] (b. Hungary, Jan. 30, 1903—d. April 2, 1967), editor, lecturer, writer on the drama. Gassner came to the United States in 1911, became a citizen in 1929. He was active in the theater, edited several anthologies of plays—among them, *A Treasury of the Theater* (4 v., 1935–1951), *Best Plays of the Modern American Theater* (1939), *Best American Plays* (5 v., 1939–1958) with *Supplement* (1961)—some collections of "best" film plays, and a *Library of Drama and Music*, which began publication in 1945. He wrote a learned and useful survey of dramatic literature, *Masters of the Drama* (1940); and his *Theater in Our Times* (1954) covers modern drama to the post-World War II theater in France. With Edward Quinn, he edited the *Reader's Encyclopedia of World Drama* (1969).

Gastonia strike. Gastonia, a city in North Carolina, is a center of textile manufacturing. In 1929 it was the scene of an unsuccessful strike which culminated in violence. The incident shocked the conscience of the country; on it were based two novels, Mary Heaton Vorse's *Strike!* (1930) and Grace Lumpkin's *To Make My Bread* (1932).

Gates, Eleanor (b. Shakopee, Minn., Sept. 26, 1875—d. March 7, 1951), novelist, playwright. Among her writings: *The Biography of a Prairie Girl* (1902); *The Poor Little Rich Girl* (first a novel, then a play, 1913); *We Are Seven* (produced, 1913); *The Rich Little Poor Boy* (1921). *The Poor Little Rich Girl* was her most important work, and its title has passed into a popular saying. It portrays with pleasing fantasy the longing of every child for a simple, natural life.

Gates, Horatio (b. England, 1728?–d. 1806), soldier. Gates served in the British army under Braddock, returned to England, then at Washington's urging came to America to live. During the Revolution he fought on the American side, received a high command, was given the credit for repulsing Burgoyne at Saratoga (1777). Out of the reputation thus won the Conway Cabal arose—an attempt to replace Washington with Gates. This failed, and when Gates was disastrously defeated in the Battle of Camden (1780), he was retired in disgrace. In 1782 he was ordered back into service under Washington, whom he served loyally to the end of the war. Gates appears often in historical novels laid in the Revolutionary period; an example is J. P. Kennedy's Horse-Shoe Robinson (1835).

Gates, Lewis F[dwards] (1860–1924), teacher, critic. Gates was famous as a teacher at Harvard; among his eminent students was Frank Norris, who wrote portions of McTeague (1899) while attending Gates' classes. Gates' lectures and essays were collected in *Three Studies in Literature* (1899) and *Studies and Appreciations* (1900). He made it his role to reconcile naturalism with academic criticism and to define the significance of impressionism; he also stressed the importance of scholarship in criticism. Van Wyck Brooks calls him "a first-rate critical writer," selecting his *Newman as a Prose-Writer* for special praise.

Gates Ajar, The (1868), a novel by Elizabeth Stuart Phelps Ward. There were three sequels: *Beyond the Gates* (1883); *The Gates Between* (1887); *Within the Gates* (1901). The first of these novels was written with the definite purpose of consoling those who had lost relatives or friends in the Civil War. It centers around a young woman who had lost her brother. She is at first inconsolable, but her aunt brings her at last to a belief in the immortality of the soul. The other stories follow a similar pattern. *The Gates Ajar* was the best seller of its day.

Gauss, Christian (b. Ann Arbor, Mich., Feb., 2, 1878—d. Nov. 1, 1951), teacher, college administrator, translator, author. Gauss taught Romance languages in several universities, finally at Princeton; he became dean of the college in 1925, dean of alumni in 1946. He received many honors for his work as a scholar and as an active fighter for democratic causes. Among his books: *The German Emperors* (1915); *Through Col-*

lege on Nothing a Year (1915); *Why We Went to War* (1918); *Life in College* (1930); *A Primer for Tomorrow* (1934). *The Papers of Christian Gauss,* edited by Katherine Gauss Jackson, appeared in 1957.

Gaut Gurley (1857), a novel by D. P. THOMPSON. The leading character is a ruthless person, animated with a spirit of revenge. He discovers that a prosperous Boston merchant, Mark Elwood, has killed a customs official and uses his knowledge to dominate Elwood, whom at last he kills. The background is mostly the Maine woods, and Thompson, as Alexander Cowie points out, "makes it clear that the primeval forest does not necessarily promote human virtues."

Gauvreau, Émile [Henry] (b. Centerville, Conn., Feb. 4, 1891—d. Oct. 15, 1956), newspaperman, editor, columnist. A first-rate reporter and editor, Gauvreau won a national reputation by his pioneer work in a somewhat dubious field—the tabloid newspaper. He was the editor and publisher of the New York *Evening Graphic* (1924–29), then became managing editor of the New York *Daily and Sunday Mirror* (1929–35). Later he became a news columnist and edited a rotogravure section for the Philadelphia *Inquirer* and *Click,* a picture monthly. His most important book is his autobiography, *My Last Million Readers* (1941), a cynical and faithful account of his experiences with noted men and with the newspaper reading public. Among his other books: *Hot News* (1931); *The Scandal Monger* (1932); and a book on Russia, *What So Proudly We Hailed* (1935). He wrote usefully on General William Mitchell and American aviation.

Gayarré, Charles Étienne Arthur (b. near New Orleans, Jan. 9, 1805—d. Feb. 11, 1895),

lawyer, public official, historian, novelist, playwright. In early life Gayarré held several public offices and was elected to the United States Senate (1835), but was obliged to resign because of ill health and went abroad for study and medical care. Always deeply interested in the history of his native state, he rendered an English work on the subject into a French abridgment (1830), some years later wrote a *Histoire de la Louisiane* (2 v., 1846, 1847), and then his most important writing, a four-volume *History of Louisiana* (1851–66), which began with a separate work, *Romance of the History of Louisiana* (1848). In this Gayarré was obviously under the influence of Sir Walter Scott, but the completed work is nevertheless soundly historical. He was also active in the composition of imaginative works—*The School for Politics* (1854); *Fernando de Lemos—Truth and Fiction* (1872), which was in part autobiographical; a sequel called *Aubert Dubayet* (1882); and a play, *Dr. Bluff in Russia* (1865). Many of his letters were reproduced in Charles R. Anderson's study of Gayarré as one of the "last literary cavaliers." Later Creole novelists found in his histories a wealth of suggestions for their stories.

Gayler, Charles (b. New York City, April 1, 1820—d. May 28, 1892), newspaperman, dramatist. Gayler worked for papers in Cincinnati and New York, but from the time that he studied law as a young man he was interested in the stage; his first play, *The Heir of Glen Avon,* was produced in 1839. From that time until 1888 he continued to write for the stage, producing numerous hits. He and the critics, as is often the case, failed to get along together. To fool them Gayler produced *The Magic Marriage* (1861) under another name, won unanimous praise in the press, and then revealed his authorship—to the further wrath of the critics. Both his industry and his speed were immense. Bull Run was fought on July 21, 1861; on Aug. 15 Gayler's *Bull Run* was on the stage of the New Bowery Theater, ran for four weeks, and was later revived. His *Hatteras Inlet, or, Our Naval Victories* was produced the same year three months after the event. From 1870 to the time he retired he is said to have written thirty plays. Among the better known were *The Buckeye Gold Hunters* (1849); *Out of the Streets* (1868); *Fritz: Our Cousin-German* (1870); *Lights and Shadows of New York* (1888).

Gayley, Charles Mills (b. China, Feb. 22, 1858—d. July 26, 1932), teacher, scholar. For the greater part of his life Gayley was associated with the University of California, where he became professor of English in 1889; he retired in 1923. His *Classic Myths in English Literature* (1893) is still a widely used textbook. He prepared a work of great scholarship, *Methods and Materials of Literary Criticism* (1899), in collaboration with FRED NEWTON SCOTT; and a sequel, dealing with lyric, epic, and allied forms of poetry, in collaboration with Benjamin Putnam Kurtz (1920). He edited several collections of plays, and in 1917 published a stimulating volume on *Shakespeare and the Founders of Liberty in America.*

Gazette of the United States. A New York weekly founded by John Fenno (1751–1798) and financed by ALEXANDER HAMILTON as an organ of the Federalists. To combat this paper "of pure Toryism, disseminating the doctrines of monarchy, aristocracy, and the exclusion of the people," as Jefferson expressed it, Philip Freneau, who at that time was editor of *The Daily Advertiser* in New York, was asked to set up a competing periodical, the NATIONAL GA-ZETTE (1791), that would "go through the states and furnish a Whig vehicle of intelligence." The two papers engaged in many lively battles, in the course of which they employed without restraint virulent and violent news stories, editorials, poems, and skits, some of them directed against the highest figures in the new Republic. In the Federalist *Gazette* appeared John Adams' *Discourses on Davila* (1790). In 1793 the paper became a daily. After Fenno's death his son became editor. In 1804 the name was changed to *United States Gazette;* later it merged with other papers and survived until 1847.

Geddes, Norman Bel (b. Adrian, Mich., April 27, 1893—d. May 8, 1958), stage designer, producer, author. Bel Geddes made his first production, *Nju,* in 1916. Thereafter he designed well over two hundred theatrical productions; his settings for Max Reinhardt's *The Miracle* (1923) attracted particular attention. He produced designs for the World's Fairs in 1929 and 1938, for the first streamlined ocean liners, for airplanes, and for many buildings and industrial productions. He also devised a scheme for national automobile highways, described in his book *Magic Motorways* (1940). Among his other books: *A Project for a Theatrical Presentation of "The Divine Comedy" of Dante* (1923) and *Horizons* (1932).

Geddes, Virgil (b. Dixon Co., Neb., May 14, 1897—   ), dramatist, poet. Geddes aroused interest and controversy with two of his plays laid in the Middle West, *The Earth Between* (1929) and *Native Ground* (1932). He also has written *The Frog* (1927) and later produced *Pocahontas and the Elders* (1933) and *Four Comedies from the Life of George Emery Blum* (1934). His two best-known plays deal with the theme of incest. John Gassner speaks of "their excellently realized, tight-lipped but passionate and suddenly explosive natives." In 1941 Geddes was appointed postmaster in Brookfield, Conn. He told of his experiences in *Country Postmaster* (1952).

Geisel, Theodor Seuss. See DR. SEUSS.

Geismar, Maxwell [David] (b. New York City, Aug. 1, 1909—   ), short-story writer, critic, teacher. One of the most esteemed of contemporary critics, Geismar devoted himself to writing a critical account of the American novel, emphasizing the 20th century. His books on the subject include *Writers in Crisis: The*

American Novel, 1925–1940 (1942); *The Last of the Provincials: The American Novel, 1915–1925* (1947); *Rebels and Ancestors: The American Novel, 1890–1915* (1953); *American Moderns: From Rebellion to Conformity* (1958).

Gelber, Jack (b. Chicago, April 12, 1932—   ), playwright. *The Connection,* the first play by this previously unknown playwright, was produced "Off Broadway" in 1959 and soon came to be regarded as an important expression of the rebellious younger generation of the fifties. Despite its frank treatment of drug addiction and its assault on the audience with long stretches of improvised jazz, the play had a popular and critical success. The "connection" is the narcotics supplier who is awaited by the addicts in the play. In 1961 there were London and Paris productions and a film version. Previously Gelber had attended the University of Illinois and had numerous jobs including sheet-metal work and ship fitting. *The Connection* was published in 1960. *The Apple,* produced in 1961, received mixed reviews in New York. As in *The Connection,* the actors mingled with the audience between the acts.

Gellhorn, Martha (b. St. Louis, Mo., 1908—   ), journalist, novelist. As a war correspondent for *Collier's* from 1938 to 1945 Miss Gellhorn experienced some of the most exciting and horrifying events of the time. She reported on the Spanish Civil War in 1937–38, Russia's attack on Finland in 1939, Japan's on China in 1940–41, and the European war from England, Italy, France, and Germany until 1945. She met ERNEST HEMINGWAY during the Spanish Civil War, was married to him in 1940, and divorced in 1945. She is said to be the original of the girl in Hemingway's play THE FIFTH COLUMN. FOR WHOM THE BELL TOLLS was dedicated to her. Miss Gellhorn's fiction mostly derives from actual events she reported on and has been praised for its immediacy and journalistic excellence. *The Trouble I've Seen* (1936) was the fictionalized result of a report for Harry Hopkins' Federal Emergency Relief agency on the living conditions of people on relief in industrial areas. Her articles as war correspondent are collected, virtually unchanged, in *The Face of War* (1959). Some other books: *The Honeyed Peace* (1954); *Two by Two* (1958); the novel *His Own Man* (1961).

General Magazine and Historical Chronicle, for all the British Plantations in America, The (Jan.–June, 1741). This magazine, issued by BENJAMIN FRANKLIN, just missed being the first magazine published in the English colonies. John Webbe, whom Franklin had engaged as editor, left him for a rival publisher, Andrew Bradford, who anticipated Franklin by three days with *The American Magazine.* The latter was published, however, for only three months. Franklin's magazine closely imitated English models and was largely devoted to discussion of foreign affairs.

General William Booth Enters into Heaven (1913), a poem by VACHEL LINDSAY. This poem was the first of Lindsay's to attract wide attention. It was written in 1912, following the death of the famous leader of the Salvation Army, and was published the next year in the magazine *Poetry* and in a collection of Lindsay's poems. The poem successfully catches the rhythm of Salvation Army chants, and it goes well to the accompaniment of banjos and tambourines. Lindsay himself often recited the poem effectively. Many of the lines are skillful examples of onomatopoeia.

"Genius," The (1915), a novel by THEODORE DREISER. The hero is a middle western artist, Eugene Witla, who becomes the art director of a large magazine corporation, has numerous love affairs, attains financial and social success, marries Angela, who dies in childbirth; Witla himself suffers a breakdown, but recovers his health and devotes himself thereafter to painting and the care of his daughter. George Snell calls the book "a long muddy narrative," in the course of which Dreiser indulges in much moralizing on platitudinous levels while he seeks to show Witla as a plaything in the "trap of circumstance." According to Helen Dreiser, in her book *My Life with Dreiser* (1951), Witla is a composite of three men—the artist Everett Shinn, an art editor Dreiser knew, and Dreiser himself.

Genteel Tradition at Bay, The (1931), an essay by GEORGE SANTAYANA. The term "genteel tradition" was applied at the close of the 19th century to a group of American writers who had set up a traditional standard, literary, social, and moral, that emphasized correctness and conventionality. These writers avoided reporting the American scene with any degree of realism. Santayana defined this tradition as a "New England disease," which sought austerity and rigid mental discipline and was opposed to pagan conceptions that tended to release the emotions. Santayana also attacked the "New Humanism" of IRVING BABBITT and PAUL ELMER MORE because of their desire to reinstate a "settled belief" in a supernatural human soul and in a precise divine revelation. (See HUMANISM.) Santayana argued rather in favor of a rational and uninhibited quest for truth. He continued his attack on New England ideals in his novel, THE LAST PURITAN (1935).

Gentle Art of Making Enemies, The (1890), a collection of essays by JAMES MCNEILL WHISTLER in which he brought together some previous publications, including *Whistler vs. Ruskin, Art and Art Critics*, and *Ten O'Clock Lectures*, all published in 1888. In this book Whistler expounded his own ideas of art and replied wittily, sometimes savagely, to his enemies.

Gentle Boy, The (1837, in TWICE-TOLD TALES, *First Series*), a story by Nathaniel Hawthorne. Hawthorne imagines what would happen if a young Quaker child had been left helpless among the Puritans. Every man is against him, his timid kindness is rewarded with treachery, and he dies inevitably. The five-year-old Ilbrahim is made an instance of innocence suffering in a world of evil. This tale has always

been regarded as among Hawthorne's best, and illustrates the sentence he set down in his notebook in 1836: "There is evil in every human heart."

Gentleman from Indiana, The (1899), a novel by BOOTH TARKINGTON. In this first lively novel, Tarkington anticipated the muckraking school of a few years later. He tells the story of John Harkless, a promising young college graduate who buys and edits a newspaper in a small Hoosier town. Harkless discovers many things that are wrong, especially in local politics, and he attacks with particular vigor a gang of "White Caps." They assault him, and his disappearance leads to the belief that he has been murdered. The girl he has fallen in love with takes over his paper and carries it on with equal vigor. Young John returns, secures a nomination to the House of Representatives, and is elected. He sees his enemies punished and the community purified. V. L. Parrington found in the story "a flabby and somewhat saccharine philosophy." Tarkington had difficulty in finding a publisher for the book; when it finally appeared it made him famous overnight.

Gentleman Johnny. See SIR JOHN BURGOYNE.

Gentleman's Agreement (1947), a novel by LAURA HOBSON. Phil Green, a member of the editorial staff of *Smith's Weekly*, is assigned to write a series of articles about anti-Semitism in America. He decides to pose as a Jew for six months, and he has some extraordinary experiences. Lewis Gannett commented on the book: "There are no Ku-Kluxers in Mrs. Hobson's story—just a lot of nice people who, more or less unconsciously, in varying minor degrees, by their 'gentlemen's code' feed the fires of Kluxism." The novel was made into a successful movie (1946) by MOSS HART, with Elia Kazan as director.

Gentlemen Prefer Blondes (1925), a novel by ANITA LOOS. This story of Lorelei Lee, a good-looking moron who managed to do pretty well for herself, is subtitled "The Illuminating Diary of a Professional Lady." The author had been working in Hollywood, where she discovered models for Lorelei and Lorelei's Mr. Gus Eisman, the Button King. H. L. Mencken held that it was full of "shrewd observation and devastating irony." It is said that chorus girls, manicurists, and others bought the book with the idea that it would be a useful handbook on how to get rich—but they merely enriched Miss Loos. The sales ran to half a million. In 1926 a successful stage version was produced, in 1928 a movie, in 1949 a musical comedy. Miss Loos wrote a less successful follow-up, *But Gentlemen Marry Brunettes* (1926).

Gentle People, The (1939), a comedy by IRWIN SHAW. This play is subtitled "A Brooklyn Fable." It tells how two harmless middle-aged men, who have bought a boat to take them to the Gulf of Mexico for some fishing, are molested by a gangster. They lure him into their boat, row out to Sheepshead Bay and drown him, then continue with their trip. The play was intended as a parable showing what to do about fascists, a burning problem in the year of its production.

Gentle Reader, The (1903), a collection of essays by SAMUEL McCHORD CROTHERS. These are mildly witty and agreeable discourses by one of the last of the Addisonian school of American essayists.

George, Henry (b. Philadelphia, Sept. 2, 1839 —d. Oct. 29, 1897), editor, lecturer, economist. George spent a year at sea when he was sixteen, then entered a printing office to learn typesetting, and acquired the beginnings of a knowl-

edge of printing and publishing, with which he was associated in one way or another for the rest of his life. He left the printing office after nine months and again went to sea, this time en route for California, where he spent more than five years in and out of work and in dire poverty. In October, 1868, the *Overland Monthly* printed the first of his articles, which anticipated his later thesis; written just before the completion of the transcontinental railroad, the article, *What the Railroad Will Bring Us,* argued that increased population and business would bring greater wealth for a few and greater poverty for many. George traveled to New York and was again struck that the most cosmopolitan and "civilized" of American cities should present a "shocking contrast between monstrous wealth and debasing want."

Upon his return to California he became editor of the *Oakland Transcript,* a newly established democratic paper. During this time he came to the conclusion that land increases in value as the population grows, and the men who work the land are obliged to pay more for the privilege. This was the germ of PROGRESS AND POVERTY (1879), in which George argued that every man has a right to work the land and enjoy the products of his labor, but when land is in private ownership he must pay a rent and thus loses some of his labor. Since the increased value of land in populated communities is due less to the owner of the land than to the community as a whole, the landlord is robbing both the worker and the community by exacting a rent. To combat this, George proposed his famous "single tax" on the land, to give back to the community the part of the land's value which the community had created. This tax— on the land and on nothing else—would relieve industry and labor from taxes, since it would be sufficient for the functioning of the state. Although initially published at George's expense, *Progress and Poverty* went through over a hundred editions and quickly reached a wide circulation. Its indictment of ownership by absentee landlords, monopolies, and land speculation was echoed by thousands of workers, farmers, and tenants, as well as by writers; HAMLIN GARLAND and WILLIAM DEAN HOWELLS, among others, were greatly influenced by George's ideas.

After the publication of *Progress and Poverty* George moved to New York, where he wrote *The Irish Land Question* (1881). He wrote a series of articles for *Frank Leslie's Illustrated Newspaper* later published as *Social Problems* (1883), and made two tours to Great Britain. In 1886, he was an unsuccessful candidate for mayor of New York City, and was called a dangerous fanatic by Tammany Hall because of his social-welfare campaign. In 1897 he again ran for mayor, in spite of ill health, but died shortly before the election. His other works include *Protection and Free Trade* (1886) and *The Science of Political Economy* (1897). His ideas have been kept alive by Henry George Schools of social science in New York City and elsewhere, and by the Robert Schalkenbach Foundation. Among his noted converts were Tolstoy, Sun Yat sen, and Ramsay MacDonald. As late as 1947 a party calling itself the Georgeists won several seats in the Danish parliament. His son Henry (1862–1916) wrote his biography, *The Life of Henry George* (1900), and Anna George de Mille, daughter of the younger George, wrote *Henry George, Citizen of the World* (1950).

George Balcombe (1836), a novel by NATHANIEL BEVERLEY TUCKER. This was a story of plantation life, published anonymously. Tucker was both a scholar and a novelist, and foresaw some of the difficulties the country was facing in disunion. Poe believed it was the best novel by an American.

George's Mother (1896), a novel by STEPHEN CRANE. This is a tale of George Kelsey, who is his mother's ideal—but she is deluded. (It is significant that Crane at first called this novel "A Woman without Weapons.") Her whole life sacrificed to his well-being, she anticipates the time when her son shall become "a white and looming king among men." She worships him with all the intensity of a sweetheart, and with the blind devotion of a religious fanatic she dies still believing in him. "It is the most heartrending picture of mother-love that I have ever seen in literature," said John D. Barry in the *Daily Tatler,* "and mother-love is a theme that ought to touch even critics. Yet the book is not for one instant either mawkish or morbid."

The New York *World* complained that this tale of east-side life in New York City can hardly be called a novel, for it is barely a novelette and there is no plot and no action. William Dean Howells praised Crane's honesty with the reader for what we would today call social realism: the pathos of the underprivileged "rendered without one maudlin touch." Whereas Crane's

MAGGIE is a full study, *George's Mother* is, says Howells, "the study of a situation merely: a poor, inadequate woman, of a commonplace religiosity, whose son goes to the bad. The wonder of it is the courage which deals with persons so absolutely average, and the art that graces them with the beauty of the author's compassion for everything that errs and suffers."

Maggie and *George's Mother*, with "An Appreciation by W. D. Howells," comprised *Bowery Tales* (1900). They are reprinted, together with other Bowery stories, in *Stephen Crane: An Omnibus* (1952), edited by R. W. Stallman.

George Washington Slept Here (1940), a farce by GEORGE S. KAUFMAN and MOSS HART. The authors satirize the city-dweller's urge to buy and completely renovate a house in the country. Although some friends of the senior author subtitled it "George Kaufman Slipt Here," the play went on to a moderate success. It was also filmed.

Georgia Scenes, Characters, Incidents, &c., in the First Half Century of the Republic (1835), eighteen humorous sketches by AUGUSTUS BALDWIN LONGSTREET; they appeared originally in the *Southern Recorder* (of Milledgeville, Ga.) and the *Augusta State Rights Sentinel* in 1827. In book form they attained great popularity and went through many editions. Longstreet was a fervent admirer of Addison, and some of his pieces follow that writer's style closely. In others he becomes a pioneer regionalist, reproducing the folkways and the language of Georgia and the Southeast in early days with faithfulness and humor.

Gerard, Richard (b. New York City, June 8, 1876—d. July 2, 1948), writer of lyrics. Gerard's full name was Richard Gerard Husch. He first studied medicine, finally became a post-office clerk. But he always wanted to be a song writer, and wrote many lyrics that were set to music and became popular—*I've Got My Eye on You, Follow the Crowd on Sunday,* and *Some Day in the Far Away* among them. But his greatest hit was SWEET ADELINE, which he wrote for a tune peddled by Harry Armstrong, a Boston pianist and composer. The name was inspired by the famous Italian singer, Adelina Patti. The song was sold and published in 1903 and became immensely popular. It was employed as a theme song by a Boston politician, John J. ("Honey") Fitzgerald, whose sweet singing of the song on every possible occasion twice convinced the Boston electorate that he would make a good mayor.

Gerhardt, Jennie. See JENNIE GERHARDT.

German-American dialect. Since the German word for "German" is *Deutsch,* it was easy for Americans to speak of Germans as "Dutch." The chief center of German dialect in the United States is Pennsylvania, and the descendants of Germans in that state, and their special form of speech, are still called "Pennsylvania Dutch." The people in this area belong to similar, rather austere religious faiths, practice their own folkways with unswerving loyalty, and are re-nowned for their thrift, solidity, and well-cooked, fattening meals. In the course of the centuries their dialect has been greatly modified by loans from English; by the middle of the 20th century it was no longer true that the Pennsylvania Dutch spoke only their dialect.

The dialect received its first literary recognition when Charles Godfrey Leland in 1856 contributed the first of his *Hans Breitmann Ballads* (see under BREITMANN) to *Graham's Magazine.* He was imitated by CHARLES FOLLEN ADAMS in a *Leedle Yawcob Strauss* series (1877–1910). In 1913 Kurt M. Stein began contributing verses in a modified German-American dialect to Bert Leston Taylor's column in the Chicago *Tribune.* In 1925 a collection, *Die Schoenste Lengevitch,* appeared, followed by *Gemixte Pickles* (1927) and *Limburger Lyrics* (1932). In all these literary uses English nouns and verbs are boldly teutonized. Thus Leland tells how Breitmann, in the uneasy atmosphere of the New World, decides that he can "solfe de infinide ash von eternal shpree." Stein clings more closely to German: "Den andern abend ging mein frau und ich a walk zu nehme."

German influence in America. German migration to North America began in the late 17th century with the arrival in Pennsylvania of Mennonite colonists, the forerunners of many groups of German Protestants—Amish, Dunkards, Moravians, and Schwenkfelders—who came to the New World during the next 150 years. Thereafter new waves of immigrants, many of them political refugees, continued to arrive during the 19th and 20th centuries, including among them many prominent artists, writers, scholars, and scientists. Today the German element in the American population is second only to the British, and many sections of the country—*e.g.,* parts of Pennsylvania, Milwaukee, St. Louis, etc.—retain a distinctly German character. The influence of German culture on American thought and institutions has been exerted through these immigrants, through American travelers in Germany, and of course also through the introduction and translation of much German literature in the United States. The chief influence has been that of the German idealists and romanticists of the late 18th and early 19th centuries, notably the influence of Kant upon American TRANSCENDENTALISM and that of Goethe and his successors upon a series of American writers including Irving, Hawthorne, Poe, Longfellow, and Whitman. In the early 19th century German, especially Prussian, theories of education began to exert a profound influence on American education, both in public schools and in universities. Indeed, the whole concept of American graduate education is German in origin. In the 20th century German EXPRESSIONISM has found some admirers among American writers and artists, particularly American Abstract Expressionists.

Recent studies of German influence on America are: H. A. Pochmann and A. R. Schultz, *Bibliography of German Culture in America to 1940* (1953); H. A. Pochmann, *German Culture* in America: Philosophical and Literary Influences, 1600–1900 (1957). Invaluable bibliographical aids in the area of literature are: B. Q. Morgan, A Critical Bibliography of German Literature in English Translation, 1481–1927, With Supplement Embracing the Years 1928–1935 (2nd ed., 1938); S. H. Goodnight, German Literature in American Magazines Prior to 1846 (1907); M. H. Haertel, German Literature in American Magazines, 1846 to 1880 (1908); Lillie V. Hathaway, German Literature of the Mid-Nineteenth Century in England and America as Reflected in the Journals, 1840–1914 (1935). Also to be mentioned are: J. Wesley Thomas, Amerikanische Dichter und die deutsche Literatur (1950); Stanley Vogel, German Literary Influences on the American Transcendentalists, 1810–1840 (1955); and P. A. Shelley et al., Anglo-German and American-German Crosscurrents, v. I (1957).

Geronimo [Indian name: **Goyathlay**] (b. Arizona, 1829—d. 1909), American Apache chieftain who in 1885–86 led a vigorous attack on white settlers, was captured by General George Crook (1829–1890), escaped, and later surrendered to General Nelson A. Miles (1839–1925). He finally settled down with members of his tribe on farmland and ranches at Fort Sill, Okla. There he joined the Dutch Reformed Church (1903) and dictated an account of his life to Stephen M. Barrett—Geronimo's Story of His Life (1906). He is described in Miles' Personal Recollections (1896); Britton Davis wrote The Truth about Geronimo (1929). A town in Arizona is named for him. During World War II American parachutists would often begin their leap downward by yelling "Geronimo!" The reason for this use of the term is unknown.

Gerontion (1920), a poem by T. S. ELIOT. The title of the poem comes from the Greek word geron which means "an old man"; the narrator, "an old man in a dry month," reviews in a series of associative images his past inaction and present inability to take action. The poem expresses Eliot's sense of the world as a cultural and emotional wasteland, and desire for some kind of salvation. Technically the poem shows a development toward SYMBOLISM; Eliot uses a tightly-packed, melodic free-verse line.

Gerould, Katharine Fuller (b. Brockton, Mass., Feb. 6, 1879—d. July 27, 1944), short-story writer, novelist, essayist. James Branch Cabell referred to Mrs. Gerould maliciously as one who tried to write like Henry James and occasionally succeeded in writing like Edith Wharton. There was, however, something more acrid and realistic in Mrs. Gerould than in either of them; perhaps the theories of Freud, then already in the air, really influenced her more. In her short stories—the best of them collected in VAIN OBLATIONS (1914), THE GREAT TRADITION (1915), and Valiant Dust (1922)—she exhibited an astonishing power of intellectualizing, with poignant restraint and irony, some extreme emotional or ethical situation. She also wrote essays (Modes and Morals, 1919; Ring-

side Seats, 1937) and novels (Lost Valley, 1922; Conquistador, 1923; The Light that Never Was, 1931), but did her best work in the short story.

Mrs. Gerould's husband, **Gordon Hall Gerould** (b. Goffstown, N.H., Oct. 4, 1877—d. April 11, 1953), taught English at Princeton (1905–1946). He was an authority on fiction, medieval and modern, and himself wrote several novels, including Youth in Harley (1920) and A Midsummer Mystery (1925). He also wrote on The Ballad of Tradition (1932).

Gerry, Elbridge (b. Marblehead, Mass., 1744—d. 1814), statesman, public official, writer on political topics. Gerry signed the Declaration of Independence and helped frame the Constitution, then wrote Observations on the New Constitution (1788), which created sentiment in favor of the proposed Bill of Rights. He held many public offices, served in Congress, was twice governor of Massachusetts, served as Vice-President (1813–14) under Madison. His name is preserved in the term gerrymander, since the cutting up of one voting district in order to preserve control for his political party was attributed to his influence as governor. GILBERT STUART took his pencil and added head, wings, and claws to an outline of the political district, and said, "That will do for a salamander." A quick-witted editor retorted, "Better say gerrymander." The term now is a standard word for irregular juggling of the boundaries of political districts.

Gershwin, George (b. Brooklyn, N.Y., Sept. 26, 1898—d. July 11, 1937), composer. He sold his first song at eighteen; two years later he wrote the classic tune Swanee for Al Jolson, and the score for a complete musical comedy, La, La, Lucille. Beginning in 1920 he composed the music for five successive George White Scandals; in the same period he wrote many popular songs, including Somebody Loves Me (1924). Part of one performance of the 1923 Scandals was a one-act opera, 135th Street, later performed independently at Carnegie Hall. It was serious in tone, even though it employed the idiom of jazz; as a result Paul Whiteman commissioned Gershwin to write the famous Rhapsody in Blue (1923). Gershwin went on to other great successes, including music for An American in Paris (1928), Strike Up the Band (1930), OF THEE I SING (1931), and Let 'Em Eat Cake (1933). Finally came his masterpiece, Porgy and Bess (1935), a folk opera based on the book by DuBose HEYWARD, with lyrics by Heyward and by IRA GERSHWIN. (See PORGY.) Jazz Piano Preludes was composed in 1936, but the last two years of his life he could not produce any more large musical compositions. Even in so short a life he attained worldwide fame for his exaltation of jazz and popular music. David Ewen's Journey to Greatness (1956) gives a full account of his life and music, as does George Gershwin: Man and Legend (1958), by Merle Armitage.

Gershwin, Ira (b. New York City, Dec. 6, 1896—   ), lyricist. He wrote the words for his brother George's earliest compositions, and continued to write lyrics cleverly and competently after George's death in 1937. A book of his personal experiences in the field of lyric writing, *Lyrics on Several Occasions,* came out in 1959. Among the Broadway shows for which he has written the lyrics are: *Lady Be Good* (1924); *Oh, Kay!* (1926); *Funny Face* (1927); *Strike Up the Band* (1930); OF THEE I SING (1931); *Let 'Em Eat Cake* (1933); *Porgy and Bess* (1935), with DuBose HEYWARD; *Lady in the Dark* (1941); *An American in Paris* (a movie, 1951, with music by GEORGE GERSHWIN); *A Star Is Born* and *The Country Girl* (both movies, 1954).

Gertrude of Wyoming (1809), a narrative poem by Thomas Campbell. The British poet (1777–1844) was one of the earliest European writers to take for a work of imagination an American setting. In skillful but uninspired Spenserian stanzas he described the devastation wrought by an Indian attack in 1778 on the quiet valley of Wyoming in Pennsylvania, and on the marriage of Henry Waldegrave and Gertrude, daughter of the patriarch Albert.

Gesell, Arnold (b. Alma, Wis., June 21, 1880 —d. May 29, 1961), clinical psychologist, child specialist. Gesell founded the Yale Child Development Clinic in 1911 and was its director until 1948. He was research consultant for The Gesell Institute of Child Development from 1950 to 1958. His studies of normal development in the embryo, the infant, and children from preschool age through adolescence have become authoritative guides for parents and social scientists. *Infant Development* (1952) is a good introduction to Gesell's method. He establishes the psychological norms of behavior at each stage of the infant's growth after pragmatically examining a large number of cases. Using this guide book, parents can determine the normalcy of their own child's behavior. Gesell's work with films is well known. He established a photographic library, The Yale Films of Child Development, in 1925, and produced *The Embryology of Human Behavior* (1949–50) for the Medical Film Institute. From 1930 he employed motion pictures in his research; he has produced a number of scientific and educational films. Among his books: *The Child From Five to Ten* (1946, with F. Ilg); *Youth: The Years From Ten to Sixteen* (1956, with Frances Ilg and Louise Ames).

Gessler, Clifford [Franklin] (b. Milton Junction, Wis., Nov. 9, 1893—   ), poet, teacher, newspaperman, critic. Gessler did newspaper work in California and Hawaii, and many of his poems and prose writings have related to Hawaiian scenes and persons. Among his publications: *Slants* (1924); *Kanaka Moon* (1927); *Road My Body Goes* (1937); *Hawaii, Isles of Enchantment* (1937); *Tropic Earth* (1944); *The Reasonable Life* (1950).

Get-Rich-Quick Wallingford (1908), a group of related stories by GEORGE RANDOLPH CHESTER. Wallingford, whose name has become part of American folklore, is a company promoter. With his satellite Blackie Daw, he engages in many dubious enterprises, but manages to escape the hand of the law. He is probably the liveliest and most engaging rascal in American picaresque fiction. Chester continued his adventures in several other books: *Young Wallingford* (1910); *Wallingford and Blackie Daw* (1913); *Wallingford in His Prime* (1913). GEORGE M. COHAN made a successful dramatization of the stories (1910), which concluded piously with Wallingford saying: "What a fool a man is to be a crook!"

Gettysburg, Pa., and the **Gettysburg Address.** Gettysburg is a town of a few thousand inhabitants in Adams Co., Pa. The Battle of Gettysburg, the turning point of the Civil War, took place on July 1, 2, and 3, 1863. Flushed with his great victory at Chancellorsville, Lee swept into Pennsylvania hoping to destroy the Army of the Potomac. At Gettysburg he met the northern army. The Union forces were driven back to heights later known as Cemetery Hill and Cemetery Ridge. Many attacks and severe artillery fire failed to bring the battle to a conclusion. In midafternoon the firing slackened, and the Confederate General George Edward Pickett directed a tremendous charge up Cemetery Ridge with fifteen thousand men. They met a deadly fire, and although some of the Confederate forces gained their objective, it was at too great a price; the attack ended in defeat. Next day the Confederate army withdrew from the bloody battlefield.

Immediately after the battle a large portion of the site became a National Cemetery. The cemetery was dedicated on Nov. 19, 1863; Senator EDWARD EVERETT was the orator of the day. President ABRAHAM LINCOLN was present to make "a few remarks." A huge crowd listened to Everett with respect and applause as he delivered his two-hour address. Then Lincoln arose and spoke for two minutes, giving what is officially known as "An Address Delivered at the Dedication of the Cemetery at Gettysburg." Exactly how Lincoln's brief remarks were received is not known. It is, at any rate, inaccurate to say that the *Address* was not appreciated for a long time, as it received warm praise from many contemporaries.

Five versions of the *Address* exist. Lincoln wrote one in the White House, revised it en route to Gettysburg or in the town itself, actually delivered a version somewhat different from the latter. A third version was written soon afterward at Everett's request, and was sold in a fair held for the benefit of survivors of the Union troops. Two more versions were written by Lincoln for a similar occasion. The address has always been regarded as Lincoln's masterpiece. Roy P. Basler points out how skillfully and subtly Lincoln employed repetition (such key words as *they, we, here*), alliteration, assonance, parallelism. William B. Hesseltine, in *Lincoln and the War Governors* (1948), shows that Lincoln during the war years moved steadily to take away powers of the states and build a nation. He reached a climax in the *Gettysburg*

Address, which was about a nation and spoken to a nation and not about a league of states.

The Battle of Gettysburg immediately inspired northern poets to some striking verses: Bayard Taylor's *Gettysburg Ode,* Edmund Clarence Stedman's *Gettysburg,* Bret Harte's *John Burns at Gettysburg.* Later, Elsie Singmaster wrote *Gettysburg: Stories of the Red Harvest and the Aftermath* (1913); but MacKinlay Kantor's novel, *Long Remember* (1934), gives the most accurate and impressive picture of the battle. Mary Raymond Shipman Andrews wrote "a sentimental footnote to history" in THE PERFECT TRIBUTE (1906), a fictional version of the delivery of the *Address.* Earl Schenck Miers and Richard A. Brown's *Gettysburg* (1948) is a careful, documented story of the battle. Clifford Dowdey has factually analyzed the campaign in *Pickett's Charge* (1957) and *Death of a Nation* (1958).

Ghent, Treaty of. This treaty, signed on Dec. 24, 1814, in effect did no more than end the War of 1812, leaving disputes for future negotiations; in April, 1817, a treaty of much greater importance was concluded. This provided, among other things, for the complete disarmament of the American-Canadian border.

Ghost of the Buffaloes, The (1917), a poem by VACHEL LINDSAY. In Lindsay's customary elocutionary style, the piece is, says Harry Haydon Clark, "an impressive illustration of his power in dealing with the primitive, colorful, vigorous, and romantic aspects of local tradition."

Giant-Killer (1928), a novel by ELMER DAVIS. A realistic and somewhat cynical retelling of the story of David and Goliath, with local color based on careful research.

Giants in the Earth: A Saga of the Prairie (published in Norwegian, 1924–25; in English, 1927), a novel by OLE E. RÖLVAAG. In a powerful depiction of the life of an immigrant family on the plains of South Dakota, Rölvaag tells how Per Hansa, whose early days had been spent on the sea, brings his family in 1873 to a farm far from any neighbors, and becomes passionately devoted to the land. But his wife continues to long for the civilized comforts of Norway, is reconciled only when a minister visits them and gives her the comforts of religion; she becomes in fact a religious fanatic. When a friend lies dying she insists that her husband go out and bring back a minister; he leaves in a blizzard and never returns. The narrative describes endless struggles with harsh nature in a new land. The English version was made by the author in collaboration with Lincoln Colcord; a stage version of the book by Thomas Job appeared in 1928. Rölvaag wrote two sequels: PEDER VICTORIOUS (1927) and THEIR FATHER'S GOD (1931).

Gibbons, Floyd P[hillips] (b. Washington, D.C., July 16, 1887—d. Sept. 24, 1939), war correspondent, author, radio commentator. Gibbons was always in the forefront of the battle and lost his left eye in the Battle of Château-Thierry. Wherever wars or revolutions took place, Gibbons was on the spot. He wrote *How the Laconia Sank* (1917); *And They Thought We Wouldn't Fight* (1918); *The Red Knight of Germany* (1927).

Gibbons, James Cardinal (b. Baltimore, Md., July 23, 1834—d. March 24, 1921), religious leader, author, memoirist. Ordained a priest in 1861, Gibbons rose steadily until he was created a cardinal in 1886. He helped establish the Catholic University of Washington. Among his writings: *The Faith of Our Fathers* (1877); *Our Christian Heritage* (1889); *A Retrospect of 50 Years* (2 v., 1916).

Gibbs, Emily. Young heroine of OUR TOWN, a play by Thornton Wilder. She dies in childbirth, returns as a grieving spirit to her New Hampshire village. What she sees and learns there in a poignant realization of life reconciles her to her eternal future.

Gibbs, Josiah Willard (b. Salem, Mass., April 30, 1790—d. March 25, 1861), linguist, Orientalist. He taught sacred literature at Yale Divinity School (1826–61). Among his works were a translation of a German dictionary, *Hebrew and English Lexicon of the Old Testament* (1824), and *Philological Studies* (1857). His son, **J. Willard Gibbs** (b. New Haven, Feb. 11, 1839—d. April 28, 1903), attained even wider fame as a mathematical physicist and philosopher. His entire career was spent at Yale, as a student and teacher. He won scientific honors all over the world. Albert Einstein called him "the greatest mind in American history." He was undoubtedly difficult, writing in a style that resembled mathematics more than English. His most important work was a "paper" that ran to 160,000 words, *On the Equilibrium of Heterogeneous Substances.* This was first published in installments in the *Transactions of the Connecticut Academy* (October, 1875; May, 1876; May, 1877), then in the *American Journal of Science* (December, 1878). P. S. Epstein, in *A Commentary on the Scientific Writings of J. Willard Gibbs* (1936), wrote: "We see here a phenomenon almost unparalleled in the history of science. A young investigator, having discovered an entirely new branch of science, gave in a single contribution an exhaustive treatment of it which foreshadowed the development of theoretical chemistry for a quarter of a century." Among his other writings: *Elementary Principles in Statistical Mechanics* (1902); *Scientific Papers* (collected in 1906); the *Collected Works,* edited by W. R. Longley and R. G. Van Name (2 v., 1928). In *Willard Gibbs* (1942) Muriel Rukeyser explores some of the philosophical and mystical implications of Gibbs' ideas.

Gibbs, Wolcott (b. New York City, March 15, 1902—d. Aug. 16, 1958), critic, short-story writer, parodist. Gibbs was closely associated with THE NEW YORKER throughout his professional career, as editor, reporter, fiction writer, and drama critic. His weekly play reviews for many years were noted for their incisively deflating eloquence, not always devoid of malice. He engaged in a feud with his fellow drama critic BURTON RASCOE, and when the latter accused Gibbs of stealing his material, Gibbs responded, "I have done many terrible things in my life, but I have never robbed the poor box." Gibbs struck out at cant and pomposity wherever he found them and did much to shape *The New Yorker's* early iconoclastic attitudes. He wrote *Bed of Neuroses* (1937), part of which was republished in *More in Sorrow* (1958), his last book. His one play, *Season in the Sun* (1950), was moderately successful; one of its leading characters was modeled on Harold Ross of *The New Yorker*.

Gibson, Charles Dana (b. Roxbury, Mass., Sept. 14, 1867—d. Dec. 23, 1944), illustrator, author. Gibson won success in his teens and held it to the end of his life. The greater part of his career was spent on LIFE. He illustrated many books and articles, notably the stories of RICHARD HARDING DAVIS. But his greatest triumph was the creation (1896) of the so-called "Gibson Girl," who appeared in innumerable drawings. (His model was his wife, the former Irene Langhorne.) She was beautiful, dignified, and fashionable—the last because everybody from the "400" to the shopgirl immediately began imitating her looks, clothes, and manners. Gibson published collections of his drawings, also travel observations; among them, *Drawings* (1894); *Pictures of People* (1896); *Sketches and Cartoons* (1898); *The Education of Mr. Pipp* (1899); *Sketches in Egypt* (1899); *The Americans* (1900); *A Widow and Her Friends* (1901); *Social Ladder* (1902); *Our Neighbors* (1905).

Gibson, William (b. New York City, Nov. 13, 1914—   ), author, playwright. After leaving the City College of New York, Gibson wrote for years without much financial success, until his novel *Cobweb* was brought for the motion pictures. The cast of his comedy *Two for the Seesaw* (1959) was kept to only two characters for reasons of economy. A bright success on Broadway, it told the story of a Bronx gamine, with ulcers and heavy emotional problems, involved with a Midwestern lawyer. Gibson's first title for this play was "After the Verb To Love," which he said "nobody liked but me." *Dinny and the Witches*, a fantasy, was produced off-Broadway in 1959. *The Miracle Worker* became a great success in 1960, after its adaptation from the original television play, which had won the Sylvania Award. It is the story of HELEN KELLER as a child, and of the heroic efforts of her tutor, Anne Sullivan, to break through the almost insurmountable barrier of her deafness and blindness and communicate to her the basic concepts of learning. *The Seesaw Log* (1959) records the adventures and misadventures of *Two for the Seesaw* on the road.

Giddings, Franklin H[enry] (b. Sherman, Conn., March 23, 1855—d. June 11, 1931), teacher, sociologist, author. For the greater part of his career Giddings was on the faculty of Columbia University. He was a man of learning and of trenchant mind, who never hesitated to say what he thought. His books on his special subjects were among the earliest to be published in this field, particularly *The Principles of Sociology* (1896). In later years he wrote *The Responsible State* (1918) and *The Scientific Study of Human Society* (1924).

Gideons, Society of the. See BIBLE IN THE U.S.

Gifford, Fannie Stearns Davis (b. Cleveland, Ohio, March 6, 1884—d. Feb. 24, 1958), poet. Mrs. Gifford's verses are marked by delicacy of feeling and skillful wording. She published *Myself and I* (1913), *Crack o' Dawn* (1915), and *The Ancient Beautiful Things* (1923).

gift books. See ANNUALS and LADY'S BOOKS.

Gift of the Magi, The (1906), a story by O. HENRY. Containing perhaps the most famous of O. Henry's trick endings, this Yuletide narrative tells how a young husband and wife each try to buy the other a suitable Christmas present. He sells his watch to buy her a set of combs; she has her beautiful hair cut off and sells the tresses to buy him a watch-fob. But O. Henry is sure that in the end they don't mind. The tale is included in THE FOUR MILLION.

Gilbert, Sir Humphrey (1539?–1583), English navigator and soldier. The half-brother of Sir WALTER RALEGH, Gilbert served in various European military expeditions, finally set out on an expedition to settle colonists in the New World (1578–79) but failed. In a second try (1583) he established the first British colony in North America at St. John's, Newfoundland. His voyage was described in Edward Haies' contemporary narrative, *Sir Humphrey Gilbert and His Enterprise of Colonization in America* (printed, 1903). Longfellow wrote a stirring ballad, *Sir Humphrey Gilbert*.

Gilbreth, Frank B[unker] (b. Fairfield, Me., July 7, 1868—d. June 14, 1924), engineer, efficiency expert. He organized the Society for the Promotion of the Science of Management and wrote a *Primer of Scientific Management* (1911). His wife, **Lillian E[velyn] Gilbreth** (b. Oakland, Calif., May 24, 1878—   ), was also an engineer and collaborated with him in writing *Fatigue Study* (1919), *Time Study* (1920), and other books. After his death she continued his work as an efficiency expert. She wrote *Psychology of Management* (1912); *The Home-Maker and Her Job* (1927); *Living With Our Children* (1928); *Normal Lives for the Disabled* (1945, with Edna Yost); *The Foreman and Manpower Managements* (1947, with Alice Rice Cook); and *Management in the Home* (1954 and 1959, with O. M. Thomas and Eleanor C. Clymer). The hilarious account of life in a family of twelve children where both parents were geniuses and the father a richly amusing eccentric besides, is CHEAPER BY THE DOZEN (1949) by two of her children, Frank B. Gilbreth, Jr., and Ernestine Gilbreth Carey. Also about the famous pair was Edna Yost's *Frank and Lillian Gilbreth* (1949).

Gilchrist, Anne (1828–1885), an Englishwoman who, with her husband **Alexander** (1828–1861), wrote a *Life of Blake* (1863) and who became greatly interested in the poetry of WALT WHITMAN. At that time the "Children of Adam" section of *Leaves of Grass* was under attack for alleged indecency. Mrs. Gilchrist found nothing morally wrong in the poems, indeed found them beautiful. With her consent her letters were sent to Whitman and were published in the Boston *Radical* as "A Woman's Estimate of Walt Whitman." George Rice Carpenter held that their influence in decreasing the attacks on Whitman was "scarcely to be exaggerated." Later Mrs. Gilchrist came with her children to live in Philadelphia (1876–78), where the poet often visited her. Through her intercession substantial help came to him from abroad. At her death Whitman wrote of her: "My noblest woman friend, now buried in an English grave." Thomas B. Larned edited *The Letters of Anne Gilchrist and Walt Whitman* (1918).

Gilded Age, The (1873), a novel by MARK TWAIN and CHARLES DUDLEY WARNER. The plot is a sensational affair, involving seduction, murder, political corruption, the destruction of a steamboat by fire, wild financial speculation, etc. The book's mixture of satire, romance, and exposure became a success, perhaps chiefly owing to the central character, Colonel Beriah Sellers (see under COLONEL SELLERS), who strongly recalls Dickens' Micawber in his optimistic schemes for getting rich and his invariable failures. Sellers persuades his friend Squire "Si" Hawkins to join him in the development of some lands in Missouri; the project ends in a fiasco. The squire's adopted daughter Laura is seduced by Colonel Selby; later, in Washington, she murders him, is tried, and acquitted. There are one or two incidental love affairs which develop more happily but could just as well have been omitted. Much of the tale is based on reminiscence; Colonel Sellers is unquestionably Twain's kinsman James Lampton, and Laura Hawkins was suggested by Mrs. Laura Fair of California, who had recently been acquitted of murder on the ground of emotional insanity. Senator Dilworthy, a corrupt politician, was modeled on Senator Pomeroy of Kansas; William M. Weed and his associates closely resembled the Tweed Ring of New York. In the dramatic version of the novel (1874) Seller's first name was changed to Mulberry, and that name was also employed in THE AMERICAN CLAIMANT (1892), a sequel to the novel. The phrase "Gilded Age" has become a common description of the hectic post-Civil War period of which Twain and Warner wrote; and the novel itself was a forerunner of many similar attacks on political corruption and financial juggling.

Gilder, Richard Watson (b. Bordentown, N.J., Feb. 8, 1844—d. Nov. 18, 1909), newspaper and magazine editor, poet. Gilder headed an important literary circle in the final decades of the 19th century—first in Newark, later in New York City. He served as a newspaper editor in Newark, later conducting SCRIBNER'S MONTHLY (1870–81), and *The Century Magazine* (1881–1909), in the metropolis. He wrote poetry, highly regarded in its time, including *The New Day* (1876) and *Five Books of Songs* (1900); his *Letters* appeared in 1916. But he showed the caliber of his mind by refusing to receive Robert Louis Stevenson when he passed through New York; he had heard rumors about Stevenson's private life and did not consider him respectable. His sister, **Jeanette Gilder** (b. Flushing, N.Y., Oct. 3, 1849—d. Jan. 17, 1916), helped to make the news of authors a literary commodity and wrote entertainingly about her encounters with writers in *The Autobiography of a Tomboy* (1900) and *The Tomboy at Work* (1904). She and her brother Joseph founded and edited *The Critic* (1881–1906); they collaborated on *Essays from "The Critic"* (1883) and *Authors at Home* (1888).

Gildersleeve, Basil L[anneau] (b. Charleston, S.C., Oct. 23, 1831—d. Jan. 9, 1924), teacher, classicist, editor. Gildersleeve was one of the best-known scholars of his day, famous as an authority on Greek and Latin, as in his *Essays and Studies* (1890) and *Hellas and Hesperia* (1909), but also a writer of vigor on *The Creed of the Old South, 1865–1915* (1915). He founded and edited the *American Journal of Philology* (1876–1915).

Giles Corey. See COREY, GILES.

Gill, Brendan (b. Hartford, Conn., Oct. 4, 1914—   ), novelist, short-story writer, poet, critic. His name is usually associated with the *New Yorker* magazine, which he joined after graduation from Yale in 1936. He was well known as a short-story writer for that magazine when he published his first novel, *The Trouble of One House* (1950). This carefully etched study of a dying woman seemed purposely to restrain the charm and humor of Gill's stories in order to sharpen the characters. The book received an award from the National Institute of Arts and Letters and a special citation from the National Book Awards. *The Day the Money Stopped* (1957) is a comedy written almost entirely in dialogue, so it was no surprise that Gill and MAXWELL ANDERSON adapted it as a play the year after it was written.

Gillette, William [Hooker] (b. Hartford, Conn., July 24, 1855—d. April 29, 1937), actor, playwright. Gillette was a capable, intelligent actor, especially effective in his own plays. The best of them was his four-act dramatization of Arthur Conan Doyle's famous stories, under the title *Sherlock Holmes* (1899). Almost equally popular were *Esmeralda* (1881), HELD BY THE ENEMY (1886), and SECRET SERVICE (1895). He also played many Shakespearean roles.

Gilligan, Edmund (b. Waltham, Mass., June 7, 1899—   ), editor, novelist. Many of Gilligan's excellent novels of the sea have been depictions of Gloucester fishermen in which realistic details have given plausibility to romantic plots. Among them: *White Sails Crowding* (1939); *The Gaunt Woman* (1943); *Voyage of the Golden Hind* (1945); *I Name Thee Mara* (1946); *Storm at Sable Island* (1948); *My Earth, My Sea* (1959).

Gillilan, Strickland (b. Jackson, Ohio, Oct. 9,

1869—d. April 25, 1954), newspaperman, editor, comic writer. Although he wrote much else of merit, Gillilan is remembered mainly for two pieces of verse. Working in 1897 for the Richmond (Ind.) *Palladium*, he ran across a story of an Irish railroad foreman who had been told to "make it brief" when reporting wrecks. His telegram on one occasion Gillilan turned into a poem with a famous refrain: "Off agin, on agin, gone agin, FINNIGIN." This became the leading poem of his collection, *Including Finnigin* (1910). In 1940 he calculated that he had recited the poem more than 11,000 times. In 1894 Gillilan published in the Baltimore *American* what he believed to be the shortest poem in the English language. It is called *Microbes* and reads: "Madam,/Adam/Had 'em." Gillilan collected his writings in *You and Me* (1917); *A Sample Case of Humor* (1918); *Laugh It Off* (1924); *Gillilan, Finnigin, & Co.* (1940).

Gillis, James Martin (b. Boston, Nov. 12, 1876—d. March 14, 1957), clergyman, teacher, columnist, editor. A member of the Congregation of Paulist Fathers, Gillis became active as a teacher and writer in the Catholic Church. In 1922 he was appointed editor of *The Catholic World*. He also wrote a syndicated column, "Sursum Corda: What's Right with the World," and gave many addresses on the radio. His books include: *False Prophets* (1925); *Christianity and Civilization* (1932); *The Paulists* (1932); *So Near is God* (1953).

Gilliss, Walter (b. Lexington, Ky., May 17, 1855—d. Sept. 24, 1925), printer, poet, memoirist. Gilliss founded the Gilliss Press in New York City in 1871, and it became noted for the beauty and excellence of its productions. He wrote *A Printer's Sun Dial* (1913); *Verses and Songs* (1916); *Recollections of the Gilliss Press* (1926).

Gilman, Arthur (b. Alton, Ill., June 22, 1837—d. Dec. 27, 1909), editor, historian. Gilman edited *Chaucer* (3 v., 1879); *Lothrop's Library of Entertaining History* (6 v., 1880–85); *A Library of Religious Poetry* (1887); and other works. He also wrote *Boston, Past and Present* (1873). He is chiefly remembered as a champion of higher education for women. He proposed the "Harvard Annex" (founded 1878), which extended Harvard College instruction to women. When this became Radcliffe College in 1893, he was promoted from executive secretary to regent of the college.

Gilman, Caroline Howard (b. Boston, Oct. 8, 1794—d. Sept. 15, 1888), poet, editor, memoirist. Mrs. Gilman, the wife of a clergyman, began writing religious verse at an early age. She was well acquainted with conditions in the North and the South and described them cheerfully and unaffectedly in *Recollections of a New England Housekeeper* (1834); *The Poetry of Traveling in the United States* (1838); and *Recollections of a Southern Matron* (1838). Her verse was collected in *Tales and Ballads* (1839); and *Verses of a Lifetime* (1849). In 1832 she commenced the publication of *The Rose Bud*,

a weekly juvenile publication, one of the earliest, if not the first, of its kind in the country.

Gilman, Daniel Coit (b. Norwich, Conn., July 6, 1831—d. Oct. 13, 1908), teacher, college administrator, editor, historian. In the course of his distinguished career, Gilman taught at Yale, was president of the University of California (1872–75) and first president of Johns Hopkins University (1876–1901), where he drew many famous scholars to the faculty. On his retirement he became the first president of the Carnegie Institution (1901–04). He was editor-in-chief of the *New International Encyclopedia* (1902); and wrote *James Monroe* (1883); *University Problems* (1898); and *The Launching of a University* (1906). His own teachings greatly promoted the acceptance of the Darwinian hypothesis.

Gilman, Lawrence (b. Flushing, N.Y., July 5, 1878—d. Sept. 8, 1939), newspaperman, critic, writer on music. In 1896 Gilman became a reporter on the New York *Herald*. Two years later he joined the staff of *Harper's Weekly* and eventually became managing editor. In 1913 he became one of the editors of *Harper's Monthly*, in 1921 went over to the *North American Review*, in 1923 was made music critic of the New York *Tribune* (later the *Herald Tribune*) and continued there until his death. Gilman wrote on music with deep enthusiasm for the objects of his special admiration. Among his books: *Phases of Modern Music* (1904); *Edward MacDowell* (1906); *Nature in Music* (1914); *Wagner's Operas* (1937).

Gilmer, Elizabeth Meriwether ["Dorothy Dix"] (b. Montgomery Co., Tenn., Nov. 18, 1870—d. Dec. 16, 1951), newspaperwoman, columnist. After her marriage Mrs. Gilmer became a reporter and feature writer on the New Orleans *Picayune*, adopting an alliterative pen name which in time became one of the most famous in the world. The readers of her column, "Dorothy Dix Talks," were scattered all over the world, and were calculated to total sixty million. Various syndicates took over the distribution of her copy. Three days a week there was a sermonette, usually sensible advice and exhortation. On the other three days letters from readers appeared together with comments. Such letters, in which readers asked help on their problems, reached "Dorothy Dix" at the rate of many hundreds a day. She published *How to Win and Hold a Husband* (1939) and other collections. Harnett T. Kane wrote a biography, *Dear Dorothy Dix* (1952).

Gilpatric, Guy (b. New York City., Jan. 21, 1896—d. July 7, 1950), aviator, advertising copywriter, short-story writer, novelist. Gilpatric was a test pilot and flying instructor before World War I; he served from August, 1917, to December, 1918, in the A.E.F. He began to write in 1918, especially stories dealing with a rough-and-ready character, "Muster Colin Glencannon," chief engineer of the S.S. *Inchcliffe Castle*, whom one reader described as "undoubtedly the biggest, drunkenst, 'fightenest' blackguard in either steam or sail, on any ocean." Gilpatric's books include *Scotch and Water* (1931); *Half Seas Over* (1932); *Mr. Glencannon* (1935); *Three Sheets in the Wind* (1936); *The Glencannon Omnibus* (1937); *The Gentleman with the Walrus Mustache* (1938); *Glencannon Afloat* (1941); *Second Glencannon Omnibus* (1942); *Action in the North Atlantic* (1943); *Guy Gilpatric's Flying Stories* (1945); *The Canny Mr. Glencannon* (1947); *The Last Glencannon Omnibus* (1953).

Gilpin, William (b. Brandywine, Pa., Oct. 4, 1813?—d. Jan. 20, 1894), soldier, public official, expounder of geopolitics. Born in a Quaker family, Gilpin nevertheless entered West Point, but left shortly to study law. However, adventure in the West and army life attracted him strongly. He joined Frémont in his Pacific explorations, served in the war with Mexico, made himself thoroughly acquainted with the West, and when Lincoln became President was appointed first territorial governor of Colorado, which he helped to save for the Union cause. He settled permanently in Denver and began to write books which Wallace Stegner describes as setting forth "not merely a new theory of property and a new economic philosophy, but the first geopolitical theorizing, the first global thought." Within what he called "the Isothermal Zodiac" all great civilizations develop, Gilpin stated, the United States lay within that belt and would in time become the great world example of unity, peace, and prosperity. He urged methods of uniting the nations; for example, intercontinental railroads at the Bering Strait and Gibraltar. These ideas were set forth in *The Central Gold Region* (1860; reissued, 1873, as *The Mission of the North American People*) and *The Cosmopolitan Railway Compacting and Fusing Together All the World's Continents* (1890).

Gingrich, Arnold (b. Grand Rapids, Mich., Dec. 5, 1903—), advertising copywriter, editor. Gingrich became editor of a trade magazine, *Apparel Arts,* and in 1933 became editor of *Esquire,* which he made into a successful combination of risqué humor and some of the best serious writing done in the United States. He also edited *Coronet.*

Ginsberg, Allen (b. Newark, N.J., June 3, 1926—), poet. Leading poet of the so-called "beat generation," Ginsberg writes a loosely structured, prophetic-sounding line. HOWL (1955) is a lament for what society did to his generation, turning some to suicide, drug addiction, homosexuality, and despair. Here and in his other work, as well as in his conversation, Ginsberg epitomized the cultural and literary nonconformity of the "beats." Writing in a highly unconventional manner, he often treats subjects some have considered obscene, though when the City Lights bookstore published *Howl,* it was cleared of an obscenity charge in San Francisco Municipal Court following a customs seizure of the first edition, printed in England. He achieved a wide notoriety beyond his poetry

as a result of popular interest in the bohemianism of the "beat generation." Ginsberg claimed a "predilection for apolitical mystic communism, homosexual romance, marijuana-high mentation, and cosmic ecstasy in Poetry." *Howl and Other Poems* (1956) has been translated into several foreign languages; *Kaddish and Other Poems* was published in 1961; *Empty Mirror: Early Poems* in 1961. See BEAT WRITING.

Ginsberg, Louis (b. Newark, N.J., Oct. 1, 1896—), poet. Father of ALLEN GINSBERG. A teacher of English in the Paterson (N.J.) Central High School for many years, Ginsberg contributed verse to magazines and newspapers. His work shows a combination of rhetoric and simplicity that is often effective. His poems have been collected in *The Attic of the Past and Other Poems* (1921) and *The Everlasting Minute and Other Poems* (1937).

Ginzberg, Louis (b. Russia, Nov. 28, 1873—d. Nov. 11, 1953), teacher, authority on the Talmud. Arriving in the United States in 1899, Ginzberg became a faculty member of the Jewish Theological Seminary in New York in 1902. Among his publications, some composed in German, are six volumes on *The Legends of the Jews* (1909–28) and many books on the Talmud, the ancient sects, and the church fathers' use of Jewish writings. He also wrote *Students, Scholars, and Saints* (1928).

Giovannitti, Arturo (b. Italy, Jan. 7, 1884—d. Dec. 31, 1959), teacher, preacher, poet. When Giovannitti came to the United States, he became a crusader for economic and social changes. He worked for a time in religious missions, then as a labor organizer. He participated in strikes, and his experiences in jail during a textile strike in Lawrence, Mass., furnished material for several impressive prose poems, including *The Walker,* which Alfred Kreymborg has called "simpler, more realistic, more potent" than Wilde's *Ballad of Reading Gaol.* Occasionally he wrote in meter and rhyme. His principal poems were collected in *Arrows in the Gale* (1914). The lynching of labor leader Frank Little inspired the poem *When the Cock Crows* (1917).

Girl I Left Behind Me, The (1893), a melodrama by DAVID BELASCO and FRANKLIN FYLES. This play is laid in an army post in the Sioux country. An Indian attack is about to succeed, the commander of the post is about to kill his daughter Kate to save her from the Sioux, when suddenly the clear bugle notes of rescuing cavalry are heard.

Girl of the Golden West, The (1905), a play by DAVID BELASCO. "The Girl" who is the heroine of this play keeps a saloon in a mining camp of the old West, but is also, as A. H. Quinn puts it, "at once pure, courageous, loyal, and passionate." The sheriff and an outlaw fall in love with her, and she with the outlaw; she gambles with the sheriff for the outlaw's life, cheats, and wins. But he is captured anyway. When the miners realize how deep her love for the outlaw is, they release him, and the two set out for another part of the country. Giacomo Puccini, the Italian composer (1858–1924) based his opera, *La Fanciulla del West* (1910), on Belasco's play—the first grand opera written on an American theme. A movie was based on the play in 1930.

Girl of the Limberlost, A (1909), a novel by Gene Stratton-Porter (see under PORTER). A continuation of Mrs. Porter's popular novel *Freckles* (1904), it tells of a girl who hunts moths in Indiana swamplands in order to earn money for an education.

Girl with the Green Eyes, The (produced, 1902; published, 1905), a play by CLYDE FITCH. This is a study of a pathologically jealous woman. After revelations of several kinds have convinced her how wrong she has been, she tries to commit suicide; Fitch manages, however, to give the play a somewhat artificial happy ending. Sculley Bradley selects this as one of Fitch's two best plays.

Girty, Simon (b. 1741—d. Feb. 18, 1818), known as "the Great Renegade." A Pennsylvanian by birth, Girty deserted from the Continental army in 1778 and fought with Indians and British against the colonists. He fled to Canada when the British gave up Detroit in 1796. He has been the subject of several books: Uriah James Jones's *Simon Girty, the Outlaw* (1846); Charles McKnight's *Simon Girty, "The White Savage"* (1880); C. W. Butterfield's *History of the Girtys* (1880). Thomas Boyd's *Simon Girty* (1928) is a fictional reconstruction.

Gist, Christopher (b. Maryland, 1706?–1759), explorer, soldier. Even earlier than Daniel Boone, Gist had explored regions in Ohio and Kentucky for the Ohio Company. He was with George Washington on his trip to Fort Duquesne (1753–54), and is credited with having at this time saved Washington's life. Later he guided Braddock's expedition (1755). He kept *Journals*, which were published in 1893.

"Give me liberty, or give me death!" Speaking in the Virginia House of Delegates, March 23, 1775, PATRICK HENRY made his famous speech in defiance of the British, concluding with the words, "I know not what course others may take, but as for me, give me liberty, or give me death!" This is according to the report of William Wirt in his *Sketches of the Life and Character of Patrick Henry* (1817).

Give Me the Splendid Silent Sun (1865), a poem by WALT WHITMAN. The poem falls into two parts. In the first Whitman tells how, tired of the city, he longs to escape to nature and solitude. But then he reverses himself and asks again for city streets and "interminable eyes." G. W. Allen has noted the skillful use of repetitive cadences in this poem.

Gladden, [Solomon] Washington (b. Pottsgrove, Pa., Feb. 11, 1836—d. July 2, 1918), clergyman, writer. Gladden had pastorates in Springfield, Mass., and Columbus, Ohio, also served on the staff of the INDEPENDENT (1871–75). He urged the practical application of religious doctrines to social problems. Among his books: *Plain Thoughts on the Art of Living*

(1868); *Art and Morality* (1897); *Recollections* (1909).

Gladiator, The (1831), a play by ROBERT MONTGOMERY BIRD. Written in blank verse, this drama furnished a vehicle for EDWIN FORREST, who appeared in it more than a thousand times. It was persistently revived till the 1890's. It tells the rousing story of Spartacus, the Thracian slave who led a revolt against Rome and was killed in battle (71 B.C.). The subject was remarkably *a propos* of the slavery question. Walt Whitman said it was "as full of 'abolitionism' as an egg is of meat."

Glasgow, Ellen [Anderson Gholson] (b. Richmond, Va., April 22, 1874—d. Nov. 21, 1945), novelist, short-story writer, memoirist. One of the greatest and most realistic of the regionalists, Miss Glasgow chose to remain placidly

within a limited area that she knew very well— not merely the South but rather the Old Dominion. She was a citizen of Virginia rather than of the world. Born at a time when the harsh conditions of the Reconstruction were at last being accepted grimly by the defeated South, she saw the defects of the South, but she makes a character in *The Sheltered Life* (1932) say, "It is all nonsense to talk as if Southerners were a special breed, all wanting the same things and thinking after the same pattern." She refused to make southernism a special mental ailment, as some other writers have done. Yet there is no doubt about the total effect of her writings; they acted like a gentle catharsis. Miss Glasgow's writing displays a sense of humor. Its effect may be described in the words of H. S. Canby: "She was a major historian of our times, who, almost singlehandedly, rescued Southern fiction from the glamorous sentimentality of the Lost Cause." Alfred Kazin has held that she was born "imprisoned in a social and physical tradition not of her making, and made her career by satirizing it." In her own words, however, she merely "tilled the fertile soil of man's vanity."

The development of Miss Glasgow's art was somewhat more subtle and uneven than these generalizations imply. Leo Gurko convincingly marks her life off into three stages. Some of her early stories belong to the very school she later satirized. Thus *The Battle-Ground* (1902) is described by Kazin as "a superior sword-and-cape romance based on the legend that the Civil War was fought between gentlemen and bounders." Nevertheless, one may see her as already a rebel against the decayed traditions of the South, what she called its "sanctified fallacies." In her early novels appear young people seeking to liberate themselves from the attitudes of their parents. But World War I and the years that followed matured Miss Glasgow's mind, for in her stories written at this time one finds an advance in complication and thoughtfulness. It was perhaps her greatest period, including such books as BARREN GROUND (1925), by many critics regarded as her best novel; THE ROMANTIC COMEDIANS (1926); *They Stooped to Folly* (1929), and *The Sheltered Life* (1932). In her third stage she became conservative. "Whereas earlier she had felt exquisitely for the doubts of the aged and the protests of the young," says Gurko, "her advice to both now, battered as they are by the depression, is to grit their teeth and bear it." The title of her chief book of this period, VEIN OF IRON (1935), is characteristic. For her story *In This Our Life* (1941) she belatedly won a Pulitzer Prize. She published a collection of stories, *The Shadowy Third and Other Stories* (1923), some of them—like *The Past*, a tale of a ghost exorcised—of great excellence. Her last book was *A Certain Measure: An Interpretation of Prose Fiction* (1943). Her books appeared in two collected editions: the "Old Dominion Edition" (8 v., 1929–33), revised and with prefaces by Miss Glasgow; and the "Virginia Edition" (12 v., 1938). Miss Glasgow never attained a wide popularity. Posthumously published were *The Woman Within* (1954), her autobiography, and a selection of *Letters of Ellen Glasgow* (1958), edited by Blair Rouse. See also VIRGINIA.

Glaspell, Susan (b. Davenport, Iowa, July 1, 1882—d. July 27, 1948), novelist, dramatist, memoirist. After working for Des Moines papers, Miss Glaspell began writing short stories, went on to write a novel, *The Glory of the Conquered* (1909). She married GEORGE CRAM COOK, a fellow writer, in 1913 and went to live at Provincetown, Cape Cod. There in 1915 she and her husband organized the PROVINCETOWN PLAYERS, an experimental theater formed to combat the standards of Broadway commercialism and to introduce serious new playwrights. In collaboration with her husband she wrote for

the first bill a satirical one-act play, SUPPRESSED DESIRES (1915; published, 1920), which was produced on a ramshackle wharf. TRIFLES (produced, 1916; published, 1920), dealing with the death of a man and the arrest of his wife on suspicion, has been, like the earlier play, a continuing favorite with little theaters and amateur groups. The Cooks ardently sponsored these theaters, encouraged young dramatists like EUGENE O'NEILL, and themselves continued to prepare plays strikingly different from the stereotyped material common of the time. Miss Glaspell wrote several novels: *The Visioning* (1911), *Lifted Masks* (1912), *Fidelity* (1915), *Brook Evans* (1928), *Judd Rankin's Daughter* (1945), and others. Among her plays are *The People* (1917), *Bernice* (1919), *The Inheritors* (1921), *The Verge* (1921), and ALISON'S HOUSE (1930). The last, a play based on the life of EMILY DICKINSON, was awarded a Pulitzer Prize. Cook, an authority on the Greek drama, emigrated to Greece, lived there for several years, died there in 1924. *The Road to the Temple* (1926) is Miss Glaspell's biography of her husband.

Glass, Hugh ([?]–1833?), western trapper. On one occasion he was attacked by a grizzly bear, left for dead, but later revived. On this legend John G. Neihardt built his narrative poem, THE SONG OF HUGH GLASS (1915). Lucy Lockwood Hazard found a resemblance between Neihardt's story and an episode in Irving's ADVENTURES OF CAPTAIN BONNEVILLE (1837), also with Hawthorne's ROGER MALVIN'S BURIAL (1832). F. F. Manfred's novel, *Lord Grizzly* (1954), gives a vivid account of this great scout and mountain man.

Glass, Montague [Marsden] (b. England, July 23, 1877—d. Feb. 3, 1934), lawyer, short-story writer. A man of many talents, Glass was forced by popular demand to specialize in the humor of New York City's garment manufacturers. So successful were his tales that in 1909 he abandoned his law practice. His collections include POTASH AND PERLMUTTER (1910), *Abe and Mawruss* (1911), *Potash and Perlmutter Settle Things* (1919), *The Truth about Potash and Perlmutter and Five Other Stories* (1924), and other books. Several of the stories found their way to Broadway, in successful collaborations with CHARLES KLEIN, R. C. Megrue, and other playwrights.

Glass Key, The (1931), a detective novel by DASHIELL HAMMETT. One of the best-known in the "hard-boiled" school of detective fiction and Hammett's own favorite among his books. A bootlegging gang is involved in the murder of a public official's son. Ned Beaumont gets himself appointed a special investigator, succeeds in running down the murderer, and takes the girl of the town's political boss away from him. It was made into a moving picture.

Glass Menagerie, The (1944), a play by TENNESSEE WILLIAMS. This play, which won the New York Drama Critics Circle Award in 1945, was Williams' first success, and is considered by many critics to be his best work. It was first produced at the Civic Theatre in

Chicago and later on Broadway. Tom Wingfield, who narrates the introduction and conclusion, describes the play as being set in memory, and therefore dimly lit, sentimental, and not realistic. The seven scenes of the play are set shortly before Tom leaves home to join the Merchant Marine. In a flat in the slums of St. Louis, while the colored lights and music of the Paradise Dance Hall intrude upon the scene, his mother, Amanda, constantly harks back to imagined scenes of her southern girlhood and her "gentleman callers." Tom's sister, Laura, slightly crippled from birth, withdraws into her private world, populated by the animals in her glass menagerie. At his mother's insistence, Tom brings his friend Jim home to dinner so that Laura may have a "gentleman caller" of her own. Jim accidentally breaks the horn on the unicorn, Laura's favorite glass animal, thus making it less of a freak and more like the other horses, and manages to bring Laura out of her shyness and isolation for a few moments. However, after kissing Laura, Jim admits that he is already engaged, and Laura's emergence from her fragile world is left in doubt.

Glencarn, or, The Disappointments of Youth (1810), a novel by GEORGE WATTERSON. Watterson was a follower of CHARLES BROCKDEN BROWN in the Gothic tradition. Misfortune follows the hero Glencarn from the time when he is laid as a foundling on someone's doorstep; at the end, however, he is rescued from his various griefs and even discovers his parents. Alexander Cowie remarks that "one can only guess that the book prevailed by the sheer bulk (three volumes) of its bizarre adventure and by the tone of heavy romantic melancholy that reverberates through the whole tale."

Glick, Carl (b. Marshalltown, Iowa, Sept. 11, 1890—   ), actor, director, playwright, teacher, author of books on China. Glick began an active career in the theater in 1909, especially in the community theaters of Waterloo, Iowa; San Pedro and San Antonio, Tex.; York, Pa.; Columbia, S.C.; and Schenectady, N.Y. Among his plays: *It Isn't Done* (1928); *The Devil's Host* (1934); *The Laughing Buddha* (1937). Among his lively books on Chinese subjects: *Shake Hands with the Dragon* (1941), *Three Times I Bow* (1943), *The Secret of Serenity* (1951), *Death Sits In* (1954). His autobiography is called *I'm a Busybody* (1949). Glick is the author of numerous children's books and editor of *A Treasury of Masonic Thought* (1953).

Glimpses of Unfamiliar Japan (1894), by LAFCADIO HEARN. Hearn arrived in Japan in 1890, obtained a position as a teacher in a small town still ruled by feudal customs, and with the help of good native interpreters and his own keen sympathy obtained an intelligent view of Japanese life and character. His observations during two years appear in this book.

Glory Trail, The (included in *Sun and Saddle Leather,* a collection, 1915), a cowboy ballad by CHARLES BADGER CLARK. It is a ballad that the cowboys themselves have adopted and sing.

Gloucester, Mass. A town (founded in 1623) on Cape Ann, noted for its fishing industry and more recently as a resort town. While Gloucester fishermen range up and down the seas from the capes of Greenland to Virginia, they have especially sought the treacherous Grand Banks. It is said that 8,000 Gloucester fishermen have lost their lives in their calling. Several novelists, particularly JAMES B. CONNOLLY and EDMUND GILLIGAN, have written stories about these fishermen. WILLIAM VAUGHN MOODY wrote *Gloucester Moors* (1901), a stirring poem in behalf of the economic underdog. A famous juvenile story, Kirk Munroe's *Dorymates* (1890), describes the life of Gloucester fishermen. Other books on Gloucester: James Babson's *History of the Town of Gloucester* (1860); C. B. Hawes' *Gloucester: By the Sea* (1923); James B. Connolly's *The Port of Gloucester* (1940). Probably the greatest of all stories based on Gloucester, however, is Rudyard Kipling's *Captains Courageous* (1897).

Glueck, Nelson (b. Cincinnati, Ohio, June 4, 1900—   ), historian, archaeologist. Dr. Glueck, President of the Hebrew Union College-Jewish Institute of Religion for Cincinnati, New York, and Los Angeles, became a rabbi in 1923. He also distinguished himself as a professor and archaeologist, and received recognition from many groups for his writing, teaching, and research. He studied at the University of Cincinnati, Hebrew Union College, and the Universities of Berlin, Heidelberg, and Jena. His archaeological explorations led to several books in which he reinterpreted Bible literature. He uncovered more than 1,000 ancient sites in Palestine and Trans-Jordan, discovered King Solomon's copper mines, and excavated Solomon's port city of Ezion-Geber on the Red Sea. *Rivers In the Desert* (1959) was the result of six years' research in the Negev. In this handsomely illustrated volume Glueck contradicted the climatic theory of historic determinism by showing that the climate of the region has been constant for 10,000 years and therefore not the cause of the catastrophes suffered by its ancient civilizations. His other books: *Explorations in Eastern Palestine* (v. I–IV, 1939–1951); *The Other Side of the Jordan* (1940); and *The River Jordan* (1946).

Goddard, Charles William (b. Portland, Me., [?], 1880—d. Jan. 11, 1951), newspaperman, playwright, scriptwriter. See PERILS OF PAULINE.

Goddard, Pliny Earle (b. Lewiston, Me., Nov. 24, 1869—d. July 12, 1928), ethnologist, authority on American Indians. Goddard became curator of the department of ethnology of the American Museum of Natural History in 1909 and continued in that office until his death. He was editor of *The American Anthropologist* (1915–20) and wrote many monographs on Indian tribes, including *Life and Culture of the Hupa* (1903), *Indians of the Southwest* (1913), *Indians of the Northwest Coast* (1922).

Godey's Lady's Book. Louis A. Godey (1804–1878) combined hard business sense with soft sentiment to make his *Lady's Book* the most successful of all American magazines before the mid-19th century; by that time it was

bringing delight to 40,000 homes and had made its publisher a millionaire. It was famous for its hand-colored fashion plates and its art reproductions through the medium of excellent steel and copper engravings. It published leading American authors (at good contributors' rates), such as Poe, Longfellow, Emerson, Hawthorne, W. G. Simms, N. P. Willis, and Mrs. Stowe, as well as endless sentimental stories and verses by popular writers. Godey founded the magazine in Philadelphia in 1830 and was sole editor for its first six years; he brought in SARAH JOSEPHA HALE as "editress" when he bought her Boston *Ladies' Magazine.* Mrs. Hale, the author of *Mary Had a Little Lamb* and many other verses, was a strong advocate of women's rights and leader of the movement that led President Lincoln to proclaim the first national observance of Thanksgiving Day. Godey, however, always shared in the editorship of his magazine. In 1877 Mrs. Hale retired. The next year Godey died, and the magazine was soon outstripped by its Philadelphia rival, *Peterson's Magazine* (1842–1898). It was moved to New York in 1892, to die there six years later.

Godfrey, Thomas (b. Philadelphia, Dec. 4, 1736—d. Aug. 3, 1763), poet, playwright. Godfrey served in the militia, was a factor in Wilmington, wrote verse (of no high quality) constantly, and had some of it published in magazines or in book form: *The Court of Fancy* (1752), *Victory* (1753), *Ode on Friendship, The Invitation, Ode to Wine* (all 1758). He also wrote a blank-verse play, *The Prince of Parthia,* published two years after his death along with *Juvenile Poems on Various Subjects;* there is no direct evidence that it was actually performed. Arthur Hobson Quinn edited a reprint of the play (1917), Thomas C. Pollock considered its relationship to Nicholas Rowe's *Tamerlane,* and Henry B. Woolf wrote on Godfrey as an "18th-century Chaucerian."

Godkin, E[dwin] L[awrence] (b. Ireland, Oct. 2, 1831—d. May 21, 1902), newspaperman, editor, author. After service on several British newspapers, Godkin came to the United States in 1856 and became a lawyer here. During the Civil War, he went back to newspaper work as correspondent for the London *Daily News.* In 1865 he became the first editor of THE NATION, of which he was one of the founders, and continued in that post till 1881. In that year the magazine became the weekly edition of the New York *Post,* with Godkin as associate editor of the newspaper; in 1883 he became editor and continued as such till 1900. He then retired to England, where he died two years later. Godkin was noted for his keen intellect, his liberalism, his wide range of information, his remarkable powers of expression, and his unswerving integrity. He was an unsparing critic of the Gilded Age, but he advocated no sweeping plans for its reform. He established new standards in book reviewing, scorning mere panegyric. Some of his best writings were collected in *Reflections and Comments, 1865–95* (1895). He also wrote *The History of Hungary and the Magyars* (1853). Rollo Ogden prepared a *Life and Letters* (2 v., 1907) of the great editor, and he appears prominently in Allan Nevins' *The Evening Post* (1922).

Go Down, Moses (1940), a collection of short stories by WILLIAM FAULKNER. Set in Faulkner's mythical Yoknapatawpha County, the stories are unified by a common theme, the ritual of the hunt—whether it be a hunt for Big Ben in "The Bear," for the lovesick Negro in "Was," for buried gold in "The Fire and the Hearth," or for the Negro killer in "Pantaloon in Black." All but the last deal with the members, black and white, of the complicated McCaslin family, beginning with the second generation in "Was" and ending with the sixth in "Delta Autumn." There is, in addition, an underlying theme of initiation into manhood and the responsibility of carrying out the social traditions. Thus young Isaac McCaslin is ritually smeared with the blood of the slain deer and recognizes his responsibility to live in a way worthy of the nobility of the animal he has killed, and young Roth Edmonds comes to an awareness of the distance imposed by society between himself and Henry Beauchamp, his Negro foster-brother and cousin. The values to be found in the wilderness and those of civilization are implicitly contrasted.

"The Bear," the most famous of the stories and possibly Faulkner's best, deals mainly with the hunt for Big Ben, an enormous and elusive bear. A shorter but equally important section tells how Isaac McCaslin, through the discovery of his grandfather's Negro offspring, rejects his claim to the McCaslin plantation and the guilt of slavery with which it is stained.

God-Seeker, The (1949), a novel by SINCLAIR LEWIS. Aaron Gadd comes as a missionary to frontier Minnesota, shares in the dangers and hardships of pioneer life, experiences the religious and intellectual fervors of the time and place. Lewis sought to show that the frontier was more than a region of violence and physical daring.

God's Little Acre (1933), a novel by ERSKINE CALDWELL. A presentation of the shiftless and amoral Georgia mountaineers, the novel was filmed in 1958. The protagonist has set aside one acre of his land the income of which is to go to the church, but the acre shifts in location according to his needs at the moment.

God's Protecting Providence (1699), a diary by Jonathan Dickinson. Dickinson was a Quaker merchant who often traveled in the West Indies. This narrative tells how on one trip his ship went down off the coast of Florida. He, his wife, and their infant child, along with nine sailors, reached the shore, fell among hostile Indians, suffered many hardships, and lost five of the party before they reached St. Augustine, naked, emaciated, and half-frozen. The book, which told its story dramatically and with many vivid details, became one of the best sellers of its time, was immediately reprinted in England, and was translated into Dutch and German. American printers kept on reissuing it. It was reprinted as *Jonathan Dickinson's Journal* (1945), under the editorship of Evangeline Walker Andrews and Charles McLean Andrews.

God's Trombones (1927), a collection of seven sermons in free verse by JAMES WELDON JOHNSON. In these, Johnson took sentiments expressed ordinarily in dialect and rendered them in pure, dignified English. Of the seven, *"Go Down Death"* is usually regarded as the most beautiful. The book represents Johnson's highest achievement.

Godwin, Parke (b. Paterson, N.J., Feb. 25, 1816—d. Jan. 7, 1904), newspaperman, editor, biographer. Godwin took a position on the New York *Post* with WILLIAM CULLEN BRYANT, later his father-in-law. He was a transcendentalist (see TRANSCENDENTALISM) and a political radical, expressing his views not only in the *Post* but in other media, among them a short-lived journal, *The Pathfinder*, which he founded in 1843. His pamphlet *Democracy, Constructive and Pacific* (1844) was called by Horace Greeley the best of the contemporary studies of collectivism. That same year he published *A Popular View of the Doctrines of Charles Fourier*. He

translated books from the German, including a version of Goethe's autobiography (1846–47). In 1860 he became part owner of the *Evening Post*. In 1878, on Bryant's death, he became editor-in-chief, but in 1881 left the paper to become editor of the *Commercial Advertiser*. "No leading writer of his day makes more impression on the public mind than he," said the contemporary editor Henry Watterson. Godwin was a steadfast liberal, but also a practical man—radical in principle, but conservative in practice. He prepared a *Cyclopedia of Biography* (1866); also *A Biography of William Cullen Bryant* (2 v., 1883) and *A New Study of the Sonnets of Shakespeare* (1900). Carlos Baker wrote an account of him in *The Lives of Eighteen from Princeton* (1946).

Goetz, Ruth and **Augustus.** See THE HEIRESS.

Goffe, William (1605?–1679?), English regicide. One of the judges at the trial of Charles I, Goffe fled to New England with his father-in-law, Edward Whalley, when it became certain that Charles II would be restored to the throne. The two were received in a friendly manner by the officials of Massachusetts and Connecticut, and were concealed from royalist investigators in various homes until their deaths. Goffe, the more prominent of the pair, appears in many stories and novels, among them Cooper's THE WEPT OF WISH-TON-WISH (1829); Delia Bacon's *Tales of a Puritan* (1831); Hawthorne's *The Grey Champion* (1837), and J. K. Paulding's THE PURITAN AND HIS DAUGHTER (1849). He was likewise the subject of a play, SUPERSTITION (1824), by James Nelson Barker. Sir Walter Scott introduced him as a character in *Peveril of the Peak* (1823).

Going, Charles Buxton (b. Westchester Co., N.Y., April 5, 1863—   ), editor, playwright, poet. Going wrote stories, plays, and poems of a fanciful character. Many of his lyrics were set to music. Among his books: *Star-Glow and Song* (1909); *David Wilmot, Free Soiler* (1924); *Folklore and Fairy Plays* (1927); *Precarious Paradise and Other Plays* (1934).

Gold [1] (1913), a novel by STEWART EDWARD WHITE. It is laid in the period of the California gold rush. Four young "forty-niners" are involved in encounters with other miners, brigands, and Indians.

Gold [2] (1920; produced, 1921), a play by EUGENE O'NEILL. In 1919 O'Neill wrote a one-act play, *Where the Cross Is Made*, to help out the Provincetown Theater program. He ultimately expanded it into a full-length play, *Gold*, which deals with a search for hidden treasure and the madness it creates. The play is regarded generally as one of O'Neill's failures, despite a strong scene on an island.

Gold, Herbert (b. Cleveland, Ohio, March 9, 1924—   ), novelist, essayist, editor. The original style of his several novels and outspoken essays on contemporary subjects attracted both praise and criticism. The recipient of many academic awards and grants, and a professor at four major universities, Gold remains an uncompromisingly idiosyncratic writer. His colorful essays and stories appear in both the large circulation magazines and the literary quarterlies. Wittily critical of the "beats" in essays like his *Hip, Cool, Beat and Frantic,* he edited a book of "non-beat" short stories, *Fiction of the Fifties* (1959). Some of his novels: *Birth of a Hero* (1951), *The Man Who Was Not With It* (1956), and *Therefore Be Bold* (1960).

Gold, Michael [pen name of **Irving Granich**] (b. New York City, April 12, 1894—d. May 14, 1967), novelist, critic, editor. From the time of his editorship of THE MASSES and *The New Masses,* Gold was one of the most important figures in American "proletarian literature." The term had its first clear definition in Gold's article "Towards Proletarian Art" in the *Liberator* magazine (Feb. 1921). His novel *Jews Without Money* (1935) became a model for any aspiring proletarian novelist. This series of sketches based on Gold's impoverished childhood on New York's Lower East Side was intensely emotional, often sentimental. Later in 1930 Gold coined the term "proletarian realism"; still later appeared his essay *Wilder: Prophet of the Genteel Christ* in the *New Republic.* This fierce onslaught against literary snobbery and effeteness in the person of Thornton Wilder caused much controversy. Some of Gold's articles are collected in *Change the World!* (1937). His plays include *Fiesta* (1925), set in Mexico; and *Battle Hymn* (1930), with Michael Blankfort, about John Brown. Among his books: *The Mike Gold Reader* (1954, ed. by Samuel Sillen); *The Life of John Brown* (1960). (See PROLETARIAN LITERATURE.)

Goldberg, Isaac (b. Boston, Nov. 1, 1887—d. July 14, 1938), editor, philologist, author, biographer, translator. Goldberg's deepest interest was in language, on which he wrote learnedly and with spirit in *The Wonder of Words* (1938). He was likewise interested in wit and humor, and he wrote an excellent volume on William Gilbert and the Gilbert-Sullivan operettas (1913). Other books deal with the drama and allied arts: *The Drama of Transition* (1922); *Tin Pan Alley* (1930); *George Gershwin* (1931). Biographies of H. L. Mencken and Havelock Ellis appeared in 1925 and 1926. He devoted himself especially to the pioneer work of introducing Latin-American literature to the American public, writing *Studies in Spanish-American Literature* (1920) and *Brazilian Literature* (1922). He also prepared a collection of *Brazilian Tales* (1921).

Gold Bug, The (in *The Dollar Newspaper,* June 21–28, 1843; later in *Tales,* 1845), a story by EDGAR ALLAN POE. This was one of the earliest serious tales to use the search for buried treasure as a theme and to introduce a message in cipher. The scene is Sullivan's Island near Charleston, South Carolina; the treasure is one left by Captain Kidd; and its discovery, after much difficulty, restores the fortunes of an impoverished Southern gentleman who is the chief character. Suspense is skillfully maintained, and Poe shows dextrously how ratiocination leads to

the solution of the problem. Poe was probably partly inspired by Irving's comic *Wolfert Webber,* in which a similar team of a somewhat mysterious wonder-worker, a stolid man, and an old free Negro search for treasure on Manhattan Island.

Golden, Harry (b. New York City, May 6, 1902—   ), editor, essayist, biographer. Born of Jewish immigrant parents and brought up on New York's LOWER EAST SIDE, Golden later adopted Charlotte, N.C., as his home. These two

strikingly different environments provide the background for his humorous essays, which appear in his newspaper *The Carolina Israelite* and have been collected in three best-selling volumes: *Only In America* (1958), later adapted for Broadway (1959); *For 2¢ Plain* (1959); and *Enjoy, Enjoy!* (1960). His wide popularity stems from an ability to poke fun without offending the subjects of his humor. His famous solution for the South's Negro problem was "vertical integration." Since he had observed that whites didn't mind standing up with Negroes in bus lines, Golden proposed that the seats be removed from public school classrooms so that students could be "vertically integrated." This kind of humor has led to his being compared with Mark Twain and Will Rogers. Long a warm friend of Carl Sandburg, Golden published a biography of the poet in 1961.

Golden, John (b. New York City, June 27, 1874—d. June 17, 1955), actor, playwright, song writer, producer. Golden's was one of Broadway's most impressive careers. He wrote or had a hand in writing many plays, produced scores of others, wrote hundreds of songs, composed the librettos for at least a dozen musical shows, took a deep interest in encouraging new talent for the theater (especially through the John Golden Foundation, established in 1944), helped set up the City Center of Music and Drama in New York. Perhaps his greatest producing success was Winchell Smith and Frank Bacon's LIGHTNIN' (1918), which played for 1,291 consecutive performances. All of his productions displayed his genius for stagecraft. His most popular song was *Poor Butterfly* (1916).

Golden Book of Springfield, The (1920), a prose work by VACHEL LINDSAY. Looking at his native city (Springfield, Ill.) with a view to the future, Lindsay sketched a utopia—unconvincing in its details.

Golden Bowl, The (1904), a novel by HENRY JAMES. An early critic of this novel complained that except for the revelations made by one or two minor characters, it is difficult for a reader to follow the plot, since everyone is trying to conceal from everyone else the facts necessary to an understanding of the story. Maggie Verver, daughter of a millionaire, marries an Italian prince who previously has had a love affair with Maggie's closest friend, Charlotte Stant. Charlotte visits the pair and continues her intimacy. Then she marries Maggie's father. Everybody tries to keep it a secret from the rest that he or she ultimately knows all that has happened or is happening. The complications are more or less solved when Maggie's father goes back to America with Charlotte. James depicts with his usual subtlety the cultural and moral involvements that follow upon international marriage and irregular sex relationships. Many admirers of James regard this as one of his best works. Elizabeth Stevenson sees in the novel another illustration of one of James's favorite ideas, that goodness may provoke evil.

Golden Boy (1937), a play by CLIFFORD ODETS. Odets depicts the degeneracy of a young Italian-American who should have become a violinist but who thinks it will be easier to win fame and fortune in the boxing ring. He has an affair with his manager's mistress, becomes arrogant and conceited, kills an opponent in the ring. In a wild flight, he and the girl take a furious ride in his new automobile and are killed in a crash. This is the most successful of Odets' works.

Golden Day, The (1926), a "study in American experience and culture" by LEWIS MUMFORD. Mumford examines New England from 1830 to 1860, with special reference to Emerson, Thoreau, and Hawthorne and with an analysis of Whitman and Melville. The Civil War brought on what seems to Mumford a crisis in the competition between slave and machine, from which the machine emerged victorious. Hence came the Gilded Age, with John Dewey as one of its prophets. To Dewey, according to Mumford, a tire and a telegraph seem as high in the scale of human achievement as the works of a Whitman or a Tolstoy.

Golden Dog, The (unauthorized, 1877; auth. ed., 1896), a novel by WILLIAM KIRBY. This was the first Canadian novel to achieve widespread popularity. The story, set in old French Quebec, served as a model for numerous Canadian historical romances in the 19th century and later. The book's fascination stems, in part, from Kirby's skillful merging of Loyalist (yet democratic) sympathies and historical facts with vivid narrative and imaginative characterization.

Golden Legend, The (1872), the second part of a loosely connected trilogy called *Christus: a Mystery*, by HENRY WADSWORTH LONGFELLOW. This poem is essentially the Faust legend in its reflection of the attitudes of the Middle Ages toward Christian truths. Meant to be Longfellow's masterpiece, the poem is a very long, complex philosophical work. Despite occasional felicities, it seems only a retelling of the medieval story in a setting that Longfellow recreated through his extensive knowledge of the period. His last great attempt at a poem of epic proportions, it is probably the least successful, perhaps because he was more intent upon his message than on letting the story tell itself.

Golden Multitudes: The Story of Best-Sellers in the United States (1947), a historical study by FRANK LUTHER MOTT. Mott surveys his field with painstaking thoroughness. He deals with religion and sensationalism in the days of the Puritans, books for children, the pensive poets, politics in the Revolutionary era, Shakespeare and the Bible as perennial best sellers, the pirated European novelists and poets, the coming into popularity of American writers from Cooper and Irving on, the cheap "libraries" of 1875–93, the crusaders, the literary fevers of the 1890's, family novels, the amazing popularity of writers like CHARLES M. SHELDON and HAROLD BELL WRIGHT, westerns, juvenile stories, war books. He analyzes the secrets of best-sellerdom so far as they can be discovered. The result is a fascinating history of popular taste and social change, but it offers no particular tribute to the good sense and discrimination of the American public.

Golden Whales of California, The, and Other Rhymes in the American Language (1920), a collection of verses by VACHEL LINDSAY. The poems fall into five sections: longer pieces, with interludes; a "rhymed scenario" and some "poem games"; "cobwebs and cables"; rhymes concerning World War I; rhymes of the Middle West and Springfield, Ill. None of the poems is particularly noteworthy.

Goldman, Emma (b. Russia, June 27, 1869 —d. May 14, 1940), anarchist. She came to the United States in 1886, became known as an agitator, and in 1893 was sentenced to prison for a year. She published *Anarchism and Other Essays* (1910) and *The Social Significance of the Modern Drama* (1914). In 1919 she visited Russia, was completely disgusted with the Soviet régime, and wrote *My Disillusionment in Russia* (1925) on leaving that country. She published her autobiography, *Living My Life*, in 1931. She was an important figure in the heyday of American radicalism, and she commanded not only the respect but the affection of her fellow workers. Richard Drinnon wrote, *Rebel In Paradise: A Biography of Emma Goldman* (1961).

Gold rush. See FORTY-NINERS.

Goldwyn, Samuel (b. Poland, 1882—   ), motion picture producer. Originally Goldfish, he came to the United States in 1896. An astute judge of what a movie audience would like, Goldwyn helped found the film company of Metro-Goldwyn-Mayer, and was associated with other Hollywood enterprises. He was influential in bringing eminent writers and actors into the motion picture field. Famous for his verbal twists, one of the most famous of which was "Include me out," he wrote his memoirs, *Behind the Screen,* in 1923; Alva Johnston wrote an amusing book, *The Great Goldwyn* (1937), about him. He produced some major films, described in Richard Griffith's *Samuel Goldwyn: The Producer and His Films* (1956), and Bosley Crowther's *The Lion Roars* (1957).

Gollomb, Joseph (b. Russia, Nov. 15, 1881— d. May 23, 1950), novelist, historian, teacher, writer of books for boys. Gollomb taught English in De Witt Clinton High School in New York City (1902–12), and later made this school the scene of several of his stories, where it is called Lincoln High School. The best known of these was *That Year at Lincoln High* (1918). His narratives are marked by great storytelling skill and a sense of social values, shown also in his book *What's Democracy to You?* (1940).

Gompers, Samuel (b. England, Jan. 27, 1850 —d. Dec. 13, 1924), labor leader, economist, memoirist. Gompers came to the United States in his teens, worked as a cigar maker, rose to leadership in the feeble Cigarmaker's Union, reorganized it, was president of the American Federation of Labor from 1886 to 1924, except in 1895, and active in international labor organizations. He wrote *Labor in Europe and America* (1910); *Labor and the Common Welfare* (1919); and an autobiography, *Seventy Years of Life and Labor* (1925).

Gone with the Wind (1936), a novel by Margaret Mitchell (1900–1949). Miss Mitchell wrote only one novel, a stupendous success. At the time of her death in an accident (1949), it had won a Pulitzer Prize and had sold more than 8,000,000 copies in thirty languages and forty countries; the motion-picture version of her story (1939) was equally successful. *Gone with the Wind* shows both considerable literary skill and marked social insight. The heroine, Scarlett O'Hara, is an embodiment of the indomitable spirit of the South. She wants to marry Ashley Wilkes, but he marries Melanie Hamilton instead; and she weds Charles Hamilton in pique. Later she marries another man for his money, and then finally marries Rhett Butler, a dashing and outspoken Byronic hero. Around her surges the tumult of the Civil War, the despair of Reconstruction days, and the collapse of the old social order. Scarlett's dogged determination to restore Tara, the family estate, after Sherman destroys Atlanta, attains its goal, but at the

cost of the realization that she has sacrificed everything else for money and security.

Gonzales, Ambrose Elliot (b. Colleton Co., S.C., May 28, 1857—d. July 11, 1926), editor, authority on the Gullah dialect. Editor of *The State* at Charleston from 1891 to 1926, Gonzalez became very much interested in the GULLAH NEGRO. All his books deal with this strange group—*The Black Border* (1922), which had a glossary; *With Aesop Along the Black Border* (1924); *The Captain* (1924); and *Laguerre, a Gascon of the Black Border* (1924). Mencken says that Gullah was "admirably reported" in these stories and sketches.

Good-Bye, Proud World (composed, 1823; published, 1839), a poem by RALPH WALDO EMERSON. It echoes his familiar revolt against society and his encouragement of direct communion with nature.

Good Earth, The (1931), a novel by PEARL BUCK. It is a story of northern China, many of the details taken from Mrs. Buck's own observations while she was living in China as a child and later. It follows birth, marriage, and death in a Chinese peasant family. The story, generally regarded as Mrs. Buck's masterpiece, won universal praise for its narrative power and its sympathetic and realistic picture of life in China. It won the Pulitzer Prize in 1932 and the William Dean Howells Medal in 1935; it was largely responsible for the award to Mrs. Buck of the Nobel Prize in 1938. Many millions of copies have been sold. A spectacular motion picture based on the novel was made under the supervision of Irving Thalberg, with background shots taken in China (1937).

Good Gray Poet, The (1866), an apology by WILLIAM DOUGLAS O'CONNOR. In 1865 WALT WHITMAN was dismissed from his position in the Interior Department, ostensibly for including certain poems on sex in *Leaves of Grass*. His friend O'Connor wrote in warm indignation on Whitman's behalf, and the phrase he used as a title thereafter stuck to Whitman. In a posthumous collection, *Three Tales* (1892), O'Connor presented an idealized, Christlike picture of Whitman.

Good Housekeeping. A monthly magazine for women, founded in 1885. It was acquired in 1911 by WILLIAM RANDOLPH HEARST. It is noted for the protection it offers its readers against fraudulent or deceptive advertising through the Good Housekeeping Institute's analyses and investigations. Herbert R. Mayes, then editor, compiled *Editor's Choice: 26 Short Stories Selected from "Good Housekeeping"* (1956). A larger anthology, *A Treasury of Good Housekeeping,* came out in 1960.

Goodman, Jules Eckert (b. Gervais, Ore., Nov. 2, 1876—d. July 10, 1962), playwright. After working as an editor on several magazines, Goodman began writing plays, and a number of them were successfully produced. Among them: *The Test* (1908), *The Silent Voice* (1914), *The Man Who Came Back* (1916), *Chains* (1923). He collaborated with MONTAGUE GLASS on several plays in which Potash and Perlmutter were the leading characters.

Goodman, Nathan G[erson] (b. Philadelphia, Jan. 9, 1899—d. Aug. 22, 1953), historian. Besides his various collections of biographical sketches, such as *Famous Authors* (1943) and *Famous Pioneers* (1945), Goodman wrote some excellent biographies—of Dr. Benjamin Rush, Franklin, and others. He also edited a valuable *Benjamin Franklin Reader* (1945); and wrote *The Ingenious Dr. Franklin* (1931).

Goodman, Paul (b. New York City, Sept. 9, 1911—   ), psychoanalyst, writer. Goodman began publishing in *New Directions* in the early 40's and continued doing distinguished writing in many fields. *Communitas* (1947), written with his brother, Percival Goodman, dealt with city planning; *Gestalt Therapy* (1951) drew on the author's experience as a psychoanalyst; *Growing Up Absurd* (1960) was a brilliant analysis of the contradictions that face contemporary American youths. Goodman worked throughout his career on *The Empire City* (1959), a panoramic novel about the 30's, 40's, and 50's. In *Growing Up Absurd* he argued that young people are cut off from nature in a society which no longer offers them "honest work." He proposed work camps for youths where they could be in contact with nature and do useful work. Goodman's plays include *Faustina* (1949); *The Young Disciple* (1955); *The Cave at Machpelah* (1959) and a one-act play, *The Theory of Comedy* (1960). Among his other works: *Art and Social Nature* (1946); *Kafka's Prayer* (1947); *The Structure of Literature* (1954); *The Break-Up of Our Camp*, short stories (1949); *A Visit to Niagara* (1961).

Good Morning, America (1928), a poem by CARL SANDBURG. In it, with his usual clever and effective introduction of the vernacular and recital of folkways, Sandburg again exhibits his profound faith in the people. It is the introductory poem of a collection.

Good News from New England (1624), an account by EDWARD WINSLOW (1595–1655), one of the Pilgrims who came over on the *Mayflower*. He kept a journal and so did WILLIAM BRADFORD [1]; their accounts were first made use of in the volume known, because of its publishers, as *Mourt's Relation* (1622). *Good News* continued the latter narrative. See GEORGE MORTON.

Good Night, Sweet Prince (1943), a biography of John Barrymore (see THE BARRYMORES) by GENE FOWLER. On the basis of much private investigation Fowler composed an entertaining and truthful account of the famous actor, who is exhibited as one of the most extraordinary characters in theatrical history—a great actor who was toward the end of his career quite indifferent to his own fame and the use he made of his talents.

Goodrich, Arthur [Frederick] (b. New Britain, Conn., Feb. 18, 1878—d. June 26, 1941), novelist, playwright. Goodrich's most famous production was his dramatization of Browning's *The Ring and the Book*, called CAPONSACCHI

(1926). He also wrote *So This Is London* (1922); *The Perfect Marriage* (1932); *A Journey By Night* (1935); *I Can't Help It* (1938). *Caponsacchi* was made into a grand opera, *Tragedy in Arezzo* (1932), with music by Richard Hagerman.

Goodrich, Frank Bott. See SAMUEL GRISWOLD GOODRICH.

Goodrich, Marcus [Aurelius] (b. San Antonio, Tex., Nov. 28, 1897—   ), newspaperman, advertising copywriter, screenwriter, novelist. During World War I Goodrich served on a destroyer with the Asiatic Fleet, and his experiences suggested to him a remarkable novel, DELILAH (1941). This won the applause of critics, with its unvarnished depiction of warfare at sea, and was compared to *Moby Dick*.

Goodrich, Samuel Griswold ["Peter Parley"] (b. Ridgefield, Conn., Aug. 10, 1793—d. May 9, 1860), publisher, editor, author of children's books, memoirist. Goodrich, although like the hero of his *Travels, Voyages, and Adventures of*

Gilbert Go-Ahead he "wasn't made a Yankee for nothing," was a kindly patron of many American authors. In his magazine *The Token* (1828–42) he introduced NATHANIEL HAWTHORNE to the public, and some of the finest of the TWICE-TOLD TALES first appeared in its pages. He began the modern period of juvenile publishing in the United States when he started his endless series of "Peter Parley" books with *The Tales of Peter Parley About America* (1827). In these a deliberate attempt was made to eliminate the British background from books for children. For about thirty years he devoted himself to writing volumes of history, geography, science, and travel for children, with the help of collaborators, including Hawthorne. In what is regarded as his best book, *Recollections of a Lifetime* (1856), he enumerated his books in six closely printed pages. Millions of children learned geography from him. His PARLEY'S MAGAZINE (1833–44) had some distinguished contributors. It was taken over by *Merry's Museum* (1841–72); this in turn was merged with YOUTH'S COMPANION (1827–1929). Goodrich's son, **Frank Bott Goodrich** (b. Boston, Dec. 14, 1826—d. March 15, 1894), was a newspaperman and playwright. He wrote *Tri-Colored Sketches of Paris* (1855) and *Man Upon the Sea* (1858; republished as *Ocean's Story*, 1873). He wrote plays in collaboration with DION BOUCICAULT (*The Poor of New York*, 1858) and others. See NURSERY RHYMES.

Goodspeed, Edgar Johnson (b. Quincy, Ill., Oct. 23, 1871—d. Jan. 12, 1962), scholar, translator. Goodspeed's distinguished career, spent mainly at the University of Chicago, won him many scholarly honors. He wrote numerous papers and books on topics related to his specialty. In Paris in 1928 he made an important discovery—the so-called Codex 2400 of the Greek New Testament. Years later Goodspeed wrote a mystery story, *The Curse in the Colophon* (1935), which reflected the manuscript adventures that led to this discovery.

The work that gave Goodspeed popular fame was *The New Testament—An American Translation* (1923), followed by *The Bible, an American Translation* (with J. M. P. Smith, 1931), *The Apocrypha, An American Translation* (1938), and *The Complete Bible—An American Translation* (with J. M. P. Smith and others, 1939). He also wrote books intended to help American readers to understand the Bible: *The Story of the New Testament* (1916), *The Story of the Old Testament* (1934); *The Story of the Bible* (1936); *How Came the Bible?* (1940); *How to Read the Bible* (1946); *A Life of Jesus* (1950); *Key to Ephesians* (1956); and *Matthew, Apostle and Evangelist* (1959). Goodspeed's translation, which has sold excellently through the years, discards the alluring archaisms of the King James Version for understandability in terms of modern times; it also makes use of recent commentaries, especially in the field of Hebrew scholarship. *As I Remember* (1953) is Goodspeed's autobiography.

Goodwin, Maud Wilder (b. Ballston Spa, N.Y., June 5, 1856—d. Feb. 5, 1935), novelist, historian. Mrs. Goodwin wrote *The Colonial Cavalier* (1894); *White Aprons* (1896); *Dolly Madison* (1896); *Veronica Playfair* (1909); and other books competently based on history. See NATHANIEL BACON.

Goodyear, William Henry (b. New Haven, Conn., April 21, 1846—d. Feb. 19, 1923), archaeologist, museum director, writer on art. Goodyear devoted his life to a study of the great buildings of the past, and discovered certain structural principles previously unknown to modern authorities; in particular he was interested in the principles underlying the apparent irregularities in Gothic buildings. He was on the staff of the Metropolitan Museum of Art and then of the Brooklyn Institute. He wrote *A History of Art* (1888); *Roman and Medieval Art* (1893); *Renaissance and Modern Art* (1894); *Greek Refinements* (1912).

Gookin, Daniel (b. England or Ireland, 1612 —d. March 19, 1687), colonial administrator, writer on New England Indians. Gookin settled first in Virginia, then emigrated to New England where he held various offices of importance. At Roxbury, Mass., he helped found a free grammar school. He was greatly interested in the welfare of the Indians; in 1656 he was appointed superintendent of all the Indians who acknowledged the government of Massachusetts. He wrote *Historical Collections of the Indians in New England* (published, 1792) and *An Historical Account of the Doings and Sufferings of the Christian Indians of New England* (completed, 1674, published, 1836). See KING PHILIP.

Goops and How to Be Them (1900), by GELETT BURGESS. The Goops were strange creatures born in the author's fertile mind and designed for the entertainment of young readers and many of their elders. Burgess continued his account of them in *More Goops and How Not to Be Them* (1903); *Goop Tales* (1904); *The Goop Directory* (1913); and *The Goop Encyclopedia* (1916). The Goops have found a place in Webster, where they are defined as ill-behaved or disagreeable persons, "horrible examples" of naughtiness.

Gopher Prairie. The name given to the small town in Minnesota pictured in Sinclair Lewis' MAIN STREET (1920), with its typical narrow-mindedness and prejudices. Many readers assumed that Lewis really had Sauk Center, Minn., his birthplace, in mind. Some critics felt that Lewis had done an injustice to small town existence in his description of Gopher Prairie and that his depiction was superficial.

Gordin, Jacob (b. Russia, May 1, 1853—d. June 11, 1909), journalist, critic, novelist, translator, dramatist. Gordin emigrated to the United States in 1892. In Russia he had written novels and articles; in New York, still a contributor to Yiddish newspapers and magazines, he was gradually drawn to the Yiddish theater, where he wrote and produced many serious plays, beginning with one called *Siberia*. Altogether, about seventy pieces came from his pen, the best of which were *Mirele Efros, Gott Mensch un Teufel*, and *Der Unbekannter*. Before his time Yiddish drama had been artificial and practically worthless. Gordin made the characters genuine, the plots believable; and his humor was woven naturally into the plays. His realism was sometimes grim, and he felt rather Russian than Jewish. His adaptation of Tolstoy's *The Kreutzer Sonata* was translated into English by Langdon Mitchell and successfully produced (1907). His *Collected Works* appeared in Yiddish in 1910. While in Russia, Gordin had founded a Brotherhood to combine Christian and Jewish ethics; in New York he founded a similar Educational League.

Gordon, Caroline (b. Todd County, Ky., Oct. 6, 1895—   ), author, teacher. A graduate of Bethany College, Miss Gordon married the writer ALLEN TATE in 1924. She lectured on creative writing and the novel at Columbia University, and the universities of North Carolina, Washington, Virginia, Utah, and Kansas. Her first novel, *Penhally* (1931), told the story of three generations on a Kentucky plantation; it received both critical and popular acclaim. Her knowledge of Southern history, country, and people contributed in no small way to the success of her novels and short stories. Miss Gordon received a Guggenheim Fellowship for creative writing in 1934. Her other books include: *Aleck Maury* (1934); *The Garden of Adonis* (1936); *None Shall Look Back* (1937), a fictional study of the Confederate general, Nathan Bedford Forrest; *Green Centuries* (1941); *The Forest of the South* (1945), a collection of seventeen skillfully written short stories; *The Women on the Porch* (1946); *The House of Fiction* (with Allen Tate, 1950), a textbook; *The Malefactors* (1956); and *How to Read a Novel* (1957).

Gordon, Charles William ["Ralph Connor"] (b. Glengarry, Ont., Sept. 13, 1860—d. Oct. 31, 1937), clergyman, novelist. A liberal-minded missionary, Gordon combined preaching and gifted storytelling in his novels about Glengarry, his birthplace in Ontario, and the Canadian West in general. His books include *Black Rock* (1898), *The Sky Pilot* (1899), *The Man from Glengarry* (1901), *The Doctor* (1906), *The Rock and the River* (1931), and *The Girl from Glengarry* (1933). *Postscript to Adventure* (1938) is his autobiography.

Gorges, Sir Ferdinando (1566?–1647), English soldier, mariner, and proprietor in American colonial territory. Gorges sought to set up in the new crown territories a government definitely aristocratic, with Anglican doctrine prevailing, but the success of the Puritan colonies in Massachusetts prevented him from carrying out his designs. He received, along with John Mason (1600?–1672), grants of land in New England, in particular one section between the Piscataqua and Kennebec Rivers under the title of the Province of Maine (1622, 1639). He lacked money to develop this, and his son, of the same name (1630–1718), sold his title to Massachusetts, which then changed the name to District of Maine and continued to govern it until Maine was admitted into the Union (1820). The younger Gorges wrote *America Painted to the Life* (1658), an account that made use of EDWARD JOHNSON's *Wonder-Working Providence* (1654).

Gorman, Herbert S[herman] (b. Springfield, Mass., Jan. 1, 1893—d. Oct. 28, 1954), biographer, critic, novelist, poet. Gorman worked for newspapers in Springfield and New York, then turned to biography and novel writing, the imitation and interpretation of James Joyce, and book reviewing for the New York *Times*. His novels include *The Fool of Love* (1920), *Gold by Gold* (1925), *Jonathan Bishop* (1933), *The Mountain and the Plain* (1936), *The Wine of San Lorenzo* (1945), *The Cry of Dolores* (1947), *The Breast of the Dove* (1950). He wrote lives of Longfellow (1926), Hawthorne (1927), Dumas the Elder (1929), Mary of Scotland (1932), and James Joyce (1940).

Gorton, Samuel (b. England, 1592?—d. 1677), theological controversialist. Gorton came to Boston in 1636, moved to Plymouth and later to Rhode Island; he suffered much discomfort because of his heretical religious views. Later he served excellently as a magistrate. He wrote *Simplicity's Defence against Seven-Headed Policy* (1646), and founded a sect called Gortonists or Gortonites.

Gospel of Wealth, The. This was a general doctrine held by ANDREW CARNEGIE and first expressed in an article, "Wealth" (*North American Review*, June, 1900). He declared that the individual who by skill had amassed great wealth must do for the average man that which mediocrity prevented him from doing for himself. This doctrine of stewardship was expressed by Carnegie and many others in vast endowments to libraries, hospitals, museums, etc. *The Gospel of Wealth*, a collection of essays, appeared in 1901.

Gospels, The Four: A New Translation (1933), by CHARLES CUTLER TORREY. See BIBLE IN THE U.S.

Gotham. A name originally applied to a town in Nottinghamshire in England, the inhabitants of which deliberately played the fool in order to discourage King John from building a castle there, with its attendant taxes. Washington Irving in the SALMAGUNDI PAPERS (1807) transferred the term to New York City, but in a different sense. He intended to imply that the people of that city had unfounded and fatuous pretensions to wisdom.

Gothic melancholy, revival, and romance. In early medieval history the Goths were a single German tribe, but in later days the term Gothic became a symbol for medieval in general. A "Gothic revival" began in England when Horace Walpole settled in 1747 at Strawberry Hill, Twickenham, and made his home "a little Gothic castle." He transferred his interest in the Gothic to literature when he wrote *The Castle of Otranto* (1764), the first of the Gothic romances. Other novelists followed his lead in works full of romantic terror and melancholy. The movement spread to Germany, especially in the writings of E. T. A. Hoffmann (1776–1822) and his successors. In the United States the first great exponent of the Gothic romance was PHILIP FRENEAU, especially in his long poem, THE HOUSE OF NIGHT (1779), a meditation full of "Gothic horror" in its revolt against the conventionality of the times. Better known as a Gothic romancer is CHARLES BROCKDEN BROWN, who was deeply influenced by British writers. Brown was followed by GEORGE LIPPARD and other writers. NATHANIEL HAWTHORNE surrendered completely and employed ghosts, haunted houses, ancestral curses, hypnotism, insanity, witchcraft, and strange deaths in his stories. EDGAR ALLAN POE had similar devices, including premature burial, madness, and so on, but he mocked himself, as in *Loss of Breath*, and pointed out that his tales made use of a terror which was "not of Germany, but of the soul." They were followed by AMBROSE BIERCE and many others, down to Henry James's THE TURN

OF THE SCREW (1898). The crime and mystery stories of the 20th century have at least some of their roots in Gothic romance.

Gottlieb, Max. A character in Sinclair Lewis' ARROWSMITH (1925), unforgettably depicted as an old, disillusioned, but kindly scientist who helps to train Arrowsmith in research methods. It has been suggested that Lewis had in mind JACQUES LOEB (1859–1924), the great biophysiologist on the staff of the Rockefeller Institute for Medical Research (1910–24).

Goudy, Frederic William (b. Bloomington, Ill., March 8, 1865—d. May 11, 1947), printer, designer of printing types, founder of the Village Press. Goudy became the most famous of American type designers. More than one hundred type faces originated in his imagination and artistic skill. He printed many beautiful books, one of the earliest in honor of his master, the English poet and printer William Morris. He wrote *The Alphabet* (1918), *Typologia: Studies in Type Design and Type Making* (1940), and *Elements of Lettering* (1942), and was engaged on his autobiography at the time of his death.

Gould, John [Thomas] (b. Brighton, Mass., Oct. 22, 1908—   ), farmer, humorist, historian, memoirist. Gould has contributed to the saga of New England, especially Maine. He composed a weekly "Dispatch from the Farm" to the *Christian Science Monitor.* He wrote an excellent historical account of the *New England Town Meeting* (1940), later went on to the first of his humorous writings, *Pre-Natal Care for Fathers* (1941), described his marriage and experiences on his Maine farm in *The Farmer Takes a Wife* (1945); *Neither Hay Nor Grass* (1951); *The Fastest Hound Dog in the State of Maine* (1953). He edited *The Enterpriser,* a weekly paper for all of Maine, and often contributed to *The Christian Science Monitor, The Baltimore Sun,* and the *New York Times Magazine.*

Goulding, Francis Robert (b. Midway, Ga., Sept. 28, 1810—d. Aug. 22, 1881), clergyman, writer of books for young people. His long series of juveniles extended from *Little Josephine* (1844) to *Nacoochee* (1871). The best were those that dealt with the life of boys on the southern seaboard. Particularly good was *The Young Marooners* (1852).

Governor-General's Literary Awards, Canadian. These were first established by the famous author John Buchan when, as Lord Tweedsmuir and Governor-General of Canada in 1937, he set them up as a permanent system of recognition of literary merit. The rules and regulations are under the control of the Canadian Authors' Association, which selects the judges and frames the rules. The awards are presented to the authors of the best books in four classes —fiction, nonfiction, poetry, British Empire prizes. The authors must be residents of Canada. STEPHEN LEACOCK received an award (1938) for *My Discovery of the West.* Others honored include Gwethalyn Graham, Hugh MacLennan, E. J. Pratt, Arthur S. Bourinot, Earle

Birney. In addition a Stephen Leacock Medal for Humor was established by the Leacock Memorial Committee in 1946 and placed under the control of the Authors' Association.

"Go west, young man." This exhortation, which became the trade-mark, so to speak, of the whole pioneering and expansive spirit of America in the 19th century, seems to have been first used by John L. B. Soule (1815–1891) in an editorial or article in the Terre Haute *Express* in 1851. HORACE GREELEY used it often, particularly in a New York *Tribune* editorial (July 13, 1865) which gained wide currency, and it is usually attributed to Greeley. He himself, however, reprinted Soule's article to show the source of the phrase.

Goyen, [Charles] William (b. Trinity, Texas, April 24, 1915—   ), fiction writer, dramatist. Goyen was thirty-five when his first novel, *The House of Breath* (1950), appeared. The critics treated it as the effort of a new young writer to be unique, but, as he demonstrated in the books that followed, Goyen had already developed a personal, mature idiom. His stories take place in a poetic, mythic haze produced by his carefully written prose, and the "atmosphere" seems to be more important than either plot or character. In *The Faces of Blood Kindred* (1960), all of the stories are about chance events that reveal family ties. The author draws attention not so much to the results of these discoveries or to their effect on character as to the feeling they create. Though many of Goyen's writings were about his home state, where he taught at the University of Houston, he resisted identification as part of the "southern literary revival." He began teaching at the New School in New York City in 1957. He also published *Ghost and Flesh* (1952) and *In A Farther Country* (1955).

Grady, Henry W[oodfin] (b. Athens, Ga., May 24, 1850—d. Dec. 23, 1889), newspaper publisher, editor, orator. A fervent spokesman for the South, Grady became its most famous orator. He won national renown when on Dec. 21, 1886, he delivered a speech before the New England Society in New York City entitled "The New South." Another famous speech of his was "The Race Problem in the South" (1889). Although Grady was ardent in his devotion to the South, he pleaded constantly for fairer treatment of the Negro, since he recognized that the fate of the region depended upon establishing better racial conditions. In 1879 he bought a quarter interest in the Atlanta *Constitution,* with which paper his name was connected for the rest of his life. A posthumous collection of articles published in a New York newspaper was issued as *The New South* (1890). Edwin Du Bois Shurter edited his *Complete Orations and Speeches* (1910). Gentry Dugat wrote his life (1927).

Graham, George Rex (b. Philadelphia, June 18, 1813—d. July 13, 1894), lawyer, editor, publisher. See GRAHAM'S MAGAZINE.

Graham, Gwethalyn (b. Toronto, Jan. 18, 1913—d. Nov. 24, 1965), novelist. She wrote *Swiss Sonata* (1938), then *Earth and High*

Heaven (1944). In Canada the Governor-General's Award for Fiction was given to each of these books as it appeared; the latter in addition received the Anisfield-Wolf Award because of its contribution to a better understanding of race relations. It deals with Jews and Gentiles in Montreal, has sold more than a million copies, and has been translated into ten or more languages. A successful movie was also based on the novel (1947).

Graham, Lorenz B. (b. New Orleans, 1908—), author of folk tales, books for children. The son of a minister, Graham went to Liberia, where he taught trades and managed a general store at Monrovia College. Several years later he returned to the United States. He has a deep interest in the folk literature of African natives. His collection of tales, *How God Fix Jonah* (1946), shows how certain Biblical tales take on a local idiom and coloring as those who hear them at African missions pass them along to other natives. *Tales of Momolu* (1946) are stories of a Liberian boy who learns important lessons from the wild world of nature amidst which he lives.

Graham's Magazine. In 1826 Samuel C. Atkinson and Charles Alexander, founders of the *Saturday Evening Post,* began an attractive little monthly called the *Casket;* it was largely eclectic, with puzzles and jokes, a "School of

Flora," and articles taken over from the weekly *Post.* It carried an engraved plate in each number, and later some colored fashions in competition with *Godey's.* But it was not until George Rex Graham, an aggressive young editor-publisher, bought the *Casket* and merged it with *Burton's Gentleman's Magazine* (1837–1840) that the magazine became one of the foremost American monthlies. When Graham took over in 1839, he set out to secure the country's leading authors as contributors. He became the best paymaster in the business, and in the magazine's golden decade of the 1840's published the work of Lowell, Poe, Bryant, Longfellow, Cooper, N. P. Willis, R. H. Dana, and J. K. Paulding. Poe was literary editor for 15 months (1841–1842) and was succeeded by R. W. GRISWOLD (1842–1843). Popular writers of romance were Mrs. Emma C. Embury, Mrs. E. F. Ellett, and Mrs. Ann S. Stephens. Sartain's mezzotints and various style designs from woodcuts, as well as hand-colored fashion plates, embellished the magazine. C. H. Bodmer and other engravers contributed western scenes as well as domestic and sentimental pictures. After 1850 the competition of *Harper's New Monthly Magazine* was difficult to meet, and the 40,000 circulation claimed in 1843 dropped off. The last editor was Charles Godfrey Leland, 1857–1858.

grammar teaching in the United States. It is clear from R. L. Lyman's monograph, *English Grammar in American Schools before 1850* (1921), that schools in the American colonies shifted from Latin grammar to English and to instruction in the vernacular before British schools did, but that the change was one of subject matter only. Rules were still memorized and formally applied on the model of Latin grammar. British textbooks were at first employed. The most extensively used was *A Short Introduction to English Grammar* (1762), by Bishop Robert Lowth (1710–1787). Many of his rules were copied verbatim by American grammarians, especially by Lindley Murray in his *English Grammar* (1795), *Abridgment* (1797), *English Exercises* (1797), and *An English Grammar* (2 v., 1818). Lowth and Murray between them helped to fix prescriptive grammar—the idea that language could be made pure and logical by following highly specific rules which frequently contradicted common usage—in American schools. Other popular texts of the early 19th century were GOOLD BROWN's *Grammatical Institutes* (1823), Samuel Kirkham's *English Grammar in Familiar Lectures* (1825), and Peter Bullion's *Principles of English Grammar* (1834). Later Brown published his colossal *Grammar of Grammars* (1851). But by 1850 observation of usage was beginning to take the place of blind reliance on rules. The change was, however, accomplished exceedingly slowly and a century later was far from complete. As late as 1870 a reactionary volume, *Words and Their Ways,* by R. G. WHITE, continued to stress logic, analogy, and opposition to custom. The increase of philological studies in American universities, especially under the influence of German scholarship, helped to strengthen the forces advocating a more pragmatic treatment of grammar. The appearance of the monumental work, *A Dictionary of Contemporary American Usage* by Bergen and Cornelia Evans (1957) marked the triumph of this view. This same view governed the compilation of *Webster's Third New International Dictionary* (1961), which was accused by many scholars as abdicating its responsibility by refusing to set standards of good usage.

Among important American works which stress language as an objective phenomenon, to be examined in the light of anthropology, linguistics, history, and other disciplines, and which stress the psychological rather than the logical, are: W. D. WHITNEY's *Language and the Study of Languages* (1867); T. R. Lounsbury's *Standard of Usage in English* (1908); G. P. KRAPP's *Modern English* (1909); EDWARD SAPIR's *Language* (1921); J. B. GREENOUGH and G. L. KITTREDGE's *Words and Their Ways in English Speech* (1922); S. A. Leonard's *Doctrine of Correctness in English Usage* (1929); GEORGE O. CURME's *English Syntax* (1931); Porter Perrin's *Index to English* (1939); C. C. Fries' *What Is Good English?* (1940) and *Structure of English* (1952); R. C. POOLEY's *Teaching English Usage* (1946).

Grammatical Institute of the English Language, Comprising an Easy, Concise, and Systematic Method of Education, Designed for the Use of English Schools in America (1783), by NOAH WEBSTER. This was a combination speller, reader, and grammar, designed to teach patriotism as well as English. Ultimately it became Webster's AMERICAN SPELLER, which sold in enormous numbers.

Granberry, Edwin [Phillips] (b. Meridian, Miss., April 18, 1897—   ), pianist, teacher, novelist, short-story writer. After service in several universities, Granberry became a member of the faculty of Rollins College (1933). His stories concentrate on psychological analysis and presentation; they are often set in the wilder regions of Florida. Among his books: *The Ancient Hunger* (1927); *Strangers and Lovers* (1928); *The Erl King* (1930).

Grand Canyon of Arizona. A tremendous gorge cut by the Colorado River over millions of years. Many writers have attempted to convey some sense of the awesomeness and beauty of the canyon, including such poets as Henry van Dyke in *The Grand Canyon and Other Poems* (1914), and William H. Simpson in *Along the Old Trail* (1929). JOHN WESLEY POWELL (1834–1902) explored the Colorado River and reported his observations in *Exploration of the Colorado River* (1875), reprinted under the editorship of Horace Kephart as *First Through the Grand Canyon, 1869–70* (1915). Some vigorous descriptions are found in Frederick S. Dellenbaugh's *The Romance of the Colorado River* (1902); Lewis R. Freeman's *Down the Grand Canyon* (1924); Julius F. Stone's *Canyon Country* (1932); and Frank Waters' *The Colorado* (1946).

Grand Design, The (1949), a novel by JOHN DOS PASSOS. See GLENN SPOTTSWOOD.

Grandfather's Chair (1841), a collection of stories of colonial and revolutionary New England, told for children by NATHANIEL HAWTHORNE.

Grandfather's Clock (1876), a song by HENRY CLAY WORK, sometimes erroneously attributed to Samuel L. Milady. It has had great popularity.

Grandgent, Charles Hall (b. Dorchester, Mass., Nov. 14, 1862—d. Sept. 11, 1939), teacher, philologist. Grandgent taught Romance languages at Harvard (1896–1932). He became an authority on Dante and wrote *Dante* (1916), *The Ladies of Dante's Lyrics* (1917), and *Discourses on Dante* (1924); also *Imitations and Other Essays* (1933).

Grandissimes, The: A Story of Creole Life (1880), a historical romance by GEORGE W. CABLE. A great many picturesque and entertaining episodes are laid in New Orleans of 1803, beginning with Jefferson's purchase of Louisiana from the French. The conflicts of New Orleans society are depicted, mostly through the eyes of an American youth of German origin, Frowenfeld, who gradually learns some of the dark secrets of the lives of his aristocratic acquaintances, secrets in which he himself is ultimately involved: family feuds, race feuds, the struggle between the old order and the new "American" order, complex love affairs. The Creole mother and daughter Nancanou and the Negro ex-prince Bras-Coupé are especially vivid characters, although many critics charge that Cable's treatment of the Negro and Creole problems is incomplete and unfair.

Grandmothers, The (1927), a novel by GLENWAY WESCOTT. This is described by the author as "a family portrait." The grandmothers (three, since Alwyn Tower's paternal grandfather married twice) are fully portrayed, also Alwyn's parents and innumerable other relatives, many of whom live tragic, frustrated lives.

Granger's Index to Poetry and Recitations (1904, 1930, 1953), a compilation by Edith Granger. It gives titles of prose and verse pieces, an author index, index to first lines, etc., and includes translations as well as American and English productions.

Granich, Irving. See MICHAEL GOLD.

Grant, Anne McVickar ["Mrs. Grant of Laggan"] (1755–1838), memoirist. Mrs. Grant as a girl lived near Albany, N.Y., where her father was stationed at a post of the British army. Many years later she wrote anonymously published recollections of her experiences, *Memoirs of an American Lady* (1808). This has been described as "primary source material on contemporary manners."

Grant, Percy Stickney (b. Boston, May 13, 1860—d. Feb. 13, 1927), clergyman, poet, essayist. An Episcopalian minister, Grant was outspoken in his advanced views on social conditions and on theological controversies. He resigned his pastorate in a dispute with his bishop. Among his books: *Ad Matrem and Other Poems*

(1905); *Essays* (1922); *A Fifth Avenue Parade and Other Poems* (1922).

Grant, Robert (b. Boston, Jan. 24, 1852—d. May 19, 1940), lawyer, judge, novelist, essayist, poet. As a lawyer and jurist Grant was a liberal, although he approved of a report which led to the execution of Sacco and Vanzetti. His experience as a lawyer was reflected in his novels, including *The Average Man* (1883); *Unleavened Bread* (1900); *The Undercurrent* (1904); *The Orchid* (1905); *The Chippendales* (1909); *The Bishop's Granddaughter* (1925). Van Wyck Brooks regards *The Chippendales* as the best of Grant's books and a classic picture of the futilities and foibles of Boston at the beginning of the century. In *Fourscore* (1934) Grant wrote his autobiography, with some odd sidelights on the Sacco-Vanzetti Advisory Committee. See SACCO-VANZETTI CASE.

Grant, Ulysses S[impson] (b. near Pt. Pleasant, Ohio, April 27, 1822—d. July 23, 1885), soldier, 18th President. Grant graduated from West Point in 1843 and served in the Mexican War. But he hated the routine of soldiering, took to solitary drinking, resigned from the army in 1854. He worked as a farmer, a real estate agent, a clerk, never successfully. He entered the Union army in May, 1861, and was given the rank of brigadier-general. His rise was rapid, as he continued to win first minor, then major victories, culminating in Lee's surrender at Appomattox (April 9, 1865). From the beginning he won Lincoln's confidence. Kenneth P. Williams tells in *Lincoln Finds a General* (2 v., 1949) how the war President came to make him supreme commander.

Grant's fame was great at the close of the war; with the débâcle of Johnson's administration he became the inevitable Republican choice for President. He was elected in 1868 and again in 1872. His administration was one of corruption and graft; he was overawed by men of wealth and social station, and was a poor judge of human nature. During this time the 15th Amendment was passed (providing equal voting rights for white and colored citizens), the *Alabama* case was referred to arbitration, an amnesty act for Confederate veterans was passed, postal cards were first issued, the Centennial Exposition at Philadelphia opened.

After his years in office Grant lost all his money in an investment scheme and almost went to jail. At the suggestion of Mark Twain, then conducting a successful publishing firm, Grant wrote his *Personal Memoirs* (2 v., 1885–86), completing the manuscript while dying of throat cancer. (Horace Green's *General Grant's Last Stand*, 1936, describes this last effort.) The *Memoirs* resulted in a modest profit for Grant's estate. They have been praised for their straightforwardness and simplicity. Matthew Arnold, in *Civilization in the United States* (1888), concluded that Grant was "a man, withal, humane, simple, modest." But he reflected unfavorably on Grant's style; and Mark Twain felt it necessary to defend the *Memoirs* as one of the great works of literature, a verdict posterity has scarcely supported.

Many verse tributes were paid to Grant at the time of his death. At the end of the Civil War, John F. Poole presented at the New Bowery in New York a play called *Grant's Campaign, or, Incidents of the Rebellion* (1865). Grant appears prominently in Hamlin Garland's *Trail-Makers of the Middle Border* (1926) and incidentally in Winston Churchill's THE CRISIS (1901). A war correspondent, Sylvanus Cadwallader, kept a journal, published (1955) as *Three Years with Grant*. Adam Badeau wrote *Military History of Ulysses S. Grant* (3 v., 1868–81); HAMLIN GARLAND wrote *Ulysses S. Grant: His Life and Character* (1898); W. E. Woodward wrote *Meet General Grant* (1928); Helen Todd wrote *A Man Named Grant* (1940). Historians in the 1950's began an effort to rehabilitate Grant's reputation. Lloyd Lewis undertook a series of volumes, but died shortly after completing the first, *Captain Sam Grant* (1950). BRUCE CATTON wrote *A Stillness at Appomattox* (1953), *General Grant and the American Military Tradition* (1954), and *Grant Moves South* (1959). E. S. Miers described *Web of Victory: Grant at Vicksburg* (1955).

Grapes of Wrath, The (1939), a novel by JOHN STEINBECK. In this moving book, Steinbeck wrote a classic novel of a family's battle with starvation and economic desperation. The story also tells in vivid terms the story of the westward movement and the frontier. The JOADS, Steinbeck's central figures, are "OKIES," farmers moving west from a land of drought and bankruptcy to seek work as migrant fruit-pickers in California. They are beset by the police, participate in strike violence, are harried by death. The book belongs to the so-called PROLETARIAN LITERATURE that became more and more important in the first half of the 20th century and reflected growing economic and social unease. But Steinbeck was by no means committed merely to exploiting an ideology. His novel is one of absorbing interest, with many powerful episodes and vivid descriptions. The book was based on a careful study Steinbeck made in 1936 when he followed groups of work-seekers to California; he embodied his observations in some newspaper articles, later published as a pamphlet called *Their Blood Is Strong*. Malcolm Cowley regards it as the only American proletarian novel of the 30's to survive into the present era without losing its force. It won the 1939 Pulitzer Prize, and was made into an unprettified, realistic movie in 1940.

Grass Harp, The (1951), a novel by TRUMAN CAPOTE. An eleven-year-old orphan, Collin Fenwick, goes to live with his two elderly aunts, Dolly and Verena Talbo; Dolly, shy, tender, and imaginative, is the complete antithesis of the grasping, shrewd Verena, who finally drives Dolly, in company with Collin and Catherine, the Negro cook, to take refuge in a tree-house in a chinaberry tree. They are joined by Riley Henderson and Judge Cool, two "outcasts" from the town, and the "five fools in a tree" find their "raft in a sea of leaves," so suggestive of Huck's raft, a place where they feel they belong, where they can be honest, and where they are "free to find out who we truly are." Despite the pastoral and romantic interlude in the tree, reality dominates the end of the novel: Dolly and Verena are reunited, Dolly dies, Collin grows up to study law, and Riley Henderson becomes a public figure. But the private world of Dolly, although incompatible with the public world, is denied neither existence nor validity, and enriches the public world by its presence.

Grassroots Theatre: A Search for Regional Arts in America (1955), a personal account by Robert Gard. Gard tells of his exciting experiences in fostering the growth of regional art in the field of the drama, in New York, Alberta Province, and Wisconsin.

Grattan, C[linton] Hartley (b. Wakefield, Mass., Oct. 19, 1902—   ), lecturer, teacher, author in the fields of literature, politics, economics. Grattan, of French-Canadian descent, contributed to many magazines and newspapers, lectured in this country and Australia, and won a reputation as a fearless, well-informed critic. He took a decisive role in battling the conservative NEW HUMANISM. (See under IRVING BABBITT.) Among his books: *Bitter Bierce* (1929); *Why We Fought* (1929); *The Three Jameses: A Family of Minds* (1932); *The Deadly Parallel* (1939); *Introducing Australia* (1942, rev. ed., 1947); *In Quest of Knowledge: A Historical Perspective on Adult Education* (1955), also published in Persian, Urdu, Hindi, and Indonesian; *The United States and the Southwest Pacific* (1961); *The Southwest Pacific: A History* (1961). He edited *The Critique of Humanism* (1930).

Gratz, Rebecca (b. Philadelphia, March 4, 1781—d. Aug. 29, 1869), philanthropist. Miss Gratz, daughter of a wealthy Jewish merchant, was a woman of noble character. She was an intimate friend of Matilda Hoffman, WASHINGTON IRVING's betrothed, and nursed her in her last illness. Irving, in the course of one of his visits to Sir Walter Scott at Abbotsford (1818), told him about the death of his fiancée and told him, too, about Miss Gratz who had fallen in love with a Christian but in devotion to her own faith had refused to marry him. She gave the rest of her life and her wealth to deeds of charity. Scott made Miss Gratz the model for Rebecca in *Ivanhoe* (1819). In 1929 appeared *Letters of Rebecca Gratz*. In the same year Beatrice T. Mantel wrote a biography of her; in 1935 Rollin G. Osterweis wrote *Rebecca Gratz: A Study in Charm*.

Grau, Shirley Ann (b. New Orleans, July 8, 1929—   ), writer. The setting for most of her stories is Alabama, where she was brought up. She attended Tulane University in New Orleans, and afterward married and moved to Metairie, Louisiana, to raise a family. The world of her fiction is not the decadent South, though her writing must be put in the tradition of the southern local colorists. Her settings, local characters, and dialects are finely etched and convincing. *The Black Prince and Other Stories* appeared in 1955, and was followed by *The Hard Blue Sky* (1960); and *The House on Coliseum Street* (1961), set in New Orleans, the story of a secluded twenty-year-old girl who is one of five daughters her mother has had by five different marriages.

Graustark (1901), a novel by GEORGE BARR MCCUTCHEON. Subtitled "The Story of a Love Behind the Throne," this romance emulated Anthony Hope's popular *Prisoner of Zenda* (1894) in its account of how an American commoner named Grenfall fell in love with the Princess Yetive in a highly colored imaginary kingdom. It was followed by a series of other novels set in the same locale including *Beverly of Graustark* (1904) and *The Prince of Graustark* (1914).

Gray, Asa (b. Sanquoit, N.Y., Nov. 18, 1810—d. Jan. 30, 1888), scientist, teacher. Gray made Harvard a center of botanical study in the United States. He published a series of scientific studies of American flora, also several textbooks, including *Elements of Botany* (1836); *Flora of North America* (2 v., 1838–43, in collaboration with JOHN TORREY); *Manual of the Botany of the Northern U.S.* (1848); *How Plants Grow* (1858); *How Plants Behave* (1872); *Darwinia* (1876). He won a great following among scholars, who regarded his *Manual* as indispensable.

Gray, Harold [Lincoln] (b. Kankakee, Ill., Jan. 20, 1894—   ), newspaper artist, creator of comic strips. Gray left newspaper work in Chicago to start his own studio. In 1924 he created the popular comic strip character *Little Orphan Annie*.

Gray, James (b. Minneapolis, Minn., June 30, 1899—   ), newspaperman, critic, essayist, novelist, dramatist. Gray's writings as drama critic and book reviewer for the St. Paul *Press & Dispatch* were well received. His literary column became widely syndicated, and he moved later to the staff of the Chicago *Daily News*. A collection of his reviews was published as *On Second Thought* (1946), and he has published a number of other books, including the regional novels *Shoulder the Sky* (1935) and *Wake and Remember* (1936), a volume on *The Illinois* (1940) for "The Rivers of America Series," *The University of Minnesota 1851–1951* (1951), and several plays.

Gray Champion, The. More properly, *The Grey Champion*. See WILLIAM GOFFE.

Grayson, David. Pen name of RAY STANNARD BAKER.

Grayson, William John (b. Beaufort, S.C., Nov. [?], 1788—d. Oct. 4, 1863), lawyer, public official, poet. Grayson served ably in the South Carolina legislature, in Congress, and as port collector of Charleston. He was an ardent advocate of states' rights, but in 1850 published a pamphlet, *A Letter to Governor Seabrook*, opposing secession and pointing out the evils of disunion. His best-known poem is *The Hireling and The Slave* (1854). A work of frank and vigorous propaganda, it compares the advantages of the Negro slave in the South with the harsh life of the pauper laborer in Europe, painting an idyllic picture of the slave's share in rural life and sports. Grayson continued with this theme in *The Country* (1858).

Graysons, The (1887), a historical novel by EDWARD EGGLESTON. Into this story of pioneer life in Illinois, Eggleston successfully introduced the figure of Lincoln as a young lawyer. Lincoln wins freedom for the accused hero by proving from the almanac that, contrary to the evidence against him, there was no moonlight and hence no murder on the night in question. This episode is based on an actual event, Lincoln's successful defense of "Duff" Armstrong in a murder trial during the 1840's.

"Great American Novel, The." The frequent use of this phrase, especially during the last decade or two of the 19th century, indicated the belief that it was possible to write a genuine epic of American life which would equal the best works of other literatures. It was an expression of profound nationalistic hope in the face of what seemed to be conclusive evidence that no individual American writer possessed the requisite genius or cultural background. H. R. Brown discusses the theme in *American Literature* (March, 1935). In the period after World War I the term was more often than not used ironically.

The phrase was also used as the title of a novel (1938) by CLYDE BRION DAVIS. His hero, Homer Zigler, is a newspaperman who hopes someday to write "the great American novel"; in the meantime he works on newspapers in Cleveland, Kansas City, San Francisco, and Denver, an idealist who never achieves his great ambition.

Great Awakening, The. A religious revival movement that began with the preaching of JONATHAN EDWARDS and assumed formidable proportions in 1740–50, sweeping through New England, some of the Middle States, and the South. It was marked by an extreme emotionalism, which sometimes took erratic forms. Edwards' *Narrative of the Surprising Works of God* (1757) recorded conversions which often indicated states of mind at least temporarily not far removed from insanity. The movement was opposed by the "Old Lights," under the leadership of JONATHAN MAYHEW and CHARLES CHAUNCEY; their ideas in time led to the doctrine of Unitarianism.

Great Books Foundation, The. A nonprofit educational corporation, organized in 1947 under the laws of Illinois. This foundation seeks to promote interest in great books and to assist in their fuller comprehension. Leaders are trained for discussion groups, which have numbered many hundreds all over the country.

Great Cryptogram, The (1888), a contribution to the Shakespeare-Bacon controversy by IGNATIUS DONNELLY.

Great Dictator, The (1940), a screenplay written, produced, and directed by CHARLIE CHAPLIN, with himself in the two chief roles. For the first time in his career Chaplin played a speaking part. He was both the dictator of a mythical country (Hitler was the model) and a barber who was his double; the play showed the greater interest Chaplin was taking in social themes. Many of the episodes were among Chaplin's happiest inspirations.

Great Dismal Swamp. See DISMAL SWAMP.

Great Divide, The (in 1906 produced as *The Sabine Woman;* present title, 1909), a play contrasting East and West by WILLIAM VAUGHN MOODY. Deserting verse for prose, Moody tried to present in this play a contrast between East and West. The heroine, representing the former, is attacked by three men while alone in her brother's cabin in Arizona; she saves herself by agreeing to marry one of them, who supposedly represents the free spirit of the West. It is a vigorous, theatrical play, one that was never produced, however, as Moody wrote it; it was "discreetly toned down" by the producer.

Great Gatsby, The (1925), a novel by F. SCOTT FITZGERALD. This is Fitzgerald's most perfect work. The narrative thread is concerned mainly with marital infidelity and violent revenge, but the power of the novel derives from its sharp and antagonistic portrayal of wealthy society in America, specifically in New York and Long Island. Jay Gatsby is a man with a shady past who has achieved social rank; the world in which he moves is shown to be one of ill-breeding, moral emptiness, and desperate boredom. The "Jazz Age," Fitzgerald's constant subject, is exposed here in terms of its false glamor and cultural barrenness. Yet in the end the novel transcends its own bitter view and is probably Fitzgerald's most humane work; certainly it is his most finished and is written in a fully developed and easy style. It has enjoyed a continuous popularity since it was first published and is now considered one of the chief texts of the American literary renaissance in the post-World War I period.

Great God Brown, The (1926), a play by EUGENE O'NEILL. In this experimental work O'Neill utilized expressionistic techniques to depict the complicated relationships existing between the self-divided artist, Dion Anthony, his wife, and their friend, the successful businessman, Brown. Masks similar to those of the classic Greek theater are worn by the actors to emphasize radical shifts in the apparent characters of the protagonists.

Great Meadow, The (1930), a novel by ELIZABETH MADOX ROBERTS. In this well-written historical novel Miss Roberts tells how Kentucky was settled by emigrants from Virginia, how they fought the Indians, what hardships they endured as pioneers.

Great Rehearsal, The (1948), an account of the writing and ratification of the Constitution, by CARL VAN DOREN. Van Doren with great skill depicts the diverse interests and mental capacities of the men who took part in the Constitutional Convention, describes the conflicts that arose among them and how they were resolved in the final document, and enables the reader to draw significant parallels between the American situation in 1787 and the world situation in 1948.

Great Stone Face, The (1851), a tale by NATHANIEL HAWTHORNE included in THE SNOW IMAGE AND OTHER TWICE-TOLD TALES. The story centers around a natural rock formation on Profile Mountain in New Hampshire, sometimes called "The Old Man of the Mountain," a subject of legends since Indian days. Ernest, a simple-minded but noble inhabitant of the region, awaits the day when someone will come to visit the mountains who will really look like the Great Profile. The poet who tells the story realizes at last that it is Ernest himself who resembles the magnificent image.

Great Tradition, The (1915), a collection of stories by KATHARINE FULLER GEROULD. These tales deal mainly with family problems, especially those arising from conflict with tradition or habit. Thus a woman sacrifices her dream of happiness with someone other than her own intolerable husband in order to serve her daughter; an artist, suddenly given a large sum of money, runs away from his family.

Great Train Robbery, The (1903), a movie written and produced by Edwin S. Porter (1870–1941). Porter had already produced for Thomas A. Edison *The Life of an American Fireman* (1899? or perhaps as late as 1903), which created great excitement. But he told his story with greater skill in *The Great Train Robbery*, which established the pistol-shooting desperado as a stock figure of American cinema. It won a tremendous success, and is credited with starting the American motion picture on the path it was to follow for many years.

Great (or Gay) White Way. See BROADWAY.

Greek and Roman influence. The American colonists regarded Greek and Latin as the basis of a true education. One of the earliest schools established was the Free Grammar School set up in Boston in 1635, better known as the Boston Latin School, which has trained generation after generation for college. The earlier schools were intended only for boys, who studied Latin from the time of their admission as young children and undertook Greek usually by their fourth year. They covered a wide range of Greek and Latin literature, and were fluent in reference and quotation. The same stress was laid on the classical languages in college, perhaps with Hebrew added.

Naturally the influence of the classics on American culture was great, but it should nevertheless be stressed that American readers and thinkers found in the classics chiefly the pabulum that fed their own tendencies. Thus the American Revolution was partly guided by classical ideals; its symbols and institutions, as Gilbert Highet has pointed out, "were markedly Greco-Roman in inspiration." For example, the senior legislative body in the United States and most Latin-American countries is called the *Senate;* in the United States the Senate meets in the *Capitol.* The names of many American cities go back to Greece and Rome. Thomas Jefferson and John Adams were equally firm in their belief that the new American civilization must be based on that of ancient Greece and Rome. Monticello, Jefferson's private home, was a reminiscence of a Roman one; his plans for the University of Virginia recalled the spaciousness of a Roman villa, and its library was modeled on the Roman Pantheon. For the influence of Latin grammar on the study and teaching of English grammar, see GRAMMAR TEACHING IN THE UNITED STATES.

Well into the 20th century, a knowledge of Greek and Latin was required of every cultured person. Innumerable textbooks were produced and often attained a wide circulation. But by the second decade of the 20th century there came into the schools many young people who by a difference in tradition and home surroundings or by lack of mental endowment were quite unprepared for the study of the ancient tongues. This, combined with other educational conditions, notably the advent of the professional "educationist," resulted within a decade or two in a decay in the teaching of the classics.

Yet the influence of the classics by no means declined; those who studied them were often affected in new and vital ways. Many creative writers, going back to the ancient Hellenic world, found inspiration for compositions that reflected the present day under classic guise. Three American poets particularly under this influence were T. S. ELIOT, EZRA POUND, and HILDA DOOLITTLE. In all of these writers Greek myths, techniques, and points of view may be found; often the verse shows an unexpected kinship with choruses in Greek plays. EUGENE O'NEILL and ROBINSON JEFFERS both employed Greek legends as a means of interpreting contemporaneous life. Only in the 1950's and 1960's did the classics begin to come back into favor in secondary schools and colleges.

Translations from the classics by Americans are innumerable. Perhaps the most widely read were the dignified versions that WILLIAM CULLEN BRYANT made of Homer, especially the *Odyssey.*

Though the study of ancient languages dwindled, interest in ancient mythology persisted. During the 19th and early 20th centuries these myths furnished endless themes and allusions for poets and dramatists, from Poe's *To Helen* (1831) and Lowell's *The Shepherd of King Admetus* (1842) to T. S. Eliot's *The Cocktail Party* (1950). Even in the unscholarly field of advertising copy one hears of Ajax tires, Apollo pianos, Hercules powder, Vulcan springs, Atlas cement. Novelists have relied on their readers' familiarity with mythology, especially in a type of mocking novel bringing the ancients' problems up to date. JOHN ERSKINE wrote a whole series, beginning with THE PRIVATE LIFE OF HELEN OF TROY (1925), and ending with *Venus the Lovely Goddess* (1949); Christopher Morley's agile satire, THE TROJAN HORSE (1937), is of the same school.

Greeley, Horace (b. Amherst, N.H., Feb. 3, 1811—d. Nov. 29, 1872), printer, editor, writer, political leader. A Fourierist (see CHARLES FOURIER), Greeley advocated many reform movements, and became one of the most influential men of his time. He worked as a printer in New York and started the first penny newspaper, *The New Yorker* (1834). Later he combined this and the weekly *Log Cabin* (begun in 1840), into the New York *Tribune* (April 10, 1841), made that paper famous, and remained its editor until 1872. He exerted wide influence in both literary and political spheres, although he held elected office for only three months (Congressman, 1848–49). It was largely owing to him that Lincoln was nominated, and although many of Lincoln's ideas displeased him, he continued to support him. He was averse to the Republican policy of revenge on the South that followed the Civil War, and in 1872 ran for the Presidency against Grant in a coalition of liberal Republican and Democrats, but was defeated.

He favored the agrarian movement, with its emphasis on open land and a liberal policy for settlers. He sympathized with the laboring classes of the city and did what he could to improve their condition. He joined in the intellectual awakening of the 1840's; he employed MARGARET FULLER on the *Tribune* and even took her into his own strange household. As an editor, he showed great ability to pick brilliant correspondents, and he gave them free play. He paid no attention to I'll-stop-my-subscription letters when he expressed his liberal views; his remarkable demand for "magnanimity in triumph"—universal amnesty and universal suffrage—as the Civil War came to a close, and his willingness to put up bail for Jefferson Davis, brought him much abuse. Greeley's ideas, his radicalism, and his appearance provoked satire and insults; he often reciprocated in kind. One Henry Clapp said that he was "a self-made man who worships his creator." He is frequently credited with the admonition, "GO WEST, YOUNG MAN," but he merely made it a favorite saying of his; it originated elsewhere.

Three volumes did much to rehabilitate Greeley's reputation: Henry Luther Stoddard's *Horace Greeley, Printer, Editor, Crusader* (1946); Jeter Allen Isely's *Horace Greeley and the Republican Party* (1947); and G. Van Deusen's *Horace Greeley: 19th-Century Crusader* (1953). He appears as a character in Irving Bacheller's EBEN HOLDEN (1900). Among Greeley's own books: *Hints Toward Reform* (1850); *Glances at Europe* (1851); *The American Conflict* (1866); *Recollections of a Busy Life* (1868); *Essays on Political Economy* (1870).

Greely, Adolphus Washington (b. Newburyport, Mass., March 27, 1844—d. Oct. 20, 1935), army officer, explorer, author. Greely made many important explorations of Arctic regions. When the San Francisco earthquake and fire took place (1906), he was placed in charge of relief work. He wrote *Explorers and Travelers* (1893), *True Tales of Arctic Heroism* (1912), *Reminiscences of Adventure and Service* (1927), and other books.

Green, Adam. Pen name of LEONARD WEISGARD.

Green, Anna Katharine (b. Brooklyn, N.Y., Nov. 11, 1846—d. April 11, 1935), novelist, detective story writer, poet. Miss Green was prepared to follow the mild and decorous career of a poet; her early work in verse won the commendation of critics. Her father James Wilson Green was, however, a noted trial lawyer, and her consequent interest in crime led her to write THE LEAVENWORTH CASE (1878), the first piece of detective fiction to be written by a woman. It became a best seller overnight; her plot was logical and exciting but the style seems melodramatic and stilted by later standards. The book was dramatized successfully, and Miss Green married one of the actors, Charles Rohlfs. It was later reissued (1934), with a preface by Willard Huntington Wright ("S. S. Van Dine"). Other books of Miss Green's include *The Hand and the Ring* (1883); *The Doctor, His Wife, and the Clock* (1895); *The Filigree Ball* (1903); *The House of the Whispering Pines* (1910); and a collection of verse, *The Defense of the Bride and Other Poems* (1882).

Green, Anne (b. Savannah, Ga., Nov. 11, 1899—   ), novelist, memoirist. Miss Green's family early removed to Paris, where her father was in business. Miss Green (her brother is JULIAN GREEN) described the household in a volume of reminiscences, *With Much Love* (1948). Her novels include *The Selbys* (1930); *A Marriage of Convenience* (1933); *Fools Rush In* (1934); *The Silent Duchess* (1939); *Just Before Dawn* (1943); *The Old Lady* (1947). Her characters, many drawn from life, are treated satirically.

Green, Asa. See ASA GREENE.

Green, Joseph (b. Boston [?], 1706—d. Dec. 11, 1780), distiller, merchant, satirist. A wealthy member of Boston society, Green was an avowed loyalist in politics. He was regarded as the foremost wit of his day and exercised his talents in newspapers and pamphlets. His most widely circulated verse satire was *A Winter's Evening* (1750). He also wrote *The Poet's Lamentation for the Loss of His Cat, Which He Used to Call His Muse* (*London Magazine*, November, 1733). The poet in this case was Green's friend MATHER BYLES; the poem is sometimes called "Doctor Byles' Cat."

Green, Julian [or **Julien**] (b. France, Sept. 6, 1900—   ), novelist. Green wrote almost all his books in French, became notable in French rather than in American literature. His parents were American and he spoke English as a child; he composed one book in English, *Memories of Happy Days* (1942), nostalgic reminiscences. Green spent time in this country in the early twenties, studying at the University of Virginia, and later lived here from 1940 to 1945; he was able to perform the unique feat of writing French novels with authentic American settings. *Avarice House* (1927), his first novel, is set in Virginia; the house is modeled on one once owned by his aunt. *Moira* (1950), is obviously set at the University of Virginia. In France he is ranked among the leading French novelists. His novels are brilliant, somber studies in psychology, often set in a world of terror and violence. Among his books: *The Dark Journey* (1929); *Midnight* (1936); *The Transgressor* (1957); and *Each In His Darkness* (1961), translated by ANNE GREEN. His *Personal Record, 1928–1939* (2 v.) appeared in English in 1939. In addition to numerous studies by French critics, Samuel Stokes has written *Julian Green and the Thorn of Puritanism* (1956).

Green, Paul E[liot] (b. Lillington, N.C., March 17, 1894—   ), teacher, dramatist, motion picture scriptwriter. Green was graduated from the state university, taught dramatic art and philosophy there, and is known for plays set for the most part in North Carolina: *The Lord's Will and Other Plays* (1925); *Lonesome Road: Six Plays for Negro Theater* (1926); *The Field God* and IN ABRAHAM'S BOSOM, both of which appeared on Broadway in 1927, the latter winning the Pulitzer Prize; THE HOUSE OF CONNELLY AND OTHER PLAYS (1931); *Roll Sweet Chariot* (*Potter's Field*, 1934); NATIVE SON (with RICHARD WRIGHT, 1941); *Peer Gynt* (an American version, 1951). During the thirties he lived and worked for a time in Hollywood, but his success there was far from an unqualified one, and he returned to his teaching post in North Carolina. He did, however, write several successful scripts for Will Rogers and George Arliss. In later years he became more interested in writing what he calls "plays derived from the people's history, their legends, folk-customs and beliefs, their hopes and ideals, and producing them in hillside amphitheatres built for that purpose." Among these pieces, which he calls "symphonic dramas," are: *The Lost Colony* (1937); THE COMMON GLORY (1947); *Faith of Our Fathers* (1950); *Wilderness Road* (1955); *The Founders* (1957); *The Confederacy* (1958); *Stephen Foster* (1959). A book of essays, *Dramatic Heritage*, came out in 1953. He writes with endless variety, and with complete independence from Broadway. His natural bent is a combination of REGIONALISM and imagination; his techniques are experimental. His poetic instinct emerges even in his most realistic pictures of the South.

Green, Samuel (b. England, 1615—d. Jan. 1, 1702), printer. Green came to Massachusetts about 1633 and managed in Cambridge the only printing establishment in the colonies until 1665. He printed Eliot's INDIAN BIBLE, THE BAY PSALM BOOK, and nearly 275 other books. See THE CAMBRIDGE PRESS.

Green Bay Tree, The (1924), a novel by LOUIS BROMFIELD. Lily Shane, one of Bromfield's most successful women characters, begins life in a middle-western industrial town,

goes to Paris to bear an illegitimate child. She is shown vividly against both French and American backgrounds and as a vital force in the life of her family, of her aristocratic friends, and of some striking workmen in her native town. The novel was dramatized (1927) as *The House of Women*. It forms the first novel in a tetralogy called *Escape;* the others are *Possession* (1925), EARLY AUTUMN (1926), and *A Good Woman* (1927).

Greenberg, Samuel (b. Austria, Nov. 3, 1893 —d. Aug. 17, 1917), poet. Brought to the United States at the age of seven, Greenberg lived in a home of extreme poverty. The squalor and excitement of New York's Lower East Side nevertheless awakened the boy's imagination. In his last years "sickness closed in with his careful teeth," as he expressed it; in a charity hospital for the tubercular he began reading good literature for the first time, and writing poetry intensely and feverishly. Nothing he wrote was published in his lifetime. The manuscripts fell into the hands of HART CRANE, who was deeply impressed by Greenberg's sensuous and often striking metaphors; some of Greenberg's phrases are recognizable in Crane's poetry, although the charge of direct plagiarism sometimes leveled against Crane is without basis in fact. Greenberg's posthumous *Poems: A Selection from the Manuscripts* (1947) contains an appreciative preface by Allen Tate. His favorite themes were God and death; Horace Gregory felt that his writing held true to its Hebraic sources, and that his "flashes of insight take on the character of Isaiah's voice."

Greene, Albert Gorton (b. Providence, R.I., Feb. 10, 1802—d. Jan. 3, 1868), poet, lawyer. Greene never published a collection of his verse, but contributed to journals. He was active in municipal affairs and at one time was governor of Massachusetts. His poems are part of the Harris Collection of American Poetry at Brown University; several of them gained wide popularity, such as the Gothic and rather melodramatic piece called *The Baron's Last Banquet*. He wrote the dryly humorous OLD GRIMES at the age of sixteen and it still remains one of America's most popular humorous poems.

Greene [or Green], Asa (b. Ashby, Mass., Feb. 11, 1789—d. [?], 1837), physician, editor, bookseller, humorist. Greene came to New York about 1830, abandoned medicine, and set up as a bookseller and author. Some of his own experiences apparently appear in *The Perils of Pearl Street* (1834), adventures of a poor boy in New York. He is best remembered, however, for his satirical and burlesque novels: *The Life and Adventures of Dr. Dodimus Duckworth* (1833), which describes in mock-heroic style the experiences of a spoiled child who ultimately becomes a country doctor; *A Yankee Among the Nullifiers* (1833), a fictional account of a visit by Greene to South Carolina, also the story of tricks practiced by a crafty clock-peddler; and *Travels in America, by George Fibbleton, Esq., Ex-Barber to His Majesty, The King of Great Britain* (1833), a burlesque of Mrs. Frances

Trollope's famous book, *Domestic Manners of the Americans* (1832). Usually Greene wrote broad farce, but he had a quieter and more truly humorous side. *A Glance at New York* (1837), like *The Perils of Pearl Street,* is more realistic.

Greene, Ward (b. Asheville, N.C., Dec. 23, 1892—d. Jan. 22, 1956), newspaperman, editor, novelist. Greene's long and brilliant career as a newspaperman in the South and in New York was topped by his appointment as executive editor of King Features Syndicate (1921). In 1929 he began writing novels in the hard-boiled school, all of them marked by cool realism and exciting action. Among them: *Cora Potts* (1929); *Ride the Nightmare* (1930); *Weep No More* (1932); DEATH IN THE DEEP SOUTH (1936); *Route 28* (1940); *The Lady and the Tramp* (1954).

Greenfield Hill (1794), a descriptive poem by TIMOTHY DWIGHT. It was written in imitation of Sir John Denham's topographical poem *Cooper's Hill* (1642), and as a result of the author's residence as a minister in Greenfield, Conn. (1783–95). Unlike Denham's poem, it praises village life, at least in America, and extols the leaders of the people. Historical events are described, such as the Pequot War and the burning of Fairfield by the British (1779).

Greengroin, Artie. A character created by HARRY BROWN for the World War II magazine YANK. He is a private 1st class who is constantly getting into trouble and talks about his difficulties in a lingo that is strictly Flatbush and anything but first class. Some of the Greengroin pieces are included in *The Best from Yank* (1945) and in a gathering made by Brown, *Artie Greengroin* (1945).

Green Grow the Lilacs (1931), a folk play by LYNN RIGGS. This is in part a cowboy opus, in part a historical drama that describes Indian Territory (later Oklahoma) not long before its admission to the Union. A cowboy named Curly McLain is in love with a pretty and spoiled young woman who is attracted by him but makes use of her attraction for Jeeter Fry, a sinister character on the ranch where she lives, to spite Curly. The cowboy and Fry contend for her hand; she marries Curly. When Jeeter tries for revenge on their wedding night and accidentally kills himself in a fight, Curly is suspected of murder, then acquitted. The play was later transmuted into the outstandingly successful musical play, *Oklahoma!* (1943), by Richard Rodgers and Oscar Hammerstein II.

Greenleaf, Moses (b. Newburyport, Mass., Oct. 17, 1777—d. March 20, 1834), topographer, historian. Greenleaf was a real estate man who made himself thoroughly familiar with the topography and the resources of the region that he was exploiting, and then in several publications made his information available to the public. In 1810 he started a township in the interior of Maine that in time was named Williamsburg, and devoted himself to encouraging settlement in that entire region. Among his publications the most important was *A Survey of the State of Maine, in Reference to Its Geographical Features, Statistics, and Political Economy* (1829).

Green Mountain Boys. In the "war" (1775) between New York and Vermont a group of hastily organized militia under ETHAN ALLEN fought off the New York officers and declared the so-called "New Hampshire Grants" an independent state under the name of Vermont. Later these same "boys" fought in the American Revolution and captured the fortress of Ticonderoga. The play *The Green Mountain Boys* (1833), by Joseph Stevens Jones, and the novel *The Green Mountain Boys* (1839), by DANIEL PIERCE THOMPSON, were written about them. The latter was a great success and is still a "standard book" for boys. James Fenimore Cooper replied from the "Yorker" point of view in THE CHAINBEARER (1845).

Greenough, Horatio (b. Boston, Sept. 6, 1805 —d. Dec. 18, 1852), sculptor, writer on art. Greenough made busts of some of the most famous men of his time, including Lafayette, Henry Clay, and James Fenimore Cooper. His gigantic statue of Washington as Zeus, half nude, is now in the Smithsonian Institution. He became a noteworthy lecturer and writer, and was perhaps the first person in any land to develop a functional theory of art. His chief book was *Aesthetics in Washington* (1851). His *Essays on Art* were included in a *Memorial* biography of him by H. T. Tuckerman (1853); his *Letters to His Brother Henry* were collected (1887) by F. B. Greenough.

Greenough, James Bradstreet (b. Portland, Me., May 8, 1833—d. Oct. 11, 1901), teacher, linguist, editor. Greenough collaborated on a *Latin Grammar* (1873), wrote many learned articles, and helped found the *Harvard Studies in Classical Philology.* His most popular book was written in collaboration with GEORGE LYMAN KITTREDGE: *Words and Their Ways in English Speech* (1901). He taught at Harvard from 1865 until his death.

Green Pastures, The (1930), a play by MARC CONNELLY. This successful production ran for more than a year and a half and won a Pulitzer Prize. It was based on ROARK BRADFORD's retelling of Old Testament stories in *Ol' Man Adam an' His Chillun* (1928). Connelly himself stated that the play was "an attempt to present certain aspects of a living religion in the terms of its believers"; namely thousands of Negroes in the Deep South who accept the Old Testament as a guide to conduct readily adaptable to their own lives. The treatment is reverent though humorous, and H. S. Canby recorded that his "eyes were wet with tears through most of the performance. It was perhaps the great religious play of our American times." Technically it recalled Elizabethan chronicle plays. Brooks Atkinson called the words, "Gangway for de Lawd God Jehovah," spoken by the Angel Gabriel, "the greatest entrance cue in modern drama." He also remarked that the play probably caused a little rejoicing in heaven as well as jubilation on Broadway.

Greenslet, Ferris (b. Glens Falls, N.Y., June 30, 1875—d. Nov. 19, 1959), editor, publisher, literary critic, biographer. Greenslet was editor of the *Atlantic Monthly* (1902–07), then an editorial adviser and later editor-in-chief of Houghton Mifflin. He wrote *Joseph Glanville* (1900); *Walter Pater* (1903); *Life of J. R. Lowell* (1905); *Life of T. B. Aldrich* (1908); *The Lowells and Their Seven Worlds* (1946). The last is his most important literary and critical work, but probably he will be longest remembered by his memoirs, *Under the Bridge* (1943), telling of the many New England literary figures whom he knew personally.

Greenwich Village. Often called "The Village," this is a region in New York City extending approximately from Spring Street on the South to 14th Street on the North and from the Hudson River east to Broadway. It was originally a village, in fact, reached by stage coach from other parts of Manhattan. Here or nearby lived Thomas Paine, Poe, Henry James, Mark Twain, Whitman, Masefield. It attained national fame during the early decades of the 20th century as an equivalent of the Latin Quarter of Paris. The "native" population consisted of persons of Irish and Italian descent and numerous Negroes; they were joined by writers, artists, actors, newspapermen, and other bohemians from all over the country. Magazines were founded; shows were produced, often of a quality that challenged Broadway and to some extent revolutionized the theater; art flourished on the sidewalks and in garret studios; political radicalism found a foothold. The uninhibited Villagers made a point of flouting conventional garb and mores. Beginning in the later 1920's the Village became a refuge rather for exhibitionists than for serious artists. MAXWELL BODENHEIM called it "the Coney Island of the soul." Living at first was cheaper here than in other parts of the city, but its cost promptly went up; soon the artists were driven out and a new bourgeoisie took their place. In the 1950's the Village once more became a center of literary activity, when a great number of "off-Broadway" theaters opened throughout the area.

Floyd Dell wrote about the Village in his novels *Janet March* (1923) and *Love in Greenwich Village* (1926). Reminiscences of the famous locale are also found in Max Eastman's *Enjoyment of Life* (1948), Alyse Gregory's *The Day Is Done* (1948), Henry W. Lanier's *Greenwich Village Today and Yesterday* (1949), and George H. Knowles' anthology *The Jazz Age Revisited* (1955). Other names associated with the Village in the early 1920's are Theodore Dreiser, Eugene O'Neill, Susan Glaspell, George Cram Cook, George Bellows, Hendrik Van Loon, Edna St. Vincent Millay, Robert Edmond Jones, Louis Untermeyer, John Sloan, John Reed, Willa Cather, Mary Heaton Vorse.

Gregg, Josiah (b. Overton Co., Tenn., July 19, 1806—d. Feb. 25, 1850), author of travel books, government agent, newspaper correspondent. Gregg had a deep interest in exploration and science. His great life experience came when, in order to recover his health, he went to Santa Fe as a trader and for nine years traveled the plains regions nearby. He published a book on his adventures, *Commerce of the Prairies, or, The Journal of a Santa Fé Trader* (2 v., 1844). Henry Nash Smith ranks this book with the Lewis and Clark narrative as a literary monument of the westward movement. It was often reprinted in its own time and was included in Reuben G. Thwaites' *Early Western Travels* (v. 19 and 20, 1905) and again in a reprint by the Southwest Press (1933). Gregg died from the effects of an arduous trip over the Coast Range. Maurice G. Fulton edited his *Diary and Letters* (2 v., 1941, 1944), and Max L. Moorhead has prepared an annotated edition of *Commerce of the Prairies* (1954).

Gregory, Horace [Victor] (b. Milwaukee, Wis., April 10, 1898—   ), poet, critic, translator, teacher. Gregory was an unflagging and important contributor to the many little magazines of the 1920's and also to critical magazines during that period and later. W. R. Benét notes that much of his poetry criticizes middle-class life and presents dramatic studies of slum dwellers, but Gene Baro concludes that his chief concern is with the relationship of the individual to life. Among his books: *Chelsea Rooming House* (1930); *No Retreat* (1933); *Chorus for Survival* (1935); *Poems, 1930–1940* (1941); *Selected Poems of Horace Gregory* (1951); *Medusa in Gramercy Park and Other Poems* (1961). In 1931 he brought out a memorable translation of *The Poems of Catullus;* this was followed by *Ovid, The Metamorphoses* (1958). *A History of American Poetry, 1900–1940*, in collaboration with his wife MARYA ZATURENSKA, came out in 1946. He has written critical biographies of Amy Lowell (1958), and James McNeill Whistler (1959), and a study of D. H. Lawrence (*Pilgrim of the Apocalypse*, 1933). Fragments of Gregory's autobiography may be found in his essays on *James Whitcomb Riley* (1951) and his new introduction to *The Poems of Catullus* (1956). See GREEK AND ROMAN INFLUENCE.

Gregory, Jackson (b. Salinas, Cal., March 12, 1882—d. June 12, 1943), teacher, writer of western and detective stories. A prolific writer, Gregory won acclaim for the readability and accuracy of his western tales. Among them are: *The Outlaw* (1916); *Desert Valley* (1921); *Splendid Outlaw* (1932); *Across the Border* (1933); *Sudden Dorn* (1937); *Hermit of Thunder King* (1945).

Grenadine Etching (1947), a burlesque novel by ROBERT RUARK. This was a vigorous attack on the 1,000-page historical novels that were popular with American readers after the publication of ANTHONY ADVERSE (1933). Facile novelists could produce them according to a formula that mixed sex and sensation with more or less accurate historical data. Grenadine was a ravishingly beautiful girl with "long, silvery hair" and eyes that gave off "a greenish glow, like phosphorus"; she was plain poison to every man she met.

Grenfell, Sir Wilfred Thomason (b. England,

Feb. 28, 1865—d. Oct. 9, 1940), physician, missionary, adventurer, memoirist. Grenfell became a medical missionary in the barren lands of Labrador, performed great services in that region, and wrote numerous books about his experiences. Among them: *Harvest of the Sea* (1906); *A Man's Faith* (1908); *Adrift on an Ice-Pan* (1909); *Down North on the Labrador* (1911); *Tales of the Labrador* (1916); *A Labrador Doctor* (1923); *Forty Years for Labrador* (1932); *A Labrador Logbook* (1939). It is believed that Norman Duncan had Grenfell in mind when he wrote his popular novel, *Dr. Luke of the Labrador* (1904).

Grey, Zane (b. Zanesville, Ohio, Jan. 31, 1875—d. Oct. 23, 1939), dentist, writer of western stories and articles on outdoor life. In 1904 Grey made up his mind that writing rather than dentistry was to be his career, but not until the publication of *Riders of the Purple Sage* (1912) did he attain great popular success. He published many books after that, including *Desert Gold* (1913); *The Border Legion* (1916); *The U. P. Trail* (1918); *The Mysterious Rider* (1921); *The Thundering Herd* (1925); *Code of the West* (1934); and numerous posthumously published novels: *Rogue River Feud* (1948); *Lost Pueblo* (1954); etc. Possibly his best novel was *The Last of the Plainsmen* (1908), and some critics preferred one or two of his nonfiction books, like *Tales of Fishing* (1925), to any of his over-picturesque novels. He was always a first-rate storyteller and dramatizer of a region. Jean Kerr has written *Zane Grey: Man of the West* (1950).

Grey Champion, The (1837), a story by NATHANIEL HAWTHORNE. See WILLIAM GOFFE.

Greyslaer (1840), a romance by CHARLES FENNO HOFFMAN. The scene is the Mohawk Valley at the time of the Revolution, but the plot is based on the famous Beauchamp Case or Kentucky Tragedy, a "triangle" murder that attracted several novelists by its sensational aspects. (See under BEAUCHAMP.) The hero, Max Greyslaer, is a patriot agitator who falls in love with Alida De Roos, but they cannot marry until the shame of a secret (but, as it turns out, invalid) marriage has been cleared from her name. See WILLIAM JOHNSON.

Grierson, Francis. Pen name of BENJAMIN HENRY JESSE FRANCIS SHEPARD.

Griffith, David W[ark] (b. Crestwood, Ky., Jan. 23, 1875—d. July 23, 1948), actor, playwright, movie scriptwriter, producer. Griffith began as an actor, then became a dramatist; among his plays was *A Fool and a Girl* (1907). After the failure of this drama he decided to try the movies, first as an actor, then as a scriptwriter for Biograph Films. He soon turned to directing, doing work that was more convincing and exciting than any produced up to that time. He reached the peak of his reputation with the production of an epic film on the Civil War, *The Birth of a Nation* (1915), based on Thomas Dixon's novels THE CLANSMAN and THE LEOPARD'S SPOTS. Himself a Southerner whose father had fought in the Confederate Army, Griffith

poured into the picture much that was personal. The picture attained the greatest success won by any movie up to that time, but also brought Griffith violent denunciation for having caused the revival of the Ku Klux Klan. He was both astonished and hurt, and to show his real feelings he sank his entire fortune in another play, INTOLERANCE (1916), which in its uncut form ran for twenty hours and tried to prove, in four parallel episodes, that intolerance never pays. In fact, he was the first movie director to extend films beyond one reel.

His other innovations include the fade in and fade out, angle shots, back lighting, night photography, the moving camera, and many other techniques still in use. These techniques had a great influence in Germany, France, and Russia, where they were immediately appropriated. These foreign writers and producers have generally received more critical attention than did Griffith, although Seymour Stern has called him "our one really important national and native artist." Among his often revolutionary films were *Broken Blossoms* (1919), *Way Down East* (1920), *Orphans of the Storm* (1921), *One Exciting Night* (1922), *Isn't Life Wonderful?* (1924). In *Abraham Lincoln* (1930) Griffith tried out the talkies and won an award as the best director of the year. He developed many stars, including Douglas Fairbanks, Sr.; Mary Pickford; Lillian Gish; Mack Sennett.

Griffiths, Clyde. The chief character in Theodore Dreiser's AN AMERICAN TRAGEDY (1925).

Grile, Dod. A pen name of AMBROSE BIERCE.

Grimes, James Stanley (b. Boston, May 10, 1807—d. Sept. 27, 1903), phrenologist, teacher, philosopher. Grimes was a New England eccentric who devised strange theories of the universe and the human mind, helped establish evolution as an accepted hypothesis, and devised odd words to express himself. He spent many of his years teaching in Illinois colleges. Among his books: *A New System of Phrenology* (1839); *Etherology* (1845); *Outlines of Geonomy* (1858).

Gringo, Harry. See H. A. WISE.

Grinnell, George Bird (b. Brooklyn, N.Y., Sept. 20, 1849—d. April 11, 1938), explorer, Indian authority, editor. Grinnell spent his life exploring wild sections of the West, studying Indian tribes, and helping in the conservation movement. He wrote numerous books, among them *Pawnee Hero Stories and Folk-Tales* (1889), *Blackfoot Lodge Tales* (1892), *Travels of the Pathfinders* (1911), *The Cheyenne Indians* (2 v., 1923), besides a series of books for boys. He edited (and partly owned) *Forest and Stream* (1876–1911).

Griswold, Rufus W[ilmot] (b. Benson, Vt., Feb. 15, 1815—d. Aug. 27, 1857), newspaperman, critic, anthologist, editor. He was employed on various newspapers and magazines, worked with EDGAR ALLAN POE on GRAHAM'S MAGAZINE and succeeded him as assistant editor, published numerous anthologies and personality sketches of contemporary writers, and in time by mere persistence became a sort of literary dictator. Griswold began as a printer; he was licensed to preach as a Baptist minister, but seems never to have occupied a pulpit. The degrees of D.D. and LL.D. that he assumed he apparently bestowed on himself.

Griswold was the worst liar and the least likable man in the whole history of American literature. Horace Greeley, who was one of almost twenty editors and publishers who employed him, called him "the most expert and judicious thief who ever handled scissors." His worst qualities were shown in connection with Poe, who thought him his friend and made him his literary executor. Griswold repaid him by perpetrating a long series of slanders which have greatly influenced the estimate of Poe's character and writings. Killis Campbell dealt well with "The Poe-Griswold Controversy" in *The Mind of Poe and Other Studies* (1932). Arthur Hobson Quinn, in *Edgar Allan Poe: A Critical Biography* (1941), is scholarly, judicious, and fairminded in presenting the facts about Poe vs. Criswold. Griswold's anthology, *The Poets and Poetry of America* came out in 1842 (and had many later editions); his *Prose Writers of America* appeared in 1847; and his *The Female Poets of America*—made up from appropriate sections of *The Poets and Poetry of America*—was published in 1848, and had several later printings.

grocery magazines. Magazines published by food-store chains and sold primarily to their customers, usually at a low price. Among the leading specimens are *Woman's Day, Family Circle,* and *American Family.*

Grogan, Tom. See TOM GROGAN.

Grolier Club. An organization of bibliophiles, located at 47 East 60th St., New York City. Founded in 1884, it holds frequent exhibits and issues many publications. It has a large library, open to the public on application.

Gropper, William (b. New York City, Dec. 3, 1897—   ), artist, illustrator. Gropper is represented in the Metropolitan and many other museums, and has done numerous murals. He is also known as a book illustrator.

Gross, Milt (b. New York City, March 4, 1895—d. Nov. 30, 1953), cartoonist, writer, scenic artist. Gross began to work as a comic artist for newspapers in 1913, created a series of popular comic strips, including "Nize Baby," "Banana Oil," "Gross Exaggerations," "Dear Dollink," and others. Some of these appeared in book collections—*Hiawatta Witt No Odder Poems* (1926); *Dunt Esk* (1927); *Famous Females from Heestory* (1928); *I Shoulda Ate the Eclair* (1946); all with stories exploiting the comic possibilities of the Bronx variety of English.

Grosvenor, Gilbert H[ovey] (b. Turkey, Oct. 28, 1875—   ), editor. Grosvenor was successively assistant editor, managing editor, and editor-in-chief of the *National Geographic Magazine* (1899–1954). He turned it from a stodgy periodical with a circulation of only nine hundred into a famous periodical for students of

geography and lovers of nature and travel, with a circulation of over two million. He was the first United States editor to use natural color photographs. He made the NATIONAL GEOGRAPHIC SOCIETY wealthy, won contributions from many distinguished persons, and preferred to print only what was kindly. He wrote *Young Russia* (1914); *The Hawaiian Islands* (1924); *Discovery and Exploration* (1924); *Maps for Victory* (1942); and other books.

Ground We Stand On, The (1941), biographical sketches by JOHN DOS PASSOS. Dos Passos in his novels had been passionately critical of contemporary American life. In this collection of sketches he turned to the past and showed a complete reversal of attitude. The sketches affirm the American Dream as it appeared in the thinking and ideals of the men who had made or influenced our earlier era: Roger Williams, Sam Adams, Tom Paine, Jefferson, Joel Barlow, Hugh Henry Brackenridge.

Group, The (1775), a satirical play by MERCY OTIS WARREN. It is a drama in name only; the lines consist of a discussion among supporters of the British cause. The play was published the day before the Battle of Lexington.

Group [Theater], The. An association of earnest actors, playwrights, and producers, many originally associated with the THEATRE GUILD, who in 1931 decided to form their own organization to produce plays of "social significance." After several trials they produced a Broadway hit, Paul Green's THE HOUSE OF CONNELLY (1931), went on to introduce new talents to the theater, and produced some important works; among them are Maxwell Anderson's *Night over Taos* (1932); Howard Lawson's *Success Story* (1932); Sidney Kingsley's MEN IN WHITE (1933); Irwin Shaw's THE GENTLE PEOPLE (1939); William Saroyan's *My Heart's in the Highlands* (1939); and several plays by CLIFFORD ODETS, beginning with WAITING FOR LEFTY (1935). The group in time suffered internal dissension and broke up. Its history is described in *The Fervent Years* (1945), by HAROLD CLURMAN, who with Cheryl Crawford and Lee Strasberg had furnished the original inspiration for The Group.

Grove, Frederick Philip (b. Sweden, Feb. 14, 1872—d. Aug. 19, 1948), novelist, essayist, poet. Educated abroad, Grove lived mainly in Ontario. He wrote thoughtful and distinguished novels, including *A Search for America* (1927), a dramatic quest for the American ideal, and *The Two Generations* (1939), a chronicle of Ontario farmers. Other works include: *Over Prairie Trails* (1922), *Our Daily Bread* (1929), *The Yoke of Life* (1930).

Grove, Lena, a character in LIGHT IN AUGUST, by William Faulkner. Although not central to the main action of the story, Lena Grove offers an important and implicit contrast to the violence and death present in the plot. Her confinement symbolically re-enacts the confinement of Joe Christmas' mother, and her placidity and animal unconcern make her a minor kind of

Earth Mother, carrying out her natural function of reproduction in a context that seems, but for her, hostile to life and growth.

Gruelle, Johnny [**John Barton**] (b. Arcola, Ill., Dec. 24, 1880—d. Jan. 9, 1938), author of books for children. He created the character RAGGEDY ANN, who appeared in various books bearing her name; also Raggedy Andy and other popular personages. He originated the comic strip "Brutus" (1910).

Grund, Francis Joseph (b. Germany , 1798—d. Sept. 29, 1863), writer. Grund, a European who came to live in the United States, wrote several books which portray America as seen through foreign eyes. The most important of these was *The Americans in Their Moral, Social and Political Relations* (1837). In Philadelphia he worked as a journalist, later became editor of *Age;* still later he served in Antwerp, Le Havre, and the South German states in the U.S. consular service. H. S. Commager states that Grund was especially interested in observing the effect of the doctrine of equality on morals, politics, and the position of women in the United States.

Gryce, Ebenezer. ANNA KATHARINE GREEN'S favorite sleuth, who appears first in THE LEAVENWORTH CASE (1878). Portly and paternal, Gryce recalls Miss Green's father, a noted trial lawyer.

Guardian Angel, The (1867), a novel by OLIVER WENDELL HOLMES. This novel shows how heredity may conflict with environment and how a kindly guardian may prevent the wreck of a life. All this is illustrated by an orphan, Myrtle Hazard, brought from the tropics to live in New England. The book was a popular one; by 1887 it had passed through twenty-three editions. Not a good novel, the book presents some of Holmes' most thoughtful ideas, notably his opposition to Calvinism, which aroused much resentment.

Guérard, Albert Léon (b. France, Nov. 3, 1880—d. Nov. 12, 1959), teacher, philologist, critic, historian, memoirist. Guérard had a distinguished academic career, chiefly at Stanford University, and wrote widely on many subjects. He was especially notable for his advocacy of a world language (*World Languages,* 1921) and for his books on French literature and civilization, among them: *French Prophets of Yesterday* (1913); *French Civilization in the 19th Century* (1914); *The Napoleonic Legend* (1923); *The France of Tomorrow* (1941); *France, A Short History* (1946); *Napoleon III* (1955); *Joan of Arc* (1957); *France: The Biography of a Nation* (1959). He also wrote *Preface to World Literature* (1940) and recorded his own experience in *Personal Equation* (1948) and *Education of a Humanist* (1949).

Guess, George. See SEQUOYA.

Guest, Edgar ["**Eddie**"] **A[lbert]** (b. England, Aug. 21, 1881—d. Aug. 5, 1959), newspaperman, columnist, poet. Guest came to the United States in 1891, began working for the Detroit *Free Press* and made his entire career

on that paper. He became a verse columnist in 1899. He soon developed a remarkable facility for "folksy" verse, sentimental and moralistic. For several decades he wrote a poem a day, including Sundays. These verses were widely syndicated, gathered in numerous volumes, and personally recited on the air; he also collected royalties on greeting cards. He is said to have written more than 11,000 poems. His most famous line is: "It takes a heap o' livin' in a house t' make it home." Among his books: *A Heap o' Livin'* (1916); *Just Folks* (1917); *Collected Verse* (1934); *Living the Years* (1949). Royce Homes wrote Guest's biography (1955).

Guggenheim Fellowships. These are awarded by the John Simon Guggenheim Memorial Foundation. The forty or fifty annual fellowships are given to Americans in the fields of literature, stagecraft, art, music, history, philosophy, and science for the purpose of promoting scientific and cultural activity. Similar Guggenheim awards have been made in Latin America. Among those who have received awards: John Dos Passos, W. H. Auden, Jacques Barzun, Louis Adamic, Conrad Aiken, Carson McCullers, Angna Enters, Robert Pick, Theodore Roethke, Norman Rosten, Mark Schorer, Hart Crane, Countee Cullen, Lewis Mumford, Allen Tate, Stephen V. Benét, Oliver La Farge, Jerre Mangione, Delmore Schwartz, Jeremy Ingalls, Dixon Wecter, Eudora Welty.

Guild, Curtis (b. Boston, Jan. 13, 1827—d. March 12, 1911), editor, poet, memoirist. Guild founded the Boston *Commercial Bulletin,* merged several other papers with it, and called the combination the *Morning Traveler* and *Evening Traveler.* He collected his poems in *From Sunrise to Sunset* (1894), wrote *A Chat about Celebrities* (1897).

Guiney, Louise Imogen (b. Roxbury, Mass., Jan. 7, 1861—d. Nov. 2, 1920), poet, essayist, journalist, librarian. A Catholic by birth and intense faith, Miss Guiney (pronounced *guynee*) became "the champion of lost causes" and the restorer to fame of forgotten literary worthies. Many of her later years were spent in England; she lies buried near Oxford. Her delicate, musical verses won her early fame, if not much in the way of a living. They were modeled on the old English ballads and the poems of the cavaliers; sometimes even the spelling is antique. Her poems were collected in *Songs at the Start* (1884); *The White Sail and Other Poems* (1887); *A Roadside Harp* (1893); *England and Yesterday* (1898); and *Happy Ending* (1909; rev., 1927). Her essays were gathered in several books, including *A Little English Gallery* (1894) and *Patrins* (1897), and her *Letters* were collected (1926) in two volumes.

Guiterman, Arthur (b. Austria, Nov. 29, 1871—d. Jan. 11, 1943), poet, newspaperman, editor. Guiterman, a finished writer of light verse, first attracted attention with his *Rhymed Reviews* in *Life.* He rarely probed deeply, although his *Death and General Putnam* (in a collection of the same title, 1935) is a magnificent serious ballad. He adapted Molière's *L'École des Maris* for the Theatre Guild (1933), also wrote the libretto and lyrics for WALTER DAMROSCH's opera, *The Man Without a Country* (produced, 1937). Among his collections: *Betel Nuts* (1907); *The Laughing Muse* (1915); *Ballads of Old New York* (1920); *Lyric Laughter* (1939).

Gullah [sometimes called **Geechee**]. A name given to a group of Negroes, also to the dialect of English they speak. They are descendants of slaves who now inhabit islands off the coast of South Carolina, Georgia, and northeastern Florida, also portions of the coast itself. The name may come from *Gola*, the name of a tribe and language of the Liberian hinterland, or from *Ngola*, the name of a tribe in Angola. *Geechee* is probably the name of another Liberian tribe and language. The dialect itself is an anomaly among American Negro dialects, being the only one not easily intelligible elsewhere. It was at first believed to be a corruption of English, particularly the dialect of Lancashire, but research by Dr. Lorenzo D. Turner of Fisk University (1945) showed that Gullah borrows much of its vocabulary from at least twenty-eight African languages and dialects. Some of these words have now passed into the general American vocabulary: *buckra*, a white man; *gumbo*, okra; *hudu*, hoodoo. Among those who have discussed this dialect are John Bennett, *Gullah. A Negro Patois* (1908), Reed Smith, *Gullah* (1926); Lupton A. Wilkinson, *Gullah versus Grammar* (1933); and L. D. Turner, *Africanisms in the Gullah Dialect* (1949).

Gullah proverbs have been frequently collected (a selection is given in B. A. BOTKIN's *Southern Folklore*, 1949); a typical one is: "Yaas, bubbuh, uh haa'kee, but uh yent yeddy" —that is, "I hear what you are saying, but I am not paying any attention to it." About this group Charles C. Jones wrote *Negro Myths from the Georgia Coast* (1888); Ambrose E. Gonzales, *The Black Border* (1922); Guy B. Johnson, *Folk-Culture on St. Helena Island, S.C.* (1930). In the creative realm one finds DuBose Heyward's novels, PORGY (1925; made into a folk play, with Dorothy Heyward, 1927; made into an opera, with George Gershwin, *Porgy and Bess*, 1935) and MAMBA'S DAUGHTERS (1929); also Julia Peterkin's BLACK APRIL (1927).

Gullible's Travels (1917), satirical tales about the newly rich by RING LARDNER.

Gummere, Francis B[arton] (b. Burlington, N.J., March 6, 1855—d. May 30, 1919), teacher, authority on poetry. A disciple of Francis J. Child, Gummere became a faculty member of Haverford College, and remained there for thirty years. He was a great teacher, of whom Christopher Morley wrote: "Just to listen to him was a purifying of wit, an enrichment of memory, an enabling of judgment, an enlarging of imagination." In discussion and in his books Gummere engaged vigorously in the learned controversies on these ballads that raged particularly in his day. He wrote a *Handbook of Poetics*

(1885), collected *Old English Ballads* (1894), discussed *The Beginnings of Poetry* (1901); *The Popular Ballad* (1907); *The Oldest English Epic* (1909); and *Democracy and Poetry* (1911). He believed in the individual authorship of ballads, but strongly stressed communal elements and emphasized the importance of the dance and choral singing.

Gunmaker of Moscow, The (1856), a novel by SYLVANUS COBB, JR. This was a best seller in the year of its publication. A Russian armorer named Ruric Nevel loves and is loved by a young duchess. Peter the Great witnesses the skill of the young armorer in a duel and makes him one of his favorites. After many adventures Ruric is raised to the nobility, given a large estate, and permitted to wed the duchess.

Gunnar (1874), a "tale of Norse life" by HJALMAR HJORTH BOYESEN. Gunnar, of lowly birth, loves the niece of a landowner, and the romantic plot relates the dangers he encounters, the devotion of the lovers, the folk customs of the Norseland, the wedding festivities.

Gunter, Archibald Clavering (b. England, Oct. 25, 1847—d. Feb. 24, 1907), civil engineer, chemist, broker, novelist. Gunter had a remarkable storytelling gift, accompanied by a mediocre talent for characterization and an undistinguished style. He wrote a locally successful play while attending the University of California, went on to an engineering career, then wrote a novel. He peddled it to various publishers, all of whom turned it down. Gunter decided to publish it himself; the book, MR. BARNES OF NEW YORK (1887), immediately became a best seller. Mr. Barnes was an engaging character, even if not too credibly portrayed— an excellent surgeon, a crack shot, a successful lover, and an adept at settling international complications. None of Gunter's thirty-eight later books duplicated his first success, although *Mr. Potter of Texas* (1888) and *Miss Nobody of Nowhere* (1890) did well. See FRESH THE AMERICAN.

Gunther, John (b. Chicago, Aug. 30, 1901— d. May 29, 1970), journalist, historian. Gunther became a reporter on the Chicago *Daily News* in 1922, and stuck to reporting first and foremost throughout his career. In 1924 he became a foreign correspondent for the *News*, and thereafter the world was his beat. He wrote *Inside Europe* (1936, frequent revisions) and established a worldwide reputation; thereafter he wrote *Inside Asia* (1939); *The High Cost of Hitler* (1940); *Inside Latin America* (1941); INSIDE U.S.A. (1947); *Inside Africa* (1955). Some of these seemed to critics hasty and superficial, but all of them manifested a marvelous gift for collecting and presenting data in orderly and entertaining fashion. There was, moreover, never any question of Gunther's honesty and his deep interest in human welfare. He will perhaps be best remembered by the memorial volume he wrote on the death of his young son, the deeply affecting *Death, Be not Proud* (1949). He has written also *Roosevelt in Retro-*

spect (1950); *General Douglas MacArthur* (1951); and *President Eisenhower* (1952). His important and timely *Inside Russia Today* was published in 1958. *Inside Europe Today* came out in 1961.

Gurko, Leo. See THE ANGRY DECADE.

Gurowski, Adam G. de (b. Kalisz, Sept. 10, 1805—d. May 4, 1866), writer, scholar. Count Gurowski lived a stormy life in Europe as one of those who conspired for the freedom of Poland from Russia during the abortive revolution of 1830. In 1849 he came to the United States. During the Civil War he served as a translator in the State Department, and *My Diary: Notes on the Civil War* (1862–66) reports his observations. H. S. Commager finds him at his best in his *America and Europe* (1857), with its judicious and on the whole appreciative analysis of the American character.

Gustavus Vasa (1690), a play by BENJAMIN COLMAN. Colman was the pastor of a church in Boston; he wrote verse as well as sermons and is said to have produced his play at Harvard. If this tradition is correct, his may have been the first performed play by an American writer.

Gus the Great (1947), a novel of circus life by THOMAS W. DUNCAN. The hero, "a great red-faced rogue," goes through some extraordinary adventures, meets many strange characters. Charles Poore called the novel "a pastiche of Tarkington, Sinclair Lewis, and Dreiser," but admitted that it had "something of the color and life of the two- and three-ring circus."

Guthrie, A[lfred] B[ertram], Jr. (b. Bedford, Ind., Jan. 13, 1901—   ), newspaperman, novelist, lecturer. Guthrie got his first job as a printer's devil on the Choteau *Advocate* in Montana. In 1926 he went to Lexington, Ky., where he worked on the staff of the *Leader* for twenty years, finally becoming executive editor. His first novel, THE BIG SKY (1947) earned an immediate critical and popular success. It treats the era of the 1840 mountain men with a mingling of realism and poetry, and gives a faithful and fascinating picture of Indian life in American literature. Although Guthrie was born in Indiana, his family moved to Montana when he was still an infant, and his love of the West is a rich part of his history and his writing. In 1949 he won a Pulitzer Prize for THE WAY WEST, which describes the passage of a small emigrant train over the Oregon Trail in the middle months of 1847. Here the mountain men appear again. Guthrie also wrote *These Thousand Hills* (1956), a novel of Montana, filmed in 1958, and *The Big It* (1960). He won an Oscar for the screenplay *Shane* (1953).

Guy Rivers (1834), a "tale of Georgia" by WILLIAM GILMORE SIMMS. The story is one of gold mining in the wilds of Georgia. See BORDER ROMANCES.

H

Habberton, John (b. Brooklyn, N.Y., Feb. 24, 1842—d. Feb. 24, 1921), editor, novelist, playwright. Habberton spent most of his life in editorial work; his leisure was occupied with writing for himself. He won a great popular success with *Helen's Babies* (1876), based on the author's harrowing experiences with his two young sons (called Budge and Toddie in the book) during his wife's absence. Habberton vainly tried to repeat his success, and wrote *Other People's Children* (1877); *The Worst Boy In Town* (1880); *Some Boys' Doings* (1901). He also wrote a popular play, *Deacon Crankett* (1880).

habitant. A settler of French descent in French Canada or Louisiana. They have been the subject of many amusing poems, written in a mixture of French and English. Probably the best is WILLIAM HENRY DRUMMOND's *The Wreck of Julie Plante.*

Hacker, Louis M[orton] (b. New York City, March 17, 1899—), teacher, editor, historian. Hacker became a faculty member at Columbia University in 1934; later Dean of their School of General Studies. His main interest is the history and characteristics of American capitalism. He is concerned with the impact of economics on politics, public policy, and social and individual behavior. He wrote *The United States Since 1865* (with B. B. Kendrick, 1932); *A Short History of the New Deal* (1934); *The United States: A Graphic History* (1938); *The Triumph of American Capitalism* (1940); *American Capitalism* (1957). He edited an anthology, *The Shaping of American Tradition* (2 v., 1947); and *Major Documents in American Economic History* (2 v., 1961).

Hackett, Albert (b. New York City, Feb. 16, 1900—), playwright, screenwriter, adapter, and **Frances Goodrich [Hackett]** (b. Belleville, New Jersey, —), playwright, screenwriter, adapter. In 1927, soon after they met, these two young actors decided to collaborate on a play; but it was three years before one of the several they wrote was produced. Miss Goodrich divorced HENDRIK WILLEM VAN LOON in 1929 and married Hackett in 1932. Their joint efforts resulted in a series of successful plays and movies, culminating in an adaptation of *The Diary of Anne Frank* (1956) based on *The Story of a Young Girl.* This play, the result of two years of research and writing, received a Pulitzer Prize, the New York Drama Critics Award, and the Antoinette Perry (Tony) Award. It has since moved audiences in many nations of the world. They wrote the play *Western Union, Please* (1939), and screen plays for *The Thin Man; Easter Parade; Father of the Bride; Gaby;* and *Seven Brides for Seven Brothers,* among others.

Hackett, Francis (b. Ireland, Jan. 21, 1883—d. April 24, 1962), critic, author. Hackett came to the United States in 1901, did editorial work on Chicago newspapers and the *New Republic,* and later on *The New York Times.* Some of his excellent critical essays have been collected in *On Judging Books* (1947). He has also written *Ireland, A Study in Nationalism* (1918); *The Story of the Irish Nation* (1922); *Henry the Eighth: A Personal History* (1929); *Francis the First* (1934); *Queen Anne Boleyn* (1938); *I Chose Denmark* (1940); *American Rainbow* (1953).

Hackett, James H[enry] (b. New York City, March 15, 1800—d. Dec. 28, 1871), actor, critic, scholar. Primarily a comedian, Hackett won his greatest critical success in the role of Falstaff. Later he tried more serious parts, including Hamlet. He wrote *Notes and Comments Upon Certain Plays and Actors of Shakespeare* (1863). He was the first American actor to appear as a star on the London stage (April, 1827). He was especially successful in two typical roles: a shrewd Yankee and a bluff Westerner. Like other actors of his time, he introduced Yankee parts into all kinds of plays. He was also popular as Colonel Nimrod Wildfire in THE LION OF THE WEST (1830), a play of frontier life written for him by J. K. Paulding. His son **James K. Hackett** (1869–1926) was also an actor and excelled in romantic plays such as *The Prisoner of Zenda.*

Hadas, Moses (b. Atlanta, Ga., June 25, 1900—d. Aug. 17, 1966), literary historian, translator. Professor of Greek at Columbia University from 1953, and a leading authority on classical literature, Hadas was the author of *A History Of Greek Literature* (1950); *Aristeas to Philocrates* (1950); *A History Of Latin Literature* (1952); *Ancilla To Classical Reading* (1954); *Hellenistic Culture* (1959); and *Humanism* (1960). He edited the *Complete Works of Tacitus* (1942); *The Basic Works of Cicero* (1951); and *The Greek Poets* (1952). He also translated J. Burkhardt's *Constantine The Great* (1948); Curt Vietor's *Goethe The Poet* (1949); W. E. Otto's *The Homeric Gods* (1954); and three Hellenistic tales under the title of *Three Greek Romances* (1954).

Hadden, Briton (b. Brooklyn, N.Y., Feb. 18, 1898—d. Feb. 27, 1929), editor. At Yale Hadden and his friend HENRY R. LUCE conceived an idea for a new magazine which ultimately became TIME. They started the magazine on $86,000; within two decades it was regarded as worth more than a hundred million. Hadden edited the magazine for five years, then turned to the business end. During his editorship he invented a new language. He loved odd words and coinages, especially portmanteau words (*cinemactress,* for example), but others were based on the way in which compounds are formed in Greek. He managed from the beginning to stimulate his editorial helpers to frenzied feats of verbal invention or to enthusiastic research among Webster's less frequently used words. Hadden also did a good deal to develop *Time's* letter columns, with their often acrid controversies; he wrote some of the letters himself. Toward the end of his short life he founded the advertising magazine *Tide;* and he conceived the ideas of LIFE and FORTUNE. Exactly six years after the appearance of *Time's* first issue, Hadden died, but his imprint on the magazine to a large extent had determined its character. Noel F. Busch, a *Time-Life* editor and a cousin of Hadden's, wrote a biography, *Briton Hadden* (1949).

Hadley, Arthur T[wining] (b. New Haven, Conn., April 23, 1856—d. March 6, 1930), teacher, administrator, political economist. Eminent as a teacher and expounder of political economy, Hadley published numerous books in this field, also several volumes discussing education and democracy. Hadley graduated from Yale (1876) and joined the faculty in 1879. From 1885 to 1887 he acted as Commissioner of Labor for Connecticut. He became president of Yale in 1899 and continued as such until his retirement in 1921. He composed a classic treatise, *Railroad Transportation* (1885). He also wrote *The Education of the American Citizen* (1901); *Standards of Public Morality* (1907); *The Moral Basis of Democracy* (1919); *The Conflict Between Liberty and Equality* (1925). His oldest son, Morris Hadley, wrote a mellow and entertaining biography of his father (1949).

Hagedorn, Hermann (b. New York City, July 18, 1882—d. July 27, 1964), poet, biographer. An admirer of Theodore Roosevelt, Hagedorn devoted many of his writings to that eminent figure—*The Boys' Life of Theodore Roosevelt* (1918); *Roosevelt in the Bad Lands* (1921); *Roosevelt, Prophet of Unity* (1924); *The Rough Riders* (1927); *The Bugle That Woke America —The Saga of Theodore Roosevelt's Last Battle for His Country* (1940). *The Roosevelt Family of Sagamore Hill* (1954) was a Book-of-the-Month Selection. Hagedorn edited a selection from Roosevelt's writings (1923) and the *Memorial Edition* of his works (1923–24) and was active in the Roosevelt Memorial Association. In addition, Hagedorn wrote excellent biographies of General Leonard Wood (1920), William Boyce Thompson (1935), and Albert Schweitzer (1947). *The Hyphenated Family* (1960), is "a kind of autobiography," the history of a family that tried to live in two countries, Germany and the United States. He wrote: "It didn't work, bringing conflict and tragedy." Hagedorn issued several collections of verse: *A Troop of the Guard* (1909), *Poems and Bal-*

lads (1912), *Combat at Midnight* (1940), *The Bomb That Fell on America* (1946).

Haggard, Howard W[ilcox] (b. La Porte, Ind., July 19, 1891—d. April 22, 1959), physician, teacher, writer of technical and popular books and articles on medicine. A graduate of Yale, Haggard joined its faculty in 1919, rose to the rank of professor of applied physiology in 1938. Among his capably written and widely read books: *Are You Intelligent?* (1926); *What You Should Know about Health and Disease* (1928); *Devils, Drugs, and Doctors* (1929); *Mystery, Magic, and Medicine* (1933); *The Doctor in History* (1934); *Alcohol Explored* (with E. M. Jellinek, 1942); *Alcohol, Science and Society* (1946). Dr. Haggard contributed to numerous papers on physiology and did research work on noxious gases, alcohol, and physiology of industrial fatigue and efficiency.

Hahn, Emily (b. St. Louis, Mo., Jan. 14, 1905—   ), short-story writer, newspaperwoman, biographer. Miss Hahn visited many parts of the world, but became particularly familiar with China, which appears prominently in her frank and amusing writings. Among her books: *Seductio ad Absurdum* (1927); *Beginner's Luck* (1931); *Congo Solo* (1933); *Steps of the Sun* (1940); *The Soong Sisters* (1941); *Mr. Pan* (1942); *China to Me* (1944); *Hongkong Holiday* (1946); *Raffles of Singapore* (1946); *England to Me* (1949); *Francie* (1951) and *Francie Again* (1953), two juveniles; *Chiang Kai-shek* (1955), and *Tiger House Party* (1959).

Haig-Brown, Roderick [Langmere Haig] (b. England, Feb. 21, 1908—   ), author, angler, judge. Educated in England, Haig-Brown became a logger in the western forests of the United States and Canada before he was twenty. Later he settled in Vancouver Island, farmed, fished, wrote, and tried cases in the Vancouver juvenile court. His books about fish and other wildlife include: *Silver* (1930); *Ki-Yu* (1934); *The Western Angler* (1939); *A River Never Sleeps* (1946); *Fisherman's Spring* (1951); *Fisherman's Winter* (1954); *Fisherman's Summer* (1959). *Timber* (1942) and *On the Highest Hill* (1949) are two novels of the western woods.

Hail Columbia, Happy Land! (April 25, 1798, first rendition; pub. three days later in *The Porcupine Gazette*), a lyric by JOSEPH HOPKINSON. It was adapted to the music of *The President's March,* said to have been composed by Philip Phile (or Pheil). Hopkinson's lyric was first sung by Gilbert Fox in a Philadelphia theater at a time when war with France threatened. It became very popular and remained so during the 19th century. "Hail Columbia!" became an expletive, a euphemism for "Hell!"

Hail! Hail! the Gang's All Here! (1897), a lyric by Theodore F. Morse (1873–1924). It was adapted to the music of the "Pirates' Chorus" in Gilbert and Sullivan's opera *The Pirates of Penzance* (1879).

Haines, Helen E[lizabeth] (b. New York City, Feb. 9, 1872—   ), editor, librarian, teacher, author. Miss Haines wrote two excellent volumes, *Living With Books* (1935) and *What's in a Novel?* (1942). *Living With Books* considers the art of book selection and is widely used in libraries. Miss Haines was editor of the *Library Journal* for over twenty years and a contributor to the *Saturday Review of Literature, The Bookman, New York Herald Tribune,* and other periodicals. She also served on the faculty of Columbia University.

Haines, William Wister (b. Des Moines, Iowa, Sept. 17, 1908—   ), novelist, short-story writer, playwright. Work with power and light companies, construction and gold-mining companies, and the Pennsylvania Railroad gave Haines data for his first two novels, *Slim* (1934) and *High Tension* (1938), and for numerous short stories. Service in the Army Air Force in World War II proved useful in writing COMMAND DECISION (1947), a widely read novel which became a popular play when produced in a dramatic version by the author (1947). He also wrote *The Honorable Rocky Slade* (1957).

Hairy Ape, The (1922), an expressionist play by EUGENE O'NEILL. It exhibits the brutalization of Yank, the leader of the stokers, in the hold of a transatlantic liner. Later it shows Yank in New York, where his disillusioning adventures lead him finally to the zoo. There he realizes that an ape is his nearest kin in spirit, frees him, and is crushed to death by the beast. O'Neill said he drew Yank as a "symbol of man, who has lost his old harmony with nature."

Hakluyt, Richard (1552?–1616), English clergyman, editor, geographer. Incited by a derogatory remark regarding the insularity and lack of spirit of the English, Hakluyt resolved to gather accounts of voyages made by his countrymen, and in 1582 published a collection of *Divers Voyages Touching the Discovery of America.* He continued to amass other material and to publish it from time to time. His chief collection appeared in 1589: *The Principal Navigations, Voyages, Traffics, and Discoveries of the English Nation* (greatly enlarged, 3 v., 1598–1600). In this work he described the voyages of the Cabots, Sir John Hawkins, Sir Francis Drake, Martin Frobisher, Sir Walter Ralegh, and others to the New World.

Haldeman-Julius, E[manuel] (b. Philadelphia, July 30, 1889—d. July 31, 1951), publisher, editor, writer. Although Haldeman-Julius wrote books of his own (*Dust*, a novel written with his wife, 1921; *The Art of Reading*, 1922; *Literary Essays*, 1923; *An Agnostic Looks at Life*, 1926; *The First Hundred Million*, 1928; *My First 25 Years*, 1949), he was chiefly notable as a publisher and distributor of books by others. His publications, which he sold primarily through the mails and in enormous numbers, known as LITTLE BLUE BOOKS, were small, paperbound, inexpensive volumes, sometimes of trivial material but often of excellent writing from the past and present. They introduced millions of readers to the pleasures of reading. Haldeman-Julius also edited the *American Freeman,* a rationalist magazine, and indulged freely in controversies.

Hale, Edward Everett (b. Boston, April 3, 1822—d. June 10, 1909), clergyman, short-story writer, memoirist. Hale was a man who did many things well and with ease. He preached to the pleasure of many audiences,

and for a time (1903–09) was chaplain of the U.S. Senate. Someone asked him once, "Dr. Hale, do you pray for the Senate?" "No," he replied; "I look at the senators and pray for the people." He was a kindly and understanding critic; it is believed that he was the first to print a warm approval of Walt Whitman's LEAVES OF GRASS. His originality and inventiveness are exhibited in his most famous piece of writing, THE MAN WITHOUT A COUNTRY (first pub. in the *Atlantic Monthly*, December, 1863; pub. separately, 1865; collected with other pieces in *If, Yes, and Perhaps*, 1868). Its hero, Philip Nolan, soon became a national myth. Made into an opera by Walter Damrosch, it was produced at the Metropolitan Opera (1937). Hale wrote many other books as a guide to the future, advocating new social ideas (See OLD AND NEW). He wrote accounts of his remarkable career in *A New England Boyhood* (1893, enlarged in 1900) and *Memories of a Hundred Years* (2 v., 1902). His son, **Edward Everett Hale, Jr.** (b. Boston, Feb. 18, 1863—d. Aug. 19, 1932), wrote a biography, *The Life and Letters of Edward Everett Hale* (2 v., 1917).

Hale, Lucretia Peabody (b. Boston, Sept. 2, 1820—d. June 12, 1900), author of books for children, novelist. In 1880 appeared THE PETERKIN PAPERS, which made Miss Hale's reputation as a writer for young people. These sketches originally printed in St. Nicholas and Our Young Folks, were followed by *The Last of the Peterkins, With Others of Their Kind* (1886). The Peterkins are always making ludicrous blunders (the earliest of the stories was called *The Lady Who Put Salt in Her Coffee*), and they are frequently saved by the benevolent "Lady from Philadelphia." Miss Hale (sister of Edward Everett Hale) had a lively sense of humor, and often wrote parodies of her contemporaries. She was, like her brother, deeply interested in social causes.

Hale, Nancy (b. Boston, May 6, 1908—   ), newspaperwoman, editor, novelist. This granddaughter of Edward Everett Hale wrote several lively novels, among them *The Young Die Good* (1932); *Never Any More* (1934); *The Prodigal Women* (1942); *The Sign of Jonah* (1950). Her short stories appeared in many magazines and are collected in *The Earliest Dreams* (1936), *Between the Dark and the Daylight* (1943), and *The Empress' Ring* (1955). *A New England Girlhood* (1958) is an autobiography with some fanciful touches. *The Pattern of Perfection* came out in 1960. She moved to Virginia when she married the Elizabethan scholar Fredson Bowers.

Hale, Nathan [1] (b. Tolland Co., Conn., June 6, 1755—d. Sept. 22, 1776), teacher, soldier, spy. At Yale the young soldier had been an outstanding scholar and athlete. During the Revolution he was hanged as a spy by the British; his famous regret at having only one life to give for his country was inspired by a line in Addison's play *Cato* (1713). A stirring anonymous ballad, written soon after his death, commemorated his patriotism. Clyde Fitch wrote a successful play (1898) about him, and he appears in J. R. Simms' *The American Spy* (1846), Howard Fast's *The Unvanquished* (1942), and other novels. Isaac W. Stuart (1856), Jane Tallman (1932), and George D. Seymour (1933) have written biographies of Hale. His family included the ancestors of Edward Everett Hale.

Hale, Nathan [2] (b. Westhampton, Mass., Aug. 16, 1784—d. Feb. 8, 1863), publisher, editor, geographer. Hale, a nephew of Nathan Hale [1], bought the Boston *Daily Advertiser* in 1814, edited it till 1854, and made it an influential paper. He was one of the founders of the *North American Review* and the *Christian Examiner,* and he published and edited the *Monthly Chronicle* (1840–46). He wrote *An Epitome of Universal Geography* (1830).

Hale, Sarah Josepha Buell (b. Newport, N.H., Oct. 24, 1788—d. April 30, 1879), editor, writer, feminist. Mrs. Hale is an important figure in the annals of the emancipation of women. The death of her husband David Hale, a brilliant lawyer, left her with five children to support. She turned to writing and won great success. At first she wrote verse, in which her talent was mediocre, though one poem of hers—Mary Had a Little Lamb (1830)—became a classic. In 1828 she was asked to assume the editorship of *The Ladies' Magazine,* which in 1837 was bought by Louis A. Godey and turned into a new magazine, Godey's Lady's Book. Together they made it a great success. Mrs. Hale encouraged new writers, especially women. Her novel *Northwood, or, Life North and South* (1827) was

among the first fictional denunciations of slavery. She wrote a valuable compilation, *Woman's Record, or, Sketches of All Distinguished Women from the Beginning Till A.D. 1850* (1854). She compiled *The Ladies' Wreath* (1837), a giftbook; two annuals, *The Opal* (1845, 1848) and *The Crocus* (1849); edited the letters of Madame de Sévigné and Lady Mary Wortley Montagu.

Hale, Susan (b. Boston, Dec. 5, 1833—d. Sept. [?], 1910), illustrator, writer. Miss Hale wrote, in collaboration with her brother Edward Everett Hale, a popular series of travel books. *A Family Flight Over Egypt* (1882) was followed by volumes on France, Germany, Spain, and other countries, and by *A Family Flight Around Home* (1885). She wrote a biography of Thomas Gold Appleton (1885) and an account of *Men and Manners in the 18th Century* (1898). She was a facile and humorous illustrator, and did the drawings for the limericks in Mrs. William G. Weld's *Nonsense Book.*

Hale, William Harlan (b. New York City, July 21, 1910—   ), editor, columnist, radio broadcaster, historian. Hale, a vigorous observer and critic of his times, served on the Washington *Post* and on various magazines, including *Vanity Fair, Fortune,* the *New Republic,* and *The Reporter,* and became managing editor of *Horizon* in 1958. Among his books are: *Challenge to Defeat* (1932); *Hannibal Hooker* (1938); *A Yank in the R.A.F.* (1941); *The March of Freedom* (1947); *Horace Greeley and*

His America (1950); *Innocence Abroad* (1955).

Half-Breed, The (1845), an Indian tale by WALT WHITMAN. It is one of Whitman's two experiments in writing about the red man. The other is an interpolation in Whitman's temperance novel called FRANKLIN EVANS (1842).

Half-Way Covenant, The (*c.* 1662), a document drafted by RICHARD MATHER, which indicated a decline in the rigid dogmatism of the Mather dynasty. It advocated the baptism of children of nonregenerate though baptized parents—such parents were regarded by Mather as "half-way" members of the church.

Haliburton, Thomas Chandler ["Sam Slick"] (b. Windsor, N.S., Dec. 17, 1796—d. Aug. 27, 1865), lawyer, jurist, member of Parliament, humorist, editor. Haliburton, a lawyer and judge, was critical of the United States and of democracy. In 1856 he retired and went to England, was welcomed into literary and political circles, and was elected to the House of Commons. He was a fanatic conservative, frequently expressed contempt for what he called "the lower orders," and became more and more an avowed enemy of democracy.

In 1835 Haliburton began writing in the newspaper *The Novascotian* humorous sketches about Sam Slick, an itinerant Yankee clockmaker. This lampoon on Americans was apparently intended primarily to make Nova Scotians appreciate their own country and British institutions, but also to contrast Nova Scotian indolence with Yankee industry and shrewdness. The first sketches, with others added, were collected in THE CLOCKMAKER, OR, THE SAYINGS AND DOINGS OF SAMUEL SLICK OF SLICKVILLE (1837). The first series was followed by two others (1838, 1840), and in later years by *Sam Slick's Saws and Modern Instances* (1853) and *The Attaché, or, Sam Slick in England* (2 v., 1843–44). The books became very popular, first in Canada, then in the United States and England. Sam Slick became the best known character in the field of Yankee humor, and had many imitators. English critics praised the sketches warmly; John Wilson in *Blackwood's* (November, 1837) was pleased by Haliburton's diversion from the "treacle and water" style of Washington Irving. Sam Slick even challenged the hold of Sam Weller in *The Pickwick Papers* (1837) on the affections of the British public—although not for very long. Sam Slick is a shrewd, ruthless trader, ready to trick his customers at every opportunity. He is full of wise saws and modern instances, and has an unfailing supply of humorous stories. Some of his sayings gained wide currency, such as: "Politics makes a man as crooked as a pack does a peddler; not that they are so awful heavy either, but it teaches a man to stoop in the long run."

Artemus Ward, writing in a Nova Scotian paper, is supposed to have called Haliburton "the father of the American school of humor." V. L. D. Chittick, in his authoritative *Thomas Chandler Haliburton: A Study in Provincial Toryism* (1924), challenges both the wisdom and the authenticity of this statement. Actually critics are agreed that Haliburton was no innovator. He took Franklin as a model for his aphorisms, found the Yankee peddler and wanderer in many travel books and plays. It has also been pointed out that Sam Slick is a Yankee on whom DAVY CROCKETT has been imperfectly grafted. Apparently Haliburton tried to combine the most amusing features of Crockett's *Autobiography* (1834) and other writings with SEBA SMITH's *Life and Writings of Major Jack Downing* (1833). H. L. Mencken asserted that the sketches were written "in a dialect now intelligible only to paleophilologists."

Haliburton himself was greatly interested in American humor, and edited an anthology, *Traits of American Humor by Native Authors* (1852). He wrote *The Old Judge, or, Life in a Colony* (1849) and *The Letter-Bag of the Great Western, or, Life in a Steamer* (1858). Chittick, in an article in the *Dalhousie Review* (Summer, 1953) on *The Pervasiveness of Sam Slick*, points out his influence on Melville and many others. See HUMOR IN THE U.S.

Hall, Amanda Benjamin [Mrs. John Angell Brownell] (b. Hallville, Conn., July 12, 1890—), poet, novelist. Miss Hall published several collections of her pleasing verse: *The Dancer in the Shrine* (1923); *Cinnamon Saint* (1937); *Honey Out of Heaven* (1938); *Unweave a Rainbow* (1942); *Frosty Harp* (1954). Among her novels is *The Heart's Justice* (1922).

Hall, Donald (b. New Haven, Conn., September 20, 1928—), poet, editor. Hall has been poetry editor of the *Paris Review*, and Associate Professor of English at the University of Michigan. His first book of poems, *Exiles and Marriages* (1955), won several awards, including the Edna St. Vincent Millay Award of the Poetry Society of America. His poems are carefully wrought; they speak quietly but surely. In editing *The New Poets of England and America* (1957, with Robert Pack and LOUIS SIMPSON) Hall answered the charge that academic poetry had become effete and specious. ROBERT FROST wrote an introduction to the volume and it quickly won recognition. Like Hall, whose own poems appear in the book, most of the poets skillfully employed traditional forms. It was pointed out that even though the book contained no one great poem, the combined achievement of a large number of excellent poets spoke well for modern poetry. He has edited: *Harvard Advocate Anthology* (1950); *Whittier* (1960); *The New Poets of England and America #2* (1962); *The Poetry Sampler* (1962); *Contemporary American Verse* (1962).

Hall, Florence Marion Howe (b. Boston, Aug. 25, 1845—d. April 10, 1922), biographer, memoirist. Mrs. Hall, in collaboration with MAUDE HOWE ELLIOTT, her sister, and LAURA ELIZABETH RICHARDS, wrote a biography of her famous mother, JULIA WARD HOWE (2 v., 1915), which won a Pulitzer Prize. With Mrs. Elliott she had previously written *Laura Bridgman* (1902). Her own reminiscences appear in *Memories Grave and Gay* (1918). She also wrote several books on etiquette, including *Social Customs* (1920).

Hall, G[ranville] Stanley (b. Ashfield, Mass., Feb. 1, 1844—d. April 24, 1924), teacher, psychologist, editor, administrator. Hall, educated in part in German university methods, taught at Antioch, Johns Hopkins, and Clark, where he served as president (1889–1919). He was among the most eminent psychologists of his time, reckoned many noted men among his students (including John Dewey), founded and edited the *American Journal of Psychology* (1887–1921). His books include *The Contents of Children's Minds on Entering School* (1894); *Adolescence* (2 v., 1904; abridged as *Youth, Its Education, Regimen, and Hygiene*, 1906); *Educational Problems* (2 v., 1911); *Morale: The Supreme Standard of Life and Conduct* (1920); *Recreations of a Psychologist* (1920); *Senescence, the Last Half of Life* (1922); *Life and Confessions of a Psychologist* (1923). Hall introduced the experimental methods of Wilhelm Wundt (1832–1920) to American psychology, and invited Sigmund Freud to visit the United States. He was farseeing, and although regarded as an innovator, was really middle-of-the-road and cautious. In 1904 he warned against the pressures to which youth would be subjected in America in its modern developments. He refused to accept "intelligence tests" as particularly valuable in determining mental capacity, thus anticipating the reaction that followed the heady enthusiasm with which these tests were first introduced. Hall is supposed to have been the model for the professor in *Meteor* (1929), a play by S. N. Behrman, a former student of his.

Hall, James (b. Philadelphia, Aug. 19, 1793—d. July 5, 1868), banker, lawyer, judge, editor, historian, poet. Hall, one of the first to record the legends of the frontier, founded and edited the Illinois Monthly Magazine (1830–32), the first western literary periodical, and the *Western Monthly Magazine* (1832–36). Among his books: *Legends from the West* (1828); *Legends of the West* (1832); *The Harpe's Head: A Legend of Kentucky* (1833); *The Soldier's Bride and Other Tales* (1833); *Tales of the Border* (1835); *Sketches of History, Life, and Manners in the West* (2 v., 1834–35); *The Romance of Western History* (1857). John T. Flanagan described him in *James Hall, Literary Pioneer of the Ohio Valley* (1950).

Hall, James Norman (b. Colfax, Iowa, April 22, 1887—d. July 5, 1951), novelist, short-story writer, historian, memoirist. First a social worker, Hall served in the British and American armies during World War I, was a prisoner in Germany for six months, then a resident on the island of Tahiti. These adventures contributed data for his writings. In his fiction he had as an almost constant collaborator Charles Nordhoff, with whom he wrote a famous trilogy, Mutiny on the Bounty (1932), *Men Against the Sea* (1933), and *Pitcairn's Island* (1934), based on old records. The first volume of the trilogy was made into a movie (1935) that be-

came a classic. The collaborators also wrote *The Lafayette Flying Corps* (1920); *Falcons of France* (1929); *The Hurricane* (1936); *Botany Bay* (1941). Alone, Hall wrote *Kitchener's Mob* (1916); *High Adventure* (1918); *Mid-Pacific* (1928); *Flying with Chaucer* (1930); *Dr. Dogbody's Leg* (1940), short stories; *Lost Island* (1944); *A Word for the Sponsor* (1949), a poem; *The Far Lands* (1950); *Tahiti: Voyage Through Paradise* (1953).

Hall, Samuel (b. Medford, Mass., Nov. 2, 1740—d. Oct. 20, 1809), printer, editor. Hall assisted Ann Franklin, Benjamin's sister-in-law, in publishing the Newport *Mercury* (1762). Later he founded the *Essex Gazette* at Salem (1768); the *New England Chronicle* at Cambridge (1775); the *Massachusetts Gazette* in Boston (1785).

Hall, Sam[uel] S[tone] (b. Worcester, Mass., July 23, 1838—d. Feb. 1, 1886), dime novelist. One of the few dime novelists who had a first-hand knowledge of the West, Hall wrote under the names of "Major Sam S. Hall" and "Buckskin Sam." Among his novels are *Diamond Dick, The Dandy from Denver* (1882); *Bow and Bowie; or, Ranging for Reds* (1882); *Arizona Jack; or, Giant George's Tenderfoot Pard* (1882); *Desperate Duke, the Guadaloupe "Galoot"* (1883); and *Rocky Mountain Al; or, Nugget Nell, the Waif of the Range* (1883).

Halle, Louis J. (b. New York City, Nov. 17, 1901—   ), expert on international affairs. Professor at the Graduate Institute of International Studies in Geneva, Switzerland, since 1956. Halle had previously been with the Department of State and other bureaus concerned with international and inter-American affairs. His books on diplomacy and international affairs are scholarly, analytic, and opinionated. Of *Civilization and Foreign Policy* (1955), the Chicago *Tribune* said, "It reveals a good deal of historical erudition and shrewd insights." *Choice for Survival* (1958) predicted that limited nuclear warfare could save the world from destruction. His book on nature, *Birds Against Men* (1938), won him the John Burroughs medal for 1941. Other books include *Transcaribbean* (1935); *River of Ruins* (1938); *Spring in Washington* (1947); *On Facing the World* (1949); *Dream and Reality* (1959).

Halleck, Fitz-Greene (b. Guilford, Conn., July 8, 1790—d. Nov. 19, 1867), banker, secretary to John Jacob Astor, poet. Literature was an avocation with Halleck, and the mark of that fact, as Lowell pointed out severely in his *Fable for Critics* (1848), is upon almost everything that Halleck wrote. He had a sense of fun that appeared in his association with a group of young writers in New York who called themselves the Ugly Club and advocated "ugliness in all its forms," and in his more fruitful association with Joseph Rodman Drake, with whom he wrote the still lively Croaker Papers. These appeared first in the New York *Evening Post* and the *National Advocate* and were collected as *Poems by Croaker; Croaker & Co.;* and

Croaker, Jun. (1819) and again as *Poems, by Croaker* (1860). Later Halleck wrote FANNY (1819), a burlesque in imitation of Byron. When Drake died in 1820 Halleck wrote a beautiful elegy, beginning "Green be the turf

above thee, friend of my better days." Another popular poem was MARCO BOZZARIS (1825), again an imitation of Byron. *Alnwick Castle* (1827) was an imitation of Scott. Halleck made a gathering of his *Poetical Works* in 1847.

Halliburton, Richard (b. Brownsville, Tenn., Jan. 9, 1900—d. March 21? [22?], 1939), literary adventurer, writer of travel books. Halliburton spent most of his life wandering over the world and then writing about his experiences. Some of his books became best sellers; among them are THE ROYAL ROAD TO ROMANCE (1925); *The Glorious Adventure* (1927); *New Worlds to Conquer* (1929); *The Flying Carpet* (1932); *A Book of Marvels* (1937). Halliburton swam the Hellespont and the Panama Canal; he followed the routes of Ulysses, Cortez, and Alexander the Great. In 1939, while attempting to sail in a Chinese junk from China to San Francisco, he disappeared, and was later declared legally dead. A selection of his travel writings, *The Romantic World of Richard Halliburton,* appeared in 1961.

Halper, Albert (b. Chicago, Aug. 3, 1904—   ), novelist, short-story writer. Halper writes of poor people with a wealth of naturalistic detail and with considerable power, if not style, and has been translated into many languages. Among his works: *Union Square* (1933); *Sons of the Fathers* (1940); *The Little People* (1942); *The Golden Watch* (1953);

Atlantic Avenue (1956). Most of his work stems from his personal experience of Chicago, and he edited an anthology of stories about the city, *This is Chicago* (1952).

Halpine, Charles Graham (b. Ireland, Nov. 20, 1829—d. Aug. 3, 1868), soldier, newspaperman, poet. Halpine fought in the Civil War, attaining the rank of Brigadier-General. Already famous before the war as a newspaper wit, he reached his greatest success when under the pen name of Miles O'Reilly he began using his Civil War experiences in a humorous vein. These writings were collected in *The Life and Adventures, Songs, Services, and Speeches of Private Miles O'Reilly* (1864) and *Baked Meats of the Funeral* (1866). He was a facile versifier with a keen sense of straight-faced burlesque.

Halsey, Margaret [Frances] (b. Yonkers, N.Y., Feb. 13, 1910—   ), satirist, novelist. When Miss Halsey went to England in 1936 her letters home describing her disillusionment with the English and their ways attracted a publisher's attention; he persuaded her to turn the diary she had been keeping into a book—*With Malice Toward Some* (1938), which became a best seller and aroused many Anglophiles to spluttering wrath. Her later books are more serious, directed toward combating racial and religious intolerance, as *Some of My Best Friends Are Soldiers* (1944) and *Color Blind* (1946). She also wrote *The Folks at Home* (1952) and *This Demi-Paradise, A Westchester Diary* (1960).

Halyard, Harry. Pen name of an author whose real name is unknown. He wrote historical tales, among them *The Heroine of Tampico* (1847) and *The Mexican Spy* (1848), also *The Ocean Monarch* (1848) and *Wharton the Whale-Killer* (1848).

Hamilton, Alexander [1] (b. Scotland, 1712—d. May 11, 1756), physician, essayist, diarist. Hamilton came to America in 1738 and established a medical practice in Annapolis, Md. He was one of the founders of the Annapolis Tuesday Club, an organization "designed for humor," for which Hamilton kept facetious minutes. His fame is, however, chiefly preserved by the entertaining record of a trip to Portsmouth, N.H., in 1744, *Itinerarium* (1744; reprinted, 1948).

Hamilton, Alexander [2] (b. British West Indies, Jan. 11, 1757 [1755?]—d. July 12, 1804), soldier, statesman, economist. Because of his father's business failures Hamilton was sent to work at the age of twelve; his energy and ambition soon brought him to the attention of friends and relatives, who sent him to New York in 1772 in order that he might have a college education. He entered King's College (now Columbia), but interrupted his studies to offer his support to the growing colonial feelings against England. In December he published two anonymous pamphlets, *A Full Vindication of the Measures of Congress from the Calumnies of Their Enemies* and *The Farmer Refuted: or a More Comprehensive and Impartial View of the Disputes Between Great Britain and the Col-*

onies, which were first thought to be written by John Jay or another well-known leader, so great was the understanding they showed of the issues in question.

Early in 1776 Hamilton was given a commis-

sion as commander of an artillery company; during the remainder of that year he fought with Washington in the battles of Long Island, White Plains, Trenton, and Princeton. In 1777 he was made an aide-de-camp to Washington and promoted to the rank of Lieutenant Colonel. He was a valued advisor to his commander during the remainder of the war, but resigned because of a reprimand given him by Washington in 1781. He was elected a member of the Continental Congress in 1782, but found the Congress disorganized and inefficient; he retired after a year to practice law, but did not give up his interest in government. In 1786 he was a delegate from New York to the Annapolis convention, at which he proposed that a convention meet the following May in Philadelphia to draft a constitution. Although his contributions to the Constitutional Convention were slight, he helped secure the ratification of the Constitution in New York, even though two-thirds of the delegates had initially opposed it. Even more important was his work with John Jay and James Madison on THE FEDERALIST (1787–88), the most important and influential work of the post-Revolutionary era; Hamilton contributed more than two-thirds of the essays. *The Federalist* expressed the fundamental principles

behind the Constitution and argued for a government based on centralization, conservatism, and unity.

The Department of the Treasury was established by Congress in 1789, and Hamilton was immediately asked to be Secretary. With his characteristic ability to quickly find the root of the problem he began to organize the Treasury, made plans for the establishment of a mint and a bank, arranged for the government to take over state debts, and set up a system of taxation; his *Report on Industry and Commerce* (1791) showed his full grasp of the economic and financial problems of the time. Although Hamilton presented his plan for a national bank in 1790, the bank was not established until 1792; the constitutionality of the bill had been challenged by Thomas Jefferson and James Madison. In answer to the arguments of Jefferson and Madison, Hamilton presented his doctrine of the implied powers and of the loose construction of the Constitution, an interpretation which has since proved to be one of the cornerstones of American government.

Hamilton resigned as Secretary of the Treasury in 1795 and returned to his law practice, but continued his interest in government and used his influence to throw the disputed election of 1800 to Jefferson rather than AARON BURR; although Burr, like Hamilton, was a Federalist, Hamilton distrusted the man, believing him to be "dangerous." When Hamilton again opposed Burr's candidacy for governor of New York in 1804, Burr challenged him to a duel in which Hamilton was mortally wounded.

Although Hamilton's financial policies have often been criticized as being overly stringent or tending to favor commerce and industry at the expense of agriculture, his contribution to American government remains on a par with that of the other great statesmen of the Republic. His distrust of the "common people" and their ability to rule themselves, his desire for a strong central government, and his general political philosophy, which was based on aristocracy, power, and wealth, needed the counterbalance offered by the philosophies of Jefferson and Madison; but in the same way Jefferson's agrarianism and democratic idealism needed the political realism of Hamilton.

A dramatic study of Hamilton was made in Gertrude Atherton's novel, THE CONQUEROR (1902), based on a careful study of sources. He appears frequently in other historical fiction, including Jeremiah R. Clemens' *The Rivals* (1860); Charles F. Pidgin's *Blennerhassett* (1901); Joseph Hergesheimer's *Balisand* (1924); Howard Fast's *The Unvanquished* (1942).

As a political economist, Hamilton was strongly influenced by Thomas Hobbes' *Leviathan* (1651) and Adam Smith's *Wealth of Nations* (1776). Numerous volumes discuss his economic views, notably Charles A. Beard's *Economic Origins of Jeffersonian Democracy* (1915) and Lynton K. Caldwell's *The Administrative Theories of Hamilton and Jefferson*

(1944). Arthur H. Vandenberg wrote *Hamilton, The Greatest American* (1921), and some of his most important activities are discussed in Robert A. East's *Business Enterprise in the American Revolutionary Era* (1938). Hamilton's own writings (collected in the Federalist Edition, 12 v., 1904, edited by Henry Cabot Lodge) have great historical, little literary importance. He was a clear, concise, logical, and convincing writer on economic subjects, in the form of reports and letters; he wrote most masterfully in *The Federalist* papers; he undoubtedly provided ideas and phrases for Washington, as in the FAREWELL ADDRESS. Important collections of Hamilton material have been gathered for the Library of Congress and for the Stevens Institute of Technology. The first two volumes of Alexander Hamilton's complete works were published by Columbia University Press in 1961 as *Papers of Alexander Hamilton*, edited by Harold Syrett. *The Mind of Alexander Hamilton* (1958) is a selection of Hamilton's writings edited by Saul K. Padover. Hamilton's economic policies form the basis for several acerbic passages in Ezra Pound's *Cantos*. See also FEDERALIST PARTY.

Hamilton, Clayton [Meeker] (b. Brooklyn, N.Y., Nov. 14, 1881—d. Sept. 17, 1946), teacher, lecturer, critic, playwright. After teaching at Columbia College under BRANDER MATTHEWS, Hamilton went on to a career as a lecturer on the drama and the novel, a professional critic, and the author of several persuasive volumes on the theory of playwriting. He wrote a number of plays, none very successful. The best was *The Better Understanding* (1917), done in collaboration with AUGUSTUS THOMAS. More notable were Hamilton's critical writings, which include *Materials and Methods of Fiction* (1908); *Studies in Stagecraft* (1914); *Problems of the Playwright* (1917); *Seen on the Stage* (1920); *So You're Writing a Play!* (1935); and *Theory of the Theater* (1939).

Hamilton, Edith (b. Germany, Aug. 12, 1867 —d. May 5, 1963), essayist, classical scholar, translator. Miss Hamilton began reading Latin at the age of seven and has devoted many books to helping modern readers toward a better understanding of Greek, Roman, and Hebrew life. Among her books: *The Greek Way* (1930); *The Roman Way* (1932); *The Prophets of Israel* (1936; rev. as *Spokesmen for God: The Great Teachers of the Old Testament,* 1949); *The Echo of Greece* (1957). She also translated *Three Greek Plays* (1939). Scholars have praised Miss Hamilton's learning, general readers her skill in making ancient ideals live.

Hamlet, The (1931), **The Town** (1957), and **The Mansion** (1960), a trilogy by WILLIAM FAULKNER. Spanning almost fifty years in time, the trilogy is centered on the innumerable and vicious SNOPES family, the first of which invades Yoknapatawpha County in the early years of the 20th century. In the hamlet of Frenchman's Bend, Flem Snopes begins as a clerk in Will Varner's store, and, through usury, conniving, and thrift, becomes part owner of the store and the husband of Varner's daughter Eula. In the town of Jefferson Flem works his way into Colonel Sartoris' bank, finally becoming vice-president. In order to enrich himself still further, he drives the bank president, Manfred De Spain, from town. In *The Mansion* Flem moves into the now-vacant De Spain mansion, one of the largest and oldest houses in Jefferson. Flem is purely mercenary, without human feelings of any kind, caring only for money and for the outward appearance of respectability. He imports a number of cousins— Mink, I. O., Lump, Ike, Eck—whom he installs in various positions in the community, until the local citizens feel they are overrun with Snopeses.

The novels are loosely episodic, humorous, and ironic; *The Hamlet* is made up of stories dealing alternately with horse-trading and with love—economic life vis-à-vis emotional life. *The Town* continues this contrast on a more sophisticated level, centering on the hopeless and almost comic love of Gavin Stevens first for Eula Varner Snopes and then for her daughter, Linda, and on the machinations used by Flem to acquire more money. *The Mansion* departs from this scheme, dealing primarily with the attempts of Mink Snopes to return to Jefferson and murder Flem, and with the relationship between Gavin and Linda. Each of the novels is made up of sections narrated for the most part by characters whose main purpose is to observe the action rather than take part in it. V. K. Ratliff, the ubiquitous sewing-machine salesman; and Chick Mallison, the young nephew of Gavin Stevens.

Hamlet of A. MacLeish, The (1928), poem by ARCHIBALD MACLEISH. In this dramatic monologue of fourteen sections in accentual meter the story of Hamlet is used as a symbol for the way "the knowledge of ill is among us" and the ways in which man tries to deal with it. But MacLeish contrasts Hamlet's situation with his own (using himself as symbol for modern man), in that "in the old time" there at least was a name for the evil, i.e. a murder, an incest, a revolution, whereas now the sensitive man is distressed by something he cannot fight because he cannot know what it is.

Hamlin, Jack. A professional gambler who appears in BRET HARTE'S GABRIEL CONROY (1876) and about twenty of his short stories. He is courteous, melancholy underneath his gaiety, dissatisfied with the life he leads. He resembles JOHN OAKHURST (*The Luck of Roaring Camp* and *The Outcasts of Poker Flat*). Both characters were apparently modeled on a real person, about whom Harte wrote in *Bohemian Days in San Francisco* as a handsome man, pale and scrupulously elegant, always genial, who nonchalantly set forth for the duel that ended in his death.

Hammerstein, Oscar [Greeley Glendenning] II (b. New York City, July 12, 1895—d. Aug. 23, 1960), librettist. The nephew of a famous impresario, Oscar Hammerstein I (1847?–1919), Hammerstein began working backstage at an early age, learning by a process of trial and error what elements make up a successful book and singable lyrics for a musical play. His best guide and tutor was the librettist OTTO HARBACH, with whom he collaborated on several plays. He also collaborated with Frank Mandel and Laurence Schwab. His lyrics (well over a thousand in number) have been set to music by some of the most celebrated composers of the day—Jerome Kern, Sigmund Romberg, Rudolf Friml, Herbert Stothart, and above all RICHARD RODGERS. Among the plays in which his songs have been featured are *Rose Marie* (1924); *Sunny* (1925); *The Desert Song* (1926); *Show Boat* (1927); *New Moon* (1928); OKLAHOMA! (1943); *Carmen Jones* (1943); *Carousel* (1945); *South Pacific* (1949); *The King and I* (1951); *Flower Drum Song* (1958); *The Sound of Music* (1959). Some of these became motion-picture hits as well, and Hammerstein also wrote lyrics for a number of movies which had had no previous ancestors on the stage. Among the songs that have made Hammerstein famous are *Old Man River; When I Grow Too Old to Dream; All the Things You Are; The Last Time I Saw Paris; Oh, What a Beautiful Morning; The Surrey with the Fringe on Top; Only Make Believe; Some Enchanted Evening; Younger than Springtime.* Hammerstein won a Pulitzer Prize (1944) for *Oklahoma!* His collection of *Lyrics* (1949) shows him as an adroit metrist, an unsophisticated sentimentalist, and a clever satirist. Deems Taylor has told the story of Rodgers and Hammerstein in *Some Enchanted Evenings* (1953).

Hammett, [Samuel] Dashiell (b. St. Mary's County, Md., May 27, 1894—d. Jan. 10, 1961), writer of detective stories and movie scripts. Hammett worked as a newsboy, freight clerk, railroad laborer, messenger boy, stevedore, advertising manager, and Pinkerton detective. Up to 1922 he had published nothing but some verse; then his career turned mostly to Hollywood. One of his notable scripts was for Lillian Hellman's WATCH ON THE RHINE (1943). Hammett is best known as the creator of the so-called "hard-boiled" detective story. His books include: *Red Harvest* (1929); *The Dain Curse* (1929); *The Maltese Falcon* (1930), in which he created his most famous sleuth, Sam Spade; THE GLASS KEY (1931); THE THIN MAN (1932); *Adventures of Sam Spade* (1944); *Hammett Homicides* (1946); *The Creeping Siamese and Other Stories* (1950). On the air the Thin Man and Sam Spade have proved very popular. (See HARD-BOILED FICTION.) His books were removed from many libraries during the McCarthy era (1953).

Hammett, Samuel Adams ["Philip Paxton," "Sam Slick"] (b. New London, Conn., Feb. 4, 1816—d. Dec. 24, 1865), frontier humorist, memoirist. Hammett was one of the earliest to set down in print his observations of the southwestern frontier. *A Stray Yankee in Texas* (1853) was followed by *The Wonderful Adventures of Captain Priest* (1855) and *Piney Woods Tavern, or, Sam Slick in Texas* (1858). His hero, Sam Slick, is derived from T. C. Haliburton's

character of the same name.) W. Stanley Hoole's *Sam Slick in Texas* (1945) shows Hammett as well worthy of study and as a typical humorist of the South and Southwest in the decades preceding the Civil War. See HALIBURTON, T. C.

Hammon, Jupiter (b. [?], 1720?—d. [?], 1800?), a Negro slave who wrote verses that won publication in his own lifetime and gained the praise of white critics. He lived in Long Island and Connecticut. He antedated PHILLIS WHEATLEY by several years, and one of his poems was *A Poetical Address* (1778) inscribed to her. Much of his poetry was of religious content, such as his *Address* (1787) urging patience on his fellow slaves. Oscar Wegelin wrote a study, *Jupiter Hammon* (1915).

Hammond, John (mid-17th century), English colonist. Hammond lived in Virginia and Maryland for twenty-one years. He wrote glowingly of the new land in LEAH AND RACHEL, OR, THE TWO FRUITFUL SISTERS, VIRGINIA AND MARYLAND: THEIR PRESENT CONDITION, IMPARTIALLY STATED AND RELATED (1656).

Hammond, Percy (b. Cadiz, Ohio, March 7, 1873—d. April 25, 1936), drama critic, sports writer, war correspondent. Hammond first built up a nationwide reputation on Chicago papers, then worked for the New York *Tribune*. As a drama critic he was often in trouble with producers, but his papers supported him staunchly. He wrote *But—Is It Art?* (1927) and *This Atom in the Audience* (1940).

Hampden [Dougherty], Walter (b. Brooklyn, N.Y., June 30, 1879—d. June 11, 1955), actor. Hampden's career was one of the most distinguished on the American stage. He made his first appearance in England and was a leading man there for three seasons. In 1907 he returned to the United States. Some of his most popular roles were in *The Yellow Jacket, Macbeth, Romeo and Juliet, Hamlet, Cyrano de Bergerac,* CAPONSACCHI, *An Enemy of the People, The Admirable Crichton, The Rivals,* OUR TOWN, ETHAN FROME, *Trilby, Henry VIII.* He also appeared in motion pictures and on the air.

Hancock, John (b. Braintree [now Quincy], Mass., Jan. 23, 1737—d. Oct. 8, 1793), businessman, public official. Hancock's name is chiefly preserved by his bold signature on the Declaration of Independence. It is likely that his ability was greater than has generally been conceded and that he performed useful services in trying to keep the Continental Congress unified and active. Herbert S. Allan wrote *John Hancock: Patriot in Purple* (1948).

Handbook to Literature, with an Outline of Literary History, English and American, A (1936), by William Flint Thrall and ADDISON HIBBARD. Many items of American interest appear in this authoritative and well-written dictionary, from *almanacs* to *wit and humor.*

Hand But Not the Heart, The (1858), a novel by TIMOTHY SHAY ARTHUR. This was one of the earliest American novels to treat the divorce problem. Possibly Arthur was stimulated to write the story because of the success of his temperance novel *Ten Nights in a Bar Room* (1854).

Handlin, Oscar (b. Brooklyn, N.Y., Sept. 29, 1915—   ), social historian. Handlin's background was one of struggle for education and success as the son of immigrant parents in a big city. His historical and sociological investigations usually concerned the problems of first and second generation immigrants in modern American cities. He studied at Brooklyn College and then at Harvard, where, under the influence of Arthur M. Schlesinger, he became interested in American history and in social history. *Boston's Immigrants* (1941, 1959), which won the Dunning Prize of the American Historical Association, was his doctoral dissertation. Handlin joined the Department of History at Harvard in 1939. *The Uprooted* (1951), a study of the great immigration movements to America after 1820, received the Pulitzer Prize in History (1952). Editor of the Library of American Biography series, he wrote *Al Smith and His America* (1958) as volume eighteen. The book is a study of Smith as a son of Irish immigrant parents, and examines the difficulties of a Catholic seeking the presidency. As usual, Handlin enlivened his study with his fine sense of the pace of twentieth-century urban America. *The Newcomers* (1959), the third volume in the New York Metropolitan Area Study series, deals with Negroes and Puerto Ricans and their struggle for the good life in New York City. Some other books: *American People in the Twentieth Century* (1954); *Harvard Guide to American History* (1954); *Readings in American History* (1958).

Handy, W[illiam] C[hristopher] (b. Florence, Ala., Nov. 16, 1873—d. March 28, 1958), composer, orchestra leader, publisher. The son of a Negro preacher, Handy was always deeply absorbed in the characteristic music of his people and had opportunity to obtain a good musical education. He did a great deal to popularize the "blues," although he also incorporated elements of other folk tunes into his compositions. His more notable pieces include the *Memphis Blues* (1909); the *St. Louis Blues* (1914); the *Joe Turner Blues* (1915); the *Beale Street Blues* (1917); *Loveless Love* (1921); *Got No Mo' Home Dan a Dog* (1926). Handy became his own publisher and an active worker in theatrical circles. His songs were popular all over the globe; he made a collection of pirated versions of the *St. Louis Blues,* including phonograph records in Japanese and Russian. Among his books: *Negro Authors and Composers of the U.S.* (1935); *Negro Spirituals* (1938); *Father of the Blues* (an autobiography, 1941). He edited an anthology, *Blues* (1926), which was reissued as *A Treasury of the Blues* (1949) with a critical text by Abbe Niles and pictures by Miguel Covarrubias.

Hanford, James Holly (b. Rochester, N.Y., March 19, 1882—   ), teacher, Milton scholar. Hanford taught at several universities. At North Carolina, where he taught from 1914 to 1921, Paul Green and Thomas Wolfe were among his pupils; he may be "Old Sanford" in the latter's LOOK HOMEWARD, ANGEL (1929). Among his books: *A Milton Handbook* (1926); *The Teaching of Literature* (with C. C. Fries, 1925); *John Milton, Englishman* (1949). He also edited selections from Milton (1923), Milton's *Poems* (1936), and a *Restoration Reader* (1954).

Hanna, Mark [Marcus Alonzo] (b. New Lisbon, Ohio, Sept. 24, 1837—d. Feb. 15, 1904), businessman, political leader, legislator. Hanna made a large fortune, became interested in WILLIAM MCKINLEY and helped elect him President, dispensed Federal patronage as his adviser, was appointed senator from Ohio (1897) and served till his death. He was a frank representative of business interests but maintained excellent relations with his own employees. Thomas Beer wrote an ironic biography of him (1929).

Hannibal, Mo. A town on the Mississippi River, an important river port and industrial center. MARK TWAIN spent his boyhood there, and his experiences provided the background for *Tom Sawyer* and *Huckleberry Finn,* as well as for chapters in *Life on the Mississippi.* Here he wrote for the Hannibal *Journal,* bought by his brother Orion Clemens in 1851. Many places in the town and nearby are Mark Twain memorials: his boyhood home, the Mark Twain Museum, the Mark Twain Cave, a statue of Twain in Riverview Park, a Tom and Huck Monument at the foot of Cardiff Hill. Dixon Wecter's *Sam Clemens of Hannibal* (1952) demonstrates the enduring influence of his youth in Hannibal on most of Twain's writing.

Hansberry, Lorraine (b. Chicago, May 19, 1930—d. Jan. 12, 1965), playwright. *A Raisin in the Sun* (1959), her first play, won the New York Drama Critics Circle Award and was filmed. It was remarkable as a play about Negroes which treated them with understanding and humor as individuals, rather than merely as illustrations of a theory about race relations. It concerned the effect on the various members of a Chicago Negro family of their economic struggles, their desire for education, and their plan to move into a white neighborhood. Miss Hansberry attended the University of Wisconsin, came to New York in 1950, and married Robert Nemiroff, also a writer.

Hans Brinker, or, The Silver Skates (1865), a story for children by MARY MAPES DODGE. It tells about Hans and his sister Gretel, children in a Dutch village, whose father is injured in an accident. They engage in a skating contest in which Gretel wins the prize. Their father is cured by a famous doctor, and many other happy results ensue. The story became a great favorite and is still one.

Hansen, Harry (b. Davenport, Iowa, Dec. 26, 1884—   ), newspaperman, editor, biographer, historian. Hansen served as war correspondent for the Chicago *Daily News* during World War I and wrote *The Adventures of the 14 Points* (1919) about the peace negotiations. Later he joined the staff of the New York *World,* continued with the New York *World-Telegram,* mainly as literary editor. He wrote *Midwest Portraits* (1923); *Carl Sandburg, the Man and His Poetry* (1924); *The Chicago* [River] (1942); *The Aspirin Age* (1949); *The Fighting Constitution* (1955); *The Story of Illinois* (1956); *A History of the Civil War* (1961). In 1949 he became editor of the *World Almanac*.

Hanson, Joseph Mills (b. Yankton, S.D., July 20, 1876—), farmer, soldier, public official, historian. Hanson has been active in historical research, especially on the West and on war. Among his books: THE CONQUEST OF THE MISSOURI (1909; reprinted, 1946); *Frontier Ballads* (1910); *Historical Pageant of Yankton* (1916); *America's Battles in the Great War* (1920); *History of South Dakota in the World War* (1931). He edited the *Journal of the American Military Institute*, 1936–38.

Hans Pfaal. See THE UNPARALLELED ADVENTURES OF ONE HANS PFAAL.

Hapgood, Hutchins (b. Chicago, May 21, 1869—d. Nov. 18, 1944), newspaperman, student of social conditions, novelist. Hapgood worked on the staffs of several New York newspapers, wrote actively for magazines, and in his books did much to interpret the spirit of his day. Among his writings: *The Spirit of the Ghetto* (1902); *The Autobiography of a Thief* (1903); *The Spirit of Labor* (1907); *Types from City Streets* (1910); and his autobiography, *A Victorian in the Modern World* (1939).

Hapgood, Norman (b. Chicago, March 28, 1868—d. April 29, 1937), lawyer, newspaperman, editor, political and social crusader, diplomat, biographer, drama critic. This brother of Hutchins Hapgood exerted considerable influence not merely on the general thought of the time but also on some of its leading persons, among them ALFRED E. SMITH, about whom (in collaboration with Henry Moscowitz) he wrote a campaign biography, *Up from the City Streets* (1927), and Woodrow Wilson, whom he strongly supported as President. After a brief practice of the law, he turned to newspaper work. Later he became editor of COLLIER'S and carried on several effective campaigns against harmful drugs and foods. He served for a while as minister to Denmark. He was always interested in the drama, and knew Mark Twain and other literary figures intimately. Among his books: *Literary Statesmen and Others* (1897); *Daniel Webster* (1899); *Abraham Lincoln: The Man of the People* (1899); *George Washington* (1901); *The Stage in America* (1901); *Industry and Progress* (1911); *Why Janet Should Read Shakespeare* (1929); and his autobiography, *The Changing Years* (1930).

Hapless Orphan, The (1793), an anonymous novel by "an American Lady." Caroline Francis, the heroine, a sort of Becky Sharp, follows her own path pretty selfishly, but when she tries to take away another girl's young man and the young man commits suicide, Caroline becomes the victim of a vendetta.

Happy Birthday to You (1893), a song by Mildred J. Hill. It originated as *Good Morning to All* for the children Miss Hill taught, and has become a sort of folk song.

Happy Days (1940), one of three volumes of reminiscence by H. L. Mencken. See DAYS OF H. L. MENCKEN.

Happy Hooligan. A hobo who appeared in a comic strip by FREDERICK B. OPPER. Maude the Mule frequently abetted Hooligan; the strips were decidedly low-comic.

Happy Mountain (1928), a novel by Maristan Chapman (pen name used by John Stanton Higham Chapman [1891—] and his wife Mary Hamilton Illsley Chapman [1895—]. The story is set in the hills of Tennessee and revolves around Wait-still-on-the-Lord Lowe (generally called "Waits"), who leaves home to see the world, is astounded at the manners and lack of kindness of the low-people (as opposed to the hill-folk), buys a fiddle, learns that his girl may marry another man, goes back and woos her over again. It is a well-written novel, neglected by critics but a favorite with the public.

Happy Time, The (1945), a novel by Robert Fontaine. This is the story of a French-Canadian boy whose mother comes from a strait-laced Presbyterian family and whose father is a gay French musician. The family is frank and uninhibited, and young Bibi goes through some typical and funny adolescent experiences. The book was made into a Broadway hit by Samuel Taylor (1950) and a motion picture (1952).

Harbach, Otto [Abels] (b. Salt Lake City, Utah, Aug. 18, 1873—d. Jan. 24, 1963), newspaperman, playwright, librettist. After teaching English and working for newspapers and advertising agencies, Harbach turned to the stage. He became a noted librettist, working either alone or with collaborators. His plays include: *The Three Twins* (1907); *Bright Eyes* (1909); *The Fascinating Widow* (1910); *The Firefly* (1912); *High Jinks* (1913); *Katinka* (1915); *You're in Love* (1917); *No! No! Nannette* (1925); *Rose Marie* (1924); *The Desert Song* (1927); *Cat and the Fiddle* (1931); *Roberta* (1933).

Harbaugh, Henry (b. Franklin Co., Pa., Oct. 28, 1817—d. Dec. 28, 1867), clergyman, hymn writer, editor, poet. A busy pastor and the editor of several magazines, Harbaugh wrote fluently in English and published a collection of *Poems* (1860), *Hymns and Chants* (1861), and *The Religious Life of Washington* (1863). But he is chiefly remembered for his poems in German dialect, posthumously collected as *Harbaugh's Harfe* (1870). Among these the best known were *Das Alt Schulhaus an der Krik* and *Die Schlofschtub*.

Harbaugh, Thomas Chalmers ["Capt. Howard Holmes"] (b. Middletown, Md., Jan. 13, 1849— d. Oct. 28, 1924), poet, dime novelist. Harbaugh published at least two collections of verse, *Maple Leaves* (1884) and *Ballads of the Blue* (1892). But such fame as he won depended on his DIME NOVELS, issued mainly by Beadle & Adams, whose dates and exact authorships are far from fixed. Harbaugh undoubtedly had a hand in the NICK CARTER series. From the 1880's into the first two decades of the 20th century he wrote many other thrillers, including *Judge Lynch, Jr.; Navajo Nick; The Pampas Hunters; The Silken Lasso; Dodger Dick; The White Squadron; The Withered Hand; Kit Carson's Chum.*

Harben, Will[iam] N[athaniel] (b. Dalton, Ga., July 5, 1858—d. Aug. 7, 1919), novelist, short-story writer. One of the early regional novelists, Harben made Georgia the background for some of his widely read stories, notably *White Marie: A Story of Georgian Plantation Life* (1889); *Northern Georgian Sketches* (1900); *The Woman Who Trusted* (1901); *Abner Daniel* (1902); *The Georgians* (1904); *Ann Boyd* (1906); *Mam' Linda* (1907).

Harbor, The (1915), a novel by ERNEST POOLE. From his home on Brooklyn Heights the hero of this story looks out on New York harbor; the changes in this view over the years become symbolical of changes in his own mind and heart. He is himself an artist, but is divided between the viewpoint presented by his father-in-law, who helps to build up the harbor into a great commercial center, and that of a college friend, who presents the side of the workers. In time he chooses the latter standpoint. Poole himself had worked in the cause of the unions, and was one of the earliest to set forth their views in fiction.

Hard, Walter (b. Manchester, Vt., May 3, 1882—   ), poet, historian, folklorist. Hard may be regarded as the most representative voice of his native state, who, especially in his free verse vignettes and narratives, has told compact life-stories, etched social attitudes, speech manners, and folkways, in what Richard M. Dorson calls "a 20th-century backwash society." Hard wrote for local papers, dabbled in politics, published four volumes of verse: *Salt of Vermont* (1931); *A Mountain Township* (1933); *Vermont Vintage* (1937); *Vermont Valley* (1939). Other books of his are *Some Vermonters* (1928); *This Is Vermont* (1936), an informal guidebook written with his wife Margaret Hard; *Walter Hard's Vermont* (1941); *The Connecticut [River]* (1947), *A Matter of Fifty Houses* (1952).

hard-boiled fiction. A type of detective or crime story in which an air of realism is generated through laconic and often vulgar dialogue, through the depiction of cruelty and bloodshed at close range, through the use of generally seamy environments. The genre was perhaps a product of the prohibition era; but it was also a reaction against the attenuated prettifications of the Conan Doyle school and an attempt to apply the literary lessons taught by such serious American novelists as ERNEST HEMINGWAY and JOHN DOS PASSOS. Hard-boiled fiction seems to have appeared first in a magazine called the BLACK MASK (founded 1919), and its development was closely associated with the editor, Joseph T. Shaw. Many critics today feel that the first full-fledged example of the hard-boiled

method was DASHIELL HAMMETT's story *Fly Paper*, which appeared in August, 1929, in *Black Mask*. In 1946 Shaw compiled *The Hard-Boiled Omnibus: Early Stories from Black Mask*, including stories by Hammett, RAYMOND CHANDLER, Raoul Whitfield, and GEORGE HARMON COXE. To these names should be added those of W. R. BURNETT, Jonathan Latimer, and Peter Cheyney. More recently the hard-boiled method has degenerated into mere displays of wild sensationalism and undisguised sadism, as in the works of Mickey Spillane.

Harder They Fall, The (1947), a novel by BUDD SCHULBERG. In this story the so-called manly art of boxing is presented as a brutal sport transformed into a corrupt industry. The "hero" is an Argentinian named Toro Molina, a fighter of gigantic size, but readers of the book immediately identified him with the Italian fighter Primo Carnera, who became heavyweight champion of the world, earned more than $3,000,000 for his promoters, but returned sick and partly paralyzed to his native land. It was made into a motion picture.

Harding, Warren G[amaliel] (b. Blooming Grove, Ohio, Nov. 2, 1865—d. Aug. 2, 1923), newspaper editor and publisher, public official, 29th President. Harding came to be half-owner, editor, and publisher of a Marion, Ohio, newspaper. He was elected to the Ohio Senate, became lieutenant governor in 1904, United States Senator in 1915. In 1920 he was nominated for the Presidency. Once elected, Harding made his chief contribution to political thinking by advocating a return to "normalcy." In this period of seeming prosperity, corruption became rampant to a degree never before or since existent in American history, except perhaps in the Grant administration. During the Congressional investigation of Albert B. Fall, Secretary of the Interior, who had accepted a bribe of $100,000 for turning over oil-lands to private interests, Harding was stricken with a fatal illness, the nature of which has never been established.

From the beginning of his administration the figure of Harding was lost in a cloud of criticism and slander. H. L. Mencken declared that Harding's English (he called it "Gamalielese") was the worst he had ever encountered, and William G. McAdoo once remarked that Harding's speeches, "left the impression of an army of pompous phases moving over a landscape in search of an idea." Sensational and sometimes inaccurate books were written about the Harding administration, including Nan Britton's *The President's Daughter* (1927); Gaston B. Means' *The Strange Death of President Harding* (1930); SAMUEL HOPKINS ADAMS wrote *Revelry* (1926), *The Incredible Era* (1930), and *The Life and Times of Warren G. Harding* (1939). Harry M. Daugherty, of the "Ohio gang," told in collaboration with Thomas Dixon *The Inside Story of the Harding Tragedy* (1932), depicting Harding as "a modern Abraham Lincoln." Other books in which Harding appears are Joe Mitchell Chapple's *Life and Times of*

428

Warren G. Harding (1924); Elizabeth Jaffray's Secrets of the White House (1927); Frederick Lewis Allen's Only Yesterday (1931); Irwin Hood (Ike) Hoover's Forty-Two Years in the White House (1934). The Gang's All Here (1959), a play by Jerome Lawrence and Robert E. Lee, was thought to be based on the Harding administration.

Hardy, Arthur Sherburne (b. Andover, Mass., Aug. 13, 1847—d. Mar. 13, 1930), civil engineer, diplomat, editor, novelist, poet. Hardy graduated from West Point, spent a year in the army, taught and practiced civil engineering, served in diplomatic posts for several years in several parts of Europe and in Persia, edited the COSMOPOLITAN for two years, wrote poetry and novels. The best known of his poems is *Francesca of Rimini* (1878). His most widely read novel was *Passe Rose* (1889), the story of a dancing girl at the court of Charlemagne. He also wrote *But Yet a Woman* (1878); *The Wind of Destiny* (1886); *Aurélie* (1912); *Diane and Her Friends* (1914); his autobiography, *Things Remembered* (1923); and some mathematical texts.

Hare, Robert (b. Philadelphia, Jan. 17, 1781—d. May 15, 1858), chemist, teacher, writer. Hare invented the oxyhydrogen blowpipe and various laboratory devices. He wrote a *Brief View of the Policies and Resources of the U.S.* (1810) and *Spiritualism Scientifically Demonstrated* (1855); and two romances, *Standish the Puritan* (1850) and *Overing, or, The Heir of Wycherly* (1852).

Hare, Walter Ben (b. [?], 1870—d. June 30, 1950), actor, meteorologist, playwright. A weatherman by vocation, Hare first wrote plays for amateur groups. He attained an extraordinary success with some of his two hundred or so dramas, particularly a rural melodrama called *Aaron Slick from Punkin Crick* (1919), which made him a wealthy man. Hare wrote under three names, according to himself: "I used the pen name Lt. Beal Carmack for the plays I'm ashamed of, the name Mary Modena Burns for religious plays, and the other stuff I wrote under my own name." The lieutenant received the credit for *Aaron Slick*.

Hargrove, [Edward Thomas] Marion [Lawton] (b. Mt. Olive, N.C., Oct. 13, 1919—   ), newspaperman, novelist. Hargrove was working for the Charlotte (N.C.) *News* at the outbreak of the war, and while in the army (1941–45) continued to contribute material for a column called "In the Army Now." From this column was drawn the book entitled *See Here, Private Hargrove* (1942), which became an immediate best seller. In the meantime Hargrove was assigned to the New York office of *Yank*, then became an army overseas reporter. After the war he wrote *Something's Got to Give* (1948), a satire on the radio industry, and *The Girl He Left Behind* (1956), a humorous account of draftees.

Hariot [sometimes Harriot], Thomas (b. 1560—d. July 2, 1621), English naturalist, mathematician, astronomer, explorer. Hariot,

an able Oxford scientist, accompanied Sir Richard Grenville on a trip to the New World in 1585. He collected specimens of animals and plants on Roanoke Island, studied the Indians there, and later published his *Brief and True Report of the New-Found Land of Virginia* (1588), the first English book on the first English colony in America. The book, accurately and clearly written, was often reprinted and occasionally plagiarized. A facsimile reproduction of the 1588 edition, with an introduction by Randolph G. Adams, appeared in 1931; Stefan Lorant, in *The New World* (1946), reprinted Hariot's texts and the original water color drawings of John White.

Harland, Henry ["Sidney Luska"] (b. Russia, of American parents, March 1, 1861—d. Dec. 20, 1905), novelist, short-story writer, editor. Harland began writing under a pen name as an immigrant of Jewish background, although he was actually of English descent. These writings, well-done but artificial, include *As It Was Written: A Jewish Musician's Story* (1885); *Mrs. Pexeida* (1886); *The Yoke of the Thorah* (1887); *My Uncle Florimond* (1888); *A Latin Quarter Courtship and Other Stories* (1889); *Grandison Mather* (1889).

Then Harland went to England, came under Henry James' influence, also became associated with a group of writers ostensibly in revolt against Victorian respectability. Harland was enough of a leader in this group to found a quarterly magazine called *The Yellow Book* (1894), which had as early contributors James, George Saintsbury, Richard Garnett, Max Beerbohm, William Watson, Aubrey Beardsley. In his English period Harland wrote gay and witty romances. Best known was THE CARDINAL'S SNUFF BOX (1900), now undeservedly forgotten. Among the others: *Mademoiselle Miss and Other Stories* (1893); *Grey Roses* (1895); *Comedies and Errors* (1898); *The Lady Paramount* (1902); *My Friend Prospero* (1904).

Harland, Marion. Pen name of MARY VIRGINIA TERHUNE.

Harlem. A section of New York City extending roughly from East 96th and West 110th Streets on the south, to West 155th Street on the north, with Morningside and St. Nicholas Avenues as its boundaries on the west, and the East and Harlem Rivers on the east. It began as an idyllic Dutch settlement founded by Peter Stuyvesant in 1658 and called by him Nieuw Haarlem. All through the 19th century Harlem was a fashionable district. At the break of the century new racial groups moved in: Italians, Negroes, Latin Americans. When a New York real estate boom collapsed, an alert Negro real estate dealer took advantage of the financial difficulties of many Harlem apartment houses to make them available to Negro tenants. Soon they began to pour into Harlem and made it in time the capital of Negro America.

Negro Harlem contains slums among the worst in the world, but also has "Sugar Hill," where notables and wealthy people live in fine, comfortable houses. The rates of sickness, death, and crime are fairly high in Harlem. An increase in the number of Negro police, however, together with carefully planned social and economic services, have helped to make the district less explosive.

Italian Harlem borders on the East River; the shops and streets reproduce to a large extent the appearance of Italian marketing centers. In Latin-American Harlem, Puerto Ricans are in a great majority. Due to poverty, overcrowding, and exploitation, many of them live in deplorable physical conditions. The environment, the customs, the food, and the shops remain Spanish in character. A study of *The Puerto Rican Journey to New York* (1950) was made by C. WRIGHT MILLS, Rose Kohn, and Clarence Senior. OSCAR HANDLIN has written *The Newcomers* (1959); Dan Wakefield, *Island in the City* (1959).

Harlem has been a powerful stimulant for the artistic capabilities of its Negro residents as well as of some sympathetic white observers, including Carl Van Vechten, who wrote NIGGER HEAVEN (1926). A large group of Negro actors, singers, and dancers developed in Harlem, including such figures as Roland Hayes, Bill Robinson, Ethel Waters, and Josephine Baker. Numerous Negro magazines, such as *The Crisis* and *Opportunity*, have voiced racial aspirations and hopes. In 1929 appeared *Harlem*, a play by WALLACE THURMAN and William Jordan Rapp depicting life in black Harlem. CLAUDE MCKAY wrote poems, *Harlem Shadows* (1922), a novel, *Home to Harlem* (1928), and short stories, *Gingertown* (1932). Other fiction includes Thurman's *The Blacker the Berry* (1929); COUNTEE CULLEN's *One Way to Heaven* (1932); ANN PETRY's *The Street* (1946); JAMES BALDWIN's *Go Tell It on the Mountain* (1953); Warren Miller's *The Cool World* (1959). Nonfictional works about Harlem include JAMES WELDON JOHNSON's *Black Manhattan* (1930); LANGSTON HUGHES' *The Big Sea* (1940); McKay's *Harlem: Negro Metropolis* (1940); ROI OTTLEY's *New World A-Coming* (1943).

Harmonie, Harmony, New Harmony. Communal experiments established in Pennsylvania and Indiana by followers of George Rapp (1757–1847), a German religious leader. He led a migration of six hundred adherents to the United States in 1803, settling in a town in Butler Co., Pa., that he called Harmony. In 1815 the Rappites moved to Harmonie or New Harmony in Indiana. In 1825 they sold the colony to the Owen Community founded by Robert Owen (1771–1858), Welsh humanitarian and author of *A New View of Society* (1813). His colony failed (1828), but New Harmony became a cultural center and a weekly magazine published there, *The New-Harmony Gazette* (in 1829 called *The Free Enquirer*), continued from 1825 to 1835 to preach Owen's kind of Socialism. Meanwhile the Rappites returned to Pennsylvania and settled at Economy Town (now Ambridge), near Pittsburgh. In 1831 an adventurer who called himself "Count Maximilian De Leon" set up a secessionist movement and

got away with most of the funds of the colony; in 1832 Bernard Mueller, who opposed Rapp's doctrine of celibacy, withdrew with 250 members to Monaca, a nearby town. After Rapp's death the colony declined; in 1906 its property was taken over by the state.

Harmonium (1923), the first volume of poems by WALLACE STEVENS. It consists of works printed in little magazines beginning with the "War Number" of *Poetry* in 1914. Possibly because it included such words as girandoles, fiscs, princox, and funest, the first edition sold less than one hundred copies, although some of its poems—PETER QUINCE AT THE CLAVIER and LE MONOCLE DE MON ONCLE—have since become anthology pieces. *Harmonium* was reissued in 1931 with three poems omitted and fourteen new poems added.

Harmony, Pa. See HARMONIE, above.

Harper, George McLean (b. Shippensburg, Pa., Dec. 31, 1863—d. July 14, 1947), teacher, historian, critic. Harper taught mainly at Princeton University, first in Romance languages, later in English literature. His specialty was Wordsworth. He wrote *William Wordsworth: His Life, Works, and Influence* (1916) and *Wordsworth's French Daughter* (1921); and he edited Wordsworth's poems (1923, 1933). He also wrote *Masters of French Literature* (1901), *Sainte-Beuve* (1909), *Literary Appreciations* (1937), and other books.

Harper, William Rainey (b. New Concord, Ohio, July 24, 1856—d. Jan. 10, 1906), teacher, Hebraist, educational administrator. A great Hebrew and Biblical scholar, Harper had taught at Yale, served as educational director of the Chautauqua, and had won a reputation as the most eminent scholar in the Baptist denomination when John D. Rockefeller (1839–1937) asked him to take the presidency of the newly established University of Chicago, a Baptist school. Harper expanded the university far beyond Rockefeller's original conception. He called to the faculty some of the most noted scholars of the country, persuaded Rockefeller to raise the endowment to more than a hundred million, and made Chicago one of the great universities of the world. Himself a great teacher, he continued to hold Hebrew classes that were renowned for liveliness. He introduced many educational innovations, including the division of the collegiate instruction period into two sections, junior and senior. Among his books: *Religion and the Higher Life* (1904) and *The Trend in Higher Education* (1905). Thomas W. Goodspeed wrote his biography (1928). He appears as President Harris in Robert Herrick's novel CHIMES (1926).

Harper's Bazaar. A weekly magazine for women founded Nov. 2, 1867, by Harper & Brothers. It became a monthly in April, 1901; the spelling was changed from *Bazar* in 1929. Early numbers had contributions by some of the foremost of American writers; in recent years it has specialized in women's fashions, but still attracts some good writing. In 1913 it became a Hearst publication.

Harpers Ferry, W.Va. See JOHN BROWN.

Harper's Magazine. *Harper's New Monthly Magazine* was founded by Fletcher Harper, of Harper & Brothers, in 1850. It featured serials by the popular English novelists of the time (Dickens, Bulwer, Trollope, Thackeray, Lever,

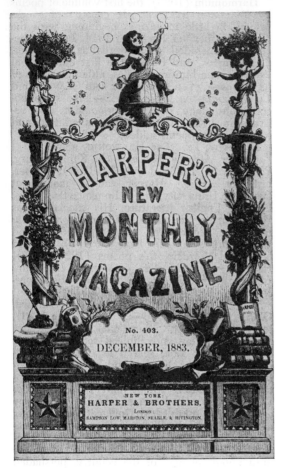

and George Eliot) and copious woodcut illustrations. It was a sensational success; it reached 200,000 circulation by 1860, an unprecedented figure for a three-dollar-a-year magazine.

For the first year or two, the English serials that furnished the body of the magazine were pirated; thereafter, "advance sheets" were purchased from the London publishers. *Harper's* long continued to draw heavily on English writers. In the 1850's, *Harper's* carried some non-English material, but mostly in the departments. "The Easy Chair," devoted to comment on literature, art, music, and "the higher politics," was first filled by Donald G. Mitchell, and then in 1859, by the urbane and erudite George William Curtis. (See EDITOR'S DRAWER.)

Henry Mills Alden began a half-century editorship in 1869. The new editorship and the competition of the new SCRIBNER'S MONTHLY caused some changes in *Harper's.* Illustrations by Edwin A. Abbey, John W. Alexander, Howard Pyle, and Winslow Homer; and serials by W. D.

Howells, Henry James, C. D. Warner, and Constance Fenimore Woolson brought distinction to the magazine. In the "Editor's Study" department, begun by Howells in 1885, an important campaign for the new realistic fiction was waged; Warner succeeded Howells in that department in 1894, though the latter returned to the magazine to occupy the "Easy Chair" in 1901–1921.

At the end of the century, color had come into the illustrations, and more attention was being given to contemporary problems. Mark Twain (whose *Joan of Arc* had been an anonymous contribution in 1895–1896) continued to be an occasional contributor, as did Mary Johnston, Booth Tarkington, Frank R. Stockton, and other leading writers. Woodrow Wilson's *History of the American People* was serialized in 1901. The Harper bankruptcy and change in ownership of 1900 had little effect on the magazine. Alden retired in 1919, turning the editorship over to Thomas B. Wells, long an assistant editor and now vice-president of the publishing company.

After World War I, it became apparent that the old "quality" magazine was losing ground. Wells virtually abandoned illustration, and concentrated on thoughtful articles about current social and moral problems, though he did not eliminate fiction. Lee F. Hartman was editor from 1931 to 1941; Frederick Lee Allen, editor from 1941 to 1953, stressed economic, political, and social problems. This emphasis continued under his successor, John Fischer.

Harper's Weekly. Fletcher Harper of the publishing house of Harper & Brothers was responsible for the founding of the *Weekly* in 1857, as he had been for that of the *Monthly* seven years before. See HARPER'S MAGAZINE. Its editors were Theodore Sedgwick (1857–1858), John Bonner (1858–1863), GEORGE WILLIAM CURTIS (1863–1892), CARL SCHURZ (1892–1894), Henry Loomis Nelson (1894–1898), John Kendrick Bangs (1898–1901), George Harvey (1901–1913), and NORMAN HAPGOOD (1913–1916). *Harper's Weekly* was a small folio, originally of 16 pages, well printed on good paper and fully illustrated. In the early 1870's it had a circulation of over 400,000; though it ran below that figure through most of its life, it was always a paper of prestige and influence. It was especially distinguished in four fields:

(1) In reports, editorials, and pictures, it gave much attention to current events.

(2) It was a journal of opinion; most of its editors were mainly concerned with politics, leaving the general content to their managing editors. Henry Mills Alden, managing editor (1863–1869), called it "the fighting arm" of the House of Harper. At first a Buchanan paper, it came strongly to Lincoln's support by the middle of the war; later it battled for Grant, Cleveland, and Wilson. Its most spectacular campaign was the one against the Tweed Ring in New York in 1871; later it gave sturdy support to civil service reform, tariff reduction, and maintenance of the gold standard.

(3) It was notable for its illustrations (wood-cuts, later halftones). It carried full- and double-page pictures of news events and slashing cartoons. Its Civil War illustration by Thomas Nast, A. R. and William Waud, and others made it a great pictorial history of that conflict. The Nast drawings that pilloried the Tweed Ring mark a high point in the history of American political cartooning. Later artists, such as Edwin A. Abbey, William T. Smedley, and Howard Pyle gave the paper distinction. R. F. Zogbaum's pictures of the War with Spain were memorable, and there was a fine pictorial record of the 1893 Columbian Exposition in Chicago. Pictures of the American girl by Charles Dana Gibson and James Montgomery Flagg were features after the turn of the century.

(4) Throughout most of its career, the *Weekly* carried serial fiction and short stories—at first, like its sister monthly, the work of Dickens, Read, Collins, and Lever, and later that of Kipling, Barrie, Conan Doyle, Hamlin Garland, Howells, and James. In 1913 the old "Journal of Civilization," as it had loved to call itself, having made no profits for some two decades, was sold to the McClure organization (see MCCLURE'S MAGAZINE), but it survived the change; it was sold again two years later, and in 1916 it was merged with the INDE-PENDENT.

Harp-Weaver, The (1923), a collection of poems by EDNA ST. VINCENT MILLAY. This volume won the Pulitzer Prize in poetry, and was especially praised for the excellence of the thirty-nine sonnets included, especially the one beginning: "Euclid alone has looked on Beauty bare."

Harrigan, Edward (b. New York City, Oct. 26, 1845—d. June 6, 1911), comedian, playwright, producer, lyricist. Harrigan made a happy theatrical connection with Anthony Cannon (1855–1891), who called himself Tony Hart. Harrigan and Hart developed a special form of drama, usually a group of related sketches written by Harrigan and featuring kindly burlesques of various racial types. The main lead was usually Irish. Their first great success, *The Mulligan Guard Picnic* (1878), contained a tune called *Mulligan's Guard* that became world-famous. A series of Mulligan plays followed, and others equally successful. The partnership broke up in 1885, but Harrigan continued to produce plays until 1896. E. J. Kahn has written a vivacious account of the team in *The Merry Partners* (1955). See DAN MULLIGAN.

Harriman, Edward H[enry] (b. Hempstead, N.Y., Feb. 20, 1848—d. Sept. 9, 1909), railroad magnate. Harriman sponsored and participated in an expedition to Alaska in 1899; a report of the expedition's observations is given in the *Harriman Alaska Series* (14 v., 1902–14), including chapters by John Burroughs and John Muir. Muir wrote Harriman's biography (1912).

Harriot, Thomas. See THOMAS HARIOT.

Harris, Benjamin (b. England [?]—d. 1716[?]), publisher, bookseller, editor, writer for children. Harris began publishing pamphlets and newspapers in England in the late 1670's. In 1686 he sailed for New England, where he seems to have stayed until around 1695. He opened a bookshop in Boston and began printing writings of his own. He issued an almanac for 1687, then sometime before 1690 printed the famous NEW ENGLAND PRIMER, of which more than 5,000,000 copies were ultimately sold. For it he wrote the rhymed alphabet, intended to give young children some idea of the Calvinist universe. It had pictures and seems to have delighted children, who up to that time had had to be content with the lengthy and dreary sermons of the time for listening and reading matter. The book was a revision and improved version of Harris' *Protestant Tutor*, published in London (1679). On Sept. 25, 1690, Harris put out the first newspaper in America, *Publick Occurrences Both Forreign and Domestick*. It had only three small pages, but was immediately suppressed for "reflections of a very high nature." Back in England, Harris issued a *Bible in Verse* (1701?).

Harris, Caleb Fiske (b. Warwick, R.I., March 9, 1818—d. Oct. 2, 1881), bibliophile, cataloguer. Harris made a specialty of American poetry and drama, gathered a large collection of books in these fields, and published (1874) a useful catalogue. His collection was bought by Henry B. Anthony and presented to Brown University (1884). With additions made since then, it is probably the best collection of its kind now in existence.

Harris, Charles K[assel] (b. Poughkeepsie, N.Y., May 1, 1865—d. Dec. 22, 1930), song writer, memoirist. Harris' first published song was *Kiss and Let's Make Up* (1891). In 1892 he wrote a tremendous success, AFTER THE BALL; his next big hit was BREAK THE NEWS TO MOTHER (1897). His last hit capitalized on a new invention: *Hello, Central, Give Me Heaven* (1901). Harris wrote an autobiography, *After the Ball: 40 Years of Melody* (1926). He established a successful music-publishing firm in New York City. The claim has been made that he invented the term "Tin-Pan Alley"; but according to Edward B. Marks, the expression was invented by Monroe H. Rosenfeld, author of *Take Back Your Gold* and other maudlin lyrics.

Harris, George Washington ["Sut Lovingood"] (b. Allegheny City, Pa., March 20, 1814—d. Dec. 11, 1869), jeweler, river pilot, railroad superintendent, humorist. Harris became a skilled river pilot while still in his teens. He was a natural-born storyteller who liked to spin earthy yarns in a racy dialect. His first full-length sketch, *The Knob Dance*, was contributed to *The Spirit of the Times* in 1845. Later his newspaper and magazine pieces were collected in *Sut Lovingood: Yarns Spun by a "Nat'ral Born Durn'd Fool"* (1867), which immediately became popular and was frequently reprinted. Harris wrote definitely for a male audience; Mark Twain knew the yarns well and was an admiring follower of his contemporary. Donald

Davidson has pointed out that Harris' language was actually Devonshire, with some admixture of Scots and something that was pure American. It was far from being what the ignorant called "negroid" or "illiterate." A selection from Harris' writings was made in 1955 by Brom Weber, but with changes and expurgations that made the book, said Edmund Wilson, "all but valueless to the serious student of literature." Both Wilson and Weber agreed that in his depiction of the "southern poor white" Harris in some ways anticipated William Faulkner and Erskine Caldwell. (See SUT LOVINGOOD YARNS.)

Harris, Joel Chandler (b. near Eatonton, Ga., Dec. 9, 1848—d. July 3, 1908), journalist, humorist, short-story writer, novelist. At thirteen Harris went to work as a printer's devil on *The Countryman,* a weekly newspaper published at

the plantation "Turnwold," and received much of his education through the help of the paper's owner, Joseph Addison Turner. Harris soon began printing some of his own writing anonymously in the paper, and, through his work on the estate, became acquainted with the plantation Negroes and their folklore. After two years at Turnwold Harris worked on newspapers in Macon, New Orleans, Savannah, and finally, in 1876, joined the staff of the Atlanta *Constitution,* where he remained for twenty-four years. For his first assignments on the *Constitution*— humorous sketches of the Negro—Harris drew

on his boyhood knowledge of Negro life at Turnwold, reproducing the Negro dialect with utmost accuracy, and creating, as his main character, a Negro named Uncle Remus. The following year an article by William Owens on Negro folklore in *Lippincott's Magazine* awakened Harris to the literary possibilities of the tales to which he had listened as a boy, and on July 20, 1879, the first of Uncle Remus' animal stories appeared in the *Constitution*. Entitled "Negro Folklore. The Story of Mr. Rabbit and Mr. Fox, as Told by Uncle Remus," the sketch later became the introduction to UNCLE REMUS, HIS SONGS AND HIS SAYINGS (1880).

Although Harris claimed to have chosen one version of each tale and presented it "without embellishment and without exaggeration," his literary ability, his ear for dialect, and his masterful characterization of Uncle Remus, who tells the tales to a small boy, turned the unvarnished folktale into a work of art. The difference between the characters of "Buh Rabbit" as recorded by Owens and Brer Rabbit in Harris' tales is significant; from a vain, sharp, yet foolish character he becomes shrewd, mischievous, and one of the most lovable of Harris' animal folk. The first sketch was immediately popular, and Harris continued the tales with "Brer Rabbit, Brer Fox, and the Tar Baby" (see THE TAR BABY) in the *Constitution* on November 16, 1879, dividing the tale into three installments— a technique he often used—to arouse the curiosity of the reader as to Brer Rabbit's ultimate escape.

Nights with Uncle Remus, a second series of tales, appeared in 1883; in it Harris introduced the Coast Negro Daddy Jack as a storyteller, but his Gullah dialect is difficult to understand and his stories were less successful than those of Uncle Remus; unlike the tales in the first collection, which are set after the Civil War, these take place during the days of slavery. There is little evidence of anything but affection between the Negroes and their masters, although the life of the plantation is not idealized or treated as a part of the grand and gracious past. Unlike the prevalent Negro character in the literature of this period, Uncle Remus is not a sentimental stereotype of the devoted slave, but an individual character of warmth, humor, superstition, and shrewdness.

Harris published several more collections of Uncle Remus stories, including *Uncle Remus and His Friends* (1892); *Told by Uncle Remus* (1905); and *Uncle Remus and the Little Boy* (1910), which appeared posthumously. He also wrote a series of stories specifically for children: *Little Mr. Thimblefinger* (1894); *Mr. Rabbit at Home* (1895); *The Story of Aaron* (1895); *Aaron in the Wildwoods* (1897); and *Plantation Pageants* (1899).

Although Harris is best known as the creator of Uncle Remus, he also wrote many stories, two novels, and three novelettes on Southern life. MINGO AND OTHER SKETCHES IN BLACK AND WHITE (1884) deals with whites and Negroes and with the contrast between the aristocracy and the middle class; perhaps the best story of the collection, "At Teague Poteet's," deals with the mountaineers of north Georgia. "Free Joe and the Rest of the World," in *Free Joe and Other Sketches* (1887) is an argument neither for nor against slavery, but a study of the tragic situation of the individual—in this case a freed slave—for whom society has no place. Harris' other collections of stories include *Balaam and His Master* (1891); *Tales of the Home Folks in Peace and War* (1898); *The Chronicles of Aunt Minervy Ann* (1899); *On the Wing of Occasions* (1900); and *The Making of a Statesman* (1902).

Harris published two novels, *Sister Jane, Her Friends and Acquaintances* (1896), a rather placid story of Georgia life before the Civil War, and *Gabriel Tolliver* (1902), which deals primarily with the Reconstruction period. *On the Plantation* (1892), a novelette, is largely autobiographical and contains vivid descriptions of Harris' boyhood and his experiences at Turnwold. Less interesting are two later novelettes, *A Little Union Scout* (1904) and *Shadow Between His Shoulder Blades* (1909, published posthumously), both of which deal with the Civil War.

In 1907 Harris and his son Julian established *Uncle Remus' Magazine,* with DON MARQUIS as an associate editor. The magazine was later merged with the *Home Magazine,* in which Harris continued to publish new Uncle Remus stories. His daughter-in-law, Julia Collier Harris, wrote *The Life and Letters of Joel Chandler Harris* (1918); R. L. Wiggin's *The Life of Joel Chandler Harris from Obscurity in Boyhood to Fame in Early Manhood* (1918) includes all his important early writings. Other books on Harris are A. F. Harlow's *Joel Chandler Harris, Plantation Storyteller* (1941) and S. B. Brookes' *Joel Chandler Harris, Folklorist* (1950).

Harris, Roy [Ellsworth] (b. Lincoln Co., Okla., Feb. 12, 1898—   ), composer. One of America's most distinguished musicians, whose compositions include symphonies, string quartets, choral compositions, piano solos, and music for bands, Harris has often worked folk and literary motifs into his works. Thus his Fifth Symphony takes as its basis the song *Johnny Comes Marching Home;* another of his symphonies uses lines from Whitman; and still another is dedicated to the memory of Lincoln.

Harris, Thomas Lake (b. England, May 15, 1823—d. March 23, 1906), poet, Christian socialist, mystic. Harris came to the United States when still a young child. He was always deeply religious, contributed to religious magazines, became a Universalist minister at the age of twenty. In 1850 he became a member of a religious community in West Virginia, and there began dictating poems which had come to him, he said, from "divine wisdom." He organized a succession of agricultural, socialist, and spiritual societies at Amenia, N.Y., and Fountain Grove, Cal. He explained his ideas in a prose work, *The Brotherhood of the New Life* (1891). Among his verse collections are *The Epic of the Starry Heaven* (1854); *A Lyric of the Golden Age* (1856); *The Wisdom of the Adepts* (1884); and *The Song of Theos* (1903).

Harris, William Torrey (b. near Killingly, Conn., Sept. 10, 1835—d. Nov. 5, 1909), teacher, educational administrator, philosopher, editor. Harris rose rapidly as a teacher in St. Louis, where he became superintendent of schools. With Henry C. Brokmeyer (1828–1906) and DENTON J. SNIDER (1841–1925) he founded the St. Louis School of Philosophy, based mainly on German idealistic writings. It became largely a defense of the American system of free enterprise as one in which the individual could, at his leisure, develop "the good life." Harris founded the *Journal of Speculative Philosophy* (1867–93), to which Charles Peirce, William James, Josiah Royce, and John Dewey contributed; in 1879 he and BRONSON ALCOTT founded the CONCORD SCHOOL of Philosophy and Literature. In 1889 Harris was made U.S. Commissioner of Education. He was a fervent believer in the public schools as the foundation stone of American society, opposed religious instruction in the public schools, advocated coeducation, and believed that each child should participate in the culture of the race through "the five windows of the soul"—grammar, literature, art, mathematics, and history.

Harris was made editor-in-chief of a revised edition of the G. & C. Merriam Company *Webster's New International Dictionary* (1909). He wrote prefaces to the fifty-eight volumes of the *International Education Series;* a complete list of his writings runs to more than five hundred titles. Among his books: *Hegel's Doctrine of Reflection* (1881); *Introduction to the Study of Philosophy* (1889); *Hegel's Logic* (1890); *The Psychologic Foundations of Education* (1898). J. S. Roberts wrote his biography (1924), and further studies have been made by Edwin L. Schaub (1936) and Kurt F. Leidecker (1946). See IDEALISM.

Harrison, Benjamin (b. North Bend, Ohio, Aug. 20, 1833—d. March 13, 1901), lawyer, public official, 23rd President. Harrison's grandfather WILLIAM HENRY HARRISON had been ninth President of the United States. Harrison served with distinction in the Civil War, and thereafter became one of Indiana's leading lawyers. In 1880 he was elected to the United States Senate, and was chosen to run against Cleveland (1888), whom he defeated. During his Presidency he made some excellent appointments and increased the prestige of the country abroad; Idaho and Wyoming were admitted as states, and Oklahoma Territory was opened to settlement. He lost the 1892 election to Cleveland and retired to his law practice. His biography was written by General Lew Wallace (1888). He published one book that had a wide sale, *This Country of Ours* (1897). *Views of an Ex-President* (1901) was compiled by his wife.

Harrison, Charles Yale (b. Philadelphia, June 16, 1898—d. March 17, 1954), newspaperman, soldier, writer. Harrison, a lively, outspoken writer, often selected controversial topics for his books. Among them: *Generals Die in Bed* (an anti-war novel, 1930); *Clarence Darrow* (1931); *There Are Victories* (1933); *Public Housing* (1937); *Nobody's Fool* (1948), a fictional study of the advertising business.

Harrison, Constance [Cary] (b. Fairfax Co., Va., April 25, 1843—d. Nov. 21, 1920), novelist, memoirist. Mrs. Harrison first won a reputation with her story *A Little Centennial Lady* (1876), derived from the diary of an aunt. She went on to other popular works, the best known of which was a satire on American social climbers abroad, *The Anglomaniacs* (1890). Others are *Bellhaven Tales* (1892); *Sweet Bells Out of Tune* (1893); *A Bachelor Maid* (1894). She wrote her memoirs in *Recollections Grave and Gay* (1911).

Harrison, Henry Sydnor (b. Sewanee, Tenn., Feb. 12, 1880—d. July 14, 1930), newspaperman, novelist, short-story writer. Dissatisfied with journalism, Harrison wrote a novel in six months, discovered he had created a best seller. This was QUEED (1911), the story of a radical who is sobered by a spell of newspaper work. Among his later stories are *V.V.'s Eyes* (1913); *Angela's Business* (1915); *Andrew Bride of Paris* (1925).

Harrison, William Henry (b. Berkeley, Va., Feb. 9, 1773—d. April 4, 1841), soldier, public official, diplomat, 9th President. Harrison served in the army, then as an official in the Northwest Territory; for twelve years he was governor of the Indiana Territory. He attacked TECUMSEH's forces in that leader's absence, and although successful at Tippecanoe (1811) in temporarily driving them away, sustained serious losses. He served during the War of 1812; was elected to the House of Representatives (1816), the Ohio senate (1819), the U.S. Senate (1824); was named minister to Colombia (1828). In 1840 he ran for President with JOHN TYLER as his running mate, and died in office a month after his inauguration.

Harrison's messages and letters were gathered in the *Indiana Historical Collections* (2 v., 1922). Dorothy B. Goebel (1922) and Freeman Cleaves (1939) have written biographies of him. He has figured occasionally in historical fiction: Samuel Woodworth's *The Champions of Freedom* (1816); Louis Zara's *This Land Is Ours* (1940); Howard Breslin's *The Tamarack Tree* (1947).

Harrisse, Henry (b. France, [?], 1830—d. May 13, 1910), international lawyer, historian, bibliographer. For many years Harrisse lived in the United States, but some of his books were written in French. He became a specialist in the age of discovery and exploration of America. He compiled a bibliography of three hundred books relating to America between 1493 and 1551 (1866), studied Columbus in several volumes (1866, 1871, 1884), investigated the voyages of the Cabots (1892, 1896), wrote on Amerigo Vespucci (1895).

Harry Franco, The Adventures of (1839), an autobiographical novel dealing with financial affairs in New York by CHARLES FREDERICK BRIGGS. He wrote other novels of similar autobiographical character under the pen name Harry Franco.

Hart, Albert Bushnell (b. Clarksville, Pa., July 1, 1854—d. June 16, 1943), teacher, historian, editor. A graduate of Harvard, Hart taught there from 1883 to 1926. He was a specialist in American history and government. Among his many books: *Introduction to the Study of Federal Government* (1891); *The Formation of the Union* (1892); *The Foundations of American Foreign Policy* (1901); *Slavery and Abolition, 1831–41* (1906); *National Ideals Historically Traced* (1907); *The Monroe Doctrine: An Interpretation* (1915); *We and Our History* (1923). He was editor of *The American Nation, a History* (28 v., 1904–18).

Hart, Frances Noyes (b. Silver Springs, Md., Aug 10, 1890—d. Oct. 25, 1943), novelist. Mrs. Hart introduced novelties such as legal proceedings and scientific detection to the detective story. The most famous of her books was *The Bellamy Trial* (1927); others were *Hide in the Dark* (1929) and *The Crooked Lane* (1934).

Hart, Fred H. (fl. 1873–78), frontier humorist. There are no facts available on Hart's life. He wrote a book called *The Sazerac Lying Club: A Nevada Book*, which Walter Blair declares the best book of tall tales published from 1855–1900. The only extant edition seems to be the fifth, published in San Francisco (1878).

Hart, James David (b. San Francisco, Calif., April 18, 1911—   ), teacher, editor, historian. Long a member of the English department of the University of California at Berkeley, he compiled THE OXFORD COMPANION TO AMERICAN LITERATURE (1941; rev. ed., 1948, 1956). In THE POPULAR BOOK (1950) he has given an informative and provocative study of changing taste in America from the 17th century to the present as shown in the records of best-selling books. *America's Literature*, written in collaboration with Clarence Gohdes, came out in 1955.

Hart, John S[eely] (b. Stockbridge, Mass., Jan. 28, 1810—d. Jan. 26, 1877), teacher, editor, historian. Hart was among the pioneers in teaching American literature and in realizing the importance of American authors such as Melville and Whitman. He edited *The Female Prose Writers of America* (1852; rev. ed., 1856) and *A Manual of American Literature* (1873). It is believed that in 1872 Hart taught, at Princeton, the first collegiate course in American literature.

Hart, Joseph C. (1798–1855), lawyer, novelist, public official. Hart lived at Nantucket for a while and in 1834 published MIRIAM COFFIN, OR, THE WHALE-FISHERMAN. This is said to be the first novel on whaling; its chief aim was to propagandize for the whaling industry. Later he issued a collection of essays on travel and literature, *The Romance of Yachting* (1848). He was at the time of his death consul in the Canary Islands.

Hart, Lorenz (b. New York City, May 2, 1895—d. Nov. 22, 1943), lyricist, translator.

For a time Hart made his living as a translator; he did (1921) the standard English version of Ferenc Molnár's *Liliom*. He and RICHARD RODGERS formed a partnership, and began a brief, fertile collaboration by writing shows successfully produced by amateurs. In 1925 their songs for the *Garrick Gaieties* helped the show run for a year and a half, instead of the one-night performance that had been planned. Further successful Rodgers and Hart collaborations were *Dearest Enemy* (1925); *Garrick Gaieties* (1926); *The Girl Friend* (1926); *Connecticut Yankee* (their greatest hit, 1927); *Jumbo* (1935); *I Married an Angel* (1938); THE BOYS FROM SYRACUSE (1939); PAL JOEY (1940), and several musical plays for the movies.

Hart, Moss (b. New York City, Oct. 24, 1904—d. Dec. 20, 1961), playwright, librettist. Hart began his theatrical career with *The Hold-Up Man* (1925). His first great success was *Once in a Lifetime* (1930, in collaboration with GEORGE S. KAUFMAN). He wrote the libretto for Irving Berlin's *Face the Music* (1933) and for Kurt Weill's *Lady in the Dark* (1941). Collaborating again with Kaufman, he wrote *Merrily We Roll Along* (1934); YOU CAN'T TAKE IT WITH YOU (1936), which won a Pulitzer Prize in 1937; *I'd Rather Be Right* (1937); *The American Way* (1939); and THE MAN WHO CAME TO DINNER (1939). He also wrote *Winged Victory* (1943); *Light Up the Sky* (1948); *The Climate of Eden* (1952). He won the Antoinette Perry Award for his direction of the musical *My Fair Lady*. His autobiography, *Act One*, became a best seller in 1959. Hart said of himself that he had "the soul of a beachcomber" and left to himself would not write another line. But what he wrote, especially in combination with Kaufman, is one of the wittiest and most effective series of plays ever to appear on the American stage. His inclination to introduce some of his contemporaries into his plays, began, it was said, with *Once in a Lifetime*. Brooks Atkinson called *The Man Who Came to Dinner* "a merciless cartoon of ALEXANDER WOOLLCOTT's bad manners, shameless egoism, boundless mischief, and widely assorted friendships." When *Light Up the Sky* was produced the air was rife with rumors that the comedy caricatured actual Broadway personages. See also GEORGE WASHINGTON SLEPT HERE.

Hart, Tony. See EDWARD HARRIGAN.

Hart, Walter M[orris] (b. Philadelphia, Nov. 23, 1872—   ), teacher, authority on the ballad. Hart began teaching at the University of California in 1895, later served as dean. Among his books: *Ballad and Epic* (1907); *Kipling the Story-Writer* (1918). He edited *English Popular Ballads* (1916).

Harte, [Francis] Bret[t] (b. Albany, N.Y., Aug. 25, 1836—d. May 5, 1902), editor, poet, short-story writer, novelist, dramatist, consul. Harte left school early, read widely, published his first poem in *The Sunday Morning Atlas* (1847). In 1854 he and his sister sailed for San Francisco to join their mother. Here Harte worked an unsuccessful claim on the Stanislaus River, taught, may have served as a guard on a pony express carrying Wells Fargo valuables. He finally entered the field of journalism; his earliest extant piece, *The Valentine*,

was contributed to San Francisco's *The Golden Era* (March 1, 1857). At this time he began using the signature "Bret Harte." Jessie Benton Frémont, herself an able writer, assisted him in developing his style of writing, meeting influential people, and finding a position at the San Francisco mint.

Harte began his literary career with humorous sketches, went on to attract attention with his verses, some humorous and some serious, finally won worldwide fame through his short stories. He helped C. H. WEBB start *The Californian* (1864), edited THE OVERLAND MONTHLY until 1870. He also edited a controversial anthology of California verse, *Outcroppings* (1865), and published a collection of his own, *The Lost Galleon and Other Tales* (1867). His CONDENSED NOVELS (1867) revealed his satirical and critical powers in parodies of various contemporaries. *The Overland Monthly* published many literary nuggets from Harte's California experiences: THE LUCK OF ROARING CAMP (1868), the comic verse narrative PLAIN LANGUAGE FROM TRUTHFUL JAMES (1870; often called *The Heathen Chinee*), and enough others to round out the collection *The Luck of Roaring Camp and Other Stories* (1870).

In 1871 Harte accepted an offer of $10,000 a year from the *Atlantic Monthly* for whatever stories and verses he chose to write, and left California for Boston. The Boston experience in the end ruined him. He produced little worthwhile writing, and the *Atlantic* became weary of the sentimentality of his stories, perhaps even more so of his "unmoral treatment of immoral subjects." The contract was not renewed. Harte soon found himself in desperate financial straits, from which a lecturing tour and the publication of a novel, GABRIEL CONROY (1875–76), did not rescue him; nor did the writing and production of a play, AH SIN (1877), in collaboration with MARK TWAIN, even though the drama was based on the popular *Heathen Chinee*. He served for a while as consul at Krefeld, Germany, and at Glasgow. Thereafter he lived in and around London; he was a favorite in literary and social circles and added to his income by lecturing. He produced numerous short-story collections, several plays, and a second series of *Condensed Novels* (1902).

Much that Harte wrote was merely a Dickensian version of the Far West. Like Dickens, he found melodrama, sentimentality, sordidness, picturesqueness, eccentricity in the scenes he was familiar with. He had a talent for mimicry, most obvious in his *Condensed Novels* and some of his verse. American local humor—stories told in barrooms, country stores, and elsewhere—had an immense influence on Harte's style and subject matter. In prose and meter he created a picturesque and idiosyncratic Bret Harte country; he could be astonishingly realistic and unconventional, though Mark Twain once remarked that the dialect employed by his characters was one that "no one on heaven or earth had ever used till Harte invented it." He was undoubtedly repetitive; he made too much use of coincidence; he was often over-romantic. Bernard De Voto called him "a literary charlatan whose tales have greatly pleased the second-rate." On the other hand, Henry Adams claimed that Harte and Whitman were the only American writers to insist on the power of sex, using it for force rather than sentiment. Harte was also a pioneer in his sympathy for minority groups. Two studies have been made of his attitude toward the Chinese: W. P. Fenn's *Ah Sin and His Brethren in American Literature* (1933) and M. L. Kleim's *The Chinese as Portrayed in the Works of Bret Harte* (1940–41). He helped make San Francisco the literary capital of the West, and was the mentor of a group of early writers there, which included Mark Twain. His influence on Western stories and movies has been potent, as R. R. Waterhouse points out in *Bret Harte, Joaquin Miller, and the Western Local Color Story* (1939).

Like Twain, Harte wanted to be a playwright, and sometimes dramatized his stories. *Two Men of Sandy Bar* was produced in 1876; *Sue* (written with T. Edgar Pemberton) in 1902; *Salomy Jane* (dramatized by Paul Armstrong) in 1907. Many of his stories have been filmed. His other works include: *Poems* (1871); *East and West Poems* (1871); *Stories of the Sierras* (1872); *Tales of the Argonauts* (1875); *Thankful Blossom* (1877); *The Twins of Table Mountains* (1879); *Poetical Works* (1880); *Cressy* (1889); *Colonel Starbottle's Client* (1892); *A Protégée of Jack Hamlin's* (1894); *Poetical Works of Bret Harte* (1896); *Some Later Verses* (1898); *Tales*

of *Trail and Town* (1898); *From Sand Hill to Pine* (1900); *Trent's Trust* (1903); *The Story of Enriquez* (1924). Material from *The Californian* by Harte and Mark Twain was collected in *Sketches of the Sixties* (1926). His son Geoffrey Bret Harte edited his *Letters* (1926) and other letters were edited by B. A. Booth (1944). An authoritative account of Harte has been written by George R. Stewart in *Bret Harte: Argonaut and Exile* (1931). See also M'LISS.

Hartford Wits, the. Known also as the Connecticut Wits, this loosely confederated group of writers collaborated, in various combinations, to produce a roughly homogeneous body of political satire during the last two decades of the 18th and the first decade of the 19th centuries. Chief among them were JOHN TRUMBULL (1750–1831), RICHARD ALSOP (1751–1816), TIMOTHY DWIGHT (1752–1817), DAVID HUMPHREYS (1753–1818), and JOEL BARLOW (1754–1812), all of Yale College, together with Dr. LEMUEL HOPKINS (1750–1801), an eccentric and talented physician of Hartford; they were later joined by THEODORE DWIGHT (1764–1846) and two other literary physicians, Mason F. Cogswell (17[?]–18[?]) and ELIHU HUBBARD SMITH (1771–1798). Barlow, Hopkins, Humphreys, and Trumbull were probably mainly responsible for THE ANARCHIAD: A POEM ON THE RESTORATION OF CHAOS AND SUBSTANTIAL NIGHT, which appeared in twelve installments (1786–87) in the *New-Haven Gazette* and the *Connecticut Magazine*. Alsop and Theodore Dwight, with some assistance from Hopkins, Cogswell, and Smith, contributed twenty numbers of THE ECHO to the *Hartford American Mercury* (1791–1805). Alsop, Theodore Dwight, and Hopkins were the principal authors of THE POLITICAL GREENHOUSE FOR THE YEAR 1798 (1799). Each of these satires was written in a strong, sometimes coarse burlesque style, modeled on the acrimonious tone of Pope's *Dunciad* or the broad ridicule of Butler's *Hudibras*, seasoned with the sharp political consciousness of such contemporary English satires as *The Rolliad*. The Wits were staunch Federalists, opposed to every threat of change. They drove sharp-pointed barbs of ridicule and recrimination deep into all opponents of established New England ways. To them French infidelism and Jeffersonian republicanism seemed equally disastrous, and against these tendencies the Wits fought a strenuous, though in the end a losing, battle. (See THE FEDERALIST PARTY.)

Each of these talented New Englanders was in his own right an author of some pretensions, and several are better remembered today for individual writings than for collaborations. Trumbull, for example, had gathered about him, when he was a tutor at Yale in the early 1770's, a group of somewhat younger men, including Dwight, Humphreys, and Barlow. He himself was soon known as the author of Addisonian essays called *The Medler* and *The Correspondent* which reproved his contemporaries from the pages of the *Boston Chronicle* and the *Connecticut Journal*. He was more widely known as a satirist in rhyme when his THE PROGRESS OF DULNESS appeared in three parts from 1771 to 1773. His principal fame, however, came in 1775 with M'FINGAL, a favorite satire of early Revolutionary times. After expanding the poem in 1783, Trumbull virtually dropped from the literary scene and devoted himself to a career in the law.

Timothy Dwight, though he seems seldom to have collaborated in satire, is remembered as the second principal figure among the Wits. A man of supreme confidence, Dwight was for several years a clergyman and schoolmaster in Greenfield, Conn. In 1795, he accepted the presidency of Yale College, a post which he held with honor until his death. His most important belletristic writings were THE CONQUEST OF CANAAN (1785), a Biblical allegory in which his contemporaries read the triumphs of their own revolutionary armies, and GREENFIELD HILL (1794), a pastoral poem descriptive of New England. His *Triumph of Infidelity* (1788) was a satirical outburst against irreligion in America, so outspoken that in later years Dwight would not acknowledge it as his own. Many volumes of sermons and a posthumous account of *Travels in New-England and New-York, 1796–1815* complete his works.

David Humphreys, less talented as a writer, made up for his lack of imaginative skill by his industriousness in everything he did. An aide-de-camp to Washington, he later undertook a number of diplomatic missions abroad and from 1791 to 1802 was minister to Lisbon and Madrid. Returning to Connecticut, he devoted himself to agriculture, especially the raising of Merino sheep. During his younger years he had written voluminously and with patriotic fervor—*A Poem Addressed to the Armies of the United States* (1780), *A Poem on the Happiness of America* (1780), *The Glory of America* (1783), and *A Poem on Industry* (1783), all of which sound didactic and imitative to modern ears. Richard Alsop of Middletown, Conn., said to have been one of America's first millionaires, was in many respects the most scholarly and bookish of the Wits. His published poems are chiefly graceful translations from the French, Italian, or Spanish, a *Versification of Ossian* (1793), and *The Twilight of the Gods* (1793), adapted from the Norse Eddas.

Joel Barlow, the youngest of the original group, was the most active and ultimately perhaps the most successful. Educated at Dartmouth and Yale under the influence of Trumbull and Dwight, he worked for years on an epic which would display the wonders of the New World. As published in 1787 it was called *The Vision of Columbus*, but for twenty years longer he worked at revising it and published it again in 1807 as THE COLUMBIAD, full of fine intention but without much fine poetry. After a varied career as chaplain, teacher, storekeeper, and editor, Barlow left New England in 1788 for France as agent for the ill-fated Scioto Land Co. Soon he was caught up by enthusiasm for the liberal ideas which he saw in the French Revolution and joined forces with Thomas Paine and such Englishmen as Horne Tooke. He produced in verse *The Conspiracy of Kings* (1791) and in prose *Advice to the Privileged Orders* (1791), both inflammatory, even radical, which made him seem apostate to his former friends in Connecticut. Perhaps the best-known of Barlow's works is the *jeu d'esprit* called HASTY PUDDING (1796), which he composed in France in nostalgic memory of New England cornmeal. As time went on he grew far beyond his former friends, became a confidant of Jefferson and Madison, a sponsor of young Robert Fulton, an American consul at Algiers, and in 1811 minister to France.

Other members of the group, each gifted within his limits, are perhaps of less individual importance. A good study of the whole group is Leon Howard's *The Connecticut Wits* (1943), and V. L. Parrington edited an anthology with the same title (1926), which includes a bibliography.

LEWIS LEARY

Hartley, Marsden (b. Lewiston, Me., Jan. 4, 1877—d. Sept. 2, 1943), poet, painter. Hartley spent his boyhood in Maine, moving at the age of fifteen to Cleveland. He studied painting in that city and in Paris and Berlin, gaining his first successes as a painter in European exhibitions. In later life he lived in New Mexico, Nova Scotia, Bermuda, New York City, and Maine, winning recognition as one of America's most talented painters, one who particularly excelled in depicting the land and seascapes of his native state. For Hartley poetry was mainly an avocation, and the three small collections published during his lifetime—*Twenty-Five Poems* (1925), *Androscoggin* (1940), and *Sea Burial* (1941)—neither sought nor received publicity. After his death a selection was made of these volumes and some five hundred poems left in manuscript: *Selected Poems of Marsden Hartley* (1945). Hartley wrote about many of the things he painted, Maine landscapes, the sea, animals, persons contemporary and historical. His verse, however, is as integral, individual, and technically sophisticated as if it had been his main endeavor.

Hartmann, [Carl] Sadakichi (b. Japan, Nov. 8, 1869—d. Nov. 21, 1944), playwright, poet, art critic. Hartmann's father was German, his mother Japanese. He came to the United States at an early age, was naturalized in 1894. Among his books: three plays, *Christ* (1893), *Buddha* (1897), and *Moses* (1934); several collections of poetry, including *Drifting Flowers of the Sea* (1906) and *My Rubaiyat* (1926); and some volumes of art criticism, including *Shakespeare in Art* (1901), *A History of American Art* (1902), and *Japanese Art* (1904). Gene Fowler described him at length in *Minutes of the Last Meeting* (1954).

Harum, David. See DAVID HARUM.

Harvard Advocate, The. A literary magazine edited, written, and published by students at

Harvard University. It was founded in 1866. Donald Hall, who edited *The Harvard Advocate Anthology* (1950), called the magazine a "nursemaid of genius." Its distinguished contributors have included T. S. Eliot, Conrad Aiken, E. A. Robinson, James Agee, and Wallace Stevens.

Harvard Classics. See CHARLES W. ELIOT.

Harvard Dictionary of Music (1944), edited by Willi Apel. A reference book dealing with the history, the aesthetics, and the appreciation of music; also with its instruments, festivals, kinds, forms, and composition.

Harvard Guide to American History (1896, 1912, 1954). In its 1954 revision the *Guide* came out under the editorship of OSCAR HANDLIN, A. M. SCHLESINGER, SAMUEL ELIOT MORISON, FREDERICK MERK, A. M. SCHLESINGER, JR., and Paul Herman Buck. Recognized as one of the most useful reference works in the field, its articles are highly readable. The remarkably detailed index runs to 143 pages. The book is a guide to history writing as well as to the study of American history.

Harvard Lampoon, The. A humorous magazine published by Harvard University students. Originally modeled after *Punch*, it was founded in 1876 by Ralph W. Curtis, John T. Wheelwright, Samuel Sherwood, and others. Its contents consist primarily of cartoons, anecdotes, and satirical pieces. "Lampy's" staff is traditionally fond of playing pranks on the Harvard community. Bernice O'Hara wrote *The Adventures of Bob Lampoon* (1939). It has done numerous spoofs of popular magazines; the July, 1961 issue of *Mademoiselle* was written by the college magazine staff in typical *Lampoon* style.

Harvard Workshop. A course in drama writing popularly known as "English 47" or "47 Workshop." (See GEORGE PIERCE BAKER.) It has had many eminent alumni: playwrights Edward Sheldon, Josephine Preston Peabody, Percy MacKaye, Eugene O'Neill, S. N. Behrman, Philip Barry, Sidney Howard; directors George Abbott, Theresa Helburn; critics Kenneth Macgowan, Heywood Broun, W. P. Eaton, Robert C. Benchley, John Mason Brown; designers Robert Edmond Jones, Lee Simonson; novelist Thomas Wolfe; and many actors.

Harvey (1944), a play by MARY C. CHASE. Harvey is a rabbit who possesses two distinctions: he is six feet tall, and he is visible only to the amiable drunkard who is the play's human protagonist. The point of the comedy turns on the futile attempts of eminent psychiatrists to dispel Harvey forever. Psychiatrists and others are generously debunked, and there is a hint of the wisdom possible to the apparently crazy. The play enjoyed a long success on Broadway, and won a Pulitzer prize.

Harvey, William Hope (b. Buffalo, W. Va., Aug. 16, 1851—d. Feb. 11, 1936), lawyer, economist. He was known as "Coin Harvey," vigorously advocated bimetallism, expressed his views in several volumes: *Coin's Financial School*, 1894; *Coin on Money, Trusts, and Imperialism*, 1899; *The Remedy*, 1915; and others. He was the presidential candidate of the Liberty Party (1932). He strongly influenced WILLIAM JENNINGS BRYAN, whose ideas on finance are said to have come almost entirely from Harvey. His books had a wide audience, fired some to enthusiasm, thoroughly frightened all conservatives.

Haskell, Daniel (b. Preston, Conn., 1784—d. Aug. 9, 1848), clergyman, teacher, gazetteer. Haskell did some historical writing, is chiefly remembered for one of the earliest books giving descriptive data on the United States: *A Complete Descriptive and Statistical Gazeteer* [sic] *of the United States of America* (1843).

Hastings, Thomas (b. Washington, Conn., Oct. 15, 1784—d. May 15, 1872), musician, editor, composer. Hastings was active in New York City churches, conducting choirs, editing collections of hymns, composing hymns of his own. He wrote *A Dissertation on Musical Taste* (1822), gathered his own compositions in *Devotional Hymns and Religious Poems* (with Lowell Mason, 1850), and edited *Spiritual Songs for Social Worship* (1831–32); *Musical Miscellany* (2 v., 1836); *The Sacred Lyre* (1840); and other similar compilations.

Hasty Pudding, The (1793), a mock-heroic poem by JOEL BARLOW. This was written in a French inn, where Barlow happened to be served a dish of Indian corn-mush, a favorite dish in his native Connecticut. He wrote three nostalgic cantos of four hundred lines in heroic couplets in which he described how he came to write the poem, how the famous dish was made, how to eat it, why it was worthy of praise. Although the verse often has all the false clangor of the heroic couplet at its worst, this clangor at moments greatly heightens the burlesque of the poem. The scenery in many passages is typically American—the sly raccoon, the bolder squirrel, the corn-husking ceremonies, the molasses, the pumpkins.

Hasty Pudding Club. A Harvard student dramatic organization which gave its first production in 1844 and its hundredth in 1944. The club believes it is the oldest dramatic group in America. The plays produced are burlesques. Some of the university's most eminent graduates have taken part in these performances, from George Santayana to Robert Benchley. At early meetings hasty puddings (made of corn meal) were served.

Hatcher, Harlan [Henthorne] (b. Ironton, Ohio, Sept. 9, 1898—   ), educator, historian, novelist. Hatcher studied at Ohio State University, receiving his Ph.D. in 1928, and remained there as teacher and administrator until 1951, when he became president of the University of Michigan. He wrote two novels set in Kentucky, *Tunnel Hill* (1931) and *Patterns of Wolfpen* (1934); a critical work, *Creating the Modern American Novel* (1935); and another novel, *Central Standard Time* (1937). Then as state director of the Federal Writers Project (1937–39) he turned to the history and literature of Ohio. He edited the Project's publication of *The Ohio Guide* in 1940, and the same year published *The Buckeye Country: A Pageant of Ohio*, which became a best seller. These books were followed by *The Great Lakes* (1944); *Lake Erie* (1945); *The Western Reserve: The Story of New Connecticut in Ohio* (1949); *A Century of Iron and Men* (1950). Hatcher's narratives are praised for combining serious scholarship with readability and an affectionately humorous perspective. He also wrote *The Versification of Robert Browning* (1928); contributed to *The History of Ohio, Vol. VI* (1943); and edited (with critical introductions) *Modern Continental, British, and American Dramas* (3 v., 1941; shorter edition, 1944).

Hatrack (*American Mercury,* April, 1926), a story by HERBERT ASBURY. This account of a small-town prostitute who seeks penitence shocked some readers, and the issue was suppressed in Boston.

Haunted Bookshop, The (1919), a novel by CHRISTOPHER MORLEY. A sequel to PARNASSUS ON WHEELS, it describes spy activities carried on in an old bookshop in Brooklyn, N.Y.

Haunted Palace, The (1839), a poem by EDGAR ALLAN POE. It appeared first in the *Baltimore Museum* (April, 1839). Later it became one of the "rhymed verbal improvisations" which Poe attributes to Roderick Usher in THE FALL OF THE HOUSE OF USHER (*Burton's Gentleman's Magazine,* Sept., 1839). It is one of the most melodious and dreamy of Poe's poems. Poe frankly admits an "under or mystic current" in its meaning, and suggests that in it may be perceived "a full consciousness, on the part of Usher, of the tottering of his lofty reason upon her throne." Later, in one of his letters, Poe stated, "By *The Haunted Palace* I mean to imply a mind haunted by phantoms—a disordered brain." Some have seen in the poem a subjective description of Poe himself. Poe charged, unjustly, that Longfellow had plagiarized this poem in his BELEAGUERED CITY (1839); the latter was based on a footnote in Scott's *Border Minstrelsy.* The only resemblance seems to be that there are ghosts in both poems.

Havighurst, Walter [Edwin] (b. Appleton, Wis., Nov. 28, 1901—   ), teacher, historian, novelist. Havighurst has taught mainly at Miami University and has written numerous regional books, both fiction and nonfiction. Among his historical works: *Upper Mississippi* ("THE RIVERS OF AMERICA" SERIES, 1937); *The Long Ships Passing* (1942); *The Land of Promise: The Story of the Northwest Territory* (1946); *Annie Oakley of the Wild West* (1954), a biography particularly well received by the critics; *Wilderness for Sale* (1956); *The Miami Years* (1959), a history of Miami University in Ohio; and *Land of the Long Horizons* (1960). His novels include *Pier 17* (1935); *The Quiet Shore* (1937); *The Winds of Spring* (1940); *Signature of Time* (1949).

Having Wonderful Time (1937), a play by ARTHUR KOBER. This comedy about the attempts of a group of vacationers in the Berkshires to improve themselves culturally and socially ran for a year on Broadway and was later made into a successful musical called *Wish You Were Here* (1952).

Hawes, Charles Boardman (b. Clifton Springs, N.Y., Jan. 24, 1889—d. July 15, 1923), teacher, writer. After teaching for a while, Hawes joined the staff of *Youth's Companion,* later became associate editor of *The Open Road.* All his life he was interested in and wrote about the sea. He published three long stories for boys: *The Mutineers* (1920); *The Great Quest* (1921); *The Dark Frigate* (1923). The last won a Newbery Award. He also wrote *Gloucester: By Land and Sea* (1923). *Whaling* (1924) was completed by his wife.

Hawks of Hawk-Hollow, The: A Tradition of Pennsylvania (1835), a novel by R. M. BIRD. A story of a Tory family in Pennsylvania the year after the battle of Yorktown. The plot is highly involuted; a case of false identities is cleared up in complex explanations and the Tories turn out to be patriotic.

Hawthorne, Julian (b. Boston, June 22, 1846 —d. July 14, 1934), novelist, historian, biographer. The son of NATHANIEL HAWTHORNE was a fluent writer of stories, none of which attained much success. Among them: *Idolatry* (1874); *Garth* (1877); *Fortune's Fool* (1883); *John Parmelee's Curse* (1886). He also wrote *Nathaniel Hawthorne and His Wife* (2 v., 1884). His daughter, **Hildegarde Hawthorne** (b. New York City, 1871—d. Dec. 10, 1952), wrote stories and biographies for young readers, as well as verse, essays, and histories for adults; among them biographies of Emerson, O. W. Holmes, John C. Frémont, and Matthew Fontaine Maury.

Hawthorne, Nathaniel (b. Salem, Mass., July 4, 1804—d. May 19, 1864), novelist, short-story writer. Hawthorne was the son of Capt. Nathaniel Hathorne, a sea captain (the author added the "w" to his name), and Elizabeth

(Manning) Hathorne, daughter of a merchant. When the boy was four his father died. Mrs. Hathorne and her three children moved to her father's house. At seven Hawthorne suffered a foot injury during a ball game, and during several years of lameness acquired the habit of

reading. For a time the family lived in Raymond, Maine, and Hawthorne graduated from Bowdoin College in 1825; among his classmates were HENRY WADSWORTH LONGFELLOW and Horatio Bridge, and another close friend, FRANKLIN PIERCE, was in the class before him.

After college Hawthorne returned to Salem and remained there for twelve years, writing tales and sketches which appeared anonymously in gift annuals, magazines, and newspapers. He published privately a novel, FANSHAWE (1828), but later withdrew it from circulation and destroyed all the copies he could find. Another book, *Seven Tales of My Native Land*, he burned before publishing. In 1837, encouraged by Horatio Bridge, who secretly financed it, he published TWICE-TOLD TALES, which Longfellow enthusiastically reviewed; the book won for Hawthorne a small audience of appreciative readers. At this time, too, he met Sophia Peabody. The favorable response to his book and his desire to marry encouraged him to seek a position, and he was appointed Measurer of the Boston Custom House. In Boston he developed his friendship with Longfellow and through him met Lowell and other members of the Cambridge group.

In 1841 Hawthorne, who had met Emerson, Thoreau, Margaret Fuller, and other Transcendentalists through Sophia Peabody, invested his savings in the BROOK FARM experiment, in the hope that the community would provide a good place to begin married life. When he realized that the lack of privacy there was repugnant to him and harmful to his work as a writer, he withdrew. He and Sophia were married in July, 1842, and went to live in the Old Manse at Concord, where the author enjoyed the happiest years of his life. Here he wrote MOSSES FROM AN OLD MANSE (1846). Later the Hawthornes moved back to Salem, where he became Surveyor of the Salem Customs House; he was removed from office in 1849 by scheming local politicians. In 1850 he published THE SCARLET LETTER, which brought him immediate fame and a certain degree of financial independence.

Hawthorne moved to Lenox, and the year and a half spent there were the most prolific of his life. (See LENOX, MASS.) He wrote THE HOUSE OF THE SEVEN GABLES (1851); THE BLITHEDALE ROMANCE (1852), drawn from his experience at Brook Farm; THE SNOW IMAGE AND OTHER TALES (1851), another book of short stories; and two classics for children, A WONDER-BOOK FOR GIRLS AND BOYS (1852) and TANGLEWOOD TALES (1853), retellings of Greek myths. In 1852 Hawthorne purchased Bronson Alcott's house in Concord, which he rechristened "The Wayside," and that summer he wrote a campaign biography for Franklin Pierce. When Pierce won the Presidency, he appointed Hawthorne consul at Liverpool and Manchester, and the author spent seven years abroad (see ENGLISH NOTE-BOOKS), first in England (1853–57), then in Italy (1857–59), where he began THE MARBLE FAUN (1860), completing it in England in 1859. After his return to Concord in 1860 his health declined, he published only one complete book, OUR OLD HOME (1863), and he began four novels which he did not complete. He died in his sleep in Plymouth, N.H., while on a trip with Franklin Pierce. He was buried in Concord in Sleepy Hollow cemetery on May 23.

In his personality Hawthorne was reticent. Although he had many acquaintances among the members of his own profession and corresponded with them, *e.g.*, with Melville about the problems of writing, Longfellow was the only writer with whom he was on intimate terms; his closest friends were Franklin Pierce and Horatio Bridge. Longfellow once remarked in his journals that with a group Hawthorne was silent; when with two or three good friends he spoke well. Yet it is evident that he did not suffer from shyness. In his youth he often made walking tours through New England, mingling freely with crowds in taverns and at country fairs, talking openly with those he met. He was, at least in his own view, a provincial, not accustomed to the usages of urban society, unable to discourse on the fashionable themes—he was never at ease with Emerson. He was a New Englander of the sea coast, of the country, ultimately of the past, not of Boston's dinner tables or Concord's philosophical parlors.

In the past Hawthorne found not only the substance of many of his stories and novels but the abiding, almost obsessive theme of all his adult work—the nature of sin. His own ancestors interested him greatly. His first American ancestor, William Hathorne, had arrived from England in 1630 and was remembered in Salem history for having given orders to have the Quakers whipped through the streets. William's son John was one of the Witchcraft Judges and had drawn a curse from one of the victims upon himself and descendants. Hawthorne read much colonial history, delighted in old documents. He studied the psychology of the Puritans and peopled his stories with characters who are either outright Puritans or who possess Puritanical traits.

Hawthorne's theme was the "unpardonable sin." He found it in many places, pre-eminently in the presumptiveness and bigotry of the Puritans themselves. The sin of *The Scarlet Letter* is not the adultery of Hester Prynne and Arthur Dimmesdale, but the attempt of Roger Chillingworth to master Dimmesdale's soul. In *The Marble Faun* it is the effects of the sin of murder rather than the murder itself. In ETHAN BRAND the "unpardonable sin" is Ethan's deliberate attempt to make an intellectual and psychological experiment on the soul of another human being, "to invade the sanctity of the human heart."

Hawthorne's other preoccupation was the literary use of the symbol, the significant object which could be manipulated to reveal ever deeper sources of meaning. Some of his stories, such as THE CELESTIAL RAILROAD and DR. HEIDEGGER'S EXPERIMENT, are outright allegories, but in his most successful works Hawthorne avoided abstract equivalents and instead concentrated the forces of conflict on a single, often ambiguous object—a flower, a statue, Hester's embroidered "A." Thus Hawthorne developed, by means largely independent of European or other American writers, a native symbolism that greatly influenced the later course of American fiction and probably had a good deal to do with the development of Melville's narrative method. (Cf. Charles Feidelson, Jr., *Symbolism and American Literature*, 1953.) Since his death Hawthorne's tales have maintained their reputation and most are considered American classics. They have been a constant source of new ideas for critics, and biographers have made the author's enigmatic personality a favorite subject.

Hawthorne's *Complete Works* were edited by G. P. Lathrop (1883). His letters and journals have appeared in incomplete editions. Biographies have been written by Henry James (1879), Moncure Conway (1890), George E. Woodberry (1902), Newton Arvin (1929), A. Mather Jackson (1940), Randall Stewart (1948), Mark Van Doren (1949). Robert Cantwell made a study of *Nathaniel Hawthorne: The American Years* (1948), and Vernon Loggins wrote an account of *The Hawthornes* through seven generations (1951). Selections from Hawthorne's short stories were made by Newton Arvin (1946) and Mark Van Doren (1951). William Bysshe Stein in *Hawthorne's Faust* (1953) analyzed the domination, as he saw it, of the Faust myth in Hawthorne's work. Rudolph von Abele wrote *The Death of the Artist: A Study of Hawthorne's Disintegration* (1955), and Randall Stewart has studied the relationship between Hawthorne and Faulkner (*College English*, February, 1956). Recent and valuable works of criticism include H. H. Waggoner's *Hawthorne, A Critical Study* (1955); Roy R. Male, Jr.'s *Hawthorne's Tragic Vision* (1957); Edward Wagenknecht's *Hawthorne: Man and Writer* (1961).

MANNING HAWTHORNE

Hay, John [Milton] (b. Salem, Ind., Oct. 8, 1838—d. July 1, 1905), lawyer, secretary to Lincoln, diplomat, Secretary of State, writer. Hay took his degree at Brown University and studied law with his uncle in Springfield, Ill., next door to the law firm of Lincoln and Herndon. When Lincoln was elected President, JOHN G. NICOLAY, his secretary, persuaded Lincoln to "let Hay come along" as his assistant. Hay admired Lincoln but was disturbed by his way of speaking, writing, and perhaps acting. He served him faithfully and well, nevertheless; Lincoln usually employed him for the more personal side of his correspondence. In later years there arose the legend that Hay had actually written some of Lincoln's most famous pieces, particularly the letter to Mrs. BIXBY. F. Lauriston Bullard thoroughly analyzed the story in his *Abraham Lincoln and the Widow Bixby* (1946) and strongly maintained that there was no truth in it. After the war Hay was made Secretary of Legation at Paris (1865–67), at Vienna (1867–

68), and at Madrid (1869–70). Out of his Spanish experiences he drew CASTILIAN DAYS (1871).

On Hay's return to the United States he joined for five years the staff of the New York *Tribune;*

among his contributions were the *Pike County Ballads*, six poems in Western dialect that were later included in PIKE COUNTY BALLADS AND OTHER POEMS (1871). In 1874 he married and later moved to Cleveland. The strike and riots of 1877 profoundly disturbed him, and he later wrote and published anonymously a novel, THE BREADWINNERS (1884), which sought to defend property against the "dangerous classes." Meanwhile he had been appointed First Assistant Secretary of State, and moved to Washington. He and Nicolay wrote *Abraham Lincoln: A History* (1890), a frankly partisan book but one making use of much valuable new material. Fifteen years later the two men edited the *Complete Works of Abraham Lincoln*. McKinley appointed Hay ambassador to Great Britain (1897–98), then secretary of state, an office he continued to hold under Theodore Roosevelt, helping effect the Open Door policy in China and the negotiations for the Panama Canal.

After Hay's death his wife edited (poorly) *The Letters of John Hay and Extracts from His Diary* (3 v., privately pub., 1908). In 1939 Tyler Dennett, author of *John Hay: From Poetry to Politics* (1933), issued the first public printing of this material in a properly edited volume, *Lincoln and the Civil War in the Diaries and Letters of John Hay*. Clarence L. Hay edited his father's *Complete Poetical Works* (1916), and *Addresses of John Hay* (1907) gave some of his speeches. Nonpolitical letters appear in Caroline Ticknor's *A Poet in Exile: Early Letters of John Hay* (1910) and in *A College Friendship: A Series of Letters from John Hay to Hannah Angell* (1938). Further biographies have been written by Lorenzo Sears (1914), William Roscoe Thayer (2 v., 1915), and Donald G. Herzberg (1946). See also JIM BLUDSO; LITTLE BREECHES.

Hayakawa, S[amuel] I[chiye] (b. Vancouver, B.C., July 18, 1906—   ), teacher, semanticist. Hayakawa, who took his Ph.D. at the University of Wisconsin, has been a resident of the United States since 1939. He has taught at the Armour Institute, the Illinois Institute of Technology, the University of Chicago, and San Francisco State College. As a student of linguistics, he became interested in the science of meaning, studied general semantics with ALFRED KORZYBSKI, and has been editor of *ETC, a Review of General Semantics* since 1943. He has written a number of lively books on semantics: *Language in Action* (1941); *Language in Thought and Action* (1949); *Language, Meaning, and Maturity* (1954).

Haycox, Ernest (b. Portland, Ore., Oct. 1, 1899—d. Oct. 13, 1950), writer of Western stories. Haycox wrote a speedy story with some regard for verisimilitude; he had a strong sense of the historical development of the West. Among his books: *Free Grass* (1929); *Starlight Rider* (1933); *Sundown Jim* (1938); *Saddle and Ride* (1939); *Rim of the Desert* (1940); *Action by Night* (1943); *The Wild Bunch* (1943); *Long Storm* (1946). Several of his stories have been filmed.

Haycraft, Howard (b. Madelia, Minn., July 24, 1905—   ), editor. Haycraft joined the H. W. Wilson Co. in 1929 and became its president in 1953; he has been editor or co-editor of several of its valuable reference works. Among these: *Authors Today and Yesterday* (1933); *The Junior Book of Authors* (1934); *British Authors of the 19th Century* (1936); *American Authors, 1600–1900* (1938); *Twentieth-Century Authors* (1942). In addition Haycraft has made himself what Helen Haines calls a "connoisseur, historian, and bibliographer" of the detective story. He has edited several anthologies in the field and has written *Murder for Pleasure: The Life and Times of the Detective Story* (1941), published to commemorate the centennial of Poe's *Murders in the Rue Morgue*, "the world's first detective story." Haycraft's *Treasury of Great Mysteries* came out in 1957; and *Ten Great Mysteries* in 1959.

Hayden, Joseph. See HOT TIME IN THE OLD TOWN TONIGHT.

Haydn, Hiram (b. Cleveland, Ohio, Nov. 3, 1907—   ), teacher, editor, novelist. After a career in teaching, Haydn became an executive officer for Phi Beta Kappa, editor of the *American Scholar*, editor for Crown Publishers, for Bobbs-Merrill, and for Random House. He has edited anthologies and written three novels: *By Nature Free* (1943); *Manhattan Furlough* (1945); *The Time Is Noon* (1948). The last

was especially commended for its sharp and subtle college scenes. In 1959 he joined with Alfred Knopf, Jr., and Simon Michael Bessie to found Atheneum Publishers.

Hayes, Alfred (b. England, 1911—   ), poet, novelist, playwright. Hayes grew up in New York City and worked there as a newspaperman, magazine and radio writer. His first book of poems, *The Big Time* (1944), made extensive use of the city background. In 1943 Hayes went into the Army, serving in Italy. During this period he worked with Roberto Rossellini on the movie, *Paisan* (1946), and gathered material for his two most successful novels, *All Thy Conquests* (1946) and *The Girl On The Via Flaminia* (1949). The latter, originally a play, was rewritten as a novel, and later readapted into a play (1954) and a movie (*Act of Love,* 1954). Two of Hayes' later novels are *Shadow of Heaven* (1947) and *In Love* (1953). These books are notable for their complex Jamesian prose style, differing from Hayes' earlier work which was distinguished by its economy of detail and taut, poetic style. His most recent volume of verse is *Welcome to the Castle* (1950), a book which critics have generally commended for force and honesty, while noting an indifference to music and verbal brilliance.

Hayes, Carlton J[oseph] H[untley] (b. Afton, N.Y., May 16, 1882—d. Sept. 3, 1964), historian, teacher. Hayes' long and distinguished career includes service in the army in World War I and as ambassador to Spain (1942–45), and professor at Columbia University. An account of his Spanish experiences is given in *Wartime Mission in Spain* (1945). Among his numerous historical writings: *British Social Politics* (1913); *History and Nature of International Relations* (1922); *Essays in Intellectual History* (1929); *Historical Evolution of Modern Nationalism* (1931); *Political and Cultural History of Modern Europe* (1932–36; rev. ed., 1939); *Spain* (1951); *Modern Europe to 1870* (1953); *Christianity and Western Civilization* (1954); *Contemporary Europe Since 1870* (1958).

Hayes, Isaac I[srael] (b. Chester Co., Pa., March 5, 1832—d. Dec. 17, 1881), physician, explorer, writer. Among Dr. Hayes' books were several that described his own experiences and observations in the Arctic—*An Arctic Boat-Journey* (1860); *The Open Polar Sea* (1867); and *The Land of Desolation* (1872). Unfortunately almost forgotten is his best book: *Cast Away in the Cold: An Old Man's Story of a Young Man's Adventures, As Related by Captain John Hardy, Mariner* (1868). The tale is moralistic, but it tells pleasantly and accurately what can happen to shipwrecked mariners in the Arctic.

Hayes, Joseph [Arnold] (b. Indianapolis, Ind., Aug. 2, 1918—   ), novelist, playwright, radio-TV writer. Hayes is best known for *The Desperate Hours* (1954), a suspense thriller which he originally wrote as a novel, and later adapted into a Broadway play and a screenplay (both 1955). "The desperate hours" are those a family in an Indianapolis suburb spend terrorized by three convicts who have chosen their house as a temporary hideout. Hayes skillfully probed the behavior of the convicts and the reactions of each member of the family without letting up on the suspense. The play received the Antoinette Perry Award for the best play of the season, and the screenplay received the Edgar Allan Poe Award. Besides his suspense dramas—*The Hours After Midnight* (1958) is another—Hayes has written comedies, short stories for national magazines, and novels and plays in collaboration with his wife, Marrijane Hayes (1919—   ). These include *Bon Voyage* (1956), and a number of one- and three-act plays for high school and college production.

Hayes, Rutherford B[irchard] (b. Delaware, Ohio, Oct. 4, 1822—d. Jan. 17, 1893), lawyer, governor, 19th President. Hayes practiced law in Ohio, was city solicitor of Cincinnati, served in the Northern Army during the Civil War. He was elected to the House of Representatives, became governor of Ohio, and ran for President in 1876 against SAMUEL J. TILDEN. The election was not decisive, but was finally decided in favor of Hayes by a commission of Supreme Court Justices, Senators, and Representatives, although Tilden had actually received a majority of popular votes. Hayes' chief actions in office were to withdraw troops from three southern states, to clean up scandalous conditions in the New York Customs House, and to resume specie payments. He appears as "Old Granite" in Henry Adams' anonymously published novel of life in Washington, DEMOCRACY (1880). Harry Barnard has written *Rutherford B. Hayes and His America* (1954).

Haymarket Square Riot. A clash between Chicago police and labor unionists on May 4, 1886, in which a bomb, thought to be thrown by anarchists, caused the death of seven policemen and wounded sixty-eight others. The arrest of eight anarchist leaders followed; although nothing could be proved, they were convicted of "constructive conspiracy to commit murder" and four of them were hanged; the others were imprisoned, and one committed suicide. The case caused widespread controversy, brought about a temporary setback to the labor union movement, and resulted in much adverse criticism of the judicial proceedings. A petition bearing the names of prominent persons all over the country led Governor JOHN PETER ALTGELD to pardon the three men still in jail. Among the petitioners was WILLIAM DEAN HOWELLS, who from that time began to take a strong interest in American social and political reforms. In 1907 Frank Harris visited Chicago to study the case, then wrote his novel *The Bomb* (1908), which is sympathetic to the convicted men.

Hayne, Paul Hamilton (b. Charleston, S.C., Jan. 1, 1830—d. July 6, 1886), poet, biographer, editor. From the beginning Hayne was destined for a literary career, although he made an attempt to study law; he began contributing to the *Southern Literary Messenger,* joined the

staff of the *Southern Literary Gazette,* and by 1855 had written enough verse for a collection, *Poems.* This was followed by *Sonnets and Other Poems* (1857) and *Avolio: A Legend of the Island of Cos* (1860). In 1857 Hayne founded

Russell's Magazine, named after Russell's Bookstore in Charleston, a gathering place for young men of literary ambition, including HENRY TIMROD. The magazine was terminated with the coming of the Civil War, in which Hayne saw only limited service. But his ardent patriotism expressed itself in a group of fervent poems, such as *The Battle of Charleston Harbor.* During Sherman's "march to the sea" Hayne's mansion was destroyed, and all he had left was a small piece of ground on the Savannah River in the pines of Georgia. There, after the war, Hayne lived with his family, making his livelihood entirely from his writings. He published *Legends and Lyrics* (1872); *The Mountain of the Lovers* (1875); *Lives of Robert Young Hayne and Hugh Swinton Legaré* (1878); *The Broken Battalions* (1885); and he edited the *Poems* of his friend Timrod (1873), with a sketch of his life. All through his later years he maintained an active correspondence with literary men and women in both the North and the South. Some of his letters have been collected by Daniel M. McKeithan, Charles Duffy, Aubrey H. Starke, Jay B. Hubbell, J. DeLancey Ferguson, and Rufus A. Coleman. Hayne's poetry is notable chiefly for its landscapes of the South, as in *Aspects of the Pines* and *The Cottage on the Hill.* His craftsmanship is marred by a tendency toward diffuseness.

Hazard, Ebenezer (b. Philadelphia, Jan. 15, 1744—d. June 13, 1817), public official, his-

torian. Closely associated with JEREMY BEL-
KNAP, early American historian, Hazard made
it his business to collect material likely to
be of use to future chroniclers. As surveyor of
post roads and later postmaster-general, Hazard
became well acquainted with places and conditions all over the colonies. He copied many documents and had it in mind to publish a documentary history of the Revolution. Congress gave
him permission to make copies of its own
papers and voted him £ 1,000 for expenses; apparently he never drew on the money and never
published the history. He finally issued two
volumes of *Historical Collections, State Papers,
and Other Authentic Documents* (1792, 1794),
which have been useful as source materials.

Hazard, Shepherd Tom [**Thomas Robinson**]
(b. S. Kingstown, R.I., Jan. 3, 1797—d. March
26, 1886), sheep-farmer, manufacturer, spiritualist, reformer, folklorist, humorist. Having
made a fortune, after a life of great hardship,
Shepherd Tom made it his business to denounce
Puritanism at every turn, to do his best to communicate with the next world, to lend his help
to worthy causes (such as better asylums for
the insane), to collect all the tall tales he heard
throughout Rhode Island. He was a writer as
well, noted for his extraordinarily long parentheses. Among his books: *Recollections of Olden
Times* (1879); *The Jonny-Cake Letters* (1882);
Miscellaneous Essays and Letters (1883). In
1915 appeared *The Jonny-Cake Letters of "Shepherd Tom."*

Hazard of New Fortunes, A (1890), a novel
by WILLIAM DEAN HOWELLS. This is the longest of Howells' works. The plot involves the relationship of a rich man, Dryfoos, to the magazine he has casually bought and also the difficulties he and his family encounter, after becoming suddenly wealthy, in scaling the social
barriers of New York. Basil March, who had
already appeared in THEIR WEDDING JOURNEY
(1871), is made the editor of the magazine; he
resigns rather than discharge a freespoken radical from his staff. Dryfoos' son Conrad turns
radical, and both he and the outspoken staff
member die from injuries received in a labor
riot. The book is one of Howells' most thoughtful commentaries on modern social and economic problems.

Hazel Kirke (1880), a play by STEELE MAC-
KAYE (1842–1894). Hazel, against the wishes
of her father, an English miller, refuses to marry
Squire Rodney, runs off instead with Carringford, who is really a lord. The latter's mother,
bitterly opposed, tells Hazel her marriage to
Carringford isn't legal, and Hazel tries to drown
herself. She is rescued by her husband and all
ends happily. The play was a revision of an
earlier one by MacKaye, *An Iron Will* (1879).
It had a consecutive run of about two years in
New York, was constantly revived for more than
thirty years, and was produced frequently
abroad.

Hazeltine, Mayo Williamson (b. Boston, April
24, 1841—d. Sept. 14, 1909), lawyer, newspaperman, book reviewer. Hazeltine had the

opportunity of practicing law, but preferred
literary criticism. He reviewed thousands of
books for the New York *Sun.* He was perhaps
the first to introduce the works of Joseph Conrad to the American public. He published *Chats
About Books* (1883).

Hazlitt, Henry (b. Philadelphia, Nov. 28,
1894—   ), newspaperman, editor, critic, authority on finance and economics. Hazlitt has
served on the staffs of various New York papers
and magazines, and began writing a regular
feature, "Business Tides," for *Newsweek* in
1946. His books are noted for their clear presentation of frequently abstruse topics. Among
them: *Thinking as a Science* (1916); *The
Anatomy of Criticism* (1933); *Economics in
One Lesson* (1946); *The Great Idea* (1951);
The Free Man's Library (1956); *The Failure
of the "New Economics": An Analysis of Keynesian Fallacies* (1959); *What you Should Know
About Inflation* (1960).

H.D. Pen name of HILDA DOOLITTLE.

Head, Sir Edmund Walker (b. England,
1805—d. Jan. 28, 1868), Canadian official,
poet, translator, art critic. Walker became
prominent first in New Brunswick, where he
was poor-law commissioner and then governor.
He was made Governor-General of Canada
(1854–61), then retired to England. He was
noted as a linguist, with special facility in German and Icelandic; he made translations from
both languages, among them *The Story of Viga
Glum* (1866). He wrote a *Handbook of Painting of the German, Dutch, Spanish, and French
Schools* (1848) and gathered his verses in
Ballads and Other Poems (1868).

Headless Horseman, The. See BROM BONES.

Headsman, The (1833), a novel by JAMES
FENIMORE COOPER. This is the third novel in
a series that began with THE BRAVO (1831)
and THE HEIDENMAUER (1832), the whole
being an expression of some of Cooper's political views. The scene is Switzerland, and Cooper,
following his long-continued attack on feudal
society and aristocratic traditions, shows the
folly of a custom that the son of a headsman
must follow his father's vocation. The horror
felt toward an executioner and his family is
skillfully described, but Cooper spoils his social
idea by letting the plot develop along absurdly
conventional lines—the executioner's son turns
out to be really the son of the Doge of Genoa.

Heald, Henry (1779–[?]), surveyor, letter-
writer. Heald made a trip with two others into
the unbroken West, ending his journey in Illinois.
The letters he wrote home were so vivid and
entertaining that they were printed as *A Western Tour in a Series of Letters* (1819).

Hearn, [Patricio] Lafcadio [Tessima Carlos]
(b. in the Ionian Islands, June 27, 1850—d.
Sept. 26, 1904), journalist, novelist, travel
writer, teacher. The son of a British army
surgeon who was of English, Irish, and Gypsy
ancestry, Hearn was born on the Greek island
of Santa Maura, in ancient times called Leucadia
(the source of his given name). His mother was
Greek, probably with a strain of Arabic and

Moorish blood. In 1852, his father was ordered to the West Indies while Hearn and his mother were left with relatives in Dublin. His mother soon abandoned him to an aunt, who placed the boy in St. Cuthbert's College to study for the

priesthood. Here he suffered the loss of his left eye. A lover of books, he overstrained his other eye, which swelled to twice its normal size. Hearn's biographers account for the eccentricities of his later character by ascribing to him an inferiority complex derived from what he considered his "repulsive" appearance. Hearn was withdrawn from St. Cuthbert's for financial reasons, and later he ran away from a Jesuit school in France.

Hearn's aunt, tired of his escapades, at last paid his passage to the United States, where he arrived, penniless and friendless, in 1869. He went to Cincinnati, Ohio, where he obtained work as an assistant in the public library, but he was dismissed for reading the books that he should have been dispensing to others. He had various other jobs before he found work as a feature writer for the Cincinnati *Enquirer,* to which he contributed much vivid writing, notably a macabre description of the charred body of a murder victim. At this time Hearn formed a liaison with a mulatto woman who had been kind to him. When he applied for a license to marry her he was rebuffed on the grounds of an Ohio law forbidding miscegenation. There is evidence of an unsanctioned ceremony; at any rate, Hearn lived with her for some time and as a result lost his job with the *Enquirer.* Shortly afterwards the editors of a rival paper, the *Commercial,* hired him.

In the course of his Cincinnati days Hearn

read assiduously, especially the mid-century French authors, Baudelaire, Flaubert, Gautier. He made a careful translation of Gautier's *Avatar.* Though he later destroyed the manuscript, the work of translating probably had a good deal to do with sharpening and polishing the cameo delicacy of his own literary style.

In 1877 Hearn was sent to New Orleans to write a series of articles for the *Commercial* on Louisiana politics. He neglected to do the political articles, and spent his time observing romantic haunts and writing colorful descriptions of the sights. As a result the *Commercial* fired him. One of his biographers has described him during this period: "He was only five feet three inches tall; the peajacket he affected was much too large and his very low collar with its black string tie much too big, giving him the appearance of a miniature but serious minded scarecrow." In addition he was no doubt hungry: for seven months he nearly starved in New Orleans. Employed at last by the New Orleans *Item,* he did much miscellaneous writing for his new editors—features, editorials, book reviews, a series of ephemeral sketches called *Fantastics.* Later he went to work for the New Orleans *Times-Democrat,* where he was a well-paid writer and was given a free hand; he devoted most of his time to translations from Spanish and French literature, which the paper apparently welcomed. His first book, *One of Cleopatra's Nights* (1882), is a translation of six of Gautier's stories. His second book, *Stray Leaves from Strange Literatures* (1884), was a collection of articles based on out-of-the-way legends and stories from many sources. His work was now well enough known to gain him admittance to the pages of eastern magazines, notably the *Century* and *Harper's Weekly.*

Though he had never been in China, he published *Some Chinese Ghosts* (1887), a series of Oriental legends. His first important novel was CHITA (1889), a beautifully moving tale of Last Island, which lies off the coast of Louisiana. The story centers on the plight of a young girl who is the last survivor of a tidal wave. In 1887 Hearn obtained a commission from *Harper's* to write a series of articles on the West Indies, and he spent the following two years in the Caribbean. Out of his experience came a travel book, *Two Years in the French West Indies* (1890), and a novel, YOUMA (1890). The latter is a story of a slave insurrection and one of the most original works in 19th-century American fiction. In 1889 Hearn returned to New York and Philadelphia, where he wrote *Karma,* one of his least successful books.

Harper's now commissioned Hearn to write a series of articles on Japan. He sailed in the spring of 1890, intending to return in a year or two. He never came back. He quickly severed his relationship with *Harper's,* quarreling with the editors over the question of relative payment for him and for an illustrator who accompanied him (the unprintable letter he wrote to *Harper's* was kept in the publishing office for a number of years as a curiosity), and he was forced to resort to free-lancing to earn a living. He had the good fortune to become friends with Capt. Mitchell McDonald, paymaster of the United States Navy in Yokohama. McDonald, who recognized and admired Hearn's genius, helped the writer to organize his financial affairs and to obtain a teaching position at a normal school in Matsue. There Hearn married Setsuko Koizumi, the daughter of a Japanese Samurai family. It was a happy marriage, bringing him a stability and serenity he had never known, as well as the only real home he had ever had. Mrs. Hearn bore him three sons and a daughter, and Hearn, to avoid legal difficulties, adopted his wife's family name. He also became a Buddhist. He found, however, that in marrying a woman of the Samurai class he had assumed the responsibility for more than a dozen of her kinsmen, including her tyrannical, eighty-year-old grandfather. Hearn's oldest son has written an amusing account of this period in his father's life. For the last ten years of his life Hearn supported his family by lecturing on English literature at the Imperial University of Tokyo.

Hearn wrote hundreds of letters, scores of articles, and more than a dozen books about Japanese life. His viewpoint shifted from his first eager acceptance to bewilderment and finally to disillusionment; at the end he lamented the passing of old Japanese ways and the coming of a new militaristic nationalism—he was one of the first to see the danger of a coming struggle between Japan and the West. GLIMPSES OF UNFAMILIAR JAPAN (1894) expresses the captivating charm of the land and its people. His last book on the subject, *Japan: An Attempt at Interpretation* (1904), is a much more sober analysis and perhaps the best book of his last period. In the same year he made plans to return to the United States, but before he could arrange the trip he died of a heart attack in Tokyo.

Hearn's other books on Japan afford a comprehensive view of their customs and culture, religion and folklore, drama and poetry. Among them: *Kokoro* (1896); *Gleanings in Buddha Fields* (1897); *Exotics and Retrospectives* (1898); *In Ghostly Japan* (1899); *Shadowings* (1900); *Kwaidan* (1904); and the posthumous *Romance of the Milky Way* (1905). See CHITA.

Hearn was a writer who combined the *fin-de-siècle* love of the exquisite with a touch of primitive vigor that led him to strange places and gave his writing a hardness that that of his British contemporaries often lacked. Elizabeth Bisland published his *Life and Letters* in 1906, his *Japanese Letters* in 1910. Nina H. Kennard wrote another biography (1911), and Edward L. Tinker described *Lafcadio Hearn's American Days* (1924; rev., 1925). The standard biography is by Vera McWilliams (1946); more recent is Elizabeth Stevenson's (1961). A bibliography prepared by P. D. and Ione Perkins (1934) lacks much newly discovered material from Japan. Hearn's wife, Setsuko Koizumi, wrote *Reminiscences* of her husband (1918), and his

son Kazuo Koizumi wrote *My Father and I: Memories of Lafcadio Hearn* (1935).

ELDON C. HILL

Hearst, William Randolph (b. San Francisco, April 29, 1863—d. Aug. 14, 1951), newspaper and magazine publisher. Hearst began his career on the San Francisco *Daily Examiner* (1887) and made it a financial success. He bought the New York *Morning Journal* (1895) and in active competition with JOSEPH PULITZER developed a sensational type of newspaper, characterized by what its opponents called "yellow journalism," that proved very popular. In 1900 he bought the Chicago *American,* in 1904 the Boston *American.* Thereafter he became owner of the largest newspaper combine in the United States. He served in Congress (1903–07), sought the governorship of New York (unsuccessfully), acquired a group of magazines (including COSMOPOLITAN and GOOD HOUSEKEEPING), bought large properties in Mexico. In World War I he opposed the United States participation; in later years attacked communism. John K. Winkler has written two books on Hearst, *Hearst: An American Phenomenon* (1928) and *W. R. Hearst: A New Appraisal* (1955). Other books about him include *Hearst, Lord of San Simeon* (1936), by Oliver Carlson and E. S. Bates, and John Tebbel's rather journalistic *The Life and Good Times of William Randolph Hearst* (1952). W. A. Swanberg's *Citizen Hearst* (1961) is considered definitive. Hearst's life is thought to have suggested Orson Welles' film *Citizen Kane* (1940).

Hearth and Home. A magazine founded in 1868. Among its editors were Donald G. Mitchell, HARRIET BEECHER STOWE, FRANK R. STOCKTON, MARY MAPES DODGE. Aimed at first at a rural audience, the magazine went into financial decline and was rescued by EDWARD EGGLESTON, its literary editor, who contributed to it his famous novel THE HOOSIER SCHOOLMASTER (1870–71). The magazine enjoyed an immediate increase in circulation. It ceased publication, however, in 1875.

Heart Is a Lonely Hunter, The (1940), a novel by CARSON McCULLERS. The story of a deaf-mute in a small southern town, this novel has been highly praised by critics as the work of a thoroughly skilled writer.

Heart of Maryland, The (1895), a Civil War play by DAVID BELASCO. This play was inspired by Rose Hartwick Thorpe's poem CURFEW MUST NOT RING TONIGHT! (1870). Belasco visited Maryland and made good use of realistic details in his background. The heroine, Maryland Calvert, falls in love with a northern officer, and when he is condemned to die and his execution is scheduled for the time of the curfew bell, she seizes the bell's clapper and swings out from the tower in a successful stratagem to stop his execution. The play was Belasco's first great success.

Hearts and Flowers (1899), a tune by Theodore Moses Tobani (1855–1933). The composer claimed a sale of 23 million copies—according to Sigmund Spaeth, either an outrageous exaggeration or a world's record. The title has become a synonym for sticky sentimentality.

Hearts of Oak (1879), an adaptation of an English melodrama, H. L. Leslie's *The Mariner's Compass* (1865), by DAVID BELASCO and J. A. HERNE. The adaptation was made without Leslie's consent, but he did not succeed in stopping the production of the play nor in being allowed to call his own play *Hearts of Oak*. Herne later bought all rights to the play, and he and his wife appeared in it many times. (See SAG HARBOR.)

Heath, James Ewell (b. Northumberland Co., Va., July 8, 1792—d. June 28, 1862), public official, novelist, playwright. Heath held various state and national posts. He had a great interest in literary matters, was an adviser for the SOUTHERN LITERARY MESSENGER, and interceded in Poe's behalf with the publisher of that magazine. Both he and the publisher concurred, however, in rejecting *The Fall of the House of Usher*. Heath himself, so far as we know, wrote only two books: *Edge-Hill, or, The Family of the Fitzroyals* (1828), a story of plantation life; and *Whigs and Democrats, or, Love of No Politics* (1839), a clever play that is a satire on rural elections in Virginia. The play was produced and published anonymously.

Heathen Chinee, The. The name popularly given to Bret Harte's humorous poem PLAIN LANGUAGE FROM TRUTHFUL JAMES (1870).

Heathen Days (1943), reminiscences by H. L. Mencken. See DAYS OF H. L. MENCKEN.

Heaven Will Protect the Working Girl (1909), a satirical song by Edgar [McPhail] Smith (1857–1938), with music by A. Baldwin Sloane. Sigmund Spaeth says the basis for the tune of the chorus was Stanley Carter's [Harry B. Berdan's] *She Was Bred in Old Kentucky* (1898). The lyric was first sung by Marie Dressler in *Tillie's Nightmare*, and immediately became a folksong, especially the lines, "You may fool the upper classes with your villainous demi-tasses,/ But heaven will protect the working girl."

Hecht, Ben (b. N.Y.C., Feb. 28, 1893—d. Apr. 18, 1964), dramatist, journalist, novelist. Hecht began writing for the Chicago *News* and lived in Chicago during its "literary renaissance," (1911–30) in which he took part, publishing stories in the *Little Review* and *Smart Set*. His first novel, *Erik Dorn* (1921) made use of his experiences as Berlin reporter for the *News* (1918–19); it is the story of a jaded intellectual who throws over both wife and mistress for the excitement of European revolution. He returns, shoots his mistress' new lover in self-defense and finds that his wife no longer wants him. The novel caused a great deal of furor, and shows influences of Huysmans, whom Hecht admired. He left the *News* in 1923 to begin his own paper—the *Literary Times*. He published more novels: *Gargoyles* (1922); *Fan-*

tazius Mallare (1923); *Count Bruga* (1926); *A Jew in Love* (1930); the latter two are lampoons of MAXWELL BODENHEIM, who had drawn a rather unflattering portrait of Hecht in *Ninth Avenue* (1926). Thirty-two years later Hecht wrote a play about Bodenheim: *Winkelberg* (1958). His short stories are considered much better; *A Thousand and One Afternoons in Chicago* (1922) and *Tales of Chicago Streets* (1924) were early collections, and many are gathered in *The Collected Stories of Ben Hecht* (1945).

He collaborated with Charles MacArthur on two plays: *The Front Page* (1928); *Twentieth Century* (1933), both made into successful films. They also wrote the scenario for *Wuthering Heights* (1939). *Spectre of the Rose* (1946), Hecht's most original scenario, is about a ballet dancer who commits suicide. He was very active in Hollywood during this period; *Notorious* (1946) and *A Flag is Born* (1946) are typical Hecht pictures.

He publicly analyzed himself in *A Guide for the Bedeviled* (1944), then bitterly attacked anti-Semitism and advocated an extreme form of Zionism at the time Israel was being formed. *Perfidy* (1961) was a study of Israel. His autobiography, *A Child of the Century* (1954), was thoroughly frank and amusing.

Heckewelder, John Gottlieb [Ernestus] (b. England, 1743—d. 1823), missionary, authority on American Indians. Heckewelder came to America as a boy, became a Moravian missionary to the Indians of Ohio and interested himself in other settlements nearer the Atlantic seaboard. With other Moravian missionaries he succeeded in converting a considerable number of Delawares and Mohegans. He became very fond of them, whereas he felt a strong antagonism to their traditional enemies, the Iroquois. This partiality appears strongly in his *Account of the History, Manners, and Customs of the Indian Nations of Pennsylvania and the Neighboring States* (1822). The book had an important literary influence. First of all it captured Cooper's imagination, and on it he based his attitude toward Indian tribes, as manifested in THE LAST OF THE MOHICANS (1826) and the later books in the LEATHER-STOCKING TALES. He also borrowed many factual details and the name Chingachgook. When he was in college Longfellow read the book and was greatly impressed by it; his *Song of Hiawatha* (1855) shows its influence (see HIAWATHA). The book has often been attacked for its partisanship, however, by those well acquainted with the actual qualities of the various Indian tribes.

Hedge, [Frederic] Henry (b. Cambridge, Mass., Dec. 12, 1805—d. Aug. 21, 1890), clergyman, poet, translator, editor, teacher. Hedge was an infant prodigy, memorized Virgil at seven. At thirteen, in the company of GEORGE BANCROFT, he went to Germany, which became the home of his mind. He became facile in German and was initiated into the realm of German idealism, which he was the first to introduce authoritatively in America. He returned to take a degree at Harvard, went on to four years in the Divinity School, became a Unitarian clergyman. In March, 1833, he wrote an article on Coleridge for the *Christian Examiner*, which he later described as "the *first word*, so far as I know, which any American had uttered in respectful recognition of the claims of transcendentalism." He knew Kant, Hegel, and Schelling at first hand; he was a transcendentalist of a sober sort, with no romantic ecstasies; he remained a conservative and a churchman, espousing idealism as a creed which taught both love and duty. Yet he was firm in his views, and when he was told that the facts were against him, he said, "So much the worse for the facts." He saw transcendentalism as a social philosophy, giving a viewpoint on institutions, and anticipated Emerson's AMERICAN SCHOLAR (1837). On September 16, 1836, was founded the Transcendental Club, often called the Hedge Club—perhaps because it met only when Hedge was in town. Hedge wrote numerous books, including *Conservatism and Reform* (1843); *Prose Writers of Germany* (1848); *Ways of the Spirit and Other Essays* (1877); *Atheism in Philosophy* (1884); *Martin Luther and Other Essays* (1888). Perry Miller calls his *Reason in Religion* (1865) "perhaps the classic statement of transcendentalized religion." He wrote one greatly admired poem, called *Questionings* when it first appeared in the *Dial* (January, 1841), later renamed *The Idealist*—a combination of Kant and Emerson. See TRANSCENDENTALISM.

Hegan, Alice. See ALICE HEGAN RICE.

Heggen, Thomas [Orlo] (b. Fort Dodge, Iowa, Dec. 23, 1919—d. May 19, 1949), novelist. Heggen left the staff of the *Reader's Digest* to serve five years in the Navy during World War II, mainly on sea duty in the Pacific. Then he returned to the *Digest*. Using his experiences as a basis he wrote *Mister Roberts* (1946), which sold more than a million copies in its original form, many hundreds of thousands more as a Pocket Book; it was adapted for the stage by Joshua Logan (1948), and was also filmed. It is an uninhibited, uncensored depiction of the boredom of the men on a Navy cargo carrier during the war. The captain, universally detested, is known as "Stupid," whereas everyone likes Mr. Roberts, the cargo officer. The book veers later from satire and ribaldry to pathos and the heroic.

Heidenmauer, The (1832), a novel by JAMES FENIMORE COOPER. The second of three novels that express Cooper's ideas on government. It succeeded THE BRAVO (1831) and was followed by THE HEADSMAN (1833). The scene is the Palatinate in the 16th century, and the plot turns on the conflict between the dominant Benedictine order and the increasing strength of Lutheranism.

Heilprin, Angelo (b. Hungary, March 31, 1853—d. July 17, 1907), geologist, explorer, author, painter, inventor. The son of Michael Heilprin (1823–1888), a noted Hebrew scholar who brought him to this country when the son

was three years old, Heilprin studied in England under eminent scientists, on his return explored the Florida Everglades, Mexico, Bermuda. He joined the staff of two Philadelphia institutions for the study of science in 1890, with the rank of professor and curator, but resigned to continue his exploration: with Peary in the Arctic, in North Africa, in Alaska, on Mount Pelée, along the Orinoco River. He published numerous technical books on geology and paleontology, also some more general writings. Among these were *Explorations on the West Coast of Florida* (1887); *The Animal Life of Our Seashore* (1888); *The Geological Evidence of Evolution* (1888); *The Bermuda Islands* (1889); *The Arctic Problem and Narrative of the Peary Expedition* (1893); *The Earth and Its Story* (1896); *Alaska and the Klondike* (1899); *Mont Pelée and the Tragedy of Martinique* (1903).

Heinlein, Robert A. ["Anson MacDonald"] (b. Butler, Mo., July 7, 1907—   ), novelist, author of science fiction and nonfiction, TV and screen writer. A prodigious writer, Heinlein has been called the dean of science fiction writers. He was graduated from Annapolis in 1929, did advanced study in mathematics and physics at U.C.L.A. graduate school, and wrote his first story in 1939. His fertile imagination was the source for many of the major themes in science fiction writing. A story about nuclear fission, written while the Manhattan Project was still a secret, had to be suppressed because of its too advanced ideas. Many of his novels written for juvenile audiences received reviews recommending them to adults as well. They were usually published simultaneously in French, German, and Italian, and often in other languages, so that they number over a hundred editions in twenty-eight foreign languages.

Heinlein's novels, even when stylistically flawed, are so original in conception that they rarely fail to hold the reader's attention. Some of his books: *The Green Hills of Earth* (1951), short stories; *The Puppet Masters* (1951); *Rocket Ship Galileo*, which was made into the movie *Destination Moon* under the author's technical supervision; *The Door Into Summer* (1957); *The Menace From Earth* (1960).

Heiress, The (1947), a play by Ruth and Augustus Goetz, based on Henry James' novel WASHINGTON SQUARE (1880). It was warmly praised by critics, had a long run, and was adapted for the screen in 1949 by the same authors.

Helburn, Theresa (b. New York City, Jan. 12, 1887[?]—d. Aug. 18, 1959), director, producer, writer. Always deeply interested in the drama, Miss Helburn became a student in G. P. BAKER's "English 47" at Radcliffe, came to New York and published some stories and verse, tried to become an actress but was dissuaded by her family, wrote some plays and dramatizations. In 1919 she found a career when she became associated with the Theatre Guild. In that year she became its executive director, then in 1933 its administrative head. Along with LAWRENCE

LANGNER she was responsible for many of the great hits of that organization. She and Langner produced *Oklahoma!* (1943); *Jacobowsky and the Colonel* (1944); *Carousel* (1945); *Come Back Little Sheba* (1950).

Held, John, Jr. (b. Salt Lake City, Utah, Jan. 10, 1889—d. March 2, 1958), cartoonist, artist. Held began his career as a cartoonist, went on to more serious work, but was always noted for his effective satire, especially of the flapper era. His collections include: *Grim Youth* (1930); *Saga of Frankie and Johnny* (1931); *Women Are Necessary* (1931); *The Flesh Is Weak* (1932); *The Works of John Held, Jr.* (1932); *A Bowl of Cherries* (1933); *Crosstown* (1934).

Held by the Enemy (1886), a Civil War play by WILLIAM GILLETTE. The action takes place in a southern city captured by northern forces. Eunice McCreery, a southern girl, is betrothed to a Confederate lieutenant, but two northern officers are also in love with her. The plot becomes complicated when the lieutenant enters the city as a spy. When he is tried, the two northerners are in direct conflict as to whether he shall be saved. Then the Confederate is wounded and apparently killed; and once more Gillette manages some striking scenes. A. H. Quinn calls this play "the first important drama of the Civil War."

Helen of Troy, The Private Life of. See PRIVATE LIFE OF HELEN OF TROY, THE.

Helicon Hall [Helicon Home Colony]. An experiment in community living which UPTON SINCLAIR founded near Englewood, N.J., and in which he invested his royalties from *The Jungle* (1906). Among the literary rebels who joined him was SINCLAIR LEWIS, who is said to have served as a somewhat indifferent janitor. Everyone worked, and outsiders who had to be called in to do this or that job were treated as equals. Prominent persons, including William James and John Dewey, visited the colony, but to the reporters it became merely a "free-love nest." A fire of mysterious origin burned the Hall to the ground in 1907, and the project was abandoned. Sinclair described his ideals for the colony in an article in *The Independent* (June 14, 1906).

Hell-Bent for Heaven (1924), a play by HATCHER HUGHES. This Pulitzer Prize-winning play is set in the North Carolina mountains; the central character is a religious fanatic, "hell-bent for heaven," who is adept in using a religious camouflage to cloak his selfish desires. He is in love with Jude Lowry, who is engaged to marry Sid Hunt, just returning from service overseas in World War I. To prevent the marriage the fanatic employs all means, mostly foul, including a declaration of love in religious symbols. He is, however, permitted to escape, to save "a run-in with the sheriff." The play adroitly mingles comedy and realism.

Hell-Fire Club, The. Actually this was a group called "the Couranteers," informally assembled by JAMES FRANKLIN to contribute to his magazine, the NEW-ENGLAND COURANT (founded Aug. 14, 1721). They attacked the MATHER family savagely, and in return the

Mathers gave the group this nickname, implying a resemblance to the Hell-Fire Clubs of London in the early 18th century—groups of reckless and dissolute young men who made the streets of London a peril and a nuisance. The contributors to the *Courant* imitated the *Spectator* papers, but not too successfully. Only occasionally is the material of native content.

Hellinger, Mark (b. New York City, March 21, 1903—d. Dec. 21, 1947), newspaperman, columnist, movie producer. A prodigious worker, Hellinger crowded several careers into his short lifetime. He wrote for the *Daily Mirror*, was a syndicated columnist for King Features who eventually produced an entire feature page of mainly sentimental gossip and stories. Then he went to Hollywood and became an ace producer; he was a specialist in screen violence. Among his movie successes were THE KILLERS (1946), based on the Ernest Hemingway story, and *The Naked City* (1948). He wrote *Moon Over Broadway* (1931), *The Ten Million* (1934), and *I Meet a Lot of People* (1940). A Broadway theater was renamed in his honor.

Hellman, George S[idney] (b. New York City, Nov. 14, 1878—d. July 16, 1958), editor, author, critic. Active in various public causes related to art and letters, Hellman became a particular student of Washington Irving. He collected his letters and other material, published a two-volume collection of letters (1915) and a biography (1925). He also wrote numerous essays, a collection of verse (1909), a play called *Esther* (1917), studies of R. L. Stevenson (1925) and Justice Benjamin Cardozo (1940), and other volumes. His Irving collection is now in the New York Public Library. His son **Geoffrey T[heodore] Hellman** (b. New York City, Feb. 13, 1907—   ), a member of the staff of *The New Yorker*, has written numerous Profiles for that weekly.

Hellman, Lillian (b. New Orleans, June 20, 1905—   ), playwright. For a time a play-reader and book reviewer, Miss Hellman took to writing plays herself; her first performed work was THE CHILDREN'S HOUR (1934), based on an obscure Scottish scandal. She went on to many remarkable plays: THE LITTLE FOXES (1939); THE WATCH ON THE RHINE (1941); *The Searching Wind* (1944); *Another Part of the Forest* (1946); *The Autumn Garden* (1951); the book for a musical adaptation of Voltaire's *Candide* (1955); *Toys in the Attic* (1960). *The Little Foxes* was made into a very popular movie by Miss Hellman in 1940, and in 1949 it became the basis for a musical drama by Marc Blitzstein called *Regina*. Many of Miss Hellman's other dramas have been made into screenplays. All of the dramas are noted for their intensity of psychological conflict and the demonic motivations of their characters.

Helper, Hinton Rowan (b. Davie Co., N.C., Dec. 27, 1829—d. March 8, 1909), memoirist, crusader. One of the most influential writers of the ante-bellum era, Helper is now almost forgotten. He was a southerner devoted to the South, brought up on a plantation run by slave labor. He worked at miscellaneous jobs in his early years; in 1849 he went to California and didn't like what he saw there, as he told in *Land of Gold: Reality vs. Fiction* (1855). This book discussed what was to become the first and greatest of his causes: free labor. But the publisher deleted the passages on this topic.

Helper began doing research work in the South for a book that was to create an immense sensation, *The Impending Crisis of the South: How to Meet It*, which he finally published at his own expense in 1857. The book had a simple thesis: the South was economically and culturally far behind the North because of its slave labor. Make slavery impossible by taxing it out of existence, said Helper, and send all black men back to Africa. The South, he added, is "fast sinking into a state of comparative imbecility and obscurity," filled with "illiterate chevaliers of bowie-knives and pistols." He denounced the authors, clergymen, and politicians of the South in unmeasured language. As a result it became illegal in most parts of the South to own the book. In the North, on the contrary, the book was an immediate success; it is believed that it went through 114 printings, in addition to a pamphlet summary produced and circulated by the Republicans.

In 1861 Helper was made a consul at Buenos Aires. On his return he published three books denouncing Negroes and all colored races as inferior and urging their deportation; one was called *The Negroes in Negroland* (1868). He also urged a project for a great north and south intercontinental railroad: *The Three Americas Railway* (1881).

Helton, Roy [Addison] (b. April 3, 1886—), poet. Helton's verse has been collected in *Youth's Pilgrimage* (1914); *Outcasts in Beulah Land and Other Poems* (1918); *Lonesome Water* (1930); *Come Back to Earth* (1946). Critics have felt that Helton's fine gift of melody and description shows to greatest advantage in his earlier poems.

Hemingway, Ernest [Miller] (b. Oak Park, Ill., July 21, 1899—d. July 2, 1961), novelist, short-story writer. The son of a doctor, Clarence Edmonds Hemingway, known for his devotion to hunting and fishing, and of Grace Hall Hemingway, whose interests were musical and religious, Hemingway made an unusual combination of these outdoor and indoor interests in his life and career. Educated at the local public schools, he was particularly active at Oak Park High, where he played football and began writing news columns, chiefly in imitation of Ring Lardner. He also wrote some light verse and several short stories, a few of which contain hints of the style he was later to make famous. He spent many summers on Walloon Lake in upper Michigan, where he was later to set several of his better-known short stories. He decided against college, and went to Kansas City after graduation from high school. There he found employment on the Kansas City *Star*, then one of the country's leading newspapers, and received valuable training for his eventual

career. He was repeatedly rejected by the army, but finally was able to get into the war as an ambulance driver, and was very severely wounded at Fossalta di Piave, Italy, just before his nineteenth birthday. He was decorated by

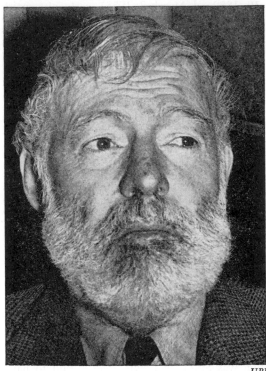

UPI

the Italians for heroism, and after hospitalization in Milan he served with the Italian infantry until the Armistice.

Following a period of recuperation in northern Michigan and employment as a foreign correspondent for the Toronto *Star*, Hemingway settled in Paris, determined, under the informal guidance of GERTRUDE STEIN, EZRA POUND, and others, to become a writer. Before long his stories, several of them reflecting his boyhood, were collected in a volume called *In Our Time* (1925) and began to attract excited attention for the attitudes and technique that were soon to become famous. His next published work was a "satirical novel," THE TORRENTS OF SPRING (1926), a parody of Sherwood Anderson, who had exerted an early influence on him. Although highly amusing to those familiar with Anderson's manner, the book was written in haste and is not of primary significance. But *The Sun Also Rises*, published in the same year, made his reputation and set him, at the age of twenty-six, in the limelight which he both enjoyed and resented for the rest of his life.

Public attention was often attached to Hemingway for extraliterary reasons. His first three marriages—to Hadley Richardson, the mother of his first son; to Pauline Pfeiffer, mother of his second and third boys; and to MARTHA GELL-

HORN, the novelist—all ended in divorce. His fourth wife was the former Mary Welsh of Minnesota, whom he met in England in 1944, and who remained with him until his death. Widely traveled, Hemingway lived for extended periods in Spain and Africa, and for most of the 1930's in Key West, Florida; he was frequently as much identified with sporting and fighting activities as with literature. In his prime he was an amateur boxer of some stature and a record-holding deep-sea fisherman, as well as an expert big-game hunter and a bullfight *aficionado*. He also fought informally in two wars, first on the Loyalist side in the Spanish Civil War, and then in World War II, particularly with the Fourth Division of the First Army, where, ostensibly a correspondent, he led a small, irregular, and colorful unit of his own in several battles in Europe. Following the war and further decoration, he settled more quietly on an elaborate farm or estate called Finca Vigía, at San Francisco de Paula, near Havana, Cuba, until the Castro revolution displaced him. He traveled once more to Spain to follow the bullfights, and finally settled in Ketchum, Idaho, near Sun Valley. Here, in very poor health, and following two periods of hospitalization in the Mayo Clinic, he died of a possibly self-inflicted gunshot wound, and here he is buried.

Despite a highly colorful, at times flamboyant, career, Hemingway will of course be remembered for his books, as soon as it is possible to separate them from the forceful, occasionally overriding personality of their author. He always considered himself primarily a writer, and he was deeply serious, dedicated, and hardworking. For many years he was probably the most famous American writer. His style, his attitudes, and some of his characters became widely recognized throughout the world. He was possibly the most influential writer of English prose in the first half of the twentieth century.

His first wholly mature and important work, IN OUR TIME, reveals at the start many of the qualities for which he was to become known. In this aspect almost a novel, the book particularly established, in a series of "chapters," a fragmentary but careful early biography of Nick Adams. This biography became the prototype for the boyhoods of most of his later, better-known protagonists. Most important, it recorded Nick's various exposures to a series of violent or otherwise upsetting experiences, beginning in Michigan and culminating with the wound he received in World War I. This was an event with far-reaching psychological and ideological implications; the "Hemingway hero," far from being the simple, wooden primitive he was often mistaken for, was in reality quite the reverse, an inordinately sensitive figure. The decision of the wounded Nick Adams that he had made a "separate peace" with the enemy and was not a "patriot" forecast a long estrangement from organized society for both the author and his typical protagonist.

THE SUN ALSO RISES presents this protagonist, now Jake Barnes, as having been wounded in the war in such a way as to make sexual experience impossible. Partly as a result, he is a member of the "lost generation," as Gertrude Stein termed it, which is represented in Paris by an international collection of entertaining but aimless expatriates, collected mainly about the novel's promiscuous heroine, Lady Brett Ashley. They are a miscellaneous group that includes Jake, an American newspaper correspondent; Robert Cohn and Bill Gorton, who are writers; Mike Campbell, whom Brett intends to marry when her divorce is final; and an unusual Greek count. The action involves considerable amounts of drinking, fishing, and going to the bullfights at a Spanish fiesta in Pamplona. Brett passes from Cohn to Romero, a young and gifted bullfighter whom she soon renounces for fear she will harm him, and finally she returns, hopelessly, to Jake. The fact that nothing really leads anywhere in the novel points to its central theme; the action comes full circle to imitate the sun which, as described in Ecclesiastes, also rises only to hasten to the place where it arose. An extraordinarily fresh and sparkling novel, it is scrupulously planned and executed, lively and entertaining. Its message is clearly that for these people, at least, life is futile, unavailing, and essentially empty.

Similarly successful and equally pessimistic was Hemingway's next novel, A FAREWELL TO ARMS (1929). Based on the sketch and the story that make up Chapter VI of IN OUR TIME, the novel presents the account of the unhappy adventures of Frederic Henry, an American lieutenant in the Italian ambulance service in World War I. After falling in love with an English nurse, Catherine Barkley, he is wounded and hospitalized in Milan, where he and Catherine are again together. Following his recuperation, he returns to his company, which is suffering badly from the war, in time for the disastrous retreat from Caporetto, in the course of which he is forced to desert in order to avoid a useless sacrifice of his life. He flees to Switzerland with Catherine, who is now pregnant with his child, and is left with nothing when she dies in childbirth. "If people bring so much courage to this world the world has to kill them to break them, so of course it kills them," the author says in comment. "The world breaks everyone and afterward many are strong at the broken places. But those that will not break it kills." Catherine is one of "the very good and the very gentle and the very brave" who are killed "impartially"; Henry, on the other hand, is broken at the end of the novel, and becomes strong only in a later appearance as the Hemingway protagonist under a different name.

Once again a cleanly and sparely written and impeccably constructed novel, it manages as few have done to fuse a war story with a love story by taking them in turn through subtly parallel stages of development. Incorporating a famous disillusionment with war—if not indeed, by extension, with modern society itself—the book is founded firmly on such moral values as belief in order, discipline, competence, and, most of all, love. But it is nonetheless a tragic, desperate novel which portrays mankind as biologically and socially trapped and doomed. It ranks with *The Sun Also Rises,* in general critical opinion, as his best novel.

These early triumphs were followed by a marked decline, for although Hemingway published regularly during the 1930's and continued to have a very wide following, none of his book-length efforts measured up to the high standard his work of the 1920's had set. First came two books of non-fiction, DEATH IN THE AFTERNOON (1932) and *Green Hills of Africa* (1935), which represent the author in escape from the society he had by implication renounced in *A Farewell to Arms.* The African book is an account of a big-game expedition, interspersed with numerous passages having to do with literature, Africa, and America, and punctuated by the author's repeated insistence that he has a right to do what he pleases where he pleases. The former book is about bullfighting in Spain, an activity to which Hemingway was long attracted—but more, he argued, as a tragic ritual in which the fighter is the high priest of a ceremonial, administering the death men seek to avoid, than as a sport. (Substantial extracts from a work on the same subject, called *The Dangerous Summer,* saw magazine publication in 1960.) A remarkably learned book for one to whose country the sport, or rite, is not native, it also contains some amusing conversations with an Old Lady and some excellent discussions of the problems of writing good prose. But it remains a minor work.

In 1937 Hemingway returned to Spain, then in the throes of civil war, as a reporter. During his visit he became ardently pro-Loyalist, and soon found himself involved in yet another "war for democracy." This fact had an important bearing, at first indirect, on his next three book-length works. A radical change in his attitudes began with the novel TO HAVE AND HAVE NOT (1937), which evidences entirely different notions about the society he had scrupulously been avoiding in his recent work. This is a "depression novel" in which the author is for the first time concerned with social problems. The story is about Harry Morgan, who, finding it impossible to earn an honest living for himself and his family, strikes out on his own as an outlaw, smuggling rum and Chinese nationals into Cuba. At the end he is killed, but not before learning that a man has no chance alone. This message, which has some appearance of having been tacked on to the novel's action, is consonant with the burden of Hemingway's next work, a play called THE FIFTH COLUMN (1938). The play was written in praise of the fighters with whom the author had associated in Madrid, and whose cause had become his own. It is the story of an American in Spain, a seemingly dissolute but attractive newspaperman who is in reality deeply involved in the war. Despite some good dialogue, the work has never been counted a success. The most remarkable thing about it is the distance

that Philip, the protagonist, has come since the days when his likeness, as Frederic Henry, said that he was "always embarrassed by the words sacred, glorious, and sacrifice and the expression in vain . . ." and that "abstract words such as glory, honor, courage, or hallow were obscene. . . ."

The best work that came out of Hemingway's reconversion to the world was his next novel, FOR WHOM THE BELL TOLLS (1940). The title, which refers to a devotion by John Donne, establishes the general theme of all men's involvement in mankind, as well as the more specific thesis that the loss of liberty anywhere reduces liberty everywhere. The novel, longest of Hemingway's works, deals with three days in the life of an American named Robert Jordan, who is fighting as a volunteer guerrilla in the Spanish civil war. It is his assignment to blow up a strategic bridge located near Segovia. As he awaits the event, he falls in love with the daughter of a Republican mayor, María. Their affair is promoted by a powerful woman named Pilar, who is in reality the leader of the little band of Spanish patriots which includes, as do all Hemingway's better novels, several colorful and memorable minor characters. Signs of imminent disaster slowly pile up. After failing, because of Communist stupidity, to get a message to Loyalist headquarters warning that the advance will not succeed, Jordan blows the bridge as he had been instructed. The attack is not successful, as the generals realize too late; Jordan is badly wounded in the retreat and is left to die. But he has learned the purpose of such a sacrifice, and he faces his destruction at the end without bitterness: "I have fought for what I believed in. . . . If we win here we will win everywhere." Marred, in the opinion of some critics, by the idealized and romantic love story, as well as by the protagonist's somewhat rhetorical expressions of faith, this was the most successful of Hemingway's books as far as sales are concerned, and it is counted among his better novels.

Following it, however, the author lapsed into a silence that lasted for an entire decade. His next novel, *Across the River and into the Trees* (1950), met with a very poor reception. This is the story of a peace-time army colonel, closely resembling the author, who comes to Venice on leave to go duck shooting, to see the young Italian countess he loves, and to make a significant pilgrimage to the place where he, Richard Cantwell (and Nick Adams, Frederic Henry, and the author himself), was wounded in World War I. Apparently written during a period of ill health, the novel is Hemingway's weakest. It points up sharply the importance of that war injury in the author's life and work, but in some of its postures and mannerisms it seems to read like a parody of his better fiction, and the hero, Cantwell, seems at times a caricature of his creator.

Only two years later, however, Hemingway published THE OLD MAN AND THE SEA (1952), a short novel widely acclaimed as a triumph and partly responsible for his winning the Nobel Prize for literature in 1954. The story, which is based on fact, concerns an old Cuban fisherman who, after a protracted spell of bad luck, ventures far into the Gulf Stream and hooks a giant marlin. He fights it for two days and nights before bringing it alongside, and then the sharks, which he fights until he has nothing left to fight with, eat all but the skeleton, which he tows home. The sense some critics had that the author was trading on, rather than any longer creating, the style for which he became famous was probably compensated for by the abundance of meaning to be found in the narrative. Primarily the tale seems to emphasize that, given the fact of death, a man must always lose his battle in life; nevertheless he can, by the manner and dignity of his losing, win his own special victory. On another level the story may be read as an allegory of the author's own literary vicissitudes; on the broadest level the short novel seems a representation of life itself as a potentially epic struggle in which man has the opportunity, while undergoing a sort of crucifixion, to establish his stature.

Following this success the author continued to write, but no more significant work was published during his lifetime. The main reason appears to have had to do with his upper-bracket tax situation; furthermore, he is said to have felt that the best inheritance he could bestow on his wife and children was manuscript. Indeed, the profits from a single short story, THE SNOWS OF KILIMANJARO, have run far into six figures.

Despite the fact that Hemingway published no important work in the shorter form after the 1930's, it is as a writer of short stories that some critics have primarily esteemed him. By that time three collections, *In Our Time*, MEN WITHOUT WOMEN (1927), and WINNER TAKE NOTHING (1932)—which were compiled and published with his one play in 1938 as *The Fifth Column and the First Forty-Nine Stories*—had established him as one of the most widely admired and imitated of short-story writers. Such pieces as THE KILLERS, THE SHORT HAPPY LIFE OF FRANCIS MACOMBER, and "The Snows of Kilimanjaro" are as well known as the novels, and have become American classics. His influence on the form in America has been incalculable, and very likely has been exceeded by no writer since Edgar Allan Poe, who substantially originated the genre.

Hemingway's stories are remarkable for their objectivity and economy, occasionally for their complexity, and frequently for their subtlety. Many of them, though admired for the cleanness and freshness of the prose and the vigor and swiftness of the action, were long poorly understood. Sometimes the difficulty arose from a failure to discern their focus: "The Killers" and "Indian Camp," for notable instances, are not primarily about gangsters or Indians, as was often believed, but about the effect of certain highly unpleasant experiences, involving gangsters and Indians, on the central figure of Nick Adams. Further, the failure to consider Nick a

consistent, developed character has caused difficulty; without remembering the fact that he was badly wounded in World War I, for example, the reader can scarcely understand what is going on beneath the curiously tense surface of "Big Two-Hearted River." Another problem has been the frequent failure to detect the author's purposes, which are never simply to shock, and are frequently subtle; neither the structure nor the essential meaning of a story like "The Sea Change" is entirely available to one who has not perceived that the author is skillfully manipulating passages from Shakespeare's *Tempest* and Pope's *Essay on Man*. "The Snows of Kilimanjaro" makes use of Dante, Flaubert, and Ambrose Bierce, and though widely regarded as a masterpiece and perennially struggled with, it still resists a complete and definitive analysis.

Hemingway's stories are of a piece with his novels in that most of the truly distinctive features of his longer works of fiction appear in them. The several protagonists who have been grouped together and called the "Hemingway hero"—Jake Barnes, Frederic Henry, Robert Jordan, and Richard Cantwell—have their genesis in Nick Adams, who appears only in the stories. Much less important in the work as a whole, and making no appearance in the stories although well known outside them, is the "Hemingway heroine," who is presented as mistress of the hero, as the British Catherine Barkley in *A Farewell to Arms*, the Spanish Maria of *For Whom the Bell Tolls*, and the Italian Renata of *Across the River and into the Trees*. An idealized woman, selfless and compliant, she changes nationality as the hero never does, and grows younger as he ages; with each successive appearance she also becomes less of a person and more of a dream.

A slightly less consistent but greatly more significant figure who appears in the stories as well as in the novels is a man who introduces and exemplifies what is often called the Hemingway "code." This is a set of controlling principles having to do with honor, courage, and endurance which, in a life of tension and pain, define a man as a man and distinguish him from people that are undisciplined and without a knowledge of the rules of the game. In a highly compromising world these principles enable certain figures in the author's work to conduct themselves extremely well in losing battles, and to show, in a well-known phrase for it, "grace under pressure." The character who exemplifies the code, sometimes called the "code hero," is often confused with the Hemingway hero, but is in reality very distinct from him. The distinction is important, because the man with the code often presents the solution to the problems that the hero, in his extreme though muted sensitivity, regularly encounters. (In a story called "The Gambler, the Nun and the Radio" both figures are presented in clear and contrasted form.) Jack, the compromised but heroic prize fighter of FIFTY GRAND, is a man who illustrates the code, as are Manuel, the bullfighter of "The Undefeated," and Harry Morgan, the smuggler and protagonist of *To Have and Have Not*. Better known representatives are Wilson, the professional hunting guide of "The Short Happy Life of Francis Macomber," and Romero, the bullfighter in *The Sun Also Rises*. Best known is old Santiago, of *The Old Man and the Sea*, who is also the most rounded and complete personification of the code. Behaving perfectly while catching and losing his great fish, he expresses most effectively Hemingway's belief that what counts most in human existence is the dignity and courage with which the individual conducts himself in the process of being destroyed by life and the world.

The violence with which Hemingway was preoccupied in his life and work has proved the core of him. The very first short story in his first significant book, *In Our Time*, has turned out to be an uncanny forecast of this preoccupation and most of its eventual implications. Called "Indian Camp," it relates the visit of Dr. Adams and his young son Nick to a camp of Indians in northern Michigan. Here the doctor delivers a baby by Caesarean section, with a jackknife and without anesthetic. When the operation, which Nick attends, is over, they look in the bunk above and discover that the husband of the patient, who has been listening to her screams for two days, has cut his head nearly off with a razor. This violence exists not for its own sake but, as it eventually transpires, so that its effect on the little boy who witnessed it can be studied; this exposure is one of the sources of the bad nerves that the hero has to contend with later on. Of equal interest is the fact that, not unnaturally, the story ends with the boy and his father discussing suicide. Readers are now unable to avoid the hindsight that the prototypes for both these figures were themselves destined, like the Indian who "couldn't stand things," to take their own lives. Dr. Hemingway shot himself with a Civil War pistol in 1929; it was a shotgun that took his son's life in 1961.

There was something fictionally appropriate about the latter's swift, wordless, and explosive departure, for seldom, anywhere in his work or life, was the author far from the essential fact of violence, and especially the fact of violent death. In DEATH IN THE AFTERNOON, while discussing how he really began his career, Hemingway related how he "was trying to learn to write, commencing with the simplest things," and how he had decided to begin with violent death, which, now that the war was over, was best observed in the bullring. Throughout his work the central theme was man in the face of violence, whether in war, in the bullring, or the hospital, whether the violent deaths of men or fish in the sea or big game or bulls on land. A line runs straight and true from "Indian Camp" through the hero's— and the author's—own repeated injuries in warfare and elsewhere, to Hemingway's own violent and final destruction.

But as the author's own life and personality begin to fade, as they must, from the public interest, it is highly doubtful that his work will fade with them. In all probability Hemingway's technical achievement has been great enough so that his better books would survive if only for the style in which they are written. The Nobel Prize committee seemed to reflect this view when they cited in 1954 "his powerful style-forming mastery of the art of modern narration. . . ."

This prose style had a long and essentially American evolution. In *Green Hills of Africa* the author made the famous remark that "all modern American literature" comes from Mark Twain's *Adventures of Huckleberry Finn* (1884). This is a broad overstatement, but Twain's successful attempt to write as an American boy might speak was indeed the beginning of a widespread contemporary style, informal and colloquial, fresh and occasionally poetic, to which Hemingway, after Twain, made the most notable contribution. However, a striking list of parallels between the lives and careers of Hemingway and Stephen Crane may help account for the fact that in Crane, to whom Hemingway has also acknowledged his debt, are also to be found several of the characteristics which mark this general tradition in American prose. At its best Crane's work shows the same intensity as Hemingway's, as well as the same terse and "unliterary" tone, the same understatements, and several of the features of the dialogue. In the days of his apprenticeship the efforts of Gertrude Stein and Sherwood Anderson to write simply, sparely, concisely, and yet repetitively are also known to have been instructive. A pamphlet published by Hemingway in Dijon in 1923, THREE STORIES AND TEN POEMS, contains two stories, "Up in Michigan" and "My Old Man," later reprinted in *In Our Time*, that reflect the debts to Stein and Anderson. (The third, called "Out of Season," is in its subject matter a little reminiscent of Scott Fitzgerald; the poems suggest debts to Stephen Crane and Vachel Lindsay.) It is here that one must turn to study the earliest manner of his adult work, since all the rest of it was stolen from Hadley Richardson, his first wife, and appears to be permanently lost. Taken together with a short pamphlet of "sketches" called *in our time* (1924), which were also reprinted in the book *In Our Time*, these fragments and stories show clearly the author's earliest purposes; in their rigorous objectivity and extreme economy, and in the sharpness, clarity, and simplicity of the prose, they illustrate the principle that the author was later to state in *Death in the Afternoon*. Writing of the early days in Paris he said: "I was trying to write then and I found the greatest difficulty, aside from knowing what you really felt, rather than what you were supposed to feel, and had been taught to feel, was to put down what really happened in action: what the actual things were which produced the emotion that you experienced . . . the real thing, the sequence of motion and fact which made the emotion. . . ." A striking equivalent to the better-known theory of the "objective correlative," previously formulated by T. S. Eliot in his *Sacred Wood* (1920), this is a key to an understanding of Hemingway's method of writing fiction.

Once Hemingway had begun to command a wider following than any of those who had had an immediate influence on him, he became an extraordinary influence himself. First in English, and then gradually in other languages, the hard, spare prose made itself felt. It functioned chiefly as a purifying agent, acting against embellishment, padding, all forms of superficial artfulness, and any surface or self-conscious sign of "thinking" on the part of the author. In addition Hemingway did more than any single writer in English to vitalize the writing of dialogue. All his life a good listener, he managed, by stripping speech to the essentials typical of the speaker, and by building patterns of mannerisms and responses peculiar to him, to produce the illusion that the people conversing in his work are actually speaking and not, as for instance in the work of Henry James, that he is speaking for them. Although the influence of his style has extended to the realms of subliterary fiction, particularly the "tough-detective school" where his effects have been radically cheapened and most of his meanings lost, his total effect has been generally applauded. Though some modern writers appear to have got stuck in it, many have been quick to concede that Hemingway was the gate through which they passed.

Another feature of his considerable significance as a 20th-century American writer has been the extraordinary way in which his views of life and the world have represented the shifting, evolving attitudes of his contemporaries, so that he became the bellwether of his age. *In Our Time* was an obscure but accurate forecast of the role that violence was to play in this century, and of the breakdown of peace in our time. In *A Farewell to Arms* the protagonist stood for countless Americans as he proceeded from complicity in a world war to bitterness to escape; in the development of his attitudes America as a whole could read its own history in the crucial period of Wilson to Harding. *The Sun Also Rises* is a memorable expression of the responses of a whole generation thrown off balance by the war and disillusioned of faith in many of the values that heretofore had sustained Western civilization. *Green Hills of Africa* and *Death in the Afternoon* are telling expressions of a resultant widespread desire for escape from social and international problems. *To Have and Have Not* reveals what the nation had learned in the great depression about the ultimate impossibility of the completely individualistic, even antisocial, existence the author, like many of his countrymen, had pursued since the war. A reborn concern for society coincided, in Spain, with a new realization of international responsibilities and a recognition of the necessity of resuming a democratic society's perennial war against tyranny. Thus in *The Fifth Column* and *For Whom the Bell Tolls* his protagonist takes up the battle again, just as his compatriots were

soon to involve themselves in World War II. And finally, as the American people began, following that war, to show a tendency to turn once again from public to private preoccupations, the Hemingway protagonist was once again a man alone, fighting his own timeless battle far from the view of his fellows in *The Old Man and the Sea*. It would be hard, if not impossible, to find a reflection, or rather refraction, of modern American experience at once as accurate and artful in any other writer.

At the same time, viewed from a different perspective, the world of Hemingway's fiction has not been broad and comprehensive. Since he concentrated on the significance of violence in our age and penetrated to what he found essential and distinctive, his world has been a narrow and limited one which has conscientiously excluded a great deal of experience that would seem normal and representative to his readers. There are no families in Hemingway, no lasting marriages, no everyday lives, few ordinary places; indeed, most of the routine facts of average existence are conspicuously absent. His world is ultimately a world at war, either literally, as involved in calculated armed combat, or figuratively, as impregnated with violence—present, expected, or just past. The perpetually uprooted inhabitants of this world are limited to the urgencies of war; their lives are dictated by emergency, their pleasures seized in a hurry. They are in combat or transit or on leave, never at home; things about them do not grow or develop for long, but break or die off, or are lost or eaten away. Misery is not universal, because there are visions of stamina, courage, and competence; the body when it is not in pain can give great pleasure; and love, though never more than a temporary condition, profoundly exists. It is a fragmentary and special world which, although most of them do not live in it, his readers have found to be valid in some essential, important way.

Accused of lacking ideas, or more often and worse, of having adolescent ones, Hemingway actually kept his thoughts for the most part from showing in his fiction, as he believed proper. Unless a deep and abiding interest in hunting, fishing, and certain sports is to be considered a sign of immaturity, the attitudes that can be found in his work are less often legitimately to be called adolescent than simply timeless or perennial. Despite the fact that he was technically a convert to Roman Catholicism, though not for many years a practicing one, and that scattered through his work there is a certain amount of Christian symbolism, such occasional thoughts about the human condition as he permitted himself tended toward the stoical and pragmatic or, as more recently urged, the existential. Fundamentally Hemingway believed that fiction and ideas are antithetical to each other, and the notion, sometimes encountered, that he was anti-intellectual stems from that belief. Read *War and Peace*, he once remarked, and see how you will skip the "Big Political

Thought passages" that Tolstoi "undoubtedly thought were the best things in the book when he wrote it . . . and see how true and lasting and important the people and the action are. . . . That is the hardest thing of all to do." At his best he did manage to do what he is here calling attention to, and he may on occasion have managed to do it in the prose that he labored so intensely to attain—the kind that "would be as valid in a year or in ten years or, with luck and if you stated it purely enough, always." His techniques, his attitudes, his sensitivity to the spirit of his age, and to violence, which has played such a role in it, conspired to establish him as one of the greatest of modern writers, and the best of his work seems likely to secure him a permanent and prominent place in the history of American letters.

Hemingway has attracted a great deal of critical attention. Carlos Baker has two books concerning his work: *Hemingway: The Writer as Artist* (1952) contains an extensive bibliography of his writing; Baker edited *Hemingway and His Critics: an International Anthology* (1961), to which is appended a detailed check list of Hemingway criticism. Philip Young also has two full-scale treatments: a book, *Ernest Hemingway* (1952), and a pamphlet with the same title (1959), both of which have been widely translated. Other useful studies are Charles A. Fenton's *The Apprenticeship of Ernest Hemingway* (1954); *Ernest Hemingway: The Man and His Work*, John K. M. McCaffery, ed. (1950); John Atkins' *The Art of Ernest Hemingway* (1952); John Killinger's *Hemingway and the Dead Gods* (1961); and S. F. Sanderson's *Ernest Hemingway* (1961).

PHILIP YOUNG

Hémon, Louis (b. France, Oct. 12, 1880— d. July 8, 1913), French newspaperman, novelist, short-story writer. Hémon emigrated from France to England, where he wrote fiction; then in 1911 he came to Quebec. He became acquainted with Eva Bouchard and made her the heroine of a novel called MARIA CHAPDELAINE; her parents were modeled after a man and wife who had employed Hémon on their farm. After sending the manuscript to the editor of the Paris newspaper *Le Temps*, Hémon set out in search of further literary material, but was killed by a train in Ontario. When his novel was published as a serial in *Le Temps* (1914), it attracted little attention. Then it appeared as a book (1916; English translation, 1921); it was a great success, and Hémon's papers were searched for additional novels and stories. These appeared as *My Lady Fair* (1923), *The Journal of Louis Hémon* (1924), *Blind Man's Buff* (1925), *Monsieur Ripois and Nemesis* (1925). Hémon was deeply impressed with the opportunities that Quebec offered the literary artist; in his appealing novel he did a great deal to realize them.

Henderson, Alice Corbin (b. St. Louis, Mo., [?], 1881—d. July 18, 1949), poet, editor, writer.

Mrs. Henderson was a poet of originality and charm and published three collections of verse: *The Spinning Woman of the Sky* (1912); *Red Earth* (1920); *The Sun Turns West* (1933). But her chief service to poetry was rendered as associate editor of the magazine POETRY (1912– 16), of which she was a co-founder. She is credited with having discovered for the magazine Carl Sandburg and Edgar Lee Masters. In her later years she became interested in New Mexico, owned a ranch not far from Santa Fe, and edited an anthology of New Mexico poetry, *The Turquoise Trail* (1926). She also wrote an account of the Penitentes there, *Brothers of Light* (1937). With HARRIET MONROE she edited an anthology, *The New Poetry* (1917).

Henderson, Archibald (b. Salisbury, N.C., June 17, 1877—d. Dec. 6, 1963), mathematician, biographer, essayist, historian. After studying under Albert Einstein in Germany he returned to North Carolina and became head of the mathematics department at the state university. He published learned writings in his field, such as *The Derivation of the Brianchon Configuration of Two Special Point-Triads*. His secondary interest was literature, particularly the works of George Bernard Shaw. He made himself Shaw's American Boswell, writing such books as *George Bernard Shaw: His Life and Works* (1911), *Bernard Shaw: Playboy and Prophet* (1932), and *George Bernard Shaw: Man of the Century* (1956), even though he also asked *Is Bernard Shaw a Dramatist?* (1929). Henderson also wrote books on Einstein, technical and popular; an immense volume on Mark Twain (1911); and a massive history of North Carolina (2 v., 1941). He described *The Conquest of the Old Southwest* (1920) and *Washington's Southern Tour* (1923); discussed *The Changing Drama* (1914); edited Thomas Godfrey's *The Prince of Parthia* (1917); and wrote the history of his own university (1949). William Lyon Phelps testified admiringly, "He's the only man in the world who can talk professionally on equal terms with Einstein and Shaw." In 1949 thirty eight of Henderson's friends and admirers presented him with a *Festschrift*—warm tributes to *Archibald Henderson: The New Crichton*, edited by S. S. Hood.

Henderson, Daniel McIntyre [1] (b. Scotland, July 10, 1851—d. Sept. 8, 1906), bookseller, poet. Henderson came to America in 1873 and established himself in Baltimore, where he was a friend and guide to many persons of literary ambition and to students and teachers at Johns Hopkins. He wrote numerous lyrics that attained considerable popularity; some were set to music. He published *Poems: Scottish and American* (1888) and *A Bit Bookie of Verse* (1906).

Henderson, Daniel [McIntyre] [2] (b. Baltimore, Md., May 27, 1880—d. Nov. 12, 1955), poet, editor, biographer, novelist. Henderson, son of the foregoing Henderson, continued the family tradition of poetry and published several volumes of graceful, sincere verse: *Life's Minstrel* (1919); *A Harp in the Winds* (1924);

Frontiers (1933). He served on the editorial staff of several magazines, in particular some in the Hearst group (1924–48). He wrote biographies of Theodore Roosevelt, Daniel Boone, Mary Tudor and Admiral Charles Wilkes, and numerous works dealing with American history; also several juveniles and a historical novel, *A Crown for Carlotta* (1929). In 1943 he edited *Reveille*, war poems by members of our armed forces. With his wife Ernestine he wrote a biography of Alice and Phoebe Cary (1950).

Henderson, William J[ames] (b. Newark, N.J., Dec. 4, 1855—d. June 5, 1937), music critic, authority on ships. Henderson became one of the country's most respected music critics, writing mostly for the New York *Sun*. He wrote fluently on his two specialties: *The Story of Music* (1889); *Elements of Navigation* (1895); *What is Good Music?* (1898); *Richard Wagner* (1901); *The Art of the Singer* (1906); and other books.

Hendrick, Burton J[esse] (b. New Haven, Conn., Dec. 8, 1871—d. March 24, 1949), biographer, historian. Hendrick, who at Yale had edited both the *Courant* and the *Literary Magazine*, became a newspaperman, joined the staff of crusaders on *McClure's Magazine*, then *World's Work*. He produced a series of important volumes, three of which won Pulitzer Prizes: *The Life and Letters of Walter H. Page* (1922); *Victory at Sea* (1920, in collaboration with Admiral William S. Sims); and a book on Ambassador Page's earlier years, *The Training of an American* (1928). Among his other books: *The Jews in America* (1923); *The Life of Andrew Carnegie* (1932); *The Lees of Virginia* (1935); *Bulwark of the Republic* (1938); *Statesmen of the Lost Cause* (1939); *Lincoln's War Cabinet* (1946).

Hennepin, [Johannes] Louis (1640–1701[?]), Flemish missionary, explorer, historian, geographer. A Franciscan friar, Hennepin preached successfully in the Low Countries, in 1665 joined LA SALLE's expedition to Canada and began working with the Iroquois Indians at Fort Frontenac, now Kingston, Ontario. In 1678 he accompanied La Salle's expedition toward the Great Lakes and then, as leader of an independent party, explored the upper Mississippi. He was captured by Sioux Indians, but rescued in 1681. He returned to France and there published accounts, believed exaggerated by historians, of his explorations: *Description de la Louisiane* (1683); *Nouveau Voyage* (1696); *Nouvelle Découverte d'un Très Grand Pays Situé dans l'Amérique* (1697). He wrote egotistically but well, and thirty-five editions of Hennepin's books appeared in five languages. An English version of his *Description de la Louisiane* was made in 1880, a more authoritative one in 1938 by Marion E. Cross.

Hennessy. A character who appears frequently in the "MR. DOOLEY" sketches of Finley Peter Dunne. Hennessy is believed to have been modeled on John J. McKenna (1853–1941), one of Dunne's friends in James McGarry's public house in Chicago. But McKenna appears in person in at least one of the Dooley pieces, *The Idle Apprentice*.

Henningsen, Charles Frederick (b. Belgium, Feb. 21, 1815—d. June 14, 1877), soldier, historian, memoirist. Henningsen, of Scandinavian descent, went to England with his parents, became a British citizen, adopted a military career, fought in Spain with the Carlists, joined the Hungarian revolutionary movement under Lajos Kossuth. He accompanied Kossuth to America (1851), married an American woman, and resided in the South. In 1856 he joined WILLIAM WALKER's filibuster in Nicaragua and during the Civil War fought in the Confederate Army. He was a man of intellect as well as a hardy adventurer, and described his experiences in *Scenes from the Belgian Revolution* (1832); *Revelations of Russia* (2 v., 1844); *Analogies and Contrasts* (2 v., 1848); *Kossuth and the Times* (1851).

Henri, Robert (b. Cincinnati, Ohio, June 25, 1865—d. July 12, 1929), artist, teacher, art critic. A leader in the group called "the Eight" (or the "Ash Can School"), which revolted against academic art, Henri painted some distinguished pieces and exerted much influence on JOHN SLOAN, William James Clackens, and others. He taught classes at the Art Students' League in New York (1915–23) and wrote *The Art Spirit* (1923), compiled from his lectures and expressing his progressive ideas.

Henry, Caleb Sprague (b. Rutland, Mass., Aug. 2, 1804—d. March 9, 1884), Episcopal clergyman, teacher, editor, philosopher. Henry taught philosophy at New York University (1838–52) and sought to popularize his own version of transcendentalism. Spirituality was synonymous in his mind with morality, and the "voice of reason" conveyed an absolute concept of right and obligation. He took an active role in the abolitionist movement and in fighting political corruption in New York City. He also opposed Unitarianism. Among his books: *On the Foundation of Morals* (1839); *Dr. Oldham at Greystones* (1860); *About Men and Things* (1873).

Henry, John, legendary, Bunyanesque Negro hero of numerous folktales and ballads. Born supposedly in the "Black River country," he was employed in the building of railroads or as a roustabout on river steamboats. Always depicted as a man of gigantic strength, he even competed with a steam drill in driving steel on the railroad. The tales are apparently based on the exploits of a giant Negro who worked on the Chesapeake & Ohio Big Bend Tunnel in the early 1870's. One of his earliest appearances in print was when Louise Rand Bascomb published a railroad song in the *Journal of American Folklore* (1909), beginning, "Johnnie Henry was a hard-workin' man, / He died with his hammer in his hand." Other collectors followed with additional material; Guy B. Johnson, in *John Henry: Tracking Down a Negro Legend* (1931), made a collection of ballads and variants. ROARK BRADFORD utilized the legend for his novel, *John Henry* (1931), which was converted into a play with music by Jacques Wolfe (1931).

Henry, Joseph (b. Albany, N.Y., Dec. 17, 1797—d. May 13, 1878), teacher, scientist, administrator. Henry was professor of natural philosophy at the College of New Jersey (Princeton) from 1832 to 1848; he left to become secretary of the newly founded Smithsonian Institution and directed its activities until the time of his death. He made many highly important discoveries in the field of electromagnetism; the *henry*, a unit of inductance, is named for him. He founded important societies, encouraged many scientists, suggested the setting up of a weather bureau, helped the country with his scientific knowledge during the Civil War. His researches, experiments, and discoveries helped lay the foundations of the technological age. He was, however, inclined to be dilatory in setting down his discoveries and theories. The Smithsonian Institution published his *Scientific Writings* (2 v., 1886). Thomas Coulson wrote an authoritative account in *Joseph Henry: His Life and Work* (1950).

Henry, O. Pen name of **William Sydney** [earlier spelled **Sidney**] **Porter** (b. Greensboro, N.C., Sept. 11, 1862—d. June 5, 1910), short-story writer, poet, newspaperman, editor. Porter grew up in Greensboro and held his first job in

his uncle's drugstore. Then he drifted off to Texas, where he spent ten years as a clerk, a draftsman in a state land office, finally a bank teller. He made a romantic elopement, and he began writing pieces for newspapers in Texas and Michigan and for a magazine of his own called THE ROLLING STONE. Then came the great tragedy in Porter's life. He was charged with embezzling funds. In a panic, Porter did not wait to stand trial, but left hastily for Central America (the scene of CABBAGES AND KINGS, 1904). There he met other "refugees," such as the outlaw Al Jennings and his brother; Al later

told about their friendship in *Through the Shadows with O. Henry* (1921). When Porter heard that his wife was ill he returned to the United States, attended her deathbed, and gave himself up to the authorities. He was tried and convicted, was sentenced to serve five years in the Federal penitentiary at Columbus, O., and was released, with time off for good conduct, after three years and three months.

There has been virtually ceaseless debate about Porter's trial and conviction. There is a certain amount of unclear evidence to indicate that Porter may have been shielding someone else. The most persuasive analysis of the accusation and conviction is contained in E. Hudson Long's *O. Henry: The Man and His Work* (1949). The records of the trial have been reproduced from the originals of the U.S. circuit court of appeals at New Orleans in W. S. *Porter, Plaintiff in Error, vs. United States, Defendant in Error* (1940).

In jail Porter was well treated by the officials and was made the prison pharmacist. To support his little daughter he turned to writing again. The first of his new stories to be signed O. Henry appeared in *McClure's Magazine* in 1899 and was called *Whistling Dick's Christmas Stocking.* Apparently he sold twelve stories while in jail; there may have been more, since he used other pseudonyms, among them Oliver Henry and S. H. Peters. Where he got the name O. Henry has been much disputed, but he probably adopted it to avoid questions about his term in prison. The most plausible derivation is that Porter found his pen name in the U.S. *Dispensatory,* a reference work consulted daily by every American drug clerk. It was the name of a celebrated French pharmacist, Etienne-Ossian Henry, abbreviated to O. Henry.

Porter's *Wanderjahre* in Texas and Central America contributed much to his storehouse of incidents and personalities; in prison he heard many stories that were the germs of his later narratives—among them the tale of Jimmy Connors, the thief who became the hero of A RETRIEVED REFORMATION and of Paul Armstrong's successful dramatization, ALIAS JIMMY VALENTINE (1909). The stories he had written in jail had made an impression on editors; when he was released he made his way to New York and soon won acclaim as America's greatest short-story writer. Although he wrote extensively of the Southwest and occasionally of other writers, Porter became the prose laureate of Manhattan. To him the city became an opportunity for writing a new series of Arabian Nights stories; in several of his tales he calls it "Bagdad-on-the-Subway."

Porter was a marvelous spinner of yarns who possessed endless inventiveness of plot and character. C. Alphonso Smith, who in his *O. Henry Biography* (1916) was the first scholar to deal with Porter's career and writings, traced four stages in the telling of an O. Henry story: the arrestive beginning; the reader's first guess as to how the story will come out; the stage in which the reader discovers that his first forecast is wrong; the triumphant conclusion with a sudden surprise. Porter's enormous success and the seeming facility of his formula turned critics and some writers against him. The continued popularity of his works, however, indicates that readers agree with his notion of what makes a good story.

In his own lifetime these collections of Porter's stories were published: THE FOUR MILLION (1906); *The Trimmed Lamp* (1907); *Heart of the West* (1907); *The Voice of the City* (1908); *The Gentle Grafter* (1908); *Roads of Destiny* (1909); *Options* (1909); *Strictly Business* (1910); *Whirligigs* (1910). After his death appeared *Let Me Feel Your Pulse* (1910); *Sixes and Sevens* (1911); *Rolling Stones* (1912); *Waifs and Strays* (1917); *Seven Odds and Ends, Poetry and Short Stories* (1920); *Letters to Lithopolis* (1922); *Postscripts* (1923); *O. Henry Encore* (1939). *The Collected Works of O. Henry* (2 v., 1953) includes all his stories and some of his poems. Porter was interested in the theater, and in collaboration with FRANKLIN P. ADAMS he wrote a fairly successful play called *Lo* (prod., 1909). In 1952 a group of Hollywood scriptwriters produced *O. Henry's Full House*, a movie based on five of his stories. In 1953, in one of the most extensive deals in publishing history, Doubleday & Co. licensed some two hundred O. Henry stories for television.

Robert H. Davis and Arthur Bartlett Maurice wrote *The Caliph of Bagdad* (1931) about the Porter they knew well. Paul S. Clarkson prepared *A Bibliography of William Sydney Porter* (1938). Two recent treatments are Dale Kramer's *The Heart of O. Henry* (1954) and Gerald Langford's definitive biography *Alias O. Henry* (1957). In 1918 was established a series of prizes known as the O. Henry Memorial Awards, given to the authors of the best stories each year; these stories are published annually in a collection that includes numerous other tales. See also THE GIFT OF THE MAGI; THE LAST LEAF [2].

Henry, Patrick (b. Hanover Co., Va., May 29, 1736—d. June 6, 1799), lawyer, orator, statesman, public official. In 1760 Henry began to practice law and soon won renown as a fiery patriotic orator. His speeches on the Stamp Act increased his renown; especially the one delivered on May 29, 1765, in the Virginia House of Burgesses. He had introduced seven resolutions, and in his peroration he shouted, "Caesar had his Brutus; Charles the First, his Cromwell; and George III—may well profit by their example!" At this point the Speaker of the House remonstrated with an interruption of "Treason! Treason!" and others echoed his words. But Henry replied, "If that be treason, make the most of it!" Even more famous was his address to the Virginia Assembly of Delegates, March 23, 1775. Henry advocated the immediate arming of the colony, and at the close of his speech said solemnly, "I know not what course others may take, but as for me, give me liberty, or give me death!" In May, 1775, the Royal Governor of Virginia proclaimed him an outlaw. With the

years after the Revolution, Henry became more conservative. He served five useful terms as governor of Virginia, declined to serve a sixth after he had been elected. He also declined to accept the positions of Secretary of State and of Chief Justice of the Supreme Court offered to him by Washington. Virginia named a county after him, and when it was split into two parts, one was called Patrick, the other Henry.

Aside from some striking phrases, Henry's fame is precarious. He wrote pamphlets, but none of great importance. In Virginia he became a folklore hero whose shrewdness was sometimes represented as passing the boundaries of honesty. Even as an orator Henry's fame would have been obscured without the cleverness of his first biographer, William Wirt, whose *Sketches of the Life and Character of Patrick Henry* (3 v., 1817) immortalized him. Wirt, no mean speaker himself, apparently transformed Henry into a notable orator. The speeches he put into Henry's mouth he did not himself invent; he gathered as well as he could memories of Henry's addresses and wove them into his narrative. Henry's grandson, William Wirt Henry, edited a useful work: *Patrick Henry: Life, Correspondence, and Speeches* (3 v., 1891). Robert D. Meade's *Patrick Henry, Patriot in the Making* (1958) is the first of two authoritative volumes. Henry has appeared often in historical novels, including John Esten Cooke's THE VIRGINIA COMEDIANS (1854); Robert W. Chambers CARDIGAN (1901); Irving Bacheller's *In the Days of Poor Richard* (1922); Hildegarde Hawthorne's *Rising Thunder* (1937); Elizabeth Page's *The Tree of Liberty* (1939); John Erskine's *Give Me Liberty* (1940); Kenneth Roberts' OLIVER WISWELL (1940). See also "GIVE ME LIBERTY OR GIVE ME DEATH!"

Henry St. John, Gentleman (1859), a novel by JOHN ESTEN COOKE. This is a sequel to THE VIRGINIA COMEDIANS (1854), involving some of the same characters as that novel of colonial life in Virginia. But the leading character is St. John, a descendant of Pocahontas who joins the opposition to Lord Dunmore, arrogant governor of the colony. A love story involves beautiful Bonnybel Vane, in whose behalf St. John fights a duel.

Henson, Josiah (b. Charles Co., Md., June 15, 1789—d. May 5, 1881), clergyman, lecturer. This Negro notable escaped from slavery, went to Canada, became a Methodist minister. He traveled widely and met many celebrities, lectured frequently on his experiences. His fame rests chiefly on the fact that HARRIET BEECHER STOWE, by her own acknowledgment in her *Key to Uncle Tom's Cabin* (1853) and in her introduction to Henson's *Truth Stranger Than Fiction* (1858, originally published as *Life of Josiah Henson* or as *Autobiography* in 1849), used the incidents of his life for "many of the finest conceptions and incidents of Uncle Tom's character." She altered and augmented them, however, so that Henson and Uncle Tom are by no means identical. Brion Gyson's *To Master, A Long Goodnight* (1946) examines Henson's career, analyzes Mrs. Stowe's employment of his character and experiences, shows the effect of her book in its own time and since then. In particular it describes the reaction of the freed black man to what has come to be called "Uncle-Tomism," and the extent to which Henson himself, in his later years, was an exemplar of this despised attitude. See UNCLE TOM'S CABIN.

Hentoff, Nat (b. Boston, June 10, 1925—), writer, critic. Hentoff graduated from Harvard and studied at the Sorbonne under a Fulbright grant. In 1960 he became a staff writer for *The New Yorker* magazine. He contributed drama reviews and articles on race relations and politics to various magazines, but he is best known as a jazz critic. His commentaries are written in a lively contemporary idiom. His books are *Hear Me Talkin' To Ya* (1955); *The Jazz Makers* (1957); *Jazz* (1959); *Jazz Street* (1960).

Hentz, Caroline Lee [Whiting] (b. Lancaster, Mass., June 1, 1800—d. Feb. 11, 1856), novelist, dramatist. Mrs. Hentz lived for many years in the South, and one definite aim of her fiction was to alleviate northern prejudice against the South, especially in respect to slavery. Her books include: *Linda, or, The Young Pilot of the "Belle Creole"* (1850); *The Planter's Northern Bride* (2 v., 1854); *Ernest Linwood, or, The Inner Life of the Author* (1856).

Herald of Gospel Liberty. This is believed to have been the first weekly in this country devoted to religious topics. It was founded in 1808 by Elias Smith, an event commemorated in J. Prester Barrett's *The Centennial of Religious Journalism* (1908).

Herbert, Henry William ["Frank Forester"] (b. England, April 7, 1807—d. May 17, 1858), teacher, translator, editor, poet, novelist, writer on sports and nature, artist. Herbert emigrated to America in 1831. For several years he taught school, then became a newspaperman; he also did some translating from the Greek and helped found the *American Monthly Magazine.* Then he began writing conventional historical romances: *The Brothers: A Tale of the Fronde* (1835); *Cromwell* (1838); RINGWOOD THE ROVER (1843); *The Roman Traitor* (1846); *The Cavaliers of England* (1852); *The Cavaliers of France* (1852). He composed and published sketches of hunting and sporting life, under the pen name Frank Forester; in so doing he became the first sports writer in the United States. Under his pen name he wrote *The Warwick Woodlands* (1845); *My Shooting Box* (1846); *The Deer-stalkers* (1849); *Field Sports of the United States and British Provinces of North America* (2 v., 1849); *The Quorndon Hounds* (1852); *The Complete Manual for Young Sportsmen* (1856); and *Horses and Horsemanship of the United States and British Provinces of North America* (1857). In 1858 Herbert, lonely and tired of life, committed suicide.

Herbert's books are still fresh and readable, the work of a genuine lover of nature and sports. Perhaps the best of his sporting novels was *The Warwick Woodlands* (reprinted 1934). His *Sporting Sketches* were collected in 1879, his

Poems in 1888. David W. Judd prepared a volume called *Life and Writings of Frank Forester* (1882), but the best biography is William S. Hunt's *Frank Forester: A Tragedy in Exile* (1933). Luke White, Jr., wrote an interesting study, *Henry William Herbert and the American Publishing Scene* (1943), which gives an account of Herbert's literary career with some hitherto unpublished details. A. R. Beverley Giddings edited a selection from Herbert's books, *Frank Forester on Upland Shooting* (1951).

Herbert, Victor (b. Ireland, Feb. 1, 1859—d. May 26, 1924), musician, composer. Herbert came to the United States in 1886 to join the orchestra of the Metropolitan Opera Company. A few years later he began conducting bands and orchestras, organized an orchestra of his own, helped found ASCAP. He was always deeply interested in composing, especially light operas. His first opera to be performed was *Prince Ananias* (1894), and for the remainder of his career he became the leading representative in this country of light, tuneful, memorable music. Between 1894 and 1917 Herbert wrote thirty-five operas and operettas, besides incidental music for other theatrical pieces. Among the operettas are *The Wizard of the Nile* (1895); *The Fortune Teller* (1898); *Babes in Toyland* (1903); *Mlle. Modiste* (1905); *The Red Mill* (1906); *Naughty Marietta* (1910); and *Sweethearts* (1913). His two grand operas are *Natoma* (1911), an Indian play, and *Madeleine* (1914), a one-act drama. In 1939 Russel Crouse and Robert Lively prepared a motion-picture play, *The Great Victor Herbert,* which included hits from many of his operettas. E. N. Waters wrote a minutely detailed life of Herbert (1955).

Herbst, Josephine [Frey] (b. Sioux City, Iowa, March 5, 1897—d. Jan. 28, 1969), novelist. Miss Herbst was firmly a proletarian novelist. Although her depiction of life among the lowly is powerful, she often forgets her story in her too minute accumulation of physical and psychological details. Among her books: *Nothing is Sacred* (1928); *Money for Love* (1929); *Pity is Not Enough* (1933); *The Executioner* (1934); *Rope of Gold* (1939); *Satan's Sergeants* (1941); *Somewhere the Tempest Fell* (1947); *New Green World* (1954); *The Watcher with the Horn* (1955). See PROLETARIAN LITERATURE.

Herford, Oliver (b. England, Dec. 12, 1863 —d. July 5, 1935), poet, illustrator, playwright, wit. Herford came to the United States as a child, studied in London and Paris, also at Antioch College. He established himself in this country as a contributor of verse and drawings to magazines. He wrote many books, illustrating most of them himself; among them were *Pen and Inklings* (1892); *The Bashful Earthquake and Other Fables and Verses* (1898); *An Alphabet of Celebrities* (1899); *A Child's Primer of Natural History* (1899); *The Cynic's Calendar* (with ETHEL WATTS MUMFORD and Addison Mizner, 1902–17); *Rubáiyát of a Persian Kitten* (1904); *A Little Book of Bores* (1906); *The Simple Jography* (1908); *Cupid's Encyclopedia* (1910); *The Kitten's Garden of Verses* (1911);

The Mythological Zoo (1912); *Confessions of a Caricaturist* (1917); *This Giddy Globe* (1919); *The Herford Aesop* (1921); *Excuse It Please* (1929); *The Deb's Dictionary* (1931). Poems he had written for *Life* were collected in 1923. He adapted *The Devil* (1908) from a play by Ferenc Molnár and wrote plays of his own, among them *The Florist's Shop* (1909) and *The Love Cure* (1909).

Hergesheimer, Joseph (b. Philadelphia, Feb. 15, 1880—d. April 25, 1954), novelist, short-story writer, historian, biographer, travel writer. In the first stage of Hergesheimer's career he won the esteem of critics in this country and

abroad. He began with an unimportant novel, *The Lay Anthony* (1914), went on to *Mountain Blood* (1915); THE THREE BLACK PENNYS (1917); two books of short stories, *Gold and Iron* (1918) and *The Happy End* (1919); LINDA CONDON (1919); JAVA HEAD (1919); CYTHEREA (1922); THE BRIGHT SHAWL (1922); and BALISAND (1924). Here Hergesheimer expressed vividly his love of beauty, his adherence to old ideals of chivalry, his melancholy at the passing of a world he loved, his interest in people who dared to be individuals. Some of the novels—*The Three Black Pennys, Java Head, Balisand*—have become classics of American fiction.

But he loved beauty in its outward aspects, seemed content with the mere appearance and feel of things; he became the antiquarian and the interior decorator rather than the artist, and his prose was deluged with languid adjectives and the perfume of luxury. Furthermore his cult of the luxury-loving aristocrat tended to vitiate his skill as a storyteller. His work degenerated in *Tampico* (1926), *The Party Dress* (1930), and *The Limestone Tree* (1931). Hergesheimer also wrote a description of the social life of

Havana, *San Cristóbal de la Habaña* (1920); a life of General Sheridan (1931); *Berlin* (1932), the record of a trip abroad; and two volumes of autobiography, *A Presbyterian Child* (1923) and *From an Old House* (1925). James Branch Cabell, a friend and fellow yearner after aristocratic ideals, wrote a book on Hergesheimer (1922) in which he tempered his admiration with suspicions that Hergesheimer had lowered his ideals in his quest for best-sellerdom. See also TOL'ABLE DAVID.

Hermannsson, Haldor (b. Iceland, Jan. 6, 1878—d. Aug. 29, 1958), teacher, historian. Educated in Iceland and Denmark, Hermannsson became in 1905 the curator of the Fiske Icelandic Collection at Cornell University and at the same time an instructor, later a full professor, on the Cornell faculty. He published numerous important works in his special field, also volumes on *The Norsemen in America* (1909), *Icelanders in America* (in Danish, 1922), and *The Problem of Wineland* (1936), and edited *The Vinland Sagas* (1944).

Herndon, William Henry (b. Greensburg, Ky., Dec. 25, 1818—d. March 18, 1891), lawyer, politician, biographer of Lincoln. In 1842 Herndon entered the office of Logan and Lincoln in Springfield, Illinois, as a student. When that firm was dissolved in 1844, Lincoln invited him to become his junior partner, and the firm of Lincoln and Herndon continued to exist until Lincoln's death.

Lincoln's assassination gave Herndon a mission in life—to preserve Lincoln for posterity. He wrote down his own reminiscences, travelled to Kentucky and talked to men who had known Lincoln as a boy, and gathered a great mass of material. Because of financial setbacks he was forced to sell much of his data to WARD HILL LAMON in 1870. In the 1880's Jesse W. Weik, an ardent student of Lincoln's life, began a correspondence with Herndon, and in 1889 the two men published *Herndon's Lincoln: The True Story of a Great Life*. The work aroused a good deal of controversy because of the inclusion of facts concerning Lincoln's mother, his religious unorthodoxy, his marriage to Mary Todd and his romance with Ann Rutledge, but recent critics have felt that Herndon's work contributed a good deal to the demythologizing of Lincoln's life. Herndon himself was the subject of David Donald's biography, *Lincoln's Herndon* (1948).

Herne, James A. [originally **James Ahern**] (b. Cohoes, N.Y., Feb. 1, 1839—d. June 2, 1901), actor, playwright. A capable actor (his daughters Julie and Chrystal also attained prominence on the stage), Herne developed as a writer into an impressive realist. Among his plays: HEARTS OF OAK (with DAVID BELASCO, 1879); *Drifting Apart* (1888); MARGARET FLEMING (1890); SHORE ACRES (1892); THE REV. GRIFFITH DAVENPORT (1899). A collection, *Shore Acres and Other Plays*, was made in 1928 by Mrs. Herne. Herne's dramas dealt often with unsophisticated characters in rural environments, and they exerted a considerable influence on succeeding dramatists,

Herold, Don (b. Bloomfield, Ind., July 9, 1889—d. June 1, 1966), humorist, artist. He wrote: *So Human* (1924); *Bigger and Better* (1925); *There Ought to Be a Law* (1926); *Our Companionate Goldfish* (1927); *Typographical Handbook* (1946); *Drunks Are Driving Me to Drink* (1953).

Herrick, Robert (b. Cambridge, Mass., April 26, 1868—d. Dec. 23, 1938), teacher, novelist, short-story writer. Herrick joined the English Department of the University of Chicago in 1893, became a full professor in 1905, retired in 1923. In his fiction he sought to describe and analyze the problems of modern industrial society, especially the corruption of the middle-class soul by commercialism. He himself drew a distinction between most of his novels as realistic and a limited group that were, as he said, idealistic, manifesting a kind of broadminded Puritanism. Among his more notable novels: *The Web of Life* (1900); THE COMMON LOT (1904); *The Memoirs of an American Citizen* (1905); *A Life for a Life* (1910); *The Healer* (1911); ONE WOMAN'S LIFE (1913); *Clark's Field* (1914); CHIMES (1926); *The End of Desire* (1932). His most widely read book was THE MASTER OF THE INN (1908), in which a cure for modern ills is sought in contemplation, quietude, and physical labor.

Herriman, George (b. New Orleans, 1880—d. April 25, 1944), cartoonist. Originally a house painter, Herriman fell from a scaffold one day and concluded that his vocation was too strenuous. He decided to become a cartoonist, and created Krazy Kat and his pals for King Features syndication. It is said that the idea for his famous cartoon strip came from an office boy named Willie, who looked over his shoulder one day at a cartoon of a cat and mouse playing marbles. "Why don't you make the mouse chase the cat?" he suggested; and Krazy Kat and Ignatz Mouse were born, along with Offisa Pup, the minion of the law. Krazy Kat loves Ignatz, whereas the Pup loves Kat. Ignatz's constant joy is to "crease Kat's bean with a brick." Krazy Kat regards this as a mark of affection, but Offisa Pup is always trying to protect the Kat.

The highbrows of the 1920's waxed ecstatic about Herriman's comic strip.

Herring, Hubert (b. Winterset, Iowa, Dec. 29, 1889—), historian, writer on international relations. Executive director of the Committee on Cultural Relations with Latin America since 1928 and professor of Latin American Civilization at Pomona and Claremont colleges since 1944, Herring has long been recognized as an expert in his field. His most extensive work is *A History of Latin America* (1955). Here he examines politics, culture, economic questions and personalities, providing a handbook on Latin America up to 1954. Other works: *Good Neighbors* (1941); *America and the Americas* (1944).

Herschberger, Ruth (b. Philipse Manor, N.Y., Jan. 30, 1917—), poet, author. Miss Herschberger grew up in Chicago and studied at the University of Chicago, Black Mountain College, and the University of Michigan. In 1948 she published her first volume of poetry, *A Way of Happening*. In the same year her *Adam's Rib* appeared, a witty prose analysis of the place of women in modern society. She is also the author of two verse plays, *A Ferocious Incident* and *Andrew Jackson* (both produced in Chicago in 1953), and has frequently contributed short stories and criticism to little magazines.

Hersey, Harold Brainerd (b. Bozeman, Mont., March 2, 1893—d. March 13, 1956), editor, poet. Much of Hersey's verse has a Montana background. Among his collections: *Gestures in Ivory* (1919); *Cylinders* (1925); *Singing Rawhide* (1926); *Bubble and Squeak* (1927); *Verse* (2 v., 1939). He tells his own story in *Pulpwood Editor* (1937). He was the first editor (1917) of *The Quill: A Magazine of Greenwich Village* and with Elinor Hersey, of *Main Street* (1929).

Hersey, John [Richard] (b. China, June 17, 1914—), magazine writer, war correspondent, editor, historian. At one time secretary to SINCLAIR LEWIS and later a writer for *Time* and *The New Yorker,* Hersey published his

first book, *Men on Bataan* (1942), as a war correspondent's report. *Into the Valley* (1943) showed his increasing mastery of language and ideas in its brief, well-written account of a skirmish on Guadalcanal. *A Bell for Adano* (1944) was based on Hersey's careful observation of the American occupation of Italy; it shows deep sympathy with an understanding of the Italian people, and was awarded a Pulitzer Prize.

HIROSHIMA (1946) made Hersey famous; in China as a correspondent for *Time* and *The New Yorker,* Hersey had made a visit to the A-bombed city to see what had happened to the inhabitants. The remarkable report he sent back appeared in *The New Yorker* on August 31, 1946. Once again Man's inhumanity and courage are the theme of Hersey's novel *The Wall* (1950), his most ambitious work—the story of the extinction of the Warsaw ghetto by the Germans. Reading the novel becomes an intense participation in the horrors and the heroism of a three-year tragedy. *The Wall* was made into a play produced on Broadway (1960), and in Europe (1961). Later publications include *The Marmot Drive* (1953); *A Single Pebble* (1956); *The War Lover* (1959); *The Child Buyer* (1960).

Herskovitz, Melville Jean (b. Bellefontaine, Ohio, Sept. 10, 1895—d. Feb. 25, 1963), anthropologist, explorer. Herskovitz taught at Columbia, Howard, and Northwestern Universities, became professor of anthropology at Northwestern. He led scientific expeditions to Dutch Guiana, Haiti, West Africa, Trinidad, and Brazil, with his wife Frances Shapiro Herskovitz as his assistant. Together they wrote *The Outline of Dahomean Religious Belief* (1933); *Rebel Destiny: Among the Bush Negroes of Dutch Guiana* (1934); *Surinam Folklore* (1936); *Trinidad Village* (1947); *Dahomean Narrative, A Cross-Cultural Analysis* (1958). In addition Herskovits wrote *The American Negro: A Study in Racial Crossing* (1928); *Life in a Haitian Valley* (1937); *Dahomey* (1938); *Acculturation* (1938); *The Economic Life of Primitive Peoples* (1940); *The Myth of a Negro Past* (1941); *Man and His Works* (1948); *Economic Anthropology* (1952); *Cultural Anthropology* (1955). The special province of Herskovitz is the Negro in Africa and the New World, and he has established some astonishing facts about the relationship that still prevails between the Negro in West Africa and in Brazil.

Hertz, Emanuel (b. Austria, Sept. 2, 1870—d. May 23, 1940), lawyer, Lincoln specialist. Hertz, who came to the United States in 1884 and practiced law in New York, gathered an immense amount of Lincoln material, most of which he presented to the Library of Congress. He gave some of his well-informed impressions of Lincoln in *Abraham Lincoln: A New Portrait* (1931), and *Lincoln Talks* (1939). He edited William H. Herndon's letters and papers in *The Hidden Lincoln* (1938).

Hertzler, Arthur E[mmanuel] (b. West Point, Iowa, July 26, 1870—d. Sept. 12, 1946), physician, medical writer, autobiographer. In addition to a long list of writings on tumors, abdominal surgery, the thyroid gland, and similar topics, Dr. Hertzler wrote several books for the lay public. One of these—*The Horse and Buggy Doctor* (1938)—became a best seller. He also wrote *Grounds of an Old Surgeon's Faith* (1944) and *Always the Child* (1944). In 1948 the Hertzler Research Foundation was set up at Halstead, Kan., his home for many years.

Hervey, Harry C[lay] (b. Beaumont, Tex., Nov. 5, 1900—d. Aug. 12, 1951), newspaperman, explorer, novelist, short-story writer. Hervey has traveled extensively in Asia and Africa and among the islands of the Pacific; he led an archaeological expedition (1925) in upper Indo-China. He sold his first story when he was only sixteen to H. L. Mencken; his first novel, *Caravans by Night* (1922), appeared when he was twenty-one. Among his other novels: *The Black Parrot* (1923); *Ethan Quest* (1925); *Congai* (1927); *Red Hotel* (1932); *The Damned Don't Cry* (1939); *School for Eternity* (1941); *Veiled Fountain* (1947).

Herzberg, Max J. (b. Brooklyn, March 29, 1886—d. Jan. 21, 1958), educator, editor, author. Herzberg was a teacher and principal in the Newark, N.J., school system for forty-four years. He reviewed books for the Newark *Evening* and *Sunday News* from 1913 until his death, and was literary editor from 1920 on. For many years he was also the editor of *Word Study,* a magazine on word usage. He edited many school texts, ranging from Shakespeare's plays to comprehensive anthologies suitable for providing material for an entire high-school course. He was also influential in increasing the works by American writers in school curricula. A founder of the Stephen Crane Association, he was its president from 1924 to 1930. His introduction to *The Red Badge of Courage* appeared in many editions and his biography of Crane appears in the *Encyclopaedia Britannica. Insults: a Practical Anthology* (1941) is another of his works for the general public.

Herzberg's influence as a critic was widespread; during his forty-four years with the Newark *News,* he estimated that he personally reviewed five thousand books and handled twenty thousand more written by others. At the time of his death, he had just turned over to the publishers the manuscript of this *Encyclopedia of American Literature,* which had been in preparation for five years.

Hesperus, The Wreck of the. See WRECK OF THE HESPERUS, THE.

Hethushka Society of the Omahas. The object of this Indian society, as recorded by Alice Fletcher and FRANCIS LAFLESCHE, was "to stimulate an heroic spirit among the people and to keep alive the memory of historical and valorous deeds." When such a deed was performed, it was recorded in song. See AMERINDIAN PROSE AND POETRY.

Hewat, Alexander (b. Scotland, 1745[?]—d. 1829), clergyman, historian. Hewat lived in South Carolina from 1763 until the outbreak of the Revolution, whereupon his Tory views led him to return to Scotland. He wrote *An Historical Account of the Rise and Progress of the Colonies of South Carolina and Georgia* (2 v., 1779), reliable except as to the Revolution.

Hewitt, James (b. England, June 4, 1770—d. Aug. 1 [?], 1827), musician. Hewitt came to America in 1772 and became active as a performer, conductor, and composer. He wrote one of the earliest of American operas, *Tammany, or,*

The Indian Chief, which was performed under the auspices of the Tammany Society of New York. The libretto was written by Anne Julia Hatton. Hewitt's son, **John Hill Hewitt** (b. New York City, July 11, 1801—d. Oct. 7, 1890), wrote many popular songs, including the *Minstrel's Return from the War* (1827) and *All Quiet Along the Potomac Tonight* (1864). He is sometimes called "the Father of American Ballad Poetry." He published *Miscellaneous Poems* (1838) and an autobiography, *Shadows on the Wall, or, Glimpses of the Past* (1877), which gives vivid pictures of the musical personalities of the mid-19th century. He edited several Baltimore periodicals and at one time successfully competed against Edgar Allan Poe in a poetry contest. He won, partly because Poe had already taken the prose prize.

Heyliger, William (b. Hoboken, N.J., March 22, 1884—d. Jan. 15, 1955), novelist, author of books for boys. Heyliger told wholesome tales that appealed to the interests of his young readers. Some of them continued to sell steadily for decades, particularly *High Benton* (1919). Others included *Captain of the Nine* (1912); *Against Odds* (1915); *Don Strong of the Wolf Patrol* (1916); *Jerry Hicks and His Gang* (1929); *Boys Who Became President* (1932); *Steve Merrill, Engineer* (1935); *Top Lineman* (1943). He also wrote a novel for adults, *Dark Conquest* (1936).

Heym, Stefan (b. Germany, April 10, 1913—), historian, novelist, dramatist. Heym came to the United States in 1935, fought in the United States Army in World War II, and won several decorations. Before the war he had written a book of warning, *Nazis in the U.S.A.* (1938); thereafter he published *Hostages* (1942); *Of Smiling Peace* (1944); *The Crusaders* (1947); *Eyes of Reason* (1951). He wrote of war realistically and yet not without admiration for heroism, and *The Crusaders* particularly won praise for its dramatic plot.

Heyward, Dorothy (b. Wooster, Ohio, June 6, 1890—d. Nov. 19, 1961), playwright, novelist. Mrs. Heyward collaborated with her husband DuBose Heyward on the dramatic versions of Porgy and Mamba's Daughters. Her most effective work as a dramatist was done in collaboration with her husband. There was a remarkable similarity between them, even in appearance, so that they were often mistaken for brother and sister. A product of the Harvard Workshop (see G. P. Baker), Dorothy Heyward won a prize at Harvard for her play *Nancy Ann,* which was produced on Broadway in 1924. Other plays by her are *Love in a Cupboard* (1926); *Jonica,* which won the MacDowell Fellowship and was produced on Broadway in 1929; and *Little Girl Blue* (1931). With Howard Rigsby she wrote a play called *South Pacific* (1944), which had a brief run on Broadway— it has no relationship to the recent hit musical by the same name based on James A. Michener's *Tales of the South Pacific* (1947). Another play is *Set My People Free* (1948). Mrs. Heyward

also wrote fiction: *Three-a-Day* (1930) and *The Pulitzer Prize Murders* (1932). The many revivals of *Porgy and Bess* occupied a good deal of her time, and she traveled abroad with it.

Heyward, DuBose (b. Charleston, S.C., Aug. 31, 1885—d. June 16, 1940), poet, novelist, playwright. With Hervey Allen, Heyward published a collection of poems, *Carolina Chansons* (1922), which revived the legends and dreams of an extinct feudal aristocracy and included many poems about pirates, Indians, historical figures. Heyward struck a more personal note in *Skylines and Horizons* (1924) and included some of his verse in *Jasbo Brown, and Selected Poems* (1931). But he had before this time turned to novel writing, and his first book was his most famous: Porgy (1925), which presented Negro life in Charleston with truthfulness and sympathy. He knew the Negro because he had lived beside him and worked beside him. Orphaned of his father in early life, and with no means of obtaining an education, he had started working while in his teens, and one of his jobs had been on the docks along with a large proportion of Negro manual laborers. With his wife Dorothy, Heyward turned the book into a play which was successfully produced in 1927. It was always a compliment to him, after the success of *Porgy,* when those who did not know him said that the play had been written by a Negro. It was Heyward's warmth and deep sympathy which misled them. Yet he belonged to that innermost core of Southern society which ignores wealth or lack of it among its own and includes only portions of Virginia, Maryland and Charleston. He was a direct descendant of Thomas Heyward, Jr., a signer of the Declaration of Independence. A foreshadowing of *Porgy* was in an account of the customs that prevailed among the Charleston Negroes, and which he sent to *The Reviewer.* In it he wrote with evident sadness: "They will be cleaned, married, conventionalized. They will be taken from the fields and given to the machines, their instinctive feelings for the way that leads to happiness, saved as it is from selfishness, by humor and genuine kindness of heart, will be supplanted by a stifling moral straitjacket."

In 1935 the play was made into an opera, *Porgy and Bess,* by George Gershwin, and it became a tremendous hit. Mamba's Daughters (1929) is another novel of Charleston Negro life and was also dramatized (1939). *Peter Ashley* (1932) is a story laid in Charleston during the Civil War, and *Star-Spangled Virgin* (1939) is about the Virgin Islands with the coming of the New Deal. Frank Durham has given an account of *DuBose Heyward: The Man Who Wrote "Porgy"* (1954).

H. H. Pen name of Helen Hunt Jackson.

Hiawatha (1855), a long narrative poem by Henry Wadsworth Longfellow. This poem, in addition to the earlier Evangeline (1847) and the later Courtship of Miles Standish (1858), was an attempt on Longfellow's part to supply America with a legendary past. A long, rambling poem, *Hiawatha* is in the form of an Indian epic; however, Longfellow's personal cultivation and knowledge of European literature led him to impose a sophisticated form on a naïve subject. The plot deals with the adventures of Hiawatha, an Ojibway Indian raised by Nokomis, the daughter of the Moon. After detailing his hero's accumulation of natural wisdom, the poet recounts the deeds of Hiawatha in revenging his mother, Wenonah, against his father, the West Wind. Hiawatha eventually becomes the leader of his people and teaches peace even in the face of the encroaching white man. When his wife, MINNEHAHA, becomes ill, he leaves with her for the land of the Northwest Wind, and departs with a message to accept the religion of the white man.

Longfellow used several prose narratives and Indian histories as his sources, notably the *Account of the History, Manners, and Customs of the Indian Nations of Pennsylvania and the Neighboring States* (1819) by the Rev. JOHN HECKEWELDER, and ALGIC RESEARCHES (1839) and other writings by HENRY R. SCHOOLCRAFT. By 1854 Longfellow had decided upon both the plan of the poem and its meter, although in June he was still calling the chief character Manabozho, apparently under the impression that Manabozho and Hiawatha were identical. The former was the name of a tricky Ojibway and Algonquin demigod, whereas Hiawatha was actually an Iroquois chieftain and reformer of the 16th century. Many of Manabozho's wiles were transferred in the poem to the villain Pau-Pau-Kee-Wis. The language and the names of Indian tribes were similarly confused.

Aside from the doubtful authenticity of the Indian elements, the poem aroused much controversy over the extent to which it owed both its meter and its incidents to the Finnish epic Kalevala. The resemblance between the two was early noted, especially in regard to the meter, but Longfellow was highly indignant at the charge of borrowing and pointed out the common employment of trochaic tetrameter lines in some earlier poems on Indians, and the use of parallelism in Indian poetry itself.

The poem has been endlessly parodied, beginning with Lewis Carroll's *Hiawatha's Photographing* (1857). T. R. Henry wrote *Wilderness Messiah: The Story of Hiawatha and the Iroquois* (1955).

Hibbard, [Clarence] Addison (b. Racine, Wis., Aug. 29, 1887—d. May 17, 1945), teacher, editor. Long a member of the staff of Northwestern University, Hibbard prepared with William F. Thrall of North Carolina the useful *Handbook to Literature* (1936). He also compiled *The Lyric South* (1929) and *Stories of the South* (1931).

Hibben, Paxton [Pattison] (b. Indianapolis, Ind., Dec. 5, 1880—d. Dec. 15, 1928), newspaperman, soldier, diplomat, biographer. In the course of his varied career Hibben wrote several excellent biographies: *Constantine I and the Greek People* (1920); *Henry Ward Beecher*

(1927); *The Peerless Leader, William Jennings Bryan* (1929). See HENRY WARD BEECHER; LYMAN BEECHER.

Hickok, Wild Bill [James Butler] (b. Troy Grove, Ill., May 27, 1837—d. Aug. 2, 1876), soldier, scout, and United States Marshal. Hickok fought in many frontier and Indian battles under Generals Custer and Sheridan. As Marshal at Hays City and later at Abilene, Kansas, he faced some of the toughest men on the frontier, killing only in self-defense or the line of duty. In 1872 he toured the east with Buffalo Bill (WILLIAM F. CODY). Four years later he was murdered by the notorious Jack McCall, and was buried in Mount Moriah cemetery in Deadwood, S.D. He became a legend in his lifetime and a folk hero after his death. CAPTAIN JACK CRAWFORD, the poet scout and one of Hickok's close friends, dedicated a ballad to him, *The Burial of Wild Bill*. Many books and articles have been written about him, including Frank J. Wilstach's *Wild Bill Hickok, the Prince of Pistoleers* (1926); William E. Connelley's *Wild Bill and His Era* (1933); Mari Sandoz' *The Buffalo Hunters* (1954).

Hicks, Elias (b. Hempstead Township, N.Y., March 19, 1748—d. Feb. 27, 1830), religious leader, memoirist. A Quaker by birth, Hicks advocated views that led him to leave the orthodox Quakers and form a sect of his own, the "Hicksites." They stressed "the inward light." Hicks was an ardent worker, is said to have traveled ten thousand miles on foot, another fifteen hundred by carriage after he was eighty, and to have preached in the open air more than a thousand times. He was a poor man, but would accept no money for his services and made his living by working his farm on the outskirts of Jericho, Long Island. He wrote and preached constantly against Negro slavery and by his efforts brought about the passage of a law in New York that abolished slavery in that state (1827). WALT WHITMAN as a boy heard him preach; his Quaker family were friends and neighbors of the Hickses. The poet's religious views were deeply influenced by those of Hicks, and in NOVEMBER BOUGHS (1888) he paid a warm tribute to the preacher, *Notes on Elias Hicks*. Among Hicks' writings: *Observations on the Slavery of the Africans* (1811) and *The Quaker* (4 v., 1827–28). His *Journal* appeared after his death (1832). In 1910 Henry W. Wilbur wrote *The Life and Labors of Elias Hicks;* in 1956 Bliss Forbush wrote *Elias Hicks, Quaker Liberal*.

Hicks, Frederick Charles (b. Auburn, N.Y., Oct. 14, 1875—d. March 30, 1956), lawyer, librarian, bibliographer. Hicks practiced law for a time; served in various libraries, including the Library of Congress, the Brooklyn Public Library, and the Columbia University Law Library; joined the Yale faculty as professor of legal bibliography and law. He published many books, among them *Aids to the Study and Use of Law Books* (1913); *Men and Books Famous in the Law* (1921); *Materials and Methods of Legal Research* (1923; 3rd ed., 1942); *Organization* and *Ethics of the Bench and Bar* (1932); *William Howard Taft, Yale Professor of Law and New Haven Citizen* (1945). He edited *Famous American Jury Speeches* (1925) and *Bermuda in Poetry* (1915).

Hicks, Granville (b. Exeter, N.H., Sept. 9, 1901—   ), teacher, editor, radio broadcaster, writer. Hicks taught in various colleges and served on the editorial staff of the *New Masses*. For years on the far left politically, he resigned from the Communist Party in 1939 and from that time on became a strong opponent of Communist doctrines and Soviet policies; he was at the same time an ardent advocate of "the American way." (See PROLETARIAN LITERATURE.) Among his books: *The Great Tradition* (1933), *John Reed—The Making of a Revolutionary* (1935), *I Like America* (1938), *The First to Awaken* (1940), *Where We Came Out* (1954). He edited *Proletarian Literature in the U.S.* (1935) and (with Ella Winter) *The Letters of Lincoln Steffens* (1938). Also he wrote three novels: *Only One Storm* (1942), *Behold Trouble* (1944), and *There Was a Man in Our Town* (1952). *Small Town* (1946) is a candid study of the New York community where he lives. He began conducting a regular department of fiction criticism in the *Saturday Review* in 1958.

Hidden Hand, The (1859), a novel by E. D. E. N. SOUTHWORTH. Mrs. Southworth, one of the most popular and tawdry novelists of her day, won her first success with this novel. It was published originally in the *New York Ledger*, the second half under the title *Capitola's Peril*. Nine years later the *Ledger* reprinted the story and again fifteen years later—probably a unique record. When Mrs. Southworth visited England in 1859, she found London shops displaying "Capitola hats" and "Capitola suits," while three London theaters simultaneously showed dramatic versions of her novel. The play was likewise popular in the United States. The novel was translated immediately into several European languages. The villain "grinds his teeth in impotent rage" and has a "dastard heart," but he is unable to "meet the eagle eye" of the hero.

Hidden Persuaders, The. See VANCE PACKARD.

Higginson, Francis (b. England, 1586—d. Aug. 6, 1630), clergyman, memoirist. Higginson came to Salem, Mass., in 1629 and became its first Congregational minister; he died the next year as a result of the rigorous New England winter. From his *Journal* was taken for publication a section called *New-England's Plantation* (1630); the entire *Journal* was included in the *Life* (1891) of him by his descendant, T. W. Higginson. *New-England's Plantation* was perhaps the earliest of a long line of publications, cultural and commercial, to boost the reputation of New England's climate.

Higginson, Thomas Wentworth (b. Cambridge, Mass., Dec. 22, 1823—d. May 9, 1911), clergyman, soldier, editor, writer. Higginson held pastorates for a number of years in several Massachusetts towns, was a strong abolitionist,

and when the war came raised a company of volunteers. But he was offered the command of the first "slave regiment" and accepted the offer; he related his experiences in *Army Life in a Black Regiment* (1870). He left the army in 1864, and thereafter (aside from a term in the legislature, 1880–81) devoted himself to writing. He knew all the prominent writers of his day and told about many of them in *Cheerful Yesterdays* (1898). He edited (with MABEL LOOMIS TODD) Emily Dickinson's *Poems* (1890). He had a constant desire to discover new talent. He wrote in an easy, pleasant style, starred with occasional epigrams, like his remark that "to be really cosmopolitan, a man must be at home even in his own country."

Higginson was greatly interested in furthering the general welfare and the higher education of women. He wrote a book entitled *Common Sense About Women* (1881). His collection in this field is now the Galatea Collection in the Boston Public Library. He also wrote biographies of Margaret Fuller (1884), his ancestor Francis Higginson (1891), Longfellow (1902), and Whittier (1902); several collections of essays, including *Atlantic Essays* (1871) and *Carlyle's Laugh and Other Surprises* (1909); histories of the United States and of its literature; a novel; and some verse. His *Writings* were collected in seven volumes in 1900, his *Letters and Journals* published in 1921.

Highet, Gilbert (b. Scotland, June 22, 1906—   ), teacher, classical scholar, writer. Highet came to this country in 1937 to teach classics at Columbia University. He became a professor of Latin there in 1950; was naturalized in 1951. He has distinguished himself in both his life and his writings by straddling the dangerous straits between public praise and scholarly recognition. Besides Latin textbooks, Highet wrote *The Classical Tradition* (1949); *The Art of Teaching* (1950); *People, Places, and Books* (1953); *The Migration of Ideas* (1954); *Juvenal the Satirist* (1954); *A Clerk of Oxenford* (1954); *Man's Unconquerable Mind* (1954); *Poets in a Landscape* (1957); *Talents and Geniuses* (1958); *The Powers of Poetry* (1960).

High Tide at Gettysburg (in the *Century Magazine*, July, 1888), a poem by WILL HENRY THOMPSON. It was a rousing battle-piece which immediately won popularity as one of the best Civil War poems.

High Tor (prod., 1936; pub., 1937), a play in prose and verse by MAXWELL ANDERSON. The play mingles realism and satire, ghosts and real persons, the past and the present. A modern young man removes to High Tor, a mountain overlooking the Hudson, as an escape from modern civilization. He can sell his property for a good price, and his fiancée urges him to do so, but he is stubborn. A gang of robbers, ghostly sailors from an old Dutch ship, an old Indian, two rascally lawyers, and other characters add to the amusing and ingenious plot. The hero finally sells his land, marries, and goes West.

Hildreth, Richard (b. Deerfield, Mass., June 28, 1807—d. July 11, 1865), lawyer, historian, economist, editor, novelist. Hildreth began as a lawyer, but soon turned to journalism as offering a wider field for his exploitation of various causes. He was a Federalist, also a decided rationalist. In the field of economics he was a Benthamite, and worked out in his own mind an elaborate philosophical system that applied Jeremy Bentham's ideas to society, politics, ethics, and religion. He planned to expound this philosophy in a series of books, but published only *Theory of Morals* (1844) and *Theory of Politics* (1853), neither very well received. He anticipated modern ideas in his emphasis on increased productivity as a way of solving social ills, rather than a mechanical distribution of wealth after a revolution; he also stressed social and scientific planning. A fanatical abolitionist, he edited two antislavery papers while in British Guiana for his health. But his views were more effectively expressed in a novel, THE SLAVE, OR, MEMOIRS OF ARCHY MOORE (1836), often reprinted as *Archy Moore*. Archy, a slave of mainly white descent, tells the harrowing story of his adventures in the South, of his marriage and the birth of his son, and of his escape to the North. It is a bitter, realistic indictment of slavery, called by Alexander Cowie "the first full-blown antislavery novel." It recalls an earlier English novel, Aphra Behn's *Oroonoko, or, The Royal Slave* (1678), laid in Surinam, then a part of British Guiana. It went through several editions, was translated into French and Italian, was then forgotten.

A magazine editor and contributor for many years, Hildreth joined HORACE GREELEY's New York *Tribune* in 1855 and stayed till 1861 when Lincoln appointed him to a consulship at Trieste; he held this office until 1864. The most important work of Hildreth, written during his 40's, was a six-volume *History of the United States* (1849–52), which discussed events till 1821 from a strongly Federalist viewpoint and which was solid, accurate, and dull. Donald Emerson, in his *Richard Hildreth* (1946), reveals Hildreth as in many ways a typical New Englander.

Hill, David J[ayne] (b. Plainfield, N.J., June 10, 1850—d. March 2, 1932), educational administrator, historian, diplomat, biographer. Hill was president first of Bucknell University, then of Rochester University, later taught in Washington, D.C., and then served as assistant secretary of state there. He also served as United States minister to Switzerland and the Netherlands and as ambassador to Germany. Among his books: *Washington Irving* (1879); *William Cullen Bryant* (1879); *The History of Diplomacy in the Development of Europe* (3 v., 1905–14); *The People's Government* (1915); *The Problem of a World Court* (1927).

Hill, Frank Ernest (b. San Jose, Calif., Aug. 29, 1888—   ), poet, teacher, editor, radio scriptwriter. Hill taught at Illinois, Stanford, and Columbia Universities; worked for the New York *Globe* and New York *Sun;* has been active as a radio writer and lecturer. He published *Stone Dust* (1928), a collection of verse, and rendered Chaucer's *Canterbury Tales* into mod-

ern verse (1930, 1935). His *The Winged Horse* (1927) is a history of poetry, written with JOSEPH AUSLANDER; later he edited *The Winged Horse Anthology* (1929). He also wrote *What Is American?* (1933), *Listen and Learn* (1937), *Radio's Listening Groups* (1941), *To Meet Will Shakespeare* (1949); and two accounts of Henry Ford and his motor company (1954, 1957).

Hill, Frederic Stanhope (b. Boston, 1805—d. April 7, 1851), editor, poet, playwright, actor. Hill abandoned the study of law to become the editor of two Boston periodicals, published *The Harvest Festival and Other Poems* (1826), then went on the stage, first as an actor, later as a stage manager. Ill health forced his retirement, but he wrote two popular plays: *The Six Degrees of Crime, or, Wine, Women, Gambling, Theft, Murder, and the Scaffold* (1826) and *The Shoemaker of Toulouse* (1834).

Hill, George Handel ["Yankee Hill"] (b. Boston, Oct. 9, 1809—d. Sept. 27, 1848), actor, humorist, memoirist. Hill, only fifteen or sixteen at the time, saw Alexander Simpson play the role of Jonathan Ploughboy in Samuel Woodworth's THE FOREST ROSE (1825) and made up his mind to become a comedian in Yankee roles. He appeared first in such a role in 1826, but not until he played Jonathan Ploughboy some years later was he recognized as the leading interpreter of the Yankee on the stage. In 1836 Hill went to England, later to Paris, and won a huge success as Hiram Dodge, a Yankee sharper in Morris Barnett's extravaganza, *The Yankee Peddler, or, Old Times in Virginia* (1834). As he grew more popular, Hill tended more and more toward monologues, with occasional interruptions by the other players. Then he adopted the monologue outright, anticipating a modern tribe of performers. Thus he would give, alone on the stage, an account of "A Learned Society," a satiric presentation of the New England thirst for abstruse discussion. His biography was written by W. K. Northall (*Life and Recollections of Yankee Hill,* 1850). In his own lifetime Hill published *Little Hill's Yankee Story Book* (1836), a gathering of monologues. After his death appeared *Scenes from the Life of an Actor, Compiled from the Journals, Letters, and Memoranda of the Late Yankee Hill* (1853).

Hill, Grace Livingston (b. Wellsville, N.Y., April 16, 1865—d. Feb. 23, 1947), novelist. At the time of her death Mrs. Hill had published her seventy-ninth volume and was at work on her eightieth; her books were said to have sold in excess of 4,000,000 copies. She had the knack of writing pleasant, wholesome, sentimental stories that many American women liked to read. Her first book was *A Chautauqua Idyl* (1887). Others were: *Katherine's Yesterday* (1896); *Phoebe Dean* (1909); *Exit Betty* (1920); *Rainbow Cottage* (1934); *Head of the House* (1940). Jean Kerr described *Grace Livingston Hill: Her Story and Her Writings* (1948).

Hill, John Alexander ["Jim Skeever"] (b. Bennington, Vt., Feb. 22, 1858—d. Jan. 24, 1916), printer, railroader, editor, essayist, publisher.

Hill started to work in a print shop, later was an engineman, finally entered newspaper work on the Pueblo (Col.) *Daily Press*. Later he became editor of a railroad periodical, *Railroad Engineering*. For this he composed essays, often in story form, giving advice to enginemen. These were gathered into book form as *Jim Skeever's Object Lessons*. He also published *Stories of the Railroad*, and wrote a textbook for locomotive engineers and firemen. In his final years he was president of the Hill Publishing Company, predecessor of the present McGraw-Hill Book Company.

Hill, Billy [William Joseph] (b. Boston, 1898—d. Dec. 24, 1940), song writer. Hill wrote numerous tunes that have become folk songs. He became famous in 1933 with *The Last Round-Up*, with its partial use of traditional cowboy material. Among his other songs are *The Old Spinning-Wheel, There's a Cabin in the Pines, Wagon Wheels, Colorado Moon, Chapel in the Moonlight, For Molly and Me, Sleepy Head*.

Hillhouse, James A[braham] (b. New Haven, Conn., Sept. 26, 1789—d. Jan. 4, 1841), poet, dramatist, member of Congress, merchant. Hillhouse was a devout admirer of the Middle Ages, rejecting in its behalf both the ancient classical world and his own times. For fifty years a congressman and a wealthy merchant, Hillhouse made poetry and drama his avocation. His drama in verse, *Demetria* (composed, 1813; pub., 1839), is considered his best piece. *Percy's Masque* (1819) was based on Bishop Percy's ballad, *The Hermit of Warksworth*. *Sachem's-Wood* (1838) is a sentimental and humorous description of his own beautiful estate in New Haven. He made a two-volume collection of his writings in 1839—*Dramas, Discourses, and Other Pieces*. C. T. Hazelrigg's *American Literary Pioneer* (1953) is a "bibliographical study" of Hillhouse.

Hillquit, Morris (b. Latvia, 1869—d. 1933), lawyer, Socialist leader, writer. Hillquit came to the United States in 1886, was twice an unsuccessful candidate for mayor of New York City, wrote several books: *A History of Socialism in the U.S.* (1903); *Socialism Summed Up* (1912); *From Marx to Lenin* (1921); and an autobiography, *Loose Leaves from a Diary* (1934).

Hillyer, Robert [Silliman] (b. East Orange, N.J., June 3, 1895—d. Dec. 24, 1961), essayist, poet, translator. Hillyer taught at Harvard, Trinity, and Kenyon. His first book was *Sonnets and Other Lyrics* (1917), followed by many others—among them *Hills Give Promise* (1923); *The Seventh Hill* (1928); *A Letter to Robert Frost and Others* (1937); *Pattern of a Day* (1940); *The Death of Captain Nemo* (1949); *The Relic and Other Poems* (1957); *In Pursuit of Poetry* (1960); *Collected Poems* (1961). His *Collected Verse* (1933) won a Pulitzer Prize. In *Poems for Music* (1947) he gathered what he considered his seventy best lyrics. He wrote several novels and made a rendering of the Egyptian *Book of the Dead—The

Coming Forth by Day (1923). Henry W. Wells calls Hillyer a "neoclassicist"; he often writes with humor and ease in a revival of the eighteenth-century heroic couplet.

Hilton, James ["Glen Trevor"] (b. England, Sept. 9, 1900—d. Dec. 20, 1954), newspaperman, textbook author, novelist. Hilton first came to the United States in 1936, took up residence in California and applied for naturalization in 1948. Chiefly known as a novelist, he wrote such great successes as *And Now Goodbye* (1931); *Rage in Heaven* (1932); *Lost Horizon* (1933); *Goodbye, Mr. Chips* (1934); *Catherine Herself* (1935); *We Are Not Alone* (1937); *Random Harvest* (1941); *So Well Remembered* (1945); *Nothing So Strange* (1947); *Time and Time Again* (1953). Many of his books were distributed by the Literary Guild, which sold more than two million copies of them.

him (1927), a play by E. E. CUMMINGS. Taking hints from German expressionism, James Joyce, and other literary pioneers, Cummings produced an extraordinary conglomeration of techniques and effects in this "phantasmagoria." The play was produced by the PROVINCETOWN PLAYERS in 1928.

Hindus, Maurice [Gershon] (b. Russia, Feb. 27, 1891—   ), free-lance writer, author of books on Russia, novelist. Hindus came to the United States in 1905, attended Colgate and Harvard Universities, began contributing articles to various magazines. He visited Russia on numerous occasions to secure materials for articles and books. Among the latter: *Russian Peasant and Revolution* (1920); *Broken Earth* (1926); *Humanity Uprooted* (1929); *Red Bread* (1931); *The Great Offensive* (1933); *Mother Russia* (1943); *The Cossacks* (1945); *Crisis in the Kremlin* (1953). He has also written an account of his youth, *Green Worlds* (1938), and several novels, among them *Moscow Skies* (1936); *To Sing with the Angels* (1941); *Magda* (1951).

Hinkle, Thomas C[lark] (b. Laclede, Ill., June 12, 1876—d. May 13, 1949), author of juveniles. Hinkle was one of the best writers for young people in the mid-20th century. Most of his stories deal with animals. He began with numerous books for very young readers, about Tiny Cottontail and Doctor Rabbit; went on to *Tawny, A Dog of the Old West* (1927); *Shag, the Story of a Dog* (1931); *Silver, The Story of a Wild Horse* (1934); *Old Nick and Bob, Two Dogs of the West* (1941), and many others.

Hintz, Howard William (b. New York City, June 10, 1903—   ), educator, clergyman. Hintz was a high-school teacher and a Presbyterian pastor before becoming an instructor of English at the College of the City of New York (1929) and at Brooklyn College (1930), where he became a professor in 1951 and chairman of the Philosophy Department in 1953. His lectures and his contributions to professional journals are in the fields of religion, philosophy, education, and literature. His books show the combination of these interests, and include: *Basic

Necessity for Spiritual Reconstruction (1936); *Religion and the Crisis of Democracy* (1938); *Thomas Wentworth Higginson, Disciple of the Newness* (1939); *Modern American Vistas* (1940); *The Quaker Influence in American Literature* (1940); *Adventures in Living, An Introduction to the Study of Biography* (1947); *Religion and Higher Education* (1955). Hintz was also general editor of *Knowledge and Values: An Introduction to Philosophy* (1958).

Hiroshima (1946), a report by JOHN HERSEY. Hersey went to the Japanese city in May, 1946, to report the results of the explosion of the first A-bomb on Aug. 6, 1945. He wrote a 30,000-word account for *The New Yorker*, which devoted its entire editorial space to the report in its issue of Aug. 31, 1946. The issue sold out immediately, and there was a tremendous demand for reprints. To satisfy popular interest the American Broadcasting Company canceled all its regular 8:30–9:00 broadcasts on four successive evenings to read the entire piece to listeners all over the country. In November the account was published in book form, and within a year had been serialized and translated all over the world in a dozen languages and in Braille. The account was objective and horrifying; it concentrated on the lives of six representative inhabitants of Hiroshima. It was generally accepted as a masterpiece of reportage, in which the truth was allowed to make its own moral impact.

Hirst, Henry Beck ["Anna Maria Hirst"] (b. Philadelphia, Aug. 23, 1817—d. March 30, 1874), lawyer, newspaperman, poet. Hirst was one of the few male writers who have assumed the name of a woman as a pseudonym; he contributed articles to several magazines under the pen name of Anna Maria Hirst. His first book, *The Book of Caged Birds* (1843), gave hints to bird lovers and contained a few poems. ENDYMION (1848) was an imitation of Keats; a year later he published *The Penance of Roland*. He was for a time a friend of Poe, but offended him by writing a parody of THE HAUNTED PALACE. In later years Hirst became an absinthe addict and died in an asylum for the insane; at this time he began claiming the authorship of Poe's *The Raven*.

His Family (1917), a novel by ERNEST POOLE. A father and his three daughters provide Poole with material for a study in the contrasting ideals of two generations in New York City. One daughter is completely devoted to the welfare of her five children; another, the principal of a high school, sacrifices herself to the interests of her young people; the third is a devotee of pleasure. The father helps to solve the problems of the first two, can do little for the third. The novel won a Pulitzer Prize.

history, writing of. Probably the first history of America written was Captain JOHN SMITH's *The General History of Virginia, New England, and the Summer Isles* (1624), which was rather a personal narrative than a true history. Some of the other "adventurers" contributed to Smith's book. Elsewhere in the colonies, history was written chiefly in New England. The so-called *Mourt's Relation* (1622), named after its publisher, was an anonymous account of "the English Plantation Settled at Plymouth" (see GEORGE MORTON). Edward Winslow wrote GOOD NEWS FROM NEW ENGLAND (1624). There followed a phalanx of New England historians— William Bradford, Nathaniel Morton, John Winthrop, Francis Higginson, Edward Johnson, John Mason, Cotton Mather, William Hubbard, Thomas Prince, Thomas Hutchinson, Daniel Gookin. Soon historians began to appear in colonies outside New England—Cadwallader Colden, John Lawson, Robert Beverley, William Stith, William Smith, Samuel Smith.

The coming of the Revolution gave a new and inspiring theme to the historians, among whom were William Gordon, David Ramsay, William Henry Drayton, William Moultrie, John Marshall, William Wirt, Mercy Warren, and Mason Locke ("Parson") Weems, who was more inspired than accurate. Many state histories appeared, later general histories of the United States. Among those who wrote on the latter theme were Abiel Holmes, Timothy Pitkin, Richard Hildreth, John Gorham Palfrey, George Tucker, and George Bancroft. Historical documents and data were collected by Ebenezer Hazard, Jeremy Belknap, Jedediah Morse, Jaret Sparks, Peter Force. Numerous biographies of American leaders appeared. Sparks was one of the earliest to write biographies—such as his life of Gouverneur Morris (1832)—objectively and well, although flaws have been discovered in his editing of letters. In the middle of the 19th century New England gave birth to three historians, sometimes disparaged as "literary"— William H. Prescott, John Lothrop Motley, and Francis Parkman; they were notable for the grace and imagination of their style and for dealing sometimes with material outside the United States. Washington Irving should be linked with them, although history-writing was of secondary interest to him.

Since the mid-19th century the output of American historians and biographers has increased greatly. The emphasis has been increasingly on the history of the United States and of the Americas, a theme that has also attracted many writers abroad. Noteworthy names in this period are Reuben Gold Thwaites, John W. Burgess, Herbert B. Adams, John William Draper, Henry Harrisse, Justin Winsor, Edward Eggleston, John Fiske, Henry Charles Lea, Hubert Howe Bancroft, Alfred Thayer Mahan, Charles Francis Adams, Henry Adams, W. G. Sumner, James Ford Rhodes, A. B. McMaster, Frederick J. Turner, Carl Becker, Preserved Smith, A. B. Hart, Edward Channing, H. E. Von Holst, E. P. Oberholtzer, James Harvey Robinson, Charles E. Beard, Charles E. Merriam, Woodrow Wilson, James Truslow Adams, Vernon L. Parrington, Henry Steele Commager, Allan Nevins, Charles Wertenbaker, Arthur M. Schlesinger, Samuel E. Morison, James G. Randall, Dixon Wecter.

In the course of time, the viewpoint of historical scholars has altered materially. The endeavor has been to avoid being literary and to become scientific. This stress has, however, tended to deaden imagination and to produce dullness. In later eras the influence of German scholarship was all-powerful, and Henry Adams attempted to adapt its methods to a study of American democracy. Actually, aside from technical procedures, he was even more under the influence of the ideas of his brother Brooks Adams, who gloomily saw history as an ever-continuing struggle between concentration and dissipation of energy, between fear and greed; and who took over, as well as he could, the mechanical laws of physics to explain the activities of man in society. Other writers, like Beard, stressed an economic interpretation of history, some to the point of accepting Marxian economic determinism.

J. F. Jameson wrote *The History of Historical Writing in America* (1891). Michael Krause wrote on the *History of American History* (1937), and the *Writing of American History* (1953), the latter a revision of his earlier work. *Historians and Their Craft* (1951), edited by Herman Ausubel, examines the leading ideas in the credos of the fifty-nine eminent historians who from 1884 to 1945 served as presidents of the American Historical Association in an endeavor to show the development of historiography in the United States. S. E. Morison wrote a stimulating essay on *History as a Literary Art* (included in his collection *By Land and by Sea*, 1953). Marie Collins Swabey wrote on *The Judgment of History* (1954), and A. S. Eisenstadt's *Charles McLean Andrews* (1956) is a study of the changing patterns of half a century of American historical writing, especially as influenced by Andrews. See *Harvard Guide to American History*.

History and Present State of Virginia, The (pub. London, 1705; rev., 1722), by ROBERT BEVERLEY. Beverley was a wealthy planter who while in London saw an unfavorable account of the colony of Virginia written by the British historian and pamphleteer John Oldmixon. Beverley undertook to do a better book, and his *History* was the result. Fred L. Pattee describes it as "a straightforward, sensible account of the actual Virginia of his day." Jay Hubbell calls the book "a minor but genuine American classic," and Louis B. Wright charged our literary historians with neglecting it for inferior works by New England divines (*The First Gentlemen of Virginia*, 1940). Wright has also edited (1945) Beverley's *Essay Upon the Government of the English Plantations*.

History of. For books where this is the first principal word in the title, see the proper name instead, e.g. *The History of Maria Kettle*: see MARIA KETTLE.

History of the Dividing Line Between Virginia and North Carolina: Run in the Year 1728 (first pub., 1841), by WILLIAM BYRD II. A later edition of the book prepared by William K. Boyd (1929) added *The Secret History of the Line*, taken from manuscript. Writing with

gentility but zest, Byrd related his experience with a party of surveyors from Virginia. The story is spiced with humor, at moments with satire, as when he writes disparagingly of some of the inhabitants of North Carolina.

History of the United States During the Administrations of Jefferson and Madison (9 v., 1885–1891), by HENRY ADAMS. This is a work of immense detail on diplomatic and political occurrences, but it is sometimes criticized for its comparative lack of attention to economic and social aspects of the period treated. It shows great narrative skill, and Adams writes with liveliness and charm. The research done in preparation for the nine volumes was extensive, and the work has been praised as "a monument to the scientific theory of history." Adams believed that the individual is helpless to control his own destiny, and pointed the moral by showing that the dynamic leader Jefferson left the country in a state approaching ruin, whereas Madison, unable to lead others, chose to drift and restored the country's prosperity. Adams had his volumes privately printed in six copies for the comments and suggestions of his friends, before placing the work before the public; later he often followed this practice.

Hitchcock, Alfred Joseph (b. England, Aug. 13, 1899—), movie director. The direction of over forty films has made Hitchcock's name virtually synonymous with a certain type of suspense movie. A typical formula is employed in many of these films: a pair of normal, attractive people find themselves caught up simultaneously in a personal romance and a bizarre and complicated intrigue. After the various complexities of plot unfold (often against an exotic background), the film winds up with a perilous chase or a hairbreadth reprieve from imminent disaster. In addition to the elements of romance and suspense, the films have been distinguished by sophistication, humor, ingenious plotting, effective use of atmosphere and secondary characters, and superior acting. Among his films are *The 39 Steps* (1935); *Sabotage* (1937); *The Lady Vanishes* (1938); *Rebecca* (1940); *Suspicion* (1941); *Lifeboat* (1943); *Spellbound* (1944); *Stage Fright* (1950); *Strangers On A Train* (1951); *Rear Window* (1954); and *Psycho* (1960). He has also lent his name to a successful television series "Alfred Hitchcock Presents"; to *Alfred Hitchcock's Mystery Magazine*, and to a number of anthologies of suspense stories.

Hitchcock, Edward (b. Deerfield, Mass., May 24, 1793—d. Feb. 27, 1864), geologist, teacher. Hitchcock taught at Amherst College, engaged in official geological surveys, returned to Amherst as president (1845–54). Hitchcock's theological leanings influenced his scientific views; he sought earnestly to find evidence for Mosaic conceptions in his researches and to reconcile theology and Darwinism. His views were expressed in *The Religion of Geology and Its Connected Sciences* (1851). He spent three years exploring Massachusetts, and in 1833 published his *Report on the Geology, Mineralogy, Botany, and Zoology of Massachusetts,* with a *Final Report* in 1841.

Hitchcock, Enos (b. Springfield, Mass., March 7, 1744—d. Feb. 26, 1803), clergyman, novelist, biographer. Hitchcock served as a chaplain in the Continental army and wrote a life of Washington (1800). He is chiefly remembered as the author of the second American novel published in book form, *Memoirs of the Bloomsgrove Family* (1790; see BLOOMSGROVE). The book is full of moral discourses, but Alexander Cowie praises Hitchcock's advanced educational doctrines. The book is also noteworthy as an early protest against imitation of the British. Hitchcock wrote a *Treatise on Education* (1790) and another story, *The Farmer's Friend, or, The History of Mr. Charles Worthy* (1793).

Hitchcock, Ethan Allen (b. Vergennes, Vt., May 18, 1798—d. Aug. 5, 1870), soldier, teacher, critic, philosopher. Hitchcock graduated from West Point, taught there for many years, served in the Mexican and Civil Wars, reaching finally the rank of major general. A report that he wrote (1830) on mistreatment of the Indians was suppressed. All his life Hitchcock was deeply interested in literature and theology, and published a number of books in these fields—among them *The Doctrines of Spinoza and Swedenborg Identified* (1846); *Swedenborg: A Hermetic Philosopher* (1858); *Remarks on the Sonnets of Shakespeare* (1865); *Notes on the "Vita Nuova" and Minor Poems of Dante* (1866). Two posthumously published volumes tell about his own experiences: *Fifty Years in Camp and Field* (1909) and *A Traveler in Indian Territory* (1930).

Hitchcock, [James] Ripley (b. Fitchburg, Mass., July 3, 1857—d. May 4, 1918), newspaperman, critic, editor. Hitchcock served as art critic on the New York *Tribune* (1882–90), wrote *Etching in America* (1886). He also wrote historical treatises, *The Louisiana Purchase* (1903) and *The Lewis and Clark Expedition* (1905), and edited "The Story of the West" series (7 v., 1895–1902). He served as editorial adviser for Appleton and Harper, and was instrumental in discovering several important authors, including Stephen Crane.

Hitti, Phillip K[huri] (b. Lebanon, June 24, 1886—   ), Orientalist, teacher. Hitti came to the United States in 1913, was naturalized in 1920, became a member and finally chairman of the department of Oriental languages at Princeton. He served on many learned and governmental bodies and wrote numerous books, including *Origins of the Islamic State* (1916); *The Syrians in America* (1924); *History of the Arabs* (1937, rev. 1960); *The Arabs* (1944, rev. 1960); *Lebanon in History* (1957); *Syria: A Short History* (1959); *The Near East in History* (1961). Hitti visited almost all the lands of the Arab world and so came to know personally heads of state and leading journalists and professors.

H. M. Pulham, Esq. (1941), a novel by JOHN P. MARQUAND. Unlike THE LATE GEORGE APLEY (1937), Pulham partially escapes from his Boston environment and inhibitions by way of World War I, and falls in love with a girl in New York, but like George Apley he weds the girl his family selects for him. The book goes on to explore the cost of conformity for both Pulham and his wife. The book satirizes the Boston Brahmin society and the change in their mores after the war. See BRAHMINS.

Hoagland, Edward (b. New York City, Dec. 21, 1932—   ), novelist. Hoagland graduated from Harvard in 1954, then served in the Army for two years, during which time he wrote, under a Houghton Mifflin Fellowship, *Cat Man* (1956). The book takes the reader behind the scenes of a circus into a raw, violent world, where the beasts are considerably less filthy than the human beings. *The Circle Home* followed in 1960. Hoagland obtained material by actually working in the locales of his novels, the circus and boxing gymnasiums.

hoaxes. Practical jokes and the like have played a large part in American folklore and humor. In frontier conditions, greenhorns and tenderfeet were the subject of incessant and sometimes cruel pranks; the country yokel was a favorite butt of urban tricksters; the "bad boy," immortalized by GEORGE W. PECK, was given large license in his endeavors to disrupt the dignity of his elders. In literature one of the first important figures associated with hoaxes was Edgar Allan Poe. He had a great fondness for gulling the public, as was evident especially in THE BALLOON HOAX (1844) and *The Facts in the Case of M. Valdemar* (*American Review*, December, 1845). In turn Poe was the subject of hoaxes, especially after his death, when poems written by others were passed off as his; one of the best—*Leonainie*—came from the pen of JAMES WHITCOMB RILEY. William Cullen Bryant was the similar victim of a poem called *A Vision of Immortality*.

The western humorists of the Mark Twain era constantly indulged in hoaxes and spoofs. In 1854, for example, Ferdinand Cartwright Ewer, who later became a minister, wrote a burlesque of spiritualism, then sent a reprint of the article to a magazine in New York ardently devoted to spirit communication. The editor printed the article in good faith, and one spiritualistic publication after another did the same. Ewer confessed the hoax, but the more ardent members of the cause refused to believe him. At about the same time GEORGE HORATIO DERBY, better known as "John Phoenix" and "Squibob," contributed to the San Francisco *Herald* a scientific report by one Dr. Hermann Ellenbogen on certain zoological discoveries in the mountains of Washington Territory, including living specimens of the Gyascutus and the Prock. The parody was reprinted in the East and proved to the Coast how gullible easterners were.

Not long after MARK TWAIN joined the staff of the Virginia City *Enterprise* he described the discovery in the Sierras of a petrified man, with one hand extended from the tip of his nose. The story was widely reprinted. One of Twain's most solemn and most successful hoaxes was the famous paragraph in *The Double-Barreled Detective Story* (1902) describing a spicy morning in early October, in which, among other details, he tells how "far in the empty sky a solitary oesophagus slept upon motionless wing."

In the east WITTER BYNNER and Arthur Davison Ficke fooled the literary public with their SPECTRA poems, written under the pseudonyms of Emanuel Morgan and Anne Knish, respectively. The BATHTUB HOAX of H. L. Mencken was a solemn article in the New York *Evening Mail* (1917), relating how the bathtub had been invented in Cincinnati in the 1840's and first installed in the White House by President Fillmore, and alleging that its use had been opposed by many doctors as an unhealthful practice. The tale was widely accepted, even adopted by an encyclopedia. In 1925 Mencken confessed the hoax, but it is still circulating as indubitable fact. It was reprinted with other essays in *The Bathtub Hoax* (1958). An unintentional hoax was the famous ORSON WELLES broadcast (1938) of Howard Koch's radio adaptation of H. G. Wells' *The War of the Worlds*, which panicked millions of listeners into believing the Martians were invading the earth. Curtis D. MacDougall described other instances in *Hoaxes* (1940). See HUMOR IN THE U.S.; also CARDIFF GIANT, HORN PAPERS, TALL TALES.

Hobart, Alice Tisdale [Nourse] (b. Lockport, N.Y., Jan. 28, 1882—d. March 14, 1967), writer of travel books, novelist. With her husband, an American businessman in China, Mrs. Hobart spent twenty years in the cities of that country and on the Manchurian and Mongolian frontiers. She embodied accounts of her experiences first in such books as *Pioneering Where the World Is Old* (1917) and *Within the Walls of Nanking* (1928), then in a series of novels about the experiences of white men in the world of Mongolians. Chief among these was *Oil for the Lamps of China* (1933). In *Their Own Country* (1940) the characters in the former book return and face the economic problems of America. Later Mrs. Hobart produced *The Peacock Sheds His Tail* (1945) about Mexico and *The Cleft Rock* (1948) about four generations in California; also *The Serpent-Wreathed Staff* (1951) and *Venture into Darkness* (1955). *Gusty's Child*, her autobiography, was published in 1959.

Hobomok: A Tale of Early Times (1824), a historical romance by LYDIA MARIA CHILD. The author, then aged only twenty-two, read a review by J. G. Palfrey that had appeared three years before in the *North American Review* (April, 1821) urging American writers to treat American themes. Immediately she sat down and wrote the first chapter of a novelette in which the Enoch Arden theme was treated forty years before Tennyson. The story supposedly follows an old Puritan manuscript, and relates how a young girl, betrothed to a neighbor who has

been reported lost at sea, falls in love with a handsome, refined Indian chief, marries him, and has a son by him. Then her betrothed returns, and the Indian nobly gives her up. It is one of the earliest novels laid in Puritan times, also one of the earliest to introduce an Indian character in a favorable light.

Hobson, Laura Z[ametkin] (b. New York City, June 18, 1900—   ), writer. Mrs. Hobson worked for various magazines and newspapers until 1935, when she began to write short stories. Her first novel, *The Trespassers* (1943), dealt partially with the problems of refugees denied entrance to the United States because of the immigrant quota system. GENTLEMAN'S AGREEMENT (1947), which attacked anti-Semitism, was highly praised, and made into a successful film. Mrs. Hobson also wrote *The Other Father* (1950) and *The Celebrity* (1951).

Hocking, William Ernest (b. Cleveland, Ohio, Aug. 10, 1873—d. June 12, 1966), philosopher. Hocking joined the Harvard faculty in 1914 and served there until his retirement (1943). He took a stand against the naturalistic and skeptical philosophers of the day, and won renown as "an impenitent idealist." Interested in logic, psychology, ethics, politics, world religion, he writes of them with great vitality. Brand Blanshard feels that Hocking's first principle is that the world must be taken as a systematic whole of meaning. Hocking's first important work was *The Meaning of God in Human Experience* (1912). Other books: *Man and the State* (1926); *The Lasting Elements of Individualism* (1937); *Thoughts on Death and Life* (1937); *Science and the Idea of God* (1944); *Freedom of the Press* (1947); *Experiment in Education* (1954); *Meaning of Immortality in Human Experience* (1957); *Strength of Men and Nations* (1959).

Hodge, Charles (b. Philadelphia, Dec. 27, 1797—d. June 19, 1878), theologian, teacher. Hodge taught at Princeton Theological Seminary from 1820 until his death. He founded the *Biblical Repertory* (1825), which later (1836) became the *Biblical Repertory and Princeton Review*, then in 1875 the *Princeton Review*, and in 1888 was merged with the *Political Science Quarterly*. Hodge is said to have boasted that in his fifty years at Princeton there had never been broached a new or original idea. His most important work was his *Systematic Theology* (4 v., 1872—1873), a treatise on traditional Calvinism. He also wrote *What Is Darwinism?* (1874).

Hodge, Frederick Webb (b. England, Oct. 28, 1864—d. Sept. 28, 1956), ethnologist, government official, explorer. Hodge attained great eminence as an authority on the Indians; he worked mainly with the Bureau of American Ethnology at Washington and museums in New York and Los Angeles. He conducted several ethnological expeditions in the Southwest and made important discoveries. He wrote numerous articles and monographs, and edited *Handbook of the American Indians North of Mexico* (1907–10), *Narratives of Cabeza de Vaca and Coronado* (1907), *Curtis's North American*

Indian (20 v., 1907–10), and similar volumes.

Hodgins, Eric (b. Detroit, Mich., March 2, 1899—   ), editor, novelist. An experienced hand in the magazine and advertising business, Hodgins first wrote, in collaboration with F. A. Magoun, *Sky High* (1929; rev. ed., 1935), *A History of Aircraft* (1931), and *Behemoth* (1932). His keen sense of satire and his dissatisfaction with the social scene made him turn to fiction, and he wrote *Mr. Blandings Builds His Dream House* (1946) and *Blandings' Way* (1950). The latter was in part a savage attack on advertising agencies, in part an attack on alleged liberals.

Hoe, Robert (b. England, Oct. 29, 1784—d. Jan. 4, 1833), inventor. Hoe came to the United States in 1803, and with his son **Richard March Hoe** (b. Sept. 12, 1812—d. June 7, 1886) invented the revolutionary rotary printing presses. The son invented a machine to fold newspapers as they came from the presses. His grandson, **Robert Hoe** (b. Mar. 10, 1839—d. Sept. 22, 1909), further improved the Hoe presses and was also an ardent book collector who was a founder of the GROLIER CLUB (1884) and was its first president. He wrote *A Short History of the Printing Press* (1902).

Hoehn, Matthew (b. Newark, N.J., 1883—d. May 13, 1959), teacher, librarian, biographer. Educated at St. Benedict's School in Newark, he became a member of the Order of St. Benedict and a librarian at the school. After many years of research, he compiled a volume of 620 "vignettes" called CATHOLIC AUTHORS: CONTEMPORARY BIOGRAPHICAL SKETCHES (1948), a valuable and readable work of reference. It was supplemented with a second volume (1952), containing 374 additional sketches.

Hoffenstein, Samuel [Goodman] (b. Lithuania, Oct. 8, 1890—d. Oct. 6, 1947), poet, humorist, newspaperman, screenwriter. Hoffenstein worked for the New York *Sun* after graduation from Lafayette, later became a press agent for a theatrical producer, and for the last fourteen years of his life was in Hollywood as a screenwriter. He prepared the screen versions of many important books, including Dreiser's AMERICAN TRAGEDY. But he himself felt that his Hollywood work had ruined his literary career. His first collection of verse, *Life Sings a Song* (1916), was unimportant, but when his sardonic *Poems in Praise of Practically Nothing* (1928) appeared, they created a great sensation. They were a characteristic product of the Jazz Age in their cynicism, but there was a note of gaiety that relieved them of all sourness and insincerity. Hoffenstein also revealed himself as an accomplished parodist and didn't spare some contemporary cynics. He followed this collection with *Year In, You're Out* (1930), then was silent until *Pencil in the Air* (1947). His *Complete Poetry* appeared in 1954.

Hoffman, Arthur Sullivant (b. Columbus, Ohio, Sept. 28, 1876—   ), teacher, editor, author of books on writing. Hoffman held editorial positions on numerous important magazines, was especially eminent as editor of *Adven-*

ture (1911–27), where the stories were thrillers, but always authentic in background. He founded the Adventurers' Club of New York. He was also the founder and namer of the 1915 American Legion. In 1929 he became a teacher of fiction writing. Among his books: *Fundamentals of Fiction Writing* (1922); *Fiction Writers on Fiction Writing* (1923); *Writing of Fiction* (1934); *Fiction Writing Self-Taught* (1939).

Hoffman, Charles Fenno (b. New York City, Feb. 7, 1806—d. June 7, 1884), lawyer, editor, novelist, memoirist, poet. Hoffman, who had been trained in the law, abandoned that profession for writing, first as a contributor to news-

papers and magazines (especially the *Knickerbocker*), then as a poet and novelist. He became famous for the novel he based on a Kentucky murder case, GREYSLAER: A ROMANCE OF THE MOHAWK (1840); and the lively descriptive letters he wrote during a journey across the Alleghenies and over the prairies were collected in *A Winter in the West* (1835). Later he wrote *Wild Scenes in the Forest and Prairie* (1839). He published three books of verse, later collected in *Poems* (1873). An unfinished novel, *Vanderlyn*, appeared in the *American Monthly Magazine* when he was its editor (1835–37). His last years were clouded by mental illness; in 1850 he was committed to a hospital. Homer F. Barnes wrote Hoffman's biography (1930). WASHINGTON IRVING was betrothed to Hoffman's sister Matilda, and her early death was the great tragedy of his life. See KNICKERBOCKER SCHOOL.

Hoffman, Malvina (b. New York City, June 15, 1887—d. July 10, 1966), sculptor. Miss Hoffman produced sculptures for many important projects and buildings, including the stone panel façade of World War II Memorial American Cemetery, at Épinal, France. She wrote an absorbing biography, *Heads and Tales* (1930); also *Sculpture Inside and Out* (1939) and *American Sculpture Series* (1948).

Hofstadter, Richard (b. Buffalo, N.Y., Aug. 6, 1916—d. Oct. 24, 1970), educator, specialist in the history of politics. After teaching at City College and Brooklyn College in New York, Hofstadter was appointed to the Columbia University faculty, and reached professorial rank in 1952. His interest in American history was first quickened by the writings of CHARLES A. BEARD. Over the years he progressively defined his views of American history by differentiating them from Beard's until the accumulated differences became considerable. Among his books: *Social Darwinism in American Thought* (1944, second ed. 1960); *The American Political Tradition* (1948); *The Development and Scope of Higher Education in the U.S.* (1952); *The Age of Reform: From Bryan to F.D.R.* (1955), which won the Pulitzer Prize in 1956; *The Development of Academic Freedom in the United States*, with Walter P. Metzger (1955).

Holbrook, Josiah (b. Derby, Conn., 1788—d. 1854), educational and social reformer. Holbrook founded an industrial school on his father's farm, in order to combine manual training and farming with knowledge drawn from books. This school failed, as did other early projects. He then became a lecturer on science and farming, and conceived the idea of an "association of adults for mutual education." The result was the famous American Lyceum, which developed a vast army of readers, gave employment to many authors, and made lectures popular in the United States.

Holbrook founded the first branch at Millbury, Mass., in 1826, established more than a hundred branches before 1829, and within the next seven years set up nearly three thousand more. He wrote *The American Lyceum, or, Society for the Improvement of Schools and Diffusion of Useful Knowledge* (1829); issued *Scientific Tracts Designed for Instruction and Entertainment* (beginning 1832); and established and edited the *Family Lyceum* (1832). He secured as speakers many of the most eminent men of the country, including Daniel Webster, Emerson, Lowell, Holmes. Some of the LYCEUMS were still in existence at the end of the 19th century. They encouraged the foundation of libraries and museums, and were influential disseminators of knowledge. The CHAUTAUQUA, Stewart H. Holbrook says, "was a sort of stepchild of the lyceum."

Holbrook, Stewart H[all] (b. Newport, Vt., Aug. 22, 1893—d. Sept. 3, 1964), newspaperman, historian, lecturer. Holbrook spent his early years in Vermont and New Hampshire, and for a time worked in his father's logging camps. Later he went to the West Coast, where he worked as a newspaperman, editor, and free-lance writer. He has earned a wide reputation for his ability to make history entertaining yet still accurate, and he has lectured on American historical subjects at Harvard, Boston University, and other educational institutions. His first book

was *Holy Old Mackinaw: A Natural History of the American Lumberjack* (1938); his first book to gain a large audience was LOST MEN OF AMERICAN HISTORY (1946). Among his other publications: *Ethan Allen* (1940); *Burning an Empire: America's Great Forest Fires* (1943); *Little Annie Oakley and Other Rugged People* (1948); *Yankee Exodus: An Account of Migration from New England* (1950); *Far Corner: A Personal View of the Pacific Northwest* (1952); *Down on the Farm* (1954); *The Columbia* (1956); *The Rocky Mountain Revolution* (1956); *Dreamers of the American Dream* (1957); *Mr. Otis* (1958); and a satire, *The Golden Age of Quackery* (1959).

Hold Autumn in Your Hand (1941), a novel by GEORGE SESSIONS PERRY. The protagonist, Sam Tucker, is a poor tenant farmer in Texas who scratches a living from the soil. The book centers on his struggle with a catfish.

Holden, Raymond ["Richard Peckham"] (b. New York City, April 7, 1894—   ), writer of mystery stories, novelist, poet. Holden began publishing verse at an early age; his first collection, *Granite and Alabaster* (1922), was followed by *Natural History* (1938), *The Arrow at the Heel* (1940), and *Selected Poems* (1946). Holden has also written fiction, but this failed to win the praise that his poetry evoked. Among his more serious novels are *Chance Has a Whip* (1935) and *Believe the Heart* (1939). His mystery novels are written under the pseudonym Richard Peckham.

Holiday (prod., 1928; pub., 1929), a play by PHILIP BARRY. This is a dissection of a rich man's family, one member of which, Julia, shares her father's drab and conventional ideas, while her brother and sister seek freedom in a wider experience. A young lawyer falls in love with Julia, learns that she is really not what he wants, marries her sister.

Holiday. A magazine published by the Curtis Publication Company. It first appeared in March, 1946, and is devoted to travel and other pursuits of leisure. In 1956 an anthology of pieces from the magazine was published, *Ten Years of Holiday*, which included work by many distinguished authors.

Holland, Edwin Clifford (b. Charleston, S.C., 1794?—d. Sept. 11, 1824), poet, dramatist, editor, essayist. Holland became an editor of the Charleston *Times,* contributed to the *Port Folio* of Philadelphia. He won distinction as a poet with his *Odes, Naval Songs, and Other Occasional Poems* (1813), and his romantic drift was further displayed in a dramatization of Byron's *The Corsair* (1818). This was produced in Charleston in 1818. *Essays; and a Drama in Five Acts* was posthumously published (1852).

Holland, Josiah Gilbert ["Timothy Titcomb"] (b. Belchertown, Mass., July 24, 1819—d. Oct. 12, 1881), editor, novelist, poet, historian. Holland was editor of the Springfield *Republican,* then with Roswell Smith helped found SCRIBNER'S MONTHLY (1870), which he edited until his death. He wrote with frank didacticism, and his stories, poems, essays, and sayings made a great appeal to his generation. Among his novels were *The Bay-Path* (1857), *Miss Gilbert's Career* (1860), ARTHUR BONNICASTLE (1873), and SEVENOAKS: A STORY OF TODAY (1875). He wrote effective verse; his *Poems* were collected in 1873. His *Timothy Titcomb's Letters to Young People, Single and Married* (1858) gave practical advice. His *Life of Abraham Lincoln* (1866) was among the most important of the earlier biographies of Lincoln. See BITTER-SWEET.

Holland, Rupert Sargent (b. Louisville, Ky., Oct. 15, 1878—d. May 4, 1952), lawyer, historian, writer. Holland wrote many excellent and accurate books of historical and other fiction for young people. Among them: *The Boy Scouts of Birch-Bark Island* (1911); *Knights of the Golden Spur* (1912); *Blackbeard's Island* (1916); *The Pirates of the Delaware* (1925); *The Rider in the Green Mask* (1926); *Drake's Lad* (1929); *The Pirate of the Gulf* (1929); *A Race for a Fortune* (1931); *The Sea-Scouts of Birch-Bark Island* (1936); *Secret of Blennerhassett* (1941). Popular also were Holland's *Historic Boyhoods* (1909) and *Historic Girlhoods* (1910) and his *Plays of the American Colonies* (1937).

Hollander, John (b. New York City, Oct. 28, 1929—   ), poet, critic. Winner of the Yale Younger Poets Series Award in 1958, Hollander has had poems published in various periodicals. A collection of his verse, *A Crackling Of Thorns*, appeared in 1958. He is also the author of numerous stories and critical essays and a book of criticism, *The Untuning of The Sky: Ideas of Music in English Poetry, 1500–1700* (1961). He has taught English at Howard and Yale universities.

Holland's: The Magazine of the South. Founded in 1876 as *Street's Weekly*, this magazine took its present name in 1904. It became a monthly, published at Dallas, Tex., by the Farm & Ranch Publishing Co.

Holley, Marietta ["Samantha Allen"] (b. Jefferson Co., N.Y., July 16, 1836—d. March 1, 1926), humorist, essayist, verse writer, novelist. "Josiah Allen's wife" had a practical and moralistic purpose in her many collections of humorous sketches and philosophizings. For example, she was an ardent advocate of temperance and women's suffrage. She believed that "you have to hold up the hammer of a personal incident to drive home the nail of Truth." Her Samantha made occasional errors in spelling and grammar, she indulged in malapropisms, and her knowledge of city ways was deficient, but she was a wise woman in contrast to several fools introduced into the sketches. Among Miss Holley's books: *My Opinions and Betsy Bobbet's* (1873); *Samantha at the Centennial* (1877); *Samantha at Saratoga* (1887); *Samantha Amongst the Colored Folks* (1892); *Samantha at the World's Fair* (1893); *Samantha in Europe* (1895); *Josiah Allen on Women's Rights* (1914). See SAMANTHA.

Holley, Mary [Austin] (b. New Haven, Conn., Oct. 30, 1784—d. Aug. 2, 1846), biographer, author of books on Texas. The wife of a clergyman who became president of Transylvania University, Mrs. Holley was led by accident to the writing of two books on Texas. After the death of her husband, she wrote *A Discourse on the Genius and Character of the Rev. Horace Holley* (1828) and tried to sell it to subscribers. In 1831 she made a trip to Texas to visit a place settled by a distant relative, the famous Stephen Austin. She became deeply interested in the new region and wrote numerous letters about it. These became a book, *Texas: Observations Historical, Geographical, and Descriptive* (1833), the first book on the subject. Later this was expanded into a fuller account, *Texas* (1835).

Holliday, Carl (b. Hanging Rock, Ohio, March 2, 1879—d. Aug. 16, 1936), teacher, poet, historian, critic. Holliday taught at the University of Toledo and at the California State College at San Jose. He published *The Cotton-Picker and Other Poems* (1907), thereafter devoted himself to history, particularly literary history. Among his books: *The Literature of Colonial Virginia* (1909); *The Wit and Humor of Colonial Days* (1912); *Woman's Life in Colonial Days* (1922).

Holliday, Robert Cortes (b. Indianapolis, Ind., July 18, 1880—d. Dec. 31, 1946), editor, critic, essayist, teacher. For a time Holliday edited the BOOKMAN; during the last decade of his life he taught the art of writing. His genial essays were collected in several volumes: *Walking Stick Papers* (1918); *Peeps at People* (1919); *Broome Street Straws* (1919); *Men and Books and Cities* (1920); *Turns about Town* (1920); *Literary Lanes and Other Byways* (1925). He also wrote books on Booth Tarkington (1918) and Joyce Kilmer (1918).

Hollister, Gideon Hiram (b. Washington, Conn., Dec. 14, 1817—d. March 24, 1881), lawyer, poet, novelist, historian. Hollister wrote two novels, *Mount Hope, or, Philip, King of the Wamapanoags* (1851) and *Kinley Hollow* (1882). He also wrote a *History of Connecticut* (1855) and a considerable amount of verse. A poem by him on Thomas à Becket (1866) was dramatized by Edwin Booth.

Holloway, Emory (b. Marshall, Mo., March 16, 1885—   ), teacher, biographer, editor. Holloway joined the faculty of Brooklyn College in 1937, became chairman of the English department in 1939. His best-known work is *Whitman—An Interpretation in Narrative* (1926), which won a Pulitzer Prize. He edited Whitman's uncollected prose and verse (1921), *Leaves of Grass* (1924), his FRANKLIN EVANS (1929), and a complete edition of Whitman (1938).

Hollow Men, The (1925), a poem by T. S. ELIOT. Occupying a position between THE WASTE LAND and ASH-WEDNESDAY, both with respect to content and the order in which the poems were written, *The Hollow Men* begins with references to human paralysis and ends with a juxtaposition of the human world of illusory dreams and the divine Kingdom beyond death. The first four sections of the poem deal respectively with the general sterility of the "living dead," the particular fear of reality and of the eyes of judgment, the desolation of the world between birth and death, and the faint hope for the appearance of the "perpetual star" and "multifoliate rose"; the fifth section recapitulates the themes of the first four in alternation of fragmentary phrases. The ending is ambiguous, both a cry of despair at the emptiness of human life and a simultaneous assertion "For Thine is the Kingdom."

Holm, John Cecil (b. Philadelphia, Nov. 4, 1904—), actor, playwright. Holm went on the stage in 1925. His first play, *Three Men on a Horse* (1935), was written in collaboration with GEORGE ABBOTT. Other plays of his include *Best Foot Forward* (1941); *Banjo Eyes* (1941); *Brighten the Corner* (1945); *Gramercy Ghost* (1947). He also wrote scripts in Hollywood.

Holmes, Abiel (b. Woodstock, Conn., Dec. 24, 1763—d. June 4, 1837), clergyman, historiographer, biographer. The father of OLIVER WENDELL HOLMES was pastor of a church in Cambridge for forty years, a man of strict Congregational faith, though he often exchanged pulpits with the Unitarian clergymen of the community. He wrote (1798) a life of Ezra Stiles, the father of his first wife, president of Yale, and his highly revered teacher. His most important production was *American Annals, or a Chronological History of America* (1805; rev. ed., 1829), a scholarly collection of data in two volumes. "The prevailing character of his preaching was practical," his famous son testified. One listener described his sermons as being as placid as his appearance.

Holmes, [John] Clellon (b. Holyoke, Mass., March 12, 1926—), novelist, critic. Kenneth Rexroth has written, "Holmes is famous as the inventor of the Beat Generation." Several years before the phenomenon became known to the American public, Holmes' novel *Go* (1952) had depicted a new, lost, wandering "beat" generation. Though he obviously knew his characters at first hand, he wrote about them objectively. Holmes has written articles on the beats for *Esquire, Holiday, The New York Times,* and others; his article, *The Philosophy of the Beat Generation,* appears in the paperback anthology, *The Beats.* Holmes' poetry has appeared in little magazines since 1948. In 1958 appeared *The Horn,* a novel about jazz.

Holmes, John (b. Somerville, Mass., Jan. 6, 1904—d. June 22, 1962), teacher, poet. Holmes began teaching English at Tufts in 1934. His publications include several volumes of excellent verse: *Address to the Living* (1937); *Fair Warning* (1939); *Map of My Country* (1943); *The Double Root* (1950); *The Symbols* (1955); *The Fortune Teller* (1961). He speaks of the "tight rhythm, harsh metaphor, disturbed or deliberately ambiguous or very private reference" in his poems, but readers have not found them as hermetic as the poetry of some other mid-20th century writers. *Writing Poetry* appeared in 1960.

Holmes, John Haynes (b. Philadelphia, Nov. 29, 1879—d. April 3, 1964), minister, reformer. Holmes graduated from the Harvard Divinity School in 1904. His long life of service to religious and social causes was marked by the publication of numerous books, among them *The Revolutionary Function of the Modern Church* (1912); *Marriage and Divorce* (1913); *Religion for Today* (1917); *New Churches for Old* (1922); *Palestine Today and Tomorrow* (1929); *The Sensible Man's View of Religion* (1933); *Rethinking Religion* (1938); *The Affirmation of Immortality* (1947); *My Gandhi* (1953); an autobiography, *I Speak for Myself* (1959); and *Collected Hymns of John Haynes Holmes* (1960). His play *If This Be Treason* was produced by the New York Theatre Guild in 1935.

Holmes, Mary Jane [Hawes] (b. Brookfield, Mass., April 5, 1825—d. Oct. 6, 1907), novelist. Mrs. Holmes began writing when she was only fifteen, and in her long lifetime published thirty-nine novels, all of them sentimental in tone and moral in purpose. She was very popular; it is said that the sale of her books passed the two-million mark. Her first book was *Tempest and Sunshine* (1854); LENA RIVERS (1856), her best known book, was called by E. Douglas Branch a "lachrymal classic." She often wrote of small-town life and of down-to-earth characters with real skill. Among her other books were *Ethelyn's Mistake* (1869), *The Tracy Diamonds* (1899), and *Rena's Experiment* (1904).

Holmes, Oliver Wendell, Sr. (b. Cambridge, Mass., Aug. 29, 1809—d. Oct. 7, 1894), physician, teacher, scientist, poet, essayist, novelist, biographer, critic, lecturer, epigrammatist. Holmes was a descendant of ANNE BRADSTREET. His grandfather was a surgeon, his father the clergyman ABIEL HOLMES. He was educated at Harvard, and became what may be called a professional Harvardian—of his 408 poems, at least 108 have some reference or relationship to Harvard. Holmes was short of stature, vivacious in inverse ratio to his height. Once he attended a meeting at which a number of tall men were present, and an acquaintance remarked, "Well, Dr. Holmes, I suppose you feel rather small among all these big fellows." "I do," replied Holmes. "I feel like a dime among a lot of pennies." A man of wide and varied tastes, Holmes loved (among many other things) horses, racing, and boxing, and was a compendium of information on these subjects. He was an inveterate conversationalist, and in prose and verse was the 19th-century Boston Brahmin version of the 20th-century wisecracker.

At first Holmes studied law, then turned to medicine. After study at home and in Paris, he was given his degree by Harvard (1836). Meanwhile verse-writing had already become his constant preoccupation, and in 1830 he won nationwide acclaim with his passionately expressed resentment against the destruction of *The Constitution,* a famous war vessel from the War of 1812. His poem, OLD IRONSIDES, appeared in the Boston *Daily Advertiser* (Sept. 16, 1830), was reprinted all over the country, and influenced the government not to destroy the vessel.

As a physician Holmes had a memorable career. He was a teacher (at Dartmouth, later at Harvard, where he became dean of the Medical School), a practitioner, and a research man. He was an enthusiastic and informative lecturer. In dealing with patients, he himself feared that they regarded him with some suspicion because of his lack of solemnity and his reputation as a wit. In the classrooms and hospitals of Paris he

said he had learned three principles: "Not to take authority when I can have facts; not to guess when I can know; not to think a man must take physic because he is sick." He brought back from Paris emphasis on the use of the microscope in medicine. More important was a momentous conclusion he set forth in a paper that he read before a medical society and published in 1843: *The Contagiousness of Puerperal Fever*. This study of childbed fever contained the charge that physicians themselves, careless about personal cleanliness, were the vehicles by which the fever was transmitted. Holmes was bitterly attacked by leading obstetricians, but republished his paper. He was fortunate to escape the fate of the Hungarian obstetrician Ignaz Philip Semmelweis (1818–1865), who a few years later expressed the same ideas, was dismissed from his hospital, and ended his life in a lunatic asylum. Many lives were saved by Holmes' methods, and he was proved right by the researches of Pasteur and Lister. He published many other medical papers and collected some of them in book form, including *Boylston Prize Dissertations* (1838), *Homeopathy and Its Kindred Delusions* (1842), and *Medical Essays, 1842–82* (1883).

Holmes had a keen aesthetic delight in the intricate order and symmetry of nature, especially of the human body. Some of this delight was expressed in one of his best poems, *The Living Temple* (1858), and his medical experiences were reflected also in *The Stethoscope Song* (1849) and *La Grisette* (1863). A more important link between Holmes the physician and Holmes the writer may be found in his three so-called "medicated" novels—ELSIE VENNER (1861), THE GUARDIAN ANGEL (1867), and A MORTAL ANTIPATHY (1885). No critic ever was inclined to rate these as superior fiction, but they reflect Holmes' pioneering interest in psychiatry. This was made clear by Clarence P. Oberndorf, professor of psychiatry at Columbia University, in his edition of *The Psychiatric Novels of Oliver Wendell Holmes* (1944; rev. ed., 1946). Oberndorf makes abridgments of the three novels in a way that emphasizes the medical and psychiatric aspects of the plots. *Elsie Venner* is shown to be a brilliant study of a schizophrenic girl, *The Guardian Angel* a study of multiple personality, *A Mortal Antipathy* a portrait of a severe phobia.

Holmes the scientist and Holmes the man of imagination are inextricably interwoven when one considers his attitude toward religion and his general philosophy of life. By descent Holmes belonged to the strictest sect of Calvinistic Puritans, although his father had been kindly in his attitude toward sinners and persons of different views from his own. Holmes nevertheless hated Calvinism to the point of obsession. He attacked the creed again and again, in prose and verse. Most famous of all the attacks was THE DEACON'S MASTERPIECE (1858), whose wonderful "one-hoss shay" went to pieces all at once, like the Calvinistic system with its reliance on logic. Similarly, in *Elsie Venner* he sought to test the doctrine of "original sin" and human responsibility. Yet he once wrote to Harriet Beecher Stowe: "I do not believe you or I can ever get the iron of Calvinism out of our souls."

Barrett Wendell called Holmes New England's "one uncompromising rationalist." He was a Brahmin of Brahmins and in the main a conservative, but in his hatred of Calvinism and in his free-thinking rationalism he was an ardent rebel. But he was not a transcendentalist, nor in politics anything but a Federalist. He loved wealth, but sincerely and actively preached humanitarianism. Minute philosophical distinctions occupied him little. As for religion, he said he could sum it up in the first two words of the Lord's Prayer.

As a poet and an essayist, Holmes seems derivative: he submitted himself to many influences, particularly Horace, Alexander Pope, and Dr. Samuel Johnson. Van Wyck Brooks holds that he was a "poet laureate" by vocation. He was in fact always ready with his neat and entertaining verses at a reunion or a celebration. At his best he is America's finest writer of *vers de société*. He usually chose such familiar media as the ballad, the octosyllabic couplet, and the heroic couplet, although he also wrote blank verse and sonnets with great skill. His most original poems were THE LAST LEAF (1833) and THE CHAMBERED NAUTILUS (1858). The latter poem Holmes preferred above all his other verses. The salt of wit still preserves many of his other poems, among them *The Height of the Ridiculous* (1830), THE BALLAD OF THE OYSTER-MAN (1830), *To an Insect* (1831), MY AUNT (1831), *Contentment* (1858), *Dorothy Q.* (1871). As a scientist, Holmes interested himself in what he called *The Physiology of Versification* (1883), an exposition of his belief that there is a vital connection between the laws of versification and the laws of respiration and the pulse.

In view of his own temperament, Holmes was bound to be more at home in the casual and discursive essay than in the more formally planned novel. Yet in the "Autocrat" series (THE AUTOCRAT OF THE BREAKFAST TABLE, 1858; *The Professor at the Breakfast Table*, 1860; THE POET AT THE BREAKFAST TABLE, 1872; *Over the Teacups*, 1891) Holmes developed what was almost a genre of his own, one based largely on his own fondness for dominating a conversation and his lighthearted gaiety and gift of phrase. It was a genre probably influenced by Boswell's *Life of Samuel Johnson*. Holmes had the idea for the series early; the two "Autocrat" papers he contributed to the *New England Magazine* (November, 1831; February, 1832) are close in manner to the series more formally begun in the *Atlantic Monthly* in 1857. The papers mix verse and narrative, speculation and homily. In them, Holmes said, "I have unburdened myself of what I was born to say," and there is no doubt that he was at his best in this peculiar amalgam of soliloquy, conversation, anecdote, epigram, and story. The topics are multifarious, just as they were in Holmes' conversation or in his popular lectures.

Of course Holmes was above all a wit. Like Irving, he managed to combine sentiment and satire, pathos and ridicule. His flow of epigram was endless: "Apology is only egotism wrong side out." "Easy-crying widows take new husbands soonest; there's nothing like wet weather for transplanting." "Man has his will, but woman has her way." "Nature, when she invented, manufactured, and patented her authors, contrived to make critics out of the chips that were left." "Grave: a sure cure for hay fever when taken eight feet deep." "I was always patient with those who thought well of me, and accepted all their tributes with something more than resignation."

Holmes' reputation declined in time, possibly because of the rising star of his son, OLIVER WENDELL HOLMES, JR. It was clear even during the elder Holmes' lifetime that there was a conflict of ideals and personalities between father and son. Some overeager advocates of the younger man have sneered at the father. Eleanor M. Tilton, writing her biography of *The Amiable Autocrat* (1947), suspected that "no house would be big enough for two vain men, both of whom liked to talk and both of whom liked

an audience of pretty women." John Greenleaf Whittier thought Holmes was "Montaigne and Bacon under one hat." To Bernard De Voto, however, Holmes "must be seen as the happiest triumph of the second-rate in our literature." Odell Shepard points to his fierce attacks on Calvinism: "His works carried the concentrated force of a hornet." Dorothy Canfield Fisher finds him "an enchanting American of noble character and fine disciplined intelligence."

Collections of Holmes material are found in the Library of Congress, the Morgan Library, and the Henry E. Huntington Library. W. L. Schroeder wrote an English appreciation of Holmes (1909). Mark A. DeWolfe Howe did an important biography of him, *Holmes of the Breakfast Table* (1939). T. F. Currier's *Bibliography* of Holmes (1953) runs to 707 pages, including an index of 46 pages. John T. Morse's *Life and Letters* of Holmes was a two-volume addition to the 13-volume Riverside edition of Holmes' *Writings* (1892, 1896). See BREAKFAST TABLE SERIES; THE BOYS.

Holmes, Oliver Wendell, Jr. (b. Boston, Mass., March 8, 1841—d. March 6, 1935), lawyer, jurist, writer on law. The younger Holmes had a deep pride in his New England background; nevertheless he had to escape "the shadow of his father." Philip P. Wiener speaks of their basic clash of ideas. Although Dr. Holmes accepted the new theories of physics and biology as presented in Darwinism, he argued eloquently against the extension of them to the realm of moral freedom and spirit. The younger Holmes on the contrary welcomed that extension. The father called mechanical force "the Deity himself in action." The younger man regarded the conservation of energy as in no need of divine concurrence.

Before he completed his senior year at Harvard, Holmes enlisted in the Union army. He served for three years and was wounded three times, twice severely. He was lost to sight for a while, and the elder Holmes reported his adventures in search of him in *My Hunt After "The Captain"* (*Atlantic Monthly*, November, 1862). In *Touched with Fire* (1946) Mark De-Wolfe Howe collected Holmes' war letters and his diary. These writings are marked by boyish enthusiasm mixed with the outbursts of a man growing older; there are complaints and many brief and vivid descriptions.

Holmes began to practice law in Boston in 1867, on his return from the first of many trips to England, and began to teach at the Harvard Law School in 1870. His lectures on *The Common Law* (1881) became a classic. In the next year he was appointed to the Supreme Judicial Court and became chief justice in 1899. In 1902 he was appointed by President Theodore Roosevelt to the Supreme Court, and after a notable series of opinions and dissents was regarded as the leading exponent of law in Anglo-Saxon countries. He retired in 1932.

Holmes deeply impressed himself upon the law and greatly influenced political and economic conditions in the United States. He had certain fixed ideas, the chief of which was that the law was made for society, not society for the law; and that judges must not allow their own opinions and prejudices to interfere with social changes, even if they know these changes are harmful. He held that the life of law was not logic but experience, that law was not an absolute but "what the courts will enforce," that the law "must found itself on actual forces," that "the first call of a theory of law is that it should fit the facts." It was an axiom of his that "certainty generally is an illusion, and repose is not the destiny of man." He said, "The best test of truth is the power of thought to get itself accepted in the market." "Our Constitution," he once explained, "is an experiment, as all life is an experiment," and he believed that courts must allow experimentation to continue.

It was customary after a while to call Holmes "the great dissenter," but some of his dissents shaped history. He was also regarded as a great liberal, although it is generally held today that Holmes by no means abandoned his father's and his native region's orthodoxy in political and economic realms. His dissents often had great influence, so that in time many of his views were accepted as good law, such as his pronouncements, always based on the Constitution, on the plenary power of Congress over commerce, on the taxing power of Congress, on the meaning of "police power," on the provisions of the Bill of Rights.

In addition to *The Common Law* Holmes published in his own lifetime a small volume of *Speeches* (1891; rev., 1913) and *Collected Legal Papers* (1920). Mark DeWolfe Howe, in addition to his edition of the letters and diary mentioned above, edited the *Holmes-Pollock Letters: The Correspondence of Mr. Justice Holmes and Sir Frederick Pollock, 1874–1932* (2 v., 1941). In 1953 appeared an extraordinarily interesting collection, *The Holmes-Laski Letters, 1916–35* —really a long-range debate between Holmes and Harold J. Laski in England. Some of Holmes' opinions as a judge appear in *The Dissenting Opinions of Mr. Justice Holmes* (1929), edited by Alfred Lief; *The Judicial Opinions of Oliver Wendell Holmes* (1940), edited by Harry C. Shriver; and Max Lerner's *The Mind and Faith of Justice Holmes* (1943). A Pulitzer Prize biography of him was Catherine Drinker Bowen's YANKEE FROM OLYMPUS (1944). Emmet Lavery's play, *The Magnificent Yankee* (1946), was also made into a movie (1951).

Holmes, William Henry (b. near Cadiz, Ohio, Dec. 1, 1846—d. April 20, 1933), artist, geologist, anthropologist, government official. Holmes was a member of the staff of the U.S. Geological Survey, later was head curator of anthropology of the U.S. National Museum and chief of the Bureau of American Ethnology. In 1920 he became director of the National Gallery of Art. He was greatly interested in the aesthetic side of the ancient American cultures he studied. Among his publications: *Art in Shell of the Ancient Americans* (1883); *Ancient Art of the Province of Chiriqui, Colombia* (1888); *Archaeo-*

logical Studies among the Ancient Cities of Mexico (1895–97); and *Handbook of Aboriginal American Antiquities* (1919). *The Holmes Anniversary Volume* (1916) paid tribute to him on his 70th birthday.

Homage to Clio (1960), a volume of poetry by W. H. AUDEN. It consists of thirty poems, a prose interlude, and some humorous "academic graffiti," short verse pieces on such poets and philosophers as Blake, Kierkegaard, Marx, and Eliot. While maintaining a great range of verse form and technique, in this volume Auden turns away from political preachments and reveals himself as a light poet and a gifted satirist, always diverting, as one reviewer noted, but seldom striking.

Homage to Mistress Bradstreet (1956), a long poem by JOHN BERRYMAN. Its subject is the Puritan poetess ANNE BRADSTREET, whose sexual tenderness Berryman sets against the sternly chaste background of Puritan New England. Conrad Aiken has called it "one of the finest poems ever written by an American."

Home, Sweet Home (1823), a lyric by JOHN HOWARD PAYNE, with music by Sir Henry R. Bishop (1786–1855). Originally Bishop wrote the music for a poem by a young English poet, Thomas Haynes Bayly (1797–1839). This version was published as a "Sicilian Air" in Bishop's collection *Melodies of Various Nations* (1822). Payne had been living in England and France for about ten years, and was throughout his life a wanderer, dying in exile as American consul in Tunis (1852). How he came to write the poem when another lyric already existed is not known. The text of Bayly's poem inspired Payne, also the meter of the first four lines, but in general Payne's poem is more poetical and more effective. It was first sung in an opera by Bishop called *Clari, or, The Maid of Milan* (1823). It reached the United States the same year. It has been a favorite number of many prima donnas. Payne seems to have received no adequate remuneration for the poem; and Bishop, as usual, had to defend himself in court against pirates.

Five years before Payne composed his song J. K. Paulding wrote these lines in his poem THE BACKWOODSMAN (1818). "Whate'er may happen, wheresoe'er we roam,/ However homely, still there's naught like home."

Home as Found (1838), a novel by JAMES FENIMORE COOPER. See HOMEWARD BOUND.

Home Book of Verse, The (1912), edited by BURTON E. STEVENSON. The first of a series of "home books" edited by Stevenson, all ample collections of material that librarians and others found exceedingly useful as reference guides and for reading.

Home Journal, The. A weekly magazine founded (1846) by N. P. WILLIS and G. P. MORRIS. It contained much miscellaneous material—verse, essays, gossip. Willis edited the magazine until his death in 1867. In 1901 the name of the magazine was changed to *Town and Country*.

Home on the Range. JOHN LOMAX first recorded this song in COWBOY SONGS (1910) and thereby saved it from oblivion. He got the ditty from a Negro singer who had often made the trip up the Chisholm trail. Then in 1934, after Franklin D. Roosevelt's supposed liking for the song had made it enormously popular, one William Goodwin and his wife claimed its authorship and ownership, and brought suit against thirty-five individuals and corporations for royalty fees amounting to half a million dollars. To combat them the Music Publishers Protective Association engaged a lawyer, Samuel Moanfeldt, to investigate the sources of the song, an assignment that took him on a three-month tour of nearly every state west of the Mississippi. On the basis of an old newspaper clipping and other evidence he concluded that Dr. Brewster Higley and Daniel E. Kelley, both of Kansas, had composed the words and music, possibly as early as 1873, under the title "My Western Home." It was published for the first time in the Kirwin (Kans.) *Chief*, March 21, 1874. Because of Moanfeldt's investigation the suit was dropped.

Homer, Sidney (b. Boston, Dec. 9, 1864—d. July 18, 1953), composer, memoirist. Homer was particularly fond of writing musical settings for poems by noted authors, including Tennyson, Stevenson, O. W. Holmes, Browning, W. E. Henley, Vachel Lindsay, John Masefield, Christina Rossetti. His wife, **Louise [Dilworth Beatty] Homer** (b. 1895—d. 1947), contralto, had a distinguished career in opera, much of it at the Metropolitan.

Homer, Winslow (b. Boston, Feb. 24, 1836—d. Sept. 29, 1910), painter. Homer was apprenticed to a lithographer in Boston and later studied at the National Academy of Design in New York. Commissioned by Harper and Brothers, he made drawings of Lincoln's inauguration (1861), then was sent to Virginia to sketch the war. Upon his return to New York he painted pictures on war subjects, of which "Prisoners from the Front" is his best known. In 1876 he visited Europe and began painting rural scenes, which he continued to produce in the United States. Finally he turned to marine painting, depicting storms, shipwrecks, and men who work close to the sea. His paintings can be seen at almost every art museum in the United States. Later works are *The Gulf Stream, Watching the Tempest, Perils of the Sea, The Life Brigade,* and *The Ship's Boat.*

Homeward Bound, or, The Chase (1838), a novel by JAMES FENIMORE COOPER. The same year he published a sequel, *Home as Found.* Originally he intended the book to be a commentary on American manners, as dissected by a person lately resident in Europe. But he did not stick very closely to this intention, instead made the book one of sea adventure. He made use in his narrative of a book by Capt. Judah Paddock, *A Narrative of the Shipwreck of the Ship "Oswego" on the Coast of South Barbary* (1818). For most part *Homeward Bound* is an entertaining account of life on an ocean liner, with nice social distinctions among the passengers and with a captain competent as a mariner and as a social arbiter. The book has

made some critics think of Cooper as a forerunner of Henry James. In *Home as Found* the leading characters of the earlier book, themselves descendants of Judge Temple of THE PIONEERS, really come to grips with Cooper's theme —American manners. In addition, much of the plot is devoted, in fictional guise, to some of Cooper's personal controversies; Edward Effingham is obviously a self-portrait. The book is severely critical of American dress, social intercourse, men of letters, businessmen, lawyers, America in general. A contemporary review by William Gilmore Simms regretted the querulous tone of the book. Another critic, Thurlow Weed, called it "a skinning alive"; Cooper sued him for libel. In fact, the novel shows Cooper at his worst.

Homony Club. An Annapolis organization. See JONATHAN BOUCHER.

Hone, Philip (b. New York City, Oct. 25, 1780—d. May 5, 1851), merchant, public official, diarist. Hone, an ardent Whig and sturdy defender of American ideas and institutions, became mayor of New York (1825), was a friend

of most of the prominent persons of his day. From 1828 until his death he kept a diary in which he recorded many vivid details of the social and cultural life of the times. The manuscript (twenty-eight quarto volumes) is in the New York Historical Society Library. Only parts of it have been published, one selection in two volumes by Bayard Tuckerman (1889) and another, also in two volumes, by Allan Nevins (1927).

Honest John Vane (1875), a novel by J. W.
DE FOREST. The title is ironical; the chief
character is a dishonest congressman who nevertheless manages to get himself re-elected. A
realistic attack on inefficiency and corruption in
national politics.

Honey in the Horn (1935), a novel by
HAROLD L. DAVIS. A realistic narrative of life
among the pioneers of early Oregon, it won a
Pulitzer Prize and debunked many popular
notions of frontier gallantry.

Honorable Peter Stirling, The (1894), a novel
by PAUL LEICESTER FORD. A portrait of an
honest and fearless politician, it enjoyed a great
vogue in its time, partly because readers believed that Stirling was modeled on Grover
Cleveland. This was denied by Ford.

Hook, Sidney (b. New York City, Dec. 20,
1902—   ), essayist, philosopher, educator.
Regarded as an outstanding educator, Hook
studied at the College of the City of New York
and Columbia University where, while working
for his doctorate, he came under the influence of
JOHN DEWEY. Basing his own thinking on
Dewey's concepts, Hook has contributed illuminating insights to many social and political problems. In *Education for Modern Man* (1946)
Hook lucidly illustrates his belief in the Socratic
doctrine of instruction, which lets the student
reach a familiar conclusion with a sense of making his own discovery. Other books: *The Metaphysics of Pragmatism* (1927); *Towards the Understanding of Karl Marx* (1933); *From Hegel
to Marx* (1936); *John Dewey, an Intellectual
Portrait* (1939); *The Hero in History* (1943);
Heresy, Yes—Conspiracy, No (1953); *Common
Sense and the Fifth Amendment* (1957). He
edited *Religious Experience and Truth* (1961),
a symposium.

Hooker, [William] Brian (b. New York City,
Nov. 2, 1880—d. Dec. 28, 1946), song writer,
opera librettist, translator, novelist. Although
Hooker wrote some excellent libretti and in 1911
won a prize of $10,000 offered by the Metropoli-
tan Opera Company, his greatest success was
a translation of Edmond Rostand's *Cyrano de
Bergerac* made in 1923. This was produced on
Broadway with WALTER HAMPDEN in the leading role; by 1937 Hampden had appeared in the
play 1,000 times. In 1950 it became a movie and
was issued in a paperback edition. Hooker collaborated with HORATIO PARKER on *Mona*
(1911) and *Fairyland* (1915). He published a
collection of *Poems* (1915). *White Bird* (1924)
was another opera. Hooker and W. H. Post gave
Rudolf Friml the text for a version (1925) of
Justin H. McCarthy's novel, *If I Were King*
(1901); this was called *The Vagabond King*.
For it Hooker wrote some of his best lyrics,
among them *Song of the Vagabonds* and *Only a
Rose*. *White Eagle* (1927) was a musical version of Edwin Milton Royle's THE SQUAW MAN
(1905) for which Hooker supplied the text; he
performed the same service in *Through the Years*
(1932), based on A. L. Martin's *Smilin' Through*
(1919).

Hooker, Thomas (b. England, July 7[?],

1586—d. July 7, 1647), Congregational clergyman, author of treatises on religion and government. Hooker was a great forerunner of American democracy who asserted the freedom of the
individual to make his own decisions in politics
and religion. He sought the abolition of all
property and religious tests for the franchise,
contended that "the foundation of authority is
laid . . . in the free consent of the people,"
and brought about (1643) a defensive organization of "United Colonies of New England" that
prefigured the United States.

Hooker was a Cambridge man and held doctrines so strongly opposed to those of Archbishop
Laud that the latter planned to silence him. But
Hooker fled to Holland, where he remained three
years until his former congregation could emigrate to Newtown (later Cambridge), Mass.,
and settle there. Later he and his congregation
moved to Connecticut and founded Hartford,
not without opposition from an autocratic governor. He was a preacher of such fire and energy
that he has been called perhaps "the most powerful pulpit orator among the ministers of New
England." Under his guidance there were
adopted by the General Assembly at Hartford
on Jan. 14, 1639, certain "Fundamental Orders"
which Charles Borgeaud called "the first written constitution of modern democracy." At the
behest of his fellow-ministers he undertook, with
JOHN COTTON, a *Survey of the Sum of Church
Discipline* (1648), a strong defense of the New
England Congregational way against the criticisms of English Presbyterians.

Other compositions have come down to us
only from the shorthand notes of admiring
listeners. Among them: *The Poor Doubting
Christian* (1629); *The Equal Ways of God*
(1632); *The Soul's Exaltation* (1638); *Four
Godly and Learned Treatises* (1638); *The
Saint's Guide* (1645); *The Saint's Dignity and
Duty* (1651); *The Application of Redemption*
(1656).

Hooper, Ellen [Sturgis] (b. Boston[?],
1812[?]—d. Nov. 3, 1848), poet. Mrs.
Hooper's fame is based largely on a six-line poem
which appeared, untitled, in the first issue of
The Dial (July, 1840). Its opening lines immediately became famous: "I slept, and dreamed
that life was Beauty;/ I woke, and found that
life was Duty." Mrs. Hooper also wrote some
hymns.

Hooper, Johnson Jones (b. Wilmington, N.C.,
June 9, 1815—d. June 7, 1862), humorist,
newspaperman, lawyer, public official. Hooper
drifted from North Carolina to Alabama, and
became identified with that state. He established
the Montgomery *Mail* in the 1850's and edited
it until 1861. His reputation as a humorist was
founded chiefly on his account of SOME ADVEN-
TURES OF CAPTAIN SIMON SUGGS, LATE OF THE
TALLAPOOSA VOLUNTEERS (1846). Simon was
depicted as an unmitigated rascal whose guiding
principle was, "It is good to be shifty in a new
country." The tales Johnson told about him were
rowdy and uninhibited, and ridiculed many institutions and folkways of the South. Of similar

character was *The Widow Rugby's Husband and Other Tales of Alabama* (1851). When war broke out Hooper became secretary of the Provisional Congress of the Southern States.

Hoosier. The word means "Indianan," and may be applied to a resident, to locutions or pronunciations, to customs, vocations, etc.; Indiana is "the Hoosier state." John Finley (1797–1866), a Virginian who spent most of his life in Indiana, claimed to have written a poem called *The Hoosier's Nest* and to have published it in the Richmond (Ind.) *Palladium* in 1830, but no verification of this claim has ever been found. On Jan. 3, 1832, the word was used in a carrier's poem, *i.e.*, a poem addressed to readers of the paper by newsboys, in the *Indiana Democrat*. The earliest known publication of Finley's poem took place on Jan. 1, 1833, when it appeared in the Indianapolis *Journal* as a similar New Year's greeting from the carrier boys. The poem gave a realistic picture of the life of the backwoodsman. In 1865 Finley published a collection entitled *The Hoosier's Nest and Other Poems,* in which the title-poem was somewhat revised. (See CAR-RIERS' ADDRESSES.)

The derivation of the term is unknown; all of the suggested etymologies are pure guess-work. Some think it means "husher" and is connected with *whoosher;* others that it is a corruption of *hussar.* Still others believe it comes from a greeting, "Who's yere?" Apparently *Hoosier* at first did not signify an Indianan particularly, but any rough-and-ready fellow of the then Wild West. But after 1833 it was confined to Indianans, at first contemptuously; to-day the term is merely descriptive.

Hoosier Chronicle, A (1912) a novel by MEREDITH NICHOLSON. A romantic tale of an Indiana girl of mysterious parentage, a politician's secretary who falls in love with him, the politician himself.

Hoosier Holiday (1916), THEODORE DREISER'S recollections of his childhood and youth in Indiana.

Hoosierisms. The inhabitants of Indiana seem from an early period to have been especially fertile in the invention and wide use of dialectal forms. EDWARD EGGLESTON said that his novel THE HOOSIER SCHOOLMASTER (1871) was the first American dialect novel to deal with a variety of speech other than that of New England. Many studies have since been made of this dialect. Albert H. Marckwardt concluded in 1939 that it was largely southern in pronunciation; others have reported on Indianan similes and folk-metaphors in general. See DIALECT IN AMERICAN LITERATURE.

Hoosier Poet. A name often given to JAMES WHITCOMB RILEY.

Hoosier School. Around 1900 so many writers born in Indiana were active in the literary world that the term "Hoosier School" was given to them. These writers included EDWARD EGGLESTON, GEORGE CARY EGGLESTON, JAMES WHITCOMB RILEY, GEORGE ADE, THEODORE DREISER, JOHN JAMES PIATT, JAMES MAURICE THOMPSON, BOOTH TARKINGTON. MEREDITH

NICHOLSON discussed the Hoosier School in *The Hoosiers* (1900).

Hoosier Schoolboy, The (1883), a novel by EDWARD EGGLESTON. This story deals unfavorably with conditions in Indiana's rural schools in Eggleston's day.

Hoosier Schoolmaster, The (1871), a novel by EDWARD EGGLESTON. This was probably based in part on the experiences of Eggleston's brother George. It tells of a young man who takes a job in a one-man school and soon discovers that his success will depend more on muscle than on book learning. He manages to win the friendship of the worst bully in the school and gets along well. Boarding around in the neighborhood, he meets people of many kinds, falls in love, finds himself suspected of being an ally of some "night riders," and has other entertaining adventures. Famous scenes in the book are the spelling bee and the trial scene. The book has a strong religious undercurrent and exhibits Eggleston's interest in Indianan dialect. The story was first published in serial form in HEARTH AND HOME, of which Eggleston was editor, and boosted its circulation fourfold; it was widely pirated all over the world. Eggleston wrote the book partly as a protest against the preoccupation of contemporary writers with New England; and he found inspiration in the axiom of the French critic Hippolyte Taine (1828–1893) that "the artist of originality will work courageously with the materials he finds in his own environment."

Hooton, E[arnest] A[lbert] (b. Clemansville, Wis., Nov. 20, 1887—d. May 3, 1954), anthropologist, teacher, curator. Hooton taught mainly at Harvard, where he became head of the Department of Anthropology and curator of the Peabody Museum. His books, written with great literary skill, are notable for their frank statements of not always palatable truths. Especially noteworthy are *Up from the Ape* (1931, 1946); *Apes, Men, and Morons* (1937); *Crime and the Man* (1939); *Why Men Behave Like Apes and Vice Versa* (1940); *Man's Poor Relations* (1942); *Young Man, You Are Normal* (1945). Hooton believed, as a result of careful investigation, that crime is the result of heredity rather than environment, and that people of differing national and racial descents tend to commit different kinds of crimes. He also argued that man is allowing himself to degenerate and is doomed to destruction unless he sterilizes the unfit.

Hoover, Herbert [Clark] (b. West Branch, Iowa, Aug. 10, 1874—d. Oct. 20, 1964), administrator, author, 30th President. Early orphaned, Hoover managed to enter Stanford University to study mining engineering. Thereafter his career represents Horatio Algerism at its best. He became an international businessman, working at important enterprises in the United States and all over the world. During World War I President Wilson asked him first to head the Commission for Relief in Belgium, and then to become Food Administrator for the United States.

President Harding made him Secretary of

Commerce in 1921; he completely reorganized the Department of Commerce in a way to make it serve business interests more efficiently. He was elected President on the Republican ticket in 1928. In the fall of 1929, after a period of unexampled prosperity, the stock market collapsed, launching the country into a disastrous economic depression. John D. Weaver describes this tragic era in his novel *Another Such Victory* (1948), especially the episode of the Bonus Expeditionary Force of World War I veterans, whom Hoover, from the viewpoint of public relations, mishandled so badly. Hoover was deeply concerned at the terrible devastation wrought by the depression, but his policies were largely futile, though they actually anticipated in many ways the policies of his successor Franklin D. Roosevelt. He was badly defeated in the 1932 election, and since then has become an "elder statesman" of the Republican Party. He performed a great public service as head of a bipartisan commission to study ways of simplifying and improving the structure of the Federal government; some of the commission's recommendations have been enacted into law.

Hoover has published several books, all informative and earnest. Among them are *American Individualism* (1922); *The Challenge to Liberty* (1934); *American Road* (1938); *Further Addresses on the American Road* (1940); *America's First Crusade* (1941); *The Problems of Lasting Peace* (1942); *Memoirs* (3 v., 1951–52); *The Ordeal of Woodrow Wilson* (1958); *The American Epic* (2 v., 1959–60), and *Addresses upon the American Road* (1961). Eugene Lyons' *Our Unknown Ex-President* (1948) sought to present him as "the warm, whimsical, and tender Hoover—the very human and deeply humane Quaker behind the solemn façade."

Hoover, J[ohn] Edgar (b. Washington, D.C., Jan. 1, 1895—   ), lawyer, criminologist, administrator, author. John Edgar Hoover was educated in the public schools of the District of Columbia and received LL.B. and LL.M. degrees from George Washington University. He entered the Department of Justice in 1917, was appointed Special Assistant to the Attorney General in 1919, served as Assistant Director of the Federal Bureau of Investigation from 1921 to 1924, and on May 10, 1924 was named its Director. He was admitted to the bar of the United States District Court for the District of Columbia, the United States Court of Claims, and the Supreme Court. On May 27, 1955, President Eisenhower presented Hoover with the National Security Medal for his outstanding service in the field of intelligence relating to national security. His two published books are: *Persons in Hiding* (1938) and *Masters of Deceit* (1958). The first described the crime situation that faced the FBI in the 1930's. The second tells of the problems which Communism presents to the social order in the United States and abroad, documenting the facts of Communism in America.

Hopalong Cassidy. See CASSIDY, HOPALONG.

Hope, Laura Lee. See THE BOBBSEY TWINS.

Hope Leslie (2 v., 1827), a novel by CATHARINE MARIA SEDGWICK. It is a story of the Pequod War in Massachusetts, about 1636; Governor Winthrop and Thomas Morton are among the historical characters. At the same time it portrays the character and grievances of the disappearing Indians, and the men and manners of the 17th century. It was exceedingly popular in its day; critics agree that its merits justified its vogue.

Hopi Indians. A small tribe in northeastern Arizona, part of the Pueblo group. They are so deeply devoted to certain philosophical and religious ideas that missionaries have found them difficult to deal with. They were called by Oliver La Farge "one of the strangest, most intriguing, most admirable, and at times most irritating groups in America, if not in the world." An intimate view of the Hopi way of thinking is found in *Sun Chief, the Autobiography of a Hopi Indian*, edited by Leo W. Simmons (1942). A sympathetic portrayal of the Hopis is Walter C. O'Kane's *Sun in the Sky* (1950). They appear imaginatively in Edna Dean Proctor's *Song of an Ancient People* (1892), Willa Cather's DEATH COMES FOR THE ARCHBISHOP (1927), and Dama Margaret Smith's *Hopi Girl* (1931).

Hopkins, Arthur [Melancthon] (b. Cleveland, Ohio, Oct. 4, 1878—d. March 22, 1950), producer, playwright. Hopkins began his remarkably successful career as a Broadway producer with *The Poor Little Rich Girl* (1913), closed it with *The Magnificent Yankee* (1946). He put on seventy-eight plays, including the work of Shakespeare, Ibsen, O'Neill, and was the first to star many notable actors. He wrote a few plays, including *The Fatted Calf* (1912), *Burlesque* (with G. M. Watters, 1927), and *Conquest* (1933); also several books: *How's Your Second Act?* (1918); *The Glory Road* (1935); *Letters to a Lonely Boy* (1937); and *Reference Point* (1948).

Hopkins, Lemuel (b. Waterbury, Conn., June 19, 1750—d. April 14, 1801), physician, poet, satirist. Hopkins was an eminent physician whose own tendency toward tuberculosis led

him to the study of medicine; he was one of the founders of the Connecticut Medical Society. He practiced in Hartford, became intimate with the group of literary men who were called the HARTFORD (or Connecticut) WITS, and contributed satiric verses to some of their enterprises—THE ANARCHIAD (1786–87), THE ECHO (1791–1805), and THE POLITICAL GREENHOUSE (1798). Among his separate writings were *The Democratiad* (1795), *The Guillotina, or, A Democratic Dirge* (1796), and numerous short poems; his works were never collected. At first he admired, later detested Jefferson; he wrote bitterly against Ethan Allen; he denounced Rhode Island as a "realm of rogues."

Hopkins, Mark (b. Stockbridge, Mass., Feb. 4, 1802—d. June 17, 1887), physician, teacher, clergyman, administrator, essayist, philosopher. A notable teacher, Hopkins became president of Williams College in 1836 and served till 1872. In an address in New York (Dec. 28, 1871), James A. Garfield, later President, made a famous remark: "Give me a log hut, with only a simple bench, Mark Hopkins at one end and I on the other, and you may have all the buildings, apparatus, and libraries without him." Although Hopkins was highly rated in his own day as a thinker who stressed the rationality of the universe and of God, his writings are now largely forgotten. Among them are *Miscellaneous Essays and Discourses* (1847); *Lectures on Moral Science* (1862); *Baccalaureate Sermons and Occasional Discourses* (1862); *Teachings and Counsels* (1884). J. H. Denison wrote his biography (1935).

Hopkins, Samuel (b. Waterbury, Conn., Sept. 17, 1721—d. Dec. 20, 1803), clergyman, author of books on theology. Hopkins lived austerely, showed constant unselfishness, freed his slaves, wrote profoundly on theology. But he was also an atrocious preacher, noted for his dullness and dogmatism even in an age that expected preachers to be dull at great length; and his writings are equally unattractive. He was a disciple of JONATHAN EDWARDS, in whose home he lived for several years. The best of his writings were those directed against slavery, *A Dialogue Concerning the Slavery of the Africans* (1776) and *A Discourse upon the Slave Trade* (1793). Widely read was his book on *A System of Doctrines Contained in Divine Revelation Explained and Defended* (1793). His theology was expounded most definitely in the posthumous *Dialogue Between a Semi-Calvinist and a Calvinist* (1805), in which the true believer is willing "to be damned for the glory of God." His *Works*, edited by Sewall Harding in three volumes, appeared in 1854. Hopkins unquestionably inspired Harriet Beecher Stowe to write THE MINISTER'S WOOING (1859).

Hopkins, Stephen (b. Providence, Rhode Island, March 7, 1707—d. July 13, 1785), governor, pamphleteer. Hopkins wrote a pamphlet, *The Rights of Colonies Examined* (1765), which investigated the origin and nature of law, rejected the claims of parliamentary authority over the colonies, and claimed for them as "much

freedom as the mother state from which they went out." See MARTIN HOWARD.

Hopkinson, Francis (b. Philadelphia, Oct. 2, 1737—d. May 9, 1791), lawyer, signer of the Declaration of Independence, musician, writer. Hopkinson is said to have been the first student of the Academy of Philadelphia, later the Uni-

versity of Pennsylvania. He was an eminent lawyer, later a Federal judge. He was also an excellent musician, and claimed to have been the first native American to produce a musical composition. Among his later works was *The Temple of Minerva* (1781), a "dramatic allegorical cantata." He also published some pieces for the harpsichord.

Hopkinson was deeply involved in the Revolution and was a member of the first CONTINENTAL CONGRESS. He wrote prose and verse assiduously in the cause of the colonies. Perhaps his most famous piece was the scurrilous but amusing BATTLE OF THE KEGS (1778), in which he told how panic-stricken the British in Philadelphia were when the Americans floated down the river some kegs filled with gunpowder and intended to blow up the British fleet. When the British captured Bordentown they burned Hopkinson's home in revenge. In the same cause he wrote A PRETTY STORY (1774), *A Political Catechism* (1777), and a *Letter to Joseph Galloway* (1778). In addition to his other accomplishments Hopkinson was an artist; he designed the state seal of New Jersey and helped design the American flag. He was a gay and charming writer. He prepared a collection of his works, *The Miscellaneous Essays and Occasional Writings of Francis Hopkinson* (3 v., 1792), but many of his writings are available only in their original periodical or manuscript forms. (See also LIBERTY'S CALL; MODERN LEARNING.) His son, **Joseph Hopkinson** (b. Philadelphia, Nov. 12, 1770—d. Jan. 15, 1842), was likewise a lawyer and judge, served in Congress, took an active part in community life, and wrote a famous patriotic song, HAIL COLUMBIA (1798).

Hopwood, Avery (b. Cleveland, Ohio, May 28, 1882—d. July 1, 1928), newspaperman, playwright. Hopwood wrote *Clothes* (1906) in collaboration with CHANNING POLLOCK. Its success led him to a career on the stage in the course of which he wrote many farces and mystery plays. The best known of the former were *The Gold-Diggers* (1919), *The Demi-Virgin* (1921), *Getting Gertie's Garter* (with Wilson Collison, 1921), and *Why Men Leave Home* (1922). The most famous of his plays was, however, the mystery melodrama THE BAT (with MARY ROBERTS RINEHART, 1920). After his death his mother established the Hopwood Literature Prizes at the University of Michigan, of which he was an alumnus. These have been awarded to promising students since 1931, and range from $75 to $2,500; many books have been published by recipients of the rewards.

Horace Chase (1894), a novel by CONSTANCE FENIMORE WOOLSON. Chase is a businessman, intelligent but rather vulgar. He makes money on a large scale but is in danger of losing his wife; in the crisis Chase unexpectedly proves he has a fineness of character that wins back his wife's love. The scene, faithfully portrayed, is the South.

Horgan, Paul (b. Buffalo, N.Y., Aug. 1, 1903 —), librarian, historian, novelist. Much of Horgan's literary work centers in New Mexico. He won the Harper Novel Prize in 1933 with his *The Fault of Angels*. Among his other books: *Men of Arms* (1931); *From the Royal City* (1934); *No Quarter Given* (1935); *Main Line West* (1936); *New Mexico's Own Chronicle* (with M. G. Fulton, 1937); *Far from Cibola* (1938); *Habit of Empire* (1938); *A Tree on the Plains* (an opera, 1942, music by Ernst Bacon); a biographical introduction to *Diary and Letters of Josiah Gregg* (2 v., 1941–44). His greatest literary achievement is undoubtedly *Great River: The Rio Grande in North American History* (2 v., 1954), for which he won a Pulitzer Prize. It was followed by *The Centuries of Santa Fe* (1956); *Rome Eternal* (1959); *A Distant Trumpet* (1960); and *Citizen of New Salem* (1961).

Horizon (prod., 1871; pub., 1885), a play by AUGUSTIN DALY. It deals artifically and conventionally with an American army post at the frontier, introducing a West Pointer as the hero and including among its characters a girl who is loved by a gambler, an Indian chief, and the officer. There is also a Chinese, obviously imitated from Bret Harte's *The Heathen Chinee*.

Horn, William F. See THE HORN PAPERS.

Hornaday, William T[emple] (b. Plainfield, Ind., Dec. 1, 1854—d. March 6, 1937), zoologist, author of books on animals and travel. An ardent conservationist, Hornaday battled for the preservation of wild life. He served as director of the Bronx Zoo in New York from 1896 to 1926. His books are vivid and vigorous, some for scholarly use, others for the general public. Among them: *Two Years in the Jungle* (1885); *The Extermination of the American Bison*

(1887); *Taxidermy and Zoological Collecting* (1892); *Guide to the New York Zoological Park* (1899); *The American Natural History* (1904); *Camp-Fires in the Canadian Rockies* (1906); *Our Vanishing Wild Life* (1913); *Minds and Manners of Wild Animals* (1922); *Tales from Nature's Wonderlands* (1924); *A Wild-Animal Round-Up* (1925); *Thirty Years' War for Wild Life* (1931).

Horn Papers, The. A set of diaries and documents gathered by William F. Horn of Topeka, Kans. He alleged that they were the results of his researches into family papers dealing with events and persons in 18th-century Pennsylvania. When they were published in a three-volume set by a local historical society, their authenticity was attacked on numerous grounds. The *William & Mary Quarterly* (October, 1947), which summed up the findings of a committee of historians, held that the papers will "beyond a doubt become collectors' items, treasured with comparable fabrications on the grand scale."

horse operas. A term used to describe movies laid in the Wild West. See WESTERNS.

Horses and Men (1923), a collection of short stories by SHERWOOD ANDERSON, for the most part about horse racing.

Horse Sense in American Humor (1942), an account of certain aspects of American humor, from Benjamin Franklin to Ogden Nash, by WALTER BLAIR. Blair, a specialist in American literature, devotes himself in this volume to a consideration of horse sense, the horse laugh, homespun philosophy, pawkiness, cracker-barrel philosophy, gumption, and mother-wit. In addition to Franklin and Nash, he writes about Davy Crockett, Jack Downing, James Russell Lowell, Johnson J. Hooper, Artemus Ward, Lincoln, Mark Twain, Josh Billings, Benjamin P. Shillaber, Mr. Dooley, Abe Martin, Will Rogers, Robert Benchley, and others. He thus makes "horse sense" the common denominator of practically all American humor.

Horse-Shoe Robinson (1835), a novel by J. P. KENNEDY. Using James Fenimore Cooper as a model, Kennedy wrote this historical romance of the South in the period of the American Revolution. The hero and the heroine favor the Revolution; the girl's father is a Tory. The most engaging character is Robinson himself—a hearty, salty, uninhibited old campaigner. The novel became popular immediately, won the praise of Irving and Poe, and continued a favorite for several decades.

Hosmer, James Kendall (b. Northfield, Mass., Jan. 29, 1834—d. May 11, 1927), clergyman, teacher, librarian, historian, biographer. Hosmer was in the ministry for six years, then taught at various universities. He became librarian of the Minneapolis Public Library in 1892 and resigned in 1904 to devote himself to writing. His many books, both scholarly and popular, include *A Short History of German Literature* (1878); *The Story of the Jews* (1885); *Samuel Adams* (1885); *A Short History of Anglo-Saxon Freedom* (1890); *A Short History of the Mississippi Valley* (1901); *The History of* *the Louisiana Purchase* (1902); *The Appeal to Arms, 1861–63* (1907); *Outcome of the Civil War, 1863–65* (1907). He wrote his reminiscences in *The Last Leaf* (1912).

Hosmer, William Howe Cuyler (b. Avon, N.Y., May 25, 1814—d. May 23, 1877), lawyer, poet, historian. Hosmer became acquainted with the Indians of western New York, Wisconsin, and Florida, and he wrote sympathetically about them in prose and verse. Among his books: *The Pioneers of Western New York* (1838); *The Themes of Song* (1842); *Yonnondido, or, Warriors of the Genesee* (1844); *Bird Notes* (1850); *Legends of the Senecas* (1850); *Poetical Works* (1854); *Later Lays and Lyrics* (1873).

Hospital Sketches (1863), memories of LOUISA MAY ALCOTT's experiences as an untrained army nurse in Washington during the Civil War. The book won her wide recognition as a writer of power and promise, and earned her the money for a trip to Europe.

Hotel Universe (1930), a play by PHILIP BARRY. The play revolves around Stephen Field, an old man whose experience of life and depth of philosophy enable him to act as a sort of mystic psychiatrist for a number of guests in his home in southern France.

Hot Plowshares (1883), a novel by ALBION W. TOURGÉE. The story is laid in the Reconstruction period, and is one of the earliest to employ the miscegenation theme. The heroine is believed to have Negro blood in her veins; she has considerable difficulty in disproving this, but finally marries the hero.

Hot Time in the Old Town Tonight, A (1896), popular song. The music is attributed to Theodore Metz (1848–1936), the words (about a camp meeting) to Joseph Hayden. Rumor attributed the tune, however, to a notorious St. Louis resort, although Metz claimed that as bandmaster for the minstrel show of McIntyre & Heath he had heard someone use the title sentence and immediately made up a march to fit the words. It remained an instrumental piece for several years, and then Hayden added the words. The song won immense popularity during the Spanish-American War, and was played when Roosevelt's Rough Riders made their San Juan Hill assault. Later it became Roosevelt's campaign song, although after he became President he repudiated the tune and resented its constant use whenever he made a public appearance.

Hough, Donald (b. St. Paul, Minn., June 29, 1895—   ), public relations counselor, editor, advertising and sales promotion manager, writer. Hough's service in World Wars I and II furnished the background for an engaging volume of reminiscences, *Captain Retread* (1944), and a novel, *The Camelephamoose* (1946). *Snow Above Town* (1943) was warmly praised for its original humor, frankness, and racy and colloquial style. Hough also wrote *Big Distance* (1945); *Darling, I Am Home* (1946); *Cocktail Hour in Jackson Hole* (1956); *Streetcar House* (1960).

Hough, Emerson (b. Newton, Iowa, June 28, 1857—d. April 30, 1923), teacher, newspaperman, lawyer, novelist. Hough did not care for teaching or the law; he gave them up for what he called "outdoor journalism" and became acquainted with many parts of the country. His first successful book was *The Story of the Cowboy* (1897), but it was not until the publication of a novel, THE MISSISSIPPI BUBBLE (1902), that he was able to rely on writing for an income. *The Law of the Land* (1904) followed, then four volumes of "The Young Alaskans" series (1910–18), *The Magnificent Adventure* (1916), *The Man Next Door* (1917), and other novels. His greatest success came in 1922 with THE COVERED WAGON, an exciting story with carefully studied historical background. NORTH OF THIRTY-SIX (1923) was also very popular. Hough wrote his recollections of the old West in *The Passing of the Frontier* (1923). *The Covered Wagon* has often been reprinted; it was made into a picturesque movie in the year of its publication. Hough's significance as a writer on the frontier has been evaluated in Lee A. Stone's *Emerson Hough: His Place in American Letters* (1925). See also FIFTY-FOUR FORTY OR FIGHT.

Hough, Henry Beetle (b. New Bedford, Mass., Nov. 8, 1896—   ), public relations counselor, editor, publisher. In 1920 Hough and his wife, Elizabeth Wilson Hough, took over the publication of the *Vineyard Gazette* at Edgartown, Martha's Vineyard. His best books are concerned with his experiences as an editor, particularly *Country Editor* (1940) and *Once More the Thunder* (1950). He also wrote *Martha's Vineyard, Summer Resort* (1936); *Thoreau of Walden* (1956); *The New England Story* (1956); *Lament For A City* (1960); and several novels: *That Lofty Sky* (1941); *All Things Are Yours* (1942); *Roosters Crow in Town* (1945); *Long Anchorage* (1947); *Singing in the Morning* (1951).

Houghton, Mrs. Hedwin. See CAROLYN WELLS.

House-Boat on the Styx, The (1895), a burlesque on history by JOHN KENDRICK BANGS. Bangs humorously mingled historical figures of several ages, also some fictional and mythical characters, in a gay mélange of episodes. The dialogues and escapades are very amusing, and the book has suffered an unjust eclipse. A sequel, *The Pursuit of the House-Boat* (1897), continued the fun; and there were other Stygian episodes in *The Enchanted Typewriter* (1899).

House by the Side of the Road, The. A poem by SAM WALTER FOSS, included in his collection *Dreams in Homespun* (1897). Two lines have become famous: "Let me live in my house by the side of the road/ And be a friend of man."

House Divided (1947), a historical novel by Ben Ames Williams. This massive romance took four years and endless research to write. It follows the fortunes of a wealthy Virginia family during the Civil War. Although Southern in its point of view, the novel is not dogmatically partisan; Williams sees the war itself as a major crime and disaster.

House of Connelly, The (1931), a play by PAUL GREEN. The action is laid in the South, with a strong contrast between the landowners, who have gradually lost their vigor, and the tenant farmers, still close to the soil. The daughter of such a farmer tricks Will Connelly, of the more aristocratic stock, into marrying her, but in the end serves him well and saves him.

House of Earth. A trilogy of novels by PEARL BUCK. They include THE GOOD EARTH (1931), *Sons* (1932), and *A House Divided* (1935). All are laid in China.

House of Mirth, The (1905), a novel by EDITH WHARTON. This famous story satirizes and reveals the weaknesses of the "high society" of New York that Edith Wharton knew so well. Its heroine is LILY BART, a poor relation who endeavors to secure a wealthy husband, becomes involved with a man who tries to blackmail her, is falsely accused of an intrigue with another woman's husband, retires from the vain contest and becomes a milliner, commits suicide just as the man she loves arrives with an offer of marriage. The book is a vivid picture of social life in New York in the days of the hansom cab. Clyde Fitch turned the novel into a play (1906), considerably altering the plot.

House of Night, The (1779, 1786), a poem by PHILIP FRENEAU. The poem runs to 136 quatrains. It belongs to the so-called Graveyard School of poetry. It is called by Harry Hayden Clark "one of the most original and romantic poems of early American literature."

House of the Seven Gables, The (1851), a novel by NATHANIEL HAWTHORNE. The story focuses on the house itself and on actions which took place in the past and have consequences in the present. The house was built two centuries before the story opens on land fraudulently obtained by the ancestral Pyncheon from an ancestral Maule, whom Pyncheon caused to be executed for witchcraft. Maule's dying curse on the Pyncheon family continues to be effective through several generations, and the last surviving Pyncheons are still under its influence as the story opens.

Hepzibah Pyncheon, an old maid, and her brother, Clifford, are chained to the house, their link with the family and the past, and view the outside world only through closed windows and curtains. Clifford, a sensitive but ineffective man, has just returned from jail, where he spent thirty years for the supposed murder of his uncle, and Hepzibah is forced to open a cent-shop to support herself and him. Their cousin, Judge Jaffrey Pyncheon, the last affluent member of the family, dies as the last victim of the curse and is revealed to be the man who wrongfully sent Clifford to prison and cheated him of his inheritance. Phoebe Pyncheon, a young and pretty country cousin, is saved from the curse by having been raised away from the house and having none of its taints. Holgrave, the boarder, is revealed to be a descendant of the executed Maule, and proves himself worthy of Phoebe when he refuses to exert mesmeric power over her, as one of his ancestors had done to enslave an earlier

Pyncheon. Thus a member of each family is raised above the curse and manages to find love.

The House of the Seven Gables is more than a blend of old curses, isolated men, past events, and a happy love story. It is a creation of life and time caught in a house, a family, and a generation of men. Scenes such as the trainride of Hepzibah and Clifford, and especially the death of the Judge, in which time stops while the author discusses its tyranny over men, are outstanding examples of Hawthorne's skill.

House of Usher, The Fall of the. See FALL OF THE HOUSE OF USHER.

house organs. Periodicals published by business firms and sent, usually without charge, to (1) employees, (2) potential or actual customers and stockholders, (3) the general public, particularly schools, in order to promote better public relations. In 1950 the total circulation of these house organs ran close to fifty million a month, a circulation double that of the country's four leading magazines. Books in this field include Robert E. Ramsay's *Effective House Organs* (1928); Garth Bentley's *How to Edit an Employee Publication* (1944); Paul F. Biklen and Robert D. Breth's *The Successful Employee Publication* (1945). There is a *Printers' Ink Directory of House Organs*, and *Stet: The House Magazine for House Magazine Editors* is issued at Hamilton, Ohio, by the Champion Paper and Fibre Company.

Houston, Sam[uel] (b. Rockbridge Co., Va., March 2, 1793—d. July 26, 1863), soldier, lawyer, public official. In the War of 1812 Houston served under Jackson. He studied law and was elected district attorney in the Nashville district, then went to Congress for two years, thereafter became governor of Tennessee. An unhappy marriage caused him to resign, and he went west into Indian country. He became friendly with the Cherokees, was appointed their agent, and was adopted into the tribe. Around 1833 he settled in Texas, became commander-in-chief of the Texan army in the War for Independence, defeated Santa Anna at the Battle of San Jacinto (April 21, 1836), and was elected president of the Republic in 1841. In 1845 Texas became a state of the Union, and Houston served as U.S. Senator until 1859, when he was elected governor. But he resigned on March 18, 1861, because he was unable to approve the entrance of Texas into the Confederacy. He took refuge in Oklahoma for a while and acquired the nickname of "Big Drunk." His was a dramatic and brilliant personality, especially as revealed in Donald Day and Harry Herbert Ullom's edition of his *Autobiography* (1954), containing many passages from his writings. Marquis James wrote a life of him called *The Raven* (1929). Houston, Tex., is named for him.

Hovey, Richard (b. Normal, Ill., May 4, 1864 —d. Feb. 24, 1900), poet, dramatist. A precocious boy, Hovey was educated at home and at Dartmouth College, where he earned a reputation among the students for his poetry, his exaggerated behavior, and his school patriotism. At some point in his undergraduate year he seems to have experienced a religious awakening; he became an Anglican, fasted, prayed, and conducted elaborate ceremonies in his room. After graduation in 1885 he studied painting for a while at the Art Students' League in Washington, then became a candidate for priest's orders. He did not complete his training, however, and later turned to newspaper work in Boston. He lectured at the Farmington School of Philosophy, especially on questions of aesthetics, and turned to the serious writing of poetry.

Hovey was an exceedingly self-conscious poet. For a time he played hard at being the American Oscar Wilde, wore a silk shirt, knee breeches, and buckled shoes. To the end he was bearded and picturesque. "Art is life," he held passionately. In 1891 he published LAUNCELOT AND GUENEVERE: A POEM IN DRAMAS, and went to England and France. He met Mallarmé and became interested in symbolism, which he thought held the key to a proper synthesis of realism and idealism. He was attracted also to Maurice Maeterlinck, and translated eight of his plays into English.

In 1892 Hovey went to Nova Scotia and New Brunswick with his friend BLISS CARMAN. There the two wrote SONGS FROM VAGABONDIA (1894), *More Songs from Vagabondia* (1896), and *Last Songs from Vagabondia* (published after Hovey's death in 1901). In 1893 *Seaward,* an elegy on the death of the poet and translator THOMAS WILLIAM PARSONS, appeared; in 1898 *Along the Trail* was published; and in 1900 Curtis Hidden Page proclaimed *Taliesin, A Masque* "the greatest poem of this sort in the English Language." *To the End of the Trail* (1908) was a posthumous collection of verse.

The best remembered of Hovey's poems are his *Men of Dartmouth, Eleazar Wheelock,* the widely popular *Stein Song, Hanover Winter Song, Barney McGee, The Kavanagh, Comrades, Here's a Health to Thee, Roberts,* and *Spring.* His revolt against convention took the guise of natural vagabonding and good fellowship. Part of his creed was a faith in an optimistic and vital America, and he was less the *littérateur* than he liked to imagine. Allan H. MacDonald of the Dartmouth faculty wrote *Richard Hovey, Man and Craftsman* (1956), which includes a bibliography prepared by Edward C. Lathem.

HERBERT FAULKNER WEST

Howadji, The. Pen name of G. W. CURTIS.
How Annandale Went Out (1910), a sonnet by EDWIN ARLINGTON ROBINSON. In his compact fourteen lines Robinson presents a drama of the conscience. A physician is called upon to attend a dying friend, a wreck of a man with "hell between him and the end." He uses "a slight kind of engine" (a hypodermic?) and puts him out of his misery. This vivid anecdote was one of the earliest realistic poems of the new poetic era to which Robinson belonged.
Howard, Bronson [Crocker] (b. Detroit, Mich., Oct. 7, 1842—d. Aug. 4, 1908), newspaperman, playwright. Howard had few the-

ories about the drama, and was indifferent to fame as an author; only a few of his plays were

published. He said bluntly, "A dramatist is a man who writes plays." But he took pride in his craft, founded the American Dramatists' Club (later the Society of American Dramatists and Composers), was an active worker in the cause of better international copyright protection. He won his first success with the farce *Saratoga* (1870). In general his plays deal with American life, particularly in the so-called upper classes. Among his notable successes were THE BANKER'S DAUGHTER (1878); *Young Mrs. Winthrop* (1882); *One of Our Girls* (1885); *The Henrietta* (1887); SHENANDOAH (1888); *Aristocracy* (1892). He produced an interesting analysis of his art in *The Autobiography of a Play* (1914), which presents three versions of a play. A. H. Quinn feels that Howard advanced from the superficial character-drawing of his earlier plays to subtle studies of the social order in his later productions. His predominant theme, Quinn feels, was the great power of social laws and conventions in shaping human lives.

Howard, George [Fitzalan] Bronson (b. Howard Co., Md., Jan. 7, 1884—d. Nov. 20, 1922), newspaperman, novelist, playwright. Howard's best book is the novel *God's Man* (1915), a scarcely veiled attack on a New York City magistrate named Joseph Corrigan. He also wrote *Birds of Prey* (1918) and *The Black Book* (1920). Among his plays were *The Snobs* (1911) and *The Alien* (with Eric Howard, 1927). Alva Johnston called him "New York's literary bad man, the Billy the Kid of the typewriter."

Howard, John Tasker (b. Brooklyn, N.Y., Nov. 30, 1890—d. Nov. 20, 1965), musicologist. Howard served as music expert for various magazines, committees, encyclopedias, broadcasting networks, and libraries; in 1940 he became curator of the Americana Music Collection at the New York Public Library. Among his extensive writings: *Our American Music* (1931; rev. ed., 1945); *Stephen Foster, America's Troubadour* (1934; rev. ed., 1953); *Ethelbert Nevin* (1935); *Our Contemporary Composers* (1941); *A Treasury of Stephen Foster* (1946); *The World's Great Operas* (1948). He has composed music in many forms and has prepared numerous radio scripts dealing with music.

Howard, Martin (b. R.I., [?]—d. 1781), lawyer, Loyalist, writer. In the heat of the controversies preceding the Revolution there appeared, on the Loyalist side, a temperate and well-reasoned pamphlet, *A Letter from a Gentleman of Halifax, to His Friend in Rhode Island* (1765). It was anonymously published, but was known to be by Howard, a Newport lawyer. It was in the main a reply to *The Rights of Colonies Examined* (1765), by Governor STEPHEN HOPKINS of Rhode Island. Howard argued that if Parliament had given the colonies certain rights, Parliament could take them away. His pamphlet was answered by Hopkins and by JAMES OTIS, and Howard retorted with a *Defense* (1765). But Howard stood alone; a mob burned him in effigy at Newport and he fled to England.

Howard, Sidney [Coe] (b. Oakland, Calif., June 26, 1891—d. Aug. 23, 1939), dramatist. Howard was a member of G. P. BAKER's "47 Workshop" at Harvard. He began with an effort in blank verse, *Swords* (1921), went on to adaptations from foreign plays, then to collaboration with EDWARD SHELDON in *Bewitched* (1924). His first original play to attract wide attention was THEY KNEW WHAT THEY WANTED (1924), which won a Pulitzer Prize with its depiction of an aging Napa Valley vintner who marries a mail-order wife and later magnanimously condones a momentary infidelity. *The Most Happy Fella* (1957) is a musical version of this play. Howard went on to one success after another. Perhaps the best of his plays are THE SILVER CORD (1926), a study of maternal possessiveness which, Brooks Atkinson said, "brought the theater up-to-date in the science of human behavior," and *Yellow Jack* (with Paul de Kruif, 1934), a documentary which tells with dramatic effectiveness how the army conquered yellow fever. He also wrote *Lucky Sam McCarver* (1925); *Ned McCobb's Daughter* (1926); *Salvation* (with CHARLES MACARTHUR, 1928); *Lute Song* (with WILL IRWIN, 1930); *The Late Christopher Bean* (an adaptation from the French of René Fauchois, 1932); DODSWORTH (with Sinclair Lewis, 1934). John Gassner called Howard a craftsman of the first order and praised his keen ear for American dialect, his keen eye for local characters. In 1939, after Howard's untimely death, the Playwrights' Company (Maxwell Anderson, S. N. Behrman, Elmer Rice, Robert E. Sherwood, and John F. Wharton) established the Sidney Howard Memorial Award of $1,500, to be given annually to a new and promising playwright.

Howe, E[dgar] W[atson] ["The Sage of Potato Hill"] (b. Treaty, Ind., May 3, 1853—d. Oct. 3, 1937), newspaperman, editor, novelist, aphorist, memoirist. Howe was always primarily the newspaperman and small-town editor. He owned and edited the Atchison (Kansas) *Daily Globe* (1877–1911), later started *E. W. Howe's Monthly* (1911–37). In 1883, after numerous rejections, his best novel, THE STORY OF A COUNTRY TOWN, appeared. It was, someone at the time said, "a petard set off under American respectability," a pioneer work whose frankness of tone in the depiction of a Midwestern community was not equaled for three or four decades. *Plain People* (1929) was Howe's autobiography, but he was best known for various collections of his editorials and aphorisms—*Lay Sermons* (1911), *Ventures in Common Sense* (1919), and *The Indignations of E. W. Howe* (1933).

Howe was one of the bitterest writers in American literature; he was a thoroughgoing cynic, pessimist, and iconoclast, a man of harsh common sense and abrupt, pithy, effective utterance. He wrote: "A woman is as old as she looks before breakfast." "There never was a radical writer honest enough to admit that the underdog often starts the fight, and that occasionally the upper dog deserves to win." "About all some men accomplish in life is to send a son to Harvard." Other works include: *An Ante-Mortem Statement* (1891); *Country Town Sayings* (1911); *The Anthology of Another Town* (1920).

Howe's son, **Gene Howe** (b. 1886—d. 1952), was a successful editor and publisher in Amarillo, Texas, especially through his column signed "Old Tack" in the Amarillo *News-Globe*.

Howe, Helen (b. Boston, Jan. 11, 1905—   ), monologuist, novelist. Miss Howe made solo appearances in army and navy hospitals, New York and London theaters, and night clubs. Her literary fame is based on her satiric novels about the foibles of New York, New England, and Hollywood society. They include: *The Whole Heart* (1943); *We Happy Few* (1946); *The Circle of the Day* (1950); *The Success* (1956); *Fires of Autumn* (1959).

Howe, Irving (b. New York City, June 11, 1920—   ), literary critic, social historian, educator. Howe's literary criticism is informed by a social point of view. In addition to his critical works, *Sherwood Anderson: A Critical Biography* (1951), and *William Faulkner: A Critical Study* (1953), he wrote *The UAW and Walter Reuther* (1949, with B. J. Widick), and *The American Communist Party: A Critical History* (1957, with Lewis Coser). Howe contributed articles and reviews on literary and political subjects to magazines like PARTISAN REVIEW. He demonstrated his ability to synthesize his social and literary interests in *Politics and the Novel* (1957), a distinguished book of essays on Stendhal, Dostoevsky, Conrad, Turgenev, Hawthorne, Henry James, Henry Adams, Malraux, Silone, and Orwell. The book is concerned not with defining "the political novel," but with examining what happens to novels that deal with politics; how they may be ruined by ideology or made truly significant by dealing with it. Howe edited, with Eliezer Greenberg, *A Treasury of Yiddish Stories* (1955).

Howe, Joseph (b. Halifax, N. Scot., Dec. 13, 1804—d. June 1, 1873), statesman, poet, journalist. The son of a Loyalist *émigré*, from whom he learned printing and literature, in 1828 Howe bought a newspaper, the *Nova Scotian*, and began his fight for a responsible government. The authorities sued him for libel, and in 1835 he won the case with magnificent oratory and established freedom of the press for Canada. This eloquence characterized his subsequent political career, which continued through several reformed governments and culminated in his acceptance of the lieutenant-governorship of Nova Scotia in 1872. His most valuable work is contained in *Speeches and Public Letters of Joseph Howe* (2 v., 1858). His literary efforts, especially his few poems, *Poems and Essays* (1874), suffer by comparison. However, he enthusiastically encouraged local poets and wits and held regular literary gatherings at his home. Thomas Chandler Haliburton's famous "Sam Slick papers" (see THE CLOCKMAKER) were first printed in the *Nova Scotian*. A representative selection of the many biographies of Howe should include: *Joseph Howe* (1904), by George Munro Grant; *The Tribune of Nova Scotia* (1914), by W. L. Grant; *Joseph Howe; A Study in Achievement and Frustration* (1935), by J. A. Roy.

Howe, Julia Ward (b. New York City, May 27, 1819—d. Oct. 17, 1910), poet, dramatist, writer of travel books, biographer, memoirist. In 1843 she married the noted humanitarian and

teacher of the blind, SAMUEL GRIDLEY HOWE, and soon came to know many of New England's

distinguished men and women; she formed a cultural link between New York and Boston. After her husband's death she continued his work and lectured on woman suffrage, prison reform, and international peace. She was an excellent linguist and a passionate lover of music. Among her writings were several collections of verse: *Passion Flowers* (1854); *Words for the Hour* (1857); *Later Lyrics* (1866); *From Sunset Ridge: Poems Old and New* (1898). She also wrote *A Trip to Cuba* (1860); *Sex and Education* (ed., 1874); *Memoir of Samuel Gridley Howe* (1876); *Modern Society* (1881); *Reminiscences* (1899); *At Sunset* (1910). Many of her letters appear in the Pulitzer Prize-winning biography of her prepared (2 v., 1915) by her two daughters, LAURA E. RICHARDS and Maud Ward Howe. Mrs. Howe is chiefly remembered for the famous BATTLE HYMN OF THE REPUBLIC, written December 1861, to a Civil War soldiers' tune, published in the *Atlantic Monthly* (February, 1862), and included in her *Later Lyrics*. She appears in the setting of her father's and her own family in Louise Hall Tharp's vivacious book, *Three Saints and a Sinner* (1956).

Howe, M[ark] A[ntony] DeWolfe (b. Bristol, R.I., Aug. 28, 1864—d. Dec. 6, 1960), biographer, historian, editor, poet. Howe worked on the staffs of *Youth's Companion*, the *Atlantic Monthly*, the *Harvard Alumni Bulletin*, and the *Harvard Graduates' Magazine*, and served as vice-president of the Atlantic Monthly. He was an active author well into his nineties. In addition all three of his children became writers— HELEN HOWE, QUINCY HOWE, and Mark De-Wolfe Howe. The last-named, a teacher of law, edited several volumes of Justice Oliver Wendell Holmes' letters.

Howe's books have a wide range, but he was pre-eminent in the field of biography. He wrote lives of Phillips Brooks (1899), George Bancroft (1908), Bishop Hare, apostle to the Sioux (1911), Charles Eliot Norton (1913), Mrs. James T. Fields (1922), Barrett Wendell (1924, a Pulitzer Prize book), James Ford Rhodes (1929), John Jay Chapman (1937), Oliver Wendell Holmes (1939), and edited the letters of many of these. He also wrote about Boston (1903, 1910) and about *The Atlantic Monthly and Its Makers* (1919), edited the "Beacon Biographies" (31 v., 1899–1910), wrote and published six volumes of verse, the last—*Sundown*—when he was ninety-two. Van Wyck Brooks said that even in his biographies Howe "was a poet all the time." His autobiography is *A Venture in Remembrance* (1941).

Howe, Quincy (b. Boston, Aug. 17, 1900—), historian, editor, radio news analyst. Howe helped edit the *Atlantic Monthly* and *Living Age*, then was editor-in-chief of Simon and Schuster. He wrote *World Diary* (1929–34); *England Expects Every American to Do His Duty* (1937); *Blood Is Cheaper Than Water* (1939); *The News and How to Understand It* (1940). The first of a projected three-volume work, *A World History of Our Own Times*, surveying the years from 1900 to 1919, was published in 1947; the second, published in 1953, covers 1918–1941. In 1961 he became senior editor of *Atlas,* a magazine of reprints from the world press.

Howe, Samuel Gridley (b. Boston, Nov. 10, 1801—d. Jan. 9, 1876), physician, teacher, crusader, welfare worker. Gridley was the husband of JULIA WARD HOWE and a great teacher of the blind. He trained the blind deaf-mute girl Laura Bridgman (1829–1889) by means of a raised type that he had devised and by other methods that later proved successful with Helen Keller. He was also interested in helping other handicapped persons. He was active in anti-slavery movements and with his wife founded an abolitionist paper, *The Commonwealth;* he later interested himself in the cause of various groups in revolt against the Turks. He served on various commissions and was in charge of several institutions. He prepared manuals for the blind, and wrote a *Historical Sketch of the Greek Revolution* (1828). His wife wrote a memoir of him (1876), his daughter Laura E. Richards edited his *Letters and Journals* (2 v., 1906–09). He appears in Louise Hall Tharp's *Three Saints and a Sinner* (1956), in John Jennings' novel *Banners Against the Wind* (1954), and in a biography (1956) by Harold Schwartz.

Howe, Will D[avid] (b. Charleston, Ind., Aug. 25, 1873—d. Dec. 8, 1946), teacher, editor. Howe taught English at Indiana University, was a member of the publishing firm of Harcourt, Brace & Howe, became an editor and director on the staff of Charles Scribner's Sons. He prepared several scholarly texts, including *The Howe Readers* (1909) and *The Literature of America* (2 v., 1929); and he compiled, in collaboration with W. J. Burke, a useful reference volume, *American Authors and Books, 1640–1940* (1943).

Howe, Sir William (1729–1814), English general. Howe took part in the engagement at Bunker Hill, then in October, 1755, succeeded Gage as commander of British troops in America. He won several battles against Washington, but failed to follow up his victories. Severe criticism led to his resignation in 1778, and the following year he appeared before Parliament and was cleared of the charges against him. He published a *Narrative of Sir William Howe Before a Committee of the House of Commons* (1778). In 1793 he was made a full general.

Howe appears several times in American writings. In reply to General Burgoyne's play, THE BLOCKADE (1775), which ridiculed the Continental soldiers, some anonymous person (probably MERCY OTIS WARREN) wrote *The Blockheads* (1776), concerned with Howe's unsuccessful attempt to storm Dorchester Heights. Francis Hopkinson made an amusing but scurrilous reference to Howe's amorousness in THE BATTLE OF THE KEGS (1778). Hawthorne wrote *Howe's Masquerade* (in *Twice-Told Tales,* 1842), the story of a ball given by Howe in Boston, at which suddenly appeared a procession of ghostly figures representing the early Puritan governors whose coming presaged the

end of royal authority in New England. Howe also appears in Richard P. Smith's *The Forsaken* (1831); S. Weir Mitchell's HUGH WYNNE, FREE QUAKER (1897); Irving Bacheller's *In the Days of Poor Richard* (1922); and Kenneth Roberts' OLIVER WISWELL (1940).

Howells, William Dean (b. Martin's Ferry, Ohio, March 1, 1837—d. May 11, 1920), novelist, poet, editor, critic. The son of a newspaperman and journeyman printer, Howells grew up in various towns in Ohio, went to school irregu-

larly, and by the time he was fifteen was a contributor of poems, tales, and essays to Ohio papers. He gave an account of his boyhood in Ohio in *A Boy's Town* (1890), and in *Years of My Youth* (1916) related his early life and his experiences after he went to work for the *Ohio State Journal* in Columbus. By the time he was twenty-three he had published two books, *Poems of Two Friends* (1860) and a campaign life of Lincoln (1860). His poetry had also appeared in the *Atlantic Monthly,* and when he made a literary pilgrimage to Boston in 1860 he was well received as a promising young writer. When he dined with Lowell, Holmes, and Fields, Holmes described the event as "the apostolic succession . . . the laying on of hands."

The life of Lincoln resulted in Howells' appointment as consul in Venice, where he spent the Civil War years and enjoyed an opportunity to observe European culture and manners. He wrote a series of travel letters to the Boston *Advertiser,* which, much revised, were published after his return to America as *Venetian Life* (1866). The book was a popular success and won him the further respect of the Cambridge group, particularly Lowell. Howells went to work for the newly-founded *Nation,* then for the ATLANTIC, of which he became editor in 1871. During this period his power as a literary figure grew steadily; he maintained an alliance with the older New England group and regularly printed contributions from Lowell, Emerson, and Longfellow in his magazine, but at the same time he encouraged new writers, notably Henry James, Mark Twain, and many of the local colorists. In part out of his friendship with James and Twain, Howells evolved his theory of realistic fiction, which he elaborated in his reviews and essays and put into practice in his own novels. As early as 1872 in his first novel, THEIR WEDDING JOURNEY, he had announced his program: "Ah! poor Real Life, which I love, can I make others share the delight I find in thy foolish and insipid face?" Later he further developed this realism of the commonplace in the tradition of the novel of manners in such works as A MODERN INSTANCE (1882) and THE RISE OF SILAS LAPHAM (1885). By this time he was recognized as one of the leading exponents of serious writing in America and as one of its most rewarding novelists.

Meanwhile Howells had left the *Atlantic* and had begun to contribute the "Editor's Study" (1886–92) to *Harper's Monthly.* Influenced by Tolstoy and by the American socialist Laurence Gronlund, he took up a sharply liberal view to supplement his realism. In his "economic novels," especially A HAZARD OF NEW FORTUNES (1890) and A TRAVELER FROM ALTRURIA (1894), he made close studies of American political and social conventions. After 1894 his militant phase subsided, though he continued to be interested in reform. Now nearly sixty, he continued to write fiction, approaching in *The Landlord at Lion's Head* (1897) and *The Kentons* (1902) the best of his earlier work. But most of his books during his later years were collections of articles that had been turned out for the several Harper magazines. *Literary Friends and Acquaintances* (1900) and *My Mark Twain* (1910) have charm and insight, and even his slighter essays are relieved by a delightful prose style. His reputation continued to grow and in 1908 he was elected president of the American Academy of Arts and Letters. Until the last ten years of his life he remained alert to new men and influences; he reviewed enthusiastically the posthumous poems of Emily Dickinson, he championed the work of Stephen Crane, and he recognized the potentialities of Frank Norris. Yet in spite of himself he had become for such younger men as Dreiser, Mencken, and Sinclair Lewis the personification of the old gentility. Mencken's disdainful description, "a contriver of pretty things . . . an Agnes Repplier in pantaloons," is typical of the dislike that the new generation felt for him.

During his career Howells wrote thirty-five novels, thirty-five plays, four books of poetry, six books of criticism, and thirty-four miscellaneous volumes. Among important works not mentioned above are: *Suburban Sketches* (essays, 1871); A CHANCE ACQUAINTANCE (1873); THE LADY OF THE AROOSTOOK (1879); *The Undiscovered Country* (1880); INDIAN SUMMER (1886); *The Minister's Charge* (1887); *The Shadow of a Dream* (1890); *Criticism and Fiction* (1891); *The Quality of Mercy* (1892); *Stops of Various Quills* (poems, 1895); *The Son of Royal Langbrith* (1904); *The Leatherwood God* (1916); *The Vacation of the Kelwyns* (1920). The critical recognition of this work when it was published, the more than fifty years of editorial activity, the close relationship with most of the important authors of the time, and the championship of early realism in American fiction, these give Howells unquestioned historical importance. Beyond that, his best novels remain eminently readable, and are more and more widely recognized as American classics. See also ANNIE KILBURN; AN IMPERATIVE DUTY.

The Life in Letters of William Dean Howells, edited by his daughter Mildred Howells, was published in 1928. Among recent critical evaluations of Howells' works are: J. L. Woodress, Jr., *Howells & Italy* (1952); Everett Carter, *Howells and the Age of Realism* (1954); E. H. Cady, *The Early Years of W. D. Howells, 1837–1885* (1956) and *The Realist at War: The Mature Years of William Dean Howells* (1958); O. W. Fryckstedt, *In Quest of America: A Study of Howells' Early Development as a Novelist* (1958); G. H. Bennett, *William Dean Howells* (1959); Van Wyck Brooks, *Howells: His Life and World* (1959).

GEORGE ARMS

Howells Medal, William Dean. An award established by the American Academy of Arts and Letters in 1921 on the eighty-fourth anniversary of Howells' birth. The medal was first presented in 1925, the winner being Mary E. Wilkins Freeman, and it has been presented each fifth year thereafter. Among those honored have been Willa Cather, Pearl Buck, Ellen Glasgow, Booth Tarkington.

Howes, Barbara (b. Boston, May 1, 1914—), poet. Miss Howes was educated in Boston and at Bennington College. She traveled extensively in England and Italy and for several years was editor of the literary quarterly *Chimera,* contributing poems and stories to numerous magazines and anthologies. In recent years such volumes as *The Undersea Farmer* (1949), *In the Cold Country* (1955), and *Light and Dark* (1960) have gained her a position among the foremost of the younger women poets in America. Her verse is careful, coherent, with subtle nuances of thought and feeling underlying its surface clarity.

Howl. A poem by ALLEN GINSBERG (1955). *Howl* is probably the most characteristic product of the beat poetry of the nineteen-fifties. It was revolutionary in both form and content. Its long, Whitmanesque line stood in sharp contrast to the tightly-wrought poetry in vogue at the time; the violence of its highly personal lament for American civilization was strikingly different from the quiet, measured voice of most modern poetry. In 1957, San Francisco customs authorities seized part of the English-printed edition of *Howl and Other Poems* on the charge that it was "obscene" literature. The book was ultimately cleared in a court case brought by LAWRENCE FERLINGHETTI's City Lights publishing company. In the course of the trial, critic Mark Schorer summarized *Howl:* "The theme of the poem is announced very clearly in the opening line, 'I saw the best minds of my generation destroyed by madness, starving hysterical naked.' . . . In the second section the mood of the poem changes and it becomes an indictment of those elements in modern society that, in the author's view, are destructive of the best qualities in human nature and of the best minds . . . the third part is a personal address to a friend . . . who is mad and in a mad house, and is the specific representative of what the author regards as a general condition . . ." (from *Horn on Howl* by Lawrence Ferlinghetti in *A Casebook on the Beat*, 1961). See BEAT WRITING.

How to Win Friends and Influence People (1936), by DALE CARNEGIE. This has been probably the most widely circulated book in the history of American writing and has been equally popular in this country and abroad. Carnegie, who was originally a teacher of public speaking, became a popular lecturer on "getting along," and he was persuaded to turn his lectures into a book, comprising such headings as "Six Ways to Make People Like You," "Twelve Ways to Win People to Your Way of Thinking," and "Seven Rules to Make Your Home Life Happier."

How to Write Short Stories (1924), a collection of ten stories by RING LARDNER. Lardner had won a wide public but little critical recognition, until this volume, with its sardonic preface, woke up the critics. He pretends to discuss the art of short-story writing; the stories included are "samples." He ridicules current formulas, as when he says, "How to begin—or, as we professionals would say, how to commence? . . . Blasco Ibáñez usually starts his stories with a Spanish word, Jack Dempsey with an 'I,' and Charley Peterson with a couple of quick, declarative sentences about his leading character, such as 'Hazel Gooftree had just gone mah jong. She felt faint.'" The stories themselves are marked by what one critic called "bitter veracity." Several, such as *Alibi Ike* and *Champion,* have become classics.

Hoyt, Charles Hale (b. Concord, N.H., July 26, 1860—d. Nov. 20, 1900), critic, playwright. Hoyt wrote drama criticism for the Boston *Post,* and became greatly interested in the stage. He began to write plays, first romantic dramas (*Cezalia,* 1882, among them), then farces; he became the foremost composer of the latter type of play, satirizing topical subjects such as woman suffrage, U.S. Senators, spiritualism, small-town life, the woes of train-travelers, the ways of plumbers. For many years he wrote and produced at least a play a year. He made large sums of money; his most famous play, A TRIP TO CHINATOWN (1891), held the stage for 650

performances. The plays were often plotless, and were intended as vehicles for songs and specialties. At least two of the songs are still familiar: *The Bowery* (words by Hoyt, music by Percy Grant) and *The Man Who Broke the Bank at Monte Carlo,* an English song by Fred Gilbert. Among other plays by Hoyt were *A Bunch of Keys* (1882); *A Parlor Match* (1884); *A Tin Soldier* (1886); *A Hole in the Ground* (1887); *A Texas Steer* (1890); *A Temperance Town* (1893); *A Milk-White Flag* (1893); *A Contented Woman* (1897); *A Stranger in New York* (1897); *A Day and a Night in New York* (1898). His plays remain in manuscript, with the exception of *A Texas Steer,* published in a collection of *Representative American Dramas* (1925).

Hrdlička, Aleš (b. Bohemia, March 29, 1869— d. Sept. 5, 1943), physician, anthropologist. Hrdlicka came to the United States when he was thirteen years old; he later joined several expeditions (1899–1903) sponsored by the American Museum of Natural History. He was appointed to the staff of the U.S. National Museum in 1903, was named curator in 1910. He founded the *American Journal of Physical Anthropology* (1918) and became its editor. He was widely known for important works on anthropometry and the evolution of man, also for his contention that American Indians are of Asiatic origin and that the cradle of mankind is in Europe, not Asia. He was a prolific writer; among his books are *Physiological and Medical Observations Among the Indians of the Southwestern U.S. and Northern Mexico* (1908); *Early Man in South America* (1912); *Physical Anthropology, Its Scope and Aims* (1919); *Anthropometry* (1920; rev. as *Practical Anthropometry,* 1939); *Old Americans* (1925); *Anthropology of the American Indian* (1927); *The Skeletal Remains of Early Man* (1930).

Hubbard, Elbert [Green] (b. Bloomington, Ill., June 19, 1856—d. May 7, 1915), businessman, printer, editor, writer. As a young man Hubbard sold soap, and might easily have become a millionaire. But he wanted to sell ideas instead, and he prospered in that business, too. He toured Europe to see what was salable in the intellectual field, was deeply impressed by William Morris' Kelmscott Press and his interior decoration ideas, and resolved to imitate them in the United States. On his return he founded the Roycroft Press at East Aurora, N.Y., and issued innumerable "arty" productions—books in imitation leather, booklets, magazines; he also produced household objects—pottery, metal and leather work, furniture—supposed to carry out Morris' ideas. As stock in trade Hubbard used familiar sentiments from Thoreau and Emerson. He made a specialty of biography, in accordance with Emerson's doctrine of "hero worship," wrote 170 LITTLE JOURNEYS to the homes of notable men and women. He also published THE PHILISTINE (1895–1915), largely devoted to his own effusions and epigrams, later issued *The Fra* (1908–17). He himself, a somewhat self-conscious aesthete in appearance, was known

as "Fra Elbertus" or "the Fra." His most successful publication was A MESSAGE TO GARCIA
(1899), a sermon on a Spanish-American War
episode. Hubbard capitalized on his fame by
appearing on the vaudeville stage and by delivering lectures which were an adroit blend of the
serious and the comic. He made East Aurora a
profitable center for worshippers who wanted
to come and stay as boarders. The place had five
hundred employees, joined in a pseudo-com-
munal enterprise. He befriended both famous
Cranes of American literature—Stephen and
Hart. He died when the S.S. *Lusitania* was sunk
by a German submarine.

Hubbard's publications include *One Day: A
Tale of the Prairies* (a novel, 1893); *Time and
Chance* (1899); *Life of Ali Baba* (1899); *Thou-
sand and One Epigrams* (1911); *The Roycroft
Dictionary* (1915); *Memorial Edition of Little
Journeys* (14 v., 1915); *Selected Writings* (14
v., 1923). Two biographies are Frank Shay's
Elbert Hubbard of East Aurora (1926) and
David Arnold Balch's *Elbert Hubbard—Genius
of Roycroft* (1940).

**Hubbard, [Frank Mc]Kin[ney] ["Abe Mar-
tin"]** (b. Bellefontaine, Ohio, Sept. 1, 1868—d.
Dec. 26, 1930), cartoonist, humorist. After
working for his father, a newspaper publisher,
Hubbard joined the Indianapolis *News* as staff
artist, cartoonist, and columnist. In 1914 he
created the character of ABE MARTIN, Hoosier
rustic, whose ungainly figure adorned the top of
a column quoting some of his shrewd cracker-
barrel epigrams. Occasionally there would be an
essay of some length in the same style, occasionally references to and quotations from other
rustics—Miss Fawn Lippincutt, the village belle;
Tell Binkley, the village failure; Young Lafe
Bud, who fancied himself a dandy.

Abe Martin would drawl: "Nobuddy works
as hard for his money as the feller that marries
it." "The safest way t' double your money is t'
fold it over once an' put it into your pocket."
"Of all th' home remedies a good wife is th'
best." "Ther's some folks standin' behind th'
President that ought t' get around where he kin
watch 'em."

Hubbard, William (b. England, [?], 1621—
d. Sept. 14, 1704), clergyman, historian. Hubbard came with his father to New England,
graduated in Harvard's first class (in 1684 he
substituted for a while as president), was ordained in 1658, served as minister of the Congregational Church in Ipswich until 1703. He
was orthodox to an extreme, but opposed the
persecution of alleged witches and protected
some of the victims. His best-known book was
his *General History of New England from the
Discovery to 1680*, first printed in part in 1815,
in fuller versions 1848, 1878. The history was
based on earlier documents by Thomas Morton,
William Bradford, and John Winthrop, but also
included material obtained by Hubbard's own
research. As might be expected, it was written
from Hubbard's special viewpoint, as Kenneth
B. Murdock shows in *William Hubbard and the
Providential Interpretation of History* (1943).

Hubbard also wrote a NARRATIVE OF THE TROU-
BLES WITH THE INDIANS IN NEW ENGLAND
(1677) and collected his *Sermons* (1684).

Hubble, Edwin Powell (b. Marshfield, Mo.,
Nov. 20, 1889—d. Sept. 28, 1953), astronomer.
As a Rhodes scholar Hubble became interested in
the common law of England and the United
States, was admitted to the bar, and practiced
law for a year. Then, turning back to an older
interest, he became an astronomer. His career
thereafter was joined with the work of the Yerkes
Observatory, Chicago, and the Mt. Wilson Observatory, Pasadena. His revolutionary discoveries are chiefly embodied in *Realm of Nebulae*
(1936) and *Observational Approach to Cosmology* (1937). His work is especially important in
extra-galactic research. His observations and
conclusions excited much controversy, often metaphysical rather than scientific in tone.

Huckleberry Finn, The Adventures of (1884),
a novel by MARK TWAIN. This sequel to TOM
SAWYER (1876), given in Huck's own words,
tells how Huck, escaping from his blackguardly
father, who had imprisoned him in a lonely

cabin, meets Jim, a runaway slave, on Jackson's
Island in the Mississippi River. Together they
float on a raft down the mighty stream, are
separated when a steamer wrecks the raft, meet
again a little later and continue their journey on
the raft. Two confidence men join them and
they drift into many extraordinary adventures,
in the course of which Tom Sawyer reappears.
Tom's Aunt Sally wants to adopt Huck, who

decides he had better disappear again, lest he be "sivilized."

The book is not only Mark Twain's greatest literary performance; it is, in the opinion of some, the greatest American novel—certainly the most characteristic in its characters, plot, and style. The dialect is reproduced with keen linguistic sense. Writing an introduction for a new edition of the novel (1950), T. S. Eliot calls Huck "one of the permanent symbolic figures of fiction, not unworthy to take a place with Ulysses, Faust, Don Quixote, Don Juan, Hamlet, and other great discoveries that man has made about himself." In the London *Times* a reviewer of Eliot's edition spoke of Huck as "a Rousseauesque figure: the 'noble savage' of the 18th century: the 'natural man' with his cold, realistic rationalism. He cannot put up with convention, manners, politeness; in a word, Society." In this figure Clemens himself is reflected, the man against society, the rationalist who scorned conventional religion and its platitudes. The two major figures in *Huckleberry Finn* are, of course, Huck and the River, the latter as much a personage as the former; the narrative, someone has said, shows how the River happened to Huck. The relationship between Huck and the Negro, Jim, is also of great importance —the struggle in Huck's soul between his "respectable" Southern prejudices and his growing appreciation of Jim's value and dignity as a human being is an ironic and powerful indictment of the moral blindness of a slaveholding society. Many modern authors have testified to the influence of the book. H. L. Mencken, for instance, said that the discovery of *Huckleberry Finn* was "the most stupendous event of my whole life"; and Ernest Hemingway has declared that "all modern American literature stems from this one book."

Hudson, Henry [sometimes **Hendryck,** a folk etymology owing to his association with the Dutch East India Co.] (b. England, [?]–d. 1611), navigator, explorer. In 1607 the Muscovy Company hired Hudson to discover a northeast passage to the Far East; he reached Greenland and Spitzbergen. In his later journey for the Dutch (on the *Halve Maen* or *Half Moon*) he discovered the river later named for him and sailed up it as far as present-day Albany (1609). In another voyage on the *Discovery,* for English interests, he reached Hudson Bay, where his ship was frozen in for the winter. His crew mutinied, set him and eight others adrift in a small boat (June 23, 1611); nothing further was ever heard of them.

Hudson, Henry Norman (b. Cornwall, Vt., Jan. 28, 1814—d. Jan. 16, 1886), clergyman, Shakespearean scholar, historian, lecturer, editor. Hudson became a Protestant minister in 1849 and edited some church magazines. But his main career lay elsewhere. He had a much-appreciated gift for explaining the plays of Shakespeare, often lectured on the plays, wrote about the dramatist profusely, and edited his *Complete Works* (20 v., 1880–81). Among his other books: *Lectures on Shakespeare* (1848);

Shakespeare: His Life, Art, and Characters (2 v., 1872); also a savage attack on a Civil War general, *A Chaplain's Campaign with General* [B. F.] *Butler* (1865).

Hudson's Bay Company. An important enterprise organized in the 17th century by a group of English businessmen to obtain furs in North America for the British market. It obtained a charter from King Charles II on May 2, 1670, and has operated continuously in Canada since then. It made many adventurous explorations, overcame opposition by the French, earned large dividends, established a continent-wide monopoly, gave up some of its powers and privileges to the Dominion of Canada (1868), continues to do a great business at the present time. The company appars in Edison Marshall's *Seward's Folly* (1924), Vardis Fisher's *Pemmican* (1956), and H. S. M. Kemp's *Northern Trader* (1956). George Bryce related the *Remarkable History of the Hudson's Bay Company* (1900), the subject also of Douglas MacKay's *Honorable Company* (1936).

Hueston, Ethel (b. Iowa, Dec. 3, 1887—), novelist. Mrs. Hueston has a long list of fiction to her credit; best known of her novels was *Prudence of the Parsonage* (1915), which had several sequels. Her liking for her characters is obvious, and her endings are invariably happy. Among her other books: *The People of This Town* (1929); *That Hastings Girl* (1933); *A Roof Over Their Heads* (1937); *Preacher's Wife* (1941); *The Family Takes a Wife* (1950).

Huggins, John Richard Desborus (b. [?]—d. [?]), a New York City barber who early in the 19th century was, as he described it, "Empereur du Friseurs, Roi du Barbières [sic]" for the wits and fops of his day. He created much amusement by the parodies and flights of fancy in his professional advertisements in the *Evening Post,* the *Morning Chronicle,* and other papers. He had a reputation as a wit, but many of his quips were undoubtedly originated by others and fastened on him. His effusions were collected in *Hugginsiana, or, Huggin's Fantasy* (1808).

Hughes, Charles Evans (b. Glens Falls, N.Y., April 11, 1862—d. Aug. 27, 1948), teacher, lawyer, public official. Hughes' distinguished legal career led to his being elected Governor of New York in 1906 and again in 1908. In 1910 he was appointed by President Taft an associate justice of the Supreme Court, but resigned six years later to run against Woodrow Wilson for the Presidency. Defeated by a narrow margin, he returned to law practice, but became Secretary of State under both Harding and Coolidge until 1925, when he became a member of the courts of international arbitration and justice at the Hague. In 1930 President Hoover appointed him Chief Justice of the Supreme Court; he served until 1941. He supported many of the measures and social advances proposed by President Roosevelt, although opposed to government agencies that usurped the functions of courts. He made the statement: "We are under a Constitution, but the Constitution is what the judges say it is." He was an eminent jurist, a great and sincere public servant. Among his books: *Conditions of Progress in Democratic Government* (1909); *The Pathway of Peace and Other Addresses* (1925); *The Supreme Court of the U.S.* (1927); *Pan-American Peace-Plans* (1929). His papers are in the Library of Congress. Dexter Perkins analyzed *Hughes and American Democratic Statesmanship* (1956).

Hughes, Dorothy [Belle Flanagan] (b. Kansas City, Mo., 1904—   ), mystery writer, poet, critic. Dorothy Hughes worked on newspapers in Missouri, New York, and New Mexico, wrote poetry, mystery stories, and criticism. Her books *The Fallen Sparrow* (1942) and *The So Blue Marble* (1940) are taut thrillers. *The Delicate Ape* (1942) is a story of foreign intrigue set in a future time. Some of her other books: *Ride the Pink Horse* (1944); *The Big Barbecue* (1949). Poetry: *Dark Certainty* (1931); *Green Loving* (1953).

Hughes, Glenn [Arthur] (b. Cozad, Neb., Dec. 7, 1894—   ), teacher, dramatist, critic. Hughes became director of the school of drama at the University of Washington in 1930. There he mingled practice with teaching, writing many plays (mostly comedies) as well as critical essays and poems. Among his plays: *Happiness for Six* (1928); *Green Fire* (1932); *Miss Millions* (1937); *Suspense* (1942); *Head First* (1947); *On the Side of the Angels* (1953); *The Magic Apple* (1954). Among his critical and historical works: *The Story of the Theater* (1928); *Imagism and the Imagists* (1931); *The Penthouse Theater: Its History and Technique* (1942); *A History of the American Theater, 1700–1950* (1951). Other works: *Notion Counter* (poems, 1953); *Trivia, Poetic Footnotes for an Unwritten Autobiography* (1956).

Hughes, Hatcher (b. Polkville, N.C., Feb. 12, 1881—d. Oct. 17, 1945), teacher, dramatist. For the greater part of his career Hughes taught at Columbia University. He also wrote several successful plays, among them *A Marriage Made in Heaven* (1918); *Wake Up, Jonathan* (with Elmer Rice, 1921); Hell-Bent for Heaven (Pulitzer Prize, 1923); *Ruint* (1924); *The Lord Blesses the Bishop* (1932). The best of these present North Carolina mountaineers. *Hell-Bent for Heaven* deals with their superstitions and feuds.

Hughes, [James] Langston (b. Joplin, Mo., Feb. 1, 1902—d. May 23, 1967), poet, editor. Hughes, one of the most eminent Negro poets of the mid-20th century, dealt with the tribulations of his race as well as their consoling joys. Often his poems have a documentary tone. Even so, there is an inherent timbre in his style, and he brought to his work an ear attuned to folk speech and song. He also made highly literate use of the blues and the ballad. Among his collections of verse: *Weary Blues* (1926); *The Dream Keeper* (1932); *Shakespeare in Harlem* (1942); *Fields of Wonder* (1947); *One Way Ticket* (1949); *Montage of a Dream Deferred* (1951); *Ask Your Mama* (1961). From

his own poem called *Cross* he made the play *Mulatto* (1935); this in turn was produced in a musical version entitled *The Barrier* (1950). He wrote the libretto for the opera *Troubled Island* (1949). Hughes' satirical sketches written for a Negro newspaper were collected in *Simple Speaks His Mind* (1950). *Not Without Laughter* (1930) is a novel, *The Ways of White Folks* (1934) a short story collection. In addition he edited an anthology, *The Poetry of the Negro* (1949), and wrote his autobiography in *The Big Sea* (1940)—part of his early life was spent as a sailor—and in *I Wonder as I Wander* (1956). Other books are *Famous Negro Music Makers* (1955), and *The Best of Simple* (1961).

Hughes, Rupert (b. Lancaster, Mo., Jan. 31, 1872—d. Sept. 9, 1956), editor, novelist, short-story writer, playwright, biographer. Hughes was a prolific and successful producer of popular literary and dramatic entertainment, occasionally ventured into other fields, as in his *Music Lovers' Cyclopedia* (1914) and his biography of George Washington (3 v., 1926, 1927, 1930). Among his stories: *The Lakerim Athletic Club* (1898); *What Will People Say?* (1914); *We Can't Have Everything* (1917); *Souls for Sale* (1922); *The Uphill Road* (1933); *Triumphant Clay* (1951). Among his plays: *Alexander the Great* (1903); *Excuse Me* (1911); *Uncle Zeb* (1913). To Hughes is credited the line: "Her face was her chaperone."

Hugh Selwyn Mauberley (1920), a poem by Ezra Pound. This is probably the first important modern American poem. Through his persona, Mauberley, Pound expresses his hatred of war, of commercialism in the arts, and his views of such contemporaries as Arnold Bennett ("Mr. Nixon") and Ford Madox Ford (the "stylist"). At the same time, *Mauberley* is Pound's farewell to London and to the period in which almost alone he championed Robert Frost, T. S. Eliot, D. H. Lawrence, and James Joyce. Eliot himself has called the poem "a document of an epoch," and the influence of its virtuosity in sound and rhythm may be seen two years later in *The Waste Land*.

Hugh Wynne, Free Quaker (1897), a historical novel by S. Weir Mitchell. One of the best stories about the American Revolution, this book was seven years in the making, owing to Dr. Mitchell's careful research. In the first-person narrative, the young hero describes the Philadelphia of his childhood and youth, his service in the American army, his captivity in a British prison, his acquaintance with Washington, Lafayette, and other heroes of the day, his own somewhat complicated love affair. Rivalry with a cousin is part of the plot, the harm inflicted by too strict religious control part of the lesson that Mitchell preaches.

Huie, William Bradford (b. Hartselle, Ala., Nov. 13, 1910—   ), novelist, journalist. During the war Huie served in the Navy on several war fronts as an officer and a correspondent. One of his early books, *The Fight for Air Power* (1942), was controversial and made the emphatic point that our long range airpower had been slowed "by army and navy groundhogs." In *The Case Against the Admirals* (1946), another critical broadside, he tried to establish that the Navy and Army had so hamstrung the Air Corps that, when Hitler started his drive for conquest, we had no airpower at all. The Navy made vigorous efforts to refute this book. *The Execution of Private Slovik*, a realistic description of the execution of an American army deserter, caused a furor after its publication in 1954. Huie was editor and publisher (1951–52) of the AMERICAN MERCURY. Some other books: *From Omaha to Okinawa* (1945); *The Revolt of Mamie Stover* (1951); *The Americanization of Emily* (1959).

Hulton, Ann (b. [?]–d. 1779), letter-writer. The sole work of this Loyalist, a resident of Brookline, Mass., is a series of letters addressed to an English correspondent. First printed in 1927 as *Letters of a Loyalist Lady*, they are useful documents of the Revolutionary period.

Human Comedy, The (1943), a novel by WILLIAM SAROYAN. This is a rather sentimental and ebullient narrative in which the protagonist is a messenger boy, Homer Macauley, who lives with his family in a California town. The novel was preceded by a film of the same name (1942) for which Saroyan produced the original scenario.

human interest story. A newspaper account of an event which is of itself not necessarily newsworthy, but which throws a certain light —sentimental, pathetic, or humorous—on human nature.

Humanism, or **The New Humanism.** A movement of literary and philosophical orthodoxy begun in the early 1900's. It combined an attack on modern literature and a plea for classical standards of taste with a call for conservative moral values. IRVING BABBITT and PAUL ELMER MORE, the leaders of the movement, saw in Humanism a preservative against the decadence of modern life. In *Literature and the American College* (1908) Babbitt upheld the *frein vital*, the "inner principle of restraint," as a curb to NATURALISM, the gospel of progress, and the romanticism of Rousseau. Less given to invective than Babbitt, More shared with his friend a general contempt for modern literature, describing Dos Passos' *Manhattan Transfer* as "an explosion in a cesspool." Both writers looked back to Emerson's distinction between "law for man" and "law for thing" to loosen the hold of utilitarian science over human activity. More developed his position in SHELBURNE ESSAYS (1904–21) and *New Shelburne Essays* (1928–36); Babbitt furthered his ideas in *The New Laokoön* (1910), *Democracy and Leadership* (1924) and most notably in *Rousseau and Romanticism* (1919).

In the 1920's Norman Foerster gathered a Humanist symposium, including T. S. Eliot, "to consider the requirements of Humanism in the various activities of modern thought and life." To the Humanist cause Foerster rallied the names of Homer, Aristotle, Buddha, Jesus, Shakespeare, and Emerson, but added little to the ideas of More and Babbitt. The symposium, published as *Humanism and America, Essays on the Outlook of Modern Civilization* (1930), was attacked by a group of rising critics, among whom were some exponents of the NEW CRITICISM. Their response filled American literary magazines in the early 1930's and was anthologized in C. Hartley Grattan's *The Critique of Humanism* (1930). They chided the Humanists for their genteel standards, exclusive tastes, and unbudging hatred of the modern world. Kenneth Burke detected fascist overtones in their doctrine, R. P. Blackmur found them defective in aesthetic appreciation, Edmund Wilson showed how Babbitt sometimes distorted and mistranslated his authorities. George Santayana continued the attack in THE GENTEEL TRADITION AT BAY (1931).

The heated debate over Humanism grew cold in the 1930's when, with a return to social themes in the novel, criticism looked toward Marx and Engels for principles. Despite the excitement it once generated, the Humanist controversy and its literature have been characterized by Howard Mumford Jones as "vast, repetitious, and abusive."

Humble-Bee, The (composed, 1837; pub., 1839), a poem by RALPH WALDO EMERSON. This famous poem is notable for its skillful use of a trochaic tetrameter couplet, with an occasional irregularity that prevents melodic monotony. It contains some of Emerson's most charming phrases. Emerson recorded in his journal (May 9, 1837), "Yesterday in the woods I followed the fine humble-bee with rhymes and fancie fine."

Humble Romance, A, and Other Stories (1887), by MARY E. WILKINS FREEMAN. These are grim stories of New England; the characters are closemouthed, joyless, unattractive.

Hume, Cyril (b. New Rochelle, N.Y., March 16, 1900—   ), novelist, screenwriter. The author of five novels and two collections of short stories and poems, all of which appeared in the space of about a dozen years after 1923, Hume was notable for a exuberant, rather florid prose style and a preoccupation with sexual tragedy. The novels are *Wife of the Centaur* (1923); *Cruel Fellowship* (1925); *The Golden Dancer* (1926); *A Dish for the Gods* (1929); and *My Sister My Bride* (1932). His short stories are collected in *Street of the Malcontents* (1927) and *Myself and the Young Bowman* (1932, includes poetry).

Humoresque (1919), a collection of eight stories of Jewish life in New York City, by FANNIE HURST. The title story tells of a lad who became a great violinist; the idea occurred to Miss Hurst at a violin recital by Mischa Elman. This was turned into a play (1923) by the author.

humor in the United States. At the beginning American humorous writers imitated 17th- and 18th-century English models, and many long continued to do so. But American humor became an independent creation when in New England at some indefinable moment the Puritan strangely spawned the YANKEE. By the time that Yankee humor, revealed in eccentric characters and rustic apothegms, reached its height, it was complemented by the frontier humor of the South, the Southwest, and the Far West, with its shrieking exaggerations, naïve fantasies, and constant irony. Then in the later 19th and 20th centuries Yankee and frontier humor were merged in an extraordinary cultural complex, in which may be found traditional elements transplanted from Europe, a persistence of crackerbarrel philosophy and of TALL TALES, verbal exuberance, funny business as a profession, a cult of the wisecrack and the insult, and mass production of laughter in movies, radio, television, and syndicated columns.

In their dealings with one another the Puritans used "sarcastic chaffing and a dry, sharp sort of humor," says Sidney George Fisher. NEW ENGLAND'S ANNOYANCES (1630), an anonymous piece of uninspired verse, discourses not too painfully on Puritan discomforts. An early teller of tall tales was John Josselyn, an Englishman who reported on the Puritan colonies in NEW ENGLAND'S RARETIES DISCOVERED (1672) and An Account of Two Voyages to New England (1675). He averred, for example, that "Indians commonly carry on their discussions in perfect hexameter verse, extempore." The greatest Puritan humorist was NATHANIEL WARD, an English clergyman who lived in Massachusetts from 1634 to 1647, then returned to England. In 1647 appeared in England his book called THE SIMPLE COBBLER OF AGAWAM (the original name of Ipswich, Mass.). Ward is so completely and viciously intolerant that he is funny, whether by intention or not. His style is Elizabethan—whimsical, figurative, allusive. Moses Coit Tyler called The Simple Cobbler "the most eccentric and amusing book produced in America during the colonial period."

During these formative years the transformation of Puritan into Yankee was proceeding. The simplest explanation is that the Puritan suppressed Elizabethanism for a while, then it came exuberantly to the surface again, but hardened, suspicious, and worldly. Vernon L. Parrington saw the Puritan as a creation of the rugged idealism of the English Reformation, the Yankee as a creation of the practical economics of native conditions. The reign of the saints passed, the rule of the lawyers and the merchants began. The people developed an ingenuity that gave birth to the resourceful, thrifty Yankee. A third cause was the decay of faith. Stephen Leacock claimed that the Puritan went to New England determined not to laugh and ultimately, grown irreverent from over-piety, turned into a humorist. There is also the notion that Yankeeism was a psychological escape from the repressions of the Puritan. The fact of the matter seems to be, however, that the strict Puritan was always in a minority in the New England population. Perhaps, therefore, the secret of the emergence of the Yankee is that he existed from the beginning.

There is, however, a sixth explanation of the way in which the Puritan turned into an avowed humorist. The Puritan, according to this theory, became a Yankee when he mixed blood with the Scotch-Irish. The resemblance of Scots and Yankees was noted as early, at least, as T. C. Haliburton, who in the preface to his anthology Traits of American Humor (1852) maintained that the humor of both was "sly, cold, quaint, practical, and sarcastic." RICHARDSON WRIGHT wrote in his entertaining account of early America, Grandfather Was Queer (1933): "[The American] wag is a horse of a different color. His wit and quixotic notions, nine times out of ten, are part of his racial inheritance. Waggery, in early America, did not get under way until the Scotch-Irish and the Irish had infiltrated the ranks of those middle-class English who formed the bulk of the first arrivals."

Whatever the road the Puritan followed, he emerged a different man, a neo-Puritan. The Yankee was shrewdness as against godliness, an assumed naïveté as against theocratic arrogance, pretended illiteracy as against pedantic learning, bucolic wit as against Latin dullness, affected taciturnity as against four-hour sermons, stubborn individualism as against conformity, unsmiling humor as against unsmiling repression. But the Puritan never really disappeared, and the thread of his influence winds in and out of American humor. It is inescapable, however faint at times, in Lowell and Lincoln but also in the artificial Bret Harte, the rebellious Mark Twain, the smiling Mr. Dooley, the bitter Ring Lardner, the sophisticated Dorothy Parker, and scores of wry aphorists.

It wasn't long before someone discovered the possibilities of the Yankee in humor, and in time he became a stereotype. Yankee ALMANACS helped to establish the traditions of a special type of humor. The anecdotes they contained were often merely adaptations of jests already current in England. The aphorisms were similarly in a new style, even if the substance was old. One of the greatest almanac-makers was R. B. Thomas (1766–1845), whose OLD FARMER'S ALMANAC, first issued in 1793, is still going strong a century and a half later. General John Burgoyne's farce THE BLOCKADE OF BOSTON (1775) portrayed a Yankee rustic, presented as Washington's orderly-sergeant. Royall Tyler, in THE CONTRAST (1787), first gave a Yankee character an important role; he was followed by a large number of other dramatists whose plays featured comic Down East characters. Meanwhile the newspapers and magazines published essays, stories, letters, and poems in rural Yankee dialect. Royall Tyler and THOMAS GREEN FESSENDEN (1771–1837) both wrote amusing verses of this sort. Newspapers also first popularized Yankee wit in the form of letters to the editor. Earliest to gain nation-wide fame were those of SEBA SMITH (1792–1868), whose JACK DOWNING letters appeared in the Portland Courier, were widely reprinted, and were imitated by C. A. DAVIS in the "Major J. Downing" letters. Famous also were the writings of the Nova Scotian T. C. HALIBURTON (1796–1865), with his Sam

Slick. (See THE CLOCKMAKER.) These Yankee types reached their apotheosis in James Russell Lowell's BIGLOW PAPERS (1848), in which Lowell revealed himself simultaneously as a notable poet, satirist, folklorist, linguist, and crusader. The type persisted into the 19th and 20th centuries. ARTEMUS WARD and JOSH BILLINGS wrote as Yankees. Billings was perhaps most Yankee in invariably following an old New England folkway: the dead-pan style of telling a joke, a trick the Puritan may have learned from the Indian.

Throughout this period the earlier academic tradition continued to prevail with numerous writers. The wittiest and merriest were that mad pair, MATHER BYLES (1707–1788) and JOSEPH GREEN (1706–1780). TIMOTHY DEXTER makes all other Yankee eccentrics seem pale by contrast. A straight-faced account of the *General History of Connecticut* (1781) by the Rev. SAMUEL ANDREWS PETERS is full of tall tales and historic burlesques. In the South one finds GEORGE ALSOP, with his jocular *Character of the Province of Maryland* (1666); Ebenezer Cook, with his SOT-WEED FACTOR (1708), another satire on Maryland; and WILLIAM BYRD (1674–1744), whose private papers were published long after his death. The HARTFORD WITS produced at least two triumphs, John Trumbull's *M'Fingal* (1781) and Joel Barlow's THE HASTY PUDDING (1793). Washington Irving added a new type to humor with his humorous Dutchmen in the HISTORY OF NEW YORK BY DIEDRICH KNICKERBOCKER (1809) and RIP VAN WINKLE (1819), while at the same time he followed Queen Anne and romantic models of humor in many of his writings. From his pen came also the burlesque portrait of a Yankee, Ichabod Crane, in the LEGEND OF SLEEPY HOLLOW (1819). With him was associated JAMES KIRKE PAULDING, an imitator of Addison, Swift, and Goldsmith. The CROAKER PAPERS (1819) of Joseph Rodman Drake and Fitz-Greene Halleck gracefully followed British tradition in their satire of New York dignitaries. An early and able satirist was Hugh H. Brackenridge (1748–1816), whose MODERN CHIVALRY (1792–1815) is an exposé of the follies of democracy and the dishonesty of frontier life, done in the style of Cervantes and Swift. In 1801 JONATHAN M. SEWALL wrote a *Eulogy on Laughter*.

The expanding frontier ushered in the new humor of the South, the West, and the Southwest. DAVY CROCKETT's tall tales set the pattern for a huge crop of such stories; he loved racy sayings, metaphoric proverbs. The generic figure of a frontiersman, the Kentuckian, loved to boast and prided himself on his rudeness. The Kentuckian soon gave way to other more westerly frontiersmen, the Nevadan and the Californian in particular, as portrayed by more sophisticated humorists such as MARK TWAIN and BRET HARTE. The "tall story" gave birth to another folk hero in MIKE FINK, kneelboatsman.

The Yankee and the Westerner both loved a quickly told story, with a snap at the end drowned in the guffaws of the audience. This sort of humor was largely oral at first, and had to be produced casually. Lincoln was a great master of this sort of tale, told with a purpose. From the social gatherings of the frontier it was transferred to the lecture platform; even in print it was best read aloud. Yankee admiration for the clever trickster continued as a tradition in frontier humor. Mark Twain in his earlier days could never resist the temptation of perpetrating a hoax. (See HOAXES.) EUGENE FIELD, a later humorist trained in the frontier tradition, was an incorrigible joker and was something of a trial to his friends. A classic of the American love of practical jokes is G. W. PECK's *Peck's Bad Boy* (1883).

Frontier humor pretended to be illiterate, but was usually produced by well-educated men. H. L. Mencken notes the naive but spontaneous hyperboles of the common folk of the West, but argues that their playing with words was soon reinforced by the deliberate inventions of a more sophisticated class. He also says that when the humor came from the frontiersmen themselves, it was a "loutish humor."

American fiction was a great gainer from the development of humor. The intrusion of comic relief into early 19th-century drama and novels produced the earliest realism in our fiction, since these characters were usually drawn from our own population, no matter how unreal the rest of the cast was. The novelists who created vigorous comic characters came mostly from the South and the Southwest—AUGUSTUS BALDWIN LONGSTREET (1790–1870), WILLIAM TAPPAN THOMPSON (1812–1882), GEORGE W. HARRIS (1814–1869), JOHNSON JONES HOOPER (1815–1862), JOSEPH G. BALDWIN (1815–1864), THOMAS B. THORPE (1815–1878). Others followed this trend: for example, Harriet Beecher Stowe in her OLDTOWN FOLKS (1869), Bret Harte in THE LUCK OF ROARING CAMP AND OTHER SKETCHES (1870), and Edward Eggleston in THE HOOSIER SCHOOLMASTER (1871). Harte held that the local color story derived from American humor. The supreme example of the humorist, the funny man turned novelist, is of course Mark Twain. His humor ranged in time and place from the rude frontier of the 1860's to all parts of the earth, and backwards and forwards in the centuries. The careless Nevadan hoaxer became the profound pessimist of THE MYSTERIOUS STRANGER.

American humorists in more recent years do not fall into any very clearly defined groups. The "funny man" is a characteristic figure of the American scene, a direct descendant of the clown of earlier days. At first he tended to be anonymous—the compiler of some almanac or jokebook. Beginning with the latter 19th century he appears as the conductor of a "column." (See COLUMNISTS.) Harold Thompson has spoken of the American funny man's "dead-pan solemnity, meandering stream-of-consciousness, burlesque, anticlimax, puns, bad spelling, and skillful timing." As with Yankee humor, there is often a concealment of sophistication and cynicism under a mask of eccentricity and illiteracy.

This is merely a continuation of the tradition of CRACKER-BARREL PHILOSOPHY so potent in American humor: Artemus Ward, FRANK MC-KINNEY ("Kin") HUBBARD, and E. W. HOWE are three widely different examples. An excellent history is Jennette Tandy, *Crackerbox Philosophers in American Humor and Satire* (1925).

Much of the humor of the United States has found a medium in newspapers and magazines, sometimes in periodicals devoted exclusively (and sometimes rather boringly) to humor. Under the so-called "exchange" system—a general understanding that an editor may borrow what he pleases from any other periodical, provided credit is given—national reputations were sometimes built up. While the system lasted it produced a vast mass of sometimes first-rate humor, especially in the form of aphorisms and wisecracks. A collection of about 2,500 such sayings was made by C. O. and E. E. Frederick in *Wisecracks* (1929). The humor magazine played an important role for about a century. It is believed that the first such periodical was *The Genius of Comedy, or, Life in New York, a Ludico-Comical Medley*, which made its appearance in 1830. Much more important was THE SPIRIT OF THE TIMES, a weekly published in New York City by William T. Porter from 1831 to 1858. It became, oddly, a prime vehicle for Southwestern and Southern humor; Porter collected some of the best stories of this genre in *The Big Bear of Arkansas and Other Sketches* (1845). Other early humor magazines were *Yankee Blade* (1845–90), CARPET BAG (1851–53), *The Lantern* (1852–53), *Comic Monthly* (1859–76), and VANITY FAIR (1859–63). The last-named magazine, whose name was taken later by another periodical, was probably the best.

A new generation of humor magazines came in the 1870's and 1880's—PUCK (1877–1918), JUDGE (1881–1939), ARKANSAS TRAVELER (1882–1916), and LIFE (1883; metamorphosed, 1936). *Puck, Judge,* and *Life* during their heyday wielded a tremendous influence, politically and socially. In their pages appeared skillful, sophisticated verses by such writers as HENRY CUYLER BUNNER (editor of *Puck*), GUY WETMORE CARRYL, ARTHUR GUITERMAN, SAMUEL HOFFENSTEIN, FRANKLIN P. ADAMS, CHRISTOPHER MORLEY, DON MARQUIS, LOUIS UNTERMEYER, PHYLLIS McGINLEY, DOROTHY PARKER, and EDNA ST. VINCENT MILLAY. Humor found new vehicles in the 1920's and thereafter, particularly in the columnists, the movies, radio and television, and night-club shows. The "comic" strips, too, were highly popular. (See THE COMICS.) One new magazine could be called a humor magazine, THE NEW YORKER, founded in 1925 by Harold Ross.

Dialect as a form of humor has long flourished in American writings. It began with the comic use of Yankee ways of speech, went on to the recording of Western forms of speech in sketches, tales, and verse such as John Hay's PIKE COUNTY BALLADS (1871). The Irishman in American humor was usually represented un-favorably until the master figure of Irish humor made his bow, F. P. Dunne's MR. DOOLEY (1898–1910). Similarly, the comic Negro of fiction and the theater received more sympathetic attention after JOEL CHANDLER HARRIS' eight books on Uncle Remus, beginning 1880. The Italian immigrant received friendly yet smiling treatment in T. A. DALY's *Canzoni* (1909) and in his later verse. The Jews in this country were portrayed humorously by themselves and others. Jewish writers, like MONTAGUE GLASS in the Potash and Perlmutter stories and L. C. ROSTEN in the Hyman Kaplan stories, interpreted Jewish immigrants humorously. Myra Kelly published some amusing tales in *Little Citizens* (1904) and *Little Aliens* (1910). Much more satiric were the stories of ARTHUR KOBER. Geoffrey Gorer, keen British observer, noted incidentally that "American Jews are chiefly responsible for the peculiarly American humor, ironical, satirical, and detached." The best known of the productions in German dialect are C. G. Leland's HANS BREITMANN ballads (1857 and later). There may also be mentioned the specialized dialects in GEORGE ADE's *Fables* (1900), in RING LARDNER's baseball stories such as YOU KNOW ME, AL (1916), and in DAMON RUNYON's Broadway *Guys and Dolls* (1932). (See DIALECT IN AMERICAN LITERATURE.)

A hybrid form was the minstrel show, which displayed synthetic Negroes—white men in blackface. The shows, beginning as early as the 1830's, developed a folklore and technique of their own; collections of their jokes were published, such as *Bones: His Gags and Stump Speeches* (1879).

Political satire entered the scene with the Connecticut or Hartford Wits. Striking combinations of political satire and poetry were made by J. R. Lowell in the *Biglow Papers* (1848) and by John Greenleaf Whittier in ICHABOD (1850). Political satire in the United States is called by Bernard De Voto "realistic, disenchanted, completely devoid of reverence." In no country in the world has the head of a nation been so roughly ridiculed as our Presidents have been by American satirists.

Comedies on the American stage present a long chronicle of adaptations, plagiarisms, imitations, then the slow development of a truly American theater. In the beginning, comedies were few: Mercy Otis Warren wrote her political satire THE GROUP (1775); Royall Tyler, THE CONTRAST (1787). James K. Paulding presented Americans against a European background in *The Bucktails* (pub., 1847). Anna Cora Mowatt's FASHION (1845) was a social satire and a great hit. Even after the Civil War comic portrayals of stereotyped rustics held the stage; then EDWARD HARRIGAN introduced urbanized versions of similar characters. BRONSON HOWARD's social comedies prepared the way for many later dramatists, among them Clyde Fitch, Rachel Crothers, Philip Barry, GEORGE S. KAUFMAN, George Kelly, SIDNEY HOWARD, S. N. Behrman. In the meantime less serious writers like George M. Cohan, Ben Hecht, Charles Mac-

Arthur, Howard Lindsay, Russel Crouse, Preston Sturges, Moss Hart, Clare Boothe, Gore Vidal produced lively plays occupied with the adventures and misadventures of American characters. A special sort of humorous fantasy often appeared in the writings of MARC CONNELLY and WILLIAM SAROYAN. ROBERT SHERWOOD adroitly mingled comedy and more serious matters. A long succession of musical comedies and light opera supplemented those imported from abroad. They range in time and merit from *The Black Crook* (1866) to OF THEE I SING (1932) and OKLAHOMA! (1943). In 20th-century American comedy the range of satire is wide; no subject is sacred. The public taste has been catholic, welcoming everything from saccharine comedy to rude Rabelaisian realism. S. N. BEHRMAN, in *No Time for Comedy* (1939), discussed the dilemma of the comic dramatist in a tragic world. (See MUSICAL COMEDY IN THE U.S.)

Since the American novel tends to be a mixed type, there are few purely comic masterpieces in American fiction. But there are many novels and stories in which humor plays a leading role: Mark Twain's HUCKLEBERRY FINN (1884) and PUDD'NHEAD WILSON (1894), for example. Other humorous fiction includes E. N. Westcott's DAVID HARUM (1898); II. L. Wilson's RUGGLES OF RED GAP (1915); Sinclair Lewis' BABBITT (1922); Ring Lardner's YOU KNOW ME AL (1916); Nathaniel West's novels; most of John P. Marquand's novels and those of Erskine Caldwell; Gertrude Stein's THE AUTOBIOGRAPHY OF ALICE B. TOKLAS (1933). Notable recent humorous fiction includes THE CATCHER IN THE RYE by J. D. Salinger (1951), *Sweet Thursday* by John Steinbeck (1954), *The Tunnel of Love* by Peter de Vries (1954), *Pnin* by Vladimir Nabokov (1957), *Rally Round the Flag Boys* by Max Shulman (1957), *Turvey* by the Canadian Earle Birney (1958), *Henderson the Rain King* by Saul Bellow (1959), *Goodbye Columbus* by Philip Roth (1959), and *The Sot Weed Factor* by John Barth (1960).

The family saga—illustrated by Clarence Day, Jr.'s LIFE WITH FATHER (1939), RUTH MC-KENNEY's *My Sister Eileen* (1938), the Gilbreths' CHEAPER BY THE DOZEN (1948), and Jean Kerr's *Please Don't Eat the Daisies* (1957)—has furnished rich humorous material. Techniques peculiarly their own were devised by JAMES BRANCH CABELL, master of the sly innuendo; by Ambrose Bierce, who distilled his bitterness in the unique DEVIL'S DICTIONARY (1881–1906); by GELETT BURGESS, one of the wisest of our humorists; by OGDEN NASH, who wildly distorts meter and rhyme to mask his shrewdness; and by S. J. PERELMAN, who made topsy-turviness a profession.

The humorous essay has been a perennial in American literature. Its most prominent early representative, JOSEPH DENNIE, was criticized by some of his Puritan readers as "sprightly rather than moral." Other essayists of similar character were WILLIAM WIRT, later a staid historian, and the group that centered around

Washington Irving and James K. Paulding or followed them, R. H. DANA and N. P. WILLIS in particular. The New England transcendental group produced more humor than is usually realized, in for instance Emerson's aphorisms and Thoreau's essays. James Russell Lowell was an urbane satirist, OLIVER WENDELL HOLMES agilely witty in many of his essays and in the "Breakfast Table" series. In a later day pleasantly humorous essays came from Brander Matthews, Harry Thurston Peck, Agnes Repplier, Samuel McChord Crothers, Christopher Morley, Robert Benchley, Heywood Broun, Simeon Strunsky, Will Cuppy, John Mason Brown. More mordant humor marks the writings of H. L. Mencken, George Jean Nathan, GELETT BURGESS, Corey Ford, Ben Hecht, H. Allen Smith. At the opening of the 20th century humorous essay-writing began to take new forms—the newspaper editorial and feature "story," the article, the book and theatrical review, the humorous advertisement. Examples of these new forms of humor abounded in *The New Yorker*—articles by Alexander Woollcott, JAMES THURBER, E. B. White, E. J. Kahn, Jr., A. J. Liebling; reviews by Dorothy Parker, Wolcott Gibbs, John Lardner, Clifton Fadiman; profiles by Alva Johnson, Russell Maloney, Geoffrey T. Hellman.

Glancing back over the multifarious details of what is undoubtedly our most significant literary development, one realizes certain outstanding aspects of American humor. Whether this humor is "a new birth of our new soil," as Lowell said of Lincoln, has been argued. Constance Rourke, deepest of all students of the subject, feels that a certain "creative fancy" completely set off our humor from that of England. Everyone notes a tendency toward exaggeration as one mark of American humor. We are rather more prone to make satirical and insulting remarks than is common in European humor. Much typically American humor has been autobiographical: the author makes himself one of the comic characters. Because of the nature of our national development, the new groups from abroad have offered one inevitable and often poignant subject for humorous treatment; reinforcing the trait just mentioned, these groups have tended toward self-insult, a common defense of minority groups everywhere.

Some excellent collections and analyses of American humor have been made. Among them may be mentioned: Carl Holliday's *The Wit and Humor of Colonial Days* (1912); T. L. Masson's *Our American Humorists* (1922); Constance M. Rourke's AMERICAN HUMOR: A STUDY OF NATIONAL CHARACTER (1931); William Murrell's *A History of American Graphic Humor* (2 v., 1933–38); Stephen Leacock's *The Greatest Pages of American Humor* (1936); Arthur P. Hudson's *Humor of the Old Deep South* (1936); Walter Blair's NATIVE AMERICAN HUMOR (1937) and his HORSE SENSE IN AMERICAN HUMOR (1942); E. B. and Katharine White's *A Subtreasury of American Humor* (1941); Thomas Craven's CARTOON CAVALCADE (1943); Max J. Herzberg and Leon Mones' *Humor of*

America (an anthology, 1945); Homer Croy's *What Grandpa Laughed At* (1948); Bennett Cerf's *Encyclopedia of Modern American Humor* (1954); Steve Allen's *The Funny Men* (1956). There are some good pages on the subject in Max Eastman's ENJOYMENT OF LAUGHTER (1936). Louis Untermeyer started an annual series, in collaboration with Ralph E. Shikes, entitled *The Best Humor of 1949-50* (1950).

Humphrey, William (b. Clarksville, Tex., June 18, 1924—   ), novelist. Humphrey's first novel *Home From the Hill* (1958) received critical acclaim, was an immediate best-seller, and was made into a motion picture. The book's distinction lies in the effective contrast between its finely etched prose and its subject matter— the passions of men who are remembered in legends, the excitement of a wild-boar hunt, cars speeding across the Texas flats. Humphrey's writing has nothing of the academic, yet he is obviously a careful craftsman. His first book was *The Last Husband and Other Stories* (1953).

Humphreys, David (b. Derby, Conn., July 10, 1752—d. Feb. 21, 1818), diplomat, manufacturer, writer. A man of varied abilities, Humphreys served in the Continental army as an aide to Washington, who employed him on

several important missions abroad. He foresaw America's industrial development and wrote a pedestrian *Poem on the Industry of the United States* (1783); he established a woollen mill after introducing Spanish merino sheep into Connecticut. A *Poem on the Happiness of the United States* (1780), a satire called THE ANARCHIAD (1786-87), a life of General Israel Putnam (1788), and two plays—*The Widow of*

Malabar (1790) and *The Yankey in England* (1814)—were among his other productions. He was reckoned a member of the HARTFORD WITS.

Humphries, [George] Rolfe (b. Philadelphia, Nov. 20, 1894—   ), poet, teacher, critic, translator. Humphries' verses have appeared in many magazines and a number of collections. His best work is in the graceful smaller forms, in which he shows a skillful use of verse-sounds and cadence. A linguist, Humphries has done translations from Virgil (the *Aeneid*) and Ovid (the *Metamorphoses*), as well as from the works of modern European authors, and he has made pleasing adaptations from Celtic medieval poetry. Among Humphries' published volumes are: *Europa and Other Poems* (1929); *Out of the Jewel* (1942); *Forbid Thy Ravens* (1948); *The Wind of Time* (1949); *Poems Collected and New* (1954); *Green Armor on Green Ground* (1956).

Huneker, James Gibbons (b. Philadelphia, Jan. 31, 1860—d. Feb. 9, 1921), biographer, short-story writer, novelist, memoirist. Of Irish ancestry, Huneker gravitated slowly but surely toward his life work—criticism in many fields, generally directed toward the discovery of new talent or toward the recognition of non-American musicians, dramatists, and writers. But Huneker was also a dissenter and damned certain persons vigorously. He wrote at first for Philadelphian periodicals, then came to New York (after a fruitful stay in Paris studying music), where he served on various newspapers and magazines, including the *Musical Courier,* the *Sun,* the *Times,* and the *World.* All his writing had, as H. L. Mencken pointed out, the "quality of infectious gusto"; in fact, Huneker was the chief American exponent of critical IMPRESSIONISM and wrote always with subjective luxuriance, leaving textual analysis to others. He introduced many new ideas and techniques to the United States and was undoubtedly an influence on the young writers who began to publish after World War I.

Among Huneker's collections of critical and biographical pieces: *Mezzotints in Modern Music* (1899); *Chopin* (1900); *Overtones* (1904); ICONOCLASTS (1905); *Egoists* (1909); *Promenades of an Impressionist* (1910); *Franz Liszt* (1911); *Old Fogy: His Musical Opinions and Grotesques* (1913); *The Pathos of Distance* (1913); *New Cosmopolis* (1915); *Ivory, Apes, and Peacocks* (1915); *Unicorns* (1917); *Bedouins* (1920); *Variations* (1921). His only novel, PAINTED VEILS, appeared in 1920, as did his autobiography, STEEPLEJACK. Huneker published two collections of short stories which have never received their critical due: *Melomaniacs* (1902) and VISIONARIES (1905). As Mencken noted, the point of view in these tales is essentially the aesthetic one; in "The Eighth Deadly Sin" he even writes a paean to perfume. Huneker himself esteemed these stories above all his other writings. His wife, Josephine Huneker, collected his *Letters* (1922) and his *Intimate Letters* (1924; reprinted, 1936).

Hunt, Helen. See HELEN HUNT JACKSON.

Hunt, Isaac (b. Barbados, 1742?—d. 1809), lawyer, political writer, clergyman. Hunt was first a student, then a tutor at the University of Pennsylvania. He wrote a series of satires which he called *A Humble Attempt at Scurrility* (1765), and the college as a result refused him his degree, finally granting it in 1771. When dissension arose between the colonies and the mother country, he took the Tory side, issuing *The Political Family* (1775) and engaging in other political activities. He was threatened with violence, escaped to Barbados and then to England. There he became a clergyman, and his son Leigh Hunt became a noted writer. But the elder man lost his position as a tutor in a ducal family because he tried to intervene in behalf of the American painter John Trumbull, who was charged with being a spy. He was arrested for debt and lived in great poverty for the rest of his life. One of his later writings was called *The Rights of Englishmen: An Antidote to the Poison Now Vending by Thomas Paine* (1791).

Hunt, William Gibbes (b. Boston, Feb. 21, 1791—d. Aug. 13, 1833), editor, publisher. After graduation from Harvard, Hunt went to Lexington, Ky., where he founded two magazines, among the earliest to be established in the West: *The Western Monitor* (1815–19) and *The Western Review and Miscellaneous Magazine* (1819–21). The contents of the latter were meritorious. Hunt included biography, fiction, verse, and history in his magazine, also digests of English novels. He also ran a series of scientific articles by CONSTANTINE S. RAFINESQUE, a traveler from Turkey in the United States.

Hunter, Dard (b. Steubenville, Ohio, Nov. 29, 1883—), printer, papermaker, writer. Hunt established a press of his own at Chillicothe, Ohio (1919), after working for several years as art director with Elbert Hubbard's Roycroft Press. In Chillicothe he made his own paper, designed his own fonts, did his own printing, wrote and published a number of books. Among them were *The Etching of Figures* (1915); *The Art of Bookmaking* (1915); *The Etching of Contemporary Life* (1917); *Primitive Papermaking* (1927); *The Literature of Papermaking, 1390–1800* (1925); *The Story of Paper* (1937); *Papermaking: The History and Technique of an Ancient Craft* (1943); *Papermaking By Hand in America* (1950); *Papermaking in Pioneer America* (1952); *My Life with Paper, An Autobiography* (1958).

Hunter, Evan (b. New York City, Oct. 15, 1926—), novelist. Hunter attended Cooper Union and Hunter College, and afterward did a stint as a high school teacher, out of which grew the sensational *Blackboard Jungle* (1954), described by *Time* magazine as a "nightmarish but authentic first novel." As a dramatic exposé of the brutal underworld of a big city high school, the book jolted Americans. Its effect was redoubled when it was turned into a realistic, hard-hitting film. Hunter investigated marital infidelity in Suburbia in *Strangers When We Meet* (1958). *Matter of Conviction* (1959) won less critical favor; some challenged its believability. The book was made into a film, *The Young Savages* (1961). Hunter worked as a literary agent for several years before turning to full-time writing as a novelist. Other books: *Second Ending* (1956); *Mothers and Daughters* (1961).

Hunter, Robert. See ANDROBOROS.

Huntington, Archer M[ilton] (b. New York City, March 10, 1870—d. Dec. 11, 1955), poet, editor, Hispanic scholar, art collector. As the son of Collis P. Huntington (1821–1900), pioneer American railroad builder, Huntington inherited a large fortune, part of which he used to found thirteen museums. These include a magnificent group in New York City at Broadway and 155th to 156th Sts., among them the AMERICAN ACADEMY OF ARTS AND LETTERS. Huntington wrote verse (*Alfonso the Eighth Rides By*, 1934), books of travel (*A Note Book in Northern Spain*, 1898), and edited *The Poem of the Cid* (3 v., 1897). His wife is the noted sculptor Anna Hyatt Huntington (1876–).

Huntington, Ellsworth (b. Galesburg, Ill., Sept. 16, 1876—d. Oct. 17, 1947), teacher, geographer, explorer, social scientist. Huntington, a member of the Yale faculty for thirty-eight years, won renown for his research on the effect of climate on man, and the relationship of heredity to environment. Among his more important writings in these fields are *Civilization and Climate* (1915), *Principles of Human Geography* (1920); *The Character of Races* (1924); *The Human Habitat* (1927); and *Mainsprings of Civilization* (1945). He had several favorite ideas. One was that as civilization advances it moves toward colder regions. Another was that the human intellect works best in a variable climate with plenty of storms. In his explorations Huntington ranged all over the world, producing such accounts as *Explorations in Turkestan* (1905); *The Pulse of Asia* (1907); *Red Man's Continent* (1919); and *West of the Pacific* (1925). He wrote with unusual skill and with no pedantry; his books reached a wide public.

Huntington [Henry E.] Library. Henry E[dwards] Huntington (b. Oneonta, N.Y., Feb. 27, 1850—d. May 23, 1927) was the nephew of Collis P[otter] Huntington (1821–1900), wealthy builder of railroads, and inherited a large fortune from him. He began to collect art objects and books, moved his valuable collection to two immense buildings on a 550-acre estate at San Marino, Cal., and in 1919–22 deeded it all to the public and provided funds for upkeep and additions. The noted collector A. S. W. Rosenbach called Huntington's purchases of 100,000 rare books and 1,000,000 manuscripts of such great value that it made him "without doubt the greatest collector of books the world has known." Important research work goes on constantly in the library, which issues *Bulletins*.

Huron Indians (more exactly, **Wyandot**). They were of the same speech and culture family as the Iroquois, but did not reach as high a degree of political development. Early writers

gave them a bad reputation: JOHN HECKE-
WELDER's influential book emphasized their
cruelty in a way that determined Cooper's attitude toward them in his LEATHER-STOCKING
TALES. They lived in Ontario and nearby sections of what was later the United States, often
fought the Iroquois but were vanquished by
them. They also fought the United States during
the Revolution and the War of 1812. There are
survivors of the Hurons in Canada, Michigan,
Ohio, and Oklahoma. The "death-song" was a
favorite form in such poetry as their bards produced. See AMERINDIAN PROSE AND POETRY.

Hurst, Fannie (b. Hamilton, Ohio, Oct. 19,
1889—d. Feb. 23, 1968), writer of fiction and
plays. She won her first fame with several
collections of short stories, particularly *Every
Soul Hath Its Song* (1916), *Gaslight Sonatas*
(1918), and HUMORESQUE (1919). Among her
books: *Star-Dust* (1921); LUMMOX (1923); *A
President Is Born* (1928); *Back Street* (1931);
Hallelujah (1944); *Man With One Head*
(1954); an autobiography, *Anatomy of Me*
(1958); *Family!* (1959); and *God Must Be Sad*
(1961). Her books have been translated into
sixteen languages; many have been made into
successful plays and motion pictures. Her stories
are well told, in a lush style, but lack depth in
characterization and are overly sentimental. Her
civic interests through the years were numerous
and varied. In 1952 she become United States
Delegate by presidential appointment to the
United Nations World Health Assembly in
Geneva and in 1953 she visited Israel at the invitation of the Israeli Government.

Hurston, Zora Neale (b. Eatonville, Fla., Jan.
7, 1901—d. Feb. 4, 1960), folklorist, teacher,
storyteller, playwright. On grants from several
foundations Miss Hurston studied folklore and
folkways, and in 1934, in *Jonah's Gourd Vine*, began making use of her observations in appealing
accounts and stories. Among her other books:
Mules and Men (1935); *Their Eyes Were
Watching God* (1937); *Tell My Horse* (1938);
Moses, Man of the Mountain (1939); *The
Voice of the Land* (1945); *Seraph on the
Suwanee* (1948). In these may be found tales
from Haiti, Jamaica, and the United States, told
naturally and skillfully, with accurate reproduction of Negro dialect and rhythm. *Dust Tracks
on a Road* (1942) is an autobiography.

Huston, John (b. Nevada, Mo., Aug. 5, 1906
—   ), actor, writer, motion-picture director.
Huston, son of the actor Walter Huston (1884–
1950), early in life picked up a wide knowledge
of the theater. He became a writer in his
twenties, some of his work appearing in the old
American Mercury. But most of his work was in
Hollywood, first as a scriptwriter, then as a director of notable films. He wrote and collaborated in the production of *Key Largo* (1948)
and *The Treasure of Sierra Madre* (1949),
among others, and directed *The Asphalt Jungle*
(1950) and *Moby Dick* (1956). He also prepared government documentary films.

Hutchins, Robert Maynard (b. Brooklyn, N.Y.,

Jan. 17, 1899—   ), lawyer, teacher, university official, fund executive, writer on education.
After service in the Army during World War I,
Hutchins graduated from Yale, became a lecturer
at the Law School there, later its dean and a
professor of law. He was made president of the
University of Chicago at the age of thirty, and
its chancellor in 1945. He resigned in 1951 to
become an associate director of the Ford Foundation, then president of the Fund for the Republic. During his two decades at Chicago he
upset many traditional procedures. He abolished
intercollegiate football at the University and
set up a program allowing a gifted student to
start college after two years' high school, then to
further shorten his course by examinations.
Hutchins also deprecated scientific thinking as
inconclusive in itself, although his faculty included some of the most eminent scientists of
the day. He is a militant and effective speaker,
with a flair for wisecracks. Among his books:
No Friendly Voice (1936); *The Higher Learning in America* (1936); *Education for Freedom*
(1943); *St. Thomas and the World State*
(1949); *The Conflict in Education* (1953);
What's a College For? (1960).

Hutchinson, Anne (b. England, 1591—d.
1643), religious teacher. The daughter of a
clergyman, Mrs. Hutchinson emigrated in 1634
with her husband and children to Boston. There
her kindliness and forceful character won a following for the antinomian doctrines she advocated. She asserted the possibility that "the
person of the Holy Ghost dwells in a justified
person," and that there was salvation by personal intuition of divine grace. She was tried
for her beliefs, and banished (1637). She emigrated first to Rhode Island, then to Pelham
Manor, a settlement near New York City, where,
the following year, she died in an Indian massacre. Near the site of her home is the present
Hutchinson Parkway, named in her honor. She
was probably the first woman in America who
dared to take the lead in discussing questions of
religion. She is the subject of a number of biographies, including Edith Curtis' *Anne Hutchinson* (1930), Winnifred Rugg's *Unafraid: A Life
of Anne Hutchinson* (1930), and R. P. Bolton's
*A Woman Misunderstood: Anne, Wife of Wil-
liam Hutchinson* (1931).

Hutchinson, Thomas (b. Boston, Mass., Sept.
9, 1711—d. June 3, 1780), public official, historian. Hutchinson entered Harvard at the
age of twelve. By the age of twenty-one he had
accumulated a modest fortune in business and
thereupon entered public life. He developed
strong Tory tendencies and was made by George
III first chief justice, then royal governor of
Massachusetts. One of his decisions caused James
Otis to utter his famous statement that "taxation
without representation is tyranny." He did not
like the Stamp Act but accepted it as legal, and
a mob destroyed his home. As governor his authority was so generally ignored that martial law
had to be proclaimed (1774). When General
Gage and his troops arrived the following year,

Gage assumed the governorship, and Hutchinson went to England to render an account of his administration. It is said that he tried in vain to induce the king to consider methods of conciliation. He never returned to America.

Hutchinson's *Diary and Letters* were published (2 v., 1884–86). His most important writing was *A Collection of Original Papers Relative to the History of the Colony of Massachusetts Bay* (2 v., 1764, 1767); a third volume appeared after his death (1828). He included some invaluable documents, wrote with restraint and in a philosophic vein, and is regarded as the best historian of his time. The so-called *Hutchinson Letters* were written allegedly to the British Foreign Office in 1768–69 and advocated strong measures against the colonies. Somehow they came into the possession of Benjamin Franklin and, apparently against Hutchinson's wishes, were published in 1772, causing much bad feeling against him. The publication brought about Franklin's removal from the office of deputy postmaster-general. Hutchinson was attacked in Mercy Otis Warren's play THE ADULATEUR (published, 1773), and he was a prominent character in Lydia M. Child's novel *The Rebels* (1825).

Hutton, Joseph (b. Philadelphia, 1787—d. 1828), actor, playwright. One of the first American dramatists to obtain a hearing, Hutton was imitative, rarely used American settings. Among his plays: *The School for Prodigals* (1808); *The Wounded Hussar* (1809); *Fashionable Follies* (1809); *The Orphan of Prague* (1810).

Hutton, Laurence (b. New York City, Aug. 8, 1843—d. June 10, 1904), critic, writer, bibliophile, editor. Hutton served as drama critic of the New York *Mail*, later became literary editor of *Harper's Magazine*. He was widely acquainted with the authors of England and the United States, and traveled a great deal in Europe. He wrote nearly fifty books, all of considerable merit, but none noteworthy enough to preserve his contemporary fame. Among them: *Plays and Players* (1875); *Literary Landmarks of London* (1885); *Curiosities of the American Stage* (1891); *Literary Landmarks of Edinburgh* (1891); *Edwin Booth* (1893); *Literary Landmarks of Rome* (1897); *Talks in a Library* (1905).

hymns. Two books of psalms were widely used in 17th century New England. The Plymouth colonists brought with them from England the *Ainsworth Psalter,* a collection of about thirty tunes from Dutch, Swiss, and English sources. The colonists of Massachusetts Bay brought the less colorful Sternhold and Hopkins psalter and, dissatisfied with its unfaithful rendering of the Hebrew text, produced in 1640 the *Whole Book of Psalms Faithfully Translated into English Meter,* usually known as the BAY PSALM BOOK. It was the first book printed in the colonies. Some later translations of the Biblical poems were metrically smoother, such as COTTON MATHER's *Psalterium Americanus* (1718)

and Thomas Prince's *The Psalms, Hymns, and Spiritual Songs of the Old and New Testaments* (1758). But late in the 17th century, largely under the influence of Methodism, a transition began which favored hymn singing over psalmody. As the strict Puritan code everywhere lost its hold, the Puritans' insistence on literal translation of the Psalms gave way to free translation and paraphrase. Often such paraphrase could scarcely be distinguished from original hymn writing. The works of Isaac Watts, an English nonconformist divine who objected to literal renditions of the Psalms, were influential in the shift toward hymnody. Watts' *Hymns and Spiritual Songs* was published in an American edition in 1739, and his method of free paraphrase was soon imitated, notably by MATHER BYLES and the Connecticut Wits. TIMOTHY DWIGHT's hymn *I Love Thy Kingdom, Lord* (1801), a paraphrase of the 137th psalm, is widely used today. Two important collections in the manner of Watts were James Lyons' *Urania, or, A Choice Collection of Psalm-Tunes, Anthems, and Hymns* (1762) and William Billings' *The New England Psalm Singer* (1770).

Of the greatest importance in the rise of hymn singing was John Wesley. After studying the hymn books of the Pennsylvania Moravians, who were especially enthusiastic over hymnody, Wesley made a *Collection of Psalms and Hymns* and published it in Charleston in 1737. Brought into frontier camp meetings, these Methodist hymns became known as spiritual songs, a term already in use in such collections as Watts' *Hymns and Spiritual Songs* (1709). Out of these were born the revivalist or gospel hymn and, at least in part, the Negro spiritual (see NEGRO SPIRITUAL). In the 19th century, hymn writing remained a popular form of literature. Almost every major American poet of the century wrote literary hymns. The religious hymn was written by LOWELL MASON, sometimes called "the father of American church music," among whose many popular works is *Bethany* ("Nearer my God to Thee"). THOMAS HASTINGS, another important hymn writer, edited with Mason *Spiritual Songs for Social Worship* (1831–32). Hosea Ballou edited collections of hymns and composed many of his own. An influential compilation was Francis P. Greenwood's *Collection of Psalms and Hymns for Christian Worship* (1830), which by 1850 had passed through fifty editions. PHILLIPS BROOKS wrote numerous hymns, among them *O Little Town of Bethlehem* (1868). A special kind of hymn is found in the patriotic anthem of the 19th century, poems such as FRANCIS SCOTT KEY's *The Star-Spangled Banner* (1814), Samuel F. Smith's AMERICA (1831), Julia Ward Howe's BATTLE-HYMN OF THE REPUBLIC (1861), and Katherine Lee Bates' AMERICA THE BEAUTIFUL (1893).

In the upland South today there is an interesting remnant of the earlier revival hymnodists: the Sacred Harp singers, who take their name from a collection of melodies sung by early Baptist settlers and published in 1844 by Benjamin Franklin White and Joel King. Unlike those pioneers who adhered to established religions, the "Old Baptists" had no written music of their own. Instead they used folk tunes. The current Sacred Harp singers follow the shape-note singing of their ancestors, a system by which square, triangular, hollow, or filled notes are used to establish relative pitch and to facilitate sight reading. Among the best known Sacred Harp hymns are *Old Ship of Zion* and *Old-Time Religion*. Many of the Sacred Harp tunes have found favor with contemporary composers. In his screen score for *The River*, Virgil Thomson used several Sacred Harp melodies, and others have been arranged by Henry Cowell, Elie Siegmeister, John Jacob Niles, and John Powell.

Hymnology in America has been treated in Edward S. Ninde's *The Story of the American Hymn* (1921), F. J. Metcalfe's *American Writers and Compilers of Sacred Music* (1925), and Henry Wilder Foote's *Three Centuries of American Hymnody* (1940).

Hymns of the Marshes (1878–82), four of six projected hymns by SIDNEY LANIER. Planned on a grandiose scale, they were only moderately successful, but contain some fine flights of imagination and often striking melody.

Hymn to Death (1820; published, 1825), a poem by WILLIAM CULLEN BRYANT. This is another of the poet's meditations on death, written five years after THANATOPSIS. It begins as a vindication of death; after 133 lines Bryant pays tribute to his father (who had died at this point in the poem's composition), questions death's justice, yet is still sure of immortality.

Hymn to the Night (1839), a poem by HENRY WADSWORTH LONGFELLOW. One of Longfellow's most melodious and famous poems, this *Hymn* was praised by Poe (no indiscriminate eulogist of Longfellow): "No poem ever opened with a beauty more august."

Hyperion (1839), a romance by HENRY WADSWORTH LONGFELLOW. Stemming from Longfellow's studies of German romanticism, *Hyperion* has been called his *Wilhelm Meister;* it narrates in thin disguise his love for Frances Appleton, later his wife. The plot, which is almost peripheral to the author's interests, is not carefully developed. Paul Flemming, a typical romantic hero, is traveling in Europe when he falls in love with Mary Ashburton. She spurns him, and he continues his quest for the mythical blue rose, long a symbol of the unattainable in German legend. During his picaresque travels he is accompanied by Berkley, an older and more experienced man who attempts to cure Paul of his romantic love. Berkley's counsel as well as unfavorable circumstances keep Paul from the attainment of his dreams. The book is studded with many of the old legends Flemming hears in his travels, which foreshadows Longfellow's use of legend in such later works as *The New England Legends* and TALES OF A WAYSIDE INN.

I

Iberville, Sieur d' [Pierre Le Moyne] (b. Quebec, July 16, 1661—d. July 9, 1706), explorer. Iberville has been called the first great Canadian. His achievements, both as an explorer and on the field of battle, were great, but he is chiefly remembered as one of the founders of Louisiana. He fought against the English as a member of the French navy, later in expeditions to Hudson's Bay (1690). He was commissioned (1698) to found a colony in Louisiana, made the first permanent settlement at what is now Biloxi, Miss. While preparing a naval expedition against England he died of yellow fever at Havana. He had planned to capture New York and Boston.

Icebound (1923), a play by OWEN DAVIS. This Pulitzer Prize-winner depicts the Jordan family, a clan of assorted scoundrels who await the death of Mother Jordan. The mother disappoints them by leaving her money to Jane Crosby, a poor relative. Jane ultimately marries a reformed member of the family, for whom she has secretly been holding the money in trust.

Iceman Cometh, The (1947), a play by EUGENE O'NEILL. In this, one of O'Neill's more esoteric efforts, a misty symbolism is worked out through the despondent characters who congregate in the End of the Line Café. Vivian C. Hopkins has pointed out some striking resemblances in the play to Maxim Gorky's *The Lower Depths* (1903).

Ichabod (1850), a poem by JOHN GREENLEAF WHITTIER. The title of the poem is a Hebrew word meaning "inglorious"; it is sometimes translated "The glory hath departed." The title may have been suggested to Whittier by a remark of James Russell Lowell's in the NATIONAL ANTI-SLAVERY STANDARD (July 2, 1846) concerning DANIEL WEBSTER: "Shall not the Recording Angel write *Ichabod* after the name of this man in the great Book of Doom?"

The poem was provoked by Whittier's hot anger at Webster when he read the latter's famous "Seventh of March" (1850) speech, delivered in support of the COMPROMISE OF 1850 and of the Fugitive Slave Law. Webster preached a doctrine of moderation, although he knew the speech would lose him many supporters. He was denounced by many New Englanders, including Emerson, Holmes, W. L. Garrison, and Wendell Phillips. *Ichabod* is surely one of the most powerful poems of denunciation ever written. Yet thirty years later Whittier repented of his violence, and in THE LOST OCCASION paid a tender tribute to Webster.

Ichabod Crane. See CRANE, ICHABOD.

Ickes, Harold L[eclaire] (b. Frankstown Township, Pa., March 15, 1874—d. Feb. 3, 1952), lawyer, public official, writer. Wellknown as a crusader for political reforms, Ickes came into national prominence when Franklin D. Roosevelt appointed him Secretary of the Interior (1933–46). He was forthright, sometimes violent and vituperative in speech. Writing an article about him in *Collier's* (1941) under the title *Holy Harold*, Walter Davenport described him as "a barrel-chested, cat-eyed badger of a man, who has almost no faith in his fellowbeings." Among his books: *The New Democracy* (1934); *Back to Work* (1935); *America's House of Lords* (1939); *The Third Term Bugaboo* (1940); *Autobiography of a Curmudgeon* (1943); *Fightin' Oil* (1943). His *Secret Diary* was published posthumously (2 v., 1953–54).

Iconoclast, The. A sobriquet sometimes given to WILLIAM COWPER BRANN. Also the name of a magazine founded by him at Austin, Tex. (July, 1891), later published at Waco.

Iconoclasts: A Book of Dramatists (1905), a collection of essays by JAMES HUNEKER. Huneker called attention to many European playwrights up to that time little known in the United States, and performed useful service in bringing fresh ideas from the Old World to the New.

Ide, Simeon (b. Shrewsbury, Vt., Sept. 28, 1794—d. June 22, 1889), printer. Ide was one of the earliest of American printers. At Claremont, N.H., he printed *The New England Farmer's Diary and Almanac*, as well as many books. Among the latter was *Scraps of California History Never Before Published: A Biographical Sketch of William B. Ide* (1880). His son Lemuel formed a publishing firm with E. P. Dutton: Ide & Dutton (1852). Edith Flanders Dunbar wrote a biography of Ide (1931).

idealism. A system of philosophy which emphasizes mind or ideas as the central reality of the universe. In various forms it is identified with Plato, Plotinus, Kant, Fichte, Hegel, Schelling, Berkeley, and other Old World metaphysicians, all of whom have exerted great influence on American philosophers. It was not until American writers and teachers became familiar with the names and works of the great German idealists of the 18th and 19th centuries that the movement made much headway in the United States. According to Herbert W. Schneider, the first American theologian and professor to become a systematic expositor of German idealism was Laurens Perseus Hickock (1798–1888) of Union College, whose principal writings were *Rational Psychology, or, The Subjective Idea and the Objective Law of All Intelligence* (1848), *Moral Science* (1853), and *Empirical Psychology* (1854). His influence was continued in Amherst, principally by Charles Edward Garman (1850–1907), whose *Letters, Lectures, and Addresses* were collected in 1909. Other notable teachers who spread the idealist gospel were

GEORGE HERBERT PALMER at Harvard, George Holmes Howison at Massachusetts Institute of Technology, John Bascom at Williams, A. C. Armstrong at Wesleyan, NOAH PORTER and GEORGE TRUMBULL LADD at Yale, GEORGE SYLVESTER MORRIS at Johns Hopkins and Michigan, John Grier Hibben at Princeton, JACOB GOULD SCHURMANN at Cornell, NICHOLAS MURRAY BUTLER at Columbia, Bowden P. Bowne at Boston University, and James E. Creighton at Cornell. Greatest of them all was JOSIAH ROYCE of Harvard, who advanced from what may be called a pure idealism to one which underwent the strong influence of the pragmatist CHARLES SANDERS PEIRCE.

Numerous schools of idealism flourished. First and most important was the St. Louis School, joined with the names of Henry Brokmeyer, WILLIAM TORREY HARRIS, and DENTON J. SNIDER; for a time it formed an alliance with the CONCORD SCHOOL of BRONSON ALCOTT. Later came THOMAS DAVIDSON's Summer School of the Cultural Sciences at Glenmore in the Adirondacks and the Breadwinner's College in New York City. Widely influential was the Society for Ethical Culture, founded in 1876 by FELIX ADLER in New York City; branches were established in other cities and it is still active. Idealism was important in the intellectual development of HENRY JAMES, SR., G. STANLEY HALL, JOHN DEWEY, WILLIAM JAMES, ALFRED H. LLOYD, and others generally not reckoned as professed idealists. Its influence was potent in the transcendentalist movement and in the development of what Schneider calls "idealistic democracy," particularly in the writings of the St. Louis School and in those of the Rev. ELISHA MULFORD. WALT WHITMAN, though probably not directly acquainted with the works of Hegel, professed a strong adherence to his doctrines. In general, American idealists have been greatly interested in the applications of idealist doctrines to government, law, the workings of society, the uses of logic, education, and behavior. See TRANSCENDENTALISM.

Idell, Albert E[dward] (b. Philadelphia, June 21, 1901—d. July 7, 1958), novelist. Widely experienced in many professions, including prize fighting, Idell used autobiographical materials in many of his novels. They include *Pug* (1941); *Centennial Summer* (1943); *Bridge to Brooklyn* (1944); *The Great Blizzard* (1948); *The Corner Store* (1953).

Ides of March, The (1948), a novel by THORNTON WILDER. One of the best fictionalizations of the life of Julius Caesar, this novel deals with the dictator's last months and his assassination. The story is told through documents—letters, extracts from diaries, snatches of verse, proclamations, circulars—which reveal Wilder's intimate knowledge of Roman antiquity. The book falls into four sections, each covering the same period of time. Thus the novel presents four views of the same events. Wilder's Caesar is a sort of 20th-century agnostic, perhaps Wilder in a toga. J. M. Lalley has said that Wilder's Caesar, unable to convert his contemporaries

to his views, "acquiesced in his own murder out of sheer chagrin."

Idiot's Delight (1936), a play by ROBERT E. SHERWOOD. In it Sherwood argues the issues of the oncoming World War II. Among the characters, all isolated in an Alpine hotel, are a young English couple, a German scientist, a French munitions manufacturer, and some American actors. After seeing the futility of the efforts of "the little people" to stop a war, one of the actors and a mysterious Irene resume an old love affair. The play reveals Sherwood's gloomy belief in the decay of western civilization. It won a Pulitzer Prize.

If I Should Die Tonight (published in the *Christian Union,* June 18, 1873), a meditative poem usually attributed to Arabella Eugenie Smith (1844–1916). It became very popular, but the parody that BEN KING (1857–1894) wrote under the same title did much to destroy the vogue of the verses.

I Have a Rendezvous with Death (*North American Review,* October, 1916), a poem by ALAN SEEGER. The young poet had enlisted in the French Foreign Legion and wrote this poem shortly before he was killed in the Battle of the Somme. It immediately became popular and was perhaps better known than any other World War I poem by an American. It was included in Seeger's *Poems* (1916).

I Hear It Was Charged Against Me (1860), a poem by WALT WHITMAN. Whitman here replies to the charge that he was preaching destructive, anarchistic doctrines. He denies the charge, says that he has no interest in being either for or against institutions, believes only in "the institution of the dear love of comrades."

Ile (1919), a one-act play by EUGENE O'NEILL. This is the story of a sea-captain who insists on continuing his hunt for whale oil (ile) at the cost of his wife's sanity and the risk of a mutiny. It is a powerful melodrama and has been a favorite of little theater and amateur groups. It was first produced (1917) by the PROVINCETOWN PLAYERS.

Iliad, The American (1947), the story of the Civil War narrated by eye-witnesses and contemporaries, as edited by Otto Eisenschiml and Ralph Newman. With the help of several hundred contributors, chosen from both sides of the Mason and Dixon Line, the editors present a vivid and complete picture of the great struggle. Edward F. Bataille described the volume as "a distinguished work of research and scholarship, presented with the rapid movement of a newsreel, the immediacy of a radio broadcast or this morning's newspaper."

Illinois Monthly Magazine. Founded October, 1830, in Vandalia, Ill., by JAMES HALL, the magazine moved first to Cincinnati, then to Louisville, where it became widely known as the *Western Monthly Magazine*. It ceased publication in 1837. Hall wrote most of the contents: stories, poems, history, criticism, gossip.

I'll Take My Stand: The South and the Agrarian Tradition, by Twelve Southerners (1930), a symposium in which a group of eminent Southerners, including ALLEN TATE, JOHN GOULD FLETCHER, ROBERT PENN WARREN, STARK YOUNG, and DONALD DAVIDSON participated. Most had been members of "The Fugitives," a group at Vanderbilt University who published a little magazine of poetry, *The Fugitive* (1922–25). In this *Agrarian Manifesto*, as they called the book, they outlined an anticapitalist movement, drawing their inspiration from the past—from Plato, Jefferson, and Carlyle. They favored an intellectual aristocracy.

I'll Take You Home Again, Kathleen (1876), a favorite song, words and music by Thomas Paine Westendorf. Westendorf's wife was visiting her home in New York, while he had to stick to his schoolteaching job in Plainfield, Ind.; hence this plaintive song.

I Love You Truly (in *Seven Songs*, 1001; separately published, 1906), a song by CARRIE JACOBS BOND, who also wrote the music. It became one of her greatest hits, and is frequently sung at weddings.

Images or Shadows of Divine Things (1948), by JONATHAN EDWARDS. These itemized manuscript notes by Edwards were gathered and published by PERRY MILLER, who saw in them an attempt "to work out a new sense of the divinity of nature and the naturalness of divinity." Miller argued that they established Edwards as "the first American empiricist," a theologian who was willing to subordinate Biblical revelation to the authority of natural reason.

imagism. A theory of poetry adopted by a number of young radical poets, English and American, who followed the leadership of T. E. Hulme and EZRA POUND (c. 1910). The movement confessed to a number of predecessors— e.g., medieval philosophy, the aesthetics of Henri Bergson, Japanese poetry, etc.—but it was primarily a reaction against the stultified form and diction of Georgian verse. It demanded absolute precision in the presentation of the individual image; in metrics it proposed the cadence of "the musical phrase," by which was meant a controlled free verse. Generally speaking, imagist poems were short, pointed observations, often no more than four or five lines in length and usually balanced on a single radically original metaphor. All poeticisms were sedulously eschewed.

Pound and Hulme were joined by a number of other poets, notably HILDA DOOLITTLE, Richard Aldington, WILLIAM CARLOS WILLIAMS, and, later, AMY LOWELL. They called themselves *Imagistes*. In 1912 Pound edited the first imagist anthology, *Some Imagiste Poets*. Meanwhile he and the others propagandized vigorously for their beliefs, and Pound, who had become foreign editor of Harriet Monroe's POETRY magazine, published therein a number of manifestoes as well as his own and his friends' poems. Other writers, mostly inferior to the original group, were attracted to the imagist technique, within a short time imagist poems were flooding the American press. Pound abandoned the movement, saying it had become "Amy-gism," and with Wyndham Lewis went on to VORTICISM

and the publication of the magazine *Blast*. Amy Lowell carried on for a few years and published three more anthologies, but by 1917 or 1918 the movement, as an institutional device, had expired. It had, however, exerted an enormous influence on the development of modern poetry and had provided the main break with the immediate past which was necessary before a new literature could appear. Some of imagism's most enduring monuments have been translations, such as those made by the English poet Arthur Waley from Chinese poetry and by FRANCIS DENSMORE from American Indian poetry. Studies of imagist theory and achievement have been made by René Taupin (1929), GLENN HUGHES (1931), and Stanley K. Coffman, Jr. (1951). See FREE VERSE.

Imlay, Gilbert (b. Monmouth Co., N.J.?, c. 1754—d. Nov. 20, 1828?), novelist, writer of travel books, soldier, surveyor, adventurer. Had Imlay written a full and frank account of his own extraordinary career, it would unquestionably have been superior to his novel THE EMIGRANTS, OR, THE HISTORY OF AN EXPATRIATED FAMILY (1793). He fought in the Revolution and assumed the title of "captain." In 1783 he went to Kentucky, where he bought land and became a surveyor. But he became entangled in financial and legal difficulties, fled to England (1792), later to France; in the latter country he sought to persuade the government to seize Louisiana from the Spaniards. In France also he formed an attachment to Mary Wollstonecraft, and was the father of her illegitimate daughter Fanny. But he deserted her and his daughter, though he seems to have continued to see them; his last meeting with Mary was recorded in 1796, shortly before her marriage to William Godwin. From this time on, there is no definite information about Imlay. In 1828 a Gilbert Imlay was buried on the island of Jersey.

Imlay wrote two books, *A Topographical Description of the Western Territory of North America* (1792) and *The Emigrants*. Both are enthusiastic eulogies of the United States. The poet Thomas Moore called the former a romantic work "which would seduce us into a belief that innocence, peace, and freedom had deserted the rest of the world for Martha's Vineyard and the banks of the Ohio." *The Emigrants* describes the adventures of an English family in America, drawing many invidious comparisons between the evils of the Old World and the wonders of the New. In the spirit of English radicalism, Imlay argued in his novel for women's rights and advocated easier divorce.

Impending Crisis of the South, The (1857). See HINTON ROWAN HELPER.

Imperative Duty, An (1891), a novel by WILLIAM DEAN HOWELLS. This was probably the first novel which centered on a characteristically American social problem, the sudden discovery of Negro ancestry by a person of apparently unmixed Caucasian blood. Rhoda Aldgate, the beautiful heroine, discovers that she is one-sixteenth Negro. She has pangs of conscience, finally decides to tell the man who wishes to marry her. He is already aware of the fact, and when Rhoda gasps, "I am a Negress!" he replies with a smile, "Well, not a very black one. Besides, what of it, if I love you?"

Imperial Purple, The (1892), a chronicle by EDGAR SALTUS. In this book about ancient scandals, written in a lyrical, sensational, and crudely colored style that matches the subject, Saltus describes the extravagant splendor and theatrical vices of the Roman emperors from Julius Caesar to Heliogabalus.

Imp of the Perverse, The (*Graham's Magazine*, July, 1845), a story by EDGAR ALLAN POE. This is the last of the group called "Tales of Conscience." Including a discourse on phrenology, the story seeks to explain by morbid example the principle of "perversity." It is obviously in part a study of Poe himself, and is done honestly and skillfully.

impressionism. This is a term for an artistic method emphasizing sense impressions of experience on the observer rather than objectivity. In painting it is applied to the French Impressionists of the 1870's who experimented with light effects, in literature to a branch of realism. Gustave Flaubert used impressionist techniques to produce the illusion of reality; he described carefully selected details of a character or scene and left it to the reader to organize these impressions for himself. Impressionism later became a part of the technique of any writer who employed SYMBOLISM, NATURALISM, or EXPRESSIONISM, and was never really thought of as a separate school of writing. Joseph Conrad was an impressionist in the tradition of Flaubert and Maupassant; among American authors, HENRY JAMES and STEPHEN CRANE have been called impressionists. A parallel technique in poetry was IMAGISM. In criticism, impressionism—often associated with fine writing like that of Walter Pater—emphasizes the individual response to a work of art; it has been described as "the adventures of a soul among masterpieces."

In Abraham's Bosom (1926), a play by PAUL GREEN. It is a play of mingled pity and terror, in which a mulatto, Abraham McCranie, tries to help Negroes by establishing a school for them in a North Carolina town. His white father helps him, but after the father's death his white half-brother Lonnie declines to give any further assistance and Abraham kills him. The play has been praised for its tragic intensity; it won a Pulitzer Prize.

Independence Hall. This famous building, situated in Independence Square, Philadelphia, was first erected as a capitol building for the colony of Pennsylvania. In 1775 the Continental Congress met here and chose Washington as commander-in-chief; in 1776 the same body adopted the DECLARATION OF INDEPENDENCE in this building. The ARTICLES OF CONFEDERATION and the CONSTITUTION were drawn up in sessions held in Independence Hall. Here is housed the Liberty Bell, which was cast in England in 1752. Harold Donaldson Eberlein and Cortlandt Van Dyke Hubbard prepared an entertaining *Diary of Independence Hall* (1949), containing extracts from memoirs, letters, histories, and newspapers.

Independent, The. A weekly periodical published in New York City from 1848 to 1923, then in Boston until 1928. Originally a Congregationalist journal, it became in later years interdenominational and in the 20th century engaged in much political discussion. It had some notable editors, including HENRY WARD BEECHER (1861–64), WILLIAM HAYES WARD (1896–1914), and Hamilton Holt (1914–20). Many of the famous writers of the day contributed to its pages. In 1916 it absorbed HARPER'S WEEKLY, in 1928 was merged into THE OUTLOOK.

Index to Periodical Literature. See WILLIAM FREDERICK POOLE.

Indian and Oklahoma Territory. A region long possessed by the "Five Civilized Tribes," lying north of Texas. By Presidential proclamation the land in this territory was thrown open to white settlement, as of noon on April 22, 1889; at the sound of a bugle, 50,000 persons made a wild rush to stake out claims. Approximately a year later the Territory of Oklahoma was organized, but a small section continued to be called Indian Territory. In 1907 the two were combined to make the State of Oklahoma. Many portions of this region have appeared in romantic fiction, as in COURTNEY RYLEY COOPER's *Oklahoma* (1926), Edna Ferber's CIMARRON (1930), and Dora Aydelotte's *Trumpets Calling* (1938).

Indian Bible (New Testament, 1661; entire Bible, 1663), a translation of the Scriptures into the dialect of the Naticks, a Massachusetts tribe of the Algonquins, by JOHN ELIOT.

Indian Burying Ground, The (1788), a poem by PHILIP FRENEAU. Always sympathetic to the Indians, Freneau in this poem portrays the red huntsman who at his death is buried in a sitting posture, with venison, images of birds, bow and arrows, and other reminders of his life kept handy at his side. The next-to-the-last stanza closes with two striking lines: "The hunter still the deer pursues,/ The hunter and the deer, a shade!" The English poet Thomas Campbell liked the last line so well that he concluded the fourth stanza of his *O'Connor's Child* (1809) with these exact words.

Indian captivity narratives. Stories, supposedly factual, of white people abducted by Indians. These narratives constituted a definite early American literary genre, and continued to appear from the colonial period to the last quarter of the 19th century. The subject matter was monotonously similar—sudden attacks on cabins and the burning of settlements, the scalping of men and women and the killing of children, horrible tortures of the captives carried away alive and frightful sufferings as they went with the red men from one camp to another, sometimes starving, often beaten, occasionally (it was alleged) even eaten.

The earliest narratives, simple, direct, and religious, begin with Mrs. Mary Rowlandson's book CAPTIVITY AND RESTAURATION OF MRS. MARY ROWLANDSON. Other examples are found in Increase Mather's ESSAY FOR THE RECORDING OF ILLUSTRIOUS PROVIDENCES (1684), Cotton Mather's MAGNALIA CHRISTI AMERICANA (1702), and John Williams' REDEEMED CAPTIVE RETURNING TO ZION (1707). The narratives became more "literary," as in Samuel Bownas' version (1760) of Elizabeth Hanson's *God's Mercy Surmounting Man's Cruelty* (1728). Then hacks began to provide these narratives, supplanting pious individuals who were thankful to God for their rescue. Hatred is expressed for white men (especially Frenchmen and priests) as much as for the Indians, as in William Fleming's *Narrative of the Sufferings and Surprising Deliverances of William and Elizabeth Fleming* (1750) and Robert Eastburn's *The Dangers and Sufferings of Robert Eastburn* (1758). Even more popular was the gory and sensational volume, *French and Indian Cruelty Exemplified in the Life and Various Vicissitudes of Peter Williamson* (1757). The material becomes a mélange of fact and fiction with salability rather than truth the main object. Charles Brockden Brown legitimatized the captive narrative in EDGAR HUNTLY (1799) by transferring it into the realm of avowed fiction.

In the 19th century the problem of authenticity became a genuine, often insoluble one, especially as historians began to turn to these narratives as a basis for their chronicles. Some of the earlier collections were still frankly sensational. More objective were the editions prepared by Samuel Gardner Drake (1832 and 1839), J. Pritts (1839), HENRY R. SCHOOLCRAFT (1844). Collections of narratives of captivity are to be found at the Newberry Library, the Huntington Library, and the Library of Congress. H. H. Peckham's *Captured by Indians* (1954) contains fourteen true tales of pioneer survivors.

Indian Girl's Lament, The (1823; published, 1826), a poem by WILLIAM CULLEN BRYANT. An Indian maiden mourns for her dead lover, slain in battle, and prepares him for his long journey to "the land of light." She hopes his thoughts will occasionally stray earthward to her, where she waits longingly to join him. The poem is sentimental and lacks verisimilitude—it also lacks the terseness characteristic of Indian poetry.

Indian [Amerindian] languages. Philologists both amateur and professional have been attracted to the Indian languages ever since white men first came in contact with the American natives. Thus an early theory developed to the effect that the Indians were the lost tribes of Israel and their languages variants of Hebrew; much ingenuity was expended in the pursuit of this conjecture. Later philologists attempted to reduce the confusing number of Indian languages to an acceptable order. One classification, made by J. W. POWELL for the Bureau of Ethnology (1891), listed fifty-six different linguistic families among the tribes living north of Mexico. EDWARD SAPIR later reduced these to

six: Eskimo-Aleut, Algonquian-Wakashan, Na-Dene, Uto-Aztecan, Penutian, and Hokan-Siouan. In all more than two hundred separate languages have been defined. In spite of much speculation, the derivation of most Indian languages remains in doubt, although it is now thought that the Eskimo-Aleut family belongs to the Uralic group along with Finno-Ugric. Central and South American Indian languages are almost equally numerous and complex, and much research remains to be done before they can be classified.

Words borrowed from the Indians were the earliest "Americanisms" and fell largely into two groups, those borrowed indirectly through Spanish and Portuguese, and those directly borrowed after the establishment of English colonies in North America. Among the former are *cacao* (cocoa), *canoe, hammock, hurricane, potato, tobacco, tomato, buccaneer, avocado, cashew, tapioca, cougar, coyote.* Direct borrowings include *opossum, moccasin, terrapin, moose, powwow, wigwam, hominy, wampum, squaw, hickory, tomahawk, toboggan, chipmunk, tepee.* In addition many American place names are of Indian origin, some of them exceedingly complex; a lake in Massachusetts now called Webster was formerly called Charugoggagaugmanchaugagoggchaubunagungamaugg.

Indian poetry. Although various 18th- and 19th-century American poets had professed an interest in Indian poetry and had pretended to imitate Indian forms in their own works, it was not until almost 1900 that scholars and critics began a large-scale study of Indian poetry for its own sake. By far the greatest of those who have entered the field has been FRANCES DENSMORE, whose many books and monographs, beginning in 1893, have made Indian poetry and music accessible to everyone. Her translations have been highly praised for both their accuracy and their literary quality. Others who have worked in the field are WASHINGTON MATTHEWS (*The Mountain Chant: A Navaho Ceremony,* 1887; *The Night Chant,* 1902; *Navaho Myths, Prayers and Songs,* 1907); FRANZ BOAS (*The Central Eskimo,* 1888; *Chinook Songs,* 1888; *Eskimo Tales and Songs,* 1894); NATALIE CURTIS BURLIN (*The Indians' Book,* 1908; rev., 1923); Eda Lou Walton (*Navajo Traditional Poetry,* 2 v., 1920); Nellie Barnes (*American Indian Verse: Characteristics of Style,* 1921; *American Indian Love Lyrics,* 1925); William Thalbitzer (*The Ammassalik Eskimo,* 1923); Constance Lindsay Skinner (*Aztec Poets,* 1925; *Songs of the Coast Dwellers,* 1930); Ruth Underhill (*Singing for Power, The Song Magic of the Papago Indians,* 1938); Paul Radin (*The Road of Life and Death: A Ritual Drama of the American Indian,* 1945). See AMERINDIAN PROSE AND POETRY.

Indian Princess, The, or, La Belle Sauvage (1808), a play by J. N. BARKER. This was the first play dealing with Indians to be produced; it was the first to introduce POCAHONTAS as the leading character; it was the first original American play to be produced in England after its initial performance in America. Barker, a good dramatist and a poet of merit, saw that the historical rescue of JOHN SMITH by the Indian princess came too early to serve as a climax and made the love affair between her and JOHN ROLFE an important part of the plot. Her saving of the colonists became the climax. For a time Pocahontas and her fellow Indians talk rhythmically in an imitation of Indian speech; later they speak in blank verse.

Indian Prophecy, The (1827), a play by George Washington Parke Custis (1781–1857). Custis, George Washington's stepson, treated in this play an early incident in Washington's life. The Indian chiefs who brought about Braddock's defeat and death (1755) killed two horses under the young Virginian officer and pierced his clothing with bullets, but at last gave up the attempt to kill him. They believed him invulnerable. This play started a vogue for Indian drama.

Indians, Tales of the North American (1929), selected and annotated by Stith Thompson (1885 —). He divides his tales into nine groups: mythological stories, mythical incidents, trickster tales, hero tales, journeys to the other world, animal wives and husbands, miscellaneous tales, tales borrowed from Europeans, Bible stories. These are further analyzed in his valuable notes into a whole series of motifs. A map indicates cultural areas.

Indians in American literature. The Indian in literature, and in American literature, particularly, has been studied in detail. In an article in *Modern Philology*, November, 1913, Gilbert Chinard analyzed the influence of the Indian on 17th- and 18th-century French literature, Hoxie N. Fairchild in *The Noble Savage* (1928) considered the Indian in English literature, and ALBERT KEISER made a careful analysis of *The Indian in American Literature* (1933).

The contact of white man and red man on American soil produced several stereotypes that had considerable basis in reality. Naturally, as the Indian resisted the advance of the European invader, there grew up for the latter the image of a ruthless savage. To deal with this savage there appeared likewise the image of the wilderness explorer who was also an "Injun fighter." Daniel G. Brinton wrote on these figures in *The Myths of the New World* (1868) and edited the *Library of Aboriginal American Literature* (8 v., 1882–90). Much important information was gathered in R. G. THWAITES' edition of *The Jesuit Relations* (73 v., 1896–1901). Musicians and students of literature in the last quarter of the 19th century joined ethnologists and linguists in the study of Indian culture. A study of folk-tales was made by Stith Thompson in TALES OF THE NORTH AMERICAN INDIANS (1929); other tales were analyzed in studies made by John R. Swanton, Grenville Goodwin, RUTH BENEDICT, Leonard Bloomfield, GEORGE A. DORSEY, ROBERT H. LOWIE, EDWARD SAPIR, CLARK WISSLER, and others. Particularly important for its widely informed and scientific viewpoint was FRANZ

BOAS' *Tsimshia Mythology*, made for the 1916 report of the Bureau of Ethnology. FRANCES DENSMORE has published many important studies of Indian music and literature.

GEORGE CATLIN, a native of Pennsylvania who was a painter, became interested in the Indians and in 1832 began a series of journeys to the West and South, in the course of which he made portraits of the Indians, and published an account of *Manners, Customs, and Conditions of the North American Indian* (1841). HENRY R. SCHOOLCRAFT initiated the study of Indian culture with his *Algic Researches* (1839) and numerous later volumes. More recently R. H. Pearce's study *Savages of America* (1952) appeared.

The Indian enters American literature with the Pocahontas legend. PHILIP FRENEAU was the first poet to portray him in native haunts with melancholy respect. Soon he appeared in fiction in varying guise, in the writings of CHARLES BROCKDEN BROWN, JAMES K. PAULDING, J. F. COOPER, and the vast host of Cooper's imitators. Travelers and historians like WASHINGTON IRVING and FRANCIS PARKMAN began to present more objective treatment of the Indian. Indian figures became common in story and drama, particularly POCAHONTAS, KING PHILIP, Conanchet, PONTIAC, JAMES LOGAN, TECUMSEH, and Sitting Bull. Still recalled are two later stage hits, William De Mille's *Strongheart* (1909) and MARY AUSTIN's *The Arrow Maker* (1911). Out of the writings of Schoolcraft, Longfellow took the figure of HIAWATHA, who assumed a place alongside Cooper's "good" Indians. W. G. SIMMS in his numerous novels presented a more balanced but less influential view. Among later writers MARK TWAIN was grossly unjust, HAMLIN GARLAND well-informed and sympathetic in portraying the red man.

Other writers in whose works the Indian appears in a friendly role are HELEN HUNT JACKSON, indignant champion of the red man; JOAQUIN MILLER, most romantic of his portrayers; and JOHN G. NEIHARDT, who sees him in relation to a destined white conquest of America. On the whole it is the Indians of the West, on the coast and toward the Mexican border, who have chiefly benefited from the new attitude toward the Indian. Oliver La Farge's LAUGHING BOY (1929), Edna Ferber's CIMARRON (1930), Dana Margaret Smith's *Hopi Girl* (1931), and D'Arcy McNickle's *The Surrounded* (1936) illustrate this point.

Other works dealing with American Indians include, to name only a few: H. H. Brackenridge's MODERN CHIVALRY (1792); Ann Eliza Bleecker's HISTORY OF MARIA KITTLE (1793); Gilbert Imlay's THE EMIGRANTS (1793); Charles Brockden Brown's EDGAR HUNTLY (1799); J. F. Cooper's LEATHER-STOCKING TALES, and other novels; James K. Paulding's THE DUTCHMAN'S FIRESIDE (1831); W. G. Simms's *The Yemassee* (1835), THE WIGWAM AND THE CABIN (a collection of short stories, 1845), *The Cassique of Accabee* (a poem, 1849), VASCONSELOS (1853), and *The Cassique of Kiawah* (1859);

Helen Hunt Jackson's *Ramona* (1884); STEWART E. WHITE's *The Westerners* (1901); Hamlin Garland's THE CAPTAIN OF THE GRAY-HORSE TROOP (1902); FREDERIC REMINGTON's *John Ermine of the Yellowstone* (1902); HONORÉ MORROW's *Lydia of the Pines* (1917); ZANE GREY's *The Vanishing American* (1925); JAMES BOYD's *Shadow of the Long Knives* (1928), *Simon Girty* (1928), and *The Long Hunt* (1931); David Garnett's *Pocahontas* (1933); MARY AUSTIN's *One-Smoke Stories* (1934); Walter D. Edmonds' DRUMS ALONG THE MOHAWK (1936) and *In the Hands of the Senecas* (1947); ESTHER FORBES' *Paradise* (1937); OLIVER LA FARGE's *All the Young Men* (1935) and *The Enemy Gods* (1937); KENNETH ROBERTS' *Northwest Passage* (1937); AUGUST DERLETH's *Wind Over Wisconsin* (1938) and *Bright Journey* (1940); EVELYN EATON's *Quietly My Captain Waits* (1940); Louis Zara's *This Land Is Ours* (1940); Marguerite Allis' *Not Without Peril* (1941); HOWARD FAST's *The Last Frontier* (1941); ELSIE SINGMASTER's *High Wind Rising* (1942); ODELL and Willard SHEPARD's *Holdfast Gaines* (1946); A. B. Guthrie, Jr.'s THE BIG SKY (1947); Robert Wilder's BRIGHT FEATHER (1948); PAUL I. WELLMAN's *Broncho Apache* (1951) and *The Comancheros* (1952); Conrad Richter's *The Light in the Forest* (1953); Harry James' *Red Man, White Man* (1957); Janice Giles' *Johnny Osage* (1960). See additional entries under names of individual tribes. See also INDIAN LANGUAGES; INDIAN POETRY; AMERINDIAN PROSE AND POETRY; MISSION INDIANS.

Indian Student, The, or, Force of Nature (1788), a poem by PHILIP FRENEAU. Shalum, an Indian boy living on the banks of the Susquehanna, is persuaded by a priest to leave "Satan's waste" and attend Harvard. There he submits for a while to the boredom of studies, determines at last to leave those "gloomy walls" and to return to the delights of nature.

Indian Summer (1886), a novel by WILLIAM DEAN HOWELLS. Theodore Colville, a journalist of forty, meets in Florence a boyhood acquaintance, the widow Mrs. Lina Bowen. He becomes engaged to her young ward Imogene Graham. When she realizes she is in love with a younger man, Colville at last recognizes the maturer love grown up between himself and Mrs. Bowen, who had been helpless to interfere in what she knew to be a mismatch. Howells considered the book one of his best.

In Dubious Battle (1936), a novel by JOHN STEINBECK. One of the more important books to come out of the proletarian movement and Steinbeck's first successful novel, *In Dubious Battle* deals with a fruit strike in a California valley and the attempts of the radical leaders to organize, lead, and provide for the striking pickers. Perhaps the most important, although not the central, character is Doc Burton, an uncommitted sympathizer who helps the strikers and is concerned with seeing things as they exist, without labels of good and bad attached. The strike fails, and Jim, one of the two leaders, is senselessly killed. The title of the novel is taken from Milton's *Paradise Lost* and refers to the "dubious battle" of Satan and his angels with the hosts of heaven.

Industrial Valley (1939), a factual narrative by RUTH McKENNEY. In it she employs the techniques of fiction, especially those introduced by JOHN DOS PASSOS. Miss McKenney tells the story of the strike of the rubber workers at Akron, Ohio, which ran from January, 1932, until March, 1936. She introduces actual persons, scenes, incidents, newspaper headlines, and other contemporary data.

Industrial Workers of the World. See I. W.W.

Infidel, The (1835), a historical novel by ROBERT M. BIRD. A sequel to his CALAVAR (1834), it continues the story of Cortez' conquest of Mexico. Bird describes vividly the picturesque scenery of Mexico and tells excitingly the sensational events that marked Cortez' advance.

Influence of Sea Power upon History, 1660–1783, The (1890), a historical analysis by Alfred Thayer Mahan (1840–1914), supplemented by *The Influence of Sea Power upon the French Revolution and Empire, 1793–1812* (1892). In 1885 Captain Mahan, an experienced officer, was unexpectedly detailed to lecture on tactics and naval history at the newly established Naval War College at Newport. As a consequence, he began to think out the philosophy of naval power, and came to the conclusions expressed first in lectures, then in his celebrated books. He showed that the Roman defeat of Carthage was due largely to sea power, then traced world history within the time boundaries of his titles to prove how determinative sea power had been. His books, which were both scholarly and entertaining, exerted a remarkable influence on the political and military ideas of his time. They became propaganda for a greater American navy, confirmed the British faith in their naval superiority, and incited Germany to rival Great Britain on the sea as well as on the land. Mahan's book has become regarded as a classic of military theory, the only American work to attain this distinction.

Information Please. A radio program which began May 17, 1938, with Dan Golenpaul as producer, CLIFTON FADIMAN as master of ceremonies, and a varying "board of experts" to reply to queries from listeners; the board usually included JOHN KIERAN, OSCAR LEVANT, and FRANKLIN P. ADAMS. It was immensely popular for a decade. In 1947 appeared the first volume of a new general fact-book, the *Information Please Almanac*, prepared by "Dan Golenpaul Associates" and edited by Kieran; in 1954 Golenpaul became editor, Kieran remained as consultant.

Ingalls, [Mildred Dodge] Jeremy (b. Gloucester, Mass., April 2, 1911—   ), poet, teacher. Her first collection, *The Metaphysical Sword*, won the 1941 prize of the YALE SERIES OF YOUNGER POETS. Her major work, *Tahl* (1945), is a long poem in blank verse, contemporary in subject matter. In 1953 she published *The Galilean Way*, a synthesis of her philosophic and religious views.

Inge, William (b. Independence, Kansas, May 3, 1913—   ), teacher, critic, playwright. Inge taught at Stephens College for Women in Columbia, Missouri, from 1938 to 1943; three of these five years were spent in the drama department, then headed by MAUDE ADAMS. In 1943, he became drama, music, and movie critic for the St. Louis *Star Times*. In December, 1944, he reviewed the Chicago opening of Tennessee Williams' *Glass Menagerie*, "which," says Inge, "I found so deeply moving that I felt a little ashamed for having led so unproductive a life." His first play, *Farther Off from Heaven* (1947), was produced by Margo Jones in her Dallas Theatre; *Come Back Little Sheba* (1950) won the George Jean Nathan and the Theatre Time Awards; *Picnic* (1953), later a movie, won the Pulitzer Prize; *Bus Stop* (1955) was a successful play and also later a movie, as was *The Dark at the Top of the Stairs* (1957); *A Loss of Roses* was produced in 1960.

Inge explores in his plays the "average" people of the Midwest, and "the surprising depths of feeling that lie just below the public surface of human personality."

Ingersoll, Charles Jared (b. Philadelphia, Oct. 3, 1782—d. May 14, 1862), lawyer, public official, writer. Ingersoll was an able man with a deep interest in the philosophy of law and politics and a considerable literary gift. He began by writing *Edwy and Elgiva*, a tragedy in blank verse produced in Philadelphia in 1801. Though his family held conservative political views, Ingersoll became a Jacksonian Democrat who served in Congress and in other public capacities. In 1808 he wrote *A View of the Rights and Wrongs, Power and Policy of the United States of America*, which attacked the British, and urged a tariff war to achieve true independence. *Inchiquin, The Jesuit's Letters* (1810) denied the views of British travelers in America and provoked a bitter notice in the English *Quarterly Review* as well as important defenses of Ingersoll in this country. In 1823 Ingersoll, speaking before the American Philosophical Society in Philadelphia, delivered *A Discourse Concerning the Influence of America on the Mind*, in which he advocated a literature true to the utilitarian American character. He wrote a tragedy, *Julian* (1831), various historical works, and his *Recollections* (1861).

Ingersoll, Ernest (b. Monroe, Mich., March 13, 1852—d. Nov. 13, 1946), naturalist, museum curator, writer. A profound student of birds and animals, Ingersoll frequently attacked persons "who would not deal honestly with nature." He was greatly admired by Theodore Roosevelt and by other naturalists, particularly JOHN BURROUGHS and WILLIAM BEEBE. He obtained his first important position as curator of the Oberlin College Museum; later he was on the staff of the Smithsonian Institution, the U.S. Geological Survey, the U.S. Fish Commission, and other

official organizations. He contributed data to encyclopedias and dictionaries, wrote for newspapers and magazines, and published a series of important and well-written books, among them *Knocking 'Round the Rockies* (1882); *Country Cousins* (1884); *Wild Neighbors* (1897); *Nature's Calendar* (1900); *The Wit of the Wild* (1906); *Primer of Bird Study* (1916); *Dragons and Dragon Lore* (1928).

Ingersoll, Ralph M[cAllister] (b. New Haven, Conn., Dec. 8, 1900—   ), mining engineer, newspaperman, writer, editor. Ingersoll began as a successful mining engineer, became managing editor of *The New Yorker*, then managing editor of *Fortune*, and later vice-president and general manager of Time, Inc. He saw active service in World War II and wrote several war books, particularly *Top Secret* (1946), which attacks all the war generals except Jacob Devers and Omar Bradley. In 1940 he helped to found *PM*, a liberal tabloid newspaper in New York City, and edited and published it, so far as his military engagements and activities as a war correspondent permitted, from 1940 to 1945, when it was purchased by Marshall Field. His tendency toward reminiscence and comment turned in 1948 to fiction, when he published a novel, *The Great Ones;* this deals with a magazine publisher and his second wife, an actress who becomes active in Republican politics. He published another novel, *Wine of Violence*, in 1951.

Ingersoll, Robert G[reen] (b. Dresden, N.Y., Aug. 11, 1833—d. July 21, 1899), lawyer, orator, lecturer, soldier, public official, agnostic. The son of a strict Congregational minister in the Middle West, Ingersoll became a brilliant lawyer, an active Republican politician, the country's most renowned orator and lecturer, and one of the world's most fervent enemies of religion; he earned the title of "The Great Agnostic." His life was exemplary, and he devoted his large earnings mainly to charity. His rationalistic views prevented his progress in politics, but he became a constant orator at Republican meetings, particularly after his eloquent nomination (1876) of James G. Blaine for President. His orations on Burns, Shakespeare, and Lincoln won wide praise; as an agnostic he gained a notoriety that did not displease him. David Saville Muzzey, in an introduction to an edition of Ingersoll's *Letters* (1951) prepared for publication by his granddaughter Eva Ingersoll Wakefield, holds that Ingersoll "exposed with matchless oratory and trenchant wit the orthodox superstitions of his day," and that his influence helped lead to a kindlier and saner conception of religion.

Ingersoll was no great philosopher; his ability lay in his brilliant phrasing of ideas by no means original with him. He was under the influence of Voltaire and even more of THOMAS PAINE. His writing is sprinkled with aphorisms, such as: "An honest God is the noblest work of man." "Calvin was as near like the God of the Old Testament as his health permitted." "Many people think they have religion when they are merely troubled with dyspepsia." "A mule has neither pride of ancestry nor hope of posterity." "Religion has not civilized man, man has civilized religion." "With soap, baptism is a good thing." Among his books are *The Gods* (1872), *Some Mistakes of Moses* (1879), *Why I Am an Agnostic* (1896). After his death appeared *The Works of Robert G. Ingersoll* (12 v., 1900).

Ingraham, Joseph Holt (b. Portland, Me., Jan. 25, 1809—d. Dec. 18, 1860), sailor, newspaperman, teacher, minister, novelist. Ingraham's early career is obscure; in his later years he became a clergyman and also ran a boys' school at Holly Springs, Miss. In his youth Ingraham was a tremendously rapid writer and prepared serials for newspapers in the style of the French fictionists. Later he became ashamed of these productions and tried to destroy them. He composed numerous historical romances, many now collectors' items. The best was *Lafitte, the Pirate of the Gulf* (1836). Another book of his, *The Prince of the House of David* (1855), likewise became a best seller; other books with a Biblical setting were *The Pillar of Fire, or, Israel in Bondage* (1859) and *The Throne of David* (1860). His enormous output has never been adequately surveyed, but two more items may be noted: *Jemmy Daly, or, The Little News Vendor. A Tale of Youthful Struggles and the Triumph of Truth and Virtue over Vice and Falsehood* (1843) and *The Beautiful Cigar Girl, or, The Mysteries of Broadway* (185[?]). See also BRUISING BILL; JEAN LAFITTE.

Ingraham, Prentiss (b. near Natchez, Miss., Dec. 22, 1843—d. Aug. 16, 1904), soldier, adventurer, author of dime novels. Son of JOSEPH HOLT INGRAHAM, he was an even more prolific writer than his father. After service in the Confederate Army, he went west, became acquainted with "Buffalo Bill" Cody (see WILLIAM F. CODY) and turned to writing stories about the frontier. He is said to have composed about six hundred—a third of them devoted to Col. Cody. Books attributed to him are *The Beautiful Rivals* (1884), *Cadet Carey of West Point* (1890), and *The Girl Rough Riders* (1903).

In His Steps (1896), a novel by CHARLES M. SHELDON. The subtitle of this famous and immensely popular novel was "What Would Jesus Do?" and the story attempts to answer the question. A Protestant minister is shocked by conditions in his community. He asks his congregation to do what they think Jesus would do in all their activities and relationships; the book goes on to give various examples of how they carry out their pledge. After publication in a Congregational weekly called *The Advance*, the novel appeared (1897) in book form. Its popularity brought forth a swarm of pirated editions, since the book, in its serial form, had not been copyrighted. Frank Luther Mott cites eighteen publishers who have had the book on their lists, only four of whom paid royalties to the author. He calls the book amateurish as literature, first-rate as a social document.

Initial, Daemonic, and Celestial Love (1847; rev., 1876), a poem by RALPH WALDO EMERSON. In this lengthy work Emerson describes the progress from physical to intellectual to spiritual love; the ideas are derived mainly from Plato's *Symposium*. The poem is written for the most part in four-stress lines arranged in couplets.

Inman, Henry (b. New York City, July 30, 1837—d. Nov. 13, 1899), soldier, newspaperman, historian. Son of a notable painter, Henry Inman (1801–1846), the younger Inman joined the army and rose to the rank of lieutenant-colonel by the time he was thirty-one, when he was dismissed from the service. His ability was marred by eccentricities that led to an estrangement from his family. He began writing about the frontier, with which he had become familiar in the Indian campaigns; among his books were *Stories of the Old Santa Fe Trail* (1881); *The Old Santa Fe Trail* (1897); *Tales of the Trail* (1898); *The Great Salt Lake Trail* (1898); *Buffalo Jones' Forty Years of Adventure* (1899).

Inman, Samuel G[uy] (b. Trinity, Tex., June 24, 1877—d. Feb. 19, 1965), teacher, author. A specialist in Latin-American affairs, Inman taught at many universities and served on many committees and commissions dealing with inter-American problems. His books include: *Intervention in Mexico* (1919); *South America Today* (1921); *Ventures in Inter-American Friendship* (1925); *Trailing the Conquistadores* (1930); *Latin America, Its Place in World Life* (1937; rev. ed., 1947); *A History of Latin America for Schools* (1944); *A New Day in Guatemala* (1951); *The Ever Nearer Near East* (1955); *Rise and Fall of Good Neighbor Policy* (1957).

In Mizzoura (1893), a play by AUGUSTUS THOMAS. Thomas began writing the play as a vehicle for the actor Nat Goodwin. A plausible sheriff tries to win the hand of the heroine; the courtship proceeds amidst local complications. George C. D. Odell found the play "a rich comedy of rural life."

Innocents Abroad, The, or, The New Pilgrim's Progress (1869), a travel book by MARK TWAIN. This volume is a crucial one in Mark Twain's career and his personal life. The book—or the letters to the San Francisco *Alta California*, the New York *Tribune*, and the New York *Herald* on which it was largely based—made him famous and assured his financial success; his meeting with Charles Langdon, one of the passengers, led in time to his marriage with Langdon's sister Olivia.

Twain had written widely-read letters on his trip to the Sandwich Islands in 1866; the *Alta California* agreed with him that a similar trip to Europe might furnish even better material, and paid his passage money on a "pleasure excursion" to the Old World, June 8 to November 19, 1867. Twain kept up a steady stream of letters about the trip—the sights and scenes, his fellow passengers, European manners as against American. He became close friends with some of the other voyagers, including Mary Mason Fairbanks, the wife of the proprietor of the Cleveland *Herald;* in 1949 Dixon Wecter edited *Mark Twain to Mrs. Fairbanks,* an account of their long continued friendship.

Two days after Twain's return, the American Publishing Co. of Hartford proposed making a book out of the letters. Twain made considerable revisions, striking out a good deal of the slang, toning down the burlesques of Scripture, touching up the descriptions. Previous to the book's appearance, he made a lot of money lecturing on his European experiences and incidentally touting the book in every way he could. On a lecture engagement in Pittsburgh he played against FANNY KEMBLE, and had two thousand auditors to her two hundred. When the book came out it was a great success, and for the first time Twain felt himself a professional author. The book was just as popular with foreign as with American readers.

The style of the book is breezily western in the frontier tradition and shows Twain maturing in a technique he was to follow for the rest of his career. The book was in part intended as a burlesque of the sentimental travel writing of the time. Gladys Carmen Bellamy, in her *Mark Twain as a Literary Artist* (1950), stresses the degree to which Twain injected criticism of American civilization into his account of his trip abroad. He found Europe, for example, infinitely superior to America in the leisure Europeans allowed themselves. In *Traveling with the Innocents Abroad: Mark Twain's Reports from Europe and the Holy Land,* edited by D. M. McKeithan (1958), the original texts of the newspaper dispatches are restored.

In Old Kentucky (1893), a play by Charles Turner Dazey. One of the most popular plays of its era was this melodrama of a horse race, with plenty of local color. The details were based on personal observation, and presented an effective contrast between the mountaineers of Kentucky and the bluegrass people. The heroine almost loses a young patrician's love by appearing in public in riding breeches.

In Ole Virginia (1887), a collection of short stories by THOMAS NELSON PAGE. Several of them, particularly MARSE CHAN and *Meh Lady,* have become favorites of anthologists. These, like some of the other tales, deal with Negroes.

In Our Time (1924 in France, 1925 in the United States), a collection of fifteen tales by ERNEST HEMINGWAY, his second book. The style is strongly under the influence of GERTRUDE STEIN and reveals some of Hemingway's characteristic moods and themes, such as his interest in sports and in American expatriates. Some of the sketches speak of his own boyhood. *A Very Short Story* introduces a plot later more fully utilized in A FAREWELL TO ARMS.

In Praise of Johnny Appleseed (*Century Magazine,* August, 1921), a poem by VACHEL LINDSAY; later printed in *Collected Poems* (1923). Lindsay follows JOHN CHAPMAN's career over the Appalachian barricade, his wanderings among the Indians and in the wilderness,

his vigorous old age. The lines are rhymed, but the meter is irregular, with the customary exultant, leaping rhythm of Lindsay's verses, as well as his usual naïveté and artificiality.

Inquiry into the Principles and Policy of the Government of the United States (1814), a treatise by JOHN TAYLOR. The author, a radical agrarian, put into this important work many concepts which later became commonplaces of American liberalism.

Inquiry on the Freedom of the Will, The (1753). See FREEDOM OF THE WILL.

Inscription for the Entrance to a Wood (composed, 1815; published in *North American Review,* September, 1817; in *Poems,* 1821), a poem by WILLIAM CULLEN BRYANT. Bryant wrote this poem under two strong and not completely reconciled influences—Calvinism (one notes the reference to "the primal curse") and Wordsworth. As he revised the poem, the former influence somewhat declined. Retiring from the guilt and misery of the world, the poet finds solace in the tranquility and gladness of nature.

Inside of the Cup, The (1913), a novel by WINSTON CHURCHILL. In this story about the minister of a wealthy church, Churchill attacks outworn church dogmas and the lack of democracy in much modern religious practice.

Inside U.S.A. (1947), a survey of the states and the state of the Union by JOHN GUNTHER. A musical revue was "suggested" by the book to Howard Dietz and Arthur Schwartz; it opened April 30, 1948, and had a moderate run.

International Documents Service. A department of Columbia University Press, organized in 1937 to serve as a distribution center for publications of a number of international organizations. As a convenience to scholars, libraries, government offices, and business firms the IDS has made available reports, studies, periodicals, and official documents. A monthly news-sheet containing a checklist, *The International Reporter,* provides data about publications.

Intervals of Robert Frost, The (1947), a critical bibliography by Louis and Esther Mertins. This is more exactly described as a "biographical bibliography." It was prepared by two friends and admirers of Frost on the basis of their own unique collection of books, magazines, newspapers, and Frost miscellany. The book falls into seven ages or sections, which are called the San Francisco, Lawrence, Derry, Dymock, Amherst, Cambridge, and Hanover "Intervals." The genesis of many of Frost's poems is described, and often odd bits of information are given. Frost himself was helpful in furnishing data.

In the American Grain (1925), a volume of essays by WILLIAM CARLOS WILLIAMS. Under the influence of D. H. Lawrence's *Studies in Classic American Literature,* Williams portrays the developing American conscience in sketches of such major figures as Columbus, Cotton Mather, Washington, Franklin, and Poe, and such minor ones as Champlain, Thomas Morton, Père Sebastian Rasles, and Jacataqua. He seeks the "grain" of American character especially in homely, rather than in heroic, incidents of national history. The critic Yvor Winters finds the style of the essays "superior in all likelihood to nearly any other prose of our time and to most of the verse."

In the Baggage Car Ahead (1896), a song by Gussie L. Davis (1863–1899). Davis had once been a Pullman porter, at another time had swept the halls of the New York Conservatory of Music, incidentally acquiring some knowledge of musical composition. The lyric tells the story of a father accompanied in a train by several troublesome children; he explains to the protesting fellow passengers that "Their mother is in a casket in the baggage car ahead." The song became the most popular "sob ballad" of the Gay Nineties, and later was often employed as a burlesque.

In the Clouds (1887), a novel by Charles Egbert Craddock (MARY NOAILLES MURFREE). As in most of Miss Murfree's novels, the background is Tennessee, and a peak of the Great Smoky Mountains dominates the scene. The characters are "poor whites," the plot deals with moonshining and a love affair that encounters difficulties.

In the Evening by the Moonlight (1880), a song by JAMES A. BLAND. It is sometimes called "Southern Melodies," and is, says Sigmund Spaeth, "still a favorite with devotees of close harmony."

In the Good Old Summer Time (1902), a song with words by Ren Shields (1868–1913) and music by George ("Honey Boy") Evans, a blackface comedian. It was first sung by Blanche Ring, and became a song that immediately inspired audience participation.

In the Midst of Life (published as *Tales of Soldiers and Civilians*, 1891; retitled, 1898), a collection of twenty-six stories by AMBROSE BIERCE. These are not merely tales of grim horror in the manner of Poe; they are Bierce's commentaries on life as he saw it. The ten tales of soldiers in the first edition all end, for example, with the death of "the young, the beautiful, the brave." All the stories imply that life is dreadful, subject to frightening accidents and horrible coincidences. They show astounding powers of imagination and ingenuity; they have "twist" endings rarely surpassed in literature. Among the most famous are *A Horseman in the Sky, An Occurrence at Owl Creek Bridge, The Man and the Snake,* and *The Eyes of the Panther.* George Sterling wrote of these tales: "No easy optimism is here, but one is made aware of the possible horrors of life, like cobras hidden in heaped orchids. Dislike the stories one may; forget them one cannot."

In the Shade of the Old Apple Tree (1905), a song with words by Henry Williams (1879–1922), music by EGBERT VAN ALSTYNE. They were a popular team, and this song was their greatest hit.

In the Tennessee Mountains (1884), eight short stories by Charles Egbert Craddock (MARY NOAILLES MURFREE). These were the first writings to bring Miss Murfree national renown;

they appeared originally in the *Atlantic Monthly.* Many of the stories have a tragic cast. All are realistic, if sometimes too long-drawn-out, depictions of existence in the Great Smoky Mountains, and the dialect is reproduced with scrupulous exactness. The stories created a sensation; when the fact was revealed that "Charles Egbert Craddock" was a well-educated, partially crippled Tennessee spinster, she was promptly compared to George Eliot.

In the Valley (1890), a historical novel by HAROLD FREDERIC. This is a realistic description of the bloody campaign around Oriskany. The battle there (1777) is made by Frederic the turning point of the war.

Intolerance (1916), a film written, directed, and produced by DAVID W. GRIFFITH. A successor to Griffith's *The Birth of a Nation* (1915), this was conceived and executed on an even more grandiose scale. It was in part an answer to criticisms against the earlier film. The plot ran in what Griffith called "four currents looked at from a hilltop," which in the last act mingled in one mighty river of drama and emotion. One stream of scenes dealt with the fall of Babylon, another with Christ, a third with the massacre of the Huguenots on St. Bartholomew's Eve, the last with a modern story involving the ruthless killing of strikers in an industrial dispute. The sections were joined by a repeated sequence suggested by Walt Whitman's line about "the cradle endlessly rocking." The film was sentimental and overdramatized; the overemphasis on spectacle blurred the message. At first the film created bewilderment, but modern criticism has been increasingly favorable.

In Tragic Life (1932), a novel by VARDIS FISHER. This is the opening novel of a tetralogy which includes *Passions Spin the Plot* (1934), *We Are Betrayed* (1935), and *No Villain Need Be* (1936). The chief character is Hunter Vridar, whose life is traced from a frontier boyhood, through a long period of self-doubt, to final serenity. The plot is probably in part autobiographical.

Intruder in the Dust (1948), a novel by WILLIAM FAULKNER. LUCAS BEAUCHAMP, an aging Negro who has long nettled the townsfolk of Jefferson because of his refusal to adopt the servile attitude of the Negro toward white people, is wrongfully accused of murdering a white man and is threatened with violent death at the hands of a mob. Through the efforts of sixteen-year-old CHICK MALLISON, Aleck Sander, Chick's Negro friend, and seventy-year-old Miss Eunice Habersham, Lucas' innocence is proved and the real murderer captured. Having once failed to establish the barrier between white and black when Lucas refused to accept money for a meal, Chick is tormented by his obligation to Lucas. In defying the conventions of white society, both by attempting to defend a "stiff-necked nigger" and by violating a grave in his search for evidence, Chick rises above the restrictions of society and comes into manhood able to recognize other human beings as individuals, regardless of their color.

In Tune with the Infinite (1897), a discussion of personal problems by Ralph Waldo Trine (1866–   ). Trine sought to apply religion and philosophical concepts to the difficulties of everyday life. The book became a best seller.

Invisible Man (1952), a novel by RALPH ELLISON. This first novel is the record of a Negro boy's going from youthful affirmation to a sense of total rejection; his final invisibility—that is, his loss of social identity—gives him a point of view often compared with that of the hero of Dostoevsky's *Notes from the Underground*. Both men finally view society from an external position, despite their desire to function within it.

The unnamed hero at first has a rather unrealistic trust in the motives of others. He is dismissed from a southern Negro college for disillusioning one of the founders by showing him the world in which the southern Negroes really live. In New York City he distinguishes himself by rousing a crowd at an eviction, and is picked by Communist leaders for a political role. Ultimately, he realizes that the Communists are merely using him as a symbol of the Negro; also, a person he is as invisible to them as to anyone else. During a surrealistic Harlem riot (treated with humor and authority that prove Ellison's writing skill), the hero realizes that he must contend with both the white people and the leaders of his own race.

The book is powerful and honest, despite some fuzziness and overwriting. With no trace of forgiveness or even hope for the future, he merely records what happened, concluding with the hero's frightening sense that he speaks for others as well as himself, that he is not the only invisible man.

Ioor, William (b. Dorchester, S.C., 1780?—d. 1830), playwright. Ioor was one of a group of dramatists who made Charleston, S.C., something of a theatrical center in the early 19th century. The names of two of his plays have survived. One, a comedy based on an English novel, was called *Independence: Or, Which Do You Like Best, the Peer or the Farmer?* (produced, 1805). The other, a historical play of patriotic character, was called *The Battle of Eutaw Springs and Evacuation of Charleston* (1813).

Ireland, Joseph Norton (b. New York City, April 24, 1817—d. Dec. 29, 1898), merchant, stage historian. Ireland was related to the notorious William Henry Ireland, who forged a number of documents allegedly Shakespearian, including plays that he himself had written. His American relative loved the theater more legitimately. He made an important collection of data about the New York theater from 1750 to 1860, and prepared a book on the subject, published in two volumes in 1866–67. He also wrote lives of two actors prominent in his day, Mrs. Mary Ann Duff (1882) and Thomas Abthorpe Cooper (1888), and he contributed many articles on the theater to magazines and newspapers.

Iron Heel, The (1907), a novel by JACK LONDON. Following the lead of Edward Bel-

lamy, London peered into the future, but only so far as the years 1912–18 when, as he saw it, a right-wing revolution would occur, followed by an upsurgence of the socialists; much later would come a golden age.

Ironquill. The pen name of EUGENE FITCH WARE.

Iron Woman, The (1911), a novel by MARGARET DELAND; a sequel to THE AWAKENING OF HELENA RITCHIE (1906).

Iroquois Indians. A group of Indian tribes who came closest of all the red men to developing a stable form of government, and whose customs, legends, and rituals greatly influenced American writers. About 1570 the Mohawk, Onondaga, Oneida, Cayuga, and Seneca Indians formed a confederacy to abolish war among themselves—but not to prevent them from making war on others. They became known as the "Five Nations." In 1720 or thereabouts the related tribe of the Tuscaroras of North Carolina joined them, and their league was then called the "SIX NATIONS." The lands they occupied or raided extended from the Valley of the St. Lawrence southward to the Carolinas and westward to the Great Lakes, but they were mainly a group resident in New York state. They were all of the same blood, spoke the same language, had similar social and religious customs. Their alliances played an important role in determining the destiny of the continent. They became bitter enemies of the French and strong allies of the British, and helped the latter in dominating North America. When the American Revolution broke out they continued their alliance with the British until their power was broken by General Sullivan in August, 1779.

The formation of the ancient Iroquois Confederacy was always attributed to a great chieftain and reformer, Hayenwatha or Hiawatha, who lived around 1550. When Longfellow took his name and deeds as the subject for his well-known poem, he did Hiawatha and his people a grave injustice by making Hiawatha an Ojibway.

Before Longfellow the Iroquois had already appeared in American writing and oratory. CADWALLADER COLDEN wrote *History of the Five Indian Nations* (1727). De Witt Clinton gave an elaborate *Discourse on the Iroquois* in an address (1811) before the New York Historical Society. James Fenimore Cooper introduced the Iroquois into the LEATHER-STOCKING TALES as the worst enemies of Chingachgook and his tribe. HENRY ROWE SCHOOLCRAFT wrote *Notes on the Iroquois* (1845; rev., 1847), but L. H. Morgan's *League of the Ho-dé-no-sau-nee, or Iroquois* (1851) was superior. Before Longfellow, a seven-thousand-line poem called *Frontenac, or, The Atotarho of the Iroquois* (1849), by Alfred B. Street, had appeared. An important volume was Horatio Hale's *Iroquois Book of Rites* (1883), based on written documents in the possession of chieftains who were in charge of these ancient ceremonies. Other studies include: Alex T. Cringan's *Pagan Dance Songs of the Iroquois* (1900); Harriet M. Converse's *Myths and Legends of the New York State Iroquois* (1908); J. M. B. Hewitt's *The Requickening Address of the League of the Iroquois* (1916, 1944); George T. Hunt's *The Wars of the Iroquois* (1940); Paul A. W. Wallace's *The White Roots of Peace* (1946, an account of the Confederacy). The six tribes were in time widely dispersed. The Cayugas moved to Canada, Wisconsin, and Ohio; the Mohawks to Canada; the Oneidas now live on a small reservation in New York, although some fled to Canada, some to the West; some of the Onondagas removed to Canada and others to the West, but most of them remained in New York; the Senecas now reside on three small reservations in New York. The Confederacy's present-day conflict with New York State officialdom is recounted in Edmund Wilson's *Apologies to the Iroquois* (1960).

Irvine, William (b. Carson Hill, Calif., June 9, 1906—   ), writer, teacher. In 1935 he joined the faculty of Stanford University and was made a full professor in 1948. Irvine referred to himself as "a native American Wild Westerner who has devoted his life to the study of sedate and sedentary English Victorians." He wrote of Victorian personalities such as Darwin and Huxley (*Apes, Angels, and Victorians*, 1955), as if he had been born to the period. In *The Universe of G. B. Shaw* (1949), Irvine produced one of the most unbiased and thorough studies of Shaw and his times. He also wrote *Walter Bagehot* (1939) and edited *Bernard Shaw: Selected Plays and Other Writings* (1956).

Irving, John Treat (b. New York City, Dec. 2, 1812—d. Feb. 27, 1906), lawyer, broker, author of travel books, novelist. Irving, a nephew of WASHINGTON IRVING, was a member of an expedition to the West in 1833 led by Henry L. Ellsworth; his experiences formed the basis for his *Indian Sketches* (1835; rev. ed., 1888) and *Hunters of the Prairie, or, The Hawk Chief* (1837). He contributed to the KNICKERBOCKER MAGAZINE under the pen name John Quod, a pseudonym also employed for several of his novels, including *The Quod Correspondence, or, The Attorney* (1842).

Irving, Peter (b. New York City, Oct. 30, 1771—d. June 27, 1838), physician, editor, merchant, writer. This older brother of WASHINGTON IRVING was deeply devoted to him, an associate with him in business and authorship. He edited a daily paper, *The Morning Chronicle* (1802–05), to which Washington Irving contributed. He assisted his brother in writing a HISTORY OF NEW YORK (1809). He himself published only one book, *Giovanni Sbogarro* (2 v., 1820), a romance laid in Venice, issued under the pen name of Percival G——.

Irving, Pierre [Munro] (b. New York City, 1803—d. Feb. 11, 1876), lawyer, editor, biographer. Pierre was the son of WASHINGTON IRVING's oldest brother, WILLIAM. He became Irving's secretary and agent, collaborated with him on *Astoria* (1836), recorded their conversations, became his literary executor. After his un-

cle's death he published an official biography, *The Life and Letters of Washington Irving* (4 v., 1862–64; 1869), which has remained the basis for all later biographies. He also edited some unpublished materials of Irving's and reprinted others in *Spanish Papers and Other Miscellanies* (2 v., 1866).

Irving, Washington (b. New York City, April 3, 1783—d. Nov. 28, 1859), essayist, historian, biographer, humorist. Irving's formal education was brief; he was an indifferent scholar but an assiduous reader in his father's library, which

contained a good assortment of the English classics. Instead of attending college, he read law and then he practiced until 1803. When his health was threatened, he went to Europe and remained for two years—the first of many visits. Throughout his life his interests were mainly historical and his influences were found among British writers, especially the 18th-century essayists.

Irving's first published writings were newspaper pieces done under the pseudonym of JONATHAN OLDSTYLE, Gent. In 1807 appeared SALMAGUNDI, a series of satirical essays done in collaboration with his brother William and their friend JAMES PAULDING; the essays had little of permanent value, but their reception encouraged Irving to continue. In 1809 he published A HISTORY OF NEW YORK, using the pseudonym of Diedrich Knickerbocker, and the book brought him immediate fame. He was greatly depressed, however, by the death of his fiancée, and entered a period of aimlessness, eventually sailing again to England, where he remained for seventeen years. His best-known book was published there in 1820, THE SKETCH BOOK OF GEOFFREY CRAYON, GENT., a collection of stories and sketches done in the 18th-century manner and mostly concerned with the scenes he had known during his childhood rambles in the New York countryside; RIP VAN WINKLE and THE LEGEND OF SLEEPY HOLLOW, two of the most famous selections from the book, are an inseparable part of our national heritage.

Irving now called himself Geoffrey Crayon, and his popularity was at its height. His reputation spread at home, in England, and on the Continent, where French and German translations brought him to a wide public, and he became the first American writer to achieve international fame, the first professional American writer in the full sense of the word. In 1822 he published BRACEBRIDGE HALL, a feeble book which nevertheless enjoyed a good sale among admirers of *The Sketch Book,* and this was followed by his least successful work, TALES OF A TRAVELER (1824), which evoked nothing but scorn from the critics. Financial worries began to plague Irving, and once again his spirits were low. He gladly accepted ALEXANDER HILL EVERETT's invitation to join him in his embassy in Madrid, thereby fulfilling a lifelong desire to go to Spain. Everett suggested that Irving translate Navarrete's *Voyages of Columbus.* In 1826 Irving settled in Madrid and began his Spanish studies, which resulted, not in a direct translation, but in four original books: HISTORY OF THE LIFE AND VOYAGES OF COLUMBUS (1828); A CHRONICLE OF THE CONQUEST OF GRANADA (1829); *The Companions of Columbus* (1831); THE LEGENDS OF THE ALHAMBRA (1832). Irving wrote enthusiastically, perhaps naively, about Spanish life and history; his narrative technique was lively and readers took well to his new work. In 1842 Irving became minister to Spain, a post he occupied for four years.

In the meantime, during a brief stay in the United States, Irving had written ASTORIA (1836; rev., 1849), a history of the Astor family done on commission from them. It earned him $4,000 but little respect. *The Adventures of Captain Bonneville, U.S.A.* (1837) gives a fairly accurate picture of the times. (See CAPTAIN BONNEVILLE.) After completing his Spanish mission, Irving settled at his home, called SUNNYSIDE, in Tarrytown, N.Y., and there spent his old age. Far from inactive, he published his *Life of Oliver Goldsmith* in 1849 and a year later his two-volume biography, *Mahomet and His Successors.* In 1855 appeared WOLFERT'S ROOST, a collection of essays, some of them revised from previous publications. His final years were spent in hard work on his life of George Washington (for whom he had been named), the fifth and final volume of which was published only a few weeks before he died.

Irving's style has been described as insipid, sentimental, prettified, and in spite of his use of American themes in some of his best work, he has been judged harshly for his dependence on British fashions. He was not a highly original writer—his style was modeled on the work of such British authors as Scott, Addison and Goldsmith; his subjects were often appropriated from English and German collections of legends and folktales; and his later books were frequently merely pallid imitations of his earlier successes. One also looks in vain in his work for the moral concern, the intellectual vitality and acuteness,

which marked such contemporaries as Hawthorne, Melville, Emerson, and Poe. However, the grace and humor of Irving's prose, its delicate pictorial quality united with a strain of antiquarian romance and a strong sense of the melancholy of change, have given his best work lasting value. His importance is twofold: first, he greatly stimulated American cultural life by showing that American writers could become genuine men of letters in the great European tradition; second, he provided in a few of his works on indigenous themes a base for the future development of American literature as well as a stock of permanently appealing native lore.

The definitive *Life of Washington Irving* has been written by Stanley T. Williams (2 v., 1935). *The Life and Letters of Washington Irving* (4 v., 1862–64; 1869) was edited by Irving's nephew, PIERRE IRVING. Best collections of Irving manuscripts and other materials are at the New York Public Library, the Sterling Memorial Library at Yale, and the Henry E. Huntington Library, San Marino, Calif.

FRANCIS V. LLOYD, JR.

Irving, William (b. New York City, Aug. 15, 1766—d. Nov. 9, 1821), Indian trader, merchant, poet, public official. The oldest brother of WASHINGTON IRVING was described by him as "the man I loved most on earth." He was primarily a businessman, but served several terms in Congress and was deeply interested in writing and in the welfare of his younger brother. He was a member of the Cockloft Hall group, and contributed verses and two letters to SALMAGUNDI (1807). He had undoubted talent and wrote urbanely and amusingly.

Irwin, Inez Haynes [Gilmore] [Mrs. Will Irwin] (b. Brazil, March 2, 1873—   ), novelist, short-story writer, writer of books for girls. An adroit and ingenious story teller, Mrs. Irwin early won a reputation. The best of her books is *Angel Island* (1914), an allegory in which angels, once married, turn into women. Among her other books: *June Jeopardy* (1908); *The Californiacs* (1916); *Gertrude Haviland's Divorce* (1925); *Family Circle* (1931); *Murder Masquerade* (1935); also the "Maida" series (1910–54) for girls and the "Phoebe and Ernest" stories (1910–12) for adolescents. Mrs. Irwin was an active campaigner in the cause of woman suffrage, and she wrote *The Story of the Woman's Party* in 1921 and *Angels and Amazons* in 1933.

Irwin, Violet [Mary] (b. Toronto, 1881—   ), novelist, short-story writer. Irwin's work often describes Indian life. Among her books: *Wits and the Woman* (1919); *Kak, The Copper Eskimo* (with VILHJALMUR STEFANSSON, 1924); *The Shaman's Revenge* (1925); *The Mountain of Jade* (1926).

Irwin, Wallace [Admah] (b. Oneida, N.Y., March 15, 1875—d. Feb. 14, 1959), newspaperman, verse writer, humorist, novelist. Irwin worked for the San Francisco *Examiner,* for a time edited the *Overland Monthly,* won his first national fame with *The Love Sonnets of a Hood-*

lum (1902), Petrarchan verses in slang. He migrated to New York in 1904 and later joined *Collier's* staff. There, under the pen name of Hashimura Togo, he began writing the *Letters of a Japanese Schoolboy*, which reached book form in 1909 and continued to be popular for at least twenty years in magazines and syndicated reprints. Later he wrote *Mr. Togo, Maid of All Work* (1913); a number of detective stories; *The Rubaiyat of Omar Khayyam Jr.* (1902); various other collections of light verse; and *Seed of the Sun* (1921), a serious novel about the conflict of Japanese and white men in California. He collaborated with Dr. Sylvester Lambert on *Yankee Doctor in Paradise* (1941).

Irwin, Will[iam Henry] (b. Oneida, N.Y., Sept. 14, 1873—d. Feb. 24, 1948), newspaperman, war correspondent, writer. The brother of WALLACE IRWIN was equally quick and skilled at all kinds of writing, a reporter above all else; his autobiography was fittingly called *The Making of a Reporter* (1942). He began by writing *Stanford Stories* (1900), in collaboration with C. K. Field, and with GELETT BURGESS he wrote two books of adventure in Californian settings. For a while he edited the San Francisco *Wave*, then served on the staff of the *Chronicle* (1901–04). In 1904 he joined the New York *Sun*. Two years later, when news of the great San Francisco earthquake and fire reached New York, there was little real news available. Irwin sat down at his typewriter and with his memory of the California city and such scraps of information as came over the wires, he tapped out an astounding amount of copy per day for eight days. The story ran under the head, "THE CITY THAT WAS," and won Irwin national renown. The articles were published in a book by that title in 1907.

S. S. McCLURE called Irwin to *McClure's Magazine*, where he did "muckraking" stories, then he went on to *Collier's*, and later he became a war correspondent. His war reports were collected as *Men, Women, and War* (1915) and *Reporter at Armageddon* (1918). He worked with HERBERT HOOVER on the Commission for Relief in Belgium, years later wrote the first biography of Hoover (1929). He wrote much fiction, an analysis of *Propaganda and the News* (1936), two successful plays called *The 13th Chair* (with BAYARD VEILLER, 1916) and *Lute Song* (with SIDNEY HOWARD, 1930).

Isaacs, Edith J[uliet] R[ich] (b. Milwaukee, Wis., March 27, 1878—d. Jan. 10, 1956), newspaperwoman, editor, public relations specialist, authority on the theater. Mrs. Isaacs did newspaper work on the Milwaukee *Sentinel* and various publicity jobs during World War I, came to her chief interest when she began editing the quarterly *Theatre Arts Magazine* (1918–23), then *Theatre Arts Monthly* (1924–46). She is credited with having exerted a great and beneficial influence on theater activities in the United States, since she saw the theater as a social and historical development, was deeply interested in discovering new talent, understood the economic problems of the theater, was an excellent judge of plays. She won many notable contributors to her magazine. Among her books: *Theatre* (1927); *Plays of American Life and Fantasy* (1929); *The Negro in the American Theatre* (1947).

Isham, Ralph Heyward (b. New York City, July 2, 1890—d. June 13, 1955), businessman, bibliophile. Isham went into business as president of a securities company and vice-president of a water power company; during World War I he volunteered for service in the British army and received the permanent rank of lieutenant-colonel. An ardent collector of Boswelliana, he managed to uncover vast amounts of hitherto unpublished material in the possession of Boswell's great-grandson, Lord Talbot de Malahide, and elsewhere. This material, ultimately presented to the Yale University Library, is being published in what may amount to thirty or forty volumes; the first volume, *The London Journal*, appeared in 1950. The preparation of the volumes has been placed under the care of FREDERICK A. POTTLE of Yale.

Isherwood, Christopher (b. England, Aug. 26, 1904—   ), novelist, playwright, biographer. Isherwood attended the Repton School, then Corpus Christi, Cambridge, and afterward worked as a tutor and studied medicine until he joined his friend W. H. AUDEN in Germany. His stories, based on this period, were collected in *Goodbye to Berlin* and later dramatized by John Van Druten for a Broadway play *I Am a Camera*, which won the New York Drama Critics Award and became also a successful movie. He also wrote an autobiography, *Lions and Shadows* (1938), collaborated with Auden on several plays, and after extensive travel settled down finally in Santa Monica, California. There he became profoundly interested in the Vedanta Society, editing several anthologies on Vedanta, and for a time lectured at the Los Angeles State College. He was elected in 1949 to the National Institute of Arts and Letters. His novel *The World in the Evening* (1954) frankly disappointed reviewers, who found it "commonplace." In 1960 he collaborated with Charles Laughton in a dramatic project based on the dialogues of Plato. Some other books: *All the Conspirators* (1928); *The Memorial* (1932); *The Last of Mr. Norris* (1935); *Prater Violet* (1945); *The Condor and the Cows* (1949); *Vedanta for Modern Man* (ed., 1951). In collaboration with Auden he wrote *Journey to a War* (1939) and several verse plays, the best known of which are *The Dog Beneath the Skin* (1935) and *The Ascent of F6* (1936). *Down there on a Visit*, a novel, appeared in 1962.

Ishmael, or, In the Depths (1863), a novel by Mrs. E. D. E. N. SOUTHWORTH; it was the first part of a novel called *Self-Made*, the second part published as *Self-Raised, or, Out of the Depths* (1864), a rags-to-riches romance which occasionally displays a sense of humor. Mrs. Southworth, describing her hero, says that he spoke "in the pure, sweet, modulated tones of a highly cultivated nature." The book was very popular.

I Shot an Arrow into the Air (1845), a poem by HENRY WADSWORTH LONGFELLOW; it was included in THE BELFRY OF BRUGES *and Other Poems* (1845). It became one of the best known of Longfellow's poems, with its mixture of melody and moralizing.

I Sing the Body Electric (1855), a poem by Walt Whitman which was given its present title in the 1867 edition of LEAVES OF GRASS. Whitman had included the poem in the first edition of his book, without a title, and then worked it over repeatedly, making the final changes in 1881. A candid poem of sexuality, it shocked many readers and no doubt repelled some New Englanders and others who for a time had admired Whitman's work.

Israel Potter: or, Fifty Years of Exile (1855), a novel by HERMAN MELVILLE. A satirical novel set at the time of the Revolution, *Israel Potter* was based on the biographical *Life and Remarkable Adventures of Israel Potter* (1824). Melville's Israel is a young man who, having left home in search of adventure and freedom, finds himself embroiled in the Battle of Bunker Hill. Thereafter he meets three men who are representative of his time and country: the sly, conniving Benjamin Franklin, who robs Israel as he seemingly befriends him; the cultivated barbarian John Paul Jones, who genuinely likes the lad; and Ethan Allen, Christian and Westerner, who represents America's best hope for nobility and greatness. Israel himself has qualities which suggest, at one time or another, each of the three: he is shrewd, gentle, daring, predatory, freedom-loving, self-reliant, chivalrous, and gentlemanly. He is, in short, the quintessence, the archetype, of the American and of America.

Taken as a prisoner of war to England, Israel grows old as a brickmaker in an industrial town, and then moves to London, a Dantean hell, all the while longing for "America the Promised Land." When he finally does return, after forty years and more of wandering, his brains are somewhat addled and his memory dimmed. He has come home, in effect, to die.

Although the ending is bathed in an Irvingesque sentimentality, Melville's irony drives home his final point: the saga of Israel is the saga of America; his decline mirrors what Melville feels to be America's decline. Melville suggests that if there is hope for America, it must come from the still youthful West, the land of Christian gentlemen, the new Promised Land. See JOHN BEAUCHAMP JONES.

Israfel (1831), a poem by EDGAR ALLAN POE. Poe prefaced this poem with a motto ascribed to the Koran: "And the angel Israfel who has the sweetest voice of all God's creatures." In 1845 the note was changed to read: "And the angel Israfel whose heartstrings are a lute, and who has the sweetest voice of all God's creatures." The original line was taken from George Sale's *Preliminary Discourse* to his translation of the Koran (1734); a lute, of course, is shaped like a heart. The poem expresses Poe's belief that poetry must be impassioned, and that a

poet like himself might under other conditions sing as well as Israfel. It is a bold assertion of the power of a human poet.

Israfel: The Life and Times of Edgar Allan Poe (1926; rev., 1934), a biography by HERVEY ALLEN. This is a full account, written by a novelist of imagination and artistry. Allen emphasizes Poe's environment, the influence of the opium he took, the handicaps of his character traits. Allen avoids literary analysis, was criticized as unscholarly and prolix.

Italian Father, The (produced, 1799; published, 1810), a play by WILLIAM DUNLAP based on Thomas Dekker's *The Honest Whore, Part II* (1630). Dunlap considered this the best of his sixty-odd plays. It tells how a father in disguise watches over his errant daughter.

Italian Journeys (1867), travel sketches by WILLIAM DEAN HOWELLS. Howells was appointed consul in Venice at the outbreak of the Civil War. With his newly wed wife he spent four years of almost undisturbed leisure in Italy, visiting places of interest, studying Italian literature, writing poetry, forming the habit of close and sympathetic observation. Out of this long stay in a country he liked came two of his best books, *Venetian Life* (1866) and *Italian Journeys*. Among the places he describes in the latter are Padua, Genoa, Pompeii, Naples, Capri, Trieste, and Rome. His keen humor is as much in evidence as his sense of the picturesque.

It Can't Happen Here (1935), a novel by SINCLAIR LEWIS. The novel deals with the rise and establishment of a fascist dictatorship in the United States. Doremus Jessup, a liberal Vermont newsaper editor, sees with sorrow and horror the partisanship—not only of many of his friends and neighbors, but even of members of his own family—to the cause of Berzelius Windrip. Upon election to the Presidency in (presumably) 1936, Windrip resections the United States into eight "provinces," gains control of both Congress and the Supreme Court by sheer force, and effectively overcomes all resistance by means of the "Minute Men," his personal storm troopers. With members of an underground organization established by Walt Trowbridge, Windrip's opponent in the election, Jessup sets out to overcome the dictator's power. He is discovered and sent to a concentration camp, but eventually escapes to join Trowbridge in Canada. By the end of the novel, however, his own family has completely disintegrated. The novel was dramatized by Sinclair Lewis and John C. Moffitt in 1936, for production by the Federal Theater Project.

Ives, Brayton (b. Farmington, Conn., Aug. 23, 1840—d. Oct. 22, 1914), book collector, cofounder of the GROLIER CLUB (1884).

Ives, Burl [Icle Ivanhoe] (b. Hunt, Ill., June 14, 1909—   ), singer, balladist, actor. Ives traveled extensively over the country, collecting folksings and rendering them to the accompaniment of his guitar. More recently he had a distinguished acting career in movies and plays. He gave an entertaining account of his experiences as a singer in *Wayfaring Stranger* (1948), which

Katherine Scherman said had "the color and naïveté of an American primitive painting." He compiled *The Burl Ives Song Book* (1953), and collected *Tales of America* (1954).

Ives, Charles Edward (b. Danbury, Conn., Oct. 20, 1874—d. May 19, 1954), composer, essayist. A Yale graduate, son of a bandmaster, Ives went into the insurance business to make a living, worked passionately in his leisure time at composing music. His pieces, more than two hundred songs and other compositions, reveal him as a pioneer American musical genius. His most famous work is his second piano sonata, called *Concord, Mass., 1840–1860* (1920), a long, complex work "of satanic difficulty," according to Paul Moor. Ives called the sonata "one person's impressions of the spirit of transcendentalism that is associated with Concord of over half a century ago." The four movements bear the names of Emerson, Hawthorne, the Alcotts, and Thoreau. Ives wrote a slim accompanying volume called *Essays Before a Sonata*. The work was not performed *in toto* until 1939; Lawrence Gilman called it "the greatest music composed by an American." In 1947 Ives was awarded a Pulitzer Prize for his *Third Symphony,* written in 1911.

Henry and Sidney Cowell point out in *Ives and His Music* (1955) that the composer expressed himself in a new symphonic speech that includes evangelical hymns, dance hall melodies, college songs, the music of the world of nature. Some of his atonal works antedate those of Schönberg and other Europeans. Ives' manuscripts are liberally salted with such directions as *ffffff* and "play as you will." He never willingly copyrighted anything and refused all fees.

Ives, James Merritt (1824–1895). See CURRIER & IVES.

I.W.W. Familiar abbreviation for the organization called Industrial Workers of the World, but read by their enemies as "I Won't Work." "Their tactics, songs, and slogans made middle-class citizens shiver," says W. H. Hale; and their militancy brought down on them many brutal persecutions. The "Wobblies," as they were often called, appear in several novels, including Winston Churchill's *The Dwelling Place of Light* (1917) and Josephine Herbst's *The Executioner* (1934).

J

Jack Downing. See Downing, Jack.

Jackson, A[braham] V[alentine] W[illiams] (b. New York City, Feb. 9, 1862—d. Aug. 8, 1937), scholar, authority on Iranian philology and culture. Jackson taught at Columbia University, first Indo-Iranian languages, then English, then Indo-Iranian again. He traveled widely in Asia and wrote important accounts of his observations, among them *Persia, Past and Present* (1906) and *From Constantinople to the Home of Omar Kháyyám* (1911). He also published *An Avesta Grammar* (1892); *Zoroaster* (1899); *Early Persian Poetry* (1920); *Zoroastrian Studies* (1928).

Jackson, Andrew (b. Waxhaw, near border of S.C. and N.C., March 15, 1767—d. June 8, 1845), lawyer, soldier, public official, seventh President. Jackson spent his young boyhood in a frontier region near the borders of North and South Carolina. The settlement was invaded by the British during the Revolution, and at thirteen Jackson fought in the battle of Hanging Rock, was captured and imprisoned by the British, and left an orphan at the end of the war. Although his early schooling had been sporadic at best, he began to read law at seventeen and was admitted to the bar before he was twenty, having learned little law but a great deal about gambling, duelling, and horseracing, skills which undoubtedly served him well in his new position as public prosecutor of Nashville, Tennessee. In 1789, frontier Tennessee was even wilder and had less regard for law and order than the Waxhaw settlement; courage and common sense, rather than a thorough knowledge of Blackstone, were needed to tame it. In 1791 Jackson married Mrs. Rachel Donelson Robards, believing that her husband had obtained a divorce; the divorce was not granted until 1793, and although Jackson and Mrs. Robards were legally remarried immediately after, Jackson's political enemies found food for scandal in the marriage, and hounded him with it until Mrs. Jackson's death in 1828.

Jackson was a delegate to the convention which drew up the Constitution of Tennessee in 1796, and was elected to the House of Representatives. He resigned his seat in the house the following year to fill a vacancy in the Senate, and again resigned to become a Supreme Court Judge in Tennessee from 1798 to 1804. From then until 1811 he was engaged in several business ventures and in the management of his plantation, "The Hermitage," near Nashville. When war with England broke out in 1812 Jackson, who had been a major general in the Tennessee militia since 1802, was ordered to subdue the Creek Indians, who had recently gone on the warpath as a result of their friendship with the British and the incitement of Tecumseh. His victory over the Creeks at Horseshoe Bend (March 27, 1814) won him a commission as major-general in the United States Army. In December, 1814, he entered New Orleans and prepared the almost defenseless city for attack by the British. The British attack was successfully repulsed with almost no losses to the Americans. Although a peace treaty with Britain had been signed before the battle was fought, it made Jackson a national hero.

In 1818 Jackson was sent to put down Seminole uprisings in Florida, and again acting without direct orders he pursued the Indians into Pensacola, seized the Spanish town, hanged two British citizens who he believed had incited the Indians, and nearly brought on war with England and Spain. Hostilities were avoided by diplomacy on both sides, and Jackson was made governor of Florida in 1821 after the territory was purchased from Spain.

Jackson was elected Senator from Tennessee in 1823 and ran unsuccessfully for President in 1824; although he received more electoral votes than any other candidate, his votes were short of the majority necessary for election, and the decision was given to the House of Representatives, which elected John Quincy Adams. Jackson won the election of 1828 by a large majority, becoming the first President from a region west of the Appalachians. The "common people," aroused for the first time by an election based on personality rather than on principles, cheered Jackson as he rode to the White House, feeling that he, as a frontiersman and a soldier, was "one of them." Jackson reciprocated by initiating the "spoils system," whereby about one in ten government officials were removed and replaced by Jackson's friends. Many of the abuses of the spoils system have been exaggerated. Nevertheless, the advantages of the frequent rotation of officers introduced by the spoils system, which prevented a particular faction from becoming too long entrenched, were probably offset by a general lowering of the standard of officialdom as a result of Jackson's belief that a "man of intelligence" needed no special training or experience to fill a government post.

Jackson's policy, which was largely unknown when he was elected, occasioned much surprise and some criticism. His informal "kitchen cabinet" gave him unofficial advice and strengthened his power as president, leaving the regular Cabinet with less influence. He surprised those who assumed him to be, as a southerner, a partisan of states' rights, with his, "Our Union, it must be preserved!" to Vice-president Calhoun's "The Union, next to our liberty, most dear." He threatened South Carolina with a charge of treason if she persisted in defying the "tariff of abominations," a high tariff of 1828 thought by some to be unconstitutional and particularly unfair to the South. Although a man of property himself, Jackson opposed the Second Bank of the United States, chartered in 1816, which he believed tended to be monopolistic and against the interests of the agricultural South and West. The election of 1832 centered around the Bank issue, and Jackson interpreted his popular victory to mean the people empowered him to dissolve the Bank. He ordered government money to be deposited in various "pet" banks, which encouraged speculation; as a result of high tariffs the national debt was liquidated, and Jackson ordered surplus funds divided among the states as loans, thus withdrawing government money from the pet banks and resulting in a sudden tightening of credit that created a financial panic. At the end of his second term he retired to The Hermitage, still the idol of his followers and still reviled by his opponents.

Jackson's official documents are included in the *Messages and Papers of Presidents* (edited by J. D. Richardson, 1896), v. II and III. His letters were gathered by J. S. Bassett in *The Correspondence of Andrew Jackson* (7 v., 1926–35). His *Farewell Address* (1837) is a review of his two Presidential terms. Biographies of Jackson include James M. Parton's *Life of Andrew Jackson* (3 v., 1860); W. G. Sumner's *Andrew Jackson* (1882); J. S. Bassett's *The Life of Andrew Jackson* (1911); Marquis James' *Life of Andrew Jackson* (2 v., 1938). Studies on the Jacksonian period include Arthur Schlesinger, Jr.'s THE AGE OF JACKSON (1945); J. W. Ward's *Andrew Jackson; Symbol for an Age* (1955); G. G. Van Deusen's *The Jacksonian Era, 1828–1848* (1959). Novels in which Jackson appears as a character include Joseph B. Cobb's *The Creole, or, Siege of New Orleans* (1850); Winston Churchill's THE CROSSING (1904); Ellery H. Clark's *The Strength of the Hills* (1926); Samuel Hopkins Adams' *The Gorgeous Hussy* (1934); Alfred Leland Crabb's *Breakfast at the Hermitage* (1945); Odell and Willard Shepard's *Holdfast Gaines* (1946); Irving Stone's *The President's Lady* (1951). Laurence Stallings' and Maxwell Anderson's play, *First Flight* (1925), deals with an episode in Jackson's youth.

Jackson, Charles [Reginald] (b. Summit, N.J., April 6, 1903—d. Sept. 21, 1968), newspaperman, writer. Jackson's first novel was *The Lost Weekend* (1944), an immediate best seller and later a striking movie (1945). The novel describes the adventures, tragic and ridiculous, of an alcoholic; Jackson averred that the events were one-third autobiographical, one-third experiences of a friend, one-third "creative imagination." *The Fall of Valor* (1946) pictures the disintegration of a marriage because of the husband's homosexual tendencies. *The Outer Edges* (1948) tells of a sex maniac's murder of two children and how it affects various people. *The Sunnier Side* (1950) contains twelve stories reminiscent of Jackson's early days in an upstate New York village; *Earthly Creatures* (1953) is another collection of short stories. Lee

Rogow says that Jackson's novels resemble personally conducted travelogues through the realm of psychopathology.

Jackson, George Pullen (b. Monson, Me., Aug. 20, 1874—d. Jan. 19, 1953), folklorist, writer, teacher. Jackson studied philology in Dresden and at the University of Chicago (Ph.B. 1904; Ph.D. 1911) and for twenty-five years taught at Vanderbilt University, Nashville, Tenn. Through his curiosity about the Sacred Harp hymnals with their square, triangular, and diamond-shaped notes to indicate pitch, and his subsequent research on it, Jackson became a leading authority on American religious folksongs. He was the founder of the Tennessee State Sacred Harp Singing Association and became president of the Tennessee Folklore Society in 1942. Among his books: *Spiritual Folksongs of Early America* (1937); *White and Negro Spirituals—116 Country Folk Songs as Sung by Both Races* (1943); *Down-East Spirituals* (1943), a supplement to his 1937 book; *The Story of the Sacred Harp, 1844–1944, Religious Folk Songs as an American Institution* (1944); *Another Sheaf of White Spirituals* (1952), which he collected, edited and illustrated. See HYMNS.

Jackson, Helen [Maria Fiske] Hunt ["Saxe Holm"] (b. Amherst, Mass., Oct. 15, 1830—d. Aug. 12, 1885), poet, novelist, essayist. Some of Mrs. Jackson's early work appeared anonymously or under the pseudonym of Saxe

Holm. Widowed in 1863, she turned to writing poetry: *Verses by H.H.* (1870), *Sonnets and Lyrics* (1886). She first won a wide public with *Bits of Travel* (1872). After her second marriage in 1875 Mrs. Jackson made her home in Colorado Springs, where her ardent nature could not remain indifferent to the plight of the local Indians. She wrote a tract, A CENTURY OF DIS-

HONOR (1881), dealing with the U.S. government's injustices toward the Indians, and circulated it at her own expense to every member of Congress. As a result, she was appointed to a special commission studying the status of the Mission Indians. RAMONA (1884) was her fictional plea for the Indian, although the personal romance of Ramona and Alessandro overshadows the fate of the race as depicted in the book. The novel is still widely read and loved for its picture of the old Spanish life of southern California in its Indian summer.

Mrs. Jackson's friendship with EMILY DICKINSON, about which not much is known because most of their correspondence is lost, affords several clues to the life of the poet. *Esther Wynn's Love Letters*, the last one of the Saxe Holm stories (1874), and MERCY PHILBRICK'S CHOICE (1876), a novel, both made use of her knowledge of her friend's life, personality, romantic attachment, and talents, apparently with Emily Dickinson's knowledge.

Jackson, Joseph Henry (b. Madison, N.J., July 21, 1894—d. July 15, 1955), editor, radio broadcaster, novelist, author of travel and historical volumes. Jackson became prominent early in the 1920's in San Francisco literary circles, particularly as literary editor of the San Francisco *Chronicle* and as one of the first to broadcast literary commentaries. He served on the board of judges of the O. Henry Memorial Awards and the Harper Prize Novel contests. He was described in Gertrude Atherton's *My San Francisco* (1946). Among his books: *Mexican Interlude* (1936); *Tintypes in Gold* (1939); *Anybody's Gold* (1941); *The California Story* (1949); *Bad Company* (1949). He edited *The Gold Rush Album* (1949).

Jackson, Shirley (b. San Francisco, Dec. 14, 1919—d. Aug. 8, 1965), fiction writer. Miss Jackson's work, embracing such varied forms as the novel, the short story, and the semiautobiographical sketch, is notable for its strong contrasts both in subject matter and in mood. She and her husband, the critic, Stanley Edgar Hyman, live in Vermont. Her two autobiographical books, *Life Among the Savages* (1953) and *Raising Demons* (1957), offer a humorous chronicle of the life of a middle-class intellectual family in a small New England town. These books have been commended for their narrative grace and wit, their accurate representation of the speech of children, and their warm but unsentimental tone. With a degree of social commentary, this vein of polished realism is also present in Miss Jackson's shorter pieces, but a large proportion of these and virtually all her novels contain a strong element of the fantastic and terrifying. Typically, in such stories, supernatural happenings, or the eerie phenomena of morbid mental states, occur disturbingly against the most ordinary backgrounds, among the most ordinary people. *The Road Through the Wall* (1948), *Hangsaman* (1951), and *The Bird's Nest* (1954) are novels about young people in abnormal mental conditions. THE LOTTERY (1949), a collection of short stories, *The*

Sundial (1958), and *The Haunting of Hill House* (1959) feature fantastic and sometimes elusive allegories. *The Witchcraft of Salem Village* (1956) is a book for young people about the Salem witch trials. Her books have been praised for brilliance of style and their perceptive, suspenseful delineation of strange psychological states.

Jackson, Thomas Jonathan ["Stonewall"] (b. Clarksburg, Va. [now W. Va.], Jan. 21, 1824—d. May 10, 1863), soldier. A graduate of West Point and a veteran of the Mexican War, Jackson gained fame as a general in the Civil War. Robert E. Lee had the highest regard for him, and his men followed him with devotion and courage to a degree that earned for him and them the epithet "Stonewall." He was largely responsible for the Southern victories at the first Battle of Bull Run and in later battles and campaigns. While following up a victory at Chancellorsville he was accidentally wounded by his own men, and died several days later.

A great poet of the North, John Greenleaf Whittier, paid tribute to Jackson after his death in BARBARA FRIETCHIE (1863), based on an apocryphal incident. Jackson's last words as he lay dying, "Let us cross the river and rest in the shade of the trees," have inspired three fine poems: *Under the Shade of the Trees*, by his sister-in-law, Margaret Junkin Preston; *The Dying Words of Stonewall Jackson*, by Sidney Lanier; and *In Which General Jackson Accompanied by His Foot Cavalry Crosses Jordan*, by Martha Keller. The same words suggested the title of Ernest Hemingway's novel *Across the River and into the Trees* (1950). An Englishman, Col. G. F. R. Henderson, composed an excellent biography, *Stonewall Jackson* (2 v., 1898; reprinted 1 v., 1949). Burke Davis has written *They Called Him Stonewall* (1954). Others who have written on Jackson include Mary Ann Jackson, Robert L. Dabney, and Thomas J. Arnold. He appears as a leading character in several novels: John Esten Cooke's *Surry of Eagle's Nest* (1866); B. K. Benson's *Bayard's Courier* (1902); Mary Johnston's THE LONG ROLL (1911); Randall Parrish's *The Red Mist* (1914); Henry Kyd Douglas' *I Rode with Stonewall* (1940).

Jacobs, Joseph (b. Australia, Aug. 29, 1854—d. Jan. 31, 1916), historian, folklorist, Jewish scholar. Jacobs went to England early in life, took a degree at Cambridge, and won a reputation both as a scholar and as a popularizer of scholarly material. He came to the United States in 1900 and spent the rest of his life here, as editor of a revision of the *Jewish Encyclopedia* and of a magazine, the *American Hebrew*. He also taught English at the Jewish Theological Seminary. His literary output was enormous. His most widely read books were for children: *English Fairy Tales* (1890); *Celtic Fairy Tales* (1891); *The Fables of Aesop* (1889); *The Book of Wonder Voyages* (1896); *Europa's Fairy Book* (1916); and similar volumes. He also wrote *Studies in Jewish Statistics* (1891); *Tennyson and "In Memoriam"* (1892); *Barlaam and*

Josephat: English Lives of Buddha (1896); and *Jewish Contributions to Civilization* (1919).

Jaffe, Bernard (b. New York City, March 5, 1896—   ), chemist, teacher, writer on science. Long a teacher of science in secondary schools, Jaffe has written authoritatively on the development of science and on great scientists. *Crucibles* (1930; rev. ed., 1948), a series of biographical sketches, received the Francis Bacon award for "humanizing knowledge." Other books: *Chemical Calculations* (1926; rev. ed., 1958); *Outposts of Science* (1935); *New World of Chemistry* (1935; rev. ed., 1959); *Men of Science in America* (1944); *Chemistry Creates a New World* (1957); *Michelson and the Speed of Light* (1960).

Jalna (1927), a novel by MAZO DE LA ROCHE. This story of the Canadian family of the Whiteoaks in their family seat won the *Atlantic Monthly* novel prize and instantaneous success with the reading public. It was the first of a series of "Jalna" books, making at last a family saga of a dozen volumes. The Whiteoaks are a vigorous, individualistic lot, diverse from generation to generation.

James, Edwin (b. Weybridge, Vt., Aug. 27, 1797—d. Oct. 28, 1861), explorer, physician, geologist, compiler of travel accounts. As a young man James accompanied Major Stephen H. Long in exploring the upper Arkansas. Using his own notes and manuscript journals kept by others, he compiled a valuable and voluminous narrative, *An Account of an Expedition from Pittsburgh to the Rocky Mountains* (2 v., 1822–23); it was reprinted in R. G. Thwaites' *Early Western Travels* (1905). James also issued *A Narrative of the Captivity and Adventures of John Tanner* (1830).

James, Henry, Sr. (b. Albany, N.Y., June 3, 1811—d. Dec. 18, 1882), theologian, philosopher, lecturer. The father of HENRY JAMES, JR., and WILLIAM JAMES originally intended to become a lawyer, for a while attended Princeton Theological Seminary, left because of an irreconcilable dissent from Calvinism. He adopted the religious ideas of Robert Sandeman, but later became to some extent a Swedenborgian (see SWEDENBORGIANISM). He was wealthy enough to do as he pleased and to write as he pleased. He traveled abroad, knew many eminent men personally, and enjoyed a rich family life, including the company of a daughter, Alice, as remarkable as his two sons. This family life is described in vivid detail in F. O. Matthiessen's *The James Family* (1947).

Among James' books: *Christianity the Logic of Creation* (1857); *Substance and Shadow* (1863); *The Secret of Swedenborg* (1869); *Society the Redeemed Form of Man* (1879). His *Literary Remains* were edited (1884) by William James. His system of philosophy was discussed by J. A. Kellogg (1885) and by Frederic Harold Young (1951); the latter finds him one of the few American thinkers whose metaphysics is Neo-Platonic and Gnostic in its genius, while his social philosophy "stands between, or more accurately beyond, the Calvin-

istic and Emersonian extremes." Herbert W. Schneider believes his aim was to reconcile individualism and collectivism, "but in practice he achieved little more than to be a mild gad-fly." Austin Warren wrote *The Elder Henry James* (1934), Frederic H. Young *The Philosophy of Henry James Sr.* (1951).

James, Henry, Jr. (b. New York City, April 15, 1843—d. Feb. 28, 1916), novelist, writer of short stories and *nouvelles*, literary criticism, accounts of his travels, autobiography, and a wealth of extraordinary letters. James has been

most widely celebrated as the novelist whose concern with form gave to novelists writing in English a compelling example of the fruits of structural consistency. Joseph Warren Beach's emphasis (in *The Method of Henry James*, 1918, rev. 1954) on the "point of view" has been most influential in this respect. Beach made plain James' principle: never to allow anything to enter the novel or story which was not represented as a perception or experience of one of the characters.

Important though it is, this aspect of James does not of course account for the powers which made him a major novelist of the late 19th and early 20th centuries and assuredly one of the greatest who has written in English. He was the grandson of one of the first American millionaires, William James of Albany, and the son of HENRY JAMES, SR., whose share of the paternal fortune was large enough to enable him to live comfortably in New York, Newport, and Cambridge, with extended intervals abroad. The novelist's father lost a leg as a consequence of fighting a fire while a child. He failed to complete his studies at the theological seminary at Princeton, but his interest in theology persisted. After a period of enthusiasm for Fourier, he undertook a new theological system, only to fall into a severe depression, which began with a bout of panic. A friend recommended the works of Swedenborg, whom James was later to call "insipid with veracity." He accepted the doctrine, and tried, in his own extensive writings, to combat the insipidity. His books harp so insistently on a few strings, however, that they are almost as boring as those of Swedenborg. In conversation and in his letters he was both gayer and wittier, though he was forever illustrating his all-inclusive system. (See *The Thought and Character of William James* by R. B. Perry and *The James Family* by F. O. Matthiessen, in which many of his letters appear.) "Father's ideas" were made game of by his lively family, although both WILLIAM JAMES (1842–1910), the future psychologist and philosopher, and Henry testified to their force and appeal when presented by their father, whose aberrant brilliance was recognized by Emerson and other well-known contemporaries.

Henry, Jr., recorded memories of his childhood and youth in two autobiographical volumes, *A Small Boy and Others* and *Notes of a Son and Brother*. The latter title is suggestive. As his biographer Leon Edel (*Henry James: The Untried Years, 1843–1870*) insists, William, a vigorous and quick-witted elder brother, must have posed a formidable challenge. The father stood ready to interpret the whole world; William was busy testing and exploring it. In these circumstances what the novelist calls his "visiting mind" took command. He became rather consciously a spectator. Though New York had much to offer his infant sensibility (in particular its theaters, in which he acquired a lifelong passion for the stage), the chief spectacle (which absorbed the whole family) was "Europe." Abroad, there was a world of high complexity and distinction, while America offered only three kinds of people: "the busy, the tipsy and Daniel Webster." The father of the family was somewhat nervously anxious to secure the best possible education for his brood (there were eventually four boys and a girl). The boys went to a bewildering succession of schools, and, in pursuit of what their father described as a better "sensuous education," were taken to Europe a number of times, where, under tutors and in Swiss and German schools, they acquired a cosmopolitan culture without a trace of cosmopolitan weariness. The passage in James' work most sharply suggestive of what Europe meant to him is an account of a visit to the Galerie d'Apollon at the Louvre in *A Small Boy and Others*.

William had thrown himself into painting (which he was soon to give up for biology), and Henry briefly tried to emulate him. But he had always scribbled, and in 1860 he found needed encouragement from the artist John La Farge, who urged him to write more seriously. He undertook some translations from the French, and got his first editorial rejections. James was eighteen in this year. The two younger brothers fought with distinction in the Civil War, but William and Henry did not enter the army. Henry's memoir of the period suggests that an "obscure hurt" received while helping to put out a fire in Newport had incapacitated him. Edel's conclusion is that James had suffered a strained back, by no means incapacitating, but emotionally linked with his father's loss of a leg. The injury filled an emotional need. It was an excuse to be passive. He need not fight; more important, he need not assert himself sexually. In 1862 James entered Harvard Law School, but left at the end of the school year. In 1864 his first story, "A Tragedy of Error," was printed, and the *North American Review* published his first book review. The columns of the *Nation* and the *Atlantic Monthly* were soon open to him, and he profited much by the friendship and encouragement of William Dean Howells, who became editor of the latter magazine in 1871. James' early fiction was rather more gloomy and subtle than the popular taste would allow, but Howells stood by him staunchly. The reviews James wrote in these early years were biting and full of discrimination, which reflected not simply an early immersion in English fiction but a close acquaintance with contemporary French practice as well.

In the early stories Hawthorne counts for much, but the emotional state of the young author counts for more. James could not escape the theme of young love, but he handled it with elaborate detours suggestive of his own feeling of incapacity for the male role. This is particularly apparent in his first novel, *Watch and Ward*, which was serialized in the *Atlantic* in 1871. (Most of James' novels first ran in magazines. However, the dates of publication given below are those of their publication as books.) James' work improved greatly after his first independent journey to Europe in his twenty-sixth year (1869). The effect of this visit was overwhelming. Florence, Venice, and Rome swept him off his feet. Yet he saw all these wonders as an American. "Travelling Companions" (1870) makes this very clear. A mere immersion in Europe was to be deplored. What is the right use of European experience for an American? is a question which is handled in many ways by the stories of the seventies. "A Passionate Pilgrim" (1871), the most ambitious of James' works up to that time, is unhappily affected by his use of the rather clumsy device (which had haunted Hawthorne) of the American who returns to find his English heritage. After James returned home in 1870, stories and travel sketches poured forth in profusion. During a second trip to Europe (1872–74) James wrote his best story to date, "A MADONNA OF THE FUTURE," and began his first novel of consequence, *Roderick Hudson*.

During these years James was much concerned with the question of taking up a permanent residence abroad. Edel suggests that to his sense that the European scene offered the cultural complication necessary to a writer we ought to add James' embarrassed response to the demand of the elder Henry James that his boys marry and settle down. Marriage was never in question for the novelist, whose only serious interest in a woman had taken the form of a rather distant worship. His passionately admired cousin, Minny Temple, had died in 1870 while he was abroad. Minny had posed an awkward challenge, but her death enshrined her for him. She became in retrospect a kind of priestess of possibility, of "moral spontaneity," whose gift for life seemed to him as great as any he had ever known. The passages in *Notes of a Son and Brother* which describe Minny as he had known her in the summer of 1865 name her "the heroine of our common scene." She was to remain *his* heroine and to appear in *The Portrait of a Lady* and *The Wings of the Dove*.

For whatever complex of reasons, the son and brother took flight from the paternal roof in 1875, settling first in Paris, where he knew Edmond de Goncourt, Maupassant, Flaubert, and —most important to him—Turgenev. In 1876 he moved to England, where he was to spend the rest of his life. *Roderick Hudson* was published as a book in that year. A list of the notable works of the seventies would include, in addition to those named above, "Madame de Mauves," THE AMERICAN (1877), "Four Meetings," *The Europeans* (1878), "An International Episode," "Daisy Miller," "A Bundle of Letters," and "The Pension Beaurepas." (A rather weak novel, *Confidence*, was published in 1879.) James' first book, A PASSIONATE PILGRIM AND OTHER TALES, had come out in 1875.

The international theme dominates the period. It represents not simply a rewarding device for making use of James' talents and personal history, but an adjustment to the question of expatriation. In juxtaposing his Americans with Europeans James was (sometimes a bit anxiously) preserving his native note. He had a delightful gift of hitting off the consequences of an encounter between characters of differing national origins (as in "A Bundle of Letters," and more ambitiously in "An International Episode"). "Madame de Mauves" had earlier demonstrated his insight into the dramatic possibilities of such collisions. The American girl in this story is a frightening figure who cares for nothing but status and external propriety. Her profligate husband, a member of the French aristocracy, is finally driven to suicide, and the young American who had admired her gives a thankful shiver at his escape.

James' first full-scale effort, RODERICK HUDSON, though it has fine passages of social observation of Northampton, Massachusetts, and presents us with a striking little group of Romans, including, of course, American expatriates, does not quite hold together. Rowland Mallet, who launches a talented American youth on his career as a sculptor, is too closely akin to the psychically disabled figures who had represented James himself in earlier work, and were fortunately

to vanish after the publication of *Confidence*. Roderick himself is too giddy and savage a figure for his creator to handle.

To find the right scale and the right situation for the sort of thing he was prepared to do at this stage was James' problem. He solved it brilliantly in THE EUROPEANS, which, though less ambitious than *Roderick Hudson*, is almost perfectly done. The encounter of Felix Young and the Baroness Münster, the "Europeans" of the title, with their New England relatives, the Wentworths, is sparely rendered, but it is not, as William James called it, "thin." Every stroke tells; it is a comedy of manners, but the manners are, as they are everywhere in James, the index of moral commitment or the lack of it.

DAISY MILLER, a long story which was serialized in England while *The Europeans* was being published month by month in the *Atlantic* (1878), was an immediate popular success and was quickly pirated in America. The American girl, armored and blinded by her innocence, who does what she likes—to the horror of the American colony in Rome, which is full of "European" suspicions of her conduct—became a figure all too representative of James' work for his own comfort. The pathos of Daisy, who dies of fever partly because the fatally expatriated Winterbourne had not found it possible to believe in her or discover her love for him, made her attractive to a wide public, and editors who kept asking for more international tales with attractive American girls were to plague James for years. Since he lived by his pen, he often found ingenious ways of satisfying them, but he was careful to provide no more dolls for the public to take to its grossly beating heart.

James' *Hawthorne* (1879) is a tempered tribute to an American writer who had done much despite the provincial limitations of his residence. It ought to be borne in mind that Hawthorne's background is that of New England, and James always felt himself a New Yorker.

WASHINGTON SQUARE (1880), laid in the neighborhood in which James had grown up in New York City, is concerned with a struggle between father and daughter over the unattractive daughter's unworthy suitor. It is as close to Balzac as James was to come, depending as it does on characters whose beliefs and capacities are initially posited by the author and allowed to work themselves out to an inevitable consequence. It is much more characteristic of the later James to make character emerge as the felt consequence of actions described in the story itself.

James' life in London during this period is very sketchily chronicled in *The Middle Years*, a posthumously published fragment of what was to have been a third autobiographical volume. But here as elsewhere his letters furnish much evidence. (No complete collection is available. Percy Lubbock edited two volumes [1920]; aside from volumes devoted to letters to individuals, there is a recent short collection, *The Selected Letters of Henry James*, 1960, ed. by Leon Edel.) James floated on a rising tide of social success in these years. In one letter he reports that he dined out 107 times during the current season. Summer tours to France and Italy and visits to the great country houses whose amenities he celebrated in his fiction filled the time he could spare from writing in the succeeding years.

Frederick W. Dupee (*Henry James*, 1951, rev. 1956) suggests that in the eighties James was forced to come to terms with the fact that he was living the life of an Englishman. His American characters reflect the change. They no longer afford a test of European culture by simple juxtaposition (as in "Daisy Miller"), but are themselves tested and found to be complex and equivocal in their own fashion. It is Dupee's point that this recognition accompanied a development on the part of James from high accomplishment to authentic greatness.

Whatever the causes, THE PORTRAIT OF A LADY (1881) is one of the finest novels in English. James launches the charming Isabel Archer on a great flight from the Albany of his childhood years to Europe, the scene of infinite possibilities. Endowed with a fortune by her disabled cousin, Ralph Touchett, she is caught by a fortune-hunting aesthete and condemned to a horrible marriage. The novel functions in terms of inverted perspectives: Isabel had seemed to demand and deserve a creative moral freedom; yet her demand is logically answered by spiritual enslavement, and the reader is made to realize how self-engrossed the original desire had been. James' fine prose comes fully into its own in this novel. It is graceful, flexible, powerful, and metaphorically denser than his preceding work. He seems almost magically to find under his hand the very word which will make for a figurative extension and deepening of his meaning. Few can write English with the exquisite sense of its exact force and of every nuance which gives us the sense of complete mastery. This perfection of control is usually accorded to the masters of French prose, whom we imagine to have an instrument of small range at their command. The great theme of James' preceding decade, the question of how one is to take possession of the great world, is handled here by a finished novelist who succeeds in giving to his central character a fullness of existence which defies abstract definition. Some critics, notably F. R. Leavis (*The Great Tradition*, 1949), find no greater achievement in the whole of James' work. If, as many have supposed, James has here imagined how it would have been had *he* died (in the person of Ralph Touchett) and Minny Temple had been endowed with the fullness of opportunity, he has not in the least compromised with his sense of actuality in imagining a career for his cousin.

Two other major works of the eighties, THE BOSTONIANS and THE PRINCESS CASAMASSIMA, are likewise novelistic in the sense that they offer more "news of life" than can be tidily summed up. The first, James' only big work with a wholly American setting, embraces a remarkable range of American experience without compelling it to the ends of form in the rigorous fashion of *The Portrait* or its other successors. Speaking generally, James, once he had finished his apprenticeship, never dealt with society panoramically, or as background, and this unaccustomed relaxation in *The Bostonians* must qualify our conclusions about the meaning of his uses of American and European experience. *The Princess Casamassima*, though it embraces much material which has to do with anarchist activity, the expression of widespread social unrest in the eighties, does so in stricter subservience to James' structural ends. While *The Bostonians* is a success in its kind, the success of *The Princess* is more questionable. James imposes on one character the task of discovering whether the glories of Europe's cultural accomplishments had been worth their cost in suffering and blood. Hyacinth Robinson has indeed had "more news of life than he knew what to do with," and the reader finds himself all too conscious of James' wide intention. Lionel Trilling's praise of the novel's dramatic fidelity to the atmosphere of revolution at the time is an answer worth noting to the charge so often repeated that James never dealt with social actuality (*The Liberal Imagination*, 1950).

James made two journeys to America during the early eighties. His mother died during the first, and the second was occasioned by the fatal illness of his father. He was not thereafter to see his own country until his visit of 1904 and 1905. London was steadily his residence until, in 1898, he bought Lamb House in Sussex. The publication of THE TRAGIC MUSE (1890) is felt by some to mark the beginning of that elaboration of his style which, though both attacked and defended by his critics, is admitted by all to have changed the character of his work, if only in the sense that it demanded a fuller measure of attention from his readers. The fact that during the nineties James adopted the habit of dictating his extraordinarily long and complicated periods is a wonder, but not in itself an explanation of the increasing complexity of his prose. (This question will be discussed below in connection with *The Wings of the Dove* and *The Golden Bowl*.)

It is not an accident that at the end of the eighties James wrote a novel (*The Tragic Muse*) which explores the meaning of pursuing the arts against the philistine background of contemporary English life. Both *The Bostonians* and *The Princess* had been commercial failures. He had done some other fine things during the eighties (THE ASPERN PAPERS, for example), but the novels succeeding *The Portrait* in which he sought to come to terms with a mass of social observations had been meat too strong for both England and America. The question posed by Hyacinth Robinson is apocalyptic, truly radical, and the Boston of *The Bostonians* is shown to be spiritually bankrupt and threatened by mere money worship. This judgment on the Athens of America found no favor there.

The public had more of an excuse to ignore *The Tragic Muse*, which is somewhat awkwardly managed as narrative. James' interesting study of his "muse," an actress, is a prelude to his serious theatrical ventures of the first half of the nineties. These were not uniformly unsuccessful, but they did not bring the returns James hoped for, nor was the stage much enriched by his plays. When, in 1895, he was hooted from the stage at the opening night of *Guy Domville*, he was moved to rededicate himself to fiction, although he never quite abandoned his hope of theatrical success. (The story is told at length in Leon Edel's introduction to *The Complete Plays of Henry James*, 1949.)

James' work in the later nineties can be grouped in various ways. He produced an extraordinary group of stories having to do with artists, among them *The Real Thing, The Lesson of the Master, The Middle Years,* and *The Death of the Lion*. (This last story, although it brings its artist to a pitiable end, contains some of the funniest passages in James, in whom humor is not nearly so rare as most people seem to think.) *The Real Thing* is a parable about fiction which may be taken to illustrate what Dorothy Van Ghent calls "the identity of the aesthetic and the moral" in James. Between 1896 and 1901 larger works emerged steadily: *The Other House, The Spoils of Poynton, What Maisie Knew, The Awkward Age,* and *The Sacred Fount*. In addition James wrote two *nouvelles,* "The Turn of the Screw" and "In the Cage."

The least intrinsically interesting, "THE TURN OF THE SCREW" is the most famous of the lot. James meant to mystify and alarm us, and he did, employing his principle that the imagined horror was worse than any that could be clearly specified. (The reader is invited to supply his own sense of the most terrible possibility.) More critical articles have been written about this *nouvelle* than anything else James wrote (the most famous is Edmund Wilson's "The Ambiguity of Henry James" in *The Triple Thinkers*). To put a stop to all this one has only to ask: What would be the result of certain knowledge that the governess imagined the horrors *or* equally certain knowledge that they were real? On two counts, nil. First, an amusing yarn (James called it a "*jeu d'esprit*") would be less amusing; second, and more important, no substantial illumination of the practice of a great artist would result.

James' choice of theme and method in the group of longer works listed above is more radically experimental than before. He had entered upon what for most writers would have been a fourth career. After his apprenticeship of the sixties, his fine and enduring work of the seventies, the achieved greatness of the eighties had been followed by five years of dogged effort to learn the craft of the stage, interspersed with the writing of some highly distinguished stories. His rededication to fiction was accompanied by a resolution to make use of what he had learned in the theater. In *The Other House,* literally adapted from one of his plays, he achieves a hair-raising theatrical directness of effect, but formally the work is halfway between theater

and book. To the anti-Jamesians, the most infuriating of this series of experiments is the last in the order of production, THE SACRED FOUNT (1901). In this parable on the wrong uses of the imagination the reader seldom knows where to pin his sentiments. But there is little doubt as to James' general moral intention, common to this work and many others, among which we may mention *The Spoils of Poynton* and *The Birthplace* (1903).

In James the great sin is, to use St. Augustine's term, *cupiditas,* which takes many forms, most simply the greed for "things," as in "the spoils" of Poynton, a collection of precious bric-a-brac. James' work is full of collectors who entertain the delusion that they may grow spiritually fatter by grasping the creations of truly imaginative men. Another form is mere lust which denies the creative uses of the other partner. Still another is the "tourist's vice," as we may call it, the attempt to make a possession of one's exquisitely cultivated sensibility. A completely frozen and dead form of this vice is to think of one's social status as aristocrat or man of wealth as a guarantee of one's value. The opposed value we may call *caritas,* though in this use we somewhat extend Augustine's term. It is not simply a wide spiritual generosity, but the acts of the generous *imagination,* particularly the power of the artist to celebrate life rather than to try to possess things, or the power of the young American girl, a Milly Theale or a Maggie Verver, to sacrifice herself in the interests of life and growth. Either the artist or the girl carries the burden of asserting this value for James; never both in the same work, for their functions are analogous. This broad opposition is the root of the theological system of the elder James, which the novelist appears to have absorbed without being fully aware of the measure of his debt. James' own way of putting the nature of the highest possible value involves the term *consciousness,* the furthest possible extension of which would attest the fullest realization of our common humanity.

The narrator of *The Sacred Fount* does not so much celebrate life as attempt to appropriate the events in the lives of those around him as material for his fantasy. Even the most ardent Jamesians are content to call this a minor work. The battle rages much more hotly over WHAT MAISIE KNEW and THE AWKWARD AGE. Critics have pointed out that Maisie, the telegraphist of "In the Cage," Nanda Brookenham of *The Awkward Age,* and the narrator of *The Sacred Fount* are all outsiders, excluded from the scene on which they seek, with or without success, to interpose. Moreover, the scene from which they are excluded is predominantly the grown-up world in which sex plays a large part. *What Maisie Knew* is an extraordinary technical tour de force in which a child seeks to make sense of a world of sexual intrigue among her elders, and emerges not only unscathed, but equipped with a burgeoning moral sense. This took a supreme deftness on James' part, but the question is whether the choice of a central consciousness so bereft leads to more than a display of virtuosity. *The Awkward Age,* for which higher claims have been made, is clearly the greater work. The title refers to the moment at which the adolescent girl must be allowed to leave the nursery and enter the drawing room, where she will inevitably stifle "good," that is, sexually tinged, conversation. "Mrs. Brook" is wonderfully done. She is the center of a circle which prides itself on its conversational tone, and her efforts to maintain it against poverty and the shifting needs and desires of those who surround her might be thought of as a touching and poetic exploration of the fate of any established scene of communication—if only there were anything to talk about. Unfortunately, there is not. The substance of the talk may be described as "the higher sniggering," and has in it so little of the meat of the converse of adult men and women that it is reminiscent of the dog's view of the family dinner as he lies under the table. Frederick W. Dupee, whose book is certainly the best on the whole range of James' work, feels that the novel reflects insight into the quality of the drawing-room life of the period. Another point of undeniable interest about this novel is its fictional method. It is not (like *The Other House*) a play turned into a novel; rather it is a novel scenically conceived, with very little interstitial tissue. As James puts it in his preface, each scene is to be a separate light on the total situation.

The stories of writers and artists have an obvious thematic tie with these longer works, since in each instance save one, *The Middle Years,* the artist suffers from the blankness of his uncomprehending audience. That James underwent an inner turmoil in these years and that he somehow came to terms with himself after writing *The Sacred Fount* seems clear. This resolution was, according to some critics, including F. R. Leavis and the present writer, achieved at some cost to the range of his concern with the actual world. One of the possibilities is that his identification with his system-making father deepened (see Saul Rosenzweig, "The Ghost of Henry James," *Partisan Review,* XI [Fall, 1944], 435–55). This, however, is the view of a minority.

The three novels James composed just after the turn of the century, THE AMBASSADORS (1903), THE WINGS OF THE DOVE (1902), and THE GOLDEN BOWL (1904), named here in the order of composition, are thought by many to be James' greatest works. James himself believed *The Ambassadors* to be the most perfectly constructed of his novels. The elaboration of the prose reaches its full measure in these three books; to an extraordinary degree it isolates his characters from the felt pressures of the commonplace in order to clear the ground for James' exquisite notation of their awareness of each other's consciousness. Perhaps the most suggestive of literary comparisons ranges them not beside precedent novels, but the dramas of Racine (see Francis Fergusson, "The Drama in

The Golden Bowl," Hound and Horn, VII [April–June, 1934], 407–13).

Of course the "awareness" of these characters is not given to all alike. Strether, the central consciousness of *The Ambassadors,* who has a measure of imagination, is dispatched by a New England matriarch to rescue her son, Chad, from a (presumably) designing woman in Paris. From Mrs. Newsome's point of view, that of "fine cold thought," or New England righteousness, Strether's mission fails. Strether discovers Chad vastly improved in *appearance;* he discovers in fact the whole vast and enticing realm of appearance, most significantly in Madame de Vionnet, Chad's mistress, and seeks finally to persuade him *not* to desert her. This inversion of perspective is of course reminiscent of that of *The Portrait of a Lady,* the work which, after *The Ambassadors,* James thought most "rounded." Strether, not being an artist or an American girl, has no means with which to reconcile appearance and morality; he retires ruefully with his capital of experience and the sense that his moral rightness depends on his not, out of the whole affair, having gotten anything for himself. Many critics have found in this essentially puritanical conclusion a momentous Jamesian affirmation of "life." They cite the germinal passage in James' notebooks (see *The Notebooks of Henry James,* ed. by F. O. Matthiessen and Kenneth Murdock, 1947). A friend had reported that William Dean Howells had, on the Parisian scene, urged a young man to "live" before it was too late, and these are the very words which Strether employs in Gloriani's garden. But James clearly saw around this wholesale injunction. All his great invokers and encouragers of life are artists or young girls, whose actions are in some way morally creative. Indeed, it may be said that the strength of this novel *as* a novel derives from the fact that James had chosen a restricted consciousness, a "comparatively" imaginative man, as he calls him in his notebooks, for his hero. It is on this lonely particularity of Strether's, lost as he is between the realms of appearance and morality, that the novel founds its appeal to us. Isabel Archer and Strether may for this reason be called James' finest central characters. They are not used up when the book ends.

There is dispute as to James' success in avoiding this danger in *The Wings of the Dove,* which reminds some of Gide's dictum that James too fully knew his characters (see *The Question of Henry James: A Collection of Critical Essays,* ed. by F. W. Dupee, 1947). For F. O. Matthiessen (*Henry James: The Major Phase,* 1944) and R. P. Blackmur (see his introduction to *The Golden Bowl*) the three last novels are the summit of James' achievement. Part of the problem for the critic here is a semantic one. If these are novels, they are certainly novels with a difference. For one thing there is the element which one commentator has called "structural imagery" and the present writer (with a differing view of its nature and importance) has described as the "emblematic" element in these novels. An abstract statement of a complicated kind of artistic process must suffice here. What James has done is to make the novel, not a dramatic poem, but functionally akin to a dramatic poem, a new literary kind in which figurative definition has the same force and is to be apprehended on the same plane as his most explicit dialogue. When, in *The Golden Bowl*, Adam Verver likens the Prince to a smooth and golden surface, a bowl in fact, his metaphor is not tributary to his actions; it *is* one of his actions. When Densher sees the plaza at Venice as the "drawing-room" of Europe "profaned and desecrated" by the storm, he is putting forward something which is to be as immediately apprehended as a part of the meaning of the book as the report of a pistol shot. A more general way of stating the matter is to say that just as in a medieval bestiary the meaning of the pictured beasts is their exhibition of a particular divine purpose, so in the James of these final novels appearance is completely at the service of consciousness. What this ultimately means is that every least thing that appears is figurative, because only in this guise does appearance have meaning. All is foreground; there is no background.

The Wings of the Dove has to do with a pair of lovers who conspire to secure the wealth of a dying American heiress. The scheme to have the young man marry Milly Theale is thwarted by a disappointed suitor who gives away the plot. Milly nonetheless leaves a fortune to the young man, who finds himself unable to accept it or to marry his fellow conspirator if she does. He is left with his memory of Milly, and his mistress, who had wanted everything, gets nothing. The emblematic elements are more to the fore in this novel than in *The Ambassadors*. The temptation is to sort them out and call them allegorical. But in allegory things stand for abstract qualities or values. James' intention is to achieve an identity between what is represented and its value. Milly Theale is quite commonly called a "redeemer" by James' readers. But those who understand his work best are using the word as a sign, a pointer, not making an analogy with Christ. Milly is a redeemer insofar as she is seen to function as one. When she sees those who copy paintings in the National Gallery as living under water, submerged in appearance, far from the (creative) sacred fount, we recognize her authority as quasi-divine, just as we recognize it in her descent from the high places of the Alps upon London, and her inescapable spiritual power when her wings "cover" the lovers at the end. The actual difficulty is that the force of these emblems depends upon intensive reading, and that this novel does not by itself establish all the emblematic elements it employs. It does not stand upon its own feet as a work of art. (The difficulty is at least in part avoided if one accepts the contention of R. P. Blackmur that the last three novels are in fact a trilogy, and therefore interdependent.)

Surely James' most difficult work, *The Golden Bowl* has the simplest possible germ. James set down in his notebook an anecdote about a father and daughter who married, only to discover that their spouses were lovers. This germ exfoliated into a very big novel, in which an apocalyptic pair of marriages, consummating a union between America and Europe, are saved by James' final "redeemer." Adam Verver and his daughter, Maggie, are inexhaustibly wealthy Americans, engaged in one of those colossal raiding expeditions which, at the turn of the century, were common among American millionaires. Adam proposes to make the museum at American City unsurpassed. Fanny Assingham, herself a partner in an international marriage of an earlier day, brings together Maggie and Prince Amerigo, in whom Adam recognizes a collector's piece of the highest order. Maggie marries, and Adam finds himself by this stroke detached and vulnerable to prowling females. At this juncture Charlotte Stant returns from America. She and the Prince had (like the conspiratorial pair in *The Wings of the Dove*) earlier found themselves too poor to marry. The matter is arranged. Adam marries Charlotte. Yet the old intimacy of father and daughter persists, despite Maggie's love for her husband. The Prince and Charlotte are thrown together—in this book it is the sexually alive who are excluded—and exclaiming, "What in the world else can we do?" they become lovers.

The work is largely composed of conversations among these four and Fanny Assingham, who resumes the whole situation for her husband, the Colonel, at the end of the first volume. Her summary is masterly and conclusive from the viewpoint of appearance. But in the second volume it is Maggie's consciousness that presides; the reality of a saving love must arrange appearances afresh. The process is initiated when, by an ironic inversion, Fanny destroys the golden bowl to preserve the appearances she had created in bringing about the marriages— but the bowl, evidence of the liaison between Charlotte and the Prince, is an index of reality, as its destruction shows. Maggie's blank American "good faith" becomes knowledge of the sinful world; she is in a position to help the Prince, though she must protect Adam at all costs. Her function as redeemer is to deny herself; knowing the reality, she must affirm the appearances to save them all; she goes into "society," and undergoes her Calvary at Fawns when, charged by Charlotte, she repudiates all her knowledge. In the end she wins. Charlotte, isolated, is led off to America as cicerone of the collection at American City. Adam's taste is vindicated.

Some of those who have praised *The Golden Bowl* most highly have questioned the relation of Adam and Maggie as approaching the incestuous, and have quarreled with James' failure to question the sources and meaning of Adam's wealth. Knowing James' work as we now do, we must assume that these things make sense within the novel as he conceived it. Dorothea

Krook (in *Interpretations of American Literature,* ed. by Feidelson and Brodtkorb, 1959) has suggested that we must think of the late James as employing the neo-Hegelian "doctrine of internal relations." The world of each novel is exhaustively understood. Whether we like what happens in it or not, we must grant that everything in it plays its defining part in relation to everything else.

After completing these three novels, James returned to America for a visit of ten months, during which he lectured widely and collected material for the book published in 1907 as THE AMERICAN SCENE. Upon his return to Lamb House in 1905 he began the extensive task of revising and prefacing his works for the New York Edition (1907–1909) of his works. He excluded certain novels and stories. The whole finally ran to twenty-six volumes, including two posthumously published novels left incomplete, *The Sense of the Past* and *The Ivory Tower,* added in 1917. The important prefaces to this edition, which detail the circumstances of composition and supply data as to the origin of many of his works, comprise an extended commentary on the craft of fiction. They were edited separately by R. P. Blackmur (*The Art of the Novel,* 1934). The general effect of the revision, or "reseeing," as James called it, was simply to tease more out of the work as originally conceived by adding qualifications and metaphors —never by changing his original intention. It must not be inferred that all James' finest work is listed here. The tale is too long. In the year of the publication of *The Ambassadors* he also issued a volume containing two of his best stories, "The Beast in the Jungle" and "The Birthplace." Much later, in 1910, a striking and in some ways quite distinctive collection of stories, *The Finer Grain,* was published. (See the chapter on James in *The Literary History of the United States,* 1948, v. II, by R. P. Blackmur.)

In 1908, while still engaged on the New York Edition, James undertook a further theatrical venture. In 1909 a serious illness left him unable to work. He journeyed to Germany with his brother William, who was gravely ill; they returned to America together and William died there in 1910. In the following year James published a minor novel, *The Outcry,* and Harvard awarded him an honorary degree, as Oxford did in 1912. This was another year of grave illness for James. *A Small Boy and Others* appeared in 1913; *Notes of a Son and Brother* in the following year. When the war broke out, James found himself unable to continue *The Ivory Tower,* an ambitious novel with an American setting. He threw himself into the work of propaganda, hospital visiting, and so forth, anxious to serve his adopted country as best he could. In order to signalize his sense of the importance of the cause, he became a naturalized British subject in 1915. He died in London in the following year.

Judged externally, the importance of James has been steadily increasing since the centennial of his birth in 1943. At that time it was difficult to obtain many of his works. At the opening of the sixties almost all his important works were readily available in inexpensive editions, and the publisher of the New York Edition took the unusual step of beginning to reissue its sumptuously printed volumes. The James vogue of the forties has passed, and major critics have not lately been so much concerned with him, but this largely means that his position is now taken for granted.

Among the most important books for the student of James not mentioned in the body of this article are: Leroy Phillips, *A Bibliography of the Writings of Henry James* (rev. ed., 1930); Lyon N. Richardson, *Henry James: Representative Selections* (1941), which has a useful chronology; Morton Dauwen Zabel, *The Portable Henry James* (rev. 1951), which has an annotated bibliography; *Eight American Authors,* issued by the Modern Language Association (1956), which has an extended bibliographical essay by Robert E. Spiller; and Leon Edel and Dan Laurence, *Bibliography of Henry James* (1957).

QUENTIN ANDERSON

James, Jesse [Woodson] (b. Kearney, Mo., Sept. 5, 1847—d. April 3, 1882), bandit. Sympathizers with the South, Jesse and his brother Frank joined a guerrilla band and served with it until the end of the Civil War. In 1866 Jesse was declared an outlaw, and for the next sixteen years was a desperado who committed daring crimes, stole from banks and railroads, caused the deaths of a number of people, and managed nevertheless to become a popular hero, an American Robin Hood. A price of $10,-000 was placed on his head, and a member of his band earned it by shooting him while his back was turned. His murder was narrated in an anonymous ballad called *Jesse James,* and he became the hero of innumerable dime novels, e.g., *Life and Death of Jesse James* (1901) in *The James Boys Weekly.* William Rose Benét wrote a poem called *Jesse James* describing the bandit's career. Jesse James, Jr., wrote *Jesse James, My Father* (1899); other biographical material appeared in Robertus Love's *The Rise and Fall of Jesse James* (1926). Three recent works are Will Henry's *Death of a Legend* (1954), Homer Croy's *Jesse James Was My Neighbor* (1949), and Carl Breihan's *Complete and Authentic Life of Jesse James* (1953).

James, Marquis (b. Springfield, Mo., Aug. 29, 1891—d. Nov. 19, 1955), journalist, biographer. James spent his childhood in and near Enid, Okla., and early worked on the local newspaper. From 1915 on, he lived in New York City. He was twice awarded the Pulitzer Prize, in 1930 for his biography of Sam Houston and in 1938 for his two-volume biography of Andrew Jackson. His published works also include: *A History of the American Legion* (1923); *They Had Their Hour* (1934); *Mr. Garner of Texas* (1939); *Alfred I. DuPont: The Family Rebel* (1941); *Biography of a Business* (1942) and

Metropolitan Life (1947), two histories of insurance companies; *The Cherokee Strip* (1945), which describes his Oklahoma boyhood.

James, William (b. New York City, Jan. 11, 1842—d. Aug. 26, 1910), physiologist, psychologist, philosopher, teacher. After an education that offered him every cultural opportunity, this son of HENRY JAMES, SR., began in 1872 to teach at Harvard, his alma mater. He first taught physiology, then psychology, finally philosophy; and the three were definitely correlated in his thinking. He continued to teach until 1907, meanwhile producing works on psychology, theology, ethics, and metaphysics that deeply influenced his contemporaries. James had considerable stylistic gifts and tried to shock his listeners and readers into awareness. Many of his phrases were memorable, as when he spoke of "the bitch goddess success," or when he wrote, "A great many people think they are thinking when they are merely rearranging their prejudices."

James was distinctly American in the concepts he advanced. His approach to metaphysics was frankly commonsensical. He objected to the pure and highly "logical" but unreal systems of so many metaphysicians. He emphasized strongly the part that the nature of the knower plays in the character and validity of the knowledge he gathers. Any concept of the world around us, he felt, is a compromise between the objectively given and the personally desired. He was led in the end to the concept of PRAGMATISM, the subject of a series of lectures by him at the Lowell Institute and later at Columbia that were published as *Pragmatism* in 1907; a sequel was *The Meaning of Truth* (1909). He urged that one must turn away from abstractions, verbal solutions, fixed principles, and pretended absolutes and look for concreteness and facts, action and power. He argued that "the ultimate test for us of what a truth means is the conduct it dictates or inspires." To many persons this all seemed a sort of crass materialism, but actually the doctrine took on in time an almost mystical quality. Among those who strongly felt James' influence was Oliver Wendell Holmes, Jr.: his most celebrated judicial opinions, according to Lloyd Morris, "reflected his pragmatic philosophy of law."

Something of the same revolt against absolutes is seen in James' deeply interesting THE VARIETIES OF RELIGIOUS EXPERIENCE (1902), which contends that any article of religious faith is "true" when it provides emotional satisfaction. THE PRINCIPLES OF PSYCHOLOGY (2 v., 1890; abridged as a school text, 1892) shows James as a keen observer of the world of sense; one remembers that his first ambition had been to become a painter. One chapter, devoted to "The Stream of Thought," advances the concept of the "STREAM OF CONSCIOUSNESS" that was to become an important and revolutionary fictional technique. In other books he discusses THE WILL TO BELIEVE (1897); *Human Immortality* (1898); *The Sentiment of Rationality* (1905); *A Pluralistic Universe* (1909). A shorter piece,

Energies of Men (1907), is a magnificent exhortation to courage.

Most notable of all the writers on James is RALPH BARTON PERRY, whose Pulitzer Prize-winning *The Thought and Character of William James* (2 v., 1935) was issued in a briefer version in 1948. Others who have written on James include Horace M. Kallen, Ralph H. Gabriel, and Lloyd Morris. His son Henry edited his *Letters* (2 v., 1920), and Elizabeth Hardwick edited *The Selected Letters of William James* (1961). See BENJAMIN PAUL BLOOD; PLURALISM.

James, Will[iam Roderick] (b. Great Falls, Mont., June 6, 1892—d. Sept. 3, 1942), rancher, cowboy, western writer and illustrator. James' simple, adventurous stories of the western "cow country" enjoyed great popularity. From his first book, *Cowboys, North and South* (1924), to his last, *The American Cowboy* (1942), he wrote about what he knew and loved; he also illustrated his own works. Among his other books, several of which were made into movies: *The Drifting Cowboy* (1925); *Smoky* (1926), which won a Newbery Medal; *Cow Country* (1927); *Sand* (1929); *Lone Cowboy: My Life Story* (1930); *Sun-Up* (1931); and *Horses I've Known* (1940).

Jameson, John Franklin (b. Boston, Sept. 19, 1859—d. Sept. 28, 1937), historian, editor, teacher. Jameson taught at Johns Hopkins, Brown, and the University of Chicago; he was director of research at Carnegie Institution (1905–28) and chief of the Manuscripts Division, Library of Congress (1928–37). He and John H. Finley were among the early originators of the DICTIONARY OF AMERICAN BIOGRAPHY. They secured the aid of Adolph S. Ochs and *The New York Times* in carrying out the project; Jameson was chairman of the committee of management. He wrote a *History of Historical Writing in America* (1891), a *Dictionary of U.S. History* (1894), and *The American Revolution Considered as a Social Movement* (1926); he edited ORIGINAL NARRATIVES OF EARLY AMERICAN HISTORY (19 v., 1906–19). He was one of the founders (1884) of the American Historical Association.

Janeway, Elizabeth [Hall] (b. Brooklyn, N.Y., Oct. 7, 1913—   ), short-story writer, novelist. While a student at Barnard College, Mrs. Janeway won the *Story* magazine intercollegiate short-story contest. She has made her career as a novelist of psychological perception. Among her works: *The Walsh Girls* (1943); *Daisy Kenyon* (1945); *The Question of Gregory* (1949); *The Vikings* (1951); *Leaving Home* (1953); *The Third Choice* (1959).

Janice Meredith (1899), historical novel by PAUL LEICESTER FORD. Ford was both a first-rate story teller and an accurate historian. His sprightly romance was a best seller. The heroine is the beautiful, vivacious, and somewhat fickle daughter of a Tory in the Province of New Jersey in 1774. A mysterious and handsome bond-servant turns out to be Col. John Brereton of the Continental army; Janice ultimately marries him. In the Philadelphia and Virginia scenes

General and Mrs. Washington are portrayed. At the turn of the century girls wore the "Janice Meredith curl" over the right shoulder, in imitation of the medallion portrait on the book's front cover. Mary Mannering, in a successful dramatic version of the story (1900), helped the vogue.

Janney, Russell [Dixon] (b. Wilmington, Ohio, April 14, 1883—d. July 14, 1963), writer, press agent. Out of the experiences of a varied career in the theater, Janney wrote a best-selling novel, *The Miracle of the Bells* (1947). The hero is a press agent whose publicity stunt for a strange actress turns out to be a "miracle." Critics found *The Vision of Red O'Shea* (1949) and *Curtain Call* (1957) too sentimental.

Janvier, Thomas A[llibone] (b. Philadelphia, July 16, 1849—d. June 18, 1913), short-story writer, journalist. Janvier traveled widely, and in his fiction used the four backgrounds he knew best: Philadelphia, New York, Mexico, and the south of France. His first book, *Color Studies* (1885), gave sketches of life in Mexico, where he had gone on a journalistic assignment. There followed *The Mexican Guide* (1886); THE AZTEC TREASURE-HOUSE (1890); *Stories of Old New Spain* (1891); *The Uncle of an Angel, and Other Stories* (1891); *Embassy to Provence* (1893); *In Old New York* (1894); *In the Sargasso Sea* (1898); *In Great Waters* (1901); *The Passing of Thomas* (1900); *The Christmas Kalends of Provence* (1902); *The Dutch Founding of New York* (1903); *Henry Hudson* (1909); *Legends of the City of Mexico* (1910); *From the South of France* (1912); *At the Casa Napoleon* (1914).

Jarrell, Randall (b. Nashville, Tenn., May 6, 1914—d. Oct. 14, 1965), teacher, critic, poet. In the intervals of teaching and while he was serving in the air force during World War II, Jarrell produced poetry which is often difficult,

often purposely phantasmal, but always skillful, and in some of his war poems he writes with stark simplicity. He served as consultant in poetry at the Library of Congress from 1956 to 1958. Among his collections of verse are: BLOOD FOR A STRANGER (1942); *Little Friend, Little Friend* (1945); *Losses* (1948); *The Seven-League Crutches* (1951); *Selected Poems* (1955); *The Woman at the Washington Zoo* (1960). Some of his critical essays have been collected in *Poetry and the Age* (1953) and *A Sad Heart at the Supermarket* (1962). *Pictures from an Institution* (1954) is a novel satirizing life at a women's college.

Jarves, James Jackson (b. Boston, Aug. 20, 1818—d. June 28, 1888), newspaperman, editor, author of travel books, art critic, diplomat. Jarves' father, Deming Jarves, called "Founder of American Glass," established glassworks at Sandwich, Massachusetts, to utilize the fine Cape Cod sand. The younger Jarves traveled extensively, settled for a while in Hawaii. He founded the first newspaper there, *The Polynesian* (1840), and was made director of the government press. While on a diplomatic mission for Kamehameha III he passed through Italy, resigned his post, and settled down in that country; from 1879 to 1882 he was United States vice-consul at Florence. He made collections of numerous art objects, some of which are now at Yale, the Cleveland Museum of Art, and the Metropolitan Museum. He sought to educate the public in sound art principles, especially in the appreciation of Italian art. He was a pioneer in urging that industry, too, should seek to become aesthetic. Among his books: *Scenes and Scenery in the Sandwich Islands* (1843); *History of the Hawaiian or Sandwich Islands* (1843–47); *Parisian Sights* (1852); *Art Hints* (1855); *Italian Sights* (1856); *Art Thoughts* (1869); *A Glimpse of the Art of Japan* (1876). Four of Jarves' six children predeceased him, and he wrote in memory of one of them, a talented artist who died at the age of fifteen, *Pepero: A Brief Memoir of James Jackson Jarves, Jr.* (1891).

Jasper, John J. (b. Fluvanna Co., Va., July 4, 1812—d. March 28, 1901), Negro preacher. For many years Jasper attracted large audiences, black and white, to the Sixth Mount Zion Church in Richmond, Virginia. He was decidedly antebellum in mood and principle; the Bible was his rock of belief and he had no use for newfangled notions of science or theology. A white listener said that "his eloquence was beyond description." His most famous sermon, called "De Sun Do Move," was printed (1850), along with introductory matter, by the Dietz Press of Richmond as one of its *Southern Masterpiece Series*.

Jastrow, Joseph (b. Poland, Jan. 30, 1863—d. Jan. 8, 1944), psychologist, popularizer of science. Jastrow came to the United States when very young. He was graduated from the University of Pennsylvania, took his doctorate at Johns Hopkins, taught there and at the University of Wisconsin. He wrote numerous books and articles intended to educate the public in

Library of Congress

psychological concepts. He wrote *The House that Freud Built* (1932), in criticism of Freud's doctrines. Among Jastrow's other books: *Fact and Fable in Psychology* (1900); *The Subconscious* (1906); *The Psychology of Conviction* (1918); *Keeping Mentally Fit* (1928); *The Betrayal of Intelligence* (1938).

Java Head (1919), a novel by JOSEPH HERGESHEIMER. In his examination of the American past, Hergesheimer turned to the China trade that helped make New England rich, and wrote *Java Head,* probably his best novel. Gerrit Ammidon, the son of a famous Salem shipowner and retired captain, whose home is called Java Head, brings back from a trip to the Orient a Chinese wife, Taou Yuen, of aristocratic family. But she is received with kindness only by the wife of her husband's brother, and in addition has the misfortune to arouse passion in a dissolute neighbor. He manages to lure her into a room; to escape him she commits suicide by taking opium. Other misfortunes follow; in the end the bereaved husband marries a girl he had once been fond of and sails back to the Orient.

Jay, John (b. New York City, Dec. 12, 1745—d. May 17, 1829), lawyer, public official, judge. Jay was admitted to the bar in 1768, five years later was a royal commissioner to settle the boundary line between New York and New

Jersey. His career is a list of offices: delegate to the First and Second Continental Congresses; chief justice of New York; minister to Spain; joint commissioner with Benjamin Franklin in making peace with England; secretary of foreign affairs under the Confederation; Chief Justice of the U.S. Supreme Court; governor of New York. Daniel Webster said of him, "When the spotless ermine of the judicial robe fell on John Jay, it touched nothing less spotless than itself." As a member of the Continental Congress Jay wrote a famous *Address to the People of Great Britain* and composed appeals to Canada, Jamaica, and Ireland to rebel. He dealt with foreign affairs in five papers he contributed to THE FEDERALIST. His *Correspondence and Public Papers* (4 v., 1890–93) were edited by Henry P. Johnston. See HARVEY BIRCH.

jayhawkers. Members of a band of guerrillas who engaged in a border war involving Kansas and Missouri in the antebellum period on the question of free soil and slavery. The jayhawkers were antislavery. The name in time came to be applied to the inhabitants of Kansas. Thompson B. Ferguson wrote *Jayhawkers: A Tale of the Border War* (1892); Adela Orpen, *The Jayhawkers* (1900); and John A. Martin, *The Jayhawker* (1908). In collaboration with Lloyd Lewis, Sinclair Lewis wrote a play, *Jayhawker* (1934).

jazz. The type of music known today as jazz arose in the United States in the early 20th century, primarily among the Negroes. It has acquired widespread popularity throughout the world and has influenced literature and other arts by its spontaneity and rhythmic force.

Several predecessors of jazz are the spiritual, the work song, the blues, and ragtime. All these combine some of the rhythmic and melodic subtleties of African music with simple European harmonies. The blending of these elements took place among both the slaves of the South and the West Indies and the Creoles of New Orleans, the city generally regarded as the birthplace of jazz.

The American Negroes first heard harmony in the hymns and anthems of Christian services, and hymns such as "When the Saints Go Marching In" still form part of the jazz repertoire. Ragtime, the immediate precursor of jazz, grew out of the band style of playing these hymns in funeral processions; first as a slow march, then, after the burial, fast and "jazzy."

Early in the 20th century attempts were made to write down and publish jazz and blues—a famous example is W. C. HANDY's *St. Louis Blues* (1914)—but they could not be transcribed precisely. Jazz has always been essentially an improvised art, and cannot be conveyed accurately by musical notation. Therefore it has depended on the migrations of its exponents and the sale of records for recognition. After World War I jazz troupes went north to cities like Chicago and New York, and with the help of the growing recording industry, soon spread the music all over the world. At different periods various styles have emerged to dominate performance of jazz: hot jazz, or Dixieland, in the twenties, swing in the thirties, bebop in the forties, cool and progressive styles in the fifties. The basic form and technique, however, has persisted: improvised variations, primarily rhythmic and melodic, above a recurring harmonic pattern and steady rhythmic pulse.

Probably the development of jazz is best shown in the numerous biographies of its famous performers: *Mr. Jelly Roll* (1950) by Alan Lomax; *Father of the Blues: An Autobiography* (1941) by W. C. Handy; Louis Armstrong's *Satchmo* (1954) and *Swing that Music* (1936); *King Joe Oliver* (1955) by Walter C. Allen and Brian A. L. Rust; *A Journey to Greatness: The Life and Music of George Gershwin* (1956) by David Ewen; *The Kingdom of Swing* (1939) by Benny Goodman and Irving Kolodin; *Lady Sings the Blues* (1956) by Billie Holiday with Bill Dufty; *In Person, Lena Horne* (1950) as told to Helen Arstein and Carlton Moss by Lena Horne; *His Eye Is On The Sparrow* (1951) by Ethel Waters, with Charles Samuels; *Famous Negro Music Makers* (1955) by Langston Hughes; *Mood Indigo* (1946) by Denis Preston; *The Jazz Makers* (1957), Nat Shapiro and Nat Hentoff, editors; and *Duke Ellington* by Barry Ulanov. More comprehensive surveys include: Marshall Stearns' *The Story of Jazz* (1956); *Shining Trumpets, a History of Jazz* (1946) by Rudi Blesh; *The Book of Jazz* (1957) by Leonard Feather; and *Jazz, Its Evolution and Essence* (1956) by Andre Hodeir.

Hot jazz became the rage in the twenties. Classical composers such as AARON COPLAND, Igor Stravinsky, Darius Milhaud, and Paul Hindemith tried to imitate it, but the only musician able successfully to combine jazz with classical music was GEORGE GERSHWIN. Paul Whiteman, whose orchestra first performed Gershwin's *Rhapsody in Blue* in 1924, was responsible for the introduction of jazz in "sweeter" and therefore more socially acceptable arrangements. Many jazz devotees of the twenties first glimpsed the new style in his popular dance band.

Even literature was affected by the sudden jazz craze. F. SCOTT FITZGERALD felt the new style embodied the character of the "flapper" era to such an extent that he called it the "Jazz Age." His contemporaries, John Held, Jr., James T. Farrell, and John Dos Passos, interpreted their surroundings with a strong awareness of its pervasive aura. Beginning with Samson Raphaelson's play *The Jazz Singer* (1925), the flood of fiction about jazz musicians began with books like: *Sweet Man* (1930) by Gilmore Millen; *Jazz Band* (1935) by Wyatt Rundell; *Young Man With a Horn* (1938), based on the life of Bix Beiderbecke, by Dorothy Baker; *Strictly Ding-Dong and Other Swing Stories* (1941) by Richard English; *Jazz Parody* (1948), a collection of short stories edited by Charles Harvey; *Go* (1952) and *The Horn* (1958) by JOHN CLELLON HOLMES; *Ride Out* (1954) by SHELBY FOOTE; ON THE ROAD (1957) and *The Subterraneans* (1958) by Jack Kerouac. Of the many short stories about jazz, EUDORA WELTY's *Powerhouse* deserves special mention.

Neither prose nor drama could benefit directly from the stimulus of jazz rhythms in the way poetry could. Early in this century Vachel Lindsay built such poems as THE CONGO (1914) and "The Daniel Jazz" (1920) upon the insistent throb of American and African Negro rhythms, and read them aloud with dramatic effect. LANGSTON HUGHES' *The Weary Blues* (1926) and most of his later poetry exhibits the forms and styles of jazz, especially blues. The

rhythmic vitality in the works of Hart Crane and E. E. CUMMINGS derived partly from jazz. Recently the Beat poets, such as Gregory Corso, Allen Ginsberg, and Gary Snyder, have made jazz their credo, the unifying spirit of all BEAT WRITING.

Some mention should be made of the jazz slang, often employed by writers of the Beat generation. Jazz performers and their admirers have developed a vocabulary to communicate exclusively among themselves. Some "words" originate from meaningless syllables interjected for percussive effect in jazz performances—a technique called "scat" singing. Most jazz words, however, are simply standard English reinterpreted, often with an amusing or ironical twist: a *Godbox* is an organ; a *spook* is a white musician; *bread* is money. Like most slang words these occasionally change their meanings; the word jazz itself admits many connotations, several of them obscene.

Obviously the lyrics of blues, the only successful jazz vocal style, are themselves poetry. In its strictest literary sense *blues* means a folk poem of three-line stanzas. The second line repeats the first, sometimes in a slightly varied form. As Marshall Stearns points out in *The Story of Jazz*, the third line resolves the tension caused by this repetition:

I'm goin' down and lay my head on the railroad track,
I'm goin' down and lay my head on the railroad track,
When the train come along, I'm gonna snatch it back.

The mood invoked in blues is generally balanced between melancholy and humor, as often stoic as it is self-pitying. The figures of speech are often original if at times strained as in:

My gal's got teeth lak a lighthouse on de sea,
My gal's got teeth lak a lighthouse on de sea,
Every time she smiles she throws a light on me.

These songs, in such greatly modified and unimaginative forms as rock 'n' roll, have unfortunately become common fodder for commercial radio, television, and records.

Numerous encyclopedias and discographies of jazz have been published. Only a few can be listed: *A Treasury of the Blues* (1949) by W. C. Handy and Abbe Niles; *The Encyclopedia of Jazz* (1955) by Leonard Feather; *Guide to Jazz* (1956) by Hugues Panassié and Madeleine Gautier; *A Handbook of Jazz* (1957) by Barry Ulanov; *The Collector's Jazz, Traditional and Swing* (1958) by John S. Wilson.

J.B. (1958), a verse drama by ARCHIBALD MACLEISH. Suggested by and constantly contrasted with the Biblical story of Job, this play shows modern man in a universe whose laws he cannot understand, and comments upon the various attitudes of faith and despair which he may choose. A successful businessman, J.B. gives thanks for his happiness without claiming to have deserved it, while his wife Sarah believes that God directly rewards or punishes man's actions as they merit. As the pointless catastrophes strike them, their positions change. Sarah will not believe her children "guilty"; she almost commits suicide in her despair at the absence of justice. In his agony, J.B., on the other hand, now demands to know a reason, a justification. A priest, a psychologist, and a cynical social historian offer unsatisfactory explanations. Even the Voice from the Whirlwind, while impressive, is not an answer relevant to the human problem of how to live. The ending affirms man's capacity to "endure and Love."

Noted for its circus tent setting and play-within-a-play structure, the play received a Pulitzer Prize, MacLeish's third. Elia Kazan directed the Broadway production, the success of which, along with that of T. S. Eliot's *The Cocktail Party*, proved that poetry on the American stage could be popular.

Jeffers, Robinson (b. Pittsburgh, Pa., Jan. 10, 1887—d. Jan. 20, 1962), poet. Jeffers, a minister's son, was educated in the classics from early childhood, attended schools at home and abroad, including the medical school of the

University of Southern California and the School of Forestry at the University of Washington. As his broad education indicates, his interests could not be confined to any single area of study, and are reflected in his poetry, much of which is based on classical and Biblical literature and which reveals Jeffers' concern with the introverted failure of modern life. Although the majority of his characters are drawn from contemporary life, they are presented in situations and against settings of relative permanence; thus Jeffers situated most of his poems near his home in Carmel, California, a region of steep mountains overhanging the sea in which he found elements of timelessness and permanence absent in the commercial and industrial life of cities. His own

home, a house and tower built of granite Jeffers himself quarried, is a monument to his love of the endurance and repose of stone. Similarly, the motifs of classical mythology, present in almost all of his work, lend his poems a universality and depth of meaning.

His first two volumes, *Flagons and Apples* (1912) and *Californians* (1916), short poems with California settings, attracted little attention. TAMAR AND OTHER POEMS (1924) first brought Jeffers recognition. Based on the Biblical story of the seduction of Tamar by her brother Amnon, it was the first of Jeffers' attempts to embody his feelings of the failure of man to look beyond himself and act creatively in the world. Jeffers uses the incest motif as a symbol of man's turning inward upon himself, and the resultant tragedy of Tamar as a symbol of its destructiveness. *Tamar and Other Poems* also includes THE TOWER BEYOND TRAGEDY, a long narrative poem based on the first two plays of Aeschylus' Oresteia; the poem, which some critics consider Jeffers' best, was dramatized by Robert Ross in 1950. The title-poem of ROAN STALLION, TAMAR AND OTHER POEMS (1925), based on a Monterey County incident in which a man was killed by his own horse, contrasts the power, beauty, and sexuality of the stallion with the civilized lusts of man. *The Women at Point Sur* (1927), which Jeffers considers his most inclusive and intense poem, deals with a minister who has outgrown traditional orthodoxy and seeks to build a new religion on the Carmel coast but is driven mad because of his conflicting desires. Jeffers intended the tragedy of the minister to embody the dangers of misunderstanding what Jeffers called the "breaking out of humanity" in the *Roan Stallion*. The title-piece of CAWDOR AND OTHER POEMS (1928) recalls Euripides' story of Phaedra and Hippolytus. The first poem of DEAR JUDAS AND OTHER POEMS (1929) is based on the Biblical story of Judas and Jesus; Jeffers views Jesus and Judas as embodying, respectively, extroversion and introversion, passion and pity, the conflicting attitudes that either drive men out into the world to live and create or into themselves to die. *Descent to the Dead* (1931), based on Greek mythology, contains "At the Fall of an Age," a dramatic poem dealing with the execution of Helen by Polyxo twenty years after the fall of Troy. The title poem of THURSO'S LANDING AND OTHER POEMS (1932) reveals, perhaps more than any other of Jeffers' poems, his dislike of "progress" and modern civilization. *Give Your Heart to the Hawks and Other Poems* (1933) reiterates Jeffers' idea that humanity is but the starting-place of the race, that man must go beyond humanity if he is to live, toward either the passivity and peace of stones or the loneliness of the hawks, who "serve God,/ Who is very beautiful, but hardly a friend of humanity." The title-poem of *Solstice and Other Poems* (1935) is a resetting of the Medea legend on the California coast; later in *Medea* (1946) he made a free adaptation of the ancient play for the modern stage that proved to be his greatest popular success when it was produced in New York in 1947.

Such Counsels You Gave to Me and Other Poems (1937) includes a dramatic poem entitled *At the Birth of an Age* based on the Volsung Saga and set in time at the end of the Graeco-Roman era and the beginning of the Christian age. The characters of the poem embody the contradiction and frustration Jeffers felt to be characteristic of the modern world. Jeffers' *Selected Poetry* appeared in 1938, and was followed by *Two Consolations* (1940), *Be Angry at the Sun* (1941), *The Double Axe* (1948), and *Hungerfield and Other Poems* (1954).

Full-length studies of Jeffers and his poetry include the following: L. C. Powell, *Robinson Jeffers, the Man and his Work* (1934); M. B. Bennet, *Robinson Jeffers and the Sea* (1936); R. Gilbert, *Shine, Perishing Republic* (1936); Radcliffe Squires, *The Loyalties of Robinson Jeffers* (1956).

Jefferson, Joseph (b. Philadelphia, Feb. 20, 1829—d. April 23, 1905), actor, playwright, memoirist. Born in the fourth generation of a theatrical family, Jefferson first appeared on the stage at the age of four and continued to play

JOSEPH JEFFERSON IN *Rip Van Winkle*

almost to the day of his death. His first great hit was Tom Taylor's *Our American Cousin* (1858). The following year it occurred to Jefferson that he might find a suitable vehicle in Washington Irving's RIP VAN WINKLE, which had already been dramatized and altered by several writers. After some experimentation he asked DION BOUCICAULT to doctor it further. He appeared in 1865 in London for 170 nights in Boucicault's version, then brought it to New York in 1866 and scored a huge success. Rip was a standard role for him for forty years. Jefferson's composite version of *Rip Van Winkle* is still current; it is reprinted in Bennett Cerf and Van H. Cartmell's *The Most Successful Plays of the American Stage* (1944) without credit to any author,

not even Irving. Jefferson became one of the most popular actors of his day, especially as a comedian. He set down his reminiscences in his gracefully written *Autobiography* (1890), which was reprinted in 1950 as *"Rip Van Winkle."*

Jefferson, Thomas (b. Albemarle Co., Va., April 13, 1743—d. July 4, 1826), statesman, diplomat, lawyer, scientist, architect, third President. Jefferson graduated from the College of William and Mary in 1762. He was well read in classical literature, science, and philosophy, and after his graduation studied law under George Wythe, one of the finest teachers of law in Virginia. He was admitted to the bar in 1767 and continued to practise until just before the Revolution. He was elected a member of the Virginia House of Burgesses in 1769 and remained in the House until 1775; his greatest contributions were made in committees and in the drafting of documents. Unable to attend the Virginia convention of 1774 because of illness, he sent a paper entitled *A Summary View of the Rights of British America*, in which he argued for the "natural rights" of emigration and settlement, for an end of British taxation and a commercial agreement between England and America based on trade. The paper was rejected as being too advanced, but was probably instrumental in gaining Jefferson's election to draft the DECLARATION OF INDEPENDENCE two years later. Jefferson's clear, concise, and subtle prose made the *Declaration* the foremost literary work of the Revolution, as well as the most important single political document in American history. Based to a large extent on the philosophy of Locke, the *Declaration* emphasized the "natural" and "inalienable" rights of man, rather than those derived from the existing body politic.

Although Jefferson did not believe in absolute human equality, neither did he believe in the artificial aristocracy of birth and wealth then ruling in Virginia; accordingly, while in the Virginia House of Delegates from 1776 to 1779, he successfully worked for the abolition of the right of primogeniture and land held in entail; he also introduced a bill for the establishment of religious freedom, separating religious opinions from civil authority. Although his *Bill for the More General Diffusion of Knowledge*, a summary of his views on education, was not adopted, he succeeded in establishing professorships of anatomy, medicine, modern languages, and law at the College of William and Mary.

Jefferson was governor of Virginia from 1779 to 1781, but had little power, due to the wartime limitations placed on his office, and in effect resigned when the British invaded Virginia. His conduct was investigated by the Assembly, and, although his actions were fully vindicated, he suffered a loss of political prestige for some time after. His dislike of publicity, which had been apparent earlier in his career, was intensified after his governorship, and he retired to his home at MONTICELLO, where he organized and enlarged memoranda about Virginia on which he had been at work for a number of years. These NOTES ON THE STATE OF VIRGINIA, published in France in 1784–85 and later pirated in the United States, established his reputation as a scientist and scholar, and are still considered a valuable source of information about the natural history of Virginia, as well as about 18th century political and social life.

Jefferson was elected a delegate to Congress in June, 1783, and his voluntary retirement thus came to an end. During his six months' service he drafted thirty-one state papers, among them his *Notes on the Establishment of a Money Unit* in which he advocated the adoption of a decimal system, and his reports on the western territory. These reports, which anticipated the famous *Northwest Ordinance of 1787*, would, had they been adopted, have forbidden slavery in the western territory after 1800.

In 1784 Jefferson was appointed to assist Benjamin Franklin in the negotiation of commercial treaties with France, and the following year became Franklin's successor as minister to France. He was an excellent diplomat, succeeded in gaining several commercial concessions from the French, and contributed to the awakening French interest in America. He observed the beginning of the French Revolution with interest, and was particularly sympathetic to the moderate reformers, although he disliked the later violence of the Revolution and the open imperialism of Napoleon. During his stay in Europe, Jefferson traveled to northern Italy, where he studied agriculture and classical architecture, and with his plans for the new state capitol of Virginia helped initiate the growth of classical architecture in America.

Jefferson's work in France prevented his attendance at the framing of the American Constitution, and on his return he was concerned that the Constitution did not include provisions regarding the rights of individuals, and did not limit the number of times a president might be re-elected. He was satisfied when a Bill of Rights was added to the Constitution, and accepted Washington's offer of the Secretaryship of State.

While Jefferson was Secretary of State he came into repeated conflict with ALEXANDER HAMILTON, Secretary of the Treasury, first over a movement for commercial discrimination against the British, which Hamilton opposed, and later because of Jefferson's fears that the Treasury was favoring commerce and finance at the expense of agriculture. Many of the basic differences between the two secretaries came to a head in 1791, when the Bank of the United States was established. Jefferson questioned the constitutionality of the Bank bill, arguing that it assumed powers not granted to the Federal government by the Constitution, but Hamilton's broad construction of the Constitution and the implied powers of the Federal government was finally accepted. By 1792 Hamilton's financial program had brought about a split in the cabinet that formed the foundation of an opposing political party, the Republicans (later Democrats), whose recognized leader was Jefferson. In the summer of 1792 Jefferson complained of Hamilton's financial policy to Wash-

ington, and the President presented Hamilton with a formal list of the objections cited against him, to which Hamilton made formal reply. Probably because of the campaign being waged against him by PHILIP FRENEAU, the editor of the *National Gazette,* Hamilton attacked Jefferson in a series of vituperative articles in the *Gazette of the United States,* with the deliberate intent of driving Jefferson from office. However, the crisis following the outbreak of the war in Europe of 1793 brought a measure of unity into the cabinet and put at least a temporary end to the Jefferson-Hamilton hostilities.

Jefferson retired from his position as Secretary of State in December, 1793 and returned to Monticello, where he devoted himself to agriculture and improvements upon his estate. Although he wrote to Madison in 1795 that he had no desire to run for president, he did not refuse when the Republican party proved determined to support him. He lost the election to JOHN ADAMS [2], and under the election system at that time became Vice-president. Jefferson took little active part in the administration, but his presiding over the Senate gave him the experience to write his *Manual of Parliamentary Practice* (1801), which is still considered a basic work on parliamentary procedure. Probably his most important contribution to American democracy during the Adams administration was his work with James Madison on the Kentucky and Virginia Resolutions, which presented the "compact" theory of the Union, in which the states were authorized to attack unconstitutional laws in protest against the abuse of civil liberties.

Jefferson and his running mate, AARON BURR, were tied in the presidential election of 1800, and the choice between them was given to the House of Representatives. Due to dissension in the Federalist party and the fact that many abstained from the voting, Jefferson was elected, despite the Federalist majority in the House. Finding almost all minor governmental offices filled with Federalist appointees, Jefferson proceeded to remove all officers whose appointment seemed to him to be of doubtful legality. He revoked the commissions of the "midnight judges" appointed by Adams at the very end of his term; the case of Marbury vs. Madison, which arose as a result of Jefferson's action, was the first instance in which the Supreme Court asserted its right to declare an act of Congress unconstitutional. Jefferson also opposed the renewal of the Alien and Sedition Acts, liberalized the Naturalization Act, and eased the national debt by cutting Federal expenses. Probably his most important contribution to the growth of America was made with the purchase of the Louisiana Territory from France in 1803, thus giving the United States not only complete control of the Mississippi river and its 800,000 acres of surrounding land but making possible the expansion of America from coast to coast.

Jefferson was easily re-elected in 1804. War between Britain and France broke out shortly after and, in an attempt to prevent the United States from being forced to enter the war, Jefferson passed the Embargo Act (1807), thus closing American markets and depriving the combatants of American supplies. The Act was particularly unpopular in New England, where shipbuilding and trade had been rapidly growing, and Jefferson was forced to repeal the Act in 1809.

After forty years of public service, Jefferson was at last able to retire permanently to Monticello and enjoy the peace of a private existence. He improved his lands by crop rotation, experimented with new farming methods and implements, studied, and pursued his varied interests. In 1814 he sold his personal library of ten thousand volumes to Congress to replace the books burned by the British during the Revolution. His advice was sought by his successors, Monroe and Madison; he was reconciled to his old friend, John Adams, and the two men, from 1811 until their deaths in 1826, carried on a voluminous correspondence which is perhaps the most interesting in American letters. Jefferson continued his interest in public education, and from the end of his presidency until his death he advocated a university "based on the illimitable freedom of the human mind to explore and to expose every subject susceptible of its contemplation." The University of Virginia—for which he had drawn plans, supervised construction, and designed the curriculum—was opened in 1825, a year before his death. Along with the *Virginia Statute for Religious Freedom* and the *Declaration of Independence,* Jefferson regarded it as one of his three greatest achievements.

Jefferson's writings fall into four classes: (1) state papers and political pamphlets, (2) the *Notes on Virginia,* (3) letters, (4) miscellaneous pieces. In the first group, aside from the *Declaration,* formal publication was given to his *Address to the Senate on the 4th of March, 1801,* his First Inaugural; both this and his Second Inaugural Address are notable and eloquent documents. Sidney Kingsley made use of Jefferson's addresses in his play, *The Patriots* (1943). *Notes on Virginia* has been constantly reprinted. The number of Jefferson's letters still in existence runs to more than 18,000; letters written to him number more than 25,000. P. Wilstach edited *The Correspondence Between John Adams and Thomas Jefferson* (1925). J. G. de Roulhad Hamilton made a selection of *The Best Letters of Thomas Jefferson* (1926). The miscellaneous writings cover a vast range: *Notes on the Establishment of a Money Unit* (1784); *Report on French Protests Against the Tonnage Laws* (1791); *Life of Captain [Meriwether] Lewis* (1817); *Autobiography* (1821; published, 1829). Gilbert Chinard edited *The Commonplace Book of Thomas Jefferson* (1926); *The Literary Bible of Thomas Jefferson* (1928).

The most complete edition of Jefferson's writings is the *Papers of Thomas Jefferson,* edited by Julian P. Boyd and others. The first volumes of the projected 52-volume work appeared in 1950; others have been steadily issued. Earlier editions include *The Writings of Thomas Jefferson,* edited by P. L. Ford (10 v., 1892–99;

20 v., 1903–04) and *The Complete Jefferson,* edited by Saul Padover (1943).

The most important recent biographies include: C. G. Bowers, *Jefferson and Hamilton* (1925); A. J. Nock, *Jefferson* (1926); G. Chinard, *Thomas Jefferson: Apostle of Americanism* (1929); C. G. Bowers, *Jefferson in Power* (1936) and *Young Jefferson* (1945); Dumas Malone, *Jefferson the Virginian* (1948) and *Jefferson and the Rights of Man* (1951). There are innumerable special studies, including the following: Adrienne Koch, *The Philosophy of Thomas Jefferson* (1943); John Dos Passos, *The Head and Heart of Thomas Jefferson* (1954); Phillips Russell, *Jefferson: Champion of the Free Mind* (1956); and M. D. Peterson, *The Jefferson Image in the American Mind* (1960). See also FEDERALIST PARTY.

Jemison, Mary (born at sea, 1743—d. Sept. 19, 1833), "the White Woman of the Genesee." When she was fifteen Mary Jemison, living in western Pennsylvania, was captured by Indians. She adopted the name "Deh-hewo-mis," married twice into the Delaware tribe, and regarded herself as one of them for the rest of her life. In 1797 the Indians granted her a large tract of land in the Genesee valley in New York state. Her story was told in James E. Seaver's *A Narrative of the Life of Mrs. Mary Jemison* (1824).

Jenks, George Charles ["W. B. Lawson"] (b. London, April 13, 1850—d. Sept. 12, 1929), newspaperman, editor, novelist. Jenks wrote innumerable dime novels; he created the popular character of DIAMOND DICK and many of the NICK CARTER stories, some of these written under his pseudonym. Typical titles are: *Diamond Dick's Decoy Duck* (1891); *The Dalton Boys in California* (1893); *Out with the Apache Kid* (1894). He worked mainly for Pittsburgh newspapers.

Jenks, Tudor [Storrs] (b. Brooklyn, N.Y., May 7, 1857—d. Feb. 11, 1922), lawyer, writer of children's books. Jenks practiced law, was on the staff of ST. NICHOLAS, and saw a whole generation of young people brought up on his books. He combined amusement with instruction in his popular treatments of historical, literary, and scientific subjects; he also wrote stories. Some of his titles: *The Century World's Fair Book for Boys and Girls* (1893); *The Boys' Book of Explorations* (1900); *In the Days of Chaucer* (1904); *In the Days of Shakespeare* (1905); *Our Army for Our Boys* (1906); *The Dolls that Talked* (1906); *Electricity for Young People* (1907); *In the Days of Goldsmith* (1907); also a comedy in collaboration with his wife, *Dinner at Seven Sharp* (1917).

Jennie Gerhardt (1911), a novel by THEODORE DREISER. Jennie's harsh German father forces her to leave home when he discovers that she is pregnant; an Ohio senator had promised to marry her but died before he could carry out his intention. She becomes the mistress of the scion of a wealthy family, who marries in his own "class," becomes ill, and is nursed by Jennie. When he dies she steals in to his funeral, afraid to speak to his family. Oscar Cargill sees the influence of George Moore's *Esther Waters* (1894) on the novel, but compares the two books to Dreiser's disadvantage. He also remarks: "It is a pretty story, wherein the heroine exhibits all those Christian virtues in which Dreiser can see so little merit." On the other hand, George F. Whicher says the book is in some respects Dreiser's best.

Jennifer Lorn (1923), a novel by ELINOR WYLIE. Mrs. Wylie's first novel and one of her most amusing works, this "sedate extravaganza" is laid mainly in the England and India of Warren Hastings' 18th century. The chief character is a pompous, aristocratic Englishman, seen through the eyes of his satiric wife as they go on a picaresque journey. Sinclair Lewis called it "the first truly civilized American novel," and Carl Van Vechten organized a torchlight parade through the streets of New York in its honor. Its punning title means "Jenny Forlorn."

Jennings, John Edward, Jr. (b. Brooklyn, N.Y., Dec. 30, 1906—), deckhand, salesman, historian, novelist. Jennings won his first success with *Next to Valour* (1939), a story of New Hampshire in the days of the Rogers Rangers. Most of his later novels have a historical basis; they include *Call the New World* (1941); *Gentleman Ranker* (1942); *The Shadow and the Glory* (1943); *The Salem Frigate* (1946); *River to the West* (1948); *The Pepper Tree* (1950); *The Sea Eagles* (1950), *Banners Against the Wind* (1954); *Shadows in the Dusk* (1955); *The Wind in His Fists* (1956). He has also written *Our American Tropics* (1938); *Boston, Cradle of Liberty* (1947); *Clipper Ship Days* (1953); *The Golden Eagle* (1959).

Jensen, Merrill. See NEW NATION.

Jessup, Philip C. (b. New York City, Jan. 5, 1897—), lawyer, teacher, public official. Jessup became a member of the bar in 1925, soon acquired a great reputation as an authority on the law of nations. Having served on many American and international bodies of law, he was United States delegate to the United Nations General Assembly (1948–52). In 1961 he was appointed to the International Court of Justice. Among his books: *The Law of Territorial Waters and Maritime Jurisdiction* (1927); *The U.S. and the World Court* (1929); *Neutrality, Its History, Economics, and Law* (2 v. contributed by Jessup, 1935, 1936); *Elihu Root* (1938); *A Modern Law of Nations* (1948); *Transnational Law* (1956). Recently he edited *Atoms For Power* (1957); and with H. J. Taubenfeld wrote *Controls For Outer Space* (1959).

Jesuits in North America. A Catholic missionary order, the Jesuits were founded by St. Ignatius of Loyola in 1540 to combat Moslem influence. In later days its chief aim has been the propagation of the faith in many parts of the world. The Jesuits accompanied or closely followed conquest of the New World by the Spanish, French, and Portuguese. Often the Jesuit missionaries, especially among the Indians, suffered torture and martyrdom. The phrase "Jesuit Martyrs of North America" is applied to eight priests, including Isaac Jogues and John De Brébeuf, whom Indians killed in the 17th century in New York and Canada, and who were canonized by Pope Pius XI (1930). Around them an epic poem, *Brébeuf and His Brethren* (1940), was written by the Canadian poet E. J. PRATT. A group of Pratt's friends rearranged the poem for presentation as a musical and dramatic pageant.

The chief early literary account of the Jesuits in their North American missionary endeavors was the famous *Jesuit Relations* (see FRENCH INFLUENCE IN AMERICA). Francis Parkman wrote *The Jesuits in North America in the 17th Century* (1867). J. H. Kennedy, in *Jesuit and Savage in New France* (1950), maintains that despite the tortures and the martyrdoms the Jesuits were a principal factor in building up the concept of the "noble savage." Richard M. Dorson, in *America Begins* (1950), expresses his admiration for "the Jesuit Fathers, cultured, aesthetic, France-loving, [who] could plunge into the North American forests to live the punishing life of the savages, with often their ridicule and possibly their tortures for thanks." These men were often keen observers who gathered in their reports many geographical, ornithological, anthropological, and other data. Edna Kenton made a selection of passages in *The Jesuit Relations* (1925, 1954).

In the middle of the 18th century came severe attacks on the Jesuits, in Portugal, France, Italy, and elsewhere; in 1773 the order was suppressed by Pope Clement XIV and went out of existence in all countries except Russia. It was universally restored by Pope Pius VII in 1814, but has continued to suffer from exile and confiscation in several nations. In the United States it is an important teaching order; among universities under its control are Fordham and Georgetown. John La Farge, S.J., made *A Report on the American Jesuits* (1956) on the many activities of Jesuits today.

Jewett, Sarah Orne (b. South Berwick, Me., Sept. 3, 1849—d. June 24, 1909), short-story writer, novelist, poet. One of the best writers of the regional and local-color movement in the late 19th century, Jewett attracted attention with her first story when she was scarcely twenty. Eight years later, William Dean Howells, then the editor of the *Atlantic Monthly*, persuaded her to publish a collection of her sketches of life in rural Maine in DEEPHAVEN (1877). She drew the subjects and backgrounds of her stories from the locale in which she was born and spent her life; her knowledge of the country and its people was supplemented by accompanying her father, a doctor, as he made his calls. She treats her characters with a tender and humorous sympathy that is both idyllic and realistic, although lacking in the harsher aspects of realism. She was influenced at first by Harriet Beecher Stowe and Rose Terry Cooke, but later, and more fruitfully, by Flaubert, Zola, Tolstoy, and Henry James. Her best writing can be found in her short stories: *A White Heron* (1886); *The King of Folly Island* (1888); *A Native of Winby* (1893);

The Life of Nancy (1895); and in her finest work, THE COUNTRY OF THE POINTED FIRS (1896), a series of tales only loosely bound together by plot. She wrote three novels: *A Country Doctor* (1884) deals with a woman doctor;

A Marsh Island (1885) is the love story of a farmer's daughter and a wealthy planter; *The Tory Lover* (1901) is based in part on the adventures of John Paul Jones. *Verses* (1916), a collection of poems, was published posthumously.

Jews in United States literature. The history of the Jews in the United States is said to begin in 1654, when twenty-three Jews from Brazil arrived in what is now New York City. From then until well into the 19th century, more Jews—from England, France, and Germany—came to America to escape political and economic oppression. The New World, with its philosophy of civil rights for all, regardless of race, creed, or religion, spelled glorious opportunities for them and, even more, for their children.

The stream of immigrants, however, was relatively thin, and even as late as 1880 there were only about 700,000 Jews in America. They had synagogues and charitable organizations, newspapers and magazines, and they produced a few books, but as a community they could not be considered of great moment in the national life.

Toward the end of the 19th century a momentous event occurred: massive and sustained immigration from the East European countries—Russia, Poland, Rumania, Bulgaria, Austria—all of which had made the Jew's life increasingly difficult. The mounting number of pogroms forced hundreds of thousands of Jews to leave the lands where their ancestors had lived for so long; by 1920, when the first major United States Immigration Act went into effect, the Jewish population had risen to well over 2,000,000.

Thereafter, especially in New York City, Boston, Chicago, and Philadelphia, a Jewish culture developed that for a while rivaled that which had prevailed in Eastern Europe, and American-Jewish journalism, theater, music, and literature came into being. The Jewish writing before this time—novels, stories, poems, plays, essays, sketches—reflected the strivings of their authors but did not reflect anything significant about the local Jewish communities, much less about the national Jewish community. The first major Jewish-American novel was THE RISE OF DAVID LEVINSKY (1917), by ABRAHAM CAHAN, for a half century the editor of the *Jewish Daily Forward*. An immigrant from Russia in the early years of the present century, David Levinsky is the prototype of many East European Jewish immigrants: eager, enterprising, successful, and fully conscious of the dreadful price he has paid for his success. All in all, it is perhaps the best of all Americanization novels. But while this book won the accolade of no less a novelist-critic than William Dean Howells, it did not gain much of a reading public. The book that did win such a public was THE PROMISED LAND (1913), by MARY ANTIN. It is a hymn of gratitude to America, as well as, in part, a plea for assimilation. Another writer of the same era who wrote knowingly of Jewish life in America was ANZIA YEZIERSKA. Her *Hungry Hearts* (1920) and *Children of Loneliness* (1923) deal largely with the same people as Abraham Cahan's work, although her books are more connected sketches than full-bodied integrated novels.

Until well into the thirties and early forties, Americanization was a major subject of Jewish-American fiction. One of the most important of such novels is *The Old Bunch* (1937), by MEYER LEVIN. Others include: *Aaron Traum* (1930), by Hyman and Lester Cohen; *One Foot in America* (1950), by Yuri Suhl; *By the Waters of Manhattan* (1930), by Charles Reznikoff; *Call It Sleep* (1934), by Henry Roth; *Blessed Is the Man* (1935), by LOUIS ZARA; and *Journey to the Dawn* (1950), *In the Morning Light* (1952), and *The Sun at Noon* (1954), all by Charles Angoff. MICHAEL GOLD's *Jews Without Money* (1930), though more a series of semi-fictional sketches of Jewish life on the East Side than an integrated work of fiction, enjoyed a temporary fame as a major proletarian literary work at the time that the Communists and fellow travelers had an influence in the New York book, magazine, and newspaper world.

Anti-Semitism, assimilation, and racial prejudice in general have occupied many writers. Books that achieved either critical acclaim or wide popularity or both were *Focus* (1945), by ARTHUR MILLER; *Wasteland* (1946), by Jo Sinclair; and GENTLEMAN'S AGREEMENT (1947), by LAURA Z. HOBSON. *Wasteland* saw the introduction, on a large scale, of psychoanalysis into Jewish-American fiction. *Gentleman's Agreement* enjoyed a huge sale and was made into a commercially successful motion picture. Its chief theme was the *sub rosa* anti-Semitism practiced by realtors in suburbia. A more serious attempt to shed light upon the anti-Semitic disease was *The Victim* (1947), by SAUL BELLOW. Mention must also be made of Norman Katkov's *Eagle at My Eyes* (1948) and *A Little Sleep, A Little Slumber* (1950).

Katkov's books, like the others just mentioned, deal with intermarriage. The novel on this subject that achieved perhaps the widest popularity and considerable critical acclaim was *The Island Within* (1928), by LUDWIG LEWISOHN. It is still considered superior to Jerome Weidman's recent novel about intermarriage, *The Enemy Camp* (1960). Most books on intermarriage are written by Jews who were once or still are married to a spouse of another faith. Margaret Abrams, who wrote *Awakened* (1954), was a convert from Christianity to Judaism, the religion of her husband. Another book that merits attention is Beatrice Levin's *The Lonely Room* (1950), which analyzes as few other books do the distaste many Jewish girls have for their background.

As more Jews have gone into industry and professions, more novels dealing with these subjects have appeared. *The Rise of David Levinsky* is as much a study of Jews in the American garment industry as it is of Americanization. The same is true of *Aaron Traum*. Charles Angoff's *In the Morning Light* contains a detailed fictional analysis of the garment industry. *My Son, The Lawyer* (1950), by Henry Denker, is not only a depression story but an exposition of the eagerness of Jewish parents to have their children enter a profession. WHAT MAKES SAMMY RUN? (1941), by BUDD SCHULBERG, is perhaps the best-known novel about Hollywood. While it is brash and in some parts unfair, it has impact and there is some truth in it. *Tomorrow's Bread* (1938) by Beatrice Bisno deals with Jews in the garment trade and in the labor-union movement. The American rabbinate, which lately has come in for sharp examination, has not brought forth a novel worthy of the subject. *God's Gentleman* (1932), by Gary August, concerns the rabbinate, but appears to have been written in anger; nevertheless, it does have power and there are scenes that are depressingly true. JEROME WEIDMAN's *I Can Get It for You Wholesale* (1937) and *What's in It for Me?* (1937) aroused controversy because of their searing indictment of the occasional unscrupulousness of the tycoons and their henchmen in the garment industry. The two books lack overall understanding, but some of their reporting is all too true.

American Jews have been involved in all the wars waged by the United States. How they fared, as Jews, in the wars before World War I has not been dealt with fictionally to any serious extent either by Jews or non-Jews, and there is no single major novel of World War I that deals with the actual life of Jewish soldiers in camp and on the war front. World War II brought forth several important novels wherein Jews as soldiers are treated with serious intent. Perhaps the most celebrated is THE NAKED AND THE DEAD (1948), by NORMAN MAILER. Although not specifically a Jewish novel, two of its main characters are Jewish soldiers who reflect the bewilderment and haunting pride of the Jew in contemporary America. IRWIN SHAW's *The Young Lions* (1948) deals with a Jewish soldier who is buffeted by the overt and covert anti-Semitism of some of his Army buddies. Louis Falstein's *Face of a Hero* (1950) is on a plane with *The Young Lions* and is artistically perhaps above it, though it did not achieve the same popularity. There are scenes in *Face of a Hero*, however, that are done with a profound understanding of why the Jew fought so heroically on the side of the Western democracies. Joseph Landon's *Angle of Attack* (1952) is concerned with a Jewish navigator who engaged in air battles over fascist and Nazi territory; there is a stirring scene of the bombing of a concentration camp crowded with desperate Jewish men, women, and children.

The Jews are celebrated for their humor, which has comforted them through centuries of persecution. East European Jewry produced many humorists and satirists, chief among them three of the pillars of Yiddish literature: Sholom Aleichem, Mendele Mocher Sforim, and Y. L. Peretz. But American Jewry is deficient in major works that are dominantly humorous. Those that have achieved popularity—*Thunder Over the Bronx* (1935), by ARTHUR KOBER, and THE EDUCATION OF H*Y*M*A*N K*A*P*L*A*N (1937), by Leonard Q. Ross—are caricatures, in the main deficient in understanding. The sequel to Mr. Ross' book, *The Return of H*y*m*a*n K*a*p*l*a*n* (1961), signed by the author's real name, LEO ROSTEN, is no better as authentic Jewish humor. Ethel Rosenberg's two books, *Go Fight City Hall* (1949) and *Uncle Julius and the Angel with Heartburn* (1951), are hardly serious works of humor; they are folksy, at times gaggy, sometimes embarrassing in their obviousness; but they may be read with some pleasure.

The tensions of Jewish youth, living in a civilization within a civilization, have naturally occupied fiction writers. However, they still have to produce a major work about them. Perhaps the best-known attempt—and in the opinion of many the most successful—is Henry Roth's *Call It Sleep* (1934). *Unquiet* (1935), by Joseph Gollomb, concerns itself to a large extent with the Americanization experiences of a Jewish boy. The most extensive treatment of the Americanization and maturing of a Jewish boy, an immigrant from Russia, is to be found in CHARLES ANGOFF's Polonsky chronicle, a continuing series of novels dealing with Jewish life in America since the beginning of the 20th century. The first three volumes, *Journey to the Dawn, In the Morning Light,* and *The Sun at Noon,* especially deal with Jewish youth—the last with Jewish youth at Harvard. David Lord's *Joey* (1949) concerns itself with an adolescent in Los Angeles. There are also Isaac Rosenfeld's *Passage From Home* (1946), Paul Rosenfeld's

The Boy in the Sun (1928), Sam Ross's *The Sidewalks Are Free* (1950), and Albert Halper's two books, *Sons of the Fathers* (1940) and *The Golden Watch* (1953). Daniel Fuchs' readable *Three Novels* (1961), recently rediscovered and republished, deal with slum life on New York's lower East Side. The novels were originally published as *Summer in Williamsburg* (1934); *Homage to Blenholt* (1936); and *Low Company* (1937).

Jewish-American literature has been especially rich in short stories. The three best anthologies of them have been compiled, with informative and interpretive introductions, by Harold U. Ribalow: *This Land, These People* (1950), *These Your Children* (1954), and *The Chosen* (1959). Mr. Ribalow's *A Treasury of American Jewish Stories* (1958) is substantially an omnibus collection of the stories in the first two anthologies, but its special introduction merits attention. The two collections of stories by Charles Angoff, *When I Was a Boy in Boston* (1947) and *Something About My Father and Other People* (1956), cover the whole range of Jewish life in America—from childhood and adolescence through the period of young manhood and womanhood to old age, and from the points of view of various degrees of acceptance of the Jewish-American situation. *The World is a Wedding* (1948), by Delmore Schwartz, is a collection of *avant-garde* stories, many of them depicting Jewish discomfort in a non-Jewish environment. Irwin Shaw's *Mixed Company* (1950) is perhaps a more authentic collection, as are *The Common Thread* (1944), by Michael Seide, and *Poor Cousin Evelyn* (1951), by James Yaffe. Two of the latest short-story collections are Bernard Malamud's The Magic Barrel (1958) and Philip Roth's *Goodbye, Columbus* (1959). The first contains thirteen stories, at least half of the first quality. The book confirmed the high opinion of Mr. Malamud expressed by several critics on the occasion of the publication of his novel, The Assistant (1957). Mr. Roth's book contains one novella and five shorter tales.

Jewish-American poetry, in the main, has not been distinguished. The didactic poetry produced by some rabbis is seldom of high literary worth. The name of Emma Lazarus (1849–1887), a part of whose poem "The New Colossus" is inscribed on a bronze tablet at the foot of the Statue of Liberty, is often mentioned, but her two collections of verse, *Admetus and Other Poems* (1871) and *Songs of a Semite* (1882), do not stand up very well after all these decades, nor does Peninia Moise's *Hymns Written for the Use of Hebrew Congregations* (1856). Jean Starr Untermeyer, Karl Shapiro, Muriel Rukeyser, Eve Merriam, Alter Brody, and Delmore Schwartz, among others, have written occasional readable verse about Jewish life. The only poet of recent times who has written Jewish poetry of haunting impact is Abraham M. Klein, whose *Hath Not a Jew* . . . (1940) holds up remarkably well after nearly a generation.

The American theater can boast of many Jews on all levels—writers, directors, producers, composers, librettists. They have, inevitably, injected much Jewish humor and satire into plays and musicals, but so far there has not been a single first-rate truly Jewish play. Elmer Rice's Street Scene (1929), The Adding Machine (1923), Counsellor-at-Law (1931), and *We, the People* (1933) contain many Jewish characters, but none of these characters has entered the stream of Jewish literary history. Clifford Odets' plays, especially Awake and Sing (1935) and *Paradise Lost* (1936), are filled with Jewish men and women, but only a rash critic would claim a long fictional life for any of them. In *Rain from Heaven* (1935), *Wine of Choice* (1938), and No Time for Comedy (1939), S. N. Behrman deals with the plight of Jewish intellectuals and of the refugees from pogroms, but his one collection of semifictional sketches, *The Worcester Account* (1952), has more life in it than all his plays put together. Arthur Kober's Having Wonderful Time (1937), dealing with life in the borsht circuit of the New York Catskills, is more vaudeville than full-blown theater, and its portrayal of Jewish life is, at best, superficial.

The past decade has brought forth several astonishing best sellers in the world of Jewish-American fiction, including Marjorie Morningstar (1955), by Herman Wouk; *Remember Me to God* (1957), by Myron Kaufman; and *Exodus* (1958), by Leon Uris. The first two deal with American Jewish life, in New York and in Boston respectively, and both are of little literary value, as is *Exodus*, which is concerned with the birth of the state of Israel. Harry Golden's *Only in America* (1959), *For Two Cents Plain* (1960), and *Enjoy, Enjoy* (1961) are collections of facile, nostalgic essays; no one claims high literary merit for them, but in small doses they make harmless and occasionally refreshing reading.

The Hitler holocaust and the establishment of the state of Israel have stimulated the writing of Jewish *belles lettres* in the United States, so that during the past twenty years probably more novels and short stories about Jewish life have been published than in all the preceding three hundred years. Poor books continue to appear, but the number of good books is increasing, such as *The Human Season* (1959), by Edward Lewis Wallant, and *The Time of the Peaches* (1959), by Arthur Granit.

For studies of Jewish writers in America see the chapter by Harold U. Ribalow entitled "American Jewish Writers and Their Judaism," in *Jews in the Modern World*, edited by Jacob Fried (1962). Leslie Fiedler presents a different point of view in *The Jew in the American Novel* (1959). The most comprehensive, up-to-date, and fully annotated bibliography of Jewish-American fiction is Harold U. Ribalow's *Books on American-Jewish Life* (1962). An indispensable source for a running bibliography of all Jewish-American literary productions can be found in the *Jewish Books Annual*, volume 19 of which appeared in 1961. The *Annual* also contains articles by various authorities in American Jewry on Jewish-American novels, poetry, essays, and plays. For contrasting points of view on the Jewish writer in America, see Charles Angoff's "Jewish Literature in English," in *Jewish Life in America*, edited by Robert Gordis (1955); and Leslie Fiedler's "The New Jewish Writer in America," in *Jewish Heritage*, v. 4, #3, Winter, 1961–62.

CHARLES ANGOFF

Jim Bludso of the Prairie Belle (in PIKE COUNTY BALLADS, 1871), a poem by JOHN HAY. This tale of a Mississippi steamboat engineer who sacrifices himself to save his passengers when his boat catches fire was based on a real incident; the engineer was named Oliver Fairchild. The poem is in Western dialect, which Hay and Bret Harte began using in verse at about the same time; Mark Twain had already made it popular in prose.

Jim Crow. T. D. Rice, an American vaudeville performer and Negro impersonator, was famous for his song *Jump, Jim Crow*, which he based on a song and shuffling dance done by an old Negro while grooming a horse. Rice's version was first given in Louisville in 1828; the song was published and sung all over the country. The term "Jim Crow" soon became an insulting epithet for Negroes. It is now generally applied to segregation in the South—"Jim Crow" cars, schools, sections, etc. See NEGROES IN AMERICAN LITERATURE.

Joad. The name of the family of "Okies" (former residents of Oklahoma) who in John Steinbeck's THE GRAPES OF WRATH (1939) make their way to California as migrant workers. Tom Joad is the chief of them; there are also his grandparents, his parents, his Uncle John, and others.

Joan of Arc, Personal Recollections of. See PERSONAL RECOLLECTIONS OF JOAN OF ARC.

John Brown: The Making of a Martyr (1929), a biography by ROBERT PENN WARREN. Warren, born in Kentucky, has little sympathy with Brown. Analyzing his treatment, Oscar Cargill wrote that Warren's "tendency to explain each revealing episode by whatever is least creditable to Brown turns the old man into an authentic monster, more giant squid than human and more amorphous than defined."

John Brown's Body [1]. A famous Civil War song of obscure origin. The tune, originally known as "Glory Hallelujah," dates back as far as 1856 and is generally credited to William Steffe, a South Carolinian who composed many camp-meeting tunes. The tune was especially popular with the soldiers of Fort Warren in Boston harbor; Sigmund Spaeth says it is possible the "John Brown" words were written there. John Tasker Howard says one of the soldiers was named John Brown and the words were intended as a joke on him. The "John Brown" verses have been attributed to Charles Sprague Hall, Frank E. Jerome, T. B. BISHOP, and others. They were first popularized by Col. Fletcher Webster's 12th

Massachusetts Regiment, which used them as a marching song; soon the song was adopted by all Union soldiers. There was, however, objection to the words, which have been largely supplanted by Julia Ward Howe's BATTLE HYMN OF THE REPUBLIC (1862), written to the "Glory Hallelujah" tune.

John Brown's Body [2] (1928), an epic poem by STEPHEN VINCENT BENÉT. The poem follows the course of events leading to the Civil War, beginning in a Prelude with the introduction of slavery and going on to John Brown's raid on Harper's Ferry and his execution. Looking at both sides of the conflict with deep sympathy, Benét eloquently sketches the great figures of the war, its momentous battles, the hardships endured by those on the home front, events on the frontier, occasional romantic moments, the men of various types and origin who served in both armies, the coming of peace. The poem has many notable portraits—of Lincoln, Grant, Stonewall Jackson, Lee, "Beauty" Stuart, Jefferson Davis, Judah P. Benjamin, and others. The narrative is based on extensive research. It was awarded a Pulitzer Prize on publication, and won numberless readers. A successful dramatic version made by Charles Laughton appeared on Broadway in 1953. See JOHN BROWN.

John Bull and Brother Jonathan, The Diverting History of (1812), a satire by JAMES KIRKE PAULDING. This satire was inspired by Francis Hopkinson's A PRETTY STORY (1774), and by the feeling that led to the War of 1812. Bullock Island represents England; Jonathan has thirteen farms; and there are references to the Manor of Frogmore of Lewis Baboon (Louis XVI). There is a British traveler in the United States, who is called Corporal Smellfungus. The satire of England is, however, so good-humored that the work was reprinted in a British journal. It ran through several editions in the United States and in revision was doubled in length. It was followed many years later by an inferior sequel, THE HISTORY OF UNCLE SAM AND HIS BOYS (1835), in which Jonathan becomes Uncle Sam, with twenty-four sons.

John Bull in America (1825), a satire by JAMES KIRKE PAULDING. In this work Paulding continued his defense of the United States against the attacks of British writers, especially travelers who returned home with sneering descriptions of this country. The subtitle of his book is *The New Munchausen*, and the book purports to be a narrative of a tour in America made by a Cockney. Paulding satirizes broadly the ignorant blunders and silly prejudices of British travelers.

John Marr and Other Sailors (1888), a collection of twenty-five poems by HERMAN MELVILLE. *John Marr* is roughly divided into four parts: Sea-Pieces, Minor Sea-Pieces, Pebbles, and a prefatory section introduced by an essay on John Marr, who has lived most of his years on the prairies in stoic frustration, away from the seas of his young manhood. Marr and the "other sailors" invoke the spirits of their long-ago shipmates, Bridegroom Dick, Tom Deadlight, Jack Roy, etc. Although Marr's resemblance to his creator is fictitious rather than autobiographical, Melville, too, was somewhat sentimental, and here expresses his own heartfelt nostalgia.

Sea-Pieces ("The Haglets" and "The Aeolian Harp") posits the ironic indeterminacy of the universe and the vanity of human wishes; Minor Sea-Pieces, the major poetic achievement of John Marr, reaffirms that wisdom. In "To Ned" he musingly recalls events of forty years before, when he and Richard Greene, "the Typee-truants," roved the Marquesas, and he wonders "if mortals twice / Here and hereafter, touch a Paradise." Another of the Minor Sea-Pieces, "The Tuft of Kelp," is, like the poetry of Emily Dickinson, gnomically expressive, a nugget of pure intelligence. Pebbles, the last section, proposes not merely the acceptance of wisdom but the wisdom of acceptance.

Johnny Appleseed. See APPLESEED, JOHNNY.

Johns, Orrick (b. St. Louis, Mo., June 2, 1887—d. July 8, 1946), editor, reviewer, dramatist, biographer, poet. Johns favored drastic changes in literature and in life and was associated with radicals in politics, labor movements, and writing. He wrote poetry that had a deliberate social consciousness, as in the poem *Second Avenue* which won a first prize of $1,000 in the *Lyric Year* contest (1912). His life ended in suicide. He made collections of his verses in *Asphalt* (1917); *Black Branches* (1920); *Wild Plum* (1926). He was at first a writer of free verse in the style of Whitman, later came under the influence of A. E. Housman and wrote in his crisper style. He had a gift for warm specific detail and for spontaneous feeling. But he disappeared from importance as a poet long before his death. In addition to poetry he wrote *Time of Our Lives: The Story of My Father and Myself* (1937), an able biography of his father George S. Johns, a crusading St. Louis editor. A play of his, *A Charming Conscience,* was produced by Margaret Anglin in 1923.

Johnson, Allen (b. Lowell, Mass., Jan. 29, 1870—d. Jan. 18, 1931), teacher, historian, biographer. Johnson taught at Yale from 1910 to 1926; he had previously been on the faculties of Grinnell and Bowdoin. He was an authority on American history and edited the monumental Yale University Press CHRONICLES OF AMERICA (50 v., 1918–21), since augmented by new volumes covering recent years. He also edited the first seven volumes of the DICTIONARY OF AMERICAN BIOGRAPHY with DUMAS MALONE (1928–31). Among his books: *Stephen A. Douglas* (1908); *Union and Democracy* (1915); *Jefferson and His Colleagues* (in the *Chronicles* series, 1921); *The Historian and Historical Evidence* (1926).

Johnson, Alvin S[aunders] (b. near Homer, Neb., Dec. 18, 1874—   ), economist, teacher, administrator, editor. A professor of economics at several universities, Johnson edited the NEW REPUBLIC from 1917 to 1923, was founder and editor-in-chief of *Social Research,* and chief working editor of the *Encyclopedia of the Social Sciences.* He was largely responsible for the founding of the New School for Social Research in New York City (1919), and was its director (1923–45). Among his books: *Rent in Modern Economic Theory* (1903); *Introduction to Economics* (1909); *The Professor and the Petticoat* (novel, 1914); *John Stuyvesant, Ancestor* (short stories, 1919); *Deliver Us from Dogma* (1934); *Spring Storm* (novel, 1936); *The Public Library: A People's University* (1938); *The Clock of History* (1946); *Pioneer's Progress* (autobiography, 1952).

Johnson, Andrew (b. Raleigh, N.C., Dec. 20, 1808—d. July 31, 1875), tailor, public official, Vice-President, 17th President. Johnson belonged to the despised "poor white" class of his native state (he settled in Tennessee in 1826) and up to the time of his marriage was practically illiterate. Under his wife's guidance he acquired a fair education, became interested in politics, was elected successively to the state legislature, the House of Representatives, the governorship of Tennessee, and the United States Senate. When the Civil War broke out, he alone of the twenty-two Senators representing the eleven seceded states remained true to the Union; when Lincoln was renominated in 1864, Johnson was deliberately chosen as his running mate to represent the South. He was in politics a Jacksonian Democrat.

On Lincoln's assassination he became President. All his measures for the reconciliation of the South were ignored or nullified. A violent contest between the President and the Congress ensued, coming to a climax in the spring of 1868 when the House of Representatives impeached Johnson. On the 5th of March began the greatest trial in the history of the United States, when formal charges against Johnson were presented in the form of eleven articles. The voting began on May 16; the Senate acquitted him by one vote. It has been said that the vote by which Johnson escaped conviction "marks the narrow margin by which the Presidential element in our system escaped destruction." Shortly afterward, Grant was nominated for the Presidency. Johnson returned home, sought for seven years to be returned to the Senate, finally succeeded in 1875. He took his seat and lived to make one more attack on his enemies on the floor of the Senate.

It is generally admitted that Johnson was a man of great courage, integrity, and common sense. Yet historians, without denying his virtues, call him egotistical, belligerent, tactless. Frank Moore edited his *Speeches* (1865). John Savage wrote about *The Life and Public Services of Andrew Johnson* (1866), and other biographies have been done by James S. Jones (1901), Robert W. Winston (1928), Lloyd Stryker (1929). Joseph W. McSpadden's *Storm Center* (1947) is a fictionalized biography.

Johnson, Burges (b. Rutland, Vt., Nov. 9, 1877—d. Feb. 23, 1963), newspaperman, teacher, editor, writer. A professor of English, Johnson is best known for his humor. Among his books are *Beastly Rhymes* (1906); *The Well of English* *and the Bucket* (1917); *As I Was Saying* (1923); *New Rhyming Dictionary and Poets' Handbook* (1931; rev., 1957); *Sonnets from the Pekinese* (1935); *Professor at Bay* (1937); *As Much As I Dare* (1944); *Campus Versus Classroom* (1946); *The Lost Art of Profanity* (1948).

Johnson, Charles Spurgeon (b. Bristol, Va., July 24, 1893—d. Oct. 29, 1956), teacher, editor, author. A teacher for many years, Johnson became president of Fisk University in 1946; he won many honors for his work in Negro culture and history. Among his books are *The Negro in American Civilization* (1930); *Shadow of the Plantation* (1934); *Preface of Racial Understanding* (1936); *Growing Up in the Black Belt* (1941); *Into the Main Stream* (1946); *Education and the Cultural Crisis* (1951).

Johnson, Clifton (b. Hadley, Mass., Jan. 25, 1865—d. Jan. 22, 1940), editor, author of travel books, illustrator. Among his books: *The New England Country* (1892); *Among English Hedgerows* (1899); *The Isle of the Shamrock* (1901); *The Picturesque Hudson* (1909); *What to See in America* (1919).

Johnson, Edgar (b. New York City, Dec. 1, 1901—   ), biographer, critic, editor, teacher. A specialist in nineteenth century literature, Johnson taught at a number of Universities before becoming chairman of the department of English at the College of the City of New York. He edited recent editions of novels of Dickens, Walter Scott, and Bulwer-Lytton, but is best known for his biographical and critical studies of Charles Dickens. These include *The Heart of Charles Dickens* (1952) and *Charles Dickens: His Tragedy and Triumph* (1952). The first is a collection of Dickens' letters to Angela Burdett-Coutts, and the latter has become the definitive modern biography of Dickens. Among his other books are *Unweave a Rainbow* (1931); *The Praying Mantis* (1937); *One Mighty Torrent* (1937), a survey of American and British biography; and two anthologies, *A Treasury of Biography* (1940) and *A Treasury of Satire* (1945). His critical articles and reviews have appeared frequently in magazines and newspapers.

Johnson, Edward (b. England, Sept. [?], 1598—d. April 23, 1672), historian. A joiner by trade, Johnson came to Boston in 1630; in 1650 he began writing a history of the Massachusetts colony. He called it *The Wonder-Working Providence of Sion's Saviour in New England,* although it was first published anonymously in England in 1654 as *A History of New England.* It was the first published large-scale history of the Puritan colonies.

Johnson, Gerald W[hite] (b. Riverton, N.C., Aug. 6, 1890—   ), newspaperman, editor, teacher, historian, biographer. H. L. Mencken called him "the best editorial writer in the South, a very excellent critic and a highly civilized man." His many books began with an unconventional biography, *Andrew Jackson, An Epic in Homespun* (1927). Other biographies are about Randolph of Roanoke (1929); Franklin D. Roosevelt (1941); Woodrow Wilson (1944); *By Reason of Strength* (1930) and *Number*

Thirty-Six (1933) are novels. Always Johnson writes from a fervent desire to preserve and promote what he considers the American virtues, his great passion being the Bill of Rights; he writes with crusading ardor about the American achievement. Among his later books are *American Heroes and Hero-Worship* (1943); *Liberal's Progress* (1948); *Incredible Tale* (1950); *This American People* (1951); *Pattern for Liberty* (1952); *America is Born* (1960); *America: A History for Peter* (1959, 3 v., a juvenile); *The Man Who Feels Left Behind* (1961).

Johnson, James Weldon (b. Jacksonville, Fla., June 17, 1871—d. June 26, 1938), lawyer, poet, teacher. Johnson became the first Negro admitted to the Florida bar since Reconstruction days. Thereafter he enjoyed a various career, including successful song-writing in New York, a term as consul in Venezuela and Nicaragua, teaching at Fisk University. Among his books: *The Autobiography of an Ex-Colored Man* (a novel, 1912); *Fifty Years and Other Poems* (1917); GOD'S TROMBONES (1927); *Black Manhattan* (1930); *Along This Way* (autobiography, 1933). He edited *The Book of Negro Poetry* (1922) and two collections of Negro spirituals (1925, 1926). *Saint Peter Relates an Incident; Selected Poems* appeared in 1935.

Johnson, Josephine W[inslow] (b. Kirkwood, Mo., June 20, 1910—   ), painter, teacher, writer. After writing short stories successfully for several years, Miss Johnson won a Pulitzer Prize with her first novel, *Now in November* (1934), a realistic but poetic story of life on a Middle-Western farm. The award occasioned the collection of her short stories in *Winter Orchard and Other Stories* (1935). *Jordanstown* (1937) shifted the scene to an industrial region during the depression; and *Wildwood* (1946) sympathetically described a girl's loneliness. Miss Johnson also published a book of verse, *Year's End* (1937), and a book for children, *Paulina* (1939). Critics have commended her "quiet and beautiful prose."

Johnson, Martin (b. Rockford, Ill., Oct. 9, 1884—d. Jan. 13, 1937), explorer, author of travel books. Accompanied on many expeditions by his wife OSA JOHNSON, this explorer of little-known regions invariably brought back entertaining and exciting accounts of his experiences. These books were usually prepared in collaboration. Among them: *Through the South Seas with Jack London* (1913); *Cannibal-Land* (1917); *Camera-Trails in Africa* (1924); *Safari* (1928); *Lion: African Adventures with the King of Beasts* (1929); *Congorilla* (1931); *Over African Jungles* (1935). In some of their later expeditions Mr. and Mrs. Johnson gathered material for motion-picture productions.

Johnson, Nunnally (b. Columbus, Ga., Dec. 5, 1897—   ), newspaperman, columnist, freelance writer, writer and producer of screenplays, humorist. Johnson worked on papers in Georgia and New York City until 1932, meanwhile writing stories and articles for magazines. He wrote the scripts for many important movies, including *The House of Rothschild, The Prisoner of Shark*

Island, The Grapes of Wrath, and *Tobacco Road.* He wrote and directed the movie versions of *The Three Faces of Eve* and *The Man in the Gray Flannel Suit.*

Johnson, Osa [Helen] (b. Chanute, Kans., March 14, 1894—d. Jan. 7, 1953), explorer, author of travel books, motion-picture producer, memoirist. With her husband MARTIN JOHNSON, Mrs. Johnson made photographic expeditions to the South Seas (1912), the Solomon Islands and the New Hebrides (1914), Borneo (1917–19), the African jungles (1921), Borneo again (1935–36). In collaboration with her husband she wrote books on these expeditions, produced motion pictures based on their travels. After his death she continued to write. Among her books: *Osa Johnson's Jungle Friends* (1939); *Four Years in Paradise* (1941); *Tarnish, The True Story of a Lion Cub* (1945). Her two volumes of autobiography had a very wide sale: *I Married Adventure* (1940) and *Bride in the Solomons* (1944).

Johnson, Owen [McMahon] (b. New York City, Aug. 27, 1878—d. Jan. 27, 1952), novelist, writer for boys. The son of the poet ROBERT UNDERWOOD JOHNSON, Owen Johnson is probably best remembered for *Stover at Yale* (1911), a campus story which mingles criticism with entertainment and which created something of a sensation. Lawrenceville School in New Jersey is the setting for THE VARMINT (1910), *The Tennessee Shad* (1911), and *Skippy Bedelle* (1923), all concerning ingenious young rascals. Johnson also wrote several novels for adult readers, including *Children of Divorce* (1927) and *The Coming of the Amazons* (1931). See DINK STOVER.

Johnson, Philander Chase (b. Wheeling, W. Va., Feb. 6, 1866—d. May 18, 1939), newspaperman, editor, drama critic, humorist. Johnson created two popular characters, Uncle Eben and SENATOR SORGHUM; the latter in particular amused readers and his name is still used occasionally to signify a pompous, illiberal southern senator. Johnson wrote daily verses for the Washington *Star.* Among his books: *Sayings of Uncle Eben* (1897); *Now-a-Day Poems* (1900); *Senator Sorghum's Primer of Politics* (1906).

Johnson, Robert Underwood (b. Washington, D.C., Jan. 12, 1853—d. Oct. 14, 1937), poet, editor, public official. Johnson performed outstanding services in securing better copyright protection for authors, in helping (with JOHN MUIR) to create Yosemite Park, in establishing the Hall of Fame at New York University (he was its director from 1919 to 1937), and in the American Academy of Arts and Letters. During World War I he originated the movement to provide "American Poets' Ambulances in Italy," and he was ambassador to Italy, 1920–21. As a poet he wrote rather stiff formal verses and was called upon to provide poems for public occasions. His *Poems* was published in 1902, enlarged in 1908, 1919, 1931. His memoirs are contained in *Remembered Yesterdays* (1923).

Johnson, Rossiter (b. Rochester, N.Y., Jan. 27, 1840—d. Oct. 3, 1931), poet, editor, essayist,

historian. Johnson edited *The World's Great Books* (40 v., 1898–1901) and *Appleton's Annual Cyclopedia* (1883–1902). His verse was collected in *Three Decades* (1895).

Johnson, Samuel (b. Guilford, Conn., Oct. 14, 1696—d. Jan. 6, 1772), theologian, philosopher, teacher, college administrator. Johnson, a graduate of Yale, became a Congregational minister, then went to England and was ordained in the Protestant Episcopal Church. On his return to America he won a wide reputation as a clergyman and a scholar. He became the first president of King's (later Columbia) College (1753), served for ten years, then returned to his old church at Stratford, Conn. As a thinker Johnson moved away from harsh Calvinism toward the rationalism of some of his English instructors. Later he turned toward Bishop George Berkeley, becoming his friend and disciple during the years that the English prelate lived at Newport, R.I. Johnson wrote *An Introduction to the Study of Philosophy* (1731); *A System of Morality* (1746); *Elementa Philosophica* (1752); *English and Hebrew Grammar* (1767). H. W. and C. Schneider edited *Samuel Johnson: His Career and Writings* (4 v., 1929), the first volume of which contains his readable *Memoirs,* together with selections from his personal correspondence.

Johnson, Thomas. See THE KENTUCKY MISCELLANY.

Johnson, Sir William (b. Ireland, 1715—d. 1774), colonist. Johnson was a land and fur trader in the colony of New York. During the French and Indian War (1754–63) he headed a force of Indians and colonial militia that defeated the French at Lake George. He was made a baronet, and in 1756–74 was Superintendent of Indian Affairs for all colonies north of the Ohio River. His estate was a large one, near the city of Johnstown, which he founded. He knew the Iroquois and their language well, married a Mohawk woman, and was made a sachem of the Mohawk tribe. He was greatly impressed by the "Attic elegance" of diction and compelling rhythm of the Indian orators. Johnson appears in several historical novels, among them James Kirke Paulding's THE DUTCHMAN'S FIRESIDE (1831); C. F. Hoffman's GREYSLAER (1840); Robert W. Chambers' CARDIGAN (1901); Kenneth Roberts' NORTHWEST PASSAGE (1937); John Tebbel's THE CONQUEROR (1951); Margaret Widdemer's *The Golden Wildcat* (1954).

Johnston, Alexander (b. Brooklyn, N.Y., April 29, 1849—d. July 20, 1889), teacher, lawyer, authority on the American political system. Johnston taught in private schools, then at Princeton University from 1883 till his death. He was a highly esteemed teacher and one of the first to realize the need for authoritative works on American politics. He wrote a *History of American Politics* (1879); *The United States: Its History and Constitution* (1889); *American Political History* (1905; 2 v., ed. by J. A. Woodburn), besides contributing important articles to the *Encyclopaedia Britannica* and editing *Repre-*

sentative Orations to Illustrate American History (3 v., 1884).

Johnston, Alva (b. Sacramento, Cal., Aug. 1, 1888—d. Nov. 23, 1950), newspaperman, writer, humorist. While working on *The New York Times* (which he later left for the New York *Herald Tribune*) he won a Pulitzer Prize for his reporting. Afterward he became well known as a writer of profiles for *The New Yorker*. Several of his lengthier profiles were printed in book form: *The Great Goldwyn* (1937); *Wilson Mizner, the Legend of a Sport* (privately printed, 1943); *The Case of Erle Stanley Gardner* (1947).

Johnston, Annie Fellows (b. Evansville, Ind., May 15, 1863—d. Oct. 5, 1931), children's writer. Famous for *The Little Colonel* (1895) and subsequent volumes in the same series for children, Mrs. Johnston spent the latter part of her life in Pewee Valley, Ky., the prototype of the Lloydsboro Valley in her books. She was a woman of deep religious interests and independent spirit; at the age of seventeen she had already begun to teach school. She wrote a number of books for children besides her famous "Little Colonel Series," and a volume of reminiscence, *The Land of the Little Colonel* (1929).

Johnston, Mary (b. Buchanan, Va., Nov. 21, 1870—d. May 9, 1936), novelist. Miss Johnston wrote some of the best of the historical romances that were so popular at the beginning of the 20th century. Her second novel, To Have

AND TO HOLD (1900), was her most popular. Of her twenty-three romances fifteen have their backgrounds in Virginia; most of the others are set on the ocean and in Great Britain. Toward the middle period of her career Miss Johnston became interested in mysticism, feminism, and

socialism, and these found their way into books, such as *Silver Cross* (1922). Among her books: *Prisoners of Hope* (1898); AUDREY (1902); *Sir Mortimer* (1904); *Lewis Rand* (1908); THE LONG ROLL (1911); *Cease Firing* (1912); *Foes* (1918); *Croatan* (1923); *The Slave Ship* (1924); *Miss Delicia Allen* (1933); *Drury Randall* (1934). The best study of Miss Johnston's work is by Edward Wagenknecht in *The World and Mary Johnston* (*Sewanee Review*, April–June, 1936).

Johnston, Richard Malcolm (b. near Powelton, Ga., March 8, 1822—d. Sept. 23, 1898), teacher, lawyer, writer, lecturer, humorist. A disciple of AUGUSTUS BALDWIN LONGSTREET, Johnston was more discreet and gentlemanly than his master in the stories he did in imitation of Longstreet's *Georgia Scenes* (1835); Johnston called his book *Georgia Sketches* (1864). Like Longstreet he learned the art of storytelling as a lawyer on circuit. In an enlarged form his book was renamed DUKESBOROUGH TALES (1871). Comic, sympathetic, nearly plotless, these dialect pieces have been called "inexpert anecdotes." They were reprinted in 1883, in the heyday of southern dialect humor, and became widely popular; as a result Johnston enjoyed a new spurt of creative activity and produced *Old Mark Langston* (1884); *Two Gray Tourists* (1885); *Mr. Absalom Billingslea and Other Georgia Folk* (1888); as well as several other books. Walter Blair sees him as establishing a clear relationship between the older humor and the newer local color writing. His *Autobiography* appeared in 1900.

Johnston Smith. See SMITH, JOHNSTON.

John Street Theater. The first permanent playhouse in New York City. It opened Dec. 7, 1767. The first play given there was George Farquhar's *The Beaux' Stratagem;* it also saw the first production in New York of plays by Shakespeare, Ben Jonson, and Congreve, as well as contemporary plays and afterpieces. When the British occupied New York the playhouse was rechristened the Theater Royal, and officers of the English garrison, especially the talented Major John André, used it for amateur productions; a professional company also occupied the theater. In 1785 an American company again occupied the theater for regular seasons. They produced British plays, but their stage also saw the premières of two important American works: Royall Tyler's THE CONTRAST (1787), in the course of which Jonathan, the Yankee bumpkin, describes his first visit to a playhouse (the John Street Theater); and William Dunlap's THE FATHER (1789). The theater was used for the last time on Jan. 13, 1798; it was then sold and demolished.

Jolas, Eugene (b. Union City, N.J., 1894—d. May 26, 1952), journalist, magazine editor. Jolas, raised in Lorraine, was trilingual from childhood, an ability he put to good use later as an editor of English, French, and German texts. In his youth he returned to the United States, worked on various newspapers, became passionately interested in contemporary *avant-garde* literature, and went to Paris with his wife, Maria MacDonald. There in 1927 he founded *transition*, a magazine of experimental literature which became the chief rallying point for symbolists, surrealists, and other advanced writers throughout the Western world. Excerpts from James Joyce's *Finnegans Wake* were published in the magazine, 1927–30. The magazine continued publication until 1938.

Jolas was a brilliant editor. In the pages of his magazine he gave encouragement to many writers who became the literary leaders of their generation—Gertrude Stein, Hart Crane, Kay Boyle, Malcolm Cowley, Allen Tate, Horace Gregory, Matthew Josephson, many representatives of the Irish school, as well as important writers from France, Germany, Italy, and Russia. In 1949 he published an anthology, *Transition Workshop*, which contains a representative selection of materials from his magazine.

Jonas, Carl (b. Omaha, Neb., May 22, 1913—), novelist. Jonas graduated from Williams College in 1936, worked as a cub reporter on an Omaha newspaper, then went to New York, where he wrote free lance radio scripts. With the outbreak of World War II, he joined the Coast Guard and continued writing during his service. His first two works attracted minor appreciation from critics and practically no notice from the public. However, *Jefferson Selleck* (1951) won instant appreciation from both. Writing with almost surgical realism, Jonas gave the portrait of a dying Midwestern business man. James Hilton wrote, "This time, although the author's scalpel is razor-sharp, Babbitt is presented with real compassion." Among his other books: *Beachhead on the Wind* (1945); *Riley McCullough* (1954); *Our Revels Now Are Ended* (1957).

Jonathan. A character in Royall Tyler's play THE CONTRAST (1787), the earliest stage Yankee.

Jonathan, Brother. See BROTHER JONATHAN.

Jonathan Corncob, Loyal American Refugee, Adventures of. Written by Himself (London, 1787). One of the earliest novels based on the American Revolution, this story describes—in the manner of Fielding and sometimes of Rabelais—the nautical and amatory adventures of the hero. This Massachusetts youth, whom chance throws into the British camp, participates in the occupation of New York City by Lord Howe and takes part in other episodes in Providence, in the Barbados during a hurricane, on a prison ship in Boston harbor, and in a naval court-martial.

Jonathan Draws the Long Bow (1947), an account of New England folklore by Richard M. Dorson (1916–   ). Dorson shows that New England in literature is more than Emerson, Longfellow, and their fellows, transcendentalists and Brahmin culture, for the region is also fertile in folktales. In his affectionately written volume he gives an account of New England popular tales of varied character: stories of witches, Munchausens, Indian tragedies, buried treasure, tricksters, specters and apparitions, eerie sea happenings, legends of places. He

closes his survey with a description of "literary folktales," as created by John G. C. Brainerd, Whittier, Daniel P. Thompson, Mrs. Stowe, Rowland E. Robinson, Holman F. Day, George S. Wasson, Robert P. Tristram Coffin, and Walter Hard. See BROTHER JONATHAN.

Jonathan to John (1861), a poem by JAMES RUSSELL LOWELL which formed part of the *Second Series* of the BIGLOW PAPERS. Published in February, 1862, it was a vigorous protest against England's action when a Northern warship seized two Confederate envoys en route to Europe on the British mail steamer *Trent*. The British government demanded immediate return of the envoys and began to mobilize armies. Lincoln yielded, rather than risk war with Great Britain, but there was great anger throughout the North, voiced by Lowell in his vigorous but overlengthy poem.

Jones, Casey. See CASEY JONES.

Jones, Howard Mumford (b. Saginaw, Mich., April 16, 1892—   ), teacher, poet, critic, historian, translator, editor. Jones taught successively at the University of Texas, at North Carolina, at Michigan, at Harvard since 1936. In 1955 he was appointed chairman of The American Council of Learned Societies. His first important scholarly work was *America and French Culture, 1750–1848* (1927). *The Romanesque Lyric* (1928), done in collaboration with P. S. Allen, included some excellent translations. About this time Jones' interests turned toward American literature, always seen in the light of European influences. His later writings include: *The Life of Moses Coit Tyler* (1933); *They Say the Forties*, a collection of his poems (1937); *Ideas in America* (1944); *The Theory of American Literature* (1948). He translated Heinrich Heine's *The North Sea* (1918), edited *Major American Writers* (with E. E. LEISY, 1935) and *Oliver Wendell Holmes* (with S. I. HAYAKAWA, 1939). He wrote a *Primer of Intellectual Freedom* (1950) and compiled a *Guide to American Literature and Its Background Since 1890* (1953). In his most influential work, *The Theory of American Literature*, he notes that critics have begun to feel the importance of rediscovering "the rooted strength and classic formularies of the American ideal." *American Humanism* was published in 1957.

Jones, Idwal (b. Wales, Dec. 8, 1892— d. Nov. 14, 1964), prospector, rancher, teacher, newspaperman. Jones' wide experience has led him to the writing of several kinds of books, on folklore, California history, viticulture and mining. Among them: *The Splendid Shilling* (1926); *Steel Chips* (1929); *Black Bayou* (1941); *The Vineyard* (1942); *Vermilion* (1947). Jones has a deep interest in California, his *Vines in the Sun* (1949) being a history of grape-growing there and his *Ark of Empire* (1951) an account of a block of houses in San Francisco. His love of fine cooking has been expressed in *High Bonnet* (1945), the fictional autobiography of a chef, and in *Chef's Holiday* (1952).

Jones, James (b. Robinson, Ill., Nov. 6, 1921—

), novelist. Jones had never written seriously until, after joining the Regular Army, he read Thomas Wolfe. Then it came to him that "he had been a writer all his life without knowing it." In 1945 Jones submitted a manuscript to Maxwell Perkins who, though he returned it, detected prodigal gifts in the unpublished writer, and offered him an advance on an unwritten second book. Thus was projected the massive novel, FROM HERE TO ETERNITY (1951), an immediate best-seller, selected for the National Book Award, and made into a successful film in 1953. A brutal, almost ugly picture of the peacetime army in Hawaii, the book aroused a critical storm, many deploring the lurid language and shocking incidents, others admiring its vitality and force. C. J. Rolo spoke of it as a "spectacular achievement because of its tremendous driving power." *The New Yorker*, however, seemed to sum up the majority of opinion: "If it is a realistic and forceful novel, it is because the English language is capable of absorbing and condoning a good deal of abuse from a man who has something to say and desperately wants to say it." Dealing with less charged material in 1957, Jones wrote *Some Came Running*, which was almost unanimously condemned as a world of "flawless tedium." But in 1959, *The Pistol*, a novella with few of the vices and most of the virtues of *From Here to Eternity*, gained much critical favor, with *The New York Times* describing it as "an incisively written, superbly short novel."

Jones, James Athearn (b. Tisbury, Mass., June 4, 1791—d. Aug. [?], 1854), novelist, folklorist. Jones wrote some novels, but his main contribution to American literature was a collection of Indian legends, *Tales of an Indian Camp* (3 v., 1829), revised as *Tradition of the North American Indians* (1830).

Jones, John Beauchamp (b. Baltimore, Md., March 6, 1810—d. Feb. 4, 1866), editor, novelist, diarist. Jones saw enough of frontier life in Kentucky and Missouri to write about it familiarly in his novels. He went back East, married, and edited the Baltimore *Sunday Visiter* [sic] at about the time Edgar Allan Poe won a prize from the magazine for his *MS. Found in a Bottle*. Later Jones edited the *Madisonian*, President Tyler's personal organ. He also began writing fiction, but had to publish his *Wild Western Scenes*, in which Daniel Boone appears as a character, at his own expense (1841); it sold 100,000 copies in his lifetime. He followed with a second volume in 1856 and with *Wild Southern Scenes* in 1859, but none of his later books equaled the success of his first. He also wrote *The Life and Adventures of a Country Merchant* (1854) and *The Monarchist* (1853). As the Civil War neared, he began the *Southern Monitor* (1858) in Philadelphia; with the outbreak of the war he retreated to Montgomery, Ala., and became a clerk in the Confederate War Department. He lived in Burlington, N.J., after the war, where he prepared for publication his most valuable book, *A Rebel War Clerk's Diary* (1866).

Jones, John Paul (b. Scotland, July 6, 1747— d. July 18, 1792), naval officer. John Paul was his original name; Jones was added to conceal some difficulty he got into. In 1773 he emigrated to Virginia and in 1775 was commissioned a lieutenant in the American navy. He distinguished himself in a number of engagements, was given command of the *Bon Homme Richard* and two other vessels, with which he attacked the *Serapis* and the *Countess of Scarborough*, British convoy escorts. After a desperate battle the *Serapis* surrendered. It was during this battle that Jones, called on to surrender by the British captain, replied, "I have not yet begun to fight!" Walt Whitman admiringly described this combat in *Leaves of Grass:* "Serene stood the little captain,/ He was not hurried . . . his voice was neither high nor low,/ His eye gave more light to us than our battle-lanterns." The *Bon Homme Richard* was so badly damaged that it sank while the ships were on their way to refuge in the Netherlands. Later Jones took service in the Russian navy as a rear admiral, won several victories against the Turks, went to Paris in 1790 and remained there till his death.

Jones was a great but boastful naval commander. His earliest biographer, Alexander S. Mackenzie, said of him (1841): "No hero ever sounded his own trumpet more unremittingly or with a louder blast." He wrote well on professional subjects, and was obviously a man of intelligence as well as courage, self-confidence, and skill. He wrote *Memoirs* (2 v., 1830). Jones has attracted numerous other biographers, among them Anna F. De Koven (1913), Phillips Russell (1927), and Valentine Thomson (1939). He has figured in numerous novels, including James Fenimore Cooper's THE PILOT (1823); Allen Cunningham's *Paul Jones: A Romance* (1827); Herman Melville's ISRAEL POTTER (1855); Frederick Whittaker's *The Sea King* (1873); Winston Churchill's RICHARD CARVEL (1899); Sarah Orne Jewett's *The Tory Lover* (1901); James Boyd's DRUMS (1925); Samuel Spewack's *Mon Paul* (1928); Inglis Fletcher's *Raleigh's Eden* (1940); Edward Ellsberg's *Captain Paul* (1941); John Jennings' *Sea Eagles* (1950); Walter Karig's *Don't Tread on Me* (1954); Pearl Frye's *Gallant Captain* (1956).

Jones, Joseph Stevens (b. Boston, Sept. 28, 1809—d. Dec. 29, 1877), actor, physician, playwright. Jones' career began as an actor, then he studied medicine, receiving his degree in 1843 from Harvard. He practiced medicine for a time, became city physician of Boston, lectured on physiology. But his love of the stage led him to become manager of the Tremont Theater and begin writing plays; the number credited to him varies from 150 to 200, of all kinds—melodramas, farces, local color plays (here he was something of a pioneer), historical plays. He created a famous Yankee character in SOLON SHINGLE, a country teamster in *The People's Lawyer* (1839). Possibly the best of Jones' plays was *The Silver Spoon* (1852), which was revised and produced as late as 1911; it may have influenced Augustin Daly in *Hori-*

zon (1871) and James A. Herne in *Shore Acres* (1892). Jones turned the play into a novel, *The Life of Jefferson S. Batkins* (1871).

Although other plays by Jones are occasionally recalled—*The Liberty Tree* (1832) and *Paul Revere* (1875) among them—the strangest and one of the most popular of his productions was *Captain Kyd, or, The Wizard of the Sea* (1830). It may be noted that Jones' father was a sea captain, killed by savages on his last voyage. With its "gross similarities" to a popular drama by Edward Fitzball, *The Flying Dutchman* (1827), Jones' play is a lurid tale of hatred, piracy, and love, with the "Witch of Hell Gate" playing a leading role and with numerous Dutch characters obviously taken from Washington Irving.

Jones, Major Joseph. The pen name of WILLIAM TAPPAN THOMPSON.

Jones, Nard [Maynard Benedict] (b. Seattle, Wash., April 12, 1904—   ), newspaperman, editor, novelist. A specialist in the Pacific Northwest, Nard Jones has won particular praise for two novels, *Oregon Detour* (1930) and *Swift Flows the River* (1940). The former is set in a small wheat-farming community, the latter portrays pioneering days on the Columbia River. Among his other novels are *The Petlands* (1931); *Wheat Women* (1933); *Scarlet Petticoat* (1942); *Still to the West* (1946); *The Island* (1948); *I'll Take What's Mine* (1954); *Ride the Dark Storm* (1955); *Great Command* (1959). He has also written *Evergreen Land* (1947), a factual account of the state of Washington.

Jones, Robert Edmond (b. Milton, N.H., Dec. 12, 1887—d. Nov. 26, 1954), stage designer, author of books on the theater. Jones designed sets for some of the most notable theatrical productions of the first half of the 20th century, especially in connection with experimental troupes—the Washington Square Players, the Provincetown Players, the Greenwich Village Theater, the Theatre Guild. Jones expressed his doctrines in *The Dramatic Imagination* (1941).

Jones, Rufus [Matthew] (b. China, Me., Jan. 25, 1863—d. June 16, 1948), teacher, college preacher, philosopher, historian. For many years Jones was professor of philosophy at Haverford College. Brand Blanshard called him "the most considerable thinker that American Quakerism has produced." His teaching was chiefly Emersonian in spirit. Among his books: *Practical Christianity* (1899); *Studies in Mystical Religion* (1909); *The Inner Life* (1916); *The Church's Debt to Heretics* (1925); *Flowering of Mysticism* (1939); *A Call to What Is Vital* (1948). Elizabeth Gray Vining has written *Friend of Life: The Biography of Rufus M. Jones* (1958).

Jones, Thomas S[amuel], Jr. (b. Boonville, N.Y., Nov. 6, 1882—d. Oct. 16, 1932), poet. A dedicated poet, Jones had sufficient means to devote his life to the cultivation of his art. He produced much verse in a Georgian vein, some of it ranking beside that of his English cohorts. He was particularly fond of sonnets. Among his

books: *The Path of Dreams* (1905); *The Rose Jar* (1906); *The Voice in the Silence* (1911); *Shadow of the Perfect Rose: Collected Poems* (1937, published posthumously).

Jordan, David Starr (b. Gainesville, N.Y., Jan. 19, 1851—d. Sept. 9, 1931), physician, teacher, scientist, college administrator, writer. Jordan began teaching botany at Cornell University, was appointed president of Stanford in 1891, became chancellor in 1913, retired in 1916. His specialty was ichthyology, and he often assisted the government in its investigations of fisheries. He was also greatly interested in furthering the cause of peace, and was an official of many organizations working in that field. He wrote, among other books, *Science Sketches* (1887); *Care and Culture of Men* (1896); *To Barbara* (poems, 1897); *Fishes* (1907); *The Human Harvest* (1907); *Stability of Truth* (1909); *War's Aftermath* (1914); *The Days of a Man* (autobiography, 2 v., 1922). Alice N. Hays has edited *David Starr Jordan: A Bibliography of His Writings, With an Appreciation by Robert E. Swain* (1952).

Jordan, Elizabeth (b. Milwaukee, Wis., May 9, 1867—d. Feb. 24, 1947), newspaperwoman, editor, playwright, memoirist, novelist, short-story writer. Miss Jordan was on the staff of the old New York *World* for ten years, editor of the *Sunday World* for three years more. She was then a "sob sister," writing "True Stories of the News" for each issue of the paper and covering many murder cases. Her stories on the LIZZIE BORDEN murder trial were avidly read. She was convinced that the defendant was innocent (though the account in her autobiography is full of errors). She became editor of HARPER'S BAZAAR, later literary adviser to Harper & Brothers. She was a close friend of Henry James, Mark Twain, William Dean Howells, and other literary and journalistic leaders; she "discovered" SINCLAIR LEWIS, whose first book she accepted and whose manuscripts she rigorously edited. She also wrote books and plays of her own: *Tales of the City Room* (1898); *Tales of the Cloister* (1901); *The Lady from Oklahoma* (a comedy, 1911); *The Story of a Pioneer* (with ANNA HOWARD SHAW, 1915); *Black Butterflies* (1926); *Page Mr. Pomeroy* (1933); *The Life of the Party* (1935); *The Real Ruth Arnold* (1945). She told her own story in *Three Rousing Cheers* (1938), depicting a life of great literary and editorial activity but also of devotion to many causes, especially woman suffrage and the welfare of authors.

Joseph, Chief (b. Idaho, 1840?—d. Sept. 21, 1904), NEZ PERCÉ Indian chieftain, military strategist. His Indian name was Hin-Ma-Too-Yah-Lat-Kekht, meaning "Thunder Coming from Water Up Over the Land." When the Federal government went back on its treaty with the Nez Percé in Idaho in 1863, Chief Joseph led his people in revolt. He won high praise from his antagonists for his extraordinary military skill. He was finally forced to surrender, on promise of good treatment. He was an outstanding spokesman for his race, especially through the medium of an article in the *North American Review* (April, 1879).

Josephson, Matthew (b. Brooklyn, N.Y., Feb. 15, 1899—), editor, biographer. Josephson was one of the group of rebels and expatriates who made the 1920's exciting in New York and Paris. He was even a member of a group, including Gorham Munson, that rebelled against the other rebels by founding a magazine called *Secession* (Spring, 1922—April, 1924). The magazine was called, on retrospect, "a queer mixture of juvenility, arrogance, and good sense." Josephson later joined the staff of BROOM, which had been fairly conservative up to that time, but thereafter was exciting, erratic, and short-lived. Still later he was the American editor of *transition*, then assistant editor of the *New Republic;* in 1948 he was elected a member of the National Institute of Arts and Letters. Meanwhile he had turned to well-written biographies and to muckraking books on business and politics. Among them: *Zola and His Time* (1928); *Portrait of the Artist as an American* (1930), biographical sketches joined by a thesis that industrial society defeats art; *Jean-Jacques Rousseau* (1932); *The Robber Barons* (1934); *The Politicos* (1938); *The President Makers* (1940); *Victor Hugo* (1942); *Stendhal* (1946); *Sidney Hillman* (1952); *Edison* (1959); *Life Among the Surrealists* (1962).

Josiah Allen's Wife. The pen name of MARIETTA HOLLEY.

Journal of a Visit to London and the Continent, 1849–50 (1948), a journal kept by HERMAN MELVILLE during a trip abroad, edited by Eleanor Melville Metcalf and published a century after it was written.

Journal of Julius Rodman (*Burton's Gentleman's Magazine,* January to June, 1840), an unfinished novel by EDGAR ALLAN POE. It was an inferior production, published anonymously.

Journals of Madam Knight and the Rev. Mr. Buckingham, The (1825). See SARAH KEMBLE KNIGHT.

Journey to the Land of Eden, A (1841), a journal by WILLIAM BYRD. Byrd kept this record of his trip to North Carolina in 1733; in it he set down his frank, often satirical observations on many subjects, including the country folk in the regions he visited.

J. S. of Dale. The pen name of FREDERIC JESUP STIMSON.

Judah, Samuel B[enjamin] H[elbert] (b. New York City, 1799?—d. July 21, 1876), dramatist, novelist, poet, lawyer. Judah tried hard to win fame in the theater, and then as a novelist, but succeeded only moderately. The ridicule and strictures that he received offended his vanity greatly, and in a satire, *Gotham and the Gothamites* (1823), he sought revenge on his critics. The result was a suit for libel, which he lost; he was fined and imprisoned. Plays of his produced up to that time included *The Mountain Torrent* (1820); *The Rose of Arragon* (1822); *A Tale of Lexington* (1822); *Odofriede the Outcast* (1822). He boasted that it took him only two or three days to write a play. Unable to gain a

reputation, Judah studied for the bar and was admitted in 1825. In 1827 he published *The Buccaneers, A Romance of Our Own Country in Its Ancient Day,* one of the earliest novels to make use of the legend of Captain Kidd. It was not, however, a straightforward narrative: Judah continued to harp on the vices of his own time.

Judd, Sylvester, III (b. Westhampton, Mass., July 23, 1813—d. Jan. 26, 1853), teacher, clergyman, novelist, poet. Judd broke with the rigid Calvinism of his ancestors by becoming a Unitarian clergyman. He seems to have exercised keen powers of observation during his pastoral calls, for some of his novels contain passages of considerable realism. But the books are more notable for their utopian ideas, especially those of Fourier, then popular with the transcendentalists. Judd published anonymously MARGARET, A TALE OF THE REAL AND IDEAL, INCLUDING SKETCHES OF A PLACE NOT BEFORE DESCRIBED, CALLED MONS CHRISTI (1845; rev., 2 v., 1851), a book designed "to promote the idea of a liberal Christianity." The heroine is the daughter of a German musician who completely transforms a New England village; the book strongly suggests the influence of Goethe's *Wilhelm Meister.* Judd espoused all the "causes" of his day—antislavery, pacifism, temperance, opposition to capital punishment—but always in a mild, nonaggressive spirit. He also wrote *A Young Man's Account of His Conversion from Calvinism* (1843); and in his biography, *The Life and Character of the Rev. Sylvester Judd* (1854), by Arethusa Hall, is preserved a document for private family use that he called *Cardiography,* an exposition of his theological difficulties and conclusions.

Judge. This comic weekly was founded in 1881 by a group of writers and artists who had resigned from the staff of PUCK not long after H. C. BUNNER became the editor of that magazine; James Albert Wales (1852–1886), a cartoonist, was the leader of the group. It had financial difficulties until it was recognized, two or three years later, as an organ for the Republicans, in opposition to *Puck* and the Democrats, but did not reach the height of its influence till the first decade of the next century. During the depression period of the 1930's it became a monthly, but ceased publication in 1939. Occasional wisecracks from its pages have survived: "Women are like money—keep them busy or they lose interest." "A go-getter once became his own boss: in two months he worked himself to death." An unsuccessful attempt to revive *Judge* was made in 1953.

Judgment Day. See YOUNG LONIGAN.

Judson, Adoniram (b. Malden, Mass., Aug. 9, 1788—d. April 12, 1850), clergyman, missionary, linguist. As a missionary to Burma, Judson suffered great hardships, including imprisonment and the death of his first two wives and five of his twelve children. He wrote the first section of an English-Burmese dictionary (1849); the Burmese-English part was later completed by Edward A. Stevens. He also made a translation of the Bible into Burmese (1834) and wrote many hymns. His third wife, **Emily [Chubbuck] Judson ["Fanny Forester"]** (b. Aug. 22, 1817—d. June 1, 1854), wrote moralistic sketches and a novel, *Allen Lucas, The Self-Made Man* (1842), later reprinted along with two other tales as *How to Be Great, Good, and Happy;* also a memoir of her husband's second wife, an unfinished memoir of Judson, and *Alderbrook* (1847), popular for several years. Both Judson's first and second wives likewise wrote books. Judson is the subject of Honoré Willsie Morrow's romance, *The Splendor of God* (1929).

Judson, E[dward] Z[ane] C[arroll] ["Ned Buntline"] (b. Stamford, Delaware Co., N.Y. March 20, 1823—d. July 16, 1886), midshipman, soldier, fur-trader, magazine editor, organizer of the Know Nothing party, playwright, dime novelist. Judson's career is more incredible than any of the four hundred dime novels he is said to have written. He served in the navy and won a reputation as an inveterate duelist. Later, in Nashville, he fought a duel with the husband of his mistress, killed him, was taken out by a mob and actually lynched—but was rescued at the point of death. He led the Astor Place Riots in New York against the English actor Macready, and was sent to jail for a year. He was a bitter anti-Catholic, and invented the name Know Nothing (a signal for secrecy) as the name of a faction against the Catholics. Although dismissed from the Union army for drunkenness during the Civil War, he later claimed the title of colonel and stated that he had been Chief of Scouts for the Army of the Potomac.

In the meantime he had become a prolific writer of dime novels, a genre that he is credited with originating. Some he published in a magazine he founded, *Ned Buntline's Own*, which preceded Beadle & Adams by at least a decade; in later years Judson worked for the latter firm. (See ERASTUS F. BEADLE.) On a trip to the West he met Col. WILLIAM F. CODY and wrote a play, *The Scouts of the Plains* (1872), for him; it was Judson who named the famous scout Buffalo Bill. Judson also wrote hymns and lectured on temperance. He undoubtedly had an astonishing knack with words, and once wrote a novel of more than six hundred pages in sixty-two hours. His original Buffalo Bill story, written in 1869 after a hasty interview with the then unknown Cody, was called *Buffalo Bill, the King of the Border Men;* it was later brought out in book form and was repeatedly reprinted.

Judson's dime novels have become collectors' items. These are a few characteristic titles: *Magdalena, The Beautiful Mexican Maid* (1847); *The Black Avenger* (1847); *The Gals of New York* (1848); *Norwood, or, Life on the Prairie* (1849); *Stella Delorme, or, The Comanche's Dream* (1860). Jay Monaghan has written a biography of Judson called *The Great Rascal* (1952). See THE DIME NOVEL.

Judson, Emily [Chubbuck]. See ADONIRAM JUDSON.

Julius Rodman. See JOURNAL OF JULIUS RODMAN.

Jumel, Mme. Eliza (b. at sea, 1769—d. July 16, 1865), lady of fortune. She was known as Eliza Brown or Betsey Bowen before she became the wife of a wealthy French wine merchant, Stephen Jumel, who had been driven out of his Haitian estates by a slave insurrection. In 1810 Jumel purchased and restored a Georgian mansion in New York City, at one time used as a military headquarters by Washington and by the British. Jumel died in 1832, and in 1833 Mme. Jumel married AARON BURR, then in his eightieth year. He managed to lose most of her fortune, and they separated not long before his death in 1836. The Jumel mansion was acquired by New York City as a museum in 1903. Mme. Jumel appears in Gertrude Atherton's THE CONQUEROR (1902). William H. Shelton described *The Jumel Mansion* (1916) and William C. Duncan wrote *The Amazing Madame Jumel* (1935).

Jump, Jim Crow. See JIM CROW.

Jumping Frog of Calaveras County, The Celebrated. See CELEBRATED JUMPING FROG.

Jungle, The (1906), a novel by UPTON SINCLAIR. Rarely has a book had such direct influence upon people's lives as did Sinclair's appalling vivid account of the Chicago stockyards. Sinclair takes Jurgis Rudkus, a poor Slav immigrant, as his central character, depicting with revolting realism his experiences as a worker in the stockyards. Jurgis becomes debased, and then, in accordance with Sinclair's own creed, turns to Socialism as a way out.

The book's two theses—that the so-called Beef Trust was knowingly selling diseased meat to the public, and that it held its employees down to a bare subsistence wage level—attracted tremendous attention. Theodore Roosevelt, then President, read the book and was profoundly shocked. He sent for Sinclair, who was able to give him exact information based on long research in Packingtown. Sinclair, it is said, wanted to give other ideas to Roosevelt, who remarked, "Tell Sinclair to go home and let me run the government."

The book became the *Uncle Tom's Cabin* of its generation. The stockyards were cleaned up, literally; a Pure Food and Drug Act was passed; labor conditions were ameliorated. Sinclair used the money he made to start a Socialistic colony called HELICON HALL in New Jersey, where Sinclair Lewis served briefly as a janitor. The book was translated into seventeen languages. In 1946 a new edition was issued, with an introduction by Sinclair.

Jungle Days (1925), an account of scientific experiences by WILLIAM BEEBE. The scene is British Guiana. The studies of flora and fauna are given a dramatic turn by an imagination which distinguishes Beebe as much as his scientific accuracy and insight. He sees the strange workings of nature as an endless chain of life and death, describes the adaptability of the jungle creatures, brings into his pages the rich coloring of tropical nature.

Junior Literary Guild. An offshoot of the LITERARY GUILD, this club was founded in 1929, with HELEN FERRIS as editor-in-chief. An anniversary volume, *To Enrich Your Life* (1939), describes its extensive operations, especially in the schools.

Junípero, Serra. See Miguel José Serra.

Jurgen (1919), a novel by James Branch Cabell, which became a *cause célèbre* and established the author's fame. This book forms part of an elaborate series of novels laid in the imaginary realm called Poictesme. Jurgen is a middle-aged pawnbroker married to a nagging wife who suddenly disappears. Jurgen goes in search of her, but really is in quest of his lost youth. By magic he finds himself twenty-one again, and sets out on strange adventures, including visits to Heaven and Hell, in which he meets a lost sweetheart and encounters a host of mythical persons. At the end he goes home, finds his wife there, and is glad to be a middle-aged, henpecked husband again.

Cabell mingles figures of ancient and medieval legend and creatures of folklore and his own imagination with persons of Christian faith, indicating that he believes in the latter just about as much as in the former. Jurgen discovers that all is vanity. Fifteen years later, in writing an introduction for a reissue of the book in the Modern Library, Cabell said that the indecency which so many persons read into *Jurgen* was an invention of the prurient, and that the novel really was "a convinced plea for monogamy, an exposure of the ultimate folly of any extra-matrimonial relations of a married man." Cabell was in fact a realist who deliberately wrote romance exaggerated to such a degree that it burst like an overblown bubble. He discussed domestic felicity, standards of morality, and political conceptions with an irony reminiscent of Anatole France. He clothed obscenities in erudition; one critic commented that Cabell's sexuality was "more truly a reaction against the South's sentimental deification of 'pure womanhood' than a call to passionate experience."

The New York Society for the Suppression of Vice, of which John S. Sumner was the executive, banned *Jurgen* from the bookshops, an act which aroused the literati. For two years the novel was supposedly out of circulation—to the great profit of the booksellers. An emergency committee was organized to battle for the book; it published a report, *Jurgen and the Censor*. When the case came to court, the judge advised acquittal. Sumner did not give up his cause, but the way was cleared for the publication of books compared with which *Jurgen's* veil of symbolism and remote phrasing were mere prudery.

Jusserand, Jean Jules (b. France, 1855—d. 1932), historian, diplomat. Jusserand, who had won fame with his books on English literature and history, was appointed ambassador to the United States in 1902. Not long afterwards appeared the last part of his most famous work, *Literary History of the English People* (3 v., 1895–1909). He was a great favorite with Washington society, including presidents. One book of his, *With Americans of Past and Present Days* (1916), received the first Pulitzer Prize for history, and he was the only non-American ever elected president of the American Historical Society.

Just A-Wearyin' for You (1909), a poem by Frank Stanton that was set to music by Carrie Jacobs Bond and won immediate popularity.

Just Before the Battle, Mother (1863), a favorite Civil War song by George Root (1820–1895). A sequel, *Just After the Battle*, was less successful.

K

Kafka, Franz. See AMERIKA.

Kah-ge-ga-gah-bowh, Chief [George Copway] (b. Canada, 1818—d. 1863), Ojibway chieftain, writer. A great hunter noted for his strength, this chieftain obtained an education in Illinois, became a writer of considerable reputation. Among his works: *The Life, Letters, and Speeches of Chief Kah-Ge-Ga-Gah-Bowh* (1850); *The Ojibway Conquest, A Tale of the Northwest* (an epic poem, 1850); *Running Sketches of Men and Places in Europe* (1851); *Traditional History and Characteristic Sketches of the Ojibway Nation* (1850). He was a close personal friend of Longfellow.

Kahler, Hugh M[acNair] (b. Philadelphia, Feb. 25, 1883—   ), editor, novelist, short-story writer. Among his novels: *Babel* (1921); *The East Wind* (1922); *Father Means Well* (1930); *The Big Pink* (1932); *Bright Danger* (1941). Kahler was for some years a contributing editor of the *Ladies' Home Journal*.

Kahn, Otto H[ermann] (b. Germany, Feb. 21, 1867—d. March 29, 1934), banker, patron of the arts. See HART CRANE.

Kalashnikoff, Nicholas S. (b. Russia, May 17, 1888—d. Aug. 17, 1961), writer. The first of Kalashnikoff's five books, *They That Take the Sword* (1939), was a "Harper Find" and won him a MacDowell Fellowship. This passionate fictionalized history of the Russian Revolution and the early years of the Communist regime was based on the author's own experiences. At Moscow University, he had been arrested for revolutionary activities and, after a year of solitary confinement, sent to northern Siberia. Later he fought in the Czar's army in World War I with the rank of captain; during the Russian Civil War he was for a time a general. *Jumper,* his debt of gratitude to war horses, was published in 1944 and acclaimed a classic to stand beside *Black Beauty.*

Kallen, H[orace] M[eyer] (b. Germany, Aug. 11, 1882—   ), teacher, editor, translator, dramatist, philosopher. He served mainly as Research Professor in Social Philosophy at the New School for Social Research in New York. As the most important advocate of WILLIAM JAMES' pragmatism, he edited an unfinished work by James. He himself is known as the exponent of a system of thought he called "cultural pluralism." Kallen prepared an acting version of the Book of Job as a Greek tragedy which has been widely performed. On his seventieth birthday was published *Vision and Action* (1953), a group of essays in his honor edited by S. Ratner, with a bibliography by Earle F. Walbridge. Among his books are *Culture and Democracy in the U.S.* (1924); *Art and Freedom* (2 v., 1942); *The Liberal Spirit* (1948); *Patterns of Progress* (1950); *Cultural Pluralism and the American Idea* (1956); *Utopians at Bay* (1958); *The Book of Job as Greek Tragedy* (1959); *A Study of Liberty* (1959).

Kalloolah (1849), a novel by WILLIAM STARBUCK MAYO. Mayo, a physician affected by wanderlust, went off to the Barbary States, determined to explore Inner Africa. He never got far, and soon returned home to practice his profession and write. His first book—undeservedly forgotten—is *Kalloolah*, the narrative of Jonathan Romer, a young American who makes up his mind to explore Africa. After varied adventures he reaches the fictitious city of Killoam, a sort of utopia utilized by Mayo to make fun of some of the usages of civilization.

Kalm, Peter (b. Sweden, 1716—d. 1779), botanist. Kalm was sent to America in 1748–51 by the Swedish Academy of Sciences. His observant, if somewhat naive, account of his experiences appeared in Sweden (3 v., 1753–61), in English translation as *Travels into North America* (2 v., 1770–71). He prepared a fourth volume, but this was destroyed in a fire. Notes on which this volume was based, however, have been incorporated in Adolph B. Benson's *The America of 1750: Peter Kalm's Travels in North America* (2 v., 1937).

Kaltenborn, H. V. [Hans von] (b. Milwaukee, Wis., July 9, 1878—d. June 14, 1965), editor, teacher, radio news analyst. Kaltenborn won his reputation after he became a news broadcaster and interpreter (1929), first for the Columbia Broadcasting System, later for the National Broadcasting Company. He covered many important events, received citations for "outstanding services" to radio and journalism. Among his books: *We Look at the World* (1930); *I Broadcast the Crisis* (1938); *Kaltenborn Edits the War News* (1942); *Europe Now* (1945); *Fifty Fabulous Years* (1950); *It Seems Like Yesterday* (1956).

Kane, Elisha Kent (b. Philadelphia, Feb. 3, 1820—d. Feb. 16, 1857), surgeon, explorer, writer. As assistant surgeon in the U.S. Navy, Kane in 1850 went as senior medical officer on board a rescue expedition that searched in vain for Sir John Franklin (1786–1847), Arctic explorer; Franklin was not given up for dead until 1857. Kane's account of the futile search was published as *The U.S. Grinnell Expedition in Search of Sir John Franklin* (1853). Kane made a second expedition in search of Franklin, this time as commander of the *Advance*. His party made some important explorations, made an overland journey to a Danish settlement in Greenland, and returned to New York City in October, 1855. Kane's *Arctic Explorations: The Second Grinnell Expedition* (2 v., 1856) is rich in scientific data and is written in a forcible style that is often unexpectedly poetic. It became an immediate best seller.

Kane, Harnett Thomas (b. New Orleans, Nov. 8, 1910—   ), newspaperman, novelist. Kane graduated from Tulane University, was a reporter on the New Orleans *Item-Tribune* (1928–43), and taught journalism at Loyola University in New Orleans. He is perhaps best known for *Louisiana Hayride: American Rehearsal for Dictatorship* (1941), an account of the career of Huey Long from his rise to power until his death and the victory of the opposition forces in 1940. Other non-fiction works are *Bayous of Louisiana* (1943); *Gentlemen, Swords and Pistols* (1951); and *Spies for the Blue and Gray* (1954). His novels, which are based on fact, include *Bride of Fortune* (1948), the story of Varina Howell, the wife of Jefferson Davis; *The Lady of Arlington* (1953), a story based on the life of Mrs. Robert E. Lee; *The Gallant Mrs. Stonewall* (1957).

Kang, Younghill (b. Korea, 1903—   ), teacher, translator, memoirist, novelist. In the United States since 1921, Kang has endeavored to serve as an interpreter of the Far East to America. He taught at New York University, served on the staff of the *Encyclopaedia Britannica* and the Metropolitan Museum. His first book was *Translations of Oriental Poetry* (1929). He went to Europe for two years on a Guggenheim fellowship. An account of his own experiences appears in his best-known book, *The Grass Roof* (1931). *East Goes West* (1937) is a novel dealing in a more general way with the life of Orientals in America.

Kanin, Garson (b. Rochester, N.Y., Nov. 24, 1912—   ), actor, playwright, director, writer. Kanin has been actively connected with the theater, on Broadway and in Hollywood, and has acted in many Broadway successes. He was an assistant to GEORGE ABBOTT, and in 1937 joined the production staff of SAMUEL GOLDWYN. During World War II he and Carol Reed of England were appointed to direct General Eisenhower's *The True Glory,* a documentary of the war which received an Academy Award in 1945. One of Kanin's most notable plays was *Born Yesterday* (1946), which ran nearly four years, and was made into a motion picture; others are *A Double Life* (1948), in collaboration with his wife, Ruth Gordon; *Smile of the World* (1949); *The Rat Race* (1949). He wrote an English libretto for Johann Strauss' *Die Fledermaus,* directed it for the Metropolitan Opera. In 1955 he directed *The Diary of Anne Frank.* He also wrote short stories, and he published his first novel, *Blow Up a Storm,* in 1959.

Kantor, MacKinlay (b. Webster City, Iowa, Feb. 4, 1904—   ), newspaperman, columnist, writer. Kantor wrote competently in many fields. He began as a reporter, became a free-lance writer, won success with his early novels, occasionally worked in Hollywood. He told the story of his childhood in *But Look, the Morn* (1947). His first novel, *Diversey* (1928), is a story of Chicago gangsters. *Long Remember*

(1934, rev., 1956), is a realistic novel about the Battle of Gettysburg. *The Voice of Bugle Ann* (1935), the engaging story of a hound, was very popular; later came *Arouse and Beware* (1936) and *The Romance of Rosy Ridge*

Tim Kantor

(1937), the former laid in the Civil War period, the latter immediately after it. In *Valedictory* (1939), a high-school janitor watches a class receive its diplomas and remembers incidents in their school lives. Among his other novels: *The Jaybird* (1932); *Gentle Annie* (1942); *Happy Land* (1943); *Midnight Lace* (1948); *Signal 32* (1950). Kantor also wrote a novel in spirited verse, *Glory for Me* (1945), a story of three discharged service men; and *Turkey in the Straw* (1935), ballads and other verse. He was the scenarist for an excellent movie, *The Best Years of Our Lives* (1947), and some critics have felt that his later books have been written chiefly with an eye on Hollywood. His ANDERSONVILLE (1955), the story of the infamous Confederate prison, became a best seller; it was followed by *Spirit Lake* (1961) and others.

Karig, Walter ["Keats Patrick"] (b. New York City, Nov. 13, 1898?—d. Sept. 30, 1956), newspaperman, artist, novelist, writer of juvenile stories, naval officer. Karig worked for the Newark (N.J.) *News,* part of the time as Washington correspondent. Under his own name, the pen name of Keats Patrick, and other pseudonyms, he began writing books in the late 1920's, and won critical approval with *Lower Than Angels* (1945), probably his best novel. Among his other novels are *Caroline Hicks* (1951); *Neely* (1953); *Don't Tread on Me* (1954). Attached to the Navy Department during World War II as a public relations man, he attained the rank of captain (1946) and became co-author of an excellent series of *Battle Reports* (1944 and later).

Kate Beaumont (1872), a novel by JOHN W. DE FOREST. Based on De Forest's experience as an official of the Freedmen's Bureau in the Reconstruction period, this novel dealt with plantation society in Charleston and with the "poor whites" in South Carolina. De Forest's depiction of the latter anticipated that of William Faulkner and Erskine Caldwell. William Dean Howells regarded this as De Forest's best novel, but it sold poorly.

Katharine Walton (1851), a novel by W. G. SIMMS. See THE PARTISAN.

Kauffman, Reginald Wright (b. Columbia, Pa., Sept. 8, 1877—d. April 25, 1959), editor, drama critic, novelist, poet. Many of his numerous books have been popular in languages other than English. Among his writings: *Jarvis of Harvard* (1901; rev., 1923); *What Is Socialism?* (1910); *The House of Bondage* (1910); *Jim* (1915; reissued, 1929, as *Jim Trent*); *The Mark of the Beast* (1916); *Our Navy at Work* (1918); *The Blood of Kings* (1926); *The Alabama Case* (1927); THE OVERLAND TRAIL (1927); *Impossible Peace* (1943). Kauffman served on many government commissions and in numerous cultural and social welfare groups.

Kaufman, George S[imon] (b. Pittsburgh, Pa., Nov. 16, 1889—d. June 2, 1961), columnist, playwright. The list of Kaufman's plays is a long one; most were Broadway hits and cordially received by the critics. Brooks Atkinson, writing an introduction for *Six Plays* by Kaufman and Moss HART (1942), described Kaufman as "master of the destructive jest," and adds that "the fury of the gags, the bitterness and speed of the attacks upon stupidity, the loudness of the humor, the precision of the phrasing are remarkable in the field of popular comedy." Kaufman began contributing to F. P. Adams' column, THE CONNING TOWER, through Adams' influence became a columnist on the Washington *Mail*, succeeded Adams as columnist on the New York *World*, joined the staff of the New York *Tribune* as a theatrical reporter, and then served capably on the New York *Times* in the same capacity.

Kaufman almost always did his plays with a collaborator, and frequently his expert services as a "play doctor" were utilized for plays that needed reworking. He was the sole author of *The Butter-and-Egg Man* (1925), which perhaps used some of his own experiences. His long series of collaborations with MARC CONNELLY included: DULCY (1921), a satire on a stupid, cliché-mouthing woman who had appeared first in F.P.A.'s column; *To the Ladies* (1922), a comedy of home life; BEGGAR ON HORSEBACK (1924), a satire on big business and its relation to art, based on a German comedy by Paul Apel; and MERTON OF THE MOVIES (1922), a merciless satire of Hollywood in which Kaufman himself took a role as an actor. Kaufman and Connelly were ideal collaborators; Kaufman never did better work than in these plays.

With Moss HART, Kaufman wrote *Once in a Lifetime* (1930), another satire of Hollywood; *Merrily We Roll Along* (1934); YOU CAN'T TAKE IT WITH YOU (1936), a harum-scarum farce which won a Pulitzer Prize; *I'd Rather Be Right* (1937), a satire on the New Deal; *The American Way* (1939), a paean to democracy; THE MAN WHO CAME TO DINNER (1939), an unflattering portrait that suggested ALEXANDER WOOLLCOTT, called "Sheridan Whiteside" (Woollcott himself toured in the leading role); and GEORGE WASHINGTON SLEPT HERE (1940), a saga of a house in the country.

With EDNA FERBER Kaufman wrote *Minick* (1924), based on one of Miss Ferber's finest short stories; *The Royal Family* (1927), an amusing revelation of the vagaries and eccentricities of a theatrical family resembling the BARRYMORES; DINNER AT EIGHT (1932), an adroit exposé of high society; *Stage Door* (1936), a sympathetic picture of the difficulties of young actresses; *The Land is Bright* (1941); and *Bravo!* (1948). With Morrie Ryskind he wrote OF THEE I SING (1932), a Gilbertian satire on American politics that won a Pulitzer Prize. GEORGE GERSHWIN wrote the music for the show, his brother Ira the lyrics. The year before, Kaufman had written the book for a musical show called *The Band Wagon* in collaboration with HOWARD DIETZ; this is called by Cecil Smith "one of the most perfect revues in the history of Broadway." Another show with Ryskind, *Let 'Em Eat Cake* (1933), was a sequel to *Of Thee I Sing*, but was less successful. With RING LARDNER, Kaufman wrote *June Moon* (1929), a farce about Tin-Pan Alley. With Alexander Woollcott he wrote *The Dark Tower* (1933); with Katharine Dayton *First Lady* (1935), about Washington society. With NUNNALLY JOHNSON he wrote a musical play, *Park Avenue* (1946). *The Small Hours* (1951), also about married life, was done with his second wife, Leueen MacGrath. He wrote *The Solid Gold Cadillac* (1952) with Howard Teichmann, and *Silk Stockings* (1953) with Abe Burrows. See also THE LATE GEORGE APLEY.

Kavanagh (1849), a romance by HENRY WADSWORTH LONGFELLOW. The central value of *Kavanagh* is the idyllic atmosphere it creates. It is a story of unfulfilled dreams, and of literary as well as amatory aspirations. The most believable character is the local schoolmaster, Mr. Churchill. The book opens on his literary reflections, but his incapacity to be the poet of his dreams is made obvious by his failure to see the drama going on around him. Kavanagh is the new minister in the town of Fairmeadow, and two girls, initially great friends, fall in love with him. Alice Archer is poor and tied to a blind mother; in contrast, Cecilia Vaughn is both beautiful and rich. Kavanagh, ignorant of Alice's love, marries Cecilia and leaves Fairmeadow; Alice wastes away and dies. When the couple returns, Kavanagh has a long discussion with Mr. Churchill on the nature of affairs in town, and the latter has to report that his romance has not yet been written.

The book delighted many discerning readers, among them Emerson and Hawthorne; the latter recognized the quietness of the book to be its chief quality. It has many quick realistic observations of small town life and character, and creates, on the whole, an amusing and romantic vision of a small New England town in which passions are either satirized or sentimentalized.

Kazan, Elia (b. Turkey, Sept. 7, 1909—   ), director. One of the most gifted of present-day directors, Kazan turned to stage directing in 1940 after seven years of acting with the turbulent and vital GROUP THEATER. He has worked with some of the most distinguished plays of the American theater: *The Skin of Our Teeth, A Streetcar Named Desire, Deep Are the Roots, All My Sons, Death of a Salesman, Cat on a Hot Tin Roof, J.B.* In 1944 he also began to direct motion pictures: *A Tree Grows in Brooklyn, Gentlemen's Agreement, Pinky, A Streetcar Named Desire, On the Waterfront* (for which he received an Academy Award for 1954), *East of Eden.* Kazan also co-founded the famous Actors Studio, to teach the controversial "method acting," which demands greater realism from the actor.

Kazin, Alfred (b. Brooklyn, N.Y., June 5, 1915—   ), critic, teacher, editor, memoirist. A perceptive critic of modern literature, Kazin is known primarily for *On Native Grounds: An Interpretation of Modern American Prose Literature* (1942; reprinted, 1956) and *The Inmost Leaf* (1955), a similar later collection. In 1951 he published an appealing book of autobiographical memories and reflections, *A Walker in the City.* He was co-editor of *Emerson: A Modern Anthology* in 1958; edited *The Portable William Blake* (1946); also wrote *F. Scott Fitzgerald: The Man and His Work* (1951) and *Contemporaries* (1962).

Keats, John C. (b. Georgia, June 12, 1920—   ), author. Keats is the author of three hard-hitting critiques of various aspects of contemporary American life. *The Crack In The Picture Window* (1957) is a study of life in low-down-payment suburbia. *Schools Without Scholars* (1958) is a discussion of follies and failures in primary and secondary education. The *Insolent Chariots* (1958) is an analysis of the big car complex as it affects Detroit and the American consumer. Notable for their intense conviction, wit, and information, the books have had a considerable popular success.

Keefe, Jack. The supposed writer of the letters by a baseball player that appear in Ring Lardner's satiric YOU KNOW ME, AL: A BUSHER'S LETTERS (1916). They describe the adventures of a baseball rookie.

Keenan, Henry Francis (b. Rochester, N.Y., May 4, 1850—d. March 7, 1928), novelist. He is remembered for THE MONEY-MAKERS (1885), which was published anonymously. He also wrote *Trajan* (1885), *The Aliens* (1886), and other novels. *The Money-Makers,* called in a subtitle "A Social Parable," sought to show the corrupting influence of big business and was intended as a reply to John Hay's attack on labor unions, THE BREADWINNERS (1884).

Keep Cool: A Novel Written in Hot Weather by Somebody (1817), by JOHN NEAL. This was Neal's first novel and one of the earliest of all American novels. It tells the story of a man who suffers deep remorse after killing a man in a duel. Neal admitted later that it contained much that was childish.

Keimer, Samuel (b. England, Feb. 11, 1688—d. 1739?), printer, publisher, editor, poet, writer of religious tracts. Keimer was an eccentric, the author of *A Brand Pluck'd from the Burning* and *A Search after Religion* (both 1718). In 1722 he came to Philadelphia and set up a printing shop. When BENJAMIN FRANKLIN came there in search of work he met Keimer, who later employed him. Franklin discovered that Keimer's religion was a mixture of French philosophical and Biblical ideas, sometimes carried to ridiculous extremes.

Later the men quarreled; and when word came to Keimer that Franklin was about to start a newspaper, Keimer hurriedly produced one of his own, *The Universal Instructor in All Arts and Sciences: and Pennsylvania Gazette* (December, 1728). When Franklin realized he had been betrayed, he joined forces with Andrew Bradford in the *American Weekly Mercury* and in February, 1729, began contributing to it his BUSY-BODY PAPERS, with an occasional attack on Keimer. The latter ran his newspaper for thirty-nine numbers, then sold out to Franklin; he gave up his printing business and left for Barbados. Franklin called the newspaper THE PENNSYLVANIA GAZETTE and ran it successfully until 1766. Because the *Saturday Evening Post* was first issued (1821) from an office at one time occupied by the *Gazette,* the *Post* chose for a while to claim that it was "founded" by Franklin.

Keimer appeared in 1734 as the editor of the *Barbados Gazette.* On one occasion he expressed his views too freely, was convicted of libel and bound over to keep the peace for six months. A collection of papers from this periodical was published in London in 1741 in two quarto volumes under the title *Caribbeana*—supposedly as an imitation of *The Tatler.* Keimer is chiefly remembered today through Franklin's vivid, mocking portrait of him in his *Autobiography.*

Keiser, Albert (b. Germany, Dec. 7, 1887—   ), clergyman, missionary, teacher. Keiser came to the United States as a child and was educated in American schools and colleges. He became a clergyman of the Lutheran Church, worked as a missionary among Indians in Montana, was for a time a pastor in Beloit, Wis., but for the greater part of his life has taught English in numerous colleges. Since 1925 he has been department chairman at Lenoir-Rhyne College in North Carolina. Under the Indian name Ho-chun-ka he was made an honorary member of the Thunderbird clan of the Winnebago tribe for meritorious service. His best-known book is a judicious and comprehensive account of

The Indian in American Literature (1933). He also wrote *The Influence of Christianity upon the Vocabulary of Old English Poetry* (1920); *Lutheran Mission Work Among the American Indians* (1922); and *College Names: Their Origin and Significance* (1952). His *Autobiography* was published in 1961.

Keith, Agnes Newton (b. Oak Park, Ill., July 6, 1901—   ), newspaperwoman, author of books about Borneo. In 1934 Mrs. Keith accompanied her husband, a Canadian citizen who had been appointed Conservator of Forests and Director of Agriculture for North Borneo. He persuaded her to write an account of her experiences and submit it in the 1939 *Atlantic Monthly* Non-Fiction Contest. She did so, under the title *Land Below the Wind*, won a $5,000 prize, and saw her book become a best seller and perennial favorite. In January, 1942, the Japanese came ashore in Borneo, and Mrs. Keith, her husband, and her young son lived in a horrible captivity. She told the story of her experiences in *Three Came Home* (1947), which was later made into a successful movie. In 1950, after a visit to the Keith family in British Columbia, the Keiths returned to Borneo. Mrs. Keith described what she saw in *White Man Returns* (1951). *Bare Feet in the Palace* was published in 1955.

Keith, George (b. Scotland, 1638?–d. 1716), clergyman, teacher, controversialist. Keith put out more than a hundred publications, in the course of which he attacked many personages, especially in the colonies, to which he came after being persecuted in England after turning Quaker. In the colonies he organized a separate sect called Keithians or Christian Quakers, then took Anglican orders and bitterly attacked the Quakers who refused to become converted with him. He was denounced by WILLIAM PENN (1692) and replied in *The Deism of William Penn and His Brethren* (1699). He wrote *A Journal of Travels from New Hampshire to Caratuck* (1706).

Kelland, Clarence Budington (b. Portland, Mich., July 11, 1881—d. Feb. 18, 1964), newspaperman, public relations expert, writer of boys' stories, novelist. Kelland worked as a reporter in Detroit, later became editor of the AMERICAN BOY there (1907–15). To this period belongs the popular series of books for boys about "Mark Tidd" (1913–18), also other books in the juvenile field. Then Kelland turned to the writing of fiction for adults and in 1921 won fame with his stories about "Scattergood Baines," still his most vivid creation. Baines is a fat Yankee promoter, apparently guileless but in reality hard and shrewd, who gets in and out of all kinds of scrapes. More of his adventures were related in *Scattergood Pulls the Strings* (1941). A storyteller of constant ingenuity and humor, Kelland is always careful to study backgrounds and present them accurately. Among his numerous later books: *Dynasty* (1929); *Hard Money* (1930); *Jealous House* (1934); *Great Crooner* (1933); *Skin Deep* (1938); *Archibald the Great* (1943); *Stolen Goods* (1950); *The Key Man*

(1952); *Murder Makes an Entrance* (1955); *West of the Law* (1958).

Keller, David H[enry] (b. Philadelphia, Dec. 23, 1880—   ), physician, writer. Keller is famous for his hundreds of contributions to science fiction magazines, in addition to more than seven hundred medical articles printed in professional journals and a series on *Sexual Education* (10 v., 1929). In 1948 two admirers, Sam Moskowitz and Will Sykera, compiled *Life Everlasting and Other Tales of Science, Fantasy, and Horror,* a collection of the best of Keller's tales, with an introduction by Moskowitz. Keller also wrote *Devil and the Doctor* (1940) and *The Lady Decides* (1950). He has a remarkable gift for strange turns in plot and a great knowledge of psychopathology that is by no means without humor.

Keller, Helen [Adams] (b. Tuscumbia, Ala., June 27, 1880—d. June 1, 1968), counselor on international relations for the American Foundation of the Blind, essayist. Born a normal child, but deprived of sight and hearing at nineteen months by a disease, Miss Keller grew half-wild in her isolated state. When she was seven, Anne Sullivan Macy (1866–1936) undertook to educate her through a system of spelling a touch alphabet into her hand. But the basic concept of communication, that of a relationship between words and things, was hard to teach. Understanding of this concept came suddenly. She and her teacher were standing by an outdoor pump while someone was pumping water; Miss Sullivan placed the child's hand under the spout while she spelled out the word water in the palm of her other hand. At last joining the thought of the fresh flowing liquid and the word, Helen stooped down and touched the earth, showing her desire to know its name. By nightfall she had learned thirty words. When she was ten years old she surprised "Teacher" by asking to be taught to speak. She received an A.B. degree *cum laude* at Radcliffe in 1904. Her teacher was her constant companion throughout her school years and after, until "Teacher's" death in 1936. Miss Keller received several honorary doctors' degrees and other honors from universities all over the world. She also wrote numerous books, among them the inspiring *Story of My Life* (1902; reissued, 1947). Among her other writings: *Optimism* (1903); *The World I Live In* (1908); *The Song of the Stone Wall* (1910); *Out of the Dark* (1913); *My Religion* (1927); *Midstream—My Later Life* (1930); *Helen Keller's Journal* (1938); *Let Us Have Faith* (1940); *The Open Door* (1957). She paid a warm tribute to her instructor in *Helen Keller's Teacher: Anne Sullivan Macy* (1955). Van Wyck Brooks wrote *Helen Keller: Sketch for a Portrait* (1955), an intimate and revealing work done in honor of her seventy-fifth birthday. He suggested that she might have taken as the motto of her devoted life Disraeli's sentence: "Life is too short to be little." Mark Twain, to whom she was drawn because his talk was "fragrant with tobacco and flamboyant with profanity," called her the most marvelous woman since Joan of Arc. In 1954 a movie, *The Unconquered*, was made of her life; it was accompanied by a sensitive narration by Katharine Cornell. *The Miracle Worker*, a successful play by William Gibson (1959), dramatized Anne Sullivan Macy's initial success in communicating with Helen as a child.

Kelley, Edgar Stillman (b. Sparta, Wis., April 14, 1857—d. Nov. 12, 1944), composer. Stillman taught in Europe and America, composed many works on American themes, among them *Puritania* (1892), an opera, and a symphonic poem (1925) based on Poe's *The Pit and the Pendulum*.

Kellogg, Elijah (b. Portland, Me., May 20, 1813—d. March 17, 1901), clergyman, novelist, poet. Kellogg wrote much juvenile literature, but is remembered only for SPARTACUS TO THE GLADIATORS (1846), a declamatory poem favored for recitations by school children of the last century.

Kelly, Eric P[hilbrook] (b. Amesbury, Mass., March 16, 1884—d. Jan. 3, 1960), teacher, author. Kelly taught at Dartmouth College and later in Poland, where he spent some time during World War I. His writing falls into two categories—authoritative books on Poland, books for young people. His titles include *The Trumpeter of Krakow* (1928), *The Blacksmith of Vilno* (1930); *The Golden Star of Walloch* (1931); *From Star to Star* (1944); *The Amazing Journey of David Ingraham* (1949).

Kelly, George [Edward] (b. Philadelphia, [?], 1887—   ), actor, playwright. Beginning in vaudeville, Kelly began to write sketches, then full-length plays. The first was THE TORCH BEARERS (1922). Two years later Kelly sprang into sudden fame with THE SHOW-OFF, an amusing and timeless study of a braggart. Then came CRAIG'S WIFE (1925), an unpitying study of a cold, nagging woman that won a Pulitzer Prize. Later plays were *Behold the Bridegroom* (1927); *Maggie the Magnificent* (1929); *Reflected Glory* (1936); *The Fatal Weakness* (1946). An uneven writer, Kelly is at his best in portraying designing women; he won the praise of George Jean Nathan, who said that "he never gives the impression that the box-office is his place of worship."

Kelly, Jonathan Falconbridge (b. Philadelphia, Aug. 14, 1817—d. July 21, 1855?), humorist. Kelly worked as a grocer, a perfumer, a farm hand before he became a writer; he was also an actor and a hotel manager. Eventually he founded a magazine in New York, bought one in Boston, founded another there, managed a paper in Waltham, Mass., conducted the *Great West* in Cincinnati, founded the *American Platform* for the American party. All these enterprises failed. Meanwhile, however, he was contributing humorous sketches to the *Spirit of the Times*, and they brought him a good income and much praise. His work was often done under pseudonyms—"Falconbridge," "Jack Humphries," "O.K.," "Cerro Gordo." After his

death some of his stories and skits were collected as *The Humors of Falconbridge* (1856), but he is scarcely remembered today.

Kelly, Walt (b. Philadelphia, Aug. 25, 1913—   ), cartoonist. Pogo, the possum, hero of Kelly's comic strip, ran for president in 1952 on an independent ticket (*I Go Pogo*). While Pogo failed to win the election, he lost none of his tremendous popularity with readers. From the first *Pogo* (1951) to the *Pogo Extra* (1960) were twenty-two Pogo books. *Ten Ever Lovin' Blue-Eyed Years with Pogo*, an anthology, came out in 1959. A year after Pogo's first appearance in 1949, the cartoon was hailed as the seventh most popular in the United States; its syndication spread to over five hundred papers throughout the country. His animal characters from the Okefenokee Swamp have earned their fame by being of a generally pleasant disposition and not averse to an occasional barbed comment on contemporary life and politics. Kelly has also worked as a commercial artist, an animator for Walt Disney and, both before and since Pogo, has gained prominence as a liberal political cartoonist.

Kemble, Edward Windsor (b. Sacramento, Calif., Jan. 18, 1861—d. Sept. 19, 1933), cartoonist, illustrator. This highly esteemed artist worked for *Life* and for newspapers; he became noted for his portrayals of Negroes. He had a sharp perception, says Thomas Craven, of the resilient humor which makes the black man's life (sometimes) bearable. Kemble also illustrated many books, including *Huckleberry Finn*, *Pudd'nhead Wilson*, *Uncle Tom's Cabin*, and other classics. When Twain saw Kemble's pictures for *Huckleberry Finn* he said: "Perfect! My dear immaculate family as I created them!"

Kemble, Fanny [Frances Anne Kemble Butler] (b. England, 1809—d. 1893), actress, poet, dramatist. Mrs. Butler, born into the famous theatrical family, the Kembles, married an American, Pierce Butler (1834), and came to the United States to live on his plantation in Georgia, unaware that her husband was a slaveowner. At first she thought his Negroes were contented, gradually she became convinced that this was not so. She recorded her enlightenment in *A Journal of a Residence on a Georgian Plantation in 1838–39* (1863, reprinted 1961), written as letters to a friend, Elizabeth Dwight Sedgwick. She was particularly incensed by the practice of driving women back to work with whips only three weeks after childbirth, and she records a dreary list of the ailments, miscarriages, and mortalities that were the consequence. Yet she says: "The people of this plantation are well-off, and consider themselves well-off, in comparison with the slaves on some of the neighboring estates." She divorced Butler in 1848, but continued to live in the United States from 1849 to 1868 and again from 1873 to 1878, giving Shakespearean readings to earn a living. She was a vivacious woman, always active, often tactless, popular with audiences. Her own play, *The Star of Seville*, was published in 1837

Henrietta Buckmaster has written a well-documented novel, *Fire in the Heart* (1948), that tells the story of Fanny Kemble's life. Margaret Armstrong's *Fanny Kemble: Passionate Victorian* (1938) is an excellent biography. Hawthorne is said to have drawn on Fanny Kemble for his portrait of Zenobia in THE BLITHEDALE ROMANCE.

Kemp, Harry [Hibbard] (b. Youngstown, Ohio, Dec. 15, 1883—d. Aug. 8, 1960), poet, novelist, editor, dramatist, biographer. Kemp, who had previously written quiet, competent poetry, broke out in the exhibitionist 1920's with verse of quite different quality and content, particularly his *Chanteys and Ballads* (1920), and with prose accounts of his life in fictional form—*Tramping on Life* (1922) and *More Miles* (1927). The basis of these novels was a trip around the world; he made special studies of night life in London and New York City and traveled over North America as a tramp. Kemp began his writing career with a four-act play called *Judas* (1910); in later years he also wrote *Boccaccio's Untold Tale and Other One-Act Plays* (1924). Among his other books: *The Thresher's Wife* (1914), a narrative poem; *The Sea and the Dunes* (1926); *The Golden Word: An Outline of a Non-Ascetic Religion* (1930); *Harry Answers Omar: A Counterblast to the Rubaiyat* (poem, 1945); *The Poet's Life of Christ: Songs of the Living Lord* (1946); *Rhyme of Provincetown Nicknames* (1954).

Kemp Morgan. See MORGAN, KEMP.

Kendall, G[eorge] W[ilkins] (b. Mt. Vernon, N.H., Aug. 22, 1809—d. Oct. 21, 1867), newspaperman, war correspondent, historian. A printer by trade, Kendall and a fellow printer in New Orleans, Francis A. Lumsden, founded *The Picayune* (1837). It was a four-page sheet, well written, and at once established itself. Kendall and Lumsden went on to what some authorities regard as the beginning of war correspondence and the gathering of news data under war conditions. In 1841, restless and desirous of establishing the fact that the people of New Mexico yearned for independence from Mexico, he set out in a trip in which he suffered harrowing hardships, was imprisoned in Mexico, and barely escaped with his life. On his return, he wrote an excellent account of his experiences in A NARRATIVE OF THE TEXAN SANTA FÉ EXPEDITION, COMPRISING A DESCRIPTION OF A TOUR THROUGH TEXAS AND ACROSS THE GREAT SOUTHWESTERN PRAIRIES (2 v., 1844; reprinted in facsimile in the *Original Narratives of Texas History and Adventure*, 2 v., 1935). When war broke out, Kendall accompanied the Texas Rangers to the border, volunteered to serve as an aide, and saw most of the major actions of the war. His dispatches occasionally anticipated official bulletins and certainly were far in advance of any other newspaper correspondence. Kendall wrote an account of *The War Between the U.S. and Mexico* (1851). His own achievement is described in Fayette Copeland's *Kendall of the Picayune* (1943); he also appears in F. Lauris-

ton Bullard's *Famous War Correspondents* (1914).

Kendrick, Baynard [Hardwick] (b. Philadelphia, April 8, 1894—   ), publisher, hotel manager, lawyer, writer. His varied experiences have given Kendrick much material for his fiction-writing. Service in World War I and welfare work with veterans in hospitals led to the creation of Duncan Maclain, a blind sleuth who appears in *The Last Express* (1937), *Blind Man's Bluff* (1943), and others of his mystery novels. He was the first president of the Mystery Writers of America, Inc. Out of his work for blinded veterans also came his first general novel, *Lights Out* (1945). Long fascinated by Florida, Kendrick wrote a historical novel about that state, *The Flames of Time* (1948), laid in an era when it was a battleground for the Spanish, English, Indians, and Americans. Other books include: *You Die Today* (1952); *Reservations for Death* (1957). His films include: *The Last Express* (1938); *Eyes in the Night* (1942); *Bright Victory* (1952); *Clear and Present Danger* (1958). His books have been transcribed into Braille, and he received a plaque from General Omar Bradley for work with blinded veterans during World War II.

Kennan, George (b. Norwalk, Ohio, Feb. 16, 1845—d. May 10, 1924), newspaperman. Kennan wrote widely on foreign subjects. The Century Co. commissioned him to visit Russia and Siberia, a trip which involved a 5,000-mile trek by dogsled; the OUTLOOK sent him to the front in the Spanish-American and Russo-Japanese Wars. He visited Mt. Pelée after its eruption in 1902. He wrote *Siberia and the Exile System* (2 v., 1891); *Campaigning in Cuba* (1899); *The Tragedy of Pelée* (1902); *E. H. Harriman* (2 v., 1922).

Kennan, George F[rost] (b. Milwaukee, Wis., Feb. 16, 1904—   ), diplomat, historian. Experience as a diplomat at strategic posts made Kennan a noted political authority, especially on the Soviet Union. In 1926, a year after graduating from Princeton, he entered foreign service, holding posts of increasing importance, climaxed in 1952 with the ambassadorship to the USSR. In 1956 he was appointed permanent professor in the School of Historical Studies at the Institute of Advanced Study. His books are astute analyses of foreign policy. *Russia Leaves the War* (1956), an investigation into the aims of Soviet policy, won for him the National Book Award and a Pulitzer Prize. *Russia, The Atom, and the West* (1958) was at first a series of lectures given over the BBC, with the specific aim of changing the climate of opinion from one favoring a military containment of Russia to one favoring co-existence. Among his books are: *Realities of American Foreign Policy* (1954); *The Decision to Intervene* (1958); *Soviet Foreign Policy* (1960); *Russia and the West Under Lenin and Stalin* (1961).

Kennedy, Charles Rann (b. England, Feb. 14, 1871—d. Feb. 16, 1950), actor, theatrical manager, writer, teacher. Kennedy made his first appearance in New York in 1903 in the medieval play *Everyman*, as revised for modern presentation. In the same cast was his equally famous actress wife, Edith Wynne Matthison, who later appeared in many of her husband's plays. With her he ran the drama department of Bennett Junior College. In 1917 he became a naturalized citizen. In 1908 he wrote a play which attained world-wide fame, *The Servant in the House*, in which a figure symbolical of or actually representing Jesus helps a family today to solve its problems through love and goodness. He wrote other plays of a religious or moralistic character —*The Winterfeast* (1908); *The Terrible Meek* (1911); *The Army with Banners* (1917); *The Chastening* (1922); *Flaming Ministers* (1932); *Face of God* (1935); *The Seventh Trumpet* (1941). One or two of these plays have been given theatrical performances, usually in "little theaters." *The Terrible Meek*, which is performed almost entirely in the dark, was a favorite vehicle for the author himself, and had thousands of performances in churches and auditoriums. Aside from *The Servant in the House*, Kennedy did not win enthusiastic praise from critics, who regard him as sensational and as carrying the study of ethics far beyond the bounds of effective drama.

Kennedy, John Fitzgerald (b. Brookline, Mass., May 29, 1917—d. Nov. 22, 1963), 35th president. Son of Joseph P. Kennedy, Boston financier and former Ambassador to the Court of St. James, and the grandson of a popular mayor of Boston, John Fitzgerald, Kennedy was born into an atmosphere of wealth and prominence. After attending the London School of Economics (1935–1936), he entered Harvard University, from which he graduated with honors in 1940. Later, he did graduate work at Stanford University. During World War II, Kennedy served as the commander of a PT boat in the South Pacific and was decorated by the Navy for the courage and leadership he displayed after his boat was rammed by a Japanese destroyer during a night action in the Solomons. His political career began in 1946 when he was elected as a Massachusetts representative to Congress. He was re-elected in 1948 and 1950, and in 1952 defeated Henry Cabot Lodge for a seat in the Senate. As a Senator, Kennedy quickly became a popular leader of the moderate liberal faction of his party and won prominence as a member of the Senate Foreign Relations Committee and the Select Senate Committee on Improper Labor-Management Activities. In 1956 he was Senator Estes Kefauver's leading rival for the Democratic vice-presidential nomination and in 1959, after impressive victories in a number of State Presidential primaries, he became the Democratic nominee for president, winning the election by a narrow margin over Vice-President Richard Nixon. He is the author of *Why England Slept* (1940), an analysis of the causes of England's failure to rearm before World War II; *Profiles In Courage* (1956), a

Pulitzer Prize-winning collection of essays dealing with congressional leaders who, in historically critical moments, placed conscience over political expediency; and *The Strategy of Peace* (1960), which presented a statement of his general aims in the area of international affairs. Kennedy's books have been praised for their literary quality as well as their depth of historical knowledge and political idealism—a tribute which has been extended to his major speeches and addresses. A widely-read man whose taste embraces poetry and fiction as well as works on history, politics, and government, Kennedy desired to create a larger role in the national life for individuals of an intellectual or literary background. This desire was reflected symbolically when he gave ROBERT FROST, the poet, a prominent place in the ceremonies attending his inauguration and, more concretely, by numerous appointments drawn from the academic field, and his reliance on the opinions of a number of writers and scholars. Among the books written about Kennedy and his family are Joseph Dinneen's *The Kennedy Family* (1959); James MacGregor Burns' *John Kennedy: A Political Profile* (1960); Joseph W. McCarthy's *The Remarkable Kennedys* (1960); and *PT 109: John F. Kennedy in World War II* (1962) by Robert J. Donovan.

Kennedy, John Pendleton ["Mark Littleton"] (b. Baltimore, Md., Oct. 25, 1795—d. Aug. 18, 1870), lawyer, public official, writer. Kennedy practiced law for several years, served in Congress, was Speaker of the House and, under

Millard Fillmore, secretary of the navy. In the latter capacity he organized the Perry expedition to Japan and Elisha Kent Kane's second Arctic expedition. He was greatly interested in

education, and was active in the affairs of the University of Maryland and the Peabody Institute.

Yet writing, always an avocation, was perhaps his deepest interest. He wrote on politics, often satirically; frequently his writing assumed the form of fiction, as in QUODLIBET (1840), a light satire on Jacksonian democracy. His fiction he published under the pen name Mark Littleton. SWALLOW BARN (1832), held together by a thin thread of story, was Kennedy's first novel and has been described as the first important fictional treatment of Virginian life. HORSE-SHOE ROBINSON (1835) was based on the personal recollections of its hero, a veteran of the Revolution whom Kennedy met while visiting South Carolina. *Rob of the Bowl* (1838), which many critics consider his best work, is laid in St. Mary's City, Maryland's first capital, in 1681; among the incidents is an attempt of Protestants to overthrow Catholic rule. Kennedy also wrote *Memoirs of the Life of William Wirt* (1849).

Kennedy, in his friendly way, helped Poe after he had read the *Ms. Found in a Bottle* (1833) as a contest judge. He furnished Thackeray data for *The Virginians* (1857–59); a legend long current credited him with having written a chapter of that book. J. B. Hubbell edited *Swallow Barn* (1929); E. E. Leisy, *Horse-Shoe Robinson* (1937). H. T. Tuckerman wrote Kennedy's biography (1871); Charles H. Bohner wrote another, *John Pendleton Kennedy: Gentleman from Baltimore* (1961).

Kennicott, Carol. Leading character in Sinclair Lewis' MAIN STREET (1921). It is she who tries to bring "culture" to Gopher Prairie.

Kent, Charles Foster (b. Palmyra, N.Y., Aug. 13, 1867—d. May 2, 1925), teacher, Biblical scholar. For the greater part of his active career Kent was professor of Biblical literature at Yale. He wrote numerous books in his special field, including *A History of the Jewish People* (1899) and *The Great Teachers of Judaism and Christianity* (1911); he also edited *The Student's Old Testament* (6 v., 1904–27), *The Historical Bible* (6 v., 1908–16), and *The Shorter Bible* (2 v., 1918–21).

Kent, Frank R[ichardson] (b. Baltimore, Md., May 1, 1877—d. April 14, 1958), newspaperman, syndicated columnist, writer on political topics. Kent joined the *Sunpapers* of Baltimore in 1898 and thereafter was connected with them in many capacities, particularly as a political reporter. He staunchly espoused the conservative side in his later years. He wrote *The Story of Maryland Politics* (1911); *The Great Game of Politics* (1923); *History of the Democratic Party* (1925); *Political Behavior* (1928); *Without Gloves* (1934). Kent seemed to Charles Fisher, when he discussed *The Columnists* (1934), "the most fastidious of the ax-men who have observed the outlandish doings in Washington."

Kent, James (b. Putnam Co., N.Y., July 31, 1763—d. Dec. 12, 1847), lawyer, public official, jurist, writer on law. Kent practiced law after his graduation from Yale and admission to the bar, and served as professor of law at Columbia; Kent Hall at that university is named for him. He also served as a judge in New York courts. It is said that Kent was the first to deliver his opinions in writing, and his views as a result became more influential on later cases. He became known as "the American Blackstone" because of his COMMENTARIES ON AMERICAN LAW (4 v., 1826–30), which have gone through many editions. He was himself a disciple of John Locke and Blackstone, and was Federalist in his viewpoint, with a strong faith in property rights. He was a great lover of literature and a friend of Charles Brockden Brown. See BREAD AND CHEESE CLUB and FRIENDLY CLUB.

Kent, Louise Andrews (b. Brookline, Mass., May 25, 1886—d. Aug. 6, 1969), novelist. Miss Kent's many books include a number of novels for children, a series of humorous books about life in New England, and two cookbooks. In 1935 *He Went With Marco Polo* became the first of six historical novels for boys, the most recent of which is *He Went With Champlain* (1959). Her three Mrs. Appleyard books—*Mrs. Appleyard's Year* (1941), *Country Mouse* (1945), and *With Kitchen Privileges* (1953) were praised for their witty and knowledgeable depiction of life in Boston and rural Vermont. Mrs. Kent's interest in New England is also evident in her cookbooks—*Mrs. Appleyard's Kitchen* (1942) and *The Summer Kitchen* (1942, with Elizabeth Kent Gay)—which combined favorite New England recipes with a running commentary by "Mrs. Appleyard." Among her other books are *Douglas of Porcupine* (1931); *Two Children Of Tyre* (1932); *The Red Rajah* (1933); *The Terrace* (1934); *He Went With Vasco Da Gama* (1938); *Paul Revere Square* (1939); *He Went With Christopher Columbus* (1940); *He Went With Magellan* (1943); *Village Greens of New England* (1948); *He Went With John Paul Jones* (1958).

Kent, Rockwell (b. Tarrytown Heights, N.Y., June 21, 1882—d. March 13, 1971), painter, travel writer. A rebel in politics as well as in painting, Kent has often stirred up controversies. He began to show in public in 1910, and thereafter wrote and illustrated numerous books based on his own experiences in various sea voyages. Among them: *Wilderness* (1920); *Voyaging Southward from the Strait of Magellan* (1924); *N. by E.* (1930); *Salamina* (1935). He also wrote *Rockwellkentiana* (1933), *This Is My Own* (1940), and *It's Me, O Lord* (1955). Among classics he has illustrated are: *Candide* (1928); *The Bridge of San Luis Rey* (1929); *The Canterbury Tales* (1930); *Moby Dick* (1930); *Beowulf* (1931).

Kenton, Simon (b. Virginia, April 3, 1755—d. April 29, 1836), Indian fighter, scout, soldier in the Revolutionary War and the War of 1812. Kenton, because of his many daring adventures and exploits, became a frontier legend. He was one of Boone's chosen company, served with George Rogers Clark and Anthony Wayne. A biography of him was written by Edna Kenton

(1930), and he appears in Robert Montgomery Bird's *Nick of the Woods* (1837); Maurice Thompson's ALICE OF OLD VINCENNES (1900); Winston Churchill's THE CROSSING (1903); and Thomas Boyd's *The Shadow of the Long Knives* (1928).

Kentuckians, The (1898), a novel by JOHN FOX, JR. One of Fox's better novels, this story contrasts the two main groups in the population of Kentucky—the richer, better educated group, mainly centered in the bluegrass region, and the illiterate, improverished group of the mountains. The story centers around leaders from each group, rivals in politics and in love. Fox draws an accurate picture of life in Kentucky, reproduces well some of the Elizabethan survivals in customs and speech among the mountaineers.

Kentucky, Keats of. A name given to MADISON CAWEIN.

Kentucky Cardinal, A (1894), a novelette by JAMES LANE ALLEN. Adam Moss, more interested in birds than in human beings, falls in love with a neighbor's daughter of somewhat capricious character. Jealous of his interest in birds, she demands that he make captive one of the Kentucky cardinals who frequent the bird refuge he has set up and present it to her in a cage. He does so, reluctantly, and the bird dies. Both are greatly distressed, quarrel for a time, are reconciled. In a sequel, *Aftermath* (1896), the lovers are married, and the wife wins the husband to some interest in social life. But she dies in giving birth to a son, and he returns to his deep absorption in nature. Both novels are written in a delicate if somewhat sentimental style, although not without humor. The Kentucky landscape is pleasingly sketched.

Kentucky Miscellany, The (1789), a collection of verses by Thomas Johnson, Jr. It is said to be the first book of poems written and printed in the state.

Kentucky Poems (1902), a collection of poems by MADISON CAWEIN. This was published in England with a laudatory introduction by Sir Edmund Gosse, and included a selection from Cawein's shorter lyrics.

Kentucky Tragedy. See BEAUCHAMPE.

Kenyon Review, The. A quarterly founded in 1939 at Gambier, Ohio, by members of the faculty of Kenyon College with JOHN CROWE RANSOM as editor. The magazine stressed close structural criticism and reviews of important new trends in music, literature, painting, and aesthetics, as well as studies of classic forms, stories, and poetry. Its initial advisory board included ALLEN TATE, MARK VAN DOREN, ROBERT PENN WARREN, and other writers of reputation. Its early circulation was aided by the purchase of the subscription list of the *Southern Review* upon that magazine's expiration in 1942. From its beginning the *Kenyon Review* presented some of the most thoughtful and capable writers of our times: R. P. Blackmur, Marianne Moore, Eliseo Vivas, and others. In 1951 an anthology, *The Kenyon Critics: Studies in Modern Literature from the "Kenyon Review,"* was prepared

by Ransom, who selected eighteen critical essays and fifteen reviews from the twelve volumes of the magazine. In 1961 it was edited by Robie Macauley, and among those on its staff were George Lanning, Robert Penn Warren, Lionel Trilling, and Eric Bentley.

Keppler, Joseph (b. Austria, Feb. 1, 1838—d. Feb. 19, 1894), cartoonist, publisher. Keppler came to the United States in 1867, founded *Die Vehme*, a German-language comic weekly, in St. Louis. In 1871 he also founded, in the same city, *Puck, Illustrierte Wochenschrift*. In 1876 he helped found in New York a weekly called *Puck, Humoristisches Wochenblatt;* the following year it became an English-language weekly, the famous PUCK that continued for some decades to purvey humor and commentary to the American audience. Cartoons prepared from lithographs rather than woodblocks were an early feature of the magazine.

Kern, Jerome [David] (b. New York City, Jan. 27, 1885—d. Nov. 11, 1945), composer. Kern's musical talents in childhood led to professional training, and his first musical comedy, *Mr. Wix of Wickham*, was done in 1910. Thereafter he wrote a long series of songs for musical shows and movies, including *Very Good, Eddie* (1915); *Leave It to Jane* (1917; revived, 1959, for a long "off-Broadway" run); *Sally* (1920; revived, 1948, with borrowings from *Leave It to Jane*); *Sunny* (1925); SHOW BOAT (1927); *The Cat and the Fiddle* (1931); *Music in the Air* (1932); *Roberta* (1933); *Very Warm for May* (1939). Among his most successful songs are *They Didn't Believe Me, I've Told Every Little Star, The Last Time I Saw Paris, Look for the Silver Lining, My Bill, Old Man River, Smoke Gets in Your Eyes.* His songs set new standards for Broadway and greatly influenced later songwriters like George Gershwin, Cole Porter, Vincent Youmans, and Richard Rodgers. *The Jerome Kern Song Book* (1955) collected fifty of his best-loved songs, with an introduction by Oscar Hammerstein II.

Kerouac, Jack (b. Lowell, Mass., Mar. 12, 1922—d. Oct. 21, 1969), novelist, poet. ON THE ROAD (1957) introduced Kerouac as one of the leading "beat" writers. His "spontaneous prose" is a type of novelistic composition parallel to the long, loose line employed by many of the beat poets. Like the poets he has been sharply criticized for lack of organization and for extolling the amorality of his characters, who seem concerned only with self-gratification. They spend their lives in search of the next "kick" which may come from drugs, drink, sex, jazz, or fast cars. Kerouac's characters also do a great deal of talking in a search for spiritual truth, especially in *The Dharma Bums* (1960), where the characters are in search of Zen Buddhist *dharma* or truth.

Kerouac has lived the "beat" life he writes about; much of his work is autobiographical. With ALLEN GINSBERG and GREGORY CORSO, he brought attention to the beat phenomenon through public appearances, reading from manuscripts and discussing the meaning and origins of the beat generation. Among his books: *The Town and the City* (1950); *The Subterraneans* (1958); *Doctor Sax* (1959); *Mexico City Blues*, verse (1959); *Tristessa* (1960). See BEAT WRITING.

Kerr, Orpheus C. The pen name of ROBERT HENRY NEWELL.

Kerr, Walter (b. Evanston, Ill., July 8, 1913 —   ), drama critic. Kerr attended Northwestern University, and taught at the Catholic University of America in Washington, D.C., until 1950, at which time he took the position of drama critic for the New York *Herald Tribune*. His reviews were fresh, vigorous, and penetrating, which helped establish him as one of the foremost critics of the Broadway theater. In 1955, disheartened by what he considered the sad state of playwriting, he wrote *How Not to Write a Play*, which, with fighting words, called on playwrights to restore the theater to its original vitality. His wife is **Jean Kerr** (b. Scranton, Pa., July, 1923—   ), who is the author of *Please Don't Eat the Daisies* (1957); *The Snake Has All the Lines* (1960); *Mary, Mary* (1961). Together they wrote the book for a musical, *Goldilocks* (1958). Other books by Walter Kerr: *Criticism and Censorship* (1956); *Pieces at Eight* (1957); *The Decline of Pleasure* (1962).

Kesselring, Joseph. See ARSENIC AND OLD LACE.

Kester, Paul (b. Delaware, Ohio, Nov. 2, 1870—d. June 20, 1933), playwright. Kester was one of the most skillful "play doctors" and playwrights of his age. He had a wide knowledge of foreign languages and adapted foreign plays to the American and English stages. In the 1890's the vogue for historical novels led him to dramatize many of them. He often wrote or adapted plays for particular players, among them JULIA MARLOWE, Marie Tempest, E. H. SOTHERN, Margaret Anglin. Of his original plays his first great success was *Sweet Nell of Old Drury* (1901), produced in England, the United States, Australia, and the Far East, and frequently revived. Other plays were *Zamar* (1893); *Mademoiselle Mars* (1902); and a dramatic version of Charles Major's *When Knighthood Was in Flower*, with Julia Marlowe playing Mary Tudor. His brother, **Vaughan Kester** (b. New Brunswick, N.J., Sept. 12, 1869—d. July 4, 1911), with whom he occasionally collaborated, was a novelist; his best-known work was *The Prodigal Judge* (1911). This tale of a boy's adventures in Ohio and western Tennessee continued to be reprinted for two decades; well supplied with deep-dyed villains, it is a well-told, if melodramatic tale.

Kettell, Samuel (b. Newburyport, Mass., Aug. 5, 1800—d. Dec. 3, 1855), editor, essayist, public official. Kettell is chiefly remembered for the three-volume reply that he made to Sydney Smith's query, "Who reads an American book?" His reply took the form of an anthology, SPECIMENS OF AMERICAN POETRY, WITH CRITICAL AND BIOGRAPHICAL NOTICES (1829), which began with Cotton Mather and continued to

Kettell's own day. He also assisted SAMUEL G. GOODRICH in the preparation of his *Peter Parley* series and translated one volume into modern Greek. As an original writer he assumed at least two pen names—Timo Titterwell for *Yankee Notions: A Medley* (1838) and Sampson Short-and-Fat for *Daw's Doings, or, The History of the Late War in the Plantations* (1842). See LITERARY HISTORIES OF THE U.S.

Key, Francis Scott (b. Carroll County, Md., Aug. 1, 1779—d. Jan. 11, 1843), lawyer, poet, author of "The Star Spangled Banner." Key received his education at St. John's College, near Annapolis. In 1801, after a period of reading law under the tutelage of Judge J. T. Case, he began practicing in Frederick, Maryland, in partnership with R. B. Taney. The latter was later to become Key's brother-in-law, as well as one of the best-known chief justices of the Supreme Court.

The War of 1812 found Key living in Georgetown in the District of Columbia, where he practiced law with an uncle, Philip Barton Key. When the British evacuated Washington in 1814, they took with them as a hostage a prominent physician, Dr. William Beanes, and Key was asked to undertake Beanes' release. Traveling through the British lines, Key was successful in his negotiations, but was detained by the British commander, Admiral Cockburn, until after a planned attack on the city of Baltimore. It was after watching the attack on Fort McHenry, one of the defenses of Baltimore, on the night of September 13–14, 1814, that Key wrote his famous poem.

"The Star Spangled Banner" was first published in the Baltimore *American* for Sept. 21, 1814, and was soon thereafter set to the music of "Anacreon in Heaven," a song composed by John Stafford Smith, an Englishman, as the anthem of the Anacreontic Societies, groups of amateur musicians. The tune was well known in America, having been current during the Revolution as "Adams and Liberty."

Key went on to become a prominent lawyer in the nation's capital. Rejecting a notion of entering the ministry, he served as United States Attorney for the District of Columbia from 1833 until 1841. His collected works were published posthumously (1857); they comprise religious and love poems and some light humorous verses. His greatest work was finally adopted as the United States' national anthem in 1931, after years of being sung as such, unofficially, by the public.

Keystone Comedies (see SENNETT, MACK).

Kid, The (1947), a poem by CONRAD AIKEN. There is a legend that a solitary bookish recluse named William Blackstone greeted Boston's first settlers on what is now the Boston Common. Aiken, in a series of nine quietly written but eloquent poems, takes Blackstone as an emblem of the "free spirit" in American life, describes his later wanderings, tells of other heroes, legendary and factual, who appear as America moves west. Aiken discussed in his USHANT (1952) his discovery of Blackstone's "magical figure" in Justin Winsor's *Memorial History of Boston* (4 v., 1880–81).

Kidd, William ["Captain Kidd"] (b. Scotland, 1645?—d. May 23, 1701), British privateer and pirate. As a shipowner in New York Kidd saw an excellent chance for personal profit in joining British ships engaged against French privateers in the West Indies; later he was sent out against the pirates who infested the Indian Ocean. In all these expeditions Kidd had royal warrants and was paid for his services. He was a man of means; he helped build Trinity Church in New York City. In 1696 he set out from New York on an expedition against pirates off Madagascar. The story goes that a mutinous crew caused him to turn pirate himself. He joined forces with two other sea marauders, and orders were issued for his arrest. He captured a number of vessels, and in 1699, on his way back from the West Indies, he was induced to land at Boston. He expected to receive a pardon, but was sent back to England, put on trial, convicted not of piracy but of murder, and hanged. The trial was a famous one, and *A Full Account of Proceedings in Relation to Captain Kidd* (1701) went into several editions.

Justly or unjustly, Captain Kidd became the leading pirate of legend in both England and the United States. Many ballads were written and printed about him, for example a *Dialogue Between the Ghost of Capt. Kidd and a Kidnapper* (1704). There was also *Captain Kidd's Farewell to the Seas* (1701), called in its American version *The Dying Words of Captain Robert Kyd*. It appeared in several broadsides, from the pre-Revolutionary period to 1820. For some reason Kidd was also supposed to have been more skillful than most pirates in concealing his wealth, and as far back as 1699 a New Jersey wag created great excitement by declaring that Kidd, during a visit to Cape May, had buried money there. That was the first of a number of similar hoaxes, among them the famous letter found in 1849 in a field near Palmer, Mass., signed "Robert Kidd." In 1894 another hoax mentioned Deer Island in Maine as a treasure-site. Kidd's ghost has also occasionally appeared, as at Clark's Island, Mass. His spirit broods over other parts of the country; in 1950 a mining engineer bought Oak Island, N.S., and said he would begin hunting a treasure cache supposedly left there by Captain Kidd.

Willard Hallam Bonner, in *Pirate Laureate: The Life and Legends of Captain Kidd* (1947), usefully re-examines the entire Kidd saga, with some attempt at the rehabilitation of Kidd's character. One section of his book analyzes the literary uses that have been made of the Kidd legends. These legends found their way into American writing, particularly fiction, between 1824 and 1849. Irving was perhaps the first to make literary use of Kidd, in TALES OF A TRAVELER (1824) and WOLFERT'S ROOST (1855); Kidd was a part of the Knickerbocker tradition. Samuel B. F. Judah wrote *The Buc-*

caneers (1827), a pretentious novel in which "Richard" Kidd becomes mixed up in all sorts of affairs. Then came Cooper, who refers to Kidd favorably in his *History of the Navy* (1839) and THE DEERSLAYER (1841), again in the 1850 Preface to THE RED ROVER. In *The Sea Lions* his conception of the plot and characters was obviously influenced by incidents in Kidd's career. But his most important use of the Kidd saga was in THE WATER WITCH (1830), where the pirate is frequently mentioned. Joseph Holt Ingraham wrote *Capt. Kidd, or, The Wizard of the Sea* (1839). Harriet Beecher Stowe's *Captain Kidd's Money* appeared in the *Atlantic Monthly* for November, 1870, and was reprinted two years later in *Sam Lawson's Oldtown Fireside Stories*. A long-lasting tribute to the fascination that Kidd exerted was a play by J. S. Jones, *Captain Kyd, or, The Wizard of the Sea*, first shown in 1830 and published in 1857. Possibly the most famous reference to the Kidd legend is in Poe's THE GOLD BUG (1843); and Poe's idea, Kidd and all, was taken over bodily by R. L. Stevenson when he came to write *Treasure Island* (1883)—the alluring chart clearly shows "Capt. Kidd's Anchorage."

Kieft, Willem (b. Sept., 1597—d. Sept. 27, 1647), governor of New Netherlands from 1638 to 1647. He appears as "William the Testy" in Washington Irving's first important work, *Knickerbocker's History of New York* (1809), and was irascible, unpopular, and unsuccessful. His administration and character were defended by J. W. Gerard, who stressed the great difficulties Kieft faced; but when he was lost at sea on his homeward voyage, JOHN WINTHROP, in his *Journal* (which later became a *History of New England*, published in 1790), proclaimed his death a "judgment of God."

Kielty, Bernardine (b. Fitchburg, Mass. [?], 189[?]—   ), columnist, editor, anthologist. Miss Kielty (Mrs. Harry Scherman) was one of the original editors of the influential magazine STORY. She participated in the "discovery" of many an author since famous. She became a senior editor at the LADIES' HOME JOURNAL in 1943, in 1944 started an "Authors Between Books" column for the *Book-of-the-Month Club News*, and in 1945 began something similar for the *Journal*. In 1947 she prepared a *Treasury of Short Stories*. Most recently she has been writing books for children.

Kieran, John [Francis] (b. New York City, Aug. 2, 1892—   ), newspaperman, columnist, radio broadcaster, editor. Kieran worked on *The New York Times*, then on the *Herald Tribune*, on the *Times* again, afterwards on the *Sun*. He became a noted columnist in the field of sports. He also became an authority on Shakespeare and bird life, and was renowned for his knowledge in general; he displayed his prodigious memory on the radio program INFORMATION PLEASE. Among his publications: *Story of the Olympic Games* (1936); *Nature Notes* (1941); *American Sporting Scene* (1941); *Footnotes on Nature* (1947); *Introduction to*

Wild Flowers (1952); *Introduction to Nature* (1957); *Natural History of New York City* (1959).

Killers, The (first published in *Scribner's Magazine,* March, 1927; reprinted in MEN WITHOUT WOMEN, 1927), a short story by ERNEST HEMINGWAY. The first of Hemingway's works to win wide popularity, this story is a study in violence, revealing the effect of urban toughness on the mind of a small-town youth. It had an enormous influence on the development of HARD-BOILED FICTION and writing about gangsters.

Kilmer, [Alfred] Joyce (b. New Brunswick, N.J., Dec. 6, 1886—d. July 30, 1918), poet, teacher, editor, essayist. After teaching for a while in the Morristown (N.J.) High School, Kilmer worked as an editor, a book reviewer, and a lecturer on poetry. A collection of his verse, *Summer of Love,* appeared in 1911 without attracting much attention. Then his poem TREES was published in the August, 1913, issue of *Poetry* and won him national fame; it became the title-piece of his second collection, *Trees and Other Poems* (1914). His last collection came out in 1917, *Main Street and Other Poems,* but in the meantime Kilmer, an enthusiastic advocate of the cause of the Allies in World War I, had enlisted in the army and was later killed in France. He was awarded a posthumous Croix de Guerre. Kilmer's literary sensitivity made him readily susceptible to many influences and one hears in his verse Yeats and other Celtic poets, some of the great Catholic poets, A. E. Housman, Edwin Arlington Robinson, and others. Someone called his verse "a bundle of broken mirrors." He seems most likely to be remembered for TREES. His wife, **Aline Kilmer** (b. Norfolk, Va., Aug. 1, 1888—d. Oct. 1, 1941), wrote good verse, perhaps superior to her husband's. Among her collections: *Candles That Burn* (1919); *The Poor King's Daughter and Other Poems* (1925); *Selected Poems* (1929).

Kilpatrick, Major General Judson. See ALLATOONA.

Kilpatrick, William Heard (b. White Plains, Ga., Nov. 20, 1871—d. Feb. 13, 1965), educator. After teaching in Georgia schools and at Mercer University, Kilpatrick joined the faculty of Teachers College at Columbia and won wide renown as a teacher of dramatic quality and as a pioneer in educational movements. Among his books: *Foundations of Method* (1925); *Education for a Changing Civilization* (1926); *Our Educational Task* (1930); *Education and the Social Crisis* (1932); *Remaking the Curriculum* (1936); *Selfhood and Civilization* (1941); *Philosophy of Education* (1951). Kilpatrick has argued that a child learns by living; his educational theory stems from the teachings of the pragmatists. Samuel Tenenbaum has written *Kilpatrick: Trail Blazer in Education* (1951).

Kimbrough, Emily (b. Muncie, Ind., Oct. 23, 1899—   ), editor, humorist, travel writer. Prior to the start of her writing career in 1932, she was editor of *Fashions of the Hour,* 1922–27, fashion editor of *Ladies' Home Journal,* 1927, and its managing editor, 1927–29. Her first of many humorous books, *Our Hearts Were Young and Gay* (1942), was written in collaboration with CORNELIA OTIS SKINNER. *We Followed Our Hearts to Hollywood* (1943) was an amusing memoir of her adventures in Hollywood with Miss Skinner after they had been asked to adapt their novel for the screen. Miss Kimbrough attracted a large and faithful readership, and became well known as a writer of travel books like *A Right Good Crew* (1958), and *Water Water Everywhere* (1956). Among her other books: *The Innocents From Indiana* (1950); *Forty Plus and Fancy Free* (1954). *Pleasure by the Busload* (1961) is another travel book.

King, Alexander (b. Austria, Nov. 13, 1900—d. Nov. 16, 1965), painter, writer, editor. King came to America in 1913; in his varied career he worked as an editor of *Life* and *Vanity Fair* and as an illustrator of special editions of plays of Eugene O'Neill. He recounted many of his activities in his extravagant, anecdotal autobiography, *Mine Enemy Grows Older* (1958), a witty and occasionally tender account of his unconventional life. *May This House Be Safe from Tigers* (1960) is also autobiographical and written in much the same ironic and strangely sensitive vein as the earlier book. In *I Should Have Kissed Her More* (1961) King continued his autobiographical journey, stopping to remember the women he had known and loved. He translated and edited poems of the German poet Peter Altenberg in *Peter Altenberg's Evocations of Love* (1960).

King, [William Benjamin] Basil (b. Charlottetown, Pr. Ed. Is., Feb. 26, 1859—d. June 22, 1928), a novelist. King served as an Episcopal minister in Halifax, then accepted a call to Cambridge. His first novels attracted no special attention, but *The Inner Shrine,* serialized in *Harper's,* then published anonymously in 1909, became a best seller. King's sight began to fail, but he was able to continue writing. His great interest in his later writings was in spiritualism and life after death. Among his books: *The Street Called Straight* (1912); *The Way Home* (1913); *The Lifted Veil* (1919); *The Discovery of God* (1923); *Adventures in Religion* (1929).

King, Ben[jamin Franklin] (b. St. Joseph, Mich., March 17, 1857—d. April 7, 1894), writer of light verse. King is remembered chiefly for his poem, IF I SHOULD DIE TONIGHT; his eight-line lament, *The Pessimist,* has also been widely quoted.

King, Clarence (b. Newport, R.I., Jan. 6, 1842—d. Dec. 24, 1901), geologist, mining engineer, author. After graduation from Yale, King crossed the continent on horseback and began working as a mining engineer at the Comstock Lode and in California, then worked on a government survey and wrote a report, with collaborators, in seven volumes. It was he who first explored and who defined the boundaries of the Yosemite Valley. For several years he was in charge of the U.S. Geological Survey as its first head and wrote technical works on geology. A lover of nature, King expressed himself most fully in *Mountaineering in the Sierra Nevada* (1872; rev. ed., 1902), which appeared first in the *Atlantic Monthly*. The scientific description is accompanied by vivid narratives of exciting experiences and by keen impressions of frontier characters. Van Wyck Brooks calls the book the equal of Parkman's *Oregon Trail* and Dana's *Two Years Before the Mast*.

In 1871 King met HENRY ADAMS in Colorado, and he has been credited with determining the noticeable turn toward scientific thinking that occurred thereafter in Adams' work. Adams found in King's pioneering geology and creed of nature "a starting point for a philosophy of energetic happiness," says Robert E. Spiller. In *The Education of Henry Adams* (1907) Adams says that King knew more than he did of art and poetry, but that, besides, he knew America. To his friends King seemed an ideal American, "the richest and most many-sided of his day," in Adams' words. Yet King was in part wasted; he spent part of 1894 in an asylum (Bloomingdale) and died, alone and uncared for, in an Arizona tavern. He was secretly married to a Negress, who bore him several children. King's biography has been written (1958) by Thurman Wilano.

King, Martin Luther, Jr. (b. Atlanta, Ga., Jan. 15, 1929—   ), Baptist minister, author. King, a Montgomery, Ala., minister, achieved national prominence at the time of the successful Negro boycott of the Montgomery busses in 1956. He became recognized as a leader of the Southern Negroes in their campaign for civil rights. In 1957 he attended the Independence Celebration of the new state of Ghana in West Africa, at the Prime Minister's personal invitation. He visited India in 1959 at the invitation of the Gandhi Memorial Trust. King's books received wide and enthusiastic acclaim. The first, *Stride Toward Freedom* (1958), is the story of the Negro boycott of the Montgomery bus lines. *The Measure of a Man* appeared in 1959.

King attended public schools in Atlanta, where his father was a Baptist minister. He received his Ph.D. degree from Boston University in 1955, and was subsequently awarded many honorary degrees. L. D. Reddick wrote a biography of King entitled *Crusader Without Violence* (1959).

King, Stoddard (b. Jackson, Wis., Aug. 19, 1889—d. June 13, 1933), newspaperman, columnist, writer of humorous verse. King's column, "Facetious Fragments," often interspersed with verses, in the Spokane *Review* (1916–33), was widely read and quoted all over the country. He collected some of his pieces in *What the Queen Said* (1926), *Listen to the Mocking Bird* (1928), and *The Raspberry Tree* (1930). While he was an undergraduate at Yale he won a prize with a poem entitled THERE'S A LONG, LONG TRAIL A-WINDING. A tour with the Yale Glee Club was offered to the undergraduate who wrote the best tune to the words; this award was

won by Zo [Alonzo] Elliott, who tried in vain to find a publisher for the song. Elliott, in Oxford for graduate work when World War I broke out, had taught the song to his fellow students. They took it into the army, and it soon was a great hit. It was published in London in 1913, M. Witmark & Sons took it over for the United States a year later. It is still popular.

King, Thomas Starr (b. New York City, Dec. 17, 1824—d. March 4, 1864), clergyman, poet, editor. King is chiefly remembered for his descriptive account, *The White Hills: Their Legends, Landscape, and Poetry* (1860), one of the earliest regional analyses. His lectures were collected by Edwin P. Whipple under the title *Substance and Show* (1877). In his later years a resident of California, he used his influence to keep that state on the Union side. In that cause he wrote some effective crusading poems.

King Cotton. A term current in the controversies preceding the Civil War. It was meant to indicate not merely the dominance of cotton in the southern economy, but also its potent sway over the rest of the nation and Europe as well. David Christy (1802–[?]) is believed to have originated the phrase in the title of his book *Cotton Is King* (1855). James Henry Hammond (1807–1864), Senator from South Carolina, popularized it in a taunting speech before the Senate: "You dare not make war on cotton . . . , Cotton is king." David L. Cohn has written a vivid account of *The Life and Times of King Cotton* (1956).

King David (1923), a narrative poem by STEPHEN VINCENT BENÉT. In ballad style Benét tells again the startling story of sin and repentance related in *2 Samuel* 11–12. The poem won the *Nation's* Poetry Prize for 1923 and was separately printed that year.

Kingdon, Frank (b. England, Feb. 27, 1894—   ), clergyman, college administrator, radio news analyst, writer. Kingdon came to the United States in 1912, was naturalized in 1918. After serving in Methodist churches from 1912 to 1934, he became president of Dana College, Newark, N.J., later of the University of Newark (1934–40). Then he devoted his time to lecturing, writing, and radio broadcasting. Among his books: *Humane Religion* (1930); *Life of John Cotton Dana* (1940); *Our Second War of Independence* (1942); *That Man in the White House* (1944); *Architects of the Republic* (1947).

King Features Syndicate. A news-gathering, feature-article, and cartoon strip organization founded in 1913 by MOSES KOENIGSBERG, the first part of whose family name, translated into English, furnished a name for the organization. It is very successful, representing many important writers and cartoonists in the syndicate field. Koenigsberg told its story in his autobiographical volume *King News* (1941).

King Philip and **King Philip's War.** The date of birth of King Philip, whose Indian name was Metacom or Metacomet, is unknown; he died in battle Aug. 12, 1676, after serving as sachem of the WAMPANOAGA INDIANS. His father, Massasoit, had been friendly to the whites; Philip realized that their encroachments would in the end drive out the red man. He therefore called for an alliance of all the Indian tribes in New England, and when the war (1675–76) broke out, the issue for a time looked doubtful. But there was dissension within the Indians' ranks; Philip was killed by an Indian, not a white man. It was many years before New England recovered from the economic and agricultural setback the conflict brought about.

Contemporary Puritan historians were viciously bitter in their attacks on Philip and fiercely exulted when he was killed. Examples are INCREASE MATHER in his *Brief History of the War with the Indians* (1676) and William Hubbard in his NARRATIVE OF THE TROUBLES WITH THE INDIANS (1677). DANIEL GOOKIN, a missionary, was more humane in his attitude, but was reviled for "taking the Indians' part" and denounced as a traitor. He took a calm historian's view in his *Historical Account of the Doings and Sufferings of the Christian Indians in New England* (dated by him Dec. 18, 1677). Benjamin Tompson, first American poet born on this continent, in his NEW ENGLAND'S CRISIS (1676), described in skillful heroic couplets some of the episodes and actors in King Philip's War and flayed the degeneracy and backsliding of the colonists as responsible for the sufferings God had inflicted upon them.

When writers in the early 19th century began to rehabilitate the red man's reputation and to exhibit the wrongs he had suffered at the hands of the white man, King Philip became a popular theme. For a time a poem in six cantos called *Yamoyden: A Tale of the Wars of King Philip* (1820) was the most popular literary production of its day. It was the work of two friends, both under twenty, JAMES W. EASTBURN and ROBERT C. SANDS; the poem exhibits Philip as a wise, bold hero who "fought because he would not yield his birthright." Although his piece was not generally known until the appearance of his *Sketch-Book* (1819), WASHINGTON IRVING had even earlier written *Philip of Pokanoket* (1814), in which Philip appears in heroic proportions. James Fenimore Cooper made use of the story in THE WEPT OF WISH-TON-WISH (1829). In a plot that involves the kidnaping of a young white girl, the emphasis is laid on Philip's noble ally Conanchet, chief of the Narragansetts.

King Philip was effectively exalted in a prize play by John Augustus Stone called METAMORA, OR, THE LAST OF THE WAMPANOAGS (produced, 1829). Edwin Forrest played the role magnificently for many years; sometimes delegations of Indians attended his performances and were deeply impressed. The grandiloquence of this and other plays about Indians irritated James Rees into writing a rather weak burlesque, *Metamora, or the Last of the Pollywoags* (1847). King Philip found a natural defender in WILLIAM APES, a Pequod Indian who became a Methodist minister in 1829. In 1836 Apes delivered a stirring address, printed the same year, on the Indian monarch. He included in his address an

oration such as Philip might have delivered in council to his chiefs and warriors.

Two early novels that dealt principally with King Philip's War were G. H. Hollister's *Mount Hope* (1851) and Daniel P. Thompson's *The Doomed Chief* (1860). Neither can be rated very highly. William G. Schofield's *Ashes in the Wilderness* (1942), which is concerned with the same war, is based on a colonial diary. Esther Forbes' *Paradise* (1937) tells the story of a family nearly destroyed in the war with the Indians. See ALGONQUIN INDIANS.

Kingsblood Royal (1947), a novel by SINCLAIR LEWIS. Lewis sought in this controversial novel to show the absurdity of the taboo against mixed white and Negro blood by depicting a man who suddenly discovers that a supposed Indian ancestor was really a black man. Lewis is savagely satiric in his depiction of types in an average American community; he views the advocates of race prejudice as not only wicked but appallingly dull. The book caused a stir, but was an inferior work by this author.

King's Henchman, The (1927), an opera by DEEMS TAYLOR for which EDNA ST. VINCENT MILLAY wrote the libretto. The events take place in the 10th century, with an Anglo-Saxon king and his foster brother as the leading characters. They woo the same woman, unworthy of both; the play ends in the tragical death of the foster brother. The opera was effective as drama, and the music won warm praise.

Kingsley, Sidney (b. New York City, Oct. 18, 1906—   ), actor, playwright. After playing small parts in stock companies and on Broadway, Kingsley secured production for a play called *Crisis*. The title was changed to MEN IN WHITE (1933); the play won a Pulitzer Prize and has been frequently revived both here and abroad. Even more successful was DEAD END (1935), which was an equal hit as a movie (1937). The play, like most of Kingsley's productions, had a social purpose, and to it was ascribed some of the credit for important laws aimed at slum clearance. Later Kingsley wrote *Ten Million Ghosts* (1936); *The World We Make* (1939); *The Outward Room* (1939); *The Patriots* (with his wife, Madge Evans Kingsley, 1942); *Detective Story* (1949; movie version, 1951); *Darkness at Noon* (1951, an adaptation from the novel by ARTHUR KOESTLER); *Lunatics and Lovers* (1954), a farce.

Kinney, Elizabeth C[lementine Dodge Stedman] (b. New York City, Dec. 18, 1810—d. Nov. 19, 1889), poet, author of travel books, essayist. Although Mrs. Kinney's tenuous hold on fame is largely based on the fact that she was the mother of the poet, critic, and anthologist EDMUND CLARENCE STEDMAN, she was also a pleasing if minor author in her own right. She published *Felicita* (1855), a romance in verse, and *Poems* (1867).

Kino, Eusebio Francisco (b. Italy, 1644—d. March 15, 1711), Jesuit missionary, explorer, map maker. Kino came to Mexico in 1681, did missionary work in Lower California, northern Mexico, southern Arizona, and was instrumental in the return of the Jesuits to the California peninsula in 1697. For nearly twenty-five years he labored as missionary, cattle raiser, and map maker, opened a road around the head of the Gulf to save the difficult passage by water, determined that California was not an island but a peninsula, and made a map which was widely circulated in Europe. He established a score of towns in California, in the river valleys of San Miguel, Magdalena, Sonóita, and Santa Cruz; among them Loreto, named after a famous shrine in central Italy. Kino discovered and described the Casa Grande ruins in Arizona, and died at Magdalena. His autobiography, *Favores Celestiales*, was found, edited and published by Herbert E. Bolton as *Kino's Historical Memoir of Pimería Alta* (2 v., 1919). Also by Bolton are *Father Kino's Lost History, Its Discovery and Its Value* (1911); *The Padre on Horseback* (1932); *Rim of Christendom* (1936). With *Padre Kino on the Trail and A Guide to His Mission Chain* (1933) by F. C. Lockwood came out in 1933; *Pioneer Padre* by Rufus Kay Wyllys in 1935.

Kinsey, Alfred Charles (b. Hoboken, N.J., June 23, 1894—d. Aug. 25, 1956), taxonomist, biological researcher. A graduate of Bowdoin College and Harvard University, Kinsey taught biology at Harvard, then at Indiana University, becoming a professor there in 1920. He published a number of textbooks on biology, as well as reports on his research, and led biological explorations in Mexico and Central America in 1931–32 and 1935–36. In 1938 he took charge of the study on human sexual behavior sponsored by the Institute for Sex Research at Indiana University and the National Research Council. He published the results of the study in *Sexual Behavior in the Human Male* (with W. B. Pomeroy and C. E. Martin, 1948) and *Sexual Behavior in the Human Female* (with Pomeroy, Martin, and P. H. Gebhard, 1953). These books were written as biological reports on patterns of physical and psychological response, but the fact that the research data consisted of confidential interviews with thousands of United States citizens gave them wide appeal in the fields of social science and literature as revelations of morals and mores in American culture, despite critical charges that the interviews did not represent a statistically accurate sampling of the American population.

Kirby, William (b. Eng., Oct. 13, 1817—d. June 23, 1906), poet, newspaper editor, novelist. Kirby came to Canada in 1832 and settled in Niagara seven years later, where he edited the Niagara *Mail* for the next twenty-five years. In 1871 he was appointed customs collector. His first major publication was *The U. E., a Tale of Upper Canada* (1859), an epic poem. *Canadian Idylls* (1894) and *Annals of Niagara* (1894) are nature poems. Kirby is mostly famous for his single novel, THE GOLDEN DOG (1877; rev. ed., 1896). He is the subject of biographies by W. R. Ruddell (1923) and by Lorne Pierce (1929).

Kirkland, Caroline [Matilda Stansbury] ["Mrs. Mary Clavers"] (b. New York City, Jan. 12, 1801—d. April 6, 1864), a novelist, author of travel books, essayist, editor. Mrs. Kirkland's husband was a teacher and missionary who finally settled in a frontier village in Michigan. Mrs. Kirkland had gone to the West with the idea that Chateaubriand and Basil Hall had pictured it accurately; she expressed her disillusionment in three books, partially fictional: *A New Home—Who'll Follow? or, Glimpses of Western Life* (1839; new edition edited by John Nerber, 1953); *Forest Life* (1842); and *Western Clearings* (1845). These books, which in part were modeled on Mary Russell Mitford's sketches of English life, *Our Village* (1824–32), were very popular. Mrs. Kirkland, used to Eastern comforts, was shocked by the frontier, particularly by its lack of culture. She has been called a forerunner of Sinclair Lewis in her depiction of "the small-town mind." See also THE UNION MAGAZINE.

Kirkland, Joseph (b. Geneva, N.Y., Jan. 7, 1830—d. April 29, 1894), editor, novelist. Kirkland, son of CAROLINE KIRKLAND, is known for one novel, ZURY: THE MEANEST MAN IN SPRING COUNTY (1887); in it he continued his mother's attempt to portray the West, particularly the life of western farmers, realistically. Its sequel, *The McVeys* (1888), was by no means so good; a third novel, *The Captain of Company K* (1891), a Civil War story, was even poorer. But Kirkland influenced others, especially HAMLIN GARLAND. He has been praised for the accuracy of his representations of western speech.

Kiss Me Kate (1948; published, 1953), a play-within-a-play by BELLA and SAMUEL SPEWACK, based on Shakespeare's *Taming of the Shrew*, with music by COLE PORTER. It is probably Porter's best work and contains many excellent songs.

Kiss the Boys Good-Bye (1938), a play by CLARE BOOTHE LUCE. This amusing travesty on Hollywood is a satirical account of a movie producer's search for someone to play Scarlett O'Hara in his version of *Gone with the Wind*. The play was itself made into a movie.

Kit Carson's Ride (published in *Poems of the Sierras*, 1871), a poem by JOAQUIN MILLER. In this stirring poem, probably the best that Miller wrote, the famous scout rescues his Indian bride from pursuing tribesmen and from a prairie fire—with the help of his good steed, 'Pache. The poem is obviously in the meter and manner of Robert Browning's *How They Brought the Good News from Ghent to Aix* (1846).

kitsch. A term taken over from the Germans to describe contemporary debased art. In *Partisan Review* articles (1939, 1946), Clement Greenberg attributed it to the industrial revolution and its establishment "of what is called universal literacy," and included in the term "popular, commercial art and literature with their chromeotypes, magazine covers, illustrations, ads, slick and pulp fiction, comics, Tin-Pan Alley music, tap dancing, Hollywood movies, etc., etc." He held that *The New Yorker* was "fundamentally high-class kitsch for the luxury trade," and said "kitsch has in the last ten years become the dominant culture in Soviet Russia."

Kittredge, George Lyman (b. Boston, Feb. 28, 1860—d. July 23, 1941), teacher, scholar. Kittredge graduated from Harvard in 1882 and taught there from 1888 until his retirement in 1936. He was familiar to generation after generation of Harvard students, many of whom took one or another of his courses as a matter of tradition. A popular, dramatic lecturer, Kittredge was famous for his fiery readings of Shakespeare and his stinging satire of delinquent students. Oscar Cargill has taken exception to the universal adulation of Kittredge. He feels that Kittredge standardized the doctoral examination and the form of the doctoral dissertation to an extent that "killed the last spark of sensibility in the future teacher of literature." Kittredge taught his disciples his own method of explication, and they taught theirs his device of a word-by-word analysis of Shakespeare's plays.

In his scholarly techniques and the fields he chose, Kittredge largely followed FRANCIS J. CHILD, his predecessor at Harvard. Among his important writings were: *The Language of Chaucer's "Troilus"* (1894); *Words and Their Ways in English Speech* (with J. B. GREENOUGH, 1901); *English and Scottish Popular Ballads* (with H. C. Sargent, 1904); *The Old Farmer and His Almanack* (1904); *English Witchcraft and James I* (1912); *Chaucer and His Poetry* (1915); *A Study of Gawain and the Green Knight* (1916); *Shakespeare* (1916); *Sir Thomas Malory* (1925); *Witchcraft in Old and New England* (1929); and an edition of *The Complete Works of Shakespeare* (1936).

In 1913 a group of Kittredge's pupils and colleagues presented a series of papers in his honor on the twenty-fifth anniversary of his teaching career at Harvard. The bibliography was superseded by James Thorpe's *Bibliography of the Writings of G. L. Kittredge* (1948). Beginning with a boyhood journal of Kittredge's in 1869 and continuing to 1946, Thorpe found that the list of Kittredge's published works numbered more than four hundred books, articles, and reviews, and demonstrated the wide range of his interests.

Kitty Foyle (1939), a novel by CHRISTOPHER MORLEY. It chronicles a love affair between a young man of one of Philadelphia's Main Line families and an Irish office girl. Helen E. Haines described the story as "the natural history of a woman only according to male research," and called it "ebullient, stream-of-consciousness retrospect, witty, often ribald, and warmly sentimental." The novel was filmed in 1940.

K-K-K-Katy (1918), a song by Geoffrey O'Hara (1882—   ). It was very popular with the soldiers in World War I and later with civilians.

Klein, Abraham Moses (b. Montreal, Feb. 14, 1909—   ), poet, novelist. Klein received his bachelor's degree from McGill University in 1930, and was admitted to the bar of Quebec in 1933, after receiving a law degree from Toronto University. His poetical works include: *Hath Not A Jew* (1940), *The Hitleriad* (1942), and *Poems* (1944). He won the Governor-General's Award in Poetry in 1948, and has contributed poetry to the *Canadian Forum* and *Poetry*, a Chicago publication. A novel, *The Second Scroll*, was published in 1951.

Klein, Charles (b. England, Jan. 7, 1867—d. May 7, 1915), actor, playwright. Klein came to the United States when he was fifteen, played juvenile roles on the stage, won his first popular success with *Heartsease* (1897). His best plays were written for production by DAVID BELASCO and performance by the noted actor David Warfield, among them *The Auctioneer* (1901) and *The Music Master* (1904). Other plays of popular appeal written by Klein were *The Lion and the Mouse* (1905), *The Third Degree* (1908), and *The Gamblers* (1910). Klein was a skillful and facile stage craftsman, but of little literary note.

Klinck, Carl F[rederick] (b. Elmira, Ont., March 24, 1908—   ), literary historian, teacher. Klinck earned degrees at the University of Western Ontario and Columbia University and returned to his first alma mater to teach English until 1956 when he became Professor of Canadian Literature. He is an authority on the literature of his native land as is shown by his critical studies and editions of Canadian works, including: *Wilfred Campbell: A Study in Late Provincial Victorianism* (1942); *Edwin J. Pratt: The Man and His Poetry* (1947, with H. G. Wells); *Canadian Anthology* (1955, 1957; ed. with R. E. Watters); *William "Tiger" Dunlop, "Blackwoodian Backwoodsman"* (ed. 1958); *Tecumseh: Fact and Fiction in Early Records* (ed. 1961).

Klipstein, Louis Frederick (b. Winchester, Va., Jan. 2, 1813—d. Aug. 20, 1878), philologist. Son of a surgeon who came to America with Hessian troops and then settled here, Klipstein was educated here and in Germany and became a devoted student of languages. He published *A Grammar of the Anglo-Saxon Language* (1848) and edited various Anglo-Saxon writings. These texts were among the earliest, if not the earliest, in this field issued in the United States. He also edited in 1844 a magazine called *Polyglot*.

Klondike gold rush. In 1896 George Washington Carmack, a "squaw man," made a bonanza strike of gold in the Klondike territory in northwest Canada. The subsequent rush reached its climax in 1898 and continued during the following years. By 1900 about $22,000,000 had been taken out of the frozen ground. Dawson became a boom city, full of queer and sometimes sinful characters, but not so sinful as ROBERT W. SERVICE made them out; he did not get to the Klondike until 1906. Even more fantastic were the newspaper reports sent home by JOAQUIN MILLER.

Numerous authors found the gold rush a literary bonanza. Probably the most famous Klondike story is Jack London's THE CALL OF THE WILD (1903); WHITE FANG (1906) and *Smoke Bellew* (1912) used the same background. Service's *Songs of a Sourdough* (1907; later called *The Spell of the Yukon*, 1908), his *Ballads of a Cheechako* (1907), and his novel *Trail of '98* (1912) recall the Klondike scene. The most famous of his Yukon poems are THE SHOOTING OF DAN MCGREW and *The Law of the Yukon.* The latter lays down Service's solemn version of Darwinian doctrine: "This is the law of the Yukon, that only the Strong shall thrive; / That surely the Weak shall perish, and only the Fit survive." Service's poems threw the spotlight on "120-proof types"—with names like Muck-Luck Mag, Gum-Boot Ben, Claw-Fingered Kitty, and Blasphemous Bill Mackie. Rex Beach set out for the Klondike but never reached it; his novels are laid in nearby Alaskan scenes. A good novel of the North was Elizabeth Robins' *The Magnetic North* (1905), written after a stay in the Klondike region.

Many factual books have been written about the Klondike gold rush; one of the best is Kathryn Winslow's *Big Pan-Out* (1950), based in part on the notes and diaries of Howard V. Sutherland, a professional writer and adventurer. It begins with the early Russian settlements and gold prospectors, goes on to give a comprehensive picture of the wild stampede into the Yukon. Miss Winslow's narrative is factual but colorful. Richard O'Connor has written *High Jinks on the Klondike* (1954), and Pierre Berton *The Klondike Fever* (1958).

Kluckhohn, Clyde K[ay] M[aben] (b. Le Mars, Iowa, Jan. 11, 1905—d. July 29, 1960), anthropologist, archaeologist, teacher, writer. Kluckhohn received his A.B. degree from Princeton in 1922, did postgraduate work at various schools, including the University of Vienna and Oxford, obtained his Ph.D. from Harvard in 1936, and began teaching there in 1935. Through the years he was active in several government agencies, especially during World War II. His interest centered to a large extent in the American Indian. Six years spent among the Navahos resulted in numerous papers and books. Among his books: *To The Foot of the Rainbow* (1927); *Beyond the Rainbow* (1933); *The Navaho* (1946); *The Children of the People* (1946, with Dr. Dorothea Leighton); *Personality in Nature, Society and Culture* (1948, rev. ed. 1953, with H. A. Murray); *Mirror for Man* (1949); *Navaho Means People* (1951, with Leonard McCombe and E. Z. Vogt). *How the Soviet System Works,* which he wrote in collaboration with Raymond Bauer and Alex Inkeles, was published in 1956.

Knapp, Samuel Lorenzo (b. Newburyport, Mass., Jan. 19, 1783—d. July 8, 1838), lawyer, editor, miscellaneous writer. The Duyckincks call Knapp "voluminous and useful," an adequate description of his numerous books and articles on the lives of eminent lawyers, men of letters, statesmen, and "females," on freemasonry, naval history, the "picturesque beauties" of the Hudson River (2 v., 1835–36), and other subjects. He also wrote *Extracts from a Journal of Travels in North America* (1818) under the pen name Ali Bey, and *The Bachelor and Other Tales, Founded on American Incident and Character* (1836). He edited various magazines, but for a time found law practice more profitable. Such of

his reputation as survives is based on the fact that he was a pioneer historian of American literature in his *Lectures on American Literature, With Remarks on Some Passages of American History* (1829).

Kneass, William (b. Lancaster, Pa., Sept. 25, 1780—d. Aug. 27, 1840), engraver. He contributed to several magazines of his time, including the *Port Folio* and the *Analectic Magazine.* See BEEF STEAK CLUB.

Knevels, Gertrude (b. Fishkill, N.Y., April 2, 1881—), playwright, author of mystery stories and books for children. In addition to short stories and plays for amateurs, Miss Knevels has written pleasant books for young people, among them *The Wonderful Bed* (1911) and *Molly Moonshine* (1930), and some cleverly contrived mystery stories, including *Octagon House Mystery* (1926); *Out of the Dark* (1932); *Death on the Clock* (1940).

Knickerbocker, Diedrich. See THE HISTORY OF NEW YORK, BY DIEDRICH KNICKERBOCKER.

Knickerbocker, H[ubert] R[enfro] (b. Yoakum, Tex., Jan. 31, 1898—d. July 13, 1949), newspaperman, war correspondent, author of books about Europe. Knickerbocker was one of the best-informed correspondents of his day; his travels, as one contemporary phrased it, "were like a synopsis of his times"; and he had a knack for being on hand at the great critical moments in history. He was killed in the crash of an airliner near Bombay, along with several other American correspondents. He received a Pulitzer Prize in 1939. Among his books: *Fighting the Red Trade Menace* (1931); *The German Crisis* (1932); *Can Europe Recover?* (1932); *Will War Come in Europe?* (1934); *Siege of Alcatraz* (1937); *Is Tomorrow Hitler's?* (1941).

Knickerbocker Holiday (1938), a musical comedy with text by MAXWELL ANDERSON and music by Kurt Weill. The play was suggested to Anderson by Washington Irving's *Knickerbocker's History of New York* (1809); the leading role of Peter Stuyvesant was played by Walter Huston. The lines and lyrics show Anderson at his best, although Weill's music is only remembered for one of the hits of the show, *September Song.*

Knickerbocker Magazine, The. The "Old Knick," founded in 1832, was New York's first monthly of wide national prestige. It almost perished in its first 16 months under inept management (though CHARLES FENNO HOFFMAN and TIMOTHY FLINT were engaged editing it); and not until May, 1834, when LEWIS GAYLORD CLARK took over as editor and part owner, did it begin to show the brilliance that later characterized it. Clark's own chatty and humorous "Editor's Table" was for many years an important part of the magazine; though it borrowed much of its varied fare, it was nearly always genial and entertaining. Clark was a likable person, and despite the fact that he was never able to pay as well as Graham or Godey, he attracted a distinguished list of contributors. Among them were such New Yorkers as WASHINGTON IRVING (a contributing editor 1839–1841), Cooper, Bryant, James K. Paulding, N. P. Willis, R. H. Stoddard, and G. W. Curtis, as well as Philadelphians Robert Montgomery Bird, Charles Godfrey Leland, Mathew Carey, and Bayard Taylor. New England was represented most prominently by Longfellow, Hawthorne, Whittier, and Holmes. Clark came to pay much attention to the West, enlisting such writers as James Hall, Mrs. Caroline Kirkland, H. R. Schoolcraft, and Francis Parkman; most important of the western *matériel* (as Clark loved to call it) was Parkman's *Oregon Trail* (1847). Most prominent among the magazine's associate editors was Clark's brother, Willis Gaylord Clark. The *Knickerbocker,* suffering from too many changes of ownership, deteriorated toward 1850, and after that date the *Harper's* competition was too much for it. It barely survived the Civil War, perishing in 1865.

Knickerbocker School. A name given to a loosely associated group of writers living and working in New York City or nearby during the first half of the 19th century. Their chief point of relationship was not unity in doctrine or practice but rather the fact that they were all helping to make New York an important literary center. Among the members of the group were Washington Irving, J. K. Paulding, James Fenimore Cooper, William Cullen Bryant, J. R. Drake, Fitz-Greene Halleck, John Howard Payne, Samuel Woodworth, Epes Sargent, Lydia M. Child, George P. Morris, G. C. Verplanck, Robert C. Sands, William Cox, N. P. Willis, Lewis G. and Willis G. Clark, C. F. Hoffman, Clement Moore, Bayard Taylor. Kendall B. Taft has made an exhaustive study of the *Minor Knickerbockers* (1947), and shows that the group indulged in self-criticism as well as in creative activity and sought to foster a national literature.

Knight, Eric ["Richard Hallas"] (b. England, April 10, 1897—d. Jan. 15, 1943), a writer, newspaperman, and cartoonist. Knight came to the United States in 1912 and remained in this country during the rest of his life, except for service in the Canadian Army during World War I and the American Army during World War II and an occasional visit to Yorkshire. His best-known tales are laid in Yorkshire, particularly *The Flying Yorkshireman* (collected with other novellas, 1936). Other books of his include *Invitation to Life* (1934); *The Happy Land* (1940); *Lassie Come Home* (a juvenile, 1940); *This Above All* (1941); *Sam Small Flies Again* (short stories, 1942).

Knight, George Wilson (b. England, Sept. 19, 1897—   ), teacher, critic, producer. After teaching mathematics in England for several years, Knight was appointed in 1931 professor of English at Toronto University, and became a resident of Canada. His chief interest is in Shakespeare's plays, some of which he has produced in Toronto. Among his books: *Myth and Miracle* (1929); *The Wheel of Fire* (1930); *The Imperial Theme* (1931); *The Shakespearean Tempest* (1932); *Principles of Shakespearean Production* (1936); *The Burning Oracle* (1939);

This Sceptered Isle (1940); *Atlantic Crossings* (1936) is "an autobiographical design."

Knight, Henry Cogswell ["Arthur Singleton, Esq."] (b. Newburyport, Mass., Jan. 29, 1789 —d. Jan. 10, 1835), clergyman, writer, lecturer. Knight, a clever versifier, published his first collection, *The Cypriad* (1809), while a sophomore at Harvard; this was later reworked as *The Trophies of Love.* He also issued *The Broken Harp* (1815) and *Poems* (2 v., 1821). After a wide tour of the country he wrote a series of amusing *Letters from the South and West* (1824) under the pen name of Arthur Singleton, Esq. In 1831 appeared some of his *Lectures and Sermons.* Knight is remembered for two curious instances of parallel phrasing. In *The Cypriad* appears a poem, *The Little Sweep,* that parallels two verses in William Blake's *Songs of Innocence and Experience* (1794), although no one knows how Knight could have seen a copy of Blake by 1809. Similarly in *The Broken Harp* there is an odd resemblance between his *Earl Kandorf and Rosabelle* and Coleridge's at that time unpublished *Christabel* (1816).

Knight, Sarah Kemble (b. Boston, April 19, 1666—d. Sept. 25, 1727), diarist, businesswoman, conductor of a dame's or writing school, humorist. Madame Knight was the daughter of a merchant who was one of Oliver Cromwell's agents in America. Her husband died in London in 1706(?), but she took over many of his and her father's responsibilities, was a shrewd business adviser, and signed many public documents. One tradition is that Benjamin Franklin attended her school.

In 1704 Madame Knight made a trip to New York to expedite the settlement of a wealthy relative's estate. She kept a diary of her journey on horseback—in those days a difficult if not dangerous undertaking—which was published in 1825, with Theodore Dwight as editor; in 1920 George Winship edited it again, and in 1935 a facsimile edition was published. This *Journal of Madame Knight* has always been regarded as one of the most vivid and authoritative pictures of the colonial period. Madame Knight was both realistic and a humorist. She speaks of the steep and rocky hills, the tottering bridges, the hard straw beds of the inns, the fricassees that could not be swallowed, the country bumpkin who "spit a large deal of aromatic tincture." There appear such comic character types as the gawky Connecticut Yankee and awkward Joan, the mendacious Quaker, the shiftless back-countrymen, the slatternly tavern hostess, and the debauched Indians.

Knight's Gambit (1939), a book of related stories by WILLIAM FAULKNER. Dealing with the various inhabitants of YOKNAPATAWPHA COUNTY, *Knight's Gambit* is a collection of detective stories in which GAVIN STEVENS, the county attorney, ferrets out the real culprits and saves the innocent. The book is ingenious and skillfully narrated; perhaps the best story is "Monk," which deals with an idiot who is imprisoned for a murder he did not commit and who finally is incited to kill the warden who has befriended him.

Knoblock [originally Knoblauch], Edward (b. New York City, April 7, 1874—d. July 19, 1945), actor, dramatist. Knoblock, long familiar with England, became a British citizen in 1916. His best-known play was *Kismet* (1911), an Arabian Nights fantasy that was very successful in England and New York; it was turned into a popular musical comedy (1953). Also a Broadway hit was *Marie-Odile* (1915), a drama of the Franco-Prussian War. In England, Knoblock worked as a collaborator on dramatizations with many novelists, including Arnold Bennett (MILESTONES, 1912), J. B. Priestley (*The Good Companions*, 1931), Vicki Baum (*Grand Hotel*, 1931); also on translations of French plays.

Knopf, Alfred A. (b. New York City, Sept. 12, 1892—   ), publisher. Knopf graduated from Columbia University in 1912, and founded a publishing firm in 1915 with Blanche Wolf, whom he married a year later. He became president of Alfred A. Knopf, Inc., in 1918, and chairman of the board in 1957, when his wife became president. In 1960 Random House, Inc., acquired the stock of the company, but the firm continued as an independent imprint. His son, Alfred, Jr., founded Atheneum Publishers in 1959 with Simon Michael Bessie and Hiram Haydn.

Knott, Thomas A[lbert] (b. Chicago, Jan. 12, 1880—d. Aug. 16, 1945), teacher, philologist, editor, lexicographer. Knott, after teaching in high schools and several universities, resigned his professorship at the State University of Iowa in order to become general editor of the Merriam-Webster dictionaries (1926–35). It was his particular task to prepare the famous "Second Edition" of *Webster's New International Dictionary* (1934), one of the soundest and most widely circulated dictionaries in the history of lexicography. He established firmly the principle that Webster, as interpreted by modern philology, was not a law-giver, but a recorder; it was the function of the editor to discover the best usage as found among reputable speakers and writers and to set it down. After the completion of this task, Knott resigned to become professor of English at the University of Michigan, a post he occupied at the time of his death. Knott saw words as always related in actual use to one another; the phrase rather than the single word created sense. In his later academic years he worked on a *Middle English Dictionary* and gave courses in Chaucer and medieval literature. With Samuel Moore he wrote *Elements of Old English* (1919; 9th edition, 1942).

Knox, Thomas W[allace] (b. Pembroke, N.H., June 26, 1835—d. Jan. 6, 1896), newspaperman, traveler, author of books for boys. Believed to be a descendant of John Knox, this member of the family followed various occupations until he settled down in newspaper work. Then he became a traveler who made that his chief occupation. The first of his journeys was across Siberia; later he visited many other parts of the earth. He turned out, ordinarily, two books a year, including a popular series, "The Boy Travelers in the Far East" (1881) and many sequels, also "The Young Nimrod" series. As a Civil War correspondent he collected his dispatches in *Camp-Fire and Cotton-Field* (1865). He composed biographies of Robert Fulton (1886), Henry Ward Beecher (1887), and other noted men; and a manual, *How to Travel* (1881). He was a wholesome, entertaining writer.

Kober, Arthur (b. Poland, Aug. 25, 1900—   ), press agent, producer, columnist, writer, playwright. Kober was brought to the United States in 1904 and was brought up in New York City. He served as a press agent for various producers, tried his own hand as a producer in 1925, became a contributor of theater and other gossip to the *Morning Telegraph,* wrote and adapted about thirty motion pictures in Hollywood. At the same time he had begun contributing to the *New Yorker,* mostly dialect stories set in the Bronx or Hollywood, and from these emerged several books: *Thunder Over the Bronx* (1935); HAVING WONDERFUL TIME (1937); *Pardon Me for Pointing* (1939); *My Dear Bella* (1941); *That Man Is Here Again* (1946); *Oooh, What You Said!* (1956). A comedy based on *Having Wonderful Time* was produced in 1937. In addition, Kober has written a successful play, *Wish You Were Here* (1952), with Joshua Logan and Harold Rome. *Mighty Man Is He,* another play, written in collaboration with George Oppenheimer, came out in 1960. Brooks Atkinson has described Kober as "a tender and sympathetic writer with considerable affection for the little people who are trying to find a place for themselves in a cold world," but others have found that his satire is often ruthless. He has an accurate ear for folk speech, especially urban speech, and a quick eye for eccentric character. He was for a time married to LILLIAN HELLMAN, the playwright.

Koenigsberg, Moses (b. New Orleans, April 16, 1878—d. Sept. 21, 1945), newspaperman, short-story writer, historian, memoirist. Koenigsberg was an inveterate newspaperman, who began writing at nine, was offered a job as a reporter at thirteen, published a paper in San Antonio at sixteen, and went on to a varied career as a reporter, an editor, and a publisher. Ultimately he became the founder and manager of the Newspaper Feature Service (1913), then of the KING FEATURES SYNDICATE, Inc. (1916), which took its name from a translation of the first part of his own family name. He later was connected with other feature and syndicate services. He wrote an autobiography, *King News* (1941). Koenigsberg wrote two other books: *Southern Martyrs* (1898); and *The Elk and the Elephant* (1899), a collection of short stories.

Kohn, Hans (b. Czechoslovakia, Sept. 15, 1891—   ), historian, lecturer, teacher. Kohn came to the United States in 1933, has taught at Smith College and the City College of New York. Among his authoritative books: *A History of Nationalism in the East* (1929); *World Order in Historical Perspective* (1942); *The Twentieth*

Century (1949); *Panslavism, Its History and Ideology* (1953); *The Mind of Modern Russia* (1955).

Kolodin, Irving (b. New York City, Feb. 22, 1908—), music critic. Kolodin was educated at the Institute of Musical Art. In 1936, Kolodin wrote *Metropolitan Opera*, a second edition appearing in 1940. He wrote again about the Metropolitan in 1953, this time a spicy account of seventy years of opera history. Between 1952 and 1958 Kolodin annotated the program for the New York Philharmonic Orchestra. Since 1950 he has served as music editor for the *Saturday Review*. *The Musical Life* (1958) is a collection of thirty essays. Other books: *Guide to Recorded Music* (1941); *New Guide* (1947, rev. 1950); *Orchestral Music on LP* (1955); *The Musical Life* (1958); *The Composer as Listener* (1958).

Komroff, Manuel (b. New York City, Sept. 7, 1890—), writer, editor, war correspondent. Notable chiefly as a historical novelist, Komroff wrote novels of various kinds, many short stories, and a manual, *How to Write a Novel* (1950), and composed at least one play, *Don Quixote and Sancho* (1942). His first novel was *Juggler's Kiss* (1927); others were *Coronet* (1930); *Two Thieves* (1931); *Waterloo* (1936); *The March of the Hundred* (1939); *The Magic Bow* (1940); *Feast of the Jesters* (1947); *Echo of Evil* (1948); *Jade Star* (1951); *The Story of Jesus* (1955); *Mozart* (1956, a juvenile). Two story collections are: *The Grace of Lambs* (1925), *All in One Day* (1932). A pleasant autobiography is *Big City, Little Boy* (1953).

Köningsmarke, the Long Finne: A Story of the New World (1823), by JAMES KIRKE PAULDING. Under somewhat disparate influences—Irving, Cooper, Shakespeare, Henry Fielding—Paulding wrote a book remarkable in many ways but not an artistic success. His story tells the adventures of a Finnish immigrant to the colony of New Sweden on the Delaware. He is a noble fellow in appearance, and the daughter of the governor falls in love with him. Both are kidnapped by the Indians, other obstacles arise, but all is well in the end. Paulding sometimes writes as a historical novelist and sometimes as a satirist of Cooper; sometimes he burlesques the Swedish officials as Irving did the Dutch rulers and sometimes he is much more serious. In his treatment of the Indians, Paulding seeks to be fair. Their orations are perhaps too philosophical, but descriptions of their savagery alternate with others in which they are treated, as Albert Keiser says, with "affectionate tenderness."

Korzybski, Alfred [Habdank] [Count] (b. Poland, July 3, 1879—d. March 1, 1950), teacher, founder of "general semantics." Korzybski came of a noble Polish family, studied in Germany, Italy, and the United States, and taught for a time in Warsaw. In World War I he served with the cavalry, and other branches of the army, and lectured in the United States. He first came to the United States in 1915 or 1916; in 1919 he married the American portrait painter Mira Edgerly, and in 1940 was natural-

ized. In 1938 he became president and director of the Institute of General Semantics, first located in Chicago, later in Lakeville, Conn. Meanwhile he had formulated his theories of what he called "general semantics," a branch of semantics, the science of meaning. He published *Manhood of Humanity: The Science and Art of Human Engineering* (1921), then a massive tome, *Science and Sanity: An Introduction to Non-Aristotelian Systems and General Semantics* (1933; 3rd ed., 1948). Korzybski and the general semanticists also publicized their views in a magazine called *ETC.: A Review of General Semantics*, founded in 1943 and edited by S. I. HAYAKAWA.

Korzybski felt that "in the old [or Aristotelian] construction of language, you cannot talk sense." As Hayakawa once explained it in *ETC.*, in the Aristotelian language structure one finds (1) the so-called *is* of identity, the confusion of words with things, and the neglect of differences between the individuals of any class of objects or persons; (2) such division of the indivisible as the distinction between "substance" and "form" or between "cause" and "effect" or between "mind" and "body"; (3) two-valued orientation, making propositions either "true" or "false" and an action either "right" or "wrong"; (4) neglect of the indefinite number of levels of abstraction. Life, said Korzybski, is made up of nonverbal facts, each one different from another and each forever changing. A man's nervous system abstracts each of these facts or a part of the fact; then he will abstract it again to make a verbal statement about it; then he'll make a statement about the statement and so on. Afterward he will react to the statements as if they were facts. The man must realize that he never knows all about a "fact"; there is always the "etc."

Korzybski believed that if the word could be distinguished from the thing and one moment from the next moment, the world would become sane. At his Institute sessions, an amazing attempt was made to apply this philosophy widely. Thus in the *Papers from the Second American Congress on General Semantics* (1943) one found not merely papers that dealt with language (like Benjamin Lee Whorf's *Languages and Logic*), but others on semantics and physiotherapy, vision and visual research, the dilemma of mental hygiene, social work, marital counseling, democracy, verbalizations in finance, nutrition, medicine, the motion-picture business. There were pieces on horticulture as a field for the investigation of semantic reactions, the application of semantics to a case of stage fright, and semantic dementia and semi-suicide. The Institute also published monographs: for example, W. Burridge's *A Colloidal-Physiological Psycho-Logic* (1938).

Krapp, George Philip (b. Cincinnati, Ohio, Sept. 1, 1872—d. April 21, 1934), teacher, historian, philologist. Krapp was among the earliest of American philologists to emphasize the new developments of English in the United States. During his career as professor of English at Columbia University (1910-34) he inducted many students into an accurate estimate of these developments as well as into a knowledge of English generally. Among his books: *America, the Great Adventure* (1924); *The English Language in America* (2 v., 1925); *The Knowledge of English* (1927); *Anglo-Saxon Reader* (1929). His book on *The English Language in America,* based on much exhaustive research, dispelled many false notions about pronunciation and usage; H. L. Mencken often acknowledged his debt to it. Krapp did a skillful, appealing version in modern English verse of Chaucer's *Troilus and Cressida* (1932).

Krause, Herbert (b. Fergus Falls, Minn., May 25, 1905—   ), farmer, newspaperman, teacher, writer. Well acquainted with the farms and farmers of Minnesota and neighboring states, Krause in his novels depicts this farm life with tragic realism and pity. His first novel, *Wind Without Rain* (1939), won the award of the Friends of American Writers. *The Thresher* (1946) is another regional novel, with strong emphasis on local folkways, morals, landscapes. Other books by Krause are: *The Oxcart Trail* (1954); *The Builder and the Stone* (1958); *The Big Four* (1960). Also regional in texture is Krause's one-act play, *Bondsmen in the Hills* (1936). *Neighbor Boy* (1939) is a book of verse.

Krey, Laura [Lettie Smith] (b. Galveston, Tex., Dec. 18, 1890—   ), novelist. Mrs. Krey is the descendant of a southern planter and is strongly under the influence of STARK YOUNG. In her novel *And Tell of Time* (1938), she is on the side of the Old South in her depiction of some unpleasant Yankees who during the Reconstruction period bring corruption and brutality, as well as demagoguery, to a community on the Brazos River. Essentially a family chronicle, "the book is dynamic in defense of a decadent feudalism," says Ernest Leisy. *On the Long Tide* (1940) is a story of the beginnings of Texas.

Kreymborg, Alfred (b. New York City, Dec. 10, 1883—d. Aug. 14, 1966), poet, editor, critic. Kreymborg has been called a patron saint of the modern "little magazine" movement. (See LITTLE MAGAZINES.) He founded *The Glebe* in September, 1913, as an organ of the Imagist movement; it pioneered for ten issues in experimental writing and published contributions by Ezra Pound, James Joyce, Richard Aldington, and William Carlos Williams. The following year he began publishing *Others;* this magazine lasted until July, 1919. It aimed to publish poems by "others" than those who were finding a place in *Poetry;* it was bolder and more experimental than the latter magazine. Kreymborg gathered the best of its verse in *Others, An Anthology* (1916). In 1921 he was persuaded by the bookseller Harold Loeb to start still another "little magazine"—BROOM, an elaborate and sumptuous affair, edited first at Rome, then in Berlin, finally in New York. While he and Loeb were in charge, it was conservative; thereafter it became erratic and exciting; it ceased publication in January, 1924. In 1927 Kreymborg established an annual publication, THE AMERICAN

CARAVAN, an experiment carried on, along with Paul Rosenfeld, Van Wyck Brooks, and Lewis Mumford, until 1936.

The poetry of Kreymborg himself is not as stimulating as was his personality and his fervor as an editor, critic, and historian. He made collections of his verses in *Mushrooms* (1916), *Funnybone Alley* (1927), and *Selected Poems, 1912–1944* (1945). Kreymborg was also interested in the experimental theatre. A charter member of the Provincetown Players and managing director of the Manhattan-Bronx Federal Theatre Project, he wrote *Plays for Merry Andrews* (1920), *Rocking Chairs and Other Comedies* (1925); *Puppet Plays* (1926); *Manhattan Men* (1929); *Ballad of Youth* (1938); *The Ballad of Valley Forge* (1944), with music by Alex North; *Man and Shadow: An Allegory* (1946), a verse allegory; *No More War and Other Poems* (1950), a ballad-play. Kreymborg told his own story twice: once in *Troubadour* (1925) in prose, again in *Man and Shadow* in blank verse.

Kroll, Harry Harrison (b. Hartford City, Ind., Feb. 18, 1888—   ), teacher, novelist, memoirist. Kroll was brought up in a farming community. A teacher all his life in high schools and universities, mainly in the West and South, his earliest literary production was *A Comparative Study of Southern Folk Speech* (1925). His first novel, *The Mountainy Singer* (1928), depicts the people of the Tennessee mountains. *Cabin in the Cotton* (1931) is set in West Tennessee; *The Keepers of the House* (1940) and *The Rider on the Bronze Horse* (1942) are set in Mississippi. Alabama is the setting for *Waters Over the Dam; Their Ancient Grudge* (1946) is another retelling of the Hatfield-McCoy feud; *Darker Grows the Valley* (1947) is an account of life in the Tennessee Valley from 1778 to TVA. *Last Homecoming* (1950) tells of a novelist who returns to his home community. Later novels include *The Long Quest* (1953); *Summer Gold* (1955); *My Heart's In The Hills* (1956); *Cloi* (1957); *For Cloi, With Love* (1958). Kroll tells the story of his life in *I Was a Sharecropper* (1937).

Kronenberger, Louis (b. Cincinnati, Ohio, Dec. 9, 1904—   ), drama critic, historian, essayist, novelist, editor. Kronenberger worked on the staff of two publishing houses, then of *Fortune,* before joining *Time* as its drama critic. He began lecturing on drama at Columbia University in 1950 and at Brandeis University in 1953, and editing an annual volume of *The Best Plays* in 1953. His other publications include an anthology of light verse (1934); a delicately satirical novel, *Grand Right and Left* (1952); *The Thread of Laughter* (1952), an account of English stage comedy; *Company Manners* (1954), "a cultural inquiry into American life" both honest and witty; and *The Republic of Letters* (1955), appreciative essays on various writers.

Krutch, Joseph Wood (b. Knoxville, Tenn., Nov. 25, 1893—d. May 22, 1970), critic, essayist. A drama critic for the *Nation* for many years, as well as a professor of English at Columbia and other universities, Krutch achieved renown for his critical work on the modern drama, his literary criticism, and his philosophic essays on the condition of modern man. He discussed the makers of modern drama in *The American Drama Since 1918* (1939, rev. 1957) and *Modernism in Modern Drama* (1954). His literary criticism includes *Edgar Allan Poe: A Study of Genius* (1926), which was one of the first psychoanalytical interpretations of literature; *Five Masters, a Study in the Mutations of the Novel* (1930); *Samuel Johnson* (1944); and *Henry David Thoreau* (1948). In *The Modern Temper* (1929), a series of essays centered on the antithesis between man and nature, he analyzed the scientific orientation of the age and its effect on man's need for extrascientific values. *The Measure of Man* (1954), a mellower and less pessimistic work, is partially an extension of *The Modern Temper* and shows the abandonment of Krutch's earlier belief that modern philosophy must be based on the deterministic and materialistic findings of science. He contributed to the symposium *Is the Common Man Too Common?* (1954), a series of essays originally printed in the *Saturday Review* on the resources of contemporary culture. *Human Nature and the Human Condition* (1959) is a critical analysis of modern society and its standards, and a clear and well-argued exposition on the necessity of humanistic values in a mechanized world. Krutch also wrote a number of meditative essays on nature and reflections on man's relationship to the universe, such as *The Twelve Seasons* (1949); *The Desert Year* (1952); *The Best of Two Worlds* (1953); *The Great Chain of Life* (1956); *The Grand Canyon: Today and All its Yesterdays* (1958); and *The Forgotton Peninsula* (1961). He edited *The Gardener's World* (1959), a collection of essays on gardens and related subjects from the writings of authors ranging from Homer to John Burroughs.

Kubly, Herbert Oswald (b. New Clarus, Wis., April 26, 1915—   ), author, teacher, newspaperman, playwright. Kubly began his career as a newspaperman in Pittsburgh and New York and ultimately became a music critic and editor of *Time*. His first nonjournalistic works to receive public attention were two plays, *Men To The Sea* (1944), and *Inherit The Wind*, produced in London in 1948 (not to be confused with the American *Inherit The Wind* by Jerome Lawrence and Robert Lee). Later, while traveling in Europe under a Fulbright grant, he wrote two travel books, *American In Italy* (1955) and *Easter in Sicily* (1956). Both were praised for their humor and shrewd observation; the first received the National Book Award for nonfiction in 1956. A collection of Kubly's short stories, *Varieties of Love* (1958), was commended for its graceful and perceptive writing. Other works include travel pieces for a number of magazines. His book *Italy* (1961) appeared in *Life* magazine's *World Library;* and two unproduced plays, *The Cocoon* (1954) and *Beautiful Dreamer* (1956).

Ku Klux Klan, a name from the Greek word *kuklos* (band or circle) given to two secret societies. The original Ku Klux Klan was formed about 1866 in Pulaski, Tennessee, as a social organization for ex-Confederates; however, because of the growing lawlessness of the freed Negroes and the political threat to white supremacy in the South, the Klan quickly developed into a secret organization intent upon frightening the superstitious and uneducated Negroes into submission. The Klan spread rapidly throughout the South, and in April, 1867, Nathan Bedford Forrest, the Grand Wizard or Cyclops of the Pulaski group, called a convention of delegates from all groups to meet at Nashville for reorganization. One important result of the Nashville convention was a declaration of principles of the Klan, which included the recognition of the supremacy of the Constitution, its laws, and the Union; the Klan further stated that its purposes were to protect the weak from the depredations of the lawless, to protect the Constitution and to aid in the execution of its laws. The Klan was formally disbanded by Forrest in 1869 when it became clear that it was being used as an instrument of violence rather than as a check to it. Despite the official disbandment, the Klan continued its activities; Congress passed the Ku Klux Klan acts of 1870 and 1871 in order to deal with the offenders. The power of the Klan was broken, and as Reconstruction came to an end and the white Southerners regained a measure of political control, the need for such an organization ceased to exist.

In 1915 a new group, modeled on the structure of the original Klan, was organized in Georgia. The new Klan did not restrict its antipathies to Negroes but attacked Catholics and Jews, as well as such ideas as birth control, Darwinism, pacificism, and the repeal of Prohibition. In the early twenties the Klan was reputed to have a membership of five million throughout the United States, and had considerable political power in Indiana, Oklahoma, and Texas. After a series of newspaper exposés of its terroristic activities, beginning in 1923, the Klan began to decline.

The Klan has furnished ample material to novelists. In Thomas Nelson Page's RED ROCK (1898) the hero, Steve Allen, leads the Klan when he returns after the war. The Klan was sensationally employed by a clergyman, THOMAS DIXON, JR., in a series of novels—THE LEOPARD'S SPOTS (1902), *The Clansman* (1905), and *The Traitor* (1907), all laid in the Reconstruction era. *The Clansman* became the basis of one of the most famous of all movies, David W. Griffith's *The Birth of a Nation* (1915), which probably helped to establish the temporary vogue of the second Klan. The earlier group appears again in T. S. Stribling's *The Store* (1932). In Laura Krey's *And Tell of Time* (1938), Ernest E. Leisy notes, "the members of the Ku Klux Klan are likened to Arthurian knights." Ward Greene's *King Cobra* (1940) warns against the dangers of these secret organizations. Howard Fast's *Freedom Road* (1944) is decidedly anti-Klan. J. C. Lester and D. L. Wilson wrote *Ku Klux Klan* (1905), Eyre Damer *When the Ku Klux Rode* (1912), S. F. Horn *Invisible Empire* (1939) about the earlier group. J. M. Mecklin's *Ku Klux Klan* (1924) deals with the later group.

Kunitz, Stanley J[asspon] (b. Worcester, Mass., July 29, 1905—   ), poet, editor, biographer. Kunitz for many years made his living as a compiler of reference books, especially as a member of the staff of the H. W. Wilson Co. Under the pen name of Dilly Tante he has edited *Living Authors* (1931) and *Authors Today and Yesterday* (1933). In collaboration with Howard Haycraft he compiled *The Junior Book of Authors* (1934; rev. ed., 1951); *British Authors of the 19th Century* (1936); *American Authors* (1938); and *Twentieth Century Authors* (1942). With Vineta Colby as his assistant he compiled the *First Supplement* (1955) to the last-named volume. For his poetry Stanley Kunitz deserves a high place among contemporary American authors. He writes mainly in conventional forms, with a tough but graceful mastery of rhythm and diction; he is one of the most highly regarded of the American "metaphysical" poets. The title of one of his volumes, *Intellectual Things* (1930), is accurate but a little misleading, until one realizes that it is taken from a line by William Blake: "For the tear is an intellectual thing." Kunitz' *Collected Poems* (1958) was awarded a Pulitzer Prize in 1959. He taught at the New School for Social Research (1950–1957) and at Brandeis University (1958–1959).

Kyne, Peter B[ernard] (b. San Francisco, Oct. 12, 1880—d. Nov. 27, 1957), soldier, clerk, editor, novelist, short-story writer. After serving with the Army in the Philippines and later in World War I, Kyne turned to miscellaneous occupations, finally decided to be a writer. He published about thirty books, among them a dozen best sellers. He was noted for his "CAPPY RICKS" stories about a wealthy shipowner, descendant of a long line of New England sailing masters.

L

Labat, Jean Baptiste (b. France, 1663—d. 1738), French missionary, explorer, memoirist. Labat in 1693 joined a mission leaving for Martinique. In the West Indies from 1695 to 1705, he kept a voluminous diary. Like the diarist Pepys he had a devouring couriosity, a sense of humor, a gift for the practical; also, comments Patrick Lee Fermor, "the same lucid and indefatigable garrulousness." He published his *Nouveau voyage aux îles de l'Amérique* (8 v., 1724–1742).

labor problems and industry. The development of the labor movement in the United States has been reflected strikingly in literature. The early equalitarians were essentially mercantile in their attitude, including TOM PAINE; they were more antifeudal than prodemocratic. Among the earliest literary men to give public support to labor doctrines were WILLIAM CULLEN BRYANT and WALT WHITMAN, in the 1830's and 1840's. In New England GEORGE BANCROFT, NATHANIEL HAWTHORNE, and RALPH WALDO EMERSON took the part of the laborer. Much that was said in behalf of freedom for the slaves also applied to labor working under degrading conditions. It was by no accident that JOHN GREENLEAF WHITTIER sympathized with labor as well as with the bound man. As the 19th century closed, thoughtful people everywhere saw the need for reforming economic conditions, and the Catholic prelate, Bishop John Lancaster Spalding (1840–1916), wrote books that opposed socialism but sought to throw the power of religion against economic evils; among his writings were *Lectures and Discourses* (1882) and *Socialism and Labor* (1902).

Numerous novels and plays have described the struggle between capital and labor. Some were written by novelists or dramatists interested chiefly in their stories and characters; others belong to what is called PROLETARIAN LITERATURE, which is often Marxist and takes no account of the great gains American labor has won. Probably the first "labor novel" was Elizabeth Stuart Phelps Ward's *The Silent Partner* (1871), a New England story. Also New England in setting was Thomas Bailey Aldrich's THE STILLWATER TRAGEDY (1880), laid in a factory town. The great debate began, however, with two novels that were both published anonymously: John Hay's THE BREADWINNERS (1883), on the side of capital; and H. F. Keenan's *The Money-Makers* (1885), a reply to it that espoused the cause of labor. In the same era came Edward Bellamy's LOOKING BACKWARD (1888) and *Equality* (1894). At the turn of the century was published Mary E. Wilkins' *The Portion of Labor* (1901), set in a New England town.

Among later novels these may be mentioned: Stewart Edward White's THE BLAZED TRAIL (1902); Upton Sinclair's THE JUNGLE (1906), *King Coal* (1917), OIL! (1927), "*Co-op*" (1936), and *Little Steel* (1938); Ernest Poole's THE HARBOR (1915); Winston Churchill's *The Dwelling Place of Light* (1917); Rex Beach's *Flowing Gold* (1922); Garet Garrett's *The Cinder Buggy* (1923); Max Eastman's *Venture* (1927); Mary Heaton Vorse's *Strike* (1930); Robert Cantwell's *Laugh and Lie Down* (1931) and *Land of Plenty* (1934); Grace Lumpkin's *To Make My Bread* (1932); Olive T. Dargan's *Call Home the Heart* (1932) and *A Stone Came Rolling* (1935); L. W. Gilfillan's *I Went to Pit College* (1934); Nelson Algren's *Somebody in Boots* (1935); Myron Brinig's *The Sun Sets in the West* (1935); Walter Havighurst's *Pier Seventeen* (1935); John Steinbeck's IN DUBIOUS BATTLE (1936); Leane Zugsmith's *A Time to Remember* (1936); Albert Maltz's *The Way Things Are* (1938) and *Underground Stream* (1940); Josephine Herbst's *The Rope of Gold* (1939); Ruth McKenney's INDUSTRIAL VALLEY (1939) and *Jake Home* (1943); Elliot Paul's *The Stars and Stripes Forever* (1939); Mari Sandoz' *Capitol City* (1939); Meyer Levin's *Citizens* (1940); Thomas Bell's *Out of This Furnace* (1941) and *There Comes a Time* (1946); Willard Motley's *We Fished All Night* (1951).

Edwin Markham's poem THE MAN WITH THE HOE (San Francisco *Examiner*, Jan. 15, 1899) won him immediate fame, was copied endlessly, and in the year of its publication became the title poem of a collection of Markham's verses. It crystallized the sentiment of the nation about downtrodden labor; numerous replies to the poem, including a prize poem by John Vance Cheney, attracted little attention.

During the depression period that began in 1929 proletarian drama became popular. Often the plays were one-acters and were produced by amateur or semiprofessional organizations, including the Workers' Laboratory Theater, the Theater of Action, the New Theater League, and Labor Stage. Some of the one-act plays became widely popular, for example Clifford Odets' WAITING FOR LEFTY (1935) and Paul Green's *Hymn to the Rising Sun* (1936). Among longer plays were George Sklar and Albert Maltz's *Peace on Earth* (1933); Maltz's *Black Pit* (1935); Albert Bein's *Let Freedom Ring* (1935); and John Howard Lawson's *Marching Song* (1937). Unusual were two other labor plays in which leftism was effectively joined with music and humor: *Pins and Needles* (1937), a revue presented by members of the International Ladies' Garment Workers' Union; and Marc Blitzstein's THE CRADLE WILL ROCK

(1938). Budd Schulberg wrote a powerful movie about labor conditions entitled *Waterfront* (1954). Unions have developed their own songs, like *Which Side Are You On?* (1921), *Roll the Union On* (1936), *Horse with a Union Label* (1939), *Picket Line Priscilla* (1939), and *Union Train* (1947).

Granville Hicks' *Proletarian Literature in the U.S.* (1935) is an anthology that gives a useful survey. John R. Commons wrote, with others, *A History of Labor in the U.S.* (4 v., 1918–35), Samuel Yellen described *American Labor Struggles* (1936), F. R. Dulles discussed *Labor in America* (1949, rev. 1961).

Lacy, Ernest (b. Warren, Pa., Sept. 19, 1863—d. June 17, 1916), lawyer, teacher, dramatist, poet. Lacy was admitted to the bar, preferred the theater to legal practice, but spent his life teaching English at the famed Central High School in Philadelphia. His life in the theater was incidental, although his plays have been highly praised. He was deeply interested in Thomas Chatterton, about whom he wrote a one-act play in verse, *Chatterton* (produced, 1894, by Julia Marlowe, and published, 1900, in Lacy's *Plays and Sonnets*). Lacy expanded this play into a five-act tragedy, *The Bard of Mary Redcliffe*, as a vehicle for E. H. Sothern; it was never produced, but was published in 1916. Christian Gauss called it "the greatest poetic drama written in the U.S." Another poetic tragedy, *Rinaldo, the Doctor of Florence*, was produced in 1895; *The Ragged Earl* was produced in 1899.

Ladd, George Trumbull (b. Painesville, Ohio, Jan. 19, 1842—d. Aug. 8, 1921), clergyman, philosopher, psychologist. Ladd preached in Milwaukee until 1879, when he accepted the chair of Mental and Moral Philosophy at Bowdoin College, then moved in 1881 to a similar post at Yale, where he founded a psychological laboratory and remained until his retirement in 1905. He also taught and lectured at many other institutions. Like William James, Ladd was interested in reconciling the scientific attitude toward nature with the idealistic view of its appreciation. He was distinguished as an interpreter and systematizer. He introduced from Germany the study of psychology as an experimental science based on physiology. His *Elements of Physiological Psychology* (1887) was the first, and after its revision by R. S. Woodworth in 1911, the most inclusive handbook on the subject in the English language. He was one of the founders of the American Psychological Association in 1892 and is regarded as a pioneer in experimental psychology. The titles of some of his many books reveal a wide range of interests: *The Doctrine of Sacred Scripture* (1883); *Philosophy of Mind* (1895); *Philosophy of Conduct* (1902); *Knowledge, Life, and Reality* (1909); *What Should I Believe?* (1915); *The Secret of Personality* (1918).

Ladd, Joseph Brown (b. Newport, R.I., July 7, 1764—d. Nov. 2, 1786), physician, poet. See DELLA CRUSCANISM.

Laddie (1913), a novel by GENE STRATTON-PORTER. This is an autobiographical account of Mrs. Porter's childhood; the title character is based on her brother Leander, who was drowned at eighteen. Like some of her earlier books, it has as its setting the Limberlost Swamp of Indiana. In the course of the next thirty years or so, the book sold more than a million and a half copies.

Ladies' Companion, The. A monthly magazine founded in New York City in May, 1834, by William W. Snowden, in imitation of GODEY'S LADY'S BOOK. Among its contributors were J. K. Paulding, Longfellow, W. G. Simms, and Poe; *The Mystery of Marie Rogêt* by Poe appeared in its pages in 1842–43. It ceased publication in October, 1844.

Ladies' Home Journal, The. In December 1883, the women's section of Cyrus H. K. Curtis' Philadelphia *Tribune and Farmer* began separate publication as a cheap small-folio monthly "conducted by Mrs. Louisa Knapp," who was in fact Mrs. Louisa Knapp Curtis. The paper looked like a success from the start, and Curtis was soon able to employ well-known contributors such as Elizabeth Stuart Phelps, Harriet Prescott Spofford, Rose Terry Cooke, Mary Jane Holmes, Will Carleton, and Robert J. Burdette. By 1893 the *Journal* was excluding patent-medicine advertising entirely, and a decade later it was a leader in the campaign that resulted in the enactment of a federal Food and Drug Act. The magazine prospered, and by 1903 it became the first high-class monthly to reach a million circulation.

In 1889 EDWARD W. BOK began his thirty-year editorship of the *Journal*. The magazine became famous for its chatty, intimate advice on personal and household matters, revealing personality sketches of famous men (sometimes autobiographical), and the fiction and poetry of such well-known writers as W. D. Howells, Mark Twain, Rudyard Kipling, Conan Doyle, Bret Harte, Mary E. Wilkins, Sarah Orne Jewett, Anthony Hope, and Hamlin Garland. The *Journal* was one of the first magazines to adopt four-color illustrations, and it was distinguished by the art work of Edwin A. Abbey, W. L. Taylor, Howard Pyle, Charles Dana Gibson, and W. T. Smedley. Beginning in 1912, the magazine published the best series of art works in color that had yet appeared in any magazine. During World War I the *Journal* published the writings of such leaders as F. D. Roosevelt, Taft, Hoover, McAdoo, and Queen Elizabeth of Belgium.

Bok retired in 1919. Though something of the old "intimacy" of the *Journal* went with him, the magazine continued its circulation advances and its use of big-name authors, including Calvin Coolidge, H. G. Wells, John Galsworthy, Booth Tarkington, and Willa Cather. To the editorship in 1935 came a husband-and-wife team, Bruce and Beatrice Blackmar Gould. They increased the *Journal's* attention to public affairs, national and international. Among popular serials in the 1940's were Franz

Werfel's *The Song of Bernadette*, Margery Sharp's *Cluny Brown*, and John P. Marquand's *Melville Goodwin, USA*. But nonfiction serials by John Gunther, Margaret Mead, and Pearl Buck were even more important; and the contributions of Mrs. Eleanor Roosevelt (which began while her husband was still president) and of Dorothy Thompson underlined the increasing emphasis on public affairs. In 1960 circulation passed six-million and advertisers paid $38,500 for the back cover of a single issue.

Ladies' Repository. A magazine founded in 1841 by Samuel Williams and published in Cincinnati by the Western agents of the Methodist Book Concern. It has listed many noted literary personages, including Alice and Phoebe Cary, among its contributors. Women's fashions and advocacy of temperance were frequent topics, and Frances E. Willard, founder of the Women's Christian Temperance Union, wrote articles for its pages. It ceased publication in December, 1876.

Lady Baltimore (1906), a novel by OWEN WISTER. Despite the title (the name of a cake), the scene of this novel is a city called Kings Port, which may be Charleston, S.C. The story is concerned with a man engaged to a girl whom he no longer really cares for and who wants to marry somebody richer than he is; and another girl, whom he ultimately marries.

Lady Eleanore's Mantle (originally published in the *Democratic Review*, December, 1838; reprinted in the second series of *Twice-Told Tales*, 1842), a short story by NATHANIEL HAWTHORNE. This story is a study in pride and its fearful punishment. Lady Eleanore Rochcliffe comes to live in Boston, at the home of her guardian. She is a haughty beauty, perpetually draped in a strange mantle, and spurns all her suitors. Then an epidemic of smallpox sweeps through the community, and she is somehow associated with it, but is herself stricken and dies, repentant. Her mantle is burned; the epidemic ends. The picture of pride is clear, though the medical lesson seems obscure.

Lady of the Aroostook, The (1879), a novel by WILLIAM DEAN HOWELLS. The *Aroostook* is a vessel on its way to Europe; the lady is a young, beautiful, and delicate teacher, on a trip abroad for her health. The only female on board, she suffers the attentions of a drunken (but patrician) passenger; she is rescued by another Boston blue blood, who gradually perceives the nobility beneath her native rusticity. When they get to Europe and Lydia meets the relatives she has come to visit, their sole question is whether the young man is good enough for her.

Lady or the Tiger?, The (*Century Magazine*, November, 1882; in book form, 1884), a story by FRANK R. STOCKTON. Stockton called the story originally *The King's Arena* and read it at a party given by a friend. Its reception there was so good that he elaborated it and sent it to the *Century Magazine;* it was the most famous story the magazine ever published. It was translated into a dozen languages, and travelers in India heard solemn discussions of the denouement, so enigmatically complicated by the mysterious nature of woman. The plot is simple but unique: in a barbaric land a handsome youth is audacious enough to fall in love with the king's daughter and she with him. His offense is discovered, and he is condemned: in a great arena he must walk up to two great doors and open one of them. Behind one door is a beautiful maiden who would be given to him in marriage; behind the other is a ravenous tiger. The princess learns the secret of the doors and signals the young man to open the door on the right. Who comes out, asked Stockton, the lady or the tiger? Stockton wrote another story supposed to solve the puzzle, *The Discourager of Hesitancy* (*The Century*, July, 1887), which, too, cleverly left the query still hanging.

lady's books. The most famous was GODEY'S LADY'S BOOK, established in 1830; it captured a wide market through the use of many devices that had made ANNUALS popular, *e.g.* elaborate title pages, steel engravings of romantic scenes, expensive fashion plates. Among Godey's predecessors were *The Weekly Visitor and Ladies' Museum* (founded 1817); *The Ladies' Literary Cabinet* (1819); *The Ladies' Magazine* (1819); *The New York Mirror and Ladies' Literary Gazette* (1823); *The Album and Ladies' Weekly Gazette* (1826); *The Philadelphia Album and Ladies' Literary Portfolio* (1827); *The Ladies' Magazine and Literary Gazette* (1828). The last-named magazine was Godey's chief competitor; he took it over in 1837, acquiring its capable editor, Mrs. SARAH JOSEPHA HALE (1788–1879), who was the author of MARY HAD A LITTLE LAMB (1830).

Laet, Johann De ([?]–[?]), a director of the Dutch West India Company and a director of the famous publishing house of the Elzevirs. A learned man with a gift for style, De Laet wrote and had Abraham Elzevir publish his account of the *Nieuwe Wereldt* (1625), the first report on the various Dutch colonies in North America.

La Farge, Christopher (b. New York City, Dec. 10, 1897—d. Jan. 5, 1956), poet, novelist, architect, water colorist, war correspondent. He was, like his brother OLIVER, a grandson of John La Farge (1835–1910), the famous architect and writer. At Harvard his interests were literary, although he specialized in architecture. His studies were interrupted by service in World War I; in World War II he served as a correspondent in the Pacific.

The 1929 depression put an end to his architectural career, and he took his family to England, where he wrote a narrative poem, *Hoxsie Sells his Acres* (1934), a "restrained tour de force" of his recollections of childhood in Rhode Island. He returned to the United States shortly thereafter. He published *Each to the Other* (1939), a highly praised novel in verse about a happy marriage; *Poems and Portraits* (1940); *The Wilsons* (1941), short stories about a snobbish family; and *East by Southwest* (1944), stories about the South

Pacific. Like his brother Oliver, Christopher was interested in the American Indian. *Mesa Verde* (1945), a play in verse, expresses this interest. *The Sudden Guest* (1946) is a prose novel in which a selfish and domineering woman recalls, during the hurricane of 1944, the ravages of the "sudden guest"—the hurricane of 1938. *All Sorts and Kinds* (1949) is a collection of eighteen of his best short stories. La Farge lacked the impact and storytelling force of his brother Oliver, but his work is intelligent, sensitive, and skillful.

La Farge, Oliver [Hazard Perry] (b. New York City, Dec. 19, 1901—d. Aug. 2, 1963), novelist, short-story writer, anthropologist. La Farge was always fascinated with Indian lore; at Harvard he specialized in anthropology

and archaeological research and after graduation made a number of archaeological and ethnological expeditions to Arizona, Mexico, and Guatemala for Harvard, Tulane, and Columbia Universities. La Farge is an exceptionally able spokesman for the Indians, since he understands their complicated psychology, appreciates their culture, and is a gifted writer. President of the American Association on Indian Affairs, his particular interest is the Navajos. LAUGHING BOY (1929), a novel about a Navajo, won a Pulitzer Prize. *Laughing Boy* was followed by *Sparks Fly Upward* (short stories, 1931); *The Year Bearer's People* (1931); *Long Pennant* (1933); *All the Young Men* (short stories, 1935); *The Enemy Gods* (1937); and *The Copper Pot* (1942), one of his few novels not concerned with Indians. He also wrote *The Eagle in the Egg* (1949), based on his experiences as an officer in the army's air transport

command; *The Mother Ditch* (1954), a juvenile; and *Behind the Mountains* (1956), a nonfiction account of simple village folk in New Mexico; *A Pictorial History of the American Indian* (1956); and *Santa Fe, The Autobiography of a Southwestern Town* (1959). *Raw Material* (1945) is autobiographical.

Lafayette, [Marie Joseph Paul Yves Roch Gilbert du Motier], Marquis de (b. France, Sept. 6, 1757—d. May 20, 1834), general, friend of America. A man of great wealth, Lafayette entered the French army and was active in French court life. When the American Revolution broke out, he offered his services and was given a major-generalship. He saw action in many battles and proved valuable as an intermediary with France; he served as an aide to Franklin in the peace negotiations.

In France, in the years that followed, Lafayette showed strongly the influence of the ideas he had absorbed in the United States. During the French Revolution he sought to be a moderating force, strove to retain the monarchy with constitutional restraints, helped bring about the adoption of laws that resembled the ones favored in the new American nation. He served in the French army but left when it was obvious that his moderate ideas were not in favor. Captured by the Austrian army, he remained in prison until his release was obtained by Napoleon. During the latter's control of the French régime, Lafayette, who disapproved of his ideas and methods, remained in retirement. After 1815 he again became politically active, invariably taking sides against reactionary rulers and régimes. He visited the United States in 1824–25, and his visit became a great triumphal tour.

Lafayette's tour inspired a number of song writers. Samuel Woodworth wrote *Lafayette's Welcome*, and the same title was used for *Grand March and Quick*, by A. Clifton. Col. W. H. Hamilton composed *The Chivalrous Knight of France*, W. Strickland wrote *Come Honor the Brave* (to the tune of *My Heart's in the Highlands*), and Major J. H. Barker presented *Hail Lafayette* as a tribute of respect. Several novels have introduced Lafayette as a character in stories of the Revolution: J. E. Heath's *Edge-Hill* (1828); Catherine Sedgwick's *The Linwoods* (1835); John Esten Cooke's *Canolles* (1877); Howard Fast's *Conceived in Liberty* (1939).

Lafitte [also Laffite], Jean (b. France, 1780? —d. 1826?), pirate, soldier. Lafitte seems to have reached the neighborhood of New Orleans around 1809 as the head of a band of smugglers and privateers. When the War of 1812 broke out, the British sought his co-operation, but he declined their offers and was accepted by General Jackson as an aid in resisting the invaders; Jackson gave him amnesty for his crimes. He took part in the Battle of New Orleans (Jan. 8, 1815), and Jackson stated that Lafitte "was one of the ablest men on that morning." But after the war was over Lafitte returned to his freebooting in Texas.

He disappears from view historically around 1826.

During his lifetime and thereafter Lafitte was regarded as a hero by the people of Louisiana, and as a legend he seems to have entered literature when Lord Byron, in a note to *The Corsair* (1815), suggested some likenesses between his hero and Lafitte. In 1826 the anonymous *Lafitte, or, The Baratarian Chief* gave a sentimental account of his life. Somewhat similar was a serial published (1831) in *The Casket* called *The Baratarian Chief*. The most noteworthy of all the stories was Joseph Holt Ingraham's *Lafitte: or, The Pirate of the Gulf* (1836). Ingraham showed him at the beginning of his career as a ruthless buccaneer, and at the end as a spiritualized hero converted by a woman's beauty to a realization of his crimes. The book was, naturally, immensely popular. Ingraham's son, the dime novelist Prentiss Ingraham, wrote *Lafitte, The Pirate of the Gulf* (1931) and *La Fitte's Lieutenant* (1931). Lafitte appears also in Joseph B. Cobb's *The Creole* (1850); Mary Devereaux' *Lafitte of Louisiana* (1902); Meredith Nicholson's *The Cavalier of Tennessee* (1928); Lyle Saxon's *Lafitte. The Pirate* (1930); Hervey Allen's *Anthony Adverse* (1933); Mitchell V. Charnley's *Jean Lafitte* (1934); Sallie Bell's *Marcel Armand* (1935); Laura Krey's *On the Long Tide* (1940); Odell and Willard Shepard's *Holdfast Gaines* (1946); Paul T. Williams' *The Iron Mistress* (1951); and Madeleine Kent's *The Corsair* (1955). Harold W. Thompson found in circulation in New York a ballad called *The Brave Lafitte*, which recounts the story of the pirate's strange bride.

La Flesche, Francis (b. Omaha Reservation, Nebraska, c. 1860—d. Sept. 5, 1932), ethnologist, lecturer, autobiographer. Francis La Flesche was the son of a chief, and was educated on the reservation. He became later an ethnologist of the Bureau of American Ethnology and with Alice Cunningham Fletcher, who adopted him as her son, was joint author of *The Omaha Tribe* (1911). He made other studies of the Osage tribe which resulted in *A Dictionary of the Osage Language* (1932) and *War Ceremony and Peace Ceremony of the Osage Indian,* printed six years after his death. He translated many Indian poems. His one work of literary interest and general appeal is *The Middle Five—Indian Boys at School* (1900), a charming account of his boyhood on the reservation. See also SUZETTE LA FLESCHE.

La Flesche, Suzette (b. Omaha Reservation, 1854—d. May 26, 1923), lecturer, essayist, biographer, sister of FRANCIS LA FLESCHE. Miss La Flesche, whose Indian name was Bright Eyes, was educated on the reservation and at a private school in Elizabeth, N.J., and returned to her birthplace to teach in the government school. In 1877 when the Poncas, a tribe related to the Omahas, were exiled from South Dakota and sent to Indian Territory, Suzette and her father, learning of their dreadful sufferings, visited them and began a campaign to acquaint the public with the injustice done to them. They were largely responsible for the abandoning of the cruel policy of driving tribes from one place to another. See STANDING BEAR.

In 1881 Suzette married Thomas H. Tibbles, an Omaha newspaperman, and assisted him with editorials and essays. She edited and wrote an introduction to an anonymous narrative, *Ploughed Under, the Story of an Indian Chief* (1881).

La Follette, Robert M[arion] (b. Primrose, Wis., June 14, 1855—d. June 18, 1925), U.S. Senator, leader of the Progressive Party movement, orator. La Follette ascended steadily from District Attorney to Congressman to Governor of Wisconsin to Senator. He was in constant battle with "the interests," and brought about striking reforms in railroad regulation, taxation, tariffs, and instituting the direct primary. He sought the Presidency as the leader of the newly formed Progressive Party, but lost the nomination to Theodore Roosevelt, who was defeated (1912) by Woodrow Wilson. La Follette was an unceasing insurgent, and in 1924 again sought the Presidency on a third-party ticket. He received about 5 million votes but was defeated by Calvin Coolidge. He was a remarkable orator; his addresses, particularly in the Senate, received wide attention. His *Autobiography* appeared in 1912; a collection of his writings, entitled *Political Philosophy,* in 1920. Bella Case La Follette, his widow, and his daughter Fola wrote a biography of him (2 v., 1953). See PROGRESSIVE PARTY.

Lahontan, Louis-Armand De Lom D'Arce, Baron de (b. France, 1666—d. 1713?), soldier, official, traveler, memoirist. Lahontan was in Canada for ten years (1683–93), and held some important official posts. In fact, his *Nouveaux Voyages de M. le Baron de Lahontan dans l'Amérique Septentrionale* (1703) gave Chateaubriand some of his notions about the "noble savage." His book was immediately translated into English, with the addition of some supposed *Dialogues* with a Huron chieftain, Adario. There have been at least fifty editions of the book; a reprint of the 1703 English version was edited by R. G. Thwaites (2 v., 1905).

Laing, Alexander [Kinnan] (b. Great Neck, Long Island, Aug 7, 1903—), poet, seaman, radio specialist, teacher, librarian, editor. Laing wandered around and filled many posts before he settled down at Dartmouth College as an English teacher and later as an assistant librarian. He wrote several volumes of verse —including *Fool's Errand* (1928) and *The Flowering Thorn* (1933)—also a discourse on poetry and language, *Wine and Physic* (1934). An epic of the clipper-ship era, *The Sea Witch* (1933; new eds., 1944, 1958), was supplemented by a prose work, *Clipper-Ship Men* (1945). He edited an anthology of horror stories, *The Haunted Omnibus* (1937), and wrote a macabre novel, *The Cadaver of Gideon Wyck* (with T. Painter, 1934).

Lamar, Mirabeau Buonaparte (b. Louisville, Ga., Aug. 16, 1798—d. Dec. 19, 1859), editor, soldier, statesman, diplomat, planter, poet, second president of Texas. Lamar was private secretary to the governor of Georgia, then became editor of the *Columbus Enquirer*, a states' rights newspaper; later he moved to Texas and joined SAM HOUSTON's army. He was promoted to major general; became secretary of war in the provisional cabinet of Burnet; served as vice-president of Texas under Sam Houston (1836–1837), and became president of Texas in 1838. Though hotheaded and ruthless in many respects, he was not without some statesmanlike qualities. He established a public school system, founded the city of Austin, and obtained formal recognition of the Lone Star Republic from the leading countries of Europe. His highly romantic *Verse Memorials* (1857) is called by W. P. Trent "the most extraordinary repository of extempore effusions addressed by a gallant gentleman to lovely ladies in the whole range of our literature." Herbert P. Gambrell wrote of him as *Mirabeau Buonaparte Lamar, Troubadour and Crusader* (1934).

Lamb, Harold [Albert] (b. Alpine, N.J., Sept. 1, 1892—d. April 10, 1962), writer. Lamb discovered historics of Asia in the Columbia University Library and his college studies went neglected. In 1914 when his father's health failed he worked as a make-up man for a trade weekly and on the financial pages of another newspaper, and began publishing stories in *Adventure* magazine. One very positive influence in Lamb's life was an editor, ARTHUR SULLIVAN HOFFMAN, a perceptive man who saw his possibilities and allowed him to write anything he chose—and accepted it. His early books were highly colored, romantic, historically accurate, and very popular. Two of them, *The Plainsman* (1936), and *The March of the Barbarians* (1940), were made into successful movies. *Genghis Khan* (1927), his earliest full-length biographical narrative, was followed by many others, among them: *Tamerlane* (1928); *Alexander of Macedon: Journey to World's End* (1946); *Charlemagne: The Legend and the Man* (1954); *Cyrus the Great* (1960); *Babur —The Tiger. First of the Great Moguls* (1961). Among his historical narratives: *The Crusades: Iron Men and Saints* (1930); *The Crusades: The Flame of Islam* (1931); *The March of Muscovy: Ivan the Terrible* (1948); *New Found World: How North America Was Discovered and Explored* (1955); *Constantinople: Birth of an Empire* (1957). Lamb spent a number of years traveling in the Near East and China and at one time repeated Marco Polo's route.

Lambert, Janet Snyder (b. Crawfordsville, Ind., Dec. 17, 1894—   ), author of books for children. Mrs. Lambert has written a large number of books for teen-age girls, beginning with the Parrish Series in 1941 which included *Star-Spangled Summer*, her first book; *Don't Cry Little Girl* (1952); and *A Song in their Hearts* (1956). Among her other books: *A Dream for Susan* (1954); *The Precious Days* (1957); *Spring Fever* (1960); *Forever and Ever* (1961).

Lamb in His Bosom (1933), novel by Caroline Miller (b. Aug. 26, 1903—   ). Study of pioneer life in the back country of Georgia in the Civil War period. It won a Pulitzer Prize.

Lambs, The. Taking as a model a London organization of the same name, The Lambs was formed in 1874 as a supper club of theatrical folk and their admirers. In 1904 it moved to its present headquarters at 128 W. 44th St., New York City. The head of the club is called "The Shepherd," and it has numerous traditional functions, usually of a gay and uninhibited character. The clubhouse is adorned with numerous paintings and statues of famous actors, and there is a collection of masks.

Lamon, Ward Hill (b. Frederick Co., Va., Jan. 6, 1828—d. May 7, 1893), lawyer, collector of Lincolniana. In 1852 Lamon became Lincoln's law partner in Danville, Illinois; he later joined the Republican party, campaigned for Lincoln's nomination and election, and was selected as a bodyguard to accompany Lincoln to Washington in 1861 when rumors of assassination plots threatened the President-elect's safety. He was appointed marshal of the District of Columbia in 1861, a post he retained until 1865, when he became a law partner of Jeremiah S. Black. He was devoted to Lincoln and was in close personal contact with him during his Presidency, sleeping in the next room when plots against Lincoln's life were rampant in 1864.

After Lincoln's death, Lamon began a collaboration with his partner's son, Chauncy F. Black, on a "true life" of Lincoln, with the agreement that only Lamon's name would appear as author; Lamon and Black bought a mass of material from WILLIAM H. HERNDON, Lincoln's one-time law partner in Springfield, who had collected the personal reminiscences of men who had known Lincoln during his boyhood. The Herndon material formed the basis of *The Life of Abraham Lincoln from His Birth to His Inauguration as President* (1872); although it was written almost entirely by Black, Lamon's name appeared as author. The book's "realistic" treatment of Lincoln was received unfavorably, and possibly for this reason a projected second volume was never completed. Many of the biographical controversies concerning Lincoln originated in Lamon's book; critics disagree over the accuracy of the work but generally feel that it was often unnecessarily scandalous. Lamon's *Recollections of Abraham Lincoln*, edited by Dorothy Lamon, appeared in 1895.

Lamont, Corliss (b. Englewood, N.J., March 28, 1902—   ), writer, teacher. Lamont, son of the millionaire banker Thomas W. Lamont, taught courses in philosophy and Russian civilization at Cornell, Columbia, and Harvard. However, his political activity and his writings were his primary interest. He is on the left politically, and, consequently, a highly controversial figure. Such books as *You Might Like Socialism* (1939), and pamphlets like *The Myth of Soviet Aggression* (1953), *Challenge to McCarthy* (1954), and *The Congressional Inqui-*

sition (1954) show his left-wing allegiance.

Other books by Lamont: *Issues of Immortality* (1932); *Russia Day by Day* (1933); *The Peoples of the Soviet Union* (1946); *A Humanist Funeral Service* (1947); *The Independent Mind* (1951); *Soviet Civilization* (1955); *Freedom is as Freedom Does: Civil Liberties Today* (1956); *Philosophy of Humanism* (1957); *The Illusion of Immortality* (1935, rev. 1950, 1959). His Basic Pamphlet Series, begun in 1952, includes: *Back to the Bill of Rights* (1952); *The Civil Liberties Crisis* (1954); *The Assault on Academic Freedom* (1955); *To End Nuclear Bomb Tests* (co-author with Margaret I. Lamont, 1958); *A Peace Program for the U.S.A.* (1959); *My Trip Around the World* (1960); *A Humanist Symposium on Metaphysics* (1960).

Lampell, Millard (b. Paterson, N.J., Jan. 10, 1919—   ), song writer, radio producer and script writer, novelist. Lampell has written many songs, including ballads for the Almanac Singers, a troupe noted for its performances at union meetings. In 1943 he wrote a poem, THE LONESOME TRAIN, which became a cantata with music by Earl Robinson; the train was Lincoln's funeral train journeying to Springfield. Later another cantata, *Morning Star* (1946), was read at a New York *Herald Tribune* forum by the actor Robert Montgomery. Lampell's experiences with wounded veterans went into a series of broadcasts that were published in book form as *The Long Way Home* (1946). He did a series of ballads for *A Walk in the Sun* (1946), a movie depicting infantry warfare in Italy during World War II, based on Harry Brown's novel (1944) of the same title. His first book, *The Hero* (1948), a novel, portrays the difficulties that face the son of an immigrant seeking to rise above his environment. In 1961 he made a successful dramatization of John Hersey's *The Wall*, for Broadway.

Lamplighter, The (1854), a novel, anonymously published, by MARIA SUSANNA CUMMINS (1827–1866). This was the author's first book; it made an immediate success and was typical of the sentimental and yet in reality crassly materialistic stories that attracted the women readers of the day. Gerty, the heroine, spends her childhood in miserable and squalid surroundings, is rescued by a kindly old lamplighter named Trueman Flint, acquires a playmate named Willie, is taken into the family of Emily Graham, a rich blind girl, when Flint dies. She learns that her father is really Emily's brother, who had run away from home when by accident he blinded her, and marries Willie, who has become very successful and wealthy. A sequel, *The Watchman* (1855), was written by Philip A. Maitland.

Hawthorne, who was receiving very small royalties from his books at the time, wrote resentfully: "America is now wholly given over to a d----d mob of scribbling women, and I should have no chance of success while the public taste is occupied with their trash—and should be ashamed of myself if I did succeed.

What is the mystery of these innumerable editions of *The Lamplighter,* and other books neither better nor worse?—worse they could not be, and better they need not be, when they sell by the 100,000." *The Lamplighter* was still selling in 1910.

Lampman, Archibald (b. Marpeth, Ont., Nov. 17, 1861—d. Feb. 10, 1899), poet, post office official. Lampman's poems show clearly the various English poets who had influenced him—Pope, Coleridge, Keats, Tennyson, Swinburne, particularly Keats. His poems on nature are his best, and he was called in his own day Canada's greatest nature poet. His influence on the later Canadian poet BLISS CARMAN was marked. His poetry was collected in *Among the Millet* (1888); *Lyrics of Earth* (1895); *Alcyone* (1899); *Poems* (1900); *At the Long Sault and Other New Poems* (1943); *Selected Poems* (1947).

Lampoon, The Harvard. See HARVARD LAMPOON.

Lamprey, Louise (b. Alexandria, N.H., April 17, 1869—d. Jan. 15, 1951), author of children's books. Miss Lamprey devoted much time to magazine and newspaper work, also conducted a library story hour and worked at a girls' camp. Her experiences with young people led her to believe that children prefer truth to make-believe, and in 1918 she published her first children's book, *In the Days of the Guild.* This was followed, at the rate of one or two a year for twenty-odd years, by *Children of Ancient Rome* (1922), *Days of the Colonists* (1922), *Children of Ancient Greece* (1924), *Days of the Pioneers* (1924), *Children of Ancient Egypt* (1926), and many others.

An authority on architecture, she contributed articles to the *Junior Encyclopaedia Britannica* (1935) on architecture and primitive dwellings, and wrote a number of juvenile books on the subject, such as *All Ways of Building* (1926); *Days of the Builders* (1926); *Wonder Tales of Architecture* (1927). Her last years were spent in Limerick, Maine, where she wrote a *History of Limerick, Maine* (1933); *Limerick Pageant* (1937); *The Story of Cookery* (1940); and *Building a Republic* (1942).

Lancaster, Bruce (b. Worcester, Mass., Aug. 22, 1896—d. June 20, 1963), State Department official, novelist. Lancaster began writing his popular historical novels while he was a consular official in Japan. The earliest, *The Wide Sleeve of Kwannon* (1938), is set in the Far East. Several deal with American history; among them: *Guns of Burgoyne* (1939); *Bright to the Wanderer* (1942); *Trumpet to Arms* (1944); *The Scarlet Patch* (1947); *No Bugles Tonight* (1948); and *Blind Journey* (1953). The period of the American Revolution has been a special favorite with Lancaster, who writes with sound historical knowledge as well as an alert storytelling gift. His historical writing includes: *Liberty* (1955); *The American Revolution* (1957); eleven chapters of the *American Heritage Book of the Revolution* (1958); *Ticonderoga, The Story of a Fort* (1959).

Lancelot (1920), a narrative poem by E. A. ROBINSON. It forms part of a trilogy that seeks to retell the Arthurian legend in modern terms —the other two are MERLIN (1917) and TRISTRAM (1927). It describes the havoc and destruction that follows Lancelot's love affair with Guinevere and the king's discovery of the double infidelity. When Arthur orders that his queen be burnt at the stake, Lancelot and his followers save her, and the pair spend several months at Joyous Gard. Then Lancelot returns Guinevere to Arthur, takes part in a war that destroys Arthur, visits Guinevere in the convent where she has taken refuge, but departs alone —to seek the Light which may come even in darkness. The poem is not one of Robinson's best. Kreymborg comments that in the love duels of this Arthurian trilogy the men come off second-best; they seem in fact Robinsonian Americans of the intellectual class, all failures and frustrates.

Land of Eden. See JOURNEY TO THE LAND OF EDEN.

Land of Little Rain, The (1903), fourteen sketches by MARY AUSTIN. Miss Austin here depicts familiar characters of the Southwest, its winged scavengers and plants and strange places. One sketch, *Jimville—A Bret Harte Town*, indicates her opinion that Harte did not exaggerate as much as some critics believe.

Landon, Melville De Lancey ["Eli Perkins"] (b. Eaton, N.Y., Sept. 7, 1839—d. Dec. 6, 1910), journalist, humorist, lecturer. Landon served in the U.S. Treasury and the Confederate Army and was a cotton planter in Arkansas and Louisiana before he settled down to a long and successful career as journalist and lecturer. In 1871 he published *A History of the Franco-Prussian War in a Nutshell.* A humorous correspondence from Saratoga for the N.Y. *Commercial Advertiser*, originally signed "Lan," later "Eli Perkins," established him as a wit. These letters, collected as *Saratoga in 1901* (1872), were followed by *Eli Perkins at Large, His Savings and Doings* (1875) *and Eli Perkins' Wit, Humor, and Pathos* (1883), which went through many editions and was followed by the equally successful *Thirty Years of Wit* (1890), partly autobiographical. After conducting Josh Billings' lecture tour, Landon ascended the platform himself and delivered thousands of humorous lectures. In 1875 he edited the complete works of ARTEMUS WARD, in 1891 compiled *Kings of Pulpit and Platform* (reissued under slightly different titles), a treasury of information about American humorists.

Landor's Cottage (1849), by EDGAR ALLAN POE. This sketch was published as a "pendant" to Poe's DOMAIN OF ARNHEIM. It was apparently a dramatization or idealization of the cottage he and his wife occupied at Fordham. There is very little story element in the sketch. But there appears in it for a short period a woman called Annie; we know that in drawing his exquisite portrait of her Poe had in mind Mrs. Annie Richmond, with whom he was at the time deeply in love. He makes Annie's identification plain in letters to her and elsewhere. Hervey Allen feels that the landscape in *Landor's Cottage* reappears in Poe's depiction of the "ghoul-haunted woodland of Weir." Some have objected to Poe's "florid sensuousness of decoration," but Hardin Craig sees Poe in the piece attempting a difficult if not impossible task— making words and arrangements of words do what color and line do in paintings.

Lane, George Martin. See THE LAY OF THE ONE FISHBALL.

Lane, Rose Wilder (b. De Smet, S.D., Dec. 5, 1887—d. Oct. 30, 1968), novelist, short-story writer. The Ozark Mountains where Mrs. Lane was raised provided the background for many of her novels and stories. She worked as a journalist in San Francisco and in 1920 and 1922 made trips to Albania. She drew on her experiences there to write *The Peaks of Shala* (1923), numerous stories and articles, and to translate *Dancer of Shamakha* (1923). Her best and characteristic writing is journalistic. She wrote two biographies: *Henry Ford's Own Story* (1917) and *The Making of Herbert Hoover* (1920). Her novels include: *He Was a Man* (1925); *Cindy: A Romance of the Ozarks* (1928); *Hill-Billy* (1926); *Let the Hurricane Roar* (1933); *Old Home Town* (1935). She also wrote *Discovery of Freedom* (1943).

Lang, Paul Henry (b. Hungary, Aug. 28, 1901—   ), musicologist, critic. Lang received his early education at the Catholic Humanistic Gymnasium in his native Budapest, went on to the Royal Academy of Music, and from there to the Universities of Heidelberg and Paris. In 1928 he came to the United States. After teaching at Vassar and Wells Colleges, he became in 1933 Professor of Musicology at Columbia University. In 1941 he published his monumental *Music in Western Civilization,* a history of music which examined its relation to the other arts and to the culture of time and place. Lang became editor of the *Musical Quarterly* in 1945, and continued to contribute erudite, felicitously phrased critical writing to other journals. In 1954 he became music critic of the New York *Herald Tribune.*

Langer, Susanne K. (b. New York City, December 20, 1895—   ), philosopher, teacher, author. Mrs. Langer attended Radcliffe College, receiving her Ph.D. in 1926. A teacher at several colleges and universities, she joined Columbia University in 1945. Her first books were purely philosophical; her later works concerned themselves with the rational aspects of art. She expressed in them the belief that "art is a basic human need." Mrs. Langer's books: *The Practice of Philosophy* (1930); *An Introduction to Symbolic Logic* (1937); *Philosophy in a New Key* (1942); *Feeling and Form* (1953); *Problems of Art* (1957); *Reflections on Art* (1958).

Langley, Samuel Pierpont (b. Roxbury, Mass., Aug. 22, 1834—d. Feb. 27, 1906), astronomer, physicist, inventor. Langley was director of the Allegheny Observatory and directed an expedition to Mount Whitney, Calif., for the purpose of studying the spectra of the sun and moon. In 1881 he became secretary of the Smithsonian Institution and helped establish the National Zoological Park and the Astrophysical Observatory. He published numerous articles and a book, *The Internal Work of the Wind* (1893), on the subject of aerodynamics; his studies and models were an important contribution to the development of aviation. A series of popular lectures, first printed in the *Century*, appeared in 1889 as a book, *The New Astronomy*, which has become a classic. The style is gracious and literary, unlike most modern scientific writing.

Langner, Lawrence (b. Wales, May 30, 1890 —d. Dec. 26, 1962), patent agent, founder and director of the Theatre Guild. Langner came to this country in 1911, started his own firm of patent agents, then organized the Washington Square Players. In 1914 the Players produced his own play, *License*, which dealt with marriage. This was followed by a number of one-act plays, the most popular of which was *Another Way Out* (1916). *The Family Exit* (1917), a farce comedy, was Langner's first full-length drama. Out of the Washington Square Players grew the Theatre Guild, of which Langner was the founder and after 1919 the director. He also founded the American Shakespeare Festival Theatre and Academy of Stratford, Connecticut. He was responsible for the first American production of Shaw's *St. Joan* and *Back to Methuselah*. He also produced several of O'Neill's plays for the Guild. He adapted European plays for the American stage, such as *Don Juan* (1921) and Molière's *School for Husbands* (1933, in collaboration with ARTHUR GUITERMAN), and with Robert Simon rewrote *Die Fledermaus*, calling it *Champagne Sec* (1933).

His wife Armina collaborated with Langner in his most successful plays. *Pursuit of Happiness* (1934), in which a Hessian soldier becomes involved with the old American custom of bundling, was followed by *Suzanna and the Elders* (1940), a comedy on life in the Oneida colony. He wrote many articles on international law, especially as relating to patents. *The Magic Curtain: The Story of a Life in Two Fields* (1951) is not only an autobiography but a picture of many of the great playwrights and actors of today, a history of the Theatre Guild, and a fascinating record of the upsurge of creative activity which in the 1910's and 1920's gave rise to the little theater movement. The Langners conducted their own summer theater in Westport, N.Y., until 1959. He also wrote *The Importance of Wearing Clothes* (1959) and *The Play's the Thing* (1960). See THEATRE GUILD.

Langstaff, Launcelot. The pen name of J. K. PAULDING.

Lanier, Clifford Anderson (b. Griffin, Ga., April 24, 1844—d. Nov. 3, 1908), poet. The brother of SIDNEY LANIER composed excellent verse, some of which is included in Sidney's *Poems* (1884). He wrote *Thorn-Fruit* (1867)

and *Sonnets to Sidney Lanier and Other Lyrics* (1915).

Lanier, Henry W[ysham] (b. Milledgeville, Ga., June [?], 1873—d. March 10, 1958), engineer, editor, publisher, author. This son of SIDNEY LANIER served in various New York publishing offices after giving up work as a civil engineer in the West Indies, then in 1925 founded, published, and edited the *Golden Book*, an attractive monthly reprint of the world's classics, old and new. He sold the magazine in 1930 and resumed writing. Among his books: *The Romance of Piscator* (1904); *The Runaway Pearls* (1922); *O Rare Content* (1930); *A. B. Frost* (1933); *Secret Life of a Secret Agent* (1938); *The Village in the City's Heart* (1949).

Lanier, Sidney (b. Macon, Ga., Feb. 3, 1842—d. Sept. 7, 1881), poet, critic, musician. Lanier was educated at private schools and Oglethorpe University, from which he graduated in 1860. The Civil War interfered with his

plans for graduate study in Germany; he served as a volunteer in the Confederate army and in 1864 was captured and imprisoned for four months at Point Lookout, Md. He emerged from his war experiences afflicted with the tuberculosis that remained with him for the rest of his short life.

Lanier had early decided that he should devote his life to writing, but economic necessity prevented him from ever completely realizing his ambition. For a time after the war he worked at odd jobs. His marriage in 1867 to Mary Day and the birth of several children increased his responsibilities. In 1873 he finally settled in Baltimore, where he became first flutist with the Peabody Symphony Orchestra. An accomplished musician even in his youth, his work now attracted the attention of distinguished conductors. At the same time he undertook various literary pursuits, both scholarly and creative. He had already published a novel, TIGER-LILIES (1867), a Civil War story containing some of the first realistic descriptions of southern life, but the book had not been a success. It was as a poet that Lanier first achieved a reputation, especially with the publication of the poem CORN in *Lippincott's Magazine* (1875). For the remaining eight years of his life he produced a succession of important poems, including THE SYMPHONY (1875), THE SONG OF THE CHATTAHOOCHEE (1877), THE MARSHES OF GLYNN (1878), *The Revenge of Hamish* (1878), and such short lyrics as SUNRISE, THE BALLAD OF TREES AND THE MASTER, and *Opposition*.

Lanier also produced three important works of criticism. *The Science of English Verse* (1880) is an attempt to establish, through a systematic analysis of verse forms and techniques, the scientific basis of versification and to demonstrate the close identity between music and poetry. In the analogy of literary and musical theory Lanier sought precise rules of form governing rhythm, color, tone, and melodic tension. One of the most interesting books on poetic technique ever written, it is still doubtful that the book has ever proved of much value to practicing poets. *The English Novel* (1883) bears as a subtitle "From Aeschylus to George Eliot: The Development of Personality," which more nearly describes its content. Lanier traces the growth of human personality in relation to the parallel development of music, science, and the novel as a literary form. There are critical appraisals of a wide variety of authors, including Aeschylus, Plato, Chaucer, Malory, Zola, Walt Whitman, and many others. Each author is interpreted in the light of his contribution to the emergence of human personality throughout Western civilization. In the course of the book Lanier touches on many social, ethical, and aesthetic problems, and reiterates his earlier thesis that science and poetry have developed simultaneously. *Shakespeare and His Forerunners*, which was not published until 1902, is a less important work. Much of Lanier's scholarly work at this time was done in conjunction with his lectureship in English literature at Johns Hopkins University, a post to which he was appointed in 1879. From his reading in medieval and Elizabethan literature he produced four books for children, adaptations of Malory, *Gil Blas*, Percy's *Reliques*, and the *Mabinogion*.

Lanier's importance as a poet, aside from the enduring readability of his best work, lies in his skill as a technician. In this respect he was

a follower of Poe; he believed poetic effects could best be produced by a deliberate manipulation of prosodic devices. In *The Symphony*, for example, he strove for a succession of precise textures to suit the poem's content. The parts of the poem reflect the components of a symphony orchestra, the various instruments —violin, flute, clarinet, horn, bassoon—representing moods and sentiments consonant with the qualities of sound they characteristically produce. Thus the violins raise the plaintive cry of the poor and oppressed against the exploitations of industrialism and commercialism. The horn, on the other hand, sounds the challenge of the spirit of chivalry. The poem is a remarkable structure of shifting meters and tonal qualities, rich in rhyme, assonance, and alliteration. It is also a ringing protest against modern materialism. Lanier believed stoutly in the virtues of nature and love of the land, themes which he developed in *Corn*; in *The Symphony*, despite his emphasis on verbal effects, he introduced clearly realistic illustrations of the brutality of trade.

Two of the most striking examples of Lanier's lyrical genius are *Sunrise* and *The Marshes of Glynn*, both from the group called HYMNS OF THE MARSHES. Rich in sensory imagery, these poems combine lights and shadows, "emerald twilights and virginal sky lights," into a vibrant chiaroscuro of contrasting and blending scenic objects. Iambics and dactyls are interspersed in lines of varying length to produce a sustained harmony of rhythm, tone, and mood. In the same category of distinguished descriptive lyrics belong *The Mocking Bird*, *Evening Song*, and *The Song of the Chattahoochee*. The last-named ingeniously captures the spirit of the rushing mountain stream in the sprightly and rippling measures of "Out of the hills of Habersham, down the valleys of Hall."

The shortcomings of Lanier's poetry are the result partly of natural limitations of genius and partly of the difficult circumstances of his life. His essential mysticism remains always vague and amorphous. His major poems are a "criticism of life," but the criticism lacks definiteness and solidity. His fervent moral indignation too often spends itself in sentimentality. Thus there is a certain lack of depth and clarity in the philosophical content of the poetry. Sound frequently takes precedence over sense and the music overshadows the meaning. The completely right word, no doubt hurriedly sought for, is not always found. Yet despite these faults Lanier possesses a permanent place in the American literary tradition. His technical originality and skill, his sure lyrical instinct, his sweep of poetic imagination, his ingenious creation of pure music through the medium of verse, and his sensitiveness to human need and yearning— these qualities secure for Lanier a place among those who by virtue of contributing a consistently developed viewpoint and an integrated body of verse deserve the rank of "major."

A "centennial" collection of Lanier's works

(10 v., 1946) was edited by C. R. Anderson. Biographies have been written by Aubrey H. Starke (1932), Lincoln Lorenz (1935), and Edwin R. Coulson (1941). See POETRY IN THE U.S.; THE CRYSTAL; MAY THE MAIDEN.

HOWARD W. HINTZ

Lanigan, George Thomas ["G. Washington Aesop"] (b. St. Charles, Que., Dec. 10, 1845— d. Feb. 5, 1886), newspaperman, humorous poet. Lanigan worked from 1874 to 1883 on the New York *World*. He published *Canadian Ballads* (1864) and *Fables* (1878), the latter under his pseudonym. He is chiefly remembered for his poem *Threnody for the* AHKOOND OF SWAT, which was written when Lanigan read in the London *Times* (Jan. 22, 1878) an item headed "The Ahkoond of Swat Is Dead." Another poem of his, *The Amateur Orlando*, had a stanza that became famous: "A squeak's heard in the orchestra,/ The leader draws across/ The intestines of the agile cat/ The tail of the noble hoss." Lanigan also dreamed of what H. L. Mencken called "the philological millennium," when he spoke of the day "when the singular verb shall lie down with the plural noun, and a little conjunction shall lead them."

Lanman, Charles (b. Monroe, Mich., June 14, 1819—d. March 4, 1895), newspaperman, public official, artist, explorer. Lanman, of partial Indian descent, was at first in business, then worked on a newspaper, but from 1849 on was for the most part in government service, usually as librarian or secretary. He was an enthusiastic explorer and a clever artist and spent his vacations in trips to many parts of the country. His books include *Letters from a Landscape Painter* (1845); *A Summer in the Wilderness* (1847); *A Tour to the River Saguenay* (1848); *Letters from the Allegheny Mountains* (1849); and *Adventures in the Wilds of America* (1854). He also wrote a life of Daniel Webster (1852) and prepared a *Dictionary of the U.S. Congress* (1859). He wrote thirty-two books, painted more than a thousand landscapes.

Lanny Budd. See BUDD, LANNY.

Lantern in Her Hand, A (1928), a novel by BESS STREETER ALDRICH. Perhaps the best of Mrs. Aldrich's stories, this tells of a pioneer woman who comes to the Nebraska prairies in the 1860's and brings up a large family against great difficulties. The book is sentimental but not mawkish. Many of its incidents come from the experiences of Mrs. Aldrich's grandparents. It was a great success, has been frequently reprinted, and has been filmed.

Laramie Boomerang, The. See THE BOOMERANG.

Larcom, Lucy (b. Beverly, Mass., March 5, 1824—d. April 17, 1893), poet, teacher, abolitionist, autobiographer. Lucy Larcom began writing poetry at seven. Her mother moved the family to Lowell at the father's death and was forced by poverty to put the children to work at the Lowell Mills. Lucy began working at a mill when she was eleven. Later she taught school in pioneer settlements in Illinois and in 1854 at Wheaton Seminar (later College) at Norton, Mass. Miss Larcom was one of the editors of OUR YOUNG FOLKS (later merged with *St. Nicholas Magazine*) from 1865 to 1873. A collected edition of her *Poems* was published in 1869, and was reissued in a *Household Edition* in 1884. She collaborated with her friend JOHN GREENLEAF WHITTIER in his two anthologies, *Child Life* (1871) and *Songs of Three Centuries* (1883). A *New England Girlhood* (1889), her autobiography, repays reading today, not only for its idyllic picture of country life, but for the light it throws on an almost unbelievable chapter in the history of American industry.

Lardner, John (b. Chicago, May 4, 1912— d. March 24, 1960), newspaperman, columnist. RING LARDNER'S son won an early reputation as a sports writer and continued to be among the best in that field. During World War II he served as a correspondent in the Pacific, North Africa, and Italy for *Newsweek*. After the war he returned to his assignment there as a columnist, mainly in the sports field. Lardner also wrote for the North American Newspaper Alliance and was a frequent contributor to the *New Yorker*. He wrote *The Crowning of Technocracy* (1933) and *Southwest Passage: The Yanks in the Pacific* (1943); he made a selection of his occasional pieces in *It Beats Working* (1947). Among his other books: *White Hopes and Other Tigers* (1951) and *Strong Cigars and Lovely Women* (1951).

Lardner, Rex (b. Niles, Mich., Sept. 3, 1881 —d. June 23, 1941), newspaperman, editor. The brother of RING LARDNER, he was on the staff of the Chicago *Inter-Ocean* for many years, then with the New York *Times* from 1929 until his death. For brief periods he worked for *Liberty* and the *Cosmopolitan*.

Lardner, Ring[gold Wilmer] (b. Niles, Mich., March 6, 1885—d. Sept. 25, 1933), newspaperman, columnist, humorist, writer. Lardner first worked for newspapers in South Bend, Ind., and Chicago. For a year or so he edited the St. Louis *Sporting News*, then became a sports writer for the Boston *American*, the Chicago *American*, and the Chicago *Tribune*. By 1919 his reputation as a sports writer was so thoroughly established that thereafter he wrote sports articles for the Bell Syndicate. His later years were spent in New York.

Lardner began his literary career by publishing what has now become merely a rare bibliophile's item, *Bib Ballads* (1915). But about that time his YOU KNOW ME AL baseball letters, revealing an illiterate, boasting, moronic baseball player and his world, were beginning to appear in the *Saturday Evening Post*, and they created a sensation—even more so when they were collected in book form (1916; rev. ed., 1925). Lardner followed up his success with a long series of books, based usually on his newspaper and syndicated articles, many showing the haste of meeting deadlines. In his later years,

however, especially after he began his unsuccessful struggle with tuberculosis, there was more
seriousness of purpose and planning in the short
stories he had begun writing. Among his books:
Gullible's Travels (1917; rev. ed., 1925); *My*

UPI

Four Weeks in France (1918); *Treat 'Em Rough*
(1918); *Own Your Own Home* (1919); *Regu-
lar Fellows I Have Met* (1919); *The Real Dope*
(1919); *Symptoms of Being 35* (1921); *The
Big Town* (1921); *Say It with Oil* (1923);
How to Write Short Stories (1924); *What
of It?* (1925); The Love Nest and Other
Stories (1926); a satirical autobiography, *The
Story of a Wonder Man* (1927); *Love with a
Smile* (1933); *First and Last* (1934). An early
collection of *The Best Short Stories of Ring
Lardner* (1922) had an introduction by Lard-
ner. His stories were again collected in *The
Round Up* (1929). With George S. Kaufman,
Lardner wrote *June Moon* (1929), a farce about
Tin-Pan Alley. After his death the Modern
Library published *The Collected Short Stories*
(1941) of Lardner, and Gilbert Seldes edited
The Portable Ring Lardner (1946).

It was obvious early in Lardner's career that
he had two publics. On the one hand, there
was the uncritical, undiscriminating reader who
got a great many laughs out of Lardner's unquestionably funny depiction of the odd characters of the baseball diamond and the sporting
world generally, later of Tin-Pan Alley, Hollywood, and similar haunts. On the other hand,
there was the more intelligent reader who in
due time realized that Lardner was one of the
great satirists of American literature, an unsurpassed storyteller (as in those masterpieces,
Haircut and *The Love Nest*), a man with a
keen ear for the niceties of character and dialogue, and, withal, one of the bitterest pessimists in all literary annals. By the flippancy
which was partly a reaction to his pessimism
and partly integrated with it, Lardner helped
to repel the second group, at least for a while.
However, he found quite early—in 1926—a discriminating admirer in H. L. Mencken, who
was quick to see that the fire in Lardner's writing sprang from moral indignation.

Verdicts of critics on Lardner have on the
whole been strongly favorable. According to
George A. Whicher, "his specialty lay in his
ability to report with seeming unconsciousness
the appalling mediocrity and vanity of the middle-class soul." To Charles Poore he appears as
"one of the most penetrating of our short-story
writers, one of the funniest of our humorists,
one of the most inexorable of our moralists."
On the other hand, James T. Farrell deplored
the antisocial character of the people Lardner
depicts; in Lardner's world the kind and decent
person is portrayed as a sucker or a comic.

Mencken also recognized him as a master of
language and an expert in recording its varieties
and variations. He says in *The American Language* (4th ed., 1936): "My own debt to him
was very great." Lardner read the first edition
(1919) of the book and from then until his
death "made penetrating and valuable suggestions. His ear for the minor peculiarities of
vulgar American was extraordinarily keen."
Mencken numbered among Lardner's close imitators Edward Streeter, H. C. Witwer, and
Will Rogers. He was almost phonographic in
transliterating the speech of the great mass of
uneducated Americans. Until he wrote *You
Know Me Al*, says Margaret Cotton Kasten, "no
one had ever considered *of* to be an auxiliary
verb," as in "Who would of thought it?" One
critic said positively, "Lardner uses it [the ver-
nacular] as a prime means of showing up, without comment, the fuzzy, flat, miserable mind of
the American boob." Surprisingly, some of Lardner's best sayings are free of rancor; thus he says
of one young man, "He gave her a look that you
could have poured on a waffle"; and of two
young people, "They gave each other a smile
with a future in it."

A biography of Lardner prepared on the basis
of much intimate information was written by
Donald Elder (1956).

Larpenteur, Charles (b. France, 1807—d.
1872), fur trader, memoirist. Larpenteur came
to Maryland as a child, then went west to St.
Louis and worked as a clerk, later as a trader.
After his death his reminiscences were published under the title *Forty Years a Fur Trader
on the Upper Missouri* (2 v., 1898); the book
has become a rich mine of material for historians.

Lars: A Pastoral of Norway (1893), a narrative poem by Bayard Taylor. The poem describes vividly a knife duel in which Lars engages; he then escapes to America and adopts
the Quaker faith. The poem was dedicated to
John Greenleaf Whittier.

Larsen, Hanna Astrup (b. Decorah, Iowa,
Sept. 1, 1873—d. Dec. 3, 1945), editor, writer,
translator. Of Scandinavian descent, Miss Larsen was deeply interested in the literature of
Scandinavia and performed important services
in making better known the writers of that
region. She served on the staff of Scandinavian-
American newspapers and magazines, besides
contributing articles to other newspapers and
magazines. She received medals from the monarchs of Sweden, Norway, and Denmark for her
services. She wrote accounts of Knut Hamsun

(1922) and Selma Lagerlöf (1936). She translated some of the novels of J. P. Jacobsen (1917, 1919) and compiled three collections: *Norway's Best Stories* (1927); *Sweden's Best Stories* (1928); *Denmark's Best Stories* (1928). From 1921 to her death she served as editor of the *American-Scandinavian Review.*

Larsen, Wolf. Chief character in Jack London's THE SEA WOLF (1904); a sea captain. He is portrayed as an example of the ruthless superman of Friedrich Nietzsche. Several times his crew, whom he cruelly torments, try to kill him, but he always manages to escape. During a shipwreck he becomes blind; he dies on a desert island, still tough and unyielding.

La Salle, René Robert Cavelier, Sieur de (b. France, 1643—d. 1687), teacher, explorer. After spending some time as a Jesuit novitiate, La Salle set out in 1666 for New France and joined his brother in Montreal. Then he went in search of a great river about which Indians had told him, later identified as the Ohio. He went as far as what is now Lake Ontario and beyond, but seems never to have reached the Ohio. In 1679 he began new explorations to the West and South, and is known to have reached Niagara Falls and explored some of the Great Lakes. In 1681–82 he continued his explorations southward and was the first white man to descend the Mississippi River to its mouth. He took possession of the whole region in the name of Louis XIV and named it in his honor Louisiana. Back in France, he was named viceroy of the Mississippi territory. In 1684 he sailed on an expedition to establish a colony at the mouth of the Mississippi, lost his way, and came to what is now Matagorda Bay in Texas. His ships were wrecked or returned to France; La Salle tried to reach the Mississippi by land. On the way his men mutinied and murdered him.

Francis Parkman wrote memorably about this great and imaginative French explorer in his book on *La Salle and the Discovery of the Great West* (1879). Mary Hartwell Catherwood concentrated on the frustration of La Salle's dreams and ambitions in her novel *The Story of Tonty* (1890). Augusta Seaman dealt with his Mississippi explorations in her *Mamselle of the Wilderness* (1913). A more mature novel than either of these is John Tebbel's *Touched with Fire* (1952), which has La Salle as a central figure.

Laski, Harold J[oseph] (b. England, 1893—d. 1950), economist, teacher, political figure. Laski, who early won a reputation as an authority on political economy, was a lecturer at McGill University (1914–16), then at Harvard (1916–20). In 1920 he became professor of political science at the University of London and exerted a profound influence on political leaders, in the direction of moderate socialism. Laski visited this country several times to lecture and teach, and wrote some of his books on conditions and tendencies in the United States, particularly *The American Presi-*

dency (1940), *American Democracy* (1948), and *Reflections on the Constitution* (1951).

When *American Democracy* appeared, the *Harvard Alumni Bulletin* called Laski "an adopted American in the thick of the fight. He is, despite his background, a most American liberal." The editorial also saw him as a "divided soul," who knew and loved things American but denounced us for our failure "to live up to the ideals of that 18th-century Enlightenment in which we became a nation." The book itself is a general political history of the United States and a detailed analysis of American trades, professions, culture, folkways. Laski believes our chief defect lies in the American businessman, whom he regards as having "adapted the main doctrines of Machiavelli's *Prince.*" A close study of *The Political Ideas of Harold J. Laski* was made in 1955 by Herbert A. Deane. A spirited revelation of two friends of opposed views was given in the *Holmes-Laski Letters* (1953).

Lasky, Jesse L., Jr. (b. New York City, Sept. 19, 1910—   ), poet, motion-picture script writer, novelist. Lasky is the son of a veteran motion-picture producer, Jesse L. Lasky (1880–1958). The younger man left this Californian background for schools in France and for travels in many parts of the Old World. He published three volumes of verse, then turned to writing scripts for movies. He wrote a narrative for the army's documentary film called *Attack: The Battle of New Britain*. He has also written novels, among them *No Angels in Heaven* (1938); *Spindrift* (1948); *Naked in a Cactus Garden* (1961).

Lasswell, Mary (b. Scotland, Feb. 8, 1905—   ), musician, teacher, novelist. Mrs. Lasswell came to Texas at an early age. Most of her stories are concerned with a group of odd Californian characters. Her first book about their uninhibited experiences was *Suds in Your Eye* (1942), a great success; *High Time* (1944) told how they took care of some orphans in wartime, *One on the House* (1949) how they took over a beer tavern in Newark, N.J. These were printed in an omnibus, *Three for the Road* (1950). The series was continued in *Wait for the Wagon* (1951) and *Tooner Schooner* (1953). In addition, Mrs. Lasswell wrote *Bread for the Living* (1948), a novel about life along the Mexican border; *I'll Take Texas* (with Bob Pool, 1958); and edited V. C. Giles' Civil War memories, *Rags and Hope* (1961).

Last Hurrah, The (1956), a novel by Edwin O'Connor, 1918—   ). This novel of a successful machine politician depicts Mayor Frank Skeffington, the perennial mayor of his city. On his 72nd birthday he announces that he will stand for yet another re-election. The novel is veracious, though sentimental. Many critics pointed out a similarity between its protagonist and Mayor James Michael Curley of Boston.

Last Leaf, The [1] (1831), a poem by OLIVER WENDELL HOLMES. Holmes, strolling the streets of Boston, used to see an old gentleman, Major Thomas Melville, grandfather of Herman Melville, who was said to have been one of the members of the Boston Tea Party. Holmes said that "his aspect . . . reminded me of a withered leaf which . . . finds itself still clinging to its bough while the new growths of spring are bursting their buds and spreading their foliage all around it." Holmes himself suggested that the metrical form, remarkably well-suited to the half-sentimental, half-satiric mood of the poem, "owed something" to the short terminal lines in Thomas Campbell's *The Battle of the Baltic* (1802); for example, "By thy wild and stormy deep,/ Elsinore." An imitation of *The Last Leaf* was written by the English poet Frederick Locker-Lampson (1821–1895)—*My Mistress's Boots* (1857).

Last Leaf, The [2] (in *The Trimmed Lamp and Other Stories*, 1907), a short story by O. HENRY. None of O. Henry's tales is more characteristic of his technique and sentiment than this account of a girl who lies dying of pneumonia in a Greenwich Village apartment and makes up her mind to go as soon as the "last leaf" of five has dropped off a vine outside her window. One leaf hangs on, and she recovers—but there is an O. Henry twist to the ending.

Last Mile, The (1930), a play by JOHN WEXLEY. Wexley based his play on an earlier one-acter of his, *Rules*. He took suggestions for his story from Robert Blake's *The Law Takes Its Toll* (*American Mercury*, July, 1929), which gave a dramatic account of experiences in the death-house; Blake was executed April 19, 1929. The play relates the story of a mutiny in an Oklahoma prison in which the leader is killed. A. H. Quinn criticized the play for its "sentimentalized argument against capital punishment." Wexley dealt with a related theme, the Scottsboro trial, in *They Shall Not Die* (1934).

Last of the Mohicans, The (1826), a novel by JAMES FENIMORE COOPER. Second of the LEATHER-STOCKING TALES, this historical romance concerns the attempt of Alice and Cora Munro to join their father at Fort William Henry near Lake Champlain, where he is commander of the British forces fighting the French. The treacherous Magua and his Huron Indians are leagued with the French, but Uncas, "the last of the Mohicans," with his father Chingachgook and their friend NATTY BUMPPO tries to assist the girls and their official escorts, the young British soldier, Heyward, and the comic psalm-singer, David Gamut. A series of attacks, captures, fights, and rescues constitutes the smoothest-knit action in the Bumppo series.

The two sisters represent the two types of women and love stories typical of Cooper and imitated thereafter in popular fiction, particularly in the western type with its code of manly purity, honor, and heroics. The suit of the honest Heyward for the fair Alice, both generous-hearted but rather stiff and ineffectual

in practical matters, at last receives paternal blessing. The love of UNCAS for Cora, who has Negro blood, is quietly passionate and efficiently courageous; it is ended when both are killed in the last fight before victory and are buried in a double funeral in which Chingachgook and Bumppo express the identity of the noblest qualities in the red man and the white. Cooper was attacked for giving too idealistic a picture of the Indian as the "noble savage," but the conflict of the different tribes of Indians and their different kinds of pride, with Uncas and Magua as antithetical extremes, provides some of the book's most powerful scenes. It is the skilled woodsman Bumppo who is an idealistic image of the noble virtues of naturalness in contrast with those whom civilization has corrupted, like some of the French and their Indian allies, or rendered awkward, like Heyward and his fellow British. See MAHICANS; JOHN GOTTLIEB HECKEWELDER.

Last Puritan, The (1936), a novel by GEORGE SANTAYANA. The eminent philosopher had written many books on metaphysics and had composed excellent poetry, but this was his first venture into fiction. Yet his satirical account of the conflict between an inhibited New Englander and an expressive young hedonist of Latin stock was really, as George F. Whicher has said, a "concrete externalization of some aspects of his philosophy." Oliver Alden, his "last Puritan," belongs to an almost extinct type, but he has doubts about himself that Santayana explores ironically, sometimes pityingly. Oliver does his duty unflinchingly, seems at times impossibly cold and unemotional. Although he may be "the last Puritan," one suspects that some of the earlier Puritans would have disowned him. The book provides examples of Santayana's keen satiric gift and his ruthless observation of Back Bay and Harvard types.

Last Time I Saw Paris, The (1942), reminiscences by ELLIOT PAUL. After the Germans took Paris in World War II Paul set down these nostalgic memories of a wonderful city in a wonderful era—the days of Paul's youth. The title was taken from a popular song of the 1940's. Paul limned with loving care some of the odd characters of the section of Paris in which he had lived; the carefully interwoven episodes are written in novelistic style. Eight years later Paul told in *Springtime in Paris* how he had revisited the section after the close of the war, found some of his friends still alive, observed the changes in the district.

Last Will of Charles Lounsbury, A. See WILLISTON FISH.

Late George Apley, The (1937), a novel by JOHN P. MARQUAND. With this book Marquand won praise from the critics who had coolly ignored his earlier writings. The book won a Pulitzer Prize and was made into a successful play (1946, Marquand collaborating with G. S. KAUFMAN) and a movie. The novel immediately began to be compared with Santayana's THE LAST PURITAN a study of Bostonian types. The story is told as "A Novel in the Form of a Memoir"; the biographer is a staid and polished annotator who manages to satirize himself as he conveys the events of George Apley's life. Apley was born into an old and wealthy family; the first Apley had been graduated from Harvard in 1662. He falls in love with an "impossible" girl named Mary Monahan and is sent on a sea voyage. Returning home, he studies law and becomes a coupon-clipper. He marries, devotes his time to charitable enterprises and collecting Chinese bronzes, is disquieted about the younger generation, even more by the taking over of Boston by the Irish.

Charles A. Brady says the novel "draws heavily on the dry tentativeness of one of the New England scriptures, THE EDUCATION OF HENRY ADAMS"; Brady also holds that "it is a difficult trick to combine irony and pathos so unfailingly as Marquand manages to do here, especially the lambent and gentle irony of [the book's] perfect understatement."

Latham, Harold S[trong] (b. Marlboro, Conn., Feb. 14, 1887—d. March 6, 1969), author of books for boys, editor. Among Latham's books are *The Story of Tim and the Club* (1918); *Marty Lends a Hand* (1919); and *Jimmy Quigg, Office Boy* (1920). In 1909 he joined the staff of the Macmillan Company, and in time rose to be vice president and editor in chief of its Trade Department. He became a traveling editor in 1952. His great "discovery" was Margaret Mitchell and her novel GONE WITH THE WIND (1936).

Lathrop, George Parsons (b. Honolulu, Hawaii, Aug. 25, 1851—d. April 19, 1898), poet, biographer, editor. Lathrop founded the American Copyright League in 1883, was editor of the Boston *Sunday Courier* and associate editor of the *Atlantic Monthly*. He wrote a *Study of Nathaniel Hawthorne* (1876) and published several collections of verse, including *Rose and Roof-Tree* (1875) and *Dreams and Days* (1892). See ROSE HAWTHORNE LATHROP.

Lathrop, Rose Hawthorne [Mother Mary Alphonsa] (b. Lenox, Mass., May 20, 1851—d. July 9, 1926), poet, memoirist, humanitarian. The second daughter of NATHANIEL HAWTHORNE married GEORGE P. LATHROP, poet and journalist, in 1871. The marriage became unhappy and the husband took to heavy drinking. In 1891 the Lathrops were converted to Roman Catholicism. Working together, they established the Catholic Summer School of America and wrote a history of the Order of the Sisters of Visitation, published as *A Story of Courage* (1894). In 1895 they separated permanently. In 1896 Mrs. Lathrop began work in a hospital, after Lathrop's death was received into the Dominican Order as Mary Alphonsa, in 1901 bought a home in Westchester Co., N.Y., which was named Rosary Hill Home (she there became Mother Alphonsa), devoted the rest of her life to care of in··rable cases of

cancer. In 1897 she published her *Memories of Hawthorne.*

Latin influence. See GREEK AND ROMAN INFLUENCE.

Latour, Archbishop. An important character in Willa Cather's DEATH COMES FOR THE ARCHBISHOP (1927). He is one of the two missionaries who work in the Southwest, as related in the novel. His fictional career bears a close resemblance to the actual life of Archbishop John Baptist Lamy (1814–1888).

Latrobe, Benjamin Henry (b. England, 1764 —d. 1820), architect, engineer, memoirist. Latrobe came to this country in 1796 and became an intimate friend of Jefferson and of Thomas Paine. The former made him surveyor of public buildings in Washington (1803). Latrobe designed many famous buildings: the Bank of Pennsylvania building in Philadelphia, the Hall of the House of Representatives in Washington, the south wing of the Capitol, the Marine Hospital, and other structures in Washington. When the Capitol was destroyed by the British, he rebuilt it (1815–17). He also remodeled the Patent Office and made alterations in the White House, designed and built the Catholic Cathedral in Baltimore, and planned a city water-supply system in Philadelphia, the first in America. He was responsible for a Greek revival in architecture in this country. He kept a *Journal*, first published in 1905 with an introduction by his son. The elder Latrobe's journals, *Impressions Respecting New Orleans*, were published in 1951. They are a diary and sketches, 1818–20, edited with an introduction and notes by Samuel Wilson, Jr. A distinguished architect, Talbot F. Hamlin, wrote a biography of the elder Latrobe, *Benjamin Henry Latrobe* (1955). His son, **John H[azelhurst] B[oneval] Latrobe** (b. May 4, 1803—d. Sept. 11, 1891), a lawyer, artist, historian, and biographer, took a deep interest in the establishment of Liberia and suggested Monrovia as the name of the capital, by way of a compliment to President Monroe. He wrote *The History of Mason and Dixon's Line* (1855); *Personal Recollections* (1858); *Maryland in Liberia* (1885); *Recollections of West Point* (1887).

Lattimore, Owen (b. Washington, D.C., July 29, 1900—   ), teacher, explorer, authority on Asia. Lattimore has explored and written about many sections of Asia: *The Desert Road to Turkestan* (1929); *High Tartary* (1930); *Manchuria, Cradle of Conflict* (1932); *Mongol Journeys* (1941); *China, A Short History* (with Eleanor Lattimore, 1947); *The Situation in Asia* (1949); *The Pivot of Asia* (1950); *Nationalism and Revolution in Mongolia* (1955). Some of his books have aroused warm controversy because of his liberal political views. *Ordeal by Slander* (1950) describes his troubles with McCarthyism. He has taught for the most part at Johns Hopkins University. He is the brother of RICHMOND LATTIMORE.

Lattimore, Richmond (b. China, May 6,

1906—   ), poet, translator, critic. A distinguished scholar, Lattimore was graduated from Dartmouth College in 1926 and studied under Rhodes and Fulbright Scholarships at Oxford, Rome, and Greece. Though chiefly regarded as a scholar and translator, Lattimore considers himself primarily a poet. His early poetry reveals the influence of such American moderns as Cummings, MacLeish, Stevens, and Hart Crane. His translations and critical works contain an unusually broad insight into the history, philosophy, and literature of ancient Greece. His own poetic gift has contributed to the richness of his translations. Lattimore's books include: *Themes in Greek and Latin Epitaphs* (1942); *The Odes of Pindar* (transl. 1944); *The Iliad of Homer* (transl. 1951); *The Complete Greek Tragedy* (1053 58, co editor); *Greek Lyrics* (transl. 1955); *Poems* (1957); *The Poetry of Greek Tragedy* (1958); *Hesiod* (transl. 1959).

Laudonnière, René Goulaine de (b. France, 16th century), explorer, memoirist. Laudonnière attempted to found a colony in Florida, but failed; he wrote an account of his experiences, *L'Histoire Notable de la Floride* (1586). One of the expedition members, an artist named Jacques Le Moyne, brought his paintings of the American scene back to France; in 1592 Theodore de Bry, a publisher in Frankfurt-am-Main, put out an edition of *La Floride* with Le Moyne's illustrations. In 1587 Laudonnière's account was translated into English and later included in Hakluyt's *Principall Navigations*. The book is especially valuable for its depiction of the Timucuan Indians, a tribe now vanished. A fellow colonist, Jean Ribaut, also wrote an account of the enterprise in his *Whole and True Discovery of Terra Florida* (1563). Portions of these narratives and reproductions of Le Moyne's illustrations appeared in Stefan Lorant's THE NEW WORLD (1946).

"Laugh and the world laughs with you," the first line of *Solitude,* a poem by ELLA WHEELER WILCOX, published in 1883. The next line runs: "Weep and you weep alone." The poem appeared in *Poems of Passion.* John Alexander Joyce laid claim to the poem, but apparently without justification.

Laughead, W. B. See PAUL BUNYAN.

Laughing Boy (1929), a novel by OLIVER LA FARGE. Out of his knowledge of Navajo customs, La Farge wrote this Pulitzer Prize winner, a novel of love and jealousy, deception and death. Laughing Boy elopes with Slim Girl, later discovers she has a lover. He tries to kill them both, but unsuccessfully; later he is reconciled with Slim Girl, but on their way back to their people she is killed from ambush and Laughing Boy is purged of both love and grief.

Laughlin, James IV (b. Pittsburgh, Pa., Oct. 30, 1914—   ), editor, publisher, poet. Laughlin has acknowledged the influence of DUDLEY FITTS, his teacher in preparatory school, in turning him to an interest in con-

temporary literature. Later, at Harvard, he pursued his studies of *avant-garde* writing, became aware of the difficulties faced by experimental authors in search of American publishers to take on their works, and issued the first volume of *New Directions* (1936) to help overcome the deficiencies of the commercial literary marketplace. Soon Laughlin was publishing not only his annual but many books and pamphlets, and New Directions was established as the most important publishing house in the United States for current serious writing. It specializes in new writing by *avant-garde* American and English authors, translations of important modern classics from abroad, and literary criticism in various contemporary modes. Laughlin's own poems have been issued from time to time in private editions and have won the admiration of readers for their immediacy and their naturalness of form and language. Among his works: *Wild Anemone, and Other Poems* (1957); *Selected Poems* (1960).

Launcelot and Guenevere, A Poem in Five Dramas (5 v., 1907), by RICHARD HOVEY. Hovey planned this ambitious work as a cycle of three poetic trilogies, each to consist of a masque and two plays, but never lived to complete his project. He sought to avoid the sentimentality of Tennyson and other mid-Victorians and to stress psychology and idealism, often symbolically. The five parts are called *The Quest of Merlin* (1891), a masque; *The Marriage of Guenevere* (1891, 1895), a tragedy; *The Birth of Galahad* (1898), a romantic drama, probably the best of the five; *Taliesen* (1900), another masque, which employed many verse forms skillfully; and *The Holy Graal and Other Fragments* (1907), parts of the cycle never completed.

Launcelot Langstaff. The pen name of J. K. PAULDING, in his contributions to the collection of essays called SALMAGUNDI (1807–08).

Laurence, William L[eonard] (b. Lithuania, March 7, 1888—   ), translator, reporter, writer. After service on the New York *World,* Laurence joined the *Times* in 1930 as a science news reporter and gained national fame and two Pulitzer Prizes (1937, 1946) for his reports. His most significant work during the 1940's was in connection with the development of the atomic bomb. A piece called *The Atom Gives Up* (Saturday Evening Post, 1940) was the first information that atomic fission might soon be a reality. Later he wrote *Dawn Over Zero: The Story of the Atomic Bomb* (1946), described by Orville Prescott as "an authoritative account of many brilliant Frankensteins cooperating to create a fabulous monster." In 1951 he wrote *The Hell Bomb,* and in 1959, *Men and Atoms.*

Laurens, Henry (b. Charleston, S.C., March 6, 1724—d. Dec. 8, 1792), merchant, statesman, diplomat. Laurens, a leading merchant of Charleston, was greatly attached to Great Britain, but broke with its government over some of its maritime policies, against which he directed *Some General Observations on American Custom House Officers and Courts of Vice-Admiralty* (1769). He served in many official capacities in South Carolina; when the new government was formed he was president of the Continental Congress for a year. He sailed for Europe in 1780 to arrange for a loan to the American forces, was captured by the British and imprisoned in the Tower of London, was then exchanged for Lord Cornwallis. He described his experiences in a *Narrative* (published, 1857, by the South Carolina Historical Society).

Laurents, Arthur (b. Brooklyn, N.Y., July 14, 1918—   ), playwright, screenwriter, director. A graduate of Cornell University, Laurents gained prominence with his *Home of the Brave* (1946), which won for him the Sidney Howard Playwright Award and a special grant from the National Academy of Arts and Sciences. He also wrote *The Time of the Cuckoo* (1953), later filmed as *Summertime;* and the book for *West Side Story* (1957), in which he transplanted the tragedy of Romeo and Juliet from Verona to New York's West Side. Music for this highly successful musical was by Leonard Bernstein. *Gypsy* (1959) again saw him producing the book for a successful musical. His *Invitation to a March* (1960), which the author directed, was a modern comedy based on the Sleeping Beauty legend. Laurents also wrote the screenplays for *Rope, Anastasia,* and the widely acclaimed film *The Snake Pit.*

Laus Deo! (1865), a poem by JOHN GREENLEAF WHITTIER. This poem celebrating the passage of the Thirteenth Amendment and the freeing of the slaves was composed (Dec. 18, 1865) as Whittier sat in the Friends' Meeting House in Amesbury and listened to the clang of the bells and the roaring of the cannon that proclaimed the passage of the famous law. When he returned home he recited passages of the poem (not yet written down) to his family. "It wrote itself," he told Lucy Larcom.

Laut, Agnes C. (b. Ontario, Feb. 11, 1871—d. Nov. 15, 1936), biographer. As a child, Miss Laut lived in Winnipeg, where she had an opportunity to observe frontier conditions and to mingle with the half-breed descendants of the great fur traders. Her first book, *Lords of the North* (1900), deals with the latter. Later Miss Laut came to live in the United States. She was always deeply interested in the past of both countries. Among her books: *The Story of the Trappers* (1902); *Freebooters of the Wilderness* (1910); *The Fur Trade of America* (1921); *The Conquest of Our Western Empire* (1927); *The Overland Trail* (1929).

Lavery, Emmet [Godfrey] (b. Poughkeepsie, N.Y., Nov. 8, 1902—   ), lawyer, newspaperman, editor, actor, script writer. After long service on the Poughkeepsie *Sunday Courier,* Lavery was attracted to the theater in the 1930's, especially in connection with the FEDERAL THEATER PROJECT of Hallie Flanagan. At first

he was an amateur actor, later became a professional on Broadway. In Hollywood, where he went as a script writer in 1935, he became active in organizing Catholic drama groups, professional and amateur. His first stage play was *The First Legion* (1934), which dealt with the Jesuits. Later he wrote *Monsignor's Hour* (1935); *Second Spring* (on the life of Cardinal Newman, 1938); *Hitler's Children* (a dramatization of Gregor Ziemer's *Education for Death,* 1942). His most successful play was *The Magnificent Yankee* (1946), the story of Justice Oliver Wendell Holmes. He wrote also *The Gentleman from Athens* (1948); *Fenelon* (1956); *American Portrait* (1958).

Law, John (b. Scotland, 1671—d. 1729), financier and speculator. See MISSISSIPPI BUBBLE.

Law of Civilization and Decay, The (1895; with an introduction by CHARLES BEARD, 1943), a treatise on history and economics by BROOKS ADAMS. This book exerted an influence on Theodore Roosevelt, Brooks' brother Henry and his circle, and various German theorists of geopolitics. It was Adams' best book, though it made little impression on the general public. Adams foresaw chaos ahead; he blamed the "moneychangers" for the corruption of mankind and, in attempting to apply the concepts of Newton, Comte, Darwin, and Marx to the history of western civilization, discovered what he thought was a continuous movement. He saw civilization as the product of social energy, itself obeying the law of mass in physics and moving in waves between centralization and decentralization. Certain master types appear in these waves, their characters determined by two motives—greed and fear. If the former predominates, the usurer rules; if the latter, the priest. Adams stressed the importance of economics and geography in a way that greatly influenced later historians. Barbara Miller Solomon has ably discussed Adams and his circle in *Ancestors and Immigrants* (1956).

Lawrence. See also LAURENCE.

Lawrence, D[avid] H[erbert] (b. England, Sept. 11, 1885—d. March 2, 1930), novelist, essayist, poet. Lawrence and his wife Frieda traveled widely, and in September, 1922, came to America to live, staying until October, 1925, mostly on MABEL DODGE LUHAN's ranch in New Mexico. Lawrence had by this time attracted followers, some of real intelligence and artistic power, like Aldous Huxley and Mrs. Luhan, others mere eccentrics. Harry T. Moore, in his *Life and Works of D. H. Lawrence* (1951), says that the writer's three years at Taos were "spent either in the hysterical atmosphere of Mabel Luhan's ranch, usually full of captive and quarreling celebrities and *arrivistes,* or in escapes from this atmosphere—escapes to the nearby mountains, to Old Mexico, once even to Europe." He speaks elsewhere of "the preposterous guests who sometimes ascended the mountain to badger the recalcitrant prophet." In 1923 Lawrence and his wife, returning from Mexico, went by boat from New Orleans to New York, living for a while in New Jersey. (See MORNINGS IN MEXICO.)

One of Lawrence's poems written in New Mexico was about Susan the cow; he seems to have established "a symbolical relationship with Susan," says Moore. "He felt a certain balance between his individuality and hers." William York Tindall had fun with that poem and with Lawrence in general in *D. H. Lawrence and Susan His Cow* (1939). A more serious work was Lawrence's STUDIES IN CLASSIC AMERICAN LITERATURE (1923), now itself considered a classic of criticism. He was deeply impressed by Mexico and wrote some poems about primitive life or survivals there. His views are contained in *The Plumed Serpent* (1926), a powerful novel in which Lawrence tried to work out his own perplexed beliefs concerning human civilization.

Two books dealing mainly with the Lawrences in America are Witter Bynner's *Journey with Genius: Recollections and Reflections Concerning the D. H. Lawrences* (1951) and Eliot Fay's *Lorenzo in Search of the Sun: D. H. Lawrence in Italy, Mexico, and the American Southwest* (1953). Edward Nehls has edited an imposing three-volume biography, *D. H. Lawrence* (1957–59), drawn from a variety of sources.

Lawrence, David (b. Philadelphia, Dec. 25, 1888—   ), newspaperman, Washington correspondent, editor. Lawrence was employed by the Associated Press in Washington in 1910 and six years later became Washington correspondent of the *New York Evening Post*, writing the first Washington dispatches to be syndicated nationally by wire. In 1926 he founded and edited the *United States Daily*, in 1933 became president and editor of the *United States News*, and in 1946 of the *World Report*. The two latter periodicals were merged in 1948 as *U.S. News and World Report* and continued to be edited by Lawrence. During Wilson's administration he was a strong partisan of that President, was lukewarm to succeeding Presidents, including Roosevelt. Charles Fisher in his analysis of *The Columnists* (1944) remarked that Lawrence felt "light was extinguished with Wilson's death." Lawrence wrote *The True Story of Woodrow Wilson* (1924); *The Other Side of Government* (1929); *Beyond the New Deal* (1934); *Stumbling into Socialism* (1935); *Nine Honest Men* (1936); *Diary of a Washington Correspondent* (1942).

Lawrence, Josephine (b. Newark, N.J., 1897?–   ), newspaperwoman, novelist. Miss Lawrence worked for the Newark *Sunday Call* and the Newark *Evening and Sunday News*. She began her career in fiction with a series for children, some of which were among the earliest to be broadcast by radio. After 1932 she wrote only novels for adults. In that year appeared *Head of the Family*, the first of many novels considering, with common sense and sympathy as well as with storytelling skill, the everyday problems of commonplace people. She hates injustice and prejudice, believes that relatives owe one another fairness and kindness, and sees deeply enough to realize that self-sacrifice may sometimes be a form of selfishness. Her approach is both satiric and sympathetic.

Among her books: *Years Are So Long* (1934); *If I Have Four Apples* (1935); *The Sound of Running Feet* (1937); *But You Are Young* (1940); *There Is Today* (1942); *Let Us Consider One Another* (1945); *Double Wedding Ring* (1946); *The Pleasant Morning Light* (1948); *My Heart Shall Not Fear* (1949); *The Picture Window* (1951); *The Web of Time* (1953); *The Gates of Living* (1955); *The Empty Nest* (1956); *All Our Tomorrows* (1959).

Lawrence, William (b. Boston, May 30, 1850 —d. Nov. 6, 1941), Episcopal clergyman, bishop of Massachusetts, biographer. One of the most eminent divines of his time, Bishop Lawrence gained international renown when in 1927 he appealed to Governor Alvan Fuller of Massachusetts to stay the sentence of Nicola Sacco and Bartolomeo Vanzetti. On another occasion he resigned as vice-president of the Boston Watch and Ward Society because he believed it had used immoral methods in convicting a book clerk for selling an indecent book. He wrote a sturdy autobiography, *Memories of a Happy Life* (1926), also the *Life of Amos A. Lawrence* (1889); *Life of Roger Wolcott* (1902); *Henry Cabot Lodge* (1925); *Phillips Brooks* (1930).

Lawson, James (b. Scotland, Nov. 9, 1798— d. March 24, 1880), businessman, critic, editor, writer. Lawson came to the United States when he was sixteen, worked in New York City as an accountant and a newspaper editor, then went back to business and became well known in marine insurance. A friend of William Gilmore Simms and other writers, he wrote an unsuccessful play, *Giordano* (1828), and published verse and essays anonymously. His *Ontwa: The Son of the Forest* (1822) was set among the Erie Indians.

Lawson, John (b. Yorkshire? [Scotland?], [?]—d. 1711), explorer, colonial official, author of travel books. Lawson came to the Carolinas toward the beginning of the 18th century and traveled widely in that region. An account of his experiences was published in London (1709) as *A New Voyage to Carolina: Containing the Exact Description and Natural History of That Country*, later reprinted, somewhat misleadingly, as *The History of Carolina*. It was also reprinted (1711) in John Stevens' *A New Collection of Voyages and Travels* and was put out in a German translation (1712, 1722). A reprint was edited by Francis L. Harriss (1937).

Lawson is one of the best of the early travel writers. He made every effort to be both accurate and just—his account is constantly friendly to the Indians and is a plea for better treatment of them. For a while he was back in England, then returned to the Carolinas in the capacity of surveyor-general. In company with a Swiss baron he set out to make plans for a new colony, but was captured and killed by Tuscarora Indians.

Lawson, John Howard (b. New York City, Sept. 25, 1895—   ), newspaperman, playwright. Lawson has been associated with radical movements in both literature and life. His early plays were examples of expressionism—particularly *Roger Bloomer* (1923) and PROCESSIONAL (1925); his later plays were proletarian in their philosophy—*Loud Speaker* (1927); *The International* (1928); *Success Story* (1932); *The Pure in Heart* (1934); *Gentlewoman* (1934); *Marching Song* (1937). Contemporary critics praised a number of Lawson's plays for their theatrical effectiveness, intelligence, and power, but in retrospect they often seem to suffer from a preponderance of ideology over drama. Lawson also wrote scripts for several movies, including *Action In The North Atlantic* (1943), *Sahara* (1943), and *Smashup* (1947). In addition, he is the author of *The Theory and Technique of Playwriting and Screenwriting* (1949), *The Hidden Heritage* (1950), a book about the cultural history of the United States, and *Film in the Battle of Ideas* (1953).

Lawson, Sam. A shiftless Yankee in Harriet Beecher Stowe's novel OLDTOWN FOLKS (1869). His droll remarks and action furnish the comic relief.

Lawson, W. B. The pen name of GEORGE CHARLES JENKS.

Lawyer Lincoln (1936), by A. A. Woldman. This is a careful, detailed account of Lincoln's career as a lawyer, the men with whom he was associated, his important cases, the fees he charged.

Lay of Ancient Rome (1901?), a parody by THOMAS R. YBARRA. This clever bit of macaronic verse appeared in the Harvard *Lampoon* while Ybarra was a freshman, as he relates in his *Young Man of the World* (1942). It created a sensation and was immediately reprinted in newspapers all over the United States and elsewhere.

Lay of the Lone Fishball, The (1857), a song by George Martin Lane (1823–1897). Lane was a genial professor of Latin at Harvard, where his rollicking song became very popular—and still is. In 1862, supposedly staid Professor FRANCIS J. CHILD built a melodious Italian opera score around the verses, and this opera, called *Il Pesceballo*, was performed several times in Boston and Cambridge for the benefit of Civil War soldiers. Child added a note in Italian on the strange charms of the New England fishball. JAMES RUSSELL LOWELL did a burlesque translation of the libretto.

Lay of the Scottish Fiddle, The (1813), a burlesque of Sir Walter Scott's *Lay of the Last Minstrel* (1805), by JAMES KIRKE PAULDING. It appeared anonymously and was devoted mainly to criticism of the British invasion of Chesapeake Bay. Oddly enough, it was published in a handsome edition in London, with a preface highly complimentary to Paulding. But a review in the London *Quarterly* was savage in its denunciation of Paulding. This and other writings of Paulding's attracted the attention of President Madison, who appointed him (1815) secretary to the Commissioners of the Navy.

Layton, Irving (b. Rumania, March 12, 1912–   ), poet. Layton was the "angry young man" of Canadian poetry for years before his first book publication in 1945. His own voice spoke out in most of his poems, full of protest against the social inequalities he saw both in the countryside and in the city. Layton relished the role of the rebel; often he purposely shocked the reader with harsh, "unpoetic" images. Layton's family came to Canada and settled in Montreal in 1913. His city poems like "Jewish Main Street" have a Montreal setting, but Layton often draws on his remarkably diverse background for subject matter. He has a degree in agriculture, was in the Royal Canadian Air Force, and worked as a waiter, supervisor of an orphan asylum, and publisher's proofreader. For his later, more mature poetry, beginning with *In the Midst of My Fever* (1954), Layton has drawn praise from leading critics and poets, including William Carlos Williams. Layton's work has been anthologized in *Cerberus* (1952), and in *Other Canadians; An Anthology of New Poetry in Canada: 1940–1946* (1947). Layton was one of the editors of *Preview*, an experimental literary magazine published during the forties. His numerous books include: *Here and Now* (1945); *Now is the Place*, prose and verse (1948); *Music on a Kazoo* (1956); and *The Swinging Flesh* (1961).

Lazarus, Emma (b. New York City, July 22, 1849—d. Nov. 19, 1887), poet, translator. The precocious child of wealthy and cultivated parents, Emma Lazarus published a volume, *Poems and Translations* (1867), written in her teens.

A novel, *Alide: An Episode in Goethe's Life* (1874), followed, and in 1881 she published a masterly translation of Heine's poems and ballads. Nevertheless, her early work, flowery and romantic, would not have won her a permanent reputation if her indignation had not been kindled by the Russian pogroms of 1882. She became a Jewish poet with a sacred cause—to defend and glorify her people. *Songs of a Semite* (1882) contains a number of notable poems, including *The Crowing of the Red Cock, The Banner of the Jew,* and the *Dance to Death,* the last considered her best work. Her sonnet *The New Colossus* (1883) is inscribed on the pedestal of the Statue of Liberty. Her *By the Waters of Babylon,* a series of poems printed in the *Century* in March, 1887, attracted attention as an early example of the influence of Whitman. The oblivion into which Emma Lazarus has fallen until recently is partly explained by H. E. Jacobs in his biography, *The World of Emma Lazarus* (1949), by the fact that many people thought her poems too exclusively Jewish and by the curious fact that her sister forbade the printing of "anything Jewish" in any new edition of Emma's works. Eve Merriam in *Emma Lazarus: Woman with a Torch* (1956) included selections from her poetry and prose.

CHARLES CHILD WALCUTT

Lazarus Laughed (1927), a play by EUGENE O'NEILL. This play apparently was performed only once—in Pasadena, Calif., April 9, 1928. It must have placed a strange burden on the actors, because of the great amount of laughing they must do in reply to the exigencies of the theme. Irving Pichel, who took the leading role at Pasadena, on one occasion laughed without interruption for four minutes.

When Jesus brings back Lazarus from the dead he immediately begins to laugh, as a symbol of his profound joy in living, "the Eternal Life in Yes." His laughter infects others, and he goes about preaching a creed of love and eternal life, symbolized in laughter. He proceeds to Rome, where he even converts some of the Roman legionnaires—but not Caligula and Tiberius. His wife Miriam is poisoned, he himself is tortured and burnt in the amphitheater, but still affirms that there is no death. There are seven choruses, wearing masks.

O'Neill himself, it is said, considered this his most successful play, and at least one critic, Oscar Cargill, agrees with him. Cargill made a striking analysis of the relationship of the play to Carl Jung and Nietzsche, especially in the latter's stress on the Dionysian.

Lea, Fanny Heaslip (b. New Orleans, Oct. 30, 1884—d. Jan. 13, 1955), novelist, playwright. Miss Lea wrote *Quicksands* (1911); *Sicily Ann* (1914); *With This Ring* (1925); *Wild Goose Chase* (1929); *Half Angel* (1932); *There Are Brothers* (1940); *Devil Within* (1948); and other amusing, sentimental stories aimed at women readers. Among her plays: *Lolly* (1930) and *Crede Byron* (1936).

Lea, Henry Charles (b. Philadelphia, Sept. 19, 1825—d. Oct. 24, 1909), publisher, historian. The descendant of a partner in an old American publishing firm, Carey & Lea, which in his time had become Blanchard & Lea, Lea began to work for his father in 1843, succeeded him as partner in 1851. He was greatly inter-

ested in medieval history, particularly the history of the Roman Catholic Church. He wrote *Superstition and Force* (1866), *Studies in Church History* (1869), and then his three most important works: *A History of the Inquisition of the Middle Ages* (3 v., 1888); *A History of the Inquisition of Spain* (4 v., 1906–07); *The Inquisition in the Spanish Dependencies* (1908); also *The Moriscos of Spain* (1901). From his papers was gathered another book, *Materials Toward a History of Witchcraft* (1939), arranged and edited by A. C. Howland. His books on the Inquisition have been described as among "the great triumphs of American scholarship." He was objective to such a degree that his readers never could guess on which side his sympathies lay. Lea's collection of 15,000 books on the Middle Ages is part of the library of the University of Pennsylvania, where a chair in history has been named in his honor.

Lea, Homer (b. Denver, Colo., Nov. 17, 1876—d. Nov. 1, 1912), soldier, novelist. In several novels—*The Vermilion Pencil* (1908), *The Valor of Ignorance* (1909), *The Day of the Saxon* (1912)—Lea made vivid prophecies of coming World Wars, especially the danger of domination of the United States by Oriental invaders.

Lea, Tom (b. El Paso, Tex., July 11, 1907—   ), artist, novelist, poet, historian. After attending the Art Institute of Chicago from 1924 to 1926, Lea devoted himself to painting and illustrating; his work appeared frequently in the *Saturday Evening Post* and *Life* magazine, and his murals decorated several public buildings in Texas. In 1941 he became artist-correspondent for *Life.* His experiences during the war led to his first book, *Peleliu Landing,* published in 1945 when Lea was almost forty. His first novel, *The Brave Bulls* (1949), concerned bullfighting; it won enthusiastic acclaim. Other novels include *The Wonderful Country* (1952) and *The Primal Yoke* (1960). He wrote *The King Ranch* (1957), a two-volume work on Texas history.

Leach, Henry Goddard (b. Philadelphia, July 3, 1880—   ), teacher, editor, authority on Scandinavian culture. Leach received many honorary degrees and other awards for his effective efforts to promote closer relations with the Scandinavian countries. He taught at various universities and served as secretary, and later as president, of the American-Scandinavian Foundation. He was also active in peace movements, was president of the Poetry Society, and lectured on international affairs. He edited *The Forum* (1923–40). He wrote *Scandinavia of the Scandinavians* (1915), and *Pageant of Old Scandinavia* (1946). *My Last Seventy Years* (1956) is his autobiography.

Leacock, John [Joseph?]. See THE FALL OF BRITISH TYRANNY.

Leacock, Stephen [Butler] (b. England, Dec. 30, 1869—d. March 28, 1944), economist, humorist, essayist. He emigrated to Canada with his parents in 1876. He was educated at

Canadian and American universities, first specializing in languages but eventually switching to economics and political science. He received his Ph.D. in 1903 and soon became professor of economics at McGill University. He won fame both as an economist, with such erudite books as *Elements of Political Science* (1906), and as a humorist, beginning with *Literary Lapses* (1910). He is best known to the general public for his witty essays and short stories. He set the style for modern wit to such an extent that Robert Benchley said his own writings were merely rewritten Leacock. George Ade said of Leacock: "He inherits the genial traditions of Lamb, Thackeray, and Lewis Carroll and has absorbed, across the Canadian border, the delightful unconventionalities of Oliver Wendell Holmes and Mark Twain, with possibly a slight flavor of Will Rogers." Mark Twain was, in fact, the subject of a biography by Leacock, as was Charles Dickens. Among his many humorous books are: *Nonsense Novels* (1911); *Frenzied Fiction* (1917); *College Days* (1923); *Hellements of Hickonomics in Hiccoughs of Verse* (1936); *My Remarkable Uncle and Other Sketches* (1942); *Leacock Roundabout* (1946). He composed several books on writing techniques, including *Humour: Its Theory and Technique* (1935); and *How to Write* (1942). His autobiography, *The Boy I Left Behind Me*, appeared in 1946.

Leaf, Munro (b. Baltimore, Md., Dec. 4, 1905—   ), teacher, football coach, writer of books for children, artist. Leaf, possibly the most widely read writer of books for young children in the mid-20th century, was an English teacher by profession. An overheard conversation on the subject of "ain't" led him to the writing of a little book called *Grammar Can Be Fun* (1934). He did a few rough sketches to help the artist with the proposed pictures, but his sketches were used instead; and he has illustrated nearly all his later books. A whole series followed his first book—*Manners Can Be Fun* (1936); *Safety Can Be Fun* (1938); and others, including the Watchbird series begun in 1939. His biggest hit was *Ferdinand the Bull* (1936). For this book Robert Lawson (1892–1957) did some highly appropriate illustrations, and it immediately became a sensational favorite not only with children but also with many adults. It is the story of a peaceable bull who loves flowers and refuses to fight in the bullring; all kinds of symbolical meanings were read into it. Leaf also wrote *Wee Gillis* (1938), with pictures by Lawson. In 1957 he wrote *Three Promises to You* for the United Nations, and in 1958 *Science Can Be Fun*.

Leah and Rachel, or, The Two Fruitful Sisters, Virginia and Maryland (1656), a tract by JOHN HAMMOND. Hammond seems to have been a military man who spent nineteen years in Virginia and two in Maryland. He left the latter colony when he was sentenced to death by the Puritans who had taken it over. His book extols life in America, even though he criti-cizes some aspects of it. The work was reprinted in Peter Force's *Tracts*, III (1844).

Learned Blacksmith, The. See ELIHU BURRITT.

Leary, Lewis (b. Blauvelt, N.Y., April 18, 1906—   ), critic, professor, editor. Leary taught at several universities before becoming a professor of English at Columbia University in 1952. He published *Idiomatic Mistakes in English* in 1932. *That Rascal Freneau: A Study in Literary Failure* (1941) established his reputation as an exhaustively thorough research scholar. *The Literary Career of Nathaniel Tucker* appeared in 1951. Leary edited and contributed to a number of professional periodicals, and also edited *The Last Poems of Philip Freneau* (1945); *Articles on American Literature* (1947; rev., 1952); *Method and Motive in the Cantos of Ezra Pound* (1954); *The Unity of Knowledge* (1955); Herman Melville's *His Fifty Years of Exile* (*Israel Potter*) (1957); *Selections From Thoreau* (1957); *Contemporary Literary Scholarship: A Critical Review* (1958); *American Literary Essays* (1960); *Mark Twain's Letters to Mary* (1961). He is also author of *Mark Twain* (1960) and *John Greenleaf Whittier* (1961).

Leather Stocking and Silk, or, Hunter John Myers and His Times (1854), a novel by JOHN ESTEN COOKE. This is a story of the Virginia Valley at the beginning of the 19th century, with the scene in Martinsburg, really Williamsburg. The plot is complex, a labyrinth of love affairs, but one of the characters, Hunter John, shows the influence of Cooper's Natty Bumppo, as does the title.

Leather-Stocking [in common usage, **Leatherstocking**] **Tales.** Five novels by JAMES FENIMORE COOPER, in which the chief character, NATTY BUMPPO, is sometimes called "Leather-Stocking" because of his leggings. Since Bumppo was definitely a "York Stater," efforts have been made to identify him with some of the famous Indian fighters of New York in the late 18th century. A special candidate for the honor is Nat Foster (1766–1840), a trapper who is said to have called himself Leather-Stocking long before Cooper wrote. A. L. Byron-Curtiss, who wrote *The Life and Adventures of Nat Foster* (1897), was confident that Cooper knew Foster, and that he adopted for Leather-Stocking an exploit of Nat's in rescuing two girls from a panther. Another candidate is Nick (sometimes called Major) Stoner (1762 or 1763–1853), who looked like an Indian, wore gold rings in his ears from boyhood, and engaged in adventures not unlike Bumppo's.

The novels appeared in print in the following sequence: THE PIONEERS (1823), THE LAST OF THE MOHICANS (1826); THE PRAIRIE (1827); THE PATHFINDER (1840); THE DEERSLAYER (1841). But the narrative sequence, following Leather-Stocking from youth to old age, is as follows: *Deerslayer, Mohicans, Pathfinder, Pioneers, Prairie*. The changes in Bumppo's character are abrupt and obviously intended to meet the exigencies of each story. But, in the order of publication, D. H. Lawrence saw the series as exhibiting "a *decrescendo* of reality, a *crescendo* of beauty." Despite all Bumppo's faults—his inconsistency of language in the various novels, the loose synthesis of his traits, his long-winded ethical essays—Alexander Cowie holds that he "claims rank with the greatest fictional characters." Sainte-Beuve and Thackeray praised him warmly. Mark Twain, on the other hand, loathed him; he claimed that Natty at times "talks like an illustrated, gilt-edged, tree-calf, hand-tooled, seven-dollar *Friendship's Offering* in the beginning of a paragraph, and like a Negro minstrel at the end of it."

Henry Nash Smith points out in *Virgin Land* (1950) that Leather-Stocking, like Daniel Boone (whom many critics regard as the real prototype of Cooper's character), for at least one section of his public was "a symbol of anarchic freedom." James Grossman, in his book on Cooper (1949), says that Bumppo keeps clear of the responsibilities imposed by civilization by moving westward all the time, just as Boone did. He ignores the horrible deeds committed by white men and lives, says Grossman, "a kind of ideal bachelor existence." A skillful abridgment of the five novels was made by Allan Nevins in a single volume entitled *The Leatherstocking Saga* (1954), with a general introduction and special introductions, and with maps and illustrations. See John Gottlieb Heckewelder.

Leavenworth Case, The (1878), a detective story by Anna Katharine Green. The policeman in the story is believable and shrewd; the plot is good; the book became an immediate best seller. Moreover, this was the first detective story written by a woman; since then women have been prolific writers of this type of novel, sometimes under male disguise on the title page. But the number of women detectives in stories has not increased in proportion.

Leaves from Margaret Smith's Journal in the Province of Massachusetts Bay, 1678–79 (1849), a novel by John Greenleaf Whittier. This is an imaginary diary supposedly kept by a young woman from England who visited her relatives in New England in the colonial period. She visits not only Massachusetts but also what is now Maine and Rhode Island, and meets several historical characters. The material is historically correct. The novel appeared serially in the *National Era* (1848) and then as a novel —anonymously.

Leaves of Grass, a collection of poems which Walt Whitman first published in 1855 and revised and augmented until 1892. The 1855 edition was a thin quarto volume of ninety-five pages, bound in green cloth stamped with designs of roots, leaves, and small flowers. The name of the author was omitted from the title page, but the frontispiece was an engraved portrait of the poet in shirt sleeves and nonchalant posture. Fewer than eight hundred copies were bound and most of these remained unsold.

Some copies have survived, however, and today they are eagerly sought by collectors and bring high prices. This first edition contained twelve poems without titles, the first and longest of which was later called "Song of Myself." The poems were preceded by a long, oddly punctuated essay, also without title, though it is usually referred to as the "1855 Preface." It was Whitman's manifesto, often compared to Wordsworth's Preface to *Lyrical Ballads*, stating what the American poet should be and do. He is to be "commensurate" with the American people. "His spirit responds to his country's spirit," and he "incarnates" the geography and natural life of his nation. The program was thus nationalistic, but also religious, for the role of the poet was to be that of guide and example, taking over the work of the priests of the past. The inspiration of this poet shall be "real objects," and his form shall be "transcendent and new," taking shape organically like growing melons and pears, shedding "the perfume impalpable to form." This theory was not entirely new, for Coleridge had expressed it in his lecture on "Shakespeare, a Poet Generally," and the verse structure of the poems that followed the preface resembled the "thought rhythm" of Hebraic and even older poetry (see entry, Walt Whitman).

The following year (1856) Whitman published a second edition of *Leaves of Grass*, revised and expanded. He omitted the 1855 Preface but printed a long public letter to Ralph Waldo Emerson, whom he addressed as "Master." The real influence of Emerson on Whitman's poems is still in dispute, but Whitman did apply and adapt many of Emerson's transcendental ideas—cf. Emerson's essay "The Poet." The most important new poem in the second edition was "Sun-Down Poem" (title changed in 1860 to "Crossing Brooklyn Ferry").

An edition which scholars have come to regard as crucial in Whitman's development was the third, published by Thayer and Eldridge of Boston in 1860. It not only contained many new poems, the best being "Out of the Cradle Endlessly Rocking," but also three new groups (the groups being composed of new and 1855–56 poems): "Chants Democratic," "Enfans d'Adam" (later changed to "Children of Adam"), and "Calamus" [1]. The first of these groups merely exemplified the nationalistic program announced in the 1855 Preface, but the other two groups launched a new program of the importance and sacredness of sex and the power of love. Several of the sex poems, such as "A Woman Waits for Me," profoundly shocked many of Whitman's readers and stirred up controversy that lasted well into the twentieth century. In the third edition Whitman also attempted to arrange his poems in a symbolical order, beginning with the semiautobiographical "Starting from Paumanok" (Indian name for Long Island) and ending with "So Long!", in which the poet envisioned himself as "disembodied, triumphant, dead," surviving in his poems.

During the remainder of his life Whitman continued to revise, rearrange, expand, and republish *Leaves of Grass*. In 1865 he published a small volume called DRUM-TAPS, and a second edition with "Sequel to Drum-Taps," containing the Lincoln elegies, "O CAPTAIN! MY CAPTAIN!" and "WHEN LILACS LAST IN THE DOORYARD BLOOM'D." But this collection of war poems was annexed to *Leaves of Grass* in 1867, and incorporated in 1872.

In 1881 Whitman completely rearranged and extensively revised *Leaves of Grass*. This edition, published by James R. Osgood in Boston, established the final order and text of the poems included in the 1881 *Leaves of Grass*. Later poems were simply annexed without disturbing the established order. However, Whitman did make a few textual changes for a limited edition in 1888 which were not taken over into the 1892, or "Death-bed Edition." This final edition was printed while the poet was mortally ill, and friends had to do much of the proof-reading. A definitive text, incorporating the poet's revisions for the rare 1888 edition, is being prepared by Harold Blodgett and Sculley Bradley for the *Collected Writings* now in process of publication. See also I SING THE BODY ELECTRIC; A BACKWARD GLANCE.

Leaves of Grass, Preface to (1855), by WALT WHITMAN. Whitman did not reprint this *Preface* when his second (1856) edition appeared; in his later years he sometimes spoke of it in deprecatory terms. Yet in 1890, when Horace Traubel questioned him about it, he remarked, "I may have underrated the *Preface*. . . . At the moment it seemed vital and necessary: it seemed to give the book some feet to stand on." The *Preface* is written in a vein that Whitman's poetry and prose tracts were to make familiar: "The United States themselves are essentially the greatest poem. . . . Of all nations the United States with veins full of poetical stuff most needs poets and will doubtless have the greatest and use them the greatest. . . . The greatest poet does not moralize or make applications of morale: he knows the soul. . . . The English language befriends the grand American expression. . . . It is the powerful language of resistance . . . it is the language of common sense."

Beginning in 1856 and continuing thereafter, Whitman used the *Preface* as a quarry for whole units of poems. It contributed largely to at least four poems: BY BLUE ONTARIO'S SHORE, *Song of Prudence*, *To a Foil'd European Revolutionaire*, and *Poem of the Singers and the Words of Poems*, all in the 1856 edition; the last-named piece became the second part of *Song of the Answerer* (1881).

Leavitt, Dudley (b. Exeter, N.H., May 23, 1772—d. Sept. 15, 1851), maker of almanacs, editor. He compiled *Leavitt's Farmer's Almanack* (1797–1851), occasionally varying the title, also edited the *New Hampshire Register* (1811–17).

Lederer, John (b. Germany, fl. 1669–70), scholar, explorer. Nothing is known of Lederer except that he was of German origin and was described by a contemporary as "a modest, ingenious person, and a pretty scholar." He wrote in Latin an account of the geography, geology, and inhabitants of Virginia which Sir William Talbot, a member of the Virginia Council, happened to see. Talbot translated the book into English and it was published in London as *The Discoveries of John Lederer in three several marches from Virginia to the West of Carolina, March 1669—Sept. 1670* (1672).

Led Horse Claim (1883), a novel by Mary Hallock Foote (1847–1938). Mrs. Foote made a Western variation of the old Romeo-and-Juliet theme. Two rival mines stand on the opposite banks of Led Horse Gulch in Colorado. When the sister of the manager of one of them comes to visit him, she meets by chance the manager of the other, and they fall in love. The ensuing complications are straightened out sentimentally but not unplausibly. Mrs. Foote gave one of the earliest descriptions of a western mining camp, and the public liked the book.

Ledoux, Louis V[ernon] (b. New York City, June 6, 1880—d. Feb. 25, 1948), chemist, poet, critic, collector. Ledoux made his living as head of the firm of Ledoux & Co., chemists and assayers. But his pleasure was in writing poetry and meeting poets, in writing criticism, and in making collections of manuscripts and Japanese prints. His verses were pleasant, melodious, and skillful. He gathered them in several collections: *Songs from the Silent Land* (1905); *The Soul's Progress and Other Poems* (1906); *The Shadow of Aetna* (1914). He wrote a book on George Edward Woodberry (1917), another on *The Art of Japan* (1927), another on *Japanese Prints of the Primitive Period* (1942), among several on this favorite subject of his. Toward the beginning of the century Ledoux met EDWIN ARLINGTON ROBINSON and until the death of the poet remained his close friend and benefactor. Robinson often stayed with the family of Ledoux at his country home at Cornwall-on-the-Hudson. The correspondence between the two men is in the Robinson collection in Harvard's Widener Library; much other important Robinson material is in the Ledoux collection at the Library of Congress. An article by Léonie Adams describing it appeared in the *Library of Congress Quarterly Journal* (November, 1949).

Ledyard, John (b. Groton, Conn., 1751—d. Jan. 10, 1789), traveler, memoirist. After a very short college career at Dartmouth and a brief but eventful stint as a sailor, he went to England, where he enlisted as a marine on Captain James Cook's journey of exploration. He prepared from memory a *Journal of Captain Cook's Last Voyage to the Pacific Ocean* (1783), a vivacious, apparently reliable account which gives the only eye-witness story of Cook's murder in Hawaii. Ledyard became convinced that the Pacific offered great opportunities for traders. After presenting his ideas to Robert Morris, Jefferson, and John Paul

Jones, he journeyed into Russia to see the Empress Catherine about his project, but he was arrested as a spy and expelled. Undaunted, he planned an expedition to Africa, but died of a bilious attack at Cairo.

Ledyard's exciting career inspired JARED SPARKS to begin writing biography; his first sketch was a *Life of John Ledyard, the American Traveler* (1828), which passed through several editions and was later included in Sparks' *Library of American Biography* (1834–38, 1844–47).

Lee, Arthur (b. Westmoreland Co., Va., Dec. 21, 1740—d. Dec. 12, 1792), physician, lawyer, public official, writer on political topics. Lee received a medical degree at Edinburgh in 1764, was admitted to the bar in London in 1775. In the meantime he had practiced medicine at Williamsburg. In London he found himself in the midst of the controversy over the authorship of the *Letters of Junius* (1768–72) and over the recalcitrant American colonies. In London he published, using the signature "Junius Americanus," the satiric and clever *Appeal to the Justice and Interests of the People of Great Britain* (1774) and *A Second Appeal* (1775). He was made an agent of the Continental Congress in London (1775), the following year joined Benjamin Franklin and Silas Deane in Paris to negotiate a treaty with France. Highly suspicious in nature, he made violent accusations of treachery against Deane and Franklin; as a result both Lee and Deane were recalled (1779). Lee served in the Continental Congress (1782–84). He opposed the adoption of the Constitution and continued to have acrimonious controversies with numerous persons. He helped John Dickinson write THE LIBERTY SONG. C. H. Lee wrote *A Vindication of Arthur Lee* (1894).

Lee, Charles (b. England, 1731—d. Oct. 2, 1782), general in the Continental Army. Early in his career Lee fought under Braddock and in various parts of Europe. He was an ardent enemy of the Tory government, and the *Letters of Junius* have sometimes been attributed to him. During the American Revolution he was captured by the British, and documents were later discovered showing that he had made traitorous proposals to Lord Howe. At the Battle of Monmouth, contrary to Washington's orders, he retreated, and was later court-martialed. He died a bitter and half-insane man. John Richard Alden, in his judicious *General Charles Lee* (1951), presents whatever evidence he can in favor of Lee. Lee has appeared in novels about the Revolution, generally in an unfavorable light, as in J. E. Heath's *Edge-Hill* (1828); H. Morford's *The Spur of Monmouth* (1876); Howard Fast's *The Unvanquished* (1942); Willard Wiener's *Morning in America* (1942).

Lee, Hannah Farnham [Sawyer] (b. Newburyport, Mass., 1780—d. Dec. 27, 1865), novelist, biographer, historian. Her later writings were, as Evert Duyckinck put it, "domestic tales illustrating the minor morals of life and topics of education." These included *Three Experiments of Living* (1837); *Elinor Fulton* (1837); and *Sketches and Stories from Life, For the Young* (1850). She also wrote about Thomas Cranmer and the Huguenots, sculpture, and old painters; and in 1853 she published a sketch of a Negro slave (originally from San Domingo) who had been devoted to her sister— *A Memoir of Pierre Toussaint*.

Lee, [Nelle] Harper (b. Monroeville, Ala., April 28, 1926—   ), novelist. Her first novel, *To Kill a Mockingbird* (1960), won a Pulitzer Prize in 1961. It was a compassionate, gripping tale of a little girl in a small Alabama town in the 1930's whose father, a lawyer, defends a Negro accused of raping a white woman.

Lee, Henry ["Light-Horse Harry"] (b. Prince William Co., Va., Jan. 29, 1756—d. March 25, 1818), soldier, statesman. By the time he was twenty-six, Lee had terminated one of the most brilliant military careers in the annals of the American Revolution. Thereafter he tried his hand at local politics, espoused the Constitution, became governor of his state, later represented it in Congress. He tried in Baltimore to lead armed opposition to the War of 1812 and was severely mauled by a band of Federalists, who almost killed him. He spent the rest of his life in the West Indies, returning to die in the home of his close friend, General Nathanael Greene.

In December 1799 Lee wrote and introduced into the House of Representatives resolutions on the death of Washington; a week later (December 26) he delivered a eulogy on Washington. In both places occurred his memorable description of Washington: "First in war, first in peace, first in the hearts of his countrymen." (Possibly he said "fellow citizens" instead of "countrymen.") A reflected fame came from the renown of his son, ROBERT E. LEE. Another son, Henry (1787–1837), became a soldier and author; as an author he was attracted mainly to military subjects and figures, such as *The Campaign of 1781 in the Carolinas* (1824) and *Life of the Emperor Napoleon* (1835).

Lee himself wrote *Memoirs of the War in the Southern Department of the U.S.* (2 v., 1812). For the third edition of this work Robert E. Lee wrote a short biography, dealing almost entirely with his father's military achievements. *The Life and Letters of Col. Henry Lee*, compiled by John Torrey Morse, appeared in 1905. James Boyd wrote *Light-Horse Harry Lee* (1931).

Lee, Henry II. See under LEE, HENRY.

Lee, Irving J. (b. New York City, Oct. 27, 1909—d. May 23, 1955), teacher of public speaking, semanticist. In 1939 Lee became interested in general semantics, as developed by ALFRED KORZYBSKI, and thereafter applied its principles in his own special field. He had been on the staff of Northwestern University for about two decades, as Professor of public speaking. In 1941 Lee wrote *Language Habits in Human Affairs: An Introduction to General*

Semantics, a work that has been called the clearest and best in the field.

Lee, Manfred B. See ELLERY QUEEN.

Lee, Richard Henry (b. Westmoreland Co., Va., Jan. 20, 1732—d. June 19, 1794), statesman, pamphleteer. This quiet, determined man—the brother of ARTHUR LEE—was one of the most distinguished of the Virginia Lees. He was a radical, in the school of Jefferson. As early as 1759 he delivered a bold oration against slavery in the House of Burgesses; he took a leading part in the resistance to British measures; on June 7, 1776, he introduced into the Continental Congress resolutions that the colonies should be independent, form alliances, and organize a confederation; he signed the DECLARATION OF INDEPENDENCE. After the war Lee opposed the Constitution because it did not contain a Bill of Rights. He was the ablest of those who replied to the *Federalist* papers —in his *Letters of the Federal Farmer* (1787–88). When he became a senator from Virginia he helped secure the adoption of the first ten Amendments, himself writing the tenth one. J. H. Powell places his "stately petitions and official papers" on a plane with those of John Dickinson. His *Letters* (2 v., 1911–14) were edited by J. C. Ballagh.

Lee, Robert E[dward] (b. Westmoreland Co., Va., Jan. 19, 1807—d. Oct. 12, 1870), soldier. Lee was the son of HENRY "LIGHT-HORSE HARRY" LEE, a member of a distinguished Virginia family and a hero of the Revolutionary War. Young Lee early showed a talent for mathematics, and graduated from West Point second highest in his class. He served seventeen years as an engineer, was promoted for gallantry during the Mexican war, and was made superintendent at West Point from 1852 to 1855. He successfully put down John Brown's insurrection at Harper's Ferry in 1859.

As a Union soldier, a Whig, and a man deeply devoted to the Union, Lee had little sympathy with the secessionist feelings in the South; but his family's long residence in Virginia and the tradition in which he had been brought up made it impossible for him, as a man of honor, to fight against his native state. Accordingly, he declined the offer of the field command of the United States army in April, 1861, and a few days later, when he learned that Virginia had seceded and felt that war was imminent, resigned from the army completely.

Virginia lost no time in choosing Lee as a commander of her army and, although he had hoped to avoid taking part in the war, he felt obliged to accept. He was made field commander of the troops in May 1861, after two months of service as military advisor to President Davis (see JEFFERSON DAVIS), and hurriedly fortified Richmond against an attack by McClellan. Lee's strategy was highly successful during the first months of the war, in spite of the greater strength of the Union army and the relative inexperience of his own troops, but he was severely handicapped by the loss of

Stonewall Jackson (see THOMAS JONATHAN JACKSON) after the battle of Chancellorsville. After his defeat at the battle of Gettysburg, due more to the inexperience of his division commanders and the unwillingness of Longstreet to follow his orders than to his own tactics, Lee sought to resign as commander. He was persuaded to carry on, but heavy casualties, lack of supplies, and the superior strength of the Union army made victories after Gettysburg small and sporadic. He surrendered to ULYSSES S. GRANT at Appomattox Court House on April 9, 1865.

Lee became president of Washington College in September, 1865, and helped considerably to raise its standards; the school's name was later changed to Washington and Lee University in his honor.

An excellent soldier and strategist, Lee also had a rare ability to inspire confidence in his men, and was often considered the ideal of Southern manhood. He was the subject of many poems by Southerners, among them Father Abram Joseph Ryan's *The Sword of Robert Lee,* John Reuben Thompson's *Lee to the Rear,* and Donald Davidson's *Lee in the Mountains* (1938), which is set in the period of Lee's college presidency. Lee also appears in poems by Northern writers, notably Edgar Lee Masters' *Lee: A Dramatic Poem* (1926). Among novels dealing with Lee are Mary Johnston's *Cease Firing* (1912) and MacKinlay Kantor's *Long Remember* (1934). A basic biography of Lee was written (1904) by his son, Capt. Robert E. Lee. Many other lives have been written, most notably one by Douglas Freeman, which was awarded a Pulitzer Prize (4 v., 1934), and a later one by the same author, *Lee of Virginia* (1958). *The Wartime Papers of R. E. Lee* were edited by Clifford Dowdey, 1961.

Lee, Robert E[dwin] (b. Elyria, Ohio, Oct. 15, 1918—   ), playwright. Lee's greatest successes have been written in collaboration with Jerome Lawrence. *Inherit the Wind* was a thinly veiled story of the "Monkey Trial" of 1925 in Dayton, Tennessee, in which a young biology teacher, John T. Scopes, was called into court for teaching evolution, against the state law (see SCOPES TRIAL). The resulting debate between Clarence Darrow, for the defense, and William Jennings Bryan, for the prosecution, rocked the country during the Twenties. This vivid drama, which ran from 1955 to 1957 on Broadway, was later made into a highly successful movie. *The Gang's All Here* (1959) was suggested by the life of President Harding; in it a mediocre man is pushed to the forefront of public life by cynical politicians. Lawrence and Lee's *Only in America,* based on HARRY GOLDEN's book, was produced in the same year, but was not a success. On his own, Lee wrote the books for two Broadway musicals: *Look Ma, I'm Dancing* (1948), and *Shangri-La* (1956). For eight years, beginning in 1946, he wrote and produced the radio and TV program, *Favorite Story.* His book,

Television, the Revolution, was published in 1945.

Lee, William. The pen name of WILLIAM S. BURROUGHS.

Leech, Margaret (b. Newburgh, N.Y., Nov. 7, 1893—   ), novelist, biographer, historian. In collaboration with Heywood Broun she wrote *Anthony Comstock, Roundsman of the Lord* (1927), based largely on the *Reports of the Society for the Suppression of Vice.* In 1941 appeared her most widely read book, *Reveille in Washington,* a historical record of doings in the capital during the Civil War. It was based on extensive research, written in lively style and received the Pulitzer Prize in 1942. In 1959 she published *In the Days of McKinley.*

Leeds, Daniel (b. England, 1652—d. Sept. 28, 1720), almanac maker, author. The first job of the Philadelphia printer William Bradford was to do an almanac for Leeds. Leeds also wrote *The Temple of Wisdom for the Little World* (1688) and *News of a Trumpet Sounding in the Wilderness* (1697). He was a Quaker who quarreled with the Quakers of the colony. His sons, Titan and Felix Leeds, were also almanac makers. **Titan Leeds** (b. 1699—d. 1738) was the subect of a long-continued hoax by Benjamin Franklin, who solemnly prophesied in the first issue of his *Poor Richard's Almanac* (Dec. 19, 1732) that Leeds would die on Oct. 17, 1733. His joke was a repetition of one that Jonathan Swift in 1708 played on an English astrologer, John Partridge.

Lefevre, Edwin (b. Colombia, Jan. 23, 1871 —d. Feb. 22, 1943), stockbroker, newspaperman, novelist, short-story writer. As a newspaperman, Lefevre was an authority on Wall Street; he wrote *Reminiscences of a Stock Operator* (1923) and *The Making of a Stockbroker* (1925). Among his other books: *Wall Street Stories* (1901); *The Golden Flood* (1905); *Sampson, Rock of Wall Street* (1907); *The Plunderers* (1916). Lefevre was a clever storyteller, with an O. Henryish gift for the unexpected ending.

Le Gallienne, Eva (b. England, Jan. 11, 1899—   ), actress. Richard Le Gallienne's daughter made her debut in England in 1915, but since 1916 has played in American theaters. She was founder and director of the Civic Repertory Theater (1926) in New York. She has edited two plays by Henrik Ibsen, *Hedda Gabler* and *The Master Builder* (1955). *At 33* (1934) is her autobiography, continued in *With a Quiet Heart* (1953).

Legaré, Hugh Swinton (b. Charleston, S.C., Jan. 2, 1797—d. June 20, 1843), lawyer, public official, diplomat, scholar. Legaré was crippled at the age of five, a misfortune which led him to devote himself strenuously to literature and later to the law. He held various state and national offices, including the attorney-generalship in President Tyler's cabinet; when Daniel Webster resigned, he was appointed Secretary of State. He wrote learnedly on Demosthenes and Byron, assessed the significance of William

Cullen Bryant, helped start the SOUTHERN REVIEW (1828), and contributed essays to many periodicals. His writings were collected in two

volumes (1845–46) by his sister. His cousin, JAMES MATTHEWES LEGARÉ, dedicated an affecting poem to his memory, *On the Death of a Kinsman.*

Legaré, James Matthewes (b. Charleston, S.C., Nov. 26, 1823—d. Mar. 30, 1859), poet. A distant cousin of HUGH SWINTON LEGARÉ, he published only one book, *Orta-Undis and Other Poems* (1848). He had, says Edd Winfield Parks, "the precision of mind natural to a classicist." His early death prevented him from pursuing his considerable originality in verse forms and his gift of describing nature.

Legend of Sleepy Hollow, The (in *The Sketch Book,* 1820), a story by WASHINGTON IRVING. At Sleepy Hollow, now Tarrytown, N.Y., Irving places his rollicking tale. The "headless horseman" probably came from German folklore, perhaps from a story by J. K. A. Musäus (1735–1787). But the really memorable character in the story is ICHABOD CRANE. According to tradition, Irving modeled Ichabod on Jesse Merwin, a local schoolmaster who was Irving's lifelong friend; he similarly made Katrina Van Alen, a buxom girl of Kinderhook, sit for his portrait of Katrina Van Tassel. Brom Van Brunt is a well-drawn study of the extrovert (see BROM BONES). *The Headless Horseman,* adapted from the story by Stephen Vincent Benét, with music by Douglas Moore, was performed in Bronxville in 1936. See SLEEPY HOLLOW; SKETCH BOOK.

Legends of the Alhambra, The (1832; revised and enlarged, 1852), a "Spanish Sketch Book" by WASHINGTON IRVING. In 1826 Irving was appointed a diplomatic attaché to the American Legation in Madrid; his work seems to have been minimal, and he spent much of his time in traveling, research, and writing. He was deeply attracted by the romantic ruins of the Alhambra at Granada, and this book was the result. In dealing with the historic clashes of Spaniard and Moor, Irving inclines to the side of the Mohammedans who erected such a splendid civilization on Spanish soil. In writing of them Irving presents them as poetic, grotesque, heroic, picturesque. He tells tales of old times, some of them based on legends, others his own invention. There are mysterious caverns, concealed treasures, phantom cavalcades, deeds of magic and love.

Leggett, William (b. New York City, April 30, 1801—d. May 29, 1839), editor, political controversialist, teacher, poet, short-story writer. For a time Leggett's family lived in a pioneer settlement on the Illinois prairies. Later he served in the navy for more than three years; his sea experiences went into three books: two collections of poems, *Leisure Hours at Sea* (1825) and *Journals of the Ocean* (1826); also *Naval Sketches* (1834). His recollections of life in the Wild West went into *Tales and Sketches, by a Country Schoolmaster* (1829). In 1828 Leggett had established a weekly newspaper, the *Critic,* largely written and printed by himself; it ceased publication after six months. In 1829 he became an editor of the New York *Evening Post.* He sided with Jackson and wrote chiefly on such matters as free trade, the U.S. Bank, etc. A drop in the *Post's* circulation, owing to some of his articles, caused him to withdraw, and he started another paper of his own, the *Plaindealer;* but financial difficulties set in and it suspended publication after six months. Leggett became ill and died just before setting out to fill an appointment as diplomatic agent to Guatemala. His articles appear in *A Collection of the Political Writings of William Leggett* (1840). Whittier and Whitman read him eagerly, and it is likely that the latter drew many of his ideas of democracy from Leggett.

Legree, Simon. The chief villain in Harriet Beecher Stowe's UNCLE TOM'S CABIN. Brutal and mean, he flogs Uncle Tom to death when he refuses to reveal the hiding-place of two runaway women slaves. He himself dies an appropriate death in the novel, but he suffered a strange resurrection in Thomas Dixon's THE LEOPARD'S SPOTS (1902). Dixon "reconstructs" him, William S. Walsh pointed out, as a Republican leader under the carpet-bag régime. His name, as *Webster's New International* states, has become a synonym for "a cruel taskmaster, any brutal person."

Leisler, Jacob (b. Germany, 1640—d. 1691), colonial agitator. Leisler was a rabid anti-Catholic. He led a group of sympathizers in a successful rebellion (1689) to seize the government of New York City. He acted as governor for two years, but was not recognized by the British crown; he was deposed, tried for treason, and hanged. While in office Leisler called for a meeting in New York of delegates from all the colonies to make preparation for a war with Canada that he declared was coming. Seven delegates, chiefly representing New England, actually met (1690), and thus constituted the first Colonial Congress in America. Many persons were greatly offended at Leisler's execution; there were two bitterly opposed factions in New York for many years, the Leislerians and the anti-Leislerians. Leisler figured in two plays: Cornelius Mathews' *Jacob Leisler* (1848) and Elizabeth Smith's *Old New York, or, Democracy in 1689* (1853); and three novels: Joseph H. Ingraham's *Leisler* (1846), Edwin L. Bynner's *The Begum's Daughter* (1890), and Dorothy Grant's *Night of Decision* (1946).

Leisure Class, The Theory of the. See THEORY OF THE LEISURE CLASS, THE.

Leisy, Ernest E[rwin] (b. Moundridge, Kans., Dec. 22, 1887—   ), teacher, specialist in American literature. After teaching in various universities, Leisy became professor of English at Southern Methodist University in 1927. He edited various American clasics and anthologies in American literature, compiled important histories and bibliographies, particularly *The American Historical Novel* (1950). He also wrote *American Literature* (1929).

Leland, Charles Godfrey. See HANS BREITMANN.

Lemelin, Roger (b. Quebec, 1919—   ), novelist, short-story writer. Lemelin is regarded as the bad boy of present-day French-Canadian literature, and he takes it as a compliment that his stories are occasionally banned. He is a self-taught man. His novels are: *Au Pied de la Pente Douce* (1944); *Les Plouffe* (1948); and *Fantaisies sur les Péchés Capitaux* (1949). The first was translated into English by Samuel Putnam as *The Town Below* (1948). The book greatly shocked some devout readers by one scene in which the neighborhood drunk sets off a firecracker in church under the seat of his sanctimonious archenemy. After its publication he was awarded a Guggenheim Fellowship; he was also elected a member of the Royal Society of Canada. In *Les Plouffe,* which was translated by Mary Finch and published in 1950 as *The Plouffe Family,* his hero is an opera singer who enters a monastery but later leaves to fight the Nazis in Europe. His third book is a series of short stories about the seven deadly sins. Stuart Keate in 1950 noted that his "realistic spoofing marked a clean break from the simple romantic folk narratives which were as much a part of Quebec as the little hand-carved figures which American tourists purchase so doggedly each summer."

Lenape Indians. See DELAWARE INDIANS.

Lena Rivers (1856), a novel by MARY JANE HOLMES. Mrs. Holmes mixed in this sentimental story all the possible ingredients of a popular book; in her lifetime it sold more than two million copies. Lena's father has disappeared and is accused of a crime, and she goes from Massachusetts to Kentucky to live among her aristocratic relatives. But when an eligible young man appears, it is of course little Cinderella whom he chooses; moreover, Lena's father turns up—not guilty at all.

L'Enfant, Pierre Charles (b. France, 1754—d. 1825), soldier, engineer, architect. In 1777 L'Enfant volunteered in the American army. He spent his first winter at Valley Forge, was captured by the British at Charleston, S.C. (1780), was exchanged two years later, left the army in 1784. Thereafter he became a prominent architect; he remodeled New York City's old City Hall as a proposed Federal Hall, built an industrial city on the site where Paterson, N.J., now stands, and strengthened various fortifications. In 1791 Washington commissioned him to design the new Federal City in the District of Columbia, and L'Enfant drew plans for a city of radiating avenues, parks, and vistas, essentially the pattern that was later followed in the development of the city of Washington. But L'Enfant often got into trouble because of his haughtiness and his tendency to spare no expense. He quarreled with Congressional committees, was removed by Washington (1793), and spent the rest of his life trying to obtain adequate payment for his services. In 1909 his remains were removed to Arlington National Cemetery.

Lengyel, Emil (b. Hungary, April 26, 1895—), newspaperman, teacher, historian. Lengyel came to the United States in 1921, was naturalized in 1927, and served as an American correspondent for several European newspapers, then joined the staff of the School of Education of New York University (1939). His books are concerned to a large extent with Middle Europe and the Middle East: *Hitler* (1932); *Millions of Dictators* (1936); *The Danube* (1939); *Turkey* (1941); *America's Role in World Affairs* (1946); *They Came from Hungary* (1947); *The Middle East Today* (1954); *The Soviet Union, The Land and Its People* (1956); *One Thousand Years of Hungary* (1958); *The Changing Middle East* (1960).

Lennox, Charlotte Ramsay (b. New York City, 1720—d. Jan. 4, 1804), poet, novelist, dramatist. Charlotte Ramsay, daughter of the governor of the colony of New York, was sent at the age of fifteen to be educated in England, where she remained the rest of her life. She attained fame by burlesquing sentimental novels and then by writing just such novels as she had lampooned. *The Female Quixote; or, The Adventures of Arabella* (1752), which she dramatized in 1758 as *Angelica; or Quixote in Petticoats*, describes a young girl who tries to live like the heroines of fashionable French novels. *The Life of Harriet Stuart* (1750) is believed to be the first novel that had American scenes —the Hudson River, Albany, the Mohawk Valley. *The History of Henrietta* (1758, drama-

tized in 1769 as *The Sister, Sophia* (1762), and *Euphemia* (1790) were widely read sentimental novels.

Lenore (1831, 1843, 1845), a poem by EDGAR ALLAN POE. This lament on the death of a beautiful young woman passed through three drafts, each version quite different from its predecessor; and yet, as Phyllis Bartlett points out in *Poems in Process* (1951), each poem was in itself a success. Poe's theme was one that he often employed. He said in THE PHILOSOPHY OF COMPOSITION (1846) and elsewhere that the death of a woman both young and beautiful "is, unquestionably, the most poetical topic in the world." He treated this topic in verse and in his stories, among them MORELLA, BERENICE, LIGEIA.

Lenox, James (b. New York City, Aug. 19, 1800—d. Feb. 17, 1880), philanthropist, collector, editor, publisher. After graduating from Columbia Law School in 1820, James Lenox entered his father's business, until the death of his father left him sole heir to several million dollars. From that time he devoted himself to study, travel, and the collection of paintings, rare books, and manuscripts. A pioneer in the field of American history, he collected Americana as well as incunabula and Shakespeariana. In order to house his treasures, he built the Lenox Library in 1870 on Fifth Avenue between 70th and 71st Streets, and there immured himself, allowing an occasional scholar to study the collection.

He edited and privately printed a number of the books and manuscripts in his collection, among them *Washington's Farewell Address to the People of the U.S.* (1850); *Nicolaus Syllacius De Insulis Meridiani atque Indici Maris Nuper Invenius* (1859), a 15th-century account of Columbus' second voyage by Niccolò Scillacio, with a translation by John Mulligan; Shakespeare's *Plays in Folio* (1861); *The Early Editions of King James' Bible in Folio* (1861). He also published the *Letter of Columbus to Luis de Santagel* (1864), an account of the unique copy of the Spanish quarto edition in the Biblioteca Ambrosiano, Milan. His *Bibliographical Account of the Voyages of Columbus* (1861) appeared in the *Historical Magazine*.

One of New York's greatest philanthropists, Lenox founded and supported the Presbyterian Hospital, endowed the New York Public Library, and left his priceless collection of books, paintings, and manuscripts to New York City. See BENJAMIN FRANKLIN STEVENS.

Lenski, Lois (b. Springfield, Ohio, Oct. 14, 1893—), artist, illustrator, writer of books for children. After doing illustrations for other authors, Miss Lenski began writing books of her own for children; her first was *Skipping Village* (1927), and many others followed, including: *Bayou Suzette* (1944); *Boom Town Boy* (1948); *I Like Winter* (1950); *Prairie School* (1951); *Houseboat Girl* (1957); *Little Sioux Girl* (1958). Several of Miss Lenski's books won awards, among them *Strawberry Girl*

(1946), the story of a child who lives an uncertain life as a member of a central Florida "strawberry family." This was awarded the Newbery Medal.

Leonard, Daniel (b. Norton, Mass., May 18, 1740—d. June 27, 1829), political controversialist, lawyer. At first an adherent of the colonists, Leonard switched his views and went over to the Crown. He was an able writer. Under the pen name of Massachusettensis he contributed a series of letters (Dec. 12, 1774–April 3, 1775) to the *Massachusetts Gazette*, presenting the Tory side with much logic and occasional threats. JOHN ADAMS [2] replied to the letters under the pen name of Novanglus. Leonard's letters were reprinted as *The Origin of the American Contest with Great Britain* (1775). Leonard was later exiled, and was made chief justice of Bermuda.

Leonard, William Ellery (b. Plainfield, N.J., Jan. 25, 1876—d. May 2, 1944), teacher, poet, translator, critic. Leonard was a professor at the University of Wisconsin. He wrote books and monographs on literary subjects, meanwhile leading a busy private life, the best record of which is found in his autobiography, *The Locomotive God* (1927) and the sonnet sequence Two LIVES (1925). There also seems to be autobiography in the sonnets *A Man Against Time* (1945). He developed a morbid fear of going far from home, which from 1922 kept him practically a prisoner in his house. But these disturbances furnished ample food for Leonard's sonorous poetry. He published many collections of verse, including *The Vaunt of Man and Other Poems* (1912); *The Lynching Bee and Other Poems* (1920); *A Son of Earth* (his collected verse, 1928); *Man Against Time, an Heroic Dream* (posthumous, 1945). In addition he was an ardent student of Lucretius, translated his poems (1916; reprinted, 1921), wrote a study of his life and poetry (1942), and helped edit the Latin text.

Leonard, Zenas (b. Clearfield, Pa., March 19, 1809—d. July 14, 1857), fur trapper and trader, explorer, memoirist. Leonard was an intelligent and adventurous pioneer. He went west to St. Louis, joined an expedition that was making its way to California, and became a fur trapper. In 1833 he joined an expedition to Utah, Nevada, and California organized by John Reddeford Walker for Capt. Benjamin Louis Eulalie de Bonneville, a Frenchman who had graduated from West Point and held a two years' furlough to engage in exploration and the fur trade. Leonard was made official clerk of the expedition and kept a journal. Part of his account was published in the Clearfield *Republican*, later was printed as a *Narrative of the Adventures of Zenas Leonard, Written by Himself* (1839; edited by W. F. Wagner, 1904, by Milo M. Quaife, 1934). It is regarded as one of the most vivid and well-written depictions of a mountain man's life. Leonard became an Indian trader on the Santa Fe trail, at Fort Sibley, Mo.

Leopard's Spots, The (1902), a novel by

THOMAS DIXON, JR. Following his usual line of thought, Dixon endeavored to show in his story what frightful results would follow if the Negro were "lifted above his station." His title was of course derived from the Biblical verse and was intended to suggest to the reader what words preceded his quotation in *Jeremiah*, xiii, 23. There was included in the narrative the description of a Negro legislature. See SIMON LEGREE.

Le Page du Pratz, Antoine Simon (b. 1690?—d. 1775), historian. Probably a Fleming, Le Page du Pratz seems to have emigrated to Louisiana. He wrote a *Histoire de la Louisiane* (3 v., 1758), which was translated as *The History of Louisiana* (2 v., 1763).

Lerner, Alan Jay (b. New York City, Aug. 31, 1918–   ), author, lyricist, producer. After graduating from Harvard in 1940 Lerner went into freelance radio writing. He began collaborating with FREDERICK LOEWE for the musical comedy stage in 1942; their first successful production was BRIGADOON (1947). He worked with Kurt Weill on the musical *Love Life* (1948), then went to Hollywood to write the screenplays for *A Royal Wedding* and the Academy Award-winning *An American in Paris*. Again in collaboration with Loewe he wrote *My Fair Lady* (1956), which has had a long and successful run on Broadway, the movie *Gigi* (1958), and the Broadway musical *Camelot* (1960), based on T. H. White's book on King Arthur, *The Once and Future King* (1958).

Lerner, Max (b. Russia, Dec. 20, 1902–   ), teacher, lecturer, editor, radio commentator, columnist, essayist. Lerner has taught at Sarah Lawrence, at Harvard, at Brandeis, and at Williams; he helped edit the *Encyclopedia of the Social Sciences* and for two years edited the NATION; he contributed regularly to several New York newspapers and has been a popular lecturer. Described as "a neo-Marxian liberal," he has advocated social change but opposed Communism. Among his books: *It Is Later Than You Think* (1938); *Ideas Are Weapons* (1939); *The Consequences of the Atom* (1945); *Actions and Passions; Notes on the Multiple Revolution of Our Time* (1949); *America as a Civilization: Life and Thought in the United States Today* (1957); *The Unfinished Country* (1959). He edited the *Portable Veblen* (1948).

Leslie, Eliza (b. Philadelphia, Nov. 15, 1787—d. Jan. 1, 1858), short-story writer, writer on domestic science. Eliza Leslie was one of the first women in this country to realize the financial possibilities of domestic science. In 1827 she published *Seventy-Five Receipts for Pastry, Cakes, and Sweetmeats*, then turned to writing children's stories. She was also successful as a short-story writer. Her best known story, *Mrs. Washington Potts*, was awarded the *Godey's Lady's Book* prize in 1845. She wrote one novel, *Amelia, or a Young Lady's Vicissitudes* (1848), but was best known for her domestic works, such as *An American Girl's*

Book (1831), *Domestic Cookery Book* (1837), *The Lady's Receipt Book* (1846), and *The Behavior Book* (1853).

Leslie, Frank ["Henry Carter"] (b. England, March 29, 1821—d. Jan. 10, 1880). *Frank Leslie's Ladies Gazette of Fashion and Fancy Needle Work,* which was first issued in January, 1854, was started by a young engraver who had come to the United States in 1848, changing his name to avoid paternal censure. Toward the end of that year, Leslie purchased the *New York Journal,* a "story paper," and combined the two publications. In 1855, he brought out *Frank Leslie's Illustrated Newspaper,* a sixteen-page weekly modeled after the *London Illustrated News.* One of its innovations was the speed with which illustrations followed the events they portrayed: they appeared two weeks after publication of the news. This publishing achievement was not matched until after the Civil War. The weekly claimed a circulation of 100,000. Although *Harper's Weekly,* first published in 1857, offered strong competition, Leslie proceeded to issue *Frank Leslie's New Family Magazine* in 1857 and *Frank Leslie's Budget of Fun* the following year.

The *Illustrated Newspaper* was Leslie's outstanding venture. Its managing editor was Henry C. Watson, who had been an associate of Edgar Allan Poe on the *Broadway Journal.* Although fine writers such as Wilkie Collins and Walter Besant were contributors, the *Illustrated News* could not match the literary standards of *Harper's Weekly.* It never lacked variety, however. Its features ranged from a series on America's "Great West" to the "Housewife's Friend Department" to prizefight news. Although given to sensationalism, the magazine also did yeoman service in campaigns against political corruption. Unfortunate real estate investments nearly ruined Leslie and his enterprises. After his death, his astute widow continued the publications with considerable success, legally taking the name of Frank Leslie. In 1889, she sold the *Illustrated Newspaper* to W. J. Arkell and Russell B. Harrison, publishers of JUDGE. The magazine, later called *Leslie's Weekly,* never succeeded in regaining its earlier popularity. Later yet it became THE AMERICAN MAGAZINE and survived until 1956, thus covering a span of more than 100 years.

Leslie, Miriam Florence Folline Squier (b. New Orleans, c. 1836—d. Sept. 18, 1914), editor, travel writer, feminist. *Frank Leslie's Lady's Journal* was edited in 1871 by Miriam F. Squier, much-married future wife of FRANK LESLIE. In 1871 she published a translation of *Travels in Central America* by Arthur Morelet. She wrote *California: a Pleasure Trip from Gotham to the Golden Gate* in 1877, an account of a fantastically luxurious trip made with Frank Leslie after their marriage.

Leslie's death in 1880 left his widow deeply in debt, but by a number of astute moves, one of them being the legal adoption of the name "Frank Leslie," she managed his magazines so shrewdly that by her death she had built up a fortune of two million dollars. She wrote and published a number of feminist books: *Rents in our Robes* (1888); *Beautiful Women of Twelve Epochs* (1890); *Are Men Gay Deceivers?* (1893); *A Social Mirage* (1899); but she is of note chiefly for her able management and editorship of *Frank Leslie's Popular Monthly.* Joaquin Miller, meeting her on her California trip, was captivated by her charms and modeled Annette, the heroine of his novel called *One Fair Woman,* upon her. Madeleine B. Stern told her extraordinary story in *Purple Passage: The Life of Mrs. Frank Leslie* (1953).

Lester, Charles Edwards (b. Griswold, Conn., July 15, 1815—d. Jan. 29, 1890), lawyer, clergyman, consular official, translator, writer. A great-grandson of JONATHAN EDWARDS, Lester was a facile writer who wrote a number of readable books. Possibly the best were revelations of revolting living conditions in English industrial areas, made after a trip abroad: *The Glory and Shame of England* (2 v., 1841) and *The Condition and Fate of England* (1842). While serving as consul at Genoa he made translations of Italian writings and also, on his return, wrote *My Consulship* (1853). Although his books on England had aroused resentment in that country, he became New York correspondent of the London *Times.* He wrote many books thereafter—biographies of American heroes, a history of *Our First Hundred Years* (1874), a book on hospital conditions during the Civil War.

Letter to His Countrymen, A (1834), by JAMES FENIMORE COOPER. Alexander Cowie describes this as "one of the most unfortunate publications Cooper ever signed." Disgruntled with press attacks that had cost him much of his American audience, Cooper attacked the American press and charged it with subserviences to foreign opinions. Although something of a Jacksonian, he attacked the President for making certain diplomatic appointments, thereafter attacked Congress for seeking to destroy the executive branch of the government, and attacked the American people for being supine during these attempts to destroy their liberties. Cooper strongly emphasized the difference between the English governmental system, in which an oligarchy had taken away all powers from the King, and the American system, with its carefully planned system of checks. At the end he utters a farewell to writing and offers a dignified reproof to his public. But of course he did not stop writing; next year appeared THE MONIKINS, an allegory and satire that was really a continuation of the theme of his *Letter.*

Letters from a Farmer in Pennsylvania, to the Inhabitants of the British Colonies (1767–68 in the *Pennsylvania Chronicle;* in pamphlet form, 1768), twelve letters by JOHN DICKINSON, published anonymously. Dickinson, a Maryland lawyer who practiced and held public office in Delaware and Pennsylvania, assumed in these *Letters* the character of a small farmer with a few servants, a good library, and some well-read friends. He was impelled to share with his countrymen, he said, his "thoughts on some late transactions." His chief point was that, in the heated controversy between the colonies and the mother country, England, not America, was legally in the wrong. He supported his thesis with arguments taken from John Locke to the effect that the purpose of government was to protect the inalienable rights of property, in accordance with the social compact involved. He soberly urged the people to use the right of legal petition, then to employ measures against the purchase of British goods, finally—if all else failed—to resort to arms.

The *Letters* made a great sensation, and were reprinted in most colonial newspapers. There were one Irish, one French, six American, two English editions in book form. Burke probably was influenced by Dickinson, and Voltaire praised him. According to Moses Tyler, the appearance of the *Letters* was the most brilliant event in the literary history of the Revolution. Dickinson was given an honorary degree by Princeton College, was known the rest of his life as "the Pennsylvania farmer." The *Letters* were presented in a new edition (1903) by R. T. H. Halsey.

Letters from an American Farmer (1782), by Michel-Guillaume Jean de Crèvecœur writing under the pen name of J. Hector St. John (see under CRÈVECŒUR). Crèvecœur (1735–1813) was a French soldier who came to Canada to

fight under Montcalm and who later made explorations around the Great Lakes. He came to New York in 1759 after the fall of Quebec, took out naturalization papers six years later,

and became a surveyor and trader, traveling far west in the course of his work. In 1769 he married Mehitable Tippet and settled down as a farmer in Orange Co., N.Y. During the Revolution he refused to espouse either side, remained a pacifist; the rebels forced him to leave his farm, the royalists imprisoned him for two months. He finally managed to get to England, then to France. There he wrote his famous *Letters*, which were published in England (1782). Later he translated them into French, *Lettres d'un Cultivateur Américain* (1783). Franklin became his friend, he was elected to the Académie des Sciences, he was taken to visit the great naturalist Turgot. Under this new influence he veered to the side of the rebels, was appointed (1783) French consul in New York. In America he found his wife dead, his farm ruined. His children had vanished, but he found them later in Boston. He wrote an additional book dealing with his second fatherland, VOYAGE DANS LA HAUTE PENNSYLVANIE ET DANS L'ÉTAT DE NEW-YORK (1801). More than a century later some suppressed letters, a number of essays, and a short play were collected in *Sketches of 18th-Century America* (1925).

Crèvecœur was an ardent disciple of Rousseau; this strain somewhat weakens the vigor of his *Letters*, although he is realistic enough when considering the life of a frontier farmer. At times he writes merely rhetorically and elegantly, at other times he is eloquent, especially in the noted passage in which he answers his own question, "What is an American?" Many of the English Romantic poets and critics read the *Letters* with delight, and William Hazlitt found in them "not only the objects but the feelings of a new country."

Letters of a Loyalist Lady. See ANNE HULTON.

Letters of a Westchester Farmer. See SAMUEL SEABURY.

Letters of Jonathan Oldstyle, Gent. (1802–03), by WASHINGTON IRVING. Irving was only nineteen when these nine essays appeared in the New York *Morning Chronicle*, edited by his brother Peter. They were pirated by a New York publisher in 1824; at the same time five editions appeared in England. All traded on Irving's sudden burst of fame; the New York edition omitted his name and attributed the Letters to "the Author of the *Sketch Book*." All nine essays were for the first time assembled in a single book when Stanley T. Williams edited them for a facsimile edition with an introduction in 1941.

The *Letters* deal mostly with the theater, which Irving loved and wanted to improve. He satirizes the ranting plays, the vulgar audiences, the inaudible music, the critics. Some well-known personages of the day are held up for ridicule, under fictitious names. The style is obviously modeled on *The Spectator* and its American imitators, and foreshadows Irving's later writing.

Letters of the British Spy, The (published anonymously in the *Virginia Argus*, 1803; in book form, 1803), by WILLIAM WIRT. These ten *Letters* were in the best Addisonian style. They described Southern society, sometimes satirically but never offensively. Especially famous was Wirt's depiction of a blind preacher. The *Letters* were supposedly written by an English traveler in the United States, to a member of Parliament. The book became a best seller.

Letters to the Editor. These have always been a popular form of expression in the United States. In the Eighteenth and early Nineteenth Centuries the sage epistles of "Brutus" and "Vox Populi" or the more colloquial communications of a "Connecticutt Farmer," "Jonathan," or "A Kentucky Man" might occasionally gain wide circulation. Among the multitude of such correspondents, two writers stand out: BENJAMIN FRANKLIN, whose voluminous letters have been collected in Verner W. Crane's *Benjamin Franklin's Letters to the Press, 1758–75* (1950); and MARK TWAIN, whose frequent missives of protest or praise were eagerly received by editors. Today, large newspapers may receive well over a thousand letters daily, out of which six or eight will be printed, sometimes drastically shortened.

Levant, Oscar (b. Pittsburgh, Pa., Dec. 27, 1906—   ), pianist, composer, memoirist, radio performer. A thoroughly competent composer and pianist, Levant became additionally well-known for his appearances on the air (especially in the program INFORMATION PLEASE), in movies, and on television, in the course of which he built a reputation as the curmudgeon of the artistic world. This side of his character was revealed in an autobiographic volume called *A Smattering of Ignorance* (1940). Much of the book is about music, particularly as originated and played in Hollywood. He tells a good deal about George Gershwin, but is no unqualified admirer.

Levertov, Denise (b. England, Oct. 24, 1923—   ), poet. Of Welsh and Jewish parentage (her father was a convert and priest of the Anglican Church and a leading authority on the Cabala), Denise Levertov was educated at home in a background of literary activity and religious speculation. She came to this country in 1948, the bride of an American who had been studying in Europe under the G.I. Bill. Recognized in England during her early twenties as a poet of considerable promise, she has been acclaimed in recent years as one of the most accomplished and original of the younger poets. Her work, graceful, alive, wonderfully lucid and tuned, is now distinctly of the American school, deriving from the poetry of William Carlos Williams and Wallace Stevens and related to such contemporaries as ROBERT CREELEY and Robert Duncan. Among her collections are *Overland to the Islands* (1958), *With Eyes at the Back of Our Heads* (1960) and *Here and Now* (1957).

Levin, Harry T[uchman] (b. Minneapolis, Minn., July 18, 1912—   ), teacher, critic, editor. Levin, a graduate of Harvard, became a member of its faculty in 1934, and chairman of its Department of Comparative Literature in 1946. His literary criticism is austere, scholarly, and acute, especially in the more contemporary field. Among his books: *The Broken Column: A Study in Romantic Hellenism* (1931); *James Joyce: A Critical Introduction* (1941); *Toward Stendhal* (1945); *The Overreacher: A Study of Christopher Marlowe* (1952); *Symbolism and Fiction* (1956); *Contexts of Criticism* (1957); *The Power of Blackness: Hawthorne, Poe, Melville* (1958, paperback 1960); *The Question of Hamlet* (1959; paperback 1961); *The Gates of Horn: A Study of Five French Realists* (1962). Much of Levin's work has been translated and anthologized. His *James Joyce*, a pioneer work, has been particularly appreciated and won praise from Joyce himself. Levin edited Ben Jonson, the Earl of Rochester, and Flaubert, as well as *The Portable James Joyce* (1945), and *Perspectives of Criticism* (1950).

Levin, Meyer (b. Chicago, Oct. 7, 1905—   ), newspaperman, novelist, actor, writer, photographer. Levin worked for several years as a photographer, reporter, feature writer, and columnist on Chicago papers; his experiences formed the basis of his first novel, REPORTER (1929). Because of a threatened libel suit, the novel was withdrawn from circulation. In the meantime he had been writing stories of Jewish life, printed in the *Menorah Journal*. He lived in Paris for a while, with the idea of becoming a painter, went on to Palestine, returned to the United States, worked as an actor, a newspaperman, a maker of documentary films. In *The Golden Mountain* (1932) Levin retold stories of the Chassidim, a remarkable sect of medieval Jewish mystics. *The Old Bunch* (1937) is a picture of his own generation, the interwoven lives of eleven boys and eight girls who had all graduated from high school in 1921. *Citizens* (1940) is a fictional account of a tragic strike. *If I Forget Thee* (1947) is a picture pageant of modern Palestine. *In Search* (1950) tells the story of Levin's own restless career. Other books of his include *Frankie and Johnnie* (1930); *Yehuda* (1931); *My Father's House* (1947); *Compulsion* (1956), a novel about the Loeb-Leopold case which was dramatized and filmed. *Eva* (1959) concerns a Jewish girl in flight from the Nazis during World War II.

Levine, Isaac Don (b. Russia, Feb. 1, 1892—   ), newspaperman, editor, biographer, authority on Russia. Levine came to the United States in 1911, worked on the New York *Tribune*, the Chicago *Daily News*, and other papers; he wrote frequently on Russia. Many of his later works have been sharply anti-Communist. Among his books: *The Russian Revolution* (1917); *Red Smoke* (1932); *Mitchell, Pioneer of Air Power* (1943). He compiled *Letters from Russian Prisons* (1925), edited Jan Valtin's *Out of the Night* (1941), collaborated with Gen. Walter G. Krivitsky in accounts of his experiences in Russia (1939) and with Oksana Kosenkina in her story of her escape from Russian custody (1950). He also wrote *Stalin's*

Great Secret (1956) and *Mind of an Assassin* (1959).

Levinger, Lee Joseph (b. Burke, Ida., March 4, 1890—   ), clergyman, historian, memoirist. Levinger served as rabbi with various Jewish synagogues and organizations, lectured on philosophy at Ohio State University, served as a chaplain abroad in World War I. Among his books: *Jewish Chaplain in France* (1921); *Anti-Semitism in the U.S.* (1925); *History of the Jews in the U.S.* (1930); *The Jewish Student in America* (1937). He wrote *Story of the Jew* (1928) and *Folk and Faith* (1942) in collaboration with his wife, **Elma Ehrlich Levinger** (b. Chicago, Oct. 6, 1887—d. Jan. 27, 1958). Mrs. Levinger was also the author of a number of books for young readers including: *The Golden Door* (1947); *Albert Einstein* (1949); *Galileo* (1952); *They Fought for Freedom* (1953); *Leonardo da Vinci* (1954); *Jewish Adventures in America* (1955).

Levy, Newman (b. New York City, Nov. 30, 1888—   ), lawyer, humorist, playwright. Levy's comedy *$1200 a Year* (1920), written with Edna Ferber, deals with the struggle of a college profesor to live on his salary. Levy also published several volumes of clever light verse, including *Opera Guyed* (1923); *Gay But Wistful* (1925); *Saturday to Monday* (1930); *My Double Life: Adventures in Law and Letters* (1958), an autobiography.

Lewis, Alfred Henry ["Dan Quin"] (b. Cleveland, Ohio, *c.* 1858—d. Dec. 23, 1914), journalist, short-story writer. Lewis was admitted to the bar at an early age. In 1881 he went west and became a hobo cowboy, writing for the Las Vegas *Optic* and wandering about southeastern Arizona. In 1885 he attempted to practice law in Kansas City, Mo., filling his spare time with politics and journalism. In 1890 he sent a story to the Kansas City *Times*, purporting to be an interview with an old cattleman, which was copied by newspapers all over the country. A character was born.

Lewis wrote many of these stories, all told by the "Old Cattleman," whose dry philosophy and homely humor follow traditions established by the American humorists of the 19th century. WOLFVILLE (1897); *Sandburrs* (1900); *Wolfville Days* (1902); *Wolfville Nights* (1902); *Wolfville Folks* (1908); and *Faro Nell and Her Friends* (1913) were very popular in their day. In 1894 Lewis became one of the ablest editors of the growing chain of Hearst papers. He also wrote a number of fictionized biographies and two books of underworld life, *Confessions of a Detective* (1906) and *The Apaches of New York* (1912).

Lewis, Charles Bertrand ["M. Quad"] (b. Liverpool, Ohio, Feb. 15, 1842—d. Aug. 21, 1924), newspaperman, columnist, dime novelist, playwright. Originally a printer, Lewis went to college for a while, served in the Union Army, worked on various newspapers in Michigan, particularly the Detroit *Free Press* (1869–91), then on the New York *World*. Early in his newspaper career he was involved in a steam-ship fire on the Ohio, and his humorous account of *How It Feels to Be Blown Up* gave him a national reputation. As a columnist he wrote about the Lime-Kiln Club, a forerunner of humorous accounts of Negro social life. Among his books: *Quad's Odds* (1875); *Goaks and Tears* (1875); *Bessie Bane, or, The Mormon's Victim* (1880); *The Comic Biography* (1881?); *Brother Gardner's Lime-Kiln Club* (1882, 1887); *Sawed-Off Sketches* (1884); *Sparks of Wit and Humor* (1887); *Trials and Troubles of the Bowser Family* (1889, 1902). A play of his, *Yakie*, was produced in 1884.

Lewis, Estelle [or Stella]. Pen name of SARAH ANNA BLANCHE ROBINSON LEWIS.

Lewis, Lloyd [Downs] (b. Pendleton, Ind., May 2, 1891—d. April 21, 1949), newspaperman, editor, writer. Lewis was a capable and versatile newspaperman who wrote drama criticism and sports news, mainly in Chicago papers, and became managing editor of the Chicago *Sun-Times*. His books were equally versatile. He started with an excellent book on Lincoln, *Myths after Lincoln* (1929); with HENRY JUSTIN SMITH he wrote a history of Chicago (1929), then a biography of General W. T. Sherman (1932), which won a Pulitzer Prize. In collaboration with SINCLAIR LEWIS he wrote a play, *Jayhawker* (1934). With Smith once more, he wrote *Oscar Wilde Discovers America* (1936) and went on to some miscellaneous volumes. In the years before his death he concentrated on what was intended to be a comprehensive biography of Ulysses S. Grant. Only the first volume, CAPTAIN SAM GRANT (1949), appeared after Lewis' death; it won wide praise for its careful research and skillful storytelling. His publisher later issued a little book of *Letters from Lloyd Lewis* (1950); they described the steps he had taken in preparing his book on Grant.

Lewis, Meriwether (b. Albemarle Co., Va., Aug. 18, 1774—d. Oct. 11, 1809), explorer, soldier, governor. Manager of his family plantation at eighteen, Meriwether Lewis served in the suppression of the Whiskey Rebellion of 1794, joined the regular army shortly afterwards, and was stationed at several frontier posts, where he learned Indian languages and customs. When Jefferson became President he asked Lewis to serve as his private secretary. Lewis' project to search for a land route to the Pacific was encouraged by Jefferson, and Congress appropriated $2,500 for the purpose. With Capt. WILLIAM CLARK as joint commander, Lewis set out from St. Louis, Mo., in the spring of 1804 on the now-famous Lewis and Clark Expedition. Undeterred by attacks from hostile Indians and unbelievable hardships, the expedition moved on to the Pacific coast. Lewis kept a detailed diary of the expedition, remarkable for its scientific accuracy and its stately 18th-century style. He was appointed governor of the Louisiana Territory, an office he held until his death.

Lewis appears in many novels, including Eva E. Dye's *The Conquest* (1902); Emerson

Hough's *The Magnificent Adventure* (1916); Ethel Hueston's *Star of the West* (1935); Donald C. Peattie's *Forward the Nation* (1942); Odell and Willard Shepard's *Holdfast Gaines* (1946). He appears also in Robert Penn Warren's *Brother to Dragons: A Tale in Verse and Voices* (1953). John Bakeless described *Lewis and Clark; Partners in Discovery* (1947). Lewis and Clark's *History of the Expedition* was edited by Nicholas Biddle (1814). R. G. Thwaites collected all the *Original Journals of the Lewis and Clark Expedition* (8 v., 1904–05), a great work of which Bernard De Voto made a one-volume abridgment (1953). See SACAJAWEA.

Lewis, Sarah Anna Blanche Robinson [pen name **Estelle Lewis,** sometimes **Stella**] (b. near Baltimore, Md., April, 1824—d. Nov. 24, 1880), poet, dramatist. Mrs. Lewis' fame rests entirely on mentions of her by EDGAR ALLAN POE. He liked a poem of hers called *Forsaken* and praised it warmly, later wrote a eulogistic article about her in the *Democratic Review* (August, 1848). She was a mildly capable and very sentimental poet whose verses were collected in *Records of the Heart* (1844) and *Child of the Sea and Other Poems* (1848). *Sappho* (a play, 1868) was translated into Greek and played in Athens. In *The Union* (March, 1848) Poe addressed an anagrammatic poem, *An Enigma,* to Mrs Lewis; and in a letter to her in 1849 he calls her "my dear sister Anna" and "my sweet sister." There is evidence of the fact that Mrs. Lewis subsidized Poe, and that his attitude was hypocritically flattering toward what he elsewhere called her "rubbish."

Lewis, [Harry] Sinclair (b. Sauk Centre, Minn., Feb. 7, 1885—d. Jan. 10, 1951), novelist. Lewis, the son of a country doctor, was a gangling, awkward boy with few friends, self-conscious and unsure of himself, and something of a dreamer. He spent his freshman year at Oberlin College in Ohio and then transferred to Yale; his first stories and poems, in imitative 19th-century verse, were published in the college literary magazine. In his last year he interrupted his studies at Yale and for a month worked as a janitor in Upton Sinclair's socialistic colony at HELICON HALL in Englewood, New Jersey. He contributed more short stories and poems to a number of magazines, and after his graduation from Yale in 1908, spent several years in newspaper and editorial work in various parts of the country. He then returned to New York and published his first novel, *Hike and the Aeroplane* (1912), a story for boys. OUR MR. WRENN: THE ROMANTIC ADVENTURES OF A GENTLE MAN (1914) deals with an American in Europe, and was praised for its realism, humor, and mild satire; *The Trail of the Hawk,* which Lewis felt prefigured Lindbergh's career, is based to some extent on Lewis' own boyhood and young manhood. It has passages of satire that foreshadow his later work, but is primarily sentimental. It was also praised by reviewers, some of whom considered Lewis to be one of the most promising young American writers. In *The Job: An American Novel* (1917) Lewis

first presented controversial subjects, in particular the theme of the young woman entering the masculine world of business and the resultant conflicts between marriage and a career. Although better than the two preceding novels,

Bettmann Archive

The Job was viewed more unfavorably by the critics, many of whom objected to the realism of the book and its unidealized treatment of the American business world. *The Innocents* (1917), a sentimental picture of an elderly couple and of village life, and *Free Air* (1919) were neither so good nor so well received as Lewis' earlier books.

Quite different are the novels of Lewis' next period, which begin with MAIN STREET (1920), a devastatingly satiric novel of the dullness and cultural deadness of the small town. Lewis drew on his boyhood knowledge of the small midwestern town to create Gopher Prairie, which was to become a symbol of the provincialism and rigidity of small towns everywhere. The novel was immensely successful, and established Lewis as a significant American novelist, the first to so completely demolish the sentimental "myth of the happy village" which had dominated, with few exceptions, stories of American rural life since the 19th century. BABBITT (1922) is in many ways an extension of *Main Street,* with the emphasis shifted from the town to George F. Babbitt, citizen, booster, and epitome of small-town attitudes and interests. Yet Babbitt is also something more than an embodiment of an attitude; in his struggle for success, his gregariousness, his unimaginative and unperceptive acceptance of his surroundings, and in his very averageness he has become something of a negative folk hero who, though the object of scorn and ridicule, is often pathetic but never quite despicable.

Lewis spent several months traveling in the Caribbean with the bacteriologist PAUL DE KRUIF in preparation for his next book, ARROWSMITH (1925), Lewis' favorite and possibly his greatest novel. A story of a young doctor and his struggle between his personal desires and his idealistic dedication to his scientific work, *Arrowsmith* is without much of the biting satire of *Main Street* and *Babbitt* and presents in its main character a theme lacking in Lewis' earlier novels, that of a man in search of truth. *Arrowsmith* was awarded a Pulitzer Prize, which Lewis refused to accept on the grounds that the prize was awarded not for literary merit but for the best presentation of "the wholesome atmosphere of American life." Even *Arrowsmith*, though not a direct satire on the materialistic and valueless aspects of American life, could hardly be said to present its atmosphere as "wholesome."

Mantrap (1926), which was based on an expedition Lewis made into the Canadian wilderness, was dismissed by most reviewers as "Lewis in a light vein." It was followed by ELMER GANTRY (1927), a mercilessly satiric story of a Midwestern minister and evangelist. It was received with even more outraged clamor than *Main Street*, but those who liked it praised it highly for its accurate reportage and for Lewis' ability to capture precisely the atmosphere and quality of a type of midwestern revivalism. The characters of Frank Shallard and Andrew Pengilly, Lewis' "ideal" religious men, went unnoticed by those who denounced Lewis as an instrument of the devil, as did the entire import of the book, which was not so much an attack on religion itself as to the dehumanized society which made it possible for Elmer to get "everything from the church and Sunday School, except, perhaps, any longing whatever for decency and kindness and reason."

The Man Who Knew Coolidge (1928), which was extended from an original short story, was another attack on the small businessman, less successful than *Babbitt*. DODSWORTH (1929) returned somewhat to the tenor of Lewis' first books, in which the middle westerner is compared favorably to the outsider. Sam Dodsworth, a prosperous midwestern businessman who has some appreciation of literature and art, takes his shallow and well-groomed wife, Fran, to Europe, where most of the novel takes place. Fran has an affair with an Austrian count, and Sam finally leaves her to marry a more congenial woman. Sidney Howard collaborated with Lewis to produce a dramatic version of *Dodsworth* in 1934.

Lewis was awarded the Nobel Prize for literature in 1930, the first American novelist to win such an honor. After *Dodsworth*, however, his work began to decline, although he continued to write prolifically. His works of this last period include ANN VICKERS (1933), the story of a social worker; *Work of Art* (1934), on hotel-keeping; IT CAN'T HAPPEN HERE, perhaps the most arousing of Lewis' later work, a strong warning on the possibility of a fascist dictatorship in the United States; *The Prodigal Parents* (1938), on the relations between the generations; *Bethel Merriday* (1940), about a girl ambitious for success in the theater; *Gideon Planish* (1943), a satire on a certain type of materialistic college president; CASS TIMBER-LANE (1945), a story of an older man's love for his young and unsuitable wife; KINGSBLOOD ROYAL (1947), on white superiority and racial prejudice; THE GOD-SEEKER (1949), about a missionary in Minnesota in the 1840's; and a posthumously published work, *World So Wide* (1951), which returns to the theme of the American in Europe, which Lewis had treated in *Our Mr. Wrenn* and *Dodsworth*.

Lewis, always an excellent mimic and an irrepressible speaker, became interested in the theater and wrote a dramatic version of *It Can't Happen Here* (play, 1936), in which he played the leading role of Doremus Jessup, a middle-aged newspaper editor. *Jayhawker* (1934), which Lewis wrote in collaboration with Lloyd Lewis, amused audiences but was not notably successful.

Almost all Lewis' books were based either on painstaking research into the subject (as his work with Paul de Kruif in preparation for *Arrowsmith*, his study of real estate for *Babbitt*, and his visits to ministers and churches for *Elmer Gantry*) or on situations or places with which Lewis himself was well acquainted. Thus his boyhood in Sauk Center provided the background for *Main Street;* his travels in Europe contributed to *Dodsworth* and *World So Wide;* his experience as an actor and playwright, to *Bethel Merriday*. There is much disguised biography in Lewis' work, and many suggestions of Lewis himself in some of his characters. Searching for "the 'reality' of America," he found the oppression of freedom and value by rigid provincialism; for the innocence of the American ideal, the corruption of a money-oriented civilization. A romancer as well as a realist and satirist, he loved the Babbitts and Main Streets of America even as he deplored them; gifted with an amazing ability for mimicry, he could impersonate his characters or deliver a Babbitt-like Rotarian speech at will, as the accuracy of tone and verisimilitude of his novels demonstrate; yet his writing is rough and his style can best be described as reportorial.

Critics have noted Lewis' resemblance to Dickens in his caricatures, his range and variety of human types, and occasionally his humor. Mencken's influence is apparent particularly in *The Trail of the Hawk*, *Main Street*, and *Elmer Gantry;* Booth Tarkington's, in *The Prodigal Parents;* and Gustave Flaubert's, in *Main Street*. Lewis himself appears as Larry Harris in William Rose Benét's poem *The Dust Which Is God*, and as Lloyd McHarg in Thomas Wolfe's *You Can't Go Home Again*. It has been suggested that Barnaby Conrad's novel *Dangerfield* was based on Lewis' last years, during part of which time Conrad was Lewis' secretary.

Lewis' first wife, Grace Hegger Lewis, wrote of their life together in *With Love From Gracie* (1956) and in a thinly disguised novel, *Half a Loaf* (1927). Harry Maule and Melville Caine edited *The Man From Main Street: A Sinclair Lewis Reader, 1903–1950* (1952), and the same year Harrison Smith edited a collection of Lewis' letters. Mark Schorer's biography, *Sinclair Lewis: An American Life,* appeared in 1961.

Lewis and Clark Expedition. See WILLIAM CLARK, MERIWETHER LEWIS.

Lewisohn, Ludwig (b. Germany, May 30, 1883—d. Dec. 31, 1955), editor, teacher, critic, writer. Lewisohn came to the United States in 1890 and studied at the College of Charleston, S.C. Later he taught at Wisconsin, Ohio State, and Brandeis Universities. An authority on German literature, he translated books by Hauptmann, Wassermann, Rilke, and others. But he was also well acquainted with the literatures of other lands. Among his critical volumes: *The Modern Drama* (1915); *The Spirit of Modern German Literature* (1916); *The Poets of Modern France* (1918); *The Drama and the Stage* (1922); *The Story of American Literature* (1937); *Goethe* (2 v., 1949). In his later years Lewisohn turned to Jewish problems and wrote: *Israel* (1925); *Rebirth* (ed. 1935); *The American Jew* (1950); and others. The Jewish theme also entered some of his fiction. Among his novels: *The Broken Snare* (1908); *Don Juan* (1923); *The Case of Mr. Crump* (1926); *Roman Summer* (1927); *The Island Within* (1928); *The Golden Vase* (1931); *The Last Days of Shylock* (1931); *Trumpet of Jubilee* (1937); *Renegade* (1942); *Anniversary* (1948); *In a Summer Season* (1955). Lewisohn also wrote two volumes of reminiscence: *Up Stream* (1922) and *Mid-Channel: An American Chronicle* (1929).

Ley, Willy ["Robert Willey"] (b. Germany, Oct. 2, 1906—), scientist, editor, author. Willy Ley forsook the realm of science fiction —and with it his pen name, Robert Willey— to concern himself with factual science. He served as a research engineer for the Washington Institute of Technology, and is now information specialist, U.S. Commerce Department. Among Ley's books: *Rockets, Missiles and Space Travel* (17th printing revised 1960); *Exotic Zoology* (1959); *Engineers' Dreams* (4th printing 1959); and *The Exploration of Mars,* written in collaboration with Wernher Von Braun (2nd printing 1960).

Leypoldt, Frederick (b. Germany, Nov. 17, 1835—d. March 31, 1884), editor, publisher. Leypoldt, along with Henry Holt, founded the firm of Leypoldt & Holt in 1866, which became Henry Holt & Co. in 1873. Leypoldt was interested in increasing the reading of books and in supplying bibliographical information. He wrote *A Reading Diary of Modern Fiction* (1881), with Lynds E. Jones compiled *The Books of All Time* (1882), and founded such trade journals and manuals as the *Library Bulletin* (1868), the *Publishers' and Stationers' Weekly* (1872, which after several changes of name became PUBLISHERS' WEEKLY), and the *Uniform Trade List Annual* (1873, which became the PUBLISHERS' TRADE LIST ANNUAL). He was also one of the founders of the LIBRARY JOURNAL (1876) and its publisher till his death.

Libbey, Laura Jean (b. New York City, March 22, 1862—d. Oct. 25, 1924), novelist. She wrote highly sentimental, sometimes lachrymose stories that attained wide popularity. Among her books: *A Fatal Wooing* (1883); *Junie's Love Test* (1886); *Miss Middleton's Lover* (1888); *That Pretty Young Girl* (1889); *A Mad Betrothal* (1890); *Parted by Fate* (1890); *We Parted at the Altar* (1892). It is said that Theodore Dreiser was influenced by Miss Libbey as well as by Balzac.

libel. Since authors deal with words, they are often concerned with that branch of jurisprudence which deals with civil and criminal liability for personal defamation conveyed in writing and print. Aside from misstatements of facts regarding a person in a nonfiction book or article, an author is most likely to be troubled by libel suits if he introduces characters in an unfavorable light and these characters can be identified with living persons; even if he introduces them favorably, he may still be sued and restrained for "invasion of privacy." An odd case was that of Serge Koussevitzky, Boston Symphony Orchestra conductor, against Moses Smith, a Boston music critic who had written a biography of the conductor (1947). In the course of the subsequent proceedings, ultimately decided in favor of the author, Justice Bernard L. Shientag said, in part: "The right-of-privacy statute does not apply to an unauthorized biography of a public figure unless the biography is fiction or novelized in character."

There are two kinds of defamation to which an author (also any other type of artist) may be subjected. He may be accused of plagiarism or of printing a book under his own name actually written by somebody else. Calling an author a plagiarist is a libel *per se* and entitles the author to claim damages. A sensitive author always feels that an unfavorable notice is a libel, but the law is against him. One judge concluded that criticism of the works of an author is not libel "unless the criticism be grossly false and work a special damage to the proprietor of the book at which the strictures are leveled."

Three volumes which discuss the laws of libel and slander are Morris L. Ernst and Alexander Lindey's *Hold Your Tongue* (1932); Philip Wittenberg's *Dangerous Words* (1947); Samuel Spring's *Risks and Rights in Publishing, Television, Radio, Motion Pictures, Advertising, and the Theater* (1952).

Liberator, The. A name given to two magazines: [1] an abolitionist journal founded at Boston by WILLIAM LLOYD GARRISON (1831–65); and [2] a left-wing magazine founded by MAX EASTMAN which superseded the MASSES in 1918 and was absorbed in 1924 by the *Labor Herald.* Garrison's magazine aroused both enthusiasm and violent opposition, and in the South laws were passed suppressing it. The second *Liberator* was a pale imitation of the *Masses.*

Liberty's Call (*Pennsylvania Packet,* 1775), a

poem by John Mason. After its publication in the *Packet,* it appeared as a broadside. It is also attributed to FRANCIS HOPKINSON.

Liberty Song, The (Boston *Gazette,* July 18, 1768), a poem by JOHN DICKINSON. This was called originally *A Song for American Freedom.* Some of the lines were written by Dickinson's friend ARTHUR LEE. The song was written to a tune that David Garrick had made popular in England, William Boyce's *Hearts of Oak.* The direct occasion for the song was the fact that the Massachusetts legislature had endorsed a *Circular Letter* denouncing new British taxes. The song caught on immediately and became the first hit in American history; it was published on a separate music sheet, the first to appear in the colonies. The song became the official tune of the Sons of Liberty, a secret order that was organized to protest against unjust taxation. The Tories resented the song and prepared a parody, which began, "Come shake your dull noodles, ye bumpkins, and bawl." A parody replied to this parody, and then the Tories wrote another version, beginning with a threat, "Ye simple Bostonians, I'll have you beware."

libraries in the U.S. The first libraries in the United States were privately owned by colonists, some of whom donated their collections to newly founded colleges. Harvard received its first collection of 400 books from John Harvard in 1638. The libraries of Yale and William and Mary were established in 1700. In 1699 the Bishop of London authorized Dr. Thomas Bray to establish parochial libraries for missionaries, and thirty parish libraries were set up in Maryland. Other parish or church libraries were founded on this pattern, especially in the South; though designed for the clergy they were open to the public.

To secure funds for books needed by the Junto Literary Society, BENJAMIN FRANKLIN in 1731 founded the Philadelphia Library Co. This was the first of many subscription libraries developed during the next century to meet the needs of literary societies, businessmen, apprentices, and others. The Athenaeum, mercantile, and apprentice libraries were of this type. There was a fee for service, but since it was small and uniform the libraries were in effect public. As the tax-supported library developed, many of the subscription libraries gave their collections to their communities, though some are still in existence.

The first town library was established through a bequest in Salisbury, Conn., in 1803 and was briefly supported by the community. Other communities found the school district a smaller and more convenient library unit. Books, mostly adult, were kept in the schoolhouse. New York was the first state to enact legislation for free libraries but did not provide for their tax support until 1845. The town and school district in New England and the township and school district in the Middle West became and remained the popular base for libraries.

Gradually the idea of municipally supported public libraries spread. The Massachusetts General Court in 1848 authorized Boston to raise $5,000 annually for library support. In 1851 the act was extended to all Massachusetts towns; soon New Hampshire, Maine, Vermont, and Ohio passed similar laws. Today all states except Delaware permit town libraries and almost 7,000 of 7,871 public libraries in the continental United States are city-owned. CHARLES JEWETT, Boston's first librarian, had much to do with this development and is called the Father of the American Library Movement. He called the first conference of librarians in New York to discuss common problems. It was not until Oct. 6, 1876, however, that librarians formally organized the American Library Association. THE LIBRARY JOURNAL began publication the same year. Other leaders included Charles Cutter, John Cotton Dana, WILLIAM POOLE, HERBERT PUTNAM, Arthur Bostwick, R. R. Bowker, and JUSTIN WINSOR. MELVIL DEWEY established the first library school at Columbia University in 1887.

Libraries were primarily for adults until 1890, even though many were organized in school districts. A growing concern for children caused librarians to begin helping young readers. At first only a few chairs were set aside for them, then a corner, a reading room, and finally a separate children's library as well as school libraries. By 1900 service to children was extremely popular and today about half of the nation's public libraries' total circulation is in children's books, although the ratio of adult to juvenile books is 2 to 1.

As the concept of the library has changed from being a depository of books to a vital community center, librarians have broadened the range and scope of materials and services available to all ages and groups to include all those that modern technology and scholarship can provide within the financial realities of community support.

Philanthropists such as JOHN JACOB ASTOR, W. L. Newberry, and ANDREW CARNEGIE did much to promote municipal library development. Carnegie donated 1,677 buildings to communities which furnished sites and agreed to maintain service on a minimum budget of ten per cent of building costs. In recent years philanthropists have primarily assisted libraries through special projects administered by the American Library Association and designed to further general library development.

State libraries were established early in most state's histories. In the beginning the state library was usually a law and legislative library for state officials, but New York in 1818 opened its state library to public use. Soon state libraries began lending and mailing books on request to citizens, school districts, villages without local service, or even to supplement the local library's collection. Congress has authorized a special book rate to make the mailing of books relatively inexpensive.

States also began to establish commissions or agencies to aid in establishing, developing, and improving libraries through advisory or other services, by providing materials, providing cooperative services and techniques, and establishing standards and requirements of various kinds. Twenty-eight states provide state funds, each according to its own formula, to promote libraries and equalize the opportunity for library service in all areas of the state.

Services to rural areas have been made difficult and expensive by distance and a scattered population but good roads, the automobile, and the bookmobile have made possible good service at reasonable cost. The county or regional library where both rural and urban people contribute to its support and enjoy its services has necessarily been a recent development. Although the county library became legally possible in 1816 when Indiana passed permissive legislation, the municipal, township, and school district libraries remained the basic units. While some libraries had encouraged rural patrons, county-wide service and support began on April 9, 1899, when Washington County, Md., began operation of a library. In 1907, under Mary L. Titcomb, this library inaugurated the bookwagon, forerunner of the bookmobile. In 1898 Ohio passed county library legislation, and libraries were immediately established in Hamilton and Van Wert counties. California, under the leadership of James L. Gillis, began a vigorous program in 1909, and now all counties but one have county-wide systems. Other states have encouraged county and regional library service with varying techniques and success. Today there are 536 county libraries, 83 regionals, 453 city and county libraries, with 250 counties having no public library of any kind within their borders. The remainder of county residents must depend upon city and town tax supported libraries.

Economic factors have prevented some states from developing adequate libraries, particularly in rural areas. To stimulate the growth of library service in rural areas the Library Services Act was passed in 1956 to provide Federal funds for five years to the states to use according to the program and plans best suited to each state. So far the Federal government has appropriated $19,050,000 which has been effectively used for county and regional library development. The Federal government has helped libraries in other ways through the years. The Library of Congress distributes its catalog cards at a nominal price and promotes interlibrary loans, service to the blind, and bibliographic service. The statistical and advisory services of the Library Services section, Office of Education, founded in 1938, the funds of the Works Progress Administration in the 1930's, the creation of libraries in the Tennessee Valley Authority, the designation in 1895 of certain libraries as depositories of government documents, and the recognition of libraries as vital in a densely populated community under the Defense Production Act of 1951 are all helpful Federal policies.

Most public libraries and library systems are administered by boards of trustees, appointed or elected, who establish basic policy, and select a librarian who administers the library. One of the chief responsibilities of the board is securing the necessary funds for the library and preparing a budget. The American Library Association has established standards of support to aid librarians and trustees in budget-making. Postwar standards were set at $1.50 per capita for minimum service, $2.25 for good service, and $3.00 for superior service for units serving 25,000 people or more. Smaller units are of course more expensive to operate. These standards are unattained goals for most libraries as yet. Recently 6,249 of the nation's 7,871 libraries reported that 173,155,537 volumes were available to 117,607,364 people and had an annual circulation of 489,519,495, with expenses of $170,222,649, exclusive of capital outlay. Yet 25,000,000 Americans living on farms and in small communities are without access to a public library. Only Delaware, Massachusetts, and Rhode Island provide local library service to all residents. The average per capita operating expense is $1.45, with a range from 38 cents per capita in West Virginia to a high of $2.39 in Massachusetts. Most libraries are operating on inadequate budgets. Yet all but a few give bountiful service for the money spent and play an important role in the growth of American civilization.

An interesting survey is Ernestine Rose, *The Public Library in American Life* (1953). Many specialized studies of libraries and librarianship have been written; a few are: Alice E. Bryan, *The Public Librarian* (1952); Marian C. Manley, *Business Information and How to Use It* (1955); *The American Library Annual* (begun in 1956), which presents a vast amount of statistical and other information; American Library Association, *Public Library Service: A Guide to Evaluation, with Minimum Standards* (1956). See also PUBLIC LIBRARIES; PUBLIC LIBRARY INQUIRY; MERCANTILE LIBRARIES.

MARGIE SORNSON MALMBERG

library associations. There are many organized groups of librarians and libraries, of which the most active and influential is the American Library Association. The Canadian Library Association also includes libraries in French Canada as the Association Canadienne des Bibliothèques. In the United States are found also the American Association of Law Libraries, the Association of Research Libraries, the Music Library Association, the National Association of State Libraries, the Special Libraries Association, and the Theater Library Association, all affiliated with the A.L.A. In addition many states have their own library associations. Unaffiliated with the A.L.A. are the American Association of Medical Record Librarians, the American Documentation Institute, the American Theological Library Association, the Association of American Library Schools, the Bibliographical Society of America, the Catholic Library Association, the Educational Film Library Association, the Inter-American Bibliographical and Library Association (with headquarters in the Library of Congress), the Library Public Relations Council, and the Medical Library Association. The Council of National Library Associations includes the A.L.A. as a member.

Library Center, Mid-West. On a grant from the Carnegie and Rockefeller Foundations in 1947, a massive Library Center was erected in Chicago, as a combination storage, distribution, and information center for fourteen middle-western universities and the important John Crerar Science Library in Chicago. The center is a successful attempt to meet difficult problems of finance, storage, and convenience for the participating universities. Each university sends to the Center little-used but necessary books, and they buy books in common. The plan is being adopted in other regions of the United States.

Library Directory, American. A master list of more than 12,000 U.S. and Canadian libraries issued triennially by the R. R. Bowker Co. It covers libraries of all kinds and gives information about special collections within large libraries. School libraries are listed in a separate volume. The same firm also issues separate volumes on public libraries, college and university libraries, Catholic high-school libraries, law libraries, medical libraries, and other specialized collections.

Library Journal, The. A magazine for librarians and booklovers founded in 1876 by R. R. Bowker, FREDERICK LEYPOLDT, and MELVIL DEWEY, who became its first editors. It is now published by the R. R. Bowker Co. It furnishes items of interest to librarians, including excellent biographical sketches of new authors.

Library of Congress. Also called the **Congressional Library.** It is located in Washington, D.C., and faces the Capitol. As early as 1782–83 the Continental Congress debated the need for a library. On April 24, 1800, President John Adams signed "An Act to Make Provision for the Removal and Accommodation of the Government of the U.S.," in which the fifth clause provided an appropriation of $5,000 "for the purchase of such books as may be necessary for the use of Congress at the city of Washington and for fitting up a suitable apartment for containing them and placing them therein." About half the sum was promptly used to buy a collection of books in London. The books became ashes when the British burned the Capitol on the night of Aug. 24–25, 1814. The Library of Congress has managed, however, to obtain another or a similar copy of all but three of the books that were destroyed.

In 1815 Jefferson was in financial straits, and the Library purchased his excellent 6,457-volume library. This became the nucleus of the present collection, today the largest in the world in the number of items it contains. Its accretions come from many sources. The administration of the copyright law is one of the charges of the librarian of the Library of Congress, through a subordinate called the Register of Copyrights. By law he has received since 1870 two copies of every book, magazine, newspaper, brochure, circular, advertisement, or label that is copyrighted. In addition the law provides for the copyrighting of unpublished plays, movie, radio, and television scripts, film strips, and published and unpublished music, so that the library possesses the world's largest collection of such material. Furthermore, the library has been made the custodian of numerous special collections, the papers of George Washington and Thomas Jefferson, for example, the J. Pierpont Morgan collection of autographs of the signers of the Declaration of Independence, and a vast gathering of Americana. The oldest "manuscript" in the Library is a Babylonian clay tablet dating from several thousand years B.C. The oldest book printed from type is the Gutenberg Bible, printed between 1450 and 1455. The oldest newspaper of which the library has a complete file is the London *Gazette,* going back to 1665. Its collection of sources for the study of American history numbers more than eleven million items. In addition it owns the world's largest collection of maps and other cartographic material. Finally, there are the library's collections of several hundred thousand recordings and of several million photographic prints, slides, and motion-picture films. It has taken a deep interest in contemporary American poetry, has itself made recordings of readings by eminent poets and made these available to the public, at one time supervised awards to poets under the Bollingen Foundation, but ceased doing so in 1949 as a result of a dispute over an award to Ezra Pound. Yale University now conducts the awards. The total number of "pieces" in the library probably runs close to forty million.

The library now has an annual appropriation of $11,000,000, plus income from special funds. The main building was put up in 1889–97, the annex in 1939. Its twenty reading rooms make books available to the general public. Its first librarian (1802–07) was John Beckley, a Congressional clerk. Probably its most distinguished was HERBERT PUTNAM (1899–1939), who greatly expanded the services of the library. He was succeeded by ARCHIBALD MACLEISH (1939–45), who modernized the library in many ways, and he in turn by Luther H. Evans (1945–53). The present librarian (1959–62) is L. QUINCY MUMFORD.

Officially the Library of Congress still exists to help Congressmen, and the service to them is now in charge of a special Legislative Reference Department. In one year this department answered, in full detail, 22,000 questions from Congressmen. The library does research for speeches, drafts bills, even provides data for replies to constituents. To other libraries the Library of Congress also renders important services. It prints catalogue cards which they can purchase and use; it has now become a custom for all American publishers to print the Library of Congress catalogue card number on the copyright page of their books and other publications. The library also publishes a large number of special lists and guides, and for a time issued a *Quarterly Journal of Current Acquisitions*. See also NATIONAL ARCHIVES.

Library of Southern Literature (1908–23). This collection of seventeen volumes was made under the editorship of Edwin A. Alderman, JOEL CHANDLER HARRIS, and Charles William Kent. It includes selections, reading guides, bibliographies, and biographical data.

Library of the World's Best Literature (1896–97), a collection in thirty-one volumes, edited by CHARLES DUDLEY WARNER and an editorial staff. In 1917 it was reissued in thirty volumes as *The Warner Library*, edited by J. W. Cunliffe and A. H. Thorndike. With it in 1913 was joined *The Reader's Digest of Books*, compiled by Helen Rex Keller. In 1917 the *Digest* was separately published; a new and enlarged edition was published in 1929.

Lieber, Francis (b. Germany, March 18, 1800—d. Oct. 2, 1872), liberal, soldier, teacher, author of books on political economy. Lieber served under Marshal Blücher at Waterloo (1815) and as a volunteer in the Greek War of Independence (1822). Then, since he was an active liberal he left Prussia and came to the United States (1827). He edited the *Encyclopedia Americana* in Boston for five years, then taught at South Carolina College in Columbia (now the state university). He was an impressive figure to the students and to the world at large. Longfellow said of him, "He is a strong man; and one whose conversation, like some tumultuous mountain brook, sets your wheels all in motion."

All the important leaders in political science felt Lieber's influence. The ideas expressed in his books were not especially original and show the influence of Edmund Burke, Henry Hallam, and others—as his biographer, Frank Freidel, points out in *Francis Lieber: 19th-Century Liberal* (1948). But what he taught, especially his idea of many independent institutions (state, city, church, science, etc.) as a means of preventing absolutism, fitted in well with American ideas. Among his books: *The Manual of Political Ethics* (1838–39); *Essays on Property and Labor* (1841); *On Civil Liberty and Self-Government* (1853); *On Nationalism and Internationalism* (1868); *On the Rise of the Constitution of the U.S.* (1872). Thomas S. Perry compiled his *Life and Letters* (1882), and his ideas were discussed in L. R. Harley's *Francis Lieber* (1899) and Bernard Edward Brown's *American Conservatives* (1951).

Lieberman, Elias (b. Russia, Oct. 30, 1883–), teacher, administrator, editor, poet, translator. Lieberman, who came to the United States in 1891, had a distinguished career as a teacher, principal, and associate superintendent of schools in the New York City school system. He edited PUCK for a year (1917–18), compiled books for use in English classes, and wrote clever and skillful verses. Among his collections: *Paved Streets* (1917); *Hand Organ*

Man (1930); *Man in the Shadows* (1939); *To My Brothers Everywhere* (1954). A statement of personal belief, *I Am an American* (a poem of some fifty lines which appeared in *Paved Streets*), has had wide circulation. His poetry appears in numerous anthologies.

Liebling, A[bbott] J[oseph] (b. New York City, Oct. 18, 1904—d. Dec. 28, 1963), newsman, columnist, war correspondent, satirist. In *The Wayward Pressman* (1947) Liebling described some of his own experiences as a newspaperman before he became a staff member of the *New Yorker* in 1935. Expelled from Dartmouth College because he cut chapel too often, he found that the Columbia School of Journalism "had all the intellectual status of a training school for future employees of the A. & P." He was discharged from the staff of the New York *Times*, which he described as "colorless, odorless, and tasteless," because he named a basketball player, whose name he did not know, "Ignoto," "unknown" in Italian. After working for a while on the Providence *Journal*, Liebling wrote feature stories for the New York *World-Telegram* and the New York *Journal*. He was told by a Hearst executive: "The public is interested in just three things: blood, money, and sex." These experiences prepared him for a role that he filled on the *New Yorker*: gadfly to American journalism. He wrote for a column called "The Wayward Press," in which he discussed at length the shortcomings of newspapers; he maintained a long-standing feud with Col. McCormick and the Chicago *Tribune*. Liebling himself was a gifted reporter, as he showed in his war sketches, *The Road Back to Paris* (1944). Among his other books: *Back Where I Came From* (1938); *The Telephone Booth Indian* (1942); *Mink and Red Herring* (1949); *Chicago: Second City* (1952); *The Sweet Science* (1956), a series of sketches on boxers and boxing; *Normandy Revisited* (1958); *The Earl of Louisiana* (1961), a series on Governor Earl Long originally done for *The New Yorker;* and *The Press* (1961), a collection of articles.

Liebman, Joshua L[oth] (b. Hamilton, Ont., April 7, 1907—d. June 9, 1948), teacher, clergyman, lecturer, author. Liebman became a rabbi in 1930, in 1939 was called to serve at Temple Israel in Boston. He taught philosophy at several universities and was often called on to act as university preacher, to lecture on Judaism, and to broadcast messages of good will. He also wrote technical books in the field of metaphysics, and *God and the World Crisis* (1941).

Lie Down in Darkness (1951), a novel by WILLIAM STYRON. Set in the South, the novel deals with the Loftis family, and is narrated by Milton Loftis as he accompanies the coffin of his daughter Peyton to the grave. The narrative technique is a Joyce-like stream of consciousness through which the other characters in the story and the events leading to Peyton's death are revealed. Basically, the story of the Loftis family is the story of its moral and psychological breakdown, and the contrast between the Negro and white, the reaction to fundamentalist religion, and the sense of guilt are the main themes. The guilt of the Loftis family itself—Milton's incest desires, Helen's jealousy and Puritanism, Peyton's father complex—reflects the traditional southern fears of inbreeding, overgentility in ladies, and fear of the Negro. The poetic language of the novel, reminiscent of the work of Thomas Wolfe and William Faulkner, and its superb stylistic skill make it one of the finest of recent southern novels.

Life [1]. *Life* was the third of a trio of humorous magazines founded in close succession: *Puck* in 1877, *Judge* in 1881, *Life* in 1883. All three are now deceased as humorous magazines. JOHN AMES MITCHELL, an artist, founded *Life*. He had received a $10,000 legacy and wanted to try out a new zinc process for reproducing his black-and-white drawings, so he decided to start a magazine to rival *Puck* and *Judge*. He was fortunate enough to discover an excellent business manager, Andrew Miller, and a very good editor, EDWARD SANFORD MARTIN. Even more important, however, were the drawings of CHARLES DANA GIBSON, who began contributing in 1886. Books of Gibson's drawings were popular all over the world, and the circulation of the magazine increased, reaching a quarter of a million at its peak in 1920. It attracted many notable contributors: the authors John Kendrick Bangs, James Whitcomb Riley, Agnes Repplier, Brander Matthews and the artists E. W. Kemble, Palmer Cox, A. B. Frost, Oliver Herford. In 1892 Thomas L. Masson became editor. The magazine advocated causes and crusades, some of them eccentric: fulminations against doctors and vivisection, against the hobble skirt ("Don't cry, Tommy; it's only a woman"), against the marriage of American girls to foreign fortune-hunters, against ticket speculators. Some were worthwhile, such as the advocacy of a Fresh Air Fund. Mitchell hated John D. Rockefeller, Sr., J. P. Morgan, Sr., and William Randolph Hearst, and never neglected an opportunity to satirize any of them savagely in text and picture. Once he was warned that his home would be bombed, and libel suits were instituted against him, not one of which he lost.

When *Life* began to fail, Gibson purchased it and made ROBERT E. SHERWOOD editor (1924–28). For a time brilliant contributors gave it a blood transfusion: Frank Sullivan, Robert Benchley, Dorothy Parker, Franklin P. Adams, Corey Ford, Don Herold, Art Young, John Held, Jr., Ellison Hoover, Ralph Barton, Percy Crosby. In 1931 it was changed to a monthly and sold to a new group. In October, 1936, it passed into the hands of TIME, INC., which wanted only the name.

Life [2]. On Nov. 23, 1936, appeared the first issue of *Life* in its new form, as a pictorial magazine. The aim was "to see life, to see the world, to eyewitness great events." At the beginning its text consisted of captions for pictures and short expository blocks. After a while the text was expanded by having at least one sustained, signed article each week. Later close-ups or profiles of noted persons and lengthy historical and scientific articles became regular features. *Life* also features reproductions of the work of famous artists. Its circulation climbed to 6,800,000. In 1954 Wallace Kirkland wrote *Recollections of a Life Photographer;* Stanley Rayfield's *How Life Gets the Story: Behind the Scenes in Photo-Journalism* appeared in 1955. *Great Readings from Life* was published in 1960.

Life Amongst the Modocs: Unwritten History (1873), an autobiographical narrative by JOAQUIN MILLER; called in later editions *Unwritten History: Life Among the Modocs* (1874), *Paquita: The Indian Heroine* (1881), *My Own Story* (1890), and *Joaquin Miller's Romantic Life Amongst the Indians* (1898). The book is called by Albert Keiser "by far the finest and best of Miller's prose productions." He adds, however, that its account of life among the Indians "contains much more poetry than truth." There is much about Paquita, a modest, intelligent, industrious, and beautiful girl whom Miller finally married. In the course of their adventures she was fatally wounded by his enemies and died, says Miller, "in my arms." See MODOC INDIANS.

Life at the South, or, "Uncle Tom's Cabin" as It Is (1852), a novel by W. L. G. Smith (1814–1878) in reply to Harriet Beecher Stowe's UNCLE TOM's CABIN.

Life Begins at 40 (1932), a volume of exhortation and counsel by WALTER PITKIN. It appeared at the height of a great economic depression and afforded comfort to many people, who bought the book in large quantities. Pitkin, who had earlier written *The Art of Learning* (1931) followed up the book with *Take It Easy!* (1935); *Let's Get What We Want* (1935); *Careers After 40* (1937); and *Making Good Before 40* (1939).

Life in the Far West (1848; reprinted, 1951, edited by LeRoy R. Hafen), an account by GEORGE FREDERICK RUXTON. This is a description of the Rocky Mountain men of the 1840's, their battles with Indians, their women, their mode of speech, their amusements. Ruxton had come from England via Vera Cruz, making his way to Santa Fe and wintering with the mountain men in what is now South Park, Colo. He wrote his account (slightly fictionized) for *Blackwood's Edinburgh Magazine* (1847–48); his story was often reprinted during the 19th century. Ruxton has been called "the father of Westerns."

Life of Reason, The (5 v., 1905–06), a philosophical examination by GEORGE SANTAYANA. Under the influence of WILLIAM JAMES, JOSIAH ROYCE, and Georg Hegel, Santayana attempted an analysis of common sense. His fundamental thesis was that "everything ideal has a natural basis and everything natural an ideal development." He employed James' psychology as an analysis of experience, substituting for James' "stream of consciousness" the term *flux*. Knowledge has two poles: physics, which explains the concretions of existence; and dialectics, which clarifies ideas, values, and objects. The life of reason takes shape in institutions: society, religion, art, and science. Santayana exploited no original notions, but his style had great charm. Later he abandoned most of his explanations, and in the four volumes of *The Realm of Being* (1927–40), he depended more on David Hume and Schopenhauer than on the earlier influences. Yet Bernard Berenson, Santayana's fellow-expatriate in Italy, said in his *Sketch for a Self-Portrait* (1949) that *The Life of Reason* was the author's "masterpiece, fit to be placed beside the books of wisdom composed by Greek Stoics and Alexandrian and Palestine Jews in the century or two before and after the earthly life of Christ."

Life on the Mississippi (1883), an autobiographical account by MARK TWAIN. Although the book as such appeared in 1883, a considerable section had been printed in the *Atlantic Monthly* in 1875; many critics regard this earlier section as the best part of the book, possibly Twain's best writing. Chapter 26 describes a feud which, when HUCKLEBERRY FINN was published (1885), became, in expanded form, Chapter 27 of that book; it was separately published in the *Century* for December, 1884. Huck Finn himself appears for the first time in Chapter 3, but this episode was never included in *Huckleberry Finn*.

The part of the book that appeared in the *Atlantic* is called "Old Times on the Mississippi." In it Twain describes the tough apprenticeship he underwent to become a river pilot, the deference paid to him as one of a great clan, the scenes on the New Orleans levee, the furor at all the river towns when the boat came in, the racing in which the steamers indulged, the heavy gambling on board. In 1882 Twain's publisher remembered the papers and suggested that he revisit the old scenes and add to the book. But times and conditions had changed greatly since ante-bellum days; the river had been stripped of its romance. Yet Twain concluded that on the river he had become "personally and familiarly present with about all the different types of human nature." The river was moreover, a highway of American humor, and Twain derived more than his pen name from its traffic and customs; he learned the kind of talk and incident that was to make him famous.

Life on the Ocean Wave, A (1838), a poem by EPES SARGENT. It first appeared in the New York *Mirror*. Henry Russell wrote music for the lyric, and the music and words were published the same year.

Life with Father (1935), a memoir of his father, Clarence Day, Sr., by CLARENCE DAY, JR. This book is a collection of humorous sketches in which experiences of the author with his highly eccentric father were reported. They began appearing in the *New Yorker*, *Harper's Magazine*, and the *New Republic* as early as 1920. The elder Day's religious views were reported in *God and My Father* (1932). Day's affectionate but irreverent portrait of his father received favorable reviews, except in Boston.

The play based on the book by RUSSEL CROUSE and HOWARD LINDSAY opened on Nov. 8, 1939, and reached its 3,224th performance on July 12, 1947, when the producer and authors decided to "call it a day," as Sam Zolotow put it in the *Times*. A movie based on the play, with a script by Donald Ogden Stewart, opened in New York on Aug. 15, 1947. A play called *Life with Mother*, also by Crouse and Lindsay, opened in New York on Oct. 20, 1948, and ran for the rest of the season.

Writing to the *Saturday Review of Literature* on the tenth anniversary of the publication of *Life with Father*, R. H. Danielson commented on the development of what he called a "Day school" of writers: "During a period in which the family as an institution has frequently been subjected to the merciless probings of psychiatry, the gentler probings of the Day school have been generally reassuring in their portrayal of life in a family as being sometimes rapturous, occasionally dangerous, but never to be feared." Among his list of novels indicating Day's influence are Ruth McKenney's *My Sister Eileen* (1938), William Saroyan's *My Name Is Aram* (1940); Kathryn Forbes' *Mama's Bank Account* (1943); John Philip Sousa III's *My Family, Right or Wrong* (1943); Carlos Bulosan's *The Laughter of My Father* (1944); Rosemary Taylor's *Chicken Every Sunday* (1943); Miriam Young's *Mother Wore Tights* (1944); Robert Louis Fontaine's *The Happy Time* (1945). Ernestine Gilbreth Carey and Frank Gilbreth, Jr., did one of the best of all in *Cheaper by the Dozen* (1948).

Ligeia (pub. in the *American Museum*, September, 1838; included in *Tales of the Grotesque and Arabesque*, 1840), a tale by EDGAR ALLAN POE. Poe reverts to a theme he had already treated in MORELLA (1835)— metempsychosis and the return of a dead wife from the grave. But his treatment of the theme in *Ligeia* is much more convincing; it was Poe's favorite of his stories, and it has always been highly regarded by critics. Ligeia, married to the man who tells her story and who is deeply devoted to her, dies after a wasting illness despite her strong desire to live. He goes to England and remarries, but with no love for his new wife; and she too dies. But as she lies in the coffin, she suddenly comes back to life— and her husband recognizes her as Ligeia. The poem THE CONQUEROR WORM was written in 1843, added to *Ligeia* in 1845. Poe may have taken the name Ligeia from Ligea, in classic mythology one of the three Sirens.

Lighthall, William Douw (b. Hamilton, Ont., Dec. 27, 1857—d. Aug. 3, 1954), Canadian lawyer, public official, poet, editor. Lightfall was active as a lawyer, founded the important Union of Canadian Municipalities, wrote books on *Canada a Modern Nation* (1904) and *The Governance of Empire* (1910), served in military units, and founded the Great War Veterans' Association. But his great interest was poetry. He published his first slim collection, *Thoughts, Moods, and Ideals,* in 1887, with an apologetic subtitle: *Crimes of Leisure.* His "first real book" was *The Young Seigneur, or, Nation-Making* (1888), published under the pseudonym Wilfred Chateauclair. The characters were French Canadians. The following year he edited *Songs of the Great Dominion.* He organized the Society of Canadian Literature (1889), which paved the way for the Canadian Authors' Association, and edited several other anthologies. He collected his verse in *Old Measures* (1922). He had great facility in meter, and also did some good pieces in free verse. Canadian patriotism animates many of his best poems.

Light in August (1932), a novel by WILLIAM FAULKNER. *Light in August* reiterates Faulkner's concern with the southern—as well as national—society which classifies men according to race, creed, and origin. JOE CHRISTMAS, the central character, appears to be white but is purported to be a Negro; he has an affair with Joanna Burden, a spinster whom the townsfolk of Jefferson regard with suspicion because of her New England background. Joe eventually kills her and sets fire to her house; he is captured, castrated, and killed by the outraged townspeople, to whom his victim has become a symbol of the innocent white woman attacked and killed by a Negro. Others of the novel's main characters exemplify the southern preoccupation with and glorification of the past: notably Gail Hightower, the unfrocked minister, who ignores his wife and loses his church because of his fanatic devotion to the memory of his grandfather, killed during the Civil War twenty years before Hightower was born. Interwoven with the story of Joe Christmas is the contrasting, placid story of LENA GROVE, who comes to Jefferson far advanced in pregnancy, expecting to find the lover who has deserted her.

Lightnin' (1918), a play by WINCHELL SMITH and FRANK BACON. This play established a long-run record for its day—1,291 performances on Broadway. Bacon himself played the leading role, Lightnin' Bill Jones, who owns the Calivada Hotel, half of which lies in Nevada, half in California. The sheriff from the former has trouble when he tries to arrest a man for whom he has a warrant; the threatened man merely jumps over the line. Lightnin' has numerous troubles, especially when his wife sues him for divorce, but manages entertainingly to solve them all. He denies indignantly that he is a liar when he boasts that he once drove a swarm of bees over the plains in the dead of winter without losing a bee.

Lilacs (in *What's O'Clock,* 1925), a poem by AMY LOWELL. One of the better-known and better free-verse poems of Miss Lowell, in which she identifies the lilacs and herself with New England. She speaks of the "great puffs of flowers" as "holding quiet conversation with an early moon" and as "a reticent flower, a curiously clear-cut candid flower."

Lillie, Gordon W[illiam] ["Pawnee Bill"] (b. Bloomington, Ill., Feb. 14, 1860—d. Feb. 3, 1942), ranchman, hunter and trapper, interpreter, showman, writer. Lillie led a highly picturesque and varied life, first as a hunter in the wilderness, then among the Pawnee Indians as an interpreter, later as a manager of Pawnee groups with Buffalo Bill, in time as the latter's partner. He worked for the preservation of the buffalo, became president of an oil company and director of the Historical Society of Oklahoma, wrote his memoirs—*Thirty Years among the Pawnee Indians* (1928). He collaborated with COURTNEY RYLEY COOPER on *Oklahoma* (1926), with Ernest Lynn on *Blazing Horizon* (1927), with Herman Mootz on *Pawnee Bill, the Romance of Oklahoma* (1928), with J. R. Johnston on *Stampede Range* (1928). J. H. DeWolff wrote an account of him in *Pawnee Bill* (1902) and Frank Winch wrote *Thrilling Lives of Buffalo Bill and Pawnee Bill* (1911).

Lilly, Ben (b. Alabama, Dec. 31, 1856—d. Dec. 17, 1936), hunter, storyteller. Around this famous hunter of bears and panthers, who was at one time Theodore Roosevelt's favorite in his expeditions and who hunted widely in Texas, Mexico, and the Rockies, a considerable mass of stories has accumulated. J. Frank Dobie wrote *The Ben Lilly Legend* (1950).

Lily Adair (pub. in one version in *Eonchs of Ruby,* 1851; in another version in *Memoralia,* 1853, and *Virginalia,* 1853), two poems with the same title by THOMAS HOLLEY CHIVERS. The later poem may be a continuation of the earlier one. Like so much of what Chivers wrote it suggests Poe, especially ULALUME, which was published in the *American Whig Review* in December, 1847. Of *Ulalume* itself, S. F. Damon said that the idea had been taken over bodily from Chivers' *Nacoochee* (1837).

Lily Bart. See BART, LILY.

Lime-Kiln Club. See CHARLES BERTRAND LEWIS.

Lincoln, Abraham (b. Hardin [now Larue] Co., Ky., Feb. 12, 1809—d. April 15, 1865), lawyer, 16th President of the United States. Ida M. Tarbell, in her book *In the Footsteps of the Lincolns* (1924), traces the family's migrations west to Illinois. Lincoln was largely self-taught, a lover of the Bible, Shakespeare, Robert Burns, Tom Paine, *The Pilgrim's Progress,* Aesop's *Fables,* and *Robinson Crusoe.* He was a good wrestler and weight lifter and a competent rail-splitter. He learned the art of storytelling at the crossroads store and became a master of Western humor. In 1828 he helped sail a flatboat down the Mississippi, saw a slave market in New Orleans, and acquired a strong dislike for slavery. He worked as a storekeeper in Salem, Ill., later as a surveyor, as postmaster, and again as a storekeeper (unsuccessful). At this time there took place the famous affair with Ann Rutledge, who died shortly after they became engaged. Edgar Lee Masters throws doubt on the reality of this affair in his biography *Lincoln the Man* (1931).

In 1832 the Black Hawk War broke out and Lincoln served as a captain. In 1834 he was elected to the State Legislature and served four terms as one of Henry Clay's Whig followers. In 1836 he was admitted to the bar, in 1837 moved to Springfield. He married Mary Todd, a woman of good family and social standing, after a troubled courtship. Paul M. Angle feels that Herndon's account of the Lincolns' domestic difficulties is "overdrawn, though not baseless." See MARY TODD LINCOLN.

Meanwhile Lincoln was earning an excellent reputation as a lawyer and went into partnership, in succession, with some of the best lawyers of Illinois, finally in 1843 with WILLIAM H. HERNDON. He was an excellent court lawyer, with a knack for winning over juries. In 1846 he was elected to Congress, where he voted against abolitionist measures but refused to favor slavery (founded, he said, "on both injustice and bad policy"), also voted for a resolution that censured President Polk for engaging with Mexico in "an unnecessary and unconstitutional war." He did not run for re-election and his political career seemed finished.

Then came the movement that ended with the founding of the Republican party, and gradually Lincoln was drawn back into public life and away from Whiggism. When JOHN C. FRÉMONT ran for the Presidency in 1856, Lincoln was the recognized leader of the Illinois Republicans. The DRED SCOTT decision of the Supreme Court (1857) drove him further toward the antislavery cause. In 1858 he accepted a Republican nomination for the U.S. Senate, and then came the famous debates with STEPHEN A. DOUGLAS, in the course of which Lincoln became nationally known, even though he lost to Douglas. The "House Divided" speech in which he accepted the nomination and his speeches during the seven debates with Douglas were read everywhere and have become classics in the literature of argumentation. Lincoln showed a masterly command of logic and language. His reputation was heightened by the *Cooper Union Address* (1860), before an Eastern audience. At the convention held the same year to nominate a candidate for the Presidency, Lincoln won by a landslide on the third ballot. In the election campaign that followed Lincoln remained silent; he carried every Northern state except New Jersey and lost every Southern state, obtaining a majority of the electoral votes. In the popular vote he had a plurality. As soon as the results were known, Southern states began to secede, but Lincoln continued his silence.

On Feb. 11, 1861, Lincoln left Springfield and made a brief *Farewell Address* as he stood on the railroad platform. His remarks revealed a dark, foreboding mood; the whole speech has the quality of poetry. It is believed that the official version was written down by Lincoln in the train after his departure; it differs in several respects from newspaper versions published at the time. Lincoln's version tends to enhance the alliterative sequence and to strengthen the rhythmic pattern, in accordance with Lincoln's usual practice.

Lincoln delivered a conciliatory *Inaugural Address* (March 4, 1861) which made it plain that his first concern was to save the Union, even if slavery had to continue. The coming of war forced Lincoln to assume dictatorial powers. He was deeply dissatisfied with the way in which McClellan and other Union generals conducted the war campaigns, particularly in view of the great superiority of the North in men, supplies, and strategic advantages. Not until Generals U. S. GRANT and W. T. SHERMAN appeared on the military scene did he feel that he had found field leaders of sufficient audacity. Some modern commentators are of the opinion that Lincoln was his own best general, that without his bold and intelligent guidance the war would have been lost.

Lincoln's conduct during the war was exemplary. He avoided acting like a dictator although he was one by the force of circumstances; the press remained free, as was shown by the violence of the personal attacks made on Lincoln. He fought the South, but refused to hate it. He wielded immense power, but was not corrupted by it. His cabinet was mostly unsympathetic, but he managed to keep the members working for him; and he kept Congress at bay. On Jan. 1, 1863, he issued his EMANCIPATION PROCLAMATION, strictly as a military measure, although in time it became more than that. On Nov. 19, 1863, he delivered the GETTYSBURG ADDRESS, the most majestic of all his utterances. When he ran for re-election, with his old foe General GEORGE B. McCLELLAN as the Democratic candidate, many thought he would lose. But the military victories of Grant, Sherman, and PHILIP SHERIDAN turned the tide. Lincoln had a majority in the Electoral College (212 to 21); the popular vote was closer. Lincoln began planning for a lasting peace, one in which the South would again take an honorable place in the nation's activities. His *Second Inaugural Address* (March 4, 1865) was a masterpiece of noble feeling and phrasing. But he was assassinated, supposedly as an act of revenge for the South; JEFFERSON DAVIS himself acknowledged that no one suffered more than the South as a result of John Wilkes Booth's senseless deed.

Lincoln's personality was deceptively simple; on examination he proves to have been a paradoxical combination of opposites. This is partially explained by the fact that, like every man who engages in public activities, he possessed considerable histrionic ability. He was often sincerely humble, but as JOHN HAY, long his private secretary, insisted, "It is absurd to call him a modest man. No great man was ever modest. It was his intellectual arrogance and unconsidered assumption of superiority that men like Salmon P. Chase and Charles Sumner never could forgive." He took a humorous and open pride in his own homeliness, and had a natural friendliness that defeated the efforts of his secretaries, Hay and J. G. NICOLAY, to protect him against intrusions.

Lincoln's humor was the most paradoxical of his qualities but helps to explain much in his career, personality, and fame. The saddest-looking of men, Lincoln was an inveterate joker. His favorite contemporary humorists included ARTEMUS WARD, R. H. NEWELL ("Orpheus C. Kerr"), and PETROLEUM V. NASBY. A frontiersman in many ways, Lincoln keenly relished the humor of the American frontier and himself contributed to its storehouse of stories. Aside from his genius in telling a story, he had of course the gift of epigram, often more wit than humor. In his speech at Quincy, Ill. (Oct. 13, 1858), he used the famous simile, "as thin as the homeopathic soup that was made by boiling the shadow of a pigeon that had starved to death."

Lincoln seems to have tried his hand once at writing in the familiar style of the Western humorists of his day. He sent an anonymous letter to the Sangamo (Ill.) *Journal*, which it published on Sept. 2, 1841. It purported to come from Aunt 'Becca in the "Lost Townships," and it satirized James Shields, the state auditor, and other Democratic officials so severely that it resulted in a challenge to a duel. He pictured Shields as "floatin' " around among a lot of "gals," young and old, to whom he was saying, "Dear girls, it is distressing, but I cannot marry you all. Too well I know how much you suffer, but do, do remember, it is not my fault that I am so handsome and so interesting." Shields was a little man, and when the challenge reached Lincoln he replied that it must be fought with "cavalry broadswords of the largest size." Shields declined. The letter was one of several pseudonymous pieces which appeared in the same newspaper.

Lincoln's humor has been collected and studied in a number of publications, among them *Old Abe's Jokes* (1864); F. B. Carpenter's *Six Months at the White House with Abraham Lincoln* (1866); *Lincoln's Anecdotes* (1867); J. B. McClure's *Anecdotes of Abraham Lincoln* (1880); A. K. McClure's *Abe Lincoln's Yarns and Stories* (1901); Henry L. Williams' *The Lincoln Story Book* (1907); Anthony Gross' *Lincoln's Own Stories* (1912); Russell Conwell's *Why Lincoln Laughed* (1922); Benjamin P. Thomas' "Lincoln's Humor: An Analysis" (1935); CARL SANDBURG's *Abraham Lincoln* (1926, 1939); Loyd Dunning's *Lincoln's Funnybone* (1942); H. B. Van Hoesen's "The Humor of Lincoln and the Seriousness of His Biographers" (1944).

Undoubtedly Lincoln is the greatest writer by far among American Presidents. Yet he cannot as a writer be separated from Lincoln the politician or Lincoln the lawyer. His success in practical realms was in large part due to his astounding command of words. He was articulate in miraculous fashion. He made himself understood by the multitude despite his frequently poetic and archaic language and his sometimes complex thought. He was persuasive beyond any other orator in American history.

The first *Complete Works* (2 v., 1894), edited by Nicolay and Hay, ran to nearly 1,400 pages of text and 1,736 letters, speeches, and miscellaneous writings. In 1905 a new edition (12 v.) was prepared, but the actual editor was apparently Francis D. Tandy. It added 518 items, mainly letters. In the same year appeared an inferior collection, *The Writings of Abraham Lincoln* (8 v.), edited by Arthur Brooks Lapsley. In the years that followed considerable new Lincoln material was discovered and collected in book form, particularly PAUL M. ANGLE's *New Letters and Papers of Lincoln* (1930); this volume assembled 430 letters, legal opinions, and miscellaneous items not found in earlier collections. It signaled, moreover, the arrival of new standards of scholarship in the Lincoln field.

Thereafter the publication of Lincoln's writings was marked by two important events. The first was a project undertaken in cooperation by the Abraham Lincoln Association and Rutgers University Press (1946) for the publication of Lincoln's writings and of books dealing with Lincoln. The first book to appear under these auspices was Angle's invaluable *Shelf of Lincoln Books* (1946), a critical selective bibliography with full annotations. The second event was the opening to public use of the Lincoln papers which had been presented to the Library of Congress on Jan. 23, 1923, by Lincoln's son, Robert Todd Lincoln (1843–1926). From the 18,350 documents David C. Mearns, director of the Library's reference department, selected more than 500 items for *The Lincoln Papers* (2 v., 1948). Some of the material was, however, already familiar from the use made of it by Nicolay and Hay in their 10-volume *Abraham Lincoln: A History* (1890) and in their compilation of Lincoln's writings. In 1953 a definitive collection appeared: *Collected Works*, edited by Roy Basler and others.

Some excellent books of selections have been made from Lincoln's writings. The earliest was apparently Luther E. Robinson's *Abraham Lincoln as a Man of Letters* (1918). This was followed by Daniel Kilham Dodge's *Abraham Lincoln, Master of Words* (1924), which contains some keen critical analyses of Lincoln's methods of composition. Philip Van Doren Stern edited a selection entitled *The Life and Writings of Abraham Lincoln* (1940), containing 274 items with prefatory statements that place them in their contemporary setting. Then followed Roy P. Basler's *Abraham Lincoln: His Speeches and Writings* (1946), with an introduction by Carl Sandburg and a detailed analysis of Lincoln's development as a writer. It contains 228 items, each of them complete; and Basler's collection is unrivaled for the care he took in finding an authentic text and for his prefatory statements to the various items. An unusual compilation is The *Lincoln En-*

cyclopedia (1961), edited by Archer H. Shaw. This work lists quotations from Lincoln's writings in dictionary fashion. *The Lincoln Treasury* (1950), edited by Caroline Thomas Harnsberger, was more careful in its 372 pages of quotations.

Several compilations of material about Lincoln have been made, among them Osborn H. Oldroyd's *The Poets' Lincoln* (1915); Mary Wright-Davis' *The Book of Lincoln* (1919); Edward Wagenknecht's *Abraham Lincoln: His Life, Work, and Character* (1947); and Paul Angle's *The Lincoln Reader* (1947). The last two are particularly good and give a brilliant survey of Lincoln literature. Angle and Earl S. Miers also prepared *The Living Lincoln* (1955). Some recent Lincoln items include: *Lincoln as They Saw Him*, by Herbert Mitgang (1956) and the above mentioned *A Lincoln Encyclopedia*, edited by Archer H. Shaw (1961).

Lincoln would probably have achieved literary fame even if he had never entered politics and attained the White House and martyrdom. There is in almost everything he said or wrote a curious mingling of the logic of the lawyer and the soaring imaginativeness of the poet. Roy Basler, who recently made the most careful and convincing study of Lincoln's development as a writer, holds that at the age of twenty-three he wrote with a "clarity that few college graduates ever achieve today." Basler emphatically denies that Lincoln's style was "homespun." Repetition of sound, as well as of words, marks Lincoln's style at all times; this feature is accompanied by grammatical as well as logical parallelism. The result is often a distinctly poetic cadence, which to Basler suggests comparison with English prose of the 17th century.

Tributes of every character have been paid to Lincoln. Walt Whitman wrote two famous poems about him, O Captain! My Captain! and When Lilacs Last in the Dooryard Bloom'd; the former is perhaps the most frequently recited of all poems about Lincoln, the latter the greatest and most affecting of all the tributes paid to him. James Russell Lowell in his Commemoration Ode wrote a magnificent passage with the famous line: "New birth of our new soil, the first American"; and elsewhere he spoke of him as "the incarnate common sense of the people." In his poem, *Lincoln, the Man of the People*, Edwin Markham wrote, "He was a man to hold against the world,/ A man to match the mountains and the sea." Other poets who wrote memorably about Lincoln include Edwin Arlington Robinson, Witter Bynner, Maurice Thompson, Vachel Lindsay, Percy MacKaye, Herman Melville, Julia Ward Howe, Bayard Taylor, J. G. Whittier, Paul Laurence Dunbar, Rosemary Benét, Carl Sandburg.

In the realm of fiction Lincoln has been a favorite character. Some of the novels and short stories in which he appears are: Henry Ward Beecher's Norwood (1867); Edward Eggleston's The Graysons (1888); Bret Harte's *Clarence* (1895); Winston Churchill's The Crisis (1901); Upton Sinclair's *Manassas* (1904); Mary Raymond Shipman Andrews' The Perfect Tribute (1906); Ida M. Tarbell's *He Knew Lincoln* (1907); Thomas Dixon's *The Southerner* (1913); S. Weir Mitchell's *Westways* (1913); Elsie Singmaster's *Gettysburg* (1913); John Buchan's *The End of the Road* (in *The Path of the King*, 1921); Irving A. Bacheller's *A Man for the Ages* (1919) and its sequel, *Father Abraham* (1925); Honoré Willsie Morrow's *Forever Free* (1927), *With Malice Toward None* (1928), and *The Last Full Measure* (1930); Bruce Lancaster's *For Us, the Living* (1940); Ben Ames Williams' House Divided (1947); Irving Stone's *Love Is Eternal* (1954).

Among plays that deal with Lincoln these may be noted: John Drinkwater's *Abraham Lincoln* (1919); Thomas Dixon, Jr.'s *A Man of the People* (1920); Arthur Goodman's *If Booth Had Missed* (1932); Robert E. Sherwood's Abe Lincoln in Illinois (1938); Betty Smith's and Webb Chase's *Lawyer Lincoln* (pub. 1939); Philip Van Doren Stern's *The Man Who Killed Lincoln* (1939); Mark Van Doren's *The Last Days of Lincoln* (1959). D. W. Griffith made a film about Lincoln, one of the first sound pictures, *Abraham Lincoln* (1930), with Walter Huston in the title role. There has been music, too, about Lincoln, as in Aaron Copland's *Lincoln Portrait* (1942).

Forest H. Sweet compiled a *Directory of Collectors of Books, Autographs, Prints, and Other Historical Material Relating to Abraham Lincoln* (1946). One great collection, recently dispersed, was described admiringly in Carl Sandburg's *Lincoln Collector: The Story of Oliver R. Barrett's Great Private Collection* (privately printed, 1949), which included some Lincoln items never before printed.

Lincoln, Abraham, biographies of. Few other historical figures besides Lincoln have evoked such a vast amount of printed matter, a good deal of it "mythological." Lloyd Lewis wrote *Myths After Lincoln* (1929) and pictured the assassinated President as parallel to "the dying god" who is the central figure in many an ancient legend. Later Roy P. Basler told the story of the development of *The Lincoln Legend* (1935). Even honest biographers and historians were misled, as Benjamin P. Thomas makes clear in his Portrait for Posterity: Lincoln and His Biographers (1947), though Thomas feels that during the middle years of the 20th century realism began to overtake legend.

The first life of Lincoln to appear, with the exception of a forty-seven-word statement in the *Dictionary of Congress* for 1858, was an account (*Lincoln's Autobiography*, 1859) Lincoln himself wrote for Jesse W. Fell, to be used for campaign purposes. William Dean Howells wrote a campaign biography of the Presidential and Vice-Presidential candidates, *Life and Speeches of Abraham Lincoln and Hannibal Hamlin* (1860). Josiah G. Holland's *The Life* of *Abraham Lincoln* (1866) generally followed the pattern of the myth already forming and saw Lincoln as "eminently a Christian President." WARD HILL LAMON's overly frank *The Life of Abraham Lincoln* (1872) presented quite another side of the President, and aroused a storm of protest.

WILLIAM H. HERNDON, Lincoln's law partner and intimate friend for years, gathered data about Lincoln with the intention of some day writing a biography of him. In the 1880's he placed his material in the hands of Jesse W. Weik, and the resultant collaboration, Herndon's *Lincoln: The True Story of a Great Life* (1889), was worthwhile. Herndon chiefly stressed the events in which he and Lincoln had been concerned together, so that the book practically stops at 1861. Herndon's view was not precisely objective, although he honestly strove for the truth, and he undoubtedly over-emphasized, for example, Lincoln's love for Ann Rutledge and his religious infidelity. The book went through many editions.

Lincoln's chief secretaries, JOHN G. NICOLAY and JOHN HAY, wrote *Abraham Lincoln: A History* (1890), based on Nicolay's notes, Hay's diary, and the President's papers. This monumental work ran for three years as a serial in the *Century Magazine*, and in book form filled ten volumes. The authors intended it to be a history of the United States from the birth of Lincoln to the end of the Civil War, and they paid particular attention to Lincoln as the leader of a great political party. Nicolay later wrote *A Short Life of Abraham Lincoln* (1902), a compact, factual account which is still worth reading.

Ida M. Tarbell's *The Life of Abraham Lincoln* (1900) incorporates in its pages reminiscences of Lincoln coming from many persons interviewed by Miss Tarbell, together with new letters, telegrams, and other documents. Paul Angle calls her work "journalism, hastily written and without distinction"; but she helped place Lincoln securely in popular affection in this unusually readable biography. In 1908 Edwin Erle Sparks provided a vivid and picturesque account of *The Lincoln-Douglas Debates of 1858*. He included the speeches and delved into contemporary newspaper stories for his local color. Joseph Fort Newton's *Lincoln and Herndon* (1910) deals with Lincoln's relationship to the radical wing of the Republican party. Newton here collected the correspondence (1854–59) between Theodore Parker, one of the Republican leaders, and Herndon, who sympathized with their views, and has supplied a detailed and well-written commentary. Lord Charnwood's *Abraham Lincoln* (1916) is a capable British interpretation. William E. Barton, in *The Life of Abraham Lincoln* (2 v., 1925), added much important information about Lincoln's ancestry, but wrote in tedious detail.

One of the greatest biographies of Lincoln, certainly the most beautifully written, is CARL SANDBURG's *Abraham Lincoln: The Prairie Years* (2 v., 1926) and *The War Years* (4 v., 1939), which was revised and condensed to one volume in 1954. Here a notable poet, steeped in history and animated with a deep love of America, presents a shifting, dynamic panorama of American characters and folkways, the poetry and sordidness of the land, with his portrait of an American hero. Charles A. Beard called the biography "a noble monument to American literature."

Colin R. Ballard, an English general, was perhaps the earliest interpreter of Lincoln to see that he was a great military innovator, and wrote on this aspect in *The Military Genius of Abraham Lincoln* (1926); many recent writers have followed Ballard's lead. Louis A. Warren went back to public documents and other source material to produce a remarkably accurate investigation of Lincoln's family and early environment in *Lincoln's Parentage and Childhood* (1926). Albert J. Beveridge's *Abraham Lincoln, 1809–1858* (2 v., 1928) is highly regarded for its historical correctness and its literary excellence, as well as its just treatment of Stephen A. Douglas. Edgar Lee Masters' *Lincoln the Man* (1931) is a sour, carping biography, whose chief thesis is that Lincoln's acts "were against liberty, and much to the advantage of monopoly and privilege, from his first days in 1832 at New Salem to the end of his life." Masters' real hero is Stephen A. Douglas, whose election as President would, he thinks, have averted the Civil War.

Lincoln: 1854–1861 (1933), by Paul M. Angle, *Lincoln: 1847–1853* (1936), by Benjamin P. Thomas, *Lincoln: 1809–1839* (1941), by Harry E. Pratt, and *Lincoln: 1840–1846* (1939), also by Pratt, were intended to give a day-by-day account of Lincoln's life until March 4, 1861. In chronological order, the volumes begin with Thomas Lincoln's activities, thereafter shift to Lincoln himself. Each page is divided into seven equal spaces, and where no data exist, the spaces are left blank. No item is included that does not originate in court records, legislative journals, contemporary newspapers, Lincoln's own writings, or those of his contemporaries.

Based on careful research, *Lincoln and the Patronage* (1943), by Harry J. Carman and Reinhard H. Luthin, shows the large extent to which Lincoln played the game of politics. James Daugherty wrote a simple, almost lyrical text, *Abraham Lincoln* (1943), to accompany his own forty vigorous lithographs; his biography, intended for young readers, has also been a favorite with adults. James G. Randall, a noted historian, wrote one of the best biographies of Lincoln in *Lincoln the President* (2 v., 1945), which carries Lincoln up to Gettysburg; two later volumes (1952, 1955) continue to his death. Volume 4 was completed by Richard N. Current. Randall also wrote *Lincoln and the South* (1946) and *Lincoln the Liberal Statesman* (1947). Randall was convinced that the war was not inevitable, and that the triumph of the Union was spoiled by the manner in which the victory was used.

Burton J. Hendrick, in *Lincoln's War Cabinet* (1946), shows how Lincoln tried to unify his party by collecting as his advisers nearly all the men he had defeated in the convention for the nomination. This absorbingly written volume exhibits Lincoln as an extraordinary executive. *Lincoln and the War Governors* (1948), by William B. Hesseltine, is an important work which shows Lincoln's tremendous influence in weakening states' rights and increasing Federal powers. *Lincoln's Herndon* (1948), by David Donald, is an excellent biography of an extraordinary character. It first details Herndon's early association with Lincoln and his considerable influence upon him; later, Herndon's attempts—as both myth-maker and truth-teller—to present a faithful picture of Lincoln to posterity. Kenneth P. Williams presents Lincoln's military genius in *Lincoln Finds a General* (5 v., 1949–59), with special emphasis on McClellan's ineptitude. A pioneer and exhaustive study of an important subject is Robert S. Harper's *Lincoln and the Press* (1951).

The Emergence of Lincoln (1950), by Allan Nevins, constitutes Volumes 3 and 4 after Nevins' earlier *Ordeal of the Union* (1947), which covered the years from 1847 to 1857. The later volumes close with Lincoln at the helm of state. With immense learning and the use of much important new data, Nevins surveys the prewar period, deals at length and favorably with Stephen A. Douglas, tells about John Brown in great detail, is realistic in dealing with the maneuvers of the Republican Party. He describes not only the many mistakes which helped lead to war, but also the great reforms and noble thinking of the period.

Brief mention might also be made of the following: Henry C. Whitney's *Life on the Circuit with Lincoln* (1892); David Miller De-Witt's *The Assassination of Abraham Lincoln* (1909); William E. Barton's *The Paternity of Abraham Lincoln* (1920), *The Lineage of Lincoln* (1929), and *Lincoln at Gettysburg* (1930); Emanuel Hertz's *Abraham Lincoln: A New Portrait* (2 v., 1931); Benjamin P. Thomas' *Lincoln's New Salem* (1934; rev., 1954); A. A. Woldman's *Lawyer Lincoln* (1936); Otto Eisenschiml's *Why Was Lincoln Murdered?* (1937); Stefan Lorant's *Lincoln, His Life in Photographs* (1941); T. Harry Williams' *Lincoln and the Radicals* (1941) and *Lincoln and His Generals* (1952); G. Lynn Sumner's *Meet Mr. Lincoln* (1946); F. Lauriston Bullard's *Abraham Lincoln and the Widow Bixby* (1946) and *Lincoln in Marble and Bronze* (1952); Donald W. Riddle's *Lincoln Runs for Congress* (1948); *The Lincoln Nobody Knows* (1958) by R. N. Current.

Lincoln, Joseph C[rosby] (b. Brewster, Mass., Feb. 13, 1870—d. March 10, 1944), poet, novelist, playwright. Many of Lincoln's ances-

tors had been Cape Cod sailors and captains, and he knew the Cape Cod region well and loved it. At first he tried to make a living in business, then turned to writing, published a collection of *Cape Cod Ballads* (1902). But when his first novel, *Cap'n Eri* (1904), appeared and made an immediate success, his future was determined. In this still readable story three retired sea captains, weary of housekeeping together, advertise for a wife. Thereafter Lincoln's novels were sure-fire successes. They were Cape Cod stories, and did not fail to take heed of the changing times, as when he wrote *The Portygee* (1920) about the immigrant fishermen from Europe who were changing the New England scene. Invariably right triumphs pleasantly in his stories. His sense of eccentric character and humorous speech never deserted him. Among his better known stories are *Mr. Pratt* (1906); *Cy Whitaker's Place* (1908); *Keziah Coffin* (1909); *Cap'n Dan's Daughter* (1914); *Shavings* (1918); *Galusha the Magnificent* (1921); *Queer Judson* (1924); *All Alongshore* (1931); *Storm Signals* (1935). The year before his death appeared *The Bradshaws of Harniss*, with World War I as a background. A Provincetown sage once remarked that the Cape had three industries: fishing, tourists, and Joseph C. Lincoln. The Chatham Historical Society has a Joseph C. Lincoln collection.

Lincoln, Mary Todd (b. Lexington, Ky., Dec. 13, 1818—d. July 16, 1882), wife of ABRAHAM LINCOLN. Numerous stories, true and false, have clustered around the Lincolns' marriage. Dr. W. A. Evans, in *Mrs. Abraham Lincoln* (1932), feels that she was not accountable for her actions after 1861. Mrs. Lincoln was adjudged of unsound mind in 1875, but again declared competent in 1876. She received a pension from Congress in 1870 and lived mostly in Europe after 1876. CARL SANDBURG and PAUL M. ANGLE collaborated on *Mary Lincoln, Wife and Widow* (1932). Irving Stone is friendly to her in his novel *Love Is Eternal* (1954). Her most recent and favorable biographer is Ruth Painter Randall, who wrote *Mary Lincoln: The Biography of a Marriage* (1953), and *The Courtship of Mr. Lincoln* (1957).

Lincoln, Victoria (b. Fall River, Mass., Oct. 23, 1904—   ), novelist, short-story writer. Miss Lincoln's first book, *February Hill* (1934), was a kindly, sometimes ribald story of a Fall River family; it established her reputation as a writer of power and wit. For some years she wrote short stories exclusively; these were collected in *Grandmother and the Comet* (1944). *The Wind at My Back* (1946) contains three novelettes, one of which—*Before the Swallow Dares*—is autobiographical. *Celia Amberley* (1949) follows a woman's life from early childhood to maturity; *Out from Eden* (1951) returns to the manner and humor of *February Hill* in its amusing study of an artist's family. More recent are *The Wild Honey* (1953) and *Dangerous Innocence* (1958).

Lincoln Library, The (1924; rev. ed., 1961), edited by Edwin Valentine Mitchell. In this one-volume, 2,271-page encyclopedia an immense amount of information is brought together. It was named after Abraham Lincoln as "the father of self-education." It includes twelve major departments: English language, literature, history, geography and travel, science, mathematics, economics and useful arts, government and politics, fine arts, education, biography, a miscellany. It is fully illustrated and has numerous tables and maps.

Lincoln Memorial. This building in Washington, D.C., is one of the most impressive on earth. It was designed by Henry Bacon (1866–1924) and dedicated in 1922. Inside is Daniel C. French's statue of Lincoln, and on the walls are engraved the GETTYSBURG ADDRESS and the *Second Inaugural Address.*

Linda Condon (1919), a novel by JOSEPH HERGESHEIMER. In this psychological study of a man and a woman Hergesheimer analyzes the meaning of beauty to a woman, of his ideals to a sculptor. Linda is a frigid woman, intent on preserving her loveliness. All her life she has been the inspiration of Dodge Pleydon, who creates a statue inspired by her. A mob destroys this, and Linda is roused to emotion at last; but Pleydon refuses her, intent on keeping his own ideals alive. The novel has been called Hergesheimer's greatest, but some have found the descriptions of luxurious living cloying.

Lindbergh, Anne Morrow (b. [?], 1906–), author. The wife of CHARLES A. LINDBERGH is an able and often highly poetic writer, some of whose books deal with experiences shared with Lindbergh and reflect his opinions. *North to the Orient* (1935) and *Listen! the Wind* (1938) are vivid descriptions of her flying experiences. *The Wave of the Future* (1940) propounded an unfortunate creed of not resisting the advance of fascism. She also wrote a charming novelette, *The Steep Ascent* (1944); the autobiographical and philosophical *Gift from the Sea* (1955), which spoke to women all over the country; *The Unicorn and Other Poems* (1956); and *Dearly Beloved* (1962).

Lindbergh, Charles A[ugustus] (b. Detroit, Mich., Feb. 4, 1902–), aviator. Lindbergh's solo flight across the Atlantic on May 20–21, 1927, the first in history, created a world sensation. With Fitzhugh Green he wrote an account of the flight called *We* (1927); the title refers to Lindbergh and his plane, *The Spirit of St. Louis.* He became internationally known, made good-will tours of several countries, and married ANNE MORROW, the daughter of the U.S. Ambassador to Mexico, Dwight W. Morrow. The tragic kidnapping and death of their infant son, Charles, Jr., in March, 1932, resulted in the passing of "Lindbergh laws" which make interstate kidnapping a Federal offense. The Lindberghs moved to Europe, where he worked with Alexis Carrel on the mechanical heart. In the years immediately preceding World War II, Lindbergh was an advocate of American neutrality. He wrote *Of*

Flight and Life (1948) and an autobiography, *The Spirit of St. Louis* (1953), which was awarded a Pulitzer Prize.

Linderman, Frank B[ird] (b. Cleveland, Ohio, Sept. 25, 1868—d. May 12, 1938), trapper, miner, chemist, writer. Linderman went to Montana as a young man and spent most of his life there. He knew the Indians well and often wrote about them, especially for children. Among his books: *Indian Why Stories* (1915); *On a Passing Frontier* (1920); *Bunch-Grass and Blue-Joint* (verse, 1921); *How It Came About Stories* (1921); *Lige Mounts* (1922); *Indian Old-Man Stories* (1920); *American: The Life Story of a Great Indian, Plenty-Coups* (1930); *Old Man Coyote* (1931); *Blackfeet Indians* (1935).

Lindeström, Peter Mårtensson (b. Sweden, [?]—d. [?]), engineer. Lindeström visited New Sweden on the Delaware in 1653–54, then returned home. During his last years he prepared an account of the new land, calling it *Geographia Americae.* It was translated from the original manuscript and published in 1925.

Lindsay, Howard (b. Waterford, N.Y., March 29, 1889—d. Feb. 11, 1968), actor, director, playwright. Lindsay left Harvard to go on the stage, showed a talent for directing, and staged DULCY and *To the Ladies,* both by George S. Kaufman and Marc Connelly, as well as other plays. He and his frequent collaborator, RUSSEL CROUSE, produced and directed numerous plays, some of their own composition. The first play they wrote together was *Anything Goes* (1934); their first partnership in production was ARSENIC AND OLD LACE (1941). Their greatest success was with their dramatization (1939) of LIFE WITH FATHER, in which Lindsay and his wife played the leads for five years. Lindsay also worked with DAMON RUNYON on *A Slight Case of Murder* (1935); with Crouse on the Pulitzer-Prize-winning STATE OF THE UNION (1945); with IRVING BERLIN on *Call Me Madam* (1950); and with RICHARD RODGERS and OSCAR HAMMERSTEIN II on *The Sound of Music* (1959).

Lindsay, [Nicholas] Vachel (b. Springfield, Ill., Nov. 10, 1879—d. Dec. 5, 1931), poet. Lindsay at first intended to be a missionary; although he gave up this idea in any literal sense, the crusading spirit was very strong in him, and he tried to convert America to a love of poetry and to a revival of agrarian civilization. For a time he wanted to be an artist. He lectured for the Anti-Saloon League through central Illinois, and spent the summer of 1912 walking from Illinois to New Mexico, preaching the "Gospel of Beauty" and exchanging his poems for hand-out meals and shelter.

Lindsay's verse, published in Harriet Monroe's magazine *Poetry,* became highly popular. Lindsay also become widely known through his public recitals, in which he would have his audience join him in his chanted refrains, in a kind of revival of medieval folk-poetry.

Lindsay was welcomed in England, appeared at Oxford, sometimes served as "resident poet" at various small colleges, always came back to

Springfield, which he celebrated in THE GOLDEN BOOK OF SPRINGFIELD (1920). His native city was also the setting for one of his best poems, *Abraham Lincoln Walks at Midnight* (1914). Gradually his poetry faded in quality, he him-

UPI

self became weary and disillusioned. Robert Morss Lovett, who knew him well, says this and a morbid conscience brought about his suicide by drinking poison.

The study of "influences" on Lindsay sends one on strange paths. He read everything that EDGAR ALLAN POE wrote, but tried, largely in vain, to escape his and Swinburne's influences. SIDNEY LANIER was a model, also WALT WHITMAN, although Lindsay's verse was an imitation of Whitman's attitude rather than of his technique. Along with these one must reckon gospel hymns, revivalist sermons, the addresses of Lincoln, Salvation Army music, Negro jazz, and the poetry readings of Prof. S. H. Clark of the University of Chicago. Lindsay recorded some of his own readings, and the records are still available. Clement Wood felt that he had a great gift which gradually deteriorated. Others have found themselves unable to hear more than rarely the sound of poetry in his work, so much of it is posturing and mouthing. Harriet Monroe eulogized Lindsay for establishing contact with his audience; Hazelton Spencer saw him as belonging with Emerson and Whitman as both voice and critic of democracy. His reputation rests on such poems as *A Gospel of*

Beauty (1908), GENERAL WILLIAM BOOTH ENTERS INTO HEAVEN (1913), *A Net to Snare the Moonlight* (1913), THE EAGLE THAT IS FORGOTTEN (1913), THE CONGO (1914), THE SANTA FE TRAIL: A HUMORESQUE (1914), THE CHINESE NIGHTINGALE (1917), THE GHOST OF THE BUFFALOES (1917), IN PRAISE OF JOHNNY APPLESEED (1921).

Among Lindsay's books: *Rhymes to Be Traded for Bread* (1912); *General William Booth Enters into Heaven and Other Poems* (1913); *Adventures While Preaching the Gospel of Beauty* (1914); *The Congo and Other Poems* (1914); *The Art of the Moving Picture* (1915); *A Handy Guide for Beggars* (1916); *The Chinese Nightingale and Other Poems* (1917); THE GOLDEN WHALES OF CALIFORNIA AND OTHER RHYMES IN THE AMERICAN LANGUAGE (1920); *Collected Poems* (1923; rev. ed., 1925); *Going-to-the-Stars* (1926); *The Candle in the Cabin* (1926); *Johnny Appleseed* (1928); *The Litany of Washington Street* (1929); *Every Soul Is a Circus* (1929). His *Selected Poems* (1931) were edited by Hazelton Spencer.

Stephen Graham wrote about Lindsay in *Tramping with a Poet in the Rockies* (1922). Biographical and critical were A. E. Trombly's *Vachel Lindsay, Adventurer* (1929) and EDGAR LEE MASTERS' *Vachel Lindsay: A Poet in America* (1935), both based on personal knowledge. Both biography and interpretation are found in Mark Harris' *City of Discontent* (1952). A more recent biography is Eleanor Ruggles' *The West-Going Heart: A Life of Vachel Lindsay* (1959).

Lindsey, Ben[jamin] B[arr] (b. Jackson, Tenn., Nov. 25, 1869—d. March 26, 1943), lawyer, public official, writer. Lindsey had a long career as a judge in Colorado and California. He described his vehement battles against "privilege" in *The Beast* (written with Harvey J. O'Higgins, 1910) and *The Rise of Plutocracy in Colorado* (1912), also in his aptly named autobiography, *The Dangerous Life* (written with Rube Borough, 1931). In the turbulent 1920's Lindsey became involved in a violent controversy aroused by the views that he expressed in *The Companionate Marriage* (written with Wainwright Evans, 1927). Oscar Cargill called him "a full-fledged Progressive of the old school."

Line o' Type or Two, A. The heading of a column in the Chicago *Tribune*. The column was originally conducted by BERT LESTON TAYLOR from 1902 to 1921; his initials B.L.T. became famous all over the country, his verses and quips were widely copied, and his column was soon imitated in other papers. It is regarded as the ancestor of humorous columns in the American press. Taylor made several books out of the material he contributed.

Linguistic Atlas of the U.S. and Canada. A large-scale linguistic project which is slowly being carried to completion. The *Atlas* was first proposed by a committee of the Modern Language Association in 1924. In 1928 Prof. E. H. Sturdevant of Yale interested the American

Council of Learned Societies in the project, which was actively launched the following year in co-operation with the Linguistic Institute of the Linguistic Society of America. The intention is to publish "linguistic maps" of different sections of the country. The first section (1939), about New England, consists of three volumes, each in two parts, in which appear 734 double-page maps. Accompanying the first volume is a large *Handbook of the Linguistic Geography of New England,* by Hans Kurath and Miles L. Hanley. The *Atlas* records variations in vocabulary and pronunciation, and is much more detailed than the *Dictionary of American English* (1936–44). In 1949 Kurath issued *Word Geography of the Eastern U.S.* E. B. Atwood described *Verb Forms of the Eastern U.S.* (1953).

Lin McLean (1897), a group of six sketches and a poem about a "charming cowboy" by OWEN WISTER. The scene is Wyoming "in the happy days when it was a Territory with a future, instead of a State with a past." Wister had begun publishing the sketches as early as 1891 when he wrote "How Lin McLean Went West" for *Harper's.*

Linton, William James (b. England, Dec. 7, 1812—d. Jan. 1, 1897), English poet, engraver, editor. Linton, an English radical, founded (1839) a short-lived magazine called the *National,* became editor of the *Illuminated Magazine* (1845), contributed political verse to the Dublin *Nation.* He published two collections of verse (1852, 1865), then in 1866 emigrated to the United States. Near New Haven, Conn., he set up a school for the study and practice of wood engraving, also a private press, from which he issued anthologies and a collection of his own *Poems and Translations* (1889). He also wrote *The Masters of Wood-Engraving* (1889), a *Life of John Greenleaf Whittier* (1893), and *Memories* (1895). He has been praised for his epigrammatic poems and for his deft translations of Villon and other French poets, and his engravings are still remembered.

Lin Yu-t'ang [in English usually **Yutang**] (b. China, Oct. 10, 1895—   ), teacher, editor, translator, writer. Educated in China, Lin attended Harvard graduate school, later studied in Germany. He went back to China to teach, wrote for various English and Chinese periodicals (some of which he founded), and edited texts for students. Lin joined revolutionary movements, of which he says, "I have always liked revolutions, but never revolutionaries." He is chancellor of Nanyang University, Singapore, and also head of the Arts and Letters division of UNESCO.

Among the books written or edited by Lin are *My Country and My People* (1935), an analysis of China which did not altogether please the Chinese—the section on Chinese humor is particularly good; *Confucius Saw Nancy* (1936); *A Nun of Taishan* (1936); *A History of the Press and Public Opinion in China* (1936); *The Importance of Living* (1937); *The Wisdom of Confucius* (1938); *Moment in Peking* (1939); *A Leaf in the Storm* (1941); *Wisdom of China and India* (1942); *Between Tears and Laughter* (1943); *The Gay Genius* (1947); *Chinatown Family* (1948); *Wisdom of Laotse* (1948); *Wisdom of America* (1950); *Widow, Nun, and Courtesan* (three stories, one original, two translated, 1951); *Famous Chinese Short Stories* (1952); *Vermilion Gate* (1953); *Looking Beyond* (1955); *The Chinese Way of Life* (1959); *The Importance of Understanding* (1960); *The Red Peony* (1962).

Lionel Lincoln, or, The Leaguer of Boston (1825), a novel by JAMES FENIMORE COOPER. The hero is a British officer in whose family history there is a mystery which Cooper is barely able to untangle by the end of the story. Lionel arrives at Boston in time to take part in the opening events of the Revolution, goes back to England with a bride. The book has good descriptions of Lexington and Concord.

Lion of the West, The (1831), a farce by JAMES KIRKE PAULDING. The play was written as a vehicle for JAMES H. HACKETT in the leading role, Col. Nimrod Wildfire, supposedly a take-off on DAVY CROCKETT and other western hunters and pioneers (see also under RINGWOOD THE ROVER). It was rewritten several times and even renamed, finally being performed (1833) as *A Kentuckian's Trip to New York;* it may have inspired W. A. Caruthers' novel *The Kentuckian in New York* (1834). See *John Augustus Stone.*

Lippard, George (b. Chester Co., Pa., April 10, 1822—d. Feb. 9, 1854), journalist, novelist, playwright. Abandoning first the ministry, then the law, Lippard at nineteen became a journalist for the *Spirit of the Times,* a Philadelphia daily. His police court reporting, marked by originality, humor, and a warm sympathy for the underdog, was so popular that it increased the paper's circulation. His column, *Our Talisman,* is somewhat in the style of Dickens' *Sketches by Boz.* Failing in health, he turned to novel-writing. *The Monks of Monk Hall* (1844), retitled a year later THE QUAKER CITY, was a lurid story about the midnight orgies of a group of the "best people." Lippard may have been influenced by the "Gothick" romances and by accounts of the scandalous practices of the 18th-century Medmenham Abbey group. It created a furor; a dramatization by the author was withdrawn by the mayor, who feared an outraged mob might destroy the theater. A watered-down version was safely performed in New York City in 1845.

Lippard became a popular lecturer on legends of the Revolution and of Washington, and wrote a number of books on the subject, as well as many romantic historical novels; among them are *Blanche of Brandywine* (1846); *Paul Ardenheim* (1848); *Bel of Prairie Eden* (1848); *The Man with the Mask* (1852). *New York: Its Upper Ten and Lower Million* (1853) and *Eleanor: or, Slave Catching in Philadelphia* (1854) deal with vice and debauchery in the two cities. In 1850 Lippard founded the "Brotherhood of the Union," a benevolent society which aimed to eliminate poverty and crime by removing the social evils causing them.

Lippincott, Horace Mather (b. Philadelphia, April 20, 1877—   ), historian. Deeply interested in history, education, and the Quakers, Lippincott wrote many valuable special studies. Among them: *The Colonial Homes of Philadelphia and Its Neighborhood* (1912); *A Portraiture of the People Called Quakers* (1915); *George Washington and the University of Pennsylvania* (1916); *Early Philadelphia* (1917); *A History of Germantown Academy* (1935); *Benjamin West* (1944); *A Searching Time for Quakers* (1945); *Quaker Meeting Houses* (1952); *A History of the Philadelphia Cricket Club, 1854–1954* (1954); *Through a Quaker Archway* (1959).

Lippincott, Joseph Wharton (b. Philadelphia, Feb. 28, 1887—   ), publisher, author. Lippincott, grandson of Joshua Ballinger Lippincott (1813–1886), founder of J. B. Lippincott & Co., became president of the firm in 1926. He wrote many books on nature (some for children), including *Bun, a Wild Rabbit* (1918); *Red Ben, the Fox of Oak Ridge* (1919); *Striped Coat, The Skunk* (1922); *The Wolf King* (1933); *Animal Neighbors of the Countryside* (1938); *Black Wings: The Unbeatable Crow* (1947); *Gray Squirrel* (1921); *Long Horn, Leader of the Deer* (1928, rev ed 1955).

Lippincott's Magazine. J. B. Lippincott & Co. began issuing this magazine in January, 1868; it won wide recognition for the excellence of its contents and for its encouragement of Southern writers. In December, 1914, it was sold to McBride, Nast & Co. and the name was changed to *McBride's Magazine*. Two years later it merged with SCRIBNER'S MAGAZINE.

Lippmann, Walter (b. New York City, Sept. 23, 1889—   ), teacher, editor, columnist, public official, author. Lippmann taught philosophy at Harvard as an assistant to GEORGE SANTAYANA. Under Woodrow Wilson he served the government in preparation for the making of peace, and is believed to have influenced Wilson's thinking on world issues. He went on to editorial positions on the *New Republic* and the New York *World*, finally became a columnist on the New York *Herald Tribune*. Meantime he had published a number of influential books, beginning with *A Preface to Politics* (1913). Lippmann hoped for a "good society," to be reached by sweet reasonableness, but events frequently disappointed him.

Lippmann in his later stages was still regarded as something of a wild-eyed radical. But David E. Weingast, in *Walter Lippmann: A Study in Personal Journalism* (1949), concluded that Lippmann proceeded from belief in a mild socialism to what came close to a defense of the *status quo*. He feels that Lippmann should be read with attention but skeptically as a "highly literate, well-informed mind" who has been wrong before and may be so again.

Always the philosopher, Lippmann analyzed society coldly and lucidly in such volumes as *Drift and Mastery* (1914); *The Stakes of Diplomacy* (1915); *Liberty and the News* (1920); *Public Opinion* (1922); *A Preface to Morals* (1929); *Interpretations, 1933–1935* (1936); *The New Imperative* (1935); *The Good Society* (1937); *U.S. Foreign Policy* (1943); *U.S. War Aims* (1944); *The Cold War* (1947); *The Public Philosophy* (1955); and *The Communist World and Ours* (1959). In 1962 Lippmann won the Pulitzer Prize for international reporting.

Litany for Dictatorships (1935), a poem by STEPHEN VINCENT BENÉT. At the height of the terror cast on the world by Hitler, Mussolini, and Stalin, Benét wrote this passionate poem of anger against dictators, a horrifying picture of what the "perfect state" does to its people, especially those who dare to think or speak against it.

literary agents. In New York City today there are about one hundred recognized literary agents. Many of the best belong to the Society of Authors' Representatives. The traditional fee is 10 per cent of the author's royalties, though some representatives charge a reading fee of from three to thirty dollars. The literary agent —or, as some prefer to call themselves, author's representative—may be a guide and mentor, a banker, a buffer between the author and the editor or publisher, a negotiator of movie and radio rights, a public relations man, a guardian for publishers and magazines against plagiarism. Some agencies are dynastic, like that of Paul Reynolds, Jr. There are large agencies such as Brandt & Brandt, or Curtis Brown, agencies which specialize in the foreign markets, and some which are represented by a single individual. Harold Ober was one of the latter; the antithesis of the high-pressure salesman, he represented F. Scott Fitzgerald, William Faulkner, Paul Gallico, Adlai Stevenson, Agatha Christie, and John Gunther. Over the years he loaned Fitzgerald as much as twenty thousand dollars, and was father-confessor, nurse, and adviser to many other authors. The agent's miscellaneous existence is treated entertainingly in Richard Mealand's *Let Me Do the Talking* (1947). The Hollywood agent appears in Arthur Kober's *That Man Is Here Again* (1946). Jane Hardy, herself an agent once, has written revealingly about the literary market in her novel *Fann Marlow* (1954). Keen glimpses of agents and their many-faced personalities may be found in the letters of Scribner's MAXWELL PERKINS.

Literary America (1952), a chronicle of American writers from 1607 to 1952 by David E. Scherman and Rosemarie Redlich. This beautifully printed and illustrated book presents America in 173 outstanding photographs as her great writers have seen her, from Jefferson's Monticello and Natty Bumppo's cave to Carl Sandburg's Chicago stockyards and Erskine Caldwell's squalid back-country scenes. Quotations from ninety-three authors supplement the pictorial text.

literary criticism. Meyer Abrams in *The Mirror and the Lamp* (1953) says there are four general approaches to literary criticism. They are (1) theories of mimesis, (2) pragmatic theories, (3) expressive theories, and (4) objective theories. At various times in Western and American literary history, one or another has tended to be dominant. But at no time has any one of them been totally out of favor or in eclipse.

Plato and Aristotle appear to have initiated the *mimetic* theories. They assumed that a play was an imitation of an action. Up and down the ages critics have argued about the precise meanings of *imitation*—how close or how far it can or should get from actuality and from history. Probably no serious critic has ever denied it some validity.

The second, *pragmatic* theories, emphasize the audience. Aristotle's doctrine of catharsis, purging the audience of pity and fear, is pragmatic. Literary criticism throughout the Christian era emphasized the audience's response— for good or evil—to the literary work. Horace stressed the utility (*utile*) as well as the beauty (*dulce*) of art. The moralistic theories of the 19th century or of the New Humanists are pragmatic.

The third, *expressive* theories, held the largest appeal for the Romantic period and the 19th century generally. These theories stress the poet's imagination and his moral nature. It gave rise to the dictum, "*Le style, c'est l'homme.*" Coleridge is perhaps the greatest expressive critic. His American disciple is Emerson.

The fourth, *objective* theories, emphasize the work itself. Thus discussed, literature is seen impersonally, objectively, apart from the author. Formalist theories about the techniques of art are objective. Mark Schorer's "style is the subject" implies an acceptance of an objective theory of art. The major emphasis in 20th-century criticism, especially in the so-called New Criticism, is objective.

Mr. Abrams says the four theories collectively endeavor to explain "the total situation of a work of art." They also, at times, tend to run together.

The mimetic theory has not been greatly emphasized in American criticism. Aristotle's *Poetics,* however, has long been taught respectfully in American colleges and universities, and modern novelists and critics have come to see the justness of the stress he lays on plot. The so-called neo-Aristotelians at the University of Chicago have tried to build a theory of modern criticism based on the *Poetics,* centering attention on mimesis. Their work can be seen in *Critics and Criticism* (1952), edited by Ronald Crane. Imitation theories have also entered literary theory in other ways, through the historical study of literature (a "climate of opinion," a "world picture," a work's "mirroring its age") and through the study of myth. The historical method of such a scholar or critic as VERNON PARRINGTON (*Main Currents in American Thought,* 3 v., 1927–30) relates the literary work to its milieu. Parrington, like all students of the historical method in literary study, was indebted to Hippolyte Taine (1828–93), the French critic, who said that a knowledge of "race, moment and milieu" could be equated with what was to be found in a given work of literature.

Nineteenth-century critics were more given to pragmatic tests than are those of the 20th century. A reader knew a line was true poetry if it caused one to catch his breath, raised gooseflesh, or stiffened the bristles in his beard. William Wimsatt and M. C. Beardsley have, in *The Affective Fallacy* (*Sewanee Review,* 1949), vigorously opposed such tests, declaring they are vague and imprecise. They disapprove of Aristotle's catharsis doctrine, or of Longinus' discussing the "transport" of an audience. They hold that the poem itself should be the center of critical attention. As a matter of emphasis, Wimsatt and Beardsley are probably right. Yet even after reading a sophisticated, knowledgeable critical analysis of a poem or story, it remains for the small private voice inside each reader to give or deny assent to the judgment. This finally is a pragmatic test.

William Cullen Bryant, in *On the Nature of Poetry* (1826), said the term *imitation* is of doubtful usefulness. He stressed the poet's imagination, his ability to create and evoke powerful feelings from symbols, thus aligning himself with expressionist theories. But he also emphasized the role of poetry in improving the audience's morality, a pragmatic theory. Emerson once or twice mentions imitation, but generally the doctrines in "The Poet" (1844) are quite similar to Bryant's. James Russell Lowell, in *The Function of the Poet* (1855), and Walt Whitman, in the Preface to *Leaves of Grass* (1855), also saw the poet as seer, projecting great moral truths. American criticism in the 19th century tended to follow Coleridge's expressionist theories. These are stated most explicitly in *Biographia Literaria* (1817).

Coleridge's doctrine of the imagination is commonly admired by such recent American critics as Kenneth Burke and Cleanth Brooks. Modern criticism does not to any considerable extent stress the poet or novelist's moral nature, but psychoanalytical criticism is in the romantic-expressionist tradition. Edmund Wilson, in *The Wound and the Bow* (1941), for example, discusses a writer's hurt, or "wound," relating it to the writer's imaginative gifts (his "bow") and literary work.

The objective theories are sometimes related to expressionist theories. For example, Coleridge emphasizes the poet's imagination, but he also discusses patterns of imagery, metrics, characterization, and tone. Edgar Allan Poe was an objective, or formalist, critic. He stressed the beauty of the poem, not its power to teach. He said in THE POETIC PRINCIPLE (1850) that "a long poem is simply a contradiction in terms," and he insisted that the short story ("Hawthorne's Tales," 1847) be constructed after the writer had conceived what his *single* effect would be. Henry James also emphasized objective theories. In *The Art of Fiction* (1888), he is aware that fiction is an imitative art, and aware, too, that the quality of the writer's mind and his moral nature profoundly influence the work he creates. But the major emphasis is on structure, and on the techniques through which a writer may create a work of art.

Almost all the terms that are current in modern American criticism are employed in the service of one or another objective theory. John Crowe Ransom uses the term "texture," by which he means images, metaphors, and meters. Robert Penn Warren, Allen Tate, and the present writer have used the term "tension," usually to mean the unity, sometimes paradoxical, resulting from a struggle of conflicting ideas. A proposition using appropriate language, characters, or episodes justifies itself by resisting convincingly a series of ironic questions. Cleanth Brooks' belief that the language of poetry is essentially paradoxical and ironic is also an objective theory.

During the early days of the Republic, of course, neoclassical ideals were dominant. Most criticism appeared in periodicals. (See Lyon Richardson, *History of Early American Magazines, 1741–1789*). Alexander Pope and Jonathan Swift were commonly praised. College textbooks in rhetoric were those used in England: Lord Kames' *Elements of Criticism* (1762), Hugh Blair's *Lectures on Rhetoric* (1783), and Archibald Alison's *Nature and Principles of Taste* (1790).

The glories of Newtonian science were in the air, and gave rise to the belief that prose should be natural, precise, and without false ornaments. Benjamin Franklin, Thomas Jefferson, and Tom Paine held such notions. An early critic of this type was JOSEPH DENNIE (1768–1812); a conservative Federalist, he wrote for *Farmer's Weekly Museum* (1796–98) and the *Port Folio* (1801–09). Forty of his essays were published as a book in 1796, and he was acclaimed as the "American Addison." His reputation was soon eclipsed by Washington Irving's.

There were many discussions of American as opposed to English writing and literature. Walter Channing, a Harvard professor, saw no way for American literature to emerge because Americans used English, not a language of their own. Meanwhile, Noah Webster was busy standardizing American spelling, and through writers like Philip Freneau (1752–1832) and Charles Brockden Brown (1771–1801) America began to have her own literature. John Trumbull (1750–1831), a Connecticut poet, expressed the common sentiment of the day:

This land her Swift and Addison shall view
The former honors equall'd by the new;
Here shall some Shakespear charm the rising age,
And hold in magic chains the listening stage.

Literary criticism, as it is more usually understood today, began in the early 19th century in America. Bryant in his *Lectures on Poetry* (1825) derided sickly imitations of neoclassical writers. He praised the judicious combination of imagination and emotion, originality and metrical flexibility. Bryant was a transitional figure between neoclassicism and romanticism. Coleridge's influence swung the balance. James Marsh (1794–1842) wrote an elaborate introduction to Coleridge's *Aids to Reflection* (1829) and *The Friend* (1831). F. H. Hedge (1805–1890) wrote extensively about the German philosophers to whom Coleridge was indebted, and he wrote an influential essay on Coleridge in the *Christian Examiner* in 1833. These men introduced Coleridge's work to Emerson and his transcendental friends. GEORGE RIPLEY (1802–1880), one of the founders of the *Dial* and the organizer of Brook Farm, also wrote transcendentalist criticism, especially during his years as book reviewer (1849–80) on the New York *Tribune*.

Transcendental criticism, and Emerson as its chief spokesman, minimized external forms and stressed the transforming power of the writer's imagination. Having read Coleridge, Emerson borrowed Kant's distinction between Understanding (rationality) and the higher Reason (intuition, etc.). Also from Coleridge he took the distinction between fancy (which works by association) and imagination (which creates), and the organic theory of composition (in which each detail is intimately involved with and modified by every other detail and by the whole).

The most active critic in Emerson's group was MARGARET FULLER (1810–1850). She was an editor of the *Dial*, an ardent feminist, an essayist, and a reviewer. *Papers on Literature and Art* was published in 1846. She divided critics into three types, the *subjective*, who simply responds or reacts to a work; the *apprehensive*, who enters imaginatively into the work, trying to identify himself with the author's intentions; and the *comprehensive*. The latter acts as the *apprehensive* critic does, but also makes a judgment about the relative merits of the work. Critics, she said, can either apply the highest standards (Coleridge's standards, for example), or enjoy lesser works of the fancy, recognizing that they are of a humbler order.

In EDGAR ALLAN POE (1809–1849) America had its first truly original critic. Through his antididacticism and his emphasis on the poem as a work of art, he influenced the symbolist writers in France, and thereby, indirectly, the art-for-art's-sake movement in England in the 1890's. Poe believed the artist needed knowledge, an idealizing imagination, and conscious artistry of a high order. He defined poetry "as the rhythmical creation of beauty." Poe argued, in a rather confused way, with Coleridge's doctrines, but was nonetheless indebted to the *Biographia Literaria*. It was in his attack on "the heresy of the didactic" that Poe went most strongly against the drift of his time. Poetry is concerned with beauty, and if the beautiful should happen to give moral instruction, this is accidental. Taste alone, informed taste, is the basis for judgment.

The critic, Poe held, should be "frank, candid, and independent . . . giving honor only where honor is due." He should not be afraid of giving offense to an author, because his loyalty is to "the general cause of letters." He should respect tradition, but not at the expense of originality. General theory, he also said, is useful, but the practicing critic should get down to particulars, discussing a work in terms of its unique effects, its merits and defects. Poe had the courage to try to live up to these rules, and thereby alienated many literary figures, including Emerson and Margaret Fuller. Quite possibly, too, his standards and frequently caustic tone discouraged the critical movement that might have been expected to develop in his wake.

Scholars have singled out a handful of mid-19th-century critics as representative of the reviewing and criticism of the time. Two are EVERT DUYCKINCK (1816–1878) and his brother GEORGE DUYCKINCK (1823–1863), co-editors of the New York *Literary World* (1847–53), the leading literary review of its day. They were acquainted with Irving, Cooper, Bryant, and Melville, and were sometimes instrumental in getting new writers into print. The brothers edited *Cyclopaedia of American Literature* (1855). Rufus Griswold (1815–1857) was a prominent New York and Philadelphia journalist. He compiled several anthologies of poems, writing introductions for them. E. P. Whipple, a prolific and generous-minded critic, is now almost forgotten. Poe believed he was a critic of great merit.

The New England Brahmins, especially OLIVER WENDELL HOLMES, SR. (1809–1894) and JAMES RUSSELL LOWELL (1819–1891), carried great weight in the literary world. Holmes was a doctor and professor of medicine. In 1852 he prepared himself for giving a series of lectures on the English poets by reading in the files of the *Edinburgh Review* and by studying the critical works of Coleridge, the Schlegels, William Hazlitt, and Leigh Hunt. He also knew Horace's *Ars Poetica* intimately. By 1857–58, when he wrote *The Autocrat of the Breakfast Table,* he had become familiar with a wide range of poetry and criticism. He thought his own way through critical problems. For example, he did not subscribe to Wordsworth's "emotion recollected in tranquility"—he said composition was "a cold-blooded, haggard, anxious, worrying hunt" after rhymes and good effects. Holmes was a witty, sane, and undogmatic critic.

Lowell was an admirer of Emerson as a speaker, but he disapproved of the transcendentalist's desire to live "off the internal revenues of the spirit." Lowell was a born conservative, but was stirred by his first wife to investigate liberal doctrines and programs. As a young man his mind and his writings were vital and often original. He was also learned. *The Biglow Papers,* a series of satiric verses in a rustic idiom, implied an attack on bookish writing and urged a native American literature. As editor of the *Atlantic Monthly* he wrote many essays, later collected in book form as *Fireside Travels* (1864), *Among My Books* (1870), *My Study Windows* (1871), and others. Lowell has been called America's most distinguished 19th-century critic, but surely this is too great praise. Lowell may have been more judicious than Poe, but he lacked Poe's brilliance and originality.

Ernest Stedman (1833–1908), a poet and successful Wall Street broker, is rather difficult to categorize. As a poet he is clearly tepid and in the genteel tradition. As a critic he is antididactic and a follower of Poe. In *Nature and Elements of Poetry* (1892) he develops the theory that beauty is independent of moral considerations. He did not, however, possess the analytical powers necessary for serious criticism.

Walt Whitman (1819–1892) proposed a revolutionary theory in *Democratic Vistas* (1871). He treats the ideals of democracy and individualism, and condemns the degradation of democracy and the crass, vulgar wealth of the post–Civil War era. He prophesies greatness in the future and asks for a cultural declaration of independence from Europe.

As a critic WILLIAM DEAN HOWELLS (1837–1920) is a curious amalgam of his age and country. He is at once a realist and a victim of the genteel tradition, a believer in Tolstoi's evolutionary ethics and in Taine's literary determinism. Art, he said, must tell the truth, but in doing so, it should serve morality and reveal the "smiling aspects" of American life and the virtues of democracy. His critical volumes include *Criticism and Fiction* (1891), *My Literary Passions* (1895), and *Literature and Life* (1902). Howells was far from being a knowledgeable critic, but he was good at sketching the lives of his literary acquaintances, and he helped secure public favor for Emily Dickinson, Stephen Crane, Hamlin Garland, and Frank Norris.

HENRY JAMES, JR. (1843–1916) is without question America's most outstanding 19th-century critic, and possibly future generations will see that he surpassed the work of any later American critics. He had a clear understanding of the value and limitations of any "rules," and he had what Keats said Shakespeare had, "negative capability": that is, no need to force a theory or to arrive at a neat, logical conclusion when confronted by two seemingly contradictory ideas. James' *The Art of Fiction* is at once simple and sophisticated, useful and unpretentious. James does, on occasion, worry points in a sophistical manner, but generally he can be depended on to see what is essential, what is peripheral, and what is beside the point. Some of his critical volumes are *French Poets and Novelists* (1878), *Notes on Novelists* (1914), and *Notes on Reviews* (1921). The prefaces he wrote for the New York edition of his novels have been a kind of *poetics* for the modern novelist. They were collected in *The Art of the Novel* (1934) by R. P. Blackmur.

In general, 19th-century critics suffered from America's cultural involvement with the genteel tradition, which minimized the life of the body, separated spirit from flesh, ignored the actualities of American life, especially urban life, and fought off scientific knowledge. The first effective criticism of the genteel tradition was George Santayana's THE GENTEEL TRADITION IN AMERICAN PHILOSOPHY (1911). He said James escaped from the genteel tradition by comprehending it and turning it into a subject matter. Poe, Hawthorne, and Emerson, he said, were highly endowed writers who "could not retail the genteel tradition; they were too keen and independent for that. . . . In their own persons they escaped the mediocrity of the genteel tradition, but they supplied nothing to supplant it in other minds." It is no very considerable exaggeration to say that the quarrel 20th-century writers and critics have had with the 19th century was over the failure of most writers in the earlier era to come to grips with the limitations of that tradition.

Modern American criticism is indebted to 19th-century criticism, especially to that of Coleridge, Poe, and James. But it also breaks with the genteel tradition and looks abroad for other sources of inspiration.

Beginning with critics like James Gibbons Huneker (1857–1921), Lewis Gates (1860–1924), and Joel Spingarn (1875–1939), American criticism turned to Europe, to Walter Pater, Anatole France, Benedetto Croce, and others. The impressionist movement, extremely important in Europe, made some headway in America, but more with poets and fiction writers than with critics.

In *The New Criticism* (1910) Spingarn said literature is expression, and the critic should ask and answer only two questions: What did the writer intend to do? and, How well did he do it? Ethical questions, the study of sources, and all the rest are beside the point. Spingarn made a little stir, but the big movement, to be known as Modern Criticism, or the NEW CRITICISM, was getting under way in England. Ezra Pound and T. S. Eliot, through their contributions to "little magazines" here and abroad— *The Egoist, Criterion, Blast, Poetry, The Little Review, The Dial,* and so on—were undertaking to establish the modern movement. Both Pound and Eliot have declared their indebtedness to the French Remy de Gourmont.

Eliot published *The Sacred Wood* (1920), which he said was concerned with "the integrity of poetry," and Pound published *Instigations* (1920), with essays on a dozen French poets, on Henry James, Remy de Gourmont, Vorticism, Provençal poetry, and the "Chinese Written Character." In these two volumes one finds many of the preoccupations of modern criticism: the emphasis on the image, symbolism, art for art's sake, and the availability of certain earlier works from Western and English literary tradition. T. E. Hulme, a British critic with whom

Pound was friendly, influenced both Eliot and Pound in their antiromantic stand (opposition to vague expressions and grandiloquence) and in their concern with literary conventions.

Eliot, Hulme, and also Ford Madox Ford, a friend of James and a proponent of impressionist fiction, exerted a considerable influence on Allen Tate, John Crowe Ransom, Robert Penn Warren, and Cleanth Brooks, all of whom had a great deal to do with carrying modern criticism to the campus. Their criticism tends to be concerned with the language of poetry and literary structure, but also with questions of regionalism, nationalism, and traditionalism. More or less associated with them, especially through their contributions to the *Southern Review* (1935–42), *Sewanee Review* (1892—   ), and *Kenyon Review* (1939—   ), are R. P. Blackmur, Kenneth Burke, Yvor Winters, William Troy, and Morton Zabel.

Concurrently with the careers of Eliot and Pound there have been, of course, other critical movements. Randolph Bourne (1886–1916), Van Wyck Brooks (1886—   ), Ludwig Lewisohn (1882–1955), H. L. Mencken (1880–1956), Stark Young (1881—   ), Lewis Mumford (1895—   ), Carl Van Doren (1885–1950), Mark Van Doren (1894—   ), and Joseph Wood Krutch (1893—   ), may be said to have been deeply involved with what Brooks, in 1915, called "America's Coming of Age." They welcomed new talent, watched and commented as literature was influenced by Freud, Jung, Marx, and the depression, and as it fought a rear-guard action against the genteel tradition. Thanks to them, O'Neill, Lewis, Dreiser, Fitzgerald, Cather, Faulkner, and other new talents got a hearing.

The critics called the New Humanists, Irving Babbitt (1865–1933) and P. E. More (1864–1937), insisted that man is a supernatural being, and that the center of concern in literature is with ethics. More published fourteen volumes of SHELBURNE ESSAYS, and Babbitt, the more astute of the two, a number of books which are still read, notably *Rousseau and Romanticism* (1910). See HUMANISM, on THE NEW HUMANISM.

Society in the 20th century apparently could not afford men of letters, like Lowell and Howells, but Malcolm Cowley, author of *Exile's Return* (1934) and *The Literary Situation* (1954), and Edmund Wilson, critic for the *New Yorker* and author of *Axel's Castle* (1931) and innumerable other books, managed to survive as professional critics.

An academic critic who merged a number of critical traditions is LIONEL TRILLING (1905—   ), especially in *The Liberal Imagination* (1943). Associated with the *Partisan Review* (1934—   ), at first a strongly leftist journal but later independent, he examined liberal assumptions, testing them against conservative and reactionary opinions. He also carefully scrutinized Freudian theory, showing where it was, or was not, relevant to the understanding of literature. A student of Arnold, Trilling writes with a sense of high seriousness, trying to relate the study of literature to an understanding of culture.

Nowadays there are many good critics publishing articles and books: Leon Edel, Philip Rahv, John Gassner, Eric Bentley, Richard Chase, Philip Young, and perhaps twenty-five or thirty others. For the past fifteen or twenty years America has had more good critics than at any other time in her history.

The 20th century has been called an Age of Criticism and an Alexandrian Age. The latter term implies that criticism is sometimes seen as being prior to poetry or drama or fiction, and also that critical preoccupations inhibit and stultify creative impulses. It does appear to be true that some of the major figures in modern literature, such as Yeats, Joyce, Eliot, and Wallace Stevens, have written their poetry or fiction only after deliberately working out complicated rationales and symbolic systems. American criticism, of course, is a part of the modern literary milieu, a victim of whatever may be excessive in it; but it also participates in and enjoys its strengths and virtues.

For further reading about pre-20th-century American literary criticism see: Clarence A. Brown, ed., *The Achievement of American Criticism* (1954); William Charvat, *The Origins of American Critical Thought* (1936); Harry H. Clark, "The Influence of Science on American Literary Criticism, 1860–1910," *Transactions of the Wisconsin Academy of Sciences, Arts, and Letters*, 44, pp. 109–64; George De Mille, *Literary Criticism in America* (1931); Norman Foerster, *American Criticism* (1928); John P. Pritchard, *Criticism in America* (1956); John Stafford, *The Literary Criticism of Young America, 1837–1850* (1952); Floyd Stovall, ed., *The Development of American Literary Criticism* (1955). *The Idea of an American Novel* (1961), edited by L. Rubin and J. R. Moore, is a useful anthology of criticism of the novel. There are hundreds of books and articles on modern American criticism. The following are anthologies and histories only: Charles Glicksberg, ed., *American Literary Criticism, 1900–1950* (1953); Stanley E. Hyman, *The Armed Vision* (1948); Murray Krieger, *The New Apologists for Poetry* (1956); William Van O'Connor, *An Age of Criticism, 1900–1950* (1952); William Van O'Connor, ed., *Forms of Modern Fiction* (1948); Robert W. Stallman, *The Critic's Notebook* (1950); Morton D. Zabel, ed., *Literary Opinion in America* (1951). *The Shock of Recognition* (1943), edited by Edmund Wilson, contains the opinions American writers have had about the work of their contemporaries. William Elton's *A Glossary of the New Criticism* (1951) is a useful introduction to some of the terminology used in modern criticism. See REVIEWERS AND REVIEWING.

WILLIAM VAN O'CONNOR

Literary Digest. I. K. Funk founded this magazine in New York City on March 1, 1890, and edited it until 1905. William Seaver Woods,

editor from 1905 to 1933, led the magazine to a high degree of success. Emphasis was laid on current events and living persons, largely by means of quotations from newspapers and magazines; cartoons were freely reproduced, and humor was a frequent feature. The magazine reached more than 2 million in circulation, and was a favorite in schools for studying current events. In 1937 it was merged with the REVIEW OF REVIEWS as *The Digest;* later that year publication was resumed under the original name. On Feb. 19, 1938, it suspended publication, and several months later was absorbed by *Time*, which had made it obsolete.

Literary Guild, The. A book club founded in 1926. It issued its first selection—Heywood Broun and Margaret Leech's *Anthony Comstock* —in March, 1927. Initially somewhat adventurous in its selections, it became more conservative and more successful after John Beecroft assumed editorship in 1937. In later years it has sent more than 4 million books annually to its members.

literary histories of the U.S. American literature was for a long time an appendix to English literature, and American literary historians have only gradually broken loose from the mother country. The best book on the writing of literary history in the United States is the survey that HOWARD MUMFORD JONES aptly called *The Theory of American Literature* (1948).

The first detailed attempt to describe American literature was a series of papers that JOHN NEAL contributed to *Blackwood's Magazine* in 1824–25. Four years later came a series of lectures by SAMUEL L. KNAPP, and the first anthology, SAMUEL KETTELL's *Specimens of American Poetry, with Critical and Biographical Notices* (3 v.). The undependable and biased RUFUS W. GRISWOLD wrote about American poets and prose writers in the 1840's, and the DUYCKINCKS produced an excellent *Cyclopaedia of American Literature* (2 v., 1855; *Supplement*, 1866), with well-chosen selections. A milestone event was the publication of MOSES COIT TYLER's *History of American Literature, 1607–1765* (2 v., 1878), followed by his equally important *Literary History of the American Revolution, 1763–83* (2 v., 1897). Works of miscellaneous character and varied importance intervened, among them EDMUND C. STEDMAN's weighty anthology, *Poets of America* (1885); CHARLES F. RICHARDSON's pioneer *American Literature* (2 v., 1887–88); E. C. Stedman and E. M. Hutchinson's *A Library of American Literature* (11 v., 1888–90); Greenough White's *The Philosophy of American Literature* (1891), which insisted that American literature is "no mere pallid reflection of literary fashions across the Atlantic"; FRED LEWIS PATTEE's clear-sighted and original *History of American Literature Since 1870* (1915).

Such histories began to multiply; they were mostly of a conventional character, although few were as conservative as BARRETT WENDELL's *Literary History of America* (1900), which treated New England almost exclusively. Particularly sound were Walter C. Bronson's (1900) and WILLIAM P. TRENT's (1903). GEORGE E. WOODBERRY sounded a challenge in *America in Literature* (1903), as did John Macy in his *Spirit of American Literature* (1908), which sought to dethrone many of our literary idols. VAN WYCK BROOKS began his remarkable career of devotion to the history of American letters with *The Wine of the Puritans* (1909) and AMERICA's COMING-OF-AGE (1915), later continued in his *The Flowering of New England* (1936); *New England: Indian Summer* (1940), and many other similar books. The first elaborate and cooperative work in this field was the *Cambridge History of American Literature* (4 v., 1917–21), edited by W. P. Trent, JOHN ERSKINE, STUART P. SHERMAN, and CARL VAN DOREN. Much livelier and more satisfactory is the *Literary History of the United States* (3 v., including one of bibliography, 1948; rev., 1953), edited by ROBERT E. SPILLER, Willard Thorp, Thomas H. Johnson, and HENRY SEIDEL CANBY, with HOWARD MUMFORD JONES, DIXON WECTER, and Stanley T. Williams as associates.

Later productions include much discussion of the character and quality of our literature, accounts of various genres, tributes to "the American genius" or doubts concerning it, chronicles of particular ages, analyses of Puritanism or humor or "the modern temper" or other special aspects. Ideological accounts vary from the magnificent if sometimes arbitrary MAIN CURRENTS IN AMERICAN THOUGHT (3 v., 1927–1930) of VERNON L. PARRINGTON to the tendentious *Story of American Literature* (1937) of LUDWIG LEWISOHN. The history of American literature abroad has been studied in such works as Clarence Gohdes' *American Literature in 19th-Century England* (1944), Halvdan Koht's *The American Spirit in Europe* (1949), and a symposium edited by Margaret Denny and William H. Gilman, *The American Writer and the European Tradition* (1950), which analyzes influences in both directions; THE LITERATURE OF THE AMERICAN PEOPLE (1951), a survey by Arthur Hobson Quinn and others.

Literary Prizes and Their Winners (1935; rev., 1939, 1946), edited by Anne J. Richter. This useful compilation covers prizes and fellowships awarded in the United States, the British Empire, the Continent, and Latin America. It describes conditions of awards and lists past winners.

Literary Review. A magazine founded in 1920 by HENRY SEIDEL CANBY. It was later called the *Saturday Review of Literature,* then the SATURDAY REVIEW.

Literary World [1]. A weekly founded in February, 1847, in New York City by the DUYCKINCKS and CHARLES FENNO HOFFMAN. It enlisted as contributors many of the New York literati in its reports on society and literature; it ceased publication in December, 1853.

Literary World [2]. A monthly founded in Boston in June, 1870, by S. R. Crocker, who edited it until 1877; BLISS CARMAN was editor in 1903–04. It had a strong literary trend; William J. Rolfe, the Shakespearean scholar, conducted a department dealing with his specialty, and whole issues were devoted to Whittier, Emerson, and others. The magazine became a fortnightly in 1879, was absorbed by the *Critic* in 1904; the latter was absorbed by PUTNAM's MAGAZINE in 1906, and *Putnam's* in turn was absorbed by the ATLANTIC MONTHLY in 1910.

Literati, The (1850), EDGAR ALLAN POE's sketches of thirty-eight authors belonging to the KNICKERBOCKER SCHOOL or resident in New York City. The sketches had appeared in six installments in *Godey's Lady's Book* (May–Oct., 1846); a seventh appeared in 1848. Some were warmly eulogistic, others epigrammatically disparaging. THOMAS DUNN ENGLISH came off worst; he replied in scurrilous language that earned him, first, a horsewhipping by Poe, and second, a libel suit that Poe won handsomely. The sketches reveal Poe as one of our most eminent and reliable critics, although the conditions of the literary world at the time compelled him to deal mainly with minor authors. He was, as usual, gallant with the ladies. R. W. GRISWOLD prepared the material for publication in book form, and as usual he played tricks. He substituted for the paper on English one that Poe wrote after the law-suit, entitled *Thomas Dunn Brown.*

Literature of the American People, The (1951), a historical and critical survey edited by ARTHUR HOBSON QUINN. This important volume is the longest and most comprehensive one-volume history of American literature; it includes a valuable 120-page bibliography. Three scholars collaborated with Quinn. Kenneth B. Murdock wrote the section on the Colonial and Revolutionary period, Quinn did a section called "The Establishment of National Literature," Clarence Gohdes dealt with the later 19th century, and George F. Whicher with the 20th century. The book is unusually lively and readable.

Literature of the Middle-Western Frontier, The (2 v., 1925), a survey by RALPH L. RUSK. The literary beginnings of the Middle West are shown in the books produced about it and the magazines of the period. There are bibliographies of "Narratives of Adventurers and Travelers from the Eastern States and from Europe" and "Travel and Observation by Western Writers."

Littell, Eliakim (b. Burlington, N.J., Jan. 2, 1797—d. May 17, 1870), editor, publisher. Littell founded the Philadelphia *Register and National Recorder* in 1819, but is best known by the magazine called *Littell's Living Age.* It began publication on May 11, 1844, and he continued as its editor until his death. In 1897 it became the *Living Age,* and it lasted until 1941. It aimed to reprint the best fiction, essays, and verse published in magazines abroad, and has often been imitated.

Littell, William (b. New Jersey, 1768—d.

Sept. 26, 1824), lawyer, poet, essayist. Best known as a compiler of law books, Littell scandalized his associates by publishing *Epistles of William, Sur-named Littell, to the People of the Realm of Kentucky* (1806), a collection of satirical essays on prominent men of the day. His admirable and well-known *Political Transactions in and Concerning Kentucky* (1806) and the solid *Narrative of the Settlement of Kentucky* (1806) were unable to alter his reputation for levity and scurrility. In the midst of the publication of *The Statute Law of Kentucky* (5 v., 1809–19), his *Festoons of Fancy, Consisting of Compositions Amatory, Sentimental and Humorous in Verse and Prose* (1814) appeared, further convincing his detractors of his frivolity.

Little, Richard H[enry] (b. Leroy, Ill., Aug. 25, 1869—d. April 27, 1946), lawyer, newspaperman. Little worked mainly for the Chicago *Tribune* (1895–1936), after a brief experience at the bar. He was a correspondent at the front during the Spanish-American War, the Russo-Japanese War, and World War I. In 1920 he inherited Bert L. Taylor's "LINE O' TYPE OR TWO" column in the *Tribune* and conducted it till his death. He issued an annual volume called *The Line Book*, beginning in 1924, also a volume called *Better Angels* (1928).

Little Blue Books. Paper-bound, five-cent booklets sold by E. HALDEMAN-JULIUS on a mail-order basis from Girard, Kans. Thousands of titles were included, millions of copies sold, as Haldeman-Julius related in *The First Hundred Million* (1928). Books like Boccaccio's *Decameron* (sold in four sections), were of course popular, but so were *Omar Khayyám* and *A Shropshire Lad*. It was Haldeman-Julius who first published WILL DURANT's *Story of Philosophy* in a group of booklets, collected (1926) to make Simon & Schuster's first great success. Many of the booklets were didactic: *How to Improve Your Conversation, How to Play Golf, How to Write Advertising*. Some were jest-books, some were published to further the publisher's agnostic views.

Little Boy Blue (1889), a poem by EUGENE FIELD. Field commemorated in the verses a little boy who had died but whose dust-covered toys still awaited his return. Ethelbert Nevin set the poem to music that became very popular.

Little Breeches (1871), a poem by JOHN HAY. This was included in Hay's PIKE COUNTY BALLADS; it appeared first in the New York *Tribune* in 1870. It is the story of a four-year-old who is rescued from injury in a wagon accident. It became immediately popular as a piece for "recitation."

Little Caesar (1929), a novel by W. R. BURNETT. This was one of the earliest and most powerful prohibition-period stories of gangsters. It became a best seller; and Mervyn LeRoy, movie producer, used it as the basis for a movie (1930) which realistically depicted the rise of an egotistic criminal to power through aggressiveness, ruthlessness, and large-scale and well organized racketeering.

Little Colonel. See ANNIE FELLOWS JOHNSTON.

Little Eohippus, The (*Saturday Evening Post*, Nov.–Dec., 1912; published in book form as *Bransford in Arcadia*, 1913), a short novel by EUGENE MANLOVE RHODES. The magazine story created a large body of warm admirers for Rhodes. The novelette was also called *Bransford of Rainbow Range*, under which title it appears in *The Best Novels and Stories* (1949) of Rhodes. It is both a love story and a western, in Rhodes' thoroughly individual style. Throughout the story appears at intervals a humorous poem about the "little eohippus" or "dawn horse," by Charlotte Perkins Gilman.

Little Eva. A character in Harriet Beecher Stowe's UNCLE TOM'S CABIN (1852). Eva is the small daughter of Uncle Tom's kindly owner, Augustine St. Clare. Her death scene is a high point in the story.

Littlefield, Walter (b. Boston, March 17, 1867—d. March 25, 1948), newspaperman, foreign correspondent, historian, translator. Littlefield was a very competent journalist, first with the New York *World* and the New York *Tribune*, then on the staff of the *Times*. He was especially good in tying up current events with history and did many excellent "background" articles. He wrote *The Truth About Dreyfus* (1927) and *When France Went Mad: The Story of the Dreyfus Case* (1936). He also showed a connection between the Camorra of Italy and the Black Hand of New York and revealed important facts in the theft of the *Mona Lisa* from the Louvre. With Lionel Strachey he edited *Love Letters of Famous Men and Women* (4 v., 1909–10).

Little Foxes (1866), a collection of essays by HARRIET BEECHER STOWE, published under the pen name of Christopher Crowfield. Chatty and didactic, they deal with such faults of humanity as fault-finding, irritability, intolerance.

Little Foxes, The (1939), a play by LILLIAN HELLMAN. It depicts unfavorably the rise of industrialism in the South, and shows the new breed of southerners as rapacious and ruthless —like "the little foxes who spoil the vines" in the Biblical verse.

Little French Girl, The (1924), a novel by ANNE DOUGLAS SEDGWICK. The story follows the popular international pattern of the day, with a French mother and her lovers, a daughter whose presence embarrasses her, the choice of a marriage for love or money.

Little Journeys (1894–1908), a series of biographical sketches by ELBERT HUBBARD. First published separately, then together in fourteen volumes, these 170 sketches told of Hubbard's visits to the homes of famous men and women; they were immensely popular, were reprinted in a memorial edition in 1914, and appeared again in partial reprints during the 1940's.

Little Leather Library. Harry Scherman, Robert Haas, and Maxwell Sackheim, newspapermen and advertising agents, decided it might be a good idea for the Whitman Candy Co. to boost trade by giving away a tiny copy of *Romeo and Juliet* with each package of confectionery. The idea succeeded and brought business; five-and-ten-cent stores and chain drugstores fell in line and began giving away capsuled literature. The list of titles grew to a hundred, and the little books were found all over the country. The three men founded the Little Leather Library (1916), which sold 40,000,000 copies of the classics at ten cents a copy. The enterprise was eventually given up, but led shortly thereafter to the founding of the BOOK-OF-THE-MONTH CLUB, as described by Charles Lee in *The Hidden Public* (1958).

Little Lord Fauntleroy (1886), a novel by FRANCES HODGSON BURNETT. Young Cedric Errol, an American boy who falls heir to an English earldom, goes to England to claim it. He is a manly, considerate youngster with beautiful manners, long curls, and a lace-collared velvet suit, and he makes a deep impression on his selfish British relatives. Mrs. Burnett had taken the idea for the costume from one worn by Oscar Wilde when he had visited her; the curls and manners were those of her own son Vivian. Mothers all over America found in the book the complete answer to the problem of raising boys, thereby producing a generation to whom the young lord was anathema. Mrs. Burnett made a dramatization of her book, and movie versions appeared in 1921 (with Mary Pickford as Fauntleroy) and 1936.

little magazines. A name usually applied specifically to small, often short-lived avantgarde publications which serve as focal points for literary heterodoxy, are intended for a small audience, and are noncommercially oriented. These periodicals have often been the only means of expression available to young, experimental writers swimming against the current of established literary tradition.

The DIAL may be regarded as the main trunk of the family tree. It appeared first as a New England transcendentalist organ published (1840–44) by MARGARET FULLER and RALPH WALDO EMERSON, then as a fortnightly in Chicago (1880–1916), then in New York as a liberal magazine which drew contributions from many distinguished writers, and finally as a literary monthly (1920–29) which championed modern movements. A few other little magazines began to make their appearance shortly before the turn of the century. Elbert Hubbard's THE PHILISTINE (1895–1915) published the work of STEPHEN CRANE and disregarded conventional notions of printing format. William Marion Reedy's MIRROR (1893–1920) first published the SPOON RIVER ANTHOLOGY (1914–15), and the works of other writers who were later to become famous. Other early little magazines include the Chicago CHAP-BOOK (1894–98); The *Lark* (1895–97); M'LLE NEW YORK (1895–96, 1898–99); and *The Papyrus* (1903–12).

The literary revolution of 1910–20 was largely set off by new little magazines which began to appear in profusion about that time: *The Masses* (founded 1911); POETRY (1912); *Glebe* (1913); *Blast* (in London, 1914, with some American contributors); *The Little Review* (1914); *Bruno's Weekly* (1915); *Others* (1915); *Contemporary Verse* (1916); *The Seven Arts* (1916); *The Lyric* (1917); *The Quill* (1917); *The Country Bard* (1918); *The Liberator* (1918). They published the work of many writers then unknown who were to become the major voices in twentieth-century literature: Sherwood Anderson, Van Wyck Brooks, Hart Crane, E. E. Cummings, John Dos Passos, Theodore Dreiser, Robert Frost, T. S. Eliot, William Faulkner, Ernest Hemingway, Vachel Lindsay, Marianne Moore, Eugene O'Neill, Katherine Anne Porter, Ezra Pound, John Crowe Ransom, Wallace Stevens, Allen Tate, William Carlos Williams, Edmund Wilson, Thomas Wolfe, and others. Frederick J. Hoffman points out that little magazines have published "about 80 per cent of our most important post-1912 critics, novelists, poets, and storytellers. Further, they have introduced and sponsored every noteworthy literary movement or school that has made its appearance in America during the past thirty years." Between 1914 and 1929 *The Little Review*, one of the most important of the little magazines, had in its pages the early work of Carl Sandburg, Vachel Lindsay, T. S. Eliot, Wallace Stevens, Marianne Moore, and Robert Frost. Harriet Monroe's *Poetry*, the only important magazine of the period to survive until the present, has continually published new verse since its founding in 1912, though in recent years its critical articles have often seemed more vital than its verse.

Some magazines succeeded in making their influence widely felt. *The Seven Arts* publicized the important nationalism of Van Wyck Brooks and Waldo Frank. *Secession*, along with *Exile*, *Glebe*, and *Others*, represented the rebellious younger generation of the twenties, and contributed to the re-evaluation of American culture demanded by the new writers. Some magazines had more limited aims: to introduce a certain kind of new poetry; to provide a forum for the NEW CRITICISM; or to assert the literary claims of a particular region. There have been magazines specializing in a psychoanalytical approach to literature, in dadaism, in Marxism, and in obscurity.

During the 1920's the American expatriates in London and Paris published numerous little magazines, often aimed primarily at an American audience. Among these were *The Criterion* (London, 1922), which T. S. Eliot edited for a time; *transition* (Paris, 1927), in which Gertrude Stein, Hemingway, and William Carlos Williams appeared; *Exile* (edited in Paris, published in Chicago, 1927), Ezra Pound's vehicle; BROOM (Rome, then London, then New York, 1921–1924); *Secession* (Vienna, Berlin, and New York, 1922–1924). Published in the United States were: *Contact* (1920); the new form of

The Dial (1920); *The Frontier* (1920); *The Double-Dealer* (1921), which first published Hemingway and early work of Edmund Wilson and Robert Penn Warren; a new *The Lyric* (1921); *The Measure* (1921); *Voices* (1921); *The Fugitive* (1922) (see THE FUGITIVES); *Laughing Horse* (1922); *The Chicago Literary Times* (1923); *Palms* (1923); *S₄N* (1919); *Bozart* (1927); *The Blues* (1929); *The Gyroscope* (1929); *The Kaleidoscope* (1929, called *The Kaleidograph* after 1932).

The twenties were the golden age of the little magazine. By the mid-twenties the literary revolution had been effected and the new movements were well under way. The mid-twenties also saw a new form of the little magazine, which would eventually supersede the more purely literary titles of the earlier decade. Many of the magazines that began publication between 1925 and 1930 can be classified in two groups: the doctrinaire politico-literary journal, typified by the *New Masses* (1926; see THE MASSES), which became the predominant form of the little magazines published in the thirties; and the quarterly or magazine review, such as the *Prairie Schooner* (1927), which came into its own during the 1930's and 1940's, and has continued to be of wide influence in the field of literary criticism.

Only a small percentage of the magazines of the early twenties continued publication in the following decades. New titles in the thirties and forties included: *The Harkness Hoot* (1930); *Story* (1931); *The American Spectator* (1932); *Wings* (1933); THE PARTISAN REVIEW (1934); *The Spinners* (1934); *American Prefaces* (1935); *The Critic* (1934); *New Directions in Prose and Poetry* (1936); THE KENYON REVIEW (1939); *Furioso* (1939); *Accent* (1940); *Florida Magazine of Verse* (1940); *The Poet of the Month* (1941); *Chimera* (1942); *Quarterly Review of Literature* (1943); *Hudson Review* (1948); *Tiger's Eye* (1947); and *Cronos* (1947).

By the late forties the dominant form of the little magazine was the quarterly review. Strictly speaking, the reviews had ceased to be "little magazines" at all; usually supported by or affiliated with the universities, they were financially secure, primarily critical rather than creative, and drew their contributors, not from among young experimental writers, but from established professors and critics.

In reaction to the almost total demise of the earlier type of little magazine, a new group of little magazines appeared during the 1950's, attacking literary conventions, and often aiming their barbs at the established quarterlies. Many of the new magazines were associated with the "beat" movement (see BEAT WRITING). They ranged in size, frequency, and format from the bimonthly EVERGREEN REVIEW which kept a foot in both the review and the little magazine camps, to the occasional *Beatitude*, a mimeographed publication that presented little-known San Francisco poets.

Some revived the titles of defunct magazines of the twenties: *Dial, The Seven Arts, Transatlantic Review;* others had cryptic titles: *Yugen; Ark II, Moby I; Big Table* (which broke away from the *Chicago Review* in 1959). Others were notable for their sprightliness and iconoclasm: *Contact* (another revival); *The Fifties* (later called *The Sixties*); *San Francisco Review;* and *Kulchur.* With the great surge in paperback publishing, several attempts were made to reach the mass market hitherto untapped by the little magazines: NEW WORLD WRITING, DISCOVERY, *Anchor Review*, and THE NOBLE SAVAGE appeared in paperback format. The established quarterlies maintained their hold on small, select audiences for the most part, although the disappearance of *Botteghe Oscure,* a trilingual magazine published in Italy, caused some dismay.

The *Index to Little Magazines Annual* (1948 —), is a good barometer of the rapid changes brought by the fifties. The 1959 edition indexed fifty-two of the best-known titles (excluding academically supported little magazines like *The Kenyon Review*). Critical publications include: Frederick J. Hoffman's *The Little Magazine* (1946), and Alice Meacham's *Little Magazines in Twentieth-Century America, 1912–1920* (1941). A significant evaluation is Lionel Trilling's "The Function of the Little Magazine," in his collection of essays, *The Liberal Imagination* (1950).

Little Men (1871), a novel by LOUISA MAY ALCOTT. A sequel to LITTLE WOMEN.

Little Orphant Annie (1885), a poem in Hoosier dialect by JAMES WHITCOMB RILEY. It was originally called *The Elf Child.* It presented the orphan girl who told the children in whose home she lived "witch tales" and stories of "the gobble-uns 'at gits you ef you Don't Watch Out!" A comic strip by Harold Gray is called "Little Orphan Annie."

Littlepage Manuscript Series. See SATANSTOE, THE CHAINBEARER, and THE REDSKINS.

Little Regiment, The: and Other Episodes of the American Civil War (1896), six short stories by STEPHEN CRANE. Like the earlier RED BADGE OF COURAGE, the stories in this collection treat the underlying theme of the study of the feelings and emotions of fighting men under trying battle conditions.

In 1896 the reviewer for The Brooklyn *Daily Eagle* commented on Crane's characteristically unstructured style in these stories: "They are not tales, they do not describe connected events, there is no thought of plot running through them."

All the stories concern events of the Civil War except for "The Veteran." Here the reader meets Henry Fleming, hero of *The Red Badge,* as an old man. Fleming dies a heroic death in a flaming barn while attempting to rescue some colts, thus vindicating his title to the badge of courage lost and won at Chancellorsville. But, as the critic for the *Academy* remarked, the final gesture of the veteran is "a trifle theatrical and commonplace" (February 22, 1897).

Little Review, The (March, 1914–May, 1929), a "little magazine" conducted by Margaret Anderson, first at Chicago, later in New York City and Paris. It was an exciting, individualistic magazine, which proclaimed its belief in "Life for Art's sake" and announced that it was written for "intelligent people whose philosophy is Applied Anarchism." In its contributions many varying ideas and personalities were explored: Nietzsche, Bergson, anarchism, feminism, psychoanalysis, cubism, dadaism. Among the contributors were Sherwood Anderson, Vachel Lindsay, Ezra Pound, W. B. Yeats, Hart Crane, Richard Aldington, T. S. Eliot, Wyndham Lewis, Ford Madox Ford, Ben Hecht, W. C. Williams, Jean Cocteau, Guillaume Apollinaire, Kenneth Burke. Most celebrated was James Joyce. When Miss Anderson started to print *Ulysses* in her magazine in installments (1918–21), four issues were confiscated by the Post Office and burned. In December, 1920, John Sumner's Society for the Suppression of Vice brought the *Review* before a special sessions court. The judge decided against Miss Anderson and fined her $100. She told the story of her adventurous life in *My Thirty Years' War* (1930) and *The Fiery Fountains* (1951). *The Little Review Anthology* appeared in 1953. See CENSORSHIP OF LITERATURE.

Little Shepherd of Kingdom Come, The (1903), a novel by JOHN FOX. This popular story relates the adventurous experiences of Chad Buford, a shepherd, with whom two women fall in love. Of doubtful parentage, he lives for a while with the Turners in the Cumberland Mountains, at a settlement which gives its name to the book. Their adopted daughter Melissa falls in love with him, but he wants to marry Margaret Dean, a Lexington girl who isn't sure about him because of a supposed "blot on his birth." In time he becomes established socially, but they are again estranged when he enlists in the Union Army. Melissa makes a dangerous trip to warn him his life is in danger, and dies of exposure; he marries Margaret after the war. The book was dramatized by EUGENE WALTER in 1916.

Little Sister, The (1949), a detective story by RAYMOND CHANDLER. This is one of the numerous excellent crime novels by a master of the genre who is both hard-boiled and literate. There are the usual carefully planned plot and well drawn characters, but the story includes an episode that is a comic masterpiece in its satire of Hollywood manners, the effort of the detective Philip Marlowe to break through the royal bodyguard that keeps ordinary mortals away from the presence of a Hollywood agent.

Little theater in the U.S. "Little theater" is an imprecise term; the movement has many names—amateur, art, experimental, grass roots, insurgent, intimate, nation-wide, non-Broadway, noncommercial, nonprofessional, Off-Broadway, people's, regional, tributary theater, and so on. Perhaps "nation-wide" would be a more adequate description for the interest in and activity of theater groups which have spread from coast to coast; however, since the early literature on the subject accurately described the movement as little, this designation is kept here. Certainly, the little-theater movement was small when it had its beginnings some half a century ago in inexpensive productions housed most often in tiny hideaway buildings, some of them seating scarcely fifty people, and few, more than two hundred.

The earliest drama in America dates back to the 16th century. In January, 1568, Father Villareal, a Spanish Jesuit priest at the fort at Biscayne Bay, Florida, wrote as follows: "We hold fiestas with litanies to the cross. We have put on two comedies, one on the day of St. John when we were expecting the governor. This play had to do with the war between men and the world, the flesh, and the devil. The soldiers enjoyed it very much." (An English translation of this letter first appeared in the United States Catholic Historical Society *Historical Records and Studies*, v. XXV, 1935.) St. John's Day was June 24; thus the first play on record so far as having been produced in the present confines of the United States was in 1567 in Florida, and not in 1598 on the Rio Grande, as theater historians have heretofore claimed. These plays were no doubt of the type of *autos sacramentales* common to the Spanish church in the 15th and 16th centuries, and were used by the fathers in their long wilderness struggle in the New World for interpreting holy scripture and teaching the ways of the cross and the mysteries of faith to the ignorant. When England won the new land from the Spanish and the business of colonization went on, some sort of drama, however crude, went with it.

At the end of the 19th century, some three and a half centuries after Father Villareal had put on his first play, American theater had grown in size and activity, but its content remained for the most part secondhand, romantic, remote, and uninspired, in spite of the fact that the country was overflowing with native material for drama—folk tales, superstitions, legends, heroes, historical events, and the like. The nation continued in the main to depend for its theatrical entertainment and diversion on importations from Europe or on homemade imitations of same by American playwrights. In *A History of American Drama* (v. 1, 1936) Arthur Hobson Quinn lists some fifteen hundred American plays written before the Civil War—most of them published and produced—of which not one has endured as dramatic literature. The American theater produced a few first-rate actors but not a single playwright, up to the time of William Vaughn Moody, of lasting and literary significance. Many of the playwrights of the late 19th century—Augustin Daly, Bronson C. Howard, James A. Herne, David Belasco, Clyde Fitch, and others—had tried to do better things, to write plays of truth and honesty, of imagination and poetic reach, and now and then there were bits and flashes on some of their pages, but these were no more than glimmers that were smothered by ignorance, lack of will, or cold neglect.

A few imaginative theorists and practitioners in Europe were the first to bring real vitality into the theater; in France, André Antoine launched his *Théâtre Libre,* which brought honesty and a sense of life to the stage in the productions of Henry François Becque, Eugène Brieux, Henrik Ibsen, Leo Tolstoi, and others. Antoine wanted the feel of actuality, and used three-dimensional properties and furnishings instead of the usual painted backdrops and materials. In Germany the Freiebühne group dedicated itself to the production of plays of the people—plays of hardy vigor and imaginative realism; on this stage the prophets of the new age—Ibsen, August Strindberg, Tolstoi, Gerhart Hauptmann, Hermann Sudermann, and Frank Wedekind—sent their voices out over the footlights. In Russia, the Moscow Art Theatre, founded by Stanislavsky and Nemirovich-Danchenko, began its fervidly human productions of great classics and the new dramas of Anton Chekhov. It was this theater group that finally revolutionized not only the art of acting but theater production itself, both in Europe and in the United States. In London Jacob T. Grein established his Independent Theatre to "give special performances of plays which have a literary and artistic rather than a commercial value." Except for the qualification "special," his credo was identical with that of the coming little-theater movement in America.

Of all the European groups, however, it was the Abbey Theatre of Dublin which gave most stimulation to the birth and development of the little-theater movement in the United States. Founded by William Butler Yeats and Lady Augusta Gregory for the writing and production of "native poetic drama," the Abbey Theatre soon gained a world-wide reputation. It was fervently Irish and national, yet it stood above politics and any show of chauvinism. The Irish playwrights caught a vision and followed it, doing exactly what the American playwrights through the decades had failed to do: they went back to the life of the people for their subject matter. There could hardly be a better philosophy of dramatic art than that laid down by Yeats and Lady Gregory and illustrated in the work of the Abbey Theatre. The living language, the living imagination, the living life were the important matters, as Yeats vehemently kept declaring.

The Irish influence, added to that of the other new theater groups, began to make itself felt in the United States. The yearnings and hopes of many a theater worker were strengthened and corroborated by what he had seen taking place elsewhere in the world. Gradually, on university campuses and in community centers, the voice of revolt turned into action. Before long the movement was in full swing; its philosophy and aim was the imaginative and noncommercial production of good plays and the encouragement of native playwrights to create them.

Courses in drama and the history of the theater had long been taught in the United States as a part of the college English literature curriculum, but GEORGE PIERCE BAKER took the lead in university theater by going a step further. In 1905 he started a course in playwriting at Radcliffe College, a thing unheard of at that time. Later he founded his "47 Workshop" at Harvard, where plays written under his guidance were staged and opened to the public. In 1925 he removed to Yale University, and remained there until his death ten years later. The list of his students reads like a modern Who's Who in the American Theater—playwrights, scenic artists, designers, technicians, theater historians and critics. The following are only a few of the hundreds of outstanding people who came from his classes: Winthrop Ames, Philip Barry, John Mason Brown, Walter Pritchard Eaton, Theresa Helburn, Sidney Howard, Frederick H. Koch, Elia Kazan, Kenneth MacGowan, Hiram Moderwell, Eugene O'Neill, Edward Sheldon, Lee Simonson, Maurice Wertheim, and Thomas Wolfe.

One of the most outstanding little-theater men was Frederick H. Koch. In 1918 he began his playwriting course and his Carolina Playmakers at the University of North Carolina. (See CAROLINA FOLK PLAYS.) Like Baker, Koch was an inspiring teacher, and, like Yeats, he believed that the best materials for poetic and imaginative drama were to be found among "the folk." If proportionate attention were paid to all the other important leaders in the university theater movement, a large historical and critical volume would have to be written. It must suffice to say that by the middle of the 20th century the university theater movement had abundantly proved itself.

PERCY MACKAYE deserves first praise for promoting the community-theater idea. His plays, primarily pageants and masques, illustrate his belief in art among the people. His first big community activity, THE CANTERBURY PILGRIMS, was produced in 1909 with fifteen hundred participants. In 1914, in collaboration with Thomas Wood Stevens, he produced the *Masque of St. Louis,* in which more than seven thousand people took part. Two years later, in a New York City stadium, he staged his huge CALIBAN BY THE YELLOW SANDS, in which he used several thousand actors and a great corps of assistant directors.

In 1912 Maurice Browne established his Little Theater in Chicago, thus giving the name to the entire movement, and Mrs. Lyman Gale opened her Toy Theater in Boston. Other groups in different parts of the country followed rapidly: the Little Theater of Philadelphia; the Vagabond Players of Baltimore; the Cleveland Playhouse; the Pasadena Playhouse; Le Petit Théâtre du Vieux Carré; and many others. In New York, the dwelling place of the ogre of commercialism, several community-theater groups rose up and proclaimed their cause. In 1916 the PROVINCE-TOWN PLAYERS and the Washington Square Players were started—the one group to become the first producer of O'Neill's plays, the other, his main later producer after becoming the THEATER GUILD. Then came the Neighborhood Playhouse, the Civic Repertory Theater, the American Laboratory Theater, the Actors' Theater, and the Equity Players. These theaters operated on professional standards, but their creative organization and drive came out of a community feeling and spirit.

Statistics gathered in 1962 showed that there were some thirty-five hundred community theaters in the nation actively engaged in producing plays the year around, as compared to some six hundred university theaters. The small community theaters, too, were numbered by the thousands. With the inclusion of church groups, labor groups, YMCA, YWCA, YMHA, and the like, the number went well beyond a hundred thousand.

By the early thirties and on into the forties it seemed that the imaginative American theater, the theater of the poet, of honesty and native strength which the rebelling little theater had set itself to create, was becoming a fact. Numerous playwrights—Maxwell Anderson, Philip Barry, S. N. Behrman, Marc Connelly, Lillian Hellman, Sidney Howard, George Kelly, Sidney Kingsley, Clifford Odets, Elmer Rice, Lynn Riggs, Robert E. Sherwood, Thornton Wilder, and later William Inge, Arthur Miller, Tennessee Williams—had answered the call and were coming into some prominence, to join the already arrived O'Neill; their work was often lyrical and high-powered, the kind of thing in which the Irish theater excelled and in which Yeats delighted.

In the thirties the movement began to extend its creative forces into the domain of the summer theater production. A striking development in this summer-theater work was the outdoor historical drama or symphonic drama, a term employed to denote the organic and interwoven use of music, dance, mime, folk song, pageantry, masks, etc., in telling the dramatic tale. The first of these dramas was PAUL GREEN's *The Lost Colony*, produced on Roanoke Island in 1937 by the Carolina Playmakers. In 1947 Green's THE COMMON GLORY opened at Williamsburg, Virginia. Kermit Hunter's *Unto These Hills* was produced in a beautiful mountainside amphitheater at Cherokee, North Carolina, in 1950.

Unfortunately, by the middle of the century there were many things beginning to go wrong with the little-theater movement; it grew academic and formal; standards of production began to go down; it became commercial—the very evil against which it once most fiercely rebelled; it became more a social organization than a creative force; and, in the majority of cases, the urge for daring experiment died out. In 1953 an editorial in *Theatre Arts Magazine* reported on a poll of little-theater productions across the country: it showed that more than 50 per cent were copies of Broadway hits, and almost 30 per cent were old standby classics that cost little and went nowhere; less than 10 per cent were new plays of any kind, and less than 6 per cent were in any way experimental. However, in recent years, particularly in New York's Off-Broadway theaters, a new growth of and interest in experimental drama has been evidenced. Although operating on a commercial and professional basis, the Off-Broadway theaters have made available to American audiences the best work of modern experimental European playwrights—Beckett, Brecht, Genêt, Ionesco, Pinter—and the American experimentalists EDWARD ALBEE, Arthur Kopit, and JACK GELBER. (See DRAMA IN THE U.S.)

PAUL GREEN

Littleton, Mark. See JOHN PENDLETON KENNEDY.

Little Willie. This purely fictional character undoubtedly was the most frequently epitaphed person in literary history; he was also known by other names. He is believed to have appeared first in *The Sweet Singer of Michigan Salutes the Public* (1876), by JULIA A. MOORE, from whose writings the humorists of several decades delighted to quote when they ran short of material. Harry Graham ("Col. D. Streamer"), an English versifier, wrote a poem in *Ruthless Rhymes for Heartless Homes* (1901) that was slightly altered later to read: "Little Willie, in bows and sashes,/ Fell in the fire and got burned to ashes./ In the winter, when the weather is chilly,/ No one likes to stir up Willie." Possibly the most admired verse was: "Little Willie hung his sister./ She was dead before we missed her./ Willie's always up to tricks./ Ain't he cute! He's only six!" A collection of some of the best of the rhymes was made in Dorothy Rickard's *Little Willie* (1953).

Little Women, or, Meg, Jo, Beth, and Amy (in two parts, 1868, 1869), a novel for young readers by LOUISA MAY ALCOTT. A suggestion by Thomas Niles, an editor with a Boston publishing firm, induced Miss Alcott to write this book, a fictionalized account of life in her own family; it made her famous and wealthy. Although intended for girls, it became popular with older readers too, and many of the scenes in the book have entered folklore. The story concerns four sisters of varying dispositions. Jo March, the heroine, is a tomboy and wants to become an author. Her older sister Meg, very pretty, aspires to be a young lady. Beth is shy and loves music. Amy hopes to be a great artist and also to overcome her selfishness. The rich boy next door, Theodore Lawrence or "Laurie," would like to marry Jo, but marries Amy instead; Jo marries an elderly professor, Mr. Bhaer (see under WILLIAM RIMMER); Meg marries John Brooke, Laurie's tutor. The story had a number of sequels.

Livesay, Dorothy (b. Winnipeg, Manit., Oct. 12, 1909—   ), Canadian poet. For her contribution to literature, Dorothy Livesay was awarded in 1947 the Lorne Pierce Gold Medal of the Royal Society of Canada, the highest literary honor for a Canadian. Two of her books of poems—*Day and Night* (1944), and *Poems for People* (1957)—received Governor-General's Medals. Her poetry often sounds surprisingly like Emily Dickinson's, but the comparison is only superficial. Livesay has been a social worker in Montreal, New Jersey, and Vancouver, and has also been active in radio work. While in Paris in 1931, studying at the Sorbonne and writing a thesis titled "The Influence of French Symbolism on Modern English Poets," she became interested in social problems. At the same time she discovered T. S. Eliot's poetry. She has absorbed Eliot's influence and projects a deep social consciousness as well. Her books of poems include: *Signposts* (1932); *The Outsider* (1935); *Seven Poems 1934–1940* (1940); *West Coast* (1943); and *Call My People Home* (1950).

Lloyd, Alfred H[enry] (b. Montclair, N.J., Jan. 3, 1864—d. May 11, 1927), teacher, administrator, philosopher, historian. Lloyd was originally headed for the ministry, but as his philosophic ideas developed he turned to other paths, continuing to "believe half-heartedly in Unitarianism," says Herbert W. Schneider. He joined the faculty of the University of Michigan, became a dean in 1915. He stressed *doubt* as the surest sign and source of idealism; to live critically was to him the essence of mental activity. His notions of religion were unorthodox; he held that "the universe itself lives; the universe thinks." Schneider speaks of "the brilliance and irony of Lloyd's expositions and the futility of his conclusions." He wrote four important books: *Citizenship and Salvation, or, Greek and Jew: A Study in the Philosophy of History* (1897); *Dynamic Idealism* (1898); *The Philosophy of History* (1899); *The Will to Doubt* (1907).

Lloyd, Henry Demarest (b. New York City, May 1, 1847—d. Sept. 28, 1903), journalist, reformer, economist. Lloyd was admitted to the bar in 1869 and became an active reformer, contributing to the defeat of Tammany in 1871. One year later he moved to Chicago to write for the Chicago *Tribune*. His articles pointed out the dangers of monopoly, the abuse of grain speculations, and the machinations of the railroads and of the Standard Oil Co. He investigated industrial oppression in the Spring Valley coal strike, championed the anarchists convicted in the Haymarket massacre of 1886, and succeeded in having two of the death sentences commuted. *A Strike of Millionaires against Miners* (1890) was a plea for the rights of labor; *Wealth against Commonwealth* (1894), his best known book, pointed out that the natural wealth was in the hands of the few, rather than controlled by the nation. He was responsible for calling the public's attention to the need for antitrust legislation and for a fairer treatment of labor.

local color. See REGIONALISM.

Locke, Alain [LeRoy] (b. Philadelphia, Sept. 13, 1886—d. June 10, 1954), sociologist, teacher, art critic, philosopher, editor. Locke was educated at Harvard and at Oxford, then became professor of philosophy at Howard University. In 1910 he toured the South to study at close hand the problems of his race. He became prominent as an authority on Negro culture with the publication of *The New Negro* (1925). An art movement called the "New Negro Renaissance" sprang up as the result of the ideas expressed in this book. *The Negro in America* (1933), a social study, was soon followed by *Frederick Douglass, a Biography of Anti-Slavery* (1935); *The Negro and his Music* (1936); *Negro Art—Past and Present* (1936); and *The Negro in Art* (1940). With Bernard Stern he edited a symposium entitled *When People Meet: A Study in Race and Culture Contact* (1942). He edited a number of anthologies of Negro stories and plays.

Locke, David Ross. See P. V. NASBY.

Locke, John (b. England, 1632—d. 1704), philosopher. Locke was one of the most influential thinkers and writers who ever lived, furnishing ideas for three revolutions—that of 1688 against James II of England, that of 1776 of the American colonies against George III, and that of 1789 of the French masses against Louis XVI. He was a highly respected adviser to many English statesmen, held some minor government offices, and published numerous writings on philosophy, the human mind, education, religion, and economics, among them *Letters Concerning Toleration* (1689, 1690, 1692); *Two Treatises of Civil Government* (1690); *An Essay Concerning the Human Understanding* (1690); *Some Thoughts Concerning Education* (1693); and *The Reasonableness of Christianity* (1695). Locke rejected the notion of "innate ideas" and held that "there is nothing in the mind except what was first in the senses"; the mind at birth is nothing but a *tabula rasa*, a blank sheet of paper. Everything in the mind is the result of environment and experience. In his two *Treatises* on government he argued for natural rights and natural law, with government resting on a "social contract" and on inalienable rights of life, liberty, and property. Locke expounded the ideas of Whiggism and the dissenters: constitutional rights, toleration, security, the sovereign will of the majority.

When Locke became secretary to the Earl of Shaftesbury in 1667 he was asked to draw the *Fundamental Constitutions of Carolina* in a way "most agreeable to the monarchy" and as an antidote to "a numerous democracy." His outline provided for a strong aristocracy sharing power with small landowners. The plan was never carried out; its real purpose seems to have been the desire to attract capital toward a new enterprise.

Jonathan Edwards read the *Essay Concerning Human Understanding* when he was only fourteen and was impressed by Locke's doctrine of sense as the ultimate source of reflection; he worked out an empiricist argument for supernatural or holy love. Benjamin Franklin, too, read Locke's *Essay*, and later was influenced by Locke's ideas on education. Tom

Paine naturally followed Locke. Samuel Adams held he was "one of the greatest men who ever lived." Richard Henry Lee said the DECLARATION OF INDEPENDENCE was copied from Locke's treatise on government. In this Locke wrote: "The state of nature has a law to govern it, which obliges every one; and reason, which is that law, teaches all mankind, who will but consult it, that being all equal and independent, no one ought to harm another in his life, health, liberty, or possessions." Jefferson gave the words a new "felicity of expression," as John Adams phrased it, but the ideas are Locke's.

Merle Curti wrote an extensive analysis of *The Great Mr. Locke: America's Philosopher, 1783–1861 (Huntington Library Bulletin,* April, 1937).

Locke, Robinson (b. Plymouth, Ohio, March 15, 1856—d. April 20, 1920), drama critic. Locke served for years on the Toledo *Blade.* At his death he left his entire collection of drama material to the New York Public Library. It consists of 494 bound scrapbooks and more than 4,700 portfolios of unmounted material.

Lockridge, Richard [Orson] (b. St. Joseph, Mo., Sept. 26, 1898—   ), newspaperman, drama critic, novelist. Lockridge worked on Kansas City papers, joined the New York *Sun* in 1923, became drama critic in 1928. In 1932 he wrote a biography of EDWIN BOOTH called *Darling of Misfortune.* In 1936 he began writing, in collaboration with his wife **Frances Lockridge** (b. [?]—d. Feb. 18, 1963), a series of detective stories that feature a married couple, the Norths, who, somewhat blunderingly, manage to be of great assistance to the police. The stories began as a series in the *New Yorker.* They became very popular and also furnished radio with some amusing episodes. Their books include: *Mr. and Mrs. North* (1936); *The Norths Meet Murder* (1940); *Murder Out of Turn* (1941); *A Pinch of Poison* (1941); *Death on the Aisle* (1942); *Killing the Goose* (1944). In collaboration with G. H. Estabrook, Lockridge wrote *Death in the Mind* (1945). The Lockridges' later works include: *Cats and People* (1950) and *The Faceless Adversary* (1956).

Lockridge, Ross [Franklin, Jr.] (b. Bloomington, Ind., April 25, 1914—d. March 6, 1948), teacher, novelist. Lockridge, the son of a teacher at Indiana University whose specialties were history and folklore, studied at the Sorbonne, did graduate work at Harvard, taught at Indiana University and Simmons College. Over a period of years he wrote a lengthy novel, *Raintree County* (1948). It was immediately accepted by Houghton Mifflin, selected by the Book-of-the-Month Club, and given the Metro-Goldwyn-Mayer Literary Award. The book was hailed as a major triumph, and the author was in particular compared to Thomas Wolfe. Lockridge's future seemed secure, but he committed suicide, apparently the victim of too great strain in repeatedly rewriting his book.

July 4, on which the entire action of the book takes place, is a great day in Raintree County, an imaginary county in Indiana. John Wickliff Shawnessy, principal of the local high school, is the chief actor; flashbacks to earlier episodes of his life vividly illuminate the history.

Lockwood, Francis Cummins (b. Mt. Erie, Ill., May 22, 1864—d. Jan. 12, 1948), teacher, historian. Lockwood taught at various universities, joining the faculty of Arizona in 1916 and continuing there, for a time as acting president, until 1930. He became interested in the background of Arizona history and, although a specialist in English literature, he wrote mainly on the southwestern region. Among his books: *Arizona Characters* (1928); *Pioneer Days in Arizona* (1932); *With Padre Kino on the Trail and A Guide to His Mission Chain* (1934); *The Apache Indians* (1938); *More Arizona Characters* (1943).

Lodge, George Cabot (b. Boston, Oct. 10, 1873—d. Aug. 21, 1909), poet, dramatist. This son of Henry Cabot Lodge was a Bostonian of Bostonians, but also a rebel. His rebellion was expressed in several collections of fine poems and two striking dramas, *Cain* (1904) and *Herakles* (1908). He was deeply under the influence of Schopenhauer and of Buddhist thought. Among his publications were *The Song of the Wave* (1898); *Poems* (1902); *The Great Adventure* (1905), and *The Soul's Inheritance* (1909). His sonnets were particularly well-written.

Lodge, Henry Cabot (b. Boston, May 12, 1850—d. Nov. 9, 1924), lawyer, editor, historian, public official. Following service in the Massachusetts legislature, Lodge was elected to the House of Representatives in 1886, to the U.S. Senate in 1893, and served till his death. He is remembered chiefly for his opposition to the League of Nations, which he prevented the United States from entering. A harsh historic verdict on him was rendered in Karl Schriftgiesser's *The Gentleman from Massachusetts* (1944). He wrote biographies of Alexander Hamilton (1882), Daniel Webster (1883), and George Washington (2 v., 1888–89), also several historical works.

Loeb, Jacques (b. Germany, April 7, 1859—d. Feb. 11, 1924), biologist. Loeb published books in both English and German. He came to the United States in 1891 after teaching at various European universities, taught at Bryn Mawr, Chicago, and California, became head of the division of experimental biology at the Rockefeller Institute. His specialty was comparative physiology and psychology. He formulated a theory of animal tropism, and artificially induced parthenogenesis. His researches were in general directed toward the explanation of life behavior on a physico-chemical basis. Among his books: *The Dynamics of Living Matter* (1906); *The Mechanistic Conception of Life* (1912); *The Organism as a Whole* (1916). It is generally believed that Sinclair Lewis used him as a model for the biologist MAX GOTTLIEB in *Arrowsmith* (1925).

Loeb, James (b. New York City, Aug. 6, 1867—d. May 28, 1933), banker, philanthropist. After a successful career in the firm of Kuhn, Loeb & Co., Loeb conceived a great scholarly project, the publication of the Loeb Classical Library, and laid aside a large endowment for it. The Library was to consist of about three hundred volumes, each to contain a reproduction of an ancient Greek or Latin text with an English translation on the facing pages. Many scholars were involved in carrying out the plan. At his death Loeb left his collection of Arretine pottery to the Fogg Museum at Harvard and helped endow several philanthropic projects.

Loewe, Frederick (b. Austria, June 10, 1904 —), composer. Loewe was a prodigy who played the piano at five and wrote music at seven. In 1924 he came to the United States, intent on a musical career, but had disappointing luck. Deciding to quit music entirely he drifted about America working at a variety of jobs—gold-mining, cattle-branding, even boxing as a bantamweight. A chance encounter with ALAN JAY LERNER at the Lambs Club was the spark that ignited his career, resulting in one of the great teams of contemporary theater. In 1947 BRIGADOON completely charmed Broadway critics, won the New York Critics Award, and ran for 581 performances. This was followed by *Paint Your Wagon* (1951). In 1956 Loewe and Lerner, taking George Bernard Shaw's *Pygmalion* as a basis, wrote one of the all-time musical favorites, *My Fair Lady*; it won the New York Critics award for the "best play" and seems destined to become an American classic. *Gigi*, written for the screen in 1959, proved another box-office bonanza, winning nine Academy Awards. The production of *Camelot* (1961) had large audiences but did not win comparable acclaim.

Lofting, Hugh (b. England, Jan. 14, 1886—d. Sept. 26, 1947), children's story writer, illustrator. After completing his training at the Polytechnical Institute of London, Lofting settled in the United States in 1912. The "Doctor Dolittle" stories, adventures of an unusual doctor who learned the language of the animals, originated in illustrated letters written to his children while he served with the British Army in World War I. *The Story of Doctor Dolittle* (1920), which went into twenty-three printings in ten years, has been translated into twelve languages. Its sequel, *Voyages of Doctor Dolittle* (1922), a Newbery Prize winner, was followed by eight more Dolittle books, all popular with young readers.

Logan, Cornelius Ambrosius (b. Baltimore, Md., May 4, 1806—d. Feb. 22, 1853), sailor, newspaperman, actor, playwright. Though originally intended for the priesthood, Logan turned to business and to roving the seas. In 1825 he appeared as an actor and toured the country successfully. In 1834 he wrote a play that proved a hit, *Yankee Land, or, The Foundling of the Apple Orchard*. Similar plays in the tradition of the Yankee rural wag were *The*

Wag of Maine (1834) and *The Vermont Wool Dealer* (1840). Logan himself appeared as Aminadab Slocum in his *Chloroform, or, New York a Hundred Years Hence* (1849).

Logan, James [1] (b. Ireland, 1674—d. 1751), public official, scholar. In 1699 Logan, a Quaker, accompanied WILLIAM PENN to the New World as his secretary and trusted adviser. In Pennsylvania, Penn made him Secretary of the Province and Commissioner of Property and Receiver-General; he left his young son under his guidance when he went back to England on business. As land agent for the proprietors, Logan negotiated skillfully with the Indians and manged to obtain huge tracts of land for settlement. He himself became rich, but always retained his scholarly interests. He published several books in Latin abroad. Benjamin Franklin issued for Logan a translation in verse of the *Moral Distiches* (1735) of Dionysius Cato and of Cicero's *De Senectute* (*M. T. Cicero's Cato Major, or, His Discourse of Old Age*, 1744). Franklin described the former as "the first translation of a classic which was both made and printed in the British colonies"; he spoke of the latter as "a happy omen that Philadelphia shall become the seat of the American Muses." By 1751 Logan had made a collection of nearly three thousand volumes, which he bequeathed to the city for public use.

Logan, James [2] (b. 1725?—d. 1780), Mingo chief. His Indian name was Tahgahjute, but he took the name of James Logan in admiration for the Pennsylvania official (see above). He was long a great friend of the English, but the murder of his family in the Yellow Creek massacre of April, 1774, changed his attitude completely, and he made it his business to kill as many whites as he could. He became a drunkard and was finally killed in a family quarrel. Brantz Mayer in 1851 published a *Discourse* called *Tah-gah-jute, or, Logan and Captain Michael Cresap* vindicating the captain from the charge of the murder.

In 1774 Logan sent a remarkable document to Lord Dunmore, then governor of Virginia. This is frequently described as an oration, but seems to have been in written form. John Gibson translated it, and it immediately gained wide currency. In his *Notes on the State of Virginia* (1784) Jefferson printed it as proof that the American Indian, contrary to European belief, was not a degenerate savage. Dr. Joseph Doddridge's play, *Logan, The Last of the Race of Shikellemus, Chief of the Cayuga Nation* (1823), and John Neal's novel, *Logan, A Family History* (1822), both seek to do justice to the Indian chief.

Logan, Olive (b. Elmira, N.Y., April 22, 1839—d. April 27, 1909), actress, playwright, newspaper correspondent, lecturer. The daughter of CORNELIUS LOGAN tried for a time to be an actress. Under the influence of ARTEMUS WARD she became a lecturer, and her talks on social and political topics proved very successful. She made frequent trips abroad and contributed to newspapers in this country, England, and France, writing under the pen name Chroniqueuse. She wrote two plays that Augustin Daly produced, *Surf* (1870) and *Newport* (1879), both social satires, also some novels and miscellaneous books; among the latter were *Apropos of Women and Theaters* (1869) and *The Mimic World* (1871).

Log of a Cowboy, The (1903), a narrative by ANDY ADAMS, based on Adams' own experiences in a five-month cattle drive from Texas to Montana in 1882. It gives a vivid and veracious account of the picturesque characters of the frontier.

Lomax, Alan (b. Austin, Tex., Jan. 31, 1915 —), ballad collector, author. Working with his father, JOHN LOMAX, and independently, Alan Lomax recorded folk songs all over the United States, in the Bahamas, Haiti, England, Scotland, Ireland, Spain, and Italy. From 1937 to 1942 he was in charge of the American Folk Music Library of the Library of Congress. During the Forties he produced a number of radio programs for C.B.S. and the B.B.C., lectured at the universities of Indiana, Chicago, Texas, and at New York University and Columbia, and continued to gather folk songs. He has also served as folk song editor for Decca and Columbia Records. He has written *Mister Jelly Roll* (1950); *Folk Songs of North America* (1960); *The Penguin Book of American Folk Songs* (1961); and *Folk Song Style* (1960). His folk song collections include: *The Southern Heritage* (1960); *Folk Songs of Britain* (1961).

Lomax, John A[very] (b. Goodman, Miss., Sept. 23, 1867—d. Jan. 26, 1948), teacher, businessman, ballad collector, memoirist. Lomax began collecting ballads as a young man; when he was a graduate student at Harvard, BARRETT WENDELL arranged for a three-year fellowship so he could go on collecting. Thomas H. Johnson holds that "with the publication of Lomax's COWBOY SONGS AND OTHER FRONTIER BALLADS in 1910 the serious and widespread study of folk literature in America had its beginning." Lomax related his experiences as a collector in his *Adventures of a Ballad Hunter* (1947). *Songs of the Cattle Trail and Cow Camp* (1918) followed the *Cowboy Songs*. With the capable assistance of his son ALAN LOMAX, he gathered together *American Ballads and Folk Songs* (1934), *Negro Folk Songs as Sung by Lead Belly* (1936), the songs in *Our Singing Country* (1941) and revised *Cowboy Songs* (1938). Lomax also took advantage of technological advances, and helped establish the Archive of American Folk Song at the Library of Congress.

London, Jack [John Griffith] (b. San Francisco, Jan. 12, 1876—d. Nov. 22, 1916), novelist, short-story writer, political essayist, propagandist. London was the illegitimate son of W. H. Chaney, descendant of colonial New Englanders, self-taught lawyer, journalist, and, eventually, astrologer; and Flora Wellman, rebellious daughter of a wealthy Ohio family, spiritualist, and

teacher of music. London never saw his father, and took the name of his stepfather, John London.

Bettmann Archive

The poverty and attending bleak prospects of London's youth determined to a great extent his choice of vocation. Knowing he must earn his living, he sought the least onerous employment but found only unskilled jobs; disgusted, he escaped to more exciting ways of life only to reject these in turn. Thus, from the age of 14, he became successively cannery worker, oyster pirate, state fish patrolman, hobo, seaman, jute-mill worker, and coal shoveler. Finally, at 18, he joined the western contingent of "Coxey's Army," crossed the continent with the unemployed, and was jailed for vagrancy; then, shocked into sober thinking by the poverty and misery he saw on every hand, he faced his own situation and made two decisions: he would train his brain to make his living, and he would try to help others escape to a better life.

The first decision carried him through a year in high school and one semester as a special student at the University of California; the second led him to socialism and party membership. Thenceforth, determined to write, he taught himself, his general education being guided by the Socialist movement. Inevitably, Marx and Engels, Spencer and Nietzsche, eagerly but hastily read, became the cornerstones of his thinking. His uncritical acceptance of Nietzsche's superman concept was, however, unfortunate, and certain of his works are marred by racism.

The Alaskan gold rush launched London as a writer. He spent the winter of 1897–98 in the Klondike, found no gold, but returned with story material for a reading public avid for tales of America's last frontier. His struggle for recognition was intense but brief; success and fame came quickly. He was soon the highest paid author in America, but this brought him little satisfaction; in time, he frankly disliked his profession. His interest in socialism, too, slowly waned, although he had been an active Socialist—as speaker, writer, and candidate—for years. He roamed the South Seas in his yacht, the *Snark;* he lived on his ranch in the Valley of the Moon, but left it frequently for sailing trips around the Horn or, in later years, lengthy stays in Hawaii. His health deteriorated rapidly toward the end, and he committed suicide in his fortieth year.

In less than two decades of writing, London produced 50 volumes of novels, short stories, essays, and plays. The quality of this large output is uneven. The best of his work ranks high, however, and explains his worldwide renown, greater today than during his lifetime. America's most extensively translated author, his books appear in nearly 50 foreign languages. Within the context of his time, he dealt with timeless themes: man's struggle against hostile nature and against hostile society for a better world and the nobility of the human spirit. His universal idiom still evokes a universal response.

Personal experiences and interests furnish the background of much of his writing. Largely autobiographical are: MARTIN EDEN (1909), in which a struggling writer achieves success, but having rejected Socialist aims and comradeship finds life meaningless and commits suicide; *The Road* (1907), a chronicle of his hobo period; and *John Barleycorn* (1913), an argument for prohibition. Socialism and social criticism dominate THE IRON HEEL (1908), a prophetic extrapolation depicting the growth of fascism in the United States in uncanny anticipation of its rise years later in Europe; *The People of the Abyss* (1903), an account of life in the London slums at the turn of the century; the first portion of THE VALLEY OF THE MOON (1913); *The War of the Classes* (1905), collected essays; and *Revolution and Other Essays* (1910).

Alaska and the South Seas are the settings of many short-story collections, including *The Son of the Wolf* (1900), London's first published book; *South Sea Tales* (1911); *Smoke Bellew* (1912); *The House of Pride and Other Tales of Hawaii* (1912); and several novels, among them THE CALL OF THE WILD (1903), which has become an American classic; WHITE FANG (1906); and *Burning Daylight* (1910). Alaska is also the background of two of his best-known short stories, "Love of Life," in *Love of Life and Other Stories* (1907), and "To Build a Fire," in *Lost Face* (1910). Among his sea stories are THE SEA WOLF (1904), in which his insistence upon Anglo-Saxon superiority is most fully developed; and *The Mutiny of the Elsinore* (1914),

inspired by his voyage around the Horn. Two short novels, THE GAME (1905) and *The Abysmal Brute* (1913), deal with prizefighting, as does the superb short story, "The Mexican" in *The Night Born* (1913). BEFORE ADAM (1907) and scattered short stories reflect his early readings in anthropology. THE STAR ROVER (1915) is a brilliant *tour de force,* combining his storytelling gift at its best, much of his philosophy, and his skill as a propagandist. *The Scarlet Plague* (1915) is early science fiction.

As a short-story master, London has been widely anthologized. Two collections contain most of his finest work in this form: *Best Short Stories of Jack London* (1945) and *Tales of Adventure* (1956). The bulk of his socialist writing has been compiled by Leonard D. Abbott in *London's Essays of Revolt* (1926) and by Philip S. Foner in *Jack London: American Rebel* (1947). Biographies include *The Book of Jack London* (2 v., 1921) by his second wife, Charmian London; *Jack London and His Times* (1939) by Joan London, a daughter of his first marriage; and *Sailor on Horseback* (1938) by Irving Stone.

Joan London

Lonesome Trail, The (1907), a collection of short stories by JOHN G. NEIHARDT. This collection was reissued, with some changes, as *Indian Tales and Others* (1926). The material came from Neihardt's experiences as an Indian trader among the Omahas in Nebraska. SUZETTE LA FLESCHE, herself an Omahan, once said that Neihardt was the only white writer who had discovered the real Indian. Many of the stories deal with aspects of Indian life unfamiliar to white men.

Lonesome Train, The (composed, 1942; performed, 1944; published in Erik Barnouw's *Radio Drama in Action,* 1945), a "folk cantata" by MILLARD LAMPELL, with music by Earl Robinson. It was recorded with Raymond Massey as Lincoln, Burl Ives as the singing narrator, Robinson as the speaking narrator. The train is the one that carried Lincoln's body back to Springfield after his assassination.

Long, Huey [Pierce] (b. Winnfield, La., Aug. 30, 1893—d. Sept. 10, 1935), lawyer, politician, public official. One of the most unabashed cynics ever to appear on the American political scene, Long made himself master of Louisiana by attacks on allegedly corrupt corporations and by a vicious system of rewards for himself and his followers. He provided the state with excellent highways and good schools during his term as governor, built a new state capitol, and helped the Louisiana State University; but his financing methods were bizarre or worse. Attempts to impeach him failed. He was elected to the U.S. Senate in 1930. He called himself "the Kingfish," announced a "Share-the-Wealth Plan," proposed to run for President. Long was assassinated by Dr. Carl A. Weiss, Jr., even though the dictator was surrounded by his armed bodyguards at the time. Weiss was immediately killed.

Long wrote two books, *Every Man a King*

(1933) and *My First Days in the White House* (posthumously published, 1935). The latter tells exactly what he intended to do as President; his account sounds like what Hitler actually did. Novelists have found Long a rewarding subject for fiction. Joseph E. Baker has suggested that Sinclair Lewis wrote IT CAN'T HAPPEN HERE (1935), a novel warning against native fascism, with Long in mind. Hamilton Basso's *Sun in Capricorn* (1942) is a savage attack on a scoundrel and dangerous demagogue not unlike Long. In John Dos Passos' NUMBER ONE (1943) Long appears as a charlatan with a lust for power matched only by his lust for women. Adria Locke Langley sentimentalized Long in *A Lion in the Streets* (1945). Although Robert Penn Warren has denied that the character of Willie Stark in his ALL THE KING'S MEN (1946) should be identified with Long, the similarity is striking. Irving Berlin's *Louisiana Purchase* (1940) is a satire of the Long régime.

Long, John Luther (b. Hanover, Pa., Jan. 1, 1861—d. Oct. 31, 1927), lawyer, short-story writer, playwright. A story entitled MADAME BUTTERFLY by John Long, published in the *Century* magazine for January, 1898, caught the eye of DAVID BELASCO, who was searching for play material. The two collaborated on a drama which, following the original story, had a long successful run. Giacomo Puccini used it as a basis for his famous opera. A second collaboration, THE DARLING OF THE GODS (1902), a Japanese melodrama, was followed by ADREA (1904), a Roman tragedy with a blind princess for heroine. Long then began to write alone, but his own plays were less successful. *Dolce* (1906), founded on his short story, and *Kassa* (1909) were followed by *Crowns* (1922), a drama of ideas. Throughout his literary career Long continued to practice law. Although *Madame Butterfly* is still appealing, *The Darling of the Gods* and *Adrea* are too melodramatic for modern taste.

Long, Sylvester. See LONG LANCE.

Long Day's Journey into Night (1956), a play by EUGENE O'NEILL. This extraordinary autobiographical drama, which was performed impressively shortly after its publication, was apparently written some time before July 22, 1941, when O'Neill presented the manuscript to Carlotta, his third wife, with a letter paying tribute to her for the way in which she had helped him "to face his dead at last and write this play—write it with deep pity and understanding for all the four haunted Tyrones." The Tyrones were the O'Neills—his father, his mother, the older son, himself. The father is the celebrated actor, the older son is a drunkard and ne'er-do-well. The only other character is Cathleen, a servant girl. A harrowing domestic tragedy, the play offers a clear insight into the character of O'Neill himself and shows again his eminence among American dramatists.

Longfellow, Henry Wadsworth (b. Portland, Me., Feb. 27, 1807—d. March 24, 1882), poet, teacher, translator, writer of prose romances. The steel engraving of Longfellow that once

hung in many American schoolrooms showed a serene countenance with a white flowing beard, the patriarch of popular sentiment. This was the writer of THE PSALM OF LIFE, THE CHILDREN'S HOUR [1] and THE VILLAGE BLACK-

SMITH. Less well known is the Longfellow who wrestled with the problems of life and suffered much sorrow and frustration, the poet of MY LOST YOUTH, MEZZO CAMMIN, and *The Cross of Snow.*

Longfellow derived from sturdy New England stock; on his mother's side he was descended from John and Priscilla Alden. He graduated from Bowdoin College, where his fellow students had included Franklin Pierce, Horatio Bridge, and Nathaniel Hawthorne. After his graduation his *alma mater* financed his first trip to Europe to study foreign languages in preparation for a teaching position. After three years abroad, he returned to become professor of modern languages at Bowdoin. But he soon became discontented with life at Brunswick, even his happy marriage in 1831 to Mary Potter of Portland failing to reconcile him to it. He turned to recollecting his pleasant experiences on the Continent in a prose narrative called OUTRE-MER: A PILGRIMAGE BEYOND THE SEA (1833–34), a work reminiscent of Washington Irving's SKETCH BOOK (1819). Finally Longfellow obtained an appointment to succeed George Ticknor in the chair of modern languages at Harvard, and again he journeyed to Europe to prepare himself. The illness and death of Mrs. Longfellow at Rotterdam dimmed the joys of his travel, but he continued to explore the glory of Old World culture, especially at Heidelberg.

Months later, on a tour in Switzerland, Longfellow met Frances Appleton, daughter of a Boston merchant, and fell in love with her. When he returned to Harvard in 1836 he began to court her seriously, but she received his attentions with coolness. Longfellow pressed his suit by portraying Miss Appleton as the heroine of his prose romance HYPERION (1839), but the effort only offended her. In the same year he published also VOICES OF THE NIGHT, his first book of poetry. The contents of this volume and of its successor BALLADS AND OTHER POEMS (1842) were chiefly lyrical, including such favorites as HYMN TO THE NIGHT, A *Psalm of Life*, THE WRECK OF THE HESPERUS, THE SKELETON IN ARMOR, and EXCELSIOR. His health failing, Longfellow sailed for Germany in 1842 to seek to regain it. On the return voyage he wrote *Poems on Slavery* (1842) as an answer to his friends and critics who deplored his Irving-like aloofness from the controversy over abolition. His book, however, is a long way from the humanitarian fervor and fighting spirit of Whittier.

Longfellow at last married Frances Appleton in 1843. As a wedding gift her father presented the couple with a deed to the Craigie house, in which the poet-professor had been rooming in Cambridge. This beautiful old mansion, now the most famous Longfellow shrine, had once been a headquarters for General Washington and was now to be the poet's home for the rest of his life. In the year of his wedding he published a drama, THE SPANISH STUDENT, began his translation of Dante, and at his wife's suggestion wrote his most effective piece of social protest, THE ARSENAL AT SPRINGFIELD, a poem inveighing against war.

The Longfellow of Craigie House, though by no means abandoning the lyric, especially the sonnet, became increasingly interested in writing long narrative verse. One by one came such well-known works as EVANGELINE (1847), THE GOLDEN LEGEND (1851), HIAWATHA (1855), THE COURTSHIP OF MILES STANDISH (1858), and TALES OF A WAYSIDE INN (1863). To these he added a long prose romance, KAVANAGH (1849), which is noteworthy for its advocacy of literary nationalism.

Longfellow was at the height of his fame when the greatest tragedy of his life occurred. One day in 1861 he saw his wife accidentally burn to death when her dress was ignited by a match that had fallen to the floor. He himself suffered severe burns in attempting to save her. For a time his shock and grief interrupted his creative life, but at length he turned for consolation back to his tasks of completing *The Divine Comedy* (1865–67), of completing his deeply religious poem CHRISTUS (1872), and of adding to *Tales of a Wayside Inn*. He wrote also many sonnets in his last years, none of which was stronger or more beautiful than *The Cross of Snow*, a poem expressing his intense sorrow over his wife's death eighteen years after it occurred.

Longfellow's contribution to American culture lay less in originality or profundity of insight than in his skillful rendering of a European tra-

dition for the American audience. Most of his poems are kindly and rather sentimental; they derive, indirectly if not directly, from foreign models, especially from the early German romantics and the Spanish poets of the Renaissance. His work for the most part is rooted in literature rather than in life, and he failed to capture the American spirit that animated such great contemporaries as Whitman or Whittier. Yet Longfellow's achievements should not be overlooked. First of all, he was a genuine singer, a master of his craft who seldom wrote an awkward or unmusical line. His sonnets are among the finest in our literature. Secondly, he made a major contribution to the American interest in and understanding of European cultures as well as to the European perception of 19th-century American civilization. He was immensely popular, commanding a larger and more loyal audience than any other American poet in his own time or since his death, and he used his popularity to promulgate a canon of quiet good taste in the arts and a recognition of proficient craftsmanship. He did much to spread the appreciation of poetry in the United States. Finally, though Longfellow is not remembered primarily as a nationalistic writer, he nevertheless did much to memorialize American history and folklore in his narrative verse. Some of his poems, such as THE MIDNIGHT RIDE OF PAUL REVERE, *The Wreck of the Hesperus*, *Evangeline*, and many others, whatever their merit as poetry may be, have become virtually inseparable parts of the American heritage, touchstones of American cultural life. Today the scales of literary taste, which for so long were unbalanced in Longfellow's favor, are swinging in the other direction, toward the 19th-century symbolists and away from Longfellow and his Cambridge friends; but it will be unfortunate if this trend completely obliterates Longfellow's contributions to the national consciousness.

The standard edition of Longfellow is Samuel Longfellow's *Works* (14 v., 1886–91), including a *Life* by the editor. A one-volume edition of the poems was prepared by H. E. Scudder (1893). Herbert Gorman sought to depict Longfellow in *A Victorian American* (1926). A fresh estimate of the poet is Edward Wagenknecht's *Longfellow: A Full-Length Portrait* (1955). Wagenknecht also edited *Mrs. Longfellow: Selected Letters and Journals of Fanny Appleton Longfellow* (1956). Harvard University Library possesses a large collection of Longfellow correspondence and other materials. See also THE BATTLE OF LOVELL'S POND; THE BELEAGUERED CITY; THE BUILDING OF THE SHIP; THE BELFRY OF BRUGES; THE ARROW AND THE SONG; MASQUE OF PANDORA; MORITURI SALUTAMUS; EMMA AND EGINHARD; THE FALCON OF SER FEDERIGO; THE BIRDS OF KILLINGSWORTH; THE DAY IS DONE; POETRY IN THE U.S.; THE BUILDERS; SANTA FILOMENA; SEAWEED; NEW ENGLAND'S TRAGEDIES.

ELDON C. HILL

Long Lance. "Chief Buffalo Child Long Lance," who claimed to be a Blackfoot Indian, was really Sylvester Long, who was a mixed-blood of Croatan Indian and Negro descent and who was born in Montana (d. 1932) around 1893. He did not know the Blackfoot Indians at first hand, but published an autobiography, *Long Lance* (1928), which was immediately accepted as an authentic description of this Indian tribe. The book became popular and Long Lance was asked to be the star in a motion picture about the Indians, *The Silent Enemy*, and to lecture on Indian life. Soon afterward he committed suicide. His book, despite the deceit that Long committed, is excellent, based on information obtained from good sources. Roberta Forsberg edited *Redmen Echoes* (1933), a collection of letters and fugitive writings by Long Lance.

Long Roll, The (1911), a novel by MARY JOHNSTON. This story of the Civil War, laid in the South, involves both battle action and a love affair. Stonewall Jackson is a leading character, and the Battle of Chancellorsville furnishes the climax of the book. In *Cease Firing* (1912), a sequel to *The Long Roll*, Miss Johnston went on to the period from Vicksburg to the close of the war. The books were based on much careful research and on personal information; Miss Johnston's father, Major Albert Johnston, was himself a participant in the war. She stresses the futility of war, feels the Confederacy failed because it was an agrarian society and lacked an adequate currency.

Longstreet, Augustus Baldwin (b. Augusta, Ga., Sept. 22, 1790—d. July 9, 1870), lawyer, clergyman, college administrator, editor, writer. Longstreet was quick at fighting, playing, dancing; alert in revival meetings and on the political stump, of ready wit and no squeamishness. He was trained at Yale and the Litchfield Law School; his chief interests were politics, religion, and money-making. He was a judge and a clergyman, a president of Emory College, of Centenary College, of the University of Mississippi, of South Carolina College. He wrote first for the Milledgeville *Southern Recorder*, then founded the *States Rights Sentinel* at Atlanta in 1834 and continued as editor until 1836.

His GEORGIA SCENES, CHARACTERS, INCIDENTS, ETC., IN THE FIRST HALF CENTURY OF THE REPUBLIC (1835, frequently reprinted) has become a classic of down-to-earth humor and regionalism. This is Georgia at its most intimate; Longstreet knew his Georgians, especially the poor whites; he could put over an anecdote and reproduced dialogue well. His favorite character is Ransy Sniffle, who excites no admiration. He moralizes heavily about the vices he portrays. Fighting, baby talk, drunkenness, modern dancing, dueling, horse racing, and the undomestic wife are severely reprimanded. One of the best pieces deals with *Georgia Theatrics*. Poe, reviewing the volume, was struck by its resemblance to the *Spectator* papers. It is said that in later years Longstreet was ashamed of the book and tried to suppress it. It set the stage

for similar regionalists, especially in the field of humor.

Later Longstreet wrote *Stories with a Moral* (posthumously published, 1912) and a novel, *Master William Mitten* (1864), which was

largely autobiographical. J. D. Wade made a study of Longstreet (1924).

Longstreet, James (b. Edgefield District, S.C., Jan. 8, 1821—d. Jan. 2, 1904), soldier, cotton broker, public official, memorist. Longstreet rendered important service during the war with Mexico and was one of Lee's most trusted generals during the Civil War. However, when he was given independent commands, he did not do as well, and he was severely criticized for his part in the defeat of the South at Gettysburg. After the war he became a cotton broker in New Orleans, later a Republican politician and office-holder in Louisiana and Georgia. He wrote an account of his life and defended his record in *From Manassas to Appomattox* (1896). Donald Bridgman Sanger and T. R. Hay wrote *James Longstreet: The Soldier* and *James Longstreet: the Politician* (1952).

Longstreet, Stephen (b. New York City, April 18, 1907—   ), novelist, playwright, editor, historian, artist, film critic. Longstreet wrote the award-winning book and screenplay for Broadway's *High Button Shoes* (1947) and Hollywood's *The Jolson Story* (1947). His interest in art and jazz produced such histories as

The Real Jazz, Old and New (1956); *Encyclopédie Du Jazz* (1958); and *Never Look Back* (1958). Out of his travel experience Longstreet wrote the best-selling *The World Revisited* (1953), and *The Boy in the Model-T* (1956), an account of his transcontinental tour of the United States at the age of twelve. In such novels as *The Pedlocks* (1951), *The Lion at Morning* (1954), and *The Promoters* (1957), he embarked upon a long series of novels that he called "a kind of native Human Comedy" covering all our history. Longstreet's novels include: *Decade* (1940); *Sound of An American* (1941); *The Beach House* (1952); *Man of Montmartre* (1958); *Geisha* (1960). Among his travelogues are: *Last Man Around the World* (1941); *Chico Goes to the Wars* (1943); and *Last Man Comes Home* (1942). He also wrote *Nine Lives With Grandfather* (1944); *The Sisters Liked Them Handsome* (1946); and *A Century on Wheels* (1952).

Long Tom Coffin. See COFFIN, LONG TOM.

Long Valley, The (1938), a collection of thirteen stories by JOHN STEINBECK. They are realistic and deal with the life of people in the Salinas Valley in California, especially in relation to the migrants who have come into the valley. Best known of the tales is *The Red Pony*, separately printed in 1945 and often reprinted.

Lonigan, Studs, the "hero" of three novels by JAMES T. FARRELL. The background is the Irish district of Chicago, Lonigan (his first name is William) is a young tough whose career reveals the conflict between ancient ideals and modern corruption. YOUNG LONIGAN (1932) follows Lonigan in his middle teens, *The Young Manhood of Studs Lonigan* (1934) takes him from his high-school days to ten years later. *Judgment Day* (1935) shows him more and more corrupt until he dies at the age of 29, destroyed by alcohol and venereal disease. He starts with good impulses, but becomes a tough and ruthless hoodlum. The stories were collected (1935) in a single volume. Farrell employs the stream-of-consciousness technique without losing sight of his story. Oscar Cargill, in *Intellectual America* (1941), commented that *The Young Manhood of Studs Lonigan* was "perhaps the most terrifying book which has been written in America" in its picture of Studs' spiritual degeneration.

Look. This picture magazine was founded by Gardner Cowles, Jr. It emerged from a 1925 Gallup survey of the Des Moines *Register and Tribune*, a newspaper owned by the Cowles family, which showed that pictures were preferred to text. Following a good deal of experimenting in the Sunday roto section of the paper, the first editor of *Look*, Vernon Pope, clinched the success of this experimental phase by syndicating a picture series to twenty-six other newspapers. *Look* was first a monthly, then a biweekly, later a weekly. It featured fashions, personalities (including some interesting animal personalities), photo-quizzes, cheesecake, and often showed good shock technique. Not long after its first appearance as a magazine in

February 1937 it began to move away from strict entertainment; since then has made excellent contributions to civic reporting with photographic essays on subjects ranging from gambling, housing, and education, to movie stars, modern art, and international events. In 1955 it won the Benjamin Franklin Magazine Award for the "best article on science or health": an account of the Salk polio vaccine. Its circulation is over 6 million.

Look Homeward, Angel: A Story of the Buried Life (1929), a novel by THOMAS WOLFE. Many critics believe that this first novel by Wolfe remains his best. It is autobiography in a thin disguise; Eugene Gant, in appearance, early environment, parentage, domestic surroundings, education, and so on, is Tom Wolfe. Always a voluble writer, Wolfe produced a veritable deluge in this first effort, and at least a little credit for the book's success must be assigned to MAX-WELL PERKINS of Charles Scribner's Sons, who edited the manuscript. The chief credit belongs to Wolfe, however, who made his book a powerful comedy—sometimes affectionate, sometimes satirical—of the life of a sensitive youth coming of age in North Carolina and later in the North. In 1957 a play was made from portions of the book by Ketti Frings.

Looking Backward 2000–1887 (1888), a novel by EDWARD BELLAMY which offered a future utopia into which Bellamy projected all his ideas for the realization of a good society. It has sold widely throughout the world and continues to be read today. In 1897 Bellamy wrote a sequel, *Equality*, in which he replied to attacks upon the earlier book and offered detailed suggestions for the carrying out of his plans.

Loomis, Alfred F[ullerton] (b. Brooklyn, Aug. 23, 1890—d. March 26, 1968), editor, writer. A yachting enthusiast, Loomis served as an editor on *Country Life* and *Motor Boating*, and participated in both World Wars as a naval officer. Among his books: *The Cruise of the Hippocampus* (1922); *Fair Winds in the Far Baltic* (1928); *Yachts Under Sail* (1933); *Ocean Racing* (1936; rev., 1946); *Ranging the Maine Coast* (1939); *The Hotspur Story* (1954); *What Price Dory* (with Chon Day 1955); also numerous excellent juveniles.

Loomis, Charles Battell (b. Flatbush, N.Y., Sept. 16, 1861—d. Sept. 23, 1911), poet, humorist. The father of ALFRED F. LOOMIS wrote a number of amusing volumes: *Just Rhymes* (1899); *Cheerful Americans* (1903); *More Cheerful Americans* (1904); *Cheer Up!* (1906); *A Holiday Touch* (1908); *Just Irish* (1909); and others.

Loon Feather, The (1940), a novel by Iola Fuller. It won the Avery Hopwood Award (1939) at the University of Michigan. It begins in the early 1800's in the Great Lakes region. The heroine, an Ojibway Indian, recalls faintly the War of 1812; her memories become more vivid when Black Hawk enters the story. The smoothly written narrative closes in an interracial love match.

Loos, Anita (b. Sisson, Cal., April 26, 1893 —), novelist, motion picture script writer. Anita Loos began writing film scripts for D. W. Griffith at the tender age of fifteen, and subsequently (with her husband, John Emerson) wrote for Douglas Fairbanks and Constance Talmadge. In later years she prepared scenarios for such films as *Red Headed Woman, San Francisco, Saratoga, Alaska, The Women, Blossoms in the Dust,* and *I Married an Angel.* But her greatest fame came from the novel GENTLEMEN PREFER BLONDES (1925), an amusing story about the travels of a predatory blonde flapper. The novel inspired a play (1925); a sequel, *But Gentlemen Marry Brunettes* (1928); a musical comedy (1949); a movie (1953); and the title of an autobiography, *This Brunette Prefers Work* (1956). She is also the author of two successful plays, *Happy Birthday* (1946) and *Gigi* (1951, from the novel by Colette).

Lord, Phillips H[aynes] ["Seth Parker"] (b. Hartford, Vt., July 13, 1902—), educational administrator, radio and television dramatist and producer. After two years as a high-school principal, Lord went into radio and later television and created the characters in a number of popular sketches; he also produced some important discussion programs. Among these productions: *Seth Parker, Country Doctor, G-Men, Gang Busters, We the People, Mr. District Attorney, Counterspy.* He has also written hymns. Some of this material has appeared in book form: *Seth Parker's Album* (1930); *Way Back Home* (1932); *Seth Parker's Scrap Book* (1935); and others.

Lord, Walter (b. Baltimore, Md., Oct. 8, 1917—), writer. Lord graduated from Princeton in 1939 and received an LL.B. from Yale in 1946. While pursuing a career in advertising and publishing, he continued his interest in dramatic events of history. *A Night to Remember,* the story of the sinking of the *Titanic,* appeared in 1955. In *Day of Infamy* (1957), another best-seller, Lord reconstructed the incidents that preceded the Pearl Harbor attack. Other books: *The Fremantle Diary* (1954); *The Good Years* (1960).

Lord, William Wilberforce (b. Madison Co., N.Y., Oct. 28, 1819—d. April 22, 1907), clergyman, poet. Upon the publication of his *Poems* (1845), Long was hailed as "the American Milton," in spite of a castigating review by Poe, who had been infuriated by Lord's burlesque of his *Raven. Christ in Hades* (1851), a religious epic, and *André* (1856), a historical narrative in blank verse, both rather thin and unMiltonic, were Lord's only other important publications. He served as chaplain in the Confederate army during the Civil War. His *Complete Poetical Works* were published in 1938.

Lorentz, Pare (b. Clarksburg, Va., Dec. 11, 1905—), movie writer. In the 1930's, when the government sponsored many serious theatrical productions, Lorentz wrote and produced two important informational and educational films. *The Plow That Broke the Plains* (1936) explained the disintegration of the wheat country by annual droughts and told what measures were being taken to prevent further damage. Even more impressive was *The River* (1938), "a tragedy of a land twice impoverished" as a result of erosion caused by Mississippi Valley floods; it showed the work of rehabilitation then going on. Lorentz is able to take an economic and social theme, on the surface merely statistical, and give it dramatic vitality. He has a sense of style, and often his text is true poetry. See DOCUMENTARY.

Lorimer, George Horace (b. Louisville, Ky., Oct. 6, 1867—d. Oct. 22, 1937), businessman, reporter, editor, author of "inspirational" books. After working for Philip Armour in the canning business and then for himself in the wholesale grocery business, Lorimer became a reporter in Boston, went to work for the SATURDAY EVENING POST in 1898, within a year was its editor. The *Post* had been on the point of expiring, but Lorimer made it into a tremendous success. He was convinced that big business and its ways spelled true romance and was able to translate this conviction into the weekly stuff of his magazine, both fiction and nonfiction. He was strict in his censorship of advertising. He encouraged bright young authors, and paid them well. He wrote two "inspirational" books, *Letters from a Self-Made Merchant to His Son* (1902) and *Old Gorgon Graham* (1904), as well as one or two others. An admiring account is John Tebbel's *George Horace Lorimer and The Saturday Evening Post* (1948).

Loring, Emilie [Baker] (b. Boston, [?]— d. March 14, 1951), novelist, writer on domestic science, playwright. Mrs. Loring began to write articles for women's magazines under the pseudonym Josephine Story. *For the Comfort of the Family* (1914) and *The Mother in the Home* (1917) are collections of essays on home-making. Her first novel, *The Trail of Conflict* (1922), was followed by twenty-eight more books of fiction, among them *It's a Great World!* (1935); *When Hearts are Light Again* (1943); *Bright Skies* (1946); *Love Came Laughing By* (1949); and *To Love and To Honor* (1950). The author said her formula for success was "a wholesome love story." *Where's Peter?* (1928), a comedy, is still occasionally performed by amateur groups.

lost generation, the. "You are all a lost generation," said GERTRUDE STEIN to ERNEST HEMINGWAY in Paris, as he recorded in the preface to THE SUN ALSO RISES (1926), still the best representation of the group of "lost" young people to whom she referred. This "lost generation" took two severe blows, some years apart: World War I and the great depression that began in 1929. Toward the last stage their muse was likely to be Nostalgia. By the middle 1920's many of them had established a place in the literary world and a fairly steady income. Blow number two was often disastrous financially and emotionally. One result was a tendency toward extremes of rightism or leftism in politics.

Not all the "artistic" Americans in Paris were artists or writers; many just had money and liked France. SAMUEL PUTNAM recorded his vivid impressions in *Paris Was Our Mistress: Memoirs of a Lost and Found Generation* (1947). He described the American colony of the 1920's as a pretty disreputable crowd who constituted, he says, a demimonde, "half French, half American, a sort of weird amalgam of Brooklyn and Montmartre." Paris was enormously exciting for anyone interested in writing, what with James Joyce and the interior monologue, EUGENE JOLAS's *transition* and "the revolution of the word," Gertrude Stein's verbal manipulations, and the impact of such varied personalities as Jean Cocteau, Louis Aragon, Pablo Picasso, Luigi Pirandello, and other writers and artists.

Some members of the lost generation found their Paris elsewhere: KATHERINE ANNE PORTER in Mexico; THOMAS WOLFE traveled widely in Europe, but preferred Germany to France; JOHN DOS PASSOS never stood still; while SCOTT FITZGERALD, after frenetic wandering over the Continent, spent his last years in California as a film writer. EZRA POUND abandoned Paris for Rapallo, Italy. KAY BOYLE stayed longer in France than most of the others, and GERTRUDE STEIN made her home there after 1902, placidly waiting for the years of chaos and disaster. Malcolm Cowley described *The Lost Generation* (1931). According to EXILE'S RETURN: A NARRATIVE OF IDEAS (1934; rev., 1951, as *Exile's Return: A Literary Odyssey of the 1920's*), Hemingway's *The Sun Also Rises* set the pattern for the lost generation of writers and their naive followers in the United States, but Fitzgerald's *Tender Is the Night* (1934) is perhaps the most poignant analysis of its spiritual climate.

The later sector of the lost generation, caught in the economic blizzard of the 1930's, stayed at home, and were glad to find shelter in the WPA projects of the Roosevelt years. The lot of writers was a hard one, as WILLIAM SAROYAN described it in THE DARING YOUNG MAN ON THE FLYING TRAPEZE (1934) and in his later collection, *Inhale and Exhale* (1936). PAUL ENGLE vented his wrath against the way people were forced to live in his *Break the Heart's Anger* (1936), as did STEPHEN VINCENT BENÉT in *Burning City* (1936). Other writers of this group included ARCHIBALD MacLEISH, KENNETH FEARING, JAMES T. FARRELL, and a host of novelists who turned to economic themes— ERSKINE CALDWELL, for example, and JOHN STEINBECK; the stage too felt the influence of this deep new interest. An account of these later writers was given by Maxine Davis in *The Lost Generation* (1936).

Lost Lady, A (1923), a novel by WILLA CATHER. This story is sometimes accounted Miss Cather's masterpiece. It shows her powers of style, subtle characterization, and moral import at their highest. The "lost lady" is Mrs. Marian Forrester, the young wife of a great western pioneer and builder of railroads. She is seen, with a naïveté that becomes the most delicate irony and revelation, through the eyes of Niel Herbert, an adoring young boy. Beautiful, charming, seemingly the perfect lady, her

passionate nature and her weakness for drink and cheap men lead her astray. When her husband dies, her chief protection against the world around her is taken away. She slowly coarsens, the placid existence to which she has been accustomed crumbles around her, she disappears and is heard of again only by rumor as the cherished wife of a wealthy Englishman in South America. To Neil she represents the great age of the pioneers. But Miss Cather saw in her life the way in which a generation of "shrewd young men," who had never dared anything, drove out "the dreamers, the great-hearted adventurers" who had won the Old West.

Lost Men of American History (1946), biographical sketches by STEWART H. HOLBROOK, an astonishing gallery of forgotten, underrated, sometimes misunderstood Americans, beginning with Alexander Young, who by misunderstanding a word started the myth of the log cabin, and going on to others like Sam Adams, our first propagandist; David Bushnell, who built a submarine; Henry Rowe Schoolcraft, who began the practice of giving melodious Indian names to lakes, hills, and rivers; and Robert Gibbon Johnson, who publicly ate a tomato, till then considered a deadly poison.

Lost Occasion, The (1880), a poem by JOHN GREENLEAF WHITTIER. In 1850 Whittier, at a white heat of anger because of Daniel Webster's famous "Seventh of March Speech," which sought by compromise with the South to avoid the disaster of a civil war, had written his great poem called ICHABOD, a flaming denunciation of Webster. He implied that Webster, hopeful of winning the Presidency, had deliberately broken faith with his Northern followers. Actually Webster had sacrificed ambition to patriotism. In 1880, long after Webster's death, Whittier apologized in *The Lost Occasion*, a fine poem, but not a classic like *Ichabod*.

Lost Pleiad, The (1829, 1859), a poem by WILLIAM GILMORE SIMMS. The first and shorter version of this poem was written, according to Simms, between his eighteenth and twentieth years. The later version was greatly revised and lengthened. Edd Winfield Parks describes the poem as "an orchestrated expression of the transiency of the most stable objects, a poem which cuts through the conventionalities of that overused subject and gives it a lasting freshness and significance." THOMAS HOLLEY CHIVERS published a collection of poems with the same title in 1845.

Lost Weekend, The (1944). See CHARLES JACKSON.

Lothrop, Amy. Pen name of ANNA BARTLETT WARNER.

Lothrop, Harriett Mulford Stone ["Margaret Sidney"] (b. New Haven, Conn., June 22, 1844 —d. Aug. 2, 1924), children's story writer. Harriett Lothrop began to write stories at an early age, although her first contributions to WIDE AWAKE magazine did not appear until 1878. Her FIVE LITTLE PEPPERS AND HOW THEY GREW (1881) sold over 2 million copies; it is the story of a lively, courageous family of children whose widowed mother works as a seamstress to keep her family together. In spite of the author's tendency to sentimentalize and instruct, the book is written with a simple, cheerful gusto and reality that appealed to young readers. *So As by Fire* (1881); *The Pettibone Name, a New England Story* (1882); *A New Departure for Girls* (1886); *Dilly and the Captain* (1887); *How Tom and Dorothy Made and Kept a Christian Home* (1888); *Rob, a Story for Boys* (1891); and several further adventures of little Peppers did not approach the spectacular success of the original *Five Little Peppers*.

Lottery, The (1949), a story by SHIRLEY JACKSON, originally in the *New Yorker* magazine. Miss Jackson's best known story has become a small classic in the few years since its publication. It has been widely anthologized and is on many college reading lists. "The lottery" is part of a spring ritual observed by everyone in a small American town. Most of the procedures of the ritual have been forgotten and no one any longer knows the reason for the lottery, but it goes on without question. Until the last lines of the story, the reader does not discover why everyone must pick a slip of paper, nor why the family that gets the one with a spot on it is disturbed. Then the horror is revealed, heightened by the almost festive air that has surrounded the proceedings throughout the story: the woman chosen by the lottery is stoned to death by her fellow townsmen.

Loudon, Samuel (b. Ireland?, 1727?—d. Feb. 24, 1813), bookseller, printer, pamphleteer. After arriving in America, Loudon became an ardent patriot, although his *The Deceiver Unmasked* (1776), an anonymous reply to Thomas Paine's COMMON SENSE, offended some radicals. He published *The New York Packet*, which later printed some of the FEDERALIST papers, and printed THE AMERICAN MAGAZINE, edited by Noah Webster. Alexander J. Wall wrote an account of *Samuel Loudon* (1922).

Louisiana Purchase. Louis XV ceded the Louisiana territory to Spain in 1762, to avoid losing it to England. Napoleon forced Spain in 1800 to yield it again to France, on condition that France would never cede the territory to another country. The terms of the treaty soon became known, and England made it clear that Napoleon would never be permitted to occupy the territory. Restrictions on American commerce on the Mississippi became an issue, and efforts were made to buy the region. Going beyond their instructions from President Jefferson, the American commissioners in France, Robert R. Livingston and James Monroe, agreed to buy the entire territory; the cost in the end amounted to about $27,267,000. The 885,000 square miles extended from the Mississippi to the Rockies and from the Gulf of Mexico to the British border in the north. Ultimately thirteen states or portions of states were carved from the territory. It was transferred on Dec. 20, 1803. Among recent accounts of the event are books by Robert Tallant (1952) and John

Chase (1960), both entitled *The Louisiana Purchase*.

Love Affairs of a Bibliomaniac, The (1896), a novel by EUGENE FIELD. In this tale Field, himself an ardent booklover, satirized the lengths to which a bibliophile could go in his passion for books.

Love and Friendship, or, Yankee Notions (produced, 1807; published, 1809), a comedy by A. B. Lindsley. This play revealed several Yankee characters against the background of Charleston, S.C. The Yankee is presented in vigorous style, displaying more "greenness" and more honesty than was customary in the stage Yankees of later vintage.

Lovecraft, H[oward] P[hillips] (b. Providence, R.I., Aug. 20, 1890—d. March 15, 1937), short-story writer, novelist. Lovecraft died when only two small books of his had been published, but he was recognized in a small circle of admirers as a master of the Gothic tale of terror and as a pioneer in science-fiction. Since his death his fame has increased. Lovecraft was a shy recluse and ill most of his life, learned in the lore of the 18th century, a master of several languages, and well versed in the sciences. He drew upon "the problematic possibilities of science" for what Donald A. Wollheim calls "his Poesque tales of cosmic dread." He had marked gifts of language, often poetic in phrasing, kindly of manner himself, he expressed in his writings mainly the cruelty of nature.

In his lifetime he published *The Shunned House* (1928) and *The Shadow Over Innsmouth* (1936). Many of his other tales had appeared in the magazine *Weird Tales*. His writings were further collected in *The Outsider and Others* (1939); *Beyond the Wall of Sleep* (1943); *Marginalia* (1944); *The Lurker at the Threshold* (1945); *The Best Supernatural Stories of H. P. Lovecraft* (1945); *Supernatural Horror in Literature* (1945); *Something About Cats and Other Pieces* (1949); *Selected Letters* (1948). August Derleth wrote a biography, *HPL: A Memoir* (1945).

Lovejoy, Arthur O. (b. Germany, Oct. 10, 1873—d. Dec. 30, 1962), philosopher. The field of inquiry known as "the history of ideas" came into being as a result of Lovejoy's work. He set out its methods and materials in *The Great Chain of Being* (1936). Here Lovejoy examined and compared views of the world held from ancient times through the eighteenth century. He often focused on the changes in meaning undergone by a particular word. His study of the different meanings of the word "nature" in the eighteenth century is probably best known. In addition to its importance for philosophy, the picture of an intellectual climate and the method of examining words for their changing content proved particularly useful to literary critics and scholars. Stanley Edgar Hyman devotes a chapter to the importance of Lovejoy in *The Armed Vision*, a book of essays on modern literary critics. Educated at the University of California, Harvard, and the

University of Paris, Lovejoy later taught at Stanford, Washington (St. Louis), Missouri, and Johns Hopkins University (for 28 years), retiring in 1938. He founded and edited *The Journal of the History of Ideas,* and wrote *The Revolt Against Dualism* (1930); *Primitivism and Related Ideas in Antiquity* (with George Boas, 1935); *Essays in the History of Ideas* (1948); *Reflections on Human Nature* (1961); and *The Reason, The Understanding, and Time* (1961).

Lovejoy, Elijah P[arish] (b. Albion, Me., Nov. 9, 1802—d. Nov. 7, 1837), teacher, clergyman, newspaper editor. Lovejoy taught school in St. Louis, then became a newspaperman. But he decided to go into the ministry, studied at the Princeton Theological Seminary, and was ordained in 1833. On returning to St. Louis, Lovejoy founded *The Observer,* which fought both slavery and intemperance. His strong views on lynching aroused so much feeling that Lovejoy removed from St. Louis and continued his newspaper at Alton, Ill., as the Alton *Observer.* By this time he had become a strong abolitionist, and mobs in Alton on four occasions destroyed his presses. The fourth time Lovejoy and the mob exchanged shots, and Lovejoy was killed. His death strengthened abolitionist feeling throughout the North. His brother, **Owen Lovejoy** (b. 1811—d. 1864), also a clergyman, continued to fight slavery, became a strong supporter of Lincoln, served in the House of Representatives (1856-64). Elijah P. Lovejoy's career may have furnished details for Katharine H. Brown's novel *The Father* (1928), which depicts an abolitionist forced out of New England to new beginnings in Illinois; his fiery editorials attract the attention of Lincoln.

Lovelace, Maud Hart (b. Mankato, Minn., April 25, 1892—　　　), author. A graduate of the University of Minnesota, Mrs. Lovelace began her literary career with *The Black Angels* (1926). Married to a journalist, she devoted her talents to the novel, short story, and children's books. Best known of her many books are the series that began with *Betsy Tacy* (1940). Later works include: *The Tune is in the Tree* (1950); *Emily of Deep Valley* (1950); *The Trees Kneel at Christmas* (1951); *Winona's Pony Cart* (1953); *Betsy's Wedding* (1955); *What Cabrillo Found* (1958).

Loveman, Amy (b. New York City, May 16, 1881—d. Dec. 11, 1955), book reviewer, editor. Miss Loveman did much of her work for the SATURDAY REVIEW OF LITERATURE. In 1938 she became head of the editorial department of the Book-of-the-Month Club, in 1951 a member of the Board of Judges. She wrote *I'm Looking for a Book* (1936) and was a co-author of *Saturday Papers* (1921) and *Designed for Reading* (1934).

Loveman, Robert (b. Cleveland, Ohio, April 11, 1864—d. July 10, 1923), poet. Loveman published several collections of verse: *Poems* (1897); *A Book of Verses* (1900); *The Gates of Silence* (1903); *On the Way to Willowdale*

(1912); *Verses* (1912). But his fame rests entirely on one poem—*April Rain* (*Harper's Magazine,* May, 1901), which begins: "It is not raining rain to me,/ It's raining daffodils."

Love Nest, The, and Other Stories (1926), a collection of nine tales by RING LARDNER. In it appear two of Lardner's most bitter stories, the title story (dramatized by Robert E. Sherwood, 1927), and *Haircut,* a story on the theme of cruelty.

Love Song of J. Alfred Prufrock, The (*Poetry* magazine, June, 1915; collected in *Prufrock and Other Observations,* London, 1917, and *Poems,* 1920), a poem by T. S. ELIOT. Said to have been written when Eliot was still an undergraduate at Harvard, this poem was not published until he had become an expatriate in England. It is a dramatic monologue which presents, with somewhat Browningesque irony, the musings of a young man whose youth is beginning to slip away from him and who is still unable to bring himself to the point of speaking frankly to the lady of his choice. The poem can be read as a study in neurotic impotence and at the same time as a contrived specimen of the cultural decay which Eliot ascribed to the controlling bourgeois classes of the Edwardian period. Except for a few scraps of juvenilia, this was Eliot's first published work, and it is doubtful that any other poet in modern times has won such admiration with his first poem. In it Eliot used many of the devices —associative progressions, precisely controlled free verse, indirect allusions, etc.—which he developed more fully in his later work. It is a brilliant example of symbolist technique and remains one of Eliot's most effective poems.

Lovett, Robert Morss (b. Boston, Dec. 25, 1870—d. Feb. 8, 1956), teacher, literary historian, educational administrator, public official, writer. Lovett might have had a career teaching at Harvard, but chose to go to an exciting new institution, the University of Chicago; he found Chicago "both unpleasant and invigorating." There he served from 1892 to 1936. He held liberal views on political topics, although he avoided discussing them in class; he favored freedom for Ireland and India, battled for peace and civil liberty, was a warm friend of JANE ADDAMS and her Hull House. During this period he collaborated with WILLIAM VAUGHN MOODY on *A History of English Literature* (1902); wrote *Richard Gresham* (1904) and *A Winged Victory* (1907), two novels that attracted little attention; published an analysis of *Edith Wharton* (1925) and a *History of the Novel in England* (with Helen Sard Hughes, 1932); edited anthologies. In 1948 Lovett published his memoirs, *All Our Years,* a frank and amusing account of an unusual career.

Lovewell, John (b. Mass., 1691—d. 1725), Indian fighter. Lovewell fought Indians skillfully until he was finally ambushed and killed in Maine at what is now called Lovell's or Lovewell's Pond. His exploits were celebrated in several ballads; Longfellow's first published poem was THE BATTLE OF LOVELL'S POND (1820). Frederic Kidder wrote *The Expeditions of Captain John Lovewell and His Encounters with the Indians, Including a Particular Account of the Pequauket Battle, and a Reprint of Rev. Thomas Symmes's Sermon* (1865). There is also an account of him in Francis Parkman's *Half-Century of Conflict* (1892). Hawthorne devoted a somewhat melodramatic story, ROGER MALVIN'S BURIAL (*The Token*, 1832; *Mosses from an Old Manse*, 1846), to two survivors of the battle.

Low Cloud, Charles Round (1873–1949), newspaperman. It was said of Low Cloud that he "thought in Winnebago and wrote in English." From 1919 to the time of his death he was a columnist for the Black River Falls (Wis.) *Banner-Journal*. He had a style all his own, in which punctuation was notable for its absence. Thus he pondered, when it was suggested that it might be well to have an Indian for President: "Yes. It would take a good thinking man because some man you will think always a good fellow everywhere." His comments were widely quoted in other papers.

Lowell, A[bbott] Lawrence (b. Boston, Dec. 13, 1856—d. Jan. 16, 1943), lawyer, teacher, political economist, university administrator. Lowell was one of the important descendants of the remarkable Percival Lowle who settled in Newbury, Mass., in 1639, and whose progeny through many generations have been ably described in Ferris Greenslet's *The Lowells and Their Seven Worlds* (1946). His older brother was PERCIVAL LOWELL, the famous astronomer; his sister was the poet AMY LOWELL. He practiced law from 1880 to 1897, meanwhile wrote his *Essays on Government* (1889), *Government and Parties in Continental Europe* (2 v., 1896), *The Influence of Party upon Legislation in England and America* (1902), and his most important work, *The Government of England* (2 v., 1908). The year before this book appeared Lowell was appointed a lecturer on government at Harvard, rose steadily in academic rank, became president of the university (1909–1933). He modified the elective system inherited from Charles W. Eliot by introducing the system of concentration and distribution and by instituting general examinations. He encouraged the advancement of scholarship by setting up and endorsing the Society of Fellows of Harvard University. He stressed a liberal education in preparation for any profession, especially public service; and he restored the primacy of Harvard College in the university set-up. He secured large endowments for buildings and instituted the house system, which did much to destroy the earlier social distinction between Harvard's "Gold Coast" and "the great unwashed." But an uprising of Harvard alumni frustrated Lowell in his efforts to introduce a quota system for minority groups.

Meanwhile Lowell was active in numerous public causes, especially the League to Enforce Peace, which sought to help Woodrow Wilson in his crusade for the League of Nations. He was one of a commission of three eminent Massachusetts citizens whom Governor Alvan Fuller appointed to review the SACCO-VANZETTI CASE; the commission ruled against them and they were executed. Greenslet concludes that "Lowell was the ablest member of the commission and largely influential in its unanimous report."

Lowell continued to write and publish. Among his many books were *Public Opinion and Popular Government* (1913); *Public Opinion in War and Peace* (1923); *At War with Academic Traditions* (1934); and a free-spoken autobiography, *What a College President Has Learned* (1938). Immediately after his retirement he completed a biography of his brother Percival (1935). Henry Aaron Yeomans, Lowell's intimate friend, wrote his official biography (1948).

Lowell, Amy [Lawrence] (b. Brookline, Mass., Feb. 9, 1874—d. May 12, 1925), poet, critic, biographer, editor. A. LAWRENCE LOWELL's sister had the same background of wealth and social distinction. She was a woman

Houghton Mifflin Company

of egotistic aggressiveness, determined to become as eminent as the other members of her illustrious family. Ultimately she hit upon literature as the sphere for her activities; she announced her greatness as a writer and critic imperiously, flooded magazine editors with manuscripts which were less submissions than commands to publish. At one point she said, "I am the only member of my family who is worth a damn." In spite of her arrogance, however, she was well liked by her friends; Ellery Sedgwick described her as "impossible manners with a golden heart." Miss Lowell was a very stout woman who smoked cigars in private and public and was well aware of her own shock-value. "Arguing with Amy," said Carl Sandburg, "is like arguing with a big blue wave."

On a trip to England Miss Lowell discovered EZRA POUND and IMAGISM, and promptly took over the latter, which thereafter became, Pound said, "Amygism." She is remembered today chiefly for her sponsorship of other Imagist and experimental poets and for her editorship of a number of Imagist anthologies. In her own work she was imitative; in Oscar Cargill's judgment she was particularly influenced by "the minor French Decadent experimentalist, Paul Fort. . . . Miss Lowell was as Decadent as the inhibitions of a mind that was at once puritanical and provincial would let her be. Like Fort, she went in, mainly, for the pretty-pretty." The English Romantics also were important in her work, and she produced a two-volume biography of Keats (1925).

The critics have not been kind to Amy Lowell, and it seems safe to say that her talent was both small and spoiled by her pretentiousness. Nevertheless, of the six hundred poems she published between 1910 and her death in 1925, a few won wide popularity and were widely reprinted in anthologies, most notably, perhaps, the familiar "Patterns." No doubt her vigorous press-agentry was largely responsible for her success, yet some of her poems, especially from her last years, today seem greatly better than most of the effusions of other American female vers librists of her period. Among her books are SWORD BLADES AND POPPY SEEDS (1914); *Men, Women, and Ghosts* (1916); *Can Grande's Castle* (1918); *What's O'Clock* (1925). She also published anonymously A CRITICAL FABLE (1922), in close imitation of her cousin James Russell Lowell's FABLE FOR CRITICS. Her *Complete Poetical Works* were edited by Louis Untermeyer (1955). Horace Gregory has written a study of her life and work in *Amy Lowell: a Portrait of the Poet in Her Time* (1958). See LILACS.

Lowell, James Russell (b. Cambridge, Mass., Feb. 22, 1819—d. Aug. 12, 1891), poet, editor, teacher, critic, diplomat. Born into a distinguished New England family, Lowell possessed an unfailing patrician reserve, yet he thought his way through to democratic ideas, took a firm stand on slavery, and was one of the first writers to recognize the greatness of Lincoln, to whom he paid tribute in his *Ode Recited at the Harvard Commemoration* (1865). (See COMMEMORATION ODE.) As a student at Harvard, Lowell preferred following his personal tastes in reading to plowing through the prescribed lists in his courses, and as a consequence he was "rusticated" for six months to Concord, where he took a critical attitude toward Emerson and came to regard Thoreau as a crank. Later he revised his estimate of Emerson, but continued to look down on the author of *Walden*. Lowell took a postgraduate course in the law school, received a degree, but did not find the practice of law congenial. He turned to journalism, contributed to the DIAL, and became editor of a high-minded but short-lived magazine, THE PIONEER.

In 1844, after a long engagement, Lowell married Maria White, herself a poet of strongly abolitionist tendencies. She encouraged her husband in his writing, and she is credited with deepening his humanitarian impulses, which found expression in antislavery articles and

blasts against the evil of war. The first work to bring Lowell national fame was THE BIGLOW PAPERS, FIRST SERIES (1848). The poems in this collection were interlarded with many prose passages, the whole forming a sort of dialogue between Hosea Biglow, a Yankee farmer, and his friends. Lowell's use of Yankee dialect, which had of course been anticipated by previous satirists, nevertheless was more authentic and at the same time funnier than anything by his predecessors. The fault of the book is its prolixity, a fault which can be charged against most of Lowell's writing.

In direct contrast was a poem published in the same year, THE VISION OF SIR LAUNFAL, long a favorite in school readers. It is a story of a medieval knight, a proud man, who spends his life seeking abroad for the Holy Grail in vain, only to find it at home when he humbly gives a crust of bread and a cup of water to a leper.

Lowell also published in 1848 his exuberant, diverting, and penetrating A FABLE FOR CRITICS. In this long work of literary comment in verse Lowell set down, frankly and often wittily, his views of his elders and his contemporaries, including himself. He had some harsh verdicts—on Poe, for example, and Bryant. His estimate of Emerson was kinder. The poem is clever and entertaining, though the criticism today seems rudimentary.

With these three books, all published in a single year, Lowell achieved a high reputation;

he became, in fact, one of the leaders of the popular, conservative school in American literature. In 1851–52 he traveled in Europe, spending his time principally in France, Germany, Italy, and England. His return to Cambridge was caused by the illness of his wife, who died in 1853. Two years later, when Longfellow decided to give up his chair as Smith Professor of Modern Languages at Harvard, Lowell was chosen as his successor.

In 1857 when the ATLANTIC MONTHLY was founded, Lowell was appointed its first editor, a position which he filled with distinction while still continuing his teaching. In 1861 he resigned his editorship to devote his whole time to teaching and writing, but three years later he joined his friend Charles Eliot Norton as co-editor of the NORTH AMERICAN REVIEW, at that time probably the most distinguished magazine in America. During this period he published two volumes of literary essays, Among My Books (1870) and My Study Windows (1871).

Lowell's devotion to his study and his classroom did not, however, prevent him from taking an active part in public life. Travel abroad, during which he had received honorary degrees from Oxford and Cambridge, prepared him admirably for his career as a diplomat. President Rutherford B. Hayes appointed him minister to Spain and a few years later minister to England. In these posts he made many friends, both for himself and for his country; he was as ardent a patriot as ever served in the United States foreign service and an able and witty spokesman for democracy.

Lowell's stature in literature has diminished in the past quarter-century. Still, despite his faults, the solid core of his work deserves attention. He once wrote: "It is the soul which makes men rich or poor, and he who has given a nation a truer conception of beauty, which is the body of truth, as love is the spirit, has done more for its happiness and to secure its freedom than if he had doubled its defenses or its revenues." The best of Lowell's poems and essays contribute to this end. See THE CATHEDRAL; COLUMBUS; THE COURTIN'; ENDYMION; THE FUNCTION OF THE POET; JONATHAN TO JOHN; ON A CERTAIN CONDESCENSION IN FOREIGNERS; SUNTHIN' IN THE PASTORAL LINE; STANZAS ON FREEDOM; THE WASHERS OF THE SHROUD.

Lowell's works today are chiefly found in anthologies. Democracy and Other Papers, a selection of essays edited by Max J. Herzberg, appeared in 1931. Representative Selections, edited by H. H. Clark and Norman Foerster, appeared in 1947. Among biographies and critical studies are: F. H. Underwood, James Russell Lowell: A Biographical Sketch (1882); E. E. Hale, James Russell Lowell and His Friends (1899); H. E. Scudder, James Russell Lowell: A Biography (2 v., 1901); Ferris Greenslet, James Russell Lowell (1905) and The Lowells and Their Seven Worlds (1946); G. W. Cooke, A Bibliography of James Russell Lowell (1906); W. H. Hudson, Lowell and His Poetry (1912); J. J. Reilly, James Russell Lowell as a Critic (1915); L. M. Shea, Lowell's Religious Outlook (1926); R. C. Beatty, James Russell Lowell (1942).

ELDON C. HILL

Lowell, Percival (b. Boston, March 13, 1855 —d. Nov. 12, 1916), astronomer. At first engaged in business, Lowell became deeply interested in astronomy, established the Lowell Observatory at Flagstaff, Ariz., and began extensive research there. He published Mars as the Abode of Life (1908) and later demonstrated the existence of a trans-Neptunian planet, which in 1930 was discovered and named Pluto. He also wrote several books on the Far East, particularly Japan. A. Lawrence Lowell, his brother, wrote Biography of Percival Lowell (1935).

Lowell, Robert [Traill Spence], Jr. (b. Boston, March 1, 1917—), poet, teacher. One of the Boston Lowells, he became a leading poet of his generation. James Russell Lowell was his great-grandfather's brother, Amy Lowell his cousin. Robert Lowell is a stubborn, idiosyncratic, maverick New Englander. Like Thoreau, he went to jail for his convictions; he declined to be drafted because he objected to Allied bombing of civilians during World War II, and was jailed for a year despite the fact that he had earlier twice tried to enlist and been rejected.

For a while, his own individualism took the form of rebellion against Protestantism; Lord Weary's Castle and The Mills of the Kavanaughs show the influence of Lowell's current Roman Catholic beliefs. Subsequently Lowell turned away from Catholicism. He has taught at Boston University and at Kenyon College, where he took his undergraduate degree in 1940. Lowell's verse is dense, witty, and resonant. His sense of rhythm and his feeling for the sounds of words mark him as an outstanding poet. His first collection of verse was Land of Unlikeness (1944), followed by Lord Weary's Castle (1946), which won a Pulitzer Prize. The Mills of the Kavanaughs, the title poem of which was a dramatic narrative set in a Maine village, appeared in 1951, and Life Studies, an autobiographical volume in prose and verse, was published in 1959. Imitations (1961) is a collection of his translations and adaptations of verse from other languages.

Lower East Side. A section of New York City below 14th Street and east of Broadway. The area is approximately two square miles. It was for many decades the haven of poor immigrants, a slum with picturesque aspects, and a community that produced many notable men and women. Its sweatshops, its tenements, its schools and welfare centers, its theaters and cafés, its political clubs all produced a myriad of industrialists, teachers, artists, musicians, gangsters, politicians, civic leaders, labor leaders, prize fighters, actors, theatrical producers, and writers of many different national origins. These nationalities came to the East Side in successive waves; it was perhaps the greatest "melting pot" in our annals.

Identified with the East Side by birth or residence were Alfred E. Smith, the sculptors Jo Davidson and Jacob Epstein, the painter George Luks; the actors Eddie Cantor, Fannie Brice, Milton Berle, and the Marx Brothers; the prominent Yiddish actors, Bertha Kalich, Jacob Adler, Molly Picon; the composers Edward Mac-Dowell, Irving Berlin, and George Gershwin; the writers Jacob A. Riis, Ernest Poole, Konrad Bercovici, James Oppenheim, Alfred Kreymborg, Myra Kelly, Michael Gold, Abraham Cahan.

Typical books dealing with the region are JACOB RIIS's *How the Other Half Lives* (1890) and *Out of Mulberry Street* (1898); Oppenheim's *Dr. Rast* (1909); Cahan's THE RISE OF DAVID LEVINSKY (1917); Fannie Hurst's HUMORESQUE (1919); Bercovici's *Dust of New York* (1919); Alexander Woollcott's *Story of Irving Berlin* (1925); ALFRED E. SMITH's *Up to Now* (1929); MICHAEL GOLD's *Jews Without Money* (1930); Harry Golden's *Only in America* (1958) and *For Two Cents Plain* (1959). Popular songs associated with the East Side are *Maggie Murphy's Home* (1890), THE SIDEWALKS OF NEW YORK (1894), and *The Sunshine of Paradise Alley* (1895). Important community agencies are Christodora House, the Church of All Nations, the Educational Alliance, the Grand Street Settlement, the Henry Street Settlement, Neighborhood House, and the University Settlement.

Lowes, John Livingston (b. Decatur, Ind., Dec. 20, 1867—d. Aug. 15, 1945), teacher, scholar, editor, essayist. Lowes took his first degree at Washington and Jefferson College (1888) and taught mathematics there for three years, then taught English at several institutions, finally at Harvard (1918–39). He published several noteworthy books: CONVENTION AND REVOLT IN POETRY (1919), a perspicuous and persuasive account of action and reaction in the history of poetry; THE ROAD TO XANADU (1927), a widely influential examination of the sources of Coleridge's *Kubla Khan* and *The Ancient Mariner* and of the nature of inspiration; two books on Chaucer (1931, 1934); two collections of essays, *Of Reading Books and Other Essays* (1930) and *Essays in Appreciation* (1936). Lowes wrote with grace, imagination, wit. He was a great classroom teacher who carried over the power of his personality into his writings. C. J. Furness wrote of him in *Word Study* (February, 1939).

Lowie, Robert H[arry] (b. Austria, June 12, 1883—d. Sept. 21, 1957), teacher, ethnologist, curator. Lowie, who came to the United States at the age of ten, became an assistant in the American Museum of Natural History in 1908, thereafter went on to positions in other museums and at various universities, eventually becoming professor of anthropology at the University of California. He took part in various expeditions among the Indians and wrote many learned papers. Among his books are *The Assiniboine* (1909); *Social Life of the*

Crow Indians (1912); *The Sun Dance of the Crow Indians* (1915); *Culture and Ethnology* (1917); *Primitive Society* (1920); *Primitive Religion* (1924); *The Origin of the State* (1927); *Are We Civilized?* (1929); *The Crow Indians* (1935); *History of Ethnological Theory* (1937); *The German People* (1945); *Social Organization* (1948); *Indians of the Plains* (1954).

Lowry, Malcolm (b. Eng., July 28, 1909—d. June 27, 1957), novelist. The son of an English cotton broker, Lowry went to sea at eighteen. His year-long voyage on a China-bound freighter furnished the basis for his first novel, *Ultramarine* (1933), which he wrote while at Cambridge. In 1939 he moved to Canada. His second novel, *Under the Volcano* (1947), which was highly praised, revolved around an alcoholic British consul in a small Mexican town who found himself powerless to control his fate. This book, Alfred Kazin has written, "is not only a profoundly sustained history of a man's disintegration, but also a positive statement in defense of basic human values and human hope." When he died in England in 1957, Lowry, whose life has been compared to that of Dylan Thomas, was completing a collection of three short novels and four stories which was published posthumously as *Hear Us O Lord From Heaven Thy Dwelling Place* (1961).

Luccock, Halford E[dward] (b. Pittsburgh, Pa., March 11, 1885—d. Nov. 5, 1960), clergyman, editor, author. Luccock joined the faculty of Yale Divinity School in 1928 as professor of homiletics. Among his books: *Studies in the Parables of Jesus* (1917); *The Christian Crusade for World Democracy* (1918); *The Story of Methodism* (1926); *Jesus and the American Mind* (1930); *Christian Faith and Economic Change* (1936); *In the Minister's Workshop* (1944); *Like a Mighty Army* (1954); *Out of this World* (1959); *365 Windows* (1960); *Never Forget to Live* (1961).

Luce, Clare Boothe (b. New York City, April 10, 1903—   ), playwright, diplomat. Miss Boothe served on the staff of *Vogue* and *Vanity Fair*, then turned to writing satirical plays: *Abide with Me* (1937); THE WOMEN (1937); KISS THE BOYS GOOD-BYE (1938); MARGIN FOR ERROR (1939). Her observations of travel abroad in a dangerous time are keenly conveyed in *Europe in the Spring* (1940). She also wrote a novel, *Stuffed Shirts* (1931, as Clare Boothe Brokaw). Increasing interest in public affairs led her to stand for Congress, and she was elected for two terms from a Connecticut district (1943–47). Her plays and her political career, in neither of which Miss Boothe restrained her potent gift for sarcasm, brought her many enemies. An attack on Franklin D. Roosevelt in particular seemed to many observers unfair. In 1953 Mrs. Luce (her second husband is HENRY LUCE, publisher of *Time, Life,* and *Fortune*) was appointed ambassador to Italy; she resigned in 1956.

Miss Boothe's literary reputation rests on her plays. *Abide with Me* makes a study of a psychopath. *The Women* is devastatingly antifeminine; the play ran for 657 performances in New York. *Kiss the Boys Good-bye* is a warning of coming fascism, and *Margin for Error* is an anti-Nazi mystery melodrama. Margaret Case Harriman gives a frank account of Clare Boothe in *Blessed Are the Debonair* (1956).

Luce, Henry R[obinson] (b. China, April 3, 1898—d. Feb. 28, 1967), publisher. Shortly after Luce's graduation from Yale he and BRITTON HADDEN raised $86,000 between them and founded TIME magazine. A quarter century later this nucleus had become a news empire which consisted of six magazines and had a combined circulation of 10 million. After *Time* began publication, it took the two young men four years to get out of debt. They had been planning to start a de luxe magazine aimed at executives as soon as they were clear of their first financial commitments. But Hadden died suddenly, in 1929. Luce carried on and brought out FORTUNE in 1930. Then came the newsreel *March of Time,* an immensely popular feature which remained a catch phrase, and in 1936 LIFE was launched. Luce also published *Architectural Forum, House and Home,* and *Sports Illustrated.* His company, Time, Inc., also operated radio and TV stations and a book division. Luce retired in 1964.

Lucifer: A Theological Tragedy (1899; rev., 1924), a play in verse by GEORGE SANTAYANA. Finding his Christian faith no longer tenable, Santayana turned to "natural religion" and to defiance. In *Lucifer* he tries to bring the Greek and Christian gods together, but neither convinces the other; both in the end show themselves powerless. Lucifer at the end invokes Truth, eternal bitter Truth, whose "joyless bosom never was unkind to him who loved thee."

Luckett, Worth. The pioneer head of a family whose story, and that of his descendants, is told in a trilogy by CONRAD RICHTER: *The Trees* (1940), *The Fields* (1946), *The Town* (1950). Luckett leads his family from Pennsylvania into the Ohio Wilderness in the early days of westering.

Luck of Roaring Camp, The (*Overland Monthly,* Aug., 1868; included in *The Luck of Roaring Camp and Other Sketches,* 1870), a story by BRET HARTE. This sentimental story reveals that the hard-boiled and irreverent miners of the gold-rush era are not so tough after all. Cherokee Sal is a prostitute who frequents a miners' camp. A child is born to her, but she dies in giving birth. The miners adopt the child and call him Thomas Luck, but the following year the camp is destroyed in a flood, and Kentuck, one of the miners, dies holding the infant in his arms. Harte was editor of the OVERLAND MONTHLY, and when *The Luck* was in proof, a female proofreader objected that the story was profane and immoral. Harte insisted that it be printed, and it was a great success with the public. The story is significant as an early example of local color and humor. Its publication made the public realize that

a new literary star had risen. Often Harte dreamed of a dramatization of the tale, was in fact working on one when he died. But the dramatic version that actually reached production in 1894 was by Dion Boucicault.

Ludlow, Fitz Hugh (b. New York City, Sept. 11, 1836—d. Sept. 12, 1870), editor, teacher, lawyer, writer. Ludlow had a brilliant mind and great talent, but was destroyed by his use of narcotics, to which he became addicted early in life. He wrote *The Apocalypse of Hasheesh* for *Putnam's Magazine* while he was a senior at Union College; the article was expanded into a book, *The Hasheesh Eater,* in 1857. He taught for a while, was admitted to the bar but never practiced, worked as a critic on several New York magazines, and as a free lance contributed to others. For the *Atlantic Monthly* he did in 1863 a series of travel sketches about the West, including a eulogistic account of a then unknown author, Mark Twain. The sketches were collected as *The Heart of the Continent* (1870). Some of his short stories appeared in *Little Brother and Other Genre-Pictures* (1867).

Ludlow, Noah Miller (b. New York City, July 3, 1795—d. Jan. 9, 1886), actor, memoirist. Ludlow combined with his histrionic ability excellent business and administrative sense. He ran companies and theaters of his own and formed one of the earliest "chains" on record, along with Sol Smith, managing theaters in St. Louis, New Orleans, Mobile, and other towns simultaneously, and seeing to it that companies with good stars performed in them. He gave the first English plays in New Orleans and was the first actor to reach some remote regions in the West and South. He told of his experiences in *Dramatic Life As I Found It* (1880). He relates that while playing in Nashville he met "a small black-eyed widow," subsequently his wife, who traveled with him and bore eight children despite her professional engagements.

Luhan, Mabel Dodge (b. Buffalo, N.Y., Feb. 26, 1879—d. Aug. 13, 1962), art patron, memoirist. Born of the wealthy Ganson family, she might have continued to lead a leisurely life of high society but for the early death of her first husband, Carl Evans. Soon afterwards she married the architect, Edwin Dodge, later divorced him and married the artist, Maurice Sterne, finally settled in Taos, New Mexico, with her fourth husband, Tony Luhan, a Pueblo Indian. She is famous for her salons in Italy and New York where many artists and intellectuals gathered, among them, Gertrude Stein, Lincoln Steffens, Bernhard Berenson, John Reed, Max Eastman, and Carl Van Vechten. Her best known protégé was probably D. H. Lawrence, about whom she wrote *Lorenzo in Taos* (1932). Lawrence and John Collier, among others, were influenced by her love of the Pueblo Indians—their ancient creed, their strange and brilliant rhythms of speech, and their simple values. Her *Intimate Memories* are valuable records of her experiences among many great artists and writers. They comprise: *Background* (1933); *European Experiences* (1935); *Movers and Shakers* (1936); *Edge of the Taos Desert* (1937). Other additions to her memoirs are *Winter in Taos* (1935) and *Taos and Its Artists* (1947). She is said to be the model for characters in Eastman's *Venture*, Lawrence's *The Woman Who Rode Away*, Van Vechten's *Peter Whiffle*, and, of course, Gertrude Stein's *A Portrait of Mabel Dodge*.

Luks, George [**Benjamin**] (b. Williamsport, Pa., Aug. 13, 1867—d. Oct. 29, 1933), painter, caricaturist, producer of comic strips. Luks, one of the most gifted American artists, sought to reproduce the contemporary scene, especially in New York, in canvases such as "Spielers," "New York Cabby," and "Bread Woman." When R. F. Outcault went over from Pulitzer to Hearst in the 1890's, Luks took over the comic strip "Hogan's Alley." Luks had a satiric gift, shown in his drawings for *Vanity Fair*.

lumberjacks in American literature. The great era of the lumber industry started about 1840. Many myths grew around the so-called lumberjack "comic gods," like PAUL BUNYAN and TONY BEAVER. It is not known whether Bunyan ever existed in more than casual allusions until W. B. Laughead made himself the Homer of the Bunyan *epos*. Tony Beaver appears in Margaret Prescott Montague's *Up Eel River* (1928). Lumberjack ballads have been found all across the country. Lumberjack tales, songs, and ballads have been collected in Roland P. Gray's *Songs and Ballads of the Maine Lumberjacks* (1925); F. L. Rickaby's *Ballads and Songs of the Shanty Boy* (1926); F. H. Eckstorm and M. W. Smyth's *The Minstrelsy of Maine* (1927); Charles E. Brown's *Whiskey Jack Yarns: Short Tales of the Old-Time Lumber Raftsmen of the Wisconsin River and Their Mythical Hero* (1940); Harold W. Thompson's *Body, Boots, and Britches* (1940); and Earl C. Beck's *Songs of the Michigan Lumberjacks* (1941). Robert E. Swanson wrote *Rhymes of a Western Logger* (1942). Some more recent works on the subject include: William M. Doerflinger's *Shantymen and Shantyboys* (1951) and Earl Clifton Beck's *They Knew Paul Bunyan* (1956). Studies have been made of the language and special terms of the loggers—in Guy Williams' *Logger-Talk* (1930), Stewart H. Holbrook's *Holy Old Mackinaw* (1938), and numerous studies in *American Speech*.

Lummox (1923), a novel by FANNY HURST. This is the story of a servant girl with an essential greatness of soul which shines amid sordid surroundings. As her life goes on she sinks lower and lower in the economic scale, but finally Miss Hurst manages to find her some consolation for a humble existence well spent. The story was made into a successful play and movie.

Lundy, Benjamin (b. Sussex Co., N.J., Jan. 4, 1789—d. Aug. 22, 1839), editor, abolitionist. Lundy was ardent in his opposition to slavery, although he would not countenance the violent verbal attacks of WILLIAM LLOYD GARRISON when he appointed the latter associate editor of a magazine he founded in 1821, *The Genius of Universal Emancipation*. Lundy traveled all over the country and also visited Canada and Haiti, the latter when he was in search of places in which colonies of freed Negroes might be established. Wherever he went he agitated against slavery. He was assaulted in Baltimore by slave dealers, and in Philadelphia a mob destroyed his property. He organized in St. Clairsville, Ohio, the Union Humane Society (1815), one of the first antislavery societies. In his book, *The War in Texas* (1836), he gave details of a plot on the part of slaveholders to have that region secede from Mexico. In 1836 he founded the *National Enquirer and Constitutional Advocate of Universal Liberty*, which JOHN GREENLEAF WHITTIER edited for a while. Thomas Earle edited Lundy's *Life, Travels, and Opinions* (1847).

Lusitania, The. On May 7, 1915, this Cunard liner was torpedoed off the coast of Ireland by a German submarine. She sank in eighteen minutes with a loss of 1,198 lives, 124 of them Americans. Indignation over this ruthless act was a contributing factor to the subsequent United States entry into the war. A. A. and Mary Hoehling have told the story of *The Last Voyage of the Lusitania* (1956).

Luska, Sidney. The pen name of HENRY HARLAND.

Lustra (1916), a collection of poems by EZRA POUND. The title, from the Latin, refers to the offerings made by Roman censors "for the sins of the whole people." The book contains some of Pound's finest early work, though the poet himself dismissed the poems as "those of a *maître de café*." Pound also issued a collection called *Lustra of Ezra Pound* (1917), an extension of the earlier volume, containing *Near Perigord*.

Luther, Seth (b. Providence, R.I., fl. 1817—d. 1846), carpenter, pamphleteer, labor reformer. Luther was a very early crusader in behalf of better conditions for industrial workers. Himself a workman, he traveled extensively throughout the country, knew the frontier well, and was ardent in his devotion to democracy. He saw the mill system of New England as a cruel exaction "on the bodies and minds of the producing classes." His *Address to the Workingmen of New England* (1832) apparently helped bring about the passage of a child labor law in Massachusetts (1842). He also wrote *An Address on the Right of Free Suffrage* (1833) and *An Address on the Origin and Progress of Avarice* (1834). He believed in extending the privileges of free public education and in abolishing monopolies, capital punishment, and imprisonment for debt. In 1834 he was made secretary to the General Trades Convention in Boston and in 1835 helped to draw up the *Boston Circular*, which advocated a ten-hour day.

lyceums. The Lowell Institute was probably the first of these, and is still in existence. A lyceum was a system of adult education through lectures by noted persons. Often a library or a collection of minerals or other objects was part of the lyceum, and often local groups studied some subject, scientific at first, historical or literary later on, in connection with the lyceum.

JOSIAH HOLBROOK, of Derby, Conn., formally started the movement when in 1826 he published an article in the *Journal of Education* outlining his plan for informal popular education. He hoped to see a lyceum in every American town, and he envisioned lyceums as a national influence. The American Lyceum, a national group, was organized in 1831. In two years a hundred lyceums had been started under Holbrook's inspiration in nearly every state of the Union; there were nearly 3,000 before the movement died down. The Civil War exerted an unfavorable effect on the lyceums, and by 1870 they had mainly degenerated into what Bayard Taylor, once a highly popular lecturer, resentfully called "nonintellectual diversion." But in the intervening years they had exerted a great educational influence, encouraged reading, helped to unify the nation. Holbrook published a book, *The American Lyceum* (1829), describing his plan, and in 1830 began issuing a number of *Scientific Tracts Designed for Instruction and Entertainment.* He also edited the *Family Lyceum* as a weekly newspaper.

Possibly the most famous of all lyceum lecturers was RALPH WALDO EMERSON. He gave up the ministry but made the lyceum platform his pulpit; his prose style is definitely oral, and he needs to be read aloud to be understood and appreciated. Despite his success and the fact that he earned his living as a lecturer over a long period of years, he does not seem to have been a particularly effective speaker.

The audiences had variety, of course. John Godfrey Saxe read them his new humorous verses, Bayard Taylor took them with him on his lively travels, John B. Gough warned them against the terrors of intemperance, mesmerists and phrenologists inducted them solemnly into these sciences, Anna Dickinson championed reforms, Henry Ward Beecher delivered his eloquent sermons, J. R. Lowell lectured amiably and wittily as far west as Wisconsin, Margaret Fuller produced learned "conversations" for Boston audiences, Theodore Parker talked eagerly to what he called "glorious phalanxes of old maids," Horace Greeley was a popular figure, W. G. Simms came up from the South, and many British lecturers were welcomed by large audiences—Dickens, Thackeray, Matthew Arnold.

In time commercial lecture bureaus began to take over the field. The comic lecturers—Mark Twain, Artemus Ward, David Ross Locke, Bill Nye, Will Rogers—formed a tribe of their own and were highly successful. The lyceum was also in large part replaced by CHAUTAUQUA, founded in 1874, and by the women's clubs, which have provided financial sustenance for innumerable lecturers. Lyceums have sprung up in many parts of the United States in a new form: adult education schools, frequently sponsored by local boards of education and offering courses in many fields. Universities, too, offer popular lecture courses. Carl Bode wrote *The American Lyceum* (1956).

Lydenberg, Harry Miller (b. Dayton, Ohio, Nov. 18, 1874—d. April 16, 1960), librarian, translator, editor, biographer. Lydenberg took his degree at Harvard in 1897. His career after graduation was chiefly with the New York Public Library, where he was chief of the reference department and director from 1934 to 1941. On his retirement he acted as director of the Biblioteca Benjamin Franklin in Mexico City for two years. He wrote a vivacious life of his predecessor at the New York library, John Shaw Billings (1924); a *History of the New York Public Library* (1923); *Paper or Sawdust: A Plea for Good Paper for Good Books* (1924); *The Care and Repair of Books* (with John Archer, 1931); a translation of André Blum's *On the Origins of Printing and Engraving* (1940). His *Crossing the Line* appeared in 1957.

Lyell, Sir Charles (b. England, 1797—d. 1875), geologist. Lyell visited America twice on scientific expeditions and wrote two books which contain his general observations as well as his scientific ones, *Travels in North America, Canada, and Nova Scotia, With Geological Observations* (1845) and *A Second Visit to the United States of North America* (1849). In contrast to the accounts written by most British travelers in America, his books praised the United States.

Lynd, Helen Merrell (b. La Grange, Ill., [?] —), teacher, author. Mrs. Lynd studied at Wellesley College and Columbia University. She taught at Vassar College and New York University before becoming a professor of social philosophy at Sarah Lawrence College. With her husband ROBERT LYND, she made two classic sociological studies, MIDDLETOWN (1929), and *Middletown in Transition* (1937). Her other writings: *England in the 1880's: Toward a Social Basis for Freedom* (1945); *On Shame and the Search for Identity* (1958).

Lynd, Robert S[taughton] (b. New Albany, Ind., Sept. 26, 1892—), teacher, sociologist, editor. With his wife HELEN, Lynd made studies of typical American communities which he made into a composite picture, MIDDLETOWN (1929). Later *Middletown in Transition* (1937) indicated changes that had occurred. Lynd became a professor of sociology at Columbia University in 1931.

Lynes, [Joseph] Russell [Jr.] (b. Great Barrington, Mass., Dec. 2, 1910—), editor, critic, writer. A Yale graduate, Lynes served as Director of Publications at Vassar College and principal at the Shipley School, Bryn Mawr, Pa., before becoming managing editor of *Harper's Magazine.* The bulk of his writing has been in the magazine field. His best-known piece was *Highbrow, Lowbrow, Middlebrow*

(*Harper's,* Feb. 1949). His books include: *Snobs* (1950); *Guests* (1951); *The Tastemakers* (1954); *A Surfeit of Honey* (1957); and the fictional *Cadwallader* (1959).

Lyon, Harris Merton (b. Santa Fe, N.M., Dec. 22, 1883—d. June 2, 1916), free-lance writer, drama critic, short-story writer. Lyon was a brilliant writer who died young. Two collections of his stories and sketches were published: *Sardonics* (1909) and *Graphics* (1913). It is believed that Theodore Dreiser, who knew him well, was thinking of Lyon when he wrote the remarkable sketch called *De Maupassant, Jr.* in his *Twelve Men* (1919).

Lyon, James (b. Newark, N.J., July 1, 1735—d. Oct. 12, 1794), hymnologist. Lyon, a graduate of Princeton in 1759, seems to have become interested in hymns at an early stage of his career in the ministry. In 1761 he published an anthology, *Urania, or, A Choice Collection of Psalm-Tunes, Anthems, and Hymns,* a book which is described as having inaugurated "a new epoch in church music." It marked the passing of the Bay Psalm Book and itself lasted for a century. Lyon himself wrote hymn music that later anthologists reprinted.

Lyons, Eugene (b. Russia, July 1, 1898—   ), editor, foreign correspondent, columnist. At one time warmly sympathetic to Soviet Russia, Lyons later became disillusioned and bitterly attacked the Soviet régime. He was editor of the American Mercury (1939–44) and then a "roving editor" for the *Reader's Digest.* Among his books: *The Life and Death of Sacco and Vanzetti* (1927); *Moscow Carrousel* (1935); *Assignment in Utopia* (1937); *The Red Decade* (1941); *Our Unknown Ex-President: A Portrait of Herbert Hoover* (1948); *Our Secret Allies: Peoples of Russia* (1953).

Lytle, Andrew [Nelson] (b. Murfreesboro, Tenn., Dec. 26, 1902—   ), writer, teacher. Lytle attended Vanderbilt University and was a member of George Pierce Baker's "47 workshop" at Harvard. He worked as an actor in New York for a time, then returned to Tennessee and contributed to the Agrarian symposium I'll Take My Stand (1930). He taught at several universities, was managing editor of the Sewanee Review (1942–43); and became its editor in 1961. Most of his writing is set in the South and is largely concerned with the impact of the prevailing Northern way of life on the old Southern traditions of strong family ties, matriarchy, and agrarianism. *The Long Night* (1936) and *The Velvet Horn* (1957) are historical novels, the former taking place during the Civil War and the latter shortly after. *A Name for Evil* (1947, reprinted in *A Novel, a Novella and Four Stories,* 1958) is a modern ghost story dealing with the spirit of a dead man and his eerie effect on his living heirs.

Lytle, William Haines (b. Cincinnati, Ohio, Nov. 2, 1826—d. Sept. 20, 1863), poet. On July 29, 1858, there appeared in the Cincinnati *Commercial* a poem by Lytle called *Antony to Cleopatra.* It began with Shakespeare's line, "I am dying, Egypt, dying." The poem became a great favorite with those who love to "recite" and with editors of anthologies. Lytle served in the Mexican War and was killed during the Civil War at the Battle of Chickamauga. His *Poems of William Haines Lytle* were collected and published in 1894 by William H. Venable and reprinted in 1912.

M

Mabbott, Thomas O[llive] (b. New York City, July 6, 1898—d. May 15, 1968), teacher, authority on Poe, numismatist. Mabbott taught for many years at Hunter College, New York City. He was a Walt Whitman enthusiast, but his principal interest was the life and writings of Poe. On the latter subject he published several books: *Poe's Politian* (1923); *Selected Poems of Poe* (1928); *Poe's Doings of Gotham* (1929); *Poe's Tamerlane* (1941); *Selections from Poe* (1951); and others. Books on other subjects include: *Walt Whitman's Half-Breed* (1927); *Wilmer's Merlin* (1941); *Bryant's Embargo* (1955). He was editor from 1943 to 1948 of *Numismatic Review*.

Mabie, Hamilton Wright (b. Coldspring, N.Y., Dec. 13, 1845—d. Dec. 31, 1916), editor, critic, essayist. One of the last of the gentlemanly Victorian critics, Mabie, with his gracious style, high moral tone, and fondness for platitudes, seems further removed from the literary world of today than his dates would indicate. Mabie was a moderately successful lawyer for eight years, but in 1879, when EDWARD EGGLESTON asked him to help edit the *Christian Union*, later called the OUTLOOK, he found an occupation much better suited to his taste and ability. Editor of church news at first, he progressed to literary editor, editorial writer, and associate editor. He published a children's book, *Norse Stories Retold from the Eddas* (1882); *My Study Fire* (1890); *Books and Culture* (1896); *The Life of the Spirit* (1899), a popular "up-lift" book; *William Shakespeare, Poet, Dramatist and Man* (1900); and *Heroines that Every Child Should Know* (1908). He also edited the *After-School Library* (1909), a twelve-volume set sold by subscription. His biography was written in 1920 by E. W. Morse.

McAlmon, Robert [Menzies] (b. Clifton, Kans., March 9, 1896—d. Feb., 1956), lawyer, cowboy, lumberjack, artist's model, writer. McAlmon was one of the earliest expatriates of the "lost generation." His career developed mostly in Paris, and most of his books were published in France. He helped edit some of the LITTLE MAGAZINES of the 1920's, including *Contact*, and contributed to others. A radical and a rebel, he infused his writing with a quality which Régis Michaud has called "pathetic nihilism." He published several volumes of verse: *Explorations* (1921); *The Portrait of a Generation* (1926); *North America, Continent of Conjecture* (1929); *Not Alone Lost* (1937). His best work is probably the semifictional sketches in *Village: As It Happened Through a Fifteen-Year Period* (1924), an account of a place called Westworth that recalls Sinclair Lewis' GOPHER PRAIRIE and Sherwood Anderson's WINESBURG, OHIO. He also composed an autobiography, *Being Geniuses Together* (1938). Robert E. Knoll has written *Robert McAlmon: Expatriate Publisher and Writer* (1957).

McArone Papers. Satires of war correspondence contributed by GEORGE ARNOLD (1834–1865), a promising young poet of the time, to *Vanity Fair*, the *Leader*, and the *Weekly Review* from 1860 to 1865.

MacArthur, Charles (b. Scranton, Pa., Nov. 5, 1895—d. April 21, 1956), newspaperman, editor, dramatist, writer and producer of motion pictures. MacArthur was a reporter on the Chicago *Herald and Examiner*, the Chicago *Tribune*, and the New York *American* from 1914 to 1923, and faithfully lived up to the romantic American tradition of the uninhibited newspaperman. This period of his life is reflected in THE FRONT PAGE (1928), the frequently revived play about newspaper life that he wrote in collaboration with BEN HECHT. In New York City he became a member of the famous ROUND TABLE at the Hotel Algonquin, and married the actress Helen Hayes. In 1924 he began doing free lance magazine work and writing plays; among the latter were *Lulu Belle* (with EDWARD SHELDON, 1926), about a Negro Carmen; *Salvation* (with SIDNEY HOWARD, 1927), about a lady evangelist; *Twentieth Century* (with Hecht, 1932), a satire on Hollywood; *Ladies and Gentlemen* (with Hecht, 1939); *Johnny on the Spot* (1941); *Swan Song* (with Hecht, 1946). In 1929 he began writing and producing movies in Hollywood. Beginning in 1948 he edited *Theatre Arts Magazine*.

McCall's Magazine. Founded in 1870 as *The Queen of Fashion*, this magazine took its present name in 1897. It fell into the doldrums in the 1920's, but Otis L. Wiese (1905–   ) brought it back to a position of leadership; he became editor in 1928, publisher in 1949. At the beginning of the 1960's, *McCall's* had climbed above six million circulation and continued to dominate the market.

McCarthy, Mary (b. Seattle, Wash., June 21, 1912—   ), novelist, short-story writer, critic. Orphaned at the age of six, Mary McCarthy was raised by an aunt and uncle and two sets of grandparents of Catholic, Jewish, and Protestant backgrounds. Her childhood is minutely and memorably recalled in *Memories of a Catholic Girlhood* (1957). She graduated from Vassar College in 1933, began writing book reviews for *The Nation* and the *New Republic*, and became drama critic for the *Partisan Review*. *Sights and Spectacles, 1937–1956* (1956) is a collection of her theater pieces, revealing her as an informed, witty, and generally accurate, if severe, critic. After her divorce from EDMUND WILSON, she taught for a few years at Bard College (1945–1946) and Sarah Lawrence College (1948), drawing upon this experience in her satirical novel, *The Groves of Academe* (1952). In this book, as in such novels as *The Company She Keeps* (1942), *The Oasis* (1949), and *A Charmed Life* (1955), her special subject is the follies of the contemporary intellectual. To the treatment of this theme she brings keen powers of observation, a polished and brilliant style, and merciless, somewhat malicious wit. She is the author of a collection of short stories, *Cast a Cold Eye* (1950), as well as *Venice Observed* (1956), *The Stones of Florence* (1959), pictorial studies of the two cities, and *On the Contrary* (1961), a collection of articles on contemporary subjects.

McCarthyism. In its narrow sense McCarthyism is the name given to the attitudes and practices of Senator Joseph McCarthy (1908–1957) and his followers employed in investigating possibly undesirable governmental employees or "security risks," especially former Communists. However, in its broadest sense the term is applied to any inquisition which attempts to prove guilt by association, misstatement, and other procedures inimical to the guarantees of human rights implied in the Constitution. These practices are generally justified by supposed danger to the nation. This latter definition would apply to many investigations of alleged Communists preceding those carried on under McCarthy, including those begun in 1938 by the first House Un-American Activities Committee, headed by Congressman Martin Dies, and also some aspects of the loyalty investigations of teachers during the 1940's and 1950's.

Much of the damning evidence during these investigations was obtained from apostate Communists testifying against their former friends and acquaintances. One former Communist, Whittaker Chambers, the prime witness against Alger Hiss, attempted to explain his own checkered career in *Witness* (1952), an autobiography. McCarthy himself defined McCarthyism in the title of his book, *McCarthyism: the Fight for America* (1952). With the help of his staff he also wrote *America's Retreat from Victory: The Story of George Catlett Marshall* (1951). Two members of his staff, William F. Buckley and L. B. Bozell, collaborated on McCarthy's most eloquent vindication, *McCarthy and His Enemies* (1954).

Most of the writing about McCarthy, however, has been severely critical, even vitriolic: *McCarthy; the Man, the Senator, the Ism* (1952), by J. Anderson and R. W. May; *Joe Must Go* (1954), by L. Gore; *Trial by Television* (1954), by Michael W. Straight; *Senator Joe McCarthy* (1959), by Richard Rovere. *McCarthy and the Communists* (1954), by James Rorty and Moshe Decter, is probably the most objective and complete analysis of the man and his methods.

Writers and intellectuals with more or less radical opinions did not escape the contumely of McCarthy and his investigating staff. CORLISS LAMONT, Harvey O'Connor, ARCHIBALD MAC-LEISH, MAXWELL GEISMAR, G. Bromley Oxnam, and OWEN LATTIMORE are a few of those who were accused of disloyalty. Two of these men bitterly recorded their ordeals: Bishop Oxnam in *I Protest* (1954) and Lattimore, who was for several months McCarthy's chief victim, in *Ordeal by Slander* (1950).

McCarthyism has even managed to influence creative literature. Before McCarthy espoused McCarthyism in 1951, many school faculties were being upset by what seemed a restriction of academic freedom: teachers were required to sign oaths of loyalty disclaiming membership in the Communist Party. This conflict was an important theme in HERMAN WOUK's play *The Traitor* (1949), later in Molly Kazan's melodrama, *The Egghead* (1957), and in HOWARD FAST's novel, *Silas Timberman* (1954).

ARTHUR MILLER's play, *The Crucible* (1953), invited timely comparison of the Salem witch trials with irresponsible investigations of "subversives." WILLIAM L. SHIRER's *Stranger Come Home* (1954) is a direct outgrowth of McCarthyism; one of the novel's main characters, O'Brien, could be McCarthy's alter ego. THE TROJAN HORSE (1952), a verse radio play by Archibald MacLeish, treats McCarthyism allegorically.

Other works, both fiction and nonfiction, which comment on this subject include: *But We Were Born Free* (1954), by ELMER DAVIS; *Crucial Decade* (1956), by Eric F. Goldman; *Revolt of the Moderates* (1956), by Samuel Lubell; *Rededication to Freedom* (1959), by Benjamin Ginsburg; *The Waist High Culture* (1959), by Thomas Griffith; *Advise and Consent* (1959), by Allen Drury.

McCaslin family, the. Characters in works by WILLIAM FAULKNER. Its members appear in the short stories in Go DOWN, MOSES. Lucas Beauchamp appears also in the novel INTRUDER IN THE DUST. Among the first families to settle in YOKNAPATAWPHA COUNTY, the McCaslins evidence, more directly than any other of Faulkner's people, the guilt of slavery which continues to influence their lives after the Civil War. The members of the McCaslin family include:

Lucas Beauchamp. Part-Negro grandson of the first McCaslin. (See entry under BEAUCHAMP, LUCAS.)

Sophonsiba Beauchamp. After Uncle Buck McCaslin stumbles accidentally into her bed, her brother, Hubert, insists he marry her, but wins her back in a poker game. Years later Buck plays another poker game in which the winner, his brother, Buddy, goes to war and the loser, Buck, has to marry Sophonsiba after all.

Tennie Beauchamp. The mother of Lucas, Tennie was won at poker by Uncle Buck McCaslin from Hubert Beauchamp in 1859.

Carothers ["Roth"] Edmonds. Roth has an affair with a very light-colored Negro woman who bears him a child, but whom he refuses to marry. The woman reveals to old Ike McCaslin that she is the great-great-granddaughter of the original McCaslin.

Carothers McCaslin ["Cass"] Edmonds.

Great-grandson of the first McCaslin, Cass inherits the entire McCaslin property after Isaac McCaslin, his cousin and heir of half the property, refuses his inheritance.

Issac ["Zack"] Edmonds. Friend and rival

that his young relative, Roth Edmonds, should marry a girl who has a trace of Negro blood, even though she has borne him a child.

[Lucius Quintus] Carothers McCaslin. The founder of the McCaslin family, old Carothers

McCASLIN GENEALOGY

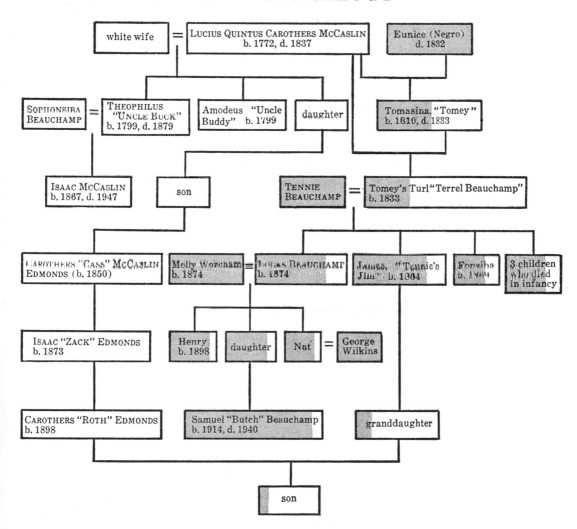

of his part-Negro cousin, Lucas Beauchamp, Zack commandeers Lucas' wife Molly to care for his infant son after the death of the child's mother. After Zack has kept Molly for six months Lucas demands that she be returned to him.

Isaac ["Ike"] McCaslin. Son of Uncle Buck and the last male McCaslin to bear the name, Isaac marries but has no children. He refuses to inherit his half of the McCaslin plantation after he learns that his grandfather had seduced his own mulatto daughter, Tomasina, whose mother commited suicide in shame, and by whom he had a son, Tomey's Turl, or Terrel. In spite of his feeling that he cannot accept the property of a man guilty both of slavery and of incest, Ike still expresses horror at the thought

is the father of a daughter and twin sons by his white wife. He seduces a Negro slave, Eunice, who bears him a daughter, Tomasina; he later seduces Tomasina, thus compounding the amount of McCaslin blood carried by the later Negro members of the family.

Theophilus ["Uncle Buck"] McCaslin. A bachelor until his sixties, Uncle Buck and his twin brother, Uncle Buddy, do not believe in slavery and invent a system whereby their father's Negro slaves can earn their freedom; most of the Negroes, however, refuse to leave the plantation after they have been freed. Buck and Buddy increase the thousand-dollar legacy of their father to his Negro son, Turl, to a thousand dollars for each of Turl's three surviving children. Uncle Buck appears as a character in THE UNVANQUISHED, in which he helps young Bayard Sartoris and his Negro companion hunt down the murderer of Bayard's grandmother.

McChesney, Emma. An attractive saleswoman in EDNA FERBER's many stories about a woman's experiences in the business world. Emma sells Featherbloom Petticoats in the Middle West. These stories pioneered treating women in business as a fictional subject. One popular collection was *Emma McChesney & Co.* (1915). The author dramatized her in *Our Mrs. McChesney* (1915).

McClellan, George B[rinton] (b. Philadelphia, Dec. 3, 1826—d. Oct. 29, 1885), soldier, engineer, public official, memoirist. McClellan attended the University of Pennsylvania and graduated from West Point in 1846, second in his class. He gained his first familiarity with combat in the Mexican War and study of the European forces in the Crimean War. He showed a particular talent for military engineering, which he taught at West Point for three years and which gained him a federal appointment as adviser on the construction of the Pacific railroad. In 1857 he resigned from the army to become chief engineer of the Illinois Central Railroad and later president of the eastern division of the Ohio and Mississippi Railroad.

When the Civil War broke out in 1861, McClellan was commissioned a major-general. He rallied a great force of men from the Western territory, with which he gained control of the northwestern part of Virginia (later to become West Virginia). He performed the same feat of organization with the Army of the Potomac when he was asked to come to Washington that same year.

He became general-in-chief of the Washington forces when General Scott retired, but did not keep this rank for long. His reluctance to take offensive action, even after a retreating enemy, and his general indecision aggravated the impatience of his superiors. He was relieved of one command after another, and finally retired. He attempted to vindicate himself by running against Lincoln in the presidential campaign of 1864.

After a brief sojourn in Europe, he returned to New Jersey to become an engineer and a public official. He was elected governor of New Jersey in 1878 and served for three years. After this he retired to write *McClellan's Own Story* (1887), in which he attempted to defend his military career. His *Mexican War Diary* (1917) was edited by William Starr Myers.

Historians have varied in their opinions of McClellan's merits and demerits, but most of them agree with Kenneth P. Williams' *Lincoln Finds a General* (1949), which claims McClellan was boastful, untrustworthy, incompetent, perhaps even a coward. There is no question regarding the deep personal antagonism that arose between McClellan and Lincoln. At one time Lincoln wrote McClellan: "My dear McClellan: If you don't want to use the Army I should like to borrow it for a while. Yours respectfully, A. Lincoln."

McClellan appears in occasional poems of his own day, admiringly so in such ones as Thomas Dunn English's *The Charge by the Ford* and Herman Melville's *Malvern Hill*. But George Henry Boker wrote of him as *Tardy George* (1865). Charles King introduced him in his lurid tale, *The General's Double* (1897). Most earnest and partisan of the efforts to restore him to public esteem was W. S. Myers' *General George B. McClellan* (1934). Clarence E. N. Macartney wrote of him in *Little Mac* (1940).

McCloskey, Robert (b. Hamilton, Ohio, Sept. 15, 1914—   ), author of children's books, illustrator. McCloskey attended Vesper George School of Art in Boston and the National Academy of Design in New York. His books have been extremely popular with children, and two of them, *Make Way for Ducklings* (1941) and *Time of Wonder* (1957) won the Caldecott Award of the American Library Association. The drawings in *Make Way for Ducklings* were considered by one reviewer to be "prophetic of future work in the picture book field." McCloskey has also written and illustrated *Lentil* (1940); *Homer Price* (1943); *Blue Berries for Sal* (1948); *Centerburg Tales* (1951); and *One Morning in Maine* (1952).

McClung, John A[lexander] (b. Washington, Ky., Sept. 25, 1804—d. Aug. 7, 1859), novelist. McClung, patterning himself on Scott and Cooper, wrote *Camden: A Tale of the South* (1830), in which he depicts events during the Revolution after the fall of Charleston. More important, because more original, was his collection *Sketches of Western Adventure* (1832).

McClure, Alexander K[elly] (b. Sherman's Dale, Pa., Jan. 9, 1828—d. June 6, 1909), newspaper editor, author of travel books, historian. McClure's most original work was an account of *3000 Miles Through the Rocky Mountains* (1869). In 1875 he and Frank McLaughlin founded the *Philadelphia Times*, which he edited forcefully until 1902, when the paper was merged with the *Public Ledger*. In 1878 the paper published a Sunday edition, the first in the city. McClure in the meantime continued to write and edit books. Among them were *Abraham Lincoln and Men of War Times* (1892) and *Old-Time Notes of Pennsylvania* (2 v., 1905). He edited a series called *Famous American Statesmen and Orators* (6 v., 1902). In 1902 he published *Recollections of Half a Century*.

McClure, S[amuel] S[idney] (b. Ireland, Feb. 17, 1857—d. March 21, 1949), editor, historian. One of the greatest editors who have lived in the United States, McClure came here in 1866, worked his way through Knox College, where he edited the campus newspaper, landed a job with *The Wheelman*, house organ of a bicycle manufacturing firm, and developed its advertising section, worked for the De Vinne Press and then for the *Century Magazine*. When the *Century* editors proved inhospitable to McClure's ideas, he resigned. He created a revolution in publishing when he started the first newspaper syndicate, the purpose of which was to reprint in serial form material that had already appeared in books, to print articles, fiction, verse, and pictorial material in newspapers all over the country, and to have simultaneous publication for both kinds of material. McClure started his syndicate in 1884, and it continued till mid-20th century. It provided mass audiences for many important new and old authors and greatly increased the financial returns from literary work.

In 1893 McClure founded MCCLURE'S MAGA-ZINE, which became the most influential periodical in the country, inspired Theodore Roosevelt to some of his reforming crusades and later to a hot denunciation for its "muckraking," brought to the fore as able a corps of assistants as any magazine has ever had, and published much enduring literature. McClure made it his mission to convince the American people of the corruption that had invaded many aspects of American life. He ran sensational "muckraking" articles on the Standard Oil Company, on the "shame of the cities," on the sins of the railroads and the insurance companies. In 1906, at its peak, McClure's partner, JOHN S. PHILLIPS, along with IDA M. TARBELL, RAY STANNARD BAKER, and LINCOLN STEFFENS, resigned and founded the American Magazine, which continued the policies of McClure's and became equally influential. In 1914 McClure suspended his own magazine, later revived it briefly. It became part of the New Smart Set in 1929, and expired in 1933. His last years McClure spent in retirement. My Autobiography (1914) was ghost-written by Willa Cather. He also published The Achievements of Liberty (1935) and What Freedom Means to Man (1938); he was himself not a particularly good writer.

McClure appears twice in fiction. R. L. Stevenson, whom he helped to win an audience, presented him as Jim Pinkerton in The Wrecker (1892). Less friendly is the characterization of him as Fulkerson, an aggressive Westerner, in W. D. Howells' A Hazard of New Fortunes (1890). Material on McClure appears in Ida M. Tarbell's All in the Day's Work (1939); Lincoln Steffens' Autobiography (1931); and Ray Stannard Baker's Native American (1941) and American Chronicle (1945). There is also a vivid portrayal of McClure in Lloyd Morris' Postscript to Yesterday (1947). See MUCKRAK-ING LITERATURE.

McClure's Magazine. JOHN S. PHILLIPS began McClure's Magazine in 1893 with SAMUEL S. MCCLURE as editor. The magazine made its first hit with Ida M. Tarbell's serial life of Napoleon, followed by her Early Life of Lincoln, both lavishly illustrated. R. L. Stevenson, Rudyard Kipling, Anthony Hope, Conan Doyle, and Thomas Hardy were leading English contributors; later William Allen White, Cy Warman, and Joel Chandler Harris joined them. Circulation reached 370,000 by 1900 (larger than that of any other general monthly except Munsey's),

with more than 100 pages of advertising in each issue.

Railroading and popular science were McClure specialties but from 1903 to 1911 it was a leader in the exposés of corruption in politics and business known as MUCKRAKING. Staff contributors in this field were Miss Tarbell, Lincoln Steffens, and Ray Stannard Baker. This group, with Phillips and others, seceded from the Mc-Clure organization in 1906 because of differences with the editor. Meanwhile Booth Tarkington, Willa Cather, and Rex Beach became leading contributors of fiction.

McClure retired in 1913 because of ill health, and the famous periodical was never the same again. McClure's was sold to Hearst, then to the Magus Publishing Company, and finally merged with the New Smart Set in 1929.

McConnel, John Ludlum (b. Morgan [now Scott] Co., Ill., Nov. 11, 1826—d. Jan. 17, 1862), lawyer, soldier, novelist. McConnel's short life was devoted mainly to the Army (he participated in the war with Mexico) and the practice of law. His most important story was Talbot and Vernon (1850), which describes the Battle of Buena Vista as McConnel himself saw it and tells the story of a romance jeopardized by an accusation of forgery.

McCord, David [Thompson Watson] (b. New York City, Nov. 15, 1897—), poet, editor, critic, painter. McCord was on the staff of the Harvard Alumni Bulletin and served as executive secretary of the Harvard Fund Council. He was drama and music critic for the old Boston Evening Transcript (1923–28). He published numerous collections of his light verse, among them Oddly Enough (1926); Floodgate (1927); Stirabout (1928); The Crows (1934); Bay Window Ballads (1935); Twelve Verses from XII Night (1938); On Occasion (1943); A Star by Day (1950); The Old Bateau and Other Poems (1953); Odds Without Ends (1954). McCord is a learned poet with quick humor and an agile command of meter and rhyme. As an editor he is particularly noted for his superb collection of humorous verse, What Cheer (1945), part of which was reprinted as the Pocket Book of Humorous Verse (1946) and again, revised, in the Modern Library (1955). Selected Poems came out in 1957; McCord wrote an amusing introduction to the book and provided humorous notes for the poems he selected.

McCormick, Anne [Elizabeth] O'Hare (b. England, 1882—d. May, 29, 1954), newspaperwoman, columnist, specialist in foreign affairs. Mrs. McCormick was born in Yorkshire of American parents, came to the United States as a child. Later she accompanied her husband, an engineer and importer, on his European trips, began writing for the New York Times Magazine, finally asked to be allowed to send dispatches. They proved so able and so rich in insight that she became a permanent member of the Times' staff, for years conducted a column on foreign affairs on the editorial page, was the first woman to win a Pulitzer Prize in journalism, won many other awards, and became a member of the small governing council of the *Times*. She had a profound sense of the essential and wrote with eloquence. She prophesied the rise of Mussolini well ahead of other forecasters. She chose to gather her writings and reflections into a book only once: *The Hammer and the Scythe* (1928). Later Marion Sheehan edited selections from her writings, *The World at Home* (1956), with an introduction by James B. Reston.

McCormick, Robert R[utherford] (b. Chicago, July 30, 1880—d. April 1, 1955), newspaperman, writer. McCormick studied law, but took over the editorship and publication of the Chicago *Tribune*, which was previously controlled by his grandfather and his father. Under his aegis, the *Tribune* was doggedly rightwing. He published several books, including *The American Revolution and Its Effect on World Civilization* (1945).

McCosh, James (b. Scotland, April 1, 1811—d. Nov. 16, 1894), clergyman, educator, philosopher. McCosh was a minister of the Established Chuch in Scotland until he left to join in the Free Church movement. The exclusion of the supernatural in J. S. Mill's *System of Logic* led him to write a refutation, *The Method of the Divine Government: Physical and Moral* (1850). He taught logic and metaphysics at Queen's College, Belfast, for sixteen years, and in 1868 was appointed president of the College of New Jersey (now Princeton).

McCosh was one of the first theologians to accept Darwin; he saw no clash between science and religion, but contended that the doctrine of evolution proved God's method of creation. As an administrator he raised standards, organized graduate studies, increased the size of the faculty, and encouraged research. He was an excellent teacher; his philosophical writings, while not original, were for the most part lucid and vigorous restatements of William Hamilton's doctrines. Among his works are: *Typical Forms and Special Ends in Creation* (1855); *The Supernatural in Relation to the Natural* (1862); *An Examination of Mr. J. S. Mill's Philosophy: Being a Defense of Fundamental Truth* (1866); *The Laws of Discursive Thought* (1870); *Christianity and Positivism* (1871); *The Scottish Philosophy* (1875); *Realistic Philosophy Defended in a Philosophical Series* (2 v., 1887).

McCoy, Horace (b. Pegram, Tenn., April 14, 1897—d. Dec. 17, 1955), newspaperman, shortstory writer, novelist. McCoy began as a sports writer on the Dallas (Texas) *Journal,* but was interested in the theater, often made pilgrimages to Paris, knew F. Scott Fitzgerald and other expatriates, and began writing stories somewhat in their manner. Some of them were printed in small magazines and attracted the attention of Edward J. O'Brien and other anthologists. He also became a screenwriter in Hollywood. His first novel, *They Shoot Horses, Don't They?* (1935), is the story told on the eve of his execution by a man who had, at her request, killed his marathon-dance partner. *No Pockets in a*

Shroud (1937), a study of corruption in a small town, followed; then came *I Should Have Stayed Home* (1938); *Kiss Tomorrow Good-Bye* (1948); and *Scalpel* (1952).

MacCracken, Henry Noble (b. Toledo, Ohio, Nov. 19, 1880—d. May 7, 1970), college president, scholar. McCracken taught English at various universities and was president of Vassar College (1915–46). He has written textbooks on English composition, edited Shakespeare, and helped prepare a manual on good usage. He also edited the *Minor Poems of Lydgate* (1910, 1934), and *The College Chaucer* (1913). Among his books: *Old Dutchess Forever* (1957) and *Blithe Dutchess: The Flowering of an American County* (1959).

McCrae, John (b. Guelph, Ont., Nov. 30, 1872—d. Jan. 28, 1918), physician, poet. McCrae received a medical degree from the University of Toronto and was made a fellow at McGill University. During World War I he served in the medical corps until his death from pneumonia. His rondeau *In Flanders Fields,* which appeared in *Punch* in 1915, soon became the best-known poem of the war. A posthumous volume, *In Flanders Fields and Other Poems,* was published in 1919.

McCullers, Carson [Smith] (b. Columbus, Ga., Feb. 19, 1917—d. Sept. 29, 1967), novelist, short-story writer, playwright. Carson McCullers studied at the Juilliard School of Music and at Columbia University. Her musi-

Louise Dahl Wolfe

cal career ended when she lost her tuition money in the subway. Her first novel, The Heart is a Lonely Hunter (1940), a parable on the subject of Fascism, was acclaimed by critics. It is the story of a deaf-mute's associations with various people in a small southern town, among them a Negro and an adolescent girl. Her second novel, *Reflections in a Golden Eye* (1941), was a more obscure and experimental work that puzzled many readers and critics; it deals with violence at a peacetime army post in the South. Her third novel, THE MEMBER OF THE WEDDING (1946), again attracted a wide audience with its exploration of the loneliness and isolation of a twelve-year-old girl, Frankie, who wants to go along on her brother's honeymoon. Mrs. Mc-Cullers wrote a brilliant dramatization of the novel (1950) which was later made into a movie (1952). Though her output was not great, Carson McCullers was recognized as a leading American writer. She explored her theme of the lonely individual's search for love among children and misfits in society and skillfully gave it universal significance. *The Ballad of the Sad Café* (1951) contains the novelette and a selection of short stories. *The Square Root of Wonderful*, a play, appeared in 1958; the novel *Clock Without Hands* in 1961.

McCulley, Johnston (b. Ottawa, Ill., Feb. 2, 1883—   ), novelist, playwright, screenwriter. McCulley, one of the most prolific writers on record, began as a newspaperman, turned to fiction with *The Land of Lost Hope* (1908), the first of a series of more than sixty romantic novels that appeared under his own name and several pen names, including *The Jungle Trail* (1917); *The Masked Woman* (1920); *The Crimson Clown* (1927); *Who Killed the Caretaker?* (1930); *Zorro Rides Again* (1931); *Reckless Range* (1937); *Range Lawyer* (1942); *The Caballero* (1947). He also wrote several plays, radio dramas, and screenplays.

McCutcheon, George Barr (b. Lafayette, Ind., July 26, 1866—d. Oct. 23, 1928), newspaperman, novelist. McCutcheon resigned his position with the Lafayette *Courier* in 1893 after the success of his second novel. His first, GRAUSTARK (1901), which he sold for $500, made a fortune for the publisher. BREWSTER'S MILLIONS (1902), which sold more than 5,000,000 copies, was made into a successful play by WINCHELL SMITH (1906) and was filmed a number of times. McCutcheon sandwiched realistic novels among his many swashbuckling money-makers, and claimed an affection for *Mary Midthorne* (1911), a quiet tale of Indiana life; but he is best known for *Graustark* and its sequels, *Beverly of Graustark* (1904) and *The Prince of Graustark* (1914).

McCutcheon, John T[inney] (b. South Raub, Ind., May 6, 1870—d. June 10, 1949), cartoonist, writer. The brother of GEORGE BARR MC-CUTCHEON was one of the greatest American cartoonists. He began working for the Chicago *Record* in 1889. GEORGE ADE joined him, and together they wrote and illustrated a striking series called *Stories of the Streets and of the Town*. In 1903 McCutcheon switched to the *Tribune* and remained there until his retirement in 1946. He saw many wars as a war correspondent, traveled widely in Asia, and hunted in Africa with the Carl Akeleys and with Theodore Roosevelt.

For many years McCutcheon's cartoons were a front-page feature of the *Tribune*. He drew some powerful political cartoons, one of which won a Pulitzer Prize in 1931, but preferred the gentler and kindlier aspects of life, as in his "Bird Center" extravaganzas and his "Boy in Springtime" drawings. Among his books: *Stories of Filipino Warfare* (1900); *Cartoons by McCutcheon* (1903); *Bird Center Cartoons* (1904); *The Mysterious Stranger and Other Cartoons* (1905); *Congressman Pumphrey, the People's Friend* (1907); *In Africa* (1910); *T.R. in Cartoons* (1910); *John McCutcheon's Book* (1948); *Drawn from Memory* (autobiography, 1950).

MacDonald, Betty [Anne Elizabeth Campbell Bard] (b. Boulder, Colo., March 26, 1908—d. Feb. 7, 1958), government official, memoirist. Mrs. MacDonald served as a labor adjuster with the government, later worked in other official capacities. She took to writing and turned out a number of extremely popular books of comic reminiscence: THE EGG AND I (1945); *Mrs. Piggle-Wiggle* (1947); *The Plague and I* (1948); *Anybody Can Do Anything* (1950); *Onions in the Stew* (1955). The first of these sold more than a million copies.

McDonald, Harl (b. near Boulder, Colo., July 27, 1899—d. March 30, 1955), musician, composer, teacher, essayist. McDonald published more than a hundred musical compositions in a great variety of forms. In some he drew inspiration from what he called the "Hispanic-Indian-Anglo-Saxon combination of the Mexican border region." He joined the staff of the University of Pennsylvania in 1926; became director of the Philadelphia orchestra in 1939. He first won renown with a symphonic fantasy called *Mojave* (1922). Later came the *First Symphony—Santa Fé Trail* (1934), *Legend of the Arkansas Traveler* (1939), *Mississippi* (1943), a suite for orchestra, and other compositions based on American themes.

MacDonald, Wilson (b. Cheapside, Ont., May 5, 1880—   ), poet, etcher. MacDonald is essentially a lyric poet; his melody is constantly maintained, his metaphors are apt and effective. He regards civilization as a failure and calls for a return to the soil. Some of his best poems are in Negro dialect. He has also written French-Canadian poems. Among his books: *Song of the Prairie Land* (1918); *The Miracle Songs of Jesus* (1921); *Out of the Wilderness* (1926); *A Flagon of Beauty* (1931); *Paul Marchand* (1933, reprinted 1959 as *Armand Dussault, and Other Poems*).

McDougall, William (b. England, June 22, 1871—d. Nov. 28, 1938), psychologist, teacher. McDougall studied both science and medicine, specialized in physiology and psychophysical interaction, taught for a while in English universities, was head of a hospital for shell-shock cases during World War I. He taught at Harvard in 1920, moved to Duke University in 1927 and remained there till his death. A. A. Roback, writing in *History of American Psychology* (1952), calls Freud and McDougall "the two great dynamists in psychology." McDougall's name is particularly connected with what he called "hormic psychology"—the doctrine that purpose and not pleasure is the mainspring of action, although pleasure may accompany the winning of a goal. McDougall felt that man works toward biologically valuable aims because nature has equipped him to pursue the course of action which helps the species. Yet he felt that man was a free agent, and implicit in his psychology was a belief in a soul—even a degree of mysticism. Attacks on McDougall's ideas came chiefly after he began teaching in the United States, but his books had a profound influence, especially *Social Psychology* (1908); more than twenty-five editions of this appeared. Among his other books: *Physiological Psychology* (1905); *Pagan Tribes of Borneo* (1911); *Psychology, The Study of Behavior* (1912); *The Group Mind* (1920); *Outline of Psychology* (1923); *Outline of Abnormal Psychology* (1926); *Psycho-analysis and Social Psychology* (1936); and *The Riddle of Life* (1938).

MacDowell, Edward A[lexander] (b. New York City, Dec. 18, 1861—d. Jan. 23, 1908), composer, pianist, teacher. After studying music abroad and composing many musical pieces, particularly his symphonic poem *Hamlet and Ophelia,* MacDowell returned to the United States in 1888. For eight years he lived in Boston, writing there his famous *Woodland Sketches* for piano and his piano sonatas, *Eroica* and *Tragica;* later he composed *New England Idyls,* the *Norse* and *Celtic* sonatas, and *Fireside Tales* for piano. He occasionally employed Indian themes in his pieces. In 1896 he was called to Columbia University to head a newly established music department. His resignation in 1904 was followed by a nervous breakdown that prevented further creative activity.

After his death some of his admirers established in his honor the MacDowell Memorial Association. His widow deeded to the Association their home at Peterboro, N.H., which thereafter became the "MacDowell Colony," to which many composers and authors came for quiet and inspiration. Among the many who benefited from the colony were Edwin Arlington Robinson, Elinor Wylie, Stephen Vincent Benét, Thornton Wilder, Willa Cather, and Padraic Colum.

MacDowell, Katherine Sherwood ["Sherwood Bonner"] (b. Holly Springs, Miss., Feb. 26, 1849—d. July 22, 1883), short-story writer, novelist. Mrs. MacDowell was amanuensis to Henry Wadsworth Longfellow for a time, meanwhile contributing verse, articles, and stories to various magazines. Some of these were collected in *Dialect Tales* (1883) and *Suwanee River Tales* (1884); for the most part they have southern backgrounds. She used her memories of the Civil War and the Reconstruction Period in an autobiographical novel, *Like Unto Like* (1878). Some of her later stories, never collected, were gloomy in their depiction of human misfortunes in the Tennessee mountains and southern Illinois. Mrs. MacDowell is remembered as one of the earliest regionalists.

McElheney, Jane ["Ada Clare"] (b. Charleston, S.C., 1836—d. March 4, 1874), novelist, poet, actress. Jane McElheney, a cousin of the poet Paul Hamilton Hayne, began publishing poetic effusions, anonymously, in various New York periodicals. At the age of twenty-one she returned from France, unmarried, but with a small son. Ada's own cheerfully given explanation was that the boy, as well as all her literary creations, resulted from a love affair with the pianist and composer Louis Gottschalk.

With Harry Clapp, editor, poet, and so-called "King of Bohemia," whom she had known in Paris, she established a "Latin Quarter" in PFAFF'S CELLAR on lower Broadway, until the Bohemians were scattered by the Civil War. As her rather fragile literary career waned she became an actress, but was never a success. Her novel *Only a Woman's Heart* (1866), like her shorter works, was a thinly disguised account of her great love affair. The hero, Victor Doria, was a combination of Gottschalk and EDWIN BOOTH. The book was not a success; even the critics who admired Ada Clare as a woman attacked her as a novelist.

McEvoy, J[oseph] P[atrick] (b. New York City, Jan. 10, 1895—d. Aug. 8, 1958), novelist, playwright. McEvoy published his first book, a volume of light verse called *Slams of Life,* in 1919. In 1924, with the production of *The Potters,* he began a successful dramatic career. His life centered around Hollywood and Broadway. *The Comic Supplement* (a revue, 1925) was followed by *Americana* (1926) and *Allez Oop* (1927). *God Loves Us* (1926), a satirical comedy attacking the Babbitts and "those who put the jazz in Jesus," was extremely popular. *Show Girl* (1928) and *Hollywood Girl* (1929), novels, were followed by *Father Meets Son* (1937), a play, and *Stars in Your Eyes* (1939), a musical comedy. McEvoy wrote many magazine articles and created the comic strip "Dixie Dugan." *Charlie Would Have Loved This* (1956) is a collection of humorous sketches.

Macfadden, Bernarr [or Bernard] (b. Mill Springs, Mo., Aug. 16, 1868—d. Oct. 12, 1955), physical culturist, editor. One of the most astonishing personalities in American history, he furnished reading matter, advice, and stimulation to millions and entertainment to practically everyone. He advocated a number of physical and dietary cults, which others called "fads," but his own personal practice of them (including standing on his head and turning somersaults) continued to an extraordinary age. Among the "evils" against which he crusaded were alcohol, medicine, tobacco, corsets, prudishness, white bread, overeating, and muscular inactivity. His opinions were accepted by large numbers of persons, even in medical ranks.

Macfadden's weapons were for the most part literary, including an exuberant gift for personal publicity in print. He began with a four-page pamphlet in the 1890's, but at the height of his success he was advocating the Macfadden road to physical and mental health and happiness to nearly fifteen million readers through ten newspapers, twenty magazines, and fifty books, including a many-volumed *Macfadden Encyclopedia of Physical Culture*. He founded *Physical Culture* in 1898, followed with a string of other magazines. Most influential was *True Story* (1919). Alva Johnston said that Macfadden's "instinct for self-revelation has resulted in the founding of . . . the nudity industry and the confession industry." Macfadden's first Physical Culture Show in Madison Square Garden (1904) was the forerunner of all bathing beauty contests. Macfadden went to jail in the cause of nudity and was heavily fined; years later a bill was introduced into the Senate to hand him back his fine.

True Story started a flood of imitators; the same was also unfortunately true of another innovation of Macfadden's; in 1924 he founded the first New York City tabloid, the *Graphic* (occasionally referred to as the *Pornographic*). The paper was a failure and died in 1932. He owned several other newspapers for a time. He published fiction in which the heroines could always take care of themselves and any annoyers. His heroes often progressed from extreme emaciation and weakness to robust, handsome health—by following the Macfadden way and presumably by eating in the Macfadden Vegetarian Restaurants, of which he founded a large number.

In the early 1040's Macfadden got him progressive financial difficulties, and minority stockholders bought out his string of publications, with a proviso that he would give them no direct competition for five years. In 1943 he bought back *Physical Culture*, which had lost circulation heavily when the new management tried to make it a beauty magazine. In 1946 he started a new magazine, *Bernarr Macfadden's Detective Magazine* (Macfadden preferred to call himself "Bernarr"). His divorced first wife, Mary Macfadden, in collaboration with EMILE GAUVREAU, wrote the somewhat hair-raising story of their marriage in *Dumbbells and Carrot Strips: The Story of Bernarr Macfadden* (1952).

McFee, William [Morley Punshon] (b. England, June 15, 1881—   ), novelist, short-story writer, essayist. Apprenticed in his seventeenth year to a firm of mechanical engineers, McFee ran away to sea in 1906 and served on ships until 1911, when he settled in the United States. His first book, *Letters from an Ocean Tramp* (1908), was followed by *Casuals of the Sea* (1916), the story of an impoverished London suburban family, which he composed during his years at sea. In World War I he served as sub-lieutenant in the British navy, and his experiences in the Mediterranean area provided a background for some of his later novels.

He has been erroneously compared to Conrad, with whom he has little in common beyond an interest in the sea. He is nearer in spirit to Somerset Maugham, since he is primarily concerned with observing the behavior of people and drawing philosophical conclusions of a shrewd and amusing though not necessarily very profound nature. *Command* (1922), one of his best novels, laid in Salonika, is the story of a mediocre man's rise to heroism. Other works include *Sailors of Fortune* (1929), short stories; *Harbours of Memory* (1921), essays; *The Harbourmaster* (1932), the tragedy of a sea-loving man who stays on land; *The Beachcomber* (1935); *Derelicts* (1938); *Spenlove in Arcady* (1941); *Family Trouble* (1949); and *The Adopted* (1952). Many of the stories are told by Chief Engineer Spenlove, whom McFee acknowledges as his "garrulous, ironic, goateed *alter ego*."

M'Fingal (1775, 1782), a burlesque epic by JOHN TRUMBULL. Trumbull was urged to write a satire on the loyalists, and this poem was the result. The first part appeared anonymously in 1775; later Trumbull divided this section into two cantos and added two more cantos. It was immensely popular and ran into numerous editions; it was also widely pirated. Trumbull closely followed Samuel Butler's *Hudibras* (1663, 1664, 1678), using the same terse tetrameter couplets. The name M'Fingal recalls James Macpherson's alleged translation of the Gaelic bard Ossian; Fingal was an old Scots hero. In the poem M'Fingal is an inveterate loyalist who is such a blunderer in his arguments that they prove the opposite case; he is ultimately tarred and feathered. Toward the end of the poem M'Fingal gloomily foresees the triumph of the rebels. See HARTFORD WITS.

McGee, Thomas D'Arcy (b. Ireland, April 13, 1825—d. April 7, 1868), political agitator, editor, poet, public official. McGee was first a violent advocate of the Irish Confederation and was arrested. He escaped to the United States and wrote for and edited various magazines, gradually losing his revolutionary zeal; he even joined the notorious antipapal "Know Nothing" party. Accused of treachery, he finally removed to Montreal, where he founded the *New Era*, was elected to the Legislative Assembly, became president of the Council and was active in the movement for a Canadian Federation. When that was established he was chosen a member of the Dominion parliament and the minister of agriculture and emigration. He was assassinated by a political enemy. McGee wrote *Irish Writers of the 17th Century* (1846); *Irish Letters* (1852); *Popular History of Ireland* (1862). A collection of his *Poems* appeared in 1869.

McGinley, Phyllis [Mrs. Charles Hayden] (b. Ontario, Ore., March 21, 1905—   ), teacher, writer of light verse and children's books. Miss McGinley is a clever versifier with something to say. She loves the contemporary scene and the 20th-century foibles of people as a subject for her gracious humor; and she even reveals successfully the humor of religion (she is a Roman Catholic). She has been a favorite contributor to *The New Yorker*, the *Atlantic Monthly*, the *Saturday Review*, and other magazines. Numerous collections of her verses have appeared, among them: *On the Contrary* (1934); *Pocketful of Wry* (1940); *Husbands Are Difficult* (1941); *Stones from a*

Glass House (1946); *All Around the Town* (1948); *Blunderbus* (1951); *A Short Walk from the Station* (1951); *Love Letters of Phyllis McGinley* (1954); *Merry Christmas, Happy New Year* (1958); *Times Three: Selected Verse From Three Decades* (1960), which won a Pulitzer prize. She has also written some amusing books for children, including *The Horse Who Lived Upstairs* (1944); *The Make-Believe Twins* (1952); *Sugar and Spice* (1960). She did the lyrics for the revue *Small Wonder* (1948); and has written a collection of essays, *The Province of the Heart* (1959).

Macgowan, Kenneth (b. Winthrop, Mass., Nov. 30, 1888—d. April 27, 1963), drama critic, director, publicity director, teacher. Macgowan was a drama and movie critic on newspapers, publicity man in Hollywood, directed plays, produced movies, and taught at the University of California as professor of theater arts. Among his books are *The Theater of Tomorrow* (1921); *Continental Stagecraft* (1922); *Masks and Demons* (1923); *Footlights Across America* (1929); *The Early Stone Age in the New World* (1948); *Early Man in the New World* (1950); *A Primer of Playwriting* (1951). Macgowan became deeply interested in anthropology, an interest awakened by his book on the masks used by primitive peoples. In 1959 he edited *Famous American Plays of the 1920's*.

MacGrath, Harold (b. Syracuse, N.Y., Sept. 4, 1871—d. Oct. 29, 1932), newspaperman, novelist. MacGrath worked for various newspapers in New York state, then turned to writing novels. His third book, *The Man on the Box* (1904), became a best seller, was promptly dramatized and later made into a film. It told the story of a young man of good family who takes a position as a groom in the family of the young lady he is in love with, prevents her father from selling important documents to a foreign country, and marries the girl. Other novels followed: *The Princess Elopes* (1905); *The Carpet from Bagdad* (1920); *Drums of Jeopardy* (1911); and others. MacGrath called them "fairy-tales for grown-ups." He also wrote the famous PERILS OF PAULINE, a silent-movie serial.

McGuffey, William Holmes (b. Washington Co., Pa., Sept. 23, 1800—d. May 4, 1873), educator, textbook compiler. Until he was eighteen, McGuffey lived with his pioneer parents in the wilderness of Ohio; he was a student at Washington College, graduated with honors in 1826. He had a remarkable memory and a gift for languages; he was an excellent student of Greek, Latin, and Hebrew. He taught at Miami University in Oxford, Ohio, was president of Cincinnati College and Ohio University, later taught at Woodward College and the University of Virginia.

McGuffey was known to thousands of Americans as the author of their first schoolbook; in fact, it is said of the author of the "Eclectic Readers" that he taught America to read. The series began in 1836 with the *First* and *Second Readers*. The *Primer*, *Third*, and *Fourth Read-ers* appeared in 1837, the *Speller* in 1838, the *Rhetorical Guide* in 1841, the *Fifth Reader* in 1844, the *Sixth* in 1857. His younger brother, Alexander Hamilton McGuffey, collaborated in the "Eclectic Series," and probably compiled

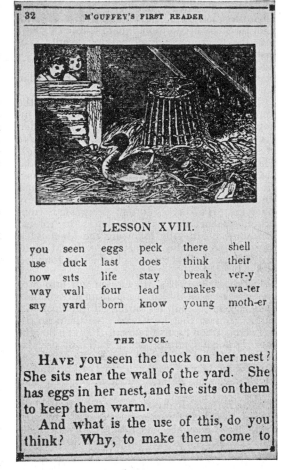

the *Speller* and the *Fifth Reader* without his brother's assistance. The books have sold 122 million copies, with new editions appearing as recently as 1920. (See READERS.)

A kind of McGuffey worship has grown up in recent years; collectors pay enormous sums for shabby first editions. In 1936, the centenary of the publication of the first *Reader*, two books appeared, *William Holmes McGuffey and His Readers* and *Old Favorites from the McGuffey Reader*, both by Harvey C. Minnich, curator of the McGuffey Museum at Miami University. In the former Minnich speaks of McGuffey as "one sent to deliver the childhood of America from the stygian night of fear and horror created by stories of the public cremation of Christian martyrs, by rhymes from Wigglesworth's THE DAY OF DOOM, [tales of] Indian massacres of their forefathers, and to create for it a renaissance in childhood's world, a world of familiar animals, familiar playthings, companions." A more significant view is given in Richard V. D. Mosier's *Making the American Mind: Social and Moral Ideas in the McGuffey Readers* (1947). He stresses the fact that Mc-Guffey had a political purpose. He was solidly enlisted on the conservative side in the recurrent feud between the Hamiltonians and the Jeffersonians.

In 1961 a new conservative-liberal controversy arose when the Wisconsin State Superintendent of Schools tried to get the Twin Lakes, Wis., School Board to stop using the 1879 edition of McGuffey's *Eclectic Reader* as a basic text in their local school. The readers were eventually kept on as supplementary texts with strongly sectarian passages excised.

McHenry, James (b. Ireland, Dec. 20, 1785 —d. July 21, 1845), novelist, dramatist, poet, critic. McHenry brought with him from Ireland (1817) a great admiration for Sir Walter Scott and Mrs. Anne Radcliffe; he added Cooper on this side of the Atlantic. His first publications were a collection of verse, *The Pleasures of Friendship* (1822), and a poem on the Revolution called *Waltham* (1823). Then appeared several historical romances, all published anonymously; in his periodical writings he sometimes used the pen name Solomon Secondsight. His two best-known novels appeared in 1823: *The Wilderness, or, Braddock's Times* and *The Spectre of the Forest.* In the former the story concerns the life of an Irish family living in the wilderness near Fort Duquesne. McHenry also wrote *O'Halloran, or, the Insurgent Chief* (1824) and *Meredith* (1831), and he published a blank-verse tragedy, *The Usurper* (1827).

McHugh, Vincent (b. Providence, R.I., Dec. 23, 1904—   ), newspaperman, poet, novelist, critic, folklorist, teacher, screenwriter. McHugh is a maverick, rich in eccentricities which he occasionally tries to rationalize, as in the somewhat pretentious introduction to a volume of poems, *The Blue Hen's Chickens* (1947). *Caleb Catlum's America* (1936) is the story of a folk hero who roams through American history, meeting everyone from Ben Franklin to the latest radio comedian. The book is an astonishing mixture, everything from pinochle to megalomania, from Latin conjugations to Yiddish slang, all charged with a kind of outlandish humor which seemed entirely agreeable to some people and mere lunacy to others. Among McHugh's other novels are *Touch Me Not* (1930); *Sing Before Breakfast* (1933); *I Am Thinking of My Darling* (1943); *The Victory* (1947); *Primer of the Novel* (1950).

MacInnes, Helen (b. Scotland, October 7, 1907—   ), novelist. Helen MacInnes is best known as the author of a series of novels of adventure and espionage that are distinguished by their literate style, faithful atmospheric detail, and credible characterization. These books include *Above Suspicion* (1941); *Assignment In Brittany* (1942); *Horizon* (1946); *Neither Five Nor Three* (1951); *Pray for a Brave Heart* (1955); and *North from Rome* (1958). Set in a wide variety of European and American backgrounds, these novels combine complex and suspenseful action with an unusually accurate rendering of the nature of the local people and their environment. She has also written *While Still We Live* (1944); *Friends and Lovers* (1947); *Rest and Be Thankful* (1949); *I and My True Love* (1953); and *Decision at Delphi* (1960).

MacInnes, Tom [Thomas Robert Edward] (b. Dresden, Ont., Oct. 29, 1867—d. Feb. 11, 1951), lawyer, public official, poet. MacInnes went to China and studied Chinese poetry and philosophy; later he wrote a book about Lao-tzu, *The Teaching of the Old Boy.* In China he persuaded the City Council to install an electric railway system, and served for several years as its director. Vancouver became his home in later years. MacInnes' poetry shows the influence of such diverse poets as Villon, Poe, and Whitman, as well as that of Chinese philosophy. Among his collections: *Lonesome Bar and Other Poems* (1909); *In Amber Lands* (1910); *Rhymes of a Rounder* (1913); *The Fool of Joy* (1918); *Complete Poems* (1923); *In the Old of My Age* (1947).

McIntyre, John T[homas] (b. Philadelphia, Nov. 26, 1871—d. May 21, 1951), newspaperman, writer. McIntyre had the knack of being able to write "down" for one part of the reading public and "up" for another part. A craftsman of great facility, he wrote detective stories (under a pen name, Kerry O'Neil), juveniles (like the "Buckskin Series"), historical novels (*Blowing Weather*, 1923, perhaps his best book; *Stained Sails*, 1928; *Drums in the Dawn*, 1932), and strongly realistic stories (*The Ragged Edge*, 1902; *Slag*, 1927; *Steps Going Down*, 1936, a story of the Philadelphia underworld that he regarded as his greatest achievement; *Ferment*, 1937; *Signing Off*, 1938). With Arnold Daly, the actor who appeared in it, he wrote *Wedding Journey*, a melodrama, the realism of which proved too strong for contemporary audiences. Later he wrote a fantasy *Young Man's Fancy*, produced in 1919, turned into a novel in 1925.

McIntyre, O[scar] **O**[dd] (b. Plattsburg, Mo., Feb. 18, 1884—d. Feb. 14, 1938), newspaperman, press agent, columnist. McIntyre, one of the shyest of men but a flamboyant dresser, became a newspaper reporter and even a city editor. He was brought up in Gallipolis, Ohio, and in 1902 began contributing to the Gallipolis *Journal*. He went on to the East Liverpool (O.) *Morning Tribune*, the Dayton *Herald*, and the Cincinnati *Post*, then reached New York City as a member of the short-lived *Hampton's Magazine*. For a time he was simultaneously writing a column and working as press agent for a New York hotel. He went on to other assignments, including work for the theatrical producer Florenz Ziegfeld, but quit the latter job because of Ziegfeld's incessant and eccentric demands.

Meanwhile his column, originally called "New York Letter," later titled "New York Day by Day," was beginning to prosper. More and more papers took it, until just before his death it was appearing in more than five hundred papers. In addition he wrote a monthly article for the *Cosmopolitan* for twenty years. McIntyre never regarded himself as a New Yorker but always as a Gallipolis boy observing the metropolis. His view of New York was distorted and melodramatic, but it gave his out-of-town readers a vivid sense of meeting the great and experiencing the incredible. He borrowed freely. When he made a collection of his pieces called *The Big Town* (1935), CHRISTOPHER MORLEY insisted that in at least thirty instances McIntyre had borrowed items from Morley's column, "The Bowling Green," in the *Saturday Review of Literature*. McIntyre's only comment was, "If it did happen, it happened unintentionally." All the popular columnists of the day sniped at him, but later columnists paid him the compliment of imitating him.

McIntyre's readers did not mind his egregious errors in spelling, nor his strange brand of French, nor his constant factual errors. They liked his oddities. Once in a while he got off good phrases, as when he asserted that "there are no illegitimate children, there are only illegitimate parents." Charles B. Driscoll wrote a *Life of O. O. McIntyre* (1938) and continued his syndicated column.

MacIver, Robert Morrison (b. Scotland, April 17, 1882—   ), teacher, political scientist, sociologist. MacIver greatly influenced two generations of students in Scotland, Canada, and the United States; he taught at Aberdeen, then at Toronto, finally joined the faculty of Columbia University in 1927. He became an American citizen in 1934. His books made him one of the most eminent of contemporary sociologists. They include: *Community—A Sociological Study* (1917); *Labor in the Changing World* (1919); *The Modern State* (1926); *Society: Its Structure and Changes* (1931); *Economic Reconstruction* (1934); *Leviathan and the People* (1939); *Social Causation* (1942); *Toward an Abiding Peace* (1943); *The Web of Government* (1947); *The Ramparts We Guard* (1950); *Democracy and the Economic Challenge* (1952); *Life: Its Dimensions and its Bounds* (1960).

McKay, Claude (b. Jamaica, Sept. 15, 1890 —d. May 22, 1948), poet, novelist. McKay was the first Negro to write a best seller—his novel *Home to Harlem* (1928), which tells how a Negro soldier returned from France after World War I. As a young man in Jamaica, McKay, a member of the native constabulary, had written dialect verses that were widely circulated in the colony. Two collections were published, *Songs of Jamaica* (1911) and *Constab Ballads* (1912). He was given an award by the National Institute of Arts and Letters, and came to the United States in 1912. He attended school for a while, worked as a Pullman porter, and began to write again. He became

an important figure in the "Negro Renaissance" of the 1920's, drifted into Communism, became disillusioned when he visited Russia. He published two more volumes of verse: *Spring in New Hampshire and Other Poems* (1920) and *Harlem Shadows* (1922); also several stories and novels: *Banjo* (1929), a story of Marseilles; *Gingertown* (1931), short stories; *Banana Bottom* (1933), set in Jamaica. His novels are often vividly realistic; *Banjo* is perhaps the best. McKay told the story of his life in *A Long Way from Home* (1937) and wrote a survey of *Harlem: Negro Metropolis* (1940).

Mackay, Isabel Ecclestone (b. Woodstock, Ont., Nov. 25, 1875—d. Aug. 15, 1928), poet, novelist. Mrs. Mackay's poems appeared in many Canadian, American, and British periodicals. They were all frankly sentimental, but the sentiment was sincere and well expressed. Her earlier poems were collected in *Between the Lights* (1904). Her novel *The House of Windows* (1912) was called by the London *Times* "an enjoyable tale, of much wholesome sentiment."

MacKaye, Percy [Wallace] (b. New York City, March 16, 1875—d. Aug. 31, 1956), teacher, poet, playwright. After an education at Harvard and Leipzig, Percy MacKaye taught in a private school in New York, then became a member of the Cornish, N.H., colony of artists and writers. THE CANTERBURY PILGRIMS (1903), a fanciful blank-verse play concerning the Wife of Bath's pursuit of Chaucer, was followed by two more poetic dramas, produced by E. H. SOTHERN and JULIA MARLOWE: *Jeanne d'Arc* (1906) and *Sappho and Phaon* (1907). THE SCARECROW (1908), a prose play based on Hawthorne's FEATHERTOP, was successful here and abroad and was made into a film. MacKaye was much interested in pageantry, community plays, and folk drama. *The Playhouse and the Play* (1909), *The Civic Theatre* (1912), and *Community Drama* (1917) deal with production problems. *St. Louis* was a community masque for 7,500 actors (1914). His other works include: *Sanctuary, A Bird Masque* (1913); *A Thousand Years Ago* (1914), a poetic drama laid in China; CALIBAN, BY THE YELLOW SANDS (1916), a community masque to commemorate the Shakespeare Tercentenary; *Rip Van Winkle* (1920), a libretto for REGINALD DeKOVEN's opera; *This Fine-Pretty World* (1923), a comedy of folk ways; *Kentucky Mountain Fantasies* (1926), one-act plays about mountaineers; *Tall Tales of the Kentucky Mountains* (1928); *Songs of a Day* (1929); *Poog's Pasture* (1938); *What We Will* (1943). He edited *The Modern Reader's Chaucer* (1912) with J. S. P. TATLOCK, wrote a biography of his father STEELE MacKAYE. His early poetic works were collected in *Poems and Plays* (2 v., 1916). MacKaye's most ambitious work was a tetralogy of verse plays, *The Mystery of Hamlet, King of Denmark—or What We Will* (1949). Here he traced the histories of the major characters in Shakespeare's tragedy up to the time the play begins. King Hamlet is the protagonist, Yorick the court jester, Claudius the jealous lover; Prince Hamlet appears as a child. MacKaye called his work "the largest continuous four-fold production of a single dramatic work in the history of the theatre since the ancient Greek productions in Athens." See LITTLE THEATER IN THE U.S.

MacKaye, [James Morrison] Steele (b. Buffalo, N.Y., June 6, 1842—d. Feb. 25, 1894), dramatist, painter, actor, inventor. Steele MacKaye studied painting with George Inness and other American painters, later in Paris. He served in the army during the Civil War, later acted at the Bowery Theater, painted, and ran an art store. After studying in Paris with François Delsarte (1811–1871), he established a school of acting in New York City at which he taught a variation of the Delsarte method. In 1872 he produced *Monaldi*, a play he had adapted from the French. In 1873 he gave *Hamlet* in French in Paris, then went on to London to give it in English.

Back in the United States, he wrote and produced plays, established theaters, initiated many new ideas. His principal innovations were overhead lighting, the moving or "double" stage, the disappearing orchestra pit, and folding chairs. Meanwhile his plays were frequently great successes, particularly HAZEL KIRKE (1880). Their merit is hard to estimate, since only *Hazel Kirke* and *Paul Kauvar* (1887) are available in print. One of MacKaye's last great achievements was the planning of a huge amphitheater, the Spectatorium, for the Chicago World's Fair (1892–93), where he gave a play about Columbus called *The World Finder*, for which Anton Dvořák wrote his *New World Symphony*. MacKaye's son PERCY MACKAYE wrote *Epoch, the Life of Steele MacKaye, Genius of the Theater* (1927).

McKenney, Ruth (b. Mishawaka, Ind., Nov. 18, 1911—   ), newspaperwoman, memoirist, novelist, sociological writer. Although primarily considered a humorist, Miss McKenney's interests are serious, and she wrote a careful investigation of economic and social conditions in Akron, Ohio, in the years 1932–36: IN-DUSTRIAL VALLEY (1939). For a time Miss McKenney was an active member of the Communist Party, but was expelled for "left deviationism." Most of her writing has been devoted to humorous accounts of her family affairs. *My Sister Eileen* (1938) was a best seller and later was made into a successful play (1941) and a musical, *Wonderful Town* (1953). The play and the musical were filmed in 1942 and 1954, respectively. Eileen and her husband, the novelist NATHANAEL WEST, were killed in an automobile accident three days before *My Sister Eileen* opened in New York. Miss Mc-Kenney wrote about her grandfather in *The Loud Red Patrick* (1947). *Love Story* (1950) is about her own marriage. The books about her sister were gathered into an omnibus vol-

ume, *All About Eileen* (1952). *Far, Far from Home* (1954) is another volume of reminiscences, and *Mirage* (1956) is a novel.

MacKenzie, Sir Alexander (b. Scotland, 1764—d. March 12, 1820), British fur trader, explorer, memoirist. An emigrant, Mackenzie entered the fur trade in Canada and made many trips of exploration in western Canada. Later he wrote *Voyages from Montreal on the River St. Lawrence, Through the Continent of North America to the Frozen and Pacific Oceans, in the Years 1789 and 1793* (1801).

McKinley, William (b. Niles, Ohio, Jan. 29, 1843—d. Sept. 14, 1901), soldier, lawyer, public official, 25th President. McKinley fought in the Civil War and practiced law in Canton, Ohio. He served in the House of Representatives (1877–82, 1884–90); he became governor of Ohio in 1891 and again in 1893. Under MARK HANNA's shrewd guidance he won a reputation for conservatism that enabled him to defeat WILLIAM JENNINGS BRYAN in the 1896 Presidential election. During his Presidency Congress passed the Dingley Tariff Act, which established the highest rates in the history of the country, and Hawaii was annexed (1898). Against McKinley's wishes, the United States entered the Spanish American War and defeated Spain. John Hay, the Secretary of State, formulated the "open door policy in China.

McKinley was easily re-elected in 1900 with Theodore Roosevelt as his running mate, but was assassinated the following year by an anarchist named Leon Czolgosz. Charles S. Olcott wrote a *Life of William McKinley* (2 v., 1916).

McLean, Sarah Pratt (b. Simsbury, Conn., July 3, 1856—d. Dec. 29, 1935), novelist. Some of Miss McLean's writings appeared under her married name, Sarah P. McLean Greene. Her first book dealt with *Cape Cod Folks* (1881), and in all her books she emphasized New England local color. Among them: *Some Other Folks* (1882); *Towhead* (1883); *Vesty of the Basins* (1892); *The Moral Imbeciles* (1898); *Flood-Tide* (1901); *Deacon Lysander* (1904); *Everbreeze* (1913).

MacLeish, Archibald (b. Glencoe, Ill., May 7, 1892—   ), poet, playwright, critic, educator, public official. Having graduated from Yale University, fought in World War I, received a law degree from Harvard University, taught in college, practiced law, and published one volume of poetry (*Tower of Ivory*, 1917), MacLeish decided in 1923 that he was dissatisfied with the life he was leading and the poetry he was writing. He moved to Paris with his family and declared later that his creative life began with that move. Except for an excursion to Persia and several to the Mediterranean, he remained in Paris until 1928, reading widely, especially among the French symbolist poets. He also read the works of his fellow expatriates Ezra Pound and T. S. Eliot.

who greatly influenced him. Pound introduced MacLeish to the poetry of ancient China and Japan, which remained a subject for allusion in MacLeish's poetry and for critical comparison in his prose.

During this period MacLeish published two volumes of short lyrics, *The Happy Marriage* (1924) and *Streets in the Moon* (1926). The first includes variations on the theme of love in experiments with various conventional poetic forms, including perfectly regular sonnets. The second reveals the development of MacLeish's own personal style through experiments with imagism, symbolism, free verse, and adaptations of older forms to the cadences of modern speech. It includes the famous *Ars Poetica* with the now proverbial lines, "A poem should not mean/ but be." Two long poems, THE POT OF EARTH (1925) and THE HAMLET OF A. MACLEISH (1928), are highly personal lyrics, yet they present their themes and establish moods by embodying them in dramatic situations revealed partly by narrative and partly through dramatic monologue. This tendency to embody philosophical questions in personal confrontations and to use actions as images appears clearly in *Nobodaddy*, a play in verse using Adam, Eve, Cain, and Abel. Written before *The Pot of Earth*, it was not published until 1926. Although the poetry is immature and often weakened by the struggle between MacLeish's attempt to write blank verse and his growing feeling for accentual meter, the play is important as the first major presentation of "the dramatic situation which the condition of self-consciousness in an indifferent universe seems to me to present," a theme dominating much of MacLeish's writing since.

MacLeish's interest in America as a subject for his writing and as an object of his vigorous personal concern began in 1929, at the time when the United States was being precipitated into a severe economic crisis. Mexico had already attracted his interest. Having read while in Europe the *True History of the Conquest of New Spain* by Bernal Díaz del Castillo, he explored Mexican history more thoroughly and in 1929 followed the route of Cortez by foot and mule-back. CONQUISTADOR was published in 1932 and received a Pulitzer prize.

MacLeish settled on a farm in Connecticut in 1928, later became one of the original editors of *Fortune,* and remained with the magazine until 1938. He continued to publish volumes of poetry every few years. But he attracted the most attention during this time by writing plays in verse rhythms that copied those of modern speech and had plots suggested by contemporary events. The "message" of each play was a timely warning apropos of a current national attitude, yet the plays portray, not specific problems, but the aspects of human nature that create these problems. Thus all three have stature as works of art more than as dated propaganda. PANIC, which appeared briefly on Broadway (1935), warned of the contagion of mob hysteria. When Hitler was only a menace, though a growing one, THE FALL OF THE CITY (1937) portrayed the populace of a unnamed city accepting through blind fear a "conqueror" whose only power was bluff. *Air Raid* (1938), on the other hand, showed the horror of the new realities of the modern world as nostalgically compared with the old—and the fate of those who refuse to face those realities.

The last two plays were written as radio scripts; both utilize the format and immediacy of the radio newscast. The Orson Welles production of *The Fall of the City* effectively demonstrated that verse drama had potential as a modern art form and that radio could have a function as its medium—as, in MacLeish's own words, the theater of "the word-excited imagination." "Only the ear is engaged and the ear is already half poet. It believes at once: creates and believes."

But MacLeish's energies were distracted from this field by the urgencies of World War II. He was appointed Librarian of Congress in 1939 and held the post until 1944; in the interim he also organized a new government agency as the Director of the Office of Facts and Figures (1941–42), then served as the Assistant Director of War Information (1942–43) and the Assistant Secretary of State (1944–45). After the war he represented the United States on several cultural missions, such as the organization of UNESCO. His poetry during this period, such as *America Was Promises* (1939) and *Colloquy for the States* (1943), was "public" and patriotic; critics complained of its bombast and rhetoric.

Deeply involved in public affairs, MacLeish published vigorous essays in numerous magazines on the social and political conditions and issues of the day, and on the poet's responsibility toward them. His controversial essay *The Irresponsibles* (1940), for instance, attacked the writers of his own expatriate generation for still using disillusionment as an excuse for non-involvement. Much of this prose was collected in *The American Cause* (1941), *A Time to Speak* (1941), and *A Time to Act* (1943).

MacLeish returned to a more purely literary life soon after the war, becoming Boylston Professor at Harvard University in 1949. The poetry published in *Actfive and Other Poems* (1948) showed again his powers as a lyricist, even when inspired by current issues, with vivid but controlled images and incisive intellectual twists. His *Collected Poems 1917–1952* won him a second Pulitzer prize (1953). Passionately convinced that poetry must serve a role *in* society, not as an escape *from* it, he began lecturing widely and publishing critical essays on the reading, teaching, appreciation, and value of poetry. He maintains that science, which is the knowledge of fact, has no quarrel with poetry, which is the feel of fact. Yet poetry is knowledge, for it alone comprehends the relationship between man as knower and the world as known; it is not the description, but rather the "experience of experience." The poet, then, recreates common experience with uncommon understanding of experience. A book length statement of his critical theory, with discussions of four major poets, is *Poetry and Experience* (1961).

The poem *Hypocrite Auteur* (1952) declared that the old metaphors of past poetry had died with their worlds, and called to modern poets to "Turn round into the actual air:/ Invent the age! Invent the metaphor!" Yet MacLeish was still, as in his earlier work, using the dramatic situations in classical and Biblical mythology as metaphors—often, however, to underline his personal vision by contrast with the familiar usage. *The Trojan Horse* (1952), another verse play for radio, satirized those who are deceived into thinking that "What takes the shape of Troy is Trojan" at a time when the Communist scare had brought forth a committee "To make official patriots of us,/ Sweating our public love by law." The "songs" in *Songs for Eve* (1954) recast the first human sinner as the heroine of intellectual and spiritual curiosity and, like the rest of the poems in the volume, use deceptively simple images from nature in deceptively quiet conversational tones to express a passionate humanism and a compulsion towards beauty, even through pain. The successfully staged verse drama *J.B.* (1958), which won MacLeish his third Pulitzer prize, stirred critical and theological controversy for months by "playing" the story of a contemporary Job in a circus tent, with comments by two actors who alternate between playing the roles of God and Satan, respectively, and being exceedingly human comedians.

Other poetry by MacLeish includes: *Einstein* (1929); *New Found Land* (1930); FRESCOES FOR MR. ROCKEFELLER'S CITY (1933); *Poems, 1924–1933* (1933); *Elpenor* (1933); *Union Pacific* (a ballet, 1934); *Public Speech* (1936); *The Land of the Free* (1938); *This Music Crept By Me Upon the Waters* (a play in verse, 1953). Other prose: *Poetry and Opinion; The Pisan Cantos of Ezra Pound; A Dialog on the Role of Poetry* (1950); *Freedom is the Right to Choose: An Inquiry into the Battle for the American Future* (1951).

McLellan, C[harles] M[orton] S[tewart] ["Hugh Morton"] (b. Maine, 1865—d. Sept. 21, 1916), playwright, librettist. With the German-born Gustave Kerker (1857–1923), McLellan collaborated in the production of several hits. He wrote the lyrics for *The Telephone Girl* (1898) and *The Belle of New York* (1898), among others; the latter was expanded and revived as *The Whirl of New York* in 1921 and again in 1945. In 1911 McLellan adapted from the French a clever farce called *The Pink Lady*, with music by Ivan Caryll (1861–1921), which was a great success. He adapted another French farce for the same composer's *Oh! Oh! Delphine* (1913). He wrote some serious plays, notably *Leah Kleschna* (1904), which describes the regeneration of a girl thief through love. After 1897 McLellan made his home in England.

McLellan, Isaac (b. Portland, Me., May 21, 1806—d. Aug. 20, 1899), poet, sportsman, lawyer. McLellan wrote verses about hunting and nature. Many of his poems appeared first in magazines such as *Forest and Stream* and the *American Angler*. Collections of his poems include *The Fall of the Indian, with Other Poems* (1830); *Mount Auburn and Other Poems* (1843); *Poems of the Rod and Gun, or, Sports by Flood and Field* (1886); and *Haunts of Wild Game* (1896).

MacLennan, Hugh (b. Cape Breton, N. Scot., March 20, 1907—   ), novelist, essayist. As a youngster MacLennan experienced the devastating explosion of Halifax Harbor during World War I; this became the theme of his first novel, *Barometer Rising* (1941). He studied at Oxford and at Princeton, taught for a while in a boys' school in Montreal, and while there began to write novels. *Barometer Rising* brought him a Guggenheim Fellowship, and in 1945 he published *Two Solitudes*, which won the Governor General's Literary Award as the best novel for that year. It reflects the tragic conflict in Canada between those of British and those of French descent. Then came *The Precipice* (1948), the story of an Ontario girl who marries a New York man. *Each Man's Son* (1951) is set in MacLennan's native island of Cape Breton. It is a study of Scots psychology and of a doctor's dilemma; the action is often tumultuous. *Time* called MacLennan "probably Canada's top novelist," but felt he had failed to attract as much notice as he deserves in the United States because "instead of crusading, shouting, or tying the English language into advance-guard knots, he quietly goes about his business, which is to write good, solid novels about Canadians." MacLennan has often spoken out on Canadian-American relations, and he has urged his own country toward greater maturity and self-confidence. *The Watch That Ends the Night* (1959) is a novel about an Enoch Arden marriage in Montreal. He also wrote *Rivers of Canada* (1961). *Scotchman's Return* (1960), contains 29 personal and critical essays.

McManus, George (b. St. Louis, Mo., Jan. 23, 1884—d. Oct. 22, 1954), cartoonist. McManus created numerous famous characters in his comic strips, "Jiggs," "Bringing Up Father," "The Newly Weds," "Let George Do It," "Panhandle Pete," "Snookums," and others. He began as a cartoonist with the St. Louis *Republic* in 1899, went on to papers in New York and to syndication. "Bringing Up Father" began *c.* 1913 and ran on endlessly, appearing in more than 750 papers all over the world and in twenty-seven languages; seven shows featuring "Father" toured the country for more than a decade, and radio programs, television shows, and movies were based upon it. McManus wrote *Fun for All* (1948).

McMaster, Guy Humphreys (b. Clyde, N.Y., Jan. 31, 1829—d. Sept. 13, 1887), lawyer, jurist, poet. McMaster varied a long and successful career as a lawyer and judge by writing occasional verses, all of which were well-turned, but only one of which attained permanent fame: *Carmen Bellicosum,* published in the *Knickerbocker Magazine* (February, 1849) under the pen name John MacGrom. This vigorously patriotic utterance is often anthologized. He wrote *Pacific Letters* for the Steuben (N.Y.) *Courier* in 1877 and other letters in 1885.

McMaster, John Bach (b. Brooklyn, N.Y., June 29, 1852—d. May 24, 1932), engineer, teacher, historian. Graduating from the College of the City of New York in 1872, McMaster, while teaching in the English department during the following year, laid his first plans for the history of the United States which was to become his life work. He was diverted from his purpose during the years 1873–77 while he practiced engineering. Later he was a member of the faculty of the University of Pennsylvania. He published two works in the field of engineering: *Bridge and Tunnel Centres* (1875) and *High Masonry Dams* (1876). He then worked for thirty years on his history, which stressed the social and economic aspects of the country rather than the military. The first volume of *The History of the People of the United States from the Revolution to the Civil War* appeared in 1883, the eighth and last in 1913. The history was hailed as both "vivacious" and "rambling." In addition to his major work he published *Benjamin Franklin as a Man of Letters* (1887); *Daniel Webster* (1902); *The Struggle for Social, Political, and Industrial Rights of Man* (1903); *The Life and Times of Stephen Girard* (2 v., 1918); *The United States in the World War* (2 v., 1918–20).

McMichael, Morton (b. Bordentown, N.J.,

Oct. 20, 1807—d. Jan. 6, 1879), editor, publisher. During the first half of the nineteenth century, McMichael was active in founding and managing magazines. He edited the SATURDAY EVENING POST (1826–1831), GODEY'S LADY'S BOOK (1842–1846), and other magazines; helped found the *Saturday News and Literary Gazette* (1836); and, with George R. Graham of *Graham's Magazine,* purchased the Philadelphia *North American* (1847), and merged the *U.S. Gazette* with it; the Philadelphia *Public Ledger* took over the newspaper in 1925.

MacMillan, Donald B[axter] (b. Provincetown, Mass., Nov. 10, 1874—   ), explorer, teacher, ethnologist, writer. One of the most eminent explorers of the twentieth century, MacMillan began his career as a teacher of classical languages, first went to the northern polar regions in 1910, and conducted ethnological investigations among the Eskimos in 1911–1912. Thereafter, he headed numerous expeditions in the Arctic region, and added greatly to geographical and ethnological knowledge. He wrote *Four Years in the White North* (1918); *Etah and Beyond* (1927); *Kahda* (1929); *How Peary Reached the Pole* (1932); and *Eskimo Place Names* (1943). His wife, Miriam, recounts her voyages with him in *Green Seas and White Ice* (1948).

MacMonnies, Frederick William (b. Brooklyn, N.Y., Sept. 28, 1863—d. March 22, 1937), sculptor. A pupil of AUGUSTUS SAINT-GAUDENS (1880–1884), he studied in Paris, where he won the Prix d'Atelier. He also won a medal in the Salon of 1891 for his statues of Nathan Hale and James Stranahan. His greatest fame came from his creation of the *MacMonnies' Fountain,* one of the sensations of the Chicago World's Fair of 1893. This was an immense boat-shaped sculpture laden with mythological figures, cherubs, caryatids and oarswomen. Later, in addition to a number of busts, figures, and equestrian statues, he produced several other massive groups: *The Wild Horses* and *The Horse Tamers* at Prospect Park, Brooklyn, and the one hundred and thirty foot *Marne Monument* near Meaux, France. The size, power, and detail of MacMonnies' work gave him immediate popularity, but the pagan exuberance of some pieces aroused controversy. Both *Bacchante,* commissioned for the Boston Public Library, and *Civic Virtue,* commissioned for New York's City Hall Park, had to be withdrawn after violent public protest. MacMonnies is recognized as one of the most important sculptors of his era and an artist with a permanent place in the academic tradition of American sculpture.

McMurtrie, Douglas Crawford (b. Belmar, N.J., July 20, 1888—d. Sept. 29, 1944), typographer. McMurtrie was on the staff of various firms until he founded his own organization in 1924. In 1927 he became director of typography of the Ludlow Typograph Co. and remained with it till his death. He was an honored figure in the world of publishing and learning, and published a great many books in his special field. Among them were *The Corrector of the Press in the Early Days of Printing* (1922); *American Type Design* (1924); *Alphabets* (1926); *Jean Guttemberg* (1926); *Type Design* (1927); *Book Decoration* (1928); *Modern Typography and Layout* (1929); *Printers' Marks* (1930); *Beginnings of the American Newspaper* (1935); *History of Printing in the U.S.* (1936); *The Book—The Story of Printing and Bookmaking* (1937); *Wings for Words: The Story of the Gutenberg Documents* (1941); *Lincoln's Religion* (1936); *The Invention of Printing: A Bibliography* (1942); besides a number of books on the history of printing in various states.

McNulty, John (b. Lawrence, Mass., 1896[?] —d. July 29, 1956), newspaperman, essayist, humorist. McNulty worked for the Lawrence *Tribune*, the Associated Press, the *Ohio State Journal*, the Pittsburgh *Press*, and *Time* magazine, but did not attract wide notice until he began contributing a series of sketches about Third Ave., New York City, to the *New Yorker*. These were chiefly reports of McNulty's observations in his favorite saloon; they were collected in *Third Avenue* (1946). Other adventures, recorded in *A Man Gets Around* (1951), concerned Bellevue Hospital, the horse-breeding regions of Kentucky, and Ireland. McNulty was effortlessly funny, perhaps because a good deal of the time he didn't try to be so. He also wrote *My Son Johnnie* (1955), a touching examination of the relationship between a father and a small boy. *The World of John McNulty* (1957) is a posthumous selection of his stories and articles.

McPheeters, Jaimie. See THE TRAVELS OF JAIMIE MCPHEETERS.

Macrae, David (b. Scotland, 1837—d. 1907), minister, missionary. Macrae visited America twice and wrote two books about his trips, *The Americans at Home* (1870; reprinted in the United States in 1952) and *America Revisited and Men I Have Met* (1908). He records his interviews with public men and authors, his observations on the post-Civil War South, and so on.

McSpadden, J[oseph] Walker (b. Knoxville, Tenn., May 13, 1874—d. Feb. 9, 1960), editor, historian, biographer. McSpadden was a reliable popularizer of historical data. He first engaged in editorial work in 1898, and published his first book, *Shakespearean Synopses*, in 1902. Among his other books: *Stories from Dickens* (1906); *Book of Holidays* (1917); *Theodore Roosevelt* (1923); *Stories from Great Operas* (1923); *Romantic Stories of the States* (12 titles, 1926–29); *How They Carried the Mail* (1930); *Storm Center* (a novel about Andrew Johnson, 1947). Two of his most valuable books, *Opera Synopses* (1911; rev. ed., 1935) and *Light Opera and Musical Comedy* (1936), were combined in a single thoroughly revised volume, OPERAS AND MUSICAL COMEDIES (1946).

MacSparran, James (b. England, 1693—d. 1757), clergyman. This Anglican minister came to Rhode Island in 1721 and became embroiled in theological arguments. The Calvinists attacked his book on *The Sacred Dignity of the Christian Priesthood Vindicated* (1751). His *America Dissected* (1753) is a description of the colonies in letter form.

McTeague (1899), a novel by FRANK NORRIS. One of the first naturalistic novels in America, *McTeague* treats the gradual degeneration of a stupid, but initially harmless, giant of a man whose instincts are nearer brute than human. McTeague practices dentistry without a licence in a poor section of San Francisco's Polk Street, and marries a girl who has just won $5,000 in a lottery. He soon loses his job and takes to drink. His wife, Trina, becomes a miser. He murders her in a fit of rage and steals her money but is tracked down and killed by her cousin. Many critics consider *McTeague* to be the finest naturalistic novel prior to the work of Dreiser. See NATURALISM.

MacVeagh, Lincoln (b. Narragansett Pier, R.I., Oct. 1, 1890—   ), publisher, diplomat, editor. MacVeagh served on the staff of Henry Holt & Co. and became president of the Dial Press (1923–33). He then entered the diplomatic service. With his wife, Margaret MacVeagh, he wrote *Greek Journey* (1937). He edited *The New Champlin Cyclopedia for Young Folks* (1924, 1925, 1930) and *Poetry from the Bible* (1925).

McWilliams, Carey (b. Steamboat Springs, Colo., Dec. 13, 1905—   ), lawyer, sociologist, public official, biographer, editor. McWilliams wrote some notable and frank books on the subject of racial minorities: *Brothers Under the Skin* (1943); *Prejudice* (on Japanese in the United States, 1944); and *A Mask for Privilege: Anti-Semitism in America* (1948). Each book is based on careful research and maintains the thesis that while prejudice cannot be outlawed by legislation, discrimination can be. McWilliams has also written *Southern California Country* (1946); *California: The Great Exception* (1949); *Witch Hunt: The Revival of Heresy* (1950).

Macy, John [Albert] (b. Detroit, Mich., April 10, 1877—d. Aug. 26, 1932), critic, literary historian, editor. Macy was literary editor of the Boston *Herald* (1913–14), of *The Nation* (1922–23). He had radical social views which influenced his judgment of trends and authors. His book on *The Spirit of American Literature* (1913) was epoch making in its attitude toward the figures reverently accepted by critics before him. He urged that we no longer put up with names that "persist by the inertia of reputation." He reviewed sixteen major authors from Irving to James and made a plea for regionalism and the use of native materials. He also wrote *Socialism in America* (1916); *The Story of the World's Literature* (1925); *About Women* (1930). His wife, Anne Sullivan Macy, was the teacher of HELEN KELLER.

Madame Butterfly (*Century Magazine*, January, 1898), a short story by JOHN LUTHER

Long, the basis for a drama by Long and Belasco (1900) and the opera (1906) by Giacomo Puccini (1858–1924). It is the story of a young Japanese woman who is tricked into believing she is the wife of an American naval officer; he deserts her and she commits suicide.

Madame Delphine (1881), a novelette by George Washington Cable. A quadroon, devoted to her almost-white daughter, attempts to assure her a happy marriage by telling her she is really the child of white parents. It did not please Southern readers opposed to miscegenation. Together with other stories on similar themes, it was responsible for the harsh treatment which drove Cable to leave the South.

Made in America (1948), a discussion of the arts in the United States by John A. Kouwenhoven. Kouwenhoven describes America as the evolution of a tremendous technological civilization established by a democratic people. Involved in this development has been a conflict between the cultivated and the vernacular. Yet Kouwenhoven firmly believes that the development of the American spirit was such that even in the field of mechanisms our products have been aesthetically superior. He emphasizes the role that humor and the American spirit of irreverence have played in "the process of clearing the ground for new growth," and holds that our vivid colloquialisms originated not on the frontier, as H. L. Mencken maintained, but in industry and technology.

Madeleva, Sister Mary. See Mary Evaline Wolff.

Madison, Charles A. See Critics and Crusaders.

Madison, Dolly [Payne Todd] (b. Guilford Co., N.C., May 20, 1768—d. July 12, 1849), wife of James Madison, memoirist. Mrs. Madison's personal recollections were published as *Memoirs and Letters* (1886). A full and authoritative biography was written by Katharine Anthony (1949). After marrying James Madison in 1794, she became an increasingly important social figure in Washington. She was the unofficial "first lady" of the widower Jefferson's administration, and the official White House hostess after her husband's inauguration in 1809. She survived her husband for more than thirteen years. She came back to Washington in 1837 as a social leader. Her means were scanty, and Congress bought some of her husband's papers for $30,000, and others, in 1848, for $25,000. She sent the first personal message over S. F. B. Morse's telegraph wires. Her domination of Washington society and her political influence has made her a popular figure in biographies and historical romances. She may be the original of the heroine of Henry Adams' Democracy, his novel about Washington society and politics.

Madison, James (b. Port Conway, Va., March 16, 1751—d. June 28, 1836), public official, pamphleteer, 4th President. Madison attended Princeton (then called the College of New Jersey) and was there converted to the doctrines of the Enlightenment and to 18th-century politi-

cal radicalism. He helped to organize the American Whig Society and became intimate with a circle that included Philip Freneau and Hugh Henry Brackenridge. When the war broke out, Madison was made chairman of the

Virginia Committee of Safety and wrote its resolutions against the British. He wrote pamphlets and was elected to the Virginia Constitutional Convention in 1776. As a member of George Mason's Committee to Prepare a Bill of Rights, he revised Mason's clause on religious freedom. He was a member of the first Virginia Assembly held under the new constitution, a member of the Governor's Council, a member of the Continental Congress (1780–83). Madison's energy, ability, and integrity were recognized by his fellow members, and he was given various important tasks. In 1784 he was back in the Virginia Assembly, and helped to secure there the passage of Jefferson's bill for religious freedom.

Madison's association with Thomas Jefferson was constantly close. Both men were outstanding exemplars of the Enlightenment, both of a philosophic turn of mind, both practical enough to know when to leave theory and consistency behind. Between them they made the Constitution what it is, especially in the provisions of the Bill of Rights. Madison's labor at the Constitutional Convention (1787) was monumental; historians today believe that he had more to do with framing the Constitution than anyone else. He devised a new type of federal state which rested solidly on majority rule while providing adequate safeguards for minorities. He won an unexpected triumph against Patrick Henry in the Virginia ratifying convention (1788) when the latter opposed the adoption of the Constitution. He contributed perhaps twenty-nine papers to THE FEDERALIST in a further attempt to get the Constitution adopted.

Madison became a member of Congress and, fearful of ALEXANDER HAMILTON's attempts to build a financial oligarchy, founded with Jefferson the Republican (later called the Democratic) Party. He is believed to have written Washington's first Inaugural Address and framed the House's reply and the responses of Washington to both the Senate and the House. Washington also consulted him about his Farewell Address. In 1794 Madison married the efficient and gracious widow Mrs. Dolly Payne Todd (see DOLLY MADISON), and in 1797 he retired from Congress. After Jefferson's election he became an able Secretary of State for his friend.

Madison was elected President in 1808, reelected in 1812. He endeavored to continue Jefferson's policies, but did not prove an able administrator. His foreign policy completely miscarried when his attempts to resist British aggression on the sea by enforcing an embargo led to the second war with England (1812–15), called by many angry citizens "Mr. Madison's War." In the later years of his administration he advocated tariff protection and a strong army.

Madison spent his last years on his estate at Montpelier, where he prepared for publication his notes on the Constitutional Convention. He was a constant supporter of the African Colonization Society, which founded Liberia, and was aware that the "dreadful calamity" of Negro slavery was incompatible with the principles of equality and freedom.

Madison's papers and writings were collected by Gaillard Hunt in *The Writings of James Madison, His Public Papers and His Private Correspondence* (9 v., 1900–1910). Writings and letters not collected by Hunt appear in other compilations. A separate edition of Madison's Constitutional Convention *Journal* was prepared by Hunt (2 v., 1908). His *Autobiography* was published in the *William and Mary Quarterly*, 1945. The fullest biography of Madison is that prepared in six volumes by Irving Brant, beginning 1941. Earlier treatments of Madison include a life by Hunt (1902) and Henry Adams' *History of the U. S. of America During the Administration of Jefferson and Madison* (9 v., 1889–91; reprinted, 1930). This is unfriendly, and—in Brant's judgment—unfair to Madison. Saul K. Padover edited *Liberty* (1950), a compilation of essays on the subject by Madison, and an anthology, *The Complete Madison* (1953). Editions of *The Federalist* lay varying stress on Madison's contributions. Adrienne Koch analyzed well *Jefferson and Madison: The Great Collaboration* (1950). Madison had no gift for striking phraseology; his literary talent was for lucidity and common sense. Novelists have found little in his career to inspire stories. He appears casually in Elizabeth Page's *The Tree of Liberty* (1939). The

sixth and final volume of Irving Brant's biography, *James Madison, Commander in Chief 1812–1836*, came out in 1961.

Madoc [**Madog ab Owain Gwynedd**] (1150[?]–1180[?]), a Welsh prince who according to old Welsh legends sailed with ten ships westward and discovered America, supposedly around 1170. Zella Armstrong, in her *Who Discovered America? The Amazing Story of Madoc* (1950), describes her collation of many references and passages in old texts and her resulting conviction that Madoc actually did cross the Atlantic and that his party left descendants here—certain blue-eyed Indians who have long puzzled anthropologists. One explorer, George Catlin, believed that the Mandans were descendants of Welsh immigrants. Robert Southey wrote an epic poem called *Madoc* (1805), which told how the Welsh chieftain sailed to America and founded a settlement, after defeating a local tribe called "Aztecas."

Madonna of the Future, The (*Atlantic Monthly*, March, 1873; in *Madonna of the Future and Other Tales*, 1879), a story by HENRY JAMES. It concerns an artist who never manages to paint his "perfect madonna," although he has dreamed of it for twenty years. F. O. Matthiessen saw in this story of an artist's frustration the expression of an anxiety that James himself felt when in the 1870's his health continued to be frail and he feared that he might never be able to complete his life's work. When the manuscript of the story was submitted to William Dean Howells for publication in the *Atlantic*, he objected to its length and to two of its episodes, which were forthwith omitted. James did not restore the rejected episodes when he reprinted the story later.

Magarac, Joe. Joe is believed to be the first legendary American hero invented by an immigrant group, the Hungarian and Slavic steel-mill workers of the Pittsburgh region; he is to them what PAUL BUNYAN is to the lumbermen. His name has become a term still applied to any man who is an especially hard worker. Owen Francis seems to have been the first to put the Magarac stories into writing, in *The Saga of Joe Magarac: Steelman* (*Scribner's Magazine*, November, 1931).

magazines. The magazines of colonial America not only were periodicals published by English settlers on a British frontier, but were frank imitations of the new and increasingly popular monthly miscellanies of the mother country. Nine years after England's first successful general monthly, the *Gentleman's Magazine*, was begun in 1731, dynamic young Benjamin Franklin was making plans to demonstrate to his countrymen on both sides of the Atlantic that such a publication could originate in the New World. This wish to exhibit American culture to the world, and especially to Britain, was transformed during and after the Revolution into a passion for developing and displaying at home and abroad a national American culture. Motives were not wholly altruistic, however; for publishers then and thereafter always had the hope, often ill founded, of making money from their ventures.

How ill founded these hopes were is shown by the fact that the sixteen magazines (nine monthlies and seven weeklies) issued before the Revolution had an average life of ten months. Though the first project for an American magazine was Franklin's, his plans were betrayed to his rival printer in Philadelphia, Andrew Bradford, who managed to get his AMERICAN MAGAZINE [1] out three days before Franklin's GENERAL MAGAZINE; both were dated January, 1741, though they were issued in mid-February. Published on the eve of the Revolution was Isaiah Thomas' *Royal American Magazine* (1774–75), with notable patriot cartoons engraved on copper by Paul Revere. Only two monthlies were issued (for limited terms) during the Revolution; both appeared in Philadelphia and both enjoyed distinguished literary editorship. Thomas Paine was editor for seven months of the *Pennsylvania Magazine* (1775–76) and Hugh Henry Brackenridge edited the *United States Magazine* throughout 1779.

In the last fifteen years of the 18th century (1786–1800), 71 magazines were begun, including 27 weekly miscellanies. They ranged from Maine to South Carolina, though Philadelphia was the leading publication center. Of the 71, only 15 lived for more than two years and only seven for more than five. Indeed, the average life of the magazines founded in the 18th century extended to only twenty months. "The expectation of failure is connected with the very name of a Magazine," observed brave Noah Webster as he began his own AMERICAN MAGAZINE [2] (1787–88).

The early monthlies were commonly modeled upon English prototypes, small octavo in size, with some 64 pages printed on the durable rag paper of the times, often with some advertising on the flimsy covers and occasionally with sparse illustration by woodcuts or copper plates. Probably three-fourths of the content was borrowed from books, pamphlets, newspapers, and other magazines. The Addisonian essay was a chief stock in trade; though these were borrowed right and left, some were notable original contributions, as CHARLES BROCKDEN BROWN's first identified work, "The Rhapsodist," in the *Columbian Magazine* and JOSEPH DENNIE's early essays in the *Farmer's Museum*, of Walpole, Vermont. Poetry, reprinted and original, was found in virtually all 18th-century magazines. Mathew Carey's *American Museum* (1787–92), perhaps the best of the magazines of its century, furnished a good anthology of early American poetry. Forerunners of the American short story are found in tales and "fragments" of the English "sensibility" and Gothic schools. Religion, news and discussions of public affairs, and science (medicine, agriculture, meteorology) held important places in the varied offerings of these magazines.

At the turn of the century Charles Brockden Brown, often called America's first man of letters, attempted four periodicals—two in New York and two in Philadelphia—but failed to win public favor for any of them; most successful of the four was the *Literary Magazine and American Register* (1803–07). The shining light of those years was Joseph Dennie's weekly PORT FOLIO (1801–27), of Philadelphia, in which that brilliant essayist discussed manners and politics with gusto—the latter from an extreme Federalist point of view.

Greatest among representatives of the review type of periodical in all the history of American journalism was the NORTH AMERICAN REVIEW (1815–1940), edited for the first half of its long life by a succession of Harvard scholars. The *North American* was for some years a participant in the third war with England—the "paper war." A considerable part of this wordy conflict was devoted to defense of the young American literature against sneers by the English Tory reviews. The famous query of Sydney Smith in the *Edinburgh Review* in 1820, "In the four quarters of the globe, who reads an American book?" continued to aggravate the tempers of American critics for nearly a hundred years. Articles by Edward Everett in the *North American* were that review's main contributions in defense of the new nationalism; but Robert Walsh, editor of a heavy Philadelphia journal called *American Quarterly Review* (1827–37), was a kind of generalissimo in the war.

Philadelphia's *Analectic Magazine* (1813–21) was chiefly notable for the brief editorship (1813–14) of Washington Irving.

With improvements in the mechanics of printing and papermaking, together with what has been called "the rise of the common man," the 1830's saw the beginnings of the first great monthlies of general circulation. GRAHAM's MAGAZINE (1826–58) of Philadelphia was distinguished in literary content and in illustration, and it set a new standard of liberal payment for contributions. The KNICKERBOCKER MAGAZINE (1833–65) was New York's most famous magazine of this period, with a list of contributors rivaling that of *Graham's*. Chief southern magazine of these years was the SOUTHERN LITERARY MESSENGER (1834–64), of Richmond, Virginia, edited by Edgar Allan Poe from 1835 to 1837. These magazines were well printed and usually ran to ninety-six pages or more.

The *Democratic Review* (1837–59) and the *American Whig Review* (1845–52), though largely political, offered a considerable amount of literary material. The former published some twenty-five pieces by Hawthorne, early tales by Walter (*sic*) Whitman, and work by Bryant, Whittier, Longfellow, and Lowell during its uneven history. Its shorter-lived Whig contemporary offered Poe, Bryant, Lowell, and Greeley, as well as such political leaders as John Quincy Adams, Daniel Webster, and John C. Calhoun.

Important quarterlies of these years were the DIAL [1] (1840–44), Boston exponent of New England transcendentalism, edited successively by Margaret Fuller and Ralph Waldo Emerson; and the *Southern Quarterly Review* (1842–57).

The latter was founded in New Orleans, but soon moved to Charleston, South Carolina, and its last few numbers were issued from Columbia, in that state. William Gilmore Simms was editor of the *Southern* from 1849 to 1855. The commercial organ of the South, and to some extent that section's political spokesman and literary voice, was *De Bow's Review* (1846–80) of New Orleans. The *Massachusetts Quarterly Review* (1847–50) was edited by Emerson, Theodore Parker, and J. Elliot Cabot, and was devoted mainly to politics and literary criticism; it was once dubbed "the *Dial* with a beard."

Though several 18th-century magazines definitely catered to women readers, the first to be specifically designed for them was the *Ladies' Magazine* (1792–93) of Philadelphia. But the first successful women's magazine, and, indeed, the most successful of all ante-bellum magazines (reaching 150,000 circulation by 1860) was GODEY'S LADY'S BOOK (1830–98), notable for its fashion plates but also for its literary fare. Though its fiction and verse often seemed sentimental in what later critics thought a ridiculous degree, its liberal pay schedule brought to its pages most of the leading American authors. The chief competitor of *Godey's* for many years was *Peterson's Ladies' National Magazine* (1842–98), long edited by Mrs. Ann S. Stephens, prolific author of serial fiction.

The urban miscellany designed for weekend reading became popular early in the 19th century. Nearly every city in the land had one or more of them in the first two-thirds of that century. They carried some news, usually emphasizing local society, sports, and amusements; but in the hands of able, idiosyncratic editors they might turn to emphasis on politics, literature of special type, or some specialized interest. Their popularity increased toward mid-century, and in 1852 Philadelphia had no less than sixteen of them. Longest-lived was the SATURDAY EVENING POST, founded in 1821 by Charles Alexander and S. C. Atkinson, two Philadelphia printers. This periodical enjoyed great success in the forties and fifties, when it published the most popular English and American writers of serial fiction and shorter pieces by several distinguished authors, thereby achieving a national circulation. After the Civil War Sunday editions of daily newspapers put many of the urban weekenders out of business; and the *Post* declined slowly toward bankruptcy until Cyrus H. K. Curtis purchased it in 1897 and brought it to what seemed like a national institution under George Horace Lorimer's editorship, 1899–1936.

Another urban miscellany of the original *Post* type was the distinguished *New York Mirror* (1823–57), edited mainly by George Pope Morris, now remembered, if at all, by his lines beginning, "O woodman, spare that tree!" and Nathaniel Parker Willis, poet and essayist. The NEW YORK LEDGER (1847–1903) was a story-paper not originally designed for weekend reading, but after the war it changed its publication day from Monday to Saturday. It reached an extraordinary popularity (it claimed 400,-000 circulation in 1860) by featuring the serials of Mrs. E. D. E. N. Southworth and Sylvanus Cobb and through the inspired advertising of Robert Bonner, its publisher. High prices lured into *Ledger* pages such contributors as Bryant, Longfellow, Mrs. Stowe, Greeley, and Everett. The SATURDAY PRESS (1838–66) was the organ of the PFAFF'S CELLAR group in New York, among whom its editor, Henry Clapp, reigned as "prince of the Bohemians." It printed early Walt Whitman poems and Mark Twain's "Jumping Frog" story.

Later distinguished examples of the weekly of parochial design were the San Francisco papers *Argonaut* (1877–   ) and WASP (1876–1935); Ambrose Bierce enlivened the former with his column for its first two years, and then transferred to the latter, where he could sting with less constraint. *Reedy's Mirror* (1891–1920) of St. Louis is best remembered for its introduction of a rising group of midwestern writers, and particularly for its publication of Edgar Lee Masters' *Spoon River Anthology* pieces (see THE MIRROR). The NEW YORKER (1925–   ) was a latecomer in the class of urban weeklies. Harold Ross, its editor until his death in 1951, declared at the beginning that his magazine was "avowedly published for a metropolitan audience," though he expected "a considerable national circulation" for it. A great national circulation was achieved, partly because New York is regarded by many as the cultural capital of the nation, and partly because of the editors' uncanny ability to attract and choose good writing on a great variety of subjects that appeal to the cultivated reader.

Returning to the field of the general monthly, we may note a new era in magazine publishing with the founding of HARPER'S NEW MONTHLY MAGAZINE in 1850. Its great success (it soon reached 200,000 circulation) was based largely on its copious illustration by woodcuts and its serial use of the work of the English novelists so popular in America at the mid-century. Though several cheaper magazines undertook for brief periods competition with *Harper's* in the new pattern, not for twenty years did another great book-publishing house challenge *Harper's* on even terms; then *Scribner's Monthly* (1870–1930), using the same lavish illustration but more American materials, became a powerful rival. In 1881 it broke away from Charles Scribner's Sons and was published as the CENTURY ILLUSTRATED MONTHLY MAGAZINE. Scribners kept out of the magazine field for five years as bound by its contract when it sold its *Monthly*, then established SCRIBNER'S MAGAZINE (1886–1939), an illustrated monthly of high quality. Another illustrated periodical issued by a New York book-publishing house was *Appleton's Journal* (1869–81). Though founded as a weekly, it turned to monthly publication in 1876. With a great variety of comments on manners and on the arts, it also published serials by English, French, and German writers, many engravings of American scenery on steel, and woodcut fold-ins of metropolitan subjects.

Meanwhile, three other book-publishing firms undertook monthly magazines of a high level, but without emphasis on illustration. PUTNAM'S MONTHLY MAGAZINE (1853–57) was, for its first three years at least, the best all-round quality magazine ever published in America. George William Curtis, Parke Godwin, Long-fellow, Thoreau, Melville, and Cooper were frequent contributors. But the competition of the times briefly drove Putnam's out of this field; after the war it issued a second series, *Putnam's Magazine* (1868–70), a brief and less brilliant attempt, followed many years later by a third series (1906–10) which was an illustrated literary-review type of magazine.

Second of the quality monthlies without illustration to appear in the mid-century era was the ATLANTIC MONTHLY (1857–   ), issued for its first half-century by a succession of Boston book publishers. It enjoyed distinguished editorship, beginning with that of James Russell Lowell. Its roll of contributors included most of the leading American authors, and its literary standards were high. By the 1960's the *Atlantic* and *Harper's* were the only survivors of the famous "quality magazines" of the 19th century.

The *Galaxy* (1866–78) was a kind of New York *Atlantic*, notable for its publication of the work of Henry James, Mark Twain, Richard Grant White, Anthony Trollope, and Justin Mc-Carthy. LIPPINCOTT'S MAGAZINE (1868–1916) of Philadelphia was a good monthly with a varied history. It printed many leading writers, with some emphasis on the South and Midwest; it used some illustration until 1885, when it adopted the policy of printing an entire novel (or novelette) in each number. The OVERLAND MONTHLY (1868–1935) of San Francisco was first edited briefly by Bret Harte; though a good literary magazine during most of its long life, it was later much given to regional promotion. The *Chautauquan* (1880–1914) was the organ of the Chautauqua Literary and Scientific Circle, and in its early years gave much of its space to readings for that great organization for adult education; eventually it introduced greater variety, with strong emphasis on public affairs.

Henry Carter was born in Ipswich, county seat of Suffolk, England, the son of a glovemaker who was unsympathetic with the boy's inclinations toward art. But Henry smuggled out some drawings to the London *Illustrated News* which were published under the name "Frank Leslie." Some years later he got away to London, there to learn the engraver's art; and when he was twenty-seven, he came to America, soon becoming chief engraver for *Gleason's Pictorial Drawing-Room Companion* (1851–59), America's first successful picture paper. Still working as "Frank Leslie," which became his legal name in 1857, he began publishing periodicals of his own in 1855. These all bore his name in the title, and all were copiously illustrated by woodcuts. They were in various fields—women's journals, juveniles, comics, etc. Most famous and longest-lived were *Frank Leslie's Illustrated Newspaper* (1855–1922) and *Frank Leslie's*

Popular Magazine (1876–1956). (See FRANK LESLIE.) The *Illustrated Newspaper* was the first important illustrated news weekly in the United States. Its pictorial coverage of the Civil War was notable. After the mid-nineties it flourished as *Leslie's Weekly*, using large pictures, short articles on general news events, personalities, sports, the theater, and humor. The monthly *Popular* became the AMERICAN MAGAZINE [5] in 1906, surviving for half a century thereafter as a good popular magazine. As for Frank Leslie, he speculated in real estate and went bankrupt in the depression of the mid-seventies; several of the dozen periodicals he was then publishing were discontinued, and he died in 1880. His wife, a remarkable woman of business acumen and energy, herself thereupon took the name "Frank Leslie" and carried on for some years with six of the original Leslie periodicals.

Begun shortly after Leslie's *Illustrated Newspaper* was HARPER'S WEEKLY (1857–1916), also distinguished for copious illustration of current events, but conducted on a higher literary level; moreover, its succession of great editors made it an important journal of opinion for many years. Later entries in this field, combining news, comment, and illustration to make popular weekly miscellanies, were COLLIER'S (1887–1957) and *Liberty* (1924–51); the latter was founded by the McCormick-Patterson newspaper organization and very popular for several years. *Collier's* was begun as *Once A Week* by Peter F. Collier and wielded no little influence under the editorship of such men as Norman Hapgood (1902–12) and William L. Chenery (1925–43).

The leading weekly journal of opinion, unsupported by either pictures or fiction, in the later 19th century was the NATION (1865–   ), founded by Edwin Lawrence Godkin, who gave it high standing, though never a large circulation. When he became editor of the New York *Evening Post,* he made it that paper's "weekly edition." It was separated from the *Post* in 1918, under Oswald Garrison Villard's ownership, and it became increasingly liberal in its social and political views. It was in the climate of fresh and radical inquiry represented by this development that the NEW REPUBLIC (1914–   ) was established by Willard D. Straight, with Herbert Croly as editor. Though it has enlisted many brilliant writers, its circulation has always been limited, and it has required subsidies from wealthy liberals to keep it going.

An early monthly of reform views, the *Arena* (1889–1909), conducted by Benjamin O. Flower, was a good index of the increasingly sensitive social conscience of the times. Another important monthly of inquiring disposition was the *Forum* (1886–1940); its long career was uneven, but it was always notable for its symposia on controversial questions. The MASSES (1911–17) was far to the left. It was founded by a group of Greenwich Village socialists and recruited a remarkable company of brilliant writers of essays, fiction, and verse. Barred from the mails during World War I, it reappeared as the Marxist LIBERATOR (1918–24), and later as the *New Masses* (1926–48).

The subject of religion was prominent in most of the early American magazines. Slightly over one-eighth of those published in the 18th century were devoted primarily to religious matters, and eventually every sect was represented not only by a monthly or quarterly review but by weeklies that were either national or regional in scope. Some denominations had a score of periodicals in publication at the same time by the mid-19th century, and by the nineties the Methodists and Baptists, most prolific in periodical literature, each had over a hundred going at one time. The earlier religious weeklies contained much secular news, but with the growth of newspaper circulations, they came to devote themselves mainly to church news and family reading. In the 20th century there were many consolidations and suspensions; Methodist periodicals, for example, were reduced again to about a score. However, in 1960 1,484 publications classified as religious were in course of publication in the United States, including Sunday-school papers and church-society organs; of these 133 were Catholic periodicals.

One of the most important of reviews in the religious field was the Unitarian bimonthly, the CHRISTIAN EXAMINER (1824–69); it was distinguished not only for its exposition of a point of view in theology, but for its literary criticism and its comment on social, philosophical, and educational problems. The CATHOLIC WORLD (1865–   ), founded and conducted for nearly a quarter-century by Isaac T. Hecker, has always been a popular type of review, but one of high standards and a notable list of contributors. Best known of 20th-century Catholic weeklies is the COMMONWEAL (1924–   ), subtitled *A Weekly Review of Literature, the Arts and Public Affairs,* and written largely by laymen.

Two famous Congregational weeklies were the INDEPENDENT (1848–1928) and the OUTLOOK (1870–1935). Among the editors of the former were Henry Ward Beecher, Theodore Tilton, and William Hayes Ward; and of the latter, Beecher and Lyman Abbott. In the early seventies the *Independent,* influenced by its contemporary (founded under the title of *Christian Union*), became more and more a secular miscellany for family reading; and the two weeklies followed that course, together with important commentary on public affairs, for many years.

Two interdenominational weeklies have long been outstanding. The CHRISTIAN HERALD (1878–   ) began as the American edition of a London journal that exploited the sermons of C. H. Spurgeon, and later featured T. DeWitt Talmage's sermons. Its good fiction and lively miscellany have long maintained its leadership in its special field. The *Christian Century* was begun by the Disciples of Christ in 1884 as the *Christian Oracle;* in 1900 it changed its name and soon thereafter declared itself "undenominational." Under able editorship it has long provided a limited readership with thought-ful commentary on social, political, international, and literary matters.

The transition between the old *Godey* type of women's magazine and the modern journals in that field was affected by (1) the dress-pattern business and (2) mail-order advertising. The path well worn by the great quartette comprising *Godey's, Peterson's, Arthur's Home Magazine* (1852–98, long conducted by the author of *Ten Nights in a Bar Room*), and *Frank Leslie's Lady's Magazine* (1857–82), with their colored fashion plates, household hints, and serial fiction, was followed by *Demorest's Monthly Magazine* (1865–99), but with one notable innovation—Demorest stapled tissue-paper dress patterns into each issue. Incidentally, *Demorest's* published many first-rate authors in its literary miscellany, and Editor Jane C. ("Jenny June") Croly made the magazine the organ of Sorosis, the mother of the whole women's-club movement in the United States. MCCALL'S (1873–   ), founded by a New York garment maker under the title *The Queen,* followed the pattern idea, and through a series of inspired changes in magazine design and illustration became by mid-20th century a leading mass-circulation monthly.

The WOMAN'S HOME COMPANION (1874–1957) began in Cleveland, Ohio, supported by mail-order advertising and called simply *The Home.* Purchased after its first decade by the Crowell Publishing Company it became famous for its excellent fiction, lively articles, and good illustration; but it finally perished from the perils of mass circulation, which will be discussed later. Paragon of cheap mail-order journals for the home was *Comfort* (1884–1942) of Augusta, Maine, which gained much of its circulation on its offer of "four years for a dollar," and was America's first million-circulation magazine, reaching that pinnacle in 1895. The LADIES' HOME JOURNAL (1883–   ), offshoot of a farm journal published by Cyrus H. K. Curtis in Philadelphia, also gained its start as a mail-order paper at fifty cents a year, but it improved its standing by paying good authors and offering much advice for home and family; and when it reached its first million circulation in 1903, its annual subscription rate was one dollar.

Three *haut-ton* fashion magazines were notable also for their literary content: HARPER'S BAZAAR (1867–   ) became a Hearst publication in 1936; VOGUE (1892–   ) began as one of the numerous class of urban weeklies of society already referred to, but under Condé Nast as publisher (1909–42) and Edna Woolman Chase as editor (1914–48) it became a magazine of excellent feature articles and a purveyor of the announcements of top stylists and garment makers. It was sold to S. I. Newhouse, the newspaper group owner, in 1959. VANITY FAIR (1913–36), edited by Frank Crowninshield, was a distinguished interpreter of the literature, theater, and arts of its period.

Though magazines for the home often carried juvenile departments, there were some outstanding periodicals designed primarily for children. The YOUTH'S COMPANION (1827–1929) was the most famous of them. Founded by the elder Nathaniel Willis as a rather preachy weekly, under Daniel S. Ford, who was associated in its management for over forty years, it printed not only some of the best fiction for children of its time but many interesting anecdotal articles by famous men and women. ST. NICHOLAS (1873–1943), edited by Mary Mapes Dodge for over thirty years, was a monthly of high quality. The *American Boy* (1899–1941), which absorbed the *Youth's Companion* in 1929, was a somewhat livelier weekly, giving more attention to adventure and sports.

Political satire was connected, throughout the whole of the 19th century, more or less closely with the humor periodicals. They came in with the partisan journalism of the new century and on the whole were a rough lot. Four of them stand out for their high quality. VANITY FAIR [1] (1859–63) was edited for a time by Artemus Ward. PUCK (1877–1918) was distinguished by Joseph Keppler's aggressive political and social cartoons, presented in bold chromolithographs. In general it was Democratic in its sympathies, and so the Republicans took over JUDGE (1881–1947), which also used colored cartoons; eventually this once-respectable weekly was lost in the ruck of low-life peep-show periodicals. LIFE [1] (1883–1936) was the greatest of American satirical weeklies; eschewing both color and political affiliation, it was superior in art, verse, and fiction.

The infinite diversity of our periodical literature is demonstrated by our most famous professional journals. The *Medical Repository* (1797–1824) was edited by Samuel Latham Mitchill and associates in New York; and the *American Journal of Medical Sciences* (1827–   ) was edited for over sixty years by Isaac Hays and his son I. Minis Hays in Philadelphia. The weekly *Journal of the American Medical Association* (1883–   ) has long exerted a powerful influence, and in the 20th century it has enjoyed the largest circulation of any medical journal in the world. The A.M.A. also publishes more than a dozen other journals in specialized fields, while all the state and large city medical societies have their own journals, supported mainly by pharmaceutical advertising. Most notable of early law reviews was the *American Law Journal* (1808–17) of Philadelphia, edited by John E. Hall, who was also a *Port Folio* editor. First of the great university law-school journals was the *Harvard Law Review* (1887–   ); it was followed by important reviews in the field from Columbia, Yale, Pennsylvania, and Michigan. Case reporters attained large circulations. *Green Bag* (1889–1914) was a unique journal devoted to the lighter side of the profession.

A very large and important group of periodicals developed in the latter half of the 19th century to represent the various industries and fields of business in the country. Earliest of these were the farm papers, represented by John S. Skinner's *American Farmer* (1819–73) of Baltimore

and Thomas Green Fessenden's *New England Farmer* (1822–46) of Boston. Later came the *American Agriculturist* (1842–   ), the COUNTRY GENTLEMAN (1853–1955), and the *Farm Journal* (1877–   ), each with its definite quality and complicated history. But by the 1870's it was evident that the varied topographical and weather conditions throughout the country gave an advantage to the many state and regional farm papers that had sprung up. Not a few of these hundreds of agricultural journals had some importance as purveyors of popular literature—essays, poetry, fiction, and humor—and were leaders in more scientific farming operations as well.

Engineering periodicals began with a group of "mechanics' magazines" in the 1820's. The *Scientific American* (1845–   ), long edited by O. D. Munn and A. E. Beach and their sons and grandsons, was a weekly for seventy-six years, then a monthly; its file contains a marvelous history of American invention and scientific ideas. POPULAR SCIENCE MONTHLY (1872–   ), founded by E. L. Youmans to introduce Herbert Spencer to America, was long continued on philosophical lines, but in 1915 turned to the more popular theme of current invention. *Science* (1883–   ) had a brief predecessor founded by Thomas A. Edison, but the new magazine was financed by Alexander Graham Bell and eventually became the official organ of the American Association for the Advancement of Science. Among specialized scientific journals the NATIONAL GEOGRAPHIC MAGAZINE (1888–   ) was notable.

Meanwhile, journals representing leading industries and trades had multiplied. Transportation, mining and oil, communications, construction—all had prosperous and increasingly specialized organs. Trade journals, later called "business papers," underwent tremendous proliferation.

Returning again to the succession of general literary monthlies (a group which most readers intended to denote by the term "magazine"), we find them revolutionized by the advent of the ten-cent magazine in the 1890's. Cheap but excellent half-tone reproduction of photographs that took the place of expensive fine-line engravings on wood, the current "hard times" that worked against the 35- and 25-cent magazines, and a lively editorial leadership that emphasized current events and public affairs all combined to turn public favor away from the older stand-bys and toward McCLURE'S MAGAZINE (1829–1929), John Brisben Walker's COSMOPOLITAN (1886–   ), *Munsey's Magazine* (1889–1929), and *Everybody's*—all selling for 10 or 15 cents. These monthlies quickly built up circulations of some half-million each, with tremendous advertising patronage.

The *Cosmopolitan* under Walker was an exciting and distinguished magazine; in 1905 it was sold to William Randolph Hearst, becoming that newspaper publisher's first venture into the magazine field, and exploited many famous names. Hearst later acquired *The World Today,* which had begun as a news magazine in 1901, later called it *Hearst's International,* but in 1925 merged it in the *Cosmopolitan.* FRANK A. MUNSEY made his debut as editor-publisher-contributor of the *Golden Argosy* (1882–   ), originally a weekly "for boys and girls," later an all-fiction monthly (dropping *Golden* from its title), and still later one of the growing list of "men's magazines." But his great and most successful venture was *Munsey's Magazine*—a failure initially as a weekly, but an overwhelming success soon after it became a fully illustrated general magazine of great variety at ten cents in 1893. *Everybody's* (1899–1930) came on later, to distinguish itself in the "muckraking" movement.

A considerable literature of exposure had developed in such magazines as the *Arena, Forum,* and *North American Review* through the 1890's; but the magazine cult of exposure of corruptions in government, finance, and society began definitely with the unexampled success of the January, 1903, issue of *McClure's,* which contained an installment of Ida M. Tarbell's history of the Standard Oil Company, an article in Lincoln Steffens' series on "The Shame of the Cities," and one of Ray Stannard Baker's exposés of labor-union "rackets." Here, more or less fortuitously, had developed an immensely popular pattern of articles on public affairs, in which *Everybody's, Cosmopolitan, Hearst's International, Collier's, Hampton's Magazine* (1898–1912), and other periodicals joined. In 1906 President Theodore Roosevelt, angered by *Cosmopolitan's* series on "The Treason of the Senate," dubbed the movement "muckraking," after the fable of the man with the muckrake in *Pilgrim's Progress.* (See MUCKRAKING LITERATURE.) The cult of obloquy in the magazines collapsed about 1912, mainly because readers had tired of its sensationalism. H. L. Mencken's AMERICAN MERCURY (1924–   ) was in its heyday a great iconoclast, but not precisely a "muckraker."

"Pulp magazines," so called because they were printed on cheap mechanical-wood-pulp paper, began with *Argosy's* experiment in that kind in 1896. They were without illustration (except occasional line-cuts) and were devoted to Westerns, mysteries, love stories, sports, wonder and horror stories, and such escape literature; they sold for ten cents a number, chiefly at the newsstands, and multiplied exceedingly until rising costs during World War II and the competition of paperback books put an end to the genre. (See the PULPS.) The "true-story" magazine, its pattern set by Bernarr Macfadden's *True Story* in 1919, purported to give true narratives of sensational incidents, particularly those involving sex. *Motion Picture* (1911–   ), eventually a member of the Fawcett group, was the first successful moving picture "fan" magazine, and the forerunner of a large, varied, and generally profitable class of illustrated periodicals, also distributed mainly by newsstands. Some of these degenerated into the vulgar mass of peep-show and "gag" magazines.

Daddy of all such was probably the *National Police Gazette* (1845–   ), which began as a crime reporter and later achieved national circulation (especially in barber shops) based on its pictures of prize fighters and burlesque queens. Comic books, based originally on newspaper comic strips, began their boom in the latter 1930's. Though mainly designed for children, they had a large readership among adults. Their frequent exploitation of crime, sex, and terror brought a considerable degree of regulation by local and state authorities and by the industry itself. This caused some decline in circulation, but at their apogee in the mid-fifties they distributed an estimated 35,000,000 copies a month.

The mid-century group of "men's magazines" began with the success of *Esquire* (1933–   ), which originated as a medium for men's clothing advertising but made a spectacular record by color pictures of ladies with very little clothing indeed (as the Alberto Varga girls); in the later 1940's it dropped this feature and came to rely upon sophisticated articles and fiction by name authors. Most of *Esquire's* herd of imitators were cheaper in content and format. *Playboy* (1953–   ) was based on the early *Esquire* formula. *Argosy* and *True* (1937–   ) turned to the "men's-magazine" class successfully, with sound editorial policies.

Another group, of greater importance from the strictly literary point of view, was made up of the LITTLE MAGAZINES. These were often published outside the metropolitan areas and always disowned a commercial motive. They wanted to survive; but they wanted even more to publish good fiction, poetry, and essays, and to break new literary ground. Among the several hundred "little magazines," not a few have been strikingly eccentric, many have striven for charm in typography and printing, most have had small circulations and short lives. Herbert S. Stone's CHAP-BOOK (1894–98) is often regarded as first of the tribe. Others were Elbert Hubbard's PHILISTINE (1895–1915), Margaret C. Anderson's LITTLE REVIEW (1914–21), John T. Frederick's MIDLAND (1915–33), Alfred Kreymborg's *Others* (1915–19), the Vanderbilt University *Fugitive* (1922–25), and another southerner, the *Double Dealer* (1921–26) of New Orleans. Harriet Monroe's POETRY (1912–   ) of Chicago holds the record for longevity in this class. The DIAL (1880–1929) became a "little magazine" in 1918. By mid-20th century most magazines of this class were sponsored by colleges and universities, as the KENYON REVIEW (1939–   ).

Eclectics had been common among American magazines from the beginning of the 19th century. Most famous was *Littell's Living Age* (1844–1941), which for many years was composed chiefly by excerpts from British periodicals. But it remained for the READER'S DIGEST (1922–   ), applying the abridgment process, spicing its pages with amusing anecdotes and sayings, and using pocket-size format, to make one of the outstanding successes in the history of American magazines.

The LITERARY DIGEST (1890–1938) was also an eclectic, but it was primarily a news magazine, taking the larger part of its content from newspapers. It was a weekly, but Albert Shaw's REVIEW OF REVIEWS (1890–1937) was a monthly and contained many valuable original articles on public affairs. Walter Hines Page's *World's Work* (1900–32) was also a monthly dealing with current events and problems, but noneclectic. All these periodicals, by a series of consolidations, came to rest in the bosom of *Time*.

TIME (1923–   ) was founded by Briton Hadden and Henry R. Luce with the object of presenting each week an orderly, condensed review of the news for intelligent readers. It was a tremendous success. After Hadden's death in 1929, Luce carried on with FORTUNE (1930–   ), a dollar-a-copy magazine of business; the great smash-hit picture weekly LIFE (1936–   ); and the weekly *Sports Illustrated* (1954–   ). *Time* had many imitators, chief of which were two launched in 1933—NEWSWEEK and the *United States News;* the latter, conducted by David Lawrence from Washington, became the *U. S. News and World Report* in 1948. Lawrence's weekly was filled chiefly with articles on national and international affairs, as was Max Ascoli's fortnightly REPORTER, begun in 1949. The SATURDAY REVIEW (first called the *Saturday Review of Literature,* 1924–   ) was an outgrowth of the book-review supplement of the New York *Evening Post;* but after Norman Cousins became editor in 1942, it challenged attention in a variety of currently interesting fields.

By the mid-20th century a certain merging of books and magazines became apparent. Some paperback series began bringing out periodical editions of original work, as NEW WORLD WRITING (1952–   ) in the Mentor Series and *New Short Novels* (1954–   ), issued simultaneously in hard and soft covers by the Ballantine Company. On the other hand the bimonthlies *American Heritage* (1954–   ) and *Horizon* (1958–   ) have been issued with lavish illustration in hard covers. Some reviews, such as the distinguished bimonthly *Annals of the American Academy of Political and Social Science,* have long been issued in both cloth and paper covers. Paperbacks and magazines crowd each other on the newsstands, and the purchasing public tend to regard them as much the same. (See PAPERBACK BOOKS.)

A survey based on *N. W. Ayer & Son's Directory* (1961) shows 8,411 nonnewspaper periodicals being published in 1960. These are divided by *Ayer* into about 900 "classes," and only about 100 are "consumer magazines," devoted to literary miscellany designed for the general public. Nearly all of the latter are more or less specialized—for example, they include the women's group and the men's group.

The total mass audience of readers, however, is no longer a guarantee of success, but an omen of disaster, primarily because a magazine with such a broad base tends to lose its identity. The failure of *Collier's* in 1957, with a circulation of 3,500,000, accented the dilemma. Such a huge mailing list is very expensive to maintain. Furthermore, with spiraling costs, the production of multimillion editions rises to a figure that only a great advertising linage at high rates can meet. But advertisers as a rule do not wish to address a mass audience of all levels and sectors, and so they incline to revolt against the high rates of mass-circulation magazines. This difficulty was partially met in the 1950's by the "split-run" device, allowing advertisers to insert their announcements in circulation sections divided geographically, or by fractions of the total. Nevertheless, the mass audience, which had seemed so necessary for competition with television, remained the "monster" of the modern magazine industry.

FRANK LUTHER MOTT

Maggie: A Girl of the Streets (privately printed, 1893; published, 1896), a novel by STEPHEN CRANE. Appearing six years before Frank Norris' MCTEAGUE, *Maggie* was the first piece of American fiction to truthfully render urban slum life. Rupert Hughes, writing in *Godey's Magazine,* called it "probably the strongest piece of slum writing we have." Crane describes the foredoomed fall of a well-meaning girl reared in an environment of drunkenness and grime. But, unlike much writing of the naturalistic school it influenced, Crane's *Maggie* is artistic, a tone-painting rather than a realistic photograph.

Crane once defined a novel as "a succession of sharply outlined pictures, which pass before the reader like a panorama, leaving each its definite impression." *Maggie*—divided into nineteen chapters or episodes—is a panorama of impressionistic vignettes, disconnected scenes reeled off with much the same jerky, nervous effect that early motion-pictures convey. Not logic but mood defines the relationship of image to image, episode to episode. Bathos and the contrast of contradictory moods form the novel's pattern. Crane's *Maggie* is thus a Bowery version of Flaubert's *Madame Bovary.*

The first edition was published under the pseudonym of Johnston Smith in paper covers early in 1893. The text of the 1893 edition is far more picturesque and melodramatic, and more blasphemous in phrasing, than that of the 1896 revision. It contains a passage that Crane expunged from Chapter 17 in later editions, in which, after Pete's rejection of Maggie, she encounters nine persons indifferent to her plight. *Maggie* and GEORGE'S MOTHER comprised *Bowery Tales,* published posthumously in England in 1900.

Magic Barrel, The (1958), a collection of short stories by BERNARD MALAMUD. With two or three exceptions, the volume is concerned with short powerful episodes concerning New York Jews. In the short-story form Malamud reveals his sensitive gift of characterization even more clearly than in his novels. His sense of the bizarre is shown in the wild Negro angel named Levine; his feel for almost demonic characters in Susskind of "The Last Mohigan" and Salzman of "The Magic Barrel."

Malamud skillfully moves from the grimly natural to the fantastic and supernatural; the world of dreams and that of the real mix in a strange amalgam. In his unusual style—a mixture of plain speech with Yiddish expressions and haunting lyrical outpourings—he is able, despite his insistence on the hard facts of reality, to imply a significant spiritual world just beyond.

Magnalia Christi Americana (1702), a history of the church in New England by COTTON MATHER. The book is in praise of "God's beautiful work," especially "the great achievements of Christ in America," but the display of erudition is at times so childlike that it is obvious Mather expected his readers also to praise the great and beautiful work of Mather. In this huge folio of nearly eight hundred pages, Mather intended to revive the spirit of religion in America. He did not succeed, but he gives a good picture of the settlement, the governors, the leading divines, the Congregational church, the "remarkable providences"—in which God showed what a deep interest He took in the New England churches—and various disturbances, theological and military, such as the wars with the Indians. Mather had three definite themes: the virtues of New England's religious way, the danger of backsliding, and the need for reform. He deals with these in highly rhetorical fashion, embellishing at every point. Barrett Wendell rated the book "among the great works of English literature in the 17th century."

Magnificent Ambersons, The (1918), a novel by BOOTH TARKINGTON which won a Pulitzer Prize. It forms part of a trilogy called *Growth* (1927), which appeared as *The Turmoil* (1915), *The Magnificent Ambersons,* and *The Midlander* (1923). The middle volume tells the story of a snob, his numerous mean actions, his final overthrow. He does a good deal to ruin the life of his mother and of other people, but is at last forgiven—by the author and some of those he has injured. The book also traces the decay of one aristocracy and the rise of another in an American city.

Mahan, Alfred T[hayer]. See INFLUENCE OF SEA POWER UPON HISTORY, *1660–1783.*

Mahicans. The Mahicans were an Indian tribe who occupied both banks of the Hudson River. During the eighteenth century, some of them went into Pennsylvania, some to Stockbridge, Mass.; those in the latter town finally settled in Wisconsin. When James Fenimore Cooper named his famous novel THE LAST OF THE MOHICANS (1826), he was confusing the Mahicans with the Mohegans, a related tribe who lived mostly in Connecticut. Many still reside there near Mohegan or Norwich. Uncas was a Mohegan, but the facts of his life and character varied greatly from Cooper's account.

Mailer, Norman (b. Long Branch, N.J., Jan. 31, 1923—   ), novelist, essayist, journalist.

After graduating from Harvard in 1943, Mailer spent two years with the Army in the Pacific theatre. His experiences as a clerk and as a rifleman provide the background for THE NAKED AND THE DEAD (1948), which became

a best-seller, was made into a movie, and is generally considered the best novel by an American about World War II. His second and third novels, *Barbary Shore* (1951) and *The Deer Park* (1955), were, however, poorly received by the critics. The former has a political theme, the latter is a sensational novel about Hollywood. Mailer has written a stage version of *Deer Park.* Its leading character, Sergius O'Shaugnessy, appears in *Advertisements for Myself on the Way Out,* part of a projected novel presented in the autobiographical collection, *Advertisements for Myself* (1959). The collection also brings together Mailer's early stories, newspaper pieces, and articles like "The White Negro," an analysis of the "hipster" (see BEAT WRITING). Mailer has also written *Deaths for the Ladies* (1962), a collection of poems.

Main Currents in American Thought, an Interpretation of American Literature from the Beginnings to 1920 (3 v., 1927–30), by VERNON LOUIS PARRINGTON. This remarkable work won a Pulitzer Prize when the first two volumes were issued in 1927. The third volume, incomplete at Parrington's death, was edited by E. H. Eby with a memoir of the author. A one-volume edition was issued in 1939.

Maine Woods, The (posthumously published, 1864), an account of three visits to Maine by HENRY D. THOREAU. Thoreau visited Maine in 1846, 1853, and 1857. This volume is a good one for introducing readers to the pleasures of

Thoreau; he intended it to be of practical help to campers. He never completed his work of preparation, and the book is a collection of three essays rather than a unified volume. Thoreau talked to the guides, rivermen, and other men of the Maine wilderness, and gives a good account of them, especially of Joe Polis, a Penobscot Indian.

Mainstream of America, The (1953 and later), edited by LEWIS GANNETT. This series aims to present "history which does not have to be memorized, but which cannot be forgotten," in a style that wins readers without loss of scholarship. Among the contributors are C. S. Forester (*Age of the Fighting Sail*); Clifford Dowdey (*The Land They Fought For*); Stewart Holbrook (*The Age of the Moguls, 1845–1920*); Bruce Lancaster (*The American Revolution, 1750–90*); Irving Stone (*The Far West, 1840–1900*); and George F. Willison (*Peopling the Eastern Shores*).

Main Street (1920), a novel by SINCLAIR LEWIS. This was the book which established Lewis as a genuinely serious writer. Its aim was to capture the American small town (here called GOPHER PRAIRIE, Minn.) *en bloc*—its pretentiousness, its fake gentility, its commercial values, its groping and often hypocritical search for "culture." Carol Kennicott's endeavor to make Gopher Prairie culture-conscious is the theme; Lewis later said that Carol was really himself.

The book is at once a satire and an affectionate portrait. Gopher Prairie is surely a fictional development of Lewis' own home town, Sauk Centre, Minn.; the naïveté of the book's characters, as they pursue the goal of "culture," was in part Lewis' own sense of awe in the presence of intellectual things. The satire is sharp and telling, yet the reader is aware of a kind of grand simplicity in the narration of the story, at least in comparison with the modern masters of European and much other American fiction. Above all the novel is accurate: many critics have pointed out that more can be learned about the American small town of the 1920's from *Main Street* than from all the studies of the sociologists combined.

The book was successfully dramatized (1921) by Harvey O'Higgins and Harriet Ford. It has been reprinted often and is without doubt one of the most influential novels ever published in America. It aroused much controversy in the 1920's; Meredith Nicholson attacked it in an essay called *Let Main Street Alone!* (1921) and Carolyn Wells burlesqued it in *Ptomaine Street, The Tale of Warble Petticoat* (1921). Many imitations were attempted by other novelists. Of all the books written during the post-World War I literary revolt, *Main Street* was the most successful in producing an American self-awareness.

Main-Traveled Roads (1891), a collection of eleven short stories by HAMLIN GARLAND. The stories were among the earliest local color studies, strikingly realistic when compared with the usual romantic fiction of the era. They drew angry criticism that Garland was "a bird willing to foul his own nest." The stories, laid in the Dakotas and Iowa, are often grim in tone. They show the farmer as often the victim of storms and devastating crop pestilences, cut off from ordinary social intercourse, in many instances crushed beneath a mortgage. Occasionally the stories portray good instead of evil, as in *God's Ravens,* an account of the kindliness of village folks to a newspaperman and his wife, and *A Good Fellow's Wife,* an engaging tale of the wife who wins back the confidence of a community where her husband, a banker, has lost all their money by his unwise speculations. Garland collected similar tales in his *Prairie Folks* (1893).

Mair, Charles (b. Lanark Co., Ont., Sept. 21, 1838—d. July 7, 1927), pioneer, government official, poet. He began to write poetry at an early age. His *Dreamland and Other Poems* (1868) received strong praise from Canadian critics, an unusual occurrence in that age of national doubt. His most famous work, *Tecumseh* (1886), describes the western movement of the white man. All of Mair's poetry shows a strong attachment to the soil and to the American pioneers. He has been praised in Canada as "the originator of our nature school of verse," and is also credited with having strongly influenced western immigration. He worked for the Dominion Immigration Service for many years. In 1891 appeared *The Last Bison,* and in 1908 *Through the Mackenzie Basin,* a travel book. His major works were republished in 1926 by John W. Garvin, together with a memoir by Robert Norwood in volume 14 of *Master Works of Canadian Authors.*

Major, Charles ["Edwin Caskoden"] b. Indianapolis, Ind., July 25, 1856—d. Feb. 13, 1913), lawyer, legislator, novelist. Major delighted in reading history as a relief from his law practice and his work as a public official. He produced a novel of the early Tudor period in England, WHEN KNIGHTHOOD WAS IN FLOWER (published, 1898, under the pen name Edwin Caskoden), which tapped a public desire for historical romance and became an immense success. It was immediately and widely imitated. Major continued writing and produced one more best seller, *Dorothy Vernon of Haddon Hall* (1902), but his other works were less successful.

Makemie, Francis (b. Ireland, 1658[?]—d. 1708), clergyman, missionary, pamphleteer. Makemie, sometimes called "the father of American Presbyterianism," came to America in 1683 and subsequently organized the first American presbytery. He engaged in many controversies. Attacked by GEORGE KEITH, founder of the so-called "Christian Quakers" or Keithians, he wrote *An Answer to George Keith's Libel* (1694). When he was attacked by the Anglican clergy, his reply was given in *Truths in a New Light* (1699). In England on a money-collecting mission, he issued *A Plain and Friendly Persuasive to the Inhabitants of Virginia and Maryland for Promoting Towns and Cohabita-*

tion (1705). Later he was fined for preaching without a license and thereupon wrote *A Narrative of a New and Unusual American Imprisonment* (1707), as a result of which he was exonerated.

Making of Americans, The (1925), a composition by GERTRUDE STEIN. Spoken of sometimes as a novel, sometimes as "the alleged history of a family's progress," this lengthy production seems to some one of Miss Stein's more intelligible books. She composed it around 1906–08, but no publisher wanted it, and it accumulated dust for twenty years. Supposedly it deals with the wanderings and experiences, mainly mental, of three generations of Miss Stein's family, but it is also supposedly the progress of everybody else. The style has many of Miss Stein's characteristic devices, particularly repetition. There is no dialogue, no action. When ERNEST HEMINGWAY first came under Miss Stein's influence, she set him to copying *The Making of Americans* for publication in Ford Madox Ford's *Transatlantic Review* and later to correcting the proofs. Hemingway is said to have stated that he learned much from this task.

Making of an American, The (1901), an autobiography by JACOB A. RIIS. Riis came to the United States from Denmark in 1870, became a police reporter, and was shocked by conditions he found in New York City slums. He wrote vigorously on the subject, attracted the attention of Theodore Roosevelt, and won his support. Riis gives a vivid account of his life in this volume, first published serially in the *Outlook*.

Malaeska, The Indian Wife of the White Hunter (1860), a novel by ANN S. STEPHENS. Well known in New York literary circles, Mrs. Stephens has gone down in fame as the first to write a Beadle Dime Novel. It sold 300,000 copies the first year, and encouraged her and others to continue producing stories for this library. See ERASTUS BEADLE.

Malamud, Bernard (b. Brooklyn, N.Y., Apr. 26, 1914—   ), novelist, short-story writer. He studied at City College of New York and Columbia University. Although he has written about a number of subjects—his first book, *The Natural* (1952), is a fantastical novel about a baseball player—Malamud's favorite subjects are impoverished American Jews: shopkeepers, shoemakers, salesmen, etc. He is not a genre writer in the ordinary sense, however, for he brings to his work distinction of style, a universalizing moral imagination, and, to a rare degree, the polar qualities of compassion and humor. Malamud is concerned with that part of the Jewish tradition which delineates what might be called "the humanism of the unfortunate"—a sense of how grief, pity, conscience, dogged suffering, and an inescapable, if reluctant, feeling of fraternity can culminate in an affirmation of the value of life and the human spirit. Complementing and conditioning this vision, and derived from the same tradition, is a strong sense of the sad and comic persistence of racial types and specific racial tragedies and an imagination which realizes itself alternately in poignant realism and bizarre parable. Milton Rugoff once referred to Malamud as a "magic realist," a phrase which suggests some of the qualities which distinguish his second novel, THE ASSISTANT (1957)—the story of an unlucky grocer and his helper—and his collection of short stories, THE MAGIC BARREL (1958), which won the 1959 National Book Award. The novel *A New Life*, which appeared in 1961, is the story of Levin, Malamud's bearded hero from New York, who goes to teach in a college in the Pacific Northwest.

Mallison, Charles ["Chick"], a character created by WILLIAM FAULKNER. The nephew of Gavin Stevens, Chick grows from childhood to young manhood in four of Faulkner's novels; as a child he narrates part of *The Town;* as a sixteen-year-old boy he is instrumental in proving Lucas Beauchamp innocent of murder in INTRUDER IN THE DUST; and as a young man he narrates part of *The Mansion* and is an interested observer in KNIGHT'S GAMBIT.

Malone, Dumas (b. Coldwater, Miss., Jan. 10, 1892—   ), teacher, historian, biographer. After teaching at various universities, Malone became professor of history at Columbia. Among his important services has been his work as editor of the DICTIONARY OF AMERICAN BIOGRAPHY. For many years he devoted himself to the study and interpretation of Jefferson, and published a series of volumes on the third President: *Jefferson the Virginian* (1948); *Jefferson and the Rights of Man* (1951); and *Thomas Jefferson and His World* (1960), with Henry Moscow; with others to follow in a work called collectively *Jefferson and His Times*. Marquis James called Malone's volumes "one of the greatest triumphs in our annals of biography." Malone also wrote *Saints in Action* (1939); *The Interpretation of History* (1943), with four collaborators; *Story of the Declaration of Independence* (1954); and, with Basil Rauch, an exhaustive two-volume history of the United States, *Empire For Liberty* (1960).

Malone, Kemp (b. Minter, Miss., March 14, 1889—   ), teacher, linguist. Malone taught in a high school and several universities before he joined the faculty of Johns Hopkins University. A noted linguistics scholar, he edited an edition of *Beowulf* (1952). Among his other books: *The Literary History of Hamlet* (1923); *The Phonology of Modern Icelandic* (1923); *Ten Old English Poems* (1941); *Studies in Heroic Legend and in Current Speech* (1959). He also edited *Deor* (1933), *Widsith* (1936), and two volumes of the Centennial Edition of Sidney Lanier's writings (1945). In his honor appeared the *Malone Anniversary Studies* (1949). He has also written some skillful verse. DUMAS MALONE is his brother.

Malone, Walter (b. De Soto Co., Miss., Feb. 10, 1866—d. May 18, 1915), lawyer, jurist, poet. Malone practiced law in Memphis, Tenn., also served as a judge. He published eight collections of verse, beginning with *Claribel and Other Poems* (1882). In *Songs of East and West* (1906) appeared his most famous poem, *Opportunity*.

Maloney, Russell (b. Brookline, Mass., June 26, 1910—d. Sept. 3, 1948), editor, broadcaster, essayist. Maloney was tutoring students at Harvard, where he received his bachelor's degree, when he was invited to join the staff of *The New Yorker*. There he wrote and rewrote over 2,500 pieces—anecdotes, sketches, stories, profiles—all marked by his own frequently vitriolic wit. The best were collected in *It's Still Maloney* (1945). After he had resigned from *The New Yorker*, he contributed articles to numerous magazines, wrote book reviews, became a featured principal on the CBS program "Of Men and Books." With his wife, Miriam Battista Maloney, he wrote the book and lyrics for a musical play, *Sleepy Hollow* (1948), based on Washington Irving's story. In collaboration with Eugene Kinkead, Maloney wrote OUR OWN BAEDEKER (1947), seventy-two capsule sketches originally published in *The New Yorker*. Many of his sketches had more than a temporary fame: for example, his satire on *Vogue*, "How to Read a Fashion Magazine," and his account of the man who set out to discover if it was true that, by the law of averages, six chimpanzees pounding six typewriters at random would in a million years type out all the books in the British Museum.

Maltz, Albert (b. Brooklyn, N.Y., Oct. 8, 1908—   ), playwright, short-story writer, novelist, movie script-writer. While studying at Yale with G. P. BAKER, Maltz and a fellowstudent, GEORGE SKLAR, wrote *Merry-Go-Round* (1932), a play on political corruption in New York City that was produced on Broadway, closed for a week in an attempted censorship, and then re-opened because of vigorous public protests. With Sklar, Maltz also wrote *Peace on Earth* (1933), a pacifist play. *Black Pit* (1935) was a play that dealt with a strike in a mining region and the psychology of a strikebreaker. Maltz's drift toward proletarian writing and propaganda is more evident in his fiction: a book of short stories, *The Way Things Are* (1938), and several novels: *The Underground Stream* (1940), *The Cross and the Arrow* (1944), and *The Journey of Simon McKeever* (1949).

His film, *The Pride of the Marines* (1945), had premières in twenty-eight cities at Guadalcanal Day banquets under the auspices of the Marine Corps, and another of his films, *Destination Tokyo* (1943), was adopted as an official training film by the Navy. *The Naked City* appeared in 1948.

Mamba's Daughters (1929), a novel by DUBOSE HEYWARD. This story of Negroes in Charleston, S.C., was turned into an effective melodrama of the same name (1939), by Hayward and his wife Dorothy.

Mammy (1921), a song with words by Sam Lewis and Joe Young, and music by Walter Donaldson, that became very popular in the 1920's, especially as sung by Al Jolson (1888–1950).

Man Against the Sky, The (1916), a poem by EDWIN A. ROBINSON. It was the title-poem in a collection of Robinson's poems that helped to consolidate his fame. Brooding on man's destiny, Robinson examines several philosophies and creeds that attempt to explain this lonely figure against the sky. He is any man—mankind symbolized. The "world on fire" that appears in the second line of the poem is World War I; it is also the sunset that stands for death, and the universe described by modern science. Then Robinson examines five attitudes toward death, and still later presents his own conclusions; Robinson was definitely not a Christian believer and seems to have looked forward to the formulation of some "non-theological religion" revealed by science. So far as one can discover, Robinson's creed is one of stoicism in the face of "the dark tideless floods of Nothingness." The attitude of critics toward the poem has varied decidedly. H. H. Clark speaks of "this rich and majestic poem." Charles Cestre refers to its "Dantesque beauty." Neff sees the affinity of the poem to the great English elegies of the nineteenth century, but he calls it "aggressive," "a mingling of laughter, scorn, and irony with pity and magnificence." Hyatt Howe Waggoner examines it respectfully, but finds it somewhat prosaic. The poem's 314 lines are loose in form, with lines of varying length and irregular rhymes.

Mandan Indians. The Mandans are a tribe belonging to the Sioux linguistic family. They were found in early times along the northern plains, and many explorers visited them, including the painter GEORGE CATLIN. Sickness decimated the tribe; in 1870 survivors settled on the Berthold reservation in North Dakota. Their songs, studied by FRANCES DENSMORE in *Mandan and Hidatsa Music* (1923), are brief, lyrical, often private rather than tribal in character.

Maney, Richard [**Sylvester**] (b. Chinook, Mont., June 11, 1892—d. June 30, 1968), press agent, writer. As an unusually successful theatrical press agent, Maney made himself into a legend. Wolcott Gibbs said that Maney, in his writings for *The New York Times* and other newspapers, sounded like "a circus barker with an Ll.D." Ben Hecht and Charles MacArthur put Maney into their play *Twentieth Century* (1932) as one Owen O'Malley, a fact affirmed by Maney himself in his autobiography, *Fanfare: Confessions of a Press Agent* (1957).

Manfred, Frederick Feikema [**"Feike Feikema"**] (b. near Doon, Iowa, Jan. 6, 1912—   ), novelist. Manfred writes in a highly personal style, which he sometimes calls "Manfredean," undisciplined but often highly effective. He wrote *The Golden Bowl* (1944); *Boy Almighty* (1945); *The Giant* (1951); *Conquering Horse* (1959); *Arrow of Love* (1961), three novelettes.

Man from Home, The (1907), a play by

BOOTH TARKINGTON and HARRY LEON WILSON. The theme contrasts the simple American with the sophisticated European. Daniel Voorhees Pike, from Indiana, goes abroad to reclaim his ward, in danger of becoming an expatriate and marrying a fortune-hunting nobleman. The plot takes, of course, an inevitable turn. The play made a great hit.

Mangione, Jerre (b. Rochester, N.Y., Mar. 20, 1909—   ), writer, government employee, editor. Mangione's writing deals mainly and happily with the life of Sicilian immigrants in the United States and with their ancestral home. *Mount Allegro* (1943) is an account of his happy childhood in Rochester and of the efforts of newcomers to adjust to American life. He also wrote *The Ship and the Flame* (1948) and *Reunion in Sicily* (1950).

Manhattan Transfer (1925), a novel by JOHN DOS PASSOS. For several years of the 1920's, the Pennsylvania Railroad maintained a station in the New Jersey meadows between Newark and Jersey City which it called Manhattan Transfer, where passengers between New York City and points south and west changed trains. The title of Dos Passos' novel is symbolic; "Manhattan Transfer" stands for the shifting and variegated life of New York City. The novel is composed with the newsreel and cinema technique Dos Passos often uses, and includes a staccato succession of descriptive and narrative scenes. The novel is in essence an imaginative sociological study, intended to give a panoramic impression of a swarming metropolis. The story revolves around an actress who marries, loves, is divorced. Many other characters appear only fleetingly. The final effect is one of frustration and defeat. It was Dos Passos' first mature work, and set the technical pattern and the philosophy for the novels that followed.

Mankiewicz, Joseph L[eo] (b. Wilkes-Barre, Pa., Feb. 11, 1909—   ), movie script-writer, director, producer. Among the many films he has directed or produced are: *Philadelphia Story* (1939); *The Late George Apley* (1947); *The Ghost and Mrs. Muir* (1947); *A Letter to Three Wives* (1948); *Five Fingers* (1951); *Guys and Dolls* (1954); *Suddenly Last Summer* (1959). Mankiewicz is also the author of the screenplays *All About Eve* (1950); *The Quiet American* (1952), *The Barefoot Contessa* (1952), and *Guys and Dolls* (1954).

Manly, John M[atthews] (b. Sumter Co., Ala., Sept. 2, 1865—d. April 2, 1940), teacher, Chaucerian scholar, literary historian, cryptographer. Originally a mathematics teacher, Manly began teaching English at the University of Chicago in 1898, and continued there for the rest of his career, mainly as head of the English Department. Although he composed manuals on composition and on *Contemporary American* and on *British Literature* (1921, 1922), his interest was mainly in Chaucer. He wrote *Some New Light on Chaucer* (1926), and *Chaucer and the Rhetoricians* (1926); and with others definitively edited Chaucer's *Works* (8 v., 1940). When the first cryptographic bureau was established by the United States Army, in World War I, Manly was called from his post at Chicago and became one of the bureau's most brilliant cryptographers. His skill as a literary sleuth became evident especially in reconstructing the original texts of lost Chaucerian manuscripts.

Mann, Horace (b. Franklin, Mass., May 4, 1796—d. Aug. 2, 1859), lawyer, legislator, educator, humanitarian. After a childhood of poverty and little education, Mann had the good fortune to meet a remarkable itinerant teacher who prepared him for Brown University in six months. After having been graduated with highest honors, he read law in Litchfield, Conn.; he was admitted to the bar in 1823, practiced in Boston and Dedham, served as State representative (1827–33), and as State senator (1833–37).

The death of his first wife left Mann without further political ambition. Instead, he espoused an unpopular cause—the care of the insane. While trying to raise funds for a state insane asylum he also sought to convince the public that insanity was no disgrace, that it was not contagious as some thought, that it might even be cured by the proper care. When, in 1837, the education bill for which he had long fought became a law, Mann gladly turned from politics to education, becoming secretary of the state board of education. He labored unceasingly to improve the public schools, increase teacher salaries, insure proper teaching. He established the first three teacher-training schools in the United States, obtained greater funds for public schools from the state and from private donors, encouraged women to go into teaching, and battled religious bigotry and sectarian control of education. The twelve annual reports (1837–48) which he made while secretary of the board of education are among the most important documents in the history of American education.

In 1848 he was elected to the House of Representatives, where his antislavery stand alienated him from his former friend Daniel Webster. His defeat as Free Soil candidate for governor of Massachusetts was followed by his appointment as president of Antioch College. Beset by money troubles, an inadequate plant, underpaid teachers, and enemies who were suspicious of nonsectarian schools, Antioch struggled along for four years, maintaining its ideals of democracy and a liberal education for the poor as well as the rich. In 1859 the college was sold for debt, and although Mann labored to reorganize it, the effort ruined his health.

Horace Mann's educational ideas represent an ideal for which educators today are still striving. In addition to the twelve *Annual Reports*, Mann published *Lectures on Education* (1845) and many magazine articles. Howard Mumford Jones says that Mann's great service is that he "persuaded the people at the grass roots to support the common schools." Mary Mann, his second wife, wrote a biography of Mann (1865) which was issued together with his works (5 v., 1891). Louise Hall Tharp wrote *Until Victory: Horace Mann and Mary Peabody* (1953).

Mann, Thomas (b. Germany, June 6, 1875—d. Aug. 12, 1955), novelist. Mann emigrated to the United States in 1938, lived for a while at Princeton, N.J., then settled in Santa Monica, Calif. He became a citizen in 1944, but in 1953 went to Switzerland and remained there the rest of his life. His daughter **Erika Mann** (b. Germany, 1905—d. 1969) has written in English, including *School for Barbarians* (1938) and *The Lights Go Down* (1940). Her younger brother **Klaus Mann** (b. Germany, 1906—d. 1949), novelist and essayist, also published a number of books in English, among them an autobiography called *The Turning Point* (1942).

Thomas Mann himself wrote no works for publication in English. He continued his writing vigorously in America, however, and wrote among other books the final volume of his *Joseph* tetralogy, *Joseph the Provider* (1944), which he characterized as reflecting the spirit of America and being essentially a "success story" —Joseph's administration of the national economy "unmistakably reflects the New Deal." *Dr. Faustus* (1948) was also written in the United States. In 1951 Mann was elected to membership in the American Academy of Arts and Letters.

Mannerhouse (1948), a three-act play with prologue by THOMAS WOLFE. When he was nineteen, long before the publication of his first novel, Wolfe wrote the first act of this play, which deals with a rebel Hamlet in the Civil War era. Later, when he was attending the classes of GEORGE PIERCE BAKER at Harvard, he wrote to his mother that Baker was "especially anxious" for him to finish the play, which was about the disintegration of a family of "the decayed southern aristocracy: it has never been adequately treated before." Such at least was Wolfe's first intention—to show "an unproductive order of society, [which] must therefore give way to the new industrialism." But when Wolfe actually completed the play and submitted it for production to the Neighborhood Playhouse in New York City, he had changed his mind about the alleged ugliness of the society he was depicting. As Guy Savino commented in a review of the play in book form: "And so Eugene, the young protagonist of the story, who in his creator's 19th year would have walked firmly away from the decaying house, instead returns and seeks tragically to identify himself again with the era that has passed—just because the author has turned a weary 25." It was first performed in German over an American sponsored radio network in Vienna, March 4, 1952.

Manners, J[ohn] Hartley (b. England, Aug. 10, 1870—d. Dec. 19, 1928), actor, playwright. Manners came to the United States in 1902, playing in Lily Langtry's company. In 1912 he married the actress Laurette Taylor, and wrote for her his greatest success, PEG O' MY HEART (1912), a comedy about a wealthy Irish girl who goes to live with her aunt in London, saves her cousin from scandal, marries the right man. The play had a long run, was produced in several languages in Europe. Manners also wrote *The House Next Door* (1909); *The Woman Intervenes* (1912); *Happiness* (1917); and *The National Anthem* (1920).

Manning, Marie. The pen name of BEATRICE FAIRFAX.

Manningoe, Nancy, a character in "That Evening Sun Go Down," a short story, and REQUIEM FOR A NUN, a novel, by William Faulkner. Although murdered by her husband after the end of "That Evening Sun," as was mentioned in *The Sound and the Fury,* Nancy was resurrected by Faulkner to play an important part in *Requiem for a Nun,* where she is Temple Drake's confidante and nursemaid to the latter's children. Because Nancy's past was as sordid as her own, she is the one person whom Temple can trust. Nancy, however, is able to face the questions of guilt and responsibility honestly, whereas Temple is not.

Man of the Hour, The (1905), a novel by Octave Thanet (pen name of ALICE FRENCH). This is one of the earliest novels to deal with labor problems and the growth of radical ideology. See GEORGE H. BROADHURST.

Mansfield, Richard (b. Germany [of English and Dutch ancestry], May 24, 1854—d. Aug. 30, 1907), actor, playwright. Mansfield was a monologist on the English stage, later took roles in Gilbert and Sullivan operas. He came to the United States in 1882. He made a great hit in *A Parisian Romance* (1883) and was thereafter one of the great stars of the American stage. He was a great romantic actor, an absolute autocrat who regarded a play primarily as a vehicle for Richard Mansfield. Mansfield won fame in the leading roles of *Dr. Jekyll and Mr. Hyde* (1887) and BEAU BRUMMELL (1890). He was magnificent in Shakespeare and helped introduce Shaw and Ibsen to the American stage.

Early in his career, when suitable material could not be found, Mansfield wrote a play called *Monsieur;* one of his greatest later successes was Booth Tarkington's *Monsieur Beaucaire.* For *The First Violin,* a play he wrote in collaboration with J. I. C. Clarke (1898), he assumed the pseudonym Meridan Phelps. He is also credited with a play entitled *Don Juan* (1891). PERCIVAL POLLARD, who adapted various plays for Mansfield, wrote a satirical novel about him, *The Imitator* (1901).

Mansion, The (1959), a novel by WILLIAM FAULKNER. See THE HAMLET.

Man That Corrupted Hadleyburg, The (1900), a story by MARK TWAIN, the title piece of a collection of stories and essays. It was one of the last and perhaps the greatest of Twain's attempts to outdo Jonathan Swift in misanthropy. It is the story of a sack of money (later the gold turns out to be lead) which a stranger leaves with a bank cashier in Hadleyburg. A note authorizes the delivery of the sack to the person who makes a certain remark, after befriending the clerk; then a secret letter comes to nineteen of the town's prominent men, telling them the supposed remark. All of them prepare to claim the treasure. In time comes exposure. The story, a brilliant piece of writing, is an excellent example of what Twain called "a tragedy-trap," a comic narrative that leads suddenly and unexpectedly to a grim outcome. The hypocrisy of American small-town culture is ruthlessly laid bare.

Mantle, [Robert] Burns (b. Watertown, N.Y., Dec. 23, 1873—d. Feb. 9, 1948), reporter, drama critic, editor. Mantle began with the Denver *Post,* first as a linotypist, later as a reporter; in an emergency he was asked to review a play and soon became well known for his excellent critiques. He migrated to Chicago papers, finally to the New York *Evening Mail* and the *Daily News.* In 1919 he began to edit an annual called *Best Plays and Yearbook of the Drama,* a reliable and useful compilation, and continued to prepare it until 1946–47. He wrote *American Playwrights of Today* (1929) and *Contemporary American Playwrights* (1938), and edited, with others, *A Treasury of the Theater* (1935). He disapproved of savage criticism and critical irresponsibility.

Manuductio ad Ministerium (1726), a manual for divinity students by Cotton Mather. In it he discusses science, experimental philosophy, the classics, modern languages, and belles-lettres. The most famous section is a treatise on style, in the course of which Mather gives his ideas on "loading the rifts with ore" by constant enlargement of the text with "touches of erudition" and "profitable references," without which the text would be "jejune and empty pages." He advises divinity students, "All your days make a little recreation of poetry in the midst of your painful studies." The book was highly esteemed, was reprinted in London (1781, 1789) as *Dr. Cotton Mather's Student and Preacher.*

Manuel, Dom. A swineherd who in James Branch Cabell's novels rises to be the Count of Poictesme, a mythical medieval realm, and who after his death is known as "the Redeemer." To Jurgen, the pawnbroker who is the titular hero of Cabell's most famous novel, are ascribed the many legends that are told of Manuel. Manuel's descendants in a complex genealogy appear in many other novels, all of which reveal Cabell's ironic view of mankind as striving, like Manuel, for the unattainable.

Manuscript Found in a Bottle. See Ms. Found in a Bottle.

Man Who Came to Dinner, The (1939), a play by Moss Hart and George S. Kaufman. This play is what an English dramatist called a "comedy of bad manners." The leading character embodies what was supposed to be a friendly burlesque on Alexander Woollcott, who was then at the height of his fame as a man who reveled in vicious insults and deliberate rudenesses. Woollcott himself was so pleased with his portrait that he played the

role on the road (Monty Woolley played it on Broadway). The main character, Sheridan Whiteside, is the guest of a Middle Western family; when he suffers an accident he is immobilized in their home for some weeks. He invites various famous and eccentric friends to visit him, meddles in family affairs, insults virtually everyone in town, and when he has earned his hosts' gratitude by at last recovering his health and is preparing to depart, he breaks his leg again. A motion-picture version was made in 1941.

Man Who Died Twice, The (1924), a blank verse narrative by Edwin Arlington Robinson. The hero of this poem is a musician who ruins his life by debauchery and, in bitter self-reproach, destroys the manuscripts of two symphonies he has written. He then prepares to die of starvation in his garret. Suddenly he feels the impulse of genius again, resolves to live, is inspired with the music of his "Third Symphony," and becomes resigned to life. He joins some street evangelists and attains salvation. The theme is that man is responsible for his own salvation; such preaching of self-reliance is characteristic of Robinson's poetry.

Man Without a Country, The (*Atlantic Monthly,* December 1863), a story by Edward Everett Hale. This story made a profound impression when it first appeared, was reprinted as a brochure in 1865, and was gathered into Hale's collection *If, Yes, and Perhaps* (1868). It was written with the intention of inspiring greater patriotism for the Union during the Civil War, and was perhaps occasioned by the remark of the Northern Copperhead Clement L. Vallandigham (1820–1871) that he didn't want to live in a country ruled by Lincoln. Lincoln banished him to the Confederacy in 1863, but he returned to campaign against Lincoln's re-election. Hale's powerful and realistic story of the naval officer who makes a hasty wish never to see America again is laid in the era of the 1805 conspiracy of Aaron Burr in the Louisiana Territory. Philip Nolan was Hale's own invention and in no way connected with a real Philip Nolan who had fought in the troubles between Texas and Mexico. Hale wrote a supplementary story, *Philip Nolan's Friends* (1876), dealing with the real Nolan. An opera, with Arthur Guiterman supplying the book and lyrics and Walter Damrosch the music, was produced in 1937.

Man with the Golden Arm, The (1949), a novel by Nelson Algren. The title refers to Frankie Machine (Francis Majcinek), a gambling-house dealer who is said to have a "golden arm" because of his sure touch with a pool cube, dice, cards, his drum sticks, and his heroin needle. It seems that he might extricate himself from the Chicago Polish slum environment he has always known, but in the end his drug addiction ruins him and drives him to suicide. As Frankie makes his way along the back streets of Chicago, the places he sees take on a phantasmagoric cast: the bars, the pool hall, the jail, inhabited by the bums and small-time criminals of Skid Row. Here society clumsily tries to deal with those it has made no room for, and fails. The book received a National Book Award in 1950 and was later made into a motion picture.

Man with the Hoe, The (1899), a poem by EDWIN MARKHAM. These famous lines, inspired by the powerful Millet painting of the same name, first appeared in the San Francisco *Examiner* on Jan. 15, 1899. The poem was immediately reprinted and translated into many languages. It is a spirited and imaginative protest against the wrongs of labor; it was the first great poetic outburst on this subject and is likely to outlast all the others.

Map of Virginia with a Description of the Country, A (1612), an account by JOHN SMITH and others. The book provides a good map of the shores of Chesapeake Bay, gives facts concerning the natural history of Virginia, adds a chronicle of occurrences in the colony from June, 1608, to the end of 1609.

Marble, Dan[forth] (b. East Windsor, Conn., April 27, 1810—d. May 13, 1849), actor. A Connecticut Yankee, Marble won early fame as a portrayer of Yankee roles. He toured the country for some years, then appeared (1836) in a play especially written for him by E. H. Thompson called *Sam Patch*. In 1844 he went on to London, where he followed J. H. Hackett in winning enthusiastic audiences for plays with Yankee parts.

Marble Faun, The (1860), a novel by NATHANIEL HAWTHORNE. This is the last great book written by Hawthorne, and in it are found the themes central to his writing: the effects of guilt and the sense of gain and loss when one attains maturity. These themes occur as early as FANSHAWE and are set forth most brilliantly in THE SCARLET LETTER.

DONATELLO, an Italian count, is the central character, and the story deals with his transition from innocence to experience. His resemblance to the Faun of Praxiteles, a symbol for Hawthorne of natural innocence, is noted by the three other important characters: the sculptor Kenyon, and the two young art students, MIRIAM and Hilda. The female characters are the blonde and dark types so familiar in Hawthorne's fiction. Miriam is an exotic, dark woman resembling Zenobia in THE BLITHEDALE ROMANCE and Hester in *The Scarlet Letter*. Hilda is a fair New England girl whose innocence is symbolized by the white pigeons in her care. Miriam's background is somehow tainted by her relation to a mysterious stranger. Hawthorne, as usual, does not attempt to clear up the ambiguity of the stranger's hold on Miriam, and her guilt becomes, in effect, the guilt of experience common to all men.

Donatello's love for Miriam and his interpretation of her desires leads him to kill the stranger; the murder is witnessed by Hilda so that, by implication, no one is free from the taint of the act. In the new maturity which comes to Donatello after the crime, and in his decision to turn himself over to the authorities,

Hawthorne develops the theme of the "fortunate fall."

The location, Rome, is an integral part of the action. In addition to its geographical and artistic landmarks, Rome figures in the story as the home of the Catholic Church; Hilda is driven to a priest by her need to confess, and the moral problems of the *felix culpa* form a focal point for the growth of experience in Donatello. It has even been suggested that the action, if plotted on a map of Rome, would form a cross.

If *The Marble Faun* lacks the artistic compression and profundity of *The Scarlet Letter*, it has a richness of texture, a sense of character and landscape, and a mastery of style which make it one of the most beautiful books written by an American.

March, Francis Andrew (b. Millbury, Mass., Oct. 25, 1825—d. Sept. 9, 1911), teacher, philologist, editor. March taught at Lafayette College from 1857 to 1906, was noted for his researches in historical English grammar and for his contributions to lexicography. Among his books: *A Comparative Grammar of the Anglo-Saxon Language* (1870) and *Introduction to Anglo-Saxon* (1870). He was a member of the Simplified Spelling Board which in 1906 attempted to reform English spelling. His son, **Francis Andrew March, Jr.** (b. Easton, Pa., March 2, 1863—d. Feb. 28, 1928), was likewise a philologist, also taught at Lafayette (1882–1928). With his father he edited a *Thesaurus Dictionary of the English Language* (1903). He was a member of the editorial staff of the *Standard Dictionary* (1893–95).

March, Jo. An important character in LOUISA MAY ALCOTT's novel LITTLE WOMEN (1868). She is in part an autobiographical portrait.

March, Joseph Moncure (b. New York City, 1899—), newspaperman, music critic, poet. While a student at Amherst College, March took part in ROBERT FROST's poetry group there, and was highly praised by Frost. He flourished briefly in the 1920's, published two remarkable narrative poems, THE WILD PARTY (1928) and *The Set-Up* (1928). Both are written in effective staccato rhythms and highly colloquial diction, the effect being "tougher" than the prose of the period's hardboiled proseurs.

March, William [pen name of **William Edward March Campbell**] (b. Mobile, Ala., Sept. 18, 1893—d. May 15, 1954), novelist, shortstory writer. March was brought up in a series of Southern sawmill towns and had little formal schooling. During World War I he served with distinction in Europe as a member of the Marine Corps; later he went to work for the Waterman Steamship Company in New York, and eventually became a vicepresident. For a time in the 1930's he lived in Hamburg, then in London.

March's reputation is based chiefly on his short stories, the best of which are collected in

Some Like them Short (1939) and *Trial Balance* (1945); but his novels, too, are of great interest, including *Company K* (1933); *Come in at the Door* (1934); *The Tallons* (1936); *The Looking Glass* (1943); and *The Bad Seed* (1954), which was dramatized by MAXWELL ANDERSON (1954).

The story *The Little Wife* (1935) is a good example of March's methods. The drummer Joe Hinckley has received a telegram from his mother-in-law telling him that his wife is dying. On the train from Montgomery to Mobile the porter brings him another telegram, which he tears to pieces without reading. He talks to two young girls at great and embarrassing length. When they reach their station, he continues talking, now to an elderly couple, who are puzzled by his loquacity. At Mobile he is met by his mother-in-law, who tells him what he has feared, that the second telegram contained news of his wife's death. The story is a careful, quiet, understated study in suppressed hysteria.

Much, though not all, of March's work is set in the South. His "Pearl County" and "Reedyville, Ala." are inhabited by farmers, mill workers, drummers, storekeepers, schoolteachers, bankers, photographers, writers, and various desiccated ladies. The whole of his writing does not represent a degenerating South, however, but rather a vigorous community in which conventional action is often the cover for ulterior purposes. If occasionally March is led into overintellectual ingenuity, nevertheless his best work is artistically and emotionally sincere. Posthumously issued was *A William March Omnibus* (1956), with an introduction by Alistair Cooke. The book contains many of his short stories and fables, *Company K,* and a novelette, OCTOBER ISLAND.

RICHARD CROWDER

Marching On (1927), a historical novel by JAMES BOYD. Set in the time of the Civil War, it is in part a love story, the narrative of a young man's attempts to win a bride above his own social station; but the book is memorable chiefly for its descriptions of the battles of Antietam and Chancellorsville and a Federal prisoner-of-war compound.

Marching Through Georgia (1865), a song by HENRY C. WORK, who wrote both the words and the music. It is a rollicking tune that celebrates General Sherman's march to the sea. Southern resentment of the song remains powerful today. See MARCH TO THE SEA.

March of Time, The. A weekly radio program, later a motion-picture feature. As early as 1924 TIME magazine had conducted radio news programs; the final title and format were adopted in 1929. The program offered enactments of memorable scenes from the news of the world, accompanied by narration in a sonorous and portentous voice that was imitated and sometimes parodied elsewhere.

March to the Sea. Gen. WILLIAM T. SHERMAN, in command of the Union Army of Tennessee, believed that only the total destruction of Southern resources and morale could bring an end to the Civil War. After his conquest of Atlanta he conducted his forces, 62,000 strong, on a march to Savannah, leaving a swathe of destruction fifty miles wide behind him; the march lasted from November 12 until December 21, 1864. Later he turned north to meet the Union forces in Virginia. (See MARCHING THROUGH GEORGIA.)

Many books describe the march and its effects: *Lincoln Finds a General* by K. P. Williams (1949); *Story of the Great March* (1865), a contemporary account by Major George Ward Nichols; *Sherman's March Through the Carolinas* (1956) by John Barrett; and *The Memoirs of William Tecumseh Sherman* (2 v., 2nd ed., 1886). *Gone with the Wind* (1936) by Margaret Mitchell is a memorable portrait of the terror and anguish of those who stood in Sherman's path.

Marcin, Max (b. Germany, May 6, 1879—d. March 30, 1948), newspaperman, dramatist, film and radio writer, short-story writer. Marcin was a prosperous newspaperman, made large sums writing fiction for popular magazines. He dealt mainly with crime, both as journalist and fictionist. His first play, *The House of Glass* (1915), was a crime story written in collaboration with GEORGE M. COHAN. He wrote many hits, either alone or in collaboration with Cohan, DONALD OGDEN STEWART, SAMUEL SHIPMAN, and others. Among them were *Eyes of Youth* (1916); *Here Comes the Bride* (1916); *The Woman in Room 13* (1917); *The Night Cap* (1921); *Los Angeles* (1927). He spent ten years in Hollywood, returned to Broadway to work as a play doctor and then on the staff of the Columbia Broadcasting System as director of various shows dealing with crime. He also wrote a four-act comic melodrama, *Cheating Cheaters* (1932).

Marco Bozzaris (*New York Review*, June, 1825), a poem by FITZ-GREENE HALLECK. Marco Bozzaris was a Greek hero of the War of Independence against the Turks, 1822–23. The battle in which he died is the subject of Halleck's spirited poem, which was an expression of the general admiration felt for the Greeks through the United States. The stirring lines and sentiments are in frank imitation of Byron. Oliver Bell Bunce wrote a play on the same theme, *Marco Bozzaris* (1850).

Marco Millions (1928), a play by EUGENE O'NEILL. The Marco of O'Neill's play is Marco Polo, who is used as a whipping-boy to express the dramatist's scorn for mercenary souls. His Marco is interested only in making his million, does not see that Kublai Khan's daughter is in love with him, serves her for the bonus he hopes to receive, marries at last a fat, commonplace Venetian. Contrasted with Marco's commercialism is the wiser insight of the Orient.

Marcosson, Isaac F[rederick] (b. Louisville, Ky., Sept. 13, 1877—d. March 14, 1961), newspaperman, editor, biographer, historian. A newspaperman and magazine editor, Marcosson did much to explain and interpret the "free-enterprise system" and its leaders. Many of his articles were collected in a long series of books. Among them: *How to Invest Your Savings* (1908); *Leonard Wood, Prophet of Preparedness* (1917); *The Business of War* (1917); *Adventures in Interviewing* (1919); *Caravans of Commerce* (1927); *David Graham Phillips and His Times* (1932); *The Romance of the Cash Register* (1935); *Marse Henry, the Biography of Henry Watterson* (1951); *Anaconda* (1957); *Before I Forget: A Pilgrimage to the Past* (1959).

Marcy, Randolph Barnes (b. Greenwich, Mass., April 9, 1812—d. Nov. 22, 1887), army officer, explorer, memoirist. Marcy had a distinguished military career; he served as a major general during the Civil War, later became Inspector General. Before the war he had explored portions of the Southwest, as related in W. B. Parker's *Notes Taken During the Expedition Commanded by Capt. R. B. Marcy, U.S.A.: Through Unexplored Texas, in the Summer of 1854* (1856). Marcy himself wrote *The Prairie Traveler* (1859); *Thirty Years of Army Life on the Border* (1866); *Border Reminiscences* (1872). W. E. Holden has written *Beyond the Cross Timbers: Travels of R. B. Marcy, 1812–1887* (1955).

Marden, Orison Swett (b. near Thornton, N.H., [?], 1850—d. March 10, 1924), newspaperman, editor, publisher, inspirational writer. In his forties Marden hit on a formula for success that brought him, if no one else, a large measure of it. All you had to do to win material prosperity was to concentrate and "think abundance." Thus, says Lloyd Morris, he "harnessed the Infinite to the national vocation of merchandising." He expounded his creed in a series of popular books: *Pushing to the Front* (1894); *Ambition and Success* (1919); *Masterful Personality* (1921). He also founded a magazine, *Success*, and was its editor from 1897 to 1912 and again from 1918 until his death.

Mardi: And a Voyage Thither (1849), a novel by HERMAN MELVILLE. In this, his third novel, Melville entertained questions of ethics and metaphysics, politics and culture, sin and guilt, innocence and experience. The complexity of the novel's content, in fact, destroys all pretensions to literary form. Originally a narrative of adventure, *Mardi* became an allegory of mind.

The most important sections of *Mardi* recount a symbolic quest for Absolute Truth, as undertaken by five men: Taji, the young monomaniacal hero; Babbalanja, a philosopher; Yoomy, a poet; Mohi, a historian; and King Media, a man of common sense. On King Media's boat, they sail through the island archipelagoes of Mardi (the World), stopping at various countries, including Vivenza (the United States), where Melville criticizes the institution of slavery and the tendency to mobocracy.

In their travels Taji, who most nearly represents Melville, kills a South Sea Islander priest, Aleema, in order to rescue Yillah, a beautiful young white woman of seemingly prelapsarian innocence. But Yillah disappears, and in seeking her, Taji undertakes a double quest: for Final Truth and for Lost Innocence.

At the same time that Taji seeks Yillah or Innocent Love, he is sought by Hautia, the incarnation of sophisticated sexuality, who speaks in the language of flowers. Hautia also represents retribution for sin, and haunts Taji for murdering the priest. Thus Taji becomes both pursuer and pursued. He is last seen alone, sailing his craft on desperate seas.

For Melville *Mardi* was a preparation for future work, which, after *Mardi*, took on new dimensions. For the first time he presented a questing hero, an analysis of metaphysical problems, and a book more important on the symbolic than on the realistic levels, in these respects anticipating *Moby Dick* and *Pierre*.

Marek, Kurt W. ["C. W. Ceram"] (b. Germany, Jan. 20, 1915—   ), critic, journalist, author. Though Marek was a prominent film and theater critic and newspaper editor in Germany, he is best known in America—under his pen name—for his three books on archaeology: *Gods, Graves and Scholars* (1951); *The Secret of the Hittites* (1956); and *The March of Archaeology* (1958). These books were successful popularizations of the history of the major archaeological discoveries in Greece, Crete, the Middle East, Egypt, and Central America. *Yestermorrow: Notes on Man's Progress* appeared in 1961.

Margaret (1849; rev. 1851), a novel by SYLVESTER JUDD. Judd depicts a Maine community that is remodeled on Fourierist lines. The novel helped to acquaint the public with the Transcendentalism and Unitarianism of Emerson and Alcott. As an early regional study, it gave an affectionate and accurate picture of the Maine landscape, human and natural.

Margaret Fleming (1890; revived 1907, 1915), a play by JAMES A. HERNE. Herne's play shocked his generation by its frank treatment of an adultery and its forgiveness; to a later generation it seems surprisingly sentimental. W. D. Howells, Hamlin Garland, Mary E. Wilkins, and other leaders of the realistic movement in fiction praised the play, which ran for only a short time.

Margaret Howth (1862), a novelette by REBECCA HARDING DAVIS. The background is an Indiana milltown. Mrs. Davis seeks to impress the reader by her picture of the drab poverty in which her characters live, and here and there definitely imitates Dickens. But her tale is a pioneer effort rather than a successful story.

Margaret Smith's Journal (1849), a story by JOHN GREENLEAF WHITTIER. Margaret is an English girl who comes to America, in 1678–

79, to visit relatives. She meets several persons of historical note, and Whittier makes use of the narrative to tell much about New England history. Margaret keeps a diary and reveals her own liberal and generous character as she speaks of slavery, witchcraft, Indian warfare, bigotry, and other matters that were Whittier's own great concern.

Marginalia. Short essays by EDGAR ALLAN POE, some of them excerpted from earlier reviews or articles that had appeared in the *Democratic Review, Godey's, Graham's,* and the *Southern Literary Messenger* from 1844 to 1849. They are of varying character and merit, sometimes merely factual in a way that reveals Poe's deep interest in science, sometimes critical, sometimes imaginative. Among other things, he defended the idea that character could be read from handwriting; he held that modern oratory was greater than that of the Greeks; he exalted the importance of punctuation; he made a keen analysis of songwriting. Dreams interested him, and he spoke of them with a touch of genius. F. O. Matthiessen called the *Marginalia* "that magnificently fertile series of suggestions on literary method."

Margolis, Max [Leopold] (b. Russia, Oct. 15, 1866—d. April 2, 1932), Biblical scholar, linguist, teacher. In 1908 he was appointed editor-in-chief of a committee to bring out a revised translation of the Bible, from the viewpoint of Reformed Judaism; he and his fellow editors took seven years to complete their task. Two books of his for popular reading were *The Story of Bible Translations* (1917) and *The Hebrew Scriptures in the Making* (1922).

Maria Chapdelaine (1921), a novel by LOUIS HÉMON, posthumously published. It is a beautiful and affecting story of French-Canadian pioneers who go out into the unbroken wilderness in the Lake St. John country beyond the Saguenay River in Quebec. Samuel Chapdelaine, his wife, and their six children work arduously at their task of "making land."

Maria Kittle, The History of (1793), a tale by ANN ELIZA BLEECKER. Probably the first piece of American fiction that deals chiefly with the American Indian, who is in general represented as cruel and bloodthirsty, this short novel relates the harrowing experiences of its heroine, who was carried off by Indians during the period of the French and Indian War. The story is believed to have been founded partly on fact.

Marie Rogêt, The Mystery of. See MYSTERY OF MARIE ROGÊT, THE.

Marion, Francis ["The Swamp Fox"] (b. probably in Berkeley Co., S.C., 1732[?]—d. Feb. 26, 1795), Revolutionary soldier. Marion commanded militia troops that practiced guerrilla action against British forces in South Carolina, living in swamps and forests. He has been a favorite figure for novelists. W. G. Simms wrote a biography of Marion (1844) and then described him in a series of seven historical romances: five related stories, beginning with

The Partisan (1835), continuing with *Mellichampe* (1836); *Katherine Walton* (1851); *The Forayers* (1855); and *Eutaw* (1856); and two novels, THE SCOUT (1841) and *Woodcraft* (1853). Marion also appears as a minor character in John P. Kennedy's HORSE-SHOE ROBINSON (1835); in an anonymous novel, *The Swamp Steed* (1852); and in Jefferson Carter's *Madam Constantia* (1919). William Cullen Bryant celebrated him in a spirited poem, SONG OF MARION'S MEN (1831).

Maritain, Jacques (b. France, Nov. 18, 1882 —), teacher, philosopher. Maritain studied in France and Germany, became a convert to Catholicism in 1906. He began the study of St. Thomas Aquinas and scholastic philosophy in 1908 and is regarded as a leading authority on Thomism. After the fall of France in 1940 Maritain and his wife fled to the United States. He taught at Toronto and Columbia Universities and became a member of the Princeton faculty in 1948. Among his books have been attacks on Bergsonism, a series called *Elements of Philosophy; The Life of Prayer* (with his wife Raïssa Maritain, 1928); *Art and Scholasticism* (1930); *The Angelic Doctor* (1931); *The Degrees of Knowledge* (1937); *Anti-Semitism* (1939); *Religion in the Modern World* (1941); *The Person and the Common Good* (1947); *Existence and the Existent* (1948); *Approaches to God* (1954); *On the Philosophy of History* (1957); *Reflections on America* (1958); and many works in French.

Marjorie Daw (1873), a short story by T. B. ALDRICH. John Fleming, confined to his home during a spell of illness, receives from his friend Edward Delaney a series of letters describing in glowing terms Edward's neighbor, Marjorie Daw. His letters in reply are so ardent that Edward tells him that Marjorie is all ready to return his love. Then John recovers, telegraphs he is coming to claim her hand—and is informed by Edward (who flees hurriedly) that there is no Marjorie Daw. When the story appeared in the *Atlantic Monthly,* it was regarded as a prime example of the new short-story techniques.

Marjorie Morningstar (1955), a novel by HERMAN WOUK. This is the story of a Jewish girl in New York and her progress via love affairs to suburbia and a family. Though a best seller, it was not highly regarded by the critics.

Markham, Edwin (b. Oregon City, Ore., April 23, 1852—d. March 7, 1940), farmer, teacher, poet, lecturer. In his boyhood Markham herded sheep and worked as a farm hand, going to school for three months during the year. After attending the State Normal School at San Jose, he taught in various parts of California. In 1899 he completed his famous poem, THE MAN WITH THE HOE, inspired by Millet's painting. Both the subject matter—a protest against the exploitation of the poor—and the style—sonorous and rhetorical—were then at the height of fashion; in a short time Markham was able to abandon teaching and devote himself to writing and lecturing on poetry and on social and industrial problems. He won another great success with his poem *Lincoln, the Man of the People*. Frank Norris is believed to have used him as the model for his sensitive, mystical Presley in THE OCTOPUS. Markham's works include *The Ballad of the Gallows Bird* (1896); *The Man with the Hoe and Other Poems* (1899); *Lincoln and Other Poems* (1901); *Gates of Paradise and Other Poems* (1920); *New Poems: Eighty Songs at 80* (1932); *Collected Poems* (1940).

Markham, Virgil (b. Oakland, Calif., April 2, 1899—   ), teacher, novelist. The son of EDWIN MARKHAM wrote some carefully constructed and entertaining novels, several of them detective stories. Among them: *The Scamp* (1926); *Death in the Dusk* (1928); *The Rogues' Road* (sequel to *The Scamp*, 1930); *Inspector Rusby's Finale* (1933); *Snatch* (1936).

Markoe, Peter (b. St. Croix, Danish West Indies, now the Virgin Islands, [?], 1752—d. Jan. 30, 1792), poet, satirist, dramatist. Markoe's father was a wealthy American with plantation holdings in the West Indies. Markoe was educated at Oxford and possibly at Trinity College, Dublin. In 1775 he was listed as a captain in the Philadelphia City Militia. He began writing verse at an early age, but all his known writings come after the war. His tragedy *The Patriot Chief* (1784), laid in Lydia, was apparently never produced but was praised by John Parke (1754–1789) in a poem, *To Mr. Peter Markoe on His Excellent Tragedy Called "The Patriot Chief,"* although Parke urged Markoe to employ native themes. His *Miscellaneous Poems* appeared in 1787. *The Times* (1788) was a topical satire praised by contemporary critics. Markoe established a "first" when he wrote a comic opera, *Reconciliation, or, The Triumph of Nature* (1790), which also never reached the boards. To Markoe are attributed *The Algerine Spy in Pennsylvania* (1787), described as "Letters Written by a Native of Algiers on the Affairs of the U.S. in America," and *The Storm, A Poem Descriptive of the Late Tempest* (1788). Sister Mary C. Diebels has written an account of *Peter Markoe, A Philadelphia Writer* (1944).

Marks, Jeannette [Augustus] (b. Chattanooga, Tenn., Aug. 16, 1875—d. March 15, 1964), writer of juveniles, poet, playwright. Educated abroad and at Wellesley College, Miss Marks taught English at Mt. Holyoke College from 1901 until her retirement. In 1911 she won the Welsh National Theater prize for *The Merry Merry Cuckoo* and *Welsh Honeymoon*, plays which have enjoyed great popularity here and in Great Britain. She organized the Play and Poetry Shop (1916) at South Hadley, Massachusetts, where poets and dramatists were invited to lecture and read from their works. In addition to writing, directing plays, and teaching, she has written children's books, poetry, and numerous scholarly articles. *The Family of the Barretts, a Colonial Romance* (1938) was the result of a study of Elizabeth Barrett Browning. As a liberal Quaker, she has worked in various causes, including seven years spent in aiding Sacco and Vanzetti (see SACCO-VANZETTI CASE); she reported the trial in *Thirteen Days* (1929). Among her other works are *The Cheerful Cricket* (1907); *Through Welsh Doorways* (1909); *Early English Hero Tales* (1915); *Three Welsh Plays* (1917); *Willow Pollen* (1921); *The Sun Chaser* (1922); *Genius and Disaster: Studies in Drugs and Genius* (1925); *The Merry Merry Cuckoo and Other Welsh Plays* (1927); *Life and Letters of Mary Emma Woolley* (1955).

Marks, Percy (b. Covelo, Calif., Sept. 9, 1891 —d. Dec. 27, 1956), teacher, novelist. A graduate of California and Harvard, Marks taught at various New England institutions, including Dartmouth and Brown, before he tossed a bombshell in the form of THE PLASTIC AGE (1924), the novel which brought him into prominence. Read today, it seems a mild enough tale of undergraduate life; in 1924 it shocked critics and readers, who accused Marks of scandalmongering and overemphasizing sex. College presidents, deans, professors, and students wrote articles and made speeches praising or damning *The Plastic Age*.

Which Way Parnassus (1926) was an attack, in many ways justifiable, on American colleges. After the success of *The Plastic Age*, which he never again approached, Marks turned to writing as a livelihood. *Lord of Himself* (1927), a sequel to *The Plastic Age*, was followed by more than a dozen novels, among them *The Unwilling God* (1929); *A Tree Grown Straight* (1936); *What's a Heaven For?* (1938); *No Steeper Wall* (1940); *Full Flood* (1942); *Shades of Sycamore* (1944); *Blair Marriman* (1949). His textbooks include *The Craft of Writing* (1932) and *Better Themes* (1933).

Mark Twain. See TWAIN, MARK.

Mark Twain's America (1932), an "essay in the correction of ideas" by BERNARD DE VOTO. A study of Twain as a product of the American frontier, this book was intended chiefly as a rejoinder to VAN WYCK BROOKS' *The Ordeal of Mark Twain* (1920; rev. ed., 1933). Brooks had seen Clemens in isolation as a man frustrated by society and by his own family (chiefly his wife), tortured by mid-Victorian morality and censorship. De Voto showed a different type of artist entirely, one who was part of a virile, vigorous environment and achieved greatness by using that environment creatively in his books. Brooks had ignored the viable aspects of frontier culture, the folk tales and music; De Voto, on the other hand, emphasized the frontier as a stimulus to imagination and poetry, vindicated America as a home for great writers. Possibly under the influence of De Voto's views, Brooks considerably altered his view of Twain when he wrote *The Times of Melville and Whitman* (1947).

Marlowe, Julia (b. England, Aug. 17, 1866 —d. Nov. 12, 1950), actress. Miss Marlowe, whose real name was Sarah Frost, was brought to this country as a child in 1871. She became especially successful in Shakespearean roles, particularly after her second marriage (1911) to E. H. SOTHERN (1859–1933). She first played opposite him in *Romeo and Juliet* (1904), which became their most popular play. Sothern gives an account of their famous partnership in *The Melancholy Tale of Me* (1916) and *Julia Marlowe's Story* (ed. by Fairfax Downey, 1954).

Marmion, or The Battle of Flodden Field (prod. at the Park Theater, New York City, April 13, 1812; pub., 1816), a play by JAMES NELSON BARKER. This historical drama in blank verse, apparently a decorous production dealing with a conflict between James IV of Scotland and Henry VIII of England, was first attributed to Thomas Morton, an English dramatist, for fear the audience would spurn a play by an American. The play was intended to symbolize the conflict between the United States and England which led to the War of 1812. It held the stage for years, was played as late as 1848.

Marmur, Jacland (b. Poland, Feb. 14, 1901 —), seaman, short-story writer, novelist. Marmur was brought to the United States in 1903. After graduation from high school, he took to the sea for thirteen years, then he settled in California. He earned a wide reputation as a writer of sea stories. Among his books: *Wind Driven* (1932); *The Sea and the Shore* (1941); *Sea Duty* (1944); *Andromeda* (1947).

Marquand, John P[hillips] (b. Wilmington, Del., Nov. 10, 1893—d. July 16, 1960), newspaperman, short-story writer, novelist, critic. In his boyhood Marquand's family moved to Newburyport, Mass., which became a frequent background for his fiction. He went to Harvard on a scholarship and was on the staff of the *Lampoon.* He worked on the Boston *Transcript* and New York *Tribune,* wrote copy for an advertising agency, and saw action as a first lieutenant in World War I. After 1921, his residence and the locale of his fiction were Newburyport, Boston, and New York City— with time off for visits to the Orient.

Marquand began his writing with *Prince and Boatswain* (1915), a collection of sketches. *The Unspeakable Gentleman* (1922) contains some good Newburyport passages descriptive of an earlier day. *Four of a Kind* (1923) is a gathering of four tales. (Marquand's shorter writings were collected in *Thirty Years,* 1954.) *The Black Cargo* (1925) is concerned with the opium trade. *Lord Timothy Dexter* (1925) is the biography of an eccentric New Englander. *Warning Hill* (1930), with its emphasis on social status, is often regarded as a precursor of Marquand's later manner. Then followed *Haven's End* (1933) and three tales set in the Orient: *Ming Yellow* (1934), *No Hero* (1935), *Thank You, Mr. Moto* (1936). Marquand also contributed stories about MR. MOTO, the polite Japanese spy, to *Collier's* and the *Saturday Evening Post.*

Marquand began his second stage with THE

LATE GEORGE APLEY (1937), which won a Pulitzer Prize with its ironic picture of a Boston family in an age of petrifaction. WICKFORD POINT (1939) carries the study a little further. In H. M. PULHAM, ESQ. (1941) a man writes

Cammann Newberry

his memoirs as he prepares to attend the twenty-fifth reunion of his Harvard class. *So Little Time* (1943) is the story of a play doctor in New York. *Repent in Haste* (1945) is the story of a wartime marriage made too quickly. *B. F.'s Daughter* (1946) describes a domineering tycoon and his domineering offspring. POINT OF NO RETURN (1949) is the almost excruciating story of a banker waiting for a promotion. In MELVILLE GOODWIN, U.S.A. (1951) a general is studied at all the stages of his development. *Sincerely, Willis Wayde* (1955) expresses satirically Marquand's disillusionment with business and its effect on human nature. *Women and Thomas Harrow* (1958) is a novel chiefly about the New York theater of the 1920's.

A Boston Brahmin of good standing, Marquand utilized his own experiences and acquaintances in his novels, although he could also write convincingly about places and people less intimately familiar to him. Like many novelists, his writing tended to fall into a pattern, which *Time* has called that of the harried American male battling his environment in successive generations, fighting a losing fight to lead the good life and be a good fellow while trying to be happy and be himself. His satire can be malicious, but is more often benign. Some critics feel that his books read too easily, but the public has recognized in

Marquand a first-rate storyteller who dealt amusingly and sometimes profoundly with the characteristic dilemmas of our era. *Timothy Dexter Revisited* (1960), published posthumously, returns to the Newburyport, Massachusetts, setting of the first Timothy Dexter book. Philip Hamburger wrote, in skillful imitation of the novelist's own techniques, an account and analysis called *J. P. Marquand, Esquire: A Portrait in the Form of a Novel* (1952).

Marquette, Jacques (1637—1675), Jesuit priest, missionary, explorer. Père Marquette came to New France as a missionary in 1666. He spent two years studying Indian languages and customs, then began work among the Ottawa Indians at Sault Ste. Marie, Mich.; in 1671 he established a mission at Mackinac Island. In 1673, in company with Louis Joliet, he began explorations that resulted in increased knowledge of many regions now part of the United States, particularly those along the Mississippi. Marquette's journal of his discoveries and observations was first published in 1681 and was reprinted in Reuben G. Thwaites' *Jesuit Relations* (1896–1901, v. 59). It reveals him as a keen observer, a practical man, an able writer. Another section of his journal, first published in 1852, is also in Thwaites. Francis Parkman included an account of him in his *Jesuits in North America* (1867).

Marquis, Don[ald Robert Perry] (b. Walnut, Ill., July 29, 1878—d. Dec. 29, 1937), newspaperman, writer. At the start of his career Marquis tried various occupations—teaching,

Lejaren Hiller

clerking, baling hay, acting, printing. He began to write for a country paper, went on to

Washington in a government job. He was intent on one goal—writing a column with a by-line. In Atlanta he worked first on the *Journal* and then as assistant editor to JOEL CHANDLER HARRIS, who gave him a chance to do a department—with a by-line—in his *Uncle Remus's Magazine*. From Harris, Marquis acquired some of his characteristic literary ways; Harris encouraged Marquis' tendency toward fantasy and perhaps toward the use of animal characters.

Marquis came to New York in 1912 and worked on various papers, particularly the *Sun*, for which he wrote "The Sun Dial," and the *Tribune*, where he wrote "The Lantern." Although he never came up to his own literary ideals, he turned out an extraordinarily large body of first-rate writing in a large number of genres. Much of it appeared first in his columns and made him one of the best-known, best-loved of the literary columnists who at that time dominated New York journalism. In the course of the years in New York, Marquis suffered many tragic losses—his son, his daughter, and his wife. He was often ill and penniless. His doctor ordered him to stop drinking completely, but Frank Sullivan reported that after holding out lugubriously for a month, Marquis appeared at The Players, advanced to the bar triumphantly, and said, "Boys, I've conquered that blankety-blank will power of mine."

Possibly Marquis will be remembered longest for his stories and verses about ARCHY AND MEHITABEL, the cockroach and the cat who inhabited the *Sun* office. The roach told these stories in the first person, without capitalizations because he could not hit the shift key on the typewriter: "coarse/ jocosity/ catches the crowd/ shakespeare/ and i/ are often/ low browed." The cat roamed widely in search of ribald adventures; she was, as she said, "toujours gai." To these two Marquis devoted *archy and mehitabel* (1927) and several sequels, all gathered from his column and collected after his death in an omnibus, *The Lives and Times of archy and mehitabel* (1940), illustrated by George Herriman. Some of the stories were made into a musical (1954) by George Kleinsinger and Joe Darion. Among other characters created by Marquis were Clem Hawley, the Old Soak, an uninhibited enemy of prohibition; Hermione and her Little Group of Serious Thinkers, all apostles of the platitudinous; the Cave Man and his battered lady love. These appeared in several books: *Hermione* (1916); THE OLD SOAK (1916; made into a play, 1926); *The Old Soak's History of the World* (1924, 1934); *Love Sonnets of a Cave Man and Other Verses* (1928).

Marquis was chiefly a poet, a master of the folk style and the satiric vein, as in *Dreams and Dust* (1915); NOAH AN' JONAH AN' CAP'N SMITH (1921); *Poems and Portraits* (1922); *Sonnets to a Red-Haired Lady* (1922); *The Awakening* (1924). Marquis deeply pondered and often rewrote a play on the last days of Jesus, *The Dark Hours* (1924), which he produced himself in 1932. But it was not a success and ruined

Marquis financially. He wrote fiction about the South in *Carter and Other People* (1921); some of his striking short stories may be found in *The Revolt of the Oyster* (1922). Deep protest is heard in *The Almost Perfect State* (1927) and *Chapters for the Orthodox* (1934). He left an incomplete novel, *Sons of the Puritans*, largely autobiographical, which was published posthumously (1939). In 1946 was issued *The Best of Don Marquis* with an introduction by his friend Christopher Morley. An exhaustive biography by Edward Anthony, *O Rare Don Marquis*, appeared in 1962.

Marryat, Frederick (b. England, 1792—d. 1848), naval officer, writer. Marryat served in the British navy for twenty-four years, retired with the rank of captain. Thereafter he wrote first-rate adventure tales such as *Mr. Midshipman Easy* (1836) and *Masterman Ready* (1841). Marryat stayed two years (1837–39) in the United States and Canada, published the book, *A Diary in America, with Remarks on Its Institutions* (3 v., England, 1839; 2 v., Philadelphia, 1839), followed by another book, *Second Series of a Diary in America* (1840). The book, like others by British authors, aroused much resentment in this country; he was hanged in effigy and his books burned.

Among Marryat's later books was a novel called *Travels and Adventures of Monsieur Violet in California, Sonora, and Western Texas* (apparently reprinted in the United States, 1849). This sensational anti-Texas story is made up largely of extracts, without credit, from JOSIAH GREGG's COMMERCE OF THE PRAIRIES (1844). There were also passages from George W. Kendall's NARRATIVE OF THE TEXAN SANTA FE EXPEDITION (1844). Marryat likewise wrote a book for boys, *The Settlers in Canada* (1844).

Marryat's son **Frank Marryat** seems to have inherited his wanderlust and gaiety. One of his books, his observations of the California gold rush, was printed as *Mountains and Molehills* (1855).

Marse Chan (*Century Magazine*, April 1884; part of the collection *In Ole Virginia*, 1887), a story in dialect by THOMAS NELSON PAGE. The tale is told by the servant of a likable Southerner, called "Marse Chan" by his faithful retainer. The hero loves a girl who returns his affection but, because of family pressure, pretends to disdain him. They are reconciled, just before he is killed on the battlefield, and she mourns him the rest of her life. It became one of the most famous of Page's nostalgic stories of the antebellum South.

Marse Henry. A name frequently given to HENRY WATTERSON (1840–1921), famous editor of the Louisville *Courier-Journal* (1868–1918).

Marsh, George Perkins (b. Woodstock, Vt., March 15, 1801—d. July 23, 1882), lawyer, public official, linguist, diplomat, conservationist. Marsh practiced law, was elected to various public offices, served in the House of Representatives (1843–49) and as minister to Turkey. In 1861 he was appointed by Lincoln as our first minister to Italy, where he served till his death. Marsh's main literary interest was the English language, its Scandinavian and Anglo-Saxon elements. He discussed these in his most noted books, *Lectures* [delivered at Columbia] *on the English Language* (1860) and *The Origin and History of the English Language* (1862). In these volumes he anticipated linguistic views of later scholars. He was also a pioneer in the field of conservation. He wrote a book (1856) advocating the domestication of the camel in the United States, and another, *Man and Nature* (1864; rev., 1874), which anticipated contemporary attempts to correct man's wasteful use of natural resources. David Lowenthal wrote *George Perkins Marsh: Versatile Vermonter* (1958).

Marsh, James (b. Hartford, Vt., July 19, 1794 —d. July 3, 1842), clergyman, teacher, educational administrator, translator, editor. Marsh studied at Dartmouth and entered the ministry. He was a German scholar, and in 1833 published his two-volume translation of Herder's *Spirit of Hebrew Poetry* (1833). He prepared young JOHN ADAMS [2] for Harvard, taught three years at Hampden-Sydney, was appointed president of the University of Vermont in 1826, later taught there as professor of moral and intellectual philosophy.

Marsh was a Calvinist, but inclined toward the mysticism of S. T. Coleridge and the Germans. He edited Coleridge's *Aids to Reflection* (1829) with a "Preliminary Essay," also the same writer's *The Friend* (1831). His writings served to bolster the new movements of Unitarianism and transcendentalism. Marsh's works were collected by Joseph Torrey in *The Remains of the Rev. James Marsh, with a Memoir* (1842). He is one of the trio discussed in Ronald V. Wells' *Three Christian Transcendentalists* (1943).

Marsh, Othniel Charles (b. Lockport, N.Y., Oct. 29, 1831—d. March 18, 1899), paleontologist, teacher, explorer. Marsh was the nephew of the renowned philanthropist George Peabody, who provided for his education at Yale, founded a museum of natural history at that university largely at Marsh's instigation, and left him a large bequest to continue his scientific investigations. At Yale Marsh became the first professor of paleontology in the United States. He began his notable collecting expeditions at a time when Indian wars were still going on in the West.

Marsh was best known for his study of the primitive horse. His principal books were *Odontornithes, A Monograph on the Extinct Toothed Birds of North America* (1880); *Dinocerata, A Monograph on an Extinct Order of Gigantic Mammals* (1884); and *The Dinosaurs of North America* (1896). C. Schuchert and C. M. LeVene wrote *O. C. Marsh, Pioneer in Paleontology* (1940).

Marshall, Christopher (b. Ireland[?], Nov. 6, 1709—d. May 4, 1797), pharmacist, public official, diarist. Marshall came to Philadelphia around 1727 and became a leading pharmacist. When the Revolutionary troubles broke out, he was an ardent supporter of the patriots, served on numerous committees, and participated (1775) in a conference that laid the groundwork for a new state. Throughout the war Marshall kept a journal which was first published in part in 1839 as *Passages from the Remembrancer of Christopher Marshall,* supplemented ten years later with passages from another year. In 1877 came a still fuller version, covering the years from 1774 to 1781. He was interested in many matters besides the war, and his diary reveals him as a man of great kindliness, faithful to Quaker principles, except in his support of the war, for which he was expelled from the Society of Friends.

Marshall, Edison (b. Rensselaer, Ind., Aug. 28, 1894—d. Oct. 29, 1967), novelist, short-story writer. A great lover of outdoor life and a traveler in Alaska, Siberia, Central Africa, and other lands, Marshall wrote excellent tales of adventure with carefully constructed backgrounds. Among his books: *The Voice of the Pack* (1920); *The Snowshoe Trail* (1921); *The Land of Forgotten Men* (1923); *The Deadfall* (1927); *Forlorn Island* (1932); *The White Brigand* (1937); *Benjamin Blake* (1941); *The Infinite Woman* (1951); *American Captain* (1954); *Inevitable Hour* (1957); *Pagan King* (1959).

Marshall, Humphry (b. Chester Co., Pa., Oct. 10, 1722—d. Nov. 5, 1801), botanist. Marshall, a cousin of John Bartram, was, like the latter, deeply interested in botany. In 1785 he published the first book on American forest shrubs and trees, arranging them in Linnaean classifications: *Arbustrum Americanum: The American Grove.*

Marshall, John (b. near Germantown [now Midland], Va., Sept. 24, 1755—d. July 6, 1835), lawyer, public official, jurist, biographer. Marshall served in the Revolution and was mustered out with the rank of captain. He became a lawyer after very little formal training. He served in the Virginia Council, the House of Burgesses, the commission to France, the House of Representatives. John Adams made him his Secretary of State in 1800, appointed him Chief Justice of the Supreme Court in 1801; he served till his death. His influence counteracted the Federalist defeat by Jefferson's Republican party and his 500-odd opinions helped to determine the course of the United States down to our own times.

Among Marshall's outstanding decisions were those in Marbury vs. Madison; Dartmouth College vs. Woodward; and the Cohens vs. Virginia. In the Dartmouth case, which involved the inviolability of contract, Marshall gave a definition of a corporation which has often been quoted: "A corporation is an artificial being, invisible, intangible, and existing only in contemplation of law." In the Cohens vs. Virginia, Marshall decided that the Federal Constitution held sway in the courts of the various states and that in forming a government under the Constitution the states had in some areas turned "large portions" of their sovereignty

over to the new national government. According to Peter R. Levin, "most of Marshall's legal dicta have been reversed long since," but nevertheless they have left a deep and permanent imprint on the country's economic and political life. John Quincy Adams said that Marshall had "settled many great constitutional questions favorably to the continuance of the Union." To Alexis de Tocqueville it seemed that without the Supreme Court "the Constitution would be a dead letter," and that it was Marshall's influence which had saved it. Marshall expressed himself with remarkable clarity in his decisions, much better than in his *Life of George Washington* (5 v., 1804–07).

Albert J. Beveridge wrote an exhaustive life of Marshall (4 v., 1916–19). An excellent and judicious account is David Loth's *Chief Justice: John Marshall and the Growth of the Republic* (1949). Henry Steele Commager wrote *John Marshall* (1954).

Marshall, Rosamund (b. New York City, Oct. 17, 1900—   ), novelist. Rosamund Marshall was educated in France, Austria, and Germany. She wrote a number of popular novels in French, under a pseudonym, then became a highly successful writer of sensational historical romances, including *Kitty* (1943); *Duchess Hotspur* (1946); *Laird's Choice* (1951); *Bond of the Flesh* (1952); *The General's Wench* (1953); *The Dollmaster* (1954); and *Rogue Cavalier* (1955). She is also the author of several juveniles, among them *None but the Brave* (1942), *The Treasure of Shafto* (1946), and *The Loving Meddler* (1954).

Marshes of Glynn, The (pub. anonymously, 1878, in *The Masque of Poets*), a poem by SIDNEY LANIER. This is frequently described as the greatest of Lanier's poems. It was contributed to a volume of 175 poems by noted authors, none of whom signed his name. In the poem Lanier reaches the height of his lifelong attempt to reconcile the techniques of music and poetry. G. W. Allen refers to its skillful and varied use of anapestic measure, "all intended primarily to produce the varying cadences of a musical composition." Its lush imagery sensuously depicts the sea marshes of Glynn County, Ga., visited by Lanier in 1875. Its philosophy is perhaps Emersonian—others have called it pagan—as Lanier welcomes his sudden freedom "from the weighing of fate and the sad discussion of sin." "A photographic interpretation" to accompany the poem was prepared by Mose Daniels (1949).

Martin, Abe. An old farmer, with scarecrow figure and shrewd homespun wisdom, who appears in the writings of FRANK McKINNEY ("KIN") HUBBARD. His pungent, often cynical sayings in Hoosier dialect were gathered from a column in the Indianapolis *News* into twenty-six volumes and two books of selections, *Abe Martin's Furrows* (1911) and *Abe Martin's Wise-Cracks* (1930).

Martin, Edward Sandford (b. Willowbrook, N.Y., Jan. 2, 1856—d. June 13, 1939), humorist, essayist, editor. As an undergraduate at

Harvard, Martin helped to found the celebrated HARVARD LAMPOON. Later he worked for the New York *Sun* and Rochester *Union and Advertiser*. With two of his Harvard friends, Thomas Masson and Andrew Miller, he helped John Ames Mitchell edit the new LIFE as a humorous weekly. For almost fifty years his temperate and witty editorials, humorous verses, and prose pieces appeared in *Life*. From 1920 until 1935 he was also the occupant of "The Easy Chair" of *Harper's Monthly*.

The War Week by Week (1914) and *The Diary of a Nation* (1917) are collections of Martin's editorials. Other works include: *Slye Ballads in Harvard China* (1882); *A Little Brother of the Rich* (1890); *Pirated Poems* (1890); *The Courtship of a Careful Man* (1905); *Reflections of a Beginning Husband* (1913); *Unrest of Women* (1913); *Abroad with Jane* (1918); *The Life of Joseph Hodges Choate* (1920); *What's Ahead and Meanwhile* (1927).

Martin, Everett Dean (b. Jacksonville, Ill., July 5, 1880—d. May 10, 1941), clergyman, teacher, sociologist. An ordained Congregationalist minister, in 1934 he became head of the department of social philosophy at Cooper Union. His *The Behavior of Crowds* (1920) was the first study of mob psychology. *The Meaning of a Liberal Education* (1926), in which he took a stand with the humanists, became a best seller in spite of its unpopular viewpoint. Other works on psychology and education by Martin are: *The Mystery of Religion: A Study in Social Psychology* (1924); *Psychology and Its Uses* (1926); *Liberty* (1930); *The Conflict of the Individual and the Mass in the Modern World* (1932); *Farewell to Revolution* (1935); *Some Principles of Political Behavior* (1939).

Martin, Helen Reimensnyder (b. Lancaster, Pa., Oct. 18, 1868—d. June 29, 1939), short-story writer, novelist. Mrs. Martin's special field was the region of the Pennsylvania Dutch. Her first and best-known novel, TILLIE: A MENNONITE MAID (1904), was set in that background. She knew well the strange customs of the Mennonites, the oddities of the males, the occasional rebellions of the women. Among her other books: *Sabina: A Story of the Amish* (1905); *The Revolt of Anne Royle* (1908); *Barnabetta* (1914); *Martha of the Mennonite Country* (1915); *Ye That Judge* (1926); *Yoked with a Lamb and Other Tales* (1930); *The Ordeal of Minnie Schultz* (1939). *Barnabetta* was turned into a play called *Erstwhile Susan* (1916), long a vehicle for Minnie Maddern Fiske.

Martin Chuzzlewit (1843), a novel by Charles Dickens. In its course the hero visits America, is fleeced in a real-estate deal, sees American manners and morals at their worst. He returns to England completely disillusioned, as Dickens himself was after his visit, recorded in AMERICAN NOTES FOR GENERAL CIRCULATION (1842).

Martin Eden (1909), a novel by JACK LONDON. This autobiographical novel told sensationally of London's contact with the "upper classes," his sudden success, his experiences with women, his disgust with society. It also prophesied, in the fate of Martin, London's own suicide. It was supplemented by the more strictly factual *John Barleycorn* (1913), an account of the power of alcohol over London.

Martyr, Peter [Pietro Martire d'Anghiera] (b. Italy, 1457–d. 1526), Italian teacher, historian, and diplomat. D'Anghiera, one time ambassador to Egypt and teacher in Spain, was one of the first to write about the early explorers, many of whom he knew personally. *De Rebus Oceanicis et Novo Orbe*, or *Decades* (1516) gives the first account of the discovery of America. Richard Willes made an English version of *Decades* (1577).

Marvel, Ik. See DONALD GRANT MITCHELL.

Marvelous Adventures of Johnny Darling, The (1949), by M. Jagendorf. An account of the exploits of John Caesar Cicero ("Catskill") Darling, about whom the folks of the Catskill Mountains like to tell tales—for example, how he harnessed enough mosquitoes to fly to China and back. He is a hero who depends more on brain than on brawn.

Mary Had a Little Lamb (*Juvenile Miscellany*, September, 1830), a poem by SARAH JOSEPHA HALE. Mrs. Hale was editor of the *Miscellany*, and published the verses over her initials; she reprinted them the same year in *Poems for Our Children, Designed for Families, Sabbath Schools, and Infant Schools*. In 1832 Lowell Mason set the words to music. They were reprinted in *McGuffey's Second Reader* (1857), and that probably established their fame. A Mary Sawyer (later Mrs. Tyler), of Sudbury, Mass., believed herself to be the original Mary and set up a claim that a certain John Roulston had written the poem. Henry Ford accepted her claim, collected two hundred "documents" to prove it, and restored the old schoolhouse at Sudbury as a memorial. In 1928 he issued *The Story of Mary's Little Lamb and Her Neighbors and Friends*. Mrs. Tyler's claim had, however, been refuted by Mrs. Hale in a letter written before her death, reprinted in a book about her, R. F. Finley's *The Lady of Godey's* (1931).

Maryland Muse, The (1731), a poem attributed to EBENEZER COOK. In the same volume appeared a revised version of Cook's satire THE SOT-WEED FACTOR, also a versified account of Bacon's Rebellion. Lawrence C. Wroth edited a facsimile version of *The Maryland Muse* (1934).

Maryland! My Maryland! (1861), a poem by JAMES RYDER RANDALL, which is sung to the tune of the German Christmas song *O Tannenbaum*. The anti-Union riots in Baltimore (1861) inspired Randall to write the poem. It was published in the New Orleans *Delta*, April 26, 1861, was widely reprinted, and was adopted as a battle song by the Confederate soldiers.

Mason, Alpheus T[homas] (b. Snow Hill, Md., Sept. 18, 1899—   ), teacher, authority on government and law. Mason took his master's and doctor's degrees at Princeton, taught at several universities, and in 1947 became professor of jurisprudence at Princeton. Among his books: *Organized Labor and the Law* (1925); *Brandeis: Lawyer and Judge in the Modern State* (1933); *The Brandeis Way: A Case Study in the Workings of Democracy* (1938); *Brandeis: A Free Man's Life* (1946); *The Fall of a Railroad Empire* (with Henry Staples, 1947); *Lectures on the American Liberal Tradition* (1948); *Free Government in the Making* (1949); *American Constitutional Law* (1954); *The Supreme Court from Taft to Warren* (1958).

Mason, Daniel Gregory (b. Brookline, Mass., Nov. 20, 1873—d. Jan. 2, 1953), composer, writer. Mason often used American themes in his musical compositions, as his *String Quartet on Negro Themes* (1918) and *Third Symphony* ("Lincoln," 1936). He was a professor of music at Columbia University from 1910 until his death. Among his books: *From Grieg to Brahms* (1902); *Beethoven and His Forerunners* (1904); *The Romantic Composers* (1906); *Contemporary Composers* (1918); *The Dilemma of American Music* (1928); *Tune In, America* (1931); *Music in My Time* (1938); *The Quartets of Beethoven* (1947).

Mason, F[rancis] Van Wyck (b. Boston, Nov. 11, 1901—   ), novelist, children's story writer. Mason served in World War I as an ambulance driver and interpreter. He graduated from Harvard in 1924 and entered business as head of his own importing firm. During World War II he served overseas, rising to the rank of colonel. His first book, *Seeds of Murder* (1930), was followed by more than a dozen other mysteries, all with exotic settings. Three juveniles, *Q-Boat* (1943), *Pilots, Man Your Planes* (1944), and *Flight into Danger* (1945), grew out of his experiences in World War II. *Captain Nemesis* (1931); *Three Harbours* (1938); *Stars on the Sea* (1940); *Rivers of Glory* (1942); and *Eagle in the Sky* (1948) are popular historical novels dealing with the Revolutionary period. *Hang My Wreath* (1941), published under the pen name Ward Weaver, is a Civil War love story. *Cutlass Empire* (1949) is a fictionalized account of the 17th-century pirate Henry Morgan. In *Proud New Flags* (1951) Mason embarked on a tetralogy devoted to naval aspects of the Civil War. Among his later novels are *Winter at Valley Forge* (1954); *Silver Leopard* (1955); *Blue Hurricane* (1958); and *Secret Mission to Bangkok* (1960).

Mason, George (b. Fairfax Co., Va., 1725—d. Oct. 7, 1792), statesman, official, author of the "Bill of Rights." Mason became a member of the Virginia House of Burgesses in 1759. Jefferson, Madison, and Washington all consulted him often during the "troubles" with England. He and Washington were particularly friendly; both served in the House of Burgesses, as "Gentlemen Justices" in Alexandria, Va., as vestrymen of Truro Parish. Mason's genius lay in his ability to take long-range views and to phrase his concepts memorably and convincingly, with the help of the Bible and John Locke. This genius was early revealed when in

1765 Mason prepared for the House a "Scheme for the Replevying of Goods under Distress for Rent," which opened with this prophetic paragraph: "The policy of encouraging the importation of free people and discouraging that of slaves has never been duly considered in this colony, or we should not at this day see one half of our best lands in most parts of the country remain unsettled, and the other cultivated with slaves; not to mention the ill effect which such a practice has upon the morals and manners of our people."

When violence broke out in Boston, Mason and Washington collected money and food for that city. A county meeting on July 18, 1774, with Washington in the chair, adopted a series of resolutions, written and read by Mason, that were thereafter known as the "Fairfax Resolves." Mason upheld the principle of "the people's being governed by no laws to which they have not given consent by Representatives freely chosen by themselves." He declared that "taxation and representation are in their nature inseparable; the right of withholding or of giving and granting of their own money is the only effective security of a free people against the encroachments of despotism and tyranny." He advocated a strong union of the colonies in "defense of our common rights." A little later Mason planned the Fairfax Independent Company of volunteers, the first such group to be formed on this continent and Washington's first command.

Mason wrote a number of documents that temporarily bore his name but became anonymous when they were adopted—for example, the VIRGINIA BILL OF RIGHTS and the Virginia Constitution. At his suggestion a statute for religious liberty was framed and adopted. When, after the war, a closer and more practical union was planned, Mason's voice was constantly heard in the debates. Yet he was one of three delegates who refused to sign the Constitution because it lacked a Bill of Rights. He published his *Objections to the Federal Constitution* in 1788. Ultimately the ten amendments which Mason proposed were adopted; he also proposed an eleventh amendment, providing a check on judicial power. Mason wished to keep the central government weak, in a strong union of the states. He finally retired to his home at Gunston Hall, today the property of the state of Virginia.

Mason's resolutions, declarations, and statutes helped to mold the Constitution, and his ideas and language greatly influenced the French Revolution. The chief "declaration" of his most important monument, the Virginia Declaration of Rights (June 12, 1776), reads: "That all men are by nature equally free and independent, and have certain inherent rights, of which, when they enter into a state of society, they cannot by any compact deprive or divest their posterity; namely, the enjoyment of life and liberty, with the means of acquiring and possessing property, and pursuing and obtaining happiness and safety."

A brother, **Thomson Mason** (1733–1785), was a Revolutionary leader, wrote nine *Letters* of a "British American" (1774) upholding the position of the colonists, and took an important part in consolidating the territory gained by George Rogers Clark in his northwest campaign.

Mason, John [1] (b. England, 1586—d. 1635), colonist. He was governor of Newfoundland (1615–21), then founded a colony he called New Hampshire. He wrote *A Brief Discourse of the New-Found-Land* (1620).

Mason, John [2] (b. England[?], 1600—d. Jan. 30, 1672), soldier, public official, town founder. Mason came to America around 1633, was active as a militiaman, and helped found Windsor and Norwich, Conn. He wrote an account of his victory over the Pequot Indians in 1637 which was included in Increase Mather's *A Relation of the Troubles That Have Happened in New England* (1677). Mather attributed the narrative to John Allyn, then secretary of the Connecticut colony, but Thomas Prince, in his *Brief History of the Pequot War* (1736), gave the correct authorship. John Bassett Moore said that it was "written in cold-blooded indifference to the feelings of compassion, and we shiver today at the vengeance of the whites; but it raised no qualms in the men of the 17th century."

Mason, John [3]. Author of LIBERTY'S CALL.

Mason, Lowell (b. Medford, Mass., Jan. 8, 1792—d. Aug. 11, 1872), teacher, hymn compiler, hymn writer. Mason left Massachusetts to work as a bank clerk in Savannah, Ga. His interest in music led him to collect psalm tunes based on Gardiner's *Sacred Melodies*. With F. L. Abel, a music teacher, he compiled a volume of hymns, published as *The Boston Handel and Haydn Society's Collection of Church Music* (1822). The great success of the hymnal led Mason to return to Massachusetts, where he had been asked to direct the music in three Boston churches. From 1827 to 1832 he was president of the Handel and Haydn Society; in 1833 he organized the Boston Academy of Music. He was interested in the Pestalozzi system of teaching, and his singing book, *Manual of Instruction* (1834), follows this method. He was influential in introducing musical education into the public schools. In 1838 he was appointed teacher of music in all the Boston schools.

Mason compiled more than fifty music books, among them *The Choir* (1832), in which AMERICA appeared for the first time. The most popular hymns of his own composition are *From Greenland's Icy Mountains* and *Nearer My God to Thee*. He moved to New York City in 1851, founded the New York Normal Institute in 1853. His fine musical library is now in the Yale University Library.

Mason, Perry. The leading character in more than sixty novels by ERLE STANLEY GARDNER. In each of these the lawyer Perry Mason gets a large case (the book titles are stranger still), sets off in search of clues with the help of his secretary Della Street and the private detective Paul Drake, indulges in a few extra-legal stunts, and ends up in an exciting trial scene in which his extraordinary knowledge of law helps him solve the case.

Mason and Slidell: A Yankee Idyll (1862), a poem in the *Second Series* (1867) of J. R. Lowell's BIGLOW PAPERS. James Murray Mason and John Slidell were sent by the Confederacy as envoys to Great Britain and France. They set sail on the British mail steamer *Trent*. On Nov. 8, 1861, the vessel was stopped by the American war vessel *Jacinto*, and the envoys arrested. The incident brought the Union to the verge of war with England. They were released on Jan. 2, 1862, and proceeded to London, but were unable to secure recognition of the Confederacy by England or France. Lowell voiced the general indignation of the North in vigorous language.

Masque of Judgement, The (1900), a play in verse by WILLIAM VAUGHN MOODY. This play was part of a trilogy; it was succeeded by THE FIRE-BRINGER (1904) and *The Death of Eve* (1912), the last never completed. The trilogy, also called *The Masque of Judgement*, is regarded as Moody's highest achievement. The plays show his preoccupation with the central theme of Puritanism in all ages of American literature—sin and the sense of sin. In this play, the archangel Raphael expresses his belief that God erred in allowing sin and then punishing the sinner; the Serpent is shown as the victor. The play is written in magnificent language that recalls Milton's. The second play is notable for its great lyric, *The Song of Pandora*. *The Death of Eve*, had it been completed, would probably have been the best of the three: it makes woman the mediator between God and man, as Eve in her wise old age returns with a new vision of the meaning of sin.

Masque of Mercy, A (1947), a poem in dialogue by ROBERT FROST. The poet wrestles, in this often amusing and always keen-witted discussion, with some ancient problems of the relation between God's mercy and God's justice. Various Biblical characters appear in slight disguises.

Masque of Pandora, The (1875), a play by HENRY WADSWORTH LONGFELLOW. This interpretation of the famous Greek myth is done with Longfellow's usual gracefulness and seriousness of purpose. He made no attempt to present inner or subtle meanings.

Masque of Reason, A (1945), a verse play by ROBERT FROST. The play, wittily written, is concerned with Job's old problem of the relationships of God and man. It presents its characters vividly, and the style attracts readers not ordinarily interested in philosophical discussions.

Masque [Mask] of the Red Death, The (*Graham's Magazine*, May, 1842), a story by EDGAR ALLAN POE. Poe's constant and pathological preoccupation with the idea of death led him here to what some critics regard as the greatest of his tales of terror. The story of Prince Prospero's attempt to isolate himself from the plague is almost pure description, with only rare and short passages of dialogue. The imagery is almost allegorical, leading finally to the overpowering figure of the Red Death. It has been conjectured that in the story Poe introduced details from his own experiences in Baltimore in 1831, when the cholera raged there.

Masquerier, Lewis (b. Paris, Ky., March 14, 1802—d. [?]), social reformer, lawyer. Masquerier started out in life by attempting to set up rigid rules for the reformation of spelling, but he was diverted to agrarian and social theorizing and ended by becoming an anarchist. He was an unsuccessful lawyer, went to New York to exploit his ideas about spelling, in 1867 published his *Phonotypic Spelling and Reading Manual*, ten years later his *Sociology, or, the Reconstruction of Society, Government, and Property*, then in 1884 *An Appendix to Sociology*. His new alphabet was phonetic and included eleven vowels and twenty-two consonants.

Massachuset Indians. This tribe was related to the Algonquian family. Webster gives the word as derived from *Massa-adchu-es-et*, a place name meaning "about the big hill." The tribe lived around Massachusetts Bay, from Salem to Plymouth. A group of them called Naticks or "Praying Indians" came under the influence of JOHN ELIOT. The tribe was practically exterminated by 1633. A remnant (called Mashpee) still lives on Cape Cod.

Massachusettensis. The pen name of DANIEL LEONARD, likewise the title of a collection of his essays (1775), in which he argued for home rule for the colonies, but also for continued allegiance to Britain. John Adams thought these essays "dangerous" because of their wit and subtlety.

Massachusetts Bay Company. This was an outgrowth of the Dorchester Company of Adventurers, which experimented with a colony on Cape Ann in 1623, was reorganized as the New England Company for a Plantation in Massachusetts Bay, then renamed the Massachusetts Bay Company. In 1626 Roger Conant and a group of colonists moved from Cape Ann to a site they called Salem. In 1628 the Massachusetts Bay Company received new grants of land. On June 12, 1630, a fleet of eleven ships carrying over 900 settlers—the beginning of what was called the "Great Migration"—reached Salem with Governor JOHN WINTHROP. Winthrop kept a record of the journey in his *Journal* (published in part, 1790; in full, 1825–26). Disagreements immediately arose with the group already established at Salem, and this group transferred itself to a settlement now the city of Beverly. The Massachusetts Bay colonists were Puritans who regarded themselves as *dissenters* from the Established Church of England, who wanted to purify the church from within—not as *separatists* like the settlers at Plymouth. They were frankly interested in the wealth of the new world. As their settlements prospered, they began to act independently of the home government, and as a consequence their charter was taken away (1684) and they remained

without legal status for two years. They then joined with Plymouth to form a single colony.

Massachusetts Centinel and the Republican Journal. A magazine founded in 1784 which in 1790 became the *Massachusetts Centinel and the Federalist Journal* and in 1840 was merged with the Boston *Daily Advertiser*. Its most noted contributor was JOHN QUINCY ADAMS, who wrote attacks on the American sympathizers (especially TOM PAINE) with French revolutionary ideas.

Massachusetts to Virginia (delivered in Ipswich, Jan. 2, 1842; printed in *The Liberator* the same month; collected in *Voices of Freedom*, 1846), a poem by JOHN GREENLEAF WHITTIER. This poem was perhaps Whittier's greatest in the cause of abolition. It is marked by a fervor that takes on the quality of a magnificent oration. The subject is the fugitive slave law, in particular the insults and threats some Virginians directed against Massachusetts for its refusal to enforce this law. The poem replies with non-Quakerish defiance, adds a strong appeal to Virginia to remember the ideals of Jefferson, and paints vividly the scandals of the slave traffic. Most powerful of all is the sweeping and imaginative panorama of Massachusetts towns responding to the appeal to save a fugitive slave: "No fetters in the Bay State! no slave upon her land!"

Massa's in de Cold, Cold Ground (1852), a song by STEPHEN FOSTER. It describes Negroes weeping at the grave of their master. Sigmund Spaeth points out the close musical resemblance between this song and Foster's *Old Folks at Home*. It still remains one of Foster's masterpieces.

Massasoit (b.[?]–d. 1661), Indian chief, sachem of the WAMPANOAGS. Massasoit was friendly to the Pilgrims and made a treaty of peace with them that was kept till the accession of his son, known as KING PHILIP. His home was in what is now Warren, R.I. He also made a treaty with Roger Williams.

Masses, The. A left-wing magazine (1911–18), originally sponsored by Piet Vlag, a restaurant manager. The first editor (January–April, 1911) was Thomas Seltzer, but neither under him nor under his immediate successors did the magazine do well. Then MAX EASTMAN took hold (December, 1912) and ran the magazine until its suppression by the Federal authorities in December, 1917. He had as his contributing editors some writers and artists who then or later were very prominent, including Floyd Dell, John Reed, Louis Untermeyer, Mary Heaton Vorse, Art Young, George Bellows, and Boardman Robinson. It was a sparkling magazine, stressing literature, art, and the spoofing of the bourgeoisie. But as the war with Germany approached, the magazine became angry and less balanced. In August, 1917, the Post Office Department barred it from the mails.

In March, 1918, *The Masses* was succeeded by THE LIBERATOR, which assumed a doctrinaire tone; Eastman was its editor for a while. In 1924 it was merged with two Communist periodicals and became *The Workers' Monthly.* In May, 1926, appeared the weekly *New Masses;* it became a monthly in 1948 under the name *Masses & Mainstream.* The editor was Samuel Sillen, and among the contributing editors were John Howard Lawson, Howard Fast, W. E. B. Du Bois, Paul Robeson, and William Gropper.

This series of magazines went through an inevitable development, losing much of their original verve as they continued. Finally, they abjectly followed changes in the Communist Party line. Floyd Dell gave particular attention to Eastman's ten years as an editor in his autobiography *Homecoming* (1933).

Master of the Inn, The (1908), a novel by ROBERT HERRICK. One of Herrick's minor works which probably will outlast his major efforts, this is the story of a physician who heals mental illness in his quiet inn, where contemplation and hard physical labor are prescribed as cures for neurotic disturbances.

Masters, Edgar Lee (b. Garnett, Kans., Aug. 23, 1868—d. May 5, 1950), lawyer, poet, writer. When Masters was one year old, his family moved to his grandfather's farm in New Salem, Ill., the country of Lincoln. His grand-

UPI

father had known Lincoln and had not thought highly of him, an attitude transmitted to the grandson. Masters' father was a lawyer and politician who wanted his son to study law, and although for a time Masters resisted and became a printer, he eventually yielded to his father's wishes, read law in his father's office, and was admitted to the bar (1891). He practiced in Chicago, established a sound reputation, and

earned a good income. Largely self-taught (he had spent one year at Knox College), Masters learned Latin and Greek by himself, read widely in philosophy and English literature. He yearned to write, and began publishing as early as 1898, when he issued *A Book of Verses.* Between this date and 1911, when *The Bread of Idleness* appeared, Masters published ten collections of poems without attracting more than perfunctory attention.

Around 1911 WILLIAM MARION REEDY, editor of *Reedy's Mirror,* handed Masters a copy of J. W. Mackail's *Select Epigrams from the Greek Anthology,* an exquisite prose translation accompanied by the original Greek. Masters was deeply impressed and was led to the writing of his own masterpiece, SPOON RIVER ANTHOLOGY (1915). His idea was to compose a series of "auto-epitaphs," or miniature autobiographies, in which the people of a village of past generations tell frankly what sort of persons they were and how they had lived. Masters' village was a combination of Petersburg, Ill., and Lewistown, Ill. The poems appeared originally in *Reedy's Mirror,* sometimes under the pseudonym Webster Ford. Masters planned to call his book *Pleasant Plains Anthology,* but Reedy protested strongly, and it appeared in 1915 under the title that made its author famous. In those sharp miniatures in free verse Masters portrays human lives with psychological insight and deep sympathy. Although some of his people, like Lucinda Matlock, have found fulfilment, most have had bitter, thwarted lives in the drab conventional surroundings of the small town. The tone and subject matter of the book were strongly influential in the literature of the ensuing decade.

As volume after volume of Masters' verse appeared (*Songs and Satires,* 1916; *Starved Rock,* 1919; *Domesday Book,* 1920; *The New Spoon River Anthology,* 1924; *Lee,* 1926; *Poems of People,* 1936; *The New World,* 1937; *Illinois Poems,* 1941; and many others), they attracted steadily lessening attention. They were, in fact, more rhetoric than poetry. Masters became a cranky one-book man who deeply resented the public and critical indifference to his works. One of his later books dealt with Mark Twain (1938) as "frustrated," but it was a case of the pot calling the kettle black. He wrote fiction, too— a historical novel about his Democratic hero, Stephen Douglas, and stories of his childhood— as well as an autobiography, *Across Spoon River* (1936), and lives of Vachel Lindsay (1935) and Walt Whitman (1937). But only one other book of his attracted any attention, *Lincoln the Man* (1931). In this he attacked Lincoln savagely, claiming that the Civil War President had destroyed American liberty. The book was roundly denounced by many critics and historians.

In 1946 Masters received the first $5,000 fellowship granted by the Academy of American Poets. When he died he was buried, with a clergymanless ceremony designed by himself, in the Petersburg cemetery, surrounded by tombstones bearing the names of many whom he had written about in the *Spoon River Anthology*.

Master Skylark (1897), a historical novel for young people by JOHN BENNETT. It depicts life in the Elizabethan era; Shakespeare is an important personage in the book.

Mather, Cotton (b. Boston, Feb. 12, 1663—d. Feb. 13, 1728), clergyman, historian, critic, folklorist. Mather was one of the most remarkable men ever born in America, an infant prodigy who entered Harvard at the age of twelve, an

expert theologian, a learned controversialist, a determined Puritan, a precursor of American deists, an indefatigable author, an able critic, a researcher in folklore and superstition, a man of scientific temperament who nevertheless inclined to believe in witchcraft, an educational theorist whose son disgraced him, and one of the most unlikable men on record. Perry Miller in *The New England Mind* (1953) calls him "the greatest intellectual in the land" and "the most nauseous human being."

Mather was born to the clerical gown; his grandfathers were RICHARD MATHER and JOHN COTTON, and his father was INCREASE MATHER. His father taught him so well that when Cotton Mather entered Harvard he was anathema to his fellow students, but the darling of the tutors. He was eighteen when he took his M.A., became his father's assistant at North Church in 1685, married the first of his three wives a year later. He became involved in one quarrel after another, some personal, some trivial, many theological, and at least one, his ardent and then dangerous advocacy of inoculation for smallpox, very much to his credit. Throughout his life he wrote unceasingly; the number of his titles has never been exactly determined, although a huge list is contained in Thomas J.

Holmes' *Cotton Mather: A Bibliography of His Works* (3 v., 1940). There is no collected edition of Mather's writings.

Mather's interests were multifarious. He had something to say on every subject. Richard M. Dorson holds that he "stands as the century's most entertaining stylist. An encyclopedic commentator on the whole range of human interests, he held his audience whether he expounded on pirates and criminals, fires and earthquakes, Quakerism and Arianism, or commerce and trading." His dexterity with words carried over into his preaching, and he would speak to a crowded church in a sermon that was not only a theological exposition but also a news analysis and an editorial. Mather was also known and recognized abroad, was elected to the Royal Society of London in 1713, and contributed to its *Philosophical Transactions*.

Some of his many writings were *Memorable Providences Relating to Witchcrafts and Possessions* (1689); *The Present State of New England* (1690); *The Wonderful Works of God Commemorated* (1690); THE WONDERS OF THE INVISIBLE WORLD (1693); *The Short History of New England* (1694); *The Life of His Excellency, Sir William Phips* (1697); *Reasonable Religion* (1700); MAGNALIA CHRISTI AMERICANA (1702); *The Negro Christianized* (1706); *The Deplorable State of New England* (1707, 1708); BONIFACIUS (1710); *Psalterium Americanum* (1718); THE CHRISTIAN PHILOSOPHER (1721); *An Account of Inoculating the Small Pox* (in collaboration with Dr. Zabdiel Boylston, 1722); *Manuductio ad Ministerium* (1726). His *Diary* was published in two volumes in 1911–12.

Mather wrote verse, too, but Lewis Leary remarks that "Cotton Mather was not quite the poet which his equivocal use of other men's lines often suggested." Of his interest in popular lore Richard Dorson notes that his *Magnalia* "accurately records folklore concepts which permeated the mind of 17th-century New England when the intellectuals shared with the folk an acceptance of the supernatural." He was greatly interested in education and drew up *Some Special Points Relating to the Education of My Children* (1708).

Some have seen in Mather "the Puritan spirit become ossified"; but actually his ideas of science and his belief in the authority of reason helped bring Puritanism to an end. He called Sir Isaac Newton "our perpetual dictator." Barrett Wendell wrote Mather's life (1891), and Kenneth B. Murdock edited *Selections from Cotton Mather* (1926). Ralph and Louise Boas wrote *Cotton Mather, Keeper of the Puritan Conscience* (1928).

Mather, Frank Jewett, Jr. (b. Deep River, Conn., July 6, 1868—d. Nov. 11, 1953), teacher, art critic. After a varied career as language teacher, art critic, and editor, in 1910 Mather became a member of the Princeton faculty in the department of art and archaeology, retiring in 1933. He was sympathetic toward new art movements, although himself especially drawn to classic art. Among his books: *Homer Martin, Poet in Landscape* (1912); *Estimates in Art* (1916); *A History of Italian Painting* (1923); *Modern Painting* (1927); *The American Spirit in Art* (1927); *Concerning Beauty* (1935); *Venetian Painters* (1936); *Western European Painting of the Renaissance* (1939); also a book of short stories, *The Collectors* (1912).

Mather, Increase (b. Dorchester, Mass., June 21, 1639—d. Aug. 23, 1723), clergyman, educational administrator, historian. Educated at Harvard, then at Trinity in Dublin, Mather first preached in England, then came home to

the pulpit of North Church (1664) and officiated there until his death. He went abroad to win a new charter for the colony, also brought about the appointment of Sir William Phips as governor. But with the coming of the Salem witchcraft trials and Phips' participation in them, Mather became increasingly subject to attack, although his own attitude was not fanatical, as is evident in his *Cases of Conscience Concerning Evil Spirits Personating Men* (1693). He accepted the presidency of Harvard and served from 1685 to 1701, retiring in a heated atmosphere of quarrels. He was a man of immense influence whose hot temper and indomitable views provoked controversy; at the beginning of his career he even opposed his father Richard Mather in a theological quarrel, although he finally changed sides. Like his son Cotton Mather he took the

unpopular scientific side in the smallpox inoculation controversy. He was deeply interested in science, but as an adjunct to theology, and sought to find the hand of Providence in many strange events, such as he chronicles in his *Doctrine of Divine Providence, Opened and Applied* (1684) and his Essay for the Recording of Illustrious Providences (1684).

Like his son he wrote endlessly; more than one hundred works are known to be his. He wrote a biography of his father, *The Life and Death of Richard Mather* (1670); his son Cotton in turn wrote a biography of Increase Mather, *Parentator* (1724). Among other writings of Increase Mather are *Some Important Truths about Conversion* (1674); *A Brief History of the War with the Indians in New England* (1676); *A Relation of the Troubles Which Have Happened in New England* (1677); *Kometographia, or, A Discourse Concerning Comets* (1683); *An Arrow Against Profane and Promiscuous Dancing* (1684); *A Narrative of the Miseries of New England* (1688); *The Order of the Gospel* (1700); *A Discourse Concerning Earthquakes* (1706); *Several Reasons Proving That Inoculating the Small Pox Is a Lawful Practice* (1721). The last was reissued, with an introduction by George L. Kittredge, in 1921. Kenneth B. Murdock wrote *Increase Mather, the Foremost American Puritan* (1925). Much material of Mather's, mainly in the form of diaries, is yet to be published. Thomas J. Holmes compiled *Increase Mather: A Bibliography of His Works* (2 v., 1931).

Mather, Kirtley Fletcher (b. Chicago, Feb. 13, 1888—   ), geologist, teacher, explorer. Mather taught geology and paleontology at numerous universities, joined the Harvard faculty in 1924, and became curator of the Harvard Geological Museum. He served with the U.S. Geology Survey from 1911 to 1945 and conducted explorations in eastern Bolivia and elsewhere for commercial organizations. He was described by the *Harvard Alumni Bulletin* (April 10, 1948) as "a scientist with a social conscience and strong convictions; he is as much bothered by the human waste implied in war and injustice as he is by the pillaging of the mines or forests." Mather's own favorite book is his *Enough and to Spare* (1944). He also wrote *Old Mother Earth* (1928); *Science in Search of God* (1928); *Sons of the Earth* (1930); *Adult Education: A Dynamic for Democracy* (with Dorothy Hewitt, 1937).

Mather, Richard (b. England, 1596—d. April 22, 1669), clergyman. Mather was an Oxford graduate, ordained about 1619, who suffered persecution like other Puritans and came to New England in 1635 as a pastor in Dorchester, Massachusetts. He is perhaps best known for the part he played in the preparation of the Bay Psalm Book (1640). He exerted great influence on church policies and the formulation of church rules, particularly the *Platform of Church Discipline* (1649). His son Increase Mather said of his preaching that it "was plain, aiming to shoot his arrows not over his people's heads, but into their hearts and consciences." Thomas J. Holmes includes a list of his writings, as well as those of twelve of his descendants, in his bibliography *The Minor Mathers* (1940). See THE HALF-WAY COVENANT.

(1856) was republished in 1877 as *The Enchanted Moccasins*. He published a small humorous weekly, *Yankee Doodle* (1846–47), and was a contributing editor of the New York *Dramatic Mirror* from 1883 until his death.

Mathews, Shailer (b. Portland, Me., May

MATHER GENEALOGY

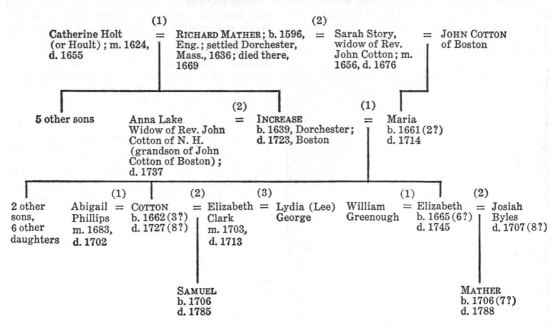

(1)		(2)	
Catherine Holt (or Hoult); m. 1624, d. 1655	=	RICHARD MATHER; b. 1596, Eng.; settled Dorchester, Mass., 1636; died there, 1669	= Sarah Story, widow of Rev. John Cotton; m. 1656, d. 1676	= JOHN COTTON of Boston

| 5 other sons | | Anna Lake Widow of Rev. John Cotton of N. H. (grandson of John Cotton of Boston); d. 1737 | (2) = | INCREASE b. 1639, Dorchester; d. 1723, Boston | (1) = | Maria b. 1661(2?) d. 1714 |

| 2 other sons, 6 other daughters | (1) Abigail Phillips m. 1683, d. 1702 | = | COTTON b. 1662(3?) d. 1727(8?) | (2) = Elizabeth Clark m. 1703, d. 1713 | (3) = Lydia (Lee) George | | William Greenough | (1) = Elizabeth b. 1665(6?) d. 1745 | (2) = Josiah Byles d. 1707(8?) |

SAMUEL
b. 1706
d. 1785

MATHER
b. 1706(7?)
d. 1788

Mather, Samuel (b. Boston, Oct. 30, 1706—d. June 27, 1785), clergyman, biographer, poet. The last of the Mathers wrote of his father in a *Life of the Very Reverend and Learned Cotton Mather* (1729). Samuel Mather was pastor for a while in the North Church, but was dismissed and formed a new congregation. He wrote a book seeking to prove that America had been known to the ancients (1773) and a poem called *The Sacred Minister* (1773). See BONIFACIUS.

Mathews, Cornelius (b. Port Chester, N.Y., Oct. 28, 1817—d. March 25, 1889), writer, editor, lawyer. Admitted to the bar in 1837, Mathews never practiced law, but turned to writing stories and poems for magazines. *Behemoth: A Legend of the Mound Builders* (1839), a romance, was followed by *The Career of Puffer Hopkins*, published serially in *Arcturus* (1841–42). This novel, like some of Mathews' later works, deals with New York politics. *Poems on Man in His Various Aspects under the American Republic* (1843) drew favorable comment from James Russell Lowell. His plays include a comedy on the New York electioneering rackets, *The Politicians* (1840); a blank verse drama, *The Martyrs of Salem* (1846), which was a hit here and abroad; a historical drama, *Jacob Leisler* (1848); and a light comedy, *False Pretenses: or, Both Sides of Good Society* (1855). His *Indian Fairy Book*

26, 1863—d. Oct. 23, 1941), teacher, editor, historian, theologian. Mathews taught rhetoric, history, and political economy at Colby College, then joined the Chicago Divinity School, where he taught systematic and comparative theology. In 1908 he became dean. He saw the Bible primarily as a social gospel, wrote *Social Teaching of Jesus* (1897). He also wrote *The French Revolution—A Sketch* (1901); *The Church and the Changing Order* (1907); *The Making of Tomorrow* (1913); *The Individual and the Social Gospel* (1914); *The Spiritual Interpretation of History* (1916); *The Faith of Modernism* (1924); *The Growth of the Idea of God* (1931); *New Faith for Old: An Autobiography* (1936).

Matthews, [James] Brander (b. New Orleans, Feb. 21, 1852—d. March 31, 1929), teacher, critic, editor, essayist, novelist. Matthews studied at Columbia College and graduated from Columbia Law School, but never practiced. He contributed to many magazines, wrote plays and fiction, became professor of English at Columbia. He specialized in drama, writing books on *The Theaters of Paris* (1880); *French Dramatists of the 19th Century* (1881); *Studies of the Stage* (1894); *The Development of the Drama* (1903); *Molière* (1910); *The Principles of Playmaking* (1919); and others. Especially noteworthy is his *Shakespeare as a Playwright* (1913), which stressed

Shakespeare's competency in the theatre rather than as a literary man. His essays ranged from the antiquity of jests to that of poker. He also stimulated the study of American literature in a history of its development (1896); wittily

fought the causes of usage as against grammatical rules, and of simplified spelling; in a brilliant study clarified the technique of the short story. He always wrote stimulatingly and informatively. His best novel was about New York City: *A Confident Tomorrow* (1899). He wrote lively short stories for *In Partnership* (in collaboration with H. C. Bunner, 1884). He left his collections and mementoes to establish the Brander Matthews Dramatic Museum at Columbia University, New York City.

Matthews, Herbert L[ionel] (b. New York City, Jan. 10, 1900—   ), newspaperman, editor, foreign correspondent. Matthews began working for *The New York Times* in 1922, and was successively reporter, foreign editor, and foreign correspondent. In his autobiographical *The Education of a Correspondent* (1946), Matthews assembled his experiences as a series of courses that made him fully aware of the evil forces in the modern world; Spain in particular proved tragically enlightening. Among Matthews' other books are: *Eyewitness in Abyssinia* (1937); *Two Wars and More to Come* (1938); *The Fruits of Fascism* (1943); *Assignment to Austerity* (with Edith Matthews, 1950); *The Yoke and the Arrows* (1956); *The Cuban Story* (1961).

Matthews, T[homas] S[tanley] (b. Cincinnati, Ohio, Jan. 16, 1901—   ), writer, editor. Matthews began as a proofreader and make-up man on the *New Republic*, then became its Assistant and its Associate Editor (1925–1929).

In 1929 he was made Books Editor of TIME, and eventually became editor. He wrote two novels early in his career, *To the Gallows I Must Go* (1931) and *The Moon's No Fool* (1936). He edited the *Selected Letters of Charles Lamb* in 1956, and wrote *The Sugar Pill* (1957) and *Name and Address* (1960).

Matthews, Washington (b. Ireland, July 17, 1843—d. April 29, 1905), surgeon, ethnologist. An early arrival in this country, Matthews became an army surgeon and served mainly in the Southwest. He became deeply interested in the Navahos and wrote several books and many papers about them, including *Navaho Legends* (1897) and *Navaho Myths, Prayers, and Songs* (1907).

Matthiessen, F[rancis] O[tto] (b. Pasadena, Calif., Feb. 10, 1902—d. April 1, 1950), teacher, critic. Matthiessen spent four years at Yale, two years in Europe as a Rhodes Scholar (1923–25), two more years at Harvard for his Ph.D. He was an instructor at Yale for two years, then returned to Harvard for the rest of his life. He taught a variety of courses in the English department, but his great teaching work was done in the tutorial system. From 1931 on he was chairman of the board of tutors in history and literature and also served as tutor at Eliot House. He lived at Eliot House until 1939, when he took an apartment in Boston with the painter Russell Cheney. Their long-standing friendship found expression in Matthiessen's book, written after Cheney's death, *Russell Cheney, 1881–1945: A Record of His Work* (1947).

In 1947 Matthiessen was teaching at Salzburg; he published his diary of the months in Salzburg and Czechoslovakia as *From the Heart of Europe* (1948). In 1949–50 he was on leave from Harvard, working on a life of Dreiser and editing *The Oxford Book of American Verse* (1950). On April 1, 1950, overcome by severe depression and "terribly oppressed by the present tensions," he committed suicide.

Matthiessen's writings were, according to Malcolm Cowley, "held together by a single concept, a search for a usable tradition in American literature." This tradition he found in the line that runs from Hawthorne through James to Eliot. Yet he was also aware of the tradition of social realism, as shown in his turning to Dreiser. George Mayberry considered his greatest achievement the understanding of the relationship between the subjective tendency and the extroverted tradition in American literature. It was his conviction that literature should be considered in its historical and social context and that, as literature cannot be severed from life, so the life of the scholar should not be cut off from the community around him. Consequently, he was concerned with social and political questions. He was active in numerous liberal and leftist organizations.

The first of Matthiessen's major works was his indispensable *The Achievement of T. S. Eliot: An Essay on the Nature of Poetry* (1935; enlarged ed., 1947). This was followed by *American Renaissance: Art and Expression in the Age of Emerson and Whitman* (1941). Then he turned to Henry James and produced *Henry James: The Major Phase* (1944) and *The James Family: Including Selections from the Writings of Henry James, Senior, William, Henry, and Alice James* (1947). In 1949 he began work on a life of Theodore Dreiser. He also contributed to anthologies and collaborative works, wrote numerous essays and reviews, and edited several books. He served as an editor for the *New England Quarterly* (1938–40).

The October, 1950, issue of the *Monthly Review,* which, according to its coeditors, Paul Sweezy and Leo Huberman, owed its foundation to the interest and generosity of Matthiessen, was a memorial issue, consisting of selections from Matthiessen's books, along with essays and statements by friends and students. The material was reissued as *F. O. Matthiessen (1902–1950): A Collective Portrait* (1950), edited by Sweezy and Huberman. *Faithful Are The Wounds* (1955), by May Sarton, is a novel said to have been suggested by Matthiessen's life. His *Theodore Dreiser* was published in 1951, and in 1952 *The Responsibilities of the Critic: Essays and Reviews,* selected by John Rackliffe, appeared. Other books are *Sarah Orne Jewett* (1929) and *Translation: An Elizabethan Art* (1931). He also edited volumes of writings by Henry James and Herman Melville.

Maud Muller (1854), a narrative poem by JOHN GREENLEAF WHITTIER, part of his collection called *The Panorama and Other Poems* (1856). The poet describes how a wealthy judge stops to talk to Maud Muller, who is raking hay. Each is deeply impressed by the other, but the judge finally rides away; each dreams of marriage to the other, but each instead marries a social equal—with regrets later on. Whittier concludes with the famous lines: "For of all sad words of tongue or pen,/ The saddest are these, 'It might have been!' " BRET HARTE, in a clever parody, *Mrs. Judge Jenkins,* imagined that the pair had really married, unhappily. His conclusion was: "More sad than these we daily see: / It is, but hadn't ought to be." According to Whittier, *Maud Muller* itself was based on an actual incident near York, Me., when he stopped to talk with a girl working in a hayfield. He may also have had in mind his own unhappy attachment to Mary Emerson Smith, who rejected him because of his poverty and social inferiority.

Mauldin, Bill [William H.] (b. Mountain Park, N.M., Oct. 29, 1921—   ), cartoonist. Mauldin worked his way through the Chicago Art Institute just in time to be drafted by the army in 1940. He fought as an infantryman in the Sicilian and Italian campaigns, was awarded a Purple Heart, and won most recognition for his cartoons of army life overseas. They appeared first in a division weekly, then in the Mediterranean edition of *Stars and Stripes,* becoming by far the most popular cartoons of the war. The two chief characters in the cartoons, Willie and Joe, are bearded, dirty G.I.'s whose attitudes toward officers, army food, the war in general, are distinctly sardonic. Mauldin shunned sentimentality and false patriotism, portrayed army life realistically. In 1945 and again in 1959 he was awarded a Pulitzer Prize.

Two collections of Mauldin's war cartoons were published, *Up Front* (1945) and *Back Home* (1946). In 1949 Mauldin published an entertaining book about his boyhood, *A Sort of a Saga.* He reported the Korean War for *Collier's; Bill Mauldin in Korea* (1952) is one of his best books.

Maum Guinea and Her Plantation Children, or, Christmas Among the Slaves (1861), a dime novel by METTA VICTORIA VICTOR (1831–1886). The book, abolitionist in sentiment, was widely read for a time, but failed to rival the vogue of *Uncle Tom's Cabin* (1852).

Maurice, Arthur Bartlett (b. Rahway, N.J., April 10, 1873—d. May 31, 1946), editor, critic, historian. During the earlier part of his career Maurice was associated with THE BOOKMAN as associate editor and editor and did much to make that magazine a widely read journal. Later he devoted himself to reviewing for New York papers and writing books, many of them historical. Among his writings: *New York in Fiction* (1901); *The History of the 19th Century in Caricature* (with F. T. Cooper, 1904); *The New York of the Novelists* (1916); *The Paris of the Novelists* (1919); *A Child's Story of American Literature* (with Algernon Tassin, 1923). In 1916 he became an assistant to Herbert Hoover on the American Relief Commission for Belgium; he recounted his experiences in *Bottled Up in Belgium* (1917).

Maury, Matthew Fontaine (b. Fredericksburg, Va., Jan. 14, 1806—d. Feb. 1, 1873), naval officer, oceanographer. Obtaining a midshipman's warrant when he was eighteen, Maury spent the next nine years at sea. His *A New Theoretical and Practical Treatise on Navigation* (1836) was extremely well received. In the summer of 1838 Maury published a series of articles in the *Richmond Whig and Public Advertiser* under the pseudonym Harry Bluff, pointing out weaknesses in the navy. Six months later he wrote more articles, signed "From Will Hatch to his old messmate Harry Bluff," which further attacked inefficiency in the navy and suggested specific reforms. He was appointed (1841) superintendent of the Depot of Charts and Instruments; this he developed into the U.S. Naval Observatory and Hydrographic Office. *Wind and Current Chart of the North Atlantic* (1847) was followed by *Abstract Log for the Use of American Navigators* (1850; later renamed *Notice to Mariners*) and *Explanations and Sailing Directions to Accompany the Wind and Current Charts* (1851).

Maury's studies in oceanography were of such value to mariners that at an international congress held in Brussels in 1853 his system of recording oceanographic data was adopted.

By the use of Maury's charts the passage from New York to Rio de Janeiro was reduced by fifteen days, passage from New York to San Francisco by forty-seven days. In 1855 his *Physical Geography of the Sea*, the first textbook on modern oceanography, appeared. In April, 1861, he resigned from his position with the United States Navy to become commander of the Confederate navy. He conducted experiments in using electric mines for harbor defense until 1862 when he was sent to England as a special agent of the Confederate government. In 1868 he returned to become professor of meteorology at the Virginia Military Institute, where he remained until his death. In his later years he published *First Lessons in Geography* (1868) and *Manual of Geography* (1870). His biography was written by C. L. Lewis (1927).

Mauve Decade, The: American Life at the Close of the 19th Century (1926), a literary and historical survey by THOMAS BEER. The book is a clever exercise in the use of irony, consisting often of the collocation of paradoxical and unrelated items, as in this sentence: "They laid Jesse James in his grave, and Dante Gabriel Rossetti died immediately." The device was effective, but after a while gave the unfortunate impression that Beer was imitating himself. Where the 90's in England had been described as characteristically "yellow," Beer tried to capture the tone of the American 90's with the term "mauve"—"pink trying to be purple."

Maverick, Samuel (1602[?]–1676[?]), public official, trader, writer on colonial America. Maverick, a shadowy figure in history, seems to have been an associate of Sir FERDINANDO GORGES, the soldier and colonial proprietor. Some time in the late 1650's he returned to England and there issued a *Brief Description of New England and the Several Towns Therein* (1660); he was back in Massachusetts in 1664 as an appointee of Charles II.

Mawson, Christopher Orlando Sylvester (b. England, 1870—d. Nov. 4, 1938), lexicographer, editor. Mawson worked on the Oxford *New English Dictionary* with Sir James Murray, was invited to come to the United States to help edit the *Century Dictionary*, later revised some of the dictionaries of the G. & C. Merriam Co. He also revised Roget's *Thesaurus*, and his *Dictionary of Foreign Terms* (1934) drew on fifty-six languages. He compiled a *Style-Book for Writers and Editors* (1926) and *The Complete Desk Book* (1939).

Maxwell, William Keepers (b. Lincoln, Ill., Aug. 16, 1908—   ), novelist, short story writer. Maxwell is noted for his sensitive evocation of the recent American past, in particular, the Mid-West of the decades before and after the First World War. Primarily concerned with the subtle and often tragic relationships existing among families and close friends, he has also written with great insight about children and adolescents. His treatment of these subjects is marked by restraint, com-passion, and a poetic fidelity to the circumstances and speech of his protagonists. Among his novels are *Bright Center of Heaven* (1934); *They Came Like Swallows* (1937); *The Folded Leaf* (1945); *Time Will Darken It* (1948); and *The Chateau* (1961). He has also written a number of short stories, some of which were collected in *Stories* (1956, with Jean Stafford, John Cheever, and Daniel Fuchs). In addition, he is the author of a children's book, *The Heavenly Tenants* (1946), and *The Writer As Illusionist* (1955).

May, Samuel Joseph (b. Boston, Sept. 12, 1797—d. July 1, 1871), Unitarian clergyman, reformer. May engaged in so many good causes and crusades that Bronson Alcott called him "the Lord's chore boy." He was active as an abolitionist, for the rights of women, as a champion of temperance. Among his books: *The Rights and Conditions of Women* (originally a sermon, 1846); *The Revival of Education* (1855); and *Some Recollections of the Anti-Slavery Conflict* (1869). He also composed *A Brief Account of His Ministry* (1867).

Mayer, Brantz (b. Baltimore, Md., Sept. 27, 1809—d. Feb. 23, 1879), lawyer, historian, editor. In 1855 Mayer ceased his law practice and began writing on historical topics. He wrote *Mexico as It Was and Is* (1844), edited the *Journal of Charles Carroll of Carrollton* (1845), also the journal of a notorious sea character, *Captain Canot, or, 20 Years of an African Slaver* (1854). The latter volume was used as a source by HERVEY ALLEN for *Anthony Adverse* (1933); the book was reprinted (1928) with an introduction by Malcolm Cowley. Another book on Mexico (1851) and a memoir of Jared Sparks (1867) were among Mayer's other writings.

Mayflower, The. On Sept. 6, 1620, the *Mayflower* sailed from Plymouth, England. The Pilgrims on the vessel had lived in Holland for eleven years and had then determined to found a settlement in America. William Brewster, John Carver, WILLIAM BRADFORD [1], and EDWARD WINSLOW were their leaders. The "strangers" in the company, men picked up in England who were not especially interested in religious dogma, apparently threatened rebellion when the land that was sighted was not Virginia, and the Pilgrims determined to form their new state on the "bleak New England shores." A violent argument broke out between the two factions; as a result came the famous *Mayflower Compact*, first of the written documents by which American history has continued the English tradition of the *Magna Carta*. Land was sighted at what was later called Cape Cod on Nov. 10 [old style], 1620 [November 20 in the modern calendar]; on the next day the *Compact* was signed by all the men of the company. They formed themselves into a "civil body politic" and pledged themselves to enact such laws and perform such actions as would be "for the general good of the colony." The *Mayflower* entered Cape Cod harbor on November 11 and made a landing on the sand dunes at what is now Provincetown. The snow was deep, there was a fierce wind, and they went back on board. On December 16 they made a landing at what was to become Plymouth. See PILGRIMS.

A beautifully wrought poem, with echoes of the old chronicles, is Conrad Aiken's *Mayflower* (in *Skylight One*, 1949). *Mayflower Heritage* (1957) by D. K. Winslow is a family record. In 1956 a reproduction of the *Mayflower* was built, based on all available documents; the following year, with Alan Villiers as captain, it duplicated as closely as possible the original voyage from England to America. *The Voyage of the Mayflower II* by Warwick Charlton was published in London in 1957, and Captain Villiers wrote *Give Me a Ship to Sail* in 1958.

Mayflower Compact, The. See THE MAYFLOWER.

Mayhew, Experience (b. Chilmark, Mass., Feb. 5, 1673—d. Nov. 29, 1758), missionary, translator, author. Mayhew was employed all his life by the Society for the Propagation of the Gospel in New England. He learned the local Indian language when he was a boy, preached to the Martha's Vineyard Indians in their own tongue and converted many of them. In 1707 he translated Cotton Mather's *The Day Which the Lord Hath Made* into the Indian language; in 1709 his translation of the Psalms and the Gospel of St. John was published, entitled the *Massachusee Psalter*. Some authorities attribute to him the *Indiane Primer* (1720), a reading book for the native children. *Indian Converts: or, Some Account of the Lives and Dying Speeches of a Considerable Number of Christianized Indians of Martha's Vineyard* (1727) gave an account of his missionary activities. A man of boundless energy, Mayhew was unable to swallow all the pessimism of the Calvinist doctrine. His *Grace Defended* (1744) acknowledged a deviation from the orthodox belief in total depravity and expressed belief in a degree of free will.

Mayhew, Jonathan (b. Chilmark, Mass., Oct. 8, 1720—d. July 9, 1766), clergyman, pamphleteer. Mayhew was the son of EXPERIENCE MAYHEW. A graduate of Harvard, he became pastor of West Church in Boston in 1647, and had already acquired such a reputation for radicalism that the more conservative clergy leagued against him. He held the post till his death.

In theology Mayhew was a forerunner of Unitarianism. One of his most trenchant writings came out of the controversies that ensued when he maintained these views in *A Letter of Reproof to Mr. John Cleaveland* (1764). In politics he espoused liberal doctrines based on Plato, Demosthenes, Cicero, Algernon Sidney, Milton, and John Locke. He was a fervent defender of the rights of man and the dignity of the individual. The Anglican clergy were wont to mark January 30, the date of Charles I's

execution, as a day of mourning, but in 1750 on that date Mayhew preached his celebrated *Discourse Concerning Unlimited Submission*, a polemic against tyranny. Mayhew became the chief clerical leader of the opposition to British repression of the colonies, as in his sermon *The Snare Broken* (1766). Joseph Green wrote an *Eclogue, Sacred to the Memory of the Rev. Jonathan Mayhew* (1766).

Mayhew, Thomas, Jr. (1621[?]—1657), Indian missionary. The grandfather of EXPERIENCE MAYHEW and the great-grandfather of JONATHAN MAYHEW, he was the owner of Martha's Vineyard and acted as governor and magistrate there. He maintained excellent relations with the Indians and sought to convert them to Christianity. He collaborated with JOHN ELIOT in writing *Tears of Repentance* (1652), reprinted by the Massachusetts Historical Society in 1834.

Maylem, John (b. Newport, R.I., Apr. 30, 1739—d. 1762[?]), soldier, poet. The dates and facts of Maylem's life are uncertain. He fought in the French and Indian Wars, described in bombastic heroic couplets *The Conquest of Louisburg* (1758), which had taken place in 1745, and later his own capture by troops under Montcalm in *Gallic Perfidy* (1758). He called himself on the title page of these poems "Philo-Bellum." Some of his verses are preserved in manuscript; they are largely celebrations of wine and Venus.

Maynard, Theodore (b. India, Nov. 3, 1890 —d. Oct. 18, 1956), teacher, writer. Maynard began residing in the United States permanently in 1920, became a citizen in 1941. He studied for the ministry and continued to preach in Unitarian churches until his conversion to Catholicism (1913). He taught at various Catholic universities, but thought of himself as primarily a poet. Among his books of verse: *Poems* (1919); *Exile and Other Poems* (1928); *Collected Poems* (1946). He also wrote, in prose, *De Soto and the Conquistadores* (1930); *The Odyssey of Francis Xavier* (1936); *The Crown and the Cross: A Biography of Thomas Cromwell* (1950); *The Long Road of Father Serra* (1954); and he has edited anthologies of Catholic verse (1926) and Catholic prose (1928). *The World I Saw* (1938) is an autobiography.

Mayo, Frank (b. Boston, April 19, 1839—d. June 8, 1896), actor, dramatist. Frank Mayo was for years one of the most popular actors of his day, both here and in England. He made a specialty of rough-and-ready character parts; thus he appeared in *Davy Crockett* (1872), written by Frank Hitchcock. Mayo wrote as a vehicle for himself a dramatization (1895) of Mark Twain's PUDD'NHEAD WILSON.

Mayo, Katherine (b. Ridgeway, Pa., Jan. 24, 1867—d. Oct. 9, 1940), newspaperwoman, historian, writer. Miss Mayo wrote militantly against social injustice. The failure of an upstate New York sheriff to apprehend three known murderers led her to write *Justice to All*

(1917), an account of the Pennsylvania State Police that led to the establishment of a similar body in New York. She investigated the workings of the Y.M.C.A. abroad during World War I and reported her favorable findings in *That Damn Y* (1920), was not as kind to the United States administration of the Philippines in *Isles of Fear* (1925). *Mother India* (1927) was a controversial study of child marriage in India. In *Volume Two* (1931) she provided documentation for her book. She was one of the best and most useful muckrakers of her generation.

Mayo, William Starbuck (b. Ogdensburg, N.Y., April 15, 1811—d. Nov. 22, 1895), physician, traveler, novelist. Mayo, in search of health and adventure, spent several years in Spain and North Africa. His observations led to the writing of some striking novels, the best of which was KALOOLAH (1849), which has been compared both to Swift's *Gulliver's Travels* and to Melville's *Typee*. *Berber* (1850) describes life among the Moors, but *Never Again* (1873) is about New York City and its social and commercial circles.

Maypole of Merry Mount, The (1836; reprinted in *Twice-Told Tales*, 1837), a story by NATHANIEL HAWTHORNE. See THOMAS MORTON. It attempts to indicate a possible reconciliation of Puritan and Cavalier ideas.

May the Maiden (1868), a poem by SIDNEY LANIER. This poem was written for *The Jacquerie*, a long poem based on Froissart's *Chronicles* that was intended to express Lanier's deep detestation of "trade" as the tyrant of the modern world. The poem was begun while Lanier was in college and was partially completed by 1868, but was never finished. It depicts an uprising in medieval France—"the first time," said Lanier, "that the big hungers of 'the People' appear in our modern civilization." But the poem is actually a love song with no relation to this central theme.

Mc. Names beginning with Mc- are alphabetized as if they began with MAC-.

Mead, Margaret (b. Philadelphia, Dec. 16, 1901—   ), psychologist, anthropologist. Before obtaining her doctor's degree from Columbia University, Margaret Mead went to Samoa as a Fellow of the National Research Council to study adolescent girls. The result of her investigations, COMING OF AGE IN SAMOA (1928), was a sound work of anthropology and a popular success. She made a number of other expeditions to distant parts of the world to study the customs of primitive peoples.

In 1926 she became assistant curator of ethnology at the American Museum of Natural History, associate curator in 1942. She has lectured on psychology at New York University, and on child care and training at Vassar, and published articles in popular magazines as well as in scholarly journals on such subjects as marriage and divorce. *Coming of Age in Samoa, Growing Up in New Guinea* (1930), and *Sex and Temperament in Three Primitive Societies* (1935) were collected in a single volume entitled *From the South Seas* (1939). Among her other works are: *An Inquiry Into the Question of Cultural Stability in Polynesia* (1930); *Changing Culture of an Indian Tribe* (1932); *And Keep Your Powder Dry* (1942); *Male and Female* (1949); *Soviet Attitudes Toward Authority: an Interdisciplinary Approach to Problems of Soviet Character* (1951); *New Lives for Old* (1956); *An Anthropologist at Work* (1959).

Meader, Stephen W[arren] (b. Providence, R.I., May 2, 1892—   ), novelist. Meader is the author of some thirty-five highly popular adventure novels for teen-age boys. Among his books are *Down the Big River* (1924); *King of the Hills* (1932); *Lumberjack* (1934); *Boy with a Pack* (1939); *Blueberry Mountain* (1941); *The Long Trains Roll* (1944); *Behind the Ranges* (1947); *Whaler 'Round the Horn* (1950); *The Buckboard Stranger* (1954); *Voyage of the Javelin* (1959); *Wild Pony Island* (1959); and *Buffalo and Beaver* (1960).

Meadowcroft, Enid LaMonte (Mrs. Donald M. Wright) (b. New York City, March 31, 1898—   ), writer, teacher, editor. Enid LaMonte Meadowcroft has chiefly written historical fiction and nonfiction for young people. Her books deal largely with events and people in the development of the United States. Among her published works: *Abe Lincoln and His Times* (with editors of *Look*, 1940); *Benjamin Franklin* (1941); *Texas Star* (1950); *On Indian Trails with Daniel Boone* (1958); *The Story of George Washington* (1957); *We Were There at the Opening of the Erie Canal* (1958); *Land of the Free* (1961).

Mearns, Hughes (b. Philadelphia, Sept. 28, 1875—d. Mar. 13, 1965), teacher, writer on educational topics, versifier. Mearns taught pedagogy in Philadelphia and then at Columbia and New York Universities; he became chairman of the Columbia Department of Education in 1926. He excelled in teaching young people to write imaginatively and in showing teachers how to encourage free expression among their students. His principles and methods are presented in *Creative Youth* (1925); *Creative Power* (1929; rev. ed., 1959); *The Creative Adult* (1940). He himself wrote expert light verse. See ANTIGONISH.

Meat Out of the Eater (1670), a poem by MICHAEL WIGGLESWORTH. The poet described his work in a subtitle: "Meditations Concerning the Necessity, End, and Usefulness of Affliction unto God's Children." The book rivals Wigglesworth's DAY OF DOOM in its lugubriousness and monotony.

Mecom, Jane [Franklin] (b. Boston, March 27, 1712—d. May[?], 1794), BENJAMIN FRANKLIN's sister. Six years his junior, Jane was, Franklin said, "ever my peculiar favorite." He kept in constant touch with her by letter for more than sixty years, and a good deal of their correspondence has survived (more of his than hers) and was capably edited by Carl Van Doren in *The Letters of Benjamin Frank-*

lin and Jane Mecom (1951); Van Doren had already written *Jane Mecom: Franklin's Favorite Sister* (1950).

Meek, Alexander Beaufort (b. Columbia, S.C., July 17, 1814—d. Nov. 1, 1865), poet, lawyer, public official, editor, historian. Meek was a successful lawyer, a judge, a Federal official, for a time Speaker of the House in the Alabama legislature; he was influential in establishing a public-school system for that state. He was a secessionist, but reluctantly. For a time he was on the editorial staff of the Mobile *Daily Register* and other papers. He wrote a history of *The Southwest* (1840), and *Romantic Passages in Southwestern History* (1857). His verses are preserved in *Songs and Poems of the South* (1857).

Meeker, Arthur, Jr. (b. Chicago, Ill., Nov. 3, 1902—   ), newspaperman, novelist. Meeker worked for newspapers until 1926, and thereafter as a free-lance writer. In his later novels, his background is likely to be either Chicago or seventeenth-century France. *American Beauty* (1929) was followed by *Vestal Virgins* (1934); *Sacrifice to the Graces* (1937); *Ivory Mischief* (1941); *The Far-Away Music* (1945); *Prairie Avenue* (1949); *The Silver Plume* (1952); and *Chicago with Love* (1955).

Meeker, Ezra (b. Huntsville, Ohio, Dec. 29, 1830—d. Dec. 3, 1928), pioneer, memoirist, historian, novelist. Six years later than FRANCIS PARKMAN, Meeker travelled the same Oregon Trail, and he related his experiences in several autobiographical volumes. Among them are: *The Ox-Team, or, The Old Oregon Trail, 1852– 1906* (1906), revised as *Ox-Team Days on the Oregon Trail* (1922); *Ventures and Adventures of Ezra Meeker, or, Sixty Years of Frontier Life* (1909), revised as *The Busy Life of 85 Years of Ezra Meeker* (1916); and *Seventy Years of Progress in Washington* (1921). He also wrote *Kate Mulhall, A Romance of the Oregon Trail* (1926).

Meeker, Nathan Cook (b. Euclid, Ohio, July 12, 1817—d. Sept. 29, 1879), newspaperman, Indian agent, memoirist. Meeker wrote a book of his experiences, *Life in the West* (1868). He was among those who became interested, through Horace Greeley, in Fourierist colonies, and for a time was active in the Union Colony in Colorado. See CHARLES FOURIER.

Megapolensis, Johannes (1603[?]—1670), clergyman. Johannes Megapolensis lived for six years on the shores of the upper Hudson, where he came into sympathetic contact with the Indians. He wrote letters about them that were made into a pamphlet (1644) entitled *Een Kort Ontwerp vande Mahakvase Indiaenen.* This was reprinted in 1651; its English versions are described in J. Franklin Jameson's *Narratives of New Netherland* (1909). Megapolensis found that the Indians were friendly to white men, though he observed they were given to lying, thieving, lewdness, murder, and drunkenness.

Meigs, Cornelia [Lynde] (b. Rock Island, Ill., Dec. 6, 1884—   ), teacher, writer of books for children, historian, biographer. Miss Meigs became professor of English at Bryn Mawr College in 1932, deeply interested in history, especially American, and in naval adventure. Her first book was a collection of short stories, *The Kingdom of the Winding Road* (1915). She won the Beacon Hill Bookshelf Prize with *The Trade Wind* (1927), the Newbery Medal with *Invincible Louisa* (1933), the latter a biography of Louisa May Alcott. Among her other books: *Master Simon's Garden* (1916); *As the Crow Flies* (1927); *The Wonderful Locomotive* (1928); *The Willow Whistle* (1931); *Railroad West* (1937); *Call of the Mountain* (1939); *Mounted Messenger* (1943). *The Violent Men* (1949) is a study of the making of the Constitution. In 1953 she was, with three associates, author of *A Critical History of Children's Literature.* She also wrote *What Makes a College? A History of Bryn Mawr* (1956).

Meiklejohn, Alexander (b. England, Feb. 3, 1872—d. Dec. 16, 1964), philosopher, teacher, educator. Meiklejohn came to the United States in 1880, taught at Brown University and became a dean there (1897–1912), was president of Amherst College (1912–24), then head of an experimental college at the University of Wisconsin (1926–38). He also taught at the San Francisco School for Social Studies and St. John's College. His experimental ideas on education aroused much controversy. He wrote: *The Liberal College* (1920); *Freedom and the College* (1923); *Education Between Two Worlds* (1942); *Education for a Free Society* (1957, 2 v.).

Mein, John (b. Scotland, [?]—d. [?]), bookseller, editor, author. Mein was the proprietor of a bookstore in Boston before the Revolution and started a circulating library in 1765. Along with John Fleming he founded the Boston *Chronicle* in 1767, but it lasted less than three years. He published *Sagittarius's Letters and Political Speculations* anonymously in 1775.

Meine, Franklin J[ulius] (b. Chicago, Ill., May 18, 1896—   ), teacher, editor, authority on American humor. In 1939 an exhibition of books and prints from Meine's extensive collection was held in the Newberry Library in Chicago, the first of its kind. In collaboration with WALTER BLAIR he wrote *Mike Fink, King of Mississippi Keelboatmen* (1933). He edited *Tall Tales of the Southwest* (1930) and *The American People's Encyclopedia* (beginning 1948).

Melanctha (1909), a story by GERTRUDE STEIN included in THREE LIVES, her first published book. It is a study of a Negro girl's mind as revealed in her natural speech-rhythms.

Melish, John (b. Scotland, 1771—d. 1822), textile manufacturer, cartographer. This Scotsman visited the United States several times and wrote *Travels in the U.S. of America in the Years, 1806 and 1807 and 1809, 1810, and 1811* (2 v., 1812). He finally settled in Philadelphia (1811). His description of this country is on the whole impartial and friendly. He sought to promote immigration from Great Britain and in 1819 issued *Information and Advice to Emigrants to the U.S.* For his travel volumes he drew numerous maps, and he published *A Military and Topographical Atlas of the U.S.* in 1813.

Mellen, Grenville (b. Biddeford, Mass. [now Me.], June 19, 1799—d. Sept. 5, 1841), lawyer, poet, storyteller, editor, historian. Mellen wrote conventional verse, largely influenced by English models and collected in *The Martyr's Triumph and Other Poems* (1833). His short stories were more meritorious. He collected and published them, under the pen name Reginald Reverie, as *Sad Tales and Glad Tales* (1828).

Mellichampe, A Legend of the Santee (1836), a novel by WILLIAM GILMORE SIMMS. See THE PARTISAN.

Melville, Herman (b. New York City, Aug. 1, 1819—d. Sept. 28, 1891), novelist, poet. Herman Melville was raised in an atmosphere of financial instability and genteel pretense. Allan, his father, a merchant who strove manfully but

fruitlessly against misfortune, died maddened and in debt when Herman was thirteen. Maria Gansevoort, his mother, herself unequal to the demands of frugal living, suffered the shame of perpetual borrowing. Her sons, as well as her less immediate family, tried to help: Gansevoort, the eldest, failed in the fur business; Herman, still in his teens, became a bank clerk and then, on the basis of less than four years of

formal schooling, an elementary school teacher. Allen apprenticed himself to a lawyer. Nevertheless the Melvilles could not overcome the accumulated debts, Maria's fiscal mismanagement, and the Depression of 1837, so in 1839, with their situation not very much improved. Melville decided to try his hand at sea; not only would he be employed for the summer but his absence would make one less mouth to feed.

Melville's voyage to Liverpool aboard the *St. Lawrence* became, sufficiently melodramatized, the substance of his fourth novel, REDBURN (1849); but, for the moment, his profits were entirely non-literary. Here, as *Redburn* indicates, innocence was initiated, kindly, but yet with brutal honesty. In England, Melville observed instances of absolute degradation, but he also experienced the exhilarating effects of the sea. When the opportunity to travel came once more, he sailed again, on January 3, 1841—this time not for England but the South Seas. The voyage became the determining experience of his life.

Deserting the *Acushnet* in the Marquesas, Melville lived several weeks among the cannibal Typee and took an island mistress; then, after participating in a mutiny on his way home and roving as a beachcomber, he spotted pins in a Honolulu bowling alley, joined the United States Navy, and visited the Galápagos Islands before reaching home by way of Cape Horn in October of 1844. Ishmael spoke true in *Moby Dick* when, as a Melville surrogate, he said that a whaleship was his Yale College and Harvard.

Although Melville had done a little writing before 1845 (notably two "Fragments from a Writing Desk" and several acidulous letters to the editor of the Albany, N.Y., *Microscope*), he had hardly considered a literary career. Nor was he considering one now, even though, at the instigation of his family and friends, he began to set down his exotic experiences. The fact is that he was at loose ends and completely untrained for any occupation on land. The result of his first efforts was TYPEE: A PEEP AT POLYNESIAN LIFE (1846), part travelog and part adventure story, but the confusion of genres is happily concealed by the pervadingly somnolent atmosphere of the "Happy Valley," the evocation of the hero's gentle inamorata, Fayaway, and by the nostalgia for innocence and first love. As for the inchoate symbolism, the unexplored conflict between conscious and unself-conscious love, and the dimly adumbrated central issue —the choice a Westerner must make between civilization and primitivism—one could hardly expect the fledgling author to be aware of such sophistications. But *Typee* was a beginning, and once having written a book that was well received, Melville saw no reason to stop. He had stumbled, quite by accident, into a career.

He stumbled into something else too: the world of books. EVERT DUYCKINCK, New York editor and literatus, opened his library to the young author, introduced him to literary society and encouraged him to continue in the vein of *Typee;* Melville took his advice and, with his next book, mined it as well as he ever would. OMOO (1847) is a realistic and superior novel of adventure, and that is one reason why Melville never wrote another: once he had conquered a genre, he did not rest content merely to exploit it further. Just as Melville realized that he could not forever exult in the sybaritic existence of beachcombing without his soul atrophying, so he also knew that he could not continue to write *Typees* and *Omoos* without serious damage to his artistic impulses. For, as he began reading the English and Continental classics, as he discovered philosophy and metaphysics, as his mind began to grow and question, he found that it was formed for stories deeper than adventure and romance.

During this same period, in August of 1847, he married Elizabeth Shaw, daughter of Lemuel Shaw, Chief Justice of Massachusetts and an old family benefactor. With his family, he moved from Lansingburg, N.Y. (where his family had gone to escape financial pressure) to New York City. Although by no means wealthy, he was an undeniably successful, even lionized, author; but his own tastes and those of his present audience would not long coincide.

MARDI AND A VOYAGE THITHER (1849), twice rewritten, was Melville's first attempt to explore the world of mind. In it he entertained questions of ethics and metaphysics, politics and culture, sin and guilt, innocence and experience. Enormously complicated, *Mardi* begins as a narrative and ends as an allegory. Its most important sections recount a symbolic quest for Absolute Truth as undertaken by five men: Taji, the monomaniacal hero; Babbalanja, a philosopher; Yoomy, a poet; Mohi, a historian; and King Media, a man of median, common sense. On King Media's boat they sail through the island archipelagos of Mardi (allegorically the world) stopping at various countries, including Vivenza (the United States), where Melville criticizes the institution of slavery and the American tendency to mobocracy. In their travels Taji kills a South Sea islander priest, Aleema, in order to rescue Yillah, a beautiful, young white woman of seemingly prelapsarian innocence. But Yillah disappears, and Taji enters upon a double quest: Lost Innocence as well as final Truth. But, as the book progresses, this Truth is revealed as relative rather than absolute, hidden, possibly nonexistent.

While Taji seeks Yillah or Innocent Love, he is sought by the arrogant Hautia, the incarnation of sophisticated sexuality, who is so overcivilized that she speaks in a symbolic language of flowers. Representing retribution for sin, she haunts Taji for murdering the priest. Thus, Taji (whom the author most nearly resembles psychologically) is both pursuer and pursued, and is last seen alone, sailing his craft on desperate seas.

Mardi is perhaps not a very good book, but for Melville it was an entirely necessary one, a preparation for the future. For the first time in his career he presents the questing hero, an analysis of metaphysical problems, and a book

more important on symbolic than realistic levels —all of which anticipates MOBY DICK and PIERRE. But *Mardi's* greatest fault was *Moby Dick's* greatest achievement: the fusion of fact and imagination.

As Melville finished *Mardi*, Elizabeth gave birth to their first child, Malcolm, who was followed by Stanwix in 1851, Elizabeth in 1853, and Frances in 1855. Thus with a wife and now a child to support and with *Mardi* a financial disaster, Melville knew he had to write another book as quickly as possible. Although writing was a conspicuously unsure way of making money, it was all he wanted to do and all he was equipped to do, but it was like running on a treadmill.

His next book, he knew, would have to be in the manner of his earlier successes—in a manner, that is, which Melville now felt he had outgrown. Not daring to indulge his philosophical passions, he dashed off his "beggarly" *Redburn: His First Voyage* (1849). As he had hoped, it was an instantaneous success, and not the bad book he imagined it to be. There are themes in *Redburn* which reverberate throughout Melville's works: the inhumanity of man to man, which provoked Melville's antimissionary propaganda in *Typee* and *Omoo*, and which would find expression again in *White Jacket*, is here denounced in the scenes of Liverpool squalor. Even the theme of the differentiation between reality and appearance, so important in *Mardi* and later in *Pierre*, Melville smuggles into *Redburn* in the hero's discovery that Captain Riga is not what he seems. The novel recounts a young man's first confrontation with the larger world, an encounter which matures him without making him cynical. Not too dissatisfied with life, but able to become righteously, if not maniacally, indignant, Redburn is the comic hero of Melville's only comic novel.

But even this novel did not help Melville to solvency; so, during New York's cholera epidemic in the summer of 1849, he sat down to write WHITE JACKET; OR, THE WORLD IN A MAN-OF-WAR (1850), a book based on his experiences in the Navy. Although writing for money, Melville could not entirely constrain himself from symbolic composition. The subtitle, for example, suggests the theme that Melville was to drive home in the final chapter: that a ship as socially complex as the *Neversink* is an apt analog for the world, with the Lord High Admiral as God. Other symbolic elements in *White Jacket* are less baldly stated. The description of the fall from the mast may be regarded as the loss of Innocence; it is the dramatic and stylistic high point in the book. The jacket, too, is susceptible of symbolic interpretation: perhaps it is ego, otherness, or innocence that Melville finally succeeds in shedding. In any event Melville was becoming interested in the meaning of whiteness, an interest which became a fascination in *Moby Dick*.

Although a vessel is hardly the place to cultivate literary acquaintances, Melville seems to have met several sailors interested in literature.

One, whom he used in the book as comic relief, is an irretrievably minor poet; but another, Jack Chase, became a major figure in Melville's imagination. Chase was a scholar-seaman, a tough-minded sailor with the soul of a poet, admired by everyone from coal-tender to captain. He is the one ideal figure in all Melville's novels, a man equally of the head and the heart. Forty years after *White Jacket*, Melville dedicated BILLY BUDD to his memory, although the hero of that later book is but a tragically flawed reflection of the original. It might also be noted that Melville remembered the hypocritical Master-at-Arms, Bland, in *Billy Budd* when he drew the portrait of Claggart.

As punishment aboard the *Neversink* was by flogging, Melville again took vociferous exception to the manner in which man treats his fellow man, and there is no question that, as propaganda, *White Jacket* helped in the abolishment of the "cat." Nevertheless, punishment for evil, evil itself, and the human system of justice continued to perplex him in the long years between this book and *Billy Budd*, where Melville arrived at his final answer.

To realize as much money as he possibly could for *White Jacket*, Melville decided to bargain with his English publishers in person, and in October of 1849 he sailed for London and the Continent. The trip was successful, not only because he received favorable terms and had the opportunity to visit museums, attend operas, meet celebrities, and buy books (one of which was the pamphlet he would transform into *Israel Potter*), but because he was able to reacquaint himself with the sea. Six times in all he sailed the ocean: in 1839, from 1841 to 1844, now in 1849, to the Mediterranean and Near East in 1856, to California in 1860, and to Bermuda in 1888. As Thoreau, like Antaeus, gained strength from contact with the land, so did Melville from the ocean. When he returned from the European voyage with vigor renewed, he was ready to begin his masterpiece.

As with *Mardi*, Melville set out to write one book and ended by writing another. Still in need of money, he began his new book as a non metaphysical narrative about whaling and the whale industry, told in lucidly realistic prose, semiautobiographical, streaked with adventure yet genially comic. The earlier chapters of *Moby Dick; or, The Whale* (1851) indicate Melville's original intention.

As Melville revised MOBY DICK he left it full of "literary" imperfections: characters who are at first important become minor and vice-versa; the narrative point of view, originally the first person, tends to become omniscient. *Moby Dick* is not a well-made book; it belongs to no classifiable genre and triumphs despite its limitations. Part of it is solid, realistic prose, part rapturous poetry; part of it is lyric, part dramatic and melodramatic; the whole is epic, the epic of a literal and metaphysical quest.

Captain Ahab, with his sturdy ship *Pequod*, his veteran crew, and his monomaniacal ambitions, is the one man completely equipped to hunt down the great white whale; if Ahab cannot succeed in his quest, then, we may suppose, no one can. All readings of *Moby Dick* must inevitably define the whale's symbolic essence, and, in the process of definition, each critic becomes his own Ahab. Opinions have ranged from Evil to God and have included Fate, Primal Good, Accidental Malice, Blood Consciousness, Nature, and the Indefinable Symbol —to name but some. The most satisfactory choice, however, would seem to be "God," and Ahab's quest, on a nonliteral level, an attempt to prove that He really exists and is knowable. Ahab's quest, however, results in his own dehumanization, the submergence of all other wills to his fiercely tyrannical spirit, and, eventually, death for all—the three American mates, one of whom, Starbuck, would restrain Ahab from his madness but cannot; the three primitive harpooners, Queequeg, Daggoo, and Tashtego; Ahab himself and all his crew—death for all save one, Ishmael, the narrator. For Moby Dick has capsized the *Pequod*, and Ahab, who has finally succeeded in harpooning the whale, is, in turn, accidentally ensnared by the harpoon line and dragged into the open sea, now in death, as in life, relentlessly pursuing the impossible.

Metaphysically tormented, desperate for recognition, near mental exhaustion from the effort of *Moby Dick*, Melville still refused to swallow the gall of unsuccess. From Pittsfield, Massachusetts, where he now lived, he brought to culmination that questing phase of his career initiated by *Mardi* and did so with a recklessness scarcely seen in American letters. *Pierre; or, The Ambiguities* (1852), his seventh novel in as many years, is a deeply personal, desperately pessimistic book, one which more nearly than any other projects Melville's own psychological conflicts and the effects of his own distraught sensibility. At times beautifully written, at times turgid, *Pierre* always suggests the author's own inner turbulence and his descent into the maelstrom of self. Indeed, its one great artistic flaw is a failure to control, or at least observe, that artistic distance proper between an author and his work.

Pierre describes how Pierre Glendinning, heir to a country estate and a pleasantly semiaristocratic life, rejects both, as well as his fiancée, Lucy Tartan, in an attempt to protect the interests of a young woman, Isabel, who, on the slimmest of evidence, has convinced Pierre that they are brother and sister. Pierre tries to establish a genuinely noble relationship with this alluring woman and, at the same time, write a book that will speak the truth at all costs. But his headstrong pursuit of principle is calamitous; he is denounced by his relatives, and forced to live in poverty. Having indirectly caused the death of his mother, Lucy, and Isabel, he commits murder and, finally, suicide. His recognition of his own incestuous passion for Isabel concludes Pierre's transformation from a charming innocent into a tempestuous cynic.

Pierre was the turning point in Melville's

career: although he wrote two more novels and the novella, *Billy Budd*, more than a dozen short stories, and five volumes of poetry (not to speak of his uncollected verse), he never again wrote with the same intensity and power. During the early 1850's he supported his family as a farmer and magazinist, turning out such remarkable tales as BARTLEBY THE SCRIVENER and "Benito Cereno" (1855). In the former, Bartleby symbolizes, in a surrealistic, whimsical, yet deadly serious fashion, the artist who refuses to compose as he is bidden by society. An extraordinarily affective story, it moves on a plane where high tragedy and low comedy meet and mingle. "Benito Cereno," in its way equally superb, is a story that gradually unfolds through the consciousness of Captain Amasa Delano who, in his innocence, observes but cannot quite plumb the evil before his very eyes. For, unlike his creator, Delano never perceives the ambiguities of the moral universe. In 1856 Melville published both stories again, with four others, in a collection of his six best and called the whole PIAZZA TALES.

During the middle 1850's Melville transformed an undistinguished biography by Henry Trumbull, *Life and Remarkable Adventures of Israel R. Potter*, into the serial ISRAEL POTTER; OR, FIFTY YEARS OF EXILE (1855), and, in his hands, it became nothing less than a fable of the American culture and polity. Although it is an exquisitely written light historical novel with some marvelously descriptive parts (as the battle between the *Bonhomme Richard* and the *Serapis*), and although the ending is bathed in an Irvingesque sentimentality, Melville's irony drives home his final point: the saga of Israel, wandering in London, the City of Dis, is the saga of America; forgetting its authentic heroes, as Israel, a fighter at Bunker Hill, is forgotten, is a sure sign that the once vibrant democracy is growing senile. If there is any hope at all for America, it must come from the still youthful West, the land of Christian gentlemen, the new Promised Land. But does this land really exist? And, if it does, can it redeem the official East? Melville asks, but does not answer these questions, and *Israel Potter* becomes an intellectual waystop in his continuing concern for the future of America, a concern first enunciated in *Mardi* and last in CLAREL (1876).

Another attempt at serialization—which, however, did not materialize—was THE CONFIDENCE-MAN, HIS MASQUERADE (1857), written with a sublimated fury, a cynicism, and an indignation beyond anger. The Confidence Man (his disguise keeps changing as the book proceeds) is a smiling, intelligent hypocrite whose single pleasure in life is in exercising his evil spells, thereby perverting the souls of others. If he succeeds it is because he knows what men want and fear most: he knows that the desperate are always in the market for false hope. As Melville was spiritual kin to the defeated Bartleby, he is, in this later novel, kin to the "gimlet-eyed" realist who tries ineffectually to expose the Con-

fidence Man. He fails because in a world without higher values the Confidence Man is king, and evil generally triumphs; good deeds are inevitably frustrated, and good men bear the bitter effects of that frustration. It is understandable, then, that Melville stopped writing for a while after *The Confidence Man;* in illness and bitterness, he had begun to anticipate "annihilation." Despairing of a spiritual reality, he had written himself into a cul-de-sac.

His family, recognizing the strain and fatigue, and recalling the fate of his father, decided that a trip abroad would be the necessary curative: his itinerary would include the Holy Land, but England was to be the first stop and a visit with Nathaniel Hawthorne, then American consul at Liverpool. Their friendship, unfortunately, had dimmed since Melville, five years before, had written letters to Hawthorne which are still the glory of American epistles, but, even so, they spent an afternoon together discussing all the old metaphysical problems.

On his return from the Near East, Greece, and Italy in 1857, Melville took to the lecture circuit with such subjects as "Roman Statuary" and "The South Seas," but he was not very successful and, after three seasons, gave up the project. Since the failure of *Pierre*, he had chosen to cultivate anonymity; but he found rejection heartbreaking. Scorned and then neglected, Melville had finally to accept a bitter truce with unsuccess and, returning to New York in 1863, he retreated to the waterfront where for nearly twenty years (1866–1885) he was a customs inspector. That he could have forgotten Hawthorne's premonitory portrayal of custom house life in *The Scarlet Letter*—its intellectual atrophy and spiritual decay—is unlikely. But Melville knew or divined what he was about; an act of will and the nearness of the ocean preserved his health and his heart. For even if during these nineteen years he did not sail the seas, still, as it did for the landsmen he described in *Moby Dick* who "of a dreamy Sabbath afternoon . . . stand thousands upon thousands . . . fixed in ocean reveries," the presence of the sea helped keep him psychically whole.

Living now an entirely private life, Melville wrote exclusively for himself, and, almost as a discipline, he turned from prose to metrical poetry. Although he had written several poems for Mardi and "Father Mapple's Hymn" for *Moby Dick*, it was not until about 1860 that he began writing poetry in earnest and not until 1866 that he published his first volume, BATTLE-PIECES AND ASPECTS OF THE WAR. It was composed of seventy-two poems in all, the last nineteen of which are frankly denoted "Verses Inscriptive and Memorial." Melville believed that the North was Right and the South Wrong—he himself capitalized both words, and, indeed, saw reflected in the civil strife nothing less than a struggle between good and apostate angels such as Milton had described in *Paradise Lost*. But, in the humane sense, Melville was not partisan or territorial; he saw the wrack of his country as something to be mourned and pitied, and, like Lincoln's, his voice was raised in compassion, not revenge.

Armed with the wisdom that "wisdom is vain, and prophecy" too, Melville looked to the human cost, to the young men irredeemably "enlightened by the volley's glare," and realized that the Civil War was the death-knell of an innocent America. In a world, as he saw it, where "God keeps the middle way," the War renewed Melville's passion for suffering humanity and human waste. "All wars are boyish," he wrote, grimly, definitively, "and are fought by boys."

In terms of length, however, *Battle-Pieces* was minuscule compared to the poem Melville began writing five years later, a poem twice as long as *Paradise Lost* and much more than twice as hard to read. *Clarel. A Poem and Pilgrimage in the Holy Land* (1876), in rhyming octosyllabic couplets, suffers, at worst, from constant inversions, lack of action and narrative flow, and a sense that some of the many characters (particularly the women) are made of cardboard. At best, however, CLAREL offers a masterly presentation of place, and verse which gleams with a hard, intellectual resonance.

Based on Melville's trip to Jerusalem, *Clarel* is, at once, a guided tour to sacred spots and a symposium on the major philosophical problems of the day. Now in his declining years—with much of the old passion spent—Melville renewed his quest for Truth with a new objectivity and a new dispassion. In addition to Clarel, a young questor oscillating between faith and doubt, the pilgrims represent virtually every religious and social persuasion possible. And there are others in profusion, some who start the trip, some who join mid-way, some who are met mid-way, some who never leave Jerusalem—prodigals, revolutionaries, Arabs, Jews, monks—the full panorama of the desert society.

Although there is an element of abortive love in *Clarel*, it is finally not a novel of sentiment but of ideas, and the final question it raises is broadly cultural: Will Western civilization, having lost its traditional faith through the incursions of science be able to revitalize itself, or is it doomed to an ultimate sterility? Melville's answer—the product of thirty years thought by one who regarded himself as a "realist"—was cautiously, qualifiedly optimistic. That it could be optimistic at all was due to his animal faith in nature and to his final conviction (spoken in the poem by Rolfe, Melville's mature image of himself) that—

Let fools count on faith's closing knell,
Time, God are inexhaustible.

As Melville moved into the last few years of his life, retired now from the customhouse, he experienced a "spontaneous after-growth," which elicited three late volumes of poetry, JOHN MARR AND OTHER SAILORS (1888), *Timoleon* (1891), and *Weeds and Wildings, with a Rose or Two* (1924), in addition to *Billy Budd* (also posthu-

mously published in 1924). *John Marr*, a collection of twenty-five poems printed in private edition, is roughly divided into four parts: *Sea-Pieces, Minor Sea-Pieces, Pebbles,* and a prefatory section introduced by an essay on John Marr, who has lived most of his years on the prairies in stoic frustration, away from the seas of his young manhood. Marr and the "other sailors" invoke their shipmate-spirits of long ago and far away, Bridegroom Dick, Tom Deadlight, Jack Roy, etc. Although his resemblance to his creator is fictive, one may safely assume that Melville, who always was somewhat tinctured with sentimentality, here expresses his own heart-felt nostalgia. Yet, in *John Marr*, he expresses much else too.

Thus *Sea-Pieces* ("The Haglets" and "The Aeolian Harp") and *Minor Sea-Pieces,* the major poetic achievement of the volume, affirm the ironic indeterminacy of the universe and the vanity of human wishes. In "To Ned" he musingly recalls roving the Marquesas forty years before and concludes wondering "if mortals twice / Here and hereafter, touch a Paradise." Another of the *Minor Sea-Pieces,* "The Tuft of Kelp" is, like the poetry of Emily Dickinson, gnomically expressive, a nugget of pure intelligence.

All dripping in tangles green,
Cast up by a lonely sea
If purer for that, O Weed,
Bitterer, too, are ye?

TIMOLEON also is a volume of miscellaneous verse, some of which had been composed in the years immediately following Melville's trip to the Mediterranean and the Near East. Although there is no thematic structure relating various poems to the whole, Melville is again a poet of high seriousness, and, unlike Poe, he seeks an intellectual, as well as an emotional, effect. However, since he was not a master metrist, his ideas—often cramped by or encased in unsuitable verse forms—lose a measure of their potency. One may gain insight into both the directions of his intellect and the hazards of his execution by reading "The Enthusiast" (on the maintenance of high ideals), "Art" (on the agonies of artistic creation), "The Garden of Metrodorus" (on the ambiguity of silence), "The Age of the Antonines" (on the sterility of Western civilization), and "After the Pleasure Party" (on the frustration of unfulfilled sexuality).

At the same time, however, that Melville could speak as the experienced revealer of truth, he could also descend into infantile fantasy, with which in *Timoleon*, as in *Pierre*, he is unable to deal without corrupting the nature of his art. Such errors of judgment and taste, however, are infrequent, and when Melville does speak from the depths of his being about a subject over which he has established artistic control, the result is unimpeachably genuine.

In WEEDS AND WILDINGS Melville recollected

a third phase of his earlier life: the early and blissful days of his marriage to Elizabeth Shaw, who is the "Madonna of the Trefoil" in the prefatory dedication. Like all of Melville's late work, this volume, too, represents him making his peace with the world and himself, but here Melville moves beyond the renunciation of the quest to the renunciation of Truth itself. It is entirely strange and more than faintly pathetic to observe Melville resurrect the ghost of Washington Irving and dedicate an entire section to that "happy shade," whose literary weight he once quite accurately compared to a grasshopper's. Although the falling off is not total, in the main *Weeds and Wildings* abjures the intellectual thrust of Melville's best poetry and does not succeed as sentimental nature verse.

Perhaps the most interesting thing of all about this volume is not its bad poetry but its loving dedication and persistently floral imagery, both of which indicate that the breach between Melville and his wife (which had gradually widened during the years) was finally healed. Here, as in *Mardi*, written during his first year of marriage, Melville employed that privately symbolic language of flowers in which Elizabeth was expert. There seems no doubt that their relationship ended, as it had begun, in devotion and love.

Like much else of Melville's "spontaneous after-growth," *Billy Budd* offers final, if finite, statements about matters Melville had pondered for a lifetime: the origin of Evil and the conflict between Evil and Good. The latter concern is presented in its starkest form, with innocent Billy and villainous Claggart as almost allegorically abstract oppositions. Their interaction admits of no ambiguity: innocence and its obverse are alone inadequate for survival. The men of extreme polarity inevitably destroy themselves or are destroyed, whereas the men who reconcile opposites and combine the Head with the Heart survive.

Not since "Bartleby" did Melville so pare and refine the action to its essentials; one reads, horror-stricken, as the plot remorselessly unfolds and Billy is carried to his death. *Billy Budd* is the last flowering of Melville the symbolist: as the Christ-like Billy mounts the yardarm, the golden sun penetrates the fleecy clouds, signifying the resurrection of the hero.

Melville's own intellectual life, buoyed as it was by the faith that "death but routs life into victory," ended on this note of potentially religious affirmation; and as he had come to accept this essentially Christian position, so he had renounced the romantic egotism of his youth and prime. Thus Captain Vere's decision to hang Billy represents the triumph of law; for Vere, allegorically the just God of the Old Testament, realizes that his first obligation is to preserve society, not self, and, therefore, however fatherly he may feel toward Billy, he dooms him nonetheless. And Billy, no less representative of the New Dispensation, willingly accedes to martyrdom, crying at the end, "God bless Captain Vere!" For Melville, *Billy Budd* was the grand finale of a great career, his own final testament, his own *requiescat*.

Herman Melville was a charter member of an artistic underground in the latter half of the 19th century, a body of seclusive individualists who included in their number Thoreau and Emily Dickinson, the painters Winslow Homer and Albert Pinkham Ryder and the sculptor William Rimmer—not to mention such dissatisfied expatriates as Henry James and James Whistler. Melville's own worst prophecy—that he would only be remembered as the man who lived among cannibals—came true in his lifetime; and although he did, in his final days, have a certain coterie following (which, unlike Walt Whitman's, kept a respectable distance), they were unable to publicize his worth. That task would not really begin until the 1920's with the publication of his complete work and the pioneering criticism of Raymond Weaver, Lewis Mumford, and others, an obligation to greatness which, once begun, has hardly ceased. See also THE APPLE TREE TABLE; THE ENCANTADAS; JOURNAL OF A VISIT TO LONDON AND THE CONTINENT.

The following is a selected list of the best critical material written about Herman Melville: Lewis Mumford, *Herman Melville* (1929); W. E. Sedgwick, *Herman Melville: The Tragedy of Mind* (1944); Charles Olson, *Call Me Ishmael* (1947); Richard Chase, *Herman Melville* (1949); Newton Arvin, *Herman Melville* (1950); Leon Howard, *Herman Melville: A Biography* (1951); M. R. Stern, *The Fine Hammered Steel of Herman Melville* (1957).

MARTIN LEONARD POPS

Melville Goodwin, U.S.A. (1951), a novel by JOHN P. MARQUAND. In a succession of sprightly and realistic episodes, a typical American military officer is depicted. The high point of the book is a journalistic interview lasting several days, to which Goodwin is subjected, a fictional description of the ordeal Marquand had endured when he was made the subject of a cover story for *Time* (March 7, 1949).

Member of the Wedding, The (1946), a novel by CARSON MCCULLERS. This is a remarkable study in child psychology. Frankie is a lonely, motherless girl whose brother is being married. Somehow she gets the notion that she will accompany him and his wife into the world. The wedding is seen through her eyes; as a chorus to her remarks and thoughts one hears her six-year-old cousin and the Negro cook. In 1950 a dramatic version of the novel by Mrs. McCullers was successfully produced in New York. It was later filmed (1952).

memoirs in the U.S. All the great events of American history have been followed by a spate of often self-laudatory and partisan memoirs. Possibly JOHN SMITH's books about his journeys in America may be considered memoirs; more veracious are WILLIAM BRADFORD's *History of*

Plimouth Plantation (1651) and JOHN WIN-THROP's *Journal* (1790). No important memoirs were produced during the Revolution, but the Civil War inspired innumerable memoirs on both sides of the Mason and Dixon line. The next era was drab, and only statemen of no great caliber reported on the course of events. The Spanish-American War produced Theodore Roosevelt's *The Rough Riders* (1899). The era of muckraking and reform brought forth some lively memoirs by William Jennings Bryan, Robert La Follette, Lincoln Steffens, and others. Military leaders like General J. J. Pershing and Admiral W. W. Sims described World War I, and Colonel E. M. House produced his *Intimate Papers* (1926–28). The New Deal era spawned a mass of memoirs written or ghost-written by notable personalities. Many leading figures of World War II have since produced memoirs.

In addition, more humble persons have written what are often fascinating versions of important happenings or equally fascinating profiles of great personages. Thus, one may mention Jonathan Boucher's *Reminiscences of an American Loyalist, 1783–1789* (1925); Anne Mc-Vickar Grant's *Memoirs of an American Lady* (1808); James T. Field's *Yesterdays with Authors* (1871); W. D. Howells' *Literary Friends and Acquaintance* (1900); Hamlin Garland's *A Son of the Middle Border* (1917); Brander Matthews' *These Many Years* (1917); Malcolm Cowley's *Exile's Return* (1934); H. L. Mencken's *Happy Days* (1940), *Newspaper Days* (1941), and *Heathen Days* (1943) (see DAYS OF H. L. MENCKEN); Gertrude Atherton's *My San Francisco* (1946); H. S. Canby's *American Memoir* (1947). More recently, an astonishing number of celebrities from the entertainment world—actors, boxers, blues singers, and others—have produced memoirs with the aid of ghost writers.

Memories (1841; published in *Lays of My Home*, 1843), a poem by JOHN GREENLEAF WHITTIER. The poet, at thirty-four, remembers his deep love for his cousin, Mary Emerson Smith. He had known her first when both were very young, and he credits her in a letter written around 1840 with awakening his mind and revealing to him "the mysteries of my own spirit." Apparently he thought of marriage, but he was too young, lacked the financial means, and above all, his Quaker beliefs differed from her Calvinist ones. She married a resident of Covington, Ky., and Whittier continued always to correspond with her.

Men Against the Sea. See MUTINY ON THE BOUNTY.

Mencken, H[enry] L[ouis] (b. Baltimore, Md., Sept. 12, 1880–d. Jan. 29, 1956), newspaperman, editor, writer. Mencken was a reporter on the Baltimore *Herald*, became city editor, then editor. He joined the *Sunpapers* in 1906 and continued with them thereafter. He became literary editor of the SMART SET in 1908, a co-editor in 1914, continuing until 1923. In 1924 he and GEORGE JEAN NATHAN

founded the AMERICAN MERCURY; he withdrew in 1933.

During the early decades of the 1900's, Mencken was at the direct center of a literary cyclone. He excited increasing vituperation from

Alfred A. Knopf, Inc.

what he called the *booboisie*, especially in the "Bible belt," another of his neologisms. His own insults were unmeasured. He denounced Hoover as "a fat Coolidge," committed innumerable instances of *lèse majesté* against Wilson and Franklin D. Roosevelt, and never minced words in talking about anybody. He flouted religion, excoriated newspapers, denounced traditionally minded authors, introduced alien ideas from Europe, eulogized radical new writers like Dreiser and Sinclair Lewis, flayed politicians. He reported the SCOPES TRIAL in a series of masterly articles, directed raucous jeers at prohibition, wrote a solemn article on the alleged invention of the bathtub in America from which President Truman quoted as if from a historical document in 1951.

Like the good newspaperman that he was, Mencken could take any subject, including linguistics, and reduce it to its elements so that everyone could understand and enjoy it. Edmund Wilson called his rather unusual prose style "a blend of American colloquial speech with a rakish literary English . . . and a tone that was humorous and brutal in the combative German manner." Oscar Cargill saw his resemblance to Shaw: "Holy Bernard taught him self-assurance, and coached him in the art of sandblasting his joshbillingsgate into the vigorous vernacular of the gentlemen's washroom." He loved satiric definitions, like these: "*Judge*—a law student who marks his own exam papers";

"*Love*—the delusion that one woman differs from another"; "*Democracy*—the worship of jackals by jackasses." He also said: "It is a sin to believe evil of others, but it is seldom a mistake."

Mencken's first book was *Ventures into Verse* (1903), a collection of pieces in conventional style. His first prose books, on Shaw (1905) and on Nietzsche (1908), exhibited him as the most belligerent literary warrior of his generation in the United States. He then wrote a play, *The Artist* (1912), followed by *Heliogabalus* (1920), which he co-authored. Meanwhile he had been writing essays on numerous topics, many of them satiric; these he collected in *A Book of Burlesques* (1916); *A Little Book in C Major* (1916); *A Book of Prefaces* (1917); *Damn: A Book of Calumny* (1918); *In Defense of Women* (1918); and a series of six books in which he vented his PREJUDICES (1919, 1920, 1922, 1924, 1926, 1927). In 1927, he amused himself by compiling a collection of *Menckeniana: A Schimpflexicon*, from some twenty-five volumes of press notices. This was a dictionary of anti-Mencken invective, some of which could be reproduced only in expurgated form. He also wrote *Notes on Democracy* (1926); *A* TREATISE ON THE GODS (1930; rev., 1946); *Making a President* (1932); and *A Treatise on Right and Wrong* (1934). See A NEGLECTED ANNIVERSARY; CHRISTMAS STORY.

His critical investigations were interrupted in 1918 by a remarkable divagation. Motivated originally perhaps by his dislike of England, Mencken had become more and more interested in the extent to which English as spoken in America was different from English as spoken in England; and with his detailed and well-organized volume called THE AMERICAN LANGUAGE, he made a reputation in an entirely new field. The book went into revised editions in 1921, 1923, and 1936. Meanwhile thousands of letters offering emendations, additions, and new viewpoints poured in from readers. The new material, carefully gathered and organized by Mencken, became too large for the fourth edition, and Mencken thereafter published two additional volumes, *Supplement One* (1945) and *Supplement Two* (1948).

Mencken wrote his autobiography in three volumes: *Happy Days* (1940); *Newspaper Days* (1941); and *Heathen Days* (1943). (See DAYS OF H. L. MENCKEN.) With this trio should be placed the irresistible *Christmas Story* (1946), a Yuletide tale to end all Yuletide tales. Out of his vast store of reading, he gathered a *New Dictionary of Quotations* (1942) that includes much fresh and unconventional material; the *Mencken Chrestomathy* (1949) offers a wide and representative selection from his writings. On September 12, 1955, his seventy-fifth birthday, his publisher presented a paperbound selection from his writings, *The Vintage Mencken*, edited by Alistair Cooke. *Minority Report: H. L. Mencken's Notebooks* (1956); *A Carnival of Buncombe* (1956), sixty-nine political pieces from the Baltimore *Evening Sun;* and *The Bath-*

tub Hoax, and Other Blasts and Bravos from the Chicago Tribune (1958) were published posthumously (see BATHTUB HOAX). *The Letters of H. L. Mencken,* edited by Guy J. Forgue, appeared in 1961.

Ernest Boyd wrote *H. L. Mencken* (1925), and Isaac Goldberg *The Man Mencken* (1925); later, Edgar Kemler wrote *The Irreverent Mr. Mencken* (1950), and William Manchester (with Mencken's assistance) *Disturber of the Peace: The Life and Riotous Times of H. L. Mencken* (1951). An acrid book was Charles Angoff's *H. L. Mencken: A Portrait from Memory* (1956). A partial biography is Carroll Frey's *Bibliography of the Writings of H. L. Mencken* (1924). According to Earle F. Walbridge, Russett Durwood in Carl Van Vechten's *Nigger Heaven* (1926) is an agreeable portrait of Mencken in thin disguise. *HLM: The Mencken Bibliography* (1961), by Betty Adler and Jane Wilhelm, is kept up to date in *Menckeniana,* a quarterly pamphlet of the Enoch Pratt Free Library.

Mending Wall (in *North of Boston,* 1914), a poem by ROBERT FROST. Possibly the most famous of Frost's poems, this piece tells how in the spring, Frost, at a Derry, N.H., farm, calls to his neighbor to come and help him mend their stone wall. Both of them contend against that natural and mysterious something "which doesn't love a wall." But the neighbor holds doggedly to a saying of his father's, "Good fences makes good neighbors," while Frost remarks, "There where it is we do not need the wall: / He is all pine and I am apple orchard; / My apple trees will never get across / And eat the cones under his pines, I tell him." The poem has, of course, a symbolical meaning, although Frost once said, "Poems can be pressed too hard for meaning." The poem is about "boundaries," and Frost honestly gives both sides.

Men in White (1933), a play by SIDNEY KINGSLEY. It presents, with strong dramatic effect, a crisis in the life of a surgeon who finds himself faced with a conflict of love and professional duty. It won a Pulitzer Prize in 1934.

Menken, Adah Isaacs (b. New Orleans, June 15, 1835[?]—d. Aug. 10, 1868), actress, poet. Adah Menken's stage career started in New Orleans in 1857; at about the same time her poems began to appear in the *Cincinnati Israelite* and the New York *Sunday Mercury*. Tongues wagged in tavern and pulpit when in the title role of Byron's *Mazeppa* she appeared half naked, strapped to the back of a horse. She was not truly beautiful, nor were her poetry and acting particularly good, yet she radiated such charm, vitality, and generosity that she attracted writers of all sorts. In San Francisco and Virginia City she captivated Joaquin Miller. BRET HARTE wrote of her as Belle Montgomery in his poetry. Mark Twain admired her and submitted his work to her criticism. In London, Dickens, Charles Reade, Swinburne, Rossetti, and Burne-Jones sat at her feet. In Paris she became the last love of Dumas *père* and was worshipped by Gautier. Her marriages and divorces were a constant subject for scandal. Her autobiographical poems, entitled *Infelicia* (1868), were full of wild romanticism. Allen Lesser's *Enchanting Rebel* (1947) is a novel based on her life.

Menninger, Karl Augustus (b. Topeka, Kans., July 22, 1893—   ), and **Menninger, William Claire** (b. Topeka, Kans., Oct. 15, 1899—d. Sept. 6, 1966), psychiatrists. Under the guidance of their father, Charles Frederick Menninger, also a physician and a pioneering psychiatrist, the Menningers conducted renowned psychiatric clinics and hospitals in Topeka. Karl Menninger wrote *The Human Mind* (1930; rev., 1945); *Man Against Himself* (1938); *Love Against Hate* (1942); also many articles to enlighten the public on psychiatric purposes and procedures. Among William Menninger's writings: *Juvenile Parests* (1936); *Psychiatry in a Troubled World* (1948); *You and Psychiatry* (1948); *Psychiatry: Its Evolution and Present Status* (1948); *How to Understand the Opposite Sex* (1956); *How to Help Your Children* (1959).

Menotti, Gian Carlo (b. Italy, July 7, 1911 —   ), composer. One of the most successful of contemporary composers of opera, Menotti is unique in that five of his works have been produced on Broadway. One of these, *The Medium* (produced in 1947 with the short comic opera, *The Telephone*), later became the only contemporary opera ever filmed and was awarded a prize at the Cannes Film Festival. Two of his works, *The Consul* (1950) and *The Saint of Bleecker Street* (1954), were recipients of the Pulitzer Prize. Menotti has had two operas commissioned by the National Broadcasting Company: *Amahl and the Night Visitors* (1951), the first opera written for television, which has become a Christmas classic, and *Maria Golovin* (1958), which was later performed on Broadway. Menotti himself wrote the libretti for all his operas, which have been notable for their unusual theatrical effectiveness as well as their music, and also wrote the libretto for Samuel Barber's opera, *Vanessa*. He has been his own stage and casting director for many of his productions. Menotti has unquestionably played a major role in creating a greater popular acceptance of opera and of operatic material in musical theater. Since the success of his first works there has been a growing demand for original American operas and English versions of standard foreign operas. It is notable, too, that the first American opera ever produced in Italy was Menotti's *The Consul* (1950).

Men Without Women (1927), fourteen short stories by ERNEST HEMINGWAY. The finest examples of Hemingway's mastery of description, dialogue, and atmosphere are to be found in this volume. The tale most often anthologized is THE KILLERS, a narrative remarkable for its atmosphere of impending doom and for the restraint with which the author handles the explosive situation. *The Undefeated* and FIFTY GRAND deal with one of Hemingway's favorite subjects—the courage of an aging man. *Hills Like White Elephants* and *A Simple Inquiry*,

both consisting of dialogue and a few vividly drawn descriptions, appear to be simple, almost trivial sketches, but have a sinister and dramatic undertone.

Mercedes (1894), a play in verse by THOMAS BAILEY ALDRICH. The scene is Spain in 1810. The play was well received on the stage, but is of small literary merit.

Mercedes of Castile (1840), a novel by JAMES FENIMORE COOPER. Cooper engaged in a great deal of research for this account of the first voyage of Columbus, interwoven with a love story.

Mercy Philbrick's Choice (1876), a novel by HELEN HUNT JACKSON. Mrs. Jackson had known EMILY DICKINSON well when both were children, then for a long time did not see her, although they exchanged many letters. Using her knowledge of Emily's life and character, Mrs. Jackson wrote a short story about her, *Esther Wynne's Love Letters*, one of the anonymously published and never acknowledged *Saxe Holm's Stories* (1874), and a novel, *Mercy Philbrick's Choice*. Mercy is morbidly diffident, has an unhappy love affair, and writes poems that she refuses to publish.

Meredith, Janice. See JANICE MEREDITH.

Merlin [1] (1874), a poem by RALPH WALDO EMERSON. Emerson, who always chafed at the rules of meter and rhyme, made a first draft of this poem for his *Journal* in 1845 and wrote it in practically free verse; later he reworked it into a somewhat more conventional form. The poem is an analysis of the methods of poetry, and in it Emerson says of the poet, "He shall not his brain encumber/ With the coil of rhythm and number;/ But, leaving rule and pale forethought,/ He shall aye climb/ For his rhyme." Elsewhere he extols the poet's great powers, bids him avoid triviality and await genuine inspiration. The poem should perhaps be paired with his essay THE AMERICAN SCHOLAR as part of Emerson's literary declaration of independence.

Merlin [2] (1917), a long blank-verse narrative poem by EDWIN ARLINGTON ROBINSON. It was followed by LANCELOT (1920) and TRISTRAM (1927). It expounds the fatalistic creed of the sage Merlin, who is called by Arthur to consult with him regarding the schemes of Arthur's illegitimate son Modred, and the illicit love affair of Guinevere and Lancelot. The poem has been criticized for its disunity, but Robinson was chiefly interested in presenting an idea— that Arthur's rotten world, and the fate it deserved and suffered, should be a mirror for later generations. The poem, published less than a month before the country entered World War I, did so badly that its publisher refused to risk *Lancelot*, and that poem had to await the close of the war.

Merriam, Charles, and **Merriam, George.** See WEBSTER'S DICTIONARY.

Merriam, Charles Edward (b. Hopkintown, Iowa, Nov. 15, 1874—d. Jan. 8, 1953), teacher, political scientist. Merriam became associated with the University of Chicago in 1900; in 1923 was made chairman of the Department of Political Science. He also served as a member of the City Council of Chicago, and in 1911 ran unsuccessfully for Mayor. Among his books are: *New Aspects of Politics* (1925); *A History of American Political Theories* (1903); *Political Power* (1934); and *Systematic Politics* (1945).

Merrill, James (b. New York City, March 3, 1926—   ), poet, novelist, playwright. James Merrill was educated at Lawrenceville School, N.J., and at Amherst College, subsequently teaching at Amherst and at Bard College. Best known as a poet, Merrill exhibits wit and great technical resource in his work, genuine feeling emerging from controlled and complicated verse. Among his collections of poetry are *First Poems* (1951) and *The Country of a Thousand Years of Peace* (1958). He is also the author of a novel, *The Seraglio* (1957), and a play, *The Immortal Husband*, performed in New York in 1955.

Merrill, Stuart [Fitzrandolph] (b. Hempstead, N.Y., Aug. 1, 1863—d. Dec. 1, 1915), poet, translator. A lifelong Socialist, Stuart Merrill was one of the early American expatriates. He lived mostly in France, and did all his writing in French. Only one book of his, a collection of admirable translations from Huysmans, Baudelaire, Mallarmé, and other French writers, appeared in English, *Pastels in Prose* (1890). He published a volume of French poems, *Les Gammes* (1887), that confirmed his leadership in the French symbolist movement. For a while, he managed the New Art Theatre in Paris, and in 1892 published a second volume of poems, *Les Fastes*. His most important work, *Une Voix dans la Foule* (1909), expresses his deep sympathy for the sufferings of mankind. M. L. Henry wrote a biography in French, *Stuart Merrill* (Paris, 1927).

Merritt, A[braham] (b. Beverly, N.J., Jan. 20, 1884—d. Aug., 1943), reporter, archaeologist, short-story writer. Merritt worked first on the Philadelphia *Inquirer*, later for the *American Weekly*, of which he became editor in 1937. In the meantime, he engaged in archaeological and historical studies relating mainly to the modern survival of ancient cults. He published several imaginative and well-written novels, something like science-fiction, including: *The Moon Pool* (1919); *The Ship of Ishtar* (1926); *The People of the Abyss* (1931); and *Dwellers in the Mirage* (1934).

Merriwell, Frank. A character credited by WILLIAM GILBERT PATTEN, who wrote under the pen name of Burt L. Standish. Patten, already a popular dime novelist, conceived this character in 1896, and continued to write weekly stories about him for eighteen years. The stories were later collected in the "Frank Merriwell Series," which ran into 208 volumes from 1900 to 1933, then was revived with *Mr. Frank Merriwell* in 1941. Patten presented Merriwell as an athletic hero at Yale; he had so many virtues that he seemed a caricature.

In 1931 he became a comic strip character. The series was the most extended in all juvenile literature, and sold more than 125,000,000 copies. It was soberly analyzed in John Levi

Cutler's *Gilbert Patten and His Frank Merriwell Saga: A Study in Sub-Literary Fiction, 1896–1913* (1934).

Merry Mount. See THOMAS MORTON.

Mertins, Louis and **Esther.** Authors of THE INTERVALS OF ROBERT FROST.

Merton, Thomas (b. France, Jan. 31, 1915 —d. Dec. 9, 1968), poet, writer, Trappist monk. Merton, born in the Pyrenees, grew up in France among artists. He received his early schooling in France. His father, a landscape painter, was British, his mother an American and a Quaker. He attended Cambridge University, England, and Columbia University, where he took his M.A. in 1939. From childhood he had a special liking for the poetry of William Blake and felt that his religious orientation owed much to Blake as well as to Jacques Maritain, St. Augustine, Dante, the 12th-century Cistercians, and the anonymous author of the *Cloud of Unknowing*. He became a convert to Catholicism in 1938, and his first book, *Thirty Poems* (1944), shows the flame of his enthusiasm for the faith he chose. In 1941 Merton entered the strict Cistercian monastery at Gethsemani, in Kentucky, as a Trappist novice. His autobiographical *The Seven-Story Mountain* (1948), became an immediate best seller. Among his books: *Man in the Divided Sea* (1946); *Figures for an Apocalypse* (1947); *Exile Ends in Glory* (1948); *Seeds of Contemplation* (1949); *Waters of Siloe* (1949); *The Sign of Jonas* (1953, autobiographical); *No Man Is An Island* (1955); *Monastic Peace* (1958); *New Seeds of Contemplation* (1961); *The New Man* (1962).

Merton of the Movies (1922), a novel by HARRY LEON WILSON, dramatized in 1922 by MARC CONNELLY and G. S. KAUFMAN, filmed in 1924. In this portrayal of Merton Gill, the small-town dry-goods clerk who finally reaches Hollywood, Wilson delightfully satirized the dreams of the average American youth as well as Hollywood itself.

Merwin, Samuel (b. Evanston, Ill., Oct. 6, 1874—d. Oct. 17, 1936), editor, novelist, director, dramatist. Merwin began his literary career by writing lively novels in collaboration with H. K. WEBSTER on American railroad-building—*The Short Line War* (1899) and CALUMET K (1901). The latter was a best-seller. Later he wrote other novels, among them two about adolescents—*Temperamental Henry* (1917), and *Henry Is Twenty* (1918). He was associate editor of *Success* from 1905 to 1909, editor till 1911; in the course of his work on this magazine he investigated the opium trade in China and wrote *Drugging a Nation* (1908).

Message to Garcia, A (1899), a hortatory essay by ELBERT HUBBARD. This was one of the most extraordinary documents ever issued in the United States. Hubbard, editor of THE PHILISTINE, needed a piece to fill out the March, 1899, issue of his magazine. He had just read a newspaper story about a certain Lt. ANDREW SUMMERS ROWAN (1857–1943), who had been given by the War Department a mission to make his way to the Cuban insurgents then in revolt against Spain, learn something about their numbers, and perhaps discuss plans of cooperation with the American Army. Rowan performed his mission against great odds. He talked to General Calixto García Iniguez, who was in command of the Cuban forces, and after encountering further difficulties, managed to reach Washington with his report.

Hubbard dressed the story up skillfully and then used it as a pretext for an industrial sermon. The issue was sold out at once, and millions of reprints were distributed during World War I. It was translated into at least twenty languages. The reason was not so much the story of Rowan's heroism as the moral that Hubbard drew from it: when you are given a job to do you ought to do it no matter what the odds against you are; be sure *you* deliver your message to Garcia. In the meantime Rowan himself was forgotten. He served in the Philippines and in 1909 resigned from the army because of ill health. In the early 1920's a movie company invited him to participate in a film based on his adventure. When he heard the plot would turn on his romance with a beautiful Cuban rebel, he refused indignantly and would not even go to see the picture.

Messer Marco Polo (1921), a novel by BRIAN DUNN-DIRNE. The story is narrated by Malachi Campbell, an Ulsterman who had fought all over the world and picked up many strange tales. He tells what he asserts to be "the real story of Marco Polo," an account of how Marco fell in love with the daughter of Kubla Khan. Through her command her magicians save him from death in the desert. He stays and marries her, and then she dies; and in his old age he goes back to Venice. A romantic tale with plenty of "Irish magic" in it, the book became a best seller.

Metamora, or, The Last of the Wampanoags (1829), a play by JOHN AUGUSTUS STONE. The play was written in response to an offer by the actor Edwin Forrest of a handsome prize for "the best tragedy, in five acts, of which the hero, or principal character, shall be an original of this country." Stone won the prize, and when the play was produced it was a great success. Forrest continued to play in it for the rest of his career; in 1836 he had R. M. BIRD revise it. However, Stone shared neither the glory nor the cash, and in despair committed suicide in 1834. The play exists in two incomplete manuscripts, printed in *America's Lost Plays* (1941). Metamora is the Indian monarch called KING PHILIP, who is portrayed as courageous, noble, and sincere, and who speaks what A. H. Quinn calls "a mixture of Indian and Ossian."

Metaphysical Club. This group of scientists, philosophers, and laymen was founded at Cambridge, Mass., some time in the 1870's. It included among its members William James, Oliver Wendell Holmes the younger, Charles Sanders Peirce, John Fiske, Chauncey Wright, Francis E. Abbot, Nicholas St. John Green, and

Joseph Warner. Green, a lawyer and a disciple of Jeremy Bentham, was credited by Peirce with having directed attention to a definition of "belief" by the British metaphysician Alexander Bain as "that upon which a man is prepared to act." From this definition, says Peirce, "pragmatism is scarce more than a corollary." He and James developed this idea when they spread the doctrine of PRAGMATISM. Peirce himself was apparently the first to put the idea down on paper, and then into print, when he drew up an article on the subject, in *The Popular Science Monthly* (1878).

Mexican War. When Texas won its independence (1836), Mexico bitterly resented the assistance the new country continued to receive from the United States. In 1845, its annexation to the United States brought on a crisis. On April 14, 1846, after attempts at negotiation had failed, Mexican troops ambushed an American force, and the war began. It was fought partly in Mexico, partly in the Southwest, and partly in California. Peace was concluded with the Treaty of Guadalupe-Hidalgo, Feb. 2, 1848. Mexico abandoned its claims to Texas, and ceded to the United States territory that now comprises most of New Mexico, Arizona, California, Colorado, Utah, and Nevada. In return the United States gave Mexico 15 million dollars and assumed claims of American citizens for 3 million dollars against Mexico.

Popular reaction to the war was unfavorable. It has often been regarded as naked aggression, imperialism at its worst. A few historians have somewhat modified this verdict, particularly George L. Rives in *The U.S. and Mexico, 1821–48* (2 v., 1913); Justin H. Smith in *War with Mexico* (2 v., 1920); Bernard De Voto in *The Year of Decision, 1846* (1943); Alfred Hoyt Bill in *Rehearsal for Conflict: The Story of Our War with Mexico* (1948); Robert Selph Henry in *The Story of the Mexican War* (1950); Otis A. Singletary in *The Mexican War* (1960). Grant, Lee, Meade, McClellan, and many other future generals received their first experience of battle in the war.

Several striking poems came out of the war: C. F. Hoffman's stirring ballad *Monterey;* General Albert Pike's *Battle of Buena Vista;* and the finest of all, Whittier's *The Angels of Buena Vista,* which foreshadows a reconciliation of the two battling nations. Fiction on the subject includes John Ludlum McConnel's *Talbot and Vernon* (1850); Mary S. Watts' *Nathan Burke* (1910); Hoffman Birney's *Eagle in the Sun* (1935); Robert L. Duffus' *Journada* (1935); Stanley Vestal's *Revolt on the Border* (1938); and Herbert S. Gorman's *The Wine of San Lorenzo* (1945).

Meyer, Annie Nathan (b. New York City, Feb. 19, 1867—d. Sept. 23, 1951), educator, dramatist, novelist. Annie Nathan prepared for college, took the Columbia University examinations, but was unable to receive credit because women were excluded from Columbia at the time. In order that other young women should not be similarly treated, she set about founding a women's branch of Columbia, after first obtaining permission from the university's trustees. The account of the founding of Barnard College in 1889 is told in her *Barnard Beginnings* (1935). *Helen Brent, M.D., A Social Study* (1892), a novel dealing with a woman's choice between love and a career, was followed by *Robert Annys, a Tale* (1901). Turning her attention to Broadway, Mrs. Meyer wrote the following plays: *The Dominant Sex* (1911); *The Dreamer* (1912); *The District Attorney* (1920); *The Advertising of Kate* (1921); *The New Way* (1925); and *Black Souls* (1932).

Mezzo Cammin (1842), a sonnet by HENRY WADSWORTH LONGFELLOW. In this poem Longfellow laments that his ambition to build "a tower of song with lofty parapet" has been defeated by "sorrow and a care that almost killed." It was written while he was on a trip to Europe for his health and was not published until 1886. The title is from Dante and refers to the fact that Longfellow, too, was in the "middle way" of his life—thirty-five years old. The sorrow was undoubtedly the death of his first wife; "the tower of song" not completed was probably his *Christus*, outlined in his notebooks of the period.

Michelson, Albert A[braham] (b. Germany, Dec. 19, 1852—d. May 9, 1931), physicist. Brought to this country as a young child, Michelson was graduated from the U.S. Naval Academy in 1873, spent the next four years as an ensign in the Navy and as an instructor in physics at the Academy. He returned to Europe to study in Berlin, Heidelberg, and Paris. In 1883 he became professor of physics in Cleveland at the Case School of Applied Science, then, after three years at Clark University, he was made head of the department of physics at the University of Chicago. He published more than eighty scientific papers and two books, *Velocity of Light* (1902) and *Light Waves and Their Uses* (1903), all dealing with light. Upon his observations and measurements of the speed of light Einstein founded his theory of relativity. He received the Nobel Prize in physics in 1907, the first American thus honored.

Michelson, Charles (b. Virginia City, Nev., [?], 1869 [1870?]—d. Jan. 8, 1948), newspaperman, correspondent, publicity director, ghostwriter. Brother of Albert Michelson, he worked for San Francisco and New York papers, was sent by W. R. HEARST to report the Cuban insurrection in 1896. Later he became one of the greatest Washington reporters. When Hoover was elected President, Michelson became the Democratic Party's No. 1 ghostwriter and phrase-maker. He hung the depression around Hoover's neck and kept it there. He also wrote first drafts for many of Roosevelt's speeches. He told his own astonishing story in *The Ghost Talks* (1944).

Michelson, Miriam (b. Calaveras, Calif., [?], 1870—d. May 28, 1942), newspaperwoman, short-story writer, novelist. Sister of CHARLES and ALBERT MICHELSON, Miss Michelson was a drama critic and special writer on several San Francisco and Philadelphia newspapers, and contributed short stories to many magazines. Her most successful novel was her first, *In the Bishop's Carriage* (1904). Among her other books: *The Madigans* (1904); *A Yellow Journalist* (1905); *The Duchess of Suds* (1911); *The Superwoman* (1912); *The Wonderlode of Silver and Gold* (1934).

Michener, James A[lbert] (b. New York City, Feb. 3, 1907—   ), short-story writer, essayist, novelist. Michener taught English at George School (Pennsylvania); he spent two and a half years in Europe studying, observing, and sailing in the Mediterranean as a seaman in the British merchant navy. During World War II, he saw active duty with the United States Navy in the South Pacific; his experiences formed the background for a collection of stories, TALES OF THE SOUTH PACIFIC (1948), which won a Pulitzer Prize and was the basis for *South Pacific,* a smash-hit musical comedy. His novel, *The Fires of Spring* (1949), describes the development of a sensitive Pennsylvania boy. The South Pacific again figures in *Return to Paradise* (1950), a volume of stories and essays. *The Voice of Asia* (1951) is nonfiction. In *The Bridges at Toko-Ri* (1953) is a fictional account of the Korean War. *Sayonara* (1954) deals sympathetically with Japanese-American relations in Japan; it became a popular motion picture. *The Floating World* (1954) is a sensitively written appreciation of Japanese wood-block prints, lavishly illustrated. He also wrote *The Bridge at Andau* (1957), about the abortive 1956 Hungarian revolution, and *Rascals in Paradise* (1957), another return to the South Seas. Among his other books are: *The Hokusai Sketchbook* (1958); *Japanese Prints* (1959); *Hawaii* (1959); *Report of the County Chairman* (1961).

Mickey Mouse. A cartoon character created by WALT DISNEY, Mickey has made his way into children's hearts all over the world—and their elders', too. Mickey, originally called Mortimer, was born Sept. 21, 1928, in a cartoon movie called *Steamboat Willie*. In *The Band Concert* (1935), he acquired color. As time went on, Mickey began to appear in more elaborate adventures, such as *Fantasia* (1940), in which Mickey was the hero of the section entitled *The Sorcerer's Apprentice*. Minnie Mouse is his staunch leading lady. His name has been given to hundreds of items of trade, and his story has been retold in scores of popular books. In his later years Donald Duck became an upstart rival.

Microbe Hunters (1926), twelve biographical sketches by PAUL DE KRUIF. On the basis of extensive investigations, de Kruif wrote this best-selling book. He began with the Dutch merchant Leeuwenhoek, whose invention of microscopes revolutionized science and led to the discovery of microbes. De Kruif then told about other scientists who continued the work of the gifted Dutch amateur, down to Walter

Reed and Paul Ehrlich. De Kruif's style is popular and yet impressive, at times overemphatic and dogmatic.

Microfilms. This development of photography is likely to have a revolutionary effect on book publishing and reading. A microphotograph is a reproduction of original material greatly reduced in size. It is read on a reading machine, which projects the film within a compact cabinet onto a viewer. Or the images can be projected on a convenient wall screen or special screen. In the world of scholarship and publishing, increasing use has been made of microphotography, with libraries as custodians of the films. More and more rare manuscripts and books are being made available for readers everywhere. Newspapers, otherwise disappointingly impermanent, are now regularly being microfilmed. One of the best collections of microfilms in the world is in the Library of Congress.

Mid-American Chants (1918), a collection of Whitmanesque verse by SHERWOOD ANDERSON.

Middle Border. See HAMLIN GARLAND.

Middleton, Drew (b. New York City, Oct. 14, 1914—   ), newspaperman, foreign and war correspondent. First for the Associated Press, and after 1942 for *The New York Times*, Middleton covered many of the most important happenings, particularly World War II and the momentous events that followed it. His articles and much new material have been gathered in *Our Share of Night* (1946); *The Struggle for Germany* (1949); *The Defense of Western Europe* (1952). He received the Overseas Press Club Citation for Excellence for *These Are The British* (1957). *The Sky Suspended, The Story of the Battle of Britain* came out in 1960.

Middleton, George (b. Paterson, N.J., Oct. 27, 1880—d. Dec. 23, 1967), editor, playwright. After graduation from college, Middleton spent two years in Paris studying the theater and writing plays. His first play, *Cavalier* (1902), was written with PAUL KESTER. *Polly with a Past* (1917), a comedy written with Guy Bolton, was one of his greatest successes. He was literary editor of *La Follette's Weekly* from 1912 until 1930. From 1929 until 1931 he was an associate producer in the Fox Film Corporation. His one-act divorce play, *Collusion*, was refused a licence by the London censor in 1921, by the Los Angeles censor two years later. Among his published plays are: *Embers* (1911); *Tradition* (1913); *Nowadays* (1914); *Masks* (1920); *The Light of the World* (1920); *Hiss! Boom!! Blah!!!* (1933); *That Was Balzac* (1936); *The Dramatists' Guild* (1939). *These Things Are Mine* (1947) is his autobiography.

Middletown (1929), a survey of a typical mid-American city in the 1920's by ROBERT S. and HELEN M. LYND. The original is usually believed to be Muncie, Ind. Later the Lynds published *Middletown in Transition* (1937).

Middle West. In general the terms *Middle West* and *Midwest* designate the region bounded on the east by the Appalachians, on the north by Canada, on the south by an extension of the Mason and Dixon Line, and on the west by the Rockies. This region would consequently include Ohio, Michigan, Illinois, Indiana, Wisconsin, Minnesota, Missouri, Iowa, Kansas, Nebraska, and the Dakotas. Frederick J. Jackson described it in *The Frontier in America* (1893) as "the economic and political center of the Republic." The literature of this region has a certain degree of unity, especially in its farm and small-town novels, in which American realism first flowered. Ralph L. Rusk described *The Literature of the Middle Western Border* (2 v., 1925). Two excellent anthologies are John T. Frederick's *Out of the Midwest: A Collection of Present-Day Writing* (1944), and John T. Flanagan's *America is West: An Anthology of Midwestern Life and Literature* (1945). In collaboration with Louis Bromfield, the editors of *Look* magazine gave a vivid textual and pictorial view of *The Midwest* (1947). Lewis Atherton wrote *Main Street on the Middle Border* (1954).

Midland, The: A Magazine of the Middle West. This was an influential "little magazine," founded by John T. Frederick in Iowa City in 1915, and edited by him until 1933, when it was absorbed by *The Frontier* (see LITTLE MAGAZINES). FRANK LUTHER MOTT was associated with him in the editorship from 1925 to 1933. The magazine was esteemed for the many fine poems and short stories that it published.

Midnight Mass for the Dying Year, The (in VOICES OF THE NIGHT, 1839), a poem by H. W. Longfellow. This melodious poem was attacked in a review by Poe as a plagiarism from Tennyson's *The Death of the Old Year* "too palpable to be mistaken."

Midnight Ride of Paul Revere, The (in *Tales of a Wayside Inn*, 1863), a ballad by H. W. Longfellow. The story is told by the Landlord, and opens the book. It narrates how Revere waited for the signal in the tower of the Old North Church, and then bore word from Boston to Lexington and Concord that British troops were approaching. Revere was not the only one to carry the warning; it was an accident of fate that made Longfellow concentrate on him and forget the others. Critics do not esteem the ballad highly. It is, however, a vivid narrative with skillful use of onomatopoeia in its anapestic tetrameter couplets.

Miers, Earl Schenck (b. Brooklyn, N.Y., May 27, 1910—   ), editor, historian, novelist, writer of juveniles. *The Ivy Years* (1945) is an account of Miers' college days at Rutgers and of the brave battle he fought against cerebral palsy, the result of a brain injury at birth. This is also the subject, frankly treated, of *Why Did This Have to Happen* (1958). Miers served on the staff of several publishing firms. His best-known books are historical, among them *Gettysburg* (with Richard A.

Brown, 1948); an account of General Sherman, *The General Who Marched to Hell* (1951); *Web of Victory* (1955), a study of Grant at Vicksburg. *Valley in Arms* (1943) is a historical novel. Among his other books: *Backfield Feud* (1936); *Composing Sticks and Mortar Boards* (1941); *Career Coach* (1941); *Bookmaking and Kindred Amenities* (1942); *Ball of Fire* (1956); *Rebel's Roost* (1956); *America and Its Presidents* (1959); *Storybook of Science* (1959); and with PAUL M. ANGLE the two volume *Tragic Years, 1861–1865* (1960).

Mifflin, Lloyd (b. Columbia, Pa., Sept. 15, 1846—d. July 16, 1921), poet, printer. Mifflin wrote a great many sonnets. He was expert and melodious, but inclined to load his lines with classical allusions. Among his collections: *At the Gates of Song* (1897); *The Slopes of Helicon* (1898); *Fields of Dawn and Later Sonnets* (1900); *Collected Sonnets* (1905); *As Twilight Falls* (1916). He made versions of Bion and other Greek poets.

Mike Fink. See FINK, MIKE.

Miles, George H[enry] (b. Baltimore, Md., July 31, 1824—d. July 24, 1871), lawyer, teacher, playwright, poet, novelist. Miles was one of the better dramatists of the mid-19th century. He disliked law, taught at Mount St. Mary's College for many years. His first play of any consequence, *Mohammed, the Arabian Prophet*, won in 1849 a prize offered by the actor Edwin Forrest, but the latter never produced it. It was finally brought to the stage in 1851. Another play by Miles dealt with a favorite theme of his day, *Hernando de Soto* (1852). It was never published, but part of the manuscript survives, and A. H. Quinn calls it "an appropriate treatment of a romantic theme." One of Miles' comedies, *Señor Valiente* (1859), was successfully produced in Baltimore and New York City. Miles wrote verse, and a poem of his, *Ave Maria*, took a prize in a competition (1866).

Milestones (1912), a play by Arnold Bennett and EDWARD KNOBLOCK. This drama, produced successfully in New York, London, Berlin, Paris, and elsewhere, and frequently revived, shows the rise and growth of a family through three generations. Wilbur D. Dunkel's study *The Genesis of "Milestones"* (1952) shows how the American playwright and the English novelist worked together: Knoblock wrote the first draft, Bennett rewrote it, together they wrote the final version.

Miles Wallingford (1844), a novel by JAMES FENIMORE COOPER. This story was really part of, rather than a sequel to, AFLOAT AND ASHORE, OR, THE ADVENTURES OF MILES WALLINGFORD, which was published several months earlier under the first part of the title. Through Miles, Cooper vents all his own peculiar notions, amid exciting adventures at sea such as Cooper described so well. The heroine has reminded biographers of Cooper's wife Susan.

Milk for Babes, Drawn out of the Breasts of Both Testaments (1646), a book of religious instruction for children by JOHN COTTON. It tended to replace early catechisms.

Millar, Margaret (b. Kitchener, Ontario, Feb. 5, 1915—), Canadian writer. Mrs. Millar makes a specialty of psychological mystery stories: *The Invisible Worm* (1941); *The Wall of Eyes* (1943); *The Iron Gate* (1945); *Vanish in an Instant* (1952); *Rose's Last Summer* (1952); *Beast in View* (1955); *An Air That Kills* (1957); *Listening Walls* (1959); *Stranger in My Grave* (1960). She is especially skillful in creating an atmosphere of sustained terror. Her husband, Kenneth Millar, also writes mysteries.

Millard, Bailey (b. Markesan, Wis., Oct. 2, 1859—d. March 20, 1941), newspaperman, editor, feature writer, poet, novelist. Millard was city editor of the San Francisco *Call*, editor of COSMOPOLITAN from 1905 to 1907, wrote feature articles for the Los Angeles *Times*. Among his books: *The Great American Novel* (1899); *Songs of the Press* (1902); *Sunland Song* (1932).

Millay, Edna St. Vincent (b. Rockland, Me., Feb. 22, 1892—d. Oct. 19, 1950), poet, dramatist. Miss Millay was fortunate to grow up in a family which encouraged her literary talents. The three Millay sisters were avid readers of

Bettmann Archive

ST. NICHOLAS magazine, as were most literate children of that generation, and it was in its pages that Edna Millay first found her welcome as a poet. Such early verses as *Forest Trees* and *Vacation Song* were published in it. RENASCENCE won publication in a poetry selection called *The Lyric Year* (1912). At eighteen, the age limit for publication in *St. Nicholas*, she bid the editors a formal farewell and thanked them for the five-dollar prize she had received. There seemed little chance that she might go to college, until one day at a party at the Whitehall summer hotel in Camden, Maine, Caroline B. Dow heard her read her poem *Renascence* and sing some of the songs she had composed. Miss Dow, head of the National Training School of YWCA, was a person of some consequence, and once her interest was kindled, she undertook to help with Miss Millay's education. After some preliminary courses at Barnard, Edna Millay entered Vassar. Her *Second April* (1921) was dedicated: "To my beloved friend Caroline B. Dow." Upon graduation from Vassar, Miss Millay went to live in Greenwich Village, New York, where the rebels of the twenties congregated with most abandon. For a while she acted with the PROVINCETOWN PLAYERS, who produced some of the plays she had written while at Vassar. Like most of her Village contemporaries, the copper-haired, green-eyed poetess was "very, very poor and very, very merry," as she described it. Although she was known in those literary circles where the sparks of genius find early recognition, the reading public in general became familiar with her work only through her second book, A FEW FIGS FROM THISTLES (1920). She was influenced particularly by Shakespeare, Keats, and to a lesser degree Gerard Manley Hopkins, and developed a special genius for the sonnet. Some of her most memorable poems were composed in this form. In 1923 she won the Pulitzer Prize for THE HARP-WEAVER AND OTHER POEMS. Her books were selling well and she made rather dramatic personal appearances that further heightened her vogue. The ardent youth of her time found in Miss Millay's verses a creed and a way of life. Undoubtedly her most quoted (and misquoted) quatrain remains: "My candle burns at both ends;/ It will not last the night;/ But ah, my foes, and oh, my friends—/ It gives a lovely light."

In 1923 she married Eugen Boissevain, a New York importer. Soon after, they purchased a farm in Austerlitz, New York, which she called Steepletop after the wildflower named Steeplebush which abounded in the region. They continued to live there for the rest of their lives. Some of Edna Millay's finest work was produced in a shack some little way from the main house.

As she approached the middle years her writing showed less impudence, more seriousness, especially when political catastrophe overtook Europe and she wrote powerful verses against the barbaric developments there, with such lines as: "God! we could keep this planet warm / By friction, if the sun should fail." Among her books are: *Aria da Capo* (1920, a play, which she considered one of her best); *Three Plays* (1926); THE KING'S HENCHMAN (1927, a play which Deems Taylor turned into an opera); *The Buck in the Snow and Other Poems* (1928); *Fatal Interview* (1931); *Wine from These Grapes* (1934); CONVERSATION AT MIDNIGHT (1937); *Huntsman, What Quary?* (1939); *Make Bright the Arrow* (1940). Her *Collected Sonnets* appeared in 1941, her *Collected Lyrics* in 1943. Published after her death were: *Mine the Harvest* (1954) and *Collected Poems* (1956). She also wrote fictional and satirical sketches, such as *Distressing Dialogues* (1924), under the pen name Nancy Boyd.

Critical opinion regarding Miss Millay is mixed. Some critics have felt that she failed to go beyond the level of her early work, and that her traditionalism made her poetry easily readable but otherwise unexceptional. Edmund Wilson, however, found her "one of the few poets writing in English in our time who have attained to anything like the stature of great literary figures in an age in which prose has predominated."

No extensive study of Miss Millay's work has as yet been made. Karl Yost compiled *A Bibliography of the Works of Edna S. Vincent Millay* (1937), which included some theretofore unpublished material. *Letters of Edna St. Vincent Millay* (1952), a selection by Allan Ross MacDougall, shows an epistolary gift that admirably supplements her poetry.

Miller, Alice Duer (b. New York City, July 27, 1874—d. Aug. 22, 1942), poet, playwright, novelist, short-story writer. Some of her light, witty novels were dramatized, in particular *Come Out of the Kitchen* (1916) and *The Charm School* (1919); another, *Gowns by Roberta* (1933), became the basis of the popular musical comedy, *Roberta*, with music by Jerome Kern and book by Otto Harbach. She conducted a column for the New York *Tribune* called "Are Women People?", wrote scripts for Hollywood, and appeared in a Hecht-MacArthur movie called *Soak the Rich*. Several collections of her short stories were published. Her great popular success came with her fervid and somewhat sentimental verse eulogy of England's resistance to the Nazis in 1940, *The White Cliffs of Dover*. In 1941 she published *I Have Loved England*. After her death her son, Denning Duer Miller, compiled a slim collection of her *Selected Poems* (1949). Reviewing the book, Sara Henderson Hay paid tribute to Mrs. Miller's passionate sense of justice and to her cleverness in light as well as serious poetry.

Miller, Arthur (b. New York City, Oct. 17, 1915—   ), playwright, novelist, scriptwriter. After high school, Miller began work in a Manhattan warehouse, but read *The Brothers Karamazov* and decided he was "born to be a writer." He entered the University of Michigan and began to write plays, won several prizes and returned to New York where he continued writing. His novel *Focus* (1945), an ironical study of racial prejudice, was followed by his first successful play, *All My Sons* (1947), a study of emotional aftermaths of World War II. DEATH OF A SALESMAN (1949) won the Pulitzer Prize for drama, had a long run on Broadway, and was made into a successful motion picture. It deals with Willie Loman, a traveling salesman who lives and believes in a world of false values in which "popularity" and "personality" are of prime importance. A realistically critical expression of American life, *Death of a Salesman* has been called an attempt "to develop a poetic drama rooted in American speech and manners." It is the best exemplification of Miller's theory that tragedy is possible in the modern theater and that its proper hero is the "common man." *The Crucible* (1953) deals with the Salem witchcraft trials of 1692 and the question of freedom

UPI

of conscience; there are pertinent parallels to the McCarthyism in America during the early fifties. *A View from the Bridge* (1955) won the New York Drama Critics' Circle Award and the Pulitzer Prize. Miller's *Collected Plays* appeared in 1958. The scenario for his film, *The Misfits* (1961), which evolved from a short story published in *Esquire* in 1957, was published in book form in 1961.

Miller, Caroline. Author of LAMB IN HIS BOSOM.

Miller, Cincinnatus Hiner [or Heine]. See JOAQUIN MILLER.

Miller, Daisy. See DAISY MILLER.

Miller, Henry (b. New York City, December 26, 1891), writer.   Born in the Yorkville section of Manhattan, Miller was brought up by his German-American parents in Brooklyn. He spent two months in City College in 1909, and took a job with a cement company. Then, with the money his father had given him to go to Cornell, he traveled in the southwest and Alaska. He returned home the next year and went to work in his father's tailor shop. In 1920 he became employment manager for the Western Union Telegraph Co.; in 1927 he was operating a Greenwich Village speakeasy; in 1930 he took up residence in France for nine

years. During this period he published *Tropic of Cancer* (1934) and *Tropic of Capricorn* (1938), as well as *Black Spring* (1936). After his return to New York in 1940, he travelled in the United States, wrote voluminously, and finally settled in Big Sur, Calif., where he has since lived.

Most of Miller's books are autobiographical. The first part of *Tropic of Capricorn* chronicles his frantic, hilarious years with Western Union; TROPIC OF CANCER covers his years of bumming around Paris; *Big Sur and the Oranges of Hieronymus Bosch* (1956) tells about his life on a secluded mountain top overlooking the Pacific Ocean. But the period he keeps returning to in most of his books is his childhood in Brooklyn's 14th Ward: "From five to ten were the most important years of my life; I lived in the street and acquired the typical American gangster spirit." Though an expatriate for many years Miller always insisted that he was "just a Brooklyn boy." "At sixty-six," he wrote, "I am more rebellious than I was at sixteen . . . now I am positive that youth is right,—or the child in its innocence." Miller is the foremost apostle of American romanticism as typified by Walt Whitman and Mark Twain. He shares with Twain the conviction that the secret of a man's life lies partly in his ability to recover his childhood innocence and purity of feeling. He has turned to the events of his own life in search of this innocence as have so many other notable American writers: F. Scott Fitzgerald, Ernest Hemingway, Thomas Wolfe. With Whitman, whom he names as a major influence, he shares a compulsion to recognize the body.

Some consider *The Colossus of Maroussi* (1941), a travel book about Greece, to be his finest work. Where thousands of tourists and scholars had sought the secrets of ancient Greece in its ruins, Miller found the spirit of Hellenism in living people, with whom he drank much wine, ate great meals, and talked long into the night. His short studies of outcasts, derelicts, and prostitutes display a warm compassion and tender humor, especially *The Alcoholic Veteran With the Washboard Cranium* and *Mademoiselle Claude*. Miller can be hilariously funny, not only about sex, but about odd characters, as in *Astrological Fricassee*, and about people he has known, as in *Max and the White Phagocytes* (1938), the story of a deracinated European Jew he befriended. His love for America comes out even in such a pointedly critical work as *The Air-Conditioned Nightmare* (1945), a collection of essays based on a nationwide tour in 1941.

Still officially unavailable in the U.S. are *Black Spring* (1936); *Tropic of Capricorn* (1939); *The World of Sex* (1940, revised ed. 1957); the three volumes of *The Rosy Crucifixion: Sexus* (1949), *Plexus* (1953), and *Nexus* (1960); and *Quiet Days in Clichy* (1956). Miller has written several pieces on literary censorship, among them *Obscenity in Literature*, *Obscenity and the Law of Reflection*, and his eloquent letter to the Supreme Court of Norway after it banned *Sexus.*

The Books in My Life (1952) lists hundreds of obscure books and authors by which Miller was profoundly affected: *The Secret Doctrine of Madame Blavatsky; She,* by H. Rider Haggard, works of Knut Hamsun and the French surrealists, to name a few. He is in constant search of philosophers and writers who deal with the world in a non-synthetic manner, and have a personal vision, as he does. Miller's vision is horrific yet optimistic. He takes his reader on a tour of the types of human degradation he himself has seen and suffered. He tells us that men have lost the art of living, and that "until this colossal, senseless machine which we have made of America is smashed and scrapped there can be no hope."

Miller has a small reputation as a watercolorist. He has done hundreds of paintings since 1928 and written a book about them, *To Paint Is To Love Again* (1960), with 14 color plates. He has exhibited in New York, San Francisco, Hollywood, at Yale, Harvard, and Dartmouth, and in Denmark, Japan, England, and Israel.

Among Miller's books: *Aller Retour New York* (1935), about a visit to the United States during his Paris period; *Scenario* (1937), "a film with sound," based on Anaïs Nin's surrealist novel *House of Incest; Money and How It Gets That Way* (1938); *The Cosmological Eye* (1939), a collection of stories and articles, his first American publication; *Hamlet* (2 v., 1939, 1941), a correspondence between Miller and his friend Michael Fraenkel. Other American publications include *The Wisdom of the Heart* (1941), a collection of sketches and essays; *Sunday After the War* (1944), thirteen sketches; *Murder and Murderer* (1944), a pacifist tract; *Semblance of a Devoted Past* (1944), letters about paintings; *Obscenity And the Law of Reflection* (1944); *The Air Conditioned Nightmare* (1945); *Remember To Remember* (1947), a continuation of *The Air Conditioned Nightmare,* containing further sketches and essays, *The Smile at the Foot of the Ladder* (1948), the story of the clown Auguste; *The Time of the Assassins* (1956), a study of Rimbaud; *A Devil in Paradise* (1956). The best anthology is *The Henry Miller Reader* (1959), edited by Miller's friend, the English novelist Lawrence Durrell, and containing a bibliography and chronology. Other collections include *The Henry Miller Miscellanea* (1945); *Nights of Love and Laughter* (1955), with an introduction by Kenneth Rexroth; and *The Intimate Henry Miller* (1959). Bern Porter compiled *Henry Miller: a Chronology and Bibliography* (1945).

Some essays on Miller: *Twilight of the Expatriates* by Edmund Wilson; *Inside the Whale* by George Orwell; *Shadow of Doom: An Essay on Henry Miller* (1944), by Wallace Fowlie; *The Strange Case of Henry Miller* (1946), by H. F. West; *Henry Miller* by Philip Rahv; *Henry Miller—The Pathology of Isolation* by

Alwyn Lee; and *The Greatest Living Author* by Karl Shapiro (see TROPIC OF CANCER). One of the most revealing books about Miller is *Art and Outrage* (1959), which contains letters about Miller by his friends Alfred Perles

Cedric Wright

and Lawrence Durrell, with letters about the letters by Miller. Alfred Perles' *My Friend Henry Miller* (1956) contains a useful checklist of Miller's books. *Henry Miller, Expatriate* (1961), by A. K. Baxter, is a recent book-length study. *The Happy Rock* (1945) is a symposium on Miller containing essays by thirty-two writers. See THE BOOSTER.

Miller, Joaquin [pen name of **Cincinnatus Hiner** (or **Heine**) **Miller**] (b. near Liberty, Ind., Sept. 8, 1837—d. Feb. 17, 1913), poet, journalist. He was christened Cincinnatus Hiner (or Heine) Miller; but when it was time for him to put his name on the title page of a book of poems, he chose the name Joaquin from Joaquin Murrietta, a Mexican brigand whom he had defended in an article.

A number of legends have grown up concerning Miller, some of them invented by the poet himself. For example, he once said that his "cradle was a covered wagon pointed West." The truth is that he was born in a house a few miles north of Liberty, Ind. His father was a farmer who turned temporarily to teaching school when the sheriff took over his farm at Liberty. By the time the boy was fifteen, the family had lived in three Indiana towns, lastly on a farm in Grant County. The father sold it, for a change, at a profit, and they finally in 1852 joined a wagon train journeying over the Oregon Trail. The Millers suffered a good deal of hardship, as did most of their fellow emigrants who made the long westward trek. However, they arrived eventually and settled on a farm in the Willamette Valley, Ore., where the boy worked at plowing and cultivating. He read on his own as many books as he could find, was drawn especially to the works of Frémont. At the age of seventeen he ran away

from home and headed for the gold fields of California.

For several years Miller wandered about the Pacific Coast, living at one time with an Indian tribe, the Diggers. According to his own story he was married to a Digger squaw. Returning to Oregon, he attended Columbia College in Eugene. Then he taught school for a while and practiced law. He helped establish a pony express route between the Washington Territory and Idaho and edited the *Democratic Register* in Eugene, a paper that was suppressed during the Civil War, probably because of Miller's Southern views. Meanwhile, he had written enough poems to fill two volumes, *Specimens* (1868) and *Joaquin et al* (1869). The books were scarcely noticed.

Disappointed, Miller went to England in the early 1870's. There he wore a sombrero and cowboy boots and posed as a representative man of the West. London took the poseur to its heart. When he smoked three cigars at once and bit the ankles of débutantes in Mayfair drawing rooms, he confirmed the image which many Britishers had formed of the American of the Pacific Coast. He was sought after as a guest by London society matrons and even became engaged to the daughter of a baronet, though the marriage never took place. In 1870 he published *Pacific Poems*, which appeared the next year in America as Songs of the Sierras. The poems were well received in England, but in the United States Miller still met with a very cool reception, although Whitman befriended him. The autobiographical Life Amongst the Modocs (1873) is in prose.

In 1886 Miller acquired a tract of land in the hills above Oakland, Calif., and built a house after his own eccentric tastes. On his estate he erected monuments to Browning, Frémont, and Moses, along with a funeral pyre readied for his own use when the time came. With the help of his friend Hamlin Garland, he published *The Building of the City Beautiful* (1893), a utopian romance; and later in the same year appeared *The Complete Poetical Works of Joaquin Miller*. His most mature work, *Light* (1907), is a narrative poem. See The Danites in the Sierras.

The poet's most famous poem is still *Columbus;* its refrain—"On, sail on!"—reflected the courage of an expanding nation and was learned by millions of school children. Kit Carson's Ride, with a galloping meter imitated from Browning's *How They Brought the Good News from Ghent to Aix,* is also well-known. *Exodus for Oregon* is a realistic description of the transcontinental migration. But a kind of oratorical extravagance mars much of Miller's verse. At his best he captured something of the sense of vastness and majesty of the West; at his worst he was noisy and dull. Harr Wagner wrote *Joaquin Miller and His Other Self* (1929), and M. M. Marberry, a biography, *Splendid Poseur* (1953).

Eldon C. Hill

Miller, John Henry (b. Germany, March 12, 1702—d. March 31, 1782), printer, publisher, editor. So far as is known, the first announcement of the Declaration of Independence was made in a German newspaper published in Pennsylvania by Miller, *Heinrich Miller's Pennsylvanische Staatsbote* (July 5, 1776), and the full text was published four days later. Though of German birth, Miller was of Swiss decent. With Samuel Holland he founded (1751) *Die Lancasterische Zeitung;* in 1762, *Der Wöchentliche Staatsbote.* Charles F. Dapp wrote a biography of Miller in 1924.

Miller, Max (b. Traverse City, Mich., Feb. 9, 1899—d. Dec. 27, 1967), reporter, author. While employed on various Pacific Coast papers, Miller turned some of his experiences to account in his first book, *I Cover the Waterfront* (1932). The book revealed him as observant, sentimental, and good-humored. Thereafter he turned out a number of similar books, among which are: *Fog and Men on Bering Sea* (1936); *Mexico Around Me* (1937); *Harbor of the Sun* (1940); *The Land Where Time Stands Still* (1943); *No Matter What Happens* (1949); *The Cruise of the Cow* (1951); *Always the Mediterranean* (1952); *Speak of the Earth* (1955); . . . *And Bring All Your Folks* (1959).

Miller, Merle (b. Montour, Iowa, May 17, 1919—   ), newspaperman, editor, novelist. Miller fought in World War II and edited Yank, came back to work for *Time,* was an editor of *Harper's Magazine* from 1947–1949. Two books of his—a novel, *Island 49* (1945), and *We*

Dropped the A-Bomb (with Abe Spitzer, 1946)—appeared before his novel *That Winter* (1948), which first won critical and popular approval for him. It was a realistic tale of three war veterans and the way they went on living in the first winter of the peace. Miller has been an active antagonist of those who seek to abridge freedom of expression in the United States: his novel *The Sure Thing* (1949) and his non-fiction *The Judges and the Judged* (1952) both deal with this topic in vigorous language. Among his later works are: *Reunion* (1954); *A Secret Understanding* (1956); *A Gay and Melancholy Sound* (1961).

Miller, Perry [Gilbert Eddy] (b. Chicago, Feb. 25, 1905—d. Dec. 9, 1963), teacher, historian. Miller became an instructor at Harvard in 1931, professor of American Literature there in 1946. His principal theme was American history as rooted in the ideas of the Puritans. He wrote his doctoral thesis on *Orthodoxy in Massachusetts* (1933). Miller saw this study as part of a larger work which would show the intellectual history of New England through the 18th and 19th centuries. He advanced many startling viewpoints, derived from careful research. With T. H. Johnson he edited a comprehensive anthology, *The Puritans* (1938), and published *The New England Mind: The 17th Century* (1939). In 1948 appeared his edition of Jonathan Edwards' IMAGES, OR, SHADOWS OF DIVINE THINGS, part of his study of New England in the 18th century. *The Raven and the Whale* (1956) is an acute literary study of Poe and Melville. *Errand into the Wilderness* (1956) is a collection of his best essays.

Miller, William (b. Pittsfield, Mass., Feb. 15, 1782—d. Dec. 20, 1849), millennialist. First a farmer, then a Baptist preacher, Miller was an eloquent and convincing speaker. He came to believe that about 1843 the world would come to an end and published *Evidence from Scripture and History of the Second Coming of Christ, about the Year 1843* (1836), originally given as sixteen lectures. It was widely read, and a new sect was formed, called Millerites; various periodicals echoing his prediction appeared, particularly *The Midnight Cry* and *Signs of the Times*. A definite date was finally set, but Oct. 22, 1844 passed without disaster. Out of the Millerites came the Seventh-Day Adventists, led by Hiram Edson.

Millett, Fred [Benjamin] (b. Brockton, Mass., Feb. 19, 1890—   ), teacher, editor, literary historian. Millett joined the faculty of the University of Chicago in 1927, and that of Wesleyan University in 1937. He became director of Wesleyan's Honors College in 1943. With J. M. MANLY and EDITH RICKERT he wrote *Contemporary American Literature* (1929) and *Contemporary British Literature* (1935). He also wrote *The Art of the Drama* (with G. E. Bentley, 1935); *Contemporary American Authors* (1940); *The Critical Process* (1940); a series of books on reading drama, fiction, and poetry (1950); *Problems and Re-*

wards in College Teaching (1961). He has edited several anthologies and a memorial to Edith Rickert (1944).

Millikan, Robert Andrews (b. Morrison, Ill., Mar. 22, 1868—d. Dec. 19, 1953), physicist. Millikan became a professor of physics at the University of Chicago in 1896, then in 1921 was made chairman of the executive council of the California Institute of Technology and director of the Norman Bridge Laboratory of Physics in Pasadena. He received the Nobel prize in physics in 1923 for isolating the electron; in 1932, he was awarded the Roosevelt Association Medal for discovering cosmic rays. Millikan was interested in the relation of science to religion, and saw no reason why they should exclude one another. Among his numerous writings are: *Mechanics, Molecular Physics, and Heat* (1903); *Electricity, Sound, and Light* (1908); *The Electron* (1917); *Science and Life* (1923); *Evolution of Science and Religion* (1927); *Science and the New Civilization* (1930); *Time, Matter, and Value* (1932); *The Religion of a Scientist* (1935); *The Human Meaning of Science* (1940). He published his autobiography in 1950.

Millis, Walter (b. Atlanta, Ga., Mar. 16, 1899—d. March 17, 1968), editor, historian. Millis, an able newspaperman, worked for Baltimore and New York City newspapers, chiefly for the *New York Herald Tribune*. He was greatly interested in the historical backgrounds of modern developments and in world political trends. His first book, *The Martial Spirit* (1931), told how the United States came to fight that strange war, the 1898 conflict with Spain. More recent events are analyzed in *Road to War* (1935); *Why Europe Fights* (1940); *The Last Phase* (1946); *This Is Pearl Harbor* (1947); *Arms and Men: A Study of American Military History* (1956).

Mills, C[harles] **Wright** (b. Waco, Tex., Aug. 28, 1916—d. March 20, 1962), sociologist. Professor of Sociology at Columbia since 1945, director of sociological studies, and author of scholarly works, Mills wrote two widely known books: *White Collar* (1951) and *The Power Elite* (1956). Both are significant contributions to the popular literature which severely criticizes contemporary American mores. *White Collar*, subtitled "America's Middle Classes," brought attention to the middle-class American society: managers, teachers, secretaries, nurses, salesgirls, insurance agents, receptionists, lawyers, even trade unionists. Mills here introduced his tendentious, flamboyant, and caustic style of relentless social criticism. In *The Power Elite* he shifted his focus to the "ruling classes" in America. Mills identified three elites who, he felt, control the country: the men of corporate wealth, the militarists, and the politicians. The book suffers to some degree from being a popularization, from sociological jargon, from its extreme opinions. Yet despite its flaws it remains an important indictment of our society. *Sociological Imagination* (1959) addresses itself to the shortcomings of contemporary sociology. Mills finds that his colleagues lack "sociological imagination," a quality in which he himself excels, and that their work suffers both from too much theory and too much research methodology. He calls for a return to "classical sociology" and provides an object lesson in an appendix called "Intellectual Craftsmanship," which details his own sociological practice. In addition to private commercial studies of mass communications, he collaborated on *New Men of Power: America's Labor Leaders* (1948); and *Puerto Rican Journey* (1950). *The Causes of World War Three* appeared in 1958. *Images of Man* in 1960. Also in 1960 appeared *Listen Yankee: The Revolution in Cuba,* his most politically oriented work, intended to correct American misconceptions about the nature of the 1958 Cuban revolution.

Mills, John (b. Morgan Park, Ill., Apr. 13, 1880—d. June 14, 1948), engineer, teacher, inventor, physicist, author. Mills made important inventions in wire and radio telephony, taught physics at Colorado College, was on the staff of the American Telephone and Telegraph Company, and other firms, and served as administrative assistant at the California Institute of Technology, Pasadena. He wrote many lucidly expressed books, both popular and technical, among which are: *Electricity, Sound, and Light* (1907); *Introduction to Thermodynamics* (1909); *Radio Communication* (1917); *Realities of Modern Science* (1919); *Within the Atom* (1921); *Letters of a Radio Engineer to His Son* (1922); *The Magic of Communication* (1923); *A Fugue in Cycles and Bels* (1935); and *The Engineer in Society* (1946).

Miln, Louise [Jordan] (b. Macomb, Ill., Mar. 5, 1864—d. Sept. 22, 1933), novelist, short-story writer, memoirist. Mrs. Miln's specialty was China. Her husband was an actor, and she herself toured many parts of the world as an actress; she wrote about her experiences in *When We Were Strolling Players in the East* (1894), and *An Actor's Wooing* (1896). She also wrote *The Feast of Lanterns* (1920), *Mr. and Mrs. Sen* (1923), *In a Shantung Garden* (1924), *It Happened in Peking* (1926), *Peng Wee's Harvest* (1933), and other stories with a Chinese background. Her view of the Orient was sentimental, her depiction decidedly less realistic than Pearl Buck's.

Milquetoast, Caspar. A character created by the cartoonist H. T. WEBSTER for the New York *Herald Tribune* and other newspapers. He is afraid of his own shadow, obeys all directions implicitly, doesn't dare call his soul his own. Hence the epithet: "a milquetoast."

Milton, George Fort (b. Chattanooga, Tenn., Nov. 19, 1894—d. Nov. 12, 1955), newspaper editor, public official, historian. Milton was an editor and owner of the Chattanooga *News* and *Tribune* and also served as an editorial writer on the Buffalo, N.Y., *Evening News.* He was active in government work and served on a number of Federal commissions. As a historian his interest was mainly in the Civil War; he wrote *The Age of Hate: Andrew Johnson and the Radicals* (1930); *The Eve of Conflict: Stephen A. Douglas and the Needless War* (1934); *Conflict: The American Civil War* (1941); *Abraham Lincoln and the Fifth Column* (1942); *The Use of Presidential Power: 1789* (1944).

Mims, Edwin (b. Richmond, Ark., May 27, 1872—d. Sept. 15, 1959), teacher, editor, biographer, critic. Mims spent most of his life teaching English at Vanderbilt University. He wrote a life of Lanier (1905); *The Advancing South* (1926); *Adventurous America* (1929); *Great Writers as Interpreters of Religion* (1945); *Chancellor Kirkland of Vanderbilt* (1952); and he edited *Southern Prose and Poetry* (1910).

Miners, Ballads of. See COAL DUST ON THE FIDDLE.

Mingo. According to Webster's *New International Dictionary,* the name is derived from the phrase, "Lenape *Mengwe* Iroquoisa," and is believed to be a term of reproach leveled by neighboring Indian tribes in the 18th century at a band of Iroquois Indians in Ohio. It seems also to have been applied by the Delaware Indians to Iroquois in general. James Fenimore Cooper employs it frequently, in his LEATHER-STOCKING TALES, to designate cruelty and treachery, as in the case of Magua the Huron in *The Last of the Mohicans.*

Mingo and Other Sketches in Black and White (1884), four stories by JOEL CHANDLER HARRIS about life in Georgia. The title story is about Mingo, a faithful black servant.

Minister's Black Veil, The (*The Token,* 1836; TWICE-TOLD TALES, 1837), a short story by Nathaniel Hawthorne. In this strange tale, a minister, on the eve of his marriage, assumes a veil and never thereafter discards it. His fiancée abandons him, his parishioners look at him with a sort of terror, and his life is one of apparent despair and gloom. As he dies, he sees on every face around him a "black veil." Still veiled, he is borne to his grave. The plot seems to have been suggested to Hawthorne by an incident he mentions in a note, telling how a clergyman in Maine had similarly worn a veil as symbol of his repentance for having accidentally killed a beloved friend.

Minister's Wooing, The (1859), a novel by HARRIET BEECHER STOWE. This was the most ambitious of Mrs. Stowe's fine group of New England stories, and was judged by James Russell Lowell to be her best book; he bought it for serialization in *The Atlantic.* Others are inclined to place OLD TOWN FOLKS (1869) higher. The setting is Newport in the latter part of the 18th century, and into the story Mrs. Stowe wove many details of New England life as she had seen it as a girl, and some of her own religious trials. SAMUEL HOPKINS is the minister, somewhat straitly orthodox. Mary Scudder is the much younger girl he woos. She is really in love with her cousin James Marvyn, but she refuses to marry him because he has not been "saved"; he goes to sea and is reported lost in a shipwreck. She accepts the minister and is prepared to wed him, when James returns. She declines to break her word to Hopkins, but he learns of her dilemma and frees her. James, in the meantime, has found his salvation in religion and, in addition, has made his fortune—thus, says Edward Wagenknecht, "illustrating the Puritan habit of making the best of both worlds."

Miniver Cheevy (1907; included in *The Town Down the River*, 1910), a poem by EDWIN ARLINGTON ROBINSON. One of Robinson's most famous poems, this character sketch depicts Miniver with sarcastic humor. He feels himself born out of his time, looks back romantically to the Middle Ages ("He missed the mediaeval grace / Of iron clothing"), scorns money but "is sore annoyed without it," and keeps on drinking. The phrasing and technical skill show Robinson at his best.

Minnehaha. A Sioux word meaning "waterfall" or "laughing water." In Longfellow's HIAWATHA (1855), Minnehaha is a Sioux maiden who becomes Hiawatha's wife.

Minnigerode, Meade (b. England, of American parents, June 19, 1887—d. Oct. 27, 1967), novelist. Minnigerode wrote popular historical novels; among the best known of them are *Laughing House* (1920); *O Susanna!* (1922); *Cordelia Chantrell* (1926); *Black Forest* (1937); *The Terror of Peru* (1940). He edited Herman Melville's letters (1929). His THE FABULOUS FORTIES (1924) is a historical survey of the 1840's. He also collaborated on writing the words to THE WHIFFENPOOF SONG.

Minor, John Lucian (b. Louisa Co., Va., April 24, 1802—d. July 8, 1858), temperance advocate. He wrote *Letters from New England* (*Southern Literary Messenger, 1834–35*); after his death J. R. Lowell printed part of his *Journal* in the *Atlantic Monthly*.

minstrel shows. In the American theater the term *minstrels* was revived early in the 19th century to designate troupes of players, primarily white men with burnt cork on their hands and faces, who presented a miscellaneous series of "acts" in the guise of Negroes. Before this period Negroes had not been unfamiliar on the American stage. The comic Negro servant appeared about the same time as the Yankee and the Irish servant, all direct descendants of comic Irish and other servants in British comedy and farce. Frequently the Negro characters danced and sang. Most of these roles were played by white men in blackface, sometimes by famous actors like EDWIN FORREST, but some Negroes became famous on the minstrel stage, particularly William Henry Lane (billed as "Juba"), a spectacular dancer.

In the 1820's it became more customary to interpolate Negro songs and dances in theatrical performances. Thomas D. Rice (1806–1860), in one of his shows, played the part of a shuffling and grotesque Negro hostler called "Jim Crow." In the early 1840's appeared DANIEL EMMETT, who wrote the tune of *Dixie* for one of his shows, and EDWIN P. CHRISTY, who used many of STEPHEN FOSTER's tunes as his own compositions (apparently at Foster's request)

and whose name became practically a synonym for Negro minstrels. The technique became stereotyped. In the first part of the show, the "olio," a row of minstrels seated on chairs, a pompous interlocutor (or "straight man") in the center, and on the corners, "Tambo" and "Brother (or Brudder) Bones," the "end men." The interlocutor was in general the butt of the end men's jokes. In the second part individual minstrels performed as singers, players, dancers, monologists, and actors. The show usually concluded with a burlesque.

Innumerable minstrel troupes toured the country. Their popularity reached its height in the years from 1850 to 1870, but the companies continued to perform well into the 1920's. The influence of these shows on the American stage was profound; Amos 'n' Andy, of radio and television fame, were their direct descendants, as was the entertainer Al Jolson.

Olive Logan sought to trace *The Ancestry of Brudder Bones* back to the medieval minstrels (*Harper's Magazine*, April, 1879). Leroy Rice told about *The Monarchs of Minstrelsy* (1911). Dailey Paskman and Sigmund Spaeth wrote *"Gentlemen, Be Seated!" A Parade of the Old-Time Minstrels* (1928), and Carl F. Wittke wrote *Tambo and Bones: A History of the American Minstrel Stage* (1930). Reports of minstrel techniques may be found in *Bones: His Gags and Stump Speeches* and similar joke books of the mid-19th century, and in *The Darkey Drama: A Collection of Ethiopian Acts, Scenes, and Interludes* (3 v., undated).

Minuit [Minnewit(?)], Peter (b. Germany, 1580—d. 1638), colonial administrator. Minuit was made director-general of the colony of New Amsterdam in 1626 and filled that post until 1631. He made peace with the Indians by buying from them the land occupied by the settlement (now the island of Manhattan) with cloth, beads, hatchets, and trinkets worth about $24 in modern money. Later Minuit fell out of favor with the Dutch and was dismissed. He led an expedition for the Swedish South Company to what is now Wilmington, Del., built Fort Christina there, and named the territory New Sweden. The following year he bought from the Indians land near the present site of Trenton, N.J. He was lost in a hurricane in the West Indies while on a trading expedition.

Miracles (1856), a poem by WALT WHITMAN. In the effective and striking lines of this poem, Whitman expresses his characteristic pantheism, his feeling that "every hour of the light and dark is a miracle, / Every cubic inch of space is a miracle." His rhythm and pattern recall the technical devices of Hebrew poetry, which influenced him greatly.

Miranda. A name used in James Russell Lowell's A FABLE FOR CRITICS (1848), for MARGARET FULLER. The portrait he draws of her is maliciously satirical. He accuses her of extreme vanity and egotism, saying that she mixes her "infinite *me*" in everything she writes, and tries to persuade her readers " 'tis something tremendously deep, / By repeating it so as to put you to sleep."

Miranda, Francisco (b. Venezuela, 1750—d. 1816), soldier, traveler, liberator. He traveled widely in Europe and America, became a profound student of European culture, knew many notables, kept copious journals. In 1780 Miranda took part in a French and Spanish expedition intended to help the rebellious American colonists. When peace came, he traveled in the United States. Later he served as a general in the French revolutionary army, renounced allegiance to Spain, and plotted freedom for his own country. He led a patriot army in Venezuela (1810), became dictator (1812), was defeated by loyalist forces (1812), and then imprisoned in Spain until his death.

His papers, carefully bound by him in sixty-three folio volumes, were left in trust in England, and lay forgotten until W. S. Robertson published a portion of them as a *Tour of the United States* (1928) and used them as a basis for a *Life of Miranda* (1929). In the meantime the papers were sold to the government of Venezuela, which began their publication in thirty-two massive volumes. Joseph F. Thorning wrote an account of *Miranda: World Citizen* (1952).

At Harvard, Miranda found religion overdone; he noted as "extraordinary" the institution's lack of a single chair for modern languages. For "pure democracy" he felt that our assemblies could hardly go further. At Sag Harbor he found a community of whale-fishers who operated off the coast of Brazil. Most of them were Indians, and Miranda gathered from the esteem in which they were held the conviction that they were, as a race, no whit inferior to any other. In Boston he met Phillis Wheatley, a Negress who had had a volume of poems published in England, and again he noted that "the rational being is the same whatever his form or aspect." When later he turned to the making of a constitution for his own New World, he always stipulated equality of rights among free men whatever their color.

Miriam. A leading character in Hawthorne's THE MARBLE FAUN (1860). She is an art student whose origin and nationality are both carefully veiled in mystery. She lives in obvious terror of Brother Antonio, a model who constantly follows her and who is killed by her friend Count Donatello. According to G. P. Lathrop, in his *Study of Hawthorne* (1876), the novelist's concept of Miriam was greatly influenced by the famous portrait of Beatrice Cenci attributed to Guido Reni. The implication left by Lathrop's suggestion (apparently based on family information, since he was Hawthorne's son-in-law) is that Brother Antonio was her father and that the motive for his murder was the same as Beatrice Cenci's. However, Julian Hawthorne, in his life of his father (1885), said that Hawthorne may have had in mind a famous French murder case in which a certain Mademoiselle Henriette Deluzy-Desportes had been implicated. According to his son, the theory had been mentioned to Hawthorne himself, and

his reply was, "I dare say she was. I knew I had some dim recollection of some crime, but I didn't know what." But he added, "The story isn't meant to be explained; it's cloudland."

Miriam Coffin, or, The Whale Fisherman (3 v., 1834), a novel by JOSEPH G. HART. This is believed to be the first work of fiction to deal with whaling. Melville was acquainted with the book and in MOBY DICK (1851) unquestionably used data from this highly factual account. The notable similarities between the two novels were first mentioned by Raymond Weaver in *Herman Melville: Mariner and Mystic* (1921), were more fully brought out by Leon Howard (*Modern Language Notes*, May, 1934), and were augmented still further by Howard P. Vincent in *The Trying-Out of Moby Dick* (1949). Colonel Hart wrote the novel principally to obtain Congressional support for the whaling industry. The book was reprinted in 1872.

Mirror, The [1]. A weekly magazine founded by GEORGE P. MORRIS in New York City in 1823. It became a widely circulated and influential magazine of high literary standards and continued so until 1842. N. P. WILLIS in 1831 merged his own magazine, *The American Monthly*, with the *Mirror*, and joined its staff as European correspondent. Selections from his articles during the next four years appeared in book form as *Pencilings by the Way* (1835). Morris and Willis attempted to revive the magazine several times. Edgar Allan Poe became a regular contributor during 1844.

Mirror, The [2]. A weekly magazine founded at St. Louis on March 1, 1891, by M. A. Fanning and James M. Calvin. For a time it seems to have been called the *Sunday Mirror*. From May 30, 1913, until Sept. 2, 1920, it was called *Reedy's Mirror*. (See WILLIAM MARION REEDY.) In 1920 CHARLES J. FINGER took it over and called it *All's Well, or, The Mirror Repolished*. It ceased publication in December, 1935. Under Reedy's editorship the magazine played an important role in the development of American, especially Middle-Western, literature. Reedy was a patron saint to the poets of the early 20th century. His greatest achievement was his publishing of Edgar Lee Masters' SPOON RIVER ANTHOLOGY (May 29, 1914—Jan. 15, 1915).

Mirror for Americans, A (3 v., 1952), edited by Warren S. Tryon (1901—   ). Tryon issued this collection as an antidote to the writings of Mrs. FRANCES TROLLOPE and other European travelers in America; it presents the travel accounts of American tourists reporting on various parts of their own country from 1790 to 1870. The East, the South, and the West are covered in the three volumes, the last being perhaps the liveliest and most readable. The texts are accompanied by contemporaneous illustrations drawn from many sources.

Mirror for Witches (1928), a novel by ESTHER FORBES. This powerful novel is a study in the application of 20th-century psychological techniques to the superstitions of the 17th century. It tells of a little girl whose parents in Brittany had been burned at the stake for witchcraft. She is brought to Massachusetts and there she, too, is accused of being in the control of demons. Under her foster mother's influence, she believes she is. Miss Forbes skillfully imitates the style of COTTON MATHER and Judge SAMUEL SEWALL in this novel which, says Ernest Leisy, "admirably conveys the unearthly mood of that strange period in our annals."

Miss Bishop (1933), a novel by BESS STREETER ALDRICH. Ella Bishop, an English teacher in a small middle-western college for fifty years, misses an opportunity for marriage, through having to care for her mother, and spends her life bringing up other women's children. *Miss Bishop* was made into a motion picture in 1941.

Mission Indians. The name is generally given to the Indians converted to Christianity by Spanish missionaries in California and the Southwest, particularly the Shoshone and Yuma tribes. The story of their conversion has been told in numerous books, among them John G. Shea's *History of the Catholic Missions Among the Indian Tribes of the U.S.* (1854); George Wharton James' *In and Out of the Old Missions* (1905); Z. Englehardt's *The Missions and Missionaries of California* (4 v., 1908–1916); Cleve Hallenbeck's *Missions of the Old Southwest* (1929); Agnes Repplier's *Junípero Serra* (1933); John A. Berger's *Franciscan Missions of California* (1941).

The mistreatment of the Mission Indians by white men was a shocking matter. Attention was first called to their plight by Helen Hunt Jackson in A CENTURY OF DISHONOR (1881), and even more forcibly in her novel *Ramona* (1884). The Mission Indians are now located on a number of small reservations in California. Other fictional depictions of them are Mary Austin's *Isidro* (1905) and Willa Cather's DEATH COMES FOR THE ARCHBISHOP (1927).

Mississippi Bubble, the. John Law (1671–1729), a Scotsman of long residence in Paris, had acquired the reputation there of being a financial wizard. He was attracted by the French settlement on the Mississippi, applied for the concession of Louisiana (1717), organized the *Compaignie de l'Occident* as the center of a stock-selling enterprise, surrounding this company with a number of others. The parent company was ultimately known as the *Compaignie des Indes*. So alluring were the prospects of profit that people stood in line to pay fifty times the par value for the stock. Law promised to exploit not only Louisiana, but also China, Africa, and other parts of the world. For a time he practically controlled the French financial system. Excitement ran high as the fever of speculation mounted, and settlement in Louisiana was encouraged. In the meantime, Law was becoming more and more entangled in the results of his speculations. As master of the French treasury, he forbade the redemption of paper money in specie (1720), and a panic resulted, in which his own and many other companies went down to ruin. He fled from France, a penniless refugee, hiding from the number-less persons who had lost all their savings when the "Mississippi Bubble" burst. EMERSON HOUGH wrote a sensational novel, *The Mississippi Bubble* (1902).

Mississippi River, the. As the most important river in the United States, the Mississippi has exerted enormous economic, political, social, military, and literary influence. Which white man first saw the Mississippi is not known. Credit for discovering it is usually given to HERNANDO DE SOTO, whose expedition reached the Mississippi in May, 1541. The French in Canada learned about the river from the Indians, and began explorations toward the middle of the seventeenth century. Among them were LA SALLE (about 1669), and HENNEPIN (1680). Settlements soon began to spring up along the river. The source of the river was not definitely determined until 1832, when an expedition led by HENRY R. SCHOOLCRAFT reached Itasca Lake in Minnesota. A large portion of the Mississippi River Valley came under American control with the LOUISIANA PURCHASE (1803).

The Mississippi, 2,470 miles long, has as its principal tributary the Missouri, which is actually longer than the Mississippi; they form one of the world's largest rivers. Flood control is extremely difficult, and floods often bring disaster to regions along the course of the various streams of which it consists. An early appeal for effective flood control was voiced in Douglas Malloch's poem *Uncle Sam's River* (1913). In 1811 the first steamboats were launched on the river and became a picturesque part of the scenery. The height of the traffic was reached in the years immediately preceding the Civil War, and that period has been immortalized in Mark Twain's LIFE ON THE MISSISSIPPI (1883); the river and its denizens also appear memorably in his HUCKLEBERRY FINN (1884). Gladys Carmen Bellamy, analyzing *Mark Twain as a Literary Artist* (1950), holds that "the great number of water images in Mark Twain's work may be explained by the fact that he spent his impressionable years in sight of the mighty Mississippi." Arthur P. Hudson, in *The Humor of the Old Deep South* (1936), calls the river in Mark Twain's ante-bellum heyday "the Midway of the longest and greatest World's Fair our country has boasted. Every barge . . . was a floating booth; every steamer, a showboat." It was also, Dr. Bellamy points out, "the highway of humor." Here lived and boasted MIKE FINK, and Mark Twain caught from him some of his flair for amusing hyperboles.

This tremendous natural phenomenon has inspired much description and nonfictional analysis. Books of this type range back to Zadock Cramer's *The Navigator* (1808) and Zebulon Pike's *Account of an Expedition to the Sources of the Mississippi* (1810) and include such later volumes as Willard Glazier's *Down the Great River* (1888); S. W. McMaster's *60 Years on the Upper Mississippi* (1893); George Cary Eggleston's *The Last of the Flatboats* (1900); Julius Chambers' *The Mississippi River* (1910);

Lyle Saxon's *Father Mississippi* (1927); Walter A. Blair's *A Raft Pilot's Log* (1930); Walter Havighurst's *Upper Mississippi: A Wilderness Saga* (1937); and Edwin and Louise Rosskam's *Towboat River* (1948).

A famous poem about a common river tragedy, the blowing up of a steamboat during a race, was John Hay's JIM BLUDSO OF THE PRAIRIE BELLE (1871). John Gould Fletcher wrote a group of poems called *Down the Mississippi* (*Selected Poems*, 1938), in which he speaks of the river as "an enormous serpent, dilating, coiling." In the field of fiction and folklore, these books may be noted: Edna Ferber's SHOW BOAT (1926); Homer Croy's *River Girl* (1931); F. J. Meine's and Walter Blair's *Mike Fink, King of Mississippi Keelboatmen* (1933); August Derleth's *Bright Journey* (1940); Cid Ricketts Sumner's *Tammy Out of Time* (1948); Katherine Bellamann's *The Hayvens of Demarest* (1951); Frances Parkinson Keyes' *Steamboat Gothic* (1952). Ben Lucien Burman has written both fiction and non-fiction about the river in the twentieth century, in *Mississippi* (1929); *Steamboat Round the Bend* (1933); *Blow for a Landing* (1945); and *Children of Noah* (1951).

Miss Lonelyhearts (1933), a novel by NATHANAEL WEST. This brief, brilliant novel is the story of a man who writes the "advice to the lovelorn" column in a New York newspaper. Haunted by the pathetic letters he receives, he tries to live the role of omniscient counselor he has assumed for the paper. He is harried on the one hand by the cynicism of his editor, Shrike, who regards religion, art, and love as attempts to escape reality; on the other hand by the demands of his girl, Betty, that he lead a normal bourgeois existence. The agonized hero's fumbling attempts to reach out to suffering humanity as a kind of modern Christ are somehow always twisted by circumstances, finally with fatal consequences. He tries to convey a message of love to the Doyles, an embittered, sordid couple; but the result is merely that Mrs. Doyle tries to seduce him and her husband murders him by mistake.

Though the novel comments strongly on the decay of religion, its theme is the helpless loneliness of the individual in modern society. However, it is the style and imagery that give the book its peculiar merit. West's language is tight and compressed; to an almost monotonous extent he uses violent images to describe commonplace events, but his treatment of actual violence is almost starkly bare. At times his brilliant precision in handling symbol and image succeed in destroying the borderline between reality and nightmare, and devastating forces are presented with great power.

Miss Lulu Bett (1920), a novel by ZONA GALE. This admirable study of a thwarted and downtrodden spinster's rehabilitation and triumph became a best-seller, and the dramatization by the author won a Pulitzer prize. As a study of small-town life, it challenges comparison with Sinclair Lewis' MAIN STREET, as showing greater insight and humor. The heroine is a plain but not unattractive woman of thirty-four, sneered at constantly by her married sister's family, and used by them as a household drudge. When her brother-in-law's brother Ninian arrives, her salvation begins, and she shows courage, initiative, and wisdom.

Missouri Compromise (1820). This famous enactment was the first of a series of legal decrees adopted in an attempt to settle peacefully the differences between the North and the South. Up to 1820, slave and free states had entered the Union together, leaving the balance of power unimpaired. Then Missouri in 1818 applied for admission alone as a slave state, though it lay within the zone of the free states of the Northwest; its admission seemed likely to bring about the admission of other states within the region of the Louisiana Purchase on the side of the South. The result was a controversy that threatened to split the Union. A compromise was reached by admitting Maine at the same time as Missouri and by providing that slavery be prohibited in the Louisiana Territory aside from Missouri. In 1854 STEPHEN A. DOUGLAS introduced a bill to repeal the Compromise when the territories of Kansas and Nebraska were being organized. It led to a rush of pro- and anti-slavery advocates into the two proposed new states. On March 6, 1857, came the Dred Scott decision; Chief Justice ROGER B. TANEY and his associates held that Scott, as a slave, could not be a citizen, and added a ruling that the Missouri Compromise had all along been void because Congress lacked power to deprive persons of their property. This legal question became a main subject for Douglas and ABRAHAM LINCOLN in their 1858 debates. Glover Moore wrote an account of *The Missouri Controversy, 1819–21* (1953).

Missouri River, the. The Missouri is a magnificent river, even longer than the Mississippi's main stream: 2,475 miles. Its headwaters rise in southwestern Montana, and it gathers the waters of many tributaries along its course. It was an early trade route, explored by the French. In 1804–1805, Lewis and Clark came to the upper Missouri (see under MERIWETHER LEWIS), and their observations appear in Lewis' *History of the Expedition Under Captains Lewis and Clark* (1814; ed. prepared by Elliott Coues, 1893). The first steamboat appeared on the river in 1819, but the fluctuations in the depth of the river made navigation difficult. Dams at the upper levels in Montana have helped to control floods and develop hydroelectric power. In the 1850's, a Weverly, Mo., newspaper bragged that the Missouri was "the muddiest, the deepest, the shallowest, the bar-iest, the snaggiest, the sandiest, the catfishiest, the swiftest, the steamboatiest, and the uncertainest river in all the world."

The Missouri has had its literary devotees. Perhaps the most ardent is JOHN G. NEIHARDT, who descended the Missouri from its headwaters in a light boat in 1906 as preparation for writing *Cycle of the West* (1949), and who wrote about it in his book of poems *The River and I* (1910). Audubon knew it, as he reports in his *Journals* (ed. by Elliott Coues, 2 v., 1897); J. F. McDermott edited *Up the Missouri River with Audubon: The Journal of Edward Harris* (1952). Henry Marie Breckenridge wrote his *Journal of a Voyage Up the River Missouri in 1811* (1814). Among other books on the river are: J. V. Brower's *The Missouri River and Its Utmost Source* (1896); Charles Larpenteur's *40 Years a Fur Trader on the Upper Missouri* (ed. by Elliott Coues, 1898); Hiram M. Chittenden's *History of Early Steamboat Navigation on the Missouri River* (2 v., 1903); Joseph Mills Hanson's CONQUEST OF THE MISSOURI (1909; reprinted, 1946), an account of the exploits and explorations of Captain Grant Marsh (1832–1916); Philip Edward Chappell's *History of the Missouri River* (1911); C. P. Deatherage's *Steamboating on the Missouri River in the 60's* (1924); Pierre A. Tabeau's *Narrative of Loisel's Expedition to the Upper Missouri* (translated from the French by Rose Abel Wright, 1939); Stanley Vestal's *The Missouri* (1945); Bernard De Voto's ACROSS THE WIDE MISSOURI (Pulitzer Prize, 1947), and his *Course of Empire* (1952).

Miss Ravenel's Conversion from Secession to Loyalty (1867), a novel by JOHN W. DE FOREST. This is now regarded as the best work of a novelist accepted today as the chief forerunner of realism in American fiction. He tells the story of a New Orleans doctor who, at the beginning of the Civil War, exiles himself and his daughter Lillie to New Boston (obviously New Haven, where De Forest lived) because he is loyal to the Union. In New Boston two men woo Lillie, a Virginian lieutenant-colonel who is likewise loyal to the Union, and a Yale scholar. The book satirizes the puritanism of society in New Boston, and it has some powerful battle scenes which anticipate Stephen Crane's *Red Badge of Courage*. It was reprinted (1939) with an introduction by Gordon S. Haight.

Mr. Barnes of New York (1887), a novel by ARCHIBALD CLAVERING GUNTER. Gunter, English-born civil engineer and stockbroker, was an enthusiastic exponent of American points of view. He wrote his novel about a wealthy and self-confident American who during his travels abroad shows himself competent to handle every situation. Gunter could not find a publisher, especially when he refused to delete certain "inelegant Americanisms." He finally published the book at his own expense; in a few months it became a great success. Gunter followed the book with *Mr. Potter of Texas* (1887) and *Miss Nobody of Nowhere* (1890).

Mr. Crewe's Career (1908), a novel by WINSTON CHURCHILL. During the era of political reform headed by Theodore Roosevelt, Churchill became interested in New Hampshire politics. His book is an account of how difficult it is for a well-meaning man to follow honest principles when they come into conflict with his personal life. The book became a best seller.

Mr. Flood's Party (1920), a narrative poem by EDWIN ARLINGTON ROBINSON. Eben Flood apparently goes on a spree once a year. He engages in a dialogue with himself, sings "Secure, with only two moons listening," but in time becomes pathetically alone again.

Mr. Higginbotham's Catastrophe (*The Token*, 1834; *Twice-Told Tales*, 1837), a story by NATHANIEL HAWTHORNE. A young tobacco peddler hears that old and wealthy Mr. Higginbotham has been hanged and spreads the story. But people tell him they have just seen the man, and he isn't dead at all. Then again he is told the same story, and goes to Mr. Higginbotham's home in time to save him from being murdered. As a reward the peddler gets Mr. Higginbotham's fortune and his niece in marriage. The story, one of Hawthorne's most light-heartedly humorous, was based on an actual murder case.

Mr. Isaacs: A Tale of Modern India (1882), a novel by F. MARION CRAWFORD. Crawford's first book became a best seller. It deals with a Persian diamond merchant named Abdul-Hafiz-ben Isak, married to three wives; he regards women in a kindly but contemptuous way. But then he meets the beautiful and noble Englishwoman, Miss Westonhaugh. He is saved from his dilemma by her death, but emerges spiritually enriched and certain that he will meet his beloved again.

Mr. Lincoln's Camera Man (1946), a biography by Roy Meredith. An account of MATHEW B. BRADY, the photographic historian of his times. Brady is noted for his photographic coverage of the Civil War. He was a pioneer in methods and in subject matter, often an artist in his results. He knew Lincoln well, and Meredith's biography reproduces pictures of that President, some little known, others familiar. There are numerous pictures of other celebrities, including a magnificent portrait of Walt Whitman.

Mister Roberts (1946), a novel by THOMAS HEGGEN concerning the men on board a cargo ship in World War II.

Mitchell, Donald Grant ["Ik Marvel"] (b. Norwich, Conn., April 12, 1822—d. Dec. 15, 1908), farmer, essayist, author. Mitchell graduated from Yale in 1841 and immediately went to New London to cultivate his ancestral farm. He left for Europe in 1844 and spent the next ten years writing stories and reports, mostly for the New York *Morning Courier and Enquirer*, and traveling in Europe and the United States. His first two books, *Fresh Gleanings* (1847) and *The Battle Summer* (1850), concern his European travels and the French revolution of 1848, respectively. However, his first popular book was REVERIES OF A BACHELOR (1850), followed by a sequel, *Dream Life* (1851). He also became the first editor of "The Easy Chair" department of HARPER'S MAGAZINE. In 1852 he married and, nostalgic for the American countryside after a year in Venice as United States Consul, he settled with his family on a Connecticut farm. His love of agriculture and the simple pleasures of rural life dominate most of his subsequent writing, which is also infused with the same warmth and candor that characterized his earlier writing. His mature work includes: *Fudge Doings* (1855); *My Farm at Edgewood* (1863); *Seven Stories* (1864); *Doctor Johns* (1866), a novel; *Rural Studies* (1867); *About Old Story Tellers* (1877); *Bound Together* (1884); *English Lands, Letters, and Kings* (4 v., 1889–97); *American Lands and Letters* (2 v., 1897–99).

Mitchell, Edward Page (b. Bath, Me., March 24, 1852—d. Jan. 22, 1927), newspaperman, editor, memoirist. Mitchell served on the New York *Sun;* from 1903 to 1920 he was its editor. He wrote *Memoirs of an Editor* (1924).

Mitchell, Isaac. See ALONZO AND MELISSA.

Mitchell, John [1] (b. England, 1680[?]— d. 1750[?] [1768? 1772?]), physician, naturalist. Mitchell seems to have settled in Virginia as a physician sometime between 1700 to 1725. He returned to England in 1746. He was interested in cartography and produced a valuable *Map of the British and French Dominions in North America* (1755). He prepared a paper on yellow fever that Benjamin Franklin turned over to Dr. Benjamin Rush, who made one of its suggestions on the use of purgatives the basis for his medical practice in that disease. He wrote an *Essay on the Causes of the Different Colors of People in Different Climates* that was published in the *Philosophical Transactions* of the Royal Society in London. To the same society he sent a paper describing thirty new genera of plants he had found around his home; *Mitchella repens*, the name of a little trailing vine, is a memorial to his deep interest in American botany.

Mitchell, John [2] (b. Braidwood, Ill., Feb. 4, 1870—d. Sept. 9, 1919), coal miner, labor leader, public official, writer. Mitchell began working in coal mines in 1882 and never had much schooling, but he developed into one of the most intellectual and articulate labor leaders of his day. He was president of the United Mine Workers of America from 1898 to 1908. He won a national reputation by his organization of the anthracite coal miners' strike in 1902. From 1915 to his death he was chairman of the New York State Industrial Commission. He wrote *Organized Labor* (1903) and *The Wage Earner and His Problems* (1913).

Mitchell, John Ames (b. New York City, Jan. 17, 1845—d. June 29, 1918), editor, artist, novelist. Mitchell studied architecture in Boston and Paris and practiced his profession for several years in Boston. Then he returned to Paris to study art and became particularly adept at black-and-white etchings. When he came back to New York in 1880, new methods of picture reproduction permitted him to use this skill to good effect. With a legacy he founded the humorous weekly, *Life*, contributing editorials, caricatures, and cartoons. He retained a controlling interest in the magazine even when later he began to write novels (see LIFE [1]). Best known of these are *Amos Judd* (1895) and *The Pines of Lory* (1901). Like all his books, which sold well in their day, but were far less important than his work on *Life*, they have

plots of sensational action and juxtapose a wide variety of often exotic characters. Other novels include: *A Romance of the Moon* (1886); *The Last American* (1889); *That First Affair* (1896); *Gloria Victis* (1897); *The Villa Claudia* (1904); *The Silent War* (1906); *Pandora's Box* (1911).

Mitchell, Margaret (b. Atlanta, Ga., [?], 1900—d. Aug. 16, 1949), novelist. Miss Mitchell is known mainly for her single, best-selling Civil War novel, GONE WITH THE WIND.

Mitchell, S[ilas] Weir (b. Philadelphia, Feb. 15, 1829—d. Jan. 4, 1914), physician, novelist, poet. After obtaining a degree in medicine from Jefferson College, Mitchell continued his studies in Paris, specializing in neurology. His

charming personality and brilliant mind soon won him a large following in this country. His writings on toxicology, neurology, and clinical medicine became known throughout the medical world. Although his first book did not appear until he was fifty, he had published short stories, poems, and stories for children anonymously from 1846 on.

His experiences as acting assistant surgeon of the Union Army during the Civil War formed the basis for *The Case of George Dedlow* (1866), a story of a quadruple amputee. *Hephzibah Guinness* (short stories, 1880) was the first volume to appear under Mitchell's own name. His first long novel, *In War Time* (1885), combined Mitchell's gift for historical narrative with his insight into human psychology in a study of an able, charming man without stamina or courage. ROLAND BLAKE (1886), another novel of the Civil War, contains a good example of the possessive woman. *Characteristics* (1891) is a novel written almost entirely in the form of conversation. HUGH WYNNE: FREE QUAKER (1897), the story of a man's struggle to live up to his Quaker ideals in war-torn Philadelphia, is thought by many to be Mitchell's finest work. *Dr. North and His Friends* (1900) is a sequel to *Characteristics*, and was followed by *Circumstance* (1901), a psychological study of the Civil War, and *Constance Trescott* (1905), the study of a woman obsessed with the desire for revenge. THE RED CITY (1907), a novel laid in the red-brick dwellings of revolutionary Philadelphia, was, like *Hugh Wynne*, the result of years of careful research. *Westways* (1913) tells of a Pennsylvania family divided by the Civil War. Dr. Mitchell depicted with remarkable skill the suffering of women in wartime.

Collections of verse occasionally interrupted the long series of novels, among them *The Hill of Stones* (1882); *The Masque and Other Poems* (1889); *The Wager* (1900). Although the poetry seems old-fashioned today, Mitchell's historical novels and psychological analyses remain fresh and modern. See THE ADVENTURES OF FRANÇOIS.

Mizener, Arthur [Moore] (b. Erie, Pa., Sept. 3, 1907—   ), critic, teacher. Mizener has written many original and graceful essays in literary appreciation and analysis, as well as book reviews, but he is chiefly known for his important studies of F. Scott Fitzgerald. In 1951 he published a biography of Fitzgerald, *The Far Side of Paradise*, which was widely praised for its scholarship, critical acuteness, and lucidity. In 1957 he edited *Afternoon of an Author*, containing fourteen uncollected short stories by Fitzgerald and six uncollected essays.

Mizner, Wilson (b. Benicia, Calif., May 19, 1876—d. April 3, 1933), miner, confidence man, entertainer, corporation promoter, gambler, hotelkeeper, prize fighter, writer, wit. For many years Mizner was just one step ahead of the vagrancy laws. He was a man of many adventures—in the Yukon and Alaska, in many parts of the United States, on shipboard and abroad, in New York City and Hollywood. He knew the underworld, Broadway, and Hollywood. He had an astounding gift of phrase, particularly of insult and hyperbole, that fitted into the mood of the 1920's and made him famous, whereas before that, his reputation had been merely shady.

His literary output consists of a few short stories, several plays written in collaboration with other dramatists, and two or three hundred anecdotes culminating in wisecracks. He experimented for a while with short dramatic pieces for use in vaudeville, then helped Paul Armstrong with his ALIAS JIMMY VALENTINE (1909) by drawing upon his knowledge of the underworld to provide characteristic incidents and language. BRONSON HOWARD persuaded Mizner to collaborate with him on an original play, *The Only Law* (1909), about a broker who kept a chorus girl, who in turn kept a gigolo. Mizner and Howard quarreled bitterly long before the play was produced, and in revenge the latter wrote a novelette, *The Parasite* (1912) for *Smart Set*, in which Mizner appears in a venomous portrayal as Milton Lizard. Mizner and Armstrong managed to compose two more plays, *The Deep Purple* (1910) and *The Greyhound* (1912). The former was summed up by Alva Johnston as "the first effective drama about modern city-bred criminals." The latter depicts confidence men on an ocean liner.

Many of Mizner's remarks were stolen. The line most often associated with the famous comic W. C. Fields, for example, "Never give a sucker an even break," was originally Mizner's. He was present in 1933 when Jim Tully's secretary told him that Calvin Coolidge was dead. "How can they tell?" asked Mizner. This line is usually attributed to Dorothy Parker.

Alva Johnston made lengthy studies of Mizner in *The New Yorker* (1942, 1950). Edward Dean Sullivan wrote *The Fabulous Wilson Mizner* (1935).

M'liss (1863–64), a novelette by BRET HARTE. This story of a neglected child, who is revealed as fiery, jealous, and pathetic, is set among the Dickensian characters Harte discovered in the California mining camps. It was an expansion of an earlier story, *The Work on Red Mountain*, which appeared in the December, 1860, issue of the *Golden Era*. None of his earlier work had attracted much attention. But Californians asked for more about M'liss, and Harte wrote this expansion as a serial in the *Era* from September, 1863, on. It was a disappointing affair and was not included in Harte's 1867 collection, but appeared in *The Luck of Roaring Camp and Other Sketches* (1870) and separately as *M'liss: An Idyl of Red Mountain* (1873).

M'lle New York. A fortnightly magazine founded in New York City in August, 1895, by VANCE THOMPSON. It appeared until April of the following year, then suspended until November 1898, when it resumed for a year. Thompson and JAMES HUNEKER made it one of the two or three most notable of the earlier experimental "little magazines." Thompson reported literary gossip and inveighed against philistinism; Huneker dealt with the theater, the fine arts, and American prejudices. *M'lle New York* introduced to American readers such writers as Ibsen, Maeterlinck, Strindberg, Verlaine, and Hamsun; and it expounded the ideas of Wagner, the Symbolists, and Nietzsche.

Moberg, Vilhelm. See THE EMIGRANTS [2].

Moby Dick, or The Whale (1851), a novel by HERMAN MELVILLE. This celebrated novel, the product of Melville's literary maturity, was almost forgotten at the time of the author's death, but in this century it has come to be regarded as the most eminent American novel. It is a tale of whales and men, drawn from the author's own experience, and a profound symbolic study of good and evil. Melville originally intended to write a relatively straightforward narrative about whaling, told in lucidly realistic prose, semi-autobiographical, yet genially comic. The first fifteen chapters of *Moby Dick* indicate Melville's original intention; the rest of the book shows just how far he departed from that intention under the influence of Shakespeare and Hawthorne.

In addition to the *Macbeth*-like touches in the plot and the *Lear*-like touches in the characterization, Melville borrowed the example of Shakespeare's rhapsodically metaphorical language, which resulted in *Moby Dick* in passages of prose poetry unrivaled anywhere in American literature. From Hawthorne (to whom the book is dedicated) Melville took a willingness to penetrate to the "axis of reality," and a courage to encounter the darkest secrets of the human heart.

The story is centered on the pursuit of Moby Dick, the great White Whale, by the monomaniacal Captain Ahab, who has lost one leg in a previous encounter with the whale. Ishmael, a young sailor, narrates the first chapters, but as the book progresses the narrative point of view repeatedly changes; it is sometimes dramatic, sometimes omniscient, and often presents scenes at which Ishmael was not present or of which he could have no knowledge. The book is interlarded with extensive sections on cetology, and presents an imposing and sometimes episodic mixture of fact, narrative, and philosophy.

The crew of Ahab's ship, the *Pequod*, is a strange mixture of races and religions, including the God-fearing, stalwart figure of Starbuck, the first mate, the three primitive harpooners—Queequeg, Daggoo, and Tashtego—the idiot Negro cabin-boy, Pip, and the strange, fire-worshipping Parsee smuggled aboard by Ahab. Although many critics find the *Pequod* and its crew to be a symbol of the world and its peoples, the major symbols of the novel—Ahab and the White Whale—are too complex to admit of any one interpretation. Ahab's quest for the whale results in his dehumanization, the submergence of all other wills to his fiercely tyrannical spirit, and, eventually, death for all except Ishmael, who floats out of the vortex left by the sinking ship on the coffin prepared by Queequeg. Ahab, snarled in the line of the harpoon which he has embedded in Moby Dick, is dragged into the open sea, in death, as in life, relentlessly pursuing the whale.

Modern American Muse, The (1950), a complete bibliography of American verse, 1900–1925, compiled by Wynot R. Irish. Using the Copyright Office's data as a basis, the compiler collected 6,906 titles of collections of verse.

Modern Chivalry (1792, 1793, 1797; rev., 1805; reprinted, with an addition, 1815), a novel by HUGH HENRY BRACKENRIDGE. This huge novel in four volumes is a sort of American *Don Quixote*, and the two main characters were obviously modeled on that work. The book

is a satire on American politics and was based in large part on Brackenridge's own embittering political experiences. The scene is western Pennsylvania and the adventures that are described, often with high humor, give a deep insight into conditions on the American frontier. Brackenridge, despite his thrusts at the defects of American life, was a staunch believer in democracy. Henry Adams called the novel "a more thoroughly American book than any written before 1833."

Modern Instance, A (1882), a novel by WILLIAM DEAN HOWELLS. One of the earliest novels of social realism in America, it deals with the marital difficulties of Bartley and Marcia Hubbard, whose "love marriage falls into ruin through the undisciplined character of both." Howells originally titled the novel *The New Medea;* there is a strong resemblance between the irrational, passionate nature of Marcia and that of her Greek counterpart. Lionel Trilling finds Bartley Hubbard to be a character who "foretells a large social actuality of the future, a man somewhat gifted but trading upon sincerity and half-truth."

Modern Learning Exemplified by a Specimen of a Collegiate Examination (1792), by FRANCIS HOPKINSON. This was a burlesque on conventional methods in education.

Modjeska [originally **Modrzejewska**], **Helena** (b. Poland, 1840—d. 1909), actress. In 1876, Madame Modjeska, who had won some renown in her native land, emigrated with her husband to California in search of health and with the idea of founding a colony. Lack of success in the latter endeavor led her to study English and go on the American stage (1877), where she attained wide popularity in both tragic and comic roles. She played a wide range —from Shakespeare to Sardou—and introduced Ibsen to America with *The Doll's House* (1883).

Modoc Indians. Their original home was in the border region between Oregon and California. By treaties with the American government they lost much of their land and retired to a reservation in southern Oregon. They attempted to return to their original home, but were defeated by government troops in the Modoc War (1872–73). Some went permanently to Oklahoma, others returned to Oregon. The Modocs are renowned for their industry and are ordinarily peaceable, but they were superior fighters in tribal days. Many today are members of the Society of Friends. Joaquin Miller wrote LIFE AMONGST THE MODOCS (1873). Other books on this tribe are A. B. Meacham's *Wi-ne-ma and Her People* (1876); Jeremiah Curtin's *Myths of the Modoc* (1912); Jeff C. Riddle's *The Indian History of the Modoc War* (1914); Leslie Spier's *Klamath Ethnography* (1930).

Moeller, Phillip (b. New York City, Aug. 26, 1880—d. Apr. 26, 1958), playwright, director. Moeller was educated at Columbia University, then traveled extensively in Europe. He helped found the Washington Square Players, and wrote dramas displaying the comedy or irony behind historical events and personages. In 1918 a collection of five of his one-act plays was published as *Five Somewhat Historical Plays*. *A Roadhouse in Arden* (1916), a three-act comedy, was followed by *Madame Sand* (1917); *Molière* (1919); *Sophia* (1919); and *Camel Through the Needle's Eye* (1929). He adapted *Fata Morgana* (1931) from the Hungarian in collaboration with J. L. A. Burrell. He was active in the Theater Guild from its founding.

Mogg Megone (*New England Magazine*, March and April, 1835), a narrative poem by John Greenleaf Whittier, published in book form in 1836. Whittier said that he intended the story merely as a framework for sketches of New England scenery. The tale is a melodramatic one of seduction and murder, involving Mogg Megone, an Indian sachem, who is killed by a white girl named Ruth Bonython. The poem includes a strong statement against war, but is in general unimpressive.

Mohawk Indians. They were one of the Iroquois confederacy of the Six Nations in what is now New York. When the Dutch settlers arrived in the 17th century, one of their "gifts" to the Mohawks took the form of guns. Thereafter the Mohawks were notorious for their insolence and their eager willingness to make war. During the Revolutionary War they sided with the British and terrorized the American border towns. During that war and again later the Mohawk chieftain Thayendanegea (Joseph Brant) visited England. Boswell called on him, Romney painted his portrait, he dined with the Prince of Wales. The white men's wars finally destroyed the Mohawks. They sold their lands to the state of New York in 1797. Some of them settled among the Senecas of Ohio, then moved with them to Indian Territory (present-day Oklahoma) in 1832. Others migrated to Ontario. Only a small number survive as recognizable units. In Indian Territory they were mostly Episcopalians, an industrious people who gave no trouble.

One meets the Mohawks frequently in history and legend. The greatest Mohawk leader was Hiawatha, who lived around 1570. H. R. Schoolcraft, writing down the myths of the Iroquois, confused him with Manabozho, the Algonquin or Chippewa deity, and Longfellow echoed Schoolcraft's confusion in his poem, The Song of Hiawatha. Ponteach, or, The Savages of America (1727), by Major Robert Rogers, which was the first American play to deal sympathetically with the Indians, introduces as a character Monelia, the daughter of the Mohawk chief Hendrik. Mohawks appear occasionally in Cooper, as in *Wyandotté* (1843) and The Redskins (1846). A group of aristocratic ruffians who infested the streets of London in the early 18th century were called *Mohocks* from the Indian tribe.

Mohawk River and Valley. About 150 miles long, the Mohawk joins the Hudson at Cohoes, above Troy; it is the largest of the Hudson's tributaries. The Mohawk Valley, today a great industrial region, was first seen by white men when Jesuit priests made their explorations. The Iroquois were driven out after the American Revolution, and a great migration of settlers poured through the valley. The so-called Mohawk Trail leads from New England in this direction.

The Battle of Oriskany (Aug. 6, 1777), near the present city of Utica, has particularly attracted historians and historical novelists, many of whom regard it as the turning point of the Revolution. The British General Barry St. Leger and his Indian allies were on their way to join General Burgoyne, but were defeated by the hardy frontiersmen of the Mohawk Valley led by General Nicholas Herkimer. Novels about this and other historical events in the Mohawk Valley include Charles Fenno Hoffman's Greyslaer (1840); Harold Frederic's In the Valley (1890); Robert Neil Stephens' *Philip Winwood* (1900); Elsie Singmaster's *The Long Journey* (1917); Walter D. Edmonds' Drums Along the Mohawk (1936). Historical accounts and descriptions are found in William Maxwell Reid's *The Mohawk Valley* (1901), Nelson Greene's *History of the Mohawk Valley* (4 v., 1925), T. Wood Clarke's *The Bloody Mohawk* (1940), and other books.

Mohegan Indians. See Mahicans.

Mohicans, The Last of the. See Last of the Mohicans.

Moïse, Penina (b. Charleston, S.C., April 23, 1797—d. Sept. 13, 1880), teacher, poet, hymnologist. Miss Moïse was obliged to leave school to help support her family, but continued her education and later conducted a school for girls. She published several volumes, among them *Fancy's Sketch Book* (1833) and *Hymns Written for the Use of Hebrew Congregations* (1856). Her *Secular and Religious Works* were collected in 1911.

Moley, Raymond (b. Berea, Ohio, Sept. 27, 1886—   ), teacher, public official, editor, author. Moley began his career as a high-school teacher and educational administrator, went on to various university posts in the field of law and government, from 1928 to 1954 was professor of public law at Columbia University. He was Assistant Secretary of State in 1933, then served on various commissions, especially in crime surveys. One of his significant contributions to contemporary political history is his *After Seven Years* (1939), which recorded with excruciating honesty the inner workings of the Roosevelt administration. In 1933 Moley founded *Today*, a journal of political affairs, and became its editor. Three years later it absorbed *Newsweek* and took its name and format. Moley was editor, then contributing editor of *Newsweek*. Among his books: *Lessons in American Citizenship* (1917, numerous new editions since then); *Lessons in Democracy* (1919); *Politics and Criminal Prosecution* (1929); *Our Criminal Courts* (1930); *Tribunes of the People* (1932); *The Hays Office* (1945); *27 Masters of Politics* (1949); *How to Keep*

Our Liberty (1952); *What Price Federal Reclamation* (1955); *Political Responsibility* (1958).

Molloy, Robert (b. Charleston, S.C., Jan. 9, 1906—   ), newspaperman, literary editor, novelist, translator. Molloy at first was a businessman, later did free-lance writing, then joined the New York *Sun* (1936) and edited its book page from 1943 to 1945. *Pride's Way* (1945), his first novel, was set in Charleston and became a best seller. Among his later stories: *Uneasy Spring* (1946); *The Best of Intentions* (1949); *Pound Foolish* (1950); *A Multitude of Sins* (1953); *An Afternoon in March* (1958). He also wrote *Charleston: A Gracious Heritage* (1947) and translated various works from Spanish and French.

Molly Maguires. This was originally an Irish secret society which used terroristic methods against landlords and their agents in Ireland. When conditions seemed to be equally oppressive in the anthracite coal regions near Scranton, Pennsylvania, a similar group was organized there, and from 1865 to 1877 it terrorized the entire region. In addition to the ballads which have been written on the subject, Francis P. Dewees wrote *The Molly Maguires* (1877); ALLAN PINKERTON described the methods employed in bringing them to justice in *The Molly Maguires and the Detectives* (1905); and J. Walter Coleman analyzed them in *The Molly Maguire Riots* (1936).

Molly Pitcher. See PITCHER, MOLLY.

Monaghan, James [Jay] (b. West Chester, Pa., March 19, 1891—   ), historian, specialist in Americana. Monaghan owned and managed several ranches, taught school on an Indian reservation, was president of a wool growers' association. He opened the cattle ranges of northwestern Colorado to sheep grazing. He made important historical explorations, was state historian of Illinois and editor of the *Journal* of the Illinois State Historical Society. His books include *Bibliography of Lincoln, 1839–1939* (1945); DIPLOMAT IN CARPET SLIPPERS: LINCOLN DEALS WITH FOREIGN AFFAIRS (1945); *The Legend of Tom Horn* (1946); THE OVERLAND TRAIL (1947); *The Great Rascal* (1952); *Civil War on the Western Border* (1955); *The Man Who Elected Lincoln* (1956). He became editor of the "American Trails Series" in 1947.

Monahan, Michael (b. Ireland, April 6, 1865 —d. Nov. 22, 1933), poet, critic, editor. He began as a journalist in Albany at the age of twenty-two. His early verses were collected in *Youth and Other Poems* (1895). In 1911 he published a biography of Heinrich Heine and in 1912 *Adventures in Life and Letters*. In the meantime he founded one of the earliest of the "LITTLE MAGAZINES"—*The Papyrus: A Magazine of Individuality*. This was a monthly which appeared from July, 1903, until May, 1912, with a suspension from September, 1906, to June, 1907. In June, 1914, Monahan founded *The Phoenix*, a similar magazine, which appeared monthly until November, 1915. Among his other books: *Benigna Vena* (1904); *Palms of Papyrus* (1908, 1909), a study of men and letters; *Nova Hibernia* (1914); *At The Sign of the Van* (1914).

Monette, John Wesley (b. near Staunton, Va., April 5, 1803—d. March 1, 1851), physician, explorer, historian. Monette is remembered chiefly for his *History of the Discovery and Settlement of the Valley of the Mississippi by Three Great European Powers* (2 v., 1846). Although he won an excellent reputation as a physician, too, a fortunate investment made him financially independent and he devoted much of his time to research and writing. During the yellow-fever epidemic of 1841 his advice to Natchez that it quarantine itself saved that city from the scourge. He was deeply interested in the effects of climate on health and civilization, and he anticipated some of Darwin's theories. What has survived from his pen is mainly medical in character, papers contributed to medical journals and observations on yellow-fever epidemics (1838 and 1842).

Money-Makers, The (1885), a novel by H. F. KEENAN. See THE BREAD-WINNERS.

Monikins, The (1835), a novel by JAMES FENIMORE COOPER. The "monikins" of Cooper's title are four monkeys, two male and two female, whose homeland is in the polar regions. They persuade Noah Poke, a Connecticut sea captain, and Sir John Goldencalf to accompany them to their homeland. The pair visit three countries which stand for England, France, and the United States; Cooper deals with all three, especially the United States, in a bitterly sarcastic vein. Obviously an imitation of *Gulliver's Travels*, it has been called by Carl Van Doren "an unbelievably dull satire"; the book was a complete failure.

Monk, Maria (b. Canada, 1817[?]—d. 1849), fraudulent nun. At the height of the anti-Catholic demonstrations of the 1830's Miss Monk made her appearance in New York City, claiming that she had escaped from a convent in Montreal. Not long afterward appeared her *Awful Disclosures of the Hotel Dieu Nunnery of Montreal* (1836), which sold 200,000 copies. Its success led her to write *Further Disclosures* (1837). Meanwhile her own dissolute behavior led many to doubt her revelations, and two Protestant clergymen went to Montreal, inspected the Hotel Dieu Nunnery, and concluded that she was an impostor. Her *Disclosures* are, nevertheless, still distributed by some anti-Catholic groups. Miss Monk died in prison in New York, after an arrest for thievery. Laughton Osborn (*c.* 1809–1878), a poet and playwright, attacked the *Disclosures* in a satirical poem, *The Vision of Rubeta* (1838).

Monks, John. Coauthor of BROTHER RAT.

Monmouth, Battle of. This famous conflict of the American Revolution was fought on June 28, 1778, in Monmouth County, N.J. It might have been decisive but for the inefficiency and misconduct of General Charles Lee, who retreated when Washington ordered him to attack General George Clinton's forces. Long suspicious of Lee's loyalty, Washington had him court-martialed and dismissed from the army. See MOLLY PITCHER.

Monocle de Mon Oncle, Le (in HARMONIUM, 1923), twelve poems by WALLACE STEVENS. In these poems, each eleven lines long, Stevens looks at faith and disillusionment, the inspiration of youth and the sadness of age, the passing of beauty and the freshness of experience, innocence and sophistication. Alfred Kreymborg thinks of his contrasts as those of a bifocal monocle, picking out things near and far.

Monroe, Harriet (b. Chicago, Dec. 23, 1860 —d. Sept. 26, 1936), editor, poet, dramatist. Miss Monroe had already attained some fame as a versifier when she was asked to write the *Columbian Ode* for the Chicago Exposition of 1893. In 1896 she published a biography of her brother-in-law, John Wellborn Root, the celebrated architect, and in 1903 five verse plays, *The Passing Show*, but it was not until 1912 that she conceived the idea that brought her fame. POETRY: A MAGAZINE OF VERSE appeared in October, 1912, and soon became a strong force in the literary world. Miss Monroe fought untiringly for many years to keep her magazine alive, to "open its pages to all sorts of experimental and unconventional work without neglecting the traditional forms," and to encourage and stimulate new poets. *Poetry* was the inspiration for dozens of ephemeral "LITTLE MAGAZINES."

As a critic Miss Monroe was not unusually gifted, and was hampered by prejudices. She published the work of a number of important poets, including T. S. Eliot, Carl Sandburg, Vachel Lindsay, and Ezra Pound, who was for a time an assistant editor. Yet she repeatedly rejected the poetry of Robert Frost until his fame had been assured elsewhere.

Her anthology *The New Poetry* (1917), edited in collaboration with ALICE CORBIN HENDERSON, was one of the early collections of FREE VERSE, as well as other verse, and was received with a great deal of interest. Both the original and the revised edition (1932) contained a large section of Miss Monroe's own verse, which she also collected in *Valeria and Other Poems* (1892), *You and I* (1914), and *Chosen Poems* (1935). Her autobiography, *A Poet's Life* (1937), gives an interesting account of her life and travels and her effort to make Chicago the literary center of the United States.

Monroe, James (b. Westmoreland Co., Va., April 28, 1758—d. July 4, 1831), soldier, lawyer, 5th President. Monroe fought in the Continental army, rising to the rank of major. After the war he studied law with THOMAS JEFFERSON and became one of his most devoted followers. He served in various legislative bodies, advocated states' rights, opposed the adoption of the Constitution, but accepted it loyally after its ratification. He was minister to France in 1794, governor of Virginia in 1799. He was sent once more as minister to France and was instrumental in bringing about

the LOUISIANA PURCHASE, but other missions to England and Spain proved failures. He became governor again, Secretary of State under Madison, then Secretary of War.

In 1816 and again in 1820 he was elected President. During his two administrations, Monroe obtained the cession of Florida from Spain, settled Canadian border disputes, and abandoned all fortifications on the Canadian border. The MONROE DOCTRINE was established, the MISSOURI COMPROMISE on slavery accepted. When Monroe retired in 1825 he went back to Virginia and tried unsuccessfully to mend his shattered finances. In 1830 he moved to New York City where he died in poverty.

Monroe's name is associated with efficiency, honesty, and mediocrity in intellect. He was an efficient builder, even if other men drew the blueprints. Two early biographies, Daniel C. Gilman's *James Monroe* (1883) and George Morgan's *Life of James Monroe* (1921), have been superseded by Arthur Styron's lively *Last of the Cocked Hats* (1945) and W. P. Cresson's *James Monroe* (1946). Monroe's writings were edited by S. M. Hamilton (7 v., 1898–1903).

Monroe, Paul (b. North Madison, Ind., June 7, 1869—d. Dec. 6, 1947), teacher, historian, editor. Monroe taught history at Columbia University Teachers College until his retirement in 1938. He became one of the leading authorities on the history of education. Among his books: *Source Book in the History of Education for the Greek and Roman Period* (1901); *The History of Education* (1905); *Principles of Secondary Education* (1914); *Essays on Comparative Education* (1927, 1932); *Founding of the American Public School System* (1940); and a volume on China (1928). He edited numerous educational texts.

Monroe Doctrine. After the fall of Napoleon, European nations on the Continent united in the Quadruple Alliance, directed against popular or democratic movements in Old World lands. But their eyes were also directed to the western hemisphere, and it was feared, both by England and the United States, that attempts would be made to seize portions of the Spanish Empire as it fell to pieces, also some of the far western and still unsettled lands. George Canning (1770–1827), the great British Foreign Secretary, suggested that a joint declaration be issued warning against any European intervention on the American continents. But Monroe's Secretary of State, JOHN QUINCY ADAMS, advocated a unilateral statement by the United States. In a message to Congress on Dec. 2, 1823, JAMES MONROE formulated his famous "doctrine," which thereafter became a cornerstone of American foreign policy. The new republics of Latin America had just been recognized by the United States and England, and Monroe warned that "we could not view any interposition for the purpose of oppressing them, or controlling in any other manner their destiny, by any European power in any other light than as the manifestation of an unfriendly disposition toward the

United States." A considerable portion of the Doctrine had been implicit or actually formulated in utterances of earlier Presidents—the doctrine of isolation from European entanglements, of the paramount interest of the United States in the fate of neighboring territory, of self-determination for American communities.

Dexter Perkins wrote *Hands Off: A History of the Monroe Doctrine* (1941). In *The Era of Good Feelings* (1952) George Dangerfield described the events and maneuvers that culminated in the formulation of the Doctrine.

Monsieur Beaucaire (1900), a novelette by BOOTH TARKINGTON. A French duke in the days of Louis XV, seeking adventure, goes to England as a barber in order to find just the right bride. He falls in love with the beautiful Lady Mary Carlisle, but after many ups and downs his true identity is revealed and he returns to France to marry his cousin. This is a fine example of Tarkington's storytelling gift and agility in characterization. It has been filmed more than once.

Monster and Other Stories, The (1899), a collection by STEPHEN CRANE. This collection contains "The Monster," "THE BLUE HOTEL," and "His New Mittens." It was reissued in 1901 with four additional stories. The *Century* rejected the title story on the grounds that it was "too horrible." "The Monster" tells the story of an amiable Negro who, in saving a child from a burning laboratory, has his face disfigured by flaming acid. He becomes an object of horror and repugnance to the townspeople, who wish to lock him up because of his transformation. Dr. Trescott, the father of the child, defends the "monster" and is consequently ostracized by his fellow-citizens. W. D. Howells said: "'The Monster' is the greatest short story ever written by an American."

Montanus, Arnoldus (b. Netherlands, 1625[?] —d. 1683), writer. He is remembered for a sumptuous volume on America, *De Nieuwe en Onbekende Weereld* ("The New and Unknown World," Amsterdam, 1671). In the year of its publication in Holland, there appeared in London a book called *America*, a large and handsomely illustrated folio ascribed to John Ogilby; according to Jarvin M. Morse, it is mostly a translation of the book by Montanus. The latter was in small part also translated by E. B. O'Callaghan, who rendered the "Description of New Netherland" for the *Documentary History of the State of New York* (1851).

Montcalm de Saint-Véran, Marquis Louis Joseph de (b. France, 1712—d. 1759), soldier. In 1756, Montcalm became field marshal of the French troops fighting to save Canada from the British. In the crucial battle of Quebec (Sept. 13, 1759), the French were defeated, and Montcalm was mortally wounded. Francis Parkman made a detailed study of the conflict in *Montcalm and Wolfe* (2 v., 1884).

Montez, Lola [stage name of **Marie Dolores Eliza Rosanna Gilbert**] (b. Ireland, 1818— d. Jan. 17, 1861), actress, adventuress. This extraordinary woman made at least three marriages but did not confine her alliances to wedlock. She went on the stage as a dancer, traveled to England and then on the Continent, became intimate with Czar Nicholas I, Franz Liszt, Dumas *père*, and King Ludwig I of Bavaria; through her influence on the King, she actually ruled Bavaria for two years. She reached the United States in 1851 and gave performances all over the country in a play called *Lola Montez in Bavaria*. She voyaged to Australia, but came back to live in New York City under the name of Fanny Gibbons from 1857 till her death. She devoted herself to helping fallen women, died in poverty, and was buried in a Booklyn cemetery under the name of Mrs. Eliza Gilbert.

In her later years, Lola Montez gave inspirational lectures, probably written for her by a clergyman, Chauncey Burr; they were published as *Lectures of Lola Montez* (1858). Under her name was also published *The Arts of Beauty* (1858). Many books have been written about her, among them Francis Lister Hawks' *The Story of a Penitent* (pub. anon., 1867); Edmund B. d'Auvergne's *Lola Montez* (1909); Horace Wyndham's *The Magnificent Montez* (1935); Isaac Goldberg's *The Queen of Hearts* (1936); Oscar Lewis' *Lola Montez: the Mid-Victorian Bad Girl in California* (1938); and Helen Holdredge's *The Woman in Black* (1955).

Montgomery, David Henry (b. Syracuse, N.Y., Apr. 7, 1837—d. May 28, 1928), clergyman, writer of textbooks. Montgomery wrote a book for the children of a friend, called *The Leading Facts of English History* (1886). This became popular at once, and he followed it with two similar books, on French history (1889) and on American history (1895). His final production was *An Elementary American History* (1904). He also edited Sir Walter Scott and Oliver Goldsmith for schools, wrote a life of Franklin (1888), edited an anthology of *Heroic Ballads* (1890). He wrote in a popular vein, but his facts were accurately compiled.

Montgomery, L[ucy] M[aude] (b. Clifton, Pr. Ed. Is., Nov. 30, 1874—d. April 24, 1942), novelist. A school teacher and the wife of a Presbyterian minister, L. M. Montgomery became by accident a popular writer of juveniles. Asked to prepare a short serial for a Sunday-School paper, she drew on her memories of a girlhood on Prince Edward Island to produce ANNE OF GREEN GABLES (1908), which became a world-wide success. This was followed by *Anne of Avonlea* (1909), *Chronicles of Avonlea* (1912), *Anne of the Island* (1915), and many other books for girls.

Montgomery, Vaida (b. Childress, Tex., Aug. 28, 1888—   ), and **Montgomery, Whitney Maxwell** (b. Eureka, Tex., Sept. 14, 1877 —   ), poets, editors. Whitney Maxwell Montgomery was a farmer and stock raiser until 1927; he had, however, been active in local and state poetry societies, and had won several awards. In 1929, two years after his marriage, he and Mrs. Montgomery founded

The Kaleidoscope, a national poetry magazine later called *The Kaleidograph,* which they published and edited. They wrote some excellent verse and also helped many poets to secure publication for their books. Among Mrs. Montgomery's own books: *Locoed and Other Poems* (1930) and *A Century with Texas Poets and Poetry* (1934); *Hail for Rain* (1948). Mr. Montgomery wrote *Corn Silks and Cotton Blossoms* (1928); *Brown Fields and Bright Lights* (1930); *Hounds in the Hills* (1934); *Joseph's Coat* (1946); and, in collaboration with his wife, edited *Bright Excalibur* (1933); *Merry-Go-Round* (1935); *Moon in the Steeple* (1937); *Blood and Dust* (1939).

Monti, Luigi (b. Italy, 1830—d. 1903), teacher, writer. Monti fled from Italian tyranny to the United States in 1850, taught at Harvard, was made American consul at Palermo. He published *The Adventures of a Consul Abroad* (1878). He was familiar with all the members of the Cambridge group of his time, and was introduced by Longfellow into the storytelling group of TALES OF A WAYSIDE INN (1863, 1872, 1874) to relate *King Robert of Sicily* and other tales.

Monticello. The home of THOMAS JEFFERSON, situated on his estate three miles east of Charlottesville, Va. Jefferson himself designed the house and supervised its construction (begun in 1770). His skill as an architect and his knowledge of architectural theory and history have been discussed in William A. Lambeth and William H. Manning's *Thomas Jefferson as an Architect and a Designer of Landscapes* (1913); Fiske Kimball's *Thomas Jefferson: Architect* (1916); Paul Wilstach's *Jefferson and Monticello* (1925; rev. ed., 1931); and Ihna T. Frary's *Thomas Jefferson, Architect and Builder* (1931). The building is of red brick with white trim, constructed in the classical or Palladian style. John S. Patton and Sallie J. Doswell made a study of *Monticello and Its Master* (1925).

Mont-Saint-Michel and Chartres (privately printed, 1904; rev., 1912; pub., 1913), a historical and philosophical work by HENRY ADAMS. Adams, a historian and student of medieval history, found in the century of 1150–1250 the Virgin of Chartres, a symbol around which he built his theory of the forces which molded history—the external forces of multiplicity and diversity, represented by modern science, and the internal force which tends toward unity and is represented by religion. Adams saw in the century of 1150–1250 man's most fully realized attempt to reconcile his outer and inner worlds, and in the Virgin the linking of masculine force and reason to feminine love and intuition. The book falls into three parts: the preparatory 12th century symbolized by Mont-Saint-Michel, the culminating moment at Chartres in the year 1200 when the opposing forces of religion and science were in perfect equilibrium, and the decline toward the middle of the 13th century when the scholasticism of St. Thomas, with its emphasis on reason, began to be in the ascendency. THE EDUCATION OF HENRY ADAMS (1907, 1918) expresses Adams' despair at the multiplicity and mechanism of the twentieth-century world—the opposite pole from thirteenth-century unity. Adams' *Letters to a Niece and Prayer to the Virgin of Chartres* (ed. by Mabel La Farge, 1920) contain some valuable supplementary material.

Moodie, Susanna [Strickland] (b. Eng., Dec. 6, 1803—d. April 8, 1885), novelist, poet. After her marriage to J. W. D. Moodie, an army officer, Mrs. Moodie sailed with him and her sister, CATHERINE PARR TRAILL, to Canada in 1832. She described the hardships experienced by pioneers like herself in the Canadian wilderness in *Roughing It in the Bush, or Life in Canada* (1852). Notable for its realism, sincerity, and dry humor, the work revealed the sentiments of a well-bred Englishwoman whose initial dislike for her new home eventually turned to affection and belief in Canada's potential greatness. Mrs. Moodie also wrote several poems and novels, including *Mark Hurdlestone* (1853) and *Geoffrey Moncton* (1856), most of which were conventionally sentimental.

Moody, Dwight Lyman (b. Northfield, Mass., Feb. 5, 1837—d. Dec. 22, 1899), evangelist. Moody was able to obtain only a few years of schooling before he went to work at the age of thirteen. He became a shoe clerk in Boston, later a traveling salesman for a wholesale shoe firm. In 1856 he moved to Chicago, where he built up a lucrative business. In 1860 he resigned from business to become an independent city missionary without salary or supervision. In 1867, 1870, and 1873 he visited Great Britain, where he preached to large numbers. On his third trip he was accompanied by Ira D. Sankey (1840–1908), his organist and singer, who collected the *Gospel Hymns* popularly referred to as "Moody and Sankey hymns." Sankey later wrote *My Life and the Story of the Gospel Hymns* (1906).

The profits from Moody's tours and the hymnal were all used for philanthropic purposes. In 1879 Moody founded the Northfield Seminary for Girls, in 1881 the Mount Hermon School for Boys, in 1889 the Chicago Bible Institute. Eighteen volumes of his sermons appeared during Moody's lifetime, with such titles as *"To the Work! To the Work!" Exhortations to Christians* (1884); *Secret Power, or, The Secret of Success in Christian Life and Christian Work* (1881); *Prevailing Prayer: What Hinders It* (1885); *Heaven: Where It Is, Its Inhabitants, and How To Get There* (1885); *Sowing and Reaping* (1896). His sermons were translated into many languages.

Moody, John (b. Jersey City, N.J., May 2, 1868—d. Feb. 16, 1958), newspaperman, financial analyst. Until 1890 Moody was a newspaperman; then he joined the staff of the banking firm of Spencer, Trask & Co. In 1900 he founded an advisory investment service that took the form of many massive annual books and a periodical, *Moody's Magazine,* which began publication in 1905. His yearbook was called *Moody's Manual of Railroads and Cor-*

porate *Securities* (founded 1900). Moody also wrote *The Truth About the Trusts* (1904); *Masters of Capital* (1919); *The Remaking of Europe* (1921); *The Long Road Home* (1933); *John Henry Newman* (1945).

Moody, William Vaughn (b. Spencer, Ind., July 8, 1869—d. Oct. 17, 1910), poet, dramatist, teacher. After receiving his M.A. at Harvard in 1894, Moody served as an assistant in the English department there. The next year he joined the faculty of the University of Chicago, where he gained a reputation among his colleagues as a brilliant and inspiring teacher. Some of his students, however, called Moody the "Man in the Iron Mask" because of the reserve he maintained in some of his relationships.

Moody's early poetry was on personal themes, modeled chiefly on the Elizabethan poets and especially Milton. Beginning with the excitements of the Bryan-McKinley Free Silver campaign, however, he became interested in political and social problems. ROBERT MORSS LOVETT, his colleague at Chicago, credited HAMLIN GARLAND with being "of influence in turning Moody's thought to social matters." A leave of absence from the university in 1899–1900 he spent in Boston and East Gloucester, Mass., writing verse, the most noteworthy being *Gloucester Moors* (1901), a lyrical work combining aesthetic power with profound comment on humanity's plight. Other poems of that time are *The Menagerie,* an ironic reflection on the theory of evolution, and two bitterly indignant protests against American imperialism, AN ODE IN TIME OF HESITATION and *On a Soldier Fallen in the Philippines.*

Moody turned his attention to the drama in the belief that modern life could best be presented on the stage. His first attempt was a closet drama in verse, THE MASQUE OF JUDGMENT (1900), an early work showing the Miltonic influence. The success of *A History of English Literature* (1904), a textbook done in collaboration with Lovett, allowed Moody to give up teaching. His second poetic drama, THE FIRE-BRINGER (1904), added to his reputation as a poet rather than as a playwright. Like *The Masque of Judgment,* it deals with man's alienation from God; and the author projected a third play, *The Death of Eve,* which was to show woman's place in bringing about a reconcilation between man and God, but the play was not completed.

Moody's most successful drama was *The Sabine Woman* (1906), later retitled THE GREAT DIVIDE (1909). Contrasting Puritan New England and the pioneering West, this prose play deals with a situation then considered daring in American drama. A young girl, alone in a cabin in Arizona, is attacked by a band of ruffians. The men bargain for her, and one of them buys her with gold from his companions. She marries her captor and comes to love him. Still, she is determined to earn enough money to repay her husband for her cost. After reimbursing him, she leaves him and returns to New England; but in the end love prevails. Moody's

last play, *The Faith Healer* (1909), a study of mysticism, had little appeal.

In May, 1909, Moody married a brilliant Chicago woman, Mrs. Harriet Brainerd, but died the next year. His *Letters to Harriet* (1935) were edited by Percy MacKaye.

Moody's reputation as a dramatist was eclipsed even in his lifetime by his reputation as a poet, and today he is remembered chiefly for a handful of powerful lyrics and for his influence on Edwin Arlington Robinson, Robert Frost, and Wallace Stevens, some of whose early blank verse masterpieces echo a Wordsworthian metric and pantheism probably transmitted through Moody. David D. Henry has written a biography of Moody (1934).

ELDON C. HILL

Moon-Calf (1920), a novel by FLOYD DELL. Dell, a middle-westerner who had been a leader in Chicago's literary set before he came to New York and became a Greenwich Village prophet, based this story largely on his own experiences. Felix Fay, a lad of "the lower classes" in a little Illinois community, is deep in daydreams as a result of reading some of the wrong books, has a love affair that goes sour, goes off to Chicago with the notion that perhaps he will find there a world closer to his heart's desire. He leaves behind him his childhood sweetheart whom he thinks he has outgrown, but in a sequel, *The Briary-Bush* (1921), he comes back and marries her, after experiencing to the fullest Chicago's literary maelstrom. The latter novel sold in large numbers when readers heard that it described, among other events, a snow bath in the nude.

Moon Hoax. See BALLOON HOAX.

Moon of the Caribbees and Six Other Plays of the Sea (1919), by EUGENE O'NEILL. This collection had been preceded by *Thirst and Other One Act Plays* (1914), a publication that O'Neill financed. Mariners of a literary turn are likely to speak enthusiastically of the realism in these plays, based on the year that O'Neill spent at sea in 1910 when he shipped aboard a vessel bound for Argentina.

Five of the plays are dramas of the sea, both realistic and poetic, dramaturgically effective yet rarely melodramatic. ILE perhaps tends that way and needs careful stage handling not to seem ridiculous, in its portrayal of a mad sea captain more intent on oil than on people. The title play describes with pathos the scene on the *Glencairn,* a British steamer, when women come aboard as she lies at a West Indian port. In BOUND EAST FOR CARDIFF a sailor of the same vessel lies dying, and a shipmate tries to cheer him up with talk of the fun they had been expecting on shore. In *The Long Voyage Home* the sailors are shown drinking in a London bar; and the *Glencairn* puts to sea in wartime for the drama of suspicion which *In the Zone* reports. WHERE THE CROSS IS MADE shifts to America to present the tragic figure of Captain Bartlett, gone mad in his dreams of a treasure that his son Nat believes never existed —but the son, too, is finally infected with the dream. *The Rope* is likewise concerned with buried treasure, supposedly buried by a father to conceal it from his sons. *Ile* and *Where the Cross Is Made* have been favorites of amateur actors and have often been anthologized.

Moore, Anne Carroll (b. Limerick, Me., July 12, 1871—d. Jan. 20, 1961), librarian, authority on children's literature. After graduating from the Library School of Pratt Institute, Miss Moore became a pioneer organizer of children's departments in libraries and Supervisor of Work with Children in the New York Public Library. She published a series of books on children's literature entitled *The Three Owls* (3 v., 1925, 1928, 1931). *My Roads to Childhood, Views and Reviews of Children's Books* appeared in 1939. Two books she wrote for children are *Nicholas: A Manhattan Christmas Story* (1924) and *Nicholas and the Golden Goose* (1932).

Moore, Brian (b. Ireland, Aug. 25, 1921—), novelist. Now a resident of the United States, Moore was educated in Ireland and later emigrated to Canada. His prize-winning first novel, *The Lonely Passion of Judith Hearne* (1956), which dealt with a middle-aged spinster in a Belfast boardinghouse, was praised as "a powerful, haunting story." Two subsequent novels, *The Feast of Lupercal* (1957) and *The Luck of Ginger Coffey* (1960), had "little men" as their subjects and were notable for their compassion and sincerity.

Moore, Charles Leonard (b. Philadelphia, March 16, 1854—d. 1923), poet. Moore wrote much poetry, little of it remembered. Most noteworthy among his poems was perhaps his ode *To America* (1896). Among his collections: *Atlas* (1881); *Poems, Antique and Modern* (1883); *Odes* (1896); *Incense and Iconoclasm* (1915).

Moore, Clement Clarke (b. New York City, July 15, 1779—d. July 10, 1863), scholar, poet. From 1823 until 1850 Moore taught Oriental and Greek literature at the General Theological Seminary in New York City. His *Compendious Lexicon of the Hebrew Language* (1809) was for years the standard authority. He published *Poems* (1844), sentimental and conventional in nature. But he is known today for a single poem, *'Twas the Night Before Christmas*, which appeared in 1823 in the *Troy Sentinel* under the title A VISIT FROM ST. NICHOLAS. See KNICKERBOCKER SCHOOL.

Moore, Douglas [Stuart] (b. Cutchogue, N.Y., Aug. 10, 1893—), teacher, composer, writer. Moore was director of music at the Cleveland Museum of Art, joined the department of music at Columbia University in 1926. His compositions include works for orchestra, chorus, chamber music and opera. Moore set many of Stephen Vincent Benét's poems to music, collaborated with him on an opera based on THE DEVIL AND DANIEL WEBSTER (prod. 1938). Of literary interest, too, are a tone poem for orchestra, *Moby Dick* (1928); an opera,

White Wings (1935), based on Philip Barry's play; an operetta, *The Headless Horseman* (1936); and *Giants in the Earth* (prod. 1951), an opera based on O. E. Rölvaag's novel, with the libretto by Arnold Sungaard. His opera *The Ballad of Baby Doe* (1955) achieved both critical and popular acclaim. Later operas include *Gallantry: A Soap Opera* (1957) and *The Wings of the Dove* (1960). Moore has also written two books, *Listening to Music* (1932) and *From Madrigal to Modern Music* (1942).

Moore, [Horatio] Frank[lin] (b. Concord, N.H., Dec. 17, 1828—d. Aug. 10, 1904), editor, anthologist. Moore was greatly interested in history, joined the staff of the New York Historical Society in 1856, edited many compilations and anthologies. Among them: *Songs and Ballads of the American Revolution* (1856); *American Eloquence* (1857); *Materials for History* (1861); *Women of the War* (1866); *Songs and Ballads of the Southern People* (1886).

Moore, George Foot (b. West Chester, Pa., Oct. 15, 1851—d. May 16, 1931), clergyman, teacher, historian. Moore was an eminent student of religion, served on the faculty of the Andover Theological Seminary from 1883 to 1904, then as professor of religion at Harvard. He wrote a commentary on the Book of *Judges* (1895); *Literature of the Old Testament* (1913); a *History of Religions* (2 vols., 1913, 1919); and *Judaism in the First Centuries of the Christian Era* (2 vols., 1927, 1930).

Moore, George Henry (b. Concord, N.H., Apr. 20, 1823—d. May 5, 1892), librarian. The elder brother of FRANK MOORE was librarian of the New York Historical Society, then of the Lenox Library (now part of the New York Public Library). He wrote on many important, and some merely entertaining, historical topics, such as *The Treason of Charles Lee* (1860); *Negroes in the Army of the Revolution* (1862); *Notes on the History of Slavery in Massachusetts* (1866); *Notes on the History of Witchcraft in Massachusetts* (1883); *Washington as an Angler* (1887); *Libels on Washington* (1889); *John Dickinson* (1890). Moore was a good public speaker and did much to stimulate interest in American history.

Moore, Grace (b. Jellicoe, Tenn., Dec. 5, 1901—d. Jan. 26, 1947), soprano, actress, memoirist. A vivacious personality, Miss Moore had a distinguished career in musical comedies, opera, and films. In her autobiography, *You're Only Human Once* (1944), she looks with candor at the famous people she has met. She was killed in an airplane accident.

Moore, John (b. Marion, Ala., Aug. 26, 1858 —d. May 10, 1929), novelist, short-story writer, poet, editor. Moore took the name of Trotwood from Dickens' *David Copperfield* and used it for a pen name, John Trotwood, later made it his middle name. His reputation as a novelist was sufficiently great in his own time for him to found a magazine, *Trotwood's Monthly*, in 1905; the following year it was renamed the *Taylor-Trotwood Monthly,* and he continued to edit it until 1911. His verses and stories are laid in the South, particularly Tennessee. Among them: *Songs and Stories from Tennessee* (1897); *The Bishop of Cottontown* (1906); *Uncle Wash, His Stories* (1910); *Hearts of Hickory* (1926).

Moore, John Bassett (b. Smyrna, Del., Dec. 3, 1860—d. Nov. 12, 1947), lawyer, authority on international law, public official. Moore was admitted to the Delaware bar in 1883, became a clerk in the State Department, in 1886–91 was Third Assistant Secretary of State, in 1898 Assistant Secretary of State. Thereafter he served in many governmental posts, was recognized as one of the greatest authorities on international law. He served for seven years on the Permanent Court of International Justice and taught at Columbia University. Among his many books: *Report on Extraterritorial Crime* (1887); *Report on Extradition* (1890); *American Notes on the Conflict of Laws* (1896); *History and Digests of International Arbitration* (6 v., 1898); *American Diplomacy, Its Spirit and Achievement* (1905); *Four Phases of American Development: Federalism, Democracy, Imperialism, Expansion* (1912); *International Law and Some Current Illusions and Other Essays* (1924); *The Works of James Buchanan* (12 v., 1908–11); *International Adjudications, Ancient and Modern* (8 v., 1929–36).

Moore, J. Owen. See ALLATOONA.

Moore, Julia A. (b. Kent Co., Mich., Dec. 1, 1847—d. June 5, 1920), known as "the Sweet Singer of Michigan." In the earlier decades of the 20th century Julia A. Moore was the toast of the literary world; the columnists always found what she wrote good for a laugh. Her first book, *The Sweet Singer of Michigan Salutes the Public* (1876), was later called *The Sentimental Song Book*. Later she issued *A Few Words to the Public with New and Original Poems by Julia A. Moore* (1878). Many years afterwards came her *Sunshine and Shadow* (1915), a historical novel. She had an unfailing instinct for the banal phrase and the irrelevant detail. See LITTLE WILLIE.

Moore, Marianne [Craig] (b. St. Louis, Mo., Nov. 15, 1887—   ), poet. One of the most highly respected and warmly admired poets of her generation, Marianne Moore established for herself an intensely personal style which yet gives the impression of a kind of public elegance; her influence on younger poets has been very great. She was graduated from Bryn Mawr and the Carlisle Commercial College and took her first job as a teacher in the Carlisle (Pa.) Indian School. Thereafter she moved to New York, became an assistant at the New York Public Library (1921–25), later was made acting editor of the THE DIAL (1925–29), which under her direction was one of the liveliest publications in the country. She has lived in Brooklyn for many years.

Miss Moore's first book, *Poems* (1921), was published without her knowledge by two friends, Hilda Doolittle ("H.D.") and Robert McAlmon. *Observations* appeared in 1924. Later came *Selected Poems* (1935), with an introduction by T. S. Eliot; *The Pangolin and Other Verse*

(1936); *What Are Years?* (1941); *Nevertheless* (1946); *Collected Poems* (1951), again with an introduction by Eliot; *The Fables of La Fontaine* (translations, 1954); *Predilections* (essays, 1955); *Like a Bulwark* (1956); *O To Be a Dragon* (1959).

A typical poem by Miss Moore is composed in stanzas of varying line-lengths, each line controlled by a strict syllabic count; the rhyme pattern is complex and the rhymes are obscure. The matter of the poem is likely to be a moral theme fleshed in intricate details which have been drawn together from diverse sources; identifications and extensions may be given in appended notes. The range of the poet's interests is astonishing, and it is not at all unusual to find the facts of her poems derived from newspapers, popular magazines, scholarly books and articles, encyclopedias, inscriptions on monuments, government leaflets, motion pictures, medieval or Oriental art, etc. She is particularly fond of animals, especially those with unusual names, and much of her imagery springs from the animal world. The whole effect of her poetry is of a strong, sometimes spinsterish integrity expressed in exquisitely meticulous language and ornamented with images of precisely blended colors.

"Her poems form part of the small body of durable poetry written in our time," said T. S. Eliot. Louise Bogan called her "now our most distinguished American poet." "She sees complacent comfort in the house-cat, the lithe strength in the leafless orangewood tree, the interlacings on the shells of turtles and snails," remarked William Van O'Connor. To Morton Dauwen Zabel she seemed "a literalist of the imagination."

Moore, Merrill (b. Columbia, Tenn., Sept. 11, 1903—d. Sept. 20, 1957), psychiatrist, poet. Moore took his medical degree at Vanderbilt Medical School (1928), taught at Harvard, became a Harvard research fellow in psychiatry, served in various hospitals and clinics in Boston. His avocation, poetry, stemmed from his college days, when he was a member of the Fugitives, the group of southern agrarians led by JOHN CROWE RANSOM. Unlike some other members of the group, who later became leaders among serious American writers, Moore in his later years took a rather lighthearted view of literature. He specialized in sonnets, claimed that he had written at least one a day every day of his adult life. His themes were often, not always, comic. He broke all traditions for sonnet-writing, used many meters and rhyme schemes, and though most of his sonnets have fourteen lines, some do not. Among his collections are *The Noise That Time Makes* (1929); *Six Sides to a Man* (1935); *Poems from The Fugitive* (1936); *M: One Thousand Autobiographical Sonnets* (1938); *Clinical Sonnets* (1949); *Illegitimate Sonnets* (1950); *More Clinical Sonnets* (1952). Henry W. Wells wrote *Poet and Psychiatrist: Merrill Moore, M.D.* (1955).

Moran of the Lady Letty (1898), a novel by FRANK NORRIS. This short adventure novel, obviously influenced by Robert Louis Stevenson, tells how a vigorous young Viking daughter of the captain of the *Lady Letty* takes over when he is drowned. She gets into rough company, from which she is protected by a shanghaied sailor who has fallen in love with her. In the hero of the story Norris portrayed himself.

More, Paul Elmer (b. St. Louis, Mo., Dec. 12, 1864—d. March 9, 1937), critic, philosopher. Reared in a Calvinistic family, More in his youth succumbed to romantic influences, notably Heine and the Schlegels, but after graduating from Washington University and teaching for five years, went to Harvard, where his fellow student in Oriental and classical languages, Irving Babbitt, who was already steadfastly antiromantic, converted him to more austere tastes; the disciple never lost his love for the Upanishads, however, which in his *Forest Philosophy of India* (*Shelburne Essays*, v. 6, 1909) he called "the childlike gropings of the practical mystic to express in language the meaning of his inner life."

More refused to take a doctorate, taught for a while at Harvard and Bryn Mawr, then decided to give up teaching. He retired to two years of seclusion at Shelburne Falls, N.H. Reading Thoreau beneath the pines may have been for More an escapist's way of dealing with the confusions and frustrations of industrialized, competitive America, but it was also a time of stocktaking and self-analysis, from which he emerged with the conviction that his role was not to create literature but to formulate "conscious and deliberate standards." For thirteen years he followed a journalistic career, laying the basis in his magazine essays for much of the doctrine of the New Humanism, the fuel for two decades of controversy. He served as literary editor of *The Independent* (1901–03) and the New York *Evening Post* (1903–07), and as editor of *The Nation* (1909–14). Thereafter he retired to Princeton, N.J., where he lived in comparative seclusion and wrote his *Greek Tradition.*

Many of More's reviews and essays were collected in the series called Shelburne Essays (11 v., 1904–21). Critics have both praised the essays for their erudition and critical insight and condemned them for outmoded psychological and sociological views. While various writers have been enthusiastic, for example, about More's interpretations of Lafcadio Hearn and Nathaniel Hawthorne, they have denounced the volume called *Aristocracy and Justice* (1915), which contains the much quoted statement that property rights are more important than the human right to life. Later, in his preface to The Demon of the Absolute (1928), More recognized his critics, particularly H. L. Mencken and Van Wyck Brooks, and replied to them. Mencken had been especially eager to draw More into open combat on the score of his social views; he had sneered at the critic's imperviousness to "the winds of anarchic doctrine that blow down his Princeton stovepipe"

and he had characterized More's critical methods as a "coroner's inquest." Brooks, riding his thesis that an acquisitive society fails both to provide a stimulating social background for the artist and to offer adequate literary leadership, had contended that More, dominated by acquisitive rather than creative instincts, represented the breakdown of intellectualism.

More's reply, *The Demon of the Absolute,* and Norman Foerster's *Toward Standards* (1930) were two broadsides from the New Humanists that precipitated the critical controversies of the early 1930's. More restated his disagreement with the behaviorists and pointed to the romantic fallacies in much contemporary writing; he particularly condemned the middle-western naturalists—Lewis, Dreiser, Sherwood Anderson. But it was his caustic epithets that won him his widest renown, as when he called Benedetto Croce an "epoptic hierophant" and described John Dos Passos' *Manhattan Transfer* as "an explosion in a cesspool." Foerster echoed More's sentiments in even more vehement terms and defended More and Babbitt as the soundest critics in America. The result was open warfare, waged in the *Bookman, The Nation,* the *New Republic,* and elsewhere. Liberal younger critics like Edmund Wilson, Kenneth Burke, and Lewis Mumford attacked the New Humanists on historical and philosophical grounds, while critics of the economic determinist school, such as Granville Hicks and Bernard Smith, maintained a predictably violent opposition.

Curiously, More now stayed aloof from the journalistic battle, allowing his followers to defend him. Perhaps he was no longer interested in polemics, but wished to concentrate on completing his body of doctrine, his permanent call to judgment. At any rate, he worked chiefly on his books. *The Greek Tradition* (5 v., 1921–31) is a notable literary monument, and the *New Shelburne Essays* (3 v., 1928–36) are a worthy addition to the preceding volumes. His *Pages from an Oxford Diary* (1937), the last of his works to be published, is a modest, graceful autobiography.

More's critical opinions were too strong not to provoke controversy; though he possessed the scholarship and sense of style that might have made him a grandee, he has not been granted either an august or a secure place in the literary hierarchy. Whereas Fred L. Pattee has eulogized More as the American Sainte-Beuve, John Dewey prophesied for him the oblivion of the misinformed. He has been called a Platonist and a Thomist, a reactionary and a revolutionary, a Puritan and an anarchist. He remains a paradoxical figure in 20th-century American criticism.

Vesta M. Parsons

Moreau de Saint-Méry, Médéric-Louis-Élie (b. Martinique, Jan. 28, 1750—d. Jan. 28, 1819), lawyer, bookseller, ambassador, writer. Moreau studied law in Paris, came back to Martinique to write on the laws of the French colonies in America (1784–90). In Paris at the time of the Revolution, he fled to this country with his family in 1792. After various travels he settled in Philadelphia as a bookseller, returned to France in 1799. His *American Journey* (*Voyage aux États-Unis de l'Amérique*) was edited by Stewart Sims; an English version was made by Kenneth and Anna M. Roberts (1947), in preparation for the former's writing of *Lydia Bailey* (1947).

Morehouse, Ward (b. Savannah, Ga., Nov. 24, 1901—d. Dec. 7, 1966), newspaperman, drama critic, columnist, biographer. Morehouse first worked for the Savannah *Press* and the Atlanta *Journal,* then for the New York *Tribune* and the New York *Sun*. After the demise of the latter paper he joined the New York *World-Telegram and Sun* (1950). In his column, "Broadway After Dark," he reported in very readable style on happenings and personalities in the theater. *Gentlemen of the Press* (1928) and *Miss Quis* (1937) are plays. His semiautobiographical volume, *Forty-Five Minutes Past Eight* (1939), was continued in a similar volume in 1953, *Just the Other Day*. Other books by Morehouse include *George M. Cohan, Prince of the American Theater* (1943) and *Matinee Tomorrow: 50 Years of the American Theater* (1949).

Morella (*Southern Literary Messenger*, April, 1835; included in *Tales of the Grotesque and Arabesque*, 1840), a story by EDGAR ALLAN POE. Again Poe tells of a strange, other-worldly beloved, dying of a disease that recalls Virginia Clemm's ailment and displaying an indomitable will to "return again." The tale is obviously a preliminary study for LIGEIA; at the time he wrote it, Poe regarded it as his best work.

More Wonders of the Invisible World (1700), by ROBERT CALEF. This attack upon COTTON MATHER and his conduct of the witchcraft investigation included some spicy details of the way in which Mather "investigated" Margaret Rule. The title is a derisive one, in imitation of Mather's WONDERS OF THE INVISIBLE WORLD (1693). Mather replied, but not very effectively. Jarvis M. Morse feels that Calef's book "stands as a landmark in 17th-century controversial writing, because of its fairness and insistence on factual accuracy."

Morgan, Sir Henry (b. Wales, 1635[?]—d. 1688), buccaneer. Commissioned by the governor of Jamaica, Morgan engaged in a series of daring exploits, finally captured Panama City after an almost incredible march across the isthmus of Panama (1671). His conduct was so ruthless that he was recalled to England to answer for it. But he won the favor of Charles II, was knighted (1674), and appointed lieutenant governor of Jamaica. He has been a favorite subject for biographers and novelists. One of the best biographies is Rosita Forbes' *Sir Henry Morgan: Pirate and Pioneer* (1946). Among the novels may be mentioned John Steinbeck's *Cup of Gold: A Life of Henry Morgan, Buccaneer, with Occasional References to History* (1929); F. Van Wyck Mason's *Cutlass Empire* (1949);

Gordon Daviot's *The Privateer* (1952). Laurence Stallings and Maxwell Anderson's play *The Buccaneer* (1925) portrays Morgan at Panama.

Morgan, John (b. Philadelphia, June 10, 1735—d. Oct. 15, 1789), physician, writer. Morgan took his medical degree at Edinburgh; returned (1765) to found the Medical School of the University of Pennsylvania. There he continued teaching while practicing medicine. He wrote *A Discourse upon the Institution of Medical Schools in America* (1765), issued four pamphlets pointing out the advantages of a continued union with Great Britain, and published *A Recommendation of Inoculation* (1776).

Morgan, Joseph (b. Connecticut, 1671—d. c. 1745), clergyman, writer. Morgan wrote many religious books, but the only one that is still remembered is the fictional *History of the Kingdom of Basaruah* (1715), an allegory that sets forth the Congregational view of the fall and redemption of man.

Morgan, J[ohn] Pierpont (b. Hartford, Conn., April 17, 1837—d. Mar. 31, 1913), banker. The Morgans, one of the leading banking families in the United States, financed numerous important business enterprises and helped support many public institutions, particularly the Metropolitan Museum of Art. J. Pierpont Morgan became a notable art and book collector, and his great library in New York City, separately housed in a beautiful building, contains some of the most notable manuscripts and rare books in the world. His son, J. Pierpont Morgan, Jr. (1861–1943), turned this library over to public use in 1924.

Morgan, Kemp. This John Bunyan of the oil-fields is a startling instance of the rapidity with which a folk hero can be born and come to full growth in the American imagination. The first oil well dug for the specific purpose of producing petroleum was drilled in 1859. How soon after that Kemp was born no one is able to say, but within a few decades a considerable saga had gathered around his name. Kemp had a remarkable nose; he could walk along and just smell the oil underground waiting to be released. He would often do the drilling himself, even run the oil into tanks. His one weakness was food, and everywhere he went he took with him the only man who could satisfy his appetite —"Bull Cook" Morrison, of Snackover, Okla. Once he drilled a "duster"—a dry well—but rather than waste the well, Kemp sawed it off into lengths, which he sold to Kansas farmers for postholes, very difficult to dig in the hard Kansan soil. Once he dug so deep that the bottom came out in Brazil, and the well spouted pure rubber. Another time the well went deep down into a tremendous lake of oil, which spouted right up to heaven; the gusher drenched the floors of Paradise with oil, the clouds slid and slithered around the sky. The angels complained to Morgan, and regretfully he put a cap on the well again. No complete book has as yet been devoted to the exploits of this good-humored hero of a characteristic American industry, but his story has been well told in tall tale anthologies like: Frank Shay's *Here's Audacity!* (1930); Anne Malcolmson's *Yankee Doodle's Cousins* (1941); Bob Duncan's *The Dicky Bird Was Singing: Men, Women, and Black Gold* (1952).

Morin, Paul (b. Montreal, 1889—   ), poet. Morin writes in French about a world far removed from his native Canada. Educated in both Montreal and Paris, he spent two years in a Jesuit school in France. He returned to Montreal to take a degree in law (1910) from the city university, and went back to France, where he earned a doctorate of letters from the Sorbonne. The subject of his studies at the Sorbonne was the sources of the work of HENRY WADSWORTH LONGFELLOW.

After his early training Morin gave up law for teaching literature and taught at McGill University (Montreal), the University of Minnesota, and Smith College. He is popular in Canada as a radio speaker on French-Canadian writers.

The substance for much of his poetry is taken from travels and wide reading. His work adds an exotic flavor to Canadian literature, evoking the beauty of antiquity and the attraction of paganism: he captures the graces of worlds gone by. His early work in particular has been criticized in Canada for being aesthetic rather than moral in point of view, and his response to paganism has been criticized by the church. Morin's most important early work was *Le Paon d'émail* (1911), a collection of short impressionistic poems. Though it sometimes verges on dilettantism, at its best it is full of descriptive power. It seems more French than Canadian, recreating the flavor and beauty of the Orient in a sumptuous, elegant, and profane image. Morin's other important book of poetry, *Poèmes de Cendre et d'Or* (1922), contains a series of moods portrayed in a more tender voice.

Morison, Samuel Eliot (b. Boston, July 9, 1887—   ), teacher, historian, biographer. A graduate of Harvard, Morison began teaching there in 1915. An ardent sailor of small boats, his specialty is American naval history. For his life of Columbus, *Admiral of the Ocean Sea* (1942; rewritten as *Christopher Columbus, Mariner*, 1955), a Pulitzer Prize winner, he gathered data by following the great navigator's course. In 1942 the Navy made him official historian of World War II, retired him with the rank of rear admiral in 1951. During the war Morison saw service and action on every type of vessel, which gave authenticity to his *History of United States Naval Operations in World War II* (15 v., 1947–62). Among his other books: *Maritime History of Massachusetts* (1921); *Oxford History of the U.S.* (1927); *Tercentennial History of Harvard University* (5 v., 1930–36); *Growth of the American Republic* (with HENRY STEELE COMMAGER, 1942); *Freedom in Contemporary Society* (1956).

Morituri Salutamus: Poem for the 50th Anniversary of the Class of 1825 in Bowdoin College (comp., 1874; read, 1875), a poem by HENRY WADSWORTH LONGFELLOW. The poet pays tribute to Bowdoin and its teachers, greets his classmates and remembers those who have died, retells an appropriate tale from the *Gesta Romanorum*, introduces many apt literary allusions, shows with what craft he can handle a verse form he rarely used, the iambic pentameter couplet. He put into the poem his philosophy of life—the injunction that it is better to be too bold than not bold at all, the reminder that many old men have continued to produce important work. However, the poem is full of pompous commonplaces.

Morley, Christopher [Darlington] (b. Haverford, Pa., May 5, 1890—d. March 28, 1957), newspaperman, editor, poet, writer. After graduation from Haverford College, where his father was professor of mathematics, Morley went to New College, Oxford, as a Rhodes scholar and while there published his first book of poems, *The Eighth Sin* (1912). Later he served on the editorial staffs of Doubleday, Page & Co. and the *Ladies' Home Journal*, then became a columnist for the Philadelphia *Public Ledger* and the New York *Evening Post*. From 1924 to 1941 he was contributing editor of the *Saturday Review of Literature*. Meanwhile his short novel, PARNASSUS ON WHEELS (1917), a story about what a later generation would have called a "bookmobile," was an immediate success, as was its sequel, THE HAUNTED BOOKSHOP (1919). A second collection of poems was *Songs for a Little House* (1917), and a book of essays was called *Shandygaff* (1918). In 1920 Morley wrote a play, *Three's a Crowd*, with EARL DERR BIGGERS, and the next year he published *One-Act Plays*.

During the 1920's Morley, along with DON MARQUIS and FRANKLIN P. ADAMS, worked in the literary spotlight of New York; all three were literary columnists of a kind that has since vanished from the journalistic scene. In addition Morley and Cleon Throckmorton founded the Hoboken Theatrical Company (1928) and produced a number of revivals. He continued to write novels, including THUNDER ON THE LEFT (1925), *Human Being* (1932), and KITTY FOYLE (1939); the last-named became a best seller. His collections of verse appeared regularly, and he edited two revisions of Bartlett's *Familiar Quotations*.

Few writers of Morley's generation possessed a more sensitive stylistic gift. He brought wit and erudition, as well as a superb ear for English syntax, to his work, and he was affectionately aware of every word's capacities. His poetry, whether free verse or rhymed and metered, was delicate, musical, and at the same time a little dry, reminding readers of the 17th-century court tradition. But somehow the critics have neglected Morley. He was too facile, too versatile, though it cannot be said that his wit was a disguise for poverty of substance. Probably what Morley lacked was the sense of an ultimate commitment which modern critics demand as the mark of true greatness. His good friend Henry Seidel Canby called him "a rusher in and out, bubbling with ideas like a soda fountain, a wit, a wagster, an Elizabethan philosopher, with one of the few minds I have known that seemed to be perpetually enjoying its own versatility."

Among Morley's other works are four books of essays: *Plum Pudding* (1921), *Streamlines* (1936), *Letters of Askance* (1939), *The Ironing-Board* (1949); five books of verse: *The Rocking Horse* (1919), *Middle Kingdom* (1944), THE OLD MANDARIN (1947), *The Ballad of New York and Other Poems* (1950), *Gentlemen's Relish* (1955); two collections of short stories: *Tales from a Rolltop Desk* (1921) and *I Know a Secret* (1927); five novels: WHERE THE BLUE BEGINS (1922), *The Swiss Family Manhattan* (1932), THE TROJAN HORSE (1937), *Thorofare* (1942), *The Man That Made Friends with Himself* (1949). *John Mistletoe* (1931) is an autobiography. G. R. Lyle and H. T. Brown, Jr., compiled a *Bibliography of Christopher Morley* (1952). See POETRY PACKAGE.

Morley, Felix [Muskett] (b. Haverford, Pa., Jan. 6, 1894—   ), teacher, newspaperman, educational administrator, writer. The younger brother of CHRISTOPHER MORLEY was, like him, a Rhodes scholar, then did newspaper and editorial work in Philadelphia, Washington, and Baltimore, and edited the Washington *Post* from 1933 to 1940. In 1936 he received a Pulitzer Prize for editorial writing. He contributed to many magazines, edited *Human Events* (1945–50) and *Barron's Weekly* (1950–54), and was president of Haverford College from 1940 to 1945. Among his books: *Our Far Eastern Assignment* (1926); *The Society of Nations* (1932); *The Power in the People* (1949); *The Foreign Policy of the U.S.* (1951); *Gumption Island* (1956); *Essays on Individuality* (1958); *Freedom and Federalism* (1959).

Morley, Frank V[igor] (b. Haverford, Pa., Jan. 4, 1899—   ), publisher, editor, author. This younger brother of CHRISTOPHER and FELIX MORLEY has been in the publishing business, mostly in London, where he is associated with Faber & Faber. Among his books: *Travels in East Anglia* (1923); *River Thames* (1926); *Lamb Before Elia* (1932); *Death in Dwelly Lane* (1951); *My One Contribution to Chess* (1946); *Great North Road* (1961).

Morley, Sylvanus Griswold (b. Chester, Pa., June 7, 1883—d. Sept. 2, 1948), archaeologist. Morley became, in time, a leading authority on Central American archaeology. Much of his information came from expeditions that he made into an almost pathless wilderness. Among his books: *An Introduction to the Study of Maya Hieroglyphs* (1915); *Inscriptions at Copan* (1920); *Guide Book to the Ruins of Quirigua* (1935); *The Inscriptions of Peten* (1937, 1938); *The Ancient Maya* (1947). In 1950 the School of American Research and the Museum of New Mexico at Santa Fe issued *Morleyana: A Collection of Writings in Memoriam Sylvanus Griswold Morley.*

Mornings in Mexico (1927), essays by D. H. LAWRENCE. In this volume Lawrence gathered sketches of two different kinds, both written in 1924. One group describes the dancing Indians of Arizona and New Mexico; the other group comprises accounts of aspects of life in Mexico. The dancing Indians appear again in *The Plumed Serpent* (1926).

Morningstar, Marjorie. See MARJORIE MORNINGSTAR.

Morrell, Benjamin (b. Rye, N.Y., July 5, 1797—d., 1839), sea captain, memoirist. Captain Morrell made some adventurous voyages, which he chronicled in *A Narrative of Four Voyages to the South Seas* (1832). Some of his experiences were also described in Thomas J. Jacobs' *Scenes, Incidents, and Adventures in the Pacific Ocean under Captain Benjamin Morrell* (1844).

Morris, Charles (b. Chester, Pa., Oct. 1. 1833—d. Sept. 6, 1922), dime novelist, editor. In addition to editing anthologies and popularizations such as *Half-Hours with the Best American Authors* (4 v., 1887); *Tales from the Dramatists* (4 v., 1893); and *Famous Orators of the World* (1903), Morris wrote many stories of the dime-novel order. Among them were *Dick, the Stowaway; Cop Colt, the Quaker City Detective;* and *Mike Merry, the Harbor Police Boy,* all published in the 1880's.

Morris, George Pope (b. Philadelphia, Oct. 10, 1802—d. July 6, 1864), editor, poet, playwright. As a youth Morris worked in a printing office in New York and wrote verses for metropolitan newspapers. At twenty-one he founded the *New York Mirror,* a weekly paper now famous for such notable contributors as W. C. Bryant, J. F. Cooper, Walt Whitman, James K. Paulding, Nathaniel Willis, and Fitz-Greene Halleck. In 1842 the *New York Mirror* became the *New Mirror* and in 1844 was superseded by the *Evening Mirror,* a daily edited by Morris and Nathaniel Willis with Edgar Allan Poe as literary critic. Poe's *The Raven* appeared in the *Evening Mirror* in February, 1845. Morris had some success as a playwright; his *Brier Cliff* (1826), a drama of the American Revolution, had a long run. *The Maid of Saxony* (1842), an operetta, was a less lucrative venture. His best known prose work was *The Little Frenchman and His Water Lots* (short stories, 1839). *The Deserted Bride and Other Poems* (1838), which contains the well-known WOODMAN, SPARE THAT TREE!, and *Poems* (1840) enjoyed great popularity. See KNICKERBOCKER SCHOOL.

Morris, George Sylvester (b. Norwich, Vt., Nov. 15, 1840—d. Mar. 23, 1889), teacher, philosopher. Originally, Morris had intended to become a clergyman, but after studying in Germany, he decided to teach philosophy. He was strongly under the influence of German idealism in its later forms. Morris returned to the United States in 1868, joined the faculty of the University of Michigan to teach modern languages and literature, in 1878 taught both at Michigan and at Johns Hopkins, and became the founder of a distinctively American school of idealism.

Morris sought to establish a connection between thought and other forms of energy, and he taught that acts of thought are literally motions. He thought of philosophy, therefore, as a science. He further argued, "That *is* which is *known*," an approach to Berkeley's views. At Michigan, he was joined by John Dewey, who became one of his chief followers. Morris' ideas and writings are described and analyzed in R. M. Wenley's *The Life and Works of G. S. Morris* (1917), and in Marc Edmund Jones' *George Sylvester Morris: His Philosophical Career and Theistic Idealism* (1948). Morris' most important books are *British Thought and Thinkers* (1880); *Kant's Critique of Pure Reason* (1882); *Philosophy and Christianity* (1883); and *Hegel's Philosophy of the State and History* (1887).

Morris, Gouverneur (b. Morrisania, N.Y., Jan. 31, 1752—d. Nov. 6, 1816), lawyer, public official, diplomat, writer. Morris went into public life at the age of twenty-three, when he represented Westchester County in the first sessions of the New York Provincial Congress, and helped draft the State constitution. He favored the Revolutionary cause from the beginning. He was elected to Congress in 1777 and served two years; helped Washington re-organize the army, and published his *Observations on the American Revolution* (1779). Defeated for re-election, he went to live in Pennsylvania; in 1787, represented that State at the Constitutional Convention. He is believed to have written the Preamble to the CONSTITUTION.

He went to France on business in 1789, became United States Commissioner to England (1790–1791), then United States Minister to France (1792–1794), serving as Washington's confidential emissary. He was thus able to observe the French Revolution in its turbulent beginnings. *The Diary of the French Revolution* which he kept was not published, however, until 1939 (edited by his great-granddaughter, Beatrix Cary Davenport). But parts of it had appeared in Jared Sparks' *The Life of Gouverneur Morris* (3 v., 1832), and in the *Diary and Letters of Gouverneur Morris* (2 v., 1888), edited by his granddaughter, Anna Cary Morris. From the beginning the *Diary* was recognized as having prime historical value and great literary and human interest. It was in part politics, in part scandal. Hippolyte Taine was one of the many historians who used it to great advantage in writing on the French Revolution.

Later Morris served as assistant to ROBERT MORRIS (no relation), then Superintendent of Finance, and drew up a plan for a decimal system of coinage, later perfected by Jefferson and Hamilton. He served in the United States Senate from 1800 to 1803. His last years were devoted to the promotion of the ERIE CANAL; he was for several years chairman of the Erie Canal Commission.

Morris was known as a man of fashion; he has been called "a courtier among courtiers, even in Paris." In the United States, he desired to keep the power in the hands of the wealthier classes. Theodore Roosevelt wrote a biography of Morris (1888); Howard Swiggett's *The Extraordinary Mr. Morris* (1952) is based on Morris' diaries and other contemporaneous data.

Morris, Lewis. See ANDROBOROS.

Morris, Lloyd (b. New York City, Sept. 23, 1893—d. Aug. 8, 1954), teacher, critic, historian. At the beginning of his career, Morris dealt mainly with literary themes, writing with insight on *The Celtic Dawn* (1917), *The Poetry of Edwin Arlington Robinson* (1923), and *The Rebellious Puritan: Portrait of Mr. Hawthorne* (1927). In *Postscript to Yesterday* (1947) and *Not So Long Ago* (1949), he worked on a broader canvas. The former is an account of the United States in the first half of the twentieth century, full of brilliant portraits and well-argued conclusions, with an entertaining mixture of trivial and weighty details. The second shows the effect of the movies, automobiles, and radio on our civilization. *Curtain Time* (1953) is a sympathetic account of the American theater from 1820 to the early 1950's. *A Threshold in the Sun* (1943) is autobiographical.

Morris, Robert (b. England, 1734—d. 1806), financier, public official. Morris came to America about 1747 and successfully engaged in the shipping business. He favored the American cause, was a signer of the Declaration of Independence and a member of the Continental Congress (1775–78). He devoted much of his fortune and his time to running the financial affairs of the new nation, organizing a national bank, and securing loans abroad. He served after the war in the Constitutional Convention, and as a senator from Pennsylvania (1789–95). But he was ruined by unwise speculations in western lands and from 1798 to 1801 was in debtor's prison. Congress never recognized his great services and sacrifices. He appears as a character in Carl Carmer's *Genesee Fever* (1942). C. L. Ver Steeg wrote an account of *Robert Morris, Revolutionary Financier* (1954).

Morris, Wright (b. Central City, Neb., Jan. 6, 1910—   ), novelist. Morris is best known for his thoughtful novel, *The Home Place* (1948), the story of a man who brings his family back to a Nebraska farm. Morris included photographs which appear as a complement to the text in *The Home Place*, as well as in *The Inhabitants* (1946). He also wrote *My Uncle Dudley* (1942); *The Man Who Was There* (1945); *The World in the Attic* (1949); *Field of Vision* (1956); *Love Among the Cannibals* (1957); *Territory Ahead* (1958); and *Ceremony in Lone Tree* (1960).

Morrison, Theodore (b. Concord, N.H., Nov. 4, 1901—   ), teacher, poet, editor. Morrison began teaching at Harvard in 1923, but took five years off to work for the *Atlantic Monthly*. He is an outstanding teacher of writing. He published several collections of reflective, melodious poems, including *The*

Serpent in the Cloud (1931); *Notes of Death and Life* (1935); *The Devious Way* (1944); *The Dream of Alcestis* (1950); also two novels, *The Stones of the House* (1953), and *To Make a World* (1957). He edited *The Portable Chaucer* (1949).

Morrissette, Pat V. (b. Cass Lake, Minn., 1901—   ), poet. Morrissette's best-known piece is *Paul Bunyan: An American Symbol* (*Folk-Say*, IV, 1932). The twenty-page poem falls into five sections: "The Birth of Paul Bunyan," "The Defiance of Paul Bunyan," "The Winter of the Blue Snows," "The Death of the Great God Bunyan," and "The Roar of the Blue Ox." (See PAUL BUNYAN.)

Morrow, Elizabeth [Reeve Cutter] (b. Cleveland, Ohio, May 29, 1873—d. Jan. 23, 1955). The wife of Dwight W. Morrow (1873–1931), lawyer, banker, and diplomat, she was at one time acting president of her alma mater, Smith College, and was always active in community affairs. She wrote numerous appealing books for children, among them *The Painted Pig* (1930); *Beast, Bird, and Fish* (1933); *The Rabbit's Nest* (1940). She wrote a book of poems, *Quatrains for My Daughter* (1931), for ANNE MORROW LINDBERGH.

Morrow, Honoré Willsie (b. Ottumwa, Iowa, [?], 1880—d. April 12, 1940), editor, novelist. From 1914 to 1919 Mrs. Willsie edited the DELINEATOR. In 1923, after divorcing her husband, she married the publisher William Morrow, and her books thereafter bore her new name. Her western stories, like *The Heart of the Desert* (1913) and *Still Jim* (1915), were highly regarded as true studies of the West. Later she turned to history; her romances offered realistic and accurate depictions of former times. The best liked was her trilogy devoted to Lincoln, collected as *Great Captain* (1935), including *Forever Free* (1927); *With Malice Toward None* (1928); *The Last Full Measure* (1930). She also defended the President's wife in *Mary Todd Lincoln* (1928). The pioneer Marcus Whitman and his wife appear authentically in *We Must March* (1925); Amos Bronson Alcott in *The Father of Little Women* (1927); John B. Gough, temperance advocate, in *Tiger! Tiger!* (1930); Daniel Webster in *Black Daniel* (1931). She wrote candidly and amusingly of her daughter in *Demon Daughter* (1939).

Morse, Edward Sylvester (b. Portland, Me., June 18, 1838—d. Dec. 20, 1925), marine zoologist, authority on ceramics, museum director, lecturer. Articulate in many fields of knowledge and with numerous publications to his credit, Morse is a characteristic example of the Yankee, more self-taught than educated, learned for the sake of learning rather than for renown, idiosyncratic to the point of unabashed eccentricity, effortlessly humorous beyond the ability of most professional funny men. He had no formal education, but some training under LOUIS AGASSIZ; as a marine zoologist he threw new light on the Darwinian theory, which he defended to the point of winning praise from Darwin himself. He was a curator in various fields at various museums, a lecturer on zoology, a conchologist, a professor at the Imperial University of Tokyo, a world-renowned authority on Japanese ceramics. He wrote *First Book of Zoology* (1875); *Japanese Homes and Their Surroundings* (1886); *Glimpses of China and Chinese Homes* (1902), also a pamphlet on *The Suppression of Unnecessary Noise* and one on the *Latrines of the East*. He worked for ten years on the monumental task of writing and editing his *Catalogue of Japanese Pottery* (1901), a classic of American scholarship. He received, late in life, honorary degrees from Bowdoin, Harvard, Yale, and Tufts. Dorothy Wyman wrote an excellent biography of the great eccentric (1942).

Morse, Jedidiah (b. Woodstock, Conn., Aug. 23, 1761—d. June 9, 1826), clergyman, teacher, geographer, editor. Morse was an important influence on his own time and had two brilliant and influential sons, Samuel F. B. Morse, inventor of the telegraph, and SIDNEY EDWARDS MORSE. He taught in Connecticut schools, in 1789 became pastor of a Charlestown, Mass., church. He was active in the New England Tract Society, the American Bible Society, the Society for Propagating the Gospel among the Indians, the Andover Theological Seminary. Early in life Morse became deeply interested in geography, and his books, including textbooks, were so popular that he was called "the father of American geography." His *American Geography* (1789) was, he said, "calculated early to impress the minds of American youth with the idea of the superior importance of their own country." Other books in this field included the first book on the subject in this country, *Geography Made Easy* (1784), which was later enlarged and called *The American Universal Geography: Elements of Geography* (1795); *The American Gazetteer* (1797). He also compiled *Annals of the American Revolution* (1824).

Morse, Sidney Edwards (b. Charlestown, Mass., Feb. 7, 1794—d. Dec. 23, 1871), inventor, editor, geographer. Like his older brother, Samuel F. B. Morse, Sidney Morse was an ingenious Yankee who made several important inventions. He devised a flexible piston pump, a bathometer for exploring ocean depths, and a special process for printing maps. Although Morse edited religious journals for the greater part of his life, his deep interest was in geography. His first important book was *The New States, or, A Comparison of the Wealth, Strength, and Opulence of the Northern and Southern States* (1813). He assisted his father JEDIDIAH MORSE in revising his popular textbooks, continued to publish similar books of his own. Among them: *An Atlas of the United States* (1823); *A Geographical View of Greece* (1824); *North American Atlas* (1842); *A System of Geography for the Use of Schools* (1844). With his younger brother Cary Morse (1795–1868) he founded the New York *Observer* and edited it from 1823 to 1858.

Morse, Theodore F. Author of HAIL! HAIL! THE GANG'S ALL HERE.

Mortal Antipathy, A (1885), a novel by OLIVER WENDELL HOLMES. This was an unsuccessful attempt to handle in fiction the theme of scars left by childhood experience. A child is dropped accidentally into a thorn bush by his cousin Laura—and thereafter has "a mortal antipathy" to good-looking young women. He is cured, many years later, when an athletic young woman rescues him from a fire, and he marries her. To many readers the novel seems a proof that Holmes had temporarily lost his sense of humor. Clarence P. Oberndorf, a clinical psychiatrist, included it in the abridgments and analyses he made of *The Psychiatric Novels of O. W. Holmes* (1943).

Morton, Charles (b. England, 1627[?]—d. 1698), clergyman, teacher, educational administrator, author. Morton, a nonconformist minister, came to Boston in 1686. Failing to become president of Harvard, he started a rival school. Harvard compromised by making him first a fellow (1692) and then vice-president (1697). He was among those who urged prosecution for witchcraft in Salem. He published a volume called *The Spirit of Man* (1693), and his textbooks on science and logic were used, in manuscript, at Harvard. His *Compendium Physicae* was partly inaccurate and clung too closely to the Aristotelian classification of physics, but it called the attention of American students to the many great changes in physical science that were stirring the Old World. This document in the history of education was edited for the *Publications of the Colonial Society of Massachusetts* (1940) by Theodore Hornberger.

Morton, Charles W. (b. Omaha, Neb., Feb. 10, 1899—d. Sept. 23, 1967), editor, humorist. Morton worked from 1928 to 1936 on Boston papers, and in 1941 became associate editor of the *Atlantic Monthly*. With the noted cartoonist FRANCIS W. DAHL, he wrote *Dahl's Boston* (1946) and *Dahl's Brave New World* (1947). He gathered some of his amusing essays in *How to Deal with Women and Other Vicissitudes* (1951) and *A Slight Sense of Outrage* (1955).

Morton, David (b. Elkton, Ky., Feb. 21, 1886—d. June 13, 1957), newspaperman, teacher, poet, editor. For six years Morton worked on various newspapers, then taught high-school English in Louisville, Ky., and Morristown, N.J. From 1924 to 1945 he was a professor of English and an instructor in boxing at Amherst. He published many collections of thoughtful, imaginative, and melodious verse, showing himself a particular master of the sonnet. Among his books: *Ships in Harbour* (1921); *Harvest* (1924); *Nocturnes and Autumnals* (1928); *Earth's Processional* (1932); *All in One Breath* (1939); *Angle of Earth and Sky* (1941); *Poems, 1920–1945* (1945); *Like a Man in Love* (1953).

Morton, George (b. England, 1585—d. 1628[?]), colonist, publisher. Morton accompanied the Pilgrims to Holland; when the rest emigrated to America in 1620, he returned to London and acted as their agent. It is conjectured that WILLIAM BRADFORD [1] and EDWARD WINSLOW prepared an account of the happenings in Plymouth, *A Relation or Journal of the Beginning and Proceedings of the English Plantation Settled at Plymouth in New England,* and sent it to Morton. He published it anonymously in 1622 and signed the preface "G. Mourt"; it is therefore generally known as *Mourt's Relation* and is the first story of the new colony. Morton himself emigrated to Plymouth in 1623. His publication or compilation was published in abridged form in *Purchas His Pilgrims* (1625). It was reissued (1865) in an edition prepared by Henry M. Dexter.

Morton, Nathaniel (b. Holland, 1613—d. June 29, 1685), colonist, public official, historian. Morton accompanied his father GEORGE MORTON to Plymouth in 1623, and after his father's death came under the care and guardianship of WILLIAM BRADFORD [1]. He became secretary of the colony, drafted its laws, was collector of taxes, member of land-survey committees, town clerk. He drew freely on the papers of Bradford and EDWARD WINSLOW in writing *New England's Memorial* (1669), the first long historical narrative published in Massachusetts. The book is a poor one, however, often summarizing important events hurriedly, with much space given to obituary verses on the Rev. THOMAS HOOKER. Morton wrote another fuller account, the manuscript of which was burned in 1674, rewritten by 1680, printed only in 1855. The original *Memorial* has been reprinted several times.

Morton, Sarah Wentworth (b. Boston, Aug. [?], 1759—d. May 14, 1846), poet. Mrs. Morton wrote under the name Philenia and was called "the American Sappho." As a member of the Della Cruscan group of poets in America she wrote with "sensibility," and her contemporaries admired the "warbling eloquence" of her verses. She collected them in *Ouabi, or, The Virtues of Nature: An Indian Tale in Four Cantos* (1790); *Beacon Hill* (1797); *The Virtues of Society* (1799). The only book she published under her own name was *My Mind and Its Thoughts* (1823), a miscellany of prose and verse. She was mistakenly thought to be the author of *The Power of Sympathy* (1789), a tale that stops at the brink of incest but reaches its climax in suicide, obviously based on occurrences in Mrs. Morton's family. At the present time the novel is usually attributed to WILLIAM HILL BROWN, but only conjecturally. Nilton Ellis and Emily Pendleton discuss the case in *Philenia, the Life and Works of Sarah Wentworth Morton* (1931); Ellis also summarizes it in a prefatory note to the Facsimile Text Society edition of *The Power of Sympathy* (2 v., 1937). See DELLA CRUSCANISM.

Morton, Thomas (b. England, 1575[?]—d. 1646 [1647?]), colonist, trader, writer. Morton, representing the Anglican and anti-Puritan faction in England, came to New England in

1622. With a group of immigrants he established a colony at what he called Merry Mount or Merrymount (now Quincy, Mass.). He alienated the neighboring Puritans because he competed successfully with them in trade with the Indians, also because he sold guns to the Indians, because he was an Anglican, and because he set up a maypole for his people—and the Indians—to dance around. The Puritans finally cut down the maypole and shipped Morton back to England in 1628. A year and a half later he returned, obstreperous as ever, but was again deported. In England he joined the foes of the Massachusetts Bay Colony and wrote *New English Canaan, or New Canaan: Containing an Abstract of New England, Composed in Three Books: Written by Thomas Morton of Clifford Inn, Gent., Upon Ten Years' Knowledge and Experiment of the Country* (Amsterdam, 1637). Morton returned to New England ten years later, was again arrested, heavily fined, and released. He made his way to York, Me., where he died.

The NEW ENGLISH CANAAN is first of all intended as a history and a memoir, of course with a bias. But it is also a geographical and ethnological description, and is full of exuberance. CHARLES FRANCIS ADAMS edited it (1883) and set forth a careful analysis of Morton in his introduction. He found that Morton's humor made the book stand out among other 17th-century American writings.

The colony at Merry Mount has been treated in Catherine Sedgwick's *Hope Leslie* (1827), Nathaniel Hawthorne's *The Maypole of Merrymount* (1836), John Lothrop Motley's *Merrymount: a Romance of the Massachusetts Colony* (1849), and Helen Grace Carlisle's *We Begin* (1932). Howard Hanson and Richard L. Stokes made an opera, *Merry Mount* (1934).

Morton's Hope, or, The Memories of a Provincial (1839), a novel by JOHN LOTHROP MOTLEY. The story describes life in a German university and is obviously based on Motley's own experiences at Göttingen and Berlin.

Mosel, Tad (b. Steubenville, Ohio, May 1, 1922—   ), playwright, poet. Mosel attended Amherst College, graduating in 1947, and the Yale School of Drama, where he studied playwriting. Five unproduced plays and a year of acting later, he achieved some recognition with a number of superior television dramas. His major success, however, came with his adaptation of JAMES AGEE's Pulitzer prize-winning novel, *A Death in the Family*, retitled *All the Way Home* (1960). His dramatic version of the novel also won a Pulitzer Prize for drama in 1961. Among his original plays are: *Star in the Summer Night* (1954); *The Lawn Party* (1954); *My Lost Saints* (1956); *The Out-of-Towners* (1957). See TELEVISION WRITING.

Mosses from an Old Manse (1846), a collection of twenty-five tales and sketches by NATHANIEL HAWTHORNE. The Manse referred to in the title and in the initial sketch was owned by Ralph Waldo Emerson, and was oc-

cupied by Hawthorne from 1842 to 1846, the first years of his marriage. The initial sketch is important in revealing something of Hawthorne's attitude toward nature as a symbol of spiritual truth. Some of Hawthorne's best stories, such as YOUNG GOODMAN BROWN, THE BIRTHMARK, RAPPACINI'S DAUGHTER, *The Artist of the Beautiful*, and THE CELESTIAL RAILROAD are included in this collection. Melville hailed it as an American masterpiece and found much of it "deep as Dante." Poe recognized Hawthorne's contribution to the art of the short story, but felt that the stories were too allegorical.

Mother (1911), a novel by KATHLEEN NORRIS. The story of a middle-western schoolteacher and her mother, this was Mrs. Norris' first novel and a long-continued best seller.

motion pictures. American contributions to the technical advances in early motion pictures included the horse-in-motion studies of EADWEARD MUYBRIDGE (1877), the photographic film of George Eastman (1889), and the ingenious sprocket system still in use to move film through a camera, developed by William K. L. Dickson (1889). THOMAS EDISON perfected the projecting Kinetoscope and demonstrated it publicly on April 23, 1896, the usual date given for the start of the American film industry.

Initially the film was modeled on stage techniques. Edwin S. Porter's THE GREAT TRAIN ROBBERY (1903) established a new pattern: scenes appeared in dramatic, rather than chronological, order; no titles separated scenes; the cut was introduced, and the two plots were developed by parallel cutting, a technique now common by which two actions are followed simultaneously by cutting from one to the other as they develop. The picture was photographed out-of-doors and consequently camera shot from different angles rather than from one position.

Within the next dozen years, the movies came of age artistically in the pictures of D. W. GRIFFITH. His work is memorable not so much for the technical devices which he introduced as for the artistry with which he treated his material; his camera functioned creatively. Under his direction, the action of a movie began to flow; he sensed that movies have a form of their own, and are a different genre from that of the theatre. *The Birth of a Nation* (1915) introduced film techniques that soon became standard practise. Although the stereotyped Negroes were a point of controversy in *Intolerance* (1916), the picture affected its audience to a degree rarely achieved by motion pictures.

Griffith was not alone even in the early days; two other important directors were Thomas Ince, whose western films with William S. Hart added a naturalness to the screen, and MACK SENNETT, whose comedies with their Keystone Kops, bathing beauties, and wild chases added a sense of fun still fresh today.

The comic film with its immediate visual humor was the vehicle for the masterful work of such men as Buster Keaton, Harold Lloyd, Harry Langdon, Ben Turpin, and "the little fellow," CHARLIE CHAPLIN's immortal tramp. Through a series of films including *The Tramp* (1915), *The Kid* (1921), and *Modern Times* (1936), Chaplin created the greatest character in American films. His recent film, *Limelight* (1952), though without the tramp, is perhaps his most profound picture.

The star system did much to shape the course of silent pictures, as, indeed, it now does with talking pictures. Mary Pickford and Douglas Fairbanks were America's idols, Chaplin its comic heart, and Valentino its romantic dream.

The two most vital film forms in the twenties were the comedy and the western film. Free from the restrictions of "messages," enormous budgets, and artistic self-consciousness, they were the training ground of such excellent directors as FRANK CAPRA, JOHN FORD, and George Stevens, and shaped the characteristic American style of speed, clean photography, sharp timing, and action impelled by a steady story line.

The Twenties and Thirties produced some pictures which must be listed in any summation of the achievements of American movies. Although directors of studio pictures were expected to follow the prevailing fashion in films, Erich von Stroheim immediately cut his own path with his uncompromising insistence on realism and his incredible attention to detail. His masterpiece, though never seen in its original length and rarely even in edited versions, was a powerful and accurate film version of Frank Norris' MCTEAGUE (1899) called *Greed* (1924). Stroheim's last appearance in films (he acted and directed) was as the old director in *Sunset Boulevard* (1950).

Rather than fight the conservative tendencies of the film business in Hollywood, Robert Flaherty, after his independently made *Nanook of the North* (1922) and studio-produced, location-shot *Moana* (1926), pursued an independent course in developing the documentary film. Flaherty's concern with people in their natural environment is seen especially in his *Man of Aran* (1934). The documentary film was given best expression while being financed by the government during the depression. The poetic technique of Flaherty influenced PARE LORENTZ' *The Plow That Broke The Plains* (1936) and his history of the Mississippi, *The River* (1937). The techniques of the documentary were effectively integrated with fiction in such pictures as De Rochemont's *The House on 92nd Street* (1945) and the earlier and more significant *Citizen Kane* (1940) of ORSON WELLES.

In 1927 *The Jazz Singer* with Al Jolson had four episodes of sound within an essentially silent picture. In very short order the silent films ceased being produced and talkies were in. When the novelty wore off, more was demanded of a picture than that it talk; quality, which in most cases seemed to have died with the silents, had to be restored. Two pictures early in the sound era used sound as an integral part of their development, and in their power and camera sweep both are memorable films: King Vidor's *Hallelujah!* (1929), with an all-Negro cast, and Lewis Milestone's *All Quiet on the Western Front* (1930), in which sight and sound blended in an effective portrayal of the horrors of war.

Comedy also learned to talk, and during the Thirties the films of the Marx Brothers and W. C. Fields often captured the pace and wild humor of the silent comedies, although they were usually without structural coherence. However, some film-makers used the advantages of sight and sound to attain a unity of structure and meaning which may be best seen in Frank Capra's *It Happened One Night* (1934). The animated comic cartoon is often (with the exception, perhaps, of the shorts of Fields and ROBERT BENCHLEY) the modern equivalent of the early one- and two-reel silent comedies. Its significant contributions have been WALT DISNEY's MICKEY MOUSE and Donald Duck, and the more recent U.P.A. development of Gerald McBoing-Boing and Mr. Magoo.

In the years before the Second World War the movies often echoed the national concern for reform and the insistence on social significance. This trend is marked in one extreme by the rash of gangster films, which, however, usually afforded a weak excuse for depicting brutality. The best of these, before a host of imitators, starred such actors as James Cagney, Humphrey Bogart and Edward G. Robinson. One of the best and also most brutal of such films was *Scarface* (1932), with Paul Muni. At the other extreme, hard, sharp realism was exploited in a true cause, often through excellent films such as the anti-lynch picture, *Fury* (1936). Occasionally a film of rare beauty was made in this genre, such as JOHN FORD's *The Informer* (1935).

As the war approached, movies tended to offer hope in the democratic way of life and the virtues of America. This often meant adding optimistic endings, as was done in John Ford's THE GRAPES OF WRATH (1939) or in celebrating great Americans as in his *Young Mr. Lincoln* (1939) and *Abe Lincoln in Illinois* (1940). Many of the best film-makers devoted themselves to documenting the war; others often made either well-intentioned propagandistic films or merely exploited enemy brutality for its own sake.

Immediately after the war, many of the best pictures returned to themes of social significance, especially problems of the transition to peace. The best of these was SAMUEL GOLDWYN's *The Best Years of Our Lives* (1946). Political corruption was openly discussed in ELIA KAZAN's *Boomerang* (1947); anti-Semitism was the theme of the provocative *Gentleman's Argeement* (1947) and *Crossfire* (1947). The concern for social questions was put aside for a number of years after this period as a result of the Congressional investigations into the political inclinations of many film-makers. The Forties also saw the return of John Huston from making films for the Army to direct the superb *The Treasure of the Sierra Madre* (1948). He soon followed this with *The African Queen* (1951), with screenplay by JAMES AGEE.

Movies in the Fifties took a new shape economically: most of the more important films were not made under the auspices of a studio but were done independently by companies formed usually for one film. Occasionally, the company was in part financed by one star who appeared in a series of films under its own aegis. Thus the star system and the production of films began to change also, for they were no longer the product of the collective controls of a studio, but a personal expression of one man's ideas. Some of the best of these films have been Hecht-Lancaster's *Marty* (1955), Robert Aldrich's *Attack* (1956) and Elia Kazan's *On the Waterfront* (1954). The independent film has also been responsible for the return of controversial themes to Hollywood, as in Otto Preminger's *The Man With The Golden Arm* (1955). During this period some excellent westerns were produced, such as Fred Zinneman's *High Noon* (1951) and George Stevens' *Shane* (1953).

New film techniques both for the making and exhibiting of films (Cinerama, Cinemascope, 3-D) are only of value to motion pictures as a creative form when they are meaningfully used in the film; otherwise they are glorified promotional stunts. An excellent example of the value of a new technique is the use of Todd A–O in the balloon sequences of *Around the World in Eighty Days* (1956). An example of imaginative use of an older technique is the technicolor photography of Bert Stern in *Jazz on a Summer's Day* (1958). Some of the most experimental films being made today are only shown to such limited audiences as New York's Cinema 16, but they demonstrate an interest in the vitality of motion pictures which transcends purely economic considerations.

Some of the best books on the history and criticism of American movies are Terry Ramsaye's *A Million and One Nights* (1926); Allardyce Nicoll's *Film and Theater* (1936); Lewis Jacobs' *The Rise of the American Film* (1939); Hortense Powdermaker's *Hollywood, The Dream Factory* (1950); Arthur Knight's *The Liveliest Art* (1958); and James Agee's *Agee on Film* (1958).

Hollywood has often fascinated American writers; it has been treated in Nathanael West's THE DAY OF THE LOCUST (1939); F. SCOTT FITZGERALD'S *The Last Tycoon* (1941); Harold Robbins' *The Dream Merchants* (1949); and Budd Schulberg's THE DISENCHANTED (1950).

Motley, John Lothrop (b. Dorchester, Mass., April 15, 1814—d. May 29, 1877), diplomat, historian. Motley entered Harvard at thirteen, obtained a doctorate from Göttingen, and returned to this country, where he published MORTON'S HOPE: OR, THE MEMOIRS OF A YOUNG

PROVINCIAL (1839), a semiautobiographical novel, and *Merry-Mount: A Romance of the Massachusetts Colony* (1849). After a few months with the United States legation in St. Petersburg, he returned home and published

a historical essay on Peter the Great in the *North American Review* in 1845. After five years of concentrated labor he completed THE RISE OF THE DUTCH REPUBLIC (3 v., 1856), a robust and spirited history on which his reputation rests. It was an immediate success; new editions and translations followed rapidly. *History of the United Netherlands* (1861–68); *Democracy the Climax of Political Progress* (1869); and *The Life and Death of Joen of Barneveld, Advocate of Holland* (1874) were the first three parts of a vast history of the Netherlands which Motley did not live to finish.

Motley, Willard (b. Chicago, July 14, 1912 —d. Mar. 4, 1965), novelist. Motley's first novel was published at thirty-five, after he had wandered across the country, from New York to California, working as a migratory laborer, dishwasher, waiter, short-order cook, ranch hand, photographer, etc. His first book, *Knock on Any Door* (1947), the story of the progressive criminal hardening of a boy in the Chicago slums, was acclaimed as a remarkably powerful and challenging novel, and compared to Dreiser and James Farrell. This was followed by *We Fished All Night* (1951) and *Let No Man Write My Epitaph* (1958), novels which effectively treated the same background of poverty and crime, but lacked the vitality of the earlier book.

Moto, Mr. A clever Japanese spy who appears in a number of stories by J. P. MARQUAND. They were collected in *Thank You, Mr. Moto* (1936). Mr. Moto also appears in *Stopover Tokyo* (1957).

Moton, Robert Russa (b. Amelia Co., Va., Aug. 26, 1867—d. May 31, 1940), teacher, administrator, writer. Moton became the head of Hampton Institute, of which he was a graduate, then in 1915 succeeded BOOKER T. WASHINGTON as principal of Tuskegee Institute. He wrote on *Racial Good Will* (1916) and *What the Negro Thinks* (1929), and gave his reminiscences in *Finding a Way Out* (1920).

Mott, Frank Luther (b. Keokuk Co., Iowa, April 4, 1886—d. Oct. 23, 1964), literary historian, editor. Mott became one of the greatest authorities on American newspapers, magazines, and best-selling books. In 1927 he was appointed professor of journalism and director of the School of Journalism at the State University of Iowa, and in 1942 joined the staff of the journalism school at the University of Missouri. For his *History of American Magazines* (3 v., 1930, 1938) he received a Pulitzer prize; volume 4 appeared in 1957. Among his other books: *Six Prophets out of the Middle West* (1917); *Literature of Pioneer Life in Iowa* (1923); *Rewards of Reading* (1926); *American Journalism: A History* (1941); *Jefferson and the Press* (1943); GOLDEN MULTITUDES: THE STORY OF BEST-SELLERS IN THE U.S. (1947); *The News in America* (1952); *Five Stories* (1957).

Moulton, [Ellen] Louise Chandler (b. Pomfret, Conn., April 10, 1835—d. Aug. 10, 1908), poet, novelist, writer of children's stories, newspaper correspondent. Mrs. Moulton began writing poems at the age of seven and was indefatigable in the production of verse, mainly in the sonnet form, that was graceful but undistinguished. She wrote about books for Boston and New York papers; composed a novel, *June Clifford* (1855), which she published anonymously; wrote short biographies of Philip Bourke Marston and Stephen Phillips, travel books, and several series of *Bedtime Stories* (1873, 1874, 1880). Her verses were collected in *The Poems and Sonnets of Louise Chandler Moulton* (1909). Lillian Whitney wrote *Louise Chandler Moulton: Poet and Friend* (1910).

Moulton, Richard Green (b. England, May 5, 1849—d. Aug. 15, 1924), teacher, critic, Biblical scholar. Moulton became professor of literary theory and interpretation at the University of Chicago in 1892 and continued teaching there until 1919. He wrote *Shakespeare as a Dramatic Artist* (1885); *The Moral System of Shakespeare* (1903); *World Literature and Its Place in General Culture* (1911); *The Modern Study of Literature* (1915). He contended that the effect of the Bible was lost by the way it was printed; that readers did not realize that the Bible was not a book but a library of books. He published some books of the Bible

separately, then all of it in *The Modern Readers' Bible* (20 v., 1896–1906). In this edition verse was written as verse, prose appeared in paragraphs. His arrangements were felicitously made, and awoke in many readers a deeper sense of the Bible as literature. Moulton's brother, William F. Moulton, himself a clergyman and able Biblical scholar, wrote his biography in 1926.

Mountaineering in the Sierra Nevada (1872), sketches by CLARENCE KING.

Mountain Interval (1916), a collection of poems, both lyric and narrative, by ROBERT FROST. This collection contains some of Frost's most enjoyable poems—THE ROAD NOT TAKEN, *Christmas Trees, In the Home Stretch, The Oven Bird,* BIRCHES, *A Time to Talk, The Cow in Apple Time,* and *Brown's Descent.*

Mountains of California, The (1894; rev. and enlarged, 1911), a description by JOHN MUIR. Muir was both a notable geologist and an ardent nature-lover. He was particularly enthusiastic about the wilder aspects of Californian scenery. In this volume he is at his best in his description of the geology, flora, fauna, and the landscapes of the Sierra Nevada, the Coast Range, the intervening Central Valley. His was a book for scientists and also one to lure others to the wilderness.

Mountain States. See ROCKY MOUNTAIN REGION.

Mount Rushmore. See GUTZON BORGLUM.

Mount Vernon. George Washington's Virginia home and burial place is situated on the Potomac, 16 miles south of Washington, D.C. Augustine Washington, father of George, bequeathed it to George's older half-brother Lawrence. Washington inherited it in 1752 on his brother's death. He enlarged his holdings to eight thousand acres and improved both the house and the estate, lived there until the outbreak of the Revolution, returned in 1783. In 1856 the grounds were purchased by the Mount Vernon Ladies' Association, which has preserved the grounds and house. Near the house is the tomb in which George and Martha Washington lie buried. Among books on Mount Vernon are Paul Wilstach's *Mount Vernon: Washington's Home and the Nation's Shrine* (1916); Paul L. Haworth's *George Washington, Country Gentleman* (1925; originally *George Washington, Farmer,* 1915); Harrison Howell Dodge's *Mount Vernon: Its Owner and Its Story* (1932); G. W. Johnson and C. C. Wall's *Mt. Vernon: The Story of a Shrine* (1953).

Mourning Becomes Electra (1931), a trilogy of plays by EUGENE O'NEILL; the parts are entitled *Homecoming, The Hunted,* and *The Haunted.* The playwright took his story from the *Oresteia* of Aeschylus, giving it a setting in 19th-century New England and a generous interlarding of Freudian theory. Agamemnon is represented by Ezra Mannon, a general returning from the Civil War. His wife Christine corresponds to Clytemnestra, his daughter (Electra) is Lavinia, his son (Orestes) is Orin. The play takes its force from the deep-rooted conflict between Puritanism and romantic passion. Many critics believe it to be O'Neill's best work. It was made into a motion picture in 1947.

Mourt's Relation. See GEORGE MORTON.

Mowatt, Anna. See FASHION, OR, LIFE IN NEW YORK.

Mowrer, Edgar Ansel (b. Bloomington, Ill., March 8, 1892—   ), newspaperman, government official, free-lance writer. Long with the Chicago *News*, Mowrer went into government service during World War II. Among his books: *Immortal Italy* (1922); *This American World* (1928); *The Future of Politics* (1930); *Germany Puts Back the Clock* (1932, Pulitzer prize); *The Dragon Awakes* (1938); *The Nightmare of American Foreign Policy* (1948); *Challenge and Decision* (1950); *An End to Make-Believe* (1961).

Mowrer, Paul Scott (b. Bloomington, Ill., July 14, 1887—   ), newspaperman, foreign and war correspondent, writer on foreign affairs, poet. Like his brother EDGAR MOWRER, Paul Mowrer was long on the staff of the Chicago *News*, at home and abroad. In 1928 he won a Pulitzer award for foreign correspondence. Among his books: *Balkanized Europe* (1921); *Our Foreign Affairs* (1924); and an autobiography, *The House of Europe* (1945). He has also published several collections of poems, among them *Hours of France* (1918); *Poems Between Wars* (1941); *Twenty-One and Sixty-Five* (1958); *The Mothering Land* (1960).

M. Quad. The pen name of C. B. LEWIS.

Mr. See MISTER.

Mrs. Wiggs of the Cabbage Patch (1901), a novel by ALICE HEGAN RICE. From childhood the author of this story about an odd, likable Southern character had two deep interests—writing and welfare work. She was active in the latter cause while living in Louisville and in the course of her experiences met the woman who suggested the character of Mrs. Wiggs. In the book she is a widow with five children to support, but she refuses to be downed by circumstances and keeps a cheerful outlook on life. She lives in a broken-down section of Louisville along the railroad tracks called, for no special reason, "The Cabbage Patch." Her three daughters are called Asia, Australia, and Europena. A wealthy young man and his former fiancée befriend the Wiggs family and become reconciled in the process. A leading personage in one of the episodes is Cuba, a half-dead horse whom Mrs. Wiggs nurses and makes a valuable member of the family. The book sold 200,000 copies in three years and continues in demand. A philanthropic enterprise in Louisville which Mrs. Rice helped to found is called the Cabbage Patch Settlement House.

MS. Found in a Bottle (*Baltimore Saturday Visiter*, Oct. 19, 1833; *Southern Literary Messenger*, Dec., 1835; *The Gift*, 1836; collected in *Tales of the Grotesque and Arabesque*, 1840), a tale by EDGAR ALLAN POE. The *Visiter* had announced a prize competition with an award of $50 for the best story, $25 for the best poem. Poe submitted a poem, THE COLISEUM, and several stories. The tales deeply impressed the judges, and they gave the award to *MS. Found in a Bottle*. This story tells how a vessel is swallowed up in a monstrous current; the narrator has been keeping a kind of journal, which survives. Poe combined the legend of the Flying Dutchman with John C. Symmes' idea that the world is hollow, with water pouring into the interior from the ocean at the poles. The descent of the wave upon the vessel is magnificently and horrifyingly described.

muckraking literature. The "literature of exposure" is almost an American genre, especially in the early 20th century. The term derives from Bunyan's *Pilgrim's Progress* (1678), in which one character is so busy raking muck that he cannot perceive the celestial crown held above him. Though used denigratingly at first, the term soon became one of praise, at least in the minds of those who favored this kind of writing.

Possibly one of the earliest muckraking novels was REBECCA HARDING DAVIS' story of wage slavery in the New England mills, *Life in the Iron Mills* (*Atlantic Monthly*, 1861). She followed this with *A Story of Today* in the same magazine (1861–62), and then wrote a novel, *John Andros* (1874), to expose the whisky trust. In the same era EDWIN LAWRENCE GODKIN founded THE NATION (1865) and devoted himself to civil service reform and attacks on protective tariff evils. Soon other novels appeared: Mark Twain and C. D. Warner's THE GILDED AGE (1873); EDWARD EGGLESTON'S *The Mystery of Metropolisville* (1873); David Ross Locke's *A Paper City* (1878); Henry Adams' DEMOCRACY (1879). When John Hay wrote his attack on labor unions, THE BREAD-WINNERS (1884), H. F. Keenan replied with an attack on big business, *The Money-Makers* (1885). W. D. Howells' RISE OF SILAS LAPHAM (1885) was the first classic study of the "big businessman." In the same decade appeared Thomas S. Denison's *An Iron Crown* (1885); JOHN T. TROWBRIDGE'S *Farnell's Folly* (1885); George T. Dowling's *The Wreckers* (1886); Martin A. Foran's *The Other Side* (1886).

The fictional exposé continued in the next decade: H. BOYESEN'S *The Mammon of Unrighteousness* (1891); HAMLIN GARLAND'S *A Member of the Third House* (1892); F. HOPKINSON SMITH'S *Tom Grogan* (1896); HAROLD FREDERIC'S *The Market Place* (1899); Margaret Sherwood's *Henry Worthington, Idealist* (1899). Charles Dudley Warner completed a stern and humorless trilogy about rich men: *A Little Journey in the World* (1889), *The Golden House* (1895), and *That Fortune* (1899). Meanwhile economists, crusaders, historians, and others were busy with factual exposures, such as HENRY GEORGE'S PROGRESS AND POVERTY (1879); HENRY DEMAREST LLOYD'S *The Story of a Great Monopoly* (*Atlantic Monthly*, 1881) and his *Wealth Against Common-Wealth* (1894); and THORSTEIN VEBLEN'S *Theory of Business Enterprise* (1899) and his THEORY OF THE LEISURE CLASS (1904). An implicit reply was made by ANDREW CARNEGIE in THE GOSPEL OF WEALTH

(1889) and his *Empire of Business* (1902).

Muckraking did not, however, really become a vocation until the turn of the century. The spearhead of the movement was *McClure's Magazine* (see S. S. McClure), with other militant periodicals following its lead. Particularly noteworthy in this era were volumes made up of material gathered from some of these magazines: Lincoln Steffens' *The Shame of the Cities* (1904), *Struggle for Self-Government* (1906), and *The Upbuilders* (1909); Ida M. Tarbell's *History of the Standard Oil Company* (1904); Samuel Hopkins Adams' *The Great American Fraud* (1906).

The fiction of the period was profuse and made a deep impression on the public. Most sensational was Upton Sinclair's The Jungle (1906); in practically all his later fiction Sinclair was still the militant reformer. An inveterate muckraker was David Graham Phillips; among his novels in this field were *The Master Rogue: The Confession of a Croesus* (1903); *The Cost* (1904); *The Deluge* (1905); *The Plum Tree* (1905); *Light-Fingered Gentry* (1907); *The Fashionable Adventures of Joshua Craig* (1909). Frank Norris' The Octopus (1901) and The Pit (1903) were widely read, as was Robert Herrick's *Memoirs of an American Citizen* (1905). Theodore Dreiser told the story of one rich man in his trilogy: The Financier (1912), The Titan (1914), and *The Stoic* (1947). Winston Churchill wrote two novels in the realm of exposure, The Inside of the Cup (1912) and *A Far Country* (1915). Jack London treated the theme in two striking novels, The Iron Heel (1908) and *Burning Daylight* (1910). Since these novels appeared, business and finance have been continuously under the scrutiny of American novelists, as in the works of Sinclair Lewis and John P. Marquand.

Accounts of the muckraking movement are found in Burton J. Hendrick's *The Age of Big Business* (1919); Norman Hapgood's *The Changing Years* (1930); John Chamberlain's *Farewell to Reform* (1932); C. C. Regier's *The Era of the Muckrakers* (1932); Mark Sullivan's *The Education of an American* (1938); *The Muckrakers: The Era of Journalism That Moved America to Reform* (1961), a collection of the most significant magazine articles of 1902–1912 edited by Arthur and Lila Weinberg.

Mudjekeewis. The father of Hiawatha in Longfellow's poem. He is given dominion over the winds for killing a great bear.

Mudville. Usually thought to be a section of Somerville, Mass. The scene of various ballads by George Whitefield D'Vys (1860–1941); also the battleground of the baseball game described in Ernest Lawrence Thayer's Casey at the Bat (1888).

Muensterberg, Hugo (b. Germany, June 1, 1863—d. Dec. 16, 1916), psychologist, teacher. Muensterberg came to the United States at the invitation of William James and remained until his death. He served as director of the newly established psychological laboratory at Harvard and as a teacher of psychology. He strongly stressed the physiological aspects of psychology and was a leader in experimental psychology and in the application of the findings of psychology to industry. Some of his important books were written in German, among them *Willenshandlung* (1888); *Beitraege zur Experimentellen Psychologie* (1889–92); and *Grundzuege der Psychologie* (1900). Among his works in English were *Psychology and Life* (1899); *The Eternal Values* (1909); *Psychology and the Teacher* (1910); *Psychology and Industrial Efficiency* (1912); *Psychology: General and Applied* (1914); *Psychology and Social Sanity* (1914). In one of his principal ideas he closely approached William James—his insistence on the motor outlet as constituting a part of consciousness; James made it a part of emotion. Always deliberately a German, Muensterberg wrote fluently on his observation of the United States: *American Traits* (1902); *American Problems* (1910); *American Patriotism* (1911). The coming of World War I brought tragedy to Muensterberg, since he fervently supported Germany. He died of a cerebral hemorrhage while lecturing at Radcliffe.

Muhlenberg, William Augustus (b. Philadelphia, Sept. 16, 1796—d. April 6, 1877), Protestant Episcopal clergyman, hymn writer. Muhlenberg served in New York City, was founder of St. Luke's Hospital, and wrote many hymns, some of which appeared in *Church Poetry* (1823). Anna Ayres prepared an account of his *Life and Works* (1889).

Muir, John (b. Scotland, April 21, 1838—d. Dec. 24, 1914), naturalist, essayist. As a small boy in Scotland, John Muir read Audubon and dreamed of exploring in the New World, a dream that was realized soon afterward when his father migrated to a farm in Wisconsin. In *The Story of My Boyhood and Youth* (1913) Muir described the hardships of his life on the farm, his boyhood delight in nature and books. Between 1863, when he left the University of Wisconsin, and 1868, when he settled for six years in the Yosemite Valley, Muir traveled thousands of miles afoot through Wisconsin, Illinois, Indiana, and Canada, and made a journey from Indiana to Mexico, the journal of which he published as *A Thousand Mile Walk to the Gulf* (1916). He had the naturalist's keen eye, a poetic appreciation of nature, and a gift for style. A lover of animals, he disliked the notion of a world made for man alone, with animals to serve him. He repeatedly expressed his wonder and admiration for the intelligence of beasts. *Stickeen* (1909) is a loving tribute to the loyalty and resourcefulness of his little half-wild dog.

Much of Muir's life was devoted to saving the natural beauties of the West from destruction by commercial exploitation. He roused the public to the need for a conservation program, and under his friend President Theodore Roosevelt the system of national parks was established. His letters report his constant, heart-breaking struggle to prevent man from ruining the beauties of nature (*Life and Letters of John Muir,* edited by W. F. Badé, 1923–24). Among his other works are THE MOUNTAINS OF CALIFORNIA (1894); *Our National Parks* (1901); *The Yosemite* (1912); *Travels in Alaska* (1915); *The Cruise of the Corwin* (1917). His *Writings* were collected by Badé (10 v., 1916–24). Linnie M. Wolfe made an excellent anthology of selections, *The Wilderness World of John Muir* (1954).

Mulford, Clarence E[dward] (b. Streator, Ill., Feb. 3, 1883—d. May 10, 1956), writer of western stories. Mulford was employed as a municipal clerk in New York City when he began writing stories. His first book was a western called *Bar-20* (1907), in which he introduced a character called HOPALONG CASSIDY, who later appeared in twenty-seven other books by Mulford. He had never been to the West, although in 1924 he finally visited the scene of his novels. Millions of copies of his books have been sold. Among them are: *Hopalong Cassidy* (1910); *The Coming of Cassidy* (1913); *Rustlers' Valley* (1924); *Hopalong Cassidy Returns* (1924); *Me an' Shorty* (1929); *The Round Up* (1933); *Hopalong Cassidy Takes Cards* (1937); *Hopalong Cassidy Serves a Writ* (1941). In 1934 the actor Bill Boyd made his first appearance in a Hopalong Cassidy movie. Hopalong became the hero of innumerable youngsters throughout the nation.

Mulford, Elisha (b. Montrose, Pa., Nov. 19, 1833—d. Dec. 9, 1885), Episcopal clergyman, teacher, writer. For the greater part of his life Mulford served as a clergyman; from 1881 he was a lecturer at the Episcopal Theological Seminary in Cambridge. He was deeply under the influence of Hegel and his English follower, Frederick Denison Maurice. His two important books were *The Nation* (1870) and *The Republic of God: An Institute of Theology* (1881). In both he preached a doctrine of democratic idealism and emphasized "natural rights," which such documents as the Constitution merely "institutionalized." Herbert W. Scheider holds that Mulford's fusion of religious language and emotion with democratic nationalism proved a powerful force which "gave a religious incentive to secular reform."

Mulford, [Amos] Prentice (b. Sag Harbor, N.Y., April 5, 1834—d. May 27, 1891), clerk, sailor, teacher, miner, newspaperman, writer, public relations counselor. Mulford's constant changes of attitude and vocation led him to many parts of the world. After working on a New York newspaper for several years, he built a small cabin in the woods near Passaic, N.J., and lived there as a hermit. He wrote an account of his experiences in *The Swamp Angel* (1888). He was an early columnist, writing for six years a piece called "The History of a Day" for the New York *Daily Graphic*. A popular work was his *Your Forces and How to Use Them* (6 v., 1888), which expounded what came to be called "the New Thought." He described humorously his western adventures in *Prentice Mulford's Story* (1889).

Mulholland, John (b. Chicago, June 9, 1898 —), magician, teacher, editor. Mulholland

developed the art of sleight-of-hand while still a child, was at first an amateur, soon became a professional. He was an editor of *The Sphinx*, a professional magazine for magicians. Among his books: *Magic in the Making* (with Milton Smith, 1925); *Quicker Than the Eye* (1932); *Story of Magic* (1935); *Beware Familiar Spirits* (1938); *The Art of Illusion* (1944); *The Early Magic Shows* (1945). Katherine Bakeless wrote about Mulholland in her book *In The Big Time* (1935).

Muller, Herbert J[oseph] (b. Mamaroneck, N.Y., July 7, 1905—), critic, teacher, scholar. Although Muller began his writings on literary criticism with *Modern Fiction* (1937), his studies led him into such widely differing subjects as semantics and the relation between science and literature, out of which evolved his book on *Science and Criticism* (1943). Some time spent with Thomas Wolfe became the basis for his book *Thomas Wolfe* (1947). At the University of Istanbul, as a visiting lecturer in American literature, Muller became interested in Byzantine history, which resulted in *Uses of the Past* (1952), perhaps his best known work. Titles of his later books show his continuing interest in history and criticism: *The Spirit of Tragedy* (1956); *The Loom of History* (1958); *Issues of Freedom* (1960); *A History of Freedom: The Ancient World* (1961).

Mulligan, Dan. Mulligan and his wife Cornelia were leading characters in a series of vaudeville sketches, later a series of plays, written by EDWARD HARRIGAN; they were performed with great success on the stage with Harrigan in the male role, his partner Tony Hart in the female. The characters were Irish immigrants sympathetically observed from life. They appeared for the first time in *The Mulligan Guard* (1873). Later plays include *The Mulligan Guard Ball* (1879); *The Mulligan Guard Chowder* (1879); *The Mulligan Guards' Christmas* (1879); *The Mulligan Guard Surprise* (1880); *The Mulligans' Silver Wedding* (1881); *Cornelia's Aspirations* (1883). All are still in manuscript, in possession of Harrigan's heirs.

Mumford, Ethel Watts (b. New York City, [?], 1878—d. May 2, 1940), novelist, playwright, humorist. Mrs. Mumford is best remembered as the co-author with OLIVER HERFORD and Addison Mizner of *The Complete Cynics' Calendar*, which made its first appearance in 1902 and continued until 1917. She wrote a novel, *Dupes* (1901); a play, *Sick-A-Bed* (1918).

Mumford, L. Quincy (1903—). See LIBRARY OF CONGRESS.

Mumford, Lewis (b. Flushing, N.Y., Oct. 19, 1895—), writer, philosopher, historian, and teacher. Mumford has brought his varied interests and learning to the writing of many books that explore the relation of man, especially modern man, to his natural and self-created surroundings. Mumford's work in city and regional planning was stimulated by reading the works of Patrick Geddes, Scottish biologist and sociologist, and in 1924 he helped found the Regional Planning Association of America. In his books, *The Brown Decades* (1931), *The Culture of Cities* (1938), *City Development* (1945), and *The City in History* (1961), he showed how the city is an expression of the growth of civilization and in turn influences that growth. *The Culture of Cities* is also a part of a four-volume study called *The Renewal of Life* that includes *Technics and Civilization* (1934), *The Condition of Man* (1944), and *The Conduct of Life* (1951). In this, his major work, he examined the emergence of the modern scientific and technological world, and he pleaded for a realization of man's obligation to create a better life from the infinite resources now at his command.

Mumford's articles in the *New Yorker* magazine have been one of the few examples of informed criticism of current architecture and planning. Some of these articles are collected in *From the Ground Up* (1956). Other books include *The Story of Utopias* (1922); Sticks and Stones (1924), one of the first histories of American architecture; The Golden Day (1926); *Herman Melville* (1929); *Green Memories* (1947), an affectionate biography of his son, Geddes, who was killed in World War II at the age of nineteen; *Art and Technics* (1952); *In the Name of Sanity* (1954); *The Transformations of Man* (1956).

Munch, Charles (b. France, Sept. 26, 1891—d. Nov. 6, 1968). Munch, one of the great contemporary conductors, studied at the Conservatory of Music of Strasbourg, made his debut in France in 1932 conducting the Orchestre Symphonique de Paris. He made his American debut in 1946 with the Boston Symphony Orchestra. Munch became its director in 1949, and brilliantly led it until his retirement in 1962. His memoirs, *I Am A Conductor* (1955) offer an insight into the exacting profession of conducting.

Mundy, Talbot (b. England, April 23, 1879—d. Aug. 5, 1940), traveler, writer. Mundy traveled extensively in Asia and Africa. He came to the United States in 1911, became a citizen in 1917. Frequently he made additional trips to the Old World and Mexico. *Rung Ho* (1914), his first book, exhibits his realism, his ability to tell a story well, his emphasis on the adventurous. Among his works: *King of the Khyber Rifles* (1916); *The Ivory Trail* (1919); *The Eye of Zeitoon* (1920); *Om* (1923); *Jungle Jest* (1932); *The Lion of Petra* (1933); *Full Moon* (1935); *Old Ugly Face* (1940).

Munford, Robert (b. Prince George Co., Va., 1730[?]—d. 1784), legislator, dramatist, poet. Munford, a Revolutionary patriot, showed the faults and virtues of both sides in the war in what may be the earliest of all American plays, The Candidates (probably 1770), and in The Patriots (1776). Munford later served as a county official in Virginia, also in the House of Burgesses and the General Assembly. During his lifetime none of his productions appeared in print, but after his death his son William (1775–1825), himself a public official, poet, and dramatist, made a *Collection of Plays and Poems* (1798) by his father. This included the two plays mentioned, also a partial translation of Ovid's *Metamorphoses* and ten poems. *The Candidates* was reprinted (1948), with an introduction by Jay B. Hubbell and Douglass Adair; *The Patriots* was reprinted in the *William and Mary Quarterly* in July 1949, with an introduction by Courtlandt Canby.

Munger, Theodore T[hornton] (b. Bainbridge, N.Y., March 5, 1830—d. Jan. 11, 1910), Congregational clergyman, inspirational essayist. Munger was perhaps the first American clergyman to popularize theological doctrines in an easy, attractive style. He addressed himself to young people in *On the Threshold* (1880), of which many thousands of copies were sold; *Lamps and Paths* (1883); and *The Freedom of Faith* (1883). He warmly praised the master who had led him away from rationalism in *Horace Bushnell: Preacher and Theologian* (1899). Some of his later writings were collected in *Essays for the Day* (1904).

Municipal Report, A (*Hampton's Magazine*, November, 1909; later collected in *Strictly Business*, 1910), a short story by O. Henry. Frank Norris once remarked that nothing worth writing about ever happened in Nashville, Tenn. O. Henry sought to prove him wrong by writing this tale, one of his best.

Munsell, Joel (b. Northfield, Mass., April 14, 1808—d. Jan. 15, 1880), printer, antiquarian, publisher, editor. As a printer Munsell followed in the footsteps of Isaiah Thomas and paid tribute to him by reprinting (1874) Thomas' *History of Printing in America* (1810). He wrote an *Outline of the History of Printing* (1839) and compiled *The Typographical Miscellany* (1850). From his establishment issued the *Lady's Magazine*, the *American Literary Magazine*, *The Spectator*, *The State Register*, and other periodicals. In 1872 appeared *Bibliotheca Munselliana*, a list of his imprints; in 1951 David S. Edelstein wrote *Joel Munsell: Printer and Antiquarian*.

Munsey, Frank A[ndrew] (b. Mercer, Me., Aug. 21, 1854—d. Dec. 22, 1925), novelist, editor, publisher. In 1882 Munsey founded a magazine for young people called *The Golden Argosy*, which in 1888 became *The Argosy*, a successful magazine for adults, and, in 1920, *The Argosy All-Story Weekly*. In 1889 he founded *Munsey's Weekly*, later called *Munsey's Magazine*. In 1929 this was merged with *Argosy All-Story*. *The All-Story Magazine* had been founded in 1904. In 1906 Munsey founded the *Railroad Man's Magazine*. In 1891 he purchased the New York *Star*, renamed it the *Daily Continent*, and published it, unsuccessfully, as a pioneer tabloid. Later he bought the Baltimore *News* (1908), the New York *Press* (1912), the New York *Sun* in both editions (1916), the New York *Herald*, the New York *Telegram* (1920), and papers in Washington and Boston. Although Munsey's habit of buying and then selling or killing distinguished newspapers earned him strong disapproval in the world of journalism, these tactics soon became standard as newspapers came to be regarded as big business. While he kept them, Munsey's papers lacked distinction, being devoted to an uninspired support of conservatism.

Munsey wrote novels, some of them stories for boys. Among them: *Afloat in a Great City* (1887); *The Boy Broker* (1888); *Derringforth* (1894); *A Tragedy of Errors* (1899). He also wrote *The Founding of the Munsey Publishing House* (1907).

Munsey's Magazine. See FRANK A. MUNSEY.

Munson, Gorham (b. Amityville, N.Y., May 26, 1896—   ), critic, editor, teacher, writer. Munson was on the staff of various publishing firms and engaged extensively in economic journalism. He founded *Secession* in 1922, an avant-garde magazine that printed poems by Hart Crane, E. E. Cummings, Marianne Moore, and many other experimental writers of the twenties. He founded and edited a fortnightly, *New Democracy* (1933–1936), devoted to the advancement of Social Credit, an economic theory that the world's ills may be cured by the public control of credit. Munson also wrote many critical articles and published numerous volumes of criticism. For over two decades he gave a popular course in creative writing at the New School for Social Research in New York City. Among his books: *Waldo Frank: A Study* (1923); *Robert Frost: A Study in Sensibility and Good Sense* (1927); *Destination: A Canvass of American Literature Since 1900* (1928); *Style and Form in American Prose* (1929); *Dilemma of the Liberated* (1930); *Twelve Decisive Battles of the Mind* (1942); *Aladdin's Lamp: The Wealth of the American Nation* (1945); *The Written Word* (1949); *The Writer's Workshop Companion* (1951); *Penobscot: Down East Paradise* (1959).

Munsterberg, Hugo. See MUENSTERBERG, HUGO.

Murat, [Napoleon] Achille, Prince (b. France, Jan. 21, 1801—d. April 15, 1847), elder son of **Joachim Murat** (b. France, 1767—d. 1815). Joachim, a French soldier who married Napoleon's sister Marie Annunciata, was made King of Naples, and was executed by the Allies after Waterloo. Achille Murat emigrated to America in 1821. He settled in Florida, became a citizen, was appointed postmaster at Lipona, practiced law, served in the militia in the Seminole War. He published three books about the United States: *Lettres sur les États-Unis* (1830); *Esquisse Morale et Politique des États-Unis* (1832; in English, *America and the Americans*, 1849); and *Exposition des Principes du Gouvernement Républicain, Tel Qu'il A Été Perfectionné en Amérique* (1833). He was a keen observer and especially useful in presenting a picture of the South. He has figured in American literature principally because of his friendly correspondence with Emerson after the latter visited the South during the winter of 1826–27. A. J. Hanna wrote *A Prince in Their Midst: The Adventurous Life of Achille Murat on the American Frontier* (1946).

Murder in the Cathedral (1935), a play in verse by T. S. ELIOT. This was Eliot's first completed drama and remains probably his most popular, although he himself expressed dissatisfaction with it. It is a work in the full tradition of the modern lyric theater, employing a herald, a lyric chorus, a cast of symbolical personages, and passages in unrestrained poetry alternating with others in prose. It was written for performance in a church and is a favorite work for amateur church theatrical groups. An operatic version, *Assassinio nella Cathedrale*, composed by Ildebrando Pizzetti in 1958, was well received; an earlier film version (1952) was not.

The action of the drama depicts the last weeks in the life of Thomas à Becket; the quarrel between church and state is the main theme. Four Tempters, representing youthful love of pleasure, yearning for power, desire for the company of wealthy men, and pride as a longing for martyrdom, importune Becket, but he rejects all four and emphasizes his wish to serve the Law of God rather than the Law of Man. Four knights (perhaps reincarnations of the Four Temptations) carry out the assassination ordered by Henry II, justifying themselves in speeches.

Both Greek and medieval antecedents are observable in the play, but it remains thoroughly modern in tone and techniques and exhibits many of the rhythms and characteristic turns of speech of Eliot's lyric verse. Whereas in his later works for the stage Eliot moved closer to the techniques of the naturalistic theater, *Murder in the Cathedral* is drawn with an ideal simplicity, visually and poetically, that lends it great force and a classical somberness of movement. On the other hand, some critics have found it too argumentative, and too strongly appealing to the mind rather than the emotions.

Murders in the Rue Morgue, The (*Graham's Magazine*, April, 1841; reprinted in *Prose Romances*, 1843, and in *Tales*, 1845), a story by EDGAR ALLAN POE. This story is called by Howard Haycraft "the world's first detective story." It was preceded by other attempts, but Poe emphasizes the detector or detective as well as the crime, and makes the interest depend on analysis rather than guesswork. In the original draft it was called *Murders in the Rue Trianon*. The plot deals with the brutal murders of a mother and a daughter. The police are baffled, but C. AUGUSTE DUPIN, like innumerable amateur sleuths to follow, is able to put the police on the track of an extraordinary solution of the crime. To this type of story Poe gave a special name, "tales of ratiocination." He regarded the *Murders* as one of his best stories.

Murdoch, Frank Hitchcock (b. Chelsea, Mass., March 11, 1843—d. Nov. 13, 1872), actor, playwright. Murdoch played in juvenile and light-comedy productions. He wrote several striking plays, none ever published. The best was produced shortly before his death—*Davy Crockett* (1872), one of his greatest successes. The leading role was taken by FRANK MAYO, who helped write the play. Murdoch also wrote *Light House Cliffs* (probably produced in

1870); *Bohemia, or The Lottery of Art* (1872); and *Only a Jew* (1873).

Murfree, Mary Noailles ["Charles Egbert Craddock"] (b. Murfreesboro, Tenn., Jan. 24, 1850—d. July 31, 1922), short-story writer, novelist. Miss Murfree, a little, soft-spoken, crippled spinster who lived most of her life in Tennessee,

published her first stories as R. Emmet Denbry, a pseudonym she later changed to Charles Egbert Craddock, the name of one of her characters. A collection of stories, IN THE TENNESSEE MOUNTAINS (1884), one of the first realistic treatments of the southern mountaineer, presented him in all his poverty, pathos, ignorance, and native wit. *The Prophet of the Great Smoky Mountains* (1885), considered her best novel, deals with the enormous Cayce family, their daughter Dorinda, a beautiful girl, and the "prophet," a local preacher who sacrifices his life to save a "revenooer." Like Miss Murfree's other works, *The Prophet* is full of poetic description, picturesque language, and difficult orthography. One character, deploring the decline of the race, remarks, "Whenst I war young, folks ez kerried rifles ter git suthin' fur supper never kem home a-suckin' the bar'l." This was followed by *Down the Ravine* (1885), a juvenile; *In the "Stranger People's" Country* (1891); *The Mystery of Witchface Mountain and Other Stories* (1895); and half a dozen other local-color books. She also wrote a series of southern historical novels, among them *Where the Battle was Fought* (1884); *The Story of Old Fort Loudon* (1889); *The Frontiersman* (1904). See IN THE CLOUDS; IN THE TENNESSEE MOUNTAINS.

Murietta. See MURRIETA.

Murphy, Gardner (b. Chillicothe, Ohio, July 8, 1895—   ), psychologist, teacher, writer. Murphy received his B.A. degree from Yale in 1916, his M.A. from Harvard a year later. On his return from France after World War I he began his long career as a teacher at Columbia University which ended in 1940 when he moved to the City College of New York. In 1952 he became Director of Research for the Menninger Foundation in Topeka, Kansas. At various times Murphy was President of the American Psychological Association and UNESCO Consultant to the Ministry of Education in New Delhi, India. Among his books are: *Approaches to Personality* (1932); *Human Nature and Enduring Peace* (1945); *Public Opinion and the Individual* (1938); *Introduction to Psychology* (1951); *In the Minds of Men* (1953); *Human Potentiality* (1958).

Murphy, Henry Cruse (b. Brooklyn, N.Y., July 5, 1810—d. Dec. 1, 1882), lawyer, public official, diplomat, historian. Murphy held important public offices, among them Mayor of Brooklyn, state senator, minister to Holland. Of Irish-Dutch descent, he was greatly interested in the Dutch settlements in America. He had a great collection of Americana, especially in this field. Among his writings were a biography of Jacob Steedam, the earliest of New Netherlands poets (1861), and an account of the voyage of Verrazano (1875). He translated David Pietersen De Vries' collection of *Voyages from Holland, 1632 to 1634* (1857) and published an *Anthology of New Netherland, or, Translations from the Early Dutch Poets of New York, with Memoirs of Their Lives* (1865).

Murphy, Robert Cushman (b. New York City, April 29, 1887—   ), ornithologist, explorer, writer. Murphy served on the staff of the Brooklyn Museum, in 1921 was appointed assistant curator of birds at the American Museum of Natural History; in 1942 he became chairman of the Department of Ornithology at the museum, research associate in 1955. He has made numerous expeditions, recording his observations in many books and papers. His writings have a grace and charm not often found in scientific records. His most notable scientific production is *Oceanic Birds of South America* (2 v., 1936). He is better known, however, for a diary he kept while navigator on a New Bedford whaling ship, *Log-Book for Grace* (1947). He also wrote *Land Birds of America* (with Dean Amadon, 1953).

Murrieta, Joaquín (1830?–1853), bandit. Probably Mexican by birth, Murrieta (also spelled Murieta) became a notorious desperado in California during the 1850's. He excited some admiration, nevertheless, and the poet who was born Cincinnatus Hiner Miller adopted the name Joaquin Miller after writing a defense of Murrieta. John R. Ridge wrote *The Life and Adventures of Joaquin Murieta* (1854; reprinted 1955), a contemporary account of the bandit's life. Although he is supposed by some to be a merely legendary figure, and by others to have successfully resisted capture, many historians believe that he was killed and his head preserved in alcohol in 1853. J. C. Cunningham wrote *The Truth About Murietta* [sic] (1938).

Murrow, Edward R[oscoe] (b. Greensboro, N.C., Apr. 4, 1908—d. Apr. 27, 1965), radio and TV broadcaster, director, producer, writer, editor. Murrow, a great reporter, never worked on a newspaper; radio and television have been his only media. One of his earliest jobs of importance was to tell America what was happening in Britain in the crucial early years of World War II. A collection of his scripts became his first book, *This Is London* (1941). Later programs were called *See It Now* and *Hear It Now*. On another program, *This I Believe,* scores of prominent persons stated their philosophy of life. One hundred of these personal creeds were collected by Murrow in a volume called *This I Believe* (1952), which became a best seller. Equally popular were his television interviews with various celebrities, *Person to Person,* suspended in 1959. In 1961 he gave up his extremely lucrative work in television to head the U.S. Information Agency.

musical comedy in the U.S., a form of entertainment that evolved gradually from the American vaudeville and burlesque and European operetta. During the 19th century, minstrel shows and variety shows performed popular songs and skits with little attempt at coherence through plot or story. However, under the mounting influence of light opera from Europe, particularly that of Gilbert and Sullivan, the modern musical comedy took shape. In 1879 Nate Salsbury produced *The Brook* in which the action and music arise, at least superficially, from the plot. Salsbury himself used the term "musical comedy" for the first time to describe this farce.

By this time entrepreneurs were beginning to realize the tremendous profits of musical productions. *The Black Crook* (1866), a five-hour extravaganza of dance, song, and show girls, had brought in over a million dollars and incidentally set the style of later spectaculars like *Evangeline* (1874) (a burlesque of the Longfellow poem). George Ade described this type of show as "disorderly conduct occasionally interrupted by talk." Nevertheless talented actors, singers, and composers were attracted to this lucrative field: Weber and Fields, and Harrigan and Hart, the famous comedy teams; Al Jolson; Fanny Brice; Dennis King; GEORGE M. COHAN; REGINALD DE KOVEN; VICTOR HERBERT; Rudolf Friml; Sigmund Romberg.

In the 20th century many people have added their improvements to the form or style of the musical comedy. Florenz Ziegfeld's *Follies* (1907–43) kept the loose form of the variety shows but introduced singers like Sophie Tucker and Eddie Cantor, and composers like JEROME KERN and IRVING BERLIN. RICHARD RODGERS and his librettists, LORENZ HART and OSCAR HAMMERSTEIN II, achieved a close unity between text and music, as in OKLAHOMA! Others that followed their lead included Frank Loesser, FREDERICK LOEWE with ALAN J. LERNER, and

LEONARD BERNSTEIN. Some composers, like Leonard Bernstein and MARK BLITZSTEIN, were able to use their classical training to escape some of the musical clichés which have always plagued musicals. GEORGE and IRA GERSHWIN broke tradition in their own way with masterpieces like OF THEE I SING and *Porgy and Bess* (see PORGY). Other names associated with the development of musical comedy include: COLE PORTER; P. G. Wodehouse; OTTO HARBACH; MOSS HART; Kurt Weill; GEORGE KAUFMAN; HOWARD DIETZ; Arthur Schwartz.

Some of the best descriptions of musical comedies are: *Operas and Musical Comedies* (1951) by J. Walker McSpadden; *Bring On the Girls!* (1953) by Guy Bolton and P. G. Wodehouse; *Musical Comedy in America* (1950) by Cecil Smith; *Complete Book of the Musical Theatre* (1958) by David Ewen.

Musser, Benjamin [Francis] (b. Lancaster, Pa., 1889—d. April 17, 1951), poet, essayist, critic. Musser was converted to Catholicism in 1908. He wrote on *Franciscan Poets* (1933), was co-founder (1931) of *The Trend,* and contributed to many of the "little magazines." *Chiaroscuro,* his first book of verse, appeared in 1923. Thereafter he published more than forty volumes, many of them collections of his own verse. His *Selected Poems* were published in 1930, his *Poems* in 1930–33. His writings were always marked by gentleness and love of mankind.

Mutiny on the Bounty (1932), a novel by JAMES NORMAN HALL and CHARLES NORDHOFF. This vivid narrative is based on the mutiny which the crew of a British war vessel carried out in 1789 against a cruel commander, Captain William Bligh. The authors kept the historical characters and background, using as narrator an elderly man, Captain Roger Byam, who had served as a midshipman on the *Bounty.* The book was followed by two others, forming a trilogy: *Men Against the Sea* (1934), which tells how Bligh and seventeen others were set adrift in an open boat; and *Pitcairn's Island* (1934), which tells of the mutineers' life on a tiny Pacific island for twenty years.

The idea for a book on the famous mutiny had occurred to Hall as far back as 1916 when he was browsing in a Paris bookstore. The two men read contemporary accounts of Captain Bligh and his great voyage over 3,600 miles of sea in an open boat, also of the arrest, trial, and execution of the mutineers. Hall wrote the English, Nordhoff the Polynesian chapters, but each contributed heavily to the work of the other. In 1935 an excellent motion-picture version of the book was made.

Muybridge, Eadweard [originally Edward James Muggeridge] (b. England, 1830—d. 1904), photographer. Muybridge came to the United States as a boy and made photography his lifework. He helped the U.S. Coast and Geodetic Survey, specialized in photographs of animals in motion, and published *The Horse in Motion* (1878) and *Animal Locomotion* (1887). Sections of the latter were reprinted in 1955 as

The Human Figure in Motion. He invented the zoopraxiscope, an early motion-picture projector.

Muzzey, David S[aville] (b. Lexington, Mass., Oct. 9, 1870—d. Apr. 14, 1965), historian. Muzzey studied here and abroad, taught at Robert College in Istanbul, the Ethical Culture School in New York City, Barnard College, and Columbia University. Among his books: *Rise of the New Testament* (1900); *The Spiritual Franciscans* (1907); *An American History* (1911); *Readings in American History* (1915); *Life of Thomas Jefferson* (1918); *The United States of America* (1922–24); *History of the American People* (1927); *James G. Blaine* (1934); *Ethics as a Religion* (1951).

My American Pilgrimage (1947), an autobiography by STOYAN CHRISTOWE.

My Ántonia (1918), a novel by WILLA CATHER. One of the first and still most successful ventures in realistic portrayal of the Middle West, this novel tells the story of an immigrant Bohemian farm family in Nebraska, especially the fortunes of Antonia Shimerda, a daughter of the family. She longs for a life of greater sensitivity than she finds on the farm. She escapes to a town, is betrayed by a philanderer, bears an illegitimate child, finally returns to the farm and marries a fellow immigrant, Anton Cuzak. *My Ántonia* is notable particularly for its lucid and moving depictions of the prairie and the people who live close to it, the farmers whose lives are controlled by storm and drought and the spring rains.

My Aunt (*New England Magazine,* October, 1831), a humorous poem by OLIVER WENDELL HOLMES. Holmes mingles mild ridicule with kindly sentiment in this account of an unmarried member of his family. It affords an amusing sidelight on oldtime education for girls of good family.

My Client Curley (1940), a radio play by Lucille Fletcher (1913—   ) and NORMAN CORWIN. based on a short story by Miss Fletcher. Curley is a caterpillar whom a youngster has taught to dance to the tune of *Yes, Sir, That's My Baby.* Curley's adventures, his climb to fame and fortune, his final disappearance make up the story; at the end he reappears as a butterfly. The piece has been revived frequently and was also made into a motion picture.

Myers, Peter Hamilton (b. Herkimer, N.Y., Aug. 4, 1812—d. Oct. 30, 1878), lawyer, writer. Myers practiced law in Brooklyn, was active as a writer in his earlier years. He began with a poem, *Ensenore* (1840), reprinted many years later in *Ensenore and Other Poems* (1875). In 1848 he published anonymously *The First of the Knickerbockers: A Tale of 1673,* followed by *The Young Patroon, or, Christmas in 1690* (1849) and *The King of the Hurons* (1850), both also anonymous. The latter was reprinted in England as *Blanche Montaigne: The Prisoner of the Border* (1857). The Duyckincks speak of him as also "an agreeable essayist."

Myers, William Starr (b. Baltimore, Md., June 17, 1877—d. Jan. 27, 1956), teacher, historian. A Johns Hopkins graduate, Myers taught mainly at Princeton, where he joined the faculty in 1906 and became professor of politics in 1918. Myers was an authority in American history. Among his books: *Socialism and American Ideals* (1919); *The Republican Party: A History* (1928); *General George B. McClellan* (1934); *The Foreign Policies of Herbert Hoover* (1940); *The Story of New Jersey* (1945).

My Friend Flicka. See MARY O'HARA.

My Heart and My Flesh (1927), a novel by ELIZABETH MADOX ROBERTS. This is a typical novel of the "New South," which anticipated William Faulkner in some of its episodes and attitudes but found a gentler and more conventional solution for its problems. The story concerns the three love affairs of Theodosia, whose father has given her two mulatto half-sisters. Her first lover is burned to death, her second deserts her. Only with the third, a simpleminded, honest stock-raiser, does she find peace. Some of the dialogue appears in the form of speeches, as in a play.

My Kinsman, Major Molineaux (*The Token,* 1832; collected in THE SNOW IMAGE AND OTHER TWICE-TOLD TALES, 1851), a story by NATHANIEL HAWTHORNE. In one of the oddest of his stories Hawthorne tells how young Robin comes to Boston in the hope that his uncle, an influential man, will help him get started on his career. The very evening he arrives in town the citizens are preparing to tar-and-feather Major Molineaux, but until the end Robin remains ignorant of this fact and merely keeps inquiring where his uncle lives. Hawthorne agreeably stresses the irony of the situation, and nothing but disappointment and disillusionment befall Robin.

My Lady Pocahontas: A True Relation of Virginia (1885), a novel by JOHN ESTEN COOKE. Elaborating on the tradition, Cooke describes the rescue of John Smith by Pocahontas, the supposed death of Smith and Pocahontas' marriage to John Rolfe, their trip to England, where POCAHONTAS finds that Smith is still alive, and the death of the Indian princess. An effective series of scenes involves Shakespeare and a performance of *The Tempest,* a play which may have been suggested to Shakespeare by incidents in the settlement of Virginia.

My Life Is Like the Summer Rose (1819), a poem by RICHARD HENRY WILDE. Wilde wrote this song as part of an epic on the Seminole War, *The Lament of the Captive.* The song was published without his consent or knowledge and reprinted all over the country. Then an Irish poet named Daniel O'Kelly and other poets claimed its composition and it was even attributed to the ancient Greek poet Alcaeus. In 1834, in the first issue of the *Southern Literary Messenger,* the poem was definitely assigned to Wilde. It was set to music by Charles Thibault in 1822 and was popular as a song. Other musical settings included one, never published, by Sidney Lanier.

My Lost Youth (1855), a poem by HENRY WADSWORTH LONGFELLOW. Written in nine-line stanzas, this lyric tells of the author's boyhood in Portland, Me. It describes Portland's history and countryside, more particularly its ships and harbor. The poem contains the well-known nostalgic refrain, "A boy's will is the wind's will,/ And the thoughts of youth are long, long thoughts." Robert Frost's *A Boy's Will* derives its title from the Longfellow poem.

My Old Kentucky Home (1853), a song by STEPHEN FOSTER, for which he wrote both lyrics and melody. Next to OLD FOLKS AT HOME it is his most popular song.

My Playmate (1860), a poem by JOHN GREENLEAF WHITTIER. One of the best of Whittier's poems, *My Playmate* was called by Tennyson "a perfect poem; in some of his descriptions of nature and wild flowers, Whittier would rank with Wordsworth." The poet recalls childhood days spent with a playmate who has been identified as Mary Emerson Smith, whom Whittier later wished to marry. Compared with Wordsworth in the "Lucy" poems, Whittier must be reckoned homelier, more realistic, and yet at least as tender and rich in sentiment. The words of the poem are mainly monosyllabic, so that the longer words are all the more effective. See MEMORIES.

Mysterious Stranger, The (written 1898, pub. 1916), a story by MARK TWAIN. Toward the end of his life Mark Twain reached a pessimism and fatalism that found voice in this story, published posthumously. The scene is Eseldorf (Jackass Village), Austria, in 1590. The narrator is a teen-age boy who is sitting on a hillside with two friends when a well-dressed young man of pleasing face and easy manners makes friends with them. It turns out that he is Satan, and he tells them that his name on earth is Philip Traum (or Dream). The boy is a willing listener to the strange ideas of Satan, since he himself has been revolted by the cruelties of life and the burning of witches. Satan denounces "morals" as the cause of wars and inequalities, tells the boys there is no heaven or hell, shows his "kindness" by killing a boy who is a hopeless cripple, insists that everything one sees or knows is an illusion, completely upsets the ideals the boys have cherished—then disappears.

The book is an expression, the bitterest in all his writings, of Twain's feeling about "the damned human race" and about religion. The book expresses, too, his delight in antique speech and in the pomp and ornament of chivalry, and his indignation against churches and monarchies. An unpublished version of the story was laid in Hannibal, Mo. Carroll D. Laverty, writing on *The Genesis of "The Mysterious Stranger"* (*Mark Twain Quarterly*, Spring–Summer, 1947), held that the germinal idea may be found in a moral tale by the English writer for children, Jane Taylor. This tale, bearing the same title, appeared in 1841 in McGuffey's *Rhetorical Guide and Fifth Reader.*

Mystery of Marie Rogêt, The (published in *Snowden's Ladies' Companion*, November and December, 1842–February, 1843; later in Poe's *Tales*, 1845), a story by EDGAR ALLAN POE. Poe's THE MURDERS IN THE RUE MORGUE, the first detective story, had attracted so much at-

tention when it was published in 1841 that Poe looked around for a successor to the tale. He found one in the murder of Mary Rogers, a beautiful girl of indifferent morals who had worked in a cigar store in lower Broadway and whose body had been found floating in the Hudson River on July 28, 1841. Poe read all the details he could find, transferred the scene to Paris, again allowed his detective C. AUGUSTE DUPIN to show his contempt for the police, and gave his own theory of the murder. It was not a particularly good story, and Poe had difficulty selling it. Arthur Hobson Quinn suggested that Poe failed in this story because his imagination was hampered as he followed the real case. Poe rightly demolished the notion Mary was killed by a gang, but did not suspect she died of an illegal operation, until a confession revealed enough for him to insert some hints when he first reprinted his story.

mystery stories. See DETECTIVE STORIES.

Mystery Writers of America, Inc. Founded in 1944, this writers' organization seeks to improve the financial returns and cultural status of writers of detective stories. American Mystery Writers Poe Awards, popularly known as "Edgars," are given yearly. A monthly bulletin, *The Third Degree*, is issued, and anthologies: *Murder Cavalcade* (1946); *Twenty Great Tales of Murder by Experts of the Mystery Writers of America* (1951); *Maiden Murders* (1952); *Crooks Tours* (1953) in which appear stories chosen by members and submitted to a board of editors.

Mystic Trumpeter, The (*Kansas Magazine*, February, 1872), a poem by WALT WHITMAN. This poem falls into eight sections. Three seem to be in the nature of invocations to "the mystic trumpeter" to bring before Whitman's eyes various scenes of the past. The next five sections have been analyzed by W. L. Werner as forming an autobiography of the poet's career. He recalls his fondness for Sir Walter Scott's pageantry, his celebration of love in LEAVES OF GRASS, the coming of the Civil War, his postwar despair at the evils of humanity, his final optimism that all will be well with the human race. The poem has both a more evident structure and greater regularity of rhythm than is customary with Whitman; portions of the final stanza fall into iambic meter that at times becomes blank verse. FREDERICK S. CONVERSE wrote a musical composition of the same title (1905), based on the poem.

My Study Windows (1871), a series of essays, mainly on literary subjects, by JAMES RUSSELL LOWELL. They show his gift for witty phrases.

My Ten Years in a Quandary and How They Grew (1936), an autobiographical lament by ROBERT BENCHLEY. Benchley describes himself as the victim of all kinds of frustrations— he cannot cure hiccoughs, wear a white suit, smoke a cigarette, or read while eating. He hopes for a total eclipse, when darkness will give him "a chance to do a lot of things I have planned to do, but have been held back from." They are all quite innocent, it turns out.

N

Nabokov, Vladimir [V. Sirin] (b. Russia, April 23, 1899—   ), novelist, poet, entomologist, critic. Nabokov, of a noble Russian family, was educated at Cambridge University, England. Between 1922 and 1940 he lived in Germany and France where he wrote poetry and prose in Russian. From 1940, when he came to America, Nabokov began to write in English, with a distinctive and lucid style. Of *Conclusive Evidence: A Memoir* (1951), George Snell wrote: "It is one of the most accomplished stylistic achievements of any *emigré* writer; in fact, it would be difficult to think of two or three writers to whom English is native who could match it in any degree." His notorious and amusing novel *Lolita* (1958), with its theme about a young "nymphet," created a literary sensation. Nabokov has taught Russian literature and creative writing at Stanford University, Wellesley College, and Cornell University. He is a recognized authority on lepidoptera. His writings in English include: *The Real Life of Sebastian Knight* (1941); *Bend Sinister* (1947); *Pnin* (1957); *Nabokov's Dozen*, a collection of short stories (1958); *Poems* (1959); *Invitation to a Beheading* (1959); *Pale Fire* (1962).

Nacoochee (1837), a poem by T. H. CHIVERS. See LILY ADAIR.

Naked and The Dead, The (1948), a novel by NORMAN MAILER about World War II. Set on an island in the South Pacific, it tells the stories of the American general directing the invasion, of Lieutenant Hearn, his assistant, and of the men in the platoon Hearn takes over after a falling out with the general. Through flashbacks into the lives of the dozen or so major characters, Mailer gives a picture of the America that went into the war; through the detailed descriptions of fighting and the men under strain he examines the immediate effects of the war; and finally, in the relationship between Lieutenant Hearn and the general, he suggests the more subtle and far-reaching effects of the war on men's minds and personalities. The book is encyclopedic yet particular, both realistic and symbolic. It is generally considered one of the best novels by an American about World War II.

Narrative and Critical History of America, The (8 v., 1884–89), edited by JUSTIN WINSOR. John Spencer Bassett called this cooperative enterprise "probably the most stimulating book on American history that has been produced in this country." Many well-known historians contributed to it. Winsor himself provided a mass of bibliographical and cartological notes that were of great value to later students. The volumes are particularly strong in material on colonial and Revolutionary history, especially of New England.

Narrative of Arthur Gordon Pym, The (1838), a novelette by EDGAR ALLAN POE. A Nantucket youth with a passion for the sea stows away in the hold of a New Bedford whaler. He helps suppress a mutiny, survives a sea storm which leaves only four men alive. At one point a vessel floats by manned only by dead men—which some may suppose a reminiscence of Coleridge's *Ancient Mariner*. In the end two survivors are left drifting in a canoe toward the South Pole, where a great human figure, its skin white as snow, stands guard.

The narrative is full of realistic details; even some of the names are real. Poe relied on a number of factual accounts of travel and sea adventures, chiefly on information supplied him by J. N. REYNOLDS, whose pamphlet *South Sea Expedition* Poe had reviewed in the *Southern Literary Messenger* (January, 1837). When Poe lay dying in Baltimore, scenes from this story apparently haunted his last dreams, and he called repeatedly, "Reynolds! Oh, Reynolds!" in a voice that echoed through the hospital corridors.

Narrative of Colonel Ethan Allen's Captivity, A (1779), by ETHAN ALLEN. Allen told how he and other prisoners of war were mistreated by the British during the Revolution. The book was frequently reprinted, and was reproduced from the original Philadelphia edition, with an introductory note by John Pell, in 1930.

Narrative of Four Voyages to the South Sea, A (1832). See BENJAMIN MORRELL.

Narrative of Surprising Conversions (1737), by JONATHAN EDWARDS. The actual title of this book was *A Faithful Narrative of the Surprising Work of God in the Conversion of Many Hundred Souls*, but the shortened title is more familiar. The book was Edwards' account of some of the manifestations of the so-called "Great Awakening" which began in 1734. The narrative takes the form of a letter to a fellow clergyman of Boston, BENJAMIN COLMAN, and describes the growth and decline of a spiritual revival in Edwards' own parish at Northampton and in neighboring towns between 1733 and the spring of 1735. There was, says Edwards, a stirring in the consciences of the young, including a child of four, who was overheard by her mother in her closet wrestling with God in prayer, from which she came out crying aloud and "wreathing her body to and fro like one in anguish of spirit." He gives other instances of the combination of spiritual exaltation and physical convulsions. But as the fervor of conversion soon began to subside, Edwards laments, "Satan seemed to be let loose and raged in a dreadful manner." An epidemic of attempted suicides swept through the community, and many suffered from strange delusions. Common sense in time got the upper hand, although Edwards continued to defend the Awakening in *Some Thoughts Concerning the Present Revival of Religion in New England* (1742). One of ROBERT LOWELL's most striking poems, *After the Surprising Conversions* (in *Lord Weary's Castle*, 1946), is based on Edwards' document.

Narrative of the Texan Santa Fe Expedition (2 v., 1844; reprinted, 1936), by GEORGE WILKINS KENDALL. The ambitious Republic of Texas sent an expedition into what is now New Mexico for the purpose of annexing towns and villages that would bring its territory down to the Rio Grande. When the expedition reached its goal, its members were immediately made prisoners by the Mexican Governor Armijo. The capture, sufferings, and release of the prisoners were described by Kendall, a New Orleans newspaperman who had joined the expedition. Fayette Copeland wrote *Kendall of the Picayune* (1943).

Narrative of the Troubles with the Indians in New England (1677), by WILLIAM HUBBARD. Hubbard's book appeared after KING PHILIP's War had ended, when the people of New England were still aroused against the Indians. But Hubbard, a clergyman, was fair-minded in his treatment of the red men, sought to give a natural rather than a providential explanation of events. He displayed a similar attitude in his *General History of New England* (completed, 1680; pub., 1815), in which he ascribes the success of the colonists to their "industry and diligent pains" and to "the salubriousness of the air in this country" as much as to "God's benevolence." His *Narrative* was reprinted in S. G. Drake's *History of the Indian Wars* (Vol. I, 1865).

narratives of captivity. See INDIAN CAPTIVITY NARRATIVES.

Nasby, Petroleum Vesuvius [pen name of **David Ross Locke**] (b. Vestal, N.Y., Sept. 20, 1833—d. Feb. 15, 1888), journalist, editor, political satirist, humorist. At the age of ten Locke worked as a printer's devil for the *Cortland Democrat,* became an itinerant printer in his early teens, and at the age of nineteen founded, with James G. Robinson, the *Plymouth Advertiser* in Plymouth, Ohio. As soon as it was well-established he left to take a position as coeditor of the *Jeffersonian* in Findlay. One evening in 1861 he met the town loafer and drunkard attempting to obtain signatures to a petition advocating the exile of all Negroes from the town. The few Negro families in Findlay were respectable, industrious citizens, and the irony of the occurrence both amused and angered Locke. A few days later a letter appeared in the *Jeffersonian* signed Petroleum V. Nasby, an alleged Copperhead, a name destined to become famous. (See COPPERHEADS.) The letter was an ironic, bitter attack on those whose views paralleled the town drunkard's.

In 1865 Locke became editor, later owner, of the Toledo *Blade,* which took over the letters of this unregenerate Copperhead and printed them for the next 16 years. He followed the type of humor associated with America at this time—bad spelling, worse grammar, braggadocio, hyperbole, and anticlimax. Funny as he seemed to the readers of his day, Nasby was a serious satirical creation. This drunken, bigoted, cowardly advocate of white supremacy and states' rights by espousing the Southern cause made it look ridiculous. Secretary of the Treasury George S. Boutwell publicly attributed the overthrow of the rebels to "the Army and Navy, the Republican Party, and the *Letters of Petroleum V. Nasby.*"

A large number of collections of Nasby letters appeared between 1864 and 1893, among them *The Nasby Papers* (1864); *Swingin' Round the Cirkle* (1867); *Inflation at the Cross Roads* (1875); *The Diary of an Office Seeker* (1881); *Nasby in Exile, or, Six Months of Travel* (1882). Cyril Clemens wrote an account of *Petroleum V. Nasby* (1936).

Nash, Isabel Jackson [Eberstadt] (b. Baltimore, Md., Sept. 30, 1934—), novelist, poet, children's writer, is OGDEN NASH's daughter. She has written children's verse with a whimsey reminiscent of her father. Among her books: *Where Did Tuffey Hide?* (1957), verses for preschool children written with her husband Frederick Eberstadt, and *The Banquet Vanishes* (1958), a novel.

Nash, Ogden (b. Rye, N.Y., Aug. 19, 1902—d. May 19, 1971), poet. Nash tried various youthful occupations—schoolteaching, editing, selling bonds, writing advertising copy—but his chief interest was in light verse, and he pursued

the comic muse with such winsome outrageousness that he soon became the most popular writer of light verse in his generation, and by 1935 was able to devote himself entirely to writing. Nash's method is an essentially Elizabethan highhandedness with the English language and the conventions of poetry. Many of his poems are in the freest of free verse, some lines being as short as one word, others as long as a paragraph. In his rhymes his verbal imagination defies the dictionary, with results that produce laughter through shock:

> In the Vanities
> No one wears panities.

Any subject suits Nash's genius, though he is especially fond of the inanities of modern urban society; his mood, entirely sardonic, stops just short of helpless exasperation. Much of Nash's writing has appeared in the *New Yorker*, and he has been one of the group that established that magazine's tone of sophisticated disaffection, as in his flint-hearted appraisal of the next generation:

> You take babies,
> I'll take rabies.

Nash's works include: *Free Wheeling* (1931); *Hard Lines* (1931); *Happy Days* (1935); *The Bad Parent's Garden of Verse* (1936); *I'm a Stranger Here Myself* (1938); *The Face Is Familiar* (1940); *Good Intentions* (1943); *Many Long Years Ago* (1945); *Versus* (1949); *Parents Keep Out: Elderly Poems for Youngerly Readers* (1951); *The Private Dining Room and Other New Verses* (1953); *The Christmas That Almost Wasn't* (1957); *Verses From 1929 On* (1959); *Boy Is A Boy* (1960). He wrote lyrics for the musical comedies *One Touch of Venus* (1943, with S. J. PERELMAN); and *Two's Company* (1952).

Nashoba Community. This was a community of slaves established at Nashoba, Tennessee, in 1825 by FRANCES [FANNY] WRIGHT. Her intention was to give the slaves a chance to earn their freedom and then colonize them in the West Indies. Though the plan succeeded it brought her more censure than praise because of the loose mores which were encouraged among the colonists.

Nassau Street Theater. New York City's first playhouse was called the Theater in Nassau Street. In 1753 Lewis Hallam, an English actor, dismantled the old theater and built a new playhouse known as the New Theater or as Hallam's in Nassau Street. After one season the theater was converted to other uses.

Nast, Thomas (b. Germany, Sept. 27, 1840— d. Dec. 7, 1902), cartoonist, illustrator. Brought to New York at the age of six, Nast began regular work with HARPER'S in 1862. At first he turned out sentimental and patriotic pictures. His first caricature appeared in January, 1863; he developed this medium until Thomas Nast and *Harper's* became the greatest power in print of the period. He chastised Andrew Johnson, supported Grant in two Presidential campaigns. However, the greatest fight of his career was his battle against the incredible Tweed Ring, which had the finances of New York City completely in its control. Numerous devastating anti-Tweed cartoons poured from Nast's pen. The circulation of *Harper's* greatly increased, and ultimately public opinion became informed enough to demand the prosecution of Tweed and some of his associates.

Nast, always conservative and usually Republican, came out strongly against race prejudice, attacked the income tax, inflation, and the reduction of the armed forces. He is credited with having first used the donkey to symbolize the Democratic Party, the elephant for the Republicans, and the tiger (emblem of Tweed's old Americus Fire Company) for Tammany Hall. (See TAMMANY.) He also illustrated books for children and the humorous writings of PETROLEUM V. NASBY.

Nast left *Harper's* in 1886, tried one paper after another unsuccessfully. With his son he had his own paper—a lifelong ambition—but *Nast's Weekly* was the most dismal failure of all. At last John Hay, Theodore Roosevelt's Secretary of State, offered him a consulship in Guayaquil, Ecuador, in 1902. Nast accepted, and died there of yellow fever within the year. Albert B. Paine wrote his biography (1904).

Natchez, Les (1826), a romance by FRANÇOIS RENÉ DE CHATEAUBRIAND. This story was originally part of the manuscript which contained the stories of ATALA and René and was written between 1797 and 1800. Like the others it was a recollection of his own experiences in America in 1791 and a restatement of his ideas of life under "natural" conditions. René, the hero, marries Celuta, a Natchez Indian girl. Celuta thinks that René has betrayed her tribe and is torn between a conflict of duties, although the real traitor turns out to be someone else. The Natchez massacre of the French settlers in 1729 forms a setting for the story. Some of Chateaubriand's descriptions were based on passages in WILLIAM BARTRAM'S *Travels* (1791).

Nathan, George Jean (b. Fort Wayne, Ind., Feb. 14, 1882—d. April 8, 1958), drama and social critic, editor, memoirist. Throughout his career Nathan was devoted mainly to the theater, and was noted for his independence of thought and his application of scholarship to the judgment of new plays. A witty drama critic for several magazines and newspapers, notably *Esquire* and the *New York Journal-American*, he collected his more important reviews in yearbooks (*The Theater Books of the Year*, 1943–51). He was a colleague of H. L. MENCKEN and WILLARD HUNTINGTON WRIGHT in editing the SMART SET during its greatest years, for a time joined Mencken in editing the AMERICAN MERCURY, later founded a periodical of his own, the *American Spectator*. With Mencken he wrote *Europe After 8:15* (1914) and *The American Credo* (1920). Among his other books: *Mr. George Jean Nathan Presents* (1917); *The Autobiography of an Attitude* (1925); *The World of George Jean Nathan* (1952); *The Theater in the Fifties* (1953).

Nathan, Robert (b. New York City, Jan. 2, 1894—   ), poet, novelist. Educated here and abroad, Nathan attended Harvard but left before graduating. *Peter Kindred* (1919), a semiautobiographical novel, was followed by *Autumn* (1921), in which he revealed an individual style, poetic, tender, mocking, occasionally vapid. *The Puppet Master* (1923), *Jonah* (1925), *The Fiddler in Barly* (1926), *The Woodcutter's House* (1927), all short novels, are close to poetry. Other books include: *The Bishop's Wife* (1928); *There Is Another Heaven* (1929); *The Orchid* (1931); *One More Spring* (1933); *The Road of Ages* (1935); *The Enchanted Voyage* (1936); *The Barly Field* (1938), a collection of five early novels; *Journey of Tapiola* (1938); *Winter in April* (1938); *Tapiola's Brave Regiment* (1941); *They Went On Together* (1941); *The Sea-Gull Cry* (1942); *But Gently Day* (1943); *Mr. Whittle and the Morning Star* (1947); *Long After Summer* (1948); *River Journey* (1949); *The Married Look* (1950); *The Innocent Eye* (1951); *Sir Henry* (1955); *So Love Returns* (1958); *The Color of Evening* (1960); *Weans* (1960); *The Wilderness Stone* (1961); *A Star in the Wind* (1962). Among Nathan's volumes of poetry are *Youth Grows Old* (1922); *The Cedar Box* (1929); *The Winter Tide* (1940); *Dunkirk; A Ballad* (1942); *The Darkening Meadows* (1945); *The Green Leaf* (1950); *Winter in April* (1958). He also wrote several plays.

Nation, Carry [usually given as **Carrie**] [**Amelia**] (b. Pope's Landing, Ky., Nov. 25, 1846—d. June 9, 1911), temperance agitator. As the result of an unfortunate experience with her intemperate first husband, Mrs. Nation became a violent crusader against liquor. She was often arrested and imprisoned, and became a national figure, storming into saloons with a hatchet and destroying liquor and furnishings. She lectured extensively and gave an account of her life in *The Use and the Need of the Life of Carry A. Nation* (1904). Herbert Asbury wrote her biography in 1929.

Nation, The. A weekly journal of politics, literature, and the arts, founded by E. L. Godkin in 1865 and still going. Although it has passed through a number of changes in ownership, *The Nation* has been a consistently liberal and sometimes radical publication; it has numbered among its editors and contributors many of the most distinguished literary figures of the United States. During the 1920's it was one of the few established periodicals open to the new literature, and much important criticism appeared in its pages. During the 1940's and 1950's it lost some of its support among intellectuals when it advocated a policy regarded as too favorable toward the Soviet Union.

National Anti-Slavery Standard. Founded in 1840, the *Standard* was insistent on immediate abolition of slavery. It won some distinguished contributors; James Russell Lowell was its editor, 1848–49, and continued to contribute to it until 1852. Some of his Biglow Papers appeared in its pages. Some of his otherwise uncollected articles have been gathered in W. E. Channing's edition of *The Anti-Slavery*

Papers of James Russell Lowell (2 v., 1902). The magazine ceased publication in 1872.

National Archives. This organization was set up by Congress (1934) for two purposes—preservation and destruction. It is given the power to decide which governmental documents shall be destroyed and which kept as historical data. Its records include such important documents as the Emancipation Proclamation and the German and Japanese surrender papers—and innumerable others, stored in the National Archives Building in Washington. Motion pictures and sound recordings are included as well. See also Library of Congress.

National Book Awards, The. These awards are given each year, in the spring. They are sponsored by the American Book Publishers Council, Inc., the American Booksellers Association, Inc., and the Book Manufacturers' Institute, Inc. A cash award is presented to each winner. The aim is to give industry-wide recognition to the most distinguished books of fiction, nonfiction and poetry of the previous year.

National Council of Teachers of English, The. Founded 1911, this organization holds annual meetings and publishes three official organs: *Elementary English, The English Journal,* and College English, all with wide circulations. It issues book lists for students in all fields. In addition it publishes special books and brochures in the English field; among them Sterling A. Leonard's *Current English Usage* (1937), C. C. Fries' American English Grammar (1941), and a group of volumes on *The English Language Arts* (beginning 1952). The Council has issued some noteworthy recordings of readings by noted authors and has shown a fruitful interest in motion pictures, radio, television, newspapers, and magazines.

National Era, The. An important abolitionist periodical, the *National Era* was founded in 1847, flourished vigorously before the war, expired in 1860. It was edited by Gamaliel Bailey, and secured as contributors some of the most prominent abolitionists of the time. The most famous of its projects was Uncle Tom's Cabin, serialized from June, 1851, to April, 1852.

National Gazette, The. This pro-Jefferson periodical, edited by Philip Freneau, engaged in heated controversy during its short existence (1791–93). The *Gazette* expressed opinions in violent opposition to those in the Gazette of the United States, a pro-Hamilton organ edited by John Fenno. The two papers engaged in campaigns of virulent party abuse, which infected their news reports, their editorials, even the poems and skits they published. In later years Jefferson asserted that the *Gazette* had "saved our Constitution, which was galloping fast into monarchy." It died when public opinion turned against the revolutionary excesses in France. Historians are still disputing whether Jefferson established and helped to manage the *Gazette,* as Hamilton and others charged.

National Geographic Society, The, and **The National Geographic Magazine.** This famous and useful Society was founded in 1888 by a small group of scientists in Washington; its membership has grown close to two million. It has financed many expeditions to unexplored or little known regions of the world, and has made deep-sea and cosmic-ray investigations. In its elaborately illustrated monthly *National Geographic Magazine* the beauties and wonders of many lands are described. The Society also prepares superb drafted maps (see HENRY GANNETT). Dr. GILBERT H. GROSVENOR (1875—), assistant editor and editor of the *Magazine* (1899–1954), was succeeded by Dr. J. O. La Gorce.

National Institute of Arts and Letters. See AMERICAN ACADEMY OF ARTS AND LETTERS.

Native American Humor, 1800–1900 (1937), a history, with many examples, by WALTER BLAIR. Professor Blair's work considers the changing attitudes of humorists toward native comic characters, the changing techniques of humor, and the changing attitudes of readers toward native humor. The range is from the *Farmer's Almanac* to Mr. Dooley, with a full section on Mark Twain.

Native Son (1940), a novel by RICHARD WRIGHT. Wright describes, vividly and bitterly, the life of a Negro boy, Bigger Thomas, against whom society conspires at every moment, largely on account of his race. He grows up in a Chicago slum, commits two murders, is captured by the police after a flight over the roof-tops, defended in court by a Communist lawyer, and condemned to death. The book is sensational, but skillfully and sensitively written; it established Wright as a leading Negro author.

naturalism. The rise of naturalistic fiction in the latter half of the 19th century was influenced by Darwin's theory of evolution, Marx's historical determinism, and the mechanistic school of philosophy. Although the term is often used synonymously with REALISM, naturalism refers particularly to works in which the author emphasizes the control which the forces of nature, heredity, and environment exert over human life, and the animalistic and instinctual elements in man. It is similar to realism primarily in its objectivity and careful attention to detail, but goes beyond realism in its tendency to take as its subject matter lower-class situations and characters, and particularly in its deterministic philosophy. Human life is pessimistically viewed as being at the mercy of uncontrollable exterior forces—the environment— or of interior drives—fear, hunger, sex. The slum girl crushed by her surroundings, such as Maggie, or the brutal and moronic superman, such as McTeague, are typical characters. Stephen Crane's MAGGIE: A GIRL OF THE STREETS (1892), Frank Norris' MCTEAGUE (1899), JACK LONDON's *The Son of the Wolf* (1900), and Theodore Dreiser's SISTER CARRIE (1900) are the earliest examples of American naturalism.

The proletarian literature of the thirties is in some ways an outgrowth of naturalism and similar to it primarily in its emphasis on the lower class; however, the only truly naturalistic novel to appear during the thirties was JAMES T. FARRELL's *Studs Lonigan* trilogy (1932, 1934, 1935). Studies of naturalism include Harry Hartwick's *The Foreground of American Fiction* (1934); ALFRED KAZIN's *On Native Grounds* (1942); RICHARD HOFSTADTER's *Social Darwinism in American Thought* (1944); Charles C. Walcutt's *American Literary Naturalism, A Divided Stream* (1956).

Nature. [1] An essay by RALPH WALDO EMERSON on which he began working around 1834, published anonymously in 1836. [2] A poem by Emerson which he used to preface his book *Nature, Addresses and Lectures* (1849); it was written in 1836. The essay has been described by David Bowers as "the original—and probably the best—systematic expression of the transcendentalist philosophy." Emerson sees nature as "Commodity" in its practical functions, as "Beauty" in the delight it arouses, as "Language" in its symbolical significance, and as "Discipline" in the education it gives the Understanding and the Reason. When man is in communion with nature he says to himself, "I become a transparent eyeball; I am nothing; I see all; the currents of the Universal Being circulate through me; I am part or parcel of God." It has been said that in *Nature* Emerson attempted to reconcile idealistic philosophy with his own practical belief in nature's existence. The essay aroused wide discussion.

Nature Atlas of America (1952), edited by E. L. Jordan. This is a beautifully illustrated record of natural phenomena in the United States and southern Canada. In connection with large-scale colored sectional maps, facts are given concerning animals, insects, birds, reptiles, fishes, rocks, trees, and wild flowers. The maps indicate where the finest observation posts for the study of nature are located and how they may be reached.

nature writing in the U.S. Inevitably the white men who came to the New World were struck by the phenomena of nature in the places they visited, and they wrote about them. The first to do so in English was THOMAS HARIOT, who visited this country in 1585 and wrote *A Brief and True Report of the New Found Land of Virginia,* an account of the flora and fauna in that region. Often the observations of these first comers were practical; SIR WALTER RALEGH, for example, was enthusiastic about the plant that we call corn and about an herb the natives called *uppowoc* and which became known as tobacco. Other early inhabitants like John Clayton, Dr. JOHN MITCHELL, Chief Justice Paul Dudley, and JAMES LOGAN, William Penn's private secretary, looked at New World products with a curious eye and reported about them to Old World learned societies. With JOHN and WILLIAM BARTRAM, writing about nature in America takes on a distinct literary flavor.

Thereafter such writing may be said to divide into two streams: objective reporting and subjective interpretation, the latter often solidly based on the former. Botanists, entomologists, zoologists, and astronomers studied the visible world with care. Among them were such outstanding figures as CONSTANTINE SAMUEL RAFINESQUE, THOMAS SAY, LOUIS AGASSIZ, J. J. AUDUBON, ASA GRAY, ALEXANDER WILSON, EDWIN POWELL HUBBLE. At the same time nature was being studied by philosophers, some of whom, like W. E. CHANNING [2], loved that "outer garment of God," the physical universe, or, like RALPH WALDO EMERSON, made nature the basis of their creed. The two groups at times mingled somewhat strangely in a favorite form of scholarly organization during the 18th and 19th centuries—the societies for the study of natural philosophy, particularly the American Philosophical Society, founded in 1742, in which BENJAMIN FRANKLIN and THOMAS JEFFERSON were so active. Herbert W. Schneider regards Jefferson's NOTES ON THE STATE OF VIRGINIA (1787) as "the first important American work on natural history." No important American poet has failed to record nature in some of its aspects, sometimes with charming verisimilitude, sometimes with cranky subjectivity. PHILIP FRENEAU is credited with writing the first important American nature poem in *The Wild Honeysuckle* (1786); he ventured into the philosophical field with his verses *On the Religion of Nature* (1815) and other poems. Bryant, Whittier, Emerson, Longfellow, Lowell, E. A. Robinson, Frost, Coffin, and a host of other poets have reported the New England landscape.

HENRY DAVID THOREAU started a school of another kind: his observations were faithful and accurate, but he used them as a springboard for his philosophizing. Among his disciples have been such men as JOHN BURROUGHS, JOHN MUIR, THEODORE ROOSEVELT, DALLAS LORE SHARP, BRADFORD TORREY, WILLIAM T. HORNADAY, WILLIAM BEEBE, DONALD CULROSS PEATTIE, EDWIN W. TEALE, JOSEPH WOOD KRUTCH.

Norman Foerster studied *Nature in American Literature* (1923), and P. M. Hicks the *Development of the Natural History Essay in American Literature* (1924). Krutch made a collection of *Great American Nature Writing* (1950).

Navahos [Navajos]. An Indian tribe of the Southwest, one of the greatest of the Indian groups. They came into early conflict with the white man and resisted him boldly. They were finally subdued by Colonel KIT CARSON in 1863. The Navahos express their intense religious feeling in long chants, usually parallel in structure. Their everyday life is inseparable from their religion; they have no formal priesthood, and everybody takes part in the ceremonies.

Fictional works dealing with the Navahos include Adolph Bandelier's THE DELIGHT MAKERS (1890), Willa Cather's DEATH COMES FOR THE ARCHBISHOP (1927), and Oliver La Farge's LAUGHING BOY (1929). Among nonfictional books are E. Sapir and H. Hoijer's *Navaho Texts* (1942); Clyde Kluckhohn and D. Leighton's *The Navaho* (1947); John Collier's *Patterns and Ceremonies of the Indians of the Southwest* (1949); A. Grove Day's *The Sky Clears* (1951);

Kluckhohn and Evon Z. Vogt's *Navaho Means People* (1951, with photographs by Leonard McCombe); Ruth Underhill's *The Navajos* (1956); and Margaret Link's *The Pollen Path* (Navaho myths, 1956).

Neal, John ["Jehu O'Cataract"] (b. Falmouth, Me., Aug. 25, 1793—d. June 20, 1876), lawyer, poet, novelist, critic. John Neal, after the most scanty education, became a clerk, an itinerant drawing teacher, a drygoods merchant. When his business failed he began to read law, while he edited *The Portico*, a monthly literary magazine published by the DELPHIAN CLUB. He wrote prose and poetry for the magazine, and in 1817 he published KEEP COOL: A NOVEL. This story of a man who suffers from feelings of guilt because he killed someone in a duel added to Neal's growing reputation as a writer, though it was not a financial success. *The Battle of Niagara: A Poem Without Notes* (1818); *Goldau: or, The Maniac Harper* (published under the pen name of Jehu O'Cataract, 1818); *Otho* (a verse tragedy, 1819); and *Logan, A Family History* (1822) increased his reputation. The last-named is an extraordinary novel combining an attack on the United States Indian policy, debtors' prisons, and capital punishment with a fantastic story, partly fact, about a Herculean Englishman who marries an Indian queen. In 1823 Neal turned out three novels; the first, *Seventy-Six*, a Revolutionary tale somewhat resembling Cooper's *The Spy*, he believed to be his best work. In *Randolph* there were some uncomplimentary references to the recently deceased father of the poet Edward Pinkney, who challenged Neal to a duel. Neal ignored the challenge, was branded a coward, and immediately turned the experience into material for his next novel, *Errata, or, The Works of Will Adams* (1823).

Sailing for England in 1823, Neal served as Jeremy Bentham's secretary for some time and acted as his spokesman years later when he returned to America. He stormed *Blackwood's Magazine*, overcame its well-known dislike for American authors, and wrote a series of sketches of American literary men, the first attempt at a literary history of the United States.

Brother Jonathan, or, The New Englanders (1824) was published in Edinburgh. On his return in 1827 to Portsmouth, Neal established *The Yankee*, a weekly newspaper. He continued to pour forth novels: RACHEL DYER (1828), the story of a Salem witch, considered by many his best work; *Authorship* (1830); THE DOWN-EASTERS (1833); *True Womanhood* (1859); *The White Pacer* (1863); *The Moose Hunter* (1864); and *Little Moccasin; or Along the Madawaska* (1865). The last three were written for the famous Beadle series of DIME NOVELS. In his autobiography, *Wandering Recollections of a Somewhat Busy Life* (1869), Neal tells the story of his energetic life in informal, rambling fashion.

Neal, Joseph Clay (b. Greenland, N.H., Feb. 3, 1807—d. July 17, 1847), essayist, humorist, editor. Neal is often placed in the school of

"CRACKER-BOX PHILOSOPHERS," but was decidedly under the influence of Charles Dickens. His first book, much of which appeared in a Philadelphia magazine he founded in 1836, *Neal's Saturday Gazette and Ladies' Literary Museum*, was *Charcoal Sketches, or, Scenes in a Metropolis* (1st series, 1838; 2nd series, 1848), a satire on Philadelphia ways and peoples. Dickens thought so highly of it that he reprinted the series in England as *The Pic Nic Papers* (1841). Several editions appeared in the United States, the last as late as 1865 (3 v.). Other writings of Neal were: *In Town and About* (1843); *Peter Ploddy and Other Oddities* (1844); *The Misfortunes of Peter Faber and Other Sketches* (1856).

Nearing, Scott (b. Morris Run, Pa., Aug. 6, 1883–   ), teacher, lecturer, sociologist. A strong advocate of economic and political reform, Nearing taught at the University of Pennsylvania, Swarthmore College, the University of Toledo, and the Rand School of Social Science. He was a Congressional candidate on the Socialist ticket in 1919. Among his books: *Social Religion* (1913); *Poverty and Riches* (1916); *The Next Stage* (1924); *Black America* (1929); *The Maple Sugar Bowl* (1950); *Economics for the Power Age* (1952); *Man's Search for the Good Life* (1954); *Freedom: Promise and Menace* (1961).

Necessary Angel, The (1951), a collection of essays on poetry by WALLACE STEVENS. Delivered mostly as speeches at various universities, the essays are difficult, serious, and contradictory: "The accuracy of accurate letters," Stevens says at one point, "is an accuracy with respect to the structure of reality." The major theme of the essays is the relation of the imagination to reality and the way the imagination, in transforming reality, enriches it. Some critics accused Stevens of using poetry as an escape from reality. He answers this charge in a discussion of the poet's "supreme fictions." These fictions of the imagination, far from an escape, invest stark reality with meaning. Thus Stevens makes poetry equal, even superior, to philosophy.

Ned Myers (1843), a narrative by JAMES FENIMORE COOPER. Although this story of a sailor's experiences is written as fiction, the book is really a factual record taken down from the lips of an old salt who in his youth had sailed with Cooper on the *Sterling*. It is a much more realistic picture of life at sea than one finds elsewhere in Cooper. Cooper himself spoke of the book as "edited by J. Fenimore Cooper." He gave as a subtitle, "A Life Before the Mast" —Dana's TWO YEARS BEFORE THE MAST had appeared in 1840 and the author had timidly sent a copy to Cooper. James Grossman compares the two books and notes that "Ned, unlike Dana, has the professional's point of view. . . . He accepts the sea as a simple fact, without grandeur or mystery, and is too casual about its hardships and perils to interest us deeply."

Neglected Anniversary, A (New York *Evening Mail*, Dec. 28, 1917), an essay by H. L. MENCKEN. This is the piece in which Mencken, with no expectation of being taken seriously, perpetrated the great BATHTUB HOAX. Ten years later he confessed it openly, and Vilhjalmur Stefansson, in *Adventures in Error* (1936), exposed the hoax in detail, but it was too late. Newspapers had reprinted the article, learned historians and authoritative encyclopedias copied down Mencken's "facts."

Mencken began his tongue-in-cheek exposition by referring to December 20, 1917, as the sadly neglected 75th anniversary of the introduction of the bathtub into These States." He placed the event in Cincinnati, gave exact details regarding the installation of the tub, depicted the controversy that arose. Dr. Oliver Wendell Holmes, according to Mencken, came out in favor of the bathtub, and 55 per cent of the members of the American Medical Association finally declared the invention harmless, but it was the example of President Millard Fillmore that gave the bathtub recognition and respectability. He took a bath in the Cincinnati contraption, liked it so much that he had a tub installed in the White House—grimly facing down all opposition. By 1860, Mencken reported, every hotel in New York City had a bathtub; some had two, and even three. The piece was reprinted in *The Bathtub Hoax* (1958).

Negroes in American literature. Because of the dispersion of Negro slaves all over the country, the ties of Negroes with their ancestral homes and habits were almost completely broken. They had no alternative but to accept the Anglo-Saxon (in some parts of the country, the French) civilization which surrounded their lives. Negroes have provided an immense body of subject matter for writers and have increasingly done writing themselves. In Negro literature there has been a constant struggle—to raise the Negro from a stereotype to an individual. That struggle is not yet altogether successful.

Writing by American Negroes began with JUPITER HAMMON and PHILLIS WHEATLEY in the third quarter of the 18th century, Hammon had no objection to slavery, and Phillis Wheatley, an extraordinary prodigy, was more interested in Alexander Pope's couplets than in the ethics of slavery. The first protest against serfdom from a Negro came from one who called himself "Othello" and who may have been Benjamin Banneker, astronomer, inventor, and almanac maker. In 1789 he published *Negro Slavery by Othello, a Free Negro*, an eloquent protest. This was followed in the next century by similar protests from Negro lips.

Poetry has continued to be a favorite vehicle of Negro expression. The best known of Negro poems are the spirituals (see entry below), largely anonymous. Anonymous Negro poets also appear in work songs, in ballads, and in various other secular folk rhymes. The words to the famous blues are often anonymous, but usually a writer is given credit on published versions; most famous was W. C. HANDY. (See JAZZ.) Among Negro poets who have won fame are George Moses Horton, PAUL LAURENCE DUNBAR, James Edwin Campbell, W. E. B. DU BOIS,

JAMES WELDON JOHNSON, JEAN TOOMER, LANGSTON HUGHES, ARNA BONTEMPS, and GWENDOLYN BROOKS, first Negro winner of a Pulitzer Prize. Their poetry has been collected in Newman Ivey White's *Anthology of Verse by American Negroes* (1924); HOWARD W. ODUM and Guy B. Johnson's *Negro Workaday Songs* (1926); COUNTEE CULLEN's *Caroling Dusk, an Anthology of Verse by Negro Poets* (1927); James Weldon Johnson's *Book of American Negro Poetry* (1931); and Langston Hughes' anthology *The Poetry of the Negro* (1949). An important modern book of verse by a Negro was Hughes' *Montage of a Dream Deferred* (1951).

In the meantime the Negro had appeared frequently in the writings of non-Negro poets, mainly in the form of protest against slavery. Among such poets were Philip Freneau, Timothy Dwight, Joel Barlow, Thomas Bradford, Stephen Foster, W. C. Bryant, H. W. Longfellow, J. G. Whittier, Walt Whitman, Ridgely Torrence, W. E. Leonard, Maxwell Bodenheim, John Gould Fletcher, William Rose Benét, Vachel Lindsay, Stephen Vincent Benét, DuBose Heyward, Sarah Cleghorn.

The first published novels by American Negro authors were William Wells Brown's *Clotel, or, The President's Daughter* (London, 1853; American ed., 1864) and Martin Delany's *Blake, or, The Huts of America* (1859). The appearance in 1892 of Francis Harper's *Iola Leroy, or, Shadows Uplifted* marked the beginning of an era of greater articulateness. Among the more important novels that followed were Paul Lawrence Dunbar's *The Uncalled* (1898), *Love of Landry* (1900), *The Fanatics* (1901), and *The Spirit of the Gods* (1904); CHARLES W. CHESNUTT's *The Wife of His Youth* (1899), *The House Behind the Cedars* (1900), *The Marrow of Tradition* (1901), and *The Colonel's Dream* (1906); W. E. B. Du Bois' *Silver Fleece* (1911) and *The Dark Princess* (1928); Jean Toomer's *Cane* (1923); Jessie Fauset's *There Is Confusion* (1924), *Plum Bun* (1929), *The Chinaberry Tree* (1931), and *Comedy, American Style* (1933); WALTER WHITE's *The Fire in the Flint* (1925) and *Flight* (1928); CLAUDE McKAY's *Home to Harlem* (1928), *Banana Bottom* (1931), and *Gingertown* (1932); Langston Hughes' *Not Without Laughter* (1930) and *The Ways of White Folks* (1934); Countee Cullen's *One Way to Heaven* (1932); ZORA NEALE HURSTON's *Jonah's Gourd Vine* (1934), *Mules and Men* (1935), *Their Eyes Were Watching* (1937), and *Seraph on the Sewannee* (1948); Arna Bontemps' BLACK THUNDER (1936), *God Sends Sunday* (1931; the basis of a musical play, *St. Louis Woman*, by Bontemps and Countee Cullen, 1946), and *Drums at Dusk* (1939); RICHARD WRIGHT's *Uncle Tom's Children* (1939), NATIVE SON (1940), and *The Outsider* (1953); Chester Bomar Himes' *If He Hollers Let Him Go* (1945), *Lonely Crusade* (1947), and *The Cord* (1953); ANN PETRY's *The Street* (1946), *Country Place* (1947), *The Narrows* (1953); FRANK YERBY's

Floodtide (1950); RALPH ELLISON's INVISIBLE MAN (1952); JAMES BALDWIN's *Go Tell It on the Mountain* (1953) and *Nobody Knows My Name* (1961).

Equally impressive is the long array of short stories and novels by white writers about Negroes. Mrs. Harriet Beecher Stowe created the most famous of Negro characters in UNCLE TOM's CABIN, OR, LIFE AMONG THE LOWLY (1852), one of the most influential books in history. She introduced Negroes into DRED, A TALE OF THE GREAT DISMAL SWAMP (1856). Other 19th-century novels in which Negroes appear include J. T. Trowbridge's *Neighbor Jackwood* (1856); G. W. Cable's THE GRANDISSIMES (1880); W. D. Howells' AN IMPERATIVE DUTY (1891); and Mark Twain's HUCKLEBERRY FINN (1884) and PUDD'NHEAD WILSON (1894). Bernard De Voto has spoken with high praise of the courage and originality with which Twain drew his Negro characters. More stereotyped were the Negroes of Thomas Nelson Page in such books as IN OLE VIRGINIA (1887).

Some later novels portrayed Negroes condescendingly or even cruelly, as in Thomas Dixon's THE LEOPARD's SPOTS (1902); Harry Stillwell Edwards' *Eneas Africanus* (1919); and Octavus Roy Cohen's *Assorted Chocolates* (1922) and its numerous successors. But many of the books that followed were more realistic and friendly, among them Mary Johnston's *The Slave Ship* (1924); Sherwood Anderson's DARK LAUGHTER (1925); Howard W. Odum's *Rainbow Round My Shoulder* (1928), *Wings on My Feet* (1929), and *Cold Blue Moon* (1931); DuBose Heyward's PORGY (1925) and MAMBA's DAUGHTERS (1929); J. P. Marquand's *The Black Cargo* (1925); Carl Van Vechten's NIGGER HEAVEN (1926); Julia M. Peterkin's BLACK APRIL (1927), SCARLET SISTER MARY (1928), and *Bright Skin* (1932); Elizabeth Madox Roberts' MY HEART AND MY FLESH (1927); ROARK BRADFORD's *Ol' Man Adam an' His Chillun* (1928), *This Side of Jordan* (1929), and *Kingdom Coming* (1933); Vera Caspary's *White Girl* (1929); Maxwell Bodenheim's *Ninth Avenue* (1930) and *Naked on Roller Skates* (1931); William Faulkner's GO DOWN, MOSES (1942) and INTRUDER IN THE DUST (1948); Hamilton Basso's *Cinnamon Seed* (1934) and *Courthouse Square* (1936); Erskine Caldwell's *Kneel to the Rising Sun* (1935); Willa Cather's SAPPHIRA AND THE SLAVE GIRL (1940); Lillian Smith's STRANGE FRUIT (1944); Cid Ricketts Sumner's *Quality* (1946) and *But the Morning Will Come* (1949); Sinclair Lewis' KINGSBLOOD ROYAL (1947); Anne Parrish's *A Clouded Star* (1948) (see HARRIET TUBMAN); Jefferson Young's *A Good Man* (1953); Jo Sinclair's *The Changelings* (1955); Warren Miller's THE COOL WORLD (1959).

The Negro's slow but sure progress in the field of drama limelights his American destiny. His appearance on the stage was early—and menial; he was almost always a comic character. The Negro MINSTRELS, white actors in blackface, began to appear early in the 19th century. In 1821 a company of Negro actors was formed in New York City and presented Shakespeare (probably *Othello*) until the police closed the theater. The first legitimate American Negro actor of any distinction was Ira Aldridge (1807–1867), who toured Europe but was not allowed to play in America. Negroes were prominent during the 1850's and 1860's as characters in anti-slavery plays or plays dealing with those of mixed blood. *The Branded Hand* (1845) preceded the dramatization of Mrs. Stowe's *Uncle Tom's Cabin* (1852) in depicting the cruelties of slavery; the stage version of *Uncle Tom's Cabin* has been presented literally hundreds of thousands of times, both in the United States and abroad. Mrs. Stowe's *Dred*, dramatized in 1856, continued her attack on slavery. Other 19th-century plays by or about Negroes include J. T. Trowbridge's *Neighbor Jackwood* (1857); William Wells Brown's *The Escape, or, A Leap for Freedom* (1858); Mrs. J. C. Swayze's *Ossawatomie Brown* (1859); Dion Boucicault's THE OCTOROON (1859); Steele MacKaye's version (1881) of A. W. Tourgee's A FOOL'S ERRAND (1879).

More serious dramas began to appear in the early 20th century. Thomas Dixon's Negrophobia was transferred to the stage with a dramatic version of *The Clansman* (1905), later the basis for the motion picture *The Birth of a Nation* (1915). Then came Joseph S. Cotter, Sr.'s *The Degenerate* (1906); William Vaughn Moody's *The Faith Healer* (1901; rev., 1910); Robert Hilliard's *Pride of Race* (1916); Ridgely Torrence's *Three Plays for a Negro Theater* (1917). Eugene O'Neill wrote of West Indian Negroes in the one-act play THE MOON OF THE CARIBBEES (prod., 1918) and a young Negro gangster in Harlem in another one-act play, *The Dreamy Kid* (1919). THE EMPEROR JONES (prod., 1920) introduces Brutus Jones, the greatest Negro character on the stage since Othello, and ALL GOD'S CHILLUN GOT WINGS (1924) deals with miscegenation. Paul Green had a more positive interest in the Negro than did O'Neill; some of his shorter pieces were collected in *Lonesome Road* (1926). Green's IN ABRAHAM'S BOSOM (1927) was a Pulitzer prize-winner. He also wrote about Negroes in *Potter's Field* (prod. in 1934, as *Roll, Sweet Chariot*) and *Hymn to the Rising Sun* (1936). DuBose and Dorothy Heyward's novel *Porgy* was dramatized in 1927, and made into a great folk opera by George Gershwin in 1935; their *Mamba's Daughters* was dramatized in 1939. Another great play was THE GREEN PASTURES (1930), based by Marc Connelly upon Roark Bradford's stories. Julia Peterkin's *Scarlet Sister Mary* was dramatized in 1930.

Hall Johnson's *Run, Little Chillun* (1933) was the first successful drama by a Negro writer to be produced on Broadway. More impressive were Johnson's arrangements of spirituals. A long array of Negro dramatists has followed, particularly Langston Hughes, Randolph Edmonds,

Zora Neale Hurston, WALLACE THURMAN, Eulalie Spence, John F. Matheus. During the 1930's the Federal Theater encouraged Negro playwrights; Negro stock companies helped produce their plays. Two effective later plays about Negroes were Philip Yordan's *Anna Lucasta* (1945) and Louis Peterson's *Take a Giant Step* (1953). In 1952 appeared a serious film, *See How They Run*, based by Emmet Lavery on a story by a young Negro schoolteacher, Mary Elizabeth Roman. Edith J. R. Isaacs wrote *The Negro in the American Theater* (1947). Two successful recent plays by Negroes were Lorraine Hansberry's *A Raisin in the Sun* (1958) and Ossie Davis' *Purlie Victorious* (1961).

The folklore of Negroes in the United States is in part a remembrance of African elements, although many of its ingredients have been taken from other cultures. William Wells Brown, that remarkable pioneer, was also the first Negro to gather folk stories, in *My Southern Home* (1880). A year later appeared the first of a long series of collections that helped to make Negro folk tales familiar all over the world: UNCLE REMUS, by the Southern white journalist Joel Chandler Harris. Later collections include C. C. Jones, Jr.'s *Myths from the Georgia Coast* (1888); Charles W. Chesnutt's *The Conjure Woman* (1899); Virginia Frazer Boyle's *Devil Tales* (1900); Ambrose E. Gonzales' *Gullah Stories of the Carolina Coast* (1922); Arthur Huff Fauset's *Negro Folktales from the South* (1927); Julia Peterkin's *Roll, Jordan, Roll* (1933); Carl Carmer's STARS FELL ON ALABAMA (1934); Zora Neale Hurston's *Mules and Men* (1935).

Early examples of "folk sermons" were collected in *Stories and Speeches of William O. Bradley* (1916). Roark Bradford collected some funny yet impressive pieces in OL' MAN ADAM AN' HIS CHILLUN (1928), later the basis for the play *The Green Pastures*. Bradford also wrote *Ol' King David an' the Philistine Boys* (1930), and made a good book out of the adventures of the Negro superman, *John Henry* (1931). Altogether different was James Weldon Johnson's GOD'S TROMBONES: SEVEN NEGRO SERMONS IN VERSE (1927). Arthur Huff Fauset and Zora Neale Hurston have reproduced other such sermons.

American literature is rich in nonfictional writings about the Negro. Among these books are: Frederick Douglass' *The Narrative of the Life of Frederick Douglass, an American Slave* (1845) and *My Bondage and My Freedom* (1855); Booker T. Washington's UP FROM SLAVERY (1900); W. E. B. Du Bois' SOULS OF BLACK FOLK (1903); James Weldon Johnson's *Autobiography of an Ex-Colored Man* (1912); Alain Locke's *The New Negro* (1925), *The Negro in America* (1933), *The Negro and His Music* (1936), *Negro Art—Past and Present* (1937), and an anthology, *Plays of Negro Life* (1927); Vernon Loggins' *The Negro Author* (1931); B. G. Brawley's *Early Negro American Authors* (1935) and *The Negro Genius* (1937);

Sterling A. Brown's *Negro Poetry and Drama* (1937) and his anthology (with others), *The Negro Caravan* (1941); Roi Ottley's *New World A-Coming* (1943), *Black Odyssey* (1948), and *The Lonely Warrior* (1955); Gunnar Myrdal's *An American Dilemma: The Negro Problem and Modern Democracy* (2 v., 1944); Langston Hughes and Arna Bontemps' *Poetry of the Negro* (1949); J. Saunders Redding's *They Came in Chains* (1950); Ethel Waters' *His Eye Is on the Sparrow* (1951); Langston Hughes' *The First Book of Negroes* (1952) and *Famous Negro Music Makers* (1955); Lillian Smith's *Now Is the Time* (1955); Walter White's *How Far the Promised Land?* (1955); Marian Anderson's *My Lord, What a Morning!* (1956); J. C. Furnas' *Goodbye to Uncle Tom* (1956).

Negro spirituals. Henry Krehbiel in *Afro-American Folk Songs* (1914) claims an African origin for the spirituals, and James W. Johnson, whose *Book of American Negro Spirituals* appeared in 1925, also claims a folk origin. Others believe that Negro spirituals originated with white people. All authorities acknowledge the strong influence of Methodist hymns and camp meeting airs. Some spirituals are sad and slow, like *Swing Low, Sweet Chariot;* others, like *Little David, Play on Your Harp,* are lively and syncopated.

The first collection with music was *Slave Songs in the United States* (1867), compiled by William Francis Allen, Charles P. Ware, and Lucy McKim Garrison. The earliest critical study, appearing in the *Atlantic Monthly* (June, 1867), was written by THOMAS W. HIGGINSON, who, as colonel of a regiment of Negro soldiers, became familiar with their songs. In 1871 the Fisk University Jubilee Singers began touring the country and aroused great interest in Negro singing. Theodore Seward's *Jubilee Songs, as Sung by the Jubilee Singers of Fisk University* appeared in 1872, G. D. Pike's *The Jubilee Singers* in 1873. Since then dozens of collections have been made; one of the largest is John Wesley Work's *American Negro Songs and Spirituals* (1940). Miles Mark Fisher's *Negro Slave Songs in the United States* (1954) delves into the historical and sociological background of the spirituals.

Neihardt, John G[neisenau] (b. Sharpsburg, Ill., Jan. 8, 1881—   ), short-story writer, dramatist, novelist, poet, professor. John Neihardt graduated from the Nebraska Normal College with a degree in science in 1897. For the next ten years he lived among the Indians, working at odd jobs. THE LONESOME TRAIL (1907), a collection of short stories of pioneering heroes and Indians, utilized his experiences during this period. In 1907 he published *A Bundle of Myrrh,* lyric poetry; in 1921, a play entitled *Two Mothers.* The first of his epic poems of the West, *The Song of Hugh Glass* (1915), was followed by *The Song of Three Friends* (1919); *The Song of the Indian Wars* (1925); *The Song of the Messiah* (1935); and *The Song of Jed Smith* (1941), which completed the series. In 1949 all five appeared in a

single volume entitled *A Cycle of the West.* He also wrote four novels: *Life's Lure* (1914); *The Splendid Wayfaring* (1920); *When the Tree Flowered* (1951); *Eagle Voice* (1953).

Neihardt was made poet laureate of Nebraska in 1921 by a special act of the state legislature; two years later he became professor of poetry at the University of Nebraska, and, later, poet-in-residence and lecturer in English at the University of Missouri.

Neilson, William Allan (b. Scotland, March 28, 1869—d. Feb. 13, 1946), teacher, college administrator, scholar, lexicographer, editor. Neilson, one of the most influential men in American education and scholarship in his time, was president of Smith College from 1917 to 1939. He showed outstanding courage on many occasions, as when he defended Sacco and Vanzetti at a public meeting in Northampton and was almost mobbed by an angry audience. He was editor-in-chief of the Merriam-Webster *Webster's New International Dictionary, Second Edition* (1934). Among his books: *Essentials of Poetry* (1912); *The Facts About Shakespeare* (1913); *A History of English Literature* (1920); *Intellectual Honesty* (1940). He was associate editor with CHARLES W. ELIOT of the "Harvard Classics" (1909), edited Shakespeare's *Complete Works* for the series of "Cambridge Poets" (1906; rev. 1942), and numerous other volumes. Margaret Farrand Thorp wrote *Neilson of Smith* (1956).

Nell, William Cooper (b. Boston, Dec. 20, 1816—d. May 25, 1874), newspaperman, historian. Nell is remembered for two historical studies: *Services of Colored Americans in the Wars of 1776 and 1812* (1851) and *The Colored Patriots of the American Revolution* (1855).

Nellie, the Beautiful Cloak Model. See OWEN DAVIS.

Nelligan, Émile (b. Montreal, Dec. 24, 1879—d. Nov. 18, 1941), poet. Educated in Montreal, he proved to be an imaginative but undisciplined student. At the age of seventeen he revealed his poetic gift in a volume of poems entitled *Le samedi* (1896), which was published under the pen name Émile Kovar. He continued to write poetry for various Montreal periodicals, and was one of the first Canadians to be influenced by the French symbolist school. In 1899 he went insane, and he spent the remainder of his life in mental institutions. His collected poems, *Émile Nelligan et son œuvre* (1903), published by Louis Dantin, have gone into several editions.

Nemerov, Howard (b. New York City, March 1, 1920—   ), poet, novelist, essayist, teacher. Graduating from Harvard just in time to enter World War II, Nemerov served as a pilot in the air force. He published his first book of verse in 1947, and afterward joined the faculty of Bennington College. He frequently contributed short stories, essays, and poems to the literary magazines. His first novel, *The Melodramatists* (1949), was described by Diana Trilling as "literate and entertaining, with a nice satiric barb." Of *Federigo or The Power of Love*

(1954), H. F. West wrote, ". . . a cutting portrait of the Hamlets who write advertising copy, of the women whose modern handbook is Freud on the one hand and *Vogue* on the other." Critics have generally praised his verse as original and vital. Among his poetry collections are *Guide to the Ruins* (1950); *Mirrors and Windows* (1958); *New and Selected Poems* (1960). *The Homecoming Game,* a novel, appeared in 1957; Nemerov's short story collection, *A Commodity of Dreams,* appeared in 1959.

Nets to Catch the Wind (1921), first publicly published book of poems by ELINOR WYLIE. In this collection Elinor Wylie manifested her outstanding traits as a poet—an interest in symbolical animals (as in THE EAGLE AND THE MOLE), and her remarkable craftsmanship. Many of the poems are in the so-called "metaphysical" manner, and the title is from the 17th century poem *The Devil's Law Case* by John Webster.

Nettels, Curtis P. See ROOTS OF AMERICAN CIVILIZATION.

Nevin, Arthur Finley. See ETHELBERT NEVIN.

Nevin, Ethelbert [Woodbridge] (b. Edgeworth, Pa., Nov. 25, 1862—d. Feb. 17, 1901), composer. Nevin won a wide reputation, especially as a composer of settings for lyrics. Perhaps the most popular of his settings were those for ROBERT CAMERON ROGERS' *The Rosary* (pub., 1894) and Frank L. Stanton's *Mighty Lak' a Rose* (1901). He also wrote several piano suites, among them *Water Scenes* (1891); *In Arcady* (1892); *May in Tuscany* (1896); *A Day in Venice* (1898). His brother, **Arthur Finley Nevin** (b. Edgeworth, Pa., April 27, 1871—d. July 10, 1943), was likewise a composer and taught music in several universities and conservatories. He composed a number of operas on Indian themes.

Nevins, Allan (b. Camp Point, Ill., May 20, 1890—d. Feb. 28, 1971), journalist, historian. Nevins did editorial work for the New York *Evening News, The Nation,* the New York *Sun,* and the New York *World.* In 1927 he accepted a professorship in American history at Cornell University, and in 1931 joined the faculty of Columbia University. He retired in 1958. Nevins wrote histories of outstanding merit and interest. His writings include: *The Life of Robert Rogers* (1914); *The Evening Post—A Century Of Journalism* (1922); *Frémont: the West's Greatest Adventurer* (2 v., 1928); *Henry White—Thirty Years of American Diplomacy* (1930); *Grover Cleveland—A Study in Courage* (1932; Pulitzer Prize, 1933); *Hamilton Fish—The Inner History of the Grant Administration* (1936; Pulitzer Prize, 1937); *Frémont, Pathmarker of the West* (1939; an enlargement and revision of *Frémont: the West's Greatest Adventurer*); *The Heritage of America* (with HENRY STEELE COMMAGER, 1939); *John D. Rockefeller: the Heroic Age of American Business* (2 v., 1940); *The Ordeal of the Union* (1946, Scribner Centenary Prize); *The Emergence of Lincoln* (2 v., 1952); *Study in Power* (1953); *Ford: the Times, the Man, the Company,* in collaboration with FRANK E. HILL (v. 1, 1954; v. 2, 1957); *The War for the Union* (1959, 2 v.). For a time, Nevins was editor of the CHRONICLES OF AMERICA.

Newbery, John, and the **Newbery Award.** Newbery (b. England, 1713—d. 1767) was a printer and bookseller who in 1744 began the publication of dozens of quaint rhymes and stories for children. The American Library Association has offered an award each year since 1922 to the best book written for children; Newbery's name was attached to the honor. Hendrik Van Loon's STORY OF MANKIND won the first award. In 1937 the CALDECOTT MEDAL (named for the English artist Randolph Caldecott) was added to the Newbery Award to honor distinguished illustrators of children's books. Irvin Kerlan prepared a descriptive catalogue, *Newbery and Caldecott Awards* (1949), which lists first editions of all books which have won these honors. See CHILDREN'S BOOKS.

New Century Cyclopedia of Names (1954), edited by Clarence L. Barnhart and others. This three-volume biographical dictionary contains information on: prominent figures in all fields and in all countries; historical events; literary works and characters; works of art; legendary and mythological persons and places. A staple reference work for most libraries, it contains about 100,000 entries, plus approximately 20,000 cross references. Its major use is as a biographical dictionary. It replaces an earlier and similar work, first published in 1894 and now outdated.

Newcomb, Simon (b. Wallace, N. Scot., March 12, 1835—d. July 11, 1909), mathematician, astronomer. At first educated by his father, Newcomb later studied at the Lawrence Scientific School of Harvard University. There he became director of the *American Ephemeris and Nautical Almanac* and greatly increased its prestige. He worked in the Naval Observatory at Washington, was professor of mathematics in the United States Navy, served as professor of astronomy at Johns Hopkins University. Newcomb was less interested in observation of the stars than in theoretical astronomy; his work on planet orbits and celestial mechanics was especially notable. Among his books: *Popular Astronomy* (1878); *The Stars* (1901); *Astronomy for Everybody* (1902); *The Reminiscences of an Astronomer* (1903).

New Criticism, The. A term used by JOHN CROWE RANSOM as the title of a critique of contemporary critical methods (1941), now a famous text. In general the New Critics seek to concentrate attention on the literary *opus* as an autonomous work of art, rather than on its author's personality or the age in which it was written. Within these limits there have been many divergencies, however, as in the study of tropes carried on by the English critic William Empson, the interest in literature as symbolic action of KENNETH BURKE, YVOR WINTERS' emphasis on the moral aspects of form and style, or R. P. BLACKMUR's investigations of larger meanings.

The principles of the New Criticism were well established before the term itself came into being. Such scholars as Caroline Spurgeon and EDITH RICKERT had been practicing the New Criticism for a decade or more; indeed, Miss Rickert stressed the need for the internal inspection of poetry in her *New Methods for the Study of Literature* as early as 1927. But in general the development of the New Criticism, at least in its early stage, was extra-academic. It derived first of all perhaps from the early writings of EZRA POUND and T. E. Hulme; T. S. ELIOT's THE SACRED WOOD (1920), a book of critical essays, was extremely influential, as was I. A. RICHARDS' *Principles of Literary Criticism* (1926). In the United States the movement found an especially receptive audience during the late 1920's at Vanderbilt University among the group, headed by Professor Ransom, which called itself The Fugitives. Although The Fugitives were primarily southern regionalists who adopted an integrated program of conservatism in politics and agrarianism in economics (cf. the joint manifesto I'LL TAKE MY STAND, 1930, and Allen Tate's REACTIONARY ESSAYS, 1936), it was chiefly the literary part of their undertaking which exerted an enduring influence. Members of the group—ALLEN TATE, CAROLINE GORDON, ROBERT PENN WARREN, DONALD DAVIDSON, and others—were exceedingly active in editing and contributing to three periodicals which became their primary outlets and, successively, the most respected literary publications in the country: THE SOUTHERN REVIEW, THE SEWANEE REVIEW, and THE KENYON REVIEW. Very quickly these writers were joined by others, critics from other parts of the country who in many cases had arrived at their literary methods independently and who in some cases professed radically different political views—in addition to Blackmur, Winters, and Burke, such men as LIONEL TRILLING, PHILIP RAHV, Frederick J. Hoffman, FRANCIS FERGUSSON, F. O. MATTHIESSEN, William Barrett, CLEANTH BROOKS, DUDLEY FITTS, Austin Warren, René Wellek, William K. Wimsatt, Jr., RANDALL JARRELL, and others. Today many younger scholars delight in calling themselves New Critics, although, paradoxically, the movement possesses less cohesion than formerly, owing to the new interests and greater divergencies among the elder critics.

A few of the most important texts of the New Criticism are Professor Ransom's *God Without Thunder* (1930), *The World's Body* (1938), *The New Criticism* (1941), and *Poems and Essays* (1955); Yvor Winters' *Primitivism and Decadence* (1937) and *Maule's Curse* (1938), both reprinted in *In Defense of Reason* (1947); Cleanth Brooks' *The Well-Wrought Urn* (1947); René Wellek and Austin Warren's *Theory of Literature* (1949); R. P. Blackmur's *The Double Agent* (1935), *The Expense of Greatness* (1940), *Language as Gesture* (1952), and *The Lion and the Honeycomb* (1955); Francis Fergusson's *The Idea of a Theater* (1948); Kenneth Burke's *The Philosophy of Literary Form* (1941); Allen Tate's *Reactionary Essays on Po-*etry *and Ideas* (1936), *Reason in Madness* (1941), and *The Forlorn Demon* (1953). Two compilations of New Criticism are R. W. Stallman's *The Critics' Notebook* (1950) and Ray B. West, Jr.'s *Essays in Modern Literary Criticism* (1952). Stanley Edgar Hyman's *The Armed Vision* (1948), an interesting critique of criticism, includes discussions of some of the New Critics. See HUMANISM.

New Dictionary of American History, The (1952), compiled by Michael Martin and Leonard Gelber. This volume contains more than four thousand entries on important names, places, events, trends, catch-phrases, laws, and other germane items in the field of American history. The articles are succinct and objective.

Newell, Robert Henry ["Orpheus C. Kerr"] (b. New York City, Dec. 13, 1836—d. July 8[?], 1901), journalist, humorist, novelist, poet. Newell contributed to New York City papers, in 1858 became assistant editor of the New York *Sunday Mercury,* for which he wrote sentimental verses and comments on current topics. During the Civil War he was a war correspondent for the New York *Herald.* He invented his pen name as a pun on the swarm of wartime office-seekers in Washington and signed it to the Orpheus C. Kerr letters, which, supposedly coming from Washington, were originally printed in the *Mercury,* later in other journals, finally as *The Orpheus C. Kerr Papers* (5 v., 1862–71). This correspondence, for the most part painfully unhumorous to the modern reader, was compounded of the same humorous devices used by the creators of Sut Lovingood and Petroleum V. Nasby—bad spelling, overstatement, anticlimax. Oddly mingled with this fashionable type of humor were, however, imaginary episodes, war incidents, and sentimental verses. Although most of the *Papers* are unreadable today, one genuinely funny letter gives the results of an imaginary contest for a new national anthem. Entries supposedly submitted by Emerson, Holmes, Aldrich, Whittier, Longfellow, and others display Newell's wit and skill as a parodist.

Newell also published *The Palace Beautiful and Other Poems* (1865) and *Versatilities* (1871), poems; *The Cloven Foot* (1870), an attempted completion of Dickens' *The Mystery of Edwin Drood; The Walking Doll, or the Asters and Disasters of Society* (1872), a novel of New York life; *There was a Man* (1884), a novel attacking the Darwinian theory. Newell was married for a short time to the actress ADAH MENKEN; from 1869 to 1874 he was an editor of the New York *World.* A nervous malady forced him to retire from active life two years later.

New England. The full, complex, and characteristic culture of New England, the region's often agonizing conflict between a Puritanical tradition and a rebellious nature, its commercial, intellectual, and social dominance, its granitic landscapes, its equally flinty humor—all this has made the home of the Yankee a favorite theme for American writers of all generations. The grass-roots culture of the region has been collected in such volumes as Richard M. Dorson's JONATHAN DRAWS THE LONG BOW (1946) and B. A. Botkin's *Treasury of New England Folklore* (1947); native Yankee wit appears in Richardson Wright's *Grandfather Was Queer: Early American Wags and Eccentrics from Colonial Times to the Civil War* (1939). The New England dialect was a stock prop of 19th-century humorists, as in SEBA SMITH's *Letters of Jack Downing* (1830) or in the Sam Slick sketches of THOMAS C. HALIBURTON (1835). James Russell Lowell used Yankee talk skillfully in his BIGLOW PAPERS (1846, 1867). A study of the English origins of Yankee speechways was made by Anders Orbeck in his *Early New England Pronunciation* (1927). The most scientific study of New England speech is to be found in *The Linguistic Atlas of New England* (1939–43). Hans Kurath, director of the *Handbook of the Linguistic Geography of New England* (1939), has also prepared a *Word Geography of the Eastern U.S.* (1949).

Until the end of the 19th century New England was undoubtedly the literary center of the United States, and writing produced there established standards for writers elsewhere. A number of studies of New England literature have been made; among them are T. G. Wright's *Literary Culture in Early New England* (1920); Samuel E. Morison's *The Puritan Pronaos: Studies in the Intellectual Life of New England in the 17th Century* (1936; rev., 1956); Van Wyck Brooks' THE FLOWERING OF NEW ENGLAND (1936); Perry Miller and Thomas H. Johnson's anthology, *The Puritans* (1938); Miller's *The New England Mind: The Seventeenth Century* (1939) and *The New England Mind: From Colony to Province* (1953); Harold S. Jantz's *The First Century of New England Verse* (1945); Louis Untermeyer's anthology, *New England Poets* (1948); Kenneth B. Murdock's *Literature and Theology in Colonial New England* (1949).

So much fiction has been written about New England that only a few outstanding titles can be mentioned: Nathaniel Hawthorne's THE HOUSE OF THE SEVEN GABLES (1851); Harriet Beecher Stowe's THE MINISTER'S WOOING (1859); Oliver Wendell Holmes' ELSIE VENNER (1861); Louisa May Alcott's LITTLE WOMEN (1868–69); Thomas Bailey Aldrich's THE STORY OF A BAD BOY (1869); Mary E. Wilkins' A NEW ENGLAND NUN AND OTHER STORIES (1891); Sarah Orne Jewett's THE COUNTRY OF THE POINTED FIRS (1896); Edith Wharton's ETHAN FROME (1911); Joseph Hergesheimer's JAVA HEAD (1919); Joseph C. Lincoln's *Head Tide* (1928); Edna Ferber's *American Beauty* (1931); Mary Ellen Chase's *Mary Peters* (1934); Rachel Field's *Time Out of Mind* (1935); George Santayana's THE LAST PURITAN (1936); John P. Marquand's THE LATE GEORGE APLEY (1937); Dorothy Canfield Fisher's *Seasoned Timber* (1939); Le Grand Cannon's *Look to the Mountain* (1942); Edwin O'Connor's THE LAST HURRAH (1956).

Additional volumes of nonfiction about New England include: Francis Higginson's *New England's Plantation* (1630); John Josselyn's *An Account of Two Voyages to New England* (1674); Nathaniel Morton's *New England's Memorial* (1721); Timothy Dwight's *Travels in New England* (4 v., 1821–22); John Winthrop's *The History of New England* (2 v., 1825–26); Charles W. Elliott's *New England History* (2 v., 1857); Lucy Larcom's *A New England Girlhood* (1889); Edward Everett Hale's *A New England Boyhood* (1900); George Lyman Kittredge's *The Old Farmer and His Almanack* (1904); James Truslow Adams' *The Founding of New England* (1921); Lewis Mumford's THE GOLDEN DAY (1926); Jonathan Daniels' *A Southerner Discovers New England* (1940); Samuel Chamberlain's *Ever New England* (1944); Perry Miller's *New England Mind from Colony to Province* (1953); Austin Warren's *New England Saints* (1956); Herbert W. Schneider's *The Puritan Mind* (1930; reissued 1958).

New England: Indian Summer, 1865–1915 (1940), fourth volume of VAN WYCK BROOKS' *Makers and Finders* series. It surveys the years between the Civil War Boston of Oliver Wendell Holmes and the New England of Robert Frost and Eugene O'Neill. Writing of New England as it merged in these years with the spirit of the nation at large, Brooks also treats Henry James, Henry Adams, and William Dean Howells. The volume drew adverse criticism for ignoring literary values in its attempt to recreate the social climate of American writers. But it was enormously popular.

New England Courant. This newspaper, founded by JAMES FRANKLIN on Aug. 7, 1721, became noteworthy for its bold attacks on the authorities and its vigorous satiric sketches in imitation of *The Spectator*. It denounced COTTON MATHER for advocating vaccination against smallpox; Mather called the contributors to the *Courant* the HELL-FIRE CLUB. Among the contributors was Franklin's younger step-brother, BENJAMIN FRANKLIN, who assumed the pen name of Silence Dogood and saw his first essay appear on April 2, 1722. James was a bit jealous, but when his attacks in the paper put him in jail he made Benjamin temporary publisher. Later the brothers quarreled, and Benjamin left for New York and Philadelphia in search of a job. The paper ceased publication June 4, 1726.

New Englander, The. This magazine was founded at Yale College (1843) by Edward Royall Tyler, son of the playwright ROYALL TYLER. Its purpose was to support evangelical Christianity. In time its interest shifted to history and economics. It became one of the best-known reviews of the mid-19th century. In 1885 its name was changed to *The New Englander and Yale Review*. In 1892 it became the YALE REVIEW. In 1911 Professor WILBUR L. CROSS of Yale took it over and made it a magazine of wide literary and general interests and of great distinction.

New England Magazine. A monthly magazine, founded by Joseph T. Buckingham and published in Boston. Its first issue appeared in July, 1831; it ceased publication in December, 1836. During its short existence it obtained a reputation for quality unrivaled until the appearance of the *Atlantic Monthly* in 1857. It had numerous noted contributors, including Hawthorne, Longfellow, Whittier, Noah Webster, Edward Everett, and Oliver Wendell Holmes, Sr. It was taken over by the *American Monthly Magazine*.

New England Nun, A, and Other Stories (1891), twenty stories by MARY E. WILKINS FREEMAN. They are written with that combination of realism and irony for which the author became famous—as in the opening story, in which a young woman's betrothed goes to Australia to make a fortune, comes back after fourteen years, and marries another woman to the relief of the heroine, who does not want her accustomed domestic ways disturbed. Carlos Baker says of the collection in general, "Miss Wilkins' refusal to overplay her hand is a sign of control rather than lack of courage."

New England Primer, The. The earliest extant edition of this famous and widely circulated "little Bible" of the colonies is dated 1727 and is a collector's item. Who prepared the Primer is not known; it was an obvious imitation of

many similar English volumes which had long been imported and circulated in the colonies. It was a tiny textbook which fitted snugly in a child's pocket. The Primer immediately won an immense popularity, circulating not only in New England but also in the other English settlements. Millions of copies were sold as late as the 19th century. Most young colonists learned to read from its pages. It was deeply religious in tone. The 1749 edition contained, among other material, an alphabet with verses and illustrations, rules for behavior, several hymns, the prayer "Now I lay me down to sleep," the shorter catechism, pious stories of several martyrs. It must have been a great relief to boys and girls, who were expected otherwise to become absorbed in the lengthy and arid sermons of that age. By 1800 the *Primer* began to look beyond the church walls for data, as when the alphabet read, "A was an Angler, and fished with a hook.

B was a Blockhead, and ne'er learned his book." The book was imitated in *The New York Primer, The American Primer,* and similar texts; only the title page was different. A *Columbian Primer* is attributed to Benjamin Franklin. See BENJAMIN HARRIS.

New England's Annoyances (1630[?]). This anonymous poem, sometimes called "the first verses by an American colonist," is said to have been taken down in 1685 from the lips of an old lady of ninety-six. The lines describe the hardships, the hazards, the privations of the New World, but bid the reader to have "a quiet and contented mind, /And all needful blessings you will find."

New England's Crisis (1676), a narrative poem by BENJAMIN TOMPSON. Probably the first epic written on American soil, Tompson's poem describes KING PHILIP's War in 650 lines of heroic couplets. The Prologue pictures New England society as being in a state of decadence sufficient to bring on the war. The narrative has many classical allusions, but the Prologue, with its lament at the passing of early American ways when "the dainty Indian maize" was eaten out of clam-shells in thatched huts, remains the most striking part of the poem.

New England's First Fruits (London, 1643), a pamphlet published anonymously but probably written by Henry Dunster, Hugh Peter, and Thomas Weld. It was in part a reply to Thomas Lechford's charges in his PLAIN DEALING (1642) that nothing was being done for the Indians in New England. The authors give a list of Indian conversions, go on to tell about the founding of Harvard College, give other data about New England.

New England's Memorial. See NATHANIEL MORTON.

New England's Prospect (1634), a guide by William Wood (1580?–1639). Wood came to New England in 1629 and remained there for four years, then returned to England and published his book in London. He makes no attempt to minimize the difficulties of living in the colonies, provides a guidebook to the country, offers suggestions on equipment needed, gives an account of the Indians. The book has considerable literary merit. It was reprinted in 1865.

New England's Rarities Discovered (1672), a description by John Josselyn. Josselyn, who made two visits to this country, was not a Puritan and was often candidly critical of the colonies. His was the first systematic attempt to record New England flora and fauna. It also gives a general description of the region, provides some medical hints, and mentions new dishes (stewed pumpkins, for example). Josselyn's book was reprinted in the *Transactions* (1860) of the American Antiquarian Society. A later book of his was *An Account of Two Voyages to New England* (1674), reprinted in the *Collections* (1833) of the Massachusetts Historical Society.

New England's Trials (1620; 2nd ed., 1622), a narrative of his experiences and observations by Captain JOHN SMITH. This was in part a tract on the fisheries, in part Smith's plea for employment to help develop them. In the 1622 edition it was enlarged to include an account of Plymouth. His story of the latter colony is strictly factual, says nothing of the religious motives that had led to the settlement. Smith's book was reprinted, in an edition edited by Charles Deane, in the *Proceedings* of the Massachusetts Historical Society (1873).

New England Tragedies, The (1868), a drama by HENRY WADSWORTH LONGFELLOW. This drama—Longfellow called it a dramatic poem —was later made part of a work called CHRISTUS (1872), a trilogy consisting of *The Divine Tragedy*, THE GOLDEN LEGEND, and *The New England Tragedies*. The plays imitated the form of medieval mystery plays, were intended to illustrate Hope in the age of Christ, Faith in the Middle Ages, Charity in modern times. Longfellow divided *The New England Tragedies* into two parts: JOHN ENDICOTT, illustrating the cruel persecution of the Quakers by the Puritans; and *Giles Corey of the Salem Farms*, portraying the witchcraft madness (see GILES COREY). Neither play has won much renown for Longfellow, who lacked skill as a dramatist.

New English Canaan (1637), an account by THOMAS MORTON. The Puritans, themselves Dissenters, did not care much for Morton, a dissenter from Puritan views. They drove him out of his settlement at Merry Mount, where apparently he had been doing what someone has called a rum-and-gun-running business with the Indians. In his *New English Canaan*, published in Amsterdam, Morton gives his side of the story. The first two sections are seriously intended, with a description of the Indians and the characteristics of the land. In the third section Morton accuses the Puritans of ousting him because they were envious of his success as a trader. Charles Francis Adams edited a reprint (1883) of *New English Canaan* for the *Publications* of the Prince Society of Boston. John L. Motley used the book as a basis for two novels, MORTON'S HOPE (1839) and *Merry Mount* (1849); Hawthorne as a basis for his story THE MAYPOLE OF MERRYMOUNT (1836).

New France. The term New France has been somewhat loosely applied to all the territories that France in time acquired in continental North America under the leadership of Champlain, Frontenac, Joliet, Marquette, and La Salle with the assistance of many zealous and fearless Jesuit missionaries. Strictly speaking, however, only the province of Quebec and a vast but ill-defined region stretching to the Alleghenies and from the Great Lakes to the Gulf of Mexico was "New France," in direct subjection to the French crown; the region of the St. Lawrence and its valley was called Canada.

New Hampshire: A Poem with Notes and Grace Notes (1923), a collection by ROBERT FROST, which won the Pulitzer Prize for poetry in 1924. This is one of Frost's greatest books and contains some of his best-known poems, including the long title poem; THE AXE-HELVE;

The Grindstone; The Onset; STOPPING BY WOODS ON A SNOWY EVENING; *Our Singing Strength; Fire and Ice.* Willard Thorp noted that in this collection the poet shows himself willing "to talk about himself and his art, somewhat defiantly."

Newhouse, Edward (b. Hungary, Nov. 10, 1911—   ), novelist, short-story writer. Newhouse came to the United States at the age of twelve and learned English at New York public school and libraries. When he was eighteen, consumed by curiosity about the United States and Mexico he set out to explore them by hopping freight trains. His first stories were published in *New Masses* and his first two novels, *You Can't Sleep Here* (1934) and *This Is Your Day* (1937), are examples of proletarian literature. However, he subsequently lost faith in the movement and disowned his early efforts as "childish." Many of his later stories appeared in *The New Yorker*. They have been collected in several books: *Anything Can Happen* (1941); *The Iron Chain* (1946); *Many Are Called* (1951). His skillful narrative and dialogue mold themes that are sometimes cynical and sometimes light-hearted but always moving. His return to the novel, with *The Temptation of Roger Heriott* (1954), was highly successful.

New Humanism, The. See HUMANISM.

New International Encyclopedia (17 v., 1902–04), edited by HARRY THURSTON PECK. (See also DANIEL COIT GILMAN.) This work was issued originally in 1886 as the *International Encyclopedia*, itself an outgrowth of the *Library of Universal Knowledge*, which was a reprint of the British reference work, *Chambers's Encyclopedia*. In 1914–16 the work was again revised, under the editorship of FRANK MOORE COLBY and Talcott Williams.

Newman, Christopher. See THE AMERICAN [1].

Newman, Louis I[srael] (b. Providence, R.I., Dec. 20, 1893—   ), rabbi, teacher, editor, biographer, playwright. Newman served in various pulpits, taught at Columbia University and the Jewish Institute of Religion, and in 1930 became rabbi of Congregation Rodeph Sholom in New York City. Among his writings are: *Jewish Influence on Christian Reform Movements* (1924); *The Hasidic Anthology* (1934); *The Talmudic Anthology* (1939); *Pangs of the Messiah and Other Plays, Pageants and Cantatas* (1957); *The Woman at the Wall* (1955).

New Masses. See THE MASSES.

New Nation, The: A History of the U.S. During the Confederation, 1781–89 (1950), by Merrill Jensen (1905–   ). Jensen gives a novel and authoritative picture of the newly freed American states from the end of the Revolution to the adoption of the Constitution. He shows the people working to improve their lot, does not find the era one of threatened bankruptcy and disintegration.

New Republic, The. A weekly, founded in New York City in 1914 by Willard D. Straight, with Herbert D. Croly as editor; he was succeeded by Bruce Bliven. It aimed to be a "liberal" magazine, at one time had what Morton D. Zabel has called "its phase of Marxist sympathies." It was strongly with Woodrow Wilson, supported him when he declared war on Germany, but later broke with him. It has always had a small but influential circulation, has been especially noted for its excellent book, drama, and moving picture reviews. Among its contributors have been Walter Lippmann, Randolph Bourne, Clarence Day, Henry Blake Fuller, Robert Morss Lovett, Stark Young, Malcolm Cowley, and James Agee. In 1936 Groff Conklin edited *The New Republic Anthology*.

News from Virginia: The Lost Flock Triumphant (1610), a ballad by Richard Rich. This is one of the earliest poems to come out of America. Its purpose was less aesthetic than utilitarian. The author was one of the Virginia pioneers and describes himself as "a soldier, blunt and plain," who to feed "his own humor" prints his impression of Jamestown in 1610. The poem was first printed in an edition (1865) edited by J. O. Halliwell.

Newspaper Days (1941), reminiscences of H. L. Mencken. See DAYS OF H. L. MENCKEN.

newspapers. The first newssheets and newspapers in the English colonies in America were a part of English journalism; published by English pioneers in a new land, they of course imitated in form and content the home papers. Thus the earliest American papers resembled the London *Gazette*, printed on both sides of a single leaf about six by ten inches, without display heads. News was derived chiefly from four sources: (1) extracts from the latest papers received from overseas, (2) extracts from papers published in other colonial towns; (3) private letters from a distance brought in by obliging readers and oral reports of travelers and sea captains; and (4) local news of general public importance (as great storms, celebrations, the governor's activities, hangings).

This last news category usually appeared under a local date line, forerunner of the editorial "flag." Purely local matters were generally disregarded as being already well known to the community, though there were brief notices of deaths and marriages. These were noted in accordance with the concept of news as historical record rather than as sensation, entertainment, human interest, or timely report.

Disregarding earlier newssheet "broadsides," the first paper designed for regular publication in America was *Publick Occurrences*, issued by Benjamin Harris in Boston, September 25, 1690. It was a three-page paper, the fourth left blank for written communications when sent to friends at a distance, thus pointing up the connection between written newsletters and early newspapers. The printed pages were packed with well-reported news, but some of it gave offense to the colonial government and no further issues were permitted. The first continuously published paper in the colonies was the Boston *News-Letter* (1704–76), founded by John Campbell, postmaster and writer of newsletters. It labeled itself conspicuously as "published by

authority." Not so the NEW ENGLAND COURANT (1721–27), also of Boston, founded by JAMES FRANKLIN, elder brother of BENJAMIN FRANKLIN. James was thrown into jail in 1722 because of a sarcastic reference to the governor; and he then named his sixteen-year-old apprentice Ben as editor, by that trick continuing publication. The next year James got out of jail and Ben broke his indentures and ran away to Philadelphia, to find fame and fortune.

In that city Andrew Bradford had founded the *American Weekly Mercury* (1719–49), for some years the town's only paper. In 1728 SAMUEL KEIMER, an eccentric printer and philosopher, began his *Universal Instructor in All Arts and Sciences and Pennsylvania Gazette*. It was not a success, and the next year Franklin, who was by this time conducting a prosperous printing business, bought the paper, decapitated the high-sounding title, and continued the PENNSYLVANIA GAZETTE until his retirement from the printing business in 1748. Franklin retained an interest in the paper until 1766, by which time his partner, David Hall, was able to buy him out; Hall, his son and grandson, and their partners continued the paper until 1815.

Meanwhile William Bradford, Andrew's father, who had been Philadelphia's first printer, moved to New York and founded that city's first newspaper, the *Gazette* (1725–44). Having had his troubles with "authority" in Philadelphia, he made his newspaper definitely a government organ. But when the popular party in New York was engaged in a struggle with avaricious Governor William Cosby, leaders of that party helped JOHN PETER ZENGER, a German immigrant, to establish his *Weekly Journal* (1733–51) and fire repeated volleys of liberal political philosophy and satire at Cosby and his supporters. Late in 1734 Zenger was jailed, though his paper continued to be issued. His trial for seditious libel in August, 1735, was a landmark in the American struggle for freedom of the press. Swayed by the oratory of Andrew Hamilton, a Philadelphia lawyer brought in to replace the attorneys who had arrogantly been disbarred for supporting him, the jury triumphantly acquitted Zenger, though the principle on which this popular action was based did not become law until many years later.

By 1750 fourteen newspapers were being published in the colonies, from Massachusetts south along the coast to South Carolina. A newspaper was commonly a by-product of a printing office, and the profit margin was represented by advertising patronage. Papers often increased to four or to six pages eleven by seventeen inches in size, and by mid-century the more successful publishers were often able to fill three or more pages with advertising, all single-column in width, with very modest headings and a few stock-cuts. All papers were printed by hand on rag paper.

Essays, in the form of letters to the editor on public affairs or moral questions, or arranged in series, *Spectator* fashion, became important in colonial journalism. The *New England Courant* was the first paper to feature imitations of the Addisonian essay; of these, Franklin's "Dogood Papers" are the most notable. Later Franklin wrote "The Busy-Body" (1729) for Bradford's *American Weekly Mercury*. Other outstanding essays were those of Mather Byles in the *New England Weekly Journal* (1727–41); some "little pieces" by Franklin in his own *Gazette;* the excellent original essay series in William Parks' papers, "The Plain Dealer" in the *Maryland Gazette* (1727–34), and "The Monitor" in the *Virginia Gazette* (1736–50). All appeared anonymously.

Proceedings of the colonial assemblies and political matters were a major concern of the colonial papers. They unanimously rebelled against the regulations requiring the use of stamped paper in 1765, and many of them encouraged the growing movement toward independence. JOHN DICKINSON's "Letters from a Farmer in Pennsylvania," published 1767–68 in William Goddard's *Pennsylvania Chronicle* (1767–74) and later reprinted in nearly all the colonial papers, were moderate, however; though they complained of taxation without representation, they did not advocate independence. Not so Thomas Paine's COMMON SENSE, first published as a pamphlet early in 1776, and later reprinted piecemeal in most American papers; It produced a greater sensation than anything ever before published in the country and forced American public opinion to face the idea of separation from the mother country.

Newspapers gained in influence during the Revolution, though the war represented a great ordeal for all of them. At the time of the battle of Lexington thirty-seven colonial newspapers were in course of publication, of which only twenty survived (some with suspensions) through the six and a half years to the surrender at Yorktown; but thirty-three new papers made courageous beginnings during the war, of which thirteen survived. Thus at the end of the war there were almost as many papers as at the beginning. Leading patriot spokesmen were the *Massachusetts Spy* (1770–1904), founded in Boston by twenty-year-old Isaiah Thomas, but moved to Worcester when the British occupied that city; the Boston *Gazette*, published by those "trumpeters of sedition" Benjamin Edes and John Gill, and written largely by such members of the Caucus Club as Samuel and John Adams, Josiah Quincy, and Joseph Warren; the *Pennsylvania Journal* (1742–93), conducted by William Bradford III, outstanding soldier-editor of the war; and John Holt's New York *Journal* (1766–1800), which was chased about over the country and its plant repeatedly destroyed by the British. Leading Tory papers were [James] *Rivington's New York Gazetteer* (1773–83), which, before the war, was one of the best and most widely circulated (3,600) papers in the colonies, but whose brilliant editor became the most hated royalist of them all; and the New York *Mercury* (1752–83), published by Hugh Gaine, the turncoat.

THE FEDERALIST, a series of papers discussing the proposed constitution, written by Alexander Hamilton, James Madison, and John Jay, appeared first in the New York *Independent Journal* (1783–1840). It was widely reprinted throughout the country, and in book form it has long exerted a world-wide influence. Following Washington's inauguration, John Fenno's GAZETTE OF THE UNITED STATES (1789–1818) became a government spokesman, while the NATIONAL GAZETTE (1791–93), conducted by the poet Philip Freneau, was the organ of the dissident party. In fact, the former represented the policies of Secretary of the Treasury Hamilton, and the latter, of Secretary of State Jefferson. After the end of the brief but stormy career of Freneau's paper, the Philadelphia *Aurora* (1793–1843), conducted by Benjamin Franklin Bache (sometimes called "Lightning-Rod Junior" because of the achievement of his famous grandfather), took up the cudgels for the anti-Federalists. Bache's printing plant was wrecked by partisans who resented his criticism of Washington, and he was later attacked on the street by Fenno. Both belligerent editors died of yellow fever in the Philadelphia epidemic of 1798. Bache was followed in the editorship of the *Aurora* and its war against the Federalists by his able son-in-law, William Duane.

Washington was so highly regarded throughout the country that criticism of him personally was limited to comparatively few papers, though such was the President's sensitiveness to press attacks that these may have affected his decision to retire at the end of his second term. On the other side, William Cobbett, later a famous English writer but at this time sojourning in America, issued his *Porcupine's Gazette* (1797–99), leading the Federalist journals in stinging satire until libel suits drove the editor back home. All this marked the beginnings of what may be called the dark ages of American journalism, in which arrant partisanship distorted the reporting of public affairs. A phase of this situation was the passage of the Alien and Sedition Acts in 1798, ostensibly designed to curb seditious utterances on what seemed the brink of a war with France, and to deport dangerous aliens. These Acts failed of re-enactment in 1801, but resentment against them had helped Jefferson into the Presidency; and the spread of new papers into the country west of the Appalachians had a tendency to redress the balance between the Federalists and what was now called the Republican party in the control of the press. But it was not until the appearance of the penny press in the 1830's that bigoted partisanship showed signs of relaxing its hold.

The first daily paper in America was a rather shabby sheet issued by the egregious Benjamin Towne, who had turned his coat twice in the Revolution. His daily of 1783–84 was one phase of his *Pennsylvania Evening Post* (1775–84). A far better daily appeared when John Dunlap and David C. Claypoole transformed their *Pennsylvania Packet*, begun in 1771, by adding *and Daily Advertiser* in 1784; under various publishers the *Daily Advertiser* continued until

1839. The first New York daily was the transformed *Morning Post* (1782–92); but it was surpassed by the *Daily Advertiser* (1785–1809), which was founded about a week after the *Post* turned daily by twenty-one-year-old Francis Childs. The chief purpose of these early dailies was to furnish prompt information of the arrival of ships and the offerings of imported goods. Once started, however, the mercantile journals usually took strong partisan positions in politics and, of course, they carried general news. By 1820, of the 512 newspapers in course of publication, forty-two were dailies, many of them carrying the word *Advertiser* in title or subtitle.

In the next decade the number of dailies increased by a third or more, some of them mainly political organs. Andrew Jackson developed a press that would "wheel and fire at word of command," and there was much outrageous scurrility in political comment on both sides. Less combative was the Washington *National Intelligencer* (1800–69), long conducted by JOSEPH GALES, JR., and W. W. Seaton, and depended upon by other papers for Washington news. Jefferson had encouraged Samuel Harrison Smith to establish it when the government was first transferred to the new capital, but it was later superseded as an administration organ by Jacksonian papers.

These papers, at $8.00 or $10.00 a year, were too expensive for common laborers, who received perhaps less than $1.00 a day in wages; but with the advent of power presses and machine-made paper, and with the rise of the common people, papers of smaller size selling on the street at a penny a copy gradually gained the ascendancy over the mercantile "blanket sheets." Benjamin Day's New York *Sun* was the first of these small four-page penny papers to make a resounding success. Its emphasis on local news (including its police-court reports in witty vein) set the pattern for the penny press. Begun in 1833, it kept its price, while increasing its page size, until Civil War times. After the war CHARLES A. DANA became its editor (1868–97), emphasizing human-interest stories and an entertaining editorial page. In 1916 Frank A. Munsey bought it; and in 1950, twenty-five years after Munsey's death, it was merged with the *World-Telegram*. Some of the 19th-century's greatest papers began at one cent, though the *Sun* was the only one to keep that price after it became successful. Five more that started at a penny will be mentioned here.

After several false starts in pursuit of fame and fortune in America, JAMES GORDON BENNETT, Scottish born and bred, founded the New York *Herald* in 1835, gaining for it by 1860 a circulation of 77,000 (the largest in the world) and profits which, by his death in 1872, had made him one of the country's wealthiest men. The *Herald* was inclined to sensationalism in news. Bennett was a great innovator, having more "firsts" in newspaper techniques to his credit than any other publisher in the history of American journalism. Upon his death, James Gordon Bennett, Jr. edited the paper from 1872 to 1918,

operating for many years by cable from his Paris residence. The *Herald* was merged with the *Tribune* in 1924.

Three New York printers, William M. Swain, Aruna S. Abell, and Azariah H. Simmons pooled interests and founded the Philadelphia *Public Ledger* (1836–1942), and in 1937, the Baltimore *Sun*. After Simmons' death Swain ran the *Public Ledger* and Abell, the *Sun*. Both were outstanding successes, encouraging the new "magnetic telegraph" and other improvements. Swain retired with a fortune in 1864, and George W. Childs was the *Public Ledger's* distinguished editor for thirty years. The *Sun* had its troubles during the Civil War, but it managed to retain outstanding editorship even after the administrations of Abell's son and grandson had ended, and it is still highly regarded by many.

HORACE GREELEY had tried a cheap-for-cash newspaper in New York several months before the *Sun* was begun, but he and his printer partner failed dismally in the attempt; in 1841 when he founded the *Tribune*, he tried again, and was losing money when he brought in the astute Thomas McElrath as business partner. From then on things went better, and the *Tribune* and *Herald*, each now sold at two cents, became great competitors for many years. The latter was always ahead in circulation, but the former's *Weekly Tribune* was remarkably popular and influential, especially in transplanted New England groups settled now from New York State westward to Kansas. Greeley himself, with all his eccentricities, stands out as probably the greatest editor in the history of American journalism. Distinguished as an enterprising newsman, even more distinguished as an effective editorial writer with a style that makes his *Tribune* articles as fresh, lucid, and persuasive today as when they were penned, he was most notable for a lifelong devotion to the principle of giving a hearing to all, minorities and majorities alike. Following Greeley's death in 1872 (after his defeat for the Presidency in that year), another great editor, WHITELAW REID, came to the *Tribune*; and the Reid family controlled it until the sale to John Hay Whitney in 1958 of what had become the *Herald Tribune*.

The *New York Times* was founded by HENRY J. RAYMOND and two financiers, George Jones and Edward B. Wesley, in 1851. During its first year it was a penny paper, then raised to two cents. Raymond, an experienced journalist, made the paper a news success, and editorially tried to avoid the "low moral tone" of the *Herald* on the one hand and the "isms" of the *Tribune* on the other. His brilliant career was cut short at the age of forty-nine (1869), and Jones took over, making his most spectacular contribution by a crusade against the Tweed Ring. But in competition with the new Pulitzer-Hearst journalism of the eighties and nineties the *Times* had declined to a a friendly receivership, with a daily $1,000 loss, when ADOLPH S. OCHS took it over in 1896. Only two years later, when he challenged the "yellow papers" on their own price level of one-cent per copy, did Ochs start the upsurge that was to make the *Times* (in some respects, at least) America's foremost newspaper. His policy was to forego sensationalism as such, print a large quantity and great variety of important news, and include in full many public documents. On the death of Ochs in 1935, ARTHUR HAYS SULZBERGER, a son-in-law, came into control.

One other great New York journal, a survivor from the early partisan era and never a penny paper, was the *Evening Post,* founded by Alexander Hamilton and friends in 1801 and edited for half a century (1829–78) by the poet WILLIAM CULLEN BRYANT. As editor, Bryant was a great liberal, ever defending free commerce, free speech, free soil. Henry Villard bought the paper in 1881 and soon placed Edwin Lawrence Godkin in charge as editor; Godkin, English born and educated, had a critical mind, was a moderate liberal, and doubtless exerted no little influence. In its later phase the New York *Post,* under the management of Dorothy Schiff, daughter of the banker Mortimer L. Schiff, became a tabloid of strongly liberal tendencies.

Meanwhile some great papers had grown up in the West and South. The earliest western papers were precarious weeklies designed to promote settlement in their regions, or to uphold party doctrines, or both. Pioneer adventurers were the Pittsburgh *Gazette* (1786–   ), sponsored in its early years by Hugh Henry Brackenridge, author of *Modern Chivalry,* a classic picaresque novel of early American politics; and the Lexington *Kentucky Gazette* (1787–1848).

By the 1890's Chicago had grown to be a great newspaper center second only (if at all) to New York. John Calhoun founded its first paper, the *Weekly Democrat,* in 1833; three years later "Long John" Wentworth bought it, edited it aggressively, made it a daily, and sold it in 1861 to the burgeoning *Tribune.* The latter paper was begun in 1847 and had a hard time until Joseph Medill, Dr. Charles H. Ray, and three other partners gained control in 1855. Ray and Medill did much to promote the political fortunes of Abraham Lincoln. The able Horace White was the *Tribune's* editor from 1866 to 1874; but it was not until Medill, who had been serving as the city's mayor, bought complete control and took over as editor in 1874 that it began to win the dominance in Chicago journalism that it still retains. Fifteen years after Medill's death in 1899 two of his grandsons, ROBERT R. McCORMICK and Joseph Medill Patterson, came into management of the paper and ran it successfully as a strong local ("Chicagoland") and Republican newspaper. Patterson's interests were eventually drawn away mainly to New York journalism, but Colonel McCormick's control did not falter until his death in 1955. Chief competitor of the *Tribune* in the pre-Medill years was the *Times* (1854–95), which, under Wilbur F. Storey's editorship (1861–78), was a sensational and eccentric paper; for a few days during June, 1864, it was suspended by the military on account of its Copperhead sym-

pathies. Outstanding among other Chicago papers was the *Daily News,* founded by Melville E. Stone in 1876.

Among the South's great papers was the New Orleans *Picayune,* begun in 1836 by GEORGE W. KENDALL and Francis Lumsden, who named it for the coin at which it was sold. In the war with Mexico (1846–47) Kendall became the first outstanding regularly employed war correspondent in history; and much of the news of that war came to eastern papers through New Orleans. Through a series of mergers, New Orleans, which for half a century had several competing newspapers at a time, became in the 20th century a city with a single newspaper ownership—the *Times-Picayune* in the morning and the *States* in the evening. In Atlanta the *Constitution* (1868–   ) gained much prestige through the editorship of HENRY W. GRADY in the eighties, and later of Evan P. Howell and his son Clark. In Louisville, Kentucky, GEORGE D. PRENTICE, poet, wit, and journalist, founded the *Journal* in 1831; after the war it gained wide recognition as the *Courier-Journal* under the editorship of the brilliant HENRY WATTERSON.

No previous war in history had been covered so thoroughly by eyewitness correspondents as was the American Civil War. More than 150 "specials" served northern papers during the conflict, and at least that many more wrote occasional reports of military operations for newspapers or magazines. The New York *Herald* was said to have had thirty or forty correspondents on various fronts during the last year of the war, and several other papers sent out more than a dozen each. Telegraph facilities were not always available, and correspondents often had to make long journeys on horseback or on foot to get their reports through. Although the great papers were limited in size to eight six-column pages, they often gave more than a dozen columns to war reports, and some were able to provide occasional front-page maps of the war areas.

In the booming decade following the Civil War the number of daily papers in the United States increased by about three-fourths; but it was not until the mid-eighties, under the stimulation of JOSEPH PULITZER's New York *World,* that what came to be called the New Journalism was developed. Pulitzer had come to St. Louis from Hungary in 1865, a penniless immigrant boy, and soon distinguished himself as a reporter on the *Westliche Post* (1857–1938), then conducted by CARL SCHURZ and Emil Preetorius. By 1878 he was able to combine the expiring *Dispatch* and the recently established *Post* to form the *Post-Dispatch,* which soon became the leading morning paper of St. Louis and a strong competitor of the morning *Globe-Democrat* (1872–   ), then under the able editorship of Joseph B. McCullagh. But Pulitzer was not satisfied with success in a midwestern city; his eyes were upon the country's greatest journalistic forum—New York. He was thirty-seven when he came to that city in 1883 and bought the *World.* The *World* had been begun as a religious type of daily in 1860, and was ably edited with a political emphasis by Manton Marble in the seventies; now it was rescued from the doldrums (and the grasp of Jay Gould) and made into the most sensational, newsy, stunt-loving, and crusading paper the country had yet seen. It was soon issuing the largest paper (sixteen pages for two cents) to the largest circulation, and had the largest advertising patronage of any American newspaper. Its editorial page was strong and advocated many reforms; the record-breaking Sunday supplements promoted, by degrees, newspaper illustration.

WILLIAM RANDOLPH HEARST, son of a California mining magnate, George Hearst, studied the Pulitzer methods with care and first experimented with them on a paper his father had bought for political purposes, the San Francisco *Examiner* (1865—   ). Journalism in that city had begun in 1847; chief papers in the early period had been the *Alta California* (1849–91), notable for contributions of such literary figures as Mark Twain and Bret Harte; and the *Chronicle* (1865—   ), founded by Michel H. and Charles de Young. But young Hearst's *Examiner* soon outdistanced competition, and when, after his father's death, his mother made available to him cash resources of $7,500,000, W. R. Hearst invaded New York to challenge Pulitzer's supremacy. In 1895 he bought the *Journal,* which had been founded in 1882 by Joseph Pulitzer's estranged brother Albert, hired away from the *World* some of its best talent, outdid that paper in its sensational news and Sunday features and also in its large-type "scare heads." By 1897 the *World* and the *Journal* were running rival series of comic pages in their Sunday supplements, featuring the "Yellow Kid," and plastering the town with advertisements of this curious figure. This practice gave rise to the expression "yellow journalism," denoting a formula that included scare-head make-up, lavish use of pictures, frauds of various kinds (faked interviews, pseudo science, "composite" photography), Sunday supplements with colored comics, and ostentatious crusades in behalf of the common people. Shortly after the turn of the century, with the *World's* gradual withdrawal from this kind of rowdy competition and Ochs' success with the *Times,* which confined itself to "all the news that's *fit* to print," "yellow journalism" as a movement tended to subside.

The Spanish-American War received much of the "yellow" treatment, however. Indeed, it is probable that the sensational handling of Spanish "atrocities" in Cuba by a number of papers had much to do with provoking that conflict. For several months during and after the war the circulations of the *Journal* and *World* ran well above the million mark.

A western paper that long followed the "yellow" formula was the Denver *Post* (1892–   ), conducted for many years by Fred G. Bonfils and Harry H. Tammen. The first Denver paper was the *Rocky Mountain News,* established at the time of the Colorado gold rush in 1859; but when Bonfils and Tammen bought the little *Post* in 1895, they proceeded to make it blatant with red headlines and sensational in content and treatment. It was, however, decidedly paternalistic in its attitude toward the people of the "Rocky Mountain Empire." Tammen died in 1924, but Bonfils continued his belligerent career until his death in 1933. Under E. P. Hoyt the *Post* maintained a position of less obstreperous but no less real influence in its region.

A distinguished paper that attained success, as did the *New York Times,* on the basis of an opposition to "yellow" journalism was the CHRISTIAN SCIENCE MONITOR, founded by Mary Baker Eddy in Boston in 1908. Though sectarian in only a page or two, the *Monitor* gave minimal attention to crime and disaster, and emphasized the arts and mutual understanding of peoples.

A postscript to the "yellow journalism" period was the one marked by what was dubbed the "gutter journalism" of some of the early tabloid newspapers. Small page-size was, of course, nothing new in the long history of American papers; but when Joseph M. Patterson and Robert R. McCormick (of the Chicago *Tribune*) started the New York *Daily News* in 1919 with sixteen four-column pages containing copious illustration and emphasis on crime-and-sex sensation, it was a new departure. Easy to read on the subway, lively and entertaining, by the early forties it reached 2,000,000 circulation—largest ever attained by an American daily. By that time Patterson, the paper's manager, had toned down its sensationalism very considerably. Not so the competitive "tabs" that had sprung up, however—BERNARR MACFARDDEN's *Daily Graphic* (1924–32), nicknamed the "Pornographic"; Hearst's *Daily Mirror* (1924—   ), which immediately became a strong competitor in "the war of the 'tabs'"; and eleven papers appearing in nine other cities in the five years following the appearance of the *Daily News.* After the reform of Patterson's paper, however, the tabloids began to lose their more sensational character and to be distinguished by (1) smaller page size, (2) copious illustration, and (3) condensed and lively news presentation. Among the later tabloids established on this formula was the Chicago *Times* (1929), combined in 1948 with Marshall Field's *Sun* (1941) as the *Sun-Times.*

Coverage of two world wars and an undeclared war in Korea was an ordeal by fire for the United States press. Old-style war correspondence was impossible, it was soon learned, in a new-style war. In the early stages of World War I only one correspondent was accredited to accompany British forces in France—Frederick Palmer of the Associated Press. Nevertheless, many American correspondents were working out of Paris, Brussels, and "somewhere in France," and more came with the American Expeditionary Force. By 1915 it was estimated that as many as five hundred men were at work on the various fronts for American newspapers and periodicals. During World War II the U.S. War Department accredited 1,186 American correspondents and news officials, and the Navy Department 460 more. (These figures are for the whole of the war, and there were probably not much over five hundred on duty at any one time.) Press coverage of the Korean conflict was expensive in lives, in suffering, and in money. Semiofficial estimates place the number of those who visited the war area during the hostilities at six hundred, of whom seventeen were killed.

Critics of the press had much to say in the 20th century about the disappearance of "personal journalism." It is true that the increased complexity of newspaper organization (with publishers, editors, managing editors, executive editors, news editors, and assorted types of managers) has tended to reduce the prestige of any "top man," but nevertheless many newspaper personalities became well known nationally in this century. The syndicated columnists writing on public affairs represented one phalanx of this new personal journalism—such men as David Lawrence, Mark Sullivan, Walter Lippmann, Arthur Brisbane, Heywood Broun, Westbrook Pegler, Drew Pearson, Marquis Childs, and James Reston. Another phalanx—this one of publisher-editors—was equally well known through individual personalities. W. R. Hearst and Colonel McCormick were famous, although they did comparatively little writing; on the other hand, John S. Knight, of the Knight Newspapers, Erwin D. Canham, of the Christian Science Monitor, and Roy Roberts, of the Kansas City Star, were highly articulate. Roberts carried forward the tradition of the Star, which had been founded in 1880 by William Rockhill Nelson, a man of strong personality; its policy through the years had been low circulation rates, heavy regional coverage, and strong advocacy of local progress and reforms.

The small-city daily field also developed some interesting personalities. This had been true in earlier years, when SAMUEL BOWLES made the Springfield, Massachusetts, Republican (1844–1947 as a daily) a paper of high prestige and influence, and Joseph R. Hawley made the Hartford Courant (1837—   as a daily) respected and powerful. In the latter decades of the 19th century two Kansas editors became famous for their writing in small-city dailies—WILLIAM ALLEN WHITE, of the Emporia Gazette (1890—   ), and EDGAR WATSON HOWE, of the Atchison Globe (1877—   ). Both these men distinguished themselves also in the fields of fiction and the essay. Editors of community weeklies (once known as the "country weeklies" of the smaller towns) were, naturally, well-known personalities to their readers. These papers (including weeklies, semiweeklies and triweeklies) reached their largest number, close to 14,000, in 1928. By 1960 they had declined, largely through mergers, to about 10,000; but they were, in general, far better equipped and better edited than in the twenties.

The great wire news agencies were, of course, more impersonal, though the increasing use of by-lines helped to overcome that detriment. The New York Associated Press was organized by six papers of that city in 1848 to co-operate in news-gathering, and it was soon selling its service to groups in other cities and regions. In the eighties the growth of one of these groups, the Western Associated Press, and the competition of an independent service called the United Press forced a realignment and the organization in 1893 of the modern Associated Press. The old U.P. collapsed in 1897, and immediately the Scripps-McRae papers set up their own Press Association, to become ten years later the modern United Press. Hearst set up his International News Service in 1909; it was merged with the U.P. in 1958 to become the United Press International.

The first general syndicates handling newspaper materials were those conducted by IRVING BACHELLER and S. S. McCLURE, begun in 1883 and 1884 respectively. They specialized in fiction, humor, and news and gossip letters. By 1960 the number of such services had increased to over two hundred, and the kinds of matter offered had proliferated amazingly. There were more than five hundred "columns" of one kind or another and about the same number of cartoons, panels, and comic strips, as well as more than a thousand specialized offerings ranging from astrology to outboard boating.

Those who deplore a decay in "personal journalism" commonly link with that complaint a criticism of sameness in American newspapers, caused by the use of the wire news services and syndicates and also by the growth of "chains" and consolidations.

Newspaper "chains," later to be called "ownership groups," doubtless began with the interests that Benjamin Franklin, James Parker, and Isaiah Thomas held for a time in papers they had helped their apprentices to set up in various colonial towns. But the first spectacular group was the one organized by E. W. SCRIPPS in the last two decades of the 19th century. Scripps' first paper was the Cleveland Press (1878—   ), originally called the Penny Press. He bought the Cincinnati Post (1881—   ) in 1883 and put Milton A. McRae in as business manager, but it was not until 1895 that the Scripps-McRae League began to expand rapidly. By 1914 it was publishing twenty-three dailies. The Scripps formula was to choose a city of 50,000 to 100,000, start a new paper at one cent, put in a promising young man as manager on a stock-ownership basis, and champion the causes of labor and the common people. If the paper appeared to be a failure after a year or two, it was dropped. In 1920 Roy W. Howard was brought in as a partner; when Scripps retired in 1922 in favor of his son Robert P. Scripps, the firm became Scripps-Howard. Altogether, E. W. Scripps, Scripps-McRae, and Scripps-Howard founded or purchased fifty-seven daily papers (many of them the results of mergers), twenty of which remained to the group in 1960. Scripps-Howard entered the New York field in 1927 by the purchase of the Telegram, famous evening associate of the Herald; and four years later they created the sensation of those times by buying the World from the

Pulitzer heirs. The morning *World* was killed at once and the evening edition was merged in the *World-Telegram;* then in 1950 the *Sun* was also purchased, merged, and its name added to the title.

The *Telegram* and the famous old *Sun* had been the only papers left of the ambitious attempt of Frank A. Munsey to build a great newspaper group of his own. Munsey made, in fact, two such attempts. The first, pursued during the first fifteen years of the century, consisted of buying, founding, merging. and killing papers in Boston, New York, Philadelphia, and Baltimore. Though this first round was unsuccessful, Munsey soon returned to the game, this time not so much with the intention of putting together a chain of papers as of "cleaning up" the New York newspaper field by buying, killing off, and merging properties in order to create a more profitable situation for the industry. His manipulations, in which he destroyed four papers, ended with his death in 1925. He left a fortune of $20,000,000, mostly to the Metropolitan Museum of Art.

The basis of the great Hearst group comprised the San Francisco *Examiner,* the New York *Journal* (with the *American* as morning edition 1901–37), the Boston *American* (1904—   ), and the Chicago *American* (founded as *Journal,* 1900, then called *American* and since 1937, *Herald-American*); but in the years 1913–29 Hearst bought or founded twenty-seven more papers, as well as six magazines, two wire services, a leading feature syndicate and a syndicated Sunday supplement, a newsreel service, and a motion-picture production company. He was in financial trouble, however, when the money panic of 1929 came along, and in 1937 he was forced to turn over his newspaper and magazine properties to a voting trust, which succeeded in bringing order out of a confusion of holding companies, and sold a number of the less profitable operations. But the Hearst group has owned, at one time or another, as many as thirty-seven dailies, chiefly in large cities. The founder died in 1951, and the group was thereafter conducted by his sons. In 1962 there were thirteen dailies in the group.

Another large group was built up, beginning in the 1920's, by Samuel I. Newhouse. By the end of 1955 there were thirteen Newhouse dailies, including the St. Louis *Globe-Democrat,* the Portland *Oregonian* (1850—   ) and the Birmingham, Alabama, *News* (1888—   ).

Newspaper mergers became, in the 20th century, a matter of concern to social observers. These mergers, or "consolidations," which followed the pattern of development in other industries, have served to reduce the number of daily papers in the United States from 2,334 at the turn of the century to 1,850 in 1960 (Ayer Directory figures for years preceding dates of Directory issue), and they have brought more than half the cities of over 100,000 population into single-ownership situations—that is, a single

newspaper, or two operated by the same corporation. Five factors combined to bring about this situation.

(1) The rise of independent journalism, which has increased steadily since the campaign of 1872, has destroyed the necessity of maintaining competitive partisan journals. Some 800 were "independent" in the campaign of 1960, and comparatively few were what might be called bigoted partisans.

(2) Advertisers found it cheaper to buy space in one paper with a general circulation, even at increased rates, than in two with overlapping coverage.

(3) Combination of a morning with an evening paper, allowing twenty-four-hour operation of a single plant, made for economy.

(4) Mounting costs, caused partly by the necessity of producing better modern papers, forced the elimination of competition.

(5) This competition became increasingly unnecessary as readers, enjoying a growing supply of news and entertainment from radio and television, news magazines, paperbacks, and other sources, tended to turn to one morning and one evening paper in each city, thereby weakening the others.

Three factors, however, seemed to indicate the beginnings of a change in this situation, and perhaps a revolution in both the business and the profession of American journalism. Technological advances pointed to eventual abandonment of expensive hot-metal processes in favor of coldtype processes and offset printing, of increased teletypesetting, and of more automation in other production departments—all of which might lead to cheaper plant facilities and an upturn in the number of papers. The phenomenal mid-century increase in suburban and exurban journalism tended to reduce the dominance of the great metropolitan papers. Finally, the rise of television has affected adversely those papers that overemphasized entertainment features, while it enhanced the prestige and prosperity of those which stress the newspaper functions of record and review.

FRANK LUTHER MOTT

Newsweek. A weekly review of the news founded in Dayton, Ohio, in 1933, *Newsweek's* first editor was Samuel T. Williamson. Three years later it was absorbed by *Today,* a journal of public affairs, founded in New York in 1933. RAYMOND MOLEY, editor-in-chief of *Today,* and Vincent Astor, its principal stockholder, decided to keep both the name and the original format of the Dayton weekly. Shortly after the merger, Malcolm Muir, then president of McGraw-Hill, became editor; in 1961 Osborn Elliott succeeded him. *Newsweek's* writers are masters of the capsule phrase, and its pages report the week's doings objectively and succinctly. In 1961 the *Washington Post* purchased the Astor Foundation's majority stock interest in *Newsweek.*

Philip Leslie Graham, president of the *Post*, became Chief Executive Officer of *Newsweek*.

New Thought, a twentieth-century nonconformist group, best described as a school of Christianity. WILLIAM JAMES in *The Varieties of Religious Experience* (1902) called it "the religion of healthy-mindedness," and the American people's "only decidedly original contribution to the systematic philosophy of life." It is closely allied to Unity, Divine Science, Science of Mind, and other such groups, which are part of the New Thought Alliance; it also has points in common with Christian Science. The healer **Phineas Parkhurst Quimby** (b. Lebanon, N.H., Feb. 16, 1802—d. Jan. 16, 1866), and particularly Emerson and his transcendental philosophy, have been channels for its expression. A notable exponent of it in England was Judge Thomas Troward, whose book, *The Edinburgh Lectures* (1909) was called by William James "Far and away the ablest statement of that philosophy that I have met." New Thought literature is abundant, and includes Troward's *The Creative Process in the Individual* (1915); Emmet Fox's *The Sermon on the Mount* (1934); C. O. Southard's *Truth Ideas of an M.D.* (1943); and Ervin Seale's *Ten Words that Will Change Your Life* (1954).

Newton, A[lfred] Edward (b. Philadelphia, Aug. 20, 1863 d. Sept. 29, 1940), businessman, bibliophile, publisher. Newton made a fortune in the electrical equipment business, thereafter devoted himself to collecting, studying, and writing about books. Among his writings are *The Amenities of Book-Collecting and Kindred Affections* (1918); *A Magnificent Farce and Other Diversions of a Book-Collector* (1921); *This Book-Collecting Game* (1928); *A Tourist in Spite of Himself* (1930); *End Papers* (1933). Two plays that he wrote—*Doctor Johnson* (1923) and *Mr. Strahan's Dinner Party* (1930)—testify to his dominant interest, which brought about his election in 1930 as the first American president of the Johnson Club in London. His genial personality was transferred to his essays. At his death his collection was dispersed by sale, so that it might not be "entombed" in a museum. His son, E. Swift Newton, paid tribute to him in a brochure entitled *A.E.N.* (1955).

Newton, Joseph Fort (b. Decatur, Tex., July 21, 1878—d. Jan. 24, 1950), clergyman, writer. Newton began as a Baptist minister, went on to found several nonsectarian churches, was finally ordained in the Protestant Episcopal Church. He became nationally known for his sermons and his books. John Haynes Holmes held that Newton's sermons were "among the great homiletical literature of our age." Newton also wrote a newspaper column called "Everyday Living." Among his books: *David Swing, Poet Preacher* (1909); *Abraham Lincoln* (1910); *Lincoln and Herndon* (1910); *Sermons and Lectures* (1912); *Wesley and Woolman* (1914); *Some Living Masters of the Pulpit* (1922); *Preaching in London* (1923); *Preaching in New York* (1924);

The Religion of Masonry (1926); *The Sermon in the Making* (1932); *River of Years* (autobiography, 1946); *The One Great Church* (1947).

New World, The (1946), edited by Stefan Lorant. The subtitle sufficiently describes this book: "The First Pictures of America made by John White and Jacques Le Moyne and Engraved by Theodore de Bry; with Contemporary Narratives of the Huguenot Settlement in Florida, 1562–1565, and the Virginia Colony, 1585–1590, edited and annotated." This book contains the first reproductions of illustrations of the New World by Jacques Le Moyne, a member of RENÉ DE LAUDONNIÈRE'S expedition to Florida (1563–65), and John White, who was sent by SIR WALTER RALEGH in 1585 to explore the territory of Virginia. The narrative is drawn from the writings of various Elizabethan explorers, which have been rewritten by the editor.

New World Writing. Beginning in 1947, this series of magazines in book form was published twice a year for sixteen issues by the New American Library; it pioneered in presenting avant-garde literature to a mass audience. It had many imitators, among them DISCOVERY, THE EVERGREEN REVIEW, THE NOBLE SAVAGE.

New York, A History of, from the Beginning of the World to the End of the Dutch Dynasty, by Diedrich Knickerbocker (1809), a satirical account by WASHINGTON IRVING. Irving began the book as a burlesque, became more serious as he advanced, and in the course of his narrative gave a good many historical facts. The work was intended as a kindly satire on the Dutch who first settled New York, but their descendants were offended by it. Book IV goes beyond the Dutch to satire of Jefferson, pictured as Governor WILLIAM KIEFT. In later editions Irving made some expurgations. Knickerbocker is a character whom Irving used later in *The Sketch Book* (1819) to tell the story of RIP VAN WINKLE. The book, as the title promises, begins ironically with the creation of the world, the discovery of America, the settlement of the New Netherlands. There are descriptions of the Battery, the "Boweric," Bowling Green, Dutch manners and morals, leading Dutch personages—some treated not too gently. Legends of an older day are recorded. Irving, defending himself against attacks, asserted justly, "Before the appearance of my work the popular traditions of our city were unrecorded; the peculiar and racy customs and usages derived from our Dutch progenitors were unnoticed or regarded with indifference, or adverted to with a sneer." The book is still good reading.

New Yorker, The. Harold Ross's *New Yorker*, begun in 1925, originally belonged to a class of urban weeklies that had long flourished in American cities by giving special attention to amusements, society, and local interests. But, like most of the more successful ventures in this field, it soon found special interests to exploit. Ross recruited a staff of distinguished talent which, under his direction, produced a brilliant and successful literary magazine. It retained its full schedules of the theater and other entertainment in New York and its "Talk of the Town" and much of its remaining contents dealt with New York activities and people, but a considerable part of its fiction, verse, reviewing, and special articles was far wider in scope. Its "PROFILES"—a type of informal biographical treatment of interesting persons—eventually included dissertations on geographical, anthropological, and historical matters that sometimes ran to serial length without losing their appeal to educated readers. A quiet satire often flavored *New Yorker* commentary and articles.

Leading contributors have been Robert Benchley, Wolcott Gibbs, Ogden Nash, John O'Hara, Dorothy Parker, S. J. Perelman, J. D. Salinger, Rebecca West, and Edmund Wilson. Ross died in 1951 and under the editorship of William Shawn, there seems to have been little change in the magazine. See HUMOR IN THE U.S.

New-Yorker, The. HORACE GREELEY'S *New-Yorker*, begun in 1834, was one of the many week-end miscellanies published throughout the first two thirds of the 19th century for Sunday reading—a genre ended only by the rise of the Sunday editions of daily papers. Greeley's paper printed tales, essays, news, reviews, statistics, and even music. Most of its contents "borrowed" from books, magazines, and newspapers. Among Greeley's editorial assistants were Park Benjamin, RUFUS W. GRISWOLD, and HENRY J. RAYMOND. An interesting periodical, the *New-Yorker* deserved more success than it ever attained. It was merged in the weekly edition of the *Tribune* when Greeley began that paper.

New York Idea, The (first prod. Nov. 19, 1906), a comedy by Langdon Mitchell. This is the story of the tangled marital affairs of two prominent social figures.

New York Ledger, The. *The Merchants' Ledger,* an illustrated weekly magazine founded in 1847, was purchased in 1851 by Robert Bonner, who changed the name in 1855 to *The New York Ledger.* He edited it until 1887 and made it the most successful magazine of its day, partly by startling innovations in advertising technique, partly by recruiting famous writers. Bryant, Tennyson, Longfellow, and the Cary sisters contributed poems; Mrs. Harriet Beecher Stowe, Mrs. E. D. E. N. Southworth, Dickens, and above all SYLVANUS COBB wrote fiction. Cobb was just the sort of storyteller Bonner liked: sentimental, sensational, and pure as the driven snow. Readers could submit their problems to Bonner, and advice would be given by men like Henry Ward Beecher and Edward Everett. In 1898 the *Ledger* became a monthly, in 1903 it ceased publication.

New York Public Library, The. Consolidated by the union of the Astor, Lenox, and other libraries in 1895, this great New York City institution consists of two main divisions: the reference department, concentrated in a massive building at Fifth Ave., and 42nd St., and a circulation division of many branches serving three boroughs. In 1948, when the library celebrated the centennial of its founding, it contained more than three million books. It is today second only to the Library of Congress in the extent of its collections. It has a print shop, does its own binding, and prints many valuable bulletins; it issues a reading list, *Branch Library Book News,* ten times a year.

New York Times. See ADOLPH S. OCHS; HENRY JARVIS RAYMOND; NEWSPAPERS.

Nez Percé Indians. The name means "pierced noses" and was given by French trappers and others to a branch of the Sahaptin or Shapahtin tribe living on the middle Columbia and lower Snake Rivers in what is now Oregon, Idaho, and Washington. They were a wandering tribe, living mainly on salmon and roots. They are described in Washington Irving's *Adventures of Captain Bonneville, U.S.A.* (1837). The discovery of gold in 1860 brought a swarm of gold-diggers and land-hungry squatters to Oregon. Some of the less farsighted Indians signed away their lands, but a group led by CHIEF JOSEPH refused to give up the beautiful Wallowa Valley in eastern Oregon. In 1877 American troops attempted to force them to leave and enter a reservation. Rather than do this, Chief Joseph and his people struck their tepees and headed for the Canadian border, a distance of nearly 1,200 miles. With less than three hundred warriors, Chief Joseph outmaneuvered and outfought American troops in fifteen engagements, but was finally obliged to surrender. He told his own story in *An Indian's View of Indian Affairs* (*North American Review,* April, 1879). Robert Payne wrote a novel about him, *The Chieftain* (1953).

The Nez Percés were settled on a reservation in Indian Territory in 1879; they were then described as a most intelligent, religious, and industrious people. But the climate was unsuitable, and their numbers shrank to 1,400 in 1885, when they moved to a reservation in Washington. They are now on an Idaho reservation. Herbert J. Spinden wrote a full account of their religion, poetry, and oratory in *The Nez Percé Indians* (1908); Lucullus V. McWhorter told the story of the Nez Percé War of 1877 in *Hear Me, My Chiefs* (1952); Francis Haines wrote on *The Nez Percés: Tribesmen of the Columbian Plateau* (1955). Franz Boas edited *Folk-Tales of Salishan and Sahaptin Tribes* (1917), and other stories were told by Archie Phinney in *Nez Percé Texts* (1934).

Nichols, Anne. See ABIE'S IRISH ROSE.

Nichols, Charles Lemuel (b. Worcester, Mass., May 29, 1851—d. Feb. 19, 1929), physician, bibliographer. Dr. Nichols specialized in the enterprises of ISAIAH THOMAS, about whose imprints he wrote a book in 1900, following it up with a full account of him (1912). He also compiled a *Checklist of Maine, New Hampshire, and Vermont Almanacs* (1929).

Nichols, Thomas Low (b. probably Orford, N.H., 1815—d. 1901), physician, novelist, reformer, memoirist. Nichols was a rebel and a radical who took refuge in England when he disagreed with the government about the Civil War. He wrote several novels, one named *Marriage* (1854, with his wife Mary Sergeant Nichols [1810–1884]); also *Ellen Ramsay* (1843); *The Lady in Black* (1844); and *Raffle for a Wife* (1845). Among his nonfictional works were *Journal in Jail* (1840); *Women, in All Ages and Nations* (1849); and his astute *Forty Years of American Life, 1821–61* (2 v., 1864). His wife also wrote an autobiographical novel, *Mary Lyndon, or, Recollections of a Lifetime* (1855).

Nicholson, Kenyon (b. Crawfordsville, Ind., May 21, 1894—   ), teacher, playwright. Nicholson was press agent for STUART WALKER's Murat Theater in Indianapolis; in 1921 he joined the Extension Division of Columbia University as instructor in dramatic composition. His play THE BARKER (1927) had a successful Broadway run. *Sailor Beware!* (1933), a farce written with Charles Robinson, was made into the musical comedy *Nice Goin'!* (1939). He also wrote *Honor Bright* (with MEREDITH NICHOLSON, 1924); *Sally and Company* (1925); *The Meal Ticket* (1926); *Here's to Your Health* (with C. Knox, 1927); *Eva the Fifth* (1928); *Taxi* (1929); *Hollywood Plays* (1930); *Words and Music* (1930); *Torch Song* (1930); *Apple of His Eye* (1945); *Out West of Eighth* (1951).

Nicholson, Meredith (b. Crawfordsville, Ind., Dec. 9, 1866—d. Dec. 21, 1947), novelist, diplomat. Meredith Nicholson is best remembered for three mystery novels, *The House of a Thousand Candles* (1905), *Rosalind at Red Gate* (1907), and *The Siege of the Seven Suitors* (1910). He was U.S. minister to Paraguay (1933–34) and Nicaragua (1938–44). See A HOOSIER CHRONICLE.

Nick of the Woods, or the Jibbenainosay (1837), a novel by ROBERT MONTGOMERY BIRD. Bird's best novel, it was extremely popular in its day. Although the writing suffers occasionally from the stilted romanticism typical of James Fenimore Cooper and other writers of frontier fiction, the complexities of plot and character are exceptional. "Bloody Nathan," scorned by pioneers as a timid Quaker who abhors all violence—his nickname is mere mockery—is later identified as the feared killer of Indians, "Nick of the Woods." Yet he is seldom aware of the conflict between his two personalities. Bird describes the causes and symptoms of Nathan's split personality with remarkable psychological insight.

Most of the other characters are stereotypes. The virtuous hero and heroine utter platitudes; the Indians are brutish savages; "Roaring Ralph" Stackpole, the picaresque horse thief, is mildly amusing. But Bird's background as a dramatist shows up in his handling of plot. He keeps the reader's interest simply by maintaining unrelieved suspense for many pages. More subtle techniques, such as the growth of minor characters, are skillfully employed to unify the story and present new crises.

Nicolay, Helen (b. France, March 9, 1866—d. Sept. 12, 1954), historian, writer for children. From her childhood Helen Nicolay assisted her father J. G. NICOLAY with his life of Abraham Lincoln. She was asked to write a boy's life of Lincoln, and the result (1906) proved so successful that she wrote a number of similar books. Among them were *The Boy's Life of Ulysses S. Grant* (1909); *Personal Traits of Abraham Lincoln* (1912); *Our Nation in the Building* (1916); *The Book of American Wars* (1918); *Lincoln's Secretary, A Biography of John G. Nicolay* (1949).

Nicolay, J[ohn] G[eorge] (b. Bavaria, Feb. 26, 1832—d. Sept. 26, 1901), journalist, historian, biographer. Nicolay was brought to this country at the age of six. His father, a flour mill operator, moved frequently; the youth had little formal schooling. Nicolay clerked in a store, then became a printer's devil for the Pittsfield (Ill.) *Free Press*. He worked his way up until by 1854 he was editor and proprietor of the paper.

In 1851 Nicolay met his future collaborator, JOHN HAY. He sold the paper to become clerk to the Secretary of State of Illinois; in 1860 he was appointed private secretary to ABRAHAM LINCOLN. Through Nicolay's efforts Hay was added to Lincoln's secretarial staff. They were intimate witnesses of most of the important acts of Lincoln's administration and were completely trusted by him. Nicolay took many notes and Hay kept a diary. The two young men, with Lincoln's approval, embarked on a projected biography of Lincoln which was also to be a history of his era. After Lincoln's death the work had to be postponed for some years while Nicolay served, from 1865 to 1869, as United States Consul in Paris, and from 1872 until 1887 as Marshal of the U.S. Supreme Court. While still holding this position Nicolay began to collaborate with Hay on *Abraham Lincoln: A History*, which appeared in ten volumes in 1890. He produced two other works, *The Outbreak of the Rebellion* (1881) and *A Short Life of Abraham Lincoln* (1902), and also edited Lincoln's *Complete Works* (12 v., 1905) with Hay, although the actual editorial work was done by Francis D. Tandy.

Nicollet, Joseph Nicholas. See BALLOON HOAX.

Nicolson, Marjorie H[ope] (b. Yonkers, N.Y., Feb. 18, 1894—   ), teacher, literary historian, editor. After having taught at various universities, Miss Nicolson was called to Smith College in 1926 and remained there until 1941, when she began teaching in the graduate school of Columbia. Her books mix learned discourse with humor and fancy, so that nonacademic readers enjoy them. The best known of her books is *Voyages to the Moon* (1948), based on a course she gave at Smith called "Science and Imagination." Her book begins with the "Invasion from Mars" broadcast of 1938, goes on to the "flying saucers" of 1947, and continues with the numerous imaginative literary voyagers of the past. She also wrote *The Art of Description* (1926); *Conway Letters* (letters of the seventeenth century Platonist Henry More and Lady Anne Conway, 1930); *The Microscope and English Imagination* (1935); *A World in the*

Moon (1937); *Newton Demands the Muse* (1946); *The Breaking of the Circle* (1950).

Niebuhr, Reinhold (b. Wright City, Mo., June 21, 1892—d. June 1, 1971), theologian. Son of the pastor of an Evangelical church in Wright City, Niebuhr took his Bachelor of Divinity degree from Yale Divinity School in 1914 and his Master's of Art in 1915. He became pastor of the Bethel Evangelical Church in Detroit, where he served for thirteen years, taking an active interest in the labor problems of the automotive workers, and indicating his sympathy for the Socialist movement. In 1928 he left Detroit to join the faculty of Union Theological Seminary in New York, and two years later became professor of Applied Christianity. Niebuhr's interest in political morality and in the failure of modern Christianity to cope with secular problems is expressed in *Moral Man and Immoral Society* (1932). He rejects the liberal Christian tendency to substitute social and economic ills for original sin, thus making the idea of redemption dependent on social or historical development, or, as in the case of Marxism, on revolution and the destruction of certain social institutions. In *The Children of Light and the Children of Darkness* (1944) he attacks the moral irresponsibility of those who fail to come to grips with the problem of power; in *Christian Realism and Political Problems* (1953) he again takes issue with secular liberalism and with the Church, which has both sheltered social evils, maintained a political neutrality which was tantamount to a tacit consent to existing injustices, and ignored the powerful realities of the political situation by "being content with an insufferable sentimentality." He sees the problem of modern man as one in which power and technocracy have brought confusion and meaninglessness, and the task of Christianity as ministering responsibility to the world as well as to the spirit. Although his criticism of American churches has sometimes been unfavorably received, he is considered to be one of the most important and influential of American theologians. His other works include *The Nature and Destiny of Man* (2 v., 1941, 1943); *The Irony of American History* (1952); *The Self and the Drama of History* (1955); *Leaves from the Notebook of a Tamed Cynic* (1956); *Structure of Nations and Empires* (1959); *Essays in Applied Christianity* (1959); *Beyond Tragedy: Essays on the Christian Interpretation of History* (1961). Among those who have analyzed his ideas are Hans Hofman in *The Theology of Reinhold Niebuhr* (1956) and June Bingham in *Courage to Change: An Introduction to the Life and Thought of Reinhold Niebuhr* (1961). A number of scholars discuss his theology and influence in *Reinhold Niebuhr: His Religious, Social, and Political Thought* (1955), a symposium edited by C. W. Kegley and R. W. Bretall.

Nigger, The (1909; pub. and prod., 1910), a play by EDWARD SHELDON. This is one of the earliest and perhaps the most effective of the plays based on the familiar plot theme: man, in this instance the governor of a state, is told that he has Negro blood. The governor is about to sign a bill that will harm the financial interests of a cousin. The latter threatens to reveal the secret, but the governor signs the bill anyway. His fiancée at first rejects him, then rejoins him.

Nigger Heaven (1926), a novel by CARL VAN VECHTEN. Set in Harlem in the jazz era, this novel has its melodramatic episodes and closes with a murder of which the hero is falsely accused. It is noteworthy as the first true literary exploration of Negro life, in this instance made by a white writer with a deep sympathy for Negro sufferings and aspirations. The book takes its title from an old term for the topmost gallery of the theater—"That's what Harlem is," says the writer. "We sit in our places in the gallery of this New York theater and watch the white world sitting down below us in the good seats." The book is generally regarded as Van Vechten's best novel.

Night Before Christmas, The (Troy *Sentinel*, Dec. 23, 1823), a poem by Clement C. Moore. See A VISIT FROM ST. NICHOLAS.

Night Over Taos (1932), a regional drama by MAXWELL ANDERSON.

Niles, Blair [Rice] (b. Charlotte Co., Va., [?], 1888[?]—d. April 13, 1959), travel writer, novelist. With her first husband, WILLIAM BEEBE, she traveled extensively. Their trip together to Mexico resulted in *Two Bird Lovers in Mexico* (1905); she collaborated on *Our Search for a Wilderness* (1910). She continued her nomadic life after her marriage to Robert Niles, an architect and expert photographer. *Casual Wanderings in Ecuador* (1923), *Colombia, Land of Miracles* (1924), and *Black Haiti* (1926) were illustrated by her husband's photographs. In 1944 she received a gold medal from the Society of Women Geographers. *Condemned to Devil's Island* (1928), a sensational account of prison life, was followed by *Free* (1930), a sequel; *Strange Brother* (1931), a fictional study of a homosexual, was praised by Havelock Ellis. Other works include *Light Again* (1933); *Day of Immense Sun* (1936); *East by Day* (1941); *The James* (1939); *Martha's Husband: An Informal Portrait of George Washington* (1951).

Niles, Samuel (b. Block Island, R.I., May 1, 1674—d. May 1, 1762), clergyman, historian, poet, writer on theology. Niles took a charge in Braintree, Mass., and won considerable renown as a preacher and writer. His *Tristitiae Ecclesiarum* (1745) is an account of the New England churches; *God's Wonder-Working Providence for New England in the Reduction of Louisburg* (1747) is a tract in verse. He also wrote *Divers Important Gospel-Doctrines* (1752); his *Summary Historic Narrative of the Wars in New England with the French and Indians* was published long after his death in the *Collections* (1837, 1861) of the Massachusetts Historical Society.

Nimrod (included in *Rose of the Wind and Other Poems*, 1910), a narrative poem by ANNA

HEMPSTEAD BRANCH. It recounts the arrogant rebellion of Nimrod, the mighty hunter, against God; his building of the Tower of Babel in defiance of God; the defeat of the hunter by the confusion of tongues that since then has plagued the earth "with differing and hostile speech." Miss Branch took her main suggestion from the Old Testament but embroidered it with many inventions of her own. To some critics it has seemed a great poem; Louis Untermeyer spoke of its "epic sweep" and its "many moments of exalted imagery."

Nims, John Frederick (b. Muskegon, Mich., Nov. 20, 1913—   ), teacher, poet. A high-school English teacher, later a professor at the University of Notre Dame, Nims published several collections of verse, among them *The Iron Pastoral* (1947); *Knowledge of the Evening: Poems 1950–1960* (1960). He edited *The Poems of St. John of the Cross* (1959). Nims is a modernist; he indulges in tumultuous and sometimes fantastic figures of speech, and loves to play with words. He concentrates on images of modern life as is, particularly urban life. "Few poets so frankly exploit their day-by-day experiences," said Richard Wilbur. Yet at times he writes with passion, as in his powerful address to Detroit called *Race Riot*. His invariable brilliance made Dudley Fitts remark: "One longs for a blessed moment of dullness from time to time."

Nin, Anaïs (b. France, 1914—   ), novelist, short-story writer, dancer. Miss Nin's Cuban-born mother brought her to the United States as a child. Her education was irregular; she was largely self-taught. At the age of ten she had begun to keep a diary which later reached voluminous proportions. Out of this diary Miss Nin has taken material for several of her books, some of which were paid for by herself or printed on her own press.

Many of her narratives are frank exercises in psychiatry, done with realism and great expressive skill. Reviewing *Under a Glass Bell*, David Steinberg found "the atmosphere of madness or near-madness expressed in prose that frequently becomes brilliantly surrealist when reality is fused with dreams." She began with a study of D. H. Lawrence (1930), went on to *Winter of Artifice* (1939); *Under a Glass Bell and Other Stories* (1944); *This Hunger* (1945); *Ladders to Fire* (1946); *Children of the Albatross* (1947); *The House of Incest* (1949); *The Four-Chambered Heart* (1950); *A Spy in the House of Love* (1954); and *Seduction of the Minotaur* (1961).

1919 (1932), a novel by JOHN DOS PASSOS. This second novel in the trilogy U.S.A. carries into World War I the careers of the characters in THE FORTY-SECOND PARALLEL, beginning with Joe Williams, the wandering, battered, and hapless sailor. Four new characters are introduced: Dick Savage, an esthetic, idealistic young Harvard man; Eveline Hutchins, bored and seeking new sensations; "Daughter" (Anne Elizabeth Trent), a relief worker; and Ben Compton, a young Jewish anarchist. The grim stories of their lives are interspersed with passages of "the Newsreel," "the Camera Eye," and short, sardonic biographical sketches, all lending historical background and social dimension to the narrative episodes, as they did in *The Forty-Second Parallel*.

Noah, Mordecai M[anuel] (b. Philadelphia, July 19, 1785—d. March 22, 1851), playwright, lawyer, editor, public official. Noah, a man of many abilities, founded two or three papers, including *Noah's Times* and *Weekly Messenger*,

studied law and was admitted to the bar, served as sheriff, surveyor of Port of New York, and a judge of the court of sessions. In 1825 Noah sought to establish a Jewish colony on Grand Island in the Niagara River, but the project never materialized. In his theatrical ventures Noah was fervently patriotic. Perhaps his best-known play was a comedy, SHE WOULD BE A SOLDIER (1819). He also wrote *Paul and Alexis* (1812; later revived as *The Wandering Boys*, 1821); *The Siege of Tripoli* (1820); *Marion, or, The Hero of Lake George* (1821); and *The Grecian Captive* (1822). His plays were popular and were often revived. In addition Noah wrote *Travels in England, France, Spain, and the Barbary States* (1819).

Noah an' Jonah an' Cap'n John Smith (1921), a poem by DON MARQUIS. Possibly Marquis' most successful poem, this piece, in folkstory style, tells how the three famous sea adventurers have a post-mortem conference in heaven and reminisce comfortably.

noble savage, The. A semiannual magazine. The first number in paperbook format similar to that of NEW WORLD WRITING and DISCOVERY appeared in March 1960. The original editors were SAUL BELLOW, Keith Botsford, and Jack Ludwig. The title and "program" of the magazine remained a mystery until publication of the third number which stated: "We did not want to have a *literary* magazine. We wanted also to print memoirs, documents, personal essays, the views of originals and eccentrics. We hoped to have a magazine for writers, edited by writers —that is, people who think and feel and express themselves in that way." Conspicuously absent from the pages was any literary criticism, though there were articles on literary subjects. A section called "Ancestors" regularly reprinted forgotten works of merit by writers of the recent past: Samuel Butler, D. H. Lawrence, Isaac Babel. *The noble savage* quickly attracted the attention of a sizable, well-informed audience.

Nock, Albert Jay (b. 1873—d. Aug. 19, 1945), clergyman, editor, writer. From his childhood Nock was a prodigy and a maverick. He opposed American participation in the two World Wars and attributed it to the malign domination of our diplomacy by England. He was theoretically a follower of Jefferson and Henry George, but did not share their humanitarianism. Although he hated British propagandists, he looked kindly on Nazi "researches." For a time he lived in Brussels, came back to the United States to become an editor of *The Freeman*, later of the NEW REPUBLIC; he contributed to numerous other magazines.

Nock was an able, lively, and cranky writer whose books had a wide range. He wrote on Rabelais and Artemus Ward and edited their writings. With Francis Neilson he wrote *How Diplomats Make War* (1915; 2nd ed., rev. 1916). Under the pen name Historicus he analyzed *The Myth of a Guilty Nation* (1922). He wrote a witty book on *Jefferson* (1926) and another on *Henry George* (1939); and under the pen name Journeyman he published *The Book of Journeyman* (1930) and *A Theory of Education in the U.S.* (1932). Collections of his essays were made in *Doing the Right Thing and Other Essays* (1928) and *Free Speech and Plain Language* (1937). Autobiographical works were *Journal of These Days: June 1932–December 1933* (1934); *Memoirs of a Superfluous Man* (1943), largely an attack on democracy; and the posthumous *Journal of Forgotten Days: 1934–35* (1949).

Nokomis. The grandmother who reared HIAWATHA and taught him the legends of the Ojibways. Her name means "Daughter of the Moon."

Nolan, Philip. See MAN WITHOUT A COUNTRY.

Nook Farm. A real-estate development on the western limits of Hartford, Conn., which attracted some notable residents. Between 1871 and 1891 they included Harriet Beecher Stowe and her husband Calvin Stowe, Isabella Beecher Hooker, the Rev. Joseph Hopkins Twichell, Frederick Beecher Perkins, Charles Dudley Warner, and others. Mark Twain brought his bride Olivia to Hartford in 1871 and built a house on the land he bought at Nook Farm. A great scandal that rocked the community was the Tilton divorce suit that involved Henry Ward Beecher as an alleged adulterer. Kenneth R. Andrews wrote a vivid description of the

group in *Nook Farm: Mark Twain's Hartford Circle* (1950).

Noon Wine (1937), a novel by KATHERINE ANNE PORTER. The scene of this book is a dairy farm in Texas which is run rather reluctantly by Mr. Thompson, who regards the chores as woman's work, but who is married to an invalid, Ellie. The silent hard work of Mr. Helton, a taciturn and rather strange new hired man, puts the farm on a paying basis. After nearly nine years, their peace is disturbed by the arrival of Homer T. Hatch, a sly and devious man who inspires distrust in Thompson at once. When he accuses Helton of being an escaped lunatic and tries to capture him for profit, Thompson kills him, believing that Hatch has knifed Helton. Although no marks of wounds are found on Helton, Thompson is acquitted of Hatch's murder. Nevertheless, he is burdened with an overwhelming guilt and finally kills himself.

The story is told in a simple, clear manner with the touches of irony usual in Miss Porter's work. Her reticence in explanation and her love of minute psychological detail force the reader to arrive at his own conclusions as to what actually happened. With the help of the author's amazing power of characterization, the everyday level of existence, which she so beautifully portrays, is contrasted with a deeper spiritual level at which she only hints.

Nordhoff, Charles (b. Prussia, Aug. 31, 1830 —d. July 14, 1901), newspaperman, author. Nordhoff came to the United States as a child, served in the United States Navy, later in the merchant marine and on sailing vessels, wrote about his experiences in *Man-of-War Life* (1856), *The Merchant Vessel* (1856), and *Whaling and Fishing* (1856). This trilogy was published in a single volume, *Nine Years a Sailor* (1857), as *Life on the Ocean* (1874), and as *In Yankee Windjammers* (1940), the last edited by his grandson CHARLES BERNARD NORDHOFF. Nordhoff was on the staff of the New York *Evening Post* (1861–71) and the New York *Herald* (1874–90). Among his other books: *Stories of the Island World* (1857); *Secession Is Rebellion* (1860); *Cape Cod and All Along the Shore* (1868); *Communistic Societies of America* (1875); *The Cotton States* (1876).

Nordhoff, Charles Bernard (b. England, Feb. 1, 1887—d. April 11, 1947), novelist. Nordhoff, born of American parents abroad, was educated at Stanford and Harvard universities. He drove an ambulance in France in 1916 and later joined the Lafayette Flying Corps, where he met JAMES NORMAN HALL. In 1920 the two future collaborators went to Tahiti, where they remained for many years. *The Fledgling* (1919) is an account, in diary form, of Nordhoff's flying experiences during World War I. Both *The Pearl Lagoon*, adventures in the South Seas, and *Picaro*, a novel about two brothers in Guadaloupe whose destinies were bound up with airplanes, appeared in 1924. *The Derelict* (1925), another novel of adventure in the South Seas, was the last book Nordhoff wrote alone. From then until his death he worked with Hall. The most famous of their collaborations was a trilogy: MUTINY ON THE BOUNTY (1932), *Men Against the Sea* (1934), and *Pitcairn's Island* (1934).

Norman, Charles (b. Russia, May 9, 1904—   ), poet, painter, biographer. Norman was brought to America when he was five. At eighteen he sailed to South America as a seaman on a freighter, later lived in Paris and served in France during World War II. For twelve years, while employed as a staff writer and editor for the Associated Press, *Time,* and *PM,* he worked on a biography of Christopher Marlowe. After its publication in 1946 he devoted himself exclusively to painting and writing. He is perhaps best known for his biographies, which include *So Worthy a Friend: William Shakespeare* (1947); *Mr. Oddity: Samuel Johnson, LLD* (1951); *Shepherd of the Ocean: Sir Walter Raleigh* (1952); *Rake Rochester: John Wilmot* (1954); *The Magic-Maker: E. E. Cummings* (1958); and *Ezra Pound* (1960). He has also written lyrical poetry: *Poems* (1929); *The Bright World* (1930); *The Savage Century* (1942); *A Soldier's Diary* (1944). *The Well of the Past* (1949) and *Dominick Dragon or The Happy Fellow* (1951) are novels.

Norman Leslie (1835), a novel by THEODORE FAY.

Norris, Charles G[ilman] (b. Chicago, April 23, 1881—d. July 25, 1945), novelist, dramatist. After graduating from the University of California, Norris worked for magazines, published his first novel, *The Amateur,* in 1916. *Salt; or, The Education of Griffith Adams* (1918) was followed in 1921 by *Brass,* a problem novel dealing with marriage. Among his other titles are *Bread* (1923); *Pig Iron* (1926); *Seed* (1930); *Zest* (1933); *Hands* (1935). Like his more famous brother (see FRANK NORRIS), Charles Norris wrote in the naturalistic tradition, dealing largely with social problems. His more romantic nature is represented by his poetic dramas, *The Rout of the Philistines* (1922); *A Gest of Robin Hood* (1929); and *Ivanhoe* (1936). He was married to the novelist KATHLEEN NORRIS.

Norris, [Benjamin] Frank[lin] (b. Chicago, March 5, 1870—d. Oct. 25, 1902), novelist. Norris grew up in Chicago and San Francisco. At the age of seventeen he acquired a serious interest in painting, and his father took him to Europe to study. The experiment did not last long, however, and Norris entered the University of California in 1890. There he read Zola, Kipling, and Richard Harding Davis, and in 1894 when he went on to Harvard he took with him the beginnings of his novel *McTeague.* Under Professor LEWIS E. GATES, who recognized his talent, he worked on this and on a second novel, *Vandover and the Brute,* though neither was published until several years later. After his year at Harvard, Norris traveled, reporting the Boer War for the San Francisco *Chronicle* and *Collier's.* Back in California he joined the staff of the *San Francisco Wave,* and

in 1898 published his first novel, MORAN OF THE LADY LETTY. He worked briefly for a publisher in New York, then went to Cuba to report the Santiago campaign for *McClure's Magazine,* an assignment which left him in poor health.

McTEAGUE appeared in 1899, followed by a sentimental romance, BLIX (1899), and a sensational story, *A Man's Woman* (1900). His most ambitious work, THE OCTOPUS (1901), heralded a great naturalistic trilogy on the production and distribution of wheat; but Norris died in 1902 after an operation for appendicitis. THE PIT, the second volume of the trilogy, appeared posthumously in 1903.

Norris' reputation as the first important naturalist in American literature rests on *McTeague, Vandover and the Brute* (the manuscript of which was lost in the San Francisco earthquake and not recovered and published until 1914), and *The Octopus.* These books embody Norris' debt to Zola, his attempt to transfer Zola's literary technique to American materials, and his great contribution to the liberation of the American novel from the vapid sentimentalism of the 1890's. *McTeague* tells of a brutal, stupid dentist who is pushed from his profession, becomes a drunkard, murders his wife, and is trapped fleeing across the California desert toward the hills where he had spent his youth. The plot is sensational, but the story is told with a care for detail and with a fairly successful use of "scientific" concepts of heredity and environment. It is also true that *McTeague* produces outsized, grotesque effects, sensational rather than scientific, and in this respect is perhaps more romantic than naturalistic; but this is the kind of romance that Norris found in Zola. *Vandover and the Brute* is a study of a degenerative disease, lycanthropy, which reduces a charming and talented young man to abject poverty, misery, and attacks of mania during which he crawls about naked, barking and snarling like a wolf. Zola had believed that such a novel could give so minute and circumstantial an account of disease that it would be a valuable scientific document, treating psychological phenomena as if they were chemical reactions. But Norris did not adhere strictly to the formula; *Vandover* is really a moral tale, somewhat confused, in which the responsibility for the protagonist's degeneracy is sometimes placed on himself, sometimes on a remorseless and purposeless universe, sometimes on society.

In *The Octopus* Norris attempted an epic portrayal of the operation of economic determinism, such as Zola had carried out so triumphantly in *Germinal*. Norris' story, however, fails to embody a consistent determinism. The reason for the failure is that his "epic" is laid on the frontier, and his ranchers, who begin the story as free agents possessed of more than the usual amount of force and self-sufficiency, engage in a heroic conflict with the forces of evil represented by the railroad. The evil of the railroad is personified by the figure of S. Behrman, whose villainous deeds are prompted by an evil within him which is not explained as the product of determining economic pressure. The uncertainty of Norris' philosophical position is brought out by the inconsistency of his economic viewpoint. At one moment the railroad is evil, at another the apathy of the voting public is to blame, at another the evils of competition are justified by the ultimate fact that the wheat is somehow grown and distributed, and at still another the wheat is presented as a force in itself which mystically *wills* to be grown and eaten. The story is continued in *The Pit*, Norris' weakest serious novel; here his renunciation of a naturalistic technique in favor of popular sentimental romance is nearly complete. The novel was written for money, in all probability, and was the author's greatest popular success. Norris' essay, THE RESPONSIBILITIES OF THE NOVELIST, was published posthumously (1903).

The accomplishment of Norris should not be underrated. He was the necessary groundbreaker for the great flowering of American fiction which followed him in the 20th century. Beyond that, his best novels remain readable and intelligent. But Norris was probably more interested in the purely novelistic aspects of Zola's technique than he was in the philosophical implications of NATURALISM. Because his novels express a confused view of reality, they fail to achieve the degree of consistency and integration that is required of permanently viable works of art.

Norris' role has been studied in Franklin Walker's *Frank Norris: A Biography* (1932); Ernest Marchand's *Frank Norris: A Study* (1942); Maxwell Geismar's *Rebels and Ancestors* (1953); Charles C. Walcutt's *American Literary Naturalism* (1956).

CHARLES CHILD WALCUTT

Norris, Kathleen [Thompson] (b. San Francisco, July 16, 1880—   ), short-story writer, novelist, memoirist. Educated at home, Kathleen Thompson went to work at nineteen. She worked as a bookkeeper, clerk, and teacher, entertaining her small brothers and sisters by telling them stories which she later sold to magazines. In 1909 she married the novelist CHARLES NORRIS and moved to New York, where she sold stories and serials to the women's magazines. Her first novel, MOTHER (1911), a sentimental tale of family life in California, was a best seller. Among Mrs. Norris' later writings: *Noon* (1925); *My San Francisco* (1932); *My California* (1933); *Victoria* (1933), a play; *Bakers' Dozen* (1938), short stories; and more than seventy novels, all appealing to the women's-magazine-reading public. *Certain People of Importance* (1922) is considered her best. Other novels by Mrs. Norris include *The Heart of Rachel* (1916); *The Barberry Bush* (1928); *The Venables* (1941); *Mink Coat* (1946); *High Holiday* (1949); *Shadow Marriage* (1952); *Dear Miss Harriet* (1955); *Family Gathering* (1959). An omnibus volume collected *The Best of Kathleen Norris* (1955).

Norsemen in America. That pre-Columbian visits to America by inhabitants of the Scandinavian countries are more than legends has long been admitted on the basis of passages in the *Eddas*. But the details of those visits have been disputed—for example, the tradition that connects the famous tower in Newport with a Norse visitor, who became Longfellow's SKELETON IN ARMOR. Three books have, in particular, explored these possibilities: Hjalmar Holland's *America 1355–1364* (1946); Edward Reman's *The Norse Discoveries and Explorations in America* (1949); and Frederick J. Pohl's *The Lost Discovery: Uncovering the Track of the Vikings in America* (1952).

North, Sterling (b. Edgerton, Wis., Nov. 4, 1906—   ), critic, poet, novelist. North began his career as a poet. His work appeared during the twenties in *The Dial*, *Poetry* magazine, and *Harper's*. In 1929 he became a reporter on the Chicago *Daily News* and from 1933 to 1943 was book reviewer. Later he became literary editor of the New York *Post*, then of the New York *World-Telegram and Sun* (1949–1956). As a critic he was influential, and widely syndicated. In 1956 he retired to become general editor of North Star Books, publishers of books on American history and biography for teen-agers. He wrote a number of novels, including *Plowing on Sunday* (1934); *Night Outlasts the Whippoorwill* (1936); *Seven Against the Years* (1939); *So Dear to My Heart* (1947, a best seller later made into a movie); and *Re-union on the Wabash* (1952). Among his juveniles are *The Birthday of Little Jesus* (1952); *Abe Lincoln, Log Cabin to White House* (1956); *George Washington* (1956); *Young Thomas Edison* (1958); *Thoreau of Walden Pond* (1959); and *Mark Twain and the River* (1960).

North American Folklore and Folksong, A Bibliography of (1949), compiled by Charles Haywood. Haywood collected more than 20,-000 titles of the most important books, studies, and articles in this field. He included all the categories of folklore: myths, legends, tales, speech, folk cures, riddles, proverbs, weather lore, games, folksongs, dances.

North American Phalanx. A Fourierist colony founded near Red Bank, N.J., by ALBERT BRISBANE in 1843. It was the most enduring of such colonies established in the United States. Conservative outsiders were horrified by the discussions and trials of saner costumes and more rights for women, of more practical methods of education, of more equitable wages. The colony lasted only until 1856. ALEXANDER WOOLLCOTT was born in the town of Phalanx in 1887. His mother, daughter of the colony's president, was born at the Phalanx in 1847. Her family continued to follow the tenets of the colony even after its dissolution and were known in the neighborhood as cranks, so that Alexander was brought up in an atmosphere of nonconformity.

North American Review. The most important of all American periodicals of the review type, the *North American Review*, was founded in 1815 and lasted until 1940. A large proportion of the country's most famous men of letters and of public affairs contributed to its pages, and its file is an unmatched repository of American thought covering a century and a quarter. It never had a large circulation (76,000 in 1891 was its peak); it changed ownership many times, and was really profitable only in the eighties and early nineties; it varied from time to time between quarterly, bimonthly, monthly, and fortnightly publication.

Editors and their terms were: WILLIAM TUDOR, 1815–1817; JARED SPARKS, 1817–1818, 1824–1830; EDWARD T. CHANNING, 1818–1819; EDWARD EVERETT, 1820–1823; ALEXANDER H. EVERETT, 1830–1835; JOHN G. PALFREY, 1836–1842; Francis Bowen, 1843–1853; A. P. Peabody, 1853–1863; JAMES RUSSELL LOWELL, 1863–1872; HENRY ADAMS, 1872–1876; Allen Thorndike Rice, 1877–1889; Lloyd S. Bryce, 1889–1896; David A. Munro, 1896–1899; George B. M. Harvey, 1899–1926; Walter Butler Mahony, 1926–1935; and John H. G. Pell, 1935–1940. Among associate editors were Charles Eliot Norton and HENRY CABOT LODGE.

The *North American* was an outgrowth of the MONTHLY ANTHOLOGY (1803–1811), conducted by a group of Harvard men organized loosely as the ANTHOLOGY CLUB. One member of the club, William Tudor, founded the *North American Review and Miscellaneous Journal* as a bimonthly in 1815. It immediately entered the

third or "paper" war with England in defense of a national American literature, although it was itself more New England than national in its scope. Bryant began his contributions to the review with *Thanatopsis* in 1817; like everything else for many years, this appeared anonymously. In its first five years the journal carried contributions from Edward and A. H. Everett, John Adams, Daniel Webster, H. W. Longfellow, and Francis Parkman; under later editors the old review became notoriously dull. As late as 1861, it was renewing its traditional opposition to immediate Negro emancipation, and it had little influence in the war years.

After the war, James Russell Lowell enlisted a group of contributors who regained much of the *Review's* former prestige: Edwin L. Godkin, Charles Francis Adams, Jr., George William Curtis, James Parton, and Goldwin Smith. Emerson appeared again, with much by the two editors. Henry Adams' editorship in the seventies gave more force to the journal; Lowell observed that Adams was making the old teakettle think it was a steam engine. Politics, science, and philology were emphasized; literary criticism came from Howells, Henry James, H. E. Boyesen, and many others.

In 1877 Allen Thorndike Rice, aged 23, wealthy, energetic, Boston-born and Oxford-educated, bought the *North American*. The next year he moved the Boston-and-Harvard journal to New York and into the arena of controversial political, industrial, social, and religious questions. Symposia by leading thinkers, such as a debate by Robert G. Ingersoll and Jeremiah S. Black on the Christian religion, were frequent. Literature was not neglected: Emerson's later essays were printed, as were several by Whitman, a debate on the Shakespeare-Bacon controversy, and work by Bryce, Anthony Trollope, and others. After Rice's untimely death in 1889, Lloyd Bryce carried forward much the same policy, with outstanding work by Gladstone, Bryce, Howells, Andrew Carnegie, and Mark Twain.

In 1899 George Harvey purchased the *North American*, making it as lively in politics and social questions as it had been under Rice. Mark Twain's *To a Person Sitting in Darkness* (February, 1901) created a sensation. Tolstoy, Maeterlinck, and d'Annunzio became contributors. Serial fiction appeared for the first time, by Henry James, Howells, and Joseph Conrad. Harvey was absentee editor in 1921–1924 while Ambassador to Great Britain, and circulation declined. W. B. Mahony, lawyer and financier, bought the *Review* in 1926; though he enlisted many famous commentators on political and literary affairs, he was unable to make headway against the newer illustrated reviews, and the "Winter, 1939–1940" issue of the *North American* was the last.

North of 36 (1923), a novel by EMERSON HOUGH. An agreeable historical novel about herding on the Chisholm Trail.

Northwest Passage (1937), a novel by KENNETH ROBERTS. This sprawling novel describes

Major ROBERT ROGERS' expedition in 1759 to destroy the Indian town of St. Francis and then his idea of finding an overland route to the Northwest. Rogers' experiences in the Northwest are described in his own *Concise Account of North America* (1765). Roberts, in preparing his novel, made extensive research, unearthed documents that historians had believed were lost. The book is one of Roberts' best works. See SIR WILLIAM JOHNSON.

Northwest Passage, the. When Pope Alexander VI in 1493 gave Spain a monopoly of the Western world, French and English expeditions tried to find a way to Cathay by sea through the "Northwest Passage." JOHN CABOT was one of the first to believe that such an all-sea route existed. Among early navigators who sought to break a way across the Arctic seas north of Canada were Martin Frobisher, George Weymouth, John Davys, Luke Fox, John Knight, and HENRY HUDSON in the 16th and 17th centuries, JAMES COOK and Sir John Franklin in the 18th. Actually no one made the passage until Roald Amundsen went through in 1906. The term was also applied to overland expeditions to the Pacific coasts. A complete history of the various expeditions is given by L. H. Neatby in his *In Quest of the Northwest Passage* (1958).

Norton, John (b. England, May 6, 1606—d. April 5, 1663), clergyman, controversialist, biographer. This learned and intolerant divine fled to New England in 1635 when Archbishop Laud launched his offensive against the Puritan preachers in England. He immediately became one of the leaders of the colony. He wrote *The Orthodox Evangelist* (1654); *Abel Being Dead yet Speaketh, or, The Life and Death of John Cotton* (1658), reprinted with notes by Enoch Pond (1834) (see JOHN COTTON); and *Heart of New England Rent, or, The Blasphemies of the Present Generation* (1659), directed against the Quakers, whom he persecuted with zeal.

Norwood (1867), a novel by HENRY WARD BEECHER. This sole novel by Harriet Beecher Stowe's brother is subtitled *Village Life in New England*. The author was not very successful as a fiction writer; his story is weighed down by his moralizing and exposition of religious doctrines. The novel is, however, noteworthy in being probably the first to introduce Lincoln as a character.

Notes on the State of Virginia (1784), a book about his native state by THOMAS JEFFERSON. It was first published in France, widely pirated there and in England. It is said that Jefferson tried to avoid a wide circulation of the *Notes* at home because he did not want his fellow Virginians to read his bitter remarks on slavery and some of his tart observations on the Constitution of the Province. No American edition appeared until 1787. The book is rich in facts, shows Jefferson's classical learning. He denounces the lack of taste and the unseemly appearance of colonial architecture in Virginia; he also expounds his agrarian philosophy.

Notes Toward a Supreme Fiction (1942), a long poem by WALLACE STEVENS. The *Notes* reflect Stevens' tendency to shift away from the rich metaphor and imagery of his earlier poetry toward a more abstract poetic statement about the nature of poetry. They begin with a flat, almost conversational statement and become progressively more metaphoric. The poem is divided into three sections labeled "It Must be Abstract," "It Must Change," and "It Must Give Pleasure." The supreme fiction, the poem, says Stevens, "refreshes life so that we share/ For a moment, the first idea." The "first idea" must be abstract, the semi-Platonic idea of the thing; it must change, since life and perspective are constantly changing; and it must give pleasure, when the abstraction is blooded by human thought.

Nothing to Wear (*Harper's Weekly*, 1857; in book form, 1857), a satirical poem about women and their love of finery by WILLIAM ALLEN BUTLER. In the mid-20th century a doll manufacturer borrowed the name of the heroine, "Miss Flora M'Flimsey," for a new creation. "Marian" (Marian Curtis Foster) has written and illustrated some charming children's books about her.

No Time for Comedy (1939), a play by S. N. BEHRMAN, concerned with a playwright who has the urge to deal with the serious problems and tragedies of his time, but the talent only for light comedy.

Notions of the Americans, Picked up by a Traveling Bachelor (1828), by JAMES FENIMORE COOPER. Lafayette asked his good friend Cooper to write an account of his triumphal American tour of 1824–25. Cooper feared that an undiluted account of official proceedings and welcomes would be dull, so he wrote a book about the United States through the letters of a supposed English traveler. This person was described as coming to the United States when Lafayette did, meeting him often, witnessing his triumphs. The book as a whole is an unconvincing glorification of this country. Cooper excuses slavery by blaming Europeans for its introduction. He defends the current treatment of the Indian. Everywhere he minimizes the wild and eccentric elements of American life in the 1820's. The book, which made many disparaging remarks about England, had a bad reception there and to it Cooper later traced the decline of his literary fortunes: he alienated Englishmen and even repelled Americans by the chauvinistic tone of the book. Cooper was later more severe in commenting on the United States.

Nott, Henry Junius (b. Union District, S.C., Nov. 4, 1797—d. Oct. 9, 1837), lawyer, teacher, humorist. Nott practiced law, then gave up that profession for literature. He served as professor of belles-lettres at the College of South Carolina. In 1834 he published *Novelettes of a Traveller, or, Odds and Ends from the Knapsack of Thomas Singularity, Journeyman Printer* (2 v.). In these picaresque sketches he made good use of local characters and incidents.

Not to Eat, Not for Love (1934), a novel by George Weller. This novel follows the happenings of a college year of forty weeks in forty chapters, is obviously modeled on John Dos

Passos and his 42ND PARALLEL (1930). Frederick L. Gwynn, of the Harvard faculty, called the book "not only the best of fables about Harvard . . . but the very best of college fiction, and one of the most engaging and thoughtful novels of the interwar period."

Novanglus. JOHN ADAMS' [2] pen name in his controversy with DANIEL LEONARD.

novel, the. Americans read and enjoyed novels before they themselves wrote them or publicly approved of them. The slow rise of native fiction was partly due to the Puritans' condemnation as immoral of anything that did not remind man of his duty to God, and, therefore of secular tales that might seduce him into idleness. But other factors were just as contributory: Americans were colonials for more than a century and a half; it took time to develop a national point of view; and the business of clearing a wilderness and settling into it meant emphasis upon practical matters and little attention to nonutilitarian, imaginative literature. The land was vast, uncultivated, and lacked sophisticated urban centers. There were printers but no publishers, and it was easier to import or to pirate fashionable works from abroad than to create, advertise, and distribute American fiction. Moreover, the novel as a genre was comparatively young, and only slowly did such a new form make its way into all areas of a distant country. If we define the word "novel" as prose fiction of extended length, then its English origins may be traced only to the beginning of the 18th century. One of its earliest exponents, Daniel Defoe, produced his first novel, *Robinson Crusoe*, in 1719; it was some years before he was followed by Samuel Richardson (*Pamela*, 1740); Tobias Smollett (*Roderick Random*, 1748); Henry Fielding (*Tom Jones*, 1749); and Laurence Sterne (*Tristram Shandy*, 1760). In the latter half of the 18th century England produced a sudden spate of popular stories: sentimental and domestic, adventure and historical, and that type of tale of terror which we call "Gothic." Some Americans were able to sample these and other new works, but only after an inevitable time lag; Benjamin Franklin, for example, offered *Robinson Crusoe* in 1734 and his own reprinting of *Pamela* in 1744.

It was natural, considering the limited resources of native writers, that American fiction should begin by being derivative. Since all our early tales were comparatively short and of inferior quality, the question of priority is not a highly important one. There had been elements of fiction in travel accounts, narratives of Indian captivities, anecdotes, and folk tales; but no one writer's name stands out until late in the 18th century. Historians have put forth several candidates for "the first American novel"; among those often named have been: JOSEPH MORGAN'S *The History of the Kingdom of Basaruah* (1715), a religious allegory; CHARLOTTE LENNOX's *The Female Quixote* (1752); Edward Bancroft's *The History of Charles Wentworth Esq.* (London, 1770); FRANCIS HOPKINSON's A PRETTY STORY (1774); and THOMAS ATWOOD DIGGES' *The*

Adventures of Alonso (London, 1775). All these fail on one or more counts: they are too short; their authors were resident in America only briefly; their scenes are not recognizably American; they do not exhibit an attitude or cast of mind that is as yet significantly American. Most critics now agree that the rise of the American novel may be dated from WILLIAM HILL BROWN's THE POWER OF SYMPATHY (published anonymously, 1789, and sometimes attributed to Mrs. Sarah Wentworth Morton). This tale, told in the form of letters and showing the marked influence of Richardson, was nevertheless set in Boston, where it was published, and was written by an American who drew his materials from a local scandal. Though dull, digressive, and piously moralistic, the tale was woven of sensational elements which included seduction, near incest, abduction, and suicide. Brown recognized that his story was open to attack; his preface contains a plea to the effect that if he had exposed vice, he had still recommended virtue.

This double quality was to remain for some years characteristic of the type of fiction most popular in the days of our early republic—the sentimental, domestic tale of a chaste heroine in regular danger of losing her virtue to a devilish seducer. Writers of such tales wanted it both ways: to lure readers by an appeal to pruriency but to haul them back to morality by sermonizing conclusions. Notable examples of the seduction story were SUSANNA ROWSON's *Charlotte Temple* (London, 1791), which has surprisingly been one of the most popular of American novels, and Hannah Foster's THE COQUETTE (1797). None of these has much more than historical interest today. Their styles were overornate, their characters insufficiently motivated, their settings poorly rendered, the motivation of their authors somewhat suspect. But they attracted readers, and their influence on popular fiction was to extend far into the next century.

A second type of novel that had been popular in England, the Gothic tale of terror, was generally beyond the power of native writers; America had no ruined castles, ancestral portraits, aristocracy, or corrupted church to portray. One sample of such a tale (with a foreign setting) is Mrs. SARAH SAYWARD WOOD's *Julia and the Illuminated Baron* (1800)—the baron is mentally "enlightened," not lighted up.

The historical novel had a rather better fate at this early period, but it did not become prominent until the first quarter of the 19th century. Though America had a past of no great depth, there was to be some attempt to mine it in the purportedly autobiographical THE FEMALE AMERICAN; OR, THE ADVENTURES OF UNCA ELIZA WINKFIELD (London, 1767), an Indian tale; JEREMY BELKNAP's *The Foresters* (1792); ANN ELIZA BLEECKER's THE HISTORY OF MARIA KITTLE (1793), set in the French and Indian wars; and JOHN DAVIS' THE FIRST SETTLERS OF VIRGINIA (1802). A fourth type of fiction, satire, was not extensively practiced by novelists; it was too sophisticated, too topical, and too ironical for the average taste. The few notable satirical novels include: GILBERT IMLAY'S THE EMIGRANTS (London, 1793), which depicted the contrast between the New and Old Worlds; ROYALL TYLER'S THE ALGERINE CAPTIVE (1797), which attacked piracy and slavery. By far the best of the lot (and one of the finest of American books before 1800) was HUGH HENRY BRACKENRIDGE'S MODERN CHIVALRY, published in installments between 1792 and 1815. Brackenridge (1748–1816) wrote an extremely long, picaresque novel with little continuous plot; although not distrustful of democracy itself, he was concerned with the failures of the American democratic experiment, and his pictures of corruption and demagoguery still have force.

Only one other American writer before 1800 ranks with Brackenridge. He is the Philadelphian, CHARLES BROCKDEN BROWN (1771–1810), who produced six novels in the astonishing space of four years. WIELAND (1798) is a tale of religious mania; ORMOND (1799) involves the conflict of a high-minded woman and a hero-villain; ARTHUR MERVYN (1799–1800) is set partly in Philadelphia during a yellow fever epidemic; EDGAR HUNTLY (1799) treats of murder and Indian adventure; *Clara Howard* (1801) and *Jane Talbot* (1801) are minor works. Brown has been called a Gothic novelist, and his use of ventriloquism, spontaneous combustion, sleepwalking, disguises, and other sensational elements gives some support to the claim. But Brown was primarily a rationalist, an enthusiast for science and the rights of women; and he was concerned with portraying the fate of reason in a not yet perfect world. His style was elaborately Latinate and balanced, and his intricate plots sometimes resemble a nested set of boxes, but his analyses of bizarre mental states and his ability to create and maintain suspense lift him far above his contemporaries. If anyone deserves the title of "father" of the American novel, it is Brown—one of the first to attempt to be a professional writer.

Before 1820 America had produced about ninety novels, but few of them ranked with the best work of Brackenridge and Brown. WASHINGTON IRVING won a reputation at home and abroad with THE SKETCH BOOK (1819–20) and with later collections of tales; he wrote no long fiction, but his style and subjects 'had some influence on Nathaniel Hawthorne and Edgar Allan Poe. The next writer of importance to appear was JAMES FENIMORE COOPER (1789–1851), who is best remembered for the five Leather-Stocking tales: THE PIONEERS (1823), THE LAST OF THE MOHICANS (1826), THE PRAIRIE (1827), THE PATHFINDER (1840), and THE DEERSLAYER (1841); these added to a growing American mythology the figures of the frontiersman NATTY BUMPPO, the Indian CHINGACHGOOK, and a host of others. Cooper was remarkable for the range of subjects in his more than thirty novels; he wrote of the American Revolution (THE SPY, 1821), the sea (THE PILOT, 1823), Europe (THE BRAVO, 1831), the Dutch background of New York (SATANSTOE,

1845); he also composed political satire (THE MONIKINS, 1835; HOME AS FOUND, 1838) and a Utopian novel (THE CRATER, 1847). Cooper, like others in the first half of the 19th century, called his books "romances"; his tales shied away from the commonplace domestic novel and concentrated on wild and exciting actions set in remote or otherwise unusual surroundings. (For the important distinction which several writers made between the "realistic" novel and the more allegorical and symbolic romance, see the studies by Richard Chase and Leslie Fiedler, listed below.) Cooper's romances were weak in style and depended too much upon coincidence for plot resolution; but they did much to awaken Americans to the significance of their own past, and they created a vogue for historical fiction similar to that which Sir Walter Scott had initiated on the other side of the Atlantic.

The followers of Scott and Cooper were numerous, and the subjects of their novels varied; among the more memorable were: JOHN NEAL, whose RACHEL DYER (1828) dealt with witchcraft in Salem; LYDIA MARIA CHILD, who wrote of the pre-Revolutionary period in *The Rebels* (1825); JAMES KIRKE PAULDING, who looked into Dutch colonialism in THE DUTCHMAN'S FIRESIDE (1831); CATHARINE MARIA SEDGWICK, whose HOPE LESLIE (1827) was concerned with Indians in 17th-century New England; TIMOTHY FLINT, who opened up interest in the West with *Francis Berrian* (1826); ROBERT MONTGOMERY BIRD, who left a fascinating portrait of an Indian hater in NICK OF THE WOODS (1837); and JOSEPH HOLT INGRAHAM, whose LAFITTE (1836) deals with the famous pirate. Southerners, too, were arousing interest in the backgrounds of their region. The best known was WILLIAM GILMORE SIMMS (1806–70), whose thirty-four works of fiction include tales of the colonial period in South Carolina (*The Yemassee*, 1835), the Revolution (THE PARTISAN, 1835), and the border areas (RICHARD HURDIS, 1838). Less notable were GEORGE TUCKER (*The Valley of Shenandoah*, 1824), NATHANIEL BEVERLEY TUCKER (GEORGE BALCOMBE, 1836), WILLIAM ALEXANDER CARUTHERS (*The Cavaliers of Virginia*, 1835), and JOHN PENDLETON KENNEDY (HORSE-SHOE ROBINSON, 1835). The Civil War added a new subject for the historical romancer, but for many years fictional treatment of the conflict was subliterary. Still worthy of note, however, are JOHN WILLIAM DE FOREST'S *Miss Ravenel's Conversion from Secession to Loyalty* (1866) and JOHN ESTEN COOKE'S more romantic view of war in *Surry of Eagle's-Nest* (1866) and other books. Antislavery sentiment accounted for RICHARD HILDRETH'S THE SLAVE (1836) and HARRIET BEECHER STOWE'S sensationally popular UNCLE TOM'S CABIN (1852).

A few authors better known as poets or short-story writers also attempted the novel in the period before 1870. EDGAR ALLAN POE wrote one extended piece of fiction, THE NARRATIVE OF ARTHUR GORDON PYM (1838), a sea adventure tale with a mysterious ending in the south polar region; HENRY WADSWORTH LONGFELLOW

contributed two mild, dreamy romances, HYPE-
RION (1839) and KAVANAGH (1849); WALT
WHITMAN produced a ludicrous temperance
tract in FRANKLIN EVANS (1842); and OLIVER
WENDELL HOLMES, SR., composed three books
that foreshadow modern psychiatric findings:
ELSIE VENNER (1861), THE GUARDIAN ANGEL
(1867), and A MORTAL ANTIPATHY (1885). To
this group may be added a few other minor
works: THEODORE FAY's *Norman Leslie* (1835),
CHARLES FENNO HOFFMAN's GREYSLAER (1839),
GEORGE LIPPARD's Gothic THE QUAKER CITY
(1844), and CORNELIUS MATHEW's *Big Abel
and the Little Manhattan* (1845).

Women had been responsible for some of our
earliest sentimental domestic fiction, and they
continued in force in the first seventy years of
the 19th century—so much so that Hawthorne
called them that "damned mob of scribbling
women." Their tear-drenched and palpitating
novels are literary fossils now, but they won a
following in their day that was not achieved by
the period's more serious writers. Most prominent were SUSAN WARNER (THE WIDE, WIDE
WORLD, 1850); Mrs. E. D. E. N. SOUTHWORTH,
who wrote more than sixty novels in her eighty-
year life span; MARIA CUMMINS (THE LAMP-
LIGHTER, 1854); and AUGUSTA JANE EVANS,
widely renowned for her *St. Elmo* (1866). Two
equally famous and prolific sentimentalists were
men: TIMOTHY SHAY ARTHUR and EDWARD
PAYSON ROE.

With the exception of Cooper and Poe, none
of the aforementioned writers contributed much
to the development of fiction as a serious art between 1820 and 1870. The discovery that the
romance could offer intellectual fare as well as
entertainment was reserved for the two men
whose names now loom above all others in this
period: NATHANIEL HAWTHORNE and Herman
Melville. Hawthorne (1804–64) produced a
number of distinguished short stories before
1850; in the next decade he wrote four important romances: THE SCARLET LETTER (1850),
THE HOUSE OF THE SEVEN GABLES (1851), THE
BLITHEDALE ROMANCE (1852), and THE MAR-
BLE FAUN (1860). Hawthorne was deeply concerned with the essential nature of man, with
his proper role in life, and with his ultimate fate.
Unlike the transcendentalists, he could come to
no optimistic conclusion; to him, man was by
nature a being in whom good and evil were
inextricably bound up. Again and again his
major fiction treats one central theme: the individual who turns away from society, either
literally or by experimentation on the souls of
others, and thus becomes isolated and convinced
that evil exists in the hearts of all. For some of
his protagonists no return to society is possible;
others find that they can live with their knowledge of evil, accept man's mixed nature, and
continue to exist in their semi-fallen state. To
portray the problem of mankind Hawthorne
developed a symbolic method which went beyond the allegory of his favorite authors, Edmund Spenser and John Bunyan, and which foreshadowed more modern fiction. He dramatized

the fundamental conflicts of the heart versus the
head, isolation versus society, innocence versus
experience, pride versus humility, introspection
versus prying into the minds of others, triumph
over sin versus destruction by it. In *The Scarlet
Letter*, set in 17th-century New England, he
examines the effect of the sin of adultery upon
HESTER PRYNNE, the Reverend Arthur Dimmesdale, and Hester's wronged husband, the
icily intellectual physician Roger Chillingworth.
In *The House of the Seven Gables* the wrong
of an ancestor is traced through seven generations of the Pyncheon family of Salem. *The
Blithedale Romance*, based loosely upon Hawthorne's connection with the utopian experiment
of Brook Farm, muses on human motivations,
interpersonal relations, and the enigma of appearance and reality. The last of the four romances, *The Marble Faun*, set in Italy, analyzes
the regenerative, educative power of experience,
through which the naïvely innocent individual,
confronted by sin and guilt, is able to rise to a
higher perception which includes the knowledge
of evil. Hawthorne's achievement was striking;
full appreciation of his subtleties has not come
until this century.

Fame was to be won early by HERMAN MEL-
VILLE (1819–1891), but as his vision of man
became increasingly deep and complex, he lost
a wide readership, his "rediscovery," beginning
in the 1920's, has been a major effort of scholarship. Melville first captivated the public with
two romances drawn from his adventures in the
South Seas, but also combined with material
from his reading and with imaginative additions;
these were TYPEE (1846) and OMOO (1847).
He tried to repeat his success with a long allegorical voyage narrative, MARDI (1849), but the
public was less interested in this first evidence
of Melville's more serious concerns. His next
book, REDBURN (1849), deals with the adventures of a young man on a voyage to Liverpool
and back to New York; WHITE-JACKET, of the
next year, has as its setting a United States Navy
vessel on a cruise from Peru to Boston. In 1851
Melville poured the fruit of his speculations on
fate, free will, evil, and reality into MOBY-DICK,
a work so vast and intricate that a whole library
of explication has grown up around it. The book
puzzled and irritated readers who had enthusiastically bought his earlier tales; Melville completed the alienation of a popular audience with
PIERRE (1852), a painful work which has a
contemporary domestic setting and which has invited psychological interpretation because of its
supposed evidence of the author's disturbed state
of mind. ISRAEL POTTER (1855), a minor tale
dealing with figures of the Revolution, was followed by the last work of fiction to appear
in Melville's lifetime, THE CONFIDENCE-MAN
(1857). This latter book, a difficult, bitter story
of the Devil and his wiles aboard a Mississippi
River boat, has recently been acclaimed by some
critics as his second greatest effort. One final
short novel, BILLY BUDD, composed 1888–91,
was not published until 1924. Melville was committed to probing the ambiguities of man's na-

ture, but he reached no conclusions he could accept with finality. As Hawthorne remarked of him, he could "neither believe, nor be comfortable in his unbelief." Melville's central image in all his best books was the voyage of discovery; of all American novelists of the first half of the 19th century, he voyaged the farthest.

During the silent years before his death in 1891, Melville lived through several new directions in fiction. Between 1870 and 1900 many writers and critics cried out regularly for more "REALISM" in the novel. The term is not susceptible of precise definition, since it meant somewhat different things to various writers; but a few characteristics of the movement can be noted: there was castigation of sentimentality and of what was called "literary lying" in contrived popular stories; there was a strong influence of the scientific method, as the author tried to study man in the crucible of life; there was increased emphasis upon reporting the American scene as it was actually observed, with more precise rendering of setting, speech peculiarities, customs, and occupations. The realistic writer tried to become both more objective and more daring in subject matter; he shied away from intrusion of himself, and he strove to open fiction to franker consideration of sex, of politics, of business, and of inequities in American society. He wanted Americans to reject servile dependence upon Europe for cultural innovations, but at the same time he was much impressed by the experiments in fiction made by foreign writers like Émile Zola, Honoré de Balzac, Gustave Flaubert, Stendhal, Leo Tolstoi, and Feodor Dostoevski. The realist was to be opposed both by the "genteel" author, who desired fiction to be idealistic and uplifting, and by the popular romancer, who continued to ply his trade with great success. But in the end he set his impress upon serious fiction for many decades.

One phase of this new insistence upon realism may be observed in the work of that group of writers loosely called "local colorists." The Civil War had made many Americans more aware of the diversity and size of the nation they had created; there was new pride in the recognition of cultural differences in New England, in the Old South, in the raw West—even in the rising melting-pot cities. And so there sprang up a group who were intent upon reporting to the rest of the nation the peculiarities characteristic of their own sections. Most were short-story writers: SARAH ORNE JEWETT and MARY E. WILKINS FREEMAN in New England; THOMAS NELSON PAGE, JOEL CHANDLER HARRIS, MARY NOAILLES MURFREE in the South; MARGARET DELAND in the Middle Atlantic States; BRET HARTE in the West. At their most effective they created believable localized settings, regional dialects, curious characters; at their weakest they were apt to fall into nostalgia or into mere quaintness or picturesqueness. A few writers attempted to expand local materials into a long novel, and a few had a notable success: GEORGE WASHINGTON CABLE (THE GRANDISSIMES, 1880, dealing with the Creoles in Louisiana); Sarah

Orne Jewett (THE COUNTRY OF THE POINTED FIRS, 1896, set in Maine); Edward Eggleston (THE HOOSIER SCHOOLMASTER, 1871); and LAFCADIO HEARN (CHITA, 1889, a tale of the Gulf Coast). As several critics have pointed out, insofar as the local colorist tended toward the "local," he emphasized the factual; insofar as he gave prominence to the "color" in locale, he veered toward a more sweetly tinged view of life. Later the movement was to evolve into the more austere work of the regionalists (see REGIONALISM).

A few other writers were to describe certain aspects of region but were to contrive to give their novels more universal application. HENRY ADAMS wrote of Washington politics in DEMOCRACY (1879); HAROLD FREDERIC depicted the narrowness of small-town New York life in THE DAMNATION OF THERON WARE (1896) and other books; EDGAR WATSON HOWE produced a biting STORY OF A COUNTRY TOWN (1883); ALBION WINEGAR TOURGÉE revealed Reconstruction turmoil in North Carolina in A FOOL'S ERRAND (1879). SILAS WEIR MITCHELL tried a more realistic approach to historical fiction in HUGH WYNNE, FREE QUAKER (1897). There was looking forward as well as back in EDWARD BELLAMY's utopian, socially oriented fantasy, LOOKING BACKWARD: 2000–1887 (1888).

As the realists were to complain, there was no dearth of best-selling romantic fiction in the period. HORATIO ALGER ("Luck and Pluck" series, 1869 ff.) and LOUISA MAY ALCOTT (LITTLE WOMEN, 1868) pacified and edified the children while parents reveled in the gaudy or touching scenes invented by LEW WALLACE (BEN HUR, 1880); FRANCIS MARION CRAWFORD (A Roman Singer, 1884); HELEN HUNT JACKSON (RAMONA, 1884); FRANCES HODGSON BURNETT (LITTLE LORD FAUNTLEROY, 1886); JAMES LANE ALLEN (A KENTUCKY CARDINAL, 1894); and hosts of others. The detective story, initiated by Poe in the 1840's, got a boost in ANNA KATHARINE GREEN's THE LEAVENWORTH CASE (1878); and the historical thriller went its dashing way in the work of CHARLES MAJOR (WHEN KNIGHTHOOD WAS IN FLOWER, 1898) and PAUL LEICESTER FORD (JANICE MEREDITH, 1899).

It is no wonder that WILLIAM DEAN HOWELLS, contemplating such productions, would ask plaintively: "Ah! poor Real Life, which I love, can I make others share the delight I find in thy foolish and insipid face?" Howells (1837–1920) was to try to rechannel public taste through reviews, articles, editorial comments, and more than forty volumes of fiction. Realism was, he said, "nothing more and nothing less than the truthful treatment of material"; he was to be somewhat timid in his own approach to fiction, but he gave willing and influential aid to the more daring realists both at home and abroad. Howells' own best work can be studied in A MODERN INSTANCE (1882), which deals unsparingly with an unhappy marriage; THE RISE OF SILAS LAPHAM (1885), one of the earliest treatments of a materialistic businessman who comes to see the light; and A HAZARD OF NEW

FORTUNES (1890), which reveals his concern for social justice. His special interest in social theory is also shown in A TRAVELER FROM ALTRURIA (1894) and a sequel, *Through the Eye of the Needle* (1907). Howells spurned the historical romance, the Gothic tale, the surprise ending, the contrived love story, and the sensational employed for its own sake. From first to last he was remarkably consistent in his approach; he wanted to photograph the plain face of America, and he succeeded admirably in creating believable characters and situations. He occasionally seems tepid to those readers steeped in the more hard-boiled realists, but critics are again discovering the worth of his panorama of social life in the latter half of the century.

Other directions in realism were to be taken by Howells' two close though utterly different friends, Mark Twain and Henry James. MARK TWAIN (1835–1910) was a southerner-westerner who was to prove one of the most popular of American authors. His career began with the freewheeling satire of the Old World in THE INNOCENTS ABROAD (1869), and he was never entirely to lose his fondness for exaggeration and brash humor. TOM SAWYER (1876) and HUCKLEBERRY FINN (1884) have been loved by generations of children, but behind the surface nostalgia for a vanished America lies a trenchant criticism of the contrarieties and failures of our civilization. Twain attacked corrupt politics in THE GILDED AGE (written with Charles Dudley Warner, 1874) and feudalism and caste in THE PRINCE AND THE PAUPER (1882) and A CONNECTICUT YANKEE IN KING ARTHUR'S COURT (1889); but many readers, conditioned by the image of the popular humorist and lecturer, were to miss his deeper satire. In later years Twain's constitutional pessimism about man's basic nature deepened; it is reflected in THE TRAGEDY OF PUDD'NHEAD WILSON (1894), a somewhat faltering study of the slavery both of body and mind in a small Mississippi River town, and in THE MYSTERIOUS STRANGER (published 1916, though written earlier), a fantasy on the theme of determinism which is set in Austria of the 1590's. Twain's interest in twin characters and in violent contrasts reveals the basic duality in his own nature; he is remembered best as a "funny man," but he was also responsible for some of the most despairing pages in our fiction.

Howells called Twain "the Lincoln of our literature," emphasizing his essential American roots. Whether one counts HENRY JAMES (1843–1916) among American authors depends somewhat upon how seriously his long residence abroad and his becoming a British subject late in life are to be counted. But James' cast of mind and the themes of his fiction show an unmistakable impress of his homeland, and his shift of allegiance was no strong repudiation of it. Critics have traditionally divided the long, highly productive career of James into three chief periods: from the middle 1860's to the 1880's he used principally American characters, in both European and American settings (RODER-

ICK HUDSON, 1876; WASHINGTON SQUARE, 1881); for the next decade or so he most often employed English characters and scenes (THE PRINCESS CASAMASSIMA, 1886; THE SPOILS OF POYNTON, 1897); after 1900 he renewed his interest in the international theme and concentrated upon Americans caught up in European situations. His style and form also underwent noticeable change: he began writing in the general tradition of the English novel, moved toward greater verbal and structural complexity in his middle period, and closed his career with works of great density and difficulty (THE WINGS OF THE DOVE, 1902; THE AMBASSADORS, 1903; THE GOLDEN BOWL, 1904). James was passionately dedicated to the art of fiction, and he contributed a valuable body of critical theory as well as practice. No brief statement can do justice to James' aesthetics, but a few of his central principles may be summarized: he was a psychological rather than a photographic realist, and he held that it was the duty of the artist to represent life, not to reproduce it. He was much concerned with technical problems, such as narrative point of view, and he developed to a high degree the symbolic method that had been initiated in America by Hawthorne and Melville. He was less interested in surface story than in the significances inherent in his plots, and he evolved an elaborate allusive style that demands the full attention of the reader. His themes were varied, but a few have been associated predominantly with his work: the conflict of societies (innocent American and cultured, decadent European), the failure of the general public to appreciate the meaning of true art, the sensitive individual in quest of an ideal society. Because he refused to compromise with the demands of popular taste, James was never a best seller, despite his general renown; but he exerted a strong influence over later writers and theoreticians of the craft of the novel. Like Melville, James has undergone a "revival"; initiated in the 1930's, it presently shows no signs of ceasing.

In the decade of the 1890's a group of younger authors began to practice a heightened form of realism that has generally been identified as "NATURALISM." Not all the writers of the group were to be equally affected, but most of them showed the influence of recent trends in science and economics which led toward a deterministic view of mankind—toward the theory that man's nature and actions were controlled by his biological inheritance and by his social environment. The naturalistic novel emphasized brutality and sordidness; it introduced elements formerly considered taboo (like sex, alcoholism, depravity, drug addiction); it became more panoramic, sprawling, documentary. Generally it preached pessimism about man's fate, but it often expressed compassion for his condition and therefore seemed to imply some lurking hope. Important in this period were: HAMLIN GARLAND, who portrayed man versus nature and a crushing social system in his stories of the Midwest (MAIN-TRAVELLED ROADS, 1891); and in novels like ROSE OF DUTCHER'S COOLLY (1895); FRANK NORRIS, whose powerful California novels combined melodrama, determinism, and a vague mysticism (MCTEAGUE, 1899; THE OCTOPUS, 1901); STEPHEN CRANE, whose MAGGIE: A GIRL OF THE STREETS (1892) is often called the first naturalistic novel, but who is better known for his antiromantic Civil War novel THE RED BADGE OF COURAGE (1895), and by far the most accomplished of the group in style and technique; and JACK LONDON, who concerned himself with class warfare, evolution, animals, and primitive men (THE CALL OF THE WILD, 1903; MARTIN EDEN, 1909). For all their obvious faults of careless writing and occasional tediousness, the naturalists performed a valuable service. Against genteelism, aestheticism, and pseudoculture they opposed a strong sense of fact, a drab reality that was for many Americans the true condition of life. They worked hard to burst the confines of fiction: to widen the vocabulary, to deal as honestly and directly with sexual matters as they could, to force greater public realization of the seamier sides of the American scene. If they themselves had few outstanding successes, they did suggest the direction that one important branch of fiction was to take in the 20th century.

THEODORE DREISER (1871–1945) was to continue naturalism both as philosophy and technique in a series of gloomy, elephantine, but still effective novels. Dreiser's career began with the frank tale of SISTER CARRIE (1900), which provoked wounded cries from genteel critics. He was to go on to write a searching trilogy about an American tycoon in THE FINANCIER (1912), THE TITAN (1914), and The Stoic (1947); in the moving AN AMERICAN TRAGEDY (1925) he analyzed social classes and the attempt of his protagonist to rise higher in the scale. Two other important books were JENNIE GERHARDT (1911) and THE "GENIUS" (1915). Upton Sinclair, a contemporary, came suddenly to notice in 1906 with his exposé of the Chicago meatpacking industry, The Jungle; he wrote a few other socially conscious studies, but in recent years he has been best known for his series of popular stories about contemporary events involving the central character of Lanny Budd.

In addition to Dreiser and Sinclair, several other significant novelists first published in the period between 1900 and 1920. SHERWOOD ANDERSON showed the influence of Freudian psychology in his sketches of the inhabitants of WINESBURG, OHIO (1919) and in later books like Poor White (1920) and DARK LAUGHTER (1925). New regionalists arose, more objective and sociological in their approach than the local colorists; among them were ELLEN GLASGOW, whose long cycle about Virginia began with The Descendant (1897) and continued through such later stories as BARREN GROUND (1925) and VEIN OF IRON (1935); and WILLA CATHER, creator of the powerful Nebraska novels O PIONEERS! (1913) and MY ÁNTONIA (1918), and of the later story of New Mexico history, DEATH COMES FOR THE ARCHBISHOP (1927). Miss Cather's distinguished work also

included THE SONG OF THE LARK (1915), A LOST LADY (1923), and THE PROFESSOR'S HOUSE (1925). EDITH WHARTON composed a brief, tragic tale of New England in ETHAN FROME (1911), but more characteristic were her novels of society, like the Jamesian THE AGE OF INNOCENCE (1920).

Highly respected in their day, but less kindly treated by modern critics, were JAMES BRANCH CABELL, a mannered romanticist who is sometimes recalled for his once scandalous JURGEN (1919), and BOOTH TARKINGTON, who captivated children with PENROD (1914) and their elders with such tales as THE MAGNIFICENT AMBERSONS (1918). Popular romancers and historical novelists charged ahead undeterred by naturalism, regionalism, or other new directions in serious fiction; representative of them were: MARY JOHNSTON (TO HAVE AND TO HOLD, 1900); JOHN FOX, JR. (THE LITTLE SHEPHERD OF KINGDOM COME, 1903); WINSTON CHURCHILL (THE CROSSING, 1904); EMERSON HOUGH (54-40 OR FIGHT!, 1909); GENE STRATTON PORTER (A GIRL OF THE LIMBERLOST, 1909); KATHLEEN NORRIS (MOTHER, 1911); and HAROLD BELL WRIGHT (THE WINNING OF BARBARA WORTH, 1911). OWEN WISTER (THE VIRGINIAN, 1902) and ZANE GREY continued to supply the craving for Western fiction, as did MARY ROBERTS RINEHART (THE CIRCULAR STAIRCASE, 1908) and others, for the detective story. EDGAR RICE BURROUGHS merits mention for his Tarzan of the Apes (1914), though it is barely above the pulp-fiction level, and for his creation of a minor science-fiction shelf. Male readers were coming into their own with such appeals to their escapist desires, and writers with their eye on the market were to pay increasing attention to them in later years.

By 1920 a number of influential forces were combining to give new shape and scope to our fiction. The findings of Sigmund Freud and other psychologists about human drives and motivations were eagerly seized upon by writers, with particular emphasis placed upon the dire effects of sexual inhibitions. World War I, the first foreign conflict in which a large number of our citizens had engaged, created some disillusionment and bitterness, but it also brought attacks upon complacency and opened up new worlds for men who had their first experience of Europe under wartime conditions. Some writers, disgusted with Prohibition and provincialism, remained in Paris to practice their art and to enjoy their membership in the "lost generation"; others remained at home to snipe at American folly, pretension, and the get-rich-quick boomtime spirit. In retrospect, the novels produced in the astonishingly fertile decade of the 1920's are most significantly characterized by their disquiet and deep questioning of America's future, despite their iconoclasm and their frequent attention to wild parties and clandestine love affairs.

The roll call of writers who first published important fiction in the twenties is a list of those who have thus far proved most influential in this century: Sinclair Lewis, F. Scott Fitzgerald,

John Dos Passos, Ernest Hemingway, William Faulkner, Thomas Wolfe, Thornton Wilder. Experimental in technique and often cynical in tone, their novels surveyed an American scene in which "normalcy" was only a catchword. SINCLAIR LEWIS (1885–1951) opened the decade with a bang with his best-selling MAIN STREET (1920), the story of a citified heroine who tried to bring some semblance of culture and intellectualism to a small Midwestern town. Lewis followed up this triumph with a sardonic portrait of a "booster" businessman, BABBITT (1922); a dissection of the career of an idealistic doctor, ARROWSMITH (1925); and a depiction of the confrontation between a self-made tycoon and superficial European high society in DODSWORTH (1929). In 1930 he won the first Nobel Prize for literature ever bestowed on an American, but his talents thereafter failed him and he went into a long creative slump from which he never managed to pull out. Lewis' baiting of the "boobs" (as the influential critic H. L. Mencken called them) now appears superficial, and his once praised slang-filled dialogue has dated painfully. There was a sentimentalist, too, behind the satirist's mask; he could never determine for himself whether he really enjoyed or despised the objects of his derision.

If any one person epitomized the spirit of the Jazz Age for most readers it was F. Scott FITZGERALD (1890–1940), who began his blazing career with two exuberantly youthful novels, THIS SIDE OF PARADISE (1920) and THE BEAUTIFUL AND DAMNED (1922). His best book, THE GREAT GATSBY (1925), a surprisingly well-controlled and symbolic tale, offers a subtle and incisive portrait of the period. Drink, easy success, and the collapse of the decade into the Great Depression effectively stultified Fitzgerald as an artist; he attempted a comeback with TENDER IS THE NIGHT (1934) and the unfinished Hollywood novel The Last Tycoon (published 1941), but he was not to return to critical favor until a decade after his early death.

JOHN DOS PASSOS (1896–   ) produced an effective war novel in THREE SOLDIERS (1921), but his panoramic view of New York City in MANHATTAN TRANSFER (1925) was better to foreshadow his major trilogy of the 1930's, U.S.A. (q.v.), made up of THE 42ND PARALLEL (1930), 1919 (1932), and THE BIG MONEY (1936). In this giant work he developed the technique of the "collective" novel, a type in which a whole city or country is the "hero." The effect at first may be that of aimlessness, but gradually the reader realizes that all the varied characters are caught up in a common social situation—which is the book's real theme. A second trilogy Dos Passos called District of Columbia; the individual works were Adventures of a Young Man (1939), NUMBER ONE (1943), and The Grand Design (1949). Midcentury (1961) was an attempt to return to some of the experimental devices he had employed in U.S.A. Dos Passos' political convictions were radical in his earlier works; in later years he swung sharply to the right, and was

unable to recapture the fire and force of the twenties and early thirties.

ERNEST HEMINGWAY (1899–1961) became one of the best-known men of his era, both as a writer and as a public figure. His first long work of fiction, THE SUN ALSO RISES (1926), definitively captured the world of the expatriate in Europe; its terse dialogue and its action scenes were to impress a generation of younger authors. Hemingway's World War I novel, A FAREWELL TO ARMS (1929), skillfully constructed and highly symbolic, now appears to be his major extended story. His record of the Spanish Civil War, a clash which attracted the attention (and presence) of a number of his contemporaries, appeared as FOR WHOM THE BELL TOLLS (1940). Far less successful were To HAVE AND HAVE NOT (1935), set in Florida and Cuba, and ACROSS THE RIVER AND INTO THE TREES (1950), a story of World War II which occasionally lapses painfully into self-parody. The final novel published in his lifetime, THE OLD MAN AND THE SEA (1952), was highly praised, but some critics felt that it did not rise to the level of his best work in the twenties (especially his excellent short stories). Hemingway's famous style, fresh and individual when it first drew notice, became less effective with imitation and his own later efforts. His subjects were somewhat limited (war, sport, love), but it is likely that future revaluation will not remove him from his place among the most significant writers of the first half of the century.

WILLIAM FAULKNER (1897–1962), who now stands with a handful of our greatest authors, began publication with two minor novels, Soldiers' Pay (1926) and Mosquitoes (1927). In 1929 he initiated what was to become his saga of the mythical Mississippi county of Yoknapatawpha in SARTORIS and THE SOUND AND THE FURY, the latter one of the most experimental works in American fiction. Other installments were published at intervals; among the longer stories the most important were AS I LAY DYING (1930), LIGHT IN AUGUST (1932), and ABSALOM, ABSALOM! (1936). Widespread recognition came slowly to Faulkner; on the basis of horrific episodes, such as those in SANCTUARY (1931), he was first considered a naturalist or a southern decadent; by the late 1940's he was acclaimed as a major symbolist in the dark tradition of Hawthorne and Melville, and his "myth of the South" received elaborate analysis and explication. Faulkner became a master of varied styles, narrative techniques, and subjects; his influence at home and abroad was one of the most powerful so far in the 20th century. Like Hemingway, he was awarded the Nobel Prize for his contributions to world literature.

Other important writers were contemporaries of these major figures. THOMAS WOLFE (1900–1938) revealed a genuine but unharnessed talent in his four massive autobiographical novels: LOOK HOMEWARD, ANGEL (1929), OF TIME AND THE RIVER (1935), THE WEB AND THE ROCK (1939), and YOU CAN'T GO HOME AGAIN

(1940)—the last two issued posthumously. THORNTON WILDER (1897—   ) wrote two mannered but impressive novels in *The Cabala* (1926) and THE BRIDGE OF SAN LUIS REY (1927). Among others of lesser rank, these drew appreciative readers: JOSEPH HERGESHEIMER (*JAVA HEAD*, 1919, and other works throughout the next decade); WALDO FRANK (*Rahab*, 1922); CARL VAN VECHTEN (NIGGER HEAVEN, 1926); and OLE EDVART RÖLVAAG (GIANTS IN THE EARTH, 1927). Representative fictionists on the popular level were: EDNA FERBER (SO BIG, 1924); FLOYD DELL (MOON-CALF, 1920); LOUIS BROMFIELD (THE GREEN BAY TREE, 1924); GERTRUDE ATHERTON (BLACK OXEN, 1923); PERCY MARKS (THE PLASTIC AGE, 1924); and JOHN ERSKINE (THE PRIVATE LIFE OF HELEN OF TROY, 1925).

The harsh depression years of the early 1930's stimulated a powerful literature of social protest, though much of it has not worn well. Several writers combined a naturalistic literary technique with a political philosophy that was leftist in sympathy—often blatantly so. JAMES T. FARRELL (1904—   ) analyzed his generation in an outspoken trilogy: YOUNG LONIGAN (1932), *The Young Manhood of Studs Lonigan* (1934), and *Judgment Day* (1935); these traced the gradual corruption of a Chicago youth by his environment. Farrell's many later works have repeated the form and themes of these books. ERSKINE CALDWELL (1903—   ) joined sexual sensationalism with a depiction of the plight of back-country Georgia farmers to produce TOBACCO ROAD (1932), GOD'S LITTLE ACRE (1933), and *Journeyman* (1935). A natural for paperback reprints, these and other stories made him one of the most widely read of American authors. The Californian JOHN STEINBECK (1902—   ) showed great promise in TORTILLA FLAT (1935), IN DUBIOUS BATTLE (1936), and the controversial THE GRAPES OF WRATH (1939), all of which depicted lower classes in conflict with a capitalistic, materialistic society. In later years he lapsed into frequent sentimentality and displayed less immediate concern for social causes. Two Negro writers who came to prominence in the period were LANGSTON HUGHES (*Not Without Laughter*, 1930) and RICHARD WRIGHT (NATIVE SON, 1940). In the hands of such men as these the novel became more documentary and proletarian, tougher in vocabulary and action, and less concerned with individual character—since the future of mankind in the mass was the author's chief interest. The movement lost force with widespread disillusionment over the direction taken by international Communism and with the outbreak of World War II at the end of the decade.

Two authors of the thirties who treated a different social level were JOHN P. MARQUAND and JOHN O'HARA. Marquand produced an excellent satiric treatment of Bostonian manners in THE LATE GEORGE APLEY (1937); his many later novels tended to be slick and conventional. O'Hara, who has written a continuing series of frank novels about the fictional community of Gibbsville, Pennsylvania, is best represented by his early *Appointment in Samarra* (1934); most critics find his later work less significant. KATHERINE ANNE PORTER wrote a short, incisive novel in NOON WINE (1937), as did NATHANAEL WEST in *Miss Lonelyhearts* (1933). Of the best-selling authors of the time, HERVEY ALLEN (*Anthony Adverse*, 1933) and Margaret Mitchell (GONE WITH THE WIND, 1936) had sensational successes with overblown and racy historical romances; other practitioners of the genre were KENNETH ROBERTS (NORTHWEST PASSAGE, 1937); MACKINLAY KANTOR (*Long Remember*, 1934); and Stark Young (*So Red the Rose*, 1934). MARJORIE KINNAN RAWLINGS wrote moving stories of Florida crackers in SOUTH MOON UNDER (1933) and THE YEARLING (1938); other regionalists were CARL CARMER (STARS FELL ON ALABAMA, 1934) and JULIA PETERKIN (SCARLET SISTER MARY, 1928). PEARL BUCK, another Nobel Prizewinner, wrote of a Chinese family in THE GOOD EARTH (1931). The rather old-fashioned "inspirational" novel was kept alive by LLOYD C. DOUGLAS (*Magnificent Obsession*, 1929; *Green Light*, 1935). WILLIAM SAROYAN began his offbeat career with short stories and plays, but went on to write novels like THE HUMAN COMEDY (1943). Detective stories and other escapist fiction generally overshadowed more serious work on the best-seller lists of the period, and book clubs and lending libraries contributed to the growth of a middlebrow art by arranging much wider distribution than most American writers had ever enjoyed before.

The decade of the 1940's was marked by America's participation in World War II and the aftermath in which the cold war began. Novels about the armed conflict started to appear even while battles still raged: JOHN STEINBECK, *The Moon Is Down* (1942); JOHN HERSEY, *A Bell for Adano* (1944). As the experience of the 1920's had indicated, many younger writers were to return from the fronts to pour out their experiences in ever franker and more profane novels: JAMES JONES, FROM HERE TO ETERNITY (1951); NORMAN MAILER, THE NAKED AND THE DEAD (1948); IRWIN SHAW, THE YOUNG LIONS (1948); HERMAN WOUK, THE CAINE MUTINY (1951). Several of these men were to continue their writing careers into the next two decades, usually with less acclaim. Older authors, too, tried their hand at wartime fiction; JAMES GOULD COZZENS (*The Just and the Unjust*, 1942) published *Guard of Honor* in 1948, then returned to other fields in *By Love Possessed* (1957).

The "southern renascence" in literature begun by Glasgow, Faulkner, Wolfe, and others continued with EUDORA WELTY (*Delta Wedding*, 1946); TRUMAN CAPOTE (OTHER VOICES, OTHER ROOMS, 1948); CARSON McCULLERS (THE MEMBER OF THE WEDDING, 1946); and CAROLINE GORDON (*Green Centuries*, 1941). Probably the best of the younger southern writers was ROBERT PENN WARREN (1905–   ), who began his career in fiction with *Night Rider* (1939) and *At Heaven's Gate* (1943), but who won his first popular and critical success with ALL THE KING'S MEN (1946), one of the finest novels of the decade; his later works, generally less well received, have included WORLD ENOUGH AND TIME (1950), *Band of Angels* (1955), and *The Cave* (1959).

NELSON ALGREN continued the big-city novel in THE MAN WITH THE GOLDEN ARM (1949) and *A Walk on the Wild Side* (1956). In the same period devotees of less intellectual fiction were reading KATHLEEN WINSOR (FOREVER AMBER, 1944); TAYLOR CALDWELL (*This Side of Innocence*, 1946); FRANK YERBY (*The Foxes of Harrow*, 1946); SAMUEL SHELLABARGER (*The Prince of Foxes,* 1947); and Frances Parkinson Keyes (*Crescent Carnival,* 1942). Science fiction, perhaps stimulated by general interest in atomic physics, attracted a growing band of enthusiasts.

One phenomenon of the 1950's was the appearance of the so-called "beat generation," a group of totally disengaged nonconformists who drew more attention to their bearded, shaggy selves than to their writing; representative was JACK KEROUAC, whose ON THE ROAD (1957) exposed their main interests: rapid and aimless travel, sex, jazz, dope, drink, Zen Buddhism (see BEAT WRITING). Much more effective as literary art were other novels of the decade: WRIGHT MORRIS (*The Field of Vision,* 1956); SAUL BELLOW (THE ADVENTURES OF AUGIE MARCH, 1953); RALPH ELLISON (*Invisible Man,* 1952); RANDALL JARRELL (*Pictures from an Institution,* 1954); and HERBERT GOLD (*The Man Who Was Not With It,* 1956). Another new talent was welcomed in WILLIAM STYRON, whose *Lie Down in Darkness* (1951) suggested discipleship to the Faulknerian method. Perhaps the greatest critical and popular triumph was that of J. D. SALINGER; his THE CATCHER IN THE RYE (1951), about a sort of citified Huck Finn, caught exactly the idiom and rhythm of speech of an outwardly hard but inwardly sensitive teen-ager. Salinger's highly individual style has won him a following which may not always have comprehended his unusual and complex combination of surface profaneness and underlying mysticism.

By the early 1960's great potentialities had been recognized in Flannery O'Connor, Harper Lee, BERNARD MALAMUD, and others, but it was still too early to assess their lasting importance. At a decade past mid-century it was fashionable to ask, "What is the matter with the American novel?"—a question that apparently stemmed from the fact that no group had arisen since World War II comparable to the formidable array which began publication in the 1920's. It was true that much creative talent was being drained off by mass media: journalism, television and radio, advertising, and films. But, paradoxically, the "paperback revolution" put a record number of both old and new books into the hands of an expanding reading audience. Even the most avant-garde younger writer often could find a publisher willing to take a risk; and

sales, owing to widespread distribution and advertising methods, were apt to exceed by far the figures for the earliest works of an author such as Faulkner.

At such close range no new "schools" or significant new directions were observable in the most recent American fiction. Many serious younger novelists were college-trained—some kept up the academic connection as teaching "writers in residence"—and they showed acquaintance with and the influence of the whole range of American and foreign literatures. If any similarity was to be noted in the rising generation it was their common interest in form (style, structure, symbol, narrative technique) over "story" as such; technically, they were often more highly accomplished than were many of their elders. They were also less committed to any particular political or religious philosophy; they were searching for answers rather than expounding them.

Finally, it seemed likely that serious creative fiction would continue to be produced in America, despite pressures toward conformity and increasing competition from other media. The novel had always been split into tales calculated to fetch a mass audience and works which, their authors realized, could be appreciated by a relative few only. As Henry James once remarked, the house of fiction has many doors. Toward the end of the second century of the American novel it still appeared probable that there were a few more for the dedicated writer to open.

Standard histories of the American novel are: Alexander Cowie, *The Rise of the American Novel* (1948); Carl Van Doren, *The American Novel, 1789–1939* (1940); and Arthur Hobson Quinn, *American Fiction* (1936). Useful bibliographies are to be found in the third volume of *Literary History of the United States* (1948), and in Lyle H. Wright, *American Fiction, 1774–1850* (1948), and *American Fiction, 1851–1875* (1957). Important recent studies are: Marius Bewley, *The Complex Fate* (1954), and *The Eccentric Design* (1959); Richard Chase, *The American Novel and Its Tradition* (1957); Leslie Fiedler, *Love and Death in the American Novel* (1960); Maxwell Geismar, *Writers in Crisis* (1942), *Last of the Provincials* (1947), *Rebels and Ancestors* (1953), and *American Moderns* (1958); Daniel G. Hoffman, *Form and Fable in American Fiction* (1961); Frederick J. Hoffman, *The Modern Novel in America* (1957); James D. Hart, *The Popular Book* (1950); Alfred Kazin, *On Native Grounds* (1942); William Wasserstrom, *Heiress of All the Ages* (1959). Other special studies are: Lars Ahnebrink, *The Beginnings of Naturalism* (1950); Joseph Blotner, *The Political Novel* (1955); Herbert R. Brown, *The Sentimental Novel* (1940); Leon Edel, *The Psychological Novel* (1955); Blanche H. Gelfant, *The American City Novel* (1954); Jay B. Hubbell, *The South in American Literature* (1954); Ernest E. Leisy, *The American Historical Novel* (1950); Harry Levin, *The Power of Blackness* (1958); R. W. B. Lewis, *The American Adam*

(1958); Perry Miller, *The Raven and the Whale* (1956); Walter B. Rideout, *The Radical Novel* (1956); Henry Nash Smith, *Virgin Land* (1950); Walter F. Taylor, *The Economic Novel* (1942); Charles C. Walcutt, *American Literary Naturalism* (1956). Good studies of symbolism are: William York Tindall, *The Literary Symbol* (1955); and Charles Feidelson, Jr., *Symbolism and American Literature* (1952).

JOSEPH V. RIDGELY

novelette. One of many terms used to describe a fictional narrative which is longer and more complex than a short story but lacks the length and the varied structure of a novel. Other terms employed are *nouvelle, novella, short novel.* William Phillips made a special study of this form in his collection of *Great American Short Novels* (1946), which includes Herman Melville's *Benito Cereno* (1855); Henry James' WASHINGTON SQUARE (1880); Stephen Crane's MAGGIE (1893); Gertrude Stein's MELANCTHA (1909); Edith Wharton's *False Dawn* (1924); F. Scott Fitzgerald's THE GREAT GATSBY (1925); Katherine Anne Porter's *Pale Horse, Pale Rider* (1936); and Glenway Wescott's *The Pilgrim Hawk* (1940). Henry James reached great distinction in other novelettes, such as *An International Episode* (1879). Edith Wharton's group of tales, OLD NEW YORK (4 v., 1924), represents another highly successful use of this art form.

November Boughs (1888), a collection of poems and prose pieces by WALT WHITMAN. Many of the poems had already appeared in the New York *Herald,* were later gathered into the 1889 edition of *Leaves of Grass.* The preface, A BACKWARD GLANCE O'ER TRAVEL'D ROADS, was likewise included in this edition.

Noyes, John Humphrey (b. Brattleboro, Vt., Sept. 3, 1811—d. April 13, 1886), Utopian, primitive communist. Noyes, trained for the ministry at Andover and Yale, lost his license to preach when it became clear that he accepted the Bible with the utmost literalness and was not prepared to compromise in any way. He urged the overthrow of the government of the United States so that Jesus Christ might take immediate control. He established a communistic colony at Putney, Vt., in 1836, but had to make a hasty departure ten years later when charges of adultery, based on the colony's system of marriages, were preferred against him. Later he founded the famous Oneida Community, where similar doctrines were preached, including both polygyny and polyandry. Again Noyes fled, this time to Canada. For a time he edited a magazine called *The Perfectionist* (founded, 1834). He was a facile and explosive writer. Among his books: *The Berean* (1847); *Male Continence* (1848); *Scientific Propagation* (about 1873); *Home Talks* (1875). His *History of American Socialisms* (1870) gives an account of colonies like his own. George W. Noyes edited *The Religious Experience of John Humphrey Noyes* (1923) and *John Humphrey Noyes: The*

Putney Community (1931); Robert Allerton Parker wrote *A Yankee Saint: John Humphrey Noyes and the Oneida Community* (1935).

Nullification, Doctrine of. A theory, held largely in the South and particularly in South Carolina, that the Constitution grants only limited powers to the Federal government, that the latter is primarily a league of states, and that any state can decide for itself whether it wants to accept an Act of Congress. The doctrine was most effectively set forth by JOHN C. CALHOUN, took active form when South Carolina tried to nullify a tariff act in 1832, became quiescent when President Jackson took prompt steps to enforce the act. E. P. Powell wrote on *Nullification and Secession* (1897), and David F. Houston made *A Critical Study of Nullification in South Carolina* (1902).

Number One (1943), a novel by JOHN DOS PASSOS. This is the second novel in the *Spottswood Series,* which begins with *Adventures of a Young Man* (1939). The book is a study of a southern politician strikingly like Huey Long. The three titles in the series appeared in one volume, *District of Columbia* (1952). See GLENN SPOTTSWOOD.

nursery rhymes. When settlers from the British Isles came to America, they brought with them old ballads and folk tales, also rhymes used to soothe or teach young children and other rhymes that children used in games. American attempts to reform these rhymes go back to SAMUEL GRISWOLD GOODRICH (Peter Parley), who almost succeeded during the mid-19th century in banishing Mother Goose from so-called "better homes," calling the pieces "coarse, vulgar, offensive." Others, disturbed by the violence and cruelty in some of the rhymes, have followed his lead, to bring about what the *Daily Mirror* of London (Nov. 3, 1948) called "Trouble in Fairyland." Meanwhile American children have invented new rhymes or new lines for older ballads. Carl Withers made an astonishing collection of these transformations and additions in *A Rocket in My Pocket: Rhymes and Chants for Young Americans* (1948).

Nuttall, Thomas (b. England, Jan. 5, 1786—d. Sept. 10, 1859), printer, botanist, ornithologist, explorer. In 1808 Nuttall came to America as a journeyman printer. BENJAMIN SMITH BARTON of the College of Philadelphia aroused his interest in botany, to such an extent that he joined an expedition to the Platte and Mandan regions and almost lost his life. In 1817 he became a member of the American Philosophical Society; the next year he published his *Genera of North American Plants* (2 v.). About this time he began explorations in Arkansas, visiting dangerous territories never before visited by white men. He published his observations in *A Journal of Travels into the Arkansas Territory* (1821). In 1824 he was called to teach botany at Harvard. He is said to have discovered more new genera and species of plants in North America than any other single scientist, with the possible exception of Asa Gray. He returned to England in the middle 1840's.

Nutting, Wallace (b. Marlboro, Mass., Nov. 17, 1861—d. July 19, 1941), clergyman, antiquarian, author. Deeply interested in history and its memorials, Nutting won a large audience with a series of gracefully illustrated and accurately written travel books: *Vermont Beautiful* (1922), *Massachusetts Beautiful* (1923), and others.

Nye, Bill [Edgar Wilson] (b. Shirley, Me., Aug. 25, 1850—d. Feb. 22, 1896), humorist, farmer, lawyer, justice of the peace, postmaster, legislator, newspaperman, playwright. Nye went to live in Wyoming, in 1881 founded the Laramie BOOMERANG, continuing as its editor until 1885. For this newspaper he wrote humorous sketches which were widely copied all over the country. In 1886 he began writing regularly for the New York *World*. About that time, too, he began his successful lecture tours. His wide variety of occupations and residences gave him plenty of material for his humorous writings and talks, which followed the tradition of Artemus Ward, Josh Billings, and others of delivering malapropisms, obvious lies, and incongruous remarks with a poker face.

Nye put out a great many books. A few of them are *Bill Nye and Boomerang* (1881); *Forty Liars and Other Lies* (1882); *Baled Hay* (1884); *Bill Nye's Chestnuts, New and Old* (1887); *Bill Nye Thinks* (1888; republished as *Sparks from the Pen of Bill Nye*, 1891); *Nye and Riley's Railway Guide* (1888; later called *Nye and Riley's Wit and Humor*, 1896); *Bill Nye's History of the U.S.* (1894). The *Railway Guide*, wrote Nye, was not "cursed by a plethora of facts or poisoned by information." "Wagner's music," he once remarked, "is better than it sounds." Nye's drama *The Cadi* (1891) was successfully produced; *The Stag Party*, written with PAUL POTTER (1895) was a failure. Everybody knew Nye in the last quarter of the 19th century; he was one of the chief public figures of the American scene. Frank W. Nye edited *Bill Nye: His Own Life Story* (1926). The University of Wyoming Library at Laramie has issued some of its Nye materials in *Letters of Edgar Wilson Nye*, edited by Nixon Orwin Rush (1952).

Nye, Russel Blaine (b. Viola, Wis., Feb. 17, 1913—   ), biographer, historian. In 1945 Nye expanded his dissertation on the historian Bancroft to a full length study which brought him a Pulitzer Prize. In his view, the historian of ideas should not strive to be completely neutral, since there is a right and wrong in the past, and the writer must make moral judgements of men and movements. His works: *George Bancroft: Brahmin Rebel* (1945); *Fettered Freedom* (1949); *Midwestern Progressive Politics* (1951, 1959); *William Lloyd Garrison* (1955); *The Cultural Life of the New Nation* (1960).

O

Oakes, Urian (b. England, 1631[?]—d. July 25, 1681), clergyman, teacher, poet. Oakes came to the Massachusetts colony around 1640, graduated from Harvard in 1649, later served as fellow and tutor at that college, but returned to England in 1650. After serving as a clergyman and teacher there for some years, he came back to this country and took over a church in Cambridge. He became a censor of the Massachusetts press, served briefly as president of Harvard.

Oakes was a man of sharp wit and great learning. Some of his highly logical sermons have survived. He expressed his emphatic views chiefly in *New England Pleaded With* (1673); he denounced freedom of worship as the "first-born of all abominations." His finest literary production was his *Elegy Upon the Death of the Rev. Mr. Thomas Shepard* (1677), the best of the funeral elegies which Puritan writers turned out with such facility and dullness.

Oakes-Smith, Elizabeth [Mrs. Seba Smith]. See ELIZABETH OAKES SMITH.

Oakhurst, John. A character in Bret Harte's THE OUTCASTS OF POKER FLAT, THE LUCK OF ROARING CAMP, and other tales of early California. Oakhurst is a professional gambler who finds his victims in mining camps. He is presented as having "the melancholy air and intellectual abstraction of a Hamlet," and he is capable of noble acts, one of which brings him death in the story of Poker Flat. Like Harte's other gambler, Jack or John Conroy, who appears in GABRIEL CONROY and some short stories, Oakhurst seems to have been modeled on a real person.

Oakley, Annie [stage name of Phoebe Anna Oakley Mozee (or Moses)] (b. Darke Co., Ohio, Aug. 13, 1860—d. Nov. 3, 1926), actress, sharpshooter. Early in life Miss Oakley became an expert marksman. She met and beat a professional named Frank Butler and then married him. She became a star in Buffalo Bill's "Original Wild West Show." (See WILLIAM F. CODY.) After recovering from an injury received in a train wreck, Miss Oakley went back to show business, but this time worked in vaudeville. Courtney R. Cooper wrote *Annie Oakley: Woman at Arms* (1927); Stewart H. Holbrook wrote *Little Annie Oakley and Other Rugged People* (1948); Walter Havighurst wrote *Annie Oakley of the Wild West* (1954). She was the heroine of the rollicking musical comedy, *Annie Get Your Gun* (1946), which starred Ethel Merman as Annie. Free passes to theatrical performances are sometimes called "Annie Oakleys" because of the holes usually punched in them.

Oath of a Free Man (1639). This document was the first piece of printing done in the English settlements in America. It has come down to us in the form given it by Major John Child in his *New England's Jonas Cast up at London* (1647). Child in this tract upheld the laws of England, which permitted non-Puritan religious worship, for the colonies. In reply the General Court of Massachusetts declared: "Our allegiance binds us not to the laws of England any longer than while we live in England." This declaration was simultaneously a declaration of independence and for intolerance.

Oboler, Arch (b. Chicago, Dec. 6, 1907—   ), radio and movie playwright, director, producer. Prolific in ideas and in composition, Oboler's work includes an enormous number of scripts. He was the first radio dramatist to publish an entire book of radio plays—*Fourteen Radio Plays* (1940), with an introduction on "The Art of Radio Writing." Other collections include *Ivory Tower* (1940); *This Freedom* (1941); *Plays for Americans* (1942); *Free World Theater* (1944); *Oboler Omnibus* (1945); *Night of the Auk* (1958).

O'Brien, Edward J[oseph] (b. Boston, Dec. 10, 1890—d. Feb. 25, 1941), newspaperman, writer, editor. Although O'Brien published a volume of poems and wrote several plays, he was best known for a long series of collections in which he passed judgment on contemporary short stories. His first collection, *The Best Short Stories of 1915* (see BEST AMERICAN SHORT STORIES), was followed by annual volumes until 1940, after which the series was continued by other hands. In 1921 he began a similar series of *Best British Short Stories*. He likewise edited *The Great Modern English Stories* (1919), *Elizabethan Tales* (1937), and other compilations.

O'Brien, Fitz-James (b. Ireland, *c.* 1828—d. April 6, 1862), poet, playwright, short-story writer. Before he was twenty-four, O'Brien had published a large number of stories, poems, and articles in Irish and English periodicals. In 1852 he arrived in New York and soon established himself as a member of the Bohemian circle that met in PFAFF'S CELLAR at 647 Broadway. He was as prodigal of his energies as of his money, turning out a flood of stories, poems, plays, and sketches, the best of which appeared in *Putnam's Magazine, Harper's,* and the *Atlantic*. His plays, mostly in one-act form, were written for James W. Wallack (1791–1864), a noted actor-manager. The most successful, *A Gentleman from Ireland*, was revived as late as 1895. When the Civil War broke out, O'Brien volunteered, and died of a wound received in the battle of Bloomery Gap.

O'Brien had remarkable inventiveness and was a forerunner of the science fiction writer. His best known tales, THE DIAMOND LENS, WHAT WAS IT?, and *The Wondersmith*, reveal a lively and unusual fancy and a fine style. His poetry has not stood the test of time so well.

Poems and Stories of Fitz-James O'Brien, Collected and Edited, With a Sketch of the Author, by William Winter, appeared in 1881.

O'Brien, Frank Michael (b. Dunkirk, N.Y., March 31, 1875—d. Sept. 22, 1943), editor, writer. O'Brien was city editor of the Buffalo *Express,* editor of the New York *Sun,* secretary to the Mayor of New York City, and served on the staff of the New York *Press* and the New York *Herald.* He wrote *The Story of the Sun* (1918) and *New York Murder Mysteries* (1932), also numerous short stories. He won a Pulitzer Prize (1921) for his editorial "The Unknown Soldier."

O'Brien, Frederick (b. Baltimore, Md., June 16, 1869—d. Jan. 9, 1932), newspaperman, author. As a youth O'Brien shipped out in a cattle boat, tramped through several South American countries, hoboed in the United States. Then he began working for newspapers, and ended as the publisher of two California papers. He spent a year in the South Seas and wrote a book on his adventures, *White Shadows in the South Seas* (1919). Its success started a controversy when ROSE WILDER LANE claimed to have written the book for O'Brien; he replied that she had merely typed it. He wrote two similar books, in which Mrs. Lane had no share: *Mystic Isles of the South Seas* (1921) and *Atolls of the Sun* (1922). His books brought about a revival of interest in the South Seas, perhaps helped with the Melville revival.

O'Brien, Howard Vincent (b. Chicago, July 11, 1888—d. Sept. 30, 1947), editor, novelist, autobiographer. In 1911 O'Brien founded the magazine *Art,* serving as editor from 1911 to 1914. From 1928 to 1932 he was literary editor of the Chicago *Daily News,* and wrote a column for it from 1932 until his death. Among his published works are: *New Men for Old* (1912); *Trodden Gold* (1922); *The Terms of the Conquest* (1923, under the pseudonym Clyde Perrin); *The Thunder Bolt* (1923); *The Green Scarf* (1924), a novel; *What a Man Wants* (1925); *Wine, Women and War: A Diary of Disillusionment* (1929, pub. anonymously); *An Abandoned Woman* (1930), a novel; *Folding Bedouins* (1936), dealing with trailer travel; *Memoirs of a Guinea Pig* (1942); *So Long, Son* (1944), a personal narrative; *All Things Considered: Memories, Experiences and Observations of a Chicagoan* (1948).

O'Brien, Seumas (b. Ireland, April 26, 1880—   ), sculptor, short-story writer, dramatist. O'Brien lived in America from 1913 to 1949 and did much of his attractive and whimsical writing and sculpture here. Among his plays: *Duty and Other Comedies* (1916); *Blind* (1918); *The Bird Catcher* (1918); *The Wild Boar* (1927); *Christmas Eve* (1928); *The Well* (1937); *Queen Puff-Puff* (1937). He also wrote *The Whale and the Grasshopper and Other Fables* (1916).

O Captain! My Captain! (1865; rev., 1867), a poem by WALT WHITMAN. This memorial on the death of ABRAHAM LINCOLN was first published in DRUM-TAPS, then included in the 1867 and 1871 editions of LEAVES OF GRASS. One of the few poems that Whitman wrote using conventional rhyme and meter, *O Captain! My Captain!* is somewhat suggestive of the verse of Poe in its use of emphatic rhythm and internal rhyme. It was highly popular at the time of its publication and continues to be widely anthologized.

Occom [also spelled **Occum** and **Ockum**], **Samson** (b. 1723—d. July 14, 1792), missionary, hymn writer, editor. A Mohegan Indian, Occom was converted in 1739 and thereafter educated by Eleazar Wheelock, who later became the first president of Dartmouth. Occom became a clergyman in 1759 and went out as a missionary to various Indian tribes, later visited England to raise money for the founding of Dartmouth, originally a college for Indian students. In 1774 he published *A Choice Collection of Hymns and Spiritual Songs.* He was credited with the authorship of several of these, particularly *Awaked by Sinai's Awful Sound,* and is therefore regarded as the first Presbyterian hymn writer in America. Harold W. Blodgett gave an account of him in *Samson Occom* (1935).

Ochs, Adolph S[imon] (b. Cincinnati, Ohio, Mar. 12, 1858—d. April 8, 1935), publisher, editor. Ochs began his newspaper career at the age of eleven as a carrier and printer's apprentice in Knoxville, Tenn. Three years later he became a newspaper compositor. In 1878, borrowing 250 dollars, he bought the *Chattanooga Times* and built it into a prosperous and influential paper. When the panic of 1893 swept away most of Ochs' fortune, his brilliant career might have come to an end but for a magnificent gamble: he went to New York and, using promises to supplement a moderate amount of cash, in 1896 bought *The New York Times,* which competition with Pulitzer and Hearst papers had very nearly killed. He was keen enough to realize that the *Times* could not compete with yellow journalism. So with a new slogan, "All the news that's fit to print," the *Times* made a point of shunning sensationalism and this appeal to the better nature of readers succeeded. Dignified, nonpartisan, offering additional features like financial coverage, book reviews, and improved foreign reporting, the *Times* increased its circulation by leaps and bounds, soon becoming one of the most influential papers in the country. It became noted particularly for its documentation of the news. Ochs gave the *Times* his own dignity, fearlessness, and strength of character. At his death he was succeeded by his son-in-law, ARTHUR HAYS SULZBERGER. Ochs also published the Philadelphia *Times* (1902–12) and the Philadelphia *Public Ledger* (1902–12). Ochs' interest in public welfare led him into such widely diverse philanthropies as founding the Chattanooga Lookout Mountain Park and making possible the publication of the DICTIONARY OF AMERICAN BIOGRAPHY. In 1946 Gerald W. Johnson wrote *An Honorable Titan: A Biographical Study of Adolph S. Ochs.*

O'Connor, Edwin (b. Providence, R.I., July

29, 1918—d. March 23, 1968), novelist. After graduation from college in 1939, O'Connor became a radio announcer; and his first novel, *The Oracle* (1951), was derived from his experiences in that field. THE LAST HURRAH (1956), a fictitious portrait of a Boston political machine boss, was a best-seller subsequently made into a motion picture. *The Edge of Sadness* (1961), which received the 1962 Pulitzer Prize for fiction, was a perceptive study of the working of God's grace in the lives of a pastor and his charges, second- and third-generation Irish immigrants, in a decaying parish in a thinly disguised Boston.

O'Connor, Flannery (b. Savannah, Ga., Aug. 12, 1925—d. Aug. 3, 1964), novelist, short story writer. Her novels *Wise Blood* (1952) and *The Violent Bear It Away* (1960) are somber tales of southern religious fanaticism. Her colorful description and realistic dialogue are combined to produce a fascinating picture of Georgia backwoods society. *A Good Man Is Hard to Find* (1955) is a collection of grotesques which show the writer's talent in treating traditional Southern themes.

O'Connor, William Douglas (b. Boston, Jan. 2, 1832—d. May 9, 1889), newspaperman, government clerk, writer. O'Connor, himself a government employee, secured for WALT WHITMAN a similar position in the Department of the Interior; and when James Harlan, head of the department, dismissed Whitman because he had written an "obscene" book (LEAVES OF GRASS), O'Connor wrote a vigorous pamphlet in Whitman's behalf, THE GOOD GRAY POET: A VINDICATION (1866), and secured him another job in the Attorney General's office. O'Connor was a smooth but sometimes hasty writer. He also wrote an antislavery novel. *Harrington* (1860). After his death Whitman wrote a preface for a posthumous collection, *Three Tales* (1892), by O'Connor.

O'Connor, William Van (b. Syracuse, N.Y., Jan. 10, 1915—d. Sept. 26, 1966), critic, writer. During his graduate work in English at Columbia, O'Connor felt troubled by what he called "the animus between scholars on the one hand, and poets, novelists, and critics on the other." For him the NEW CRITICISM, which he came on while teaching at Ohio State in 1940, solved the problem by promising the "union of literary and scholarly interests." A friendship with the poet Karl Shapiro sharpened his interest in modern poetry and criticism. O'Connor's work has been predominantly criticism, and he has made frequent contributions to literary journals. His works include the following: *Sense and Sensibility in Modern Poetry* (1948); *Forms of Modern Fiction* (1948, ed.); *The Shaping Spirit: A Study of Wallace Stevens* (1950); *An Age of Criticism* (1952); *Modern Prose, Form and Style* (1959, ed.); *A Casebook on Ezra Pound* (co-editor with Edward Stone, 1959).

October Island (1952), a novel by WILLIAM MARCH. March tells the story of a staid missionary's wife who is transformed unexpectedly into a modern goddess by the admiration of the natives on a South Sea island. The tale is March's sardonic comment on religion—or one kind of religion.

Octopus, The (1901), a novel by FRANK NORRIS. Inspired by the naturalistic studies of Zola, Norris tried to write the Great American Novel in *The Octopus*, which depicts the struggle for power between California wheat ranchers and "the Railroad," the octopus which encircles and strangles them. The climax of the novel, a pitched battle between farmers and railroad men, was founded on a historic incident known as the Mussel Slough affair. A love affair is woven into the main plot. In spite of many faults, *The Octopus*, with its epic sweep, its vivid descriptions, its thoughtful presentation of social and economic problems, was a landmark in the development of the American novel. THE PIT (1903) was a sequel; the third volume of a proposed trilogy was never written.

Octoroon, The (1859), a play by DION BOUCICAULT. This popular play on a favorite theme of American fiction and drama was based by the Irish dramatist on a novel, *The Quadroon* (1856), by the English author Captain Mayne Reid. Zoe, a slave of mixed blood, must be sold by a man who loves her to a man they both hate. It was the ancestor of many other treatments of the social effect of the presence of Negro blood. It was revived in New York in 1961, at the Phoenix Theatre.

Ode Inscribed to W. H. Channing (1847), by RALPH WALDO EMERSON. This is a key statement of Emerson's thoroughly individual views regarding the practicality of humanitarian reform. He had apparently been asked by W. H. CHANNING, a nephew of WILLIAM ELLERY CHANNING and like him a Unitarian minister and ardent humanitarian, to make a definite pronouncement on slavery. But Emerson refused (though later he changed his mind). In his poem he lamented that "Things are in the saddle,/ And ride mankind"; and he said he did not believe, as seemingly Channing did, that it would do any good to "rend the Northland from the South." Yet he was confident that "the over-god" would somehow bring good things to pass: "Wise and sure the issues are." In a paper on *New England Reformers* Emerson remarked that "society gains nothing whilst a man, not himself renovated, attempts to renovate things around him." On another occasion he said: "I have quite other slaves to free than those Negroes; to wit, imprisoned spirits, imprisoned thoughts." In his address on John Brown he nevertheless spoke out vigorously against slavery, as he did in the BOSTON HYMN (1863).

Ode in Time of Hesitation, An (*Atlantic Monthly*, May, 1900), a poem by WILLIAM VAUGHN MOODY. The imperialistic spirit aroused by our easy victory in the Spanish-American War threatened to result in the annexation of the Philippines. A vigorous voice raised against imperialism was that of Moody in this noble poem, which is a tribute to Robert

Gould Shaw as well as a plea to "let the island men go free."

Odell, George C[linton] D[ensmore] (b. Newburgh, N.Y., March 19, 1866—d. Oct. 17, 1949), teacher, authority on the drama. Odell was associated with Columbia University, first as an undergraduate, then as a teacher, and from 1895 as professor of English and dramatic literature. In 1893 he compiled *Simile and Metaphor in the English and Scottish Ballads,* in 1920 published *Shakespeare from Betterton to Irving* (2 v.). He is best known for his invaluable *Annals of the New York Stage* (1927–45), of which fourteen of the projected sixteen volumes appeared. This encyclopedic work contains photographs of actors, playbills, excerpts from contemporary criticism, and the history of the New York stage in minute detail.

Odell, Jonathan (b. Newark, N.J., Sept. 25, 1737—d. Nov. 25, 1818), clergyman, physician, satirist. Odell became a physician, was admitted to orders as an Anglican clergyman, during the Revolution served in the British forces as both chaplain and physician. He wrote songs for the British soldiers to sing, directed violent satires against American leaders, was an important underground agent for the British government. His most prolific year seems to have been 1779, when he wrote *The Word of Congress; The Congratulation; The Feu de Joie;* and *The American Times.* In 1783 Odell went to England as assistant secretary to Sir Guy Carleton; the following year he settled in the loyalist province of New Brunswick in Canada.

Ode Recited at the Harvard Commemoration (July 21, 1865), by James Russell Lowell. See COMMEMORATION ODE.

Ode Sung on the Occasion of Decorating the Graves of the Confederate Dead (1867), by HENRY TIMROD. This pathetic and melodious poem, printed in Timrod's *Poems* (1873), praises the "martyrs of a fallen cause." It was delivered at Magnolia Cemetery in Charleston, S.C. Edd Winfield Parks describes it as throbbing with vibrant emotion, yet as also possessing "a classic coolness of phrase"; he holds it to be the noblest of Timrod's poems.

Ode to the Confederate Dead (*The American Caravan,* 1927; rev. in *Mr. Pope and Other Poems,* 1928; rev. again in *Selected Poems,* 1937), by ALLEN TATE. Probably the best known of Tate's poems, this is a meditation in a Confederate graveyard, less a tribute to dead soldiers than an ironic comment on death, change, and modern times. It is an obscure poem, as Tate himself admitted implicitly by writing a prose commentary, and reminiscent of T. S. Eliot in tone and cadence. F. O. Matthiessen concluded that in the *Ode* Tate deliberately contrasts the "active faith" of the Southern past with the contemporary "solipsism . . . that denotes the failure of the human personality to function properly in nature and rhythm."

Odets, Clifford (b. Philadelphia, July 18, 1906—d. Aug. 14, 1963), playwright. Odets grew up in New York City and on leaving high

school turned to acting and writing. He worked for the Theatre Guild until the Group Theatre was formed to apply the methods developed by Stanislavski and the Moscow Art Theatre. In 1931 he joined the Group Theatre and his early plays well suited its naturalistic methods. His first two plays, which are often considered his best, dealt with social conflicts: WAITING FOR LEFTY (1935) and AWAKE AND SING (1935). They brought him fame. He continued to treat socialistic themes in his succeeding plays, but his ideology obscured his talent in most of them: *Till the Day I Die* (1935); *Paradise Lost* (1935); *I Can't Sleep* (1936); GOLDEN BOY (1937); *Night Music* (1940); *Clash By Night* (1941). These were for the most part failures and Odets turned to writing screen plays for Hollywood. His distaste for the commercialism and corruption in filmland is evident in *The Big Knife* (1948).

Odets main problem has been to live up to the triumph of his early works. With *The Country Girl* (1950) he managed to renew his success. The play marks the end of his preoccupation with political themes and centers on the struggle of a young woman to remain faithful to her dissolute husband. *The Flowering Peach* (1954) did not do so well.

Odets' style is theatrically very effective, occasionally rhetorical and even hysterical, sometimes poignantly lyrical. He has claimed kinship with Chekhov, and Joseph Wood Krutch agrees that in style and character portrayal there is a great similarity between the two playwrights.

Odiorne, Thomas (b. 1769—d. 1851), poet, philosopher. Odiorne was deeply influenced by the philosophy of John Locke; Leon Howard wrote about him as *An American Predecessor of Wordsworth* (*American Literature,* 1939). He is remembered for his long poem, *The Progress of Refinement* (1792).

Odum, Howard Washington (b. Bethlehem, Ga., May 24, 1884—d. Nov. 8, 1954), sociologist, teacher, writer, administrator. Howard Odum received two Ph.D. degrees: one from Clark University (1909); one from Columbia University (1910). He taught at many different universities, primarily in North Carolina and Georgia. In his writings he attempted to explain the racial and regional dilemmas of the South by analyzing its history; he proposed various solutions to the problems which have been the inspiration of Southern liberals. He also wrote fiction and collected folklore. His works include: *Social and Mental Traits of the Negro* (1910); *Sociology and Social Problems* (1925); *The Negro and His Songs* (1925), with G. B. Johnson; *Rainbow Round My Shoulder* (1928), *Wings on My Feet* (1929), and *Cold Blue Moon* (1931), all novels; *Southern Regions of the United States* (1936); *American Social Problems* (1939); *Race and Rumors of Race* (1943); *The Way of the South* (1947); *American Sociology* (1951), a history of the subject.

Of Mice and Men (1937), a novel by JOHN STEINBECK, dramatized by the author the same year. As Steinbeck consciously wrote this short novel "like a play," the dramatic unities are apparent throughout. The plot concerns George and his powerful, simple-minded friend Lennie, casual laborers who travel from one ranch to another, dreaming constantly of a place of their own. Written with great compassion and simplicity, *Of Mice and Men* was an outstanding success as a novel; as a drama it won the Drama Critics Circle Award for 1937. It was also made into a film (1939).

Of Thee I Sing (prod. 1931; pub. 1932), a musical comedy with music by GEORGE GERSHWIN and text by GEORGE S. KAUFMAN, IRA GERSHWIN, and Morris Ryskind. This amusing political satire and collection of first-rate songs is built around a Presidential campaign with John P. Wintergreen as the leading candidate. His running mate is Alexander Throttlebottom, a retiring and insignificant little man who aptly satirizes the Vice-Presidency. The campaign managers decide that Wintergreen must marry, and his mate is to be the winner of an Atlantic City beauty contest. It was the first musical to win a Pulitzer prize. Some of the lyrics linger in the popular memory, especially "Wintergreen for President" and "Of Thee I Sing, Baby."

Of Time and the River: A Legend of Man's Hunger in His Youth (1935), a semiautobiographical novel by THOMAS WOLFE. A sequel to LOOK HOMEWARD, ANGEL, this novel appeared at the publisher's office as an enormous, diffused manuscript of several thousand pages entitled *The October Fair*. Working long hours with editor MAXWELL PERKINS of Scribner's, Wolfe was persuaded to prune away a good part of the manuscript and divide the remainder into two works. The second half was included in THE WEB AND THE ROCK, published posthumously in 1939. *Of Time and the River* deals with Eugene Gant's studies in a playwriting course at Harvard, work as an English instructor at New York University, and his European tour. Wolfe's powerful and exuberant style, his poignant descriptions, his "chants and soliloquies and prose poems," and the violence of his reactions make this novel an exciting and important work.

Carl Van Doren believes, as do most critics, that Thomas Wolfe's four novels are really only one, "a tumultuous series of scenes held together by the unity of a single giant hunger and desire . . . haunted by the perpetual image of time as an infinite river in which men lead their short and trifling lives, so soon to be forgotten in the universal flood."

Oglethorpe, James Edward (b. England, 1696—d. 1785), philanthropist, colonist, administrator, member of the House of Commons. In 1722 Oglethorpe was elected to Parliament. In 1729 he acted as chairman of a parliamentary committee to investigate debtors' prisons; three years later he obtained a charter for the foundation of a colony in America—to be called Georgia after George II—which would be an asylum for persons newly released from debtors' prison and unemployed. He obtained many private contributions in response to an appeal, *A New and Accurate Account of South Carolina and Georgia* (1732). In October he sailed for this country with 120 settlers and founded Savannah. He acted as governor of Georgia until 1743, when he returned to England. He was again elected to Parliament, spent thirty-two years there. He was also a member of the Johnson circle in London. In her novel *Dark Sails* (1945), Helen T. Miller relates how Oglethorpe, defying Spanish threats, tried to settle the island of St. Simons, Ga.

O'Hara, John [Henry] (b. Pottsville, Pa., Jan. 31, 1905—d. Apr. 11, 1970), journalist, novelist, short-story writer. O'Hara worked on newspapers in Pennsylvania and New York City, also for *Newsweek, Time,* and *The New Yorker.*

Ann Zane Shanks

His first publication, a novel entitled *Appointment in Samarra* (1934), won him immediate fame. He went on to write many short stories, gathered into several collections, and several novels. The short story collection called PAL JOEY (1940) is perhaps the best known; the leading character became the central figure of a successful musical by that name for which O'Hara wrote the libretto (1940); the music and lyrics were by Richard Rodgers and Lorenz Hart. O'Hara is considered a master of the short story, an able commentator on a civilization he doesn't much care for, and an amusing portraitist of types not always particularly attractive. O'Hara has also published a collection of essays entitled *Sweet and Sour: Comments on Books and People* (1954). Among his other books: *Butterfield 8* (1935); *Hope of Heaven* (1938); *Files on Parade* (1939); *Pipe Night* (1945); *A Rage to Live* (1949); *Ten North Frederick* (1955); *A Family Party* (1956); *From the Terrace* (1958); *Ourselves to Know* (1960); *Assembly* (1961); *Sermons and Soda-Water* (1961).

O'Hara, Mary [Mary O'Hara Alsop] (b. Cape

May Point, N.J., July 10, 1885—   ), novelist, composer. After her first marriage Mary O'Hara Alsop moved to California, where she wrote scenarios. In 1930 she moved to a ranch in Wyoming which formed the background for her three novels about horses, *My Friend Flicka* (1941), *Thunderhead* (1943), and *The Green Grass of Wyoming* (1946). Flicka is a colt belonging to Ken McLaughlin, a boy who appears as a young man in the later novels. She discusses her own *The Son of Adam Wingate* (1952) in *Novel-in-the-Making* (1954). She has composed a number of popular musical works, of which *Wyoming Suite for Piano* (1946) is the most ambitious.

O'Hara, Scarlett. The heroine of Margaret Mitchell's best seller GONE WITH THE WIND (1936).

O'Hara, Theodore (b. Danville, Ky., Feb. 11, 1820—d. June 6, 1867), poet, teacher, editor, lawyer, soldier. O'Hara taught Greek, was admitted to the bar, edited newspapers in Alabama and Kentucky. He fought in the Mexican War, was wounded during the Cuban rebellion against Spain (1849), commanded a regiment in the Civil War. He was a favorite orator and wrote verse fluently. *The Bivouac of the Dead* and *The Old Pioneer* are almost the only poems of his remembered today. George W. Ranck wrote about *O'Hara and His Elegies* (1875), E. E. Hume on *Colonel Theodore O'Hara* (1936).

O. Henry. See HENRY, O.

O. Henry Memorial Prize Stories. In 1918 the Society of Arts and Sciences founded the O. Henry Memorial Awards for the best American short stories published each year; since 1919 an annual volume of the prize-winning stories —and others considered worthwhile—has been issued. In 1954 a special collection of thirty-four *First-Prize Stories from the O. Henry Memorial Awards, 1919–54* was edited by Harry Hansen.

Oh Promise Me (1889), a song by REGINALD DE KOVEN. This was composed as a single piece and was De Koven's first entry into the popular field. Later it was added as an aria to his opera *Robin Hood* (1890).

Oh, Susanna! (1848), a song by STEPHEN FOSTER. Written in Negro dialect and with catchy music that craved a banjo setting, this song became the great hit of its year and is one of Foster's most famous works. It was first performed by the Christy Minstrels and became a favorite with similar companies. Next it was picked up in the Gold Rush of 1849 as a sort of theme song for the gold hunters and by all the pioneering groups of the years that followed. Foster gave it outright to the music publisher W. C. Peters, along with several other songs. Peters made a fortune out of them; Foster never received any financial benefit. It was first published, with no credit to Foster, in a volume called *Music of the Original Christy Minstrels* (1848).

Oil! (1927), a novel by UPTON SINCLAIR. The Teapot Dome oil scandal of the Harding administration, which broke in the middle 1920's, resulted in Sinclair's best novel, *Oil!* Its plot is the familiar and not unrealistic one: a son breaks away from his father's "old-fashioned" ideas. In this instance, in a California milieu, the son of a wealthy oil operator, an independent doing his best to resist the encroachments and deadly competition of the big corporations, discovers that politicians are insidious creatures, that oil magnates are unscrupulous, that public officials are venal. With Sinclair's own ideological slant it is inevitable that Bunny Ross should become in time a socialist. The book is described as "a picture of civilization in Southern California."

Okie. An inhabitant of Oklahoma, used specifically in reference to the many who fled the state in the mid-1930's because of dust storms, the depression, and farm foreclosures. John Steinbeck's THE GRAPES OF WRATH (1939) deals with such a group who fled to California. The book vividly describes the migration and brought the term "Okie" into common usage. Among the other factual accounts of these people are: *Deserts on the March* (1935) by Paul Sears; *Rich Land, Poor Land* (1936) by Stuart Chase; *Factories in the Field* (1939) by Carey McWilliams; *An American Exodus* (1940) by Dorothea Lange and Paul Schuster Taylor.

Oklahoma! (1943), a folk musical with music by RICHARD RODGERS and book and lyrics by OSCAR HAMMERSTEIN II. This remarkable musical comedy is an adaptation of LYNN RIGGS' *Green Grow the Lilacs* (1931), a folk comedy set in the Indian Territory. The musical, with its memorable songs (especially "Oh, What a Beautiful Morning," "People Will Say We're in Love," "Pore Judd" and "The Surrey with the Fringe on Top"), opened on March 31, 1943, and closed on May 19, 1948. Its imaginative choreography, wrought by Agnes De Mille, brought her to the first rank and still remains a milestone in Broadway choreography. The musical received a Pulitzer Prize and has been performed all over the world.

Olcott, Chauncey [real name: **Chancellor John Olcott**] (b. Buffalo, N.Y., July 21, 1860— d. March 18, 1932), song writer, minstrel. This versatile performer appeared as a blackface minstrel, then made a specialty of dramas with an Irish background. He both wrote and sang *My Wild Irish Rose* (1899), which was first sung in the musical, *Romance of Athlone*, for which he wrote the libretto. He later assisted in the writing of *Mother Machree*, first sung in another of his operas, *Barry of Ballymore* (1910). For this Rida Johnson Young supplied the words; Olcott collaborated with Ernest Ball on the music. Olcott wrote and produced many other light operas, and himself appeared in some.

Olcott, Frances Jenkins (b. France, 188[?]—), librarian, children's writer. Miss Olcott became assistant librarian of the Brooklyn Public Library and later was chief of the children's department of the Carnegie Library of Pittsburgh. After her retirement she compiled many valuable book lists and pamphlets for teachers, parents, and professional storytellers. Among her numerous books for children are: *The Arabian Nights Entertainments* (1913); *Bible Stories to Read and Tell* (1916); *Wonder Tales from China Seas* (1925); *Wonder Tales from Baltic Wizards* (1928); *Island of Colored Shells* (1934); *The Book of Nature's Marvels* (1936); *The Bridge of Caravans* (1940); *In the Bright Syrian Land* (1946).

Old and New (1870–75), a magazine founded by EDWARD EVERETT HALE. In the magazine he exemplified the principles of his famous story, *Ten Times One Is Ten,* which led to the establishment of philanthropic societies all over the world and to the widespread "Lend a Hand" movement. Hale wrote articles and stories of many kinds for its pages; it was regarded as one of the leading magazines of the day. In 1875 it was absorbed by *Scribner's.*

Old Chester Tales (1898), short stories by MARGARET DELAND. Old Chester is actually Manchester, now a part of Pittsburgh. At the time this book was written it was a small, independent town populated by families of Scotch, Irish, and English descent. The different stories make up a single picture, with all the action revolving around Dr. Lavender, the elderly rector who appears in a number of Mrs. Deland's books.

Old Clock on the Stairs, The (1845), a poem by HENRY WADSWORTH LONGFELLOW. It was a favorite piece of the elocutionary era.

Old Corner Bookstore. A famous bookstore in Boston that was opened in 1828 by Timothy Carter. Many noted authors and publishers have made it a favorite rendezvous.

Old Creole Days (1879), short stories by GEORGE W. CABLE. The setting for all seven of these stories, and for the novelette MADAME DELPHINE which was included in the later editions, is 19th-century New Orleans. Although the plots are not particularly distinguished, Cable's blend of romance and realism, legend and local color, his skilful manipulation of the Creole dialect, and above all his ability to create fascinating characters combine to make a work that has now become a classic. His women, with their air of decadent nobility, their charming absurdity, their courage and coquetry, are not easily forgotten.

Old Farmer's Almanac, The (1793–   ). Published first in Massachusetts by Robert Bailey Thomas and originally called *The Farmer's Almanac,* this annual compilation was the backbone of many an old-time farmer's library. The *Almanac* consists of the "Farmer's Calendar," adorned with old-fashioned cuts and short poems; weather forecasts for the entire year; planting, gestation, and reproductive tables; digests of fish and game laws; anecdotes, recipes, charades, astrological lore (told with a sceptical note), and other odd bits of information. G. L. Kittredge's entertaining account of *The Old Farmer and His Almanack* (1904) points out the importance of this publication to the student of early American life.

Old Folks at Home (1851), also called *Swanee River,* by STEPHEN FOSTER. This, per-

haps Foster's greatest song, was at first attributed, at the author's wish, to the minstrel E. P. Christy, who paid Foster ten or fifteen dollars for the immediate rights. Six months later Foster asked Christy to let him put his own name to the song. Apparently Foster received royalties thereafter. Its enormous success convinced Foster that he should aim at becoming "the best Ethiopian song writer."

Old Grimes (*Providence Gazette,* Jan. 16, 1822), a humorous elegy by ALBERT GORTON GREENE. "Old Grimes" was the eccentric Ephraim Grimes, of Hubbardston, Mass., who actually did not die until twenty-two years after this alleged tribute to his virtues.

Old Homestead, The (1887). See DENMAN THOMPSON.

Old Ironsides (Boston *Daily Advertiser,* Sept. 16, 1830), a poem by OLIVER WENDELL HOLMES, SR. "Old Ironsides" was the popular name for the famous United States frigate *Constitution,* which played a notable part in the War of 1812, especially in a fight with the British frigate *Guerriere,* Aug. 19, 1812. In 1830 the navy decided the ship was no longer seaworthy, and she was condemned to be broken up and sold. Holmes saw the announcement and in great indignation sat down and wrote *Old Ironsides,* which made him famous and saved the *Constitution* from destruction. The ship was rebuilt and remained in active service for many years. It is now on exhibition at the Charleston (Mass.) naval yard.

Books about the famous vessel include C. W. Denison's *Old Ironsides and Old Adams* (1846); Justin Jones' *Mad Jack and Gentleman Jack, or, The Last Cruise of "Old Ironsides" Around the World* (1850); F. Alexander Magoun's *The Frigate Constitution and Other Historic Ships* (1928); Edward Buell's *Fighting Frigate* (1947).

Old Judge Priest (1915), stories by IRVIN S. COBB. The wise old Kentucky judge, operating in a town very much like Cobb's home town of Paducah, is a local Solomon who gets people out of all sorts of trouble by his deep insight into human nature and his profound sympathy with human beings, including those of a different pigmentation. At times he doesn't mind forgetting the letter of the law. These stories became the most famous of all Cobb's writings. He told other tales of the judge in *Down Yonder with Judge Priest and Irvin S. Cobb* (1932). Will Rogers played in a film based on the stories.

Old Kentucky Home. See MY OLD KENTUCKY HOME.

Old Maid, The (1924), a novelette by EDITH WHARTON. Appearing originally as one in a series of four small volumes entitled OLD NEW YORK, this tells the story of Tina, Charlotte Lovell's illegitimate daughter, who is brought up by Charlotte's cousin Delia in ignorance of her parentage. As she grows up she regards "Aunt Chatty" as a typical old maid; her devotion is given to Delia. The situation is almost too much for Charlotte, but to save the girl's happiness she finally reconciles herself to it. The story was ably dramatized by Zoë Akins in 1935, won a Pulitzer prize, and was later filmed.

Old Man and the Sea, The (1952), a novelette by Ernest Hemingway. Considered by many critics to be one of Hemingway's finest works, *The Old Man and the Sea* deals with an old Cuban fisherman who has had eighty-four days without a catch. Far from port on the eighty-fifth day he hooks a gigantic marlin, and, against great odds in a battle lasting two days, brings the fish alongside and harpoons it. Soon sharks appear, and the old man breaks his knife after he has killed only a few; during the last night of the voyage home the sharks devour all but the head of the great fish. The story is often interpreted as an allegory of man's inevitably losing struggle with existence; though the old man fights the great fish with courage and stoicism he is defeated in the end not by the fish—or by life itself—but by the sharks, or death. Hemingway, always a concise and economical writer, according to Malcolm Cowley here "gives words a new value . . . as if English were a strange language that he had studied or invented for himself, and was trying to write in its original purity."

Old Mandarin, The (1922, 1927, 1933, 1947), "translations" from the Chinese by Christopher Morley. Morley created the figure of a supposititious Chinese mandarin, to whom he credited short and usually witty pieces in free verse that it is not impossible to imagine a wise Chinese uttering. In the 1947 volume, *The Old Mandarin: More Translations from the Chinese*, Morley had a group called "Translations from the South American," and remarked concerning them that they are "probably as Chinese as the others."

Oldmixon, John (b. England, 1673—d. 1742), poet, historian, dramatist. Oldmixon published two volumes of verse in 1696 and 1697, and had a play produced in 1703. Thereafter he seems to have devoted himself mainly to writing history, in which the Tories came off badly. His *British Empire in America* (2 v., 1708; rev., 1741) is the first work in which the British settlements on the Atlantic coast are examined as a unit, including the West Indies. Oldmixon examined critically all available authorities, checking one against the other; in his revision he made use of new data. No one has made more trenchant comments than Oldmixon on the Puritan persecution of Roger Williams and other dissenters; he called the Massachusetts "executioners" "as real bigots in their way as Archbishop Laud are in his." Jarvis Morse says that Oldmixon "wrote well-rounded history rather than mere geographical description, brief episodical narratives, or controversial tracts."

Old New York (4 v., 1924), four historical novelettes by Edith Wharton. In this series, as often, Mrs. Wharton deals with people who come into conflict with conventional mores. It was written to present a chronological sequence from 1840 to 1880, each novelette dealing with a decade. In the first, *False Dawn*, the young New Yorker Lewis Raycie goes on the grand tour of Europe, buys pictures so far in advance

of the taste of his time that his father disinherits him. He leaves the pictures to his descendant, who sells them at auction for five million dollars. The second is The Old Maid, always considered the most successful of this quartet. *The Spark* tells of a simple, chivalrous elderly man who comes under the strong spiritual influence of Walt Whitman. *New Year's Day* relates the heroic self-sacrifice of a wife who needs to obtain money for her ailing husband and is exposed to the scorn of New York's rigid society of the day.

Old North Church. A name given to the Christ Episcopal Church of Boston, built by William Price in the style of Sir Christopher Wren and dedicated in 1723. From the belfry of Old North the lanterns were hung on April 18, 1775, the lanterns that signaled to Paul Revere. The church has been in continuous use.

Old Oaken Bucket, The (printed in the New York *Republican-Chronicle*, 1817; in *Poems, Odes, Songs*, 1818; in *Melodies, Duets, Trios, Songs, and Ballads*, 1826), by Samuel Woodworth. The poem, originally called *The Bucket*, was inspired, it is said, by a well in Scituate, Mass., where Woodworth was born. The lyric was first sung to the tune of *Jessie, the Flow'r o' Dumblane*, a lyric by Robert Tannahill with music by Robert Archibald Smith. In the 1830's E. Ives, Jr., wrote a parody on *The Old Oaken Bucket* that he called *Farewell to Home*, but set to the tune associated with Thomas Moore's poem, *Araby's Daughter*. This tune was composed by George Kiallmark. Ives' joke was a boomerang; people forgot his parody but thereafter sang *The Old Oaken Bucket* to Kiallmark's tune. George S. Kaufman and Marc Connelly took from the poem the name of their short-lived satirical play, *The Deep-Tangled Wildwood* (1923).

Old Sleuth, The. The central character in a series of dime novels put out by the firm of George P. Munro, who with Irwin P. Beadle had left the firm of Beadle & Adams (see Erastus F. Beadle) and formed a new concern. The author of the "Old Sleuth" series was Harlan P. Halsey; the stories antedated Sherlock Holmes and continued popular even after that more sophisticated and skillful detective appeared. The first number in the series came out in 1872.

Old Soak, The (1921), sketches by Don Marquis. Much of the material in this book appeared originally in Marquis' famous column *The Sun Dial*, in the New York *Sun*. They were for the most part laments—largely autobiographical—on the prohibition era. The success of the book led Marquis to write an equally successful dramatization of the sketches under the same title (1922).

Old Soldiers Never Die (1870), anonymous. This song, popular among soldiers generally, has been sung in numerous versions, some of them unprintable, to the tune of an old hymn, "Kind Words Can Never Die" (1855). Both songs are English in origin. When General Douglas MacArthur addressed the Congress at the time of his retirement in 1951, he made dramatic use of the song and for a few weeks catapulted it into wide popularity—and equally wide parody.

Old Stormalong. Captain Alfred Bulltop Stormalong was a folk hero of the Atlantic Coast in the days before the steamer. He sailed to England often, and once was in a boat so big that he barely scraped through the Cliffs of Dover, in fact rubbed off a bit of his topside paint and left the cliffs all white. His favorite vessel was a clipper ship so large that it was Wednesday in the fo'c's'le when it was still Monday aft. It is said that the initials *A.B.*, which attached to a sailor's name allegedly mean "able-bodied," are really derived from Stormalong's initials.

The Stormalong saga still remains to be explored, but Charles Edward Brown has in a pamphlet collected *Old Stormalong Yarns* (1933); Joanna C. Colcord has included the ballad of *Stormalong* in her *Songs of American Sailormen* (1938); Frank Shay has told his story at some length in *Here's Audacity! American Legendary Heroes* (1939); and Walter Blair has joined him with other early folk heroes in *Tall Tale America* (1944).

Oldstyle, Jonathan. A pen name employed by WASHINGTON IRVING in nine letters he contributed to the New York *Morning Chronicle* (1802–03) when only nineteen. The letters satirized duelling, dress, marriage customs, ranting actors, vulgar audiences, inaudible music, and the critics of the day; they foreshadow the more mature Irving. They were reproduced in facsimile in *Letters of Jonathan Oldstyle* (1941), an edition prepared by Stanley T. Williams.

Old Sweetheart of Mine, An (1877), a poem by JAMES WHITCOMB RILEY. In this popular sentimental piece, composed by an inveterate bachelor, the poet recalls an old love.

Old Swimmin' Hole and 'Leven More (1883), a book of poems by JAMES WHITCOMB RILEY. The original edition was signed "Benj. F. Johnson, of Boone," with Riley's name after it. It was the first of Riley's books in Hoosier dialect and contains *When the Frost is On the Punkin*, one of the author's best known works. In *The Old Swimmin' Hole* was the first appearance of that sentimental nostalgia for boyhood scenes that was to make Riley's fortune, influence newspaper versifiers for years to come, and cause a violent reaction in writers like HAMLIN GARLAND.

Oldtown Folks (1869), a novel by HARRIET BEECHER STOWE. "It is more to me than a story. It is my resume of the whole spirit and body of New England," wrote the author of this saga of life in Oldtown (actually South Natick, Mass., the birthplace of her husband). The action, which takes place not long after the Revolutionary War, verges on melodrama, but the characters are depicted with skill. The story is related by Horace Holyoke, a young man with a mystical turn of mind whose spiritual visions are based on similar experiences of the author's husband, Calvin Stowe. See SAM LAWSON.

Oliver Wiswell (1940), a novel by KENNETH ROBERTS, telling of the American Revolution as experienced by a Tory. Every effort is made to present the cause of the Tories in a favorable light, that of the patriots unfavorably. See SIR WILLIAM HOWE.

Ol' Man Adam an' His Chillun (1928), a book of stories about Negroes by ROARK BRADFORD. On this book Marc Connelly based his famous play, THE GREEN PASTURES (1930).

Olmsted, Frederick Law (b. Hartford, Conn., April 26, 1822—d. Aug. 28, 1903), landscape architect, author. Olmsted designed such notable landscapes and parks as Central and Riverside Parks in New York City, the World's Fair in Chicago (1893), the grounds of the Capitol in Washington. He was a highly observant writer who reported his conclusions about the South in three separately published volumes that were combined as *The Cotton Kingdom* (1856, 1857, 1860; 2 v., 1861–62; reprinted, 1953). He also wrote *An American Farmer in England* (1852). Theodora Kimball wrote his biography (2 v., 1922, 1928).

Olney, Jesse (b. Union, Connecticut, Oct. 12, 1798—d. July 30, 1872), teacher. Olney developed new ways of teaching geography. He started with the familiar in his *Practical System of Modern Geography* (1828), went on to the unfamiliar; he emphasized acquaintance with the student's own environment.

Olsen, Elder (b. March 9, 1909—   ), poet, critic. Long associated with the University of Chicago, Mr. Olsen is a notable critic of the Neo-Aristotelian school whose essays on poetry and literature in general have been published in many magazines and anthologies. Among his collections of poetry are *The Cock of Heaven* (1940), *Things of Sorrow* (1943), and *The Scarecrow Christ* (1945). A thoughtful poet of a religious and humanist orientation, Olsen has produced much vivid and powerful verse of notable content.

Olson, Charles (b. Worcester, Mass., Dec. 27, 1910—   ), poet, translator, teacher. Olson holds B.A. and M.A. degrees from Harvard and has taught at Clark University, Harvard, and Black Mountain College. The small body of poetry he began publishing relatively late in his career greatly influenced a group of poets who came into prominence in the late 1950's. Their aesthetic was found in Olson's essay *Projective Verse* (1959, first published in 1950 in shorter form), where he writes: "The poem itself must, at all points, be a high energy-construct and, at all points, an energy discharge." Olson adds to this the notion of breath as a unit of prosody; the poetic phrase, he feels, should correspond to the length of the poet's exhalation of breath as he creates it. Though *Projective Verse* is technical and obscurely written, it has been carefully read by such poets as Robert Duncan, Robert Creeley, Denise Levertov, and Allen Ginsberg. Olson wrote *Call Me Ishmael* (1947), a study of the literary influences on Melville's *Moby Dick*, and *Mayan Letters* (1953), as well as two books of poetry. In 1953 appeared the first *Maximus Poems,* followed by two more books of *Maximus Poems* (1956 and 1960). *The Distances* was published in 1961.

O'Malley, Frank Ward (b. Pittston, Pa., Nov. 30, 1875—d. Oct. 19, 1932), newspaperman, playwright, memoirist. Ward Greene says in his *Star Reporters* (1948) that O'Malley, who was on the staff of the New York *Sun* from 1906 to 1920, deserved the epitaph "greatest reporter." He left the newspaper field to write for the *Saturday Evening Post* and the *American Mercury*. Ultimately he went to France, as a protest against prohibition, and died there. He wrote several plays in collaboration with E. W. Townsend, a fellow reporter on the *Sun,* among them *The Head of the House* (1909) and *A Certain Party* (1910). He also wrote *The War-Whirl in Washington* (1918) and *The Swiss Family O'Malley* (1928). He appears in Irvin S. Cobb's "Judge Priest" stories as "Malley of the *Sun.*"

Omoo: a Narrative of Adventures in the South Seas (1847), a novel by HERMAN MELVILLE. The beginning of *Omoo* recapitulates the ending of TYPEE (1846) with Melville's rescue by the whaler *Julia* from captivity on the island of Nukaheva. Melville, still suffering from an old wound in his leg, meets the ship's doctor, a tall, ashen-faced man nicknamed Doctor Long Ghost, and the two become fast friends. A mutiny breaks out and Melville and his friends are temporarily imprisoned on Tahiti. After their release Melville and the Doctor explore Tahiti, work for a time in a potato field, and have various adventures with the natives.

Omoo is relatively free of the stylistic faults of *Typee*, and is superior in the description of character. No major figure in *Typee* is so vividly drawn as Bembo, Jermin, or Doctor Long Ghost; moreover, Melville created a host of minor characters in *Omoo* who, unlike the minor figures in *Typee*, are clearly defined individuals. *Omoo* is a straight and superior novel of adventure; nowhere in it does Melville deviate from the narrow path of realism, and in no other book does he so exult in the beachcombing life and the life of the senses.

Omoo is a Polynesia word meaning "a rover, a person wandering from one island to another," and was later used by Dion Boucicault in *Omoo, or, The Sea of Ice* (1864), which has no relation to Melville's novel. Some critics have felt that *Omoo* shows Melville at "his best, his happiest." The book has many comic episodes, and presents with great adroitness some striking and amusing characters.

On a Certain Condescension in Foreigners (1869), an essay by JAMES RUSSELL LOWELL. This is possibly the most famous of Lowell's essays, certainly one of the most amusing and incisive. Lowell, writing in an age when Europe still dominated the cultural landscape, expressed his resentment at the condescension with which Americans were received, both personally and in print.

On a Note of Triumph (1945), a radio play by NORMAN CORWIN. When the Germans surrendered in World War II, the Columbia Broadcasting System had this one-hour play by Corwin ready for production, having requested Corwin late in 1944 to prepare it. The play is a fervent celebration, an effective mixture of slang and poetry, history and exhaltation, doubt and joy.

Once I Pass'd Through a Populous City (1860, in *Leaves of Grass*, 3rd ed.; present title given, 1867, 4th ed.), a poem by WALT WHITMAN. The city is New Orleans, which Whitman and his brother visited in 1848, and where he stayed long enough to edit the New Orleans *Crescent* for three months. On the basis of this poem it has been conjectured that he had a love affair with an octoroon; one romantic biographer, Frances Winwar, went so far in her *American Giant: Walt Whitman and His Times* (1941) as to identify Whitman's mistress. But Emory Holloway found the original manuscript, which indicates how far astray these conjectures had gone. In the manuscript it is a man whom Whitman remembers; possibly he altered the poem in order to prevent charges of homosexuality.

One-Hoss Shay. See THE DEACON'S MASTERPIECE.

O'Neill, Eugene [Gladstone] (b. New York City, Oct. 16, 1888—d. Nov. 27, 1953), playwright. The son of the actors JAMES O'NEILL and Ella Quinlan, Eugene O'Neill was educated in Catholic and private schools; in 1906 he went

Pinchot, New York

to Princeton, but remained only one year, being suspended for "general hell-raising." In 1909 he married Kathleen Jenkins, from whom he was divorced in 1912; much of the period of his marriage was spent in vagabonding on the high seas and among the waterfront slums of the world's chief cities. In 1912 he became a reporter on the New London (Conn.) *Telegraph,* to which he contributed his first creative writing, mostly light verse. In the same year his health broke down, and on Christmas Eve he entered a tuberculosis sanitarium. During a year of enforced leisure he became interested in drama and read the Greeks, the Elizabethans, and the moderns, especially Ibsen and Strindberg. But after fifteen months of writing one-act plays, many of which he destroyed (publishing only *Thirst and Other One-Act Plays,* 1914), he realized the necessity of training and enrolled in GEORGE PIERCE BAKER's "47 Workshop" at Harvard.

In 1916 O'Neill was in Provincetown, Mass., where he formed his important association with SUSAN GLASPELL, GEORGE CRAM COOK, and the PROVINCETOWN PLAYERS. His first mature play, the one-act BOUND EAST FOR CARDIFF, was produced by them in 1916. Others followed: *The Long Voyage Home* (1917); ILE (1917); THE MOON OF THE CARIBBEES (1918). All of these early works reflected O'Neill's experiences as a seaman. They were collected in *Bound East for Cardiff and Other Plays* (1916) and *The Moon of the Caribbees and Other Plays* (1919). The critical attention which these plays received in New York opened the way for the production of his first full-length play, BEYOND THE HORIZON (1920), which won a Pulitzer Prize. It is a drama in conventional form about two brothers who deny their natural inclinations; the one who is by instinct a farmer goes to sea, the one who yearns to see "beyond the horizon" stays at home on the farm. It is, in a sense, a tragedy of fate, but here the hostile forces are in the environment and in the the characters themselves.

In 1918 O'Neill married Agnes Boulton, by whom he had two children; they were divorced ten years later. (She describes this period in *Part of a Long Story,* 1958.) Carlotta Monterey, a well known actress, was his third wife. Toward the end of his life O'Neill suffered greatly from Parkinson's disease, which made it virtually impossible for him to write.

THE EMPEROR JONES (1920) revealed strikingly O'Neill's originality as a stage innovator. Its structure is that of a monologue preceded and concluded with dialogues. The main interest is what happens to the soul of Emperor Jones, the self-imposed dictator of a West Indian island, when he is forced to abandon his rule and flee through the woods; the progress of his emotions from uneasiness to fear and then to hysteria is portrayed in speech, setting, and notably by the incessant beating of a drum. The psychology of fear is studied in the individual and racial memories evoked in Jones' monologue. Thus the play is an example of expressionism, the outward representation of purely subjective states.

ANNA CHRISTIE (1921), which won a Pulitzer prize in 1922, emphasizes the grip which the sea has on those who spend their lives upon it. Salty characters and spicy dialogue helped to make the play a theatrical success. Another ex-

pressionistic play, THE HAIRY APE (1922), dramatizes the problem of a stoker on a merchant ship whose self-possession is undermined by the sudden realization that he is regarded by some as a mere animal. His search to regain his self ends with a confrontation in the zoo—the protagonist on one side of the bars, an ape on the other. In DESIRE UNDER THE ELMS (1924) a domestic tragedy on a New England farm is unfolded in the elemental passions that tear a family apart. The play is powerful, but lacks the ultimate sublimation found in significant tragedy. He also wrote ALL GOD'S CHILLUN GOT WINGS (1924), a play about a white woman who marries a Negro.

The most baffling and also one of the most important of O'Neill's plays is THE GREAT GOD BROWN (1926). It deals with the inner conflicts of its main characters as contrasted with their external conflicts. In the play the actors use masks, which they put on and off to distinguish between their assumed and their real personalities. The result is a continual subtle mutation of personalities that causes a certain amount of confusion, and the critics were not altogether pleased. Yet the acute character analysis of the play, together with its vivid clash between spirituality and materialism, poetic sensitivity and philistine mediocrity, combine to make this a play of sharp insight into contemporary life.

MARCO MILLIONS (1928) is unique among O'Neill's works, both in its satirical approach and its use of anachronism for comic effect. The title character is a contemporary American high-pressure salesman in the guise of the Venetian trader; his materialism and rationalism are satirically set against the wisdom and majesty of the Orient. A more important play is STRANGE INTERLUDE (1928), a psychological study of a neurotic woman deprived of her lover. The play is notable for its successful use of soliloquy and continual asides, an innovation in 20th-century drama. For sustained characterization it is unsurpassed in American drama. It won the 1928 Pulitzer prize.

Another facet of O'Neill is brought out in MOURNING BECOMES ELECTRA (1931). The playwright here takes the Agamemnon-family story of Aeschylus and retells it in terms of a New England family immediately following the Civil War. Details and episodes, as well as the conception of fate, differ from the Greek original; but much of the basic theme is retained. The dramatic transmutation is convincing and the story as such is one of the most exciting among all O'Neill's plays. AH, WILDERNESS! (1933) provides a rich contrast; it is a light-hearted play about an adolescent boy, full of typically American humor. *Days Without End* (1934) was one of the dramatist's rare failures, both commercially and artistically.

For twelve years after 1934 O'Neill did not have a Broadway play, though he was awarded the Nobel Prize in 1936. Then came THE ICEMAN COMETH (1946), a vivid but very long portrait of social misfits and outcasts. Critics have been divided on its merits, some claiming for it a place among O'Neill's best works. But it is difficult to see in it the playwright's former imaginative brilliance. Later plays include *A Moon for the Misbegotten* (1957), and *A Touch of the Poet* (1958), both part of a long sequence of dramas upon which O'Neill was at work during his last years.

Few critics today will dissent from the general opinion that O'Neill was the greatest American dramatist of his time or, for that matter, in all American literary history. Indeed, he was one of the genuinely significant writers for the stage from any Western culture in the 20th century. He was the first to bring into the drama of the English-speaking world many of the devices invented by the rebel poets of the Continent; he was to the drama what Joyce and Eliot were to nondramatic literature. O'Neill did not repeat himself. Each play bears the impress of its own fully integrated style and technique, the result of deep immersion in the content. Beyond his boldness as an innovator of technique lay O'Neill's emotional power, lyrical skill, imaginative ingenuity, and insight into character. If he occasionally faltered in the direction of prolixity in his last years, he nevertheless possessed during most of his career a sensitive mastery of verbal effects. In short, his greatness represents a combination of all the qualities requisite to dramatic artistry, at least so far as was permitted by the restrictions and confusions implicit in his native culture.

One of the plays produced on Broadway after O'Neill's death, LONG DAY'S JOURNEY INTO NIGHT (1956), is a deeply impressive autobiographical play in which the members of the playwright's family are thinly disguised as the chief characters. Biographical and critical works by others include: Sophus Winther's *Eugene O'Neill: A Critical Study* (1934); Barrett H. Clark's *Eugene O'Neill, The Man and His Plays* (1947); Edwin Engel's *The Haunted Heroes of Eugene O'Neill* (1953); *O'Neill and His Plays: Four Decades of Criticism* (1961), edited by Oscar Cargill, N. Bryllion Fagan, and William J. Fisher; Arthur and Barbara Gelb's *O'Neill* (1962). See also THE FOUNTAIN; GOLD [2]; LAZARUS LAUGHED; S. S. GLENCAIRN.

ALLAN G. HALLINE

O'Neill, James (b. Ireland, 1847—d. 1920), actor. O'Neill was brought to the United States in 1850, became a leading player in the theatre, and won his fame playing the title role in *The Count of Monte Cristo*. He appears as James Tyrone in his son EUGENE O'NEILL'S autobiographic drama LONG DAY'S JOURNEY INTO NIGHT (1956).

One of Ours (1922; Pulitzer Prize, 1923), a novel by WILLA CATHER. It tells of a Nebraska farmer who enters the army and goes to France, where he loses his life in battle. The book was in part based on the letters of a relative of Miss Cather's who died in World War I. Heywood Broun commented that it seemed to Miss Cather that "the war was not without purpose, since it gave a significance to the life of farm boys in Nebraska. The hero of the book loses his life and finds his soul." But Broun felt that "war is too high a price."

One Woman's Life (1913), a novel by ROBERT HERRICK. The protagonist is socialite Milly Ridge, an almost completely selfish woman, who brings her husband to an early death from overwork and deserts her best friend.

Onondaga Indians. This tribe was part of the Iroquois Confederacy, sided with the British in the French and Indian Wars, and now lives mostly in Ontario. It figures occasionally in JAMES FENIMORE COOPER's novels, especially those composing the *Littlepage Manuscripts* (1845–46). The Onondagas had some interesting myths, but their most important literary memorial is the so-called *Onondaga Book*, translated by Horatio Hale in the *Iroquois Book of Rites* (1883). This was first taken down in the Onondaga language in the late 18th century by Protestant missionaries. It gives the ritual employed by the tribe when a chief was mourned at his death. Hale notes that the book, sometimes called the *Book of the Condoling Council*, might be called an "Iroquois Veda." It comprises speeches, songs, and other ceremonies, beginning with a long prose address.

On the Banks of the Wabash, Far Away (1899), a song by PAUL DRESSER. Theodore Dreiser's brother wrote this song, one of the great hits of the Spanish American War period. It is possible that Dreiser gave his brother the idea and helped him to write the words. It later became Indiana's official state song.

On the Death of Joseph Rodman Drake (1821), an elegy by FITZ-GREENE HALLECK. Halleck composed this poem soon after the death of his close friend and collaborator in 1820. The poem is written with simplicity and sincerity, and is undoubtedly Halleck's finest production.

On the Road (1957), a novel by JACK KEROUAC. This story of young men and women rushing frantically back and forth across the United States and Mexico was immediately recognized as a major document of the "Beat Generation." It was severely criticized for praising youthful aimlessness, promiscuity, and destructiveness, and for its sprawling lack of structure. To this Kerouac replied that his characters' journey is really an inner one in search of something they cannot express in words, perhaps a kind of Nirvana; he asserted also that formlessness is part of his method, a way of achieving spontaneity. Certainly the exuberantly confused writing is an apt style to evoke the character of Dean Moriarty, the protagonist. Dean, who can never move fast enough to satisfy his appetite for drinking, love-making, jazz-listening, and talking, is a fantastic, ludicrous, half-insane character; yet he seems to personify the desperate hilarity, the loneliness, and the searching that many young people experienced in the years after World War II. The manuscript of the book, originally titled "Jazz of the Beat Generation," went the rounds of publishers for several years, acquiring a notoriety even before it was finally published. *Visions of Cody* continues the adventures of Dean Moriarty; an excerpt from the novel was published in 1960.

On the Transient and Permanent in Christianity (May 19, 1841), a sermon by THEODORE PARKER. This sermon, delivered in South Boston Church, was one of the most powerful and controversial ever delivered in America and one of the most influential in the development of TRANSCENDENTALISM and Unitarianism. Parker summed up the conclusions of the "high Criticism" in tones as little inflammatory as he could make them. He urged that "the former authority of the Old Testament can never return . . . Compare the simpleness of Christianity as Christ sets it forth on the Mount with what is sometimes taught and accepted in that honored name, and what a difference! One is of God, one is of man." The commotion that followed, says Perry Miller, "made the furor over Alcott and Emerson seem very pale indeed." Parker's own congregation stood by him, also some ministers, but no other minister would exchange pulpits with him.

On Trial (1914), "a dramatic composition" by ELMER RICE. This story of a noble assassin who wants to be sentenced without a trial and of a much harassed female was written by a young law clerk who abandoned the law after this play made a great hit on Broadway. He made good use of his legal knowledge in the play but, as John Chapman put it, had the good sense to use the law as a background, not as a chief character. He was also among the first to use the "flashback" as a dramatic device. The drama was originally called *According to the Evidence*, and dealt with a Kentucky mountain feud. Arthur Hopkins persuaded Rice to shift the locale to New York City with a banker as the victim.

Opal, The Story of. See OPAL WHITELEY.

Open Boat and Other Tales of Adventure, The (1898), a collection of stories by STEPHEN CRANE. The title story is based on Crane's own experience after the wreck of the steamer *Commodore*, on which he had sailed for Cuba as a war correspondent. He was later praised by his fellow-survivors for his courage and coolness during the wreck and the trip through the surf in the small boat. Accounts of the wreck in dispatches to the New York *Press* and the Florida *Times-Union*, together with "Stephen Crane's Own Story," were collected for the first time in *Stephen Crane: An Omnibus*, edited by R. W. Stallman (1952).

In the short story that Crane reconstructed from his experience each detail is charged with significance and patterned into a scheme of relationships; hence the difference between what happened and what he reconstructed is immense. Realistic details have been converted into symbols, and their sequence forms a designed whole possessing a life of its own.

The collection was published in England as *The Open Boat and Other Stories* (1898). Besides the title story, the best story in it is "The Bride Comes to Yellow Sky." This Western tale anticipates in theme and in structure Ernest Hemingway's "The Short Happy Life of Francis Macomber." "The Bride" is structurally a paradoxical reversal of situation and has close affinities, therefore, with Crane's "A Mystery of Heroism," "The Upturned Face," and "An Episode of War." In all four Crane stories, that which is predictable—a code, a theory, or an ideal—is discovered to be unpredictable when faced with unexpected realities.

Operas and Musical Comedies (1946), a guide by J. WALKER McSPADDEN. In 1911 McSpadden published his *Opera Synopses* which went into numerous printings and was completely revised in 1935. In 1936 he published a similar work on *Light Opera and Musical Comedy*, a pioneer in its field. The present work is a combination of the two volumes, with revisions and additions.

O Pioneers! [1] See PIONEERS! O PIONEERS!

O Pioneers! [2] (1913), a novel by WILLA CATHER. Following Sarah Orne Jewett's suggestion that she write of half-forgotten childhood memories, Willa Cather set her second novel in Nebraska. Alexandra Bergson's devotion to the land dominates the book. Her successful struggle with the farm is contrasted with her Swedish family's unsuccessful struggle with American ways. The pain of her youngest brother's death is finally relieved by a happy marriage. Miss Cather compares the national character of Swedes, French, and Bohemians in the United States.

Oppenheim, James (b. St. Paul, Minn., May 24, 1882—d. Aug. 4, 1932), poet, essayist, novelist, editor, welfare worker. Oppenheim attended Columbia University but left before graduating. He was employed as a clerk from 1896 until 1903, when he became head of the Hudson Guild Settlement on the lower East Side. Two years later he headed the Hebrew Technical School for Girls in the same district. The teeming life of the slums furnished him with the material for his first book of short stories, *Dr. Rast* (1909); it also developed in him a passionate idealism, one phase of which was pacifism. Two potboiling novels were the products of these early years: *Wild Oats* (1910) and *Idle Wives* (1914). In *Songs for the New Age* (1914) Oppenheim found himself. Louis Untermeyer described these as "loose cadences" which "were psalms rather than songs . . . the Bible retranslated by Walt Whitman in collaboration with Dr. Freud." In 1916 Oppenheim founded and edited *The Seven Arts*, a magazine which, during its brief span, printed some of the finest writing of the time. The magazines ceased when its editor's pacifism conflicted with his sponsor's patriotism. Poems from *Songs for the New Age* (1914), *The Solitary* (1919), *The Mystic Warrior* (1921), and *The Golden Bird* (1923), strung together with newly written connecting lines, were collected in *The Sea* (1923).

During the war Oppenheim became interested in psychiatry, a subject to which he turned in his misery over increasing domestic troubles, disappointment over the death of his magazine, and a growing despair. *The Book of Self* (1917), a poetic treatment of psychiatry, was followed by *Your Hidden Powers* (1923) and *Behind Your Front* (1928), popular and oversimplified essays on psychoanalysis. Oppenheim's sense of mission combined with a complete lack of humor to make his later poems both dull and long-winded. He is remembered largely for one poem, "The Slave."

Oppenheimer, J[ulius] Robert (b. New York City, April 22, 1904—d. Feb. 18, 1967), physicist. Oppenheimer attended Harvard and Cambridge and received his Ph.D. from Göttingen University in 1927. He taught at the University of California at Berkeley and at the California Institute of Technology, and in 1942 was placed in charge of the project to develop the atomic bomb at Los Alamos, New Mexico. In 1954 he was investigated by the Atomic Energy Commission as a security risk, having been charged with associating with Communists and opposing the development of the hydrogen bomb. He was found a "loyal citizen" but was dismissed as a member of the Commission. Charles P. Curtis analyzed the hearing in *The Oppenheimer Case* (1955). Oppenheimer was re-elected director of the Institute for Advanced Study at Princeton in 1954. He is the author of *Open Mind* (1960).

Opper, Frederick Burr (b. Madison, Ohio, Jan. 2, 1857—d. Aug. 29, 1937), cartoonist. Opper was regarded by many as "the funniest man ever connected with the daily press of America." For a quarter of a century Opper did his famous cartoons for PUCK, then worked for the Hearst papers. His most famous cartoon was the bloated and repulsive picture of Big Business that he called "the Trusts." His most noted comic strips were the hobo "HAPPY HOOLIGAN" and his comic Frenchmen "Alphonse and Gaston." He published collections of some of his productions, among them *Our Antediluvian Ancestors* (1902), *Happy Hooligan* (1902), and *Alphonse and Gaston* (1902); in addition he did excellent illustrations for books by Mark Twain, Finley Peter Dunne, and Bill Nye. His drawings for Nye's *History of the U.S.* (1894) were particularly funny. Thomas Craven says that his pen-and-ink technique was "a mixture of barbed wire and chicken scratches," but was highly appropriate.

Oppression (1765), a poem by "an American," with notes by "a North Briton." This violent attack on the Stamp Act was printed in London; it is directed largely against John Huske of New Hampshire. The author characterizes Huske as a "Portsmouth Yankee" and in a footnote gives an explanation of the word *Yankee*. It is believed that this was the first appearance of the word in print. The author has not been identified.

Optic, Oliver. The pen name of W. T. ADAMS. His periodical for young people, *Oliver Optic's Magazine,* was founded in 1867 and ceased publication in 1875. It ran many popular serials, written mainly by Adams.

Options (1909), a collection of sixteen short stories by O. HENRY. Among the better known ones are *The Third Ingredient* (later dramatized), *The Rose of Dixie,* and *Rus in Urbe.*

Oralloossa, Son of the Incas (1832), a tragedy by ROBERT MONTGOMERY BIRD. Bird was one of the first North American writers to interest himself in South America; his play, based on careful research, deals with Peru immediately after the Spanish conquest. Bird created Oralloossa, the son and heir of the emperor Atahualpa, who leads a rebellion against Pizarro and kills the invader. (The incident is not historical.) But his own people finally betray him and bring about his death. The play has some potent scenes, and EDWIN FORREST made it one of his favorite acting vehicles. It was first printed in Clement E. Foust's *Life and Dramatic Works of Robert Montgomery Bird* (1919).

orators and oratory in the U.S. The Indian tribes orated freely in their own tongues both before and after the arrival of the white man. KING PHILIP and Chief JAMES LOGAN of the Cayuga tribe are only two of the many outstanding Indian orators praised by their white contemporaries. The primary form of oratory among English settlers was the sermon. Some of the Puritan preachers were thunderous, others were sweet and persuasive; all were unbelievably long-winded. The pulpit continued to attract many great speakers—THEODORE PARKER, RALPH WALDO EMERSON, HENRY WARD BEECHER—but their techniques changed with the spirit of the age. See SERMONS.

After the Golden Age of the sermon came the Golden Age of the political oration, approximately from 1765 to 1865. Two issues were debated endlessly: first independence, then union. During the momentous debate over the Union and slavery, we produced a great race of orators who spoke in conscious emulation of the classic orators of Greece, Rome, and England. First came a great trio: DANIEL WEBSTER, HENRY CLAY, and JOHN C. CALHOUN; then ABRAHAM LINCOLN, greatest of them all. F. O. Matthiessen wrote disapprovingly "of the kind of rhetoric that overflowed into poetry from the oratory" of the 19th century, especially in the case of OLIVER WENDELL HOLMES, JOHN GREENLEAF WHITTIER, and JAMES RUSSELL LOWELL.

Many addresses of those days were inflated pomposity. From their unconvincing rhetoric the next age reacted in favor of a simpler, more human and humorous, less long-winded treatment of important political subjects. The greatest orator of modern times was WILLIAM JENNINGS BRYAN. His eloquence won him the Democratic nomination for the Presidency three times, carried him around the country in whirlwind campaigns that brought him millions of fanatic admirers, but did not send him to the White House. The number of words uttered in any

Presidential campaign, then or now, is not only incalculable but not worth calculating. Some of the political candidates, of course, are very good speakers.

Campaign oratory has often taken the form of debates, such as the Webster-Hayne exchanges in the Senate, the Lincoln-Douglas series, or the Kennedy-Nixon television confrontations of 1960. Another kind of debate takes place in the law courts, especially when constitutional issues are at stake. Early American debaters set a high standard of excellence in reasoning and presentation, especially such speakers as PATRICK HENRY, RICHARD HENRY LEE, George Wythe, THOMAS JEFFERSON, GEORGE WASHINGTON, BENJAMIN FRANKLIN, and the best of all, JOHN ADAMS [2]. Debating societies flourished on American soil from early days, and are still a common feature of the undergraduate landscape. Cooper Union Institute in New York City gave courses in debating and oratory, gained national fame when Lincoln delivered there his *Cooper Institute Address* (Feb. 27, 1860). The 19th century produced some notable legal orators, among them RUFUS CHOATE, Joseph Hodges Choate, WILLIAM M. EVARTS, and CHAUNCEY M. DEPEW. In the 20th century no lawyer has surpassed CLARENCE S. DARROW in his verbal as well as legal dexterity.

The Puritan fondness for informational sermons was in the 19th century transformed into a love of lectures. The American Lyceum, established by Josiah Holbrook, and the Chautauqua Assembly, established by Lewis Miller and John H. Vincent, offered highly organized procedures for lectures and lecture courses. During the mid-19th century Emerson seems to have been the lecturer in greatest demand. Another common form of oratory in America is after-dinner speaking. (See LYCEUMS; CHAUTAUQUA.)

Among books on American oratory these may be noted: J. Q. Adams' *Lectures on Rhetoric and Oratory* (2 v., 1810); E. B. Williston's *Eloquence of the U.S.* (5 v., 1827); Josiah Holbrook's *The American Lyceum* (1829); E. G. Parker's *The Golden Age of American Oratory* (1857); Alexander Johnson's *Representative American Orations* (3 v., 1884); Thomas Wentworth Higginson's *American Orators and Oratory* (1901); Constance M. Rourke's *Trumpets of Jubilee* (1927); William N. Brigance's *History and Criticism of American Public Speaking* (2 v., 1943); Lew Sarett, W. T. Foster, and James H. McBurney's *Speech* (1943); F. P. Gaines' *Southern Oratory* (1946); David Mead's *Yankee Eloquence in the Middle West: The Ohio Lyceum* (1951); A. Craig Baird's *Representative American Speeches, 1901–1956* (19th ed., 1956).

Ordeal of Mark Twain, The. See VAN WYCK BROOKS.

Oregon Trail, The (1849), by FRANCIS PARKMAN. An autobiographical narrative of a tour of the West, originally called *The California and Oregon Trail*. It was first published serially in the *Knickerbocker Magazine* in 1847, and has since become a classic. It is an account of a trip made in 1846 by the author and his cousin Quincy Adams Shaw. They traveled together from St. Louis to Fort Laramie; there they separated, Parkman going to live for some weeks with a tribe of Sioux Indians among whom he found plenty of danger and excitement. *The Oregon Trail* contains valuable descriptions of the prairies at the most fascinating period of their history and a remarkable ethnological study of the Indians. On the basis of his own close observations, Parkman charged Fenimore Cooper with lack of realism in his portrayals of Indian characters, especially UNCAS. The book was republished in 1943 in an edition prepared by Mason Wade from Parkman's notebooks.

A much earlier account of the Oregon trail is found in *On the Oregon Trail: Robert Stuart's Journey of Discovery*, first published in 1953 in an edition prepared by K. A. Spaulding. Stuart made the journey in reverse, leaving Fort Astoria on June 29, 1812, and arriving at St. Louis, after many dangers and privations, on April 30, 1813. He and his companions established the route later used by wagon trains.

O'Reilly, John Boyle (b. Ireland, June 28, 1844—d. Aug. 10, 1890), journalist, poet, novelist. O'Reilly was imprisoned for his activities in the Fenian movement; he was transported to Australia, in 1869 made a daring escape to the United States. He became a citizen, bought a part interest in the *Pilot*, the most influential "Irish" paper in America at the time, and was its manager and editor-in-chief until his death. He published some books of poems, among them *Songs from Southern Seas* (1873); *Songs, Legends, and Ballads* (1878); *Poems and Speeches* (1891); *Selected Poems* (1913). *Moondyne* (1879), a powerful novel of convict life in Australia, helped secure the freedom of all Irish military prisoners in Australia by calling attention to their plight. He also wrote *Ethics of Boxing and Manly Sport* (1888). W. C. Schofield wrote a biography of O'Reilly entitled *Seek for a Hero* (1956).

Original Narratives of Early American History, The (19 v., 1906–1919), edited by J. FRANKLIN JAMESON. This valuable set of volumes was prepared under the auspices of the American Historical Association. The material ranges in time from the *Saga of Eric the Red* (985) to John Olamixon's *History of the British Empire in America* (1708). Included are Bradford's HISTORY OF PLYMOUTH PLANTATION; Captain John Smith's *A True Relation;* Francis Yeardley's *Narrative of Excursions in Carolina;* William Penn's *A Further Account of the Province of Pennsylvania;* Champlain's *Voyages;* Johnson's *Wonder-Working Providence;* Father Vimont's *Journey of Jean Nicolet;* Pedro de Castenada's *Narrative of the Expedition of Coronado;* and many other articles of great interest and importance.

Ormond, or, The Secret Witness (1799), a novel by CHARLES BROCKDEN BROWN. A melodramatic narrative in which the hero, Ormond, returning from travel abroad and contact with the French philosophers, feels himself **freed**

from all ethical considerations. But when he tries to violate the heroine, Constantia, she kills him. Fortunately there is a "secret witness" to her crime, and she is acquitted. The novel has been criticized for its lack of coherence and for its constant employment of coincidence. Nevertheless it enjoyed a wide audience abroad. According to the testimony of Thomas Love Peacock, Percy Bysshe Shelley found in Constantia "a perfect combination of the purely ideal and the possibly real."

Orphan Angel, The (1926; in England 1927, as *Mortal Image*), a novel by ELINOR WYLIE. Many of Mrs. Wylie's admirers find this their favorite novel and consider it unjustly neglected by the critics. The novel reflects Mrs. Wylie's passionate admiration of Shelley. Wagenknecht has called her attachment a "long-distance love-affair: there were times when she was more Shelley than Shelley was himself." In this romantic story she imagines that Shelley, instead of drowning, was picked up by a Yankee brig and carried to America. The year is 1822 and Shelley, a profound republican, is delighted by the land and the people. His romantic search for Silver Cross (Sylvie La Croix) carries him across America on a journey that Mrs. Wylie depicts with a mixture of realism and poetry that she never surpassed.

Orphic Sayings (*The Dial*, July, 1840, and later issues), by AMOS BRONSON ALCOTT. The first fifty of these *Sayings*, printed in a single issue, created an immediate sensation—and a good deal of laughter. Alcott dealt, as clearly as he could, with such topics as enthusiasm, hope, vocation ("Engage in nothing that cripples or degrades you"), temptation, conscience, speech, originality, nature. Herbert Schneider holds that the *Orphic Sayings* were at first in Coleridge's manner and spirit, later became increasingly esoteric; his "idealism was corrupted by mysticism."

O'Ruddy, The (1903), a romance by STEPHEN CRANE and Robert Barr. Crane's intentions in this last, unfinished work were mixed. He wrote it primarily for financial gain, in order to pay off his debts and provide for Cora Crane. As a romance this picaresque tale of an Irishman's adventures in England might perhaps have been a rousing success, had he lived to complete it; but he had intended it as a "satiric romance." Here and there Crane's characteristic style can be found, but according to Robert Barr, the English novelist who completed the novel, Crane had written only one fourth of it. The book was reprinted (1926) in *The Work of Stephen Crane* (v. 7 and 8), with an introduction by Thomas Beer.

Osage Indians. These Indians belong to the Sioux linguistic group and are among the original hunting tribes of the Great Plains. They were widely feared for their courage and aggressiveness. They liked merriment, good food, and horses; they were gentle with children and had developed a highly symbolic religion; they were tall, dignified, and sometimes haughty. Their history is a long and strange one, beginning with the earliest French and Spanish trade with the Indians, and concluding in the present with their accumulation of enormous wealth from the gas and oil fields in Oklahoma—to which place they had reluctantly migrated under pressure from the white men. Their number is about 5,000, as compared with a probable 6,500 when Lewis and Clark first discovered them in 1804. Missionaries first appeared among them in 1820. They are at present strongly Roman Catholic. Full-blooded Osage number only 11 per cent of the tribe; many of the others bear names handed down from the days of the French traders. They have produced notable figures; among these are John Joseph Mathews, a graduate of Oxford and an author of books dealing with Indian life, and Maria Tallchief, a prominent ballerina.

The most extensive study of the Osages was made by a member of the Omaha tribe, the excellent ethnologist and writer FRANCIS LA FLESCHE. His volumes, issued by the Bureau of American Ethnology: *Rite of the Chiefs; Sayings of the Ancient Men* (1921); *The Rite of Vigil* (1925); *Two Versions of the Child-Naming Rite* (1928); *Songs of the Wa-xó-be* (1930); *War Ceremony and Peace Ceremony of the Osage Indians* (1939). Some of their chants show an extraordinary maturity of thought. Washington Irving refers often to the Osage in his *Tour of the Prairies* (1835). In CIMARRON (1930), Edna Ferber portrays the Osage Indians as wealthy parvenus who act like anyone who has suddenly struck it rich. Time has subdued this flashiness.

Osborn, Bradley Sillick (b. Rye, N.Y., Aug. 16, 1828—d. May 6, 1912), naval officer, newspaperman, editor. As an authority on naval subjects, Osborn was for a time war correspondent for the New York *World* and the New York *Herald*. His story of the fall of Fort Sumter was a notable "scoop." After the war he founded the *Nautical Gazette* (1871). He wrote *Osborn's Handbook of the U.S. Navy* (1863).

Osborn, Chase Salmon (b. Huntington Co., Ind., Jan. 22, 1860—d. April 11, 1949), newspaperman, publisher, public official, geologist, writer. Osborn's extraordinary career included the holding of many offices (he was governor of Michigan, 1911–12) and a deep interest in iron mining and Indians. He began his career as a newspaperman and publisher, wrote numerous books, among them *The Andean Land* (2 v., 1909); *The Iron Hunter* (1919); *The Law of Divine Concord* (1921); *Madagascar* (1924); *History of Michigan* (1926); *Following the Ancient Gold Trail of Hiram of Tyre* (1932); and two books on Hiawatha (1942, 1944, with S. B. Osborn).

Osborn, Henry Fairfield (b. Fairfield, Conn., Aug. 8, 1857—d. Nov. 6, 1935), paleontologist. Osborn graduated from Princeton University, then went to Europe, where he met Huxley and Darwin. He became professor of science at Princeton University in 1881, later was invited to organize the department of biology at Columbia University. In 1891 he became head of the department of mammalian paleontology at the American Museum of Natural History, where he built up a remarkable collection of fossil vertebrates and arranged striking displays. From 1909 until 1925 he was president of the New York Zoological Society. The most popular of his books were *Men of the Old Stone Age* (1915) and *The Origin and Evolution of Life* (1917). Other works include *The Age of Mammals in Europe, Asia, and North America* (1910); *Impressions of Great Naturalists* (1924); *Evolution and Religion in Education* (1926); *Cope, Master Naturalist* (1931).

Osborne, Letitia Preston (b. Union, W. Va., Aug. 9, 1894—   ), lecturer, novelist. An inveterate traveler, Mrs. Osborne was particularly familiar with the West Indies and Central and South America. Two of her best novels, *They Change Their Skies* (1945) and *The Little Voyage* (1949), are set in Latin America. *Through Purple Glass* (1946) is about Boston. Mrs. Osborne has a deft hand in portraying character; she is satirical yet sympathetic.

Osbourne, Lloyd (b. San Francisco, April 7, 1868—d. May 22, 1947), novelist, short-story writer. At the time of his mother's marriage to ROBERT LOUIS STEVENSON, Lloyd Osbourne, then a boy of twelve, received a toy printing press with which he and his stepfather spent long hours printing stories, poems, and woodcuts. After trying to live in California, Switzerland, England and France, the Stevensons set out in 1887 on a cruise to the South Seas. In 1888 both Osbourne and his stepfather were adopted by one of the native tribes. Lloyd Osbourne grew into a man of charm and tact. His ability to handle the natives, as well as his skill in the Samoan language, fitted him admirably for his post as United States vice-consul in Samoa. He collaborated with Stevenson on *The Wrong Box* (1889), *The Wrecker* (1892), and *The Ebb Tide* (1894). After Stevenson's death in 1894 he returned to his country, where he continued to write light fiction, detective stories, and plays. Among his titles are *The Queen vs. Billy* (1900); *The Motor Maniacs* (1905); *Three Speeds Forward* (1906); *Wild Justice* (1906); *The Grierson Mystery* (1928). Of more importance are his *Memoirs of Vailima* (1902), a valuable account of Stevenson in the South Seas which he wrote with his sister Isobel Strong, and *An Intimate Portrait of R.L.S.* (1924).

Osceola (b. Creek Co., Ga., 1800?—d. 1838), Seminole Indian warrior. When the United States tried to force the Seminoles to leave Florida, they withdrew from their villages under Osceola's leadership and took refuge in the Everglades. They were never defeated, never made a peace treaty, and still live in the Everglades. Osceola was treacherously seized while negotiating with army officers under a flag of truce, and he died a prisoner in Fort Moultrie, S.C. He is the chief figure in J. B. Benton's *Osceola, or, Fact and Fiction: A Tale of the Seminole War* (1838) and Theodore Pratt's *Seminole* (1954).

Osgood, Charles G[rosvenor] (b. Wellsboro, Pa., May 4, 1871—d. July 27, 1964), literary his-

torian. Osgood joined the English department at Princeton University in 1905 and became a professor in 1913. He was an authority on Dr. Samuel Johnson and James Boswell. He also wrote on Boccaccio (1930) and Virgil (1930), and edited *Edmund Spenser* (1932–57, 10 v.), in collaboration with Edwin Greenlaw. Other books by him include: *Spenser's English Rivers* (1920); *The Voice of England* (1935); *Poetry As a Means of Grace* (1941).

Osgood, Frances Sargent (b. Boston, June 18, 1811—d. May 12, 1850), poet. Mrs. Osgood wrote simple, sentimental verses, published in *Wreath of Wild Flowers from New England* (1838), *The Casket of Fate* (1840), and other collections. Her name lives chiefly because of her association with Edgar Allan Poe, who praised her verses far beyond their worth. Mary E. Hewitt wrote her biography (1851).

Osgood, Herbert L[evi] (b. Canton, Me., April 9, 1855—d. Sept. 11, 1918), teacher, historian. Osgood taught at Columbia University from 1890 until his death. He wrote a three-volume history of the American colonies in the 17th century (1904–07), and four volumes on American colonial history in the 18th century (1924). He belonged to what is sometimes called the "Imperial School" of American historians, men who around 1900 began to modify the highly patriotic viewpoint of earlier historians and to see colonial development against the background of the British Empire. Osgood's son-in-law, Dixon Ryan Fox, wrote *Herbert Levi Osgood: An American Scholar* (1924).

O'Sheel [Shields], Shaemas (b. New York City, Sept. 19, 1886—d. May 9, 1954), poet. An American follower of the Irish renaissance, O'Sheel wrote one poem that became famous: "They Went Forth to Battle, but They Always Fell." Among his collections: *The Blossomy Bough* (1911); *The Light Feet of Goats* (1915); *Jealous of Dead Leaves* (1938); *Antigone and Selected Poems* (posth. pub., 1960).

Osler, Sir William (b. Bondhead, Ont., July 12, 1849—d. Dec. 29, 1919), physician, teacher, writer. Osler taught first at McGill University and then at the University of Pennsylvania. In 1888 he became chief physician at Johns Hopkins Hospital and professor of medicine at Johns Hopkins University, where he remained until 1904 when he accepted a chair at Oxford. Osler was distinguished for his clinical methods. It was said of him that he could see more with a microscope than had ever been seen before; and his eminent colleague, Dr. John M. T. Finney, referred to his "exquisite hands." He criticized the lax standards of the United States medical schools of his day, and was largely responsible for their improvement. Among his best-known works are: *The Principles and Practice of Medicine* (1891); *Lectures on Abdominal Tumors* (1895); *Cancer of the Stomach* (1900); *Science and Immortality* (1904); *The Student Life* (1905); *A Way of Life* (1914). Dr. Harvey Cushing's *Life of Sir William Osler* (2 v., 1925) is a tribute to a great teacher by one of his most distinguished students.

Ostenso, Martha (b. Norway, Sept. 17, 1900—d. Nov. 24, 1963), novelist. Brought here at an early age, Martha Ostenso lived in Minnesota, South Dakota, and Manitoba. Her first book, *A Far Land* (1924), was a collection of verse; it was followed by *Wild Geese* (1925), a prize-winning novel and her best known work. Among her other novels are *The Dark Dawn* (1926); *The Mad Carews* (1927); *The Young May Moon* (1929); *The Waters Under the Earth* (1930); *The White Reef* (1934); *Milk Route* (1948); *Sunset Tree* (1949); *A Man Had Tall Sons* (1958). They are for the most part set in scenes familiar to Miss Ostenso and realistically described, even though the plots are romantic.

Otero, Miguel Antonio (b. St. Louis, Mo., Oct. 17, 1859—d. Aug. 7, 1944), banker, public official, historian, memoirist. Otero led an active life in business and as a public official. In 1897 he was appointed governor of New Mexico Territory and served until 1906. He wrote *Conquistadores of Spain and Buccaneers of England, France, and Holland* (1925), *The Real Billy the Kid* (1935), also several autobiographical works.

Other Voices, Other Rooms (1948), a novel by TRUMAN CAPOTE. Thirteen-year-old Joel Knox arrives at the dilapidated mansion called Skully's Landing, and enters a world imbued with dream and fantasy. The house is inhabited by the perfumed, effeminate Randolph, the Negroes Jesus Fever and his daughter, Zoo, and Joel's invalid father. Beyond lies the Cloud Hotel, the mysterious retreat of the lunatic Negro Little Sunshine, the place "folks go . . . when they died but were not dead," and where Joel discovers self-awareness and a precocious wisdom that enables him to see the emptiness and paralysis of the inhabitants of Skully's Landing. Essentially a story of initiation, *Other Voices, Other Rooms* has been viewed by some critics as analogous to the quest for the Holy Grail and the archetypal Search for the Father.

Otis, Harrison Gray (b. Boston, Oct. 8, 1765—d. Oct. 28, 1848), lawyer, statesman, political writer. The nephew of JAMES OTIS was elected to the House of Representatives, later to the Senate, and served as mayor of Boston. He was an ardent member of the FEDERALIST PARTY, but his influence waned with his stubborn support of the unpopular Hartford Convention (1814–15), which opposed the War of 1812. Otis spoke constantly in favor of Federalist ideas and issued two volumes of *Letters Developing the Character and View of the Hartford Convention* (1820, 1824). The noted architect Charles Bulfinch designed three houses for him on a tract of land in Boston that Otis developed, which became known as Beacon Hill. Samuel E. Morison wrote his biography (2 v., 1913).

Otis, James (b. West Barnstable, Mass., Feb. 5, 1725—d. May 23, 1783), politician, pamphleteer. Otis was an ardent patriot during the Revolutionary period whose pamphlets attracted much attention. He is depicted as Brutus in his sister MERCY OTIS WARREN's play, THE ADU-

LATEUR (pub. 1773). Among his writings: *A Vindication of the Conduct of the House of Representatives of the Province of Massachusetts Bay* (1762); *The Rights of the British Colonies Asserted and Proved* (1764). The

University of Missouri Studies for 1929 contains his pamphlets, edited by C. F. Mullett.

Ottley, Roi (b. New York City, Aug. 2, 1906—d. Oct. 1, 1960), newspaperman, broadcaster, author. Ottley wrote for numerous magazines and New York City newspapers. He won fame with his first book *New World A-Coming* (1943), a brilliant description of Negro life in Harlem and elsewhere. Ottley went abroad during the war as correspondent for *Liberty*, *PM*, and the Pittsburgh *Courier*. *Black Odyssey* (1948) is a history of the Negro in America; *No Green Pastures* (1951) is a survey of race relations in Europe and Africa. *The Lonely Warrior* (1955) is the story of Robert S. Abbott, the founder of a crusading newspaper which greatly influenced the Negro press in the United States.

Ouâbi, or, The Virtues of Nature (1790), by SARAH WENTWORTH MORTON. See DEATH SONGS, INDIAN.

Our Mr. Wrenn (1914), a novel by SINCLAIR LEWIS. Aside from *Hike and the Aeroplane* (1912), a story for boys written under the pen name of Tom Graham, this was Lewis' first book. It is the story of a New York clerk who is a meek bachelor, a "Caspar Milquetoast." He makes a trip to England in a cattleboat, falls in love with a red-haired art student, finds it won't do, comes back and marries a department store buyer, and is shown at the end as a meek married man. The book has notes of the later Lewis in it, with its attacks on "the live wire," business slogans, "highbrows," and the average businessman. It was reprinted in 1951, with an introduction by Harrison Smith.

Our Old Home (1863, pub. in part in the *Atlantic Monthly* in 1862), a series of sketches by NATHANIEL HAWTHORNE. The book was drawn from the period between 1853 and 1858 which Hawthorne spent in England, first as American Consul at Liverpool and later as a tourist. It gives artistic form to many of the details recorded in Hawthorne's *English Notebooks* and is one of the best works written by an American about England.

After a brief description of his consular duties and the people he encountered in fulfilling them, Hawthorne's narrative takes the reader through the country of his beloved Dr. Johnson and some of the haunts of Burns. The book concludes with sketches of English poverty and a satiric view of civic banquets. It is a view of England through honest eyes, and is worth attention for its revelations of 19th-century England and America.

Our Own Baedeker (1947), seventy-two sketches of places outside the United States by Eugene Kinkead and RUSSELL MALONEY. These pieces appeared originally in the *New Yorker* and were done with that magazine's passion for the casual, in this case taking the form of startling and unrelated facts. The sketches are both informative and entertaining, despite the fact, revealed by Geoffrey Hellman in a spoofing introduction, that Maloney had never been outside the United States "and not very far inside," while Kinkead "summers on Fire Island, facing Portugal."

Oursler, [Charles] Fulton (b. Baltimore, Md., Jan. 22, 1893—d. May 24, 1952), editor, author, critic. Oursler was a versatile writer who composed successful detective stories under the pen name of Anthony Abbot and wrote many plays and motion-picture scenarios, including *The Spider* (with LOWELL BRENTANO, 1927), which had a long run on Broadway. He was associated with many magazines in important editorial capacities and as a contributor, in 1944 became a senior editor of the *Reader's Digest*. In his early years Oursler was a Baptist, for a while was an agnostic, in his later years was a devout Catholic. His most famous books were those on the Bible and Christianity, particularly *The Greatest Story Ever Told* (1947, as a series of radio broadcasts; 1949, in book form) and *The Greatest Book Ever Written* (1951). Oursler had a great gift for popularization.

Our Times: The United States, 1900–1925 (6 v., 1926–35), a history by MARK SULLIVAN. Sullivan, a capable newspaperman and editor, described events that had come under his own observation, and his informal account gave a clear vista of a quarter of a century. The volumes were lavishly illustrated.

Our Town (1938), a play by THORNTON WILDER. Presented without scenery of any kind, utilizing a narrator and a loose episodic form, adventurous and imaginative in style, this unique play won the Pulitzer prize for Drama in 1938 and is one of the most distinguished in the modern repertoire. It deals with the simplest and most touching aspects of life in a small town and contains nothing like the brutal realism of O'Neill's New England plays. A stage manager casually introduces the characters and his narration bridges the gap between the audience and the play's action. At times he also enters the scene and becomes part of the play. The play's action centers around the life of the Webb family and the Gibbs family, their neighbors. George Gibbs and Emily Webb fall in love, marry, she dies, as the life of the town continues to move about them. Burns Mantle said of the play: "*Our Town* . . . impressively combined a homely and sensitive study of native character with a novelty of form that completely detached it from the ordinary drama of commerce." See EMILY GIBBS.

Our Young Folks. An excellent magazine for younger readers, founded in January 1865 by Ticknor and Fields; it merged with ST. NICHOLAS eight years later. Its chief editors were LUCY LARCOM, Mary Abigail Dodge, and J. T. TROWBRIDGE; the latter printed in it his serial, *Jack Hazard and His Fortunes*, thereafter one of his most popular books. Other contributors included Harriet Beecher Stowe, John Greenleaf Whittier, T. W. Higginson, T. B. Aldrich, Elizabeth Stuart Phelps, E. E. Hale, Rose Terry Cooke, Bayard Taylor, Mayne Reid, "Oliver Optic," Horatio Alger.

Outcasts of Poker Flat, The (*Overland Monthly*, January, 1869), a short story by BRET HARTE. This most famous of Harte's tales is a characteristic mixture of Dickensian sentimentality and Wild West sardonics. In it a group of ne'er-do-wells—the gambler JOHN OAKHURST, two prostitutes, and a drunkard—are expelled from Poker Flat, a western mining camp. They are joined by a naive young couple who are eloping. A blizzard traps them on a mountain pass, and the outcasts, one after another, sacrifice themselves for the young woman, who dies with them. Her lover in the meantime has left to bring help, but returns too late. Whatever the merits or demerits of the story, it helped to found the local-color school of American fiction, and its influence is still to be observed in current writing.

Outcault, R[ichard] F[elton] (b. Lancaster, Ohio, Jan. 14, 1863—d. Sept. 25, 1928), cartoonist. Outcault created some famous comic strips, including "Hogan's Alley" (1895) for the New York *World*, the "Yellow Kid" (1896) for the New York *Journal* (the term "yellow journalism" was first applied to the *Journal* as a result of Outcault's drawings), and "Buster Brown" (1902) for the New York *Herald*. A little before any of these, Outcault had published in the Sunday supplement of the New York *World* a colored sequence that in six boxes unfolded the singular transformation of an anaconda which swallowed a succulent yellow dog. The sequence was entitled "The Origin of a New Species," which it was indeed—the first comic strip in color. Among his books: *Tige—His Story* (1905), a juvenile book with illustrations; *My Resolutions: Buster Brown* (1906).

Outlook, The. A famous weekly magazine which appeared from 1870 until 1935. Originally it was called the *Christian Union* and was edited by HENRY WARD BEECHER, who had announced in THE INDEPENDENT (1861) that he "would assume the liberty of meddling with every question which agitated the civil or Christian community." In 1893 the name was changed to *The Outlook;* by that time LYMAN ABBOTT was editor. A great sensation was created when THEODORE ROOSEVELT joined its staff in 1909; he wrote articles agitating for many reforms. HAMILTON WRIGHT MABIE was another noted staff member. In 1928 the magazine absorbed *The Independent.* It became a monthly in 1932 as *The New Outlook.*

Out of the Cradle Endlessly Rocking (pub. 1859 in the New York *Saturday Press* as *A Child's Reminiscence;* in 1860 ed. of LEAVES OF GRASS as *A Word Out of the Sea;* included under its present title in *Sea-Drift* section of 1881 ed.), a poem by WALT WHITMAN. Many critics find the poem to have at least three levels: a memory of childhood, a mature expression of love, and a philosophical discovery. The poem describes how a child, walking the beach on Long Island, hears the call of a bird, a "visitor from Alabama," mourning his lost mate, and ends with the poet being given the "word out of the sea," the word "death." The moment of the revelation from the sea becomes a turning- or maturation-point for the poet, who can never again be the child he once was, having come to an understanding of the real meaning and beauty of death. The poem is highly melodious, and is considered one of Whitman's best. It is thought to have provided the inspiration for the brief scenes of the cradle in D. W. Griffith's classic film, INTOLERANCE (1916). PAUL CRESTON used it as the basis for an orchestral composition of the same title.

Out of the Hurly Burly (1874), humorous sketches by CHARLES HEBER CLARK (Max Adeler), for which A. B. FROST did his first illustrations. The sketches had the humorous exaggerations typical of the period. A German version was published in New York as *Fern vom Weltgetuemmel* (1874); and Karl Knortz, in his *Geschichte der Nordamerikanischen Literatur* (1891), called the book "a display of almost every facet in an Eastern American village."

Outre-Mer (1835), a series of travel sketches by HENRY WADSWORTH LONGFELLOW. The material for the sketches was gathered during Longfellow's years of study and travel through Europe, in particular, Germany. The attitude of the sketches is best characterized as picturesque. The book added little to Longfellow's fame and is all but forgotten today.

Outside Looking In (1925), a play by Maxwell Anderson. See BEGGARS OF LIFE.

Overland Monthly (July 1868—July 1935), a magazine founded by a San Francisco bookseller, Anton Roman, and first edited by BRET HARTE. The magazine was intended to be regional, although Harte took care to transcend the bounds of the Pacific Coast in his search for authors and material; in fact, he made the *Atlantic Monthly* his model. Harte was then comparatively unknown; in a short time the *Overland* made him famous, since in its second issue he printed his own story THE LUCK OF ROARING CAMP. The story was a new departure for Harte; he followed it up with three great stories: THE OUTCASTS OF POKER FLAT, *Miggles*, and TENNESSEE'S PARDNER. In the *Overland* also appeared his most famous poem, "The Heathen Chinee" (called in the magazine PLAIN LANGUAGE FROM TRUTHFUL JAMES). Harte conducted a column called "Etc.," in which he satirized local peculiarities like the suppression of news of earthquakes and municipal corruption. He was adroit in winning noted contributors, including Mark Twain, and was particularly friendly to young writers.

When Harte left the *Overland* to go east on a tempting offer from the *Atlantic*, he became something of a lost soul. The *Overland*, too, began to decline. However, it continued to attract notable names: George Sterling, Joaquin Miller, Josiah Royce, Frank Norris, Robinson Jeffers, Edgar Lee Masters, and Jack London. London tells of his experiences as a contributor in his autobiographical novel MARTIN EDEN (1909), where the magazine is called the *Transcontinental Monthly.* See AMBROSE BIERCE.

Overland Trail, The (1947), a historical account by JAY MONAGHAN. What Monaghan calls in this volume "the Overland Trail" most historians designate as "the Oregon Trail." He rejects the common name because parts of it "were traveled by many more Mormons and Argonauts than by Oregon-bound pioneers." He gives a good account of western migration from Gray's discovery of the Columbia (1792) to the completion of the Union Pacific Railroad (1869). Prominent in his narrative are Lewis and Clark, the agents of J. J. Astor, the missionaries, Frémont, the Donner party, Parkman, the Mormons, the gold-seekers, the men of the Pony Express.

Over-Soul (1841), an essay by RALPH WALDO EMERSON. It was included in the *Essays, First Series.* The central thought of a primal mind, a cosmic unity in its Platonic sense, is one found everywhere in Emerson's writings. Here he defines it again: "It is the soul of the whole; the wise silence; the universal beauty to which every part and particle is equally related; the Eternal One."

Overstreet, H[arry] A[llen] (b. San Francisco, Oct. 25, 1875—   ), teacher, writer, lecturer. Overstreet taught philosophy at the University of California for ten years, then became head of the philosophy department at the College of the City of New York. He retired in 1939 and became a lecturer at Town Hall and a master of ceremonies of *The Town Meeting of the Air.* He saw in the latter an answer to the need for "hard-bitten, disciplined, grown-up citizen intelligence." Among his books are: *Influencing Human Behavior* (1925); *About Ourselves: Psychology for Normal People* (1927); *The Enduring Quest: A Search for a Philosophy of Life* (1931); *We Move in New Directions* (1933); *A Guide to Civilized Leisure* (1934); *A Declaration of Interdependence* (1937); *Let Me Think* (1939); *Our Free Minds* (1941). His writings have been outstanding as popularizations of philosophy. In collaboration with his wife **Bonaro Overstreet** (b. Geyserville, Calif., Oct. 30, 1902—   ), author of much distinguished poetry, he wrote *The Mature Mind* (1949); *The Mind Goes Forth* (1956); *What We Must Know About Communism* (1958); *The War Called Peace: Krushchev's Communism* (1961).

Over the Hills to the Poor House (*Harper's Weekly*, June 17, 1871), a poem by WILL CARLETON, included in his *Farm Ballads* (1873). "Over the hills to the poor-house I'm trudgin' my weary way," says the speaker in the poem; and includes details of his family life: "She had an edication, an' that was good for her;/ But when she twitted me on mine, 'twas carryin' things too fur."

Over There (1917), a song by GEORGE M. COHAN. The tune is an adaptation of a bugle call; the words exhort American soldiers to enthusiasm as they embark for overseas. Cohan received a Congressional Medal of Honor for composing it, and undoubtedly it is one of the most effective war songs ever written. When it was first performed at the New York Hippodrome, late in 1917, it was received with "frenzied enthusiasm," and it was revived with equal popularity during World War II.

Owen, Robert Dale (b. Scotland, Nov. 9, 1801—d. June 24, 1877), social reformer, author, statesman. Robert Dale Owen was the eldest son of the English reformer, Robert Owen. He represented his father's ideas in the United States in numerous articles and pamphlets beginning with his editorship of the New Harmony *Gazette* from 1825 to 1827. Soon after the failure of his father's utopian community at New Harmony, Indiana, Dale Owen came under the influence of Frances (Fanny) Wright and became editor of her paper the *Free Enquirer*, which was patterned after the defunct *Gazette*. This too failed, he turned to politics, and served in Congress and in the Indiana Legislature. He managed to effectuate some of his educational and legal reforms and is responsible for the bill which established the Smithsonian Institute. While he was U.S. Minister at Naples (1855–58) he became interested in Spiritualism and wrote two explanatory books: *Footfalls on the Boundary of Another World* (1860) and *The Debatable Land Between This World and the Next* (1872). His most influential work, however, is in the field of social or political reform: *The Policy of Emancipation* (1863); *The Wrong of Slavery* (1864); *The Future of the Northwest* (1863); *Divorce: Being a Correspondence Between Horace Greeley and Robert Dale Owen* (1860). Miscellaneous works in other fields include: *Hints on Public Architecture* (1849); *Pocahontas: An Historical Drama* (1838); *Beyond the Breakers* (1870), a novel. His autobiography is called *Threading My Way* (1874).

Owen, Russell (b. Chicago, Jan. 18, 1889—d. April 3, 1952), newspaperman, special correspondent. One of the most esteemed newspapermen of his day, Owen worked for the New York *Sun*, then for *The New York Times*. Among his famous stories were those on various Arctic and Antarctic expeditions which he accompanied personally, the early air races, the Lindbergh and many other pioneering flights, many major sporting events. For his articles covering the first Byrd Antarctic Expedition (1929–30) he received a Pulitzer prize and a medal presented by Congress to members of the expedition. He wrote *South of the Sun* (1934) and *The Antarctic Ocean* (1941).

Ox-Bow Incident, The (1940), a novel by WALTER VAN TILBURG CLARK. Set in Nevada in 1885, this powerful story tells how three supposed cattle rustlers are lynched—just as word comes that they are innocent. The novel had implications of World War II and the struggle between democracy and totalitarianism, justice and ruthlessness. In 1942 an equally powerful motion picture with the same title was produced.

Oxford Companion to American Literature, The (1941; rev. and enlarged ed., 1948, 1956), compiled by JAMES D. HART. This reference work duplicated for American letters the valuable service rendered by Sir Paul Harvey's *Oxford Companion to English Literature* (1932). Hart includes artists, musicians, noted statesmen, and other persons not strictly literary. His summaries of important books are concise and accurate.

Oz, The Land of. This was an imaginary realm created by L. FRANK BAUM and made the scene of fourteen stories for children. The first, THE WONDERFUL WIZARD OF OZ (1900), was the most famous, and was made into a very popular musical comedy, *The Wizard of Oz* (1901), and an equally successful film (1939). The series was continued almost indefinitely by Ruth Plumly Thompson and other writers.

Ozark Mountains, the. These mountains constitute an eroded tableland that extends from southwestern Missouri across northwestern Arkansas into eastern Oklahoma. It is part of the speech region called Appalachia; for centuries it has been a backwater of American culture, in which have survived many folk beliefs, folktales, and locutions not found elsewhere in the United States. It has been said erroneously that these survivals are Elizabethan in origin. At least in language, according to Harold B. Allen, the survivals must be traced to 18th-century northern English. Ethnologists and sociologists have tended to regard the people of the Ozarks as of low intelligence and initiative. But the linguists and folklorists have found the Ozarks one of their happiest hunting grounds, and a whole series of books has appeared in which Ozarkian stories are reproduced and special locutions recorded.

Among books on the Ozarks: Charles Morrow Wilson's *Backwoods America* (1934); Vance Randolph's *The Ozarks* (1931), *Ozark Mountain Folks* (1932), *Ozark Superstitions* (1947), *Ozark Folksongs* (1950), *Tall Tales from the Ozarks* (1951), *Who Blowed Up the Church House?* and *Other Ozark Folk Tales* (1952), *Down in the Holler: A Gallery of Ozark Folk Speech* (with George P. Wilson, 1953), *The Devil's Pretty Daughter* (1955); Jean Bell Mosley's *The Mocking Bird Piano* (1953); William Byron Mowrey's *Tales of the Ozarks* (1954); *The Ozarks and some of Its People* (1956) by the Ozark poet, Rosa Marinoni; *Arts and Crafts of the Ozarks* (1957) by Bonnie Lek Coump; *Land of the Oldest Hills* (1957) by Daisy Pat Stockwell; *Stars Upstream: Life Along an Ozark River* (1958) by Leonard Hall; *The Bodacious Ozarks: True Tales of the Backhills* (1959) by Charles Morrow Wilson. Fiction includes H. B. Wright's *That Printer of Udell's* (1903) and *The Shepherd of the Hills* (1907); MacKinlay Kantor's *The Voice of Bugle Ann* (1935) and *Daughter of Bugle Ann* (1953).

Pacing Mustang, the. A widespread legend of a magnificent stallion who was often seen but never captured. The first printed report of his presence is found in Washington Irving's TOUR ON THE PRAIRIES (1835). JOSIAH GREGG heard "marvelous tales," reported in his *Commerce of the Prairies* (1844), of a stallion of "perfect symmetry, milk-white, save a pair of black ears." These stories circulated, he said, in the northern Rockies, on the Arkansas, near the borders of Texas. In 1851 Melville introduced the Pacing Mustang into MOBY DICK in his famous chapter "The Whiteness of the Whale."

Pack, Robert (b. New York City, May 19, 1929—   ), poet, critic, editor. As co-editor, with DONALD HALL and LOUIS SIMPSON, of the anthology *The New Poets of England and America* (1957), Pack's name has come to be associated with modern poetry. Like many of the other poets in the anthology, Pack writes reflective, carefully structured verse. In addition to his books of poetry, *The Irony of Joy* (1955) and *A Stranger's Privilege* (1959), he has written the perceptive *Wallace Stevens: An Approach to His Poetry and Thought* (1958).

Packard, Vance [Oakley] (b. Granville Summit, Pa., May 22, 1914—   ), social critic. Packard obtained his A.B. at Pennsylvania State College in 1936, and his M.A. at Columbia University the following year. He did a stint as columnist for the Boston *Herald* in 1938, worked as a feature editor for the Associated Press until 1942. His books, hard-hitting yet entertaining critiques of the American social scene, have become best sellers. *The Hidden Persuaders* (1957), which Auguste Spectorsky called a "frightening, entertaining and thought-stimulating book," deals critically with the use and abuse of motivational research by advertising agencies to manipulate mass markets. *The Status Seekers* (1959) is an analysis of the often wasteful symbols utilized by certain groups to acquire social status. *The Waste Makers* (1960) is a criticism of the theory of built-in-obsolescence by which big business strives to increase consumption and production. Packard's books touched a raw nerve among many advertising and business executives, thereby stimulating heated controversy.

Padover, Saul K. (b. Austria, April 13, 1905—   ), historian, editor, biographer, teacher, journalist. Beginning as a purely historical writer with a special interest in the Founding Fathers of the American Republic, Padover gradually extended his writing to include contemporary politics and political theory. He had a varied career in government, serving as a consultant and official in the Department of the Interior (1938–1944), a political analyst for the OSS (1944), and an intelligence officer in the United States Army (1944–1946). From 1946 to 1948 he was an editorial writer for the newspaper *PM*. In 1949 he became Dean of the School of Politics at the New School for Social Research. The liberal bent and readability of his books have given them a greater currency than is common for scholarly works. Among the books that he wrote or edited are *Jefferson* (1942); *Wilson's Ideals* (1942); *The Complete Jefferson* (1943); *Experiment In Germany* (1946); *The Living U.S. Constitution* (1953); *The Complete Madison* (1953); *French Institutions: Values and Politics* (1954); *The Washington Papers* (1955); *The Mind of Alexander Hamilton* (1958); *Nehru On World History* (1960); *The World of the Founding Fathers* (1960); and *The Genius of America* (1960). He also wrote a number of studies for the "Foreign Policy Association Headline" series, including *France* (1950); *Psychological Warfare* (1951); *Europe's Quest for Unity* (1953); and *Foreign Policy and Public Opinion* (1958).

Page, Elizabeth (b. Castleton, Vt., Aug. 27, 1889—   ), teacher, welfare worker, novelist. The diary of her great-uncle Henry Page, who was a Forty-Niner, gave Miss Page data for one of her best-known novels, *Wagons West* (1930). Her most admired work is *The Tree of Liberty* (1939), which portrays the conflict between the Jeffersonians and the Hamiltonians. Miss Page favors the former and, says Ernest E. Leisy, "gives an unsurpassed picture" of Jefferson. Among her other books: *Wild Horses and Gold* (1932) and *Wilderness Adventure* (1946).

Page, P[atricia] K[athleen] (b. England, Nov. 23, 1916—   ), Canadian poet and short-story writer. P. K. Page has been called the most brilliant member of the group of experimental writers who were associated with the magazine *Preview* during the 1940's. Her work appeared in their anthology, *Unit of Five* (1944). Though she shares with the other poets of this group a concern with social realities, "her flair," it has been pointed out, "is psychological rather than political." T. S. Eliot's poetry was an important influence; in addition, it may be said that her language and imagery are chiseled and often obscure, in the manner of Wallace Stevens. In these respects she differs sharply from most socially oriented Canadian poets. Miss Page was appointed to the Canadian National Film Board. Her poems and short stories have appeared in numerous magazines; her publications include: *As Ten As Twenty* (1946) and *The Metal and the Flower* (1954).

Page, Thomas Nelson (b. Hanover Co., Va., April 23, 1853—d. Nov. 1, 1922), lawyer, diplomat, novelist, historian, essayist. Page, brought up on a plantation, was related to many Southern "first families," and imbibed their ideas of chivalry. He practiced law in Richmond, but soon found himself as a romantic writer. After his dialect story MARSE CHAN was printed in the *Century Magazine* (April, 1884) he wrote other stories collected in IN OLE VIRGINIA (1887). His RED ROCK (1898), long a best

seller, thrilled readers with its picture of the Southern revolt against Reconstruction, which gave rise to the Ku Klux Klan. The same sentimental and romantic spirit is seen in *The Old Gentleman of the Black Stock* (1897), a love story; TWO LITTLE CONFEDERATES (1888), a story for children; the novels *Gordon Keith* (1903) and *John Marvel, Assistant* (1909); and *The Red Riders* (1924), finished by his brother Rosewell Page. Other books of his are *The Old South* (1892); *Social Life in Old Virginia* (1897); *The Old Dominion* (1908); and *Robert E. Lee, Man and Soldier* (1911). From 1913 to 1919 Page was ambassador to Italy. His writings were collected in 1906–18 (18 v.). A biography, *Thomas Nelson Page*, was published in 1923 by Rosewell Page.

Page, Walter Hines (b. Cary, N.C., Aug. 15, 1855—d. Dec. 21, 1918), journalist, diplomat. Page edited the St. Joseph (Mo.) *Gazette*, then worked on the New York *World* from 1881 to 1883. Gaining control of the Raleigh (N.C.) *State Chronicle*, he advocated drastic reforms in the South. In 1891 he took over the *Forum;* in 1898 he became editor of the ATLANTIC MONTHLY, revitalizing that periodical. The next year he launched the publishing firm of Doubleday, Page (now Doubleday & Co.). In 1913 Woodrow Wilson appointed him ambas-

sador to England. His enthusiasm for the Allied cause and his generally pro-British bias are evident in his *Letters* (1922–25). His other writings include *The Rebuilding of Old Commonwealths* (1902); *A Publisher's Confession* (1905); and, under the pen name Nicholas Worth, *The Southerner* (1909).

Pageant of America. A series of fifteen volumes (1925–29) edited by RALPH HENRY GABRIEL. They present American history strikingly under various heads: *Adventures in the Wilderness, The Lure of the Frontier, The March of Commerce, The Epic of Industry, The Winning of Freedom, The American Spirit in Letters, Annals of American Sport*, etc. The volumes are well illustrated.

Paine, Albert Bigelow (b. New Bedford, Mass., July 10, 1861—d. April 9, 1937), biographer, editor, novelist, writer for children. At the end of the Civil War the Paine family moved to Xenia, Ill., where Albert attended school in a one-room shack and helped his father in the village store. While still in his teens, his first rhymes were accepted by the *New York Weekly*. He became interested in photography in 1881 and traveled in the South taking pictures. For the next three years he was employed by a photographers' supply company in Kansas, but in 1895, when a number of his prose pieces were accepted by *Harper's Weekly*, he set out for New York. There he wrote some unsuccessful novels and started a newspaper syndicate which failed. His biography *Thomas Nast* (1904, see THOMAS NAST) proved so successful that he was asked to write other biographies.

Paine will be remembered chiefly for his connection with MARK TWAIN. In January, 1906, he approached Twain with the proposition that he become the great man's secretary and official biographer. Twain, who liked the Nast biography, was willing, and the two set to work, using a stenographer to catch Twain's memories and anecdotes. Out of these sessions emerged Twain's *Speeches* (1910), edited by Paine; Paine's *Mark Twain, A Biography* (3 v., 1912); *Mark Twain's Letters* (2 v., 1917); and *Mark Twain's Autobiography* (2 v., 1924), edited by Paine. Paine also wrote *Moments with Mark Twain* (1920) and edited *The Family Mark Twain* (1935). Paine was adulatory rather than critical in his work, and modern critics have spoken of him disparagingly. Nevertheless, he performed a valuable service in preserving materials that might otherwise have been lost.

Paine's long list of titles includes: *The Bread Line* (1900); *The Van Dwellers* (1901); *The Great White Way* (1901), which gave its name to Broadway; *The Commuters* (1904); *Joan of Arc—Maid of France* (1925), for which he received the decoration of the Legion of Honor in 1928; and *Life and Lillian Gish* (1932). He also wrote more than twenty volumes of stories and rhymes for children, the best known being *The Arkansaw Bear* (1898).

Paine, Ralph D[elahaye] (b. Lemont, Ill., Aug. 28, 1871—d. April 29, 1925), newspaperman, novelist, short-story writer, historian.

Paine wrote more than thirty books, at least twenty dealing with the sea. His own life was full of exciting experiences, many of which he described in *Roads of Adventure* (1922). He wrote both fiction and nonfiction for young people, wholesome books now neglected. Among them were *The Praying Skipper and Other Stories* (1906); *The Ships and Sailors of Old Salem* (1909); *The Book of Buried Treasure* (1911); *The Judgments of the Sea and Other Stories* (1912); *The Adventures of Captain O'Shea* (1913); *The Long Road Home* (1916); *Lost Ships and Lonely Seas* (1921); *Joshua Barney* (1924).

Paine, Robert Treat [the younger] (b. Taunton, Mass., Dec. 9, 1773—d. Nov. 13, 1811), poet, drama critic, editor, lawyer. Paine was a younger son of Robert Treat Paine (1731–1814), the noted patriot, and was an ardent supporter of the Federalists. He wrote facilely and in his own time was highly esteemed; today his productions seem dull. His most important poems were *The Invention of Letters* (1795), *The Ruling Passion* (1797), and ADAMS AND LIBERTY (a campaign song, 1798). His drama criticism is probably the best of his writing. Much of it is included in *The Works in Verse and Prose of the Late Robert Treat Paine, Jr.* (1812). See DELLA CRUSCANISM.

Paine, Thomas (b. England, Jan. 29, 1737—d. June 8, 1809), editor, writer. Paine's father was a Quaker (Paine liked to think of himself as a Friend), his mother a member of the Church of England. He left school at the age of

thirteen and entered upon a series of vocations, in none of which he achieved any great success. For a time he was a tax collector, a job which left him with a clear hatred of social inequality. During one of BENJAMIN FRANKLIN'S visits to England the two met; Franklin was impressed with Paine and persuaded him to emigrate to America. Paine arrived in Philadelphia in 1774 and on Franklin's recommendation was made editor of the *Pennsylvania Magazine*, the first issue of which appeared in January, 1775. In his essays for the magazine Paine showed his customary fearlessness and originality of thought, advocating ideas far in advance of his time, among them women's rights, freedom for Negroes, a system of international arbitration, national and international copyright, kindness to animals.

When the Battle of Lexington was fought, Paine's course was set. He left his editorship and gave all his energy to the new cause. He joined Washington's army in its retreat across New Jersey in 1776 and seems to have won at once the esteem of the commander-in-chief. When the troops reached Newark, Paine sat on a log alongside a campfire and with a drumhead for a desk wrote the first of the famous series of pamphlets called THE AMERICAN CRISIS. The opening lines of the first number became the most famous that Paine ever wrote: "These are the times that try men's souls. The summer soldier and the sunshine patriot will, in this crisis, shrink from the service of his country, but he that stands it now deserves the love and thanks of man and woman. Tyranny, like hell, is not easily conquered; yet we have this consolation with us, that the harder the conflict, the more glorious the triumph. . . ." Washington ordered the words read to his shivering men, and no doubt the pamphlet helped to inspire the surprising defeat of the British at Trenton a few days later. When the first number of *The Crisis* was published, it continued to exert a great effect, prepared for by Paine's earlier publication COMMON SENSE (1776), which had made him a leading propagandist of the patriot cause. Paine continued to write further issues of *The Crisis* at Morristown and perhaps at Trenton. To commemorate his stay at the former town a statue by George J. Lober which shows Paine writing on his drumhead was unveiled July 4, 1950.

The last number of *The Crisis* was published in 1783. All the issues had had a considerable effect on public opinion, because they spoke for the man in the street or on the field; they were a passionate expression of all men's desire for freedom. Struthers Burt has called Paine "the spark plug of the American Revolution." Paine, though poor, refused all royalties, gave the copyright to the United States.

In 1787 Paine began a new career in Europe. A man of considerable inventive ability, he returned to the Old World with an entirely peaceful intention—to perfect an iron bridge. But he soon found himself in the midst of a new revolutionary turmoil. He was invited by the French to become a member from Pas-de-Calais in the National Assembly, an honor which made him the first modern international. To Franklin's remark, "Where Liberty is, there is my country," came Paine's amendment, "Where Liberty is not, there is mine. My country is the world; to do good, my religion."

The French Revolution divided opinion in America almost as deeply as in Europe. Among those affected were Paine and THOMAS JEFFERson; and the difference in their outlook—Paine an internationalist, Jefferson still a nationalist—caused a break between them. Elsewhere Paine met violent opposition. JOHN ADAMS [2] had once said of him: "Washington's sword would have been wielded in vain had it not been supported by the pen of Paine. History is to ascribe the American Revolution to Paine." But now Adams called him "the filthy Tom Paine," starting a vicious epithet down the centuries. In London clubs men wore TP nails in their boot heels to bear witness to their trampling on his principles. He was proscribed and his books burnt by the hangman. Yet he kept on writing. When Edmund Burke published his *Reflections on the French Revolution* (1790), Paine wrote a reply that he called THE RIGHTS OF MAN (1791), which appeared with a dedication to George Washington. It was a vindication of the republican form of government of the United States, whose constitution he declared was "to liberty what a grammar is to language." Against Burke's theory of a single, static contract, Paine reaffirmed the doctrine of natural rights, arguing that each new generation has the right to decide how it shall be governed. The book was widely circulated and a *Second Part* appeared in 1792.

Vituperation against Paine reached such heights that his life was in danger. He managed to escape from England and return to France, where he was enthusiastically received in the convention drafting a constitution for the new Republic. He was one of the few persons active in the early years of the Revolution who escaped the guillotine. But it was not because he ceased to be free-spoken. One of his most courageous acts was to vote and write against the execution of the French monarch. He lined up with the moderates and incurred Robespierre's suspicions, was imprisoned, and escaped death only because the French tyrant himself was executed just as he was about to order Paine's death.

At this time Paine was writing his last important book, THE AGE OF REASON (Parts I & II, 1794, 1796), part of it in prison. It was his most controversial work and his most misunderstood. Actually his views were those held by many who shared in the 18th-century Enlightenment; he was emphatically not an atheist. But he undertook a rational scrutiny of the Scriptures, much in the spirit of the later "higher criticism," and his analysis of Biblical revelation offended many readers deeply. Yet he was sincere, even impressive, in his affirmation of faith as a product of Nature and Reason. One English bishop held that many of Paine's ideas of God have a "philosophical sublimity."

Paine returned to America in 1802. He lived in New York City, Bordentown, N.J., and New Rochelle, N.Y. He was poverty-stricken and in poor health; he was ostracized and attacked bitterly and unjustly. Even when he died he was not allowed to rest in peace. He had asked to be buried on his little farm at New Rochelle, but William Cobbett, the eccentric English pamphleteer, visited America in 1819 and dug up the coffin and took it to England. There he was not allowed to bury the body; what became of Paine's bones is unknown.

What happened to Paine after his death made Dixon Wecter call him a *Hero in Reverse* (*Virginia Quarterly Review,* Spring, 1942). One of Paine's earliest biographers was James Cheetham, a personal enemy whose *Life of Thomas Paine* (1809) was, says Wecter, "libelous"; it was Cheetham who first coined the phrase "filthy little atheist," an epithet that made Americans forget that Congress on Aug. 26, 1785, had "*Resolved,* That the early and continued labors of Thomas Paine and his timely publications merit the approbation of this Congress." It was *The Age of Reason* that primarily caused the trouble, along with Paine's uncomplimentary letter of 1796 to Washington, written because Washington, like Burke, saw anarchy in the French Revolution. When Paine came to the United States in 1802, Jefferson, then President, was embarrassed to receive him publicly, even though he, better than most, understood Paine's views and motives. Unfounded, ridiculous stories of Paine's drunkenness and personal slovenry proliferated; a frightened stage driver refused to give him a seat; in 1806 he was denied the right to vote; and he was reported to have been overcome by horror and remorse on his deathbed. During his own lifetime two unfriendly biographies were published, Cheetham's and one by George Chalmers (London, 1791). These were somewhat corrected by Thomas C. Rickman's *Life* (London, 1819). Even friendlier was a biography by Calvin Blanchard (1860, 1877). But the ideas of the revilers were long-lived, in spite of defenses by such men as Lincoln and Whitman. On the eve of the Civil War the City Council of Philadelphia refused a portrait of Paine for Independence Hall. For a long time the New York Historical Society kept a bust of Paine hidden in order to protect it. Theodore Roosevelt repeated the epithet "filthy little atheist." The first energetic attempt at rehabilitation was made by Rev. Moncure D. Conway, a Congregationalist minister, in his biography of Paine (1892) and his four-volume *Writings of Thomas Paine* (1894–96). Since then, despite outcroppings of the old calumnies, Paine's reputation has continued to grow, and today there is a considerable Paine cult. His cottage in New Rochelle has been made a memorial under the care of the Huguenot and Historical Society; and his home in Bordentown is also a memorial.

Besides the publications mentioned above, these writings by Paine may be listed: *The Case of the Officers of Excise* (1772, 1793); *Epistle to the People Called Quakers* (1776); *Public Good* (1780); *Reasons for Wishing to Preserve the Life of Louis Capet* (1793); *Dissertation on First-Principles of Government* (1795); *The Decline and Fall of the English System of Finance* (1796); *Agrarian Justice* (1797); *Letter to the People of France and the French Armies* (1797); *Letters to the Citizens of the United States of America* (1802–03); *Miscellaneous Poems* (1819). In addition to Conway, the following have edited collections of Paine's writings: Daniel E. Wheeler (10 v., 1908); William M. Van der Weyde (10 v., 1925); Philip S. Foner (2 v., 1945).

Books on Paine include Ellery Sedgwick's *Thomas Paine* (1899); Mary A. Best's *Thomas Paine, Prophet and Martyr of Democracy* (1927); Hesketh Pearson's *Tom Paine, Friend of Mankind* (1937); Frank Smith's *Thomas Paine, Liberator* (1938); H. H. Clark's *Six New Letters of Thomas Paine* (1939); John Dos Passos' *The Living Thoughts of Tom Paine* (1940); W. E. Woodward's *Tom Paine, America's Godfather* (1945); Hildegarde Hawthorne's *The Mighty Pen: A Life of Thomas Paine* (1949). Howard Fast's *Citizen Tom Paine* (1943) is a fictionalized biography, of which E. E. Leisy judiciously says that Fast "writes sensitively, but trims his stories always to a proletarian thesis." Some Paine manuscripts are in the Rutgers University Library.

HERBERT FAULKNER WEST

Painted Veils (1920), a novel by JAMES HUNEKER. Huneker used as background the art world of New York City that he knew so well, introducing many real people under their own names. In addition he digressed readily into discussion of the art movements of the day. The morals of the fictional characters are for the most part free-and-easy. The book was privately printed and was regarded as very daring in its day.

Painting in America: The Story of 450 Years (1956), by E. P. Richardson. Richardson, director of the Detroit Institute of Art and author of numerous books on American painting and painters, gives in this handsome volume a complete account of American painting from the earliest examples to the present.

Palfrey, John Gorham (b. Boston, May 2, 1796—d. April 26, 1881), clergyman, historian, editor, teacher. Palfrey owned and edited the NORTH AMERICAN REVIEW (1835–43), was professor of sacred literature at Harvard (1831–39), delivered and published the *Lowell Lectures on the Evidences of Christianity* (2 v., 1843), analyzed the *Relation Between Judaism and Christianity* (1854), wrote an elaborate *History of New England* (5 v., 1858–90). A man of liberal thought, he was well liked by intellectual Bostonians and in his political activities won the active help of Emerson and Longfellow. In his later years he was a friend and adviser of Henry Adams.

Pal Joey (1940), a collection of twelve stories by JOHN O'HARA. Famous stories about an infamous character, "a tap-dancing heel," these first appeared in *The New Yorker* (Oct. 22, 1938—July 13, 1940), then in book form. They were transformed into a hit musical (1940), with music and lyrics by RICHARD RODGERS and LORENZ HART, the book by O'Hara. When the play was revived in 1952, the book of the show was published. It is discussed by Clifton Fadiman in his *Party of One* (1955).

Palmer, Alice Freeman (b. Colesville, N.Y., Feb. 21, 1855—d. Dec. 6, 1902), educator, poet. In 1882 she was appointed president of the young Wellesley College. Under her administration the Academic Council was formed, entrance examinations were stiffened, courses of study standardized, and the faculty strengthened. She founded the Association of Collegiate Alumnae, the forerunner of the American Association of University Women, in 1882. In 1887 she married Professor GEORGE HERBERT PALMER of Harvard. After her death her husband published a little volume of her poetry entitled *A Marriage Cycle* (1915), a touching tribute to the felicitous partnership of two extraordinary individuals. He wrote *The Life of Alice Freeman Palmer* in 1908.

Palmer, Frederick (b. Pleasantville, Pa., Jan. 29, 1873—d. Sept. 2, 1958), newspaperman, war correspondent, biographer, memoirist. Beginning at the age of twenty-two, Palmer covered all the important events in several continents down to World War II. He wrote *Going to War with Greece* (1897); *With Kuroki in Manchuria* (1904); *Central America and Its Problems* (1910); *My Year of the War* (1915); *The Folly of Nations* (1921); *Newton D. Baker* (1931); *With My Own Eyes* (1933); *It Can Be Done This Time* (1944); *John J. Pershing* (1948); also several novels.

Palmer, George Herbert (b. Boston, March 19, 1842—d. May 7, 1933), philosopher, teacher. After graduating from Harvard, Palmer studied at Andover Theological Seminary and taught Greek at Harvard, where he was transferred to the Philosophy Department in 1872. By 1883 he was a full professor and one of the great men of the Harvard faculty. Never an innovator, Palmer excelled as critic and expositor of other men's philosophy. He taught a social ethic intended to mediate between Puritanism and Hegelianism. He was one of the first professors at Harvard to abandon textbooks and work out his ideas in lecture form. Among his numerous philosophical works were: *The Field of Ethics* (1901); *The Nature of Goodness* (1903); *The Problem of Freedom* (1911); *Altruism: Its Nature and Variety* (1919). His literary and critical works include: *The English Works of George Herbert* (3 v., 1905); *The Life of Alice Freeman Palmer* (1908); *Intimations of Immortality in the Sonnets of Shakespere* (1912); *Formative Types in English Poetry* (1918). A much admired translation was his version of the *Odyssey* (1884). His *Autobiography of a Philosopher* appeared in 1930.

Palmer, Ray (b. Little Compton, R.I., Nov. 12, 1808—d. March 29, 1887), teacher, clergyman, hymn writer. At first a teacher in New York and Connecticut, Palmer served in Congregational pulpits in Maine, New York, and New Jersey. He wrote extensively in prose on religious topics, but is chiefly remembered for his hymns, especially *My Faith Looks Up to Thee*. His hymns and other verses were collected in *Hymns and Sacred Pieces* (1865), *Hymns of My Holy Hours* (1867), and *The Poetical Works by Ray Palmer* (1876).

Palóu, Francisco (b. Majorca, 1722[?]—d. 1789[?]), missionary. In 1749 Palóu accompanied JUNÍPERO SERRA to Mexico. He was one of the Franciscan group that replaced the Jesuits in Lower California (1768). Five years later he moved northward and founded the Mission Dolores (1776), still standing in San Francisco as its oldest building. He wrote a *Life of Junípero Serra* (1787; English translation, 1913); his numerous reports and letters have been gathered as *Historical Memoirs of New California* (4 v., 1926).

Pancoast, Henry S[packman] (b. Germantown, Pa., Aug. 24, 1858—d. March 25, 1928), teacher, literary historian. For many years a member of the faculty of the University of Pennsylvania, Pancoast wrote *An Introduction to American Literature* (1898) and *A First Book in English Literature* (in collaboration with Percy Van Dyke Shelly, 1910); he also edited several anthologies.

Panic (1935), a verse play by ARCHIBALD MACLEISH. The plot and imagery evoke the financial crashes of the depression of the early thirties, demonstrating the way human panic transforms them into catastrophes as inevitable and unopposable as fog or a hurricane or a thread spun by the fates. One banker, McGafferty, resists panic, but the pounding, echoing rhythms of the crowd's speeches cause hysteria as they represent it and make it true that "Man's fate is a drum." A preface to the play outlines MacLeish's new approach to poetic language for the modern stage. Rejecting blank verse as a medium for contemporary American speech, he chooses accentual meter, in which stresses are counted instead of syllables.

Papashvily, George (b. Russia, Aug. 23, 1898 —   ), and **Papashvily, Helen [Waite]** (b. Stockton, Calif., Dec. 19, 1906—   ), humorists, essayists, memoirists. George Papashvily (a sculptor), and his wife collaborated on several popular books, and Mrs. Papashvily has done other writing of her own, especially juveniles. Their books together are humorous in tone, dealing mainly with the husband's experiences as an immigrant: *Anything Can Happen* (1945); *Yes and No Stories* (1946); *Thanks to Noah* (1951); *Dogs and People* (1954). Mrs. Papashvily wrote *All the Happy Endings* (1956), which analyzes the "scribbling women" of the 19th century—female authors of sentimental novels who, according to Mrs. Papashvily, injected much antimasculine material into their stories.

paperback books. In the early 1960's there were more than 20,000 paperback book titles currently in print in the United States, at prices ranging from 25 cents to more than $3.00. They were issued by scores of publishers and sold through a variety of retail outlets. Broadly, they could be divided into two categories—those sold largely through so-called mass-market distribution (*i.e.* magazine wholesalers and chain stores) and those sold in much smaller quantities at a higher price, almost exclusively through traditional book shops and college bookstores. The

editorial range of the popular-priced mass-distributed books matched that of the higher priced paperbacks in coverage of scholarly disciplines—the physical, natural, and social sciences, religion, history, art, philosophy, language, and reference—but included a wider choice of fiction, especially in the areas of pure entertainment: mysteries, Western Americana, science fiction, cartoons, games, and crossword puzzles. The higher priced paper books, on the other hand, included a larger percentage of highly specialized, even esoteric, titles, and a growing number of educational outline series and textbooks.

However, among the higher priced paperbounds, more widely distributed than has even been the case with hard cover editions, there developed an extraordinarily fine choice of poetry; not only of the established classics, but volumes by Hart Crane, T. S. Eliot, William Empson, E. E. Cummings, Robert Frost, Robert Lowell, Lawrence Durrell, Theodore Roethke, Donald Hall, and a great many other significant contemporaries. The higher-priced volumes in the early 1960's also included many volumes of literary criticism and bibliography not previously available in inexpensive paperback form. The inexpensive paperback books had tended in the 1950's to give wider currency to the more popular established poets and critics, including many excellent new translations of Greek, Latin, and later European poets and dramatists.

In book shops—college book shops particularly—Joyce, Ezra Pound, Auden, Thomas Merton, and Boris Pasternak appeared alongside Poe, Byron, Wordsworth, and Kipling. There was scarcely a novelist from Defoe and Jane Austen to J. D. Salinger and C. P. Snow who was not represented, along with all the principal philosophers from Plato and Aristotle to Sir Isaiah Berlin, John Dewey and A. J. Ayer.

This 20th-century phenomenon of paperbound books derives from many examples, at home and abroad, in the 19th century. (See DIME NOVELS and CHAPBOOKS.) In Germany, for example, Tauchnitz books, founded in Leipzig around 1840, developed some 5,000 English-language titles during the century before World War II. Tauchnitz licensed copyright material from British and American publishers on a royalty basis, and sold their "continental editions" throughout the world except in the United States and the British Commonwealth. In 1932, in Hamburg, Germany, Albatross Books, better designed and stressing contemporary authors, made such a dramatic entry into the English-language field that three years later Albatross took over the management of Tauchnitz. Almost immediately Penguin Books in England copied the Albatross format and, at a price of sixpence, soon dominated the English-language areas of the world everywhere except in the United States. Penguin Books represented a vast improvement on many British predecessors, such as Benn's Sixpenny Library, in format, design, and quality of editorial content. Penguin had a vast influence upon the subsequent American developments in paperbound publishing. Bantam Books were founded, with the financial backing of Curtis Publishing Company and the Grosset and Dunlap hard-cover reprinters, by Ian Ballantine, Penguin's first American representative; he subsequently left Bantam to organize his own Ballantine Books. The New American Library of World Literature, Inc., publishers of Signet Books, Signet Classics, and Mentor Books, derived directly from Penguin Books when the chairman and president, respectively, Victor Weybright and Kurt Enoch, who had built up the American branch, acquired full ownership and changed the corporate name and imprints to avoid confusion with the former parent company in England. Thereafter Penguin organized, on a more modest scale, a new American company based in Baltimore; in 1960 New American Library was acquired by the Times-Mirror Company. Pocket Books, founded in 1939 by Simon and Schuster and Robert de Graff, were the first of the large paperback publishers and first to use magazine wholesalers and drug and variety chain stores to achieve widespread distribution. They were soon followed, during World War II, by Dell Books and Avon Books (now owned by Hearst) in 1943. Even Fawcett Publications indirectly derived their books from Penguin by copying many of the book features of New American Library, for whom they served as a distributor in the decade after the war.

However, the United States was not without a considerable historical background in the publication of paperbound books prior to the mid-20th-century burgeoning of the industry. In the 1880's one out of every three books published in the United States or imported from England was paperbound. They ranged from imports of leading 19th-century British writers from Cassell and Company in London, frequently priced at ten cents per volume, to Chapman and Hall sixpenny volumes of Carlyle and other notables of the period. Meanwhile, Harper and Brothers were publishing paperbound editions of hundreds of outstanding books by foreign authors without paying royalties. Scribner's published a series of miniature pocket books, derived from *Scribner's Magazine.* The American Book Exchange issued classics and translations, often abridged, at a price of five cents. The Munro Library of Popular Novels, priced at twenty-five cents, included Conan Doyle, Kipling, Stevenson, Bulwer Lytton, Scott, and Dickens; and the Atlas series, issued by A. S. Barnes, represented the scholarly and literary scene from history to belles-lettres. Butler Brothers, with their Eclectic Series, published a number of classics at a low price made possible by paid advertising on the back cover for such products as the "braided-edge hammock—no stretch, no knots, strongest made."

The International Copyright Act of 1891 practically extinguished overnight this once-thriving industry, then approaching bankruptcy through overproduction of the works of Continental authors to whom no royalties were paid.

Except for the dime novels of the Wild West and adventure, which continued to be produced in the category of the later wood-pulp (*i.e.* newsprint) magazines, the entire 19th-century development, based on piracy of foreign authors' works, was at the expense of American authors, who were often neglected. Two years before the International Copyright Act, John W. Lovell, a successful operator, formed the United States Book Company and absorbed most of the competition. Five years later, except for certain school readers and some Wild West dime novels, there was hardly a paperbound book published in the United States.

The significant factors which encouraged the paperbound industry in the United States just before, during, and after World War II, were:

(1) The development of rotary-press book production in standard format, using rubber plates, and "perfect" binding—that is, binding not sewn but glued at the spine by automatic machines, which held the cover in place as well as holding the pages together.

(2) The pioneering of distribution through magazine wholesalers and non-book-shop outlets, rather than confining the marketing to a dwindling number of book shops—thus ensuring the economy of large printings and widespread distribution.

(3) The cumulative effect of Armed Forces Editions, provided for American troops in World War II, which developed the habit of reading books in millions of young Americans who were normally not book readers; followed by the GI Bill of Rights and other educational programs that resulted in 3,500,000 college registrants in the 1960's, with 7,000,000 predicted for the early 1970's, and with high-school education almost universal.

The leaders in the field of inexpensive paperbound books—Pocket Books, New American Library, Bantam Books, and others—at first licensed reprints of established books, and their varied wares were more or less a by-product of the major complex of hard-cover publishers. In theory and in practice paperbound books were distributed to sales outlets which did not ordinarily handle hard-cover books; hence they were an extension of the market to a new audience which, like that of the book clubs, did not patronize book shops. It was not long, however, until book shops—and college book shops especially—became interested in the high-quality books that were available, usually at a price of 25 cents. Higher prices were introduced in the 1950's. The higher prices—35 cents, 50 cents, even 75 cents and subsequently 95 cents—enabled the inexpensive paperbound industry to publish big books, fiction and nonfiction, and to move from pure mass appeal to a widely diversified audience which, in the words of one eminent critic, represented "class appeal with mass circulation."

As a result of the expansion and diversification of the inexpensive paperbound industry, paperbound reprints soon were not an ephemeral by-product but a basic contribution to the best tradition of book publishing—that is, the back list. Many books which were out of print when licensed from hard-cover publishers and university presses prospered and flourished when attractively produced in paperback form and put on sale in drugstores, chain stores, bus terminals, airports, book shops, and college bookstores.

The astonishing demand for good books for every mood and taste and within reach of every purse encouraged many publishers to enter the field. As a result the competition became and has remained fierce. There is competition for display space at the retail level, and equally fierce competition for publication rights.

The phenomenal success of quality paperback books at a low price brought about an inevitable reaction on the part of many trade publishers and university presses. They decided to start their own paperbound series, often by terminating short-term reprint licenses to the low-priced field and issuing the books at ninety-five cents and upward.

The significant discovery of the publishers of widely distributed inexpensive paperbacks was that their own taste, judgment, flair, courage, and experience coincided, generally, with the attributes of the hard-cover publishers from whom they licensed reprint rights. As reprint rights became more expensive, or were terminated by publishers who were developing their own higher-priced paperbound series, the inexpensive sector of the industry was forced to develop original material. It happened gradually, first of all in the "category" books—Westerns, thrillers, science fiction, cartoon books, reference —and then moved ineluctably in the direction of scholarly material and general fiction.

In order to demonstrate that paperback production does not necessarily represent vulgarization, most paperbound publishers in the 1950's developed literary publications to attract and discover new talent. NEW WORLD WRITING, published by New American Library, led the way in 1952, followed by DISCOVERY, an anthology devoted to the work of American writers only, which was published by Pocket Books for two years. The first issue of Anchor Review (Doubleday) appeared in 1955. Subsequently, the lively EVERGREEN REVIEW, Noonday, and others sponsored by paperback publishers appeared. In 1959 New World Writing, still in paperbound form, was transferred to Lippincott. New American Library had launched this book-format "little magazine" and harnessed it to its distribution system to achieve an average circulation of 100,000 copies. Once its mission was accomplished and dozens of "little magazines" appeared—some, like Dial, "reappeared"—the editors decided they could contribute more to the cause of literature by concentrating on books rather than literary criticism, stories, and fragments of novels.

In the postwar years paperbound books were nearly all of standard format, manufactured by four or five specialized printers, and displayed in racks which were adapted to a standardized product. Eventually many improvements—such as the use of higher quality paper, better cover

design, and especially more flexible glue than the older kind, which had tended to deteriorate under various conditions of temperature or humidity—made many inexpensive paperback volumes indistinguishable from the more expensive paperback books. The price was held down by printings of 100,000 copies up to 2,000,000 or 3,000,000 copies, compared with the more normal printing of 10,000 or 20,000 copies for the higher-priced paperbounds which are not mass distributed. Many higher-priced paperbounds cost more to produce than a case-bound hard-cover book, but readers seem to prefer them for many reasons—ease of handling; brightness of display which makes them an impulse purchase; and a feeling that in urban society one doesn't necessarily have to preserve every book forever. Paperback readers cull their libraries, making room constantly for new books.

Unlike the 19th-century paperbound phenomenon, which was based more or less on "piracy" of foreign authors, the mid-20th-century paperbound book, at every price level, often provides the author with a genuinely substantial audience and concomitant income. Paperbound publishers, nevertheless, frequently discover or develop literary properties which deserve to be reprinted in durable library editions, and they then usually place the hard-cover rights for prior publication.

Most of the major newspapers of the United States now review paperback books. Annually or more often, many produce a paperback supplement to their regular weekend book review sections—notably the New York Times, the New York Herald Tribune, the Chicago Tribune, the San Francisco Chronicle, and the Los Angeles Times.

Paperback books are universally applauded by libraries, especially college libraries, which, when students purchase their supplementary reading in paperback form, can devote their budgets to many more expensive scholarly series and reference books instead of reserving multiple hard-cover copies for classroom assignments. Paperback books have favorably influenced the availability of American literature abroad because of a price within reach of the student or general reader in even economically undeveloped areas of the world. The paperback industry in the United States seldom produces "export editions," except occasionally in cooperation with United States Government programs overseas; but Penguin Books, in England, which are austerely produced for the home market, use a garish dust jacket, with colored illustrations, to capture the mass market in such areas as Australia. The trend in American design of paperback books is toward greater simplicity and more artistic, even abstract, cover designs. Better paper and less cramped typography are also favored, and the price is somewhat higher than in the 1940's and 1950's.

A simple bibliography of "Paperbound Books in Print" is issued quarterly by R. R. Bowker; "Paperbound Books in America" by Freeman Lewis, the "16th Bowker Lecture," was published by the New York Public Library in 1952; and "The Paper-Bound Book: Twentieth Century Publishing Phenomenon," by Kurt Enoch, was reprinted from *The Library Quarterly* (XXIV), No. 3, July, 1954. However, no serious student of American letters or American publishing has yet covered paperback books in the United States comprehensively and adequately in any one monograph or book.

In relation to the literary scene, there is scarcely a notable author, contemporary or classical, who is not listed in the quarterly volumes of "Paperbound Books in Print." *Publishers' Weekly,* the organ of the book trade, gives special attention to paperback books. The spring, 1961, "Paperbound Books in Print" lists 239 publishers, many of which have several imprints, so that the scope of paperback publishing appears to be endless. It would not be appropriate to speculate upon the future except to point out that the circumstances which resulted in the collapse of the paperbound industry in the 1890's do not exist today. Paperbound publishers pay royalties, and their costs are premised upon a fair, sometimes even an excessive, return to the holder of the rights, whether a publisher or an author. One thing which the industry has, as a whole, demonstrated is that it exists in necessary co-operation with all other publishers, and with authors and agents. The trade association of general publishers in the United States, the American Book Publishers Council, continuously includes on its board representatives of the paperback sector of the industry. Some publishers are drifting away from the nomenclature of "paperback" or "paperbound," preferring to use the term "soft cover" in the event that some synthetic cover material may supersede the predominant paper covers in use today. A few publishers have designed their paperback books so that they may be rebound for durable preservation, but this does not reflect a trend.

Many well-established series of hard-cover reprints and classics are being transformed in whole or in part into paperback form—notably Everyman's Library, which has sold some 44,-000,000 books since it was launched at a shilling a volume in London at the turn of the century. Several American publishers of soft-cover books average close to 44,000,000 copies annually, at least half of which compare favorably in quality with the works of the 1,260 authors of "Everyman." Random House and Alfred A. Knopf have merged the Vintage paperbounds of Knopf and the paperbound editions of Modern Library. The university presses, even when there is no great economy in producing a small printing of a book in soft covers rather than in boards, find that paper covers give them a unique opportunity to employ modern design treatment.

The American branches of the great university presses of Oxford and Cambridge provided a number of significant critical works on world literature, including studies of Goethe, Juvenal, Cervantes, Chaucer, and Shakespeare. The American university presses, although stressing science, education, psychology, history, and reli-

gion, also made a tremendous contribution to the wider dissemination of important literary criticism, drama, biography, and poetry. Some major general publishers developed a variety of imprints for books in special categories. Doubleday, for example, publishes Anchor, intellectual; Image, Catholic; and Dolphin, a wide variety of novels, essays, travel books, and even outstanding mysteries. Macmillan, Scribner's, and Harcourt, Brace and World developed special paperback series. Farrar, Straus and Cudahy acquired Noonday, and World Publishing Company purchased Meridian. But it remained for the lower-priced paperbacks, widely distributed beyond the conventional book trade—in drugstores, supermarkets, airports, and bus terminals —to pioneer in the massive diffusion of literary and scholarly works by the millions of copies.

The effect of this twofold development— cheaper books in the book shops and much cheaper books universally available in every neighborhood throughout the nation—was to give new prestige and importance to books as compared with popular periodicals and to widen the intellectual horizon of ordinary readers as well as students. A secondary effect, which began to become discernible in the late 1950's, was a decline in the number of book writers in fields of ephemeral entertainment and an increase in the number of serious authors undertaking important novels, biographies, translations, critical works, and important readable books in many areas of science and mathematics. The reading of books and the writing of books tended to become a significant sign of sophisticated status, as they were in elite families and communities in the 19th century. Books on architecture, art, psychology, religion, and science, including the social sciences, became part of the current and casual continuing education of adults as well as students. The effect of this diffusion of learning and literature is not readily measurable, but ultimately it should have a constructive influence upon domestic education and culture, and upon world understanding generally.

The economic consequences on hard-cover publishing of this wide distribution of literature in soft-cover form have happily not been adverse. On the contrary, the paperback expansion of book production was obviously necessary to keep pace with the increase of education and population throughout the world.

Victor Weybright

Parents' Magazine. Founded in 1926 as *Children—The Magazine for Parents*, the magazine took its present name in 1929. The founder was George Hecht. Parents' Institute, an organization, publishes the magazine and several others later established by Hecht. The editor from the start was Clara Savage Littledale. Her resourcefulness and common sense gave the magazine a wide appeal. She crusaded for women's votes, better pay for teachers, school lunches, better health examinations for children, less lurid comics, training for mothers, also gave advice on marriage problems and housing, books, movies, and records. She followed the changed attitudes of child psychologists, from the era when it was fashionable to let children alone to the new era when showing them love and tenderness is no longer regarded as an intellectual crime.

Parke, John (b. Dover, Del., April 7, 1754—d. Dec. 11, 1789), soldier, poet, translator. Parke attended Newark College in Delaware and the College of Philadelphia, and became an excellent classical scholar. He served in the Continental Army from 1775 to 1778 in the Quartermaster's Department, lived thereafter in retirement. He published only one volume, which also contains contributions by his friend David French. The collection was called *The Lyric Works of Horace, to Which Are Added a Number of Original Poems* (1786). His renderings of Horace anticipate some of the later efforts of American verse writers like EUGENE FIELD and FRANKLIN P. ADAMS, who take their themes and viewpoints from Horace but give the renderings a contemporaneous setting. The collection included some original verses in the then current neo-classical style; also a play, *Virginia*.

Parker, Arthur Caswell (b. Iroquois, N.Y., April 5, 1881—d. Jan. 1, 1955), ethnologist, archaeologist, writer. Parker was born on the Cattaraugus Reservation of the Senecas. His great-uncle General Ely S. Parker was the "last grand sachem of the Iroquois and General Grant's military secretary," according to a biography of his kinsman that Parker published in 1919. Parker occupied important posts as an archaeologist and ethnologist, being especially interested in American Indians. Among his books: *Erie Indian Village* (1907); *Maize and Other Plant Foods* (1909); *Code of Handsome Lake* (1913); *Constitution of the Five Nations* (1916); *Archaeological History of N.Y.* (1922); *Seneca Myths and Folk Tales* (1923); *Indian How Book* (1927); *Gustango Gold* (1930); *Manual for History Museums.*

Parker, Cornelia Stratton. See AN AMERICAN IDYLL.

Parker, Dorothy [Rothschild] (b. West End, N.J., Aug. 22, 1893—d. June 7, 1967), poet, short-story writer. Mrs. Parker began her career by writing occasional verse, playing the piano in a dancing school, and writing captions for a fashion magazine; to her is credited the advertising epigram: "Brevity is the soul of lingerie." She became drama critic of *Vanity Fair* in 1917, but was discharged in 1920 because her reviews were too harsh. Thereafter she frequently wrote drama and book reviews for *The New Yorker*, which turned a deaf ear to the cries of the wounded. Mrs. Parker is noted for the sharpness of her critical sallies, as when she described Katherine Hepburn in *The Lake* as running "the whole gamut of emotion from A to B." A good many other trenchancies, dispensed in prose, verse, or random discourse, earned her a reputation for caustic wit probably unequaled by any other female American of her generation.

Mrs. Parker's publications include ENOUGH ROPE (verse, 1926; new ed., 1933); *Sunset Gun* (verse, 1928); *Laments for the Living* (stories, 1930); *Death and Taxes* (verse, 1931); *After Such Pleasures* (stories, 1933). The verse has been collected in *Not So Deep as a Well* (1936), the stories in *Here Lies* (1939). She also wrote a play with ELMER RICE, *Close Harmony* (1924). *The Viking Portable Dorothy Parker*, which contains all her major works, appeared in 1944.

In her verse Mrs. Parker loved to write on departed or departing love, the fickle female, various types of suitors, memories of love, and occasionally more weighty themes. She was sardonic, rather limited in range, and drily elegant in meter and rhyme, although she could at times leave this realm and write a beautiful Christmas poem like *Prayer for a New Mother*. Her stories are as profound in their knowledge of human nature as they are deep in disenchantment. Some, like *Big Blonde*, have become classics; others, like *Lady with a Lamp, Glory in the Daytime*, and *A Telephone Call*, are almost as good. They are often dramatized wisecracks at the expense of sentimentality. Only RING LARDNER can be compared with her, says Mark Van Doren, in hatred of stupidity, cruelty, and weakness. Her stories are often a concentrated essence of loathing.

Parker, Sir [Horatio] Gilbert (b. Ont., Nov. 23, 1862—d. Sept. 6, 1932), novelist. Parker wrote verse at sixteen, studied for the ministry at Trinity College, Toronto, and taught English there. In poor health, he went around the world, and for four years was associate editor of the Sydney (Australia) *Morning Herald*. Returning to Canada, he wrote short stories, collected in *Pierre and His People* (1892), and became the Dominion's best-known novelist. THE SEATS OF THE MIGHTY (1896), a novel of the fall of Quebec, was a best seller, and so was *The Right of Way* (1901). From 1898 on he lived in England, where he was knighted in 1902. He also wrote *A Ladder of Swords* (1904); *The Weavers* (1907); *The Judgment House* (1913); *The Power and the Glory* (1925); many short stories; and much propaganda for the Allied cause during World War I.

Parker, Horatio William (b. Auburndale, Mass., Sept. 15, 1863—d. Dec. 18, 1919), organist, teacher, composer. Parker was professor of music theory at Yale University, later dean of the Yale Music School. He won fame with the oratorio *Hora Novissima* (1893), received a prize of $10,000 from the Metropolitan Opera House for his opera *Mona*, on which he collaborated with BRIAN HOOKER as librettist (1911). He and Hooker also wrote another prize-winning opera, *Fairyland* (1915). Parker composed many church pieces, cantatas, hymns, and oratorios. His choral works, such as *A Star Song*, are regarded as his best works. G. W. Chadwick wrote his biography (1921).

Parker, Samuel (b. Ashfield, Mass., April 23, 1779—d. March 21, 1866), Congregational clergyman, missionary. For several years Parker preached in western New York and engaged in missionary activities there. He represented the American Board of Commissioners for Foreign Missionaries in Oregon, and his activities there helped to establish American claims to that region. He explored the countryside, established friendly relations with the Indians, and chose sites for missions. His literary fame rests on his excellent *Journal of an Exploring Tour Beyond the Rocky Mountains* (1838).

Parker, Theodore (b. Lexington, Mass., Aug. 24, 1810—d. May 10, 1860), clergyman, abolitionist, writer. Parker graduated from Harvard Divinity School, became pastor of the Unitarian congregation of West Roxbury, Mass., and married Lydia Cabot. A member of the Transcendental Club, he expounded its philosophy in his *Discourse of Matters Pertaining to Religion* (1842). A famous sermon, ON THE TRANSIENT AND PERMANENT IN CHRISTIANITY (1841), was the first statement of his unorthodox beliefs. Here he rejects the scriptures and the established church as the source of divinity and instead invokes personal intuition with God. These apparent heresies earned him the censure of his fellow clergymen but he refused to resign and retained a loyal congregation. In 1845 he became preacher to the new Twenty-Eighth Congregational Society with 7000 members. He actively supported abolitionism, hiding slaves in his own house and aiding John Brown. His *Letter to the People of the United States Touching the Matter of Slavery* (1848) attempts to prove the evil of that system. Mr. Power, the inspired preacher in Louisa May Alcott's novel, *Work* (1873), derives from Parker. His sermons were collected in three volumes (1853–5) and his collected works in fourteen volumes (1863–70). He is the subject of a biography (1936) by Henry Steele Commager and he appears in the novel, *The Sin of the Prophet* (1952) by Truman John Nelson.

Parkinson, Thomas Francis (b. San Francisco, Feb. 24, 1920—   ), teacher, critic, poet. Parkinson received a doctoral degree in 1948 from the University of California, and has been on the faculty there since 1945. His publications include *W. B. Yeats, Self-Critic* (1951), a study of the poet's early verse; *Men, Women, Vines* (1959) a book of poems; and *A Casebook on the Beat* (1961), a compilation of writing by and about the "Beat generation" (see BEAT WRITING). He has also contributed poems and articles to the *Pacific Spectator,* the *Nation,* the *Sewanee Review,* and other periodicals.

Parkman, Francis (b. Boston, Sept. 16, 1823 —d. Nov. 8, 1893), historian, horticulturalist. Early in life Parkman contracted a serious case of what he called "Injuns on the brain." His boyhood was spent on the Middlesex Fells, hunting, fishing, trapping, becoming an expert shot and an authority on woodcraft and Indian lore. Following his graduation from Harvard University he obtained a law degree from the Harvard Law School, but never practiced. In 1846 he set out with his cousin Quincy Adams Shaw on an expedition to Fort Laramie, Wyo. There he heard that a nearby encampment of Sioux

were preparing an attack on the Snake Indians. Parkman determined to join the Sioux warriors and observe Indians on the warpath. He found the tribe after a hazardous mountain journey, and for the next few weeks lived with the war-

riors under the most primitive and strenuous conditions. All during the journey he kept a detailed record which was published in the *Knickerbocker Magazine* as THE OREGON TRAIL (1847). In 1849 the record was published as *The California and The Oregon Trail.*

On his return, Parkman's health suffered a complete breakdown. Unable to endure light for more than a few minutes at a time, he constructed a wire frame that enabled him to write with his eyes closed. In this fashion, or by dictation, he wrote HISTORY OF THE CONSPIRACY OF PONTIAC (1851). In 1856 he wrote a curious semiautobiographical novel, VASSALL MORTON. Two years later he journeyed to Europe in search of a cure for his nervous disorders, and on his return took up the culture of roses, the results of which he published in *The Book of Roses* (1866). His health improved as he worked in his garden. In 1871 he was appointed professor of horticulture at Harvard.

In spite of these interruptions he continued to write histories: *Pioneers of France in the New World* (1865); *The Jesuits in North America in the Seventeenth Century* (1867); *The Discovery of the Great West* (1869; reprinted in 1879 as *La Salle and the Discovery of the Great West*); *The Old Regime in Canada* (1874); *Count Frontenac and New France Under Louis XIV, Montcalm and Wolfe* (1884); *A Half Century of Conflict* (1892). *The Journals of Francis Parkman* (2 v., 1947), a recent discovery, contains important material on Parkman as historian and man of letters. *The Works of Francis Parkman* (21 v., 1897–1901) has a long introductory essay by John Fiske. The most recent edition of his complete works is the Centenary Edition of *The Works of Francis Parkman* (12 v., 1922). *The Parkman Reader* (1955), edited by S. E. Morison, is an excellent introduction to his writings. Another abridgment is John Tebbel's *Battle for North America* (1948). Parkman's *Letters* were collected in two volumes edited by W. R. Jacobs (1960); C. H. Gardiner collected *The Literary Memoranda of Francis Parkman* (1961).

Like JOHN MOTLEY, Parkman saw history in terms of a constant struggle between progress and reaction: England, the democracy, battling France, the military despot. Unlike Motley, he had little admiration for either side. His books often have what Clarence Gohdes called "an implicit romantic radiance." Otis A. Pease, in *Francis Parkman's History* (1953), sought to evaluate Parkman as a historian. Howard Doughty wrote a biography, *Francis Parkman* (1962).

Parley, Peter. See S. G. GOODRICH.

Parley's Magazine. See S. G. GOODRICH.

Parnassus on Wheels (1917), a novel by CHRISTOPHER MORLEY. The title is derived from a wagon bookshop drawn by Pegasus, a sleek, well-fed horse. The owner of this wandering bookstore is ROGER MIFFLIN, who takes his affectionate dog, Boccaccio, along with him on his journeys. He sells the outfit to Helen McGill, who describes herself disparagingly as a fat spinster of thirty-eight; Mifflin goes along to show her the business, successfully fights off her big brother who wants her back as his maid-of-all-work, gets thrown into jail wrongfully, and is duly rescued to marry Helen. The book has stayed in print continuously since its appearance, has been called the best novel ever written about books and bookmen. An edition in 1956 has an introduction by John T. Winterich. In 1919 appeared a sequel, THE HAUNTED BOOKSHOP, which told another love story enacted in Mifflin's Brooklyn bookshop. Both books were printed together (1948) in an edition with an introduction by Joseph Margolies.

Parrington, Vernon L[ouis] (b. Aurora, Ill., Aug. 3, 1871—d. June 16, 1929), teacher, historian, biographer, critic. Parrington was brought up in the heart of Kansas Populism, a movement whose ideas moulded his own development. After attending the College of Emporia, Parrington went to Harvard University for two years and emerged with an intense desire to get "the last lingering Harvard prejudices out of my system." Then he began his long teaching career, beginning at the College of Emporia, then at the University of Oklahoma (which he left as the result of a "political cyclone"), finally at the University of Washington.

He was a superb teacher and theorist, reaching the climax of his career with THE COLONIAL MIND (1927), which received a Pulitzer prize and became the opening section of his great work MAIN CURRENTS IN AMERICAN THOUGHT (1927–1930), left unfinished at his death. Up to that time his only publication, aside from articles, had been a college anthology, *The Con-*

necticut Wits (1926). Parrington's main aesthetic quality was a sense of architecture. This was everywhere evident in the harmony, balance, and proportion of his work. He refused, however, to write a belletristic account of American literature; he attempted instead a history of America in terms of the writings, of whatever kind, produced on its soil. He was deeply influenced by Hippolyte Taine's hypothesis that the literature of a people is the inevitable outgrowth of their racial peculiarities, environment, and epoch. He made a frank avowal in the foreword to his first volume: "The point of view from which I have endeavored to evaluate the materials is liberal rather than conservative, Jeffersonian rather than Federalistic." He is at his best, therefore, when treating authors who are in some way exponents of liberalism: Roger Williams, Franklin, Tom Paine, Emerson, Thoreau, Channing, Theodore Parker, Hamlin Garland, above all Jefferson. Parrington's history has been attacked for his lack of aesthetic appreciation except where literature happens to convey an ostensible social or political message. He wrote brilliantly of General Grant but lamely of Hawthorne—Grant had made "history," Hawthorne merely "reflected" a tradition. But he has been extremely influential, especially in the 1930's.

Parrish, Anne (b. Colorado Springs, Colo., Nov. 12, 1888—d. Sept. 5, 1957), painter, novelist. Coming from a family that included some noted artists (MAXFIELD PARRISH was her cousin), Miss Parrish at first intended to become a painter. But in the early 1920's she began writing novels and proved an adept and entertaining storyteller. THE PERENNIAL BACHELOR (1925), which won the lucrative Harper's Prize, is an ironic study of a man who never marries and at sixty goes as a beau to parties of young people, unaware of their laughter. In later novels she made similarly clever and convincing studies of odd personalities. The great crises in Europe and America that came with the rise of the dictators gave her books a more serious mood, as in *Mr. Despondency's Daughter* (1938) and *Pray for Tomorrow* (1941). *A Clouded Star* (1948) centers on some of the experiences of HARRIET TUBMAN, an ex-slave who assisted many Negroes in their flight to freedom on the Underground Railroad. *The Lucky One* was published posthumously in 1958.

Parrish, Maxfield (b. Philadelphia, July 25, 1870—d. Mar. 30, 1966), painter. This great favorite of the American public was a pupil of HOWARD PYLE and an able illustrator of such classics as *The Arabian Nights*, Palgrave's *Golden Treasury*, Kenneth Grahame's *Golden Age*. His work was often sentimental, exhibiting an aura of unreality in bright colors, especially a rich shade of blue that is called by his name. He has painted some striking murals, such as the King Cole mural first hung in the Knickerbocker Hotel bar, later in the bar of the St. Regis Hotel in New York.

Parsons, Elsie Clews (b. [?], 1875—d. Dec.

19, 1941), anthropologist. Mrs. Parsons became a leading authority on Amerindian lore. Among her books were *Notes on Zuni* (1917); *Folk Tales of Andros Islands, Bahamas* (1918); *Folklore of the Sea Islands* (1923); *Ceremonial of Zuni* (1924); *Pueblo of Jemez* (1925); *Tewa Tales* (1926); *Taos Pueblo* (1936); *Pueblo Indian Religion* (1939); *Taos Tales* (1940). She began her writing career by publishing some books of a more general nature, such as *The Family* (1906); *The Old-Fashioned Woman* (1913); *Fear and Conventionality* (1914); *Social Freedom* (1915); *Social Rule* (1916).

Parsons, Louella O. (b. Freeport, Ill., Aug. 6, 1893——), Hollywood columnist. Credit for originating the column of gossip about motion-picture personalities is disputed; Mrs. Parsons may have been first when she undertook such a column for the Chicago *Herald* (1914). Since she joined William Randolph Hearst's newspaper syndicate in the Twenties, her fame has grown until her influence surpasses that of many Hollywood directors and producers. She entitled her autobiography *The Gay Illiterate* (1944).

Parsons, T[homas] W[illiam] (b. Boston, Aug. 18, 1819—d. Sept. 3, 1892), dentist, poet, translator. This gentle, meticulous, unworldly man was educated at Harvard Medical School, but before obtaining a degree he left to travel in Italy. Upon his return he buried himself in his study, began translating Dante, turned out occasional verses to celebrate the marriage or death of prominent Bostonians. Although he practiced dentistry, his great interest was in perfecting his translation of the *Divine Comedy*. In 1867 his *Inferno* was published in Boston with illustrations by Gustave Doré; between 1870 and 1883 about two-thirds of the *Purgatorio* appeared in the *Catholic World*.

Parsons' original verse was published in *Poems* (1854); *The Magnolia* (1866); *The Old House at Sudbury* (1870); *The Shadow of the Obelisk* (1872); *The Willey House, and Sonnets* (1875). In 1893 a posthumous *Complete Poems* was published. After his death C. E. Norton gathered his translations in *The Divine Comedy of Dante Alighieri* (1893). Although Parsons' work no longer appeals to the modern reader, it was highly regarded in his day.

Particular, Pertinax. Pen name of TOBIAS WATKINS.

Partington, Mrs. The name became legendary through a humorous speech made by Sydney Smith in England in 1831 in which he ridiculed the rejection of the Reform Bill by the House of Lords by inventing a Dame Partington who at a time of great storm, got out her mop and broom and vigorously pushed back the Atlantic Ocean. The speech helped to put the bill through. B. P. SHILLABER took over the name, called his character Mrs. Ruth Partington, and placed all kinds of malapropisms in her mouth as she discussed everything under the sun, from Calvinism to patent medicines. Yet she spoke often with Yankee wisdom and was, as Walter Blair puts it, "the soul of grandmotherly kindness." Shillaber was the editor of a humor-

ous magazine, THE CARPET BAG, in which his sketches first appeared, to be collected later in several volumes. The magazine was greatly admired by Mark Twain as a young man, and in it appeared his first printed sketch. Aunt Polly in Twain's *Tom Sawyer* is distinctly reminiscent of Mrs. Partington. By a strange coincidence, in fact, the picture of Shillaber's heroine, labeled "Contentment," which appeared in *The Life and Sayings of Mrs. Partington* (1854), turned up in the first edition of *Tom Sawyer* (1876) as a picture of AUNT POLLY.

Partington, Ruth. See MRS. PARTINGTON and BENJAMIN P. SHILLABER.

Partisan, The, a Tale of the Revolution (1835), a novel by WILLIAM GILMORE SIMMS. The first novel in a trilogy dealing with the Revolutionary War in South Carolina, *The Partisan* centers on the events between the fall of Charleston and Gates' defeat at Camden, and on the actions of Major Singleton and Colonel Walton, patriots and aristocratic landholders. Its sequel, *Mellichampe, a Legend of the Santee* (1836), deals with the time between the defeat at Camden and the arrival of Nathaniel Greene, and with the rivalry between Ernest Mellichampe, a patriot, and Barsfield, a Tory, for the hand of Janet Berkeley, a loyal Partisan. The military action in *Katharine Walton, Or, the Rebel of Dorchester* (1851), the third novel of the trilogy, is nearly the same as that in *Mellichampe;* the central characters are Colonel Walton, who appeared in *The Partisan*, his daughter Katharine, who marries Singleton, also the hero of both books. The most famous character in the trilogy is CAPTAIN PORGY, a "prose Falstaff" considered by some critics to be the best comic character in American romantic fiction. Porgy also appeared in *The Forayers* (1855) and was a central character in *Woodcraft* (1854).

Partisan Leader, The: A Novel, and an Apocalypse of the Origin and Struggles of the Southern Confederacy (1836; fictitiously dated 1856), by NATHANIEL BEVERLY TUCKER. Tucker published the book under the pseudonym of Edward William Sidney. His chief aim was to influence the country against the election of MARTIN VAN BUREN. His book prophesied, in a fictional projection of the future, that Van Buren would set up a dictatorial rule and would so offend the southern states that in 1849 South Carolina would secede and Virginia would be on the point of doing so. The book produced no effect on the election, but during the Civil War it was reprinted on both sides of the Mason and Dixon Line for propaganda purposes.

Partisan Review. A magazine founded in 1934. Though first closely connected with the radical left wing in politics, it soon began to diverge from orthodox Marxism. In 1936 it merged with the *Anvil*, edited by William Phillips, who joined the editorial board of the *Partisan Review*. In 1937, after discontinuing publication for fourteen months, a new board of editors was formed which took a strongly independent stand politically. In addition to

PHILLIP RAHV, one of the founders, and Phillips, it included F. W. Dupee, Dwight Mac-Donald, and MARY McCARTHY. The magazine has published creative work by most of the prominent writers of the contemporary Anglo-American literary world, without regard to private political convictions and with special emphasis on the most serious aspect of *avant-garde* literature. They also have introduced much Continental writing to American readers through translations. Lionel Trilling has done some of his most distinguished work for the *Partisan Review*, as have other critics such as Richard Chase and Robert Gorham Davis. Saul Bellow's work was first published in its pages; part of James T. Farrell's STUDS LONIGAN appeared there in installments. During its whole existence the magazine has been a primary rallying point for American intellectuals. It is particularly well known for its symposia on contemporary questions affecting writers and other intellectuals. Several volumes containing collections of material from the magazine have been published: *The Partisan Reader—1934–44* (1946), edited by Phillips and Rahv, with an introduction by Trilling; *The New Partisan Reader* (1953); *Stories in the Modern Manner* (1953); and *More Stories in the Modern Manner* (1954).

Parton, Ethel (b. New York City, Dec. 1, 1862—d. Feb. 27, 1944), writer for young people. When Ethel Thompson's parents died she was taken in by her grandmother SARAH WILLIS, who won fame under the pen name Fanny Fern. Miss Thompson adopted the name of her grandmother's third husband JAMES PARTON and later occasionally collaborated with him. She lived mostly in Newburyport, Mass., the scene of many of her stories. She was a staff member of *Youth's Companion* for more than forty years, and contributed to that magazine and to ST. NICHOLAS. She wrote *Melissa Ann, A Little Girl of the 1820s* (1931); *Tabitha Mary, A Little Girl of 1810* (1933); *Penelope Ellen and Her Friends: Three Little Girls of 1840* (1936); and similar historical narratives, based on research and on family recollections.

Parton, James (b. England, Feb. 9, 1822—d. Oct. 17, 1891), teacher, biographer, essayist. Parton, brought to America in 1827, was educated at an academy in White Plains, N.Y., where, after graduation, he remained as a teacher. He traveled for a year, then spent four years teaching at a private school in Philadelphia. In 1848 his essay demonstrating that a woman had written *Jane Eyre* brought him to the attention of NATHANIEL PARKER WILLIS, editor of the New York *Home Journal*, who gave him a position on the paper. In 1854 Parton was commissioned by the Mason Brothers Publishing Co. to write a life of Horace Greeley. This appeared a year later and was an outstanding success. Parton devoted the rest of his life to writing, turning out a long list of titles remarkable even in that age of literary industry. He was married for some years to SARA PAYSON WILLIS, better known as Fanny Fern, a lady journalist. His best books are *The Life and*

Times of Aaron Burr (1857; enlarged ed., 2 v., 1864); *Life of Andrew Jackson* (3 v., 1859–60); *Life and Times of Benjamin Franklin* (2 v., 1864); *Life of John Jacob Astor* (1865); *Life of Thomas Jefferson* (1874); *Life of Voltaire* (2 v., 1881). Although he wrote in haste and made many errors, he was an honest and charitable biographer. M. E. Flower has written *James Parton: The Father of Modern Biography* (1951).

Parton, Sara Payson Willis. See SARA PAYSON WILLIS.

Partridge, Bellamy (b. Phelps, N.Y., 1878—d. July 5, 1960), author, editor, critic. Although a prolific writer of fiction and nonfiction for many years, Partridge did not gain popular favor until his sixties, with *Country Lawyer* (1939), a book based on the life of his father, which was later made into a film. From then on, his writings, distinguished by a tender, nostalgic tone, took firmer hold on the public. As a youth, Partridge prepared for the bar, studying at Hobart College and Union University. However, when World War I broke out, he served as a war correspondent. In 1923 he joined the publishing firm of Brentano, and edited a book column for several years. His special gift for seizing the flavor of the turn of the century, that faded yet secure Victorian world, was highly marked in his more popular books. *The Big Family* (1941) related the lively story of a lawyer's household of eight children. *As We Were* (1946) recollected family life between 1850 and 1900, with pictures collected by Otto Bettmann. *January Thaw* (1945), which told the adventures of a city couple determined to renovate a Connecticut farmhouse, became a Broadway play. *The Old Oaken Bucket* (1949) was about a rundown house with a spurious past. Other books: *The Roosevelt Family in America* (1936); *Excuse My Dust* (1943); *The Big Freeze* (1948); *Salad Days* (1951); *Fill 'er Up* (1952); *Going, Going, Gone* (1958).

Passage to India (1868; pub., 1871, in "Annex" to *Leaves of Grass*), a poem by WALT WHITMAN. Three great material triumphs prompted this poem: the laying of the Atlantic cable in 1866, the opening of the Suez Canal, and the completion of the Union Pacific Railroad in 1869. Whitman felt that these events heralded a great era of peace in which a superior civilization would be created by captains and engineers, noble inventors and scientists. To him the opening of the Suez Canal meant union with India, where civilization had perhaps been born. But the whole poem rests on Whitman's recognition that his faith in democracy had been premature, that much still remained to be done before the New World could achieve the ideals he had celebrated in his earlier work. From the world as it was he turned aside in *Passage to India* to imagine a utopia still to come.

Passionate Pilgrim, The, and Other Stories (1875), a collection by HENRY JAMES. In 1873, in a letter to his mother, James mentioned his intention of making "a volume of tales on the theme of American adventurers in Europe, leading off with *The Passionate Pilgrim,"* which had appeared in 1871. This title story was one of a number of pieces stimulated by his trip abroad in 1869–70. It tells of Clement Searle, who goes to England, long the object of his dreams, to claim a rich estate. He is penniless, ill, morbid; his misadventures lead to his death just at the moment when his desire was on the point of being gratified. The tale is ironic and tragic, but full of James' own passionate love of England.

Pastor, Tony [Antonio] (b. New York City, May 28, 1837—d. Aug. 26, 1908), actor, theater manager, song writer. Pastor was still a child when he went on the stage, and the theater continued to be his intense interest. He began as a clown and a ballad singer, and many of the songs he made popular were written by himself. He "cleaned up" variety acts and made the music halls places where parents could bring their children. It was due to his stimulus that vaudeville became popular all over the country. A collection of his songs was called *Tony Pastor's New Union Song Book* (1862).

Pastorius, Francis Daniel (b. Germany, Sept. 26, 1651—d. c. Jan. 1, 1720), theologian, lawyer, colonist, public official, teacher, geographer, historian, poet. Pastorius was among the most learned of the American colonists, an adept in seven languages, well acquainted not only with legal and theological writings, but with those in the fields of science and medicine. Early in life he was greatly attracted by the teachings of a group of Quakers in Frankfurt; he has been described as a Friend who was also part Lutheran and Pietist. His ability attracted immediate attention and he was sent (1683) as an agent of the Frankfurt Quakers to buy land in Pennsylvania for a settlement. He obtained 15,-000 acres of land on favorable terms from WILLIAM PENN, founded Germantown (he was its first mayor), was a member of the Assembly (1687, 1691), taught in Germantown and Philadelphia, was a good friend of the local Indians. He wrote many important documents, particularly a noble protest against Negro slavery, the first on record in America. He married Ennecke Klostermanns in 1688; they appear as characters in John Greenleaf Whittier's important but little known poem THE PENNSYLVANIA PILGRIM (1872).

Pastorius was a prolific writer; much that he wrote, still unpublished (particularly numerous poems), is in five volumes of manuscripts in the library of the Historical Society of Pennsylvania. This collection he called his *Bienenstock* or *Melliotrophium* ("Beehive"); it bears witness to his encyclopedic learning and his skill as a linguist. But he published a considerable body of work, including his doctoral thesis on a legal topic at Altdorf (1676); a report (1684) in German on the Pennsylvania colony (printed in an English version in A. C. Myer's *Narratives of Early Pennsylvania*, 1912, as *Pastorius' First Account of Pennsylvania); Vier Kleine Doch Ungemeine und Sehr Nuetzliche Tractaetlein* (1690); an epistle to the Pietists of Germany (1697); *Henry Bernard Koster, William Davis,*

Thomas Rutter, and Thomas Bowyer: Four Boasting Disputers of This World Briefly Rebuked (a publication in the lively theological dispute with GEORGE KEITH, 1697); *A New Primmer or Methodical Directions to Attain the True Spelling, Reading, and Writing of English* (1698[?]); *Umstaendige Geographische Beschreibung der zu Allerletzt Erfundenen Provintz Pensylvaniae* (1700; in an English version in Myer's *Narratives of Early Pennsylvania*). The last is regarded as Pastorius' most important production. Jarvis Morse remarks that it gives a methodical account of Pennsylvania and in addition "no reader can fail to be charmed by the author's unobtrusive learning, his sincerity, and his humanity."

A biography of Pastorius was written by Marion Dexter Learned (1908). A full account of him appears in S. W. Pennypacker's *The Settlement of Germantown* (1899). A list of his writings was given in Oswald Seidensticker's *First Century of German Printing in America, 1728–1830, Preceded by a Notice of the Literary Works of F. D. Pastorius* (1893).

Patchen, Kenneth (b. Niles, Ohio, Dec. 13, 1911—   ), poet, novelist, painter. Patchen is noted especially for his poems, most of which are short observations or narratives, written in free forms and in strikingly original language. He is perhaps the one genuine American surrealist. Some of his work gives the impression of having been written unconsciously; it is a merging of humor and fantasy, sometimes veering toward satire, sometimes merely sentimental. He has often illustrated his poems with his own abstract paintings, and some of his verse has appeared in portfolios of hand-printed illustrated sheets. He has published many books, which found a wider audience than most of his fellow *avant-garde* poets. Among his books: *Before the Brave* (1936); *Dark Kingdom* (1942); *Sleepers Awake* (1946); *Panels for the Walls of Heaven* (1947); *Selected Poems* (1947); *Red Wine and Yellow Hair* (1949); also many prose works, including *The Journal of Albion Moonlight* (1941); *Memoirs of a Shy Pornographer* (1945); *See You in the Morning* (1948); *Because It Is* (1960). *The City Wears a Slouch Hat* (1942) is a radio play.

Paterson: Books I–V (1946, 1948, 1950, 1951, 1958), a poem by WILLIAM CARLOS WILLIAMS. This is a large poem in every respect. Williams surveys contemporary civilization in an excursive assemblage of lyrics, narrative episodes, prose interludes, notes, etc. The poem is the culmination of Williams' effort to make, not something that means, but something that is. In his "Author's Note" Williams explains that "*Paterson* is a long poem in four parts—that a man in himself is a city, beginning, seeking, achieving, and concluding his life in ways which the various aspects of a city may embody—if imaginatively conceived—any city, all the details of which may be made to voice his intimate convictions. Part One introduces the elemental character of the place. The Second Part comprises the modern replicas. Three will seek a language to make them vocal, and Four, the river below the falls, will be reminiscent of episodes—all that any one man may achieve in a lifetime." Book V, which appeared some years after the first four, is a kind of coda to the rest, carrying the development forward into new complexities. In Williams' case the city is, of course, Paterson, N.J., where he worked most of his life as a physician. The poem is shaped by the overriding metaphor: the human mind (male and female) as a city beside a river (time), constantly eroded and rebuilt, the only sound being the "language" of the waterfall (contemporary events). Into this structure Williams has morticed large chunks of history, some rough hewn from the chronicles of Paterson itself, others imaginatively reconstructed, still others drawn from different lands and cultures. Alongside are personal reminiscences, letters, love poems, stories, all pointing toward the primacy of objective experience. The whole makes a remarkable testimonial by a poet who has been called "America's greatest living primitive," a mystique of the natural world which endows the historical moment with utmost meaning. It may be that *Paterson* will eventually be seen to be the 20th-century counterpart of Whitman's *Leaves of Grass*.

Pathfinder, The, or, The Inland Sea (1840), a novel by JAMES FENIMORE COOPER. It was next to the last in order of publication of the five books making up the LEATHER-STOCKING TALES, the third in order of narrative sequence. The "Pathfinder" is, of course, NATTY BUMPPO, otherwise "Leatherstocking" and the "Deerslayer." The background is the Lake Ontario country, the time is 1760, the plot is set against the background of the French and Indian Wars. There is a love affair: beautiful Mabel Dunham's father would like her to marry Natty, but he gives her up to Jasper Western when he realizes Mabel is in love with the latter. But Jasper, too, has his troubles; he is suspected of being a traitor, mainly because he can speak French. The true villain, however, is revealed in time. D. H. Lawrence called Natty as portrayed here "a saint with a gun." Balzac was ecstatic in praise of the novel; "It is beautiful, it is grand. Its interest is tremendous." He particularly praised its descriptions. Edward Wagenknecht selected the siege of the blockhouse, which involves Dew-of-June, Cooper's best Indian heroine, as the most thrilling sequence in the novel. The combination of land and sea, says Norman Holmes Pearson in his excellent introduction to a 1952 reprint, gives it "a unique concentration of Cooper's recognized talents."

Patri, Angelo (b. Italy, Nov. 26, 1877—), teacher, children's writer. Patri came to America as a child, received an A.B. from the College of the City of New York (1897) and an M.A. from Columbia University (1904); he began his long teaching career, which continued until 1944. At Columbia he had become interested in the practical application of JOHN DEWEY's educational theories. When the supervisors of the schools where he later taught objected to his use of Dewey's methods, Patri moved on until

he found a school where he could put his ideas into practice. His first move, upon becoming principal of an elementary school, was to build up relations between school and parents; the formation of the Parents' Association resulted. Dorothy Canfield Fisher said he made "one of the finest contributions to civilized life in our nation." Of his syndicated column, President Eliot of Harvard wrote many years ago: "Whatever else Patri does, he must never stop those irreplaceable talks to teachers and parents in the newspaper." His books include *Pinocchio in Africa* (1911); *White Patch* (1911); *A School Master of the Great City* (1917); *Spirit of America* (1924); *The Parents' Counsellor* (1940); *Your Child in War Time* (1943); *How to Help Your Child Grow Up* (1948); *Biondino* (1951).

Patrick, John (b. Louisville, Ky., May 17, 1905—), playwright. Patrick attended schools in Louisiana and Texas and was a student at Harvard and Columbia before he began to write for the National Broadcasting System in San Francisco. His first play, *Hell Freezes Over,* was produced on Broadway in 1935, but was unsuccessful, as was *The Willow and I* (1942). Patrick was an ambulance driver for the American Field Service during the Second World War; his wartime experiences supplied the background for his first successful play, *The Hasty Heart* (1945). Three more plays were produced and published (*The Story of Mary Surratt,* 1947; *The Curious Savage,* 1950; and *Lo and Behold!,* 1951) before Patrick came to dramatize Vern Schneider's novel, *The Teahouse of the August Moon,* in 1953. This comedy dealing with the somewhat improbable adventures of a group of American soldiers in Okinawa during the Occupation was awarded the New York Drama Critics Circle Award and the Pulitzer Prize. Patrick has also written a number of screenplays, among them *Three Coins in the Fountain* (1954); *Love is a Many Splendored Thing* (1955); *High Society* (1956); and *Les Girls* (1957).

Patriots, The (1776), a play by ROBERT MUNFORD. The play's title is ironic. Munford detached himself from the hatreds and angers of war and depicted extremists on both sides unfavorably. Kenneth B. Murdock called it "one of the best American plays dealing with the Revolution." It was probably never produced, first appeared in print in Munford's *Collection of Plays and Poems* (1798). It was reprinted in the *William and Mary Quarterly* (July, 1949), edited by Courtlandt Canby.

patroons. On June 7, 1629, the States General of the Netherlands confirmed a Charter of Freedom and Exemptions under which the Dutch West India Company was empowered to grant certain privileges to colonists. To those who transported fifty settlers, they gave estates fronting sixteen miles along navigable rivers and extending inland as far as settlement would permit. The grantees were called patroons, were given feudal rights and granted exemption from taxation for eight years. By the end of January,

1630, five patroonships had been granted along the Hudson, Connecticut, and Delaware Rivers. The privileges of the patroons remained undisturbed during English rule and after the Revolution. It was not until the 1840's that tenants made determined efforts to end all feudal privileges. Anti-Rent Associations brought on what was called the Anti-Rent War in the manor of Rensselaerswyck in the Albany region (1839–46). Finally in 1846 a more liberal constitution was adopted by New York state, by which perpetual leases were gradually replaced by fee-simple tenure. The unrest and violence were described in James Fenimore Cooper's trilogy entitled *The Littlepage Manuscripts* (1845, 1846). See ANTI-RENT LAWS.

Pattee, Fred Lewis (b. Bristol, N.H., March 22, 1863—d. May 6, 1950), literary historian, teacher. Pattee studied at Dartmouth College and in Germany, came back to teach, mainly at Pennsylvania State College. A pioneer in the study of American literature, he viewed literature as a popular expression rather than as the production of an elite. Among his histories were: *A History of American Literature* (1896); *A History of American Literature Since 1870* (1915); *Sidelights on American Literature* (1922); *The Development of the American Short Story* (1923); *The New American Literature* (1930); *The First Century of American Literature* (1935); *The Feminine Fifties* (1940). *Penn State Yankee: The Autobiography of Fred Lewis Pattee* appeared in 1953.

Patten, William Gilbert ["Burt L. Standish"] (b. Corinna, Me., Oct. 25, 1866—d. Jan. 16, 1945), author of boys' books. Patten began to write in his late teens and won immediate success; he wrote western stories under the pen name of William West Wilder. His great fame, however, came as Burt L. Standish when he began to publish under that name a series of novels about a character named FRANK MERRIWELL, a highly virtuous, manly Yale student. All together Patten's books have sold more than 100 million copies; the Merriwell series alone numbered more than two hundred titles. Patten was often praised for the benign influence his high-minded heroes were supposed to have exerted on young readers.

Pattie, James Ohio (b. Bracken Co., Ky., 1804—d. 1850[?]), explorer, memoirist. In the 1820's Pattie undertook several expeditions to Lower California, New Mexico, and Mexico. He wrote an account of his exciting adventures in a book that was edited and probably largely written by Timothy Flint: *The Personal Narrative of James O. Pattie, of Kentucky, During an Expedition from St. Louis, through the Vast Regions Between That Place and the Pacific Ocean* (1831). Upon the book one B. Bilson, otherwise unknown, based an abridged account of adventures supposedly his own, *The Hunters of Kentucky, or, The Trials and Toils of Trappers and Traders* (1847). The *Narrative* was included in Reuben G. Thwaites' *Early Western Travels* (1905) and was edited by Milo M. Quaife

(1930). Little is known of Pattie's later life, except that he was one of the Forty-Niners.

Patton, Frances Gray (b. Raleigh, N.C., March 19, 1906—   ), short-story writer, playwright, poet. Mrs. Patton has been called "a Jane Austen of North Carolina." She is thoroughly acquainted with the Carolinian scene and writes about it with quiet irony and gracious wit. She wrote plays in her earlier days, published a few poems, but is known mainly for her short stories, some of which are collected in *The Finer Things of Life* (1951) and *A Piece of Luck* (1955). *Good Morning, Miss Dove* (1954) is a novel about a small-town schoolmarm.

Patton, George S[mith], Jr. (b. San Gabriel, Cal., Nov. 11, 1885—d. Dec. 21, 1945), soldier, diarist. Patton served in the African and European theaters during World War II, became a full general, renowned for his reckless daring and military skill. After his death in an automobile accident extracts from his diary were published as *War As I Knew It* (1947). According to Douglas S. Freeman, who wrote the introduction, Patton's diary was as fiery as he was, and to save the feelings of persons still living large parts of it had been deleted.

Paul, Elliot [Harold] (b. Malden, Mass., Feb. 13, 1891—d. April 7, 1958), journalist, editor, writer. Paul spent less than a year at the University of Maine, abandoning college to join his brother on an irrigation project in Idaho and Wyoming. After serving in World War I he remained in France to write for the Associated Press and the Paris editions of the Chicago *Tribune* and the New York *Herald Tribune*. His novels *Indelible* (1922), *Impromptu* (1923), and *Imperturbe* (1924) were hailed by a small circle of admirers. In 1927, with EUGENE JOLAS, he founded and edited the famous avant-garde periodical *transition*. *The Life and Death of a Spanish Town* (1937) tells the story of the beautiful village of Santa Eulalia, Ibiza, in the Balearic Islands, where Paul lived from 1931 until it was destroyed by Franco armies during the Spanish Civil War; it is undoubtedly his best book. Other works of this time were *Lava Rock* (1928); *Low Run Tide* (1928); *The Amazon* (1929); *Concert Pitch* (1938); *Stars and Stripes Forever* (1939); *All the Brave* (1939), written with L. Quintanilla. His most popular book was the nostalgic memoir THE LAST TIME I SAW PARIS (1942). The great success of *The Mysterious Mickey Finn* (1939), a burlesque detective extravaganza, may have led him to abandon his more solid talents and concentrate on detective fiction. *Hugger-Mugger in the Louvre* (1940), *Mayhem in B-Flat* (1940), *Fracas in the Foothills* (1941), *The Black Gardenia* (1952), and other crime novels brought Paul thousands of readers who had never heard of *transition* or the expatriate colonies in the Balearics. Paul also wrote for the films; his best-known scenario was *A Woman's Face* (1941). Paul also wrote autobiographical books, not quite so appealing, of his life in the United States: *Linden on the Saugus Branch* (1947);

Ghost Town on the Yellowstone (1948); *My Old Kentucky Home* (1949); *Desperate Scenery* (1954).

Paul, John. Pen name of CHARLES HENRY WEBB.

Paul, Louis (b. Brooklyn, N.Y., Dec. 4, 1901—), novelist, short-story writer, poet. Paul enlisted in the army during World War I, thereafter wandered all over the United States for three years, engaging in such varied occupations as road building and working as a hospital orderly, a movie extra, a motorman, an elevator operator, a typist, a miner, a ditchdigger, a sailor. His short story called *No More Trouble for Jedwick* brought him his first fame when it was accepted by *Esquire* and awarded first prize in the O. Henry Memorial Awards for 1934. His novels include *The Pumpkin Coach* (1935); *A Horse in Arizona* (1936); *The Wrong World* (1938); *A Passion for Privacy* (1940); *This Is My Brother* (1943); *Breakdown* (1946); *A Husband for Mama* (1950); *The Man Who Came Home* (1953); *Dara the Cypriot* (1959). *Breakdown,* the story of an alcoholic, was dramatized (1948) as *The Cup of Trembling.*

Paul, Maury [Henry Biddle] (b. Philadelphia, April 14, 1890—d. July 17, 1942), newspaperman, society editor. Paul worked first on a Philadelphia paper, then on several New York papers, finally joined the staff of the Hearst papers in 1919 as society editor. He was at one time writing five different columns under the names of Cholly Knickerbocker, Dolly Madison, Polly Stuyvesant, and Billy Benedict; one column was unsigned. He often wrote articles on socialites and social doings for *Cosmopolitan.* At the time of his death an obituary notice described him as "the plump, exquisite little man who rose to his place of power as a society arbiter through a combination of audacity, insolence, and charm." He supposedly invented the terms "café society" and "glamor girl." His language was all his own; he was a master of the trite circumlocution. Eve Brown, his successor as Cholly Knickerbocker, wrote an ironic biography of him, *Champagne Cholly: The Life and Times of Maury Paul* (1947).

Paulding, Hiram (b. Westchester Co., N.Y., Dec. 11, 1797—d. Oct. 20, 1878), naval officer, memoirist. Paulding had a distinguished naval career as acting lieutenant of the *Ticonderoga* in the Battle of Lake Champlain (1813), in service against the Barbary pirates (1815), in a campaign against Walker's filibusterers in Nicaragua (1857), as commandant of the New York navy yard (1861–65). He described two of his exploits in books: *Journal of a Cruise of the U.S. Schooner Dolphin* (1831), an account of his pursuit of mutineers in the South Seas, and *Bolivar in His Camp* (1834), which tells how Paulding carried dispatches to Simón Bolívar in a 1,500-mile horseback trip across the Andes.

Paulding, James Kirke ["Launcelot Langstaff"] (b. Putnam Co., N.Y., Aug. 22, 1778—d. April 6, 1860), novelist, dramatist, historian. Paulding's almost ideal boyhood was spent in

fishing, hunting, and reading omnivorously. At eighteen he worked in a public office with his brother, and there he met WASHINGTON IRVING and his brother William. A lively friendship sprang up among the young men, who formed the nucleus of a group called "The Nine Worthies of Cockloft Hall." From 1807 to 1808 Paulding and Irving published a humorous periodical, SALMAGUNDI; OR, THE WHIM-WHAMS AND OPINIONS OF LAUNCELOT LANGSTAFF, ESQ., AND OTHERS, which contained essays styled after the *Spectator.* Years later Paulding wrote a second series, *Tellers from the South, A Sketch of Old England, Salmagundi; Second Series* (1819–20). THE DIVERTING HISTORY OF JOHN BULL AND BROTHER JONATHAN (1812) was a thinly disguised allegory attacking the pugnacious old despot John Bull. Paulding later wrote a sequel to this, called THE HISTORY OF UNCLE SAM AND HIS BOYS (1835). THE LAY OF THE SCOTTISH FIDDLE (1813), a burlesque poem, ridiculed the romanticism of Scott. THE BACKWOODSMAN (1818) celebrated, in rather dull verse, the adventures of a New York pioneer in Ohio. A number of histories, some serious, some more in the spirit of the *Diverting History,* appeared between 1815 and 1825: *The United States and England* (1815); *Letters from the South* (2 v., 1817); *A Sketch of Old England, by a New England Man* (2 v., 1822); and JOHN BULL IN AMERICA; OR, THE NEW MUNCHAUSEN (1825).

KONINGSMARKE, THE LONG FINNE: A STORY OF THE NEW WORLD (1823) was his first important work of fiction, a historical romance dealing with the Swedes in Delaware in the 17th century and satirizing the popular English romances of Scott. THE LION OF THE WEST (1831), a drama of a rough American frontiersman, won a prize, was a great stage success, and laid the foundation for Paulding's popularity. THE DUTCHMAN'S FIRESIDE (1831), based, like

Cooper's *Satanstoe* (1845), on Mrs. Grant's *Memoirs of an American Lady* (1808), is believed by some critics to be Paulding's best novel. He also wrote WESTWARD HO! (1832); *A Life of Washington* (1835); *Slavery in the United States* (1836); *The Old Continental; or, The Price of Liberty* (1846); and THE PURITAN AND HIS DAUGHTER (1849). *The Bucktails: or, Americans in England* (1847), a satiric drama, portrays a shrewd Yankee type.

Paulding was a member of the Board of Navy Commissioners (1815–23) and Secretary of the Navy under Van Buren (1838–41). His novels, all but forgotten today, merit a better fate because of his impatience with false romanticism and his skillful use of the American scene. Paulding's son William Irving Paulding did a *Literary Life* of his father (1867). A. L. Herold wrote *James Kirke Paulding: Versatile American* (1926).

Paul Revere, The Midnight Ride of. See MIDNIGHT RIDE OF PAUL REVERE, THE.

Paumanok. This Indian name for Long Island became famous through WALT WHITMAN'S use of it. He employed the name in the titles of two of his poems, *A Paumanok Picture* (1881) and *Paumanok* (1888). It also appears in *Out of the Cradle Endlessly Rocking* (1859, 1881) and in *Specimen Days* (1882).

Pavilion of Women (1946), a novel by PEARL BUCK. The scene is China, but the theme—the extent to which women should confine themselves to domesticity—is not limited to that country. Mrs. Buck paints the Chinese background vividly, while preaching an effective sermon of human brotherhood and love.

Pawnee Indians. A tribe of Plains Indians who belonged to the group speaking the Caddoan language. Originally they lived in the Lower Mississippi Valley. The Pawnee enter history when one of their number served as a guide for CORONADO (1541). Great lovers of horses, they made frequent raids on Spanish territory in New Mexico up to the beginning of the 19th century. French traders managed to become friendly with them; present-day Pawnee are likely to have an admixture of French as well as English blood. Their power declined as a result of cholera and other diseases. After the cession of the Louisiana Territory to the United States (1803) the Pawnee became firm friends of the United States. They gave up all their lands except a tract in Nebraska, then removed to a reservation in Oklahoma.

The Pawnee appear in Washington Irving's *Tour of the Prairies* (1835). Even earlier the Pawnee, along with the Sioux, had supplanted the Delaware and the Hurons in the third of James Fenimore Cooper's *Leather-Stocking Series* to appear, THE PRAIRIE (1827). Cooper carefully studied the region in which the story is laid and talked to representatives of the tribes he portrayed. He gained a very favorable impression of the wisdom and moderation of these Indians. He spent more time writing *The Prairie* than any of his other novels because he was

fascinated by the natural setting and the Indian data he had accumulated; Edward Wagenknecht calls it "the most exalted of Cooper's books."

The poetry and music of the Pawnee have been explored since the close of the 19th century. A thorough survey was made by Alice C. Fletcher in *The Hako: A Pawnee Ceremonial* (1904). FRANCES DENSMORE, the best known collector of Indian poetry and music, wrote a book on *Pawnee Music* (1929). George E. Hyde, in his *Pawnee Indians* (1951), emphasizes their highly developed political and religious organization. Other books include James R. Murie's *Pawnee Indian Societies* (1914); G. B. Grinnell's *Pawnee Hero Stories and Folk Tales* (1889); W. R. Wedel's *Introduction to Pawnee Archaeology* (1936).

Paxson, Frederic Logan (b. Philadelphia, Feb. 23, 1877—d. Oct. 24, 1948), historian, teacher. After teaching in high schools Paxson was called to university work at Colorado, Michigan, and Wisconsin. He became an authority on the American frontier, about which he wrote in *The Last American Frontier* (1910) and THE HISTORY OF THE AMERICAN FRONTIER (1924), which won a Pulitzer award. He also wrote *The Independence of the South American Republics* (1903); *The Civil War* (1911); *The U.S. in Recent Times* (1926).

Paxton, Philip. See SAMUEL ADAMS HAMMETT.

Payne, John Howard (b. New York City, or possibly East Hampton, L.I., June 9, 1791—d. April 9, 1852), actor, playwright, poet. Working as a clerk to help his father support nine children, Payne at fourteen found time to edit

a weekly paper of dramatic news, the *Thespian Mirror* (1805–06); at fifteen he was the author of a drama, *Julia, or, The Wanderer* (1806). Some of his father's friends raised money to send him to Union College, but in less than a year he was back in New York in the theater. In 1809 he created a sensation as Young Norval in John Home's popular tragedy, *Douglas*. He went to England in 1813, where he continued to act and to write plays, and was always on the verge of bankruptcy. An adaptation of a play called BRUTUS, OR, THE FALL OF TARQUIN (1818) brought him some fame but little money. In debtors' prison he wrote *Therese, Orphan of Geneva* (1821), making enough money to gain his freedom. Then came his greatest triumph, *Clari, The Maid of Milan* (1823). This contained a song called HOME, SWEET HOME, with music by Sir Henry Bishop. It became immensely popular, but Payne had sold the play outright and collected no royalties. He wrote and adapted other plays but remained poor. While in England he met Mary Shelley, widow of the poet Percy Bysshe Shelley, and courted her fervently but in vain. He returned to America penniless. Theatrical benefit performances were arranged for him and brought in almost $10,000. Daniel Webster and other friends obtained for him the post of consul in Tunis, which he held on and off until his death.

Eleven plays of his were rescued from manuscripts and published in *America's Lost Plays* (v. 5 and 6, 1940), edited by Codman Hislop and W. R. Richardson. *Charles II* was included by A. H. Quinn in *Representative American Plays* (1917). This was a version of a French play, done with Payne's friend WASHINGTON IRVING. Quinn calls it his best comedy, and regards Payne as a playwright of great skill.

Biographies were written by Gabriel Harrison (1884), W. T. Hanson (1913), Rosa P. Chiles (1930), and Grace Overmyer (1957). Maude Barragan wrote a biographical novel, *John Howard Payne, Skywalker* (1953). See KNICKERBOCKER SCHOOL.

Payne, Leonidas Warren (b. Auburn, Ala., July 12, 1873—d. June 16, 1945), teacher, linguist, literary historian. After teaching on the staffs of several southern schools and acting as associate editor of a revision of Worcester's *Dictionary* (1906–08), Payne joined the faculty of the University of Texas. He was a co-founder and the first president of the Texas Folklore Society and wrote *A Survey of Texas Literature* (1928) and *Texas Poems* (with others, 1936). He edited numerous anthologies for use in secondary schools.

Peabody, Elizabeth Palmer (b. Billerica, Mass., May 16, 1804—d. Jan. 3, 1894), educator. Elizabeth Peabody's remarkable teaching career began when, still in her teens, she taught at her mother's private school in Billerica. Later she and her sister Mary opened a school in Boston. She also served as a devoted secretary for WILLIAM ELLERY CHANNING [1] during these years. In 1834 she became assistant to BRONSON ALCOTT in his famous Temple School. Difficult as Alcott was, she remained with him for two loyal years, carrying his burdens, fighting his battles, and working selflessly for the ideals of the school, overlooking the fact that Alcott fre-

quently forgot to pay her salary. *A Record of a School* (1835) gives an account of her work with Alcott.

Her early thirst for learning brought her into contact with some of the great thinkers of the day; at the age of eighteen she was tutored in Greek by RALPH WALDO EMERSON. It was through Elizabeth that NATHANIEL HAWTHORNE met her sister Sophia, his future wife. The bookstore that Elizabeth opened in Boston in 1839 became the meeting place for writers, philosophers, Harvard professors, liberal clergymen, and Transcendentalists. Here plans for BROOK FARM were laid, and THE DIAL, the organ of the Brook Farm community, was published in the rear of the store (1842–43). Miss Peabody contributed articles to the magazine that were reprinted, with some of her memoirs, as *A Last Evening with Allston* (1886). In 1844, after a fire destroyed her bookstore, she returned to teaching. At about this time she met HORACE MANN (1796–1859), with whom she entered into a platonic friendship. If she was surprised when Mann married her sister Mary, she was too generous to feel any resentment; throughout her life she remained on excellent terms with the Manns. She was a fervid Abolitionist; her antislavery feelings bound her closer to the Manns but strained her relations with the Hawthornes, who refused to enter into the controversy.

The first kindergarten in the United States was opened by Miss Peabody in 1860; it was founded upon the educational ideas of Friedrich Froebel. She studied Froebel's methods abroad, lectured and wrote books and articles on the new kindergarten methods. From 1873 until 1875 she published a magazine called *Kindergarten Messenger*, from 1879 until 1884 she lectured at Alcott's School of Philosophy in Concord. By this time she had established herself as a "character," a wonderfully energetic, keen, headstrong old lady. She was more remarkable as a teacher and a personality than as a writer. Her works include *Chronological History of the United States* (1856); *Reminiscences of William Ellery Channing* (1880); *Lectures in the Training Schools for Kindergartens* (1888).

Miss Birdseye in Henry James' *The Bostonians* (1886) may be a portrait of her, though James denied that any resemblance was intended. A delightfully humorous and sympathetic study is *The Peabody Sisters of Salem* (1950), by Louise Hall Tharp who also wrote *Until Victory: Horace Mann and Mary Peabody* (1953).

Peabody, Josephine Preston (b. Brooklyn, N.Y., May 30, 1874—d. Dec. 4, 1922), poet, playwright. From the age of thirteen Josephine Peabody wrote poems, many published in leading magazines. Her first book, *Old Greek Folk Stories* (1897), was followed by several volumes of verse: *The Wayfarers* (1898); *The Singing Leaves* (1903); *Pan: A Choric Idyll* (1904); *The Book of the Little Past* (1908); *The Singing Man* (1911); and *Harvest Moon* (1916). At Radcliffe College she came under the influence of WILLIAM VAUGHN MOODY, turned to writing poetic dramas: a one-act play,

Fortune and Men's Eyes (1900); the much more ambitious and successful *Marlowe* (1901); *Wings* (1905), a one-act play laid in medieval Northumbria; THE PIPER (1910), the author's best known work today; *The Wolf of Gubbio* (1913), about St. Francis; *The Chameleon* (1917), a comedy of modern life; and *Portrait of Mrs. W.* (1922), a prose play about the love affair of Mary Wollstonecraft and William Godwin. In 1925 her *Diary and Letters* appeared, followed in 1927 by *Collected Poems* and *Collected Plays*.

Peale, Norman Vincent (b. Bowersville, Ohio, May 31, 1898—   ), clergyman, writer, editor. After holding several charges in various cities, Peale became minister of the Marble Collegiate Reformed Church, New York City, in 1932. An effective preacher and writer, he called on the findings of psychiatry to help him inspire the troubled. He defined Christianity as "the science of successful living." Among his many widely read books *A Guide to Confident Living* (1948) and *The Power of Positive Thinking* (1952) are perhaps the best known. Arthur Gordon has written *Norman Vincent Peale, Minister to Millions* (1958).

Pearl. The child born of the adultery of Arthur Dimmesdale and Hester Prynne in Hawthorne's SCARLET LETTER (1850). She was drawn from Hawthorne's daughter Una.

Pearl, The (1947), a novelette by JOHN STEINBECK. Kino, an Indian pearl-fisher in the Gulf of California, and his wife Juana have a baby named Coyotito. The child is stung by a scorpion, and the parents appeal in vain to a mercenary physician to treat the baby. Kino, in despair, goes out to look for a pearl that will pay the doctor—and finds one, the Pearl of the World, as big as a seagull's egg. But the pearl brings only tragedy. All the violent and ruthless people of the region plot to steal the pearl, and much conflict ensues. The story is based on a folk tale that Steinbeck heard when he made a trip to the region in which his narrative is set.

Pearl of Orr's Island, The (1862), a novel by HARRIET BEECHER STOWE. Whittier called it "the most charming New England idyll ever written." Mara Lincoln, the "pearl of great price," is brought up in the Maine fishing village of Orr's Island by her grandparents, who also adopt Moses, a Spanish boy. Mara comes to love Moses, but after many complications she dies and he marries her friend Sally. It is generally held that the local-color movement in New England began with this novel.

Pearson, [Andrew] Drew [Russell] (b. Evanston, Ill., Dec. 13, 1897—d. Sept. 1, 1969), columnist, broadcaster, author. Pearson has probably engaged in more controversies than any other Washington correspondent; most notable was his feud with the columnist WESTBROOK PEGLER. Pearson's political reports, often featuring sensational revelations, are published in a column called "Washington Merry-Go-Round" that appears in many hundreds of newspapers. In his column he collaborated for a while with ROBERT S. ALLEN,

and some of their material went into three books: *Washington Merry-Go-Round* (1931); *More Washington Merry-Go-Round* (1932); *The Nine Old Men* (1936). He also wrote *U.S.A.: Second-Class Power* (with Jack Anderson, 1958). *Time* described Pearson's style as a "brand of ruthless, theatrical crusading, high-voltage, hypodermic journalism that has made him the most intensely feared and hated man in Washington." The article noted, however, that Pearson, unlike other columnists, never stooped to name-calling. He conceived the idea of a Friendship Train which collected food for Europe in huge quantities in 1947.

Pearson, Edmund Lester (b. Newburyport, Mass., Feb. 11, 1880—d. Aug. 8, 1937), librarian, editor, bibliophile, writer on crime. From 1914 to 1927 Pearson edited the valuable *Bulletin of the New York Public Library*. In an agreeable style he wrote books on many topics of a literary nature: *The Librarian at Play* (1911); *Books in Black or Red* (1923); *Queer Books* (1928); *Dime Novels* (1929). He also wrote on crime: *Studies in Murder* (1926); *More Studies in Murder* (1936); *The Trial of Lizzie Borden* (1937). He wrote biographies of Theodore Roosevelt (1920) and Henry Tufts (1930), and *The Voyage of the Hoppergrass* (1913), a story for boys.

Pearson's Magazine. A monthly equivalent of the London magazine of the same name; it was started in 1899 and ceased publication in 1925. For a time it reprinted some of the contents of the British magazine. Its chief fame comes from the fact that the brilliant and erratic Frank Harris bought it in 1916. He edited it until September 1922, but brought himself into disfavor because of his attacks on "big business" and the conduct of World War I. At the close of the war, Harris accurately prophesied World War II, but no one paid any attention to him. After he left the magazine it changed its policies, but survived for only three years.

Peary, Robert Edwin (b. Cresson, Pa., May 6, 1856—d. Feb. 20, 1920), explorer. Peary entered the United States Navy as a civil engineer. He began his Arctic explorations in 1886; on April 6, 1909, he reached the North Pole. Dr. Frederick Cook claimed that he had reached the pole a year earlier; in 1911 Congress recognized Peary's claims and made him a rear admiral, but the controversy has never been entirely stilled. Peary wrote *Northward over the "Great Ice"* (2 v., 1898); *Nearest the Pole* (1907); *The North Pole* (1910); *Secrets of Polar Travel* (1917). His biography was written by Fitzhugh Green (1926) and by W. H. Hobbs (1936). As late as 1951 F. J. Pohl edited Cook's *Return from the Pole* in the conviction that Cook's claim was justified. Peary's wife, **Josephine Diebitsch Peary** (1863–1895), accompanied him on early expeditions, wrote *My Arctic Journal* (1893); *The Snow Baby* (1901), an account of her daughter who was born farther north than any other white child; and *Children of the Arctic* (1903). His daughter, **Marie Ahnighito Peary** (1893–   ), wrote *The*

Snowbaby's Own Story (1934) and other children's books.

Pease, Howard (b. Stockton, Calif., Sept. 6, 1894—   ), short-story writer. Pease devoted himself to writing adventure tales for young people, particularly boys, although older readers enjoyed them too. The best known is perhaps his first book, *The Tattooed Man* (1926), although *The Jinx Ship* (1928) closely rivaled it. A good many of Pease's books are sea stories, and a favorite character in a number of them is Tod Moran, who is both brave and ingenious. Pease wrote his books with care, was realistic in his emphasis on contemporary problems, featured able character drawing and rapidly moving plots. Other books of his include: *Shanghai Passage* (1929); *Secret Cargo* (1931); *Wind in the Rigging* (1935); *Hurricane Weather* (1936); *Captain Binnacle* (1938); *Heart of Danger* (1946); *Bound for Singapore* (1948); *The Dark Adventure* (1950); *Mystery on Telegraph Hill* (1961).

Pease, Lute [Lucius Curtis] (b. Winnemucca, Nev., March 27, 1869—   ), cartoonist, painter, reporter, editor. Pease began as a rancher in California, prospected for gold in Alaska, served as correspondent for the Seattle *Post-Intelligencer,* and was made a district United States commissioner. He went back to the States to become a cartoonist and reporter for the Portland *Oregonian.* He then served as editor-in-chief for the *Pacific Monthly.* When Jack London's *Martin Eden* was rejected by several eastern magazines, Pease ran it serially in the *Pacific* and illustrated the installments. In 1914 he became political cartoonist for the Newark (N.J.) *Evening News,* and in 1949 won a Pulitzer award for the best cartoon of the year. In the 1930's Pease began to win distinction as a painter in oils.

Peattie, Donald Culross (b. Chicago, June 21, 1898—d. Nov. 16, 1964), naturalist. Peattie was a botanist for the Department of Agriculture from 1922 until 1926 when, with the publication of his first book—*Cargoes and Harvests,* a study of economic botany—he resigned in order to devote himself to writing. From 1926 until 1936 he conducted a nature column in the Washington *Star.* Although he published four novels—*Up Country* (1928, with his wife Louise Redfield), *Port of Call* (1932), *Sons of the Martians* (1932), and *The Bright Lexicon* (1934)—as well as a number of children's books, he is best known for his nature writings, which combine science, poetic prose, and popular philosophy. *An Almanac for Moderns* (1935) was highly praised by the critics. In *Singing in the Wilderness: A Salute to John James Audubon* (1935) the lyric prose verges on sentimentality. *Immortal Village* (1945) is a charmingly written history of the town of Vence in southern France. With his son Noel, Peattie wrote *A Cup of Sky* (1950). Among his other books: *Green Laurels: The Lives and Achievements of the Great Naturalists* (1936); *A Book of Hours* (1937); *Flowering Earth* (1939); *The Road of a Naturalist* (1941), an autobiography; *Forward the Nation*

(1942); *American Heartwood* (1949); *Sportsman's Country* (1952); *A Natural History of Western Trees* (1953); *Lives of Destiny* (1954); *Parade with Banners* (1957). He is a roving reporter for the *Reader's Digest.*

Peck, Annie Smith (b. Providence, R.I., Oct. 19, 1850—d. July 18, 1935), explorer, archaeologist, memoirist. A famed mountain climber, who made ascents of the Matterhorn (1895), Popocatepetl and Orizaba (1897), and Huascarán in Peru (the first ascent ever made, 1908), Annie Smith Peck gathered much scientific data in the course of her remarkable climbing feats. She recorded her experiences and observations in *A Search for the Apex of America* (1911); *The South American Tour* (1914); *Flying over South America* (1932).

Peck, George (b. Otsego Co., N.Y., Aug. 8, 1797—d. May 20, 1876), Methodist clergyman, editor, historian, memoirist. This able clergyman published many books in his lifetime, most of which explain and expound the Methodist views of Christianity. While serving in various pulpits, he edited the *Methodist Quarterly Review* (1840–47) and the *Christian Advocate* (1847–52) and wrote *Wyoming [Valley]: Its History* (1858). Late in life he published an autobiographical volume: *The Life and Times of the Rev. George Peck, D.D.* (1874). His daughter Mary Holon inherited his literary gifts and wrote vigorously for newspapers and church magazines; she married another Methodist clergyman, Jonathan Townley Crane, and became the mother of fourteen children, the youngest of whom was STEPHEN CRANE.

Peck, George Wilbur (b. Henderson, N.Y., Sept. 28, 1840—d. April 16, 1916), newspaperman, public official, humorist. Peck made his reputation in LaCrosse, Wis., as a humorous writer; he collected some of his sketches in *Adventures of One Terence McGrant* (1871). He founded a newspaper of his own called *The Sun* in 1874; four years later he moved the paper to Milwaukee. There his views as an editor proved so popular that he was elected mayor of the city and then governor of the state (1890–94). Meanwhile he had continued to publish in his paper, and then in book form, many humorous sketches. The most popular of them dealt with two characters he called *Peck's Bad Boy and His Pa* (1883). Peck, whose books sold in the hundreds of thousands, continued to write and produced *Peck's Bad Boy and His Pa, No. 2* (1883); *Peck's Boss Book* (1884); *Peck's Irish Friend, Phelan Geohagan* (1887); *Peck's Uncle Ike and the Red-Headed Boy* (1899); *Peck's Bad Boy with the Cowboys* (1907). *How Private George W. Peck Put Down the Rebellion* (1887) gave humorous memories of the Civil War. *Mirth for the Million* (1883) was later reprinted as *Peck's Fun* (1887). In his *Diary* for 1885 Thomas A. Edison spoke of *Peck's Bad Boy* as "a sponge-cake kind of literature." *Peck's Bad Boy* is no longer read, but the title remains as a popular by-word.

Peck, Harry Thurston (b. Stamford, Conn., Nov. 24, 1856—d. March 23, 1914), teacher, classical scholar, editor, writer. Peck taught Latin at Columbia University, where he was a highly regarded scholar, from 1882 to 1910. He did not limit himself, however, to scholarship alone, but in some of his writing sought a popular audience; and in his personal life he was more the man of the world than a staid academician. Writing of him in *The Mauve Decade* (1926), Thomas Beer noted that he "wrote Tennysonian verses and a book for children, tabulated the Semitic legends of creation, edited Latin grammars, and reviewed novels for newspapers," and that he did much to introduce French literary notions to the American public. He edited THE BOOKMAN (see BEST SELLERS) from 1895 until 1902 and made it the liveliest literary journal of the period. Peck's life ended in scandal when his conduct with a young lady became the subject of a court action; he committed suicide shortly afterward.

Peck was the author of many books. Some of his titles are *The Personal Equation* (1897); *What Is Good English?* (1899); *Greystone and Porphyry* (poems, 1899); *William Hickling Prescott* (1905); *Twenty Years of the Republic* (1906); *Studies in Several Literatures* (1909); *Hilda and the Wishes* (1907); and in addition he edited *Harper's Dictionary of Classical Literature and Antiquities* (1897); the *Acta Columbiana* (1892–1903); the NEW INTERNATIONAL ENCYCLOPEDIA (1892, 1900–03), and *A History of Classical Philology* (1911).

Peck, Samuel Minturn (b. Tuscaloosa, Ala., Nov. 4, 1854—d. May 3, 1938), poet, writer of sketches. Peck wrote sugary verses, mainly about the South. Among his collections: *Cap and Bells* (1886); *Rings and Love Knots* (1892); *Rhymes and Roses* (1895); *Fair Women of Today* (1896); *The Autumn Trail* (1925). He also gathered his prose sketches in *Alabama Sketches* (1902) and *Swamp Tales* (1912).

Peckham, Richard. A pseudonym of RAYMOND HOLDEN.

Peck's Bad Boy. See GEORGE WILBUR PECK.

Pecos Bill. This folk hero of the Southwest is the cowboy's equivalent of the logger's PAUL BUNYAN. He cleared Texas of badmen, taught the broncos to buck, invented tarantulas and scorpions as a joke on his friends, dug the Rio Grande river, and invented roping. His horse, Widow-Maker, was raised on a special diet of nitroglycerin and barbed wire and killed everyone who rode him except Bill. Pecos Bill's exploits are told in *Tall Tales from Texas* (1934), by Mody C. Boatright, and in shorter pieces by Edward O'Reilly and J. Frank Dobie. Carl Sandburg in *The People, Yes* (1936) calls him Pecos Pete.

Peder Victorious (1923; translated from the Norwegian, 1929), the second in a trilogy of novels by OLE RÖLVAAG, the first being GIANTS IN THE EARTH and the third THEIR FATHER'S GOD. The scene is the Dakotas. The story involves the experiences of a family of Norwegian immigrants, their difficulties, their church affairs, their social diversions, etc. The hero is Peder Victorious Holm, who is urged by his mother

and the local minister to enter the clergy; instead, as a result of a love affair, he chooses to become a farmer.

Peet, Stephen Denison (b. Euclid, Ohio, Dec. 2, 1831—d. May 24, 1914), clergyman, archaeologist. Peet made a second vocation of archaeology, directed his interest chiefly toward the mound-builders and the ancient remains of the cliff and pueblo dwellers. He produced a noteworthy work in five volumes entitled *Prehistoric America* (1890–1905). He was the founder of the *American Antiquarian and Oriental Journal* (1878) and a co-founder of the Ohio Archaeological Society (1875).

Pegler, James Westbrook (b. Minneapolis, Minn., Aug. 2, 1894—d. June 24, 1969), journalist. Pegler began as a reporter and sportswriter, and at one point was sent to Washington by the Chicago *Tribune* to cover political activities there from a sportsman's point of view. He wrote some irreverent dispatches in which the government leaders were treated as if they were prize-fight managers, and these attracted the attention of Roy Howard, who in 1933 hired Pegler and began to run his column, called "Fair Enough," in all the Scripps-Howard newspapers. At the end of six months the local editors unanimously requested Pegler's withdrawal, but after a year a taste for Pegler had apparently been created in the public mind, and his column became a popular feature.

Pegler's political views are conservative in the extreme. Although he has in his own way frequently combatted corruption and tyranny—he was awarded a Pulitzer prize in 1941 for his exposure of corrupt practices in the labor movement—he is noted particularly for his fervent objection to liberal movements and to any expansion of Federal authority. He was a foe of Franklin D. Roosevelt, and frequently attacked the President and his family. Pegler's prose is vigorous and frequently vituperative; he does not refrain from personal contumely in his pursuit of his enemies. One victim, QUENTIN REYNOLDS, struck back and sued for libel; he was awarded a very large amount in damages. Other fellow columnists have deplored Pegler's journalistic deportment. DREW PEARSON and WALTER WINCHELL, both special targets of Pegler's sarcasm, long feuded with him in their columns.

Peg o' My Heart (1912), a very successful comedy by J. HARTLEY MANNERS. It was written as a vehicle for his wife Laurette Taylor, and it became a hit in both New York and London. It is included in Bennett Cerf and Van H. Cartmell's anthology *S.R.O.: The Most Successful Plays in the History of the American Stage* (1944).

Pei, Mario A. (b. Italy, Feb. 16, 1901—), linguist, teacher, novelist. Pei learned his first foreign language when his parents brought him to this country in 1908. He is one of the foremost living authorities on language. During the war and after, he wrote and broadcast in half a dozen languages for several government agencies, the Voice of America, and Radio Free Europe. Since 1937 he has taught at Columbia University, where he was appointed Professor of Romance philology in 1952. His famous thirty-seven-language "War Linguistics" course was published as *The World's Chief Languages* (1948). Active in professional language-teaching circles, he has contributed to most of the major professional journals here and abroad. He has also written articles for *The New York Times Magazine,* the *New Leader, Reader's Digest, Holiday,* and other well known magazines. His best known book, *The Story of Language* (1949), was a Book-of-the-Month-Club selection. Also popular were *The Story of English* (1952), and *Getting Along in French (Spanish, Italian, German, Portuguese, Russian)* (1957–59). Among his other books: *The Italian Language* (1941); *Dictionary of Linguistics* (1954); *One Language for the World* (1958); and *Talking Your Way Around the World* (1961).

Peirce, Benjamin [1] (b. Salem, Mass., Sept. 30, 1778—d. July 26, 1831), librarian, historian, public official. Peirce represented Salem in the Massachusetts legislature for several years, in 1826 was made librarian of Harvard University. He compiled a *Catalogue* (4 v., 1830–31) of the library, also a *History of Harvard University* (1833).

Peirce, Benjamin [2] (b. Salem, Mass., April 4, 1809—d. Oct. 6, 1880), astronomer, mathematician, teacher, public official. The son of the earlier Benjamin Peirce (see above) became a tutor at Harvard University two years after his graduation in 1829. In 1842 he was made Perkins Professor of Astronomy and Mathematics. His popular lectures on astronomy led to the founding of the Harvard Observatory. He served as consultant for the *American Nautical Almanac* and as superintendent of the U.S. Coast Survey, then as consulting geometer to the Survey. He was a founder of the American National Academy of Sciences, one of the organizers of the Dudley Observatory in Albany, wrote numerous textbooks. Among his texts were *Tables of the Moon* (1853); *Physical and Celestial Mechanics* (1855); *Linear Associative Algebras* (1870). With his associate Joseph Lovering (1813–1892), Peirce began to publish in 1842 the *Cambridge Miscellany,* a periodical devoted entirely to mathematics. It was so novel that only five issues appeared. He had a profound belief in mathematics as in itself a philosophy and once defined it as "the science which draws necessary conclusions." In his lectures he would often turn aside from equations to discourse on the greatness of the Creator and on the beauty and grandeur of mathematics.

Peirce, Charles Santiago Sanders (b. Cambridge, Mass., Sept. 10, 1839—d. April 19, 1914), logician, scientist, philosopher. Peirce attributed his abilities and ideas to the influence of his father, the second BENJAMIN PEIRCE, a brilliant mathematician, who supervised much of his education. After his graduation from Harvard, where he developed an interest in philosophy, he joined the United States Coast Survey, which employed him for thirty years (1861–91). His scientific work on astronomy, gravity, and geodetics was original and competent, but did not attract much notice. During the same period he studied under LOUIS AGASSIZ, lectured at Harvard on the philosophy of science (1864–65), was a member of the group which gave the Harvard lectures in philosophy (1869–70), and published a number of papers on logic which were of great importance.

His connection with the Cambridge META-PHYSICAL CLUB in the 1870's and his friendship with Chauncey Wright and WILLIAM JAMES contributed to his formulation of the philosophy of PRAGMATISM. A paper in the *North American Review* (Oct. 1871), in which he defended the philosophical realism of Duns Scotus and attacked Berkeley's nominalism, contains some elements of pragmatism, but Peirce did not publish a full statement of pragmatism until 1878. His article entitled *How to Make Our Ideas Clear,* which appeared in *Popular Science Monthly* in January, 1878, is considered to be the progenitor of the philosophy of pragmatism in the United States. William James, to whom pragmatism owes its fame as a movement, first used the term in 1898, crediting Peirce as the originator; however, Peirce's pragmatism is a different variety, more similar to the idealism of Josiah Royce, and including universals and an Absolute which James and his followers rejected.

Peirce's teaching was sporadic, and by far the majority of his papers—on logic, metaphysics, mathematics, religion, psychology, science, and a wide range of other subjects—were not published in his lifetime. He devoted the last twenty-five years of his life to writing, hampered toward the end by financial difficulties and poor health. Never given much recognition, outside of small professional circles, before his death, he has since come to be regarded as one of the most brilliant minds of his time and one of the most outstanding American philosophers. Charles Hartshorne and Paul Weiss edited the *Collected Papers of Charles Sanders Peirce* (6 v., 1931–35). Works on Peirce include W. B. Gallie's *Peirce and Pragmatism* (1952) and James K. Feibleman's *Introduction to Peirce's Philosophy* (1946).

Peirce, William (b. England, 1590[?]—d. 1641), shipmaster, almanac compiler. In 1638 Peirce issued his *Almanac for the Year of Our Lord 1639,* probably the first almanac put out in America. It was printed by the Stephen Daye Press.

Peixotto, Ernest [Clifford] (b. San Francisco, Oct. 15, 1869—d. Dec. 6, 1940), artist, historian, author of travel books. Peixotto was one of the best known painters and illustrators of his time, serving during World War I as official artist with the American Expeditionary Force and preparing drawings for such books as Theodore Roosevelt's *Life of Cromwell* (1900) and H. C. Lodge's *Story of the Revolution* (1898); he also did the murals for the Cleveland Public Library. In addition Peixotto was a prolific author, writing *By Italian Seas* (1906); *Through the French Provinces* (1910); *Romantic California* (1910); *Our Hispanic Southwest* (1916); *A Revolutionary Pilgrimage*

(1917); *A Bacchic Pilgrimage* (1932); and other books.

Pelican, The (1907), by Dixon Merritt. One of the most celebrated of all limericks, which Don Marquis once collected and printed in sixty-four versions, but which ran originally: "A wonderful bird is the pelican!/ His bill will hold more than his belican./ He can take in his beak/ Enough food for a week,/ But I'm damned if I see how the helican!" It first appeared in the Nashville *Banner*.

P.E.N. A world association of writers which preserves international ties among men of letters. P.E.N. was founded in London on October 6, 1921, by Catherine Dawson Scott, an English writer, and John Galsworthy, who became its first president and who established a trust fund for the organization with the Nobel prize money awarded to him in 1932. At the first meeting it was pointed out that the initial letters of "poet," "essayist," and "novelist" were the same in most European languages, and so might serve as a title. Since its founding P.E.N. clubs have been established in almost every country in the world. There is also a center known as P.E.N. Writers in Exile, notable because its members preferred homelessness to dictatorship. The first P.E.N. center in the United States was opened in New York City (1922) under the presidency of BOOTH TARKINGTON.

Pendexter, Hugh (b. Pittsfield, Mass., Jan. 15, 1875—d. June 11, 1940), teacher, newspaperman, novelist. After twelve years of writing for newspapers in Rochester, N.Y., Pendexter wrote many excellent historical novels of a sort young people especially like, also numerous short stories. Among his books: *Tiberius Smith* (1907); *Young Timber Cruisers* (1911); *Young Sea Merchants* (1917); *Red Belts* (1920); *Harry Idaho* (1926); *The Red Road* (1927); *Bush Lopers* (1931); *The Trail of Pontiac* (1933); *Long Knives* (1937). Many of them ran in series.

Penhallow, Samuel (b. England, July 2, 1665 —d. Dec. 2, 1726), merchant, public official, historian. Penhallow originally studied to be a minister, but marriage into the governing class of New Hampshire, to which he emigrated (1686), turned his thoughts to trade and he became a very wealthy man. He also served the colony as chief justice. He became greatly interested in the Wars with the Indians, wars that he accounted for as a punishment from God for the sins of the Puritans, particularly for their not Christianizing the Indians. He prepared a book on the subject which became popular: *The History of the Wars of New England with the Eastern Indians* (1726; reprinted, 1859).

Penn, William (b. England, Oct. 14, 1644— d. July 30, 1718), statesman, religious and political writer. After his expulsion from Oxford University in 1662 because of his religious convictions, Penn traveled in France and Italy until recalled by his father Sir William Penn. He had some difficulty in choosing a career. He followed the sea briefly, but gave up his naval career to study law. When he wearied of Lincoln's Inn, his father sent him in 1666 to manage his Irish estates. In Ireland Penn was imprisoned for his avowal of Quaker beliefs. When released, he returned to London, where he continued to express them. His first important work, *No Cross, No Crown* (1669), was a powerful plea for the Friends' religion and a scathing attack upon the established clergy. During the next three years he was imprisoned a number of times but did not cease his activities. *The Great Case of Liberty of Conscience* (1670), written in prison, is a noble defense of religious toleration. Upon his release in 1671 he visited Holland and Germany, founding a Quaker society at Emden. He married in 1672 and settled down in Hertfordshire, where he wrote the *Treatise of Oaths, England's Present Interest Considered,* and a number of other tracts.

Penn acted as arbitrator in a dispute between Fenwick and Byllinge, two Friends who had bought land in America from the Crown. When a portion was put up for sale, Penn bought it, becoming one of the five proprietors. He visited the new colony, drew up a constitution, and soon a large number of Quakers settled in what became West Jersey. In 1677 he returned to Holland and Germany to continue his missionary work, this time accompanied by George Fox. As a result of this expedition, a number of Germans from Kirchheim were drawn to the New World, where they settled in Germantown, the earlier name for Philadelphia. When in 1678 a new threat of "popish terror" appeared, Penn wrote his *Epistle to the Children of Light in This Generation,* followed a year later by *An Address to Protestants of All Persuasions,* then several lively and timely political tracts. But things looked grave for all dissenters, and he once more thought of America. He asked King Charles II for territory in America in payment of a debt owed to his father. On March 14, 1681, Penn received "a tract of land in America north of Maryland" which he named Sylvania—to which the king, over the new owner's protests, prefixed the name Penn in honor of Penn's father. Penn spent the next year drawing up a constitution. In September, 1682, after writing his *Farewell to England,* he sailed without his family to the New World. On arrival he gathered together an assembly and passed "The Great Law of Pennsylvania," which stated that the territory was to be a Christian state on a Quaker model. His *Some Account of the Province of Pennsylvania* was published in 1681. Penn was notable for his just and friendly relations with the Indians. Voltaire said that his pact with the Indians was the only treaty made with them which was never sworn to and never broken.

Trouble with LORD BALTIMORE over the treatment of Quakers in Maryland brought Penn back to England in 1684; five months later King Charles died and Penn found himself in a powerful position. He managed to obtain the release of 1,200 imprisoned Quakers, as well as a pardon for John Locke. *Information and Direction to Such Persons as Are Inclined to America* was published in 1684. He undertook a third mission to Holland and Germany in 1686; on his return he set out on a preaching tour in England. *Good Advice to the Church of England, Roman Catholics, and Protestant Dissenters* appeared at this time.

During the absence of her governor troubles were brewing in Pennsylvania, and finally the Council in London removed Penn as governor. He lived for some time in retirement, during which he wrote *Some Fruits of Solitude* (1693), a book of maxims often regarded as the most literary of his writings. On Aug. 20, 1694, his governorship was restored. He did not, however, return to Pennsylvania until 1699, when he was forced to wrestle with the problem of slavery, which he was unable to abolish. In 1700 he made another successful treaty with the Indians, and worked with Lord Bellomont in New York on a consolidation of the laws in America. He was forced to return to England in 1701, and once again affairs in America went from bad to worse. Penn decided to give his province back to the Crown, if Queen Mary would take the Quakers under her protection. His mind was affected by a stroke before arrangements could be completed, and he died a few years later. A remarkable scheme for establishing *The Present and Future Peace of Europe* through a European parliament appeared in 1693.

Among Penn's other works are *Fruits of a Father's Love* (1727); *An Account of W. Penn's Travails in Holland and Germany* (1694); *A Brief Account of the Rise and Progress of the People Called Quakers* (1694); *The Harmony of Divine and Heavenly Doctrines* (1696); and *The Christian Quaker and His Divine Testimony* (1674). H. J. Cadbury and Isabel Grubb have edited Penn's *My Irish Journal* (1952). The most nearly complete edition of Penn's works is *A Collection of the Works of William Penn* (2 v., 1726), with a biography by Joseph Besse. An illuminating book is Violet Oakley's *Holy Experiment: Our Heritage from William Penn, 1644–1944* (1950), and there are good biographies by William Hull (1937), Edward C. O. Beatty (1939), and Catherine Owen Peare (1956). Penn appears in Anna L. B. Thomas' novel *Nancy Lloyd, The Journal of a Quaker Pioneer* (1927). Pennsbury Manor, Penn's home in Bucks County, has been "re-created" as a memorial.

Pennell, Joseph Stanley [1] (b. Philadelphia, July 4, 1857—d. April 23, 1926), artist, teacher, critic. Pennell studied art at the Pennsylvania School of Industrial Design, where he learned the technique of etching. He was commissioned by the art editor of *Scribner's* to make etchings of Philadelphia's historic buildings. Charles Godfrey Leland (see HANS BREITMANN), who was asked to write the accompanying text, suggested his niece, **Elizabeth Robins** (b. Philadelphia, Feb. 21, 1855—d. Feb. 8, 1936), as collaborator. Three years later Pennell married her. He illustrated Cable's *The Creoles of Louisiana* (1884), and was sent to Italy to illustrate William Dean Howells' articles on Tuscan cities. After an outbreak of cholera,

the Pennells went to England, where a bicycle trip to Canterbury resulted in *A Canterbury Pilgrimage* (text by Elizabeth, illustrations by Joseph, 1885).

They decided to settle permanently in London, where they became popular figures in a literary group that included Sir Edmund Gosse, Henry James, George Bernard Shaw, and James McNeill Whistler. In 1884 Mrs. Pennell published the *Life of Mary Wollstonecraft*. Pennell became art editor of the *Star* in 1888, but turned over his column to his wife, who conducted it, as well as her own in the *Daily Chronicle*, for many years. Whistler gave various private papers to the Pennells and asked them to write his biography; the *Life of James McNeill Whistler* appeared in 1908 followed by *The Whistler Journal* (1921). In 1912 the Pennells visited America. A series of superb lithographs of the Panama Canal was followed by others of Yosemite, the Grand Canyon, Washington, and Philadelphia. *Our Philadelphia*, by Elizabeth and Joseph Pennell, appeared in 1914. During World War I Pennell made a series of drawings of British factories, later published as *Pictures of War Work in England* (1917), as well as lithographs for war posters.

When his health broke down as a result of his strenuous war work, Pennell returned to America with his wife, taught at the Art Students' League in New York, and served as art critic for the Brooklyn *Eagle*. In 1925 he published *The Adventures of an Illustrator*. Mrs. Pennell was the author of *Charles Godfrey Leland* (1906); *Our House and London Out of Our Windows* (1912); *Nights* (1916); and *The Life and Letters of Joseph Pennell* (2 v., 1929).

Pennell, Joseph Stanley [2] (b. Junction City, Kan., July 4, 1908—), newspaperman, teacher, writer. After working on newspapers in Denver and California, Pennell wrote a novel, THE HISTORY OF ROME HANKS (1944), the narrator of which seeks to discover how he came to be what he is by an inquest into his forebears. The background is mostly the Civil War, in which Pennell's ancestors had fought on both sides. The book made a decided sensation, with most critical reaction favorable. Similar novels were *The History of Nora Beckham* (1948) and *The History of Thomas Wagnal* (1951).

Pennsylvania Farmer. The pen name of JOHN DICKINSON.

Pennsylvania Gazette, The. SAMUEL KEIMER, BENJAMIN FRANKLIN's first employer and later his constant rival, issued on Dec. 24, 1728, a weekly periodical *The Universal Instructor in All Arts and Sciences and Pennsylvania Gazette*. After nine ponderous and unsuccessful months, Keimer was glad to get rid of the paper and sold it to Franklin, who published the first issue under his editorship on Oct. 2, 1729, and continued to own and edit the weekly until 1766. Franklin promptly dropped the adult education section of the paper's title and issued it simply as *The Pennsylvania Gazette*. In 1732 he began to issue a German edition called *Die Philadelphische Zeitung*, but this soon failed. The

English version was very successful. It was as lively as Franklin could make it. He himself contributed his *Dialogue Between Philocles and Horatio Concerning Virtue and Pleasure;* the letters of Anthony Afterwit and Alice Addertongue; *The Meditation on a Quart Mug; A Witch Trial at Mount Holly;* and *An Apology for Printers,* the last being a statement (June 10, 1731) on freedom of the press. He introduced weather reports and wrote obviously for the man in the street. In 1754 he published in the *Gazette* what was probably the first cartoon in an American paper. David Hall and his descendants continued the paper. The last issue appeared on Oct. 11, 1815.

Pennsylvania Pilgrim, The (1872), a narrative poem by JOHN GREENLEAF WHITTIER. Next to *Snow-Bound,* this is Whittier's longest poem, and he regarded it as greater. It tells the story of the Quaker settlement in Pennsylvania under the leadership of the gifted and noble FRANCIS DANIEL PASTORIUS. The poem is soundly historical yet truly poetic. In Pastorius' life Whittier found the first antislavery protest.

Penrod (1914), a novel by BOOTH TARKINGTON. This account of the humorous adventures of a twelve-year-old boy in a Middle-Western community (drawn from the author's nephews) won wide popularity and was followed by *Penrod and Sam* (1916) and *Penrod Jashber* (1929). All three were gathered in an omnibus volume, *Penrod: His Complete Story* (1931). Edward Wagenknecht spoke appreciatively of these amusing adventures as coming "close to folklore," although critics agree that in their analysis of the psychology of adolescence they fall far below Mark Twain's *Tom Sawyer* and *Huckleberry Finn* and Stephen Crane's *Whilomville Stories.* They were as true to their period, however, as these books to theirs.

Peony (1948), a novel by PEARL BUCK. This is a narrative concerning racial conflict, exemplified in the story of a Jewish family living in China.

People, Yes, The (1936), a poem by CARL SANDBURG. This is a conglomerate poem, composed in alternating passages of prose and free verse, narrative and homily, copybook English and slang. The whole is intended to present the poet's faith in the United States and democracy in general. Oscar Cargill finds the book "diffuse, occasionally rambling, and sometimes long-winded," nevertheless "still a splendid organic whole." The book expresses not merely a series of sincere enthusiasms but also the character of a people—the nation's moods, occupations, amusements, its shrewd philosophy of life. Cargill holds that nowhere can one find a better collection of adages, riddles, and fence-rail syllogisms: *e.g.,* "How can you compete with a skunk?" and "The coat and the pants do the work, but the vest gets the gravy." Sandburg by no means overlooks the faults of Americans; indeed, he ridicules them with wit and acumen. Babette Deutsch finds the poem unsuccessful, feels that it is largely composed of "cant phrases,

slang, stale jokes, tall stories, the jargon of Main Street."

Pepper, George Wharton (b. Philadelphia, March 16, 1867—d. May 24, 1961), lawyer, public official, teacher, writer. Pepper, an erudite man of agile mind, became one of the most distinguished of American lawyers. He taught law at the University of Pennsylvania (1893–1910) and lectured at Yale. He was a member of the Pennsylvania Commission on Constitutional Revision and served in the United States Senate (1922–27). His books reflect his wide range of activities. Among them are *The Borderland of Federal and State Decisions* (1889); *A Voice From the Crowd* (1915); *Men and Issues* (1924); *In the Senate* (1930); *Family Quarrels* (1931); his autobiography, *Philadelphia Lawyer* (1944); and *Analytical Index to the Book of Common Prayer* (1948).

Pepperell, Sir William (b. Kittery Point, Me., June 27, 1696—d. July 6, 1759), public official, soldier. In 1722 he became a colonel in the Maine militia; in 1727 he was elected to his majesty's Council for the Commonwealth of Massachusetts, and held this office for 32 years. Pepperell was a successful merchant, a member of the governor's council, for a time chief justice of the colony. In 1745 he led an expedition against Fort Louisburg at Cape Breton and helped capture it. In the French and Indian War he raised a regiment and was appointed lieutenant general. He kept a *Journal* of the Louisburg expedition (pub. 1911).

Pequod. The whaling ship in Melville's MOBY DICK (1851).

Pequot Indians. The Pequots were an Algonquian tribe who moved out of northern New England into Connecticut, Rhode Island, and Long Island under pressure from Puritan settlers. When a trader named John Oldham was murdered by the Pequots (July 20, 1636), JOHN MASON led a group of Puritans and Indians in an attack (1638) on the Pequots at Fort Mystic, which they burned to the ground. Mason wrote a plain, unvarnished *Brief History of the Pequot War,* which was included (without his name) in Increase Mather's *Brief History of the War with the Indians in New England* (1677) and separately published in an edition prepared by Thomas Prince (1736). One of his lieutenants, John Underhill, in *News from America* (1638), gave a less reliable account. Philip Vincent, a young English clergyman in New England at the time, wrote *A True Relation of the Late Battle Fought in New England* (1637) that was free from personal bias. Lion Gardiner, an observer rather than a participant, gave some important additional information in his *Relation of the Pequot Wars* (about 1660). All of these form the basis of Howard Bradstreet's *The Story of the War with the Pequots* (1933). The picture of cruelty being met with even greater cruelty is not a pleasant one.

Perch, Philemon. The pen name of R. M. JOHNSTON.

Percival, James Gates (b. Kensington, Conn.,

Sept. 15, 1795—d. May 2, 1856), poet, geologist. One of the most learned men of his time, Percival distinguished himself in several fields, most notably those of literature and geology. He was a competent physician, and for a time

was both medical officer and teacher of chemistry at West Point. His literary efforts included original poetry in both English and German, translations from Russian, Serbian, and Hungarian, a play (*Zamor*, 1815), Phi Beta Kappa addresses at Harvard and Yale, and magazine contributions as editor of the Connecticut *Herald* and Bond's *American Athenaeum*. His long poem, "Prometheus" (published in *Poems*, 1821), was compared favorably by critics to Byron's *Childe Harold*. Though modern taste would not support the judgement, in his day Percival was generally recognized as the leading American poet before Bryant.

Yet Percival was doomed by his mental instability to perpetual failure. Conflicts arising from his delusions of persecution repeatedly lost him positions, and he lived much of his life in squalor. For ten years he resided on the grounds of the State Hospital at New Haven, Connecticut.

Percival also published *Prometheus Part II with Other Poems* (1822); *Clio I and II* (1822); *Clio No. III* (1827); and *The Dream of a Day, and Other Poems* (1843). For a while he assisted Noah Webster in the preparation of the latter's famous dictionary, but the two quarreled, and the association was broken. He made several important technical contributions in the field of geology, surveyed the lead fields of the midwest, and was state geologist of both Wisconsin and Connecticut.

Percy, Florence. The pen name of Elizabeth Akers.

Percy, George (b. England, 1580—d. 1632), colonist. Percy, a son of the Earl of Northumberland, was deputy governor of Virginia Colony in 1609–10 and again in 1611. He prepared three manuscripts on his experiences (1608, 1612, around 1622). His *Observations Gathered out of a Discourse of the Plantation of the Southern Colony in Virginia* seems to have combined the 1608 and 1622 manuscripts and was printed in *Purchas His Pilgrims* (1652). The second manuscript was printed in 1922. In the opinion of Jarvis Morse, Percy gives in the first section of his *Observations* the best account of the voyage of the first colonists to Jamestown.

Percy, William Alexander (b. Greenville, Miss., May 14, 1885—d. Jan. 21, 1942), lawyer, poet, memoirist. Percy began the practice of law at Greenville in 1908, served with the Commission for Relief in Belgium in 1916, then with the American Expeditionary Forces in World War I. He published none of his verse in book form until 1915 when *Sappho in Levkas* appeared; then followed *In April Once* (1920); *Enzio's Kingdom* (1924); *Selected Poems* (1930). *Lanterns on the Levee* (1941) is an autobiography. Hodding Carter called the latter "the sad, lyric autobiography of a man who belonged rightly to an earlier century." David L. Cohn described Percy as "cultivated and compassionate, a cosmopolitan and an enlightened provincial." His poems are written in traditional forms and with alluring melody, expressing love of nature and detestation of the city.

Perelman, S[idney] J[oseph] (b. Brooklyn, N.Y., Feb. 1, 1904—   ), humorist. Perelman graduated from Brown University in 1925 and wrote for various humor magazines until 1929, when his first book, *Dawn Ginsbergh's Revenge*, precipitated a national paroxysm and secured, apparently indefinitely, its author's fame. He was immediately offered a job in Hollywood, where he was a gag- and scriptwriter. In recent years much of his work has been first published in such magazines as the *New Yorker* before appearing in book form. Perelman claims to have been influenced primarily by James Joyce, whom he considers to be "*the* great comic writer"; Perelman's own extraordinary vocabulary and verbal facility are perhaps the most impressive aspects of his humor. If it were not for the intrepid exaggeration upon which his humor turns he would probably deserve a place among the distinguished stylists of 20th century American writing. At the root of his comedy lies a rather hard-bitten moral integrity and a sardonic wisdom; he has little patience with any nonsense but his own. He has poked a sharply satirical finger at nearly every foolishness of contemporary society, and his scrutiny of the entertainment and advertising industries in particular has been shrewd.

Among his books: *Parlor, Bedlam, and Bath* (1930); *Strictly from Hunger* (1937); *Keep it Crisp* (1946); *Crazy Like a Fox* (1944); *Acres and Pains* (1947); *The Best of S. J. Perelman* (1947); *Westward Ha! or, Around the World in 80 Cliches* (1948); *Listen to the Mocking Bird* (1949); *The Swiss Family Perelman* (1950); *The Ill-Tempered Clavicord* (1953); *Perelman's Home Companion* (1955); *The Road to Miltown, or, Under the Spreading Atrophy* (1957); *The Rising Gorge* (1961). He has written three plays, the best known of which is *One Touch of Venus* (with Ogden Nash, 1943). A collection,

The Most of S. J. Perelman, was published in 1958.

Perennial Bachelor, The (1925), a novel by ANNE PARRISH. A winner of the Harper Prize, this work relates the story of the Campions, a family whose welfare is sacrificed to that of Victor, the only boy; he grows up a spoiled and ungrateful fop.

Perfect Tribute, The (1906), a story of the delivery and effect of Lincoln's *Gettysburg Address,* by MARY RAYMOND SHIPMAN ANDREWS. Lincoln, incognito, visits a Washington hospital the next day and hears a dying Confederate soldier read the Address.

Perils of Pauline, The (1914[?] and thereafter), a series of movies produced in weekly installments for many years; the script writer was CHARLES WILLIAM GODDARD (1880–1951) and the leading actress was PEARL WHITE. Pauline is always in danger, but always manages to escape. She hangs at the edge of cliffs, is caught in quicksand, is swept down millraces —and enjoys it all. Goddard also wrote or helped to write *The Exploits of Elaine, The Mysteries of Myra,* and similar movie series. See HAROLD MACGRATH.

Perkins, Eli. The pen name of MELVILLE DE LANCEY LANDON.

Perkins, Frederick Beecher (b. Hartford, Conn., Sept. 27, 1828—d. Jan. 27, 1899), librarian, editor, biographer. Perkins was a nephew of Henry Ward Beecher and Harriet Beecher Stowe, a brother-in-law of Edward Everett Hale. He worked on newspapers for a while, later became librarian of the Connecticut Historical Society (1857–61), then of the San Francisco Public Library (1880–87). He was an associate editor of the LIBRARY JOURNAL (1877–80). Among his books: *Charles Dickens* (1870); *The Best Reading* (1872); a novel, *The Lost Library* (1874); DEVIL PUZZLERS AND OTHER STUDIES (1877).

Perkins, Lucy Fitch (b. Maples, Ind., July 12, 1865—d. March 18, 1937), artist, writer for children. Mrs. Perkins was both a clever writer and a capable illustrator. In 1911 she wrote *The Dutch Twins,* and this was so successful that she followed it up with a whole series of similarly named stories: *The Japanese Twins* (1912); *The Irish Twins* (1913); *The Eskimo Twins* (1914); *The Belgian Twins* (1917); and many others. Among them were some historical tales such as *The Puritan Twins* (1921) and *The Colonial Twins of Virginia* (1924). Mrs. Perkins sought to promote friendliness with other nations by her portrayal of their young people. Her daughter Eleanor Ellis Perkins wrote her biography, *Eve Among the Puritans* (1956).

Perkins, Maxwell Evarts (b. New York City, Sept. 20, 1884—d. June 17, 1947), newspaperman, editor, publisher. Perkins worked from 1907 to 1910 for *The New York Times,* then joined the staff of Charles Scribner's Sons, ultimately becoming a vice-president and editor-in-chief. The firm, when he joined it, was decidedly conservative; Perkins had the insight to welcome writers of a newer type, such as Ring Lardner, F. Scott Fitzgerald, Ernest Hemingway, and Thomas Wolfe. Wolfe's inchoate first manuscript of 800,000 words, which later became LOOK HOMEWARD, ANGEL (1929), had already been rejected by several publishers. Perkins labored arduously with him and his manuscript and produced a finished novel. Wolfe dedicated his next novel, OF TIME AND THE RIVER (1935), to Perkins in glowing terms. But he took his third book to another publisher. In *You Can't Go Home Again* (1940) he introduced a character named Foxhall Edwards who was obviously patterned— fondly or maliciously according to the reader's own bias—on Perkins. Clearly Wolfe suffered from a growing resentment of the continual linkage of his name with Perkins' throughout the book trade; he wanted to prove that he could write a good novel by himself. Just before Wolfe died in 1938 he wrote a handsome apology to Perkins. Perkins very freely forgave him, but it was later said by many of Perkins' friends that Wolfe's ingratitude had been a serious disappointment to him. The controversy revived when *Editor to Author: The Letters of Maxwell E. Perkins* appeared in 1950, and it was developed further in Struthers Burt's essay called *Catalyst for Genius: Maxwell Perkins, 1884– 1947,* published in the *Saturday Review of Literature* (June 9, 1951). Burt's essay was a warm tribute to Perkins as both man and editor.

Perley. The pen name of BENJAMIN PERLEY POORE.

Perrot, Nicholas (b. France, 1644—d. 1718[?]), fur trader, explorer. He acquired great skill in Indian languages and was used by Frontenac as an envoy to encourage the Sioux and other tribes to make war on the Iroquois, who were unfriendly to the French. In the name of France he took possession of the Upper Mississippi region. He wrote a *Mémoire* on the Indians and their habits and religions (pub., 1864; translated, 1911).

Perry, Bliss (b. Williamstown, Mass., Nov. 25, 1860—d. Feb. 13, 1954), teacher, editor, writer. During his early years of teaching at Williams College and at Princeton University Perry published three novels and a collection of short stories. He became editor of the *Atlantic Monthly* in 1899, a position which he held until 1909. He left the *Atlantic* for Harvard, where he taught English until 1930, and was known to generations of students as one of the most inspired and lovable teachers in America. He edited *Little Masterpieces* (18 v., 1895–1900) and was the general editor of the *Cambridge Edition of the Poets* (1905–1909). His most important critical works are *Walt Whitman: His Life and Works* (1906) and *Emerson Today* (1931); he also wrote *The Amateur Spirit* (1904); *Whittier* (1907); *The American Mind* (1912); *Carlyle* (1915); and *The American Spirit in Literature* (1918). His works of fiction include *The Broughton House* (1890); *The Plated City* (1895); *Salem Kittredge and Other Stories* (1894); and *The Powers at Play* (1899).

And Gladly Teach (1935) is a modest, urbane, and delightful autobiography.

Perry, George Sessions (b. Rockdale, Tex., May 5, 1910—d. Dec. 13?, 1956), war correspondent, writer, editor. Perry wrote chiefly of life in the United States. His best known book was *Cities of America* (1947), an account of twenty-one cities that appeared chapter by chapter in the *Saturday Evening Post*. *My Granny Van* (1949) is a biography of his grandmother. *Families of America* (1949) describes nine American families of varying national origins. He also wrote two good novels—*Walls Rise Up* (1939) and HOLD AUTUMN IN YOUR HAND (1941)—and *The Story of Texas A. & M.* (1951).

Perry, Matthew Calbraith (b. Newport, R.I., April 10, 1794—d. March 4, 1858), naval officer. Perry was a younger brother of Commodore OLIVER HAZARD PERRY. His naval activities included valuable service during the Mexican War. While in command of a fleet in Asiatic waters he opened communication with Japan by entering the Bay of Yedo (or Tokyo) to deliver a letter from President Fillmore to the Emperor of Japan. The following year (1854) he returned and concluded a treaty of amity with Japan, bringing about the entrance of that country into world affairs. In 1952 Sidney Wallach edited Perry's *Expedition of the American Squadron*, the story of his Japanese exploit.

Perry, Nora (b. Dudley, Mass., [?], 1831—d. May 13, 1896), poet, author of books for girls. She wrote conventional and simple lyrics, also books for girls, including *Hope Benham* (1894) and *Mary Bartlett's Step-Mother* (1900). Her verse was collected in *After the Ball and Other Poems* (1875).

Perry, Oliver Hazard (b. South Kingston, R.I., Aug. 20, 1785—d. Aug. 23, 1819), naval officer. Perry took part in the naval war against France and in the Tripolitan War. When the War of 1812 broke out he was given command of the naval forces on Lake Erie. On Sept. 10, 1813, he defeated the British fleet with vessels he had himself constructed and sent a famous message to General W. H. Harrison, "We have met the enemy and they are ours." While completing a diplomatic mission to Venezuela he died of yellow fever. Perry's shipbuilding exploit is well described in Carl D. Lane's novel *The Fleet in the Forest* (1943); the Battle of Lake Erie appears vividly in Irving Bacheller's D'RI AND I (1901) and Robert S. Harper's *Trumpet in the Wilderness* (1940). A. S. Mackenzie wrote *The Life of Commodore Oliver Hazard Perry* (2 v., 1840); more recent lives have been written by James C. Mills (1913) and Charles J. Dutton (1935).

Perry, Ralph Barton (b. Poultney, Vt., July 3, 1876—d. Jan. 22, 1957), teacher, philosopher, biographer. Perry, a Princeton and Harvard graduate, taught philosophy at Williams and Smith Colleges, went to Harvard in 1902, became a full professor in 1913. He became the chief authority on his friend and teacher WILLIAM JAMES, preparing *An Annotated Bibliography of the Writing of William James* (1920), *The Thought and Character of William James* (2 v., 1935, a Pulitzer prize winner), *In the Spirit of William James* (1938), and numerous articles on the man whose ideas he chiefly followed. He called his own version of pragmatism "neo-realism." He also wrote *The Approach to Philosophy* (1905); *The New Realism* (1912); *General Theory of Value* (1926); *A Defense of Philosophy* (1931); *On All Fronts* (1941); *Puritanism and Democracy* (1945); *Characteristically American* (1949); *Realms of Value* (1953); and other books—all showing James' influence in the vigor and vitality of his style.

Perry, Thomas Sergeant (b. Newport, R.I., Jan. 23, 1845—d. May 7, 1928), critic, teacher, biographer, historian. Edwin Arlington Robinson, who edited his letters in 1929, called Perry "one of the great appreciators." He wrote *The Life and Letters of Francis Lieber* (1882), *English Literature of the 18th Century* (1883), *From Opitz to Lessing* (1885), *The Evolution of a Snob* (1887), *A History of Greek Literature* (1890), *John Fiske* (1906), and many articles and book reviews. He taught at Harvard University for two brief periods (1868–72, 1877–82) and in Japan (1898–1901). Perry was deeply interested in foreign literatures, and was particularly active in popularizing Turgenev and other Russian novelists, as well as some of the naturalistic French novelists. Biographies of Perry were written by John T. Morse, Jr. (1929), and by Virginia Harlow (1951).

Pershing, J[ohn] J[oseph] (b. Linn Co., Mo., Sept. 13, 1860—d. July 15, 1948), soldier, teacher, lawyer. A graduate of West Point, Pershing spent his entire life in the army. During the Spanish American War he served in Cuba. In 1913 he suppressed an insurrection in the Philippines, in 1916 took part in the pursuit of the Mexican bandit Francisco Villa. That year he became a major general. In 1917 he was placed in command of the American Expeditionary Forces in France. When the great offensive of July 1918 began, the American Army under Pershing opened the way for the collapse of the German forces. He became Chief of Staff in 1921. In 1931 he published *My Experiences in the World War* (2 v.), a work for which he received a Pulitzer Prize in history.

Personae (1909), the second volume of poems by EZRA POUND. The title means "masks of the actor," recalling W. B. Yeats' demand that the poet objectify his experience through an imagined personality, a mask. It also reveals Pound's indebtedness to the monologues of Browning's *Men and Women*. Pound also used *Personae* as the title for later collections of verse.

Personal Recollections of Joan of Arc (1896), a semifictional biography by MARK TWAIN. In order to avoid unsuitable comparisons with his comic writing, Twain published this as a French work by "The Sieur Louis de Conte." It is for the most part factual and serious, since Twain had a deep reverence for the French heroine. But he introduced occasional episodes of fiction, and the book is not without moments of characteristic humor. Twain stated that in the first two-thirds of the book there was much "fancy and invention." Mary A. Wyman made an interesting study (1946) of a marked similarity between the character of Edmond Aubrey (called "the Paladin") in the book and Mark Twain himself. Changed from a braggart into a hero by Joan's confidence in him, he is cut down by her side with the standard in his hand.

Perspectives U.S.A. A quarterly magazine founded in October, 1952, and published in five editions in the United States, England, France, Germany, and Italy. The materials in the English-language editions were translated into French, German, and Italian for the Continental editions; all editions were sold at a nominal price through a world-wide circulation system. *Perspectives U.S.A.* was published by Intercultural Publications, a nonprofit organization, under the terms of a grant from the Ford Foundation, and its aim was to bring the intellectual and artistic life of the United States closer to the peoples of foreign lands. Much of the content of the magazine was reprinted from materials previously published in other American magazines, but some special articles were directly commissioned. The originator and director of the project was JAMES LAUGHLIN, head of the publishing firm of New Directions. The last issue of *Perspectives U.S.A.* appeared in the summer of 1956; its file comprises the most distinguished collection of American creative and critical work in the post-World War II period. In addition Intercultural Publications carried on a number of other projects, including the publication of supplements on various foreign cultures in the *Atlantic Monthly,* the publication of anthologies of American writing in foreign countries not reached by *Perspectives U.S.A.,* and the organization of traveling exhibitions of American painting and sculpture in Europe and Asia.

Peterkin, Julia [Mood] (b. Laurens Co., S.C., Oct. 31, 1880—d. Aug. 10, 1961), novelist, short-story writer. Mrs. Peterkin became a specialist in the life and strange language of the Gullah Negroes of the South Carolina coast and regions further south. Her treatment of them is sympathetic and yet realistic in its depiction of their hard, humble, often tragic lives. Her novel SCARLET SISTER MARY (1928) won a Pulitzer prize and was dramatized (1930) by Daniel Reed; the play was performed by a white cast, headed by Ethel Barrymore, in blackface. Mrs. Peterkin's other books include *Green Thursday* (1924); BLACK APRIL (1927); *Bright Skin* (1932); *Roll, Jordan, Roll* (1933, a collection of photographs with text by Mrs. Peterkin); *Plantation Christmas* (1934). Francis Butler Simkins felt that in *Scarlet Sister Mary* Mrs. Peterkin had created one of the major characters of American literature, and that her treatment of the country Negro revealed "an almost native comprehension."

Peterkin Papers, The (1880), by LUCRETIA PEABODY HALE. Miss Hale established her literary fame with these humorous stories of family life. One of the best was *The Peterkins' Christmas Tree.* Miss Hale told the stories to the little daughter of a friend of hers, then published them in OUR YOUNG FOLKS and ST. NICHOLAS. Later she issued another collection, *The Last of the Peterkins, with Others of Their Kind* (1886).

Peter Quince at the Clavier (in HARMONIUM, 1923), a poem by WALLACE STEVENS. Sitting at the clavier, the poet retells the story of Susanna and the elders, from the *Apocrypha* of the Bible, and draws the conclusion that "beauty is momentary in the mind . . . /But in the flesh it is immortal"; it is, too, a kind of music, and in the case of Susanna "plays/On the clear viol of her memory,/And makes a constant sacrament of praise." The poem is one of Stevens' most limpid and melodious.

Peter Rugg, the Missing Man (1824), a story by WILLIAM AUSTIN. It appeared first in the *New England Galaxy* (Sept. 10, 1824), since then has been reprinted in numerous anthologies. Peter Rugg, driving to Boston and overtaken by a severe squall, stubbornly refuses to take shelter, and is condemned to go on driving for fifty years. The tale bears obvious resemblances to *Rip Van Winkle* (1819) and the story of the Wandering Jew. Austin wrote a sequel in which Peter, like Rip, gets home and finds everything changed. Nathaniel Hawthorne makes reference to the tale in the gathering of curious odds and ends that he called A Virtuoso's Collection (*Boston Miscellany,* May, 1842). Louise Imogen Guiney and Amy Lowell both used the tale as a basis for ballads.

Peters, Samuel Andrew (b. Hebron, Conn., Nov. 20, 1735—d. April 19, 1826), Anglican clergyman, historian, teller of tall tales. As rector of the Anglican church at Hebron, Conn., Peters tactlessly fulminated against the growing discontent with the British government. In October 1774, he fled to England.

In 1781 Peters published his *General History of Connecticut.* With great plausibility he mixed true statements with inventions and exaggerations. Peters was strongly critical of Puritan bigotry, and indulged his fancy for spinning yarns in a fashion that truly made him the forerunner of the tall tales of the Wild West. All was told with proper historical garniture and dignity. The book was widely denounced. In 1805 Peters returned to America to establish some land claims of the heirs of the English explorer Jonathan Carver. His claims were disallowed by Congress in the year of his death. J. H. Trumbull wrote *The Rev. Samuel Peters: His Defenders and Apologists* (1877).

Petersham, Maude (b. Kingston, N.Y., Aug. 5, 1889—   ), and **Petersham, Miska** (b. Hungary, Sept. 20, 1888—d. 1960), illustrators and writers of books for children. Mr. and Mrs. Petersham became two of the most esteemed of contemporary writers and illustrators for children. Some of their books were written for their own child, some grew out of recollections of Hungary; to prepare *The Christ Child* (1931) they spent several months in

Palestine. Among their other books: *Get-a-Way and Háry János* (1933); *Miki and Mary* (1934); *The Story Book of Aircraft* (1935); *The Story Book of Wheat* (1936); *The Rooster Crows* (1945), which was awarded the Caldecott Medal.

Peterson, Charles Jacobs (b. Philadelphia, July 20, 1819—d. March 4, 1887), editor, historian, novelist, publisher. Peterson was a powerful figure in Philadelphia literary life when that city was at the height of its prosperity as a publishing center. He was an editor of *Atkinson's Casket*, which later became GRAHAM'S MAGAZINE (1842), and of the SATURDAY EVENING POST. He founded the *Ladies' National Magazine* (1842), later called *Peterson's Magazine*, and with ANN S. STEPHENS edited it until his death. Meanwhile he wrote several historical novels: *Grace Dudley; or, Arnold at Saratoga* (1849); *Kate Aylesford* (1855); and others. He also wrote popular histories, including *The Military Heroes of the Revolution* (1848) and *Naval Heroes of the United States* (1850).

Peterson, Henry (b. Philadelphia, Dec. 7, 1818—d. Oct. 10, 1891), editor, publisher, poet, novelist. Like his cousin CHARLES JACOBS PETERSON, Henry Peterson was an important figure in the magazine world of Philadelphia. He was on the editorial staff of the *Saturday Gazette*, then became editor of the SATURDAY EVENING POST, which he and Edmund Deacon purchased in 1848. He also wrote a good deal of verse and several novels. In 1863 he collected his *Poems*, in 1869 published *The Modern Job* in free verse. Among his novels were *Pemberton* (1873), *Confessions of a Minister* (1874) and *Bessie's Lovers* (1877). In 1864 Deacon and Peterson bought the *Lady's Friend*, which Peterson's wife Sarah edited until 1874.

Peterson, Houston (b. Fresno, Calif., Dec. 11, 1897—   ), teacher, biographer, lecturer, broadcaster. As a college professor at Columbia and Rutgers universities, as chairman and director of the Cooper Union Forum, Peterson did much to make philosophy and literature familiar to a constantly increasing public. His valuable and vigorously written books include: *Havelock Ellis, Philosopher of Love* (1928); *Huxley, Prophet of Science* (1932); *The Lonely Debate* (1938). He has compiled several anthologies: *The Book of Sonnet Sequences* (1929); *Poet to Poet* (1945); *A Treasury of the World's Great Speeches* (1954). *Great Teachers* (1946) is a striking symposium edited by Peterson.

Peterson, Roger Tory (b. Jamestown, N.Y., Aug. 28, 1908—   ), nature writer, artist, teacher. Tory, who combines artistry with science, has published authoritative books on birds, for which he has received numerous awards. Among his books: *Field Guide to Birds* (1934); *Junior Book of Birds* (1939), a guide to twenty-three common North American birds and one of the best available for young ornithologists; *A Field Guide to Western Birds* (1941), for which he traveled 20,000 miles in search of material; *Birds Over America* (1948);

How to Know the Birds (1949); *Wildlife in Color* (1951). He edited the *Bird Watcher's Anthology* (1957) and has illustrated many books on birds.

Petrified Forest, The (1935), a play by ROBERT E. SHERWOOD. The background of this powerful play is an Arizona desert. To a gasoline station and cheap lunchroom comes Alan Squier, an unsuccessful New England author who is hitchhiking to California. At his own request a gangster kills Alan, but not before the latter has altered his insurance policy to make the daughter of the proprietor his beneficiary, so that she can escape from her sordid environment. Edmond Gagey said of the play: "No dramatic work better expresses the complete disillusionment of the postwar [post-World War I] era."

Petry, Ann (b. Old Saybrook, Conn., Oct. 12, 1911—   ), pharmacist, advertising agent, newspaperwoman, editor, short-story writer, novelist. In 1945 a Houghton Mifflin scholarship made it possible for her to complete her first book, *The Street* (1946), one of the best novels ever written about Harlem. Two later novels show Mrs. Petry's familiarity with Connecticut, both its Negro and white inhabitants: *Country Place* (1947) and *The Narrows* (1953). *Harriet Tubman: Conductor on the Underground Railway* (1955) was a juvenile.

Pfaff's Cellar. A famous tavern at 653 Broadway near Bleecker St., New York City, this was the meeting place for the "Bohemians" of the 1850's. WALT WHITMAN, Henry Clapp, Ada Clare, FITZ-JAMES O'BRIEN, BAYARD TAYLOR, GEORGE ARNOLD, ADAH MENKEN, and WILLIAM WINTER were among the regular members. The group was scattered by the Civil War, but the Bohemians had written so much in praise of Pfaff's that it flourished as a tourist attraction for many years. A lively account of Pfaff's Cellar is found in Albert Parry's *Garrets and Pretenders* (1933).

Phaenomena Quaedam Apocalyptica ad Aspectum Novi Orbis Configurata (1697), an interpretation of *Revelations* by SAMUEL SEWALL. Some political events of the day, particularly the difficulties with Governor Andros, turned Judge Sewall to the prophecies of St. John. He published this pamphlet as tending "toward a description of the New Heaven," namely, New England. For the most part he wrote of defects and weaknesses, but despite its blemishes Sewall foresaw a great future for the country he loved. While contemporary New England writers were still talking about English landscapes, Sewall wrote in loving detail about Plum Island, where he had played as a boy.

Phalanx. See NORTH AMERICAN PHALANX.

Phelps, Elizabeth [Stuart] ["H. Trusta"] (b. Andover, Mass., Aug. 13, 1815—d. Nov. 30, 1852), novelist. Using her own experiences as a basis, Mrs. Phelps wrote many popular books, largely religious in content: *Sunny Side, or, The Country Minister's Wife* (1851); *A Peep at Number Five, or, A Chapter in the Life of a City Pastor* (1851); *The Angel Over the*

Right Shoulder (1852); *The Tell-Tale* (1853); and others. She also wrote books for children, including the four-volume "Kitty Brown" series (1850 and later). Her daughter, Elizabeth, also became an author. See ELIZABETH STUART PHELPS WARD.

Phelps, William Lyon (b. New Haven, Conn., Jan. 2, 1865—d. Aug. 21, 1943), teacher, critic, essayist, lecturer. Phelps' long career teaching from 1891 until 1933 was spent almost entirely at Yale. His industry, wit, and enthusiasm for athletics and college life in general, as well as for literature, made him a popular figure. His early work *The Beginnings of the English Romantic Movement* (1893) is still an important study. Phelps was one of the first champions of the Russian novel; his *Essays on Russian Novelists* (1911) was widely influential. From 1922 until his death he conducted a section for *Scribner's* magazine entitled AS I LIKE IT, selections of which were published under the same title in 1923, 1924, and 1926. He also wrote a widely syndicated newspaper column. In later years his criticism tended to become overpopular and overfacile.

Teaching in School and College (1912) is a lively account of his experiences as student and teacher. He also published *Browning: How to Know Him* (1915); *Essays on Modern Dramatists* (1921); *Some Makers of American Literature* (1923); *Essays on American Authors* (1924); *Adventures and Confessions* (1926); *Happiness* (1927); *Love* (1928); *Memory* (1929); *The Excitement of Teaching* (1931); *What I Like in Prose: An Anthology* (1933). He wrote a frank and amusing *Autobiography with Letters* (1939).

Philadelphia Story, The (1939), a play by PHILIP BARRY. It tells the story of Tracy Lord, a young heiress who finds her old Philadelphia family traditions too restrictive, especially after an escapade with a reporter on the eve of her second marriage. The action is hilarious and often startling, and Barry aims some sharp barbs at Philadelphia society. Yet his most sympathetic and tolerant character is C. K. Dexter Haven, a man of Tracy's own social set. He was her first husband, and when everything becomes mixed up on the morning of the second wedding, he takes the place of the pompous, priggish new bridegroom and remarries Tracy. The play made a hit on Broadway and was also filmed.

Philenia. The pen name of SARAH WENTWORTH MORTON.

Philip, King. See KING PHILIP.

Philistine, The. A monthly magazine founded in 1895 at East Aurora, N.Y., by ELBERT HUBBARD. A disciple of the British poet and storyteller William Morris (1834–1896), Hubbard sought to do for the American public what Morris seemed to be doing in England, namely, to stigmatize modern machine culture as unesthetic and revive an interest in the arts and crafts. The magazine, a vehicle especially for Hubbard's apothegms, was an instrument of adult education. The most famous piece to appear in it was A MESSAGE TO GARCIA (1899), an inspirational exhortation that was later reprinted many times. The magazine suspended publication in 1915, shortly after Hubbard went down with the *Lusitania.*

Phillips, David Graham ["John Graham"] (b. Madison, Ind., Oct. 31, 1867—d. Jan. 24, 1911), journalist, novelist. Phillips worked for the Cincinnati *Times-Star,* the New York *Tribune,* the New York *Sun,* and the New York *World.* From 1901 to 1911 he published many muckraking articles; the series entitled *The Treason of the Senate* was published in *Cosmopolitan* in 1906. He also wrote twenty-three "problem" novels, among them *The Great God Success* (1901); *The Cost* (1904); *The Deluge* (1905); *Light-Fingered Gentry* (1907); *The Fashionable Adventures of Joshua Craig* (1909); *The Conflict* (1911); *George Helm* (1912). A number of his novels, as well as his only play, *The Worth of a Woman* (1908), deal with his era's changing attitudes toward women. His most important novel, SUSAN LENOX: HER FALL AND RISE (1917), a well-documented account of a country girl who becomes a prostitute, led his friends to call him an American Balzac.

Phillips wrote speedily but with care, and if his novels are not literature they are journalism at its best. His career was cut short by a madman who shot him when he was walking near Gramercy Park in New York; the assailant believed Phillips had maligned his sister in *Joshua Craig.* I. F. Marcosson published *David Graham Phillips and His Times* in 1932. In the symposium *Eighteen from Princeton* (1946), Eric F. Goldman wrote of Phillips as a "Victorian Critic of Victorianism."

Phillips, Henry Wallace (b. New York City, Jan. 11, 1869—d. May 23, 1930), miner, teacher, writer. Phillips was one of the best writers of Western stories, although his work today is almost entirely neglected. He created a cowboy hero named "Red Saunders" who contrived to get himself, his friends, and his foes into innumerable difficulties, mostly funny. The stories were illustrated by a master artist, A. B. FROST. Phillips was a good friend of another writer of western tales, EUGENE MANLOVE RHODES, and occasionally collaborated with him. Among Phillips' books: *Red Saunders* (1902); *Plain Mary Smith: A Romance of Red Saunders* (1905); *Mr. Scraggs: Introduced by Red Saunders* (1906); *Red Saunders' Pets and Other Critters* (1906); *The Mascot of Sweetbriar Gulch* (1908); *Trolley Folly* (1909).

Phillips, John S[andburn] (b. Council Bluffs, Iowa, July 2, 1861—d. Feb. 28, 1949), editor, publisher, syndicate owner. In 1886 Phillips and SAMUEL S. MCCLURE founded a newspaper syndicate, in 1893 MCCLURE'S MAGAZINE, which became one of the most influential publications of the muckraking era. In 1906 Phillips took over the AMERICAN MAGAZINE and remained with it until 1938. He was also a book publisher, first with the firm of McClure, Phillips & Co. (1900–1906), then as president of the Phillips

Publishing Co. (1906–10). He published a book of his own called *The Papers: Occasional Pieces* (1936).

Phillips, Wendell (b. Boston, Mass., Nov. 29, 1811—d. Feb. 2, 1884), lawyer, orator, reformer. Phillips graduated from Harvard Law School and was admitted to the bar in 1834. In 1835 he witnessed the mobbing of WILLIAM LLOYD GARRISON by proslavery sympathizers, an incident that changed the course of his life. Joining Garrison in the Anti-Slavery Society, he devoted all his time to lecturing in favor of abolition, even though sometimes threatened with the lunatic asylum. A brilliant and gifted speaker, he introduced a direct and colloquial manner of public speaking as opposed to the elaborate and flowery style then in vogue. After the Civil War he labored for prohibition, women's suffrage, prison reform, and various administrative changes. The first volume of his *Speeches, Lectures, and Letters* appeared in 1863, the second in 1891. George L. Austin's *Life and Times of Wendell Phillips* (1884) and Lorenzo Sears' *Wendell Phillips* (1909) throw additional light on this great Bostonian. His achievements, along with those of Garrison, are also described in Ralph Korngold's *Two Friends of Man* (1950).

Philosophy 4 (1903), a humorous—and snobbish—story of undergraduate life at Harvard by OWEN WISTER. Alexander Woollcott excoriated it in *While Rome Burns* (1934).

Philosophy of Composition, The (*Graham's Magazine*, April, 1846), an essay by EDGAR ALLAN POE. This is perhaps the most famous piece of criticism in American literature. It seeks to explain the nature of literary composition by taking the reader into the workshop of Poe's mind when he was composing THE RAVEN. Poe insists that careful planning must precede the writing of any poem, and that the plan must foresee the *dénouement* from the beginning. A pattern must be elaborated, the exact nature of the effect to be produced must be analyzed. To show what he means, Poe explains how in planning *The Raven* he deliberately kept the poem brief, included a refrain in order to achieve the poetic effect he wanted, chose a single word ("nevermore") for this refrain, selected the death of a beautiful woman as the most poetic of all topics. Poe's rational dissection of the poem has injured the esthetic sensibilities of some readers, and others have scoffed at Poe's claim to deliberate objectivity in the composition of poetry. Poe may have juggled his data a bit to make his point, but he performed a valuable service in analyzing the actual processes of inspiration.

Philo Vance. See VANCE, PHILO.

Phips [or Phipps], Sir William (b. Maine, Feb. 2, 1651—d. Feb. 18, 1695), soldier, governor. A skilled mariner, Phips was knighted for recovering treasure from a vessel sunk off Haiti. He commanded Massachusetts troops in the capture of Port Royal (1690) and in an unsuccessful attack on Quebec, and was made royal governor of Massachusetts Bay Colony. He was among those responsible for the execution of twenty innocent persons during the Salem witchcraft trials. Phips appears as an animal character in Cotton Mather's *Political Fables* (1692) and under his own name in Nathaniel Hawthorne's *Fanshawe and Other Pieces* (1876). Alice Lounsbury wrote *Sir William Phips* (1941).

Phoenix, John. The pen name of GEORGE HORATIO DERBY (1823–1861), California newspaperman. One of his books, a volume of sketches and burlesques, was called *Phoenixiana* (1856).

Piatt, John James (b. James' Mills, Ind., March 1, 1835—d. Feb. 16, 1917), newspaperman, writer, editor, consul. Piatt first worked for the *Ohio State Journal* when WILLIAM DEAN HOWELLS was a member of the staff. They published together *Poems of Two Friends* (1860). Thereafter Piatt wrote for the Louisville (Ky.) *Journal*, the Cincinnati (Ohio) *Chronicle*, and the Cincinnati *Commercial*, and edited *The Midland* and *Uncle Remus' Home Magazine*. From 1882 to 1893 he served as American consul at Cork, then at Dublin. Meanwhile he published many pleasant volumes of carefully written verse, including *Poems in Sunshine and Firelight* (1866); *Western Windows and Other Poems* (1869); *Idyls and Lyrics of the Ohio Valley* (1881); *Odes in Ohio and Other Poems* (1897). His wife, Sarah Morgan [Bryan] Piatt (b. Lexington, Ky., Aug. 11, 1836—d. Dec. 22, 1919), wrote similar pleasing, conventional verse; they often published volumes together, like *The Nests at Washington and Other Poems* (1864) and *The Children Out-of-Doors: A Book of Verses by Two in One House* (1885).

Piazza Tales, The (1856), a collection of six stories by HERMAN MELVILLE. All the tales except "The Piazza," which Melville wrote as an introductory sketch for the collection, were selected from among fifteen stories that had been previously published in magazines; the five that comprise *The Piazza Tales* all appeared in *Putnam's Monthly Magazine*, and are among the finest stories he ever wrote.

"The Bell Tower" is a story of the artist Bannadonna, who, in creating a mechanical man, strives to rival the power of God; but Bannadonna is destroyed by his own creation, and Melville invokes the obvious moral: "And so pride went before the fall." Somewhat similar in theme to "The Bell Tower" is "The Lightning-Rod Man," which tells how a lightning-rod salesman tries to sell his wares one stormy afternoon. But the householder refuses to purchase a rod, believing that, though man cannot control the acts of Deity, he should not fear Him.

"THE ENCANTADAS, OR, THE ENCHANTED ISLES" is a collection of ten sketches set in the Galápagos Islands, which Melville visited as a seaman in 1841. The sketches are uneven in quality; probably the best are the powerfully sentimental tale of the Chola Widow and the magnificent descriptions of "The Isles at Large."

In this latter sketch Melville describes the general appearance of the Encantadas—ashy, barren, inhabited by enormous tortoises—until he transforms them into symbols of hell on earth.

"The Piazza" and "Benito Cereno" bear some resemblance to one another in their investigation into the difference between appearance and reality, but "The Piazza" is by far the less important of the two. "Benito Cereno" is a minor triumph, flawed only by its ending, which is delivered as a document rather than integrated as art. Most of the action takes place aboard the *San Dominick,* a slave ship commanded by Benito Cereno. Although the captain appears to be in command, in reality he is the prisoner of the slaves, who are led by the Senegalese Babo, posing as Cereno's valet. The narrative gradually unfolds through the consciousness of Captain Amasa Delano of Massachusetts, who, in his innocence, never more than suspects the evil he cannot quite plumb. Eventually the conspirators are undone and Babo put to death, but Cereno dies soon afterward. Melville based the story on facts taken from *A Narrative of Voyages and Travels in the Northern and Southern Hemispheres* (1817), by AMASA DELANO.

BARTLEBY THE SCRIVENER, considered by some critics to be the best story of the collection, deals with an enigmatic young scrivener who refuses to work but will not leave his employer's office. Strongly disturbed by Bartleby, for whom he feels somehow responsible, the employer moves his office elsewhere, and Bartleby is taken to prison, where he dies.

Pickens, William (b. Anderson Co., S.C., Jan. 15, 1881—d. Apr. 6, 1954), teacher, government official, writer. Pickens taught the ancient languages, German, and other subjects at several universities, was an officer of the National Association for the Advancement of Colored People, and wrote books in several fields. Among them: *Abraham Lincoln* (1909); *The Heir of Slaves* (1910); *Frederick Douglass* (1912); *50 Years of Emancipation* (1913); *American Aesop* (1926).

Pickering, John (b. Salem, Mass., Feb. 7, 1777—d. May 5, 1846), lawyer, diplomat, linguist. Pickering was attached to the legations in Lisbon and London, then returned to the United States and was admitted to the bar. In 1829 he became City Solicitor in Boston. He became adept in many different tongues; Franklin Edgerton described him as "one of the two greatest general linguists of the first half of the 19th century in America." His two greatest linguistic interests were the languages spoken by American Indians and the special locutions that English-speaking residents of the United States had adopted. On the former subject he wrote an article for the *Memoirs* (1820) of the American Academy entitled *On the Adoption of a Universal Orthography for the Indian Languages of North America.* On the other subject he wrote the first formal work on American: *A Vocabulary, or, Collection of Words and Phrases Which Have Supposed to Be Peculiar to the*

U.S. of America (1816). In 1817 Noah Webster wrote *A Letter to the Honorable John Pickering on the Subject of His Vocabulary.* In this he took exception to some of Pickering's assertions. See TIMOTHY PICKERING.

Pickering, Timothy (b. Salem, Mass., July 17, 1745—d. Jan. 29, 1829), public official. Pickering served in the Pennsylvania Constitutional Convention, became postmaster-general, secretary of war, secretary of state, United States Senator, and Congressman. The best known of his writings is the *Political Essays Series of Letters Addressed to the People of the U.S.* (1812), in connection with his ideas for a New England Confederacy. JOHN PICKERING was his son. Octavius Pickering and C. W. Upham wrote *The Life of Timothy Pickering* (4 v., 1867–73).

Pickthall, Marjorie L[owrey] C[hristie] (b. England, Sept. 14, 1883—d. April 19, 1922), Canadian poet, novelist. Miss Pickthall was brought by her parents to Toronto in 1890. She worked for a short time as a librarian, published short stories and some novels, including *Little Hearts* (1915), but it was her poetry that won a wide reputation. She issued several collections: *Drift of Pinions* (1912); *Lamp of Poor Souls* (1916); *The Wood Carver's Wife and Other Poems* (1922). Her father Arthur C. Pickthall edited her *Collected Poems* (1927). Her verses are melodic, in traditional forms, with a constantly wistful note. She came under the influence of the Celtic Renaissance, but often employed Canadian themes and backgrounds.

Picturesque Word Origins (1933), a collection of articles on the etymology of words, compiled by the editorial staff of G. & C. Merriam Co. The words selected for treatment range from *abet,* which has its origin in the baiting of wild animals, to *yuletide,* which meant "jolly" plus "time," just as it does now. Words used today are shown to be derived from the slang of Roman soldiers or the lingo of Malay savages.

Pidgin, Charles Felton (b. Roxbury, Mass., Nov. 11, 1844—d. June 3, 1923), newspaperman, public official, novelist. Pidgin wrote some entertaining and accurate historical and regional novels. The best known is *Quincy Adams Sawyer, or, Mason's Corners Folks* (1900), a study of Yankee idiosyncrasies said to have been inspired by James Russell Lowell's *The Courtin'.* Pidgin also took a chivalrous interest in Aaron Burr and wrote three books in his defense— *Blennerhassett* (1901), *Little Burr: The Warwick of America* (1905), and *Theodosia* [Burr], *The First Gentlewoman of Her Time* (1907). *Quincy Adams Sawyer* was dramatized as *The Courtin',* a comic opera successfully produced in 1913.

Pier, Arthur Stanwood (b. Pittsburgh, Pa., April 21, 1874—d. Aug. 14, 1966), editor, writer. On winning a short-story competition, Pier abandoned his studies of law for an editorial position with the YOUTH'S COMPANION. He was also editor of the *Harvard Graduates' Magazine* from 1918 until 1930. From 1930 until 1944 he taught English at St. Paul's School, Concord, N.H., which he had attended as a boy and which was the inspiration of many of his stories: *The Boys of St. Timothy's* (1904); *Harding of St. Timothy's* (1906); *The New Boy* (1908); *The Jester of St. Timothy's* (1911). In 1913 he published a brief *Story of Harvard*. His later boys' books emphasized sport: *The Coach* (1928); *The Captain* (1929); *The Rigor of the Game* (1929); *The Cheer Leader* (1930); *The Champion* (1931). In 1934 he wrote *St. Paul's School, 1855–1934*. Among his other books are *American Apostles to the Philippines* (1950) and *Forbes, Telephone Pioneer* (1953).

Pierce, Franklin (b. Hillsboro, N.H., Nov. 23, 1804—d. Oct. 8, 1869), 14th President. Pierce graduated from Bowdoin College in the same class with Longfellow and Hawthorne, then studied law. After a few years in the State Legislature, he was elected to Congress. In 1837 he became a United States Senator, in 1842 district attorney of New Hampshire. He enlisted in the Mexican War, became a brigadier general in 1847. A "dark horse" Democratic candidate in the 1852 Presidential campaign, Pierce defeated General WINFIELD SCOTT, the Whig candidate. His administration was marred by an imperialistic foreign policy and by a conciliatory attitude toward slavery that culminated in the Kansas-Nebraska bill, which allowed settlers to decide whether or not to have slaves and which would have repealed the Missouri Compromise. Pierce did not seek re-election, but retired to Concord, N.H. When the Civil War broke out he supported the Northern cause.

William Rufus King and NATHANIEL HAWTHORNE both wrote campaign biographies of Pierce in 1852. Hawthorne's biography was an act of friendship and loyalty; Pierce, however weak as a President, was as a man honest, generous, charming, well-educated. Some of his writings have been published in *Messages and Papers of the Presidents* (1897) by J. D. Richardson and in the *Calendar of the Papers of Franklin Pierce* (1917). Some of his correspondence was published in *American Historical Review* (Vol. 10). R. F. Nichols wrote a life (1931), reissued in a second revised edition (1958).

Pierce, Lorne (b. Delta, Ont., Aug. 3, 1890—d. Nov. 27, 1961), editor, biographer, literary historian. Pierce received degrees in theology and letters from various Canadian and American universities, was ordained in 1916, and became editor-in-chief of the Ryerson Press in 1920. In this latter capacity he encouraged numerous young Canadian writers and published their work. He also founded several awards for literature. He wrote numerous articles and textbooks as well as many volumes about the Canadian people and their arts, including: *Marjorie Pickthall, a Book of Remembrance* (1925); *William Kirby: the Portrait of a Loyalist* (1929); *Master Builders* (1937); *A Canadian People* (1945); *Grace Coombs: Artist* (1949). He also edited collections of Canadian prose and poetry, such as: *The Makers of Canadian Literature* (13 v., 1922); *Alfred Lord Tennyson and William Kirby* (1929), correspondence between the two

poets; and *Bliss Carman's Scrapbook* (1931).

Pierpont, John (b. Litchfield, Conn., April 6, 1785—d. Aug. 27, 1866), clergyman, poet. Like many other unsuccessful lawyers, Pierpont turned from the bar to literature, publishing *Airs of Palestine*, his first book of poems, in 1816. He attended Harvard Divinity School and became pastor of the Hollis Street Church in Boston in 1819. His antislavery views and advocacy of temperance and other unpopular causes led to his transfer to a Unitarian church in Troy, N.Y., and then to West Medford, Mass. From 1861 until his death he served as clerk in the Treasury Department in Washington. He published two later books of poetry, *Airs of Palestine and Other Poems* (1840) and *The Anti-Slavery Poems of John Pierpont* (1843). He also edited two school readers, *The American First Class Book* (1823) and *The National Reader* (1827).

Pierre, or The Ambiguities (1852), a novel by HERMAN MELVILLE. *Pierre* is a deeply personal, desperately pessimistic book, one which more nearly than any other projects Melville's own psychological conflicts and the effects of his own tormented sensibility. At times beautifully written, at times turgid, *Pierre* always suggests the author's own inner turbulence; its one great artistic fault is a failure to observe that artistic distance proper between an author and his work.

Pierre describes how Pierre Glendinning, a young writer, heir to a country estate and a pleasantly semiaristocratic life, rejects both, as well as his fiancée, Lucy Tartan, in an effort to legitimize the claim and protect the interests of a young woman, Isabel, who, on the slimmest of evidence, has convinced Pierre that they are brother and sister. Removing from the country to New York City, Pierre tries to establish a genuinely noble relationship with this alluring woman and, at the same time, write what he regards as truth at all costs. Pierre's collision with society is nothing short of calamitous; he is disowned by his relatives, forced to live in the poverty of a social bohemia, and eventually dies in prison. In the disastrous pursuit of principle, he indirectly causes the death of his mother, Lucy, and Isabel; he is directly responsible for the death of his cousin before he himself commits suicide. Furthermore, his decision to regard Isabel as a sister and to treat her with honor and respect backfires completely, for he recognizes the onset of incestuous passions—a recognition which concludes Pierre's transformation from a charming innocent into a tempestuous cynic.

Pike, Albert (b. Boston, Dec. 29, 1809—d. April 2, 1891), lawyer, soldier, editor, writer. This remarkable man had several careers, first as a hunter and trapper in the Southwest, then as an editor and lawyer in Arkansas and as the compiler of many volumes of reports of law cases, thereafter as a soldier in the Mexican War and in the Confederate army. He was accused of atrocities in his use of Indian troops, and for a time was forced to flee to Canada; his property was confiscated in 1865. He practiced law not only in Little Rock but also in New Orleans, Memphis, and Washington. He became a Mason in 1850 and after the Civil War devoted himself to making revisions of the Scottish Rite ceremonials.

Pike was a fluent and energetic writer who hoped to be remembered for his poetry. His *Prose Sketches and Poems Written in the Western Country* (1834) has been praised for its vivid depiction of the early Southwest. The attacks on him during the Civil War led to his *Letter to the President of the Confederate States* (1862). As a Mason he wrote *The Morals and Dogma of the Ancient and Accepted Scottish Rite* (1872). Two collections of Pike's verse appeared: *Nugae* (1854) and *Hymns to the Gods and Other Poems* (1872; pub. in enlarged form, 1873, 1882). These and many uncollected poems were gathered by his daughter in three volumes (1900, 1916, 1916). One of Pike's poems, *The Widowed Heart*, appeared two years before Poe's THE RAVEN, which bears some striking resemblances to it. Pike accused Poe of plagiarism; Poe may have been familiar with the poem, but he certainly used his own material and handling.

Pike, Zebulon Montgomery (b. Lamberton, N.J., Jan. 5, 1779—d. April 27, 1813), explorer, soldier. The son of an army officer, Zebulon Pike entered his father's company at fifteen; at twenty-six he was commissioned by James Wilkinson, governor of the Louisiana Territory, to explore the West. He made several important expeditions, on one of which he caught his first glimpse of the mountain that bears his name and declared it unclimbable. He died in battle during an invasion of Canada in the War of 1812. His *Account of an Expedition to the Sources of the Mississippi and through the Western Parts of Louisiana* was published in 1810. The standard edition (3 v., 1895) has a memoir and notes by Elliott Coues. *Zebulon Pike's Arkansaw Journal* was edited by S. H. Hart and A. B. Hulbert in 1932. Pike was a man of vivid imagination and considerable gift of style. W. Eugene Hollon wrote *The Lost Pathfinder: Zebulon Montgomery Pike* (1949).

Pike County Ballads (1871), a collection of poems by JOHN HAY. These verses were written in western dialect and immediately became very popular, starting a fashion in regional literature. According to Bayard Taylor (1860), "A *pike* in the California dialect is a native of Missouri, Arkansas, northern Texas, or southern Illinois. The first emigrants that came over the plains were from Pike Co., Mo. . . . He is the Anglo-Saxon relapsed into semi-barbarism. He is long, lathy, and sallow; he expectorates vehemently; he takes naturally to whisky." Many eastern aesthetes objected bitterly to the popularity that Hay and BRET HARTE gave to the Pike County personalities and their dialect. This attitude affected Hay himself, who wanted people to forget that he had ever written the half-dozen or so poems in dialect that made him famous. The best known of the *Ballads* are JIM

BLUDSO OF THE PRAIRIE BELL and LITTLE BREECHES. Undoubtedly MARK TWAIN learned much from both Hay and Harte, and his Missouri characters are likely to talk the Pike dialect. See GEORGE HORATIO DERBY.

Pike County Puzzle (Aug. 28, 1894), the first and only issue of a magazine written and edited by STEPHEN CRANE. It is four pages folio, unbound. It was prepared at a summer camp, with the help of some of Crane's friends, and was intended as a burlesque of a country newspaper. It is one of the rarest of Stephen Crane items.

Pilgrims, The. A name given to English settlers who landed from the *Mayflower* at what is now Provincetown, Mass., on Nov. 21, 1620, and who on Dec. 21 went on to what is now Plymouth. They were one of the most courageous, free-spirited, and sturdy groups that ever landed on American shores. Often confused with the Puritans, who settled other parts of Massachusetts, they have perhaps been most thoroughly revealed in GEORGE F. WILLISON's *Saints and Strangers* (1945). Willison demonstrates that in creed and historical experiences they differed greatly from the Puritans. Theologically the Puritans, whatever their criticism of the Established Church, remained a part of it at first and in general accepted its religious beliefs and practices. But the Pilgrims were Separatists who sought to restore the church "to its primitive order, liberty, and beauty." Unlike the Puritans of Boston, they passed no laws against "gay apparel," often had large and varied wardrobes.

The Pilgrims had a difficult time during their first year; half of them died during that period. The Indians were on the whole kind to them, and made treaties which were better kept, as usual, by the red men than by the palefaces. When the first anniversary of their landing was celebrated, they did not eat turkey, contrary to the legend, but venison, eel, and other delicacies. A legendary romance flourished in the case of the trio whom Longfellow celebrated in THE COURTSHIP OF MILES STANDISH (1858)—John and Priscilla Alden and Standish—and who have since been favorites of many novelists.

The earliest published account of the Plymouth Colony was Robert Cushman's *A Sermon Preached at Plymouth* (1622). *Mourt's Relation* (1622) is a document with a strange history that gives WILLIAM BRADFORD's [1] account of his experiences. Several novelists have endeavored to tell the "truth" about the colony, among them Helen Grace Carlisle in *We Begin* (1932), which introduces Freud to a strange company, and Ernest Gebler in *The Plymouth Adventure* (1950). Willison also edited *The Pilgrim Reader* (1953), in which the Pilgrims were allowed to tell their own story in a group of carefully arranged extracts. See THE MAYFLOWER.

Pilot, The (1823), a novel by JAMES FENIMORE COOPER. With this book Cooper entered the third of the fictional realms in which he did his greatest work: first, history, in THE SPY (1821); then the frontier, in THE PIONEERS

(1823); finally, the sea, which Cooper himself knew best of all from his own experience. He was attempting to demonstrate that he could write a sea story better than Sir Walter Scott's *The Pirate* (1822)—at least in nautical details. The mysterious central figure, Mr. Gray, is obviously modeled on JOHN PAUL JONES. There is some of the customary inept love-making which Cooper always thought necessary to bring into his stories, but the exciting action at sea makes the novel great. The notable character-drawing is found in lesser figures, especially LONG TOM COFFIN of Nantucket, usually regarded as a counterpart at sea of NATTY BUMPPO on land. The book, with its patriotic appeal and its breezy sea episodes, was an immediate success in the United States and England.

Pinchot, Gifford (b. Simsbury, Conn., Aug. 11, 1865—d. Oct. 4, 1946), forester, public official, author. Pinchot rendered inestimable services to the cause of good government and of conservation and inspired some of Theodore Roosevelt's most fruitful activities. He studied forestry abroad, returned to become the first professional American forester, served as chief of the Forest Service in the U.S. Department of Agriculture (1898–1910). He taught forestry at Yale University (1903–36) and with his brother Amos founded the Pinchot School of Forestry there. He was commissioner of forestry in Pennsylvania from 1920 to 1922, governor of that state from 1923 to 1927 and from 1931 to 1935. Pinchot wrote numerous technical works on forestry, including *A Primer of Forestry* (1899, 1905). He also wrote *The Fight for Conservation* (1909); *To the South Seas* (1930); *Just Fishing Talk* (1936); *Breaking New Ground* (1946). His best known work is *The Training of a Forester* (1914), which was rewritten for its fourth edition (1937).

Pinckney, Charles (b. Charleston, S.C., Oct. 26, 1757—d. Oct. 29, 1824), soldier, public official. After serving in the Continental Army and the Continental Congress, Pinckney was elected to the Constitutional Convention. There he submitted, in what became known as the "Pinckney Draught," more than thirty provisions later incorporated in the Constitution. Later he served as governor of South Carolina, as United States Senator, as Minister to Spain, as a member of the House of Representatives. In his later years he veered from Federalist allegiance to Jeffersonianism. His *Speeches* were collected in 1800. His services in drafting the Constitution have been studied in C. C. Nott's *The Mystery of the Pinckney Draught* (1908) and A. J. Bethea's *Contribution of Charles Pinckney to the Formation of the American Union* (1937).

Pinckney, Charles Cotesworth (b. Charleston, S.C., Feb. 25, 1746—d. Aug. 16, 1825), soldier, lawyer, public official, diplomat. Pinckney, a cousin of Charles Pinckney, was educated in England and admitted to the bar there; he also studied at the Royal Military College at Caën, France. On his return to America he was admitted to the South Carolina bar and began a successful practice in Charleston. He was a member (1775) of the first South Carolina Provincial Congress; in 1779 was chosen president of the South Carolina Senate and served in the war. He was a delegate to the Constitutional Convention and helped in obtaining ratification of the Constitution by South Carolina.

He went to France in 1797 with a mission that included JOHN MARSHALL and ELBRIDGE GERRY. French agents demanded a bribe before they would proceed with negotiations, but Pinckney is said to have replied, "Not a sixpence!" The mission's official report identified the men simply as Messieurs X, Y, and Z. The report was made public, excited wide comment, and the episode became known as the "XYZ affair." On June 18, 1798, a banquet was given in Marshall's honor in Philadelphia, with defiance to France uttered in all the toasts and speeches. The eleventh toast was offered by Robert Goodloe Harper: "Millions for defense, but not one cent for tribute!" The words were erroneously attributed to Pinckney, and were inscribed on his cenotaph in St. Michael's Church in Charleston. Pinckney was an unsuccessful candidate for the Vice-Presidency (1800) and for the Presidency (1804, 1808).

Pinckney, Josephine [Lyons Scott] (b. Charleston, S.C., Jan. 25, 1895—d. Oct. 4, 1957), poet, novelist. Miss Pinckney began as a poet, went on to write novels, both mainly about Charleston and the Carolinian scene; her poems are melodious and decorative, but always there is an intellectual, often a comic content. The instinct for comedy, rare in a poet, comes out strongly in her novels, which are amusing studies of manners, keenly observed. Her collection of verse, made in 1927, was called *Sea-Drinking Cities*. Among her novels: *Hilton Head* (1941); THREE O'CLOCK DINNER (1945); *Great Mischief* (1948); *Splendid in Ashes* (posthumous, 1958).

Pinkerton, Allan (b. Scotland, Aug. 25, 1819—d. July 1, 1884), detective, memoirist. Pinkerton came to the United States in 1842 and established a detective agency, said to be the first in this country, in Chicago in 1850. He gained great fame by solving express company thefts and by guarding President-elect Lincoln against an attempted assassination. He organized the Secret Service of the North during the Civil War and did important espionage and counterespionage work. Later he won notoriety, rather than fame, by his ruthless suppression of labor agitations, especially in the Homestead Strike (1892); his methods occasioned a Congressional investigation. He helped break up the renowned gang called the MOLLY MAGUIRES. He wrote many memoirs, but Howard Haycraft speaks of these as "semifictional." Among them were *The Expressman and the Detective* (1874); *The Molly Maguires and the Detectives* (1878); *Criminal Reminiscences and Detective Sketches* (1879); *The Spy of the Rebellion* (1883); *Bank Robbers and Detectives* (1883); *30 Years a Detective* (1884). R. W. Rowan wrote an account of *The Pinkertons* (1931).

Pinkney, Edward Coote (b. England, of

American parentage, Oct. 1, 1802—d. April 11, 1828), midshipman, lawyer, teacher, poet. At the age of nine Pinkney was brought to this country by his father William Pinkney (1764–1822), a distinguished lawyer and diplomat who had been serving his country abroad as a minister dealing with controversial issues between the United States and England. The younger Pinkney entered the navy at the age of fourteen, and served until he challenged his commander to a duel and was forced to resign. He studied law and was admitted to the bar, edited *The Marylander,* taught at the University of Maryland, and published some small collections of verse: *Look Out Upon the Stars, My Love* (1823); *Rodolph: A Fragment* (1823); *Poems* (1825). His poems are melodious and openly derivative. T. O. Mabbott and F. L. Pleadwell, who wrote and compiled *The Life and Works of Edward Coote Pinkney* (1926), feel that Pinkney's originality and power have been underrated.

Pinto, Isaac (b. June 12, 1720—d. Jan. 17, 1791), scholar. Pinto compiled *Prayers for Shabbath, Rosh-Hashanah, and Kippur* (1765–66), intended for descendants of Spanish and Portuguese Jews. The translation is admirably idiomatic, characterized by dignity and simplicity of diction, and is the first Jewish prayer book printed in America, in English.

Pioneer, The (January, February, March, 1843), a magazine founded by JAMES RUSSELL LOWELL and Robert Carter. The importance of this periodical is much greater than its short life would indicate; it ran through only three issues. Lowell hoped that he could put out a magazine superior to the vapid women's magazines then so popular. He also hoped that it might give him economic independence and enable him to marry his beloved Maria White. But the magazine failed, not so much for want of popular support as because the publishers were dishonest, Lowell's eyesight failed, and the subeditor he left in charge was tactless and inefficient.

Some striking contributions appeared in the magazine, among them Nathaniel Hawthorne's *The Birthmark* and *The Hall of Fantasy,* Edgar Allan Poe's *The Tell-Tale Heart* and *Notes Upon English Verse,* and much excellent poetry by John Greenleaf Whittier, Elizabeth Barrett, and others. Some writings by Lowell appeared anonymously. In the February issue appeared, anonymously, the first published poems of Maria White, two sonnets addressed to Lowell. The three issues were reprinted in facsimile (1947) in an edition edited by Sculley Bradley.

Pioneers! O Pioneers! (in *Drum-Taps,* 1865; in *Annex to Leaves of Grass,* 1867), a poem by WALT WHITMAN. In twenty-six stanzas, Whitman addresses a paean to the pioneers of America. The stanzas consist of four lines—the first short, the next two long, the last a refrain, "Pioneers! O pioneers!" The poem is unusually regular in its metrics, compared to most of Whitman's writing.

Pioneers, The, or, The Sources of the Susque-hanna (1823), a novel by JAMES FENIMORE COOPER. This was the first of the LEATHER-STOCKING TALES to be published, but in the order of events in NATTY BUMPPO's life, it is next to the last of the five. In it the conceptions of both the hero and the frontier are not yet clear. Cooper was especially fond of the book because of the many memories of COOPERS-TOWN, New York, and his own youth found in the story. Judge Temple is drawn from his father. The main plot is concerned with the ownership of an estate in upper New York, in 1793. More important is the scrape Natty—now an elderly man—gets into when he shoots a buck out of season, and still more important are the incidental details of background and time.

Piper, Edwin Ford (b. Auburn, Neb., Feb. 8, 1871—d. May 14, 1939), poet, teacher. From 1905 to 1939 Piper taught English at the University of Iowa. His great interest was in folk balladry, especially cowboy songs. He was stimulated to write poems that have much of the tang of popular songs, especially those collected in *Barbed Wire and Wayfarers* (1924). He also wrote *Paintrock Road* (1927) and *Canterbury Pilgrims* (1935) and contributed to *Poetry* magazine and the *Journal of American Folklore.*

Piper, The (1907), a play by JOSEPHINE PRESTON PEABODY. In 1910 this play in verse was awarded first prize among 315 dramas submitted for the opening of the Shakespeare Memorial Theater at Stratford-on-Avon. It was produced that year in Stratford, in 1911 in New York City. The play, skillfully written, was based on the old legend of the Pied Piper of Hamelin, a legend which Miss Peabody turned into a lively version of the conflict between good and evil.

Pisan Cantos, The (1948), ten sections of the longer *Cantos* of EZRA POUND. These sections were written while the poet was imprisoned in an army stockade in Italy for his Fascist radio broadcasts. Many of the obscurities of the poems are to be explained as allusions to personnel of the detention center. "The ripper," for example, represents a sergeant who tore unfastened buttons from the uniforms of trainees. The volume created a furious controversy when a group of poets chosen by the Library of Congress, and including Conrad Aiken, W. H. Auden, and T. S. Eliot, selected *The Pisan Cantos* for the library's Bollingen Prize of 1948. Many critics found it difficult to separate Pound the poet from the poem, as Dwight Macdonald called him, "Mr. Pound the Fascist, Mr. Pound the anti-Semite, Mr. Pound the traitor, Mr. Pound the funny-money crank."

Piston, Walter (b. Rockland, Me., Jan. 20, 1894—   ), composer, painter, teacher. A graduate of Harvard University, Piston began teaching there in 1926. He has composed numerous orchestral and chamber music works; his best known composition is *The Incredible Flutist* (1938), an orchestral suite composed for a ballet showing a country circus. His *Partita for Violin, Viola, and Organ* (1944) was based on passages chosen by Archibald MacLeish from

Carl Sandburg's THE PEOPLE, YES. In 1948 he was awarded a Pulitzer prize for his *Symphony No. 3*. His books include several on harmony and counterpoint. Aaron Copland describes him as "a representative of New England who speaks an international language."

Pit, The (1903), a novel by FRANK NORRIS. The second part of the unfinished trilogy *Epic of the Wheat*, of which THE OCTOPUS was the first, this posthumously published novel is composed of three distinct elements: the adventures of Curtis Jadwin, who attempts to corner the Chicago wheat market; the love story of Jadwin's wife Laura; and the story of the wheat itself, the life force which Norris intended as the great central theme of the trilogy. *The Pit*, lacking the power of *The Octopus*, is more of a conventional melodrama, and much less successful than Norris' other novels. It was dramatized by Channing Pollock in 1904.

Pit and the Pendulum, The (written, 1842; pub. in *The Gift*, 1843), a story by EDGAR ALLAN POE. In this tale suspense is carried to the point of cruelty inflicted on the reader. Poe imagines a man who, after long suffering, is dragged before a court of the Spanish Inquisition in Toledo and given a death sentence—with tortures that have been ingeniously and fiendishly contrived. Exploring his rat-infested cell, he almost plunges into a deep pit. Later, as he lies bound, he perceives above him a knife-edged pendulum that gradually swings lower and lower. He smears food on his ropes; in the nick of time the rats gnaw them through. Even this is not enough torment; the walls of the cell become heated and force him in terror to the edge of the pit—but he is saved at the very last moment when French soldiers capture the city. Poe gathered elements of his plot from several sources: Juan Antonio Llorente's *Critical History of the Spanish Inquisition;* Charles Brockden Brown's EDGAR HUNTLY (1799); William Mudford's story *The Iron Shroud*, from *Blackwood's Magazine*, and two other stories in the same periodical: *The Iron Bell* and *The Involuntary Experimentalist*.

Pitcairn's Island. See MUTINY ON THE BOUNTY.

Pitcher, Moll. A woman whom Richard M. Dorson calls "more celebrated than any other witch of modern times." She lived in Lynn, Mass., died in 1813. Whittier knew about her and wrote a poem in her honor entitled *Moll Pitcher* (1832).

Pitcher, Molly. The heroic young woman who brought water to the exhausted American troops in the battle of MONMOUTH (June 28, 1778) and who herself served at a cannon all that hot Sunday. She was born Mary Ludwig, Oct. 13, 1754. She married John Caspar Hays, who in 1775 enlisted in the colonial artillery, and replaced him at the cannon when he was overcome by heat. The soldiers, who heard her called "Molly" by her husband, called out, "Here comes Molly and her pitcher!" Hence the name. Hays died in 1789; she was remarried to George McCauley. She died Jan. 22, 1832.

Pitkin, Walter B[roughton] (b. Ypsilanti, Mich., Feb. 6, 1878—d. Jan. 25, 1953), teacher, editor, writer. From the University of Michigan Pitkin went abroad to study, came back to teach psychology at Columbia University (1905–09) and in the School of Journalism there (1912–43); in the years between he had worked on newspapers and magazines. He served as editor or adviser to several enterprises —an encyclopedia, the *Farm Journal, Parents' Magazine*, Universal Pictures among them. He wrote many articles and more than forty books. The most successful of these was LIFE BEGINS AT FORTY (1932), the sale of which reached several hundred thousand copies. Among his other books was one on a favorite theme: *Short Introduction to the History of Human Stupidity* (1932). He never went on to write the projected chronicle, but the *Introduction* was translated into fifteen languages. Among his other books: *The Art and Business of the Short Story* (1913); *Must We Fight Japan?* (1920); *The Twilight of the American Mind* (1928); *The Art of Rapid Reading* (1929); *The Psychology of Achievement* (1930); *The Art of Learning* (1931); *More Power to You* (1933); *Take It Easy!* (1935); *Careers After 40* (1937); *Escape from Fear* (1940); *On My Own* (1944); *Road to a Richer Life* (1949).

Plain Dealing (1642), a treatise by Thomas Lechford (fl. 1629–1642). The author came to Boston around 1638, returned to England in 1641. He was a lawyer, the first in New England, but he was no Puritan and had little sympathy for the way in which the colony was administered. In 1641 he was debarred from practice for trying to influence a jury out of court. His *Note-Book Kept by Thomas Lechford, Esq., Lawyer* was first published in an edition prepared by E. E. Hale. It gives a record of his activities and of the group in which he lived from June 27, 1638, to July 21, 1641. In his own lifetime Lechford published *Plain Dealing, or, Notes from New England*. The book was reissued in 1644 as *New England's Advice to Old England;* J. Hammond Trumbull edited it in 1867. Replies were made to some of Lechford's criticisms in an anonymous pamphlet, NEW ENGLAND'S FIRST FRUITS (1643), which was probably written by Henry Dunster, Hugh Peter, and Thomas Weld. This includes an important section on the founding of Harvard University.

Plain Language from Truthful James (*Overland Monthly*, September, 1870), a humorous poem by BRET HARTE. It tells how the humorist BILL NYE and the mining camp character "Truthful" James try to get the better of a Chinese named Ah Sin in euchre. The Chinese player is too good for them, until they discover that he has a card or two up his sleeve—including twenty-four jacks. An agile parodist, Harte cast his poem in Swinburnian rhythms. The poem is believed to have influenced the earlier writings of Kipling. It was included in the first edition of Harte's *Poems* (1871), but immediately was widely reprinted and pirated, usually under the title *The Heathen Chinee*. It has itself been parodied; David McCord regards as particularly good Arthur C. Hilton's *The Heathen Passee*, which deals with cribbing in a Cambridge examination (included in Walter Jerrold and R. M. Leonard's *A Century of Parody*, 1913). It was unsuccessfully dramatized as AH SIN by Harte and MARK TWAIN in 1877.

Plains Indians. A term that includes a large number of Indian tribes. According to Muriel H. Wright, it is sometimes confined to the "Hunters of the Plains," who lived between the Mississippi River and the Rockies; sometimes it also includes "the Woodsmen of the Forests" or "Woodland Tribes," among them the Kiowa, Comanche, Apache, Cheyenne, and Arapaho Indians. Originally they employed dogs for transportation, but they took so quickly to the use of horses that they are sometimes designated as "the Horse Nations of the Plains." They spoke several languages, had numerous differences in culture, but also had some traits in common, such as their nomadic existence and bison-hunting. They were warriors, depended little on agriculture, were expert in leather work, lived in tepees, in general answered to the concept of the Indian presented by Cooper, Longfellow, Neihardt, Parkman, Garland, and Wild West stories and films. Within these tribes much poetry originated: war songs, dream songs, hunting songs, curing spells, game songs, ceremonial chants. See AMERINDIAN POETRY AND PROSE.

Plains or Great Plains, The. Roughly, the region extending from the Mississippi to the Rockies, but excluding the arid portions of the Southwest and the Dakota badlands. Before the white man came, the plains were covered with tough grass which supported huge herds of bison; there were few trees. Today it comprises one of the most important agricultural regions of the world. Two important works on the history of the region are Walter Prescott Webb's *The Great Plains* (1931) and Henry Nash Smith's *Virgin Land: The American West as Symbol and Myth* (1950).

Plastic Age, The (1924), a novel by PERCY MARKS. While on the faculty of Brown University, Marks wrote this fairly realistic narrative of college life, with a vivid description of the manners and morals of the 1920's. It shocked many readers, especially the authorities at Brown.

Players, The. A New York City club, located in the former residence of Edwin Booth at 16 Gramercy Park. Booth donated his home to the club, and after its dedication on Dec. 3, 1888, continued to live there until his death in 1893. His library, bedroom, and working quarters have been preserved intact. The club has a striking collection of theatrical relics, and a fine library, which was opened in 1959 to qualified researchers.

Pledge to the Flag, The. The 400th anniversary of the discovery of America (1892) was celebrated by special exercises in American schools. The program contained the *Pledge to the Flag*, which had been prepared in tentative form by James B. Upham (1845–1905), a member of the publishing firm which issued YOUTH'S COMPANION. It was printed for the first time in the *Companion* (Sept. 8, 1892), has since then been recited in schools everywhere in the United States.

Plimpton, George A[rthur] (b. Walpole, Mass., July 13, 1855—d. July 1, 1936), publisher, bibliophile, historian. Plimpton was from 1914 to 1931 the president of the important Boston textbook firm, Ginn & Co. He was greatly interested in textbooks as a medium of education and in their history and was believed to have made the largest collection of textbooks in the world. He also specialized in Italian literature; his collection was given to Wellesley College. He wrote *The Education of Shakespeare, Illustrated from the Schoolbooks in Use in His Time* (1933) and *The Education of Chaucer, Illustrated from the Textbooks Used in His Time* (1935).

Plummer, Jonathan (b. Newbury, Mass., July 13, 1761—d. Sept. 13, 1819), preacher, pawnbroker, professional writer of love letters, balladist, peddler. Plummer was appointed by TIMOTHY DEXTER as his poet laureate and responded by writing, among other pieces, *The Author's Congratulatory Address to Citizen Timothy Dexter on His Attaining an Independent Fortune* (1793). Another piece of his was called *Parson Pidgin, or, Holy Kissing, Occasioned by a Report That Parson Pidgin Had Kissed a Young Woman* (1807). He peddled in Newbury's Market Square an odd conglomeration of sermons, poems, and notions. His poems were the familiar "broadsides" of his time, providing both news and scandal. He wrote an autobiography in three successive pamphlets, *A Sketch of the History of the Life of Jonathan Plummer* (1797[?]). He is described in John P. Marquand's *Lord Timothy Dexter* (1925).

Plunder (1948), a novel by SAMUEL HOPKINS ADAMS. As in REVELRY (1926), which exposed the corruption of the Harding era, Adams aims a shaft at Washington two decades later—and not much changed. But Adams set the time forward to 1950 and imagined an administration elected by a new party called the "Free Enterprise Non-Political Association." The crooks ride high until they try to take over the football "racket." It is satire done somewhat hastily but with exuberance and wit.

pluralism. A general metaphysical term (meaning a belief in the diversity of ultimate reality) which is often applied specifically to the philosophical system of WILLIAM JAMES. James set forth his beliefs in a series of lectures at Oxford University (1908), then published them (1909) in *A Pluralistic Universe*. He was influenced by BENJAMIN PAUL BLOOD's *Anaesthetic Revelation* (1874). The last work of James' published during his lifetime was an essay on Blood called *A Pluralistic Mystic*, and Blood, who had conducted an active correspondence with James, wrote as his final work a book called *Pluriverse* (1920). Another influence on James may have been George H.

Howison (1834–1916), who developed what he called a personalistic pluralism. James' pithiest statement of his creed was: "*Prima facie* the world is a pluralism; as we find it, its unity seems to be that of any collection."

Plymouth Plantation, A History of (pub. 1856), chronicle by WILLIAM BRADFORD [1]. This work was begun about 1630 and tells of the aspirations and trials of the settlers of Plymouth from 1609 to 1649. Though it remained unpublished until 1856, the *History* reflects the devout character of the greatest of our earliest historians. "Spetiall providences" of God are alluded to throughout the book.

Bradford's style, adapted from that of the Geneva Bible of 1560, is studiously clear. The 1609–1620 section is by far the best from the stylistic point of view; it is relieved by humor, irony, and alliteration. The author's sense of justice and striving for freedom inspired him to become eloquent in parts of this first section. Once Bradford's hard-won freedom was secure, however, he lapsed into keeping a plodding chronicle of the important events of his colony. As the years progressed, the noble artist became more the clever politician and able governor. This is further revealed when Bradford reverts to using letters to further his narrative, rather than original writing. Because of the inclusion of such primary material, however, the book was an important source for other early historians, notably Nathaniel Morton, Thomas Prince, and Cotton Mather. The reader of the *History* comes upon familiar historical incidents in their first recorded form, notably discussions of the actions of Roger Williams and the voyage of the *Mayflower*. The original manuscript was owned by Prince, who bequeathed it to the Old South Church. It disappeared during the Revolution, was discovered in 1855 in the library of the Bishop of London and returned to America.

Pocahontas (b. 1595[?]—d. 1617), Indian girl who befriended white settlers in Virginia. The correct name of this daughter of King Powhatan was Matoaka, Pocahontas being a pet name meaning "playful" which Powhatan applied to several of his children. According to John Smith's *General History of Virginia* (1624), the princess saved him from death at the hands of her father's men. In 1613 she was taken as a hostage by the British but was treated with courtesy. Converted to Christianity and baptized Rebecca, she married JOHN ROLFE in 1614. Shortly afterward she accompanied him to England, where she captivated London society with her beauty and intelligence. She died on shipboard just after leaving England to return to America. She was mentioned by Ben Jonson in his *Staple of News* (1625). Thomas Fuller in his *Worthies of England* (1662) was apparently the first to question Smith's account of his narrow escape; later historians rejected it altogether. However, Bradford Smith in *Captain John Smith, His Life and Legend* (1953) suggests once again that there may have been some truth in the romantic story.

Pocahontas figures in the following works: *Travels* (1803), *Captain Smith and Princess Pocahontas* (1805), and a novel, THE FIRST SETTLERS OF VIRGINIA (1805), by John Davis; THE INDIAN PRINCESS, OR, LA BELLE SAUVAGE (1808), a drama by James Nelson Barker; *Pocahontas, or, The Settlers of Virginia* (1830), a drama by George Washington Parke Custis; *Pocahontas: A Historical Drama in Five Acts* (1837), by Robert Dale Owen; *Powatan, a Metrical Romance* (1841), by Seba Smith; *Pocahontas and Other Poems* (1841), by Lydia H. Sigourney; *Po-ca-hon-tas! or, The Gentle Savage* (1855), a satiric drama by John Brougham; MY LADY POKAHONTAS (1885), a novel by John Esten Cooke; *Pocahontas: A Pageant* (1912), by Margaret Ullman; *Pocahontas, Our Mother* (1917), a poem by Vachel Lindsay; *Pocahontas and the Elders* (1933), a folkpiece in four acts by Virgil Geddes; *Pocahontas* (1933), a novel by David Garnett; *The Bridge* (1930), an epic poem by Hart Crane. See POWHATAN INDIANS.

Poe, Edgar Allan (b. Boston, Jan. 19, 1809— d. Oct. 7, 1849), poet, short-story writer, critic. Poe was the son of a talented actress, Elizabeth Arnold, and her second husband, David Poe, Jr.,

an actor and the son of a prominent officer in the Revolution. Orphaned in Richmond late in 1811, Poe was taken into the home of John Allan, a wealthy merchant. Allan, who regarded the boy as a genius, became his godfather but did not formally adopt him.

The Allan family went to England in 1815, where Poe attended the classical academy of Dr. John Bransby at Stoke Newington. In the summer of 1820 the family returned to Richmond, where the boy entered the school of Joseph H. Clarke, and composed a number of verses in honor of local schoolgirls. These are lost, but a satire, written when Poe was enrolled at the school of William Burke in 1823 and 1824, has survived.

Poe fell in love with Elmira Royster and was secretly engaged when he went to the University of Virginia in February, 1826; however, the engagement came to nothing, for Miss Royster's family intercepted the letters of the pair, and shortly thereafter arranged for her to be married to Alexander Barrett Shelton of Richmond. At the University Poe stood high in Greek, Latin, French, Italian, and Spanish, but remained only one term; apparently Allan had refused Poe spending money, and the young man gambled in hopes of raising funds. When he acquired only debts, Allan withdrew his godson from the university. Tales of Poe's heavy drinking at that time are probably exaggerated; however, Poe was constitutionally unable to tolerate liquor, and even small amounts often had disastrous effects upon him.

On his return to Richmond Poe quarreled with his godfather and ran away to Boston, where he arranged for his first volume, TAMERLANE AND OTHER POEMS (1827), to be published anonymously. Some of the poems concerned his unhappy love affair with Miss Royster; the best one, "The Lake," is about the legends told of the Lake of the Dismal Swamp, near Norfolk. Poe was unable to find employment, and, in desperate financial straits, enlisted in the army under the name of "Edgar A. Perry"; he was sent to Fort Moultrie on Sullivan's Island, the scene of his later story, "The Gold Bug." He wrote to Allan, asking him to help secure his release from the army, but Allan refused until the death of his wife, who pleaded Poe's cause on her deathbed. Allan sent for Poe on the condition that Poe would enter West Point, and the two were reconciled, at least temporarily.

Poe published another volume, *Al Aaraaf, Tamerlane, and Minor Poems* (see AL AARAAF), in Baltimore in 1829. Included is "Fairyland," an archly humorous poem owing something to *A Midsummer Night's Dream* and entirely unlike anything else Poe wrote. He returned to Richmond and quarreled again with John Allan before entering West Point in the summer of 1830. When Allan remarried in October of that year, it was apparent to Poe that he could expect little further aid from that quarter; shortly thereafter Allan disowned him because of a disparaging remark made by Poe in a letter that reached Allan's hands. With no immediate financial resources and no hope of any from the Allan family, Poe set about getting himself expelled from West Point.

Poe came to New York, where he published *Poems* (1831). The preface to this volume shows he took an interest in Coleridge's critical theories, by which some critics feel Poe was influenced. Others find in Poe a kinship to Byron, Moore, and Shelley alone among the great romantics. The influence of the Baltimore lyrist, Edward Coote Pinckney, also seems sure. But Poe was already very much his own man, as is evidenced in the great brief lyric TO HELEN, in ISRAFEL, and in THE SLEEPER, a macabre verse of which its author was curiously fond. The two strange landscapes, THE CITY IN THE SEA, which describes the ruins of Gomorrah, and the "Valley of Unrest," about the Hebrides, show great originality.

Poe went to Baltimore and began to write short stories. Some of these, submitted in a prize contest, were published in the Philadelphia *Saturday Courier* in 1832. In 1833 the MS. FOUND IN A BOTTLE won a $50 prize from the Baltimore *Saturday Visiter* and brought Poe some national recognition. He went to work on a play, POLITIAN, which he never finished. Through the novelist JOHN P. KENNEDY he established a connection with the SOUTHERN LITERARY MESSENGER of Richmond; he became its assistant editor and then, in December, 1835, its editor. He urged high literary standards, and during his editorship the *Messenger's* subscription list increased from 500 to over 3,500. However, his castigations of unimportant books led to literary quarrels from which he was never to be free thereafter. Meanwhile Poe's aunt, Mrs. Maria Poe Clemm, with whom he had resided in Baltimore, arranged a marriage there in September between Poe and her daughter Virginia, who was then only thirteen years old (see VIRGINIA CLEMM). The couple lived for two years as brother and sister, but the marriage led to some social disapproval. Virginia was a devoted and sometimes a tolerant wife, but "never read half" of her husband's poetry. During her life Poe addressed no poems to her. He was apparently very much attached to Mrs. Clemm, who was the mainstay of the family during their long bouts of poverty and Virginia's illness; Poe wrote for her his charming sonnet "To My Mother" (1849).

For the *Messenger* Poe wrote BERENICE and MORELLA, as well as *Hans Pfaal*, a comic tale of a voyage to the moon. (See THE UNPARALLELED ADVENTURES OF ONE HANS PFAAL.) Two poems, "Bridal Ballad" and "To Zante," may have related to a meeting with his first love, Elmira Royster, now Mrs. Shelton. Poe also began a serial, "Arthur Gordon Pym" (see THE NARRATIVE OF ARTHUR GORDON PYM), installments of which appeared in January and February of 1837; however, he then resigned from the *Messenger* and came to New York, where he published the complete serial as a book in 1838. An account of sea adventures based on fact, *The Narrative* is a grotesque and imaginative tale that ends in wildly incredible scenes near the South Pole. It was greatly admired by Charles Baudelaire, though Poe himself called it a silly book.

In the summer of 1838 Poe was in Philadelphia, helping a Professor Thomas Wyatt bring out two books on natural history. Finally he became an editor of *Burton's Gentleman's Magazine* in May, 1839. The magazine was owned by the comedian WILLIAM E. BURTON, with whom Poe remained until they quarreled in June of 1840. Poe had plans for a magazine of his own to be called, punningly, the *Penn*, and later the *Stylus;* beyond several prospectuses, the last in 1848, nothing came of it. He also solved ciphers in a paper called *Alexander's*

Weekly Messenger, and wrote miscellaneous papers, including a few news articles. In the *Saturday Evening Post* for May 1, 1841, Poe predicted the ending of Dickens' *Barnaby Rudge* from the first chapters.

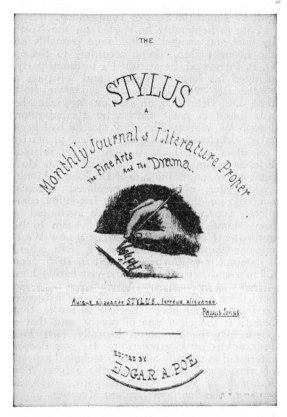

George R. Graham bought Burton out and established GRAHAM'S MAGAZINE in December of 1840. Poe became an editor in charge of reviews with the April issue, and remained until May, 1842. As had been the case with the *Southern Literary Messenger,* the circulation of the magazine increased dramatically while Poe was associated with it.

Although TALES OF THE GROTESQUE AND ARABESQUE (1840), containing twenty-five pieces, sold badly, Poe was busy with short stories, and produced some of his masterpieces. THE MURDERS IN THE RUE MORGUE was in *Graham's* for April, 1841; if not the first DETECTIVE STORY, it was certainly that which set the form. Poe was also to invent almost all the species of the genus; he made an attempt (not wholly successful) to solve a real crime in THE MYSTERY OF MARIE ROGÊT in 1842; he dismissed the crime itself as of no interest in THE PURLOINED LETTER (1844); and in the same year he wrote the little-read "Thou Art the Man," the first story in which the criminal is at first undetected because he looks like a wholly respectable person. Other notable stories written between 1838 and 1843 include LIGEIA, THE FALL OF THE HOUSE OF USHER, WILLIAM WIL-

SON, the enigmatic ELEONORA, THE MASQUE OF THE RED DEATH, THE TELL-TALE HEART, THE BLACK CAT, THE PREMATURE BURIAL, and the most popular of all, THE GOLD BUG, perhaps the greatest of all tales of buried treasure.

Misfortune struck the Poe household in January of 1842 when Virginia broke a blood vessel in singing. Her life was despaired of, and although she recovered somewhat, her health continued to be poor until her death from tuberculosis five years later.

Poe met Charles Dickens in Philadelphia in 1842 and hoped, vainly, to form some connection in England through him. Poe was also in correspondence with JAMES RUSSELL LOWELL; they met in 1845, and did not like each other.

In April of 1844 Poe, with Virginia, Mrs Clemm, and the celebrated pet, Cat-erina, came to New York. He sold his BALLOON-HOAX to the New York *Sun,* and went to work on the genial Major Mordecai M. Noah's paper, the *Sunday Times.* In October he joined N. P. Willis and General George P. Morris on the new "paper for the upper ten thousand," the *Evening Mirror.* He lived for a time "in the country" (near what is now Eighty-seventh St. and Broadway), and there wrote a final draft of THE RAVEN. After it was rejected by Graham, it was sold to George H. Colton for pseudonymous publication in the February issue of a new magazine, the *American Review.* Willis saw it in proof and published it in the *Mirror* on January 29, 1845, with an enthusiastic introduction and the author's name. Success was instantaneous; "Mr. Poe the poet" was to be world famous, permanently.

He became an editor of a weekly paper, the *Broadway Journal,* and published a series of papers on Longfellow's "plagiarisms"—although Poe meant only that Longfellow was a derivative poet. He lectured on poetry at the Society Library. He met Mrs. FRANCES SARGENT OSGOOD (temporarily separated, though not publicly, from her husband), and fell in love with her—perhaps platonically, and in any case with Virginia's approval. He also frequented the salon of Anne Charlotte Lynch, later Mrs. Botta. And he was pursued by Mrs. Elizabeth F. Ellet, a woman of bad character—vain, ambitious only of reputation, and given to writing anonymous letters. This all led to complicated quarrels which may be left to the major biographers. He published *The Raven and Other Poems* and a selection of a dozen of his *Tales.* He went to Boston to lecture, became drunk, and read his poem "Al Aaraaf," which the audience found baffling, although T. W. Higginson testified to its beauty. He became the sole proprietor of the *Broadway Journal,* in which he published revised versions of most of his stories. But the paper collapsed, the last issue being that of January 3, 1846.

At the advice of the eccentric through melodious poet, Dr. THOMAS HOLLEY CHIVERS, he moved again from the city to the cottage at Fordham, his last home. He published THE PHILOSOPHY OF COMPOSITION in *Graham's Magazine* in April of 1846. For *Godey's Lady's Book* he wrote a series of papers called THE LITERATI OF NEW YORK, most of which were innocuous; however, one on Dr. THOMAS DUNN ENGLISH, with whom Poe had had a fist fight (remotely connected with Mrs. Ellet and Mrs. Osgood), led to bitter controversy. Poe ultimately sued for libel and won his case, but at the expense of all reputation for sobriety or reliability. Godey gave up the *Literati* series, but printed THE CASK OF AMONTILLADO, a story of revenge now thought to be in part inspired by the author's own bitter quarrels. The story is ironic—a villain murders his enemy and is not found out; but at the end he realizes that the victim has rested in peace, while he has not.

Early in 1847 Virginia died. Poe was also very ill, and was nursed by Mrs. Clemm and Mrs. Marie Louise Shew; the latter was the daughter of a physician and had been trained as one at home. To her Poe wrote several poems; one, "The Beloved Physician," of some length, is lost save for ten lines. She is supposed to have suggested THE BELLS to him. Mrs. Shew consulted the famous Dr. Valentine Mott about her patient; she was told Poe had had a brain lesion in youth and would not live long. The lesion is thought to have produced manic and depressive periods, which might account for some of Poe's wild freaks and for occasional references to his being kept under sedation. All medical men who knew the poet or have studied his case agree that he did not use drugs habitually. Poe's one important work of 1847 was ULALUME.

Early in 1848 Poe gave a lecture on the universe, which was revised as a book, EUREKA. In September he went to Providence and became engaged to the local poetess, SARAH HELEN WHITMAN, to whom he had written a second "To Helen" (now sometimes called "To Helen Whitman") before their meeting. This affair produced a number of impassioned and very literary letters, but soon ended. Poe had visited Lowell, Massachusetts, in July and lectured on the "Poetic Principle"; while in Lowell he first met Mrs. Annie Richmond, with whom he fell in love. In 1849 he addressed to her a long poem, "For Annie," ascribing his recovery from illness to the thought of the beloved lady's presence.

Poe began to write for the Boston *Flag of Our Union,* a cheap paper that paid well. To it he sent his last horror story, "Hop-Frog," his sonnet "To My Mother," and the short poem "Eldorado," which is about a search for beauty rather than gold. Poe also found a patron, Sarah (or Estelle) Anna Lewis, who employed him as her press agent. Poe and Mrs. Clemm spent a good deal of time visiting the Lewis home in Brooklyn.

Late in June of 1849, after having composed a final version of "The Bells" and ANNABEL LEE, Poe went south. He had a horrible spree in Philadelphia, but was rescued by C. Chauncey Burr, a minor writer, and John Sartain, the engraver who now ran the *Union Magazine.* They sent the poet to Richmond, where he had a happy summer, becoming engaged again to the sweetheart of his youth, the widowed Elmira Royster Shelton. He was also received in society, and enjoyed the friendship of the young poetess Susan Archer Talley, later Mrs. Weiss. Poe lectured both in Richmond and Norfolk. He went on two sprees, however, and on August 27 joined the Sons of Temperance.

Late in September he started for the North by boat and arrived in Baltimore probably on the twenty-eighth. There, according to Bishop O. P. Fitzgerald, he attended a birthday party, pledged his hostess in wine, and went on a spree. His whereabouts are unknown from then until October 3, an election day, when he was found in great distress by a compositor, Joseph W. Walker. The story that he had been taken, drunken or drugged, to polling places by "repeaters" is a hoax, though widely related. Friends brought him to the Washington Hospital where, under the care of Dr. John J. Moran (who later published overcolored reminiscences), he died without ever becoming completely conscious. The last words attributed to him, "Lord, help my poor soul," seem to be authentic. He was buried in what is now Westminster Churchyard on October 8, 1849, where a monument to him was erected in 1875. Mrs. Clemm and her daughter now rest beside him.

Poe was primarily and by choice a poet. He held three important ideas besides his insistence on brevity: that poetry is close to music, that beauty is the chief aim of poetry, and that a poem may be composed logically (see THE PHILOSOPHY OF COMPOSITION). He was deeply interested in prosody and other technical aspects of verse, and published on the subject *The Rationale of Verse* (Oct. and Nov., 1848, in issues of the *Southern Literary Messenger*).

For reasons of economic necessity, Poe wrote little verse between 1831 and 1845, concentrating instead on the tales. Nevertheless, THE HAUNTED PALACE, an allegory of madness, and THE CONQUEROR WORM, the most pessimistic yet the most powerful of all his poems, belong to this period. With the sudden recognition brought by the publication of "The Raven" in 1845, he turned more to poetry. In the last years of his life he wrote the cheerful short lyric "Eulalie"; "The Bells," which had been begun by Mrs. Shew; "For Annie," the simplest of his ballads; and the courageous brief lyric "Eldorado."

Poe cared less for his tales than for his poems. Nevertheless, he had a firm and workable theory about the short story, which he expounded in his famous review (GRAHAM'S MAGAZINE, April–May, 1842) of Hawthorne's *Twice-Told Tales.* A skillful literary artist, said Poe, does not fashion his thoughts to accommodate his incidents, "but having conceived, with deliberate care, a certain unique or single *effect* to be wrought out, he then invents such incidents—he then combines such events as may best aid him in establishing this preconceived effect. . . . In the whole composition there should be no word written, of which the tendency, direct or indirect, is not to the one pre-established design."

He insisted on unity of mood as well as of time, space, and action. Poe is credited with the invention of the modern detective story with its amateur sleuth. He was similarly original in his version of the treasure hunt, "The Gold Bug," particularly in his introduction of a cryptogram.

Although Poe fancied his humorous work, the best of it is too much taken up with the faults and foibles of the world around him. "Some Words with a Mummy," for instance, deals with a brief American fad for Egyptology, and "The Literary Life of Thingum Bob," the best of the humorous tales, was a satire on the magazines of his day. Both are too dated to give pleasure to any but a few students of the period. He also wrote a gentle little love story, "Three Sundays in a Week," but his great stories, beyond any doubt, are the tales of horror, ratiocination, or pure beauty.

The style of Poe's stories progressed from one highly decorated and elaborate, as in "THE AS-SICNATION," to one of straightforward simplicity, as in THE IMP OF THE PERVERSE and "Hop-Frog." He said that the stories of pure beauty, most notably THE DOMAIN OF ARNHEIM, had in them much of his soul. Toward the end of his life he remarked that he thought he had accomplished his purpose in poetry, but that he saw new possibilities in prose. These were almost certainly in the realm of pure beauty.

Besides the books of criticism mentioned above, there is a great deal extant of Poe's work as a day-to-day critic. Much of it is about works that came unchosen to a reviewer's table. It often contains keen remarks of great significance, although too much of it is devoted to the examination of flies in amber.

Poe had a tremendous influence abroad. His special kind of poetry was echoed by Tennyson, Swinburne, and Rossetti; his stories influenced Stevenson, Conan Doyle, Jules Verne, Huysmans, and many others. It was in France that Poe's influence attained its widest range, largely owing to the deep respect of Charles Baudelaire for Poe's poems, stories, and aesthetic theories. Between 1856 and 1864 Baudelaire wrote three articles on Poe and translated, with singular felicity, several of his works. Lois and Francis E. Hyslop, Jr., translated and edited *Baudelaire on Poe* (1952), which contains Baudelaire's three major essays and various prefaces and notes. Mallarmé, Valery, and Rimbaud, as well as the whole flock of Parnassians, symbolists, and surrealists, exhibit the influence of Poe. (See SYMBOLISM.) Covering the entire range of "influences" is a volume on *Poe in Foreign Lands and Tongues* (1941), edited by John C. French.

Poe was given to telling romantic stories of himself, and the construction of an accurate biography has been fraught with the greatest difficulties. The first formal biographer, R. W. GRISWOLD, published in the *Works* a memoir (1850) which was bitterly unfriendly to the poet, but which cannot be wholly neglected. In 1859 SARAH HELEN WHITMAN published *Edgar Poe and His Critics*, the first full-length defense of her fiancé. John H. Ingram, an Englishman, wrote many biographical articles and a full-length book, *Edgar Allan Poe* (1880). He had access to many friends of Poe, especially ladies, but in his zeal to defend Poe's memory he sometimes disregarded plain facts. Most of Ingram's papers are now at the University of Virginia; an annotated check list (1960) of them by John C. Miller is of great value. In 1885 appeared GEORGE EDWARD WOODBERRY's very valuable *Edgar Allan Poe* (rev. ed., 2 v., 1909). The biography (1902) by James A. Harrison was highly favorable to Poe; it contained much new information, but is in some ways superficial. In 1926 HERVEY ALLEN published ISRAFEL, the most widely read of Poe's biographies, but one which is nevertheless misleading; it was begun as a novel, and the author never completely eliminated all fictional passages. In the same year appeared *Edgar Allan Poe the Man* by Mary E. Phillips, which, though uncritical and prejudiced, contains a repository of stories and pictures that, if used discerningly, is of great value. One of the most controversial of all books on Poe was JOSEPH WOOD KRUTCH's *Edgar Allan Poe: A Study in Genius* (1926). Krutch found the key to Poe's morbidity in the fact that his stories were marked by a "complete sexlessness." Killis Campbell has written often and significantly on Poe. His most important book is *The Mind of Poe and Other Studies* (1932). His title essay is an invaluable summing up. Particularly important is Campbell's evidence on Poe's constant use of contemporary life in America. Campbell also produced a most valuable edition of *The Poems of Edgar Allan Poe* (1917).

The best single life of Poe is ARTHUR HOBSON QUINN's *Edgar Allan Poe* (1941), though it is too much for the defense to be wholly satisfactory. He also prepared in collaboration with R. H. Hart an edition of *Edgar Allan Poe Letters and Documents* in the Enoch Pratt Free Library.

Most of the many editions of Poe's works are founded on Griswold's (1849–56). Ingram's edition (1874–75) made a few additions to the canon, as did that of Stedman and Woodberry (1895). The only edition that even approached completeness was the seventeen-volume work (1902) of James A. Harrison. In 1962 the first volume of a new edition appeared under the general editorship of T. O. Mabbott; the series promised to contain 20 per cent more material, mostly in the area of criticism. *The Letters of Edgar Allan Poe* (2 v., 1948) were edited by John Ward Ostrom. *A Concordance of the Poetical Works* appeared in 1941.

Other important books on various aspects of Poe and his works include: Susan Archer Talley Weiss, *The Home Life of Poe* (1907); C. Alphonso Smith, *Poe, How to Know Him* (1921); N. Bryllion Fagin, *The Histrionic Mr. Poe* (1949); Haldeen Braddy, *Glorious Incense* (1953); Patrick H. Quinn, *The French Face of Edgar Poe* (1957); Vincent Buranelli, *Edgar Allan Poe* (1961). See also: POETRY IN THE U.S.; LITERARY CRITICISM; SHORT STORY; BON

Bon; The Coliseum; A Descent into the Maelstrom; The Devil in the Belfry; Duc de L'Omelette; A Fable for Critics; Gothic Melancholy; Journal of Julius; Landor's Cottage; Lenore; Marginalia; The Pit and the Pendulum; The Poetic Principle.

Thomas Ollive Mabbott

Poems in Process (1951), an analysis by Phyllis Bartlett. This valuable volume studies the mental processes involved in the composition and revision of poems. Miss Bartlett makes excellent use of many manuscript collections that indicate both the process of writing and of revision.

Poet at the Breakfast Table, The (1872), essays and dialogues by Oliver Wendell Holmes, Sr. This is the third in the series of rambling talks that began with The Autocrat of the Breakfast Table (1858), continued with *The Professor at the Breakfast Table* (1860), and closed with *Over the Teacups* (1891). The chief persons at the table are the Poet; the Old Master, given to philosophy; the Scarabee, an entomologist; the young astronomer, with his poetic outlook; Scheherazade, a young girl who writes stories; and the Lady. But Holmes often writes his ideas directly instead of placing them in the mouths of his characters. He admits in the *Epilogue* that one may find in it "one actor in a dozen parts." He talks on many topics, with an occasional interspersed poem. The papers, like the earlier ones, first appeared in the *Atlantic Monthly*. See Breakfast Table Series.

Poetic Mind, The (1922), an analysis by Frederick Clarke Prescott. Prescott, a specialist in American literature who taught at Cornell University, was deeply interested in the nature of poetry and the manner of its creation, an interest stemming perhaps from his study of Edgar Allan Poe; he published an anthology, *Critical Writings of Poe* (1909). Before writing *The Poetic Mind* he had written *Poetry and Dreams* (1912); he followed it with *Poetry and Myth* (1927). Prescott particularly studied those poets "disposed to introspection and self-analysis," including Emerson and Poe. He used the term *poetry* to include what he called "inspired" writing in prose. He discussed daydreams, mystical vision, primitive imagination and the imagination in childhood, the subjects of poetry, the unconscious mind in poetry, the desires and emotions in poetry, the nature and function of imagination, symbols and figures, impulse and control as factors in inspiration, poetic madness and its catharsis, the "uses" of poetry. He leaned somewhat upon Freud, in general furnished a stimulating analysis of the inner meaning and outward forms of poetry.

Poetic Principle, The (1850), by Edgar Allan Poe. Poe lectured on this subject in several cities during 1848–49. The essay was published posthumously in *Sartain's Union Magazine* (October, 1850). The ideas expressed in it were favorites with Poe and may be found in

some of his earlier writings, including Al Aaraaf, one of his longest poems, written in 1827–29. Both *Al Aaraaf* and *The Poetic Principle* completely negate the notion that Poe was a fanatical believer in art for art's sake or that he opposed moral and spiritual elements in poetry. George E. Woodberry interpreted the poem to mean that "beauty is the direct revelation of the divine to mankind, and the protection of the soul against sin." In the essay Poe criticized the inartistic didactic elements in the literature of his day, but included as material suitable for true poetical effect "all noble thoughts—all unworldly motives—in all holy impulses—all chivalrous, generous, and self-sacrificing deeds." The essay contains eleven poems, English and American, offered as examples of fine poetry.

Poet Lore. A monthly magazine founded at Philadelphia in 1889 by Charlotte Endymion Porter, poet and Shakespearean scholar, and Helen Archibald Clarke, an ardent student of Browning. The magazine discussed English and American poets and "the comparative study of literature." In 1892 it removed to Boston and became a quarterly. It expired in 1953, after publishing much verse of merit.

Poetry: A Magazine of Verse. An important American magazine of verse founded in October, 1912, by Harriet Monroe, who edited it until her death in 1935. It is published in Chicago. Succeeding editors have been Morton Dauwen Zabel (1936–37), George Dillon (1937–42, 1946–50), Peter De Vries (1942), Jessica Nelson North (1942–43), Marion Strobel (1943–45), Hayden Carruth (1950–51), Karl Shapiro (1952–55), Henry Rago (1955—   ). In addition other distinguished poets and critics have served as associate editors, foreign editors, contributing editors, etc.—*e.g.* Ezra Pound, Yvor Winters, Wallace Fowlie. When it was founded in 1912 the magazine quickly became the foremost spokesman for the new movement in American literature, though Harriet Monroe herself was doubtful about some of the new writers. It published much of the early work of such poets as Ezra Pound, T. S. Eliot, Wallace Stevens, William Carlos Williams, D. H. Lawrence, Edna Millay, Elinor Wylie, Robinson Jeffers, Marianne Moore, and many others. Since then the magazine has been generally open to all groups of poets; occasionally it has tended to be stodgy, but on the whole has been lively and progressive. Much distinguished as well as controversial criticism has appeared in its pages. See Imagism.

Poetry and Drama (1951), a lecture by T. S. Eliot. In this lecture at Harvard University, Eliot chose to unite his deep interests in poetry, drama, and criticism. For the most part, however, he confined himself to poetic drama as exemplified in his own Murder in the Cathedral, The Family Reunion, and The Cocktail Party. He made the point that prose can be just as antiquated and mannered as verse; prose is no more "natural" than poetry. In writing his own plays Eliot discovered that "the essential was to avoid any echo of Shakespeare." He has avoided blank verse, preferring lines of irregular length and a varying number of syllables.

Poetry and Dreams (1912), also **Poetry and Myth** (1927), analyses by Frederick Clarke Prescott. See POETIC MIND, THE.

Poetry Explication. A Checklist of Interpretations Since 1925 of British and American Poems, Past and Present (1950), edited by George Arms and Joseph M. Kuntz. This valuable checklist approaches "the new criticism" from its most useful viewpoint. Much of this criticism has been devoted to close analysis of literary works rather than to literary history. It seeks to make clear the *density* of words—the fashion in which interpretations may vary through error or chance, or according to the varying backgrounds of the user, the listener, and the reader. The fact that such varying interpretations are possible is probably the legitimate basis for the refusal of many contemporary poets to "explain" their frequently obscure poems.

poetry in the U.S. American historians, whether their province has been literature or some other department of the national accomplishment, have customarily interpreted the evolution of our civilization in terms of its relationship to Europe. A pretty tedious business by now, as everyone agreed. But any attempt to escape these terms is bound to end in failure: we can no more dismiss our provincialism— and its effects—than a hunchback can dismiss his hump. For example, a far higher proportion of American poets have been motivated by specifically national feeling than one finds in culturally autonomous regions. These poets have dwelt, specifically and insistently, upon the entire range of provincial attitudes—from self-negation to self-glorification—and, even among the relatively few major poets who have not devoted themselves explicitly to the issues of national consciousness, close analysis invariably reveals the warp of parochialism in one or another disguise. It is the national neurosis *par excellence*. Though what the poets have said— their cries of vindication and moans of unworthiness—may be vastly important in other connections, for any such survey as the one attempted here they remain valuable more as attitudinal data than as objective judgments. Hence the history of American poetry ultimately reduces itself to a study in the cultural sociology of provincialism, and there is very little the student of poetry can do about it, however aesthetically minded he may be. Does this militate against the individual reader's pleasure in American poetry, or abrogate the poetry's intrinsic value? The fact is, many readers are deterred from the enjoyment of American poetry by their inability to separate the poetry from their own sense of cultural provincialism. Then again, many readers aren't.

At first, of course, not provincialism but colonialism was the controlling factor. In the cultural sense there was no "America" during the first years of occupation by Europeans: there were only Europeans living, for one reason or another, away from home, and at what point you choose to say that a genuinely American cultural differentiation emerges depends more upon your subjective insight than upon the calculable data. In the prose of the 17th century one may perhaps discern an American element before the century runs out: in Bradford's HISTORY OF PLYMOUTH PLANTATION (written before 1650; published 1856), for instance, or Samuel Sewall's *Diary* (written 1674–1729; published 1878–82) or Robert Beverley's *History* (mostly written before 1700; published 1705). In poetry, however, not even these slight indications of a rising native genius can be found. One may say two things about colonial poetry in America: all of it copied English models; almost all of it was very bad.

Neither point is unexpected when one considers the cultural milieu of the English colonies. The highly cultivated strata of British society did not emigrate to America. Yes, there were a few brilliant adventurers, gentlemen like Raleigh; but very few. Most of the colonists, north and south, were literate but far from intellectual; sufficiently interested in reading to follow the literary fashions but rarely knowledgeable in the technical aspects of literary theory. Hence their taste was often second-rate. They imported books, including some good books, but the biggest trade, outside purely doctrinal materials, was in the works of inferior poets, and this continued until well after the Revolution. In 1732, for instance, the Bostonian bookseller Richard Fry imported twelve hundred copies of the works of Stephen Duck, the Wiltshire poet; and ANNE BRADSTREET, whose poetic talent and devotional fervor ought to have brought her close to John Donne or George Herbert or Richard Crashaw, or at least to Giles Fletcher or the honest Puritan George Wither, seems instead to have chosen as her models the labored conceits of Francis Quarles and Josuah Sylvester's uninspired translations from the uninspired French verse of Seigneur Du Bartas. Shakespeare was well known in America, though the Bay colonists were generally unfriendly to the theater, but *Paradise Lost* was apparently (and surprisingly) not known to more than a handful of colonists until well after 1700. The most popular work of versification by far among those written by colonists was Michael Wigglesworth's DAY OF DOOM (1662), an execrably written tract on damnation, the government of hell, and allied horrors. Terrified children were still required to memorize its choice bite in the 19th century.

Nevertheless, Mistress Bradstreet was a talented poet. Her poems were published in London in 1650 as THE TENTH MUSE LATELY SPRUNG UP IN AMERICA, a title which she had no part in choosing. Occasionally the sense of her religious conviction comes to us through her verses with genuine force, and if her metaphors were not notably original in conception, her imagination at least found turns of phrase which could give them the appearance of independent generation. But although she was a colonial housewife who lived with the wilderness scarcely a stone's throw from her back door, not much in her work betrays an American origin: the poems could have been written in any dissenting household of Dorset. Today she is famous, the heroine of novels, the tutelary spirit of poets (see John Berryman's HOMAGE TO MISTRESS BRADSTREET, 1956), but only because her poems were the first to be published by an American author. Nobody reads them.

EDWARD TAYLOR has fared somewhat better; he enjoyed the advantage of being "discovered" 250 years after his death. A preacher at Westfield, Mass., he wrote verses for private ends alone, and kept them in a manuscript which his heirs were enjoined to leave unpublished. He wrote in the metaphysical manner, notably after Donne, and got into his poems a sensuousness of feeling that Donne would have recognized; perhaps this explains Taylor's reticence about publication—fear that the poems, though mostly religious in theme, were still too agreeable to accord with the reputation of a dissenting minister. What is more important, Taylor also got into his poems a certain amount of detail—for us the "local habitation" without which no poetry can endure. Taylor's manuscript turned up in the Yale Library in 1937, and was promptly published (*The Poetical Works of Edward Taylor*, Thomas H. Johnson, ed., 1939); since then the poems have been studied and read more than any other American poetry of the time, and the book has already become scarce—a new edition is needed. Kenneth Murdock has called Taylor the "greatest poet of New England before the nineteenth century." This still isn't saying much; against the crushing dullness of the rest, the slightest talent would stand out. But in fact Taylor deserves a place with his colleagues overseas, the minor English poets of the 17th century who wrote much that we now consider the best the language affords, and beyond this he was the first poet to capture anything at all of the local temper in America.

As the 18th century wore on, American poets became somewhat less preoccupied with doom and somewhat more aware of the new spirit in English poetry which was represented by Dryden and Pope. Suppose, for the sake of the narrative, that the classical impetus in modern literature reached its height, its moment of splendid poise, in 1666, the year of *Le Misanthrope*. Impossible to say precisely when the moment broke upon America. Certainly not before 1745, however, when *Poems on Several Occasions* by JOHN ADAMS [1] (not the future President) appeared; these contained a trace of classical delicacy and regularity. Hence there was a lag of at least seventy-five years; and it would be possible to write the whole cultural history of North America in terms of the progressive means by which this lag was shortened. In 1747 William Livingston, later a prominent Revolutionary figure, published his *Philosophical Solitude*, a poem in tolerable heroic couplets.

The young Philadelphian THOMAS GODFREY also showed talent in classical meters, though he died too young to develop them; his friend Nathaniel Evans, also a poet, edited a posthumous edition of Godfrey's *Juvenile Poems on Various Subjects* (1765). Joseph Shippen wrote an allegedly graceful poem, "The Glooms of Ligonier," which acquired a long (gloomy?) popularity. In all these poets, however, classicism was never more than a password to the *haut ton*, sincerely as it may have been imitated on occasion. In America the taste for classicism existed, but never the need; the land itself did not ask for it; and hence its meaning for the pre-Revolutionary American mind must have been—in the full sense—problematical.

As Revolutionary sentiment grew in strength, however, one element of the English classical movement was seized by American poets and put to an immediately practical use—the element of satire, turned inevitably against the country of its flowering. Even in this case American poets preferred, not the toughness of Dryden or the suavity of Pope, but the boisterousness of Charles Churchill and the bathos of Mark Akenside. The type can be seen in its full vigor among the HARTFORD WITS, a group of Connecticut poets led by JOHN TRUMBULL, TIMOTHY DWIGHT, and JOEL BARLOW, the authors respectively of M'FINGAL (1775), THE CONQUEST OF CANAAN (1785), and THE COLUMBIAD (first version, 1787; final version, 1807). These were patriotic verses, as fiery in their way as any oration by John Adams or Patrick Henry, and as full of bad rhetoric. But they were popular and they served their admirable purpose admirably; moreover, in the terms of this article there can be no doubt that they constituted the first effective, large-scale adaptation of native materials to the ends of self-conscious literary composition in verse. The mark of provincialism is still abundantly upon them; but it was now definitely provincialism, not colonialism. Nor should the Wits be downgraded on account of their rough technique; they were outstanding men—Barlow a diplomat, Dwight a president of Yale, Trumbull a prodigy and one of the most brilliant men in America.

The Wits by no means exhaust the topic of Revolutionary poetry, for a finer talent than any of them was also producing patriotic verses. PHILIP FRENEAU is the first American poet in Richard Aldington's *Viking Book of Poetry of the English-Speaking World;* and if Freneau is the first American poet who may be taken seriously by a European editor, he was also the first who pointed the way toward a genuinely *poetic* solution to the dilemma of provincialism. He was a soldier, a politician, a journalist; much of his verse was written for patriotic or political ends. But there remains a body of work which is poetic in the fullest sense, a personal amalgam of experience and feeling. After the Revolution, Freneau continued to write poetry—nature poems, love poems, some important experiments with themes from Indian life. Beginning with a neoclassical metric, he loosened his verse, made it a personal vehicle, introduced natural diction (independently of Wordsworth). Neither Romantic nor Gothic, Freneau drove his technique before him toward the goal of style. Here is the opening of his THE HOUSE OF NIGHT:

Trembling I write my dream, and recollect
A fearful vision at the midnight hour;
So late, death o'er me spreads his signal wings,
Painted with fancies of malignant power!

Much in American poetry, to the present day, stems from this plain line. Not another major poet in America before Emily Dickinson, not even Edgar Allan Poe, would have resisted the temptation to rhyme the first and third lines—a significant resistance. In America, Freneau occupies something like the stage that Chatterton, Smart, Gray, and Blake occupy in England: pre-Romantics freed of neoclassical academicism. Freneau did not go as far in most respects as his English contemporaries—this would have been impossible in the circumstances—but he did well. Americans should honor his work by reading it more than they do.

Freneau leads directly into the Romantic movement and the American 19th century in general with its two great figures, Poe and Walt Whitman, whose influence extends throughout world literature, and a third, Emily Dickinson, who in a less direct way has exerted an equal force. But a word or two must be said first about literary activity below this level. In the eastern cities the beginning of the 19th century was a time of relaxation and refinement; the wilderness was tamed, independence was won, the great urban fortunes had been founded. Women, emancipated from domestic chores by their husbands' wealth, became the poet's chief readers —a condition from which American poetry has yet to emerge. The romantic, subjective poetry of Wordsworth and Coleridge, and more especially of Shelley, Byron, Leigh Hunt, Joseph Blanco White, Thomas Moore, Thomas Hood, etc., found an ardent audience among such readers, as did a number of American versifiers ready to embark on imitation. FITZ-GREENE HALLECK wrote mainly sentimental verses, though a Byronesque satire, FANNY (1817), has been praised (rather unaccountably) by Ezra Pound. Halleck's friend JOSEPH RODMAN DRAKE wrote technically unobjectionable verses full of fays and sprites. Eaglesfield Smith wrote verse romances in the manner of Scott, fake dialect and all, and Samuel Woodworth wrote THE OLD OAKEN BUCKET (1826). Gothic melodrama flourished on the stage in New York, Philadelphia, and Charleston—Boston still took a dim view of theatrical entertainments—and the mood was sustained in architecture by Joseph Latrobe and his followers.

In 1820, Sydney Smith, the English critic and wit, asked: "In the four quarters of the globe, who reads an American book? or goes to an American play? or looks at an American picture or statue?" The taunt was widely circulated in America, and widely approved by citizens who comprised the self-appointed elite. When JAMES N. BARKER dramatized in 1812 for production Scott's Marmion in a New York theater, the playbill read, "By Thomas Mortan, an Englishman." The public took well to the play; but when word leaked out that the adapter was really Barker, an American, the production folded in three weeks. In the face of this, no wonder American poets seldom were able to take their own work seriously.

Yet some of these poets may have been geniuses, and a few undoubtedly were. Washington Allston, for instance, rebelled against his family's decision that he become a doctor, and ran off to London to study. The British acclaimed him. Clearly he was one of the most brilliant young men of the age, both a painter and a poet; but in the long run he was paralyzed by his sense of being an American, and he failed to produce anything like the important work that was expected of him, though he left some charming fugitive pieces. WILLIAM CULLEN BRYANT is another case in point. His THANATOPSIS (1817), written when he was seventeen though not published until six years later, leaves no doubt of his high gift, and a few of his later poems are unequivocally good. But these few are scarcely vigorous enough to clamber above the dull, pedantic mishmash of the rest—imitative works written under a compulsion to bring European culture to America. As lifelong editor of the New York Post, Bryant made this his main concern; no doubt his learned, fluent editorials, articles, and reviews did a good deal to elevate the cultural tone of 19th-century America, but the same energy put into the shaping of American experience in verse might have resulted in something more important. Finally, the case of HENRY WADSWORTH LONGFELLOW. Of course, the question of a neurotic personality cannot be altogether evaded, here or elsewhere. Longfellow's genius was enormous. Some of his love poems and other personal lyrics are quite good enough to deserve more readers than they have today. Moreover, he obviously did not shirk his responsibility toward the American scene: his verse narratives almost all sprang from native sources. Yet in nearly everything he wrote one detects a weakness, a failure of aesthetic daring or aesthetic faith at the heart of the poem; the poet retreats at the point where a bold word or exceptional meter might win victory, i.e. in a full unified poem. Longfellow was an assiduous scholar, particularly attracted to German and Scandinavian literatures. Too much of his work is imitative and lacks realism: the spirit of locality is not much in evidence in EVANGELINE (1847), for instance, or HIAWATHA (1855), though both purport to be American experiments in American mythology. His best effort in narrative was no doubt his slightest, Paul Revere's Ride (1861), tossed off quickly and with no thought of foreign models. In the end Longfellow became the most popular American poet of the century and the cultural arbiter of the American middle class, deeply committed to gentility. He presided in Cambridge, the leader of the New England school of poets—prosperous, gentle, kindly, and conventional; and he ended as a bearded countenance gazing benignly down from ten thousand classroom walls, the worst fate that can befall a writer. These three provincial poets, judged by strict critical standards, lost their way. To what extent their provincialism can be blamed for the misadventure, no one will ever determine precisely; but aside from any other historical or biographical considerations, the texts of their poems alone give plenty of evidence that provincialism was an important factor. Nor was the loss to American poetry limited to these three.

"What does the poet make and what does his work create?" The question was asked by I. A. Richards, and he supplied his own answer: "Himself and his world first, and thereby other worlds and other men." Clearly no poet who has been considered here so far thought of his role in any such terms as these. On the contrary, these poets took themselves and their worlds as given, inalterable, fixed, in a sense the reliable components of an existence fraught with the contingency of God's will, certainly not in need of self-creation; and for this reason, perhaps, they failed very largely to affect the selves or worlds of their readers. Professor Richards' statement of the poet's office is crucially modern, the base of modern literary theory; and it is significant that the first American poet who regarded himself as in any sense a "maker" or "creator" was also our first modern poet, EDGAR ALLAN POE. No one who has studied Poe's poems in relation to his life can doubt that the latter was as deeply influenced by the former as the other way round. Experience was meaningless for Poe until it had been poeticized; poetry was valueless until it had been lived. Beyond this, he buttressed his poetry with a critical theory that was both personal and prescriptive. No American writer before him had attempted anything so comprehensive. Poe hadn't the integrative sensibility which has become almost second nature for poets today; his verse and criticism were not always congruent; but both were illuminating and both—but especially the criticism—produced effects which have been pervasive in all Western literature.

Coleridge defined the twofold force of poetry as "the power of exciting the sympathy of the reader by a faithful adherence to the truth of nature, and the power of giving the interest of novelty by the modifying colours of imagination." Conceivably Poe read these words as a boy, for he attended school in England not long after the publication of the *Biographia Literaria*. In any case, he was an admirer of Coleridge, and in theory subscribed to the sound Romantic doctrine contained in the elder poet's critical precept. In practice, however, Poe was attracted more by the second half of Coleridge's definition than by the first. Poe's criticism says little about nature, but much about the use of language to sustain a mood, both through the meanings of words, considered primarily under their connotative aspects, and through the sounds of words. He came close to advocating automatic writing. If he fell short of that, he at least insisted on the primacy of the subconscious mind as the source of poetry's images and symbols, and he was an unquestioning believer in the efficacy of affective form. His trouble was that he failed to achieve in his poetry the spontaneity that his critical precepts required. His mood in verse was generally narrow, confined at one limit by melancholy and at the other by the macabre; and he attempted to sustain this mood in studied meters and assonances which too often strained his technique. Modern readers are likely to find his effect more a contrived euphoniousness than a genuine liberation of feeling, with the result that they prefer his short stories to his poetry. Even so, a dozen or more of Poe's lyrics succeed marvelously, and are probably the best things of their kind in Anglo-American literature. Together with his stories, they have become so deeply ingrained in American culture that they are touchstones of the historical consciousness.

Poe's theories of language and symbolism were almost completely ignored by succeeding American poets for a hundred years, and the art of symbolism, so natural to American temperament and civilization, was left in the hands of the novelists, particularly Hawthorne and Melville. In part this was owing to the ascendancy of the Pre-Raphaelite movement in England and its consequent acceptance in America. The failure of the Rossettis and their friends to understand the real nature of the symbol in art permitted them to neglect Poe. But the French poet Charles Baudelaire was more receptive—and more astute. He read and translated Poe's work, and expanded Poe's concepts of the poetic act. Thus Poe's theories passed into French literature at a point where they could be most usefully absorbed, combining with the effects of Baudelaire's *Fleurs du Mal* (1857) and Gautier's *Émaux et Camées* (1852) to produce, in the ensuing works of Mallarmé, Rimbaud, the Parnassians, and the Symbolists, a literary development of great intrinsic vitality. In the course of time, the English Pre-Raphaelites declined, the Rhymers ascended; and when Arthur Symons brought the French poets to the Anglo-American audience in his *The Symbolist Movement in Literature* (1899), which was widely read by young poets in the first years of the 20th century, Poe's influence re-entered American literary life. At the same time it was spreading elsewhere by analogous means, until today the Poesque element in Western poetry taken as a whole is incalculably large.

Behind Poe, in a manner of speaking, the ordinary work of literary production went on, centered chiefly in New England. The transcendentalists and abolitionists used verse for their lucubrations when the mood to do so overtook them, and RALPH WALDO EMERSON turned out occasional poems which possessed a certain intellectual vividness, though his verse-writing technique was slap-dash; his friend HENRY DAVID THOREAU did nothing in poetry of any account. Probably the best of the transcendental poets was JONES VERY, whose brilliant, anxiety-ridden, intense mind was capable of only a small output of compressed and tightly formal poems, testimonials of ecstatic mysticism less akin to Emerson's religion than to the Mathers'. JOHN GREENLEAF WHITTIER, a low-born New Englander, wrote crudely but with a nice attention to homely detail, as in his minor masterpiece of descriptive verse, SNOW-BOUND (1866); but much of his ability was lost in volatile anti-slavery diatribes. JAMES RUSSELL LOWELL was the epitome of Brahminism, urbane, learned, and mostly dull—a writer of pretentious doggerel. These men formed a close and usually closed circle, the Academy of their day, headed by Longfellow, deriving a locus from Longfellow's graciously appointed home in Cambridge. (See BRAHMINS.) Among them, they controlled the editorial policies of the NORTH AMERICAN REVIEW and the ATLANTIC MONTHLY, and hence the literary tastes of most of cultivated America. Their book reviews could make or break young writers. Probably the most likable of them was OLIVER WENDELL HOLMES, SR., who wrote entertaining essays and several novels that remain interesting for their pre-Freudian excursions into psychotherapeutics; but he did not try seriously to write poetry. When WILLIAM DEAN HOWELLS came East as a young man to seek his literary fortune, he went to Cambridge, for he knew his career hung in the balance until Lowell had condescended to pronounce a judgment. A favorable judgment was given, as it turned out, and eventually Howells succeeded to Lowell's kingdom. But the American writer who most needed and most deserved the help of the Cambridge circle never got it: HERMAN MELVILLE worked all his life in a state of almost total critical neglect, and his poems, which are highly regarded today, were mainly published at his own expense and read by no more than a few dozen people during his lifetime.

Meanwhile, southern poets of the middle 19th century wandered into an attenuating dilettantism. As the crisis of Fort Sumter approached, the patriarchal planters and their more or less humanistic, late 18th-century culture gave way to the newly rich cotton kings, western farmers, and red-necked politicos. "The southern farmer of this period had neither the culture, the breadth of view, nor the tolerance of the Virginia planter of the eighteenth century," wrote Jay B. Hubbell, the South's chief modern apologist in literature. It can be argued that culture, breadth of view, and tolerance are no guarantors of good writing and may even be inimical to it; but in the South of 1830 to 1865, at any rate, the point seems well taken. By and large, southern taste of the period, like western taste, was subliterary—there was no one for poets to write *for*. Southern scholars usually claim Poe as their own, on the strength of his having been brought

up in Richmond, but the claim is tenuous; and aside from Poe what was there? JAMES RYDER RANDALL, HENRY TIMROD (the most popular proslavery poet), FRANCIS ORRAY TICKNOR, ABRAM JOSEPH RYAN, Innes Randolph, WILLIAM J. GRAYSON—forgotten figures, no better than pretty poets, except in the minds of a few southern scholars. This is not to say that there was no vigorous writing in the South; but most of it was prose, the work of WILLIAM GILMORE SIMMS, JOHN PENDLETON KENNEDY, WILLIAM ALEXANDER CARUTHERS, JOHN ESTEN COOKE and Philip Pendleton Cooke, etc., strong trinomial writers who among them contributed more than is sometimes thought to the progress of fictional realism in America. Nor should the western southerners and the humorists be forgotten—DAVY CROCKETT, AUGUSTUS B. LONGSTREET, GEORGE W. HARRIS. But the attempt to find still readable southern poetry from this period is distressingly tedious. Professor Hubbell and others have tried to resurrect JAMES M. LEGARÉ, on the strength that his prosodic technique was firmer than the others', but a look at his work shows it to be only watered-down, fifth-rate Tennysonianism, like the rest.

WALT WHITMAN was no Tennysonian. He said his "God be with you" to the European poets and then parted company with them irrevocably, at the same time and in consequence parting company with his American colleagues, too. He sang no sweet songs, but long, loosely metered chants; he put no history in his poems, but only the broad democratic present and the radiant future; he cared nothing for empire, unless it was the empire of free men—and women. Yes, sex was overt in Whitman's poems; not the coy naughtiness of most previous erotic poetry, but an open, even naïve acclamation of joy in sexual love, accompanied sometimes by an implicit recommendation of indiscriminateness. His aim was the perfection of the individual person through immersion in the commonalty of persons, and the anointing oil of the ritual was love. Whitman dealt more frankly with the physiological aspects of existence than any poet had before. With him, universal nature was a generative force, moving confidently forward toward the realization of Democratic Man. Even in death, nature retained its somewhat inscrutable *élan*. Of all the optimistic philosophies and literatures that derived from the general 19th-century ferment over evolutionary theory, Whitman's was, by and large, the happiest; and perhaps also the most successful. Spencer fell into confusion, Nietzsche into shameless posturing, Huxley into witticism, Marx into ward-heeling pettifoggery. Whitman, with only the flimsiest conceptualizing apparatus, outlives them all—read today not only with pleasure but with a sense of shared conviction by millions of like-minded people in every part of the world. This fact does not by any means place Whitman above the flaws of his own insight, the shortcomings of his historical consciousness. The critic Edward Dahlberg has written: "By taking original sin out of Hebraic Christianity, [Whitman] disavowed pitiable human folly . . . and so annulled redemption. He annihilated the Savior, the Word, the Image, without which the world becomes an insensate medley of hideous flying atoms." Even allowing for Dahlberg's iconoclastic rhetoric, his barb strikes home, and one need not be a theological formalist (Dahlberg is not) to recognize it. Whitman's zeal, enthusiasm, fervor, his grand cadences and liturgical phrasings, his irrepressible, highhanded love of word-making, cannot entirely conceal the shallowness of his insight. In spite of his tender, moving funeral song for President Lincoln, in spite of his invocations to nature's darker forces, Whitman lacked the tragic sense; and to the extent that knowledge of tragedy is prerequisite to the composition of genuinely and humanly affective poetry, Whitman failed. In the context of 19th-century American optimism and expansionism, the failure seems slight; but in the context of the longer comparative view that we are inclined to take today (even if we do not go as far as Dahlberg), we cannot help but notice it. Nor can we help but notice the evidence from Whitman's personal life that appears to indicate a homosexual temperament. The failure of sympathy in the poet—for that, ultimately, is the source of a defective tragic vision—may be related to the failure of authority in the man.

Whitman published his poems first in 1855 as LEAVES OF GRASS, a small pamphlet which he printed and sold himself. It did not attract much notice. Most people who did read it didn't like it. Nevertheless, Whitman persevered, and in the course of his life published a number of further editions, each an expansion and revision of its predecessor. Gradually his audience formed. Before his death he had acquired a gratifyingly enthusiastic following, both at home and abroad. Other poets began imitating him. To what extent his unmetered but highly rhythmical lines affected later experiments in vers libre it is, of course, impossible to say, for other poets during Whitman's lifetime were writing unmetered verse, especially in France. Probably in the long run Whitman's influence has been less than Poe's. But influence is not the only measure of a poet's success, nor even the chief one; and there is no doubt whatever that Whitman's acceptance throughout the world has been very wide and very appreciative. Considering the nature of Whitman's poetic materials, this is nothing less than astonishing. For what personality was Whitman offering to view? Precisely that which had been the butt of the world's ridicule for decades—the naïve, optimistic, self-assured, democratic American, the Yankee Doodle, the Generals Scadder and Choke. The measure of Whitman's genius is the degree to which he—Walt Whitman, the singer, the poet, the public personality, the collective "I" —converted this image of ridicule into one of the modern world's most compelling identities: Everyman as the principle of promise and faith.

The difference between Whitman's poetry and that of EMILY DICKINSON is so great that it scarcely seems possible the two were con-temporaries. Perhaps the fact that they lived and worked at about the same time is as good an indication as any of the floundering quality of American literature before the 20th century. No conceivable "movement" or "school" or even "period" (in the usual literary sense) could unite two so dissimilar poets. Where Whitman was the democratic poet, the public poet, the celebrator of men's collective motives, Miss Dickinson was personal, introspective, private. Where Whitman was optimistic, Miss Dickinson was wryly pessimistic. Where Whitman was credulously pantheistic, Miss Dickinson was apprehensively Calvinistic. Where Whitman rewrote and polished his poems continually, and did all that he could to secure their acceptance, Miss Dickinson jotted down her poems on odd scraps of paper, scarcely ever went back to them, and left them concealed in a drawer, where they remained until after she died. Where Whitman was expansive, rhetorical, long-winded, Miss Dickinson was lyrical, cryptic, compressed. Where Whitman acclaimed sex and freedom, implying at least that the two were necessary concomitants, Miss Dickinson was so disturbed by her one mildly incorrect attachment to a married man that she buried herself in neurotic seclusion for the rest of her life. And so on and so on—the disparities are almost endless.

In an important sense, Emily Dickinson was a profoundly American poet, although she seldom incorporated any explicitly American materials in her poems. But, owing to her spiritual locus in the center, so to speak, of the conflict between New England's early and later theologies, she felt and expressed, often in dimly realized terms, a characteristically American anguish. She lived in Amherst, Mass. As a child she learned the Calvinist creed and the Calvinist morality of her forebears; but she also picked up in her adolescent reading a smattering of the 19th-century revolt. Not enough of it, clearly, to fix her unequivocally with the transcendentalists or the Unitarians, but enough to turn her mind toward problems of doubt, guilt, purpose, etc. Her own neurotic anxieties gave her general quest a driving personal force. Without much formal education and with few intellectually disposed friends, she lacked the means of conceptualizing these cultural and moral conflicts as they were conceptualized by other troubled New Englanders of the time—Nathaniel Hawthorne, Harriet Beecher Stowe, or Henry Adams. Hence she never attempted anything on the grand scale, but instead captured her fears and resolutions in fugitive scraps of verse, shaped on the rhythms of the hymn tunes she remembered from childhood, cast up in images taken from her garden, her house, her reading. The result was a large body of mediocre verse surrounding twenty or thirty poems of shattering brilliance. The faults of the poems are easy to pick out: huge abstractions left unwedded to the context; allegories either flatly obvious or unanchored and cryptic; exoticisms (from her reading) tagged on without meaning or necessity; and, worst of all, what the critic Yvor Winters has called her "quality of silly playfulness," an apparently deep-rooted need to meet questions of ultimacy with an attitude of childish irresponsibility and coquetry. Yet in the twenty or thirty brilliant poems—and some critics would say thirty or forty; the number is open to dispute, though the general proportion of good to mediocre is not—she transcended these defects of poetic skill and temperament with an accession of genius probably greater than anything of its kind elsewhere in English literature. These poems offer much of value to readers and critics; but the manner of their composition offers even more to those who are willing to speculate about the psychology of the procedural imagination.

After Miss Dickinson's death, a considerable tangle developed in respect to the publication rights to her literary remains, and in consequence the poems were published only gradually, a little at a time, in a number of succeeding volumes, and sometimes the texts were inaccurate. The final, scholarly, variorum edition didn't appear until early in the 1950's, and much critical work remains to be done. But the main impact of her poems on readers and other poets was immediate. Her influence spread through American poetry like—for once the simile is not exaggerated—wildfire, especially among poets who came to prominence after World War I and more especially among female poets—Léonie Adams, Louise Bogan, Edna St. Vincent Millay, Elinor Wylie, and many others. Today her style is so widely disseminated through American poetry (the figure is apt though bizarre) that it has become virtually indistinguishable from *the* American style, and Whitman's chanting sentences have almost vanished from the poetic consciousness. Styles wear out; anyone who has examined the alternations of literary fashion in the past can be sure that the balance will swing back in the other direction, probably before long. But if he is also sensitive to intrinsic values, the student will be confident, too, that these twenty or thirty or forty of Emily Dickinson's poems will remain classics of American literature as long as American literature exists.

Southern intellectual life was as seriously disrupted by the Civil War as any other aspect of existence. The fact is that the main intellectual and artistic currents in the United States during the first half of the 19th century—TRANSCENDENTALISM, Unitarianism, Owenism, the various other ramifications of Romantic theory—had been closely and doubtless inevitably tied to abolitionism, while at the same time abolitionism itself had been driven into such an uncompromising position by its radical wing, men like Whittier, Garrison, and the supporters of John Brown, that southern intellectuals who might have desired to align themselves with a less bellicose but nevertheless progressive program of national development in the arts were prevented from doing so and were left instead to cultivate their own turnip patches. In some respects these turnip patches turned out to be remarkably fertile. But not for poetry. After 1865, prose was able to break from the gracile 18th-century sen-

timentalism which dominated southern taste, and the new prose writers who sought their inspiration in the language they heard around them, instead of in Addison or Walpole, gave to American literature a very necessary infusion of local color and folk symbolism. This ranged from the subliterary (though culturally important) dialect tales of JOEL CHANDLER HARRIS and THOMAS NELSON PAGE to such formal masterpieces as HUCKLEBERRY FINN and THE GRANDISSIMES. Even in music Louis Gottschalk could make something like the same break, introducing Creole materials into his highly sophisticated compositions. But poetry, bound in a tight prosodic heritage, could not manage it. With one exception, the South produced not a single important poet between 1860 and 1900, and it is significant that the one who did succeed in creating, in a few poems, a serious modern southern style was a northern Negro, PAUL LAURENCE DUNBAR. These forty years of southern literary history form a lucidly heightened illustration of the whole predicament of provincial culture— provincialism with a vengeance—for the South was, during this period, a provincial culture within a provincial culture.

Of course the exception was SIDNEY LANIER. Today his poetry, with its Pre-Raphaelite and Swinburnian affinities, is unpopular; many readers would be inclined to deny that Lanier actually is an exception to the run of southern mediocrity. The last popular edition of his poems was issued in 1915. Nevertheless, Lanier must be accorded wide respect for the quality of his mind and the seriousness of his intent, since both of these, aside from his poems themselves, have entered and augmented the main current of American poetry. It is tempting to say that Lanier was a kind of second-rate Poe, since like his predecessor he was deeply interested in the musical elements of verse and the techniques by which they are manipulated. But in reality he pursued a highly individual course. In the first place, he was both a professional musician and a creditable literary scholar, and was able to give to his essays in criticism an authenticity which Poe's more fanciful cerebrations might never have achieved on their own. In the second place, Lanier was more deeply committed than Poe to the content of his work, at least in the sense that he was concerned not only for its emotional coherence but for its social and philosophical utility. Charles Anderson, the editor of Lanier's *Works* (1945), has observed that Lanier inclined toward the Emersonian conception of the poet as a religious seer "in charge of all learning to convert it into wisdom." This conversion, provided we use "learning" in the philosophical sense to mean all cognized experience, lies also at the heart of the modern or symbolist conception of the poet's role; and it seems fair to say that Lanier, however old-fashioned his poems may seem now, came close to our view of the poetic act. But, working apart from the center of literary activity, he gave much of his energy to poetically tangential enterprises. He was convinced that poetic technique could be reduced to a science if only prosodists would apply the analogy of music, and he wrote two books, *The Science of English Verse* (1883) and *Music and Poetry* (1889), to prove his point. They are tedious books, though here and there they contain interesting technical analyses. In his own poetry he applied his principles as well as he could, ending up too often with an exaggerated onomatopoeia that obscures his metrical experiments and novel imageries. In spite of this, however, there is enough substance in some of his poems to suggest that they may survive their present eclipse and come into favor again as taste in literature continues on its spiral course.

In the North, meanwhile, affairs were not much better. The old Cambridge school declined, and was replaced by a new one, more cosmopolitan, more refined, and occasionally more daring. William Dean Howells advocated a judicious realism in prose fiction. WILLIAM VAUGHN MOODY faced up intelligently to sexual taboos, as in THE GREAT DIVIDE (1906), a drama which won considerable success. But he didn't really go far in this direction; neither did TRUMBULL STICKNEY nor GEORGE SANTAYANA, who were the two other most distinguished members of the group. These men were without question excellent poets and truly critical intellects—they were perhaps the first Americans who constructed literary careers which exhibited in some degree the qualities we attach to the great Europeans, men like Arnold, Leconte de Lisle, Carducci; in other words, they were the first American men of letters. Moreover, they may have had more influence on their successors than most readers now suspect. The intense originality of the poetry of WALLACE STEVENS, for instance, has led critics to seek its origins, no doubt with reason, in distant sources—Rimbaud and Laforgue; but the movement of his verse is often prefigured in passages from the works of Moody, whose poems were popular when Stevens was a young man. The case awaits the investigations of the scholars. This is not to insinuate that the end of the century in America brought forth much memorable poetry: it didn't. Moody, Stickney, and Santayana were gifted poets, they gave American readers a touch of salutary professionalism at a high level, and they dealt often enough with themes from American life. Good writers in certain circumstances can make themselves useful by other means than the production of masterpieces. If these poets had not yet found the combination of matter and manner which could raise American poetry to the level of English, this is to say that beneath their veneer they were still provincial poets.

There were poets residing in the rest of the country too, of course. But they didn't bring much to the main task at hand. Indiana had JAMES WHITCOMB RILEY, Chicago had EUGENE FIELD, Kentucky had MADISON CAWEIN; BLISS CARMAN and RICHARD HOVEY worked mainly in the East; in California a curious mixture of frontier roughhouse and yellow-book preciosity,

stemming from AMBROSE BIERCE, issued in the poetry of GEORGE STERLING, JOAQUIN MILLER, C. W. STODDARD, EDWIN MARKHAM, and others; two women whose poems remain readable were LIZETTE WOODWORTH REESE and ANNA HEMPSTEAD BRANCH; other poets who were notable for one reason or another were EDWARD ROWLAND SILL, Philip Henry Savage, JOHN B. TABB, FRANK DEMPSTER SHERMAN, LOUISE CHANDLER MOULTON, Henry Jones; and PERCY MACKAYE wrote admirably for the verse theater and the opera. By the end of the 19th century, cultural life in the United States, in its aspects of organization and management, had become as extensive as cultural life anywhere. But although these poets and others produced works which have value as folklore, history, entertainment, social commentary, or occasionally as still valid poems in their own right, none made an enduring contribution to the development of a soundly based and balanced American poetry.

Success in removing the burden of provincialism from American poetry fell finally to the men and women who created the "revolution of the word," as it is often called, or more simply the "modern poetry," as we still refer to it nearly two generations after its inception. Conventionally, the date of the revolution is given as 1912, when HARRIET MONROE founded POETRY: A MAGAZINE OF VERSE in Chicago; the magazine quickly became the principal organ of the "new poetry" (another common designation). But without in the least diminishing the importance of *Poetry* or extenuating the genuinely revolutionary effects of much that the new poets did, one may believe that the movement did not occur overnight. The old turn-of-the-century poets in America, as noted already, were sophisticated writers, like their contemporaries in England; and they were aware of Baudelaire and the Symbolists. At the same time, the new poets did not acquire much following until after World War I. Thus the period of emergence for the new poetry lasted at least fifteen years, probably longer; and moreover, one important transitional poet, like Yeats in England, spanned the whole era, and one proto-revolutionary preceded it. EDWIN ARLINGTON ROBINSON's first book was published in 1896, his last in 1935. In its toughness and psychological daring, his verse foreshadowed many elements of the revolutionary poetry, while his metric remained fixed in conventional usage. He wrote with power, often of themes from New England history and society; his work has been dimmed by Robert Frost's success with similar themes, which is an unfortunate outcome, for whereas Frost's attitudes have generally been ironic and metaphysical and touched with Emersonian softness, Robinson conceived his subjects in terms of tragic purity. No poet has brought lyrical narrative, that difficult form invented by Wordsworth, to a tenser development, and such poems of Robinson's as "Luke Havergal" and "Eros Turannos" should not be forgotten. STEPHEN CRANE, whose poems embodied a tough, realistic content in an ironic free verse that owed something to Whitman and something to journalese, would not have earned much of a reputation on the ground of his verse alone: he didn't write enough of it and his technique was primitive. But there is no doubt that he anticipated many innovations of the new poetry in the small number of poems he did write and publish, all before 1900. Moreover, because his novels attracted widespread attention and were praised by Howells, Huneker, and other influential critics, his verse undoubtedly was read and studied by the young writers who came along in the early years of the new century.

The new poets began their revolution as a rebellion against poetic practices and purposes that had gone stale. Their motives were for the most part negative rather than affirmative. They reacted against Victorianism, Georgianism, genteelism, the academy, the establishment, the rules and conventions, Wordsworth, Tennyson, Swinburne, Bridges, the whole suffocating past. Off they went, hellbent for leather, unfurling their banners as they rode—female emancipation, abolition of sexual taboos, down with American commercialism, abolition of deans and professors, and—at the head, resplendent in gory hues—vers libre! As the ranks swelled, some banners were torn down and replaced by others, divisive (not to say derisive) slogans were hurled back and forth, squadrons wheeled away on new lines of march, platoons were lost and never heard from again, and the scene took on the appearance of a melee. Naturally, anything like a complete disentanglement of the conflicting elements is beyond the scope of an encyclopedia article. From here on, these observations will be abbreviated, exclusive, and general.

In geographical terms, the charge of the revolutionaries was more in the nature of an exodus—away from the former centers of culture in the East, particularly Cambridge and New York. The new poets were fed up with the conservative policies of the established publishing firms and the universities. The new centers of American poetry were two: Chicago and Europe. They represented two broadly divergent forces in American poetry; and for a quarter of a century a conflict between them invigorated the literary scene, though the two parties were so equally drawn that much of the time the conflict was subdued and antagonists from either side could mingle together on terms of mutual respect. Only when the Chicagoan school finally succumbed to the European were cries of triumph, anger, and misery plainly heard.

In Chicago, HARRIET MONROE ruled. Although she welcomed members of the European school to the pages of *Poetry*, it is clear in retrospect that her sympathies lay first with the westerners, the Whitmanians, the ebullient democrats. Miss Monroe was a good editor and a sensitive reader, she recognized the great verbal talents of Ezra Pound and his friends; but she lacked their erudition. Like many others in the same fix, she was unwilling to commit herself to an unreserved judgment—which was of course what the Poundians wanted. CARL SANDBURG was the leader of the Chicago group; others were EDGAR LEE MASTERS (whose candid SPOON RIVER ANTHOLOGY, 1915, used to be cited as a liberating force for American letters, though today its importance seems less decisive), VACHEL LINDSAY, LEW SARETT, STEPHEN VINCENT BENÉT, FLOYD DELL. The historical importance of these poets, together with that of their colleagues who wrote in prose—HAMLIN GARLAND, FRANK NORRIS, THEODORE DREISER, SINCLAIR LEWIS, ERNEST HEMINGWAY—cannot be overemphasized. In a very real sense they were the van of the *avantgarde*, without whom the less aggressive combatants could have made no headway; and besides, they represented an aspect of the American character, its expansive and progressive mood, which is never submerged for long.

But a significant omen of the future was the migration of THE LITTLE REVIEW, founded in 1914 by Margaret Anderson, from Chicago to New York and then to Europe. Miss Anderson took a more esoteric line than Miss Monroe; soon she was attracting away from *Poetry* the American writers of the European branch whose sophisticated nostrils had begun to detect the aroma of prairie dust that clung to some of Miss Monroe's protégés. The most important were EZRA POUND, who had been *Poetry's* foreign editor, and T. S. ELIOT. Pound had gone to Europe in 1908, had settled in London; there he and T. E. Hulme, a minor English philosopher, had established the imagist movement, advocating extreme precision of imagery and realism of outlook, together with free metric. They chose as models the verse of Greek antiquity, the ideographic poems of the Orient, the song forms of the troubadours and Villon, the associative and evocative techniques of the symbolists; and they attracted to their group such poets as H. D. (HILDA DOOLITTLE), JOHN GOULD FLETCHER, WILLIAM CARLOS WILLIAMS, and MARIANNE MOORE. Soon IMAGISM was taken over by AMY LOWELL and turned into a universal society for vers-librists; and Pound, a very fast-moving young man, went on to other affairs. Eliot, also in London, found himself attracted to the older man's tough intellectuality, and the two became friends and collaborators.

Two main points should be emphasized about these American poets who lived in London and Paris during the years immediately before and after World War I. First, Pound had a knack of attracting to himself some of the finest writers who have ever appeared in the English-speaking world, and he had the further knack of bringing out their best and publicizing it to any part of the literate community that would listen. Besides the poets already mentioned, Pound worked with such writers as Hemingway, James Joyce, E. E. Cummings; and even older writers—Robert Frost, W. B. Yeats, Ford Madox Ford—have acknowledged his example. Pound insisted on clarity, precision, a reasoned technique; it wasn't so much that he enforced these notions on unwilling followers as that he gave other writers who already shared his ideas an aggressive sense of solidarity and support, poetry in the U.S. (cont.)

which was just what they needed at that point. Secondly, many of these poets and novelists were fine critics too; and here they enjoyed a considerable advantage over the Chicagoans. Pound and Eliot especially were important. Between them they had produced by 1925 a core of critical theory, announced chiefly in short essays and reviews, which established not only the tone but the main areas of interest for the whole half-century of literary activity to come. It has been called by its enemies the cult of form. This is unfair so far as it suggests a denial of feeling; but it is true that Pound and Eliot and the critics who have followed their example have been profoundly interested in the way the poem works on the page, and hence have insisted on close textual analysis as the beginning of all literary appreciation, however it may be followed up by ancillary methods of interpretation.

By 1920 or thereabouts the main lines were drawn, and the rest may be very quickly and roughly sketched in. Back in the United States various writers, mostly in the East, were following in the footsteps of the European school. ROBERT FROST, who had published his first book in England in 1913, soon returned to the United States, where he found an appreciative audience for his work, and took up a career which led ultimately to the popular leadership of American letters. WALLACE STEVENS entered upon his determinedly individualistic course. William Carlos Williams also refused to be classified; admiring Pound but detesting Eliot, he used the symbolist and imagist techniques to develop an ideologically American aesthetic, which has had a very wide influence on younger poets. The female poets who became popular in the twenties mostly favored the formalists—EDNA ST. VINCENT MILLAY and ELINOR WYLIE, both of whom successfully feminized the decade's attitude of sentimental bitterness, and LOUISE BOGAN and LÉONIE ADAMS, who came later and were more reserved. The expatriate groups in London and Paris included CONRAD AIKEN, who had begun publishing his poems before the war and was now clearly a leader of the new movement; E. E. CUMMINGS, whose lyric intensity and formal eccentricity quickly attracted an audience; and ARCHIBALD MACLEISH, whose early poems were gently metaphysical in tone. In the South a considerable renaissance was under way, particularly in Nashville, where the group variously known as the FUGITIVES, the Secessionists, and the Southern Agrarians was active in literature and political philosophy. The literary branch included JOHN CROWE RANSOM, ALLEN TATE, ROBERT PENN WARREN, MERRILL MOORE, and the novelist CAROLINE GORDON. These were all writers of the first rank, who put not only learning but good tough thinking back into southern poetry, and their reputations quickly ascended from the regional to the national plane. In criticism they exerted an enormous influence, especially Ransom, Tate, and Warren, who extended and refined the policies of Pound and Eliot, working closely with such

British critics as I. A. Richards, William Empson, and F. R. Leavis. In politics, under the leadership of DONALD DAVIDSON, the group took a frank stand for the social values of the Old South, advocated the re-establishment of an agrarian aristocracy, and then gradually relaxed its dogmatism, or at any event ceased to argue for it publicly, when no one took it seriously. The two strongest personalities of the decade, however, were HART CRANE, whose stormy, dense, splendidly eloquent poems attracted much attention, and YVOR WINTERS, a young Chicagoan living in California who turned from Chicagoesque experiments in imagist technique to a strict classical form, in which he has composed poems of great perspicuity and force—among the best written in America. At the same time Winters devoted himself to a hot-tempered, trenchant criticism of his contemporaries, making Crane his special anathema; and he bore down heavily on what he called the fallacy of expressive form, which he found infecting the work of virtually every major 20th-century poet.

In the thirties, the proletarian impulse turned many poets away from narrow concern with form and expression. Such expatriates as Archibald MacLeish and MALCOLM COWLEY returned home and put their poetic skill to the service of frankly political ends. New poets like MURIEL RUKEYSER and ALFRED HAYES took up proletarian themes, betraying in their style the great influence of W. H. AUDEN on American literature. Others, like KENNETH FEARING, leaned toward Whitman and Sandburg in their use of language. Louis Zukofsky and the objectivists followed Pound and Williams in treating social themes in the larger context of cultural history. A group of young Californian poets, associated with Winters, included J. V. Cunningham and Howard Baker, whose formally quiet poems often conveyed acute social bitterness. The older poets, of course, continued their work; Eliot's ASH WEDNESDAY (1930) was received with mixed feelings by many admirers who found his acceptance of literal dogma too easy, and the new installments of Pound's Cantos aroused considerable debate. Marianne Moore found among younger poets many who praised her elegant, intricate poems.

The forties introduced two fine Jewish poets, DELMORE SCHWARTZ and KARL SHAPIRO, who dealt with urban themes in a clipped rhetoric that owed at least something to the style of political writing adopted by the Anglo-American left. Other poets who chose somewhat the same tone were RANDALL JARRELL, JOHN FREDERICK NIMS, HARRY BROWN, RICHARD EBERHART, and John Malcolm Brinnin; bitter war poems predominated in the early part of the decade. THEODORE ROETHKE became one of the few poets who have successfully cultivated two distinct styles, in his case a freely metered, highly metaphorical, Rimbaud-like abstractionism, used for the evocation of dream states and the psychology of children, and a more formal, metered and rhymed lyricism, recalling Waller or Sir John Davies and used for expressions of self-conscious feeling. After the war ROBERT LOWELL marked a return to the strict metaphysical style of Tate and Eliot. ELIZABETH BISHOP revealed the influence of Marianne Moore, and JEAN GARRIGUE of the Surrealists. RICHARD WILBUR pushed the classical motif in the direction of rococo minuteness, and at the other end of the scale KENNETH PATCHEN and KENNETH REXROTH worked in strictly ametrical forms, often very beautifully. But after World War II there could be no doubt that the European element in modern American writing had triumphed over the Chicagoan. The examples of Pound, Eliot, Joyce, Yeats, and Ford Madox Ford—to name only English-speaking contemporaries—were too powerful to be overcome or denied. The internationally oriented criticism of John Crowe Ransom and Allen Tate was supreme in the country, and the KENYON REVIEW, edited by Ransom, was regarded as the fount of authority, though its editor was actually a good deal more open-minded than many of his admirers (and detractors) liked to believe.

This disposition of forces persisted in the fifties, already called the decade of academicism. Ransom's prosy style in verse was imitated by Anthony Hecht and HOWARD NEMEROV, his lighter moods by Daniel Hoffman and W. S. Merwin, his moral vigor by Donald Justice and W. D. Snodgrass. Reed Whittemore turned to openly mock-critical verse (on the analogy of Dryden's mock-heroics) with considerable success. DONALD HALL, who edited the *Paris Review* (an American magazine in spite of its name), became a leader of the young academicians. By the end of the decade a strong reaction set in against academicism, chiefly among the Beats, as they proclaimed themselves. This was a vestigial outcropping of Chicagoism, but too debilitated by bad writing and false sentimentality to produce much lasting effect, though the best of the central group, GREGORY CORSO, wrote some well-conceived and moving poems. Other poets who had already been working successfully in the broadly Williamsesque tradition were for a while attracted to the Beats by their claim to marshal the forces of anti-academicism; but it is significant that the best of these writers —Kenneth Rexroth, Denise Levertov, Robert Creeley, Robert Duncan—had renounced the association, openly or privately, by the end of the decade.

At the end of so brief an account of the American poetry written since 1920, one thinks of names, a great many, that ought to have been included if simple justice were to be served —such individualists as Adelaide Crapsey, ROBINSON JEFFERS, José Garcia Villa, Samuel Greenberg, R. P. BLACKMUR, Mina Loy; such important poets as STANLEY KUNITZ, WITTER BYNNER, MARK VAN DOREN, THOMAS MERTON, MARYA ZATURENSKA; such minor but often marvelous poets as Norman Macleod, John Wheelwright, THEODORE SPENCER, James Merrill, PAUL ENGLE, JESSE STUART, Josephine Miles, JOHN PEALE BISHOP, Phelps Putnam, GENEVIEVE TAGGARD, WINFIELD TOWNLEY

SCOTT, COUNTEE CULLEN, WILLIAM ELLERY LEONARD, ROBERT FITZGERALD, LANGSTON HUGHES, EUNICE TIETJENS, ALFRED KREYMBORG, SARA TEASDALE, EDMUND WILSON, Henry Rago, Marsden Hartley, Rosalie Moore, GEORGE DILLON, Barbara Howes, ROLFE HUMPHRIES, Ruth Stone, BABETTE DEUTSCH, Elder Olson, Reuel Denney; such young poets as Theodore Holmes, Carolyn Kizer, Stanley Burnshaw, James Dickey, or Vassar Miller. Even in the earlier periods, many poets who merit discussion have been omitted; RICHARD ALSOP, THOMAS FESSENDEN, EMMA LAZARUS, FREDERICK TUCKERMAN, STEPHEN FOSTER—these names must at least be set down. And it is too bad that nothing could be said about translations.

But there simply isn't room. There couldn't be enough room in anything less than a large book.

May anything be added about the point raised at the beginning? Have the poets of the modern era overcome American provincialism? The answer must be no and then yes. No, provincialism will never be overcome, if by this one means eradicated: it is as much a part of American culture as our accent. But yes, provincialism has been overcome, if one means that the poets of the 20th century have turned all American culture, and specifically its provincialism, into material for a mature, authentic literature. Some poets, *e.g.* Wallace Stevens, have indeed virtually eradicated provincialism by being denationalized personalities, ignorant of cultural relativity. Such is the ingenuousness of total cosmopolitanism. Others, like Dr. Williams, have been determinedly provincial, aggressively aware of national cultural values. But most, like Tate and Jarrell and Miss Bogan, have simply assumed that the American is what he is, that he must write about himself, and that he may at last do so without hostility and in self-confidence and self-respect. They have created a national, not a provincial, poetry—and this, as has been remarked elsewhere, makes all the difference. A national poetry is one, equal, indwelling, receptive. The poets were not the first to secure such a cultural identity. Henry James in the novel, Edward A. MacDowell and Charles Ives in music, Louis Sullivan in architecture, Flood and Charles Sanders Peirce in philosophy—all these came before the poets. But a good case could be made for the hypothesis that the poets have done more than the rest to consolidate the position. In any event, the pleasure of reading American poetry need not be diminished again by the fear that it somehow betrays an inferior national genius. This was undoubtedly the fear that distorted much of the cultural life of our forefathers.

Many resources are available to the reader who wishes to make further inquiries. The two standard histories of American literature are THE CAMBRIDGE HISTORY OF AMERICAN LITERATURE (1917–21) and LITERARY HISTORY OF THE UNITED STATES (1948), each edited by a committee of scholars and containing serviceable bibliographies. Histories of American poetry, in whole or part, have been written by Horace Gregory and Marya Zaturenska, William B. Otis, Henry W. Wells, Babette Deutsch, Louise Bogan, Bruce Weirick, James L. Onderdonk, Samuel L. Knapp, and others. Other useful studies which bear on the intent of this article are: De Witt Clinton, *An Introductory Discourse Delivered Before the Literary and Philosophical Society of New York* (1815); Charles J. Ingersoll, *A Discourse Concerning the Influence of America on the Mind* (1823); R. W. Emerson, "The American Scholar" (an address delivered in 1837); Eugène A. Vail, *De le Littérature et des Hommes de Lettres des États-Unis d'Amérique* (1841); E. A. Poe, *The Literati* (1850); William T. Coggeshall, *The Protective Policy in Literature* (1859); Greenough White, *A Sketch of the Philosophy of American Literature* (1891); Moses C. Tyler, *A History of American Literature During the Colonial Period and The Literary History of the American Revolution* (both 1897); John Macy, *The Spirit of American Literature* (1908); Van Wyck Brooks, *America's Coming of Age* (1915—salt well); D. H. Lawrence, *Studies in Classic American Literature* (1923); V. L. Parrington, *Main Currents in American Thought* (1927–30—not much about poetry); Matthew Josephson, *Portrait of the Artist as American* (1930); Gorham B. Munson, *The Dilemma of the Liberated* (1930); Kenneth Burke, *Counter Statement* (1931) and *Permanence and Change* (1935); Malcolm Cowley, *Exile's Return* (1934); Yvor Winters, *Primitivism and Decadence* (1937); Josephine K. Piercy, *Studies in Literary Types in Seventeenth-Century America* (1939); Perry Miller, *The New England Mind* (1939); Jay Saunders Redding, *To Make a Poet Black* (1939); George S. Gordon, *Anglo-American Literary Relations* (1942); Alfred Kazin, *On Native Grounds* (1942); Jay B. Hubbell, *The South in American Literature* (1954); William K. Wimsatt, Jr., and Cleanth Brooks, *Literary Criticism: A Short History* (1957); Louis B. Wright, *The Cultural Life of the American Colonies* (1957). There are no complete bibliographies of American poetry; for partial bibliographies, consult Tom P. Cross, *Bibliographical Guide to English Studies* (various editions).

HAYDEN CARRUTH

Poetry Package (1950), poems by W. R. B. and C. M. The former initials stand for WILLIAM ROSE BENÉT, the latter for CHRISTOPHER MORLEY. Benét's publishers once issued a collection of his poems priced at $3.50; Morley's publishers issued a collection of his poems at $2.50. One day in a bookshop Morley found both books tied together and offered at $1 under the label "Poetry Package." The two poets got together and published forty-three new poems at the $1 price, eliminating the humiliating first step. There is no indication of who wrote which poem; the reader is left the puzzle or pleasure of guessing.

Poetry Society of America, The. This organization, established in 1910, became the parent of scores of regional groups throughout the country, suggests the Pulitzer prize in poetry, has set up many encouraging prizes of its own. Its membership has included some of the most distinguished poets of the country—ROBERT FROST became its honorary president. It issued *The Poetry Society of America Anthology* (1947) and *In Fealty to Apollo* (1950).

poetry workshops and summer conferences. In the 20th century in the United States there suddenly appeared poetry (and sometimes fiction) workshops and "summer conferences" at the universities, in which famous poets gave instruction to many eager students. In February, 1952, POETRY devoted an issue to describing two notable workshops: THEODORE ROETHKE's at the University of Washington and PAUL ENGLE's at the University of Iowa. Roethke and Engle told how they taught poetry, and drew some significant conclusions; both presented impressive selections from their students' work. At Iowa, Engle issued a brochure, *Poems from the Iowa Poetry Workshop* (1951), containing the best poems written by members of his class in a single season.

Poets and Poetry of America, The. See RUFUS W. GRISWOLD.

Poets and Poetry of the West, The (1860), an anthology edited by William Turner Coggeshall. This collection, with its biographical and critical commentaries, was one of the earliest to explore and arrange the poetic productions of the Middle West. Coggeshall made a plea for recognition of literary regions in the United States in his ironically named volume, *The Protective Policy in Literature* (1859). His only predecessor in the field was WILLIAM D. GALLAGHER, who had issued *Selections from the Poetical Literature of the West* in 1841.

Poets at Work (1948), an analysis by W. H. AUDEN, KARL SHAPIRO, DONALD STAUFFER, and Rudolf Arnheim. The basis of this volume is the poetry collection at the Lockwood Memorial Library of the University of Buffalo, one of the most important repositories of manuscripts and worksheets of contemporary verse in existence today. Stauffer discusses *Genesis, or, The Poet as Maker;* Shapiro analyzes *The Meaning of the Discarded Poem;* Arnheim contributes *Psychological Notes on the Poetical Process.* Auden, taking as his title *Squares and Oblongs,* makes what Herbert J. Miller described (*Poetry,* July, 1948) as "a self-conscious repudiation of any high or holy function of poetry."

Poets of America, The (1885), a collection of critical essays by EDMUND CLARENCE STEDMAN. Stedman was among the first to establish the claim of American poetry to systematic and appreciative consideration. Ten years earlier he had established his critical reputation with his *Victorian Poets.* In his new book he discussed the New Englanders, Poe, Bayard Taylor, Whitman. He did full justice to the first group, but went far beyond them in estimating the worth of Poe and Whitman. The book made a deep impression on readers of his day. Stedman followed up his book by preparing, with Ellen M. Hutchinson, *A Library of American Literature from the Earliest Settlements to the Present Time* (11 v., 1889–90) and then by editing his celebrated collection of poems, An American Anthology, 1787–1900 (1900).

Pogo. A comic strip by Walt Kelly.

Poictesme. An imaginary region in the Middle Ages which is the setting for several novels by James Branch Cabell.

Point of No Return (1949), a novel by John P. Marquand. The theme of this story is the ambition of a businessman, Charley Gray, to win promotion in the bank in which he is employed. While he waits anxiously for the announcement of the promotion, he revisits his home town, Clyde, Me., a close fictional study of Newburyport, Mass. From 1930 to 1934 W. Lloyd Warner and a team of Yale sociologists and social anthropologists had made a study of Newburyport, published in 1941 as *The Social Life of a Modern Community;* in Marquand's novel there is a similar sociological study of Clyde. As the story of this research project unrolls, Marquand analyzes and reveals some of the hidden human puzzles that Warner could not explain. The novel, unquestionably one of Marquand's best, was dramatized successfully by Paul Osborn (prod., 1951; publ., 1952). Both novel and play express regret that business success can kill much that is spiritual in a man.

Politian: A Tragedy (1835–36), an unfinished drama in verse by Edgar Allan Poe. Three scenes were published by Poe in the December 1835 *Southern Literary Messenger* as *Scenes from an Unpublished Drama.* Two more were added in January. Actually he wrote eleven scenes, one of them a poem called *The Coliseum* which had already appeared in the *Saturday Visiter* (Oct. 26, 1833) and was later reprinted in magazines and in *The Raven and Other Poems* (1845). The other omitted scenes were of varied character, some of them low comedy. The text of all the scenes was first published complete (1923) by Thomas O. Mabbott, who later made some corrections (*Notes & Queries*, July 14, 1945). Poe took the plot of his play from a famous murder case known as the "Kentucky Tragedy." His scene is Italy, the lover who takes revenge is not yet the husband of the injured heroine, the medium is blank verse. Poe found neither drama nor blank verse congenial. See under Beauchampe.

Political Greenhouse, The (*Connecticut Courant*, 1799), a satire in verse by Richard Alsop, Lemuel Hopkins, and Theodore Dwight. It represented the prevailing Federalist point of view among the Hartford writers active at that time. See Hartford Wits.

Political Litany, A (1775), a satire by Philip Freneau. This is an attack on the British, cast into the mold of *Libera Nos, Domine.* Freneau begs for the colonies in revolt to be delivered from the British nation and its scoundrels and rascals, its soldiers and sailors, its statesmen and bishops. It is a lively piece, Freneau at his partisan best.

political parties and literature. In the United States there have been what can reasonably be called two political philosophies. One, represented by the Federalist, Whig, and Republican parties, is characteristically conservative, and has been to a large extent identified with financial, commercial, and industrial interests; the other, represented by the Democratic-Republican and Democratic parties, is traditionally liberal, and has appealed especially to the working classes.

The sharpest division of political opinion during colonial times emerged from the frequent clashes between the royal governors and the colonial assemblies. Critics of the King's policy were many. The Boston lawyer James Otis asserted the privileges of the colonies under the British constitution in his first political pamphlet, *A Vindication of the Conduct of the House of Representatives* (1762), and raised the question of taxation without representation in *The Rights of the British Colonies Asserted* (1764). The Stamp Act prompted John Adams' *A Dissertation on the Canon and Feudal Law* (1768) and John Dickinson's notable pamphlet, *Considerations upon the Rights of the Colonists to the Privileges of British Subjects* (1765). Most vigorous of the New England clergy in opposing Parliamentary measures was Jonathan Mayhew, who wrote his *Discourse Concerning Unlimited Submission* (1750) and, on repeal of the Stamp Act, *The Snare Broken* (1766). Dickinson's *Letters from a Farmer in Pennsylvania to the Inhabitants of the British Colonies* (1768) was issued to protest the passage of the Townshend Acts. Most influential of all Revolutionary pamphlets were Thomas Paine's Common Sense (1776) and The American Crisis (1776–83).

The Reverend Samuel Seabury presented the British argument in a series of pamphlets attacking the aims and policy of the First Continental Congress; Daniel Leonard stressed the unconstitutional character of the Revolutionary position in a series of letters to the newspapers under the pen name of "Massachusettensis." With the outbreak of the War of Independence the rift between these two colonial factions opened wide.

The achievement of self-government brought new differences of opinion to light, and shortly after the conclusion of the war the patriots found divisions within their own ranks. These appeared notably in the Constitutional Convention (1787) over the form of government to be established by the Constitution. The large states were determined to establish a strong national government, while the smaller ones desired to continue the existing system under which the states possessed supreme power. Inasmuch as the system finally adopted was of the federal type, the champions of the Constitution were known as the Federalists, and the opponents, as Anti-Federalists. The opinions of the former were set forth by Alexander Hamilton, John Jay, and James Madison in The Federalist (1788); their essays constitute some of the most valuable records in all American political literature.

The first presidential election (1789) was free from partisan division, and all sixty-nine electors cast their ballots for GEORGE WASHINGTON. The chief issue of Washington's first term was the fiscal program devised by Alexander Hamilton. His program was nationalistic in character, broadly construing the Constitution, and thereby strengthening the central government at the expense of the states. He advocated a diversified economic order and active governmental encouragement of finance, industry, commerce, and shipping; he expressed sympathy for creditor interests and distrusted the people's capacity to govern. A group in opposition to the Hamiltonians appeared in Congress, organized by THOMAS JEFFERSON and led in Congress by James Madison. Jefferson expressed a sympathy for the debtor class, a distrust of centralized government, and a belief in the perfectibility of man; he desired a democratic agrarian order and relative freedom from organized finance. This political breach was widened with the establishment of the NATIONAL GAZETTE (1791), an anti-administration organ under the editorship of PHILIP FRENEAU, which soon entered into battle with the Federalist GAZETTE OF THE UNITED STATES, edited by John Fenno.

By 1792 Jefferson had nearly perfected the organization of his opposition party, the Democratic-Republican party, drawing its membership chiefly from the southern states, which were in favor of strict construction of the Constitution and states' rights, i.e., sovereignty of the states as opposed to a strong federal government. The strength of the Democratic-Republican party increased rapidly, so that it nearly captured the election of 1796; John Adams, the Federalist candidate, won by a narrow margin. In 1800 and again in 1804 Jefferson was elected as a Republican, and the party remained in power until 1825. The election of 1816 marked the disappearance of the Federalist party from the political field. The Republican party, which had come into power in 1801, emphasizing a strict construction of the Constitution and a faith in the ability of the people to govern themselves, emerged from the War of 1812 greatly changed. Nevertheless, Jefferson had enunciated the fundamental principles associated with American democracy.

During the administration of JOHN QUINCY ADAMS (1825–29) the Republican party split into the National Republicans, a conservative group led by Adams, and the Democratic Republicans, a liberal group upholding the western agrarian interests, led by ANDREW JACKSON. Triumphant in 1828 and again in 1832, Jackson's party became known as the Democrats.

Jackson's elevation of the Presidency to real political power and his exercise of party leadership led to the organization of the Whigs, an opposition party led by Henry Clay, Daniel Webster, and John C. Calhoun. The Whigs were a heterogeneous collection—the Anti-Masonic party, National Republicans, ardent states' rights

men, and personal opponents of Jackson. Jackson was soon engaged in bitter battle with Calhoun over the doctrine of nullification expounded in Calhoun's South Carolina Exposition and Protest (1828). WILLIAM CULLEN BRYANT, who had assumed the editorship of the New York Evening Post in 1829, steadily supported the Democratic position. JAMES FENIMORE COOPER, in his Letter to His Countrymen (June, 1834), vehemently attacked the United States Senate, which had declared Jackson's removal of central bank deposits unconstitutional. Cooper also wrote two novels, Homeward Bound (1838) and Home as Found (1838), which illustrated his political philosophy and indirectly supported Jackson's policies; through John Effingham, one of the characters, he satirized the commercial standards and attitudes in New York.

Lack of Whig unity in the election of 1836 gave Martin Van Buren, a Democrat, an easy victory. The Whig candidate, William Henry Harrison, was swung into office in 1840 on a wave of popular enthusiasm for his Indian military successes, but of the next three elections two were won by the Democrats, in spite of the growing opposition to their support of slavery.

It was over the issue of slavery that American writing exerted its greatest influence on the course of politics. JOHN GREENLEAF WHITTIER left the Whigs and helped to found the Liberty party. He attacked the Union in his poem "Texas" (1844), believing it to be the institution that was keeping slavery alive. Some of his strongest verse was written with the object of forcing leaders of the Whig party to take a stand against slavery; in his poem ICHABOD (1850) he bitterly attacked Daniel Webster for his support of the Fugitive Slave law. "Justice and Expedience" was a poetic appeal to the conscience of New England to break its financial and commercial connections with the South.

In the first of his BIGLOW PAPERS, JAMES RUSSELL LOWELL addressed a stirring appeal to the conscience of New England: "Massachusetts, God forgive her, She's akneelin' with the rest. . . ." The third paper, "What Mr. Robinson Thinks," and the fifth paper, "The Debate in the Sennit," voice Lowell's indignation at the attitude of John Calhoun toward the northern Senators. RALPH WALDO EMERSON objected vehemently to the Whigs' attempts at compromise with the pro-slavery elements and wrote in his Journals: "Ah, thou damnable Half-and-Half! Choose, I pray you, between God and the Whig Party, and do not longer strew sugar on this bottled spider." The passage of the Fugitive Slave law in 1850 roused him to fury and a denunciation of Webster. HENRY WADSWORTH LONGFELLOW also contributed to the cause of the abolitionists in his "Poems on Slavery" (1842). However, in The Building of the Ship (1849) he considered the preservation of the Union to be of greater importance than the abolition of slavery: "Thou, too, sail on, O Ship of State! Sail on, O Union, strong and great!" Agitation over the Fugitive Slave law prompted Harriet Beecher Stowe's UNCLE TOM'S CABIN

(1852). Other influential abolitionists were WILLIAM LLOYD GARRISON, editor of the *Liberator,* and WENDELL PHILLIPS. Henry David Thoreau voiced his protest in CIVIL DISOBEDIENCE (1849).

The compromises of the Whigs and the Democratic administration's support of the southern cause forced the strongly antislavery elements into independent political organizations. On July 6, 1854, a convention held at Jackson, Michigan, adopted a resolution demanding the repeal of the Kansas-Nebraska Act and the Fugitive Slave law, denouncing slavery as a moral, social, and political evil, and agreeing to oppose its extension. The convention took the name Republican.

The new party selected John C. Frémont, who was unknown in political life, as its candidate in the election of 1856. James Buchanan, a Democrat, won the Presidency. Lowell, who had greeted the birth of the Republican party with enthusiasm, used the *Atlantic Monthly* as a vehicle for his attack on Buchanan's administration for its lack of vigor. In 1860 the lines were sharply drawn over the slavery issue. The Democrats split into two factions; the more conservative nominated John C. Breckinridge; the more liberal named STEPHEN A. DOUGLAS. The Republican party won the election with ABRAHAM LINCOLN. During the war Lowell's *North American Review* dealt with the need to preserve the Union; his *E Pluribus Unum* (1861) was an able exposition for a strong central government. Emerson pointed out the necessity of emancipation in "American Civilization" (*Atlantic Monthly,* 1862), and, in January, 1863, read his "Boston Hymn" to celebrate Lincoln's EMANCIPATION PROCLAMATION.

The close of the war and the adoption of Reconstruction policies left a void in party issues. The original mission of the Republican party had been accomplished and the Democratic party stood discredited. Grant's two Republican administrations (1869–77) produced a general distrust of government officials, but another Republican, Rutherford B. Hayes, was elected in 1876.

The period of business activity that had followed the close of the war had ended with the crash of 1873. Hard times split the country politically. In 1879 Henry George published PROGRESS AND POVERTY, in which he held that taxes should be confined to the economic rent derived from land. The debtor classes in the West seized on a policy of inflation to rescue them from depression. Grant's veto of the bill to increase the greenbacks in circulation and the passage of the Resumption Act drove the West to independent movement. In 1876 the Greenback party was organized; the forerunner of the Populist party, it was the first political expression of agrarian discontent. Second in importance to the money question was the tariff issue. The Republicans had begun an alliance with the business interests of the nation and were committed to a policy of protective tariff. The South and the Southwest, areas of Demo-

cratic strength, had the least to gain from a protective tariff and therefore advocated either a revenue tariff or free trade. In the election of 1884 Grover Cleveland, a Democrat, won the Presidency; the Republicans returned to power in 1888, but Cleveland was re-elected in 1892 on a clear-cut tariff revision platform.

The disintegration of the Greenback party after the election of 1880 had left agrarian interests stranded politically. Both major parties were responsive to eastern financial opinion, and not until 1892 did the farmers and laborers combine to form a Populist party, voicing grave dissatisfaction with eastern financial and commercial policies. The Populists' policy of free and unlimited coinage of silver and gold at the existing legal ratio of 16 to 1 became the dominant issue of the 1890's. William H. Harvey's *Coin's Financial School* (1894) and Ignatius Donnelly's *The American People's Money* (1895) became guides for the bimetallists. Among the magazines that served as a platform for the silverites were the *Arena* and the *National Bimetallist.* President Cleveland's repeal of the Silver Purchase Act and his aggressive action in sending federal troops against the Pullman and railroad strikers in Chicago split his party in two. The campaign of 1896 developed into a violent class contest between the great holders of wealth and the lower middle class and working classes.

The Republican convention adopted a platform opposing the free coinage of silver except by international agreement, and nominated William McKinley. The Democrats, after hours of debate, during which WILLIAM JENNINGS BRYAN delivered his "CROSS OF GOLD" oration, adopted the silver platform and nominated Bryan. The leaders of the Populist party supported Bryan; their party thus dropped from sight, but not before it had proved a potent factor in emphasizing conditions and demands of the western section of the country. The ensuing election, in which McKinley was the victor, indicated that the party of Jefferson and Jackson had again come under the domination of the radical social democracy of the West. It was also apparent that the Republican party had become conservative, that it possessed great strength among the commercial and industrial interests of the country, and that it was to be associated with conservative business policies, a sound dollar, and a protective tariff. McKinley was re-elected in 1900, but served only a few months before he was assassinated. He was succeeded by Theodore Roosevelt who was re-elected in 1904, and chose William Howard Taft as the successful Republican candidate of 1908.

During this period the nation's chief concern was with domestic issues. If a 19th-century novelist chose a political theme, he generally did so to expose the evils of corruption in government (see MUCKRAKING) or to bemoan the vulgarities of public life, as in HENRY ADAMS' DEMOCRACY. During Roosevelt's administration a group of journalistic writers aroused public opinion with exposures of corruption; they also attacked social evils like slums and juvenile delinquency. Notable among these works were: IDA M. TARBELL's *History of the Standard Oil Company* (1903), LINCOLN STEFFENS' *The Shame of the Cities* (1904), and UPTON SINCLAIR's *The Jungle* (1906).

In the spring of 1912 liberal and conservative elements were found in both major parties. The Republican convention nominated the conservative William H. Taft; the disaffection of liberals within the party led to the formation of the Progressive party, which nominated Theodore Roosevelt on a platform which included demands for prohibition of child labor, minimum-wage standards for working women, and the direct election of Senators. In the Democratic convention the liberals dominated the situation, with Woodrow Wilson winning the nomination; however, the conservatives refrained from taking separate political action. Wilson won the election and was re-elected in 1916.

In the election of 1920 Warren G. Harding's slogan "back to normalcy" caught the popular imagination and the Republicans won by a landslide. The next presidential election turned wholly on domestic questions. The chief topics of debate were tax revision, agricultural relief, regulation of railroads, tariffs, and economy in the government. The Progressive party nominated Robert La Follette for President on a platform of radical character; Calvin Coolidge, a Republican, was elected, defeating John W. Davis (Democrat), and La Follette, who polled a surprising 4,800,000 votes.

Although there was agricultural and liberal dissatisfaction with the Republican administration of Coolidge, Hoover was elected in 1928, Al Smith having been defeated on issues of religion, bossism, and Prohibition. The issues of the election of 1932 primarily concerned the depression and how to combat it, the serious plight of the farmers, relief of unemployment, foreign trade and tariff revision, and national fiscal policies. Franklin D. Roosevelt, a Democrat, won by a landslide; he was re-elected in 1936, 1940, and 1944. His New Deal caused great controversy, and resulted in the reappearance of strictly political or governmental questions after their having been submerged during seventy years of post–Civil War life. Of greatest significance is the Democratic policy advocating the assumption by the national government of powers heretofore held by the states or not exercised by either authority.

Upon Roosevelt's sudden death Harry S. Truman became President in 1945, and was re-elected in 1948, although he had to face the opposition of two splinter parties: the States' Rights Democrats nominated J. Strom Thurmond, and a new Progressive party nominated Henry A. Wallace, who ran on a platform of friendship for Russia and numerous radical doctrines. Dwight D. Eisenhower, a Republican, was elected in 1952 and 1956. John F. Kennedy's election in 1960 returned the Democrats to the White House.

The novels that touch upon the political ex-

perience of contemporary America most often raise the specters of totalitarianism, defeated radicalism, or disabled liberalism: John Dos Passos' *U.S.A.* (*q.v.*) (1938); Lionel Trilling's *The Middle of the Journey* (1947); and Robert Penn Warren's ALL THE KING'S MEN (1946). HENRY STEELE COMMAGER edited an excellent collection, *Documents of American History* (1934).

Politician Outwitted (prod., 1788; pub., 1789), a patriotic drama attributed to Samuel Low. It dramatized the great contest for and against the new Constitution.

Polk, James Knox (b. Mecklenburg Co., N.C., Nov. 2, 1795—d. June 15, 1849), eleventh President. Polk graduated from the University of North Carolina in 1818, studied law, set up practice in Nashville, Tenn. In 1825 he became a member of the House of Representatives, where he remained for seven terms, a staunch supporter of ANDREW JACKSON. He was Speaker of the House, 1835–39, then left to become Governor of Tennessee, 1839–41. He was nominated as a "dark horse" candidate at the 1844 Democratic Convention, triumphed over the Whig candidate, HENRY CLAY. As President, Polk made his aims clear from the start: "One, a reduction of the tariff; another, the independent treasury; a third, the settlement of the Oregon boundary question; and lastly, the acquisition of California." All this was accomplished, plus the war with Mexico. George Bancroft, who planned to write a life of Polk but died before he could do so, asserted that Polk was the best statesman of his group and was "prudent, far-sighted, bold, excelling any Democrat of his day in undeviatingly correct exposition of his democratic principles."

Eugene Irving McCormac's excellent biography, *James K. Polk* (1922), supplanted John S. Jenkins' *James Knox Polk and a History of His Administration* (1850). Perhaps a too admiring account is Martha Morrel's *Young Hickory* (1949). Allan Nevins' *Polk: The Diary of a President* (1952) is made up of selections from *The Diary of James K. Polk During His Presidency, 1845 to 1849*, edited by M. M. Quaife (4 v., 1910). Emerson Hough depicted Polk, not very favorably, in his novel *Fifty-four Forty or Fight!* (1909).

Pollard, Edward A[lfred] (b. Albemarle Co., Va., Feb. 27, 1831—d. Dec. 16, 1872), editor, historian, biographer. Pollard edited the *Daily Richmond Examiner* from 1861 to 1867. An ardent supporter of the South, he wrote *Southern Spy, or Curiosities of Slavery in the South* (1859); *Letters of the Southern Spy* (1861); *Southern History of the War* (1863; enlarged, 1866); *The Lost Cause* (1866); and a life of Jefferson Davis (1869).

Pollard, [Joseph] Percival (b. Germany, Jan. 29, 1869—d. Dec. 17, 1911), critic, playwright, novelist. Pollard received his education in England, came to the United States in 1885, began to write critical articles in the 1890's, was a reviewer for *Town Topics* from 1897 until his death. He established a reputation as an authority on European, especially German, literature, and wrote about American authors. The best of his critical writing was gathered in *Their Day in Court* (1909). *Masks and Minstrels of New Germany* (1911) introduced American readers to many little known German writers. He also wrote plays of his own, adapted others for RICHARD MANSFIELD, satirized Mansfield in a novel called *The Imitator* (1901). He made American Puritanism a favorite target.

Pollock, Channing (b. Washington, D.C., March 4, 1880—d. Aug. 17, 1946), critic, playwright. Pollock was first of all a man of the theater. He wrote plays of every possible kind, from farces to thesis dramas, and fought both censorship and salaciousness. He began as a drama critic for the Washington *Post* and the Washington *Times,* then wrote drama reviews for several New York magazines, including *Smart Set.* He wrote more than thirty plays, most of them successful. Among them were *A Game of Hearts* (1900); *Napoleon the Great* (1901); a dramatization of Frank Norris' THE PIT (1904); *In the Bishop's Carriage* (1902); *The Little Gray Lady* (1906); *Clothes* (with AVERY HOPWOOD, 1906); *The Sign on the Door* (1919); and *The Fool* (1922). Later plays such as *Mr. Moneypenny* (1928) and *The House Beautiful* (1931) struck a more serious and sentimental tone. Pollock also wrote many books and several popular songs, including "My Man" for Fannie Brice, lectured widely, edited the Columbia Broadcasting System's *Magazine of the Air* and wrote several radio plays, devised a system of twenty-seven form letters for replying to critics, and wrote his memoirs in *The Adventures of a Happy Man* (1939; enlarged, 1946), and *Harvest of My Years* (1943).

Pollyanna (1913), a children's novel by ELEANOR HODGMAN PORTER. This resolutely cheerful story of an appealing orphan who invents the "glad game" when she is sent to live with a stern aunt sold over a million copies; apartment houses, a brand of milk, a game, and innumerable babies were named for "the Glad Girl." *Pollyanna* was dramatized in 1916 by Catherine Chisholm Cushing, later made into a movie for Mary Pickford. *Pollyanna Grows Up* (1915), the only sequel by Mrs. Porter, was followed by a series of Pollyanna books by Harriet Lummis Smith, Elizabeth Borton, and Virginia May Moffitt. "Pollyanna" is now a part of the language, defined in *Webster's New World Dictionary* as "an excessively or persistently optimistic person."

Pomfret, John Edwin (b. Philadelphia, Sept. 21, 1898—   ), teacher, college administrator, historian. Pomfret taught at the universities of South Carolina, Princeton, and Vanderbilt, was appointed president of William and Mary in 1942, then became director of the Huntington Library, San Marino, Calif. He wrote *The Struggle for Land in Ireland* (1930) and *The Geographical Pattern of Mankind* (1935), and edited *California Gold Rush Voyages* (1954).

Ponceau, Pierre Étienne Du. See DU PONCEAU, PIERRE ÉTIENNE.

Ponce de Leon, Juan (b. Spain, 1460[?]—d. May[?] [June?], 1521). See FOUNTAIN OF YOUTH.

Pond, Frederick Eugene ["Will Wildwood"] (b. Packwaukee, Wis., April 8, 1856—d. Nov. 1, 1925), sportswriter, editor. An authority on field sports, Pond wrote a *Handbook for Young Sportsmen* (1876) and *Memoirs of Eminent Sportsmen* (1878), also edited HENRY WILLIAM HERBERT's *Sporting Scenes and Characters* (2 v., 1881). When he came east to edit *Turf, Field, and Farm,* he immediately got in touch with E. Z. C. JUDSON (Ned Buntline) as a possible contributor, and after Judson's death Pond wrote *The Life and Adventures of Ned Buntline* (1888), containing much information obtained from personal conversations with that remarkable person. Pond edited other books about sports and several magazines, including *Wildwood's Magazine.*

Pond, James B[urton] (b. Cuba, N.Y., June 11, 1838—d. June 21, 1903), lecture manager, memoirist. Pond was the most successful lecture manager of his day; among his clients were Mark Twain, Henry Ward Beecher, George W. Cable, James Whitcomb Riley, Ralph Waldo Emerson, William Dean Howells, and Bill Nye. He wrote amusing reminiscences in *A Summer in England with Henry Ward Beecher* (1887) and *Eccentricities of Genius: Memories of Famous Men and Women of the Platform and Stage* (1900).

Ponteach, or, The Savages of America (1766), a play by Major ROBERT ROGERS. Rogers had fought Indians since his boyhood and as commander of "Rogers' Rangers" had played a leading role in the siege of Detroit by the Ottawa chieftain PONTIAC. *Ponteach* was not only the first American play about Indians but also the first friendly treatment of them. The plot is complicated and includes a love affair; the medium is the somewhat pompous blank verse of the period. It was never produced, and in published form met with severe strictures from critics. But unquestionably Rogers' portrait of Pontiac helped establish his reputation as a "noble savage" and a great leader. Another play on the same subject was Gen. Alexander Macomb's *Pontiac, or, The Siege of Detroit* (1835), produced in 1838 at the National Theater in Washington. Macomb also exhibited Pontiac in a noble light, introduced Major Rogers as a leading character, and gave the worst of it to the British officers.

Pontiac (b. 1720[?]—d. 1769), Ottawa Indian chieftain. Pontiac was probably born in northwestern Ohio. After he became leader of his tribe, he seems to have conceived the idea of forming a loose confederacy of several Algonquian tribes. According to recent historians, his influence was greatly exaggerated by Francis Parkman in *The History of the Conspiracy of Pontiac* (1851). When the French were defeated in the French and Indian Wars, Pontiac and his fellow chieftains distrusted the new British rulers. War broke out in 1763, and Detroit was besieged by Pontiac and his allies.

Pontiac was a clever tactician, but was defeated by the British and signed a treaty of peace on July 25, 1766. He was murdered by another Indian in 1769.

The "conspiracy's" most recent historian, Howard H. Peckham, has put together in *Pontiac and the Indian Uprising* (1947) a fully documented account of what happened, although he could find little about Pontiac personally. The chieftain appears in several novels: Mary C. Crowley's *The Heroine of the Strait* (1902); Randall Parrish's *A Sword of the Old Frontier* (1905); Louis Zara's *This Land Is Mine* (1940); Hervey Allen's *The Forest and the Fort* (1943). For plays about him see PONTEACH.

Pony Express. A postal enterprise, undertaken under private auspices, which carried mail from St. Joseph, Mo., to Sacramento, Calif., for seventy-nine weeks (April 3, 1860, to Oct. 24, 1861, with a four-week suspension because of the Pah-Ute War). The chief dividends it paid were those of the imagination, quickening the pulse of everyone who thought of the bold and reckless men who raced over plain and mountain in all kinds of weather, against all kinds of odds. At its height the service employed 125 riders, 400 station men and assistants, 420 horses. It guaranteed delivery of the mail in ten days between St. Joseph and Sacramento, and rarely failed. Horses were changed every ten or twenty miles. Letters were carried at first at $5 apiece; later the charges were reduced and never at any time paid the costs of operation. Two of the most famous riders were Buffalo Bill (see WILLIAM F. CODY) and WILD BILL HICKOK.

Among books that tell about the Pony Express are Frank A. Root and W. E. Connelley's *The Overland Stage to California* (1901); Frank J. Visscher's *A Thrilling and Truthful History of the Pony Express* (1908); Glenn D. Bradley's *The Story of the Pony Express* (1913); Henry James Forman's *The Pony Express* (1925); LeRoy Hafen's *The Overland Mail* (1926); Alvin F. Harlow's *Old Post Bags* (1928); G. D. Brewerton's *Overland with Kit Carson* (1930); J. Frank Dobie's *On the Open Range* (1931) and *The Mustangs* (1952); Arthur Chapman's *The Pony Express* (1932); Howard R. Driggs' *The Pony Express Goes Through* (1935); Samuel Hopkins Adams' *The Pony Express* (1950); Lee Jensen's *The Pony Express* (1955).

Poole, Ernest (b. Chicago, Jan. 23, 1880—d. Jan. 10, 1950), journalist, novelist. The strong social interest which appears in Poole's novels showed itself early in his life when, after graduating from Princeton University in 1902, he went to live in a settlement house in the slums of New York. He wrote articles for magazines exposing child labor, sweat shops, and the horrible conditions of the East Side; he covered the Chicago stockyard strike in 1904 for *The Outlook*, and traveled in Russia the following year reporting on the abortive revolution of 1905. His first novel, THE HARBOR (1915), an outstanding proletarian novel, deals with the America of the immigrant's dream—a land young, powerful, growing, with space for everyone. The harbor is a symbol of the business world, now friendly, now menacing. HIS FAMILY (1917), a Pulitzer prize winner, shows the problems arising from the flow of immigrants into old New York. In 1917 Poole returned to Russia after serving as war correspondent in France and Germany. From this visit came *The Village* (1918) and *The Dark People* (1918), accounts of Russian life, and *The Little Dark Man* (1925), Russian tales and sketches. Other novels are *His Second Wife* (1918); *Blind* (1920); *Beggar's Gold* (1921); *Millions* (1922); *Danger* (1923); *With Eastern Eyes* (1926); *The Destroyer* (1931); *Great Winds* (1933); *The Nancy Flyer* (1949). *Nurses on Horseback* (1932) is an account of the remarkable work done in the Kentucky mountains by the Frontier Nursing Association. *The Bridge* (1940) is an autobiography. Although many of his novels have a vigor that owes much to his reporter's training, Poole did not quite live up to his early promise.

Poole, William Frederick (b. Salem, Mass., Dec. 24, 1821—d. March 1, 1894), librarian, historian. While still a student at Yale University, Poole became interested in library work, was appointed to the staff of the university library, and in 1848 published his very useful and most famous work, *Poole's Index to Periodical Literature*, which he enlarged in later editions and which was continued after his death by other compilers. He became head librarian of the Boston Athenaeum (1856), of the Cincinnati Public Library (1871), of the Chicago Public Library (1874), of the Newberry Library in Chicago (1887). Among his books: *The Battle of the Dictionaries* (1856); *Cotton Mather and Salem Witchcraft* (1869); *Anti-Slavery Before 1800* (1887); *Columbus and the Founding of the New World* (1892).

Pooley, Robert C[ecil] (b. Brooklyn, N.Y., March 25, 1898—   ), teacher, linguist. Pooley joined the faculty of the University of Wisconsin in 1931, and became chairman of the department of integrated studies in 1947. Long active in the NATIONAL COUNCIL OF TEACHERS OF ENGLISH, he prepared for that association a volume on *Teaching English Usage* (1946) which provides a sensible guide to modern scholarly views of language. In 1957 he wrote *Teaching English Grammar*.

Poor, Henry Varnum (b. Andover, Me., Dec. 8, 1812—d. Jan. 4, 1905), railroad man, economist, statistician. Poor, a friend of Emerson, Theodore Parker, and other intellectual leaders of the day, helped his brother John Alfred Poor build the Atlantic and St. Lawrence Railroad. He was interested above all in gathering practical data about this enterprise as it developed, and in discovering, as he put it, the form or soul of the enterprise. With his son Henry William Poor, he founded the firm of H. V. & H. W. Poor, which published annually, beginning with 1868, *Poor's Manual of Railroads;* this became in 1925 *Poor's Railroad Section.* The firm also developed other manuals and reference books.

In addition Poor wrote on *Money and Its Laws* (1877); *Twenty-Two Years of Protection* (1888); *The Tariff* (1892); and edited *The American Railroad Journal* (1849–62).

Poore, Benjamin ["Perley"] (b. near Newburyport, Mass., Nov. 2, 1820—d. May 29, 1887), newspaperman, biographer. Poore was one of the most widely known Washington correspondents of his day. Under the pen name "Perley" he wrote newspaper columns for the Boston *Journal* (1854–84), in the meantime preparing numerous popular biographies. Among others, he wrote lives of Zachary Taylor, U. S. Grant, General A. E. Burnside, Louis Philippe. He also edited the first issue of the *Congressional Record.*

Poor Richard's Almanack (1733–57), an annual compilation prepared by BENJAMIN FRANKLIN. He ascribed the almanac to Richard Saunders, the publisher of an English compilation, *Apollo Anglicanus,* and also a Philadelphia customer of his. The *Almanack* became a vehicle for Franklin's common-sense philosophy, and many of his maxims have become familiar sayings, for example: "Nothing but money is sweeter than honey." "Approve not of him who commends all you say." He also drew upon the proverbs of all ages. The *Almanack* was very popular. Franklin sold it in 1757, and it continued to be published until 1790. There have been numerous reprints of selections from the *Almanack,* one edited by Paul Leicester Ford (1890).

Popeye, a character in SANCTUARY, a novel by William Faulkner. An embodiment of pure evil, Popeye is a reptilian and perverted gangster and murderer who rapes Temple Drake and kills the halfwit Tommy. Popeye is finally hanged in Alabama for a murder he did not commit, having been busy, at the time of the supposed crime, murdering a man in Memphis.

Popular Book, The (1950), "a history of America's literary taste" by JAMES D. HART. Hart's stimulating and original volume usefully supplements Frank Luther Mott's GOLDEN MULTITUDES: THE STORY OF BEST-SELLERS IN THE U.S. (1947), since the points of view of the two books differ. Mott is interested in sales over a long period, Hart in popular reading taste as related to social changes and pressures. The general public, Hart concludes, wants certain services: the clarification of ideas already in circulation (Paine's *American Crisis*), the emotional statement of attitudes people are prepared to accept (Mrs. Stowe's *Uncle Tom's Cabin*), the popularization of desirable information theretofore obscure (Durant's *Story of Philosophy*), the satisfying appeal in terms of various forms of entertainment currently considered amusing or exciting (Erle Stanley Gardner's *The Case of the Curious Bride*).

Popular Mechanics. A monthly magazine founded in 1902 by Henry Haven Windsor, who made its motto from the beginning, "Written so that you can understand it." It has always relied heavily on pictures and lays claim to having been America's pioneer picture magazine. In its exceedingly practical articles on how to make or do things, its home workshop section has been especially popular. It also has issued millions of "how to do it" books and pamphlets since 1904. Among notable contributors have been Guglielmo Marconi, Thomas A. Edison, Alexander Graham Bell, Theodore Roosevelt, Pierre Curie, Roy Chapman Andrews. In 1951 was issued Edward L. Throm's compilation *Fifty Years of Popular Mechanics,* with text and pictures in facsimile taken from more than six hundred issues of the magazine.

Popular Science Monthly. A magazine founded in May, 1872, by Edward Livingston Youmans. Youmans had been editing the famous "International Scientific Series" for D. Appleton & Co. He had persuaded Herbert Spencer to write a book for the series, and when the book, *The Study of Sociology,* reached him, he persuaded the publishing firm to undertake the magazine so that Spencer's work could be published serially. Its contributors have included many notables, among them Henry George, Charles Darwin, William James, Thomas A. Edison, Havelock Ellis. It uses many illustrations, has tended in recent years to relegate "how to do it" material to sections at the back.

Populist party. See POLITICAL PARTIES.

Porgy (1925), a novel by DuBose HEYWARD. It is a powerful story of the Charleston, S.C., waterfront and the Negroes who live on Catfish Row. Most notable among them is the crippled beggar Porgy, who becomes involved in a murder and is jailed as a witness by a white detective. Other important characters are Bess, Sportin' Life, Crown, and Serena. Heyward and his wife Dorothy adapted the novel into a successful play called *Porgy* (1927).

The effective use of spirituals in this play suggested to GEORGE GERSHWIN the possibility of turning it into a folk opera. The libretto was prepared by Heyward in collaboration with IRA GERSHWIN. Then George Gershwin began writing the music; in order to get the "feel" of the background, he lived for several weeks in a shack on the Charleston waterfront and sought in particular to absorb the music of the Gullah Negroes. The opera *Porgy and Bess* opened in 1935 and has since been recognized as an American classic. Its songs have become universally known—*Summertime, I Got Plenty of Nuttin'; It Ain't Necessarily So; Bess, You Is My Woman Now;* and others. It has often been revived, and the novel has frequently been reprinted. In 1952 the State Department used the opera as an instrument in cultural relations, sending it on a tour of Europe and Asia with an all-Negro cast.

Porgy, Captain. A comic character appearing in WILLIAM GILMORE SIMMS' trilogy of the Revolutionary War—THE PARTISAN (1835); *Mellichampe* (1836); *Katharine Walton* (1851) —and in *The Forayers* (1855) and *Woodcraft* (1854). Porgy combines a Falstaffian paunch and love for food and drink with the more typical Southern virtues of bravery, gallantry, and generosity. He is bawdy, humorous, inventive, and a tireless practical joker. Many critics felt Simms was at his best when describing the exploits of Porgy, although others (notably Edgar Allan Poe) found Porgy "an insufferable bore."

Porter, Cole (b. Peru, Ind., June 9, 1893—d. Oct. 15, 1964), composer, lyricist. Musically inclined from childhood, Porter went to Yale, then to Harvard to study law. But he soon switched to music and obtained a thorough musical education in Cambridge and Paris. A wealthy playboy, it took him a long time to convince Tin-Pan Alley that he could write first-rate songs, and Broadway that he had a keen sense of the theater. His first musical was *See America First* (1916). He won his first great success with his lyrics in *Hitchy Koo* (1920), then went on to such other great hits as *Greenwich Follies* (1925); *Paris* (1928); *50 Million Frenchmen* (1929); *Anything Goes* (1934); *Red Hot and Blue* (1936); *Panama Hattie* (1940); *Something for the Boys* (1943); *Kiss Me, Kate* (1948); *Can-Can* (1953); *Silk Stockings* (1955); also, some films, such as *Night and Day* (1946); *High Society* (1956); *Les Girls* (1957). These musical comedies and films included such successful songs as "Night and Day," "Begin the Beguine," "Everything I Love," "In the Still of the Night," "I've Got You Under My Skin," "It's De-Lovely," "I Get a Kick Out of You," "C'est Magnifique," "True Love," and many others. He has also written a good deal for TV. His melodic genius is evident in all Porter's music. He is a witty versifier, infectiously gay. In 1954 Random House published *103 Lyrics by Cole Porter* with an introduction by Fred Lounsberry.

Porter, David (b. Boston, Feb. 1, 1780—d. March 3, 1843), naval officer, memoirist. Porter saw sea duty during the War of 1812, and later in the Caribbean, but was court-martialed because of difficulties with the Spanish authorities in Puerto Rico. He served in the Mexican navy, 1826–29, then received from President Jackson consular and diplomatic appointments in Algiers and Constantinople. His memories of the Pacific were published as *A Journal of a Cruise Made to the Pacific Ocean, 1812–1814* (2 v., 1815), a book read with profit by Herman Melville. Porter also wrote *Constantinople and Its Environs* (2 v., 1835), in which he included letters he had written to James K. Paulding.

Porter, David Dixon (b. Chester, Pa., June 8, 1813—d. Feb. 13, 1891), naval officer, historian. The son of DAVID PORTER entered the navy at the age of sixteen, served under his father in the West Indies and in the Mexican navy. During the Civil War he commanded the mortar fleet under Farragut and helped bring about the surrender of Vicksburg. After the war Porter was made superintendent of the Naval Academy, became an admiral in 1870, and held important positions in the Navy Department. He edited *Memoir of Commodore David Porter* (1875), wrote his own memoirs of the Civil War (1885) and a *History of the Navy during the War of the Rebellion* (1887), and two novels.

Porter, Edwin S. Author and producer of THE GREAT TRAIN ROBBERY.

Porter, Eleanor H[odgman] (b. Littleton, N.H., Dec. 19, 1868—d. May 21, 1920), teacher, singer, novelist. Mrs. Porter wrote sentimental novels, beginning with *Cross-Currents* (1907). She created two particularly popular characters, *Miss Billie* (1911), whose fortunes she continued to relate in *Miss Billie—Married* (1914), and POLLYANNA (1913), about whom she wrote one sequel, *Pollyanna Grows Up* (1915). Later she published *Just David* (1916), also a best seller. Since her death at least five sequels by other writers have given further details of Pollyanna's persistently glad disposition and have carried the sale of the "Pollyanna" series to well beyond two million.

Porter, Gene[va] Stratton (b. Wabash Co., Ind., Aug. 17, 1863—d. Dec. 6, 1924), naturalist, novelist. Just south of Wabash, where Mrs. Porter's farmer-clergyman father moved when she was eleven, is the great Limberlost Swamp. There she studied birds, feathers, bees, moths, eggs, other forms of nature. Her LADDIE (1913) tells in fiction the story of her own childhood in the Limberlost country; *Freckles* (1904) portrays a lad whose days are spent in the Limberlost Swamp; and A GIRL OF THE LIMBERLOST (1909) has the same background. Other books of hers are *The Song of the Cardinal* (1902); *At the Foot of the Rainbow* (1908); *The Harvester* (1911); *Michael O'Halloran* (1915); *The Keeper of the Bees* (1925). Her books sold in millions. The nature lore which, as one critic said, "mitigated the fatuity of her novels," did not restrain contemporary reviewers from denouncing her super-saccharine sentimentality. Her daughter Jeanette Porter Meehan wrote her biography, *The Lady of the Limberlost* (1928).

Porter, Horace (b. Huntingdon, Pa., April 15, 1837—d. May 29, 1921), soldier, diplomat. After graduating from West Point, Porter served in the Army of the Potomac, becoming Grant's aide-de-camp near the end of the war. In 1867–68 he was Assistant Secretary of War; during Grant's presidency he was his military secretary. He served as Ambassador to France from 1897 to 1905. In April, 1905, he recovered the body of JOHN PAUL JONES and returned it to the United States, a service for which he received the thanks of Congress and the privileges of the floor of both houses for life. As a delegate to the Hague Peace Conference (1907) he propounded the "Porter Proposition," imposing restrictions upon debt collection by strong nations from weaker ones. *West Point Life* (1860) and *Campaigning with Grant* (1897) recount his military experiences.

Porter, Katherine Anne (b. Indian Creek, Tex., May 15, 1890—   ), short-story writer, novelist. Miss Porter once described herself as "precocious, nervous, rebellious, untractable," to which one could also add "individualistic." Perhaps her most distinguished writing has been done in the form of the short novel rather than the short story or long novel; she is regarded as one of the most intelligent and thoughtful practitioners of modern fiction. Her meaning is not always immediately apparent, and she appeals to a limited audience willing to delve for hid-

UPI

den significances. She prefers to treat characters, as Leo Gurko has said, "in disharmony with their environment." Ray B. West, Jr., considers *Flowering Judas* (1930) her most successful single work of fiction. He locates three kinds of symbols in it and concludes that "social consciousness" is central in Miss Porter's thinking, but in a wider sense than any particular political creed. Other books by Miss Porter are *Hacienda* (1934); NOON WINE (1937); *Pale Horse, Pale Rider* (1939); *The Leaning Tower* (1944). She has also translated stories from the Spanish and wrote an introduction to an anthology of South American stories, *Fiesta in November* (1942). Miss Porter has been very conscious of her own art and of the art of fiction in general; an able critic, in *The Days Before* (1952) she made a gathering of her essays on life and art written over a period of thirty years. *Ship of Fools,* her first new novel in twenty years, appeared in 1962.

Porter, Noah (b. Farmington, Conn., Dec. 14, 1811—d. March 4, 1892), clergyman, philosopher, educator. Porter was graduated from Yale University in 1831, served as a tutor there while studying divinity. He preached in New Milford, Conn., and in Springfield, Mass., accepting the Clark professorship of moral philosophy and metaphysics at Yale in 1846. In 1871

he became president of Yale, a position he held until 1886, when ill health forced him to resign. He continued to teach philosophy, although his scholarship far outshone his pedagogy. A champion of conservatism, he believed that education should be "distinctively and earnestly Christian." He denounced Herbert Spencer, advocated Latin and Greek as the only sound basis of liberal education. His views are set forth in *The American Colleges and the American Public* (1870, 1878).

Porter was universally respected at Yale, although he did not always succeed in persuading his listeners. Henry Holt told of a lecture in which Porter, vigorously attacking Darwinism, inadvertently converted his entire class to the theory of evolution. In spite of his conservatism, however, his writings were probably more widely read than those of any other American philosopher of his time. *The Human Intellect* (1868), his chief work, reissued many times, was widely praised. He edited the 1864 edition of *Webster's American Dictionary of the English Language* as well as *Webster's International Dictionary* (1890). *The Sciences of Nature Versus the Science of Man* (1871); *Science and Sentiment* (1882); *The Elements of Moral Science, Theoretical and Practical* (1885); *Kant's Ethics* (1886); and *Fifteen Years in the Chapel of Yale College, 1871–1886* (1888) are his other principal works.

Porter, William Sydney. See O. HENRY.

Porter, William Trotter (b. Newbury, Vt., Dec. 24, 1809—d. July 19, 1858), humorist, newspaperman, editor. Porter worked on newspapers in Vermont and New York City. In 1831 he founded a weekly sporting journal called SPIRIT OF THE TIMES and edited it until 1856, at which time the magazine was sold to George Wilkes and the name changed to *Porter's Spirit of the Times.* It continued to be published until 1861. Porter's magazine was in part a reprint periodical, and he daily searched through newspapers and magazines in his quest for material, particularly comic material. In his pages appeared the best of southwestern and a good deal of national humor. Porter compiled from his magazine three collections: *The Big Bear of Arkansas and Other Tales* (1845); *A Quarter Race in Kentucky* (1847); and *Colonel Thorpe's Scenes in Arkansaw* (1858). Francis Brinley wrote a *Life of William T. Porter* (1860). Mark Twain undoubtedly read and enjoyed *Spirit of the Times.* Bernard De Voto feels certain that a story in that magazine influenced Twain when he wrote his *Jumping Frog* story.

Port Folio, The. JOSEPH DENNIE, Harvard graduate, lawyer, dandy, and essayist, founded the *Port Folio* in Philadelphia in 1801. It was a weekly miscellany devoted chiefly to literature and politics. John Quincy Adams, Charles Brockden Brown, Alexander Wilson, Thomas G. Fessenden, and William Dunlap were among the contributors to the early volumes of the magazine; but Dennie himself, often using his pen name "Oliver Oldschool," was the chief writer throughout his editorship. He was an extreme

Federalist; his eloquent denunciation of the democratic system in his series "The Progress of Democracy" (1803) caused him to be tried for seditious libel, but he was acquitted through a brilliant defense by Joseph Hopkinson. Dennie attacked Jefferson with poison-pen brilliance in 1802–1803, but in 1809 he abandoned political discussion. Commentary on English, classical, and Continental writers was important in the *Port Folio*, with travel, biography, American speech, and social customs lending great variety to the contents of the journal.

Dennie died in 1812, and was succeeded by Nicholas Biddle, who made the *Port Folio* a monthly review, but the magazine declined in popularity. Later editors were Charles Caldwell (1814–1816) and John E. Hall (1816–1827). In 1816 it was taken over by the Halls; Sarah Ewing Hall had four literary sons, all of some distinction, but their united efforts failed to save the *Port Folio* from extinction in 1827.

Portrait for Posterity: Lincoln and His Biographers (1947), a critical treatise by Benjamin P. Thomas. It is apparent from Thomas' excellent survey that there is a fascinating drama in the history of his biographers' accounts of Lincoln. As in any drama, there is conflict: between the romanticists and the realists, even between truth and distortion of the truth. There is still argument on important points; Thomas shows what answers were given to these questions by Lincoln's biographers. His analysis and Paul M. Angle's *A Shelf of Lincoln Books* (1946) are the best guides to the vast number of books about Lincoln.

Portrait of a Lady, The (1881), a novel by HENRY JAMES. Isabel Archer, thought to be modeled on James' memory of his cousin Minnie Temple, is the heroine of the novel; her character determines the action that gives it form. In this sense *The Portrait of a Lady* is contrary to James' usual conception of the well-made novel, in which the action and the situation determine the characters who are to carry out the action. Isabel is one of James' most finely realized characters, and *The Portrait* is a highly unified novel. The action begins when Isabel rejects the proposal of Lord Warburton, a wealthy and cultivated Englishman. Isabel, a relatively poor but spiritually independent American girl, inherits a large sum of money from her uncle largely as a result of her rejection of Warburton, and, financially independent, is at liberty to make further choices. Feeling that she wants a man for whom she can do something, she chooses to marry Gilbert Osmond, a superficially attractive but weak man enslaved by poverty and by his former mistress, Madame Merle, by whom he has had a child, Pansy. Isabel realizes, too late, that she cannot help Osmond, but chooses to remain with him for the sake of the child when Caspar Goodwood, an old admirer, begs her to flee with him and escape from Osmond. By sacrificing her own freedom of action in order to make freedom of choice possible to Pansy, Isabel asserts her inner freedom from material and emotional states of dependence.

Posey, Alexander Lawrence (b. near Eufaula, Indian Territory (Okla.), Aug. 3, 1873—d. May 27, 1908), Creek Indian poet, humorist, editor. Posey edited the *Indian Journal* from 1901 to 1903, and published in it some of his verses and his satirical *Fus Fixico Letters*. The latter were written in Indian-English dialect.

Post, Emily [Price] (b. Baltimore, Md., Oct. 3, 1873—d. Sept. 25, 1960), novelist, writer on etiquette. Born to wealth and social position, Emily Price grew up in New York, made her debut in 1892, and married the dashing Edwin Post the same year. Later she parted from him and turned to writing fiction. Her novels *The Flight of the Moth* (1904), *Purple and Fine Linen* (1906), and others, all dealt with Americans living elegantly in Europe.

When her publisher asked Mrs. Post to write a manual of etiquette she indignantly refused. He pointed out that her novels were "nothing but manners," sent her an etiquette book which so horrified her with its inaccuracies that she agreed to write one. *Etiquette* (1922) sold half a million copies, establishing its author as social arbiter of America. It was revised in 1927 and frequently thereafter. Although details have changed since the first edition, the fundamentals remain the same: kindness is the source of all manners. Mrs. Post also wrote *How to Behave Though a Debutante* (1928), *The Personality of a House* (1930), and *Children Are People* (1940). In 1929 she made her radio debut. Her daily syndicated column on good taste was carried by nearly two hundred newspapers beginning in 1932.

Post, Melville Davisson (b. Romines Mills, W. Va., April 19, 1871—d. June 23, 1930), lawyer, storyteller, novelist. Post was a skillful and literate writer of detective and mystery stories, the best known of which had a shrewd character named UNCLE ABNER as sleuth. Abner is described by Howard Haycraft as "a rock-hewn Virginia squire of the Jeffersonian era." Post created other sleuths, but none as good a Uncle Abner, with his rugged ability to protect the innocent and the wronged. Post had literary ability beyond the average in style and characterization. Out of observations during his legal practice he wrote *The Strange Cases of Randolph Mason* (1896), adventures of an unscrupulous lawyer who knew how to find loopholes in the law. Among his other books: *The Man of Last Resort* (1897); *Dwellers in the Hills* (1901); *The Corrector of Destinies* (1908); *Uncle Abner, Master of Mysteries* (1918); *The Mystery at the Blue Villa* (1919); *The Man Hunters* (1926); *The Silent Witness* (1930).

Postl, Karl Anton. See CHARLES SEALSFIELD.

Postman Always Rings Twice, The (1934), a novel by JAMES M. CAIN. This is a celebrated specimen of the hard-boiled school of American fiction, the story of a plot by a young wife and her lover to murder her aging husband and collect his insurance. The scene is primarily a roadside café in California. The novel opens with a famous sentence: "They threw me off the hay truck about noon."

Potash and Perlmutter. The chief characters in numerous stories by MONTAGUE GLASS. They are partners in the cloak-and-suit business, later in motion pictures; their joys and troubles, skillfully conveyed in dialect, amused a host of readers. For years there was a steady demand for the tales, which were collected in *Potash and Perlmutter* (1910); *Abe and Mawruss* (1911); *Potash and Perlmutter Settle Things* (1919); and other volumes. The characters were even more popular on the stage, beginning with *Potash and Perlmutter* (1913, in a dramatization by CHARLES KLEIN), *Abe and Mawruss* (1915, Glass in collaboration with Roi Cooper Megrue), and *Keeping Expenses Down* (1932, in collaboration with Dan Jarrett). In the last the heroes were given new names.

Potiphar Papers (1853), seven essays by GEORGE WILLIAM CURTIS, dramatized as "Our Best People" (1854). Curtis, an ardent reformer, in these papers satirizes the so-called high society of his times; the newly rich, the old families, the young hangers-on who are good for such emergencies as a dance or a dinner. The chief character is Mrs. Potiphar, a climber, whose husband endures her as best he can.

Pot of Earth, The (1925), a long poem by ARCHIBALD MACLEISH. Taking its action and dominant imagery from the description of an ancient fertility rite in Sir James Frazer's *The Golden Bough*, this poem describes the life cycle in three parallel movements that intertwine as one: a plant seed sprouting in the springtime and being discarded by the new plant, the fertility god Adonis being killed that the new Spring may grow from his body, and the sexual maturation, marriage, and death in childbirth of a contemporary young girl. The girl, however, is aware of the direction of the forces of growth, and although she approaches and accepts each new stage with wonder, she resists the constant movement, feeling that if she were not being hurried so much, she would find more in life "than just to die of living."

Potter, Paul [Meredith] (b. England, June 3, 1853—d. March 7, 1921), dramatist. Potter was a skillful adapter of novels for stage production, as in his dramatizations of Du Maurier's *Trilby* (1895), Ouida's *Under Two Flags* (1901), and Balzac's *Honor of the Family* (1907). He also wrote some original plays, among them *The Ugly Duckling* (1890), *The American Minister* (1892), and *The Conquerors* (1898); the first of these was the most successful.

Pottle, Frederick A[lbert] (b. Lovell, Me., Aug. 3, 1897—   ), teacher, editor. Pottle began to teach at Yale University in 1925, became a full professor in 1930. When the Boswell papers were brought to the United States by R. H. ISHAM and finally placed in the Yale library, Pottle was appointed to supervise the publication of *The Private Papers of James Boswell*, a project still in progress. A number of the early volumes in the series became best sellers.

Pound, Ezra [Loomis] (b. Hailey, Idaho, Oct. 30, 1885—   ), poet, translator, critic,

editor. Pound attended the University of Pennsylvania, transferred to Hamilton College, returned to Pennsylvania for graduate work, left before obtaining his Ph.D. to live in Europe, first in Italy, then in England and France, and finally in Italy again, where he became a permanent resident at Rapallo after 1924. His first book, a small collection of poems entitled *A Lume Spento*, was published in Venice in 1908. Since then he has published many books and much periodical writing; he is one of the most voluminous writers of the 20th century.

Pound's genius for linguistics led him as a young man to the study of medieval and early Renaissance literature, especially the Provençal and Italian poets. He translated many poems from this period, wrote several excellent critical

essays which cut through the academic accumulations of traditional scholarship and revealed the literature freshly. Meanwhile in England Pound had helped to inaugurate IMAGISM, had proclaimed a number of principles of verse composition which have since become famous. Briefly, he insisted on the use of fresh and, if appropriate, colloquial language; composition on the model of music, *i.e.* the free phrase rather than the forced metric; utter clarity of image and metaphor. Pound soon became dissatisfied with the unskillful poets who were attracted to imagism and went on to other concerns, but the critical concepts he propounded during his imagist period probably had more to do with the development of modern poetry in England and America than any other single influence.

Critics have praised him for "giving us a living language again."

Pound's early poems and translations attracted much attention among serious writers. At the same time he undertook to champion modern poetry in every way he could. He became foreign editor of POETRY magazine and bombarded the Chicago office with manifestoes, letters, manuscripts of poetry (his own and others'). In 1917 he also became London editor of THE LITTLE REVIEW and carried on his attack in the pages of that magazine. In 1927 he founded and edited *The Exile*. He played the role of impresario, sought publishers for the early works of T. S. ELIOT, Wyndham Lewis, James Joyce, WILLIAM CARLOS WILLIAMS, and others. He became a friend of William Butler Yeats and greatly influenced the direction of the Irish poet's later work.

Pound became dissatisfied with London, moved to Paris, then on to Italy. In 1917 he published the first of his *Cantos*, an epic poem done in the manner of an anthology and taking for its theme all of civilization. Pound's adaptations of ERNEST FENOLLOSA's translations of the poems of Li Po, published in *Cathay* (1915), had been widely praised. T. S. Eliot called Pound "the inventor of Chinese poetry for our time." Pound made a study of the classical stage of Japan and wrote *Noh, Or Accomplishment* (1916). In 1919 appeared *Homage to Sextus Propertius*, a broad adaptation of Propertius, a very influential work; and in 1920 he published HUGH SELWYN MAUBERLEY, a series of satirical poems that are regarded by many critics as his finest work.

In the early 1920's Pound began to discover an interest in economics, stemming chiefly from a study of "social credit" theories. During the 1920's and 1930's a large number of polemical works on economics came from Pound's pen, and the continuation of the *Cantos*, particularly large sections devoted to Chinese and early American politics, showed the influence of his economic beliefs. In Italy Pound felt that some of the practices of Mussolini were in accord with the doctrines of social credit, and he espoused Fascism, at least in some of its general applications. During World War II he broadcast, on the Italian radio, a series of programs addressed to Allied troops; as a result he was indicted for treason and brought to the United States to stand trial after the war. However, he was adjudged mentally incompetent to prepare a defense, and in 1946 he was committed to St. Elizabeth's Hospital in Washington, D.C., under the custody of the Federal government. In 1958 he was at last released when the indictment against him was withdrawn; this action was taken after a concerted appeal to the government by American poets, led by ROBERT FROST. Upon his release Pound returned to Italy.

Always a controversial figure, Pound has been denounced vehemently by some critics, warmly praised by others. Though scholars have found occasional flaws in his learning, there is no doubt that he is an immensely erudite poet. The *Cantos* are constructed of materials drawn from many languages and literatures, including Italian, German, Spanish, Greek, Latin, and Chinese; the difficulties of reading them are considerably complicated for the reader who is ignorant of these languages. But Pound is much more than a pedant. In his early poems he displayed a lyrical finesse perhaps never equaled by another American poet, and although in his later works he has often been inclined to expostulation and rather prosy ranting, there are still lyrical interludes which prove that the old skill has not been lost. In addition to his poetry, Pound has continued to publish occasional prose works; most of his criticism has been impromptu, aimed at an immediate problem of contemporary taste or technique, and in consequence his critical beliefs have not been presented as systematically as some would like. On the other hand, his criticism is among the liveliest and most vigorous we have, often witty and always shrewd. The purely polemical works on economics have no real significance compared to the rest.

Pound's books of poetry include *A Lume Spento* (1908); *Exultations* (1909); PERSONAE (1909); *Provença* (1910); *Canzoni* (1911); *Riposte* (1912); LUSTRA (1916); *Quia Pauper Amavi* (1919); *Umbra* (1920); CANTOS I–XVI (1925); *Selected Poems* (1928); *A Draft of XXX Cantos* (1930); *Eleven New Cantos, XXXI–XLI* (1934); *Fifth Decad of Cantos* (1937); *Cantos LII–LXXI* (1940); *Cantos* (1948); PISAN CANTOS (1948); *Collected Poems* (1950); SECTION: ROCK DRILL, CANTOS 85–95 DE LOS CANTARES (1956); *Thrones: 96–109 De Los Cantares* (1959). His essays and works of literary criticism include *The Spirit of Romance* (1910; rev. 1953); *Pavannes and Divisions* (1918); *Instigations* (1920); *Indiscretions* (1923); *Antheil and the Treatise on Harmony* (1924); *How to Read* (1931); *ABC of Reading* (1934); *Make It New* (1934); *Polite Essays* (1937); *Guide to Kulchur* (1938; rev. 1951); *The Literary Essays of Ezra Pound* (with an introduction by T. S. Eliot, 1954); *Patria Mia* (written 1913, pub. 1950); *Pavannes and Divagations* (1958).

Among the most important discussions of Pound's work are the following: T. S. Eliot's *Ezra Pound: His Metric and Poetry* (1917); Alice Amdur's *The Poetry of Ezra Pound* (1936); Charles Norman's *The Case of Ezra Pound* (1948); Hugh Kenner's *The Poetry of Ezra Pound* (1951); Harold H. Watts' *Ezra Pound and the Cantos* (1952); Lewis Leary's *Motive and Method in "The Cantos" of Ezra Pound* (essays by several authors, 1954); John J. Espey's *Mauberley: A Study in Composition* (1955). The first full-length biography, by Charles Norman, appeared in 1960.

Pound, Louise (b. Lincoln, Neb., June 30, 1872—d. June 28, 1958), teacher, sportswoman, editor, linguist. One of the great figures of American scholarship, Dr. Pound taught mainly at the University of Nebraska. She was active in many learned societies and in community affairs, and she also won a series of tennis championships. Her contributions to periodicals ranged from essays on slang and the linguistics of dreams to criticisms of Poe and Whitman. Her chief interests were the American language and the ballad. Aside from editions of the classics and several anthologies, she produced three books: *Poetic Origins and the Ballad* (1921); *American Ballads and Songs* (1922); and *Selected Writings of Louise Pound* (1949). The latter volume reprints articles in six divisions: literary, linguistic, on vocabulary and diction, on folklore, educational, and miscellaneous; it has a complete bibliography and an account of Dr. Pound's life and writing by Mamie Meredith and Ruth Odell. H. L. Mencken once asserted that "her early work and that of her students put the study of American English on its legs." See DIALECT IN AMERICAN LITERATURE.

Pound, Roscoe (b. Lincoln, Neb., Oct. 27, 1870—d. July 1, 1965), legal writer. LOUISE POUND'S brother began his career as director of the Botanical Survey of Nebraska. He soon turned to the law, however, was admitted to the bar in 1890, and began a long and distinguished career as a professor of law at Nebraska, Northwestern, Chicago, and Harvard Universities, finally as dean of the Harvard Law School. After 1937 he taught for a while at the University of California Law School in Los Angeles and acted as adviser to the Ministry of Justice of the Republic of China. His books on our legal system and the philosophy of law are regarded as among the most important ever written in the United States. Among them are *Spirit of the Common Law* (1921); *Introduction to the Philosophy of Law* (1922); *Law and Morals* (1924); *Criminal Justice in America* (1930); *The Formative Era of American Law* (1938); *Contemporary Juristic Theory* (1940); *Social Control Through Law* (1942); *The Task of Law* (1944); *New Paths of the Law* (1950); *Justice According to Law* (1951).

Powderly, Terence [Vincent] (b. Carbondale, Pa., Jan. 22, 1849—d. June 24, 1924), memoirist. Powderly joined the Knights of Labor in 1874, in later years tried to reconcile controversies between that organization and the American Federation of Labor. He was one of the first labor men to hold public office, as mayor of Scranton, Pa., in 1878–84, as Commissioner of Immigration in 1897–1902, and as chief of the Division of Information of the Bureau of Immigration in 1907–21. He was notable for his conciliatory policy in labor disputes. He helped in the adoption of an alien contract-labor law, in establishing labor bureaus, and in setting up public arbitration systems. He described his experiences in *Thirty Years of Labor, 1859–1889* (1889) and *The Path I Trod* (1940).

Powell, Dawn (b. Mt. Gilead, Ohio, Nov. 28, 1897—d. Nov. 14, 1965), press agent, writer. An often ruthlessly realistic writer, Miss Powell's chief fame has come from her novels. Some are laid in small towns in the West, others are satires of the literary and entertainment world

of Manhattan. Among them: *Whither* (1925); *She Walks in Beauty* (1928); *The Bride's House* (1929); *Dance Night* (1930); *The Tenth Moon* (1932); *Turn, Magic Wheel* (1936); *The Happy Island* (1938); *A Time to Be Born* (1942); *My Home Is Far Away* (1944); *The Locusts Have No King* (1948); *Sunday, Monday, and Always* (short stories, 1952); *The Wicked Pavilion* (1954); *Cage for Lovers* (1957).

Powell, John Wesley (b. Mt. Morris, N.Y., March 24, 1834—d. Sept. 23, 1902), geologist, teacher, ethnologist. Powell taught at Illinois Wesleyan and the Illinois Normal University, then because of his deep interest in geology he became a pioneer explorer of the Green and Colorado Rivers, joined the staff of the U.S. Geological Survey and in 1880 succeeded CLARENCE KING as its director. His interests then turned to ethnology and he became director of the Bureau of Ethnology (1879–1902). He was a far-seeing and yet practical man who sought to reform the outmoded and corrupt administration of public lands in the post-Civil War period. He advanced his ideas in *Exploration of the Colorado River of the West* (1875; edited in part by Horace Kephart as *First Through the Grand Canyon,* 1915) and in his revolutionary *Report on the Arid Region of the United States* (1878). William Culp Darrah wrote a life of *Powell of the Colorado* (1951), showing his great services to conservation and to knowledge of the Indians. Powell's work is discussed also in Walter P. Webb's *The Great Plains* (1931); Harold H. Dunham's *Government Handout* (1941); Bernard De Voto's *The Literary Fallacy* (1944). The most authoritative and satisfactory account of Powell is Wallace Stegner's *Beyond the Hundredth Meridian: J. W. Powell and the Second Opening of the West* (1954).

Powell, Thomas (b. England, Sept. 3, 1809—d. Jan. 14, 1887), playwright, editor, biographer, poet. Powell, a bohemian and hack writer of unreliable character, came to the United States in 1849 after he had assisted several English authors in the production of a modernized Chaucer. In this country he associated with the group that met in PFAFF'S CELLAR and edited or helped to edit several periodicals, among them *Frank Leslie's Illustrated Newspaper.* He wrote verse with facility, sometimes ascribing his work to authors more famous than himself. He collected a series of *Dramatic Poems* (1844) and wrote a play, *The Wife's Revenge* (1842). His books on *The Living Authors of England* (1849) and *The Living Authors of America* (1850) had some value. Another of his works was *Chit Chat by Pierce Pungent* (1857).

Power of Fancy, The (1770), a poem by PHILIP FRENEAU. With overtones of Milton, Freneau combines a budding romanticism with an older deistic faith in the divinity of nature. Fancy, a "vagrant, restless" spirit, can roam freely through the world and discover there, rather than in the Bible, the word of God. Many critics have called attention to the poem's form which, in a musical tetrameter, anticipates Keats and departs from the artificialities of American and English verse of the time.

Power of Sympathy, The (1789), by WIL-LIAM HILL BROWN, is often called the first American novel. It was long attributed to Sarah Wentworth Morton because a seduction in it corresponds to one in her family. The main plot concerns the suicide of a youth who discovers his betrothed is his half-sister.

Powers, Hiram (b. Woodstock, Vt., July 29, 1805—d. June 27, 1873), sculptor. When his "The Greek Slave" (1843) was shown at the International Exhibition of 1851 in London, Powers became the first American sculptor to achieve a European reputation. Its classic beauty moved Elizabeth Barrett Browning to write a sonnet beginning "They say Ideal beauty . . ." Though none of Powers' other work equaled this, nevertheless he did excellent work and is known for his portrait busts of John Q. Adams, Jackson, Webster, Calhoun, Longfellow, Gen. Sheridan, and Van Buren.

Powers, James Farl (b. Jacksonville, Ill., July 8, 1917—   ), writer, teacher. Powers attended Northwestern University, was employed in Chicago bookshops for a time, and taught at Marquette University. His first collection of short stories, *Prince of Darkness* (1947), is made up in large part of stories dealing with the Catholic clergy, which he treats with critical sensitivity and wry humor. *The Presence of Grace* (1956) also deals predominately with the life of the clergy, but such stories as *Fire Island* or *The Poor Thing* show Powers to be equally capable of evoking the petty miseries and frustrations of life outside the rectory. Though his characters are slight, they are sensitively drawn, and his pervasive irony is subtle and well handled.

Powhatan Indians. This tribe belonged to an Algonquian confederacy in Virginia and Maryland and came into immediate relationship with the settlers at Jamestown (1607). Their name derived from their residence at Powhata. The English seem to have persuaded the chieftain, whom they also called Powhatan, although his Indian name was Wahusonacook, that they had been shipwrecked and would leave as soon as other English vessels came. When it became apparent that they had no intention of leaving, Powhatan became hostile. According to what may be a legend, his daughter POCAHONTAS prevented warfare and brought about a truce. When Powhatan died in 1618, his successor Opechancanough led a rebellion against the English. In 1641 the confederacy was thoroughly defeated.

Pownall, Thomas (b. England, 1722—d. Feb. 25, 1805), English colonial administrator. Pownall was secretary to the governor of New York, later lieutenant governor of New Jersey, then governor of Massachusetts. In 1760 he returned to England and was elected to Parliament. He was against all attempts at curtailing American liberties and proposed a centralized administration and union of the colonies in a book called *The Administration of the Colonies* (1764).

pragmatism. A form of philosophy of which WILLIAM JAMES, its most prominent representative, said that "it has no dogmas and no doctrine save its methods." James is largely responsible for its formulation and ideas; he gave much of the credit for it to CHARLES S. PEIRCE and F. C. S. Schiller. Pragmatism rejects absolutes, substitutes pluralism for monism, sees everything in the context in which it occurs, believes that truth is not something to be found but something to be forever sought, that ideas must be put to work in order to see the results—and if they work, they are good. James described it, not without irony, as "a method of settling metaphysical disputes that might otherwise be interminable." Philip Wiener, in *Evolution and the Founders of Pragmatism* (1949), discusses its background in science and natural theology, its birthplace in Peirce's METAPHYSICAL CLUB and Peirce's own ideas, the contributions of Chauncey Wright, Darwinism in James' psychology and pragmatism, its relationship to John Fiske's philosophy of history, the pragmatic legal philosophy of Nicholas St. John Green, evolutionary pragmatism in the legal theory of the younger OLIVER WENDELL HOLMES, the philosophical legacy of the founders of pragmatism. Among the most prominent of James' followers was JOHN DEWEY.

Pragmatism has often been identified with Americanism. As H. S. Commager has said, "Practical, democratic, individualistic, opportunistic, spontaneous, hopeful, pragmatism is wonderfully adapted to the temperament of the average American." It seems to be another name for horse sense. Use was made of the doctrine to justify all the malpractices of business and politics; it became a sponsor for the "success school" of American thought and writing.

The beginning of the school may be found in an article of Peirce's, *How to Make Our Ideas Clear* (*Popular Science Monthly*, January, 1878). James wrote *Pragmatism: A New Name for an Old Way of Thinking* (1907). Other books on the subject include J. B. Pratt's *What Is Pragmatism?* (1909); H. Heath Bawden's *The Principles of Pragmatism* (1910); Addison W. Moore's *Pragmatism and Its Critics* (1910); John Dewey's *Creative Intelligence* (a symposium, 1917); Eduard Baumgarten's *Der Pragmatismus: R. W. Emerson, W. James, J. Dewey* (1938).

Prairie, The (1827), a novel by JAMES FENI-MORE COOPER. It was the third of the LEATH-ER-STOCKING TALES to be published, but chronologically is last in NATTY BUMPPO's life. As befits the mood of tranquillity which Cooper creates for the Deerslayer's old age, there is less excitement in this story than in the others, but the buffalo stampede and the prairie fire have been praised as stirring episodes. The dog Hector, Leatherstocking's companion and helper, is an engaging character. Involved in the action are the good Pawnee and the bad Sioux Indians. The book adds a new realm to Cooper's imagination: the prairie rivals the sea and the forest of his other books. His knowledge of the prairies was not based on direct observation; he relied a good deal on the Lewis and Clark *Journals* (1814). A truthful but unlovely portrait was drawn of the squatter Ishmael Bush and his family; doubtless Cooper's ideas on property influenced his attitude toward the Bush family.

Prairies, The (1833), a poem by WILLIAM CULLEN BRYANT. This eloquent description of the prairie lands was suggested to the poet by a visit to his brothers in Illinois. Ralph N. Miller feels that Bryant's choice of certain details may have been determined by "the American response to European sneers"—particularly his stress upon the immensity of the plains, the character and history of the ancient Indians, the startling beauty of the reptiles, the presence of the honey-bee.

Prairie Schooner, The. Founded at the University of Nebraska in 1927, this magazine announced itself as the interpreter of the prairie country, but its contributors came from all sections. It has been one of the best of the "little magazines," and one of the longest-lived. In 1955 Paul R. Stewart told *The "Prairie Schooner" Story: A Little Magazine's First 25 Years.* In 1958, when KARL SHAPIRO became editor, the name was changed to *The Schooner.*

Pratt, Edwin J[ohn] (b. Western Bay, Newf., Feb. 4, 1883—d. April 26, 1964), poet. Pratt was for a time a salesman, then a manufacturer of a cough remedy; he took courses in theology and wrote a thesis, *Pauline Eschatology.* Thereafter he taught in various Toronto colleges, in the meantime publishing several collections of verse that have won much praise in Canada and the United States. His career and his writing are ably analyzed in *Edwin J. Pratt: The Man and His Poetry* (1947), by Henry W. Wells and Carl F. Klinck. Wells calls Pratt an "Aristophanic Newfoundlander," stresses the "minimum of evidence of literary indebtedness" in his poetry. On the other hand, the poetry, says Wells, "probably contains more allusions to geology, zoology, and paleontology than that of any other writer of repute today." Pelham Edgar, a Canadian commentator, sees Pratt's greatness chiefly in the field of heroic narrative, where may be found a "compound of whimsy, humor, and seriousness, of tenderness and playful satire, that is original in no usual degree."

Pratt's first important work was a huge five-act play in blank verse called *Clay*, which he could not get published and which he ultimately burned. In 1925 came *Witches' Brew*, called by Edgar "hilarious extravagance." An ode on the theme of death was called *The Iron Door* (1927). The collection called *Newfoundland Verse* (1923) also appeared before two of Pratt's best known narratives, *The Roosevelt and the Antinoë* (1930) and *Brébeuf and His Brethren* (1940). The latter sums up material in two volumes of the *Jesuit Relations* (see JESUITS IN AMERICA). The poem was turned by friends of Pratt into a dramatic and musical pageant, with music by Healey Willan. Then came *Dunkirk* (1941), *Behind the Log* (1947), and *Towards the Last Spike* (1952). Pratt's work has been

gathered in *Collected Poems* (Toronto, 1944; in somewhat briefer form, New York, 1945).

Pratt, Fletcher (b. Buffalo, N.Y., April 25, 1897—d. June 10, 1956), newspaperman, free-lance writer. With a strong gift for the assimilation of facts in any field and an even greater gift for popularizing information, Pratt was possibly the best known expert on military matters of his time. His first book, *The Heroic Years: 14 Years of the Republic, 1801–1815*, appeared in 1934. Thereafter he wrote more than thirty books, ranging from a much-praised volume on the Civil War, *Ordeal by Fire* (1935), to books on the Napoleonic Wars, Japanese card games, cooking, weapons of war, and great generals, in addition to much science fiction and a volume or two for children. His last book was a *Compact History of the U.S. Navy* (1957).

Pratt, Theodore (b. Minneapolis, Minn., April 26, 1901—   ), novelist, playwright. Pratt was educated at Colgate and Columbia Universities, where he contributed to magazines. He worked as a columnist and play reviewer for *Variety*, wrote for *The New Yorker.* Settling down in Florida, at Boca Raton, he composed many books, nine of them about Florida. His play *Big Blow* (1938), dramatized from his book, ran on Broadway. He wrote a trilogy about Florida: *The Barefoot Mailman* (1943), *The Flame Tree* (1950), and *The Big Bubble* (1951). His other books include: *Spring From Downward* (1933); *Not Without the Wedding* (1935); *Mercy Island* (1941); *Mr. Limpet* (1942); *Mr. Winkle Goes to War* (1943); *Thunder Mountain* (1944); *Miss Dilly Says No* (1945); *The Tormented* (1950); *Cocotte* (1951); *Handsome* (1951); *The Golden Sorrow* (1952); *Escape to Eden* (1953); *Smash-Up* (1954); *Seminole* (1954); *The Lovers of Pompeii* (1961). Short story collections are *Perils in Provence* (1944) and *Florida Roundabout* (1959).

Prattler, The. A column conducted by AMBROSE BIERCE in the San Francisco *Argonaut*, the San Francisco *Wasp*, and the San Francisco *Examiner.*

Prayer to the Virgin of Chartres (1920), by HENRY ADAMS. This piece was found among Adams' papers and was published after his death by his niece, Mabel La Farge, in her compilation *Letters to a Niece.* It is in verse and concludes with a *Prayer to a Dynamo*, which Adams describes as "the last/ Of the strange prayers humanity has wailed." So far as is known, Adams wrote only two poems: this one and *Buddha and Brahma*, published in 1915 but written much earlier. The latter piece indicated his failure to find in Eastern creeds any center of unity. Returning from the Orient, he traveled in France, and there he discovered in the cathedral splendors of Mont-Saint-Michel, Amiens, Coutances, Paris, and especially Chartres, the symbols that he sought. To Adams the Virgin of Chartres was the symbol of his belief that intuition, love, and art speak deeper lessons than reason or science. The poem was probably written around 1904.

Precaution, or, Prevention Is Better Than Cure (2 v., 1820), a novel by JAMES FENIMORE COOPER. Many persons have exclaimed in disgust after reading some novel or other, "Why, I could write a better one myself!" but Cooper went ahead and did it. The name of the novel he was reading is not known, but it was some sort of tea-table romance. However, when Cooper sat down to write *Precaution* he took Jane Austen's *Persuasion* (1818) as his model. Cooper maintains the thesis that the selection of a husband or a wife is the business of the parents as much as of those immediately involved. The setting is England, the book was published anonymously, and it was assumed to be the work of an English gentlewoman.

Prejudices (1919, 1920, 1922, 1924, 1926, 1927), essays by H. L. MENCKEN. A volume of selections appeared in 1927; some of the essays were reprinted in *The Mencken Chrestomathy* (1949). The essays appeared originally in the *Smart Set*, the *American Mercury*, the Baltimore *Sun*, and the New York *Mail*. They show Mencken in the role of the bad boy of American literature and as a ruthless iconoclast. Mencken lauded Germany, denounced the condition of American letters, but espoused such new writers as Theodore Dreiser, James Branch Cabell, and Sinclair Lewis.

Premature Burial, The (*Dollar Newspaper*, July 31, 1844), a "tale of terror" by EDGAR ALLAN POE. A man subject to cataleptic seizures, which to anyone unacquainted with them may seem like death itself, takes every possible precaution against being buried alive. He awakens from one such seizure in a berth in a small sloop; the coffin lid that he imagines above him is really the bottom of the berth above. The terror that has him in its grip disappears, and he is cured of his ailment. Poe cites in his story cases of premature burial, but W. T. Bandy suggests the most likely source of the story (*American Literature*, May, 1947), a poem by Mrs. Seba Smith called *The Life-Preserving Coffin* which appeared in the *Columbian Lady's and Gentleman's Magazine* (January, 1844). Another source often suggested is *Buried Alive* (*Blackwood's Magazine*, October, 1821).

Prentice, George Dennison (b. Preston, Conn., Dec. 18, 1802—d. Jan. 22, 1870), newspaperman, editor. Prentice was the first editor of the *New England Review*, published at Hartford; later he edited the Louisville *Daily Journal*, which became the Louisville *Courier-Journal*. Under Prentice's able editorship the Louisville newspaper became one of the most esteemed papers of the day. Some of his contributions were collected as *Prenticeana, or, Wit and Humor in Paragraphs* (1860). The 1870 edition contains a biographical sketch by G. W. Griffin. Prentice also wrote a biography of Henry Clay (1831); his *Poems* were collected in 1876. HENRY WATTERSON, his famous successor as editor of the *Journal*, delivered a *Memorial Address* (1870); W. L. Visscher wrote of him in *Ten Wise Men and Some More* (1909).

Prescott, Frederick C[larke]. See THE POETIC MIND.

Prescott, Orville (b. Cleveland, Ohio, Sept. 8, 1906—   ), critic. Educated at Williams College, Prescott early entered the field of criticism. After work on the staffs of *Newsweek* and *Cue*, he became well known as the daily literary critic for *The New York Times*. He published civilized literary commentary and edited anthologies. Of *In My Opinion* (1952), a systematic analysis of American fiction, the San Francisco *Chronicle* said "[Mr. Prescott has] literary and ethical stands and he applies them courageously." The title of his autobiography, *The Five Dollar Gold Piece* (1956), was inspired by the author's memory of his grandmother who promised him a five-dollar gold piece if he learned to read at the age of six. Other books: *Mid Century: An Anthology of Outstanding American Short Stories* (1958) and *The Undying Past* (1961).

Prescott, William Hickling (b. Salem, Mass., May 4, 1796—d. Jan. 28, 1859), historian. In his junior year at Harvard University, Prescott was hit by a crust of bread thrown by a romping classmate, an accident which cost him the sight

of his left eye. He graduated in 1814 and began reading law, but was forced to abandon it when his other eye began to fail. From that time he was never able to use his sight for more than ten minutes at a stretch. He was sent to visit his grandfather in the Azores, the nearest he ever came to Spain or Peru. Returning home in 1817, he decided to become a writer.

The first of a number of articles by Prescott appeared in the *North American Review* in 1821, followed in 1834 by a life of Charles Brockden Brown. These and other articles were collected in *Biographies and Critical Miscellanies* (1845). From 1829 until 1836 Prescott worked diligently on the first of his great histories. He was wealthy enough to pay research assistants and readers, and with the aid of an instrument called a *noctograph*, much like the one Francis Parkman invented for himself, he was able to work and still spare his eyes. During this time he also learned French, Italian, and Spanish. The *History of the Reign of Ferdinand and Isabella the Catholic* (1838), seven years in preparation, sold out the first edition in a few weeks and received praise from historians throughout the world. Irving, who had intended to write a history of Mexico, magnanimously left the field to Prescott, who in turn cut short his work on Philip II so as not to encroach on John Motley's territory. The writing of the later histories came more easily. HISTORY OF THE CONQUEST OF MEXICO (1843), HISTORY OF THE CONQUEST OF PERU (1847), and *History of the Reign of Philip II* (1855–58), which was incomplete at Prescott's death, maintain a high level of excellence. Prescott was more interested in action than in theory. He delighted in thrilling narrative and vivid descriptions; unlike other great historians, he expounded no philosophy of history. He wrote primarily for the reader's enjoyment, without ever thinking of himself as a serious historian.

The Life of William Hickling Prescott (1864), by his lifelong friend George Ticknor, is still the authoritative biography, although Harry Thurston Peck wrote a readable life in 1905. The *Correspondence of William Hickling Prescott, 1833–1847* (1925) was selected and edited by Prescott's great-grandson Roger Wolcott. The Montezuma Edition of *The Works of William H. Prescott* (22 v.) appeared in 1904. C. H. Gardiner wrote *Prescott and His Publishers* (1959) and edited *The Literary Memoranda of William Hickling Prescott* (1961).

Preston, Keith (b. Chicago, Sept. 29, 1884—d. July 7, 1927), teacher, poet, columnist. Preston was a professor of Latin and as such was well acquainted with the Latin breed of epigram that he himself especially cultivated. His best known piece was a quatrain on *The Liberators*: "Among our literary scenes/ Saddest this sight to me:/ The graves of little magazines/ That died to make verse free." He conducted a weekly column of literary criticism and a daily humorous column, both for the Chicago *Daily News*. His published works include *Studies in the Diction of the Sermo Amatorius of the Latin Comedy* (1916); *Types of Pan* (1919); *Splinters* (1921); *Top o' the Column* (1925).

Preston, Margaret Junkin (b. Milton, Pa., May 19, 1820—d. March 28, 1897), memoirist, poet. Mrs. Preston was born in the North but married John T. L. Preston, a professor of Latin in the Virginia Military Institute, and thereafter she was devoted to the South. Her husband joined the Confederate Army and became Adjutant-General on the staff of his brother-in-law "Stonewall" Jackson. When Jackson was killed in battle, Mrs. Preston took his last words as the refrain of her most famous poem, "Under the Shade of the Trees." One of the last military statements of Robert E. Lee suggested her poem

"Gone Forward." *Silverwood: A Book of Memories* (1856) was her first book. She collected her verses in *Old Songs and New* (1870) and *For Love's Sake* (1886). Elizabeth P. Allan prepared *The Life and Letters of Margaret Junkin Preston* (1903).

Pretty Story, A: Written by Peter Grievous, Esq. (September, 1774), a pamphlet by FRANCIS HOPKINSON. Published while the Continental Congress was assembling in Philadelphia, this satirical allegory was intended to portray the events leading to the establishment of the Congress. The pamphlet went into three editions before 1775.

Price, Carl F[owler] (b. New Brunswick, N.J., May 16, 1881—d. April 12, 1948), businessman, hymnologist. Price, an ardent Methodist, made the study and writing of hymns a long-continued avocation. Among his books: *The Music and Hymnody of the Methodist Hymnal* (1911); *Curiosities of the Hymnal* (1926); *Wesleyan's First Century* (1932). He also edited *The Wesleyan Song Book* (1901); *A Year of Song* (1916); *Wesleyan Verse* (1927); *Intercollegiate Song Book* (1931); and several hymnals. He composed more than two hundred hymn tunes.

Priest, George Madison (b. Henderson, Ky., Jan. 25, 1873—d. Feb. 17, 1947), teacher, scholar. Priest studied in Germany, served as professor of Germanic languages at Princeton University. He wrote *A Brief History of German Literature* (1909) and *Germany Since 1740* (1915), translated Goethe and other writers, edited an *Anthology of German Literature in the 18th Century* (1934).

Priest, Judge. See IRVIN S. COBB.

Prime, Benjamin Youngs (b. Huntington, N.Y., Dec. 9, 1733—d. Oct. 31, 1791), physician, poet. Dr. Prime, who practiced in New York, published two somewhat antithetical collections of poems. *The Patriot Muse* (1764), dealing principally with the French and Indian Wars, was ardently pro-British; *Columbia's Glory, or, British Pride Humbled* (1791) upheld the American cause during the Revolution and one fine passage paid tribute to General Washington.

Prince, Morton (b. Boston, Dec. 21, 1854—d. Aug. 31, 1929), psychologist, teacher, editor. Prince was a pioneer in psychopathology and initiator of the Harvard Psychological Laboratory. He began with a deep interest in metaphysics and wrote a book on psychical monism shortly after he left college. He studied the ideas of Dr. Silas W. (S. WEIR) MITCHELL and worked in Paris and Nancy. He is regarded as essentially an empiricist—"in the lineage of Locke, Hume, John Stuart Mill, and Huxley," according to A. A. Roback. He evolved a concept of the *coconscious* that resembled Freud's *unconscious*. In some of his investigations he reached results that ally him to Pavlov and the conditioned-reflex school. He held that a division between the normal and the abnormal was artificial, always sought to determine a physical basis for a mental phenomenon. His therapy consisted essentially of re-education, in supplying new meanings to patients; Roback finds this approach closer to Jung than to Freud. One of his great services was to found the *Journal of Abnormal Psychology* (1906), which he edited till his death. Among his books: *The Nature of Mind and of Human Automatism* (1885); *The Dissociation of a Personality* (1906); *The Unconscious* (1913); *Clinical and Experimental Studies in Personality* (1929).

Prince, Thomas (b. Sandwich, Mass., May 15, 1687—d. Oct. 22, 1758), clergyman, historian. Prince studied law, theology, and medicine in England, was co-pastor of Old South Church in Boston until his death. He was a conservative in thought, but an ardent colonial patriot and a defender of civil liberties. He issued many publications, including twenty-nine sermons. His most important work was his *Chronological History of New England in the Form of Annals* (1736), which was continued with three pamphlets in 1755. He collected a vast library of data and was scrupulous in putting down his sources. The book is a world history from the time of Adam to the Puritan colonies. Prince has been called the earliest of objective historians, also one of the dullest.

Prince and the Pauper, The (1881), a novel by MARK TWAIN. The idea for this book came to Twain when he was reading Charlotte M. Yonge's *The Prince and the Page* (1865), in which a medieval nobleman lives for years disguised as a blind beggar. As early as Nov. 23, 1877, Twain set down this idea for a story in his notebook: "Edward VI and a little pauper exchange places by accident a day or so before Henry VIII's death. The Prince wanders in rags and hardships and the pauper suffers the (to him) horrible miseries of princedom, up to the moment of crowning in Westminster Abbey, when proof is brought and the mistake rectified." He read the book to his two little girls as it progressed and dedicated it "To Those Good-Mannered and Agreeable Children, Susy and Clara Clemens." They always regarded it as the best of his books. Gladys Carmen Bellamy calls it "his finest achievement, so far as structure is concerned."

Prince of India, The, or, Why Constantinople Fell (1893), a novel by LEW WALLACE. It took Wallace approximately twelve years to compose this 300,000-word novel. President Garfield, who was a great admirer of *Ben Hur* and who had appointed Wallace minister to Turkey, suggested a book with Constantinople as its setting. Wallace fixed on the Princess Irené as his heroine, decided to introduce the Wandering Jew as a main character, did endless research on historical details. Irving McKee, in his life of Wallace, feels that the Prince—the Wandering Jew—is "very much a projection of Wallace himself." The plot presents the Prince's endeavor to fuse religions and sects into a peaceable botherhood. The historic scenes, greatly influenced by Sir Walter Scott, lack the pungent sophistication of Gibbon. The book had a cool critical reception, sold very well for six months, then fell out of favor. An elaborate and costly dramatization was denounced by critics as "a pious bore." A charge of plagiarism against Wallace, since his novel had some purely coincidental similarities to James M. Ludlow's *The Captain of the Janizaries* (1886), caused a mild sensation.

Prince of Parthia, The (prod., 1767), a play by THOMAS GODFREY. See DRAMA.

Prince of Peace, The. A popular lecture by WILLIAM JENNINGS BRYAN, given innumerable times all over the United States, especially at Chautauqua gatherings.

Princess Casamassima, The (1886), a novel by HENRY JAMES. The Princess Casamassima is the former Christina Light, the beloved of the sculptor in RODERICK HUDSON (1876); now, separated from her husband, she decides to make a firsthand study of poverty and radicalism in London. In the novel James offers his own commentary on socialism, which was then just beginning to be a factor in political life. The real hero of the book, however, is Hyacinth Robinson, the illegitimate son of an English nobleman and a Frenchwoman, who, though brought up in the London slums and a member of a radical underground movement, makes his way into upper-class society, where he meets the Princess. He is selected by the revolutionaries to commit an assassination, and, torn between the opposing interests of socialism and society, ends his life in suicide. The book is notable for its satire, its descriptions of London, and its comedy scenes. It was reissued in 1948 with an introduction by Lionel Trilling.

Principles of Psychology, The (2 v., 1890), a treatise by WILLIAM JAMES. A biologist and physiologist as well as a philosopher, James was particularly qualified to establish psychology as a science in its own right, rather than as a subdivision of philosophy; and *The Principles of Psychology* both represents the achievements of psychology at the end of the 19th century and asserts its right to be considered an independent science, based on the physiology of the nervous system, but withal exceeding the bounds of both physiology and philosophy.

The primary literary significance of the *Principles* lies in the chapter on the "stream of thought," which was a germinal factor in the development of the STREAM OF CONSCIOUSNESS technique of writing. In describing thought as a "stream" James broke with the prevalent theory of the association of ideas, which was atomistic and considered all ideas to be reducible to simple ideas, out of which complex ideas were built, and which retained a distinct identity in different combinations. James felt that thoughts were comparable to pulses or waves which are unique and have a transitory existence, but cannot be analyzed into separable components. James was also concerned with the perceptions of time and space, and with nativism, the belief that an individual is born with certain innate abilities and attitudes. Nativism, and the conclusion that the mind is the means by which the organism adapts itself to the environment, led James to attempt to reconcile the deterministic tendencies of evolutionary science with choice and free will. James' work greatly influenced JOHN DEWEY's theory of education as adjustment to life.

Pringle, Henry F[owles] (b. New York City, Aug. 23, 1897—d. April 7, 1958), newspaperman, teacher, biographer. Pringle worked from 1920 to 1927 for several New York newspapers, then became a free-lance writer and a teacher at the Columbia School of Journalism. He wrote biographies of Alfred E. Smith (1927), Theodore Roosevelt (1931, awarded a Pulitzer prize), and William Howard Taft (1939).

Private Life of Helen of Troy, The (1925), a novel by JOHN ERSKINE. In this Greenwich Village version of an ancient scandal, Helen, "unrepentant, but too beautiful to kill," is brought home by Menelaus. In her conversations she sets forth spiritedly the notions of morality fashionable among young intellectuals in 1925. Telemachus, looking for his father Odysseus, promptly falls in love with her.

Problem, The (1840), a poem by RALPH WALDO EMERSON. The poet here discusses a paradox in his own nature that somewhat disturbs him. He had expressed the same idea in his *Journals* (1838): "It is very grateful to my feelings to go into a Roman cathedral, yet I look as my countrymen do at the Roman priesthood. It is very grateful to me to go into an English church and hear the liturgy read. Yet nothing would induce me to be the English priest." Emerson in fact had taken orders, and then later had retired from the pulpit. What made him retire was, as his poem indicates, the feeling that lovely as churches may be, there is something higher and nobler in the world of nature. The poem contains one of Emerson's most famous sayings: "He builded better than he knew—/ The conscious stone to beauty grew."

Processional (1925), a play by JOHN HOWARD LAWSON. This play was an indication of the changing mood of the American theater. It was also a good American example of the European movement called expressionism—an endeavor to "externalize" inner emotions in some physical manifestation. The setting is a West Virginian town in the grip of martial law during a coal strike. The characters are satiric versions of vaudeville racial and social types, and the Ku Klux Klan is the butt of many jokes. The play had a definite leftist attitude, but the mood was on the whole humorous. It was only later that Lawson, as J. W. Krutch put it, "turned to a Marxian denunciation of American decadence in *Gentlewoman* (1934)."

Proctor, Edna Dean (b. Henniker, N.H., Sept. 18, 1829—d. Dec. 18, 1923), poet, travel writer. Her youth was spent in the small New England town where she wrote antislavery poems and articles during the Civil War. After the war she traveled in Russia, writing a series of letters to the New York *Independent* which were published as *Russian Journey* (1872). During the 1870's she lived in Brooklyn, writing articles for the *Tribune*. *Poems* (1866) was followed by *The Song of the Ancient People* (1892); *The Mountain Maid and Other Poems of New Hampshire* (1900); *Songs of America* (1906); and *The Glory of Toil* (1916). In a trip to the West she was roused by the plight of the Indians and wrote a flurry of newspaper articles urging more humane treatment of them. *The Complete Poetical Works of Edna Dean Proctor* appeared in 1925.

Professor at the Breakfast Table, The (1860), the first of the three sequels to Oliver Wendell Holmes' *Autocrat of the Breakfast Table*. See BREAKFAST TABLE SERIES.

Professor's House, The (1925), a novel by WILLA CATHER. Houses are in this novel made the symbol of varying attitudes toward life; a principal episode is concerned with Professor St. Peter's doubts when his wife wants him to move to a new and supposedly better house. The Southwest, in which Miss Cather had become increasingly interested, contributes numerous incidents and motifs, and also the cliff-dwellers' homes which her characters find beautiful and deeply significant. St. Peter's is a troubled mentality. He comes to a crisis at the age of fifty-two, "exactly the age the author reached in the year of the novel's appearance," as Leon Edel recalls in his *Willa Cather* (1953). It is a sad, pessimistic, despairing book, a reflection of Miss Cather's own mood at the time. It records four types of corruption, failure, and betrayal: St. Peter as the victim of his wife's ambition and his daughter's desire for social position; his own realization that the university at which he teaches has lost its integrity; Tom Outland's inability to interest government archaeologists in his discovery of an ancient mesa city; the commercialization of the airplane invention that Outland had made.

Professor's Story, The (1860), a novel by OLIVER WENDELL HOLMES. This appeared serially in the *Atlantic Monthly*. In book form it was renamed ELSIE VENNER. See also the BRAHMINS.

profile. A variety of biographical sketch, variously called *character, description, interview, psychograph, close-up, cover story, personal sketch.* It is likely that the great popularization of the personal sketch came when JAMES GORDON BENNETT in the 19th century developed the newspaper interview in the New York *Herald.* Successive generations of reporters began to augment their reports with bits of intimate description. In the early 20th century the British biographer Lytton Strachey (1880–1932) turned the hackneyed trade of biography writing into an art. Equally good and even more clever in phraseology was Philip Guedella (1889–1944). The Irish writer Ernest Boyd (1887–1946) undoubtedly furnished suggestions for *The New Yorker* type of profile in sketches such as *Portraits: Real and Imaginary* (1924). A specialized form of the personal sketch was GAMALIEL BRADFORD's *psychograph,* exemplified in his *Damaged Souls* (1923).

Then came THE NEW YORKER, which adopted the term *profile* for the sketches that appeared in its pages. Other magazines followed: *Time* with its *cover stories*, *Life* with its *close-ups*, and many other magazines with feature stories intent on personalities. Often the "sketches" proved voluminous enough to make a full-sized book. Occasionally the subject was a thing rather than a person, as with John Bainbridge's analysis of the *Reader's Digest*. A profile is not formal biography, but includes the essentials. It aims to explore and reveal eccentricity of personality and performance, almost always ironically and often satirically. A typical collection is Robert Lewis Taylor's *Doctor, Lawyer, Merchant, Chief* (1948), which comprises twenty-two pieces, many of which first appeared in *The New Yorker*.

Progress and Poverty (1879), a treatise by HENRY GEORGE. This volume became one of the most influential books ever written, not merely because of the novelty and force of its ideas, but because of the glow of George's style —almost unique in a book of this type. George's fundamental idea was easily grasped. He stressed the lamentable fact that progress and poverty seem to go hand in hand. He found the secret of this undesirable partnership in the systems of taxation practiced everywhere, which in his judgment shackled labor and punished capital and allowed landlords to profit through increased rents when the value of their property went up because of social advances. He advocated a simple remedy: impose only a *single tax* (the two words became the symbol of the movement he founded), a tax on land; confiscate all unused land. "Appropriate all rent by taxation," he urged. The ideas expressed by George were not original, even if the combination of them was novel. He derived from Jefferson, Emerson, Comte, Condorcet, Fourier, John Stuart Mill, and other reformers. His voice was, however, the voice of a great crusader, of an economic evangelist, rather than an objective scientist. He deeply influenced thoughtful and sensitive persons all over the world, even if they usually refused to accept the panacea he proposed. Innumerable persons paid tribute to his sincerity and cogency, among them John Dewey, Nicholas Murray Butler, Woodrow Wilson, Lloyd George, George Bernard Shaw, Leo Tolstoy, Louis D. Brandeis, and Aldous Huxley. His book won instantaneous popularity and was translated into many languages. Organizations sprang up to carry his ideas into effect; some are still in active existence. One of the things that attracted people everywhere to George and his book was his strong conviction of man's innate goodness. He sought to infuse economics with the Golden Rule and love of one's neighbor. In 1954 appeared a seventy-fifth anniversary edition of the book.

Progressive, The. A liberal magazine founded in 1909 by ROBERT M. LA FOLLETTE in furtherance of his various policies and his candidacies for office and in support of his Progressive Party. It ceased publication in October, 1947, though a magazine of that name still exists.

Progressive party. Three American political parties have borne this name: (1) The Progressive party of 1912, also known as the Bull Moose party, which consisted of Republicans who had withdrawn from their party when it nominated W. H. TAFT and not THEODORE ROOSEVELT for President. In the ensuing election Woodrow Wilson became President, but Roosevelt, with eighty-eight electoral votes, ran ahead of Taft. (2) The Progressive party of 1924, which likewise represented a secession from the Republican party. It nominated ROBERT LA FOLLETTE for President on a platform of radical character. He received almost five million votes in the ensuing election. (3) The Progressive party of 1948, which consisted mainly of Democrats opposed to the election of HARRY S. TRUMAN. It nominated HENRY A. WALLACE for the presidency on a platform of friendship for Russia and of numerous radical doctrines. Wallace polled 1,156,103 votes.

Progress of Dulness, The (1772–73), a satirical poem by JOHN TRUMBULL. This poem in three parts deals with three typical characters —Tom Brainless, a shallow and conservative clergyman; Dick Brainless, a dissipated and stupid fop; and Miss Harriet Simper, a modish young woman who takes her code of life from romantic novels. Harriet, in love with Dick, loses him and marries Tom. The poem entertainingly satirizes college education, long sermons, the fiction of the day, religious bigotry, oddities of dress and manners. Readers of that day immediately identified certain local institutions (such as Yale University) and some notables as the real objects of Trumbull's satire, and he was viciously attacked in the press and even threatened with violence.

Progress to the Mines (1841, 1928), a journal by WILLIAM BYRD. This portion of Byrd's account of his various journeys was composed in 1732. He visited Fredericksburg and the iron mines around Germanna and gave careful descriptions of the methods of manufacturing iron in his time, also the fear among colonial manufacturers that England planned to restrict their industry, a fear realized in 1750. The commentary, although a spirited one, is not as rich in humor as some other accounts that Byrd wrote; it is more a businessman's analysis of his situation.

Prokosch, Frederic (b. Madison, Wis., May 17, 1908—), teacher, poet, novelist. Prokosch taught English literature at various universities in the United States and England, and was in government service during World War II. His writings include erudite, sensitive, melancholic poetry and a number of novels which at first inclined toward the poetic and the impressionistic, later were more sharply realistic. Among them: *The Asiatics* (1935); *The Seven Who Fled* (1937); *Night of the Poor* (1939); *The Conspirators* (1943); *Age of Thunder*

(1945); *The Idols of the Cave* (1946); *Storm and Echo* (1948); *Nine Days to Mukalla* (1953). His *Chosen Poems* appeared in 1947. His acquaintance with many parts of the earth is reflected in the numerous countries that form the background of his writings. *A Tale for Midnight* (1955) is a brilliant but frightening study of the Cenci. His most recent work is *Ballad of Love* (1960).

proletarian literature. The combined effect of the great depression and the socioeconomic emphasis of the New Deal fostered the only significant outbreak of proletarian literature and criticism the United States has known. Although a handful of writers, notably William Dean Howells and Edward Bellamy, had expressed some mildly socialistic and utopian ideals toward the end of the nineteenth century and Frank Norris argued against economic exploitation in THE OCTOPUS (1901), these writers must be considered advocates of social reform rather than writers committed to radical political change. The earliest well-known example of a proletarian novel is Upton Sinclair's THE JUNGLE (1906); like most of Sinclair's books it was socialist rather than Marxist in sympathy. Most proletarian writing from this time until the onset of the depression is forgotten today, with the exception of Abraham Cahan's THE RISE OF DAVID LEVINSKY (1917) and MAX EASTMAN's *Venture* (1927).

With the onset of the depression a number of writers and intellectuals began to turn to theoretical Marxism as a possible solution to the evils of American economy, and within a ten-year period at least seventy proletarian novels appeared. The proletarian novel portrayed the struggle between workers and employers, living conditions of poor workers, and often more specific themes which showed the benefits of Marxism and disparaged capitalism. However, few novels which were entirely propagandistic or adhered closely to party lines were successful as literature; as might be expected, the best writing of the period was often the work of authors whose books were more than vehicles for their political beliefs. A representative selection of proletarian literature may be found in GRANVILLE HICKS' *Proletarian Literature in the U.S.* (1935), which contains Clifford Odets' play, WAITING FOR LEFTY (1935) and selections from several novels, among them *Jews Without Money* (1930) by MICHAEL GOLD. Daniel Aaron wrote an extensive study: *Writers on the Left: Episodes in American Literary Communism* (1961).

Among the memorable novels of the period are James T. Farrell's STUDS LONIGAN trilogy; John Dos Passos' U.S.A. (1938); JOSEPHINE HERBST's trilogy *Pity is Not Enough* (1933), *The Executioner Waits* (1934) and *Rope of Gold* (1939); Henry Roth's *Call It Sleep* (1935); and John Steinbeck's IN DUBIOUS BATTLE (1936) and THE GRAPES OF WRATH (1939). Other proletarian writers include NELSON ALGREN, SHERWOOD ANDERSON, MAXWELL BODENHEIM, ERSKINE CALDWELL, WALDO FRANK, MEYER LEVIN, Grace Lumpkin, IRWIN SHAW, DALTON TRUMBO, and RICHARD WRIGHT.

After 1940 there were relatively few proletarian novels. Disillusion with communism as a result of the Soviet-Nazi pact of 1939, the end of the depression, and the outbreak of World War II ended proletarian writing as a movement. The best post-depression proletarian writing includes Richard Wright's NATIVE SON (1940); JAMES T. FARRELL's *Father and Son* (1940); HOWARD FAST's *The Unvanquished* (1942); Norman Mailer's THE NAKED AND THE DEAD (1948); Nelson Algren's THE MAN WITH THE GOLDEN ARM (1949). See LABOR PROBLEMS AND INDUSTRY.

Prometheus Pyrphoros (*Harvard Monthly,* November, 1900; *Poems*, 1905), dramatic scenes by TRUMBULL STICKNEY. The story was based directly on Greek sources, sought to present Prometheus as a sort of hero of scientific progress, and was somewhat pessimistic in tone, in accordance with the ideas of Stickney's friend HENRY ADAMS. In the poem, says Thomas Riggs, Jr., "we can perceive the crumbling consciousness of Newton's world, the world of infinite progress."

Promised Land, The (1912), an autobiography by MARY ANTIN. When she was still a child the author wrote an account in Yiddish of her early life in Polotzk, Russian Poland, where she lived inside the Jewish Pale with her parents. As the anti-Jewish feeling grew and pogroms began, the family managed to travel steerage to America, where they settled in the Boston slums. In 1899 Miss Antin translated her story into English, adding her later experiences. It appeared first in serial form in the *Atlantic Monthly;* later it was expanded into book form. The naive style of *The Promised Land* conveys admirably the child's bewilderment and terror in Plotzk, the hopes and dreams in the new country, and finally the emerging delight as the young girl learns English from kindly teachers in the public schools and even has a poem to George Washington accepted by a Boston newspaper. The book has become a classic and has been widely read in American schools. Miss Antin also wrote *They Who Knock at Our Doors* (1914).

Proper Bostonians, The (1947), a historical and satirical treatise by CLEVELAND AMORY. One of the elect, Amory writes about his peers in a tone far from reverent. He debunks, among other legends, that of the famed Boston Cabot family's connection with the aristocracy. He shows how solidly the Boston oligarchy is founded upon wealth accumulated by merchant princes whose children make careful marriages. Yet these men and women are often philanthropic; Arthur Train claimed that the true Bostonian combines "wholesale charity and retail penuriousness." According to Amory, eating oatmeal is a Boston custom, like the morning lecture and the afternoon walk, the trustee meeting and the charity bazaar, the daily tea and the anniversary dinner, the funeral, the formal call, and the Friday Symphony.

Prophet of the Great Smoky Mountains, The (1885), a novel by MARY NOAILLES MURFREE (Charles Egbert Craddock).

Prose Writers of America. See RUFUS W. GRISWOLD.

Proud Miss MacBride, The (1850), a satirical poem by JOHN G. SAXE. An attack on snobbery in New York City, the poem tells of Miss McBride who, feeling that MacBride was more ostentatious, changed her name. She rejects worthy suitors whose social station seems not high enough to her, and in the end is humiliated when the man she finally accepts turns out to be a worthless fortune hunter.

Prouty, Olive [Higgins] (b. Worcester, Mass., Jan. 7, 1882—   ), novelist. Best known for her novel STELLA DALLAS (1922), Olive Prouty wrote a number of other competent works, none of which matched its popularity. Her first book was *Bobbie, General Manager* (1913); *Home Port* appeared in 1947, *Fabia* in 1951.

Providence Plantations. The name given to a group of settlements made by ROGER WILLIAMS and others in what is now Rhode Island. Williams, an expatriate from Massachusetts because of his religious views, founded the first colony (1636) at what is now Providence. Later came ANNE HUTCHINSON, William Coddington, John Clark, and SAMUEL GORTON, the last-named a secessionist from Williams' colony. In 1644 all the settlements were united by a royal charter as Providence Plantations.

Provincetown Players. An influential group of actors, producers, and playwrights who in various forms of organization from 1915 to 1929 produced almost a hundred plays by close to fifty playwrights and brought about the greatest era in American drama. The group started as an acting company in Provincetown, Mass., under the direction of GEORGE CRAM COOK; their first theater, called the Wharf Theater (1916), was an abandoned fish house on a pier that was owned by Mary Heaton Vorse. Among the plays given were SUPPRESSED DESIRES, by Cook and his wife SUSAN GLASPELL; *Change Your Style*, by Cook; and *Contemporaries*, by Wilbur Daniel Steele. Even more important was the first production of a play by EUGENE O'NEILL, BOUND EAST FOR CARDIFF. Later the group moved to New York City, where it established the Playwrights' Theater in a private home on Macdougal St., two years later the Provincetown Playhouse on the same street. In 1929 the group moved to the Garrick Theater uptown, and after an unsuccessful season disbanded.

In New York the Players continued to produce plays by O'Neill, as well as works by FLOYD DELL, THEODORE DREISER, EDNA ST. VINCENT MILLAY, Miss Glaspell, SHERWOOD ANDERSON, PAUL GREEN, E. E. CUMMINGS, and EDNA FERBER. The great service of the group was the attention it focused on native writers. Helen Deutsch and Stella Hanau wrote *In Provincetown* (1931), and Miss Glaspell gave some account of her and her husband's experiences in *The Road to the Temple* (1926). Agnes Boulton, Eugene O'Neill's second wife, has also given a valuable account in her *Part of a Long Story* (1958).

Prue and I (1856), seven sketches by G. W. CURTIS. A middle-aged bookkeeper, living with his devoted wife on a meager salary, meditates on various lands he will never visit, records some of his daily observations in New York City, follows some of the great people of legend he has met, remembers some of his relatives, throughout makes clear the compelling power of love and goodness. The style is reminiscent of Washington Irving's SALMAGUNDI.

Prufrock and Other Observations (1917), poems by T. S. ELIOT. This was Eliot's first collection of verses, a paperbound pamphlet containing only twelve poems. The title is derived from the first poem in the collection, THE LOVE SONG OF J. ALFRED PRUFROCK.

Prynne, Hester. The heroine of Hawthorne's THE SCARLET LETTER (1850). She is condemned to wear a scarlet *A* on her dress because she has committed adultery.

Psalm of Life, The (in *Voices of the Night*, 1839), a poem by HENRY WADSWORTH LONGFELLOW. The poet stated that the poem came to him in a flash and was quickly written on the morning of July 26, 1838. It was extremely popular and widely anthologized, although most critics have considered it to be jingly and sentimental. It contains the well-known lines, "Life is real! Life is earnest!" and, "Footprints in the sands of time."

psychoanalysis and literature. Several American magazines (the *Forum, McClure's*, the *Century*, the *Dial, The Nation*) carried articles on Freudian psychoanalysis as early as 1915, although it did not achieve any great literary importance until after the first World War. Its over-all influence, however, must be considered as part of the spirit of the time, which had its beginnings in the attempt of the Romantic movement of the 19th century to explore the irrational, to remove as much as possible the limitations of human experience. The influence of psychoanalysis on the literature of the Twenties is thus difficult to pinpoint except with a few writers who were definitely "converted" to Freudianism. For the most part, the concepts of Freudian psychoanalysis were so highly assimilated in the iconoclastic temper of the Twenties that it is almost impossible to say where Freudianism began and individual insight and predilection left off.

Among the writers who deliberately adopted psychoanalytical theory was CONRAD AIKEN. He had studied Sigmund Freud, WILLIAM JAMES, and Henri Bergson. His BLUE VOYAGE (1927) and *Great Circle* (1933) reflect his psychoanalytic knowledge in their intense subjectivity and subtle character realization. The "STREAM OF CONSCIOUSNESS" technique used by Aiken and others is to a large degree an outgrowth of Freud's discovery of the unconscious and the resultant attempt on the part of writers to approximate the "flow" of the unconscious psychic life, although it must be borne in mind that the "stream of consciousness" itself was first suggested by James.

Freud's most significant contribution to literature was his *Interpretation of Dreams* (1900, English trans. 1913). The dream has a symbolic language all its own brought about by the distortion and "censorship" needed to disguise dream thoughts unacceptable to the conscious mind. It has become a rich field of investigation both for the psychologist and the artist. By revealing the unconscious, to which dreams are often the key, Freud provided the artist (particularly the symbolist) with new territory and new images; the unconscious itself, freed from conscious control, became the particular playground of the surrealists. (See SURREALISM.)

The use of dream as a literary and psychological device is found in the novels of ARTHUR KOESTLER, WALDO FRANK, and LUDWIG LEWISOHN. Frank's *Our America* (1919) is filled with Freudian terminology; the heroes of Lewisohn's *The Island Within* (1928) and of F. Scott Fitzgerald's TENDER IS THE NIGHT (1934) are psychoanalysts, the hero of Koestler's *Arrival and Departure* (1943) a patient undergoing analysis. During the Twenties SHERWOOD ANDERSON was called the "American Freudian," although it is not known that Anderson directly or deliberately borrowed from Freud. The characters of WINESBURG, OHIO (1919) all suffer to a greater or lesser degree from some kind of frustration or repression, particularly sexual, which indicates not so much that Anderson was using Freud but that he was working along parallel lines with Freud. Anderson also frequently uses dream symbolism, and shifts from the world of fact to the "large world of fancy."

In 1930 EUGENE JOLAS introduced Carl Jung to American readers in *transition*, a magazine published in Paris but usually made up of works by American writers. Jolas felt that Jung, rather than Freud, gave dream symbols their importance for the artist. Jung, who had begun as a disciple of Freud, had found Freud's concept of the symbol ("a product of the unconscious imagination") too limiting; Jung himself saw the symbol as the best way of expressing that for which there is no verbal equivalent, and found it to be a link between the conscious and unconscious mind. The major cause of dissension between Freud and Jung, however, arose when Jung declared symbols to be the property not only of the personal unconscious of the individual but to arise from the collective unconscious of the entire race. These symbols, or archetypes, are, according to Jung, "more or less the same everywhere and in all individuals." A common expression of the archetypes is myth or fairy tale, although these forms are not psychologically so important as archetypes which have not received such conscious elaboration. Sir James G. Frazer's extensive study of primitive mythology in *The Golden Bough* (16 v., 1890–1915) presents an interesting corroboration of Jung's theory in showing the similarities and complex interrelationship of myth and ritual in cultures far separated not only geographically but in time. T. S. Eliot has acknowledged his debt to *The Golden Bough*, which provided some of the material used in *The Waste Land* (1922). A recent study is Leon Edel's *The Psychological Novel, 1900–1950* (1955).

psychographs. A term devised by Gamaliel Bradford. See AMERICAN PORTRAITS; GAMALIEL BRADFORD; PROFILE.

Public Libraries in the U.S.: Their History, Condition, and Management (1876). This special report of the Bureau of Education in the Department of the Interior was made as a contribution to the World's Fair celebration at Philadelphia of the 100th anniversary of the signing of the Declaration of Independence. At this celebration, the American Library Association was founded and the LIBRARY JOURNAL established. See LIBRARIES IN THE U.S.

Public Library Inquiry, The (1949–50). In 1947 the Social Science Research Council, at the suggestion of the American Library Association, undertook an inquiry into the basic problems facing public libraries at mid-century. A grant of $200,000 was made available by the Carnegie Corporation of New York. The inquiry was carried out under the direction of Dr. Robert D. Leigh, political scientist and former president of Bennington College. The reports, based on investigations in sixty communities, give much useful information not only on the main subject of the inquiry, but also on the main factors that influence the spread of information to the public, including book publishing, information films, and government publications.

The seven volumes in the *Inquiry* were: (1) *The Book Industry*, by William Miller; (2) *The Information Film*, by Gloria Waldron; (3) *The Library's Public*, by Bernard Berelson, dean of the Graduate Library School at the University of Chicago; (4) *The Public Library in the Political Process*, by Oliver Garceau; (5) *Government Publications for the Citizen*, by James L. McCamy; (6) *The Public Librarian*, by Alice I. Bryan and Dr. Leigh; (7) *The Public Library in the United States*, by Dr. Leigh, as director of the *Inquiry*, who summarized its findings. The volumes were frankly critical of certain conditions. It was noted that the people of the United States spent for all their libraries only two-thirds of what they spent on bowling alleys and billiards. Only one person in ten is a regular library user. See also LIBRARIES IN THE U.S.

Publicola. The pen name used by JOHN QUINCY ADAMS for eleven articles that appeared in the *Columbian Centinel* of Boston from June 8 to July 27, 1791. Adams, then in his early twenties, was opposing such doctrinaires as Thomas Paine in their argument that the majority had an absolute right to rule. Adams, as a Federalist, appealed to an ethical absolute, as represented in the judiciary, in behalf of the minority.

public speaking. See ORATORS AND ORATORY.

Publishers' Trade List Annual. In this consolidated catalogue, first issued in 1873, publishers contribute their own catalogues, which are bound along with others to make a single large volume.

Publishers' Weekly. The first issue of this indispensable journal of the book publishing business appeared on Jan. 18, 1872. The founder and first editor was FREDERICK LEYPOLDT, who had earlier conducted two short-lived periodicals, the *Literary Bulletin* (founded, 1868) and the *Monthly Book Trade Circular* (founded, 1869). He called his new magazine the *Publishers' and Stationers' Weekly Trade Circular;* in 1873 it took its present name. Very early in the magazine's career Leypoldt secured the able assistance of Richard Rogers Bowker, who on Leypoldt's death in 1884 succeeded him as editor and continued in charge of the *Weekly* until his death in 1933. In 1918 Frederic G. Melcher became co-editor; he is also president of the R. R. Bowker Co., which issues the *Weekly*, the *Library Journal*, and other publications useful in the book trade. The *Weekly* is an exhaustive record of the book trade from week to week and season to season. Through Melcher it has sponsored some important awards in the field of children's literature. It is the one magazine consulted by members of all branches of the book business. In its seventy-fifth anniversary issue (Jan. 18, 1947) the *Weekly* pointed out that the number of new titles issued in a year was nearly ten times that of 1872; moreover, the number of copies issued had increased about fiftyfold. Distribution methods had also greatly changed, with stores other than bookstores, as well as book clubs, accounting for more and more sales.

publishing. See BOOK PUBLISHING IN THE U.S.

Publius. The pen name attached to essays by the three contributors to THE FEDERALIST papers (1787–88): Alexander Hamilton, James Madison, and John Jay.

Puck. This humorous weekly was originally a German-language publication, founded in St. Louis by JOSEPH KEPPLER in 1869 as *Puck, Illustrierte Wochenschrift* and then issued in New York City in 1876, still in German, as *Puck, Humoristisches Wochenblatt*. In March, 1877, an English edition began to appear, with Sydney Rosenfeld as editor for one year. He was succeeded by its most famous and long-lasting editor, H. C. BUNNER (1878–96); he in turn by HARRY LEON WILSON (1896–1902), JOHN KENDRICK BANGS (1904–05), A. H. Folwell (1905–16), and Karl Schmidt (1916). The magazine was sold in 1917 to WILLIAM RANDOLPH HEARST and ceased publication the next year, although the name was used for many years as the title of a Hearst Sunday magazine section. In Bunner's day the magazine was a famous one, with Bunner writing about half of each issue—stories, poems, essays, even supplying captions for the cartoons. Bunner's stories, many of them clever in a Gallic fashion, were collected in SHORT SIXES (1891) and MADE IN FRANCE (1893); his verses in AIRS FROM ARCADY AND ELSEWHERE (1884). Keppler, a

capable illustrator, brought in new methods of reproduction of drawings that greatly helped the weekly. Among the contributors were Dana Burnet, James Huneker, Richard K. Munkittrick, F. P. Adams, Arthur Guiterman, George Jean Nathan, and the cartoonists "Hy" Mayer and Frederick Opper.

Pudd'nhead Wilson, The Tragedy of (1894), a novel by MARK TWAIN. David Wilson is called "Pudd'nhead" by the townsfolk because his wisdom and eccentricity is beyond their comprehension. He redeems himself in their eyes by solving simultaneously a murder mystery and a case of transposed identities.

The plot is simple and convincing. On the same day in the 1830's in Mississippi two children are born: a white boy and a boy of part Negro parentage. The latter's mother, Roxy, a slave, is given charge of both children, and in fear that her own child will be sold down the river, interchanges them in the cradle. When they grow up the whites of the region accept the Negro as an equal and treat the white boy as a mulatto bound to be sold sooner or later. As it happens, the boy of mixed breed grows up to be a scalawag, sells his own mother, and robs and murders his uncle. He accuses Luigi, one of a pair of twins who have wandered into the neighborhood, of the murder. Pudd'nhead, who is a lawyer, undertakes Luigi's defense and proves his innocence by comparing fingerprints, a novel police technique in those days. The real murderer and his identity is exposed and the white boy takes his rightful place.

Throughout his life Twain was interested in the dichotomies of human nature, the personalities of twins, and the influence of heredity and environment on individuals. Perhaps this interest derived from his own nature: he tended to alternate moods of extreme elation or depression. In 1869 he wrote a sketch about the original Siamese twins, Chang and Eng, who join opposite sides in the Civil War, and take each other prisoner at Seven Pines. Another set of twins appears in the comedy, *Those Extraordinary Twins* which was bound with *Pudd'nhead Wilson* in 1894 and in which Pudd'nhead and Roxy are also introduced. THE PRINCE AND THE PAUPER is probably the best known of Twain's "twin" stories.

Twain makes it clear in the book how he regards human servitude. It is clear, too, that he would have society take more heed of environment and training as affecting character. He used the book as an opportunity to create a wonderful group of epigrams, which appear as headpieces for the chapters and are given as taken from *Pudd'nhead Wilson's Calendar*. They are a distillation of Twain's wit and wisdom. Commentators have found Calvinism, melodrama, a fearless treatment of the theme of miscegenation, and great artistic courage in the book, undoubtedly one of Twain's masterpieces.

Pueblo Indians. A name given to Indian tribes who lived in a certain type of dwelling in the southwestern United States, Mexico, and

South America. The dwellings were built of stone or adobe, usually were several stories high, often in the form of terraces, and had entrances on the roof, reached by ladders. There was also a subterranean *kiva*, a ceremonial chamber. Generally the pueblos were communal, housing several families. In the United States the region of the pueblos is in "the Four Corners," where the Arizona, New Mexico, Utah, and Colorado boundaries intersect.

The tribes who lived in these pueblos vary somewhat in the accounts of differing authorities. Generally the term is confined to the Zuñi and Hopi Indians. They were mostly farmers but were also skilled in pottery, textiles, carvings, and silverwork. Their architecture and handicrafts have influenced neighboring white groups; the Museum of New Mexico and associated institutions, artists, and collectors have fostered these crafts, also Indian dancing and painting. Much poetry of the Pueblo Indians has been collected and has won admiration for its delicacy, spirituality, and frequent tenderness. Their hymns and prayers and their cradle and children's songs are especially distinguished. Erna Fergusson described Pueblo rituals in *Dancing Gods* (1931).

Other books on the peoples of the Pueblo region include Frank Hamilton Cushing's *Zuñi Folk Tales* (1901) and *My Adventures in Zuñi* (1941); Walter Hough's *The Hopi Indians* (1915); A. F. Bandelier's THE DELIGHT-MAKERS (1890); C. F. Lummis' *Mesa, Canon, and Pueblo* (1925); Edgar L. Hewett's *Ancient Life in the American Southwest* (1930) and *The Pueblo Indian World* (with Bertha P. Drutton, 1945); John Louw Nelson's *Rhythm for Rain* (1937); Leo W. Simmons' *Sun Chief: the Autobiography of a Hopi Indian* (1942); Stanley A. Stubbs' *Bird's-Eye View of the Pueblos* (1950), and Ruth Benedict's *Patterns of Culture* (1934).

Pulham, H. M. See H. M. PULHAM, ESQ.

Pulitzer, Joseph (b. Hungary, April 10, 1847 —d. Oct. 29, 1911), newspaper editor and publisher. Pulitzer came to New York in search of adventure and served briefly in the 1st New York Cavalry. In St. Louis he became a reporter on a German daily, the *Westliche Post*. He went into local politics, first as member of the Missouri legislature, then as one of the three police commissioners of St. Louis. By 1871 he was part owner of the *Post*, but sold out his interest to travel abroad. In 1878 he bought the *St. Louis Dispatch* and built it up into one of the most profitable papers in the West. In its columns he launched a campaign against political corruption in St. Louis. A prominent lawyer who was involved in the exposure stormed into the office of Pulitzer's assistant during Pulitzer's absence from town, and a furious quarrel ensued which ended in the shooting of the lawyer.

As the result of the wave of popular feeling against him, Pulitzer went to New York and bought the New York *World* from Jay Gould. In less than seven years the circulation of the *World* jumped from under 20,000 to over 200,-000; the paper proved to be a gold mine. WIL-LIAM RANDOLPH HEARST challenged Pulitzer's supremacy in 1896 when he bought the New York *Journal,* but the *World* continued to flourish. Pulitzer professed a love for truth, a set of lofty ideals, and a contempt for political pressure. He was shrewd enough to know that he could fight corruption and Hearst together under the banner of "idealism." The ensuing struggle for power resulted in some of the dirtiest fighting ever known in the history of journalism. At last the public revolted, clubs and libraries banned the *World,* and Pulitzer decided to clean up his paper. In the meantime his health was failing and he became blind. He retired from active life, left Columbia University $2,000,000 to found a School of Journalism and to award the now famous PULITZER PRIZES.

David Graham Phillips, a former *World* reporter, drew an acid portrait of Pulitzer in his novel *The Great God Success* (1901). Alleyne Ireland's *Joseph Pulitzer, Reminiscences of a Secretary* (1914); Don C. Seitz's *Joseph Pulitzer, His Life and Letters* (1924); and James Wyman Barrett's *Joseph Pulitzer and His World* (1941) throw light on this paradoxical figure who exerted so great a force, both for good and for ill, in the newspaper world. Pulitzer's son Joseph (1885–1955) inherited the St. Louis *Post Dispatch* and continued it with striking success. The New York *World* was merged with the New York *Telegram.*

Pulitzer Prizes. JOSEPH PULITZER set aside a fund of $500,000 to provide for these awards, which were to be given "for the encouragement of public service, public morals, American literature, and the advancement of education." The first prizes were awarded in 1917. Eight prizes are awarded in journalism: for the most meritorious service rendered by a newspaper, the best local reporting, the best local reporting with no edition-time pressure, the best reporting on national affairs, the most distinguished international reporting, the most distinguished editorial writing, the best cartoon, and the outstanding example of news photography. Five awards are given in letters: for the most distinguished novel, preferably about American life; for the American play best showing the power and educational value of the stage; the finest book on American history; the best biography or autobiography teaching patriotic and unselfish services to the people; the most distinguished volume of verse. A prize is also awarded in music, usually to a work of some magnitude such as an opera or long orchestral piece. All the awards are made annually under the control of the School of Journalism at Columbia University and the university trustees. Juries make reports to an Advisory Board which then makes recommendations to the trustees.

pulps, the. There are three types of material used in making paper: rag pulp, straw pulp, and wood pulp. The last, the least expensive, has been used extensively in the so-called "pulp" magazines, as opposed to the "slick" magazines. The "pulps" publish mainly escape fiction— westerns, sensational love and equally sensational "true" stories, sports stories, horror and wonder tales. Among the recent "pulps" are *Jungle Stories, Black Mask, F.B.I. Detective, True Police Cases, Thrilling Love, Fate, Other Worlds, .44 Western, Pecos Kid Western, Ranch Love Stories,* to name only a few.

Pulsifer, Harold Trowbridge (b. Manchester, Conn., Nov. 18, 1886—d. April 8, 1948), poet, editor. Pulsifer's maternal grandfather was a co-founder of THE OUTLOOK with LYMAN ABBOTT, and when Pulsifer left Harvard University he joined the staff of that magazine, acting as managing editor from 1923 to 1928. He introduced many new poets to the public through *The Outlook* and himself wrote verse. It was collected in *Mothers and Men* (1916); *Harvest of Time* (1932); *Elegy for a House* (1935); *Rowen* (1937); and other volumes. In 1931–32 he served as president of the Poetry Society of America.

Pumpelly, Raphael (b. Owego, N.Y., Sept. 8, 1837—d. Aug. 10, 1923), geologist, explorer, memoirist. Pumpelly made important geological expeditions to Siberia, China, and Central Asia. He also explored the copper and iron resources of Michigan and the Lake Superior region and investigated the mineral resources of the United States for the 10th United States Census. He was a lively writer and recounted his experiences in several books, including *Across America and Asia* (1869); *Explorations in Central Asia* (1905); and *My Reminiscences* (2 v., 1918).

"Punch, boys, punch with care! Punch in the presence of the passinjare!" (Sept. 27, 1875), a poem by Isaac Hill Bromley (1833–1898), attributed sometimes to Noah Brooks (1830–1903). It is said to have been inspired by a notice to conductors posted in New York horsecars. Moses P. Handy added to it; it appeared with a musical score in *Scribner's Monthly* (April, 1876). In February, 1876, Mark Twain made it nationally famous by using it as the basis for a humorous article for the *Atlantic Monthly* entitled *A Literary Nightmare;* he tells of the acute sufferings inflicted on him by the persistence of the verses in his memory, although he quotes them inexactly. Many readers thought he had invented the jingle.

Pupin, Michael I[dvorsky] (b. Hungary, Oct. 4, 1858—d. March 12, 1935), physicist, inventor. Pupin sailed to America in 1874 to escape from Austrian tyranny, landed in New York with a fez on his head and five cents in his pocket. After working at a number of odd jobs, he was able to save enough money to enter Columbia University, graduating in 1883, the year in which he was naturalized. In 1885 he went abroad to study mathematics at Cambridge and in Germany. He was appointed instructor in mathematical physics at Columbia in 1889; in 1901 he became professor of electromechanics. Pupin's most important work was his research into electric resonance and the magnetization of iron. The "Pupin coil," which he invented, was essential to the development of

the long-distance telephone. He was also a pioneer in the use of the X ray. His beautifully written autobiography, *From Immigrant to Inventor* (1923), received a Pulitzer Prize.

Among his other books are: *New Reformation* (1927), which suggests the possible transition from physical to spiritual realities; *Thermodynamics of Reversible Cycles in Gases and Saturated Vapors* (1894); *Serbian Orthodox Church* (1918); *Yugoslavia* (1919); *The Romance of the Machine* (1930); and more than sixty-five articles on scientific subjects.

Purdy, James (b. 1923—   ), novelist, short-story writer. Purdy was born in rural Ohio, a region that provides the setting for his latest novel, *The Nephew* (1960), and was educated in the Midwest. After receiving an M.A. from the University of Chicago, he went abroad, where he spent some time at the University of Madrid. His collection of short stories, *Color of Darkness* (1957), brought him considerable attention, which was more than justified by his first novel, *Malcolm* (1959). In tracing his hero's course through a series of picaresque adventures, Purdy comments on the lack of values in urban American life. In *The Nephew* he turned to rural life, following the attempts of Alma, a retired school teacher, to write a memorial booklet for her beloved nephew, who has been reported killed. In gathering material, she learns many questionable facts about the young man's life— and is forced to re-examine her own empty existence. She returns to the cares of daily life in a small town with more awareness of the complexity of life. Purdy's wit and linguistic skill, his nostalgia and surrealistic sense of time and place combine in an often powerful style.

Puritan and His Daughter, The (1849), a novel by JAMES KIRKE PAULDING. The story is a depiction of Puritanism in the Old World and the New. It shifts from England in the days of Cromwell to Virginia and then to a locality on the Connecticut River that Alexander Cowie identifies as probably Hadley, Mass. The tale makes an attack on religious prejudice and bigotry. The Puritan's daughter falls in love with the Cavalier's son; when the girl is accused in the Salem witchcraft madness, the young man manages to save her.

Puritan in Babylon, A (1938), a biography of Calvin Coolidge by WILLIAM ALLEN WHITE. White disliked Coolidge, but did his best in this carefully written and entertaining biography to treat him fairly.

Puritans and Puritanism. The Puritans were first of all Presbyterians who followed the Swiss method of controlling their churches by committees of ministers and laymen. They also believed in a single church and creed, with no room for outsiders or other beliefs, but their difficulties with the British crown and Anglican officials led a considerable percentage of them to advocate separatism, and numerous Independent or Separatist congregations were set up. Attempts to suppress them led many Puritans to become refugees, first in Holland

and then in America. The short rule of British Puritans in the time of Cromwell ended in the return of the Stuarts; and the Puritans, Separatists, and Independents then became Nonconformists. Ralph Barton Perry summarizes the essential doctrine of Puritanism as "theocratic, Congregational-Presbyterian, Protestant, medieval Christianity."

Nathaniel Hawthorne has a celebrated passage in THE SNOW-IMAGE (1851) on his own forebears: "Such a life [in the New England frontier settlements] was sinister to the intellect and sinister to the heart; especially when one generation had bequeathed its religious gloom, and the counterfeit of its religious ardor, to the next; for these characteristics, by being inherited from the example and precept of other human beings, and not from an original and spiritual source, assumed the form both of hypocrisy and exaggeration." It was mainly the ministers who were blamed. "Are you, sir, the person who serves here?" a stranger asked a minister whom he met in the streets of Rowley, Mass. "I am, sir, the person who rules here," the minister responded. Richardson Wright has called the ecclesiastical history of New England "the dreariest of all subjects." Yet Ola Elizabeth Winslow, in *Meetinghouse Hill, 1630–1783* (1952), tilts a useful and well-aimed lance against the popular notion that New England was ruled by its ministers. She stresses the overwhelming importance of the town meetings; in these workshops of democracy New England learned to be intolerant of British rule.

The Puritans felt themselves to be the heirs of the Old Testament, and to some extent built their polity and commonwealth upon it. The frequent sternness of that section of the Bible matched the sternness of the New England landscape and the stern men who found that landscape congenial. They deftly managed to pick out from the Old Testament all its more dour and harsher portions, overlooking many passages of divine love and love for one's neighbors. But, as W. E. H. Lecky remarked, "It is an historical fact that in the great majority of instances the early Puritan defenders of civil liberty derived their political principles chiefly from the Old Testament." (See also under SALEM WITCH-CRAFT TRIALS.)

It has been easy to neglect or sneer at the nobler aspects of Puritanism, to ridicule its less lovely aspects. Although New England writers protested violently against slavery and capital punishment, the common conscience of the region was untouched. For respectability was founded on property, and respectability was mightier than John Calvin. Confidence in their own elect righteousness gave the Puritans their intense bigotry and intolerance. At his best the Puritan was, as Ralph Barton Perry calls him, "a moral athlete"; at his worst, a complacent hypocrite. Rigid laws against adultery led to some of the worst cases of sex perversion imaginable, according to Richardson Wright's *Hawkers and Walkers in Early America* (1927).

Wright adds that "the private diaries of the early Fathers and pious New England clergy would have made Rabelais white with envy." The Puritans took to the sea with vigor, and were shrewd and diligent businessmen. They frowned upon idling and found it easy to identify economic success with moral qualities. Perry and others identify Puritan doctrine with our doctrine of individualism and our capitalistic and free enterprise system.

The influence of the Puritans was very great because of their numbers and their concentration in one area. An important factor in the population, however, was the non-Puritan element among the settlers along the seacoast from Maine to Cape Cod. They were fishermen, traders, and nonconformists who showed a constant indifference to school, church, politics, and other characteristic New England institutions. Firmly founded, intractable Puritanism did not, in fact, last very long. By 1690 it was becoming evident that the reign of the saints was passing, largely as a result of the increasing dignity and strength of the Boston merchants. The charter of 1691, moreover, guaranteed freedom of worship to all Christian sects. The power of the clergy was waning and among the greater ministers a definite rationalism was appearing. Metaphysically, the battle was between determinism and free will, and congregations preferred the latter.

The Puritans were almost fanatic in their love of learning, and produced more books than the people in any other colony. Theology was of course the predominant subject. History was another favorite topic, sometimes in the form of autobiographical reports by early settlers. NATHANIEL WARD was an early Yankee aphorist, the MATHER family produced books profusely, there were arid laureates of Puritanism in verse like MICHAEL WIGGLESWORTH; other poets, principally EDWARD TAYLOR and ANNE BRADSTREET, wrote more pleasingly. Keeping diaries was a common habit with the Puritans. As Puritan influence decreased there came a more literary flowering in the transcendental movement and in what Van Wyck Brooks calls "New England's Indian Summer." Meantime they built beautiful ships and houses, laid out lovely farms and gardens; contrary to the popular notion, they did not lack aesthetic graces.

Perhaps the most ardent and intelligent defender of Puritanism as an intellectual, cultural, and spiritual force has been a European critic, Régis Michaud, in *The American Novel of Today* (1928). Other scholarly discussions of Puritanism and the Puritans include Van Wyck Brooks' *The Wine of the Puritans* (1909); J. T. Adams' *The Founding of New England* (1921); V. L. Parrington's THE COLONIAL MIND (1927, as the first volume of *Main Currents in American Thought*); Henry W. Lawrence's *The Not-Quite Puritans* (1928); S. E. Morison's *The Puritan Pronaos* (1936); Perry Miller and T. H. Johnson's *The Puritans* (an anthology, 1938); Ralph Barton Perry's *Puritanism and Democracy*

(1944); Kenneth B. Murdock's *Literature and Theology in Colonial New England* (1949); George M. Stephenson's *The Puritan Heritage* (1952); Perry Miller's *The New England Mind: From Colony to Province* (1953).

A vast amount of fiction has been written about the Puritans in their various historical epochs, including Puritan influences in New England down to the present day. Some of the more outstanding novels are: J. F. Cooper's THE WEPT OF WISH-TON-WISH (1829); Delia Bacon's *Tales of the Puritans* (1831); J. K. Paulding's *The Puritan and His Daughter* (1849); J. L. Motley's *Merrymount: A Romance of the Massachusetts Colony* (1849); John Greenleaf Whittier's MARGARET SMITH'S JOURNAL (1849); Nathaniel Hawthorne's THE SCARLET LETTER (1850); Harriet Beecher Stowe's THE MINISTER'S WOOING (1859) and PEARL OF ORR'S ISLAND (1862); Rose Terry Cooke's *Rootbound and Other Sketches* (1885); William Dean Howells' THE RISE OF SILAS LAPHAM (1885); Mary E. Wilkins' A NEW ENGLAND NUN AND OTHER STORIES (1891); Alice Brown's *Meadow Grass* (1895); Sarah Orne Jewett's THE COUNTRY OF THE POINTED FIRS (1896); Edith Wharton's ETHAN FROME (1911); Esther Forbes' MIRROR FOR WITCHES (1928) and *Paradise* (1937); Mary Ellen Chase's *Silas Crockett* (1935); George Santayana's THE LAST PURITAN (1935); Stephen Vincent Benét's THE DEVIL AND DANIEL WEBSTER (1937); J. P. Marquand's THE LATE GEORGE APLEY (1937) and WICKFORD POINT (1939); Frances Winwar's *Gallows Hill* (1937); Ruth Moore's *Spoonhandle* (1946).

Poems that are characteristically Puritan are innumerable, from the earliest days in New England to the present time. Among them: Anne Bradstreet's THE TENTH MUSE (1650); Michael Wigglesworth's THE DAY OF DOOM (1662[?]) and MEAT OUT OF THE EATER (1669); THE NEW ENGLAND PRIMER (1681); Edward Taylor's *Poetical Works* (late 17th century; first printed, 1939); Henry Wadsworth Longfellow's COURTSHIP OF MILES STANDISH (1858); Oliver Wendell Holmes' THE DEACON'S MASTERPIECE (1858); Edwin Arlington Robinson's THE CHILDREN OF THE NIGHT (1897); Robert P. Tristram Coffin's *Yoke of Thunder* (1932), *Saltwater Farm* (1937), and other collections.

Among plays that throw light on Puritan character and events in their history are H. W. Longfellow's NEW ENGLAND TRAGEDIES (1868); James Herne's SHORE ACRES (1893); Eugene O'Neill's ILE (1917), DESIRE UNDER THE ELMS (1924), and MOURNING BECOMES ELECTRA (1931); Arthur Miller's *The Crucible* (1953). James Russell Lowell wrote tolerant essays on the Puritans in *New England Two Centuries Ago* (1865) and *Witchcraft* (1868).

Purloined Letter, The (*The Gift*, 1845), a story by EDGAR ALLAN POE. This is usually regarded as the greatest of Poe's three detective stories, with his French detective C. AUGUSTE DUPIN displaying even more than his customary acumen. A woman of royal rank has been blackmailed by a cabinet minister; she appeals to the police and they to Dupin. He visits the blackmailer and promptly finds the letter—"hidden" where everybody can see it. Dupin manages to retrieve the letter by substituting a facsimile and receives a large reward. Howard Haycraft calls it "structurally and aesthetically" the most satisfying of Poe's detective tales.

Purple Cow, The. See GELETT BURGESS.

Pusey, Merlo J[ohn] (b. Woodruff, Utah, Feb. 3, 1902—   ), newspaperman, teacher, writer. Pusey worked first for the Salt Lake City *Deseret News*, then for the Washington *News* and the Washington *Post*, becoming the associate editor of the latter in 1945. From 1939 to 1942 he taught journalism at George Washington University. He wrote some authoritative works on current events, history, and biography: *The Supreme Court Crisis* (1937); *Big Government: Can We Control It?* (1945); *Charles Evans Hughes* (2 v., 1951), which won a Pulitzer prize.

Putnam, George Haven (b. England, April 2, 1844—d. Feb. 27, 1930), soldier, publisher, historian, biographer, memoirist. After serving in the Union army during the Civil War, Putnam became a partner in the publishing firm which his father, **George Palmer Putnam** (1814–1872), had organized in 1866. He became head of the firm and remained in charge until his death. He was also an energetic author. Among his books: *Authors and Their Public in Ancient Times* (1894); *Books and Their Makers During the Middle Ages* (2 v., 1896–97); *A Prisoner of War in Virginia* (1912); *George Palmer Putnam* (1912); *Memories of a Publisher* (1915); *Some Memories of the Civil War* (1924).

Putnam, George Palmer. See PUTNAM, GEORGE HAVEN.

Putnam, Herbert (b. New York City, Sept. 20, 1861—d. Aug. 14, 1955), librarian. Putnam was admitted to the bar and practiced in Boston until 1895. In 1895 he was appointed librarian of the Boston Public Library, in 1899 of the Library of Congress, a post he held until his retirement in 1939. He received many honorary degrees for his distinguished work in Washington, where the Library of Congress under his guidance attained a collection of more than five million volumes and ranked with the greatest European libraries.

Putnam, Israel (b. Salem Village [now Danvers], Mass., Jan. 7, 1718—d. May 29, 1790), Revolutionary soldier and hero. When the Revolutionary agitations began, Putnam became one of the Sons of Liberty, was commissioned a brigadier general, then a major general, and participated in many important actions in 1776–77. He wrote an account of an expedition against Havana (1762), and a trip to Florida published in 1931 as *The Two Putnams*. Nathaniel Harrington Bannister wrote a play about him, *Putnam* (prod., 1844; pub. *c.* 1859). He is mentioned in James Fenimore Cooper's LIONEL LINCOLN (1825) and was the inspiration for Arthur Guiterman's poem *Death and General Putnam* (1935).

Putnam, [Howard] Phelps (b. Boston, 1894—

d. 1948), poet. Born into a literary Boston family—his grandfather was a noted journalist; his father, a writer on metaphysical subjects— Putnam was educated at Phillips Exeter and Yale. After graduating, he engaged in a wide variety of enterprises, from working in an Arizona copper mine to serving as an assistant editor on the *Atlantic Monthly*. Putnam published only two collections of verse, *Trinc* (1927) and *The Five Seasons* (1930), leaving at his death a long incomplete philosophical poem, "The Earthly Comedy." He is best known for his early poetry, which, in ballad, song, or sonnet form, combines lyric delicacy and hard-bitten, colloquial satire in a distinctive and often effective way.

Putnam, Samuel (b. Rossville, Ill., 1892— d. Jan. 15, 1950), newspaperman, critic, literary historian, editor, translator. Putnam worked for a time on a Chicago newspaper, lived in Paris from 1927 to 1934. From 1929 to 1933 he wrote a weekly "Paris Letter" for the book page of the New York *Sun* and a letter on art for *The New York Times* and the Chicago *Daily News*, at the same time contributing to and sometimes helping to edit various "little magazines." He told the amusing and often significant story of his experience in *Paris Was Our Mistress. Memoirs of a Lost and Found Generation* (1947). While abroad Putnam acquired French, Spanish, Italian, and Portuguese, and by his translations, critical essays, and historical accounts won a prominent position as a literary man. Best known of his books was *Marvelous Journey* (1948), an admirable account of Brazilian literature. He did a translation of *Don Quixote* (1949) which was reprinted in *The Portable Cervantes*, along with other writings. He also translated Rabelais, Pirandello, and others.

Putnam's Monthly Magazine. Founded in January, 1853, with the imprint of a distinguished publishing house, this magazine included among its contributors Herman Melville, Henry Wadsworth Longfellow, James Russell Lowell, Henry David Thoreau, James Fenimore Cooper, William Cullen Bryant. After two years Putnam's sold it. It merged with another magazine, which itself soon ceased publication (1857). Then came *Putnam's Magazine*, founded in January, 1868; Frank R. Stockton, W. D. Howells, and John Burroughs contributed to its pages. In 1870 it was merged with the newly founded SCRIBNER'S. In 1906 *Putnam's Monthly and The Critic* appeared, a new magazine that absorbed an older one. It attracted some good authors,

mainly humorists; among them were Don Marquis and Gelett Burgess. In 1910 it was merged with the ATLANTIC MONTHLY.

Pyle, Ernie [Ernest Taylor] (b. Dana, Ind., Aug. 3, 1900—d. April 18, 1945), newspaperman, war correspondent, columnist. Pyle was a great newspaperman whose homely columns were read all over the country before World War II. His war correspondence was regarded as the best written by any of the reporters who covered the battle action. He was killed by Japanese machine gun fire on Ie Jima, a small island off the coast of Okinawa. The army in general regarded him as its best friend, one who told the truth sympathetically to the folks at home. During his lifetime and posthumously several volumes by Pyle were published: *Ernie Pyle in England* (1941); *Here Is Your War* (1943); *Brave Men* (1944); *Last Chapter* (1946); *An Ernie Pyle Album* (1946); and *Home Country* (1947), a collection of Pyle's prewar newspaper columns, rich in folklore and Americana. In 1944 he was awarded a Pulitzer prize for distinguished reporting. Lee G. Miller wrote *The Story of Ernie Pyle* (1950).

Pyle, Howard (b. Wilmington, Del., March 5, 1853—d. Nov. 9, 1911), illustrator, art teacher, children's author. Pyle studied art while helping with his father's leather business. When in 1876 *Scribner's Magazine* accepted some sketches he had written and illustrated, he moved to New York and, after nearly starving, managed to maintain himself as writer and illustrator. In 1880 he returned to Wilmington to write children's books. He taught at the Drexel Institute in Philadelphia from 1894 until 1900, when he opened his own art school in Wilmington. Among his pupils were N. C. WYETH (who copied his methods) and MAXFIELD PARRISH. Among the books he wrote and illustrated are *The Merry Adventures of Robin Hood* (1883); *Pepper and Salt* (1885); *The Wonder Clock* (1887); *Otto of the Silver Hand* (1888); *Men of Iron* (1892); *The Ghost of Captain Brand* (1896); *The Price of Blood* (1899); *The Story of King Arthur and His Knights* (1903); *The Story of the Champions of the Round Table* (1905); *The Story of Sir Launcelot and His Companions* (1907). He revivified colonial life and medieval legends in his strongly individual paintings, many of which were reproduced in *Harper's Magazine*.

Pyncheon. The Pyncheon family plays the chief role in Hawthorne's THE HOUSE OF THE SEVEN GABLES (1851).

Q

Quad, M. The pen name of CHARLES BERTRAND LEWIS.

Quaife, Milo Milton (b. Nashua, Iowa, Oct. 6, 1880—d. Sept. 1, 1959), teacher, historian, editor. Quaife taught for a while at the Lewis Institute, lectured at other institutions, and was an official of various historical societies. In the field of history he dealt mainly with the West. Among his books: *The Development of Chicago* (1916); *Wisconsin—Its History and Its People* (1924); *Lake Michigan* (1944); *This Is Detroit* (1951); *Forty-Six Years: The Published Writings of Milo M. Quaife* (1955). He served as an advisory editor of the DICTIONARY OF AMERICAN HISTORY and of the "American Lake" series (1941–49).

Quaker City, The, or The Monks of Monk Hall (1844), a novel by GEORGE LIPPARD. This was possibly the first muckraking novel in the history of American fiction. Lippard himself claimed, with some pride, that the book had been "more attacked and more read than any [other] work of American fiction published for the last ten years." Alexander Cowie calls it "probably the most extravagant compound of Gothic terror, intense melodrama, and social invective ever written on this continent." It was an exposé of vice in Philadelphia; there are three main plots, and the action takes place in three days. The book was fittingly dedicated to CHARLES BROCKDEN BROWN. Lippard was a sincere champion of the poor and oppressed, but he seemed to take a psychopathic pleasure in depicting sensational events.

Quaker Poet, The. A name frequently given to JOHN GREENLEAF WHITTIER.

Quantrill [sometimes **Quantrell**], **William Clarke** (b. Canal Dover, Ohio, July 31, 1837—d. June 6, 1865), farmer, schoolmaster, soldier. Quantrill was mustered into Confederate service in 1862 after operating as a guerrilla in Kansas and Missouri; he defeated a Federal cavalry unit (October, 1863) and brutally murdered all the men captured. He was himself mortally wounded in action. Many books have been written in which he appears; among them are W. E. Connelley's *Quantrill and the Border Wars* (1910); John McCorkle's *Three Years with Quantrill* (1914); Alice Nichols' *Bleeding Kansas* (1954). Quantrill became a folklore hero; Charles J. Finger has recorded a ballad entitled *Quantrell* (*Frontier Ballads*, 1927).

Quayle, Mary Jane Ward. See MARY JANE WARD.

Queechy (1852), a novel by SUSAN WARNER. This sentimental and pious book became an immediate best seller, although never quite so popular as the same author's THE WIDE, WIDE WORLD (1850). It was highly praised by Elizabeth Barrett Browning. It depicted the life of orphan Fleda Ringgan whose virtues overcome all her misfortunes, so that she marries well and happily. The scene is Queechy, Vt., a town not mentioned in the gazetteers.

Queed (1911), a novel by HENRY SYDNOR HARRISON. This best seller told the story of an absent-minded and likable newspaperman who takes lessons from a pugilist and finds himself entangled in several amusing love affairs. H. L. Mencken called it "William J. Locke diluted with vast drafts from *Laddie* and *Pollyanna.*"

Queen, Ellery. The pseudonym of **Frederic Dannay** (b. Brooklyn, New York, Oct. 20, 1905—   ), and **Manfred B. Lee** (b. Brooklyn, New York, Jan. 11, 1905—d. Apr. 3, 1971), detective writers, editors, critics of crime fiction, publishers. Lee and Dannay, who are cousins, became known the world over as "Ellery Queen," author of the series of mystery novels and stories featuring the detective, Ellery Queen. As a detective Ellery Queen is described as the son of a police inspector in New York City. He is often permitted to solve a murder or other mystery on his own, with incidental help from police officials. Lee and Dannay, under the pseudonym "Barnaby Ross," also created detective Drury Lane. Since their first mystery novel, *The Roman Hat Mystery* (1929), they have been responsible for the publication of nearly a hundred books; in 1941 they began to edit *Ellery Queen's Mystery Magazine*, the finest periodical of its kind. They stated: "Queen has waged an unceasing battle . . . on two fronts: to raise the sights of mystery writers generally to the target of a genuine and respected literary form . . . and to encourage good writing among our colleagues by offering a practical market not otherwise available among American magazines of high or low stature, as well as to develop new writers seeking expression in the genre." Queen has achieved victory on both these fronts; he has also given the DETECTIVE STORY a respectable place in serious writing. Queen's magazine often carries mystery stories by well-known authors both current and past and has made it seem as if every writer of note in history produced at least one such story. Eight Nobel and twenty-seven Pulitzer prize-winning authors have been published. Queen compiled the definitive detective anthology, *101 Years' Entertainment* (1941). Now housed at the University of Texas, the Queen collection of crime fiction is the finest and largest of its kind in the world. *Ellery Queen's 15th Mystery Annual* appeared in 1960. Among their best-known books: *Drury Lane's Last Case* (1933); *The Adventures of Ellery Queen* (1934), short stories; *The Origin of Evil* (1951); and *The Glass Village* (1954). Anthony Boucher has written a pamphlet, *Ellery Queen: A Double Portrait.*

Questing Spirit, The (1947), an anthology edited by HALFORD E. LUCCOCK and Frances Brentano. These extensive passages in prose and verse, fiction and drama, essay and epigram, give a view of religion in the literature of our time. See LOWELL BRENTANO.

Quick, Herbert (b. Grundy Co., Iowa, Oct. 23, 1861—d. May 10, 1925), teacher, lawyer, novelist, editor. Long engaged in teaching and law practice, Quick's fame is preserved by two of his many books: *Vandemark's Folly* (1921) and *The Hawkeye* (1923). Both stories have Iowa as a background and have helped make readers conscious of the historical significance of that state. Quick wrote his autobiography in *One Man's Life* (1925).

Quiet Cities (1928), a collection of sketches by JOSEPH HERGESHEIMER. He treats, with vivid detail, Pittsburgh, Natchez, New Orleans, Lexington, Albany, and Boston. Included also is an interesting story about Brook Farm.

Quillen, Robert (b. Syracuse, Kans., March 25, 1887—d. Dec. 19, 1948), newspaperman, humorist. Quillen worked for the Baltimore *Sun*, wrote editorials and feature material for the *Saturday Evening Post*. His column "Quillen's Quills" was used in some three hundred newspapers; his comic features "Aunt Het" and "Willie Willis" likewise appeared in many papers. Among his sayings: "A hick town is one where there is no place to go where you shouldn't be" and "Character is made by what you stand for; reputation by what you fall for." He wrote *One Man's Religion* (1923) and *The Path Wharton Found* (1924).

Quimby, Phineas Parkhurst. See NEW THOUGHT.

Quin, Dan. The pen name of ALFRED HENRY LEWIS.

Quincy, Josiah (b. Braintree, Mass., Feb. 4, 1772—d. July 1, 1864), lawyer, public official, educator. Quincy served in the House of Representatives, in the Massachusetts Senate, as mayor of Boston, finally as president of Harvard (1829–45). He opposed the Embargo Act, the acquisition of Louisiana, and the War of 1812. He wrote a *History of Harvard University* (2 v., 1840) and *A Municipal History of Boston* (1852). His grandson, **Josiah Phillips Quincy** (1829–1910), wrote poetry, novels, short stories, and many essays.

Quinn, Arthur Hobson (b. Philadelphia, Feb. 9, 1875—d. Oct. 16, 1960), teacher, critic, literary historian, biographer, editor. Quinn's long and distinguished career was spent mostly at the University of Pennsylvania where he was a specialist in drama, particularly American drama. His *Edgar Allan Poe* (1941) is an important critical evaluation which also presents much new information. In addition Quinn wrote a *History of the American Drama* (3 v., 1923, 1927; 1st v. rev., 1943; 2nd v. rev., 1936). He edited THE LITERATURE OF THE AMERICAN PEOPLE (1951), writing the second section, called *The Establishment of National Literature*. He has edited several collections of plays and also, with R. H. Hart, *Edgar Allan Poe Letters and Documents* (1941).

Quivera. See CIBOLA, SEVEN CITIES OF.

Quodlibet (1840), a satire by JOHN PENDLETON KENNEDY. Jacksonian democracy is Kennedy's target in this story, and he directs some very sharp shafts against it. As Vernon Parrington points out, Kennedy applies "exuberant raillery" to what the Whigs regarded as the follies of Jacksonism—its deification of the majority vote, its glib talk about "the people," its hatred of aristocrats. Kennedy lays the scene in the Borough of Quodlibet, which is supposed to attain great prosperity under benign Democratic finance. What actually was taking place in the country at the time was a battle between the rising money power and the agrarian group. Jackson, as the Old Hero, is not an admirable figure, Van Buren an even sorrier one.

R

Rabble in Arms (1933), a novel by KENNETH ROBERTS. This is a continuation of the history of the Revolution which Roberts began in ARUNDEL (1930), his story of Benedict Arnold's expedition against Quebec. *Rabble in Arms* describes Arnold's stopping Burgoyne's invasion. Both stories undertake to humanize the Revolution by exploring the factual basis that underlies the myths.

Rabinowitz, Solomon J. See SHOLOM ALEICHEM.

Rachel Dyer (1828), a novel by JOHN NEAL. Unlike some of Neal's earlier novels, which tended toward sensationalism and triviality, this is a serious study of the Salem witch trials. It is regarded as his best work. His treatment is objective rather than denunciatory; he calls for charity toward the deluded men who erred so gravely. The hero is a minister, the heroine a Quaker woman condemned to death who refuses to save herself by a fake confession.

Radin, Max (b. Poland, March 29, 1880—d. June 22, 1950), lawyer, professor, author. Radin came to the United States in 1884. After teaching Latin in various Eastern high schools, he became an instructor at Columbia University and at the College of the City of New York, then was appointed professor of law at the University of California. He was admitted to the New York bar and the California bar. He won a wide reputation for the liberalism and humaneness of his views and for his profound learning. Among his writings: *The Legislation of the Greeks and Romans on Corporations* (1909); *Handbook of Roman Law* (1927); *Life of the People in Biblical Times* (1929); *The Lawful Pursuit of Gain* (1931); *The Trial of Jesus of Nazareth* (1931); *Handbook of Anglo-American Legal History* (1936); *Manners and Morals of Business* (1939); *Law as Logic and Experience* (1940).

radio writing. Probably no form of creative writing is under such strict commercial control as that of writing for radio (or television). The writer is often the party least important in the production of a successful program. His role has become subservient to the sponsor's appeal. A result of this is the relative unimportance of scripts as literature.

The most important literary figure connected with radio has probably been ARCHIBALD MACLEISH. His impressive verse dramas for radio include THE FALL OF THE CITY (1937), AIR RAID (1938), and *The States Talking* (1941). NORMAN CORWIN began publishing his radio plays in 1939 (*The Fly Through the Air*) and has been the most prolific writer of radio scripts with distinct literary value. ARCH OBOLER for a time rivaled him, particularly with his *14 Radio Plays* (1940). STEPHEN VINCENT BENÉT wrote numerous effective scripts, some collected in *We Stand United and Other Radio Scripts* (1945). Eric Barnouw's *Radio Drama in Action: 25 Plays of a Changing World* (1945) includes works by ORSON WELLES, PEARL BUCK, ALAN LOMAX, Benét, NORMAN ROSTEN, Corwin, ARTHUR MILLER, LANGSTON HUGHES, ROI OTTLEY, Oboler, and others. Joseph Liss, in *Radio's Best Plays* (1947), includes some important authors not in Barnouw's gathering: MacLeish, MARC BLITZSTEIN, THOMAS WOLFE, and Lucille Fletcher. See TELEVISION WRITING.

Radisson, Pierre Esprit (b. France, 1636—d. 1710[?]), fur trader, explorer. Radisson came to Canada around 1651, was for a time a captive of the Iroquois Indians. Later he formed an exploring partnership with his brother-in-law Médart Chouart, Sieur des Groseilliers. In a manuscript, various parts of which are in the Bodleian Library at Oxford, in the Hudson's Bay House, and in the British Museum, he described "four voyages"—some first-hand, some from the descriptions of others. Part of the account is in French, part in English. Radisson was a keen observer, not unsympathetic to the Indians, and his writings have a vivid interest surpassed by few other early narratives. His *Voyages* were printed in 1885, again in 1943.

Rafinesque, Constantine Samuel (b. Turkey, Oct. 22, 1783—d. Sept. 18, 1840), naturalist, historian, economist, author. Rafinesque's father was French, his mother German. He spent many years in Italy, later lived in the United States. He was completely lacking in tact and lost his chief teaching job, at Transylvania College, but as Bernard Jaffe points out in *Men of Science in America* (1944), "There was scarcely a realm of human knowledge which entirely escaped this inquisitive man. His thinking and his writing invaded the fields of archaeology, architecture, banking, botany, cartography, and conchology," with strong interests in economics, engineering, ethics, geography, history, ichthyology, Indian lore and languages, morals, paleontology, philology, philanthropy, philosophy, religion, sericulture, and surveying. He was guilty of exaggerations and at times of flimsy reasoning, but he had a hazy glimpse of the germ theory of disease half a century before Pasteur and of the theory of evolution two decades before Darwin.

Rafinesque's personal life was unhappy but he took a keen enjoyment in his numerous expeditions, his contributions to learned journals, and his correspondence with scientists everywhere. Among his writings: *Annals of Nature* (1820); *Ichthyologia Ohiensis* (1820); *History of Kentucky* (1824); *Medical Flora, or, Manual of the Medical Botany of the U.S.* (1828–30); *American Manual of the Grape Vines* (1830); *American Florist* (1832); *A Life of Travels and Researches in North America and South Europe* (1836; reprinted, 1944); *New Flora and Botany of North America* (1836); *Safe Banking, Including the Principles of Wealth* (1837). Richard E. Call prepared *The Life and Writings of Rafinesque* (1895); T. J. Fitzpatrick wrote *Rafinesque, A Sketch of His Life, with a Bibliography* (1911); and Harry B. Weiss told of *Rafinesque's Kentucky Friends* (1936). See W. G. HUNT.

Ragged Dick (1867), a novel by HORATIO ALGER. This was Alger's first successful book —it was preceded by *Frank's Campaign* (1864) —and started the immense vogue for his stories. *Ragged Dick* was first published serially in Oliver Optic's *Student and Schoolmate* and became the title of two series. It has sometimes been called Alger's best story. Dick starts out as a bootblack in New York City, makes the most of his chances, saves the little daughter of a rich man from drowning, and advances to inevitable success.

Raggedy Ann. A character who first appeared in JOHNNY GRUELLE's book (1918) by that name and immediately became very popular with children. The first book was followed by *Raggedy Andy* (1920) and other books about both characters. Dolls made up to look like the illustrations in the books have long been popular.

Raggedy Man, The (1890), a poem by JAMES WHITCOMB RILEY. Written in the dialect of a little boy, the poem tells of a hired man who performs odd jobs around a farm and wins the child's admiration through his storytelling and little favors. The poem has the rather jarring refrain: "Raggedy! Raggedy! Raggedy man!" The Raggedy Man is also the beau of "Lizabuth Ann" in Riley's "Our Hired Girl."

Rahv, Philip (b. Russia, March 10, 1908—), critic, editor, teacher. Rahv came to America as a boy and went to school in Providence, R.I. Stimulated by ideas and books even as a youth, he became a political theorist in the Thirties. His reviews and articles appeared in the liberal magazines, and in 1933 he and others founded the PARTISAN REVIEW. Ten years after its birth, this magazine was called by T. S. Eliot "America's leading literary magazine." Writers of vitality appeared in its pages, to gain later recognition from the publishers and the public. In 1949 Rahv wrote *Image and Idea*, a collection of essays about writers such as James, Hawthorne, Tolstoy, and Kafka. Rahv's critical method places strong emphasis on the cultural milieu. *The Great Short Novels of Henry James* (1944), which Rahv edited, did much to help bring on the Jamesian revival. In 1950 Rahv received a Guggenheim Award. Some other books: *The Short Novels of Tolstoy* (1946); *Literature in America* (1957). See DISCOVERY OF EUROPE.

railroad folklore and literature. Railroads have from their earliest beginnings fascinated Americans. B. A. Botkin and Alvin F. Harlow, in their *Treasury of Railroad Folklore* (1953), quote W. Fred Cottrell as saying that "around this young giant there grew up a mythology that made a romance of railroading. No matter how humble his own role, a railroader long felt himself in some degree superior for being a soldier in so glorious an army." The contents of this book reveal the richness of railroad folklore: its heroes (including the saga of CASEY JONES), the hold-up gangs (including that of JESSE JAMES), the railroad "stiffs" and the rail fans, tools and tricks of the trade, strange tales told in the roundhouse, work songs, ballads, names and nicknames. The language of the railroad men was often rich in new colloquialisms and imaginative phrases.

Fiction and nonfiction on railroads include: S. R. Smith's *Romance and Humor of the Rail* (1873); Cy Waram's *Tales of an Engineer* (1895), *Snow on the Headlight* (1899), *Short Rails* (1900), and *The Last Spike and Other Railroad Stories* (1906); Frank Norris' THE OCTOPUS (1901); Francis Lynde's *Empire Builders* (1907), *Young Blood* (1929), and *The Fight on the Standing Stone* (1925); Robert Horrick's *Together* (1908); Upton Sinclair's *Money* (1908), Theodore Dreiser's THE TITAN (1914); Bruce V. Crandall's *After 40 Years* (1925), *Railroading on the Rails and Off* (1927), and *Reveries of an Editor* (1932); Lucius M. Beebe's *High Iron: A Book of Trains* (1938) and *Highliners: A Railroad Album* (1940); Frank P. Donovan, Jr.'s *The Railroad in Literature: A Brief Survey* (1940); Taylor Caldwell's *Never Victorious, Never Defeated* (1954). The most famous railroad ballad is, of course, *Casey Jones*. Another ballad, *I've Been Workin' on the Railroad*, was first printed in *Carmina Princetonia* in 1894. See also JOHN HENRY.

Raine, William MacLeod (b. England, June 22, 1871—d. July 25, 1954), teacher, novelist. Raine, who came to the United States at the age of ten, first wrote short stories and historical novels, taught school for a while, then after some experience with the Arizona Rangers turned to writing spectacularly successful Westerns. Beginning with *Wyoming* (1908), he averaged two novels a year, and all eighty of his books maintained freshness and considerable literary appeal. Among them: *Ridgway of Montana* (1909); *A Texas Ranger* (1911); *The Yukon Trail* (1917); *Gunsight Pass* (1921); *Bonanza* (1926); *Colorado* (1928); *The Fighting Tenderfoot* (1929); *Roaring River* (1934); *Sons of the Saddle* (1938); *Justice Deferred* (1942); *The Bandit Trail* (1949); *Dry Bones in the Valley* (1953).

Râle [or Rasles], Sebastien (b. France, 1657[?]—d. 1724), Jesuit missionary, explorer, lexicographer. Assigned to New France in 1689, Father Râle established a mission among the Abnaki Indians in Maine. He wrote a *Dictionary of the Abnaki Language*, not published until 1833. Nathaniel Deering, Maine editor and dramatist, wrote a tragedy entitled *Carabasset* (1830), in which a Jesuit priest named Rallé, apparently based on Father Râle, appears most favorably.

Ralegh [Raleigh], Sir Walter (b. England, 1552[?]—d. 1618), soldier, explorer, poet, historian. Ralegh attended Oxford, fought for the Huguenots in France and against the Irish, led privateering vessels against the Spaniards, gained Queen Elizabeth's favor. In 1583 he took part in his half-brother Sir HUMPHREY GILBERT's expedition to America; Gilbert's ship was lost on the homeward voyage. The queen's patent for exploration was then given to Ralegh. He organized several expeditions to a region called by him "Virginia," a tribute to Queen Elizabeth, the "Virgin Queen." It included all of the land between Florida and Newfoundland. William S. Powell held that "credit for the development of America as an English-speaking nation undoubtedly belongs more to Ralegh for his vision of empire than to any other man." Several groups under Ralegh's leadership settled on Roanoke Island off the coast of North Carolina, but they finally disappeared—killed or taken captive by Indians. This became known as "The Lost Colony"; every year since 1937 a pageant by PAUL GREEN called *The Lost Colony* has been given on the island.

Ralegh helped in the defeat of the Spanish Armada (1588), engaged in literary pursuits, wrote in 1591 his *Report of the Truth of the Fight about the Islens of Azores*, the story of the defeat of *The Revenge*. He also wrote some very good verse, collected as *The Poems of Sir Walter Ralegh* (1591). In 1595 he led an expedition to Guiana, and on his return wrote *The Discoverie of the Large, Rich, and Bewtifyl Empyre of Guiana* (1596). When James I ascended the throne in 1603 Ralegh lost favor, was accused of conspiracy against James, and spent thirteen years in the Tower of London. There he made chemical experiments and wrote portions of a *History of the World* (1614), which got as far as 130 B.C. James released him for another expedition to Guiana, but when he returned home without any gold he was again arrested, given a biased hearing, and beheaded.

Many books have been written about Ralegh, among them Increase N. Tarbox's *Sir Walter Ralegh and His Colony in America* (1884); Irvin Anthony's *Ralegh and His World* (1934); and Ernest A. Strathmann's *Sir Walter Ralegh: A Study in Elizabethan Skepticism* (1951). Barrett Wendell wrote a play about him, *Ralegh in Guiana* (1902). A series of novels set in Ralegh's Roanoke and neighboring regions was composed by Inglis Fletcher. Ralegh also appears in Charles Kingsley's *Westward Ho!* (1855); Van Wyck Mason's *The Golden Admiral* (1953); and Rosemary Sutcliff's *Lady in Waiting* (1957).

Raleigh, Sir Walter. See SIR WALTER RALEGH.

Ralph, James (b. N.J.[?] [Philadelphia?], 1695[?]—d. Jan. 24, 1762), editor, teacher, writer, pamphleteer. Ralph was a boon companion to BENJAMIN FRANKLIN, with whom he sailed to London in 1724. His efforts at literary success failed and he went off to teach in the provinces. He composed long poems, attacked Pope in *Sawney* (1728), was the first American-born author to have plays produced on the London stage—*The Fashionable Lady* (1730) and others. He wrote a *History of England* in two huge folios (1744–76), a treatise on *The Use and Abuse of Parliaments* (1744), another—his last book and based on his own experiences—on *The Case of Authors by Profession or Trade Stated, with Regard to Booksellers, the Stage, and the Public* (1758). He was in the employ of the politician George Bubb Dodington (1691–1762) and of Frederick, Prince of Wales, as a pamphleteer. He knew enough about government intrigues to be given a pension in 1753 to purchase his silence, but did not live to enjoy it long.

Ralph, Julian (b. New York City, May 27, 1853—d. Jan. 20, 1903), newspaperman, short-story writer, autobiographer. Ralph joined the New York *Sun* in 1875, after serving on the New York *World* and the New York *Daily Graphic;* in 1895 he went over to the New York *Journal.* He became a famous war correspondent, reporting, among others, the Greco-Turkish War and the Boer War. Among his books: *The Sun's German Barber* (1883); *On Canada's Frontier* (1892); *Our Great West* (1893); *Dixie, or, Southern Scenes and Sketches* (1895); *A Prince of Georgia and Other Tales* (1899); *The Making of a Journalist* (1903).

Ramona (1884), a novel by HELEN HUNT JACKSON. This famous work appeared serially in the *Outlook,* and was published in book form in 1885; it has continued to be widely read. Ramona, an orphan of mixed Scottish and Indian blood, is brought up as a foster sister to Felipe Moreno, who falls in love with her, as does Alessandro, a Mission Indian of noble character. Her foster mother opposes the attentions of the latter, but the pair elope and undergo horrible experiences because of his Indian descent. He is driven mad by these experiences and dies; later Ramona marries Felipe. The story is believed to have been based on the life of a real person whose last descendant, Condino Hopkins, died on an Indian reservation near Banning, Calif.; Ramona herself is said to be buried in the Cahuilla Indian Reservation near San Jacinto. The book, which has many striking scenes, undoubtedly had a powerful influence in bringing about a change in the attitude of white men toward the Indians. Mrs. Jackson treated the same theme earlier in a nonfiction work, A CENTURY OF DISHONOR (1881).

Ramsay, David (b. Lancaster Co., Pa., April 2, 1749—d. May 8, 1815), teacher, physician, legislator, writer. Ramsay, an ardent supporter of colonial rights, served in the South Carolina legislature and for a time as an army surgeon. For two years he served in the Continental Congress, and later was again in the state legislature. He became best known for his *History of the American Revolution* (1789), although later research showed that he had depended too much on the British *Annual Register*. He also wrote pamphlets in defense of the American cause, several medical works, a *Biographical Chart, on a New Plan, to Facilitate the Study of History,* and several histories, among them *A History of the Revolution in South Carolina* (1785), *A History of the United States* (1816–17), and *Universal History Americanized* (1819). The last was his most ambitious work and appeared posthumously in twelve volumes.

Ramsaye, Terry (b. Tonganoxie, Kans., Nov. 2, 1885—d. Aug. 19, 1954), newspaperman, editor, motion picture producer, historian. Ramsaye worked for several newspapers in the Middle West, then went into the motion-picture business. He had considerable experience in that industry before he became an editor of the *Motion Picture Herald* and other periodicals (1931–50). He wrote a comprehensive and reliable history of motion pictures, *A Million and One Nights* (2 v., 1926).

Rand, Ayn (b. [?], Russia—   ) novelist, philosopher. *For the New Intellectual: The Philosophy of Ayn Rand* (1961) sets forth, in an essay and in philosophical excerpts from her novels, Miss Rand's "objectivist" philosophy. Her

Phyllis Cerf

central argument is a defense of capitalism and an attack on government controls because they may frustrate the self-interested, supermanlike individual she pictures in her novels. In a strong attack on this book, Sidney Hook said, "Despite the great play with the word 'reason,' one is struck by the absence of any serious argument in this unique combination of tautology and extravagant absurdity." Miss Rand also wrote a mystery play, *The Night of January 16th* (1935), as well as three novels—THE FOUNTAIN-

HEAD (1943), *Atlas Shrugged* (1957), and *We The Living* (1959)—which are polemical and melodramatic vehicles for her ideas. *The Fountainhead,* later filmed, is a rhapsody on the lone genius who stands out against by the common herd; the hero was modeled on Frank Lloyd Wright. *Atlas Shrugged* hinges on a revolt by a group of superior men within industry who express Miss Rand's philosophy.

Randall, James Garfield (b. Indianapolis, June 24, 1881—d. Feb. 20, 1953), teacher, historian. Randall taught at several institutions, finally at the University of Illinois from 1920 until his retirement. There he earned a wide reputation as a sound scholar. He became a specialist in Lincoln and the Civil War. He manifested strong sympathy with the South and refused to regard the war as really "an irrepressible conflict," rather as the tragic error of an emotional and "blundering" generation. He planned a definitive four-volume biography of Lincoln as President, but only three volumes appeared in his lifetime: *Lincoln from Springfield to Bull Run* (1945); *Lincoln the President: from Bull Run to Gettysburg* (1945); and *Midstream: Lincoln the President* (1952). He wrote eight chapters for the fourth volume, which was completed from his notes after his death by Richard N. Current and published in 1955 as *Last Full Measure.* Randall wrote many other books on Lincoln and the Civil War, including *Constitutional Problems Under Lincoln* (1926); *Civil War and Reconstruction* (1937); *Lincoln and the South* (1946); *Lincoln the Liberal Statesman* (1947).

Randall, James Ryder (b. Baltimore, Md., Jan. 1, 1839—d. Jan. 14, 1908), poet, teacher, newspaperman, editor. Randall taught at Poydras College in Louisiana and there, on the outbreak of the Civil War, wrote his most famous poem, MARYLAND, MY MARYLAND, first printed in the New Orleans *Delta* (April 26, 1861) and reprinted all over the South. After 1865 Randall worked for the Augusta (Ga.) *Constitutionalist* and other papers. His *Poems* were published in 1910.

Randolph, Edmund [Jennings] (b. near Williamsburg, Va., Aug. 10, 1753—d. Sept. 12, 1813), lawyer, public official. Randolph served his state and his country in many capacities—as a member of the Virginia Constitutional Convention (1776), in the Second Continental Congress (1779, 1780, 1782), and in the Federal Constitutional Convention (1787); as attorney-general of Virginia (1776–86), as governor of Virginia (1787–88), as Federal attorney-general (1789–94), and as secretary of state under Washington (1794–95). He was an eminent lawyer, served as senior counsel for AARON BURR in his trial for treason (1807) and secured his acquittal. At the Constitutional Convention he advocated a plan known as the Virginia or Randolph plan, which would have greatly centralized the government and included a triumvirate of executives from three regions. He wrote a *Vindication* (1795). His *Essay on the Revolu-*

tionary History of Virginia appeared in the *Virginia Historical Magazine* (1935–37).

Randolph, John (b. Cawsons, Va., June 2, 1773—d. May 24, 1833), statesman, orator. After a sound classical education, Randolph became interested in politics and was elected to Congress in 1799. Thereafter he served in the House and in the Senate. For a time he was a floor leader for Jefferson's followers; later he broke with Jefferson on various issues. He was a man of many eccentricities, outspoken prejudices, and scathing invective. The difficulties of his personality, which finally passed into insanity, may be explained by his constant poor health, the early death of his parents and then of a beloved brother, and the apparent impossibility of marriage.

His ability in Congress received early recognition; he became chairman of the powerful Ways and Means Committee and virtual leader of the House when only twenty-eight. But his fierce individualism produced a break when he began to write letters signed "Decius" in the Richmond *Enquirer* beginning Aug. 15, 1806. He and his followers formed what is believed to be the first "third party" in American history. They named themselves the "Tertium Quids" and called for a return to "the principles of '98." He opposed the acquisition of Florida, the War of 1812, and other measures. He was an opponent of slavery and freed his own slaves in his will, but did not favor the emancipation of slaves by the state. His ideas, which stressed his love for Virginia, paved the way for secession. In later years he was constantly in opposition to HENRY CLAY, and finally fought a duel with him, which ended harmlessly. Jackson made him minister to Russia (1830), but illness forced his resignation.

There are several accounts of Randolph's extraordinary career, among them those by Lemuel Sawyer (1844), Hugh A. Garland (2 v., 1850), W. Cabell Bruce (2 v., 1922), Gerald W. Johnson (1929), and Russell Kirk (1952).

Randolph, Vance (b. Pittsburg, Kans., Feb. 23, 1892—), teacher, folklorist, scenario writer. Randolph taught at the University of Kansas, wrote scripts in Hollywood, collected material for the Archive of American Folklore at the Library of Congress. His specialty is the Ozarks. Among his books: *The Ozarks* (1931); *Ozark Mountain Folks* (1932); *From an Ozark Holler* (1933); *Ozark Outdoors* (1934); *Ozark Anthology* (1940); *Ozark Folksongs* (4 v., 1946–50); *Ozark Superstitions* (1947); *We Always Lie to Strangers* (1951); *Who Blowed Up the Church House?* (1952); *Down in the Holler* (with George P. Wilson, 1953); *The Devil's Pretty Daughter and Other Ozark Folk Tales* (1955); *Talking Turtle and Other Ozark Folk Tales* (1957); *Sticks in the Knapsack, and Other Ozark Folk Tales* (1958). See OZARK MOUNTAINS.

Rankin, Jeremiah Eames (b. Thornton, N.H., Jan. 2, 1828—d. Nov. 28, 1904), clergyman, writer of hymns and other poems, teacher.

Rankin is best remembered for his hymn *God Be With You Till We Meet Again,* popularized by Dwight Lyman Moody and Ira D. Sankey. Rankin was pastor of the First Congregational Church in Washington, D.C. and later became president of Howard University (1889–1903). He loved to write in Scots dialect, of which he had a familiar command. He collected some of his verses in *The Auld Scotch Mither and Other Poems* (1873) and *Ingleside Rhaims* (1887).

Ransom, John Crowe (b. Pulaski, Tenn., April 30, 1888—), poet, critic, teacher. One of the most distinguished American authors of the 20th century and a leader of the Southern regionalists, Ransom was raised in Tennessee. He graduated from Vanderbilt University, then went to Oxford as a Rhodes scholar. For twenty-three years (aside from service in World War I) he taught at Vanderbilt; in 1937 he became professor of poetry at Kenyon College and continued there until his retirement in 1958. In 1939 he founded the KENYON REVIEW, a highly respected quarterly of critical and creative writing. As a young instructor at Vanderbilt, Ransom was a member of the group that called itself "The Fugitives"; he became known for his aggressive belief in Southern agrarianism and he contributed to the symposia I'LL TAKE MY STAND (1930) and *Who Owns America?* (1936). As a critic Ransom originated the term "NEW CRITICISM" and did much to establish the tone and quality of American literary analysis in the 1930's, 1940's, and 1950's. His volumes of literary essays include *God Without Thunder* (1930); *The World's Body* (1938); and *The New Criticism* (1941). He also edited a collection from the pages of the *Kenyon Review: The Kenyon Critics* (1951). His most recent essays have appeared in *Poems and Essays* (1955), a paperbound collection.

Ransom reached his widest audience, however, as a poet. Although his output is small, some of his poems are among the most famous produced in the United States in the present century. His books of verse include *Poems About God* (1919); *Chills and Fever* (1924); *Grace After Meat* (1924); *Two Gentlemen in Bonds* (1927); *Selected Poems* (1945). Commentators tend to emphasize Ransom's irony, his gentle mixture of wit and feeling. Edd Winfield Parks, in *Southern Poets* (1936), felt that Ransom expressed his "philosophy largely by exposing the insufficiency of people in a world devoid of grace and myth." Yet Ransom keeps his roots in the soil; local Tennessee scenery and idiom often form the texture of his work. On him, as on other poets of his generation, the influence of the metaphysical poets of England has been pronounced, but he has never succumbed to stylistic limitation as have some of his fellows. Mortality is his favorite theme, always treated with an ironical respect; one of his loveliest poems, *Bells for John Whiteside's Daughter,* is an elegy for a little girl which masks but does not conceal its deep feeling in a light tone, and *Here Lies a Lady* treats the same theme somewhat more philosophically. In 1951 Ransom received the BOLLINGEN AWARD in poetry, in 1958 the gold medal of Brandeis University. See AGRARIANS; THE EQUILIBRISTS.

Raphaelson, Samson (b. New York City, March 30, 1896—   ), newspaperman, teacher, writer, film director. Raphaelson worked for a newspaper and then for an advertising agency, taught for a year at the University of Illinois, contributed short stories to popular magazines, wrote his first successful play, *The Jazz Singer*, in 1925, began writing screenplays in 1929, later became a movie director. His list of notable screenplay credits includes *Suspicion* (1941); *Heaven Can Wait* (1943); *Green Dolphin Street* (1947). Two of his plays, *Accent on Youth* (1934) and *Jason* (1942), aim to let the public in on the psychology and attitudes of dramatists. Another play was *Hilda Crane* (1950).

Rappaccini's Daughter (*Democratic Review*, 1844; in *Mosses from an Old Manse*, 1846), a story by NATHANIEL HAWTHORNE. This is one of the most fantastic and effective of Hawthorne's short stories, in which a brooding symbolism pervades the incidents of an ingenious plot. A scientist whose absorption in his experiments is deeper than his love for his child feeds his daughter poison to study its effects. A young student falls in love with her and seeks to cure her with an antidote, but it kills her. As his *American Notes* testifies, Hawthorne had found the germ of his story in Sir Thomas Browne's *Vulgar Errors;* Browne had discovered the idea as far back as the medieval *Gesta romanorum*. *Rappacini's Daughter* forms the basis for CHARLES WAKEFIELD CADMAN's opera, *The Garden of Mystery* (1925).

Rascoe, [Arthur] Burton (b. Fulton, Ky., Oct. 22, 1892—d. March 19, 1957), editor, critic, columnist, historian, memoirist. After work on the Shawnee (Okla.) *Herald*, Rascoe became literary and drama editor of the Chicago *Tribune* (1912–20), entered on the heyday of his career in the 1920's when he went to New York City to work for various newspapers, magazines, and syndicates; from 1927 to 1928 he was editor of the BOOKMAN. He ran a syndicated column, "The Daybook of a New Yorker" (1924–28). In later years he was a free-lance writer. Among his books: *Theodore Dreiser* (1925); *A Bookman's Daybook* (1929); *The Joys of Reading* (1937); and two autobiographical volumes, *Before I Forget* (1937) and *We Were Interrupted* (1947). As a critic of books and plays, Rascoe never hesitated to be caustic. His *Titans of Literature, from Homer to the Present* (1932) caused much protest and elicited the correction of numerous errors. He collaborated on various volumes, edited many classics, directed attention to many eminent foreign writers.

Ratcliffe, Senator. A character in Henry Adams' anonymous novel DEMOCRACY (1880). He was recognized by readers as a composite portrait of several men in public life, particularly

JAMES G. BLAINE. A review in *The Nation* (April 22, 1880) charged the author with gross exaggeration and started that "to represent such a man as the probable Republican candidate for President is a perversion which must detract from the force of any picture of American politics."

Rauschenbusch, Walter (b. Rochester, N.Y., Oct. 4, 1861—d. July 25, 1918), Baptist minister, teacher, author. Rauschenbusch, descendant of a long line of clergymen, saw religion in terms of human welfare; he had expert training in sociology and economics. For many years he taught church history at the Rochester Theological Seminary and was widely influential in the rise of the "social gospel" movement. Among his books: *Christianity and the Social Crisis* (1907); *Christianizing the Social Order* (1912); *The Social Principles of Jesus* (1916); *Theology of the Social Gospel* (1917).

Ravage, Marcus Eli. See AN AMERICAN IN THE MAKING.

Raven, The (*American (Whig) Review*, Feb., 1845; *The Raven and Other Poems*, 1845), a poem by EDGAR ALLAN POE in which the poet, steeped in melancholy memories of a lost love, is haunted by death in the guise of a raven. This poem made Poe famous and aroused much discussion because of Poe's account of how he wrote it (THE PHILOSOPHY OF COMPOSITION, 1846). It has sometimes been regarded as a mere tour de force, and has been often parodied. In his essay on the poem Poe explained how he had selected his theme, how he had chosen the meter and refrain, his theories about the most suitable topics for poetry. Phyllis Bartlett offers the reader of the essay three choices in her *Poems in Process* (1951); one may accept Poe's account of his writing methods literally, one may dismiss it as a hoax, or one may accept it as Poe's genuine theory of composition which he himself was unable to live up to.

There is much argument among Poe's biographers as to whether *The Raven* developed slowly or was dashed off in a white heat. Both views are probably right. Poe said he pondered the poem for years. But the final draft was written at a sitting, late in 1844. He admitted that the metrical form was a modification of that used in *Lady Geraldine's Courtship* by Mrs. E. B. Browning. The poem depends less on onomatopoeia than THE BELLS, but is rich in alliteration. John H. Ingram discussed *The Raven, With Literary and Historical Commentary* (1885); H. E. Legler examined *Poe's Raven, Its Origin and Genesis* (1907); Oscar Cargill and J. R. Moore found new sources for the poem (cf. *American Literature*, November, 1936, and January, 1951). See also ALBERT PIKE.

Rawlings, Marjorie Kinnan (b. Washington, D.C., Aug. 8, 1896—d. Dec. 14, 1953), newspaperwoman, poet, novelist. Mrs. Rawlings began as a reporter for the Louisville (Ky.) *Courier-Journal* and the Rochester (N.Y.) *Journal*, then wrote syndicated verse for United Features (1925–27). Throughout this period she kept on writing short stories. Her greatest triumph was THE YEARLING (1938), a novel which won a Pulitzer prize and was made into a movie. Her best work dated from the time (1928) she settled at Cross Creek, Fla., where she had bought an orange grove. Thereafter she told stories rich in Floridian atmosphere, assembling hitherto unused materials of folklore and folkways. She wrote with an earthy humor and with deep respect for her characters. For the most part her work took the form of fiction: SOUTH MOON UNDER (1933); Golden Apples (1935); When the Whippoorwill (stories, 1940); The Sojourner (1953). She described the region in which she lived through an entertaining nonfiction work, Cross Creek (1942), and gathered some of its fine recipes in Cross Creek Cookery (1942).

Raymond, George Lansing (b. Chicago, Sept. 3, 1839—d. July 11, 1929), scholar, poet, dramatist, editor. Raymond taught at Princeton and George Washington universities. He was deeply interested in the rationale of poetry, as is shown in various publications, particularly Poetry as a Representative Art (1886); his works on pure esthetics include Art in Theory (1894) and Comparative Aesthetics (8 v., 1909). His books of verse are The Aztec God and Other Dramas (1900) and Dante and Collected Verse (1909).

Raymond, Henry Jarvis (b. Lima, N.Y., Jan. 24, 1820—d. June 18, 1869), newspaperman, editor, historian. Raymond began his career under HORACE GREELEY, first on the latter's weekly, The New Yorker, later as his assistant on the Tribune. After a brief stay on the Courier, Raymond and George Jones founded (1851) a new paper in New York City: the Times. His fame is based chiefly on his association with this paper. Charles A. Dana summed up Raymond's policy by saying that he "aimed at a middle line between the mental eccentricity of the Tribune and the moral eccentricity of the Herald." From the beginning Raymond sought three stylistic qualities: neatness, dignity, and correctness; the paper still follows his principles. Readers also liked his full news coverage and special articles. He hated zealots and in journalism and politics preferred the middle road.

Raymond wrote Disunion and Slavery (1860) and a History of the Administration of Lincoln (1864). Much has been written about him, especially in histories of the Times. An excellent biography is E. Francis Brown's Raymond of the Times (1951).

Raynolds, Robert (b. Santa Fe, N.M., April 29, 1902—d. Oct. 24, 1964), novelist, poet, essayist. Raynolds attended Princeton University and received a B.A. degree from Lafayette College in 1925. He taught and lectured at various times, but writing soon became his chief occupation. He once commented: "I was born to sing that life is good." His song of the good life stretched into a number of highly successful books. His novel Brothers in the West (1931) was a Harper Prize novel. It was followed by

Saunders Oak (1933); Fortune (1935); May Bretton (1944); The Obscure Enemy (1945); Paquita (1947); The Sinner of Saint Ambrose (1952), a Book-of-the-Month-Club selection; The Quality of Quiros (1955); Far Flight of Love (1957); and two books of essays, The Choice to Love (1959) and In Praise of Gratitude (1961). Whether writing of the dying days of the Roman Empire as in The Sinner of Saint Ambrose, or the seemingly harmless confines of a New England town as in May Bretton, a fervent sympathy and a sense of beauty are hallmarks of Raynolds' writing. In 1941 he wrote a drama in verse: Boadicea.

Reactionary Essays on Poetry and Ideas (1936), a book of critical essays by ALLAN TATE. In this early example of the NEW CRITICISM Tate tried to remove the discussion of poetry from the realm of human experience into that of pure form. Though he felt that moral convictions and political-social considerations were superfluous to the consideration and evaluation of poetry, Tate managed to discuss some social, political, and educational problems along the way. The word "reactionary" in the title refers to Tate's professed opposition to science, positivism, and scientific criticism.

Read, Opie [Percival] (b. Nashville, Tenn., Dec. 22, 1852—d. Nov. 2, 1939), newspaperman, humorist, novelist, editor, lecturer. Read was an extraordinary character, as amusing as any of the eccentrics he wrote about in his hastily composed fifty-two books or talked about in his popular lectures. He was a huge man, described by Clyde Brion Davis as a man of drawling and sometimes purposely illiterate speech, with an amazing talent for storytelling and an unlimited capacity for corn whiskey, also a poker player of great ability. Read claimed he had lectured in every county in the country. He edited a magazine, The Arkansas Traveler, founded by him in 1882. It became very popular and lasted till 1916. The Jucklins (1895) sold about two million copies. Later he wrote The Kentucky Colonel (1890); Judge Elbridge (1899); My Young Master (1896); Son of the Sword-Maker (1905); "By the Eternal" (1906); The Gold Gauze Veil (1927); and other stories. I Remember (1930) and Mark Twain and I (1940) are autobiographical. Maurice Elfer wrote Opie Read (1940).

Read, Thomas Buchanan (b. near Guthriesville, Pa., March 12, 1822—d. May 11, 1872), painter, poet. Read began as a grocer's clerk and cigarmaker, went on to become a painter of canal boats and signs, finally earned a living as an itinerant portrait painter. He made his way to Boston and gained the favor of rich patrons. He turned to writing verse, was encouraged by Longfellow, and his poems began to appear in Boston papers. His work was collected in Poems (1847). He went abroad, was well received by literary men, and won new patrons as a portraitist. During the Civil War he was attached to the staff of General Lew Wallace; he rendered a great patriotic service in his speaking and reciting tours throughout the North in company with the actor James Edward Murdoch. It was Murdoch who recited the famous *Sheridan's Ride* on the very day that Read wrote it. *The Wagoner of the Alleghenies* was a popular narrative poem (1862). His *Summer Story, Sheridan's Ride, and Other Poems* appeared in 1865, his *Poetical Works* (3 v.) in 1866. He wrote gracefully and melodiously.

readers. In early days children had no special provision made for their reading. During the Victorian era, however, more and more books were written especially for children, and carefully prepared readers—collections of miscellaneous material chosen for its moral, literary, or patriotic value—were published. Such books seem to have been a characteristically American product, with W. H. McGuffey's *Eclectic Readers* (6 v., 1836–57) as the pioneer and most famous instance. These books were "graded" according to the age of the children concerned. They exerted wide influence, which is studied in revealing detail by Richard D. Mosier in *Making the American Mind: Social and Moral Ideas in the McGuffey Readers* (1947).

The McGuffey readers had innumerable competitors. In one form or another, books of this type are still popular in American schools. In high schools, during the 1920's and thereafter, they often took the form of anthologies which united the study of brief selections with the analysis of important classics reproduced in full. These anthologies were likewise arranged progressively. See TEXTBOOKS.

Reader's Digest, the. In 1922 the husband-and-wife team of DeWitt and Lila Acheson Wallace founded in a Greenwich Village basement a small pocket-size eclectic monthly adapted to the growing passion for brevity that affected readers of American magazines and newspapers. Its 64 pages were filled with skilfully condensed articles from other American magazines. It specialized in human-interest pieces dealing with health, family, common life, and personal recollections. It soon came to print occasional articles on economic, social, and international matters, always with a strong rightist trend. It liked light comment, and in the 1920's used much of WILLIAM LYON PHELPS' "As I Like It" from *Scribner's* and E. B. WHITE's "Talk of the Town" from the *New Yorker*. Gradually it built up its own small departments of wit, humor, and anecdotes by offering payment to readers who contributed such material. Eventually it added a book section in which a current book was condensed. Generally optimistic, it advocated the basic virtues, and offered instruction as well as amusement.

Originally, other magazines allowed their pages to be rifled *in petto* on the theory that this was good promotion; later, payments were made to both magazine and author. By mid-century a large proportion of the *Digest's* material was written for it on order and published without subterfuge as original material, or

"planted" in other magazines to be transplanted to the *Digest's* pages.

After the first year the Wallaces left Greenwich Village for Pleasantville, 40 miles north of New York. There the *Digest* was edited in humble quarters until 1939, when it moved into its new $1,500,000 building at nearby Chappaqua. Before World War II it had a circulation of about 7,000,000, which increased to over 12,000,000 after the war—the largest attained by any magazine. It began publishing editions in foreign countries in 1938, multiplying them until by the end of the 1950's it had 26 foreign editions in 13 languages, with an aggregate circulation of over 7,000,000.

By this time, however, mass circulations were not profitable without commensurate advertising, and in 1955 the *Reader's Digest*, which had originally prided itself on a certain independence supposed to rest upon its freedom from commercial announcements, opened its pages to advertisers. The next year it declared a policy limiting them to 20% of its pages, but by 1961 it went beyond 30%, or 100 pages of a total of 280. First distributed only by subscriptions, the magazine took to the newsstands in 1929, but its mail distribution has always far exceeded that from the stands.

Shortly after the end of its first decade the *Reader's Digest* had established itself as a popular American institution; it was easy to pick up for a few minutes or a few hours, often looked down upon by the intelligentsia, but always amusing here and there, and often genuinely informative and educational.

Reader's Encyclopedia, The (1948; 2nd ed., 1965), an encyclopedia of world literature and the arts edited by WILLIAM ROSE BENÉT. It includes plots and characters of novels, plays, and poems; biographies of American and foreign authors from ancient times to the present; analyses of trends in literature; explanations of classical and Biblical references; definitions of literary terms; brief sketches of artists and historical personages who figure in literature.

Readers' Guide to Periodical Literature. A cumulative bibliography begun in February, 1901, and published by the H. W. Wilson Co. It originally covered the contents of seven magazines. In 1903 it absorbed an earlier guide, the *Cumulated Index to a Selected List of Periodicals*. The Guide now publishes biweekly, monthly, quarterly, annual, and biennial indexes to a very wide range of American magazines, and is an indispensable tool for students, researchers, and librarians. In 1935 a smaller edition for school and small public libraries, *Abridged Readers' Guide*, was established.

Realf, Richard (b. England, June 14, 1834— d. Oct. 28, 1878), newspaper correspondent, poet. A born versifier, Realf began writing in meter at a very early age, and attracted the attention of Harriet Martineau and others, who paid for the publication of a collection of his poems, *Guesses at the Beautiful*, when he was only eighteen. But he got into difficulties with one family that patronized him, and came to the United States practically as a refugee in 1854. He became involved in the JOHN BROWN conspiracy and was to have been secretary of state in Brown's proposed commonwealth. He married several times, not taking the trouble to divorce his first wife; he was an alcoholic and lectured on temperance. He served in the Union Army during the Civil War, worked on the Pittsburgh *Commercial* (1872–77), and toward the end of his life went to San Francisco, where he obtained a petty job in the Mint and became acquainted with AMBROSE BIERCE. The sudden reappearance of his second wife, who spent most of her time trying to ruin him, was too much for him, and he took poison and died, leaving three sonnets to explain his suicide. Twenty years after his death appeared *Poems by Richard Realf, Poet, Soldier, Workman.* It is believed that the character of Hayden Douglas in Mary E. Jackson's novel *The Spy of Osawatomie* (1881) is modeled on Realf.

realism. A term used to designate a theory of artistic practice which proposes that the work of art should present an objective rendering of actual life, of literal fact, without idealization or the alteration of given actuality in the interest of moral or religious preconceptions. The distinction between realism and naturalism is often difficult to make in practice, but in general the realists hold that (in the case of literature) the writer may manipulate his materials to meet esthetic needs as long as his end effect conforms to a realistic conception of life and nature, while the naturalists hold that the writer must render an exact report of his subject, whatever the artistic exigencies may be. The latter have been more prone to didacticism than the former, and their works, as in the "proletarian" novels of the 20th century, have frequently been revelations of social injustice accompanied by implicit exhortations to reform. Both terms, and the modern formulations of the concepts they signify, originated chiefly among 19th century French writers and critics, and they have exerted a strong influence on the American novelists of the 20th century.

On the other hand, a native American realism can be traced back to the Puritans, who were not opposed to facing the facts of life and fate. The Yankee in literature, though frequently a comic character, was also eminently a realist, and he continued throughout the 18th and early 19th centuries. Mark Twain was a realist in his best work, especially in HUCKLEBERRY FINN, though he probably was not conscious, at least in his early career, of practicing any particular literary credo. WILLIAM DEAN HOWELLS was a much more self-conscious theorist, and he more than any other deserves the title of the first American realist in the modern sense. Some of the scenes in his *Rise of Silas Lapham* (1885) shocked his contemporaries; he was among the first to praise such writers as Stephen Crane and Theodore Dreiser. Today the concept of realism has become so pervasive in modern writing that the term itself scarcely retains any distinct or

sectarian import. In a philosophical connection the term has been used by various anti-idealists, including the American pragmatic and pluralistic philosophers, to signify a "common sense" attitude toward metaphysical problems. See NATURALISM; PRAGMATISM.

Reaney, James [Crerar] (b. Stratford, Ont., Sept. 1, 1926–   ), Canadian poet and teacher. Reaney was educated at the University of Toronto and has taught creative writing at the University of Manitoba. He writes plays and short stories as well as poetry. Reaney's poems are deceptively simple in subject and language; often he writes of children or childlike matters (as in a poem titled "The Katzenjammer Kids") with a seeming innocence, behind which lurks a wry wit. Some of his more nonsensical sounding verses are reminiscent of the work of Lewis Carroll. Reaney's first book of poems, *The Red Heart* (1949), received the Governor-General's Medal. Since then he has published *The Kildeen* (1959) and *A Suit of Nettles* (1959).

Reason the Only Oracle of Man; or, A Compendious System of Natural Religion (1784), a work attributed to ETHAN ALLEN. The author attacks impostures of the church, revelation and miracles, appeals to authority, Christianity in general. But he believed in God and immortality and seeks to justify his belief on rational, *i.e.* deistic, principles. In his youth Allen had come under the influence of Dr. Thomas Young (1732–1777), a freethinker; moreover, while a prisoner of the British he had heard many infidel discussions. His book is sometimes called "Ethan Allen's Bible." It is believed that most of it is actually the work of Dr. Young, to whose manuscripts on these subjects Allen had access. See DEISM.

Rebecca of Sunnybrook Farm (1903), a story for girls by KATE DOUGLAS WIGGIN. Rebecca Rowena Randall, ten years old, leaves her impoverished and widowed mother and her sisters and brothers and goes to live with two maiden aunts, Miranda and Jane, in Riverboro. She makes friends, eventually wins an admirer, graduates from an academy, and in general radiates unquenchable charm and good humor in the face of considerable harshness from Aunt Miranda. The story was successfully dramatized (1910) and was followed by *New Chronicles of Rebecca* (1907). It was also made into a Shirley Temple film in 1937.

Reconstruction, the. At the end of the Civil War, Lincoln's policy toward the South, which was also followed by Johnson, was one of leniency. The radical Republicans, however, desired to punish the South and forestall the attempts of the Southern states to reduce the Negro to peonage by means of the Black Codes. They overcame the lenient faction and passed the Reconstruction Act (March 2, 1867), with other legislation and Constitutional Amendments that protected the new rights of the Negroes and guaranteed them the ballot. To enforce these laws the Republicans sent officials to the South whom the people there called "carpetbaggers."

Their misrule and corruption, together with the humiliation of having Northerners and former slaves in power, produced as a reaction, the KU KLUX KLAN and a new spirit of unity creating "the Solid South." For more than a decade the Southern states were socially, politically, and economically ruined. Finally President Hayes ordered the troops removed from the South in April, 1877. The carpetbag governments immediately fell and the native whites came back into power. Except for providing a Constitutional basis for future Negro emancipation, the radical Republicans had done little more than insure that for more than two generations the South would vote solidly Democratic.

Historians and others have described the Reconstruction Era in detail. Among nonfiction works on the period: G. W. Cable's *The Silent South* (1885); W. A. Dunning's *Reconstruction, Political and Economic* (1907); Claude Bowers's *The Tragic Era* (1929); J. G. Randall's *The Civil War and Reconstruction* (1937); W. E. B. Du Bois's *Black Reconstruction* (1935); C. V. Woodward's *Reunion and Reaction* (1956); Hodding Carter's *Angry Scar* (1959); and Paul Buck's *Road to Reunion* (1937). Novels dealing with the period include, among many others: A. W. Tourgee's *A Royal Gentleman* (1881), *A Fool's Errand* (1879), and BRICKS WITHOUT STRAW (1880); John W. De Forest's *The Bloody Chasm* (1881); Mary Noailles Murfree's *Where the Battle Was Fought* (1884); G. W. Cable's *John March, Southerner* (1894); T. N. Page's RED ROCK (1898) and *The Red Riders* (1924); Ellen Glasgow's *The Voice of the People* (1900) and *The Deliverance* (1904); Thomas Dixon, Jr.'s THE LEOPARD'S SPOTS (1902), *The Clansman* (1905), and *The Traitor* (1907); Joseph Hergesheimer's *The Limestone Tree* (1931); Margaret Mitchell's GONE WITH THE WIND (1936); Ben Ames Williams' *The Unconquered* (1953).

Red Badge of Courage, The: An Episode of the American Civil War (1895), a novel by STEPHEN CRANE. In shortened form, *The Red Badge of Courage* appeared first in the Philadelphia *Press* in December, 1894.

Crane's realism and unconventional treatment of military subjects were favorably noted in early reviews. The insight into the feelings and fears of fighting men revealed in the book provided a new reading experience for a public unaccustomed to the revelation of the "seamy" side of battle, the very human, "nonheroic" aspects of men at war. Reviewers were quick to note and appreciate the frank treatment of human emotions under stress. "The story is not pleasant by any means," said the *Outlook* (December 21, 1895), "but the author seems to lay bare the very nerves of his character; practically, the book is a minute study of one man's mind in the environment of war in all its horrible detail."

The Red Badge of Courage deals (though the conflict is not named in the book) with the battle of Chancellorsville (see BATTLE OF CHANCELLORSVILLE), one of the bloodiest conflicts of the American Civil War, and the conversion from cowardice to heroism of a Union soldier, Henry Fleming. The story involves not only the conflict between Confederate and Union soldiers, but that found in the mind of Henry Fleming himself. As a psychological study of the mind of a man under extreme tension and anxiety, the novel has few peers.

The book stirred up critical warfare that still rages. Widely reviewed in England, it won for Crane the personal friendships of H. G. Wells and Henry James. Ernest Hemingway called *The Red Badge* "one of the finest books in our literature." The definitive text—the final manuscript and the earlier draft of *The Red Badge,* with five new manuscript pages—appears in *The Red Badge of Courage and Other Stories,* edited by R. W. Stallman (1960).

Redburn (1849), a novel by HERMAN MELVILLE. Almost all of *Redburn* is semiautobiographical; the author, with gentle, ironic detachment, remembers and playfully distorts the memory of his own first trip across the Atlantic. The major theme of *Redburn* is expressed through the figure of the alert young man who wanders the path from innocence to experience. Other themes in the novel are found frequently in Melville's work: the inhumanity of man to man, which provoked Melville's anti-missionary propaganda in TYPEE and OMOO and which would find expression again in WHITE JACKET, is here eloquently denounced in the scenes of Liverpool squalor. Another significant theme is the distinction between appearance and reality, though it is less emphasized here than in MARDI and later in PIERRE. Redburn discovers to his chagrin and the reader's amusement that Captain Riga is not what he seems. Thus Redburn recounts a young boy's first confrontation with the larger world, an encounter which matures him but does not render him cynical. Redburn becomes the man satisfied—or not too dissatisfied —with life, a man who can become righteously —but not maniacally—indignant. The result in *Redburn* is a comic hero, and Melville's only comic novel.

Red City, The (1907), a novel by S. WEIR MITCHELL. This story is about Philadelphia during Washington's second term. Mitchell in writing it drew on the journal of Elizabeth Drinker. The yellow fever epidemic is realistically described. There is an attractive picture of Washington, as a man rather than a statesman. The hero is a French émigré whose father has been murdered by the Jacobins; he takes revenge on the man responsible when he arrives as Citizen Genêt's secretary. See THE ADVENTURES OF FRANÇOIS.

Red Cross. See CLARA H. BARTON.

Redeemed Captive Returned to Zion, The (1707), a narrative of captivity among the Indians written by JOHN WILLIAMS. Next to Mary Rowlandson's CAPTIVITY AND RESTAURATION (1682), this was the best seller among the widely read captivity narratives. Frank Luther Mott says that Williams' narrative was not as "tough-minded" as that of Mrs. Rowlandson, but Williams gives a vivid account of a massacre and of the sufferings undergone on long forced marches to the north. Williams made much of his resistance to attempts by Jesuits to convert him. See INDIAN CAPTIVITY NARRATIVES.

Redlich, Rosemarie. See LITERARY AMERICA.

Redman, Ben Ray (b. Brooklyn, N.Y., Feb. 21, 1896—d. Aug. 2, 1961), critic, writer. Redman's large literary output includes literary columns, editions of classics, translations from the French and Italian; he worked in publishing houses, wrote a critical biography of Edwin Arlington Robinson (1925), published a collection of poems called *Masquerade* (1923), worked in Hollywood. Some of his work (especially some detective stories) were written under the pen name Jeremy Lord.

Redpath, James (b. Scotland, Aug. 24, 1833 —d. Feb. 10, 1891), newspaperman, manager of a lecture bureau, school official, writer. When Redpath was seventeen his parents emigrated to Michigan. He began to write for newspapers and attracted the attention of HORACE GREELEY; he continued to work for the New York *Tribune* for thirty years. He was especially interested in Kansas, in John Brown, in slavery, and in obtaining a refuge for Negroes in Haiti; he acted as a consular official for Haiti for several years. He was a correspondent during the Civil War, then superintendent of schools at Charleston, S.C. A good speaker, he decided (1868) to organize a lecture bureau; his agency became famous in this country and abroad. For a time he edited the NORTH AMERICAN REVIEW. In the 1880's he became deeply interested in Ireland and agitated for its freedom. Among his books: *Tales and Traditions of the Border* (with his father, 1849); *The Roving Editor* (1859); *Echoes of Harper's Ferry* (1860); *The Public Life of Captain John Brown* (1860); *A Guide to Hayti* (1860); *Talks About Ireland* (1881).

Red Rock (1898), a novel by THOMAS NELSON PAGE. This was probably the first novel in which a Southerner spoke frankly about "the good old days" of the South and about the cruel wrongs inflicted in the Reconstruction Era. The book was, moreover, very favorably received in the North as well as the South. For Page wrote without violence, and he was not crude in THOMAS DIXON's fashion. He pictured the effect of the war and Reconstruction on two old families. The beginnings of the KU KLUX KLAN are described and its motives and acts justified; it is through influence on Northern friends, however, that reforms are brought about. Some minor romances lend sentimentality to the plot.

Red Rover, The (1827), a novel by JAMES FENIMORE COOPER. The plot of this romance is somewhat tortuous, with the hero taking three names during its course. At first he is Lt. Henry Ark, an officer in the British Navy about the middle of the 18th century, who takes the name Wilder and enlists as a common sailor on board the *Dolphin* in the hope of tracking down a mysterious pirate, "the Red Rover." He finally encounters the latter, who actually saves his life, at the same time rescuing Gertrude Grayson and

her governess Mrs. Wyllys. Later it turns out that the lieutenant is really the son of the latter and that his name is Paul de Lacey. The Red Rover turns out to be a punctilious gentleman who left the service of his Britannic Majesty because of indignation over the wrongs inflicted on the colonies. In an epilogue it is revealed, twenty years later, that he had joined the American patriots and fought with them against England. There are some good sea scenes and one fierce battle. Comic relief is furnished by an admiral's widow who constantly commits malapropisms with maritime terms. There is an affecting death scene, that of Black Scipio. Cooper wrote the novel in France and it attained popular success both in America and abroad. In 1828 it was dramatized by S. H. Chapman.

Redskins, The, or, Indian and Injin (1846), a novel by JAMES FENIMORE COOPER, the third of the *Littlepage Manuscripts*. It deals with the dangerous situation created in New York state when bands of agitators uprose against the patroon system; the result was the Anti-Rent War (1839–46). The agitators disguised themselves as "Injins"; one of the important characters in Cooper's book is a real Indian, Susquesus. The big landlords wanted the patroon system to continue; the renters wanted to buy the land outright. In 1846 a constitutional convention provided measures whereby the great manors were broken up. Cooper himself sympathized with the patroons and strongly favored them in his novels on the subject. *The Redskins* was the most polemical of these novels, although Cooper worked in enough action and love-making to keep the story going. See ANTI-RENT LAWS.

Reece, Byron (b. Choestoe, Ga., 1917—d. June 3, 1958), poet, novelist, farmer. After leaving college, Reece taught for a while, then decided to be a farmer in northern Georgia. He also continued to write and publish ballads and lyrics which show the influence of A. E. Housman, but strike an individual note. His collections include *Ballad of the Bones and Other Poems* (1945) and *Bow Down in Jericho* (1950). *Better a Dinner of Herbs* (1950) and *The Hawk and the Sun* (1955) are novels.

Reed, John (b. Portland, Ore., Oct. 22, 1887—d. Oct. 19, 1920), newspaperman, poet. A wealthy young man and a graduate of Harvard (1910), he joined the staff of the AMERICAN MAGAZINE in 1911, at which time his already serious interest in social problems was further aroused by his friendship with LINCOLN STEFFENS. In 1913 he joined the staff of THE MASSES, edited by Max Eastman. Sent to Mexico by the *Metropolitan Magazine* to report the Mexican revolution, he won national fame for his reporting, and out of this experience grew his first book, *Insurgent Mexico* (1914). His news reports on World War I, written for the same magazine, were republished as *The War in Eastern Europe* (1916). During 1916, also, a book of his poems was published, entitled *Tamburlaine and Other Poems*. He was an enthusiastic observer and supporter of the October Revolution in Russia, became a friend of Lenin, and wrote propaganda material for the Bolsheviks. After his subsequent return to the United States, he was continually under fire for his radical ideas and was arrested several times. During this period he wrote *Ten Days That Shook the World* (1919), an eloquent eyewitness account of the Russian revolution and his most important book. After his expulsion from the Socialist Party in 1919, Reed founded the Communist Party in America, wrote its manifesto, and edited its paper, *The Voice of Labor*. (See POLITICAL PARTIES AND LITERATURE.) Again he left America for Russia, was refused readmission to the United States, and remained in Russia until he was stricken by typhus and died in 1920. His verses are no longer remembered, but he was a brilliant journalist of the old romantic school rather than a merely objective reporter. Mabel Dodge Luhan wrote at length about him in *Movers and Shakers* (1936), as did Lincoln Steffens in his *Autobiography* (1931). He appears as the chief character in Max Eastman's novel *Venture* (1927). John Stuart edited a volume of selections from his writings, *The Education of John Reed* (1955).

Reed, Myrtle (b. Norwood Park, Ill., Sept. 27, 1874—d. Aug. 17, 1911), novelist, essayist, poet. Popular in her own day and endowed with some literary graces, Miss Reed is best known for her *Lavender and Old Lace* (1902). She was handled severely by the critics because of her saccharine sentimentality; as late as 1941 her book inspired the title of Joseph Kesselring's satiric play, *Arsenic and Old Lace*. Among Miss Reed's other books are *Love Letters of a Musician* (1899); *Love Affairs of Literary Men* (1907); *Sonnets of a Lover* (1910); *The Myrtle Reed Year Book* (1911).

Reed, Sampson (b. West Bridgewater, Mass., June 10, 1800—d. July 8, 1880), Swedenborgian. On his graduation from Harvard College, Reed began attending the Harvard Divinity School, but left when he was converted to the doctrines of Swedenborg (see SWEDENBORGIANISM). He is remembered chiefly because of his deep influence on RALPH WALDO EMERSON, who strongly admired him. When he received his M.A. degree at Harvard (1821) he delivered an *Oration on Genius* (printed, 1849), which Emerson heard and was impressed by. Emerson also read his *Observations on the Growth of the Mind* (1826). Reed stressed the "doctrine of correspondences," which he later analyzed at length in his *Correspondence of the Sun, Heat, and Light* (1862). His writings were an avocation. Reed earned his living as a pharmacist, finally became a wealthy wholesale druggist. He gave much money to the Swedenborgian church in America and to the *New Jerusalem Magazine*, which he and his brother Caleb edited.

Reedy, William Marion (b. St. Louis, Mo., Dec. 11, 1862—d. July 28, 1920), newspaperman, editor, critic. Reedy was one of the great literary influences of his time. For many years he worked on St. Louis newspapers, among others the MIRROR [2], which went through several bankruptcies and reorganizations, finally was presented (1896) to Reedy. Thereafter it was known as *Reedy's Mirror*, and became the medium through which Reedy introduced many new writers. A true Jeffersonian liberal, Reedy was no dogmatist like some of the leftist editors who appeared later. He published little in book form: *The Law of Love* (1905) and *A Golden Book and the Literature of Childhood* (1910).

Reese, Lizette Woodworth (b. Waverly, Md., Jan. 9, 1856—d. Dec. 17, 1935), teacher, poet, memoirist. Miss Reese taught school for forty-five years, chiefly as an English teacher in the Western High School in Baltimore. Poetry was her private passion and avocation. She published several small collections: *A Branch of May* (1887); *A Handful of Lavender* (1891); *A Quiet Road* (1896); *A Wayside Lute* (1909); *Spicewood* (1920); *Wild Cherry* (1923); *Selected Poems* (1926); *Little Henrietta* (1927); *White April and Other Poems* (1930); *Pastures and Other Poems* (1933); *The Old House in the Country* (1936). She also wrote two autobiographical volumes: *A Victorian Village* (1929) and *The York Road* (1931).

Miss Reese had the gift of melody and phrasing and the power to discriminate between sentiment and sentimentality. Often she resembles Herrick and other 17th century poets; often Sara Teasdale and Edna St. Vincent Millay resemble Miss Reese. One sonnet of hers, *Tears*, became overwhelmingly popular.

Reeve, Arthur B[enjamin] (b. Patchogue, N.Y., Oct. 15, 1880—d. Aug. 9, 1936), editor, writer of detective stories. Reeve worked for several magazines, and wrote a series of articles on crime detection for the *Survey*. This turned him toward fiction on the subject. He contrived an entertaining sleuth named Professor Craig Kennedy, who made his first appearance in *Cosmopolitan* in 1910, and in 1912 in a story called *The Poisoned Pen*. Craig Kennedy became known as "the American Sherlock Holmes," and in the person of Reeve himself was sometimes called on to help solve actual cases, *e.g.* the Lindbergh kidnaping. It is said that Kennedy was modeled on Dr. Otto H. Schultze, an able New York physician who was medical adviser to the New York district attorney. Reeve made good use of current mechanical inventions. His clever style and inventiveness lured many readers to their first acquaintance with the detective story. Among Reeve's other books: *The Silent Bullet* (stories, 1912); *The Dream Doctor* (1917); *The Clutching Hand* (1934).

regionalism in American literature. The concept of regionalism is as old as the first colonies. The geographical, religious, national, and commercial differences of the original settlements inspired sentiments of separateness among the settlers, these being accentuated by the formation of separate states and the settlement of new lands to the West. The states still jealously guard their "rights," and the study of state and regional cultures is a flourishing intellectual pursuit in America today.

From the point of view of the arts, regionalism seems to have developed in four stages: sectionalism, the local-color mania, regionalism proper, and the folk revival. *Sectionalism,* as Fulmer Mood has shown in his *Origin, Evolution, and Application of the Sectional Concept, 1750–1900* (in Merrill Jensen's symposium *Regionalism in America,* 1951), reveals itself in some of the so-called "schools" of American literature—the New England school, the Knickerbocker school, the South Carolina school, and others. Later, toward the end of the 19th century, *local color* became the concern of many writers who studied native manners and speech in order to lend verisimilitude or humor to their writing. Literary *regionalism* as a movement reached its height in the late 1920's and the 1930's, a period of great political, economic, and social turmoil; sometimes it was a wavering drift toward Marxism in the depiction of "proletarian" life, sometimes it was a conservative revolt and an insistence on the indigenous values of former times. With a return to prosperity, regionalism died away as an ideology, and was replaced, especially after World War II, by a new emphasis on *folklore.* Many writers continued to describe distinct regions, from Cape Cod to the western wheatlands, from New Orleans to the boss-ridden cities of the North, but chiefly the writers dealt with their subjects historically and culturally rather than morally or politically.

Regionalism may be found in the very beginnings of creative writing in America, in the novels of JAMES FENIMORE COOPER and C. B. BROWN, in the Dutch settings of WASHINGTON IRVING, in the New England backgrounds of NATHANIEL HAWTHORNE. Sometimes BRET HARTE is singled out as the first post-bellum local colorist; one may add EDWARD EGGLESTON, HELEN HUNT JACKSON, JOEL CHANDLER HARRIS, G. W. CABLE, MARY NOAILLES MURFREE, T. N. PAGE, JOHN FOX, JR., SARAH ORNE JEWETT, MARY E. WILKINS FREEMAN, MARK TWAIN, HAMLIN GARLAND, BOOTH TARKINGTON, MARY ELLEN CHASE, EDITH WHARTON, STEWART EDWARD WHITE, DOROTHY CANFIELD FISHER, RUTH SUCKOW, OLIVER LA FARGE, to mention only a few.

Regionalism has been found mainly in novels, but is present also in American plays. Felix Sper made a useful survey in *From Native Roots: A Panorama of Our Regional Drama* (1948). Among American playwrights utilizing regionalistic elements may be cited Eugene O'Neill (New England), William Inge (the West), and Tennessee Williams (the South). One of the pioneers in the encouragement of this type of writing and its production by amateur groups was Professor Frederick H. Koch, who worked with such groups at Rutgers, North Dakota, and North Carolina Universities. He trained some playwrights of national renown—PAUL GREEN, for example. Poetry has, of course, many regional representatives: JOHN GREENLEAF WHITTIER, JAMES RUSSELL LOWELL, JOHN HAY, JAMES WHITCOMB RILEY, CARL SANDBURG, E. A. ROBINSON, ROBERT P. TRISTRAM COFFIN, ROBINSON JEFFERS, JOHN CROWE RANSOM, and numerous others.

Among nonfiction publications on regionalism, two series are outstanding. RIVERS OF AMERICA was planned and begun by Constance Lindsay Skinner, after her death was edited by Carl Carmer. It has reached about fifty volumes and has covered all parts of the country. The *American Folkways* (begun 1941, with Duell, Sloan & Pearce as publishers) is edited by Erskine Caldwell. Each of the volumes—about thirty-five in all—describes a particular "country," as *Golden Gate Country,* by Gertrude Atherton; *Corn Country,* by Homer Croy; *Mormon Country,* by Wallace Stegner; *Short Grass Country,* by Stanley Vestal. Other regional books include: F. J. Turner's *Significance of the Frontier in American History* (1893), THE FRONTIER IN AMERICAN HISTORY (1920), and *The Significance of Sections in American History* (1932); R. L. Rusk's THE LITERATURE OF THE MIDDLE WESTERN FRONTIER (2 v., 1925); J. C. Ransom's *The South and the Agrarian Tradition* (with others, 1938); B. A. Botkin's *Treasury of American Folklore* (1944), *Treasury of New England Folklore* (1947), *Treasury of Southern Folklore* (1949), and *Treasury of Western Folklore* (1951); Stewart H. Holbrook's *Promised Land: A Collection of Northwestern Writing* (1945); Edith and Frank Shay's *Sand in Their Shoes: A Cape Cod Reader* (1951); Vance Randolph's *Who Blowed Up the Church House? and Other Ozark Folk Tales* (1952). An important study of linguistic regionalism, especially as represented in the surveys and atlases, has been made by a group headed by Hans Kurath. See also DIALECT IN AMERICAN LITERATURE; THE FAR WEST; FOLKLORE IN AMERICAN LITERATURE; GULLAH; HUMOR IN THE UNITED STATES; MIDDLE WEST; THE MISSISSIPPI RIVER; THE MISSOURI RIVER; NEW ENGLAND; THE OZARK MOUNTAINS; ROCKY MOUNTAIN REGION; THE SOUTH; THE SOUTHWEST; TALL TALES AND TALL TALK; YANKEE IN AMERICAN LANGUAGE AND LITERATURE.

Regulators of Arkansas, The (1857). See FREDERICK GERSTAECKER.

Reid, [Thomas] Mayne (b. Ireland, April 4, 1818—d. Oct. 22, 1883), soldier, actor, writer. In 1840 Reid set sail for the United States, landed in New Orleans, and visited many places in the interior, earning his living in varied occupations. He finally drifted to Philadelphia where he made his living by writing. He was a loyal friend of Edgar Allan Poe and wrote a sympathetic article called *A Dead Man Defended,* which appeared in a magazine he edited, *Onward* (April, 1869). In 1845 Reid accepted a commission in the United States army and joined the forces fighting against Mexico. While recovering from a severe wound, he worked on a novel called *The Rifle Rangers: Adventures of an Officer in Southern Mexico* (2 v., 1850). In 1853 he married Elizabeth Hyde, then fifteen years old; she inspired his novel *The Child Wife,* and after his death wrote a *Memoir* (1890).

Reid's novels were mainly stories of adventure. Among them were *The Scalp Hunters* (1851); *The Boy Hunters* (1852); *The War Trail* (1857); *The Headless Horseman* (1866); *The Castaways* (1870); *Forest Exiles* (1854). Especially popular was *Afloat in the Forest* (1866), the story of a white family adrift on a huge log down the Amazon. His play *The Quadroon* (1856), based on one of his own novels, seems to have suggested Dion Boucicault's *The Octoroon*.

Reid, Whitelaw (b. near Xenia, Ohio, Oct. 27, 1837—d. Dec. 15, 1912), newspaperman, editor, diplomat, historian. Reid began his career in Ohio, where he edited the Xenia *News* for two years. From the first he was keenly interested in the Republican party. He became a legislative correspondent in 1861 and won admiration for the vigor of his writing. Then he was sent to the front and to Washington and wrote notable dispatches on the fall of Richmond and the assassination of Lincoln. With the close of the fighting he toured the South, reporting his observations in *After the War* (1866). For a time he owned and supervised cotton plantations in two southern states. He then returned to the North and completed a history of *Ohio in the War* (1868).

In 1868 Reid joined the staff of the New York *Tribune*, then edited by HORACE GREELEY. He was made managing editor the following year. Reid greatly improved the literary quality and raised the national standing of the *Tribune*. When Greeley ran for President against Grant (1872), Reid took charge of the paper and campaigned vigorously in its columns for him. Greeley died that year and Reid continued in full charge. In 1881 he placed JOHN HAY in charge of the paper and turned much of his attention to politics. He was appointed minister to France by Benjamin Harrison; McKinley and Theodore Roosevelt both sent him on special missions abroad; Roosevelt appointed him ambassador to England.

Reid's other books include *Our New Duties* (1899); *Problems of Expansion* (1900); *American and English Studies* (1913). Royal Cortissoz wrote *The Life of Whitelaw Reid* (2 v., 1921). Reid's son, Ogden Mills Reid (1882–1947), became editor of the *Tribune* after his father died. He did much to continue the paper as a leader in the liberal wing of the Republican party. He was succeeded by his widow, Helen Rogers Reid, as president of the New York Tribune, Inc; their son, Whitelaw Reid, was editor of the *Tribune* until 1958.

Reik, Theodor (b. Austria, 1888—d. Dec. 31, 1969), psychoanalyst. Reik, a contemporary psychoanalyst, studied with Freud in 1910. He wrote his dissertation on psychoanalysis in 1911 and, the year following, obtained his Ph.D. degree from the University of Vienna. A paper on applied psychoanalysis in 1914 won for Reik a first prize awarded by Freud himself. For years he lectured in Vienna, Berlin, and The Hague, until 1938 when he came to America. Although a star pupil of Freud's, Reik ultimately

parted from orthodox Freudianism. In *Listening with the Third Ear* (1948), he goes into the process by which Freud discovered psychoanalysis. He also presents in detail cases from his own three decades of practice. The "Third Ear" is the creative intuition of the analyst who perceives the unconscious thoughts of patients. Reik veered sharply from Freud in *The Psychology of Sex Relations* (1945) by rejecting the concept that neuroses have sexual roots and by insisting that the sublimation of the sexual urge is a fiction. Neurosis, for Reik, is "an emotional disturbance caused by a shake-up of the self-trust and confidence of a person." In *Fragment of a Great Confession* (1949), his autobiography, he analyzes his own obsession with the writings of Goethe; he also gives his views on the psychoanalytic problems of authors. In *The Secret Self* (1952), Reik applies his insights to the works of the great writers. *The Haunting Melody* (1953) is a study of his psychoanalytic reactions to music, particularly to Gustav Mahler's *Second Symphony*. Other books: *Psycho-Analytic Studies* (1931); *The Ritual* (with preface by Freud, 1931); *Unknown Murderer* (1936); *Surprise and the Psychoanalyst* (1937); *From Thirty Years with Freud* (1940); *Dogma and Compulsion* (1951); *The Search Within* (1956); *Of Love and Lust* (1957); *The Compulsion to Confess* (1959); *The Creation of Woman* (1960).

Reinterpretation of American Literature, A: Some Contributions Toward the Understanding of Its Historical Development (1928), a symposium edited by NORMAN FOERSTER for the American Literature Group of the Modern Language Association. The contributors were Foerster, Fred Lewis Pattee, Jay B. Hubbell, H. M. Jones, K. B. Murdock, Paul Kaufman, V. L. Parrington, Arthur M. Schlesinger, Sr., and H. H. Clark. The contributors all accepted Foerster's hypothesis that American literature was the product of European culture and the American environment, and that the four primary factors that shaped its development were the Puritan tradition, the frontier spirit, romanticism, and realism. Jones, looking back at the book in his *Theory of American Literature* (1948), felt that the note of the volume was humility and that this was the key to much about American literature that has been written since. Probably as a result of discussion of the volume the magazine *American Literature* was founded in 1929.

Reitzel, Robert (b. Germany, 1849—d. 1898), poet, polemicist, lecturer, editor, translator. Reitzel has sometimes been considered the most brilliant of German-American writers. Educated as a clergyman, he became a freethinker and gave up his ministry. He wandered all over the country as a lecturer, finally settled down in Detroit as the editor of a weekly called *Der arme Teufel* (1884). This served as an appropriate medium for his writings, in prose and verse, on all sort of subjects. He was a fiery and witty crusader who espoused social democracy, world citizenship, materialism, the workers' movement, and other causes. Long after his death a collection of his writings in this magazine was made, *Des armen Teufels gesammelte Schriften* (1913). A posthumous autobiography also appeared, *Abenteuer eines Gruenen* ("Adventures of a Greenhorn," 1902). His translations did much to acquaint German readers with Thoreau and Emerson, but the paramount influence on Reitzel himself was Heinrich Heine.

The Reivers (1962), a novel by WILLIAM FAULKNER. Set in 1905, this is a humorous tale involving eleven-year-old Lucius Priest; Boon Hogganbeck, the Priest family's moronic retainer; and Ned, their Negro coachman. These three "reivers," or plunderers, "steal" Lucius' grandfather's new motorcar and set off for Memphis, where they stay at a brothel. They swap the car for a race horse, and the intrigue which follows is the basis for the plot of this comic, near-farcical addition to the saga of YOKNAPATAWPHA COUNTY.

religion in U.S. literature. Many European settlers migrated to America to secure freedom of religious worship, but this quest was no guarantee of their toleration of other faiths. Of all the colonies Maryland, with its mixture of Protestants and Catholics, and Pennsylvania, with its Quaker creed, came closest to complete tolerance of other religions; also the Dutch in New Amsterdam allowed freedom of worship. According to W. W. Sweet in *Religion in the Development of American Culture, 1765–1840* (1952), the Baptists first preached the need for the separation of church and state. Their efforts bore fruit in the writing of this great principle into state constitutions, except in New England. Sweet and Anson Phelps Stokes, in the latter's monumental *Church and State in the U.S.* (3 v., 1950), also feel that all the rights mentioned in the First Amendment are interrelated, and all have to do primarily with religion.

The history of religion in the United States has been, for practically all sects, a movement away from formal theology toward what is most often a placid and nondogmatic faith. Theologically this has meant a revulsion against the doctrine of man's insignificance and innate depravity, a greater acceptance of the majesty and loving-kindness of God. In the days of the so-called Enlightenment, of which THOMAS JEFFERSON is a major representative, reason was stressed in matters of belief and Biblical interpretation. Pragmatism and other "practical" forms of thinking have made a great appeal; some clergymen have gladly sought a union between theology and psychiatry. The Bible is still our greatest best seller, although there is no longer the close reading of its verses that characterized the Puritan era. With the weakening of sectarianism and a deeper realization of the essential unity of mankind, the clergy have led Americans toward fellowship with other creeds and toward a deeper interest in social and economic problems.

Religious education is conducted outside the classrooms of public schools. In the churches themselves, aside from parochial schools, instruction is generally given in Sunday School classes. To assist in such instruction a vast literature has grown up. During the 19th century "Sunday school books" acquired an unfavorable reputation because of their frequent saccharinity and lack of realism. More recent books of this type are much more skillfully composed.

Religious writing in America began with Puritan, Quaker, and other refugees. The native-born theologians began with men like the later Mathers, and have been vigorously represented by a long line of writers, down to Reinhold Niebuhr. A brief selection of outstanding books in this field might include: John Cotton's *A Model of Church and Civil Power* (1634) and *The Keys of the Kingdom of Heaven* (1644); Thomas Hooker's *A Survey of the Sum of Church Discipline* (1648); John Eliot's *The Christian Commonwealth* (1659); Increase Mather's *The Order of the Gospel* (1700); Cotton Mather's MAGNALIA CHRISTI AMERICANA (1702); Jonathan Edwards' SINNERS IN THE HANDS OF AN ANGRY GOD (1741); John Woolman's *Works* (including his *Journal*, 1774); Ethan Allen's REASON THE ONLY ORACLE OF MAN (1784); Joseph Priestley's *Discourses on the Evidences of Revealed Religion* (1794); Timothy Dwight's *Theology* (5 v., 1818); Mary Baker Eddy's SCIENCE AND HEALTH (1875); Asa Gray's *Natural Science and Religion* (1880); H. W. Beecher's *Evolution and Religion* (2 v., 1885); Robert G. Ingersoll's *Why I Am an Agnostic* (1896); William James' VARIETIES OF RELIGIOUS EXPERIENCE (1902); George Santayana's LIFE OF REASON (5 v., 1905–06; 1 v., 1954); Josiah Royce's *Sources of Religious Insight* (1912); Felix Adler's *An Ethical View of Life* (1918); Harry Emerson Fosdick's *Christianity and Progress* (1922); Rufus M. Jones' *New Studies in Mystical Religion* (1927); Alfred North Whitehead's *Religion in the Making* (1926); Reinhold Niebuhr's *Moral Man and Immoral Society* (1932) and *Beyond Tragedy* (1938); John Dewey's *A Common Faith* (1934); Jacques Maritain's *The Person and the Common Good* (1947) and *Existence and the Existent* (1948); Paul Blanshard's *American Freedom and Catholic Power* (1949); H. W. Schneider's *Religion in 20th-Century America* (1952).

Inspirational volumes have enjoyed a tremendous sale; those with a psychiatric slant have found special popularity in recent years. Most of them are sincere endeavors to help people in mental or spiritual distress, but their language is closer to the brisk business world than to either the ministry or medicine.

Religion has naturally always fascinated the storyteller. (Novels about the BIBLE have already been noted under that heading.) Some of those more directly concerned with life in the Americas are: Nathaniel Hawthorne's THE SCARLET LETTER (1850) and THE BLITHEDALE ROMANCE (1852); Harriet Beecher Stowe's THE MINISTER'S WOOING (1859); Edward Eggleston's THE CIRCUIT RIDER (1874) and ROXY (1878); Harold Frederic's THE DAMNATION OF

THERON WARE (1896); Charles Sheldon's IN HIS STEPS (1897); Helen R. Martin's TILLIE, A MENNONITE MAID (1904); Winston Churchill's THE INSIDE OF THE CUP (1913); William Dean Howells' *The Leatherwood God* (1916); Sinclair Lewis' ELMER GANTRY (1927); Willa Cather's DEATH COMES FOR THE ARCHBISHOP (1927) and SHADOWS ON THE ROCK (1931); Thornton Wilder's THE BRIDGE OF SAN LUIS REY (1927) and *Heaven's My Destination* (1935); Oliver La Farge's LAUGHING BOY (1929) and *The Enemy Gods* (1937); O. E. Rölvaag's THEIR FATHER'S GOD (1931); Lloyd Douglas' *Green Light* (1935); Pearl Buck's *The Exile* (1936); LeGrand Cannon's *A Mighty Fortress* (1937); Gwethalyn Graham's *Earth and High Heaven* (1944); Jessamyn West's *The Friendly Persuasion* (1945); Theodore Dreiser's *The Bulwark* (1946); Henry Morton Robinson's THE CARDINAL (1950).

The clergy have as a rule been handled tenderly on the stage and in the movies. An early and sympathetic treatment was James A. Herne's THE REVEREND GRIFFITH DAVENPORT (1899). During the 1920's, however, ministers (rarely priests) were sometimes shown in all too human roles—like the minister in John Colton and Clemence Randolph's *Rain* (1922), based on Somerset Maugham's story. Other plays on religious themes are Percy MacKaye's *Jeanne d'Arc* (1905); Charles Rann Kennedy's *The Servant in the House* (1908) and *The Terrible Meek* (1912); William Hurlbut's *The Bride of the Lamb* (1926); Eugene O'Neill's LAZARUS LAUGHED (1927) and *Days Without End* (1933); Sidney Howard and Charles MacArthur's *Salvation* (1928); Marc Connelly's THE GREEN PASTURES (1930); and T. S. Eliot's MURDER IN THE CATHEDRAL (1935) and THE COCKTAIL PARTY (1949). Radio has proved hospitable to a friendly presentation of religious themes, both in direct discourses by clergymen of all faiths and in occasional dramatizations. Probably the best of the latter was the long series presented during the 1940's under the auspices of the Jewish Theological Seminary and later called *The Eternal Light*. Morton Wishengrad wrote many of the scripts, which were based on Biblical and Talmudic stories.

In poetry one finds early examples such as Michael Wigglesworth's THE DAY OF DOOM (1662), but often its ecstatic Calvinism, as in Jonathan Edwards, reached poetic heights in prose more strikingly than in verse. But in the 19th century spiritual insight is manifest in Ralph Waldo Emerson, Walt Whitman, and John Greenleaf Whittier; and H. W. Wells sees it equally in 20th-century poets like Stephen Vincent Benét, Carl Sandburg, Hart Crane, and Mark Van Doren.

The first periodical devoted exclusively to news of religion was probably the *Christian Magazine,* founded in 1802 by the Rev. Elias Smith. It lasted for two years, then was replaced in 1806 by the HERALD OF GOSPEL LIBERTY, the precursor of innumerable similar magazines.

Among important contemporary religious magazines are the following: *America, American Judaism, American Lutheran, Catholic World, Chicago Jewish Forum, Christian Advocate, Christian Century,* CHRISTIAN HERALD, *Christian Register, The Churchman, Commentary,* COMMONWEAL, *Forward, Jubilee, The Living Church, The Lutheran, Messenger of the Sacred Heart, The Pastor, Presbyterian Life, Presbyterian Outlook, Pulpit Digest, The Pulpiteer, Religion in Life, The Sign, Voice of St. Jude.* One great newspaper, the *Christian Science Monitor,* strikingly represents a religious viewpoint in the selection and description of news. See also under THE BIBLE IN THE U.S.

Remarkable Providences (1684), an essay by INCREASE MATHER. See AN ESSAY FOR THE RECORDING OF ILLUSTRIOUS PROVIDENCES RELATING TO WITCHCRAFTS AND POSSESSIONS.

Remarque, Erich Maria (b. Germany, June 22, 1898—d. Sept. 26, 1970), newspaperman, novelist. Remarque was a sports writer in Germany when he wrote his first and most famous novel, *All Quiet on the Western Front* (1929), a realistic picture of war based on the author's own experiences. He lived in Switzerland for a while and was permanently exiled by the Nazis. He came to the United States in 1939, became a citizen in 1947. Among his later books: *The Road Back* (1931); *Three Comrades* (1937); *Flotsam* (1941); *Arch of Triumph* (1946); *A Time to Love and a Time to Die* (1954); *Black Obelisk* (1957); *Heaven Has No Favorites* (1961). He usually writes about the sufferings of soldiers and of veterans after the wars.

"Remember the Alamo!" See ALAMO.

"Remember the Maine!" On Feb. 15, 1898, the American battleship *Maine* was blown up in Havana harbor; only sixteen crew members escaped uninjured. A wave of fury swept the country, largely set in motion by hysterical journalism. Some attributed the slogan "Remember the Maine!" to Fred J. Gould, who published a poem by that name in the Youngstown (Ohio) *Vindicator.* The poet Richard Hovey used the phrase in his poem *The Word of the Lord from Havana.* A naval court of inquiry declared itself unable to fix any responsibility for the explosion; but a strong pro-war party forced President McKinley's hand, and the United States finally made a formal declaration of war against Spain. See SPANISH-AMERICAN WAR.

Remembrance Rock (1948), a novel by CARL SANDBURG. This narrative of gigantic scope is a mixture of philosophy and story, of prose, poetry, and sermon, of biography and history. It begins in England in 1608 with Oliver Windrow, follows his descendants to Plymouth and down through the course of American history to the battle of Okinawa. Everywhere the protagonists follow the American dream, and Sandburg comments on it voluminously and wisely. In structure the narrative is really three novels.

Remington, Frederic [Sackrider] (b. Canton, N.Y., Oct. 4, 1861—d. Dec. 26, 1909), artist, writer. Remington attended the Yale School of

Fine Arts, then worked on ranches in the West and brought back many striking sketches of cowboys and Indians in action. He soon began to write stories and sketches intended largely as vehicles for his illustrations. When he did the drawings for Theodore Roosevelt's *Ranch Life and the Hunting Trail* (1888) he became famous. He became a roaming correspondent whose coverage of the Spanish-American War was especially noteworthy. Because of his dashing and sometimes juvenile prose, some critics looked down upon his work as an artist. He was remarkably accurate in his depictions of horses in motion; his paintings and sculptures today command high prices. It is said that he produced altogether more than 2,730 pictures and twenty-five sculptures, illustrated more than seventy books (aside from hundreds of magazine illustrations), including seventeen of his own (among them portfolios of his pictures). Friendly critics hold that as an artist he evolved from a somewhat garish illustrator to a notable painter. Undoubtedly he helped create the idea of the West held by people from the 1880's on.

Remington's books include *Pony Tracks* (1895); *Crooked Trails* (1898); *Sundown Leflare* (1899); *Stories of Peace and War* (1899); *Men with the Bark On* (1900); *John Ermine of the Yellowstone* (1902); *The Way of an Indian* (1906). Collections of his pictures include *Drawings* (1897); *Remington's Frontier Sketches* (1898); *A Bunch of Buckskins* (1900); *Western Types* (1902); *Done in the Open* (1902); and others. Harold McCracken's biography *Frederic Remington: Artist of the Old West* (1947) gives an accurate picture of the man and his accomplishments, and includes many reproductions of his drawings and paintings.

Remus, Uncle. See UNCLE REMUS.

Renascence (1912), a poem by EDNA ST. VINCENT MILLAY. Thought to have been written when Miss Millay was seventeen, *Renascence* was one of two hundred poems published in *The Lyric Year,* an anthology of winning poems in a national contest sponsored by the publisher Mitchell Kennerley, in which *Renascence* took the second prize.

The poem first describes the poet's sense of physical boundaries and the oppressive closeness of the earth and sky. Then, confronted by infinity, she experiences all sin and suffering, desires death, and at last the weight of infinity presses her down into the grave. She is content to be dead until she hears the rain and thinks of the "drenched and dripping apple-trees"; she prays for a "new birth" and is released from the grave into a comprehension of the "radiant identity" of God. Edmund Wilson feels that the poem gives the central theme of all Miss Millay's work—her loneliness, her fear that the world will crush her, and the necessity of summoning strength to assert herself and to embrace the world with love.

Reporter, The (1929), a novel by MEYER LEVIN. This was Levin's first novel and was a direct reflection of his early experience on a Chicago newspaper. It was immediately suppressed, perhaps because Levin had given an unflattering account of the methods of one newspaper and a libel suit was threatened.

Report from Paradise (1952), two tales by MARK TWAIN. This small volume, edited by Dixon Wecter, contains one previously published story, CAPTAIN STORMFIELD'S VISIT TO HEAVEN (originally *An Extract from Captain Stormfield's Visit to Heaven,* 1909), and one published for the first time, *Letter from the Recording Angel.* The former is here printed as it was originally written, with no suppressions. It was Mrs. Clemens who urged her husband to suppress the other, although he thought very highly of it. Together, they give Twain's attitude toward religion, which seemed more sacrilegious in its day than it actually was. What Twain detested was people who talked a lot about the forms of religion but never practiced its principles.

Repplier, Agnes (b. Philadelphia, April 1, 1855—d. Dec. 15, 1950), essayist, historian, biographer, poet, memoirist. One of the most urbane, intellectual, and witty essayists of her time, Miss Repplier maintained her high standards from her first essay in the *Atlantic* in 1886. She was an inveterate Philadelphian and wrote *Philadelphia—The Place and the People* (1898).

In later years she wrote *In Our Convent Days* (1905); she also wrote several biographies that showed the deep influence of her convent training: *The Life of Père Marquette* (1929), *Mère Marie of the Ursulines* (1931), and *Junípero Serro* (1933; rev., 1947). She began her writing career by working for a newspaper and doing children's stories and religious articles. Later she contributed almost a hundred essays to the *Atlantic.* She wrote an affectionate volume about *The Cat* (1912).

In her book *In Pursuit of Laughter* (1936)—in effect a history of her main subject—she sought to explain humor. She wrote with keen pleasure about medieval gaiety, the joyous beggars and Feasts of Fools, the naively funny miracle plays, and the wise court jesters. Today, she concluded, "we make scant pretense of cheerfulness." Among her other books: *Books and Men* (1888); *Points of View* (1891); *Essays in Miniature* (1892); *Essays in Idleness* (1893); *Compromises* (1904); *The Fireside Sphinx* (1901); *A Happy Half-Century* (1908); *Americans and Others* (1912); *Counter Currents* (1915); *Points of Friction* (1920); *Under Dispute* (1924); *Eight Decades* (1937). Not long before her death George Stewart Stokes prepared a biography of Miss Repplier (1949), based on many conversations with her.

Representative Men (1850), biographical sketches by RALPH WALDO EMERSON. These were lectures delivered in the United States and England during 1845–48. The volume discusses Shakespeare the Poet, Plato the Philosopher, Goethe the Writer, Swedenborg the Mystic, Napoleon the Man of the World, Montaigne the Skeptic; there is an introductory piece "On the

Uses of Great Men." The book obviously resembles Thomas Carlyle's *On Heroes, Hero Worship, and the Heroic in History* (1841). But Carlyle was an idolator of the Great Man and adulated his ruthlessness in seeking power and dominating the masses, whereas Emerson saw him as the product and the representative of his time and his people.

Republican party. See POLITICAL PARTIES AND LITERATURE.

Requiem for a Nun (1951), a novel by WILLIAM FAULKNER. Written in three prose sections, which provide the background, and three acts which present the drama in the courthouse and the jail, *Requiem for a Nun* centers on TEMPLE DRAKE, one of the main characters of SANCTUARY. In the interval of eight years separating the events of the two novels, Temple has married Gowan Stevens and borne two children; she is being blackmailed by Pete, brother of her lover in *Sanctuary*, and is planning to run away with him when NANCY MANNINGOE, her Negro servant, kills Temple's youngest child. Her attempts to gain a pardon from the governor for Nancy finally bring out Temple's own involvement in and responsibility for the crime.

Resistance to Civil Government (1849), an essay by HENRY DAVID THOREAU. The title is usually shortened to CIVIL DISOBEDIENCE.

Responsibilities of the Novelist, The (1903), an essay by FRANK NORRIS. Like his contemporary Hamlin Garland, Norris proclaimed that fiction has a purpose beyond mere narrative. The realism of William Dean Howells and Henry James he rejects as concerned with trivia, "the drama of a broken teacup." In its place Norris offers "romance," which portrays characters larger than life controlled by forces greater than they. Romance, he argues, will appeal not to the aesthete or the artist alone, but to the "people." It is in appealing to the people that the responsibility of the novelist lies.

Reston, James (b. Scotland, November 3, 1909—   ), reporter. Brought to the United States in 1910, Reston was educated in the public schools of Dayton, Ohio, and the University of Illinois, where he graduated in 1932. He began his career as a journalist for the Springfield (Ohio) *Daily News*, working also as a sports publicity director for Ohio State University. For a year he served as traveling secretary for the Cincinnati Baseball Club under Larry MacPhail. After another year spent with the Associated Press, he was sent to London in 1937 to cover major sports events in summer, and the foreign office in winter. In 1939 he joined the London Bureau of *The New York Times* and in 1941 was shifted to their Washington Bureau. During the war Reston served as head of the Information Service of the Office of War Intelligence in the American Embassy in London. He won a Pulitzer Prize for his news dispatches and interpretative articles in 1944 on the Dumbarton Oaks Conference. He won another Pulitzer award in 1956 for national reporting. With Marquis Childs, he edited *Walter Lippman and His Times* (1959).

Retail Bookseller, The. A magazine founded in 1898 as the *Monthly Bulletin of the Baker & Taylor Company*. It took its present name in 1923. The magazine carries news of books and publishers, lists best-selling and best-renting books, contains a calendar of dates of publication (with annotations), prints articles on booksellers, etc.

Retrieved Reformation, A (in *Roads of Destiny*, 1909), a story by O. HENRY. It relates the ironic fate of Jimmy Valentine, a burglar who makes up his mind to reform but is foiled when he shows his skill in opening a safe during an emergency. Jimmy is said to have been modeled on O. Henry's fellow prisoner in the Ohio State Penitentiary, Jimmy Connors. Paul Armstrong based his successful play ALIAS JIMMY VALENTINE (1909) on the story.

Return of Peter Grimm, The (1911), a play by DAVID BELASCO. Grimm, a botanist and old bachelor, completely mistakes the character of his worthless nephew Frederik and even extracts a promise from his foster daughter Kathrine that she will marry him. Peter dies suddenly at the end of Act I, then comes back to earth determined to prevent or undo the mischievous marriage he has arranged. He is successful in the end. The play is full of fanciful episodes, but Belasco, with his skillful stagecraft, manages to make them plausible, and his sentimentality is not offensive. The play had a long run with DAVID WARFIELD as Peter Grimm. CECIL B. DE MILLE is credited with help on the play.

Reunion in Vienna (1931), a play by ROBERT E. SHERWOOD. An exiled Hapsburg archduke returns to Vienna and there arranges a rendezvous with his former mistress who has married a psychiatrist during his absence. The doctor is too involved in psychoanalytic theories to notice the foolishness of his own cuckoldom: he believes the affair will cure his wife of an obsession. Joseph Wood Krutch claims that the play is "perfectly in the Continental tradition."

Revelry (1926), a novel by SAMUEL HOPKINS ADAMS. Adams dealt with contemporary oil scandals in this story of life in Washington during the Harding administration, and his book created a great sensation. The portraits were quite recognizable. All sales were banned in Washington, and it was attacked elsewhere, but Adams' later book on Harding (1939) showed how accurate it was.

Revere, Paul (b. Boston, Jan. 1, 1735—d. May 10, 1818), patriot, craftsman, cartoonist. Revere was a successful silversmith, experimented with engraving and portrait painting, carved frames, and manufactured false teeth. His greatest interest, however, was in politics, and when trouble arose between England and her colonies he turned out crude but effective cartoons for the Revolutionary cause. Of his many patriotic services the most famous was his midnight ride from Boston to Lexington on April 18–19, 1775, to warn the colonists that the Redcoats were approaching from Boston. There are probably few poems as famous in America as Longfellow's account of the ride (see THE MIDNIGHT RIDE OF PAUL REVERE). As a military man Revere was less successful than as courier and craftsman. After the war he spent his time making beautiful gold and silverware, experimenting with engraving processes, casting church bells, making cannon, and discovering a process for rolling sheet copper. His silverware is some of the finest that America has produced, and many examples are displayed in the Boston Museum of Fine Arts.

Paul Revere's Own Account of his Midnight Ride, April 18–19, 1775, with a short account of his life by S. E. Morison, was printed in *Old South Leaflet no. 222* (1922). Other accounts are *The Life of Colonel Paul Revere* (2 v., 1891) by Elbridge H. Goss; *Paul Revere and His Engravings* (1901) by William L. Andrews; *The True Story of Paul Revere* (1905) by Charles F. Gettemy; *Paul Revere and the World He Lived In* (1942) and *America's Paul Revere* (1946) by Esther Forbes; and *Paul Revere and the Minute Men* (1950) by Dorothy Canfield Fisher. Revere figures vividly in Esther Forbes' novel *Johnny Tremaine* (1943).

Reverend Griffith Davenport, The (1899), by JAMES A. HERNE. Herne founded this play on a novel, *An Unofficial Patriot* (1894), by Helen H. Gardener. Of the manuscript of the play nothing survives except Act IV, but the plot has been reconstructed from contemporary accounts and from data supplied by some of the surviving actors. The play, laid in the Civil War period, showed a Methodist circuit rider who owns a large plantation in the South but hates slavery. Davenport frees his slaves and incurs the ill will of his neighbors. He has numerous misadventures, including capture by a confederate contingent of which his son is captain.

Reveries of a Bachelor, or, A Book of the Heart (1850), by "Ik Marvel" (DONALD G. MITCHELL). The book contains four "reveries," the first of which appeared in the *Southern Literary Messenger* (1849). A sequel entitled *Dream Life* appeared in 1851. All the papers are mildly sentimental, gently humorous. They reveal a bachelor's thoughts of love and marriage; the last tells of a happy conclusion when "Caroline" becomes his wife. The scenes are in city and country, in America and abroad. The book became widely popular.

reviewers and reviewing. In America the first literary editor and the first man to conduct a daily book-review column was GEORGE RIPLEY, who in 1849 began to write a daily review for the New York *Tribune*. In 1850 he also became literary editor of Harper's *New Monthly Magazine*. In 1896 *The New York Times* established the *Times Saturday Book Review*, later transferred to the Sunday edition. The New York *Herald Tribune Books* began to appear in 1924; in 1960 it changed its title to the *Lively Arts and Book Review*, absorbing theatre, art, radio, and television, but soon returned to its original form. American magazines continued to give space to reviews of books, in addition to more formal articles of literary criti-

cism. Among some that achieved a high reputation in this field were the *North American Review*, the *Southern Literary Messenger*, *The Dial*, *Harper's Monthly Magazine*, *Godey's Lady's Book*, the *Atlantic Monthly*, the *Sewanee Review*, the *Yale Review*, the *New Republic*, *The Nation*, the *American Mercury* (in its earlier form), the *Virginia Quarterly Review*, *Commonweal*, *Poetry*, the *Partisan Review*, the *Kenyon Review*. Several magazines were founded specifically for the purpose of printing reviews and articles on current literature, including *The Book Buyer*, *The Bookman*, and the *Saturday Review* (formerly *Saturday Review of Literature*). *Book Review Digest* (1905 —) is a compilation of selected reviews from about seventy-five American periodicals.

One literary editor who was also a novelist and playwright was WILLIAM DEAN HOWELLS. As subeditor and editor of the *Atlantic Monthly* (1866–81) he had done considerable reviewing. From 1886 to 1891 he contributed the "Editor's Study" to *Harper's*, went to the *Cosmopolitan* for a year, returned to *Harper's* in 1900 and continued there till his death (1920). Howells wrote his articles on new and old books as a crusader for realism in fiction; his articles were collected in *Criticism and Fiction* (1891), *My Literary Passions* (1895), and *Literature and Life* (1902). Out of magazine articles JAMES RUSSELL LOWELL made such volumes as the two series called *Among My Books* (1870, 1876); long after his death, nine of his uncollected reviews were reprinted as *The Round Table* (1913), still others in *The Function of the Poet and Other Essays* (1920). A similar volume was E. P. Whipple's *American Literature and Other Papers* (1887). Other influential reviewers have been Alexander Woollcott, H. L. Mencken, Edmund Wilson, and Anthony West.

On the larger publications, the editor may have on call paid reviewers. On many newspapers the book review editor does all the reviewing himself, with occasional assistance from others, often unpaid. During the mid-20th century syndicates were organized to furnish reviews to newspapers. See LITERARY CRITICISM.

Review of Reviews, The. Founded at first (1890) as an American complement to a British magazine of the same name, this periodical took on an independent existence when ALBERT SHAW became editor (1894). It was always greatly interested in European affairs. It was influential for many years, but gradually faded away. In 1937 it merged with a similarly dying magazine, THE LITTLE DIGEST; the combination was called *The Digest*, which suspended publication in 1938.

Revised Version of the Bible. See BIBLE IN THE U.S.

Revolt of Mother, The (1890), a short story by MARY E. WILKINS FREEMAN. A typical Yankee farmer faces a revolt by his wife, who insists that some of the money he spends on agricultural equipment and big barns be spent instead on her and their young son and daughter. He yields, after she and they set up house-keeping in the new barn, and his surrender exemplifies a general change which has transformed the rural countryside. The story has been frequently anthologized.

Revolutionary War. See AMERICAN REVOLUTION IN U.S. LITERATURE.

Revolution of the Word, The. A manifesto that appeared in the magazine *transition*. See EUGENE JOLAS.

Rexford, Eben E[ugene] (b. Johnsburg, N.Y., July 16, 1848—d. Oct. 18, 1916), poet, writer on gardening. Rexford published several collections of verse, *Brother and Lover* (1886), *Pansies and Rosemary* (1911), and others; also several books on gardening. He is chiefly remembered for his poem *Silver Threads Among the Gold*, set to music by Hart Pease Danks (1873). Mary L. P. Smith wrote a life of Rexford (1930).

Rexroth, Kenneth (b. South Bend, Ind., Dec. 22, 1905—   ), poet, translator, critic. Largely self-educated, Rexroth knows some of Latin, Greek, Italian, French, classical Japanese, German, Spanish, and Chinese—enough of the

Arthur Knight

last to publish a fine book of translations from Chinese poetry, *One Hundred Poems from the Chinese* (1956). In addition to poetry he wrote a ballet, *Original Sin*, performed in 1961 by the San Francisco Ballet. Among his books: *In What Hour?* (1940); *The Phoenix and the Tortoise* (1944); *The Art of Worldly Wisdom* (1949); *The Signature of All Things* (1950); *Beyond the Mountains* (four verse dramas, 1951); *The Dragon and the Unicorn* (1952); *In Defense of the Earth* (1956); *The Minority of One* (1961). He has also edited the *Selected Poems of D. H. Lawrence* (1947), *New British Poets* (1948),

and *Nights of Love and Laughter* by Henry Miller.

Reynolds, Jeremiah N. (b. 1799[?]—d. 1858), explorer, writer. Reynolds is chiefly remembered for the influence he exerted upon research in the Antarctic and upon two authors —Herman Melville and Edgar Allan Poe. The former probably read Reynolds' account of a fierce white whale called *Mocha Dick* in the *Knickerbocker Magazine* (1839). Poe introduced Reynolds' polar theory into his UNPARALLELED ADVENTURES OF ONE HANS PFAAL (1835), and used a portion of an address that Reynolds made to Congress (published in 1836) in his NARRATIVE OF ARTHUR GORDON PYM (1838). Reynolds' fantastic notions apparently stirred Poe deeply; when he lay dying in a Baltimore hospital, he cried "Reynolds! Reynolds!" many times. Reynolds wrote about the *Voyage of the U.S. Frigate Potomac, 1831–34* (1835). He prepared a pamphlet, *A South Sea Expedition* (1837), and undoubtedly stimulated interest in exploring the southern parts of the Atlantic and Pacific oceans.

Reynolds, Quentin (b. N.Y.C., Apr. 11, 1902 —d. Mar. 17, 1965), newsman, short story writer. After taking a degree in law, Reynolds entered newspaper work as a reporter, a sportswriter, and staff writer. From his observations of wartime England he wrote the best seller *The Wounded Don't Cry* (1941). Assigned to Moscow as a press officer for W. Averill Harriman, he resigned after six months to show his repugnance for Soviet censorship. A slur against Reynolds cost WESTBROOK PEGLER and the Hearst corporations $175,000, the biggest libel penalty to date on record. His books are written in crisp, racy prose and deal with timely subject matter. A partial list: *London Diary* (1941); *Only the Stars are Neutral* (1942); *The Curtain Rises* (1944); *Courtroom* (1950); *Man Who Wouldn't Talk* (1953); *Headquarters* (1955); *Fiction Factory* (1955); *They Fought for the Skies* (1957); *Operation Success* (1957); *Known But to God* (1960); *Minister of Death* (1960).

Rhodes, Eugene Manlove (b. Tecumseh, Neb., Jan. 19, 1869 d. June 27, 1934), cowboy, government scout, writer. Rhodes is regarded as one of the leading writers of western stories. He knew the ranches well, had studied cowboys all his life, wrote with realism and sympathy. It was not until he was close to forty that he began writing. Many of his stories appeared in the *Saturday Evening Post* and created a Rhodes cult. The best known of them was called THE LITTLE EOHIPPUS (*Saturday Evening Post*, November–December, 1912), which later was expanded into a novel and published as *Bransford in Arcadia* (1914); in 1917 it was reprinted as *Bransford of Rainbow Range*. It is still probably the favorite of most admirers of Rhodes, although Frank V. Dearing, when he edited *The Best Novels and Stories* (1949) of Rhodes, reported that most critics regarded *Paso Por Aqui* (1926) as his masterpiece. J. Frank Dobie spoke of the vivacity of the cowboys' talk, and Walter Van Tilburg Clark praised Rhodes' "enormous landscapes—all so lovingly done that no other purveyor of the western can even touch them." Rhodes was also a facile verse writer. Among his principal books are *Good Men and True* (1910); *West is West* (1917); *Beyond the Desert* (1934); and *The Proud Sheriff* (1935). His wife, May Davison Rhodes, wrote a biography of him, *The Hired Man on Horseback* (1938), and W. H. Hutchinson wrote *A Bar Cross Man: The Life and Letters of Eugene Manlove Rhodes* (1956).

Rhodes, James Ford (b. Cleveland, Ohio, May 1, 1848—d. Jan. 22, 1927), newspaperman, businessman, historian. All through his life as a businessman in the coal and iron industries, Rhodes was deeply interested in American history, which he viewed against the background of Henry Thomas Buckle's scientifically written *History of Civilization* (1857–61). His fame rests chiefly on his most elaborate production, done after his retirement from business, a *History of the United States* (7 v., 1893–1906), which covered the years from 1850 up to the administration of Theodore Roosevelt. Two later volumes continued the narrative to 1908 (1919, 1922). His one-volume *History of the Civil War* (1917) won a Pulitzer prize. He was regarded as a great authority on the Civil War and the postwar period.

Rhodora, The: On Being Asked, Whence Is the Flower (comp., 1834; first pub. in the *Western Messenger,* July, 1839), a poem by RALPH WALDO EMERSON. The poem has been variously interpreted. One critic explained that the poem represents Emerson's most effective expression of "the relations of the Primal Mind to the Individual Mind," and others have marked its transcendental flavor. On the surface the poem seems simple enough. Emerson says that the rhodora is beautiful even if no one sees it, but he is thankful that God brought him there to see it. H. H. Clark believes the poem is a reply to didactic moralizers about the claims of beauty. The poem is among the most beautiful and melodious of Emerson's verses.

Ribaut [Ribault?], Jean (b. 1520[?]—d. 1565), French navigator, explorer. See RENÉ GOULAIN DE LAUDONNIÈRE.

Rice, Alice Hegan [Caldwell] (b. Shelbyville, Ky., Jan. 11, 1870—d. Feb. 10, 1942), novelist. Mrs. Rice spent most of her life in Louisville, except for extensive travels. She is known chiefly for her first book, MRS. WIGGS OF THE CABBAGE PATCH (1901), which shows her interest in settlement work, her keen appreciation of character, and her sense of humor. The book was an immediate success, was translated into French, German, Spanish, Norwegian, Danish, Japanese, and Braille, also produced as a play. Later Mrs. Rice was one of the founders of the Cabbage Patch Settlement House in Louisville. In 1902 she married CALE YOUNG RICE, a rising young poet, and for the rest of her life they successfully combined matrimony, travel, and writing. She produced more than a dozen novels, three volumes of short stories, to which her husband also contributed, and an autobiog-

raphy, *The Inky Way* (1940). *Happiness Road* (1942), a little book of personal philosophy, was completed and brought out after her death by her husband. Her books include: *Lovey Mary* (1903); *Sandy* (1905); *Captain June* (1907); *Mr. Opp* (1909); *A Romance of Billy Goat Hill* (1912); *Miss Mink's Soldier and Other Stories* (1918); *Quinn* (1921); *The Buffer* (1929); *Mr. Pete and Co.* (1933); *The Lark Legacy* (1935).

Rice, Cale Young (b. Dixon, Ky., Dec. 7, 1872—d. Jan. 23, 1943), poet, dramatist, novelist, critic. Rice studied at Cumberland and Harvard universities. He taught for one year (1901) at Cumberland, but upon marrying Alice Hegan, the popular novelist (see above), gave up teaching to devote himself to poetry. He published twenty-six volumes of verse and poetic drama, among them *From Dusk to Dusk* (1898); *Song Surf* (1900); *Many Gods* (1910); *Far Quests* (1912). *Yolanda of Cypress* (1907), a poetic drama, was made into an opera in 1929. *Turn About Tales* (1920) and *Winners and Losers* (1925) are books of short stories written in collaboration with his wife. He also wrote novels and an autobiography, *Bridging the Years* (1939). After his wife's death he committed suicide.

Rice, Elmer (b. New York City, Sept. 28, 1892—d. May 8, 1967), playwright, director, novelist. Rice gave up his law career early, although he continued to be interested in questions of censorship, arbitration, and legal rights. ON TRIAL (1914), his first play and the first

stage production to employ motion-picture techniques, was a hit. Other successful plays followed. THE ADDING MACHINE (1923) dextrously adapts German expressionist techniques in a satire on the growing robotization of man. Rice stressed sheer realism, however, in STREET SCENE (1929, a Pulitzer prize play), which depicts slum conditions; *The Left Bank* (1931), a portrayal of ineffectual expatriates; COUNSELOR-AT-LAW (1931), a not-too-flattering picture of the legal profession. The depression and the Nazi and Soviet menace produced *We, the People* (1933); *Judgment Day* (1934); *Between Two Worlds* (1934); *Two on an Island* (1940); *Flight to the West* (1940). These later plays were less successful, but *Dream Girl* (1945) and an operatic version of *Street Scene* (1947), for which Kurt Weill supplied the music, were very popular. Brooks Atkinson called the latter "a musical play of magnificence and glory."

The drama critics on the whole, however, were not too kind to Rice. Arthur Hobson Quinn remarked that "he can talk about the drama, but he really is not a creative artist." In the 1930's Rice was so irritated with the critics that he composed a satire on them and the stage, *Not for Children* (pub., 1935) and for a year or two retired from the theater. He returned with *American Landscape* (1938), *The Grand Tour* (1951), and *The Winner* (1954). In 1950 Rice made a selection of his work in *Seven Plays*, chosen from twenty four that he had produced in thirty-five years: *On Trial, The Adding Machine, Street Scene, Counselor-at-Law, Judgment Day, Two on an Island, Dream Girl*. Rice also wrote several novels, including *A Voyage to Purilia* (1930) and *The Show Must Go On* (1949). His autobiography, *Minority Report*, was published in 1963.

Rice, Grantland (b. Murfreesboro, Tenn., Nov. 1, 1880—d. July 13, 1954), newspaperman, sportswriter, poet. Rice worked for several southern and New York City newspapers, wrote a popular column called "The Sportlight," which became a syndicated feature in 1930. He also wrote verse with facility and wit; two collections (1917 and 1941) contain a number of pieces that have been very popular. Rice was reckoned one of the leading sportswriters of the day. He described his own life entertainingly in *The Tumult and the Shouting: My Life in Sport* (1954). John Kieran made a final gathering of his verses in *The Final Answer and Other Poems* (1955).

Rice, T. D. See JIM CROW.

Rich, Louise Dickinson (b. Huntington, Mass., June 14, 1903—   ), teacher, writer. Mrs. Rich's specialty is the perils and pleasures of life in close contact with nature, especially in Maine. She and her husband, Ralph Eugene Rich, lived for six years in the deep woods. Her account of her experiences, *We Took to the Woods* (1942), became a nonfiction best seller. Among her later books: *Happy the Land* (1946); *The Start of the Trail* (1949); *My Neck of the Woods* (1950); *Trail to the North* (1952); *Only Parent* (1953); *Innocence Under the Elms* (1955); *The Peninsula* (1958).

Rich, Richard. See NEWS FROM VIRGINIA.

Richard Carvel (1899), a historical novel by WINSTON CHURCHILL. One of the most popular novels about the Revolution, *Richard Carvel* is an account, narrated by the hero, of his adventures aboard a slaver from which he is rescued by JOHN PAUL JONES. The book describes sea warfare, a London interlude, and a successful love affair. Churchill was influenced by Thackeray, and some of the plot seems to be patterned after *Henry Esmond*. For the London portion he drew upon Boswell's *Life of Johnson*.

Richard Cory (1897), a poem by EDWIN ARLINGTON ROBINSON. This sixteen-line Browningesque portrait is one of the poet's most famous works. It is not only a portrait but also a narrative and an epigram, telling of the suicide of a supposedly successful man.

Richard Hurdis (1838), a novel by WILLIAM GILMORE SIMMS. See BORDER ROMANCES.

Richards, Laura Elizabeth (b. Boston, Feb. 27, 1850—d. Jan. 14, 1943), writer of children's books, poet. Laura Elizabeth Richards, daughter of Samuel Gridley and JULIA WARD HOWE, was born to a tradition of literature, started writing at the age of ten, and continued all her life, producing more than eighty books, most of them for children. *Tirra Lirra* (1932) was a Junior Literary Guild selection for that year, and *Captain January* (1890) was made into a movie in 1936 and experienced a second success. In 1917 Mrs. Richards won a Pulitzer prize for biography with her life of her mother, *Julia Ward Howe* (1916), written in collaboration with MAUDE HOWE ELLIOTT and with help from FLORENCE HOWE HALL. She edited her father's letters and journals (1906–09) and wrote a life, *Samuel Gridley Howe* (1935). *E. A. R.* (1936) is a brief life of Edwin Arlington Robinson, and *Stepping Westward* (1931) is autobiographical. She also contributed verse, chiefly ballads, to the *Atlantic Monthly*, the *Century*, and other periodicals. She lived most of her married life in Gardiner, Me., where her home was a center for the state's literary circle. Some of her other books are: *Five Mice* (1881); *Rita* (1900); *Snow White* (1900); *Geoffrey Strong* (1901), *Grandmother* (1907), *Florence Nightingale* (1909); *Miss Jinny* (1913); *Abigail Adams and Her Times* (1917); *Joan of Arc* (1919); *Honor Bright* (1920); *Star Bright* (1928); *Laura Bridgman* (1928).

Richardson, Charles Francis (b. Hallowell, Me., May 29, 1851—d. Oct. 8, 1913), teacher, poet, literary historian. Richardson, after doing newspaper work and editing a magazine called *Good Literature*, became professor of Anglo-Saxon at Dartmouth College. He published several miscellaneous volumes, including a collection of poems, *The Cross* (1879), but he is remembered chiefly as a pioneer in the study of American literature. He published a primer on the subject (1878), then his *American Literature, 1607–1885* (2 v., 1887–88). Although Howard Mumford Jones found flaws in Richardson's major work, he praised it for its comprehensiveness and its excellent analytical interpretations. Richardson was influenced by Hippolyte

Taine, Matthew Arnold, and to a certain extent by Charles Darwin.

Richardson, Jack C[arter] (b. New York City, Feb. 18, 1934—   ), playwright, novelist, short-story writer. Upon the presentation of Richardson's first play, produced off Broadway, *The Prodigal* (1960), critics agreed that the young playwright brought a keen intellect, wit, and objectivity to the theatre. He was, moreover, willing to tackle themes with a broad scope. *The Prodigal* was based on the Orestes theme, interpreted as a struggle between idealism and political opportunism, and treated with wry, sophisticated humor. *Gallows Humor,* a tragicomedy, was seen in 1961. In the same year Richardson published a novel, *The Prison Life of Harris Philmore.* He has contributed short stories to many literary magazines such as *Transatlantic Review* and *New World.*

Richardson, John (b. Queenstown, Upper Canada [now Ont.], Oct. 4, 1796—d. May 12, 1852), Canadian soldier, writer. Richardson fought for the British in 1812, after the war went to England and joined the British army, wrote a careful account of *The War of 1812* (1842). A quarrel with a commanding officer led him to write a book attacking him and the army, but the general was sustained and Richardson returned to Canada, where he became Canadian correspondent of the London *Times.* He also for a time edited a magazine and was superintendent of police on the Welland Canal. He died in New York City in extreme poverty. His best-known work was a novel, *Wacousta, or, The Prophecy* (1832), which deals somewhat romantically with the PONTIAC conspiracy and is regarded as the beginning of Canadian fiction. He also wrote *Personal Memoirs* (1838); *Eight Years in Canada* (1847); and a poem, *Tecumseh* (1828).

Richie, Helena. Chief character in MARGARET DELAND's novels THE AWAKING OF HELENA RICHIE (1906) and *The Iron Woman* (1911), usually regarded as her best work.

Richler, Mordecai (b. Montreal, 1931—   ), novelist. After attending Sir George Williams University in Montreal for two years, Richler went to Europe, where he wrote his first novel, *The Acrobats* (1954). Since then he has made his home in London. His fourth book, *The Apprenticeship of Duddy Kravitz* (1959), dealt with the early career of a clever, ambitious Jewish boy from a Montreal slum. Praised for its vitality and for the richness of its characterization, the novel has been called "the Canadian *What Makes Sammy Run.*" Other novels by Richler are *Son of a Smaller Hero* (1955) and *A Choice of Enemies* (1957).

Richman, Arthur (b. New York City, April 16, 1886—d. Sept. 10, 1944), dramatist, screenwriter. Richman wrote numerous plays, some of them adaptations. His most highly esteemed play was *Ambush* (1921), the poignant story of a family tragedy. Other dramas include *The Serpent's Tooth* (1922); *The Awful Truth* (1922); *A Proud Woman* (1927); and *The Season Changes* (1935).

Richter, Conrad [Michael] (b. Pine Grove, Pa., Oct. 13, 1890—d. Oct. 30, 1968), editor, short-story writer, novelist. Richter followed a miscellany of occupations as a young man, finally turned to writing as his chosen vocation. At first he wrote juveniles for *John Martin's Book* and for a magazine of his own, the *Junior Magazine Book.* He became deeply interested in the Southwest, lived there for many years. In his writings he became an interpreter of America in the light of its past. But historical details, personages, and happenings are thoroughly subordinated to the characters and the events in their lives. Critics still regard his first novel, THE SEA OF GRASS (1937), as perhaps his greatest, but his work as a whole, rather than any single production, marks him as an outstanding American novelist.

His earliest publication was *Brothers of No Kin and Other Stories* (1924). His most elaborate production was a trilogy depicting a pioneer group over the years: *The Trees* (1940); *The Fields* (1946); *The Town* (Pulitzer prize, 1950). *Always Young and Fair* (1947) is based on Richter's own recollections of Spanish American War days. *The Freeman* (1943) is laid in Ohio during the Revolution. *Tracey Cromwell* (1942) is about a woman in Arizona in the 1890's. Among his later books: *The Light in the Forest* (1953); *The Mountains and the Desert* (1955); *The Water of Kronos* (1960). See WORTH LUCKETT.

Rickert, [Martha] Edith (b. Dover, Ohio, July 11, 1871—d. May 23, 1938), scholar, writer. Miss Rickert taught at Vassar College and at the University of Chicago, where she did her best work in collaboration with J. M. MANLY, producing the definitive edition of Chaucer's *Canterbury Tales* from a collation of all known manuscripts. She also edited a number of other early English texts, wrote several novels, collaborated again with Manly on *The Writing of English* (1919), *Contemporary British Literature* (1921), and *Contemporary American Literature* (1922).

Ricketson, Daniel (b. New Bedford, Mass., July 30, 1813—d. July 16, 1898), poet, historian. One of the minor transcendentalists, Ricketson is chiefly remembered for his associations with Emerson, Alcott, and particularly Thoreau (see TRANSCENDENTALISM). He wrote a *History of New Bedford* (1858); his *New Bedford of the Past* (1903) appeared posthumously. He also published two collections of poems (1869, 1873). Some miscellaneous and autobiographical pieces of his were compiled for publication (1910) by his daughter Anne and his son Walton, who also edited *Daniel Ricketson and His Friends* (1902).

Ricketts, Edward F. (b. May 14, 1897—d. May 11, 1948), marine biologist. Ricketts is remembered chiefly for his friendship with JOHN STEINBECK, for his collaboration with him on *The Sea of Cortez* (1941), a book on marine biology, and for his appearance as "Doc" in Steinbeck's CANNERY ROW (1945). The novelist also wrote a foreword for the revised edition of

Ricketts' *Between Pacific Tides* (1952), the first edition of which had been prepared (1939) with the literary and photographic collaboration of Jack Calvin. The book was revised after Ricketts' death by Joel W. Hedgpeth. Steinbeck said Ricketts had "the profoundest mind I know." His knowledge of the tidepool dwellers along the Pacific coast was comprehensive.

Riddell, John. See COREY FORD.

Rider, [Arthur] Fremont (b. Trenton, N.J., May 25, 1885—   ), librarian, writer. Having edited a number of magazines (*The Delineator* in 1907; *The New Idea Woman's Magazine* in 1908; *The Monthly Book Review* in 1904–17; *The Library Journal* in 1914–17; *Business Digest* in 1917–21), Rider became librarian of Wesleyan University in 1933. He was active in developing new functions for libraries; among his books in the field of librarianship are *A Study of Library Policy* (1943); *Melvil Dewey, A Biography* (1944); *Compact Book Storage* (1949). He also edited travel guides to New York City, Bermuda, Washington, and California.

Ridge, John R[ollin] (b. near Rome, Ga., March 19, 1827—d. Oct. 5, 1867), poet. Ridge was the son of John Ridge, a Cherokee chieftain who negotiated, with others, a treaty with the government giving away tribal lands. The father was murdered by resentful tribesmen on June 22, 1839, in the presence of his family. His son later described the scene. At the same time, in another part of the reservation, his grandfather, also a prominent leader of the tribe, was murdered. As a writer Ridge was known as "Yellow Bird," a translation of his Indian name, Cheesquat-a-law-ny. His *Poems* (1868) and *The Life and Adventures of Joaquin Murieta* (1854) were his chief publications. He served on the staffs of several California newspapers.

Ridge, Lola (b. Ireland, 1883—d. May 19, 1941), poet. Born in Dublin and brought up in Australia, Miss Ridge came to the United States in 1907. She was always a woman of frail health and always a rebel. She took her inspiration and something of her poetic technique from WALT WHITMAN, but was also influenced by the imagists (see IMAGISM). Fame came to her with the publication of *The Ghetto* in the *New Republic* in 1918. It was a long poem giving a pitiless picture of the poverty and foulness in New York's slums. The poem gave its title to her first collection (1918). Later came *Sun-Up* (1920), with its memories of Australia; *Red Flag* (1927), a sonnet sequence; *Firehead* (1929), inspired by the SACCO-VANZETTI CASE but in its lines recording the Crucifixion; *Dance of Fire* (1935). Miss Ridge was a skillful painter, earned her living by illustrating, writing advertising copy, modeling, working in a factory, writing stories for which she herself cared little. Llewelyn Powys once said that the beauty of her face was "like the impassive death-mask of a saint." Her poems have been almost completely forgotten; they expressed the anger and fears of her day with considerable technical skill but not memorably.

Ridgely, Joseph Vincent (b. Montgomery, Ala., June 23, 1921—   ), literary historian, teacher. Ridgely received degrees from the University of Florida and Johns Hopkins University and began teaching literature in colleges and universities in 1946. Since that time he has specialized in America literature and has become known for his studies of early American novelists, such as *William Gilmore Simms* (1962). His edition of Simms' *The Yemassee* is carefully annotated.

Riding, Laura (b. New York City, Jan. 16, 1901—   ), poet, essayist, biographer, novelist. Brought up in a politically radical household, Miss Riding has been from the beginning a poet who does her own thinking, is more inclined to write intellectually than "poetically," and bends her form to suit her thought and feeling. Alfred Kreymborg found in her approach a distinct resemblance to Gertrude Stein; he added that whether Miss Riding "is a genius, an eccentric, or a dilettante, I am as yet unable to determine." Although Miss Riding ironically declares that she has a "jokeless modern mind," her writing is often more playful than solemn. Among Miss Riding's books: *The Close Chaplet* (1926); *A Survey of Modernist Poetry* (with Robert Graves, 1927); *Contemporaries and Snobs* (1928); *Poems: A Joking Word* (1930); *Four Unposted Letters to Catherine* (1933); *Poet: A Lying Word* (1933); *A Trojan Ending* (a novel, 1937); *Collected Poems* (1938); *Lives of Wives* (biographical sketches, 1939).

Ridpath, John Clark (b. Putnam Co., Ind., April 26, 1840—d. July 31, 1900), teacher, historian, editor. Ridpath taught English and history at Indiana Asbury College, later at De Pauw University, while he wrote "popular histories" (his term) about the United States, the world in general, the "great races of mankind." In 1898 he edited "The Ridpath Library of Universal Literature" (25 v.). He also wrote numerous biographies. He was personally as popular as his writings became, and was greatly esteemed as a teacher.

Riesenberg, Felix (b. Milwaukee, Wis., April 9, 1879—d. Nov. 19, 1939), master mariner, engineer, novelist. Riesenberg spent twelve years at sea; he was an officer of the U.S. Coast and Geodetic Survey and a member of the Wellman Polar expedition. In September, 1902, he was navigator of the airship *America* in the first attempt to reach the North Pole by dirigible. He then went to Columbia University and took a degree in civil engineering in 1911. He was assistant engineer on the Catskill Aqueduct, resident engineer in the construction of the Columbia-Presbyterian Medical Center. He wrote two technical books on the merchant marine, *The Men on Deck* (1918) and *Standard Seamanship* (1922); they are authoritative works in a neglected field. He also wrote a number of novels: *P.A.L.* (1925), later issued as *Red Horses* (1928), is laid between World War I and the boom of the 1920's; *East Side, West Side* (1927) is a novel of New York; *Passing Strangers* (1932) is a story of the depression.

Other books tell of the sea: *Under Sail* (1915); *Vignettes of the Sea* (1926); *Shipmates* (1928); *Log of the Sea* (1933); *Mother Sea* (1933). *Living Again* (1937) is autobiographical. He also wrote for the screen, stage, and radio, edited the *Nautical Gazette*.

Riesman, David, Jr. (b. Philadelphia, Sept. 22, 1909——   ), sociologist, writer, lecturer. Riesman attended Penn Charter, a Quaker preparatory school, then Harvard University, graduating in 1931. Continuing on to Harvard Law School without any real legal ambitions, Riesman came under the influence there of Felix Frankfurter and James McLaughlin. Although he practiced law for a while, he became strongly drawn to the "newer" social sciences. His work with ERICH FROMM and his wide readings in psychoanalytic literature finally diverted him from law and brought him fully into the social sciences. At the University of Chicago he sought to fulfill his aim of becoming an "all-around social scientist" by working with sociological, psychological, economic, political, and historical materials. The Committee on National Policy at Yale University in 1948 offered him an opportunity to do research on American character and community which later nurtured *The Lonely Crowd* (1950, with others) and *Faces in the Crowd* (1952, with N. Glazer). *The Lonely Crowd,* after its republication as a paperback, achieved the status of a modern classic. It is a multilevel investigation of the social character formation of the middle class of America. Jacques Barzun, in seeking an explanation for its brilliant public reception, wrote: "Riesman never forgets that he lives among those he has studied and that before reducing them to types, he feels their feelings and understands them." Other books: *Civil Liberties in a Period of Transition* (1942); *Democracy and Defamation* (1942); *Thorstein Veblen: A Critical Interpretation* (1953); *Individualism Reconsidered and Other Essays* (1954). In 1958 he became professor of Social Science at Harvard.

Riggs, Lynn (b. Claremore, Okla., Aug. 31, 1899—d. June 30, 1954), poet, playwright. Before entering the University of Oklahoma in 1921, Riggs worked on miscellaneous jobs all over the country. When he finally enrolled in college he made up for lost time by teaching freshman English in his sophomore year. His first play, *Knives from Syria* (1921), was produced in 1925. In 1926 he went to New York and devoted himself to writing. *Big Lake* was produced in 1927 by the American Laboratory Theater. He also wrote *Rancor* and *Domino Parlor* at this time; both were produced but failed to reach Broadway. *Borned in Texas,* a romantic comedy written in Paris on a Guggenheim Fellowship, was staged as *Roadside* (1930) but was not successful. A volume of verse, *The Iron Dish,* appeared the same year. Riggs' first successful play, GREEN GROW THE LILACS, a remarkably fresh and appealing folk drama, formed the basis for the even more successful musical comedy OKLAHOMA! (1943), by Oscar Hammerstein and Richard Rodgers. *Russet*

Mantle (1936), a comedy, and *The Cherokee Night* (1936), a tragedy, were followed by *The Cream of the Well,* which closed in 1941 after a few performances. Riggs enlisted as a private in the army in 1942, settled in New Mexico after the war. He issued *Four Plays* (1947), wrote *Hang on to Love* (1948) and *Toward the Western Sky* (1951), was working on a novel at the time of his death.

Riggs, Stephen R[eturn] (b. Steubenville, Ohio, March 23, 1812—d. Aug. 24, 1883), missionary, translator, memoirist. Riggs recorded his experiences as a missionary in *Mary and I: 40 Years with the Sioux* (1880). He became well acquainted with the Sioux language and issued grammars and dictionaries in that language. With John P. Williams he translated and compiled a book of hymns, *Dakota Odowan* (1853).

Rights of Man, The (1791–92), a tract by THOMAS PAINE. This was published in two parts in London. It was a reply to Edmund Burke's *Reflections on the Revolution in France* (1790), an attack on the doctrine of natural rights which lamented that "the age of chivalry is gone." Paine's rejoinder was dedicated to George Washington and sold so widely that the British government suppressed it and prosecuted Paine for treason. The suppression merely increased the underground circulation of the tract; to escape prosecution Paine fled to Paris and became a French citizen. In the United States the tract made a similar sensation and was immediately adopted by the Republicans (later called Democrats). Its ideas were commonplace with men like Jefferson; for example, that no man or government had a right to bind succeeding generations. Jefferson wrote a letter which was used as an introduction for the Philadelphia edition of the tract without his authorization and embarrassed him greatly; it was regarded as a direct attack by the secretary of state (as Jefferson then was) upon Vice-President John Adams. The pamphlet set up numerous other repercussions in this country.

Riis, Jacob A[ugustus] (b. Denmark, May 3, 1849—d. May 26, 1914), journalist, reformer. Riis' father was a teacher in a Latin School, but the boy showed no interest in an academic career and was apprenticed to a carpenter. The man whom Theodore Roosevelt called the best American he knew did not come to this country until he was twenty-one. His first seven years in the United States were difficult ones, in which he worked at many jobs, often suffered from hunger and cold, and learned at first hand the squalor of the slums of New York City and the iniquities of the police lodging-house system. Finally in 1877 he was employed as a reporter by the New York *Tribune,* with which he remained until 1888, going then to the New York *Evening Sun.* In 1899 he retired from newspaper work and devoted himself to lectures, articles, and books.

As a police reporter he waged for more than ten years a single-handed battle against the terrible conditions in the New York City tenements.

Finally his book *How the Other Half Lives* (1890) brought Theodore Roosevelt to his assistance, and reform was begun, resulting ultimately in improved water supply, child labor laws, playgrounds, the closing of the police lodging-houses, and the elimination of the worst slum, the notorious Mulberry Bend. Riis remained a close friend of Roosevelt, but refused to hold any public office. THE MAKING OF AN AMERICAN (1901) is Riis' own account of his life and crusades and his most famous book. Other books are: *The Children of the Poor* (1892); *Out of Mulberry Street* (1898); *The Battle with the Slum* (1902); *Children of the Tenements* (1903); *Theodore Roosevelt the Citizen* (1904); *Is There a Santa Claus?* (1904); *The Old Town* (1909); *Hero Tales of the Far North* (1910).

Riley, James Whitcomb (b. Greenfield, Ind., Oct. 7, 1849—d. July 22, 1916), poet, lecturer, newspaperman. Riley attended the public schools in the little town where he was born, but showed little interest in his books, except Mc-

Guffey's *Sixth Reader.* His real education was acquired at the courthouse, the cobbler's shop, and other popular spots in Greenfield where his active mind stored up tales of the local people and his accurate ear noted the peculiarities of the local dialect. He was a gifted musician, actor, and painter, as well as a writer, and he traveled about Indiana, first painting advertisements on barns and fences, later as a musician and actor for a traveling patent medicine show. He joined the staff of the Greenfield *Times,* going later to the Anderson *Democrat* as local editor.

In 1877, while Riley was on the *Democrat,* he perpetrated the famous *Leonainie* hoax, publishing in the Kokomo (Ind.) *Dispatch,* with the connivance of the editor, a poem supposedly by EDGAR ALLAN POE but in reality a skillful imitation by Riley. This escapade brought him much notoriety and caused him embarrassment the rest of his life; the immediate result was that he lost his job. However, he soon found employment with the Indianapolis *Journal,* where he worked from 1877 to 1885. Eventually he moved to Indianapolis and lived there the rest of his life.

While he was with the *Journal* Riley began contributing to it a series of poems in the Hoosier dialect, dealing with homely subjects. These were written under the pen name "Benjamin F. Johnson, of Boone." A group of these poems was published in 1883 as "*The Old Swimmin'-Hole*" and 'Leven More Poems. This book and his subsequent ones launched him on a wave of popularity which brought him greater financial returns than any other American poet had known to that time. This popularity Riley increased by his lecture tours, where—despite habitual intemperance—he displayed his abilities as an actor and humorist. He also wrote humorous sketches and nondialect poems, but is chiefly remembered for his dialect poems. Richard Crowder calls them "comforting, familiar platitudes restated in verse." His most popular poems are: *When the Frost Is on the Punkin',* *The Old Man and Jim,* LITTLE ORPHANT ANNIE, *Knee-Deep in June,* THE RAGGEDY MAN. See also OLD SWEETHEART OF MINE.

Riley's collections include: *Afterwhiles* (1887); *Pipes o' Pan at Zekesbury* (1888); *Old-Fashioned Roses* (1888); *Rhymes of Childhood* (1891); *Green Fields and Running Brooks* (1892); *Poems Here at Home* (1893); *Riley Child Rhymes* (1899); *Book of Joyous Children* (1902). A Biographical Edition was issued in six volumes in 1913, in one volume in 1937. His *Letters* were edited (1930) by W. L. Phelps. Marcus Dickey wrote *The Youth of James Whitcomb Riley* (1919) and *The Maturity of James Whitcomb Riley* (1922). A centennial volume (1951) included three addresses given at Indiana University in 1949 by James T. Farrell, Horace Gregory, and Jeanette Covert Nolan. Richard Crowder wrote *Those Innocent Years: The Legacy and Inheritance of a Hero of the Victorian Era, James Whitcomb Riley* (1957).

Riley, [Isaac] Woodbridge (b. New York City, May 20, 1869—d. Sept. 2, 1933), teacher, historian, philosopher. Riley taught at Vassar College from 1908 to 1933. His most important books are those he wrote on American philosophical thought and religious movements, among them *The Founder of Mormonism* (1902); *American Philosophy: The Early Schools* (1907); *American Thought from Puritanism to Pragmatism* (1915). He also wrote *From Myth to Reason* (1926); *Men and Morals* (1929); *The Meaning of Mysticism* (1930).

Rimmer, William (b. England, Feb. 20, 1816—d. Aug. 20, 1879), physician, artist, teacher, author. Rimmer was brought to the United States in 1826 by his father, a French refugee who Rimmer claimed was the lost Dauphin. Rimmer was a physician who painted for his own amusement. But his work attracted attention, and in 1870 he opened a studio in Boston. Some of his paintings and sculptures are found in our leading museums. In 1876 he became professor of anatomy and sculpture at the Boston Museum of Fine Arts, publishing the lectures he delivered as *Art Anatomy* (1877). Earlier he had written *Elements of Design* (1864). One of his students was Louisa May Alcott, and some scholars believe Rimmer was the inspiration for the character of Professor Bhaer in LITTLE WOMEN.

Rinehart, Mary Roberts (b. Pittsburgh, Pa., Aug. 12, 1876—d. Sept. 22, 1958), novelist, detective-story writer, playwright. After finishing high school, Mary Roberts entered the Pittsburgh Training School for Nurses, but as soon as she received her diploma she married Dr. Stanley Rinehart. Financial troubles brought on by the stock-market crash of 1903 started her writing. At first she wrote verses, short articles, and children's stories, but THE CIRCULAR STAIRCASE (1908) and *The Man in Lower Ten* (1909) established her as the writer of a new type of detective story, one in which a well-knit plot was combined with lifelike, sometimes humorous characterizations of normal people.

During World War I Mrs. Rinehart served as war correspondent for the *Saturday Evening Post* on the Belgian and French fronts. As a correspondent she had the honor of interviewing Queen Mary of England, a privilege until then granted to no reporter; also the king and queen of the Belgians. The Belgian Medal of Queen Elizabeth was awarded to her in recognition of her hospital and relief work.

In addition to her detective stories Mrs. Rinehart was also the author of a series of amusing stories about a dauntless spinster and her two friends: *The Amazing Adventures of Letitia Carberry* (1911); TISH (1916); *More Tish* (1921); *Tish Plays the Game* (1926); *Tish Marches On* (1937); *The Best of Tish* (selected stories, 1955). Of her more serious novels, *K* (1915) and *The Breaking Point* (1922) are considered her best. AVERY HOPWOOD collaborated with her on four plays, one of which, THE BAT (1920), based on *The Circular Staircase*, had a phenomenal run. Some of her novels have been dramatized by other playwrights, and many have been translated into foreign languages. *My Story,* which is autobiographical, was written in 1931 and revised in 1948; one critic called it her finest book.

Among her other books: *When a Man Marries* (1909); *The Street of Seven Stars* (1914); *Kings, Queens, and Pawns* (1915); *Through Glacier Park* (1916); *The Amazing Interlude* (1918); *Love Stories* (1919); *The Out Trail* (1923); *Temperamental People* (1924); *The Red Lamp* (1925); *The Door* (1930); *The Wall* (1938); *A Light in the Window* (1948); *The Frightened Wife* (1953).

Ringwood the Rover: A Tale of Florida (1843), a novel by H. W. HERBERT (Frank Forester). This is a fictional account of the actual experiences of Governor William Pope Duval of Florida, who supplied material for several stories by WASHINGTON IRVING and who is believed by some to be the original of Nimrod Wildfire in J. K. Paulding's play THE LION OF THE WEST (1831). In his life of Herbert (*Frank Forester: A Tragedy in Exile,* 1933), William Southworth Hunt characterizes the novel as "not far removed from the dime novel of subsequent generations."

Ripley, George (b. Greenfield, Mass., Oct. 3, 1802—d. July 4, 1880), editor, reformer, literary critic. After graduating from Harvard University in 1823 Ripley taught mathematics there while attending the Divinity School. He became a Unitarian minister in Boston. For fifteen years he remained at the same church, studying German theology and editing the *Christian Register.* In 1838 Ripley began to edit *Specimens of Foreign Standard Literature* (14 v., 1838–52), translations of Victor Cousin, Théodore Simon Jouffroy, and Friedrich Ernst Schleiermacher, whose philosophies formed part of the basis for the American transcendental movement. Andrew Norton's *The Latest Form of Infidelity* (1839), a reply to Ralph Waldo Emerson's *Divinity School Address,* contained an attack on Ripley's *Discourses on the Philosophy of Religion* (1836). Ripley answered in a series of letters, later published as *Letters on the Latest Form of Infidelity* (1840). A year later he resigned from the ministry.

On April 1, 1841, Ripley, with twenty other members of the Transcendental Club, moved to West Roxbury, where he became president of the famous experiment in communal living, BROOK FARM. There he taught mathematics and philosophy, edited THE DIAL, and worked on the farm. (See TRANSCENDENTALISM.) After the disastrous fire of 1846, Ripley, loaded with debts, moved to Flatbush, L.I., where he edited *The Harbinger.* In 1849 he abandoned *The Harbinger* and became literary critic of the New York *Tribune.* He soon became an outstanding influence in the world of letters. He recognized at once the value of such works as *The Scarlet Letter* and *The Origin of Species* and rarely allowed a single important publication to escape his notice. He became one of the founders of *Harper's New Monthly Magazine,* and with the income from this, the *Tribune,* and his *History of Literature and the Fine Arts* (1852), prepared with BAYARD TAYLOR, he managed to work his way out of his crushing debts. In 1858 he brought out the first volume of the *New American Cyclopedia* (16 v., 1858–63), later revised as the *American Cyclopedia* (1873–76). He traveled extensively in Europe in 1866, 1869, and 1870, meeting many of the authors whose works he had praised.

Although Ripley was too modest to collect his critical essays, he was a great influence on American thought and letters. In 1870 W. E. Channing wrote of him, "It was George Ripley, and Ripley alone, who truly originated Brook Farm, and his should be the honor through all time." O. B.

Frothingham's *George Ripley* (1882) appeared in the "American Men of Letters" series. J. T. Codman's *Brook Farm, Historical and Personal Memoirs* (1894), Lindsay Swift's *Brook Farm, Its Members, Scholars, and Visitors* (1900), and Katherine Burton's *Paradise Planters* (1939) contain additional information.

Ripley, Robert L[eroy] (b. Santa Rosa, Cal., Dec. 25, 1893—d. May 27, 1949), cartoonist. At the age of sixteen Ripley began working as a sports cartoonist for the San Francisco *Bulletin*, later went on to the *Chronicle* and the New York *Globe*. In December, 1918, Ripley drew for the *Globe* the first of his *Believe It or Not* cartoons, showing seven unusual if not incredible achievements. The cartoon soon became a daily feature, several years later was syndicated by King Features, which at one time needed a staff of eighty to collect material and handle the letters that Ripley received. His first book of *Believe It or Not* cartoons appeared in 1928; several others followed, with paperback reprints. Ripley turned his home at Mamaroneck, N.Y., into a museum of curios; he called the place Bion after the initials of his cartoons. Bob Considine wrote *Ripley, the Modern Marco Polo* (1961).

Rip Van Winkle (1819), a tale by WASHINGTON IRVING. This most famous piece in Irving's *Sketch Book* immediately became a popular favorite. Irving tells how henpecked Rip Van Winkle, in the days before the Revolution, wanders into the Catskills with his faithful dog Wolf and there meets a dwarfish and strangely costumed man whom he helps to carry a keg of liquor. They go into the mountains and come to a gathering of other strange persons who are playing nine-pins, but no one says a word. Rip takes a nip or two at the keg, soon falls into a stupor, and sleeps for twenty years. He awakens to find his beard full-grown and white, returns to his village to find his wife dead, his daughter married and a mother, the whole country changed; now George Washington's image, and not George III's, adorns the village inn's signboard. Rip goes on to a happy old age.

The plot is an ancient folk theme. Although it appears in many times and places, Irving presumably based his story particularly on the German folk tale of Peter Klaus. Some critics rather unfairly accused him of plagiarism, in a field where the idea of copyrights would be ridiculous. Irving made the story, as he said, "a frame" for "the play of thought, and sentiment, and language," with "a half-concealed vein of humor." Harold W. Thompson called Rip "a genuine American character, but he is the universal type of the indolent, henpecked man." Herman Melville, who had great respect for Irving, wrote *Rip Van Winkle's Lilac* (1890), relating a final episode in Rip's life. A lilac he had planted in his youth had furnished shoots for hundreds of bushes nearby, turning the neighborhood into a garden of lilacs.

Like Rip's lilac bush, the story of his life has also sprouted freely in the theater. A pirated version of Irving's tale was played in Albany,

N.Y., in 1828. Another version was produced in 1829, one copy of which has survived; this was the work of John Kerr, an English actor and play adaptor. It is held to be the basis of all later adaptations. Another version was made by WILLIAM BAYLE BERNARD in 1832 or 1834. Charles Burke made a new version in 1850. In 1855 appeared an opera by G. F. Bristow based on the tale. Then the famous actor JOSEPH JEFFERSON commissioned DION BOUCICAULT to do a revision. The resulting version, first produced in London in 1865, became the standard form of the play, and was Jefferson's major vehicle until 1904. JAMES A. HERNE made a version around 1874. In 1920 PERCY MACKAYE composed a folk opera for which REGINALD DE KOVEN wrote the music. A French composer, Robert Jean Planquette, wrote still another opera, produced in 1881 and given in the United States in a modernized version in 1933.

Rise of American Civilization, The (2 v., 1927), by CHARLES A. and MARY R. BEARD. A third volume was called *America in Midpassage* (1939). A fourth volume usually joined with these is *The American Spirit: A Study of the Idea of Civilization in the U.S.* (1942). The first two volumes carried the story down to the middle 1920's. In the third the narrative was continued to 1938. The fourth volume sought a central theme in American history, tracing American principles from 18th-century France through colonial times to the New Deal. Perhaps a fifth volume should be added, *A Basic History of the U.S.* (1944), noteworthy because in it Beard revised his earlier ideas of the "economic interpretation of history."

Rise of David Levinsky, The (1917), a novel by ABRAHAM CAHAN. Cahan, who escaped from Czarist persecution in 1882 and fled to New York City, established himself as a successful editor of a Yiddish daily and an excellent novelist. His David Levinsky, sometimes ruthless and unscrupulous, becomes a rich man. But he does not attain happiness, and ends up without a family or a real home. The book presents a vivid picture of the needle trades in New York City and the unions in their early days, and is recognized as the first important immigrant novel. See LOWER EAST SIDE.

Rise of Silas Lapham, The (1885), a novel by WILLIAM DEAN HOWELLS. The best known of Howells' works, this was also one of the earliest novels about the world of business, depicting the money-getting methods of Lapham, a newcomer to Boston, as he proceeds toward wealth and ends in final ruin. In another sense it is a social novel, showing Lapham's efforts to introduce himself into the older Brahmin society of the metropolis; the novel's most famous scene is that in which Silas attends an important dinner party and disgraces himself by drinking too much. At its deepest level, however, the novel is a work of morality, showing Lapham's moral "rise" from ruthlessness to a recognition of ethical standards. In the end Silas even contributes to his own financial defeat by refusing to engage in practices which he now considers immoral.

Throughout the story is woven a love affair between the son of a Brahmin family and Penelope Lapham, the daughter of Silas; at the end the two find happiness by escaping to Mexico.

The novel is without doubt Howells' best and one of the triumphs of American fiction. The figure of Silas is skillfully drawn and presents an important American type: the self-reliant businessman, tough and shrewd and ambitious, although essentially honest, willing to accept the right so far as he can understand it. The novel is a complex of social and moral feeling that probes the significance of American civilization in its growing aspect.

Rise of the Dutch Republic, The (3 v., 1856), a history by J. L. MOTLEY. Motley continued his account of the history of the Netherlands in later volumes, but this section was perhaps his most dramatic. He saw two antagonistic ideas in the person of two antagonists: William of Orange, the hero, representing freedom and Protestantism, and Philip II of Spain, representing absolutism and Catholicism. Motley overdramatized the conflict, but remains in some passages one of the most literary of American historians. He wrote in the contemporary manner of Carlylean hero worship.

Rittenhouse, Jessie B[elle] (b. Mt. Morris, N.Y., 1869—d. Sept. 28, 1948), poet, teacher, editor, critic. Miss Rittenhouse taught for a while in private schools, then began contributing to newspapers and syndicates. She lectured on poetry, published numerous collections of verse, including *The Younger American Poets* (1904), and wrote reviews, specializing in poetry. She was a founder of the Poetry Society of America and also a founder and president of the Poetry Society of Florida. She married the poet CLINTON SCOLLARD. Among her books: *The Door of Dreams* (1918); *The Lifted Cup* (1921); *The Secret Bird* (1930); *The Moving Tide: New and Selected Lyrics* (1939). *My House of Life* (1934) is an autobiography.

Rivers of America Series. This series began with ROBERT P. TRISTRAM COFFIN's *The Kennebec* (1937), was followed by STRUTHERS BURT's *Powder River* (1938) and CARL CARMER's *The Hudson* (1939). Since then the series has reached many volumes. Numerous noted authors have contributed. Each volume has included geographical and economic data, accounts of historical happenings, descriptions of persons and places, folklore. Until her death in 1939, Constance Lindsay Skinner was the editor. Later editors have included STEPHEN VINCENT BENÉT, HERVEY ALLEN, and Carl Carmer.

Rives, Amelie. See PRINCESS TROUBETZKOY.

Road Not Taken, The (*Atlantic Monthly*, August, 1915; the opening poem in *Mountain Interval*, 1916), a poem by ROBERT FROST. This frequently anthologized poem is obviously symbolical. Frost comes to a fork in the road and is undecided which way to go. Both roads seem very much alike, even if one "was grassy and wanted wear." He takes the one less traveled— and "that has made all the difference."

Road to Rome, The (1927), a play by ROBERT E. SHERWOOD. This was Sherwood's first produced play and, although a rollicking comedy influenced by G. B. Shaw's *Caesar and Cleopatra* (1899), it was in its way a plea against war. Hannibal is about to capture Rome. He is prevented from doing so by the allurements of Amytis, wife of Fabius Maximus, a pompous Senator; Amytis enjoys her task.

Road to Xanadu, The (1927; enlarged ed., 1930), by JOHN LIVINGSTON LOWES. Lowes subtitled his critical and psychological masterpiece "A Study in the Ways of the Imagination." His title is a combination of a bit of dialogue from Goethe's *Faust,* used as a motto (*Faust:* "Wohin der Weg?" [Whither the way?] *Mephistopheles:* "Kein weg! Ins Unbetretene." [No way, but into the unexplored.]) and the place name that S. T. Coleridge made famous in his poem *Kubla Khan* (1797). On the surface the book is a study of how Coleridge came to write some of his poems. In reality it is a unique study of the workings of the imagination, with Coleridge as an example. The learning shown in the book is prodigious, and it includes some important discoveries. Clifton Joseph Furness stated, in a profile of Lowes (*Word Study,* February 1939): "William James' essay *Stream of Consciousness* does not offer so tangible a chart of the flotsam and jetsam of mind stuff as does Lowes' concluding chapter on 'Imagination Creatrix.'" According to Robert E. Spiller, Lowes "borrowed a hypothesis and a method from the psychologist Jung."

Roan Stallion (in *Roan Stallion, Tamar and Other Poems,* 1925), a narrative poem by ROBINSON JEFFERS. Set in the mountains near Monterey, Calif., the *Roan Stallion* deals with the almost religious love of a woman named California for a magnificent red stallion, in which she sees a power and beauty equivalent to that of a divinity. When her brutal husband is trampled to death by the horse she shoots the animal "out of some obscure human fidelity," but feels that she "has killed God." Jeffers' powerful descriptions of the action and the almost mythological quality of the poem make it one of his best.

Roark, Garland (b. Groesbeck, Tex., July 26, 1904—   ), cartoonist, advertising man, novelist. Roark's writings include many fine adventure stories, which he wrote while working for advertising agencies in Dallas, Chicago, and Houston. His first success was *Wake of the Red Witch* (1946), which was made into a movie. Later books include *Rainbow in the Royals* (1950); *Star in the Rigging* (1954); *Tales of the Caribbean* (1959); *Should the Wind Be Fair* (1960).

Robb, John S. ["Solitaire"]. Robb was a Missourian newspaperman and humorist. Little is known of his life aside from the fact that he wrote humorous stories of the West and Southwest around the middle of the 19th century. Some of his contributions appeared in the SPIRIT OF THE TIMES. He prepared one or two collections of his material; the best known is *Streaks* of *Squatter Life and Far Western Scenes: A Series of Humorous Sketches Descriptive of Incident and Character in the Wild West* (1846, 1847), which was reprinted as *Western Scenes, or, Life on the Prairie* (1858). In this book were several tales of MIKE FINK, among the earliest to appear and apparently gathered from oral tradition.

Robbins, Leonard H. (b. Lincoln, Neb., April 2, 1877—d. June 24, 1947), newspaperman, humorist, columnist, poet. Robbins did newspaper work in Lincoln, Philadelphia, Newark, and New York. In *The New York Times* magazine section he conducted a column called "About." He collected some of his verses in *Jersey Jingles* (1907). His humor was keen but never bitter; he was a stickler for exactness and fairness in his satire, as in his reporting.

Robe, The (1942), a novel by LLOYD C. DOUGLAS. Douglas, a Lutheran clergyman as well as a novelist, was once asked what became of the robe for which the Roman soldiers who had crucified Jesus cast lots. Douglas wrote this novel by way of reply. *The Robe* became one of the most popular novels ever written, but received scant praise from the critics.

Robert of Lincoln (*Putnam's Magazine*, June, 1855), a poem by WILLIAM CULLEN BRYANT. A melodiously written piece about the bob-o-link, it has long been a favorite with children.

Roberts, Brigham Henry (b. England, March 13, 1857—d. Sept. 27, 1933), Mormon leader, historian, newspaperman, biographer. Roberts was brought to Utah in 1866 and became a leader of the Mormon Church. He worked on the Salt Lake City *Tribune* (1890–96) and served as an army chaplain in France (1918–19). He wrote *The Life of John Taylor* (1892); *New Witnesses for God* (3 v., 1895); *The Missouri Persecutions* (1900); *The Rise and Fall of Nauvoo* (1900); *A Comprehensive History of the Church of Jesus Christ of Latter Day Saints, Century I* (6 v., 1930).

Roberts, Sir Charles G[eorge] D[ouglas] (b. Douglas, N. Bruns., Jan. 10, 1860—d. Nov. 26, 1943), writer, teacher, editor. Roberts belonged to a distinguished literary family; his brother Theodore Goodridge Roberts was likewise a noted poet and novelist, and Bliss Carman was a first cousin. He edited *The Week* at Toronto, taught English and French literature, later economics, at King's College in Nova Scotia, was associate editor of the *Illustrated American* in New York City. He enlisted at the age of fifty-four to serve in World War I. In 1925 he resumed teaching at King's College.

When he published *Orion and Other Poems* (1880), Roberts, in the opinion of Canadian critics, began the modern era of Canadian literature. The book was strongly under English influence, but as Lorne Pierce pointed out, Roberts "sang the old songs in a new way . . . and proved that poetry was definitely taking root in Canadian soil." He was knighted in 1935. Roberts also wrote historical novels and stories about animals, usually against a background of Canadian nature. Among his novels one, *The Heart*

of *the Ancient Wood* (1900), "a deeply felt sylvan romance," may be reckoned a masterpiece. Among his books of poetry: *In Divers Tones* (1887); *Songs of the Common Day* (1893); *New York Nocturnes* (1898); *Collected Poems* (1900); *The Book of the Rose* (1903); *Selected Poems* (1936). His prose works include: *Earth's Enigmas* (1896); *A History of Canada* (1897); *The Forge in the Forest* (1897); *The Kindred of the Wild* (1902); *The Haunters of the Silences* (1907); *The Feet of the Furtive* (1912); *Children of the Wild* (1913); *Eyes of the Wilderness* (1933). James Cappon wrote an account of Roberts (1905) for the "Makers of Canadian Literature" series; E. M. Pomeroy reappraised him in a similar volume (1943).

Roberts, Elizabeth Madox (b. Perrysville, Ky., 1886—d. March 13, 1941), poet, novelist. Miss Roberts spent her youth in Kentucky and in the mountains of Colorado. Ill health delayed her schooling. It was not until 1921 that she graduated from the University of Chicago; the same year she won the Fiske Prize for poetry. Although she won two more prizes in 1928 and 1931 and published two books of verse, *Under the Tree* (1922) and *Song in the Meadow* (1940), she is known primarily for her prose. *The Time of Man* (1926), a moving and poetic novel of frontier life, was followed by MY HEART AND MY FLESH (1927), a study of the decay of a southern family. THE GREAT MEADOW (1930) was described by Carl Van Doren as "the richest and loveliest of all narratives of the settlement of Kentucky." But Granville Hicks found it and *A Buried Treasure* (1931) "diffuse and overwritten." *The Haunted Mirror* (1932), a collection of short stories, was followed by *He Sent Forth a Raven* (1935), a venture into mysticism. *Black is My Truelove's Hair* (1938), a story as simple as the folk ballad from which its title derives, scored a popular success. Edward Wagenknecht says that Miss Roberts' poetic insight and method were at once her greatest gifts as a novelist and her sharpest limitation. H. M. Campbell and R. E. Foster wrote *Elizabeth Madox Roberts: American Novelist* (1956). They regard her as more than a regionalist and select *The Time of Man* and *The Great Meadow* as her best books.

Roberts, Kenneth [Lewis] (b. Kennebunk, Me., Dec. 8, 1885—d. July 21, 1957), newspaperman, editor, translator, author. Roberts, a voluminous writer, loved battle, engaged lustily in controversy about his concept of American history and just as eagerly over whether it is possible to discover underground sources of water by waving a wooden wand ("dowsing"). Robert P. T. Coffin called him "a quicksilver mind among the leaden historians, a running almanac and encyclopedia of Maine from cookery to colonial wars." In the latter characterization he was no doubt thinking of Roberts' stimulating volume *Trending Into Maine* (1938) and his *Good Maine Food* (with Marjorie Mosser, 1939). In *I Wanted to Write* (1949) Roberts compiled a sort of autobiography in which he not only described his literary apprenticeship and early struggles but also vented his extensive dislikes and prejudices.

Some of the best historical novels in American literature came from his vigorous and vivid pen. Among them are: ARUNDEL (1930); *The Lively Lady* (1931); RABBLE IN ARMS (1933); NORTHWEST PASSAGE (1937); OLIVER WISWELL (1940); LYDIA BAILEY (1947). He made use of journals of some of the men who accompanied Benedict Arnold to Canada in writing *Arundel;* later he compiled and edited these journals as *March to Quebec* (1939). He and Mrs. Roberts did an excellent translation (1947) from the French of Morceau de St. Méry's *Voyage aux États-Unis d'Amérique*. Later historical works were *Boon Island* (1956) and *The Battle of Cowpens* (posthumously pub., 1958). The *Kenneth Roberts Reader* was issued in 1945. Two pamphlets brought out by Roberts' publisher give much interesting information: *Kenneth Roberts: A Biographical Sketch* (1936) and *Kenneth Roberts: An American Novelist* (1938).

Roberts, [George Edward] Theodore Goodrich (b. Fredericton, N. Bruns., July 7, 1877— d. Feb. 24, 1953), poet, novelist. Roberts' career was long and distinguished, as befits a member of his well-known family. The family's history is described in Lloyd Roberts' *The Book of Roberts*. Theodore Goodrich Roberts was a journalist, writing for the *Newfoundland Magazine* and serving as special correspondent for the New York *Independent* in the Spanish-American War. During World War I, Roberts was a captain in the Canadian army; he wrote several volumes of military history. In his poetry he employed traditional forms, including the ballad in English folk speech. The poems usually evoke the atmosphere of the seacoast in the Canadian Maritime Provinces, where he spent the greater part of his life. The same setting provided the backgrounds for most of his thirty romantic novels, among them: *The Red Feathers* (1907); *The Wasp* (1914); and *Stranger From Up Along* (1924). His poetry includes *Northland Lyrics* (1899); *The Lost Shipmate* (1926); and *The Leather Bottle* (1934).

Roberts, W[alter] Adolphe (b. Jamaica, Oct. 15, 1886—   ), newspaperman, author, editor. Roberts began as a reporter on Jamaican papers, then joined the staff of the New York *Tribune*. Later he edited *Ainslee's Magazine*, the *American Parade*, and *Brief Stories*. In World War I he covered the front for the Brooklyn *Eagle*. His verse was collected in *Pierrot Wounded and Other Poems* (1919) and *Pan and Peacocks* (1928). He wrote several novels, mostly set in South America and New Orleans. His factual books about the West Indies are especially noteworthy, including *Lands of the Inner Sea* (1948); *Six Great Jamaicans* (1952); *Havana: The Portrait of a City* (1953); *Jamaica: The Portrait of an Island* (1955).

Robertson, Frank C[hester] (b. Moscow, Idaho, Jan. 12, 1890—   ), farmer, author of western novels, stories, articles. Robertson's family grew up on the fringes of the Rocky Mountain frontier and was always on the go. His parents were converted by Mormon missionaries. In 1914 Robertson "located" a homestead and farmed it until 1922, when he wrote and sold his first story. His writings since then include more than a thousand short stories and more than 150 books. The latter are regarded as well above average in literary merit and authenticity and have been translated into many languages. In *A Ram in the Thicket* (1950) Robertson told his own story, a sincere, modest narrative. He was elected president (1959–60) of Western Writers of America. Among his better-known books: *Foreman of the Forty-Bar* (1925); *Fall of Buffalo Horn* (1928); *The Hidden Cabin* (1929); *Riders of the Sunset Trail* (1930); *The Mormon Trail* (1931); *Forbidden Trails* (1935); *The Pride of Pine Creek* (1938); *Longhorns of Hate* (1949); *Wrangler on the Prod* (1950); *Saddle on a Cloud* (1952); *Cruel Winds of Winter* (1954); *Life and Times of Soapy Smith* (1961). Robertson also conducts a syndicated newspaper column, "The Chopping Block."

Robertson, Morgan [Andrew] (b. Oswego, N.Y., Sept. 30, 1861—d. March 24, 1915), short-story writer. After a few years of schooling Robertson went to sea as a cabin boy; from 1877 until 1886 he was in the merchant service. He then enrolled at Cooper Union, learned the jewelry trade, and opened his own shop in a small coastal town in Maine. His eyes suffered from the close work, however, and he began to write sea stories for English and American magazines. Although his stories were better than average, he was never able to command a good price for them, and in consequence suffered greatly from debt. Bad luck dogged him. Finally he was no longer able to write at all. Some months later IRVIN S. COBB learned through his friend Bozeman Bulger, a free-lance writer, that Robertson and his wife were penniless in a room on the edge of Harlem. The two samaritans raised enough money to set Robertson and his wife on their feet, but Robertson seemed unable to earn a living. Cobb and Bulger secured the copyrights for Robertson's earlier books and contemplated a special edition, each volume with a foreword by such writers as Rex Beach, Booth Tarkington, and George Ade. When Robertson confessed that all his life he had longed for a fur coat and a gold-headed cane, Cobb and Bulger managed to obtain these for him, secondhand and somewhat battered. Not long afterwards Robertson was found dead in a shabby hotel in Atlantic City, seated before a window that looked over the sea and with his fur coat about his shoulders and his cane across his knees. Today he is regarded as one of the finest writers of sea stories in English. Among his collections of short stories: *Futility* (1898); *Spun Yarn* (1898); *Shipmates* (1901); *Sinful Peck* (1903); *Down to the Sea* (1905); *Land Ho!* (1905); *Masters of Men* (1914). One of his best tales is *The Derelict Neptune* from *Spun Yarn*.

Robins, Elizabeth [1]. See JOSEPH STANLEY PENNELL [1].

Robins, Elizabeth [2] ["C. E. Raimond"] (b.

Louisville, Ky., 1865[?]—d. May 8, 1952), actress, novelist, feminist. At sixteen Miss Robins left a school in Zanesville, Ohio, for the stage. On the death of her young actor-husband, she was taken to Norway by Mrs. Ole Bull, wife of the great Norwegian violinist, and there she made an intensive study of Ibsen. Not long afterward she settled in London, where she became acquainted with Oscar Wilde, Henry James, and George Bernard Shaw. She was the first woman to play *Hedda Gabler* in London; she also played a number of other Ibsen roles. Perhaps as the result of her many literary friendships, Miss Robins decided to write. Under the pen name of C. E. Raimond she published *Below the Salt* (1896); *The Open Question* (1898); and *The Magnetic North* (1904). She abandoned her pen name when she turned to feminist writing. She dramatized her novel *The Convert* (1906) as *Votes for Women* (1906). *My Little Sister* (1913), the story of a well-born girl who was abducted and forced into prostitution, was so alarming that many readers wrote to newspapers demanding an investigation of the white slave traffic. *Theater and Friendship* (1932), a volume of letters written by Henry James to Miss Robins and containing autobiographical notes by her, was followed by *Both Sides of the Curtain* (1940), an autobiography.

Robinson, Charles (b. Hardwick, Mass., July 21, 1818—d. Aug. 17, 1894), physician, welfare worker, political leader, public official. After practicing medicine in Massachusetts, Robinson went to California, where he tried to prevent the introduction of slavery. He returned to Massachusetts to resume his medical practice, but was sent to Kansas as an agent of the New England Emigrant Aid Committee and there became the leader of the Free-State group. In 1856 he was chosen governor, but was arrested and imprisoned on a charge of treason and usurpation. In 1861 he was again elected governor, later served in the state senate. He was a generous benefactor of the state university. While residing in Sacramento he founded and edited the *Settlers' and Miners' Tribune*. He wrote *Kansas: Its Interior and Exterior Life* (1856) and *The Kansas Conflict* (1892).

Robinson, Edwin Arlington (b. Head Tide, Me., Dec. 22, 1869—d. April 6, 1935), poet. Gardiner, Me., where his family moved shortly after his birth, is really Robinson's home town, celebrated under the name of "Tilbury Town" in his poetry. Here the boy Edwin led a quiet life; in high school he was disciplined in verse writing by Dr. A. T. Schumann, an amateur poet interested in the French forms. Later he went on to Harvard University, but did not complete the undergraduate course. He was called home because of his father's failing health, and returned to Gardiner suffering from an old ear injury and obsessed by the sense of failure that had dogged him from childhood. In 1896 he published his first book of poems at his own expense, *The Torrent and the Night Before*. Republished with changes the following year at the expense of a friend, the 1897 edition (called THE CHILDREN

OF THE NIGHT) is now considered Robinson's first "public" volume.

At this point he fell into a pattern which was never really broken, a pattern of restlessness, financial insecurity, loneliness relieved only by a

The Macmillan Company

few friends, periods of depression in which he resorted to alcohol. He went to New York in 1897, returned to Harvard (as a clerk, not a student) in 1898, went again to New York the next year. *Captain Craig* (see THE BOOK OF ANNANDALE) appeared in 1902, backed by John Hays Gardiner and Mrs. Laura Richards. Robinson was working in the subway, making just enough to keep going. Good luck beckoned when Theodore Roosevelt, then in the White House, became interested in Robinson's work and secured for the poet a sinecure in the New York Custom House at $2,000 a year. With the coming of the Taft administration (1909), however, Robinson felt he must resign his government position. The following year he brought out his third book of verse, *The Town Down the River*.

In the summer of 1911 Robinson made his first visit to the MacDowell colony at Peterboro, N.H., and found it such an inviting place to work that he returned each summer until his death. The first book of verse to come out of these summers was THE MAN AGAINST THE SKY (1916). MERLIN, the first of three long Arthurian poems, appeared in 1917. LANCELOT and *The Three Taverns* followed in 1920. AVON'S HAR-

VEST was published in 1921, the same year in which his first *Collected Poems* received a Pulitzer prize. Though now recognized as an important poet, Robinson was still largely dependent on his friends for a livelihood.

Peterboro in the summer, Boston in the spring and fall, New York in the winter—this became Robinson's routine. TRISTRAM, in 1927, brought him at last wide fame and a certain measure of financial independence, thanks to Carl Van Doren and the Literary Guild. Robinson devoted the rest of his life to the writing of long narrative poems, struggling in this way to retain his hold on financial security, but his narratives are generally thought by critics to be inferior to his earlier short poems. He entered New York Hospital in January, 1935, suffering from cancer, and died three months later, just after completing the proofreading of his final work, *King Jasper*. His ashes were buried in Gardiner.

In addition to the collections of verse already mentioned, Robinson wrote: *Roman Bartholow* (1923); THE MAN WHO DIED TWICE (1924); DIONYSUS IN DOUBT (1925); CAVENDER'S HOUSE (1929); *The Glory of the Nightingales* (1930); *Matthias at the Door* (1931); *Nicodemus* (1932); TALIFER (1933); *Amaranth* (1934). His *Collected Poems* appeared in 1937. A selection, TILBURY TOWN, was issued in 1953. The *Selected Letters,* edited by Ridgely Torrence, appeared in 1940, and another selection, edited by Denham Sutcliffe, in 1947. The two best bibliographies are Charles B. Hogan's *A Bibliography of Edwin Arlington Robinson* (1936) and Lillian Lippincott's *A Bibliography of the Writings and Criticisms of Edwin Arlington Robinson* (1937). Colby College has a collection of letters as well as some of the poet's books and personal belongings. Yale University has a small collection of letters. The most important collection of letters (about 2,500) is at Harvard. The Lewis M. Isaacs collection of Robinson materials is at the New York Public Library.

Robinson's faults were many: too often his poetry was obscure, owing to unfinished thinking, a lack of concrete imagery, or indirectness of statement; it failed generally in lyricism, though occasional bursts reveal a fine ear for metrical effects; it needed vigor. Robinson inclined toward verbosity and circumlocution, perhaps a compensation for his inarticulateness in private life. But at a time when American poetry was at a low ebb Robinson introduced a new honesty, concentration, austerity, and dignity, a precision and plainness of diction, which his successors made into a poetic renaissance. In a career which began in a time of flowery sentimentality and ended in the midst of untrammeled experimentation, Robinson himself stayed close to the conventions of form and technique; his short poems are mostly rhymed lyrics sometimes reminiscent of the 17th-century Metaphysicals, and his long poems are in rather rugged blank verse. Although Robinson denied that he was a pessimist, much of his best work deals with the themes of failure and alienation, in which the hope of the future is very nearly sub-

merged. Yet in his best and most popular short poems—*Eros Turannos, The Mill, Hillcrest, The Sheaves, Luke Havergal, The Clerks*—Robinson's stylistic strength and integrity produce an affirmative effect.

Biographical and critical studies of Robinson have been published by Ben Ray Redman (1926), Mark Van Doren (1927), Hermann Hagedorn (1938), Yvor Winters (1947), Emery E. Neff (1948), Ellsworth Barnard (1952), Edwin S. Fussell (1954). For individual poems see under title entries. See also LOUIS V. LEDOUX; UNTRIANGULATED STARS; and entries for the poems BEN JONSON ENTERTAINS A MAN FROM STRATFORD; DEMOS AND DIONYSUS; FLAMMONDE; HOW ANNANDALE WENT OUT; MINIVER CHEEVY; MR. FLOOD'S PARTY; RICHARD CORY; VETERAN SIRENS.

RICHARD CROWDER

Robinson, Edwin Meade. See TED ROBINSON.

Robinson, Harriet Jane Hanson (b. Boston, Feb. 8, 1825—d. Dec. 22, 1911), novelist, memoirist, woman suffragist. Mrs. Robinson was in her youth a mill worker in Lowell, Mass. She became deeply interested in woman suffrage in her later years, and wrote as propaganda *Captain Mary Miller* (1887) and *The New Pandora* (1889). She also wrote *Loom and Spindle; or Life Among the Early Mill Girls* (1898).

Robinson, Henry Morton (b. Boston, Sept. 7, 1898—d. Jan. 13, 1961), teacher, editor, poet, novelist, critic. At first an English teacher at Columbia University, Robinson became a freelance writer. He published three verse collections: *Buck Fever* (1929); *Second Wisdom* (1936); and *The Enchanted Grindstone and Other Poems* (1952). Verse was perhaps Robinson's favorite and natural medium. In 1935 he became an associate editor of *Reader's Digest*, in 1942 a senior editor. *A Skeleton Key to Finnegans Wake* (with Joseph Campbell, 1944) established him as a Joyce authority. His novels *The Perfect Round* (1945) and *The Great Snow* (1947) were widely read. His next novel, THE CARDINAL (1950), was a best seller over a long period. Prominent Catholic prelates appear in the story, and some critics guessed that Robinson had based his main character on the late William Cardinal O'Connell of Boston. His last novel was *Water of Life* (1960).

Robinson, James Harvey (b. Bloomington, Ill., June 29, 1863—d. Feb. 16, 1936), teacher, historian. After traveling in Europe and spending a year in business in Bloomington, Robinson decided to go to Harvard University. He graduated in 1887, studied in Germany, and received a doctorate from the University of Freiburg in 1890. The following year he became professor of European history and assistant editor of the *Annals of the American Academy of Political and Social Science at the University of Pennsylvania*. From 1895 until 1919 he taught at Columbia University, where his courses became famous. Irwin Edman, one of his students, said history as presented by Robinson was not dates and names, but "the changing fashions of adult follies taken seriously in various ages." His great heroes were Lucretius, who saw religion as diabolism; Francis Bacon, who foresaw the human potentialities of science; and Voltaire, who showed the folly of superstition. In 1919 Robinson resigned in protest against the unfair treatment of certain Columbia professors who were opposed to World War I. He helped to found the New School for Social Research, where he taught until 1921. After the success of his remarkable book *The Mind in the Making* (1921), which some critics consider one of the most influential books of our time, he resigned to devote himself to writing. Robinson's other principal works are: *Introduction to the History of Western Europe* (1903); *The Development of Modern Europe* (1907, with C. A. BEARD); *The New History* (1911, essays); *The Middle Period of European History* (1915); *Medieval and Modern Times* (1916); *The Relation of Intelligence to Social Reform* (1921); *The Humanizing of Knowledge* (1923); and *The Ordeal of Civilization* (1926).

Robinson, Rowland Evans (b. Ferrisburg, Vt., May 14, 1833—d. Oct. 15, 1900), wood carver, cartoonist, writer. Robinson's work as an engraver and cartoonist greatly impaired his eyesight and in 1893 brought on total blindness. He was, however, a prolific writer, at first on sports and country life, later in other fields. For a time he served as an editor of *Forest and Stream.* He was at his best in portraying and interpreting the folkways and humor of a pioneer Vermont community. UNCLE LISHA, a shoemaker and the autocrat of a convivial group, appears in several of his books, including *Uncle Lisha's Shop: Life in a Corner of Yankeeland* (1887; semicentennial ed., 1933); *Sam Lovel's Camps: Uncle Lisha's Friends Under Bark and Canvas* (1889); *Uncle Lisha's Outing* (1897). He also wrote *Forest and Stream* (1886); *Vermont: A Study of Independence* (1892); *In New England's Fields and Woods* (1896); *A Hero of Ticonderoga* (1898; reprinted, 1934); *Hunting Without a Gun and Other Papers* (1905); *Silver Fields and Sketches of a Farmer-Sportsman* (1921). The Centennial Edition of his writings (7 v., 1933–36) includes other books in addition to those mentioned above, also some theretofore uncollected pieces.

Robinson, Solon (b. Tolland, Conn., Oct. 21, 1803—d. Nov. 3, 1880), farmer, writer, public official. Robinson was an energetic person, well acquainted with many people, places, and vocations. He was particularly interested in agricultural problems, visited many states to observe rural conditions, himself ran a farm, wrote numerous reports and articles, published a magazine called *The Plow,* and was farm editor of the New York *Tribune.* He also wrote fiction and verse. Among his books: *Guano: A Treatise of Practical Information for Farmers* (1852); *Hot Corn-Life Scenes in N.Y.* (1854); *Facts for Farmers* (1864); *How to Live: Saving and Wasting; or, Domestic Economy Illustrated by the Life of Two Families of Opposite Character*

(a novel, 1873). *Selected Writings* of Robinson were edited by H. A. Kellar (2 v., 1936).

Robinson, Ted [Edwin Meade] (b. Lima [now Howe], Ind., Nov. 1, 1878—d. Sept. 20, 1946), poet, teacher, newspaperman. Robinson worked for Indianapolis papers, then for the Cleveland *Leader,* finally for the Cleveland *Plain Dealer.* He began conducting a column for the *Leader* in 1905, became nationally known through his "Philosophy of Folly" column in the *Plain Dealer.* He published several collections of verse, including *Mere Melodies* (1918); *Piping and Panning* (1920); *Life, Love, and the Weather* (1945). He was adept with rhythm and rhyme and clever in phrasing.

Rochambeau, Jean Baptiste Donatien de Vimeur, Comte de (b. France, July 1, 1725—d. May 10, 1807), soldier, memoirist. At seventeen Rochambeau entered the French army, early became a colonel. In 1780 he was sent, with 6,000 men, to aid the Americans in the Revolution. He remained for a year at Newport, R.I., then joined Washington for the march on Yorktown. While the French fleet controlled the Chesapeake, Washington and Rochambeau took Yorktown and forced Cornwallis to surrender. After the war Rochambeau returned to France and served in the French Revolution. Later Napoleon made him an officer in the Legion of Honor. Rochambeau's *Mémoires* (1890) were translated in part into English by W. E. Wright as *Memoirs of the Marshall Count de Rochambeau Relative to the War of Independence of the United States* (1838). Jean Jules Jusserand wrote *Rochambeau in America* (1916).

Roche, James Jeffrey (b. Ireland, May 31, 1847—d. April 3, 1908), journalist, consul, writer. Roche's family migrated to Prince Edward Island, where he was educated by his father and at St. Dunstan's College. In 1866 he moved to Boston and served as assistant editor of the Boston *Pilot,* a Catholic journal. Seven years later he succeeded John Boyle O'Reilly as editor. His first novel, *The Story of the Filibusters* (1891), was reprinted ten years later as *By-Ways of War;* it was highly praised by Richard Harding Davis. With Lady Gregory, Douglas Hyde, and others he helped prepare *Irish Literature* (1904). In 1904 Roche was appointed consul to Genoa by Theodore Roosevelt, later was consul at Berne. In 1891 he published a *Life of John Boyle O'Reilly.* Among his books of humorous verse: *Songs and Satires* (1886); *Ballads of Blue Water and Other Poems* (1895); *Her Majesty the King: A Romance of the Harem* (1898); *The V-a-s-e and Other Bric-a-Brac* (1900); *The Sorrows of Sap'ed* (1904).

Rock-a-Bye, Baby (1887), a song by Effie I. Canning Carlton. Mrs. Carlton (1874[?]–1940) was an actress. In 1886 she set to music a variation of the words of the old Mother Goose jingle; it was sung for the first time in Denman Thompson's *The Old Homestead* (1887) and was published in Boston. Since then the music has varied in different versions, but all are based on Mrs. Carlton's original.

Rocked in the Cradle of the Deep (1831), a hymn by EMMA WILLARD. The poem was written at sea and some years later was set to music by the English clergyman and composer Joseph Philip Knight (1812–1887). "A boon to the basso profundo," Sigmund Spaeth calls it. It became a favorite in Negro minstrel shows; its only rival in its special type, says Spaeth, is Arthur Lamp and H. W. Petrie's *Asleep in the Deep* (1898).

Rockefeller, John D[avison], Sr. (b. Richford, N.Y., July 8, 1839—d. May 23, 1937), industrialist, philanthropist. Rockefeller entered the oil business in 1861, gradually absorbed many oil refineries in Cleveland, and in January, 1870, formed the Standard Oil Company with himself as the largest stockholder. A ruthless entrepreneur, by 1882 he had acquired an almost complete control of the oil business. But one court decision after another somewhat reduced his empire, especially after the publication of Ida M. Tarbell's *History of the Standard Oil Company* (1904). In 1911 Rockefeller retired as head of the company. Thereafter his life was devoted to worthy causes—and to a rehabilitation of his reputation. Among his important beneficiaries were the University of Chicago (established by him in 1892), the Rockefeller Foundation, the Laura Spelman Rockefeller Memorial, and the Rockefeller Institute for Medical Research. His *Random Reminiscences* appeared in 1935.

From 1911 on his son, John D[avison] Rockefeller, Jr. (1874–1960), took charge of the family business interests and expanded them far beyond the oil industry. The Rockefeller family's most notable industrial achievement was the building of Rockefeller Center (or Radio City) in New York City. The younger Rockefeller's philanthropies have included donations to the Museum of Modern Art and the remarkable rebuilding of Williamsburg, Va. He wrote about *The Colorado Industrial Plan* (1916) and *The Personal Relation in Industry* (1924). All of his sons have been active in philanthropies, and some in public service.

Books about John D. Rockefeller, Sr., include H. D. Lloyd's *Wealth Against Commonwealth* (1894); John K. Winkler's *John D.: A Portrait in Oils* (1929); John T. Flynn's *God's Gold* (1932). Allan Nevins' *John D. Rockefeller* (2 v., 1940) was revised in 1953 as *Study in Power: John D. Rockefeller, Industrialist and Philanthropist*. Raymond B. Fosdick wrote *John D. Rockefeller, Jr.: A Portrait* (1956), and Nancy Newhall wrote *A Contribution to the Heritage of Every American: The Conservation Activities of John D. Rockefeller* [Jr.] (1957).

Rock Me to Sleep, Mother (*Saturday Evening Post*, 1860), a poem by ELIZABETH AKERS. It first appeared under the pseudonym Florence Percy, later in her *Poems* (1866) under her own name, again in *The Sunset Song and Other Verses* (1902). The most persistent competitor for the honor of having written the poem was a certain Alexander M. W. Ball. Ernest Leslie composed the musical setting.

Rockwell, Norman (b. New York City, Feb. 3, 1894—   ), illustrator. Noted particularly for his magazine covers and story illustrations, especially in the *Saturday Evening Post*, Rockwell won a national reputation for his skill in depicting the common man and familiar scenes. His pictures, filled with homely, recognizable detail, are more remarkable for storytelling qualities than for artistic merit, though he is represented in the Metropolitan Museum of Art. Arthur L. Guptill wrote a genial biography and interpretation, *Norman Rockwell, Illustrator* (1946). His autobiography, *My Adventures as an Illustrator*, was published in 1960 and ran serially in the *Saturday Evening Post*.

Rocky Mountain region. The Rocky Mountains extend for more than four thousand miles from the Mexican frontier to the Arctic in Canadian territory. In the United States Colorado, Utah, Nevada, Wyoming, Montana, and Idaho are included in this area. Highest peak in this range within the United States is Mt. Ebert in Colorado; the state contains 1,064 peaks exceeding 10,000 feet in height. The Rockies form the Continental Divide separating Pacific drainage from Atlantic (Gulf of Mexico) and Arctic drainage. They contain rich mineral deposits, fertile mountain pastures, forest wealth, and provide a refuge for much wild life. They are a great reservoir of water and power. In the United States Rockies are Yellowstone, Glacier, Grand Teton, and Rocky Mountain National Parks.

In 1540 Coronado's scouts penetrated into the region, where the Pueblo Indians had a notable civilization. There were other Spanish explorers at the beginning of the 18th century; French explorers came from Canada in 1742. But the mountain area was not very well known until the United States acquired part of it by the Louisiana Purchase, and the Lewis and Clark Expedition (see MERIWETHER LEWIS) explored it (1805–06). Their *Journal* has many references to the region, which was soon familiar to the fur traders and trappers who, along with missionaries, entered it in large numbers during the early decades of the 19th century. In 1847 the Mormons found their Zion here and introduced irrigation. After the Mexican War the United States obtained title to the whole region. Settlements were set up in portions that later became states, especially when miners who had made no finds in California came back to Colorado, Nevada, Idaho, and Montana and made discoveries as rich as those in the Pacific state. Then began a new mythology, that of the mountain miners, with Mark Twain, Bret Harte, and others as their chroniclers. The wealth of the region increased and with it a deepening interest in the arts. The states and their people are individualists, with some distrust of the capitalist East.

Mark Twain's ROUGHING IT (1872) is the literary classic of the region; in the days of the great silver-mining boom, Twain got his literary start working on the Virginia City (Nev.) *Territorial Enterprise*, now successfully and picturesquely revived by Lucius Beebe. More recent writers on the region include Lew Sarett, Vardis Fisher, Walter Van Tilburg Clark, Bernard De Voto, Wallace Stegner, Clyde Brion Davis, and A. B. Guthrie, Jr. Anthologies and nonfiction include Levette Jay Davidson and Prudence Bostwick's *The Literature of the Rocky Mountain West, 1803–1903* (1939); Ray B. West, Jr.'s *Rocky Mountain Reader* (1946); Levette Davidson and Forrester Blake's *Rocky Mountain Tales* (1947); David Lavender's *The Big Divide* (1949); *Rocky Mountain Cities* (a symposium, 1949); Elvin L. Howe's *Rocky Mountain Empire* (1950); Morris E. Carnsey's *America's New Frontier: The Mountain West* (1950); Albert N. Williams' *Rocky Mountain Country* (1950).

Roderick Hudson (1876), a novel by HENRY JAMES. This was James' first major work and was written after he had emigrated to Europe. The titular hero is a precocious sculptor from Massachusetts whom Rowland Hallett, a rich patron of the arts, takes abroad. Rowland expects Roderick to develop his talent under the influence of Classical sculpture. Roderick becomes engaged to Mary Garland before he leaves America but in Italy he falls passionately in love with the beautiful but inconstant Christina Light. Roderick abandons his art, in spite of his early success, to pursue Christina, even after she marries Prince Casamassima and travels to Switzerland. His patron denounces him, his fiancée joins him in Switzerland, yet Roderick is unable to recover his moral balance. He wanders off into the mountains during a storm and is found dead at the foot of a cliff. The ultimate tragedy is Rowland's. His hope that Mary would some day return his smoldering love for her is stifled under her silent accusation that he had abandoned Roderick. In this early novel James uses several techniques which characterize his later works: the point-of-view shifts but usually resides in Rowland's mind; the intricate but precise structure unifies the story; the style hints at the complexities of James' mature prose. James revised it extensively in later years. Christina reappears in THE PRINCESS CASAMASSIMA.

Rodgers, Richard (b. New York City, June 28, 1902—   ), composer. Rodgers has written charming and greatly varied music for a number of exceedingly popular musical comedies. Rodgers' collaboration with LORENZ HART began in the autumn of 1919 when he entered Columbia University, though they had met a year earlier. As a freshman, he wrote the music for the Varsity Show, the first freshman in Columbia's history to achieve this distinction. With Hart he created such hit shows as *A Connecticut Yankee* (1927), *I Married an Angel* (1937), *The Boys from Syracuse* (1938), *Pal Joey* (1940), and many others. His collaboration with OSCAR HAMMERSTEIN II began in 1942 when they turned Lynn Riggs' play GREEN GROW THE LILACS into a spectacularly successful folk opera, OKLAHOMA! (1943, Pulitzer prize). They went on to write *Carousel* (1945), based on Ferenc Molnár's *Liliom*; *South Pacific*

(1949), based on James A. Michener's TALES OF THE SOUTH PACIFIC (1949 New York Drama Critics Circle Award; 1950 Pulitzer prize); *The King and I* (1951); *Me and Juliet* (1953); *Flower Drum Song* (1958); *The Sound of Music* (1959). Most of these were later filmed. After Hammerstein's death, Rodgers supplied music and lyrics for *No Strings* (1962).

Among Rodgers' best known songs are "If I Loved You"; "This Can't Be Love"; "There's a Small Hotel"; "My Heart Stood Still"; "Oh, What a Beautiful Morning!"; "Some Enchanted Evening." *The Rodgers and Hart Song Book* was issued in 1951, *Six Plays* by Rodgers and Hammerstein in 1955. Deems Taylor's *Some Enchanted Evenings* (1953) is an account of the latter partnership.

Rodman, Selden (b. New York City, Feb. 19, 1909—   ), art critic, writer, editor. Rodman has been co-director of the remarkable Centre d'Art in Port-au-Prince; he was also a pioneer in encouraging Haitian primitive artists and has written two enthusiastic and stimulating books on Haiti: *Renaissance in Haiti* (1948) and *Haiti: the Black Republic* (1954). As a poet he pioneered in writing about air flight in *The Airmen* (1941). Among his other works are *Lawrence: The Last Crusade* (1937); *The Revolutionists* (a play, 1942); *The Amazing Year: A Diary in Verso* (1947); *Portrait of the Artist as an American* (1951); *The Eye of Man: Form and Content in Western Painting* (1955); *Conversations with Artists* (1957). He has also edited several verse anthologies.

Roe, E[dward] P[ayson] (b. New Windsor, N.Y., March 7, 1838—d. July 19, 1888), clergyman, novelist. Roe was ordained in 1862, was a chaplain during the Civil War, and served as minister to the Highland Falls Presbyterian Church for eight years. His curiosity and compassion were aroused by reports of the great Chicago fire of 1872. He visited the city, examined the ruins, and wrote his first novel, *Barriers Burned Away*, as a magazine serial. It was published in book form in 1872 and became an immediate best seller, one of the greatest in American literary history. His second novel, *Opening a Chestnut Burr* (1874), was so favorably received that Roe resigned his pastorate to devote himself to writing. He published seventeen more novels, most of them best sellers. Among his other titles are *From Jest to Earnest* (1875); *A Knight of the Nineteenth Century* (1877); *A Face Illumined* (1878); *Without A Home* (1881); *A Young Girl's Wooing* (1884); *Driven Back to Eden* (1885); *He Fell in Love with His Wife* (1886); *Found Yet Lost* (1888). *Play and Profit in My Garden* (1873) and *A Manual on the Culture of Small Fruits* (1880) showed his interest in horticulture. His sister Mary A. Roe wrote *EPR, Reminiscences of His Life* (1899).

Roethke, Theodore (b. Saginaw, Mich., May 25, 1908—d. Aug. 1, 1963), poet. Roethke taught at Lafayette College, Pennsylvania State, Bennington College, and the University of Washington. His poems have been collected in *Open*

House (1941); *The Lost Son and Other Poems* (1948); *Praise to the End!* (1951); *The Waking* (1953); WORDS FOR THE WIND (1958). His poems fall into two categories: those written in strict forms and employing generally witty and

Imogen Cunningham

rational modes of thought and those in free forms using irrational, sometimes surrealistic modes of thought. Among the latter are some remarkable evocations of childhood and old age. Roethke's father was a flower-grower, and the poet's childhood was deeply influenced by experiences in the greenhouse, experiences which emerge very often in the horticultural imagery of his poems. They are strong poems, strikingly original and frequently deeply moving. Roethke, who was awarded a Pulitzer prize in 1954 and the Bollingen Prize in 1958, is certainly among the foremost American poets of his generation.

Roger Malvin's Burial (*The Token*, 1832; collected in *Mosses from an Old Manse*, 1846), a story by NATHANIEL HAWTHORNE. The background of this story is the battle described in the old ballad of *Lovewell's Flight*, which, together with a prose document, Hawthorne uses to start his narrative. He relates how Roger Malvin and Reuben Bourne, the young man betrothed to Malvin's daughter Dorcas, are returning wounded from the battle. The older man knows he must die soon and begs Reuben to go on without him. But he exacts a pledge that Reuben will return and give him proper burial. Reuben fails to fulfill his promise and all through the

years is a moody, stricken man. Much later, through personal tragedy, the curse is removed. The tale seems like a morbid phantasm of Puritan conscience, with the whole cosmos working to inflict retribution. See also HUGH GLASS; JOHN LOVEWELL.

Rogers, Bruce (b. Lafayette, Ind., May 14, 1870—d. May 18, 1957), book designer. Rogers started in the art department of the Indianapolis *News*, worked with printing firms and publishers as an expert in type and page design. He received numerous awards for his skill in design and his keen aesthetic sense. Many limited editions issuing from various presses were designed by him. In 1953 appeared his *PI: A Hodge-Podge of the Letters, Papers, and Addresses Written during the Last 60 Years*. The book has humor as well as a notable mass of technical information. In 1955 he designed *Printing as an Art* for the Harvard University Press.

Rogers, J[oel] A[ugustus] (b. Jamaica, 1883—), free-lance writer. Self-educated, Rogers came to know many lands in Europe, Asia, and Africa and wrote about them in such books as *The Maroons of the West Indies and South America* (1921). He contributed to the *American Mercury, The Crisis*, the *Survey Graphic*, and the *Journal of Negro History*. Among his other books: *From Superman to Man* (1917; reissued, 1941) and *The Greatest Men of African Descent* (1931).

Rogers, Joel Townsley (b. Sedalia, Mo., Nov. 22, 1896—), poet, mystery writer. Rogers attended Harvard and Princeton universities and obtained his A.B. degree *cum laude* from Harvard in 1917. For two years after college he served in naval aviation, and from 1922 to 1925 he was editor of Brentano's *Book Chat*. In 1927 he began devoting his full time to free-lance writing. He is represented in *Eight More Harvard Poets* (first published in 1922, and reprinted several times since), and in the *Saturday Evening Post Treasury* (1954). His books include: *Once in a Red Moon* (1924); *The Red Right Hand* (1945), an unusual and well-received mystery novel; *Lady With the Dice* (1946); *The Stopped Clock* (1958); *The Cold Stone Heart* (1962).

Rogers, Robert (b. Methuen, Mass. [Dunbarton, N.H.?], Nov. 7, 1731—d. May 18, 1795), explorer, soldier, memoirist. Rogers was one of the great adventurers of American history, but a man of unstable character and doubtful morals. He loved hunting, fishing, and fighting, traded with the Indians and fought them. To escape prosecution for counterfeiting he enlisted as a scout and spy in the French and Indian War. He found favor with Sir William Johnson and became a *ranger*, a term denoting a soldier, usually mounted, whose business it was to range over an area for its protection, especially against Indians. Johnson placed Rogers in charge of a company of rangers, later of nine companies. He performed many daring and heroic deeds, helped capture Montreal, in 1763 assisted in putting down PONTIAC'S rebellion. He was a popular hero for his exploits against the Indians, but also engaged in illicit deals with them which left him heavily in debt.

In 1765 Rogers went to England, eager for political appointments and literary fame. He took three manuscripts, the first two published in 1765, the third in 1766. *A Concise Account of North America* gave, for the first time in English, a full account of the Old West, which Rogers had traversed on horse, on foot, and by canoe. His *Journals* (reprinted, 1883) are about his early years as a ranger. His play PONTEACH, OR, THE SAVAGES OF AMERICA is a curious work, the first known play to deal primarily with Indians. The hero, about whose tragic life Rogers wrote in blank verse of low merit, is Pontiac, against whom Rogers had fought but whom apparently he admired.

Rogers succeeded in getting himself appointed to a post at Mackinac from which he could send out exploring expeditions into the Northwest, but he was accused of dealing illegally with the French and aiming to set up a realm of his own. He was arrested by General Thomas Gage, tried by court-martial, acquitted, and in 1769 was again in England, where he sued General Gage unsuccessfully. In 1774 he went into the service of the Bey of Algiers. The following year he returned to America. He offered his services to both sides, but Washington had him arrested as a spy. He was paroled but nevertheless entered the service of the British as captain of a company of the Queen's American Rangers. He was defeated in a skirmish near White Plains, N.Y. In 1780 he returned to England, where he died in obscurity and poverty.

Kenneth Roberts built one of his best novels around Rogers: NORTHWEST PASSAGE (1937). The Queen's American Rangers appear in Frank Hough's *The Neutral Ground* (1941).

Rogers, Robert Cameron (b. Buffalo, N.Y., Jan. 7, 1862—d. April 20, 1912), poet. Rogers is remembered chiefly for his poem called "The Rosary" (1894), which appeared in *The Rosary and Other Poems* (1906) and was set to music by Ethelbert Nevin (1898). Rogers issued other collections, including *The Wind in the Clearing and Other Poems* (1895) and *For the King and Other Poems* (1899).

Rogers, Robert William (b. Philadelphia, Feb. 14, 1864—d. Dec. 12, 1930), teacher, Orientalist. Rogers was professor of Hebrew and Old Testament exegesis at the Drew Theological Seminary, also serving as professor of Oriental literature at Princeton University. He was a spirited teacher and an excellent lecturer. Among his books: *Outlines of the History of Early Babylonia* (1895); *A History of Babylonia and Assyria* (2 v., 1900); *The History and Literature of the Hebrew People* (2 v., 1917); *A History of Ancient Persia* (1929).

Rogers, Will[iam Penn Adair] (b. near Oologah, Indian Territory [now Okla.], Nov. 4, 1879—d. Aug. 15, 1935), rancher, actor, humorist. Rogers was one of the most striking and original figures to appear in American literature and on the American stage. He became a rancher, then sold his holdings to make a trip around the world. Partly of Indian blood, he joined a Wild West show in the Argentine in 1902 under the name of Cherokee Bill. He was a skilled horseman and an expert with the lasso; later his expertness became part of a vaudeville act in which the circlings of the lasso were interspersed with seemingly naïve, but in reality very shrewd, wisecracks. By 1905 he had reached New York, where he performed in Hammerstein's Roof Garden. In 1914 he became a leading member of the cast of the Ziegfeld Follies. His wisecracks became popular sayings and led to his starting a newspaper column (1926), speaking as a commentator on the air, and appearing in numerous motion pictures. In the latter he played characteristically homely roles and made sage and witty remarks; among these movies were *State Fair*, *A Connecticut Yankee*, *David Harum*, *Judge Priest*, *Lightnin'*, and *Steamboat Round the Bend*. He wrote a series of books: *The Cowboy Philosopher on Prohibition* (1919); *The Cowboy Philosopher on the Peace Conference* (1919); *What We Laugh At* (1920); *The Illiterate Digest* (1924); *Letters of a Self-Made Diplomat to His President* (1927); *There's Not a Bathing-Suit in Russia* (1927); *Will Rogers' Political Follies* (1929). An early enthusiast for aviation, he was killed in an airplane accident while flying in Alaska with the noted aviator Wiley Post. In 1949 Donald Day made a selection from his writings that was called *The Autobiography of Will Rogers*. It revealed him, as Catherine Brown said, as a liberal, prophet, humorist, philosopher, friend, and citizen of the world. Day also compiled selections from Rogers' newspaper columns in *Sanity Is Where You Find It* (1955).

Rogers' movie directors never bothered to write a script for his dialogue. He was given free rein and allowed to say what seemed the right thing; similarly his remarks on the stage varied from day to day. He was a brilliant exponent of the cracker-barrel tradition in American humor and spoke in a rustic dialect of indeterminate origin. He made frequent remarks on current politics; "I don't make jokes," he asserted, "I just watch the government and report the facts." He is said to have wagered that he could make Calvin Coolidge laugh the first time he met him. When he was taken to the White House and introduced to the President, he leaned over politely and asked, "What's the name, please?" He won his bet. A favorite quip was: "No, my ancestors didn't come over on the *Mayflower*. But they met the boat." Perhaps his most famous "Rogerism" was his conclusion that "the United States never lost a war or won a conference." "When I die," he once said, "my epitaph, or whatever you call those signs on gravestones, is going to read, 'I joked about every prominent man of my time, but I never met a man I didn't like.'"

Several books about Rogers have been written by people who knew him—P. J. O'Brien's *Will Rogers* (1935); Jack Lait's *Our Will Rogers* (1936); Homer Croy's *Our Will Rogers* (1953).

A movie, *The Story of Will Rogers,* in which his son, Will Rogers, Jr., played the leading role, was produced in 1952.

Rohlfs, Mrs. Charles. Married name of ANNA KATHARINE GREEN.

Roland Blake (1886), a novel by S. WEIR MITCHELL. Although Dr. Mitchell was an excellent storyteller, adept in using history as a background, he always remained the experienced physician with a special interest in psychology. This novel exemplifies his varied talents. It gives a realistic picture of the Civil War, especially the Wilderness Campaign, and tells a story with spirit. But its chief achievement is its portrait of a neurotic woman, Octopia Darnell; it was one of the earliest studies in American fiction of a Lesbian.

Rolfe, John (b. England, 1585—d. 1622), colonist. In 1609 Rolfe sailed for Virginia with his bride. After her death he began to experiment with Indian tobacco, and succeeded in producing a variety that was "pleasant, sweet, and strong." The sale of tobacco brought prosperity to Virginia and insured the permanent settlement there. In 1613 Rolfe fell in love with POCAHONTAS, who was brought to Jamestown as a hostage. He married her a year later, and in 1616 sailed with her to England. After she died in 1617 Rolfe wrote an *Account of Virginia,* which was first printed in the United States in the *Southern Literary Messenger* (June, 1839). He returned to Virginia, and is believed to have been killed by Indians. *A True Relation of the State of Virginia Left by Sir Thomas Dale in May Last 1616,* by Rolfe, was printed in 1951.

Ralph Hamor's *A True Discourse of the Present State of Virginia* (1615) and John Smith's *The Generall Historie of Virginia* (1624) show the importance of Rolfe in the development of the colony. Rolfe appears in J. E. Cooke's MY LADY POKOHONTAS (1885) and in several other plays and novels about the Indian maiden.

Rolfe, William James (b. Newburyport, Mass., Dec. 10, 1827—d. July 7, 1910), teacher, philologist, scholar. Rolfe spent twenty years as a schoolteacher, was a pioneer in introducing the study of English literature into secondary schools. He made many trips to Europe, prepared numerous school texts, and taught during the summer session at various universities. His first textbook, *A Handbook of Latin Poetry* (1866), edited with J. H. Hanson, was followed by nearly 150 more. He is best known for his two school editions of Shakespeare, each in 40 volumes (1871–84, 1903–06), outrageously expurgated. Rolfe also edited *The Poetical Works of Sir Walter Scott* (1888); *The Complete Works of Alfred, Lord Tennyson* (12 v., 1895–98); and the Cambridge Edition of *The Poetic and Dramatic Works of Alfred, Lord Tennyson* (1898). He wrote A *Life of William Shakespeare* (1904). He was co-editor from 1869 to 1893 of the *Boston Journal of Chemistry* and its successor, *Popular Science News.* The *Emerson College Magazine Rolfe Memorial Number* (November, 1910) contains his autobiography.

Rolling Stone, The. The name that William Sydney Porter (O. HENRY) gave to W. C. BRANN's *Iconoclast* when he purchased it in 1894 and began issuing it at Austin, Tex. The magazine was resold to Brann in 1895; he changed the name back to its original one. Porter's estate in 1913 published a collection of stories, poems, and sketches called *Rolling Stones,* which included some pieces from the magazine.

Rollins, Philip Ashton (b. Somersworth, N.H., Jan. 20, 1869—d. Sept. 11, 1950), lawyer, historian of the West. Rollins was deeply interested in the West, and in 1920 began collecting early Western Americana. In 1945 he and his wife presented three thousand items from this collection to his alma mater, Princeton University. Rollins also wrote *The Cowboy: His Characteristics, His Equipment, and His Part in the Development of the West* (1922), *The Cowboy: An Unconventional History* (1936), and *Gone Haywire* (1939), and edited Robert Stuart's *The Discovery of the Oregon Trail* (1935).

Rollo Books. See JACOB ABBOTT.

Rölvaag, Ole Edvart (b. Norway, April 22, 1876—d. Nov. 5, 1931), novelist. Born of fisher folk, Rölvaag was deeply impressed by the wild beauty of the Norwegian landscape. In August, 1896, he emigrated to America, reached

Elk Point, S.D., and for three years worked as a laborer. When he had saved enough money he entered Augustana College, a preparatory school, in 1899. He then attended St. Olaf's College, Northfield, Minn. He was hampered by his unfamiliarity with English and by ill health, but

managed to graduate with honors in 1905. Some of his teachers, impressed by his determination and his marked abilities, made it possible for him to return to Norway to attend graduate school at the University of Oslo. The next year he became professor of Norwegian at St. Olaf's.

Rölvaag wrote his first novel, *Nils and Astri*, during his senior year, but it was never published. All of his novels were written in Norwegian. *Amerika-Breve*, or *Letters from America* (1912), an autobiographical novel cast in the form of letters written to relatives in Norway and published under the pseudonym Paal Morck, was followed in 1914 by *On Forgotten Paths*. His masterpiece, GIANTS IN THE EARTH (1927), which was translated by Lincoln Colcord, was first published in Norway in two volumes: *In Those Days* (1924) and *The Kingdom Is Founded* (1925). Its sequel, PEDER VICTORIOUS (1929), was followed by *Pure Gold* (1930), a translation of *Two Simpletons* (published in Norway, 1920). In 1931 appeared THEIR FATHER'S GOD. *The Boat of Longing* (1933), inspired by the tragic death of Rölvaag's youngest child, is a mystical and poetic novel in which the glorious scenery of Norway is contrasted with the sordid American city.

Romance (1913), a play by EDWARD SHELDON. When a young man comes to tell his grandfather, a clergyman, of his intention to marry an actress, the older man tries to dissuade him by relating the great romance of his own youth when he fell in love with an Italian opera singer. But the grandson sticks to his resolution, and the grandfather accepts his decision. The play was one of the first to make use of the flashback as a stage device; the main part of the play occurs in the past. This became the most popular of Sheldon's plays and was performed all over the world; Doris Keane played the role of the opera singer in the original production.

Romance of Dollard, The (1888), a historical novel by MARY HARTWELL CATHERWOOD. This story of New France in 1660 was Mrs. Catherwood's first important success. It tells the romantic tale of a young woman of noble birth who comes to Quebec with a shipload of other women ready to choose husbands among the eager frontiersmen. She marries the commandant of Montreal, who had known her in France. He returns to his post, is compelled to leave her to fight an Indian invasion; she insists on joining him and is killed when the fort is taken by the Iroquois. Francis Parkman wrote a preface for the book and vouched for the truth of the main incidents.

Roman influence. See GREEK AND ROMAN INFLUENCE.

Romantic Comedians, The (1926), a novel by ELLEN GLASGOW. Like Miss Glasgow's *They Stooped to Folly* (1929) and *The Sheltered Life* (1932), this novel is a satirical comedy of manners. The marriage of the elderly Judge Honeywell to Annabel Upchurch, aged eighteen, might have made a cheap and unpleasant story in the hands of a less gifted writer. Miss Glasgow made of it a blend of wit and compassion. Judge Honeywell may be a fool, but he is such a dignified and courteous fool that the reader feels pity and affection for him even while laughing at his follies.

Rome Hanks, The History of (1944), a novel by JOSEPH STANLEY PENNELL. The story of a young man investigating the lives of his forebears in the Civil War, this novel won wide popularity and was made into a successful motion picture.

Rope, The (1919), a one-act play by EUGENE O'NEILL. See MOON OF THE CARIBBEES.

Roosevelt, [Anna] Eleanor. See FRANKLIN D. ROOSEVELT.

Roosevelt, Franklin D[elano] (b. Hyde Park, N.Y., Jan. 30, 1882—d. April 12, 1945), 32nd President. Roosevelt was a fifth cousin of THEODORE ROOSEVELT, who was also his wife's uncle. His family, of Dutch and English descent, was wealthy; he was educated at Groton and Harvard University. He then attended Columbia University Law School and there married Anna Eleanor Roosevelt (1884—1962). Admitted to the bar in 1907, he entered politics in 1910 as the leader of a group of insurgents against Tammany Hall in New York; he won election to the state legislature. He supported Woodrow Wilson in 1912, in 1913 was made an Assistant Secretary of the Navy under Josephus Daniels. In 1920 he was nominated as the Vice-Presidential candidate on the ticket with James M. Cox and battled eloquently for the League of Nations. In August, 1921, he was stricken with poliomyelitis; he went to Warm Springs, Ga., to take the cure but, although his condition was somewhat alleviated, he remained a cripple for the rest of his life. He later established a foundation at Warm Springs.

Roosevelt never gave in to his ailment. He supported Governor Alfred E. Smith of New York for the Democratic presidential nomination; Smith in turn urged Roosevelt to accept a nomination for the governorship of New York. Smith lost to Hoover, but Roosevelt was elected governor, served for two terms, and won national fame for his progressive policies. In 1932 he won the presidential nomination and was elected by a tremendous majority. He was thereafter re-elected three times—a unique and, to some opponents, a dangerous achievement in American political history. In combating the evils of the Depression, he began a series of drastic reforms, creating many new kinds of governmental agencies: the Civilian Conservation Corps, the Agricultural Adjustment Administration, the Tennessee Valley Authority, the National Recovery Administration, the Works Progress Administration, the Public Works Administration, and others. Many denounced the increasing invasion of private business by these agencies. Roosevelt suffered only one really major defeat; he was not permitted to enlarge the Supreme Court in order to facilitate the legislation of his remedial measures.

The national debt increased enormously, but so did the national income. World War II brought a new phase of the Roosevelt era. With masterly command of propaganda techniques Roosevelt aroused the country against the fascist threat. He and Sir Winston Churchill from the beginning looked beyond the war to a world in which wars would cease. America built up history's greatest fighting machine, defeated its enemies on all the continents, began preparing the atom bomb. But Roosevelt's health broke down, and he died before the end of the war. Some have complained that Roosevelt allowed Stalin to deceive him at Yalta. But David E. Weingast, in *Franklin D. Roosevelt: Man of Destiny* (1952), remarks: "If the Yalta conference had broken up in disagreement, the Russians would still have expanded at will."

Roosevelt had an extraordinary gift for communication. Even more effective than his personal appearances for political addresses were his famous radio "Fireside Chats." Although earlier Presidents had held press conferences somewhat casually, Roosevelt made them a potent instrument of communication with the public. A transcript of the proceedings was always made; these were published in the *Public Papers and Addresses of Franklin D. Roosevelt*, edited by Samuel I. Rosenman (1928–45).

Roosevelt had help with his speeches, as have many other Presidents; but, according to Robert E. Sherwood, no matter who contributed suggestions, phrases, or whole passages, the speech in its final version was Roosevelt's. His ghost-writing personnel changed from time to time, but the tone and rhythm of his speeches remained the same. Among the Presidents he stands next to Lincoln as an orator and a phrase-maker. One may recall a few of his statements: "I pledge you, I pledge myself, to a new deal for the American people" (*Address at Chicago*, July 2, 1932). "Let me assert my firm belief that the only thing we have to fear is fear itself" (*First Inaugural Address*, March 4, 1933). "I see one-third of a nation ill-housed, ill-clad, ill-nourished" (*Second Inaugural Address*, Jan. 20, 1937). "We have learned that we cannot live alone, at peace; that our own well-being is dependent upon the well-being of other nations far away. We have learned that we must live as men and not as ostriches, not as dogs in the manger" (*Fourth Inaugural Address*, Jan. 20, 1945).

Roosevelt wrote *The Happy Warrior, Alfred E. Smith* (1928); *Government—Not Politics* (1932); *Looking Forward* (1933); *On Our Way* (1934). Collections of his writings include J. B. S. Hardman's *Rendezvous with Destiny: Addresses and Opinions of Franklin D. Roosevelt* (1944); Dagobert Runes' *The American Way: Selections from the Public Addresses and Papers of Franklin D. Roosevelt* (1944); B. D. Zevin's *Nothing to Fear: The Selected Addresses of Franklin D. Roosevelt, 1932–46* (1946); *F. D. R.: His Personal Letters* (4 v., 1947, 1948, 1950); *F. D. R.: Columnist* (1947); *As FDR Said: A Treasury of His Speeches, Conversations, and Writings* (edited by Frank Kingdon, 1950); *Franklin D. Roosevelt's Own Story, Told in His Own Words from His Private and*

Public Papers (selected by Donald Day, 1951).

Roosevelt has been treated in many books, by friend and foe. Among them: Earle Looker's *This Man Roosevelt* (1932) and *The American Way: Franklin Roosevelt in Action* (1933); Charles A. Beard's *The Recovery Program, 1933–34* (with G. H. E. Smith, 1934); Rexford G. Tugwell's *The Battle for Democracy* (1935); Joseph Alsop and Turner Catledge's *The 168 Days* (1938); Emil Ludwig's *Roosevelt: A Study in Fortune and Power* (1938); Thomas E. Dewey's *The Case Against the New Deal* (1940); Robert H. Jackson's *The Struggle for Judicial Supremacy* (1941); Gerald W. Johnson's *Roosevelt: Dictator or Democrat?* (1941); Harold L. Ickes' *The Autobiography of a Curmudgeon* (1943) and his *Secret Diary* (published in 1953 and following years); Frank Kingdon's *"That Man" in the White House* (1944); Edward R. Stettinius' *Lend-Lease: Weapon for Victory* (1944) and *Roosevelt and the Russians* (1949); Josephus Daniels' *The Wilson Era* (2 v., 1944, 1946) and *Shirt Sleeve Diplomat* (1947); Frances Perkins' *The Roosevelt I Knew* (1946) and *The Roosevelt Myth* (1948); Cordell Hull's *Memoirs* (2 v., 1948); Henry L. Stimson and McGeorge Bundy's *On Active Service in Peace and War* (1948); Robert Sherwood's *Roosevelt and Hopkins* (1948); John Gunther's *Roosevelt in Retrospect* (1950); Allan Nevins' *The New Deal and World Affairs* (1950); James N. Rosenau's *Roosevelt Treasury* (a symposium, 1950); Harold F. Gosnell's *Champion Campaigner: Franklin D. Roosevelt* (1952); the correspondence of *Roosevelt and [Josephus] Daniels: A Friendship in Politics* (1952); Samuel I. Rosenman's *Working with Roosevelt* (1952); J. M. Burns' *Roosevelt: The Lion and the Fox* (1956); Arthur M. Schlesinger, Jr.'s *The Age of Roosevelt* (several volumes, 1957 and later).

In a musical satire, *I'd Rather Be Right* (1937) by George S. Kaufman, Lorenz Hart, and Richard Rodgers, George M. Cohan gave a lifelike impersonation of Roosevelt. Dore Schary wrote a moving play about him, *Sunrise at Campobello* (1958), which ran on Broadway for over a year and was made into a film. It showed the effect on Roosevelt's character of the paralysis from which he suffered.

In *The Roosevelt Era* (1947) Milton Crane collected many contemporary pieces to reveal the kaleidoscopic background against which Roosevelt moved. He speaks with admiration of the effect of the New Deal in the field of letters and art, as shown by the admirable State Guides, the Federal Theater, and the frescoes and murals all over the land. The WPA in cultural life was described in Willson Whitman's *Bread and Circuses* (1937); *Federal Theater Plays* (2 v., 1938); Grace Overmyer's *Government and Arts* (1939); Harold Clurman's *The Fervent Years: Group Theater* (1945).

A quiet, unself-conscious figure in the midst of all this turmoil was the wife of the President, whose activities continued after his death. **Mrs. [Anna] Eleanor Roosevelt** (b. New York City,

Oct. 11, 1884—d. Nov. 7, 1962), worked for social-welfare causes, held a few public offices, contributed a column to a newspaper syndicate, lectured widely. In 1945 and 1946 and from 1949 to 1952 she was the United States Representative in the General Assembly of the United Nations. Among her books: *When You Grow Up to Vote* (1932); *It's Up to the Women* (1933); *This Is My Story* (1937); *My Days* (1938); *If You Ask Me* (1946); *This I Remember* (1949); *The Moral Basis of Democracy* (1953); *It Seems to Me* (1954); *On My Own* (1958). Jeanette Eaton told *The Story of Mrs. Roosevelt* (1956).

Roosevelt, Kermit (b. Oyster Bay, N.Y., Oct. 10, 1889—d. June 4, 1943), explorer, soldier, author of travel books. Kermit Roosevelt was THEODORE ROOSEVELT's son and accompanied him on his hunting trip to Africa (1909–10) and in his exploration of the "River of Doubt" in Brazil (1914). He engaged in several business enterprises and became acquainted with various parts of the world, some of which he described in his writings. He served with the British army in World War II, later with the United States Army; he died in active service in Alaska. Among his books: *War in the Garden of Eden* (1919); *The Happy Hunting Grounds* (1920); *Quentin Roosevelt—A Sketch with Letters* (1921), an account of his brother, killed in World War I, written in collaboration with another brother, Theodore, Jr.; *East of the Sun and West of the Moon* (1926); *Cleared for Strange Ports* (1927); *American Backlogs* (1928); *Trailing the Giant Panda* (with Theodore, Jr., 1929).

Roosevelt, Theodore (b. New York City, Oct. 27, 1858—d. Jan. 6, 1919), soldier, writer, 26th President. After his graduation from Harvard University, Roosevelt turned to writing history, in which he was intensely interested all his life. His first book was *The Naval War of 1812* (1882). Then he entered politics and served from 1882 to 1884 as a Republican member of the New York legislature. His health was fragile and he fully restored it by engaging, sometimes recklessly, in strenuous physical activities; he published a book called THE STRENUOUS LIFE AND OTHER ESSAYS (1900). After the death of Alice Lee (1884), his first wife, Roosevelt went to the Dakota Territory, where he ranched and won the favor of the local inhabitants. At this time he completed several books: *Hunting Trips of a Ranchman* (1885); *Thomas Hart Benton* (1886); *Ranch Life and the Hunting-Trail* (1888). Back home in New York, he re-entered politics, married Edith Carow. He was appointed by President Harrison to the U.S. Civil Service Commission (1889–95). Then he was made police commissioner of New York City under a reform mayor, and his vigor and determination in that office won him national repute. At this time he published the last of the four volumes of THE WINNING OF THE WEST (1889–96).

In 1897 President McKinley made Roosevelt Assistant Secretary of the Navy, but when war with Spain broke out in 1898 Roosevelt resigned and organized the Rough Riders, a volunteer cavalry group which he led into battle in Cuba. Roosevelt led a charge up the famous San Juan Hill with great exuberance, although historians aver that the hill had already been captured. The commander returned to New York, was hailed as a hero, won the nomination for governor, was triumphantly elected (1898). But Tom Platt, Republican boss of the state, feared Roosevelt's independence and induced the Republican convention in 1900 to get Roosevelt out of the way by nominating him as McKinley's running mate in the presidential campaign. Roosevelt accepted with gloom, was duly elected Vice-President, but in 1901 McKinley was assassinated and Roosevelt became President.

Roosevelt had a reputation as a firebrand; he alarmed conservatives in his own party. He was the first President to recognize that a policy of isolation for the United States was dead. He realized further the primacy of economic issues and interfered actively in the business life of the nation. He was uncompromising in his viewpoint that all Americans were entitled to equal treatment, irrespective of race, creed, or color. An increasingly able politician who managed to get most of what he wanted from Congress, he was also a master of public relations, always the center of attraction. Anything economic, social, ethical, literary, scientific, historical, journalistic —in which he happened to be interested was likely to be shoved into the headlines by one of his remarks.

Opinion has varied as to the profundity of Roosevelt's mind and the importance of his measures. In general historians feel that he was not as radical as he seemed. The Square Deal which he proclaimed anticipated the New Deal in many ways and equally alarmed many contemporaries. In his "trust-busting" activities Roosevelt brought about numerous reforms that made competition at least somewhat more decorous and provided important ground rules for business practice. Aroused by Upton Sinclair's THE JUNGLE (1906), he brought about the passage of the Pure Food and Drug Act. He sought somewhat unsuccessfully to conserve natural resources. He did effect the building of the Panama Canal. He settled the Alaska boundary dispute, and helped negotiate an end to the Russo-Japanese War. He had a firm maxim for international affairs: "Speak softly and carry a big stick." As John Morton Blum shows in *The Republican Roosevelt* (1954), the President had three chief political ideas: he believed in power, in the strong executive; he believed in order, enforced by the executive; he believed in morality for everybody.

In 1908 Roosevelt decided not to run again for President, fearing "the concentration of power in one hand." In March, 1909, he turned the Presidency over to his "lieutenant," WILLIAM HOWARD TAFT, and departed on a hunting trip in Africa and a tour of Europe. He came home to find the Republican party he had hoped to make one of "sane, constructive radicalism" returned to rank conservatism, and soon it was open war. Unable to win the Republican nomination in 1912, Roosevelt organized the progressive "Bull Moose" party, ran against both Taft and Woodrow Wilson, and took enough votes away from Taft to make Wilson win. In World War I Roosevelt spoke and wrote steadily in favor of intervention. His son Quentin was killed in action; in World War II his sons Kermit and Theodore died in active service. In his last years Roosevelt was embittered and frustrated, often violent in expressing his views.

Of all American Presidents, with the possible exception of Woodrow Wilson, Roosevelt was probably the most deeply interested in books and the nearest to being a professional writer. The help that he gave Edwin Arlington Robinson when that poet was in difficult circumstances is well known. (See CHILDREN OF THE NIGHT.) He often talked about books in public; his endorsement could make a best seller. His own books sold well, especially *The Winning of the West*. He felt that historical writing must be vivid as well as accurate, although later critics have found him deficient in both respects. He also wrote, in addition to the books noted above, *American Ideals and Other Essays* (1897); *Oliver Cromwell* (1900); *Outdoor Pastimes of an American Hunter* (1905); *The New Nationalism* (1910); *History as Literature and Other Essays* (1913); *Theodore Roosevelt, An Autobiography* (1913); *Through the Brazilian Wilderness* (1914); *America and the World War* (1915); *A Book-Lover's Holidays in the Open* (1916); *The Great Adventure* (1918). His *Diaries of Boyhood and Youth* were published in 1928, selections from his *Letters* (8 v.) in 1951–54. Many of his letters, especially to his family and intimate friends, show a sense of humor and winning informality. His *Works* have appeared in several editions. Samuel E. Morison wrote an introduction for *Three Great Letters by Theodore Roosevelt* (1954) and edited *The Hunting and Exploring Adventures of Theodore Roosevelt* (told in his own words, 1955). Hermann Hagedorn edited selections called *The Free Citizen* (1956), wrote *Roosevelt in the Bad Lands* (1921), *The Rough Riders* (1927), and *The Roosevelt Family of Sagamore Hill* (1954).

Other books dealing with Roosevelt include: Henry Cabot Lodge's *Theodore Roosevelt* (1919); Corinne Roosevelt Robinson's *My Brother, Theodore Roosevelt* (1921); Earle Looker's *The White House Gang* (1929); Owen Wister's *Roosevelt: The Story of a Friendship* (1930); H. U. Faulkner's *The Quest for Social Justice* (1931); Claude Bowers' *Beveridge and the Progressive Era* (1932); G. E. Mowry's *Theodore Roosevelt and the Progressive Movement* (1946) and *The Era of Theodore Roosevelt, 1900–1912* (1958); Carleton Putnam's *Theodore Roosevelt: The Formative Years, 1858–1886* (first of four projected volumes, 1958); Edward Wagenknecht's *The Seven Worlds of Theodore Roosevelt* (1959).

John Hall Wheelock prepared a *Bibliography of Theodore Roosevelt* (1920), A. B. Hart and

H. R. Ferleger a *Theodore Roosevelt Cyclopedia* (1941). Roosevelt as "an energizing factor in American culture" is agreeably depicted in Grant C. Knight's *The Strenuous Age in American Literature* (1954). One man—FINLEY PETER DUNNE—found Roosevelt an endless inspiration for his salty humor, and Roosevelt did not seem to mind. Dunne told the President that he had reckoned up his literary assets and found that Roosevelt was seventy-five per cent of them. Roosevelt's house at Sagamore Hill, Oyster Bay, Long Island, which was used as a summer White House, was established as a memorial in 1953.

Root, Elihu (b. Clinton, N.Y., Feb. 15, 1845—d. Feb. 7, 1937), lawyer, statesman, diplomat. Root obtained a law degree from New York University and was admitted to the bar. A staunch Republican, he went into politics, and in 1883 became U.S. Attorney for the Southern District of New York. He was appointed Secretary of War by McKinley in 1899, and Secretary of State by Roosevelt in 1905. He played an important part in bringing about better relations between the United States and such countries as China, Japan, Latin America, and the Philippines. For this work and for his stand on the Panama Toll question he was awarded the Nobel Peace Prize in 1912. He was a Senator from 1909 to 1915. In 1917 Wilson sent him to Russia as Ambassador Extraordinary.

After the war Root made suggestions for changes in the Versailles Treaty and the League of Nations which Wilson adopted. Although Root favored the League, he is said to have written the anti-League plank in the Republican Platform of 1920. In 1920 he helped draft plans for the Permanent Court of International Justice. He also helped organize the Carnegie Endowment to Promote World Peace.

Charles Evans Hughes called Root the "most astute among lawyers, most shrewd among diplomats, most wise among statesmen." He was also an able writer in the cause of peace and conservatism. Among his books: *The Citizen's Part in Government* (1907); *Experiment in Government and the Essentials of its Constitution* (1913); *Addresses on International Subjects* (1916); *Addresses on Government and Citizenship* (1916); *The Military and Colonial Policy of the United States* (1916); *Latin America and the United States* (1917); *Russia and the United States* (1917); *Miscellaneous Addresses* (1917); *Men and Policies* (1924). Richard W. Leopold has written *Elihu Root and the Conservative Tradition* (1954).

Root, George Frederick (b. Sheffield, Mass., Aug. 30, 1820—d. Aug. 6, 1895), composer, music publisher. Some of the most popular martial songs of the Civil War period were composed by Root, among them *There's Music in the Air, Boys; Tramp! Tramp! Tramp!; Just Before the Battle, Mother*. In his later years he joined the publishing firm of Root & Cady in Chicago—the former was his brother. He also wrote many hymns, including *The Shining Shore*, and several cantatas, among them *The*

Pilgrim Fathers (1854). *Rosalie, the Prairie Flower* (1855) was his most successful sentimental ballad. Root wrote his autobiography in *The Story of a Musical Life* (1891).

Root, Robert Kilburn (b. Brooklyn, N.Y., April 7, 1877—d. Nov. 20, 1950), teacher, scholar. Root taught first at Yale University, then at Princeton University from 1905 to 1946; he was for a time dean of the faculty. He began his literary career with *Classical Mythology in Shakespeare* (1903), went on to much scholarly research and editing. He published *The Textual Tradition of Chaucer's "Troilus"* (1916).

Rootabaga Stories (1922), juvenile fiction by CARL SANDBURG. The author calls these whimsical sketches "moral tales." Written in a style nearer poetry than prose, rich in the language and cadence of folk songs, *Rootabaga Stories* is directed toward very young children. It was followed by *Rootabaga Pigeons* (1923).

Roots of American Civilization, The (1938), a history of American colonial life by Curtis P. Nettels (1898—   ). He argues that "the basic institutions of American government and the prevailing philosophy of today were shaped in large measure during the colonial period." He goes back to Europe for the motivation of colonial settlement and to discover the origin of the ethnological, economic, and other traits of the settlers.

Rosary, The. See ROBERT CAMERON ROGERS.

Rose, Aquila (b. England, 1696[?]—d. Aug. 22[?], 1723), sailor, printer, poet. When Benjamin Franklin applied for a job at SAMUEL KEIMER's shop, he found him setting type for an elegy on Rose, who had been Keimer's assistant. Some years later Rose's son Joseph became Franklin's assistant and collected all of his father's available poems as *Poems on Several Occasions* (1740).

Rose, Reginald. See TELEVISION WRITING.

Rosenbach, A[braham] S[imon] W[olf] (b. Philadelphia, July 22, 1876—d. July 1, 1952), bibliophile, teacher, editor, writer. Rosenbach was the most eminent bibliophile of the first half of the 20th century. He was a scholar who knew the value of a book, no matter what the language in which it was printed. At his death his Philadelphia home was turned into a museum under the care of the Rosenbach Foundation. Here are found many extraordinary articles, historical and literary; also fine furniture, paintings, early silver, and other articles of interest. He also established (1930) the Rosenbach Fellowship in Bibliography at the University of Pennsylvania, where he had taught English from 1898 to 1901.

Among Rosenbach's own books are: *The Unpublishable Memoirs* (1917); *An American Jewish Bibliography* (1926); *Books and Bidders* (1927); *The All-Embracing Doctor Franklin* (1932); *Early American Children's Books* (1933); *The Libraries of the Presidents of the United States* (1934); *A Book Hunter's Holiday* (1936); *The First Theatrical Company in America* (1939). *To Dr. R.: Essays Collected and Published in Honor of His 70th Birthday* was published in 1946, and a biography, *Rosen-*

bach, by Edwin Wolf and John F. Fleming appeared in 1960.

Rosenfeld, Monroe H. See CHARLES K. HARRIS.

Rosenfeld, Morris (b. Poland, Dec. 28, 1862 —d. June 21, 1923), poet. Rosenfeld received an orthodox Jewish education at home. He was sent to London in 1882 to learn tailoring and to Amsterdam to learn gem cutting. In 1886 he emigrated to America and was submerged in the crowded New York ghetto, where he worked as a presser in the sweat shops. Barely able to make a living, he wrote poems about the misery he saw about him; these were printed in the Yiddish newspapers. He published a collection of folk and revolutionary songs, *Die Glocke* (1888), followed in 1890 by *Die Blumenkette.* Leo Weiner published in *Songs of the Ghetto* (1898) some of Rosenfeld's poems in prose translations. He became editor of and contributor to a number of Yiddish papers, and gave readings at American colleges and in many European cities. *The Works of Morris Rosenfeld* (3 v.) appeared in 1908.

Rosenfeld, Paul (b. New York City, May 4, 1890—d. July 21, 1946), critic, essayist, novelist. Although Rosenfeld wrote a novel, *The Boy in the Sun* (1928), he was pre-eminently a critic, first of music, then of all the fine arts. A discerning and sensitive analyst, he managed to keep the esteem and affection of those about whom he wrote. At his death many of them united in a tribute to his memory, *Paul Rosenfeld: Voyager in the Arts,* edited by Jerome Mellquist and Lucie Wiese. Among his books: *Musical Portraits* (1920); *Musical Chronicle* (1923); *Port of N.Y.* (1924); *Men Seen* (1925); *By Way of Art* (1928); *An Hour with American Music* (1929); *Discoveries of a Music Critic* (1936). He helped edit the "American Caravan" series.

Rose of Dutcher's Coolly (1895; rev. ed., 1899), a novel by HAMLIN GARLAND. Garland wrote effectively of his own experiences in several nonfictional books, and seems to have utilized them again here—strangely enough with a woman to represent him. He tells about a Middle Western farm girl who attends the University of Wisconsin and then goes on to Chicago to become a writer, in rebellion against the restrictions of farm life. She rejects marriage as a hindrance to her literary development, but later changes her mind. The book is carefully written and displays Garland's style at its best. It was a forerunner of the realistic movement in American fiction and explains why Garland was able to understand and help younger writers like Stephen Crane (see REALISM). Some critics have found the ending of the book too romantic for the rest of the story.

Rose Tattoo, The (1951), a play by TENNESSEE WILLIAMS. Set in a Sicilian community on the Gulf Coast, the play deals with a passionate and earthy dressmaker, Serafina Delle Rose, whose truckdriver husband, Rosario, has just been killed. Serafina abandons herself to grief, keeps Rosario's ashes in a marble urn in the house, storms and rages and refuses to believe rumors that Rosario had been unfaithful, and finally, after three years of widowhood and frustration, meets a young truckdriver who, like the dead Rosario, wears a rose tattoo on his chest. Alternately superstitious and devoutly religious, Serafina is one of Williams' most robust and healthy characters; unlike another of his primitive heroes, Stanley in *A Streetcar Named Desire*, Serafina is basically warm-hearted and sympathetic to the needs of others. Her peasant simplicity makes her direct and violent, but not cruel. The Sicilian neighborhood women and the earnest courtship of the not-too-bright truckdriver, Mangiacavallo, provide elements of clownish humor usually lacking in Williams' work.

Rosier, James (1575[?]–1635), explorer. Rosier may have been a priest; he accompanied George Waymouth when the latter in 1605 undertook to find for Sir Thomas Arundel a refuge for Roman Catholics somewhere along the eastern shore of North America. The voyagers investigated Nantucket and various sites on the present Massachusetts coast. Rosier wrote *True Relation of the Most Properous Voyage Made This Present Year 1605 by Captain George Waymouth* (1605). His account was reprinted (1887), with notes, for the Gorges Society, also in H. S. Burrage's *Early English and French Voyages* (1906).

Ross, Alexander (b. Scotland, May 9, 1783—d. Oct. 23, 1856), explorer. Alexander Ross settled in Canada in 1804, taught school for a few years before becoming a clerk in the Pacific Fur Company. He helped establish Fort Astoria in what is now Oregon. Later he was in charge of Fort Nez Percé, but he kept up his connections with various fur companies. After fifteen years he moved to Canada, where he became the first sheriff of the Red River Colony. He was a man of considerable influence as well as a valuable recorder of Northwestern history. *Adventures of the First Settlers on the Oregon or Columbia River* (1849) was followed by *The Fur Hunters of the Far West* (2 v., 1855) and *The Red River Settlement* (1856).

Ross, Alexander Coffman (b. Zanesville, Ohio, May 31, 1812—d. Feb. 26, 1883), jeweler, songwriter. Ross is remembered for one work —to the tune of a familiar song, "Little Pigs," he wrote in 1840 the words of a campaign song, "Tippecanoe and Tyler Too," that helped win the Presidential election of that year for General WILLIAM HENRY HARRISON.

Ross, Barnaby. A pen name used by Frederic Dannay and Manfred B. Lee, whose better known pseudonym is ELLERY QUEEN.

Ross, Betsy (b. Philadelphia, Jan. 1, 1752—d. Jan. 30, 1836), flagmaker. The patriotic seamstress sewing the first American flag is as familiar a figure as young George Washington chopping down the cherry tree, and probably has about as much basis in fact. The story of Mrs. Ross making the flag at the request of Washington and John Hancock was first heard in a paper read to the Historical Society of Pennsylvania on May 29, 1870, by her grandson William Canby. It is true that the Ross family had been in the upholstery and flagmaking business for some years, and that after her husband's death Betsy Ross carried on the family business successfully. Very likely the firm did manufacture flags for the newly united colonies, but who made the first one it is impossible to tell today.

Ross, Edward A[lsworth] (b. Virden, Ill., Dec. 12, 1866—d. July 23, 1951), teacher, sociologist. Ross taught at various universities, principally the University of Wisconsin. He helped to establish the important role that economic problems and tendencies play in politics. His most widely known book, *Sin and Society* (1907), was read eagerly by President Theodore Roosevelt. He analyzed the psychology of sin, showed how inadequate our older ethical codes were to deal with child labor, stock watering, and the adulteration of foods. Ross said modern sinners were, for the most part, upright and well-intentioned gentlemen who "sin with calm countenance and a serene soul." He resigned a position at Stanford University in 1900 in opposition to restrictions on academic freedom in discussion of economic and sociological questions. Among his other books: *Honest Dollars* (1896); *Social Control* (1901); *Latter Day Sinners and Saints* (1910); *Changing America* (1912); *South of Panama* (1915); *What Is America?* (1919); *Roads to Social Peace* (1924); *Seventy Years of It* (1936).

Ross, Harold [Wallace]. See THE NEW YORKER.

Ross, Leonard Q. Pen name of LEO CALVIN ROSTEN.

Ross, Malcolm (b. Newark, N.J., June 1, 1895—   ), public official, editor, writer. Ross worked as a reporter on several newspapers in the Arizona copper mines and the Texas oil fields, and became well acquainted with labor conditions. He served as director of information for the National Labor Relations Board, and from 1943 to 1946 was chairman of the President's Fair Employment Practices Committee. Most widely known of his publications was a "personal history," *Death of a Yale Man* (1939). *All Manner of Men* (1948) is a record of Ross' experiences in dealing with discrimination in the United States. He also wrote *Machine Age in the Hills* (1933) and several novels, including *Deep Enough* (1926) and *The Man Who Lived Backward* (1950).

Rosten, Leo Calvin ["Leonard Q. Ross"] (b. Poland, April 11, 1908—   ), political scientist, teacher, research worker, consultant, humorist. As a scholar Rosten produced a number of informative studies, the best known of which is probably *Hollywood: The Movie Colony, the Movie Makers* (1941), an objective analysis of the motion-picture industry. While in Hollywood Rosten tried his own hand at scriptwriting, produced *The Velvet Touch* (1948), an effective detective story. Other books are *The Washington Correspondents* (1937), an analysis of news gathering in the capital, and *A Guide to the*

Religions of America (1955). Undoubtedly Rosten's most widely read book, however, is a book of comic sketches written under his pen name and concerned with the activities of a night school for immigrant adults, THE EDUCA-TION OF H°Y°M°A°N K°A°P°L°A°N (1937). He picked up this theme again in 1959 with *The Return of Hyman Kaplan.*

Rosten, Norman (b. New York City, Jan. 1, 1914—   ), poet, radio writer, playwright. Rosten has written vigorous poetry about life today; it has been his faith, moreover, that verse is still a natural medium for the stage and even more for broadcasting. His *This Proud Pilgrimage* was produced at the University of Michigan Theater in 1938; *First Stop to Heaven* appeared on Broadway in 1941. He has also written plays for radio, including some on American historical figures for the *Cavalcade of America.* His poems were collected in *Return Again, Traveler* (1940) and *The Fourth Decade and Other Poems* (1943). THE BIG ROAD (1946) is an ambitious and somewhat turgid poem in which Rosten describes the building of the Alcan highway to Alaska. This was followed by *Songs for Patricia* (1951) and *The Plane and the Shadow* (1953). His play *Mister Johnson,* based on the novel by Joyce Cary, was produced on Broadway in 1956.

Roth, Philip (b. Newark, N.J., March 19, 1933—   ), short-story writer. Roth obtained his M.A. at the University of Chicago in 1955 and taught English there for the next two years. In 1960 he became visiting lecturer at the Writer's Workshop, State University of Iowa. His book *Goodbye Columbus* (1959), consisting of a novella and short stories, aroused excitement in critical circles, most of which recognized the vitality of his talent. The title novella is a perceptive yet malicious treatment of a summer love affair. The short stories, which deal with contemporary Jewish life, had previously appeared in *The New Yorker,* the *Paris Review,* and *Commentary.* In 1960 he won the National Book Award for fiction. Many of his short stories have been anthologized in the *Best American Short Stories of 1956, 1959,* and *1960,* the O. Henry Prize *Stories* for 1960, and in *Stories from the New Yorker (1950–1960).*

Rouché, Berton (b. Kansas City, Mo., April 16, 1911—   ), novelist, medical reporter. Rouché graduated from the University of Missouri in 1933, and after his first novel *Black Weather* (1945), turned to narratives of medical detection. *Incurable Wound* (1958) consists of six stories of medical detection. Rouché dealt with Northeastern Americana in *Delectable Mountains* (1959), a series of offbeat interviews with unusual personalities. He won a Special Award in 1954 from the Mystery Writers of America. Other books: *Eleven Blue Men* (1954); *The Last Enemy* (1956); *The Neutral Spirit: A Portrait of Alcohol* (1960).

Rough Hewn (1922), a novel by DOROTHY CANFIELD FISHER. See THE BRIMMING CUP.

Roughing It (1872), a narrative by MARK TWAIN. In this famous book Twain relates how he and his brother Orion made their way to Nevada in the early 1860's and worked in the mining camps there. He then tells about his trip to San Francisco and the Sandwich Islands. He met numerous entertaining characters, among them western desperadoes and vigilantes, newspapermen, and Brigham Young. He gives a marvelously vivid and fundamentally veracious picture of the Far West in the early days. He fictionized himself and some of his companions, anticipating the techniques he later used in his novels. In particular, as Delancey Ferguson has noted, the dramatic personality of Mark Twain as distinct from Sam Clemens was for the first time defined in print; he made himself the butt of his story, "one of the prize asses of the asinine human race."

The book was written after INNOCENTS ABROAD had scored its great success and apparently as a result of that success. Elisha Bliss, publisher of the first book, proposed one of this kind; and on July 15, 1870, Twain wrote to Orion Clemens that he had begun the book that day and asked his brother to send him some notes he could use. Orion did so, as did Joseph Goodman and others. The book was published in February and did very well, but not as well as *Innocents.* William Dean Howells gave it a good send off with a review in which he praised the book's humor as "always amiable, manly, and generous."

Rounds, Glen (b. South Dakota, 1906—   ), rancher, painter, illustrator, writer. From the time of his youth in the Bad Lands, Rounds followed a variety of occupations and acquired a vast fund of information about the appearance, habits, and folk stories of a large number of fast-disappearing types of Americans. He painted American life as colorfully as he wrote about it. His books are mainly juveniles, and include *Ol' Paul, the Mighty Logger* (1936, 1949); *Lumbercamp* (1937); *Stolen Pony* (1948); *Hunted Horses* (1951); *Buffalo Harvest* (1952); *Swamp Life* (1957); *Beaver Business* (1960). He also illustrated books of American folk tales by other authors.

Round Table. This name was given to at least two informal groups of literary men and women and their friends who met for dinner or luncheon. The earlier one, chronicled in Brander Matthews' *Roster of the Round Table Dining Club* (1926), was founded in 1867 and continued to meet well into the present century. The other, sometimes called the "Algonquin Round Table" because its meetings were held in that famous hostelry in New York City, seems to have started around 1919 and soon included all the best-known writers, newspapermen, artists, and musicians about town. A full account of the group is found in *Tales of a Wayward Inn* (1938), by Frank Case, the hotel's able and genial proprietor, and in *The Vicious Circle* (1951), by his daughter Margaret Case Harriman.

Round Up (1929), a collection of short stories by RING LARDNER.

Rouquette, François Dominique (b. Bayou Lacombe, La., Jan. 2, 1810—d. May [?], 1890),

poet; **Rouquette, Adrien Emmanuel** (b. New
Orleans, Feb. 13, 1813—d. July 15, 1887),
priest, poet, novelist.   These two brothers, who
wrote mainly in French, were notable for their
deep interest in the Indians. As children they
frequently ran away to live among the Choctaws
in the St. Tammany forest near their home.
When they grew up they spent much of their
time in the wilds.

The elder Rouquette is usually thought the
superior poet. Educated in France, he took up
the life of a hermit on his return, writing poems
and living off the woods. Later he taught in New
Orleans, then ran a grocery store in Arkansas.
He published two collections, *Les Meschacé-
béennes* (1839) and *Fleurs d'Amérique* (1856).
He wrote about the beauty of nature and the
nobility of the Indians and the Negroes. In
France he was highly esteemed by Victor Hugo.

The younger brother became a priest who
lived among the Indians and spent his leisure
reading Chateaubriand, Ossian, Edward Young's
Night Thoughts (1742), the Bible. He wrote a
novel, *La Nouvelle Atala* (1879), which shows
the influence of Chateaubriand in more than its
title; there are fine passages on nature and the
Indians are treated with admiration. Before he
entered the priesthood he had fallen in love
with an Indian chieftain's daughter, but she
had died of tuberculosis before they could be
married. In his residence abroad his poems, *Les
Savanes* (1841), were praised by Sainte-Beuve,
and he was called an "American Ossian." He
wrote poems in English as well, collected as
Wild Flowers (1848) and *Patriotic Poems*
(1860). He also wrote poems in *gombo*, the
Negro-French dialect. At his death he was working on a dictionary of the Choctaw language.

Rourke, Constance M[ayfield] (b. Cleveland,
Ohio, Nov. 14, 1885—d. March 23, 1941),
teacher, biographer, critic, historian. Miss
Rourke taught English at Vassar College from
1910 to 1915, thereafter lived mainly at Grand
Rapids. She became a specialist in the field of
American folklore and humor, and was esteemed
as a scholar who did not think it necessary to be
dull. It was her purpose to prepare a full account
of the relation of American art, taken in its
broadest sense, to American culture. This subject she considered in her posthumously published *The Roots of American Culture and Other
Essays* (1942), which expounded the view that
the native American genius was not literary at
all. She was particularly opposed to the idea that
if Americans had enough contacts with Europe
they might be able to develop aesthetically.
Miss Rourke's most important work was AMER-
ICAN HUMOR: A STUDY OF THE NATIONAL CHAR-
ACTER (1931), which H. M. Jones described as
"cultural history from an unorthodox point of
view" and Lewis Mumford characterized as "the
most original piece of research that has appeared
in American cultural history." In originality of
thought, grace of style, and historical soundness,
her book surpasses all other attempts to analyze
our most characteristic literary product. She
gathered material not only from literature but

from traveling about the country and talking to
people. She devoted a separate book to Davy
Crockett (1934), and also wrote *Trumpets of
Jubilee* (1927); *Troupers of the Gold Coast*
(1928); *Audubon* (1936); and *Charles Sheeler:
Artist in the American Tradition* (1938).

Rousseau and Romanticism (1919), a study
of the romantic character by IRVING BABBITT.
It is a prolonged attack against Naturalism as
represented by Rousseau, treating Romanticism
as the emotional aspect of Rousseau's philosophy. In the romantic emphasis on the ego and
on whim, Babbitt saw the chief menace to
civilization. Against the romantic ideal he poses
the Humanist ideals of ethical restraint and classical standards of taste.

Rover Boys Series.   A popular series of books
for boys. The series included more than thirty
titles, the first published in 1899. The books
were written by EDWARD STRATEMEYER under
the pen name Arthur M. Winfield.

Rovere, Richard Halworth (b. Jersey City,
N.J., May 5, 1915—   ), political and literary
critic.   Rovere attended Bard College, Columbia University, obtained his A.B. in 1937. At
various times he was an editor for the *New
Masses*, *The Nation*, *Common Sense*, *Harper's*
magazine, the *Spectator* of London, the *American Scholar*, and *The New Yorker*. His books
have dealt largely with political controversy.
The General and the President (1951), which
was written with ARTHUR M. SCHLESINGER, JR.,
went into the bitter controversy between Douglas
MacArthur and Harry Truman, throwing documented support on the side of the President.
The Eisenhower Years (1956), a set of essays
describing the personalities and policies that
swirled about the president, was written from
the vantage point of Washington, where Rovere
served as correspondent for *The New Yorker*.
Other books: *Howe and Hummel: Their True
and Scandalous History* (1947); *Senator Joe
McCarthy* (1959), an incisive unfriendly portrait; *The Orwell Reader* (ed., 1956).

Rowan, Andrew Summers (b. Gap Mills, Va.
[now W. Va.], April 23, 1857—d. Jan. 11,
1943), soldier, memoirist.   Rowan was the man
who carried A MESSAGE TO GARCIA, as described by Elbert Hubbard (*The Philistine*,
March, 1899), and himself later wrote *How I
Carried the Message to Garcia* (1923). He also
wrote *The Island of Cuba* (1898). A lieutenant
when he carried the message, he was later promoted to a lieutenant colonel of volunteers, was
retired in 1909 with the rank of major.

Rowland, Dunbar (b. Oakland, Miss., Aug.
25, 1864—d. Nov. 1, 1937), historian, editor.
Deeply devoted to recording the annals of his
native state, Rowland founded (1902) the Mississippi State Department of Archives and History and edited the *Publications* of the Mississippi Historical Society. He wrote and edited
many books on the history of the state, among
them one subtitled "The Heart of the South" (2
v., 1925).

Rowland, Helen (b. Washington, D.C., Dec.
26, 1875—d. Dec. 26, 1950), columnist, lec-

turer. Miss Rowland (Mrs. William Hill Brereton) first became a columnist for the New York *World,* and her epigrams, many of them about women and their relationship to men, were widely quoted. In 1923 King Features began to syndicate her work. She also contributed to magazines and was a favorite radio speaker. Her columns were collected in several books, including *The Digressions of Polly* (1905); *Reflections of a Bachelor Girl* (1909); *The Sayings of Mrs. Solomon* (1913); *A Guide to Men* (1922); *This Married Life* (1927). Among her witticisms: "A husband is what is left of the lover after the nerve has been extracted." "Love, the quest; marriage, the conquest; divorce, the inquest." "When you see what some girls marry, you realize how they must hate to work for a living."

Rowlandson, Mary. See under CAPTIVITY AND RESTAURATION OF MRS. MARY ROWLANDSON.

Rowson, Susanna [Haswell] (b. England, *c.* 1762—d. March 2, 1824), writer, actress, educator. Susanna Haswell spent the years from 1767 to 1778 in America, where her father, a naval lieutenant, was stationed in Massachusetts. Her first novel, *Victoria* (1786), was not particularly successful, nor were *The Inquisitor, or, Invisible Rambler* (1788); *Poems on Various Subjects* (1788); *A Trip to Parnassus* (1788); or *Mary, or, the Test of Honour* (1789). In 1791 CHARLOTTE, A TALE OF TRUTH caught the popular fancy, particularly in America, where much of the sentimental and instructive romance is laid. When a business failure wiped out their fortune, the Rowsons took to the stage in plays by Mrs. Rowson, including *Slaves of Algiers* (1794); *The Female Patriot* (1795); *Trials of the Human Heart* (1795); and *Americans in England* (1796). They performed in England and America during the years 1793–96.

Mrs. Rowson left the stage in 1797 and opened a girls' school in Boston. She edited the *Boston Weekly Magazine* and wrote *Reuben and Rachel, or, Tales of Old Times* (1798), a historical novel; *Miscellaneous Poems* (1804); *Sarah, or, the Exemplary Wife* (1813), a semi-autobiographical novel; and *Charlotte's Daughter, or, The Three Orphans,* usually called *Lucy Temple* (posthumously pub., 1828).

Roxy (1878), a novel by EDWARD EGGLESTON. It presents the trials and renunciations of a noble young woman in Indiana in the early 19th century. The novel gives a warm picture of Hoosier scenes and people.

Roy, Gabrielle (b. St. Boniface, Manit., 1909—   ), novelist. After a brief teaching career, Miss Roy spent two years in Europe studying drama, and began to contribute articles and stories to French and Canadian periodicals. Her first novel, *Bonheur d'occasion* (1945; Eng. title, *The Tin Flute*), won France's Prix Femina in 1947. The story of a large French-Canadian family living in an impoverished quarter of Montreal, it was remarkable for its "vivid characterization, unflinching honesty and dry-eyed compassion." Her later works include the novels *La petite poule d'eau* (1950; Eng. title, *Where Nests the Water Hen*) and *Alexandre Chenevert*

(1954; Eng. title, *The Cashier*). *Rue Deschambault* (1955; Eng. title, *Street of Riches*) is a collection of autobiographical sketches.

Royal Family, The (1927), a play by GEORGE S. KAUFMAN and EDNA FERBER. See THE BARRYMORES.

Royall, Anne Newport (b. Maryland, June 11, 1769—d. Oct. 1, 1854), novelist, editor, travel writer. Anne Newport's early childhood was spent on the frontier of Pennsylvania. Her father died when she was thirteen, and she returned to the South, where she worked with her mother as household help for Captain William Royall of Virginia. In 1797, after educating Anne, Captain Royall married her. When he died sixteen years later, his fortune was given to another heir. His widow turned to a career of writing. From 1824 until 1831 she traveled continually, recording her impressions of the life and manners she saw around her. In 1831 she published in Washington, D.C., a newspaper called *Paul Pry,* which was succeeded by *The Huntress.* In them she constantly attacked fraud and graft in government circles; as a result she was frequently reviled and ridiculed. Her writing was honest, independent, courageous, and often charming. Her principal works are: *Sketches of History, Life, and Manners in the United States* (1826); *The Black Book, or, A Continuation of Travels In the United States* (1828–29); *Mrs. Royall's Pennsylvania* (1829); *Mrs. Royall's Southern Tour* (1830–31); *Letters from Alabama* (1830); and a novel, *The Tennessean* (1827). *The Life and Times of Anne Royall,* by Sarah Harvey Porter (1909), was supplemented by George Stuyvesant Jackson's *The Uncommon Scold, the Story of Anne Royall* (1937).

Royal Road to Romance, The (1925), a travel book by RICHARD HALLIBURTON. The author, son of a wealthy family, decided that he would go round the world the hard way and shipped as a seaman on a freighter, later did part of his traveling on foot. This continued for two years. Some years later his book was published and became a best seller.

Royce, Josiah (b. Grass Valley, Cal., Nov. 20, 1855—d. Sept. 14, 1916), philosopher, teacher, essayist. Taught at home by his mother until he was eleven, Royce entered high school in San Francisco in 1869, where he excelled in mathematics. At the newly established University of California he studied under Joseph Le Conte, the famous geologist. He received a Ph.D. from Johns Hopkins University in 1878, returning to teach English at the University of California for the next four years. In 1882 Royce went to Harvard University to replace William James, who was absent on leave, and remained there for the rest of his life. *The Religious Aspect of Philosophy* (1885) established Royce's famous theory of the Absolute. He held that if one admits the presence of evil in the world, it then necessarily follows that there is also an absolute principle of truth, an all-knowing mind or "Universal Thought." William James assailed this theory vigorously, and the two friends argued cheerfully for many years. "Different as our minds are," wrote James to Royce in 1900, "yours has nourished mine, as no other social influence ever has, and in converse with you I have always felt that my life was being lived importantly." According to George Santayana, Royce "wanted to fuse absolute idealism with social realism, with which it is radically incompatible." Royce was the leader of the post-Kantian idealistic school in this country. (See IDEALISM.) *The Spirit of Modern Philosophy* (1892), which weighs positivism and evolution and finds them wanting, was followed by *The Concept of God* (1897); *Studies in Good Will and Evil* (1898); *The World and the Individual* (2 v., 1900–01); *The Philosophy of Loyalty* (1908); *The Problem of Christianity* (2 v., 1913); and *Lectures on Modern Idealism* (1919). His *Fugitive Essays* (1920) deal with Shelley, George Eliot, and Browning. *The Feud of Oakfield Creek* (1887) was the philosopher's one attempt at fiction. Studies of Royce are found in *Papers in Honor of Josiah Royce on His 60th Birthday* (1916) and in Santayana's CHARACTER AND OPINION IN THE UNITED STATES (1920).

Royle, Edwin Milton (b. Lexington, Mo., March 2, 1862—d. Feb. 16, 1942), playwright, actor, producer. Royle graduated from Princeton University in 1883. His first play, *Friends* (1892), was based on the struggles of men like himself, musicians, singers, and writers. *Captain Impudence* (1897), a one-act sketch, had a long run in vaudeville. *My Wife's Husbands* (1903), a farce, was made into a musical comedy entitled *Marrying Mary* (1906). THE SQUAW MAN (1906), one of the most successful plays of its day, showed Royle's interest in absolute realism. The Indian chief was drawn from life; both he and his daughter spoke an authentic Ute dialect which Royle had learned from the Indians themselves. The play became Cecil B. De Mille's first movie (1914) and the first film to be made in Hollywood. *The Struggle Everlasting* (1907), a modern morality play, was followed by *The Unwritten Law*, another melodrama, and *Lancelot and Elaine* (1921), a dramatization of Tennyson's poem. Royle co-starred with his wife, Selena Fetter, and produced many of his own plays. He also dramatized a number of well known novels. He wrote *Edwin Booth as I Knew Him* (1933), as well as poems and songs. His daughter Selena became an actress.

Ruark, Robert [Chester] (b. Wilmington, N.C., Dec. 29, 1915—d. June 30, 1965), newspaper columnist, parodist, novelist. Ruark worked for the Washington (D.C.) *Daily News*, first as a sportswriter, later as assistant city editor. After serving in the navy (1942–45), he became Washington correspondent for the Scripps-Howard papers and a columnist for United Features. He has a facile gift for expressing aversion amusingly and in a facetiously ungrammatical style. He has poked fun at bankers and progressive education, psychiatrists and Texans, southern cooking and the historical novel. This last hatred was embodied in two parodies, GRENADINE ETCHING (1947) and *Grenadine's Spawn* (1952). There are forty essays lampooning the American scene in *I Didn't Know It Was Loaded* (1948), others in *One for the Road* (1949). A trip to Africa occasioned *Horn of the Hunter* (1953) and a novel, *Something of Value* (1955), which offers a melodramatic view of the conflict between whites and natives in Kenya. *The Old Man and the Boy* (1957) is autobiographical. *Poor No More* (1959), a novel, tells of the rise and fall of a North Carolina boy, Craig Price, who becomes a tycoon through unscrupulous methods.

Rudder Grange (1879), a novel by FRANK R. STOCKTON. Published serially, *Rudder Grange* was the first novel to establish the author's reputation as a notable humorist. The narrator and his wife Euphemia, after a long search to find a pleasant but inexpensive summer house, at last discover an old canal boat which they convert into a houseboat and name *Rudder Grange*. The adventures that befall the couple's maid Pomona, her faithful follower Jonas, and the humorous boarder are told in the irrepressibly droll style that later delighted readers of THE CASTING AWAY OF MRS. LECKS AND MRS. ALESHINE (1886). The secret of Stockton's humor lies in his completely grave approach to the most absurd situations. The more fantastic the plot, the more realistic the details. So popular was *Rudder Grange* that two sequels followed: *The Rudder Grangers Abroad* (1891) and *Pomona's Travels* (1894).

Rugg, Harold (b. Fitchburg, Mass., Jan. 17, 1886—d. May 17, 1960), educator. In his early years Rugg worked as a weaver before he entered Dartmouth College, getting his degree in engineering in 1908. He received his Ph.D. in education from the University of Illinois and taught there until 1920, going then to Columbia University Teachers College, retiring in 1951. In 1920 he sought a more unified method of presenting social science; the resultant textbooks sold in the millions to young students. *The Great Technology* (1933), which called for "A New Social Order," made him a controversial figure. An energetic campaign against him was begun in 1935 by ultraconservatives. Two years later, in a small town in Ohio, his books were actually burned. In spite of these attacks, his books sold even more widely than before. In 1941 he published *That Men May Understand* which combines an autobiography with an eloquent defense of his ideas. Some other works: *The Child Centered School* (1928); *Introduction to American Civilization* (1929, rev. 1938); *Culture and Education in America* (1931); *Conquest of America* (1937); *Now is the Moment* (1943); *Foundations for Education* (1947); *The Teacher of Teachers* (1952). Many of these books advocate the methods of progressive education in Rugg's typically impassioned style.

Ruggles, Eleanor (b. Boston, June 24, 1916—   ), biographer. Eleanor Ruggles studied at Vassar College where, under the auspices of Alan Porter, she discovered Gerard Manley Hopkins. Her research on Hopkins led her to study John Henry Newman, and her love for the theater ultimately brought her to Edwin Booth.

She felt that these men were cast in the heroic mold, for each became triumphant in spite of difficult lives and turbulent temperaments. Her biographies are a rare blend of scholarly research and lucid narrative. Theodore Spencer, in a review of the Hopkins biography, said: "she is both sensitive and impartial . . . and has written as good a book as we are likely to have." Among her books: *Gerard Manley Hopkins* (1944); *Journey Into Faith: The Anglican Life of John Henry Newman* (1948); *Prince of Players: Edwin Booth* (1953); *The West Going Heart: A Life of Vachel Lindsay* (1959).

Ruggles of Red Gap (1915), a novel by HARRY LEON WILSON. In this comic novel, Ruggles is a "gentleman's gentleman"—a butler—whose fond employer loses him to an American. He is taken across the Atlantic to Red Gap, a western town, and there is involved in sundry adventures which end in his complete reconciliation to the land of the "traitorous Washington." He even becomes the social arbiter of the community and is appointed to read the Declaration of Independence at a Fourth of July celebration. Harrison Rhodes wrote a play from the novel (1915), with music by Sigmund Romberg. Successful movie versions were made in 1919, 1923, and 1935, the last with Charles Laughton as Ruggles.

Rukeyser, Muriel (b. New York City, Dec. 15, 1913—   ), poet, biographer, lecturer. Miss Rukeyser's poems are acute refractions of an industrial and technological world. Often her imagery is drawn from the immediate scene; as B. Alsterlund has said of her, "Mack trucks, not meadow-larks, are city-bred Muriel Rukeyser's symbols of dawn." Her first collection, *Theory of Flight* (1935), in its title poem reflects her serious researches at the Roosevelt School of the Air. *U.S. 1* (1938) shows the poet's conviction that workmen were being exploited along that highway. Her later collections indicate a trend toward the psychological and the pathological; these include *A Turning Wind* (1939); *Beast in View* (1944); *The Green Wave* (1948); *Orpheus* (1949); *Selected Poems* (1951), *Chain Lightning* (1955); *Body of Waking* (1958); *Sun Stone* (1961); *I Go Out* (1961); *Selected Poems of Octavio Paz* (1961); *Poems 1935–1961* (1961). She is undoubtedly a subtle thinker and a skillful writer, but obscurity often mars the beauty of her work. Her intellectual strength and her interest in modern science and thought are well expressed in her biography of *Willard Gibbs: American Genius* (1942). She also paid tribute to Wendell Willkie in *One Life* (1957).

Rumford, Count. See BENJAMIN THOMPSON.

Runyon, [Alfred] Damon (b. Manhattan, Kan., Oct. 4, 1884—d. Dec. 10, 1946), journalist, short-story writer. Runyon grew up in Pueblo, Colo., where his first articles were printed in the Pueblo *Chieftain*. At fourteen he enlisted in the army and was sent to the Philippines during the Spanish American War. After ten years of reporting for western papers he became a sportswriter for the New York *American*

(1911). He was war correspondent for the Hearst papers in Mexico in 1912 and 1916, in Europe during World War I. From 1918 until his death he ran a column for the Hearst syndicate. Many of his stories about Broadway characters appeared in the *Saturday Evening Post* and other popular magazines; he had a large following long before his first book, *Guys and Dolls* (1932), was published. It was followed by *Blue Plate Special* (1934); *Money from Home* (1935); *My Wife Ethel* (1939); *Take It Easy* (1938); *My Old Man* (1939); *The Best of Runyon* (1938); *Runyon à la Carte* (1944); *Runyon First and Last* (1949). His style, so individual that it is often referred to as *Runyonese*, relies upon Broadway slang, outrageous metaphor, and a constant use of the present tense. *A Slight Case of Murder* (1935), with HOWARD LINDSAY, was Runyon's only play, although many of his stories were made into successful films. The musical comedy *Guys and Dolls* (1952), by Jo Swerling and Abe Burrows, with a score by Frank Loesser, was based on Runyon characters and incidents.

Edward Horace Weiner wrote *The Damon Runyon Story* (1948), and Clark Kinnaird wrote *A Guy Named Runyon* (1954). But the personal tragedies in his life were not truly revealed until Damon Runyon, Jr., published *Father's Footsteps* (1954). It is a revelation of the failure of his two marriages, the enslavement to alcohol he conquered only to find his wife a victim, his estrangement from his son.

Rush, Benjamin (b. near Philadelphia, Dec. 24, 1745—d. April 19, 1813), physician, chemist, teacher, public official, author. Rush was a great admirer of Thomas Jefferson and like him had an informed and worthwhile opinion on almost everything under the sun. He called agriculture "the true basis of national health, riches, and populousness." As a medical man he was overly dogmatic in his insistence on bleeding as a form of therapy. On the other hand, his theory that the yellow fever epidemic of 1793 was caused partly by poor sanitation was advanced for the times and led him to be ostracized by the medical profession. He made advances in dentistry and veterinary medicine. His *Medical Inquiries and Observations Upon the Diseases of the Mind* (1812) helped to found modern psychiatry. He argued for abolition of slavery and for women's education, opposed excessive study of Greek and Roman classics, defined man as a religious as well as a social and domestic animal. He wrote constantly, and his pamphlets compare with Benjamin Franklin's in breadth of interest. It was Rush who suggested to Thomas Paine the writing of COMMON SENSE. He was also a signer of the Declaration of Independence. He wrote *A Syllabus of a Course of Lectures on Chemistry* (1770); *Sermons to Gentlemen Upon Temperance and Exercise* (1772); *An Address to the Inhabitants of the British Settlements in America Upon Slave-Keeping* (1773); *An Inquiry into the Influence of Physical Causes Upon the Moral Faculty* (1786). He collected his *Essays: Literary, Moral, and Philosophical* in

1798, his *Medical Inquiries and Observations* in 1789. *The Autobiography of Benjamin Rush,* which included his *Travels Through Life* and his *Commonplace Book for 1789–1813* as he left it for his children, appeared in 1948 with George W. Corner as editor. L. H. Butterfield edited his *Letters* (2 v., 1951). Nathan G. Goodman wrote *Benjamin Rush, Physician and Citizen* (1934), and there is much about him in J. H. Powell's *Bring Out Your Dead: The Great Plague of Yellow Fever in Philadelphia in 1793* (1949).

Rush, James (b. Philadelphia, March 15, 1786—d. May 26, 1869), physician, psychologist, satirist. The son of BENJAMIN RUSH was a distinguished man and an eccentric. He married a wealthy woman, soon withdrew from the practice of medicine and devoted himself to a study of the human mind. In this field he published two books of some note: *The Philosophy of the Human Voice* (1827) and *A Brief Outline of an Analysis of the Human Intellect* (1865). In his *History of American Psychology* (1952) A. A. Roback deplores the neglect which these two books have suffered and calls Rush's system of psychology "bold and radical for the 1860's."

Rusk, Ralph L[eslie] (b. Rantoul, Ill., July 11, 1888—d. June 30, 1962), American literature specialist. Rusk taught literature at several universities, among them Indiana and Columbia. Among his publications: LITERATURE OF THE MIDDLE WESTERN FRONTIER (2 v., 1925); Emerson's letters for the years 1813–1881 (6 v., 1939); *The Life of Ralph Waldo Emerson* (1949).

Russell, Charles Edward (b. Davenport, Iowa, Sept. 25, 1860—d. April 23, 1941), poet, journalist, sociologist, biographer. After varied newspaper experience in Minneapolis, Detroit, and New York, Russell became city editor of the *World* in 1894 and managing editor in 1897. In 1900 he became publisher of Hearst's two Chicago newspapers, the *American* and the *Examiner*. After a breakdown in health in 1902 he shifted to magazine writing and became famous for his muckraking articles. He dealt with a number of subjects—Southern prison camps, Northern prisons, the Michigan copper strike, women's suffrage, slums owned by the Trinity Church Corporation—but his particular targets were the railroads and the meat packers. In 1908 he joined the Socialist Party; two years later he ran for governor of New York, in 1913 for mayor, and the following year for United States senator. Disagreeing with the party's pacifism during World War I, he was expelled for advocating America's entry into the war. President Wilson appointed him to Elihu Root's mission to Russia in 1917; out of his experiences came *Unchained Russia* (1918). In 1918 he went to Great Britain with the Committee on Public Information and a year later became a member of Wilson's Industrial Review Board.

Russell, an early Christian Zionist, was founder and president of the Pro-Palestine Federation of America. His interest in drama and music led him to write *Julia Marlowe: Her Life and Art* (1926) and *The American Orchestra and Theodore Thomas* (Pulitzer prize, 1927). Among his other works are: *Such Stuff as Dreams* (1902) and *The Twin Immortalities* (1904), verse; *The Greatest Trust in the World* (1905), an exposé of the meat packers; *The Uprising of the Many* (1907); *Lawless Wealth* (1908); *Thomas Chatterton: The Marvelous Boy* (1908); *Songs of Democracy* (1909); *Why I Am a Socialist* (1910); *Business: The Heart of the Nation* (1911); *Stories of the Great Railroads* (1912); *Wendell Phillips* (1918); *A-Rafting on the Mississipp'* (1928); *Blaine of Maine* (1931); and his autobiography, *Bare Hands and Stone Walls* (1933).

Russell, Irwin (b. Port Gibson, Miss., June 3, 1853—d. Dec. 23, 1879), poet. Russell was admitted to the bar at nineteen, but found the law dull. He escaped frequently on trips to Texas and New Orleans and observed life on the Mississippi. His early poems, usually in Negro dialect, were printed in *Puck, St. Nicholas,* and *Scribner's.* In 1878 he exhausted himself helping his father, a physician, in fighting a yellow fever epidemic in Port Gibson, and died some months later. Little is remembered today of his once-popular verse except CHRISTMAS NIGHT IN THE QUARTERS. *Poems by Irwin Russell* (1888) was reprinted in 1917 as *Christmas Night in the Quarters and Other Poems.*

Russell, John (b. Davenport, Iowa, April 22, 1885—d. March 6, 1956), explorer, newspaperman, short-story writer, novelist. The son of CHARLES EDWARD RUSSELL traveled widely, was a special correspondent of the New York *Herald* in Panama and Peru, later did miscellaneous writing for that paper. His reputation is based chiefly on his well-constructed short stories, which usually had exotic settings. Among his collections: *The Red Mark and Other Stories* (1919); *Where the Pavement Ends* (1921); *The Lost God and Other Adventure Stories* (1947).

Russell, Osborne (b. Hallowell, Maine[?], June 12, 1814—d. 1865[?]), frontiersman, memoirist. Russell spent the years 1834 to 1843 in the Far West and kept a *Journal of a Trapper*, not published until 1921. This is an important commentary on the mountain men and the BLACKFEET INDIANS. Russell's factual accounts are detailed and significant. Bernard De Voto makes numerous references to him in *Across the Wide Missouri* (1947).

Russell, Sir W[illiam] H[oward] (b. Ireland, March 28, 1820—d. Feb. 10, 1907), British journalist. Russell came to the United States as a correspondent for the London *Times*. His experiences in America during the first years of the Civil War and later are recorded in *Pictures of Southern Life, Social, Political, and Military* (1863); *My Diary North and South* (1863); and *Hesperothen: Notes from the West* (2 v., 1882). He was convinced that the Union could not be restored, especially after the Battle of Bull Run, which he described vividly. He had a quick eye and ready pen for description. *My*

Diary North and South was reissued in abridged form in 1954.

Rustics in Rebellion (pub., 1866, as *Campaigns of a Non-Combatant;* reprinted, 1950), war correspondence of GEORGE ALFRED TOWNSEND. A war correspondent of the New York *Herald* during the Civil War, Townsend was a brilliant pioneer of the kind of writing one finds in Stephen Crane's *Red Badge of Courage* and the dispatches written by the realistic correspondents of World War II. Like Crane's young soldier, he experienced the terror of being under fire, and he described vividly the several panics that swept the Army of the Potomac. His emphasis was on the common soldier and the sufferings of civilians.

Rutledge, Archibald [Hamilton] (b. McClellansville, S.C., Oct. 23, 1883—   ), teacher, poet, short-story writer. Rutledge, poet laureate of his native state, wrote much in prose and verse to celebrate the beauty and traditions of the region. His verse is pleasant and skillful, some of his most effective work being in quatrains. Among his poetry collections: *Under the Pines* (1907); *New Poems* (1917); *Collected Poems* (1925); *The Everlasting Light* (1949); *The Heart's Chalice* (1953). Rutledge's prose contains many effective descriptions of nature, and *Home by the River* (1941, 1955) describes a fine old house. *Those Were the Days* (1955) is autobiographical.

Ruxton, George [Augustus] Frederick (b. England, 1820—d. 1848), English traveler, soldier, ethnologist. Into his short life Ruxton compressed a dozen lifetimes of adventure. At fifteen he was expelled from the Royal Military Academy. At seventeen he was fighting in the Carlist Wars in Spain and was awarded the title of knight. At twenty he was hunting in Canada. By the time he was twenty-four he had made two trips to Africa and had contributed a paper on the Bushmen to the Ethnological Society of London. In 1846 he was in Mexico, traveled north to Colorado, and crossed the Great Plains. Back in England he published *Adventures in Mexico and the Rocky Mountains* (1847) and LIFE IN THE FAR WEST (1848). He died of dysentery before he could begin a second trip to the Rockies. Both his books are valuable accounts of life in the Rockies and are immensely readable. In 1924 the second half of Ruxton's *Adventures* was reprinted as *Wild Life in the Rocky Mountains*. *Life in the Far West* was reprinted in 1951. Clyde and Mae

Reed Porter wrote *Ruxton of the Rockies* (1950).

Ryan, Abram Joseph (b. Hagerstown, Md., Feb. 5, 1838—d. April 22, 1886), priest, poet. The son of an Irish immigrant, Abram Ryan studied at the Christian Brothers' School and at Niagara University, where he prepared for

the priesthood. He was ordained in 1856, and after a few years of teaching returned to the South, where he served as chaplain in the Confederate Army. He was deeply moved by the loss of the Confederate cause, the death of his younger brother in battle, and the suffering he saw everywhere. His grief expressed itself poignantly in his poems. After the war "the poet of the Lost Cause" served as priest in Augusta, Mobile, New Orleans, Biloxi, Nashville, Knoxville, Macon, and Mobile. He also edited, for brief periods, *The Pacificator* and the *Banner of the South* in Augusta, and *The Star,* a Catholic weekly in New Orleans. His poems were very popular in the South; many of them were set to music and sung in the schools. The best known are *The Conquered Banner, The Lost Cause,* and *The Sword of Robert E. Lee. Father Ryan's Poems* (1879) was followed by *A Crown for Our Queen* (1882), a book of religious verse. He retired in his last years to a Franciscan monastery in Louisville, where he worked on a life of Christ, but he did not live to complete it.

S

Saadi (*The Dial,* 1842; *Poems,* 1847), a poem by RALPH WALDO EMERSON. Emerson uses the Persian poet Saadi [Sadi] (1184[?]–1291[?]) as a mouthpiece for his own view of poetry. Saadi, honored as a Mohammedan saint, wrote with both simplicity and wit, qualities characteristic of Emerson himself. In the poem he praises the poet's aloofness and his search for beauty in the commonplace.

Sabatini, Rafael. See CAPTAIN BLOOD.

Sabbath Scene, A (1850), a poem by JOHN GREENLEAF WHITTIER. Nowhere else in Whittier's poetry does he speak with such violence against slavery and its friends in the North. He directs his denunciation especially against Northern clergymen who smugly urged the prompt execution of the Fugitive Slave Law and defended the system of slavery as a Biblical institution. He imagines a scene in which a poor Negress takes refuge in a church one Sabbath morning, and the parson helps to return her to her master. The poet denounces the clergyman and the church: "Down with pulpit, down with priest,/ And give us nature's teaching!" He awakes to find it all a dream. The poem was written in the hope of preventing the passage of Henry Clay's Fugitive Slave Law, which was supported by Daniel Webster.

Sabin, Edwin L[egrand] (b. Rockford, Ill., Dec. 23, 1870–   ), historian, novelist. Sabin's specialty was the West, about which he wrote fluently and often, and generally out of a fund of knowledge respected by other historians. His first book was *The Making of Iowa* (1900). Among his other writings: *When You Were a Boy* (1905); *Circle K* (1911); *Kit Carson Days* (1914; rev. ed., 1935); *On the Overland Stage* (1918); *Boys' Book of Frontier Fighters* (1919); *The Rose of Santa Fé* (1923); *Jim Bridger on the Moccasin Trail* (1928); *Wild Men of the Wild West* (1929); *Pirate Waters* (1941).

Sabin, Joseph (b. England, Dec. 9, 1821– d. June 5, 1881), bookseller, bibliographer. Sabin came to the United States in 1848 and opened a bookstore. By 1865 he was known as a specialist in rare books and prints. In 1868 he began an enterprise which took sixty-eight years to complete, his *Bibliotheca Americana: A Dictionary of Books Relating to America, from Its Discovery to the Present Time*. Of its twenty-nine volumes he edited the first fourteen; succeeding volumes were edited by WILBERFORCE EAMES and R. W. G. Vail.

Sacajawea (b. near Lemhi, Idaho, 1788[?] —d. April 9, 1884), Shoshone Indian woman, guide to Lewis and Clark Expedition. In 1800 she had been captured by an enemy tribe and sold to Toussaint Charbonneau, a French trader, who married her. Lewis and Clark persuaded her and her husband (together with their two-month-old child) to accompany them to the headwaters of the Missouri (her native home), to the Pacific, and back again. In their *Journals* Lewis and Clark make frequent and friendly mention of her. She served as interpreter, was helpful in securing horses and guides and in pointing out native food plants. Later she left Charbonneau, married a Comanche (1856), and went with him to the Wind River Reservation in Wyoming. Novels and biographies about Sacajawea include Emerson Hough's *The Magnificent Adventure* (1916); James W. Schultz's *Bird Woman* (1918); Grace R. Hebard's *Sacajawea* (1933); Ethel Hueston's *Star of the West* (1935); Donald C. Peattie's *Forward the Nation* (1942). See MERIWETHER LEWIS.

Sacco-Vanzetti case. A celebrated murder trial (May–July, 1921) in which two Italian aliens were condemned to death for killing a paymaster and a guard at South Braintree, Mass., on April 15, 1920. The trial and conviction brought repercussions throughout the country, including a review of the case by a committee appointed by Governor Fuller of Massachusetts (President Lowell of Harvard, President Stratton of the Massachusetts Institute of Technology, and Judge Robert Grant), but the two men were finally executed seven years later (Aug. 22, 1927). The case probably created more public controversy than any other criminal trial in the history of the United States, and many literary men and women engaged actively in the debate, mostly in behalf of the two defendants.

Nicola Sacco (b. 1891) and Bartolomeo Vanzetti (b. 1888) were avowed anarchists; in addition to the murder charge against them they were accused of evading the draft during World War I. They denied any part in the murder, and a witness who claimed he had participated in the crime exonerated them. The two were nevertheless condemned. As a result of the Bolshevik revolution in Russia and of the activities of the I.W.W. and other radical groups in this country, antiradical feeling ran high among patriotic elements in the United States during the early 1920's, and this feeling obviously became involved in the public response to the trial. How much this extralegal sentiment had to do with the actual court proceedings is still a matter of debate.

The two accused men knew little English at the time of their arrest, but they (especially Vanzetti) took a keen interest in learning the language during their imprisonment. They wrote hundreds of letters in Italian and English to friends, relatives, and sympathizers, and though the letters were ungrammatical they possessed considerable literary power. Vanzetti's final appeal has become a classic. A collection of *Letters of Sacco and Vanzetti* appeared in 1928; a transcript of the case appeared in five volumes in 1928–29, edited by Newton D. Baker; Felix Frankfurter wrote *The Case of Sacco and Vanzetti* (1927); and Michael Angelo Musmanno analyzed the case in *After 12 Years* (1939).

In 1948 appeared *The Legacy of Sacco and Vanzetti* by C. Louis Joughin and Edmund M. Morgan. Joughin analyzed 144 poems, six plays, and eight novels on the Sacco-Vanzetti theme. Upton Sinclair made the case the center of his novel entitled BOSTON (1928); James Thurber and Elliott Nugent introduced Vanzetti's famous letter into their social comedy *The Male Animal* (1940); Edna St. Vincent Millay (in her poem *Justice Denied in Massachusetts*, 1927), H. L. Mencken, John Dos Passos, Lola Ridge, Maxwell Anderson (whose plays *Gods of the Lightning*, 1928, and *Winterset*, 1935, were based on the case), and many others spoke in warm protest against the way the trial had been conducted. A series of paintings by Ben Shahn were published under the title *The Passion of Sacco and Vanzetti* (1961).

Sac Prairie. A fictional community in Wisconsin, the locale of a series of novels by AUGUST DERLETH depicting middle western prairie life from 1830 to 1950. A leading personage in the novels is Chalfonte Pierneau. Sac Prairie is undoubtedly based on Sauk City, Derleth's birthplace and residence. Derleth expected to write about fifty volumes in his saga, but has completed only eight.

Sacred Fount, The (1901), a novelette by HENRY JAMES. The title refers to the theory of the narrator that in an unequal marriage or liaison the older or weaker partner is refreshed and invigorated at the "sacred fount" of the younger or stronger personality, which in turn becomes depleted. The scene of the story is an English weekend house party, and the narrator attempts, by the use of his theory, to discover the relationships among his fellow guests. In the end he confides his hypothesis to one of the principals, who dismisses it as "a house of cards," leaving the narrator and the reader uncertain whether the denial is dictated by honesty or policy.

The book has been described by R. P. Blackmur as "the work in which James most nearly earned his reputation for difficulty." Almost a parody of James' own style, *The Sacred Fount* is more intellectualizing than fiction. Some critics assert, however, that in this book lies the clue to the whole intent of Henry James. A new edition (1953) had an introduction by Leon Edel.

Sacred Wood, The (1920), a collection of essays by T. S. ELIOT. The role of tradition is emphasized, both in creative writing and in literary criticism. The book was of major importance in determining the modern evaluation of the Metaphysical poets and the Elizabethan and Jacobean playwrights.

Sag Harbor (1899), a play by JAMES A. HERNE and DAVID BELASCO. The play is a revision of HEARTS OF OAK (1879), which was called *Chums* (1879) and based on an English play entitled *The Mariner's Compass* (prod. in the United States, 1865). It is a drama of rival lovers—in the earlier versions foster father and son, in *Sag Harbor* two brothers. Herne played the leading role; the play had a long run.

sailors' songs (shanties, chanteys). The practice of singing such songs is very ancient, as some of them indicate by their obsolete technical details. During the 18th and early 19th centuries the American merchant marine experienced a great growth and shantying became a well-developed art. "Forecastle songs," not sung as work songs, are largely variants of old English, Irish, and Scots ballads; other types with cadences adapted to the work at hand were "short-drag shanties," "halliard shanties," and "windlass or capstan shanties." Even on American ships Irish sailors were admitted to be the best shantymen, though in time they were outstripped by American Negroes. There was little partsinging, except occasionally among Negro crews.

Lincoln Colcord made the first collection of American sailors' songs, *Roll and Go* (1924), later revised by his daughter Joanna as *Songs of American Sailormen* (1938). Other collections: Frank Shay's *Iron Men and Wooden Ships: Deep Sea Chanties* (1924); Fannie H. Eckstorm and Mary W. Smyth's *Minstrelsy of Maine* (1927); Robert W. Neeser's *American Naval Songs and Ballads* (1938); Frank Shay's *American Sea Songs and Chanteys* (1948).

St. Clair, Arthur (b. Scotland, 1736—d. 1818), soldier. St. Clair served in the American army during the Revolution, but was court-martialed (1778) when he abandoned Fort Ticonderoga before Burgoyne's advance. He was exonerated, became a member of the Continental Congress and its president (1787). He was the first governor of the Northwest Territory (1787–1802), but when he was defeated by the Indians in a battle near Fort Wayne (Nov. 4, 1791), he resigned his army command and was later removed from his post as governor. He wrote a vindication of his conduct, *A Narrative of the Manner in Which the Campaign Against the Indians Was Conducted* (pub., 1812). His *Papers* were edited by W. H. Smith (2 v., 1882).

St. Elmo (1866), a novel by Augusta Evans Wilson. (See AUGUSTA JANE EVANS.) With the spectacular popularity of Mrs. Wilson's third novel, a kind of St. Elmo's fire ran through the South. Plantations, schools, hotels, steamboats, merchandise, infants, and thirteen towns were named for the Byronic hero of this melodrama. When Edna Earle, an impossibly gifted and erudite young prude, finally succeeded in taming St. Elmo, the South's womanhood swooned with delight and strong men wrote to the author to tell her they had been "saved" by her novel. Edward Wagenknecht calls it an unparalleled combination of trashy, hyperemotional subject matter and superelegant style, a "pious, pretentious, unwholesome book."

Saint-Gaudens, Augustus (b. Ireland, March 1, 1848—d. Aug. 3, 1907), sculptor, memoirist. Brought to the United States in his infancy, Saint-Gaudens studied art in America, France, and Italy, and produced many fine works, including the statue of Admiral Farragut in Madison Square, New York City, the equestrian monument to General Sherman at the 59th Street entrance to New York's Central Park, portrait statues of Lincoln, Robert Louis Stevenson, and many others. Two of his pieces are intimately linked with literature. One is his monument on Beacon Hill in Boston to Robert Gould Shaw (1837–1863), who was killed while storming Fort Wagner at the head of the first enlisted Negro Regiment; this monument evoked in 1900 William Vaughn Moody's An Ode in Time of Hesitation. The other is the impressive hooded and shrouded figure in Rock Creek Cemetery, Washington, D.C., dedicated to the memory of Henry Adams' wife Marian. Adams, an intimate friend of Saint-Gaudens, introduced him into his novel Esther (1884); the heroine is a portrait of Adams' wife, who had committed suicide.

Saint-Gaudens' *Reminiscences* (2 v.) appeared after his death (1913). Royal Cortissoz wrote his biography (1907). Saint-Gaudens was elected to the American Hall of Fame in 1920.

St. John, Hector. The pen name of Michel-Guillaume St. Jean de Crèvecœur.

St. Nicholas. A magazine for young people founded in November, 1873, by Roswell Smith and published in New York City. It ceased publication in February, 1940. Its most noted editor was Mary Mapes Dodge, author of *Hans Brinker, or, The Silver Skates* (1865). Practically every author of juvenile literature sooner or later contributed to the magazine; some became famous because of their contributions. Among them were Mark Twain, Kipling, Robert Louis Stevenson, Edward Eggleston, Howard Pyle, Palmer Cox (author of the *Brownie Books*), Frank Stockton, Frances Hodgson Burnett, Dorothy Canfield Fisher, Louisa May Alcott. Young, talented contributors were awarded prizes and membership in the magazine's literary society, the St. Nicholas League. Unfortunately, times and tastes changed and the magazine lost its popularity. However, the *St. Nicholas Anthology* (1948), with selections culled by Henry Steele Commager and an introduction by May Lamberton Becker, the magazine's last editor, proved very successful. This anthology was followed by a similar volume in 1950.

Saints and Strangers (1945), a history by George Willison. See Pilgrims.

Sala, George Augustus (b. England, 1828—d. 1895), war correspondent. Sala covered the Civil War for the London *Telegraph,* wrote *My Diary in America in the Midst of War* (1865). In 1879–80 he made an extensive tour of the United States; in his second report, *America Revisited* (1882), he tried to reach a better understanding of the country.

Sale, Chic [pen name of **Charles Partlow**]

(b. Huron, S.D., Aug. 25, 1885—d. Nov. 7, 1936), actor, humorist. Sale won wide acclaim on the vaudeville stage as an impersonator of rural types, from small girls to old men; later he played similar parts on the screen and was also popular in Broadway revues. He had some facility as a writer, which finally found vent in an extraordinary performance called *The Specialist* (1929). This was a small book upon a subject never before treated in print—the construction of outhouses. It sold a million copies in a very short time and is still being reprinted. Sale also wrote *A Corn-Husker Crashes the Movies* (1933) and other books.

Salem witchcraft trials. The witch hunt of 1692, in which hundreds were brought to trial, nineteen hanged, and one pressed to death, was no unique incident; it was merely the climax in America of a long history of superstition, as George Lyman Kittredge demonstrated in *Witchcraft in Old and New England* (1929). Witchcraft also "flourished in Anglican England, and survived the longest in Catholic Europe," according to Jarvis M. Morse (*American Beginnings,* 1952). The Salem trials have been particularly attractive as a subject for later authors.

The earliest account seems to be Deodat Lawson's *True Narrative of Some Remarkable Passages Relating to Sundry Persons Afflicted by Witchcraft, at Salem Village* (1692). Cotton Mather soon after published The Wonders of the Invisible World (1693), which received some indignant replies, and Increase Mather wrote *Cases of Conscience Concerning Evil Spirits* (1693). *Narratives of the Witchcraft Cases, 1648–1706,* were collected (1915) by George L. Burr. Other books on the subject are: Thomas Brattle's *A Full and Candid Account of the Delusion Called Witchcraft Which Prevailed in New England* (ms., 1692; pub., 1798); John Hale's *A Modest Enquiry into the Nature of Witchcraft* (1702), Samuel F. Haven's *The Mathers and the Witchcraft Delusions* (1874); W. S. Nevins' *Witchcraft in Salem Village in 1692* (1916); Marion Starkey's *The Devil in Massachusetts: A Modern Inquiry into the Salem Witch Trials* (1949); Margaret Alice Murray's *The God of the Witches* (1952).

Novels about the witchcraft dementia include: John Neal's Rachel Dyer (1828); J. W. De Forest's *Witching Times* (serialized, 1856–57); Mary E. Wilkins Freeman's *Giles Corey* (1893); Esther Forbes' Mirror for Witches (1928); Esther Hammand's *Road to Endor* (1940); Shirley Barker's *Peace, My Daughters* (1949); and others. J. N. Barker wrote a play about Salem, *Superstition* (1824); Cornelius Mathews (1817–1889) dramatized the subject in *Witchcraft: or, The Martyrs of Salem* (1846); Longfellow put *Giles Cory of the Salem Farms* (1868) in his New England Tragedies; Arthur Miller wrote a forceful drama, *The Crucible* (1953), which was later used as the basis for an opera. See Samuel Sewall.

Salinger, J[erome] D[avid] (b. New York City, Jan. 1, 1919—   ), novelist, short-story writer. Salinger was raised in and around New York City, attended three colleges but did not graduate, and served in France during World War II. His first story was published when he was twenty-one, and he has since published in

UPI

a number of magazines, but most frequently in *The New Yorker*. THE CATCHER IN THE RYE (1951), a novel dealing with two days in the life of Holden Caulfield, an adolescent boy on the verge of a nervous breakdown, was highly praised when it appeared and has come to be considered a work of high literary quality. Holden, who has run away from his prep school just before the start of Christmas vacations, is unwilling to go home and drifts about in New York, getting himself into a series of wryly humorous adventures; his sophistication and amazing but credible articulateness enable the "ageless adolescent" to comment, sometimes explicitly, sometimes implicitly, on the problems imposed on adolescence by modern society. Stylistically, the book is clean, concise, and particularly notable for Salinger's skillful use of colloquial speech.

Nine Stories (1953), a collection of stories which originally appeared in *The New Yorker*, was equally well received by the critics. Most of the stories deal with precocious, sometimes troubled, children, whose sensitivity is in strong contrast to the materialistic and emotionally empty adult world of their parents. The first story, "A Perfect Day for Bananafish," ends with the suicide of Seymour Glass. Salinger returned

to the Glass family in *Franny and Zooey* (1961), two long stories originally published in *The New Yorker*. Franny Glass, a pretty twenty-year-old college student, and her brother Zooey, a television actor, are the youngest of the original seven Glass children, two of whom are now dead and all of whom were child prodigies. Franny's intelligence and sensitivity leave her unable to cope with the pseudo-sophisticated and meaningless society in which she lives, and, in desperation at the spiritual barrenness of a world she cannot love, she has a nervous breakdown. In the long conversation which takes up almost half of the "Zooey" story, her brother reminds her of the "Fat Lady," a symbol of all the ugliness and pettiness of the world which she has categorically rejected but which she must nevertheless love, in order, as it were, to be saved. Although much of the story is centered on a discussion of religious mysticism Salinger claims that "Zooey" is not religious or mystical but a love story. Salinger has also written *Seymour: An Introduction*, another long story on the Glass family which appeared in *The New Yorker* in 1959 but has not yet been published in book form. F. L. Gwynn and J. L. Blotner wrote *The Fiction of J. D. Salinger* (1958). Perhaps no other author of so few works has been the subject of so many analyses in the scholarly journals.

Salisbury, Harrison E. (b. Minneapolis, Minn., Nov. 14, 1908—   ), correspondent. Salisbury attended the University of Minnesota and worked for the United Press from 1930 to 1948. A year later he joined *The New York Times*, won a Pulitzer Prize for International Correspondence in 1955. His book *American in Russia* (1955) describes his experiences and observations from 1949 to 1958. Salisbury's *The Shook-Up Generation* (1958) examined the problem of America's violent youth in congested cities. Other books: *Russia on the Way* (1946); *To Moscow—And Beyond* (1960).

Salmagundi; or, The Whim-Whams and Opinions of Launcelot Langstaff, Esq. and Others. A humorous periodical published by WILLIAM IRVING, JAMES KIRKE PAULDING, and WASHINGTON IRVING. It was issued in twenty numbers (Jan. 24, 1807–Jan. 25, 1808), and in 1808 was collected in book form. According to the preface the magazine, which stands as an American link between *The Spectator* and the *Pickwick Papers*, was designed to "instruct the young, reform the old, correct the town, and castigate the age." Under fantastic pseudonyms the writers aired their views on such topics as "the conduct of the world," politics, the theater, music, and the fashions of the day. In politics they were Federalist, in taste, aristocratic and conservative. This was the first writing of its kind to appear in the United States and was an immediate success. William Irving is known to be the author of the light verse and Paulding of the Oriental letters. In 1819 Paulding issued a second series by himself, but since it lacked the mixture of minds and variety of tastes needed to make it a true "salmagundi," it was not a success. Much of the discussion which led to the papers took place at Mount Pleasant, the home of Gouverneur Kemble on the banks of the Passaic near Newark, N.J.; in the papers it was called Cockloft Hall.

Saltus, Edgar [Evertson] (b. New York City, Oct. 8, 1855—d. July 31, 1921), essayist, novelist. Saltus studied at Heidelberg, Munich, and Paris. He graduated from the Columbia Law School in 1880, and with no intention of ever practising law, plunged into the kind of social life he later described in his novels. His first book, a biography of Balzac, appeared in 1884. There followed two epigrammatic condensations of garbled Schopenhauer and Spinoza entitled *The Philosophy of Disenchantment* (1885) and *The Anatomy of Negation* (1886). Bad as these were, they caught the popular fancy with their sophisticated pessimism. *Mr. Incoul's Misadventure,* the first of Saltus' "diabolical" novels, came out in 1887, followed by *The Truth About Tristrem Varick* (1888); *The Pace That Kills* (1889); *Vanity Square* (1906); etc. After his much-publicized divorce he wrote *Madam Sapphira* (1893), an attempt at self-justification thinly disguised as fiction.

Saltus early recognized the popular appeal of exotic and erotic history: THE IMPERIAL PURPLE (1892), a history of the Roman emperors; *Historia Amoris* (1906), a history of love; and *The Imperial Orgy* (1920), a history of the Romanoffs, found avid readers. Saltus parallels Oscar Wilde, whom he met in London and about whom he later wrote *Oscar Wilde: An Idler's Impression* (1919). Like Wilde he had a sharp wit and was vain and temperamental. His novels contain many excellent epigrams and at least one memorable character, Alphabet Jones. H. L. Mencken and Carl Van Vechten felt the magic of Saltus at his best, and both tried to re-establish his popularity. James Huneker portrayed him as a minor character in PAINTED VEILS (1920) and was influenced by his style, as was Van Vechten. *Edgar Saltus the Man* (1925) is a biography by his third wife, Marie Saltus, who, with the best of intentions, accentuated all that was petty and foolish in her husband's life, putting the kiss of death on his literary fame. See THE EROTIC SCHOOL.

Salut au Monde (called *Poem of Salutation* in *Leaves of Grass,* 1856 ed.; given its present title in 1867), a poem by WALT WHITMAN. This extraordinary composition proclaims in minute and specific detail Whitman's kinship with all mankind. Whitman reviews a multitude of scenes all over the world, sees people working and traveling, performing their religious rites and their daily tasks. Henry Alonzo Myers has commented on the poem: "He does not say, I am the equal of that man; he says, I am that man; and he says it of all the people of the earth."

Salvation Nell (1908), a drama by EDWARD SHELDON. The heroine, Nell Sanders, who supports a wastrel on her earnings as scullery maid in a barroom, goes to the Salvation Army when she loses her job, and there meets Lieutenant Maggie O'Sullivan. The highly emotional scenes that follow Nell's reformation gave an excellent opportunity for the talents of Mrs. Minnie Maddern Fiske, who played the part. Old-fashioned and sentimental, *Salvation Nell* nevertheless shows Sheldon's observation of life and a sense of theater remarkable in a man of twenty-two.

Samantha. Samantha was a leading character created by MARIETTA HOLLEY in a long series of humorous books that, in their day, were almost as popular as Mark Twain's. The humor of the character arose from her homilies, her malapropisms, and her awkward aphorisms in the course of her various excursions with her acquiescent husband, Josiah. She reflected, however, the opinions of the more advanced women of her day, and found time for a bit of pleasant propaganda in the cause of temperance and women's suffrage. The character was described by Miss Holley's publishers as "cute, wise, shrewd, and observing, with a vein of strong common sense."

Sam Clemens of Hannibal (1952), a biography by DIXON WECTER. Published posthumously, this first volume of a projected definitive biography of Mark Twain covers his boyhood years. Wecter felt that "no major artist ever made more of his boyhood than did Samuel Clemens," and his biography was praised by critics.

Sam Slick. See T. C. HALIBURTON and S. A. HAMMETT.

Samuel, Maurice (b. Rumania, Feb. 8, 1895 —   ), essayist, novelist, social historian. In his autobiographical *The Gentleman and the Jew* (1950), Samuel describes his turning away from the Jewish heritage and his return to it. His English upbringing, a ten-year stay in Palestine, and world-wide travel experience provide the background for his essays on Jewish subjects. Samuel introduced to English speaking readers the two great Yiddish humorists, Aleichem and Peretz, in *The World of Sholom Aleichem* (1943) and *Prince of the Ghetto* (1948). The former is Samuel's re-creation of Jewish life in southern Russia based on Aleichem's writings; the latter is a collection of stories with a preface and two chapters on the Yiddish language by Samuel. *Professor and the Fossil: Some Observations on Arnold J. Toynbee's A Study of History* (1956) displays Samuel's best qualities: humaneness, wit, and learning. Without being abusive he argues convincingly that Toynbee's treatment of the Jews is biased, unclear, incorrect, and incomplete. Among his books are: *The Outsider* (1921); *You Gentiles* (1924); *Web of Lucifer,* a novel (1947); *Certain Peoples of the Book,* essays on biblical characters (1955); and *Second Crucifixion,* a novel (1960).

Sanborn, Franklin Benjamin (b. Hampton Falls, N.H., Dec. 15, 1831—d. Feb. 27, 1917), teacher, biographer, editor, journalist, abolitionist. Sanborn was a friend of RALPH WALDO

EMERSON, BRONSON ALCOTT, and THEODORE PARKER and claimed he was more indebted to them for his education than to Harvard. While still an undergraduate he started a little school at Concord, at Emerson's request, where he taught the children of Emerson, Nathaniel Hawthorne, Horace Mann, and John Brown, conducting his classes according to Alcott's "progressive" methods. A staunch abolitionist, Sanborn assisted in the underground railroad and toured the West in 1856 to report on the progress of the Free Soil group. He was involved in the plans for John Brown's raid on Harper's Ferry, and for a while was in trouble with the law.

Sanborn edited the Boston *Commonwealth* and was a resident editor of the Springfield *Republican*. Much of his life was spent collecting material about the great New Englanders. He published *Henry D. Thoreau* (1882); *The Life and Letters of John Brown* (1885; the 4th ed., 1910, was called *John Brown, Liberator of Kansas and Martyr of Virginia*); *Dr. S. G. Howe, the Philanthropist* (1891); *Bronson Alcott: His Life and Philosophy* (with W. T. Harris, 2 v., 1893); *The Personality of Thoreau* (1901); *Ralph Waldo Emerson* (1901); *Hawthorne and His Friends* (1908); *Recollections of Seventy Years* (2 v., 1909); *The Life of Henry David Thoreau* (1917).

After the Civil War Sanborn retained his political interests and continued to attack the stupidity and venality of Massachusetts politicians for many years. He became secretary of the state Board of Charities in 1863 and worked tirelessly for the improvement of prisons, insane asylums, schools for the deaf, and orphanages. Appreciations of Sanborn appeared in the *Proceedings of the Massachusetts Historical Society,* one by Lindsay Swift in 1917, another by Edward Stanwood in 1918.

Sanctuary (1931), a novel by WILLIAM FAULKNER. The acts of violence—Temple Drake's rape and Tommy's murder—central to the story set the lawyer Horace Benbow on a quest for justice which ends with his realization that the law is often more closely related to public opinion than to the unbiased aims of justice. Believing the accused murderer, Lee Goodwin, to be innocent, Benbow unsuccessfully attempts to give shelter to Goodwin's common-law wife and their infant son, and to find out the truth from TEMPLE DRAKE, who witnessed the murder. Temple falsely testifies against Goodwin to protect POPEYE, the rapist and real murderer, and Goodwin is killed by the townspeople. (See REQUIEM FOR A NUN.)

Sandburg, Carl (b. Galesburg, Ill., Jan. 6, 1878—d. July 22, 1967), poet, biographer. The son of Swedish immigrants, Sandburg attended public schools until he was thirteen, then began a long series of varied jobs, in Galesburg and on a wandering tour of the West: driver of a milk wagon, porter in a barber shop, scene shifter in a theater, worker in a brick kiln, carpenter's assistant, dishwasher, house painter, etc. In the Spanish-American War he served

for eight months in Puerto Rico. After the war he entered Lombard College, where he became a student of Philip Green Wright. Sandburg's first book, a paperbound pamphlet of thirty-nine pages called *In Reckless Ecstasy* (1904),

UPI

was set up and printed on a hand press in Wright's basement. Of the fifty copies printed only two or three, now collector's items, are known to exist.

Later Sandburg traveled for a while as a representative of Underwood & Underwood, selling stereopticon slides. In 1907–08 he worked as a district organizer for the Wisconsin Social-Democratic party, then wrote for several Milwaukee newspapers, notably the *Leader.* On June 15, 1908, he married Lillian Steichen, a schoolteacher and sister of the famous photographer Edward Steichen. From 1910 to 1912 he served as secretary to Emil Seidel, first socialist mayor of Milwaukee.

Sandburg moved to Chicago to continue his newspaper career on the *Daily News* and the *Daybook.* His first poems to gain a wide audience appeared in Harriet Monroe's POETRY: A MAGAZINE OF VERSE in 1914. Two years later appeared his *Chicago Poems,* and in 1918 he published CORNHUSKERS. Both volumes were well received by fellow poets and by a fairly wide general audience.

Meanwhile Sandburg had set out to make himself an authority on Lincoln, whose personality and achievements greatly attracted the poet who had made the virtues of American democracy his principal subject. His exhaustive biography of the Civil War President, requiring many years of preparation and writing, appeared as *Abraham Lincoln: The Prairie Years* (2 v., 1926) and *Abraham Lincoln: The War Years* (4 v., 1939), which won a Pulitzer prize. The first twenty-six chapters from the biography were issued separately as *Abe Lincoln Grows Up* (1931), with an introduction by Max J. Herzberg, and an abridgment of all six volumes, *Abraham Lincoln,* appeared in 1954.

Sandburg's growing reputation during the 1920's and 1930's allowed him to give up newspaper work and live on his writing and his lecturing. He toured the country several times, reading from his poems and singing folk songs, which he accompanied on the guitar. His collections of local ballads, THE AMERICAN SONGBAG (1927) and *The New American Songbag* (1950), have been an important contribution to the literature of American folklore. For a time the poet conducted a syndicated newspaper column. He served as narrator for the radio series called "Cavalcade of America," took part in foreign broadcasts of the Office of War Information, and also contributed his services as writer to other wartime projects. For several years he lived with his wife and three daughters near Harbert, Mich., on a bluff overlooking Lake Michigan. He later retired to a farm at Flat Rock, N.C. In 1946 the Carl Sandburg Association began the restoration of his birthplace in Galesburg.

Sandburg's principal books of poetry, besides those already mentioned, are: SMOKE AND STEEL (1920); *Slabs of the Sunburnt West* (1922); *Selected Poems* (1926); GOOD MORNING, AMERICA (1928); *Early Moon* (1930); THE PEOPLE, YES (1936). In 1950 appeared his *Complete Poems,* for which he won a second Pulitzer prize. In prose, besides the Lincoln biography, Sandburg wrote the biography of his brother-in-law, *Steichen the Photographer* (1929); *The Chicago Race Riots* (1919); *Mary Lincoln, Wife and Widow* (1932); four books for children, ROOTABAGA STORIES (1922); *Rootabaga Pigeons* (1923); *The Rootabaga Country* (1929); and *Potato Face* (1930); REMEMBRANCE ROCK (a novel, 1948); *Always the Young Strangers* (1952), an autobiographical account of his youth; and *Prairie Town Boy* (1955), a reprint of one section of *Always the Young Strangers.* In 1960 he collaborated on the screen play for *King of Kings.*

In mood Sandburg's poetry ranges from his brutal attack on Billy Sunday (*To a Contemporary Bunkshooter*) to the vigor of his paeans to American democracy and the tenderness of such wispy fantasies as *Fog.* His style is made of equal parts of Whitman, the Imagists, and original Sandburg, with a passing debt to the Lincoln of the *Gettysburg Address.* Rhymeless and unmetered, his poems nevertheless employ strong cadences derived from common Middle Western speech, and the diction ranges from a strong, sometimes hackneyed rhetoric to easygoing slang. He was not above invective, for among his poems are

powerful denunciations of hypocrisy and political and commercial chicanery. He often wrote about the uncouth and the vulgar, the muscular and the primitive. Yet behind this vigor and animal force lies a large fund of pity and loving-kindness which is the primary motive for all his poetry. Sandburg is not in fashion today with the academic poets and critics who have, perhaps temporarily, captured the positions of power in the American literary world; but his work remains popular with a large and loyal audience. There is no doubt that his poems offer a representation of his time and place which is at once widely characteristic and poetically significant.

In 1961, HARRY GOLDEN wrote *Carl Sandburg,* a biographical study.

RICHARD CROWDER

Sanderson, Ivan Terence (b. Scotland, Jan. 30, 1911—   ), biologist, nature writer. After his graduation from Cambridge, Sanderson started his travels, collecting specimens for zoos and museums, covering in all about sixteen countries. He became well known to Americans with *Animal Treasure* (1937), a Book-of-the-Month Club selection illustrated with his own delicate drawings. According to *Time* magazine, "His sympathy towards animals is as rich as his eye for detail is acute, and his prose style is limpid." Other critics recognized his gift for communicating his sincere love of nature. Some of his books are: *Animal Tales* (1946); *The Monkey Kingdom* (1957); *Abominable Snowmen* (1961); and *The Continent We Live On* (1961).

Sanderson, John (b. Carlisle, Pa., [?], 1783 —d. April 5, 1844), teacher, author. At first Sanderson studied law, later taught in the Clermont Seminary. He became a well-liked contributor to several periodicals, particularly *The Port Folio* and *The Aurora.* He and his brother Joseph wrote two volumes of *Lives of the Signers of the Declaration of Independence* (1820; completed in seven additional volumes by Robert Waln, Jr.). His health failed in 1835 and he went abroad to France and then to England. His impressions of the former country were given in *Sketches of Paris: Familiar Letters to His Friends, by an American Gentleman* (2 v., 1838); those of England appeared in several papers in the *Knickerbocker Magazine.* They were genial, observant sketches; the Parisian letters were reprinted in England as *The American in Paris* (2 v., 1838).

Sandoz, Mari Susette (b. Sheridan County, Neb., 1901—d. Mar. 10, 1966), novelist, historical writer. Miss Sandoz, the daughter of Swiss emigrants, did not speak English until she started school at the age of nine, considering Swiss German her mother tongue. Her informal education, however, was strictly western American, including much contact with the Sioux Indians. When she was sixteen she passed the rural teachers' examination and taught school in western Nebraska for five years. She studied intermittently at the University of Nebraska, took a position as research worker and associate editor of the *State Journal of the Nebraska Historical Society.*

In 1935, after thirteen rejections, her biography of her father, *Old Jules,* was accepted and awarded the Atlantic Monthly prize. In 1947 she began teaching advanced fiction writing at the Writers' Institute of the University of Wisconsin. Her novels include *Slogum House* (1937); *Capital City* (1939); *The Tom-Walker* (1947); *Miss Morissa* (1955). Her best work, however, is found in her nonfiction narratives: *Crazy Horse* (1942); *Cheyenne Autumn* (1953); *The Buffalo Hunters* (1954); *The Cattlemen* (1958); and two books in 1961, *Love Song to the Plains* and *These Were the Sioux.* She also contributed articles and fiction to magazines. All her writings show her interest in history and her Nebraska background.

Sands, Robert C[harles] (b. Flatbush, N.Y., May 11, 1799—d. Dec. 16, 1832), poet, essayist, editor. Sands, a likeable and competent writer of the KNICKERBOCKER SCHOOL, wrote skillful verse, was a genial essayist, edited several magazines and yearbooks in collaboration with WILLIAM CULLEN BRYANT and G. C. VERPLANCK. His best known poem, written with JAMES W. EASTBURN, was called *Yamoyden* and was about King Philip. *The Writings of Robert C. Sands, in Prose and Verse* (2 v., 1834) was edited by Verplanck. Bryant wrote a memoir of him in the *Knickerbocker Magazine.*

Sangster, Charles (b. Point Frederick, Upper Canada [now Ontario], July 16, 1822—d. Dec. 9, 1893), poet, post office official. Sangster has been called the first poet to make appreciative use of Canadian subjects. He contributed verse and prose to several periodicals, for a time edited *The Courier* in Amherstburg, published *The St. Lawrence and the Saguenay and Other Poems* (1856); *Hesperus and Other Poems* (1860); and *Our Norland* (1893). Although Oliver Wendell Holmes said, "His verse adds new interest to the woods and streams amidst which he sings," his poetry is largely imitative of his English contemporaries.

Sangster, Margaret E[lizabeth] (b. New Rochelle, N.Y., Feb. 22, 1838—d. June 4, 1912), newspaperwoman, editor, poet, writer of juveniles. Mrs. Sangster's name was associated as editor or subeditor with many important magazines of her time, including *Hearth and Home,* the *Christian Intelligencer, Harper's Young People, Harper's Bazaar,* the *Christian Herald,* the *Ladies' Home Journal,* and the *Woman's Home Companion.* She wrote, sentimentally but not unsensibly, *Little Janey* (1855); *Poems of the Household* (1882); *Easter Bells* (1897); *Winsome Womanhood* (1900); *Good Manners for All Occasions* (1904); *My Garden of Hearts* (1913); and many other books. *An Autobiography: From My Youth Up* (1909) described her busy career.

Sankey, Ira David. See DWIGHT LYMAN MOODY.

Santa Anna [or Ana], Antonio López de (b. Mexico, 1795—d. 1876), soldier, politician. Santa Anna was a soldier in the Spanish army for a while, returned to Mexico and after several revolts gained the presidency in 1833. When Americans in Texas talked about separation from Mexico, he made himself dictator. He besieged the Alamo, a fort, and massacred all its defenders. He suffered a severe defeat by Sam Houston at the Battle of San Jacinto, was captured by the Texans, and was released only on condition that he would approve the independence of Texas. He defended Vera Cruz unsuccessfully against a French invasion and, in 1841, again became President. During the Mexican-American War he led the Mexican Army, but was severely defeated. He resigned and left the country. In 1853 he was recalled to become President again, but another revolution soon drove him out. He died in extreme poverty. His *Letters Relating to War* were edited by J. H. Smith for the American Historical Association *Report* (1917).

Santa Fe Trail: A Humoresque, The (1914), a poem by VACHEL LINDSAY. Lindsay gives in this famous poem a vehement and vivid picture of industrial civilization at the beginning of the 20th century. His details, presented with his usual heavy rhythms and his imitation of jazz cadences, have deceived some readers into believing that he endorsed this civilization. On the contrary, his intention was to make clear his preference through the contrast between images of commercialism and the frequent interruptions of the Rachel-Jane bird, which sings quietly of love and eternal youth.

Santa Fe Trail, the. The main overland route to the Southwest and southern California in the years before the railroad. Innumerable explorers, traders, military expeditions, and travelers traversed the Santa Fe Trail, and it is still the route of a transcontinental highway and the Atchison, Topeka, and Santa Fe Railroad. The trail began at Independence (originally at Franklin), Mo., proceeded along the prairie divide to the great bend of the Arkansas River, followed the river upward almost to the mountains, then turned south to Santa Fe. It was originally traced by WILLIAM BECKNELL in 1821.

Josiah Gregg's *Commerce of the Prairies* (2 v., 1844) is the classic account of the trail; additional information is contained in Gregg's *Diary and Letters* (1941), edited by M. G. Fulton. Other nonfiction is: George W. Kendall's *Narrative of the Texan Santa Fe Expedition* (2 v., 1844); G. F. RUXTON's LIFE IN THE FAR WEST (1859); Henry Inman's *The Old Santa Fe Trail* (1897); R. L. Duffus' *The Santa Fe Trail* (1930); STANLEY VESTAL's *The Old Santa Fe Trail* (1939); and *The Santa Fe Trail* (1946), compiled by the editors of *Look* magazine. Novels about the trail include STANLEY VESTAL's *'Dobe Walls* (1917); R. L. Duffus' *Jornada* (1935); HARVEY FERGUSSON's trilogy

Followers of the Sun (1936); Ottamar Hamele's *When Destiny Called* (1948).

Santa Filomena (*Atlantic Monthly*, November, 1857), a poem by HENRY WADSWORTH LONGFELLOW. A phrase that Longfellow applied in this poem to Florence Nightingale—"a lady with a lamp"—gained worldwide currency.

Santayana, George (b. Spain, Dec. 16, 1863 —d. Sept. 26, 1952), philosopher, poet, novelist, critic. There were two principal centers of attachment in Santayana's life: the Spanish town of Avila where he spent his childhood

and Cambridge, Mass., where he studied and taught. His mother, at the time of her marriage to his father, was a widow with three children; Santayana was named for her first husband, George Sturgis, a wealthy Bostonite. The boy's removal from Spain to Massachusetts when he was nine years old involved, as he later said, "a terrible moral disinheritance." He was never again to feel at home in Spain, yet he remained Spanish in nationality and sentiment.

In the Boston Latin School, Santayana acquired a love of poetry and himself began to write verse. He went on to Harvard University, then studied for two years in Berlin, where he acquired a thorough knowledge of the Greek philosophers, although he found German philosophy repugnant. He earned his M.A. and Ph.D. degrees in another year at Harvard and took a teaching position in the department of philosophy there. He loved teaching and was an eloquent lecturer. Robert Benchley, one of his students, confessed to being baffled by the meaning of his words, but enthralled by their music. Also among his students were Conrad Aiken, Felix Frankfurter, Walter Lippmann, and T. S. Eliot.

In spite of his pleasure in teaching, Santayana always hated "to be a professor," and when in

1912 he received a legacy that made him independent, he resigned from the university and spent the rest of his life in travel and study. He made occasional trips to Spain, but for the most part passed his winters in Rome and his summers in Paris. He spent the First World War in England. At the beginning of the Second, he moved into a nursing home in Rome, a retreat conducted by an English order of Roman Catholic sisters; he once said he was a Catholic in everything except faith. Here he lived the rest of his life, undisturbed by the Italian government since he had retained his Spanish citizenship. He was buried in Rome at the Verona Catholic Cemetery in the tomb of the Spaniards, thus returning symbolically to the country of his birth.

Santayana said of his own work that it might be divided into two strands, the poetic and the academic. The poetic, which is also the personal, includes such works as *Sonnets and Other Verses* (1894); LUCIFER: A THEOLOGICAL TRAGEDY (1899); *The Hermit of Carmel and Other Poems* (1901); *Soliloquies in England and Later Soliloquies* (1925); DIALOGUES IN LIMBO (1925). THE LAST PURITAN (1935), his only novel, won him popular fame. His memoirs, *Persons and Places*, were published in three volumes: *The Background of My Life* (1944); *The Middle Span* (1945); *My Host the World* (1953).

The academic strand begins with *The Sense of Beauty* (1896), an outline of an aesthetic theory. *Interpretations of Poetry and Religion* (1900) is the practical application of his concepts. His most outstanding early work is THE LIFE OF REASON; OR, THE PHASES OF HUMAN PROGRESS, published in five volumes: *Introduction and Reason in Common Sense* (1905); *Reason in Society* (1905); *Reason in Religion* (1905); *Reason in Art* (1905); *Reason in Science* (1906). Santayana called this work "only a semijudicial review of the most familiar forms of society, religion, art, and science in the western world." It is based on a materialistic view of nature and life, somewhat modified in *Scepticism and Animal Faith* (1923), which contends that, though logic compels man to skepticism, animal faith leads him to acquire knowledge. This book serves as an introduction to *Realms of Being*, which discusses the themes of man's knowledge in four volumes: *The Realm of Essence* (1927); *The Realm of Matter* (1930); *The Realm of Truth* (1937); *The Realm of Spirit* (1940).

Other works are: *Three Philosophical Poets: Lucretius, Dante, and Goethe* (1910); *Winds of Doctrine* (1913); *Platonism and the Spiritual Life* (1927); *Turns of Thought in Modern Philosophy* (1933); *Obiter Scripta: Lectures, Essays and Reviews* (1936); *The Idea of Christ in the Gospels* (1946). Works dealing with the American character are *Philosophical Opinion in America* (1918); CHARACTER AND OPINION IN THE UNITED STATES (1921); THE GENTEEL TRADITION AT BAY (1931). *Dialogues in Limbo* (1925; reissued, 1948) is a work that Santayana himself esteemed most highly. A collection of his aphorisms, *Atoms of Thought*, appeared in 1950. *Dominations and Powers: Reflections on Liberty, Society, and Government* (1951) expresses his conviction that "the world is positively crying for a universal government." *The Letters of George Santayana* (1955) were edited with a commentary and introduction by Daniel Cory.

Santayana made no claim to originality. In the introduction to *Scepticism and Animal Faith* he said, "For good or ill I am an ignorant man, almost a poet, and I can only spread a feast of what every one knows." He had a certain daemonic quality of intellect that made even his satire seem to be a kind of cold light. It has been said of him that his basic premise was, "Chaos is perhaps at the bottom of everything." Many of his other sayings are memorable: "Those who cannot remember the past are condemned to repeat it." "*Fanaticism:* redoubling your efforts when you have forgotten your aim." "Everything in life is lyrical in its ideal, tragic in its fate and comic in its existence." "It is easier to make a saint out of a libertine than out of a prig." "The young man who has not wept is a savage, and the old man who will not laugh is a fool." Willard Arnett analyzed his work in *Santayana and the Sense of Beauty* (1955).

Santee, Ross (b. Thornburg, Iowa, Aug. 16, 1888—   ), artist, novelist. Santee attended the Chicago Art Institute, ambitious to become a cartoonist. Instead, discouraged by his early experiences in New York, he went to Arizona to work on the range. After a while he resumed his drawings of cowboys, horses in action, Apache Indians, which struck the fancy of editors in the East. They bought his work, encouraging him to also "put down on paper some of his yarns." He then embarked on a long career of illustrating and writing stories mostly concerned with the West. He admired artists such as Daumier and Forain, and writers such as Mark Twain, W. H. Hudson, and Tom Lea. In a modest appraisal of his work he said: "I always have a good alibi; in the company of writers I try to pass off as an artist, in the presence of artists I swap the deck; in this way controversy can always be avoided." Some of his books: *Men and Horses* (1926); *Cowboy* (1928); *The Pooch* (1931); *The Bar X Golf Course* (1933); *The Bubbling Spring* (1949); *Rusty* (1950); *Hardrock and the Silver Sage* (1951); *Lost Pony Tracks* (1953).

Sapir, Edward (b. Germany, Jan. 26, 1884 —d. Feb. 4, 1939), anthropologist, linguist. Sapir came to the United States at an early age, graduated from Columbia University and began his learned studies in Germanics and the Indo-European languages. FRANZ BOAS gave him the opportunity to study American Indian languages, one of which—Takelma, spoken in Oregon—became the subject of his doctoral thesis. He taught at the University of Pennsylvania, was the chief anthropologist of the Geological Survey of Canada, taught at the University of Chicago, finally was head of the Anthropology Department of Yale University.

Sapir stressed the influence of culture and personality and was among the first to include semantics in his courses. He was a pioneer in the introduction of rigidly scientific methods to the study of languages and culture. He made contributions to theories of language and studies of particular languages; the best known was perhaps his division of Amerindian languages into six great stocks.

The most famous of Sapir's books is his semipopular *Language, An Introduction to the Study of Speech* (1921). He also wrote on the *Southern Paiute Language* (1931) and edited *Wishram Texts* (1909) and *Takelma Texts* (1909). His *Selected Writings* were edited by David Mandelbaum (1949). The London *Times Literary Supplement,* reviewing the latter book, said that "in spite of the necessarily formidable jargon of modern linguistics, he was a master of clear and picturesque English." Sapir was a poet as well as a scientist, contributing approximately two hundred poems to periodicals between 1917 and 1931. He was, moreover, a distinguished and prescient reviewer of poets.

Sapphira and the Slave Girl (1940), a novel by WILLA CATHER. In New Testament history Sapphira and her husband Ananias were struck dead for lying. The scene of Miss Cather's novel is Virginia, and the basis of the plot is probably a story current during her childhood there. The chief characters are several white families of distinction and a mulatto girl, Nancy Till, product of an illegitimate affair between her mother, housekeeper of the Henry Colbert household, and a painter who had done portraits of Colbert and his wife Sapphira. The latter is an invalid and becomes more and more jealous of Nancy, whom she unjustly suspects of trying to win her husband. She conspires against her unsuccessfully; the girl is assisted through the Underground Railroad to escape to Canada. Many years later she returns to visit her mother and the people who had helped her escape. The book is notable for its calm and scrupulous depiction of character.

Saracinesca (1887), a novel by F. MARION CRAWFORD. It was the first of four novels dealing with the fortunes of a great Italian family in Rome from 1865 to the 1890's. The chief figure of the novels is old Prince Saracinesca, the head of the house. The best-drawn of the characters is Corona Saracinesca, one of the most attractive of Crawford's numerous heroines. *Saracinesca* was followed by *Sant' Ilario* (1889); *Don Orsino* (1892); *Corleone* (1897).

Sarett, Lew (b. Chicago, May 16, 1888—d. Aug. 17, 1954), poet, lecturer, teacher. Sarett served as a woodsman, guide, and United States Ranger in the Rockies and Canada for several months each year for sixteen years. He became an instructor in English and public speaking at the University of Illinois in 1912 and was made head of the division of public speaking four years later. In 1920 he was appointed professor of oratory at Northwestern University.

Sarett's lyrical poetry has a wide range and is adept in its variety of rhythms and meters. It is often concerned with the American Indian and the creatures of the wild. Among his collections: *Many Many Moons* (1920); *The Box of God* (1922); *Slow Smoke* (1925); *Wings Against the Moon* (1931); *Collected Poems* (1941). He also wrote several speech manuals, in collaboration with W. T. Foster and others.

Sarg, Tony [Anthony Frederick] (b. Guatemala, April 24, 1880—d. March 7, 1942), illustrator, humorist, marionette-maker, author. Sarg, educated in Germany, served for a time in the German army, then worked as an illustrator in London. He came to the United States in 1915, was naturalized in 1921, and became famous for his marionette shows and the books he based on them. His books include *Tony Sarg's Book for Children* (1924); *Tony Sarg's Animal Book* (1925); *Tony Sarg's Wonder Zoo* (1927); *Tony Sarg's New York* (1927); *Tony Sarg's Wonder Book* (1941). He wrote a *Book of Marionette Plays* (1927) with Anne Stoddard. Among the books he illustrated were Irvin S. Cobb's *Fiddle, D.D.* and *Speaking of Operations* (both 1916).

Sargent, Epes (b. Gloucester, Mass., Sept. 27, 1813—d. Dec. 30, 1880), writer, editor. Sargent attended the Boston Latin School; his earliest literary effort, a series of letters written from Russia during a trip with his father, ap-

peared in the school paper. He worked for the Boston *Daily Advertiser* and the *Daily Atlas* for several years. In 1837 his play *Velasco* was produced in Boston and was published two years later. In New York, after working on the *Mirror* and the *New World*, he started *Sargent's New Monthly Magazine*, which lasted from January to June, 1843. He returned to Boston in 1847 to edit the *Transcript* but retired after a few years to write plays, poems, novels, and

textbooks. SPARTACUS TO THE GLADIATORS, Elijah Kellogg's famous elocution piece, was first published in Sargent's *School Reader* (1846). Among his chief works were: *Fleetwood; or, The Stain of Birth* (1845), a novel; *Songs of the Sea and Other Poems* (1847); *Change Makes Change* (1854) and *The Priestess* (1854), dramas; *Peculiar: A Tale of the Great Transition* (1864) and *The Woman Who Dared* (1870), poems. *Planchette; or, The Despair of Science* (1869); *The Proof Palpable of Immortality* (1875) and *The Scientific Basis of Spiritualism* (1880) were the results of his interest in the supernatural. See KNICKERBOCKER SCHOOL.

Sargent, John Singer (b. Italy, Jan. 12, 1856—d. April 15, 1925), painter. Born of American parents, Sargent was educated at the Academy in Florence and the École des Beaux Arts in Paris. He made his residence in England in 1884, but spent much of his time traveling in Italy, Morocco, and Spain, painting many portraits on commission. After a successful show in Boston in 1887 he remained there for two years, revisited England for a year, then returned to America in 1890. He studied in Egypt in search of background material for a series of murals for the Boston Public Library entitled "The History of Religion," which was begun in 1896 and completed in 1916.

In 1897 Sargent was elected to the Royal Academy. In spite of the sharp criticism of Roger Fry, a British critic who disdained Sargent's facile technique and easy beauty, he was very popular in England. He was besieged by ladies who wanted him to paint their portraits, and his technical ability deteriorated into superficial charm. He was a strong opponent of modern trends in painting, and was probably at his best in paintings of prim Boston matrons and white-pinafored children. Occasionally in paintings of rich upstarts he introduced a suggestion of social commentary.

John S. Sargent, His Life and Work (1925), was written by William Howe Downes. *The Lady and the Painter* (1951), by Eleanor Palffry, is a novel based on the lives of Sargent and Isabella S. Gardner, whose museum in Boston contains some of Sargent's best paintings. Charles Merrill Mount did a biography (1955); David McKibbon wrote *Sargent's Boston* (1956).

Sargent, Lucius Manlius (b. Boston, June 25, 1786—d. June 2, 1867), poet, antiquarian, translator. Sargent turned from the study of law to translating Virgil, wrote poetry of his own, engaged in antiquarian research. He was especially interested in two crusades—temperance and the defense of slavery. Among his books: *Hubert and Ellen and Other Poems* (1812); *The Stage Coach* (1838); *Temperance Tales* (6 v., 1863–64); *The Ballad of the Abolition Blunder-buss* (1861). J. H. Sheppard wrote *Reminiscences of L. M. Sargent* (1871).

Sargent, Porter (b. Brooklyn, N.Y., June 6, 1872—d. March 27, 1951), publisher, teacher, zoologist, writer. Sargent taught in California schools and at Harvard University. He then turned to the preparation of handbooks on private schools and summer camps. He was a fearless and outspoken writer, and his caustic introductions to these volumes make amusing reading. Among his other works: *Spoils: Poems from a Crowded Life* (1935); *Education: A Realistic Approach* (1939); *Between Two Wars: The Failure of Education, 1920–1940* (1945); *What's Wrong With Us?* (1949); *Is Poetry a Secretion?* (1949).

Sargent, Winthrop (b. Philadelphia, Sept. 23, 1825—d. May 18, 1870), historian, editor. Sargent was interested chiefly in historical research on the Revolutionary period. He wrote some notable works, among them *A History of an Expedition Against Fort Duquesne, Under Major General Braddock* (1855) and *The Loyalist Poetry of the Revolution* (1857). His *Life and Times of Major John André* (1861) perhaps overeulogized the British spy. He also edited the loyalist poems of Joseph Stansbury and Jonathan Odell (1860).

Saroyan, William (b. Fresno, Cal., Aug. 31, 1908—   ), short-story writer, novelist, playwright, song writer. Saroyan's early childhood was spent in an orphanage until his widowed mother was able to support her nu-

merous children. He attended Fresno Junior High School, read avidly, and left school at twelve to become a telegraph messenger. He was unable to remain at any job for long, and after he had disappeared from work repeatedly he was blacklisted by the employment bureau.

His first short story to be published (in the Armenian magazine *Hairenik*) was reprinted in O'Brien's *Best Short Stories of 1934*. In the same year THE DARING YOUNG MAN ON THE

FLYING TRAPEZE appeared. The breezy, impertinent, tender style made it an immediate success. There followed *Inhale and Exhale* (1936); *Three Times Three* (1936); *Little Children* (1937); *Love, Here Is My Hat* (1938); *The Trouble with Tigers* (1938); and *Peace, It's Wonderful* (1939). The autobiographical *My Name Is Aram* (1940) contains some of his best stories. THE HUMAN COMEDY (1942), an exuberant novel about a little boy who delivered telegrams during World War II, was largely autobiographical. It was made into a successful movie. His play *My Heart's in the Highlands* (1939) was a Broadway success, and THE TIME OF YOUR LIFE (1939) won a Pulitzer prize which the author refused to accept. *Love's Old Sweet Song* (1940) and *The Beautiful People* (1941) were less successful. In 1961, *Two by Saroyan* (including *The Cave Dwellers*, 1958) were revived off Broadway. Saroyan's stories leave behind them an aura of eccentric sentimentality. His later writings include *The Adventures of Wesley Jackson* (1946); *The Assyrian and Other Stories* (1950); *Rock Wagram and Tracy's Tiger* (1951); *The Bicycle Rider of Beverly Hills* (1952); *The Laughing Matter* (1953); *The Bouncing Ball* and *Mama, I Love You* (1956); *Papa, You're Crazy* (1957). The *William Saroyan Reader* was published in 1958. *Here Comes, There Goes You Know Who* (1961) is a volume of reminiscences.

Sarton, George [Alfred Leon] (b. Belgium, Aug. 31, 1884—d. March 21, 1956), teacher, historian of science. Sarton came to the United States in 1915 and became a citizen in 1924. His special field was chemistry, but his deepest interest was in the history of science. He lectured on the subject at Harvard University in 1916–18, became a member of the Harvard faculty in 1920, professor of the history of science after 1940. He founded two magazines devoted to his special field, *Isis* (1912) and *Osiris* (1936), and edited them both. He published many important books, among them *Introduction to the History of Science* (2 v., 1927, 1931); *The History of Science and the New Humanism* (1931); *The Study of the History of Science* (1936); *Science and Learning in the 14th Century* (2 v., 1947); *The Life of Science* (1948); *Science and Tradition* (1951); *Ancient Science Through the Golden Age of Greece* (1952); *Horus, A Guide to the History of Science* (1953); *Six Wings: Men of Science in the Renaissance* (1957). Sarton placed a strong emphasis on the contributions of Oriental science, especially in preparing for the "miracle" of Greece, and he threw new light on Greek science itself. He was an excellent writer with a strongly humanistic approach.

Sarton, [Elinor] May (b. Belgium, May 3, 1912—   ), poet, novelist. Miss Sarton and her mother came to the United States in 1916 to join her father GEORGE SARTON. She has taught literature and creative writing in several American colleges, has won numerous awards for her poetry and much critical praise for her work in both prose and poetry. Her novels include *The Single Hound* (1938); *The Bridge of Years* (1946); *Shadow of a Man* (1950); *A Shower of Summer Days* (1952); *Faithful Are the Wounds* (1955); *The Small Room* (1961). Among her collections of verse are: *Encounter in April* (1937); *Inner Landscape* (1939); *The*

picks up the beginnings of the Sartoris family in THE UNVANQUISHED.

Sartoris, Col. John. A leading character in William Faulkner's SARTORIS (1929), THE UNVANQUISHED (1938), and other novels and stories. He has numerous descendants and kinfolk. The Sartoris family is believed to be remi-

SARTORIS GENEALOGY

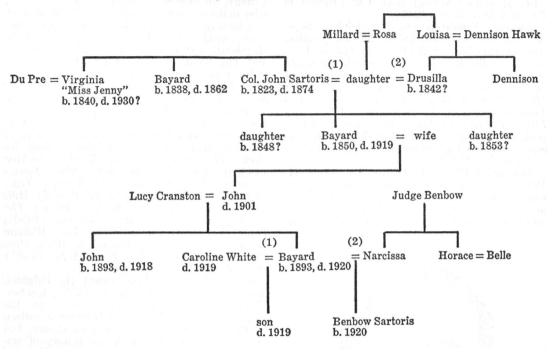

Lion and the Rose (1948); *The Land of Silence and Other Poems* (1953). Although her verses have been described as "pure poetry," she sometimes makes use of current themes and American scenes. *Fur Person* (1957) is the story of a "gentleman cat," and *I Knew A Phoenix* (1959) a collection of autobiographical reminiscences.

Sartoris (1929), a novel by WILLIAM FAULKNER. A saga of the Sartoris family, the novel deals primarily with young Bayard Sartoris' urge for self-destruction. His beloved twin brother, John, having been killed in World War I, Bayard returns home, haunted by the memories of his brother, and becomes involved in a number of accidents. Because of his reckless driving, his grandfather, old Bayard Sartoris, rides with him in an attempt to force him to drive carefully, but young Bayard runs the car off a cliff and his grandfather dies of a heart attack. Unable to face either himself or his family, Bayard goes to Ohio to become a test pilot and is killed. Faulkner's first novel to deal with YOKNAPATAWPHA COUNTY, *Sartoris* contains many of his later themes: the dying-out of the positive values of the Old South; the sterility and destructiveness of the industrial and machine age following World War I; and the inability of the heirs of the old world to adjust to the new. Faulkner

niscent of the Faulkner family, descendants of Col. William C. Faulkner (or Falkner).

Satanstoe (1845), a novel by JAMES FENIMORE COOPER. This was the first novel of a trilogy called *The Littlepage Manuscripts* which included also THE CHAINBEARER (1845) and THE REDSKINS (1846). It is autobiographical in form. Cornelius Littlepage is the heir of an aristocratic family of Dutch descent living at "Satanstoe," a strip of land in Westchester County, New York. He is educated at Princeton University, makes fun of the Yankees, is enthralled by the sights of New York City, "comes out" in society, saves a little girl from a caged lion, rescues her again from the Hudson in flood, and fights the French at Lake George. In *The Chainbearer* Cornelius' son Mordaunt works on the "patent" of land which the Littlepages hold in northern New York and comes in contact with squatters; in *The Redskins* Mordaunt's grandson takes part in the Anti-Rent War. Cooper made much use of material from Anne Grant's *Memoirs of an American Lady* (2 v., 1808). See ANTI-RENT LAWS.

Saturday Club. A Boston dinner club that came into existence in 1855, and was later called *Magazine Club* or *Atlantic Club*. Among its members were RALPH WALDO EMERSON,

HENRY WADSWORTH LONGFELLOW, JAMES RUSSELL LOWELL, LOUIS AGASSIZ, NATHANIEL HAWTHORNE, JOHN LOTHROP MOTLEY, CHARLES SUMNER, and JOHN GREENLEAF WHITTIER. They dined together once a month at the Parker House. OLIVER WENDELL HOLMES, the leader and perhaps the wittiest conversationalist of the group, immortalized the club in his poem *At the Saturday Club* (1884). Edward W. Emerson wrote about *The Early Years of the Saturday Club, 1855–1879* (1918), and M. A. DeWolfe Howe continued the narrative to 1920 in *The Later Years of the Saturday Club* (1927). The group still meets.

Saturday Evening Post, The. Volume I, Number 1, of the *Saturday Evening Post* was issued August 4, 1821, joining the scores of weekend miscellanies for Sunday reading then springing up all over the country. The founders were Charles Alexander and Samuel C. Atkinson, both ambitious young printers; the former brought to the partnership the subscription list of the *Bee*, a similar venture that had lasted only briefly, and the latter an interest in a printing plant that had once produced the defunct PENNSYLVANIA GAZETTE. During its first five years the *Post* was edited, chiefly by the use of scissors and pastepot, by Thomas Cottrell Clarke. The paper contained some tales and poems by amateur writers, a serial of the seduction novel pattern then popular, a "Dramatic Summary" reviewing plays, an essay series, some household hints, and a considerable amount of news in single paragraph form.

The paper did well. The *Casket* (later GRAHAM'S MAGAZINE), which Atkinson and Alexander began as a monthly sister publication in 1826, passed on some of its own material to the *Post* for more than twenty years, including contributions by Edgar Allan Poe, Nathaniel Parker Willis, James Kirke Paulding, and John Neal. RUFUS W. GRISWOLD was literary editor of both publications in 1842–1843.

When the *Post* absorbed the *Saturday Bulletin* in 1832, it became one of the leading weekend miscellanies in America; in the next decade it absorbed three more such papers. In 1846 HENRY PETERSON, poet, novelist, and book publisher, was called to the editorial chair of the flourishing periodical. Two years later he and his publishing partner, Edmund Deacon, purchased the business, and the golden age of the early history of the *Saturday Evening Post* began. It still had only four pages, but they measured two feet wide by four feet long. The paper's leading contributors were Mrs. E. D. E. N. Southworth, the immensely popular writer of serial fiction, and the scarcely less popular Emerson Bennett, Mrs. Mary A. Denison, Grace Greenwood and "Fanny Fern" Willis. In the 1850's it added, mostly through literary piracy, the work of such famous English novelists as Dickens (*A Tale of Two Cities* appeared in 1858), Reade, Mrs. Mulock, "Ouida," and G. P. R. James. Though virtually unillustrated in its earlier years, the *Post* made a feature of its large front-page woodcut beginning in 1863;

and during the Civil War pictures borrowed from *Frank Leslie's Illustrated Newspaper* accompanied some news of military operations.

The *Post* declined after the war. Peterson retired in 1873 and four years later the paper was sold at sheriff's sale to Andrew E. Smythe. The week-end miscellanies were being supplanted by Sunday editions of daily papers, and the *Post* had a meager existence as a cheap story-paper until, following Smythe's death in 1897, the virtually bankrupt sheet was sold to Cyrus H. K. Curtis for $1,000.

Curtis had made a spectacular success with his monthly *Ladies' Home Journal*, and at first he made the *Post* a kind of weekly version of it. By 1899 he had found a brilliant new editor, GEORGE HORACE LORIMER, and a successful new policy based on the interests of the young man in the dawning 20th century. Three types of subject matter dominated—business, public affairs, and romance—but all three were more or less oriented in the direction of business and the young man's opportunities in an era of expansion and America's "manifest destiny." Business, outdoor adventure, sports, and humor were exploited. Typical series were Lorimer's own *Letters of a Self-Made Merchant to His Son*, George Randolph Chester's *Get Rich Quick Wallingford* tales, Frank Norris' *The Pit* serial, and Arthur Train's stories of *Mr. Tutt*, the tricky lawyer. Writers of virile fiction included Kipling, Jack London, Stephen Crane, and Rex Beach; and among humorists were Irvin Cobb, Ring Lardner, George Fitch, and Montague Glass.

By 1909 the *Post's* circulation had reached a million; five years later that figure had doubled. Curtis' techniques of promotion included the use of Benjamin Franklin's name as "founder." The *Post* had long been proud of its age, and for four months after he purchased the magazine Curtis had continued the big black-face line in the front-page name-plate "Founded A.D. 1821"; then on January 29, 1898, this suddenly gave place to "Founded A.D. 1728," with the explanation that Benjamin Franklin had edited it in 1729–1765. (This was all later simplified to "Founded in 1728 by B. Franklin.") At the same time the volume number was jumped from 77 to 170. Thus in one week the *Post* gained 93 years in age, as well as a new patron saint. The claim upon Franklin was not fabricated by Curtis, however; others had prepared the myth for him, basing it on the fact that the *Post* was first issued from a shop that had formerly produced the PENNSYLVANIA GAZETTE, a newspaper famous because Franklin had conducted it from 1729 to 1748. Franklin had not founded the *Gazette*, however, nor was the *Post* a continuation of it. The *Gazette* expired in 1815, six years before the *Post* was founded, on a very different plan, by men who had not been connected with the management of the *Gazette*. All of this is a mere footnote to the promotional history of a highly successful magazine.

After its first ten years under Lorimer, the

editorial policy of the *Post* was somewhat altered, chiefly by its appeal to women as well as to men. Robert W. Chambers, David Graham Phillips, William J. Locke, G. K. Chesterton, Corra Harris, and J. P. Marquand became familiar contributors. Detective serials came to be constant fare. Illustration was copious and colorful. For years Samuel G. Blythe was the leading writer of political editorials, and the *Post* swung from what was originally a leftist position to one well to the right. Lorimer was strongly opposed to F. D. Roosevelt.

Curtis died in 1932 and Lorimer five years later. Wesley W. Stout carried on the Lorimer editorial policies for five years, but when Ben Hibbs became editor in 1942, changes in typography, illustration, and design were accompanied by a marked change in the direction of non-fiction emphasis, though C. S. Forester's serial stories of sea adventure, and Erle Stanley Gardner's and Clarence Budington Kelland's detective stories kept on. Circulation rose to 6,000,000 in 1960. However, mass circulations, sought after as they may be, bring difficult problems of high solicitation and production costs; and the early 1960's were years of trial for the old *Post*. Executive Editor Robert Fuoss was responsible for the face-lifting and policy changing that brought out a new *Post* in September, 1961. Its political policy was more liberal, its articles often more striking, and its appearance more in accord with the spirit of the times among leading American magazines.

Saturday Press. A weekly magazine founded in New York City (1858) by Henry Clapp and others; it continued to appear until 1866. The group that haunted PFAFF'S CELLAR contributed to it freely. It was known as a bohemian, and what was later called an "experimental," magazine. It won a high reputation, and to writers of a literary bent it was placed on a par with the *Atlantic Monthly*. Mark Twain's first literary appearance in the East came with the *Saturday Press'* publication (Nov. 18, 1865) of his *Jumping Frog* story. Walt Whitman liked the magazine and sent it some of his best work.

Saturday Review. A weekly literary review founded in 1924 by HENRY SEIDEL CANBY, CHRISTOPHER MORLEY, AMY LOVEMAN, and WILLIAM ROSE BENÉT. Originally named *The Saturday Review of Literature*, it changed its name in 1952 to the *Saturday Review*, since by then it covered world events, recordings, the drama, radio, television, and travel, as well as books. Canby was editor in chief until 1936; he was succeeded by BERNARD DE VOTO (1936–38), George Stevens (1938–40), and NORMAN COUSINS (since 1940). Several columns are widely read, notably "Trade Winds," first written by Christopher Morley, later by Bennett Cerf and John G. Fuller; "Broadway Postscript," once written by John Mason Brown, later by Henry Hewes; "Booked for Travel," by Horace Sutton; "Manner of Speaking," by John Ciardi. The magazine encourages controversy and receives a huge mail from readers endorsing or opposing its views,

keeping "Letters to the Editor" a lively page.

Saturday Visiter. A weekly magazine founded at Baltimore in 1832 by Charles F. Cloud; it was at first called *The Morning Visiter*. In 1833 it awarded a prize of fifty dollars to Edgar Allan Poe for his MS. FOUND IN A BOTTLE, which was published in the October 19 issue and helped to establish Poe's reputation. Around 1847 the *Visiter* was merged with the NATIONAL ERA.

Sauk Indians. A tribe of the Algonquian linguistic stock, located originally in Wisconsin. The Sauk, in alliance with the Fox Indians, warred on white settlers and in 1832 were defeated in the Black Hawk War. Today the Sauk live in reservations in Oklahoma, Kansas, and Iowa. They are strongly conservative; some continued for a long time to live in bark houses and to wear blankets. Today they are generally Christians, chiefly Methodists and Baptists. Black Hawk, their chieftain, dictated an account of his life, published in 1834. He appears in Iola Fuller's THE LOON FEATHER (1940); LOUIS ZARA's *This Land Is Ours* (1940); Charlton G. Laird's *Thunder on the River* (1949).

Saunders, Richard. The pen name under which Benjamin Franklin wrote POOR RICHARD'S ALMANACK.

Savage, Thomas (b. England, 1608—d. 1692), soldier, colonist, public official, memoirist. Savage came to America in 1635, was one of the founders of Newport, held public office in Boston, and wrote an *Account of the Late Action of the New Englanders . . . Against the French in Canada* (1691).

Sawyer, Tom. See TOM SAWYER, THE ADVENTURES OF.

Saxe, John Godfrey (b. Highgate, Vt., June 2, 1816—d. March 31, 1887), journalist, poet, humorist. Saxe was admitted to the New York bar, was superintendent of schools in Chittenden Co., Vt., and was state's attorney of Ver-

mont. He edited the Burlington *Sentinel* for six years, and later joined the staff of the Albany *Journal.* He published many humorous poems and was much in demand as a humorous lecturer. After a series of personal tragedies, Saxe withdrew from society, sinking deeper and deeper into melancholy. He wrote *Progress: A Satirical Poem* (1846); *Humorous and Satirical Poems* (1850); *The Money-King and Other Poems* (1860); *Complete Poems* (1861); *The Fly-ing Dutchman, or, The Wrath of Herr Von-stoppetnoze* (1862); *Clever Stories of Many Nations Rendered into Rhyme* (1865); and *Leisure Day Rhymes* (1875). Although he had a great vogue in his day, he was a mediocre versifier at best. See also THE PROUD MISS MACBRIDE.

Saxon, Lyle (b. Baton Rouge, La., Sept. 4, 1891—d. April 9, 1946), newspaperman, freelance writer. Saxon lived in New Orleans most of his life and was a feature writer for the *Times-Picayune.* He helped compile the volume on Louisiana for the "American Guide Series." He wrote many books on Louisiana, including *Father Mississippi* (1927); *Fabulous New Orleans* (1928); *Old Louisiana* (1929); *Lafitte the Pirate* (a novel, 1930); *Children of Strangers* (1937); *New Orleans City Guide* (1938). His short story *Cane River* won him an O. Henry Memorial Prize (1926); other stories of his appeared frequently in magazines and in one collection, *Gumbo-Ya-Ya* (1945).

Say, Thomas (b. Philadelphia, June 29, 1787 —d. Oct. 10, 1834), entomologist, explorer. Say began his career as a druggist. He became acquainted with the leading scientists of the day, was admitted to the Academy of Natural Sciences, and became curator of its museum. Opportunity to accompany an expedition into Florida and another expedition across the Rockies furnished him with many specimens and with data for scientific papers that made his reputation. For a time he joined Robert Owen's utopian settlement at New Harmony. In 1825 he published a *Narrative of an Expedition to the Source of St. Peter's River.* He began to specialize in entomology, in 1824 issued the first volume of his *American Entomology,* in 1828 two additional volumes. His papers were collected in 1869 (2 v., with notes by Joseph Le Conte). He ruined his health by his devotion to science, made no outstanding contribution, but gave a great impetus to neglected areas of research. H. B. Weiss and G. H. Ziegler wrote *Thomas Say, Early American Naturalist* (1931).

Sayers, Henry J. See TA-RA-RA-BOOM-DE-AY.

Scarecrow, The (1908), a play by PERCY MACKAYE. This drama was first produced by the Harvard Dramatic Club (1909), then at a theater in Middletown, Conn., on Broadway (1911), then in England and Germany (1914). Based on Nathaniel Hawthorne's FEATHERTOP, it tells of a scarecrow who is given life by a witch and assumes the title Lord Ravensbane. The lord is sent by the malignant witch to woo Rachel Merton, who falls in love with him. But the scarecrow is exposed and, to save Rachel further grief, dies. MacKaye introduced some striking dramatic effects and some amusing

satire. The play was filmed as *Puritan Passions* with Glenn Hunter as the Scarecrow, and was revived in New York in 1953.

Scarlet Letter, The (1850), a novel by NATHANIEL HAWTHORNE. This renowned story is preceded by a preface in which Hawthorne assumes the role of the finder of the manuscript and a scarlet letter "A," now faded and worn, in the Salem Custom House attic. He claims merely to have transcribed the story, thus creating a dispassionate role for himself.

Set in seventeenth century Salem, the novel is built around three scaffold scenes which occur at the beginning, the middle and the end. The story opens with the public condemnation of Hester Prynne, and the exhortation that she confess the name of the father of her illegitimate child, Pearl. Hester's husband, an old and scholarly physician just arrived from England, assumes the name of Roger Chillingworth in order to seek out Hester's lover and revenge himself upon him. He attaches himself as physician to the respected and seemingly holy minister, Arthur Dimmesdale, suspecting him to be the father of the child.

The Scarlet Letter traces the effect of the actual and symbolic sin on all the characters. Hester, who wears the visible sign of the sin, finally learns to live with it. She embroiders the scarlet letter she has been forced to wear with gold thread and makes it the mark of her ties with the community which shunned her. She ennobles herself by accepting her lot and devoting herself to the community, by which she is respected, although not forgiven. Dimmesdale, although his preaching helps the community, is unable to expiate his sin by mortification of the flesh, and finally confesses publicly, but dies immediately thereafter. Chillingworth is revealed as the worst sinner of the three, because he sins out of hate, while the others sin out of love. He becomes the devil's tool when he commits what is to Hawthorne the cardinal sin, the invasion of the sanctity of the human heart, in attempting to assert his will over Dimmesdale.

The novel is not about adultory, for the act occurred before the opening of the story, nor about sin *per se;* but rather it is about the effect of sin on the mind and spirit of the characters. The scarlet letter comes to stand not for adultery, but for the guilt which is the common experience of all men. No one is spared, and ultimately even those who seem most holy are implicated; it is the mark of human life. If there is any obvious moralizing it is in Hawthorne's insistence that, although punishment can only be meted out by God, not man, man must still be true to himself and reveal a sign by which his guilt may be known.

Scarlet Sister Mary (1928), a novel by JULIA PETERKIN. The heroine of this local color story is a Gullah Negress on a South Carolina plantation. Her rich and joyous spirit survives in spite of her desperate poverty, her desertion by a worthless husband, and a number of casual affairs that leave her with nine children. She is expelled from the church but readmitted after her confidence has been shaken by the death of her favorite son and by a vision of Christ's suffering. Starkly realistic throughout, the novel is written with a deep sympathy for the bitter lives of the fieldworkers. It won a Pulitzer prize in 1929 and was dramatized the following year by Daniel Reed, with Ethel Barrymore in the leading role.

Schaff, Philip (b. Switzerland, Jan. 1, 1819 —d. Oct. 20, 1893), theologian, historian, teacher. Educated in Germany, Schaff taught in the German Reformed Church Theological Seminary in Mercersburg, Pa., and in the Union Theological Seminary. In 1888 he founded the American Society of Church History. Among his books: *The Principles of Protestantism* (1845); *A History of the Christian Church* (6 v., 1858–1892); *The Creeds of Christendom* (1877); *Through Bible Lands* (1878); *Bible Dictionary* (1880). David S. Schaff wrote *The Life of Philip Schaff* (1897).

Schary, Dore (b. Newark, N.J., August 31, 1905—), playwright, motion picture producer. Schary has written fiction, articles, and plays. In Hollywood he served as head of RKO studios and as Vice President in Charge of Production for M-G-M. His tenure at M-G-M became controversial since he attempted not only films with elements of entertainment but also films that were socially probing. Among his pictures are *Bad Day at Black Rock,* which won high critical favor, and *Miss Lonelyhearts,* from the novel by NATHANAEL WEST. His play *Sunrise at Campobello* (1957), the story of Franklin D. Roosevelt's crucial and formative years, was successful on Broadway and later as a film. Other works: *Case History of a Movie* (1950) and *The Highest Tree* (1959).

Schauffler, Robert Haven (b. Austria, April 8, 1879—d. Nov. 24, 1964), poet, writer on music. Schauffler wrote several books intended to produce a better understanding of music, among them *Music as a Social Force in America* (1927); *Beethoven—The Man Who Freed Music* (1929); and *The Unknown Brahms* (1933). He is perhaps most widely known for a poem *Scum o' the Earth* (1912), a denunciation of race and religious prejudice. This was the title poem in a collection. Two other gatherings of verses were *The White Comrade and Other Poems* (1920) and *The Magic Flame and Other Poems* (1923). His second wife was MARGARET WIDDEMER.

Schechter, Solomon (b. Rumania, Dec. 7, 1847—d. Nov. 19, 1915), Hebrew scholar, administrator, editor. Schechter studied in Vienna and Germany, went to London to teach and to publish editions of Hebrew classics and write learned articles. In 1892 he was appointed reader in rabbinics at Cambridge University. At this time he made his famous explorations of the Cairo Genizah, a hidden collection of ancient Hebrew manuscripts and books, known as the Taylor-Schechter Collection. He was invited in 1902 to serve as president of the reorganized Jewish Theological Seminary in New York City, where he became influential in American Jewish life.

In his writings Schechter brought meticulous scientific method to Biblical problems and was an authoritative exponent of rabbinical theology. In addition he became an authority on Abraham Lincoln and the Civil War. Both scholarly and readable are his *Studies in Judaism* (1896, 1908, 1924); *The Wisdom of Ben Sira* (with Charles Taylor, 1899); *Some Aspects of Rabbinic Theology* (1909); and *Seminary Addresses and Other Papers* (1915). He was one of the editors of the *Jewish Encyclopedia* (12 v., 1901–06).

Schelling Felix E[manuel] (b. New Albany, Ind., Sept. 3, 1858—d. Dec. 15, 1945), editor. Schelling was a noted authority on Elizabethan literature. Among his best known books were *A History of Elizabethan Drama* (2 v., 1908); *English Literature During the Lifetime of Shakespeare* (1910); *The English Lyric* (1913); *Elizabethan Playwrights* (1925). He also edited *A Book of Elizabethan Lyrics* (1899). He served as John Welsh Centennial Professor of English Literature at the University of Pennsylvania from 1893 until 1929. Among his students was Ezra Pound.

Scherman, David E. Co-author of LITERARY AMERICA.

Schlesinger, Arthur M[eier], Sr. (b. Xenia, Ohio, Feb. 27, 1888—d. Oct. 30, 1965), historian. Schlesinger taught at Ohio State and Iowa Universities before joining Harvard University as professor of history in 1924. His many important historical works include *The Colonial Merchants and the American Revolution* (1918); *New Viewpoints in American History* (1922); *Political and Social History of the U.S.* (1925; rev. in later editions); *The Rise of the City* (1933); *Learning How to Behave: A Historical Study of American Etiquette Books* (1940); *Paths to the Present* (1949); *The American as Reformer* (1950); HARVARD GUIDE TO AMERICAN HISTORY (1954); *Prelude to Independence: The Newspaper War on Britain, 1764–1776* (1958). *The Atlantic Migration,* written with M. L. Hansen, won a Pulitzer prize (1941).

Schlesinger, Arthur M[eier], Jr. (b. Columbus, Ohio, Oct. 15, 1917—), teacher, historian. An associate professor at Harvard in 1946, a full professor in 1954, Schlesinger followed his father (see above) as a teacher and writer of books on history, but wrote extensively on current problems. He has won the Pulitzer Prize for History (1946), the Francis Parkman Prize (1957) and the Bancroft Prize (1958). He was appointed special assistant to President Kennedy in 1961. Among his writings: *Orestes A. Brownson: A Pilgrim's Progress* (1939); THE AGE OF JACKSON (Pulitzer prize, 1945); *The Vital Center* (1949); *The General and the President* (with R. H. Rovere, 1951); *The Age of [Franklin D.] Roosevelt,* now including *The Crisis of the Old Order* (1957), *The Coming of the New Deal* (1959), and *The Politics of Upheaval* (1960).

Schmitt, Gladys (b. Pittsburgh, Pa., May 31,

1909—   ), teacher, poet, novelist. For a time Miss Schmitt worked for the SCHOLASTIC PUBLICATIONS. Later she taught composition at the Carnegie Institute of Technology. Her first novel was *The Gates of Aulis* (1940), followed by *David the King* (1946), based on the Bible story. Later books include *Alexandra* (1947); *Confessors of the Name* (1952); *The Persistent Image* (1955). *A Small Fire* (1957) won approval from critics, several of whom spoke of her shrewd insights and her great narrative skill. *Rembrandt* was published in 1961.

Schneider, Herbert W[allace] (b. Berea, Ohio, March 16, 1892—   ), teacher, philosopher, historian. Schneider became an instructor at Columbia University in 1918, a full professor in 1942. His works, in addition to many articles in his special field, include *A History of American Philosophy* (1946); *Religion in 20th-Century America* (1952); and *Three Dimensions of Public Morality* (1956). The first, a detailed and stimulating survey of the whole course of American thought, includes discussions not only of professional philosophers but of many literary figures and is the standard work in its field. The valuable bibliographies in the book were compiled by Joseph L. Blau, who also compiled a complementary volume, *American Philosophic Addresses* (1952).

Scholastic Publications. *The Scholastic* was originally a biweekly magazine for high school students, founded in Pittsburgh in 1920 as the *Western Pennsylvania Scholastic.* Numerous other magazines have supplemented the original periodical, which is now called *Senior Scholastic.* Among the others are *World Week, Practical English, Junior Scholastic, Newstime, Literary Cavalcade, Scholastic Coach, Practical Home Economics.* In addition Scholastic Publications conducts annual art and literary competitions and the Teen-Age Book Club, and publishes its own paperbound books, both reprints of the classics and originals.

Schoolcraft, Henry Rowe (b. Watervliet, N.Y., March 28, 1793—d. Dec. 10, 1864), geologist, explorer, ethnologist, writer. Schoolcraft traveled in Missouri and Arkansas, accompanied the Lewis Cass expedition (1820) to Lake Superior as a geologist, was appointed an Indian agent there, and discovered the source of the Mississippi in 1832. He married the granddaughter of a Chippewa chieftain and from her gathered much Indian lore. He was Superintendent of Indian Affairs for Michigan (1836–41) and wrote about his explorations and researches in a number of influential books. He was the first white man to translate Indian poetry and among the first to report Indian legends and religious beliefs seriously. He wrote *A View of the Lead Mines of Missouri* (1819); *Travels in the Central Portions of the Mississippi Valley* (1825); *Narrative of an Expedition Through the Upper Mississippi to Itasca Lake* (1834); *Algic Researches, Comprising Inquiries Respecting the Mental Characteristics of the North American Indians* (2 v., 1839; later reprinted as *The Myth of Hiawatha*) (see

ALGIC RESEARCHES); *Oneonta, or, The Red Race of America* (8 v., 1844–45; rev. and reissued, 1851, as *The American Indians: Their History, Condition, and Prospects*); *Notes on the Iroquois* (1846); *Personal Memoirs of a Residence of Thirty Years with the Indian Tribes* (1851); *Scenes and Adventures in the Semi-Alpine Region of the Ozark Mountains of Missouri and Arkansas* (1863; in this was reprinted his *View of the Lead Mines*). *Indian Legends* (1955), based on his books, was compiled by M. L. Williams. Schoolcraft's writings, especially *Algic Researches,* had a profound influence on LONGFELLOW, who repeated Schoolcraft's great blunder—confusing the Iroquoian Hiawatha with the Chippewa Manabozho and laying on the southern shores of Lake Superior adventures that had taken place in central New York. Chase S. and Stellanova Osborne wrote *Schoolcraft—Longfellow—Hiawatha* (1943).

School Days (1907), a song by GUS EDWARDS with words by Will D. Cobb. It was Edwards' greatest popular success and is still frequently sung.

school newspapers and magazines. A customary extracurricular activity in American schools is the publication of school periodicals. The first such periodical on record was *The Students' Gazette,* published at the William Penn Charter School in Philadelphia in the 18th century. The great development of these periodicals began in the 1920's; today there are more than eighteen thousand school papers. Annual awards for the best school newspapers are now given by the Columbia Scholastic Press Association. See CHARLES B. DRISCOLL.

Schorer, Mark (b. Sauk City, Wis., May 17, 1908—   ), novelist, critic, biographer. Mark Schorer was educated at the University of Wisconsin, wrote his first novel *"A House Too Old"* (1935) a year before he acquired his Ph.D. He published short stories, mostly in *The New Yorker,* and literary articles in the quarterlies, later teaching and writing at Dartmouth College, Harvard University, and the University of California. Several grants enabled him to pursue long-range scholarship aims. His book *William Blake* (1946) took ten years to write and achieved critical acclaim. The *New Republic* described it as a "masterly analysis of the mind and art of a poet." *The Wars of Love* (1954) was called by *The New York Times* "a dark and disturbing short novel . . . [Schorer] again demonstrates his great skill as an observer of human frailty." Other books: *The Hermit Place* (1941); *The State of Mind* (thirty-two stories, 1946); and a biography, *Sinclair Lewis: An American Life* (1961).

Schramm, Wilbur (b. Marietta, Ohio, Aug. 5, 1907—   ), newspaperman, baseball player, musician, teacher, writer. This versatile author started as a newspaper reporter in the Ohio Valley, then went on to the Boston *Herald.* He was a good enough musician to win a fellowship to the New England Conservatory, to occupy a chair in the New England Symphony, and to play for John Philip Sousa. He was also a professional baseball player. He began teaching at Iowa in 1935, moved on to the University of Illinois in 1947, became dean of the division of communications there in 1950. In the meantime he had sold many stories, mostly in the tradition of the American tall tale. He has published: *Approaches to a Science of English Verse* (1935); *American Medley* (stories, 1937); *Francis Parkman* (1938); *Windwagon Smith and Other Stories* (1947). He has edited *Mass Communications* (1949); *Process and Effects of Mass Communication* (1954); *The Impact of Educational Television* (1960).

Schriftgiesser, Karl (b. Boston, Mass., Nov. 12, 1903—   ), historian, biographer. Schriftgiesser attended the famous Roxbury Latin School, in 1924 became a feature writer on the Boston *Evening Transcript,* and for ten years made contributions to such magazines as the *American Mercury, The New Yorker,* and the *New Republic. Families* (1940) traced the growth of ten outstanding families in America from the Adams to the Roosevelts, and *The Amazing Roosevelt Family* (1942) told the history of the family that produced two presidents. *The Gentleman from Massachusetts* (1944) is a critical biography of Henry Cabot Lodge, whose influence kept America out of the League of Nations. *This Was Normalcy* (1948) is an analysis of the presidential administrations of Harding and Coolidge; *The Lobbyists* (1951) is a study of pressure groups in Washington influencing legislation. Other books: *Farmer from Merna* (1955); *Business Comes of Age* (1960).

Schulberg, Budd (b. New York City, March 27, 1914—   ), short-story writer, novelist. The son of a film producer, Schulberg first observed human nature, apparently at its worst, in Hollywood, and as a result wrote his first best seller, WHAT MAKES SAMMY RUN? (1941), the satirical story of a tough movie careerist. His next novel, THE HARDER THEY FALL (1947), was an equally sardonic account of the prizefighting world, the main character being drawn from a former heavyweight champion. In THE DISENCHANTED (1950) Schulberg again obviously had a life model, in this case F. SCOTT FITZGERALD; the two had met when they worked together on a motion picture about college life and made a trip to Dartmouth College to gather background material. Schulberg's novel is the story of a gifted man who finds himself frustrated by life and his own nature. It was dramatized and produced on Broadway in 1958. Schulberg also wrote a number of spirited but thoughtful short stories, collected in *Faces in the Crowd* (1953), and his screenplay *On the Waterfront* (1954) won wide critical acclaim.

Schultze, Bunny [Carl Emil] (b. Lexington, Ky., May 25, 1866—d. Jan. 18, 1939), cartoonist. Schultze's most famous character was "Foxy Grandpa," who made his first appearance in the New York *Herald* on Jan. 7, 1900. Grandpa's grandsons continually played tricks

on him, but he invariably outfoxed them in the end.

Schuman, William [Howard] (b. New York City, Aug. 4, 1910—   ), composer, teacher. Schuman began as a popular song writer, became deeply interested in serious music, and taught at Sarah Lawrence College. In 1944 he became special publications consultant for G. Schirmer, Inc.; in 1945 was elected president of the Juilliard School of Music; he relinquished this post to become President of the Lincoln Center for the performing arts in 1961. Although his music manifests several influences —Hindemith, Copland, Sibelius, and others— he is regarded as distinctly original. He particularly likes composing for the theater and the ballet, and has done incidental music for Shakespeare's *King Henry VIII* and the ballet *Undertow,* which was produced at the Metropolitan in 1945. Other works are: *American Festival Overture* (1939); *Night Journey* (1947); *Judith* (1949); *George Washington Bridge* (1950). Schuman's choral works often have a literary content. His *Four Canonic Choruses for Mixed Voices* (1933) are based on poems by Edna St. Vincent Millay, Countee Cullen, Carl Sandburg, and Alfred Tennyson. He also wrote a chorus for Whitman's *Pioneers!* and based other pieces on poems by Genevieve Taggard. In 1943 he received a Pulitzer prize for a composition based on Whitman, *A Free Song. The Mighty Casey* (1951–1953), a popular ballet, was written with a libretto by Jeremy Gury.

Schumpeter, Joseph A[lois] (b. Austria, Feb. 8, 1883—d. Jan. 8, 1950), lawyer, teacher, economist. Schumpeter started the practice of law in Austria in 1907, began university teaching in the same country in 1909, was appointed Austrian minister of finance (1919), became professor of economics at the University of Bonn. In 1932 he came to the United States to join the Harvard University faculty, and he remained here until his death. He attained a great reputation as an authority on economics, especially with his *Theory of Economic Development* (1911; English translation, 1934). He made a major contribution to the discussion of entrepreneurship, stressing the importance of the creators, the innovators, the ruling lords who make the crucial decisions. Among his later books: *Business Cycles, A Theoretical, Statistical, and Historical Analysis of the Capitalist Process* (1939) and *Capitalism, Socialism, and Democracy* (1942).

Schurz, Carl (b. Germany, March 2, 1829 —d. May 14, 1906), soldier, statesman, journalist. Schurz entered the University of Bonn with the intention of becoming a historian, but instead joined the unsuccessful revolutionary movement of 1848 and was forced to flee the country. In 1852 he came to the United States and in 1855 settled in Watertown, Wis., where he studied law and was admitted to the bar. He soon became interested in the antislavery movement and the young Republican party. He campaigned for Lincoln against Douglas and made a tour of New England, speaking against the Know-Nothing party and in support of full rights for naturalized citizens. In the campaign of 1860 he made effective speeches in both English and German.

Lincoln appointed him minister to Spain, but he resigned to become an officer in the Union army. In the summer of 1865 he toured the South and wrote a report on conditions there. This report, although it was of extraordinary value, was suppressed by President Johnson because it recommended the extension of the franchise to Negroes as a condition of readmission to the Union of the seceding states. It was made public only at the demand of Congress.

Schurz then went into newspaper work, serving on the New York *Tribune* and the Detroit *Post*. In 1867 he became a partner and joint editor of the St. Louis *Westliche Post*. In 1868 he was temporary chairman and keynote speaker for the Republican National Convention and was elected senator from Missouri. In 1876 he was appointed Secretary of the Interior by Hayes. After his cabinet term he was co-editor of the New York *Evening Post*, and later wrote the leading editorials for *Harper's Weekly*. He was president of the National Civil Reform League in 1892–1901.

Schurz was at his best campaigning and in the Senate. Various editions of his speeches have been published, among them *Speeches of Carl Schurz* (1865) and *Speeches, Correspondence, and Political Papers of Carl Schurz* (1913), edited by Frederic Bancroft. Other works of his are: *The New South* (1865), a pamphlet; *Life of Henry Clay* (1887); *Abraham Lincoln: An Essay* (1889); *The Reminiscences of Carl Schurz* (1907–08). Among works about him are: Otto Danneke's *Carl Schurz* (1929); C. V. Easum's *The Americanization of Carl Schurz* (1929); C. M. Fuess' *Carl Schurz, Reformer* (1932).

Schuster, M[ax] Lincoln (b. Austria, March 2, 1897—   ), newspaperman, free-lance writer, editor, publisher. Schuster worked on newspapers in New York and Boston and on the Washington staff of the United Press. He was a cofounder of the publishing firm of Simon & Schuster. He wrote *Eyes on the World: A Photographic Record of History in the Making* (1935) and edited *A Treasury of the World's Great Letters* (1940).

Schwartz, Delmore (b. Brooklyn, N.Y., Dec. 8, 1913—d. July 11, 1966), poet, short-story writer. One of the most gifted of modern writers, Schwartz achieved a sudden reputation, when he was still a college student, with his fluent and richly modulated poems. He held several editorial posts, and continued to write lyrics, fiction, drama, and criticism—all of a high order. He taught at Harvard, Princeton, and New York universities, the University of Indiana, and elsewhere. His work is characterized by a deep irony. Among his works are *In Dreams Begin Responsibilities* (verse, 1938); *Shenandoah* (verse drama, 1941); *Genesis* (verse,

1943); *Vaudeville for a Princess* (verse, 1950). He translated Rimbaud's *A Season in Hell* (1939). His short stories, many of them accenting the problems of Jewish life, have been collected in *The World Is a Wedding* (1948). A volume of new and selected earlier poems, *Summer Knowledge* (1959), was awarded the Bollingen Prize in 1960, making Schwartz the youngest to have received the prize.

Science and Health, with Key to the Scriptures (1875), a devotional textbook by MARY BAKER EDDY. In 1862 Mrs. Eddy came under the influence of the mental healing system of Dr. Phineas Parkhurst Quimby and was cured of a long invalidism. Her reflections on her experience led her to the writing of *Science and Health*, which underwent some revisions until 1910 and which has circulated in millions of copies and has been translated into many foreign languages. Her doctrines attracted numerous converts; in 1879 the First Church of Christ Scientist was chartered. In 1895 Mrs. Eddy abolished personal preaching in her church and ordained the Bible and *Science and Health* as the "pastor" for her followers.

science-fiction. Science-fiction may be defined as comprising that class of stories in which the seemingly impossible is made to appear possible by the introduction of alleged scientific hypotheses and discoveries and of still uninvented mechanical contrivances. It is characteristically a dream of the future; sometimes the dream comes true. Jules Verne may be considered the first science-fiction writer. His most successful imitator was H. G. Wells.

In American literature EDGAR ALLAN POE is the first great figure of science-fiction, particularly in THE UNPARALLELED ADVENTURES OF ONE HANS PFAAL and the NARRATIVE OF ARTHUR GORDON PYM. In the Poe style was Fitz-James O'Brien's THE DIAMOND LENS (*Atlantic Monthly*, January, 1850). EDWARD EVERETT HALE definitely foreshadowed science-fiction in his novelette *The Brick Moon* (1870) and in a tale entitled *Hands Off*, which appeared anonymously in *Harper's* (March, 1881). The many later science-fiction magazines were anticipated by the dime novels of the later 19th century, such as "Noname's" *Frank Reade and His Steam Man of the Plains, or, The Terror of the West* (1883); Richard B. Montgomery's *Two Boys' Trip to an Unknown Planet* (1889); and Lu Senarens' *Frank Reade and His Queen Clipper of the Clouds* (1900). A different but favorite type of science-fiction story was Edward Bellamy's LOOKING BACKWARD (1888); also his *Equality* (1897). These were written as serious literature and indicated a way toward the achievement of a new world right here. Preceding these were the effervescent IGNATIUS DONNELLY's narratives, especially *Caesar's Column: A Story of the 20th Century* (1891). One should also note FRANK R. STOCKTON's *The Great War Syndicate* (1889) and ROBERT W. CHAMBERS' *The King in Yellow* (1895), stories that are said to have influenced a 20th-century master, H. P. LOVECRAFT.

The turn of the century brought a burgeoning of science-fiction. One of the most stimulating writers was an astronomer, GARRETT P. SERVISS, who composed stories of life in outer space, among them *Moon Metal* (1900) and *The Moon Maiden* (1915). EDGAR RICE BURROUGHS wrote ten Martian novels, followed by several with Venus as a setting. In his Tarzan stories he created a new race of apes and various lost cities, one inhabited by Atlanteans. In 1908 Hugo Gernsback founded a magazine named *Modern Electrics;* in the issue of April, 1911, he began a serial entitled *Ralph 124C41+: A Romance of the Year 2660.* Later he published other magazines, including *Science-Fiction Plus.* In 1926 he started *Amazing Stories,* the first magazine devoted entirely to science-fiction. Other early magazines had included this type of literary offering, among them *Weird Tales.* In the latter H. P. LOVECRAFT found his chief market. In some respects Lovecraft is the most literary (and at times the most rhetorical) of all science-fiction writers. One of Lovecraft's chief followers is AUGUST DERLETH.

Later writers are legion—many are true experts and specialists—and only a few can be named: Fletcher Pratt, Eric Temple Bell (John Taine), David H. Keller, Stanley G. Weinbaum, L. Sprague de Camp, Ray Bradbury, Isaac Asimov, Vardis Fisher, A. E. Van Vogt, Nelson Bond, William F. Jenkins (Murray Leinster), Robert A. Heinlein, W. A. P. White (Anthony Boucher). It is not entirely clear what factors gave the sudden spurt to the reading and publishing of science-fiction in the mid-20th century. *Life* once tried to explain the phenomenon by saying that science-fiction is "the folk literature of the machine age."

Hugo Gernsback felt that the quality of science-fiction had deteriorated and that it tended to gravitate more and more into the esoteric and sophisticated. Other charges were that science-fiction novels had become merely imitation westerns, "space operas" instead of "horse operas." Richard J. Hurley said (*Books on Trial,* June, 1953): "Examining science-fiction we find that life is cheap, cruelty is common, love of neighbor is unknown, religion is archaic if not ignored." Some good recent analyses are L. Sprague de Camp's *Science-Fiction Handbook* (1953); Reginald Bretnor's symposium *Modern Science Fiction: Its Meaning and Its Future* (1953); and Basil Davenport's *Inquiry into Science Fiction* (1955).

Among the more outstanding recent examples of s-f are: John Taine's *The Iron Star* (1930) and *Before the Dawn* (1934); Edwin Balmer and Philip Wylie's *When Worlds Collide* (1932) and *After Worlds Collide* (1934); H. P. Lovecraft's *The Shadow Out of Time* (1939); L. Sprague de Camp's *Lest Darkness Fall* (1941); A. E. Van Vogt's *Slan* (1946), *The Weapon Shops of Isher* (1951), and *Away and Beyond* (1952); Robert A. Heinlein's *Rocket Ship Galileo* (1947) and *The Green Hills of Earth* (1951); Robert Lewis Taylor's *Adrift in a*

Boneyard (a satire on books about the future, 1947); Theodore Sturgeon's *Without Sorcery* (1949) and *More than Human* (1953); Isaac Asimov's *I, Robot* (1950) and *People in the Sky* (1950); Ray Bradbury's *The Martian Chronicles* (1950), *The Illustrated Man* (1951), and *The October Country* (1955); Fletcher Pratt's *Double Space* (1951); Walter M. Miller, Jr.'s *Canticle for Leibowitz* (1960).

Excellent anthologies are: Groff Conklin's *The Best of Science-Fiction* (1946) and *Possible Worlds of Science-Fiction* (1951); Philip Van Doren Stern's *Travelers in Time* (1947); August Derleth's *Strange Ports of Call* (1948) and *Beyond Time and Space* (1950); Martin Greenberg's *Men Against the Stars* (1950); Wilson Tucker's *The Science-Fiction Treasury* (1954); Anthony Boucher's *The Best from "Fantasy and Science Fiction"* (1955). Among the popular science-fiction magazines are *Galaxy, Analog of Science Fact–Science Fiction* (formerly *Astounding Science Fiction*), and *Fantasy and Science Fiction.*

Science of English Verse, The (1879), a treatise on versification by SIDNEY LANIER.

Scollard, Clinton (b. Clinton, N.Y., Sept. 28, 1860—d. Nov. 19, 1932), poet, novelist. Scollard studied at Hamilton College and Harvard and Cambridge universities. From 1888 to 1896 he was professor of rhetoric and English literature at Hamilton, but retired to devote himself to creative work. In 1884 *Pictures in Song* was published, the first of a series of books which ended in 1932 with *Songs from a Southern Shore.* He wrote *A Boy's Book of Rhyme* (1896), *Songs of a Sylvan Lover* (1912), *The Epic of Golf* (1923), and *The Crowning Years* (1929. His gift was chiefly lyric and was distinguished more for perfection of technique than for originality. In addition to essays and travel sketches in prose, he composed historical romances: *A Man-at-Arms* (1898); *The Son of a Tory* (1901); *The Cloistering of Ursula* (1902); and *Count Falcon of the Eyrie* (1903).

In 1924 he married JESSIE B. RITTENHOUSE, poet and critic, with whom he produced two anthologies: *Bird-Lovers' Anthology* (1930) and *Patrician Rhymes* (1932). He also collaborated with FRANK DEMPSTER SHERMAN on *A Southern Flight* (1905) and edited his poems in 1917. *The Singing Heart* (1934) is a selection of his poems edited by his wife, with a memoir.

Scopes trial. A famous court contest (July, 1925) in which John T. Scopes, a Tennessee science teacher, was found guilty of having taught the doctrine of evolution. The great antagonists were CLARENCE DARROW, who defended Scopes, and WILLIAM JENNINGS BRYAN, who led the prosecution forces to a temporary victory for religious conservatism and died five days after the end of the trial. The verdict was later reversed by the Tennessee Supreme Court. H. L. Mencken reported the "monkey" trial in some famous sardonic dispatches. In 1955 the trial was turned into a successful play, *Inherit the Wind*, by Jerome Lawrence and Robert E. Lee, and was later filmed.

Scot, George (b. Scotland, 17th century), colonist. Scot had the task of encouraging emigration to New Jersey. In 1685 he embarked for America after composing a promotion tract called *The Model of the Government of East Jersey* (1685). Both he and his wife died on the voyage, but a daughter remained in the colony. His tract gave a history of colonization from Biblical days, then pictured contemporary New Jersey with the help of testimonial letters. He presented many human as well as economic and legalistic details. His book was reprinted in W. A. Whitehead's *East Jersey Under the Proprietary Governments* (1846).

Scott, Dred (b. Southampton Co., Va., 1795[?]—d. Sept. 17, 1858), Negro slave owned by Dr. John Emerson. He was taken (1834) by his master from St. Louis, Mo., to Rock Island, Ill., later to Fort Snelling in Wisconsin Territory. In Illinois slavery had been forbidden by the Ordinance of 1787, in Wisconsin slavery was forbidden by the Missouri Compromise. In 1846 Scott sued for his liberty in the Missouri courts on the ground that he had been freed by his stay in a free territory. His case reached the Supreme Court in 1857. In the famous Dred Scott decision the Court ruled upon several questions: (1) Scott as a Negro was not a citizen; (2) Congress could not prohibit a citizen from carrying any property, including slaves, into any territory; (3) the Missouri Compromise was unconstitutional since under the Fifth Amendment Congress was prohibited from depriving persons of their property without due process of law. The decision created a furor, especially in the North. In the Lincoln-Douglas debates (see under LINCOLN) Douglas tried to win northern favor by enunciating a doctrine of local sovereignty to counterbalance the Dred Scott decision; as a consequence he lost backing in the South. The Fourteenth Amendment (1868) annulled the decision. See ROGER B. TANEY.

Scott, Duncan Campbell (b. Ottawa, Ont., Aug. 2, 1862—d. Dec. 19, 1947), Canadian poet, short-story writer, public official. Well-acquainted with the Canadian wilds and the Indians who inhabited them, Scott spent many years in the Canadian department of Indian affairs. He wrote much poetry and many short stories besides contributing articles to magazines. He also knew French Canada, and his first fiction, *In the Village of Viger* (1896), was a collection of French-Canadian stories. Among his other books: *The Magic House and Other Poems* (1893); *Labor and the Angel* (1898); *New World Lyrics and Ballads* (1905); *Lundy's Lane* (1916); *Beauty and Life* (1921); *The Green Cloister* (1935); *The Circle of Affection* (1947). He issued his *Collected Poems* in 1926; in 1951 Edward Killoran Brown edited a group of *Selected Poems*. In *Leading Canadian*

Poets (1948) Pelham Edgar paid tribute to the vividness of Scott's description of Canadian landscapes and the truth of his delineation of Indians.

Scott, Evelyn (b. Clarksville, Tenn., Jan. 17, 1893—), poet, novelist, memoirist. Miss Scott's works show many innovations in fiction, seeking above all to explore the lower depths of consciousness. One of her books, *The Wave* (1929), won particular attention. She made War, specifically the Civil War, the hero of the book, and showed it as a mass movement whose progress was revealed in seventy scenes. Every type of communication was adroitly used —letters, newspaper accounts, stream-of-consciousness fragments, army reports, war songs, plantation melodies. Two of Miss Scott's other books are autobiographical: *Escapade* (1923), and *Background in Tennessee* (1937). *Migrations* (1927) is a novel about the Gold Rush of 1849; *A Calendar of Sin* (1931) is a family saga. Other books include: *Precipitations* (poems, 1920); *The Narrow House* (1921); *Narcissus* (1922); *Blue Rum* (1930); *The Winter Alone* (poems, 1930); *Eva Gay* (1933); *Bread and the Sword* (1937); *The Shadow of the Hawk* (1941).

Scott, F[rancis] R[eginald] (b. Quebec, Aug. 1, 1899—), poet. Scott's father was Canon Scott, a much anthologized Canadian poet. The son has been an influential figure in Canadian poetry since the twenties, when he was a member of the "Montreal school," a group of poets influenced by T. S. Eliot. He was instrumental in the publication of *New Provinces: Poems of Several Authors* (1936), which included some of his own experimental work, along with that of five other modernist poets. During the forties he was one of the editors of the experimental literary magazine, *Preview*. Scott's poetry is often witty and amusing, as when he pokes fun at Canadian poetic movements in "The Canadian Authors Meet." Elsewhere, however, he reveals a profound concern with social problems. Here he reflects his background, which is unusual for a poet. Educated at McGill University and at Oxford as a Rhodes scholar, Scott joined the McGill faculty of law in 1928. In 1952 he was a United Nations representative in Burma. Besides poetry, he has written on national and international affairs. W. E. Collin, the Canadian critic, included in his book *The White Savannahs* (1936) a long appreciation of Scott's poetry titled "Pilgrim of the Absolute." Scott has contributed articles on social planning and poems to numerous magazines. His books of poetry include: *Overture* (1945) and *Events and Signals* (1954).

Scott, Fred Newton (b. Terre Haute, Ind., Aug. 20, 1860—d. May 29, 1931), teacher, writer, editor, critic. Scott led a notable life in which there were two major achievements. He was among the first to provide the study of English with definite aims and techniques, especially in a book on *The Teaching of English* (1903), written with George Rice Carpenter and Franklin T. Baker. He was a member of the English department at the University of Michigan from 1889 to 1927. In addition Scott produced with CHARLES MILLS GAYLEY a monumental annotated guide and bibliography in the field of aesthetics, particularly the aesthetics of literature: *An Introduction to the Methods and Materials of Literary Criticism* (1899). He had previously written *Principles of Style* (1890). Some of his essays were collected in *The Standard of American Speech and Other Essays* (1926).

Scott, Harvey [Whitefield] (b. Groveland, Ill., Feb. 1, 1838—d. Aug. 7, 1910), journalist, editor, writer. Scott was with the Portland *Oregonian* from 1877 until his death, ultimately as editor. He wrote *Religion, Theology, and Morals* (2 v., 1917) and a *History of the Oregon Country* (6 v., 1924).

Scott, Natalie Anderson (b. Russia, Sept. 7, 1906—), novelist, painter. Miss Scott, a descendant of Russian Cossacks and a Scottish great-grandmother, spent her earlier years in several countries; her father was a liberal who found it convenient to leave Russia several times. In 1922 her family made the United States their permanent home. She published her first novel, *So Brief the Years* (1935), under her original name, Natalie B. Sokoloff; it was an account of the conflict between Whites and Reds in Russia. *The Sisters Livingston* (1946) was followed by *The Story of Mrs. Murphy* (1947), a tale of a sordid drunkard. It was a selection of the Book-of-the-Month Club. Later novels: *The Husband* (1948); *Romance* (1951); *The Little Stockade* (1954); *Salvation Johnny* (1958); *The Golden Trollop* (1961).

Scott, Winfield (b. near Petersburg, Va., June 13, 1786—d. May 29, 1866), soldier, memoirist. Scott was a distinguished soldier who fought bravely in the War of 1812 and commanded the American Army during the Mexican War. In 1852 he ran unsuccessfully against FRANKLIN PIERCE for the Presidency. He remained loyal to the Union, and when he published his *Memoirs* (2 v., 1864) he inscribed a set to General Grant. He wrote other books, among them *General Regulations for the Army* (1825) and *Infantry Tactics* (1835). M. J. Wright wrote his biography (1894) and A. D. H. Smith told of his life in *Old Fuss and Feathers* (1937).

Scott, Winfield Townley (b. Haverhill, Mass., April 30, 1910—d. April 28, 1968), teacher, poet. Scott worked for a number of years as a newspaperman, especially on the Providence (R.I.) *Journal*, and taught at Bard College. Scott's poetry is noted for its supple colloquial strength. He dealt often with New England characters and ideas, as in *Elegy for Robinson* (1936) and *Mr. Whittier and Other Poems* (1948). Other collections are *Biography for Traman* (1937); *Wind the Clock* (1941); *The Sword on the Table* (1942); *To Marry Strangers* (1945). *The Dark Sister* (1958) is a remarkable epic on the theme of Viking explorations in North America. *Poems: 1937–1962*

(1962) is a comprehensive collection of his verse.

Scout, The (1841), a novel by WILLIAM GILMORE SIMMS. Originally called *The Kinsmen*, this novel is set against the background of the Revolution and, as its original title suggests, is an episode in the life of a family—the struggle of two half-brothers in war and love.

Scoville, Samuel, Jr. (b. Norwich, N.Y., June 9, 1872—d. Dec. 4, 1950), lawyer, writer. Scoville was a successful Philadelphia attorney who conducted a popular legal column in several local papers. In addition he wrote historical works and books on nature, among them *Brave Deeds of Union Soldiers* (1915); *Boy Scout in the Wilderness* (1919); *Wild Folk* (1922); *Man and Beast* (1924).

Scribner's Magazine. When *Scribner's Monthly* was sold to the newly formed Century Company in 1881 and became the CENTURY ILLUSTRATED MONTHLY MAGAZINE, it was part of the bargain that Charles Scribner's Sons would not re-enter the magazine field for at least five years; but as soon as that time was up, in January, 1887, the new *Scribner's Magazine* appeared, obviously competing with the *Century* and *Harper's*. Edward L. Burlingame was editor; leading contributors for fifteen years or more were Robert Louis Stevenson, Harold Frederic, James M. Barrie, H. C. Bunner, W. C. Brownell, Theodore Roosevelt, and Jacob A. Riis. The magazine was strong in fiction, travel, biography, and criticism of art and letters.

Throughout its first four decades the magazine was beautifully illustrated. In its early years it was distinguished by such wood engravers as George Kruell and Frederick Juengling; in the 1890's it was quick to adopt halftones based on the work of such artists as J. W. Alexander, C. D. Gibson, Will H. Low, W. T. Smedley and Maxfield Parrish. After the turn of the century it became a leader in full-color illustration by Parrish, Howard Pyle, N. C. Wyeth, Frederic Remington, A. B. Frost, and H. C. Christy.

In 1914 Robert Bridges became editor; an excellent essayist and literary critic himself, he maintained the magazine's high quality. John Galsworthy, Edith Wharton, and Theodore Roosevelt were leading contributors. The magazine gave a good deal of attention to the World War. By 1925 it had begun to place a greater emphasis on public affairs. In the late 1920's the great fiction hits were Hemingway's A FAREWELL TO ARMS and the S. S. Van Dine mysteries. A downward trend in circulation was temporarily halted by such work, but continued after the retirement of Bridges in 1930 in spite of such newcomers to its pages as Thomas Wolfe, Sherwood Anderson, D. H. Lawrence, Erskine Caldwell, and a number of distinguished leftist non-fiction writers. In 1929 the subscription list was sold to *Esquire* and the name to the *Commentator;* in 1942 the publisher of *Scribner's Commentator* was found guilty of accepting subsidies from Japan for the publication of propaganda for that government.

Scribner's Monthly. See CENTURY ILLUSTRATED MONTHLY MAGAZINE.

Scripps, E[dward] W[yllis] (b. near Rushville, Ill., June 18, 1854—d. March 12, 1926), newspaperman, publisher, philanthropist. Scripps, together with members of his family, established or acquired numerous newspapers and set up a dynasty that exercised a wide influence on the journalism of his time. He began with the Detroit *Evening News,* ultimately becoming city editor. Then he founded the Cleveland *Penny Press,* acquired the St. Louis *Evening Chronicle,* later the Cincinnati *Post;* from these he fashioned the first newspaper chain in the United States. Other members of his family assisted him, and he was also joined by MILTON ALEXANDER MCRAE (1858–1930), who organized with him the Scripps-McRae League of Newspapers (1895) and the Scripps-McRae Press Association (1897), which in combination later became the United Press. The Newspaper Enterprise Association (NEA) was organized (1902) to furnish features and cartoons, the first syndicate in the United States. Scripps went on to acquire a large chain of Pacific coast papers and many others. He endowed the Scripps Foundation (for population research) at Miami University in Ohio, and with his sister he founded the Scripps Institution of Oceanography at La Jolla, Calif. When his son Robert Paine Scripps took on Roy Howard as his assistant and partner, the newspaper enterprises were called Scripps-Howard. In 1951 appeared *Damned Old Crank: A Self-Portrait of E. W. Scripps,* edited by Charles R. McCabe. McRae wrote *Forty Years in Newspaperdom* (1924).

Scudder, Antoinette [Quinby] (b. Newark, N.J., Sept. 11, 1898—d. Jan. 27, 1958), poet, playwright, novelist, painter, critic, theater sponsor. Miss Scudder's work includes several collections of verse, among them: *Provincetown Sonnets and Other Poems* (1925); *The Soul of Ilaria* (1926); *Huckleberries* (1929); *Out of Peony and Blade* (1931); *The Henchman and the Moon* (1934); *East End, West End* (1935); *Italics for Life: Collected Poems* (1947). Her dramatic works were published as *The Cherry Tart and Other Plays* (1938) and *The World in a Match Box* (1949). *The Grey Studio* (1934) was a novelette. Much of her work exhibits her fondness for the sea. Miss Scudder sponsored the Newark Playhouse in 1929; in 1934 it became the Paper Mill Playhouse in Millburn, N.J.

Scudder, Horace E[lisha] (b. Boston, Oct. 16, 1838—d. Jan. 11, 1902), editor, writer. Scudder's childhood was characterized by the pious and happy influences described in his book about an older brother, *Life and Letters of David Coit Scudder, a Missionary in Southern India* (1864). After graduating from Williams College he went to New York, where he taught private pupils and wrote two books for children, *Seven Little People and Their Friends* (1862) and *Dream Children* (1864), which were published anonymously. He joined Henry

O. Houghton's publishing firm (afterward the Houghton Mifflin Co.), serving mainly as literary editor. As editor of the ATLANTIC MONTHLY from 1890 to 1898 he was the author of a large body of fugitive writing, much of it published anonymously in the *Atlantic.*

Scudder did more than any other individual to raise the standards of literature for children, through his own writings and through his editorial duties. When the *Riverside Magazine for Young People* was started in 1867 he contributed stories and enlisted such distinguished writers as Hans Christian Andersen, Jacob Abbott, Frank R. Stockton, and Sarah Orne Jewett. As editor he planned the "American Commonwealth Series" and the "Riverside Literature Series." As author he wrote the *Bodley Books* (1875–1887), popular juvenile books of travel, and *Childhood in Literature and Art* (1894). He wrote biographies of Noah Webster (1882); George Washington (1890), one of the "Riverside" series; and James Russell Lowell (1901); and *Stories and Romances* (1880) and *A History of the United States* (1884).

Scudder, Vida D[utton] (b. India, Dec. 15, 1861—d. Oct. 9, 1954), teacher, critic, editor, writer. Miss Scudder joined the Wellesley College faculty in 1887, became a full professor in 1910, retired in 1927. In the course of her long career she wrote on many topics, but her most influential book was perhaps *Social Ideals in English Letters* (1898; rev., 1922, 1923), which reflected her deep humanitarian concern and her conviction that the study of literature was more than an *explication de texte.* She also wrote *The Life of the Spirit in the Modern English Poets* (1895); *A Listener in Babel* (1903); *The Disciple of a Saint* (1907); *Social Teachings of the Christian Year* (1921); *The Franciscan Adventure* (1931); *The Privilege of Age: Essays Secular and Spiritual* (1939). *On Journey* (1937) and *My Quest for Reality* (1953) are autobiographical.

Seabrook, William [Buehler] (b. Westminster, Md., Feb. 22, 1886—d. Sept. 20, 1945), newspaperman, writer. Seabrook worked for papers in Georgia and New York, later did feature articles for news syndicates, began traveling widely in 1924. He reported his experiences in somewhat sensational volumes. Among them: *Adventures in Arabia* (1927); *The Magic Island* [Haiti] (1929); *Jungle Ways* (1931); *Air Adventure* (1933); *Witchcraft* (1940). *Asylum* (1935) tells of his stay in a hospital in an attempt to cure himself of alcoholism; *No Hiding Place* (1942) is also autobiographical.

Seabury, Samuel (b. Groton, Conn., Nov. 30, 1729—d. Feb. 25, 1796), Episcopal clergyman, author. Seabury studied at Yale University and in Scotland, held pastorates in New Jersey, Long Island, and Westchester, in 1783 was elected the first Episcopalian American-born bishop. He was a Loyalist during the Revolution and his pamphlets were widely read. His *Letters of a Westchester Farmer, 1774–1775* were edited (1930), with an introduction by Clarence H.

Vance. He published *Discourses on Several Subjects* (2 v., 1793) and additional *Discourses on Several Important Subjects* (1798). His grandson **Samuel Seabury** (1801–1872) edited *The Churchman*, founded *The Protestant Churchman* (1846), wrote *The Study of the Classics on Christian Principles* (1831). His great-great-grandson, another **Samuel Seabury** (1873–1958), was a celebrated lawyer, jurist, and political reformer.

Sea Lions, The (1849), a novel by JAMES FENIMORE COOPER. Cooper had long been interested in CAPTAIN KIDD, and in his *History of the Navy* (1839) had given an account of Kidd's life and of the treasure the pirate had reputedly buried. In *The Sea Lions* novel Cooper interwove an account of whaling in the Antarctic and treasure hunting in the West Indies. The treasure hunt is based on a treasure island chart found among the belongings of a mysterious deceased sailor.

Sealsfield, Charles [also **C. Seatsfield** and **C. Sidons:** pen names of **Karl Anton Postl**] (b. Moravia, March 3, 1793—d. May 26, 1864), novelist, short-story writer, travel writer. All his life Sealsfield concealed his real name and that he was originally a monk who escaped from a Bohemian monastery and in 1822 fled to the United States. He became an American citizen, but also lived in various parts of Europe. He traveled extensively in this country, especially in the Southwest and the Mississippi Valley, and visited Mexico. He wrote his books in German and translated them himself into English. He was most widely read among German-Americans, but had a large audience in other countries. He was enthusiastic in his admiration of American institutions and was a fiery battler for freedom and against oppression everywhere.

Sealsfield wrote voluminously. The first fruits of his travels in the United States were *Die Vereinigten Staaten von Nordamerika, Nach Ihren Politischen, Religioesen, und Gesellschaftlichen Verhaeltnisse Betrachtet*, published in Germany (2 v.) in 1827. It appeared in London as *The United States of North America as They Are* (1827) and *The Americans as They Are* (1828). Most of his books deal with America, especially the southern and southwestern regions. He invented what he called the "ethnographic novel," which deals with an entire people through the depiction of individuals. Typical was *Tokeah, or, The White Rose* (1829; rewritten in German, 1833). Other novels were grouped to produce the same effect: *Die Deutschamerikanischen Wahlverwandtschaft* (4 v., 1839–40) and *Sueden und Norden* (3 v., 1842–43). One of his best books was *Das Kajuetenbuch* ("The Cabin Book," 1841), stories dealing mainly with the Texas War of Independence. His works were in part collected in a fifteen-volume edition published in Germany (1845–47). William P. Dallman analyzed *The Spirit of America as Interpreted in the Works of Charles Sealsfield* (1935); Otto

Heller studied *The Language of Charles Sealsfield as Atypical Usage* (1941). A bibliography of his writings and of works about him was prepared (1939) by Heller and Theodore H. Leon. Longfellow referred to his "favorite Sealsfield" and reread the Louisiana sections of his *Lebensbilder* (1835–37) when he was writing *Evangeline* (1847). According to Albert B. Faust, William Gilmore Simms borrowed an episode from *Ralph Doughbys Brautfahrt* (1834) for his *Guy Rivers* (1834); Helen Hunt Jackson's *Ramona* (1884) has resemblances to *Tokeah*, and Mayne Reid is said to have adapted the third and best part of his *Wild Life* from a translation of *The Cabin Book*.

Seaman, Augusta Huiell (b. New York City, April 3, 1879—d. June 4, 1950), writer for girls. Mrs. Seaman began her career as a staff member of ST. NICHOLAS, in which her earlier work appeared. She found that girls liked mystery stories, and she wrote more than forty of them in book form. Her first, *Jacqueline of the Carrier Pigeons* (1910), established her reputation. In 1927 she moved with her second husband, Francis Parkman Freeman, to Island Beach, N.J., a virgin wilderness amid the shore resorts. Thereafter she became deeply interested in New Jersey, and many of her books reflected this interest: *The Pine Barrens Mystery* (1937); *The Case of the Calico Crab* (1942); *The Vanishing Octant Mystery* (1949). Her historical backgrounds were based on careful research.

Seaman, Elizabeth Cochrane ["Nellie Bly"] (b. Cochran Mills, Pa., May 5, 1867—d. Jan. 27, 1922), journalist. Elizabeth Cochrane received her early education from her father, a judge, and began to write highly imaginative stories when still a child. She sold her first article to the Pittsburgh *Dispatch*, and George Madden, the managing editor, suggested she take her pen name from a popular song by Stephen Foster. Thereafter she was known as Nellie Bly. The death of her father left her impoverished; she moved to Pittsburgh, went to work for the *Dispatch* at five dollars a week, and wrote many crusading articles about factories and sweatshops. In 1887 she visited Mexico with her mother, financing the trip with travel articles written in the form of letters to Madden. He offered her fifteen dollars a week on her return, but her goal was New York, and she set out to conquer it.

A small woman with a deceptively meek manner, Nellie Bly was a dynamo of energy and ingenuity. By patience and bullying she pushed her way into JOSEPH PULITZER's office and laid before him her plans for sensational articles for the *World*. Pulitzer set her to work. First, feigning insanity, she had herself sent to Blackwell's Island, the city asylum. After her release the *World* printed her horrifying account of "the human rat-trap, easy to get into, impossible to get out of." A grand jury investigated her charges and appropriated three million dollars for improvements. Next she attacked Edward

Phelps, Albany lobbyist; then city prisons, old people's homes, factories, the "mashers" of Central Park. She became so formidable a muckraker that it was said public officials viewed every beggar woman and prostitute with suspicion, lest she turn out to be Nellie Bly in disguise.

In 1889 she accomplished her greatest feat —a trip around the world to break the record set by Jules Verne's hero in *Around the World in Eighty Days* (1873). She stopped in Amiens to call on Verne, who didn't think she could do it. When she landed in New York after circling the globe in seventy-two and a half days, the city went wild. In 1895 she married Robert Seaman. After his death she became involved in endless litigation which ate up most of the estate and embittered her later years. She withdrew from public life, and although she continued to write for the New York *Evening Journal* until her death, few people knew that the fabulous Nellie Bly was still alive. She published *Ten Days in a Mad-house* (1887); *Six Months in Mexico* (1888); *The Mystery of Central Park* (1889); *Nellie Bly's Book: Around the World in Seventy-Two Days* (1890). Ishbel Ross wrote of her exploits in *Ladies of the Press* (1936), and Iris Noble in *Nellie Bly: First Woman Reporter* (1956).

Sea of Grass, The (1937), a novel by CONRAD RICHTER. This story of a cattle baron of the old Southwest and his hopeless battle against progress is recounted by a young boy who watches the action but never participates in it or fully understands it. Filled with a warm, rich feeling for the land, the novel is marred, some critics feel, by an impossibly glamorous heroine.

Sears, Edmund Hamilton (b. Sandisfield, Mass., April 6, 1810—d. Jan. 16, 1876), Unitarian clergyman, editor, hymn writer. He wrote a book on immortality called *Athanasia* (1858), edited the *Monthly Religious Magazine* (1859–71), and wrote some famous hymns, including *It Came Upon a Midnight Clear* and *Calm on the Listening Ear of Night*.

Sears, Lorenzo (b. Searsville, Mass., April 18, 1838—d. March 1, 1916), teacher, critic, historian. On the faculty of Brown University from 1890 to 1906, Sears was one of the earliest historians of American literature. He wrote *American Literature in the Colonial and National Periods* (1902) and *The Makers of American Literature* (1904), also *The History of Oratory* (1896), *The Principles and Methods of Literary Criticism* (1898), and lives of Wendell Phillips (1909), John Hancock (1912), and John Jay (1914).

Seats of the Mighty (1896), a novel by SIR GILBERT PARKER. The setting of this historical romance is Quebec at the crisis of the war between the French and English. Captain Robert Moray of Lord Amherst's regiment, a hostage on parole in Quebec, is imprisoned on false charges of espionage. The usual events of the historical romance—an escape from jail, the delivery of the papers, a secret marriage, and a search for the missing bride—occupy the rest of the novel. *Seats of the Mighty* was dramatized in 1897 by the author.

Seaweed (1844), a poem by HENRY WADSWORTH LONGFELLOW. In this poem Longfellow sets forth a theory about the origin of poetry. He states that just as a storm causes seaweed to be torn from its base and tossed up on shore, so "storms of wild emotion/ Strike the ocean/ Of the poet's soul" and tear off "some fragment of a song" which is "at length in books recorded." The first four stanzas are a little masterpiece of description, meter, and rhyme, whereas the last four stanzas are merely an instance of Longfellow's compulsion to find some sort of didactic conclusion everywhere.

Sea Wolf, The (1904), a novel by JACK LONDON. The ruthless power of Wolf Larsen, captain of the sealing schooner *Ghost*, is challenged when he rescues Humphrey Van Weyden, a literary critic, and Maude Brewster, a lady poet, after the ferry boat in which they were crossing San Francisco Bay had collided with a steamer. Although Wolf cannot accurately be called a Nietzschean superman, he probably evolved from London's interest in Nietzsche. The story breaks into two parts, the first taking place on shipboard, the second on a desert island where Humphrey, Wolf, and Miss Brewster are wrecked. Years after its publication London stated that he wrote *The Sea Wolf* to show that a superman could not survive in modern society. The novel is still well thought of in Europe, although in this country it is now generally regarded as a "boys' book."

Seccomb, John (b. Medford, Mass., April 25, 1708—d. Oct. 27, 1792), Congregational clergyman, humorist. Seccomb was ordained minister of the town of Harvard in 1733. In 1757 he resigned and later became the minister of a dissenting congregation in Chester, Nova Scotia. He published an ordination sermon in Nova Scotia (1770) and a funeral sermon on the death of Governor Jonathan Belcher's wife (1771). His fame as a humorist is based on a cleverly rhymed poem, *Father Abbey's Will* (1730), written in honor of a bedmaker and sweeper at Harvard named Matthew Abdy.

Secret Service (1895), a play by WILLIAM GILLETTE. In this Civil War melodrama Gillette played the part of Lewis Dumont, a Northern spy who, during the siege of Richmond, enters the city pretending to be Captain Thorne of the Confederate Army. Edith Varney, a Southern girl who falls in love with him, secures a commission for him as major attached to the Telegraph Service. When Thorne is unmasked Edith is torn between love and patriotic duty. One reason for the play's success, according to A. H. Quinn, was that it extolled the spirit of American gentlefolk, whether Northern or Southern.

Section: Rock-Drill 85–95 de los Cantares (1956), a section of the longer *Cantos* of EZRA POUND. Here the *Cantos* move into a new phase, and Pound begins to describe his "paradise."

Sedgwick, Anne Douglas (b. Englewood, N.J., March 28, 1873—d. July 19, 1935), novelist. Miss Sedgwick married Basil de Selincourt (1908) and thereafter resided in England. Her best-known novel was THE LITTLE FRENCH GIRL (1924). She also wrote *The Dull Miss Archinard* (1898); *Franklin Winslow Kane* (1910); TANTE (1911); *Adrienne Toner* (1922); and other stories.

Sedgwick, Catharine Maria (b. Stockbridge, Mass., Dec. 28, 1789—d. July 31, 1867), novelist, biographer. Miss Sedgwick, called "the Maria Edgeworth of America," was a member of one of the most prominent families in New

England. Her interest in good works led her to write her first novel, *A New-England Tale* (1822), published anonymously. Although her original purpose was moral uplift, she was too good a writer to stop at that. Her next novel, *Redwood* (1824), was extremely popular and was reprinted in England, where it was compared with the *Waverley* novels, and in France, where Paris newspapers debated whether Cooper was the author. She is best known today for HOPE LESLIE (1827), a historical romance about the settlement of Springfield, Mass. Other novels were *Clarence* (1830); *The Linwoods* (1835); *Live and Let Live* (1837). She also wrote biographies of Lucretia M. Davidson (1837) and John Curtis (1858). Although part of Miss Sedgwick's success, particularly in Europe, lay in the novelty of her use of the American scene, her books had some solid virtues. The historical backgrounds were accurate, the characters well

conceived, and the domestic detail of village life precise and appealing. Her common sense kept her from the bombast and absurdities of many other romantic novelists. *The Life and Letters of Catharine M. Sedgwick* (1871), edited by Mary Dewey, included "Reminiscences of Miss Sedgwick" by William Cullen Bryant.

Sedgwick, Ellery (b. New York City, Feb. 27, 1872—d. April 21, 1960), editor. Sedgwick began his career as an editor of YOUTH'S COMPANION, *Leslie's Monthly Magazine,* the *American Magazine,* and finally the ATLANTIC MONTHLY (1908–38). How he felt about his vocation he told in *The Happy Profession* (1946), in which he recalled meetings with many famous persons. As an undergraduate at Harvard University, Sedgwick dreamed of becoming editor of the *Atlantic*. When he attained his ambition the magazine became in effect Ellery Sedgwick, and readers seemed to like it that way. He later edited *Atlantic Harvest* (1947), a collection of forty-seven memorable pieces from the magazine under his editorship. See also OPAL WHITELEY.

Sedgwick, Henry Dwight (b. Stockbridge, Mass., Sept. 24, 1861—d. Jan. 5, 1956), lawyer, essayist. The older brother of ELLERY SEDGWICK published *Essays on Great Writers* (1902); *The New American Type and Other Essays* (1908); *An Apology for Old Maids and Other Essays* (1916); *The Art of Happiness* (1933); *In Praise of Gentlemen* (1935); *Horace* (1947); and other volumes.

Seeger, Alan (b. New York City, June 22, 1888—d. July 4, 1916), poet. After graduation from Harvard University, Seeger set out to write, first in New York, later in Paris. When World War I broke out he enlisted in the French Foreign Legion, was killed at Belloy-en-Senterre, was awarded a posthumous Croix de Guerre and Medaille Militaire. Seeger was a thoroughgoing romanticist, fierce, handsome, rebellious, whose longings somewhat outspanned his talents. I HAVE A RENDEZVOUS WITH DEATH, which appeared in his *Collected Poems* (1916), was one of the most popular poems of the first World War.

Seitz, Don Carlos (b. Portage, Ohio, Oct. 24, 1862—d. Dec. 4, 1935), journalist, biographer, poet. Seitz began as correspondent for the Brooklyn *Eagle,* became its city editor in 1889. He went on to other newspaper jobs, and ended as business manager of Pulitzer's New York *World,* a position he held for twenty-five years. Toward the end of his life he worked for a while as associate editor of the *Outlook.* He published two books of verse, *The Buccaneers* (1912) and *Farm Voices* (1918); but chiefly he is known for his biographies: *Artemus Ward* (1919); *Joseph Pulitzer* (1924); *Braxton Bragg, General of the Confederacy* (1924); *Horace Greeley* (1926); *Charles Curtis* (1928); *James Gordon Bennett* (1928); *Lincoln the Politician* (1931). Among his other volumes are: *The Dreadful Decade (1869–1879)* (1926); *The Great Island,* a book about Newfoundland

(1926); *The Also Rans* (1927); *Famous American Duels* (1929).

Seldes, George (b. Alliance, N.J., Nov. 16, 1890—   ), journalist. Seldes was born in a "sort of Utopian society" founded by his father, who received helpful communications from Count Tolstoy and Prince Kropotkin on how to operate a co-operative idealistic colony. The experiment failed. Seldes went to Harvard University, during the war worked in the press section of the American army, obtaining credit for capturing a town. His writings are bold, sometimes brash, attempts to get behind sham and reveal truth. *Sawdust Caesar* (1932) was an exposé of Mussolini. *In Fact,* Seldes' famous liberal newsletter begun in 1940, achieved the remarkable circulation of 176,-000 before its demise ten years later. In 1953 he wrote *Tell the Truth and Run,* a record of his forty years in journalism, which he described not as a biography but as "a record of adventures and meanings." Some of his works: *You Can't Print That* (1929); *The Truth Behind the News* (1929); *The Vatican and the Modern World* (1933); *Iron, Blood and Profits* (1934); *Lords of the Press* (1938); *The Facts Are* (1942); *Facts and Fascism* (1943); *The People Don't Know* (1949); *The World's Great Quotations* (1050).

Seldes, Gilbert [Vivian] (b. Alliance, N.J., Jan. 3, 1893—d. Sept. 29, 1970), critic, journalist, writer. A brother of the journalist GEORGE SELDES, Seldes was music critic for the Philadelphia *Evening Ledger,* a foreign correspondent during World War I, and a political correspondent for *L'Echo* of Paris in Washington, D.C., after the war. He went on to various other editorial positions, including an associate editorship with *Collier's,* the managing editorship of the *Dial,* the post of critic for various New York newspapers; at one time he was director of television programming for the Columbia Broadcasting System.

Seldes' first book, *The United States and the War* (1917), was followed by his best-known critical work, *The Seven Lively Arts* (1924; 1957), an appraisal of such popular art forms as the comic strip, the motion picture, vaudeville, jazz, etc. *The Stammering Century* (1928) examines 19th-century America. *The Wings of the Eagle* (1929) is a novel. There followed *The Movies and the Talkies* (1929); *Lysistrata* (an adaptation, 1930); *The Future of Drinking* (1930), which examined the effects of Prohibition; *Against Revolution, The Year of the Locust* (1932), a study of the United States during the depression; *Mainland* (1936), another study of American life; *The Movies Come from America* (1937); *Your Money and Your Life* (1937); *The Great Audience* (1950); *Writing for Television* (1952); *The Public Arts* (1956). His work also includes many scripts for radio and television, and reviews of television and radio for the *Saturday Review.* Under the name of Foster Johns he wrote *The Victory Murders* (1927) and *The Square Emerald* (1928), detective stories.

Self-Reliance (in *Essays, First Series,* 1841), an essay by RALPH WALDO EMERSON. In this essay Emerson preached a doctrine of independence and individualism. Some of the essay's epigrammatic statements became famous immediately: "Whoso would be a man must be a non-conformist." "Society everywhere is in conspiracy against the manhood of every one of its members." "Nothing is at last sacred but the integrity of your own mind." "A foolish consistency is the hobgoblin of little minds." "An institution is the lengthened shadow of a man."

Sellers, Colonel Beriah. A character in THE GILDED AGE (novel, 1873; play, 1874) by Mark Twain and Charles Dudley Warner, and in THE AMERICAN CLAIMANT (play, in collaboration with William Dean Howells, 1883; novel, 1892). In the stage version of *The Gilded Age* the colonel's name was changed to Mulberry Sellers, and thereafter that form was employed. Mark Twain is believed to have taken hints for the character from his brother Orion, but it may be suspected that Sellers was partly autobiographical. According to other conjectures, he was Twain's father or perhaps James Lampton, a favorite cousin of Twain's mother. As depicted in the novels, he is a man of endless schemes and unwearied optimism, an American Micawber. Twain himself thought of Lampton as the model for the character; he insisted that some of the funniest episodes in the novels and the stage version were actual happenings.

The American Claimant was originally a play which Twain reworked eight years after he and Warner had written it and offered it to the actor John T. Raymond, who turned it down. Raymond later, without permission, made a play (1874) from *The Gilded Age,* though Twain was able to forbid its performance. Later Twain and Raymond agreed to the use of a version done by Twain himself, probably with help from Raymond's scenarist, Gilbert Densmore.

Sellers, Isaiah (b. Iredell Co., N.C., 1802[?]—d. March 6, 1864), steamboat pilot, newspaperman. Sellers was one of the great pilots of the Mississippi in the early days; in LIFE ON THE MISSISSIPPI (1883) Mark Twain calls him "the patriarch of the craft." Sellers had an idea that he was also a good writer and contributed "river reports" to the New Orleans *Picayune,* supposedly under the pen name of Mark Twain, although DeLancey Ferguson points out in his *Mark Twain* (1943) that "it is still to be proved that the old man ever used the signature." Clemens at this time was beginning to experiment with a burlesque style, and on May 7, 1859, he published in the New Orleans *True Delta* a satire on Sellers, which he tells about in *Life on the Mississippi.* The satire is said to have hurt Sellers greatly and to have caused him to give up his newspaper work. See MARK TWAIN.

Sellers, Mulberry. See COLONEL BERIAH SELLERS.

Selling of Joseph, The (1700), a tract by SAMUEL SEWALL. Judge Sewall was eminently conservative, but he also had a deep sense of justice. This tract was the first in America to denounce Negro slavery, and it also mentioned "women's rights."

semantics. See STUART CHASE; S. I. HAYA-KAWA; ALFRED KORZYBSKI.

Seminole Indians. The name means "separatist" and was given to a Muskhogean tribe of Florida which left the Creek tribe and was later joined by Yamassee and Yuchi Indians and runaway Negro slaves. They were under Spanish rule during the War of 1812 and were hostile to the United States. There were two Seminole Wars (1817–1818 and 1835–1842), the second led by the great warrior OSCEOLA. No treaty was signed; most of the tribe moved to Oklahoma, but several hundred remained in the Florida Everglades, farming and making souvenirs for a living. They retain their picturesque costumes. In Oklahoma they are regarded as an educated and cultured group.

Novels dealing with the Seminoles include Robert Wilder's BRIGHT FEATHER (1948); Theodore Pratt's *Seminole* (1954); Frank G. Slaughter's *The Seminole* (1956). Frances Densmore made a penetrating study of their history and culture in *Seminole Music* (1956).

Semmes, Raphael (b. Charles Co., Md., Sept. 27, 1809—d. Aug. 30, 1877), naval officer, lawyer, memoirist. Semmes was perhaps the best known Confederate naval officer during the Civil War; he commanded two raiders that inflicted great damage on northern commerce, the *Sumter* and the *Alabama*. After the war he practiced law in Mobile, Ala. He wrote several books about his experiences, including *Service Afloat and Ashore During the Mexican War* (1851); *Campaign of General Scott in the Valley of Mexico* (1852); *Cruise of the Alabama and the Sumter* (1864); and *Memoirs of Service Afloat During the War Between the States* (1869).

Senarens, Luis Philip (b. Brooklyn, N.Y., [?], 1863—d. Dec. 26, 1939), dime novelist. Senarens is said to have written more than 1,500 books—but the books were usually only sixteen pages long, three columns to the page. He employed many pen names. His most popular hero was Frank Reade, who appeared in a long series of stories, some of them published in the *Frank Reade Weekly* (1902 and thereafter). Frank had a knack for creating mechanical devices that to some extent anticipated science-fiction.

Sennett, Mack [stage name of **Michael Sinnott**] (b. Danville, Que., 1884—d. Nov. 5, 1960), actor, film producer, director. Sennett worked as an actor under the direction of DAVID W. GRIFFITH. In 1912 he joined the Keystone Co. and began producing the comic extravaganzas with which his fame is associated. In addition he developed a number of comedians who earned fame in their own right—Charlie Chaplin, Ben Turpin, Roscoe [Fatty] Arbuckle, Harold Lloyd, Harry Langdon, Buster Keaton, and others. Pretty girls (to whom no favoritism was shown in the usual roughhouse) and a corps of spectacularly ineffectual policemen (the "Keystone Cops") were invariable features of Sennett's pictures. He did not particularly favor gags for their own sake; his comedy lay in action. He joined Paramount in 1917, and his comedy began to become more refined. With Cameron Forbes he wrote *Mack Sennett, King of Comedy* (1954).

Septimius Felton, or A Romance of Immortality (1871), a novel by NATHANIEL HAWTHORNE. The existence of this story was discovered only after Hawthorne's death, and a large part of the manuscript was prepared and subsequently published by his wife. The manuscript was referred to in the preface to OUR OLD HOME, but it seems to have functioned merely as a preliminary to THE DOLLIVER ROMANCE. Never polished by Hawthorne, and indeed never intended for an audience in its existing state, *Septimius Felton* indicates a decline in Hawthorne's powers at the end of his life and is of interest primarily in its revelations as a work-in-progress.

The plot of *Septimius Felton* is set both in England and America, and centers on a hero of mixed English and Indian blood. He discovers the elixir of life, causes the death of his sweetheart and finally disappears in England. Affairs are further confused by the partial development of the characters of Rose Garfield and Robert Hagburn, and the introduction of a long episode recounting the tale of a bloody footprint.

Sequoya (b. Tennessee, [1770?]—d. Aug., 1843), CHEROKEE INDIAN, artisan, alphabet inventor. Sequoya was half-white, half-Indian. In later life he called himself George Guess, George Gist, and George Guest. He is said to have been injured in a hunting accident and therefore prevented from engaging in the customary sports and war activities of his tribe. He turned to working on silver and painting animal subjects; he is credited with having invented a painting brush without knowing that such a device existed elsewhere. Around 1809 he began to work on developing a Cherokee alphabet or syllabary. After ten years or so he produced a workable alphabet, which immediately went into general use and is still employed. It is so simple that all the Cherokees became literate in a matter of months. In 1825 a version of the New Testament was made in Cherokee with the help of Sequoya's symbols. In 1827 a Boston firm cast a font of type in Cherokee characters; this was used in the publication (1828–34) of a newspaper called the *Cherokee Phoenix*, later the *Cherokee Phoenix & Indian's Advocate*. The *Cherokee Messenger* (established August 1844) was likewise printed in the Cherokee language. Sequoya also served on the delegation that signed a treaty (1828) resulting in moving the Cherokees to Indian Territory. G. E. Foster wrote *Sequoyah, the American Cadmus and Modern Moses: A Complete Biography of the Greatest of Redmen* (1885).

Serena Blandish (1928), a play by S. N. BEHRMAN, based on a novel of the same title by Enid Bagnold.

Serling, [Edward] Rod[man] (b. Syracuse, N.Y., Dec. 25, 1924–   ), TV writer, playwright. Serling attended Antioch College, and afterward launched himself brilliantly in television with a series of plays that incisively probed contemporary themes. *Patterns* (1957) dealt with a young business executive caught between his driving ambition and the damage to his ideals; it won an Emmy Award. *Requiem for a Heavyweight* (1956), which won the George Foster Peabody Award, was a dramatic probe into the downfall of a professional pugilist. Other works: *The Comedian* (1957); *The Velvet Alley* (1959); *The Twilight Zone* (1959). See TELEVISION WRITING.

sermons. An incalculable number of sermons are delivered weekly in the United States; but the influence and literary esteem of such sermons has declined greatly since the days of the Puritans (see ORATORS AND ORATORY). At that time the carefully wrought sermons of the more able ministers took the place of modern newspapers and magazines, radio and television, library and lay lectures, even a college education. The early Puritans did not lay so much emphasis on hellfire as did the later ones. A great many sermons were printed, especially those delivered at the funerals of distinguished persons, on some civic occasion, or at ordinations. Typical publications were: Thomas Hooker's *The Soul's Preparation* (1632); Peter Bulkeley's *The Gospel Covenant Opened* (1651); Samuel Moody's *The Doleful State of the Damned* (1701); Thomas Foxcroft's *The Day of a Godly Man's Death* (1722); Joseph Morgan's *Sin Its Own Punishment* (1728).

Distinguished preachers constitute a long roll call in American literature. Among them: JOHN COTTON, NATHANIEL WARD, JOHN ELIOT, ROGER WILLIAMS, THOMAS HOOKER, the three Mathers (see COTTON MATHER), John Davenport, JONATHAN EDWARDS, JONATHAN MAYHEW, SAMUEL HOPKINS, WILLIAM ELLERY CHANNING [1], THEODORE PARKER, HENRY WARD BEECHER, PHILLIPS BROOKS, HARRY EMERSON FOSDICK. In modern times spellbinding has given way to a more informal preaching which reaches an audience vastly greater than that of any other era. Clergymen today often appear on radio or television, and many publish popular "inspirational" books. Others have found it wise to go beyond theology in their sermons, discussing, for instance, controversial political topics. Halford E. Luccock, former professor of homiletics at Yale Divinity School, co-edited with Frances Brentano THE QUESTING SPIRIT (1947), an anthology of religious literature of our time. Other recent books include Edgar DeWitt Jones' *American Preachers of Today* and *The Great Business of Preaching* (1936), and A. C. Craig's *Preaching in a Scientific Age* (1954).

One of the most notable collections of sermons ever published was that of a layman, the Negro poet JAMES WELDON JOHNSON. In GOD'S TROMBONES (1927) he gathered a group of free-verse sermons both simple and powerful. The sermons preached by Negro preachers have long

been a subject for loving burlesque. The best known is Roark Bradford's *Ol' Man Adam and His Chillun* (1928), on which the famous play THE GREEN PASTURES (1930) was based.

Serra, Miguel José [Junípero] (b. Majorca, Nov. 24, 1713–d. Aug. 28, 1784), missionary. Father Serra attended the University of Palma, where he joined the Franciscan Order, taking the name of Junípero. In 1749 he sailed for Mexico as a missionary. His first assignment was to the Pamé Indian Mission in the Sierra Gorda Mountains. He composed a catechism in the Pamé language and with the aid of his six priests taught the Indians agriculture, carpentry, ironwork, tanning, and brickmaking. One of the priests was Francisco Palou, who was later Junípero's biographer. Three years later Father Serra was recalled to Mexico City to preach. In 1769 he went with the Galvez expedition up the coast of California and founded the first mission at San Diego. The next year he founded the San Carlos mission at Monterey, in 1771 the missions of San Antonio and San Gabriel, in 1776 the mission of San Francisco, and in 1777 that of Santa Clara. These missions and several lesser ones were the first settlements in California.

Father Serra loved the Indians, converted thousands, and protected them from exploitation by the civil authorities. *Father Serra's Diary: an Account of His Journey from Loretto to San Diego, 1787* was published in 1935. Francisco Palou's *Life and Apostolic Labors of the Venerable Father Junípero Serra* was translated by C. Scott Willams in 1913. Agnes Repplier's *Junípero Serra, Pioneer of California* (1933); Ivy Bolton's *Father Junípero Serra* (1952); and Theodore Maynard's *The Long Road of Father Serra* (1954) furnish popular information. Willa Cather includes a legend about Father Serra in DEATH COMES FOR THE ARCHBISHOP (1927). Isabella Gibson Zeigler wrote a novel about him called *The Nine Days of Father Serra* (1951).

Service, Robert W[illiam] (b. England, Jan. 16, 1874–d. Sept. 11, 1958), poet, novelist. At fourteen Service started to work as a bank clerk in Glasgow, Scotland. He migrated to Canada six years later, worked on a farm in British Columbia until 1902, when he returned to banking and was transferred to Whitehorse, in the Yukon, and to Dawson. He left the bank to spend eight years traveling in sub-Arctic regions, where he accumulated material for his northland ballads. During World War I he drove an ambulance for the Red Cross, later became an intelligence officer in the Canadian Army. He settled in France after the war. In 1940 he escaped with his family from his home in Brittany just ahead of the German armies. He went to Canada, spent some time in Hollywood, where he wrote his autobiography, *Ploughman of the Moon* (1945), and returned to France for the remainder of his life. Service wrote several novels, among them *The Master of the Microbe* (1926) and *The House of Fear* (1927), but is best known for his verses, which achieved great popularity in the early part of the 20th century. Their marked rhythm and red-blooded subject matter made them a favorite target for parody writers. Among his books of verse are *Songs of a Sourdough* (1907), later retitled *The Spell of the Yukon*, which contains his best known ballad, THE SHOOTING OF DAN MCGREW; *Ballads of a Cheechako* (1909); *Rhymes of a Rolling Stone* (1912); *Rhymes of a Red Cross Man* (1916); *Ballads of a Bohemian* (1920); *Bar-Room Ballads* (1940); *Rhymes of a Roughneck* (1951); *Rhymes of a Rebel* (1952); *Carols of an Old Codger* (1954). He told the story of his life in *Harper of Heaven* (1948). Geoffrey T. Hellman wrote a lengthy profile of Service in *The New Yorker* (March 30 and April 6, 1946). See KLONDIKE GOLD RUSH.

Serviss, Garrett P[utnam] (b. Sharon Springs, N.Y., March 24, 1851—d. May 25, 1929), newspaperman, popularizer of scientific data, science-fiction writer. Among Serviss' widely read books were *Astronomy with an Opera Glass* (1888); *Astronomy with the Naked Eye* (1908); and *Curiosities of the Sky* (1909).

Sessions, Roger [Huntington] (b. Brooklyn, Dec. 28, 1896—   ), composer, teacher, author. Sessions entered Harvard University at the age of fourteen and two years later was made editor of the *Harvard Musical Review*. He studied with HORATIO PARKER at Yale University, later with Ernest Bloch and in schools abroad. At various times Sessions taught at Smith College, Boston and Princeton Universities, and the University of California. His work has been regarded as chiefly for other musicians, and he has been described as "probably the most difficult of United States composers." Among his notable compositions are the *Incidental Music to the Black Maskers* (1923); *Three Chorale Preludes for Organ* (1924–26); *First Symphony* (1927); *Pastorale for Flute* (1929); *First String Quartet* (1936); *Second Symphony* (1946); and an opera, *The Trial of Lucullus* (1947). Among his books: *The Musical Experience of Composer, Performer, and Listener* (1950) and *Harmonic Practice* (1951). His mother, Ruth Huntington Sessions, gives interesting details about Sessions in her autobiography, *Sixty-Odd* (1936). His *Turn O Libertad* (1944), a song based on a poem by Whitman, attracted particular attention, as did his *String Quintet* (1958).

Seth Jones, or, The Captives of the Frontier (pub., 1860, as No. 8 of *Beadle's Dime Novels*), by EDWARD S. ELLIS. This was called by Orville J. Victor, for thirty years editor of Beadle & Adams productions, "the perfect dime novel." The hero, of good station in life, assumes the disguise of an aged and eccentric hunter because he has heard that while he was away fighting in the Revolution his sweetheart had ceased to care for him. The story sold close to half a million copies in six months. This success determined Ellis's career; he continued for three decades to write similar stories, mainly about hunters. See DIME NOVEL, THE.

Seth's Brother's Wife (1887), a novel by HAROLD FREDERIC. This was Frederic's first novel, which appeared serially in *Scribner's Monthly*, then was published in book form. It was not a success. In this story of a triangular love affair and a murder involving two brothers and the wife of the older one, Frederic wrote realistically of soured lives and drabness, although in a later story (*The Editor and the Schoolma'am, The New York Times*, Sept. 9, 1888) he satirized the way in which Russian pessimism and gloom were penetrating American fiction. The background of his novel is upper New York State: the farmers, newspapermen, and the politicians of the region are well portrayed.

Seton, Anya (b. New York City, 1916–   ), novelist. Anya Seton, daughter of the naturalist ERNEST THOMPSON SETON, had little desire to write until 1937. Then, in her twenties, she became fired with ambition and put intense efforts into literary production. Nineteen months later she sold her first story. In 1941 she wrote a biographical novel, *My Theodosia*, the story of Aaron Burr's daughter, and realized that this genre was most satisfying for her. After that her efforts were concentrated in novels aimed at recreating the past of America. With *Katherine* (1954), a best-selling novel on which she worked four years, she entered into the world of fourteenth century England, telling of Katherine Synford, Chaucer's sister-in-law. *Dragonwyck* (1944) was a successful novel, sometimes called a "Hudson River Gothic." Some of her other books: *The Turquoise* (1946); *The Hearth and the Eagle* (1948); *Foxfire* (1951); *The Mistletoe and Sword* (1955); *Winthrop Woman* (1958). *Dragonwyck* and *Foxfire* have been filmed.

Seton, Ernest [Evan] Thompson (b. England, Aug. 14, 1860—d. Oct. 23, 1946), naturalist, illustrator, animal-story writer. Ernest Seton Thompson, as he was originally called, grew up in Ontario on a farm; in the forests nearby he studied birds and animals with a passion that lasted all his life. His studies at the Toronto Collegiate Institute were interrupted when he was stricken with tuberculosis; camping and hunting helped restore his health. He studied art at the Royal Academy in London, concentrating especially on animal sketches. After some time back in Canada and in the West, he went to New York City, where he supported himself by selling stories and drawings to magazines. In 1898 Seton collected eight of his realistic animal stories under the title *Wild Animals I Have Known*. The book was a great success, and he continued to publish as fast as he could write and illustrate. He also lectured extensively in the United States and Canada.

Among his titles are: *The Biography of a Grizzly* (1900); *Lives of the Hunted* (1901); *Two Little Savages* (1903); *Scouting for Boys* (1910); *Woodcraft and Indian Lore* (1912); *Wild Animals at Home* (1913); *Bannertail* (1922); *Lives of Game Animals* (1925); *The Gospel of the Redmen* (1936); *The Biography of an Arctic Fox* (1937); *Mainly About Wolves*

(1937); *The Trail of an Artist-Naturalist* (1940), an autobiography. *America: Selections from the Writings of the Artist Naturalist* (1954) has an introduction by Farida A. Wiley.

Seuss, Dr. [pen name of **Theodor Seuss Geisel**] (b. Springfield, Mass., March 2, 1904—   ), writer-illustrator of children's books, cartoonist, public relations counsel. Aside from Geisel's strictly literary and artistic work, he won fame as the originator and producer of several striking advertising campaigns—in particular the "Quick, Henry, the Flit!" series for the Standard Oil Company of New Jersey. His pen name is a compound of his mother's maiden name and a Ph.D. degree he said he never took the trouble to earn. His books are mainly juveniles written in verse and illustrated by the author. Among them are: *And to Think I Saw It on Mulberry Street* (1937); *The 500 Hats of Bartholomew Cubbins* (1938); *The King's Stilts* (1939); *Horton Hatches the Egg* (1940); *Horton Hears a Who* (1954); *On Beyond Zebra* (1955); *If I Ran the Circus* (1956); *How the Grinch Stole Christmas* (1957); *Yertle the Turtle* (1958); *Happy Birthday to You* (1959); *Green Eggs and Ham* (1960); *Speeches and Other Stories* (1961). *The Seven Lady Godivas* (1939) is a book for older readers—though adults have been enthusiastic readers of his fantastically comic books for children. One of the verses in *Mulberry Street* furnished the inspiration for *Marco Takes a Walk* (1942), one of Deems Taylor's "variations for orchestra." Two books for beginning readers are: *Cat in the Hat Comes Back!* (1959); *One Fish, Two Fish, Red Fish, Blue Fish* (1960).

Seven Cities of Cibola. See CIBOLA, THE SEVEN CITIES OF, and FRANCISCO VÁSQUEZ DE CORONADO.

Seven Keys to Baldpate (1913), a novel by EARL DERR BIGGERS. It describes the queer events that occur when a writer shuts himself up in a deserted hotel to produce a novel that has to meet a deadline. In the same year the novel was made into a clever melodrama by GEORGE M. COHAN, who created a collection of reporters, crooks, and politicians to spring one surprise after another, and himself appeared in the play. The play held the stage for years and in 1935 was made into a movie.

Sevenoaks (1875), a novel by JOSIAH GILBERT HOLLAND. The New England village of Sevenoaks is the scene of the machinations of Robert Belcher, an unscrupulous millionaire who obtained his wealth by stealing a patent from the inventor Paul Benedict. Edward Wagenknecht observes that it is interesting to compare the predatory Belcher, who is said to have been based on Jim Fisk, with similar later fictional characters, such as Dreiser's FRANK COWPERWOOD. The novel was dramatized by J. L. GILDER in 1876 as *Seven Oaks*. (See RICHARD WATSON GILDER.)

Seventeen (1916), a novel by BOOTH TARKINGTON. Written in much the same style as PENROD, *Seventeen* presents William Sylvanus Baxter, "Silly Billy," an adolescent in the throes of his first love affair. The creature upon whom he lavishes his attention is Lola Pratt, the "Baby-Talk Lady." The novel was dramatized in 1918 by Hugh S. Stange and Stannard Mears; it has been filmed a number of times and in 1951 was made into a musical by Sally Benson.

Seventeen. A magazine founded in Philadelphia in 1945 by the J. B. Lippincott Co. The periodical is aimed at an audience of adolescent girls, and its circulation now runs beyond a million. Three anthologies have been culled from its pages.

Sewall, Jonathan (b. Salem, Mass., Aug. 17, 1728—d. Sept. 26, 1796), lawyer, playwright. During the Revolution, Sewall advocated the Loyalist cause and to further it wrote a satirical play, *The Americans Roused in a Cure for the Spleen* (1775), using the pen name Sir Roger de Coverley. Later that year the play was reprinted as *The American's Counsel, in a Cure for the Spleen*. Sewall is described in J. H. Stark's *The Loyalists of Massachusetts* (1910).

Sewall, Jonathan Mitchell (b. Salem, Mass., [?], 1748—d. March 29, 1808), merchant, lawyer, poet. Sewall was adopted by his uncle, Judge SAMUEL SEWALL. He was at first a merchant, then studied and practiced law. He wrote much miscellaneous verse and an epilogue (1778) to Addison's *Cato*. His song called *War and Washington* was sung by the Revolutionary forces throughout America. He also tried to paraphrase the poems of Ossian. His *Miscellaneous Poems* appeared in 1801.

Sewall, Samuel (b. England, March 28, 1652—d. Jan. 1, 1730), jurist, diarist. Sewall's parents arrived in New England when the future diarist was nine. In 1671 he graduated from Harvard; two years later he was appointed

resident fellow at the college, and keeper of the library a year after. He became manager of the colony's only licensed printing press from 1681 to 1684. He was deputy to the General Court for Westfield in 1683, and from 1684 to 1686 a member of the Council. In 1691 he was named councilor for the new charter forced upon Massachusetts by the Crown. In the same year Governor Phips appointed him one of the special commissioners to try the Salem witch-craft cases. Later, convinced of the innocence of the nineteen persons condemned in court, Sewall stood up in the Old South Church in Boston while a bill was read in which he took "the blame and shame" for the miscarriage of justice. He was appointed justice of the Superior Court in 1692 and made a commissioner for the Society for the Propagation of the Gospel in New England in 1699.

Sewall was a compassionate man who believed that Indians and slaves should be kindly treated. He was also a strict Calvinist. His tract THE SELLING OF JOSEPH (1700) was the first antislavery work to be printed in America. He also wrote *Proposals Touching the Accomplishment of Prophecies Humbly Offered* (1713); *A Memorial Relating to the Kennebeck Indians* (1721); and, with Edward Rawson, anonymously, *The Revolution in New England Justified* (1691). He also produced numerous uncollected verse which he liked to read aloud, but he is chiefly known for his *Diary*, which extended from 1674 to 1729, with a break from 1677 to 1685. In it he gave a valuable and vivid account of day-to-day life in New England. *The Letters of Samuel Lee and Samuel Sewall Relating to New England and the Indians* were published in the *Massachusetts Historical Society Collections* in 1913. The *Diary* appeared in three volumes of the *Massachusetts Historical Society Collections* (1878–82), and an abridged edition, edited by Mark Van Doren, was published in 1927. G. E. Ellis' *An Address on the Life and Character of Chief Justice Samuel Sewall* (1885), N. H. Chamberlain's *Samuel Sewall and the World He Lived In* (1897), and Whittier's "The Prophecy of Samuel Sewall" give accounts of him. See PHAENOMENA.

Sewanee Review, The. A quarterly magazine founded in 1892 at the University of the South, Sewanee, Tenn. It is now reckoned the oldest quarterly of its kind in the United States and has been directed by a long succession of editors, including WILLIAM P. TRENT, Benjamin W. Wells, J. B. Henneman, GEORGE HERBERT CLARKE, William S. Knickerbocker, ALLEN TATE, John Palmer, and Monroe K. Spears. The editors have always been especially interested in southern affairs, but in later years (under Tate and his successors) the magazine has been chiefly noted as an organ of the NEW CRITICISM and of *avant-garde* writing generally.

Seward, William Henry (b. Florida, N.Y., May 16, 1801—d. Oct. 10, 1872), statesman, public official, orator. Seward began his career as a Democrat and as such served in the New York legislature. Later he switched to the Whig party and was elected (1838) governor of New York. In 1849 he became a United States Senator; in 1852 he allied himself with the Know-Nothing party to secure re-election, and in 1855 he openly and permanently joined the newly formed Republican party. A warm humanitarian and nationalist, he supported Presi-

dent Jackson against nullification, opposed imprisonment for debt, strongly opposed slavery, sought compromises that would save the country from war, championed Louis Kossuth and Irish freedom.

Seward hoped to obtain the Republican nomination for President in 1860, but when Lincoln was chosen he campaigned for him. Lincoln had a high regard for his ability and character and made him Secretary of State; Seward made an extraordinary proposition at the beginning of his term in office—that Lincoln maneuver the country into war with some foreign nation in order to save the Union. Lincoln declined, and Seward's direction of foreign affairs thereafter took a more moderate course. He negotiated the purchase of Alaska, long known as "Seward's Folly." At the time of Lincoln's assassination an attempt was made on Seward's life also, but he recovered. When Johnson became President, Seward supported him staunchly and wrote many of his addresses. He retired from office in 1869.

Seward wrote an *Autobiography* (1877); his *Works* were collected (5 v.) in 1884. Olive R. Seward edited *William H. Seward's Travels Around the World* (1873); F. W. Seward wrote an account of *Seward at Washington* (2 v., 1891). Frederic Bancroft wrote a biography of Seward (2 v., 1900). Edison Marshall in *Seward's Folly* (1924), a novel, told how an attempt to keep Alaska out of the hands of the United States was foiled. Earl Conrad wrote *Mr. Seward for the Defense* (1956).

Seymour, Charles (b. New Haven, Conn., Jan. 1, 1885—d. Aug. 11, 1963), historian, teacher, educational administrator. Long an eminent figure at Yale, where he began to teach in 1911, Seymour became president of the university in 1937, retired in 1950. He was an engaging scholar and able lecturer. Woodrow Wilson thought so highly of his *Diplomatic Background of the War* (1916) that he appointed Seymour a member of the American peace delegation. Among his other books: *Electoral Reform in England and Wales* (1915); *Woodrow Wilson and the World War* (1921); *American Diplomacy During the World War* (1934; rev., 1942). He also edited *The Intimate Papers of Colonel House* (4 v., 1926–28).

Shadows on the Rock (1931), a novel by WILLA CATHER. A product of Miss Cather's late interest in Catholicism, this work is an episodic narrative of life in Quebec during the last days of Frontenac, centered upon the life of Cécile Auclair, a child recently emigrated from Old France. The book contains some of Miss Cather's best descriptive writing—scenes of the St. Lawrence, the churches and market-places of the town, etc.

shanties or **shanteys.** See SAILORS' SONGS.

Shapiro, Karl [Jay] (b. Baltimore, Md., Nov. 10, 1913—   ), poet, critic, editor. Shapiro won a wide reputation for the poems he wrote as a soldier during World War II, and continued to produce much genuinely excellent work in the postwar period. He works chiefly in traditional forms, but in an intelligently modern and "unpoetic" diction that gives his poetry a tone of suppleness and seriousness. His best war poems appeared in *V-Letter and Other Poems* (1944). Other books of his verse are: *Person, Place, and Thing* (1942); *The Place for Love* (1943); *Trial of a Poet and Other Poems* (1947); *Poems 1940–1953* (1953); *Poems of a Jew* (1958). Shapiro has been much interested in aesthetic problems, especially in defining the role of the poet; among his critical writings are *Essay on Rime* (a disquisition in verse, 1945) and *Beyond Criticism* (1953). In addition Shapiro has been a teacher and editor, having taught for some years at Johns Hopkins University. Later he became editor of the magazine POETRY (1950–56), then teacher at the University of Nebraska and editor of *The Schooner* (formerly THE PRAIRIE SCHOONER).

Shapley, Harlow (b. Nashville, Mo., Nov. 2, 1885—   ), astronomer, writer. After obtaining his B.A. and M.A. degrees at the University of Missouri, Shapley took his Ph.D. at Princeton. He became director of the Harvard Observatory in 1921 and held that post until 1952. In that year he became Paine Professor of Astronomy at Harvard. In 1949, when the National Council of Arts, Sciences and Professions sponsored the Cultural and Scientific Conference for World Peace, he was its chairman. His special field is cosmogony, which treats of the structure and nature of the universe; a secondary interest of his is entomology. Recognized as one of the great contemporary astronomers, Shapley has also written for the general reader with vividness and lucidity. He has received numerous honorary degrees and other awards. Among his books are: *Starlight* (1926); *The Stars* (1927); *A Sourcebook on Astronomy* (with H. E. Howarth, 1929); *Star Clusters* (1930); *Flights From Chaos* (1930); *Sidereal Explorations* (1931); *Galaxies* (1943); *Treasury of Science* (1943); *Readings in the World of Science* (1948).

Sharp, Dallas Lore (b. Haleyville, N.J., Dec. 13, 1870—d. Nov. 29, 1929), teacher, naturalist, writer. Sharp taught English at Boston University for many years, but became better known through his avocation, the study of nature. He wrote numerous books, among them: *A Watcher in the Woods* (1903); *The Face of the Fields* (1911); *Beyond the Pasture Bars* (1914). He wrote about John Burroughs in *The Seer of Slabsides* (1921) and expressed a deep patriotism in *The Better Country* (1928).

Shaw, Albert (b. Shandon, Ohio, July 23, 1857—d. June 25, 1947), editor, teacher, writer. After working on newspapers in Iowa, Shaw taught at Cornell University, but left in 1891 to take charge of the influential American REVIEW OF REVIEWS until its merger (1937) with the *Literary Digest;* the magazines were then called the *Digest*, which he continued to edit. He was an ardent student of political reform, a follower of THEODORE ROOSEVELT. He

made numerous studies of municipal government in Europe, gave lectures at various universities and before civic groups, and wrote able interpretations of American political events for the *Review*. His first book was *Icaria: A Chapter in the History of Communism* (1884), an account of an ill-fated community at Icaria, Iowa. Among his other books: *Co-operation in a Western City* (1886); *History of Co-operation in the U.S.* (with others, 1888); *Municipal Government in Great Britain* (1895); *The Business Career in Its Public Relations* (1904); *Political Problems of American Development* (1907); *Abraham Lincoln* (2 v., 1929). Among Shaw's English admirers were James Bryce and John Morley. He once said that he believed in reform but was not himself a reformer; he was never an extravagant zealot.

Shaw, Anna Howard (b. England, Feb. 14, 1847—d. July 2, 1919), reformer, teacher, physician, clergyman. At the age of four Anna Shaw came with her family to Massachusetts, later to the Michigan wilderness. Her experiences are recorded in her autobiography *The Story of a Pioneer* (1915). In the face of many obstacles she attended the theological school of Boston University, and in 1878 was appointed pastor of the Wesleyan Methodist Church at East Dennis, Mass. She also obtained her M.D. degree from Boston University in 1886.

An outstanding lecturer, she was much in demand as a speaker on temperance and women's rights. Among her friends were Emerson, Alcott, Whittier, Wendell Phillips, and Julia Ward Howe. Along with Susan B. Anthony she worked for women's rights, attended conventions, and continued to lecture. In 1904 she became president of the National American Woman Suffrage Association. During World War I she served as chairman of the Women's Committee of the Council of National Defense, receiving a Distinguished Service Medal for her work. Shortly afterwards she joined William H. Taft and President Lowell of Harvard in their tour of the country for the League of Nations.

Shaw, Charles Gray (b. Elizabeth, N.J., June 23, 1871—d. July 28, 1949), teacher, philosopher, humorist. Shaw first won renown as a track athlete; in later years he walked from New York to Philadelphia in twenty-three hours and forty minutes. He taught philosophy at New York University from 1899 to 1941, and attracted wide attention with some of his barbed remarks. He campaigned for the abolition of slums and better housing. Among his books: *Christianity and Modern Culture* (1906); *The Ego and Its Place in the World* (1913); *Outline of Philosophy* (1930); *The Road to Happiness* (1937). He contributed to many encyclopedias and magazines.

Shaw, Henry Wheeler. See JOSH BILLINGS.

Shaw, Irwin (b. New York City, Feb. 27, 1913—   ), novelist, short-story writer, playwright. Shaw left Brooklyn College after failing in freshman mathematics, worked in a cosmetics factory, a department store, and a furniture company. Returning to college, he conducted a column for the student magazine and wrote plays for the dramatic society. After his graduation in 1934 he prepared serials for the radio, among them dramatizations of the comic strips "The Gumps" and "Dick Tracy." His pacifist play BURY THE DEAD (1936) was produced in a small theater and later moved to Broadway. He then went to Hollywood to write screenplays.

THE GENTLE PEOPLE: A BROOKLYN FABLE (1939), a dramatic phantasy dealing with the threat of dictatorship, was followed by *Sailor Off the Bremen* (1939), a collection of excellent short stories. Equally impressive was *Welcome to the City* (1942), another group of stories. *Sons and Soldiers* (1944), a play originally called *Labor for the Wind*, was followed by *Act of Faith and Other Stories* (1946). Shaw's first novel, THE YOUNG LIONS (1948), one of the most important novels of World War II, was highly praised by many critics. *Mixed Company*, short stories, and *Report from Israel*, the text for a volume of camera studies by Robert Capa, appeared in 1950. *The Troubled Air* (1950), a novel, deals with the plight of the well-meaning liberal caught between the threat of red-baiting and witch-hunting on the one hand, and Communist pressure on the other. This was followed by *Lucy Crown* (1956) and *Two Weeks in Another Town* (1960). See PROLETARIAN LITERATURE IN THE UNITED STATES.

Shawn, Ted [Edwin M.] (b. Kansas City, Mo., Oct. 21, 1891—), dancer, author. Shawn's professional career began in Los Angeles in 1912. He married another famous dancer, Ruth St. Denis, and with her founded (1915) the Denishawn School. He wrote *Ruth St. Denis, Pioneer and Prophet* (1920); *The American Ballet* (1926); *Fundamentals of a Dance Education* (1937); *Dance We Must* (1940); *How Beautiful Upon the Mountain* (1943); *Every Little Movement* (1954); *33 Years of American Dance* (1959). He was the guiding spirit behind the founding of the dance school and festival theater at Jacob's Pillow, Mass.

Shawnee Indians. A tribe of Algonquian stock. The name meant "southerner," although the tribe is believed to have originated in the north. One branch settled in Illinois and Ohio and along the Cumberland Valley; another went further south to the Savannah River but was forced back to Pennsylvania by the Cherokees and Catawbas around 1707. The Shawnees were a warlike people, fighting with other tribes, with the French, and later with the United States.

Early in the nineteenth century Tenskwatawa, the "Prophet," brother of the great TECUMSEH, exhorted them to return to the old order of things and collected many followers at the source of the Tippecanoe River in Indiana, where they were defeated in the celebrated Battle of Tippecanoe in 1811 by General W. H.

HARRISON. In 1825 they were sent to a reservation in Kansas, but large numbers went on to Texas, where they remained until driven out in 1850. Many of them now live in Oklahoma. An 18th-century observer described them as tall, athletic, fun-loving, courageous, intelligent, and treacherous.

Causes of Alienation of the Delaware and Shawnee Indians from British Interests (1759), by C. Thomson, listed their grievances and suggested more justice to the Shawnees. David Jones described them in *A Journal of Two Visits Made to Some Nations of Indians on the West Side of the River Ohio in the Years 1772 and 1773* (1865). *A True Account of the Sufferings of Mary Kinnan* (1795) is a Virginia woman's account of her captivity from 1791 until 1794. The Shawnees appear in such fiction as R. M. Bird's *Nick of the Woods* (1837); Emerson Bennett's *The Pioneer's Daughter* (1866); Edward Sylvester's *Footprints in the Forest* (1866).

Shay, Frank (b. East Orange, N.J., April 8, 1888—d. Jan. 14, 1954), bookseller, publisher, editor, writer. Shay owned bookshops in New York and Provincetown, also organized Frank Shay's Traveling Bookshop. He was deeply interested in the stage, organized the Caravan Theater, and was a founder of the PROVINCETOWN PLAYERS. He also at time was a publisher, particularly for some of EDNA ST. VINCENT MILLAY's early poems. He edited several play anthologies and wrote or compiled many books about the sea and sea songs, among them *Iron Men and Wooden Ships* (1924); *American Sea Songs and Chanties* (1948); *The Bos'n's Locker* (1949); and *The Ships Flying* (1953). Among his other books are *My Pious Friends and Drunken Companions* (1927); *Here's Audacity* (1930); *Incredible Pizarro* (1932); *The Best Men Are Cooks* (1938); and an anthology of Cape Cod literature, *Sand in Their Shoes* (1951, ed. with his wife Edith Foley Shay). He was the originator of the outdoor art exhibits at Provincetown.

Shays' Rebellion. This was an agrarian rebellion in Massachusetts in 1786–87; it was named for Daniel Shays, a Revolutionary War veteran. He and other debt-ridden farmers petitioned the Massachusetts legislature to issue paper money, reduce taxes and governmental salaries, and stop mortgage foreclosures. Shays led a force of 1,200 men against the government arsenal at Springfield, where Federal troops broke up the insurrection. However, the legislature avoided imposing a direct tax in 1787 and exempted clothing, household goods, and the tools of one's trade from debt process. Ralph I. Lockwood wrote a novel, *The Insurgents* (1835), about Shays and his "broomstick army." In 1879 Edward Bellamy wrote his historical novel *The Duke of Stockbridge*, with the rebellion as a background. Marion L. Starkey described the uprising in *A Little Rebellion* (1955).

Shea, John Dawson Gilmary (b. New York City, July 22, 1824—d. Feb. 22, 1892), Catholic historian, editor, philologist. Shea performed important service in gathering facts about Catholic missionaries in early days and in the field of Indian linguistics. Possibly his greatest work was his massive *History of the Catholic Church in the U.S.* (4 v., 1886–92). He also wrote *The Discovery and Exploration of the Mississippi Valley* (1853); *Early Voyages Up and Down the Mississippi* (1862); and a *Lincoln Memorial* (1865). An important linguistic work was *Library of American Linguistics* (15 v., 1860–74). He edited the original text of the *Jesuit Relations* (26 v., 1857–87) and was the founder of the U.S. Catholic Historical Society. Peter Guilday wrote his biography (1926).

Sheean, [James] Vincent (b. Christian Co., Ill., Dec. 5, 1899—   ), novelist, biographer, reporter, memoirist. After studying at the University of Chicago, Sheean entered the field of journalism and shortly became European correspondent for the Chicago *Tribune.* Stirring and troubled scenes seemed to draw him like magnets. He reported, among other events, the Fascist march on Rome and the Spanish and French wars on the Riff tribesmen.

Personal History (1935), perhaps his best known work, relates Sheean's spiritual autobiography up to that point. Other nonfiction works include: *An American Among the Riffi* (1926); *The New Persia* (1927); *Not Peace but a Sword* (1939), a denunciation of Fascism; *Between the Thunder and the Sun* (1943), which contains portraits of his father-in-law, Sir Johnston Forbes-Robertson, and his aunt, Maxine Elliott; *This House Against This House* (1946); *Lead Kindly Light* (1949), a tribute to Mahatma Gandhi; *The Indigo Bunting, A Memoir of Edna St. Vincent Millay* (1951); *Orpheus at Eighty* (1958), a tribute to Giuseppe Verdi; *Nehru, the Years of Power* (1959).

Sheean's novels reflect his varied cosmopolitan experiences and his concern with the individual's relationship to society. Among them are: *The Anatomy of Virtue* (1927); *Gog and Magog* (1930); *The Tide* (1933); *Sanfelice* (1936); *The Pieces of a Fan* (short stories, 1937); *A Day of Battle* (1938); *An International Incident* (comedy, 1940); *Bird of the Wilderness* (1941); *A Certain Rich Man* (1947); *Rage of the Soul* (1952); *Lily* (1954). In his personal narratives he gives readers, said *Time,* a mixture that "is part tract, part treatise, part I-was-right-there testimony."

Sheen, Fulton J[ohn] (b. El Paso, Ill., May 8, 1895—   ), clergyman, teacher, writer, administrator, broadcaster. Sheen attended many schools at home and abroad, taking a doctor of philosophy degree at Louvain, a doctor of divinity degree at Rome. He was ordained a priest in the Roman Catholic Church in 1919, taught and preached in England for a while, became a member of the faculty of the Catholic University of America in 1926. A great preacher, Sheen delivered a weekly sermon on the "Catholic Hour" of the National Broadcasting Co. from 1930 to 1945, and in the

1950's began conducting a television program, "Life Is Worth Living." His sermons have been printed and distributed in millions of copies. From 1931 to 1945 Sheen was preacher in St. Patrick's Cathedral in New York City. In 1951 he was appointed titular bishop of Caesariana and auxiliary bishop of New York. He has been a firm opponent of Communism. Sheen was responsible for the conversion of many well-known people to the Catholic faith— among them, Heywood Broun, Henry Ford II, Louis Budenz, and Clare Boothe Luce.

Bishop Sheen's many books include: *God and Intelligence* (1925); *Religion Without God* (1928); *Old Errors and New Labels* (1931); *Seven Last Words* (1933); *The Moral Universe* (1936); *Tactics of Communism* (1937); *Liberty, Equality, and Fraternity* (1938); *For God and Country* (1941); *Seven Pillars of Peace* (1944); *Preface to Religion* (1946); *Three to Get Married* (1951); *Life is Worth Living* (five series, 1953–57); *The Life of Christ* (1958); *This is the Holy Land* (1961).

Shelburne Essays (14 v., 1904–35), literary, philosophical, and religious essays by PAUL ELMER MORE. More, along with IRVING BABBITT, was a founder of the New Humanist movement, the aim of which was to restore classical discipline in place of what More defines as the chief modern value, romanticism: "the infinitely craving personality, the usurpation of emotion over reason . . . the confusion of the sensuous and the spiritual . . ." The essays admit to his antiromantic bias, but their measured tone and classical erudition still make them worth reading. Their name comes from Shelburne, N.H., where More began writing them. See HUMANISM.

Sheldon, Charles M[onroe] (b. Wellesville, N.Y., Feb. 26, 1857—d. Feb. 24, 1946), Congregationalist clergyman, editor, novelist, memoirist. Sheldon called himself "a Christian Socialist," meaning one who "applied the teachings of the Sermon on the Mount to everyday life." He published various volumes of exhortation and narrative but attained fame when he wrote IN HIS STEPS (1896), which sold about twenty-five million copies in sixteen languages and for which, because of a faulty copyright, he never received a penny in royalties. In 1900 he was asked to edit the Topeka *Daily Capitol* for a week. He barred crime news, even stories about the national political conventions, censored the advertisements, filled the paper with religious news and editorials. From all over the country came demands for the issue that raised the circulation from 30,000 daily to 370,-000. Later he edited the CHRISTIAN HERALD (1920–25), continuing to write for it after 1925. He wrote his autobiography in *Charles M. Sheldon: His Life and Story* (1925).

Sheldon, Edward Brewster (b. Chicago, Feb. 4, 1886—d. April 1, 1946), dramatist. At Harvard Sheldon was a student in GEORGE PIERCE BAKER's 47 Workshop and organized the Harvard Dramatic Club. While still there he wrote SALVATION NELL, which was produced in 1908. The following year he produced THE NIGGER, which created a furore; the play deals with the status of Negroes in the South and shows dramatically how the love of a white Southern girl withstands the knowledge that the man she loves has Negro blood. Later came many other successful plays: THE BOSS (1912); *The High Road* (1912); ROMANCE (1913). He adapted, in blank verse, an Italian play by Sem Benelli which was produced (1919) as *The Jest* with Lionel and John Barrymore in the leading roles. In other plays he collaborated with leading playwrights of the time, in particular with SIDNEY HOWARD on *Bewitched* (1924), with CHARLES MACARTHUR on *Lulu Belle* (1926), and with MARGARET AYER BARNES on *Dishonored Lady* (1930). In 1923 Sheldon was stricken with progressive paralysis, in 1931 with total blindness, but he remained to the last very much a part of Broadway; he was consulted about scripts and roles constantly and his apartment was a favorite meetingplace of leading actors and actresses. Eric W. Barnes wrote a sympathetic biography, *The Man Who Lived Twice* (1956).

Shellabarger, Samuel (b. Washington, D.C., May 18, 1888—d. March 21, 1954), historian, novelist. Educated at Princeton, Harvard, and Munich universities, Shellabarger taught at Princeton from 1914 to 1923, then retired to devote himself to writing. His writings fall into three categories. First are his scholarly biographies, *The Chevalier Bayard* (1928) and *Lord Chesterfield* (1935; rev., 1951). Second are mysteries and light romances written under the pseudonyms of John Esteven and Peter Loring. Third are his historical romances. Three deal with the Renaissance—Spain and Mexico in CAPTAIN FROM CASTILE (1945); Italy in *Prince of Foxes* (1947); France in *The King's Cavalier* (1950). *Lord Vanity* (1953) is a story of the fall of Quebec. Shellabarger spent much time abroad, and his careful research lent authentic detail to his fiction, though his plots were often wildly unrealistic. His historical fiction attracted a very wide public.

Shelton, Frederick William (b. Jamaica, N.Y., May 20, 1815—d. June 20, 1881), Protestant Episcopal clergyman, humorist. For a time Shelton sought to make a living by his pen, writing humorous sketches for the KNICKERBOCKER MAGAZINE. In 1837, irritated by the descriptions of America that Mrs. Trollope and other visitors had given, he wrote *The Trollopiad, or, Traveling Gentleman in America,* and dedicated the work, written in satirical couplets, to Mrs. Trollope. In 1847 he was ordained a minister of the Protestant Episcopal Church and occupied country parishes in New York and Vermont. He used some of his experiences as a preacher in his later writings. Among his books were *The Rector of St. Bardolph's, or, Superannuated* (1852); *Up the River* (1853); *Peeps from a Belfry, or, The Parish Sketch Book* (1855).

Shenandoah (1888), a play by BRONSON HOWARD. This Civil War play covers the entire period of the struggle. It involves two couples who go through many exciting experiences and present both the Northern and Southern points of view. The play was a great success and was frequently revived and sometimes imitated. It was first printed in 1897.

Shepard, Benjamin Henry Jesse Francis ["Francis Grierson"] (b. England, Sept. 18, 1848—d. May 29, 1927), musician, essayist, memoirist. Shepard was brought to the United States while an infant. He developed an extraordinary talent as a pianist and became famous in his twenties. When he decided to write, he took the pen name by which he became widely known, so that his two gifts might receive unbiased consideration without reference to one another. He lived abroad for many years, but in 1913 returned to this country to write and lecture. His essays appeared in newspapers and magazines; his first book was written in French and appeared in France, *La Révolte Idéaliste* (1889). He made his first English collection of essays in 1899, *Modern Mysticism and Other Essays.* Thereafter appeared *The Celtic Temperament and Other Essays* (1901); *The Valley of Shadows: Recollections, 1858–63* (1909); *Portraits* (1910); *La Vie et les Hommes* (1911); *The Invisible Alliance* (1913); *Abraham Lincoln, The Practical Mystic* (1921). He died in extreme poverty.

Shepard, Odell (b. Sterling, Ill., July 22, 1884—d. July 19, 1967), public official, writer. Shepard studied music at Northwestern University, received degrees in English at Chicago and Harvard. A journalist and church organist for several years thereafter, he finally settled into teaching English at the Smith Academy (St. Louis), Southern California and Harvard universities, Radcliffe and Trinity colleges. Scholarship, familiar discussion, and Connecticut lore all find expression in his published works. These include *Shakespeare Questions* (1916); *A Lonely Flue* (poems, 1917); *Bliss Carman* (1923); *The Harvest of a Quiet Eye* (1927); *The Joys of Forgetting* (1928); *The Lore of the Unicorn* (1929); *Thy Rod and Thy Creel* (1930); *Pedlar's Progress, The Life of Bronson Alcott* (Pulitzer prize, 1937); *Connecticut Past and Present* (1939). He also edited works of Thoreau, Alcott, and Longfellow, as well as several essay collections and college literature surveys. With his son Willard Odell Shepard, he wrote two historical novels: *Holdfast Gaines* (1946), whose hero is a Mohegan Indian, and *Jenkins' Ear* (1951), a narrative set in Horace Walpole's era. Shepard served as lieutenant-governor of Connecticut (1940–41) and was made an honorary chief of the Mohegan Indian tribe.

Shepard, Thomas (b. England, Nov. 5, 1605 —d. Aug. 25, 1649), clergyman, writer. Silenced in England because of his nonconformity, Shepard emigrated to New England, became pastor of a church in Newtown (later Cambridge), Mass., in succession to THOMAS HOOKER, whose daughter he married. He was active in founding Harvard College. He wrote fluently. Among his books: *The Sincere Convert* (1641), which went through twenty editions up to 1812; *New England's Lamentation for Old England's Present Errors* (1645); *Theses Sabbaticae* (1649). Other writings appeared posthumously, including a diary in 1747. N. Adams edited his *Autobiography* in 1832. His *Works* (3 v.) were gathered in 1834. He was renowned as a great preacher and a truly humble man.

Sheridan, Philip Henry (b. Albany, N.Y., March 6, 1831—d. Aug. 5, 1888), soldier, memoirist. One of the chief Northern cavalry commanders in the Civil War, Sheridan took part in numerous vital engagements, such as Chickamauga and the Battle of the Wilderness. He was an aggressive, versatile, and successful general. During the Reconstruction period he was a harsh military governor of Texas and Louisiana. In 1867 he commanded the Department of Missouri; he visited Europe to observe the Franco-Prussian War; in 1883 he succeeded Sherman as commander of the United States army.

Sheridan's *Personal Memoirs* (1888) is a literate, sustained account of his deeds. Among his biographies are those by Joseph Hergesheimer (1931) and Richard O'Connor (1953). Thomas Buchanan Read celebrated one of his more daring exploits in the Civil War in his poem *Sheridan's Ride* (1865). He also appears in Bruce Lancaster's novel *Roll Shenandoah* (1956).

Sherman, Frank Dempster (b. Peekskill, N.Y., May 6, 1860—d. Sept. 19, 1916), architect, teacher, poet. This noted architect taught graphics at Columbia University and was also a skilled writer of light verse. His wide interests were reflected in his poems, of which several collections appeared. Among them: *Madrigals and Catches* (1887); *Lyrics for a Lute* (1890); *Little Folk Lyrics* (1892); *Lyrics of Joy* (1904). Clinton Scollard edited a collection of his poems in 1917.

Sherman, John (b. Lancaster, Ohio, May 10, 1823—d. Oct. 22, 1900), lawyer, public official, financier. Sherman was the younger brother of General W. T. Sherman. He practiced law in Ohio, served in the House of Representatives (1855–61), the United States Senate (1861–77), as Secretary of the Treasury (1877–81), once more in the Senate (1881–97), and as Secretary of State (1897–98). His name was attached to two famous Congressional measures, the Sherman Anti-Trust Act (1890) and the Sherman Act for keeping up the price of silver (in force 1890–93). He was one of the founders of the Republican party, ardently supported Frémont, was a vigorous advocate of measures to prosecute the Civil War, defended the protective tariff, and helped establish financial stability after the war. Sherman's *Selected Speeches* appeared in 1879, his *Recollections of 40 Years in the House, Senate, and Cabinet* in 1895 (2 v.). A collection of his and his brother's *Letters* was published in 1894. T. E. Burton wrote his biography in 1906. C. G. Washburn

analyzed *The Sherman Law* (1910); Edward Berman discussed *Labor and the Sherman Act* (1930). He may have been the model for SENATOR RATCLIFFE, political boss in Henry Adams' *Democracy* (1880).

Sherman, Stuart P[ratt] (b. Anita, Iowa, Oct. 1, 1881—d. Aug. 21, 1926), teacher, critic, editor. Sherman, after taking degrees at Williams and Harvard, taught at Northwestern, then at Illinois (1907–1924). He wrote much and vigorously, and attracted a wide audience. As an ardent advocate of American ideas he engaged in many spirited contests with H. L. MENCKEN, who once refused to meet him. But gradually Sherman adopted a more moderate attitude. He was bitterly attacked by Burton Rascoe in the New York *Tribune*, but succeeded Rascoe as editor of the book section of that newspaper in 1924 and made it a lively place for criticism and discussion. Among his books: *Matthew Arnold: How to Know Him* (1917); *On Contemporary Literature* (1917); *Americans* (1922); *The Genius of America* (1923); *My Dear Cornelia* (1924); *Points of View* (1924); *Critical Woodcuts* (1926); *The Main Stream* (1927); *The Emotional Discovery of America* (1932). Jacob Zeitlin and Homer Woodbridge prepared *The Life and Letters of Stuart P. Sherman* (2 v., 1929).

Sherman, William Tecumseh (b. Lancaster, Ohio, Feb. 8, 1820—d. Feb. 14, 1891), soldier. Sherman served in the Mexican War, later acted as superintendent of a military academy in Alexandria, La. He was an outstanding Northern commander during the Civil War, became a major general in 1862 and succeeded Grant in the Western command. On Nov. 15, 1864, he ordered the burning of Atlanta and started his famous "march to the Sea," which cut the Confederacy in half. He so devasted the country that his name is still an anathema in the South.

After the war he performed important services in the West. He was asked to run for the Presidency, but refused. His most famous remark came in a speech made in Columbus, Ohio (Aug. 11, 1880): "There is many a boy here today who looks on war as all glory, but, boys, it is all hell."

Sherman's *Memoirs* were published in 1875 (2 v.). His letters have been published along with his brother's (see JOHN SHERMAN), and as *Home Letters of General Sherman* (ed. by M. A. DeWolfe Howe, 1909). Books about Sherman include J. D. Cox's *The March to the Sea* (1909); B. H. Liddell Hart's *Sherman—Soldier, Realist, American* (1929); Lloyd Lewis' *Sherman, Fighting Prophet* (1932); Earl Schenck Miers' *The General Who Marched to Hell* (1951); R. G. Ahearn's *W. T. Sherman and the Settlement of the West* (1956). A potent war song was Henry Work's MARCHING THROUGH GEORGIA (1865). Sherman figures in Maurice Thompson's *His Second Campaign* (1883); Winston Churchill's THE CRISIS (1901); Mary Johnston's *Cease Firing* (1912); John Brick's *Jubilee* (1956).

Sherwood, Robert E[mmet] (b. New Rochelle, N.Y., April 4, 1896—d. Nov. 14, 1955), playwright, editor, biographer. Sherwood was pre-eminently a man of the theater, but his wide interests, particularly in politics,

Karsh of Ottawa

led him into many other fields and greatly affected his outlook in his plays. His education at Harvard was cut short by World War I; he served in the Canadian Black Watch Regiment, was gassed at Vimy Ridge and wounded at Amiens. The war left him with a bitter resolution to do all he could to stop future wars. This attitude appears in *Acropolis* (1933), which lashed at Hitler, and IDIOT'S DELIGHT (1936), a pacifist drama that won a Pulitzer prize. When he returned from the war Sherwood became drama critic of *Vanity Fair* (1919–20), associate editor and then editor of the old LIFE (1920–28). He and ROBERT BENCHLEY resigned from *Vanity Fair* because DOROTHY PARKER had been discharged for writing an unfavorable review. On *Life* he also served as movie critic and was one of the first to apply serious critical standards to motion pictures.

Sherwood's first play, *Barnum Was Right*, was written while he was still at Harvard, and produced by the HASTY PUDDING CLUB. His first Broadway production was THE ROAD TO ROME (1927), an attack on the concept of military glory. Thereafter followed *The Love Nest* (1927); *The Queen's Husband* (1928); *Waterloo Bridge* (1930); *This Is New York* (1931); REUNION IN VIENNA (1931); THE PETRIFIED FOREST (1935); ABE LINCOLN IN ILLINOIS (1938, Pulitzer prize); THERE SHALL BE NO NIGHT (1940). A number of these plays contributed to the cause which Sherwood espoused in the 1930's, the endeavor to hold the lines

against European totalitarian regimes and marshal American opinion against them. He helped organize the Committee to Defend America by Aiding the Allies and gave generously of his royalties to the American Red Cross and to Finnish Relief. FRANKLIN D. ROOSEVELT made him special assistant to the Secretary of War and to the Secretary of the Navy, then director of overseas operation of the Office of War Information. Sherwood helped Roosevelt write some of his most notable speeches. He wrote about his war services in a remarkable volume, *Roosevelt and Hopkins* (1948), which won a Pulitzer prize and several other awards.

During this period Sherwood did little dramatic writing, only *The Rugged Path* (1945) and a musical comedy, *Miss Liberty* (1949, with IRVING BERLIN). With Joan Harrison he was responsible for the script of the excellent movie based on Daphne du Maurier's *Rebecca* (1940) and of the award-winning *Best Years of Our Lives* (1946). He also wrote original plays for television production during the 1950's.

In his manifold use of theatrical techniques Sherwood was melodramatic, humorous, satirical, philosophical, biographical, ideological, grim, and tender. He was a showman and sometimes wrote trivial plays. But *Reunion in Vienna*, for example, is a superb comedy; and *Abe Lincoln in Illinois* is a genuinely artistic exercise in hero worship.

She's the Sweetheart of Sigma Chi (1911), a song with music by F. Dudleigh Verner, words by Byron D. Stokes. This song made Sigma Chi the most famous college fraternity in the country. Verner and Stokes were both members of Alpha Pi at Albion College when they composed the song.

She Would Be a Soldier (1819), a play by MORDECAI M. NOAH. The setting is the invasion of Canada during the War of 1812. Christine, anxious about her sweetheart Lenox, disguises herself as a man and joins the American army. Her sex is discovered and she is accused of being a spy, but Lenox intervenes and saves her. Like all of Noah's plays, *She Would Be a Soldier* is intensely patriotic.

Shield of Achilles, The (1955), a volume of twenty-eight poems by W. H. AUDEN. In it was seen the new and more mature Auden whose interests had shifted from political problems to moral and spiritual ones; it was chosen for the National Book Award in 1956. The title poem contrasts the shield of the ancient warrior with the modern warrior's shield, where scenes of glorious battle are less important than "an arbitrary spot / Where bored officials lounged."

Shillaber, Benjamin Penhallow ["Mrs. Partington"] (b. Portsmouth, N.H., July 12, 1814—d. Nov. 25, 1890), printer, newspaperman, humorist. Shillaber, after working as a printer and on the Boston *Post*, found that a character he had created for the latter, MRS. RUTH PARTINGTON, was so popular with the public that he made a career out of reporting her misadventures and her remarks. He founded a humorous weekly named THE CARPET BAG which won a wide circulation in the West and Southwest. In it appeared the first recorded publication of MARK TWAIN, a sketch of life in Hannibal entitled *The Dandy Frightening the Squatter* (May 1, 1852). He followed up *The Life and Sayings of Mrs. Partington* (1854), a best seller, with *Partington Patchwork* (1872). Shillaber wrote an account of his life in the *New England Magazine* (June, 1893—May, 1894). This has been utilized in Cyril Clemens' *Shillaber* (1946), which also prints some of Shillaber's letters and other miscellaneous material.

Shiloh [1]. The name for Shelley in Elinor Wylie's THE ORPHAN ANGEL (1926).

Shiloh [2]. Site of famous Civil War battle.

Shipley, Joseph T. (b. Brooklyn, N.Y., Aug. 19, 1893—   ), editor, critic, teacher, lecturer. Shipley taught English in the Stuyvesant High School of New York City, the College of the City of New York, Brooklyn College, and Yeshiva College. He contributed to or edited various magazines, especially as a drama critic. He wrote *Trends in Literature* (1948), and edited several valuable compilations. Among the latter: *Dictionary of World Literature* (1943); *Encyclopedia of Literature* (1946); *Guide to Great Plays* (1952); *Dictionary of Forgotten Words* (1953); *Dictionary of Early English* (1955); *Dictionary of World Literary Terms* (1955).

Shipman, Samuel (b. New York City, Dec. 25, 1883—d. Feb. 9, 1937), playwright. Shipman, a skillful theatrical technician, wrote a number of successful plays, including *The Crooked Square* (1923); *Friendly Enemies* (with Aaron Hoffman, 1918); *Children of Today* (1926); *Cheaper to Marry* (1924); *Crime* (with John B. Hymer, 1927).

Shirer, William L[awrence] (b. Chicago, Feb. 23, 1904—   ), newspaperman, foreign correspondent, broadcaster, writer. Shirer began his newspaper career on the Paris edition of the Chicago *Tribune,* an assignment which led to his remaining abroad for more than two decades as a correspondent for various papers and syndicates. In 1937 he joined the staff of the Columbia Broadcasting System and reported on the crises of the late 1930's and thereafter. He reported them also in book form: *Berlin Diary* (1940) and *End of a Berlin Diary* (1947). Other observations and experiences appear in *Midcentury Journey* (1952) and in two *romans à clef, The Traitor* (1953) and *Stranger Come Home* (1954). In 1948 he received the One World award for radio in recognition of his activities in "awakening America to the danger of Nazism." His account of *The Rise and Fall of the Third Reich* (1960) was a best seller.

Shirley, William (b. England, Dec. 2, 1694 —d. March 24, 1771), colonial administrator, military leader. Shirley came to America (1731) with strong imperialistic views and expressed them freely when he was appointed governor of Massachusetts in 1741. He planned the expedition against Louisburg (1745), wrote *A Journal of the Siege of Louisburg* (1746). He continued as governor until 1749 when he went to England and France to serve on a commission that determined the boundary line between New England and French North America. On his return he was again appointed governor and became a major general at the outbreak of the French and Indian Wars. But his campaigns were unsuccessful. He became unpopular, was recalled to England in 1756, and from 1761 to 1767 was governor of the Bahamas. He defended himself in a publication called *Conduct of General William Shirley* (1758). His *Correspondence, 1731–60,* was edited by C. H. Lincoln (2 v., 1912). G. A. Wood wrote *William Shirley, Governor of Massachusetts* (1920).

Shock of Recognition, The (1943), an anthology edited by EDMUND WILSON. This is a gathering of literary documents which chronicle the progress of literature in this country by presenting important essays, poems, parodies, biographical sketches, letters, and other materials. It begins with James Russell Lowell and Edgar Allan Poe, concludes with H. L. Mencken, John Dos Passos, and Sherwood Anderson. The writers included often comment on one another, sometimes mildly, sometimes savagely.

Sholom Aleichem [pen name of **Solomon J. Rabinowitz** (b. Russia, Feb. 18, 1859—d. May 13, 1916), author of Russian, Yiddish, and Hebrew short stories, etc. Born in Russia, where his parents were storekeepers and later innkeepers, Rabinowitz had an opportunity to observe many eccentric types. Well educated in local Hebrew institutions, he began teaching at the age of seventeen, served as a rabbi for several years, lost a fortune left to him by his father, fled from Russia at the time of the 1905 pogrom. Thereafter he lived in several European countries, especially in Italy and Switzerland. When World War I broke out, he went to Denmark, then in 1906 to New York.

At an early age Rabinowitz adopted as a pen name the Hebrew greeting *Sholom Aleichem*— "Peace be with you." He won wide fame under this pseudonym. He wrote in three languages, but was especially insistent on establishing Yiddish as a tongue well suited to literary expression. He contributed to Yiddish newspapers in Russia, and at a time when he had considerable means he established a year book, the *Yiddische Volk-Bibliothèque,* which helped to give dignity to writings in Yiddish. He managed to capture on paper the expressiveness and variety of the language, particularly its humor. He liked especially to be known as the "Yiddish Mark Twain." It is said that on one of Rabinowitz's early visits to New York, Mark Twain was among the first to call on him. "I wanted to meet you," said Twain, "because I understand that I am the American Sholom Aleichem." But Rabinowitz's humor always had an undertone of tragedy or of pathos. His best work was done informally in the *skitze* or sketch; he often told his stories in a monologue or a letter. He wrote about the Old World and the New, often hurriedly as a journalist. His collected writings in Yiddish comprise twenty-three volumes. *Eisenbahn Geschichte* (2 v., 1909) is a story of the life of actors—Rabinowitz himself wrote frequently for the stage. One of his plays, *She Must Marry a Doctor,* is included in Isaac Goldberg's *Six Plays of the Yiddish Theater* (1916). Numerous English translations of Rabinowitz's works have appeared: *Stempenyu* (1913) and *Jewish Children* (1920); a collection of twenty-seven short stories translated by Julius and Frances Butwin as *The Old Country* (1946); *The Great Fair: My Childhood and Youth* (1955), an autobiography in the form of a novel translated by the author's granddaughter, Tamara Kahana. A play, *The World of Sholom Aleichem* (1953) was based in part on his stories. Recent editions of his work in translation include *Inside Kasrilevke* (1948); *Tevye's Daughters* (1949); *Wandering Star* (1952); *The Adventures of Mottel, The Cantor's Son* (1953); and *Stories And Satires* (1959).

Shoo, Fly, Don't Bodder Me. A song popular in the late 1880's, especially as sung by the minstrel Billy Reeves, to whom the words were frequently attributed. They were also attributed to THOMAS BRIGHAM BISHOP, and their actual authorship, like that of the music, which may have been composed by Frank Campbell or Jasper Rose, remains doubtful. The song was revived in the musical version of Clyde Fitch's CAPTAIN JINKS OF THE HORSE MARINES (1925).

Shooting of Dan McGrew, The (1907), a poem by ROBERT W. SERVICE. The poem, which has circulated in millions of copies, concerns the fate of "Dangerous Dan McGrew," a Yukon desperado (see KLONDIKE GOLD RUSH). It is said that Service wrote the poem when asked to contribute something to be read at a church service; the poem was turned down as hardly suitable for the occasion, but it set Service off on his career as a modern balladist. He said later that the poem had been based on actual events, but that the names were fictitious.

Shore Acres (1893), a play by JAMES A. HERNE. This was a radical revision of his earlier play called *The Hawthornes* (1889) and was itself first performed as *Shore Acres Subdivision* and as *Uncle Nat.* Its success at first was only moderate; later it made a fortune for Herne. It is the story of two brothers, one self-sacrificing, the other aggressive, and is on the whole a somewhat somber study of life in Maine. It introduced what most critics regarded as "wholesome realism," one instance of which was a kitchen scene in which a turkey dinner was cooked on stage.

Short Happy Life of Francis Macomber, The (1938), short story by ERNEST HEMINGWAY. In this compact, suspenseful story, the Macombers, an American couple, are on a safari in Africa with the Englishman Wilson as their guide. When confronted with a mad, wounded lion, Macomber proves himself a coward, is saved by Wilson, and earns his wife's utter contempt. On the next hunting expedition, Macomber feels a gathering strength and his wife, who has always found gratification in his weakness, is suddenly frightened by this new Macomber. His second chance comes with a wild buffalo. Cowardice vanishes and as he heroically tries to fell the onrushing beast, a bullet fired by his wife misses the buffalo and kills Macomber. The story infuses Hemingway's favorite theme, cowardice as opposed to courage, with tragic overtones, and is perhaps one of Hemingway's best shorter pieces of writing.

Short Sixes: Stories to Be Read While the Candle Burns (1891), thirteen stories by H. C. BUNNER. It contains one of the earliest stories to ridicule extreme southernism—*Col. Brereton's Aunty.* One of the best stories in the collection is *The Love-Letters of Smith.*

short story, the. The "short story" is the most recent of recognized literary forms, and as such is the only genre in which American authors could participate from the beginning. It was in the United States, early in the 19th century, that the short story emerged as a form capable of engaging the interest of all major writers of fiction. An American author was the first to use the term "short story" to describe his collection of prose tales, and it was an American writer who attempted the first significant definition.

This does not mean that the short prose narrative was unknown before the early 1800's. We have examples from ancient cultures that go as far back as the 8th century B.C. There are, however, significant differences between early narratives, generally known as "tales," and what we have come to know as the "short story." Early tales were either parts of a larger whole (as in Boccaccio's *Decameron*), or were other than literary (as in the Greek legends and the parables of the New Testament). The concept of the short tale as an individual work of art appears to have had its origin in EDGAR ALLAN POE's review of NATHANIEL HAWTHORNE's *Twice-Told Tales* in *Graham's Magazine* (1842). Poe professed to have discovered genius of a high order in Hawthorne's book, and proceeded to generalize upon the critical principles that seemed to provide the order of the tales. The first use of the term "story," however, appears to have come somewhat later, when Henry James, also an admirer of Hawthorne, titled one of his collections *Daisy Miller: A Study; and Other Stories* (1883). Since that time the term "short story" has become the commonly accepted name for the form that Poe first sought to define.

Perhaps the most significant fact about Poe's writing on the short story (aside from his serious and sympathetic reading of Hawthorne) is his emphatic statement that this form belongs "to the loftiest region of art." He said further that the writer of short fiction should not fashion his thoughts to accommodate his incidents, "but having conceived with deliberate care a certain unique or single *effect* to be wrought out, he then invents such incidents—he then combines such events as may best aid him in establishing his preconceived effects." Poe warned that "if his very initial sentence tend not to the outbringing of this effect, then he has failed in his first step. In the whole composition there should be no word written, of which the tendency, direct or indirect, is not to the one pre-established design."

Poe's emphasis upon unity, upon economy and self-containment, is an attitude that has guided short-story writers to the present day; and it is one of Poe's concepts that so impressed the French poet Charles Baudelaire, and through him influenced a whole generation of 19th-century European writers. Less significant was Poe's method, which probably appears more mechanical than he intended and was possibly aimed at authors whose writing was too didactic to serve his higher purpose. Behind Poe's attempts at definition, however, resides the significant recognition that the importance of the short story lies in its ability to examine and portray the inner workings of the mind, either as it affects experience or is affected by it. Such well-known stories by Poe as THE GOLD BUG and THE PURLOINED LETTER exemplify the first type (which he called ratiocinative), where the mind exercises a certain control over nature. Such stories as THE FALL OF THE HOUSE USHER and LIGEIA portray the second (which Poe called "tales of atmosphere or effect"), in which the mind is affected by the unusual and the unknown.

Most of Hawthorne's tales contained the atmosphere and singleness of effect that Poe demanded. They appear, however, to have been motivated by Hawthorne's essential disagreement with the dominant New England attitude of his day, as exemplified by Ralph Waldo Emerson and the transcendentalists, the attitude that celebrated the virtue of innocence and saw in nature a fundamental benevolence. Hawthorne's short fiction examined American life, both past and present, revealed beneath its surface a world of evil, and warned against the dangers of failure to recognize and come to grips with that evil. More so than Poe's, Hawthorne's style incorporated the voice of the native American as it had come to him through the oral tradition and from his New England Yankee neighbors, a style which was to be extended by the school of native humorists culminating in Mark Twain.

Although Hawthorne was later to refer to his stories as "blasted allegories"—they contained a didactic element that sometimes troubled Poe—he produced a notable body of work, particularly in such volumes as TWICE-TOLD TALES, MOSSES FROM AN OLD MANSE, and THE SNOW IMAGE AND OTHER TWICE-TOLD TALES. The best of them convey a sense of reality that make them moving human experiences, not merely thought-provoking exercises.

Hawthorne's most immediate influence among his contemporaries was upon HERMAN MELVILLE, who read him at the time he was preparing to write his masterwork, MOBY DICK, and in the same period in which he discovered Shakespeare. In his enthusiasm for Hawthorne, Melville did not hesitate to rank him almost as Shakespeare's equal, finding in him, as he expressed it, the soul of America as well as its voice. Most significantly, Melville accepted Hawthorne's antitranscendentalist attitude, particularly as it reflected the dangers of innocence and the reality of evil.

Melville arrived at the short-story form late in his career. PIAZZA TALES appeared in 1856, ten years after his first novel, *Typee*, and five years after the publication of *Moby Dick*. His stories appeared at a time when his reputation had ebbed, so that full appreciation of such works as BENITO CERENO and BARTLEBY THE SCRIVENER, two masterpieces of the American short story, had to await the revival of Melville's reputation in the 20th century.

HENRY JAMES, probably the most prolific of all American short-story writers, was also affected by Nathaniel Hawthorne. Early in his career he wrote an appreciative study of Hawthorne that appeared as the first volume in the distinguished "English Men of Letters" series. James published two volumes of stories before producing his first novel; eight more collections followed. He also wrote brilliantly on the craft of fiction, examining both the novel and the short-story forms. At one point he stated: "To write a series of good little tales I deem ample work for a lifetime." He was concerned with the matter of the form of fiction, as Poe had been, but his interest in problems of form and style came probably from the French writers whom Poe had influenced, not directly from Poe himself. James discussed the obligations of the writer of fiction with a thoroughness, sensitivity, and erudition unusual in an American of his day.

Among James' best-known short stories are "The Real Thing," "The Liar," "The Lesson of the Master," "The Beast in the Jungle," and "The Altar of the Dead"; these are just a few of his many excellent short works.

Contemporary with James, but offering an interesting contrast, is MARK TWAIN, who emerged as a writer of fiction directly from the school of native American humorists that flourished in the popular press and on the lecture platforms of the country in the 19th century. His first and probably best-known "tale" (it is not, strictly speaking, a short story) is THE CELEBRATED JUMPING FROG OF CALAVERAS COUNTY (1867).

Much of Mark Twain's early work was more suited to the lecture platform than to the pages of literature, told as it was in the voice of the humorous narrator, relating exaggerated anecdotes and "tall tales" from the folk tradition (see TALL TALES AND TALL TALK); but it was in the telling of such crude tales that he learned the particular craft that was to produce one of America's finest novels and a group of excellent short stories. This craft, which was the use of the American voice as a mask through which significant aspects of American life could be presented and commented upon, was to have a marked effect upon most American short-story writing to follow. Twain's best stories were written late in his career, some of them colored by the pessimism that clouded that period of his life. Among them are "The £1,-000,000 Bank-Note," THE MAN THAT CORRUPTED HADLEYBURG, and THE MYSTERIOUS STRANGER.

By the close of Twain's career the first important period in American fiction had come to an end. In the years that followed (roughly, the last decade of the 19th century and the first decade of the 20th), American fiction-writing languished, and the authors who represented it were divided into two contrasting factions. One of these was marked by self-conscious aestheticism and sentimentality; the other, by a kind of energetic and rugged honesty. Among the first group were the writers of the "genteel tradition," writers for the popular press and pseudo-aesthetes—such writers as T. B. ALDRICH, LAFCADIO HEARN, AMBROSE BIERCE, O. HENRY, and BRET HARTE. Among the second were the writers of social protest, such as WILLIAM DEAN HOWELLS, HAMLIN GARLAND, FRANK NORRIS, and JACK LONDON. Occasional excellent stories are to be gleaned from among the productions of these writers, particularly the first group. Except for Jack London, the writers of the second group wrote more significantly in the novel form than in the short story.

There is, however, an outstanding exception in the person of STEPHEN CRANE, whose writing career lasted only eight years, between the publication of his novel *Maggie: A Girl of the Streets* (1892) and his death in 1900. In his early work in the short story, as in his first novel, Crane began by choosing to ally himself with the social realists, particularly Howells and Garland, because he believed them to be mostly concerned with "the truth." As his career continued, however, his subject matter broadened and his craft improved. From a preoccupation with the plight of the socially dispossessed, such as he displayed in his *Bowery Tales,* he moved to a concern with mankind confronted by a violent but impassive nature. This theme is explored most skillfully in such stories as THE OPEN BOAT, "The Bride Comes to Yellow Sky," and THE BLUE HOTEL. Crane's style contains elements of the school of native humorists, sobered and refined; and this style, as well as his concern for man's action when confronted by an indifferent nature, was to have great effect upon short-story writers to follow in the 20th century.

Before the full effects of Crane's example could be felt, however, two writers intervened whose interests were more nearly allied to those of the social realists. They were THEODORE DREISER and SHERWOOD ANDERSON. Dreiser's early novels appeared at the turn of the century, but his first collection of short stories was not published until 1918. Anderson, whose first novel appeared in 1916, published his first collection of short stories in 1917, and his most famous collection, WINESBURG, OHIO, in 1919.

Dreiser's short stories are, for the most part, less works of genuinely literary interest than they are case histories of characters suffering social injustice. Sherwood Anderson, much impressed by the new psychology and disheartened by a society moving from an agrarian culture to industrialism, likewise wrote many stories that appear to be more psychological or sociological studies than genuine short stories. At their best, however, both authors wrote a few stories of lasting interest. In "The Lost Phoebe," Dreiser presented a self-contained and pathetic instance of the failure of American rural family life. Anderson, in THE TRIUMPH OF THE EGG, displayed a genuine flair for comedy of the gentler sort, while in such stories as "I'm a Fool" and "I Want to Know Why," he portrayed the gropings and yearnings of adolescence with an understanding and an objectivity that avoided the sentimentality so obvious in much of his work.

Perhaps the greatest service Dreiser and Anderson performed in the American short story lay not so much in their own work as in the role they played in opposing the timid editorial standards that prevailed during most of their careers. By so doing, they prepared the way for the significant work that was to appear following the end of World War I, the considerable body of short stories by such authors as ERNEST HEMINGWAY, WILLIAM FAULKNER, F. SCOTT FITZGERALD, KATHERINE ANNE PORTER, RING LARDNER, and JOHN STEINBECK.

Ernest Hemingway's acknowledged masters were Mark Twain and Stephen Crane. In Twain he believed he had found the true voice of America. In Crane he saw not only a further development of Twain's style, but also an attitude toward nature that seemed more vital for his time than Twain's relative benevolence, and an attitude toward society more appropriate than that of Henry James. Hemingway chose as subject for his stories those moments of physical crisis that demand courage. Like Crane, he adopted the concept of the code as a means of achieving "grace under pressure," which represented Hemingway's definition of courage. He seems to have taken a hint from Crane's use of simple sentences and curt speech to develop his own stylistic method of ironic understatement. During his apprentice years in Europe Hemingway came under the tutelage of Ford Madox Ford, and through him was introduced to the works of Henry James, Joseph Conrad, and such French authors as Maupassant, Dumas, Daudet, Stendhal, Flaubert, Baudelaire, and Rimbaud (from whom he said he learned his craft). From these authors, particularly the French poets and novelists, Hemingway received the influence of Edgar Allan Poe in perhaps its most significant form. From this time on few Americans would take the craft of the short story more lightly than had Poe or those Europeans whom he had affected.

Hemingway published three volumes of short stories, IN OUR TIME (1924), MEN WITHOUT WOMEN (1927), and WINNER TAKE NOTHING (1933), in addition to his collected edition, THE FIFTH COLUMN AND THE FIRST FORTY-NINE STORIES (1938), in which appeared four previously uncollected stories. Among his best-known tales are "The Undefeated," THE KILLERS, "A Clean Well-Lighted Place," THE SHORT HAPPY LIFE OF FRANCIS MACOMBER, "The Capital of the World," and THE SNOWS OF KILIMANJARO.

William Faulkner, growing up in the American South, found his subject in the changes that had taken place in society as reflected primarily in pre–Civil War times and our own day. Of a generation that still felt the effects of the destruction of the old South and yet was aware of the rise of a new society, Faulkner reflects in his short stories (as in his novels) a pervading sense of loss as well as a concern for what superseded the old manners and customs. He presents a postwar southern society that is made up almost equally of characters who cling futilely to the old ideals and characters who have accepted, or come to terms with, the present. In addition, he hints at an overriding judgment based on natural virtues that will "endure" and "prevail."

Faulkner published two volumes of short stories, *These Thirteen* (1931) and *Doctor Martino, and Other Stories* (1934), in addition to his *Collected Stories* (1950). However, he wrote other collections of related short stories such as *The Unvanquished* (1938), GO DOWN MOSES, AND OTHER STORIES (1942), and *Knight's Gambit* (1949), none of which are included in the *Collected Stories*. He is best known for such stories as "A Rose for Emily," "That Evening Sun," "Wash," "Spotted Horses," and "The Bear."

F. Scott Fitzgerald, along with Ernest Hemingway, has long been considered a spokesman for the so-called lost generation, that group of writers who began their careers following World War I. Such a term as the lost generation appears today to have less significance than was once thought, but it does serve a purpose if we see it as merely another manifestation of what has existed in the writing of the American short story from the beginning. Insofar as the writers of the 1920's reflected disillusion with the past, they made common cause with earlier writers who portrayed the decay of Western traditions in the art and society of Europe—such as Hawthorne, who surveyed a world of evil in human society, or Melville, who saw the years since the French Revolution as "a crisis of Christendom," or Henry James, who portrayed the decay of the old morals and the old manners.

F. Scott Fitzgerald's "sad young men" sought meaning and beauty in a world that could provide them with only momentary sensation. Such an attitude was a reaction to the idealism and the optimism of the past, as well as a representation of the sterility of the present, but it offered little hope except the example of individual heroism at great cost and against great odds. The young men of Fitzgerald's stories generally came out of the West, as he himself came from St. Paul, to astound and captivate but finally to succumb to the weight of social restrictions of which they appeared to be unaware. That their frantic search for happiness was more innocent and less evil than the glitter that attracted them we learn from the pictures of the rich and successful in such short stories as "A Diamond as Big as the Ritz," "May-Day," and "The Rich Boy." The full consequence of that innocence is explored in a late story, "Babylon Revisited," in which Fitzgerald has his principal character recognize and acknowledge his irresponsibility. These and other stories appeared in four volumes: *Flappers and Philosophers* (1920), *Tales of the Jazz Age* (1922), *All the Sad Young Men* (1926), and *Taps at Reveille* (1935). A posthumous collection, *Selected Stories*, appeared in 1951.

Katherine Anne Porter, a native of Texas, began publishing her short stories in the late 1920's. Miss Porter's output has not been great, but she has maintained a consistently high quality in her writing. Her subjects are drawn from her own background: life in the South, in Mexico, and in Europe. Her attitude toward her material shows clearly the result of her Roman Catholic upbringing, her travels, and her interest in social causes. Her first published volume was a limited edition of a few copies published under the title *Flowering Judas* (1930). In 1935 this book was expanded and printed in a regular trade edition. A second volume, *Pale Horse, Pale Rider*, containing three long stories, appeared in 1939. *The Leaning Tower and Other Stories*, which contained eight short stories and the long title story, was published in 1944.

Ring Lardner, a midwestern sports reporter at the time he began writing stories about baseball in 1918, developed a style similar to Mark Twain's in that it utilized the vernacular as a source of ironic comment upon American society just prior to and following the First World War. His best work was contained in two volumes, *The Big Town* (1921) and *Round Up* (1929). His most widely known stories are "Haircut" and "Golden Honeymoon."

John Steinbeck, a Californian, began publishing in the late 1920's, but he remained singularly unaware of the influences that had affected most of his contemporaries. Best known for his novels, Steinbeck has nevertheless produced a respectable body of short fiction, the best of which is contained in the volume THE LONG VALLEY (1938). His stories are concerned mostly with man in his relationship to nature, but less the indifferent nature of Crane and Hemingway than the more benevolent kind of Mark Twain's *Huckleberry Finn*. Wary of sophistication and of urban social values, Steinbeck celebrates the virtues of a life lived close to the soil.

One of the most interesting features of the

American short story in the period following World War I was the rise of a body of fiction writers from the southern states, most of whom seemed more at home in the short-story form than in the novel. Aside from William Faulkner and Katherine Anne Porter, this group includes Caroline Gordon, Robert Penn Warren, Eudora Welty, Peter Taylor, Truman Capote, William Styron, and Flannery O'Connor.

In other sections of the country during this same period, significant short fiction has been produced by J. D. Salinger, Irwin Shaw, John Updike, and Harvey Swados in the East; J. F. Powers, Saul Bellow, Herbert Gold, Evan Connell, R. V. Cassill, Calvin Kentfield, John Cheever, and James B. Hall from the Midwest; Walter Van Tilburg Clark, Vardis Fisher, and Wallace Stegner from the Far West.

Anthologies of American short stories include: Robert Ramsey, ed., *Short Stories of America* (1921); Alexander Jessup, ed., *Representative American Short Stories* (1944); Bennett Cerf, ed., *Modern American Short Stories* (1945); John A. Burrell and Bennett Cerf, eds., *An Anthology of Famous American Stories* (1953); Mary and Wallace Stegner, eds., *Great American Short Stories* (1958); and Ray B. West, Jr., ed., *American Short Stories* (1959). American short stories appear annually collected in *Best American Short Stories* and the O. Henry Memorial Award *Prize Short Stories*.

History and criticism of the American short story has been sparse. Some titles are: Fred Lewis Pattee, *The Development of the American Short Story* (1923); Edward J. O'Brien, *The Dance of the Machines: The American Short Story and the Industrial Age* (1929); Ray B. West, Jr., *The Short Story in America: 1900-1950* (1952). Articles on various short stories and on various authors may be found in such volumes as *Critiques and Essays on Modern Fiction* (1952), edited by John Aldridge, and *Forms of Modern Fiction* (1948), edited by William Van O'Connor. Introductions to the various anthologies of American stories also provide valuable comment. The most valuable bibliography of critical articles on the short story is *Short Fiction Criticism* (1960), edited by Jarvis Thurston, O. B. Emerson, Carl Hartman, and E. V. Wright.

RAY B. WEST, JR.

Shoshone [Shoshoni] Indians. Members of the Shoshonean tribe, one of the three groups of the Uto-Aztecan linguistic family. They were found mainly in the mountain regions of western Wyoming and Colorado, also in Idaho, Utah, and Nevada; about 3,000 survivors now live on reservations in Idaho. They are also called Snake Indians, from the Snake River. They fall into two groups, those toward the east, who were nomadic, skilled in horsemanship, and famous as warriors and buffalo hunters, and those toward the west (sometimes called Digger Indians), who lived a sedentary life, cultivated berries and roots, and lived in brush

shelters. The Shoshones were always friendly to whites and took to life on the reservations with comparative tractability; as early as 1900 their children began attending reservation schools. During the revivalist movement of the "Ghost Dance Religion" the Shoshones were influenced by the new creed and its dances and trances. In 1857 JOAQUIN MILLER began living with the Digger Indians, took a wife among them, and had a daughter called Cali-Shasta.

Show Boat (1926), a novel by EDNA FERBER. In this popular book three theatrical generations appear. First there is Captain Andy Hawks, who runs a showboat on the Mississippi and marries Parthy Ann, a prim New England schoolmarm. They have one daughter, Magnolia, who becomes an actress and runs off with the leading man, Gaylord Ravenal. Their daughter Kim is born on the showboat. The captain dies and Parthy Ann takes over; Ravenal takes Magnolia to Chicago, but ultimately leaves her, and she returns to the showboat. Kim meanwhile grows up to be a Broadway star. The novel has been filmed twice, and was made into an operetta (1927) by the librettist OSCAR HAMMERSTEIN and the composer JEROME KERN. It is one of Kern's best scores, and includes his song *Old Man River* which has become both a classic and a folksong. The operetta is often revived.

Show-Off, The (1924), a comedy by GEORGE KELLY. The background is North Philadelphia; the hero, Aubrey Piper, is an amusing show-off, a freight clerk who manages to get the better of people even when they see through him. At the end there is, somehow, sympathy for the boaster, even for his bad jokes, since he is obviously an underdog who is trying to conceal his weakness. His wife continues to be completely devoted to him and blind to his faults. The play is in essence a satire on American success stories and those who accept them.

Shuster, George N[auman] (b. Lancaster, Wis., Aug. 27, 1894—   ), teacher, editor, author. Shuster taught English at various universities, in 1939 became acting president of Hunter College and president in 1940. He has also been an editor of COMMONWEAL. He served as a member of many important committees and commissions, was a delegate to UNESCO in 1945, and a member of the University of Chicago Commission on the Freedom of the Press (1944-47). Among his books: *The Catholic Spirit in Modern English Literature* (1922); *English Literature* (1926); *The Catholic Church and Current Literature* (1929); *The Germans* (1932); *Religion and Education* (1945); *Religion Behind the Iron Curtain* (1954); *Education and Moral Wisdom* (1960).

Shute, Henry Augustus (b. Exeter, N.H., Nov. 17, 1856—d. Jan. 25, 1943), lawyer, judge, humorist. Shute, who served as a judge in New Hampshire from 1883 to 1936, loved to reminisce about his own lively boyhood; he did so in numerous books about a character named Plupy Shute: *The Real Diary of A Real Boy* (1902), *Real Boys* (1905), *Plupy* (1911),

Plupy, The Wirst Yet (1929); and others. In addition he wrote *A Profane and Somewhat Unreliable History of Exeter* (1907) and *A Country Lawyer* (1911). The "Plupy" books are based not merely on recollections but on an actual diary that Judge Shute kept as a boy.

Sidewalks of New York, The (1894), a popular song, words by James W. Blake, music by Charles B. Lawlor. Sigmund Spaeth feels that the forerunner for the words was *Babies on Our Block* (1879) by Edward Harrigan. The song, often called *East Side, West Side,* is the unofficial anthem of New York City and was the musical signature of Al Smith.

Siegel, Eli (b. Latvia, 1902—   ), printer, poet. Siegel's fame rests on a prize poem in the *Nation* (Feb. 11, 1925), *Hot Afternoons Have Been in Montana.* The poem provoked lavish praise and some controversy at first, then both poem and poet disappeared completely from public view. William Carlos Williams resuscitated Siegel's reputation in 1952. Siegel then published *Is Beauty the Making One of Opposites?* (1955), *Art as Life* (1957), and *Hot Afternoons Have Been in Montana: Poems* (1957).

Signs, Language, and Behavior (1946), by Charles W. Morris. This volume was called by Hugh R. Walpole, Morris's fellow semanticist, "the most thorough and unbiased account of the field of semantics that has yet appeared." The volume deals with the nature of signs, the different functions of utterances, and the ideas of other semanticists such as Ogden, Peirce, Richards. Morris distinguishes sixteen types of discourse, including the *Fictive* (embracing the novel), the *Mythological,* and the *Poetic.*

Sigourney, Lydia Howard Huntley (b. Norwich, Conn., Sept. 1, 1791—d. June 10, 1865), poet. At the age of eight the future "Sweet Singer of Hartford" first broke into rhyme. She

first book appeared, *Moral Pieces in Prose and Verse.* In 1819 she married Charles Sigourney, a wealthy man who disapproved of careers for women, so for a while Lydia's pen was employed only for her private enjoyment. When her husband's business began to fail she published anonymously in magazines with her husband's consent. She was essentially a journalist, one of the first sob sisters, using her verses as a gossip writer uses his column. Items from the newspapers supplied her inspiration—the burial of an Indian maiden, the pardon of a convict after twenty years, a spectacular fire. Her favorite subject, however, was death; she burst into elegy as easily as a hired mourner bursts into tears, and a contemporary wit called her memorial verses "death's second terror." She also wrote novels, among them *Lucy Howard's Journal* (1858), and a *History of Marcus Aurelius* (1836). *The Faded Hope* (1853) is a memoir of her son, who died in 1850; *Letters of Life* (1866) is an autobiography, elegantly and piously written. Altogether she published sixty volumes, many of them verse. *Poetical Works of Mrs. L. H. Sigourney* (1850), edited by F. W. N. Bayley, was published in England. Gordon Haight's *Mrs. Sigourney, The Sweet Singer of Hartford* appeared in 1930.

Silas Crockett (1935), a novel by MARY ELLEN CHASE. See the CROCKETTS.

Silas Lapham, The Rise of. See RISE OF SILAS LAPHAM, THE.

Sill, Edward Rowland (b. Windsor, Conn., April 29, 1841—d. Feb. 28, 1887), poet, essayist, teacher. Orphaned in boyhood, Sill was

was educated at Norwich and Hartford, and in 1814 opened a girls' school. A year later her

brought up by an uncle in Cuyahoga Falls, Ohio. After graduating from Yale, he sailed around the Horn to California, tried various means of earning a living, and returned to the East in 1866. He taught in high schools and then became professor of English at the University of California, but in 1883 came back to Cuyahoga Falls. For years he contributed essays to the *Atlantic Monthly* and wrote poems under the name of Andrew Hedbrooke. *The Fool's Prayer* and *Opportunity*, his only poems familiar today, are by no means his best; he had a gentle lyric gift, suggestive of Matthew Arnold, and like the English poet he wrestled with religious skepticism. *The Hermitage and Other Poems* (1868), *The Venus of Milo and Other Poems* (1883), and *Poems* (1887) were collected in 1902. His collected *Prose* had appeared two years earlier. A. R. Ferguson wrote *E. R. Sill, The Twilight Poet* (1955).

Silliman, Benjamin (b. Trumbull, Conn., Aug. 8, 1779—d. Nov. 24, 1864), educator, scientist, travel writer. Silliman graduated from Yale at seventeen and became professor of chemistry and natural history when he was twenty-three. A few years later he journeyed to Europe, and on his return in 1806 published a *Journal of Travels in England, Holland, and Scotland* (1810), which went through many editions. He was an impressive speaker and was much in demand as a lecturer on scientific subjects. In 1818 he founded and edited the *American Journal of Science and Arts*, later edited by his son **Benjamin Silliman** (1816–85), also a professor of chemistry at Yale and the author of college texts for chemistry and physics. The younger Benjamin Silliman, with John P. Norton, helped establish a school of applied chemistry at Yale which became the Sheffield Scientific School. Both father and son were original members of the National Academy of Sciences (1863).

Silver Cord, The (1926), a play by SIDNEY HOWARD. Ths was one of the earliest and best psychological studies on the stage of a dominant mother. Mrs. Phelps has two sons, one of whom is unable to break away from her, while the other succeeds only through the help of his wife. The play deals with its subject directly and without sentimentality.

Silvers, Earl Reed (b. Jersey City, N.J., Feb. 22, 1891—d. March 26, 1948), teacher, author. Silvers, a graduate of Rutgers, returned to the university as alumni secretary, and later joined the faculty. He was head of the Rutgers University Press from 1938 to 1944, when he became dean of men. He published twenty-seven books for boys, most of them with high school or college backgrounds. Among his works are *Dick Arnold of Raritan College* (1920) and *The Hillsdale High Champions* (1925).

Simenon, Georges [pen name of **Georges Sim**] (b. Belgium, Feb. 13, 1903—   ), novelist. Simenon wrote first in France, visited much of the world, and in 1945 took up residence in the United States. He is a writer of prodigious facility, variety, and fertility who at the peak of his production was using seventeen pseudonyms and is said to have written more than four hun-

dred novels. In spite of this his work is distinguished by intelligence and sensitivity, and some of his serious novels deserve and receive serious critical attention. He is best known to the public, however, for his detective novels, especially those concerning the ratiocinative exploits of Inspector Maigret of the Paris Sûreté. A few of his best books are: *Tropic Moon* (1935); *Escape in Vain* (1937); *The Man Who Watched the Trains Go By* (1938); *First Born* (1943); *The Snow Was Black* (1948); *Satan's Children* (1953); *Tidal Wave* (1954); *Maigret in New York's Underworld* (1955).

Simms, William Gilmore (b. Charleston, S.C., April 17, 1806—d. June 11, 1870), lawyer, writer, legislator. Simms, one of the greatest Southern writers, was a man of many vocational interests, and also a man of many misfortunes,

not the least being the neglect that has befallen him today, even in the South. His mother died when he was very young, his father went bankrupt, his grandmother raised him. He went through an apprenticeship as a druggist, but later turned to the law. Meanwhile his deepest interest lay in literature; Charleston in his youth was a city of considerable literary activity. Simms, however, had no social standing and found himself excluded from the city's literary and aristocratic circles.

He began as a poet. In fact, all his life he considered himself primarily a poet, and he published eighteen volumes of poetry up to 1860, including lyric, dramatic, and narrative pieces, all done skillfully but without greatness. When he turned to writing romances he fared better. Possibly his imagination was awakened when he accepted his father's invitation to come

West and look at the country. His father, an improvident Irishman with a gift for storytelling, had led a wandering life as a soldier in Tennessee, Florida, Alabama, and finally Mississippi, where his son joined him in 1824 or 1825. The two lived on a plantation near Georgeville, and Simms saw something of Cherokee and Creek Indians there. He visited frontier settlements and became acquainted with many frontier types, especially the toughs and eccentrics who appear realistically in some of his stories.

Back home in Charleston, Simms sought to make a living as a lawyer, dabbled in politics, published verse, wrote for newspapers. He suffered misfortunes, losing his father, wife, and grandmother within a few years. His first novel, *Martin Faber: The Story of a Criminal* (1833), was favorably received; his first border romance, GUY RIVERS (1834), was an outstanding success (See BORDER ROMANCES.) *The Yemassee* (1835), a tale laid in Carolina in 1715, introduced Indians and was perhaps Simms' most widely read work. THE PARTISAN (1835), a story of the Revolution, had as sequels *Mellichampe* (1836) and *Katharine Walton* (1851). There followed a long succession of novels, including *Richard Hurdis* (1838); *Border Beagles* (1840); BEAUCHAMPE (1842); *The Forayers* (1855); *Eutaw* (1856, see EUTAW SPRINGS); *The Cassique of Kiawah* (1859). He also wrote plays: *Norman Maurice* (1851) and *Michael Bonham* (1852). One of his verse collections was *Poems: Descriptive, Dramatic, Legendary, and Contemplative* (1853). He wrote many volumes of history, including *Slavery in America* (1838); *The History of South Carolina* (1840); and *South Carolina in the Revolution* (1853); also biographies of Francis Marion (1844), Captain John Smith (1846), and Nathanael Greene (1849). His *Works*, containing much of his fiction and poetry, appeared in twenty volumes in 1853–66.

In his romances Simms was a loyal follower of Sir Walter Scott and James Fenimore Cooper. His stories preserve a wealth of local tradition and express vividly many of the aspects of the American Revolution in South Carolina. He loved a good crime story, narrated in faithful detail. His literary opinions were expressed in many essays, some collected in *Views and Reviews on American Literature, History, and Fiction* (1845). E. W. Parks pictures him as expounding valiantly the Southern ideal of agrarian life, including a defense of slavery. Simms was also steeped in Elizabethan literature, and one of his best characters, CAPTAIN PORGY, has been called "the American Falstaff." See also CHARLEMONT; THE LOST PLEIAD; THE SCOUT; VASCONSELOS; WIGWAM AND CABIN.

He was surrounded by a coterie of young men in his later years, chief among them PAUL HAMILTON HAYNE. He maintained a vast correspondence with his friends in the North and South, collected in *Letters* (5 v., 1952 and later), edited by Mary C. Simms Oliphant (his granddaughter), and others. The letters reveal,

among much else of interest, that Simms was eventually made a member of the St. Cecilia Society, the highest social honor that could come to a Charlestonian.

WILLIAM P. TRENT's biography of Simms (1892) has been made somewhat obsolete by the new facts revealed in the letters. The best bibliography is A. S. Salley's *Catalogue of the Salley Collection of the Works of William Gilmore Simms* (1943). *The Yemassee* was edited with an introduction (1937) by Alexander Cowie. JOSEPH V. RIDGELY has done a study, *William Gilmore Simms* (1962).

Simon Legree. See LEGREE, SIMON.

Simonson, Lee (b. New York City, June 26, 1888–   ), scenic designer, author. Simonson graduated from Harvard in 1908 and spent the next four years in Paris studying painting. He began designing scenery for the Washington Square Players, went on to the Theatre Guild (which he helped found) where he produced some of his best efforts. (See THEATRE GUILD.) He furnished imaginative sets, which were highly praised, for the Metropolitan Opera's production of *The Ring of the Nibelungen* in 1948. Simonson served as a director of the Theatre Guild and the Costume Institute of the Metropolitan Museum of Art; a consultant for several university theaters; an editor, art critic, and lecturer. Among his books are: *Minor Prophecies* (1927); *The Stage Is Set* (1932); *Settings and Costumes of the Modern Stage* (1933); *Theatre Art* (1934); *Part of a Lifetime* (1943); *The Art of Scenic Design* (1950).

Simple Cobbler of Agawam in America, The (pub., London, 1647), by NATHANIEL WARD under the pseudonym Theodore de la Guard. Ward was at the time a clergyman in Agawam (later called Ipswich), Mass. "Cobbler" was metaphoric; Ward said he was willing to help mend the country "both in the upper leather and sole, with all the honest stitches he can take." The book is a satirical denunciation of England and New England for being "tolerant," of England for the quarrel between Parliament and the Crown, and of the human race in general, and women in particular, for being silly. The *Cobbler* has been frequently reprinted, *e.g.*, in facsimile with an introduction by Lawrence C. Wroth in 1937.

Simpson, Louis (b. British West Indies, March 27, 1923–   ), poet. A graduate of Columbia University, Simpson taught there, at the New School for Social Research, and at the University of California at Berkeley. His poems are well constructed and intelligent; they often deal with the author's personal insight into Biblical and mythical subjects. Simpson was co-editor, with DONALD HALL and ROBERT PACK, of *New Poets of England and America* (1957). His books of poems include: *The Arrivistes* (1949); *Good News of Death and Other Poems* (1955); and *A Dream of Governors* (1959).

Sims, Lieutenant A. K. Pen name of JOHN HARVEY WHITSON.

Sinclair, Harold (b. Chicago, May 8, 1907

—d. May 24, 1966), musician, clerk, author. Several of Sinclair's novels had a wide circulation. His first, *Journey Home* (1936), was a picaresque narrative which used all of America for its background. *American Years* (1938), *The Years of Growth* (1940), and *Years of Illusion* (1941) tell the history of an Illinois town from 1830 to 1914. He wrote about Benedict Arnold's march on Quebec in *Westward the Tide* (1940). He also wrote *Port of New Orleans* (1942); *Music Out of Dixie* (1952); *The Horse Soldiers* (1956); *The Cavalryman* (1958).

Sinclair, Lister [Shedden] (b. India, Jan. 9, 1921—   ), actor, playwright, mathematician, linguist. Sinclair studied and taught mathematics in Canada, but he is best known for his contribution to radio drama. For many Canadians, works performed by the Canadian Broadcasting Company are the main source of dramatic entertainment, and Sinclair is one of the organization's most important playwrights. Such plays as *We All Hate Toronto* and *Encounter by Moonlight* are typical of his Shavian wit. His *A Play on Words* (1948) is the first selection of Canadian radio drama by a single author to be published. His stage play *Socrates* opened in 1952.

Sinclair, Upton [Beall] ["Arthur Stirling," "Frederick Garrison," "Clarke Fitch"] (b. Baltimore, Md., Sept. 20, 1878—d. Nov. 25, 1968), novelist, editor. Sinclair was more than a literary phenomenon; he was an event in nature.

The Viking Press

It is easy to laugh or sneer at him, but most American critics have done so in a good-natured way; and abroad he was invariably taken seriously. Sinclair brought about important re-

forms when he published THE JUNGLE (1906) and, with the assistance of Theodore Roosevelt, secured the passage of the Pure Food and Drug Act (1906). Most of his books were written with the immediate purpose of helping humanity; some are also first-rate novels, among them OIL! (1927). Sinclair was an adept storyteller as well as a crusader; like THEODORE DREISER, he began by writing dime novels. He was an ardent Socialist from his earliest days, and ran unsuccessfully for political office several times, notably the governorship of California. But he became an equally ardent opponent of Communism, in the years when many American liberals were being duped.

Sinclair's first novel, *Springtime and Harvest* (1901), was later given the title of *King Midas*. This was followed by *The Journal of Arthur Stirling* (1903), which was accepted for a while as factual rather than fictional; then came *Prince Hagen* (1903); *Manassas* (1904), a novel of the Civil War; and *A Captain of Industry* (1906). *The Jungle,* published in the same year, created a great sensation. Five publishers refused it, and Sinclair published it himself; it was an immediate best seller. With the money received from the sale of the book Sinclair founded a co-operative Socialist venture, the HELICON HALL at Englewood, N.J., where he himself was a resident. He organized a traveling theater for the performance of Socialist dramas and was for a while a resident of a single-tax colony. (See PROGRESS AND POVERTY.)

After *The Jungle* Sinclair had an assured reputation and continued to publish many novels, including *The Metropolis* (1908); *The Moneychangers* (1908); *Love's Pilgrimage* (1911), in part autobiographical; *King Coal* (1917); *They Call Me Carpenter* (1922); BOSTON (1928), which dealt with the SACCO-VANZETTI CASE; *The Wet Parade* (1931); *It Happened to Didymus* (1958); *Affectionately, Eve* (1961); also *Plays of Protest* (1912) and other plays; many political and industrial studies, including THE BRASS CHECK, A STUDY OF AMERICAN JOURNALISM (1919); *American Outpost: A Book of Reminiscences* (1932); and *Upton Sinclair Presents William Fox* (1933). He also edited an anthology, *The Cry for Justice* (1915).

With the rise of Mussolini and Hitler, then of the Russian Communists, Sinclair became more and more preoccupied with the European scene and the dangers the United States was facing. He then began the unprecedentedly lengthy series that deals with LANNY BUDD, a scion of a wealthy and cultured family who is so much troubled by the state of the world that he resolves to do something about it. The series began with *World's End* (1940) and continued for a lively and readable eleven volumes. Lanny knows everyone or has connections that enable him to know everyone. He penetrates into the secrets of the high and mighty everywhere and brings them back to the United States for the good of the country. He is a secret agent who initiates important actions; he gives suggestions to rulers that they adopt immediately.

In English-language editions the Budd novels have sold more than a million copies, and they have been translated into more than twenty languages, including Russian.

Floyd Dell stated in *Upton Sinclair: A Study in Social Protest* (1927) that he had introduced Sinclair into his novel *An Old Man's Folly* under the name of Sanford Peyton. Two Sinclair anthologies have been compiled, one edited by J. O. Evans in 1934, the other published in 1947. Reviewing the latter book, R. L. Duffus noted that the explanation for Sinclair's lack of humor may be found in a statement Sinclair made in 1903: "My Cause is the Cause of a man who has never yet been defeated, and whose whole being is one all-devouring, God-given holy purpose."

Single Hound, The (1914), a group of 146 poems by EMILY DICKINSON. They were published by her niece, Martha Dickinson Bianchi, and were described as for the most part verses sent, along with flowers, to Miss Dickinson's sister-in-law, Susan Gilbert Dickinson, her next-door neighbor. An analysis of the poems by Millicent Todd Bingham in *Ancestors' Brocade* (1945) shows that not all of them had previously been unpublished.

single tax. See PROGRESS AND POVERTY.

Singmaster, Elsie (b. Schuylkill Haven, Pa., Aug. 29, 1879—d. Sept. 30, 1958), novelist. Miss Singmaster lived most of her life in the Pennsylvania Dutch environment she described in her novels. She began writing when she was eleven; during her maturity she turned out over a score of novels, both juvenile and adult. Among them are *Katy Gaumer* (1914); *Keller's Anna Ruth* (1926); *The Young Ravenels* (1932); *The Loving Heart* (1937); *A High Wind Rising* (1942). Miss Singmaster's several nonfiction works include *A Short Life of Martin Luther* (1917).

Sinners in the Hands of an Angry God (July 8, 1741), a sermon by JONATHAN EDWARDS. This is perhaps Edwards' most famous statement of doctrine, particularly in its emphasis on God's alleged vindictiveness and the extreme danger of eternal hell-fire in which most human beings stand. Modern views of the sermon vary widely. Some hold that it proves what a great literary artist Edwards was. But when Lyman Beecher read aloud to his wife passages from the sermon, she exclaimed indignantly, "Dr. Beecher, I shall not listen to another word of that slander of my Heavenly Father!" The sermon is believed to have stimulated the emotional excesses of the "Great Awakening" (1725–56).

Sioux Indians. Several tribes speaking allied languages, constituting one of the major linguistic families of North America. These tribes are, in fact, so numerous that the word *Sioux* has become almost synonymous with Indians of the Great Plains. The Sioux were reputed to be bloodthirsty and were favorite antagonists in the dime novels of the 19th century. The term signifies tribes living in the Dakotas, but some southern Sioux were mingled with the Osage,

Iowa, Ponca, Omaha, Kansas, and Winnebago tribes. Army officers considered them the finest of Indian horsemen next to the Comanches. General Nelson Miles, who had often fought against them, called them the "noblemen of the plains." They had a reputation for honesty and for keeping treaties, also for cleanliness. Because the white man did not reciprocate their uprightness with respect to treaties, they fought many wars with the United States. Sioux leaders whose names became familiar were Spotted Tail, Crazy Horse, Rain-in-the-Face, Red Cloud, and above all Sitting Bull. The Sioux today live on several reservations, some in Oklahoma. They have adopted many white folkways, but still read newspapers in Siouan and retain many old customs, legends, and ceremonies.

Sioux songs recorded by ethnologists are particularly interesting in imagery and form. James Mooney rendered several for his *Ghost-Dance Religion* (1896). War and peace songs are prevalent among them, like the patriotic ode *You May Go on the Warpath*, translated by Frances Densmore. Dr. Densmore prepared a valuable bulletin on *Music in Its Relation to the Religious Thought of the Teton Sioux* (1916). Much poetry is joined to the name of Sitting Bull, as recorded in Stanley Vestal's *Sitting Bull* (1932; rev., 1957).

The Sioux appear frequently in early accounts of explorers and from time to time in imaginative literature. The Lewis and Clark *Journals* (1814) contain numerous references to them. Louis Deffebach placed the scene of his blank-verse drama *Oolaita, or, The Indian Heroine* (1821) among the Sioux. James Fenimore Cooper, journeying westward in search of new material, studied the Sioux. Washington Irving has much to say about them in ASTORIA (1836). In Stanley Vestal's biography and in W. Fletcher Johnson's *Sitting Bull* (1891) appear many details of life among the Sioux. Hamlin Garland's classic story THE CAPTAIN OF THE GRAY HORSE TROOP (1902) has its locale at old Fort Smith among the Tetongs, a Sioux tribe. Dr. Charles A. Eastman, whose Indian name was Ohiyesa, told of his life among the Sioux in *An Indian Boyhood* (1902). Chief Luther Standing Bear wrote several books about the Sioux, among them *My People the Sioux* (1928); *My Indian Boyhood* (1931); *Land of the Spotted Eagle* (1933). Similar details are given in *Black Elk Speaks* (1932), a narrative taken down by John G. Neihardt. Joseph Epes Brown edited the same medicine man's *The Sacred Pipe: Black Elk's Account of the Seven Rites of the Oglala Sioux* (1953). G. E. Hyde wrote of the last stand of the Sioux in *A Sioux Chronicle* (1956).

Siringo, Charles A. (b. Matagorda Co., Tex., Feb. 17, 1855—d. Oct. 19, 1928), cowboy, detective, memoirist, biographer. In his early years Siringo was a cowboy; in 1886 he joined the Pinkerton Agency. He looked back with constant pleasure to his cowboy days, wrote frequently about them. His book *A Texas Cowboy, or, 15 Years on the Hurricane Deck of a Spanish Cow Pony* (1885) became a classic; it was the first authentic autobiography by a cowboy. He expanded this narrative in *A Cowboy Detective* (1912); *A Lone Star Cowboy* (1919); *Riata and Spurs* (1927); and other books. A reprint of *A Texas Cowboy* appeared in 1950 with an introduction by J. FRANK DOBIE and illustrations by TOM LEA. Dobie said: "No record of cowboy life has supplanted his rollicking, restless, realistic chronicle." Siringo knew all the tough old-timers personally, wrote *A History of "Billy the Kid"* (1920).

Sironia, Texas (2 v., 1952), a novel by Madison Cooper. This was one of the longest novels ever published—1,731 pages and more than a hundred principal characters—an absorbing depiction of life in a small town, beginning in 1800 and ending in 1921. Cooper probably took much of his material from observations of Waco, Tex., where he was then living. Critics described the book as mid-Victorian in technique, but admitted its documentary value.

Sister Carrie (1900), a novel by THEODORE DREISER. The first novel of this pioneer American literary realist, *Sister Carrie* was officially published in 1900, but, because of its supposed immorality it was not readily available to readers until 1912. Carrie, an innocent country girl, is pitted against the impersonal cruelty of Chicago in the 1890's. She is rescued by a traveling salesman, Charles Drouet. Later a wealthy married man, George Hurstwood, virtually abducts her to New York. Hurstwood acts dishonorably through real love; but Carrie's weakness is closer to what Granville Hicks calls Dreiser's own "desire for the ostentatious luxury of the successful business man." Reaching still further for material comforts, Carrie goes on the stage. As her star rises Hurstwood's sinks lower until, unknown to Carrie, he becomes a destitute Bowery bum and commits suicide. Carrie herself finds no happiness, but "though often disillusioned, she was still waiting for that halcyon day when she should be led among dreams become real."

Dreiser's writing has here what Lionel Trilling calls "the awkwardness, the chaos, the heaviness which we associate with 'reality.' " His dialogue is often flat, his philosophical digressions banal. Nevertheless there is power in the spectacle of these helpless creatures in the grip of social forces they cannot control. Like so many of Dreiser's creations, Carrie and Hurstwood are always seeking to escape from the realities of life—dreaming in the midst of the Darwinian struggle for survival. The novel was filmed under the same title.

Sitting Bull. See SIOUX INDIANS.

Siwash, Old. GEORGE FITCH wrote a series of hilarious stories about this alleged freshwater college (supposedly Knox College in Illinois). They first appeared in the *Saturday Evening Post,* then in book form as *The Big Strike at Siwash* (1909) and *At Good Old Siwash* (1911). "Old Siwash" became a synonym for the small American college with lively students and loyal alumni.

Six Nations. The Indian confederacy known first as the "League of the Five Nations" (Mohawks, Senecas, Oneidas, Onondagas, Cayugas), later, after the admission of the Tuscaroras (about 1715) by its present name. See IROQUOIS.

1601 (*c.* 1876), a long unpublished sketch by MARK TWAIN. This piece had as a subtitle "Conversation as It Was by the Social Fireside in the Time of the Tudors." Making what was for his time a distinctly injudicious use of the Anglo-Saxon vocabulary, Twain wrote the sketch around 1876, and it was surreptitiously printed in his lifetime by John Hay and others. It was not offered publicly until 1939, however, when it was edited with a bibliography by Franklin S. Meine. See THE PRINCE AND THE PAUPER.

Skeever, Jim. Pen name of JOHN ALEXANDER HILL.

Skeleton in Armor, The (1841), a ballad by HENRY WADSWORTH LONGFELLOW. In Touro Park, Newport, R.I., stands a mysterious structure, a round tower of roughhewn stones, based on eight round columns. The first reference to the tower occurs in 1766, when it was called a stone-built windmill. In 1839 a Danish authority, Professor C. C. Rafn, concluded that it was an ancient Norse building. Longfellow accepted this conclusion, pretended that the skeleton of the builder could speak, and the result was a famous sentimental poem, effectively written.

Edison Marshall thought he could improve on Longfellow and used the plot of the poem for his implausible novel *The Viking* (1951). An astonishing amount of material on the Newport Tower has accumulated, much of it in the mid-20th century. One of the best books on the subject is Hjalmar R. Holand's *America 1355–1365: A New Chapter in Pre-Columbian History* (1946).

Sketch Book of Geoffrey Crayon, Gent., The (1819, 1820), a collection of stories and essays by WASHINGTON IRVING. This volume became one of the most influential in American literary history and may be regarded as marking the beginning of the American short story. In his earlier writings Irving was close to the 18th-century mood; here he moved over into the romantic realm of Sir Walter Scott and his contemporaries. Like most of the American romantic writers, Irving was heavily influenced by German authors, particularly in RIP VAN WINKLE and THE LEGEND OF SLEEPY HOLLOW; he also made pioneer and striking use of American folklore. American readers liked his travel sketches, especially *Westminster Abbey* and *Stratford on Avon.* For several generations the book was widely read in American schools.

Skinner, Charles M. See AMERICAN MYTHS AND LEGENDS.

Skinner, Cornelia Otis (b. Chicago, May 30, 1901—   ), actress, humorist, biographer. The daughter of two Thespians, Otis and Maud Skinner, it was almost inevitable that Miss Skinner should go on the stage. She attended Bryn Mawr, made her first Broadway appearance with her father in *Blood and Sand* (1921).

Four years later her play *Captain Fury* was produced, and that same year she began to appear as a solo performer in character sketches which she wrote herself. In 1937 she performed the remarkable feat of turning Margaret Ayer Barnes' novel *Edna His Wife* into a full-length drama in which she played all the parts.

When the birth of her son brought a temporary halt to her acting, Miss Skinner tried her hand at humorous writing, and over the years has turned out *Tiny Garments* (1932); *Excuse It, Please* (1937); *Dithers and Jitters* (1938); *Soap Behind the Ears* (1941); *Bottoms Up!* (1955); and *The Ape in Me* (1959). *Our Hearts Were Young and Gay* (1942), written with Emily Kimbrough, is a charming and humorous account of their European trip twenty years before. It became a best seller, and was dramatized by Jean Kerr in the same year. *Family Circle* (1948), a biography of her parents, is written with skill and taste. *That's Me All Over* (1948) is an omnibus of earlier writings.

With Samuel Taylor, she wrote *The Pleasure of His Company* (1948), a play in which she appeared on Broadway.

Skinner, Otis (b. Cambridge, Mass., June 28, 1858—d. Jan. 4, 1942), actor, author. At nineteen, Skinner was hired by the Philadelphia Museum to play in the museum stock company. He made his New York debut in 1879, and soon became one of the most popular of the younger actors. He married the actress Maud Durbin in 1895. One of his most famous roles was that of the beggar in *Kismet*, a play than ran from 1911 to 1914. He was the author of *Footlights and Spotlights* (1924); *Mad Folk of the Theatre* (1928); *One Man in His Time* (1938), which he wrote in collaboration with his wife; and *The Last Tragedian: Booth Tells His Own Story* (1939). He was the father of CORNELIA OTIS SKINNER.

skinners. See COWBOYS.

Skin of our Teeth, The (1942), a play by THORNTON WILDER. This is an amusing combination of fantasy, morality, and satire, for which Wilder won his third Pulitzer prize (1943). The play is unconventional in form; characters frequently address the audience, either explaining incidents or expressing bewilderment at their meaning. Its theme is universal; man's escape from disaster through the ages. The central character is George Antrobus, who invents the lever and the wheel and who is elected President of the Ancient and Honorable Order of Mammals (Subdivision: Humans). He is almost lured away from his wife (who, during 5,000 years of marriage, managed to invent the apron) by Sabina, the Eternal Temptress. However, he returns home in time of despair and disaster. The play has been revived frequently since its original production in New York. Some critics have found striking similarities between the play and parts of *Finnegans Wake* (1939) by James Joyce.

Skipper Ireson's Ride (1857), a ballad by JOHN GREENLEAF WHITTIER. This vigorous poem denounced a hardhearted Marblehead sea captain who "Sailed away from a sinking wreck, / With his own towns-people on her deck," and who was tarred and feathered by the women of Marblehead when he returned. Whittier based the poem on a rhyme he had heard in childhood. Later he learned that he had done Skipper Ireson an injustice; it was established by Samuel Roads, Jr., in *History and Traditions of Marblehead* (1880), that Ireson's own crew had prevented him from going to the rescue.

Sklar, George (b. Meriden, Conn., June 1, 1908—   ), novelist, playwright. Sklar was a member of GEORGE PIERCE BAKER's drama workshop at Yale University, where he wrote, in collaboration with ALBERT MALTZ, the *Merry-Go-Round* (1933). There followed five other plays, mostly in a vigorous proletarian genre typical of the postdepression era. The best of these was *Stevedore* (with Paul Peters 1934), an indictment of racial bias. An admittedly barren period spent as a Hollywood script writer lasted until he published his first novel, *Two Worlds of Johnny Truro* (1947), the story of a seventeen-year-old's emotional awakening during his love affair with a sophisticated older woman. Most reviews approved his blunt, forceful dialogue but questioned his mastery of the novel form. Other novels followed: *The Promising Young Man* (1951), which dissects the character of a "tennis bum"; *The Housewarming* (1953), which deals with a man who sells his soul for success only to find disillusion; and *Identity* (1961).

slang, American. Slang comprises terms of illegitimate or obscure ancestry which seek to break into good lexicographic society. Sometimes they succeed: *mob, bogus, encroach, reliable, nice, strenuous,* and *workmanship* were all once attacked as slang. Occasionally slang springs from the cant of thieves, as it did in the 1920's and thereafter. The jargon used in special trades or professions is not really slang, although it may become so. There was a sudden florescence of ambitious slangwrights in the 1920's and later; DAMON RUNYON, BUGS BAER, WALTER WINCHELL, GEORGE ADE, RING LARDNER, GELETT BURGESS, Rube Goldberg, MILT GROSS, WILSON MIZNER, and others. Sports writers, because of the monotony of their material, are the most determined inventors of bizarre and flowery language.

Ralph Waldo Emerson, in a notable passage in his *Journal* (June 24, 1840), said: "The language of the street is always strong. What can describe the folly and emptiness of scolding like the word *jawing?* And I confess to some pleasure from the stinging rhetoric of a rattling oath in the mouth of truckmen and teamsters. . . . Cut these words and they would bleed; they are vascular and alive; they walk and run." WALT WHITMAN felt the same way, and wrote an essay on *Slang in America* (1885). An odd development was the deliberate use of American slang in JOHN V. A. WEAVER's otherwise conventional poems, written, it is said, at the suggestion of H. L. Mencken. He published three collections: *In American: Poems* (1921); *Finders: More Poems in American* (1926); *More "In American" Poems* (1926).

The richness and picturesqueness of American slang—in such words as *O.K., stooge, phony, debunk, sugar daddy, stiff, flat-foot, bonehead, speakeasy, rambunctious, cool, endsville, crazy, pad,* the innumerable slang synonyms for drunkenness, girls, money, and other important subjects—in time convinced most linguists that slang might be regarded with pride rather than distaste. George Philip Krapp, one of the great linguists, said that American slang "is the child of the new nationalism, the new spirit of joyous adventure that entered American life after the War of 1812." Collections of American slang include: *Dictionary of American Slang* (1960), compiled by Harold Wentworth and Stuart Berg Flexner; L. V. Berrey and Melvin Den Bark's *American Thesaurus of Slang* (1942; rev., 1947; 2nd ed., 1953); H. L. Mencken's THE AMERICAN LANGUAGE (4th ed., 1936, sec. XI; and *Supplement Two*, 1948, sec. XI); W. J. Burke's *The Literature of Slang* (1939); RAMON F. ADAMS' *Western Words: A Dictionary of the Range, Cow Camp, and Trail* (1944); H. W. Horwill's *Dictionary of Modern American Usage* (1944); Arnold Shaw's *The Lingo of Tin Pan Alley* (1949); Frank O'Leary's *Dictionary of American Underworld Lingo* (1951).

Slaughter, Frank G[ill] ["C. V. Terry"] (b. Washington, D.C., Feb. 25, 1908—   ), physician, novelist. There have been many literary physicians, but few have relied so heavily upon medicine for fictional material as has Frank Slaughter. He graduated from Duke University in 1926, obtained a medical degree in 1930, and entered the Army Medical Corps in 1942. He wrote three nonfiction books: *The New Science of Surgery* (1946); *Medicine for Moderns* (1947), a treatise on psychosomatic medicine; and *Immortal Magyar* (1950), a biography of Dr. Ignaz Philipp Semmelweis. His medical novels include *That None Should Die* (1941); *Spencer Brade, M.D.,* (1942); *Air Surgeon* (1943); *A Touch of Glory* (1945); *In a Dark Garden* (1946); *The Golden Isle* (1947); *Sangaree* (1948); *Divine Mistress* (1949); *The Stubborn Heart* (1950); *The Road to Bithynia* (1951); *The Healer* (1955); *Sword and Scalpel* (1957); *Epidemic* (1961). *The Curse of Jezebel* (1961) is an Old Testament story retold.

Slave, The, or, Memoirs of Archy Moore (1836), a novel by RICHARD HILDRETH. This was the first of the antislavery novels and influenced HARRIER BEECHER STOWE. Archy, who is mostly of white descent, tells his own story; his harrowing adventures show the cruelties of the slavery system at its worst. Hildreth, a Massachusetts lawyer, obtained his facts from personal observations in Florida, where he lived for two years, and from much reading. He emphasized the economic superiority of "free enterprise" in New England as opposed to the slave system of the South.

Sleeper, The (1831), a poem by EDGAR ALLAN POE. Originally called *Irene,* this poem was regarded by Poe as one of his best. It is undoubtedly one of his most melodious poems, skillful in its use of alliteration and onomatopoeia to produce an effect of drowsiness.

Sleepy Hollow. Tarrytown, North Tarrytown, and Irvington in New York State on the east bank of the Hudson are sometimes called "Sleepy Hollow Country." The region was made famous by Washington Irving in his LEGEND OF SLEEPY HOLLOW (1819); he himself lived here in the house called Sunnyside, which is now restored.

Slichter, Sumner H[uber] (b. Madison, Wis., Jan. 8, 1892—d. Sept. 27, 1959), teacher, economist. Slichter, after study at home and abroad, taught at Princeton and Cornell Universities, then became professor of business economics at Harvard University. He served as an adviser to many institutions and firms and to the government. His works include many authoritative books on economics: *The Turnover of Factory Labor* (1918); *Modern Economic Society* (1931); *Towards Stability* (1934); *Union Policy and Industrial Management* (1941); *The Challenge of Industrial Relations* (1947); *The American Economy: Its Problems and Prospects* (1948); *What's Ahead for American Business* (1951); *Technology and the Great American Experiment* (1959).

Slick, Sam. See T. C. HALIBURTON and SAMUEL ADAMS HAMMETT.

Sloan, John (b. Lock Haven, Pa., Aug. 2, 1871—d. Sept. 8, 1951), artist, writer. Sloan was largely self-taught, had no European training, forcibly enunciated his frequently iconoclastic ideas on art, and led a famous rebellion of realistic painters who, as "The Eight," helped establish what was called "modern art" in the United States. He began by doing striking impressions of New York City streets, especially in the Chelsea and Greenwich Village sections. The conventional critics disliked his work intensely, and he and the other members of "The Eight" were described as the "Black Gang," "Apostles of Ugliness," and the "Ashcan School." The other seven, now generally accepted as important artists, were ROBERT HENRI, William Glackens, Maurice Prendergast, Ernest Lawson, GEORGE LUKS, Everett Shinn, and Arthur Davies. They felt it their job to paint the American environment honestly. It was mainly by his work as an illustrator for various magazines that Sloan was able to make a living; his painting and etching were for a long time an avocation. He exerted a great influence on other artists, both by his work and through his teaching at the Art Students League. In 1917 he organized the Society of Independent Artists. He set down his ideas in *The Gist of Art* (1939). Lloyd Goodrich wrote *John Sloan* (1951), and Van Wyck Brooks wrote *John Sloan: A Painter's Life* (1955).

Slobodkin, Louis (b. Albany, N.Y., Feb. 19, 1903—   ), architectural sculptor, designer, writer for children. Slobodkin, who studied at the Beaux Arts Institute of Design, wrote and illustrated a long list of books for children, among them: *Magic Michael* (1944); *The Seaweed Hat* (1947); *Mr. Mushroom* (1950); *Space Ship Under the Apple Tree* (1952); *The Little Owl Who Could Not Sleep* (1958); *Gogo* (1960). He also wrote articles on sculpture and a book for adults, *Sculpture Principles and Practice* (1949). From 1921 on some of his architectural sculpture appeared at the Whitney and Metropolitan Museums, the Museum of Modern Art, and many other museums around the country. He won the Caldecott Medal as a book illustrator in 1944.

Slocum, Joshua (b. Wilmot Township, N. Scot., Feb. 20, 1844—d. [?], 1909), sailor, chronicler. Slocum began as a sailor, went coasting, square sailing, fishing, sealing, etc., and reached many of the world's ports, especially in the far North. Once he lost his ship on the coast of South America, built another and sailed it home. His most famous adventure came when he was fifty-one. Again he built a ship for himself, the thirty-six-foot *Spray,* and set out all alone on a three-year voyage, venturing around both capes and across both great oceans. He was called "a Thoreau of the sea" when he told the story in *Sailing Alone Around the World* (1900), which created a sensation. Before this book he had written and published *Voyage of the Liberdale* (1890), an account of a voyage with his family along the North and South American coasts for 5,500 miles. On Nov. 14, 1909, he set forth on another voyage and was never heard from again. C. E. Slocum wrote *A Short History of the Slocums* (2 v., 1882, 1908); his son Victor Slocum wrote *Capt. Joshua Slocum* (1950). In 1956 appeared W. M. Teller's *The Search for Captain Slocum,* an account of his life and disappearance.

Sloluck, J. Milton. A pen name of AMBROSE BIERCE.

Slonim, Marc (b. Russia, March 28, 1894 —   ), literary critic, historian. Slonim was educated in Europe at the Universities of Petrograd and Florence. For several years he lectured in various European universities, and taught comparative literature at Sarah Lawrence College. His published works number more than twenty authoritative books, ranging widely over the field of Russian literature. Most of them, which critics have received enthusiastically, are lucid, detailed treatments of the Russian giants of literature. *The New Yorker,* however, remarked of his *Modern Russian Literature* (1953) that it was "fine on facts but less satisfactory on the nuances of literature that evade analysis." Other works: *The Epic of Russian Literature* (1950); *Modern Italian Short Stories* (1954); *Three Loves of Dostoevsky* (1955); *An Outline of Russian Literature* (1958); *The Russian Theater* (1961).

Smalley, George W[ashburn] (b. Franklin, Mass., June 2, 1833—d. April 4, 1916), newspaperman, foreign correspondent, memoirist. Smalley covered the Civil War for the New York *Tribune;* after the war he organized the

Tribune's London bureau and covered European events until 1895; thereupon he returned to the United States to serve as American correspondent for the London *Times.* He knew important people on both sides of the Atlantic and described them in several books, in which he did much to promote Anglo-American friendship. Among his titles: *A Review of Mr. Bright's Speeches* (1868); *London Letters* (1890); *Studies of Men* (1895); *Anglo-American Memories* (2 v., 1911–12).

Smart Set, The. A magazine founded in 1890 by William D'Alton, who called himself Colonel Mann and who had previously made large sums of money by publishing scandal sheets in New York. The colonel aimed to cater to cultured society with his new magazine, which he called "A Magazine of Cleverness." Many younger writers were attracted to the *Smart Set,* but it was not a financial success, and the colonel sold it (1900) to JOHN ADAMS THAYER. Thayer found a capable editor in WILLARD HUNTINGTON WRIGHT, who took complete control in 1912 and secured the assistance of some of the boldest young men of his day, in particular H. L. MENCKEN and GEORGE JEAN NATHAN. For one year this triumvirate made the *Smart Set,* as Burton Rascoe has said in his introduction to *Smart Set Anthology* (1934), "the most memorable, the most audacious, the best edited, and the best remembered of any magazine ever published on this continent." But the magazine shocked many readers and some authors, and Thayer let Wright go and put Mencken and Nathan in charge (December, 1914). They continued until December, 1923, when William Randolph Hearst bought the magazine; it ceased publication in 1930.

During its heyday *Smart Set* made sprightly war on gentility and the *booboisie,* especially in its department called "Americana." But it also published much serious writing and counted among its contributors many notable authors, including William Rose Benét, Frank Harris, Elinor Wylie, Lord Dunsany, William Butler Yeats, F. Scott Fitzgerald, Thorne Smith, Sinclair Lewis, James Branch Cabell, Dashiell Hammett, Aldous Huxley, Dorothy Parker, D. H. Lawrence, George Moore, Joseph Conrad, Oliver Gogarty, Maxwell Anderson, James Joyce, Eugene O'Neill, Arthur Schnitzler, Harriet Monroe, Lizette Woodworth Reese, Gelett Burgess, and others. See AMERICAN MERCURY.

Smet, Pierre-Jean de (b. Belgium, Jan. 30, 1801—d. May 23, 1873), Jesuit missionary. Father de Smet came to the United States in 1821, received training in Maryland and Missouri, and in 1827 was ordained. He began working with the Indians in 1838 and was known to them as "Blackrobe." He was also active in raising money for missions. He visited Sitting Bull in 1868 and sought to conciliate him, and he founded missions throughout the Oregon country and on the Great Plains. He wrote freely of his experiences in *Letters and Sketches, with a Narrative of a Year's Residence* among the Indian Tribes of the Rocky Mountains (1843; reprinted in R. G. Thwaites' *Early Western Travels, 1748–1846, 1904–07, Vol. XXVII*); *Oregon Missions and Travels Over the Rocky Mountains* (1847; reprinted in Thwaites, Vol. XXIX); *New Indian Sketches* (1863). H. M. Chittenden and A. T. Richardson edited the *Life, Letters, and Travels of Pierre-Jean de Smet* (1905); E. Laveille (1915) and Helene Margaret (1940) wrote biographies of him.

Smith, Alfred E[manuel] (b. New York City, Dec. 30, 1873—d. Oct. 4, 1944), political leader, public official. Born on the East Side, Al Smith joined Tammany Hall at an early age, served in the New York legislature (1903–15). He was elected sheriff of New York County in 1915, and in 1917 became president of the New York City Board of Aldermen. He was an ardent advocate of legislation to improve labor and industrial conditions, favored woman suffrage and the repeal of prohibition. In 1923 he was elected governor of the state and served for four terms. In 1928 he was nominated as the Democratic candidate for the Presidency by Franklin D. Roosevelt, who also wrote *The Happy Warrior: Alfred E. Smith* (1928). Smith was defeated by Hoover, largely because of his Catholic faith; he became an embittered man and went over completely to the conservative group.

Smith was a man of extraordinary ability, a genius in his ability to reduce governmental complexities to simple terms that people could understand. He was one of the first to use radio to reach the public. He published *Progressive Democracy* (1928); *Up to Now* (an autobiography, 1929); *The Citizen and His Government* (1935). Biographies of him were written by Norman Hapgood and Henry Moskowitz (1927), H. F. Pringle (1937), his daughter Emily Smith Warner (1956), and Oscar Handlin (1958).

Smith, Arthur James Mitchall (b. Montreal, Que., 1902—   ), Canadian poet. Smith, who formed part of a literary group at McGill University, began publishing poems that attracted attention for their wit and freshness of language and imagery. Some of his poems appeared in the *Dial*. He studied at Edinburgh, took a Ph.D. there, and taught at various North American universities, including Michigan State University. With F. R. Scott he edited an anthology, *New Provinces* (1936); in 1941 he received a Guggenheim Fellowship in order to work on another anthology, *The Book of Canadian Poetry*. He published two collections of poems, *News of the Phoenix* (1943) and *A Sort of Ecstasy* (1954), and edited *Seven Centuries of Verse* (1947), *The Worldly Muse* (1951), and *The Oxford Book of Canadian Verse* (1960).

Smith, Betty [Wehner] (b. Brooklyn, N.Y., Dec. 15, 1904—   ), playwright, novelist. Mrs. Smith left school after the eighth grade; an unsuccessful early marriage left her with two children. When the children were old

enough she studied at the University of Michigan, where she won the Avery Hopwood award in drama, which encouraged her to make a career in playwriting. Her works include more than seventy one-act plays. She acted in stock and on the radio and for the Federal Theater Project. In 1943 her partly autobiographical novel of a Brooklyn slum childhood, A TREE GROWS IN BROOKLYN, was published and became a best seller; all told, more than 2,500,000 copies were printed in this country. Later, in collaboration with GEORGE ABBOTT, she turned the novel into a successful musical play (1951). She then joined the faculty of the University of North Carolina as a drama lecturer. Two further novels, *Tomorrow Will Be Better* (1948) and *Maggie-Now* (1958), failed to equal her first success.

Smith, Chard Powers (b. Watertown, N.Y., Nov. 1, 1894—   ), poet, novelist, historian, paleontologist. Smith's deep interest in poetry is revealed in collections of verse, which include: *Along the Wind* (1925); *Lost Address* (1928); *Hamilton* (a verse drama, 1930); *The Quest of Pan* (1930); and *Prelude to Man* (1936). The author of valuable critical works such as *Pattern and Variation in Poetry* (1932) and *Annals of the Poets* (1932), he also described *The Housatonic* (1946) in the Rivers of America series. Among his novels are: *Artillery of Time* (1939); *Ladies' Day* (1941); *Turn of the Dial* (1943), a satire on advertising; and *He's in the Artillery Now* (1943).

Smith, C[harles] Alphonso (b. Greensboro, N.C., May 28, 1864—d. June 13, 1924), teacher, critic. Smith first taught at Louisiana State University, then at the University of North Carolina. In 1909 he was appointed Edgar Allan Poe Professor at the University of Virginia, and in 1917 he became head of the English Department at the U.S. Naval Academy. He was especially interested in southern literature, wrote books on O. Henry (1916) and on Poe (1921), issued a collection of *Southern Literary Studies* (1927), and edited the *Library of Southern Literature* (17 v., 1906–23). He also wrote *What Can Literature Do for Me?* (1913).

Smith, Charles H[enry] ["Bill Arp"] (b. Lawrenceville, Ga., June 15, 1826—d. Aug. 24, 1903), lawyer, humorist, newspaperman. Smith served in the Confederate Army and contributed numerous dialect letters under the pen name of Bill Arp to a newspaper at Rome, Ga., called *Southern Confederacy*. After the war he continued these letters in the Atlanta *Constitution* for more than twenty-five years. Smith at first pretended to be a Northern sympathizer and addressed some of his letters to "Mr. Linkhorn." Later he assumed the role of a good-natured and hard-working Southerner confronted with the difficulties of the postwar era. As Napier Wilt points out in *Some American Humorists* (1929), there is little satire in the later sketches, and "a genial homely philosophy takes its place." Among the collections made of Smith's material: *Bill Arp So Called* (1866); *Bill Arp's Peace Papers* (1873); *Bill Arp's*

Scrap Book (1884); *Bill Arp: From the Uncivil War to Date* (1903).

Smith, David Eugene (b. Cortland, N.Y., Jan. 21, 1860—d. July 29, 1944), teacher, historian, librarian, editor, book collector. Smith served at Teachers College, Columbia University, from 1901 to 1926. His most important work was his *History of Mathematics* (2 v., 1923, 1925). He also wrote *Rara Arithmetica* (1907) and *Number Stories of Long Ago* (1919). He helped edit *Scripta Mathematica* and the *American Mathematical Monthly*.

Smith, Elihu Hubbard (b. Litchfield, Conn., Sept. 4, 1771—d. Sept. 19, 1798), physician, poet, playwright, editor. This short-lived writer of considerable promise died of yellow fever after producing several interesting works: an anthology, *American Poems, Selected and Original* (1793), perhaps the earliest book of its kind in the United States, and an opera, *Edwin and Angelina* (1796). He was active in the HARTFORD WITS while he lived in his native state and in the FRIENDLY CLUB when he moved to New York City.

Smith, Elizabeth Oakes ["Ernest Helfenstein"] (b. North Yarmouth, Me., Aug. 12, 1806—d. Nov. 15, 1893), poet, novelist. In her own lifetime Mrs. SEBA SMITH's reputation was considerably greater than her husband's; today interest in her writing is mainly historical. She was greatly interested in woman suffrage and other causes, and frequently worked them into the plots of her novels and plays. She began as a poet; in 1845 she collected her *Poetical Writings*. Her novels include: *The Western Captive* (1842); *The Sinless Child* (1843); *The Newsboy* (1854); *The Bald Eagle* (1867). *The Newsboy* was one of the earliest sociological novels. *Selections from the Autobiography of Elizabeth Oakes Smith* was published in 1924.

Smith, F[rancis] Hopkinson (b. Baltimore, Md., Oct. 23, 1838—d. April 7, 1915), engineer, illustrator, painter, short-story writer, novelist. Smith worked in his brother's iron foundry until the end of the Civil War, then moved to New York. He entered into partnership with James Symington and turned to engineering; he built the Block Island breakwater, the Race Rock Lighthouse, and the foundation for the Statue of Liberty. He also sketched and painted. Two books of travel sketches, *Well-Worn Roads of Spain, Holland, and Italy* (1887) and *A White Umbrella in Mexico* (1889), caught the public's attention. In 1891 he published a novelette based on his famous after-dinner stories, COLONEL CARTER OF CARTERSVILLE. It was so successful that he abandoned engineering for writing. Among his principal works: *A Day at Laguerre's and Other Days* (short stories, 1892); TOM GROGAN (1896); *The Fortunes of Oliver Horn* (1902); THE TIDES OF BARNEGAT (1906); *Kennedy Square* (1911). He also published books of charcoal sketches, among them *In Thackeray's London* (1913) and *In Dickens' London* (1914). He was a competent storyteller, influenced by Dickens and Bret Harte, though more realistic than either.

Smith, Goldwin (b. England, Aug. 13, 1823 —d. June 7, 1910), lecturer, teacher, historian, journalist. Smith was educated at Eton and Oxford, then taught law and modern history at Oxford. His interest in American history took him to the United States, where in 1868 he became professor of constitutional and English history at Cornell University. He moved to Toronto in 1871 and remained there until his death. Deeply interested in Canadian politics, he was the first president of the National Club of Toronto in 1875 and was a strong advocate of commercial union with the United States. Under the signature "A Bystander" he published a series of articles in the *Canadian Monthly* from 1872 to 1878, and in the *Nation* from 1874 to 1876. In 1880 he started his own magazine, *The Bystander*. He published a large number of lectures, histories, and biographies, among them *Lectures on Modern History* (1861); *Irish History and Irish Character* (1861); *Cowper* (1881); *Jane Austen* (1890); *Canada and the Canadian Question* (1891); *Irish History and the Irish Question* (1905); *No Refuge But the Truth* (1908). His *Reminiscences* appeared in 1912.

Smith, H[arry] Allen (b. McLeansboro, Ill., Dec. 19, 1907—), newspaperman, humorist. Smith began working on newspapers at fifteen. He became a feature writer for the United Press in 1929, contributed many articles to the New York *World-Telegram,* and put together his first books from his newspaper pieces. Although primarily a humorist, Smith is at times entirely serious, and he likes to convey information in his writings. Sometimes he has made extended trips to gather material for his satire, as in his *London Journal* (1952), in part a parody of Boswell's famous diary, and in *Rebel Yell* (1954), a satire on some aspects of southern life. One of his most amusing books is *People Named Smith* (1950), a cockeyed treatise on genealogy which establishes the Smiths as a momentous clan. Fred Allen called Smith "the screwball's Boswell" whose pen is dedicated to "the riff and the raff, to those who slink through life fraught with insignificance." Critics long ago determined that the human race is parted into two groups, those who like Smith and those who don't, and that the twain are permanently divided. A taste for Smith's humor, however, is not necessarily confined to the lowbrows, as was shown when Professor Bergan Evans compiled an admiring anthology, *The World, The Flesh, and H. Allen Smith* (1954). Other books by Smith include *Low Man on a Totem Pole* (1941); *Life in a Putty Knife Factory* (1943); *Lost in the Horse Latitudes* (1945); *Rhubarb* (1946); *We Went Thataway* (1949); *The Compleat Practical Joker* (1953); *Don't Get Perconel with a Chicken* (1959); *How to Write Without Knowing Nothing* (1961).

Smith, Harry B[ache] (b. Buffalo, N.Y., [?], 1860—d. Jan. 1, 1936), librettist. Smith knew the American stage so well and was such a rapid workman that he was called on again and again to supply book and lyrics for musical comedies and light operas—three hundred times or more according to the best accounts. Some first-rate musicians worked with him, among them REGINALD DE KOVEN for *Robin Hood* (1890) and other operas. Smith also did book or lyrics or both for *The Wizard of the Nile* (1895); *The Fortune Teller* (1898); *Babette* (1899); *The Girl from Utah* (1912); *The Red Canary* (1914); *Princess Flavia* (1925); *Countess Maritza* (1926); *Cherry Blossoms* (1927).

Smith, Henry Justin (b. Chicago, June 19, 1875—d. Feb. 9, 1936), newspaperman, critic, historian. Smith was a member of the Chicago literary group of the 1920's and 1930's which included BEN HECHT, CARL SANDBURG, and other lively writers. As a member of the staff of the Chicago *Daily News* from 1901 on, Smith was able to do much for the advancement of his friends. He himself wrote *Deadlines* (1922) and *Chicago: A Portait* (1931). Hecht devotes several pages to Smith in his *A Child of the Century* (1954) and states that he borrowed Smith's exterior looks for the hero of his novel *Erik Dorn* (1921).

Smith, Henry Nash (b. Dallas, Tex., Sept. 29, 1906—   ), teacher, editor. Smith taught at Southern Methodist and Texas Universities, at the University of Minnesota, and in 1953 became professor of English at the University of California at Berkeley. He was on the editorial staff of the *Southwest Review* (1927–41). He is best known for VIRGIN LAND: THE AMERICAN WEST AS SYMBOL AND MYTH (1950) and for editing some of the works of James Fenimore Cooper and Mark Twain.

Smith, James [1] (b. Ireland, 1719[?]—d. July 11, 1806), lawyer, soldier, statesman, judge. Smith was brought to Pennsylvania when he was about ten years old, became a surveyor and then a lawyer. He raised the first company of Revolutionary volunteers in Pennsylvania and served as captain. He signed the Declaration of Independence, later helped frame a constitution for his state, served in Congress and as a judge. In July, 1774, at a meeting of the provincial conference, he read an *Essay on the Constitutional Power of Great Britain over the United States,* which spoke in favor of stopping the importation of British goods and of a congress for the colonies. Later he served frequently in Congress, in the Pennsylvania assembly, and as a brigadier general in the militia.

Smith, James [2] (b. Franklin Co., Pennsylvania, 1737[?]—d. 1814[?]), soldier, pioneer, public official, missionary. In 1755 Smith was captured by Indians and lived for four years among them. In 1760 he returned to Pennsylvania, became a farmer, and engaged in exploring and Indian fighting. In 1778 he became a colonel in the militia, in 1788 moved to Kentucky, was a member of the constitutional convention there in 1792 and a member of the

legislature. But he became interested in religion and served as a missionary to the Indians. Returning from one of his trips, he found that his son James had become a Shaker. He visited a settlement of Shakers near Lebanon, Ohio, and wrote two violent pamphlets denouncing them (1810). He also wrote *Treatise on the Mode and Manner of Indian War* (1812), but is chiefly remembered for his *Account of the Remarkable Occurrences in the Life and Travels of Col. James Smith, During His Captivity with the Indians* (1799), which has often been reprinted.

Smith, John (b. England, [?], 1580—d. June 21, 1631), explorer, promoter, soldier of fortune memoirist. Moses Coit Tyler characterized Smith as "the last professional knight-errant." The son of a prosperous farmer, he

ran away when his mother remarried after his father's death. He never married and was noted for his purity and virtue. But he made enemies right and left, and got into scrapes from which he was duly rescued by a Turkish lady and an English duchess. He traveled all over Europe, fought in Holland and then in Hungary against the Turks, was captured and sold as a slave, escaped, and journeyed to Morocco.

Smith reached Virginia, with other colonists, on April 26, 1607. After many contributions to the welfare of the Jamestown settlement, he was elected president of the colony. He made explorations nearby, in the course of which he was captured by the Indians and his life dramatically saved by Pocahontas. He ruled the colony well, but with a rigor that made him enemies. He continued his explorations, especially along the shores of Chesapeake Bay, and returned to London in 1609.

Several years later he resumed his explorations of America. In 1614 he headed an expedition to New England and explored the coast from Penobscot to Cape Cod. On another expedition the following year he was captured by

French pirates. He was unable to secure finances for any later expeditions. He wrote pamphlets and published maps to further his ideas, which were surprisingly democratic; for his settlement of New England he favored farmers, craftsmen, and fishermen, rather than gentlemen, as colonists. Jamestown had been a fortified trading post; Smith preferred a colony of landowners. The Puritans consulted his writings but refused his offer to guide them. It is noteworthy that Smith always stressed the wealth to be found in New England fishing —rather than problematical gold.

The reliability of Smith's writings has been questioned because they sounded too much like modern advertising, but now historians are more ready to credit them than once was the case. Among his books and pamphlets: A True Relation of Virginia (1608); A Map of Virginia, with a Description of the Country (1612); A Description of New England (1616); New England's Trials (1620, 1622); The General History of Virginia, New England, and the Summer Isles (1624; reprinted, 2 v., 1907); An Accidence, or, The Pathway to Experience Necessary for All Young Seamen (1626); The True Travels, Adventures, and Observations of Captain John Smith (1630); Advertisements for the Unexperienced Planters of New England, or Any Where (1631). Edward Arber collected Smith's writings as Travels and Works of Captain John Smith (1884; reprinted with some corrections by A. G. Bradley, 2 v., 1910).

Books about Smith include John Davis' Captain Smith and the Princess Pocahontas (1805); W. G. Simms' Life of Captain John Smith (1846); C. D. Warner's Captain John Smith (1881); A. G. Bradley's Captain John Smith (1905); Blair Niles' The James (1939). Bradford Smith wrote the best biography, Captain John Smith (1953); delving into records, especially those found in Hungary, he established the plausibility of many of the earlier Smith stories long believed false. In fiction Smith has appeared in John Davis' The First Settlers of Virginia (1802); John Esten Cooke's My Lady Pokahontas (1835); David Garnett's Pocahontas (1933); Edison Marshall's Great Smith (1953). For dramas about Smith see Pocahontas.

Smith, Johnston. A pen name used by Stephen Crane when he privately printed his novelette Maggie: A Girl of the Streets in 1893. When a regular edition appeared (1896), it carried his real name.

Smith, Joseph (b. Sharon, Vt., Dec. 23, 1805—d. June 27, 1844), Mormon prophet. In 1820 Smith began to have supernatural visions which appointed him the prophet of a new religion; in 1827, according to his account, he got from the angel Moroni a book written in strange characters on golden plates. He translated the message as the Book of Mormon (1830), and on this book the Church of the Latter-Day Saints was founded the same year. Smith decided to move westward with his followers, went first to Ohio (1831), then to Missouri (1838), then to Nauvoo, Ill. (1840). There on July 12, 1843, he proclaimed the doctrine of polygamy. Much opposition was aroused, especially in the columns of the Nauvoo Expositor. When Smith's followers destroyed the press of this paper, a warrant was issued for Smith's arrest. He resisted, and was ultimately placed in a jail at Carthage. A mob invaded the jail and killed him. J. H. Evans wrote Joseph Smith: An American Prophet (1933), F. M. Brodie, No Man Knows My History: The Life of Joseph Smith (1945), Ray B. West, Jr., Kingdom of the Saints (1957).

Smith, Lillian (b. Jasper, Fla., Dec. 12, 1897—d. Sept. 28, 1966), author, editor. When Lillian Smith was growing up in a small Southern town, her family befriended a homeless little girl, presumably white. Discovered to be a Negro, the child was spirited away, much to Lillian's distress. Possibly this small tragedy started her on her course of social agitation and reform. After leaving Piedmont College, she studied at the Peabody Conservatory of Music and at Teachers College, Columbia University. In a mission school at Huchow, China, where she taught music for three years, she experienced a different kind of racial conflict. Back in Georgia, she threw herself into civic work, founding and directing a girls' camp, editing and writing. With a friend she began a quarterly, South Today, that soon turned from literary to social criticism. Strange Fruit (1944), her vividly written novel of a white man and a colored girl hopelessly in love, won much critical praise and countless readers in the North and South alike, though it was banned in Boston as "obscene." The purport of the novel was frankly propagandistic. Miss Smith's nonfiction works include Killers of the Dream (1949, rev. ed. 1961); The Journey (1954); Now Is the Time (1955); One Hour (1959).

Smith, Logan Pearsall (b. Millville, N.J., Oct. 18, 1865—d. March 2, 1946), epigrammatist, critic, essayist, biographer. Smith was the son of a wealthy bottle manufacturer. His mother came of an old Quaker family; he was first cousin to M. Carey Thomas, president of Bryn Mawr; one of his sisters married Bernhard Berenson, another became the first wife of Bertrand Russell. Walt Whitman came often to Smith's home in Philadelphia and William James was a family friend. Smith himself declined to work in the family business, was given a settlement of $25,000, and went to live in England; he became a British citizen in 1913. In England he was friendly with many noted writers. The story of his life there is told with complete frankness in Robert Gathorne-Hardy's Story of a Friendship (1950). Smith's talk was as notable as his writing and greatly resembled it in "its peculiar curve and break and flow, its own phrasing and rhythm."

Smith won a remarkable reputation on both sides of the Atlantic as one of the most fastidious, pithy, and witty of writers. He loved the sentence and the brief paragraph and compressed into them thoughts ironic, cynical, sad, humorous, and wise. He began publishing these thoughts in TRIVIA (1902), *More Trivia* (1921), and *Afterthoughts* (1931), which were collected in *All Trivia* and included *Last Words* (1934).

Smith also wrote longer books. The best is his autobiographical *Unforgotten Years* (1938). He wrote two excellent books on language, *The English Language* (1912) and *Words and Idioms* (1925). An animated introduction to one of his favorite authors was his *On Reading Shakespeare* (1933), and he also wrote *Milton and His Modern Critics* (1941).

Smith, Nora Archibald (b. Philadelphia, 1859[?]—d. Feb. 1, 1934), teacher, school administrator, author of books for children. The sister of KATE DOUGLAS WIGGIN collaborated with her on fifteen books, including *Kindergarten Principles and Practice* (1897) and several books for children. She also wrote *The Message of Froebel* (1900); *The Doll's Calendar* (1909); *Action-Poems and Plays for Children* (1923). In 1925 she described *Kate Douglas Wiggin as Her Sister Knew Her*. Most of her career was spent in San Francisco, where she and Mrs. Wiggin were highly esteemed for their pioneer work with young children.

Smith, Paul Jordan (b. Wytheville, Va., April 19, 1885—   ), teacher, critic, editor. Smith taught at the University of California, and in 1933 became literary editor of the Los Angeles *Times*. Among his writings: *The Soul of Woman* (1916); *A Key to the "Ulysses" of James Joyce* (1927); *Bibliographia Burtonia* (1931); *For the Love of Books* (1934); *Samuel Butler* (1935). With FLOYD DELL he edited Robert Burton's *Anatomy of Melancholy* (1927).

Smith, Preserved (b. Cincinnati, Ohio, July 22, 1880—d. May 15, 1941), historian, teacher. Smith taught at Harvard, then at Cornell from 1922 until his death. He was a specialist in the field of religion and philosophy. Among his books: *The Life and Letters of Martin Luther* (1911); *The Age of the Reformation* (1920); *Erasmus* (1923); *A History of Modern Culture* (2 v., 1930–34).

Smith, Red [Walter Wellesley] (b. Green Bay, Wis., Sept. 25, 1905—   ), sports writer. Smith worked for Milwaukee, St. Louis, and Philadelphia papers before joining the staff of the New York *Herald Tribune* in 1945. By verdict of his own peers, he is rated the best sports writer in the country. He writes intelligently, does not consider sports sacred but likes them and writes about them with enjoyment and wit. Some of his pieces have been collected in book form. Among his books: *Out of the Red* (1950) and *Views of Sports* (1954).

Smith, Richard Penn (b. Philadelphia, March 13, 1799—d. Aug. 12, 1854), lawyer, editor, playwright, novelist. Smith practiced law, bought and edited the Philadelphia newspaper *The Aurora* (1822–27), but was greatly attracted to the theater, and wrote about twenty plays which reveal a wide variety of theme

and technique and helped to carry American drama through a period of transition. Unfortunately not all of the plays have been preserved, even in manuscript. This was owing partly to EDWIN FORREST's custom of forbidding his playwrights to publish their plays, out of a well-justified fear (in an era of literary and theatrical piracy) that his rivals would immediately produce them. Smith himself drew freely on French plays: among his adaptations were *The Disowned* (1829) and *The Sentinels, or, The Two Sergeants* (1829). Another play, *The Actress of Padua* (1836), seems to have been a free adaptation of Victor Hugo's *Angelo, Tyran de Padoue* (1835). Smith's adaptation exists only in another version he made of Hugo's play in fictional form, *The Actress of Padua and Other Tales* (1836). He also dealt with American themes, as in *William Penn* (1829) and *The Triumph at Plattsburg* (1830). He wrote THE EIGHTH OF JANUARY (1829), *The Deformed* (1830), and *Caius Marius* (1831). He wrote a novel about the Revolution, *The Forsaken* (1831).

Smith made one other odd contribution to literary history: he is supposed to have ghostwritten DAVY CROCKETT's autobiography, *Col. Crockett's Exploits and Adventures in Texas* (1836); the title is sometimes given as *Davy Crockett and His Adventures in Texas, Told Mostly by Himself* and the date as 1834. Smith's *Miscellaneous Writings* (1856) were edited by his son Horace W. Smith. *The Triumph at Plattsburg* was printed from manuscript by A. H. Quinn in his *Representative American Plays* (1917); several other plays were edited by R. W. Ware and H. W. Schoenberger for v. 13 of *America's Lost Plays* (1941). Bruce W. McCullough wrote *The Life and Writings of Richard Penn Smith, with a Reprint of His Play, "The Deformed"* (1917).

Smith, Samuel (b. 1720—d. 1776), public official, historian. Smith was the author of a pioneer history of New Jersey, *History of the Colony of Nova-Caesaria, or New Jersey* (1765). He prefaced his narrative with speculations on pre-Columbian history, and began the history itself with an account of what happened after the English took over the Jerseys from the Dutch in 1664. He discussed the confused Jersey land titles, Indian culture, local resources, the governors of the colony, and concluded with an account of the "present state" of the region.

Smith, Rev. Samuel Francis. See AMERICA.

Smith, Samuel Stanhope (b. Pequea, Pa., March 16, 1750—d. Aug. 21, 1819), Presbyterian clergyman, college president, philosopher, historian. Smith entered the ministry in 1773, became professor of moral philosophy at the College of New Jersey (later Princeton) in 1779, and president of the college in 1795. Samuel Holt Monk said that "he was born into the deepest blue of colonial Presbyterianism, and seems to have been predestined and elected to the service of his *Alma Mater*." Smith preached with powerful eloquence and was a great fund-raiser. He was greatly interested in the natural sciences and first introduced chemistry as a separate subject in the American college curriculum. In addition, he wrote poetry and was a philosopher in his own right. Monk describes Smith as "a great teacher and a man of unusual beauty, elegance, and charm."

Among Smith's writings are: *Lectures on the Evidences of the Christian Religion* (1809); *Lectures on Moral and Political Philosophy* (2 v., 1812); and a sequel to David Ramsay's *History of the United States* (1816–1817). He had a deep interest in anthropology, which sometimes determined his views on Biblical and political questions; he wrote an *Essay on the Causes of the Variety of Complexion and Figure in the Human Species* [and] *Strictures on Lord Kames's Discourse on the Original Diversity of Mankind* (1787). S. H. Monk wrote the sketch of him included in *The Lives of 18 from Princeton* (1946).

Smith, Seba ["Major Jack Downing"] (b. Buckfield, Me., Sept. 14, 1792—d. July 28, 1868), teacher, editor, humorist, poet, teller of folktales. From early boyhood Smith was well acquainted with Maine, its villages and its people. He went to school for a little while, followed various trades, was given money to attend Bowdoin, from which he graduated in 1818. Then he taught school, wrote some poetry, and began to contribute to newspapers, especially in Portland. In 1823 he married Elizabeth Prince, who under the name ELIZABETH OAKES SMITH gained a literary reputation much greater than her husband's. In 1829 he founded the Portland *Courier*. The paper did poorly so Smith looked around for ideas and decided to become a humorist.

Under the name Major Jack Downing he began to contribute letters to the *Courier*. The first appeared on Jan. 18, 1830; it was, Fred Lewis Pattee said, "a national event." At first Smith satirized the local legislature and Maine people and ways, then went on to the national scene by sending the major to Washington, where he allegedly became an intimate of President Jackson and a member of his "kitchen cabinet." The letters were joyfully reprinted all over the country, and Smith made several successful books out of them. Several imitators sprang up; the best was CHARLES AUGUSTUS DAVIS, who turned the letters from a gentle satire on all political parties into a violent attack on Jackson and his cohorts. The public became befuddled over the rival authors, and Jackson, who chuckled over Smith's letters, told his intimates he sincerely believed that Martin Van Buren had written them.

The Downing letters, with some intervals, continued until the Civil War. In 1839 Smith and his wife moved to New York City and joined the "literati" there. Both husband and wife contributed sketches, stories, and verse to magazines; Smith in addition served as editor of various magazines. Among his publications: *The Life and Writings of Major Jack Downing of Downingville, Away Down East in the State of Maine* (1833); *The Select Letters of Major Jack Downing* (1834); *May-Day in N.Y.* (1845); *'Way Down East* (1854); *My 30 Years Out of the Senate* (1859). Davis' *Letters of J. Downing, Major, Downingville Militia* (1834) went through ten editions and was widely pirated.

Several skits about Jack Downing were performed in New York theaters. In 1834 JAMES HACKETT produced *Major Jack Downing*. In June, 1836, "Yankee" Hill appropriately appeared as Jack in *The Lion of the East;* in September Jack was a leading character in *Moonshine*. The major had numerous literary progeny: T. C. Haliburton's Sam Slick, Charles Farrar Browne's ARTEMUS WARD, James Russell Lowell's HOSEA BIGLOW, and other Yankee oracles and humorists who posed as semi-illiterate and wrote in dialect. Alice Wyman wrote *Two American Pioneers: Seba Smith and Elizabeth Oakes Smith* (1927).

Smith, Sol[omon Franklin]. See NOAH MILLER LUDLOW.

Smith, T[homas] V[ernor] (b. Blanket, Tex., April 26, 1890—d. May 24, 1964), philosopher, public official. Smith began as a teacher of literature and philosophy at Texas Christian University, went on to teach philosophy at the Universities of Texas and Chicago, then at Syracuse University. While at Chicago he was elected to Congress (1939–41) and was heard by millions on the air as a member of the "Chicago Round Table." He wrote *The Democratic Way of Life* (with Eduard Lindeman, 1925); *The Promise of American Politics* (1936); *Democratic Tradition in America* (1941); *Abraham Lincoln and the Spiritual Life* (1951); *On Being Retired* (1956). He is also author of *Ethics of Compromise and the Art of Containment* (1956).

Smith, Thorne (b. Annapolis, Md., [?], 1892 —d. June 21, 1934), humorist. Smith published an early novel, *Biltmore Oswald*, in 1918, but did not achieve success until 1926, when TOPPER appeared. Thereafter he published *The Stray Lamb* (1929); *Did She Fall?* (1930); *The Night Life of the Gods* (1931); *Turnabout* (1931); *The Bishop's Jaegers* (1932); *Topper Takes a Trip* (1932); *Skin and Bones* (1933); *The Glorious Pool* (posthumous, 1934); *The Passionate Witch* (completed by Norman Matson, 1935). Smith had a clever gift for fantasy; his plots are impish and well spiced with blandly facetious sexual episodes. He described a drunken fire engine, a man and wife who uproariously exchanged biological functions, a duck named Havelock Ellis, a pool in Greenwich Village which bestowed eternal life, a mild-mannered man named Topper whom two ribald ghosts adopt, and uninhibited Olympian gods. A number of movies and a television series have been based on *Topper*.

Smith, Walter Bedell (b. Indianapolis, Ind., Oct. 5, 1895—d. Aug 9, 1961), soldier, diplomat, writer. Smith had a distinguished military career, rising from the rank of an infantry private to that of a general. He served as ambassador to the U.S.S.R. from 1946 to 1949 and wrote an account of his observations in *My Three Years In Moscow* (1950). This plain-spoken record of a soldier-diplomat was generally well received by critics. *The New York Times* praised its "strong sense of reality." Joseph Barnes of the *New Republic*, however, called it "a disappointing book on a depressing subject." His study of *Eisenhower's Six Great Decisions* appeared in 1956.

Smith, Walter Wellesley. See RED SMITH.

Smith, William [1] (b. Scotland, Sept. 7, 1727—d. May 14, 1803), Episcopal clergyman, teacher, historian. Smith came to America (1751) as a tutor. His *General Idea of the College of Mirania* (1753) led to his appointment as teacher at the Academy and Charitable School, which presently became the College of Philadelphia (and ultimately the University of Pennsylvania). He also established a school in Chestertown, Md., which became Washington College with Smith as its president (1782–89). He helped make the College of Philadelphia a center of learning in the colonies, and was active in the Episcopal Church; but his Loyalist writings aroused great opposition among the patriotic colonists. Particularly pro-British was his *Sermon on the Present Situation of American Affairs* (1775). Earlier he had denounced the pacifism of Quakers in his *Brief State of the Province of Pennsylvania* and his *Brief View of the Conduct of Pennsylvania for the Year 1755* (1756).

Smith also had a strong literary influence. He edited the *American Magazine and Monthly Chronicle* (1757–58), which encouraged poets to write verse as art rather than for didactic purposes. He wrote for this magazine a series of essays under the pen name "The Hermit," and published his *Discourses on Public Occasions in America* in London (1762). H. W. Smith issued *The Life and Correspondence of the Rev. William Smith, D.D.* (2 v., 1879, 1880). A. G. Gegenheimer wrote *William Smith: Educator and Churchman* (1943).

Smith, William [2] (b. New York City, June 25, 1728—d. Dec. 3, 1793), lawyer, judge, historian. Known as "William Smith the Younger," Smith attended Yale, studied law, and was admitted to the bar in 1750. He was greatly esteemed for his legal ability. He was made chief justice of the province of New York in 1767. In politics he was a moderate under suspicion from both sides; he finally went over to the British. In 1786 he was made chief justice of Canada, where he lived until his death. His literary fame rests on his *History of the Province of New York, from the First Discovery to the Year 1732* (1757), which illustrates his political viewpoint in great detail. A second volume appeared in 1829.

Smith, Winchell (b. Hartford, Conn., April 5, 1871—d. June 10, 1933), actor, director, playwright. Smith first appeared on the stage in 1892; by 1904 he had become a successful producer and director. In 1906 he collaborated with Byron Ongley on BREWSTER'S MILLIONS

(based on George Barr McCutcheon's novel, 1902), which was a great success and is still sometimes revived. *The Fortune Hunter* (1909) was an equal success and first gave prominence to John Barrymore. Greatest of all Smith's hits, however, was LIGHTNIN' (1918), written in collaboration with FRANK BACON, who took the leading role. *Lightnin'* broke all theatrical records up to its time. Smith's gift for amusing caricature appears likewise in later plays: *The Boomerang* (with Victor Mapes, 1915); *Turn to the Right* (1916); *Thank You* (with Tom Cushing, 1921); and others.

Smoke and Steel (1920), a collection of poems by CARL SANDBURG. The title poem is an attempt to find some kind of beauty—if only the beauty of terror and repulsion—in modern industrialism, particularly that of the steel mills. Sandburg sees a civilization founded on smoke and steel and the blood of men.

Snake Indians. See SHOSHONE INDIANS.

Snelling, William Joseph (b. Boston, Dec. 26, 1804—d. Dec. 24, 1848), trapper, newspaperman, satirist. Snelling began as a western trapper, became well acquainted with Indian life, and wrote a widely read book, *Tales of the Northwest, or, Sketches of Indian Life and Character* (1830; reissued, with an introduction by John T. Flanagan, 1936). In 1827 he helped subdue a revolt among the Winnebago Indians, returned to Boston, and became a poverty-stricken hack writer. He made fun of poets and poetasters of his day in *Truth: A New Year's Gift for Scribblers* (1831), writing his satire in verse of his own. He made an attack on gambling in *Exposé of the Vice of Gaming as It Lately Existed in New England* (1833). He was attacked in turn, took to drinking, spent four months in prison, and wrote a defiant book *The Rat-Trap, or Cogitations of a Convict in the House of Correction* (1837). He became editor of the Boston *Herald* a year before his death. He is remembered chiefly for his *Tales* with their description of life among the Dakota Indians.

Snider, Denton J[aques] (b. near Mt. Gilead, Ohio, Jan. 9, 1841—d. Nov. 25, 1925), teacher, philosopher, poet. Snider taught in St. Louis, helped found the St. Louis Philosophical Society, and was a close associate of W. T. HARRIS. Like Harris, Snider was a follower of Hegel and did much to spread knowledge of the latter's teaching. But he did so with variations of his own, devising an ingenious system of dialectic which he called "Universal Psychology." He applied this dialectic to American history in three of his books: *Social Institutions* (1901); *The State, Especially the American State, Psychologically Treated* (1902); and *The American Ten Years' War, 1855–65* (1906). He also applied Hegelianism to American economics and sociology. He took an active part in Missouri politics, wrote often for the *Journal of Speculative Philosophy*, which he helped to edit, and published numerous books in many fields, including four collections of verse. Among his other writings: *A Walk in Hellas* (2 v., 1881–

82); *Psychology and the Psychosis* (1890); *Cosmos and Diacosmos* (1909); *A Writer of Books in His Genesis* (1910); *The St. Louis Movement in Philosophy, Literature, Education, and Psychology, with Chapters of Autobiography* (1920); and *Collected Writings* (8 v., 1921–23). He attempted to set up a "Communal University" and organized "The Denton J. Snider Association for Universal Culture" for a small group that came to hear him lecture. Frances B. Harmon discussed Snider in *The*

thieves and killers in THE UNVANQUISHED and reappears much later in "Barn Burning" (in *Collected Stories*). While a tenant on land belonging to Major De Spain, he ruins a valuable rug and is ordered to deduct the cost from his forthcoming crop. In revenge he burns De Spain's barn. Still later he is a minor character in *The Hamlet*.

Byron Snopes, a character in *The Town*. Byron, a clerk in COLONEL SARTORIS' bank, writes anonymous letters to Narcissa Benbow in

SNOPES GENEALOGY

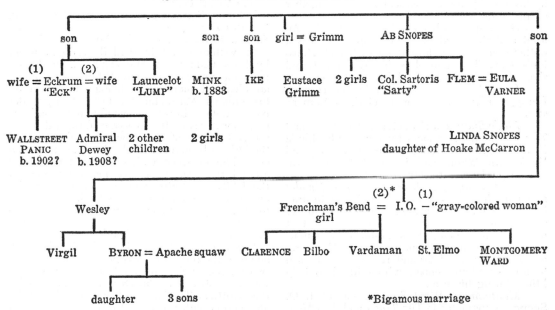

Social Philosophy of the St. Louis Hegelians (1943). See IDEALISM.

Snodgrass, W[illiam] D[ewitt] (b. Wilkinsburg, Pa., Jan. 5, 1926—   ), poet. W. D. Snodgrass was educated at Geneva College and the State University of Iowa and has taught at Cornell and the University of Rochester. His initial volume of poems, *The Heart's Needle* (1959), won the first poetry award of the Ingram Merrill Foundation and gained for its author a high position among contemporary poets. Snodgrass combines verbal brilliance with deep feeling. Not an innovator, he works in the fairly well-established contemporary tradition of meditative lyric, but his poetry is highly individual, intensely personal, finely polished.

Snopes family, the. Inhabitants of William Faulkner's mythical YOKNAPATAWPHA COUNTY, the Snopeses appear in several of Faulkner's novels (notably THE HAMLET, *The Town*, and *The Mansion*) and are representative of the vicious and inhuman aspects of modern commercial civilization. The members of the Snopes family include:

Ab Snopes. The first of the Snopeses to be mentioned, Ab is involved with a gang of horse

Sartoris and in *The Town* robs the bank and flees.

Clarence Snopes, son of I. O. Snopes, a character in SANCTUARY and *The Mansion*. Clarence is a Mississippi state Senator; in *Sanctuary* he is willing to sell to the highest bidder information to be used in a murder trial.

Colonel Sartoris Snopes ["Sarty"], a character in "Barn Burning." The only "true" Snopes whom Faulkner treats sympathetically, the boy Sarty is torn between his loyalty to his father and his knowledge of his father's meanness.

Eck Snopes, a character in *The Hamlet*. Supposedly not a "true" Snopes, Eck is a blacksmith and an honest man.

Eula Varner Snopes, a character in *The Hamlet* and *The Town*. The beautiful and voluptuous daughter of Will Varner, Eula marries Flem Snopes, who is "a crippled Vulcan to her Venus," when she is already pregnant with another man's child. She has an eighteen-year-long love affair with Manfred De Spain after her marriage to Flem, and kills herself to prevent her daughter, Linda, from being involved in a scandal.

Flem Snopes, son of Ab Snopes, a central

character in *The Hamlet, The Town,* and *The Mansion.* The most clever and most mercenary of the Snopeses, Flem works his way from clerkship in Varner's store to the vice-presidency of Colonel Sartoris' bank in Jefferson. He is largely responsible for the suicide of his wife and drives Manfred De Spain, her lover, from town in order to become president of the Bank of Jefferson and move into the De Spain mansion. He exploits the greed of others for his own gain, and is concerned with obtaining and preserving a patina of respectability.

I. O. Snopes, a character in *The Hamlet.* For a time a schoolteacher, I. O. is characterized by his lengthy and nonsensical stringing together of proverbs.

Ike Snopes, a character in *The Hamlet.* An idiot and the ward of Flem Snopes, Ike has a pathetic and tender love affair with Jack Houston's cow. The animal is finally bought and slaughtered by Ike's scandalized relatives.

Lump Snopes, a character in *The Hamlet.* Lump is Flem's successor as clerk in Varner's store.

Linda Snopes, a character in *The Town* and *The Mansion.* A Snopes by name only, Linda is the illegitimate child of Eula Varner and Hoake McCarron and is courted by Gavin Stevens, a lawyer twenty years her senior.

Mink Snopes, a character in *The Hamlet* and *The Mansion.* Mink allows his cow to stray into Jack Houston's pasture and is ordered to pay a pound fee to reclaim the animal. Feeling that he has been wronged, Mink ambushes and murders Houston and is sent to prison. He is released forty years later and returns to Jefferson to murder Flem Snopes, who refused to help Mink during his trial.

Montgomery Ward Snopes, son of I. O. Snopes, a character in *The Town* and *The Mansion.* Montgomery Ward runs a "French postcard peep-show" behind a supposed photography studio. He is discovered, but to prevent the name of Snopes from being soiled with a charge of pornography, Flem plants whisky in Montgomery Ward's studio and has him jailed on a charge of moonshining.

Wallstreet Panic Snopes, son of Eck Snopes, a character in *The Hamlet* and *The Town.* Like his father, Wallstreet is honest, therefore not a true Snopes. He buys a grocery store and becomes a prosperous wholesaler.

Snow, Edgar Parks (b. Kansas City, Mo., July 19, 1905–   ), editor, journalist. *Red Star Over China* (1938), a pioneering first-hand report of the rising Communist power in China, established Snow's reputation. As a correspondent for the *Saturday Evening Post,* Snow traveled extensively through most of the World War II areas. His book *People on Our Side,* written during the early years of the war, was a Book-of-the-Month Club selection in 1944. Over the years Snow lectured and taught, and as a correspondent interviewed most of the important political leaders. Among his many other books: *The Pattern of Soviet Power* (1945); *Stalin Must Have Peace* (1946); *Ran-*

dom Notes on Red China (1957); *China* (1957); *Journey to the Beginning* (1958).

Snow, [Charles] Wilbert (b. St. George, Me., April 6, 1884–   ), teacher, poet, public official. Snow taught English at several colleges and universities, joined the faculty at Wesleyan University in 1921. He was lieutenant-governor of Connecticut in 1945–46 and in 1946–47 was governor. The quality of his verse makes him one of the leading poets of New England; appears in *Maine Coast* (1923), *The Inner Harbor* (1926), *Down East* (1932), *Selected Poems* (1936), *Before the Wind* (1938), and *Maine Tides* (1940). Many of his poems deal with homely themes: *Advice to a Clam-Digger, Country Funeral, Mail Time, Country Dance, Prayer Meeting.* He also wrote *Sonnets to Steve, and Other Poems* (1957).

Snow-Bound, A Winter Idyll (1866), a poem by JOHN GREENLEAF WHITTIER. *Snow-Bound* begins as an excursion into Whittier's boyhood, an idealized memory of being snowed in on his father's Massachusetts farm. Sharply depicted details bring out vividly the wondrous metamorphosis of the everyday farmyard under the soft magic of the snowfall and emphasize the "Flemish pictures of old days" indoors—the cozy, homely room with everyone telling tales around the fire. A pensive mood intrudes on the jollity as Whittier looks back nostalgically on his childhood. He pays affectionate tribute to his family and their guests, and adds a heartfelt prayer, reflecting his Quaker ideals, for universal peace and brotherhood.

Whittier himself identified the family characters of the poem as his father, mother, brother, two sisters, uncle, and aunt. In addition there was the district schoolmaster, who boarded with the Whittiers. The "half-welcome guest" was the able and eccentric Harriet Livermore. The poem has often been compared to Robert Burns' *The Cotter's Saturday Night* (1786).

Snow Image, The, and Other Twice-Told Tales (1851), a collection of seventeen tales and sketches by NATHANIEL HAWTHORNE. The stories are an assemblage of early works and new material. The only unifying factor is perhaps the idea of the brevity of human life and fame. The title story, subheaded "A Childish Miracle," contrasts the practical world of the father with the imaginative world of the children, symbolized by the snow sprite which they create. The melting of the snow figure represents the transitory nature of the child's imaginative world and of art. The concluding story, MY KINSMAN, MAJOR MOLINEAUX, shows the fleeting glory of one man, and another man's subsequent initiation into life. ETHAN BRAND, the best story of the collection, deals with a man in search of the unpardonable sin who finds, after wandering across the earth, that the very search causes the sin to reside in his own heart. In his Faustian quest for knowledge, Brand represents a theme which is central to Hawthorne's writings. See THE DEVIL IN MANUSCRIPT; THE GREAT STONE FACE.

Snows of Kilimanjaro, The (*Esquire,* August,

1936; included in *The Fifth Column and the First 49 Stories*, 1938), short story by ERNEST HEMINGWAY. With a wealthy woman who has been keeping him, Harry, a writer, goes on a safari in Africa. There he hopes to "work the fat off his mind" so that he can set to work on all the things he has dreamed of writing. This dream is shattered when he develops gangrene in his leg. In the knowledge of death he reviews his life, a life which has sacrificed talent for pleasure. In a dream just before he dies he sees the legendary, gigantic, frozen leopard on the summit of Mt. Kilimanjaro, a symbol of death in the pursuit of vain, fleshly pleasures. This is probably Hemingway's best-known short story, since it appears in many anthologies and was made into a movie.

Snyder, Cary. See BEAT WRITING.

soap operas. Technically these radio programs (and their television parallels) are known as "daytime serials." Their popular name comes from the fact that many have been sponsored by soap manufacturing companies. They are essentially a direct descendant of the long-running serials in the old story weeklies. The art of the soap opera seems to have begun in Chicago around 1928; the oldest serial on the air was *Just Plain Bill*, the scripts for which ran to millions of words. Among some that ran for a long time were *The Romance of Helen Trent*, *Portia Faces Life*, *Young Dr. Malone*, *The Goldbergs*, *Life Can be Beautiful*.

The main ingredient in the plot of any soap opera is female suffering. The narrative runs in endlessly extended installments, for years and years; nothing ever comes to a positive conclusion. When a male character receives the emphasis he is likely to be a homely philosopher. A woman character in the leading role is often a Cinderella type.

One of the most frequent complaints against soap operas is their slow motion. James Thurber wrote an exhaustive series of articles for *The New Yorker* (beginning May 15, 1948) on *Soapland* and gave numerous instances of the pace of soap opera plots. Another series of satirical articles by Thomas Whiteside was published in book form: *The Relaxed Sell* (1954). But no amount of ridicule has served to halt the popularity of these operas with women. Frank and Anne S. Hummert, among the most prolific writers and successful producers of soap operas over a long period, had received more than fifty million fan letters by 1954. Robert Hardy Andrews wrote a novel, *Legend of a Lady* (1949), out of direct personal knowledge of the soap opera field. With the increasing popularity of television as a medium, many former radio serials have been transfered to the screen.

Sobbin' Women (*Country Gentleman*, May, 1926; in *Thirteen O'Clock*, 1937), a story by STEPHEN VINCENT BENÉT. Using the old Roman story of the rape of the Sabine women as a basis, Benét wrote this amusing story with the Tennessee Valley as a background. A family with seven sons moves into the valley; when father, mother, and hired maid die, it becomes evident that a woman is needed around the house. The brothers solve the dilemma by abducting their brides *en masse* from a dance. All turns out well, of course. In 1954 the story was turned into a musical-comedy film, *Seven Brides for Seven Brothers*.

Sobel, Bernard. Author of BURLEYCUE.

Sobel, Louis (b. New Haven, Conn., Aug. 10, 1896—   ), newspaperman. Sobel worked for various papers in Connecticut and New York before becoming a columnist for the Hearst chain. He has based several books on his columns. The best known is *Some Days Are Happy* (1947), largely an account of his early years.

So Big (1924), a novel by EDNA FERBER. One of Miss Ferber's best novels, this quiet story deals with the struggles of the widowed Selina DeJong to make a living for herself and her baby son Dirk. Cut off from everyone like herself (she was the village schoolteacher before her marriage), living in a community of truck farmers who do not understand her fine qualities, she beats them at their own game by becoming one of the most successful truck farmers in the district. Her son grows up to be a likable young man who comes to appreciate his mother's sacrifices for him.

sob sister. When women first entered newspaper work they were often assigned to write feature articles of a sentimental nature, and in consequence they were called "sob sisters," their reports "sob stories." William Randolph Hearst was the first to make systematic use of such materials. The term is no longer in common use.

Soby, James Thrall (b. Hartford, Conn., Dec. 14, 1906—   ), art critic. Soby attended Williams College where he developed a profound interest in illustrated books, especially those that featured works of the contemporary artists of France. He left college after two years, going to the Paris of the twenties to start collecting contemporary paintings. On his return to Hartford, he devoted himself totally to art collection. In 1942 he joined the staff of the Museum of Modern Art and later became art critic for the *Saturday Review*. He has been described as "one of the most discerning writers on modern art." Soby often expresses his view that the art critic can only arrive at an understanding of contemporary art by devotion to the art of the past. Some of his books: *After Picasso* (1935); *Salvador Dali* (1941); *Romance Painting in America* (with Dorothy C. Miller, 1943); *Georges Rouault* (1945); *Ben Shahn* (1947); *Contemporary Painters* (1948); *Modern Art and the New Past* (1957); *Joan Miró* (1959); *Recent Sculpture U.S.A.* (1959).

social criticism. The course of American social criticism has been deep and continuous, although the stream of thought has flowed in many directions. The national habit of self-criticism was inherited from Calvinism, with its sense of abasement and guilt, but it fed upon the passionate idealism which brought settlers to America from every corner of the world and sent them across the continent to build a commonwealth as well as to make a living. From the colonial sermon to the Revolutionary pamphlet, from the religious treatise to the abolitionist novel and the muckraking magazine, from the acid ironies of the Progressive writers of the turn of the century to the current analyses of the American national character, one may trace an underlying concern with the American conscience cutting across the more formal labels of liberal, conservative, and radical.

The colonial American thinkers were busy in the first phase of their history exploring the relationship between God and man; in the second phase they were busy finding intellectual reasons for the coming struggle for Independence. But in neither period were they too busy to forget their sense of a mission in the wilderness, to build a gleaming city upon a hill. Their mission in Massachusetts was to establish a holy society; in Pennsylvania, to establish a peaceful one; in Virginia, a graceful aristocratic one. But in all three areas the influence of the Old Testament and of church-making was a dominant one. The Quaker society of Pennsylvania was plagued with a continuing perfectionism which did not apply to the other two typical colonial societies: both the Puritans of Massachusetts and the Episcopalians of Virginia started as conservatives in religion and in politics, and they tempered whatever utopianism they brought with them to the practical urgencies of their situation. It was against this basic conservatism that the social critics of the time broke their lances.

The two important figures in New England social criticism of the colonial period were Roger Williams and John Wise. The theological theory of the dominant elite of the Massachusetts Bay Colony (see MASSACHUSETTS BAY COMPANY) was that of the covenant of God with man, upon which the Puritans sought to build a Bible commonwealth, fusing Church and State under the theocracy of a few men of God. COTTON MATHER expressed this theory most meaningfully when he spoke of the "covenant of grace," by which a man was admitted to the community of the Church through his own act of faith, without, however, wholly replacing the "covenant of works" by which he had to win grace through the orthodoxy of his overt behavior. Clearly there was a potential individualism in the covenant of grace. But it was some time before the individualist element emerged: for the greater part of the colonial period it was the corporate character of the covenant which was emphasized; one can look back today and see that it was linked not only with the corporate ("non-separatist") character of the New England congregation, but also with the closed economic system of mercantilism by which the British governed their colonies.

The latent individualism of the covenant was brought out in the religious teaching of ROGER WILLIAMS (c. 1603–1683). One of the Populists of his day, a lonely, tortured, sometimes crotchety, always passionately committed man, Wil-

liams was the first great radical of the American tradition. "A People," he wrote, "may erect and establish what forme of Government seemes to them most meete for their civill condition." However, the burden of his thinking was not political, but religious. He shattered the bonds that held Church and State together, and those who came after him built a wall between them. He fought for the individual conscience, resting his whole reliance upon the individual's own relation to God. He was driven out of Massachusetts Bay, built a separate settlement in Rhode Island, and attracted dissenting thinkers from every part of New England. Much of the history of American literature goes back to his fierce affirmation of the individual conscience without any corporate links.

JOHN WISE (1652–1725) was the first colonial thinker to see the democratic tendency in New England Puritanism. If religion expressed a special relationship of man to God, not dependent upon civil society in the form of the government, then the individual was endowed by Nature with a set of rights and liberties which were equally independent of government; they preceded the State and were not to be abridged by the State. Wise's theory was the first to undermine the New England theocracy, which had reached the climax of its efforts at thought control in the SALEM WITCHCRAFT TRIALS at the end of the 17th century. Wise, the son of an indentured servant, was a man of the people who broke away from the constant invoking of scripture characteristic of his time and rested his genial and often humorous writing on his own analytic powers. This tendency led to the idea of the power of men to control their social environment in their own way, and for humanist purposes.

These theological disputes, which find rather forbidding expression in the sermons and pamphlets of the time, also produced a body of personal narrative (as with SAMUEL SEWALL's *Diary*, 1878–82) and of poetry of some consequence. MICHAEL WIGGLESWORTH's *God's Controversy with New England* (1662) expresses the more orthodox view of the critical wars. ANNE BRADSTREET's (1612[?]–1672) poems have a quality of everyday expressiveness that pointed the road to the more relaxed life which the social reformers were opening up. EDWARD TAYLOR's *God's Determinations Touching His Elect* (probably written before 1690) traces, in Perry Miller's words, "the agonizing pilgrimage of man into the fellowship of the saints." But the real scars of battle, as they left their mark on the American literary tradition, are to be found among the later writers even more than the contemporaries. THE SCARLET LETTER (1850) of NATHANIEL HAWTHORNE, his HOUSE OF SEVEN GABLES (1851), his BLITHEDALE ROMANCE (1852), and the larger number of his short stories reveal the inward-turning conscience of the social critics of Puritanism, seeking to liberate itself from the Calvinist straitjacket.

The latter part of the colonial period is dominated by the very diverse figures of JONATHAN

EDWARDS (1703–1758) and BENJAMIN FRANK-
LIN (1706–1790). Edwards, whom Moses Coit
Tyler, writing more than a century later in his
classic *History of American Literature* (1878),
calls "the most original and most acute thinker
yet produced in America," was a fiery figure
who had moved away from the idea of the elect
to an intense campaign of conversion. Although
his roots were Calvinist, he based his conversion
efforts on John Locke's theory of association,
exhorting his listeners to flee the pains of hellfire
and embrace the joys they could expect from a
rediscovered faith. His massive figure thus
bridges the gap between Puritanism and deism,
and by accepting Locke's basic hedonism, he
foreshadowed in his own grim way the coming
American happiness society. His role in the Great
Awakening left its influence on much of the
later literature of religious revivalism, especially
on the moving cultural frontier.

It has been said that Benjamin Franklin embodied and expressed his society completely, in
fact, smugly. Certainly he was an integrated
man—shrewd, practical, skeptical, ironic, rational, self-improving—who carved out a successful career for himself and became the first
man whom the European world recognized as
the New American. Yet his personal character
should not blind us to the transforming effect of
his social thinking upon his society. In his Prefaces to POOR RICHARD'S ALMANACK (1732–57),
in *The Way to Wealth* (1758), and especially in
his great AUTOBIOGRAPHY (1868), he created a
literature, unsophisticated in tune, which found
its way into the secret places of the hearts of
his ordinary contemporaries and helped to demolish a body of opinion and belief which was
already crumbling. In one sense, of course, he
was a direct descendant of Cotton Mather, to
whose writings he pays a particular tribute: he
took one aspect of the Puritan ethic—the economic virtues of frugality, thrift, hard work,
persistence—and made them more palatable to
the people by stripping from them the dolorous
garment of the Puritan mentality. But he also
took the other side—the whole forbidding world
of Puritan denial, narrowness, and censorious-
ness—and swept it away with his genial irony.
Thus his writings, which are read today simply
as literature, were in their own day a devastating
form of social criticism. Despite the opinion of
D. H. Lawrence, Franklin was not himself Poor
Richard, but shrewdly used him for his purposes.
He had a feel for popular myth and, as the
apostle of the printed word for the people and
the forerunner of a hedonic middle-class way
of life, he did much to bring onto the stage of
history the practical and optimistic America that
the world recognizes today. The Puritans had
looked back nostalgically to a primitive Golden
Age in the past and longed for a new Golden
Age in the future, regarding the present as a
transitory limbo of fallen men. This is what
Franklin changed, and it never had a chance
again.

The radical political criticism of the American Revolutionary period implied a social
criticism as well. Lawyers like JAMES OTIS and
SAMUEL ADAMS, and intellectuals like THOMAS
JEFFERSON and JAMES MADISON, rummaged
through the classics of antiquity and the French
and British writers for the arguments that would
nail down a theory of man's natural rights and
thus bolster the struggle for independence from
England. The CONSTITUTION itself has been
considered a conservative document, as compared with the democratic radicalism of the
DECLARATION OF INDEPENDENCE. Yet the Founding Fathers who framed it were actually practical politicians who stretched the democratic
assumptions as far as they would go in the direction of authentic and effective representative
government, with a strong relationship between
President and demos. This was also the spirit in
which the greatest single contribution to American political thinking, THE FEDERALIST PAPERS,
was written. The Bill of Rights, which was a set
of reservations to the Constitution and therefore
an implied criticism of the vulnerable polity it
set up, was forced through at the urging of
Jefferson and his followers. These three together
—the Declaration, the Constitution, and the Bill
of Rights—have continued to function through
the whole of American history as an instrument
of social criticism, in the sense that they were
used as a yardstick of an achievable constitutional democracy by which the contemporary
institutions of every generation could be measured.

The early generations of the republic conducted the life of the mind largely in the shadow
of the "Jefferson-Hamilton dichotomy." Jefferson had become the fountainhead for the main
stream of American radical social criticism since
his day, while ALEXANDER HAMILTON's political
and social philosophy has been invoked by the
conservative tradition. Like a banyan tree, Jefferson has stunted many who have grown up in
his shadow. Actually there is not one Jefferson
but many—the Jefferson who cared about the
liberties of the individual and the rights of states
as against centralized and oligarchical power,
the Jefferson who (for all his optimism about
man's nature) distrusted strong government, the
Jefferson who wanted to cling to a republic of
small farmers and craftsmen and feared cities
and manufactures, the Jefferson who was obsessed with the iniquities of a European society
of privilege and thus became an isolationist in
his foreign policy, the Jefferson who hated the
"dead hand of the past" and had faith only in
the living present and the future it can create,
the Jefferson who felt that no democracy could
survive without a "natural aristocracy" of "virtue
and talent," the Jefferson who was broadly cosmopolitan in his tastes and an inspired amateur
in his own activities, and who made the life of
the mind his central concern and a system of
rational optimism his basic philosophy. The generations that followed him invoked one or another of the many Jeffersons, depending on their
taste, the political ax they had to grind, and the
nature of the crisis in which America found itself.

The strain of Jeffersonianism will be found not only in American thought from JOHN TAYLOR to CHARLES A. BEARD and VERNON PARRINGTON, but also in American literature from PHILIP FRENEAU and JAMES FENIMORE COOPER to JOHN DOS PASSOS and ROBERT PENN WARREN. Jefferson as a symbol has replaced Jefferson as a democratic thinker: as a symbol he has become a sharper instrument for social criticism today than he ever was as a thinker, except for the more unrestrained aspects of the radical doctrine which he took over from the French.

But while Jefferson has remained a symbolic force in social criticism, it was Alexander Hamilton who left the practical imprint on American society and who is currently being revived by the "new conservative" critique of present-day America. It was Hamiltonian policy —with respect to the currency, the development of manufactures and industrialism, the maintenance of an effective central government—which built the society of the early "happy republic." It was Jeffersonian thinking and Jefferson's appeal to the common man which gave the republic and also the later American society its dynamic, and thus a measure of stability. History has rarely offered an example of two opponents whose thinking fitted together so neatly to shape a society and a state. Herbert Croly, in *The Promise of American Life*, written in the generation of the First World War, gave the clearest exposition of a philosophy of "Jeffersonian ends and Hamiltonian means," but he expressed what American society had already moved toward.

The first great American social scientist— HENRY C. CAREY, whose *Principles of Social Science* defended a policy of American protectionism against foreign imports and also a cohesive American society—wrote in the Hamiltonian spirit. Many of the great later sociologists have written in a Jeffersonian one. The contest between the two has been the implicit theme of a number of political novels. But, as suggested, there was confluence as well as contrast. Jefferson's "Great Revolution" was based on the rise of the common man, on the extension of his right to vote, on his getting a property freehold and equal access to educational opportunity. It was not achieved in his own time, but by the time Alexis de Tocqueville visited the new republic in the 1830's this was the kind of society he observed, noted down, and described in his great work *Democracy in America*, and from which he drew the principles of democratic egalitarianism which augured the American "new man" and the new society.

What may be called the Left Wing of Jeffersonian social criticism was followed by a similar Left Wing of Jacksonian thought. In every area of American life—prison reform, women's rights, educational reform, sexual codes, religious thought—there was a burst of sharp and imaginative criticism of the possessing and governing groups. From abroad came the Fourierist and other Utopian thinkers who found in the New World an appropriate setting for their communalist experiments. Such settlements as BROOK FARM, New Harmony, and others became the theme of social controversy and literary comment from the time of Emerson and Thoreau up to Aldous Huxley in his later American phase. These radical currents, largely associated with the Jacksonian West, mingled with those of New England thinkers like WILLIAM ELLERY CHANNING, ORESTES BROWNSON, RALPH WALDO EMERSON and HENRY DAVID THOREAU, and with new currents of doctrine from German mysticism and Carlylean England to produce a renascence of American social criticism. Lewis Mumford has called this phase of the history of American thought and literature the "Golden Day"; F. O. Matthiessen has called it the "American Renaissance." It had its start in the latter part of the Great Enlightenment, in which both Jonathan Edwards and Thomas Jefferson had, each in his own way, participated. It extended through the period of the Concord thinkers and New England transcendentalism into the period immediately preceding the Civil War. (See CONCORD SCHOOL, TRANSCENDENTALISM.)

If the Jacksonian radicals represented one prong of this revival, and the transcendentalists (stretching them to include Hawthorne), a second, the third prong forked out into the dark vision of HERMAN MELVILLE and the leaves-of-grass democracy of WALT WHITMAN. In its Jacksonian phase social criticism focused on the propertied interests and the business oligarchy. In its millenarian phase, of the communist societies, it premised human perfectibility, thrusting aside the daily compromises with a fallible human nature. In its transcendentalist phase, especially in the acid writings of Thoreau and Benjamin Andrews, it rejected the complacent rationalism of the Enlightenment and moved into the area of civil disobedience and of anarchism. In the DEMOCRATIC VISTAS of Whitman it sought a mystique of human connection between the humblest units of a democracy, and in consequence rejected the institutional cement of recognized property, authority, and power.

What is being suggested here is the cyclical development of American social criticism. In its origins the dominant temper was that of rejection of theocratic authoritarianism. During the founding of the republic it took the form of wiping the slate clean of the residues of European feudalism and mercantilism, and building a working American democracy on an almost virginal continent. During the renascence of the Jacksonian revolution, it took the form of a radical political romanticism, which tried to work out the implications of the new social experiment in every area of social thought.

The struggle over slavery and the Union was an interlude in this cyclical movement, for not much else could happen in American social thought until these two issues were resolved. It was necessary to clear them away in order to rediscover the main stream of social direction. The great opponents on the issue of unity were JOHN C. CALHOUN and the Nationalists, from Jackson to Lincoln. Calhoun, whose mind was one of the subtlest and sharpest in the history of American political thought, was fighting a losing battle. He did not understand that the logic of his theory of "concurrent majorities"—really a theory of minority veto—could lead to a multinational America in which each section would become a nation of itself. Nor did he understand that his vision of a Greek society based on the plantation system and slavery was powerless against the "march of the iron men" in the form of technology. Yet there were many writers who came after Calhoun, even as late as the southern agrarian FUGITIVES who wrote I'LL TAKE MY STAND in Calhoun's spirit. Some of the most memorable products of recent American literature, especially those coming out of the Deep South and culminating in the novels of William Faulkner, would have been impossible without the conflict of nostalgia and conscience with which the best southern writers seem possessed.

The struggle over southern reconstruction produced considerable pamphlet literature, but nothing with the power of the great abolitionist tracts of WILLIAM LLOYD GARRISON and JULIA WARD HOWE. By contrast, it was the corruptions of a triumphant northern capitalism that served as the targets of the most drastic social criticism between the ending of the Civil War and the coming of the Populist movement. Few American social critics had foreseen that the idealist passion of the abolitionists would usher in a society based not only on freedom but on capitalist power. Whitman saw it later, if he did not foresee it earlier, and the gravamen of his great tract *Democratic Vistas* (1871) rests on the corrosions and corruptions of the Gilded Age: he carried on the transcendentalist tradition by calling for a mighty "Literatus"—a prophetic poet—who would bring American society out of its doldrums into the fullness of its potential strength. Mark Twain, not only in THE GILDED AGE (1874) but also in A CONNECTICUT YANKEE AT KING ARTHUR'S COURT (1889), attacked the same targets, but without Whitman's rolling periods and his mystique. It was left to William Dean Howells, almost alone among the novelists, to say explicitly (in A TRAVELER IN ALTRURIA) that the enemy was "the Accumulation"—that is to say, the concentration of corporate power which threatened to snuff out the Jeffersonian dream. HENRY GEORGE, at once less literary and more programmatic, tried to get at the same "accumulation" preventively through his "single tax" on the accretions of land value. It is rarely that what might otherwise seem a crotchety proposal exerts the influence that George's did, not only on his own day but on later generations: the phenomenon indicates how strongly so many Americans felt that the American promise had been bilked.

It was the same disenchantment that led to another renascence of American social criticism —that of the "Progressive Era," a term which must be used broadly to refer to the heyday of the Populists, the muckrakers (see MUCKRAKING LITERATURE), the intellectual liberals and radicals of the universities, as well as the Progressives themselves in the time of Theodore Roosevelt and Woodrow Wilson. (See PROGRESSIVE PARTY.) The most powerful of the Populist social critics was HENRY DEMAREST LLOYD, whose *Wealth Against Commonwealth* (1894) was an effort to generalize the case of the oil monopoly into a theory of the impact of the new plutocracy. Lloyd wrote in the tradition of WENDELL PHILLIPS and THEODORE PARKER, the great preachers who had prepared the ground for the abolitionist struggle against slavery: in the case of Lloyd, whose preaching was through his research and pamphleteering, it was a new abolitionism that he was preparing—the struggle to tame, if not eradicate vested capital.

One of the crucial questions about American social criticism in the Progressive era is why the European socialist movements failed to establish themselves in the American soil and climate. There was no lack of anticapitalist writers and thinkers in this period; there were strong tradeunion movements—stronger, in fact, than in Europe; there was the insistent thrust of the American conscience; there were movements of "twenty-four-hour violence," ranging from SHAYS' REBELLION in the early republic to the syndicalist "direct action" of the I.W.W. Wobblies in the Northwest after World War I: there were scattered settlements of Christian Socialists as well as of the secularist utopian movements. Yet the dominant fact about the radicalism of the period from the 1880's until World War I was that it never coalesced into a genuine and unified ideological movement. The reasons for this fact are still obscure, although the best lead is probably the social mobility of an open class society and the cohesiveness which this gave to that society in the folk mind: all the pulls of success and power were active not only in the middle-class mentality but that of the working class as well. Whatever the reasons, the fact itself cannot be doubted, and its consequences were felt in the whole of American literature of the past seventy-five years, in which the themes of social protest are sporadic and isolated, however intense.

It was natural for much social protest to take the form of journalism in a society as restless as the American, with its advanced technology of the printed word. The most influential of the muckrakers who used this form were IDA TARBELL (who used the same target as Henry Demarest Lloyd, the history of Standard Oil) and LINCOLN STEFFENS, whose explorations of civic corruption (*The Shame of the Cities*, 1904) gave a mighty propulsion to similar forays into every other area of American life, including child labor, prostitution, educational method, national politics, high finance. In his later *Autobiography* (1931) Steffens traced his intellectual pilgrimage beyond his muckraking days, and in it, as in his two volumes of *Letters* (1938), one can find an odyssey stretching from exposés of local graft to an identification with the Russian Revolution.

Young men like JOHN REED, working in the spirit of Steffens, went far beyond him: one of the three founders of the American Communist Party, Reed died disillusioned and broken-hearted in Russia. On the other hand, Upton Sinclair, who made his reputation by exposing conditions in the Chicago stockyards, never went beyond a democratic socialism, and modified even that sufficiently to run for governor of California. The two American novelists who owe most to the Populist and "muckraker" movements were FRANK NORRIS and THEODORE DREISER: each of them wrote a trilogy on the theme of capitalist power, Norris using as his primary symbol the "octopus" of capitalism that held a stranglehold upon the small farmer and the common man, while Dreiser's symbol was the Titan of capitalist industry and finance who showed his power-thrust in both corporate and amatory intrigue. See THE OCTOPUS and THE TITAN.

The academic writings of the Progressive period have proved a more abiding influence than the more journalistic and political ones. There was a strong conservative strain, perhaps best typified by WILLIAM GRAHAM SUMNER, of Yale, who expressed most vigorously the creed of social Darwinism: that the same laws operate in the social world as in the natural world, that "natural selection" necessarily discards the weak and ineffectual and leads to the survival of the "fit," and that their survival is the test of their fitness. This represented a transposition of Herbert Spencer's doctrines, as well as of Darwin's, across the sea. Its most powerful impact was not so much on literature (although Dreiser, for all his radicalism, was a Darwinian as well as a Nietzschean) as upon constitutional thought. Although Justice Oliver Wendell Holmes insisted in his famous dissent in the Lochner case (1905) that "the Fourteenth Amendment does not enact Mr. Herbert Spencer's *Social Statics,*" a succession of American Supreme Court majorities from the end of the Civil War until well into the New Deal era used exactly the premise that there was such a relation between the Constitution and the doctrine of *laissez faire*. The resulting sense of frustration among American liberals and radicals led to their stress on the jungle character of the economic struggle—a stress which was reflected in at least a half-century of American literature.

The intellectual phase of the Progressive movement was in part a response to the lack of planning in American life, especially in the thinking of LESTER F. WARD, whose prolific writings added up to a plea for a "sociocracy," that would proceed by rational planned social change and would control the economic and social environment as science and technology controlled the natural environment. Much of Thorstein Veblen's "institutional economics" was also a protest, more ironic and more sophisticated than that of Ward, against the economic anarchy.

But in a more important sense the academic thinkers protested against the formalism and rigidity of their own scholarly tradition, especially in philosophy, education, and law. The towering position of JOSIAH ROYCE as the spokesman for an idealist philosophy which went too far in accepting the social *status quo* became the target for attack by the philosophers of the "pragmatic revolt." The triad of the great pragmatic philosophers—CHARLES S. PEIRCE, WILLIAM JAMES, and JOHN DEWEY—became the strongest influence of the whole Progressive period, and gave an intellectual frame not only to the protest against philosophic idealism and formalism but also to the struggles against the social *status quo*. Peirce, who possessed the most original of the three minds, left it to others to follow up the implications of his doctrine. James, whose artless fluency of style and genial polemical manner concealed a powerful social intent, was probably the greatest single intellectual influence of the whole Progressive period: his PRINCIPLES OF PSYCHOLOGY (1890) gave the period new psychological guide lines just as his lectures on *Pragmatism* (see PRAGMATISM) gave it a new philosophical approach, and his *Talks to Teachers* proved powerful in using those carriers of doctrine effectively. John Dewey followed out the implications of pragmatism, especially in scientific method and aesthetic theory, but most notably in educational theory and method. He was responsible for the currents of thought that brought about "progressivism" in education, although the movement went far beyond his intent.

Perhaps the most powerful single mind among the social critics of the Progressive era—indeed, of modern American social thought—was that of THORSTEIN VEBLEN. Detached, ironic, astringent, a marginal man who was largely alienated from his culture and could therefore be savagely destructive of it, Veblen came closer than any other thinker to being the American counterpart of Karl Marx, although he wrote some sharp criticism of Marxist economic doctrine and used a drastically different terminology. His first and greatest book, THE THEORY OF THE LEISURE CLASS (1899), left an impact on several generations of novelists and short-story writers, as did his attack on the business culture in *The Theory of Business Enterprise* (1904) and *Absentee Ownership* (1923): one can, for example, trace much of Sinclair Lewis, especially MAIN STREET (1920), BABBITT (1922), and DODSWORTH (1929), and also much of Dos Passos' *U.S.A.* (*q.v.*) (1938), to Veblen's writing and animus. His *Higher Learning in America* (1918) has also inspired a host of novels, most of them minor, about college campus life and university politics. Veblen's primary targets were neoclassical economics and the power of the American "captains of industry," and while he did not succeed in developing a social program other than that of a "soviet of engineers and technicians," some of the implications of his thinking were used in the legislative constructions of the New Deal and the Fair Deal. An economic thinker who was more fertile in influencing legislation was John R. Commons, who fathered the "Wisconsin school" of welfare legislation.

One of the notable figures of the period was Louis D. Brandeis, a successful lawyer who became a "people's attorney," an antagonist of high finance who masterminded the Pujo Committee investigation and wrote scathingly of financial intrigue in *Other People's Money* (1914), a Supreme Court justice of striking judicial ability who mastered and transmitted the economic and sociological approach to juristic problems. While Justice Oliver Wendell Holmes had a more graceful and epigrammatic literary style and more of a philosophical sweep, along with a more sophisticated mind, it is the influence of Justice Brandeis that has remained pervasive in constitutional struggles against social injustice, and one may trace a direct line from the "Brandeis brief" to the opinion of Chief Justice Warren for a unanimous Court in the school desegregation decision.

One does not ordinarily think of historians as carriers of social protest and criticism, yet the American historians of the Progressive period were an integral part of its whole political stance. Frederick J. Turner's classic essay, "The Significance of the Frontier in American History" (see The Frontier in American History), was in its underlying premises a product of a democratic critique of the exhausted institutions of the eastern seaboard, and in its impact it influenced a school of literary writing about the frontier spirit. Henry Adams, who had used a federalist interpretation of the era of the Jeffersonian revolution in his great History of the United States (1885–91), went on to a much more fundamental critique and prophecy of modern industrial life in his "Rule of Phase," which applied the theories of physics to the course of history. His brother, Brooks Adams, applied his own variant of the economic interpretation of history to the new forces of corporate concentration and economic imperialism. Working largely in the same spirit of economic determinism, but reaching back to Jefferson and Madison for his sources, Charles A. Beard embodied in his magisterial The Rise of American Civilization (1927) the whole intellectual universe of progressivism, and used it for revaluing the American past. Vernon L. Parrington, taking his cue partly from Beard's work and partly from that of his own master, J. Allen Smith, performed much the same task for the sweep of American intellectual history in his three-volume Main Currents in American Thought (1927–30). James Harvey Robinson's *The New History* (1912) and *The Humanizing of Knowledge* (1926) exerted an influence far beyond his own historical contributions. Randolph Bourne, not a historian but a literary and a social critic, worked in much the same spirit and, as a "literary radical," left a sharp impress on the younger writers of the World War I generation.

Among the sociologists proper—those who called themselves by that term and who built up sociology as a systematic social study—the men who were the most critical of American society were Edward Allsworth Ross and Charles H. Cooley, both of them working along the lines of a theory of social control as against an individualist and laissez-faire society. In a more practical way Jane Addams embodied the same viewpoint in her creative impact upon the social work and social welfare movement; Samuel Gompers expressed the angle of vision of a job-conscious nonideological trade unionism which was shrewd in adapting to American social reality; while Eugene V. Debs was one of the isolated figures who spent his own warm human generosity on a socialist crusade in terms of a bitter class struggle. Closely allied with these welfare and reform movements was the "Social Gospel" movement in American theology, which got much of its impetus from Walter Rautenstrauch's *Christianizing the Old Order* (1912).

The period between World War I and the present has proved as prolific in social criticism as did the Progressive period, but it is still difficult to get enough perspective to measure the relative stature of the social thinkers. In legal theory, Justices Black and Douglas have carried on much of the work of Justice Brandeis, while Justice Felix Frankfurter has worked in the tradition of Holmes. In economic thought Alvin Hansen has carried over the basic Keynesian approach to the American economy, while John K. Galbraith, especially in *The Affluent Society* (1958), has continued with the institutional economics of the Veblen tradition, although with greater literary grace and with a less lumbering irony. Easily the sharpest mind, however, was that of a transplanted Austrian economist, Josef Schumpeter, whose studies of imperialism, capitalism, and democracy will outlive many others, and whose criticism of the disintegrating role of the intellectuals in a democratic capitalist society may serve to set in a withering perspective the whole guilt-ridden tradition of American social criticism.

In sociology the most comprehensive and the densest work—dense both in depth and difficulty—has been that of Talcott Parsons, who has aimed at a total theory of human society, and, while critical of many aspects of American life, has worked in the liberal rather than in the radical tradition. The work of Robert E. Park and, even more, that of Robert and Helen Lynd in their *Middletown* and *Middletown Revisited* evoked a spate of studies of American communities. Along with the *Yankee City* series of W. Lloyd Warner, they awakened a new interest among American fiction writers in the class and status structure of their city and small-town settings. A book which had a considerable impact on American attitudes toward popular culture and conformity was David Riesman's *The Lonely Crowd* (1950), a study of the shifting frames in which the American national character has expressed itself. Riesman's typology of American personality types has brought into the everyday vocabulary such phrases as the "inner-directed" and the "other-directed" man, although his real strength must be sought not so much in a typology as in the searching explanation of the ambiguities of American society.

Similarly the title of W. H. WHYTE, JR.'s book, *The Organization Man* (1956), has also come into the everyday literary vocabulary, marking the readiness of the American creative and critical writers for Whyte's analysis of the corrosion of the Puritan ethic and the substitution of impersonal and economic virtues for the older ones. In the theory of class and stratification it was mainly C. WRIGHT MILLS who applied the merged viewpoints of Veblen and of the German theorist, Max Weber, to the American class structure, notably in his books, *White Collar* (1951) and *The Power Elite* (1956); again it is a mark of the impact of Mills' thought that the latter term has become part of the working vocabulary of the American writer. In the wake of these men, a school of sharp criticism of mass culture, mass leisure, and the mass media has developed with representatives on almost every campus. Much of this critique of mass culture goes back to the earlier work of VAN WYCK BROOKS during the 1920's, in his classification (in *America's Coming of Age*) of "high-brow," "low-brow," and "middle-brow" culture. Much of the dissatisfaction with American life today is channeled both in social criticism and in contemporary fiction into the scorn of the high culture for the popular culture.

One of the striking developments in American social criticism has been its sense of anthropological detachment, largely the work of a remarkable group whose first notable figure was FRANZ BOAS, who studied the primitive mind but tried to apply his results to modern life. RUTH BENEDICT's *Patterns of Culture* and *The Chrysanthemum and the Sword* taught a generation of writers to look for the revealing symbolic attitudes of a culture. MARGARET MEAD's many books shuttle between primitive culture and contemporary America, ranging over sexual mores, growing patterns of behavior, political and economic attitudes, and education; always impatient of cant, they show a growing critical maturity of viewpoint.

Behind each period of American literary expression one can find a school of philosophic and social thought. In fact, one might trace the history of American literature in terms of the successive influence of Puritan divines, revolutionary French and British political philosophers, transcendentalist German thinkers, Darwin, Nietzsche, Marx and Marxism. But in the contemporary period the influence of Freud and of his rivals and collaborators has come to occupy a central place. Without this influence the seminal theology and social thinking of REINHOLD NIEBUHR would have been impossible; Niebuhr's *The Nature and Destiny of Man*, and a host of books on history, politics, and belief embody the tradition of the American conscience without its political and intellectual naïveté. Among the American psychoanalysts, the most influential writings have been those of HARRY STACK SULLIVAN, ERICH FROMM, and Erik Erikson. Fromm's earlier works—*Escape from Freedom* (1941) and *Man for Himself* (1947)—have

been more formative than his later writings, and Riesman's concept of the other-directed personality owes much to Fromm's "marketing orientation." Sullivan's relation to Freudianism is much like that of Veblen's to Marxism: In both cases the doctrine suffered a sea change in being transported from Europe, and the American variant developed its own characteristic vocabulary. While Sullivan's writings about "interpersonal relations" are difficult, they have proved full of insights for poets and novelists alike. Erikson, in his *Childhood and Society* (1950) and in later books, has stressed the crises of identity in the life cycle of the individual, and it is likely that much of the fiction of the 1960's will concern itself with the search for identity. These themes, of course, must be taken along with the more fundamental themes of *eros* and *thanatos* with which Freud dealt— the basic life force and death thrust in man himself—and, along with the related theological speculation of Kierkegaard and REINHOLD NIEBUHR, they are likely to form a frame within which much of American literature will be written.

General works of social criticism include: Van Wyck Brooks' *Makers and Finders: A History of the Writers in America, 1800–1915* (1936–42); Roger Burlingame's *The American Conscience* (1957); Morris R. Cohen's *American Thought: A Critical Sketch* (1954); Carl N. Degler's *Out of Our Past* (1959); Merle Curti's *The Growth of American Thought* (1943); Louis Hartz's *The Liberal Tradition in America* (1955); Vernon L. Parrington's *Main Currents in American Thought* (3 v., 1927–30); Max Lerner's *America as a Civilization* (1957), *Ideas Are Weapons* (1939), *Ideas for the Ice Age* (1941), "Notes on Literature and American Civilization" (*American Quarterly Supplement*, v. XI, Summer 1959); Stow Persons' *American Minds* (1958); William A. Williams' *The Contours of American History* (1961).

Among the outstanding books dealing with specific periods are: (1) Colonial: D. J. Boorstin's *The Americans: The Colonial Experience* (1958); Clinton Rossiter's *Seedtime of the Republic* (1953); Moses C. Tyler's *A History of American Literature 1607–1765*, ed. by Perry Miller (a new 1-v. ed., 1962). (2) Early Republic: Merrill Peterson's *The Jefferson Image in the American Mind* (1960); F. O. Matthiessen's *The American Renaissance* (1941); Lewis Mumford's *The Golden Day* (new ed., 1957). (3) Modern: Daniel Aaron's *Men of Good Hope: A Story of American Progressives* (1951); Henry Steele Commager's *The American Mind* (1950); Louis Filler's *Crusaders for American Liberalism* (1930); Eric F. Goldman's *Rendezvous with Destiny* (1952); Ralph H. Gabriel's *The Course of American Democratic Thought* (1956); Richard Hofstadter's *Social Darwinism in American Thought* (1944) and *The Age of Reform* (1955); Charles A. Madison's *Critics and Crusaders* (1947); Morton G. White's *Social Thought in America: The Revolt Against*

Formalism (1949); *Sociology Today: Problems and Prospects*, ed. by R. K. Merton, L. Brown, and L. S. Cottrell, Jr. (1959).

The following works express special viewpoints or cover special areas of social criticism: *The New American Right*, Daniel Bell, ed. (1955); *Socialism and American Life* by D. D. Egbert and Stow Persons (1952); Theodore Draper's *The Roots of American Communism* (1957) and *American Communism and Soviet Russia* (1960); Clinton Rossiter's *Conservatism in America* (2nd ed., rev., 1962); *Series on Men and Movements*, pub. by Syracuse University Press; Harry E. Barnes' and Howard Becker's *Social Thought from Lore to Science* (2 v., 1938); J. Dorfman's *The Economic Mind in American Civilization* (5 v., 1946–1959); Charles H. Page's *Class and American Sociology* (1940); Maurice Stein's *The Eclipse of Community* (1960); Harvey Wish's *The American Historian* (1960).

Several anthologies have been compiled on various aspects of social thought, among them: Ray Ginger's *American Social Thought* (1961); *American Radicals*, Harvey Goldberg, ed. (1957); Louis M. Hacker's *The Shaping of the American Tradition* (1947); Perry Miller, ed., *The American Puritans: Their Prose and Poetry* (1956), *The Transcendentalists: An Anthology* (1950), *American Thought: Civil War to World War I* (1954); Bernard Smith's *The Democratic Spirit* (1941).

MAX LERNER

Soglow, Otto (b. New York City, Dec. 23, 1900—   ), cartoonist. Soglow began drawing cartoons for leading magazines in 1925, and in 1933 joined King Features Syndicate. A number of his drawings have been collected in books: *Pretty Pictures* (1931); *Everything's Rosy* (1932); *The Little King* (with David Plotkin, 1933); *Wasn't the Depression Terrible?* (1934). Soglow's illustrations appear in books of verse by OGDEN NASH and others including some of his own.

Soldiers of Fortune (1897), a novel by RICHARD HARDING DAVIS. Following the formula made popular by Anthony Hope's *Prisoner of Zenda* (1894), this romance describes dashing intrigue in an exotic setting, with an honest Yankee love story. The novel was dramatized by the author and AUGUSTUS THOMAS in 1902.

Solon Shingle. A character in *The People's Lawyer* (1839), a play by JOSEPH STEVENS JONES. Shingle, a Yankee teamster, proved so popular that the play, which enjoyed a long run and was often revived, was sometimes called *Solon Shingle.*

Some Adventures of Captain Simon Suggs (1845), by JOHNSON J. HOOPER. Hooper was a rising young lawyer, politician, and newspaperman, who later became the highly respected Secretary of the Confederacy. He was twenty-nine when he contributed the first of the Suggs sketches to the *East Alabamian*, a newspaper of which he was editor. Captain Suggs was a hard-drinking, ready-witted backwoodsman whose philosophy was summed up in the maxim "It's good to be shifty in a new country." He was modeled on a well-known character, Bird H. Young, a farmer who might have been regarded as a leading citizen, but who loved to drink and gamble and was an inveterate practical joker.

William T. Porter began picking up the sketches for his *Spirit of the Times*, and recommended them to Carey & Hart for book publication. The collection was quite popular; by 1856 it had gone into an eleventh printing. Both Dickens and Thackeray read Hooper and liked him, as did Mark Twain, Bret Harte, and Artemus Ward, who learned some tricks of humor from him. In an introduction to W. Stanley Hoole's life of Hooper called *Alias Simon Suggs* (1952), Franklin J. Meine holds that Hooper's book is a masterpiece of American humor. According to Bernard De Voto, chapter 20 of *Huckleberry Finn* is "all but identical" with a chapter in *Simon Suggs.*

Song of Marion's Men, The (1831), a poem by WILLIAM CULLEN BRYANT. This stirring patriotic poem celebrates the achievements of General FRANCIS MARION (1732[?]–1795), known as the "Swamp Fox."

"Song of Myself," the longest poem in WALT WHITMAN's LEAVES OF GRASS, running to nearly two thousand lines. This poem is often regarded as Whitman's most important and most characteristic work. It was first published without title in 1855; in 1856 it was called "A Poem of Walt Whitman, an American"; in 1860, simply "Walt Whitman"; and finally in the 1881 edition, "Song of Myself." In the first lines the poet states that, though he sings himself, "what I assume you shall assume . . ." The "I" is the fictional poet-messiah roaming through time and space, dilating with pride and joy in the mystery and beauties of creation, until finally: "I bequeath myself to the dirt to grow from the grass I love, / If you want me again look for me under your bootsoles." In no other poem did Whitman exhibit such intense ecstasy, such original and sharply focused imagery. In some passages the images pile up in long lists or "catalogs," but even these give a sense of space and plenitude. And yet the poem is so loosely constructed that many critics have been unable to find any order in it. The fifty-two sections may be considered as separate poems, but they do supplement each other in an esthetic progression. Most critics now agree that the first (1855) version was best. As Malcolm Cowley puts it, "the text of the first edition is the purest text for 'Song of Myself,' since many of the later corrections were also corruptions of the style and concealments of the original meaning." In some of his revisions Whitman weakened the imagery, and the insertions of allusions to the Civil War seem out of place. However, the poem was not fundamentally changed from 1855 to 1881 (the final revision). All versions justify one in calling this one of the great lyrics of cosmic emotion in world literature.

Song of the Broad-Axe (1856), a poem by WALT WHITMAN. This poem appeared first in the 1856 edition of *Leaves of Grass* and was considerably revised in later editions. It describes the use of the axe in feudal lands abroad and in democratic lands at home.

Song of the Chattahoochee, The (probably comp. in 1877; pub., 1883; in posthumous poems, 1884), a poem by SIDNEY LANIER. Throughout his career Lanier, a skilled musician, sought constantly to arrive at an artistic marriage of verse and music, perhaps never more successfully than in this poem. It is a triumph of alliteration, onomatopoeia, and melody.

Song of the Lark, The (1915), a novel by WILLA CATHER. The author said this was both her favorite novel and the one that satisfied her least. It deals with the transformation of Thea Kronborg, daughter of a Swedish preacher in Moonstone, Col., from a passionate, troubled, eager adolescent into a famous opera singer. Thea is to some extent drawn from the famous Wagnerian singer Olive Fremstad.

Song of the Open Road (1856), a poem by WALT WHITMAN. In the 1856 and 1860 editions of *Leaves of Grass* this poem was called *Poem of the Road*. It was given its present title in 1871. Other revisions were made in subsequent editions. Whitman's attitude toward the world as he travels the open road seems to be deliberately and defiantly undiscriminating—everything is just as good and valuable as everything else. The poet is delighted that there are so many impressions competing for his attention. The opening lines are famous: "Afoot and light-hearted, I take to the open road, / Healthy, free, the world before me, / The long brown path before me leading wherever I choose."

Songs from Vagabondia (1890), poems by BLISS CARMAN and RICHARD HOVEY. These poems are melodious songs in the bohemian tradition, and were widely popular, especially in college circles, during the last years of the 19th century. Carman wrote *A Vagabond Song* that set the key. Hovey contributed the celebrated *Stein Song*, also *Comrades* and *At The Crossroad*. The two poets later issued *More Songs from Vagabondia* (1898) and *Last Songs from Vagabondia* (1901).

songs in American culture. Naturally the early settlers brought along their favorite songs. Had they been interested, they would have found an indigenous music among the Indians of considerable bulk and value, but it was not until centuries later that an attempt was made to study this music. Meanwhile the Pilgrims and Puritans had their psalters, and the colonists at Jamestown remembered and sang old English ballads. Folk tunes were in the mental baggage of the Spaniards and the Dutch, and black men in the slave ships did not forget the rhythms of Africa, which long afterward fascinated the white man too. French songs were carried to Quebec and to French possessions in the West and South.

Songs of a political cast were among the first tunes of the more or less unified colonies. The most famous was of course YANKEE DOODLE. Church songs continued to be written; hymn production has never been low in the history of American music. Patriotism sometimes chose the form of hymns, as with S. F. Smith's AMERICA, or appropriated one of hymnology's best tunes, as with AMERICA THE BEAUTIFUL. The War of 1812 inspired the composition of our national anthem THE STAR-SPANGLED BANNER.

Songs were an invariable part of all home gatherings. Many collections were made and widely distributed—one of the first was the *American Musical Miscellany* (1789). Tunes were freely borrowed from English, Irish, and Scots sources. The words reflected the social, political, patriotic, economic, and other interests of the times. Sentimental songs were constantly popular, like WOODMAN, SPARE THAT TREE. Along with these arose songs that are truly indigenous. Some were work songs like *Blow, Boys, Blow*. Westward emigrants sang *Promised Land*. Some songs celebrated remarkable events such as the discovery of gold. The songs of the Negroes became a paramount influence, culminating in the songs of STEPHEN FOSTER. In addition the black man was the pretext for the popular Negro minstrel shows.

A great war brought forth the BATTLE HYMN OF THE REPUBLIC and popularized DIXIE. In the course of the massive expansion after the war, various songs reflected the railroad, the cowboy, the immigrant. Meanwhile, the musical tastes of the American people seemed to become more and more sentimental. There was a craze for ditties like *Will You Love Me in December As You Do in May?* and *Silver Threads Among the Gold*. College songs, sometimes maudlin and sometimes ribald, were heard on campuses and at sporting events. Spanish War veterans were welcomed with an old song, WHEN JOHNNIE COMES MARCHING HOME, and in World War I our soldiers were inspired by George M. Cohan's OVER THERE, which won its composer the Congressional Medal. Jazz spread over the land, and then even more eccentric tunes. More and more the songs that became popular were first heard on the stage, the screen, or the air. Phonographs and juke boxes inundated neighborhoods with endlessly repeated tunes. Songs as sheet music or recordings sold millions of copies apiece. Great song writers appeared: Victor Herbert, Reginald De Koven, Jerome Kern, Irving Berlin, George Gershwin, Rudolph Friml, Sigmund Romberg, Cole Porter, Rodgers and Hammerstein, Lerner and Loewe, W. C. Handy.

Only a few of the many books dealing with American songs can be mentioned here: Frank Moore's *Songs and Ballads of the American Revolution* (1856); W. W. Newell's *Games and Songs of American Children* (1903); Helen K. Johnson's *Our Familiar Songs and Those Who Made Them* (1907); H. W. Odum and G. B. Johnson's *The Negro and His Songs* (1925); Alexander Woollcott's *The Story of Irving Ber-*

lin (1925); Carl Sandburg's THE AMERICAN SONGBAG (1927); Sigmund Spaeth's *They Still Sing of Love* (1929) and *A History of Popular Music* (1948); Cecil J. Sharp's *English Folk Songs from the Southern Appalachians* (1932); S. Sherwin and L. Latzman's *Songs of the Gold Miners* (1932); John Tasker Howard's *Stephen Foster* (1932; rev., 1953); E. B. Marks' *They All Sang* (1934); S. Damon Foster's *Series of Old American Songs* (1936); G. P. Jackson's *Spiritual Folk Songs of Early America* (1937); Helen L. Kaufman's *From Jehovah to Jazz* (1937); John and Alan Lomax's *Our Singing Country* (1941); W. C. Handy's *The Father of the Blues, an Autobiography* (1941); Carl Carmer's *America Sings* (1942) and *Songs of the Rivers of America* (1942); Edward Dolph's *Sound Off! Soldier Songs from the Revolution to World War II* (1942); Arthur Loesser's *Humor in American Songs* (1942); Olin Downes and Elie Singmaster's *A Treasury of American Songs* (1943); David Ewen's *Songs of America* (1947); John and Alan Lomax's *Folksong: U.S.A.* (1948); Cecil Smith's *Musical Comedy in America* (1950); Russell Ames' *Story of American Folksong* (1960); Pete Seeger's *American Favorite Ballads* (1961). See also BALLADS; MINSTREL SHOW; MUSICAL COMEDY; NEGRO SPIRITUALS; SAILOR SONGS, OSCAR GEORGE THEODORE SONNECK.

Songs of Labor and Other Poems (1850), poems by JOHN GREENLEAF WHITTIER. Whittier called these verses "my simple lays of homely toil." The *Dedication* (in verse) is followed by *The Ship-Builders, The Shoemakers, The Drovers, The Fishermen, The Huskers, The Corn-Song,* and *The Lumbermen.* The poems express much of the poet's philosophy of life, especially his belief in the nobility of manual labor; the lines are spirited and musical. Perhaps the best is *The Shoemakers,* in which he celebrates various shoemakers who had become poets. Whittier himself had earned his way through Haverhill Academy by making women's slippers and was known as "the Shoemaker Poet." The *Songs* appeared originally in the *Democratic Review* and the *National Era* in 1845–47. John A. Pollard notes that Whittier was "ahead of Whitman in celebrating the American workingman," but always with a stern emphasis on "duty done."

Songs of the Sierras (1871), poems by JOAQUIN MILLER. These were published in London as *Pacific Poems* while the Oregon poet was making a sensation by satisfying the British notion of what a Westerner should be. The poems brought him the acquaintance of many noted English writers, and reverberations reached America. In the collection Miller included poems that had already appeared in his three earlier gatherings; the verses have his characteristic rapidity of rhythm and facility of narrative.

Sonneck, Oscar George Theodore (b. Jersey City, N.J., Oct. 6, 1873—d. Oct. 30, 1928), musicologist. Educated in Germany, Sonneck returned to the United States and became active as a student and chronicler of music. In 1902 he was appointed as the first chief of the Music Division of the Library of Congress. He made many researches into early American music and gathered material for the Library that made it one of the leading music collections in the world. In 1915 he founded and was the first editor of the *Musical Quarterly.* In 1917 he left the Library to become a director and later vice-president of G. Schirmer Co. Among his books: *Bibliography of Early Secular American Music* (1905); *Early Concert Life in America* (1907); *Early Opera in America* (1915); *Beethoven Letters in America* (1927). In 1909 he prepared a careful historical report on *The Star-Spangled Banner* and other national songs.

Sonnichsen, Albert (b. San Francisco, May 5, 1878—d. Aug. 15, 1931), newspaperman, war correspondent. Sonnichsen served on the staff of the New York *Tribune,* the New York *Evening Post,* and other papers. He gathered some of his articles, with additions, in several volumes, among them *Deep Sea Vagabonds* (1903); *Ten Months a Captive Among the Filipinos* (1901); and *Confessions of a Macedonian Bandit* (1909).

Son of the Middle Border, A (1917), an autobiographical narrative by HAMLIN CARLAND. It is the most interesting volume in a series in which Carland described his own pioneering experiences in the Middle West. Garland here demonstrates the qualities that made his works unpopular at first but ultimately led to their recognition as among the earliest truthful depictions of the middle western scene. He writes feelingly of the grandeur of the prairie, but also of the endless round of chores that aged women before their time, and he reveals the selfish landholding policies that forced men like his father into what was by then a fruitless quest from frontier to frontier—the "sunset regions" of the heroic pioneers of old. The book was succeeded by A DAUGHTER OF THE MIDDLE BORDER (1921); *Trail-Makers of the Middle Border* (1926); *Memories of the Middle Border* (1926); and *Back-Trailers of the Middle Border* (1928).

Sorghum, Senator. A satirical character in the writings of PHILANDER CHASE JOHNSON, particularly his *Senator Sorghum's Primer of Politics* (1906).

Sorokin, Pitirim [Alexandrovitch] (b. Russia, Jan. 21, 1889—   ), sociologist, teacher, writer. Educated in Russia, Sorokin taught there for a while, came to this country in 1923, and was naturalized in 1930. In 1924 he began teaching at the University of Minnesota, and in 1930 was appointed to the faculty of Harvard University, where he became director of a Research Center in Creative Altruism. Among his books: *Sociology of Revolution* (1925); *A Source Book in Rural Sociology* (3 v., 1930–31); *Social and Cultural Dynamics* (4 v., 1937–41); *Crisis of Our Age* (1941); *Russia and the U.S.* (1944); *Society, Culture and Personality* (1947); *Altruistic Love* (1950); *S.O.S.: The Meaning of Our Crisis* (1951); *The Ways and*

Powers of Love (1954); *American Sex Revolution* (1957).

Sothern, E[dward] A[skew] ["Douglas Stuart"] (b. England, April 1, 1826—d. Jan. 20, 1881), English actor. Known best for his eccentric roles, Sothern became famous in 1858 when he played Lord Dundreary in Tom Taylor's *Our American Cousin*. Some critics thought he did even better in a later play, *Brother Sam*.

Sothern, E[dward] H[ugh] (b. New Orleans, Dec. 6, 1859—d. Oct. 28, 1933), actor, memoirist. Sothern was a son of E. A. Sothern; his name is closely associated with that of Julia Marlowe, whom he married (1911) after a divorce from the actress Virginia Harned. He was educated in England, originally intended to become a painter, but was irresistibly drawn to the theater. A handsome, dignified man, he proved ideally suited to light, romantic roles and won great success in such plays as *The Prisoner of Zenda, Under the Red Robe, Henry Esmond, If I Were King*. He also played Dundreary in a revival of *Our American Cousin*. He appeared with Miss Marlowe in a number of Shakespearean productions. Sothern continued on the stage until 1927, thereafter gave much of his time to lecturing and public readings. He recorded his life in an autobiography called *The Melancholy Tale of "Me"* (1916). He also wrote *Julia Marlowe's Story*, published posthumously in 1954.

Sot-Weed Factor, The; or, A Voyage to Maryland (1708), a satire by Ebenezer Cook. The author may have been, as he says in this poem, an Englishman who came to Maryland in order to act as a "factor," or agent, of a British merchant dealing in tobacco, but his true identity is problematical. The poem is a Hudibrastic narrative of the author's dealings in America, his effort to recover property stolen from him, his mistreatment in the courts; it ends with a trenchant curse on America and all its inhabitants. In 1730 appeared a sequel, *Sotweed Redivivus, or The Planter's Looking-Glass*, by "E. C. Gent." It is a much more serious and less readable production, directed against the overproduction of tobacco. In a revised version this was also printed in The Maryland Muse (1731), which was edited by Lawrence C. Wroth for the *Proceedings of the American Antiquarian Society* (1934). In 1960 John Barth published a novel, *The Sot-Weed Factor*, based on the poems.

Soule, George Henry, Jr. (b. Stamford, Conn., June 11, 1887—   ), economist. Soule served as editor on the *New Republic*, also taught economics at Rutgers, Columbia, and Bennington. In 1952 he published *Economic Forces in American History*, which Louis Hacker reviewed as "the best analysis we have of the contemporary American economic scene." Among his many other works is *American Economic History* (1957).

Souls of Black Folk, The (1903), a collection of essays by W. E. B. Du Bois. This influential volume gives, affectingly and impressively, the point of view of a Negro who believes it is beneath the dignity of a human being to beg for those rights that belong to all mankind. Du Bois presents with courage and insight the cause of the Negro in America.

Sound and the Fury, The (1929), a novel by William Faulkner. Faulkner's fourth novel, his first radical experiment in form and technique, is one of his most successful works. Three of the book's four sections are interior monologues of the three Compson brothers, who, with their hypochondriac mother and their vanished sister Caddy, are the sole surviving members of a decaying aristocratic family in Mississippi. The first section, seen through the eyes of the idiot Benjy, is literally "a tale told by an idiot, full of sound and fury." The second follows the thoughts of Quentin, a Harvard student whose world, built on a dying view of family honor and on his abnormally close ties to his sister Caddy, has been shattered by her seduction and hasty, loveless marriage. In their cryptic, often confusing changes of period, these two sections reflect respectively the disorder and the hypersensitivity of their protagonists' minds.

The third section is related in straightforward language by greedy, petty-minded Jason, who has kept for himself the money Caddy has been sending for the support of her illegitimate daughter Quentin. Quentin manages to steal it back and runs off with a traveling carnival performer. The final section is a third-person narrative focused on Dilsey, the Negro cook, whose patience and compassion are implicitly contrasted with the self-absorption and self-destructiveness of the Compsons.

Sousa, John Philip (b. Washington, D.C., Nov. 6, 1854—d. March 6, 1932), bandmaster, composer. Well educated in music, Sousa in 1880 became the bandmaster of the U.S. Marine Corps band stationed at the White House; the band soon won national fame. In 1892 he was released from duty and formed his own band, with which he toured here and abroad. He wrote music of much variety but won fame particularly with his marches: *Semper Fidelis* (1888), *Washington Post March* (1889), *The Stars and Stripes Forever* (1897), and others. He also wrote two comic operas, *El Capitan* (1896) and *The Bride Elect* (1897); and two novels, *Pipetown Sandy* (1905) and *The Fifth String* (1907). His autobiography *Marching Along* was published in 1928.

South, the. The South is the most unified, most discussed, and most self-conscious region of the United States. Ordinarily eleven states are included—Virginia, North Carolina, South Carolina, Georgia, Florida, Alabama, Mississippi, Louisiana, Kentucky, Tennessee, and Arkansas—and sometimes also Maryland, Delaware, and Missouri. The region is homogeneous partly because of the nature of the population: the majority of the whites are Protestant and of Anglo-Saxon stock. Another factor is the economic one. The South until the World Wars was an agricultural region specializing heavily in one crop—cotton. The wars cut off the demand for cotton, and the destructiveness of the boll weevil forced a rotation in crops. The result was a much more stable economic system and a tendency for the South to conform more with the other states of the Union.

The early Southern colonies were founded by English, Spanish, and French settlers with traditions and attitudes quite different from those of the English, Dutch, and German settlers of the North. Carl Bridenbaugh, in *Myths and Realities* (1952), distinguishes three "societies of the colonial South": the Chesapeake Society, which developed a firmly rooted aristocratic culture; the Carolina Coastal Society, in which a plutocracy with no sense of social and political responsibility grew up; and the "back country," the first "melting pot" of America. In early days, Southerners predominated in the winning of the West; much of the West was Southern in population and folkways during the pioneer period, as Everett Dick has shown in *The Dixie Frontier* (1948). The Reconstruction Era, bringing hardship and humiliation, gave the South a unity it had never before really possessed. The industrialization of the South was, nevertheless, inevitable, and by the mid-20th century had assumed proportions that brought the South into direct competition with New England, although the "new South" still remained largely rural.

Certain traits and ideals have characterized Southern society and culture: assumption of aristocracy, with a chivalrous code strongly under the influence of Sir Walter Scott; romanticism and sentimentality, nurtured by the plantation system and finding expression especially in the idealization of Southern womanhood; courtesy and lavish hospitality; hatred of the Yankees and Yankee ways; devotion to the Democratic Party; intolerance and violence in such matters as religious faith, states' rights, white supremacy, labor unions. The middle decades of the 20th century saw a southern literary revolt in which realism in the raw exposed much of the earlier sentimentality as unreal and insincere. Particularly on the issue of white supremacy, the number of persons who have the courage to speak against the prevailing bias is increasing constantly. However, the legend of the romantic South, the South of the chivalrous Virginia planter, persists. Writers such as ELLEN GLASGOW and WILLIAM FAULKNER have sought to dispel the legend, but Miss Glasgow found herself increasingly in sympathy with the ideals of the Old South, and Faulkner has virtually created a new legend.

The South has produced many notable writers. During the early days of the Union some of the greatest governmental documents were written by southerners—George Wythe, Thomas Jefferson, James Madison, James Monroe, John Marshall, and others. Somewhat later came W. G. Simms, Edgar Allan Poe, Thomas Holley Chivers, as well as frontier types like Davy Crockett and humorists like Augustus Baldwin Longstreet. Political and religious oratory found an especially enthusiastic audience in an area where large numbers were unable to read. The recognized master of invective in Southern oratory was John Randolph, who gave his bitter gibes a high literary polish. The greatest Southern thinker was John C. Calhoun, a persuasive orator and an original philosopher.

The Civil War produced surprisingly little first-rate imaginative writing. John Esten Cooke, Charles Henry Smith (Bill Arp), Henry Timrod, Paul Hamilton Hayne, John B. Tabb wrote during this period; Joel Chandler Harris' Uncle Remus tales and Roark Bradford delved fruitfully into Negro folklore. Some years later came such writers as Sidney Lanier, T. N. Page, George W. Cable, and Mary Noailles Murfree.

In the 20th century a host of Southern authors suddenly appeared. In fiction there were Elizabeth Madox Roberts, DuBose and Dorothy Hayward, Ellen Glasgow, William Faulkner, Thomas Wolfe, Erskine Caldwell, James Branch Cabell, Eudora Welty, Katherine Anne Porter, Jesse Stuart, Stark Young, Caroline Gordon, Irvin S. Cobb, James Boyd, Robert Penn Warren, Carson McCullers, Hamilton Basso, Truman Capote, Josephine Pinckney, and many others. Outstanding poets included Conrad Aiken, John Peale Bishop, Lizette Woodworth Reese, Madison Cawein, John Gould Fletcher, John Crowe Ransom, James Weldon Johnson, Allen Tate, Robert Penn Warren, Randall Jarrell. There was also a fine crop of Southern critics. Tate, Ransom, Warren, Bishop, Cleanth Brooks, Robert B. Heilman. Paul Green and Tennessee Williams are the most famous modern Southern playwrights.

The Negro music of the South exerted a general influence and was widely imitated by white musicians. Ironically enough, the most popular "songs of the South" were written by northerners: Stephen Collins Foster, a native of Pittsburgh, and D. D. Emmett, who wrote *Dixie*. Jazz and the blues began in the South, particularly in New Orleans and Memphis; most of the most famous jazz musicians and composers have been southern-born Negroes like Louis Armstrong and W. C. Handy.

Fictional works on the South abound, and only a few can be mentioned: Richard Hildreth's THE SLAVE (1836); Harriet Beecher Stowe's UNCLE TOM'S CABIN (1852) and DRED (1856); G. W. Harris' SUT LOVINGOOD YARNS (1867); Mark Twain's TOM SAWYER (1876), HUCKLEBERRY FINN (1884), and PUDD'NHEAD WILSON (1894); G. W. Cable's OLD CREOLE DAYS (1879), THE GRANDISSIMES (1880), *Bonaventure* (1888), and *John March, Southerner* (1894); F. Hopkinson Smith's COLONEL CARTER OF CARTERSVILLE (1891); James Lane Allen's A KENTUCKY CARDINAL (1894); Lafcadio Hearn's CHITA (1889); John Fox, Jr.'s THE LITTLE SHEPHERD OF KINGDOM COME (1903) and THE TRAIL OF THE LONESOME PINE (1908); Thomas Dixon's *The Clansman* (1905); Irvin S. Cobb's OLD JUDGE PRIEST (1915); Julia Peterkin's SCARLET SISTER MARY (1928); William Faulkner's SARTORIS (1929), THE SOUND AND THE FURY (1929), INTRUDER IN THE DUST (1948), and others; Thomas Wolfe's LOOK

HOMEWARD ANGEL (1929); Marjorie Kinnan Rawlings' SOUTH MOON UNDER (1933) and THE YEARLING (1938); Zora Neale Hurston's *Jonah's Gourd Vine* (1934); Margaret Mitchell's GONE WITH THE WIND (1936); Stark Young's *So Red the Rose* (1938); Carson McCullers' THE HEART IS A LONELY HUNTER (1940), *Reflections in a Golden Eye* (1941), THE MEMBER OF THE WEDDING (1946), *The Ballad of the Sad Café* (1951), and *Clock Without Hands* (1961); Lillian Smith's STRANGE FRUIT (1944); Eudora Welty's *Delta Wedding* (1946); Robert Penn Warren's ALL THE KING'S MEN (1946), *The Cave* (1950), and *Wilderness* (1961); Calder Willingham's *End as a Man* (1947); Lael Tucker's *Lament for Four Virgins* (1952); Jefferson Young's *A Good Man* (1953); Tennessee Williams' THE GLASS MENAGERIE (1944), A STREETCAR NAMED DESIRE (1947), THE ROSE TATTOO (1951), *Orpheus Descending* (1957), and *Suddenly, Last Summer* (1958); William Styron's LIE DOWN IN DARKNESS (1951), *The Long March* (1952), and *Set This House on Fire* (1960); Flannery O'Connor's *A Good Man Is Hard to Find* (1955) and *The Violent Bear It Away* (1960); James Agee's *A Death in the Family* (1957); Harper Lee's *To Kill a Mockingbird* (1960).

Nonfiction about the South includes, among many other books: William Byrd's HISTORY OF THE DIVIDING LINE (written, 1729; pub., 1841) and A JOURNEY TO THE LAND OF EDEN (written, 1733; pub., 1841); William Bartram's *Travels* (1791); J. K. Paulding's *Letters from the South* (2 v., 1817); John T. Trowbridge's *The South* (1866); Thomas Nelson Page's *The Old South* (1892); Edwin P. Shurter's *Oratory in the South* (1908); John T. Faris' *Seeing the Sunny South* (1921); N. I. White's *American Negro Folk Songs* (1928); Allen Tate's I'LL TAKE MY STAND (a symposium, 1930); Virginius Dabney's *Liberalism in the South* (1932); and *Below the Potomac* (1942); Arthur Palmer Hudson's *Humor of the Old South* (an anthology, 1936); Stark Young's *A Southern Treasury* (an anthology, 1937); Jonathan Daniels' *A Southerner Discovers the South* (1938), *Tar Heels* (1941), and *Frontier on the Potomac* (1946); W. J. Cash's *Mind of the South* (1941); Wendell M. Stephenson and E. Merton Coulter's *A History of the South* (10 v., 1947 and later); Lilliam Smith's *Killers of the Dream* (1949); R. G. Osterweis' *Romanticism and Nationalism in the Old South* (1949); B. A. Botkin's *A Treasury of Southern Folklore* (1949); Hodding Carter's *Southern Legacy* (1950); C. Vann Woodward's *Origins of the New South, 1877–1913* (1951); Avery O. Craven's *The Growth of Southern Nationalism* (1953); William T. Polk's *Southern Accent* (1953); Jay B. Hubbell's *The South in American Literature, 1607–1900* (1954); Clement Eaton's *History of the Southern Confederacy* (1954); Cornelia Hancock's *After Gettysburg* (letters, 1956); Robert Penn Warren's *Segregation: The Inner Conflict* (1956).

Southern Literary Messenger, The. This magazine was founded in Richmond, Va., by T. W. White in August, 1834. EDGAR ALLAN POE's *Berenice* was printed in the March, 1835, issue, *The Unparalleled Adventures of One Hans Pfaal* in June, 1835; in December of that year Poe assumed the editorship. His scathing book reviews and stimulating critical essays gave the magazine a wide reputation, as did the stories he contributed; he raised its circulation from 500 to 3,500. But he received small compensation and smaller appreciation from White, and he left the magazine in 1837. He was succeeded by Matthew F. Maury, who served until 1843. Maury, a celebrated naval officer and oceanographer, contributed a series of articles under the pen name Harry Bluff which brought on a much-needed reorganization of the Navy. George W. Bagby was editor from 1860 to 1864, when the magazine ceased publication. Revived in 1939 by the Dietz Press, it frequently reprinted contributions of Poe to the original magazine. Benjamin B. Minor wrote *The Southern Literary Messenger, 1834–64* (1905); David K. Jackson described *Poe and the Southern Literary Messenger* (1934) and *The Contributors and Contributions to the Southern Literary Messenger* (1936).

Southern Review [1] The first of the magazines so-called was founded in 1828, at Charleston, S.C., by Stephen Eliott and HUGH SWINTON LEGARÉ, and expired four years later. The two men gave their quarterly magazine a high literary tone and sought to foster literature in the South without becoming chauvinistic.

[2] A quarterly with the same name was published in Baltimore from January, 1867, to October, 1879. It was founded by A. T. Bledsoe and Sophia Bledsoe Herrick and was an ardent advocate of southern ideas and writers, with PAUL HAMILTON HAYNE as its chief critic.

[3] The third magazine called *Southern Review* was also a quarterly, published at Louisiana State University from July, 1935, to April, 1942, under a succession of editors—C. W. Pipkin, CLEANTH BROOKS, and ROBERT PENN WARREN. It became one of the more important "little magazines." In its critical essays it aligned itself with the New Critics and their techniques of close textual examination of poems. It had many notable contributors, among them John Crowe Ransom, F. O. Matthiessen, Yvor Winters, Wallace Stevens, W. H. Auden, Randall Jarrell, Donald Davidson, Mark Van Doren, Caroline Gordon, Katherine Anne Porter, and Eudora Welty. *Stories from the Southern Review* (1953) was edited by Brooks and Warren.

Southern Vanguard, A. See JOHN PEALE BISHOP.

South in American Literature, The (1954), a literary history by Jay B. Hubbell. A carefully documented but sometimes pedantic history of Southern writing from the beginning until 1900. This is probably the best work of its kind, and though written with obvious affection for the subject, is an impartial study; Professor Hubbell considers only two Southern writers, Poe and Mark Twain, as artists of the first rank.

South Moon Under (1933), a novel by MAR-JORIE KINNAN RAWLINGS. Mrs. Rawlings' first novel makes use of her favorite setting—Florida. Her hero, Lant Jackson, is a hunter and prefers the wilds to the urban communities that encroach upon his domain.

South-Sea Idyls (1873), a travel book by CHARLES WARREN STODDARD. William Dean Howells described it as "the lightest, sweetest, wildest things that ever were written about the life of the summer ocean." It is still one of the best books about life in the South Seas.

Southwest, the. This region comprises Texas, Oklahoma, Arizona, and New Mexico. John W. Caughey, a specialist in western history, also includes much of Colorado, Utah, Nevada, and southern California. The region contains a great area of desert land; it is also a land of mountains and in recent years has outstripped the Northwest in building urban areas. Much of it is arid, but irrigation has turned large sections into fertile farmland. The cowboy, the oil millionaire, and more recently the atomic scientist are three characteristic inhabitants of the area.

The Grand Canyon and other places of extraordinary beauty and appeal attract millions of tourists annually. But the historic sites of the Southwest are of equal interest. Remnants of four cultures are found almost everywhere in the region. First was the Indian culture. Many of the Indians dwelt in villages consisting of flat-roofed communal dwellings called *pueblos*, and were thus called Pueblo Indians; among these were the Hopi and the Zuñi tribes, whose legendary riches in the "Seven Cities of Cibola" attracted CORONADO. Today many other tribes are found in the Southwest, particularly in Oklahoma, once known as Indian Territory. The Spaniards came north from the conquered lands of Mexico. These expeditions, it has been said, began "the winning of the West." The Spanish influence altered with the years and became Mexican—part Caucasian, part Amerindian. As the Anglo-Saxon "mountain man" penetrated farther south and west, conflict was inevitable, as Robert Glass Cleland shows in THIS RECKLESS BREED OF MEN: THE TRAPPERS AND FUR TRADERS OF THE SOUTHWEST (1950). The clash, which came in Texas, ended with the foundation of a republic now part of the United States and a war that brought about the annexation of a rich territory in the Southwest. Since then the culture of the United States has dominated the region—without, however, destroying the cultures that preceded it. One student of the Southwest spoke of it as "the least American of all the regions."

There are many fine art museums in the Southwest, and creative art centers are found in many places, particularly in New Mexico at Taos, Albuquerque, and Santa Fe. Since the beginning of the 20th century, Southwestern

universities have moved to the front in educational and scientific activity. Architecture has been deeply influenced by Indian and Spanish styles and techniques. Frank Lloyd Wright worked with the Taliesen Fellowship in studios and workshops near Phoenix to produce a typical Southwestern style in architecture.

Fiction about the Southwest for many decades followed the tradition of the dime novel and Wild Western story, with novels like Stewart Edward White's *Arizona Nights* (1907) and Zane Grey's *The Thundering Herd* (1925). During the 1920's, however, New Mexico was "rediscovered," particularly under the influence of the English writer D. H. LAWRENCE. Some of the better novels about the region include: Mary Austin's *Isidro* (1905); Harvey Fergusson's *Blood of the Conquerors* (1921), *In Those Days* (1936), and *Conquest of Dom Pedro* (1954); Willa Cather's DEATH COMES FOR THE ARCHBISHOP (1927); Oliver LaFarge's LAUGHING BOY (1929); Edna Ferber's CIMARRON (1930); Paul Horgan's *Return of the Weed* (1936), *Far from Cibala* (1938), and other books; Conrad Richter's THE SEA OF GRASS (1937) and other books; Stanley Vestal's *Revolt on the Border* (1938); John Steinbeck's THE GRAPES OF WRATH (1939); Paul I. Wellman's *Jubal Troop* (1939) and *The Iron Mistress* (1951); Virginia Hersch's *The Seven Cities of Gold* (1946).

There are many nonfiction works dealing with the history, literature, and local color of the Southwest. Among them: Zebulon M. Pike's *Southwestern Expedition* (1810); Josiah Gregg's *Commerce of the Prairies* (2 v., 1844) and *Diary and Letters* (2 v., 1941, 1948); Mary Austin's LAND OF LITTLE RAIN (1903) and *The American Rhythm* (1923); Ernest Peixotto's *Our Historic Southwest* (1916); H. E. Bolton's *Spanish Exploration in the Southwest, 1542–1706* (1916) and *Coronado* (1949); Constance Lindsay Skinner's *Pioneers of the Old Southwest* (1919); E. Douglas Branch's *The Cowboy and His Interpreters* (1926); Mabel Major and Rebecca W. Smith's *The Southwest in Literature* (an anthology, 1929); J. Frank Dobie's *Coronado's Children* (1931); *The Longhorns* (1941); *The Voice of the Coyote* (1949); and *The Mustangs* (1952); Paul I. Wellman's *Death in the Desert* (1934) and *Glory, God, and Gold* (1954); G. W. Kendall's *Narrative of the Santa Fé Expedition* (2 v., facsimile reproduction, 1935); Erna Fergusson's *Our Southwest* (1940) and *New Mexico: A Pageant of Three Peoples* (1952); G. P. Hammond and Agapito Rey's edition of *Narratives of the Coronado Expedition, 1540–42* (1940); Cleve Hallenbeck's *Alvar Nuñez Cabeza de Vaca* (1940) and *Sun Chief: The Autobiography of a Hopi Indian* (1942); George Sessions Perry's *Roundup Time, a Collection of Southwestern Writing* (1943); *Southwesterners Write* (an anthology, 1947); Joseph Wood Krutch's *The Desert Year* (1952). Paul Horgan's *Great River: The Rio Grande in North American History* (2 v., 1954) is a magnificent survey of the region, and J. Frank Dobie's *Life and Literature of the Southwest* (1942, rev. 1952) is the best introduction to Southwestern writing. Edwin W. Gaston, Jr., wrote *The Early Novel of the Southwest* (1961). In addition, the Southwest has produced a great body of folklore and song, some of which was collected by B. A. Botkin in *The Southwest Scene* (1931) and *A Treasury of Western Folklore* (1951).

Southwick, Solomon (b. Newport, R.I., Dec. 25, 1773—d. Nov. 18, 1839), poet, editor. Southwick was editor of the Albany *Register* from 1808 to 1817. In 1819 he founded *The Ploughboy,* one of the earliest newspapers intended for farmers, and wrote articles for it under a pen name that became famous—Henry Homespun, Jr. In 1823 he published a long didactic poem, *The Pleasures of Poverty,* and, in 1837, *Five Lessons for Young Men.*

Southworth, E[mma] D[orothy] E[liza] N[evitte] (b. Washington, D.C., Dec. 26, 1819 —d. June 30, 1899), novelist. One of the most prolific and most widely read novelists of her day, Mrs. Southworth is now hardly remembered. She married in 1841, was deserted two years later by her husband, and with two children to support turned to teaching and writing to make a living. Her first novel, *Retribution,* was published in 1847. THE HIDDEN HAND (1859), her greatest triumph was serialized in *The New York Ledger* and was dramatized by Robert Jones (1867, pub. 1889). She went on to write more than sixty novels which sold altogether millions of copies. Her earlier work showed the realistic influence of her own harsh experience, but she was gradually led into what Mary Noel calls "heaven-sent catastrophes, paired off with equally heaven-sent deliverances" by her editor, Robert Bonner. Among her books: *The Curse of Clifton* (1852); *The Missing Bride* (1855); ISHMAEL, OR, IN THE DEPTHS (1863); *Self-Raised, or From the Depths* (1864); *The Fatal Marriage* (1869); *The Maiden Widow* (1870); *A Leap in the Dark* (1881). In 1872 her *Works* (42 v.) were published. Regis Louise Boyle wrote *Mrs. E. D. E. N. Southworth, Novelist* as a doctoral dissertation in 1939.

Sovereignty and Goodness of God, The. See under CAPTIVITY AND RESTAURATION OF MRS. MARY ROWLANDSON.

Sowerby, Leo (b. Grand Rapids, Mich., May 1, 1895—d. July 7, 1968), composer. Sowerby began in somewhat conventional style, but under the influence of Percy Grainger and English folk singers he developed a style of his own. Many of his compositions stem from American scenes and from literature. *Come Autumn Time* (1916), and overture, was inspired by Bliss Carman's poem *Autumn.* A choral work with orchestra was based (1925) on Lowell's *Vision of Sir Launfal.* One of his finest works is an orchestral piece entitled *Prairie* (1929), based on a poem by Carl Sandburg. In 1946 another choral work, based on St. Francis of Assisi's *Canticle of the Sun,* was awarded a Pulitzer prize.

Spaeth, Sigmund (b. Philadelphia, April 10, 1885—d. Nov. 11, 1965), musicologist. Spaeth took a Ph.D. degree at Princeton University with a thesis on *Milton's Knowledge of Music,* went on to serve as a music critic on the old *Life,* several New York City newspapers, and several magazines. He went into business, conducted tours to music festivals in Europe, ran a syndicated column on music, conducted a program on the air in which he dissected various popular songs. He became known as "The Tune Detective." He wrote or edited many informative and vivacious books on music. Among them: *The Common Sense of Music* (1924); *Barber Shop Ballads* (1925); *Words and Music* (1926); *Read 'Em and Weep* (1926, rev. 1960); *American Mountain Songs* (1927); *Gentlemen, Be Seated* (1928); *The Art of Enjoying Music* (1933); *Great Symphonies* (1936); *Music for Fun* (1939); *Guide to Great Orchestral Music* (1943); *History of Popular Music in America* (1948); *Dedication: The Love Story of Clara and Robert Schumann* (1950); *Fun with Music* (1951); *Real Book About Music* (1953); *Fifty Years with Music* (1959).

Spain and Spanish influence in the New World. Spain's conquest of the greatest empire in all history presents two figures side by side, the conquistador and the Jesuit priest. Columbus' discoveries were consolidated by the conquistadors. Portugal seized a great realm on the east coast of South America; and when word of the richness and extent of the new lands reached other European nations, the French, English, and Dutch began to loot the Spanish Empire. The last Spanish outposts in the New World fell in the SPANISH-AMERICAN WAR. However, Spanish culture survives vigorously in the eighteen Latin-American republics which were carved from the Empire; together they occupy about 4,500,000 square miles of territory and possess a population of about 100 million.

The history of Mexico over the centuries is approximately typical. For three hundred years it was a Spanish colony. During this period education was promoted and printing presses established; more than 10,000 churches were built, some of great beauty. Fierce conflict between the white man and the Indian marked Spanish advances on every frontier, as Philip Wayne Powell showed in *Soldiers, Indians, and Silver: The Northward Advance of New Spain, 1550–1600* (1952). But it should also be pointed out that the Spaniards were more successful in assimilating native populations and cultures than the Anglo-Saxon conquerors to the north.

In the United States Florida was one Spanish outpost, the Southwest another, California still another. Spain sent its viceroys to organize governmental control. The Jesuits and Franciscans hastened on their missions among the Indian tribes; their *Relations* are among the most important early documents about the New World.

The Southwest is still deeply imbued with Spanish influence. In New Mexico the legislature is officially bilingual. Through Mexico, as J. Frank Dobie points out in *Life and Literature of the Southwest* (rev. ed., 1952), "the Spaniards have had had an abiding influence on the architecture and language of the Southwest. They gave us our most distinctive occupation, ranching on the open range. They influenced mining greatly, and our land and irrigation laws still go back to Spanish and Mexican sources."

Spanish-speaking groups have offered some problems of assimilation. Mexicans in search of work have sought entry across the Mexican border, sometimes by swimming the Rio Grande (the so-called "wetbacks"); legal and illegal entrants are found in considerable numbers in Texas, California, and elsewhere. Great numbers of Puerto Ricans, who are American citizens, though most have clung to Spanish as a mother tongue, have entered the United States to congregate in New York City and other cities. The Puerto Ricans have often lived under wretched conditions in the worst urban slums. John H. Burma wrote a documented account of *Spanish-Speaking Groups in the U.S.* (1954).

Useful accounts of Spanish influence are Aurora Lea's *Literary Folklore of the Hispanic Southwest* (1953) and Stanley T. Williams' *Spanish Background of American Literature* (2 v., 1955).

Devoted to Spain and its conquests is Archibald MacLeish's poem CONQUISTADOR (1932). This was based on Bernal Díaz Castillo's account (1632) of the Spanish conquest of Mexico. Eugene O'Neill made good use of the Ponce de León story of the Fountain of Youth in his play THE FOUNTAIN (prod., 1925). Novels about the Spaniards in the New World include: Charles Kingsley's *Westward Ho!* (1855); Lew Wallace's THE FAIR GOD (1873); Joseph Conrad's *Nostromo* (1904); Peter B. Kyne's *Tide of Empire* (1927); Thornton Wilder's THE BRIDGE OF SAN LUIS REY (1927); Vicente Blasco Ibáñez's *Unknown Lands* (1929) and *Knight of the Virgin* (1930); Gladys Malvern's *If Love Comes* (1932); Honoré Willsie Morrow's *Beyond the Blue Sierra* (1932); Blair Niles' *Maria Paluna* (1934) and *Day of Immense Sun* (1936); John Steinbeck's TORTILLA FLAT (1935) and THE PEARL (1948); Kyle Crichton's *The Proud People* (1940); James Branch Cabell's *First Gentleman of America* (1942); Samuel Shellabarger's CAPTAIN FROM CASTILE (1945).

Spanish-American War. This conflict marked the definite appearance of the United States as a leading world power. The war was brought on by various causes, particularly the oppressive rule of Spain in Cuba. Soon after WILLIAM McKINLEY became President in 1896 a new Cuban rebellion broke out. It was ferociously suppressed by the Spanish General Valeriano Weyler, and the American "yellow press" fanned public opinion against Spain. After further provocative incidents came the sinking of the United States battleship *Maine* (Feb. 15, 1898) in Havana harbor (see entry REMEMBER THE MAINE). Despite his sincere efforts to avoid war, the President was forced by popular clamor to send a message to the Congress asking for the "forcible intervention" of the United States to establish peace in Cuba. This was done in a joint resolution, which stated that Cuba would be left to its own people after peace had been declared. McKinley signed the resolution on April 20; a blockade of Cuba was inaugurated on April 22; Spain declared war on the United States April 24.

On May 1 Admiral George Dewey won the resounding victory of Manila Bay, as a result of which the Philippines fell into American hands. Cuba was invaded and Spanish forces were defeated at the Battles of El Caney and San Juan Hill (June 30, 1898). A great naval victory was won in Santiago Harbor (July 3). Santiago surrendered on July 17. On July 26 Spain sued for peace. In the treaty of peace the United States gave Spain 20 million dollars in payment for the Philippines; Puerto Rico and Guam were ceded to this country. After the war came a strong anti-imperialist movement, fostered by such diverse personalities as Senator George F. Hoar of Massachusetts, Samuel Gompers, Andrew Carnegie, Jane Addams, and William Vaughn Moody. THEODORE ROOSEVELT's dramatic participation in the war brought him the vice-presidential nomination in 1900 and, after McKinley's death, the presidency. The war made him one of the great folk heroes of American history.

The finest piece of literature that arose out of this conflict was published before the war began, Stephen Crane's THE OPEN BOAT (1897). This narrative relates Crane's experiences in a lifeboat after the vessel in which he was trying to get to Cuba was wrecked off the Florida coast. Later Crane served as war correspondent in Cuba, helped wounded men under fire, and wrote some memorable stories, collected in *Wounds in the Rain* (1900). Richard Harding Davis, a war correspondent on the same front, wrote about Crane in *Notes of a War Correspondent* (1910) and in several articles. He also wrote *Cuba in War Time* (1897) and *The Cuban and Puerto Rican Campaigns* (1898). Frank Norris was also on the scene, reporting the war for *McClure's Magazine*. Two contemporary poems, Richard Hovey's *Unmanifest Destiny* (1898) and John Jerome Rooney's *The Men Behind the Guns* (1898), have definitely survived the war; Elbert Hubbard's A MESSAGE TO GARCIA (1899) had a circulation of more than forty million copies. The favorite marching song of the soldiers in the war was A HOT TIME IN THE OLD TOWN TONIGHT (1896), by Joe Hayden and Theodore A. Metz.

Unquestionably the best treatment of the Spanish-American War is Walter Millis' *The Martial Spirit* (1931). Other nonfiction books on the conflict include Stephen Bonsal's *The Fight for Santiago* (1899); George Kennan's

Campaigning in Cuba (1899); Harry Thurston Peck's *Twenty Years of the Republic* (1906); George Dewey's *Autobiography* (1913); C. E. Chapman's *The Cuban Republic* (1927); M. M. Wilkerson's *Public Opinion in the Spanish-American War* (1932); J. W. Pratt's *Expansionists of 1898* (1936). Among novels on the war are Joseph Hergesheimer's THE BRIGHT SHAWL (1922); Hermann Hagedorn's *The Rough Riders* (1927); Elswyth Thane's *Ever After* (1945); Conrad Richter's *Always Young and Fair* (1947).

Spanish Bayonet (1926), a historical novel by STEPHEN VINCENT BENÉT.

Spanish Main, the. Originally this term was applied to the *mainland* of South America or to a portion bordering on the Caribbean Sea from the Isthmus of Panama to the Orinoco River. The term is also customarily applied to the whole Caribbean area, through which Spanish ships loaded with gold would sail on their way home. With the defeat of the Spanish Armada by England (1588), this region became the happy hunting ground of buccaneers who in the name of England looted the Spanish galleons. Their cry was "Westward Ho!"—a slogan which Charles Kingsley adopted as the title of a novel (1855) that depicts the spirit of these Elizabethan adventurers. Later pirates who invaded this region are presented in Rafael Sabatini's CAPTAIN BLOOD (1922). Philip Ainsworth Means' *The Spanish Main* (1935) is a good account of the region.

Spanish Student, The (pub. serially, 1842; in book form, 1843), a dramatic poem by HENRY WADSWORTH LONGFELLOW. It was one of several poems which Longfellow wrote on Spanish themes. In the introduction he acknowledges his indebtedness to *La Gitanilla*, a story by Cervantes, also to three Spanish plays. Preciosa, the daughter of a nobleman, is stolen by gypsies, becomes a dancer, is wooed by a young man of high birth, and marries him when she is discovered to be of good family. The work contains a pleasing lyric, *Serenade*, which was set to music and became the best known of Longfellow's songs. Edgar Allan Poe, when he reviewed the play, attacked Longfellow as a plagiarist, charging that it contained passages stolen from his own dramatic fragment, *Politian.* Longfellow's play was never produced in his lifetime in this country, but was staged in the city of Dessau in Germany (1855) in a German version by Adolf Boettger.

Spargo, John (b. England, Jan. 31, 1876 —), socialist reformer, museum director, historian. Spargo came to the United States in 1901. In England he had been identified with the socialist cause, and in this country he continued to write and lecture in behalf of reform and as a Socialist party worker. In 1917, however, he left the party because of its opposition to World War I, founding, with Samuel Gompers, the "American Alliance for Labor and Democracy" and the Nationalist Party; in the 1920's he became director and curator of the Bennington, Vt., Historical Museum and Art Gallery. He wrote a great many books, among them *The Bitter Cry of the Children* (1906); *Forces That Make for Socialism in America* (1906); *The Socialism of William Morris* (1908); *Karl Marx, His Life and Works* (1909); *Americanism and Social Democracy* (1918); *Bolshevism, The Enemy of Political and Industrial Democracy* (1919); *Russia as the American Problem* (1920); *The Bennington Battle Monument and Its Story* (1925); *The Epic of Fort Massachusetts* (1933); *Behold the Splendor of Champlain* (1938); *Covered Wooden Bridges of Bennington and Vicinity* (1953).

Sparks, Jared (b. Willington, Conn., May 10, 1789—d. March 14, 1866), clergyman, historian, teacher, editor. Sparks taught at Harvard, his alma mater, from 1817 to 1819, while editing the NORTH AMERICAN REVIEW. Then he served as pastor of a Unitarian church in Baltimore, also as chaplain of the House of Representatives. In 1823 he bought the *North American Review* and edited it until 1829; under his control it became one of the most influential magazines in the United States. In the meantime he had become deeply interested in the history of the American Revolution, editing the diplomatic correspondence of the Revolution (12 v., 1829–30), the writings of Washington (12 v., 1834–38), the works of Benjamin Franklin (10 v., 1836–40), and other collections; he also wrote lives of Benedict Arnold, Ethan Allen, Marquette, La Salle, and others, and edited two series of a *Library of American Biography* (10 v., 1834–38); 15 v., 1844–47), himself contributing eight of the sixty sketches. In addition Sparks founded and edited the *American Almanac and Repository of Useful Knowledge* (1830–61). In 1839 he became professor of history at Harvard, and in 1849 president of the university.

Sparks did much in his own day to make the writing and reading of American biography and history popular. He was one of the first to go to manuscript sources. However, he has fallen into disrepute as a scholar, chiefly because he sometimes presented bowdlerized or incomplete texts of the works he edited without indicating his part in the final product. H. B. Adams edited the *Life and Writings of Jared Sparks* (2 v., 1893). See JOHN LEDYARD.

Sparrowgrass Papers, The (1856; reprinted, 1869), humorous sketches by FREDERICK SWARTHOUT COZZENS.

Spartacus to the Gladiators (1846), a declamation composed by ELIJAH KELLOGG. Spartacus, a Thracian gladiator, organized a slave revolt in Rome (72 B.C.) which for a time appeared as if it might be successful; he was finally defeated and killed. Kellogg, a Congregational minister who wrote many books for children, published his declamation first in Epes Sargent's *School Reader.* It became immediately popular and remained for several generations a favorite piece for recitations.

Spaulding, Solomon (b. Ashford, Conn. [?], 1761—d. Oct. 20, 1816), clergyman, businessman, novelist. Spaulding occupied pulpits in several New England towns, but left the ministry in 1795 and went into commercial pursuits. In 1812 he published a romance entitled *The Manuscript Found*, an account of pre-Columbian America; the manuscript itself was supposed to have been discovered in an ancient mound. The charge was later made that JOSEPH SMITH and Sidney Rigdon had seen the manuscript before its publication and had used it in writing *The Book of Mormon* (1830). Spaulding's book was reprinted by the Mormons (1885).

Specimen Days and Collect, a collection of WALT WHITMAN's diaries, notes, and essays first published in 1882 by Rees Welsh in Philadelphia and republished later that year by David McKay as *Specimen Days*. The book begins with accounts of the poet's ancestry and boyhood on Long Island, but more extensive coverage is given to his experiences during the Civil War. Many of these paragraphs were transcribed from the notebooks he carried with him through the hospitals on his visits to the soldiers; others were jotted down during visits to recent battlefields or while staying in army camps. Although Whitman finally decided that "the real war will never get into the books," his own accounts of the war have both historical and literary value. In calmer mood, *Specimen Days and Collect* then shifts to the Indian summer of Whitman's old age, when, after suffering paralysis on his left side, he partly regained his health by sunbathing and mild exercise at Timber Creek, on a farm several miles from Camden, New Jersey. Many of the nature notes recorded under these circumstances have real charm. The "Collect" is a miscellaneous collection of essays on many subjects, but mostly literary. They have less value than the more personal "Specimen Days" of the war years and old-age invalidism. This book also contained, as an appendix, some samples of Whitman's juvenilia.

Specimens of American Poetry, with Critical and Biographical Notices (3 v., 1829), edited by SAMUEL KETTELL. This was one of the earliest collections of American verse; it also contained a "Catalogue of American Poetry" in the third volume. Its selections ranged from Cotton Mather to Whittier.

Specimens of the American Poets, with Critical Notices and a Preface (1822). This anthology, printed in London, does not give the name of the editor, but Jay B. Hubbell identified him as Israel Keech Tefft. The collections included the whole of William Cullen Bryant's *Poems* (1821) and almost the whole of Fitz-Greene Halleck's *Fanny* (1819).

Speck, Frank G[ouldsmith] (b. Brooklyn, N.Y., Nov. 8, 1881—d. Feb. 6, 1950), teacher, anthropologist. Speck concentrated on the ethnology and linguistics of the Indian, and was also an authority on archaeology, religion, primitive art, and sociology as these were related to the red man. He served for many years as professor of anthropology at the University of Pennsylvania. Among his books: *Ceremonial Songs of the Creek and Yuchi Indians* (1911); *Penobscot Shamanism* (1920); *The Rappahannock Indians of Virginia* (1925); *Native Tribes and Dialects of Connecticut* (1926); *A Study of the Delaware Indian Big House Ceremony* (1931); *The Midwinter Rites of the Cayuga Long House* (1949).

Spectorsky, Auguste Comte (b. France, Aug. 13, 1910—), editor, author, publisher. Spectorsky's *The Exurbanites* (1955), a sardonic look at the social and moral behavior of the counties just outside of suburbia, brought him his greatest success. He was an associate editor on *The New Yorker* (1938–41), an editor of *Charm, Playboy,* and *Park East* magazines, and a story editor for 20th Century-Fox, for whom he purchased *Letter to Three Wives* and *Gentlemen's Agreement.* He edited *The College Years* (1958), an anthology intended, he wrote, to hold up "the literary mirror to college life in all its aspects." Among his books: *Invitation to Skiing* (1947); *Man into Beast* (1948); *The Book of the Sea* (1954); *The Book of the Mountains* (1955); *The Book of the Sky* (1956); *The New Invitation to Skiing* (1958).

Spectra and the Spectrist School. This alleged school and the poems published as *Spectra: A Book of Poetic Experiments* (1916) constitute one of the most amusing hoaxes in literary history. The hoaxers were WITTER BYNNER, who called himself Emanuel Morgan, and ARTHUR DAVISON FICKE, who called himself Anne Knish. Bynner told the story of the hoax in a letter to *Word Study* (October, 1948): "In 1915, irked by the prevalence of what seemed to me pretentious poetic groups calling themselves 'Imagist,' 'Vorticist,' etc., I was prompted to found a school myself. . . ." Inspired by Nijinsky's performance in *Le Spectre de la Rose*, he and Ficke wrote their "Spectric" poems. "The school attained fame and following," Bynner continued, "and was taken seriously for nearly two years. . . . I myself actually wrote a glowing review of the book for the *New Republic*—by request." Anne Knish and Emanuel Morgan composed a panegyric *The Spectric School of Poetry*, which *Forum* published in June, 1916. William J. Smith told the story in *The Spectra Hoax* (1961).

Spectre Bridegroom, The (1819), a story by WASHINGTON IRVING, included in *The Sketch Book.* It tells how Sir Hermann von Starkenfaust gains the bride supposed to marry a friend of his by playing the role of a spectre; his friend is dead. It is one of the tales that shows the strong influence of German romanticism on Irving at this time.

Speiser, Ephraim Avigdor (b. Spain, Jan. 24, 1902—), Orientalist, archaeologist, teacher. Speiser came to the United States in 1920, was naturalized in 1926. He joined the faculty of the University of Pennsylvania in 1924. He did important research work as an archaeologist in Iraq and Mesopotamia, and during World War II he was chief of the Near East Section of the Office of Strategic Services. Among his books: *Mesopotamian Origins* (1930); *Excavations at Tepe Gawra* (1935); *The U.S. and the Near East* (1947; rev., 1950); *Akkadian Myths and Epics* (1950).

Spence, Hartzell (b. Clarion, Iowa, Feb. 15, 1908—   ), novelist, biographer. Spence helped found and edit the army weekly, YANK, in 1942. His best-known books are mellow reminiscences of his early youth and of his father, a Methodist minister. Typical are the autobiographical *One Foot in Heaven* (1940) and *Get Thou Behind Me* (1942), which described humorously and lovingly life in a small town. *Happily Ever After* (1949) is an attempt to evaluate the spiritual contributions he had received from his father. Also on religion, a theme of constant interest to Spence, are *The Story of America's Religions* (1960) and *The Clergy and What They Do* (1961). Other books include: *Radio City* (1941); *Faint Shadow* (1947); *The Big Top* (1951); and *Bride of the Conqueror* (1954).

Spencer, Cornelia Phillips (b. Harlem, N.Y., March 20, 1825—d. March 11, 1908), historian. Mrs. Spencer was an outspoken advocate of the South. She lived and wrote in the village of Chapel Hill; and Zebulon B. Vance, governor of North Carolina, called her "the smartest woman in North Carolina—and the smartest man too." Among her books: *The Last 90 Days of the War in North Carolina* (1866); *First Steps in North Carolina History* (1889). Her *Selected Papers* were edited (1953) by Louis R. Wilson. Hope S. Chamberlain wrote *Old Days in Chapel Hill: Being the Life and Letters of Cornelia Phillips Spencer* (1926).

Spencer, Elizabeth [Mrs. John Rusher] (b. Carrollton, Miss., July 19, 1921—   ), novelist. A precise stylist whose stories are often set in her native Mississippi, Elizabeth Spencer is one of the best Southern regionalist writers. Some of her writing in *Fire in the Morning* (1948) and *This Crooked Way* (1952) is comparable to the work of Eudora Welty or Carson McCullers. *The Light in the Piazza* (1960) is a short, delicate, Jamesian novel of a woman and her daughter traveling in Italy. Miss Spencer's short stories, which have appeared in the *Virginia Quarterly, The New Yorker,* and *McCall's,* have been anthologized in a *New Southern Harvest; Stories from the New Yorker: 1950–1960;* and *Prize Stories: The O. Henry Awards* (1960).

Spencer, Theodore (b. Villanova, Pa., July 4, 1902—d. Jan. 18, 1949), poet, teacher, critic, editor. Spencer joined the Harvard faculty in 1927 and became one of the most popular lecturers and teachers. He was appointed to the Boylston Chair of Rhetoric and Oratory in 1946. Spencer especially excelled in interpreting Elizabethan drama and metaphysical poetry. In connection with this specialty he wrote *Death and Elizabethan Tragedy* (1936); *Studies in Metaphysical Poetry* (with MARK VAN DOREN, 1939); and *Shakespeare and the Nature of Man* (1942). He was him-

self strongly under the influence of the metaphysical poets, and edited *A Garland for John Donne* (1931). Despite his wide learning he could write affecting lyrics in simple terms. He published five collections: *The Paradox in the Circle* (1941); *The World in Your Hand* (1943); *An Act of Life* (1944); *Poems: 1940–47* (1948); *An Acre in the Seed* (posthumous, 1950). Dudley Fitts described the kind of poems he wrote best as "philosophical light verse."

Sper, Felix. Author of FROM NATIVE ROOTS.

Spewack, Bella (b. Hungary, 1899—   ) and **Samuel Spewack** (b. Russia, 1899—   ), playwrights, film scenarists. The Spewacks met while both were in newspaper work; they are best known for their plays. In addition, Mrs. Spewack wrote short stories, and her husband wrote detective stories and served with the Office of War Information. Among plays the Spewacks wrote or produced together: *Solitaire Man* (1926); *Poppa* (1928); *War Song* (1928); *Clear All Wires* (1932); *Spring Song* (1934); BOY MEETS GIRL (1935); *Leave It to Me* (1938); *Miss Swan Expects* (1939; pub. 1941 as *Trousers to Match*); KISS ME, KATE (1949); *My Three Angels* (1953), adapted from the French; *Festival* (1955). COLE PORTER composed the songs for *Leave It to Me* and KISS ME, KATE; the latter was undoubtedly the best of all the Spewack productions. They also wrote many screenplays.

Speyer, Leonora (b. Washington, D.C., Nov. 1872—d. Feb. 10, 1955), poet, violinist. Mrs. Speyer wrote poems of deep feeling and melodic beauty. Among her collections; *Canopic Jar* (1921); *Fiddler's Farewell* (1926, Pulitzer Prize); *Naked Heel* (1931); *Slow Wall* (1939); *Nor Without Music* (1946, as part of a reprint of *Slow Wall*).

Spiller, Robert E[rnest] (b. Philadelphia, Nov. 13, 1896—   ), teacher, literary historian, editor. Spiller joined the faculty of Swarthmore College in 1921 and in 1945 became a professor of English at the University of Pennsylvania. An authority on American literature, he was one of the four editors of *The Literary History of the United States* (1945, 1953). Among his writings: *The Americans in England During the First Half-Century of Independence* (1926); *Fenimore Cooper, Critic of His Times* (1931); *The Cycle of American Literature* (1955). He edited several of Cooper's books; Henry Adams' *Esther;* an anthology, *The Roots of National Culture* (1933); *Social Control in a Free Society* (1960); and with Eric Larabee *American Perspectives: The National Self-Image in the Twentieth Century* (1961).

Spingarn, Joel E[lias] (b. New York City, May 17, 1875—d. July 26, 1939), teacher, critic. Spingarn was most influential as a theoretical critic. His address "The New Criticism," delivered at Columbia University in 1910, opposed shifting the emphasis from the work of art to other matters, such as biography, history, or philosophy. Spingarn argued for a consideration of a poem in terms of what the poet tried to express and how well he expressed it; he in some ways anticipated the theories of the New Critics of the thirties and forties. (See NEW CRITICISM.) His books include *A History of the Literary Criticism in the Renaissance* (1899); *Creative Criticism* (1917; expanded and rev., 1931). He edited *Critical Essays of the 17th Century* (3 v., 1908–09) and *Criticism in America* (1924). A man of independent wealth, he was greatly interested in the welfare of Negroes and established the Spingarn Medal for the highest accomplishment by an American Negro each year. He helped found the publishing firm of Harcourt, Brace & Co.

Spirit of the Times. A magazine founded on Dec. 10, 1831, by WILLIAM T. PORTER and devoted to sports and humor. It became highly influential and published contributions by many leading humorists and sports writers of the era, including Thomas B. Thorpe, Henry William Herbert (Frank Forester), Albert Pike, W. T. Thompson, J. J. Hooper, J. M. Field, George W. Harris, and Richard Malcolm Johnston. Porter also encouraged contributions from non-professional writers, especially tales and anecdotes from the frontier, with the result that the files of his magazine are today a primary source of American folklore. It is said that Mark Twain learned much of his narrative technique from reading the *Spirit*, and his famous story THE CELEBRATED JUMPING FROG OF CALAVERAS COUNTY is an excellent example of the magazine's contents. Porter made two collections of material from his magazine: *The Big Bear of Arkansas and Other Sketches, Illustrative of Characters and Incidents in the South and Southwest* (1845, 1855); *A Quarter Race in Kentucky* (1846, 1847; reprinted as *Colonel Thorpe's Scenes in Arkansas*, 1858). In 1856 Porter sold the magazine to George Wilkes but continued to edit it until 1858. Wilkes, founder of the *National Police Gazette*, changed the name to *Porter's Spirit of the Times*, then in 1859 founded *The Spirit of the Times and Sportsman*; in 1861 he ceased publication of Porter's magazine. His own became *Wilkes's Spirit of the Times* and continued until 1902, when it was merged with *The Horseman*.

spirituals. See NEGRO SPIRITUALS.

Spock, Benjamin [McLane] (b. New Haven, Conn., May 2, 1903—   ), pediatrician, educator. For millions of American parents, the name of Dr. Spock is synonymous with child rearing. His *Common Sense Book of Baby and Child Care* first appeared in 1946, while he was teaching pediatrics at Cornell Medical College. Including paperback editions, it has sold over 11 million copies. From 1947 to 1951, Spock served as a consultant in psychiatry at the Mayo Clinic in Rochester, Minnesota. In 1955 he became Professor of Child Development at Western Reserve University. His books on child care established Dr. Spock as America's leading pediatrician. Among them are *A Baby's*

First Year (1954, with J. Reinhart and W. Miller), *Feeding Your Baby and Child* (1955, with M. Lowenberg), and *Dr. Spock Talks with Mothers* (1961).

Spofford, Harriet [Elizabeth] Prescott (b. Calais, Me., April 3, 1835—d. Aug. 14, 1921), novelist, poet, short-story writer, essayist, autobiographer. Mrs. Spofford was one of the most productive and popular writers of the later 19th century. She wrote novels, including *Sir Rohan's Ghost* (1860) and *Marquis of Carabas* (1882); verse, collected in *Poems* (1881) and *Ballads About Authors* (1887); short stories, gathered in *The Amber Gods and Other Stories* (1863); and much else. None of it was very good, none very bad. She was regarded as important enough to be denounced by Henry James, who (then twenty-two years old) said of her novel *Azarian* (1864) that the "fine writing" in which it abounded was "the cheapest writing of the day." She knew English and American literature well, wrote too much because of the need to support her family, took Charles Reade as her master but followed Keats in the lavishness of her imagery. Her stories attracted the attention of William Dean Howells and others of note, and have now disappeared completely.

Spoon River Anthology (1915), a series of verse epitaphs by EDGAR LEE MASTERS. In 1914 WILLIAM MARION REEDY began publishing in his *Reedy's Mirror* a series of poems by a Chicago lawyer who hid his identity under the pen name Webster Ford. They continued until Jan. 15, 1915. In that year the Macmillan Co. published them under Masters' name and created a tremendous sensation. Masters had lived near Lewiston, Illinois for years, and the cemetery at Spoon River is apparently the one he had in mind when he wrote his collection: the names of characters in the *Anthology* may be read on the tombstones there, and Masters himself was buried there in 1950.

Reedy was in a way responsible for the idea of the poems. He gave Masters a copy of the famous *Greek Anthology;* Masters was deeply impressed by the Greek poems and began to write epitaphs of his own. Masters' poems have been described as a mingling of drama, cynicism, and compassion. In each, someone who actually lived tells his or her own story briefly. The most famous poem is that in which Ann Rutledge tells of her love for Lincoln (whom Masters hated and often denounced).

Later Masters tried to repeat his success in the *New Spoon River* (1924), but it never attained the eminence of the first collection. The *Anthology* was Masters' outstanding work as a poet, and he never forgave the American public because it overlooked everything else he had written. His mood of contrariness is evident in the poems themselves, which deliberately violate the Latin maxim *De mortuis nil nisi bonum*. Helen Choate Bell, daughter of Rufus Choate and a famous wit, said of the *Anthology*, "I did not know anyone could make death vulgar."

Other critics saw in the collection an attack on life in small middle-western towns. Everywhere in the poems Masters shows his skill in using the basic living speech which E. A. Robinson, Carl Sandburg, and others were then reintroducing into poetry. The collection was made the basis of an opera presented in Italy in 1947. Masters discussed *The Genesis of Spoon River* in the *American Mercury* (January, 1933).

Spotswood, Alexander (b. Morocco, [?] 1676 —d. June 7, 1740), British soldier, administrator. Spotswood was appointed lieutenant governor of Virginia in 1710 and remained in America for the rest of his life. As acting governor (his superior refused to cross the Atlantic) he was in general alert for the welfare of the colony, but was disliked by the Virginian upper class and was finally dismissed. He served as deputy postmaster general of the American colonies from 1730 to 1739. R. A. Brock edited his *Official Letters, 1710–1722* (2 v., 1882–85), and Leonidas Dodson wrote an account of him (1932) as governor. He appears in W. A. Caruthers' *The Knights of the Horseshoe* (1845).

Spottswood, Glenn. Hero of the first novel in JOHN DOS PASSOS' trilogy about the Spottswood family, *Adventures of a Young Man* (1939). Dos Passos tells in this novel how Glenn grows up, adopts Communism, and becomes disillusioned after fighting in the Spanish Civil War. NUMBER ONE (1943) and THE GRAND DESIGN (1949) complete the trilogy which appeared in one volume as *District of Columbia* (1952).

Sprague, Charles (b. Boston, Oct. 26, 1791 —d. Jan. 22, 1875), banker, poet. Sprague was particularly under the influence of the more meditative poets of the latter 18th century in England. His much admired *Ode to Shakespeare,* for example, plainly exhibits his study of Thomas Gray and William Collins. His poetry was mainly occasional; the *Shakespeare Ode* was a prize address delivered at the Boston Theater (1823) in connection with a pageant in honor of the dramatist. Another was a *Centennial Ode* which paid tribute to the Pilgrim Fathers. He also wrote well in prose, as in his piece called *The American Indian.* His *Writings* were collected in 1841, again in 1876.

Springs, Elliott White (b. Lancaster, S.C., July 31, 1896—d. Oct. 15, 1959), pilot, writer, businessman. Springs served with the British and American air forces in World War I; in World War II he was a lieutenant colonel in the United States Army Air Corps. After the first war he started in business with his father, an owner of cotton mills, but left and wrote several books: *Nocturne Militaire* (1927); *Leave Me with a Smile* (1928); *Contact: A Romance of the Air* (1930); *Pent-Up on a Penthouse* (1931); *Warbirds and Ladybirds* (1931). After his father died in 1931 he took back the business. In 1948 Springs published *Clothes Make the Man.*

Spy, The (1821), a historical novel by JAMES FENIMORE COOPER. This was the first of

Cooper's three great successes in three different kinds of fiction; it was followed by THE PIONEERS (1823), the first of his Indian stories, and THE PILOT (1823), his first sea story. *The Spy* is an entertaining mixture of fighting, espionage, and love. The central character is Harvey Birch, a Yankee peddler on whom George Washington (here called William Harper), relies strongly. The action takes place in Westchester County, N.Y., where two rival bands operate, the Americans and the British. Captain Henry Wharton, of the British faction, visits his Westchester home and is almost captured, but his patriotic sister Frances persuades Mr. Harper to aid her brother. Leader of his pursuers is Major Payton Dunwoodie, betrothed to Frances. Urged by Frances to delay his pursuit, Dunwoodie uses an immediate marriage ceremony as a pretext for the delay. Birch is active in all these events, sometimes in the manner of a Yankee peddler, sometimes in the lofty style of the aristocrats. But he is depicted throughout the book as a man of noble instincts and deep patriotism who refuses all rewards.

Birch was admittedly based on a real personage. Cooper's friend, Judge JOHN JAY, told Cooper of a secret agent employed during the Revolution to gather information on British activities. This man ran a double risk: both the Americans and the British were likely to hang him. Many conjectures have since been advanced as to this man's real identity. Tremain McDowell in *American Literature* (March, 1930) examined the question at great length, and his conclusion was that "Harvey Birch is the original creation of Cooper's imagination."

James Grossman described Cooper's methods of composition in writing *The Spy,* methods that he continued to employ throughout his career. Cooper persuaded his publisher to set his novel in print as he went along. After volume one was printed the publisher began to fear that Cooper would go on forever. To reassure him, Cooper wrote the final chapter before several earlier ones were ready; it was printed and even paged immediately. That held Cooper down rigidly. As a consequence, the book's conclusion leaves unanswered several important questions, the most important of these being Birch's future. The novel illustrates the fact that Cooper was always, as Grossman calls him, a "loose, slovenly author."

Sir Walter Scott's *Waverley* (1814) influenced Cooper in writing this novel and later ones. At times he makes the somewhat primitive Westchester seem like a land of chivalry transported from the Scotch Highlands or the Middle Ages. Mr. Harper resembles Bonnie Prince Charlie, says Grossman, rather than the actual commander of the American armies.

Although Cooper was not especially concerned with Negro rights, he enjoyed describing Negro characters, and in the character of the servant Caesar he presented the first of his numerous full-drawn portraits of Negroes.

Squaw Man, The (1905), a play by EDWIN MILTON ROYLE. This romantic drama, one of the most successful of its day, concerns an English aristocrat and the Indian girl he marries after she has saved his life. The girl bears him a son, but commits suicide in order to avoid standing in his way when he becomes heir to an English title.

Squibob Papers, The (1865), a series of humorous sketches by GEORGE DERBY, who often employed Squibob as a pseudonym. The sketches represent one of the earliest developments in American humor, employing puns, grotesqueries, exaggerated understatement, and rowdy burlesque. A number of them originally appeared in the San Francisco *Pioneer*. George R. Stewart wrote about Derby in *John Phoenix, Esq., The Veritable Squibob: A Life of Captain George H. Derby, U.S.A.* (1937).

Squier, E[phraim] G[eorge] ["Samuel A. Bard"] (b. Bethlehem, N.Y., June 17, 1821—d. April 17, 1888), newspaper editor, diplomat, archaeologist, writer. Squier was one of the first to investigate the ancient mounds of Ohio, and later became interested in similar mounds in New York. Appointed as special chargé d'affaires in Peru, he made investigations of that country's archaeological remains (1849–50), returning in 1853 and 1863–64 for further surveys. Among his books: *Ancient Monuments of the Mississippi Valley* (with E. H. Davis, 1848); *Antiquities of the State of New York* (1851); *Travels in Central America* (1852); *The States of Central America* (1858); *Peru* (1877). Around 1857 Squier met an actress named Miriam Follen; they were married in 1858, but were divorced in 1873 when she fell in love with Frank Leslie. (See under MIRIAM LESLIE). Much about Squier is to be found in Madeleine Stern's amusing biography *Purple Passage: The Life of Frank Leslie* (1953). He suffered a mental breakdown after the divorce proceedings and was committed to an insane asylum.

Squirrel-Cage, The (1912), a novel by DOROTHY CANFIELD FISHER. In the contrasted characters of a husband and wife Mrs. Fisher effectively showed the difference between the materialistic attitude of a social-minded and avaricious woman and the more altruistic attitude of the man she loved. This was the author's first successful novel.

S. S. Glencairn (1948), the collective title given to a revival of four one-act plays by EUGENE O'NEILL. All of the plays were written before 1919 and printed in his MOON OF THE CARIBBEES of that year. The action of three of the plays takes place on the British tramp steamer *Glencairn*. George Jean Nathan, reviewing this new production, found that O'Neill had created marine characters destructive of the earlier stereotypes. He denied that the plays were great, but said that they foreshadowed O'Neill's greatness to come.

Stafford, Jean (b. Covina, Cal., July 1, 1915—), novelist, short-story writer. Jean Stafford's works include three highly praised novels and a number of short stories. She particularly excels in the rendering of the minds and speech of children, with a notable grasp of what the New York *Herald Tribune* called their "recurrent sense of pain and apprehension." For this reason, perhaps, her most successful book was *The Mountain Lion* (1947), a story of a brother and sister in the years between childhood and adolescence, which was commended for its brilliance of language and imagery as well as its subtlety and understanding. Her first novel, BOSTON ADVENTURE (1944), was praised as a striking and original book which stood up "amazingly well" to comparison with the work of Marcel Proust (*New Yorker*). *The Catherine Wheel* (1951) was described as "a novel of great accomplishment" (in *The New Statesman & Nation*). In her collection of short stories, *Children Are Bored on Sunday* (1953), her gift for precise, evocative prose and impeccable form was evident. She also wrote a short novel, *A Winter's Tale* (1954).

Stallings, Laurence (b. Macon, Ga., Nov. 25, 1894—d. Feb. 28, 1968), playwright, scenarist, drama critic, novelist. Much of Stallings' early life is related in his novel *Plumes* (1924), which tells its hero's experiences at a college called Woodland (really Wake Forest College), where he falls in love with a professor's daughter. He joins the marines, has embittering war experiences, and loses a leg after being wounded at Belleau Wood—exactly as Stallings had done. Stallings put his war experience to use again in *What Price Glory?* (1924), done in collaboration with MAXWELL ANDERSON, with whom he also wrote *First Flight* (1925), a play about Andrew Jackson in his youth, and *The Buccaneer* (1925), about Sir Henry Morgan. The three productions were collected in *Three American Plays* (1926). The war figured again in a photographic, antiwar account of *The First World War* (1933), which became a best seller. Thereafter Stallings wrote operas, motion-picture scenarios and dramatizations, none of which attained the popularity of his earlier writings. He was one of the first to use jazz in an operatic production, *Deep River* (1926), with New Orleans as a background; *Rainbow* (with OSCAR HAMMERSTEIN, 1928), was another opera, set in the Far West. In 1930 he made a dramatic version of Hemingway's *A Farewell to Arms*. Perhaps the best known of his movies was *The Big Parade* (1925).

Stallman, R[obert] W[ooster] (b. Milwaukee, Wis., Sept. 27, 1911—), teacher, critic, poet. Stallman holds a doctoral degree from the University of Wisconsin, and joined the faculty of the University of Connecticut in 1949. An expert on the work of STEPHEN CRANE, he was coeditor with Lillian Gilkes of *Stephen Crane: Letters* (1960), which was praised for its completeness and for the sharpness of its insights into the writer's life. Other books edited by Stallman include *Critiques and Essays in Criticism, 1920–1948* (1949), *Stephen Crane: an Omnibus* (1952), and *The Art of Joseph Conrad: a Critical Symposium* (1960). In addition, he has written *The Art of Modern*

Fiction (1960) with RAY B. WEST, JR., and *The Houses that James Built and Other Studies* (1961); he frequently contributes poems and articles to such periodicals as *The Kenyon Review, New Republic,* and *The Sewanee Review.*

Standard Dictionary of the English Language, The (1893–95; rev., 1913, 1934, 1942, 1946, 1949, 1952, etc.), a dictionary published by Funk & Wagnalls Co., with FRANK H. VIZETELLY as the first managing editor and with Charles Earle Funk as supervisor of later revisions. This dictionary provides "reformed" as well as standard spellings, gives the present meaning of words first in its definitions, prints Greek words in the English alphabet, and includes several hundred thousand words. A number of abridgments have been published, including a *New College Standard Dictionary* and a *New Desk Standard.* The later revisions of the unabridged are called *New Standard Dictionary.*

Standing Bear, Luther (b. South Dakota, Dec. [?], 1868—d. [?] 1947), Sioux chieftain, writer on Indian life. Standing Bear spent his boyhood on the plains of Nebraska and South Dakota, and at the age of eleven was sent to Carlisle, Pa., where he was the first student to step inside the doors of its famous Indian school. On leaving he became first a clerk, later a teacher at the Rosebud Agency in South Dakota. In 1898 he became a member of Buffalo Bill's Wild West Show, acting as an interpreter. His branch of the Sioux family, the Ponca tribe, was given a land allotment in Indian Territory, but when the members of the tribe moved there they were mistreated and many of them died. Standing Bear, accompanied by Joseph La Flesche and his young daughter SUZETTE LA FLESCHE, made a lecture tour and enlisted the support of Henry Wadsworth Longfellow and HELEN HUNT JACKSON. As a result the government investigated the plight of the Poncas and made some restitution to them. Standing Bear was often called upon for lectures and also acted in the movies. He wrote a number of informative and vivid books, among them *My People, The Sioux* (1928); *My Indian Boyhood* (1931); *Land of the Spotted Eagle* (1933); *Twenty True Stories* (1934).

Standish, Burt L. The pen name of GILBERT PATTEN.

Standish, Miles [or Myles] (b. England, 1584 [?]—d. Oct. 3, 1656), soldier, colonist, public official. Standish was a professional soldier who fought in the Netherlands. The Pilgrims evidently had a high respect for him, since they hired him to accompany them to the New World in the *Mayflower.* He showed marked ability as a soldier, engineer, and administrator. He lives in history, however, largely because of his military clash with rollicking THOMAS MORTON, whom he twice ejected from New England as a public nuisance; Morton retaliated by his sneering references to Standish in THE NEW ENGLAND CANAAN (1632). Less historically, he comes alive in Longfellow's poem THE COURTSHIP OF MILES STANDISH,

which has no basis in fact. Standish seems to have had no difficulty in obtaining brides; he was twice married. Neither he nor his second wife was a member of the church, and unlike most other colonists, he believed in tolerance of other people's religion. Tudor Jenks wrote a biography of him, *Captain Myles Standish* (1905). Standish appears in many works of fiction, including John Lothrop Motley's *Merry-Mount* (1849); Jane Austin's *Standish of Standish* (1889); Helen Carlisle's *We Begin* (1932); Ernest Begler's *Plymouth Adventure* (1950).

Stanley, Sir Henry M[orton] (b. Wales [?], 1841—d. May 10, 1904), newspaperman. His name was originally John Rowlands; he adopted that of Stanley in tribute to a merchant in New Orleans by whom he was employed when he worked his way as a cabin boy to that city. He served in the United States Navy and the Confederate Army and went on various expeditions as a newspaperman. In 1869 the New York *Herald,* which had previously employed him in Ethiopia, sent him in search of David Livingstone (1813–1873), a Scots missionary and explorer who was lost somewhere in the heart of Africa. Stanley started from Zanzibar in 1871, found Livingstone in November at Ujiji. When the men met, Stanley uttered the now famous words, "Dr. Livingstone, I presume?" The following year Stanley published a book, *How I Found Livingstone.* He remained in Africa as a *Herald* correspondent, made some important explorations, and gave up his American citizenship to become a British citizen again (1892); he was knighted and became a member of Parliament. His *Autobiography,* edited by his widow, appeared in 1909. Among his books: *Through the Dark Continent* (2 v., 1878); *The Congo and the Founding of Its Free State* (2 v., 1885); *In Darkest Africa* (2 v., 1890).

Stansbury, Joseph (b. England, Jan. 9, 1742 [1743?]—d. Nov. 9, 1809), merchant, poet. Stansbury, who emigrated to Philadelphia in 1767, was against independence and became a British agent. He wrote numerous songs intended to encourage the British soldiers. After the war he took refuge in Nova Scotia, and later settled down in New York City. Unlike his fellow loyalist poet, the Rev. Jonathan Odell, Stansbury was never insulting or vindictive. *The Loyal Verses of Joseph Stansbury and Jonathan Odell* were collected by Winthrop Sargent in 1860.

Stanton, Elizabeth Cady (b. Johnstown, N.Y., Nov. 12, 1815—d. Oct. 26, 1902), woman suffragist, editor, writer. When her brother died, Mrs. Stanton was allowed to take his place at the Johnstown Academy—the only girl in the school—and won a prize in Greek, but no college would admit her. She studied law in her father's office but could not take the bar examinations or practice. When she accompanied her husband, an abolitionist, to London to attend an antislavery conference, she saw Lucretia Mott denied the floor. She and Mrs. Mott became the first agitators for woman suffrage; in 1848 the first women's rights convention was held at her home in Seneca Falls, N.Y. In 1851 she and Susan B. Anthony joined forces and worked together for many years. In 1868 she ran for Congress, although ineligible to sit, and garnered twenty-four votes. The next year she became president of the National Woman's Suffrage Association, in the late 1860's edited, with Miss Anthony, a militant magazine called *Revolution*. All these labors on behalf of woman suffrage and other causes did not prevent her from rearing a large family of sons and daughters. One of the latter, Harriet Stanton Blatch, likewise became a leader in the woman's suffrage movement. Mrs. Stanton wrote *A History of Woman Suffrage* (with Susan B. Anthony and M. J. Gage, 6 v., 1881–1922) and her autobiography, *Eighty Years and More* (1898). Theodore Stanton and Harriet Blatch edited *Elizabeth Cady Stanton, As Revealed in Her Letters, Diary, and Reminiscences* (2 v., 1922).

Stanton, Frank L[ebby] (b. Charleston, S.C., Feb. 22, 1857—d. Jan. 7, 1927), newspaperman, poet. Stanton was perhaps the earliest of the columnists in the modern style. He joined the staff of the Atlanta *Constitution* in 1889 and soon after began a column called "Just from Georgia," which was widely read and reprinted all over the country. A compilation of selections from this column was made by his daughter under the title of his column (1927). He wrote facile and melodious verses and has sometimes been called "Poet Laureate of Georgia." One of his verses, *Mighty Lak' a Rose* (1901), became nationally known as set to music by ETHELBERT NEVIN. His lyrics were collected in 1892, 1898, 1900, 1902, and 1904.

Stanzas on Freedom (1843), a poem by JAMES RUSSELL LOWELL. This great antislavery poem appealed to Americans, particularly those living in New England, to free the slaves.

Starbottle, Colonel Culpeper. A character who appears in many of BRET HARTE's stories. He is a southern stereotype, fond of women, liquor, and oratory.

Starch, Daniel (b. La Crosse, Wis., March 8, 1883—), psychologist. Starch taught at the University of Wisconsin and Harvard University. He specialized in educational psychology and psychometrics, applying these techniques to business practices. Among his books: *Advertising: Its Principles, Practices, and Technique* (1914); *Principles of Advertising* (1923); *An Analysis of 5,000,000 Inquiries* (1929); *Buying Power of the American Public* (1931); *Faith, Fear, and Fortunes* (1934); *How to Develop Your Executive Ability* (1943). He developed special techniques for measuring the "readership" of newspaper and magazine advertisements and founded the firm of Daniel Starch and Staff.

Starr, Frederick (b. Auburn, N.Y., Sept. 2, 1858—d. Aug. 14, 1933), anthropologist. Starr was an authority on the Indian civilizations of Mexico, and taught for many years at the University of Chicago. Among his books: *American Indians* (1898); *Truths About the Congo* (1907); *In Indian Mexico* (1908); *Philippine Studies* (1909); *Liberia* (1913). He also compiled *Readings from Modern Mexican Authors* (1904).

Starrett, [Charles] Vincent [Emerson] (b. Toronto, Ont., Oct. 26, 1886—), newspaperman, critic, editor, writer. Starrett began as a reporter for the old Chicago *Inter-Ocean*, went on to the Chicago *Daily News*. He lived in many other towns, including New York, London, Paris, Rome, Reno, St. Louis, and Peking. His writings include well over a hundred books of every kind: poems, short stories, detective novels, books about Sherlock Holmes, a bibliography of Stephen Crane's writings, humorous sketches, biographies, novels. Among them: *Arthur Machen* (1918); *Ambrose Bierce* (1920); *Buried Caesars* (essays, 1923); *The Private Life of Sherlock Holmes* (1933); *The Great Hotel Murder* (1934); *Books Alive* (1940); *Bookman's Holiday* (1942); *Autolycus in Limbo* (poems, 1943); *Murder in Peking* (1946); *Great All-Star Animal League Ball Game* (1957). See BAKER STREET IRREGULARS.

Star Rover, The (1915), a series of related stories by JACK LONDON. A California convict, in prison for life, learns how to escape by leaving his body and incarnating himself in another person; in each case he undergoes strange adventures. Some of London's best short stories are in this underrated volume, especially *The Engraved Oarblade*. The collection has sometimes been interpreted as a turning away from the materialism London had expounded in BEFORE ADAM (1906). The chief character was apparently based on a strange Californian named Ed Morrell, who professed to have taken part in many train holdups and made off with numerous sacks of gold. During the latter part of his life Morrell lectured and wrote on "The Folly of a Life of Crime"—based on a short stretch in San Quentin; he also headed the Honor League of Reformed Criminals. So C. B. Glasscock explains in *Bandits and the Southern Pacific* (1929). Morrell himself wrote *The 25th Man: The Strange Story of EM, the Hero of Jack London's "Star Rover"* (1924; reprinted, 1956).

Stars Fell on Alabama (1934), a volume of folklore by CARL CARMER. While teaching at the University of Alabama (1921–27), Carmer became greatly interested in recording local folkways, folk tales, folk songs, and proverbs. He made a selection of them in this book, which became very popular. It was followed by similar volumes by Carmer on other sections of the country, especially his native New York.

Star-Spangled Banner, The. See FRANCIS SCOTT KEY.

Starting from Paumanok (1860), a poem by WALT WHITMAN. This first appeared in the 1860 edition of *Leaves of Grass* under the title *Proto-Leaf*. The present title was substituted in the 1867 edition. The poem was frequently revised, mainly in 1867, but some further changes were made in 1881 when a section was transferred to SONG OF MYSELF. *Paumanok* was the Indian name for Long Island; it means "fish-shaped."

The poem is one of Whitman's most characteristic, in matter and manner. It is primarily a celebration of comradeship. Gay Wilson Allen, in his *American Prosody* (1935), uses a passage from the poem to demonstrate an important point about the imagery in *Leaves of Grass:* "It expresses emotion either by naming the sensations of which the emotion consists, or it indirectly portrays the emotion by naming the concrete objects which may be counted upon to produce the sensation." The diction is often characteristic—the use of such words and phrases as *Americanos, libertad, omnes, camerado, ma femme, oratresses,* and so on. Whitman revels in exclamation points and catalogues. He insists on his doctrine of total equalitarianism: "All the things of the universe are perfect miracles, each as profound as any." He makes the poem, as he promises, "an evangel-poem of comrades and of love."

State Fair (1932), a novel by PHIL STRONG. Strong portrays sentimentally but not mawkishly the consequences of an Iowa state fair at which the Frake family wins various prizes and two younger members fall temporarily in love. The novel was widely read and was filmed three times.

State of the Union (1945), a play by HOWARD LINDSAY and RUSSEL CROUSE. This amusing and effective political satire won a Pulitzer prize (1946), ran on Broadway for 765 performances, and was filmed in 1948. It is said that the idea of the play was suggested by the actress Helen Hayes when she asked the authors if they had ever thought of doing a play about a Presidential candidate. The authors deny that WENDELL WILLKIE was the model for the hero, but there is an unquestionable resemblance. Mossback conservatism and wild-eyed radicalism were equally the butts of the satire, and the authors made a point of ridiculing the American electorate's political apathy.

Status Seekers, The. See VANCE PACKARD.

Stauffer, Donald A[lfred] (b. Denver, Colo., July 4, 1902—d. Aug. 8, 1952), critic. Stauffer, a graduate of Princeton and a Rhodes scholar, went back to Princeton to teach, eventually became chairman of the English department. He won an outstanding reputation as a biographer, an acute critic, and a sensitive poet. He served during the war with the marines in the Pacific. Among his writings: *English Biography Before 1700* (1930); *The Art of Biography in the 18th Century* (1941); *The Intent of the Critic* (1941); *The Nature of Poetry* (1946); *The Saint and the Hunchback* (a novel, 1946); *The Golden Nightingale* (lectures on poetry, 1949); *A World of Images* (1949).

Stedman, Edmund Clarence (b. Hartford, Conn., Oct. 8, 1833—d. Jan. 18, 1908), stockbroker, poet, critic, anthologist. Stedman's boyhood was spent in Connecticut and New Jersey. He matriculated at Yale in 1849, but was expelled two years later for neglecting his studies. His reading in the poetry of the English Romantics and early Victorians, especially Ten-

nyson, aroused an ambition to write, and he acquired a reputation as a minor versifier, meanwhile making his living as a journalist and as a stockbroker on Wall Street. His best known poem is *Pan in Wall Street* (1867).

The abolitionist movement and the Civil War evoked his best early verse, including *Honest Abe of the West,* one of the earliest, if not the first, of the Lincoln campaign songs. As a correspondent for the New York *World* he took an active part in the Battle of Bull Run, in which he showed considerable valor under fire.

It was as a critic, a leader of New York literary society, and especially as an anthologist that Stedman achieved his main reputation. In collaboration with GEORGE EDWARD WOODBERRY he edited a ten-volume edition of *The Works of Edgar Allan Poe* (1894–95). Two volumes of criticism, *Victorian Poets* (1875) and POETS OF AMERICA (1885), were supplemented by two anthologies, *A Victorian Anthology* (1895) and AN AMERICAN ANTHOLOGY (1900), both of which became widely popular. In *The Nature and Elements of Poetry* (1892) he proclaimed his aesthetic creed, inveighing against the "heresy of the didactic." He wrote: "A prosaic moral is injurious to virtue by making it repulsive." He was one of the first important critics in the country to recognize the merit of Walt Whitman's poetry. Nevertheless, like his English contemporary Francis Turner Palgrave, he became a symbol of Victorian gentility for the young revolutionary poets of the

20th century, and his reputation has suffered greatly, and perhaps unjustly, in the past three or four decades.

In addition to the books mentioned Stedman was the author of *Poems, Lyrical and Idyllic* (1860); *Alice of Monmouth, An Idyll of the Great War, With Other Poems* (1864); *The Blameless Prince and Other Poems* (1869); *The Poetical Works of Edmund Clarence Stedman* (1873). With Ellen M. Hutchinson he edited *A Library of American Literature from the Earliest Settlement to the Present Time* (11 v., 1888–90). It is worth noting that Stedman made his hobby aviation long before manned flight was regarded as a practicality by most men. As early as the 1870's he published essays in which he predicted, with remarkable accuracy, the designs that dirigibles and other airships were eventually to take.

ELDON C. HILL

Steegmuller, Francis (b. New Haven, Conn., July 3, 1906—   ), writer, biographer. While still a student at Columbia University, Steegmuller began contributing to *The New Yorker* magazine. Later, as a member of its staff, he wrote the column "Talk of the Town." An intense interest in the psychology of the creative process and in the nature of painting turned him to biographies of Flaubert, Maupassant, and James Jarves. His works also include neatly plotted, fast-moving murder mysteries, under two pseudonyms: Byron Steel and David Keith. His biographies include: *O Rare Ben Jonson* (1927); *Sir Francis Bacon* (1930); *Flaubert and Madame Bovary* (1939); *Maupassant, A Lion in the Path* (1949); and *The Two Lives of James Jackson Jarves* (1951). He also translated and edited *The Selected Letters of Gustave Flaubert* (1954) and translated *Madame Bovary* (1957). Steegmuller also wrote *States of Grace* (1946), a novel about "uncharitable behavior in supposedly religious circles."

Steele, Wilbur Daniel (b. Greensboro, N.C., March 17, 1886—   ), short-story writer, novelist, playwright. Steele graduated from the University of Denver in 1907, studied art at home and abroad, and in 1910 began publishing stories which won both popular and critical approval. He has been called the "No. 1 short-story writer for the medium-browed." He won the O. Henry Memorial Award four times for *For They Know Not What They Do* (1919); *Bubbles* (1926); *The Man Who Saw Through Heaven* (1927); and *Can't Cross Jordan* (1931). Other outstanding stories are *The Marriage in Kairwan* (1923); *La Guiablesse* (1923); *For Where Is Your Fortune Now?* (1929). Two collections of his stories are *The Best Short Stories of Wilbur Daniel Steele* (1946) and *Full Cargo* (1952), which levied on earlier gatherings: *Land's End* (1918); *The Shame Dance* (1923); *Urkey Island* (1926); *The Man Who Saw Through Heaven* (1927); *Tower of Sand* (1929); and others. Steele's stories are notable for their great variety of background, their con-

stant ingenuity, and their grasp of psychopathology.

Steele's first novel was *Storm* (1914). Later came *Isles of the Blest* (1924); *Taboo* (1925); *Meat* (1928); *Undertow* (1930); *That Girl from Memphis* (1945); *Diamond Wedding* (1950); *Their Town* (1952). *That Girl from Memphis* is the best among these. It has been said that Steele's novels tend to be overlong and overwritten, and that his invention flags in a long narrative. He also wrote one-act plays, and with his second wife, Norma Mitchell, a full-length drama, *Post Road* (1935). In collaboration with Anthony Brown he dramatized one of his best known short stories, *How Beautiful with Shoes* (1935).

Steendam, Jacob (b. Netherlands, 1616[?]– d. 1672[?]), Dutch poet. Usually regarded as New York's first poet, Steendam, who came to the New Netherlands around 1650, may perhaps also be regarded as one of the earliest writers of real-estate advertising in the New World. Before coming to America he had been in the service of the West India Co. in Africa. He was on his own, however, as a trader in New Amsterdam. His family came with him when he bought land on Long Island. His poetical works were issued in three volumes: *Den Distelvink* ("The Goldfinch," 1649–50); *Klacht van Nieuw Nederlandt tot Haar Moeder* ("Complaint of New Netherlands to Her Mother," 1659); and *'T Lof van Nieuw Nederlandt* ("The Praise of New Netherlands," 1661). In the second volume he urged better treatment for the Dutch colony, in the third he praised the colony in warm terms. Later he published a collection, *Zeede-Zanger voor de Batavische Jonkheyt* ("Moral Songs for Batavian Youth," 1671). Henry Cruse Murphy wrote a biography of Steendam (1861) and included his poems; they may also be found in Murphy's *Anthology of New Netherlands* (1865).

Steeplejack (2 v., 1919), an autobiographical narrative by JAMES HUNEKER. In rambling style Huneker expresses his enthusiasm for the many arts in which he was interested and tells of the artists he has known. His criticisms are most valid when he is talking about music, an art he himself studied as a professional pianist. He expresses his lack of esteem for American painters, as when he speaks of "the superstitious veneration entertained for second-rate painters like Gilbert Stuart, Copley, Peale." He himself popularized many of the foreign artists and writers who were to influence the new generation.

Steere, Richard (b. England, [?] 1643—d. June 22, 1721), colonist, poet. Nothing is known of Steere's early life except that he was a "Citizen of London" and that he published a narrative poem *The History of the Babylonish Cabal* (1682), which took the Earl of Shaftesbury's part in the Whig dispute with the King's Party. He came to New England around this time, lived for a while in Providence, R.I., then removed to Southold, Long Island. A wealthy man, he had the leisure to indulge his talent for poetry. In this country he published *A Monumental Memorial of Marine Mercy* (1684) and *The Daniel Catcher* (1713). The latter volume contains his two most striking poems, *Earth Felicities, Heavens Allowances* and *On a Seastorm Nigh the Coast. Earth Felicities* is written in blank verse, unusual at that time, and both poems reflect a protoromantic appreciation of nature, also unusual for that period.

Stefansson, Vilhjalmur (b. Arnes, Manitoba, Nov. 3, 1879—d. Aug. 26, 1962), explorer, anthropologist, writer. Reared as a farmer and cowboy in North Dakota, he studied at various universities, concluding with three years' postgraduate work in comparative religion and anthropology at Harvard. Most of his life thereafter was spent in exploration and in arguing effectively about his observations and conclusions. He became interested particularly in the Arctic regions and made many explorations in the north. He also made an expedition to tropical Australia. He won gold medals from many geographical societies and honorary doctorates from several universities.

Stefansson was not content with merely reporting scientific observations, but sought constantly to find practical uses in his discoveries. He was convinced, for example, that people could live comfortably in northern regions, and expressed his views forcibly in *The Northward Course of Empire* (1922) and *Not by Bread Alone* (1946). Among his other books: *My Life with the Eskimos* (1913); *The Friendly Arctic* (1921); *The Adventure of Wrangel Island* (1925); *The Standardization of Error* (1927); *The Three Voyages of Martin Frobisher* (1938); *Arctic Manual* (1941); *The Arctic in Fact and Fiction* (1945); *Great Adventures and Explorations* (an anthology, 1947); *New Compass of the World* (1949); *Northwest to Fortune* (1958).

Steffens, [Joseph] Lincoln (b. San Francisco, April 6, 1866—d. Aug. 9, 1936), newspaperman, muckraker, memoirist. After a somewhat restless and unrestrained youth, Steffens studied philosophy abroad, married, and on his return to this country went into newspaper work in New York, serving on the *Evening Post,* the *Commercial Advertiser, McClure's,* the *American,* and *Everybody's* during the years from 1892 to 1911. This was the muckraking era, and Steffens became a leader in exposing the sins of politicians and business leaders (see MUCKRAKING LITERATURE). He was adept in winning the confidence and friendship of the men he exposed.

In an article that appeared in *McClure's* in October, 1902, Steffens set down his observations of the fight district attorney Joseph W. Folk was waging against bribers and grafters in St. Louis. The article attracted much attention and has been regarded by many as the beginning of the muckraking movement. Steffens went on to many similar articles and books: *The Shame of the Cities* (1904); *The Struggle for Self-Government* (1906); *Upbuilders* (1909); *The Least of These* (1910); *Out of*

the Muck (1913); *Lincoln Steffens Speaking* (1936). He reminisced freely and entertainingly in his *Autobiography* (2 v., 1931); his *Letters* (2 v., 1938) are likewise revealing. When the Russian Revolution overthrew the czars he visited Russia, came back convinced that Utopia was at hand, and thereafter espoused the Communist cause.

Stegner, Wallace [Earle] (b. Lake Mills, Iowa, Feb. 18, 1909—), teacher, writer. Stegner attended high school and college in Salt Lake City and did graduate work at the universities of Iowa and California. He taught at Iowa, Utah, Wisconsin, Harvard, and Stanford universities. In 1937 he won the Little, Brown Novelette Contest with his *Remembering Laughter,* and he twice won the O. Henry Memorial Award. Among his other novels: *The Potter's House* (1938); *On a Darkling Plain* (1940); *Fire and Ice* (1941); *The Big Rock Candy Mountain* (1943); *Second Growth* (1947); *Country Dance* (1948); *The Preacher and the Slave* (1950). These novels, like his excellent short stories, some of which have been collected in *Women on the Wall* (1950), *City of the Living* (1956), and *A Shooting Star* (1961), have varied and realistic settings and give an animated, impressive picture of American rural life.

Stegner's work also includes nonfiction of great interest. Under the auspices of *Look* magazine he undertook a survey of national and religious tensions in the United States and published the results in a frank, polemical, trenchant volume entitled *One Nation* (1945). Also under the auspices of *Look,* he prepared an informative volume called *The Central Northwest* (1947) in the "Look at America" series. Earlier he had written about *Mormon Country* (1942). Undoubtedly the best of his nonfictional works, however, is *Beyond the 100th Meridian* (1954), a biography of a great explorer, engineer, and conservationist, John Wesley Powell. As director of the creative writing center at Stanford, Stegner analyzed *The Writer's Art* (1950) and in collaboration with Stuart Brown and Claude Simpson compiled *An Exposition Workshop* (1939).

Steichen, Edward (b. Luxembourg, March 27, 1879—), photographer, painter, plant breeder. Although Steichen refers to himself in *Who's Who* as a "plant breeder" and although his excellent paintings are hung in many prominent galleries, the major part of his fame rests upon his highly imaginative photography. He was one of the first photographers to explore the aesthetic possibilities of the camera, and has won many awards for his achievements. His brilliant use of light and shadow in black and white photography and his crafty choice of the "right moment" have produced astonishing effects. His unique portraits of noted personalities in the arts are now famous. He was chief photographer of the Conde Nast publications from 1923 to 1928, and served in World War I as commander of the photographic division of the air service. In World War II he served in a similar capacity with the Navy, and out of this experience came *The Blue Ghost* (1947), a photographic log and personal narrative of the U.S.S. *Lexington* in combat operation. In 1947 he became director of the department of photography at the Museum of Modern Art, where his photographic exhibits added greatly to the acceptance of photography as an art form. Most notable of these exhibits was *The Family of Man*, later published as a collection (1955). His brother-in-law, CARL SANDBURG, wrote an account of him, *Steichen the Photographer* (1929).

Steig, William (b. New York City, Nov. 14, 1907—   ), artist, cartoonist. Steig developed his special style of humor in the pages of *The New Yorker*, *Vanity Fair*, *Collier's* and other magazines. At the same time he won a notable reputation as a serious artist for his water colors and wood sculpture. His cartoons have been published in a number of collections: *About People* (1939); *The Lonely Ones* (1942); *All Embarrassed* (1944); *Small Fry* (1944); *Persistent Faces* (1945); *Till Death Do Us Part* (1947); *The Rejected Lovers* (1951); *Dreams of Glory* (1953); *The Steig Album* (1959).

Stein, Gertrude (b. Allegheny, Pa., Feb. 3, 1874—d. July 27, 1946), writer, art critic. Miss Stein once said that America was her country and Paris her home town. She came of a wealthy family, in which she was one of five children;

UPI

throughout her life, her older brother LEO STEIN jealously contended with her for the rank of first genius in the family. She attended Radcliffe College, where she was influenced by WILLIAM JAMES and showed evidence of literary ability, then apparently intended to become a physician. Psychology was her chief interest; as a student she wrote a paper on spontaneous automatic writing—possibly the chief source of her later literary hypotheses and procedures. She studied medicine at Johns Hopkins University for four years, specializing in brain anatomy, but took no degree—she said she was bored by examinations. Thereafter she lived abroad, mainly in France. In 1903 she went to

Paris with Alice B. Toklas, who became her nurse, secretary, chef, confidant, and in her later years the supposititious author of THE AUTOBIOGRAPHY OF ALICE B. TOKLAS (1933), actually a book by Gertrude Stein about Gertrude Stein. Miss Stein returned to the United States only once, in 1934, when she undertook a lecture tour. W. G. Rogers, an admiring newspaperman, who was literary editor of the Associated Press, had suggested the visit; later he wrote a memoir of Miss Stein, *When This You See Remember Me: Gertrude Stein in Person* (1948).

Miss Stein's manner of life abroad was as extraordinary as her own personality. She had plenty of money, and at first had to pay for the publication of her writings or submit them with the understanding that she expected no fee. Later in life some of her books began to make money. She was, from the beginning, a contributor to *transition*, but later feuded with the editor, EUGENE JOLAS, who was apparently never very enthusiastic about her "solution of language," resented her capitulation to "a Barnumesque publicity," and disliked her refusal to tolerate any relationship unaccompanied by adulation. Miss Stein also followed what was almost a career as an art critic and patron. Her ideas in the field of painting were as unorthodox as in the field of literature. She became a patron of some of the leading art innovators of the period, including Picasso, Matisse, and Bracque. She bought some of their work and sometimes was presented with important productions of theirs. Picasso painted a renowned portrait of her.

After her reputation spread to the United States, it became necessary for any literary aspirant to visit her if he was in Paris. She had an especial attraction for the American soldiers of both World Wars; she gives an account of them in *Brewsie and Willie* (1946). The literati who surrounded her were to her "the lost generation," in a famous phrase she coined. She spoke with the utmost confidence as she espoused various theories of life, art, literature, politics, humanity, and language. In guarded moments she wrote in a fashion that her publisher, Bennett Cerf at Random House, often frankly described in the blurb as something he couldn't understand; but she could write lucidly when she chose, as in *Wars I Have Seen* (1945). Naturally no writing man could resist the opportunity of writing about her if he had met her; some were influenced by her, although Babette Deutsch wisely points out that it was novelists rather than poets who gained something in the way of directness from her techniques. ERNEST HEMINGWAY's case has been most often discussed, most understandingly in Charles A. Fenton's *The Apprenticeship of Ernest Hemingway: The Early Years* (1954).

Miss Stein's writings make a long list; posthumous works continued to be published long after her death. She was experimental from the beginning, but not all of her works conform to the idea the public had of her and her literary techniques. She was particularly interested in an experiment to discover the character of sub-conscious thought; she was interested in auto-matic writing, also in the primitive mind. Some years elapsed after her flight to Europe before she was willing to publish her early and, in some respects, most impressive literary experi-ments. The two books that established her repu-tation for a special kind of literary eccentricity were THREE LIVES (1909) and *Tender Buttons* (1914). The former, Oscar Cargill notes, "was to revolutionize American primitivistic writing"; the latter was "regarded as the most absurd of efforts at creating a 'new' poetry." Although these early books confirmed the conviction of her special circle that she was a great writer, the public found in them an endless opportunity for ridicule. Clifton Fadiman labeled her "the Mama of DADA." Yet her influence increased through the 1920's. Some of her characteristic phrases were: "In the United States there is more space where nobody is than where any-body is. This is what makes America what it is." "It is better than a little thing that has mel-low real mellow. It is better than lakes whole lakes, it is better than seeing." "*Chicken.* Alas a dirty word, alas a dirty third, alas a dirty bird." The most famous of her lines was, of course, "Rose is a rose is a rose is a rose," which appears in *Sacred Emily* (*Geography and Plays*, 1922).

Miss Stein favored a disconnectiveness that often gave the effect of inscrutability, if not al-ways of profundity. In her love of refrain and rhyme she revealed an outlook of the poet and the child. Metaphysically it was part of her search for rhythm and balance in the universe. She loved to emphasize certain words. Miss Deutsch feels that she stressed *as, and, or* to represent abstract relations and liked participles for their "suggestion of continuity." She also preferred the verb to the noun. She had a grim dislike for punctuation. She remarked plain-tively: "A comma by helping you along hold-ing your coat and putting on your shoes keeps you from living your life as actively as you should live it."

Miss Stein wrote what some people called "nonobjective prose." Possibly the best clue to her intentions is to compare her with James Joyce, of whom she was envious. Whereas Joyce, with supreme linguistic genius, trans-mogrified worn-out and lifeless *connotations* of words into something new and strange, Miss Stein assaulted the *denotations* of words. They looked the same as they had always looked, they sounded the same, but the customary and conventional significance of the words had leaked away and disappeared.

It may be that the most sensible and coherent view of Miss Stein was taken when Oliver Evans discussed her as a humorist (*Prairie Schooner,* Spring, 1947). He even went so far as to relate her to our traditional "Western humor"—in her exaggerations and grimness, her lack of malice, her *non sequiturs,* and her slyness. Evans' view

had been somewhat portentously anticipated by James Feibleman in his book *In Praise of Com-edy* (1939). Her trick of putting together ideas which do not belong together, Feibleman claims, ridicules the commonest error of bad thinking. She avoids any real denotation, is a proponent of irrationalism, but really succeeds in defend-ing reason. He grants that "her books have helped to reacquaint us with the naked sound of our language, hitherto only available to for-eigners."

A host of eminent people wrote to Miss Stein and, for the most part, expressed admiration for her work. Out of 20,000 such letters, Don-ald Gallup selected nearly 450 to make a book called *The Flowers of Friendship* (1953). The writers include every variety of literary, politi-cal, and philosophical creed, from Richard Wright to T. S. Eliot. Even such sturdy indi-vidualists as Israel Zangwill, who told her frankly that one of her early books had made him "tremble for her reason," praised another writing as "revealing a beautiful sympathy with humble lives." Robert McAlmon, also at first a doubter, found "the zip of intelligence and the whoop of personality" in her MELANCTHA (in *Three Lives*). Sherwood Anderson, always sympathetic, expressed a slight doubt: "She may be, just *may* be, the greatest word-slinger of our generation."

The very titles of her writings are a revela-tion of Miss Stein's mental and rhetorical slant. The following is a list of her publications not already mentioned, including some posthumous issues: THE MAKING OF AMERICANS (1925); *A Book Concluding with As a Wife Has a Cow* (1926); *Composition as Explanation* (1926); *A Village: Are You Ready Yet Not Yet: A Play in Four Acts* (1928); *Useful Knowledge* (1928); *An Acquaintance with Description* (1929); *Lucy Church Amiably* (1930); *Dix Portraits* (1930); *How to Write* (1931); *A Long Gay Book* (1932); *Operas and Plays* (1932); *Matisse, Picasso, and Gertrude Stein, with Two Shorter Stories* (1933); FOUR SAINTS IN THREE ACTS (set to music, 1934, by VIRGIL THOMSON, and produced at Hartford, Conn., with an all-Negro cast, by the Friends and Ene-mies of Modern Music); *Portraits and Prayers* (1934); *Narration: Four Lectures* (1935); *Lec-tures in America* (1935); *The Geographical History of America* (1936); *Everybody's Auto-biography* (1937); *A Wedding Bouquet: Ballet* (1938); *Anciens et Modernes: Picasso* (1938); *The World Is Round* (1939); *Paris France* (1940); *What Are Masterpieces* (1940); *Ida: A Novel* (1941); *In Savoy or "Yes" is for Yes for a Very Young Man* (1946; prod. on Broad-way, 1949, as *Yes Is for a Very Young Man*); *Selected Writings of Gertrude Stein* (1946); FOUR IN AMERICA (1947); *The Mother of Us All* (1947, produced as an opera at Columbia University, with music by Virgil Thomson); *First Reader and Three Plays* (1948); *Blood on the Dining-Room Floor* (1948); *Last Operas and Plays* (1949); *Two (Gertrude Stein and*

Her Brother) and Other Early Portraits (the first volume of the *Yale Edition of the Unpublished Writings of Gertrude Stein,* 1951); *Mrs. Reynolds and Five Earlier Novelettes* (1952); *Bee Time Vine and Other Pieces* (1953); *The Alice B. Toklas Cookbook* (a book dominated by Miss Stein, although without indication that it was ghost-written, 1954); *Stanzas in Meditation and Other Poems* (1956).

Among books devoted to the elucidation of her works and ideas are Bravig Imbs' *Confessions of Another Young Man* (1936); Rosalind S. Miller's *Gertrude Stein: Form and Intelligibility* (1949); Donald Sutherland's *Gertrude Stein* (1952); Elizabeth Sprigge's *Gertrude Stein: Her Life and Work* (1957); John Malcolm Brinnin's *The Third Rose: Gertrude Stein and Her World* (1959). See also THE LOST GENERATION.

Stein, Leo (b. Allegheny, Pa., 1872—d. July 29, 1947), painter, art critic, essayist. Leo was GERTRUDE STEIN's older brother. He escaped to France in 1902 and immediately began the business of his life by "discovering" Cézanne. Gertrude followed him in 1903 and the pair lived, separately or together, either in Italy or France for the rest of their lives. They engulfed themselves in the latest experiments or eccentricities in art, psychology, philosophy, and literature. But an estrangement developed between the two, largely because of jealousy. Leo, who perhaps had the better intellect and ideas, sank into the background. He married in 1916 and lived happily thereafter.

Leo criticized his sister freely. He wrote to a friend: "Both Picasso and Gertrude are using their intellects, which they ain't got, to do what would need the finest critical tact, which they ain't got neither; and they are in my belief turning out the most Godalmighty rubbish that is to be found." He himself, however, was not a particularly good writer, and in his lifetime published only one book, *Appreciations: Painting, Poetry, and Prose* (1947), which gave final evidence of the soundness of his judgments in the field of art. Much more revelatory was his *Journey into the Self: Being the Letters, Papers, and Journals of Leo Stein* (1950, ed. by Edmund Fuller).

Steinbeck, John [Ernst] (b. Salinas, Calif., Feb. 27, 1902—d. Dec. 20, 1968), writer. Some of the best scenes in Steinbeck's stories are set in Monterey County, in which he was born and spent most of his life. He attended Stanford University for a time, specializing in marine biology, then went east in a freight boat via the Panama Canal, learning enough about the buccaneer Sir Henry Morgan to write his first book, *Cup of Gold: A Life of Sir Henry Morgan, Buccaneer, with Occasional References to History* (1929). In New York City Steinbeck worked for a while as a newspaperman, then as a hod carrier, but soon returned to California. For two winters he lived alone in the high Sierras, then worked in a trout hatchery, on fruit ranches, as a surveyor, an apprentice

painter, and a chemist, but always kept on writing. Out of this period he emerged with a profound understanding of manual laborers that has manifested itself in many of his books.

His next book, *Pastures of Heaven* (1932),

UPI

was a collection of short stories dealing with the inhabitants of the secluded valley of that name, and the first evidence of Steinbeck's interest in half-wits, the "unfinished children of nature," and the "simple" man uncorrupted by a money-grubbing civilization. In spite of the lovely natural setting of the *Pastures of Heaven,* all of its inhabitants are in some way warped by failing to come to terms with themselves, or by failing to see themselves as part of a larger whole of humanity. *To a God Unknown* (1933), a mixture of pantheism and mysticism, is Steinbeck's strongest statement about man's relationship to the land, a theme present to a lesser degree in most of his writings. TORTILLA FLAT (1935) and IN DUBIOUS BATTLE (1936) established Steinbeck's reputation. The former dealt with the humorous affection of the Paisanos (Mexican-Americans) of Monterey, California. The latter told of a violent strike among California fruit pickers. Partially a protest against the conditions under which the picker worked, it was another link in his developing philosophy of the relationship between man and man. OF MICE AND MEN (1937) is especially notable for its depiction of the simple-minded giant Lennie, another of nature's "unfinished children." It was first conceived as a play and was dramatized in the year of its publication, winning the Drama Critics' Circle Award. THE LONG VALLEY (1938) was a book of short stories.

In 1939 Steinbeck published THE GRAPES OF WRATH, sometimes described as "the 20th-century *Uncle Tom's Cabin*." In its depiction of the Joad family fleeing the disastrous dust bowl of Oklahoma, this book summed up the despair of the early 1930's. Possibly it was as effective as Upton Sinclair's *The Jungle* (1906) had been in crystallizing public opinion against allowing such conditions to continue. Beyond its importance as a social document, however, it was also an affirmation of the solidity of mankind and the sanctity of life; "Everything that lives," says Tom Joad, "is holy." The novel was awarded a Pulitzer prize and was made into a motion picture in 1940.

Following the *Grapes of Wrath* Steinbeck's interest in marine biology led him to publish two books primarily about sea life, but interspersed with other observations on men and nature: *Sea of Cortez* (with EDWARD F. RICKETTS, 1941) and *The Log from the Sea of Cortez* (1951), a reissue of the narrative part of the former volume with a short biographical sketch of Ricketts, who was killed in 1948. Doc, a leading character of *Cannery Row* (1945), strongly resembles Ricketts. Both CANNERY Row and its sequel *Sweet Thursday* (1954) deal with "Mac and the boys," a group of happy indigents whose lack of sophistication and acquisitiveness permits them to live in a state of nature. *The Red Pony* (1945) is an account of four episodes in the life of a boy on a California ranch. *The Wayward Bus* (1947) describes the sexual misadventures of a group stranded overnight at a California wayside station. THE PEARL (1947) is a novelette that shows how the finding of a magnificent pearl by a simple Mexican fisherman brings him only misfortune. *Burning Bright* (1950) tells of a wife who, when she finds her husband sterile, seeks to have a child by another man. Perhaps the best—and certainly the most ambitious—novel after *The Grapes of Wrath* is EAST OF EDEN (1952). The novelette *The Short Reign of Pippin IV* (1957) is an amusing satirical "fabrication" of French politics today. His novel *Winter of our Discontent* appeared in 1961.

In general, Steinbeck's shorter fiction is humorous, warm sometimes to the point of being sentimental, and concerned with the small tragedies in the lives of simple people; it implicitly contrasts the "good life" of the natural man close to the soil with the depersonalization and dehumanization of the commercial world. His longer fiction is often subject to a philosophic tendentiousness, but is primarily concerned with the growth and development of men to whom it is necessary to be good "group-men" in order to be good individuals.

Steinbeck wrote three non-fiction works: *Bombs Away: The Story of a Bomber Team* (1942); *Russian Journal* (1948, with Robert Capa as photographer); and *Once There Was a War* (1958), excerpts from his work as a war correspondent. Two books were privately printed: *Saint Katy the Virgin* (1936) and *How Edith McGillicudy Met R. L. S.* (1943).

Besides dramatizing *Of Mice and Men* (1937), he wrote a dramatization of his novel *The Moon Is Down* (1942), dealing with the Nazi threat. As a novel, *Burning Bright* was already so close to theatrical techniques that little was needed to make it ready for production in the year of its publication. Steinbeck also wrote the film scripts for *The Forgotten Village, The Pearl,* and *Viva Zapata!*

Two collections of Steinbeck's writings have been made: *The Portable Steinbeck* (1943; rev., 1946) and *The Short Novels of John Steinbeck* (ed. by Joseph Henry Jackson, 1953). In the latter Jackson wrote: "He earnestly wishes to make people understand one another, and he is able, like Blake, to 'seek love in the pity of others' woe.'" He noted the frequent disagreements about Steinbeck among critics: "They have called him a naturalist, a mystic, and a primitive. They have described him as brilliant, perceptive, wise, and also as childlike. Some of his tenderest scenes have been called vile; many of his more subtle humors have been missed entirely." Steinbeck's work has been studied in Lewis Gannett's *John Steinbeck, Personal and Bibliographical Notes* (1939); George T. Miron's *The Truth About John Steinbeck and the Migrants* (1939); Harry T. Moore's *The Novels of John Steinbeck* (1939); Peter Lisca's *The Wide World of John Steinbeck* (1958); and Warren French's *John Steinbeck* (1961). He won the 1962 Nobel Prize for Literature.

Steiner, George (b. France, April 23, 1929 —), critic, fiction and poetry writer, political journalist. Steiner was educated at the universities of Chicago, Harvard, and Oxford. His articles in English and American periodicals such as *Encounter, Harper's, The Atlantic, Yale Review,* and *Kenyon Review* reveal a remarkable range, from political commentary to literary history. Steiner is able to write about a new book of fiction or a new translation of the Bible with equal felicity and authority. *Tolstoy or Dostoevsky* (1959) tried something rare in contemporary criticism: the comparison of two great figures in the context of their times and their literary heritage. Steiner subtitled the book "An Essay in the Old Criticism." *The Death of Tragedy* (1961) traces and analyzes the development of tragedy from the ancient Greeks to the present.

Stella, Joseph (b. Italy, June 13, 1880—d. Nov. 5, 1946), painter. Stella came to the United States in 1896, won a notable reputation for his "futurist" drawings and paintings of miners, steel-mill workers, bridges, and other city landmarks. He seems to have exerted a strong influence on Hart Crane, who admired him greatly. Stella secured the publication of an article by Crane, *The Brooklyn Bridge*, in the spring, 1929, issue of *transition*. Stella's futurist-cubist painting of Brooklyn Bridge attracted much attention in the avant-garde world. Brom Weber, in his book on Crane (1948), traces many resemblances in thought and attitude between Crane and Stella. He feels that Stella's painting is "an admirable plastic representation of the *Atlantis* section" in Crane's *The Bridge* (1930).

Stella Dallas (1923), a novel by OLIVE HIGGINS PROUTY. It is a story of a New England woman who sacrifices herself for her daughter's happiness. The novel began as a serial, went on to become a best seller as a book, was made into a play with Mrs. Leslie Carter as the star, then was turned into a silent movie, later into a talking picture, finally into a long-lasting radio serial of the soap-opera type.

Stephansson, Stephan G[udmundsson] (b. Iceland, Oct. 3, 1853—d. Aug. 10, 1927), farmer, poet, social agitator. Stephansson emigrated to North America in 1873 and settled as a farmer in Alberta, Canada, in 1889; he remained there the rest of his life. His poems are ranked among the best written in Icelandic in his day. His collected poems, *Andvokur* ("Wakeful Nights," 1909) appeared in six volumes. He also wrote freely in prose. All his work reveals him as an ardent lover of nature and a bold opponent of social wrongs.

Stephens, Alexander Hamilton (b. near Crawfordsville, Ga., Feb. 11, 1812—d. March 4, 1883), lawyer, public official, writer. Stephens studied law and in 1836 was elected to the Georgia state legislature. Thereafter he occupied many posts of importance, serving as a member of Congress (1843–59), as Vice President of the Confederacy, as a member of the United States Senate (who was not allowed to take his seat), again as a member of Congress (1873–82), and finally as governor of Georgia (1882 until his death). Stephens was always a moderate, but the heat of the prewar controversies led him to take an intransigent stand on slavery. He later served as editor and part owner of the Atlanta *Southern Sun*.

Stephens discussed the war issues in his *Constitutional View of the War Between the States* (2 v., 1868, 1870), later replied to his critics in *The Reviewers Reviewed* (1872). He also wrote a *History of the United States* (1882) and his *Recollections* [and] *Diary Kept When a Prisoner, 1865* (1910). Louis Pendleton (1908), Rudolph Von Abele (1946), and Eudora R. Richardson (1932) wrote biographies of Stephens.

Stephens, Ann S[ophia Winterbotham] (b. Derby, Conn., 1813—d. Aug. 20, 1886), novelist, humorist, poet, short-story writer, editor. One of the most popular authors of the mid-19th century, Mrs. Stephens seems to have begun her career when she was widowed. Often her books had a vague historical flavor and were laid in past eras of either the United States or England. They were written to make suspenseful serials. *Mary Derwent* (1838), for example, was run twice as a serial in one magazine, run again as a serial in another magazine, was then lengthened and published as a book (1858), came out in a uniform set of Mrs. Stephens' writings (1886); in the meantime the novel had appeared as a serial in the London *Family Herald* (1866) and in the Pittston *Gazette*

(1878), and was finally reprinted (1908) for its alleged historical interest. The story tells how an English noblewoman, fleeing to America and taking refuge with a Shawnee tribe, receives a proposal of marriage from a Shawnee chieftain. She refuses, but yields to save a white man and his wife and child.

Mrs. Stephens' most famous book was MALAESKA (1860), the first number issued in the Beadle Dime Novels. *Esther, A Story of the Oregon Trail* (1869) introduces one of "Nature's noblemen," an amalgam of DANIEL BOONE and James Fenimore Cooper's LEATHERSTOCKING. Like some other writers of the day, she imitated T. C. Haliburton's Sam Slick and wrote a book supposedly by Jonathan Slick called *High Life in New York* (1843), which was reprinted in London in 1844 and in this country in 1854, 1859, 1863, 1873. Walter Blair notes that Mrs. Stephens "had a flair for Yankee dialect, vivid descriptions, and scenes in which the scent of onions was important." She also wrote *Alice Copley* (1844); *Fashion and Famine* (1854); *The Rejected Wife* (1863); *The Indian Queen* (1864). She founded the *Portland Magazine* (1834) and *Mrs. Stephens' Illustrated New Monthly* (1856) and served on the editorial staffs of other magazines.

Stephens, John Lloyd (b. Shrewsbury, N.J., Nov. 28, 1805—d. Oct. 12, 1852), lawyer, diplomatic agent, railroad builder, archaeologist. Van Wyck Brooks called Stephens "the greatest of American travel writers." In his late twenties Stephens traveled extensively in Europe and the Near East, and on his return published *Incidents of Travel in Egypt, Arabia Petraea, and the Holy Land* (2 v., 1837) and *Incidents of Travel in Greece, Turkey, Russia, and Poland* (2 v., 1838). In 1839 President Van Buren appointed him a diplomatic agent to the Federation of Central American Republics. What Stephens accomplished as a diplomat is less important than the fact that he made use of his residence in Central America to explore the jungles of that region and its Mayan ruins. With Frederick Catherwood he made extensive explorations, and their observations were vividly set down by Stephens in *Incidents of Travel in Central America* (2 v., 1841) and *Incidents of Travel in Yucatan* (2 v., 1843), with drawings by Catherwood. These two publications went through twenty-three printings between 1841 and 1871, and were reprinted (1949) in two volumes edited by Richard L. Predmore. Stephens was undoubtedly the first to recognize the grandeur and significance of the Mayan ruins. He also laid out the course for a future Nicaraguan Canal and was the president of the Panama Railway Co. He designed the plan for the railroad, which was completed three years after his death. Victor W. von Hagen wrote about him in *Maya Explorer* (1947).

Stephens, Robert Neilson (b. Bloomfield, Pa., July 22, 1867—d. 1906), newspaperman, theatrical agent, playwright, novelist. After working for several business firms, Stephens joined the staff of the Philadelphia *Press,* and within a year became its drama critic. This job eventually led to his writings plays of his own; they were popular and melodramatic. E. H. SOTHERN appeared in the most popular of them, *An Enemy to the King* (1896), which appealed to the current vogue for history viewed romantically. At the suggestion of a Boston publisher Stephens turned his play into a novel (1897). He also wrote other novels, including *A Gentleman Player* (1899); *Captain Ravenshaw* (1901); *The Bright Face of Danger* (1904). Stephens was warmly welcomed in England, and his books were eagerly imitated by Charles Major, Maurice Thompson, and other writers.

Stereotype of the Single Woman in American Novels, The (1951), by Dorothy Yost Deegan. This valuable social study goes from the pre-Hawthorne period, when British influence was strong, through the decades when an American pattern was slowly emerging, down to the present time with its somewhat startling new types of the single woman. Mrs. Deegan feels that American creative writers have failed signally in portraying "the successful women who build their lives apart from marriage." She selects eight women characters for special study, including Hepzibah Pyncheon in *The House of the Seven Gables* (1851), Theodore Dreiser's *Jennie Gerhardt* (1911), Mattie Silver in Edith Wharton's *Ethan Frome* (1911).

Sterling, George (b. Sag Harbor, N.Y., Dec. 1, 1869—d. Nov. 17, 1926), poet, dramatist, critic. Sterling was one of JOHN B. TABB's pupils in Maryland, became a clerk in a real estate office in Oakland, Calif., and was freed from the necessity of earning a living by a gift from an aunt. Thereafter he devoted himself entirely to writing, and spent most of his life in Carmel and San Francisco. He was an active member of the Bohemian Club in the latter city, wrote plays for its famous "high jinks" in Bohemian Grove, and died by his own hand in one of the rooms of the club. Western admirers, especially Ambrose Bierce, thought Sterling on a level with the greatest writers of the past; the East scarcely knew his name, except as the author of A WINE OF WIZARDRY, a poem which appeared in the *Cosmopolitan* (September, 1907) and created a sensation with its lush imagery and melancholy melody. He had no compensating humor, and struck bottom with a poem called *Willy Smith at the Ball Game,* in which Willy listens to the brass band and hears "music adrift from Samarkand."

Among Sterling's books: *The Testimony of the Suns and Other Poems* (1903); *The Triumph of Bohemia: A Forest Play* (1907); *A Wine of Wizardry and Other Poems* (1909); *Beyond the Breakers and Other Poems* (1914); *Yosemite: An Ode* (1916); *The Caged Eagle and Other Poems* (1916); *The Play of Everyman* (1917); *Thirty-five Sonnets* (1917); *Lilith: A Dramatic Poem* (1919); *Rosamund* (a play, 1920); *Sails and Mirage and Other Poems* (1921); *Truth* (a play, 1923); *Strange*

Waters (1926); *Sonnets to Craig* (1928); *After Sunset* (1939). He wrote a prose work that shows his breadth of sympathy as he viewed the pioneering poetry of his day—*Robinson Jeffers: The Man and the Artist* (1926).

Mary Austin wrote about *George Sterling at Carmel* (*American Mercury,* May, 1927), and reminiscences and appreciations of Sterling are to be found in *The Letters of Ambrose Bierce* (1921) and Joseph Noel's *Footloose in Arcadia* (1940). Cecil Johnson prepared *A Bibliography of the Writings of George Sterling* (*Publishers' Weekly,* April 18, 1931; separately published, 1931). Jack London introduced Sterling into *Martin Eden* (1909) as Russ Brissenden.

Sterling, James (b. Ireland, 1701 [?]—d. Nov. 10, 1763), clergyman, writer, public official. Sterling wrote plays, including *The Rival Generals* (1722) and *The Parricide* (1736), produced a poetic version of *The Loves of Hero and Leander* (1728), and indulged in pamphleteering and newspaper writing. In 1733 he was ordained as an Anglican clergyman; the next year he issued *The Poetical Works of the Rev. James Sterling.* He came to America in 1737 and held charges in several Maryland parishes. In 1752 he was appointed collector of customs at Chester. He had a strong love for the American scene and wrote verses for numerous periodicals. Among his later writings were *An Epistle to the Hon. Arthur Dobbs in Europe* (verse, 1752) and *Zeal against the Enemies of Our Country, Pathetically Recommended* (1755).

Stern, Joseph William (b. New York City, Jan. 11, 1870—d. March 31, 1934), song writer, song publisher. Originally a salesman in the music business, Stern formed a music publishing firm with Edward B. Marks in 1894. The two men wrote some well-known songs, including *The Little Lost Child* (1894) and *My Mother Was a Lady* (1896), and published many other famous ditties of the turn of the century.

Stern, Philip Van Doren (b. Wyalusing, Pa., Sept. 10, 1900—), advertising agent, historian, novelist, anthologist. Stern worked for an advertising agent, later for various publishing firms; he was also general manager of "Editions for the Armed Services," which provided good books inexpensively during World War II. His own varied literary works include an authentic historical novel, *The Drums of Morning* (1942); *The Man Who Killed Lincoln* (1939); *The Life and Writings of Lincoln* (1940); and *An End to Valor: the Last Days of the Civil War* (1958), a long, thoroughly documented account of the period between March 4 and May 24, 1865. He also compiled numerous anthologies, and a *Pictorial History of the Automobile* (1953).

Steuben, Baron Friedrich Wilhelm Ludolf Gerhard Augustin von (b. Prussia, Sept. 17, 1730—d. Nov. 28, 1794), soldier. Steuben served in his own country during the Seven Years' War, reaching the rank of captain. In 1777, heavily in debt and looking for employment, he came to America and offered his services to Congress. By March, 1778, he was at Valley Forge doing a job of training soldiers; his *Regulations* (written, 1778–79) became the standard guide for the Continental Army. In May he was given the rank of major-general. At the Battle of Monmouth he rallied the retreating troops of Charles Lee and re-formed them for action. In 1780 he assisted General Greene in the South, later commanded a division at Yorktown and received Cornwallis' proposal of surrender. After the war, by acts of

in the Royal Institution of Great Britain. Material relating to America was also collected for the British Museum. The older brother wrote *Historical Nuggets* (1862); *Bibliotheca Historica* (1870); and *Recollections of Mr. James Lenox of New York and the Formation of His Library* (1886).

Stevens, Gavin, a character created by WILLIAM FAULKNER. Stevens, a lawyer and later the county attorney in Jefferson, appears in several of Faulkner's novels. Educated at Harvard and Heidelberg, he is a philosophic observer and

STEVENS GENEALOGY

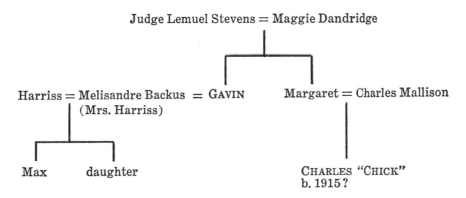

Judge Lemuel Stevens = Maggie Dandridge

Harriss = Melisandre Backus = GAVIN   Margaret = Charles Mallison
         (Mrs. Harriss)

Max   daughter   CHARLES "CHICK"
                                             b. 1915?

the Pennsylvania and New York legislatures, he became an American citizen. He submitted to Washington a plan for a small standing army and a military school in *A Letter on the Subject of an Established Militia* (1784).

Stevens, Abel (b. Philadelphia, Jan. 17, 1815—d. Sept. 11, 1897), Methodist clergyman, historian, biographer, editor. Stevens, who served as editor of *Zion's Herald* (1840–52) and the *National Magazine* (1852–56), wrote numerous works of historical character. Among them were *A History of the Religious Movement of the 18th Century Called Methodism* (3 v., 1858–61); *A History of the Methodist Episcopal Church in the U.S.* (4 v., 1864–67); and *Madame De Staël* (2 v., 1881). He also wrote *Sketches and Incidents* (2 v., 1844–45).

Stevens, Benjamin Franklin (b. Barnet, Vt., Feb. 19, 1833—d. March 5, 1902) and his brother **Henry Stevens** (b. Barnet, Vt., Aug. 24, 1819—d. Feb. 28, 1886), booksellers, bibliographers. These Americans became London booksellers, specializing in Americana. They acted as agents for American bibliophiles and for the Library of Congress; some of their research material is now deposited in the latter institution. The younger Stevens prepared an *Introduction to the Catalogue Index of Manuscripts in the Archives of England, France, Holland, and Spain Relating to America, 1763 to 1783,* also a *Report on American Manuscripts*

commentator on events in YOKNAPATAWPHA COUNTY, although he rarely is directly involved in them. He develops a hopeless love for Eula Varner Snopes in *The Town,* and later for her daughter, Linda, in *The Mansion;* he solves murders in KNIGHT'S GAMBIT, and is a somewhat ineffectual but philosophic presence in INTRUDER IN THE DUST. Finally, to cure himself of his unrewarded love for Linda Snopes, he marries Melisandre Backus Harriss, a wealthy widow who appears in the title story of *Knight's Gambit.*

Stevens, James [Floyd] (b. near Albia, Iowa, Nov. 15, 1892—   ), public relations counsel, storyteller, columnist. Stevens won a notable success with his first book, *Paul Bunyan* (1925), then dealt with Paul in three other works, *Saginaw Paul Bunyan* (1932), *Paul Bunyan's Bears* (1947), and *Paul Bunyan's Tree Farm* (1954). He also wrote novels, based largely on his experiences in the Northwest. Among them: *Brawny-man* (1926) and *Big Jim Turner* (1948). *Mattock* (1927) describes experiences in World War I, and *Homer in the Sagebrush* (1928) contains thirteen short stories about the West. *Green Power* appeared in 1958.

Stevens, Thaddeus (b. Danville, Vt., April 4, 1792—d. Aug. 11, 1868), teacher, lawyer, industrialist, public official. Stevens taught school in York, Pa., practiced law at Gettysburg, made investments in local industries. He was elected six times to the Pennsylvania legislature and became known for his attacks on Free Masonry and slavery and his advocacy of public education, banking interests, and tariff protection. He was elected as a Whig to the House of Representatives in 1849, then switched to the Republican party in 1859. His strong views on slavery led him to become a leader of the radical wing of the Republican party, which initiated "carpetbag" rule in the reconstructed South, passed the 14th Amendment, and tried to impeach President Johnson. The evil done by Stevens' harsh policy in the South has never been erased. There have been several biographies of Stevens, by J. A. Woodburn (1913), T. F. Woodley (1934), R. N. Current (1942), and Ralph Korngold (1955). He appears as "Stoneman" in Thomas Dixon's *The Clansman* (1905), consequently in D. W. Griffith's movie *The Birth of a Nation* (1915), based on the book.

Stevens, Wallace (b. Reading, Pa., Oct. 2, 1879—d. Aug. 2, 1955), poet, lawyer. Stevens was a lawyer who served for most of his life as an executive in an insurance company in Hartford, Conn. He wrote poetry in his spare time, won an early reputation as an experimentalist, and became one of the most influential and widely revered poets of his generation in America. He did not publish his first collection, HARMONIUM (1923; reprinted with additions, 1931), until he was forty-three years old; thereafter came *Ideas of Order* (1935); *Owl's Clover* (1936); *The Man with the Blue Guitar and Other Poems* (1937); *Parts of a World* (1942); NOTES TOWARD A SUPREME FICTION (1942); *Esthétique du Mal* (1945); *Transport to Summer* (1947); *Three Academic Pieces* (two poems and a prose address, 1947); *The Auroras of Autumn* (1950); THE NECESSARY ANGEL (essays and addresses, 1951); *Collected Poems* (1954); *Opus Posthumous* (ed. by Samuel French Morse, 1957).

In his youth Stevens was addicted to the more opulent manifestations of reality, particularly the West Indies, and he invested his poems with a Caribbean exoticism of sea and jungle. He employed a recondite vocabularly, lavish imagery, metaphors of brilliant originality, and a rhetoric whose intricate stylizations were designed not only to please but to shock. At the level of prosody he was always the master; in some of his early poems he produced blank verse of a quality unmatched elsewhere in the twentieth century, and in his less conventional poems he was nearly uniformly superb. In his later work he turned away from the tropical splendors of the South and devoted himself more to the harsher landscapes of New England, where he made his home. But until the end of his life his poetic style remained marked by a kind of intelligent dandyism, never soft or merely pretty, always hard as a diamond and regally controlled.

Critics unfailingly point out the great influence of the French Symbolist movement on the development of Stevens' verse. What is less often noticed is Stevens' affinity to the English Romantics, especially Wordsworth and Coleridge. In substance his poems range through an extraordinary variety of topics, but his continuing theme was the exploration of man's aesthetic experience as the key to fundamental reality. He emphasized the role of the imagination as a way of knowing and posited metaphor as the chief form, not only of expression, but of knowledge. Beneath Stevens' surface elegance there is often a sense of brooding, especially in his later poems, an ethical discontent which is not always made explicit or even clear. In a review of one of his books a critic for *Time* once wrote: "Few living poets can be as vivid and as vague, both at once."

In December, 1940, the *Harvard Advocate* issued a "Wallace Stevens Number." William Van O'Connor's *The Shaping Spirit: A Study of Wallace Stevens* (1950) is a critical study. A number of analytical and eulogistic essays were collected in a special issue of the *Trinity College Review* (May, 1954) in honor of the poet's seventy-fifth birthday. Samuel French Morse compiled *Wallace Stevens: A Preliminary Checklist of His Published Writings* (1954). Robert Pack's *Wallace Stevens*, an extended critical study, was published in 1958.

Stevenson, Adlai E[wing] (b. Los Angeles, Calif., Feb. 5, 1900—d. July 14, 1965), lawyer, statesman. Stevenson was graduated from Princeton, attended Harvard Law School and Northwestern University Law School, and was admitted to the bar in 1926. He worked in various government agencies in Washington, practiced law in Chicago, served as special assistant first to Secretary of the Navy Frank Knox, later to two Secretaries of State, Edward Stettinius and James Byrnes. He handled press relations at the San Francisco United Nations Conference, was senior adviser to the United States delegation to the United Nations General Assembly. In 1947 he was elected governor of Illinois and instituted many vigorous reforms. He was Democratic nominee for President in 1952 and again in 1956, but both times lost the election to Dwight D. Eisenhower. He was appointed Ambassador to the United Nations by President Kennedy in 1961.

Stevenson's campaign speeches established him as one of the most brilliant orators in United States history; someone remarked, "They can keep Stevenson out of the White House, but not out of Bartlett." His addresses have been remarkable for their sincerity, their fairness to his opponents, their insight, their incisive humor. John K. Hutchens in the New York *Herald Tribune* (May 11, 1953) spoke of "their combination of style and sense, those infrequent political bed-fellows." The Republican party's slogan, Stevenson remarked, was to "throw the rascals in"; more seriously he stated: "My definition of a free society is a society where it is safe to be unpopular." His speeches have been published in *Speeches of Adlai Stevenson* (1952); *Adlai's Almanac; The Wit and Wis-*

dom of Stevenson of Illinois (1952); *Major Campaign Speeches of Adlai E. Stevenson* (1953); *Call to Greatness* (1954).

During the 1952 campaign, biographies were written by Noel F. Busch and John Bartlow Martin; later books on Stevenson were written by Walter Johnson (1955), Elizabeth Stevenson Ives and Hildegarde Dolson (1956), Kenneth S. Davis (1957), and Stuart G. Brown (1961). Among Stevenson's books are: *What I Think* (1956); *Friends and Enemies* (1959); *Putting First Things First, A Democratic View* (1960).

Stevenson, Burton E[gbert] (b. Chillicothe, Ohio, Nov. 9, 1872—d. May 13, 1962), newsman, librarian, compiler of reference works, novelist. At first a member of the staff of two Chillicothe newspapers and a correspondent for the New York *Tribune*, Stevenson became librarian of the public library in his home town in 1899. He also founded the American Library in Paris and acted as its director at various times. His works include about forty novels, mystery stories, books for children, and a play (*A King in Babylon*, pub. 1955); but his chief reputation came as the compiler and editor of a number of useful reference works. Among them: *Poems of American History* (1908); THE HOME BOOK OF VERSE (1912); *The Home Book of Verse for Young Folks* (1915); *The Home Book of Modern Verse* (1925); *The Home Book of Quotations* (1934); *The Home Book of Proverbs, Maxims, and Familiar Phrases* (1948); *The Home Book of Bible Quotations* (1949); *Standard Book of Shakespeare Quotations* (1953). The eighth edition, revised, enlarged, of the *Home Book of Quotations* appeared in 1956.

Stevenson, Robert Louis (b. Scotland, Nov. 13, 1850—d. Nov. 13, 1894), novelist, short-story writer, essayist, writer of travel books, poet. Stevenson had numerous connections with the United States. He fell in love with an American woman, Mrs. Fanny Osbourne, and after she divorced her first husband he married her (1880). One of her sons, LLOYD OSBOURNE, became Stevenson's helper and collaborator and later led an independent literary existence. Stevenson first came to the United States in 1879, and went to California to be near Mrs. Osbourne. While walking from San Francisco to Monterey he lost his way, and the resultant exposure permanently damaged his delicate constitution. At Monterey he managed to write *The Pavilion on the Links*, his famous essay on Thoreau, and drafts of *The Amateur Emigrant* (1895) and *Prince Otto* (1895). ACROSS THE PLAINS (1892) recounts his trip across the country. *The Silverado Squatters* (1883) describes his honeymoon trip (accompanied by Lloyd Osbourne) to the abandoned mining town of Silverado, Calif. Anne Roller Issler wrote *Stevenson at Silverado* (1939), and a trilogy published by the Stanford University Press commemorates Stevenson's stay in California: Anne B. Fisher's *No More a Stranger* (1946), and Mrs. Issler's *Happier for His*

Presence (1949) and *Our Mountain Hermitage* (1949). Stevenson made use of some San Francisco background material in his novel *The Wrecker* (1892), written with Osbourne; he also pictured S. S. MCCLURE, the magazine publisher, as Jim Pinkerton in that book. Other details of the city appear in *The Ebb-Tide* (1894), also written with Osbourne; and he wrote a picturesque essay on San Francisco.

In August, 1880, the Stevensons returned to Scotland, and thereafter Stevenson published some of his most famous books. In 1887 they returned to the United States, and Stevenson stayed for a time at the Trudeau sanitarium at Saranac, N.Y., in a vain effort to overcome his tubercular condition. He hated the climate, but wrote a number of essays there, as well as most of *The Master of Ballantrae* (1889). Subsequently he made a pleasanter stay at Manasquan on the New Jersey coast. Charlotte Eaton, the wife of an artist friend, recorded her memories of this time in *Stevenson at Manasquan* (1921). Finally the Stevensons set out for the South Seas, stopping in Honolulu for five months, where Stevenson finished *The Master of Ballantrae*. They settled in Apia, in the Samoan Islands, in October, 1890, and Stevenson died there four years later.

Edwin J. Beinecke collected a vast amount of valuable material relating to Stevenson, and in 1951 presented the collection to Yale University. This is undoubtedly the most important collection of Stevenson material to be found anywhere, and has been catalogued in several volumes by George L. McKay.

Stewart, Donald Ogden (b. Columbus, Ohio, Nov. 30, 1894—   ), actor, humorist, author of movie scripts. Stewart won his first success as an actor, particularly in Philip Barry's HOLIDAY (1928–29) and in his own play *Rebound* (1930). After a spell in the Navy in World War I he began writing screenplays and books of humor, some of which became best sellers. Among them: *A Parody Outline of History* (1921); *Aunt Polly's Story of Mankind* (1923); *Mr. and Mrs. Haddock Abroad* (1924); *Mr. and Mrs. Haddock in Paris, France* (1926); *Father William* (1929). After fifteen years in Hollywood, he returned to Broadway with a fantasy called *How I Wonder* (1947), which received unfavorable critical notices.

Stewart, George R[ippey] (b. Sewickley, Pa., May 31, 1895—   ), teacher, writer. A graduate of Princeton University in 1917, Stewart taught English and American literature at Columbia University, the University of Michigan, the University of California, and elsewhere. He wrote some conventional fiction, particularly *Doctor's Oral* (1939), a harrowing account of what happens when a graduate student come up for his oral examination. *East of the Giants* (1938) is also a novel, a tale of the gold rush; and *Storm* (1941) is a fictionalized account of a huge weather disturbance as it travels eastward from the Orient to the Atlantic ocean. *The Years of the City*, a novel, appeared in 1955. Stewart's writing shows a remarkable gift for popularizing abstruse scholarly and scientific information without in any way cheapening it; among his nonfiction writings are a life of Bret Harte (1931); *Ordeal by Hunger* (1936); *Names on the Land* (1945); *Man, an Autobiography* (1946); *Fire* (1948); *U.S. 40* (a biography of a highway, (1953); *American Ways of Life* (1954); *Pickett's Charge* (1959); *Donner Pass and Those Who Crossed It* (1960).

Stewart, Randall (b. Fayetteville, Tenn., July 25, 1896—   ), teacher. With degrees from Vanderbilt, Harvard, and Yale Universities, Stewart began teaching English at Oklahoma, taught later at Idaho and Vanderbilt, and joined the faculty of Brown in 1937. He is noted for his work on Hawthorne's life and writings, preparing authoritative editions of *The American Notebooks of Nathaniel Hawthorne* (1932) and Hawthorne's *English Notebooks* (1941), also a biography of Hawthorne (1948). He edited *Letters to Sophia* [Hawthorne] for the *Huntington Library Quarterly* (VII, 1944). Stewart performed a great service to Hawthorne scholarship by reinstating many frank words and phrases from the *Notebooks* which Mrs. Hawthorne had bowdlerized after her husband's death. Along with Walter Blair and Theodore Hornberger, Stewart edited an anthology, *The Literature of the United States* (1946). In 1958 he published *American Literature and Christian Doctrine*.

Stickney, [Joseph] Trumbull (b. Switzerland, June 20, 1874—d. Oct. 11, 1904), poet, dramatist. Stickney's parents brought him to the United States when he was five years old; his father was head of the Latin department at Trinity College. His father was his only teacher, and under his instruction Stickney was able to enter Harvard, from which he graduated in 1895. He returned at once to Europe, studied at the Sorbonne, and was the first American to receive that institution's *Doctorat des Lettres*. He went back to teach at Harvard, and died of a brain tumor at the age of thirty.

In his studies and in his general philosophy Stickney was closely associated with WILLIAM VAUGHN MOODY, with whom he read much Greek literature. Moody wrote THE FIRE-BRINGER (1904); Stickney preceded him with a dramatic work on the same theme, PROMETHEUS PYRPHOROS (1900). He also prepared a collection of *Dramatic Verses* (1902). After Stickney's death Moody and two other friends, George Cabot Lodge and J. E. Lodge, collected his *Poems* (1905).

Sticks and Stones (1924), a study of American architecture in its relationship to American civilization by LEWIS MUMFORD. Mumford covers a wide range, from the Puritan villages of New England, which he compares with the communal organization in Sir Thomas More's *Utopia*, to modern buildings, which he defines as establishments "devoted to the manufacture of light, the circulation of air, the maintenance of uniform temperature, and the vertical trans-

portation of its inhabitants." The book is rich in insights, novel points of view, and happy phrases.

Stieglitz, Alfred (b. Hoboken, N.J., Jan. 1, 1864—d. July 13, 1946), photoengraver, photographer, editor. Stieglitz studied engineering, chemistry, and photoengraving in Germany and the United States. His interest in three-color processes led him to experiments in photography which attracted wide attention and brought about an appreciation of the potentialities of photography as an art. His own photographs won many prizes all over the world. He established a movement called "Photo-Secession," and set up a gallery where the work of its adherents could be exhibited. He encouraged many artists outside of photography, including Georgia O'Keeffe, whom he married in 1925. He edited the *American Amateur Photographer* (1892–96); founded, managed, and edited *Camera Notes* (1897–1903); edited and published the quarterly *Camera Work* from 1903 until his death. He was recognized as the leading photographer and theorist of photographic methods in the United States. He wrote *Picturesque Bits of New York, and Other Studies* in 1897.

Stiles, Ezra (b. North Haven, Conn., Nov. 29, 1727—d. May 12, 1795), teacher, lawyer, clergyman, scholar, educational administrator. Stiles was a graduate of Yale, taught there for a while, then practiced law in New Haven. For twenty-two years he filled various Congregational pulpits in Rhode Island (where he helped found Rhode Island College, later Brown University) and New Hampshire. In 1778 he became president of Yale College and professor of ecclesiastical history, and gave instruction in Hebrew and the sciences. He had a great zeal for civil and religious liberties and was one of the earliest supporters of American independence.

He published little in his own lifetime, his chief literary production being his *History of Three of the Judges of King Charles I* (1794). He also published some of his sermons and addresses, one of which was entitled *The United States Elevated to Glory and Honor* (1783). His *Diary* and other writings are preserved at Yale in forty-five volumes. A portion of the former, called *Literary Diary*, was published in 1901 with F. B. Dexter as editor; Dexter also edited *Extracts and Miscellanies* (1916). I. M. Calder edited his *Letters and Papers* (1933). His *Life* (1798) was written by Abiel Holmes, his son-in-law and the father of O. W. Holmes.

Still, James (b. Double Creek, Ala., July 16, 1906—   ), poet, novelist, short-story writer. James Still was educated at Vanderbilt University and the University of Illinois. He worked as a librarian in rural Kentucky and became a resident of that state. Much of his writing derived from his knowledge of life in the Kentucky mountains, vividly evoking the scenery, language, and mores of the region. His volume of poetry, *Hounds on the Mountain* (1937), received critical praise; his novel,

River of Earth (1940), and his collection of short stories, *On Troublesome Creek* (1941), have been commended as recreating with great fidelity and sensual immediacy the life of simple mountain people. Since the forties many of Still's stories and poems have appeared in literary magazines and anthologies.

Still, William Grant (b. Woodville, Miss., May 11, 1895—   ), musician. Still studied music at the Oberlin Conservatory of Music and the New England Conservatory; he received the honorary degree of Mus. Dr. from Howard University. He played violin, oboe, and cello in orchestras, arranged music for various orchestras and directed them, especially on the "Deep River Hour" on radio. Still was the first Negro to conduct a major symphony orchestra in this country—the Los Angeles Philharmonic (1936) in the Hollywood Bowl. He often treated Negro or African themes, as in his symphony *Afro-American* (1930); *A Deserted Plantation* (1933); *And They Lynched Him on a Tree* (1940) for chorus and orchestra; *From the Delta* (1945).

Stillwater Tragedy, The (1880), a novel by THOMAS BAILEY ALDRICH. The novel is notable as perhaps the first to introduce a "private eye," several years before Sherlock Holmes, also for its introduction of a labor union leader (who turns out to be willing to help with a murder).

Stilwell, Joseph Warren (b. Palatka, Fla., March 19, 1883—d. Oct. 12, 1946), soldier, teacher, diarist. Stilwell, known to his colleagues as "Vinegar Joe," was a brave, capable, and outspoken officer, a graduate of West Point, later an instructor there. He served with the American Expeditionary Force in Europe in World War I, later in the Far East on various assignments. During World War II he was promoted to the rank of lieutenant general and given command of all American and some Chinese forces in the China-Burma-India theater. His outnumbered troops were driven back by the Japanese, but his retreat from Burma to India was regarded as an outstanding feat of the war. He severely criticized Lord Louis Mountbatten for not launching a full-scale offensive in Burma and had serious disagreements with the Chinese leader Chiang Kai-shek. He was therefore recalled (November, 1944) and given command of American ground forces, the 10th Army in the Pacific theater. After his death appeared the *Stilwell Papers* (1948), edited and arranged from his diaries and letters by Theodore H. White. The book contains an immense amount of data on the long-continued controversy over China and the Communists. White found his observations "quick, biting, pictorial." He wrote with integrity, telling the truth as he saw it.

Stimpson, George W[illiam] (b. Jones Co., Iowa, Nov. 3, 1896—d. Sept. 27, 1952), newspaperman, historian. Stimpson studied law for a while but found newspaper work more attractive. He was on the Valparaiso *Messenger* in 1921–22, then went to Washington to work for the *Herald*, became associate editor of *The*

Pathfinder and later Washington correspondent of the Houston *Post* and other papers. He acquired an immense amount of information, especially about American history and politics. He conducted a radio program and also a daily syndicated feature, "Information Roundup." Beginning in 1928 he published a series of popular books in which he gave carefully authenticated answers to questions of great variety. Among them: *Nuggets of Knowledge* (1928); *Popular Questions Answered* (1930); *Things Worth Knowing* (1932); *Uncommon Knowledge* (1936); *A Book About the Bible* (1945); *A Book About a Thousand Things* (1946); *Information Roundup* (1948); *A Book About American History* (1950); *A Book About American Politics* (1952). His books are not collections of arid data but fascinating symposia.

Stimson, Frederic Jesup ["J. S. of Dale"] (b. Dedham, Mass., July 20, 1855—d. Nov. 19, 1943), lawyer, teacher, diplomat, author. A distinguished lawyer and professor of law at Harvard, Stimson also served as ambassador to Argentina and Brazil. Under his own name he wrote *Government by Injunction* (1894); *Labor in Its Relation to Laws* (1895); *The American Constitution* (1908); and *My United States* (1931). Under his pseudonym he wrote lighter works of various kinds: *Rollo's Journey to Cambridge* (1879); *The Crime of Henry Vane* (1884); *The Sentimental Calendar* (1886); *King Noanett* (1896); *Jethro Bacon of Sandwich* (1902); *In Cure of Her Soul* (1906); *My Story: Being the Memoirs of Benedict Arnold* (1917).

Stimson, Henry L[ewis] (b. New York City, Sept. 21, 1867—d. Oct. 20, 1950), lawyer, public official, author. One of the ablest men ever to hold public office, Stimson was a Yale graduate who took an M.A. at Harvard and later studied law there. He was a member of distinguished law firms in New York for many years, but also served as United States attorney for the southern district of New York, as Secretary of War under Taft, Secretary of State under Hoover, and Secretary of War under Franklin D. Roosevelt and Truman. The so-called Stimson Doctrine required nonrecognition of territory taken by aggressors. He believed in increased income taxes for the rich and in universal military training. He wrote several books, among them *American Policy in Nicaragua* (1927); *Democracy and Nationalism in Europe* (1934); *The Far Eastern Crisis* (1936); and an autobiography, *On Active Service in Peace and War* (with McGeorge Bundy, 1948). Richard N. Current, in *Secretary Stimson: A Study in Statecraft* (1954), suggests that the Stimson Doctrine made Japan decide on war with the United States.

Stith, William (b. Virginia [?], 1707—d. Sept. 19, 1755), clergyman, teacher, historian, educational administrator. Stith was educated at Oxford and ordained in the Church of England. On his return to the colonies in 1731 he was elected master of the grammar school in William and Mary College, and five years later took charge of Henrico Parish, where he wrote his most famous book, *History of the First Discovery and Settlement of Virginia* (1747). In 1752 he was appointed president of William and Mary, and at the same time served as minister of York-Hampton Parish. Among his other publications were *A Sermon Preached Before the General Assembly* (1745) and *The Sinfulness and Pernicious Nature of Gaming* (1752).

Stith was a careful researcher, gathering facts for his history both in England and America. His book has been accused of verbosity on the one hand, on the other of neglecting economic factors in favor of political and personal data. Reprints appeared in 1753 and 1865.

Stobo, Robert (b. Glasgow, Scotland, 1727 —d. 1772[?]), soldier, memoirist. Stobo served under Washington at Fort Necessity (1754). Held as a hostage by the French, he was sentenced to death (1755) but escaped from Quebec, joined the British at Louisburg, and assisted Wolfe in his attack on Quebec (1759). Later he served in the West Indies and England. His *Memoirs* appeared in 1800. Meanwhile Tobias Smollett had used him as a model for the character of an eccentric Scottish soldier in his last novel, *The Expedition of Humphry Clinker* (1771). In Sir Gilbert Parker's novel *Seats of the Mighty* (1896), Stobo was similarly the model for Robert Moray.

Stockton, Francis [Frank] R[ichard] (b. Philadelphia, April 5, 1834—d. April 20, 1902), novelist, short-story writer, editor. Stockton was one of the most admired fiction writers of the later 19th century—for his humor, his ingenuity, his narrative ability. At the present his works are little read, except for a few frequently anthologized stories. He was a forerunner of O. Henry in the trick ending, but in the development of his stories is much less artificial; his style is more natural and less rhetorical. He was not particularly concerned with social, political, and economic problems, but regarded himself primarily as an entertainer.

At first a wood engraver and draftsman, Stockton early turned to writing. He worked for a while on newspapers in Philadelphia and New York, contributed humorous pieces to *Vanity Fair,* joined the staff of *Scribner's Magazine,* and later was assistant editor of *St. Nicholas.* During the period of his writing stories for children he developed his vein of fantasy and humor. Not until he was forty-five did he publish a book—RUDDER GRANGE (1879), which won national renown. The story concerns a newly married, devoted, but impecunious couple who take up residence in an abandoned canal boat which ultimately gets adrift in Newark Bay. There is little plot, but it was enough to satisfy its many readers, who demanded a sequel; Stockton obliged with *The Rudder Grangers Abroad* (1891) and *Pomona's Travels* (1894). But plot was everything in Stockton's most famous story, THE LADY OR THE TIGER?, which first appeared in the *Century* (November, 1882), took the lead in the collection called *The Lady or the Tiger? and Other Stories* (1884), and furnished material for an operetta (1888).

The success of this story made it possible for Stockton to devote all his time to writing for adults. Yet there was a close connection between his stories for a juvenile audience and his more mature work. In the latter one finds the same love of the marvelous, the same fanciful humor that appear in *Ting-a-ling* (1870); *Roundabout Rambles in Lands of Fact and Fancy* (1872); *Tales Out of School* (1875); *A Jolly Fellowship* (1880); *The Floating Prince and Other Fairy Tales* (1881); *The Story of Viteau* (1884); *The Bee Man of Orn and Other Fanciful Tales* (1887). Stockton wrote one of the earliest science-fiction stories, *A Tale of Negative Gravity* (*Century Magazine,* December, 1884). Fred Lewis Pattee praises Stockton's ability to be "humorous without being grotesque," his "whimsical unexpectedness," his tinge of irony. Among stories of his most likely to be remembered are *The Love Letters of Smith, Zenobia's Infidelity, The Remarkable Wreck of the "Thomas Hyke,"* and *The Griffin and the Minor Canon.*

The funniest of Stockton's novels is probably THE CASTING AWAY OF MRS. LECKS AND MRS. ALESHINE (1886). Other books include *The Late Mrs. Null* (1886); *The Adventures of Captain Horn* (1895); *The Great Stone of Sardis* (1898); *Kate Bonnet* (1902); also the short-story collections, *A Christmas Wreck and Other Stories* (1886); *The Clocks of Rondaine* (1892); *Fanciful Tales* (1894); *The Magic Egg* (1907). His *Novels and Stories* (23 v.) appeared in 1899–1904. Martin J. Griffin, Jr., wrote *Frank R. Stockton: A Critical Biography* (1939).

Stoddard, Charles Warren (b. Rochester, N.Y., Aug. 7, 1843—d. Apr. 23, 1909), poet, teacher, author of travel books. Stoddard attended college at Oakland, Calif., and contributed to magazines, especially Bret Harte's *Golden Era;* in 1867 Harte edited Stoddard's *Poems* for publication. Stoddard's poor health sent him abroad on travels; he wrote many books about the places he visited. The most famous and influential was SOUTH-SEA IDYLS (1873; English ed., 1874), which was read by Robert Louis Stevenson and many others and started the literary vogue for Polynesia. Among his other books: *Mashallah!* (1881); *The Lepers of Molokai* (1885 which led Stevenson to his famous Father Damien outburst); *Hawaiian Life: Lazy Letters from Low Latitudes* (1894); *A Cruise Under the Crescent from Suez to San Marco* (1898); *Over the Rocky Mountains to Alaska* (1899); *In the Footprints of the Padres* (1902); *The Island of Tranquil Delights* (1904). Ina Coolbrith edited his *Poems* in 1917. His *A Troubled Heart* (1885) tells the story of his conversion to Roman Catholicism. Stoddard was a pleasant writer but without great literary merit. Among his many friends was Mark Twain, whom he served as secretary.

Stoddard, Henry L[uther] (b. New York City, Oct. 7, 1861—d. Dec. 13, 1947), newspaperman, editor, author. Stoddard served on many newspapers in New York and Philadelphia, and was a great admirer of Horace Greeley, of whom he published a stimulating biography in 1946. He knew intimately all the great political figures of his day. Among his books of reminiscences is *Presidential Sweepstakes: The Story of Political Conventions and Campaigns* (1948).

Stoddard, John L[awson] (b. Brookline, Mass., April 24, 1850—d. June 5, 1931), traveler, lecturer, writer, editor. Stoddard began his world-wide travels in 1874 and by 1879 was winning fame as a vivid lecturer on his experiences. Later he wrote many books on his trips abroad, and on other topics: *Red-Letter Days Abroad* (1884); *Glimpses of the World* (1892); *Lectures* (10 v., 1897–98; 5 additional v., 1901); *Beautiful Scenes of America* (1902); and *Poems* (1913). He edited *The Stoddard Library* (12 v., 1910), selections from "the world's great writers." D. Crane Taylor wrote *John L. Stoddard* (1935).

Stoddard, [Theodore] Lothrop (b. Brookline, Mass., June 29, 1883—d. May 1, 1950), lawyer, writer. Stoddard was greatly interested in the influence of race, geography, and history upon nations and wrote many books discussing these matters, especially as they affected the United States. Among his titles: *Present-Day Europe—Its National States of Mind* (1917); *The Rising Tide of Color Against White World-Supremacy* (1920); *The New World of Islam* (1921); *The Revolt Against Civilization* (1922); *Racial Realities in Europe* (1924); *Re-Forging America* (1927); *Europe and Our Money* (1932); *Lonely America* (1932); *Into the Darkness* (1940). He also wrote *Master of Manhattan* (1931), a life of Tammany boss Richard Croker.

Stoddard, Richard Henry (b. Hingham, Mass., July 2, 1825—d. May 12, 1903), poet, book reviewer, editor, public official. Stoddard worked for several newspapers and magazines in New York City, after holding jobs of various

kinds in an effort to help his poverty-stricken family. In 1845 he began to win a hearing for his verse. He followed the model of the popular Romantic and Victorian poets, later began to introduce Oriental subject matter into his verses. He eked out his income by holding various government jobs, including that of inspector of customs in New York, a position obtained for him by Nathaniel Hawthorne. He wrote reviews for the New York *Mail and Express* and for a magazine called *Aldine* and edited various series of volumes. He was highly respected as a critic.

His best poem was *Abraham Lincoln: An Horatian Ode* (1865), but his poetry in general was imitative and tame. He made many contemporary authors better known to readers in his pleasantly intimate *Bric-a-Brac Series* and *Sans-Souci Series.* Among his books: *Footprints* (1849); *Poems* (1852); *The King's Bell* (1863); *The Book of the East and Other Poems* (1871); *The Lion's Cub with Other Verse* (1890); *Recollections, Personal and Literary* (1903). In 1880 appeared a collection of all his poems to that date.

Stoddard, Solomon (b. Boston, Sept. [?], 1643—d. Feb. 11, 1729), Congregational clergyman, controversialist. A graduate of Harvard, Stoddard became its first librarian (1667–74), and served as pastor at Northampton (1672–1729). He engaged in warm controversy with

INCREASE MATHER and wrote in defense of "Stoddardeanism" in *The Doctrine of Instituted Churches* (1700). He also wrote *An Answer to Some Cases of Conscience* (1722), which answered such questions as these: "Is It Lawful to Wear Long Hair?" "Did We Any Wrong to the Indians in Buying Their Land at a Small Price?" He answered no to both queries. Stoddard was the grandfather of Jonathan Edwards and therefore an ancestor of Aaron Burr, also of Charles Warren Stoddard, John L. Stoddard, and other persons of note.

Stoddard, William Osborn ["Col. Cris Forrest"] (b. Homer, N.Y., Sept. 24, 1835—d. Aug. 29, 1925), editor, public official, inventor, author. Stoddard, a man of wide interests and abilities, after graduation from the University of Rochester became associate editor of the West Urbana *Central Illinois Gazette*. In the course of his work he met Lincoln, was deeply impressed by him, and was one of the first to suggest him for the Presidency. When Lincoln was elected, Stoddard became an assistant private secretary. Later he wrote *Abraham Lincoln* (1884); *Inside the White House in War Times* (1890); *The Table Talk of Abraham Lincoln* (1894); *Lincoln at Work* (1900); *The Lives of the Presidents* (10 v., 1886–89). He served as U.S. marshal of Arkansas, patented nine inventions in the fields of telegraphy, manufacturing, and railways, and still managed to write more than a hundred books, more than seventy of them for boys. Among these juveniles were *Dab Kinzer* (1881); *The Red Mustang* (1890); *Little Smoke: A Tale of the Sioux* (1891); *The Lost Gold of the Montezumas* (1897); *The Spy of Yorktown* (1903).

Stokes, Frederick A[bbot] (b. Brooklyn, N.Y., Nov. 4, 1857—d. Nov. 15, 1939), publisher, memoirist. Stokes founded the publishing house named after him (1881), which in 1941 was consolidated with J. B. Lippincott & Co. He wrote *College Tramps* (1880) and *A Publisher's Random Notes, 1880–1935* (1935). In 1926 appeared *The House of Stokes, 1881–1926.*

Stolz, Mary Slattery (b. Boston, Mass., March 20, 1924—   ), author. Mrs. Stolz gained distinction and popularity by her portrayal of teenage girls in both novels and short stories. She presents realistic situations and problems that encourage her young readers to think rather than to dream, and she also gives much practical information on careers in which young girls might be most interested. Her books: *To Tell Your Love* (1950); *The Seagulls Woke Me* (1951); *Ready or Not* (1953); *In A Mirror* (1953); *Pray Love Remember* (1954); *The Leftover Elf* (1952); *Truth and Consequence* (1953); *Two by Two* (1954); *Rosemary* (1955); *The Day and the Way We Met* (1956); *Hospital Zone* (1956); *Because of Madeline* (1957); *Goodbye My Shadow* (1957); *Second Nature* (1958); *And Love Replied* (1958); *Some Merry-Go-Round Music* (1959); *A Dog on Barkham Street* (1960); *Emmett's Pig* (1960); *The Beautiful Friend* (1960).

Stone, Grace Zaring ["Ethel Vance"] (b. New York City, Jan. 9, 1896—   ), novelist. Mrs. Stone made two careers in fiction, writing her more serious books under her own name, her more sensational books under her pen name. Both kinds have been very popular. Among the former: *Letters to a Djinn* (1922); *The Heaven and Earth of Doña Elena* (1929); *The Bitter Tea of General Yen* (1930); *The Almond Tree* (1931); *The Cold Journey* (1934). Under her pen name she wrote *Escape* (1939); *Reprisal* (1942); *Winter Meeting* (1946); *The Secret Thread* (1948); *The Grotto* (1951). It is said that Mrs. Stone first used a pen name for *Escape*, a lurid tale of Nazi tyranny, in order to protect her daughter, at that time married to a German nobleman who was an official in the Nazi regime.

Stone, Irving ["Irving Tennenbaum"] (b. San Francisco, July 14, 1903—   ), novelist, teacher, short-story writer, playwright, theater director, biographer. Stone worked his way through the University of California by playing the saxophone in a dance band and picking fruit during the summer. He taught economics while taking his master's degree, but gave up his studies and turned to writing. He wrote short stories and plays, directed a theater in Jersey City, and made a living by writing for pulp magazines. The turning point in his career came when in 1930 in Paris he became interested in the paintings and life of Vincent van Gogh, the Dutch artist. His first novel, *Pageant of Youth* (1933), made no particular impression, but he created a sensation with *Lust for Life* (1934), a fictional biography of van Gogh, some of whose writings he also edited in *Dear Theo: The Autobiography of Vincent van Gogh* (1937).

Clarence Darrow for the Defense (1941) and *Earl Warren* (1948) are straight biographies, as is the entertaining and useful *They Also Ran* (1943), an account of Presidential nominees who failed to get into the White House. But more popular are Stone's other skillfully contrived fictional biographies: *Sailor on Horseback* (1938), about Jack London; *Immortal Wife* (1944), about Jessie Frémont; *Adversary in the House* (1947), about Eugene V. Debs and his wife; *The Passionate Journey* (1949), about the exciting and tormented artist, John Noble; *The President's Lady* (1951), about Rachel Jackson; *Love Is Eternal* (1954), about Mrs. Lincoln; and the best-selling *The Agony and the Ecstasy* (1961), about Michelangelo.

Stone also wrote a nonhistorical novel, *False Witness* (1940), edited an anthology of selections from the autobiographies of famous Americans, *We Speak for Ourselves* (1950), and wrote *Men to Match My Mountains; the Opening of the Far West, 1840–1900* (1956).

A brochure by Joseph Henry Jackson deals with *Irving Stone and the Biographical Novel* (1954). Stone has always stressed the fact that his novels are based on original research, and that sometimes he has discovered facts unknown to professional historians. But many critics have called his narratives "pseudo-biographies" which embroider too fancifully and sentimentally on the lives of their subjects. *Immortal Wife* is probably the best of Stone's biographical novels; the least convincing is *Love Is Eternal*.

Stone, John Augustus (b. Concord, Mass., Dec. 15, 1800—d. May 29, 1834), actor, playwright, poet. Stone played character roles well but won no great fame. When Edwin Forrest offered a prize for an Indian play, Stone's METAMORA (1829) won. Stone then wrote a number of similar plays: *Tancred: King of Sicily* (1831); *The Demoniac, or, The Prophet's Bride* (1831); *The Ancient Briton* (1833); *The Knight of the Golden Fleece, or, the Yankee in Spain* (1834). JAMES H. HACKETT commissioned him to revise James K. Paulding's THE LION OF THE WEST (1831), a farce, for his use, and it became one of his favorite productions, with Hackett in the role of Col. Nimrod Wildfire. The manuscript of this play, long lost, was discovered by James N. Tidwell in the British Museum and edited for publication in 1954. But Stone profited little from all his work, since Forrest, who made a fortune out of the plays by Stone, R. M. Bird, and others paid no royalties. In despair Stone committed suicide by throwing himself into the Schuylkill River. Forrest erected a handsome monument over the grave.

Stone, Melville E[lijah] (b. Hudson, Ill., Aug. 22, 1848—d. Feb. 15, 1929), newspaperman, editor, executive. With Victor F. Lawson, Stone founded the Chicago *News*, pioneered in setting the price of the paper at a penny. He made his paper an ardent defender of labor and a strong competitor for the Chicago *Tribune*. In 1888 he left the *News*, and in 1893 became the general manager of the Associated Press of Illinois, which later became the Associated Press (AP) in New York; Stone served as manager and editor from 1900 to 1921. He wrote *Fifty Years a Journalist* (1921).

Stone, William Leete (b. New Paltz, N.Y., Apr. 20, 1792—d. Aug. 15, 1844), newspaperman, editor, writer. Stone edited papers in New York and Connecticut, and in 1821 became proprietor and editor of the New York *Commercial Advertiser*. While at Hudson, N.Y., he edited a literary magazine called *The Lounger*, contributed tales to the popular "Annuals" of the period, some of which he collected as *Tales and Sketches* (1834), and showed a deep interest in history. He was particularly interested in the Indians of his own region and published several books on the subject, among them a *Life of Joseph Brant* (2 v., 1838) and *The Life and Times of Red Jacket* (1841). He took a keen pleasure in exposing impostors, as in *Matthias and His Impostures* (1833), an account of some religious delusions, and *Maria Monk and the Nunnery of Hôtel Dieu* (1836), an account of a woman who claimed to have revealed shocking practices in a convent. He was also active in politics and sometimes engaged in violent controversies, particularly one with James Fenimore Cooper, who successfully sued Stone for libel.

Stong, Phil[ip Duffield] (b. Keosauqua, Iowa, Jan. 27, 1899—d. April 26, 1957), teacher, newspaperman, editor, writer. Stong worked as a high-school instructor, an editorial writer, an instructor in journalism and debating at Drake University, served on the staffs of several magazines, several news services, and the New York *World*. In 1932 appeared what is still his best known book, STATE FAIR; the same Iowan scene and some of the characters of this novel are found in a sequel, *Return in August* (1953). The great success of *State Fair* resulted in Stong's going to Hollywood, where he worked with Will Rogers on the first of three successful movie versions of the novel. Thereafter he wrote a long succession of stories, some for young people (*e.g.*, *Farm Boy*, 1934, and *The Hired Man's Elephant*, 1939), all agreeably and skillfully written; also some nonfiction, including *Horses and Americans* (1939); *Hawkeyes* (a history of Iowa, 1940); *Marta of Muscovy* (a biography of Peter the Great's wife, 1945); and others. Among his other novels: *The Stranger's Return* (1933); *Career* (1936); *The Iron Mountain* (1942); *Jessamy John* (1947); *Blizzard* (1955); *Gold in Them Hills* (1957). *If School Keeps* (1940) is an autobiography. His best books humorously present Middle-Western scenes and people.

Stopping by Woods on a Snowy Evening (*New Republic*, March 7, 1923; in *New Hampshire*, 1923), a poem by ROBERT FROST. Frost made some interesting remarks about this famous lyric. He said on one occasion that the poem contains "all I ever knew"; at another time that it was the kind of poem he'd like to print on one page, to be followed with "forty pages of footnotes." No one has attempted any such explication, although some readers have been a little puzzled to know exactly what Frost was trying to say in this beautifully phrased and irregularly melodious poem. Possibly Henry W. Wells hit it best when he interpreted the poem (*The American Way of Poetry*, 1943) as a "symbolic epitome" of "the ancient war, nowhere waged so fiercely as in the breast of the New Englander, between duty and beauty."

Stork, Charles Wharton (b. Philadelphia, Feb. 12, 1881—   ), poet, teacher, translator, editor. Stork taught English at the University of Pennsylvania and at Bryn Mawr College. He wrote much verse (collected in *Day Dreams of Greece*, 1908; *Sea and Bay*, 1916; and *Sunset Harbor*, 1933) and, as editor of the magazine *Contemporary Verse*, encouraged others to write. From this magazine he gathered material for two anthologies (1920, 1923). As translator he helped to familiarize American readers with Swedish literature in *Modern Swedish Masterpieces* (1923) and *Anthology of Swedish Lyrics* (1928, rev. ed. 1930).

Stormalong, Old. See OLD STORMALONG.

Story. A magazine founded in Vienna in April, 1931, by WHIT BURNETT and his wife MARTHA FOLEY. It was published there and then in Majorca until 1933, when the editors and their magazine came to New York City.

There the magazine attained fame as the only periodical exclusively devoted to the short story as an art form. It was at various times a monthly, a bimonthly, a quarterly, then in 1951 began to appear twice a year. The editors had by that time separated. In *Story: The Fiction of the Forties* (1949), Whit Burnett and Hallie Burnett, his second wife, chose fifty-one stories that had appeared in the pages of *Story* over a decade. The emphasis was on psychology rather than adventure, on the novel rather than the conventional, on the newcomer rather than the old-timer, on the unhappy childhood rather than the happy ending.

Story, Isaac (b. Marblehead, Mass., Aug. 7, 1774—d. July 19, 1803), editor, poet, essayist. This writer died so young, used so many pseudonyms (Peter Quince was one of them), and was so imitative that it is hard to say whether he had genuine promise or not. As a satirist he imitated the English writer Peter Pindar; as an essayist, Joseph Dennie, editor of the *Farmer's Weekly Museum*, in which some of his essays appeared. A collection of his satirical verses was published (by Peter Quince) as *A Parnassian Shop Opened in the Pindaric Stile* (1801). He also wrote poems with patriotic and romantic themes. Among his writings: *Liberty* (1795) and *An Eulogy on the Glorious Virtues of the Illustrious George Washington* (1800).

Story, Joseph (b. Marblehead, Mass., Sept. 10, 1779—d. Sept. 18, 1845), lawyer, public official, writer. Story shares with JOHN MARSHALL the credit for establishing the strength of the Supreme Court, particularly in its power to make decisions affecting the jurisdiction of the states. He began the practice of law in 1801, was elected first to the Massachusetts legislature, then to Congress, was made associate justice of the Supreme Court in 1811. In addition he became a professor of law at Harvard in 1829. During the War of 1812 he was responsible for many important decisions on maritime prizes, later for many decisions in the realm of equity jurisprudence. He was an ardent opponent of slavery. In his twenties he published a collection of verse, *The Power of Solitude* (1804), which he tried later to suppress; his decisions and his books on the law showed considerable literary ability. Among his books: *Commentaries on the Constitution of the United States* (3 v., 1833); *On the Conflict of Laws* (1834); *On Equity Jurisprudence* (2 v., 1835–36); *Equity Pleadings* (1838); *Law of Promissory Notes* (1845). His *Miscellaneous Writings* were gathered in 1852 by his son, the sculptor and poet WILLIAM WETMORE STORY, who had previously prepared the *Life and Letters* (2 v., 1851) of his father and had also made a statue of him.

Story, William Wetmore (b. Salem, Mass., Feb. 12, 1819—d. Oct. 7, 1895), lawyer, sculptor, poet, actor, biographer, author of travel books, novelist, dramatist, author of law books. JOSEPH STORY's son was a man of many talents, in none of which he attained eminence. He was perhaps best known as a sculptor; his most famous productions were statues of John Marshall, Joseph Henry, Edward Everett, George Peabody, Cleopatra, and Semiramis. He disliked New England and lived in Italy for the greater part of his life, becoming friendly with the literary expatriates of his day. In his statues and poems Story was undoubtedly too submissive to classical traditions. His *Poems* were collected in 1845, again in *Graffiti d'Italia* (1868). They were written in almost slavish imitation of the dramatic monologues of his friend Robert Browning. One of his most popular books was a collection of essays, *Roba di Roma* (1862); he also wrote *Fiammetta* (1886), and a play, *Nero* (1875). He wrote several law books while practicing law in Boston.

One of Henry James' least known books is *William Wetmore Story and His Friends* (1903), in which James seeks to explain the expatriates of the earlier years of the 19th century.

Story of a Bad Boy, The (1870), a semiautobiographical narrative by THOMAS BAILEY ALDRICH. Aldrich tries to explain in the opening sentences that he doesn't really mean a *bad* boy, but just "a real human boy." The adventures he relates as happening to Tom Bailey more or less coincide with his own experiences in Portsmouth, N.H., but he adds to them episodes entirely fictional. The young hero spends his earlier years in New Orleans; on his way to "Rivermouth" to live with his grandfather and his great-aunt he meets "Sailor Ben," who turns out later to be the long-lost husband of his relatives' trusted servant, Kitty Collins. At Rivermouth he gets into all kinds of mischief, in a fashion quite different from the goody-goody heroes of such English novels as Thomas Day's *Sandford and Merton* (1783). The book became very popular and paved the way for Twain's *Adventures of Tom Sawyer* (1876). In 1893 Aldrich wrote *An Old Town by the Sea*, a nonfictional account of his life in Portsmouth. Alexander Cowie considers *The Story of a Bad Boy* a brilliant satire on puritanism in decay (*Rise of the American Novel*, 1948). The story ran originally for an entire year in *Our Young Folks* (1869).

Story of a Country Town, The (1883), a novel by E. W. HOWE. This story of the "Middle Border" represents another step forward in the realistic depiction of life in the Middle West during the 19th century. EDWARD EGGLESTON had been too much of an optimist to represent conditions truly. Howe was far from an optimist. His own personal life and the life he saw around him brought him to a misanthropic point of view, and in this stark, monotonous, veracious story he told the truth as he saw it. Howe tried to be impartial and present the facts as they were, but he lacked the storyteller's gift of entertaining narration. He submitted the book to several publishers, all of whom rejected it. He finally printed it himself and sent a copy to Mark Twain, who broke his invariable rule and sent him comments on the book, characterizing its style as "simple, sincere, direct." Howe wrote an introduction for the 1927 edition of the book.

Story of Mankind, The (1921), a history by HENDRIK VAN LOON. In this book Van Loon sought to provide an account of world history that would give lay readers a vivid idea of how mankind had really developed. It was told from a viewpoint of philosophic doubt and was enhanced by Van Loon's own amusing illustrations. The book was rejected by fourteen publishers; the fifteenth publisher made a fortune out of the book, which went into edition after edition.

Story of the Other Wise Man, The (1896), a Christmas piece by HENRY VAN DYKE. It was first delivered as a sermon at the Brick Presbyterian Church, where the author was pastor. It has been widely read and translated into many foreign languages.

Story Teller's Story, A (1924), an autobiographical narrative by SHERWOOD ANDERSON.

story weeklies. In the mid-19th century a special type of weekly developed—the so-called *story weekly*, to which Mary Noel devoted an amusing and instructive volume, VILLAINS GALORE (1954). These weeklies were tremendously successful. The stories were melodramatic and certain plot formulas were inevitable. If a guardian had a rich ward, into the insane asylum she went. There were forged letters, birthmarks, seductions, babies changed in the cradle, remarkable coincidences. The language was equally melodramatic and conventional. Usually the stories ran as serials, sometimes as many as five in an issue. Among the better known writers for the story weeklies were Horatio Alger, Maturin M. Ballou, Sylvanus Cobb, Fanny Fern, Joseph Holt Ingraham, E. D. E. N. Southworth, and Ann S. Stephens.

Stout, Rex [Todhunter] (b. Noblesville, Ind., Dec. 1, 1886—   ), detective-story writer. Stout followed several business occupations, served in the navy, even wrote several serious novels before he turned to the creation of his adipose orchid-fancier and avid gourmet, Nero Wolfe. Wolfe insists that all information about a crime he is expected to solve be brought to him at his New York home and office, but he employs an assistant, Archie Goodwin, the capable narrator of the stories, to seek out clues. Wolfe began his career in *Fer-de-Lance* (1934); later adventures include *The League of Frightened Men* (1935); *Some Buried Caesar* (1939); *Black Orchids* (1942); *Three Doors to Death* (1950); *Prisoner's Base* (1952); *Before Midnight* (1955); and others. Alva Johnston did an admiring profile of Stout for *The New Yorker* (July 16 and 23, 1949).

Stout Gentleman, The (1822), a tale by WASHINGTON IRVING. This famous romance of the English stagecoach was originally printed in Irving's BRACEBRIDGE HALL. When one of his reviewers remarked that even "his most comical pieces have always a serious end in view," Irving said, "I have kept that to myself hitherto, but that man has found me out. He has detected the moral of *The Stout Gentleman*."

Stover, Dink. A character in several stories by OWEN JOHNSON. He is introduced first in THE VARMINT (1910) and *The Tennessee Shad* (1911), which relate his adventures in prep school, supposedly Lawrenceville. *Stover at Yale* (1911) sounds a more serious note and attacks the character of undergraduate life, particularly the senior societies and the anti-intellectualism of many students.

Stowe, Calvin E[llis] (b. Natick, Mass., April 26, 1802—d. Aug. 22, 1886), Congregational clergyman, teacher, writer. Stowe was an eminent teacher who served as professor of Greek at Dartmouth College, then as teacher of Biblical literature at the newly founded Lane Theological Seminary at Cincinnati. There he met and married Harriet Beecher, whose father, LYMAN BEECHER, was president of Lane. In 1850 Stowe became professor of religion at Bowdoin College, later at Andover Academy. He was a great friend of the public schools. The state of Ohio in 1836 appointed him to investigate the schools of Europe; his *Report on Elementary Instruction in Europe* (1837) exerted a great influence in Ohio and was reprinted elsewhere. In 1864 the Stowes went to live at Hartford, Conn., next door to Mark Twain (see NOOK FARM). In 1866, they began spending their winters at Mandarin, Fla. Stowe's other books were *An Introduction to the Criticism and Interpretation of the Bible* (1835) and *The Origin and History of the Books of the Bible* (1867).

Stowe, Harriet [Elizabeth] Beecher (b. Litchfield, Conn., June 14, 1811—d. July 1, 1896), novelist. Mrs. Stowe was the daughter of one of the greatest of Congregational clergymen (LYMAN BEECHER), married another eminent

clergyman (CALVIN E. STOWE), and was the sister of HENRY WARD BEECHER, the most renowned pulpit orator of his day. Her intellectual life for years was a dichotomy—she was fascinated with Puritanism and at the same time repelled by its harshness; she ended by becoming an Episcopalian. Charles Foster has treated her relationship to Puritanism in *The Rungless Ladder* (1955). She was also an anomaly in her work as a writer. Her *Uncle Tom's Cabin* became internationally famous, sold millions of copies in many languages; when Mrs. Stowe visited Lincoln at the White House, the President half-seriously called it the cause of the Civil War. It convinced the North that slavery was iniquitous, while the South hated it and hated Mrs. Stowe. Yet the name of its chief character has become for Negroes a term for servility—*Uncle Tomism.* Mrs. Stowe's fame is secure as the author of one of the four or five most widely circulated books in the history of mankind. But the book itself has been attacked—justly enough—on historical, sociological, and literary grounds; and other books by Mrs. Stowe have been adjudged much superior in artistic performance. Some of her other works have been hailed as forerunners of regionalism and as among the best books ever written about New England. But the average reader has never heard of *The Minister's Wooing* (1859) or *Oldtown Folks* (1869).

When Harriet was thirteen, her sister Kate took her into her school for girls; the next year Harriet was teaching moral philosophy there. In 1832 her father became head of the newly founded Lane Theological Seminary at Cincinnati. Two years later Harriet's first story was given first prize in a contest in which a story by Edgar Allan Poe was also submitted. The story, *Uncle Lot,* appeared in the *Western Monthly Magazine.* In 1835, while teaching in Cincinnati, she published *An Elementary Geography.* In 1836 she married Calvin Stowe, who was on the faculty of Lane. Stowe was an able man, but not in money matters. He had a strong insight into his wife's abilities and urged her to keep on writing. During this period, however, Mrs. Stowe was kept busy by her housekeeping duties.

Stowe was appointed to the faculty of Bowdoin College in 1848. As Mrs. Stowe sat in the First Parish Church in Brunswick, Me., she had a sudden vision of a ragged, white-haired slave being brutally flogged. That afternoon she began her famous novel, which appeared in 1851–52 as a serial in *The National Era,* in 1852 as a book. (See also entry on UNCLE TOM'S CABIN.) Her "incendiary" book made her famous and brought in a great deal of money. In 1853 the Stowes visited Europe and were received with tremendous acclaim in England. Mrs. Stowe met Lord Byron's widow, and took her part against Byron with a true crusader's zeal. Her article *The True Story of Lady Byron's Life* appeared simultaneously in the *Atlantic Monthly* and the British *Macmillan's Magazine* (September, 1869), and was followed by a book, *Lady Byron Vindicated* (1870). Her charges of incest against Byron did not enhance her reputation in England.

Mrs. Stowe felt deeply the death of her oldest son Henry, for a short time tried to find help in spiritualism, and continued to move further away from Calvinism. During the war another son, Frederick, was severely wounded; Karl Brown wrote a novel about him, *The Cup of Trembling* (1953), which presents a highly disapproving view of Mrs. Stowe and Henry Ward Beecher. At the close of the war the Stowes removed to Mandarin, Fla., where Mrs. Stowe did what she could to alleviate the condition both of the South and of the Negroes. While living there she wrote many books, including a description of the local scene, *Palmetto Leaves* (1873). She and her husband taught in the Episcopal chapel. In 1873 they returned to New England and found a home in Hartford.

Mrs. Stowe wrote voluminously, sometimes employing the pen name Christopher Crowfield. She did much miscellaneous writing: *The Mayflower, or, Sketches of Scenes and Characters Among the Descendants of the Pilgrims* (1843); *A Key to Uncle Tom's Cabin* (1853); *Sunny Memories of Foreign Lands* (1854); *A Geography for My Children* (1855); *Religious Poems* (1867); *Our Famous Women* (1884). DRED (1856), described as "A Tale of the Great Dismal Swamp," was another attack on slavery. Some of her writing was autobiographical: *Our Charley and What to Do with Him* (1858); *My Wife and I* (1871); *We and Our Neighbors* (1875). Most critics consider her best books those with a New England scene, often based at least partly on her own experiences. These include THE MINISTER'S WOOING (1859); THE PEARL OF ORR'S ISLAND (1862); OLDTOWN FOLKS (1869); *Sam Lawson's Oldtown Fireside Stories* (1872); and *Poganuc People* (1878). She seems to have studied local legends carefully, showed a genuine gift for humorous characterization, and was greatly helped by her husband, an adept spinner of yarns with a rich store of boyhood memories. In general, however, Mrs. Stowe's prose style leaves much to be desired; she is often repetitious, and shows a defective knowledge of sentence structure and syntax; her descriptions are at times vague and inexact; often her dramatic crises sound amateurish. Yet, at its best, her storytelling drive carries everything before it.

Mrs. Stowe's *Writings* were collected (16 v.) in 1896. *Uncle Tom's Cabin* is still frequently reprinted, as in Raymond Weaver's 1938 edition. Books about her include Charles E. Stowe's *Life* (compiled from her letters and journals, 1889); Annie A. Fields' *Life and Letters of Harriet Beecher Stowe* (1897); Lyman Beecher Stowe's *Harriet Beecher Stowe: The Story of Her Life* (1911) and his *Saints, Sinners, and Beechers* (1934); Forrest Wilson's *Crusader in Crinoline: The Life of Harriet Beecher Stowe* (1941). *Harriet* (1943) was a play by Florence Ryerson and Colin Clements. See LITTLE FOXES.

Stowe, Leland (b. Southbury, Conn., Nov. 10, 1899—   ), correspondent, author. Stowe was graduated from Wesleyan University in 1921. A foreign correspondent for the New York *Herald Tribune* from 1926 to 1939, and recipient of the Pulitzer prize for foreign correspondence in 1930, he covered World War II for the Chicago *Daily News* and New York *Post*. After the war he served as foreign editor for *The Reporter*, roving editor for the *Reader's Digest*, and Professor of Journalism at the University of Michigan. Stowe's books, the result of on-the-spot observations and analysis of the major events around the world, show the same stylistic clarity and freshness for which he won renown as a correspondent. They include: *Nazi Means War* (1934); *No Other Road to Freedom* (1941); *They Shall Not Sleep* (1944); *While Time Remains* (1946); *Target: You* (1949); *Conquest by Terror: The Story of Satellite Europe* (1952); *Crusoe of Lonesome Lake* (1957).

Strachey, William (early 17th century), English colonist, public official, writer. Strachey is known only through his writings. He was on board the *Sea Adventure*, chief vessel of an expedition sent to Virginia, when a great tempest overtook the fleet. The *Sea Adventure* was separated from the other vessels and driven upon the rocks of the "still-vexed Bermoothes" (first called Somers Islands, after the ship's captain, later the Bermudas). All on board reached shore safely, remained there for nine months, then built two small boats and reached Virginia in May, 1610. Shakespeare probably read some of the subsequent accounts of the adventure, including Strachey's letter (July 15, 1610) to "an Excellent Lady" in London; there are some parallelisms of phrasing between the letter and *The Tempest*. A full discussion of the probable debt of Shakespeare to Strachey may be found in C. M. Gayley's *Shakespeare and the Founders of Liberty in America* (1917). The letter was not actually published until 1625, as part of Samuel Purchas' *Hakluytus Posthumus, or, Purchas His Pilgrims*.

Strachey served as secretary of the Virginia Company until 1611. He wrote *History of Travel into Virginia Britannia* (printed in 1849), also edited and was part compiler of the code known as Dale's Laws: *For the Colony in Virginia: Laws Divine, Moral, and Martial* (1612). C. R. Sanders wrote *The Strachey Family: Their Writings and Literary Associations* (1953).

Strange Fruit (1944), a novel by LILLIAN SMITH. Miss Smith is one of several southern authors who deal with the problem of racial tension with realism and deep sympathy for the Negro. She depicts here the tragedy of a Negro girl and a white man caught in a coil of prejudice, misunderstanding, and violence. A murder and a brutal lynching are described vividly. The book sold widely, and was dramatized (1945) by the author and Esther Smith.

Strange Interlude (1928), a play in nine acts by EUGENE O'NEILL. This sensational and very popular drama opened on Broadway Jan. 30, 1928, closed June 15, 1929. The performances began at 5:30 and were adjourned for dinner; Part Two of the play was performed in the evening. The plot concerns the emotional, especially the sexual, reactions of Nina Leeds, who subconsciously hates her father, a professor, holding him responsible for preventing her from sleeping with her fiancé before he was killed in France. She becomes a nurse, marries good-natured Sam Evans, but when she learns she is about to have a child resorts to abortion because there is a strain of insanity in his family. However, she has an affair with Dr. Darrell, and their child is very fond of his supposed father but hates his real father. When Evans dies Nina marries a childhood admirer who reminds her of her father.

To make clear the thoughts, reactions, and inner yearnings of his characters O'Neill effectively revived the asides and soliloquies of Elizabethan drama, and made them a means of revealing the stream of consciousness, which novelists at about that time were beginning to use in eager imitation of James Joyce. The play also greatly appealed to the current interest in Freud, and echoed Schopenhauer's ideas on love, women, the sex impulse, human happiness, and the denial of the will to live.

Stratemeyer, Edward ["Allen Winfield," "Arthur Winfield," "Ralph Bonehill," etc.] (b. Elizabeth, N.J., Oct. 4, 1862—d. May 10, 1930), writer of books for boys. Stratemeyer wrote a great many books, most of them in series. In 1927 he told a reporter that his most popular series, the ROVER BOYS (written under the pen name of Arthur Winfield), had sold close to 4 million copies. He had a loyal audience of boys who, when they became fathers, bought more copies of his books for their sons. TOM SWIFT gave his name to another popular series. Stratemeyer also wrote historical stories, among them *Under Dewey at Manila* (1898); the "Frontier Series"; the "Mexican War Series"; and others. In the early 20th century he found the demand for his books so great that he established the Stratemeyer Literary Syndicate and hired hardworking assistants to grind out many new volumes. This syndicate continued production years after Stratemeyer's death.

Stratton-Porter, Gene. See GENE STRATTON PORTER.

Straus, Oscar S[olomon] (b. Germany, Dec. 23, 1850—d. May 3, 1926), businessman, diplomat, writer. Straus was a member of the family of department store magnates which founded various firms and acquired others, including Abraham & Straus, R. H. Macy, and L. Bamberger & Co. Straus himself was more interested in various forms of public service and in authorship than in direct activities in business. He served as minister to Turkey and as our first ambassador to that country. In 1902 he served on the permanent court of arbitration at the Hague, then as secretary of commerce and labor under Theodore Roosevelt (1906–09). He wrote numerous books, among them *The Origin of the Republican Form of Government in the U.S.* (1885); *Roger Williams, the*

Pioneer of Religious Liberty (1894); *Reform in the Consular Service* (1894); *Our Diplomacy: A Survey* (1902); *The Hague Tribunal* (1904). *Under Four Administrations* (1922) was autobiographical.

stream of consciousness, the (interior monologue). This literary device turns to use as a revelation of character the fact that the human mind is disorderly, disconnected, impatient, obscure in its workings, cunning in deceit and concealment, yet at the same time illuminative if properly interpreted. The use of the device may be traced to the soliloquy and the aside employed in Elizabethan drama, but the interior monologue of modern fiction and drama is only distantly related to the Elizabethan form. Most Elizabethan dramatists, in fact, treated the soliloquy as a more or less disconnected lyric on a meditative topic rather than as a development of character through psychological revelation in depth. The interior monologue reached its highest form in *Ulysses* (1922), by the Irishman James Joyce.

Many later writers anticipated the development of the interior monologue, *e.g.*, Laurence Sterne in *Tristram Shandy* and Dostoevsky in *Crime and Punishment*. But the chief impetus for the modern form of the interior monologue is usually ascribed to a French writer, Édouard Dujardin, to an American psychologist, WILLIAM JAMES, and to a French philosopher, Henri Bergson. Dujardin wrote an experimental novel *Les Lauriers Sont Coupés* (1887), which appeared in the United States as *We'll to the Woods No More* (1938). Joyce acknowledged his debt to Dujardin, who published in 1931 *Le Monologue Intérieur: Son Apparition, Ses Origines, Sa Place dans L'Oeuvre de James Joyce.*

William James' PRINCIPLES OF PSYCHOLOGY (1890) contains a celebrated chapter called "The Stream of Thought." In this there occurs for the first time the phrase "the stream of consciousness." Dujardin defines the phrase he devised, "interior monologue," as a device which enables the direct introduction of the reader "into the interior life of the character, without any interventions in the way of explanation or commentary on the part of the author," and stresses the fact that the thoughts revealed lie nearest the unconscious. Studying the human mind from within, James found "a teeming multiplicity of objects and relations" and constant change. Henry James' novels show the influence of his brother's ideas. About the same time in France, Henri Bergson was emphasizing intuition and the "indivisible flux" of consciousness. He held that logical novelists had distorted reality and oversimplified it.

Joyce's brilliant use of stream of consciousness produced a host of imitators: Dorothy Richardson, Virginia Woolf, Elizabeth Bowen, Katherine Mansfield, and others in England; Sherwood Anderson, Ernest Hemingway, Conrad Aiken, Gertrude Stein, William Faulkner, James T. Farrell, W. C. Williams, Thomas Wolfe, John Dos Passos, and Eugene O'Neill in the United States. Some American novels employing this technique are E. E. Cummings' *Eimi* (1933); Conrad Aiken's BLUE VOYAGE (1927); William Faulkner's THE SOUND AND THE FURY (1929); Christopher Morley's KITTY FOYLE (1939); Josephine Herbst's *Somewhere the Tempest Fell* (1947). Some critics have felt that the use, or abuse, of this technique unduly sacrifices artistry and story line to an overly-subjective realism. Robert Humphrey analyzes the subject in *The Stream of Consciousness in the Modern Novel* (1954).

Street, James [Howell] (b. Lumberton, Miss., Oct. 15, 1903—d. Sept. 28, 1954), novelist, journalist. Street spent his youth in Mississippi. While in high school, he worked as a part time reporter for the Laurel *Daily Leader* and at the age of eighteen, without completing his high school education, he became a reporter for the Hattiesburg *American*. In 1923, he joined the Baptist ministry, but gave it up two years later feeling that he was unfitted for it, emotionally and religiously. He returned to journalism and began writing his first short stories, while reporting for the New York *World Telegram*. He is the author of several novels. *The Gauntlet* (1945), set in Missouri, is based on Street's own experiences as a Baptist minister. In the sequel, *The High Calling* (1951), the hero, London Wingo, accepts a call to a North Carolina church. The books give a sympathetic picture of a Protestant minister and his problems. Other novels include: *Look Away!* (1936); *Oh, Promised Land* (1940); *The Biscuit Eater* (1941); *In My Father's House* (1941); *By Valour and Arms* (1944); *Tomorrow We Reap* (1949); *Velvet Doublet* (1953); *Good-bye, My Lady* (1954). His two books of nonfiction are: *The Civil War* (1953) and *The Revolutionary War* (1954). His son, James Street, Jr., edited *James Street's South* (1955). See THE DABNEYS.

Street, Julian (b. Chicago, April 12, 1879—d. Feb. 19, 1947), newspaperman, novelist, essayist, author of travel sketches. Street wrote short stories, one of which won an O. Henry Memorial Award and became the title story in *Mr. Bisbee's Princess* (1925). He became an authority on wines, gastronomy, and travel, writing a number of books in these fields: *My Enemy the Motor* (1908); *Welcome to Our City* (1913); *American Adventures* (1917); *Mysterious Japan* (1921); *Where Paris Dines* (1929); *Wines* (1933; rev., 1948). He collaborated with BOOTH TARKINGTON on a comedy, *The Country Cousin* (1916).

Streetcar Named Desire, A (1947), a play by TENNESSEE WILLIAMS. The play is set in the French Quarter of New Orleans, where two streetcars, one named Desire, the other named Cemetery, run on a single track. Blanche DuBois, the central character, is a fading Southern belle who tries to maintain illusions of gentility in spite of her poverty and moral degeneration. Forced to sell what is left of the family plantation, she comes to live with her sister, Stella, who is married to Stanley, a brutal, animalistic man. Blanche's pretensions to gentility, her frilly clothing, and her affected and flirtatious behavior annoy Stanley and upset the household. Mitch, a more naïve friend of Stanley's, accepts her at face value and thinks of marrying her, until Stanley tells him of Blanche's notorious and neurotic sexual escapades. Her hopes of marriage destroyed, Blanche confronts Stanley in all her outdated finery and provokes him into raping her. Finally, completely unable to impose her illusions upon reality, she breaks down mentally and is led away to an asylum, still clinging to her fantasies and appealing to the "kindness of strangers." The play was awarded a Pulitzer prize and a film version (1951) was also widely successful.

Streeter, Ed[ward] (b. New York City, Aug. 1, 1891—   ), banker, humorist. Streeter became a vice-president of the Bank of New York in 1931. Several of his humorous books have been extremely successful. The first, *Dere Mable* (1917), was based on World War I and was followed by *That's Me All Over Mable* (1918). Since then other books, all frankly based on his own experiences, have followed, among them *Same Old Bill* (1918); *Daily Except Sunday* (1938); *Father of the Bride* (1949; made into a successful movie, 1950); *Skoal Scandinavia* (1952); *Mr Hobbs' Vacation* (1954); *Mr. Robbins Rides Again* (1958).

Street Scene (1929), a play by ELMER RICE. Here the dramatist abandoned his previous expressionist techniques and resorted to stark objectivity and naturalistic propagandizing. The play presents life in a slum tenement and was one of the first stage productions to include realistic sound effects throughout the performance. Characters of various racial and temperamental components figure in the story, which reaches its climax in a double murder. The play won a Pulitzer prize, and a musical version was made in 1947 with a score by Kurt Weill.

Streit, Clarence K. (b. California, Mo., Jan. 21, 1896—   ), editor, correspondent, author, lecturer. Streit studied at the University of Montana, the Sorbonne, and as a Rhodes scholar at Oxford. He worked primarily as a correspondent until the publication of his *Union Now* (1939). At that time he resigned from *The New York Times* to devote full time to establishing the Federal Union of Democracies which he had proposed in his book. He became president of the Inter-Democracy Federal Unionists and his cause found a number of followers both in America and England. His *Hafiz: The Tongue of the Hidden* (1928) was an adaptation of the Persian poet Hafiz. Streit's other books: *Where Iron Is, There Is the Fatherland* (1920); *Union Now in Britain* (1941); *Not Again in Vain* (1942); *Hafiz in Quatrains* (1946); *Freedom Against Itself* (1954); *Freedom's Frontier—Atlantic Union Now* (1961).

Strenuous Life, The (April 10, 1899), an address delivered in Chicago by THEODORE ROOSEVELT. It was printed in *The Strenuous Life: Essays and Addresses* (1900). Roosevelt here preached the doctrine "that the highest form of

success comes, not to the man who desires mere easy peace, but to the man who does not shrink from danger, from hardship, or from bitter toil." The word *strenuous* was thereafter associated with Roosevelt and became a catchword of the era. Grant C. Knight wrote *The Strenuous Age in American Literature, 1900–1910* (1954). The Rev. Charles Wagner intended his book *The Simple Life* (1901) to offer an alternative.

Stribling, T[homas] S[igismund] (b. Clifton, Tenn., Mar. 4, 1881—d. July 8, 1965), novelist. Stribling wrote many novels about the South, one of which, *The Store* (1932), won a Pulitzer prize. Other novels are *Birthright* (1922); *Bright Metal* (1928); *Strange Moon* (1929); *Backwater* (1930); *The Forge* (1931); *The Unfinished Cathedral* (1934); *The Sound Wagon* (1935); *These Bars of Flesh* (1938). *Teeftallow* (1926) was dramatized as *Rope* (1928). Stribling deals with the typical difficulties of the South, sometimes laying his story in the past, sometimes in the present. *These Bars of Flesh* was an attack on progressive education and New York labor unions, set on a campus which appeared to be modeled on Columbia.

Stringer, Arthur [John Arbuthnott] (b. Chatham, Ont., Feb. 26, 1874—d. Sept. 14, 1950), writer. Stringer was at first a clerk in a railroad office, later a writer for newspapers and magazines and literary editor of the magazine *Success*. In 1917 he went to Hollywood to work on movie scenarios; one of his earliest scripts was prepared (1918) for the serial PERILS OF PAULINE. He became a citizen of the United States in 1937. In his long literary career Stringer wrote more than fifty novels, among them *The Man Who Couldn't Sleep* (1919); *Prairie Child* (1922); *Star in a Mist* (1943). One of his best books is a biography of the English poet Rupert Brooke, *Red Wine of Youth* (1948). But his favorite writings were his poems, some of the best of which were in Irish dialect; he had a gift for melody and a sense of the magic of words. While Canadian scenes often figure in his poems, he also wrote a pleasant collection of *New York Nocturnes* (1948). His first book was *Watchers of the Twilight and Other Poems* (1894). *Irish Poems* (1911) and some free-verse poems, *Open Water* (1912), were other collections. Victor Lauriston wrote his biography (1941).

Strode, Hudson (b. Cairo, Ill., Oct. 31, 1893 —   ), author, teacher, lecturer. Strode was a popular professor at the University of Alabama, where he taught a course in creative writing that produced several successful young writers. Over the years he traveled widely, writing appreciatively of foreign lands. These books were received with enthusiasm by critics. After reading *Timeless Mexico* (1944), Thomas Mann described it as "a brilliant and fascinating literary work and probably the best book ever written on Mexico." The Chicago *Daily News* called *South by Thunderbird* (1937) "unquestionably the best book on modern South America." One of Strode's major works is a two-volume biography of Jefferson Davis; the first volume, *Jefferson Davis: American Patriot* (1955), was highly praised. For the second volume, *Jefferson Davis: Confederate President* (1959), Strode received the 1960 Award of the American Academy of Public Affairs. Among his books: *The Story of Bermuda* (1932); *The Pageant of Cuba* (1934); *Sweden, Model for a World* (1949); *Denmark Is a Lovely Land* (1951).

Strong, Austin (b. San Francisco, April 18, 1881—d. Sept. 17, 1952), architect, playwright. Strong worked as a landscape artist until 1905. His first plays were written in collaboration with Robert Louis Stevenson's stepson, LLOYD OSBOURNE, who was Strong's uncle, *The Exile* (prod. in London, 1903) and *The Father of the Wilderness* (prod. in London and New York, 1905). One of his most famous plays is a one-act drama, *The Drums of Oude* (1906). Later plays were *Rip Van Winkle* (1911); *Three Wise Fools* (1918); *Seventh Heaven* (1920); *A Play Without a Name* (1928). A collection, *The Drums of Oude and Other One-Act Plays*, appeared in 1926. Strong was esteemed as a skillful playwright who gave full opportunity to the talents of his actors. He also contributed to the *Atlantic* and other magazines.

Strong, George Templeton. See THE DIARY OF GEORGE TEMPLETON STRONG.

Strunsky, Simeon (b. Russia, July 23, 1879 —d. Feb. 5, 1948), newspaperman, essayist, novelist. Strunsky was brought to this country at the age of seven, and later made a brilliant record at Columbia University. He first worked on the staff of an encyclopedia, then for the New York *Post*, where he conducted a column called "Post Impressions," selections from which were made into a book (1914) with the same title. He became editor of the editorial page in 1920, left to join the New York *Times* staff in 1924, and remained with that paper until his death. As a newspaperman he was chiefly noted for the anonymous column the *Times* called "Topics of the Times." This daily column was originated by F. C. Mortimer in 1896; in 1932 Strunsky took it over. He has been called the "last of the essayists." Often his topic was some aspect of life in New York City, but he ranged with quiet humor over the cosmos—from the Marshall Plan to Herodotus and from Eva Peron to best sellers. At the same time he conducted a column in the *Times Book Review*.

Strunsky wrote numerous books, occasionally semifictional, as in *Professor Latimer's Progress* (1918). Among his other books: *The Patient Observer* (1911); *Belshazzar Court* (1914); *Little Journeys to Paris* (1918); *Sinbad and His Friends* (1921); *The Living Tradition* (1939); *No Mean City* (a book about New York, 1944); *Two Came to Town* (1947).

Stryker, Lloyd Paul (b. Chicago, June 5, 1885—d. June 21, 1955), lawyer, public official, writer. Stryker served as assistant district attorney for New York County, practiced primarily as a trial lawyer. He wrote—with much literary skill—*Andrew Johnson: A Study in Courage* (1929); *Courts and Doctors* (1932); *For the Defense* (a biography of Thomas Erskine, 1947); and *The Art of Advocacy* (1954).

Stuart, Gilbert [Charles] (b. No. Kingston, R.I., Dec. 3, 1755—d. July 29, 1828), portrait painter. It was said that Stuart left Rhode Island and fled to England because of his Tory sympathies. In London he studied under Benjamin West and won a reputation that placed him on a par with the great English portraitists of that age. In 1793 he returned to America. He painted the first five Presidents and did three original studies of Washington, the most famous of which hangs in the Pennsylvania Academy of Fine Arts in Philadelphia. He painted many other famous men and women, including George III and George IV, Mrs. Siddons, Sir Joshua Reynolds, and Benjamin West. Stuart's biography was written by W. T. Whitely; an illustrated, descriptive list of his works by Lawrence Parks.

Stuart, J[ames] E[well] B[rown] [Jeb] (b. Feb. 6, 1833—d. May 12, 1864), soldier. A graduate of West Point in 1854 and thereafter an officer in the United States Army, Stuart resigned his commission in 1861, took a cavalry command in the Confederate Army, and was made a brigadier general. He engaged in some of the most spectacular exploits of the war—in his raid on McClellan's forces (June, 1862), in the Seven Days' Battles, at Manassas, in the raid into Pennsylvania, at Fredericksburg, at Chancellorsville, at Gettysburg. He was mortally wounded at Yellow Tavern, Va., and died in Richmond the next day. J. W. Thomason, Jr., wrote a biography *Jeb Stuart* (1930). He appears in fiction as a character in C. T. Brady's THE PATRIOTS (1906) and Joseph S. Pennell's THE HISTORY OF ROME HANKS (1944).

Stuart, Jesse [Hilton] (b. W-Hollow, Ky., Aug. 8, 1907—), poet, novelist, teacher, editor. Stuart wrote more than a score of books which show his passionate love for the mountain country of Kentucky, the region where he was born. He is also known for his verse, and published in this medium *The Man With a Bull-Tongue Plow* (1934), *Album of Destiny* (1944), and *Kentucky Is My Land* (1952). He won his earliest successes, however, with short stories, first collected in *Head o' W-Hollow* (1936); later collections include *Men of the Mountain* (1941); *Tales from the Plum Grove* (1946); *Clearing in the Sky* (1950); *Plowshare in Heaven* (1958). His first novel, *Trees of Heaven* (1940), describes a typical disagreement between two mountain men. *Taps for Private Tussie* (1943) is a hilarious, honest, and not very favorable depiction of Kentucky life which was very popular when it came out. *Mongrel Mettle* (1944) is a dog's-eye view of the same scene. *Foretaste of Glory* (1946), *Hie to the Hunter* (1950), and *The Good Spirit of Laurel Ridge* (1953) are other novels.

Throughout these fictional works Stuart shows his ability to tell a good story, but his well-drawn characters and their wit and wisdom mingled with simplicity are the chief attraction. *Beyond Dark Hills* (1938) is autobiographical; *The Thread That Runs So True* (1949) describes his school experiences. *The Year of My Rebirth* (1956) movingly depicts Stuart's comeback from a nearly fatal heart attack.

Stuart, Robert (b. Scotland, Feb. 19, 1785 —d. Oct. 29, 1848), fur trader, explorer, diarist. After Stuart and others had made their way by sea to found Astoria (1811), he made an eastward journey to St. Louis over a route at that time practically unknown to white men. In the course of his explorations he discovered South Pass, later part of the route used by immigrants to California and Oregon. Washington Irving tells about him in ASTORIA (1836), and P. A. Rollins edited *The Discovery of the Oregon Trail: Robert Stuart's Narratives, 1811–13* (1935).

Stuart, Ruth McEnery (b. Marksville, La., May 21, 1849—d. May 6, 1917), short-story writer, novelist. Well acquainted with all Southern types, Mrs. Stuart's specialty was Louisiana; her command of dialects was especially accurate. Her gift was in the writing of short stories rather than sustained narratives. Among her books: *A Golden Wedding and Other Tales* (1893); *Carlotta's Intended and Other Tales* (1894); *Solomon Crow's Christmas Pockets and Other Tales* (1896); *Sonny* (1896); *In Simpkinsville: Character Tales* (1897); *Aunt Amity's Silver Wedding and Other Stories* (1909).

Stuck, Hudson (b. England, Nov. 11, 1863 —d. Oct. 10, 1920), Protestant Episcopal clergyman, missionary. In 1885 Stuck came to the United States, served in Texas, then in 1904 was appointed archdeacon of the Yukon; he labored in that region until his death. He recorded his experiences in *Ten Thousand Miles with a Dog Sled* (1914); *Voyages on the Yukon and Its Tributaries* (1917); *The Alaskan Missions of the Episcopal Church* (1920); *A Winter Circuit of Our Arctic Coast* (1920).

Studies in Classic American Literature (1923), a series of essays by D. H. LAWRENCE. After an essay on "The Spirit of Place," Lawrence goes on to examine Benjamin Franklin, whom he despises; Hector St. John Crèvecœur, whom he seeks to interpret; James Fenimore Cooper, whom he analyzes first in his "white novels," then in the Leatherstocking Tales; Edgar Allan Poe, whom he regards as above all a scientist; Nathaniel Hawthorne, whom he considers from two viewpoints—as the author of *The Scarlet Letter* and of *The Blithedale Romance;* Richard Henry Dana, whose *Two Years Before the Mast* he turns into a metaphysical document, at the same time taking a morbid interest in the flogging scenes; Herman Melville, seen as "the greatest seer and poet of the sea"; finally Walt Whitman, with his love of comrades. Edmund Wilson regards it as "one of the few first-rate books that have ever been written on the subject," even if it

has "shots that do not hit the mark and moments that are quite hysterical" (*Shock of Recognition,* 1943).

Studs Lonigan. See LONIGAN, STUDS.

Sturgeon, Theodore [Edward Hamilton Waldo] (b. Philadelphia, 1918—   ), science-fiction writer. Hardly a science-fiction collection exists that does not include at least one story by this prolific author. He favors the ironic surprise ending but is better known for his imaginativeness than for "fine writing." Perhaps most noteworthy of his stories is *Baby Is Three.* Here Sturgeon introduced to science-fiction writing the idea of a group of humans forming a symbiotic relationship so close that they are able to function as a super organism. Under the pseudonym Frederick R. Ewing he wrote to order a novel called *I, Libertine* (1956) to satisfy the demand for an imaginary novel of that title; a New York disc jockey had hoaxed his audience into believing such a novel existed. Among his other books: *More Than Human* (1953); *E Pluribus Unicorn* (1953); *Venus Plus X* (1950, published originally as *Dreaming Jewels*); *The Way Home* (1955, stories edited by Groff Conklin); *The Synthetic Man* (1961).

Sturges, Preston (b. Chicago, Aug. 29, 1898—d. Aug. 6, 1959), playwright, scriptwriter, movie director and producer, inventor. Sturges was at first in his mother's cosmetics business, invented various products and devices, including a kissproof lip rouge and a vibrationless engine; wrote songs; became an assistant stage manager to Brock Pemberton; and began writing plays of his own—the most successful of which was *Strictly Dishonorable* (1929). Then he went to Hollywood and wrote movie scripts. After a while he began to direct and if possible produce his own scripts. His movie *The Great McGinty* (1940) received an Academy Award. Among his other successful motion pictures: *The Power and the Glory* (1932); *The Green Hat* (1933); *If I Were King* (1938); *Remember the Night* (1939); *Sullivan's Travels* (1941); *The Miracle of Morgan's Creek* (1944); *Hail the Conquering Hero* (1944); *The Sin of Harold Diddlebock* (1946). Bosley Crowther has said that Sturges has restored "to the art of the cinema a certain graphic velocity which it has missed since the turmoils of Mack Sennett went out with the talking film."

Stuyvesant, Peter (b. Netherlands 1592— d. Feb. [?] 1672), soldier, colonial administrator. Stuyvesant was employed as a colonial administrator by the Dutch West India Co. In 1643 he was made governor of Curaçao and adjacent islands belonging to the Dutch. In 1644, while making an attack on the Portuguese island of St. Martin, he lost his right leg and was forced to return to Holland. There he was provided with a wooden leg which he decorated with silver bands and called his "silver leg." In 1646 he was appointed director-general of New Netherland. From the very start he announced and carried out a policy in which the interests of the colonists were bluntly subordinated to those of the company, and he was not popular. But he was successful for a while in settling disputes with other colonies, sometimes by force. He attacked and captured New Sweden in 1655. In 1664 he was obliged to surrender his colony to England because he lacked local support. In 1665 he returned to Holland, but came back in 1667 and lived on his farm on the Bowery until his death. He was a man of violent temper, strong prejudices, and stubborn will. Washington Irving drew a satirical portrait of him as Peter the Headstrong in A HISTORY OF NEW YORK BY DIEDRICH KNICKERBOCKER (1809).

Styron, William [Clark, Jr.] (b. Newport News, Va., June 11, 1925—   ), novelist. Styron's first novel, LIE DOWN IN DARKNESS (1951), the story of the degeneration of a Southern family, won critical acclaim. Written in the "stream of consciousness" technique, it reveals Styron's indebtedness to James Joyce, Thomas Wolfe, and particularly William Faulkner. Styron also wrote *The Long March* (1952), a novella which appeared in *discovery* and has come to be regarded as a small classic. *Set This House on Fire* was published in 1960.

Suckow, Ruth (b. Hawarden, Iowa, Aug. 6, 1892—d. Jan. 23, 1960), novelist, short-story writer, teacher, apiarist. Although her works cover many themes and settings, Miss Suckow's specialty was stories set in small Iowan towns and other parts of the Middle West, usually with German-American characters. COUNTRY PEOPLE (1924), her first novel, told the story of three generations of German-Americans in a rural setting. It remains her most highly esteemed work. She wrote two sympathetic stories about ministers, *The Bonney Family* (1928) and *New Hope* (1942); her father was a liberal-minded Congregational minister. Young women often occupied her attention, as in *The Odyssey of a Nice Girl* (1925) and *The Kramer Girls* (1930). Among other titles: *Iowa Interiors* (1926); *Cora* (1929); *Children and Older People* (1931); *The Folks* (1934). Much that is autobiographical appears in *Some Others and Myself: Seven Stories and a Memoir* (1952). In 1959 she published *The John Wood Case*.

Sugrue, Thomas (b. Naugatuck, Conn., May 7, 1907—d. Jan. 6, 1953), newspaperman, critic, writer. Sugrue worked for the Naugatuck *Daily News*, then for the New York *Herald Tribune*, later was on the staff of various magazines and contributed articles to them, particularly excellent book reviews. In 1938 he was afflicted with a crippling arthritic condition and never walked again. But he continued to be active and to write books. In 1949 he flew to Israel, where he gathered material for *Watch for the Morning* (1950). He had previously written *Such Is the Kingdom* (1940); *There Is a River* (1943); *Starling of the White House* (1946); *We Called It Music* (with Eddie Condon, 1947). He wrote a stimulating, adult, witty

autobiography, *Stranger in the Earth* (1948), which describes his search for God. Several months before his death appeared *A Catholic Speaks His Mind on America's Religious Conflict* (1952). The book deplores the lack of true religious tolerance in the United States, analyzed the two natural elements in religion—the mystical and the ethical—and offers a plan for progressive cooperation among religious groups.

Sullivan, A[loysius] M[ichael] (b. Harrison, N.J., Aug. 9, 1896—   ), advertising executive, poet. For a time a free-lance writer, then with an advertising agency, Sullivan in 1934 joined the firm of Dun & Bradstreet as associate editor of *Dun's Review*. He was for several years president of the Poetry Society of America and published many collections of verse. Among them: *This Day and Age* (1944); *Tim Murphy Morgan, Rifleman, and Other Ballads* (1948); *Incident in Silver* (1950); *Choral Poems for Radio* (1951); *Psalms of the Prodigal and Other Poems* (1953); *The Three-Dimensional Man* (1956). Although fond of history, he is equally interested in new developments of science and technology and has dwelt on their imaginative aspects. He writes often about nature, about Irishmen and Irish scenes, about religion.

Sullivan, Frank [Francis John] (b. Saratoga Springs, N.Y., Sept. 22, 1892—   ), columnist, free-lance writer. Sullivan was long a columnist for the New York *World*. He is perhaps best known for his satiric collection of clichés in various professions and vocations, but his wit ranges over a multitude of themes. His remarks are sometimes likely to pain his subjects, as when he wrote his superb parody *A Garland of Ibids for Van Wyck Brooks*. But even at his sharpest Sullivan is mellow. He can write with equal tongue-in-cheek on the Bach family, the hobby of collecting paper rompers for lamb chops, the days we celebrate (Sullivan suggests that we add Honey for Breakfast Day, Want Ad Week, and Leave Us Alone Week). His writings often appeared in *The New Yorker* magazine. Among his books: *Life and Times of Martha Hepplethwaite* (1926); *The Adventures of an Oaf* (with Herbert Roth, 1927); *Innocent Bystanding* (1928); *Broccoli and Old Lace* (1931); *In One Ear* (1933); *A Pearl in Every Oyster* (1938); *Sullivan at Bay* (1939); *A Rock in Every Snowball* (1946); *The Night the Old Nostalgia Burned Down* (1953); *Sullivan Bites News* (with Sam Berman, 1954); *Moose in the Hoose* (1959).

Sullivan, Harry Stack (b. Norwich, N.Y., Feb. 21, 1892—d. Jan. 15, 1949), psychologist, psychiatrist. At the Sheppard-Pratt Hospital in Baltimore, Sullivan undertook his important work on schizophrenia. In 1934 he became the head of the William Alanson White Foundation in Washington, later also of the Washington School of Psychiatry. In his teaching, which became deeply influential, he laid strong emphasis on the effects of cultural forces on personality and on what he called *interpersonality*. Sullivan was not a good writer, *e.g.*, in his *Conceptions of Modern Psychiatry* (1940), but he was an excellent, lively lecturer. His later lectures at the Washington School of Psychiatry were recorded and posthumously published as *The Interpersonal Theory of Psychiatry* (ed. by Helen Swick Perry and Mary Ladd Gawel, 1953). Previously Patrick Mullahy had edited *A Study of Interpersonal Relations* (1949), a symposium on Sullivan's concept by Harold Lasswell, Edward Sapir, Ruth Benedict, Sullivan himself, and others. Mullahy likewise edited *The Contributions of Harry Stack Sullivan* (1952), a record made by his students and associates of the essence of his work.

Sullivan, John (b. Somersworth, N.H., Feb. 17, 1740—d. Jan. 23, 1795), public official. Sullivan was a member of the Continental Congress and took an active part in many important Revolutionary battles, attaining the rank of general. Along with James Clinton he was sent to northern New York to punish the Six Nations for their part in the massacre of Wyoming. He defeated the Indians and their English allies, but failed to follow up his advantage, and engaged in a controversy with Washington. In 1779 he resigned from the army, became attorney general and then "president" of New Hampshire. His *Journals of the Expedition Against the Six Nations* appeared in 1887, his *Letters and Papers* (2 v., ed. by O. G. Hammond) in 1930–31.

Sullivan, John L[awrence] (b. Boston, Oct. 15, 1858—d. Feb. 2, 1918), heavyweight boxing champion. The "Boston Strong Boy," the great "John L.," was the winner of many tremendous bouts that made him the hero of his generation. He lost his title to "Gentleman Jim" Corbett (Sept. 7, 1892). In his heyday and in the years after his downfall Sullivan was the great hero of the American saloon, although toward the end of his life he became a temperance lecturer. He published his *Life and Reminiscences* in 1892. R. F. Dibble wrote his biography (1925).

Sullivan, Louis Henri [or Henry] (b. Boston, Sept. 3, 1856—d. April 14, 1924), architect. While perhaps not the inventor of the American skyscraper, Sullivan was undoubtedly a pioneer in recognizing the steel skeleton as integral and in avoiding traditional and nonfunctional ornamentation. He repudiated the slavish following of classical precepts common in his day and set a model for our tall structures that has been closely followed. His buildings are found all over the United States, from the Chicago Auditorium (1889) and the Transportation Building at the World's Columbian Exposition (1893) to the Guaranty Building in Buffalo (1895). Sullivan also promoted his ideas in lectures and in writings. Among his books are *The Autobiography of an Idea* (1924) and the posthumously published *Kindergarten Chats on Architecture, Education, and Democracy* (1934). FRANK LLOYD WRIGHT was a student

and disciple in Sullivan's workshop and for a time his partner. With the help of many photographs John Szarkowski presented *The Idea of Louis Sullivan* in 1956.

Sullivan, Mark (b. Avondale, Pa., Sept. 10, 1874—d. Aug. 13, 1952), newspaperman, historian, memoirist, editor. Sullivan began working on a paper he owned in Phoenixville, Pa., when he was nineteen, sold it to go to Harvard University, completed a course in the law school but never practiced. Thereafter he worked for newspapers and magazines in New York, in 1923 joining the New York *Herald Tribune*, with which he stayed until his death. His three-times-a-week column was widely syndicated. In 1926 he began writing OUR TIMES: THE UNITED STATES 1900–1925, annals of the 20th century which reached six volumes. He also wrote the autobiographical *Education of an American* (1938). He made a great hit with muckraking articles in the early years of the century, but grew more placid and conservative in later years.

Sullivan County Sketches (1949), ten pieces by STEPHEN CRANE, collected and edited by Melvin Schoberlin. Only three of these stories or sketches appear in Crane's collected writings; the editor found the others in newspapers and magazines in which they had originally been published. One paper in which some of the sketches were printed was the New York *Tribune*. Crane's brother Townley was New Jersey correspondent for the *Tribune* and Stephen was pinch-hitting for him when a Labor Day parade took place. Stephen's report, written ironically so that his sympathy for the marching workers was not immediately obvious, caused a great furor and the discharge of both brothers, although Townley was later reinstated. But later Crane took a dislike to the Sullivan County sketches and apparently did his best to destroy all copies of them he could find. They are nevertheless often striking in their humor and freshness of descriptive detail and for their "boisterous, outdoor masculinity"— they are obviously allied to the tall tales of western humor in the American literary tradition. Robert Halsband (*Saturday Review of Literature*, July 9, 1949) felt the sketches anticipated Crane's "later psychological intensity, verbal brilliance, and rich symbolism."

Sulzberger, Arthur Hays (b. New York City, Sept. 12, 1891—d. Dec. 11, 1968), publisher. The son-in-law of ADOLPH S. OCHS entered the newspaper business in 1919, became the publisher of *The New York Times* in 1935. His nephew, **Cyrus L[eo] Sulzberger** (b. New York City, Oct. 27, 1912—   ), joined the staff of the *Times*, was its chief foreign correspondent, and then became its foreign affairs columnist. In the days before World War II he was banned successively from Hungary, Rumania, Bulgaria, and Italy. Early in his career he wrote *Sit Down with John L. Lewis* (1938).

Sumner, Charles (b. Boston, Jan. 6, 1811—d. March 11, 1874), lawyer, public official, orator. Sumner, one of the Boston BRAHMINS, took his undergraduate degree and then studied law at Harvard. After a trip abroad he became active in politics, especially as an abolitionist. In 1851 he was elected to the United States Senate and was re-elected for three further terms. His speeches were sometimes inflammatory; his Senate address (May 20, 1856) on *The Crime Against Kansas* resulted in an assault on him two days later by Representative Preston S. Brooks. He hated the South and was a leading figure in the attempt to remove President Johnson from office. He was the most conspicuous figure in the Senate during the Civil War and Reconstruction years; Carl Schurz, who knew him well, called him both "a Puritan idealist" and "a moral terrorist." Sumner was primarily an orator; he collected his *Orations and Speeches* (1850) and his *Speeches and Addresses* (1856); his *Works* (15 v.) appeared in 1870–83. E. L. Pierce wrote an elaborate biography of him, *Memoir and Letters of Charles Sumner* (4 v., 1877–93). Other biographies include Moorfield Storey's (1900) and G. H. Haynes' (1909). In 1874 Henry Wadsworth Longfellow wrote a memorial poem, *Charles Sumner*.

Sumner, William Graham (b. Paterson, N.J., Oct. 30, 1840—d. April 12, 1910), clergyman, teacher, economist, writer. Sumner was a tutor at Yale for three years, then was ordained a priest in the Episcopal Church. For a time he served in New York and Morristown churches. In 1872 he was called to teach at Yale as professor of political and social science. Sumner's classes attracted listeners who were fascinated but not always persuaded. He loved to shock his mid-Victorian students, as when he defined man as "an ape grown rusty at climbing who yet feels himself to be a symbol and the frail representative of Omnipotence."

Sumner was an unrestricted free-enterpriser, a firm believer in the survival of the fittest, a courageous defender of the *status quo*, an advocate of the social utility of wealth and of the ancient virtues of self-reliance, thrift, prudence, and a sense of duty. Though still Puritanic and theological, he added Darwin to the decalogue. So much did he detest state interference in the activities of the individual that he would have preferred to abolish public education and public control over sanitation and child labor. "Do not coddle the weak," he preached, or you will have "the survival of the unfittest." It particularly amused him to show how temporary and transitory were the ethical ideas of mankind. His most famous book, FOLKWAYS (1907), is a sardonic analysis of mankind's customs and ideas. Lloyd Morris feels that this book "explicitly denied the central doctrines of American democratic faith" and undermined "ancient national traditions and inherited attitudes." Yet Sumner was bitter against those who took him too literally by making Mammon their God.

At the same time Sumner was a learned historian, economist, and sociologist in such works as his *History of American Currency* (1874);

American Finance (1875); *Andrew Jackson as a Public Man* (1882); *Alexander Hamilton* (1890); *Robert Morris* (1892); *History of Banking in the U.S.* (1896). In *The Forgotten Man* (a lecture, pub. 1883) he spoke of the industrious taxpayer who had to meet all the bills of "progress." Sumner's collected essays and addresses appear in *What Social Classes Owe to Each Other* (1883); *The Challenge of Facts and Other Essays* (1914); *The Forgotten Man and Other Essays* (ed. by A. G. Keller, 1918). His *Selected Essays* (1924) were edited by Keller and M. R. Davie, who also prepared for publication *The Science of Society* (4 v., 1927) and *Essays* (2 v., 1934). Keller edited *The Forgotten Man's Almanac* (1944), described as "rations of common sense by W. G. Sumner." H. E. Starr wrote a biography of Sumner (1925), and Keller, *Reminiscences* of his friend (1933).

Sun Also Rises, The (1926), a novel by ERNEST HEMINGWAY. This is a novel about "the lost generation," as Gertrude Stein called them, meaning those Americans who had fought during World War I in France and then had expatriated themselves from the America of Calvin Coolidge. They were heavy drinkers and completely disillusioned. The story is told by Jake Barnes, rendered impotent from a wound received in the war. Lady Brett Ashley, who is divorcing her husband, is in love with him; her frustrated and uninhibited search for satisfaction elsewhere brings unhappy complications to most of the characters in the book. Part of the scene is Hemingway's favorite Spain, and bullfighting and a matador are part of the story. Oscar Cargill suggested (*Intellectual America*, 1941) that Hemingway, in creating and describing his characters, was influenced by Gertrude Stein's "type psychology" of classifying people by "the way they love."

The book was a best seller and probably influenced people's lives to a much greater extent than is usually true of novels. It was widely believed to be a *roman à clef*, and Paris wits asserted that its title should have been "Six Characters in Search of an Author—with a Gun Apiece." Carlos Baker, reviewing the book twenty-five years after its appearance, spoke of its "desperate gaiety," but felt that it had become a classic because it was so well written and constructed and because of "its richness in symbolic suggestiveness." He also spoke of "its sturdy moral backbone." See also THE LOST GENERATION.

Sunnier Side, The (1950), twelve stories by CHARLES JACKSON.

Sunnybank. The home of ALBERT PAYSON TERHUNE, famous for his stories of collie dogs. Here he maintained the Sunnybank kennels and wrote widely popular stories about his favorite dogs, including *Lad of Sunnybank* (1929) and *The Book of Sunnybank* (1934). His wife Anice Terhune composed *Sunnybank Songs for Children* (1929).

Sunnyside. WASHINGTON IRVING's home on the Hudson, not far from Tarrytown, N.Y., where he lived from 1836 to 1842 and again from 1846 until his death in 1859. It was originally built as an old Dutch farmhouse in 1656, was burned by the British during the Revolution, and was rebuilt in 1785. When Irving bought it in 1835 he enlarged it from a four-room colonial saltbox to a fifteen-room mansion. John D. Rockefeller, Jr., donated half a million dollars to restore the house as a national shrine, which was opened to the public on Oct. 4, 1947.

Sunrise (1880), a poem by SIDNEY LANIER, later the first section of HYMNS OF THE MARSHES. Its 192 lines are rich in tumultuous melody and exclamatory lyricism. Gay Wilson Allen comments on the skill with which Lanier's anapests exercise "various and subtle effects on the few iambic lines." See BALLAD OF TREES AND THE MASTER.

Sunthin' in the Pastoral Line (*Atlantic Monthly*, 1862; *Biglow Papers, Second Series*, 1867), a poem by JAMES RUSSELL LOWELL. Hosea Biglow falls asleep and dreams that an old Puritan Father appears and gives him some practical ideas on how to deal with the slavery issue. In good Yankee dialect he talks to him on how Charles I was beheaded because he was a tyrant and urges that Hosea, his descendant, must similarly overthrow slavery. Hosea tells him that "Our Charles hez gut eight million necks," and adds, "The hardest question ain't the black man's right, / The trouble is to 'mancipate the white." The poem, as Harry Hayden Clark suggests, should be read in conjunction with Lowell's introduction to it and with his essays *New England Two Centuries Ago; Rebellion: Its Causes and Consequences;* and *Rousseau and the Sentimentalists.*

Sun-Up (1923), a play by Lula Vollmer, one of the first American folk dramas. This drama presents the hillbilly seriously but not too convincingly. It portrays the widow Cagle in the North Carolina mountains, whose husband has been killed by a "revenooer" and whose son goes off to France in World War I. A deserter takes refuge with her; when she hears her son has been killed in the government "feud," she decides to kill the deserter. But her son's voice, coming with music from the afterworld, restrains her, bids her do something to restore love in the world.

Superstition (prod., 1823; pub., 1825), a play by JAMES NELSON BARKER. This complicated play deals with the Stuart house of England and at the same time the witchcraft trials in New England, where the action takes place. The hero, Charles Fitzroy, is really the son of Charles II, but his grandfather, one of the regicides who had brought Charles I to the execution block, is a refugee in the New World, and because of his mysterious appearance and disappearance is taken for a minion of the devil. But all these matters remain unrevealed until after Charles is convicted on a clergyman's testimony and executed. The clergyman personifies for Barker the clerical tyranny over

Puritan communities. The play is regarded as Barker's best work.

Suppressed Desires (1915), a one-act play by SUSAN GLASPELL and her husband GEORGE CRAM COOK. This was one of the earliest plays produced by the PROVINCETOWN PLAYERS at their Wharf Theater. It deals satirically with the Freudian notion that suppressed desires, usually sexual, are the cause of most neurotic conditions, but if brought to the surface and allowed to express themselves, lose their harmful effect.

surrealism. A psychological, aesthetic, and philosophical concept which strongly affected literature and painting, also at times the drama and cinema, first in France, later (but less strongly) in other countries. It originated between the First and Second World Wars as a definite movement, but claimed forerunners such as Monk Lewis' Gothic novels and the poetry of Rimbaud and Saint-John Perse.

Surrealism had its roots in Freud's theory of the unconscious, particularly that expressed in *Interpretation of Dreams* (1900, English translation 1913), and flowered after the first outburst of the unconscious into Dadaism in 1916. Convinced of the meaninglessness and uselessness of Dadaism, André Breton, a psychiatrist and disciple of Freud, experimented with automatic writing and published the results as *Les champs magnétiques* in 1921; in 1924 he issued the first Surrealist manifesto. The name "surrealism" was a contribution of Guillaume Apollinaire; Herbert Read attempted to introduce a literal translation of "surrealism" as "superrealism" in England during the thirties, but the original name survived. The surrealists conceive of the unconscious as the source of beauty and truth and attempt to exploit it; the superior reality is that of the dream, and the means of attaining that reality is a psychic automatism which operates in the absence of all rational, moral, and aesthetic control. Surrealism in England was fostered by David Gascoyne (*A Short Survey of Surrealism*, 1935) and Herbert Read (*Surrealism*, 1936); Gascoyne, however, left the ranks in 1938 and Read's brand of surrealism ultimately evolved into an ideology which depends less on the absolute autonomy of the unconscious than on a romantic defense of the irrational as a necessary and active principle of art. American writers influenced by surrealism include HENRY MILLER, WILLIAM CARLOS WILLIAMS, and E. E. CUMMINGS.

Survey Graphic, The. Founded in 1897 as *Charities*, an official organ of the N. Y. Charity Organization Society, this magazine took the name *The Survey* in 1897. In 1912 the Society withdrew its support when the magazine published an article advocating the election of Theodore Roosevelt. It continued as a liberal magazine, appealing especially to social workers. In 1902 Paul Kellogg joined its staff, in 1912 became its editor, continuing in that position until 1952, when illness forced his withdrawal and the suspension of the magazine.

Susan and God (1937), a play by RACHEL CROTHERS. The most successful of this author's plays is marred by her customary sentimentalism but numerous satiric passages redeem it. Susan comes back from England infatuated with the doctrines of a new religious sect resembling the so-called Oxford Movement. Susan says that all one need do to find God in this "new way" is just show "Love—love—*love* for other people—*not* for yourself." But she completely ignores her inebriate and neglected

jokers"; jokes, corn likker, and sex were his chief preoccupations. Mark Twain knew Harris' writings and was influenced by him. Bernard De Voto employed a passage from *Blown Up with Soda* to refute what he describes as Van Wyck Brooks' "childlike" belief that "the pioneer had no sex life." Brom Weber edited the Sut Lovingood tales (1954).

Sutpen family, the. A family in ABSALOM, ABSALOM!, by William Faulkner. Its complex relationships include both Negroes and whites.

SUTPEN GENEALOGY

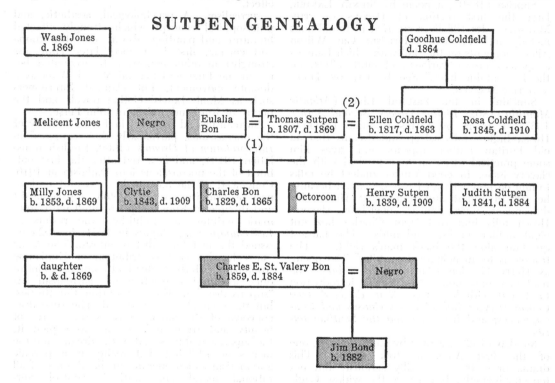

husband and her daughter. Her husband finally sees her selfishness, leaves her, and threatens divorce. However, Miss Crothers contrives a happy ending in which all are reconciled.

Susan Lenox: Her Fall and Rise (1917), a posthumous novel by DAVID GRAHAM PHILLIPS. This novel was at first suppressed because of its depiction of a girl of loose morals who is frequently a prostitute. The book eventually was recognized as an attack on society rather than an indecent story. It received warm praise from Edith Wharton. Susan is an illegitimate child whose mother dies at her birth; the revelation of this fact by a cruel cousin drives her away from the home of her aunt and uncle when she is seventeen. Thereafter her course is a checkered and complicated one, with many men of varied character in her life.

Sut Lovingood Yarns (1867), tales by GEORGE WASHINGTON HARRIS. They were originally contributed to the *Spirit of the Times,* later collected in *Sut Lovingood Yarns: Spun by a "Nat'ral Born Durn'd Fool"* (1867). Lovingood has been called "the prince of coarse practical

The following are members of the Sutpen family:

Charles Bon. Son of Thomas Sutpen and the part-Negro Eulalia Bon, Charles marries a New Orleans octoroon by whom he has a son, Charles Étienne St.-Valery Bon. He is later engaged to his half-sister, Judith Sutpen, but is killed by her brother, Henry, before the marriage can take place.

Eulalia Bon. The daughter of a Haitian plantation owner, Eulalia is divorced by Thomas Sutpen when he discovers she has Negro blood.

Jim Bond. The idiot son of Charles É. St.-Valery Bon and a Negro woman, Jim is the last remaining descendant of Thomas Sutpen. He disappears after Sutpen's house is burned in 1909.

Ellen Coldfield. The daughter of a respected merchant in Jefferson, Ellen is married to Thomas Sutpen, by whom she has two children, Henry and Judith. She is largely responsible for the engagement between Judith and her half-brother Charles Bon.

Rosa Coldfield. The spinster sister-in-law of Thomas Sutpen, Rosa narrates part of *Ab-*

salom, Absalom! She is engaged, but never married, to Sutpen, who, in his desire for male offspring to bear his name, insults her by suggesting that "they try it first and if it was a boy and lived, they would be married."

Wash Jones. Grandfather of the girl who bears an illegitimate daughter to Sutpen, Jones is a poor white squatter and handyman around the Sutpen estate. He murders his granddaughter, her newborn child, and Sutpen, and then kills himself.

Clytie [Clytemnestra] Sutpen. The daughter of Thomas Sutpen and a Negro slave, Clytie burns the Sutpen house over her own and Henry Sutpen's head in 1909 to prevent Henry from being taken to jail for the murder of Charles Bon.

Henry Sutpen. Son of Thomas Sutpen by his second wife, Ellen Coldfield, Henry meets Charles Bon at the University of Mississippi and forms an intimate friendship with him, unaware that Bon is his half brother. Learning of their relationship and of Bon's Negro blood, Henry murders him to prevent his marrying Henry's sister, Judith. Henry disappears after the murder and is discovered in 1909, ill, hiding in Sutpen's almost-deserted house, cared for by his mulatto half-sister Clytie.

Judith Sutpen. Daughter of Thomas Sutpen and Ellen Coldfield, Judith is engaged to marry her half-brother Charles Bon. After his death she brings up his part-negro son, Charles Étienne St.-Valery Bon.

Thomas Sutpen. Descended from a family of southern poor whites, Sutpen came to Mississippi in 1833 and acquired one hundred square miles of fertile bottom land from the Chickasaw chief Ikkemotubbe, on which he built a plantation called Sutpen's Hundred. He married Ellen Coldfield in order to connect himself with the local gentry and properly carry out his great design to found an aristocratic southern family. He is murdered by his handyman in 1869 after a last and futile attempt to beget a white son to become master of Sutpen's Hundred.

Swados, Harvey (b. Buffalo, N.Y., Oct. 28, 1920—   ), author, critic, teacher. Swados studied at the University of Michigan. He was a faculty member at Sarah Lawrence College and the University of Iowa before serving as visiting professor at San Francisco State College. His first novel, *Out Went the Candle* (1955), was a realistic depiction of an American family during and after the second World War. *On the Line* (1957), a more successful novel, was reminiscent of the social protest novels of the thirties; it portrayed the assembly line workers of a large automobile factory. Swados was awarded a Guggenheim Fellowship in fiction in 1961. His other books: *False Coin* (1959); *Nights in the Gardens of Brooklyn* (1960).

Swallow Barn: A Sojourn in the Old Dominion (1832), a novel by JOHN PENDLETON KENNEDY. It was described by Kennedy himself as "a series of detached sketches linked together by the hooks and eyes of a traveler's notes. . . . There is a rivulet of story wandering through a broad meadow of episode." Influenced by Addison and Irving, the book is chiefly notable as one of the earliest to present the American stereotypes of the southern gentleman and plantation life.

Swanson, Neil H[armon] (b. Minneapolis, Minn., June 30, 1896—   ), newspaperman, historian, historical novelist. A newspaperman almost all his life, Swanson early became interested in writing histories in fictional style. Two of his early books fall in this class: *The First Rebel* (1937) and *The Perilous Fight* (1945). In 1939 he began a series designed to show the development of the Middle Atlantic states during the 18th century. In the projected series he included some novels he had already published—*The Judas Tree* (1933) among them. Others are *Unconquered* (1947) and *The Calico Tree* (1955). With Anne Sherbourne Swanson he published *Star-Spangled Banner* (1958).

Swap, Solomon. A Yankee character who appears in many American comedies of the first half of the 19th century, though the name and some of the traits were taken from a farce by the English dramatist George Colman the Younger. Solomon was made famous by such actors as JAMES H. HACKETT and GEORGE HANDEL HILL.

Swedenborgianism. This small but influential religious sect was founded on the doctrines of Emanuel Swedenborg (b. Sweden, Jan. 29, 1688—d. March 29, 1772). He was in the earlier part of his life an eminent scientist. Then in April, 1744, he had a vision of Christ, and thereafter devoted himself largely to expounding a mystic doctrine of God and the world, but founded no church, in the belief that Protestant sects could incorporate his ideas into their own teaching. His writings appeared mainly in Latin; among the most well known are *Heaven and Hell* (1758) and *The Apocalypse Revealed* (1766). His doctrines include a special interpretation of the Trinity, emphasis on certain books of the Bible, three descending levels or "degrees of being in God," and the prediction of a new dispensation. Swedenborgians were first organized (1778) as a church in London. The sect was called the "Society of the New Church Signified by the New Jerusalem," more often called "the New Church." Members are few and widely scattered; their total number is believed to be 25,000.

James Glen preached Swedenborgianism in Philadelphia and Boston in 1784; a society was organized in Baltimore in 1792, a national group in 1817. Swedenborg's deepest influence was exerted on the CONCORD SCHOOL during the early 19th century. Ralph Waldo Emerson called him a "colossal soul," and the dwellers at BROOK FARM deeply revered him. His mystical doctrine of contact with the spiritual world, combined with a belief in human perfectionism, was peculiarly suited to the American intellectual genius. Henry James the elder pondered these doctrines deeply, gathering from them his concept of "divine-natural humanity," and through him they influenced his son, the novelist. The theme of natural history in the garments of spirituality also inspired Alexander Kinmont in his *Natural History of Man*, a series of lectures delivered in 1837–38, and Job Durfee's discourse *The Influence of Scientific Discovery and Invention on Social and Political Progress* (1843).

Sweeney. A character, at one point called Apeneck Sweeney, who appears in a number of poems by T. S. ELIOT, notably *Sweeney Among the Nightingales* (1918); *Mr. Eliot's Sunday Morning Service* (1918); *Sweeney Erect* (1919); THE WASTE LAND (1922); and two fragments entitled *Sweeney Agonistes* (separately pub., 1926, 1927; then together, 1932). He is intended as a satirical portrait of sensual, materialistic man, particularly in the 20th century. Eliot has said that Sweeney is a composite of several South Boston Irishmen he observed in his youth.

Critics have paid much attention to Sweeney, many seeing him as one pole of a duality in which the other pole is represented by various aristocratic and often neurotic figures. Between them they characterize contemporary life. Lloyd Frankenberg has suggested some significant parallels between Sweeney and the protagonist of an anonymous 12th- or 13th-century epic, *Buile Shuibne*, "The Frenzy of Sweeney" (Frankenberg suggests that "Sweeney Agonistes" would be a fair translation). William York Tindall wrote that "on the surface it is a picture of vulgar reality. . . . But what really matters is this: jazz rhythms, tone, and the redundant banalities of 'demotic' speech, working together, produce what [James] Joyce called an epiphany, a commonplace that reveals the depth of reality, a complex of feeling and idea that cannot be translated into critical prose." According to George Williamson, the original title of the poem was *Wanna Go Home, Baby?*

Sweeney, James J[ohnson] (b. Brooklyn, N.Y., May 30, 1900—   ), art critic, museum director. Sweeney studied at Georgetown and Cambridge Universities, as well as at the Sorbonne and the University of Siena, Italy. Sweeney planned an exhibition of 20th century painting and sculpture at the University of Chicago, and an exhibition of African Negro art for New York's Museum of Modern Art before becoming a lecturer at New York University's Institute of Fine Arts in 1935. He served as curator of painting and sculpture at the Museum of Modern Art from 1945–46. The next two years were devoted to lecturing at the Salzburg Seminar in American Studies. In 1952 he was appointed director of the Solomon R. Guggenheim Museum in New York City. He resigned in 1960 and was subsequently named director of The Museum of Fine Arts of Houston and Lecturer on Fine Arts at Harvard University. Sweeney's interest in contemporary literature was displayed as an as-

sociate editor of *transition*, and an advisory editor of the *Partisan Review*. His books include: *Plastic Redirections in 20th Century Painting* (1934); *African Negro Art* (ed., 1935); *Joan Miro* (1941); *Alexander Calder* (1943); *Three Young Rats and Other Rhymes* (ed., 1944); *Stuart Davis* (1945); *Marc Chagall* (1946); *Henry Moore* (1947); *African Folk Tales and Sculpture* (with P. Radin, 1952); *Burri* (1955); *The Miro Atmosphere* (1959); *Antoni Gaudi* (with J. L. Sert, 1960).

Sweet Adeline (1903), a ballad, words by RICHARD GERARD, music by Harry W. Armstrong. Originally the name of the heroine was Rosalie; it was changed to Adeline in honor of the famous opera singer Adelina Patti. Originally, too, it was entitled *My Old England Home*. Written in 1896, the song did not find a publisher until seven years later; then its sales steadily mounted. John F. Fitzgerald (Honey Fitz) used it in his successful campaign for mayor of Boston and felt he owed his election to the song. It likewise became the favorite ballad of the Society for the Preservation and Encouragement of Barber Shop Quartet Singing in America.

Sweet Alice. The heroine of the query addressed to BEN BOLT in THOMAS DUNN ENGLISH's famous song: "Oh, don't you remember sweet Alice, Ben Bolt?" The poem appeared in the *New Mirror*, Sept. 2, 1843.

Sweet Singer of Michigan, The. See JULIA A. MOORE.

Swift, Tom. A boy inventor, hero of a long series of novels for boys. Tom's hair-raising adventures with all kinds of contrivances, some of which anticipated actual inventions, became widely popular and brought considerable wealth to his creator, EDWARD L. STRATEMEYER. Some titles in the series are still in print.

Swinton, William (b. Scotland, April 23, 1833—d. Oct. 24, 1892), newspaperman, teacher, historian, textbook author. Swinton's parents took him to Canada in 1843. He taught as a young man in New York City and North Carolina, then joined the staff of *The New York Times* and helped cover the Civil War. Later he wrote several books about the war, one attacking General McClellan (1864), another describing *The Twelve Decisive Battles of the War* (1867). From 1869 to 1874 he was professor of English at the University of California. A disagreement with the president there led to his resignation, and he thereafter wrote successful textbooks for use in elementary schools. His *Readers* were especially popular. He won a gold medal at the Paris Exposition of 1878 for his work in this field.

Swope, Herbert Bayard (b. St. Louis, Mo., Jan. 5, 1882—d. June 20, 1958), newspaperman, editor, public official. Swope was a war correspondent for the New York *World* in World War I and was awarded the first Pulitzer prize in the field of reporting. He covered other important assignments in later years, then served as executive editor of the *World*. He held the office of chairman of the New York

Racing Commission and various appointments in other fields of public service. He wrote several books, among them *Inside the German Empire in the Third Year of the War* (1917).

Sword Blades and Poppy Seed (1914), a collection of poems by AMY LOWELL. This second collection of Miss Lowell's verse is important particularly for its inclusion of poems written in free verse and the first English examples of "polyphonic prose," rhythmical prose characterized by the devices of verse except strict meter. Although none of the poetry is particularly outstanding, the volume was one of the first indications of the growing trend away from traditional rhyme and meter toward new forms. An American leader of the imagist movement (see IMAGISM), Miss Lowell was one of the first to put her arguments for precision, clarity, and accuracy of description into practice in poetry.

Sykes, Gerald (b. Ontario, Canada, Dec. 31, 1903—   ), novelist, critic. His first novel, *The Nice American* (1951), appeared when Sykes was forty-eight. He was previously known for his articles in such magazines as *Hound and Horn, Partisan Review*, the *New Republic*, and *the Nation*. His novels received increasing praise as their fictional technique improved. Among his books: *The Center of the Stage* (1952); *The Children of Light* (1955); *The Hidden Remnant* (1962).

Sylvester, Harry (b. Brooklyn, N.Y., Jan. 19, 1908—   ), newspaperman, short-story writer, novelist. Sylvester's stories are set in varying backgrounds. The short stories in *All Your Idols* (1948) are mainly set in Mexico, his longer fiction in Maryland, New Mexico, New York City, and Peru. Sylvester became deeply interested in the problems of the Roman Catholic Church as observed in various parts of the United States. The most widely read of his books on the subject was *Moon Gaffney* (1947), a study of a Tammany politician's son. It was described in *Time* as "a blast against bias, false Irish pride, and the local little Father Coughlins."

Sylvestre, Guy Jean (b. Sorel, Que., May 17, 1918—   ), critic, librarian. Educated at the College St. Marie in Montreal and the University of Ottawa, Sylvestre was president of the Canadian Writer's Foundation and has been honored for his literary work by the Royal Society of Canada. *Anthologie de la poésie canadienne française* (1943) and *Poètes catholiques de la France contemporaine* (1944) are anthologies of poetry compiled by Sylvestre; *Impressions du théâtre* (1950) and *Sondages* (1954) —the latter, a series of literary essays on writers such as Raymond Radiguet, Louis Aragon, and Paul Valéry—are considered to be among his best works.

symbolism. Primarily a European movement, symbolism originated in France in the mid-19th century and became of great importance and influence during the 1880's. It arose largely as a part of a romantic reaction that freed French verse from the rigidity and rhetoric of the classi-

cism that had dominated French literature during the 18th century. Charles Baudelaire, who is considered one of the founders of symbolism, was deeply impressed by the poetry of EDGAR ALLAN POE; he translated Poe's works into French and brought Poe more recognition in Europe than he was receiving in America. The musicality of Poe's verse and his use of synaesthesia were influential in the development of the poetry of Baudelaire, whose sonnet *Correspondances*, treating all objects as symbols, finds a "correspondence" between visual, auditory, and sensory perceptions.

Arthur Rimbaud, seeking to become a seer through a "reasoned derangement of all the senses," took symbolism further from objective reality as his *Bateau Ivre* wobbled drunkenly through the seas of experience, and attempted to create, through incantatory language, a new world of vision. Stéphane Mallarmé, perhaps the most important of the symbolist poets, sought to divorce language from its particularity, creating poems whose obscurity became the more dense as he approached his abstract—and inaccessible —ideal. Influenced by Poe and Baudelaire, Mallarmé's salons and his aesthetic theories came closest to creating a "school" of symbolism and were highly influential, both in France and in the spreading of symbolism to England.

Disdaining nature as chaotic and repugnant, the symbolists cultivated artifice in their personal lives to complement the artifice of the work of art, thus establishing the cult of the "dandy," which was paralleled by Oscar Wilde and other English decadents of the eighties and nineties. Symbolism first made itself felt as an influence in England toward the end of the 19th century, was a factor in the development of free verse and may have had some indirect effect on EZRA POUND's and AMY LOWELL's IMAGISM. American critical and "little" magazines began to pay attention to French symbolism in the beginning of the 20th century, and American expatriates in Europe furthered the introduction of French poetry and aesthetics into America.

In *The Twenties* (1955), Frederick J. Hoffman concludes that "French symbolism was not a negligible factor in the development of modern American poetry"; however, since no American poet has been a symbolist exactly after the fashion of the French, it is difficult to differentiate between influence and individual development. Certainly during the twenties there was a marked vogue toward difficult, tightly constructed poetry in which words, singly and in combinations, were used in new or unusual ways—poetry which suggested rather than stated; which was highly evocative, often musical; or which depended (in the words of Hart Crane) on "the illogical impingements of words on the consciousness," rather than on their logical connotations. HART CRANE, particularly in his early poems, is possibly the only American poet who can be truly classified as a symbolist. Some critics consider T. S. ELIOT to have adapted some of the techniques of symbolism for his own uses; some of the poems of WILLIAM

CARLOS WILLIAMS and ARCHIBALD MACLEISH are broadly symbolic in their use of subject matter but not, like some of WALLACE STEVENS, in their technique as well.

Symbolism as a general term, and particularly with reference to prose writings, should not be confused with symbolist poetry, which refers to a particular literary movement characterized by the desire to express a state of mind by purely sensuous images, and to suggest rather than describe. Symbolism in general may refer to any one thing being made to stand for another, a literary technique that is fairly widespread. The best examples of American symbolism of this type are the novels of NATHANIEL HAWTHORNE and HERMAN MELVILLE, particularly THE SCARLET LETTER and MOBY DICK. *The Scarlet Letter* itself is a symbol, a fact which Hawthorne underlines in the chapter on the Custom House, where he finds a faded and worn letter A which still seems to exert some of its mysterious force. Hester's child, Pearl, is something of a symbolic figure, as is the wicked Chillingworth, and the scaffold and forest scenes take on symbolic significance. *Moby Dick* is almost inexhaustible in symbolic meaning; Ahab, the ship, the strange crew, Ishmael, and the whale are all susceptible of a variety of symbolic interpretations. For a further discussion of 19th-century American symbolism see *Symbolism and American Literature* (1953), by Charles Feidelson, Jr. Works dealing with the symbolist poets in France include Arthur Symons, *The Symbolist Movement in Literature* (1899) and Ruth Z. Temple, *Critic's Alchemy: A Study of the Introduction of French Symbolism into England* (1953). For a general discussion of modern symbolism see William York Tindall, *The Literary Symbol* (1958).

Symphony, The (1875), a poem by SIDNEY LANIER. In this extraordinary poem Lanier deliberately created some striking effects intended to demonstrate that close relationship between poetry and music which he constantly asserted. The poem closes with Lanier's most famous phrase, "Music is Love in search of a word." The poem is a strong denunciation of industrialism and the commercial attitude of "glozing and lying." It is a plea for greater humanity and for attention to "the poor-folks' crying." The pattern of the poem consists of the successive use of various instruments in the orchestra: the violins, the flute, the clarinet, the horn, the oboe.

syndicate features. See NEWSPAPERS.

T

Tabb, John Banister (b. Amelia Co., Va., March 22, 1845—d. Nov. 19, 1909), poet, teacher. Tabb intended to make music his profession. He was refused by the Confederate Army during the Civil War because of defective vision, but became a blockade runner. He made a number of trips to Europe before he was captured and imprisoned at Point Lookout, where he met SIDNEY LANIER, another prisoner. The two became fast friends; it was Lanier who inspired Tabb to write poetry. After the war Tabb became a teacher at St. Paul's School for Boys in Baltimore. In 1872 he joined the Roman Catholic Church and entered St. Charles' College, Md., graduating in 1875. After another stint of teaching in Baltimore, he began his studies for the priesthood at St. Mary's Seminary and was ordained in 1884; he returned to St. Charles' College to teach English and remained there the rest of his life.

Father Tabb's poetry has been compared to Emily Dickinson's, and there is a superficial resemblance. Both poets experimented with new techniques, both were deeply interested in nature and religion, both tended toward brevity. But Tabb's poems lack the freshness he admired in Emily Dickinson's work; his was a far more conventional mind. The influence of Edgar Allan Poe is more marked. Among his books are *An Octave to Mary* (1893); *Poems* (1894), which ran to 17 editions; *Lyrics* (1897); *Child Verse* (1899); *Later Lyrics* (1902); *The Rosary in Rhyme* (1904); *Quips and Quiddits* (1907). Tabb's reputation was extended to England by *Later Lyrics* (1902), and by *A Selection from the Verses of John B. Tabb*, compiled by Alice Meynell in 1907. His only prose work was *Bone Rules, or the Skeleton of English Grammar* (1897). A niece, Jennie Masters Tabb, wrote *Father Tabb, His Life and Work* (1921); Francis A. Litz wrote *Father Tabb: A Study of His Life and Works* (1923), collected his letters and other prose (1950) and collected his poems in 1928.

Tablets (1868), a miscellaneous collection by AMOS BRONSON ALCOTT. This volume contains both prose and verse, neither of a high order of merit. One typical saying is: "Who loves a garden still his Eden keeps, / Perennial pleasures plants, and wholesome harvests reaps." There are two sections, one called "Practical," the other, "Speculative."

tabloids. See NEWSPAPERS.

Taft, Lorado (b. Elmwood, Ill., April 29, 1860—d. Oct. 30, 1936), sculptor, writer, teacher. Taft did portrait busts, statues, and some military monuments, with competence but no special originality. The *Fountain of Time* and the *Fountain of the Great Lakes*, both in Chicago, are considered his best works. He also taught at the Chicago Art Institute, and wrote *The History of American Sculpture* (1903, rev. 1924); and *Modern Tendencies in American Sculpture* (1921). Hamlin Garland, Taft's brother-in-law, wrote about him in DAUGHTER OF THE MIDDLE BORDER (1921).

Taft, William Howard (b. Cincinnati, Ohio, Sept. 15, 1857—d. March 8, 1930), lawyer, judge, public official, teacher, author, twenty-sixth President of the United States. Taft went to Yale University, was graduated from the Cincinnati Law School in 1880, and was admitted to the bar. He occupied a long series of public offices: assistant prosecuting attorney, assistant county solicitor, judge of the Superior Court, U.S. solicitor general, judge of the Federal Circuit Court, head of the Philippines Commission, governor of the Philippines, Secretary of War, provisional governor of Cuba. Then, at Theodore Roosevelt's unflagging insistence, he was nominated for President and elected over William Jennings Bryan (1908). But Taft was fundamentally more conservative than Roosevelt, and offended not only his old friend, but numerous progressive voters; he ran unsuccessfully for a second term against Woodrow Wilson and against Roosevelt, who had founded the Bull Moose party in his anger against Taft. In 1913 Taft became professor of constitutional law at Yale Law School and served until 1921, when he was appointed Chief Justice of the Supreme Court.

Taft wrote several books, among them *Popular Government* (1913), and *Our Chief Magistrate and His Powers* (1916). Mrs. William Howard Taft wrote *Recollections of Full Years* (1914); H. S. Duffy wrote a biography of Taft (1930); and H. F. Pringle wrote *The Life and Times of W. H. Taft* (2 v., 1939). Taft in his pre-Presidential days appears in Frederick Palmer's novel, *The Big Fellow* (1908).

Two sons of Taft won distinction: **Robert A[lphonso] Taft** (1889–1953) and **Charles P[helps] Taft** (1897—   ). The former became a lawyer and then a distinguished public official, from 1939 till his death serving as Senator from Ohio, and from 1947 on, as leader of the Republican majority in the Senate. He wrote *A Foreign Policy for Americans* (1951). His calm courage in the face of a painful death from cancer led to the composition of Jhan and June Robbins' *Eight Weeks to Live* (1954). William S. White wrote a eulogistic biography, *The Taft Story* (1954). His younger brother, a lawyer who occasionally served in public office, wrote several able analyses of public affairs, among them: *City Management—The Cincinnati Experiment* (1933); *You and I—and Roosevelt*

(1936); *Why I Am for the Church* (1947); and *Democracy in Politics and Economics* (1950).

Taggard, Genevieve (b. Waitsburg, Wash., Nov. 28, 1894—d. Nov. 8, 1948), poet, teacher, biographer, editor. Miss Taggard's life was devoted to writing and the interpretation of poetry. She published numerous collections, among them being: *For Eager Lovers* (1922); *Hawaiian Hilltop* (1923); *Words for the Chisel* (1926); *Not Mine to Finish* (1934); *Poems, 1918–1938* (1938); *Slow Music* (1946); *Origin Hawaii* (1947). She taught English at Mount Holyoke and Sarah Lawrence Colleges, founded and edited *The Measure, a Journal of Verse* (1920–1926), wrote a biography of Emily Dickinson (1930), edited several anthologies, and wrote lyrics for composers, including Aaron Copland. She was a follower of the metaphysical school and a metrical innovator. Alfred Kreymborg described her as in love with storms and finding no peace in quietude. Hawaii, her residence during childhood and youth, was a frequent theme in her verses.

Tailfer, Patrick (fl. 1741), 18th-century physician, satirist, pamphleteer. Little is known of Tailfer save that in his sole published work he called himself an "M.D." and that in a reply to this work he was accused of cruelty to his servants, even of having murdered one of them. He and several others quarreled bitterly with Gen. JAMES OGLETHORPE of the Georgia colony and fled to Charleston, S.C. There in 1741 they issued a pamphlet of considerable length, entitled *A True and Historical Narrative of the Colony at Georgia . . . ,* by Patrick Tailfer, M.D., Hugh Anderson, M.A., David Douglas, "and Others, Landholders in Georgia." Tailfer, to whom the pamphlet is usually ascribed, indulged in scathing satire at the expense of Oglethorpe and other Georgia officials, but presented sufficient documentary evidence to make the attack effective. The pamphlet was reprinted in Peter Force's *Historical Tracts* (4 v., 1836–46), also in the Georgia Historical Society's *Collections* (Vol. II, 1842), which also reprinted an official reply by Benjamin Martyn, secretary of the Georgia trustees. Another reply was made by the Rev. William Best in a sermon to these trustees, *The Merit and Reward of a Good Intention* (1742).

Tales of a Traveller (1824), thirty-two stories and sketches by WASHINGTON IRVING. Four sets of ingeniously framed stories give this collection of Irving's a sustained interest lacking in his earlier works. The first group, told by a number of convivial English gentlemen, contains one rousingly humorous ghost story, *The Bold Dragoon.* The second part deals with the adventures of Buckthorne, a young English literary hopeful. The third is concerned with Italian bandits. In the last and best section, *The Money Diggers,* Irving is again creating his own special brand of American folklore. THE DEVIL AND TOM WALKER, which has been called "a comic New England Faust," deserves

to rank beside the best legends from THE SKETCH BOOK (1820).

Despite the romantic background and sentimental situations in many of the stories, they are all solidly based in realistic detail. And Irving frequently ends by laughing at his own romanticism, which was strongly influenced by German literature.

Tales of a Wayside Inn (1863), a collection of twenty-one long narrative poems by HENRY WADSWORTH LONGFELLOW. The tales are built around a framework similar to that used by Chaucer in the *Canterbury Tales* and Boccaccio in the *Decameron:* each is narrated by a member of a group gathered around a fireside in a New England tavern. Most of the tales reflect Longfellow's strong interest in medievalism and the early history of Europe. The best of these artificially dated stories is probably "The Saga of King Olaf," which is presented in a manner that gives it an air of mythology.

Not all the stories have an ancient setting, but even the popular "Paul Revere's Ride" is presented as a piece of dated history. For Longfellow was not able to treat a modern event poetically until it had been recast in ancient clothing; his work offers a sentimental escape from reality rather than a penetration of reality for the truths contained in it. Some of the more interesting of the other tales included in this collection are "Elizabeth," the story told by the Theologian, and "The Ballad of Carmilhan," told by the Musician. See OLE BULL; LUIGI MONTI; BIRDS OF KILLINGSWORTH; EMMA AND EGINHARD; THE FALCON OF SER FEDERIGO.

Tales of Soldiers and Civilians (1891), by AMBROSE BIERCE. See IN THE MIDST OF LIFE, the title given this collection in 1898.

Tales of the Grotesque and Arabesque (2 v., 1840), twenty-five stories by EDGAR ALLAN POE. This was Poe's first published collection and includes some of his most famous stories, notably THE FALL OF THE HOUSE OF USHER. In his preface Poe replied to the charge made frequently against him, that his work was permeated with "Germanism and gloom." He said: "If in many of my productions terror has been the basis, I maintain that terror is not of Germany but of the soul." The volumes were rather favorably received but sold slowly, and Poe received no encouragement when he proposed a second enlarged edition. See THE ASSIGNATION; BERENICE.

Tales of the South Pacific (1947), eighteen stories by JAMES A. MICHENER. Michener made rich use of his World War II naval experiences in this collection, which won the 1948 Pulitzer prize for fiction. Although each tale can be read independently, various characters, American and native, reappear from time to time to form a connecting link. Against the background of the South Pacific, Michener gives a splendid picture of the cooperation and fellowship of the United States forces. Mixed with the high excitement of the battle pieces are the comic, romantic, and ironic interludes behind the scenes. Beautiful native girls, bizarre French colonizers, even the descendants of the *Bounty* mutineers who settled on Pitcairn Island, mingle in these pages to form one of the most sympathetic and illuminating books to come out of the war. Oscar Hammerstein II and Richard C. Rodgers drew together themes from several of the stories for the spectacularly successful musical *South Pacific* (1949).

Taliaferro, Harden E. (b. Surry Co., N.C., 1818—d. Nov. 2, 1875), clergyman, writer. Taliaferro (whose name is pronounced "Toliver") was born in the mountainous western part of North Carolina and became a Baptist preacher at an early age; his book *The Grace of God Manifested* (1857) was published by the Southern Baptist Publication Society. He also wrote widely for denominational magazines. But he was a folklorist as well as a preacher, and he collected many tales, especially tall tales, among the mountain folk of his region. He made a collection, *Fisher's River: Scenes and Characters* (1859), in which the stories are retold with authentic humor and a profound knowledge of the Carolina mountaineer, and this book remains his chief claim to fame. The work was issued under the pen name "Skitt."

Talifer (1933), a novel in blank verse by Edwin Arlington Robinson. Two men—a businessman and a doctor—are deeply interested in two women—one somewhat mentally immature, the other an intellectual. The businessman, engaged to the former, gives her up and marries the latter. The marriage proves to be unhappy; a divorce is arranged, then the businessman marries his first love and lives happily. The intellectual woman, under the doctor's care, stays abroad and studies at Oxford. As analyzed by Henry W. Wells in *The American Way of Poetry* (1943), in this poem, as in later stories by Robinson, "the leading character is first depressed and later redeemed."

Talisman, The (1827–1830). This periodical, issued annually by Edam Bliss, was originally undertaken by Gulian C. Verplanck, William Cullen Bryant, and Robert C. Sands as a joint collection of miscellanies in the 18th-century fashion. It was edited by the imaginary "Francis Herbert, Esq.," and was continued until three volumes had been published. In 1833, the three volumes were republished as *Miscellanies first published under the name of The Talisman*. Each author contributed some of his best work to the annual. Verplanck wrote a piece called *Reminiscences of New York*, with help from Bryant; the latter contributed *The Indian Spring* and a poem in blank verse, *The Dream of the Princess Papantzin*.

talking books. These are books recorded on phonograph records for the use of the blind. The project was begun in 1934 by the American Foundation for the Blind; the recordings, prepared in many cases with the cooperation of the authors, are made for the Library of Congress and are distributed free throughout the United States. Among the authors who have read portions of their works on such records are Stephen Vincent Benét, Thomas Mann, Eleanor Roosevelt, Somerset Maugham, Robert E. Sherwood, and many others.

Tallant, Robert (b. New Orleans, April 20, 1909—d. April 1, 1957), folklorist, novelist. New Orleans served as the background for all of Tallant's work. In collaboration with Lyle Saxon and Edward Dryer he wrote and edited *Gumbo Ya-Ya, A Collection of Louisiana Folklore* (1945), then wrote *Voodoo in New Orleans* (1946); *Mardi Gras* (1948); and *The Romantic New Orleanians* (1950). His first novel, *Mrs. Candy and Saturday Night* (1947), is an attractive and unusual story of his native city. *Angel in the Wardrobe* (1948) and *Mr. Preen's Salon* (1949) are also laid in New Orleans.

tall tales and tall talk. Constance Rourke was probably right in setting down the Rev. Samuel A. Peters in her *American Humor* as a conscious rather than unconscious humorist, in which case his *General History of Connecticut* (1781) may be said to contain some of our earliest specimens of satirical lying. Benjamin Franklin, originator of so much else in American civilization, seems also to have written the first "spoof" for a newspaper. On May 20, 1765, he wrote a letter to a London newspaper as a satirical reply to some of the statements being made about the American colonists. He mentioned particularly the story, "in all the papers last week," that the people of Canada were preparing to set up "a cod and whale fishery this summer in the upper lakes"; he noted that "the grand leap of a whale in that chase up the fall of Niagara is esteemed, by all who have seen it, as one of the finest spectacles in nature."

The American tall tale made its formal bow in Washington Irving's History of New York by Diedrich Knickerbocker (1809), with its famous profile of Governor Wouter Van Twiller, for example, who was "exactly five feet six inches in height and six feet five inches in circumference." Generally, however, it is held that the tall tale first began to flourish on the Western frontier. The backwoodsman, represented by such historic figures as Daniel Boone and Davy Crockett, would repeat endless wild tales of his own exploits, some of them true and others exaggerated. To match the fooleries of Crockett, the West invented Mike Fink, king of the flatboatmen, whose vast hyperboles made other men's boasts seem like understatements. The Crockett *Almanacs*, about fifty of which appeared between 1835 and 1856, purported to be the work of Crockett himself or his "heirs," and told many tall tales about Crockett, Fink, Boone, and others. This tall talk had a deep influence on many writers, including Mark Twain and Walt Whitman. Some fine examples are given in Twain's Life on the Mississippi (1883).

The Yankee never went to the lengths the Westerner did; his humor was still spare and comparatively restrained. Richard Dorson finds "the casual lie" characteristic of Yankee humor today. His JONATHAN DRAWS THE LONG BOW (1946) covers a wide and constantly entertaining range of supernatural stories; yarns of greenhorns, tricksters, and originals; tall tales of hunting and fishing, strong men, and the constantly-reappearing sea serpent; also literary folk tales. Dorothy Canfield Fisher, in an article entitled *Old Salt and Old Oak* (*Saturday Review of Literature*, May 22, 1943), mentions another class of New England tales, those which give in a brief phrase a vivid glimpse into the tangled brains of somebody who isn't quite "all there." There is a familiar one about a hired man who heard someone talking about a dead body found near a river. He asked anxiously, "Did it have on a brown coat?" . . . "Yes," was the answer. He shrank back, then asked, "Did it have on black buttoned shoes?" "No." "Oh, then," he cried in relief, " 'twan't me!" The chief folk hero of New England is Captain STORMALONG, the sailor giant and hero of the sea. He appears in an old sailors' shanty and in Walter Blair's accounts in *Tall Tale America* (1944). Lewis Pendleton endeavored to rival the exploits of Stormalong in *Down East: The Remarkable Adventures on the Briny Deep and Ashore of Captain Isaac Drinkwater and Jedediah Peabody* (1937).

PAUL BUNYAN is perhaps the greatest mythical hero America has produced. Tales about him have been gathered in several books, such as H. W. Felton's *Legends of Paul Bunyan* (1947). Other folk heroes are James Bridger, FEBOLD FEBOLDSON, Gib Morgan (of the oil fields), PECOS BILL, JOHN HENRY, TONY BEAVER, BILLY THE KID, and BIG-FOOT WALLACE, some of them modeled on actual persons. Other real people whose size has been magnified in American narratives include Capt. JOHN SMITH, JOHNNY APPLESEED, WILLIAM F. CODY, ANNIE OAKLEY, JESSE JAMES, the pirate LAFITTE, and KIT CARSON. Mody C. Boatright, discussing *The Art of Tall Lying* (*Southwest Review*, Autumn, 1949), felt that the men who moved west with the frontier had "in the tall tale developed one of America's few indigenous art forms." H. L. Mencken found in the grotesque metaphors and far-fetched exaggerations of American tall talk the source of a great many Americanisms (*The American Language*, 4th ed., 1936).

There have been numerous collections of regional tall tales, or stories about individual heroes. Among these: J. H. Ingraham's *Lafitte, the Pirate of the Gulf* (1836); John C. Duval's *Adventures of Big-Foot Wallace* (1870); W. N. Burns' *The Saga of Billy the Kid* (1926); Percy MacKaye's *Tall Tales of the Kentucky Mountains* (1926); Frank Shay's *Here's Audacity! American Legendary Heroes* (1930); F. J. Meine's *Tall Tales of the Southwest* (1930); Roark Bradford's *John Henry* (1931); Walter Blair and F. J. Meine's *Mike Fink* (1933); Bernard De Voto's MARK TWAIN'S AMERICA (1932); James H. Daugherty's *Their Weight

in Wildcats* (1936); A. P. Hudson's *Humor of the Old Deep South* (1936); Vincent McHugh's *Caleb Catlum's America* (1936); J. C. Bowman's *Pecos Bill, the Greatest Cowboy of All Time* (1937); *Davy Crockett: American Comic Legend* (1939, ed. by Richard Dorson); Thomas D. Clark's *The Rampaging Frontier* (1939); Harold W. Thompson's *Body, Boots, & Britches* (1940); B. A. Botkin's TREASURY OF AMERICAN FOLKLORE (1944), *Treasury of New England Folklore* (1947), and *Western Folklore* (1951); M. C. Boatright's *Gib Morgan, Minstrel of the Oil Fields* (1945); Ben C. Clough's *The American Imagination at Work: Tall Tales and Folk Tales* (1947); Paul R. Beath's *Tall Tales from the Great Plains* (1948); Vance Randolph's *We Always Lie to Strangers: Tall Tales from the Ozarks* (1951); J. Frank Dobie's *Tales of Old-Time Texas* (1955); Bill Gulick's *White Men, Red Men, and Mountain Men* (1955); John T. Flanagan and Arthur Palmer Hudson's *American Folklore Reader; Folklore in American Literature* (1958).

Talmage, T[homas] De Witt (b. Bound Brook, N.J., Jan. 7, 1832—d. April 12, 1902), clergyman, editor. Talmage began to study law at the College of the City of New York, but shifted to the New Brunswick Theological Seminary, graduating in 1856. His first pulpit was in the Dutch Reformed Church of Belleville, N.J. In 1862 he was called to the Second Dutch Reformed Church of Philadelphia, where his eloquence and zeal attracted great crowds. His sermons were directed against card playing, theatergoing, books and newspapers he didn't like, Mormonism, ruinous extravagance, wicked sports, but especially against strong drink. He became so famous that at the Central Presbyterian Church in Brooklyn in 1869 he drew the largest congregation of churchgoers ever assembled in America up to that time, and his sermons were printed in more than 3,000 newspapers.

Talmage edited *The Christian at Work* from 1874 to 1876 and *Frank Leslie's Sunday Magazine* from 1881 to 1889. He became editor of the CHRISTIAN HERALD in 1890; nine years later he resigned his pulpit to give all his time to this periodical. Among his many volumes of sermons are *Crumbs Swept Up* (1870); *Every-Day Religion* (1875); *The Marriage Tie* (1890); and *Fifty Short Sermons* (1923). *T. De Witt Talmage as I Knew Him* (1912) is an autobiography.

Tamar (in *Tamar and Other Poems*, 1924), a narrative poem by ROBINSON JEFFERS. Jeffers' first attempt at a narrative poem, *Tamar* contains many themes which were developed more successfully in the writer's later work. The poem, loosely based on the Biblical story of Tamar, a daughter of King David who was seduced by her brother, deals with a modern Tamar living on the Monterey coast, who seduces her brother, a neighbor, and her father, communicates with the dead and finally brings down destruction on her entire family. Tamar is both the avenger, expiating the bloodguilt incurred by her father's incestuous love for his sister, and a symbol of the destructiveness of narcissism and introversion.

Tamerlane and Other Poems (1827), the first published collection of verses by EDGAR ALLAN POE. His name was not on the title page, which read simply, "By a Bostonian." It is one of the rarest of his books; copies have sold for as much as $17,500. *Tamerlane* proved unpopular, however, and in desperation Poe enlisted in the army as Edgar A. Perry. The Byronic title poem is a narrative based on Poe's love affair with Sarah Elmira Royster of Richmond. The speaker is the famous Mongol conqueror, who here describes a love affair of his own time, though the poem does not aim at historical accuracy. In the poem Poe stressed the four themes that later dominated his work: pride, love, beauty, and death. The collection also includes *Visit of the Dead, The Lake, Evening Star*, and *Imitation*. The last, after much revision, was later called *A Dream Within a Dream*. In his introduction Poe implied that he had written the title poem when he was fourteen, but few have believed it.

Tammany. Tamanend was the name of a 17th-century chief of the Lenni-Lenape (DELAWARE) Indians. He was friendly to the white men, made a treaty with William Penn, and appears in James Fenimore Cooper's *Last of the Mohicans*. Because of his sentiments he was adopted by a group of societies as a representative of American patriotism and democracy. Using the common form of his name they called themselves the Sons of King (sometimes Saint) Tammany. Society of Tammany, founded in New York City in 1786, reorganized in 1789, is the only one to survive. The Society at first espoused the Federalist cause, later went over to the Republican side and helped bring about the election of Jefferson, and has been important in Democratic politics ever since. It is generally known now as "Tammany Hall." To the public it has represented "bossism" at its worst. Its best known "boss" was William M. Tweed (1823–1878), who headed what was called "the Tweed Ring," broken up by a reform Democrat, SAMUEL J. TILDEN. During the crusade against Tweed, THOMAS NAST produced (1869–72) a series of destructive cartoons for *Harper's Weekly*. Later Tammany officials have often been accused of crimes similar to Tweed's. The organization has, however, become somewhat more discreet in its activities and remains a powerful force in the city, state, and nation.

Anne Julia Hatton wrote an opera *The Songs of T-a-m-m-a-n-y, or, The Indian Chief* (prod., 1794; pub., 1808), for which James Hewitt wrote the music. Gus Edwards wrote the music for a lyric by Vincent P. Bryan, *Tammany* (1905), which has become Tammany Hall's official anthem. Many books have been written about Tammany Hall and its leaders, among them S. J. Tilden's *New York City "Ring"* (1873); Gustavus Myers' *History of Tammany Hall* (1901); D. T. Lynch's *"Boss" Tweed*

(1927); Gene Fowler's *Beau James* (about Mayor James J. Walker, 1949).

Taney, Roger B[rooke] (b. Calvert Co., Md., March 17, 1777—d. Oct. 12, 1864), lawyer, public official, Chief Justice of the Supreme Court. Taney was a successful lawyer, was appointed Attorney General of the United States, then nominated for Secretary of the Treasury by President Jackson. Jackson's controversy with the Bank of the United States had aroused sufficient enmity in the Senate to prevent Taney's confirmation for the post of Secretary. In 1836 he was, however, confirmed as Chief Justice and held that office till his death. His decisions were of varying character, but his most famous one, in the case of DRED SCOTT, resulted in violent condemnation by Northern opponents of slavery. He also wrote a decision that only Congress had the right to suspend the writ of *habeas corpus*. Samuel Tyler wrote a *Memoir* (1872) of Taney; C. B. Swisher, a biography (1935); C. W. Smith, an analysis: *Roger B. Taney, Jacksonian Jurist* (1936).

Tanglewood Tales (1853), six Greek myths retold by NATHANIEL HAWTHORNE. Issued as a sequel to Hawthorne's A WONDER-BOOK FOR GIRLS AND BOYS (1851), the *Tanglewood Tales* happily dispenses with the saccharine Eustace Bright, the narrator in the earlier volume. The new book includes *The Minotaur, The Pygmies, The Dragon's Teeth, Circe's Palace, The Pomegranate Seeds*, and *The Golden Fleece*, all carefully purified for a juvenile audience. The stories are told straightforwardly and charmingly, and seem to reflect the author's tranquil state of mind when he was writing them.

Tannehill, Wilkins (b. Pittsburgh, Pa., 1787 —1858), literary historian, bank official, public official, newspaperman, bookseller. In all his varied occupations, which included being mayor of Nashville (1825–26), taking part in Masonic activities and publishing a Masonic manual (1824), editing newspapers in Nashville and Louisville and also a Masonic magazine, Tannehill was deeply absorbed in the study of "comparative literature." In 1827 there appeared in Nashville, from the press of John S. Simpson, Tannehill's 844-page *Sketches of the History of Literature, from the Earliest Period to the Revival of Letters in the 15th Century*, a truly astounding book to have been published at that early date in a city west of the Alleghenies. Tannehill says in his introduction that he had had only "occasional leisure" to write the book and was able to consult no extensive libraries.

Tannenbaum, Samuel A[aron] (b. Hungary, May 1, 1874?—d. Oct. 31, 1948), physician, Elizabethan scholar, handwriting expert. Richard D. Altick calls Tannenbaum "a New York physician who was a passionate student of Elizabethan handwriting and bibliography and a stormy petrel in scholarly circles" (*The Scholar Adventurers*, 1950). Tannenbaum wrote *Problems in Shakspere's Penmanship* (1927); *The Assassination of Christopher Marlowe* (1928); *Shakspere's and "Sir Thomas More"* (1930); *The Handwriting of the Renaissance*

(1930); *Shaksperian Scraps and Other Elizabethan Fragments* (1933); *Was Shakspere a Gentleman?* (1909); and other books in this field. He also prepared numerous bibliographies of Elizabethan writers. Tannenbaum came to the United States in 1886, was naturalized in 1895, and practiced medicine successfully in New York City. In his professional field he wrote *The Psychology of Accidents* (1924) and *The Patient's Dilemma* (1935).

Tanner, John (b. Kentucky, 1780[?]—d. 1847), Indian scout. Tanner was captured by the Indians, and in 1830 published his *Narrative of the Captivity and Adventures of John Tanner During 30 Years' Residence Among the Indians*. The book became one of Henry Wadsworth Longfellow's chief sources when he was composing HIAWATHA (1855).

Tante (1911), a novel by ANNE DOUGLAS SEDGWICK. Madame Okraska, a great pianist, is the guardian of Karen Woodruff, who calls her "Tante." Possessive and jealous, she manages for a time to break off Karen's happy marriage.

Tappan, Eva March (b. Blackstone, Mass., Dec. 26, 1854—d. Jan. 30, 1930), teacher, biographer, historian, anthologist. Miss Tappan wrote for young readers (and often for their elders as well) authoritative, sensible, and literate accounts of Charles Lamb (1896), the people in the Elizabethan (1902) and Victorian (1903) eras, the Greek people (1908), the days of knighthood (1912), and other persons and nations. She also edited several anthologies. Before beginning her writing career, Miss Tappan had been a high school English teacher in Worcester, Mass.

Tar: A Midwest Childhood (1927), a fictional autobiography by SHERWOOD ANDERSON. It is complementary to his *Story-Teller's Story* (1924).

Ta-ra-ra-boom-de-ay! (1891), a song by Henry J. Sayers. The refrain is a jumble of nonsense syllables which formed part of the song, *A Sweet Tuxedo Girl Am I, Queen of High Society*. It was not original with Sayers, but was part of an obscene song popular in St. Louis. The tune of the refrain has been traced so far back in musical history that, when a suit for breach of copyright was entered against the owners of the song, Judge Robert Patterson decided that both the music and the nonsense syllables were in the public domain. It first became popular in England, then in the United States. Christopher Morley interpolated it in his Hoboken production of *The Black Crook*, and in 1892 James Thornton wrote a song, *I'm the Man That Wrote Ta-ra-ra-boom-de-ay*.

Tar Baby, The. A character immortalized in JOEL CHANDLER HARRIS' Uncle Remus stories. The Tar Baby appears in *The Tar Baby Story and Other Rhymes by Uncle Remus* (1904), and elsewhere in Harris' prose tales, for example the story "How Mr. Fox caught Mr. Rabbit" (in *Uncle Remus, His Songs and His Sayings*, 1880). Variants of the story have been found all over the world. The Tar Baby, a tar doll set up by the roadside, irritates Br'er Rabbit to such an extent that he strikes him until he himself is stuck tight.

Tarbell, Ida M[inerva] (b. Erie County, Pa., Nov. 5, 1857—d. Jan. 6, 1944), author, editor, journalist. Miss Tarbell was graduated from Allegheny College, taught at Poland Union Seminary (Ohio), and was associate editor of *The Chautauquan*. She did free-lance writing in Paris for three years, came back in 1894 as a staff member of *McClure's Magazine*, for which she wrote some famous exposés. (See also S. S. McCLURE.) She wrote a magazine series on Napoleon, which soon appeared as her first published book, *Short Life of Napoleon Bonaparte* (1895); her *Life of Madame Roland* (1896) followed. Then came a series on Lincoln that was later published as *Early Life of Abraham Lincoln* (2 v., 1900).

Miss Tarbell had literally grown up in the emergent oil industry, and as the muckrakers came into prominence at the turn of the century, she spent five years of research for a series of articles on the Standard Oil Company. These articles, with further documentary additions, appeared as *The History of the Standard Oil Company* (2 v., 1904), and created an immediate sensation. Her style was prosaic, but public opinion was undoubtedly ripe for such an exposé of what she called "a compact body of a few able, cold-blooded men . . . to whom anything was right that they could get."

From 1906 to 1915, Miss Tarbell was associate editor of *The American Magazine*, later resumed free-lance writing, and took up lecturing. By this time she could see the positive significance of certain new types of business titans, as evident in her *New Ideals in Business* (1916); *Life of Judge Gary* (1925); *Owen D. Young: A New Type of Industrial Leader* (1932); and *The Nationalizing of Business, 1878–1898* (1936). Her other books include: *The Business of Being a Woman* (1912); *The Ways of Women* (1915); *The Rising of the Tide* (1919); and *He Knew Lincoln, and Other Billy Brown Stories* (1924). *All in the Day's Work* (1939) is an autobiography.

Tarkington, [Newton] Booth (b. Indianapolis, Ind., July 29, 1869—d. May 19, 1946), novelist, playwright. Tarkington attended Purdue University, transferred to Princeton University, where he founded the Triangle Club, but left without graduating. In 1902–03 he was a member of the Indiana House of Representatives. The cynicism and dishonesty of the lawmakers affected him profoundly, and his first novel, THE GENTLEMAN FROM INDIANA (1899), deals with political corruption. His legislative experiences also figure in a later political novel, *In the Arena* (1905). MONSIEUR BEAUCAIRE (1900), a romantic confection that caught the popular fancy, and *Cherry* (1903), an amusing satire on a college professor, were largely imitative. THE CONQUEST OF CANAAN (1905) depicts life in a small town. Tarkington's greatest success was PENROD (1914), a story about a twelve-year-old boy who for a time rivaled Tom Sawyer and Peck's Bad Boy in the esteem of the American reading public, though many critics were quick to point out the shallowness of Tarkington's conception of

UPI

adolescence. SEVENTEEN (1916) concerns Willie Baxter, a somewhat older Penrod, in the throes of his first love affair. Tarkington went on to other adult novels, achieved success as a local colorist, as in *Growth* (1927), a trilogy of urban life in the Middle West. He wrote many novels, more than forty altogether, won Pulitzer prizes for THE MAGNIFICENT AMBERSONS (1918; filmed by Orson Welles, 1941) and for *Alice Adams* (1921). He also wrote twenty-five plays, eleven of them in collaboration with HARRY LEON WILSON. In spite of the speed with which he worked, writing was never easy for him. Speaking of *The Plutocrat* (1926), a novel about a self-made man abroad, Tarkington said it was "a very painful job, worse than having the measles." In 1930 his eyesight, never strong, failed completely, and only after a series of operations did he partly regain it. He was fond of travel, often lived abroad, and liked to think of himself as an eccentric. *The World Does Move* (1928) is his autobiography. He left an uncompleted novel, *The Show-Piece* (1947). In 1949 appeared *Your Amiable Uncle*, letters (mostly about European travel) to his nephews, charmingly illustrated by himself. In *Booth Tarkington: Gentleman from Indiana* (1955) James Woodress wrote a sympathetic

account of Tarkington's contribution to an understanding of our own society in his epoch. See also ALICE ADAMS.

Tarzan. A fabulous character appearing in stories and novels by EDGAR RICE BURROUGHS. Burroughs once said that he had created Tarzan out of stories he told himself in attempting to overcome insomnia. A hero of the jungle, Tarzan is described as the son of an English nobleman, abandoned in Africa in infancy; he is brought up by apes, becomes a man of prodigious strength and agility, learns apese, elephantese, and other jungle languages, and pursues a hair-raising series of incredible adventures. Tarzan first appeared in *Tarzan of the Apes* (1914); more than thirty sequels followed, in the course of which the hero married, had a son and eventually a grandson. By the early 1940's more than 25 million copies of the Tarzan books had been sold in fifty-six languages. In 1918 a film based on *Tarzan of the Apes*, with Elmo Lincoln as Tarzan, made a tremendous hit. In 1930 the same book became a sound film, and thereafter a long series of Tarzan movies appeared, the leading role passing among a succession of more than a dozen actors—the first was Johnny Weissmuller, a popular Olympic swimming champion. Since 1929 Tarzan has also been the central figure of a popular comic strip. His exploits have been frequently narrated in radio and television broadcasts. This figment of an author's sleepless nights became one of the most popular folk heroes of the mid-20th century.

Tate, [John Orley] Allen (b. Winchester, Ky., Nov. 19, 1899—   ), poet, critic, biographer, novelist, editor, teacher. Tate graduated from Vanderbilt University (1922), where he was a founding member of the "Fugitives," a group which included DONALD DAVIDSON, JOHN CROWE RANSOM, MERRILL MOORE, and others. They published a remarkable literary periodical, *The Fugitive*, from 1922 to 1925. Essentially southern literary men who were social and political conservatives seriously stirred by their region, the Fugitives turned their major attention to the new literature and the more precise critical theory which came into notice after World War I. From their deepened interest in southern history and culture came the symposium I'LL TAKE MY STAND (1930), to which Tate contributed *Remarks on the Southern Religion*.

Tate married CAROLINE GORDON, the novelist, in 1924; they were divorced thirty years later. He held Guggenheim Fellowships in 1928 and 1929, taught English literature at Southwestern College, the University of North Carolina, Columbia and Princeton Universities, was southern editor of *Hound and Horn* (1931–34), edited the SEWANEE REVIEW (1944–46), was an editor for Henry Holt and Co., and on the faculty of the University of Minnesota.

Tate is known equally for his poetry, in which he has combined a classical severity of form with a deeply felt, often religious symbolism, and for his criticism. His essays show a remarkable range; Latin literature, the modern poets, and especially Edgar Allan Poe have attracted his attention. His best known poem is the much anthologized ODE TO THE CONFEDERATE DEAD, although others, such as *The*

Rollie McKenna

Mediterranean, Seasons of the Soul, Sonnets at Christmas, Death of Little Boys, and *Mr. Pope,* are widely known. Among his books of verse are *Mr. Pope and Other Poems* (1928); *Poems: 1928–1931* (1932); *The Mediterranean and Other Poems* (1936); *Poems: 1922–1947* (a collected ed., 1948). His books of essays include REACTIONARY ESSAYS ON POETRY AND IDEAS (1936); *Reason in Madness* (1941); *The Forlorn Demon* (1953). He published one novel, *The Fathers* (1938). In addition he edited several anthologies and (with Francis Cheney) *Sixty American Poets, 1896–1944* (1945) and *Language of Poetry* (1960), a critical and bibliographical checklist issued by the Library of Congress. See NEW CRITICISM.

Tatlock, John S[trong] P[erry] (b. Stamford, Conn., Feb. 24, 1876—d. June 24, 1948), teacher, editor, scholar. Tatlock taught English at the Universities of Michigan, Stanford, Harvard, and California. Although he worked in other fields as well, he was known primarily as a leading authority on Chaucer. He prepared, in collaboration with PERCY MACKAYE, *The Modern Reader's Chaucer: The Complete Works Now Put into Modern English* (1912). He also produced for use by scholars books on

The Development and Chronology of Chaucer's Works (1907) and *The Scene of the Franklin's Tale Revisited* (1915). With A. G. Kennedy he compiled a *Concordance to Chaucer* (1927).

Taussig, Frank W[illiam] (b. St. Louis, Mo., Dec. 28, 1859—d. Nov. 11, 1940), teacher, political economist, editor. Taussig taught at Harvard University from 1882 until 1935 and was one of the founders of the Harvard School of Business Administration. He was noted as an authority on the tariff and served (1917–19) as chairman of the U.S. Tariff Commission. He edited the *Quarterly Journal of Economics* (1896–1937) and wrote a *Tariff History of the United States* (1888) that went through numerous editions. He also wrote *The Silver Situation in the United States* (1892); *Wages and Capital* (1896); *Principles of Economics* (1911); *International Trade* (1927).

Taylor, [James] Bayard (b. Kennett Square, Pa., Jan. 11, 1825—d. Dec. 19, 1878), journalist, lecturer, poet, translator, novelist, diplomat. As a boy Taylor was apprenticed to a printer, but left this work for a European walk-

ing tour with two friends. Some of his letters from Europe were printed in the New York *Tribune,* others in the *Saturday Evening Post* and other periodicals. They were published in book form as *Views Afoot; or, Europe Seen with Knapsack and Staff* (1846); their competent descriptions and conventional touristic awe made the book an immense success, the twentieth edition coming out in 1855. The *Tribune* then sent Taylor to California to report on the 1849 gold rush and whatever else came to hand; these experiences were published as *Eldorado, or, Adventures in the Path of Empire* (1850), the most recent edition of which appeared in 1949. Taylor remained in journalism for the rest of his life, also held diplomatic posts in St. Petersburg and Berlin, served as a historian on Commodore Perry's expedition to Japan, and as a nonresident Professor of German literature at Cornell University (1869–77).

Taylor's travel pieces were so popular that HORACE GREELEY sent him to many far-off places, about which Taylor later lectured with considerable success. But he insisted on thinking of himself as primarily a serious poet. In his Whittieresque *Home Pastorals* (1875) he dealt realistically with his own experience; but mostly his verse is hopelessly overromantic, as in his *Poems of the Orient* (1855). His best known poem today is the BEDOUIN SONG. He was at his best in the adroit parodies of *The Echo Club and Other Diversions* (1876). He also wrote several novels, only one of which, *The Story of Kennett* (1866), deserves serious attention as a realistic depiction of the people and countryside Taylor knew best. He was always an eager student of German, and his competent and still widely used translation of Goethe's *Faust* (1870–71) finally brought him the academic recognition he had always longed for, as well as his appointment as minister to Germany (1878).

Taylor's works, beyond those mentioned above, include *Ximena* (1844); *Rhymes of Travel, Ballads, and Poems* (1849); *A Journey to Central Africa* (1854); *Hannah Thurston: A Story of American Life* (1863); *John Godfrey's Fortunes, Related by Himself: A Story of American Life* (1864); *The Picture of St. John* (1866); *Studies in German Literature* (1879). Two collections of Taylor's works were made in 1880: *The Dramatic Works of Bayard Taylor* and *The Poetical Works of Bayard Taylor*. Marie Hansen-Taylor and Horace E. Scudder wrote *Life and Letters of Bayard Taylor* (2 v., 1884); Richmond C. Beatty wrote *Bayard Taylor: Laureate of the Gilded Age* (1936); Richard Cary wrote *The Genteel Circle: Bayard Taylor and His New York Friends* (1952). John R. Schultz edited *The Unpublished Letters of Bayard Taylor in the Huntington Library* (1937). See also LARS, A PASTORAL OF NORWAY.

Taylor, Bert Leston ["B. L. T."] (b. Goshen, Mass., Nov. 13, 1866—d. March 19, 1921), newspaperman, poet, columnist. After working for several Eastern newspapers, Taylor joined the Chicago *Tribune*. He began writing his famous column, "A Line o' Type or Two," and continued it until shortly before his death, except during the years 1903–09, when he worked for *Puck* and the New York *Morning Telegraph*. His column was a pioneer for the more decorous columns of later days. It encouraged contributors, including Franklin P. Adams. Taylor was a clever verse writer as well. He published numerous books based on his columns, among them *Line-o'-type Lyrics* (1902); *A Line-o'-Verse or Two* (1911); *Motley Measures* (1911); *The So-Called Human*

Race (1922). His column was continued after his death under the same heading.

Taylor, [Joseph] Deems (b. N.Y.C., Dec. 22, 1885—d. July 3, 1966), composer, critic. Taylor graduated from New York University, studied with Oscar Coon, then turned to composition. During World War I he served as European correspondent for the New York *Herald Tribune*, then became associate editor of *Collier's*. Two years later he was appointed music critic of the New York *World*. In 1927 he became editor of *Musical America* and in 1936 commentator for the New York Philharmonic Sunday broadcasts. He wrote the music for two operas, both performed at the Metropolitan Opera House: THE KING'S HENCHMAN (with libretto by EDNA ST. VINCENT MILLAY, 1927) and *Peter Ibbetson* (1931). Other well-known works are an orchestral suite, *Through the Looking Glass* (1918), and a symphonic poem, *Jurgen* (1936). He revised his Sunday broadcasts and published them as *Of Men and Music* (1937); *The Well-Tempered Listener* (1940); *Music to My Ears* (1949). *Some Enchanted Evenings* (1953) is a book about the composer Richard Rodgers. See also BEGGAR ON HORSEBACK.

Taylor, Edward (b. England, 1645[?]—d. June 24, 1729), Puritan divine, physician, poet. Taylor came to Boston in 1668, graduated from Harvard University, and became a minister and physician in Westfield, Mass. His poetry, similar to that of the 17th-century English metaphysical poets John Donne and George Herbert, has been judged superior to any produced by his colonial contemporaries. Taylor requested that none of his works be published, and his grandson, Ezra Stiles, deposited his manuscripts in the Yale University library. Some of the poems were discovered in 1937, and in 1939 *The Poetical Works of Edward Taylor*, edited by Thomas H. Johnson, was published. This included a long verse sequence, *God's Determinations*, and several *Sacramental Meditations*, as well as other poems. *Some Edward Taylor Gleanings* were published in the *New England Quarterly* (v. XVI, 1943); *The Topical Verses of Edward Taylor* in the *Publications of the Colonial Society of Massachusetts* (v. XXXIV, 1943). Extracts from Taylor's diary were printed in *Proceedings of the Massachusetts Historical Society* (v. XVIII, 1881), and a letter of his to Increase Mather in *Collections of the Massachusetts Historical Society* (4th ser., v. VIII, 1868). Thomas H. Johnson wrote *Edward Taylor: A Puritan "Sacred Poet"* (*New England Quarterly* [v. 10, 1937]). Donald E. Stanford's *Poems of Edward Taylor* appeared in 1960, Norman S. Grabo's *Edward Taylor* in 1962.

Taylor, Henry Osborn (b. New York City, Dec. 5, 1856—d. April 13, 1941), lawyer, historian. After graduating from Harvard University and Columbia Law School, Taylor studied law in Leipzig. In 1884 he published a *Treatise on the Law of Private Corporations* which went through five editions. It was revised in 1902. During the next ten years he immersed himself in the study of ancient literature, history, and philosophy, in preparation for an extensive two-volume work entitled *Ancient Ideals, a Study of Intellectual and Spiritual Growth from Early Greek Times to the Establishment of Christianity* (1896; 2nd ed., 1913). *The Classical Heritage of the Middle Ages* (1901) was followed by his most famous work, *The Medieval Mind* (2 v., 1911). Regarded by many historians as one of the greatest books on the period, it is widely used in colleges today. There followed *Deliverance: The Freeing of the Spirit in the Ancient World* (1915); *Freedom of Mind in History* (1922); *Human Values and Verities* (1928); *A Layman's View of History* (1935); and *A Historian's Creed* (1939). Although never on the staff of any university, Dr. Taylor delivered lectures at Columbia, Harvard, and Stanford.

Taylor, John (b. Orange or Caroline County, Va., Dec. 19[?], 1753—d. Aug. 21, 1824), agronomist, statesman. Taylor spent two years at the College of William and Mary, read law in his uncle's office, and was licensed to practice in 1774. At the outbreak of the war he entered the Continental Army and rose to the rank of major, later resigned in disgust at the botched administration of the Army and completed his military career serving as lieutenant colonel in the Virginia militia. After the war he married and settled on a plantation on the Rappahannock. Always a staunch believer in a society based upon the self-dependent rural freeholder, he was never reconciled to the social and political developments of the 19th century. His splendid but unsystematic INQUIRY INTO THE PRINCIPLES AND POLICY OF THE GOVERNMENT OF THE UNITED STATES (1814) became the gospel of states' rights and agrarian liberalism; it was a searching indictment of the Hamiltonian system. His *Arator, . . . a Series of Agricultural Essays, Practical and Political* (1813) shows Taylor to be the greatest American agronomist before Edmund Ruffin.

Taylor's political career was extensive. He served in the Virginia House of Delegates from 1779 to 1782, and again for four years beginning in 1796. He also served in the Senate three times. He opposed the Constitution at first, on the grounds that the rights of states and persons were insufficiently guaranteed, but loyally supported it after its passage. He entered pamphlet warfare in an attempt to defeat Hamilton's banking and funding measures. His other published works include *Definitions of Parties* (1794); *A Defense of the Measures of the Administration of Thomas Jefferson* (1804); *Construction Construed and Constitutions Vindicated* (1820); *Tyranny Unmasked* (1822); and *New Views of the Constitution of the United States* (1823). A collection of Taylor's *Letters* appears in the *John P. Branch Historical Papers of Randolph-Macon College* (v. II, 1908). H. H. Simms wrote *Life of John Taylor* (1932) and E. T. Mudge wrote *The Social Philosophy of John Taylor of Caroline* (1939).

Taylor, Peter Hillsman (b. Nashville, Tenn., 1917—), novelist, short story writer. Taylor was educated at Kenyon College, graduating in 1940. After serving in World War II and teaching for a few years at the Woman's College of North Carolina, he returned as a teacher to Kenyon. Taylor's stories of middle-class family life in the upper South are marked by subtle intelligence, humor, and an unobtrusive distinction of style. He is an original and craftsmanlike writer whose work has been especially appreciated by other authors of Southern origin for its quietness and absence of regional exhibitionism. Taylor's published works include three collections of short stories: *A Long Fourth and Other Stories* (1948), *The Widows of Thornton* (1954), and *Happy Families Are All Alike* (1960); a short novel, *A Woman of Means* (1950); and a play, *Tennessee Day in St. Louis* (1957).

Taylor, Robert Lewis (b. Carbondale, Ill., Sept. 24, 1912—), newspaperman, biographer, humorist. Taylor began as a newspaperman in St. Louis. From 1939 to 1948 he worked for *The New Yorker*, becoming one of its most adept writers of profiles. One collection of these profiles, *Doctor, Lawyer, Merchant, Chief* (1948), also includes four short stories and some war sketches. He wrote a number of full-length biographies with skill, accuracy, and vivacity, among them *W. C. Fields: His Follies and Fortunes* (1949) and *Winston Churchill, An Informal Study in Greatness* (1958). His novels *Adrift in a Boneyard* (1947), THE TRAVELS OF JAMIE MCPHEETERS (1958), and *A Journey to Matecumbe* (1961) are admired as examples of the modern use of picaresque technique.

Taylor, Rosemary (b. Phoenix, Ariz., May 8, 1899—), memoirist, radio writer. Mrs. Winchcombe-Taylor's family (she married another writer, John Winchcombe-Taylor) came to Arizona as pioneers. Many of her books are descriptive of conditions in her native region, and especially in her own household. They include *Chicken Every Sunday* (1943) and *Ridin' the Rainbow* (1944); also *Bar Nothing Ranch* (1946) and *Ghost Town Bonanza* (1954). *Chicken Every Sunday* was made into a successful play, later a movie. A novel, *Come Clean, My Love* (1949), lacked the appeal of her lively reminiscences.

Taylor, Zachary (b. Montebello, Va., Nov. 24, 1784—d. July 9, 1850), soldier, 12th President. Taylor steadily rose in the U. S. Army, winning fame in numerous engagements with Indians in the West and South. In the Battle of Buena Vista (Feb. 22, 1847), in the Mexican War, he defeated an overwhelmingly larger Mexican force; his victory made him the most popular figure in the country. Though he had no strong political opinions, he was nominated for the Presidency by the Whig party. He was elected, took office in 1849, and died a little more than sixteen months later.

Although a Virginia slaveowner, Taylor shocked the southerners of his day by opposing the great compromise on which HENRY CLAY and DANIEL WEBSTER agreed. He did not believe in abolishing slavery, but opposed its extension; he favored the admission of California as a free state. He was also a firm Union man. His chief biographer, Holman Hamilton, in his life of Taylor (2 v., 1941, 1951), believes that the Civil War might have been averted had Taylor continued to be President. Silas Bent McKinley and Silas Bent, in their biography called *Old Rough and Ready* (1946), praise Taylor as a soldier admired by Ulysses S. Grant, George B. McClellan, Pierre Beauregard, and Robert E. Lee, who had all fought under him. Other biographies are by C. Frank Powell (1846), John Frost (1847), J. Reese Fry and R. T. Conrad (1847), Oliver O. Howard (1892), and Brainard Dyer (1946). Taylor appears as a character in Robert W. Chambers' *Gitana* (1931), much more memorably in Herbert Gorman's *The Wine of San Lorenzo* (1945).

Teach, Edward ["Blackbeard"] (b. England [?]—d. Nov. 22, 1718), pirate. This famous marine bandit obtained letters of marque from England during the War of the Spanish Succession, and after the peace continued to rove the seas in search of prey. He made the Spanish Main and the Atlantic his chosen territory as far north as the coast of the Carolinas. He became famous for his ferocity in battle and for his cruelty; he was finally killed in a battle at Ocracoke Inlet, North Carolina, and most of his crew members were hanged. Don Tracy introduced him into his novel *Carolina Corsair* (1955).

Tead, Ordway (b. Somerville, Mass., Sept. 19, 1891—   ), business consultant, teacher, editor, author. Tead started as a consultant on business problems, taught in this and other fields, acted as the director of business publications for McGraw-Hill Book Co., and in 1925 became editor of social and economic books for Harper & Bros. He served as an officer of many associations. Among his books: *Instincts in Industry* (1918); *The People's Part in Peace* (1918); *Personnel Administration—Its Principles and Practice* (with H. C. Metcalf, 1920); third ed., 1933); *The Art of Leadership* (1935); *Creative Management* (1935); *The Case for Democracy* (1937); *Democratic Administration* (1945); *Equalizing Educational Opportunities Beyond the Secondary School* (1947); *College Teaching and College Learning* (1949); *The Art of Administration* (1951); *Character Building and Higher Education* (1953); *Climate of Learning* (1958).

Teale, Edwin Way (b. Joliet, Ill., June 2, 1899—   ), teacher, editor, free-lance writer, naturalist. Teale taught public speaking for a while, became an editorial assistant to Dr. FRANK CRANE, from 1929 to 1941 worked for *Popular Science Monthly*, and in 1941 became a free-lance writer, writing popular books on nature and the out-of-doors. Among his books: *Grassroot Jungles* (1937; rev., 1944); *Boys' Book of Insects* (1939); *Byways to Adventure* (1942);

Dune Boy, The Early Years of a Naturalist (1943); *Insect Life* (1944); *The Lost Woods* (1945); *North with the Spring* (1951); *Circle of the Seasons* (1953); *The Wilderness World of John Muir* (1954); *Autumn Across America* (1956); *Journey into Summer* (1960). He also edited *Green Treasury* (1952), a nature anthology, and wrote the introduction to an edition of William H. Hudson's *Green Mansions* (1949).

Teasdale, Sara (b. St. Louis, Mo., Aug. 8, 1884—d. Jan. 29, 1933), poet. A delicate and neurotic child of elderly, overprotective parents, Miss Teasdale was educated at home and in private schools. When she finished her brief schooling she traveled extensively in this country and abroad, always well chaperoned. From her earliest years she was torn between a passion for life and a terror of it, a longing to escape from her parents and a morbid dependence upon them. Her first book, *Sonnets to Duse and Other Poems* (1907), was privately printed; *Helen of Troy and Other Poems* (1911) was warmly praised by Louis Untermeyer and other critics for its delicate craftsmanship and its feminine point of view.

Although she could not break away from her parents until after her marriage in 1914, Miss Teasdale visited Chicago frequently, becoming a part of the literary groups that gathered around HARRIET MONROE and Mrs. William Vaughn Moody. She also went to New York often, where she entered into a mild love affair with the poet JOHN HALL WHEELOCK. In 1913 VACHEL LINDSAY met her and fell in love with her, wooing her with a vehemence that both attracted and repelled her. Perhaps her fears drove her into the safety of a marriage with Ernst Filsinger, a kindly St. Louis businessman, but she became more and more withdrawn until in 1929 she divorced her husband and moved to New York, where she lived in seclusion. As her life grew more austere and virginal, her poetry became more passionate. *Rivers to the Sea* (1915) was followed by *Love Songs* (1917), which received a special Pulitzer Prize in 1918 and went through five printings in a single year. *Flame and Shadow* (1920) contains the often anthologized *Let It Be Forgotten* and other well-known lyrics. For young people she edited an anthology, *Rainbow Gold* (1922), also made a selection of her own poems, *Stars Tonight* (1930). Her book of verse, *Dark of the Moon* (1926), was translated into several languages, including Japanese. *Strange Victory* (1933) and *Collected Poems* (1937) were published posthumously.

At the time of her death from an overdose of sleeping tablets Miss Teasdale was at work on a life of Christina Rossetti, her favorite poet. Louis Untermeyer wrote of her at some length in his autobiography, *From Another World* (1939). She appears in Mark Harris' biographical novel, *City of Discontent* (1952), which deals with Vachel Lindsay.

Tecumseh (b. Miami Valley, Ohio, 1768[?] —d. Oct. 5, 1813), Indian statesman, orator, fighter. Tecumseh was a member of the Shawnee tribe, and with his twin brother Tenskwa-tawa did all he could to withstand the advance of the white man. When in 1795 a treaty was contracted that took away more than half of what is now Ohio, Tecumseh and his brother led a movement to reverse the agreement. While Tecumseh was absent on a recruiting trip, General WILLIAM HENRY HARRISON defeated the Indians at the Battle of Tippecanoe (Nov. 7, 1811), at which Tecumseh's brother, known as "The Prophet," was killed. In the War of 1812 Tecumseh became an ally of the British. At the Battle of the Thames (Canada), Oct. 5, 1813, Harrison defeated the British and Indians, and Tecumseh was killed.

Tecumseh is regarded as the greatest of all Indian leaders and was a notable orator. Dr. William Emmons wrote a pamphlet about him in 1822 and devoted to him the seventeenth canto of his long epic poem about the War of 1812, *The Fredoniad* (1827); in 1836 he published *Tecumseh, or, the Battle of the Thames,* which he called "a national drama." Benjamin Drake wrote a biography in 1841. *Tecumseh, a Drama* (1886), by the Canadian poet Charles Mair (1838–1927), was one of the first works produced in the Dominion to win wide praise. Tecumseh appears in several novels, but none gives a notable portrait. Among them: Samuel Woodworth's *The Champions of Freedom* (1816); Edward S. Ellis' *The Forest Spy* (1861); Odell and Willard Shepard's *Holdfast Gaines* (1946). Nonfictional works include J. W. Oskison's *Tecumseh and His Times* (1938); Marion Campbell's *The Boyhood of Tecumseh* (1940); Glenn Tucker's *Tecumseh, Vision of Glory* (1956). See SHAWNEE INDIANS.

television writing. Television as a dramatic medium, as opposed to the stage, motion pictures, or radio, has both limitations and advantages which have made television plays a distinct dramatic genre. Although most television plays are written in the standard three-act form, they are short (usually fifty minutes in length, less frequently, seventy-five), mechanically limited both in the size of the cast and the scope of the action portrayed, and usually restricted by commercial sponsors to uncontroversial subjects. However, within these limitations the best television writers have explored the possibilities of subtle and intimate analysis of character and of human relationships, and, in the words of Paddy Chayefsky, of a "meticulous literalness" and attention to mundane detail that is possible in no other medium.

Unfortunately, the large majority of television plays have been things of the moment, without depth of meaning, written and produced in a very short time under difficult conditions. Quality is too often sacrificed to quantity, art to entertainment, and even entertainment to advertising. Inasmuch as the sponsor's first concern is with the sale of his product, the trend has been to discourage plays that might offend any member of a potential audience; the appeal is to mass taste, and the plays that result are often indifferent as works of literature.

Since most plays are "live" rather than filmed and since most studios can accommodate only a few sets, playwrights have generally given close attention to the unities of time and space. In many plays the time elapsed during the action is exactly the amount of time necessary for the performance; rarely does the action of a play cover more than a few days. As a result, there is a compactness and intensity, a sense of immediacy and dramatic power, in the best television drama not often found on the stage or in motion pictures. Furthermore, the intimacy of the television screen seems to demand a realistic rather than an experimental or impressionistic approach; one of the main advantages of television drama is the sense of physical proximity of the characters to one another and to the audience; the dialogue, which has sometimes been criticized for its lack of metaphor or lyricism, is reflective of this tendency toward realism; usually simple, direct, and easily understandable, it is the language of "ordinary" people.

Foremost among television playwrights is PADDY CHAYEFSKY, whose *Marty* (1954) is an excellent example of the best uses of television's potential. A story of loneliness and love, it is a subtle, searching, low-keyed drama focused on Marty, an Italian butcher, a representative of the thousands who are in no way exceptional and who are surrounded by false conventions and values which they have been taught to accept. Through the relationships of the characters, Chayefsky is able to present both the literal reality of mundane life and the depth of human need beneath it. *The Bachelor Party* (1955), more episodic and less structurally coherent than *Marty*, again deals with the relationships of average people, pinpointing the commonplace in order to reveal the most basic aspects of human nature.

Somewhat similar to Chayefsky in his use of realism and in his choice of "typical" small people and their small conflicts and failings is TAD MOSEL; *The Out-of-Towners* (1957), set in the anonymity of a postal employees' convention, deals with a lonely, unattractive woman, her frustrated dreams of romance, and her poignant and pathetic meeting with a married man. ROD SERLING's plays frequently depend more on situation and external forces for their action than on the characters themselves; *Requiem for a Heavyweight* (1956) combines the realism and concern for human needs and loyalties of Chayefsky and Mosel with the more stock setting of the fight ring, yet it is nonetheless a study in depth of the desires and fears of an ex-boxer and his manager, of their conflicts and of their search for themselves. *Noon on Doomsday* (1955), an attack on provincialism and prejudice, is almost entirely centered on events and uses stock characters as a vehicle for its message.

Reginald Rose has tended toward the suspense story, rather than the penetration of character, as a means of dramatic expression. *Tragedy in a Temporary Town* (1955), which deals with a supposed attack on a hysterical fifteen-year-old girl, explores racial prejudice and mob violence in a trailer camp; *Twelve Angry Men* (1954) again takes a situation—the unwillingness of the jurors to question the guilt of an accused murderer—and probes toward the human indifference behind it.

GORE VIDAL, better known as a novelist and Broadway playwright, has written a number of television plays, of which the best known is *Visit to a Small Planet* (1956), a mildly satirical fantasy on American politics. *Honor* (1957), a somewhat romantic tragedy set in the South during the Civil War, deals with the unrealistic and incompatible moral values held by the main character, a lately established southern gentleman.

Collections of television plays include the following: Paddy Chayefsky, *Television Plays* (1955); Reginald Rose, *Six Television Plays* (1956); Gore Vidal, *Visit to a Small Planet and Other Television Plays* (1957); Writers Guild of America, *The Prize Plays of Television and Radio, 1956* (1957); A. S. Burack, ed., *Television Plays for Writers* (1957); William I. Kaufman, ed., *The Best Television Plays, 1957* (1957). See also RADIO WRITING.

Telling the Bees (1858; collected in *Home Ballads*, 1860), a poem by JOHN GREENLEAF WHITTIER. The title is derived from the old New England custom of "telling the bees" and dressing their hives in mourning when a person has died. A young man, coming to visit his beloved, sees the hired girl draping each hive "with a shred of black." He thinks his fiancée's grandfather has died, but then he hears the hired girl singing to the bees, "Stay at home, pretty bees, fly not hence!/ Mistress Mary is dead and gone!"

Tell-Tale Heart, The (1843), a story by EDGAR ALLAN POE. A homicidal maniac murders an old man and buries the dismembered body beneath the floor of the room in which he lives, putting the victim's watch with the body. The police come to make inquiries, and as they talk to the murderer he hears what he believes to be the beating of the dead man's heart; in a frenzy he confesses his crime, the police dig up the body, and the watch is found to be still ticking. The story, one of Poe's best, has been called a forerunner of modern fictional treatments of the subconscious. It was contributed to the first issue of a magazine called THE PIONEER, edited by James Russell Lowell. The magazine did not prosper, and Poe never received the $13 promised him for the story.

Tender Is the Night (1934), a novel by F. SCOTT FITZGERALD. In the decadent setting of post-World War I Europe, a wealthy mental patient, Nicole, falls passionately in love with Dick Diver, a young psychiatrist. She finds her cure in marrying him; but as she achieves independence he deteriorates. Finally Nicole leaves him for a man who will be her lover, not her caretaker. Diver is perhaps a reflection of Fitzgerald's own painful experiences with his mentally disturbed wife Zelda. Despite the book's many terrifying scenes, the warm tenderness

of its writing lifts it into the realm of genuine tragedy. Fitzgerald was not satisfied with the book and kept reworking it, never completing his task. After his death Malcolm Cowley examined all the manuscripts and made a new version (1951), carefully based on Fitzgerald's intentions, in which the episodes were placed in chronological rather than semidramatic order.

Tennessee's Pardner (*Overland Monthly*, June, 1869; in THE LUCK OF ROARING CAMP, 1870); a story by BRET HARTE. Having struck gold with his first mining camp stories in the *Overland*, Harte continued with this tale, a mixture of sentimentalism and cynicism. Tennessee runs off with his "pardner's" wife but soon returns when she abandons him too. When Tennessee is being tried for robbery, his partner silently strides into the courtroom and empties all his money on the table in payment for Tennessee's life. But Tennessee is hanged and his partner dies a few months after burying him. Harte sentimentalized the relationship between the two men, but in Tennessee's partner he created the type of the strong silent cowboy hero so prevalent in fiction and movies.

Tenney, Tabitha [Gilman] (b. Exeter, N.H., April 7, 1762—d. May 2, 1837), novelist, anthologist. Mrs. Tenney's rearing was devout, bookish, and somewhat rural. In 1788 she married Dr. Samuel Tenny, who had been a surgeon in the Continental Army. Her husband served as a congressman from 1800 to 1807. Mrs. Tenney's first book, *The Pleasing Instructor* (1799[?]), was an anthology of elevating selections from the poets and from classical authors. But she is chiefly known for her one novel, FEMALE QUIXOTISM: EXHIBITED IN THE ROMANTIC OPINIONS AND EXTRAVAGANT ADVENTURES OF DORCASINA SHELDON (1801). It is written in the picaresque tradition and pokes fun at the sentimental novels so popular with female audiences at the time, who were all too apt to mistake them for life. Fred Lewis Pattee calls it the most popular American novel before *Uncle Tom's Cabin*.

There is no biography of Mrs. Tenney, but Arthur Gilman's *The Gilman Family* (1869) and M. J. Tenney's *The Tenney Family . . . , 1638–1904* (1904) supply pertinent facts. Herbert Ross Brown's *The Sentimental Novel in America, 1789–1860* (1940) gives a detailed account of the school which Mrs. Tenney subjected to derision.

Ten Nights in a Bar-Room and What I Saw There (1854), a story by TIMOTHY SHAY ARTHUR. Described by Carl Van Doren as a lurid romance in which weak tears mingle with strong drink, this melodramatic story held the attention of readers for more than twenty years and was a favorite with temperance lecturers. It was dramatized in 1858 by William W. Pratt, and as a drama was more in demand than any other play except *Uncle Tom's Cabin;* it precipitated the passage of many "temperance" laws. The climax was little Mary's song at the saloon door, "Father, dear Father, come home with me now," and when she was accidentally killed by the saloonkeeper, there was rarely a dry eye in the house. The play is still a favorite with college and amateur groups, though seldom presented in the spirit of its author's intention. As late as 1952 an eccentric schoolmaster left $25,000 to the school libraries of Stroudsburg, Pa., with the proviso that they each contain at least ten copies of the story. Offers to sell copies came from all over the country—some at $2,000 apiece—but finally the requisite number of texts was donated.

Tenth Muse, The. A description sometimes given to ANNE BRADSTREET, Puritan pioneer and the first poet to write in English on the North American continent. In 1650 a collection of her poems was published in England, without her knowledge, by her brother-in-law. It was called *The Tenth Muse Lately Sprung Up in America.*

Tenting on the Old Camp Ground (1864), a song by Walter Kittredge (1834–1905). Kittredge, a soldier in the Civil War in the Union Army, wrote these words out of his own experience. The song was taken up by the famous singing Hutchinson family of New Hampshire —the so-called "Tribe of Jesse." It has never lost its appeal.

Terhune, Albert Payson (b. Newark, N.J., Dec. 21, 1872—d. Feb. 18, 1942), novelist. Terhune was the son of Albert Payson Terhune, a clergyman, and MARY VIRGINIA TERHUNE (Marion Harland), a novelist. His childhood was divided between Newark and Europe. After graduating from Columbia University, Terhune traveled in Europe and the Far East, then returned to the United States and published *Syria From the Saddle* (1896). In 1900 he and his mother wrote *Dr. Dale,* a novel much publicized as the first mother-and-son collaboration (though the pair had been preceded in England by Hesketh Prichard and his mother Kate). Terhune became a reporter for the New York *World,* but disliked his work and resigned in 1916. He wrote a number of novels before he hit on the subject that was to make him famous. After the success of *Lad: A Dog* (1919), he wrote almost exclusively of dogs, usually collies. There followed *Bruce* (1920); *Buff: A Collie* (1921); *Further Adventures of Lad* (1922); *His Dog* (1922); *Black Caesar's Clan* (1923); *The Heart of a Dog* (1925); *Treasure* (1926); *The Luck of the Laird* (1927); *Lad of Sunnybank* (1928). In his autobiography, *To the Best of My Memory* (1930), Terhune described himself as "the Apostle of the Obvious and the Writer for the Very Young," but he was overmodest; no one could write a better dog story than he. After abandoning the newspaper profession, he devoted himself to writing and to raising collies. His kennels at SUNNYBANK in Pompton, N.J., became famous, and his pedigreed dogs were sold all over the world. A selection of his dog stories was made in *The Terhune Omnibus* (1937) by Max J. Herzberg.

Terhune, Mary Virginia [Hawes] ["Marion Harland"] (b. Dennisville, Va., Dec. 21, 1830—

d. June 3, 1922), novelist, home economist. Mrs. Terhune began to write at the age of nine; at fourteen she was a regular contributor to Richmond newspapers. Two years later, under the name Marion Harland, she published *Alone* (1854), a novel, the first of a long series of successes, among them *Sunnybank* (1866) and *A Gallant Fight* (1888). She married a clergyman, raised a family, and continued to write. At the request of her publisher she produced *Common Sense in the Household* (1871), which was so successful that for many years she abandoned fiction for home economics. No Victorian kitchen was complete without her *National Cookbook* (1896). She wrote syndicated articles for newspapers and magazines on home management, edited the magazine *Babyhood,* and was for a time in charge of the children's department of *St. Nicholas. The Home of the Bible* (1895) was the result of a trip through the Holy Land with her son ALBERT PAYSON TERHUNE, who collaborated with her on a novel, *Dr. Dale* (1900). She also wrote *Charlotte Brontë at Home* (1899); *Hannah More* (1900); *Everyday Etiquette* (1905); and *Marion Harland's Autobiography* (1910). She dictated her last novel, *The Carringtons of High Hall* (1919), when she was almost ninety and totally blind. Two of her daughters, as well as her son Albert and her grandson Frederic F. Van de Water, were also writers. See SUNNYBANK.

Terman, Lewis M[adison] (b. Johnson Co., Ind., Jan. 15, 1877—d. Dec. 21, 1956), teacher, psychologist. After teaching in public schools and normal schools, Terman joined the faculty of Stanford University in 1910, became a full professor in 1916, and head of the psychology department in 1922. He became greatly interested in psychometrics and devised the so-called Stanford revisions of the Binet-Simon intelligence tests (1916), which are now more frequently known by his own name. Terman developed another special interest, measuring intelligence and fostering the development of gifted children; his ideas, procedures, and books exerted a wide influence. Among his writings: *The Teacher's Health* (1913); *Health Work in the Schools* (1914); *The Measurement of Intelligence* (1916); *The Intelligence of School Children* (1919); *The Terman Group Test* (with T. L. Kelley and G. M. Ruch, 1920); *Genetic Studies of Genius* (with others, 3 v., 1925, 1926, 1930); *Children's Reading* (with Margaret Lima, 1925); *Marital Happiness* (1938); *The Terman-McNemar Test of Mental Ability* (with Q. McNemar, 1942); *The Gifted Child Grows Up* (with Melita Oden, 1947).

Terminus (1867), a poem by RALPH WALDO EMERSON. Terminus, in the religion of Rome, was the god who presided over boundaries and landmarks. This striking poem, rich in fine phrases, has usually been accepted as a poem on old age. "It is time to be old," says Emerson, "to take in sail." He was then sixty-four, lived fifteen years longer, but in his last days was senile. C. F. Strauch has argued, however, that the date of composition usually given for the poem is wrong; the first draft, he says, was composed before 1860, and in its inception the poem was not chiefly about old age. It then treated three themes: growing old, an Emersonian variation of the *carpe diem* injunction, and integrity.

Territorial Enterprise. A Nevada newspaper founded Dec. 18, 1858, at Mormon Station. It removed to Carson City for a while, then in 1860 settled down in Virginia City. It is still in existence, although occasionally suspended. In 1952 LUCIUS BEEBE became its publisher, with Charles Clegg as editor. Beebe became the paper's historian and enthusiastic celebrator. His *Comstock Commotion: The Story of the Territorial Enterprise* (1954) states his conviction that from the paper's first beginnings it was "destined to become the pattern and archetype of all Western newspapers in pioneer times." Among those who contributed to it in early days were Mark Twain, Dan De Quille, and Joe Goodman. It still uses the old-fashioned type face and antiquated advertisements, and is popular for its colorful and somewhat satirical accounts of local happenings.

Terror and Decorum (1948), a volume of poems by PETER VIERECK. This first collection of poems deals largely with Viereck's war experiences and generally, according to Richard Eberhart, "with the problem of the formalizing of knowledge." Critical attitudes towards his work have been mixed. The book was awarded a Pulitzer prize.

Testut, Charles (b. France, 1818[?]—d. July 1, 1892), physician, newspaperman, poet, novelist, biographer. A resident of New Orleans from an early age, Testut led a busy literary as well as medical life, writing many books, writing for newspapers, becoming a leader in the city's literary activities. Probably his most frequently consulted book today is not his fiction or poetry but his *Portraits Littéraires de la Nouvelle-Orléans* (1850), sketches of fifty-two contemporary writers. He published two collections of poems, *Les Echos* (1849) and *Fleurs d'Été* (1851). He wrote many novels, of which three received the chief attention: *Saint-Denis* (1845); *Calisto* (1849); *Le Vieux Salomon* (written 1858, pub. 1877). Testut was not above reproducing whole pages from authors he liked in his own novels.

Texas Rangers. The "Big Three" of Texan legendry are Davy Crockett, Sam Houston, and Big-Foot Wallace. Alongside them stand those six-gun men, the Texas Rangers. Although the storytellers have turned the Rangers into huge, handsome swashbucklers, their leaders were frequently not that type of man at all. Their reputation for incredible courage was established early in the 1830's while the struggle to found a republic was going on. Indians and Mexicans early learned to fear them, and their approach often scared their opponents into surrender. During the Mexican War, Taylor used them frequently but did not care much for their complete disregard of military formalities. During the Civil War the Rangers fought as units of the Confederate Army and continued to maintain their reputation. At the close of the war Texas was infested with desperadoes, and the Texas Rangers took care of them with cool efficiency. As private wars and desperadoes became less common in a state of many large cities, the need for the special services of the Texas Rangers diminished. In 1935 the Rangers became a part of the State Highway Patrol.

The best book about the Rangers is undoubtedly Walter Prescott Webb's *The Texas Rangers: A Century of Frontier Defense* (1935). Other nonfiction works include S. C. Reid's *Scouting Expeditions of the Texas Rangers* (1859; rep., 1936); James Pike's *Scout and Ranger* (1865; rep., 1932); N. A. Jennings' *The Texas Ranger* (1899; rep., 1930); J. B. Gillett's *Six Years with the Texas Rangers* (1921) and *The Texas Ranger* (with H. R. Driggs, 1927). The Rangers have appeared frequently in novels, such as Joseph Holt Ingraham's *The Texas Ranger, or, The Maid of Matamoras, a Tale of the Mexican War* (1846); H. W. Herbert's *Pierre the Partisan: A Tale of the Mexican Marches* (1848); C. W. Webber's *Old Hicks the Guide* (1848) and *The Prairie Scout* (1852); William MacLeod Raine's *A Texas Ranger* (1911); Clarence Budington Kelland's *This Is My Son* (1949); Paul I. Wellman's *The Comancheros* (1952).

Texas Steer, or "Money Makes the Mare Go" (1890) by CHARLES H. HOYT. A Texan congressman is made the butt of the jokes in this farce. It is the only one of Hoyt's plays ever to be published—in M. J. Moses' *Representative American Dramas* (1925).

textbooks. In the schools of the colonists the Bible was not merely a spiritual and ethical guide but also a medium of instruction. English textbooks found their way immediately into the colonies: for example, Coote's *The English Schoolmaster* (1596) and Nat. Strong's *England's Perfect Schoolmaster* (1676). The hornbook, a one-page rudimentary primer protected by a sheet of transparent horn, taught the alphabet, a benediction, and the Lord's Prayer. The second piece of printing in the British colonies was a textbook, Ezekiel Cheever's *Short Introduction to the Latin Tongue* (1645). Then came a more famous and more successful textbook, the NEW ENGLAND PRIMER, printed some time between 1685 and 1690. It went through many revisions and editions and was widely imitated.

With the American Revolution textbook importation from England ceased. For a while American textbooks were difficult to come by, and a real beginning was not made until NOAH WEBSTER began producing his momentous books. His famous *Speller* was printed at his own expense; the 1829 edition—*The Elementary Spelling Book*—sold millions of copies. It produced many imitations, instigated the production of arithmetic, grammar, and other textbooks, fixed the textbook habit upon American education as the most efficient method of inculcating knowledge, and created the race of textbook publishers. The next tremendous success was made with what came to be called readers (later superseded by anthologies and collections)—the famous *Eclectic Readers* for various grades edited by WILLIAM H. McGUFFEY. These *Readers* turned away from sectarian religious teaching but laid strong emphasis on ethical training. They also introduced the idea of graded selections, so that a series of volumes was prepared to meet the needs of successive age groups.

Myriads of textbooks of all sorts have followed the three great forerunners. There have been fashions in textbooks as in everything else. Authors of Latin grammars and editions of Latin classics, for example, were once sure of a comfortable income; today such books are much less popular. On the other hand, textbooks on stenography and economics are now widely used. Compulsory education has necessitated the production of reading material for what are now called, euphemistically, "reluctant readers." The teaching of GRAMMAR has been the subject of much controversy.

The notion that there are ideal vocabularies for a particular grade caused books to be rewritten accordingly. Some of the great children's classics were for a time subjected to this indignity.

College textbooks offer somewhat different problems. They lay less stress on pedagogical procedures, often are entirely factual, sometimes prove so readable that, as with Harvey Wish's *Contemporary America* (1948, 1955), the book is popular with the general public.

After World War II textbook publishers faced a new problem which took on harmful dimensions—the censorship of books. Previously publishers had faced objections to books mainly because they offended religious groups. Shakespeare's *Merchant of Venice*, for instance, disappeared from some English classrooms. But after 1945 censorship took amazing new forms. Expressions that seemed critical of American practices, attempts to deal with Russia objectively, mention of international organizations, brought vehement objections from superpatriot groups. (See McCARTHYISM.) Textbook publishers were astounded at these attacks. They are among the most conservative and cautious of all mercantile groups, and their work has always been subject to a minute and searching scrutiny. The competition among them is intense. It was unfortunately true that a mere charge against a book was sufficient to cause timorous states and communities to drop it immediately. HAROLD RUGG's *The Great Technology* suffered typical abuse but retained its popularity. The National Council of Teachers of English took official notice of such attacks by appointing a Committee on Censorship of Teaching Materials for Classroom and Library, which issued a report, *Censorship and Controversy* (November, 1953).

An excellent article summing up both the deficiencies and the advantages of textbooks in the United States, *What Is Wrong with Text-*

books?, was written by P. A. Knowlton for *The School Executive* (October, 1950). Other historically important textbooks and books about textbooks are: W. D. Whitney's *Language and the Study of Language* (1867) and *Essentials of English Grammar* (1877); Etta Griffith's *Education in McGuffey's Time* (1894); Paul L. Ford's *The New England Primer* (1897); Clifton Johnson's *Old-Time Schools and School Books* (1904); T. R. Lounsbury's *Standard of Usage in English* (1908); G. P. Krapp's *Modern English* (1909) and *Comprehensive Guide to Good English* (1909); Edward Sapir's *Language* (1921); J. B. Greenough and G. L. Kittredge's *Words and Their Ways in English Speech* (1922); Otto Jespersen's *Philosophy of Grammar* (1924) and *Growth and Structure of the English Language* (1929); Merle Curti's *Social Ideas of American Educators* (1935); E. C. Shoemaker's *Noah Webster, Pioneer of Learning* (1936); Anne Lyon Haight's *Banned Books* (2nd ed., 1955); L. M. Myers' *Guide to American English* (1955).

Thacher, James (b. Barnstable, Mass., Feb. 14, 1754—d. May 23, 1844), physician, historian. Thacher's wartime journal, later published as *A Military Journal During the American Revolutionary War* (1823), is one of the best contemporary accounts of the Revolution. After the war he practiced and taught medicine in Plymouth, Mass., where his reputation soon spread through the country and to Europe. His *The American Dispensatory* (1810) and *American Modern Practice* (1817) became standard medical texts, and his pioneer *American Medical Biography* (1828) is a valuable account of early American medicine and its practitioners. He also wrote an *Essay on Demonology, Ghosts, and Apparitions* (1831).

Thacher, John Boyd (b. Ballston Spa, N.Y., Sept. 11, 1847—d. Feb. 25, 1909), bibliophile, public official, historian. Thacher conducted a successful business in Albany and served that city as mayor for two terms, was also an ardent book and autograph collector. His collection of incunabula is in the Library of Congress; he had a complete set of signatures of the signers of the Declaration of Independence. Among his own writings the most important was the three-volume *Christopher Columbus* (1903–04). He also wrote *The Continent of America* (1896) and *The Cabotian Discovery* (1897). F. W. Ashley prepared a catalogue of his collection in the Library of Congress (1915).

Thanatopsis (comp., 1811; pub., 1817), a poem by WILLIAM CULLEN BRYANT. Like many young poets, Bryant as an adolescent tended toward gloomy thoughts of death, and in his reading preferred the melancholy poets. He was greatly influenced by a group of 18th-century English poets, known collectively under the name of the Graveyard School, who anticipated the romantic movement by their carefully cultivated love of melancholy. Henry Kirke White, whose *Remains* was a collection republished in this country, undoubtedly influenced Bryant most in some of his early work, including *Thanatopsis*. In 1817 Bryant's father, while clearing out a desk, found the manuscript of *Thanatopsis* and some other poems by his son. Without consulting the young author, he copied the poem, also INSCRIPTION FOR THE ENTRANCE TO A WOOD, and presented them to his friend Willard Phillips, one of the editors of the *North American Review*. The poems were printed in the September, 1817, issue of the *Review*—by an odd mistake as a single poem. Not until 1821 did the board of editors learn that the son, not the father, was the author.

When Bryant published a collection of *Poems* in 1821 he included *Thanatopsis*, but with numerous revisions. Carl Van Doren, in an article entitled *The Growth of "Thanatopsis"* (*The Nation*, Oct. 7, 1915), analyzed these changes. Most important of the changes was the passage of sixteen and a half lines which he inserted at the beginning; this passage places the entire poem in the mouth of Nature, which is made responsible for its philosophy. Thus the poem becomes one of courage rather than fear as Bryant accepts the democracy of death. This message is even more evident in the last nine lines of the poem, also added in the 1821 version.

The poem immediately became famous and by some is regarded as the first important poem to be written by an American. In 1820 Sydney Smith asked his contemptuous question, "Who reads an American book?" Two years later a writer in *Blackwood's Magazine* prophesied, on the strength of To A WATERFOWL and *Thanatopsis*, that Bryant would assume a high rank among English poets. Critical comments on the poem range from G. W. Curtis and W. A. Bradley's opinion that it expresses the general spirit of Puritanism to Carl Van Doren's view that it is "as pagan as Lucretius."

Thane, Elswyth [Mrs. William Beebe] (b. Burlington, Iowa [?], 1900—   ), novelist. Her first novel, *Riders of the Wind* (1925), was followed by many more, down to *Homing* (1957). She is also the author of five nonfiction works and several plays. Two summers' research in the British Museum (1928–29) resulted in a number of historical novels. Two of her plays were produced: *The Tudor Wench* (1934) and *Young Mr. Disraeli* (London, 1935; New York, 1937). Beginning with *Dawn's Early Light* (1943), she wrote a "pentalogy" of historical novels that ended with *Kissing Kin* (1948), tracing an American family from 1774 to 1934, for the most part in Williamsburg, Va. *Washington's Lady* (1960) continued her novels of America.

Thanet, Octave. See ALICE FRENCH.

Thatcher, Benjamin Bussey (b. Warren, Me., Oct. 8, 1809—d. July 14, 1840), lawyer, abolitionist, historian, editor. Thatcher belonged to the group of antislavery crusaders who favored colonization in Liberia. He was an opponent of WILLIAM LLOYD GARRISON in this respect, edited the *Colonization and Journal of Freedom,* and lectured in behalf of the Liberia project. He also prepared *Memoirs* (1834) of PHILLIS

WHEATLEY, the Negro poet, published in conjunction with an edition of her verses. Thatcher was likewise interested in the Indians, wrote *Indian Biography* (2 v., 1832) and *Indian Traits* (2 v., 1833). His *Boston Book* (1837) was an anthology. He wrote numerous poems for periodicals, but no collection of them was made.

Thaxter, Celia [Laighton] (b. Portsmouth, N.H., June 29, 1835—d. Aug. 26, 1894), poet. Educated by her father and the tutor (later a lawyer) who became her husband, Mrs. Thaxter spent much of her life on Appledore Island

off the New Hampshire coast, where her father ran a summer hotel. Her poetry and prose reflect her abiding interest in the sea. Her first published poem, *Land-Locked* appeared in the *Atlantic Monthly* (March, 1861), after which she contributed regularly to that magazine. *Poems* (1872) was followed by *Among the Isles of Shoals* (1873), a collection of sketches previously published in the *Atlantic; Drift-Weed* (1879); *Poems for Children* (1884); *The Cruise of the Mystery* (1886); *Idyls and Pastorals* (1886); *An Island Garden* (1894). Her poems are graceful and pleasing, but today are mostly unknown.

Thayer, Alexander Wheelock (b. S. Natick, Mass., Oct. 22, 1817—d. July 15, 1897), music critic, biographer, American consul. Thayer lived for many years in Germany and Austria (serving as American consul at Trieste, 1862–82), and had his most important work published in German before it appeared in English. For a time he was music critic for the New York

Tribune. His specialty was Beethoven; he wrote an incomplete biography of the great composer in English, which was translated into German and published in Germany (3 v., 1866, 1872, 1879). The translator collaborated on the succeeding volume, *The Life of Ludwig van Beethoven* (1921), with a German music authority, who in turn worked on the fifth volume and completed it. Henry E. Krehbiel, also a music critic for the *Tribune*, edited the work in English.

Thayer, Ernest Lawrence. See CASEY AT THE BAT.

Thayer, John Adams (b. Boston, Feb. 20, 1861—d. Feb. 21, 1936), publisher. Thayer was connected with some notable magazine publications and was a cofounder (1903) of the firm of Ridgway-Thayer, which published *Everybody's Magazine.* He also published THE SMART SET from 1911–14. His memoirs appeared in three editions under different titles: *Astir: A Publisher's Life-Story* (1910); *Getting On: The Confessions of a Publisher* (in England, 1911); and *Out of the Rut: A Business Life Story* (1912).

Thayer, William Roscoe (b. Boston, Jan. 16, 1859—d. Sept. 7, 1923), historian, biographer. Thayer received an M.A. from Harvard University (1886), taught English there (1888–1889), and edited the *Harvard Graduates' Magazine* (1892–1915). Since his youth he had studied history, and in 1893 he published *The Dawn of Italian Independence. The Life and Times of Cavour* (1911) won him the highest awards the Italian government had to bestow. Thayer also wrote *The Life and Letters of John Hay* (1915); *Theodore Roosevelt, An Intimate Biography* (1919); and *The Art of Biography* (1920).

Theatre Arts. A magazine founded as a quarterly in 1916; it became a monthly in 1924. SHELDON CHENEY was the first editor and was succeeded by Edith J. R. Isaacs and John D. MacArthur. It has published many excellent articles and has strongly fostered experimentation in the theater. In addition, it publishes a complete play, usually contemporary, each month.

Theatre Guild. The Theatre Guild, which asserted it existed "for drama, for beauty, for ideas," presented its first play, Jacinto Benevente's *Bonds of Interest,* April 14, 1919. It opened the Guild Theater, April 13, 1925, with G. B. Shaw's *Caesar and Cleopatra.* Subscribers were the first to see new plays; later the general public bought seats. In the course of the years that followed, it had a considerable number of hits, some failures. Many first-rate actors appeared, many dramatists obtained a hearing for plays not likely to be commercial successes. See THE GROUP.

Their Fathers' God (1931), a novel by O. E. RÖLVAAG. This last volume of a trilogy including GIANTS IN THE EARTH (1927) and PEDER VICTORIUS (1929) is set in the Dakotas during the late 19th century and treats the conflict between Peder Holm, a Norwegian farmer of Lutheran faith, and his Irish Catholic wife

Susie Doheny over the raising of their infant son Petie. It is a bleakly realistic study of antagonism.

Their Wedding Journey (1871), a novel by WILLIAM DEAN HOWELLS. This first novel, describing Basil and Isabel March's honeymoon trip by boat and train to New York City, Rochester, Niagara Falls, and Canada, is largely autobiographical and treats with loving fidelity the people and scenes of everyday American life. Theodore Dreiser remarked of the book that there was "not a sentimental passage in it, quarrels from beginning to end, just the way it would be, don't you know, quite beautiful and true."

Theory of the Leisure Class, The (1899), a treatise by THORSTEIN VEBLEN. Described in the subtitle as "An Economic Study of Institutions," this work was an early and exceedingly influential examination of the concept of status. Veblen held that the feudal subdivision of classes had continued into modern times, the lords employing themselves uselessly (as in killing animals) while the lower classes labored at industrial pursuits to support the whole of society. The leisure class, Veblen said, justifies itself solely by practicing "conspicuous leisure and conspicuous consumption"; he defined *waste* as any activity not contributing to material productivity. Veblen took a sternly economic view, refused to consider cultural values, though he himself was not an uncultivated man. Mainly his book was a passionate rejection of the economic system he saw flourishing in America during the late 19th century, before the great industrial baronies had been brought under control and before the day of meliorative labor legislation. He wrote well and vigorously and had a knack for choosing pointed examples to illustrate his theme.

Veblen was attacked by various opponents, but it was not until twenty years later that he met an adversary of equal powers in H. L. MENCKEN—no economist but an ardent believer in aristocratic values. In a piece called *Professor Veblen and the Cow,* first published in *Smart Set* (May, 1919) and later included in *Prejudices I* (1919), Mencken called the theory of conspicuous waste "one per cent platitude and 99 per cent nonsense"; he complained that Veblen's style "affected the higher cerebral centers like a constant roll of subway expresses"; he called Veblen's book "simply socialism and well water." He took particular offense at Veblen's criticism of urban dwellers for not keeping cows: Mencken pointed out sarcastically that Veblen had ignored the effect of bovine excrement in a crowded environment. In spite of Mencken's ridicule, however, *The Theory of the Leisure Class* was and is widely recognized as an American classic in economics and sociology, and it is still one of the most popular works of scholarly literature ever produced in the United States.

theosophy. The word means "divine wisdom," and its concepts go back to early idealistic philosophy, particularly to Plato, Plotinus, and the Christian gnostics. Theosophy also makes a deliberate attempt to include ideas from the world's great scriptures, especially of India, also of China and Egypt. It is mystical in tone, accepts the possibility of communication with another world, characterizes God as a causeless One Cause, promulgates the doctrines of reincarnation. In modern times theosophy has become a widely taught and accepted body of belief, especially in connection with the famous Theosophical Society, founded in 1875 by Madame Helena Petrovna Blavatsky in New York City and now an international body. Among Madame Blavatsky's chief followers were Annie Besant, president of the Society from 1907 to 1933, and William Butler Yeats. Madame Blavatsky's *The Secret Doctrine* (2 v., 1888) is a fundamental document of the sect.

There'll Be a Hot Time in the Old Town Tonight. See HOT TIME IN THE OLD TOWN TONIGHT.

There's a Long, Long Trail A-Winding (pub. 1913, London; 1914, U.S.), a song, words by STODDARD KING, music by Alonzo (Zo) Elliott. The lyric was written for a smoker of the Zeta Psi fraternity at Yale, was given a literary prize, and when a tour with the Glee Club was offered to the person who wrote the best music for the words, Elliott won the award. The song was taken to England by Elliott when he did graduate work at Oxford, and was immediately taken up by the British Army. It became popular in the United States thereafter.

There Shall Be No Night (1940), a drama by ROBERT E. SHERWOOD. Inspired by a wartime broadcast by William L. White, *There Shall Be No Night* tells of Kaarlo Valkonen, a brilliant neurologist who refuses to face the threat of war. When his native Finland is invaded and his only son is killed, Valkonen too is drawn in. At his death his American wife is left to a last-ditch defense of their home. When the play opened in the uncertain spring of 1940, Sherwood was accused of being a warmonger, and even a Communist. He replied with a pointed reference to the United States' "ostrich-escapism." Transcending contemporary issues, however, is his message that "we have within ourselves the power to conquer bestiality . . . with the power of light that is in our minds." When Finland became unpopular, Sherwood changed the locale of the play. It won the Pulitzer Prize (1941).

There Was a Child Went Forth (1855; considerably revised in succeeding editions of *Leaves of Grass*), a poem by WALT WHITMAN. The poem had no title in the first edition, was called *Poem of the Child That Went Forth, and Always Goes Forth, Forever and Forever* in 1860; the present title was given in 1871. It is obviously intended to be autobiographical, calls the months by the Quaker names with which Whitman was familiar in his childhood, shows how he pantheistically identifies himself with the objects around him. There are sharply etched profiles of his mother, whom he loved,

and his father, whom he apparently did not; and he describes the familiar landscape of the sea front.

Thériault, Yves (b. Quebec, Nov. 28, 1916 —), French-Canadian writer of fiction. Thériault, regarded as one of the leading 20th-century novelists and short-story writers of French Canada, is not particularly interested in straightforward storytelling, stresses rather the depiction of persons in tragic or ironic situations, the use of symbolism. He wrote *Contes pour un homme seul* (1944); *La Fille laide* (1950); *Le Dompteur d'Ours* (1950); *Les Vendeurs du Temple* (1953).

These Thirteen (1931), a collection of short stories by WILLIAM FAULKNER. This volume contains perhaps the best known of all of Faulkner's stories, "A Rose for Emily," which deals with an eccentric and aging southern spinster. After the death of her father, Miss Emily Grierson is courted by Homer Barron, a Yankee construction foreman, who mysteriously disappears. Many years later, after she has become a town legend, seldom seen but often speculated about, Miss Emily dies and the townspeople find the skeleton of Barron locked in an upstairs bedroom. The book also contains "Red Leaves" and "A Justice," two stories dealing with the Chickasaw Indians of Yoknapatawpha County in the days before the coming of the white man. The latter story is narrated to young Quentin Compson (see THE COMPSON FAMILY).

They All Played Ragtime (1950), a chronicle by Rudi Blesh and Harriet Janis. This is a scholarly history of ragtime, its composers and performers, up to and including the early phases of jazz. The book contains bibliographies of musical compositions, phonograph recordings, and player-piano rolls.

They Knew What They Wanted (1924), a play by SIDNEY HOWARD. Tony Patucci, a middle-aged Napa Valley winegrower, misleads his mail-order bride, Amy, with a picture of his handsome young hired man Joe. On the wedding day Tony breaks both his legs. Amy, humiliated and confused, allows Joe to seduce her and becomes pregnant. Tony nearly kills the younger man when he finds out what has happened; then his nobility of heart prevails and he asks Amy to stay. "Den evrabody say Tony is so goddam young an' strong he's break both his leg' an' having baby just da same!" The play won a Pulitzer prize in 1925 and was Howard's first popular success. It was filmed and later became the basis of an equally successful musical, *The Most Happy Fella* (1957) by Frank Loesser.

Thin Man, The (1934), a novel by DASHIELL HAMMETT. Nick Charles, a former detective, solves a murder by discovering that the suspected killer, the "thin man," had himself been slain many months earlier by the real murderer. A Pinkerton detective himself for eight years, Hammett originated in the novel a tough, hard-drinking hero who set a style in detective stories that has been widely imitated; the humor in the story was also a novelty. As a motion picture, *The Thin Man* (1936), with William Powell as Nick and Myrna Loy as his wife Nora, was very popular and had a series of profitable sequels. Connoisseurs rate *The Thin Man* below Hammett's *The Maltese Falcon* (1930) and THE GLASS KEY (1931).

Third Violet, The (1897), a novel by STEPHEN CRANE. The story is about an impecunious landscape painter's love for a rich girl, Grace Fanhall, whom the artist meets at a mountain summer resort. She gives him two violets during their stay out of town, and then he calls upon her in New York City to tell her that he can never forget her or the violets; whereupon she contemptuously gives him a third violet and cries, "Oh, do go! Go! Please! I want you to go!" *The Third Violet,* Wilson Follett said, "consists almost entirely of two strands of autobiography which intersect but are never twisted into complete unity." The major strand is Crane's hopeless love affair with Helen Trent in September, 1891, when he was not yet twenty, and the secondary strand is refashioned from Crane's 1893 period when he lived in New York. The book was poorly received. The *Critic* bluntly stated the majority opinion: "The author not only shows no grasp of character, but omits to present any characters to grasp . . . the author has practically left the entire novel to the reader's imagination . . . taking the book as a whole, the author has prepared for those who would gladly be his admirers as many kinds of disappointment as 200 pages can possibly hold."

Thirst and Other Plays (1914), a collection of one-act plays by EUGENE O'NEILL. See MOON OF THE CARIBBEES.

Thirteenth Chair, The (1916), a melodrama by BAYARD VEILLER. A man is murdered in the course of a séance, and one of his friends hires a medium to discover the criminal. During the course of a second séance another man is killed but the medium finally catches the murderer. The play was a great hit.

Thirty Years' View, or History of the Working of the American Government from 1820 to 1850 (2 v., 1854–56), by THOMAS HART BENTON. This is really the political autobiography of a remarkable man, known as "Old Bullion" because of his support of "sound money" and his opposition to the National Bank along with Andrew Jackson. He opposed nullification, voted for the annexation of Texas, took part in all the political controversies of his day. But his valuable book is also an account of frontier conditions. Seba Smith (Major Jack Downing) parodied the book in *My Thirty Years Out of the Senate* (1859).

This Land is Ours (1940), a novel by LOUIS ZARA. This historical adventure narrates the life of frontiersman Andrew Benton from the defeat of Braddock to the founding of Chicago. Benton is captured by Indians, accompanies the Clark expedition, and survives many hardships and dangers.

This Reckless Breed of Men: The Trappers and Fur Traders of the Southwest (1950), a historical account by Robert Glass Cleland. This volume, by a capable scholar who does not neglect the human side, studies the fur trade mainly in the California–Arizona–New Mexico region. The author concludes that this trade reached its height in 1830 or 1832 and the era of the fur traders and the mountain men was finished when China opened its five Treaty Ports (1835) and silk began to be imported for the making of men's hats, which previously had been made of beaver pelts.

This Side of Paradise (1920), a novel by F. SCOTT FITZGERALD. Amory Blaine, a wealthy and snobbish young man from the Middle West, attends Princeton University and acquires a refined sense of the proper "social" values. A series of flirtations with some rather predatory young ladies culminates in a genuine but ill-fated love for Isabelle Borgé, who rejects Amory to marry a wealthier young man. The novel became a best seller, its characters models for the young men and women of the 1920's. As in his later novel THE GREAT GATSBY (1925), Fitzgerald treats the characteristic theme of true romantic love blighted by money lust. Most important in the novel is the honest and detailed description of the incipient "Jazz Age"; Fitzgerald writes here of the "lost generation" in its college days. Arthur Mizener suggested in *The Far Side of Paradise* (1949) that Fitzgerald wrote as if he were "some kind of impassioned and naïve anthropologist."

Thomas, A[lbert] E[llsworth] (b. Chester, Mass., Sept. 16, 1872—d. June 18, 1947), newspaperman, playwright. From 1895 to 1909 Thomas worked on various newspapers in New York, including the *Times,* the *Sun,* the *Evening Post,* and the *Tribune.* But his deep interest was in the theater, and he wrote some lively plays, including *Thirty Days* (with CLAYTON HAMILTON, 1910); *Her Husband's Wife* (1910); *What the Doctor Ordered* (1911); *The French Doll* (1922); *Our Nell* (with BRIAN HOOKER, 1922); *White Magic* (1926); *The Big Pond* (with GEORGE MIDDLETON, 1928); *Her Friend the King* (with Harrison Rhodes, 1929); *No More Ladies* (1934); *Merely Murder* (1937). The *Times* at the time of his death lauded him as an all-around master craftsman and as "the brightest wit among our writers for the stage in the second and third decades of this century."

Thomas, Augustus (b. St. Louis, Mo., Jan. 8, 1857—d. Aug. 16, 1934), actor, manager, playwright. Thomas was almost entirely self-educated, reading widely, drawing, and writing sketches. He joined the Marion Place Dramatic Club, which produced his first play, *Alone* (1875). In the summer he acted with a traveling company, meeting some of the great actors of the day. In 1876 he began to read law, but his heart was in the theater. He joined another amateur group, the McCullough Club, for which he dramatized FRANCES HODGSON BURNETT'S *Editha's Burglar;* later he expanded it into a four-act play, *The Burglar* (1889). In

1885 he joined the staff of the St. Louis *Post-Dispatch,* wrote articles and drew cartoons for it. He went to New York three years later as manager for JULIA MARLOWE, but returned to St. Louis to become advance agent for Washington Irving Bishop, a mind reader. Some of the material for THE WITCHING HOUR (1907), a thriller dealing with hypnotism and clairvoyance, was obtained at this time. He returned to New York when *The Burglar,* starring Maurice Barrymore, began a ten-year run. He became adapter and reviser of foreign plays for the Madison Square Theater, a position earlier held by Dion Boucicault. During his long theatrical career Thomas wrote more than fifty plays, among them: *Alabama* (1891); IN MIZZOURA (1893); *Arizona* (1899); *The Harvest Moon* (1909); AS A MAN THINKS (1911); *Rio Grande* (1916); *The Copperhead* (1918); *Palmy Days* (1920). *The Print of My Remembrance* (1922) is an autobiography illustrated by the author's own spirited sketches. See SOLDIERS OF FORTUNE; THE EARL OF PAW-TUCKET.

Thomas, Calvin (b. near Lapeer, Mich., Oct. 28, 1854—d. Nov. 4, 1919), teacher, scholar, editor. Thomas taught at the University of Michigan (1878–96), then joined the faculty of Columbia University as professor of Germanic languages and literature in 1896. Among his writings: *Life and Works of Schiller* (1901); *A History of German Literature* (1909); *Scholarship and Other Essays* (1924). He also edited an anthology of German literature (1907) and Goethe's *Faust* (2 v., 1892–97).

Thomas, [Martha] Carey (b. Baltimore, Md., Jan. 2, 1857—d. Dec. 2, 1935), teacher, administrator, crusader. Dr. Thomas graduated from Cornell (1877) in a day when women's higher education was frowned upon, later studied at Johns Hopkins and abroad. All her life she fought for women's rights, especially suffrage and higher education. She helped organize Bryn Mawr College (1884), became dean and professor of English there (1884–94), then its president (1894–1922). Among her books: *The Higher Education of Women* (1900); *Should the Higher Education of Women Differ from That of Men?* (1901); and *The College* (1905).

Thomas, Charles Swain (b. Pendleton, Ind., Dec. 29, 1868—d. Jan. 26, 1943), teacher, author. Thomas taught in high schools for a while, was a principal and superintendent of schools in various towns in the Middle West and Massachusetts, was appointed a lecturer on education at Harvard University (1920) and became an associate professor there (1930–36). He produced several useful books: *How to Teach the English Classics* (1910); *The Teaching of English in the Secondary School* (1916; rev., 1927); *When I Write a Theme* (with J. C. Bowman, 1930). He also edited many classics for school use and directed *The English Leaflet,* a periodical published by the New England Association of Teachers of English, from 1909 to 1940.

Thomas, Edith Matilda (b. Chatham, Ohio, Aug. 12, 1854—d. Sept. 13, 1925), poet. Miss Thomas attended normal school, studied classics, and started to write poetry that reflected classical influences. In New York City she met HELEN HUNT JACKSON, who helped her to place her poems in leading magazines and newspapers. Her gentle imaginative lyrics appealed to a limited group and are almost forgotten today. Among her books: *A New Year's Masque and Other Poems* (1885); *The Round Year* (1886); *Lyrics and Sonnets* (1887); *The Dancers, and Other Legends and Lyrics* (1903); *The Flower from the Ashes* (1915).

Thomas, Frederick William (b. Providence, R.I., Oct. 25, 1806—d. Aug. 27, 1866), lawyer, editor, teacher, preacher, novelist. In 1860 Thomas became literary editor of the Richmond *Enquirer,* later joined the editorial staff of Columbia *South Carolinian.* Crippled by injuries suffered in childhood, Thomas nevertheless wrote verse (*The Emigrant,* 1833) and several novels—*Clinton Bradshaw, or, The Adventures of a Lawyer* (2 v., 1835), *East and West* (1836), *Howard Pinckney* (1840), *John Randolph of Roanoke* (1853). The novels were popular, especially *Clinton Bradshaw,* which revealed the law's seamy side. Thomas was a close friend of Edgar Allan Poe, and tried to help him.

Thomas, Isaiah (b. Boston, Jan. 19, 1749—d. April 4, 1831), printer. After serving his printing apprenticeship, Thomas founded, with Zachariah Fowle, the *Massachusetts Spy* (1770), a patriotic paper that was still appearing as late as 1904. He fought at Lexington and Concord and later did printing work for the new government. After the war he became the leading printer in the country. His retirement gave him time to write *The History of Printing in America* (1810) and to found the American Antiquarian Society. Benjamin T. Hill edited *The Diary of Isaiah Thomas, 1805–1828* (1909) for the Society. Annie R. Marble wrote a biography, *From 'Prentice to Patron* (1935), and Clifford K. Shipton wrote *Isaiah Thomas: Printer, Patriot, and Philanthropist* (1948). See also CHAPBOOKS.

Thomas, Lowell [Jackson] (b. Woodington, Ohio, April 6, 1892—   ), journalist, travel writer, lecturer, news commentator. Thomas worked as a gold miner, cook, reporter, professor of oratory, English instructor, historian, war correspondent, lecturer, magazine editor, and radio, television, and motion-picture news commentator. His many books of travel, adventure and biography include: *With Lawrence in Arabia* (1924); *The First World Flight* (1925); *Raiders of the Deep* (1928); *Out of This World* (1950); *History As You Heard It* (1957); *The Vital Spark* (1959); *Sir Hubert Wilkins: His World of Adventure* (1961). He also made several travel films in the Far East. He is best known, however, for his news broadcasts.

Thomas, Norman [Mattoon] (b. Marion, Ohio, Nov. 20, 1884—d. Dec. 19, 1968), clergyman, editor, writer. Thomas graduated from

Princeton in 1905 and was ordained as a Presbyterian minister in 1911. He founded *World Tomorrow* (1918), which he edited until 1921, was assistant editor of THE NATION (1921–22), and directed the League for Industrial Democracy (1922). Eventually he resigned from his ministerial duties in order to devote his entire time to writing and speaking for social reform and pacifism. As a Socialist Party candidate he ran unsuccessfully for many offices: Governor of New York (1924), Mayor of New York City (1925, 1929), Congressman (1930), President (1928–1948). His works include *The Challenge of War* (1925); *What Is Industrial Democracy?* (1927); *Socialism of Our Time* (1929); *The Conscientious Democracy* (1930); *The Choice Before Us* (1934); *War—No Profit, No Glory No Need* (1935); *What Is Our Destiny?* (1944); *Appeal to the Nations* (1947); *A Socialist's Faith* (1951); *The Test of Freedom* (1954); *Prerequisites for Peace* (1959); *The Great Dissenters* (1961).

Thomas, Robert Bailey. See THE OLD FARMER'S ALMANAC.

Thomason, John W[illiam], Jr. (b. Huntsville, Tex., Feb. 28, 1893—d. March 12, 1944), soldier, author, artist. Thomason's career as an army officer and his literary career were inextricably interwoven. He wrote *Fix Bayonets* (1926), a vivid first novel of fighting men in action during the first World War, made even more graphic by his own illustrations. Other writings included *Red Pants and Other Stories* (1927) and *Jeb Stuart* (1930).

Thomes, William Henry (b. Portland, Me., May 5, 1824—d. March 6, 1895), trader, reporter, publisher, novelist, memoirist. Thomes' first great experience was in going to sea on the *Admittance* when he was eighteen years old, deserting when he reached California and taking part in the fur trade and possibly in military service, then returning to Boston by way of Mexico and England and becoming a reporter. The gold rush lured him back to California, but his health became poor. Later wanderings took him to islands in the Pacific, China, and Australia. In 1855 he was back in the United States and again a reporter in Boston. In 1860 he became a partner in a publishing house that issued a weekly, *The American Union*, for which Thomes wrote adventure stories; some of them were later put out as books. It is believed that at least half a million copies of his books were sold. His firm increased in importance, and Thomes became prominent both in literary and political circles. But his sole surviving book is *On Land and Sea* (1883), which has sometimes been compared to Richard Henry Dana's *Two Years Before the Mast* (1840). It is said, in fact, that Dana's book both stimulated Thomes to become a world traveler and inspired him in his autobiography. One of his novels, *Lewey and I* (1884), is based on his experiences in California in the 1840's. Among his other books: *The Gold Hunters' Adventures, or, Life in Australia* (1864) and its sequel, *The Bushrangers* (1866);

The Whaleman's Adventures (1872); *A Slaver's Adventures on Land and Sea* (1872); *Life in the East Indies* (1873); *Running the Blockade* (1875); *The Ocean Rovers* (1896).

Thompson, Benjamin (b. Woburn, Mass., March 26, 1753—d. Aug. 24, 1814), scientist, teacher, public official, philanthropist. Thompson studied astronomy, attended classes in "experimental philosophy" at Harvard, studied medicine for a while, and taught school at Concord, N.H. He married a rich widow, but fled from his wife and daughter because of his activities as a loyalist spy. In England he was knighted for his services. Thereafter he began his career as a scientist, creating ideas and devices in every possible field, especially the military. After the Revolution he went to Bavaria, where he occupied almost every office at the Elector's court and won, through the latter's influence, the title of count of the Holy Roman Empire.

Back in England once more Thompson continued his researches. He called himself Count Rumford; Rumford was the former name of the present Concord, N.H. Perhaps the first to demonstrate that heat was motion, he carried his experiments with heat into the practical realm and experimented with kitchen utensils. He also helped found the Royal Institution and gave substantial sums to the Royal Society and the American Academy of Arts and Sciences to award prizes for discoveries in light and heat. He left a fund to establish the Rumford professorship at Harvard in the physical and mathematical sciences as applied to the useful arts.

Thompson's last years were spent in Paris, where he remarried; his second wife was the widow of the French chemist Antoine Lavoisier. He was a lonely, morose old man, sometimes called "the insufferable genius." Egon Larson wrote the best biography of him, an entertaining book entitled *An American in Europe: The Biography of Benjamin Thompson, Count Rumford* (1953). Larson believes that the work Thompson did for the Royal Institution is perhaps his best title to lasting fame. Franklin D. Roosevelt once linked Thompson with Benjamin Franklin and Thomas Jefferson as "the three greatest minds that America has produced."

The Complete Works of Count Rumford were published (1870) by the American Academy of Arts and Sciences. His *Kleine Schriften* appeared in 1797. Among his other publications were: *Proposals for Forming a Public Institution* (1799); *Philosophical Papers* (1802); *On the Excellent Qualities of Coffee* (1812). Other books about Thompson and his achievements are H. Bence Jones' *The Royal Institution, Its Founders and First Professors* (1871); T. L. Nichols' *Count Rumford: How He Banished Beggary from Bavaria* (1873); J. A. Thompson's *Count Rumford of Massachusetts* (1935); Allen French's *General Gage's Informers* (1932); Thomas Martin's *The Royal Institution* (1942).

Thompson, Charles Willis (b. Kalamazoo, Mich., March 15, 1871—d. Sept. 8, 1946), newspaperman, free-lance writer. Thompson joined the staff of *The New York Times* as a reporter, later served as head of the *Times'* Washington Bureau, as editor of the Sunday *Times Book Review,* as a traveling political correspondent, and in other capacities. He was a prolific and entertaining writer. In 1922 he began free-lancing, contributing to numerous magazines. He was the author of *Party Leaders of Our Time* (1906); *The New Voter* (1918); *Presidents I've Known and Two Near-Presidents* (1929); and *The Fiery Epoch* (1931), an interpretative history of the Civil War.

Thompson, Daniel Pierce (b. Charlestown, Mass., Oct. 1, 1795—d. June 6, 1868), lawyer, judge, novelist, historian. Thompson was reared on a frontier farm at Berlin, Vermont. He graduated from Middlebury College, tutored and studied law in Virginia. Back in Montpelier, he began to practice law and engage in politics. He served as probate judge in Washington County, compiled *The Laws of Vermont . . . Including the Year 1834,* and was a founder of the Vermont Historical Society. As "A Member of the Vermont Bar," he published a lame satire on the Masonic movement, *The Adventures of Timothy Peacock, Esquire* (1835). He also edited an antislavery paper, the *Green Mountain Freeman* (1849–65) and lectured on the lyceum circuit.

Thompson is best known for his novels, which imitate James Fenimore Cooper's but are less romantic and more exact in geographical and historical data. Thompson saw himself as a preserver of certain intrinsically romantic episodes in early Vermont history. He would use, he made clear, "little more fiction than was deemed sufficient to weave them together and impart to the tissue a connected interest." This method could result in so dreary a book as *The Doomed Chief* (1860), but at its best produced the enormously popular novel *The Green Mountain Boys* (1839). *Locke Amsden; or, The Schoolmaster* (1847) gives a lovingly detailed picture of early 19th-century Vermont frontier life. Thompson's other works include: *Lucy Hosmer, or, The Guardian and the Ghost* (1848); *The Rangers, or, The Tory's Daughter* (1851); Gaut Gurley, or, The Trappers of Umbabog (1857); *The Shaker Lovers and Other Tales* (1847); *Centeola and Other Tales* (1864); and two competent histories, *History of Vermont and the Northern Campaign of 1777* (1851) and a *History of the Town of Montpelier* (1860).

John E. Flitcroft's *The Novelist of Vermont* (1929) is the only biography of Thompson. Flitcroft published the extensive manuscript of *The Honest Lawyer,* a novel Thompson was writing at the time of his death, as an appendix to his biography. Richard M. Dorson gives a good account of Thompson in *Jonathan Draws the Long Bow* (1946).

Thompson, David (b. England, April 30, 1770—d. Feb. 10, 1857), trader, explorer. Thompson came to Canada as an apprentice to the Hudson's Bay Company and spent the rest of his life there. A trader and explorer in western Canada, he kept careful journals of his various trips and made a map of the Canadian West. Because of his skill as a surveyor he was head of the British commission that fixed and marked the United States–Canadian boundary line (1816–26). Part of his journals was published as *David Thompson's Narrative of His Explorations in Western America* (1916).

Thompson, Denman (b. near Girard, Pa., Oct. 15, 1833—d. April 14, 1911), actor, playwright. As a boy, Thompson worked as handyman in a circus in Boston, then became an actor in the Royal Lyceum Company of Toronto. He was not a great success on the stage, and turned to playwriting in 1875. His first attempt, written with George W. Ryer, was a two-scene character sketch of a Yankee farmer in which he acted the leading part. This was an immediate success at its première in Pittsburgh. Thompson expanded it into a full-length play entitled *Joshua Whitcomb.* After two successful seasons in New York, Thompson wrote The Old Homestead (1886), the same play now grown to four acts. It proved so popular that most of Thompson's remaining life was devoted to playing it. Although he wrote other plays, they have been forgotten. Thompson, together with James A. Herne, started the great vogue for rural plays.

Thompson, Dorothy (b. Lancaster, N.Y., July 9, 1894—d. Jan. 31, 1961), journalist. In 1920 Miss Thompson became foreign correspondent for the Philadelphia *Public Ledger* and the New York *Evening Post;* she remained in Vienna and Berlin until 1928. Later she started a column in the New York *Herald Tribune* which in time was syndicated in two hundred other papers. She also gave a weekly news program on the radio. From 1928 until 1942 she was married to Sinclair Lewis. She was a fearless and aggressive campaigner; at her best, according to John Chamberlain, she was able to "write rings around any other newspaper columnist." Among her books are *The New Russia* (1928); *I Saw Hitler* (1932); *Refugees* (1938); *Political Guide* (1938); *Let the Record Speak* (1939); *Listen, Hans* (1942); *The Courage to Be Happy* (1957).

Thompson, Edward Herbert (b. Worcester Co., Mass., Sept. 28, 1860—d. May 11, 1935), American consul, archaeologist. Thompson was consul in Yucatán from 1885 to 1909. He made many important archaeological explorations, particularly in the Mayan ruins at Chichen Itzá. He described his discoveries in *Children of the Cave* (1929) and *People of the Serpent* (1932).

Thompson, Ernest Seton. See Ernest Thompson Seton.

Thompson, Harold W[illiam] (b. Buffalo, N.Y., June 5, 1891—d. Feb. 24, 1964), teacher, historian. Thompson taught English at the New York State College for Teachers and at Cornell University. His interest in the collection of New York folklore led to his serving as president of the American Folklore Society and the New York Folklore Society. He wrote one of the most enjoyable books in the folklore field, *Body, Boots, and Britches* (1940), a collection of tales and verses gathered in New York state. With Edith E. Cutting he edited *Pioneer Songster, Texts from the Stevens Douglass Manuscript of Western New York, 1841–1856* (1958).

Thompson, John R[euben] (b. Richmond, Va., Oct. 23, 1823—d. April 30, 1873), editor, poet. After graduating from the University of Virginia, Thompson practiced law for two years until his wealthy father purchased for him THE SOUTHERN LITERARY MESSENGER (1847), the foremost literary organ of the South, which EDGAR ALLAN POE had edited a decade earlier. As editor of the *Messenger,* Thompson published the writings of such eminent Southern authors as John Esten Cooke, Paul Hamilton Hayne, William Gilmore Simms, John Pendleton Kennedy, and Henry Timrod, and he encouraged many young writers. Later he was appointed literary editor of WILLIAM CULLEN BRYANT's New York *Evening Post.* Thompson's own poetry was popular in his day, especially his intensely patriotic war poems. In 1920 John S. Patton edited his *Poems,* with a memoir.

Thompson, [James] Maurice (b. Fairfield, Ind., Sept. 9, 1844—d. Feb. 15, 1901), poet, novelist, editor. The son of a Baptist minister who frequently moved from one small town to another, Thompson was educated by his mother. He enlisted in the Confederate Army at seventeen, served until the end of the war, then took up civil engineering. Changing to law, he opened an office in Crawfordsville, Ind., and in his spare time he wrote poetry and prose which was published in Southern magazines for some years before it was recognized in other parts of the country. *Hoosier Mosaics* (1875), a volume of sketches in dialect, was followed by a number of children's books and nature studies. His best known work, ALICE OF OLD VINCENNES, appeared in 1900. A historical novel based on Clark's 1779 expedition, it became a best seller and is still read today. From 1889 until his death he was literary editor of the *Independent.*

Thompson, Mortimer Neal. See MORTIMER NEAL THOMSON.

Thompson, Vance [Charles] (b. [?], April 17, 1863—d. June 5, 1925), biographer, editor, poet, essayist, playwright, critic. A man of versatile but superficial talent, Thompson is best remembered as the editor of the magazine M'LLE NEW YORK. JAMES HUNEKER was his fellow editor, and together they introduced to American readers many contemporary European authors. Thompson wrote several books, among them *French Portraits* (1900); *The Life and Letters of Ethelbert Nevin* (1913); *The Night Watchman and Other Poems* (1914); *Woman* (1917); *Take It from Me* (1919); *Strindberg and His Plays* (1921); *Louisa* (1924).

Thompson, Will Henry (b. Calhoun, Ga., March 10, 1848—d. [?], 1918), lawyer, Confederate soldier, expert in archery, poet. The brother of Maurice Thompson was noted chiefly for his impressive poem HIGH TIDE AT GETTYSBURG (1888). He also wrote, with his brother, *How to Train in Archery* (1879).

Thompson, William Tappan (b. Ravenna, Ohio, Aug. 31, 1812—d. March 24, 1882), humorist, editor. Thompson worked as a printer's devil in Philadelphia, served as legal assistant to the secretary of the territory of Florida, and helped AUGUSTUS BALDWIN LONGSTREET on his newspaper in Augusta, Ga. With this training behind him, he found and edited several weekly literary journals and newspapers of his own (1838–82). It was in the last few issues of his *Family Companion and Ladies' Mirror* (1843) and in his next weekly, *The Southern Miscellany* (1843–45), that his humorous letters of "Major Jones," one of the earliest representations of the Georgia cracker, appeared. The homely and amusing misadventures of this fictitious farmer were collected in *Major Jones's Courtship* (1843), a book popular in both the North and the South. *Major Jones's Chronicles of Pineville* (1845) and *Major Jones's Sketches of Travel* (1848) continued the series. Thompson defended the institution of slavery in *The Slaveholder Abroad* (1860).

Thompson, Zadock (b. Bridgewater, Vt., May 23, 1796—d. Jan. 19, 1856), historian, naturalist. Thompson was deeply committed to his native state in his life and work. After working his way through the University of Vermont by compiling almanacs, he became a tutor there (1825–33), and taught for a time in two Canadian schools. His *History of the State of Vermont* (1833) was followed by *Geography and History of Lower Canada* (1835). But Thompson's enduring work is the *History of Vermont, Natural, Civil, and Statistical* (1842), still a standard reference work. Having assembled a famous collection of local minerals, he was chosen assistant state geologist (1845). A few years later he became professor of chemistry and natural history at the University of Vermont and state naturalist.

Thomson, Charles (b. Ireland, Nov. 29, 1729—d. Aug. 16, 1824), writer on theology, translator, secretary. Brought to America as a child, Thomson was educated in American schools and taught at the Friends School in Philadelphia. He was an active patriot and became "perpetual secretary" to Congress, serving from 1774 to 1789. In his later years he devoted himself to translations of Biblical texts, including a version of the Septuagint (1808). He also published a *Synopsis of the Four Evangelists* (1815).

Thomson, E[dward] W[illiam] (b. Toronto Township, Ont., Feb. 12, 1849—d. March 5, 1924), Canadian soldier, surveyor, newspaperman, editor, writer. Thomson entered business in Philadelphia, fought in the Union Army, practiced surveying in Canada and worked for the Toronto *Globe.* For twelve years he was associate editor of the YOUTH'S COMPANION, and in 1903 became Canadian correspondent of the Boston *Transcript.* Throughout his career he wrote short stories and poems which were highly esteemed by his contemporaries. Among his books: *Old Man Savarin and Other Stories* (1895); *Smoky Days* (1901); *Between Earth and Sky* (verses, 1897); *The Many-Mansioned House and Other Poems* (1909).

Thomson [or Thompson], Mortimer Neal ["Q. K. Philander Doesticks"] (b. Riga, N.Y., Sept. 2, 1831—d. June 25, 1875), humorist, newspaperman, editor. Expelled from the University of Michigan for belonging to a secret society, Thomson for a while appeared with a traveling troupe of actors, and in 1854 began to work for newspapers. On the New York *Tribune* he finally did some serious work as a correspondent—by reporting a slave auction in Savannah (his account became a tract translated into several languages) and by serving at the front during the war. In 1854 he began to use his famous pen name—"Q.K.," standing for "Queer Kritter." He put his earlier work mainly into the form of letters addressed to newspapers; later he wrote numerous parodies on Longfellow, Scott, and others. After the war he lived in New York City, where he edited magazines for several years. He wrote DOE-STICKS WHAT HE SAYS (1855); *Plu-ri-bus-tah* (a parody of *Hiawatha,* 1856); *Nothing to Say: A Slight Slap at Mobocratic Snobbery* (1857); *The History and Records of the Elephant Club* (1856); *The Witches of N.Y.* (1859); *Lady of the Lake* (a parody of Scott, 1860).

Thomson, Virgil (b. Kansas City, Mo., Nov. 25, 1896—   ), composer, music critic. After studying and teaching music at Harvard University, Thomson lived in Paris (1925–40), where he became acquainted with GERTRUDE STEIN. With her he collaborated on two operas, *Four Saints In Three Acts* (1934) and *The Mother Of Us All* (1947). Especially admirable are the musical scores he wrote for PARE LORENTZ's two documentary films, *The Plow That Broke The Plains* (1936) and *The River* (1937). On his return to this country, Thomson became music critic for the New York *Herald Tribune* (1940). His music often has literary overtones. One of his choral works is a setting for COUNTEE CULLEN's *Medea Choruses* (1934); he wrote incidental music for plays by Sophocles, Euripides, and Shakespeare; and he won a Pulitzer prize in music for his score for Robert Flaherty's film *Louisiana Story* (1948). Among his critical and interpretive writings are *The State of Music* (1939); *The Musical Scene* (1945); *The Art of Judging Music* (1948); *Music Right and Left* (1951). Most recently he wrote scores for two films: *The Goddess* (1955) by PADDY CHAYEVSKY and a United Nations documentary *Power Among Men* (1958), as well as a *Missa Pro Defunctis* (1960) for chorus and orchestra.

Thoreau, Henry David (b. Concord, Mass., July 12, 1817—d. May 6, 1862), transcendental-

ist, essayist, naturalist, poet. Thoreau's parents were intelligent but undistinguished people whose financial resources were small, but whose home was a center of affection and vivacity. Henry, the third of four children, was a grave

child who early showed a love of nature; he was selected as the "scholar" of the family, and, at some sacrifice, was sent to the Concord Academy and to Harvard, where, although an honor student and a speaker at Commencement, he was almost unknown. During the long winter vacation of his second year at Harvard he taught school at Canton, Massachusetts, where he lived in the home of the Unitarian minister, ORESTES BROWNSON, who introduced him to the German language and literature; his knowledge of Greek and Latin was such that he could read the languages easily, and he knew Italian, French, and, to a lesser extent, Spanish. The Greek economy of style is reflected in his writings, and his wide reading—also including the English metaphysical poets, Coleridge, Carlyle, and the Hindu scriptures—influenced the development of his philosophy.

After his graduation from Harvard he and his older brother, John, opened a school in Concord in which Henry taught for three years, until John's increasingly poor health brought the venture to an end in 1841. Previously, he and John had both fallen in love with Ellen Sewall, to whom Henry proposed—and was rejected—in 1840; both his intimate friendship with his brother and his love for Ellen found expression in his idealistic and transcendental philosophy of friendship in his later writings, particularly in WALDEN. In 1841 he went to live in the home of RALPH WALDO EMERSON, whom he had met in 1837; he and Emerson formed a close friendship which continued, with some later coolness, until the end of Thoreau's life. Thus he was introduced into the transcendentalist circle (see TRANSCENDENTALISM) of which Emerson was the hub, and met MARGARET FULLER, AMOS BRONSON ALCOTT, Theodore Parker, George Ripley, WILLIAM ELLERY CHANNING [2], and others; some of his work was published in THE DIAL, of which he edited the April, 1843, issue during Emerson's absence. Emerson in particular and the transcendentalist group as a whole were an important influence in Thoreau's life and in his philosophy of independence and self-reliance. Thoreau continued to live in the Emerson household, where he had access to the library and spent much of his time writing, until 1843, when he left to become a tutor of the children of Emerson's brother William on Staten Island. While in New York he met ALBERT BRISBANE, the elder HENRY JAMES, and HORACE GREELEY, but missed his Concord home and returned in 1844.

At the age of twenty-six, still without a profession when most of his Harvard classmates were well embarked on their careers, and still without a definite aim in life, Thoreau came back to Concord and made plans to "live away in the woods," because, as he wrote later, "I wished to live deliberately, to front only the essential facts of life, and see if I could not learn what it had to teach." Emerson had bought several acres bordering on Walden pond, where he gave Thoreau permission to clear the land and build his cabin, and on July 4, 1845, Thoreau completed his house and began a residence that lasted for over two years. Although removed from the village, he was in no sense a hermit; and though without a salaried occupation, he was never idle. He walked into Concord almost every day, stopping to talk to the Irish railroad laborers on the way, and set his chair before the door of his cabin when he wished passers-by to stop and visit with him; he boated on the pond and walked in the woods, observing the life of plants and animals, and kept almost daily records in his journal; he worked on the record of the trip he took with his brother John, who had died of lockjaw in 1842, on the Concord and Merrimack rivers in August of 1839; and he cultivated his bean patch and his philosophy. During his second summer at Walden the outbreak of the Mexican War brought to a head many of the problems which impinged on the question of slavery; deciding that he could not support a government which sanctioned slavery even implicitly, Thoreau refused to pay his poll tax and was jailed. His one-man protest ended after one night when his aunt, much to his disgust, paid his tax and secured his release. He lectured on "Civil Disobedience" (originally called "Resistance to Civil Government") and published his speech as an article in the periodical *Aesthetic Papers* (1849), protesting against the apathy of men who would not defy their government when it was in conflict with their principles.

Thoreau left Walden on September 7, 1847, having completed the manuscript of A WEEK ON THE CONCORD AND THE MERRIMACK RIVERS, and began looking for a publisher. When he found none, Thoreau worked in his father's pencil factory until he could afford to pay for the book's publication himself. During this time he again lived in the Emerson house while Emerson was in Europe. The *Week* was published in 1849, and although both George Ripley and James Russell Lowell praised the book in reviews, it sold barely more than two hundred copies. The first draft of *Walden,* completed at this time, found no publisher until 1854 because of the poor reception of the earlier book. Thoreau occupied himself with various jobs, hiring out as a mason, painter, carpenter, or day laborer, for he found "the occupation of a day-laborer was the most independent of any." He developed an interest in surveying and became one of the best surveyors in Concord; he invented a graphite flotation process which made the Thoreau pencils superior to those of competitors, and thus made the family business more profitable. He also found time to continue his habitual walks in the woods and made numerous recordings and soundings, following the scientific method of Louis Agassiz, which, unfortunately, resulted in detailed factual description, but none of the discursive philosophizing which marks so much of Thoreau's best work. He made excursions to the Maine woods (which he had first visited in 1846) again in 1853 and 1857; to Cape Cod in 1849, 1850, 1855, and 1857; to Canada for twelve days with Ellery Channing in 1850; to New York again in 1856, seeing Walt Whitman, whose poetry he admired, and Henry Ward Beecher.

The passage of the Fugitive Slave Law in 1850 made Thoreau, like many other New Englanders who helped escaped slaves on their way to Canada, a criminal. He grew increasingly concerned over the sufferance given by New England, largely for economic reasons, to slavery and to the increasingly bad conditions found in New England factories; his belief in his obligation to speak out against such social and political injustice led him to lecture on "Slavery in Massachusetts" at an antislavery meeting in Framingham in 1854, and to write "Life Without Principle" (published posthumously in the *Atlantic Monthly,* October, 1863) in his journal. In 1859, after JOHN BROWN had been captured during his raid on Harper's Ferry, Thoreau was the first person in the country to speak in his defense in two eloquent and moving speeches delivered in Concord and in Boston.

Thoreau made his last excursion in 1861, a short trip to Minnesota undertaken in hopes of improving his health, which had been irreparably damaged by bronchitis several years before. He returned from Minnesota, the closest he ever came to the West he had always wanted to visit, even weaker than he was before he had left, and died of tuberculosis shortly thereafter.

From 1837, after a suggestion by Emerson, until the end of his life Thoreau kept a journal that comprises thousands of printed pages, possibly the most extensive record of a man's inner life that we possess, a kind of quarry from which Thoreau mined everything that he wrote. His other prose works, most of them derived from excursions, include *A Week on the Concord and Merrimack Rivers* (1849), which, although a factual record of his trip, is also a kind of anthology in which reside Thoreau's verse, his observations, and his thoughts; *Walden: or, Life in the Woods* (1854), his most famous work, as much a philosophical discussion of man, society, and government as it is an account of his life at Walden pond. Posthumously published were *Excursions* (1863), nine excellent essays written at different times and intended to be used as lectures, of which the most famous is "Wild Apples"; THE MAINE WOODS (1864), which records three different excursions: Thoreau's trip to Mount Katahdin (which he called "Ktaadn"), published in the *Union Magazine* in 1848; "Chesuncook," which appeared in the *Atlantic Monthly* in the same year; and "The Allegash and the East Branch," which is a marvel of precise observation; CAPE COD (1865); A YANKEE IN CANADA (1866), which derived from the 1850 trip with Channing, and describes Montreal, Quebec, Montmorency, and St. Anne. Included in the book are eight miscellaneous social and political essays, notably CIVIL DISOBEDIENCE and "A Plea for Captain John Brown." Selections from his journal were published as *Early Spring in Massachusetts* (1881); *Summer* (1884); *Winter* (1888); and *Autumn* (1892); a selection of his poems entitled *Poems of Nature* was edited by H. S. Salt and F. S. Sanborn in 1895; the twenty-volume Walden edition (14 v. of which are filled by his *Journal*) of his writings appeared in 1906. A volume of "every available piece" of his poetry was edited in 1943 by Carl Bode.

Thoreau's view of government, "That state is best which governs least," is Jeffersonian democracy pushed to its logical end. Yet Thoreau was no proponent of anarchy, no incipient revolutionist; he was an ardent individualist who believed that man should live according to the dictates of his conscience, willing to oppose the majority when the majority lived without principle. As a transcendentalist he was unwilling to sacrifice his ideals to expediency; as a realist he could see that "from a lower point of view, the Constitution, with all its faults, is very good"; but "from a point of view . . . higher still . . . who shall say . . . that [it is] worth looking at or thinking of at all?" Seeing the imperfection of man, he could still believe in the possibility of achieving perfection. Although he found his retreat at Walden valuable for him, he never advocated that others should "go and do likewise"; though he sought to live without material possessions, he did not preach asceticism as a way of life.

The best prose writer of the CONCORD SCHOOL, Thoreau is one of the great stylists of our language. He was a master of the sentence, and at their best his sentences are sheer beauty. Like the Greek authors, whom he loved, he was also a maker of phrases, but like Emerson, he arranged his sentences round an idea, and let the paragraph take care of itself. His best style is found in *Walden* and the *Journal*. His poetry, which was virtually unread in his own day, is considered by many modern critics to be far in advance of its time, reflecting the English metaphysicals as well as the Greeks, and, by its irregular meter and boldness of imagery, anticipating the later poetry of Emily Dickinson, as well as the experimental verse of the 20th century.

The greatest heritage from Thoreau is his ideas. Though he formulated no complete system of philosophy, he believed in the existence of moral values which can be directly perceived by the individual and by which the individual should live. Like the transcendentalists, he felt that many of these values were revealed in nature, and that man should live close to nature, eschewing mere material possessions and directing his life toward intellectual or spiritual fulfillment. In the tradition of Jefferson, he believed that men's lives are more important than the state, for the state is the servant and not the master of men, and that man is duty-bound to resist the state if it encroaches upon his integrity.

Thoreau's major ideas are expressed in *Walden* and in his essay on "Civil Disobedience," his most influential works. *Walden* became a textbook of the British Labour Party, and influenced Tolstoi and Gandhi. "Civil Disobedience" was read by Gandhi in a Pretoria jail, and became the basis of his passive-resistance campaign for freeing India.

There are a number of biographies of Thoreau, including. W. E. Channing, *Thoreau, the Poet-Naturalist* (1873, rev. ed. 1902); Henry S. Salt, *The Life of Henry David Thoreau* (1896); Brooks Atkinson, *Thoreau, the Cosmic Yankee* (1927); Mark Van Doren, *Henry David Thoreau: A Critical Study* (1916); Joseph Wood Krutch, *Henry David Thoreau* (1948). Other works on Thoreau are: E. Seybold, *Thoreau: The Quest and the Classics* (1951); Walter R. Harding's edition of *Thoreau: A Century of Criticism* (1954), *Thoreau Handbook* (1959), and *Thoreau, Man of Concord* (1960); H. B. Hough, *Thoreau of Walden* (1956); J. L. Shanley, *The Making of Walden* (1957); Leo Stoller, *After Walden: Thoreau's Changing Views on Economic Man* (1957); Charles R. Metzger, *Thoreau and Whitman: A Study of Their Aesthetics* (1961).

ROBERT L. CROWELL

Thorndike, Ashley Horace (b. Houlton, Me., Dec. 26, 1871—d. April 17, 1933), scholar. An authority on Elizabethan literature, Thorndike taught English at Columbia University (1906–33), where his brothers Edward L. Thorndike, a psychologist, and Lynn Thorndike, a historian, also taught. He was president of the Modern Language Association and of the Shakespeare Association of America, as well as vice-president of the National Institute of Arts and Letters. His major writings combine painstaking accuracy and thoroughness with a lively imagination. Among his works: *Elements of Rhetoric and Composition* (1905); *Everyday English* (1913); *Shakespeare's Theater* (1916); *A History of English Literature* (1920); *English Comedy* (1929).

Thorndike, Edward L[ee] (b. Williamsburg, Mass., Aug. 31, 1874—d. Aug. 9, 1949), psychologist. Educated at Wesleyan, Harvard, and Columbia universities, Thorndike became professor of educational psychology at Columbia Teacher's College, where he was one of the first in this country to apply the scientific techniques of exact quantitative measurement to problems of learning and group behavior. His interest in the relation of vocabulary to the learning process resulted in the publication of several statistical word studies and graded word lists for pedagogic use (in collaboration with Clarence Barnhart), as well as the *Thorndike-Century Junior Dictionary* (1935) and the *Thorndike-Barnhart Comprehensive Desk Dictionary* (1951). Among his other numerous publications are *Educational Psychology* (1903); *The Psychology of Learning* (1914); *Human Learning* (1931); *Human Nature and the Social Order* (1940); and *Man and His Works* (1943).

Thorndike, Lynn (b. Lynn, Mass., July 24, 1882—d. Dec. 28, 1965), historian. The younger brother of Ashley H. and Edward L. Thorndike was also a teacher, first at Western Reserve University, later at Columbia University. He made general history his subject and wrote a number of lively books. Among them: *The Place of Magic in the Intellectual History of Europe* (1905); *A Short History of Civilization* (1926); and his principal production, *A History of Magic and Experimental Science* (8 v., 1923–58).

Thorpe, Rose Hartwick (b. Mishawaka, Ind., July 18, 1850—d. July 19, 1939), poet. Author of a dozen books of fiction and poetry, Mrs. Thorpe is best known for her popular ballad, CURFEW MUST NOT RING TO-NIGHT (1867), a melodramatic narrative poem of a girl who, in order to prevent the execution of her lover at curfew time, clings to the clapper of the bell and so silences it. The idea came from a short story called *Love and Loyalty,* published anonymously in *Peterson's Magazine* (1865). Various ballads, lyrics, and "inspirational" poems are collected in *The Poetical Works of Rose Hartwick Thorpe* (1912).

Thorpe, Thomas B[angs] (b. Westfield, Mass., March 1, 1815—d. Sept. 20, 1878), humorist, editor, painter. Thorpe was well known for his pictures of frontier scenes and for his portraits. He owned and edited several newspapers in Louisiana and co-edited the popular humorous New York journal, SPIRIT OF THE TIMES. From his experiences in the army during the Mexican War he wrote *Our Army on the Rio Grande* (1846); *Our Army at Monterey* (1847); and *The Taylor Anecdote Book* (1848). He was a colonel in the Civil War. From 1869 to his death he held a civil service post in the New York Custom House. His story *The Big Bear of Arkansas* (*Spirit of the Times,* 1841), was called by Walter Blair "the most famous tall tale of the pre-Civil War Southwest." Other sketches and tales, less vigorous than *The Big Bear,* were collected in *The Mysteries of the Backwoods* (1846) and *The Hive of the Bee Hunter* (1854). See also TOM OWEN, THE BEE HUNTER.

Three Black Pennys, The (1917), a novel by JOSEPH HERGESHEIMER. This three-part romantic novel traces the decline of intemperate power and ruthless individualism through three generations of the Penny family, owners of a rich iron works in Pennsylvania. Llewellyn Jones notes that "the unity of the blood of the Pennys . . . as well as the beautifully worked technical devices in the story give the novel a unity that is absolute."

Three Lives (1909), three stories by GERTRUDE STEIN. Her first published book, *Three Lives* is written in a clear, masterful style that is far from the obscurity of much of Miss Stein's writing. The "three lives" are those of the good Anna, a purposeful, subtly domineering German serving woman; Melanctha, an uneducated but sensitive and wise Negro girl; and the gentle Lena, a pathetically feeble-minded young German maid. Of the three, the long story of MELANCTHA is the most impressive and the most popular. For many readers, *Three Lives* is Gertrude Stein at her best.

Three O'Clock Dinner (1945), a novel by JOSEPHINE PINCKNEY. Described by the author as "a comedy of manners," this novel takes as its picturesque background Charleston, S.C., in an era of transition. It describes a family scandal with wit and drama.

Three Soldiers (1921), a novel by JOHN DOS PASSOS. One of the finest of the pacifist novels to appear after World War I, *Three Soldiers* deals with John Andrews, a musician just graduated from Harvard, who joins the army in the expectation of finding comfort by contributing to a righteous cause. Instead he encounters tyranny, aimlessness, red tape, cruelty, utter boredom. His two companions, an Italian-American and a gentle farm boy, are likewise disillusioned. The farmer, goaded beyond endurance, kills an officer; Andrews deserts with him and faces a long prison term. When shocked readers protested against the realism of the novel, Dos Passos replied that his story was nearer the truth than the romantic war novels then in vogue.

Three Stories and Ten Poems (1923), the first published volume by ERNEST HEMINGWAY. It was issued in Dijon, France, by Robert McAlmon's Contact Publishing Co. in a series devoted to the works of expatriates. Altogether three hundred copies were printed. The three stories are *Up in Michigan, Out of Season,* and *My Old Man.* Six of the poems had been first published in *Poetry* (January, 1923). The verse suggests Stephen Crane and Ambrose Bierce; the stories show the influence of Sherwood Anderson and Gertrude Stein.

Threnody (1847), an elegy by RALPH WALDO EMERSON on the death of his five-year-old son Waldo. One of Emerson's most moving poems, *Threnody* begins with a lament for

"The gracious boy, who did adorn / The world whereinto he was born." The opening 175 lines embody his lament; the rest is his attempt to find consolation in transcendental unity and in the belief that the individual, dying, is "Lost in God, in Godhead found."

Thunder on the Left (1925), a novel by CHRISTOPHER MORLEY. This fantasy compares the adult world, its complexity, duplicity, and problems, with the relatively simple, ingenuous, and secure world of childhood. On his tenth birthday Martin Richardson's wish to learn what it is like to be grown up is granted; he finds himself, still with his ten-year-old perceptions and values, among his now mature friends. When the difficulties and involvements of being grown up reach a crisis, Martin wishes again and is safely back at his tenth birthday party. The novel was dramatized under the same title in 1928 by Jean Ferguson Black.

Thunder Rock (1939), a play by Robert Ardrey. With the Second World War imminent, David Charleston, a disillusioned journalist, isolates himself in Thunder Rock lighthouse on Lake Michigan. Charleston retreats from reality, creating as imaginary companions the captain and five passengers of a boat sunk off the Rock in 1849. From the hopes and fears of these projections of his own submerged conscience, he regains his confidence. *Thunder Rock* received the Sidney Howard Dramatic Award (1940) and was made into a motion picture (1944).

Thurber, James [Grover] (b. Columbus, Ohio, Dec. 8, 1894—d. Nov. 2, 1961), essayist, short-story writer, humorist, artist, playwright. Thurber grew up in Columbus in a family which, by his own account, was addicted to absurdity; some of his funniest essays deal with events in his childhood home, events which he claims to have recounted with no more than simple veracity. At the same time, however, his boyhood produced his greatest single misfortune when, as the result of an accident to one eye, the impairment of his vision which ended in eventual blindness began. Thurber entered Ohio State University in 1913, took a year off to read texts not included in the curriculum, was refused by the army because of poor eyesight when World War I broke out, spent 1917–18 as a code clerk in the State Department at Washington and in Paris, then returned to Columbus to complete his studies in 1919.

Until 1927 he worked as a newspaper reporter in Columbus, Paris, and New York. At a cocktail party in New York sometime during 1927 he met E. B. WHITE, who became a life-long friend and introduced him to Harold Ross, editor of the recently founded and somewhat unstable NEW YORKER. Ross hired Thurber to be his managing editor; but Thurber, who apparently did not relish executive authority, with some difficulty worked himself down to a position as ordinary staff writer, and then left the organization altogether to become a contributor. During Thurber's time on the staff, however, *The New Yorker* won much popularity, and there is no doubt that he had a good deal to do with fixing the tone and style of the magazine.

Thurber was probably the only contemporary

UPI

American humorist whose work is considered by the most erudite critics to be a genuine contribution to the nation's literature. In matters of style he clearly deserved this distinction: he wrote lucidly, straightforwardly, with an artist's understanding of American prose rhythms; he never condescended to the merely verbal frivolities upon which most recent comic writers have relied. But the substance of Thurber's writing is what gives it durability. His humor conveys a depth and consistency of thought and feeling which make it eminently re-readable. He wrote with a tender cynicism which converts sex, for example, into a war, but a war from which may emerge an ultimate triumph of humility. He exposed the inevitable follies of humanity with an intelligence of heart which is seen in the end to be humanity's own saving virtue. Thurber defined humor as "emotional chaos remembered in tranquility," and though the chaos is what provokes the immediate comic response, the power of ordered remembering is what perhaps remains as the permanent effect.

Thurber ranged widely in his work. He will always be known primarily as a comic writer, but many of his stories venture into fantasy of the most delicate and thoughtful kind, and some go beyond, into the starkly macabre. Thurber possessed an acute sensitivity to internal fears and bewilderments; he used these skillfully in shaping the dramatic action of many pieces. The story "The Secret Life of Walter Mitty," for example, a favorite among Thurber readers, describes the fantasies of an average little man who pictures himself doing heroic deeds. Danny Kaye starred in the movie version.

Thurber deprecated his own drawings, but they actually make a very apt complement to his writing. The seal in the bedroom, the dogs of indeterminable breed and implacable serenity, the women whose slightest gestures betray their goal of sexual tyranny, the men in the throes of tipsy revolt—all these characters, drawn with a slightly tentative simplicity, have become central figures in the sophisticated folk art of the urban 20th century.

By the late 1940's Thurber's eyesight had become so poor that he was unable to continue his drawings, but a fairly large body of work had been completed, enough to fix the patterns which other cartoonists, imitating Thurber, have turned into stereotypes of mid-century comic art.

Thurber's books include: *Is Sex Necessary?* (with E. B. White, 1929); *The Owl in the Attic and Other Perplexities* (1931); *The Seal in the Bedroom and Other Predicaments* (1932); *My Life and Hard Times* (1933); *The Middle-Aged Man on the Flying Trapeze* (1935); *Let Your Mind Alone* (1937); *The Cream of Thurber* (1939); *The Male Animal* (a play with Elliot Nugent, 1940); *Fables for Our Times* (1940, 1956); *My World—and Welcome to It* (1942); *Men, Women, and Dogs* (1943); *The White Deer* (a fantasy for children, 1945); *The Thurber Carnival* (1945); *The Beast in Me and Other Animals* (1949); *The Thirteen Clocks* (a children's story, 1950); *The Thurber Album* (1952); *Thurber Country* (1953); *The Secret Dream of Stanley Caldwell* (1954); *Thurber's Dogs* (1955); *The Wonderful O* (a children's fantasy, 1957); *Alarms and Diversions* (1957); *The Years with Ross* (a memoir of Harold Ross, 1959). His last book of essays, *Lanterns and Lances*, was published in 1961.

Thurman, Wallace (b. Salt Lake City, Utah, Aug. 16, 1902—d. Dec. 22, 1934), editor, novelist, playwright. Thurman in his brief life gave great promise. He served on the editorial staff of *The Messenger* and a publishing firm, and helped found two short-lived magazines, *Fire* and *Harlem*. He wrote two novels, *The Blacker the Berry* (1929) and *Infants of the Spring* (1932); a play, *Harlem*, written with W. J. Rapp, was produced in 1929. He was definitely an individualist, one who turned his keen satirical powers against members of his own Negro race. *The Blacker the Berry* attacked some of the aspects of the so-called New Negro movement and lampooned the racial pride exhibited by many Negroes. Mencken and Van Vechten seem to have been strong influences on Thurman.

Thurso's Landing (in *Thurso's Landing and Other Poems*, 1932), a narrative poem by ROBINSON JEFFERS. The characters in *Thurso's Landing* embody, in varying degrees, the death wish which Jeffers feels to be a characteristic of modern civilization. The poem deals with Helen Thurso's ambivalent attitudes toward her husband, whom she alternately loves and hates, toward her crippled brother-in-law, who loves her, and toward death itself, which simultaneously fascinates and repels her.

Thurston, Lorrin Andrews (b. Honolulu, Hawaii, July 31, 1858—d. May 11, 1931), lawyer, editor, politician, memoirist. Thurston began practicing law in Hawaii, and when the revolutionary movement started there in 1887 he was one of its leaders. He was Minister of the Interior in a reform government, and when Queen Liliuokalani attempted to squelch the new administration, he led the movement which deposed her (1894). He became Hawaii's envoy to the United States and helped establish a new constitution for Hawaii. He was a member of the negotiating team that concluded the annexation of the islands by the United States in 1897. He owned and edited the Honolulu *Advertiser*. His *Memoirs of the Hawaiian Revolution* appeared in 1936, as did a collection of his *Writings*.

Thwaites, Reuben Gold (b. Dorchester, Mass., May 15, 1853—d. Oct. 22, 1913), librarian, editor, historian. In his youth Thwaites worked as a Wisconsin farmer, teacher, and a reporter on the Oshkosh *Times*. After attending Yale, he became managing editor of the Wisconsin *State Journal*, and later secretary of the Wisconsin Historical Society. With a group of assistants he collected and translated the seventy-three-volume *Jesuit Relations and Allied Documents* (1896–1901). Among his original writings were *Father Marquette* (1902) and *France in America* (1905). See also EARLY WESTERN TRAVELS.

Thwing, Charles F[ranklin] (b. New Sharon, Me., Nov. 9, 1853—d. Aug. 29, 1937), clergyman, teacher, educational administrator, historian. Ordained as a Congregational minister in 1879, Thwing became president of Western Reserve University in 1890 and served until 1921, at the same time serving as secretary of the Carnegie Foundation for the Advancement of Learning (1905–21). He wrote many books dealing with the history and the needs of American colleges and universities. Among them: *American Colleges* (1878); *Within College Walls* (1893); *The American College in American Life* (1897); *College Administration* (1900); *History of Higher Education in America* (1906); *Universities of the World* (1911); *The College President* (1925); *Education and Religion* (1929).

Ticknor, Caroline (b. Boston, [?], 1866—d. May 11, 1937), biographer, literary historian. Miss Ticknor wrote some carefully documented volumes on literary figures, among them: *Hawthorne and His Publisher* (1913); *Poe's Helen*

(1916); *May Alcott* (1928). Hervey Allen in his *Israfel* (1934) acknowledged his indebtedness to her work on Poe.

Ticknor, Francis Orray (b. Fortville, Ga., Nov. 13, 1822—d. Dec. 18, 1874), physician, poet. Ticknor studied medicine in Philadelphia and New York, then returned to Georgia to practice. He was in charge of war hospitals in and around Columbus. He loved writing verse and composed many of his poems on prescription blanks while in the saddle on the way to see patients. His *Poems* were published in 1879; a later edition (1911), prepared by Michelle Cutliff Ticknor, included some hitherto unpublished poems. Ticknor's poetry was obviously influenced by Robert Browning.

Ticknor, George (b. Boston, Aug. 1, 1791—d. Jan. 26, 1871), educator, biographer, literary historian, scholar. Ticknor studied French, Spanish, Latin, and Greek as a boy, was adjudged ready for college at the age of ten, but did not actually begin until he was fourteen. After graduating from Dartmouth, he read for the law, was admitted to the bar, and practiced for a year. But he was much more drawn to scholarly pursuits and—lured by the then superior educational methods in Germany—learned German, then joined EDWARD EVERETT in graduate work at Göttingen. After his studies there he traveled elsewhere in Europe, including six months in Spain.

In his twenty-fifth year, Ticknor accepted the new Smith Professorship of French, Spanish, and Belles Lettres at Harvard. His rich *Syllabus of the Spanish Literature Course* (1823), the first of its kind in any language, systematically covered the materials in the best form of German historical criticism. He reorganized his own department on lines patterned after Göttingen and attempted—without complete success—to reform the system of instruction in the entire university. He resigned in 1835, handing over his chair to Henry Wadsworth Longfellow.

In Boston he devoted himself to writing his great *History of Spanish Literature* (3 v., 1849, 1872), to charitable pursuits, to clubs, and to a grand effort to make the Boston Public Library the greatest in America. He returned to Europe to search out books for the Library, to which he was to leave his incomparable collection of rare books on Spanish literature. In 1864 he published a biography of his old friend, *Life of William Hickling Prescott*. For all his learning Ticknor remained a literary colonial: one searches his letters in vain for any mention of such men as Emerson or Thoreau, or of the exciting literary and philosophical movements afoot in New England at the time; they were too radical for his tastes. He brought to his *History of Spanish Literature* everything but an intuitive sympathy for the romantic Spanish genius, although it is still a standard reference work. Ticknor also wrote a *Life of Lafayette* (1824). Anna Ticknor and George S. Hillard compiled *Life, Letters and Journals of George Ticknor* (2 v., 1876). Orie W. Long's *Literary Pioneers: Early American Explorers of European Culture* (1935) describes Ticknor's stay at Göttingen.

Tides of Barnegat, The (1906), a novel by F. HOPKINSON SMITH. To protect her sister Lucy, Jane Cobden breaks off her own engagement to marry a doctor in the fishing community of Barnegat on the Jersey coast and instead takes Lucy to Paris, where Lucy bears an illegitimate son. Back in Barnegat, the son joins a lifesaving station, and tries to rescue his father in a storm; both drown. The secret comes out, and Jane and the doctor finally marry.

Tietjens, Eunice [Strong] (b. Chicago, July 29, 1884—d. Sept. 6, 1944), poet, novelist, editor, lecturer. Mrs. Paul Tietjens, later Mrs. Cloyd Head, was active in the vigorous Chicago group of writers in the early 20th century. She published collections of poems, including *Profiles from China* (1917), *Body and Raiment* (1919), and *Leaves in Windy Weather* (1929), wrote novels, including *Jake* (1921), and juvenile fiction. She was a great traveler and wrote textbooks on Japan (1924) and China (1930), prepared an anthology of *Poetry of the Orient* (1928), and lectured on the Far East at the University of Miami (1933–35). *The World at My Shoulder* (1938) is an autobiography. Among her greatest services was assisting HARRIET MONROE on the staff of *Poetry* from 1913 to her death. In her autobiography Mrs. Tietjens stressed the great influence that Miss Monroe had exerted on her development as a poet.

Tiger-Lilies (1867), a novel by SIDNEY LANIER. A tangled tale of Southern chivalry, with melodramatic incidents, stilted dialogue, and excessive literary allusions, *Tiger-Lilies* is lifted above utter banality by its heartfelt lyric passages on music and by the vivid account of young Philip Sterling's experiences as a prisoner of the Union Army. (Lanier was a prisoner of war for four months.) Also striking is the characterization of the impoverished, embittered Gorm Smallin, a Confederate deserter who shoots Philip's parents and burns down their home in his rage against "rich folks."

Tilbury Town. The imaginary scene of many of EDWIN ARLINGTON ROBINSON's poems. Drawn partly from Robinson's home town of Gardiner, Me., it is inhabited by people of the middle class, materialistic, prudish, and smugly conventional. Richard Cory, Flammonde, Miniver Cheevy, old Eben Flood, and other protagonists of Robinson's poems are either rebels against or outcasts from the town. Lawrence Thompson edited a selection of these poems in *Tilbury Town* (1953).

Tilden, Samuel J[ones] (b. New Lebanon, N.Y., Feb. 9, 1814—d. Aug. 4, 1886), governor, lawyer, philanthropist. Tilden was a staunch Democrat; he supported President Van Buren and labored for the nomination of Polk. After studying law at New York University, he became corporation counsel for New York City, gained fame as an outstanding lawyer, and accumulated a large fortune. His success in exposing and extirpating the "Tweed Ring," on which he wrote *The New York City "Ring"* (1873) (see TAMMANY), helped him to win the gubernatorial election as a reform candidate (1874). Nominated for the Presidency by the Democratic party in 1876, he was apparently elected by a majority of 250,000 votes, but an electoral committee with a Republican majority of one gave the election to RUTHERFORD B. HAYES. The Tilden Trust of $3,000,000 formed the basis for what is now the New York Public Library. John Bigelow edited *The Writings and Speeches of Samuel J. Tilden* (2 v., 1885) and wrote *The Life of Samuel J. Tilden* (2 v., 1895). A later biography is A. C. Flick and G. S. Lobrano's *Samuel J. Tilden* (1939).

Tillich, Paul (b. Germany, Aug. 20, 1886 —d. Oct. 22, 1965), philosopher, theologian. Dr. Tillich received many degrees; he studied at the universities of Berlin, Tübingen, Halle, and Breslau. He served as chaplain in the German Army during World War I; later he taught theology and philosophy at the universities of Berlin, Marburg, Dresden, and Frankfurt-am-Main. The rise of Nazism forced him to leave Germany. Coming to New York, Dr. Tillich taught at the Union Theological Seminary from 1933 until 1955, becoming an American citizen in 1940. He was appointed University Professor at Harvard—a special honor that permitted him freedom to work in any field he chose. His writings are concerned for the most part with the line dividing theology and philosophy and the relationship between religion and psychology. They reveal that his theology was built on "the method of correlation between questions arising out of the human predicament and the answers given in the classical symbols of religion." Dr. Tillich's books include: *The Religious Situation* (1932); *The Interpretation of History* (1936); *The Protestant Era* (1948); *Systematic Theology, Volume I* (1951); *The Courage to Be* (1952); *Love, Power and Justice* (1954); *The New Being* (1955); *The Shaking of the Foundations* (1948); *Biblical Religion and the Search for Ultimate Reality* (1955); *Dynamics of Faith* (1957); *Systematic Theology, Volume II* (1959); *Theology and Culture* (1959).

Tillie: A Mennonite Maid (1904), a novel by HELEN R. MARTIN. Tillie, a Pennsylvania Dutch girl hungry for the better things of life, is befriended by a sympathetic teacher and grows up to escape her father's harsh domination. The novel's melodramatic plot and fine exploitation of local color made a dramatic version of the story a perennial favorite with summer theater audiences.

Tilton, Theodore (b. New York City, Oct. 2, 1835—d. May 25, 1907), editor. Tilton is remembered chiefly for his famous damage suit against HENRY WARD BEECHER, in which he charged adultery with Mrs. Tilton. From 1883 on he lived abroad. He was the author of numerous stories and of a book of *Sonnets Addressed to the Memory of Frederick Douglass* (1895). The ancient sensation of the Beecher-Tilton scandal was vivaciously revived in Robert

Shaplen's *Free Love and Heavenly Sinners* (1954).

Time and **Time, Inc.** Time, Inc., is a corporation that publishes several magazines. The first was *Time* (1923). The others are *Life*, the name of which was acquired (1936) from the owners of the humorous magazine so called; FORTUNE; *Architectural Forum—House & Home;* and *Sports Illustrated*. At one time the corporation also owned *Tide*, an advertising magazine (sold in 1930). HENRY R. LUCE is editor-in-chief of *Time* and *Life* and director of Time, Inc.

The official title of *Time* is *Time, The Weekly Newsmagazine*. Its founders were Luce and his fellow student at Yale, BRITON HADDEN. At college Hadden often talked about how poorly informed the American people were, and how something should be done about it. He and Luce brooded about getting out some kind of paper during the three or four years after they left Yale. On March 3, 1923, the first issue of *Time* appeared and produced a sensation. On Feb. 27, 1929, Hadden died; by that time the circulation was well over 200,000. A quarter of a century later it was about 2 million. In March, 1931, the popular MARCH OF TIME program began to appear on the air; in February, 1935, appeared the first issue of the "March of Time" movie series. May, 1941, saw the first Latin-American issue of *Time*. In February, 1943, a Canadian edition appeared. In April, 1945, *Time's* European edition was started in Paris.

The departments in *Time* cover the wide range of American interests intelligently, fully, and often with material not available elsewhere. There are departments on medicine, science, religion, education, drama, books, and other areas of human endeavor, as well as more general news. Each issue begins with a sheaf of letters; these are often accompanied by acknowledgments of error or by tart replies to censure. A standing feature is the "cover story," which deals, thoroughly and not always without malice, with the person depicted on the cover. One man who had been subjected to the series of interviews which eventuated in a cover story, J. P. Marquand, turned the tables by describing the process in his novel, MELVILLE GOODWIN, U.S.A. (1951).

In the course of its picturesque and lively years three charges have frequently been made against *Time:* first, that its pages are biased; second, that it is frequently vindictive and gratuitously insulting in its description of individuals; third, that its special style is rhetorical and artificial. *Time* freely admits the first charge; its publisher, James A. Linen, acknowledged the fact that the reporters and the editor "made a critical judgment and appraisal of the meaning of events." As to the second charge, *Time* merely smiles. There is no doubt about the artificiality, sometimes carried to irritating lengths, of *Time's* style. But this style served admirably at the beginning of *Time's* career to attract wide attention and has since been somewhat modified and mellowed. Lloyd Morris pointed out (*Post-script to Yesterday*, 1947) that once readers had "mastered its peculiarities and discounted its glibness," they found *Time* a useful "blend of hard facts, owlish gossip, humor, and often shrewd analysis."

So piquant a subject as *Time* has naturally not escaped the attention of novelists and playwrights. William Saroyan gave some space to the magazine in his play *Love's Old Sweet Song* (1939). Jack Iams' *Profit by Experience* (1943) and Charles Wertenbaker's *The Death of Kings* (1954) are both novels about the magazine. George Frazier's chronicle *It's About Time* (1951) was announced as "the first full-length study" of the periodical. Geoffrey T. Hellman sharply satirized "Timestyle" in "*Time*" *Lumbers On* (*The New Yorker*, April 16, 1955).

Time of Your Life, The (1939), a play by WILLIAM SAROYAN. One of the author's most successful fantasies, a blend of social consciousness and poetic symbolism, this play surprised its backers by becoming a Broadway hit. Laid in a waterfront saloon, it takes as its themes the need to make the most of life, to be compassionate toward the weak, and to oppose the enemies of life, with force if necessary. A remarkable collection of lovable eccentrics represent the weak—a dreaming prostitute, a starving Negro musician, an ex-frontiersman, an Arab with a mouth-organ, and a young hopeful pouring nickels into a pinball machine all through the play. The forces of evil are represented by Detective Blick of the Vice Squad, whom many critics identified with Hitler. The play was given the New York Drama Critics' Award, also the Pulitzer Prize for 1940, which Saroyan refused.

Timoleon (1891), a volume of poetry by HERMAN MELVILLE. Although the last of Melville's works published in his lifetime, much of *Timoleon*—certainly all the section entitled *Fruit of Travel Long Ago*—was composed in the years immediately following his trip to the Mediterranean and the Near East in 1857.

Melville was a poet of high seriousness, and, unlike Poe, sought an intellectual as well as emotional effect. However, he is not a master metrist, and his ideas are often cramped by or incased in unsuitable verse forms, thus losing some of their potency. One may gain insight into both the direction of his thoughts and the shortcomings of his execution by reading "The Enthusiast," on the maintenance of high ideals; "Art," on the agonies of artistic creation; "The Garden of Metrodorus," on the ambiguity of silence; "The Age of the Antonines," on the sterility of Western civilization; and "After the Pleasure Party," on the frustration of unfulfilled sexuality.

Timrod, Henry (b. Charleston, S.C., Dec. 8, 1828—d. Oct. 6, 1867), poet, war correspondent. At the Coates School in Charleston Timrod met PAUL HAMILTON HAYNE, who became his lifelong friend and posthumous editor. He entered the University of Georgia, where he became absorbed in the classical writers, but illness and lack of funds forced his withdrawal

before graduation. He attempted to read for the law, but abandoned it for poetry and for several years was a private tutor.

Timrod's early work contains translations of Catullus, and his immersion in the classical

poets is clear in his poetry. In 1860 a small collection of nature lyrics, the only book of his own which Timrod ever saw in print, was published. Between 1850 and 1860 he wrote four major critical essays on poetry for a Charleston periodical, *Russell's Magazine*. His reputation rests chiefly on his war poems, which earned him the title "Laureate of the Confederacy." His best known poems are *The Cotton Boll* and ETHNOGENESIS. He was, Jay Hubbell says in *The Last Years of Henry Timrod, 1864–1867* (1941), "singularly free from Southern literary provincialism," and his skillful use of classical forms, especially the ode, gave his poems a severity that saved them from the overemotionalism of some of his contemporaries.

Timrod's health prevented combatant service, but he was for some time a war correspondent. As editor of the Columbia *South Carolinian* (1864) he felt able to marry Kate S. Goodwin, to whom his *Katie* poems are dedicated, and entered into a brief period of happiness. But the capture and burning of Columbia (Feb. 17, 1865) completely ruined him. The rest of his life was consumed in a series of ineffectual jobs, malnutrition, and despair. He was unable even to raise the few dollars necessary for a trip to New York City to meet C. B. Richardson, the publisher, and finally succumbed to the tuberculosis from which he had suffered for many years.

Paul Hamilton Hayne's collection *The Poems of Henry Timrod* (1873) contains the bulk of Timrod's poems and a *Memoir* of the poet's life. In 1942 Guy A. Cardwell, Jr., issued *The Uncollected Poems of Henry Timrod* and Edd Winfield Parks published *The Essays of Henry Timrod*, which he introduced with a long critical essay on Timrod's principles and prosody. Biographies were written by G. A. Wauchope (1915) and Henry T. Thompson (1928).

Tindall, William York (b. Williamstown, Vt., March 7, 1903–   ), teacher, critic. Tindall studied at Columbia University, receiving his Ph.D. in 1934. Prior to becoming Professor of English at Columbia, he taught at New York and Northwestern Universities. As a critic he reveals a thorough comprehension of the contemporary British and American literary scenes. It was in his work on James Joyce that Tindall particularly distinguished himself, receiving recognition as an authority on both the man and his works. Books by Tindall: *John Bunyan* (1934); *D. H. Lawrence and Susan His Cow* (1939); *Forces in Modern British Literature* (1947); *James Joyce* (1950); *Joyce's Chamber Music* (1954); *The Literary Symbol* (1955); *Reader's Guide to James Joyce* (1959); *Beckett's Bums* (1960); *The Joyce Country* (1960).

Tinker, Chauncey Brewster (b. Auburn, Me., Oct. 22, 1876–d. March 16, 1963), biographer. Tinker graduated from Yale in 1899, a year later received his M.A. while teaching English at the Sheffield Scientific School. In 1902, after earning his Ph.D., he taught English at Bryn Mawr, returning to Yale in 1903 as Emily Sanford Professor in English Literature. During World War I he served as captain in the Military Intelligence Division of the General Staff. *The Translations of Beowulf: A Critical Biography* (1903) was followed by *The Salon and English Letters* (1915). *Young Boswell* (1922), a biography, was so popular that the author became known as "Boswell's Tinker." *The Letters of James Boswell* appeared in 1924. Tinker's lectures at Harvard on fine arts in 1930 and on poetry in 1937–38 were published as *Painter and Poet* (1938). He was a much-loved teacher during his long years at Yale, broadening the horizons of his students. He was made keeper of rare books in the Sterling Memorial Library at Yale in 1931. One of his prime purposes was to gather at Yale the world's greatest collection of books on Johnson and Boswell, a purpose in which he fully succeeded.

Tinker, Edward Larocque (b. New York City, Sept. 12, 1881–   ), historian, lawyer, novelist, linguist, banker, printer. A man of inherited wealth, Tinker followed many lines of intellectual interest in addition to serving as an officer of a realty company and a banking official. He made printing a hobby and became a wood engraver. His marriage to Frances McKee of New Orleans gave him a deep interest in Louisiana; he took a doctor's degree at the Sorbonne with a thesis on *Les Écrits de Langue Française en Louisiane au XIXe Siècle* (1932), later published *Bibliography of French Newspapers and Periodicals of Louisiana* (1933) and *Gombo: The Creole Dialect of Louisiana* (1934). With his wife he wrote four novelettes, published as *Old New Orleans* (4 v., 1930). He made a large, probably unrivaled, collection of

Lafcadio Hearn's writings and wrote a book on *Lafcadio Hearn's American Days* (1924). *The Palingenesis of Craps* appeared in 1933. Tinker later became interested in literature about horses and horsemen; he described *The Gaucho and the Birth of a Literature* (1948) and *The Horsemen of the Americas and the Literature They Inspired* (1953). *Creole City* (1953) is about New Orleans. *Life and Literature of the Pampas* appeared in 1960.

Tish. A character in a group of stories by MARY ROBERTS RINEHART, beginning with *The Amazing Adventures of Letitia Carberry* (1911). Mrs. Rinehart wrote a number of books about the amusing adventures of Tish, an old maid, and her two middle-aged cronies, Aggie and Lizzie. Among the other titles are *Tish* (1916); *More Tish* (1922); *Tish Plays the Game* (1926); and *The Best of Tish* (1955).

Titan, The (1914), a novel by THEODORE DREISER. This sequel to THE FINANCIER (1912) continues the story of Frank Cowperwood, based on the life of the public utilities tycoon Charles Tyson Yerkes (1837–1905). After marrying Aileen Butler, his former mistress, Cowperwood moves from Philadelphia to Chicago, where he almost succeeds in establishing a monopoly of public utilities. Dissatisfaction with Aileen leads him to a series of affairs with other women; when the Chicago citizenry frustrates his financial schemes, he departs for Europe with Berenice Fleming, the lovely young daughter of the madam of a Louisville brothel. Cowperwood, a powerful, irresistibly compelling man, driven by his own need for power, beautiful women, and social prestige, at last experiences "the pathos of the discovery that even giants are but pigmies, and that an ultimate balance must be struck." Dreiser wrote a sequel, *The Stoic*, which was published posthumously (1947), thus concluding "the trilogy of desire" with Cowperwood's life in England.

Titchener, Edward Bradford (b. England, Jan. 11, 1867–d. Aug. 3, 1927), psychologist, teacher, editor. Educated at Oxford and Leipzig under Wilhelm Wundt, Titchener became an assistant professor of psychology at Cornell University, continued to teach there until his death. He became a noted authority in his field, edited the *American Journal of Psychology*, wrote numerous books on psychology. He was a leader in the structuralist school, which placed a strong emphasis on experiment and research. A group of psychologists whom he invited to annual meetings from 1904 on became in 1928 the Society of Experimental Psychologists. Among his books: *An Outline of Psychology* (1896); *A Primer of Psychology* (1898); *Experimental Psychology* (2 v., 1901, 1905); *Lectures on the Elemental Psychology of Feeling and Attention* (1908); *Lectures on the Elementary Psychology of the Thought Processes* (1909); *Textbook of Psychology* (2 v., 1909, 1910); *Beginners' Psychology* (1915).

Titcomb, Timothy. The pen name of J. G. HOLLAND.

To a Waterfowl (1815), a poem by WILLIAM CULLEN BRYANT. James Russell Lowell in *A Fable for Critics* (1848) accused Bryant of being "as cool and as dignified,/ As a smooth, silent iceberg, that never is ignified," but he certainly was not that in this intense, emotional poem. Written in the poet's twenty-first year, it was called by Matthew Arnold the best short poem in the language. It is said that in the winter of 1815 Bryant was journeying to Plainfield, Mass., where he expected to make his living as a lawyer. He was "very forlorn and desolate indeed, not knowing what was to become of him in the big world," as he later wrote in describing the journey. Then suddenly he saw against the sunset a solitary bird making its way across the sky. The poem tells the thoughts that occurred to him and the moral inspiration and belief in divine guidance that the bird's flight gave him. The metric form and the rhythm of the stanzas lend an effect of skimming to the poem.

Tobacco (*Penn State Froth*, November, 1915), a humorous poem by Graham Lee Hemminger. Hemminger, a student at Pennsylvania State College and editor of *Froth*, had, so the story goes, two blank inches in the middle of a column to fill up. He wrote his eight-line poem, beginning "Tobacco is a dirty weed: / I like it," as an answer to the antismoking campaign of one of the deans. The poem was widely reprinted and parodied.

Tobacco Road (1932), a novel by ERSKINE CALDWELL. Jeeter Lester, a Georgia farmer without money to plant a crop, loves the land, but the land is worn out. He lives in hopeless poverty on Tobacco Road with his starving old mother, his sickly wife Ada, and his two children, sixteen-year-old Dude and Ellie May, who has a harelip. A third child, Pearl, has been married at the age of twelve to Lov Bensey, a railroad worker. When the widowed Sister Bessie Rice induces Dude to marry her by buying him a new automobile, Dude accidentally kills his grandmother and wrecks the vehicle. Pearl runs away from Lov Bensey; Ellie May happily goes to live with him; and Jeeter and Ada, left alone one night, perish when their shack burns down. The hapless Lesters, at once comical and shockingly degenerate, became widely familiar to the public through Jack Kirkland's dramatization (1933), which ran for 3,182 performances on Broadway, and through a motion picture (1941). Caldwell, in a special introduction for the play (1948), remarked: "No one will find here the Old South or the New South, the Deep South, or the Romantic South, but perhaps he will find a broad expanse of peopled land between the Piedmont and Low Country."

Tocqueville, Alexis [Charles Maurice Henri Clérel] de (b. France, July 29, 1805—d. April 16, 1859), lawyer, sociologist, public official, writer. De Tocqueville is chiefly remembered for one of the greatest political, social, and cultural investigations ever made, his *Democracy in America* [*De la Démocratie en Amérique*],

which was published in two volumes (1835, 1840), immediately rendered into English by Henry Reeve for a British edition (1835, 1840). This edition has been reprinted many times, with corrections and revisions, in England and this country. A definitive American edition was prepared by Phillips Bradley (1945). It has also appeared in many French editions and has been translated into Danish, German, Hungarian, Italian, Russian, Serbian, Spanish, and Swedish.

Tocqueville began as a lawyer, took his final degree in 1826, and then began the travels he was so fond of—in Italy and Sicily. While still in his twenties he was appointed an assistant magistrate. The French government sent him to the United States in 1831, along with his friend and fellow magistrate Gustave de Beaumont, to study the American prison system. From New York City they traveled as far east as Boston, as far west as Green Bay, as far north as Sault Ste. Marie and Quebec, as far south as New Orleans. Back in France they wrote *Du Système Pénitentionaire aux États-Unis et de son Application en France* (1833), which appeared in the same year in the United States.

Meanwhile Tocqueville proceeded to write and publish his masterwork. He was elected to the French Academy in 1841, was a member of the Chamber of Deputies until Louis Napoleon's *coup d'état* (1851) forced him into retirement. With his new leisure he began a study of French history and democracy, publishing his *Histoire Philosophique de Règne de Louis XV* in 1846, his analysis of *L'Ancien Régime et la Révolution* in 1856.

In his great book it becomes clear that this fastidious, highly cultured young aristocrat was taken aback by some of the manifestations of Jacksonian democracy. Yet he always retains his sense of justice in his measured and brilliant analysis. The first part of his book treats specific aspects of government and politics: the principle of the people's sovereignty, the nature of the states and local communities, judicial power, the Constitution, political parties, liberty of the press, the working of suffrage, the consequences of the unlimited power of the majority, the ways in which its "tyranny" is mitigated, the present and probable future condition of the three races inhabiting American territory. The last section considers difficulties that would face the creation of an aristocracy and analyzes the causes of the commercial prosperity of the United States. The second volume is more subtle and evinces an astounding power to distinguish a pattern of American traits and tendencies. It examines the influence of democracy on American manners, religion, science, literature, and art. Tocqueville was sometimes remarkably acute in his analyses; he regarded local government as the taproot of democracy. Throughout the book it is obvious that he was not intent on instructing Americans but rather in providing data that would help the French in their quest for an efficient government.

Tocqueville's book is widely recognized as an important political treatise. Its implications and conclusions have been examined anew in each generation, and the book is still healthily alive—as witness the frequent quotation since World War II of Tocqueville's comparison of the United States and Russia: "Each of them seems to be marked by the will of Heaven to sway the destinies of half the globe," with freedom as the principle instrument of America, servitude, of Russia. Horace Greeley felt that it was "by far the most important book that has been written on the nature and influence of democracy." Harold Laski concluded that *Democracy in America* is "perhaps the greatest work ever written in one country by the citizen of another."

Numerous books and articles have been published on Tocqueville. Some of those in English include M. C. M. Simpson's *Memoirs, Letters, and Remains of Alexis de Tocqueville* (2 v., 1861) and his *Correspondence and Conversations of Alexis de Tocqueville with Nassau William Senior from 1834 to 1859* (2 v., 1872); James Bryce's *The Predictions of Hamilton and Tocqueville* (1887); G. W. Pierson's *Tocqueville and Beaumont in America* (1938); Jacob P. Mayer's *Alexis de Tocqueville* (1940) and his edition of *The Recollections of Alexis de Tocqueville* (1949).

Todd, Mabel Loomis (b. Cambridge, Mass., Nov. 10, 1856—d. Oct. 4, 1932), lecturer, editor, author. In 1879 Mrs. Todd went to Amherst College with her husband, a professor of astronomy. With her intelligence, charm, and boundless energy, she made her home a salon for music lovers, taught music in two private schools, and founded a number of clubs. She accompanied her husband on astronomical expeditions to Japan, Russia, South America, and other lands, writing accounts of her travels for *The Nation*, the *Century*, and other publications. She also wrote *Footprints* (1883), a novelette; *Total Eclipses of the Sun* (1894), popular science; *A Cycle of Sonnets* (1896); and two travel books, *Corona and Coronet* (1898) and *Tripoli, the Mysterious* (1912).

Mrs. Todd is best known, however, for her acquaintanceship with Emily Dickinson's family circle and for her editorial work on Emily Dickinson's manuscripts. After Emily's death, her sister Lavinia asked Mrs. Todd to make a selection from the manuscript poems and to prepare them for publication. With the aid of Thomas W. Higginson she edited *Poems*, first series (1890) and *Poems*, second series (1891). She was the sole editor of *Letters of Emily Dickinson* (1894) and *Poems*, third series (1896). A revised and enlarged edition of the *Letters* appeared in 1931. Because of the eccentricities of Emily Dickinson's handwriting and punctuation and because of her calculated avoidance of exact rhymes, both Mrs. Todd and Higginson engaged in "creative editing" of the texts. *Bolts of Melody: New Poems of Emily Dickinson* (1945) was completed by her daughter Mrs. Millicent Todd Bingham, who is also the author of *Ancestors' Brocades: The Literary Debut of Emily Dickinson* (1945); and two other volumes about the Dickinson circle: *Emily Dickinson, A Revelation* (1954) and *Emily Dickinson's Home* (1955).

Togo, Hashimura. The leading character in Wallace Irwin's satirical *Letters of a Japanese Schoolboy* (1909) and its sequel, *Mr. Togo, Maid of All Work* (1913). See WALLACE IRWIN.

To Have and Have Not (1937), a novel by ERNEST HEMINGWAY. Harry Morgan, a native of Key West, is forced by the depression to turn to smuggling, bootlegging, and finally to helping four Cuban revolutionaries escape. Fatally wounded in a fight, Morgan is picked up by the Coast Guard and dies, gasping, "One man alone ain't got . . . no chance." In *Ernest Hemingway* (1952), Philip Young writes, "The contrast between the Haves and the Have Nots in the novel . . . is unconvincing." But the author's new concern with social problems presaged *For Whom the Bell Tolls* (1940).

To Have and to Hold (1900), a novel by MARY JOHNSTON. The Virginia colony of 1621 forms the background of this romantic tale. When adventurous Ralph Percy goes to Jamestown to choose a wife from a shipload of girls sent over from England, he little suspects the noble birth of the beautiful woman who throws herself on his mercy. Jocelyn—fleeing the loathsome advances of Lord Carnal—at first despises her husband. But subsequent adventures on land and sea reveal his courage and devotion and love finally blossoms. In the midst of all this derring-do *To Have and to Hold* presents an animated picture of primitive America as it must have looked to colonizers from a more civilized land. It is one of the most popular historical novels ever produced in the United States.

To Helen. The title of two poems by EDGAR ALLAN POE, one published in 1831 ("Helen, thy beauty is to me"), the other in 1848 ("I saw thee once—once only—years ago"). The first was inscribed to the memory of Mrs. Jane Stith Stanard of Richmond, Va., for whom Poe had cherished, in his own words, "the first purely ideal love of my soul." It is without question one of his most beautiful lyrics, even though it contains some obscure allusions. The second poem was addressed to MRS. SARAH HELEN WHITMAN of Providence, R.I., of whom he caught a glimpse one evening when he stayed overnight in Providence. Later he became acquainted with Mrs. Whitman and was betrothed to her. She reluctantly concluded that she could not marry him, but always remained his most ardent defender. In the two poems Poe shows his equal mastery of the rhymed stanza and blank verse.

Tol'able David (1919), a short story by JOSEPH HERGESHEIMER. This tale of a West Virginia mountain boy's triumph over great odds appeared in the collection *The Happy End* (1919). Sixteen-year-old David Kinemon is forced into conflict with the Hatburns, a degenerate Kentucky family who cripple Allen,

David's older brother. When he kills all three Hatburns after a savage battle, David recalls the story of Goliath and reflects that he is just a "tol'able" David. The story was filmed in 1921.

Tom Grogan (1896), a novel by F. HOPKINSON SMITH. One of the earliest novels to deal with labor and waterfront problems, this is the story of a New York stevedore's wife whose husband dies; she conceals his death in order to conduct the business in his name and is herself the "Tom" of the title. Her great strength of will, her powerful physique, her devotion to her children enable her to succeed against attempts to destroy her business. Blackmail, arson, and attempted murder provide part of the action of the story.

Tomlinson, E[verett] T[itsworth] (b. Shiloh, N.J., May 23, 1859—d. Oct. 30, 1931), teacher, clergyman, writer of boys' books. Tomlinson graduated from Williams College, two years later became principal of the Auburn, N.Y., high school. In 1883 he was appointed headmaster at Rutgers Preparatory School, New Brunswick. He became pastor in 1888 of New York City's Central Baptist Church, where he remained for twenty-three years. His earliest publications were Latin and Greek texts, but his great interest was in writing boys' books with historical backgrounds. During his lifetime more than 2 million copies of his books were sold. Some of the best known titles are: *The Search for Andrew Field* (1894); *The Boy Soldiers of 1812* (1895); *The Colonial Boys* (1895); *Three Young Continentals* (1896); *Tecumseh's Young Braves* (1897); *Boys with Old Hickory* (1898); *The Rider of the Black Horse* (1904); *Light Horse Harry's Legion* (1910); *Champion of the Regiment* (1911); *Scouting with Daniel Boone* (1914); *The Story of General Pershing* (1917).

Tomlinson H[enry] M[ajor] (b. England, 1873—d. Feb. 5, 1958), war correspondent, novelist, author of sea stories and travel books. Tomlinson, deeply interested in the sea and ships, was invited (1910) by his brother-in-law, the master of the tramp steamer *Capella*, to accompany him on a journey to the Amazon with a cargo of coal to be delivered 2,000 miles up the river. Out of the journey came Tomlinson's first book, *The Sea and the Jungle* (1912), which made him famous. It is a literary classic, showing a marked gift for vivid phrases and exact accounts. Victor Wolfgang von Hagen includes Tomlinson in *The Green World of the Naturalists* (1948), his "treasury of five centuries of natural history in South America." Recent books include *Gallions' Reach* (1955) and *Trumpet Shall Sound* (1957).

Tom Owen, the Bee Hunter (1846), a sketch by THOMAS BANGS THORPE. This account of "mighty Tom Owen" was printed in a collection entitled *The Mysteries of the Backwoods; or, Sketches of the Southwest, Including Character, Scenery, and Rural Sports* (1846). Equipped with an axe and a pair of buckets,

the frontier hero scanned the distance for a bee, followed it with his keen eye to its hidden hive, then chopped down the tree and harvested the honey. Tom also appears in Thorpe's *The Hive of the Bee-Hunter* (1854). Tom's statement that on a clear day he could see a bee over a mile away is typical of the author; he was a pioneer in the American "tall tale," as exemplified in his *The Big Bear of Arkansas* (1841).

Tompson, Benjamin (b. Braintree, Mass., July 14, 1642—d. April 10[?], 1714), schoolmaster, physician, poet. Tompson graduated from Harvard in 1662. In 1667 he became master of the Boston Latin School, then the "Free School," then taught in Braintree and Roxbury. Though trained for the ministry, he never occupied a pulpit, but eked out his income by practicing medicine.

Tompson was much called upon for memorial elegies and other verses for special occasions, but his chief fame rests on his ambitious narrative poem on King Philip's War (1675–76), NEW ENGLAND'S CRISIS (1676). This long narrative, modeled on Francis Quarles' *History of Sampson* (1631), reflects the commonly held contemporary belief that wars were a celestial chastisement for the decline of piety. The poem is, however, laced with enough irreverence to allow some question as to whether Tompson fully believed this theory. The poem is also notable for its accurate use of Indian words and Indian English.

Tompson's standard of performance is more often crude than memorable. But his enthusiastic and satirical use of native material—colonial foibles, forms, stock attitudes, and Indians—gives him a minor place in American literary history and makes him the antiquarian's delight. Howard J. Hall edited *Benjamin Thompson, His Poems* (1924). Further material is found in Kenneth B. Murdock's *Handkerchiefs from Paul* (1927) and Harold S. Jantz's *The First Century of New England Verse* (1943).

Tom Sawyer, The Adventures of (1876), a novel by MARK TWAIN. The plot of *Tom Sawyer* is episodic, dealing in part with Tom's pranks in school, Sunday school, and the respectable world of his Aunt Polly, and in part with his adventures with Huck Finn, the outcaste son of the local ne'er-do-well. Tom's shrewdness and ingenuity are revealed in his dealings with his peers, and his romantic love of adventure in the episodes involving Huck. While hopefully curing warts with a dead cat in the cemetery under a full moon, Tom and Huck witness a murder and, in terror of the murderer, Injun Joe, secretly flee to Jackson's island. They are searched for, are finally mourned for dead, and return to town in time to attend their own funeral. Tom and his sweetheart, Becky Thatcher, get lost in a cave in which Injun Joe is hiding; Tom and Becky escape and Tom returns with Huck to find the treasure that Injun Joe has buried in the cave.

The story closely follows incidents involving Twain and his friends that occurred in Hannibal, Mo., which Twain called "St. Petersburg" in the novel. Huck Finn was modeled on Tom Blankenship; Injun Joe on a man who died in Hannibal in his nineties; Becky Thatcher was really Laura Hawkins, Twain's first sweetheart; Aunt Polly was his mother, but also bears a strong resemblance to B. P. Shillaber's Mrs. Partington.

Tom Sawyer was immensely popular with both children and adults, appeared in English editions abroad and was translated into many languages. Twain wrote a sequel, Huckleberry Finn (1884), which is considered his greatest book, and two sequels of lesser importance: Tom Sawyer Abroad (1894) and Tom Sawyer, Detective (1896).

Tom Sawyer, Detective (1896), a novel by Mark Twain. Tom Sawyer and Huck Finn revisit the Phelpses in Arkansas (scene of the end of *Huckleberry Finn*); and Tom saves Uncle Silas, who is mistakenly accused of murder, by unraveling a complicated plot of robbery, murder, and revenge. In a footnote Twain says that the incidents are based on "an old-time Swedish criminal trial," but more evident is the influence of Sherlock Holmes, whom Twain admired. The story is well contrived, but the rich humor and vivid characterizations of Twain's great books are missing.

Tom Sawyer Abroad (1894), a novel by Mark Twain. A sequel to *Huckleberry Finn*, this minor novel is a study of the provincial mind confronted with new and alien experiences. Tom Sawyer, Huck Finn, and "Negro Jim" sail in a balloon across the ocean to the Sahara Desert, Egypt, and Palestine. They encounter wild beasts, a desert caravan, and a mirage along the way. These adventures evoke lively and amusing discussions among Tom, Huck, and Jim, representing respectively three levels of intelligence: book learning, common sense, and primitive superstition.

Tom Swift. See Swift, Tom.

Tonty [or **Tonti**], **Henry** (b. Italy, c. 1650— d. Sept. 1704), Italian explorer. He was the son of the Italian banker Lorenzo Tonti, who invented the "tontine" system of insurance. The son went into the service of the French, sailed for America, and helped explore various parts of the Mississippi Valley and Canada. He was with La Salle when the French explorer sailed down the Mississippi and claimed the adjoining territory for France (1678–83). He also helped the Louisiana colony in its early days (1700–04), and died in Alabama.

Toomer, Jean (b. Washington, D.C., Dec. 26, 1894—   ), author, lecturer. Toomer's first book, *Cane* (1923), a mélange of poetry and prose, gave him an immediate reputation as a sensitive and gifted Negro writer. Probably indebted in style to Sherwood Anderson and Waldo Frank, *Cane* is exotic and lyrical. In a foreword to the book, Waldo Frank wrote: "For Toomer, the Southland is not a problem to be solved; it is a field of loveliness to be sung." Following *Cane* Toomer published *Babo; A One-Act Sketch of Negro Life* (1927); *Essentials*

(1931), a collection of aphorisms; and *Portage Potential* (1932). *The Flavor of Man* (1949) was a lecture delivered in Philadelphia to the Young Friends Society.

Topper (1926), a novel by Thorne Smith. Bawdy and boisterous, this humorous story deals with Cosmo Topper, a sober and respectable gentleman whose dull suburban existence is transformed into an extended holiday of romance, ribaldry, and countless cocktails by his adventures with two carefree young ghosts, George and Marion Kerby. Written during the era of prohibition, *Topper*, as well as its sequel, *Topper Takes a Trip* (1932), dramatizes the mood of rebellion against middle-class morality that was to form the staple of Smith's later novels. The book was made into a widely popular motion picture (1937) and a series of television shows (1953).

Torchbearers, The (1922), a play by George Kelly. This skillfully constructed farce satirizes the socialites who use the Little Theater as a playground. Kelly's first long play, it is set in the Philadelphia he knew so well.

Tories. American supporters of Great Britain in the American Revolution.

Torrence, [Frederic] Ridgely (b. Xenia, Ohio, Feb. 27, 1875—d. Dec. 25, 1950), poet, playwright, editor, library official, critic. Torrence served for several years on the staff of the New York Public Library, later on *The Critic* and *The Cosmopolitan*, then as poetry editor of the *New Republic*. At varying periods he was poet-in-residence at Antioch College and at Ohio's Miami University. His first verse collection, *The House of a Hundred Lights*, appeared in 1900; *Hesperides* in 1925; *Poems* in 1941, and again in enlarged form posthumously in 1952. He received numerous awards, among them a Fellowship of the Academy of American Poets, carrying a grant of $5,000. Among his fellow poets who esteemed and praised him warmly were A. E. Housman and Edwin Arlington Robinson. Robert Frost wrote a fine lyric about him, *A Passing Glimpse*. His collection *Plays for a Negro Theater* (1917) deepened interest in the Negro as literary material; the first play in the book, *Granny Maumee*, was produced (1914) with a white cast. It was perhaps the first serious drama about Negroes by an American writer, and the first to be acted by a Negro cast (1917). *Story of John Hope* (1948) is a biography of the Negro educator, into which Torrence injects his own personality to the point where it seems almost an autobiography.

Torrents of Spring, The (1926), a novel by Ernest Hemingway. A burlesque of Sherwood Anderson and the "Chicago school" of authors, this comic novel tells of Yogi Johnson and Scripps O'Neil, workers in a pump factory in Petosky, Mich.; of Scripps' amours with two waitresses in Brown's Beanery, and of Yogi's adventures with the Indians. F. Scott Fitzgerald suggested that Hemingway write the novel, and readers of Sherwood Anderson's Dark Laughter (1925) will admit that Hemingway's burlesque ("He went out into the night. It seemed the only thing to do. He did it.") is not too unfair; the clowning on Hemingway's part was really a literary declaration of independence.

Torrey, Bradford (b. Weymouth, Mass., Oct. 9, 1843—d. Oct. 7, 1912), ornithologist, writer, teacher, editor. Torrey taught for two years, then earned a living as a businessman, but from his earliest years he made the study of birds his hobby. In 1886 he became a member of the staff of *Youth's Companion*. In his later years, suffering from ill health, he moved to a cabin near Santa Barbara, Calif., isolated from the world. He became a noted ornithologist. Mingled with his close observation was an almost mystical philosophy of nature, and he wrote in a style of marked literary grace. He published *Birds in the Bush* (1885); *A Rambler's Lease* (1889); *A Florida Sketch Book* (1894); *A World of Green Hills* (1898); *The Clerk of the Woods* (1903); *Field Days in California* (1913); and other volumes. He also edited the writings of Thoreau (14 v., 1906).

Torrey, Charles Cutler (b. East Harwick, Vt., Dec. 20, 1863—d. Nov. 12, 1956), archaeologist, teacher, historian, translator. Torrey took a doctor's degree at Strassburg, taught at Bowdoin College and Andover Theological Seminary, became professor of Semitics at Yale University in 1900, retired in 1932. He directed archaeological expeditions in the Near East and wrote many books on that region. Among them: *The Commercial-Theological Terms in the Koran* (1892); *Composition and Historical Value of Ezra-Nehemiah* (1896); *Ezra Studies* (1910); *Mysticism in Islam* (1921); *Jewish Foundation of Islam* (1933); *Brief Introduction to the Apocryphal Literature* (1945); *Lives of the Prophets* (1946); *Chronicler's History of Israel* (1954). He made several translations, including *The Four Gospels: A New Translation* (1933). He was co-editor of the *Journal of the American Oriental Society*. See BIBLE IN THE U.S.

Torrey, John (b. New York City, Aug. 15, 1796—d. March 10, 1873), physician, naturalist, chemist. Torrey graduated from the College of Physicians and Surgeons, practiced medicine for a while, but became more deeply interested in pure science, especially botany and chemistry. He taught at West Point, the College of Physicians and Surgeons, and the College of New Jersey (later Princeton); and he was appointed assayer of the U.S. Assay Office in New York in 1853. He was also for a time New York State Geologist. His most famous pupil was ASA GRAY, with whom he wrote *Flora of North America* (1838–43). He wrote a separate account of *Flora of the State of New York* (1843) and other botanical works.

Torsvan, Berick Traven ["B. Traven"] (b. Chicago, March 5, 1890—d. March 26, 1969), novelist. Torsvan, who refused to the end to identify himself, was called "the mystery man of American letters." His books, which have been frequently translated, have made more stir abroad than in the United States; their success overseas seems to derive more from his attacks on capitalists than on literary merit, but his writings are often skillfully written narratives with vivid descriptions. Among them are *The Death Ship* (1934); *The Treasure of the Sierra Madre* (1935); *The Bridge in the Jungle* (1938); *The Rebellion of the Hanged* (1952). The second of these provided material for a movie of the same name (1948).

Tortesa, or the Usurer (1839), a play by NATHANIEL PARKER WILLIS. Written for James William Wallack, who played the lead, this romantic drama leans heavily on *Romeo and Juliet* and *A Winter's Tale* for its plot. The Florentine moneylender Tortesa desires the hand of Isabella, the Count's daughter, not for love, but as a symbol of rank and culture. In the end he gives her up to her true love, Angelo. Edgar Allan Poe declared *Tortesa* by far the best drama by an American author written up to that time.

Tortilla Flat (1935), a novel by JOHN STEINBECK. Written in a simple, lucid prose humorously reminiscent of Sir Thomas Malory's style, this episodic tale concerns the poor but carefree *paisano* Danny and his friends Pillon, Pablo, Big Joe Portagee, Jesus Maria Corcoran, and the old Pirate, all of whom gather in Danny's house, which Steinbeck tells us "was not unlike the Round Table." The novel (accepted after nine publishers had turned it down) contrasts the complexities of modern civilization with the simple life of the *paisanos*. There is in the story Steinbeck's usual glorification of irresponsibility when joined with kindness.

Totheroh, Dan (b. San Francisco, 1895 —   ), dramatist. *Wild Birds* (1922), first produced by the University of California where Totheroh was a director of dramatic performances, had a brief run in New York City and established him as a dramatist of power. The story of an orphan girl and a reform school boy who come to a tragic end reflected the concern of the 1920's with psychology and psychoanalysis. Totheroh also had a deep interest in Western themes, which he combined with a study of psychopathology. *Distant Drums* (1932) tells the story of a neurotic woman in a wagon caravan moving toward Oregon. *Moor Born* (1934) treats a whole group of neurotics —the famous Brontë family. *Mother Lode* (1934), written with George O'Neill, deals with life in early California. *Live Life Again* (1943) retells—not very successfully—*Hamlet* in terms of life on a Nebraska farm. Totheroh also wrote several novels, among them *Wild Orchard* (1927) and *Deep Valley* (1942).

Tourgée, Albion W[inegar] (b. Williamsfield, Ohio, May 2, 1838—d. May 21, 1905), lawyer, consul, novelist. In 1865 Tourgée moved to North Carolina and became active in reconstruction measures; he finally grew tired of living in a hostile atmosphere and returned north. In A FOOL'S ERRAND (1879) he sought to combine romance and propaganda about

Southern mistreatment of Northerners. The book was widely read and was followed by a sequel, BRICKS WITHOUT STRAW (1880), with much the same ideas. Tourgée was particularly distressed by the serious disabilities from which Negroes in the South suffered. His books helped to make the Southern theme a factor in American literature again. Writing in *The Forum* (December, 1888), Tourgée stated his conviction that American literature had become "distinctly Confederate in sympathy." Among his other books were *Figs and Thistles* (1879); HOT PLOUGHSHARES (1883); *An Appeal to Caesar* (1884); *Button's Inn* (1887); *Pactolus Prime* (1890). G. J. Becker wrote of him as *A Pioneer in Social Criticism* (*American Literature*, March, 1947).

Tour on the Prairies, A (1835), a travel book by WASHINGTON IRVING. This rich narrative describes Irving's journey over the country west of Arkansas from Fort Gibson to the Cross Timbers in what is now Oklahoma. It relates his experiences as a buffalo hunter, reveals his understanding of the Indians as individuals, describes the vastness and loneliness of the prairies. The characters that appear are lively but not comic exaggerations.

Tower Beyond Tragedy, The (in *Tamar and Other Poems*, 1924), a play in verse by ROBINSON JEFFERS. Based on *Agamemnon* and *The Libation Bearers*, the first two plays of the Oresteian trilogy of Aeschylus, *The Tower Beyond Tragedy* departs from its Greek models primarily in enlarging the role of the Trojan prophetess Cassandra and in giving less emphasis to the conflict between two equally compelling obligations than to the contrast between the incestuous desires of Electra, who begs Orestes to stay with her in the city and rule his people, and the desire of Orestes to break away from her and from whatever ties might bind him to humanity. The main characters are powerfully portrayed, and their speeches, which make up the body of the poem, reveal Jeffers to be a skilled dramatist as well as a poet. *The Tower Beyond Tragedy* was produced on Broadway in 1950.

Town, The. See THE HAMLET.

Town & Country. A weekly magazine called *The National Press: A Home Journal* was first issued in New York City on Feb. 14, 1846; with the November 21 issue it changed its name to *The Home Journal*. In 1901 it became *Town & Country*. Its first editors were NATHANIEL PARKER WILLIS and GEORGE POPE MORRIS, noted literati of the mid-19th century; for a time Edgar Allan Poe was their assistant. It was the announced goal of the editors to give "such a summary of news as will make our reader sure that he loses nothing worth knowing of the world's goings-on." But it early became a medium appealing particularly to the rich, whose "tastes and feelings" the editors planned to "instruct, refine, and amuse." Nevertheless, Willis and Morris took their missionary enterprise with some seriousness and included works of some of the leading British authors of the

day as well as many contemporary American writers. When in December, 1946, the magazine published an impressive 348-page retrospective issue, it proved to be not so much a literary as a social composite.

In 1925 the magazine was bought by WILLIAM RANDOLPH HEARST and placed under the editorship of the capable Harry Bull, who restored to it some of the ideals Willis and Morris had announced. Under his guidance the magazine "discovered" such authors as Ludwig Bemelmans, W. H. Auden, Oliver La Farge, Evelyn Waugh, Henry Miller, and Oliver St. John Gogarty.

Town Crier. A column conducted by AMBROSE BIERCE in the San Francisco *News Letter*.

Towne, Charles Hanson (b. Louisville, Ky., Feb. 2, 1877—d. Feb. 28, 1949), poet, editor, actor, newspaperman. Towne was sometimes gently accused of being an unofficial press agent for Manhattan Island. He had begun selling his adept and amusing verses to magazines by the time he was seventeen, and served on the staff of various magazines—*The Designer, The Smart Set, McClure's Magazine,* and *Harper's Bazaar.* He conducted a literary column for the New York *American* and contributed to other newspapers and periodicals. In 1940 he embarked on a new career, playing the role of the clergyman in *Life With Father.* His recollections of his varied career appear in his autobiography, *So Far So Good* (1945); *This New York of Mine* (1931) is likewise rich in recollections. He wrote lyrics for plays and for song cycles.

Townsend, George Alfred [Gath], (b. Georgetown, Del., Jan. 30, 1841—d. April 15, 1914), journalist, novelist, playwright. Townsend was a gifted journalist who capitalized on the articles he wrote by reworking them into volumes of biography and fiction. Two biographies, *The Life and Battles of Garibaldi* and *The Real Life of Abraham Lincoln,* appeared in 1867. His best known works are *The Entailed Hat* (1884), a novel dealing with the kidnaping and selling of free Negroes in Delaware and Maryland before the Civil War, and *Tales of the Chesapeake* (1880), local color stories. He also wrote *The Bohemians* (1861) and *President Cromwell* (1885), dramas; *Katy of Catocin* (1886) and *Mrs. Reynolds and Hamilton* (1890), novels; *Poems* (1870) and *Poems of Men and Events* (1899); and travel books. See also RUSTICS IN REBELLION.

Townsend, Mary Ashley [Van Voorhis] ["Mary Ashley Xariffa"] (b. Lyons, N.Y., Sept. 24, 1836—d. June 7, 1901), essayist, poet, novelist. Mary Ashley married in 1853 and settled in New Orleans. Under the name of Xariffa she contributed a series of essays called "Quillotypes" and "The Crossbone Papers" to the New Orleans *Delta.* As Mary Ashley she published articles in the *Crescent.* In 1881 the *Picayune* printed a group of letters written on a trip to Mexico. *Xariffa's Poems* (1870) contained her well-known sentimental *Creed. The Brother Clerks* (1857), a melodramatic novel in a New Orleans setting, was followed in 1874 by *The Captain's Story, and Other Verse.* Warmly praised by Oliver Wendell Holmes, it created a furor because it dealt with the then sensational theme of the discovery by a supposed white man that his mother was a mulatto. *Down the Bayou and Other Poems* (1882) and *Distaff and Spindle* (1895) followed.

Tracy, Dick. A famous comic strip character, the creation of Chester Gould (1901 —   ). Tracy is a detective who tracks down flamboyantly named criminals, incessantly upholds law and order, and conducts himself in a highly stylized manner which comes close to parody.

Tragedy of Pudd'nhead Wilson, The. See PUDD'NHEAD WILSON, THE TRAGEDY OF.

Tragic Muse, The (1890), a novel by HENRY JAMES. Nicholas Dormer, son of an eminent English statesman, gives up a brilliant career in Parliament, his godfather's promised fortune, and the hand of his beautiful and wealthy cousin, Julia Dallow, to become a portrait painter. He is inspired to do this partly by the example of his actress friend Miriam Rooth. The novel was originally published in the *Atlantic Monthly*, and dramatized in 1927.

Traill, Catherine Parr [Strickland] (b. Eng., Jan. 9, 1802—d. Aug. 29, 1899), author, naturalist. Mrs. Traill came to Canada with her husband and her sister, SUSANNA MOODIE, in 1832, and settled near Rice Lake, Ontario. The two sisters wrote of the many trials and occasional rewards of frontier life with a frankness designed to disillusion the dupes of land agents. Mrs. Traill's *The Backwoods of Canada* (1836), a series of letters to her mother, is a good example of her candor and dry humor. Other books, such as *Lady Mary and Her Nurse* (1850) and *The Canadian Crusoes* (1852; republished 1855 as *Lost in the Backwoods; The Female Emigrants Guide*), appealed primarily to children; Canada's natural beauties are described in *Rambles in the Canadian Forest* (1859), *Plant Life in Canada, or Gleanings from Forest, Lake, and Plain* (1885), and *Pearls and Pebbles, or The Notes of an Old Naturalist* (1894).

Trail of the Lonesome Pine, The (1908), a novel by JOHN FOX. Fox combined many popular elements in this story of the Cumberland Mountains, and the book immediately became a best seller. A young engineer comes to the mountains in one of the early attempts to industrialize them, finds himself in the midst of a mountain feud, falls in love with a beautiful but uneducated girl who is prepared to marry her cousin, sends her east to be educated, and marries her. The novel was successfully made into a silent film (1922), but before that was made into a play (1912) by EUGENE WALTER and compressed into an appealing song (1913) by Ballard MacDonald and Harry Carroll.

Train, Arthur [Cheney] (b. Boston, Sept. 6, 1875—d. Dec. 22, 1945), lawyer, public official, writer. Train was a graduate of Harvard College and the Harvard Law School, was admitted to the bar in Massachusetts and New

York. His first practice in New York City came as counsel for the New York Legal Aid Society, service that impressed him deeply and is reflected in his famous stories about Ephraim Tutt. For a while he was in private practice, then joined the staff of District Attorney Eugene A. Philbin, later worked with District Attorney William Travers Jerome. He also served the state as a special deputy attorney general, then went into private practice once more. As his books became best sellers Train devoted more time to writing, finally giving up the law entirely.

Train first appeared in print when his short story *The Maximilian Diamond* was published in *Leslie's Magazine* (July, 1904). His first book was *McAllister and His Double* (1905). But his Tutt stories, about a crafty old lawyer who uses his legal skill to help persons in trouble, won him his widest fame. They appeared in the *Saturday Evening Post* and furnished material for more than a dozen books. He wrote many other books, among them *The Prisoner at the Bar* (1906); *Confessions of Artemus Quibble* (1909); *The Earthquake* (1918); *On the Trail of the Bad Men* (1925); *Puritan's Progress* (1931); *My Day in Court* (1939); *From the District Attorney's Office* (1939); and *Tassels on Her Boots* (1940). He was a masterly storyteller, one of great ingenuity and plausibility. He was held in high esteem by his fellow lawyers; his *Mr. Tutt's Case Book* (1937) was required reading in several law schools. John Crosby praised Train's gift for creating authentic small-town characters. Many readers believed that Mr. Tutt was a real person whose pen name was "Arthur Train." This belief became especially widespread after the appearance of *Yankee Lawyer: The Autobiography of Ephraim Tutt* (1943), a marvelously plausible narrative.

Tramp Abroad, A (1880), a travel book by MARK TWAIN. Based partly upon a five-week walking tour that Twain made with the Rev. JOSEPH TWICHELL (Mr. Harris in the book) through southern Germany and Switzerland in the summer of 1878, *A Tramp Abroad* is a discursive, occasionally humorous sequence of anecdotes, descriptive sketches of German scenes and customs, and comic illustrations by the author. Although the book lacks the vigor and freshness of THE INNOCENTS ABROAD (1869), it contains passages in Twain's best vein, like BAKER'S BLUE-JAY YARN and the satire of a French duel.

Tramp! Tramp! Tramp! (1864), a war song by GEORGE FREDERICK ROOT (1820–1895). It was popular with soldiers at the end of the Civil War and was revived during the Spanish American War. It has an excellent military swing; the tune has been used with other words. The title was used for a movie in 1926, and the tune is quoted in Part II of Ernest Bloch's *America* (1927), an orchestral suite.

Transatlantic Exchanges (1952), an anthology edited by Yvonne French. The editor examines crosscurrents of Anglo-American opinion in the 19th century. In her survey she finds that the American goes to England searching for his past, the Englishman turns to the United States in quest of his future. She begins with Tom Paine's and Dr. Samuel Johnson's contradictory views, goes on to notable visitors like Harriet Martineau, Mrs. Trollope, and Bernard Shaw on the one hand and Ralph Waldo Emerson, Nathaniel Hawthorne, Mark Twain, and Henry Adams on the other. Included in the extracts are numerous insults, freely delivered on both sides.

Transcendental Club. See TRANSCENDENTALISM.

transcendentalism. In America, a movement of philosophical idealism which reached its height in New England during the 1840's and inspired the work of RALPH WALDO EMERSON, BRONSON ALCOTT, HENRY DAVID THOREAU, MARGARET FULLER, and others. Rebelling against the "coldness" of 18th-century empiricism and its reliance on sense experience, the transcendentalists asserted the supremacy of mind over matter and defended intuition as a guide to truth.

The terms *transcendent* and *transcendental* had been employed during the Middle Ages to designate concepts which "overpass" the finite. The Schoolmen had used them to describe universal truths which transcended the categories of Aristotle. Kant, who influenced the New England group, reserved the term *transcendent* for those ideas that can in no way be experienced, using *transcendental* for *a priori* elements of thought (such as the concepts of space and time) which do not arise from sense experience but are manifested in and give meaning to sense experience.

New England transcendentalism was one of several aspects of the new romanticism which stemmed from Germany and France, and its followers read widely in Kant, Hegel, Schelling, Fichte, Goethe, and Mme. de Staël, though many received their inspiration indirectly by way of Coleridge and Carlyle. Indeed, the transcendentalists often adopted the language of Coleridge in distinguishing between the old school of the "reason," which reached conclusions by observation and induction, and the new school of "understanding," which used *a priori* "pure reason" to intuit an immediate perception of truth regardless of external evidence. They caught the contagion of Carlyle's moral fervor, sometimes echoing his jagged eloquence as well as his thoughts. When Thoreau writes, "We know but few men, a great many coats and breeches," one suspects he has been reading Carlyle's *Sartor Resartus.* However, both Thoreau and Emerson were genuinely inventive and original; their chief debt to the European idealists was an attitude of antiformalism and a philosophical sanction for their own independence of thought.

Emerson's *Nature* (1836) is described by David Bowers as "the original—and probably the best—systematic expression of the transcendentalist philosophy."

The beginning of Emerson's lecture called *The Transcendentalist* (1842) is the most articulate contemporary statement of the group's position: "What is popularly called Transcendentalism among us, is Idealism; Idealism as it appears in 1842. As thinkers, mankind have ever divided into two sects, Materialists and Idealists; the first class founding on experience, the second on consciousness; the first class beginning to think from the data of the senses, the second class perceive that the senses are not final, and say, 'The senses give us representations of things,' but what are the things themselves, they cannot tell. The materialist insists on facts, on history, on the force of circumstances and the animal wants of man; the idealist on the power of Thought and of Will, on inspiration, on miracle, on individual culture. These two modes of thinking are both natural, but the idealist contends that his way of thinking is in higher nature. He concedes all that the other affirms, admits the impressions of sense, admits their coherency, their use and beauty, and then asks the materialist for his grounds of assurance that things are as his senses represent them. But I, he says, affirm facts not affected by the illusions of sense, facts which are of the same nature as the faculty which reports them, and not liable to doubt; facts which in their first appearance to us assume a native superiority to material facts, degrading these into a language by which the first are to be spoken. . . ."

New England transcendentalism was not an organized movement, nor did it produce a philosophical system; like its chief spokesman, Emerson, it stood for self-expression and so encouraged its followers to seek the light wherever their natures pointed it out. Three specific projects were closely related to the movement, however: the Transcendental Club, *The Dial,* and Brook Farm.

The Transcendental Club was organized in 1836 at the home of the Rev. GEORGE RIPLEY for "exchange of thought among those interested in the new views in philosophy, theology, and literature." Early members were Ripley, Emerson, FREDERIC HENRY HEDGE, Convers Francis, JAMES FREEMAN CLARKE, and A. Bronson Alcott. Later they were joined by THEODORE PARKER, Margaret Fuller, ORESTES BROWNSON, ELIZABETH and Sophia PEABODY, WILLIAM ELLERY CHANNING, JONES VERY, CHRISTOPHER P. CRANCH, Charles T. Follen, and others.

The DIAL and BROOK FARM both had their roots in the discussion of the Transcendental Club. The *Dial* was issued quarterly under the editorship of Margaret Fuller until 1842, thereafter under Emerson until 1844, when it suspended. It published much material that could scarcely have found an outlet elsewhere in America, and in the case of Thoreau, at least, served to launch a career of great significance. Brook Farm was organized as a joint stock company in West Roxbury, Mass., in 1841, and included among its members GEORGE RIPLEY, CHARLES A. DANA, JOHN S. DWIGHT, George P.

Bradford, NATHANIEL HAWTHORNE, and others. In 1844, influenced by ALBERT BRISBANE, it became a Fourieristic "phalanx," and in 1846 a fire destroyed much of the association's property. The group was dissolved the following year. Hawthorne's picture of the community in his THE BLITHEDALE ROMANCE (1852), though not to be accepted literally, undoubtedly reflects the attitude of one who knew the project intimately.

On the whole, however, the transcendentalists were slow to take group action; they regarded each man as a law unto himself and often looked on causes and charities with skepticism. They were somewhat slow to espouse active abolitionism, though their belief in freedom and individualism, together with their impatience with conventional ideas about property rights, made them sympathetic from the start. In the end many of them took action against the slave interests in one form or another, and both Emerson and Thoreau supported John Brown.

For a full treatment of American transcendentalism see O. B. Frothingham's *Transcendentalism in New England* (1876); H. C. Goddard's *Studies in New England Transcendentalism* (1908); Arthur Christy's *The Orient in American Transcendentalism* (1932); R. W. B. Lewis' *The American Adam* (1955). Perry Miller compiled *The Transcendentalists: An Anthology* (1950), a selection of representative statements, with commentaries and a bibliography. An important work by Charles Ives, the composer, is his *Concord, Mass., 1840–1860*, a symphony in four movements marked "Emerson," "Hawthorne," "The Alcotts," and "Thoreau." Ives explained that this immense composition was intended "to present one person's impression of the spirit of transcendentalism." See IDEALISM; SWEDENBORGIANISM.

FREDERICK T. McGILL, JR.

transition. See EUGENE JOLAS.

Traprock, Walter E. The name assumed by **George Shepard Chappell** (b. New London, Conn., Jan. 2, 1877—d. Nov. 25, 1946) when he wrote a number of travel books intended to satirize a craze during the 1920's for lurid memoirs of supposed or exaggerated adventures. Chappell's first and most successful parody was *The Cruise of the Kawa* (1921), which was followed by *My Northern Exposure* (1922), *Sarah of the Sahara* (1923), and *Dr. Traprock's Memory Book* (1931). Edmund Pearson called the first book "the most successful hoax in history." It purported to be the adventures of a Derby, Conn., doctor on a Polynesian voyage, in the course of which he acquired a native wife. He discovered a new group of islands which he named the Filbert Islands because of the remarkable filbert nuts he found on them. One photograph showed a bird's nest containing dice, allegedly laid by the bird. The book was read with openmouthed credulity, and some people wrote or telegraphed to Dr. Traprock offering to join his next voyage.

Traubel, Horace [Logo] (b. Camden, N.J., Dec. 19, 1858—d. Sept. 8, 1919), editor, biographer. Best known for his friendship with WALT WHITMAN, Traubel was deeply influenced by the poet. As a youth he worked at such varied jobs as newsboy, compositor, lithographer, bank clerk, and factory paymaster. In Philadelphia he founded and edited the monthly *Conservator* (1890–1919) and *The Artsman* (1903–07). Traubel's political philosophy, a mixture of Marxist socialism and poetic mysticism, found expression in these periodicals and in his books: *Chants Communal* (1904); *Optimos* (1910); *Collects* (1914). As one of Whitman's three literary executors, Traubel took part in the publication of several books by and about the poet. His own contribution was *With Walt Whitman in Camden* (3 v., 1906, 1908, 1914), part of a meticulously kept diary of daily conversations with Whitman. A fourth volume, edited by Sculley Bradley, appeared in 1953. Much of Traubel's own creative writings in a Whitmanesque free verse vacillate unimpressively between poetry and prose. His friend David Karsner wrote *Horace Traubel, His Life and Work* (1919).

Traveler from Altruria, A (1894), a novel by WILLIAM DEAN HOWELLS. America's social and economic shortcomings are revealed in a series of amusing conversations between Mr. Homos, a visitor from the utopian land of Altruria, and a popular novelist, a banker, a lawyer, a doctor, a professor, a minister, and a society woman. Mr. Homos expounds Howells' Christian socialist ideas in his account of the peaceful overthrow of "the Accumulation" (*i.e.*, monopolies) in Altruria by the popular vote and the establishment of a truly democratic, humanitarian commonwealth. References in the novel to Thomas More's *Utopia* (1516), Francis Bacon's *New Atlantis* (1618), and William Morris' *News from Nowhere* (1891) suggest some of Howells' literary models. The account of Altruria is continued in a sequel, *Through the Eye of the Needle* (1907). George Snell called the novel "a more literate *Looking Backward*."

Travels of Jaimie McPheeters, The (1958), a novel by ROBERT LEWIS TAYLOR. An engaging example of the late picaresque, this meandering tale follows twelve-year-old Jaimie as he sets out with his father in 1849 from Tennessee to the California goldfields. The father, Dr. McPheeters, part saint and part charlatan, is actually the chief figure in this story of cutthroats, gamblers, adventurers, and Indians. The novel received the Pulitzer Prize in 1959.

Traven, B. Pen name of BERICK TRAVEN TORSVAN.

Treasury of American Folklore, A (1944), edited by B. A. BOTKIN. In his huge and always entertaining anthology Botkin collects and records a wide variety of folk materials under such headings as "Heroes and Boasters," "Boosters and Knockers," "Jesters," and "Liars." There are also songs, legends, children's rhymes, etc.

Treatise of the New India, A (1553), the first

book about America published in England. The full title was: *A Treatise of the New India, with Other New-Found Lands and Islands, as Well Eastward as Westward, as They Are Known and Found in These Our Days.* It was a translation by the Englishman Richard Eben from Sebastian Muenster's *Cosmographia Universalis* (1544). Eben's version discusses the Spanish explorations in the New World up to the year 1501 with references to such hazards as cannibals, Amazons, and poisoned arrows.

Treatise on the Gods, A (1930; "corrected and rewritten," 1946), by H. L. MENCKEN. According to Edgar Kemler in *The Irreverent Mr. Mencken* (1950), Mencken began writing this analysis of world religion without much enthusiasm; nevertheless he did a good deal of research and by the time he finished regarded it as his masterpiece. It sold in considerable quantities, was reprinted ten times, then was revised. The book received many excellent reviews, despite its outspoken hostility to religion, and was also furiously attacked. In the *New Republic* Hazelton Spencer called it "lively without affectation, logical without sophistry, amusing, and, above all, clear and wise." In his 1946 revision Mencken left largely unchanged the first four sections, dealing with the nature and origin of religion, its evolution, its varieties, and its Christian form. But the fifth section—on the state of religion today—was elaborately reworked to bring it up to date. Mencken regarded the book as forming one of a trilogy with *Notes on Democracy* (1926) and *Treatise on Right and Wrong* (1934).

Tree Grows in Brooklyn, A (1943), a novel by BETTY SMITH. Inspired by reading Thomas Wolfe, Betty Smith put the essence of what she knew about Brooklyn into her best-selling first novel. Her heroine, Francie Nolan, is a sensitive child growing up in a slum. Francie's parents are Johnnie, a lovable drunkard misplaced in his hardboiled surroundings, and Katie, whose tenderness is often submerged by her fierce determination not to go under. The story is saved from unalloyed sordidness by its author's tender, sometimes humorous sympathy for her characters. The novel was filmed, and a musical comedy was based on it by Mrs. Smith in collaboration with George Abbott (1951).

Trees (*Poetry*, August, 1913; in *Trees and Other Poems,* 1914), a poem by JOYCE KILMER. This is probably the most widely read poem in modern American literature; it immediately became famous, and Kilmer's death in battle served to increase his popularity and the poem's. It has been set to music more than a dozen times. The most popular musical version is Oscar Rosbach's (1922), which is, according to one music publisher, "a permanent best seller—right up there with the *Star-Spangled Banner.*" The more highbrow critics generally scorn it, and it has frequently been parodied. The tree which is said to have inspired it, a white oak believed to be more than 275 years old, is still standing on the grounds of Rutgers University at New Brunswick, N.J.

Trends in Research in American Literature, 1940–50 (1951), a report by the American Literature Group of the Modern Language Association. Those engaged were Roy Harvey Pearce, Alexander C. Kern, James D. Hart, Allan G. Halline, and Carvel Collins, each of whom was assigned a chronological segment on which to make a report. The chief endeavor of the committee was to discover authors and topics that had been neglected, also to point out that some authors were getting more than their share of research. It was concluded that the early periods of American literature, particularly the colonial era, have recently been neglected. The greatest number of books and papers were written on Mark Twain, Henry James, Herman Melville, T. S. Eliot, Walt Whitman, Edgar Allan Poe, Henry David Thoreau, Nathaniel Hawthorne, Ralph Waldo Emerson, Thomas Jefferson, and Benjamin Franklin, in that order.

Trent, William Peterfield (b. Richmond, Va., Nov. 10, 1862—d. Dec. 6, 1939), teacher, historian, literary critic, poet. He received his M.A. from the University of Virginia and began teaching; in 1888 he joined the faculty of the University of the South, becoming academic dean there in 1894. In 1892 he founded and edited the SEWANEE REVIEW in an attempt to rouse the South from what he felt was its intellectual torpor. His biography of William Gilmore Simms (1892) was condemned in the South for its criticism of slavery. Paul Buck, in *The Road to Reunion* (1937), calls it "the most devastating indictment of the intellectual life of the Old South ever written by an informed scholar." Trent found a more sympathetic climate in the North and began teaching at Columbia University in 1900, where he became one of the earliest specialists in American literature. He experienced many personal difficulties because his attitude toward World War I was not unthinkingly patriotic. His monumental life of Defoe remains unpublished. He also helped edit THE CAMBRIDGE HISTORY OF AMERICAN LITERATURE (4 v., 1917–21) and sold his valuable collection of Defoe material to the Boston Museum. His other books include: *English Culture in Virginia* (1889); *Southern Statesman of the Old Regime* (1897); *Robert E. Lee* (1899); *John Milton* (1899); *Verses* (1899); *A History of American Literature: 1607–1865* (1903); *Greatness in Literature* (1905); *Great American Writers* (1912). He helped edit the Columbia edition of *The Works of John Milton* (18 v.; 1931–38).

Trent Affair, The. See MASON & SLIDELL.

Trial of Mary Dugan, The (1927), a courtroom drama by BAYARD VEILLER.

Tribune Primer, The (1882), a parody primer by EUGENE FIELD. Field wrote this, his first book, when he was managing editor of the Denver *Tribune.* The first edition of about fifty copies has become a bibliomaniac's prize. The book is chiefly full of bad advice to children to fall down wells, mutilate flies, beat up the baby, eat concentrated lye, etc.

Trifles (1916), a one-act play by Susan Glaspell. Originally produced by the Provincetown Players, this one-acter immediately became a favorite of amateur companies, especially in women's clubs. It deals with a wife's murder of her husband in a New England community, a crime apparently without motivation. But the quick observations of women neighbors are cleverly contrasted with the condescending obtuseness of their menfolk; and it becomes obvious that the husband merely got what he deserved. The play, a dramatization of Miss Glaspell's short story *A Jury of Her Peers*, was included in her collection of *Plays* (1920).

Trilling, Diana Rubin (b. New York City, [?]—   ), writer. A graduate of Radcliffe College, Mrs. Trilling married the distinguished critic Lionel Trilling in 1929. She edited and wrote the introductions for *The Portable D. H. Lawrence* (1947) and *The Selected Letters of D. H. Lawrence* (1958), in addition to contributing literary, political, and cultural essays to the *Partisan Review*.

Trilling, Lionel (b. New York City, July 4, 1905—   ), teacher, critic, writer. Trilling took three degrees at Columbia University, taught at the University of Wisconsin and Hunter College, and joined the faculty of Columbia in 1931 as a professor of English literature. He was always interested in Matthew Arnold, partly because of Arnold's lifelong effort to bridge the gap between the theory of the liberal arts and the conduct of life. This interest bore fruit in his first published work: *Matthew Arnold* (1939). He found new insight into Arnold's character and work by using the methods of modern psychology, anthropology, and political theory. In later critical works he also employed these methods: *E. M. Forster* (1943); *The Liberal Imagination* (1950); *The Opposing Self* (1955); and *A Gathering of Fugitives* (1956). His interesting novel *The Middle of the Journey* (1947) is an effort in the exercise of what Trilling called the "moral imagination." Trilling's works include several excellent short stories. His highly influential essays in *The Nation, New Republic, The New York Times Book Review, Partisan Review*, and *Kenyon Review*, have revived interest in many neglected works. As editorial adviser to the latter two of these he inspired their consistent excellence. He wrote *Freud and the Crisis of Our Culture* (1955), and edited *The Portable Matthew Arnold* (1949) and the *Letters of John Keats* (1950).

Trimmed Lamp, The, and Other Stories (1907), a collection by O. Henry.

Trip to Chinatown, A (1891), a musical farce by Charles H. Hoyt with most of the music by Percy Gaunt. The scene is San Francisco, and the characters are a rich bachelor, a widow, the bachelor's niece, and a friend who comes West for his health. Although the play was set in San Francisco, it contained the hit songs called "The Bowery" and "East Side, West Side." Sigmund Spaeth states that the famous ditty *After the Ball* was a failure at

first, but became a hit when interpolated in *A Trip to Chinatown* (1892). The musical ran for 650 performances, breaking all previous records.

Tristram (1927), a narrative poem in blank verse by Edwin Arlington Robinson. *Tristram* is the third and best of Robinson's Arthurian poems; it was preceded by Merlin (1917) and Lancelot (1920). Because it was a Literary Guild offering and because of its emphasis—unusual for Robinson—on passion rather than irony, it met with an enthusiastic audience and brought its author belated recognition and financial security, as well as a Pulitzer prize.

Tristram falls violently in love with his old uncle's beautiful wife, Isolt; but he marries Isolt of Brittany, whose adoration he can never return. Her pitiable resignation begins and ends the poem. In between come the lovers' happiness and death, full of imagery of sea and stars. Robinson cunningly opposes the two Isolts: the longed-for unattainable and the neglected attainable. His naturalistic description and superb portrayal of thwarted passion make this, in Emery Neff's opinion, the best Tristram poem in English, although not Robinson's masterpiece. It is, however, little read today.

Triumph of the Egg, The (1921), "a book of impressions from American life in tales and poems," by Sherwood Anderson. The title story tells of an unsuccessful chicken farmer whose life is dominated by eggs and who realizes his tragedy and frustration when he fails to perform a simple trick with an egg. Other stories in the book, which some critics regard as Anderson's best, relate simple incidents in everyday lives that are given poignancy by Anderson's interpretations.

Triumphs of Love, The, or, Happy Reconciliation (1795), a play by John Murdoch. This play introduced the first "stage Negro" to an American audience—with a name that became conventional thereafter: Sambo. Undoubtedly a white man took the part. Quakers and the Whiskey Rebellion also enter into the plot.

Trivia (1902), aphoristic essays by Logan Pearsall Smith. This slim volume, enlarged in subsequent years (*All Trivia*, 1934), contains the whimsical distillation of the thoughts of a fastidious and learned man. "Pieces of moral prose," their author called them; but his exquisite taste and polished style lend them a sprightliness lacking in his definition.

Trojan Horse, The [1] (as a novel, 1937; as a play, 1941), by Christopher Morley. Morley called the play a "contemporary drama laid in 1185 B.C." He utilizes Homer's story to satirize modern habits and ways of thinking—more amusingly and agilely than John Erskine had done in *Helen of Troy* (1925).

Trojan Horse, The [2] (1952), a verse play for radio. See Archibald MacLeish.

Trollope, Anthony (b. London, April 24, 1815—d. Dec. 6, 1882), postal inspector, editor, author. The famous English novelist served the British Post Office from 1834 to 1867. In the course of his service he made trips abroad, including two to the United States. Perhaps because he remembered the harsh account of America given by his mother (see next entry), Trollope published a largely favorable account in his *North America* (1862) and wrote a novel called *The American Senator* (1877). He also wrote a travel book called *The West Indies and the Spanish Main* (1859). A keen and shrewd observer, Trollope described in *North America* many American cities, was impressed by our gadgets, and also had sharp criticisms. The book was reprinted in 1951, with an introduction, notes, and new materials by Donald Smalley and Bradford Allen Booth.

Trollope, Frances [Milton] (b. England, March 10, 1780—d. Oct. 6, 1863), English novelist, author of travel books. Mrs. Trollope turned out more than fifty novels and travel books, but is best remembered for her *Domestic Manners of the Americans* (1832), written after a stay of twenty-five months in Cincinnati, then a frontier town, and sixteen months in the East. The failure of several of her schemes, including a plan to start a department store in Cincinnati, may have influenced her point of view toward things American, which ranged from mildly favorable to viciously censorious. She found us so raw and proud that our "desire for approbation" and "delicate sensitiveness under censure" constituted "a weakness which amounts to imbecility." Her criticisms of frontier crudities are tactless, but often graphic and well merited. Mark Twain paid tribute to her honesty in *Life on the Mississippi*, but this passage was suppressed.

Other Americans were more touchy; two satirical replies to Mrs. Trollope were Asa Greene's *Travels in America by George Fibbleton* (1833) and Frederick William Shelton's *The Trollopiad, or, Traveling Gentlemen in America* (1837). More serious was Francis J. Grund's *The Americans in Their Moral, Social, and Political Relations* (1837). Mrs. Trollope also appears satirically as Mrs. Wollope in J. K. Paulding's play THE LION OF THE WEST (comp., 1830; pub., 1954). Her book, however, went through four editions the first year and a fifth in 1839; the latest is that edited by Donald Smalley (1949), which includes numerous additions from the original manuscript.

Tropic of Cancer (1934), a book by HENRY MILLER. Miller's first published work, *Tropic of Cancer* was published in Paris and was immediately banned by United States customs. In 1961 the first American edition became a best seller. The book is a history of Miller's life in Paris during the early thirties. Penniless and starving, he underwent a complete physical and spiritual degradation. The numerous philosophical ruminations that intrude on his story explain the poet's "heroic descent to the very bowels of the earth, the dark and fearsome sojourn in the belly of the whale." The poet's ascent from this abyss and his final emergence as "a bright, gory sun god cast up on an alien

shore" is meant to inspire the reader with the same joy of life Miller found after his sufferings. George Orwell noted that "the callous coarseness with which the characters in *Tropic of Cancer* talk is very rare in fiction, but it is extremely common in real life." Edmund Wilson called it "the epitaph for the whole generation which migrated to France after the war." Later critics continued to defend the book against charges of immorality and have praised its comic scenes. Miller himself said of it, "Liberally larded with the sexual as was that work, the concern of its author was not with sex . . . but with the problem of self-liberation."

Troubetzkoy, Amélie Rives, Princess (b. Richmond, Va., Aug. 23, 1863—d. June 15, 1945), novelist, playwright, poet. Amélie Rives married first J. A. Armstrong, whom she divorced in 1895. She then married (1896) a portrait painter, Prince Pierre Troubetzkoy of Russia, who died in 1936. She wrote some successful novels, including *The Quick, or the Dead?* (1889), *The World's End* (1914), and *Firedamp* (1930); also several books of verse, among them *Sélené* (1905) and *As the Wind Blew* (1922); and several plays, including *Herod and Mariamne* (1888); *Augustine the Man* (1906); *The Fear Market* (1916); *Allegiance* (1918); *Love-in-a-Mist* (with Gilbert Emery, 1926). Her play *The Young Elizabeth* appeared in 1937. Her first book won her the widest fame; she never attained with any later work the popularity of this best seller of 1889. Its scenes of hysterical passion were attacked and parodied, but were highly regarded by the sentimental. See THE EROTIC SCHOOL.

Trowbridge, John Townsend ["Paul Creyton"] (b. Ogden Township, N.Y., September 18, 1827—d. Feb. 12, 1916), author, editor. Trowbridge was largely self-taught, and won early publication for his literary productions. For several years he taught school in Illinois and New York, then his contributions of short stories to Mordecai M. Noah's *Dollar Magazine* won him that editor's friendship and help. He himself began editing magazines in 1850. In 1865 he joined the staff of OUR YOUNG FOLKS, then served as its managing editor from 1870 to 1873; in October, 1873, it merged with *St. Nicholas*. In the meantime Trowbridge had been contributing material, especially his excellent verse, to the *Atlantic*, and writing his books for boys. Perhaps his best known and best written books were *Neighbor Jackwood* (1857) and CUDJO'S CAVE (1864). Like other authors of juveniles, he did some books in series, especially the widely read "Jack Hazard Series" (1871–74). His *Poetical Works* were published in 1903 and include two pieces not yet forgotten: DARIUS GREEN AND HIS FLYING MACHINE and *The Vagabonds*. *My Own Story* appeared in 1903. *Neighbor Jackwood*, a true New England novel, was dramatized in 1857.

True Relation of Virginia, A (1608), an account of the first American colony by JOHN SMITH. Largely written in a tent in the wilderness, this account was intended for the London stockholders who financed Smith's voyage, and is mostly concerned with early Indian troubles, the choice of a site for settlement, and civic organization in the colony. Smith's celebrated release by Pocahontas from the hands of Powhatan is scarcely mentioned in the narrative. It was only after Pocahontas became celebrated in England that Smith remembered her as anything but a ten-year-old girl. Although the *True Relation* is the work of a twenty-eight-year-old mercenary with no literary ambitions, it is often called the first book in American literature.

Truman, Harry S. (b. Lamar, Mo., May 8, 1884—   ), public official, Vice-President, 33rd President.   Unable to obtain a college education, Truman managed his father's farm and clerked in a bank for a while. He served in the armed forces during World War I, then started an unsuccessful business venture as a haberdasher. Through the influence of Thomas J. Pendergast, the political boss of Kansas City and the surrounding region, he won a series of public offices: county judge, presiding judge of the court, United States Senator. In the meantime he had attended the Kansas City Law School for two years.

In 1944 Truman was elected Vice-President under FRANKLIN D. ROOSEVELT, took office in January, and became President when Roosevelt died on April 12, 1945. He made many momentous decisions toward the end of World War II, the most important of which was perhaps the use of the atomic bomb to end the war against Japan. He gave unwavering support to the newly formed United Nations. At first he sought to work with Russia, but soon realized that this was impractical and formulated the "Truman Doctrine" of aid to the free peoples of the world "resisting attempted subjugation by armed minorities or outside pressures." In his domestic policies Truman generally followed Roosevelt's New Deal.

In the 1948 election Truman surprised most experts by defeating Thomas E. Dewey. In what he regarded as his own Presidency he gave United States aid to the United Nations when North Korea, assisted by Russia and China, invaded South Korea (1950). To him must be credited the Marshall Plan, aimed against Russian Communism. He refused to run for a third term, and returned to Independence, Mo., where he devoted much of his time to the preparation of his memoirs and the planning of a memorial library (now in operation) for his personal papers.

Books about Truman include Frank McNaughton and Walter Hehmeyer's *This Man Truman* (1945); Jonathan Daniels' *The Man of Independence* (1950); and William Hillman's *Mr. President* (1952). Cyril Clemens compiled a collection of speeches, *Truman Speaks* (1946); M. B. Schnapper edited *The Truman Program: Addresses and Messages by Harry S. Truman* (1949); and Louis W. Koenig made a valuable collection of speeches, documents, and press conference discussions in *The Truman Adminis-*

tration: Its Principles and Practice (1955). Truman is the author of *Years of Decision* (1955) and *Years of Trial and Hope* (1956)—his memoirs—as well as *Mr. Citizen* (1960).

Trumbo, Dalton (b. Montrose, Colo., Dec. 9, 1905—   ), novelist, film writer.   Trumbo wrote over forty screenplays. Among them are: *A Man to Remember, Kitty Foyle, A Guy Named Joe, Thirty Seconds Over Tokyo, Our Vines Have Tender Grapes, The Brave One* (1958 Academy Award), *Spartacus, Exodus.* Trumbo was a vigorous left-wing novelist, pamphleteer, and magazine writer during the Thirties. His fiction, essays, and verse have appeared in numerous magazines, among them: the *Saturday Evening Post, Vanity Fair, The Nation, New Masses, Theatre Arts,* and the *Screen Writer,* of which he was founding editor. His most striking work is *Johnny Got His Gun* (1939), a gripping, almost unbearably vivid antiwar novel which received a National Booksellers Award. In it a mutilated victim of World War I wants to be displayed to people as an object lesson in the horrors of war, but the powers-that-be will not allow it. The book was published just six days after the German invasion of Poland. For a decade after World War II, Trumbo was blacklisted by the motion-picture companies, who refused to hire him and other leftist writers because of their political views. His works include: *Eclipse* (1935); *The Remarkable Andrew* (1940); *Night of the Aurochs* (1961); the Broadway play *The Biggest Thief in Town* (1949), about a dishonest undertaker; and the pamphlets *The Time of the Toad* (1948) and *The Devil in the Book* (1955).

Trumbull, John (b. Westbury, Conn., April 13, 1750—d. May 11, 1831), poet.   A child prodigy, Trumbull passed the Yale entrance examination at the age of seven. As a student at Yale College he criticized the academic curriculum and advocated a more liberal one that would include literature. This criticism forms the subject of *An Essay on the Uses and Advantages of the Fine Arts* (1770) as well as his long satirical poem THE PROGRESS OF DULNESS (1772-73), the latter written after he had become a tutor at Yale (1772). He published a series of essays under the pseudonym of "The Correspondent" in *The Connecticut Journal* (1770-73). Having passed the bar examination, he practiced law in the office of John Adams in Boston, and took part in the political agitation of the time. Later he was a representative in the legislature of Connecticut and a judge in the Supreme Court.

The Revolution evoked the patriotic poem *An Elegy on the Times* (1774), and Trumbull's most popular poem, M'FINGAL (begun, 1775; completed, 1782). After the Revolution Trumbull became leader of the "HARTFORD WITS" and a staunchly conservative Federalist. *The Poetical Works of John Trumbull* was published in two volumes (1820).

Tubman, Harriet [Ross] (b. Dorchester Co., Md., 1821[?]—d. March 10, 1913), Negro emancipation leader, worker on Underground

Railroad. Mrs. Tubman spent her early life as a field hand, and escaped from slavery about 1849. She returned to the South on the Underground Railroad and spent the next ten years leading more than three hundred slaves to freedom. During the Civil War she worked as a cook and nurse for the Union Army, led scouting parties, and often spied behind the Confederate lines. After the war she gave shelter to children and old people in her home in Auburn, New York. Sarah Hopkins Bradford wrote *Scenes in the Life of Harriet Tubman* (1869; rev. as *Harriet the Moses of Her People,* 1886). Earl Conrad wrote *Harriet Tubman* (1943), a biography. Anne Parish's novel *Clouded Star* (1948) is centered on Mrs. Tubman's work on the Underground Railroad. Ann Petry wrote *Harriet Tubman: Conductor on the Underground Railway* (1955).

Tucker, [Nathaniel] Beverley (b. Chesterfield Co., Va., Sept. 6, 1784—d. Aug. 26, 1851), teacher, novelist. Tucker defended slavery and the Old South in his fiction and as professor of law at the College of William and Mary. His first novel, published anonymously, was GEORGE BALCOMBE (1836), a romantic tale heavily indebted to Scott. Edgar Allan Poe praised the book as *"the best* American novel." Under the pen name of Edward W. Sidney Tucker wrote THE PARTISAN LEADER (1836), a novel that achieved notoriety by its prediction of secession and civil war and its wholesale attack on Jackson, Van Buren, and northern democracy. Tucker's third novel, *Gertrude,* appeared serially in the *Southern Literary Messenger* (1844–45).

Tucker, George ["Joseph Atterley"] (b. Bermuda, Aug. 20, 1775—d. April 10, 1861), public official, economist, teacher, writer. Tucker was a friend of Jefferson and Madison and wrote a life of the former (2 v., 1837). He came to the United States in 1795, graduated from the College of William and Mary (1797), studied law with his kinsman ST. GEORGE TUCKER, and began practice in Richmond. Along with his law work he did much writing—essays, letters for publication, verse. But Richmond's social activities demanded too much of his time and he removed to southern Virginia. He continued to write and became more and more interested in economics and philosophy. In 1815 he was elected to the Virginia House of Burgesses, in 1819 to the House of Representatives, and at the age of fifty was made professor of moral philosophy at the University of Virginia. He published books in economics, history, and philosophy, among them *The Laws of Wages, Profits, and Rent Investigated* (1837); *The Theory of Money and Banks Investigated* (1837); *The History of the United States* (4 v., 1856–57); *Political Economy for the People* (1859); *Essays, Moral and Metaphysical* (1860). Tucker was also a novelist, but the only story of his to be remembered is *A Voyage to the Moon* (1827), published under the pen name of Joseph Atterley.

Tucker, St. George (b. Bermuda, June 29, 1752—d. Nov. 10, 1827), lawyer, teacher, poet, editor. In the early 1770's Tucker came to Williamsburg, Va., to study law with George Wythe. Back in Bermuda, he furnished aid to the American patriots. He returned to Virginia in 1778, married Mrs. Frances Bland Randolph, mother of John Randolph of Roanoke, and served in the Virginia militia. After the war Tucker attained eminence as a lawyer, judge, and teacher of law at the College of William and Mary. In 1796 he published *A Dissertation on Slavery: With a Proposal for the Gradual Abolition of It in the State of Virginia.* He compiled an American edition of Blackstone's *Commentaries* (5 v., 1803) which became the standard authority in the South. Washington highly esteemed his *Liberty, a Poem on the Independence of America* (1788), but of more merit were his *Probationary Odes of Jonathan Pindar, Esq.,* political satires in imitation of John Wolcot, who wrote in England under the pen name Peter Pindar. These appeared in part in Philip Freneau's *National Gazette* (1793) and then in book form (1796); they have been erroneously ascribed to Freneau. The poems are anti-Federalist and satirize Alexander Hamilton and John Adams among others. One of the most admired mansions in Williamsburg is the St. George Tucker house, still occupied by members of the Tucker family. Mary Haldane Coleman wrote *St. George Tucker: Citizen of No Mean City* (1938).

Tuckerman, Bayard (b. New York City, July 2, 1855—d. Oct. 20, 1923), critic, historian, biographer, editor, lecturer. A graceful amateur who never had to write for a living, Tuckerman engaged in careful research at home and abroad in gathering material for his books. Among them: *A History of English Prose Fiction from Sir Thomas Malory to George Eliot* (1882); *Life of General Lafayette* (2 v., 1889); *Peter Stuyvesant* (1893); *William Jay and the Constitutional Movement for the Abolition of Slavery* (1894); *Life of General Philip Schuyler* (1903); two books on genealogy. Perhaps his most important service was an edition of the *Diary of Philip Hone* (2 v., 1889). He lectured on English at Princeton University from 1898 to 1907.

Tuckerman, Frederick Goddard (b. Boston, Feb. 4, 1821—d. May 9, 1873), poet, lawyer, scientist. Tuckerman was admitted to the bar and practiced for a short time, but for the greater part of his life was a recluse at Greenfield, Mass. There he observed the skies and nature, made notes on eclipses and local fauna, and mingled little with people. In 1860 he published a slim book of *Poems,* all sonnets. He sent copies to some of the noted writers of the time; Tennyson regarded them highly.

New American editions of his *Poems* appeared in 1864 and 1869, then Tuckerman dropped out of sight until the 20th century. In 1931 WITTER BYNNER prepared an edition of *The Sonnets of Frederick Goddard Tucker-*

man, with a long and enthusiastic introduction. In 1952 Samuel A. Golden prepared an informative account of *Frederick Goddard Tuckerman: An American Sonneteer,* which includes some hitherto unpublished poems and letters. Many modern poets have praised Tuckerman for the imaginative and magical phrasing which expresses the deep melancholy of his poems. But his free use of the sonnet form, which probably repelled many of his mid-Victorian readers, is very likely what most attracts the modern reader.

Tuckerman, Henry Theodore (b. Boston, April 20, 1813—d. Dec. 17, 1871), critic, historian, writer. A man of great culture and sensitive appreciation, Tuckerman was valued more highly by his American contemporaries than his writings justify. Among his works: *Italian Sketch-Book* (1835); *Characteristics of Literature* (1840, 1851); *Rambles and Reveries* (1841); *Thoughts on the Poets* (1846); *Artist Life* (1847); *Poems* (1851); *Essays Biographical and Critical* (1857). His only book likely to be still consulted is his scholarly *America and Her Commentators: With a Critical Sketch of Travel in the U.S.* (1864). *Webster's Biographical Dictionary* notes: "The conventionality of his Petrarchan sonnets gave rise to word 'tuckermanity.'"

Tudor, William (b. Boston, Mass., Jan. 28, 1779—d. March 9, 1830), editor, merchant, diplomat, biographer, essayist. As a merchant, Tudor carried on a successful business exporting ice to South America. He was always greatly interested in literature, and wrote much that his contemporaries found amusing and informative; he also took part in at least two editorial projects and was active in the Anthology Club. This club sponsored the magazine called the *Monthly Anthology,* to which he contributed European travel letters and many miscellaneous essays. Later he was active on the NORTH AMERICAN REVIEW and not only wrote the prospectus for the first issue (May 1815) but wrote three-fourths of the first four volumes. Tudor likewise helped found the Athenaeum Library and was instrumental in bringing about the erection of the Bunker Hill Monument. In 1823 he was appointed American consul at Lima, four years later at Rio de Janeiro. He died of fever at Rio. Most of Tudor's writings remained uncollected. Some of them, however, appeared in *Letters on the Eastern States* (1820) and *Miscellanies* (1821); he also wrote a life of James Otis (1823). An odd book was published anonymously in 1829, *Gebel Teir,* a satire in which the principal nations of the world are discussed by a synod of birds.

Tuesday Club. [1] A club by this name flourished in Annapolis, Md., around the middle of the 18th century. It was a coffee-house affair, with Dr. ALEXANDER HAMILTON and Jonas Green as prominent members. [2] A similarly named club was active in Philadelphia in the early 19th century. It furnished contributions for the PORT FOLIO. [3] The Tuesday Evening Club of Boston had many brilliant (usually amateur) writers, whose contributions appeared in the earlier volumes of the *North American Review.*

Tugwell, Rexford G[uy] (b. Sinclairville, N.Y., July 10, 1891—   ), political scientist, teacher, government official, author, editor Tugwell began teaching in the University of Pennsylvania, where he had taken a degree at the Wharton School of Finance and Commerce. Then he taught at the University of Washington and at Columbia University. He interrupted his teaching to become Assistant Secretary, then Under-Secretary of the Department of Agriculture (1933–37), afterward chairman of the New York City Planning Commission. He was appointed chancellor of the University of Puerto Rico in 1941, governor of the island the same year. He joined the faculty of the University of Chicago as professor of political science in 1946.

As a "brain truster" in Washington he attracted much opposition by his somewhat radical ideas. Among his books: *The Economic Basis of Public Interest* (1922); *American Economic Life* (with others, 1925, 1930); *Industry's Coming of Age* (1927); *The Industrial Discipline* (1933); *Battle for Democracy* (1935); *Puerto Rican Public Papers* (1945); *The Stricken Land* (1946); *A Chronicle of Jeopardy, 1945–1955* (1955); *The Art of Politics* (1958); *The Enlargement of the Presidency* (co-author, 1960).

Tulley, John (b. England, 1639[?]—d. Oct. 5, 1701), almanac maker. Tulley was among the first to produce almanacs in America. He came to this country at a very early age and lived in Saybrook, Conn. He was also apparently the first to give his almanacs a humorous turn, soon widely imitated. His almanacs were issued from 1687 to 1702 and became very popular. The 1689 issue contained a road guide to New England, the first of its kind.

Tully, Jim (b. St. Mary's, Ohio, June 3, 1891 —d. June 22, 1947), hobo, farmer, prize fighter, writer, publicity man. Somehow in the course of his bitter, poverty-stricken youth Tully learned to read, then while hoboing managed to get hold of many of the world's classics, and became what someone called "a literary bum." He haunted libraries in the intervals of his pugilistic career, and began writing; he was one of the many writers whom H. L. Mencken "discovered." His life and occupations continued to be diversified, especially when he reached Hollywood. Tully looked on himself as a super-Hemingway. He once remarked, "If I ever get to the stage where I'm not interested in taxi drivers and waiters and cops and gangsters and all the miscellaneous run of human beings, I'll be lost." But as the 1920's faded his vogue began to decline; he complained that the public was "synthetic" and preferred "synthetic writers" to natural writers like himself. Among his books: *Emmet Lawlor* (1922); BEGGARS OF LIFE (1924); *Jarnegan* (1926); *The Life of Charlie Chaplin* (1926); *Circus Parade* (1927); *Shanty Irish* (1928); *Close Ups* (1930); *Adventures* in *Interviewing* (1931); *Men in the Rough* (1933); *The Bruiser* (1936); *A Dozen and One* (1943).

Tully, Richard Walton (b. Nevada City, Calif., May 7, 1877—d. Jan. 31, 1945), playwright, producer. Educated at the University of California, Tully won a prize there for a farce called *A Strenuous Life* (1900). He went on to write a large number of successful plays in which romance and picturesque backgrounds were emphasized. Perhaps the most noted of these was *The Bird of Paradise* (1912), a drama of Hawaii; a long-drawn-out suit for plagiarism brought against him on the basis of this play was eventually decided in his favor. The play was made into a musical comedy in 1930. Other plays by Tully include *Rose of the Rancho* (1906); *Omar the Tentmaker* (1914); *The Flame* (1916); and *Blossom Bride* (1927).

Tunis, John R[oberts] (b. Boston, Dec. 7, 1889 —), writer, broadcaster. Tunis' books for young people are first-rate adventure stories, but they are always animated by what is best described as a moral purpose—the inculcation of good ethics and good citizenship. Tunis also wrote some sharp analyses of the sports world, particularly *$port$: Heroics and Hysterics* (1928); *Sport for the Fun of It* (1940); and *Democracy and Sport* (1941). Other nonfiction works are *Was College Worth While?* (1936) and *This Writing Game* (1941). *American Girl* (1930) is a novel obviously based on the career of Helen Wills Moody, the tennis champion. Some of his best-known juveniles are *The Iron Duke* (1938); *The Duke Decides* (1939); *Champion's Choice* (1940); *World Series* (1941); *Million-Miler* (1942); *All-American* (1942); *A City for Lincoln* (1945); *Young Razzle* (1949); *Buddy and the Old Pro* (1955); *American Way in Sports* (1958).

Tunney, Gene [James Joseph] (b. New York City, May 25, 1897—), heavyweight boxing champion. A marine in World War I, a successful contender for the light-heavyweight championship, then for the heavyweight championship, he defeated Jack Dempsey (Sept. 23, 1926), defeated him again (Sept. 22, 1927) in the famous "long-count" bout, and announced his retirement from the ring after winning over Tom Heeney (July 26, 1928). He then engaged in business and civic enterprises and was director of athletics and physical fitness of navy personnel during World War II. He wrote *A Man Must Fight* (1932) and *Arms for Living* (1941).

Turkey in the Straw. One of the most popular of American folk tunes. This was originally a minstrel song called *Zip Coon*, sung by Bob Farrell in 1834, also claimed by George Washington Dixon (it was published about 1834 "as sung by Mr. Dixon"). *Zip Coon* inspired many parodies and imitations, the best known of which is *Turkey in the Straw*. David Guion prepared a modern setting for orchestra and piano. But it is traditionally sung and danced to the fiddle.

Turnbull, Agnes Sligh (b. New Alexandria,

Pa., Oct. 14, 1888—), novelist, short-story writer. Mrs. Turnbull taught English for a while, and shortly after her marriage to James L. Turnbull (1918) began writing short stories —her first was published in the *American Magazine* (1920). Some years later she turned to novels. Among the best known are *The Rolling Years* (1936); *Remember the End* (1938); *The Day Must Dawn* (1942); *The Bishop's Mantle* (1947); *The Gown of Glory* (1952). The most successful has been *The Bishop's Mantle*, a vivid picture of a liberal Protestant clergyman. But her earlier books also found a wide public. *Dear Me* (1941) is a book made from Mrs. Turnbull's diary. *Out of My Heart* (1958) is autobiographical.

Turner, Frederick Jackson (b. Portage, Wis., Nov. 14, 1861—d. March 14, 1932), historian, teacher. After attending the University of Wisconsin, Turner spent a year as a newspaper reporter and another year as a tutor in rhetoric and oratory at his alma mater. He took his M.A. at Johns Hopkins University, returned to Wisconsin as assistant professor of history. His doctoral dissertation, *The Character and Influence of the Indian Trade in Wisconsin: A Study in the Trading Post as an Institution* (1890), has become a standard work.

In July 1893, at a meeting of the American Historical Association, Turner read a paper which claimed the attention of his profession. *The Significance of the Frontier in American History* offered a new explanation of the process of American development. Instead of the then-usual emphasis on the East and Anglo-Saxon political institutions, Turner stressed the significance of the continually advancing frontier as a "safety valve." Turner explored his notion further in *The Rise of the New West* (1906) and in a series of papers collected in THE FRONTIER IN AMERICAN HISTORY (1920). By this time he had joined the history department at Harvard University, where he found many eager young disciples.

More recently, historians and critics have ventured to raise their voices against Turner's frontier thesis. Henry Nash Smith, for example, in VIRGIN LAND, THE AMERICAN WEST AS SYMBOL AND MYTH (1950), suggests that Turner was a captive of an American "agrarian myth," as much a part of the history of American Romanticism as James Fenimore Cooper. Among Turner's other books are *The Significance of Sections in American History* (1932) and *The United States, 1830–1850: The Nation and Its Sections* (1935). *Early Writings* (1938), compiled by E. F. Edwards, contains a complete Turner bibliography.

Turner, Joseph Addison (b. near Eatonton, Ga., Sept. 23, 1826—d. Feb. 29, 1868), planter, lawyer, printer, editor, poet, essayist. Turner, whom his protégé JOEL CHANDLER HARRIS called "a miscellaneous genius," was a wealthy man whose plantation was named Turnwold. There he conducted most of his enterprises, including the printing plant from which he published the only magazine ever issued on a plantation, *The Countryman*. Nearby lived his brother, **William Wilberforce Turner** (19th century), who wrote *Jack Hopeton and His Friends, or, The Adventures of a Georgian* (1860). In accordance with his name, Joseph Addison Turner contributed to his magazine essays in good 18th-century style. His aim was to stimulate the writing of good books in the South, a literature separate and distinct. His writings survive only in the pages of his magazine; Jay Hubbell, in *The South in Literature* (1954), prefers his amusing *Goose-Quill Essays* and a long poem in imitation of Goldsmith's *Deserted Village* called *The Old Plantation*.

Turner exerted one important influence—on Joel Chandler Harris. Harris was hired to learn the printing business, was given free access to Turner's library, and soon began to write for *The Countryman*. More important, he began to learn about Negroes at Turnwold and to listen to the older slaves as they told their folk tales. Harris' *On the Plantation* (1892) is a semificticious account of his life at Turnwold.

Turn of the Screw, The (1898), a novelette by HENRY JAMES. A haunting terror story, *The Turn of the Screw* is told in diary form by an inexperienced young governess in love with her employer on a lonely British estate. She gradually realizes that her precocious young charges, Miles and Flora, are under the evil influence of two ghosts, Peter Quint, the ex-steward, and Miss Jessel, their former governess. As the horror mounts the narrator can turn to nobody but the housekeeper for moral support in her attempt at a sort of spiritual battle for the children's souls. At the climax of the story she enters into open conflict with the children, alienating Flora and causing Miles to die of fright.

Some modern critics have attempted to relegate the ghosts to some Freudian corner of the governess' mind. But James, in his notebooks for January 12, 1895, had jotted down as a literary possibility a ghost story he had just been told by the Archbishop of Canterbury, a story of orphaned children corrupted by wicked servants who later die and haunt them. However, James kept the nature of his ghosts ambiguous. As Elizabeth Stevenson says (*The Crooked Corridor, A Study of Henry James*, 1949), "Elaborate psychoanalysis of the governess would turn her into a creature who spoils the point of the story." James' subtle artistry, his understanding of children, and what F. O. Matthiessen calls his "extraordinary command of his own kind of darkness . . . the darkness of moral evil," all help to bring out the Jamesian conclusion that ghosts may be worst when seen by daylight. The story was effectively dramatized by William Archibald as *The Innocents* (1950); made into an opera by Benjamin Britten, first performed in 1954; and into a film (1961).

Tuscarora Indians. A tribe of the Iroquoian linguistic stock, formerly living in northwestern North Carolina. They were allied with the French, and in 1711 attacked the white settlers. After a costly defeat they sued for peace in 1712, but again in 1713 they attacked and again were severely defeated. The remnants of the tribe fled to a region north of the Ohio River and in 1715 joined the Iroquois Confederacy, which then became the "Six Nations." Some descendants are found mingled with the Senecas in Ottawa County, Okla. James Fenimore Cooper introduces two prominent Tuscarora chieftains among his characters. One gives the title to his novel WYANDOTTÉ (1843); the other is Chief Arrowhead in THE PATHFINDER (1840). A modern Tuscarora, Chief Elias Johnson, wrote *Legends, Traditions, and Laws of the Iroquois or Six Nations and History of the Tuscarora Indians* (1881). The tribe's present-day conflict with New York State officialdom is recounted in Edmund Wilson's *Apologies to the Iroquois* (1960).

Tutt, Ephraim. See ARTHUR TRAIN.

Twain, Mark. The pen name of **Samuel Langhorne Clemens** (b. Florida, Mo., Nov. 30, 1835—d. April 21, 1910), newspaperman, riverboat pilot, lecturer, writer. Twain was primarily a product of the Mississippi Valley and the re-

ceding frontier. He looked back to his boyhood in Hannibal, Mo., as a golden age, and Hannibal and its people were an inexhaustible mine of material for some of his best writings, such as TOM SAWYER, HUCKLEBERRY FINN, and PUD-D'NHEAD WILSON. In these books one finds Twain's father, mother, sister, and brother, and the actual playmates of his boyhood; above all there is the Mississippi River. Here, too, are innumerable episodes based upon fact, some never suspected to be actual events until Dixon Wecter wrote a definitive version of the early part of Twain's life in SAM CLEMENS OF HANNIBAL (1952). Twain achieved in his books the distinction of creating what Wecter calls "the universal Hannibal, the home town of all boys everywhere."

In Hannibal, Clemens viewed with pity the contrast between white and black men, and his pity later came to life in *Pudd'nhead Wilson*. Here, too, he began to reject orthodox Christianity, but based his own philosophy, which became angrier as he grew older, on what De-Lancey Ferguson describes as a "mechanistic theory which was Calvinism minus God."

Twain's father died when he was about twelve, at which time his formal schooling ended and he became a printer's apprentice. For two years he worked for the Hannibal *Courier*, then joined the *Journal*, founded by his older brother, Orion. He began writing for the *Journal*, and before he left Hannibal, he saw his first story printed, *The Dandy Frightening the Squatter*, a typical piece of frontier humor. Twain also published squibs, letters, replies to his own letters, and verses, and conducted a column here. In 1853 he became a journeyman printer and worked in St. Louis, New York City, Philadelphia, again in St. Louis, then with Orion in Keokuk, Iowa, and in Cincinnati. While on his journeys he wrote occasional letters to newspapers. At this time, too, he acquired a pseudonym, calling himself "Thomas Jefferson Snodgrass" after the character in *Pickwick Papers*. His first letters were written in that most facile of all forms of humor, misspelling. He rarely used the device again.

From 1857 till the Civil War ended steamboating on the Mississippi, Twain worked on the river, first under the tutelage of the famous pilot Horace Bixby. Twain wrote in his classic account, LIFE ON THE MISSISSIPPI: "In that brief schooling, I got . . . acquainted with all the different types of human nature that are to be found in fiction, biography, or history." He was licensed a pilot on April 9, 1859. There were trials as well as thrills, including the death of his brother Henry during the burning of one of the boats. During this time, in the New Orleans *Picayune*, he burlesqued a fellow pilot, ISAIAH SELLERS, who wrote pompous articles for the *New Delta*. The parodying so affected Sellers that he never published again. Sellers may have been the first to use the pen name "Mark Twain." These words were used by rivermen as part of the vocabulary in which they called out their river soundings; they signified "safe water," that is to say, a depth of two fathoms.

After dallying with the idea of joining the Confederate army, Twain rejoined Orion who, an ardent Unionist, had been made secretary of the Territory of Nevada. There Twain worked as a miner, had a job on Joe Goodman's TERRITORIAL ENTERPRISE in Virginia City, made several friends of a literary turn, definitely decided to become a writer, and first used the pen name "Mark Twain." Nevada was still frontier territory, and during the three years Twain spent there he acquired its characteristic boisterousness and profanity. His newspaper writings were vigorous and unrefined. These experiences furnished him with material for ROUGHING IT, published ten years later. The narrative is no doubt embroidered; Twain never pretended to tell stories with dull accuracy. Here, too, he met ARTEMUS WARD and learned how a clever lecturer does his job.

In 1864 Twain moved to California. He worked for BRET HARTE and later acknowledged that he had learned much from him, but he was angered by charges that he had plagiarized Harte; the two men in later years were unfriendly. He contributed for a while to the San Francisco *Call*, but soon became San Francisco correspondent of the Virginia City *Enterprise*, writing as he pleased about the corruption present in the California city. The police were displeased, and Twain found it convenient to take refuge for a while in the hills with the miner Jim Gillis, an adept teller of tall tales. Nearby was another story teller named Ben Coon, from whom Twain heard the story of the jumping frog. When he returned to San Francisco, he contributed his story of "The Celebrated Jumping Frog of Calaveras County" to the *Sunday Press* (Nov. 18, 1865). It swept the country, established Twain's fame, and showed that he could take an old plot and produce a classic.

Then the Sacramento *Union* sent Twain to Hawaii to investigate the commercial possibilities there. He stayed four months, collected facts assiduously, but managed to work plenty of humor into his accounts. Back in San Francisco, it occurred to him that he might turn his Hawaiian experience into a lecture. On October 2, 1866, he delivered his first real public talk. He proved a born speaker, later making a tour of central California and Nevada with his competent manager, Denis McCarthy. He published his first book, THE CELEBRATED JUMPING FROG OF CALAVERAS COUNTY AND OTHER SKETCHES (1867), although he never collected a penny in royalties.

Meantime the *Alta California* financed him on an excursion to Europe in the *Quaker City*. He made many fast friends on the ship, including Charles Langdon of Elmira, N.Y. At the end of the trip Langdon invited Twain to visit the family. Twain fell in love with Charles' sister, Olivia, and married her on Feb. 2, 1870. Twain was devoted to his wife, who did her best to cure him of his slovenly habits, his profanity and drinking. As a result of some censorship she exercised over his writings, Mrs. Clemens has been seen by some critics as a malign influence on Twain's literary career. This idea was first fully set forth in VAN WYCK BROOKS' *The Ordeal of Mark Twain* (1920), and answered in Bernard De Voto's MARK TWAIN'S AMERICA (1932).

The European trip produced a series of letters that further established Twain's fame as one of America's greatest humorists. The letters were full of fun, even if to some readers they seemed a philistine's attack on the culture of Europe. THE INNOCENTS ABROAD (1869) was very successful and enabled Twain to pay his debts; it also overcame the Langdon family's scruples about his marrying their daughter.

Twain and his bride later moved to Buffalo. Again in England in 1871, Twain found himself the toast of London.

For the rest of his life, seeking to protect his family, Twain was deeply concerned with his rights as an author. He finally established a publishing firm of his own in 1883 with a nephew, Charles L. Webster. The firm was highly successful for a while, but Twain's business affairs became more and more tangled until he met Henry H. Rogers of the Standard Oil Company, who had long been an admirer of his. On Rogers' advice, the publishing concern went into bankruptcy (April 18, 1894). An agreement to pay fifty cents on the dollar was finally reached; Twain could have done better for his own advantage, but as a point of honor refused to go into personal bankruptcy. Rogers was instrumental in bringing about an agreement between Twain and Harper & Brothers (1902), by which this firm took complete charge of all Twain's works. This arrangement returned Twain to a sense of financial security.

All this hectic extracurricular activity did not interrupt the series of masterpieces Twain produced after *Innocents Abroad*. Twain was a happy member of an intimate circle of friends forming a literary colony in Hartford, Conn. Here he wrote *Roughing It* (1871); THE GILDED AGE (with CHARLES DUDLEY WARNER, 1873); his first articles in the *Atlantic; A True Story* and *Old Times on the Mississippi* (1874–75); *The Adventures of Tom Sawyer* (1876); A TRAMP ABROAD (1880); THE PRINCE AND THE PAUPER (1882); *Life on the Mississippi* (1883); *The Adventures of Huckleberry Finn* (1884); A CONNECTICUT YANKEE IN KING ARTHUR'S COURT (1889). He made several trips between 1877 and 1883 to such places as Bermuda, Europe, and Canada.

In 1884 Twain and his friend GEORGE W. CABLE joined in a lecture tour. The two men were different in every possible respect. Twain was free in language, despised religion, loved to spend money freely; Cable was a strict Sabbatarian, finicky, and very stingy. But he did Twain one great service by giving him Malory's *Morte d'Arthur* to read; this was the germ of the *Connecticut Yankee*.

In June, 1891, Twain and his family left the United States for a protracted stay abroad. In 1895–96, accompanied by his wife and their daughter Clara, Twain lectured his way around the world in a fashion that must have been exhausting to him. In England came word of their daughter Susie's tragic death. On June 5, 1905, Twain's wife died. After that Twain lived for a while in New York City, made several trips to Bermuda, and spent his last years in a house called Stormfield at Redding, Conn. Here his daughter Jean, an epileptic, died.

Through these years Twain kept writing and publishing: THE AMERICAN CLAIMANT (1892); TOM SAWYER ABROAD (1894); *The Tragedy of Pudd'nhead Wilson* (1894); PERSONAL RECOLLECTIONS OF JOAN OF ARC (1896); TOM SAWYER, DETECTIVE (1896); FOLLOWING THE EQUATOR (1897); THE MAN THAT CORRUPTED HADLEYBURG AND OTHER STORIES AND ESSAYS (1900); *A Double-Barreled Detective Story* (1902); *My Debut as a Literary Person* (1903); *Extracts From Adam's Diary* (1904); WHAT IS MAN? (1906); EVE'S DIARY (1906); *Is Shakespeare Dead?* (1909); *Extract from Captain Stormfield's Visit to Heaven* (1909); THE MYSTERIOUS STRANGER (1916); and other books. His collected works were published as *The Writings of Mark Twain* (ed. by A. B. PAINE, his secretary, 37 v., 1922–25); *Mark Twain's Works* appeared in 1933 (23 v.). *Mark Twain's Autobiography* (2 v., 1924) was likewise edited by Paine, and steadily, from time to time, other writings by Twain have been printed from the vast store of his manuscripts. Secretly printed in his lifetime was the piece called 1601; OR, CONVERSATION AS IT WAS BY THE FIRESIDE IN THE TIME OF THE TUDORS. Franklin J. Meine edited this with a bibliography in 1939. *The Love Letters of Mark Twain* (1949) were edited by Dixon Wecter. Some special editions of his writings may be mentioned: *The Family Mark Twain* (with biographical summary by A. B. Paine and foreword by Owen Wister, 1935); *Life on the Mississippi* (ed. Willis Wagner, with much new material, including "suppressed passages," 1944); *The Portable Mark Twain* (ed. Bernard De Voto, 1946); *Mark Twain's Report From Paradise* (ed. Dixon Wecter, 1952); *Mark Twain—Life as I Find It: Essays, Sketches, Tales, and Other Material* (ed. Charles Neider, 1961).

Twain had a naturally dramatic personality and was greatly interested in the theater. His most successful plays were written in collaboration: *The Gilded Age* (with G. S. Densmore, 1873) and AH SIN (with Bret Harte, 1877). He collaborated with William Dean Howells in a play about Colonel Sellers, *The American Claimant, or, Mulberry Sellers Ten Years Later* (1887). Twain used it as the basis for a book called *The American Claimant* (1892) which, like the play, proved a failure. He wrote other plays, none of which were ever published. Many of his novels, however, concentrate upon dialogue. Frank Mayo, whose favorite role had been Davy Crockett, dramatized *Pudd'nhead Wilson* in 1895. Twain thought of *The Prince and the Pauper* originally as a play, but wrote it as a novel. *Tom Sawyer* and *A Connecticut Yankee* were popular in the movies. Richard Rodgers and Lorenz Hart's first outstanding production, *A Connecticut Yankee* (1927), was based upon the novel. The American composer Lukas Foss wrote an opera called *The Jumping Frog of Calaveras County* (1950).

Since Twain was an artist, most of his effects were intentional. In two realms—as a humorist and as a lecturer—he consciously acquired a trade, and as a storyteller he obviously derived his art from the frontier raconteurs he had heard so often. His technical devices were mostly those of the humorists of his time, but he retained many of them for his more serious writings: exaggerations, odd similes, sober-faced hoaxes, irreverences, mangled quotations from the classics, a pretense of imbecility, deadpan seriousness at the funniest moments, anticlimax. Perhaps in the attempt to devise art that would seem artless, he made fun of authors who used careful technique and defended the rambling, nonclimactic story, the effect of which depends upon its manner of telling. But he revised his humorous stories carefully, making full use of the "cappers" that inevitably concluded the typical frontier yarn. His real or apparent lack of method shows up more in his longer works. Wyatt Blassingame (*Mark Twain Quarterly*, Winter, 1953) concludes that Twain "was not so interested in his novel as a compact whole as in the individual scenes on which he could release his full flamboyant genius." Twain's almost passionate interest in style is expressed in his maxim: "The difference between the *right* word and the *almost* right word is the difference between lightning and the lightning bug." He delivered other dicta on the writing trade, but his greatest service to American literature was the ability with which he used the American vulgate and introduced it into writing that was obviously literary. According to H. L. Mencken, Twain was the "first American author of world rank to write a genuinely colloquial and native American." In a preface to *Huckleberry Finn*, Twain showed a linguistic pride in having done his best to differentiate several forms of speech introduced into that book: "the Missouri Negro dialect, the extremest form of the backwoods Southwestern dialect, the ordinary Pike County dialect, and four modified versions of this last."

Although Twain began writing purely as a humorist, he later became a bitter satirist. He believed that "humor must not professedly teach, and it must not professedly preach, but it must do both if it would live forever." He testified that "against the assault of laughter nothing can stand." In *Following the Equator* he wrote: "Everything human is pathetic. The secret source of humor itself is not joy but sorrow. There is no humor in heaven." His indignation was frequently aroused, and he ridiculed religious fanaticism, politics, social stupidities, legal injustice, sentimentality, and the whole Gilded Age. Alexander Cowie remarks: "He seemed perpetually surprised that God did not stamp out evil. . . . Compared with Henry Adams, his contemporary in disillusionment, Mark Twain seems an adolescent in the throes of his despair that the world is imperfect." Of course Twain vented some of his high humor and a good deal of his bad humor on persons. James Fenimore Cooper was a favorite target for his wit. In *Fenimore Cooper's Literary Offenses* (*North American Review*, July, 1895) he piled up charges hilariously, concluding that Cooper "wrote the poorest English that exists in our language." He wrote an essay in behalf of Harriet Shelley which attacks Percy Bysshe Shelley savagely, and he belittled Mary Baker Eddy in *Christian Science*. His personal rancor on occasion knew no bounds.

Twain was one of the great epigrammatists of world literature, and it is likely that his influence has made Americans connoisseurs of the wisecrack. Brander Matthews writes (*The Tocsin of Revolt and Other Essays*, 1922): "It was toward the end of his career . . . that his indurated sadness, his total dissatisfaction with life, found relief in chiseled sentences to be set beside the sayings of Epictetus." These epigrams particularly found expression in *Pudd'n-head Wilson*. Matthews quotes from Twain's works: "Whoever has lived long enough to find out what life is, knows how deep a debt of gratitude we owe to Adam, the first benefactor of our race: he brought death into the world."

That favorite game of the scholar, the tracing of "influences," has been played with Twain, but not with outstanding success except in his relationship to the frontier and frontier humorists. Undoubtedly he knew the Bible well, also Shakespeare. He admired *Don Quixote*, and there is distinct evidence of the influence of Don Quixote and Sancho Panza on the relationship of Tom Sawyer and Huck Finn. Tom Paine's writings helped shape his thinking on religion and republicanism. He was greatly influenced by the humorists of his youth—Davy Crockett, T. B. Thorpe, and the men whose pieces he published in the *Spirit of the Times*. Then there were the newspapermen he met in Nevada, particularly Joseph Goodman and William Wright ("Dan De Quille"). In California Twain learned new tricks of the literary trade from men as diverse as the old miner Jim Gillis and the popular writer Bret Harte. Among literary men for whom Twain had a great respect were Oliver Wendell Holmes and William Dean Howells. Howells, as editor of the *Atlantic*, encouraged Twain to write for that magazine, and in 1910 wrote an affectionate book, *My Mark Twain*.

The mass of investigation of Twain's life and work has approached the monumental. Some books about him, besides those already mentioned, include: Albert Bigelow Paine's *Mark Twain, a Biography* (1921); Mary Lawton's *A Lifetime with Mark Twain* (memoirs of Katie Leary, the Clemens' housekeeper in Hartford, 1925); *Mark Twain Anecdotes* (ed. Cyril Clemens, 1929); Clara Clemens' *My Father, Mark Twain* (1931); Stephen Leacock's *Mark Twain* (1933); Edgar Lee Masters' *Mark Twain: A Portrait* (1938); Bernard De Voto's *Mark Twain at Work* (1942); Cyril Clemens' *Young Mark Twain* (1943); Gladys Carmen Bellamy's *Mark Twain as a Literary Artist* (1950); H. S. Canby's *Turn East, Turn West: Mark Twain and Henry James* (1951); *Mark Twain: Selected Criticism* (ed. Arthur L. Scott, 1955). Twain's boyhood home in Hannibal, as well as several other buildings there, and his home in Hartford have been preserved as memorials. In 1958 Charles Neider edited Twain's chaotic *Autobiography*, presenting its events in chronological order for the first time.

'Twas the Night Before Christmas. See A VISIT FROM ST. NICHOLAS.

Twenty Years at Hull House (1910), an autobiographical narrative by JANE ADDAMS. One of the earliest of social workers and directors of settlement houses, Miss Addams established the Hull House Settlement in Chicago in 1889. Many social and educational activities were carried on under Miss Addams' capable direction. But her interests went far beyond the settlement house; she spoke and worked in connection with labor troubles and legislation and problems of immigration, and contributed to civic betterment as a member of the Chicago Board of Education. The book is a lively account of a remarkably fruitful social project and reveals a woman who was profoundly concerned with the welfare of humanity. There is today a Labor Museum in Hull House.

Twice-Told Tales (1837), a collection of tales and sketches by NATHANIEL HAWTHORNE. Some of the stories originally appeared in magazines and gift books, and some were written for a proposed book to be called *Seven Tales of My Native Land,* which was never assembled. The name of the collection probably comes from the line in *King John:* "Life is as tedious as a twice-told tale." Particularly noteworthy are the picturesque historical sketches, such as *Howe's Masquerade* (see under Sir WILLIAM HOWE), *The Grey Champion* (see under WILLIAM GOFFE), THE GENTLE BOY, THE MAYPOLE OF MERRY MOUNT, and THE AMBITIOUS GUEST. Of the moral tales, *The Great Carbuncle* reveals Hawthorne's symbolism at its best. See also THE MINISTER'S BLACK VEIL.

Twichell, Joseph [Hopkins] (b. Southington, Conn., May 27, 1838—d. Dec. 20, 1918), clergyman, biographer, editor. For fifty years Twichell served as a minister in Hartford, Conn., and was an intimate member of MARK TWAIN's literary circle there. He became Twain's closest friend, often went on trips with him, and is the "Harris" of A TRAMP ABROAD (1880). He had a decided literary gift of his own, wrote a biography of *John Winthrop* (1891); he also edited *Some Old Puritan Love-Letters: John and Margaret Winthrop, 1618–1638* (1893).

Two Admirals, The (1842), a novel by JAMES FENIMORE COOPER. Cooper, an expert in naval history, had long wanted to write a story based on "the teeming and glorious naval history" of England. He finally chose the period of the Young Pretender's attempt (1745) to regain his throne, an attempt abetted by the French navy. Two British admirals are the protagonists. Admiral Oakes is loyal to the Hanoverian occupants of the throne, Admiral Bluewater believes that it belongs to the Stuarts. Oakes engages in battle with the French fleet and is near defeat when Bluewater decides to help his friend and his country. The French are defeated in a great engagement, which Cooper describes superbly. Cooper had a propagandistic motive in his discussion of fleet movements. He wanted to convince laymen and especially members of Congress that a fleet is a unit the effectiveness of which is that of its weakest member and that fleets at sea cannot be expected to obey orders from authorities on shore. He criticized, too, the lack of an American fleet. The novel is intimately related to his *History of the Navy of the U.S.* (1839); the one prepared for the writing of the other. He found additional details, however, in *The Public and Private Correspondence* (1828) of Vice-Admiral Lord Collingwood, whose great friendship for and collaboration with Lord Nelson resembled that of Bluewater for Oakes.

Two Little Confederates (1888), a story by THOMAS NELSON PAGE. This account of the adventures of two Southern lads during the Civil War, in the course of which they help Confederate troops to capture a group of marauding northerners, was a favorite juvenile book in the late 19th century.

Two Lives (1922), a sonnet sequence by WILLIAM ELLERY LEONARD. Leonard began writing these poems in 1913, published them privately and anonymously in 1922, then with his name in 1925. The book created a sensation and ran through several editions. Leonard never regarded the book as complete, but kept on adding and revising. It is his own appalling and tragic story that he tells in this sequence: he comes to the University of Wisconsin to teach English, rents a room in an old house, falls in love with the daughter of his landlord, and marries her; but two years later she commits suicide. The poem goes on to tell how friends blamed him; some even said that he had forced her to take the poison. What they did not know was that, fearing insanity, she had tried three times to commit suicide before they had met and was saved each time by her father. Leonard's intense candor, his gift of phrase, his skillful manipulation of the sonnet, his tragic awareness, all make *Two Lives* a very remarkable poem, though critics and anthologists have neglected it.

Two Orphans, The (prod. in Paris, January, 1874; New York, Dec. 21, 1874), a play by Adolphe d'Ennery and Eugene Cormon that was adapted for the American stage by N. Hart Jackson. Jackson's version was revised by GLENN HUGHES for a 1939 production at the Showboat Theater, University of Washington. Hughes' version was included in Bennett Cerf's and Van H. Cartmell's *S.R.O.: The Most Successful Plays in the History of the American Stage* (1944). John Chapman described the play as "a mixture of high life and low, of virtue and dastardy, of tears without laughter." Kate Claxton, who played the role of Louise, a blind orphan, bought the play and performed in it for twenty years.

Louise and her sister Henriette arrive in Paris and fall into the hands of abductors. Louise is made to beg on the streets; her sister is saved for a worse fate but is rescued by the Chevalier de Vaudrey, who wishes to marry her. The sisters search frantically for each other through three acts, are reunited at last to discover that they are not sisters at all.

Two Years Before the Mast (1840), a narrative by RICHARD HENRY DANA, JR. To pass the time while recovering his eyesight, impaired by a severe attack of measles, Dana shipped out of Boston in 1834 on the *Pilgrim*, sailed around the Horn to California on a hide-trading expedition. The book is based on the journal he kept during the voyage. Horrified by the brutal captain's mistreatment of the sailors, shocked by their lack of legal redress, Dana wrote with a burning indignation which did much to rouse the public to the mariners' plight. The book went through many editions, was widely translated, and was adopted by the British Board of Admiralty for distribution to the navy. Dana added a final chapter in 1859 in which he described a second trip to California and told what had happened to some of the men and ships mentioned earlier.

William Cullen Bryant, who found a publisher for Dana, considered his work "equal to *Robinson Crusoe.*" It has also been called "the *Uncle Tom's Cabin* of mariners." Melville said he read it with "strange congenial feelings" and called it unmatchable. Critics are divided in their opinion about whether Dana influenced *Moby Dick* and the psychological implications of Joseph Conrad's sea tales, but the book is a direct, powerful presentation of life at sea.

Tyler, John (b. Greenway, Va., March 29, 1790—d. Jan. 18, 1862), lawyer, public official, 10th President. After graduation from the College of William and Mary, Tyler was admitted to the bar and was elected to the Virginia legislature when he was twenty-one. Later he served his district in the House of Representatives, returned to the Virginia legislature, was elected governor (1825–27). He served (as a Democrat) in the United States Senate from 1827 to 1836. In 1839 WILLIAM H. HARRISON was nominated for the Presidency by the Whigs, with Tyler as his running mate; this was the famous campaign in which the slogan "Tippecanoe and Tyler Too" played such a great part. Harrison and Tyler won, but Harrison died a month after the inaugural exercises and Tyler became President (1841–1845).

His shift of allegiance from the Democratic to the Whig party left Tyler in a somewhat bipartisan state of mind; and his four years in the White House ended by leaving him a man without a party. Daniel Webster as his Secretary of State remained faithful to him, and continued to serve in the cabinet when all other members resigned after Tyler had vetoed bills to establish a national bank; Webster left in 1843 after completing important agreements with England. Tyler declined to join in the spoils system, signed the bill admitting Texas to the Union, negotiated a treaty with Great Britain that fixed our northern boundary and another with China that stimulated trade with that nation, reorganized the navy, rigidly supported states' rights, but was unable to control unruly Whigs like Henry Clay who did not like his independence.

In 1844 Tyler was renominated by a states' rights convention but decided it was prudent to withdraw. From 1845 on he practiced law in Virginia and took little part in politics. As the gap between North and South widened Tyler condemned secession and led a compromise movement, but his efforts failed. When Virginia seceded he approved the action and at the time of his death had been elected a member of the Confederate Congress.

Hiram Cummings wrote *A Secret History of the Tyler Dynasty* (pub. anonymously, 1845); Lyon G. Tyler published *The Letters and Times of the Tylers* (3 v., 1884–96); Oliver P. Chitwood wrote *John Tyler, Champion of the Old South* (1939); Robert J. Morgan wrote *A Whig Embattled* (1954).

Tyler, Moses Coit (b. Griswold, Conn., Aug. 2, 1835—d. Dec. 28, 1900), minister, teacher, literary historian. Tyler attended Yale College, Yale Divinity School, and the Andover Theological Seminary. He was ordained minister of the Owego, N.Y., Congregational Church and later was called to Poughkeepsie. But he was beset with doubts and conflicts, and when his health broke down he resigned his pastorate (1862). To recover his strength he resorted to Dr. Dio Lewis' system of "musical gymnastics," felt the effects to be so salutary that he traveled to London to establish an institute of physical culture. There he lectured frequently before scientists and physicians, also before literary groups.

Tyler returned to the United States in 1867 and was appointed to the Chair of Rhetoric and English Literature at the University of Michigan. In 1881 he was called to Cornell University to occupy the first chair of American history ever established in the United States. He was strongly influenced by H. T. Buckle's *History of Civilization in England* (1854, 1860), with its emphasis, as he explained in his *Journal*, on "a spirit of the age as ruling the evolution of the events of the age." With this thesis as a background he wrote his epical *History of American Literature During the Colonial Time, 1607–1765* (2 v., 1878; 1 v., 1950). This work has retained vitality but has been somewhat diminished by subsequent research. His *Literary History of the American Revolution, 1763–1783* (2 v., 1897; reprint, 1941), however, remains the basic study of American Revolutionary literature.

The long interval between his two masterpieces was devoted to efforts to establish the American Historical Association (1884), to long religious meditation which finally brought him into the Episcopal Church, to a biography of *Patrick Henry* (1887), and to his *Three Men of Letters* (1895), a discussion of Joel Barlow, Timothy Dwight, and Bishop Berkeley. *Moses Coit Tyler: Selections from His Letters and Diaries* (1911) was edited by J. T. Austen. Howard Mumford Jones wrote *The Life of Moses Coit Tyler* (1934).

Tyler, Parker (b. New Orleans, 1907 —), poet, critic. Tyler forsook his formal education to come to New York. He took Ezra Pound, T. S. Eliot, William Carlos Williams, and E. E. Cummings as masters for his poetry, some of which was printed in *transition* and *Poetry* magazines before it appeared in his collections *The Metaphor in the Jungle* (1941) and *The Granite Butterfly* (1945). These poems showed the strong influences of surrealism and symbolism, as did his prose.

An editorial staff writer for *View* from 1942 to 1947, Tyler began to write extensively on movies. *Hollywood Hallucination* (1944) was hailed by Iris Barry as "the first book in its field to deserve the name of creative criticism." *Chaplin: Last of the Clowns* (1948) was criticized for its obscurity and Freudian orientation. These highly individualistic works were intended for the serious student of the film rather than for the average moviegoer. As such, they stand as major contributions to the study of the motion picture as an art form.

Tyler's other books: *The Young and Evil* (with C. H. Ford, 1933); *Yesterday's Children* (with P. Tchelitchew, 1944); *Magic and Myth of the Movies* (1947); *The Three Faces of the Film* (1960).

Tyler, Royall (b. Boston, July 18, 1757—d. Aug. 26, 1826), lawyer, teacher, writer. Tyler was a graduate of Harvard College, and Yale gave him an honorary degree. He studied law in the office of JOHN ADAMS, [2], fell in love

with the boss's daughter Abigail, but the boss promptly removed his daughter to France; in 1794 Tyler married Mary Palmer. During the Revolution he served as aide to General Sullivan in his attack on Newport; when Shays' Rebellion broke out he was on General Lincoln's staff. Then he began the practice of law in Guildford,

Vt., from 1807 to 1813 served as chief justice of the Supreme Court of Vermont, and also served as professor of jurisprudence at the University of Vermont (1811–14).

In the meantime Tyler had been active in literary fields. He practically started the American drama on its course when his comedy THE CONTRAST was produced in New York City (1787); in this play Yankees for the first time appear as characters in comic roles, speaking an authentic dialect; it is the first comedy written by a native American. In later years he and JOSEPH DENNIE operated under a dual pen name, "Colon and Spondee," and became the first American columnists. Their contributions appeared in the *Farmer's Weekly Museum*, published at Walpole, N.Y., by Isaiah Thomas and David Carlisle, with Dennie as editor. Tyler showed remarkable skill in verse forms and a facile humor. In 1797 he wrote another comedy, *The Georgia Spec, or, Land in the Moon,* and his best-known novel, THE ALGERINE CAPTIVE. See YANKEE IN LONDON.

Typee: A Peep at Polynesian Life (1846), a novel by HERMAN MELVILLE. In January, 1841, Melville sailed on the whaler *Acushnet,* bound for the Pacific. Eighteen months later he and a friend, Toby Greene, deserted the ship at the Marquesas Islands and after incredible hardships reached the valley of the dreaded cannibalistic Typees. Melville spent four months of sybaritic imprisonment before being rescued by the *Julia,* an Australian whaler. Melville's account of his sojourn in Typee was his first novel, and was generously received, although the book would have been much better if he had clearly decided what kind of story he wanted to write: a travelogue or a novel of adventure and romance.

As an account of ship desertion, cliff descents, and cannibal islanders there is certainly much tension created at the start and much suspense at the end; in between, however, Melville wrote his travel book, interpolating anthropology, sociology, descriptions of tappa making, marriage customs, law, natural history, and much else of Polynesian life. The result is a mélange, a dispersal of Melville's energies and the novel's tensions. Even Melville admits at one point that he has been "sadly discursive."

Unified or not, however, *Typee* is not without merit. The pervadingly somnolent atmosphere of the "Happy Valley" and the hero's inamorata, Fayaway, evoke nostalgia for innocence and first love. But, in the main, *Typee* promises more than it realizes. Its symbolism (probably unconscious) remains inchoate; the conflict between conscious and unself-conscious love remains unexplored; and the central problem—the choice a Westerner must make between civilization and primitivism—is but weakly adumbrated. *Typee* is an apprentice effort, a beginning which Melville would fulfill with his next book, OMOO (1847).

U

Ulalume (*American Whig Review*, December 1847), a poem by EDGAR ALLAN POE. This was composed at the suggestion of Professor C. P. Bronson, an elocutionist who wanted "a poem suitable for recitation about the length and somewhat of the character of Collins' Ode to Passions." There is a distinct plot, as Professor T. O. Mabbott pointed out in 1948, founded on a then current ghost story. On Hallowe'en, when the dead have power, the speaker and his soul walk in the "misty-mid-region of Weir" (a painter of the Hudson River school), "by the dark tarn of Auber" (the composer of the ballet *The Lake of the Fairies*). It is the land of imagination. They follow "Astarte's be-diamonded crescent," the planet Venus, but are stopped by the door of the forgotten tomb of the narrator's beloved. Hope is vain of replacing her with a new love.

Poe discussed the poem with Mrs. Helen Whitman and with Bronson's daughter, but refused to explain it to others. Yet when the parts are explained, the whole remains an inexplicably powerful evocation of mystery. It has had great influence on symbolist poetry in France and England, as well as here. Poe pronounced the title "You-la-loom."

Ullman, James Ramsey (b. New York City, Nov. 24, 1907—   ), theatrical producer, writer, mountaineer. A graduate of Princeton University, Ullman wrote a thesis on *Mad Shelley* which the Princeton University Press published (1930). He worked for a Brooklyn newspaper, then turned to writing and producing plays. After a series of Broadway failures he went to South America, where he crossed the Andes and followed the Amazon to the sea, as the explorer Orellana had done. The result was a book, *The Other Side of the Mountain* (1938). His short stories have appeared in many magazines. *High Conquest* (1941) is a history of mountaineering; Ullman himself climbed many of the world's famous mountains. *The White Tower* (1945), a novel about mountain climbing, is perhaps the best of his books. Two years later he published an anthology of mountaineering stories, *Kingdom of Everest*. Ullman served as an ambulance driver with the British army in Africa as a member of the American Field Service (1942–43) and was awarded the African Star. His second novel, *River of the Sun* (1951), was based on his South American experiences. Among his later writings: *Windom's Way* (1952); *The Island of the Blue Macaws* (1953); *The Sands of Karakorum* (1953); *Banner in the Sky* (1954); *The Age of Mountaineering* (1954). *The Day on Fire* (1958) is a novel based on the life of Rimbaud.

ultima Thule. Thule was a land discovered by a Greek explorer named Pytheas in the 4th century B.C. and described by Polybius and other ancient historians as "an island in the northern ocean." There is no agreement as to which island was meant, Shetland, Iceland, or the Orkneys. The Latins added the adjective *ultima* and gave to the phrase "ultima Thule" a special significance as the end of the world or the end of all things. HENRY WADSWORTH LONGFELLOW called what he believed would be his last collection of verse *Ultima Thule* (1880), but later published *In the Harbor: Ultima Thule—Part II* (1882). Marguerite in Gounod's *Faust* sings an aria "Le Roi de Thule."

Uncas. A young Indian chief, hero of THE LAST OF THE MOHICANS (1826) by James Fenimore Cooper. He dies heroically while trying to save Cora Munro from Magua, the Indian villain of the story. He has no real connection with the historic character similarly named, who was a Pequot by birth. Uncas is generally regarded as a highly idealized portrait of an Indian.

Uncle Abner. A character in numerous detective stories by MELVILLE DAVISSON POST. Post created six detective characters in his popular stories, but Uncle Abner is pre-eminent among them. In *Murder for Pleasure: The Life and Times of the Detective Story* (1941), Howard Haycraft says: "No reader can call himself a connoisseur who does not know Uncle Abner forward and backward. . . ." He is definitely a rural character, a rockhewn squire who makes it his business to protect the innocent and to right wrongs in his mountain community. He began his career in 1911 in a series of stories contributed to magazines. The best of them were gathered in *Uncle Abner, Master of Mysteries* (1918).

Uncle John of Woodchuck. A nickname affectionately bestowed on JOHN BURROUGHS by his friends. He lived at Roxbury, N.Y., in a farmhouse called Woodchuck Lodge.

Uncle Lisha. A Vermont character who appears in several books by ROWLAND EVANS ROBINSON (1833–1900). They depict an amusing personality and are often rich in carefully observed details of nature. Among them: *Uncle Lisha's Shop: Life in a Corner of Yankeeland* (1887); *Uncle Lisha's Friends Under Bark and Canvas* (1889); *Uncle Lisha's Outing* (1897).

Uncle Remus, His Songs and His Sayings (1880), a collection of thirty-four stories by JOEL CHANDLER HARRIS. Told to a small white boy by Uncle Remus, an aging Negro, these stories were based on Negro tales and legends Harris himself heard as a boy, and are among the finest examples of dialect and regional writing in America. The animal characters—Brer Rabbit,

Brer Fox, Brer Wolf, and others—are cleverly drawn, and their adventures usually stress the contrast between strength and shrewdness and the conflict between characters of unequal size in which the smaller and more intelligent wins. Uncle Remus himself is one of the most accurate depictions of the Negro to emerge in the 19th century. There were many sequels to his first book.

Uncle Sam. Originally a derogatory nickname for the Federal government used during the War of 1812 by New England opponents of its war policies, and now commonly accepted as the personification of the government. Uncle Sam may have been inspired by the nickname of a government inspector in Troy, N.Y., one Samuel Wilson, or it may represent an extension of the initials of the United States. *The Adventures of Uncle Sam* (1816), by "Frederick Augustus Fidfaddy," seems to be the earliest use of the name in a book.

Uncle Sam and His Boys, The History of (1835), a satire by JAMES KIRKE PAULDING. This is a sequel to Paulding's more famous work THE DIVERTING HISTORY OF JOHN BULL AND BROTHER JONATHAN (1812). In it Brother Jonathan, who had "13 farms," becomes Uncle Sam, who has "24 sons"—some of them a bit jealous of the others. The book displays Paulding's inveterate Anglophobia.

Uncle Tom's Cabin, or, Life Among the Lowly (1852), a novel by HARRIET BEECHER STOWE. The book is an account of the trials, sufferings, and innate grandeur of Uncle Tom, a Negro slave who is cruelly mistreated by a Yankee overseer named SIMON LECREE and finally whipped to death by him. Uncle Tom is deeply devoted to LITTLE EVA, daughter of his white owner, Augustine St. Clare. Other characters include the mulatto girl ELIZA; the impish Negro child Topsy; Miss Ophelia, a precise New England spinster; Marks, the slave catcher. Two famous scenes depict Little Eva's death and Eliza's escape over the ice of the Ohio, carrying her boy Harry; her husband George follows her via the UNDERGROUND RAILROAD to Ohio and they manage to outwit the slave catchers. The background is plantation life in Kentucky and Louisiana. In 1851–52 it was serialized in Gamaliel Bailey's THE NATIONAL ERA, one of his two antislavery papers. "God wrote the book," Mrs. Stowe once declared, "I took His dictation." She wrote it as a contribution to the cause of abolition, but showed more fairness to the South than was generally realized. Her despicable villain is a Vermonter from her own part of the country; she vents her sharpest ridicule on a Yankee woman. On the other hand, she depicts in admiring colors the true southern gentleman and the genuine southern lady. Mrs. Stowe's primary fear was that the abolitionists would denounce her; she had always avoided approving their cause and she liked the South. To defend herself she wrote *A Key to "Uncle Tom's Cabin"* (1853), in which she set forth the evidence for some of the scenes and ideas in the book; and

she used some of the material in her later novel DRED: A TALE OF THE GREAT DISMAL SWAMP (1856), which discusses slavery from several new points of view and repeats some of the characters of the earlier novel under new names.

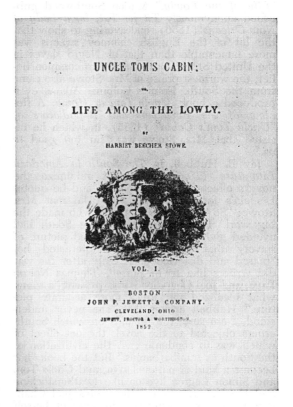

The prototype for Uncle Tom was one JOSIAH HENSON, whose life and influence is described in Brion Gysin's *To Master, A Long Goodnight* (1946). In her *Key* Mrs. Stowe identified Henson as her model, but his life varied in many details from that of Uncle Tom. Henson escaped to Canada, lectured widely, in time crossed to England. He relished the fact that he had served as Uncle Tom's model and wrote an autobiography, *Life of Josiah Henson* (1849), which was augmented as *Truth Stranger Than Fiction* (1858), with a preface by Mrs. Stowe. It is also believed that Theodore Dwight Weld's tracts *The Bible Against Slavery* (1837) and *American Slavery As It Is* (1839) greatly influenced Mrs. Stowe.

It is likely that *Uncle Tom's Cabin* has sold more widely than any other work of fiction ever written. It has been translated into every European language, as well as more remote tongues. Mrs. Stowe's literary renown became worldwide. In Scotland an "emancipation fund" was raised by penny subscribers. In Russia and Siam masters succumbed to the book's appeal by liberating their serfs. She was, of course, furiously denounced in the South. A volume published anonymously in 1852 as a reply to Mrs. Stowe was *The North and the South, or,*

Slavery and Its Contrasts: A Tale of Real Life.
Probably in the same year appeared William
L. G. Smith's proslavery novel *Uncle Tom's
Cabin as It Is, or, Life at the South. Being
Narrative, Scenes, and Incidents in the Real
"Life of the Lowly."* Marion Southwood published anonymously *Tit for Tat, by a Lady of
New Orleans* (1856), endeavoring to show that
the lot of the English chimney sweeps was
more lamentable than that of Negro slaves in
the United States. But contrary to common belief, the warmest praise of Mrs. Stowe also came
from the South. Francis Colburn Adams even
produced a book, *Uncle Tom at Home: A Review of the Reviewers and Repudiators of
"Uncle Tom's Cabin"* (1853), in which he insisted that Mrs. Stowe was "far too good to
us."

Jay B. Hubbell, in *The South in American
Literature* (1954), does not minimize the
novel's effect on public opinion, and he quotes
Lincoln's famous remark when he met Mrs.
Stowe: "So this is the little lady who made the
big war!" Hubbell holds that the South had
avoided giving the world a detailed picture of
slavery that might have counteracted her
"biased and distorted one." Only after the war
did writers like Irwin Russell, Thomas Nelson
Page, and Joel Chandler Harris present "a somewhat idealized but much more accurate picture." Hubbell argues that "she never understood, I am sure, the grounds on which Southerners objected to the novel, the net effect of
which was to condemn . . . the civilization of
the South as semibarbarous." But the book "has
become a kind of national saga, and Uncle Tom
and Simon Legree live on like Leatherstocking
and Huckleberry Finn." He quotes Joel Chandler Harris as arguing that in spite of herself
Mrs. Stowe had found a certain charm in the
slave system: "All the worthy and beautiful
characters in her book—Uncle Tom, little Eva,
the beloved Master, and the rest—are the
products of the system the text of the book is
all the time condemning."

Edmund Wilson, rereading the novel in the
1950's, praised it as the work of "a first-rate
modern social intelligence." He points out, as all
fair-minded critics have done, that Mrs. Stowe
held New Englanders to be just as guilty as
Southerners. From 1853 to the present, the
play based on the novel has never been long
off the boards; it has become the chief American folk drama. The favorite version was prepared by GEORGE L. AIKEN. In 1933 The Players
produced a version with Otis Skinner as Uncle
Tom. This was published the following year
and reprinted in Bennett Cerf and Van H.
Cartmell's *S.R.O.: The Most Successful Plays
in the History of the American Stage* (1944).
Uncle Tom and Topsy on the stage were stereotype Negroes, and the play is responsible for
many incorrect ideas about the novel. Harry
Birdoff told the story of this unique theatrical
phenomenon in *The World's Greatest Hit:
"Uncle Tom's Cabin"* (1948). The play has
also appeared frequently on motion-picture

screens. E. E. Cummings' ballet *Tom* (1935)
is a burlesque on *Uncle Tom's Cabin.*

The term "Uncle Tomism" has come to stand
for an accusation made by some Negroes against
others of exhibiting undue subservience to the
white man. An interesting modern commentary
is J. C. Furnas' *Goodbye to Uncle Tom* (1956).
See NEGROES (section on drama).

Uncle Wiggily. See BEDTIME STORY; HOW-
ARD R. GARIS.

Under Cover [1] (1903), a play by EDWARD
HARRIGAN. Its dramatis personae included,
as usual with Harrigan, characters from the
sporting crowd along with Irish, German, and
Negro types.

[2] (1914), another play with the same title
written by Roi Cooper Megrue. It was one of
the earliest of the crook plays and involved an
attempt to smuggle a valuable necklace through
the customs. The action takes place in the New
York Customs House and in a fashionable residence on Long Island.

Underground Railroad, the. The organized
secret system for transporting slaves to freedom
before the Civil War. Negroes were frequently
hidden on coastal vessels bound from the South
Atlantic seaboard to New England, where they
were helped further north, sometimes to Canada. Many Quakers served as agents of the
Underground Railroad, like the kindly Friends
who aid the fleeing Eliza in UNCLE TOM'S
CABIN. Prominent New England writers gave
money and active support to fugitive slaves.
The Railroad appears in Neill C. Wilson's *The
Freedom Song* (1955) and in many other novels
of the ante-bellum period. See HARRIET TUB-
MAN.

Underhill, John (b. 1597[?]—d. Sept. 21,
1672), soldier, public official, memoirist.
Underhill was a professional soldier who fought
first in Holland, then in 1630 came to Boston to
organize the militia. He helped the Connecticut
colonists fight against the Pequot tribe, was for
a time a deputy of the General Court, but got
into trouble over religious controversies. He
fought against the Dutch in the New Netherlands and wrote an account of this war, *News
from America* (1638), which Richard M. Dorson called "crude but classic." It was reprinted
in the *Collections* (1837) of the Massachusetts
Historical Society. John Greenleaf Whittier
greatly admired Underhill and wrote a poem
John Underhill (in *Hazel Blossoms,* 1875).

Underhill, John Garrett (b. Brooklyn, N.Y.,
Jan. 10, 1876—d. May 5, 1946), teacher, critic,
editor, translator, producer. Underhill was
greatly interested in the theater and in Spanish
literature; he combined his interests in his translations of the Spanish dramatists Jacinto
Benavente (1917–24), G. Martínez Sierra
(with Helen and Harley Granville-Barker,
1923), Lope de Vega (1936), and Calderón
(1944). He was also active in stage productions, both in English and Spanish. He wrote
Spanish Literature in the England of the Tudors
(1899) and was one of the editors of *Poet
Lore* (1918).

Understood Betsy (1917), a story for young people by DOROTHY CANFIELD FISHER. Elizabeth Ann is at first a timid and not very likable city child whose Aunt Frances cossets and tries to "understand" her. But when her aunt becomes sick she is sent to matter-of-fact cousins on a Vermont farm. There she grows to love the farm and her casual new relatives, discovers herself and her abilities, and ceases to be "Understood Betsy." The story was serialized in *St. Nicholas.*

Undertaker's Garland, The (1922), a collection of poems and prose pieces by JOHN PEALE BISHOP and EDMUND WILSON. The authors say, in a provocative preface, "We found our hymns to beauty and to love turning into funeral dirges and, instead of our old witty trifles, we fell to writing epitaphs. In a word, our environment and age have at last proved too strong for us, and, in a spirit which we honestly hope is one of loyal Americanism, we have decided that we shall best interpret our country in a book devoted to death." Among the contents: *The Death of the Last Centaur, The Death of an Efficiency Expert, The Funeral of an Undertaker, The Madman's Funeral, Emily in Hades, The Death of God, Resurrection.*

Under the Gaslight (prod. New York, 1870; London, 1868, as *London by Gaslight*), a melodrama by AUGUSTIN DALY. When Laura Courtlandt discovers that her father is a criminal, her lover deserts her and she suffers extreme poverty. She rescues a one-armed soldier from death on a railroad track and marries him. The New York background is realistically done, but the characters are conventional, the plot largely implausible. Among the characters is a blackmailer, the typical melodrama villain. The rescue scene was immediately duplicated in *After Dark* by DION BOUCICAULT; Daly sued him and won the suit. Daly used the character of the soldier as a means of criticizing the United States government for its treatment of wounded veterans. The play has been frequently and successfully revived.

Under the Old Elm (1875), a poem by JAMES RUSSELL LOWELL "read at Cambridge on the hundredth anniversary of Washington's taking command of the American Army, 3rd July, 1775." The poem, along with Lowell's *Ode Recited at the Harvard Commemoration* (1865), ranks among the best occasional poems in American literature. The *Ode* gives voice to Lowell's feeling of kindly reconciliation with the South after the Civil War and to his plea for national unity.

"Under the spreading chestnut tree." The often-quoted opening line of Henry Wadsworth Longfellow's THE VILLAGE BLACKSMITH (1844).

Union Magazine, The. This magazine was founded in July, 1847, with CAROLINE S. KIRKLAND as its editor for about eighteen months. Then John Sartain bought it and began publishing it as *Sartain's Union Magazine.* The magazine won attention for the excellence of its mezzotint reproductions. Edgar Allan Poe's second poem entitled *To Helen, The Bells,* and his *Poetic Principle* were all published in the magazine; other contributors included Henry Wadsworth Longfellow and James Russell Lowell. The magazine ceased publication in 1852.

Unknown Soldier, The (1929), a story by CONINGSBY DAWSON.

Unmanifest Destiny (1898), a poem by RICHARD HOVEY. This fervidly patriotic poem, one of the two or three best-known poems by Hovey, expresses the idea that even in our defeats the hand of destiny is present although "unmanifest."

Unparalleled Adventures of One Hans Pfaal, The (*Southern Literary Messenger,* June, 1835), a tale by EDGAR ALLAN POE. One of the earliest specimens of science fiction in American literature, this tale describes a voyage to the moon, done with tongue-in-cheek verisimilitude. The conclusion reveals it as a hoax. Three weeks later there appeared in the New York *Sun* the first of a series of articles on certain "Lunar Discoveries." These articles were supposedly reprinted from the nonexistent *Edinburgh Journal of Science* and described the discovery of life on the moon by Sir John Herschel, the eminent British astronomer. The articles made a great sensation, and were later revealed as the work of Richard Adams Locke. See BALLOON HOAX.

Untermeyer, Jean Starr (b. Zanesville, Ohio, May 13, 1886—   ), singer, poet, critic, translator, teacher. Mrs. Untermeyer, the divorced wife of Louis Untermeyer, made her debut as a singer in Vienna and London in 1924, specializing in German songs. She translated numerous works from German, taught at Olivet and the New School for Social Research, and contributed critical articles to magazines. But her reputation is based mainly on her several collections of verse: *Growing Pains* (1918); *Dreams Out of Darkness* (1921); *Steep Ascent* (1927); *Winged Child* (1936); and *Love and Need: Collected Poems* (1940). Critics have noted austerity and moral fervor as the dominant notes in her "gravely musical" poems.

Untermeyer, Louis (b. New York City, Oct. 1, 1885—   ), poet, translator, anthologist. Untermeyer's cavalier attitude toward geometry prevented his graduation from high school. After this his schooling came largely from his wide reading and from twenty years' work in various capacities in his father's jewelry factory. In 1923 he went to Europe to study for two years. He had already written *First Love* (1911), *Challenge* (1914), and several other volumes of poetry, but his more mature poems are found in *Burning Bush* (1928) and *Food and Drink* (1932). His poem *Caliban* best expresses his "social passion." He wrote some superb parodies, reissued in one volume as *Collected Parodies* (1926). He also wrote *American Poetry Since 1900* (1923); a novel, *Moses* (1928); *New Songs for New Voices* (with Clara and David Mannes, 1928); a biography of Heine (1937); an autobiography, *From Another World* (1939);

and translated Ernst Toller's *Masse Mensch* (1923). *Makers of the Modern World,* a series of compact biographies, appeared in 1955.

Untermeyer is best known, however, as an anthologist. His forward-looking anthologies molded the taste of two generations of readers. These include: *Modern American Poetry* (1919); *American Poetry from the Beginning to Whitman* (1931); *The Book of Living Verse* (1931); *New Modern American and British Poetry* (1950); *Magic Circle* (1952); *Modern American and British Poetry: Revised Shorter Edition* (with Karl Shapiro and Richard Wilbur, 1955); *Treasury of Great Poems* (1955); *Treasury of Ribaldry* (1956); *Golden Treasury of Poetry* (1959); *For You with Love* (1961).

Untriangulated Stars (1947), letters of EDWIN ARLINGTON ROBINSON to Harry de Forest Smith, 1890–1905. Smith was the only man in Gardiner, Me., who understood Robinson and could listen sympathetically to the poems he wrote. In his letters Robinson expressed himself candidly and sincerely; the result is, as Louise Dauner remarked (*American Literature,* March 1948), "an odyssey of self-doubt, artistic and economic struggle, and pain; and also of pride, faith, courage, and occasionally shy whimsicality."

Unvanquished, The (1934), a novel by WILLIAM FAULKNER. Set during the time of the Civil War, *The Unvanquished* deals with the Sartoris family, whose history Faulkner recounted in SARTORIS. Composed of seven stories that appeared first in the *Saturday Evening Post* and elsewhere, *The Unvanquished* centers primarily on the adventures of young Bayard Sartoris and his Negro companion Ringo; the Sartorises—Bayard, his father, the Colonel, and his grandmother, Miss Rosa—are treated romantically and sometimes tenderly, but never with the searching or even implicit criticism of the southern character found in Faulkner's other novels of the Old South. It is probable that Faulkner modeled COLONEL SARTORIS on William C. Falkner, his great-grandfather, who was also a colonel during the Civil War and was killed in 1889 by a former business partner under circumstances strikingly similar to those in which Colonel Sartoris was killed by Ben Redlaw.

Updike, Daniel Berkeley (b. Providence, R.I., Feb. 24, 1860—d. Dec. 28, 1941), printer, publisher, author. Updike founded the Merrymount Press in Boston in 1893 and was thereafter recognized as one of the chief influences in the improvement of typography in the United States. He lectured on printing at Harvard University, the California Institute of Technology, and the Huntington Library, and received honorary degrees from Brown University and Harvard. His most important work was *Printing Types: Their History, Forms, and Use* (2 v., 1922). He also wrote *In the Day's Work* (1924); *Notes on the Merrymount Press* (1934); *Some Aspects of Printing, Old and New* (1941). G. P. Winship wrote an account of him and his press (1948).

Updike, John Hoyer (b. Shillington, Pa., Mar.

18, 1932—   ), author, poet. A graduate of Harvard University, Updike contributed several poems and short stories to *The New Yorker* before the publication of his first book, a collection of poems, *The Carpentered Hen* (1958). These poems revealed a comic sense that pokes fun without being cruel. His acceptance as a novelist came with *The Poorhouse Fair* (1959), which won high critical acclaim. *Rabbit, Run* (1960) reached a larger audience and strengthened his reputation with the critics. Updike also wrote *The Same Door* (1959) and *Pigeon Feathers and Other Stories* (1962), both collections of short stories.

Up from Slavery (1900), an autobiography by BOOKER T. WASHINGTON. Washington is here looking back over the long, hard pull that led from a poor Southern slave cabin to the presidency of Tuskegee Institute. In his struggles for an education at Hampton Institute, Washington recognized the need of emphasizing industrial education for Negroes, rather than unrealistically concentrating on booklearning. These beliefs he put into practice when he helped found Tuskegee and rose to world fame as its president. The dignity of labor and the gospel of the toothbrush—these he constantly preached. He was a tireless worker in the cause of raising up his own race, an inspiring speaker whose fairmindedness could impress the most rabid Negro-haters. His life story, though hastily written, is an important document in the fields of education and race relations.

Upham, Charles Wentworth (b. St. John, N.B., May 4, 1802—d. June 15, 1875), clergyman, public official, historian, biographer. After graduating from Harvard University, Upham became associate pastor of a Unitarian church. His sermon *The Scripture Doctrine of Regeneration* was printed in 1840. He also served in the Massachusetts legislature, was elected to Congress in 1853, and wrote a campaign biography of John C. Frémont. More important was his careful investigation of *Salem Witchcraft* (1867). He was married to Ann Susan Holmes, sister of Oliver Wendell Holmes. Nathaniel Hawthorne apparently disliked him and is said to have modeled the second Judge Pyncheon in *The House of the Seven Gables* on Upham.

Upson, William Hazlett (b. Glen Ridge, N.J., Sept. 26, 1891—   ), novelist, short-story writer. After serving with the field artillery in France in World War I, Upson worked for a firm that sold tractors. His experiences in the war and in business served as material for groups of humorous stories, later collected in books, and for novels. Particularly popular were the misadventures of a tractor salesman, Alexander Botts, who described his experiences in letters to his firm and to others. Among Upson's books: *The Piano Movers* (1927); *Me and Henry and the Artillery* (1928); *Alexander Botts—Earthworm Tractors* (1929); *Earthworm in Europe* (1931); *Botts in War, Botts in Peace* (1944); *How to Be Rich Like Me* (1947); *Earthworms Through the Ages* (1947); *No Rest for Botts* (1951). In 1936 Joe E. Brown

starred in a movie called *Earthworm Tractors*.
Upson wrote *Middlebury Parade,* a musical
comedy, in 1949.

Uriel. The meaning of the word is "flame
of God" or "Angel of Light." It was originally
applied to an angel mentioned in the second
Book of Esdras in the Apocrypha. He was one
of the seven angels of rabbinical legend sent
by God to answer the questions of Esdras. The
Uriel legend was later incorporated into Christian legend, and appears most notably in Longfellow's GOLDEN LEGEND. Ralph Waldo Emerson invented a new legend entitled *Uriel*
(1838), which relates the dangers of enunciating a new truth, even among the divinities in
heaven.

Uris, Leon M. (b. Baltimore, Md., August
3, 1924–   ), author, screenwriter. Uris
achieved instantaneous success with his first
novel, *Battle Cry* (1953), a long, vivid account
of how the Marines were trained and fought
in World War II. *Exodus* (1958) was his best
received and most widely read novel. It traces
the history of European Jewry from the close
of the last century to the establishment of the
state of Israel. The film versions of both novels
also enjoyed tremendous popularity; Uris himself wrote the screenplay for *Battle Cry* in 1954.
Uris' other books include *The Angry Hills*
(1955), a novel; *Exodus Revisited* (1960), a
collection of essays with photographs by D.
Harissiadis; and *Mila 18* (1961), a novel set in
the uprising of the Warsaw ghetto during the
Second World War.

U.S.A. (1938). The title under which JOHN
DOS PASSOS collected, in an omnibus volume, his
trilogy of novels—THE 42ND PARALLEL (1930),
1919 (*q.v.*) (1932), and THE BIG MONEY (1936).

Ushant (1952), an autobiographical novel
by CONRAD AIKEN. It is obviously a mingling
of fact, fictionized fact, and fiction—somewhat
in the manner of Goethe's *Dichtung und Wahr-
heit.* The title comes from the name of an island off the coast of Brittany (called in French
Île d'Ouessant), an island of rocks and reefs
where Chateaubriand was wrecked on his return to France from America. The island seems
to suggest to Aiken the peril of living. Aiken,
who loves puns, even hints that the title means
to him "You-shan't."

One meets in the book the three wives of the
narrator, whom he distinguishes from one another as Lorelei I, Lorelei II, and Lorelei III.
There is, in addition, a good deal of philandering. Frequent references are made to the narrator's three children, all born of his first marriage. The literati of the era appear—his associates when he helped to inaugurate the "New
Poetry" in London—John Gould Fletcher, Harold Munro, Ezra Pound, and others. There are
fairly affectionate but occasionally satiric references to T. S. Eliot, whom he first knew when
they were classmates at Harvard University.
Chronology means nothing in *Ushant;* the landscape is that of a waking dream, the monologue
proceeds haphazardly in a manner that suggests, as some critics have pointed out, the re-
membrances of a patient on a psychoanalyst's
couch.

Usher, Roderick. The leading character in
Edgar Allan Poe's FALL OF THE HOUSE OF USHER
(in *Tales of the Grotesque and the Arabesque,*
1840). He is a deeply melancholic character,
who realizes that his twin sister Madeline has
been buried alive, but has no strength to go to
her assistance. Then she appears at the door of
his room, wounded and bleeding from her efforts to free herself, falls heavily upon him, and
in her violent and now real death agonies carries him to the floor as a corpse.

V

Vail, Henry Hobart (b. Pomfret, Vt., May 27, 1839—d. Sept. 2, 1925), editor, historian. Vail was a member of the staffs of several publishing firms and was particularly active in the editing and publishing of the McGuffey *Readers*. He wrote a *History of the McGuffey Readers* (1910) and *Pomfret, Vt.* (2 v., 1930).

Vain Oblations (in *Vain Oblations and Other Stories,* 1914), a story by KATHARINE FULLERTON GEROULD. This is an extraordinary story, with overtones of irony, about a New England woman captured by African savages. An expedition goes in search of her, but finds that she is content to remain a captive.

Valentine, Jimmy. One of O. Henry's most famous characters. See A RETRIEVED REFORMATION.

Vallentine, Benjamin Bennaton (b. England, Sept. 7, 1843—d. March 30, 1926), newspaperman, editor, humorist, playwright. Vallentine lived in Australia for several years, then returned to England, and in 1871 came to the United States. He worked for a shipping firm, studied law, finally became a civil service employee of New York City. He helped found PUCK in 1877, and for its first seven years was its managing editor. His letters written under the pen name of Lord Fitz-Noodle were satires on the British nobility. He had other newspaper and magazine connections and also wrote several plays, including *Fadette* (1892) and *In Paradise* (1899).

Valley Forge (1934), a play in free verse by MAXWELL ANDERSON. Washington is shown in 1777–78 as on the point of making peace, but his soldiers' devotion and courage make him change his mind.

Valley of Decision, The (1902), a novel by EDITH WHARTON. This story depicts the clash in late 18th-century Italy between the new antireligious ideas of Rousseau and Voltaire and the old conservative beliefs. Despite its historical setting, the plot is actually another statement of Mrs. Wharton's creed that breaks with convention are ultimately punished. Her chief character, Duke Odo, accepts the new ideas and seeks to alleviate the condition of his people. But by the time his subjects are ready to accept his ideas he has become a conservative and is exiled. The plot also involves Fulvia, daughter of an exiled philosopher, whom Odo loves. He rescues her from a convent but later on she is killed by a bullet meant for him. The book was made into a film in 1945.

Valley of the Moon, The (1913), a novel by JACK LONDON. In the fervor of his faith in socialism, London wrote this story of a strike in a California town, its consequences in the family life of Billy Roberts, a teamster and ex-prize fighter, and his final winning of happiness in the Valley of the Moon in Sonoma County. What London called the Valley of the Moon was Sonoma Valley; London himself lived on a nearby ranch and lies buried on "Little Hill" there.

Van Alstyne, Egbert A[nson] (b. Marengo, Ill., 1878—d. July 19, 1951), song writer. Van Alstyne's first major success was *Navajo* (1903). He wrote the music for more than seven hundred songs and the words for some of them. Among his greatest hits were: IN THE SHADE OF THE OLD APPLE TREE (lyrics by Harry Williams), *Pretty Baby, Your Eyes Have Told Me So, Little Old Church in the Valley,* and *Pony Boy.* Gus Kahn was one of his favorite lyricists.

Van Bibber, Cortland. Van Bibber, a favorite character in the stories of RICHARD HARDING DAVIS, is in part perhaps an incarnation of Davis himself. A Robin Hood of the social set, he has charm, courage, initiative, and a high sense of chivalry mingled with humor. He loves to get odd characters out of trouble and does so efficiently, even though he seems to be no more than an empty-headed man about town. The Van Bibber stories are included in *Van Bibber and Others* (1892) and *Episodes in Van Bibber's Life* (1899).

Van Buren, Martin (b. Kinderhook, N.Y., Dec. 5, 1782—d. July 24, 1862), lawyer, public official, 8th President. Van Buren read for the law for six years, was admitted to the bar in 1803, and practiced successfully in Kinderhook and Albany. He was surrogate of Columbia County (1808–13), state senator (1812–20), and state attorney general (1815–19). He showed himself a thoroughgoing Jeffersonian as United States Senator (1821–28) and, for a brief time in 1829, as Governor of New York, but resigned to become Jackson's Secretary of State. He left the State Department in August, 1831, to become minister to the Court of St. James, but his confirmation was effectively blocked by his enemy JOHN C. CALHOUN. Vice-President under Jackson (1833–37), he became "King Andrew's" heir apparent and defeated W. H. HARRISON for the Presidency in 1836.

Van Buren left an unoriginal Jeffersonian manuscript, published by his sons as *An Inquiry into the Origins and Course of Political Parties in the United States* (1867). Standard biographies are by E. M. Shepard (1899) and H. M. Alexander (1935), but the best recent discussion of his career is in A. M. Schlesinger, Jr.'s THE AGE OF JACKSON (1945). Elizabeth H. West's *Calendar of the Papers of Martin Van Buren* (1910) is a guide to the Van Buren manuscripts in the Library of Congress. The unfinished *Autobiography of Martin Van Buren* was edited by J. C. Fitzpatrick in the *Annual*

Report, American Historical Association for 1918 (v. 2, 1920). Van Buren appears as a villain in THE PARTISAN LEADER (1836), a novel by a Calhoun follower, N. B. Tucker.

Vance, Philo. A character in the detective stories of WILLARD HUNTINGTON WRIGHT, who published them under the pen name of S. S. Van Dine. Of the first, *The Benson Murder Case* (1926), Howard Haycraft said: "Overnight, American crime fiction came of age." The books were not merely literate, but often learned, occasionally ostentatiously so, and greatly impressed the public.

Vanderbilt, Arthur T. (b. Newark, N.J., July 7, 1888—d. June 16, 1957), lawyer, teacher, judge. A graduate of Wesleyan University and Columbia Law School, Vanderbilt was admitted to the bar in 1913, became professor of law the following year at New York University Law School and served there until 1948, became its dean in 1943. He became a judge of the circuit court in New Jersey in 1947 and was appointed chief justice in 1948. He was an active worker in numerous judicial, civil, and governmental organizations. He wrote *Studying Law* (1945); *Men and Measures in the Law* (1949); *Minimum Standards of Judicial Administration* (1949); *Cases and Other Materials on Modern Procedure and Judicial Administration* (1952); *The Doctrine of the Separation of Powers—Its Present-Day Significance* (1952); *The Challenge of Law Reform* (1955).

Vanderbilt, Cornelius (b. Staten Island, N.Y., May 27, 1794—d. Jan. 4, 1877), financier, steamship and railroad executive. Vanderbilt operated steamship lines on the Hudson, on Long Island Sound, to California during the gold rush, and to Europe. He made great sums of money, chiefly by cutting rates until his competitors were put out of business or joined him, but also by improving the speed and comfort of travel. He was equally successful in the railroad business and with his son **William H[enry] Vanderbilt** (1821–1885) was largely responsible for the organization and success of the New York Central Railroad system.

William Vanderbilt made large gifts to Vanderbilt University, originally endowed by his father, also to the New York College of Physicians and Surgeons and to the Metropolitan Museum of Art. **Cornelius Vanderbilt III** (1873–1942), a great-grandson of the first Cornelius, was an engineer and inventor who patented many devices for the improvement of locomotives and freight cars. His son **Cornelius Vanderbilt, Jr.** (1898–   ), a newspaperman and travel columnist, published several books, including *Personal Experiences of a Cub Reporter* (1922); *Experiences of a Washington Correspondent* (1924); *Farewell to Fifth Avenue* (1935); and *The Living Past of America* (1955).

W. A. Croffut wrote *The Vanderbilts and the Story of Their Fortune* (1886); A. D. H. Smith wrote *Commodore Vanderbilt* (1927); and Wayne Andrews wrote *The Vanderbilt Legend* (1941).

Vandercook, John W[omack] (b. England, April 22, 1902—d. Jan. 6, 1963), newspaperman, news commentator, writer. Vandercook came to the United States at an early age. He began his career as an actor, then served as a reporter on the Columbus *Citizen*, the Washington *News*, and the Baltimore *Post*; he became assistant editor of the Macfadden Publications and was feature editor of the New York *Graphic*. He has traveled extensively and served as a lively and persuasive news commentator. His books are sometimes straight personal narrative or history, as in *Tom-Tom* (1926); *Black Majesty* (1928); *Dark Islands* (1937); *Discover Puerto Rico* (1939); *Caribbee Cruise* (1938); *Empress of the Dusk* (1940). He also wrote some excellent detective stories laid in exotic locales, such as *Murder in Trinidad* (1933); *Murder in Fiji* (1935); *Murder in Haiti* (1953); *Murder in New Guinea* (1959).

Van der Donck, Adriaen (b. Netherlands, May 7, 1620—d. 1655[?]), colonist, historian. Van der Donck served from 1641 as an officer of the New Netherland government under PETER STUYVESANT and founded a colony along the Hudson on what is now the site of Yonkers. He returned to Holland because of a disagreement with Stuyvesant and published his *Vertoogh van Nieu-Neder-Land* ("Representation of New Netherland," 1650), which exhibited his strong prejudice against Stuyvesant. Later he returned to America. *Beschrijvinge van Nieuvv-Nederlant* ("Description of New Netherland," 1655) was partly an expansion of his earlier book.

Van de Water, Frederic F[ranklyn] (b. Pompton Lakes, N.J., Sept. 30, 1890—d. Sept. 16, 1968), editor, novelist, historian. Van de Water was the son of Virginia Van de Water, author of several books; the grandson of Mary Virginia Terhune (Marion Harland), novelist and author of books on housekeeping; and the nephew of Albert Payson Terhune. He worked for several years on newspapers in New York, then turned to free-lance writing, especially about Vermont. Among his books: *Grey Riders* (1921); *Horsemen of the Law Havoc* (1931); *A Home in the Country* (1937); *Rudyard Kipling's Vermont Feud* (1937); *Reluctant Rebel* (1948); *Catch a Falling Star* (1949); *In Defense of Worms* (1949); *Wings of the Morning* (1955); *Day of Battle* (1958).

Van Dine, S. S. The pen name of WILLARD HUNTINGTON WRIGHT.

Van Doren, Carl [Clinton] (b. Hope, Ill., Sept. 10, 1885—d. July 18, 1950), editor, anthologist, critic, writer. Carl Van Doren, the brother of MARK VAN DOREN, served on the Columbia University faculty from 1911 to 1930, was headmaster of Brearley School (1916–18), managing editor of the CAMBRIDGE HISTORY OF AMERICAN LITERATURE (3 v., 1917, 1918, 1921), literary editor of THE NATION (1919–22), editor for the Literary Guild and The Living Library, and a member of the committee on management of the DICTIONARY OF AMERICAN BIOGRAPHY (1926–36).

Van Doren was one of a vigorous group of young men who were able, after years of steady scholarship and creative academic politics, to see American history and literature established as constituent parts of regular university programs. His literary criticism was measured and avuncular, and he particularly delighted in the 18th century. His *Benjamin Franklin* (1938), a Pulitzer prize winner, comes closer than any other book to the secret of Franklin's many-sided genius; Van Doren calls Franklin "more than any single man: a harmonious human multitude." THE GREAT REHEARSAL (1948) is likewise an indispensable aid to the understanding of the 18th century. Other works of Van Doren's include *The Life of Thomas Love Peacock* (1911); *The American Novel* (1921; rev., 1940); *Contemporary Novelists* (1922); *Other Provinces* (short stories, 1925); *James Branch Cabell* (1925); *The Ninth Wave* (novel, 1926); *Swift* (1930); *Sinclair Lewis* (1933); *What Is American Literature?* (1935); *Three Worlds* (autobiography, 1936); *Secret History of the American Revolution* (1941); and *Jane Mecom, The Favorite Sister of Benjamin Franklin* (1950).

Van Doren, Dorothy [Graffe] (b. San Francisco, May 2, 1896—   ), editor, writer. The wife of MARK VAN DOREN, she served on the staff of the NATION from 1919 to 1936, the last ten years of which she spent as associate editor. During the war and later she was with the Office of War Information and the State Department Overseas Information Service. She is the author of *Flowering Quince* (1927); *Brother and Brother* (1928); *Those First Affections* (1938); *Dacey Hamilton* (1942); *Country Wife* (1950); *The Professor and I* (1959); *Men, Women and Cats* (1960).

Van Doren, Mark (b. Hope, Ill., June 13, 1894—   ), poet, critic, novelist, short-story writer, editor. Mark Van Doren graduated from the University of Illinois in 1914 and obtained his Ph.D. from Columbia University in 1920. Subsequently he taught at Columbia, lectured, and wrote in various forms. He served as literary editor and film critic for THE NATION in the twenties. In 1940 he won a Pulitzer prize for his *Collected Poems* (1939).

Van Doren's works include many volumes of poetry, stories, novels, and criticism. The very diversity of his work is proof of his lively perception and interest. His novels and short stories are distinguished by their warmth and imagination; his poetry projects universal thoughts from everyday things. L. L. Salomon said that his poems are "layered in many depths, the artifice hidden, the art revealed." His verse has sometimes been criticized, however, for lack of passion. He brought his poetic insight to critical works and biographies like *Henry David Thoreau* (1916); *The Poetry of John Dryden* (1931); *Shakespeare* (1939); *Nathaniel Hawthorne* (1949); *The Happy Critic* (1961). He edited the *Anthology of World Poetry* (1928, 1936). A few of his books of poetry: *Spring Thunder and Other Poems* (1924); *A Winter*

Diary and Other Poems (1935); *The Mayfield Deer* (1941); *Spring Birth* (1953); *Morning Worship and Other Poems* (1960). *Tilda* (1943) is a novel and *Nobody Say a Word, and Other Stories* (1953) contains some of his best short stories. He wrote one play, *Last Days of Lincoln* (1959), and an *Autobiography* (1958). His wife, DOROTHY GRAFFE VAN DOREN, wrote a biography of him, *The Professor and I* (1959).

Van Druten, John [William] (b. England, June 1, 1901—d. Dec. 19, 1957), lawyer, teacher, dramatist, novelist, director. Van Druten was teaching law in Wales when his first play, *Young Woodley* (1925), a study of adolescence, was banned by the British Censor. It was immediately produced in the United States and later opened peacefully in London. Van Druten accompanied the play to the United States and later became an American citizen. His plays are intelligent and lighthearted, nevertheless showing keen psychological insight; and have been for the most part quite successful. They include: *Old Acquaintance* (1940); *The Damask Cheek* (with LLOYD MORRIS, 1942); *The Voice of the Turtle* (1943); *I Remember Mama* (based on sketches by KATHRYN FORBES, 1944); *Bell, Book, and Candle* (1950); *I Am a Camera* (based on sketches by Christopher Isherwood, 1951). He capably directed several plays, both his own and others'; wrote several novels, including one based on *Young Woodley;* and dealt with his own craft in *The Way to the Present* (1938) and *The Playwright at Work* (1953). Several of his plays have been made into motion pictures.

van Dyke, Henry (b. Germantown, Pa., Nov. 10, 1852—d. April 10, 1933), writer, educator, diplomat, preacher. The most prominent member of a talented family, Henry van Dyke received his education at Princeton University. After serving as pastor of the United Congregational Church, New Bedford, R.I., and as minister of Brick Presbyterian Church, New York City, he became a professor of English literature at Princeton. President Wilson appointed him minister to the Netherlands and Luxembourg (1913–16), and during World War I he served in the navy as a chaplain. Back at Princeton after the war, he was active in the Presbyterian Church, exerting a strong liberal influence.

Van Dyke's first book, *The Reality of Religion* (1884), presages his lifelong attempt to fuse religion and practical, everyday living in a keen personal enjoyment of life. His wide literary range is seen in such titles as *Little Rivers* (1895) and *Fisherman's Luck* (1899), nature essays; THE STORY OF THE OTHER WISE MAN (1896); *The Builders* (1897) and *The White Bees* (1909), poetry; *The Poetry of Tennyson* (1899); *The Ruling Passion* (1901), short stories; *The Spirit of America* (1910), lectures delivered at the Sorbonne; and *The House of Rimmon* (1929), a play. *The Blue Flower* (1902) is a translation from Novalis. The "Avalon" edition of his collected works (17 v., 1920–22) was named after his home in Princeton.

Van Dyke, John C[harles] (b. New Brunswick, N.J., April 21, 1856—d. Dec. 5, 1932), art critic, librarian. A frequent contributor of articles on art to *Century Magazine*, and the author of twenty-nine books, chiefly on painting, Van Dyke was librarian at New Brunswick Theological Seminary and a professor of art history at Rutgers College. Among his numerous books are *Books and How to Use Them* (1883); *Principles of Art* (1887); *History of Painting* (1894); *New Guides to Old Masters* (12 v., 1914); *Rembrandt and His School* (1923); and *In Java* (1929). He edited *The Studio* (1883–84) and *Art Review* (1887–88).

van Dyke, Paul (b. New York City, March 25, 1859—d. Aug. 30, 1933), educator, historian, clergyman. This younger brother of HENRY VAN DYKE was ordained a Presbyterian minister (1887) and served his church for the next ten years. After the appearance of his first book, *The Age of the Renaissance* (1897), he became a professor of modern history at Princeton University. *Renaissance Portraits* (1905) was followed by *Catherine de Medicis* (2 v., 1922); *Ignatius Loyola* (1926); *The Story of France* (1928); and *George Washington* (1931).

van Dyke, Tertius (b. New York City, Jan. 18, 1886—d. Feb. 28, 1958), clergyman, poet. Van Dyke served as a Presbyterian minister in New York City, headmaster of a Connecticut private school, and dean of Hartford Theological Seminary. His chief writings are *Songs of Seeking and Finding* (1920) and *Henry van Dyke* (1935), a biography of his father. (See HENRY VAN DYKE.) With his father he wrote a series of syndicated newspaper articles, *The Guidepost* (1924–26), and a book entitled *Light My Candle* (1926).

van Gelder, Robert (b. Baltimore, Md., Oct. 19, 1904—d. April 3, 1952), newspaperman, editor, writer. Van Gelder began as a reporter on two New Haven newspapers, then went to work for the *New York Times*. He was editor of the *Times* Sunday book review section from 1943 to 1946; some of his interviews with authors were collected in *Writers and Writing* (1946). At the suggestion of W. Somerset Maugham he began writing fiction—*Important People*, a novel, appeared in 1948. He also wrote some juveniles—*Smash Picture* (1938), *Marjorie Fleming* (1940), and *The Enemy in the House* (1940). With his wife Dorothy van Gelder he edited an anthology, *American Legend: A Treasury of Our Country's Yesterdays* (1946).

Vanity Fair. [1] A comic weekly founded December 31, 1859, by three members of the Stephens family, Louis Henry, William Allan, and Henry Louis. CHARLES GODFREY LELAND was its managing editor in 1860–61, ARTEMUS WARD succeeded him (1861–62). It expired July 4, 1863. During its brief career it enlisted many contributors of note, among them Thomas Bailey Aldrich, R. H. Stoddard, William Winter, and William Dean Howells. The members of the staff and their contributors made the celebrated PFAFF'S CELLAR their meeting place. The *Vanity Fair* group appears in Albert Parry's *Garrets and Pretenders, A History of Bohemianism in America* (1933).

[2] A second magazine by the same name was founded as a monthly in New York City in 1868, but its beginnings are shadowy and it had various other names at first. It was edited by Frank Harris from 1907 to 1911. Condé Nast bought it in 1913, and under FRANK CROWNINSHIELD, its editor (1914–35), it became one of the sprightliest and most sophisticated magazines of its day. In 1935 it was absorbed by VOGUE, also owned by Nast. An elegant collection of pictures, articles, and fiction, *Vanity Fair: A Cavalcade of the Twenties*, edited by Cleveland Amory and Frederic Bradlee, appeared in 1960.

Van Loan, Charles E[mmet] (b. San Jose, Cal., June 29, 1876—d. March 3, 1919), sports editor, writer. Van Loan began by working as a secretary, contributing sports notes to the Los Angeles *Examiner*. They were so well written that in 1903 he was asked to become sports editor for the paper without having had any previous newspaper experience. The next year he moved to New York City, and for the rest of his life was known as the best American writer of sports fiction. He saw the romance as well as the humor of a game, and his material was based on close observation. His work appeared in many of the popular magazines of the time. Among the collections made of his stories were *The Big League* (1911); *The $10,-000 Arm* (1912); *Inside the Ropes* (1913); *The Lucky Seventh* (1913); *Old Man Curry* (1917); *Fore!* (1918); *Taking the Count* (1919); *Score by Innings* (1919).

Van Loon, Hendrik Willem (b. Holland, Jan. 14, 1882—d. March 11, 1944), journalist, historian. Van Loon left the Netherlands to study at Cornell and Harvard universities, then became a foreign correspondent. He received his Ph.D. at Munich in 1911 and taught history at various American universities. In the meantime he had written *The Fall of the Dutch Republic* (1913) and *The Rise of the Dutch Kingdom* (1915), both works of substantial scholarship. Much more popular were his *Ancient Man* (1920) and THE STORY OF MANKIND (1921). He became assistant editor of the Baltimore *Sun* (1924), and was a distinguished radio commentator for many years. His further literary labors included writing children's books and biographies of Peter Stuyvesant and Rembrandt, and editing several songbooks. But he is best known for his facile but never condescending surveys, enlivened by his own effective drawings: *The Story of the Bible* (1923); *Man the Miracle Maker* (1928); *Van Loon's Geography* (1932); *Ships and How They Sailed the Seven Seas* (1935); *The Arts* (1937); *The Story of the Pacific* (1940); *Van Loon's Lives* (1942); and other similar books.

van Paassen, Pierre [born **Pieter Anthonie Laurusse van Paassen**] (b. Holland, Feb. 7, 1895—d. Jan. 8, 1968), writer. After he received his education in Holland, Canada, and France, van Paassen worked as a reporter on the Toronto *Globe* and the Atlanta *Constitution,* and as a columnist and foreign correspondent for the New York *Evening World* and the Toronto *Star.* An old and bitter foe of Fascism, he was expelled from Italy, France, and Germany in the 1930's. For his lifelong devotion to the Jews and Zionism he was made an honorary citizen of Tel Aviv. Brought up a Calvinist, he was ordained a Unitarian minister (1946). *Israel and the Vision of Humanity* (1932), van Paassen's first book, reflects his identification of the fate of the Jewish people with the fate of all men. With J. W. Wise he edited *Nazism: An Assault on Civilization* (1934). *Days of Our Years* (1939), in which political history is interwoven with autobiographical reminiscences, was a best seller, as was *The Forgotten Ally* (1943), which deals with Jews during World War II. Van Paassen's other books include *The Time Is Now!* (1941); *That Day Alone* (1941); *Who's on the Lord's Side? Who?* (1942); *Earth Could Be Fair* (1946); *The Tower of Terzel* (1948); *Why Jesus Died* (1949); *Jerusalem Calling* (1955); and *Crown of Fire* (1960). Although occasionally sentimental and inaccurate, van Paassen was one of the most memorable journalist-historians of his time.

Van Twiller, Wouter [or **Walter**] (b. Netherlands, 1580[?]—d. 1656[?]), official. Van Twiller was governor of New Netherland from 1633 to 1637. He is one of the chief characters in Washington Irving's HISTORY OF NEW YORK . . . BY DIEDRICH KNICKERBOCKER. Irving described him as "exactly five feet six inches in height and six feet five inches in circumference." He typifies the "golden age" of the Knickerbocker aristocrat which Irving was satirizing in this work. Of Twiller, Irving goes on to say: "So invincible was his gravity that he was never known to laugh or even to smile through the whole course of a long and prosperous life. Nay, if a joke were uttered in his presence, that set light minded hearers in a roar, it was observed to throw him into a state of perplexity." This and other irreverent descriptions incensed the old Dutch families, but delighted Irving's contemporaries. Irving's profile of Twiller was based on the memoirs of David Pieterszen de Vries, a sea captain and colonizer who had disliked Twiller intensely.

Van Tyne, Claude Halstead (b. Tecumseh, Mich., Oct. 16, 1869—d. March 21, 1930), teacher, historian. Van Tyne studied at the University of Michigan and in various European universities, became a teacher of history at his alma mater in 1906, and department head in 1911. He was an outstanding authority on American history and won, posthumously, a Pulitzer prize for his *War of Independence, American Phase* (1929). He was a man of strong beliefs and often aroused controversy with his views. Among his other books: *The Loyalists in the American Revolution* (1902);

The American Revolution: 1776–1783 (1905); *The Causes of the War of Independence* (1922); also several textbooks.

Van Vechten, Carl (b. Cedar Rapids, Iowa, June 17, 1880—d. Dec. 21, 1964), novelist, music and dance critic, photographer. Van Vechten perhaps represents the spirit of the American intelligentsia in the 1920's, at once reckless and elegant, better than any other writer. He produced seven brittle novels, five books of music criticism, of which *Interpreters and Interpretations* (1917) is perhaps best known, numerous critical prefaces, and *The Tiger in the House* (1920), a charming book about cats. *Peter Whiffle* (1922), his first novel, is a Beerbohmesque imaginary autobiography of an aesthete and dilettante. THE BLIND BOW-BOY (1923) is a curious mixture of vulgarity, perverse intelligence, and elegance. *The Tattooed Countess* (1924) gives an authentic picture of fin-de-siècle Iowa, his native state. NIGGER HEAVEN (1926) was the first and remains one of the best novels about Harlem; Van Vechten was perhaps the first established literary man to take Negro artists seriously. *Parties* (1930) was his last novel; thereafter he turned to a career in photography. He wrote about himself in *Sacred and Profane Memories* (1932). He edited the *Selected Works of Gertrude Stein* (1946) and *Last Operas and Plays by Gertrude Stein* (1949).

Van Vogt, A[lfred] E[lton] (b. Canada, April 26, 1912—), science fiction writer. Van Vogt sold his first story when he was twenty. His name has become especially familiar to readers of science fiction and tales of fantasy. His best known book is *The World of Ā* (1948), an account of a utopian community on the planet Venus whose inhabitants have been conditioned semantically along the lines set down by ALFRED KORZYBSKI. As a consequence they are protected forever from strife and war. Science fiction enthusiasts, however, are more inclined to praise *Slan* (1946), which tells of a group of mutants known as Slans, notable for their ability to communicate thought by means of tendrils which grow in and along their hair. Among Van Vogt's other books are: *The Book of Ptath* (1947); *The Weapon Makers* (1947); *Out of the Unknown* (1948), a collection of short stories, with Edna Mayne Hull; *The Voyage of the Space Beagle* (1950); *The Weapon Shops of Isher* (1951, a sequel to *The Weapon Makers*); *Away and Beyond* (1952); *The Mixed Men* (1952); *The Hypnotism Handbook* (1956), with Charles Edward Cook; *Mind Cage* (1957); *War Against the Rull* (1959); *Siege of the Unseen* (1959).

Vanzetti, Bartolomeo. See SACCO-VANZETTI CASE.

Varieties of Religious Experience, The (1902), a work by WILLIAM JAMES. Based on the material which James had collected on the psychology and philosophy of religion for lectures at the University of Edinburgh in 1901 and 1902, *The Varieties of Religious Ex-*

perience contains numerous descriptions of religious states of consciousness, which James presented from a pragmatic point of view. He regarded the mystical experience in the light of his hypothesis of a "subliminal self" which is able to transcend the narrow limits of normal experience. The book has remained one of the most popular of James' works, and is particularly important for the evidence it gave for religious experience as a phenomenon *sui generis.*

Variety. In the language of show business at the beginning of the 20th century the word *variety* meant VAUDEVILLE. In 1905 Sime Silverman began publishing a weekly magazine named *Variety,* which became the chief trade journal of the theatrical business and one of the most successful periodicals in American history. At first it dealt mainly with vaudeville, but gradually it expanded to take in every branch of the theater; it also runs a column about the literati, who are now deeply concerned with "rights" in the theatrical field. *Variety* has always made it its business to tell the truth and not be afraid of getting into a fight. It presents an immense amount of news and comment, frequently in the form of "inside stories." In 1933 a separate edition began appearing in Hollywood as a daily. Abel Green succeeded Silverman as editor.

Variety is especially known for the spectacular language it has been fabricating over the years; sports, the underworld, and *Variety* have undoubtedly been the three greatest fertilizers of American slang. Abel Green collected some of *Variety's* neologisms, such as *big time, juve, m.c.,* the *borscht circuit, eatery, vamp, angel* (someone who finances a Broadway production), and *pix.* The greatest neologist on the staff of *Variety* was Jack Conway, who is credited with *S.A., to click, high-hat, pushover, pay-off, belly laugh, scram,* and many others. *Variety's* headline for the financial debacle of 1929 was long remembered: "Wall Street Lays an Egg." Walter Winchell freely acknowledges that he learned many of his verbal procedures from the paper.

David Stoddart told Silverman's story in *Lord Broadway* (1941). *The Spice of Variety* (1952), edited by Green, is an amusing collection of contributions from actors, critics, playwrights, and others.

Varmint, The (1910), a collection of stories by OWEN JOHNSON. These stories chronicle the adventures of DINK STOVER as a student at the Lawrenceville School in New Jersey. They became immensely popular among young readers. Stover's career was continued in *The Tennessee Shad* (1911) and *Stover at Yale* (1911).

Vasconselos (1853), a novel by WILLIAM GILMORE SIMMS. It describes colorfully the conflict between the explorer de Soto, who is unfavorably depicted, and the adventurer Vasconselos. Vasconselos thinks he has been unfairly treated by de Soto, turns traitor and marries an Indian princess.

Vashon, George (1820–1878), poet. Sterling A. Brown, in *Negro Poetry and Drama* (1937), describes Vashon as a well-educated and ambitious writer who found inspiration in the abolitionist cause. He was the first Negro to write a narrative poem of any length, "Vincent Ogé," a chronicle of the Haitian revolutionary hero; it appeared in a collection called *Autographs of Freedom* (1856).

Vassall Morton (1856), a novel by FRANCIS PARKMAN. In this narrative Parkman included some of his own experiences. He told the story of a Harvard graduate who studies races and people and who for a time is held captive by the Indians.

vaudeville. A form of amusement in the theater in which variety is the pattern. The origin of the word is obscure. *Webster's New International Dictionary* (1934) states that it was derived from the French village Vau-de-Vire in Normandy, the inhabitants of which were famous for the satirical songs they sang. In England a similar type of entertainment developed in the music halls, originally adjuncts to taverns. These music halls became popular in the early 18th century and provided programs of songs, dances, acrobatics, and pantomimes; later the links with taverns were broken. The English music hall undoubtedly influenced American vaudeville entertainments, except that pantomimes never became popular here.

TONY PASTOR gave vaudeville its real start when on Oct. 24, 1881, he opened his new 14th Street Theater in New York with a series of vaudeville acts. Competition in this area was keen, and as it continued better theaters were built, stage properties were improved, and mechanical gadgets added wonderment to the acts. Theaters were open from eleven in the morning to eleven at night, offering two complete sets of performances. Some famous vaudeville producers were Oscar Hammerstein, Alexander Pantages, and Marcus Loew. The Palace Theater in New York was formerly the principal home of vaudeville. Vaudeville became for an astonishing number of performers a training school that led to stardom. From the vaudeville theater came such actors as Eddie Cantor, the Marx brothers, WILL ROGERS, FRED ALLEN, W. C. Fields, Jimmy Durante, Fred and Adele Astaire, and Fannie Brice. Among the varieties of performers were acrobats, jugglers, ballad singers, magicians, midgets, monologists, animals, family teams, ventriloquists, sharpshooters, mind-readers, dancers of all kinds, hypnotists, minstrels, contortionists, mimics, and female impersonators.

Vaudeville flourished mightily during the 1920's, but suffered severely from the 1929 crash. Even worse, however, was the coming of the movies and radio. When television appeared after World War II, vaudeville experienced a minor revival. For the most part the vaudeville pattern has been transferred back to the numerous and flourishing night clubs of the United States. In its more earthy forms vaudeville becomes burlesque. Abel Green and Joe Laurie, Jr.'s *Show Biz: From Vaude to Video* (1951) devotes much space to the history of vaudeville.

Veblen, Thorstein B[unde] (b. Cato Township, Wis., July 30, 1857—d. Aug. 3, 1929), economist, social philosopher. Veblen was born on the agricultural frontier in Wisconsin and was reared in Minnesota among highly clannish Norwegian immigrants. Norwegian, not English, was his native language. His keen mind and biting tongue led to loneliness and unpopularity in his youth. Despite his dissent from the communal mores, however, Veblen did share deeply in the agrarian unrest of the 1870's and 1880's in which pre-Marxian utopian socialist ingredients and real grievances combined to produce the later Populist outburst against the railroads and "Eastern capitalists."

Veblen's father saw to it that his children were well educated and sent his son to Carleton College in Northfield, Minn. Afterward Veblen studied at Johns Hopkins University, then transferred to Yale University and took his Ph.D. in philosophy (1884). As academic posts in philosophy were then the private preserve of the clergy, Veblen returned to Minnesota, where he studied and translated from the Norse for seven years. In 1891 he went to Cornell University for further study, then was called to the economics department of the new University of Chicago. Later he taught at Stanford University and the University of Missouri; at Missouri he gave his most famous course, "Economic Factors in Civilization." Veblen was an eccentric and mostly unpopular teacher, but a brilliant minority found him uncommonly stimulating.

Meantime Veblen's domestic life was foundering; he was divorced from his first wife in 1911, remarried in 1914, and did not bother to hide his irregular relationships with several other women. In 1918 he became an editor of The Dial in New York and a lecturer at the New School for Social Research. In 1925 he was offered the presidency of the American Economic Association, but rejected it because, as he noted, "They didn't offer it to me when I needed it."

Veblen's first published book, The Theory of the Leisure Class (1899), won him instant fame. It was generally misunderstood as literary satire, but was actually a richly ironic evolutionary analysis of the pecuniary values of the middle and business classes. Later books included *The Theory of Business Enterprise* (1904); *The Instinct of Workmanship* (1914), his most original and baffling effort; *Imperial Germany and the Industrial Revolution* (1915); *An Inquiry into the Nature of Peace* (1917); *The Higher Learning in America* (1918); *The Vested Interests and the State of the Industrial Arts* (1919); *The Place of Science in Modern Civilization* (1919); *The Engineers and the Price System* (1921); *The Laxdaela Saga*

(translated from the Icelandic with an introduction, 1925); and *Essays in Our Changing Order* (ed. by Leon Ardzrooni, 1934). Max Lerner edited the *Portable Veblen* (1948).

Veblen's writings circulate constantly about what he defined as the two major contrasting human drives: the predatory and the productive. He distinguished sharply between "business" and "industry"; the latter was the endlessly fecund process of making goods to answer actual needs, the former a predatory scheme of "parasites" to make profits by interfering in the direct consumption of goods for use. Human nature, like human institutions, said Veblen, is not immutable; all aspects of culture, all moral standards, change with time and often with place. The development of the machine process is a free gift of evolution, and if left to the industrial factors and not to the business predators it would guarantee an abundant earthly peace for all. Veblen's main methodological point has been absorbed into the axioms of modern economics. His other contributions are usually turned aside by economists as "literary," and not without cause; his style is notable for its relentless irony and its assumption of cool neutrality.

The most original yet—in his lifetime—least openly acknowledged American economist, Veblen profoundly influenced his own time as well as later thought. Books about him include Joseph Dorfman's *Thorstein Veblen and His America* (1934); R. L. Duffus' *The Innocents at Cedro: A Memoir of Thorstein Veblen and Some Others* (1944); David Riesman's *Thorstein Veblen, A Critical Interpretation* (1953); Bernard Rosenberg's *The Values of Veblen: A Critical Appraisal* (1958); and Lev E. Dobriansky's *Veblenism: A New Critique* (1958).

Vedder, Elihu (b. New York City, Feb. 26, 1836—d. Jan. 29, 1923), painter, illustrator, writer. Vedder's paintings include some of the murals in the Library of Congress, and his best known illustrations are those for the *Rubáiyát of Omar Khayyám*, translated by Edward FitzGerald (1884). He wrote several books, some of them humorous. Among his books: *Digressions of V* (1910), a humorous autobiography; *Miscellaneous Moods in Verse* (1914); *Doubt and Other Things* (1922).

Veiller, Bayard (b. Brooklyn, N.Y., Jan. 2, 1869—d. June 16, 1943), newspaperman, dramatist. After holding jobs on Chicago and New York papers, Veiller turned to writing plays; he made a specialty of mystery dramas, and some of them were very successful. Among them were Within the Law (1912); The Thirteenth Chair (1916), which used spiritualism as a theme; The Trial of Mary Dugan (1927), which included a meticulously arranged courtroom scene; Damn Your Honor (1929); and That's the Woman (1930). In his later days Veiller became a movie executive. He wrote an autobiography, *The Fun I've Had* (1941).

Vein of Iron (1935), a novel by Ellen

GLASGOW. One of Miss Glasgow's latest novels, *Vein of Iron* is considered one of her best. It deals with the "vein of iron" in the character of a woman who meets all kinds of misfortune in the Virginia mountains where she first lives, then later in Virginia towns. The period is the years before and during the depression of the 1930's.

Venable, William Henry (b. Waynesville, Ohio, April 29, 1836—d. July 6, 1920), teacher, historian, writer. For the greater part of his life Venable was a teacher of English and science in the schools of Cincinnati. He was influential in educational circles, a popular lecturer, and a contributor to many periodicals. He wrote books of many kinds, among them a book on pedagogy entitled *Let Him First Be a Man* (1893), several novels, and much miscellaneous verse. But he is chiefly remembered today for a useful historical work, *Beginnings of Literary Culture in the Ohio Valley* (1891). This book includes historical and biographical sketches, some of them offering material on early Western writers not mentioned elsewhere; it was a pioneer regional study.

Venetian Glass Nephew, The (1925), a novel by ELINOR WYLIE. This fantasy tells how Rosalba, a woman of flesh and blood, falls in love with and marries Virginio, who is made of glass. To harmonize herself and her husband she is willingly transmogrified by fire into porcelain. The story has been interpreted as intended to symbolize the conflict between nature and art.

Venetian Life (1866), travel sketches by WILLIAM DEAN HOWELLS. See ITALIAN JOURNEYS.

Vernon, Dorothy. The heroine of a historical novel entitled *Dorothy Vernon of Haddon Hall* (1902), by CHARLES MAJOR. She falls in love with her father's bitterest enemy, Sir John Manners; sets two kingdoms at odds; runs away with Manners; and becomes the ancestress of the dukes of Rutland. Major based his story on an actual character in English history, but his book failed to duplicate the success of his WHEN KNIGHTHOOD WAS IN FLOWER (1898), which he wrote under the pen name Edwin Caskoden. However, it reached the best-seller lists.

Verplanck, G[ulian] C[rommelin] (b. New York City, Aug. 6, 1786—d. March 18, 1870), politician, editor, author. Verplanck is remembered today chiefly for his hatred of Governor DeWITT CLINTON and his friendship for WILLIAM CULLEN BRYANT. A decade-long feud with Clinton produced erudite satires in verse and prose, such as *A Fable for Statesmen and Politicians* (1815); *The State Triumvirate* (1819); *The Bucktail Bards* (1819). Verplanck founded with Charles King the New York *American*, in which many of his attacks on Clinton first appeared. With Bryant and R. C. SANDS he edited an annual giftbook, THE TALISMAN (1828–30). One of the earliest of American Shakespearean scholars, he published

Shakespeare's Plays: With His Life (3 v., 1847).

Besides his literary enterprises, Verplanck served in the New York Assembly, in Congress, and as a state senator. His public addresses were collected in *Discourses and Addresses* (1833). Bryant wrote *A Discourse on the Life, Character and Writings of Gulian Crommelin Verplanck* (1870). Robert W. July wrote a eulogistic account of *The Essential New Yorker* (1951) as an important voice of 19th-century American romanticism and nationalism. See KNICKERBOCKER SCHOOL.

Verrazano [or Verrazzano], Giovanni da (b. *c.* 1480[?]—d. 1527[?]), Italian navigator. Verrazano discovered parts of the North American continent while in the service of Francis I of France. He gave the first description of the North American coast after actually viewing it. He found the mouth of the Hudson River in 1524. He prepared a *Letter on My Voyages* (c. 1524) which appeared in Hakluyt's *Voyages* (v. 8), the New York Historical Society's *Collections, Second Series* (v. 1, 1841), and the American Scenic and Historical Preservation Society's *Report* (v. 15, 1910, Appendix).

Verrill, A[lpheus] Hyatt (b. New Haven, Conn., July 28, 1871—d. Nov. 14, 1954), naturalist, explorer, ethnologist, inventor, writer. Verrill made explorations mainly in the West Indies and Latin America and contributed data to both ethnology and zoology. He was also an expert photographer and produced a new process of color photography. He wrote more than a hundred books on natural history, Indians, and exploration, some of which were for boys. Among them: *In Morgan's Wake* (1915); *Book of the West Indies* (1917); *Panama Past and Present* (1921); *Boys' Book of Buccaneers* (1927); *Under Peruvian Skies* (1930); *Our Indians* (1935); *Along New England Shores* (1936); *My Jungle Trails* (1937); *The Real Americans* (1954).

vers libre. See FREE VERSE.

Very, Jones (b. Salem, Mass., Aug. 28, 1813 —d. May 8, 1880), poet. After teaching at Fisk Latin School to earn money for tuition, Very went to Harvard College, then the Harvard Divinity School, where he served briefly as a tutor of Greek. Licensed as a Unitarian minister he preached numerous sermons despite his shyness and otherworldliness. He lived a retired life in Salem with his sisters, occasionally contributing to the Salem *Gazette* and the *Christian Register* and writing sonnets and lyrics celebrating ecstatic religious visions and mysticism. At one time he was committed to McLean Asylum in Somerville, Mass., but his friend Ralph Waldo Emerson stoutly insisted that he was "profoundly sane." Very was associated with TRANSCENDENTALISM. Very's first book, *Essays and Poems* (1839), was edited and published by Emerson, and William Cullen Bryant and William Channing both praised his sonnets highly. His work resembles that of Montaigne and the 17th-century English metaphysical

poets. Two posthumously published collections were *Poems* (1883) and *Poems and Essays* (1886). Very was studied by Yvor Winters in *Maule's Curse* (1938).

Vespucci, Amerigo (Latinized as **Americus**) (b. Italy, 1454—d. 1512), cosmographer, navigator, explorer. Vespucci was a clerk in the commercial office of the House of the Medici when word of Columbus' success in crossing the ocean reached Italy. It inspired Vespucci to set off for Spain immediately in search of a contract to furnish supplies for Columbus' second voyage. It is probable that Vespucci did take part in fitting out Columbus' second voyage, and he himself made four voyages to the New World. During Vespucci's third voyage he landed on the coast of Brazil—some time between May and October of 1502—but in a voyage of 1497 he mentions touching upon a coast "which we thought to be that of a continent." If he was right, the fact would give him priority over both John Cabot and Columbus in reaching the mainland of America.

In 1503 Vespucci wrote a short account of his third voyage which soon appeared in a Latin version, *Mundus Novus* (1504). He gives a vivid description of the country and its inhabitants. A copy came into the hands of a German geographer named Martin Waldseemueller, who remarked in a Latin treatise entitled *Cosmographiae Introductio* (1507): "A fourth part of the earth has been discovered by

Amerigo Vespucci . . . I see no reason why anyone could justly object to naming this part *Amerige;* that is, the land of *Amerigo,* or *America,* after its discoverer." Germán Arciniegas, in *Amerigo and the New World: The Life and Times of Amerigo Vespucci* (1955), rejects the idea that Vespucci was "a sly thief who cunningly robbed Columbus of his rightful glory." He lists nine pages of titles of books about Vespucci, ranging from E. D. Adams' *America and Americans, The Name and Its Significance* (1926) to Stefan Zweig's *Amerigo, A Comedy of Errors in History* (1942).

Vestal, Stanley. The pen name of WALTER S. CAMPBELL.

Veteran Sirens (in *Collected Poems,* 1921), a poem by EDWIN ARLINGTON ROBINSON. Yvor Winters described the poem as "an expression of sympathy for old prostitutes who must continue as best they are able at their trade." Laurence Perrine disputed this view and held that the poem "deals rather, in my opinion, with middle-aged or elderly spinsters who refuse to accept either age or their spinsterhood gracefully." The diversity of interpretations suggests a certain obscurity in the poem, but probably Perrine's is close to Robinson's intention.

Vicious Circle, The (1951), an account of the Algonquin Round Table by Margaret Case Harriman. See ROUND TABLE.

Victor, Frances [**Fuller**] (b. Oneida Co., N.Y., May 23, 1826—d. Nov. 14, 1902), journalist, poet, historian. In 1856 Frances Fuller married a naval engineer, Henry Clay Victor; six years later her sister Metta Victoria (see below) married a New York editor, ORVILLE JAMES VICTOR, the brother of her sister's husband. Both sisters were protégées of RUFUS W. GRISWOLD, who edited the collection of verse they published jointly, *Poems of Sentiment and Imagination* (1851). Many years later Frances published *Poems* (1900). Her husband lost his life in a shipwreck, and her later years were full of hardship and poverty. She wrote a good *History of Oregon* (2 v., 1886, 1888), also wrote about other states in the Northwest, and was a member of H. H. Bancroft's staff in the preparation of the *History of the Northwest Coast* (1884).

Victor, Metta Victoria [**Fuller**] (b. near Erie, Pa., March 2, 1831—d. June 26, 1886), poet, dime novelist, humorist. Metta's fame and apparently her ability surpassed that of her sister Frances (see above). Together they wrote *Poems of Sentiment and Imagination* (1851). Then Metta began writing fiction and achieved fame with a temperance novel, *The Senator's Son* (1853). When she married ORVILLE JAMES VICTOR, who worked for the famous ERASTUS F. BEADLE, she became a prolific contributor of serials to the cheap magazines of the day. Oddly enough, she wrote under her own name for the New York *Weekly* and for *Saturday Night,* but her contributions to Beadle's magazines and libraries appeared under various pen names. Typical of her books were *Alice Wilde, The Raftsman's Daughter*

(1860); *The Backwoods Bride* (1861); Maum Guinea and Her Plantation Children (1862); *The Gold Hunters* (1874). Another of her books was *Lives of the Female Mormons* (1856). As the popularity of the dime novel waned she began writing humorous stories and sketches.

Victor, Orville James (b. Sandusky, Ohio, Oct. 23, 1827—d. March 14, 1910), editor, publisher, historian. Victor was originally a historian who wrote some unimportant books on the Revolution and the Civil War. He became an editor for Beadle & Smith and for them not only invented a formula for successfully writing the stories they were publishing but also proved an apt instructor for the writers they hired. In so doing he created a new genre, the DIME NOVEL.

Vidal, Gore (b. West Point, N.Y., Oct. 3, 1925—   ), novelist, playwright, poet. Vidal made use of his army experiences in World War II in his first published book, *Williwaw* (1946), the scene of which was the Aleutian Islands. There followed a rapid succession of other novels, including *In a Yellow Wood* (1947); *The City and the Pillar* (1948); *The Season of Comfort* (1949); *A Search for the King* (1950); *Dark Green, Bright Red* (1950); *The Judgment of Paris* (1952); *Messiah* (1954). As "Edgar Box" he has written mystery stories. Among his books *The City and the Pillar* has attracted the widest attention, including some severe denunciation for its picture of homosexuality. Especially notable is his story "Erlinda and Mr. Coffin" in *A Thirsty Evil and Other Stories* (1956). Vidal has also written some thoughtful verse and a number of plays, published in *Visit to a Small Planet and Other Television Plays* (1956). *Visit to a Small Planet* was rewritten as a three-act drama and successfully produced on Broadway in 1957. *The Best Man*, a successful Broadway play on a political theme, was produced in 1960. Vidal, grandson of Oklahoma's Senator Gore, had a bout with politics in 1961, when he ran unsuccessfully for office in upstate New York.

Vielé, Herman Knickerbocker (b. New York City, Jan. 31, 1856—d. Dec. 14, 1908), novelist, playwright. Vielé is best known for his novel *The Last of the Knickerbockers* (1901). His brother Egbert Ludovicus Vielé (1863–1937) lived and wrote in France under the name Francis Vielé-Griffin and was regarded as one of the great French poets of his day.

Viereck, George Sylvester (b. Germany, Dec. 31, 1884—d. March 18, 1962), novelist, essayist. Viereck settled in New York City in 1895. He was associate editor of *Current Literature* (1906–15) and editor of *International* (1912–18) and *American Monthly* (1914–27). He actively championed the German cause during World War I. Among his numerous writings are *A Game at Love and Other Plays* (1906); *Nineveh, and Other Poems* (1907); *Roosevelt: A Study in Ambivalence* (1919); *My First Two Thousand Years* (a trilogy written with Paul Eldridge,

1928–32); *The Temptation of Jonathan* (political essays, 1938); *Gloria* (a novel, 1952), and *Men into Beasts* (1952). During World War II, he served as library advisor to the German Library of Information, and was imprisoned from 1942 to 1947 for not declaring himself a German agent in the United States.

Viereck, Peter [Robert Edwin] (b. New York City, Aug. 5, 1916—   ), poet, teacher. A son of George Sylvester Viereck, Peter Viereck was educated at Harvard and taught at Harvard and at Radcliffe, Smith, and Mount

Holyoke colleges. Viereck's political attitude of "liberal conservatism" found expression in *Metapolitics* (1941), a book he called "a psychoanalysis of Nazism"; most explicitly in *Conservatism Revisited* (1949); and also in *Shame and Glory of the Intellectuals* (1953), the brief *Dream and Responsibility* (1953), and *Unadjusted Man: A New Hero for Americans* (1956). His novelette *Who Killed the Universe?* appeared in *New Directions* (1948). TERROR AND DECORUM, his first book of poems, won the Tietjens Prize for poetry and a Pulitzer prize (1948). It was followed by other collections: *Strike Through the Mask!* (1950); *The First Morning* (1952); *A Walk on Moss* (1956); *The Persimmon Tree* (1956). William Carlos Williams described some of Viereck's poems as "lyrical, sensitive, distinguished in feeling"; but other criticisms have not always been so favorable. *The Roots of the Nazi Mind* appeared in 1961.

vigilantes. The name is derived from the "Vigilance Committees" which in the West in the old frontier days and in the South during the Civil War undertook to maintain law and order through privately organized groups of civilians. Those in the South directed their activities mainly against Northern sympathizers and Negroes. Those in the West administered a rough kind of justice in a lawless time. Lynching was a frequent penalty directed against robbers, outlaws, and horse and cattle thieves. In California the vigilantes were especially active during the gold-rush period beginning in 1849. N. P. Langford wrote an account of *Vigilante Days and Ways* (1910). Four fictional stories which exhibit the vigilantes in California are Bret Harte's OUTCASTS OF POKER FLAT (1869); Frank Norris' THE OCTOPUS (1901); John Steinbeck's IN DUBIOUS BATTLE (1936); Richard Summers' *Vigilante* (1949). One story that relates poignantly the shocking injustice the vigilantes sometimes perpetrated is Walter Van Tilburg Clark's THE OX-BOW INCIDENT (1940), which is set in Nevada and was made into an excellent film. Alan Valentine's *Vigilante Justice* (1956) is an account of early days in turbulent San Francisco.

Village Blacksmith, The (1839; published in *Ballads and Other Poems*, 1841), a poem by HENRY WADSWORTH LONGFELLOW. The smithy described in this poem, one of the most popular and widely recited that Longfellow wrote, was suggested by an actual smithy that stood on Brattle St., Cambridge. But it was also Longfellow's purpose in the poem to praise one of his own ancestors, a blacksmith in Newberry. The poem is frankly moralistic and sentimental, and has been condemned on that account. But it is written with great metrical skill and melody.

Villains Galore (1954), an account of "the heyday of the popular STORY WEEKLY" by Mary Noel. Miss Noel states that "fifty years of showmanship, of advertising and fanfare, were necessary before the modern newsstand became an established institution." During the 19th century it was the story magazines that contributed most to the success of these newsstands. These story weeklies were easy to read and appealed to middle-class taste and prejudices. Editors paid high prices to authors who wrote (no doubt with tongue in cheek) their highly sentimental romances and stilted dialogues.

Villard, Henry [original name: **Ferdinand Heinrich Gustav Hilgard**] (b. Bavaria, April 10, 1835—d. Nov. 12, 1900), publisher, author. After immigration, Villard worked for the New York *Staatszeitung* (1858) and served as a Civil War correspondent for the New York *Herald* and the New York *Tribune*. He married the only daughter of William Lloyd Garrison (1866) and had a son, OSWALD GARRISON VILLARD. An aggressive financier, he controlled the Northern Pacific Railroad as president and chairman of the board of directors. In addition to his efforts to obtain a transportation monopoly in the Northwest, Villard gave financial aid to Thomas Edison, founded the Edison General Electric Company (1889), and became owner and editor of the New York *Evening Post* (1881). His earliest book was *The Past and Present of the Pike's Peak Gold Regions* (1860).

A Journey to Alaska (1899) was published in the New York *Evening Post*, and his son published a posthumous edition of Villard's *The Early History of Transportation in Oregon* (1944). Two sources of biographical information are *Memoirs of Henry Villard* (2 v., 1904) and J. B. Hedges' *Henry Villard and the Railways of the Northwest* (1930).

Villard, Oswald Garrison (b. Germany, March 13, 1872—d. Oct. 1, 1949), editor, author. Villard spent his long journalistic career championing such causes as pacifism, free trade, minority rights, and the moral responsibilities of the American press. After his education at Harvard, he worked on his father's paper, the New York *Evening Post* (1897–1918), eventually becoming editor and president. He was also the manager and owner of THE NATION (1918–32) and a contributing editor until 1940. One of the founders of the National Association for the Advancement of Colored People (1910), he wrote *John Brown: A Biography Fifty Years Afterwards* (1910). Other books of his are *Germany Embattled* (1915); *Newspapers and Newspaper Men* (1923); *Prophets, True and False* (1927); *The German Phoenix* (1933); *Fighting Years: Memoirs of a Liberal Editor* (1939); *The Disappearing Daily* (1944); *Free Trade—Free World* (1947); *How America Is Being Militarized* (1947).

Vinal, Harold (b. Vinalhaven, Me., Oct. 17, 1891—d. Mar. 9, 1965), poet, editor, teacher. Vinal is a writer of melodious and sweet poetry, which is most successful in its depiction of Maine scenery. Among his collections: *White April* (1922); *Voyage* (1923); *Nor Youth Nor Age* (1924); *A Stranger in Heaven* (1927); *Hymn to Chaos* (1931); *Hurricane* (1936); *Selected Poems* (1948); *Hurricane and Other Poems* (1957). In 1921 he founded a quarterly magazine of poetry called VOICES, which he also edited.

Vincent, Howard P[aton] (b. Galesburg, Ill., Oct. 9, 1904—   ), teacher, editor, literary historian. Vincent studied at Oberlin College and Harvard, taught at various universities, in 1942 joined the faculty of the Illinois Institute of Technology. He is the leading authority on Herman Melville. His most important publication is *The Trying-Out of Moby Dick* (1949), a critical account of the creation of the famous novel. He edited *The Collected Poems of Herman Melville* (1947) and is general editor of a twelve-volume edition of Melville's writings. He also edited Dorothy Wordsworth's *Letters* (1944).

Vinland [also called **Wineland** and **Vineland**]. A region in the New World visited by Norsemen; so named because of the wild grapes they found there. It has been identified with Cape Cod, also with many other localities from Labrador to New Jersey. It was visited by Norsemen from about 1000 A.D. on, and when Greenland became a bishopric Vinland was included in its boundaries.

Virginia (1913), a novel by ELLEN GLAS-

GOW. This story of a Southern woman is set in the years between 1884 and 1912. Her marriage is unhappy, she is unable to adapt herself to a new environment, loses the respect of her husband and daughters, but manages to retain the love of her son. Edward Wagenknecht concludes that Miss Glasgow began her portraiture of Virginia in an ironic mood, but changed as she went on to one of compassion. The book is, in essence, an analysis of the new world of women of the early 20th century.

Virginia Bill of Rights. This was drawn up by GEORGE MASON and adopted by the Virginia Convention of Delegates on June 12, 1776. The *Bill* contains sixteen articles. The first anticipates closely the DECLARATION OF INDEPENDENCE composed by Mason's friend Jefferson. Mason's work reads in part, "That all men are by Nature equally free and independent, and have certain inherent rights, of which, when they enter into a state of society, they cannot, by any compact, deprive or divest their posterity; namely, the enjoyment of life and liberty, with the means of acquiring and possessing property, and pursuing and obtaining happiness and safety." In other articles Mason anticipated also the Constitution and the Bill of Rights, for example in the Fifth Article, which declared "that the legislative and executive powers of the state should be separate and distinct from the judicative," and again in the Eighth Article, which decreed "that in all capital or criminal prosecutions a man hath a right to demand the cause and nature of his accusation, to be confronted with the accusers and witnesses, to call for evidence in his favor . . . nor can he be compelled to give evidence against himself." Julian Boyd (*The Declaration of Independence,* 1945) ascribed the similarity of language to the influence of John Locke and others.

Virginia City Territorial Enterprise, The. See TERRITORIAL ENTERPRISE.

Virginia Comedians, The (1854), a novel by JOHN ESTEN COOKE. Cooke was an imitator of James Fenimore Cooper, but his love scenes were more successful than Cooper's. In this novel Cooke manages an intertwining of love stories that captivated his own age; his principal character is a roué and a cynic who abducts an actress and (as he supposes) kills the man who tries to rescue her. He flees to Europe, returning later to make a more suitable match with his cousin. The second part was published separately as *Captain Ralph.* A sequel to both, HENRY ST. JOHN, GENTLEMAN (1859), is set in the Shenandoah Valley at the beginning of the Revolution. Jay Hubbell comments that Cooke regarded himself as a social historian who had reconstructed a great period in American history.

Virginia Company. This "adventure" was chartered in 1606 by King James I and authorized two companies: the Plymouth Company (meaning Plymouth in England), which was to colonize northern sections of North America; and the London Company, which was to be active in the southern territories claimed by England. In 1609, after the Plymouth branch had failed to show any activity, a new charter was obtained that made the London Company absolute. In the meantime energetic measures had been taken to colonize a region called Virginia. In 1612 the colony was made self-governing, in 1619 the first legislature assembled. In 1623 the Privy Council investigated the colony and alleged misrule there; in 1624 the king annulled the charter of the London Company. Accounts of the company appear in H. L. Osgood's *American Colonies in the 17th Century* (3 v., 1904–07); S. M. Kingsbury's edition of the *Records of the Virginia Company of London* (4 v., 1906–35); T. J. Wertenbaker's *Planters of Colonial Virginia* (1932); W. F. Craven's *Dissolution of the Virginia Company* (1932) and *Southern Colonies in the 17th Century* (1949).

Virginia Declaration of Rights. See VIRGINIA BILL OF RIGHTS.

Virginia Harmony (1831), a collection of songs by James P. Carrell (or Carroll). The book was a general collection, but Carrell put his name to seventeen of the tunes. Eight of these were reprinted in later collections by other compilers.

Virginian, The (1902), a novel by OWEN WISTER. One of the steadiest best sellers in American literary history, *The Virginian* has sometimes been described as the ancestor of the Western. The scene is Wyoming in pioneer days. The hero, who remains unnamed, provokes the enmity of a local bad man named Trampas. In a poker game Trampas accuses the Virginian of cheating and impugns his ancestry. Instantly the Virginian's pistol is drawn and lies on the table before him; thereupon he launches what has become the world's most hackneyed retort: "When you call me that, smile." Trampas backs down. Later the Virginian rescues a New England schoolmistress from a stage coach that has been marooned in high water by a drunken driver, and eventually they get married. The climax is a pistol duel between Trampas and the Virginian in which Trampas is vanquished, the scene constituting the first "walkdown" in American literature.

Wister, a fanatical admirer of THEODORE ROOSEVELT, had gone to Wyoming for his health at Roosevelt's suggestion and began writing stories set in that locality. He dedicated *The Virginian* to Roosevelt, many of whose traits and ideals resemble those of Wister's hero. Actually Everitt Cyril Johnson, once a fellow ranch hand with Wister, claimed to have been the original for the Virginian. But according to Wister himself, in a preface to the sixteenth edition of his book (1928), the hero was a combination of several persons he had known in Wyoming.

Wister's book undoubtedly had a deep influence on the writers of Western stories, plays, film and radio scripts, and the Virginian became the prototype of all cowboy heroes. The novel was dramatized in 1903 and was performed for ten years on the road and in New York, thereafter in stock. Several film versions have also been made. Walter S. Campbell (Stanley Vestal) says of Wister: "His work suffers more than most books by short-time visitors into the region from the fact that it was all a spectacle to him, and therefore he could not quite come to grips with or understand the life about him." But this superficiality did not prevent the book from selling more than 2 million copies within fifty years after its publication.

Virginia Quarterly Review. An influential critical magazine founded in 1925 and published at the University of Virginia. Its many contributors have included such authors as Robert Frost, Sherwood Anderson, and Thomas Wolfe.

Virginians, The (1857–59), a novel by William Makepeace Thackeray. Thackeray made two visits to the United States, one in 1852–53, the other in 1855–56. The novel appeared in monthly installments over a period of two years. On one occasion he visited the home of the historian W. H. Prescott in Boston, where he saw two swords hung in a crossed position over the mantelpiece: one sword had belonged to Prescott's father's father, the other to his mother's father, and the two grandfathers had used the swords on opposite sides in the Revolution. It is said that this suggested to Thackeray the idea of a story about two brothers, one a loyalist and the other a rebel; he made the story into a sequel for his *Henry Esmond* by placing the Esmond descendants on an estate in Virginia. Thackeray asked JOHN PENDLETON KENNEDY for help in dealing with American geography, and Kennedy supplied an outline and a map. Formerly some critics attributed some chapters to Kennedy's own hand, but this theory is now discredited. The novel contains a number of errors, as when the people of Virginia are said to be making maple sugar in the autumn, and in spite of Kennedy's map the geography in the novel is inaccurate. Eyre Crowe wrote *With Thackeray in America* (1893) and James G. Wilson compiled *Thackeray in the United States* (1904).

Virgin Land: The American West as Symbol and Myth (1950), an analysis by HENRY NASH SMITH. In this profound and influential book Smith gives a literary and anthropological interpretation of our Western movement, dealing with economic and political factors in his analysis. Characteristic chapters are those on "The Western Hero in the Dime Novel" and "The Dime Novel Heroines." He sees the degeneration of the Western novel in the face of the industrial development of the 20th century as symptomatic of changing American ideals.

Virtuoso's Collection, A (*Boston Miscellany*, May, 1842), a group of stories by NATHANIEL HAWTHORNE. See PETER RUGG, THE MISSING MAN.

Visionaries (1905), a collection of short stories by JAMES G. HUNEKER. Many of these striking stories have highly original, sometimes fantastic plots, and they have been unduly neglected. Harry Levin said that they "fall somewhere between Henry James and O. Henry."

Vision of Sir Launfal, The (1848), a narrative poem by JAMES RUSSELL LOWELL. This story of the conversion of a proud medieval knight has no connection with Thomas Chestre's 15th-century *Sir Launfal* or with the still earlier poem by Marie de France. The quest for the Grail comes of course from Malory, and Lowell may have been influenced by Tennyson's *Sir Galahad.* The poem opens with the famous line "What is so rare as a day in June," goes on to tell how Sir Launfal, riding proudly forth in quest of the Grail, spurns a leper begging for alms but tosses him a piece of gold, which the leper refuses to lift from the dust. Many years later Launfal returns to his castle, weary and disappointed. Once more he encounters the leper, shares with him his last crust of bread, and offers him water from his wooden bowl. Then the leper is transformed into Christ, who tells Launfal the bowl is the Grail—"Who gives himself with his alms feeds three:/ Himself, his hungering neighbor, and me." Launfal accepts the lesson, and his future works show that one does not need to go abroad to find the Holy Grail.

Lowell himself was deeply pleased with his poem and held, "I am the first poet who has endeavored to express the American Idea." By this he meant, according to H. E. Scudder, that just as Tennyson threw into his retelling of the Arthurian romance a moral sense, Lowell, also a moralist, made a parable of the tale and "in the broadest interpretation of democracy, sang of the leveling of all ranks in a common divine humanity." The poem is likewise an illustration of Lowell's great command of meter; he varies it constantly and skillfully in the 347 lines of the poem.

Visit from St. Nicholas, A (Troy, N.Y., *Sentinel*, Dec. 23, 1823), a Christmas ballad by CLEMENT CLARKE MOORE. This famous poem was written by a kindly New York City scholar for his own family. It marked a dividing line between the old Puritan abhorrence for Christmas celebrations and a new attitude in which the Christmas spirit was embodied in the figure of Santa Claus, a Dutch and German creation. The poem itself has been described by R. V. Halsey as the first truly original story in the literature of the American nursery. It immediately became famous; it is often called by its opening words, *'Twas the Night Before Christmas.*

Vizetelly, Frank (b. England, April 2, 1864 —d. Dec. 20, 1938), editor, author, lexicographer. Vizetelly was educated in England and France, and received several honorary doctor's degrees from American universities. He came to the United States in 1891 and became a citizen in 1926; he worked most of his life for the Funk & Wagnalls Company, publishers of the STANDARD DICTIONARY. As editor of the dictionary (1913–1938), as conductor of "The Lexicographer's Easy Chair" in the *Literary*

Digest, and as a nationally known radio broadcaster, he became the foremost authority on pronunciation, spelling, and neologisms, holding a status in America comparable to that held by H. W. Fowler in England. Some of his books: *A Desk Book of Errors in English* (1906); *A Desk Book of 25,000 Words Frequently Mispronounced* (1917); *How to Use English* (1932); *How to Speak Effectively* (1937).

Vogt, William (b. Mineola, N.Y., May 15, 1903—d. July 11, 1968), ornithologist, author. A graduate of St. Stephen's College (now Bard College), Vogt served as curator of the Jones Beach State Bird Sanctuary and chief of the Conservation Section at American Union before being named national director of the Planned Parenthood Federation of America. In his early writings he devoted himself primarily to ornithology. His later essays and books were written in support of the Planned Parenthood Federation. *Road to Survival* (1948) was a highly controversial book advocating population control. *People* (1960) was to a large degree a revision and expansion of the ideas Vogt had set forth in *Road to Survival.* Vogt's other books: *Audubon's Birds of America* (1937); *El Hombre y la Tierra* (1944).

Vogue. A fashion magazine for women, founded Dec. 17, 1892, in New York by Arthur Turnure and Harry McVickar as a weekly. In 1910 it became a semimonthly. Condé Nast bought it in 1909, and it absorbed VANITY FAIR in 1935. Edna Woolman Chase (see under ILKA CHASE) joined its staff in 1895 when it was a small weekly written by society for society, became its editor in 1914, and in 1919 was appointed editor-in-chief of the London, Paris, and New York editions. In 1952 she gave up her post as editor but continued as chairman of the board; she was succeeded as editor by Jessica Daves. By 1960 the circulation was nearing 500,000 in America alone. In 1954 Mrs. Chase, with the assistance of her daughter Ilka, published her autobiography, *Always in Vogue,* which describes her experiences in making the magazine an arbiter of taste.

The magazine has had many famous contributors. At one time Frank Crowninshield, Robert E. Sherwood, Dorothy Parker, and Robert Benchley were all on the staff. Other contributors included Marjorie Kinnan Rawlings, Rebecca West, James Hilton, Ernest Hemingway, Jules Romains, Hendrik Van Loon, Ludwig Bemelmans, Katherine Anne Porter, Thomas Wolfe, Clare Boothe Luce, André Maurois, Archibald MacLeish, William Saroyan, Paul Gallico, Max Eastman, John Mason Brown, Mary Ellen Chase, Ilka Chase. These contributors and others appear in an impressive anthology, *Vogue's First Reader* (1942), edited by Frank Crowninshield.

Voices. A magazine founded by HAROLD VINAL in 1921. It began as a bimonthly, later became a quarterly, and made itself a leading organ for new poets unable to secure an audience elsewhere. Among its contributors have

been Allen Tate, Mark Van Doren, Robert Penn Warren, Kenneth Fearing, Genevieve Taggard, Donald Davidson, and Vinal himself.

Voices of the Night (1839), a collection by HENRY WADSWORTH LONGFELLOW of poems previously published in magazines. Among them are A PSALM OF LIFE, HYMN TO THE NIGHT, and THE BELEAGUERED CITY. Edgar Allan Poe immediately accused Longfellow of plagiarism because of alleged similarities between the *The Beleaguered City* and his own HAUNTED PALACE; but there is little resemblance in their moods. This book helped establish Longfellow as the country's most popular poet.

Voluntaries (1863), a poem by RALPH WALDO EMERSON. This dirge was written in honor of Col. Robert Gould Shaw, who was killed in the Civil War while storming Fort Wagner, July 18, 1863, at the head of the first enlisted Negro regiment, the 54th Massachusetts. A statue was erected to Shaw, and William Vaughn Moody, after seeing it, composed his famous ODE IN TIME OF HESITATION (1900). Emerson's poem reflects the violent emotion of the era of disunion; he rejects the idea that the preservation of the Union is superior to the abolition of slavery and alludes scornfully to Daniel Webster. What saves the poem for later generations is the stirring third section, which begins, "In an age of fops and tops" and closes, "When Duty whispers low, *Thou must,* / The youth replies, *I can.*"

Von Hagen, Victor Wolfgang (b. St. Louis, Mo., Feb. 29, 1908—　　), explorer, naturalist, author, editor. Von Hagen, a notable authority on South America, devoted most of his forty-odd volumes to that continent. His personal explorations, sometimes with the sponsorship of organizations like the American Geographic Society, took him mainly to Central America, the west coast of South America, and along the Amazon. He made researches in biology, ethnobotany, ethnology, archaeology, and geography. Several museums contain collections made by him. He edited an informative volume called *The Green World of the Naturalists* (1948), described as "a treasury of five centuries of natural history in South America." In this book he showed that in addition to the greedy Spanish conquerors there were other Spaniards, as well as naturalists from other nations, who looked in the New World for scientific riches. Among his other books: *Off with Their Heads* (1937); *Ecuador the Unknown* (1939); *Quetzal Quest* (1940); *Jungle in the Clouds* (1940); *Riches of Central America* (1941); *South American Zoo* (1946); *Ecuador and the Galapagos Islands* (1949); *The Four Seasons of Manuela* (1952); *Highway of the Sun* (1955); *Incas, People of the Sun* (1961).

Von Tilzer, Harry (b. Detroit, Mich., [?], 1872—d. Jan. 10, 1946), composer of popular songs, music publisher, vaudeville singer, pianist. Von Tilzer wrote the music for hundreds of popular songs. It was not until 1898, however, that he made the hit parade with *My Old New Hampshire Home,* with words by Andrew B. Sterling. The song sold a million copies, and Von Tilzer soon afterward formed his own music publishing firm, which he continued successfully until his death. Some of the songs for which he wrote or sponsored the music are *A Bird in a Gilded Cage, Where the Morning Glories Twine Around the Door, On a Sunday Afternoon, Wait Till the Sun Shines, Nellie, All Alone, I Want a Girl Just Like the Girl That Married Dear Old Dad.*

vorticism. A British art movement, similar to cubism and futurism, influential also in literary circles. Among its notable literary followers were Richard Aldington, Ford Madox Hueffer (see FORD MADOX FORD), T. S. ELIOT, Rebecca West, Wyndham Lewis, and EZRA POUND. Pound seems to have embraced vorticism when Amy Lowell took imagism away from him. Two issues of the magazine *Blast* became their outlet, proclaiming the movement's mission "to destroy politeness, standardization, and academic, that is, civilized vision."

Voyage dans la Haute Pennsylvanie et dans l'état de New York (3 v., 1801), a travel book of essays and stories by HECTOR ST. JOHN DE CRÈVECŒUR. This work was rescued from comparative oblivion in an article by Percy G. Adams in *American Literature* (May, 1953). Adams later translated and published a selection of essays and stories from the *Voyage* under the title *Crèvecœur's Eighteenth-Century Travels in Pennsylvania and New York* (1961).

W

Wagenknecht, Edward (b. Chicago, March 28, 1900—   ), teacher, critic, biographer, anthologist. Wagenknecht taught at various universities, including the University of Chicago and Boston University. His works include many agreeable literary histories, among them *Cavalcade of the English Novel* (1943) and *Cavalcade of the American Novel* (1952); accounts of Bernard Shaw (1929), Charles Dickens (1929), and Mark Twain (1935); biographies of Lillian Gish (1927), Geraldine Farrar (1929), and Jenny Lind (1931); and critical essays on Chaucer. His numerous anthologies include collections of Christmas stories, ghost stories, romantic tales, and others. Most important of his books is perhaps *Longfellow: A Full-Length Portrait* (1955), a biography based on very thorough original research. It takes issue with the only other recent examination of Longfellow, Lawrence Thompson's *Young Longfellow* (1938), which examines the poet, says Wagenknecht, "with a jaundiced eye." He himself deals less with Longfellow's writings than with his life. This book was followed by *Mrs. Longfellow: Selected Letters and Journals* (1956). Some lectures delivered in the Lowell Series were published as *The Seven Worlds of Theodore Roosevelt* (1958). He also wrote *Nathaniel Hawthorne: Man and Writer* (1961) and *Washington Irving: Moderation Displayed* (1962).

Wagner, Henry R[aup] (b. Philadelphia, Sept. 27, 1862—d. March 28, 1957), lawyer, businessman, collector, editor. In the midst of a busy career Wagner found time to collect old books and maps, prepare valuable bibliographies and catalogues, and write several books. His important collection of Western Americana was acquired in 1922 by Henry E. Huntington. Among his publications: *Sir Francis Drake's Voyage Around the World* (1926); *Spanish Voyages to the Northwest Coast of America in the 16th Century* (1929); *The Cartography of the Northwest Coast of America to the Year 1800* (1937); *The Plains and the Rockies, 1800–1865* (a bibliography, 1921, 1937); *Juan Rodríguez Cabrillo* (1941); *The Rise of Fernando Cortés* (1944).

Wagstaff, Blanche Shoemaker (b. New York City, July 10, 1888—   ), critic, editor, poet. Mrs. Wagstaff engaged in many forms of literary activity, helping to edit magazines, writing reviews, writing plays, but chiefly writing poetry. Among her collections of poems are *Songs of Youth* (1906); *Narcissus* (1917); *Mortality and Other Poems* (1931). Many of her verses have been set to music and translated into French, Swedish, and other languages. She helped edit *The Mask, The Poetry Journal,* and *Contemporary Vision* among the "little magazines."

Waiting for Lefty (1935), a short play by CLIFFORD ODETS. This play, Odets' first, deals with a taxi drivers' strike. Using an impressionistic flashback technique, Odets presents six episodic scenes showing the lives of the people involved in the strike. At the climax the news that the committeeman Lefty has been murdered rouses the men to decisive action. Although the play is too violently propagandistic to have much lasting value, Odets displays here his amazing gift for dialogue, more fully developed in later plays. *Waiting for Lefty* was one of the best known of the proletarian plays of the 1930's.

Wakeman, Frederic (b. Scranton, Kans., Dec. 26, 1909—   ), advertising copywriter, account executive, novelist. Wakeman's experiences in an advertising agency, in the navy, and in the literary world directly furnished material for his novels. His first book was *Shore Leave* (1944), which in some of its sharply delineated scenes foreshadowed the approach he later took in his greatest success, *The Hucksters* (1946). *The Hucksters* combines a somewhat ineffective love story with a bitter satirical attack on the insincerity and stupidity of American advertising. The book was called "the *Uncle Tom's Cabin* of advertising." *The Saxon Charm* (1947) depicts a Broadway producer as a scoundrel. Later novels by Wakeman include *The Wastrel* (1949); *Mandrake Root* (1953); *The Fabulous Train* (1955); *Deluxe Tour* (1956).

Walam Olum [the **Red Score**]. A Leni-Lenape Indian document, the only surviving one that could be described as a book. It is something between a historical narrative and an epic, inscribed originally on birch bark in pictographs. It contains a creation myth and the account of a prehistoric migration from somewhere in the north and west to the Atlantic coast. The Leni-Lenapes were called Delawares by the white man and lived in the valley of the Delaware, mainly in New Jersey. Today the chief remnants of the tribe live in Oklahoma. (See DELAWARE INDIANS.)

The *Red Score* was discovered and translated by CONSTANTINE RAFINESQUE. The best account of it is given in Daniel G. Brinton's *The Lenape and Their Legends, With the Complete Text and Symbols of the Walam Olum* (1885). A. Grove Day, discussing the poem in *The Sky Clears: Poetry of the American Indians* (1951), finds that "the tone of the chronicle is gloomy and confused, and gives the impression of a serious and half-awakened people wandering in chaos."

Walcot, Charles Melton (b. England, [?] 1816—d. May 15, 1868), architect, actor, singer, dramatist. Walcot came to the United States in 1837 as an architect, but became very successful in the theater because of his fine singing voice and his ability as a comedian. He wrote a number of burlesques and comedies, among them *The Imp of the Elements* (1844); *Don Giovanni in Gotham* (1844); *The Don Not Done* (1844). His son Charles Melton Walcot (1840–1921) likewise became an accomplished actor.

Walden, or, Life in the Woods (1854), a narrative by HENRY DAVID THOREAU. In the spring of 1845 Thoreau built a simple cabin near Walden Pond, Concord. Convinced that "the mass of men lead lives of quiet desperation," he lived there alone from July 4, 1845, to Sept. 6, 1847, in a deliberate attempt to "front the essential facts of life." Inveighing against the slavery to material desires which he saw in 19th-century American society, he sought happiness in living as close as possible to nature, only occasionally going into town or receiving visitors at his hut. His expenses were approximately eight dollars a year.

Thoreau gives the reasons for his solitary experiment in the early chapters of *Walden*. He describes his experiences as an amateur naturalist in a lively expository style, singing praises of the changing seasons and the pleasures afforded by his little lake with enthusiasm and great literary skill. Always there is a moral emphasis on a kind of Oriental simplicity and purity. One must, says Thoreau, free oneself from social and political ties, live chastely, eat simple food, read and study seriously. "He is blessed," he writes at one point, "who is assured that the animal is dying out in him day by day, the divine being established."

Thoreau was a Yankee as well as a mystic, however, and his practical teaching was not that everyone should live alone in the woods but that each man should be true to himself and his own truest feelings regardless of the pressures of society and convention. One of the world's greatest books, *Walden* has become a classic statement of the American intellectual spirit. It is the most popular of Thoreau's works and the most often reprinted. Several editions and many critical analyses appeared in 1954, the centenary of its original publication. Among those who have acknowledged the influence of the book have been Tolstoy and Mahatma Gandhi.

Walden Pond and Thoreau's home are today a state reservation which attracts many visitors annually.

Walker, Danton [MacIntyre] (b. Marietta, Ga., July 26, 1899—d. Aug. 8, 1960), columnist. Walker described his varied career in *Danton's Inferno: The Story of a Columnist* (1955). He wrote *Some Excursions into the Supernatural* (1956) and *Guide to New York Night Life* (1958). He was an actor, dancer, theatrical director, and a member of Hoover's Belgian Relief staff. He did all kinds of newspaper writing, finally winning a nation-wide public as a Broadway columnist for the New York *Daily News*.

Walker, David Harry [Henry] (b. Scot., Feb. 9, 1911—), novelist. Walker received his education mostly in England. He was an Army officer in the Black Watch from 1931 to 1947 and a prisoner of war for five years. After the war he went to India, then retired to New Brunswick, Canada, where he began a prolific writing career. His works include: *The Story and the Silence* (1949); *Geordie* (1950), which became the film *Wee Geordie; The Pillar* (1952); *Digby* (1953); *Harry Black* (1956), which also was filmed; *Sandy Was a Soldier's Boy; A Fable* (1957); *Where the High Winds Blow* (1960).

Walker, James J[ohn] (b. New York City, June 19, 1881—d. Nov. 18, 1946), lawyer, song writer, politician, business executive. "Jimmy" Walker was elected to the New York Assembly even before he was admitted to law practice (1912). In 1915 he was elected to the New York Senate; in 1925 and 1929 he was elected mayor of New York City. He was one of the most popular politicians in the state and became a symbol of the speakeasy era. As an avocation he wrote popular songs, the most famous of which was "Will You Love Me in December as You Did in May?" (music by Ernest Ball, 1905). He allowed corruption to creep into the city government, was much criticized and suspected of illegal transactions, finally resigned in 1932 and in 1940 became an executive in the cloak and suit industry. Gene Fowler wrote an entertaining biography, *Beau James* (1949).

Walker, Mildred [Mrs. Ferdinand R. Schemm] (b. Philadelphia, May 2, 1905—), novelist, teacher. Miss Walker composed much verse and fiction before her novel *Fireweed* (1934) won the Avery Hopwood prize. Other books include *Light from Arcturus* (1935); *Dr. Norton's Wife* (1938); *The Brewers' Big Horses* (1940); *Unless the Wind Turns* (1941); *Winter Wheat* (1944); *Southwest Corner* (1951); *Curlew's Cry* (1955); *The Body of a Young Man* (1960).

Walker, Stanley (b. Lampasas, Tex., Oct. 21, 1898—d. Nov. 25, 1962), newsman. Walker served as a reporter on two Texas newspapers, then worked on the staffs of the New York *Herald*, the New York *Mirror*, the New York *American*, *The New Yorker*, and the New York *Woman*. In 1937 he returned to the *Herald Tribune*, where he was virtually czar of the news room, later served for a year as editor of the Philadelphia *Evening Public Ledger*. He then turned to free-lancing and writing books, giving up his newspaper career for a ranch in his native state. His best book is undoubtedly the well-informed and frequently satiric *City Editor* (1934). Others are *Night Club Era* (1933); *Mrs. Astor's Horse* (1935); *Dewey, an American of This Century* (1944); *Home to Texas* (1956).

Walker, Stuart (b. Augusta, Ky., March 4, 1888—d. March 13, 1941), actor, stage man-

ager, producer, playwright. Associated at first
with DAVID BELASCO in various capacities,
Walker then founded and directed repertory
companies in Indianapolis and Cincinnati. Later
he was a director and producer at Paramount
studios in Hollywood. He became especially
famous for his Portmanteau Theatre, which
began in New York City and then toured the
country. It produced plays by Lord Dunsany
and others, also many by Walker himself.
Among the latter were *Six Who Pass While the
Lentils Boil, Five Flights Up,* and *The King's
Great Aunt Sits on the Floor,* included in Walker's two collections *Portmanteau Plays* (1917)
and *More Portmanteau Plays* (1919); and *The
King's Great Aunt* (1923). He wrote *The Demi-
Reds* (1936) with Gladys Unger.

Walker, William (b. Nashville, Tenn., May
8, 1824—d. Sept. 12, 1860), adventurer.
Walker studied medicine and law, but became
one of the most remarkable military leaders
the United States has ever known. He first organized an expedition intended to turn Lower
California and Sonora into a republic. When
this failed he invaded Nicaragua with an army
of fifty-eight men, won some extraordinary successes, and was inaugurated president (1856).
But he got into trouble with Cornelius Vanderbilt, who caused a coalition of Central American powers to oust him (1857), and after several further attempts to conquer the country
he was executed by a Honduran firing squad.

Walker wrote an account of *The War in
Nicaragua* (1860). Richard Harding Davis
wrote about him in *Real Soldiers of Fortune*
(1906), Laurence Greene wrote *The Filibuster:
The Career of William Walker* (1937), and
Joaquin Miller composed a famous poem, *With
Walker in Nicaragua.* Bret Harte introduced
Walker in disguise in two of his stories, and he
appears in Darwin Teilhet's novel *The Lion's
Skin* (1955). See WILLIAM VINCENT WELLS.

Wallace, Big-Foot. See BIG-FOOT WALLACE,
THE ADVENTURES OF.

Wallace, Dillon (b. Craigsville, N.Y., June
24, 1863—d. Sept. 28, 1939), author of adventure books. For the most part Wallace's
books are set in Labrador. Among them are
The Lure of the Labrador Wild (1905) and
The Story of Grenfell of the Labrador (1922),
both very popular.

Wallace, Henry ["Uncle Henry"] (b. West
Newton, Pa., March 19, 1836—d. Feb. 22,
1916), clergyman, columnist, publisher. Wallace was ordained as a Presbyterian minister
and served as such until 1877 when the state
of his health caused him to give up the ministry
and move to Iowa. There he became deeply
interested in farming. He was contributing editor of the *Iowa Homestead* and other magazines. He bought a magazine which became
widely known as *Wallace's Farmer* and in which
his own contributions were usually signed
"Uncle Henry." Some of his writings were collected in book form: *Uncle Henry's Letters to
the Farm Boy* (1897) and *Uncle Henry's Own
Story of His Life* (3 v., 1917–19). He also
wrote *The Doctrines of the Plymouth Brethren*
(1878) and *Clover Culture* (1892). His son
Henry Cantwell Wallace (1866–1924) succeeded him as editor.

Wallace, Henry Agard (b. Adair Co., Iowa,
Oct. 7, 1888—d. Nov. 18, 1965), farm expert,
politician, editor, author. Wallace, grandson
of HENRY WALLACE and son of Henry Cantwell
Wallace, began as associate editor of the family
magazine in 1910 and continued as editor after
its merger with the *Iowa Homestead* in 1929.
As a farmer he made successful experiments in
developing new corn hybrids. In 1933 President
Franklin D. Roosevelt appointed him secretary
of agriculture; he was ardent in the support of
New Deal policies, and instituted new devices
to help farmers toward a steadier income. He
was elected Vice-President in 1940; when
HARRY S. TRUMAN succeeded him (1944) he
became secretary of commerce and continued
in that capacity after Truman became President.
His free expressions of opinion on foreign affairs, especially in an address at Madison
Square Garden (Sept. 12, 1946), led to his
dismissal from the cabinet. He served as editor
of the NEW REPUBLIC (1946–48), then as contributing editor. He became the Presidential
candidate (1948) of a newly formed Progressive party, but was defeated. He abandoned
this party in 1950 because it favored Communist views on the Korean War.

Wallace's works include numerous earnest
and free-spoken books, which reveal his idealism
rather than his political practicality. Among his
books: *Agricultural Prices* (1920); *Corn and
Corn Growing* (1923); *America Must Choose*
(1934); *Statesmanship and Religion* (1934);
Whose Constitution? (1936); *Technology, Corporations, and the General Welfare* (1937);
Paths to Plenty (1938; rev. ed. entitled *Price
of Freedom,* 1940); *The American Choice*
(1940); *The Century of the Common Man*
(1943); *Democracy Reborn* (1944); *Sixty Million Jobs* (1945); *Toward World Peace* (1948);
Corn and the Midwestern Farmer (1956). Russell Lord wrote about *The Wallaces of Iowa*
(1948). See PROGRESSIVE PARTY.

Wallace, Lew[is] (b. Brookville, Ind., April
10, 1827—d. Feb. 15, 1905), lawyer, novelist,
statesman, soldier. Wallace practiced law in
Indianapolis, was elected to the state senate
(1856), and rose to the rank of major-general
during the Civil War. After the war he was
appointed governor of New Mexico (1878–81)
and minister to Turkey (1881–85). He also
served as governor of Indiana. As early as 1843
he had begun, under the influence of Prescott's
Conquest of Mexico, to write a novel set in
Mexico. It was finally published as THE FAIR
GOD (1873). With BEN HUR: A TALE OF THE
CHRIST (1880) he achieved an almost incredible popularity. This dramatic, swiftly
moving novel sold about 2 million copies and
was translated into numerous languages. A
stage version prepared by William Young
(1899) was popular for several years, and two
spectacular motion pictures made from the book

were very successful in 1925 and 1959. The famous chariot race from the novel was long a staple of Barnum & Bailey's Circus. Later books by Wallace were *The Life of Benjamin Harrison* (1888); *The Boyhood of Christ* (1888);

THE PRINCE OF INDIA (1893); *The Wooing of Malkatoon* (poem, 1898). In *Lew Wallace, An Autobiography* (2 v., 1906) Wallace wrote of his life up to 1864; his wife completed the book. Irving McKee wrote an enthusiastic biography, *"Ben-Hur" Wallace* (1947).

Wallace, William Alexander Anderson. See BIG-FOOT WALLACE, THE ADVENTURES OF.

Wallace, William Ross (b. Kentucky, [?] 1819—d. May 5, 1881), lawyer, poet. In his own day the poems of Wallace were widely read; today only one is remembered—*What Rules the World* (c. 1865)—and that for two lines: "The hand that rocks the cradle/ Is the hand that rules the world." His verse was often intensely patriotic, and he was especially ardent in his advocacy of the North during the Civil War. In temperament and even in appearance he resembled Edgar Allan Poe, whom he claimed to have known well. Among his publications: *The Battle of Tippecanoe* (1837); *Alban the Pirate* (1848); *Meditations in America and Other Poems* (1851); *The Liberty Bell* (1862).

Waller, Mary Ella (b. Boston, March 1, 1855—d. June 15, 1938), novelist, essayist. Miss Waller lived for many years in the White River Valley in Vermont. She wrote many books, of which one made an instantaneous hit —*The Wood-Carver of 'Lympus* (1904). She

preached simplicity of living and goodwill to mankind.

Wall Street. A short narrow street in the oldest section of New York City, between Broadway and the East River. For more than a century Wall Street has been at the center of New York's financial district and has been the working address of some of the world's most powerful bankers and financiers. Originally the street was actually the site of a wall built by the Dutch in New Amsterdam as a barricade against the Indians. When the English captured New York the wall became a wagon road. Most of the official buildings of New York City clustered nearby. Federal Hall was the place where auctioneers sold stocks and bonds; ultimately a group of stock brokers set up a room of their own at 40 Wall Street, the beginning of the New York Stock Exchange.

The tremendous influence of the Stock Exchange and of Wall Street generally was demonstrated in October, 1929, when a crash of prices on this exchange tragically affected the whole world. Its history and the ramifications of finance are well described in Dorothy Sterling's *Wall Street* (1955). Novels about Wall Street and the financial world include R. B. Kimball's *Henry Powers, Banker* (1868); Charles Dudley Warner's *A Little Journey in the World* (1889), *The Golden House* (1894), and *That Fortune* (1899); Brander Matthews' *His Father's Son* (1896); John Dos Passos' THE BIG MONEY (1936); Walter D. Edmonds' *Young Ames* (1942).

Waln, Nora (b. Grampian, Pa., June 4, 1895—d. Sept. 27, 1964), journalist, writer. Miss Waln's great interest in China inspired the writing of her best seller *The House of Exile* (1933). After a stay in Germany during Hitler's regime she set down her unfavorable impressions in *Reaching for the Stars* (1939). After World War II she lived in China, Japan, and Europe as a correspondent for various American periodicals, particularly the *Atlantic Monthly.*

Waln, Robert ["Peter Atall"] (b. Philadelphia, Oct. 20, 1794—d. July 4, 1825), writer. Waln, a man of ample means, pursued literature at his leisure, writing articles of miscellaneous character, sometimes under the pen name of Peter Atall, Esq. It was under this pseudonym that he published a satire on fashionable Philadelphia, *The Hermit in America on a Visit to Philadelphia* (1819). He issued several volumes of verse, among them *American Bards* (1820) and *Sisyphi Opus* (1820). He also wrote a biography of Lafayette and biographical sketches of the signers of the Declaration of Independence.

Walsh, James Joseph (b. Archbald, Pa., April 12, 1865—d. Feb. 28, 1942), physician, writer, teacher, historian. Walsh was a graduate of Fordham University, studied abroad, and began practicing medicine in 1898. He taught in various institutions, especially at Fordham, where he was professor of neurology. He was medical director of the Fordham School of Sociology and established the Fordham University Press. Walsh was a versatile author whose works were by no means limited to medical studies. His works include *Makers of Modern Medicine* (1907); *Catholic Churchmen in Science* (3 v., 1917); *Medieval Medicine* (1920); *Religion and Health* (1920); *What Civilization Owes to Italy* (1923); *Eating and Health* (1925); *The World's Debt to the Irish* (1926); *Laughter and Health* (1927); *Mother Alphonsa, Rose Hawthorne Lathrop* (1930); *A Golden Treasury of Medieval Literature* (1931); *High Points of Medieval Culture* (1937).

Walsh, Robert (b. Baltimore, Md., Aug. 30, 1784—d. Feb. 7, 1859), journalist, editor, diplomat. The earlier part of Walsh's life was given over to work on several magazines. For a time he practiced law, and for several years taught school. In 1844 he was appointed consul-general at Paris; he served until 1851, contributed articles to American magazines, and died abroad. Perhaps his most vigorous piece was a reply to the attacks of British travelers and editors on the United States, *An Appeal from the Judgments of Great Britain Respecting the U.S.* (1819).

He engaged in another controversy with Robert Goodloe Harper, who in 1813 delivered an address at Georgetown eulogizing Russian military skill rather than the Russian winter for the victory over Napoleon. The address and Walsh's letters in opposition to it were published as *Correspondence with Robert Goodloe Harper Respecting Russia* (1813). Walsh pointed out the dangers of Russian ascendancy. He made a collection of his miscellaneous articles in *Didactics, Social, Literary, and Political* (2 v., 1837). J. C. Walsh wrote his biography (1927).

Walter, Eugene (b. Cleveland, Ohio, Nov. 27, 1874—d. Sept. 26, 1941), playwright. Beginning as a reporter in Cleveland, New York City, Cincinnati, and Seattle, Walter worked, at one time or another, as business manager of public entertainments ranging from minstrel shows and circuses to symphony orchestras and grand opera companies. He wrote more than two dozen plays, most of them melodramas that were realistic enough to become widely popular. Among them: *The Undertow* (1906); *Paid in Full* (1907); THE EASIEST WAY (1908); *Fine Feathers* (1911); and dramatic adaptations of THE TRAIL OF THE LONESOME PINE (1911) and THE LITTLE SHEPHERD OF KINGDOM COME (1916). He collected a series of ten lectures in *How to Write a Play* (1925). His dramatic technique proved readily adaptable to motion pictures and he wrote numerous film scenarios.

Walter, Thomas (b. Roxbury, Mass., Dec. 13, 1696—d. Jan. 10, 1725), clergyman, musician. Walter, a nephew of Cotton Mather, was led astray for a while from the strict Puritanical fold by John Checkley (1680–1753), who had studied in England and there had

gone over to the Church of England; but back in Boston Checkley published two books defending the Congregational Church. The Mather family quickly took care of Walter by installing him as a minister at Roxbury. Walter later engaged in controversy with Checkley over the issue of inoculation for smallpox, which Checkley opposed.

In *A Choice Dialogue between John Faustus a Conjurer and Jack Tory His Friend* (1720), an answer to Checkley's *A Modest Proof of the Order and Government in the Church*, Walter has a subordinate devil tell Checkley how much Satan liked his attempts, but accuses him of bungling the job. Walter is chiefly remembered, however, for *The Grounds and Rules of Music Explained* (1721). He also wrote *The Sweet Psalmist of Israel* (1722).

Wampanoag Indians. An Algonquian tribe that occupied eastern Massachusetts when the Pilgrims landed there. They were also called Pokanokets. Their most prominent chieftains were MASSASOIT, who gave the English a friendly welcome, and King Philip, with whom the settlers fought what is called King Philip's War (1675–76), which ended in the almost complete extermination of the tribe. The Wampanoags figure in several dramas and poems, in some of which King Philip plays a role. (See KING PHILIP.)

Wanamaker, John (b. Philadelphia, July 11, 1838—d. Dec. 12, 1922), merchant. Best known for his successful department stores in Philadelphia and New York, Wanamaker was also active in religious work and the cause of temperance. For his financial aid in Benjamin Harrison's election campaign he was made postmaster-general (1889). Besides the widely read house organ of the Wanamaker stores, his writings include *The Value of Character in Business* (1917); *Maxims of Life and Business* (1923); *Prayers of John Wanamaker* (1923). H. A. Gibbons' *John Wanamaker* (2 v., 1926) is a useful biography.

War Between the States. See CIVIL WAR.

Warburg, James P[aul] (b. Germany, Aug. 18, 1896—   ), banker, writer. Warburg was brought to this country when he was an infant but often visited Europe in his childhood. In World War I he served as a naval aviator. He entered banking, served as an official in several firms and as a government adviser during World War II; he was deputy director (1942–44) of the overseas branch of the Office of War Information. Among his numerous books: *Wool and Wool Manufacture* (1920); *Acceptance Financing* (1922); *The Money Muddle* (1934); *Hell Bent for Election* (1935); *Peace in Our Time?* (1940); *Foreign Policy Begins at Home* (1944); *Germany, Bridge or Battleground?* (1947); *Victory Without War* (1951); *Germany: Key to Peace* (1953); *The U.S. in a Changing World* (1954); *Disarmament—Challenge of the Nineteen Sixties* (1961); also several volumes of verse.

Ward, Artemus [pen name of **Charles Farrar**

Browne] (b. Waterford, Me., April 26, 1834—d. March 6, 1867), newspaperman, editor, humorist, lecturer. When Browne was thirteen his father died; he became a printer, then worked for various New England newspapers.

He sent his earliest contributions to *The Carpet Bag* of Boston and began an itinerant life, ending finally in Ohio, where he served on several newspapers. Something he wrote for the Toledo *Commercial* attracted the attention of the Cleveland *Plain Dealer* and he was asked to do a humorous column for that paper. He responded in 1858 with his first Artemus Ward letters: Ward, a shrewd and supposedly illiterate showman, wrote in what was represented to be Yankee dialect and told of adventures and misadventures with his traveling museum of wax figures (also a few "snaiks and other critturs"). The letters were widely reprinted and gave Ward a national reputation. He became city editor of the *Plain Dealer*, but had some difficulties with the manager and in 1860 resigned. He and his character, drawn in part from SEBA SMITH's Jack Downing, were by that time merged, and he became better known by his pen name than by his own name.

From Cleveland, Ward went to New York City, where he established connections with VANITY FAIR. To this magazine he contributed some of his best sketches, mostly in the form of interviews; among them was a fictitious interview with Lincoln which delighted the President. At this time Ward published his first collection, *Artemus Ward, His Book* (1862), which sold forty thousand copies in a short time.

Ward next became a lecturer. He began in 1861 with an address called *Babes in the Woods,* in which he never got around to that subject. It was a great hit. Moreover, Ward —unlike many lecturers—liked to lecture. He made a point of seeming altogether solemn, affecting what Stephen Leacock called "an intense dullness of intelligence." He was a master of sudden and prolonged pauses which emphasized the incongruity of his remarks. In the course of his travels, he stayed in Virginia City, Nev., for three weeks and had a hilarious time with MARK TWAIN and his newspaper crowd. In 1866 he departed for England, where he won great success. He was made an editor of *Punch,* led a life that was far too convivial, and died in England of tuberculosis.

In Ward's lifetime he published only one more book, *Artemus Ward, His Travels* (1865). Posthumously appeared *Artemus Ward in London* (1869), *Artemus Ward's Lectures* (1869), and *Artemus Ward: His Works Complete* (1875, 1890, 1910). Among his more famous articles and lectures were "High-Handed Outrage at Utica," "Among the Spirits," "The Showman's Courtship," "Wax Figures vs. Shakespeare," "Among the Free Lovers," "Artemus Ward in the Egyptian Hall," "The Tower of London," and "Artemus Ward Among the Mormons."

Max Eastman said that Ward seems to have possessed "the most unalloyed humorousness of all the laughter-loving immortals." Albert J. Nock, in *Free Speech and Plain Language* (1937), called Ward "the first really great critic of American society." Bernard De Voto, on the other hand, failed to understand why "that succession of labored jokes, puns, and strained similes embedded in misspellings seemed so universally laughable as it did," and labeled Ward "an object of antiquarian interest only."

When one examines Ward's techniques it becomes obvious that some of them were already being widely used in his own time, and that in general all of them are outstanding traits of American popular humor. Immediately prominent were his cacography, or humorous misspellings, and what he himself called "ingrammaticisms"—a parallel attack on grammatical conventions. A whole host of American humorists have followed Ward as specialists in cacography. Ward's deliberately bad grammar created many absurdities, as when he said: "The Mormon's religion is singular, and his wives are plural." "I now bid you a welcome adieu." "I have no politics—nary a one."

Ward loved puns and plays on words. Josh Billings thought that his best joke was his remark, talking of Brigham Young and the Mormons, that "the pretty girls in Utah mostly marry Young." Quaint gentlemanliness should be noted as another marked trait of Ward's humor. Charles Reade spoke of "the refined, delicate, intellectual countenance, the sweet grave mouth" of Ward, from which issued so many convulsing jests. He had his barbed sentences and epigrams too. To him is attributed the remark: "The trouble with Napoleon was that he tried to do too much, and did it." He also said:

"I prefer temperance hotels, although they sell worse liquor than any other kind of hotels." "Let us all be happy and live within our means, even if we have to borrow the money to do it with." He loved burlesque and anticlimax, always delivered in solemn style. He announced that "one of the principal features of my entertainment is that it contains so many things that don't have anything to do with it." During the Civil War he proclaimed, "I have already given two cousins to the war, and I stand ready to sacrifice my wife's brother." Pure absurdity was always an outstanding aspect of his style. His British audience was vastly amused when he pointed to the picture of a Nevada mountain: "The highest part of that mountain is the top." Walter Blair noted that in Ward's rigmarole about the Mormons "the sentences in his speech were put together in the vague style of a *stream of consciousness* novel. . . ." A writer for the London *Spectator*, quoted by Blair, told delightedly how Ward wandered hopelessly from one grotesque idea to another, as though he were not even a party to the transaction, although he had an earnest and rather melancholy interest in the result.

Further writings of Ward may be found in *Letters of Artemus Ward to Charles E. Wilson, 1858–61* (1900); *Artemus Ward's Best Stories* (ed. by Clifton Johnson with an introduction by William Dean Howells, 1912); and *Selected Works of Artemus Ward* (ed. by A. J. Nock, 1924). E. P. Hingston wrote *Genial Showman* (1870) and Don C. Seitz wrote *Artemus Ward: A Biography and a Bibliography* (1926).

Ward, Christopher [**Longstreth**] (b. Wilmington, Del., Oct. 6, 1868—d. Feb. 20, 1943), lawyer, humorist, historian. Ward practiced law and in 1920 became president of the Corporation Service Co. He wrote well, often in a humorous vein, as in his best-selling *The Triumph of the Nut* (1923), and in his *Twisted Tales* (1924) and *Foolish Fiction* (1925), parodies of current novels. He also wrote historical works, among them *Sweden on the Delaware* (1938) and *The Delaware Continentals* (1941).

Ward, Elizabeth Stuart Phelps (b. Boston, Aug. 31, 1844—d. Jan. 28, 1911), novelist, poet. In THE GATES AJAR (1868) Elizabeth Ward achieved an immediate national popularity, largely because the sentimental religiousness of the novel appealed to a public just recovering from the devastations of the Civil War. Such later novels as *Beyond the Gates* (1883), *The Gates Between* (1887), and *Within the Gates* (1901) were less successful. *The Gates Ajar* inspired Mark Twain to write a burlesque in CAPTAIN STORMFIELD'S VISIT TO HEAVEN. Her *Doctor Zay* (1882) was one of the earliest American novels to deal with women in the medical profession. Many of her short stories appeared in the *Atlantic Monthly* and other magazines, and her poetry was published in *Poetic Studies* (1875) and *Songs of the Silent World* (1885). *Chapters From a Life* (1896) is autobiographical.

Ward, Lester F[**rank**] (b. Joliet, Ill., June 18,

1841—d. April 18, 1913), botanist, geologist, sociologist, teacher. A pioneer in American sociology, Ward taught in such books as *Dynamic Sociology* (1883), *The Psychic Factors of Civilization* (1893), and *Outlines of Sociology* (1898) that human intelligence was a vital factor in the evolutionary process and that, given a rational, planned social order, man could actively shape the course of human progress. After working for the Federal treasury department and serving as geologist and paleontologist for the Geological Survey, he became professor of sociology at Brown University (1906). He wrote his "mental biography" in *Glimpses of the Cosmos* (6 v., 1913–18).

Ward, Mary Jane [**Mrs. Mary Jane Quayle**] (b. Fairmount, Ind., Aug. 27, 1905—   ), author. A graduate of Northwestern University, Mrs. Quayle wrote *The Tree Has Roots* (1937), and *The Wax Apple* (1938), before her best-known work, *The Snake Pit* (1946), the story of a young wife's long years in a mental hospital and her struggle to regain sanity and freedom. The book enjoyed tremendous popularity both in America and abroad, and was made into a successful movie. Her later novels, while not as popular as *The Snake Pit*, were well received, revealing as they did her insight into feminine psychology. These novels include, *The Professor's Umbrella* (1948); *A Little Night Music* (1951); *It's Different for a Woman* (1952).

Ward, Nathaniel [**"Theodore de la Guard"**] (b. England, [?] 1578—d. *c.* 1652), clergyman, lawyer, public official, writer. Ward, the son of an Essex clergyman, was educated at Cambridge, studied and practiced law, and traveled on the Continent. He became a minister, was known for his wit and his outspokenness in behalf of Puritan doctrine. In 1633 he was excommunicated by Archbishop Laud and took refuge in the Massachusetts Bay Colony. From 1634 to 1636 he served as minister at Agawam (later Ipswich). To him fell the task of writing a code restricting the autocracy of the magistrates, the so-called BODY OF LIBERTIES of 1641, which, in its recognition of fundamental human rights, is ranked by some with the Magna Carta and the Bill of Rights. Ward's most famous work is THE SIMPLE COBLER OF AGGAWAM IN AMERICA. This was written in Massachusetts in 1645 and published in London in 1647 under the pen name Theodore de la Guard. The subtitle announces that the "simple cobler" is "willing to help 'mend his native country, lamentably tattered, both in the upper-leather and sole, with all the honest stitches he can take." The book, a vehement denunciation of religious tolerance, of the strife between Parliament and King Charles, and of the frivolity of women, made a great stir and went through four editions. Ward returned to England in the winter of 1646–47, was called upon to preach before Commons, and did so with his usual uninhibited frankness. He ended his days as an active minister at Shenstone.

Moses Coit Tyler called the *Simple Cobler*

"a tremendous partisan pamphlet, intensely vital . . . full of fire, wit, whim, eloquence, sarcasm, patriotism, bigotry." *The Simple Cobler* has appeared in several editions, the most recent and best being a facsimile reprint prepared by Lawrence C. Wroth (1937). Two writings of Ward not reprinted are his *Religious Retreat Sounded to a Religious Army* (1647) and *A Word to Mr. Peters* (1647). The *Liberties* was edited for the *American History Leaflets* (1896). A biography of Ward was written by J. W. Dean (1868). See HUMOR IN THE U.S.

Ward, Samuel (b. New York City, Jan. 25, 1814—d. May 19, 1884), poet, lobbyist, miner, memoirist. Ward was the brother of JULIA WARD HOWE. He published a volume of verse (*Lyrical Recreations*, 1865) and is believed to have been the original of Horace Bellingham in Marion Crawford's *Dr. Claudius* (1883). He became a representative of the banking interests in Washington and was called "King of the Lobbyists." In mid-century Ward suffered a series of family deaths and financial reverses and went to California in the gold rush. He wrote a book about his experiences, calling himself "Midas Jr." In 1949 this book, rediscovered by Carvel Collins, was reprinted with some entertaining editorial data as *Sam Ward in the Gold Rush.* Meanwhile, entirely by coincidence, Frank Maloy Anderson was sleuthing to discover the author of the anonymous DIARY OF A PUBLIC MAN (1879). In 1948 he published a spectacular "detective story" to prove that Sam Ward was the author. Ward himself had made a second fortune, traveled all over the world, remarried, and become a well-known social figure. He appears in Louise Hall Tharp's *Three Saints and a Sinner* (1956).

Ward, Samuel A[ugustus] (b. Newark, N.J., [?], 1847—d. [?], 1903), merchant, musician. Ward is best known for his *Materna,* a melody which was used for Katharine Lee Bates' poem AMERICA THE BEAUTIFUL.

Ward, Thomas ["Flaccus"] (b. Newark, N.J., June 8, 1807—d. April 13, 1873), physician, poet, musician, philanthropist. A man of wealth, Ward studied medicine and received a degree, but pursued the profession for only a short time. He wrote much verse, collected in *Passaic, a Group of Poems Touching That River, with Other Musings* (1842). He used the pen name Flaccus. In later years he resided in New York, where he built an impressive hall for charity performances of theatricals. He wrote an opera for such a performance, *Flora, or, The Gypsy's Frolic* (1858) and a group of *War Lyrics* (1865). Edgar Allan Poe dissected his first collection elaborately and concluded that, despite some merits, Ward was "a second-rate, or third-rate, or perhaps a ninety-ninth-rate poetaster."

Ward, William Hayes (b. Abington, Mass., June 25, 1835—d. Aug. 28, 1916), Congregational clergyman, editor, archaeologist, author. Ward became most widely known in connection with an influential weekly, THE INDEPEND-

ENT, whose staff he joined in 1868; he became editor in 1896. He directed an archaeological expedition to examine Babylonian sites in 1884–85, and published a report on this in 1885; he also wrote *The Seal Cylinders of Western Asia* (1910) and *What I Believe and Why* (1915).

Warde, Frederic (b. Wells, Minn., July 29, 1894—d. July 31, 1939), book designer, editor. Warde was director of printing at the Princeton University Press, was one of the founders of the Watch Hill Press, served on the staff of the Limited Editions Club, then with the Oxford University Press. While with the Limited Editions Club he edited *The Dolphin,* founded by George Macy (1933). He wrote an account of the American printing designer Bruce Rogers (1925). His wife, also a typographer, was Beatrice Becker (Paul Beaujon).

Warde, Frederick [Barkham] (b. England, Feb. 23, 1851—d. Feb. 7, 1935), actor, authority on Shakespeare, memoirist. After giving up the idea of being a lawyer, Warde appeared in England in touring companies. He came to the United States in 1874 and starred in his own company for many years. He abandoned the stage in 1919, but appeared in several films. Shakespeare was his favorite medium; he wrote two books about the dramatist, *Shakespeare's Fools* (1913) and *Shakespearean Studies Simplified* (1925). He wrote one of the best of stage autobiographies, *Fifty Years of Make-Believe* (1925).

Ware, Eugene Fitch ["Ironquill"] (b. Hartford, Conn., May 29, 1841—d. July 1, 1911), army officer, lawyer, public official, poet, historian. Ware served throughout the Civil War and was mustered out as a captain of cavalry. He earned his living at first as a harnessmaker, but at his wife's urging studied law, was admitted to the bar, and was very successful as a corporation lawyer. He served in the state legislature and on several commissions. He was fond of history, wrote numerous papers, and prepared an account of *The Indian War of '64* (1892). He also wrote verse under the pen name of Ironquill and made several collections, among them *The Rhymes of Ironquill* (1908) and *From Court to Court* (1909).

Ware, Henry (b. Sherborn, Mass., April 1, 1764—d. July 12, 1845), clergyman, teacher, author of controversial writings on religion. Ware held a pastorate at Hingham, Mass., for eighteen years, then a professorship in the Harvard Divinity School, which he helped to organize. He helped establish Unitarianism, taking an active part in the controversies with the Trinitarians. A volume of his lectures was called *An Inquiry into the Foundation, Evidences, and Truths of Religion* (1842). He married three times; of his nineteen children three became noted men: **Henry, Jr.** (b. Hingham, Mass., April 21, 1794—d. Sept. 22, 1843), a Unitarian minister who taught at Harvard, wrote many books and articles, and edited *The Christian Disciple* (1819–23); **John** (b. Hingham, Mass., Dec. 19, 1795—d. April 29, 1864), a physician who also taught at Harvard and whose lectures were collected in *Discourses on Medical Education* (1847) and *Hints to Young Men* (1850); and **William** (b. Hingham, Mass., Aug. 3, 1797—d. Feb. 19, 1852), Unitarian clergyman and novelist who wrote ZENOBIA (originally called *Letters of Lucius M. Piso from Palmyra to His Friend Marcus Curtius at Rome*, 1837), a very popular novel, and also *Aurelian* (originally called *Probus*, 1838) and *Julian* (1841), as well as various travel sketches and biographies, and who edited *American Unitarian Biography* (2 v., 1850, 1851).

Ware, John. See HENRY WARE.

Ware, Theron. See DAMNATION OF THERON WARE.

Ware, William. See HENRY WARE.

Warfield, David (b. San Francisco, Nov. 28, 1866—d. June 27, 1951), actor. As a portrayer of character roles, Warfield was at his best in productions directed by DAVID BELASCO. Usually he played Jewish characters, and it was in one such role that he attained his first great success, in *The Auctioneer* (1901), produced by Belasco. Later he played with equal success in *The Music Maker* (1904) and THE RETURN OF PETER GRIMM (1911), both Belasco productions. Belasco starred him as Shylock in *The Merchant of Venice* (1922) and prepared *A Souvenir of Shakespeare's "The Merchant of Venice," as Presented by David Belasco* for private printing (1923).

War Is Kind (1899), a collection of poems by STEPHEN CRANE. Most of these poems are cynical ("A newspaper is a collection of half-injustices," for example); a few are built by contrast of mood (hope/despair; illusion/reality), some are syllogistic in form, and most are non-metrical. No. XXI is a typical Crane parable poem, of a kind more frequently found in his BLACK RIDERS collection (1895): "man said to the universe:/ 'Sir, I exist!'/ 'However,' replied the universe,/ 'The fact has not created in me/ A sense of obligation.'" The title poem, "Do not weep, maiden, for war is kind," which is the best poem in the volume, was scoffed at by the New York *World* as being "not poetry as Tennyson understood it."

Warman, Cy (b. near Greenup, Ill., June 22, 1855—d. April 7, 1914), farmer, railroad worker, newspaperman, writer. Warman's varied career led him to two kinds of fame. A facile verse writer, he composed a song, *Sweet Marie* (music by Raymon Moore) which became an enormous success. He also wrote numerous convincing stories and books on railroaders, including *Tales of an Engineer* (1895), *The Express Messenger* (1897); *The Story of the Railroad* (1898); *Snow on the Headlight* (1899); *The Last Spike* (1906). His poems were collected in *Mountain Melodies* (1892), and *Songs of Cy Warman* (1911).

Warner, Anna Bartlett ["Amy Lothrop"] (b. New York City, Aug. 31, 1827—d. Jan. 22, 1915), novelist, author of juveniles and books on religion and gardening. The sister of the somewhat better known SUSAN B. WARNER wrote fiction very much in her sister's style and some-

times collaborated with her. After the appearance of Susan's *The Wide, Wide World* (1851), Anna wrote *Dollars and Cents* (1852), under the pen name Amy Lothrop. The sisters collaborated on about fifteen novels, among them *Mr. Rutherford's Children* (2 v., 1853–55) and *Wych Hazel* (1876). Books Anna wrote on her own include *Stories of Vinegar Hill* (6 v., 1872), *The Fourth Watch* (a religious book, 1872), and *Gardening by Myself* (1892). After her sister's death she wrote a book about her (1909). Olivia E. P. Stokes wrote *Letters and Memories of Susan and Anna Bartlett Warner* (1925).

Warner, Charles Dudley (b. Plainfield, Mass., Sept. 12, 1829—d. Oct. 20, 1900), essayist, editor, novelist. Warner is remembered today chiefly for his collaboration with MARK TWAIN on THE GILDED AGE (1873), but in his lifetime he was a popular and prolific author in his own right. After working as a railroad surveyor in Missouri and a lawyer in Chicago, Warner settled in Hartford, Conn., and became editor of the Hartford *Evening Post* (1861), later the *Courant* (1867). His first book of essays, *My Summer in a Garden* (1871), was hailed as a worthy successor to Washington Irving's genial sketches and went through forty-four editions by 1895. Equally successful were the essays collected in BACKLOG STUDIES (1873); *Baddeck* (1874); and *Being a Boy* (1878). He also wrote travel books, among which were *Saunterings* (1872); *My Winter on the Nile* (1876); and *In the Levant* (1877). His trilogy of novels, *A Little Journey in the World* (1889), *The Golden House* (1895), and *That Fortune* (1899), satirized the era to which *The Gilded Age* had given a popular name. He also published biographies of Washington Irving and Capt. John Smith for the AMERICAN MEN OF LETTERS SERIES, of which he was editor; he wrote literary criticism in *The Relation of Literature to Life* (1896) and *Fashions in Literature* (1902); and he edited, with others, the multi-volume LIBRARY OF THE WORLD'S BEST LITERATURE (1896–97). He succeeded William Dean Howells in the "Editor's Study" of *Harper's* (1892), and was president of the American Social Science Association and the National Institute of Arts and Letters. A close friend of Mark Twain, Howells, and Thomas Bailey Aldrich, Warner was in many respects a typical New England writer of the late 19th century.

Warner, Josiah (b. Boston, 1798[?]—d. April 14, 1874), musician, teacher, social reformer. Warner for a time taught music and conducted an orchestra in Cincinnati. When Robert Owen founded his utopian colony at New Harmony, Ind., Warner joined him there with his family. But he found that in fundamental ideas and devices he differed decidedly from Owen. He started what he called an "equity store" in Cincinnati, later (1850) founded a colony called "Modern Times" on Long Island, but had to give it up in 1862 since it attracted more than the usual number of fools and eccentrics. He wrote a series of books which are regarded as the basis of philosophical anarchism in the United States. Among them: *Equitable Commerce* (1846); *True Civilization* (1863, new version 1875); also *Written Music Remodeled and Invested with the Simplicity of an Exact Science* (1860). He belonged to the tribe of Yankee inventors. One of his devices was a lard-burning lamp. He also made several inventions for use in printing, including a cylinder self-inking press. William Bailie wrote *Josiah Warren, the First American Anarchist* (1906).

Warner, Susan Bogert ["Elizabeth Wetherell"] (b. New York City, July 11, 1819—d. March 17, 1885), novelist, author of books for children. In her day Miss Warner was the most popular of American novelists, at home and abroad. Two of her books—THE WIDE, WIDE WORLD (1850), a story for girls, and QUEECHY (1852)—were surpassed in sales only by *Uncle Tom's Cabin* (1851–52). Miss Warner wrote several books in collaboration with her younger sister ANNA BARTLETT WARNER, but Anna was somewhat more cheerful in tone than Susan, who tended toward pathos and heavy moralizing. Among her other books were *The Hills of Shatemuc* (1856); *The Old Helmet* (1863); *Melbourne House* (1864); *Nobody* (1882).

War of 1812, the (1812–1814). The second war between the United States and England was fought ostensibly to maintain American freedom of the seas, but was also directed toward the American annexation of Canada and Florida. In its actual course the war was disheartening; its history is mainly an account of disasters. Important for American literary history was the morning after a British attack on Fort McHenry, when Francis Scott Key, seeing that "our flag was still there," composed *The Star-Spangled Banner,* which later became the United States national anthem.

Among historical works on the War of 1812 are H. M. Brackenridge's *History of the Late War Between the U.S. and Great Britain* (1818); J. T. Headley's *Second War with England* (1853); D. D. Porter's *Memoir of Commodore David Porter* (1875); Theodore Roosevelt's *The Naval War of 1812* (1882); Henry Adams' *History of the U.S. During the Administrations of Jefferson and Madison* (9 v., 1885–91); A. T. Mahan's *Admiral Farragut* (1892) and *Sea Power in Its Relations to the War of 1812* (1905); K. C. Babcock's *Rise of American Nationality* (1906); S. E. Morison's *Letters of Harrison Gray Otis* (1913); C. K. Webster's *British Diplomacy, 1813–15* (1921); Fletcher Pratt's *The Heroic Years, 1801–15* (1934) and *Preble's Boys* (1950); Francis F. Beirne's *The War of 1812* (1949); Glen Tucker's *Poltroons and Patriots* (2 v., 1954); and C. S. Forester's *The Age of Fighting Sail: The Story of the Naval War of 1812* (1956).

Novels on the war include J. K. Paulding's DIVERTING HISTORY OF JOHN BULL AND BROTHER JONATHAN (1812); Irving Bacheller's D'RI AND I (1901); Kenneth Roberts' *The Lively Lady* (1931) and *Captain Caution* (1934); F. Van Wyck Mason's *Captain Renegade* (1932; rewritten as *Wild Drums Beat,* 1954); James Street's *Oh, Promised Land* (1940); James Jennings' *Call the New World* (1941) and *The Salem Frigate* (1946); Marguerite Allis' *To Keep Us Free* (1953). James Nelson Barker wrote a play called MARMION, based on Sir Walter Scott's poem, which was produced in New York City April 13, 1812. Its protests against tyranny echoed the feeling against England in those days, and it was received with great enthusiasm. Mordecai M. Noah's SHE WOULD BE A SOLDIER, OR, THE PLAINS OF CHIPPEWA (1819) and Richard Penn Smith's *The Triumph at Plattsburgh* (1830) were patriotic plays. William Emmons published what he called "a national drama"— *Tecumseh, or, The Battle of the Thames* (1836). He had treated the same episode in a pamphlet published in 1822 and returned to it in one section of *The Fredoniad, or, Freedom Preserved, an Epic Poem of the Late War of 1812.* These plays were all tedious and pretentious. During the war some of our victories inspired ditties such as W. Strickland's *Decatur's Victory,* Samuel Woodworth's *Erie and Champlain* and *The Hunters of Kentucky,* and Charles Miner's *James Bird.* The most famous poem about the war, aside from *The Star-Spangled Banner,* is of course Oliver Wendell Holmes' OLD IRONSIDES (1830), dedicated to the preservation of the ship *Constitution.*

War of Independence. See AMERICAN REVOLUTION.

Warren, Austin (b. Waltham, Mass., July 4, 1899—), critic, teacher. Warren studied at Wesleyan College in Connecticut and at Harvard and Princeton universities, receiving his doctorate from the latter in 1926. His renown as a teacher came in his work at Boston and New York universities and at the Universities of Iowa and Michigan. His scholarship was attested to in such critical writings as *Alexander Pope as Critic and Humanist* (1929) and *Rage for Order: Essays in Criticism* (1947). With René Wellek he made a singularly distinguished contribution to literary study in *The Theory of Literature* (1949). Warren's other books: *The Elder Henry James* (1934); *Crashaw: A Study in Baroque Sensibility* (1938); *New England Saints* (1956). He also edited *Hawthorne: Representative Selections* (1934).

Warren, Charles (b. Boston, March 9, 1868— d. Aug. 16, 1954), lawyer, author, historian. A Massachusetts lawyer, assistant U.S. attorney general, and lecturer at various universities, Warren also wrote many books, chiefly on American law, government, and history. *The Supreme Court in United States History* (3 v., 1922) won a Pulitzer prize (1923). Among his other writings are *A History of the American Bar* (1911) and *Odd Byways in American History* (1942).

Warren, Mercy Otis (b. Barnstable, Mass., Sept. 14, 1728—d. Oct. 19, 1814), poet, dramatist, historian. Sister of the patriot JAMES OTIS and husband of General James Warren, Mercy Otis Warren devoted her literary talents to the service of the American republic. She corresponded with many prominent patriots, giving encouragement and respected advice in political matters. Her verse dramas, THE ADULATEUR: A TRAGEDY (1773) and THE GROUP (1775), were topical satires of the British and the American Tories. She also published the fervently republican *Poems Dramatic and Miscellaneous* (1790) and a *History of the Rise, Progress, and Termination of the American Revolution* (1805). Alice Brown wrote about her in *Mercy Warren* (1896). Katharine Anthony wrote *First Lady of the Revolution: Mercy Otis Warren* (1958). See also THE BLOCKADE.

Warren, Robert Penn (b. Guthrie, Ky., April 24, 1905—   ), poet, novelist, teacher. Warren is identified with the Southern agrarian movement and with the NEW CRITICISM in literature. He was educated at Vanderbilt Uni-

Peter Fink

versity, the University of California and Yale University, and has taught at Southwestern College, Vanderbilt and Louisiana State universities, the University of Michigan, and Yale. His contributions to the *Fugitive* (1922–25) while he was still an undergraduate reflected his militant interest in the South, as did his association with the group led by JOHN CROWE RANSOM; his early JOHN BROWN, THE MAKING OF A MARTYR (1929) was a determined exercise in southernism. He was one of the contributors to I'LL TAKE MY STAND (1930), the manifesto of Southern agrarianism; he helped found and edit THE SOUTHERN REVIEW (1935–42); and with Albert Erskine edited two anthologies: *A Southern Harvest* (1937) and *A New Southern Harvest* (1957).

Warren's early reputation was made, however, with his poetry, which showed him to be

a writer with a finely controlled talent for vivid metaphor and brilliant descriptions. His poems won many awards. Among his collections are *Thirty-Six Poems* (1935); *Eleven Poems on the Same Theme* (1942); *Selected Poems, 1923–1943* (1944); *Brother to Dragons* (a dramatic narrative in verse, 1953); *Promises, Poems 1954–56* (1957). Warren's prose fiction won him a wider audience. His first novel, *Night Rider* (1939), is a story of the Kentucky Tobacco War of 1904. *At Heaven's Gate* (1943) was suggested by the career of Luke Lea, a corrupt Tennessee businessman and politician. ALL THE KING'S MEN (1946), Warren's most popular novel, drew partly from the career of Huey Long (although Warren denied this) for its account of vicious politics in a Southern state; it won a Pulitzer prize and was made into a powerful motion picture (1949). CIRCUS IN THE ATTIC (1948) is a collection of two novelettes and twelve short stories. A murder in Frankfort, Ky. (1826), the famous "Kentucky Tragedy" (see under BEAUCHAMPE), gave Warren the story for WORLD ENOUGH AND TIME (1950). *Band of Angels* (1955) is a tale of miscegenation in the Civil War era. *The Cave* (1959) is a philosophical novel, and *Wilderness* (1961), a historical novel of the Civil War period. In 1961 an essay, *The Legacy of the Civil War*, was published.

Warren is known equally as well for his work as a critic and scholar. A college textbook by him and CLEANTH BROOKS, *Understanding Poetry* (1938), has probably been the most influential single factor in shaping the teaching of English in America during the 20th century. His essays have been widely published in the literary journals, and his *Selected Essays* appeared in 1958. See AGRARIANS.

Washers of the Shroud, The (1861), a poem by JAMES RUSSELL LOWELL. Lowell wrote this under pressure for publication in the *Atlantic* (November, 1861); it was regarded as one of his most important poems. The verse expresses Lowell's strong reaction to the Civil War. In earlier days he had been something of a pacifist, but here he says that sometimes justice must resort to force and that democracy is more than easy words.

Washington, Booker T[aliaferro] (b. near Hale's Ford, Va., April 5, 1856—d. Nov. 14, 1915), educator, author, lecturer. The son of a Negro slave and a white man, Washington began work in the salt furnaces and coal mines of Malden, W.Va., educating himself first at night school and later by working his way through Hampton Normal and Agricultural Institute (1872–75). After some years of teaching and advanced study, he returned to Hampton to take charge of an experimental group of Indian students and established a night school to aid especially needy aspirants. He was chosen to found Tuskegee Institute and built it up from humble beginnings to a large, influential organization. In addition he organized the National Negro Business League in Boston (1901) and gave many influential speeches.

Among his many books are *Sowing and Reaping* (1900); Up from Slavery (1901); *Character Building* (1902); *Working with the Hands* (1904); *Tuskegee and Its People* (1905); *Frederick Douglass* (1907); *The Story of the*

Negro (1909); *My Larger Education* (1911); *The Man Farthest Down* (1912). Basil Matthews wrote *Booker T. Washington, Educator and Interracial Interpreter* (1948); S. R. Spencer, Jr., wrote *Booker T. Washington and the Negro's Place in American Life* (1955). In 1946 a bust and tablet honoring him were unveiled at the Hall of Fame, New York City.

Washington, George (b. Westmoreland Co., Va., Feb. 22, 1732—d. Dec. 14, 1799), surveyor, soldier, statesman, first President. Washington had little formal education, but early showed an aptitude for mathematics, and by the time he was fifteen was a skilled surveyor. From 1753 to 1759 he was an officer in the French and Indian War, during which time the hardships under which he had to work and his difficulties with his superiors formed the beginnings of his antipathy for the British. He was elected to the Virginia House of Burgesses in 1758 and successively re-elected until the House was dissolved by the colonial governor in 1774. During the decade before the outbreak of the Revolution he became progressively more dissatisfied with British rule, particularly with the commercial regulations that required him, and other Virginia planters, to trade exclusively with Britain under conditions which he felt to be unfair to the colonists. After 1770 the increase in colonial taxation, in particular the Stamp Act, and the British prohibition against colonial paper money, further added to American grievances.

Washington was one of Virginia's delegates to the first and second Continental Congresses in 1774 and 1775, and was elected commander of the Continental Army in June, 1775. He was faced with the problem of directing an untrained and inexperienced army, composed primarily of militiamen whose terms of enlistment were short; his task was further complicated by a lack of supplies and the hesitancy on the part of Congress to establish the long-term enlistments necessary for a permanent army. In spite of his handicaps his leadership and success in the field were remarkable.

The end of the war found the newly independent country in confusion. Under the Articles of Confederation, the central government could not provide a stable currency, raise taxes to pay debts, or adequately control the problems arising in the various states. Shays' Rebellion in Massachusetts added to Washington's growing feeling that a stronger and more centralized government was necessary. He was elected president of the Constitutional Convention that met in Philadelphia in 1787. The Constitution it adopted, which provided for a balance of powers in the federal government, and allowed the separate states to manage their purely local affairs, reflects many of Washington's ideas of government. He was unanimously elected first President in 1789. During his administration he raised taxes by various tariff acts, made provisions for paying the war debts of both the Union and the states, created a sound currency and a National Bank, and encouraged the growth of industries that would decrease American economic dependence on European products. Washington's tendency, particularly during his second term, to sympathize with Alexander Hamilton and the Federalists brought charges from the Republicans that he was creating too strong a central government and was, particularly by the Bank Act and the Excise Act, favoring business and industry at the expense of agriculture. He declined a third term and prepared, with the help of several friends, a famous Farewell Address. It was never actually delivered, but was published in *Claypoole's American Daily Advertiser* (Sept. 17, 1796).

Washington was not primarily a writer. He sought help from his more articulate friends—Hamilton and Madison in particular—when it was necessary to prepare an important document, such as the *Farewell Address*. He was, however, not without skill in the composition of a narrative, as in *The Journal of Major George Washington, Sent by the Hon. Robert Dinwiddie, Esq., His Majesty's Lieutenant-Governor and Commander-in-Chief of Virginia, to the Commandant of the French Forces on Ohio*, which was printed at Williamsburg in 1754. In the course of his later life Washington kept a journal, wrote many letters, prepared army orders, and composed numerous official documents.

The bicentenary edition of Washington's writings appeared in thirty-nine volumes (1931–44), with John C. Fitzpatrick as editor. Other editions of his works include: A. B. Hulbert's *Washington and the West: Being George Wash-*

ington's Diary of Sept. 1784 (1905, 1911); J. C. Fitzpatrick's *Calendar of the Correspondence of George Washington, Commander-in-Chief of the Continental Army* (5 v., 1905–15), *Diaries of George Washington, 1748–99* (4 v., 1925), and *George Washington, Colonial Traveler* (extracts from his papers, 1927); Philip S. Foner's *George Washington: Selections from His Writings* (1944); Saxe Commins' *Basic Writings of George Washington* (1948); Saul K. Padover's *The Washington Papers: Basic Selections from the Public and Private Writings of George Washington* (1955).

Much mythology and adulation has grown up about Washington and his place in the nation's history. Jefferson said of him: "Never did nature and fortune combine more perfectly to make a man great." It is believed that General Harry Knox, Washington's close friend, was the first to call him "The Father of his Country." (See FRANCIS BAILEY.) Another good friend, Col. Henry ("Light-Horse Harry") Lee, offered resolutions in his memory (Dec. 19, 1799) in which occurs the famous phrase, "Washington, first in war, first in peace, and first in the hearts of his countrymen." The first of the myths was created by Mason Locke Weems, who wrote *A History of the Life and Death, Virtues, and Exploits, of General George Washington* (1800). His great creation was the story that the child Washington admitted having cut down a cherry tree because he could not tell a lie, and was immediately forgiven by his astonished father. Another widely repeated story showed Washington throwing stones (some claimed silver dollars) across the Rappahannock River. John Marshall's *Life of Washington* (5 v., 1804–07) is adulatory and biased toward the Federalist side when discussing Washington's presidency. Jared Sparks, a professor of history at Harvard University, produced a twelve volume edition of Washington's writings (1834–37), the first volume of which is a life of Washington; the work must be used with caution, since Sparks altered the wording of documents in order to produce a picture of a flawless man. Washington Irving's *Life of George Washington* (5 v., 1855–59) relies on Sparks' work and is therefore not entirely accurate. Less adulatory and more accurate biographies include Paul L. Ford's *The True George Washington* (1896, repub. as *George Washington*, 1924); Henry C. Lodge's *George Washington* (2 v., 1898); Woodrow Wilson's *George Washington* (1903); J. C. Fitzpatrick's *George Washington Himself* (1933); Curtis P. Nettels' *George Washington and American Independence* (1951); William Alfred Bryan's *George Washington in American Literature, 1775–1865* (1952); and Douglas Southall Freeman's biography in seven volumes (1948–1957).

Some of the works of fiction in which Washington appears directly or indirectly are H. H. Brackenridge's *Modern Chivalry* (1792–1815); Charles Brockden Brown's *Ormond* (1799); James Fenimore Cooper's *The Spy* (1821); Catharine Maria Sedgwick's *The Linwoods*

(1835); J. K. Paulding's *The Old Continental* (1846); John Esten Cooke's *Fairfax, or, The Master of Greenway Court* (1868); Bret Harte's *Thankful Blossom* (1877); S. Weir Mitchell's *Hugh Wynne, Free Quaker* (1897) and *The Red City* (1907); Paul Leicester Ford's *Janice Meredith* (1899); Gertrude Atherton's *The Conqueror* (1902); Joseph Hergesheimer's *Balisand* (1924); Elizabeth Page's *The Tree of Liberty* (1939); Kenneth Roberts' *Oliver Wiswell* (1940); Howard Fast's *The Unvanquished* (1942); Janet Whitney's *Judith* (1943). Two 20th-century plays that dealt with Washington had a quality far above that of plays about him produced earlier—Maxwell Anderson's *Valley Forge* (1934) and Sidney Kingsley's *The Patriots* (1945).

Among guides to the extensive manuscripts and printed material about Washington are W. S. Baker's *Bibliotheca Washingtoniana: A Descriptive List of the Biographies and Biographical Sketches of George Washington* (1889); A. P. C. Griffin's *Catalogue of the Washington Collection in the Boston Athenaeum* (1897); and the A. L. A. *Classified Washington Bibliography* (1931). To these may be added Gertrude R. B. Richards' *Select Critical Bibliography of Manuscript Sources* and Geneva B. Snelling's *Selective Bibliography of Printed Sources*, both prepared for Volume VI of Freeman's biography (1954). See AMERICAN REVOLUTION IN U.S. LITERATURE.

Washington Merry-Go-Round. See DREW PEARSON.

Washington Square (1881), a novel by HENRY JAMES. As a boy James had lived on Washington Square in New York, at that time the city's most fashionable residential district. The novel concerns Catherine Sloper, the shy and stolid daughter of wealthy, urbane, sardonic Dr. Austin Sloper. When young Morris Townsend, who is courting Catherine for her money, learns that her father will disinherit her if she marries him, he leaves her. Renewing his courtship after Dr. Sloper dies and leaves Catherine a small fortune, Morris is rejected sadly but firmly by Catherine, who lives on at Washington Square, an old maid. Thus Catherine, plain and unintelligent, nevertheless withstands the world's assaults. The novel was dramatized (1947) as THE HEIRESS and filmed in 1949.

Wasp, The. A weekly founded in 1856. It became famous when AMBROSE BIERCE was appointed its editor (1880–86); some of his scathing attacks appeared in its pages. Other contributors were Mark Twain and Bret Harte. It was later called *Wasp & News-Letter* and lasted into the present century.

Waste Land, The (1922), a poem by T. S. ELIOT. A work of 434 lines in five sections, *The Waste Land* is undoubtedly the most famous and influential poem written in English during the first half of the 20th century. Many of its symbols were drawn from Jesse L. Weston's *From Ritual to Romance*, a study of medieval themes and legends, and James G. Frazer's *Golden Bough,* a monumental work on anthropology and myth. Basically, *The Waste Land* is an examination of modern Western civilization in terms drawn from the Grail legend; the Fisher King is ill and impotent, and his kingdom is laid waste; only the arrival of the Grail knight, who will ask the three thaumaturgical questions, will destroy the spell and restore the kingdom to fertility. The poem is highly allusive and ironic, and consists of a panoramic juxtaposition of episodes, historical sketches, imaginary landscapes, miniature dramas, and lyrical interludes.

The first section, "The Burial of the Dead," begins with April, "the cruellest month," in which the advent of spring only serves to re-awaken the dull, sterile world to an awareness of its condition. Various protagonists and scenes are introduced which are allusively symptomatic of the living death of the 20th-century waste land. Section II, "A Game of Chess," deals primarily with lust and sterility. There is a sharp contrast between the two scenes, the one in an opulently furnished bedroom, the other in a London pub. The title of the section is taken from Thomas Middleton's play, *Women Beware Women*, in which a woman is distracted by a game of chess while her daughter-in-law is being raped. In "The Fire Sermon" (III) the 20th-century world is merged with the past by means of the figures of the fisherman and of Tiresias, the ancient seer who had seen snakes coupling and had been changed, for a time, into a woman. The theme of boredom, barrenness, and shame in sexual encounters is reiterated in the scenes between the typist and the "youth carbuncular," Elizabeth and Leicester, and the three Thames maidens. Part IV, "Death by Water," refers back to the "drowned Phoenician sailor" of Part I and to the prophecy to "fear death by water." Part V, "What the Thunder Said," suggests the approach to the Chapel Perilous of medieval legend, and, as Eliot's notes indicate, "the present decay of Eastern Europe." The thunder speaks the words of the Upanishad, "give, sympathize, control"; the final word, *shantih*, is the equivalent of the "peace that passes understanding."

Eliot has said that in its original form the poem was twice its present length and that the work of cutting it was entrusted to his friend EZRA POUND, a service Eliot acknowledges in his dedication of the poem to Pound as *"il miglior fabbro."* The poem has been widely and variously imitated by other poets, Eliot's contemporaries as well as younger writers. More has been written about *The Waste Land* than about any other work of modern poetry. No English or American critic has been able to feel that his work is complete without a consideration of the poem, which, because of its rich symbolical content, is susceptible to almost endless interpretations. A good elementary guide to the poem may be found in George Williamson's *A Reader's Guide to T. S. Eliot.*

Watch on the Rhine, The (1941), a play by LILLIAN HELLMAN. A German refugee in the United States whom Nazi agents want to inter-cept is recognized by a dissolute hanger-on at the German embassy who demands a large bribe in return for keeping silent. The refugee kills him and in so doing helps to awaken complacent Americans to the dangers of European tyrannies. The plot is strained and the characters are none too plausible, but the play effectively cultivated its author's aim. It was later made into a successful movie with a script by Dashiell Hammett.

Water Witch, The (1830), a novel by JAMES FENIMORE COOPER. This novel was written while Cooper was in Paris, far from the Sandy Hook region in which the action of the story occurs; it was first published at Dresden. The plot is laid in the time of Queen Anne's War (1702–13), and it seems to have been Cooper's intention to create a legendary history for his native New Jersey, as Washington Irving had done for New York. A phantom ship carries on illicit trade between freebooters and colonial New York, with a witch on board and a shrine in her honor in the cabin. Adventures of various kinds take place at sea, on the Atlantic highlands of New Jersey, and in a home on the Shrewsbury. The novel was several times converted into successful plays.

Watkins, Tobias ["Pertinax Particular"] (b. Maryland, [?] 1780—d. Nov. 14, 1855), physician, editor, historian. With JOHN NEAL, Watkins wrote *A History of the American Revolution* (2 v., 1819). He was one of the founders (1816) of the DELPHIAN CLUB in Baltimore and under his pen name edited *Tales of the Tripod; or, A Delphian Evening* (1821). He founded a magazine called *The Portico* (1816–18), to which members of the Delphian Club contributed.

Watson, John B[roadus] (b. Greenville, S.C., Jan. 9, 1878—d. Sept. 25, 1958), teacher, psychologist, consultant. His classic book was *Psychology from the Standpoint of the Behaviorist* (1919). He shocked his generation by asserting, "No one has ever touched a soul or seen one in a test tube." Other books are BEHAVIORISM (1925; rev., 1931) and *Ways of Behaviorism* (1928).

Watson, John Whitaker. See BEAUTIFUL SNOW.

Watterson, Henry (b. Washington, D.C., Feb. 16, 1840—d. Dec. 22, 1921), newspaper editor, politician. Watterson loved the South and fought in the Confederate cavalry during the Civil War. His father, a congressman from Tennessee, had also been a newspaper editor, and Watterson had considerable newspaper experience before he settled in Louisville, Ky. There he helped revive a dying paper, the *Journal*, then took over the *Courier* (1868), and presided over the famous *Courier-Journal* to his death. His unabashedly rhetorical editorials became known all over the country. He was bitter against Theodore Roosevelt, supported Wilson in World War I but opposed America's entry into the League of Nations. He received a Pulitzer prize (1918) for his editorials warmly supporting American ideals during World War I.

He published *Oddities of Southern Life and Character* (1882); *The Compromises of Life* (1903); and *"Marse Henry": An Autobiography* (1919). Two biographies of him have appeared: Isaac F. Marcosson's *"Marse Henry"* (1951) and J. F. Wall's *Henry Watterson: Reconstructed Rebel* (1956).

Watterston, George (b. on shipboard, New York Harbor, Oct. 23, 1783—d. Feb. 4, 1854), lawyer, librarian, novelist, poet. Many of Watterson's books were published anonymously, including a novel called *The Lawyer; or, Man As He Ought Not to Be* (1808), a story of legal chicaneries. A story in the Gothic school of fiction was GLENCARN; OR, THE DISAPPOINTMENTS OF YOUTH (3 v., 1810). He was long a resident of Washington, D.C., edited the Washington *City Gazette* for a year, was Librarian of Congress from 1815 to 1829, and wrote several books about the city. He wrote verse, too, including *The Wanderer in Jamaica* (1810) and *The Scenes of Youth* (1813).

Watts, Mary S[tanbery] (b. Delaware Co., Ohio, Nov. 4, 1868—d. May 21, 1958), novelist. Mrs. Watts was a prolific and capable novelist whose best known work was *Nathan Burke* (1910), a historical novel about Ohio. She made Thackeray and Defoe her models in attempts to secure realism in conversation and direct narrative. Among her other books: *The Legacy* (1911); *The Rudder* (1916); *Father and Son* (1919); *The Noon Mark* (1920); *The Fabric of the Loom* (1924).

Wave, The (1929). See EVELYN SCOTT.

Way Down East (1898), a play by Lottie Blair Parker. This rural drama, fitted out with conventional rustic characters, jokes, and sentiments, was a huge success, running for 361 performances in New York and thereafter as a standard play for stock companies. It was also made into a movie (1920). In its most famous scene the stern bucolic father orders the erring woman whom his son wants to marry out into the cold. The scene was always played straight and was a reliable tearjerker.

Wayne, Anthony ["Mad Anthony"] (b. Chester Co., Pa., Jan. 1, 1745—d. Dec. 15, 1796), tanner, surveyor, legislator, soldier. Wayne was elected to the Pennsylvania legislature in 1774 and to the Committee of Safety in 1775. He was commissioned a colonel in the Continental Army in 1776 and served in many important engagements, rising to the rank of brigadier general. He was most renowned for his bold storming of Stony Point on the Hudson (July 15, 1779). He retired as a brevet major general at the close of the Revolution and served in the House as representative from Georgia (1791–92). Washington appointed him commander of American forces to deal with hostile Indians in the West. He defeated an Indian army decisively in the Battle of Fallen Timbers (Aug. 20, 1794) near the present site of Toledo, Ohio, then negotiated a treaty. His nickname, Mad Anthony, was given him for his reckless bravery in action; it was also applied to him sneeringly by his enemies.

Many books have been written about Wayne, among them H. N. Moore's *Life and Services of General Anthony Wayne* (1845); J. Watts De Peyster's *Major General Anthony Wayne* (1886); F. E. Wilson's *The Peace of Mad Anthony* (1909); H. E. Wildes' *Anthony Wayne* (1941). Novels in which he appears include James Hall's *Harpe's Head* (1833); John Esten Cooke's *Canolles* (1877); J. B. Naylor's *In the Days of St. Clair* (1902) and *Under Mad Anthony's Banner* (1903); Thomas Boyd's *The Shadow of the Long Knives* (1928); and Morison Wood's *The Devil is a Lonely Man* (1946).

Wayside Inn, The. See TALES OF A WAYSIDE INN.

Way West, The (1949), a novel by A. B. GUTHRIE, JR. This story of the great westward trek to Oregon won a Pulitzer prize and is undoubtedly one of the best novels about the American migration to the Pacific Coast. The central figure of the story is Lije Evans, strong, slow, and calm; his wife Rebecca is a proper mate for him, durable and uncomplaining. Her husband has to battle for the leadership of the wagon train, and the conflict forms a main strand of the plot. The other chief strand is concerned with the love of two young people. Another impressive figure is the mountain guide, Dick Summers, a far from conventional backwoodsman who appeared also in an earlier novel by Guthrie, THE BIG SKY (1947).

We Are Coming, Father Abraham, Three Hundred Thousand More (1862), a poem by James Sloan Gibbons (1810–1892) which first appeared anonymously in the New York *Evening Post;* it was at first attributed to the editor, William Cullen Bryant. Gibbons was an Abolitionist, and the poem was written in response to Lincoln's call for 300,000 additional volunteers. Stephen Foster's musical setting of the poem became a great favorite in the North.

Weathers, W. T. See WILLIAM BYRD.

Weaver, John V[an] A[lstyn] (b. Charlotte, N.C., July 17, 1893—d. June 14, 1938), newspaperman, editor, writer. A student at Hamilton College and Harvard University, a newspaperman in Chicago and Brooklyn, an army officer in World War I, Weaver became a typical New Yorker, especially after his marriage to the actress Peggy Wood. He was a deft worker with words but wrote verse that attracted no attention until he adopted a suggestion of H. L. Mencken and wrote in slang. Several volumes of such verses were published, as well as some in straight English: *In American* (1921); *Finders* (1923); *More in American* (1926); *To Youth* (1928); *Turning Point* (1930); and *Trial Balance* (1931)—the last an autobiography in verse. He also wrote three novels and then, in collaboration with George Abbott, a play based in part on some of his rhymed tales, *Love 'Em and Leave 'Em* (1926). A collection of all the poems "in American" appeared in 1939. In the last years of his life Weaver worked in Hollywood. His novel *Joy Girl* (1932) is a satire of Hollywood life.

Web and the Rock, The (1939), a novel by

THOMAS WOLFE. Here Wolfe follows his autobiographical hero, George Webber, to the "Enfabled Rock" of New York, where, in the midst of his youthful literary struggles, he meets the gifted scenic designer Mrs. Esther Jack (modeled on Mrs. Aline Bernstein). During their turbulent love affair he is at first entranced by and then disillusioned with the magic of the city that is so much a part of Esther's personality. In passages of mingled satire and lyricism Wolfe develops the cultural conflict of Christian and Jew, yokel and city dweller. At length George breaks from Esther's web of devotion and flees abroad to seek in an older culture the stability he could not find in the American city.

Webb, Charles Henry ["John Paul"] (b. Rouses Point, N.Y., Jan. 24, 1834—d. May 24, 1905), whaler, newspaperman, inventor, humorist. After reading *Moby Dick* Webb decided to be a whaler and sailed the Arctic and South Pacific seas for almost four years. Then he helped his brother in the grain business in Illinois, wrote for New York papers as a columnist, thereafter migrated to San Francisco and joined the staff of the *Bulletin*. He founded and edited *The Californian* (1864) and established his chief title to fame, his friendship with and assistance to MARK TWAIN. Both Twain and Bret Harte were contributors to his magazine. In 1866 he settled in New York and was the publisher of Twain's first book, *The Celebrated Frog of Calaveras County and Other Sketches* (1867). For a while he was a Wall Street broker. In 1872 he began writing humorous sketches for the New York *Tribune* under the name of John Paul, compiled several volumes of sketches and verse, made various inventions, wrote plays, and traveled abroad. He parodied Charles Reade's *Griffith Gaunt* and Augusta Wilson's *St. Elmo* in his *Liffith Lank; or, Lunacy* (1866) and *St. Twel'mo* (1868). He also wrote *John Paul's Book* (1874); *Parodies, Prose and Verse* (1876); *Sea-Weed and What We Seed* (1876).

Webb, James Watson (b. Claverack, N.Y., Feb. 8, 1802—d. June 7, 1884), newspaperman, editor, diplomat. From the beginning of his career as an editor, Webb gained the reputation of a cantankerous, vitriolic, stubborn person who welcomed quarrels. After serving in the army for three years, he bought the New York *Courier* (1827) and merged it with the *Enquirer* which he bought in 1829. He became a leader in the Whig party and strongly fought arguments in the South for secession. In 1849 he began a career in the foreign service. He wrote several pamphlets including *Slavery and Its Tendencies* (1856); *A National Currency* (1875); also *Reminiscences of General Samuel B. Webb* (his father), 1882.

Webb, Walter Prescott (b. Panola Co., Tex., April 3, 1888—d. March 8, 1963), teacher, historian. In 1918 Webb joined the faculty of the University of Texas as professor of history. He is chiefly known for his philosophy of American history as expressed in his most widely read work, *The Great Plains* (1931). He also wrote *The Growth of a Nation* (with collaborators, 1928); *The Texas Rangers* (1935); *Divided We Stand: The Crisis of Frontierless Democracy* (1937); *The Great Frontier* (1952); *More Water for Texas* (1954); *An Honest Preface* (1959).

Webber, Charles Wilkins (b. Russellville, Ky., May 29, 1819—d. April [?], 1856), Texas Ranger, newspaperman, explorer, naturalist, filibuster, writer of Western stories, historian. At one time Webber studied medicine; at another time he was enrolled in the Princeton Theological Seminary. But at nineteen he joined the Texas Rangers, in 1849 led an expedition to the Colorado and Gila Rivers, and in 1854 organized a company to use camels as a means of crossing the western deserts. The following year he became a member of WILLIAM WALKER's filibustering expedition to Nicaragua, where he was probably killed in battle.

All this time Webber was writing busily, usually tales of wild and improbable invention which he tried to dignify with a philosophy of primitivism. His best known book was *Old Hicks, the Guide* (1848); the first seven chapters were based on his own journal of a trip to the headwaters of the Trinity River in Texas. He was a contributor to many newspapers and magazines, and for two years was editor and joint owner of the *American Review*, later the *American Whig Review*. He knew J. J. Audubon well and under his influence wrote *Wild Scenes and Song Birds* (1854). Among his other books: *The Gold Mines of the Gila* (1849); *The Hunter-Naturalist* (1851); *The Wild Girl of Nebraska* (1852); *Tales of the Southern Border* (1852); *The Prairie Scout, or, Agatone the Renegade* (1852); *The Romance of Forest and Prairie Life* (1853). In his own day he was much praised by the critics.

Weber, Joseph ["Joe"] (b. New York City, Aug. 11, 1867—d. May 10, 1942), comedian. Weber was the stage partner of LEWIS ("LEW") MAURICE FIELDS; they first appeared together at the age of ten in a juvenile skit satirizing German immigrants. That was their act for the rest of their lives. In 1885 they organized a company and gave their skits mainly in a New York theater. Among their productions were *Twirly-Whirly*, *The Geezer*, *Whoop-Dee-Doo*, *Hoity-Toity*, and *Higgledy-Piggledy*. Then the team broke up and the men appeared separately, though neither was as successful alone as the two had been together. They were reunited in *Hokey-Pokey* (1912), and also appeared together in movies and on the radio. Among famous actors who obtained their start in the Weber & Fields companies were David Warfield, DeWolf Hopper, William Collier, Fay Templeton, and Lillian Russell.

Weber, Max (b. Russian Poland, April 18, 1881—d. Oct. 5, 1961), painter, poet, essayist. Weber was brought to the United States in 1891, later studied in several European countries, worked with Matisse, became a cubist and later an expressionist. He began returning to realism in 1917, but in the 1930's seemed on his way back to abstractionism. Among his famous paintings are *Whither Now?*, *Two Musicians*, *Geranium*. He wrote *Cubist Poems* (1914); *Essays on Art* (1916); *Primitives* (1927); and *Woodcuts* (1957).

Webster, Daniel (b. Salisbury, N.H., Jan. 18, 1782—d. Oct. 24, 1852), lawyer, public official, statesman, orator. Webster attended Dartmouth College and became in time its most distinguished graduate. He taught school for

a time, then studied law. At first he practiced in New Hampshire and represented that state in the House of Representatives (1813–17). In 1816 he removed to Boston. He was representative from Massachusetts in 1823–27, senator in 1827–41. He gained wide renown as a statesman and lawyer, delivered many famous orations and won many important cases. He served as Secretary of State (1841–43) and negotiated the important Webster-Ashburton Treaty with Great Britain. From 1845–50 he was again senator from Massachusetts, and from 1850–52 again Secretary of State. He frequently sought the Presidential nomination, but never obtained it.

Webster represented a strong conservative tradition. He opposed the War of 1812, but was wholeheartedly against any action that would destroy the Union. By his willingness to compromise in order to avoid war he incurred the distrust of both the radical Northern abolitionists and the Southern fire-eaters. After Webster's *Seventh of March Speech* (1850) John Greenleaf Whittier wrote a poem of denunciation, ICHABOD; after the Civil War Whittier repented his harsh indictment and in THE LOST OCCASION (1880) he showed his tardy com-

prehension of Webster's motives. Oliver Wendell Holmes paralleled *Ichabod* in his poem *The Statesman's Secret* (1850); later he, too, repented and wrote sympathetically of Webster in *The Birthday of Daniel Webster*. Webster became the legal and political representative of New England "big business," secured a lucrative practice before the Supreme Court, was personally careless about his finances and usually in debt, and accepted from one of his best clients, the Bank of the United States, large sums of money while he was occupying offices of public trust.

Webster, a great orator, was also something of an actor. His appearance assisted him. Stephen Vincent Benét, in THE DEVIL AND DANIEL WEBSTER (1937), described him as having "a mouth like a mastiff, a voice like thunder, and eyes like burning anthracite." A report spread, according to Nathaniel Hawthorne's *The Great Stone Face* (1851), that "the likeness of the Great Stone Face had appeared upon the broad shoulders of a certain eminent statesman." When Webster delivered his *Eulogy of Adams and Jefferson* (1826) he said: "True eloquence does not consist in speech. . . . It must exist in the man, in the subject, in the occasion. . . . It comes, if it comes at all, like the outbreaking of a fountain from the earth, or the bursting forth of volcanic fires, with spontaneous, original, native force."

Webster's addresses may be classified in three ways: (1) addresses made in Congress, such as his replies to Robert Y. Hayne and his *Seventh of March Speech;* (2) his "ceremonial" addresses, such as the *Plymouth Oration* (1820) and the first *Bunker Hill Oration* (1825); (3) his addresses made before judges and juries, such as that in the *Dartmouth Case* (1818) and at the *White Murder Trial* (1830). He had a great faculty for putting into glowing words the ideals that inspired men. In the *Second Reply to Hayne* occurs the famous phrase: "Liberty *and* Union, now and forever, one and inseparable." Other memorable statements were: "The people's government, made for the people, made by the people, and answerable to the people." "When my eyes shall be turned to behold for the last time the sun in heaven, may I not see him shining on the broken and dishonored fragments of a once glorious Union: on States dissevered, discordant, belligerent; on a land rent with civil feuds, or drenched, it may be, in fraternal blood." "There is nothing so powerful as truth—and often nothing so strange." "Liberty exists in proportion to wholesome restraint."

Among books by and about Webster are: S. L. Knapp's *Memoir of the Life of Daniel Webster* (1831); Edward Everett's edition of *The Works of Daniel Webster* (6 v., 1851); Charles Lamman's *Private Life of Daniel Webster* (1852); Fletcher Webster's edition of *The Private Correspondence of Daniel Webster* (2 v., 1857); H. C. Lodge's *Daniel Webster* (1883); C. H. Van Tyne's edition of *The Letters of Daniel Webster* (1902); J. W. McIntyre's edition of *The Writings and Speeches of Daniel Webster* (18 v., 1903); E. P. Wheeler's *Daniel Webster: The Expounder of the Constitution* (1905); F. A. Ogg's *Daniel Webster* (1916); R. L. Carey's *Daniel Webster as an Economist* (1929); S. H. Adams' *The Godlike Daniel* (1933); Claude M. Fuess' *Daniel Webster* (2 v., 1930); Gerald W. Johnson's *America's Silver Age* (1938); Richard N. Current's *Daniel Webster and the Rise of National Conservatism* (1955). Webster appears as a character in Howard Breslin's *The Tamarack Tree* (1947).

Webster, H[arold] T[ucker] (b. Parkersburg, W.Va., Sept. 21, 1885—d. Sept. 21, 1952), cartoonist. Webster studied art in Chicago, later worked for several newspapers, including the Denver *Republican*, the Chicago *Inter-Ocean*, the Cincinnati *Post*, and the New York *Tribune*. In 1925 he joined the New York *World*, but later appeared chiefly in the *Herald Tribune*. The "hero" in his cartoons, which in his last years were widely circulated, was often a middle-class professional man, the mild-mannered victim of modern civilization. The most noted was the "timid soul," CASPAR MILQUETOAST. Another series dealt with the vagaries of bridge players. "The Unseen Audience" poked fun at radio programs. Many collections of Webster's cartoons were made; the last appeared after his death, *The Best of H. T. Webster* (1953), with an introduction by Robert E. Sherwood and a biographical sketch by Philo Calhoun.

Webster, Henry Kitchell (b. Evanston, Ill., Sept. 7, 1875—d. Dec. 8, 1932), teacher, novelist. A graduate of Hamilton College, Webster at first taught English, then began a long collaboration with SAMUEL MERWIN (1874–1936) on a series of novels, the best of which was a railroad story called CALUMET "K" (1901). He had a gift for writing pleasant, well-told yarns, not without some realistic detail, although the plots were more sentimental than profound. Among the titles that became particular favorites were *The Whispering Man* (1908); *An American Family* (1918); *Joseph Greer and His Daughter* (1922).

Webster, Jean (b. Fredonia, N.Y., July 24, 1876—d. June 11, 1916), author of children's books. Miss Webster's name was originally Alice Jane Chandler Webster, and the "Jean" was adopted in honor of Mark Twain's mother, who was her aunt. Her father was the Webster who handled Twain's business affairs and was his partner as a publisher. Miss Webster, a kindly woman always deeply interested in the problems of downtrodden and handicapped people, wrote her most famous book, DADDY-LONG-LEGS (1912), primarily to help the latter group; *Dear Enemy* (1915) was a sequel. Among her other writings were two popular collections of stories for girls, *When Patty Went to College* (1903) and *Just Patty* (1911). *Daddy-Long-Legs* was successfully filmed in 1955.

Webster, Noah (b. West Hartford, Conn.,

Oct. 16, 1758—d. May 28, 1843), lawyer, teacher, editor, author, lexicographer. Webster joined the Continental Army along with his father and was among those who marched against Burgoyne. When he took his B.A. degree

at Yale (1778) he became a teacher at Hartford and Litchfield, taught a singing school at Sharon, Conn., then a classical school at Sharon, N.Y., still later a school in Philadelphia. He engaged in lecturing and had a reputation as an orator of moderate ability. In the years following the Revolution, Webster's most intense interest was in the establishment of a strong central government. Admitted to the bar in 1781, he continued to teach and also practiced law. Irritated by the incompetence of the confederation, he wrote pamphlets arguing for national union and for a stronger central establishment, among them *Sketches of American Policy* (1785). In 1787 he advocated the adoption of the Constitution. From 1793 to 1798 he was immersed in journalistic activities, in the course of which he supported the policies of Washington and Adams. He edited a New York City daily called *The American Minerva* (founded Dec. 9, 1793) and a semiweekly called *The Herald*, which consisted of articles selected from the daily.

By this time Webster's ruling passion had become what was later called Americanism. In his *Dissertation upon the English Language* (1789) he showed the exact direction his thought was taking: "As an independent nation, our honor requires us to have a system of our own, in language as well as government." His GRAMMATICAL INSTITUTE OF THE ENGLISH LANGUAGE demanded a purely American literature. This work appeared in three parts (1783, 1784, 1785). The first dealt with spelling, the second with grammar, the third with "the necessary rules of reading and speaking." The first part, when separately published, became the famous blue-back *Speller*, an old-time best seller. Here, too, Webster demanded an American orthography. The *Speller* (see THE AMERICAN SPELLER) was undoubtedly a great help in unifying the nation culturally and establishing a national language.

Meantime Webster was hard at work on his monumental *Dictionary*. The multifariousness of his interests unquestionably assisted him when he began to define words of all sorts. He was a spelling reformer, a gardener, an experimental scientist. He wrote on literature, economics, and politics, edited Governor Winthrop's *Journal*, and wrote a revised version of the Bible. He served as committeeman of his Hartford school district and on the General Assembly of Connecticut and the General Court of Massachusetts; he was a councilman and alderman in New Haven and judge of the county court. In Amherst he was a selectman, president of the Amherst Academy, and helped found Amherst College. He was a director of the Hampshire Bible Society, a vice-president of the Hampshire and Hampden Agricultural Society, and a founder of the Connecticut Academy of Arts and Sciences. He took an active part in community affairs in New Haven, traveled widely in the United States, and studied in Paris, London, and Cambridge.

In 1825 he finally completed the work, and AN AMERICAN DICTIONARY OF THE ENGLISH LANGUAGE appeared in New Haven in 1828. He had an abridgment made a year later by JOSEPH EMERSON WORCESTER, who later was to produce a dictionary that became for a while a great rival of Webster's. In 1841 he brought out a revised form of the dictionary. In 1843 the G. & C. Merriam Co. took over all unsold copies and the right to produce further editions. From this firm in the course of more than a century have come many massive revisions and several abridgments of the dictionary, which has been acknowledged as supreme in its field.

Erwin C. Shoemaker wrote *Noah Webster, Pioneer of Learning* (1936). Harry R. Warfel, in addition to writing *Noah Webster, Schoolmaster to America* (1936), edited *Noah Webster's Poems* (1936), his *Sketches of America* (1937), his *Dissertations on the English Language* (1951), and his *Letters* (1953). An exhaustive *Bibliography of the Writings of Noah Webster*, compiled by his granddaughter Emily Ford Skeel, was edited by Edwin H. Carpenter, Jr. (1958). See also WEBSTER'S DICTIONARY.

Webster, Pelatiah (b. Lebanon, Conn., Nov. 24, 1726—d. Sept. 2, 1795), political economist. A prolific pamphleteer of the Revolutionary period, Webster wrote a series of letters on credit, free trade, and taxation for the Pennsylvania *Evening Post* (beginning Oct. 5, 1776), later collected in *Political Essays* (1791). His *A Dissertation on the Political Union and Constitution of the Thirteen United States of North-America* (1783) advocated a stronger Federal union; and he supported the adoption of the Constitution by Pennsylvania in *Remarks on the Address of Sixteen Members of the Assembly of Pennsylvania* (1787) and *The Weakness of Brutus Exposed* (1787). In *A Plea for the Poor Soldiers* (1790) Webster requested recompense for soldiers and creditors who had helped win the Revolution.

Webster's Dictionary. NOAH WEBSTER, after issuing a series of popular spelling books and a *Compendious Dictionary of the English Language* (1806), turned his attention to his *American Dictionary of the English Language* (1828), a great book in two volumes with definitions of 70,000 terms and emphasis on "the American way." It was, however, no financial success, since it sold at twenty dollars a copy. In 1840 Webster issued a corrected and enlarged second edition. When Webster died three years later, his book came into the market, and the Merriam brothers, George and Charles, purchased the publishing rights. They took immediate steps to modernize the dictionary and make it accessible to a larger public. They engaged Chauncey A. Goodrich, Webster's son-in-law and literary heir, to revise the book. In 1847 they published a one-volume edition to sell at six dollars, and won public favor immediately. The Massachusetts legislature proposed that a copy be placed in every schoolhouse in the state; New York state took similar action, and Congress made it a standard authority. In 1859 illustrations were made part of the text for the first time in any American dictionary and lists of synonyms were introduced.

The famous *Unabridged Webster* was prepared under the editorship of Dr. NOAH PORTER, later president of Yale University, in 1864, and the 1847 book was withdrawn from the market. Yet half a century later this antiquated lexicon, no longer protected by copyright, was issued by some publishers as "Webster's Dictionary," in which even the misprints were reproduced. In 1890 another complete revision was made, *Webster's International Dictionary*, with Porter again serving as editor. The next completely revised edition (1909) was called *Webster's New International Dictionary*, with Dr. WILLIAM T. HARRIS, former U.S. Commissioner of Education, as editor; it contained twice as many entries as its immediate predecessor. In 1934 appeared *Webster's New International Dictionary, Second Edition*, under the editorship of WILLIAM ALLAN NEILSON, then president of Smith College, and Thomas A. Knott, noted linguist. The *Third New International Dictionary* appeared in 1961 with Philip B. Gove as general editor. This edition generated considerable controversy chiefly because it accepted common usage as the criterion for correctness. The first edition of *Webster's Collegiate Dictionary* appeared in 1898; several new editions have appeared, the latest in 1960.

The G. & C. Merriam Co. has also issued

Webster's Dictionary of Synonyms (1942); *Webster's Biographical Dictionary* (1943); *A Pronouncing Dictionary of American English* (by J. S. Kenyon and Thomas A. Knott, 1944); and *Webster's Geographical Dictionary* (1949). In 1947, the centenary of the first Merriam-Webster Dictionary's appearance, Robert Keith Leavitt published a commemorative volume, *Noah's Ark, New England Yankees, and the Endless Quest.*

Wechsberg, Joseph (b. Czechoslovakia, Aug. 29, 1907—   ), journalist. Wechsberg's lively career includes working as a violinist on ocean liners, a lawyer, a soldier, and a writer. His first book, *Die Grosse Mauer* (1938), was a travel book. After coming to the United States to lecture and write for magazines (1938), he decided to remain and become a citizen. He was awarded a Houghton Mifflin Literary Fellowship (1943), for which he wrote his first book in English, *Looking for a Bluebird* (1945), a collection of sketches that had originally appeared in *The New Yorker* and *Esquire*. During World War II he served in the army in Europe; *Homecoming* (1946) is the story of his return as an American soldier to Prague, his original home. The best of the sketches he wrote for American magazines after the war were published in *Sweet and Sour* (1948). *The Continental Touch* (1948), *The Self-Betrayed* (1955), and *Avalanche* (1958) are novels, *Blue Trout and Black Truffles* (1953) is an account of culinary adventures, and *Melba and Her Times* (1961) tells of the famed operatic soprano Nellie Melba.

Wecter, Dixon (b. Houston, Tex., Jan. 12, 1906—d. June 24, 1950), teacher, historian, biographer. Wecter studied at Baylor, Yale, and Oxford Universities, returning to Yale for his doctor's degree (1936). He taught English at the University of Denver, the University of Colorado, and the University of California at Los Angeles; he taught American history at the University of Sydney; was appointed a research fellow at the Huntington Library, and was made literary executor of the Mark Twain estate (1946). He was a writer and a scholar, with a keen eye for the significant facts. He wrote *The Saga of American Society* (1937); *Edmund Burke and His Kinsmen* (1939); *The Hero in America* (1941); *When Johnny Comes Marching Home* (1944); and *The Age of the Great Depression* (1948). He completed four projects relating to Mark Twain: editions of Mark Twain's *Letters to Mrs. Fairbanks* (1949); *Report from Paradise*, a collection of Twain's "celestial" stories; *Love Letters of Mark Twain* (1950); and the opening volume of a projected definitive biography, SAM CLEMENS OF HANNIBAL (posthumously pub., 1952).

Weed, Thurlow (b. Greene Co., N.Y., Nov. 15, 1797—d. Nov. 22, 1882), journalist, politician. Editor of the Rochester (N.Y.) *Telegraph*, the *Anti-Masonic Enquirer*, the Albany *Evening Journal*, and the New York *Commercial Advertiser*, Weed was a powerful leader of the Whig party. He helped elect Presidents Adams, Harrison, Taylor, and Lincoln. He was one of the dominating figures in New York state politics. His chief published writings were *Letters from Europe and the West Indies* (1886) and the posthumously issued autobiography, *Life of Thurlow Weed* (1883–84).

Weeds and Wildings (posthumously published, 1924), a volume of poetry by HERMAN MELVILLE. In these late poems Melville fondly recollected the early and blissful days of his marriage to Elizabeth Shaw, the "Madonna of the Trefoil" in the prefatory dedication. Like all Melville's late work, *Weeds and Wildings* represents him making peace with the world and with himself. After a life of psychological and philosophical turbulence, he finally achieved contentment. Unfortunately, however, his newly won quiescence fatally diminishes the value of the poetry, in which he moves beyond the renunciation of the quest, even beyond the wisdom of acceptance, to a renunciation of truth itself. It is entirely strange and more than faintly pathetic to observe Melville resurrect the ghost of Washington Irving and dedicate an entire section to that "happy shade," whose literary weight he once, quite accurately, compared to a grasshopper's. Similarly, one thinks of Thomas Bailey Aldrich and the cult of sentimentality as one reads Melville's epithet for Man, "Eden's bad boy." Fortunately, however, the falling off is not total, and, at the end, Melville moves ambivalently between this tender-minded withdrawal from reality and a more or less tough-minded confrontation with it, which such poems as "Field Asters" and "Profundity and Levity" suggest. But in the main *Weeds and Wildings* abjures the intellectual thrust of Melville's best poetry, and does not succeed as sentimental nature verse, where it is somewhat reminiscent of Emily Dickinson at her second or third best.

Week on the Concord and Merrimack Rivers, A (1849), a narrative by HENRY DAVID THOREAU. Thoreau's first book describes a river voyage made in August, 1839, with his brother John. Each chapter covers a day of the week. Many passages of restrained but lyrical description make the book almost the equal of WALDEN, and there are bits of poetry, discourses on literature and history, and philosophical speculations.

Weeks, Edward A[ugustus], Jr. (b. Elizabeth, N.J., Feb. 19, 1898—   ), editor, lecturer, essayist. Weeks became devoted to books early in his life. After service in the army he began as a manuscript reader and then a salesman for a New York publisher. He became associate editor of the ATLANTIC MONTHLY (1924), editor of the Atlantic Monthly Press (1928–37), and editor of the *Atlantic* in 1938. As editor he made the magazine more vigorous and more successful, and he is known for his perceptive book reviews. He wrote *This Trade of Writing* (1935), *The Open Heart* (1955), and *In Friendly Candor* (1959), and edited *Great Short Novels* (1941), *The Pocket Atlantic* (1946), and *Jubilee: One Hundred Years of the Atlantic* (with Emily Flint, 1957).

Weems, Mason Locke (b. Arundel Co., Md.,

Oct. 11, 1759—d. May 23, 1825), biographer, bookseller, clergyman. "Parson" Weems, originator of the famous story of GEORGE WASHINGTON and the cherry tree, was an itinerant literary patriot and evangelist. Ordained a deacon

in England, he served as a preacher in Maryland, then became a traveling book agent, distributing morally uplifting and entertaining books. His own writings were fervently moral: *Philanthropist* (1799); *True Patriot* (1802); *God's Revenge Against Murder* (1807); *The Drunkard's Looking Glass* (1812); *The Bad Wife's Looking Glass* (1823). As a biographer Weems wrote with zest and imagination and absolutely no regard for facts. His *History of the Life, Death, Virtues, and Exploits of George Washington* (1800) was vastly popular in its day; its original readers accepted it as semifictional, but later in the 19th century some of its exaggerations and inventions passed into the mythology of American childhood. Weems also wrote "biographies" of Francis Marion (1809), Benjamin Franklin (1815), and William Penn (1822).

Weidman, Jerome (b. New York City, April 4, 1913—   ), novelist. Educated at the College of the City of New York and New York University, Weidman was on the editorial staff of Simon and Schuster and served with the Office of War Information during World War II. His first novel, *I Can Get It for You Wholesale* (1937), depicted such repulsive Jewish characters that the publisher for a time ceased printing the book (1938). But the novel was so popular that Weidman wrote a sequel, *What's in It for Me?* (1938). Other novels are *I'll Never Go There Any More* (1941) and *The Price Is Right* (1949). *The Horse That Could Whistle "Dixie"* (1939) and *The Captain's*

Tiger (1947) are short story collections; *Letter of Credit* (1940) describes a trip around the world. Weidman's wartime experiences furnished him with some of the material for *The*

Lights Around the Shore (1943); *Too Early to Tell* (1946), a satire on war propaganda; and *The Third Angel* (1953). After *Your Daughter Iris* (1955), another novel, came *The Enemy Camp* (1958), a story of anti-Semitism, and *Before You Go* (1960). He also wrote two Broadway plays, *Fiorello!* (1959), which was awarded a Pulitzer prize, and *Tenderloin* (1901).

Weiman, Rita (b. Philadelphia, [?] 1889—d. June 23, 1954), dramatist, novelist, short-story writer. Although Miss Weiman studied at the Art Students League in New York and worked for the New York *Herald* and the New York *Journal-American*, her real love was the theatre. *The Stage Door* (1920); *Footlights* (short stories, 1923); and *What Measure of Love?* (novel, 1935) reveal this interest. She also wrote another novel, *Playing the Game* (1910), and numerous plays.

Weisgard, Leonard [Adam Green] (b. New Haven, Conn., Dec. 13, 1916—   ), author and illustrator of juvenile books. Trained at Pratt Institute, Weisgard did numerous illustrations for magazines, then he began writing and illustrating children's books. Among them are *Down Huckleberry Hill* (1947), *Pelican Here, Pelican There* (1948), and *Treasures to See* (1956).

Welch, William Henry (b. Norfolk, Conn., April 8, 1850—d. April 30, 1934), physician, pathologist. One of America's foremost pathologists, Welch was graduated from Yale University, received his medical degree from Columbia University, and studied in Germany. He studied and taught pathology at Bellevue Hospital, New York, then at Johns Hopkins, introducing many of the latest European ideas and methods. He became the first dean of the school of Medicine at Johns Hopkins and in the same year founded the *Journal of Experimental Medicine*. Among his writings are *General Pathology of Fever* (1888); *The Biology of Bacteria, Infection and Immunity* (1894); *Bacteriology of Surgical Infections* (1895); and *Thrombosis and Embolism* (1899). W. C. Burket edited *Papers and Addresses by William Henry Welch* (3 v., 1920). An admirable biography is James T. and Simon Flexner's *William Henry Welch and the Heroic Age of American Medicine* (1941).

Weld, Theodore Dwight (b. Hampton, Conn., Nov. 23, 1803—d. Feb. 3, 1895), abolitionist. At Utica Academy, N.Y., Weld became a proselyte of the revivalist Charles Grandison Finney and left school to become an itinerant preacher. By 1830 he was a confirmed abolitionist, and he persuaded Arthur and Lewis Tappan to endow Lane Seminary in Cincinnati as an abolitionist school, LYMAN BEECHER serving as president. Here Weld converted Harriet and Henry Ward Beecher to abolitionism. He also helped found the American Anti-Slavery Society (1834), for which he trained missionaries and wrote numerous tracts: *The Bible Against Slavery* (1837); *The Power of Congress over the District of Columbia* (1837); a revision of *Emancipation in the West Indies* (1838); *American Slavery as It Is* (1839); and *Slavery and the Internal Slave Trade in the United States* (with J. A. Thome, 1841). G. H. Barnes and D. L. Dumond edited *The Correspondence of Theodore Weld* (1934) and Benjamin P. Thomas wrote *Theodore Weld, Crusader for Freedom* (1950).

Welde, Thomas. See BAY PSALM BOOK.

Weller, George [Anthony]. See NOT TO EAT, NOT FOR LOVE.

Welles, Gideon (b. Glastonbury, Conn., July 1, 1802—d. Feb. 11, 1878), journalist, politician. Welles was editor and part owner of the Hartford *Times* and a founder of the Hartford *Evening Press* (1856). Elected to the Connecticut legislature (1827–35), he later served as Secretary of the Navy under Lincoln and Johnson (1861–69). His innovation of ironclad battleships and his effective blockade of the Confederacy helped win the Civil War. Welles' *Lincoln and Seward* (1874) was based on one of of the many articles he wrote for *Galaxy* magazine. Autobiographical material is found in *The Diary of Gideon Welles* (3 v., 1911), edited by E. T. Welles, and in Welles' letters published in *The Magazine of History* (1924).

Welles, [George] Orson (b. Kenosha, Wis., May 6, 1915—   ), actor, radio and theatrical producer. Welles, a man of great originality and unpredictable temperament, began his career with the Gate Theater in Dublin, toured with Katharine Cornell, in 1934 directed the Woodstock Festival, and in 1935 played the lead in PANIC. His stage productions, especially after he founded the Mercury Theater, included an all-Negro *Macbeth* and a provocative modern-dress *Julius Caesar*. He wrote and directed several radio and television programs, including one in the interest of hemispheric relations, *Hello, Americans* (1942–43). His radio dramatization of H. G. Wells' *War of the Worlds* (1938), done in the form of a newscast, convinced many people that Martians were actually invading North America and created a panic throughout the East; it is probably the most famous single radio broadcast ever made. He collaborated with Roger Hill in compiling *Everybody's Shakespeare* (1934) and the *Mercury Shakespeare* (1939). In Hollywood, Welles wrote, directed and starred in *Citizen Kane* (1940), a story modeled on the life of William Randolph Hearst, and *The Magnificent Ambersons* (1941). During the late forties and fifties, he became even more active in movies, both as an actor in *Moby Dick* (1956), *The Long Hot Summer* (1958), and *Compulsion* (1959), and as director and star of the controversial productions of *Macbeth* (1947) and *Othello* (1955). In 1952 Welles staged *King Lear*, and due to an injury caused by an accident played the part of Lear from a wheelchair. In recent years he has acted and produced chiefly in Europe.

Welles, Sumner (b. New York City, Oct. 14, 1892—d. Sept. 24, 1961), diplomat, historian, columnist. Welles, an able diplomat, was a graduate of Groton and Harvard, traveled abroad for a while, then entered the diplomatic field. His first assignment was as secretary to the United States embassy in Tokyo; later he served in Buenos Aires and Havana, as a member of various missions, finally as assistant secretary and undersecretary in the State Department (1933–43). A highly articulate person with a command of several languages, Welles wrote a number of important books: *Naboth's Vineyard* (1928); *The U.S. and the World Crisis* (1941); *World of the Four Freedoms* (1943); *The Time for Decision* (1944); *The Intelligent American's Guide to the Peace* (1945); *Where Are We Heading?* (1946); *We Need Not Fail* (1948); *Seven Decisions That Shaped History* (1951).

Welles, Winifred (b. Norwichtown, Conn., Jan. 26, 1893—d. 1939), poet, historian. This sensitive poet published several collections: *The Hesitant Heart* (1919); *This Delicate Love* (1929); *Skipping Along Alone* (1931); *Blossoming Antlers* (1933); *A Spectacle for Scholars* (1935); and *The Park That Spring Forgot* (1940). Posthumously published were *The Shape of Memory* (1944) and a prose work, *The Lost Landscape: Some Memories of a Family and a Town in Connecticut, 1659–1906* (1946).

Wellman, Paul I[selin] (b. Enid, Okla., Oct. 14, 1898—d. Sept. 16, 1966), newspaperman, writer. When Wellman was a child his parents settled for ten years in West Africa. Returning to this country, he lived mainly in Utah. He served in the army during World War I, and for the next twenty-five years worked on the Wichita *Beacon*, the Wichita *Eagle*, and the Kansas City *Star*. He spent two years writing scripts in Hollywood. He wrote four histories: *Death on the Prairie* (1934); *Death in the Desert* (1935); *The Trampling Herd* (1939); *Glory, God, and Gold* (1954). His historical fiction includes *Broncho Apache* (1936); *Jubal Troop* (1939); *Angel with Spurs* (1942); *The Bowl of Brass* (1944); *The Walls of Jericho* (1947); *The Chain* (1949); *The Iron Mistress* (1951); *The Comancheros* (1952); *The Female* (1953). In 1950 his two earlier histories were issued in one volume as *Death on Horseback*. Later works include *Ride the Red Earth* (1958) and *Stuart Symington* (1959).

Wells, Carolyn (b. Rahway, N.J., 1869 —d. March 26, 1942), anthologist, author. Past mistress of parody and the author of almost 170 books ranging from detective stories to juvenile fiction, Carolyn Wells is probably best known for *A Nonsense Anthology* (1902). Her first book, *At the Sign of the Sphinx* (1896), was a collection of charades. Other of her popular anthologies are *A Parody Anthology* (1904); *A Satire Anthology* (1905); *A Whimsy Anthology* (1906). *The Patty Books* (1911) is a series of her children's stories, while the *Fleming Stone Omnibus* (1933) is a good example of her work as a detective story writer. Her autobiography is entitled *The Rest of My Life* (1937). She was a collector and editor of the writings of Walt Whitman and Edward Lear, the influence of the latter being evident in her own nonsense verse.

Wells, [Grant] Carveth (b. England, Jan. 21, 1887—d. Feb. 16, 1957), lecturer, explorer, author. Wells worked as a civil engineer in Canada and on the Malay Peninsula. After coming to America (1918), he led expeditions to Uganda, Lapland, Panama, Mexico, Pakistan, the Caucasus, Kashmir, and Thailand for the American Museum of Natural History and the Geographic Society of Chicago. Except for his first book, *Field Engineer's Handbook* (1913), he wrote travel books such as *Six Years in the Malay Jungle* (1925); *In Coldest Africa* (1929); *Exploring the World* (1934); *The Road to Shalimar* (1951); and *Introducing Africa* (1953). Wells lectured about his travels and produced several motion pictures.

Wells, William Vincent (b. Boston, Jan. 2, 1826—d. June 1, 1876), sailor, government official, writer. Wells spent his early years at sea and was said to have been shipwrecked five times. He followed various vocations in California—miner, farmer, engineer, businessman, newspaperman. In 1854 he visited Honduras, and the following year went back as American consul. He sympathized with WILLIAM WALKER and wrote an account called *Walker's Expedi-* *tion to Nicaragua* (1856). During the Civil War he acted as clerk of the naval office in San Francisco. In 1856 he headed a propaganda agency for the Emperor Maximilian of Mexico. He based his *Explorations and Adventures in Honduras* (1857) on his personal diary, and wrote a biography of his great-grandfather Samuel Adams (3 v., 1865). He also contributed to *Harper's Magazine* and other periodicals and acted as foreign correspondent for several newspapers while in Honduras.

Welty, Eudora (b. Jackson, Miss., April 13, 1909—   ), novelist, short-story writer. Eudora Welty attended Mississippi State College for Women and graduated from the University of Wisconsin. She studied advertising at Columbia University and worked at miscellaneous writing and publicity jobs before she began to write seriously. In her works she concentrates on the small-town Mississippi life she knows so well. Her first stories won instant critical acclaim, but it was some time before the reading public recognized her talents. Her published works include *A Curtain of Green* (1941), *The Wide Net* (1943), and *The Golden Apples* (1949), short story collections; two novelettes, *The Robber Bridegroom* (1942) and *Music from Spain* (1948; later included in *The Golden Apples*); *Delta Wedding* (1946), a sensitive novel about Southern family life; *The Ponder Heart* (1954), a delightful short novel which was dramatized successfully in 1956; and *The Bride of the Innisfallen* (1955).

Miss Welty's stories are "offbeat" accounts of extraordinary happenings in seemingly ordinary lives. Coupled with the uncanny accuracy of her colloquial speech, which she uses with richly comic effect, is a sense of the mysterious which gives her work an almost mythological dimension. Some of her most characteristic stories are "Why I Live at the P.O."; "Livy's Back"; and "The Petrified Old Mr. Marble Man."

Wemyss, Francis Courtney (b. England, May 13, 1797—d. Jan. 5, 1859), actor, stage manager, author. Wemyss was a capable comedian who became a member of the Philadelphia stock company in 1822. He recorded his memories in *Twenty-Six Years of the Life of an Actor and Manager* (2 v., 1847; reprinted as *A Theatrical Biography*, 1848) and wrote *A Chronology of the American Stage, from 1752 to 1852* (1852).

Wendell, Barrett (b. Boston, Aug. 23, 1855— d. Feb. 8, 1921), teacher, scholar, writer. After graduating from Harvard, Wendell made an unsuccessful attempt to pass a bar examination (1880). That same year he was appointed to the Harvard faculty and taught there until 1917. He gave the first course at Harvard in American literature. Many years later (1904) he gave a series of lectures at the Sorbonne on American literature and traditions. His first published books were two novels. He then went on to scholarly books (*Cotton Mather, The Puritan Priest*, 1891; *William Shakespeare*, 1894; *The Temper of the 17th Century in English Literature*, 1894); textbooks (*English Composition*, 1891); essays (*Stelligeri and Other Essays Con-*

cerning America, 1893); and three short plays (*Raleigh in Guiana, Rosamund,* and *A Christmas Masque,* 1902). He also wrote *The Traditions of European Literature* (1920), based on a comparative literature course he gave at Harvard.

But his principal work was his *A Literary History of America* (1900). The book gave him three opportunities: to extol New England, to vent his prejudices against democracy, and to exercise his wit against American authors and tendencies. Unquestionably an able writer, he was obsessed by Anglophilism and Brahminism in their most violent form. He often seemed more interested in phrasing than in accuracy of judgment, as when he described Whitman's *Leaves of Grass* as "confused, inarticulate, and surging in a mad kind of rhythm which sounds as if hexameters were trying to bubble through sewage."

M. A. DeWolfe Howe prepared *Barrett Wendell and His Letters* (1924).

Wept of Wish-ton-Wish, The (1829), a novel by James Fenimore Cooper. This narrative is at once a story of King Philip's War and an unfriendly study of Puritan theocracy in a small Connecticut community. The villain is the Rev. Meek Wolfe, who preaches the murder of Indian women and children as a religious duty and pries into everyone's private affairs. The hero is Conanchet, a "noble savage," of the Narragansett tribe. King Philip of the Wampanoags is one of the chief characters, but the action centers around Conanchet, who for a while is captured by the whites and becomes a member of the Heathcote family; later he kidnaps the young daughter of the family. The daughter is "the wept" of the title. Wish-ton-Wish is the valley where the Heathcotes live. Later in the course of the war the Heathcotes are captured by the Indians, and Conanchet reveals to them that he has married their daughter. She has in the meantime become entirely Indian in viewpoint. James Grossman notes in his life of Cooper (1949) that Cooper makes both Conanchet and the Puritans derive their speech from the same model, the King James Bible. A short play based on the novel was performed in 1851.

Wertenbaker, T[homas] J[efferson] (b. Charlottesville, Va., Feb. 6, 1879—   ), teacher, historian, editor. Wertenbaker taught in Texas and Virginia and after 1910 at Princeton University. His specialty is American history. Among his books: *Patrician and Plebeian in Virginia* (1916); *Planters of Colonial Virginia* (1922); *The First Americans* (1927); *The Founding of American Civilization* (1938); *The Golden Age of Colonial Culture* (1942); *Princeton, 1746–1946* (1946); *The Puritan Oligarchy* (1947); *Father Knickerbocker Rebels* (1948); *Bacon's Rebellion* (1951); *The Shaping of Colonial Virginia* (1958).

Wertham, Frederic (b. Germany, 1895—   ), psychiatrist, author, teacher. Wertham studied medicine at the Universities of Erlangen, Würzburg and Munich, and at Kings College, London. Coming to America, he served as senior psychiatrist in the Department of Hospitals,

New York City; director of the mental hygiene clinic at Bellevue Hospital; and as chief psychiatric consultant to the Kefauver Committee for the Study of Organized Crime. Wertham's writings reflect his interest both in the psychological problems of contemporary intellectuals and in the effects of violence in films and comic books on youth. His indictment of comic books, *Seduction of the Innocent* (1954), is perhaps best known of his many books. Others include *The Show of Violence* (1949); *Social Meaning of Legal Concepts: Criminal Guilt* (1950); *Why Do They Commit Murder?* (1954); *The Sexual Offender and His Offenses* (1956); *Psychiatry and Censorship* (1957).

Wescott, Glenway (b. Kewaskum, Wis., April 11, 1901—   ), poet, novelist. Wescott attended the University of Chicago. His first book, *The Bitterns* (1920), was a volume of poems; for a time he wrote reviews for *Poetry*.

His first novel, *The Apple of the Eye* (1924), was originally published serially in the *Dial*. Although he lived abroad for many years, he turned to Wisconsin for material and mood in *Goodbye Wisconsin* (1928), a collection of short stories. The Grandmothers (1927), his best known novel, and *The Babe's Bed* (1930) are also set in Wisconsin. *A Calendar of Saints for Unbelievers* and *Fear and Trembling* were published in 1932. *The Pilgrim Hawk* (1940) and *Apartment in Athens* (1945) are novels with European settings.

West, Andrew F[leming] (b. Alleghany, Pa., May 17, 1853—d. Dec. 27, 1943), teacher, educational administrator. A professor of Latin at Princeton University and dean of the graduate school there, West wrote *Alcuin and the Rise of the Christian Schools* (1893); *The American College* (1899); *American Liberal Education* (1907); *American General Education* (1932). His interest in classical literature yielded, among other works, a *Latin Grammar* (1902) and an edition of Terence (1888). He also wrote *Stray Verses* (1931).

West, Benjamin (b. Rehoboth, Mass., March [?], 1730—d. Aug. 26, 1813), mathematician, astronomer, almanac publisher. Entirely self taught, West became learned enough in science to be elected a fellow of the American Academy of Arts and Sciences. In 1788 he was made professor of mathematics and astronomy at Rhode Island College (later Brown University). He wrote *An Account of the Observation of Venus Upon the Sun the Third Day of June 1769* and similarly reported an eclipse of the sun in 1781. He began issuing almanacs in 1763, using for some of them the pen name Isaac Bickerstaff. This was probably a reference to Jonathan Swift's fictitious astrologer and almanac maker of the same name. West's first issue was called simply *An Almanack*. In 1765 he issued *The New-England Almanack*, which continued to appear until 1781. *Bickerstaff's Boston Almanac* appeared in 1768, 1779, and 1783–93, and was the first illustrated almanac in Massachusetts. West also issued *The North-American Calendar, or Rhode Island Almanac* (1781–87) and *The Rhode Island Almanac* (1804–06).

West, Herbert Faulkner (b. Jamaica Plain, Mass., Jan. 6, 1898—   ), professor, critic. West began teaching English and comparative literature at Dartmouth College in 1925. His specialties are essays on book collecting, such as those in *Modern Book Collecting for the Impecunious Amateur* (1936) and *The Mind on the Wing* (1947), and writers on nature, as in *The Nature Writers* (1939). *Rebel Thought* (1953) includes chapters on diverse philosophers of Western civilization. West founded Westholm Publications (1955), and is also known as a book reviewer. Other works include: *Modern Conquistador: Robert Bontine Cunninghame Graham* (1933); *A Stephen Crane Collection* (1948); *W. H. Hudson's Reading* (1947); *John Sloan's Last Summer* (1952); *What Price Teaching?* (1957); *Learning My ABC's* (1958); *For a Hudson Biographer* (1958).

West, Jessamyn (b. [?] Indiana, [?]—   ), novelist, short story writer. A resident of California since the age of six, Jessamyn West studied at Whittier College, a small Quaker institution, and the University of California. She began to write while confined to a sanatorium with tuberculosis; her first book, *The Friendly Persuasion*, was published in 1945. This consisted of a series of sketches of the life of a Quaker family in southern Indiana during the Civil War, and was praised by reviewers. Her subsequent books —*The Witch Diggers* (1951), a novel about life on an Indiana poor farm at the turn of the century; *Cress Delehanty* (1953), sketches about an adolescent girl; a collection of short stories, *Love, Death and the Ladies' Drill Team* (1959);

and a novel set in southern California, *South of the Angels* (1960)—have almost without exception received similar accolades. She is also the author of *Mirror for the Sky* (1948), a script for an opera on the life of Audubon; *To See The Dream* (1957), an account of her experiences in Hollywood during the filming of *The Friendly Persuasion* (1956); and *Love is Not What You Think* (1959).

West, Mae. See DIAMOND LIL.

West, Nathanael [pen name of **Nathan Wallenstein Weinstein**] (b. New York City, 1904 —d. Dec. 22, 1940), novelist. *The Complete Works of Nathanael West* was published in 1957 with an introduction by Alan Ross. It

By permission, Estate of Nathanael West

contains just four short novels, yet it represents the work of a major figure in American fiction. West's vision of the horror and emptiness of modern life is established most effectively in his two acknowledged masterpieces, MISS LONELYHEARTS (1933) and THE DAY OF THE LOCUST (1939). The former is about a newspaper writer who conducts an agony column and gradually succumbs to the real agony that underlies the absurd letters he receives in great numbers daily. *The Day of the Locust* is about Hollywood as West saw it; a disturbingly surrealistic vision culminating in a riot at a movie premiere. West had been in Hollywood writing movie scripts for three years when he began his last novel. One of his films was *Advice to the Lovelorn*, an adaptation of *Miss Lonelyhearts*. In 1940, West and his wife, Eileen McKenney, were killed in an automobile accident in California.

West, Ray B., Jr. (b. Logan, Utah, July 30, 1908—   ), educator, short-story writer. After receiving his undergraduate and Master's degrees at the University of Utah, West took his Ph.D. in American literature at the University of Iowa in 1935. He has taught at many colleges, among them Kansas State and the University of

Iowa, where he taught writing with PAUL ENGLE; he is now professor of English at San Francisco State University.

His own writings include a large number of prize-winning short stories, the critical text *The Rise of Short Fiction 1900–1950* (1952); a biography of the Mormon adventure in Utah, *Kingdom of The Saints* (1957). He has been the editor of *The Western Review* as well as of numerous anthologies of short stories.

Westcott, E[dward] N[oyes] (b. Syracuse, N.Y., Sept. 27, 1846—d. March 31, 1898), novelist. Until ill health forced him to retire from business, Westcott was an obscure New York banker, for a time secretary of the Syracuse Water Commission, and an amateur musician. He began writing, chiefly for his own amusement, a humorous novel about a small-town banker named David Harum. When DAVID HARUM: A STORY OF AMERICAN LIFE finally appeared in 1898, its author had died, just a few months too soon to see his novel become a great national favorite. It was later filmed with Will Rogers in the title role. A posthumously published story, *The Teller* (1901), is accompanied by some of Westcott's letters and a brief biographical sketch.

Westendorf, Thomas Paine. Composer of I'LL TAKE YOU HOME AGAIN, KATHLEEN.

Western Messenger, The. A magazine issued from June, 1835, to April, 1841, in Cincinnati by a group of Unitarian ministers. R. L. Rusk called it "perhaps the highest point in the literary achievement of early western magazines," and C. H. Gohdes ranked it as an outstanding transcendental publication. Among its contributors were W. H. Channing, Elizabeth Peabody, Margaret Fuller, Jones Very, Francis Parkman, and Ralph Waldo Emerson.

westerns. A genre of popular fiction, unique in many of its stylized properties, though not in its general characteristics, to the United States. The western derives from the purportedly true narratives of adventure in the West that were widely circulated in the mid-19th century in popular magazines and cheap books. Often these narratives were built around historical characters, frontiersmen, Indian scouts, and the like. As the West was opened to cattle ranchers and miners in the post-Civil War period, the tendency among sensational writers was to make the cowboy their hero and to model their villains on the outlaws who had infested the West after the demobilization of the Union and Confederate Armies. In one direction the western degenerated into a highly stylized yarn punctuated regularly by gunfire; in another direction it was used by serious novelists as a convention within which they could write about themes of enduring importance. Both kinds of westerns became standard fare for Hollywood producers, and today the "horse opera" is one of the most characteristic forms of television entertainment.

Owen Wister's THE VIRGINIAN (1902), the first western to win literary fame, solidified the pattern. Many have competed with Wister, but no single western has ever equaled his in sales.

Many western writers have adopted several pen names and have been immensely prolific. FREDERICK FAUST used at least five pseudonyms, among them Max Brand, and wrote more than 100 westerns, as well as numerous other books. ZANE GREY wrote so many books that his publisher did not issue them all as he wrote them, and some continued to appear for several years after his death.

In recent years some writers of westerns have resented the low critical status of their art. An association, the Western Writers of America, was formed on May 16, 1952. In April, 1953, it began issuing a monthly publication, *The Roundup*. The association also set up an "Ernie"—in memory of ERNEST HAYCOX, "who did so much to raise the level of the western." The award is given to the best western published each year.

Many westerns first appear in specialized western magazines, occasionally in the smooth-paper periodicals. The titles of these magazines run true to form: *Ace-High Western Stories, Dime Western, Double Action Western, Lariat Story Magazine, Masked Rider Western, Pecos Kid Western, Rodeo Romances, Six-Gun Western, Texas Rangers.* Some of these are still in print and there are many new ones.

One of the earliest and in some respects most notable of all writers of westerns was the dime novelist EDWARD ZANE CARROLL JUDSON. He called himself Ned Buntline. Jay Monaghan wrote a biography of him entitled *The Great Rascal* (1952), J. Frank Dobie, in *Guide to the Life and Literature of the Southwest* (1942, 1952), feels that if one reads the best writers of westerns—he names W. M. RAINE, Dane Coolidge, Eugene Cunningham, B. M. BOWER, Clay Fisher, and Ernest Haycox—one "would find, spottedly, a surprising amount of truth about land and men, a fluency in genuine cowboy lingo, and a respect for the code of conduct."

Western Words: A Dictionary of the Range, Cow Camp, and Trail (1944), compiled by RAMON F. ADAMS. This readable and informational volume was preceded by *Cowboy Lingo* (1936), also compiled by Adams.

Weston, Christine (b. India, Aug. 31, 1904—), novelist, short-story writer. Mrs. Weston lived in India until 1923, when she married an American, Robert Weston, and came to the United States. Her books deal mainly with India, and include *Be Thou the Bride* (1940); *The Devil's Foot* (1942); *Indigo* (1944); *The Dark Wood* (1946); *There and Then* (short stories, 1947); *The World Is a Bridge* (1950).

West-Running Brook (1928), by ROBERT FROST. This fifth book of Frost's poems is divided into six sections, the poem *West-Running Brook* standing alone as one of the sections. The reviewers neglected the book, and this fact seems to have discouraged the poet, who made no new collections until 1936. The gathering does not in fact contain any poem that attracted special attention, aside from the title poem. Even that has puzzled commentators. It relates a somewhat metaphysical conversation between a husband and wife, newly married, about a New England brook that perversely flows west instead of east.

Westward Ho! (1832), a novel by J. K. PAULDING. This early best seller combines an account of pioneering in western Virginia and Kentucky with a love story. The latter is also a study of a religious fanatic who fears that he has inherited a strain of insanity. Paulding was both fascinated and repelled by religious fanaticism; he had already treated it in KÖNINGS-MARKE (1823) and did so later in THE PURITAN AND HIS DAUGHTER (1849). In *Westward Ho!* the girl Dudley Rainsford loves helps to cure him of his phobia. Some of its material was drawn from Timothy Flint's *Recollections of the Last Ten Years* (1826).

Westward the Briton (1953), an anthology compiled by Robert G. Ahearn. Practically every literate Britisher who visited the United States in the early days felt it his duty to write a book about the country. Ahearn made a collection from the books of nearly three hundred travelers who visited our West between 1865 and 1900. His book provides an excellent and frequently amusing perspective of an important section of our country in a formative era.

Wetherald, [Agnes] Ethelwyn (b. Rockwood, Ont., April 26, 1857—d. March 9, 1940), poet, periodical writer. Miss Wetherald contributed to the Toronto *Daily Globe*, then went to Philadelphia to work for the *Ladies' Home Journal.* Her *Lyrics and Sonnets* were collected in 1931; most noteworthy are her bird songs and her poems for children; among them *The Last Robin* (1907) and *Tree Top Morning* (1921).

Wetherell, Elizabeth. Pen name of SUSAN BOGERT WARNER.

Wetjen, Albert Richard (b. England, Aug. 20, 1900—d. March 9, 1948), sailor, newspaperman, writer. Wetjen went to sea at the age of thirteen, fought in the British army during World War I, was twice shipwrecked, went to Canada in 1920. In 1921 he came to the United States and lived here thereafter, although he continued to wander to many places all over the world. He worked for Oregon newspapers, then began writing fiction. His own experiences gave him material for many good stories of adventure. These were collected in *Captains All* (1924); *Way for a Sailor* (1928); *Beyond Justice* (1936); *In the Wake of the Shark* (1939); and *Outland Tales* (1940). He was co-founder and editor of a magazine, *The Outlander* (1933).

Wexley, John (b. New York City, Sept. 14, 1907—   ), playwright. Wexley is noted for his treatment of social problems on the stage. The best known of his plays is THE LAST MILE (1930), a strong plea for prison reform. Other plays of his are *Steel* (1931); *They Shall Not Die,* built around the Scottsboro Trial (1934); *Running Dogs* (1938). His work also includes movie scripts.

Weybright, Victor (b. Keymar, Maryland, March 16, 1903—   ), writer, publisher. Weybright attended the universities of Pennsylvania and Chicago, and worked in various writing and editing capacities. In 1945 he became editor-in-chief of the New American Library of World Literature, Inc., publishers of Signet and Mentor paperbound books. Besides numerous contributions to periodicals, he wrote *Spangled Banner* (1935), the story of Francis Scott Key; and *Buffalo Bill and the Wild West* (with Henry B. Sell, 1955).

Weygandt, Cornelius (b. Germantown, Pa., Dec. 13, 1871—d. Aug. 1, 1957), teacher, literary and social historian, editor, newspaperman, memoirist. Weygandt, a graduate of the University of Pennsylvania, worked on the Philadelphia *Record* and the Philadelphia *Evening Telegraph,* then went back to his alma mater as an instructor in English, rose to the rank of professor in 1907, and retired in 1942. His writings fall for the most part into two groups. Some deal with literary themes, like his *Irish Plays and Playwrights* (1913), in which he made Irish drama known in America; *Century of the English Novel* (1925); *The Time of Tennyson* (1936); and *The Time of Yeats* (1937); others with the history, appearance, and genius of places, like *The Red Hills* (1920); *The White Hills* (1934); *The Blue Hills* (1936); *New Hampshire Neighbors* (1937); *Philadelphia Folks* (1938); *The Dutch Country* (1939); *Down* (1940); *The Plenty of Pennsylvania* (1942); *The Heart of New Hampshire* (1944). He wrote a pleasant and frank autobiography, *On the Edge of Evening* (1946).

Wharton, Edith [Newbold Jones] (b. New York City, Jan. 24, 1862—d. Aug. 11, 1937), novelist, short-story writer, memoirist. Edith Wharton's life is a brilliant exception to the cliché that writers do their best work starving in a garret. Born into one of New York's best families, she was early taken abroad, and was educated at home by governesses. As a child she tried her hand at poetry, some of which was published, and novels, which were not. After her marriage to Edward Wharton she divided her time between foreign travel and her Newport, R.I., home, "Land's End." Accustomed as she was to the artistic glories of Europe, she despaired of improving the ugly exterior of the house, but she and the architect Ogden Codman decided to decorate the interior to express the owners' personalities, a new idea for those days. Their subsequent book, *The Decoration of Houses* (1897), sold widely. Bored with her stuffy social and cultural milieu and troubled by her husband's mental and physical ill health, Mrs. Wharton had already turned to unfashionable intellectual pursuits. Now—with her family's full disapproval—she found herself launched on a career of distinguished prose writing.

She moved to Lenox, Mass., finding happiness there in her work and her many literary friendships. In 1899 a volume of short stories, *The Greater Inclination,* was published, followed by *The Touchstone* (1900), a novelette reflecting her admiration for Henry James and his interest in ethical values; THE VALLEY OF DECISION (1902), a panoramic novel set in 18th-century Italy; and *Sanctuary* (1903). A keen and critical observer of the New York society she knew so well, she found her chief literary problem in extracting human significance from this seemingly shallow soil. Out of this social milieu came LILY BART, the heroine of her first

major work, THE HOUSE OF MIRTH (1905), which dramatizes the dangers of varying from a set social pattern.

In 1907 she moved permanently to France. After writing *Madame de Treymes* and *The Fruit of the Tree* (both 1907) she turned to the "derelict mountain villages of New England" in her least typical but most single-mindedly tragic novel, ETHAN FROME (1911). Although contemporary sentimentalists disliked her grim picture of inarticulate farm people, *Ethan Frome* remains her best known work and a classic of its kind.

She divorced her husband in 1912, mainly because of his mental difficulties. After another minor novel, *The Reef* (1912), came THE CUSTOM OF THE COUNTRY (1913), illustrating the gradual breakdown of traditional New York culture.

During World War I Mrs. Wharton remained in Paris, where her extensive relief work won her a Cross of the Legion of Honor. She described her wartime experiences in two novels, *The Marne* (1918) and *A Son at the Front*

(1923). Meantime she had returned to a simple New England scene in *Summer* (1917). In 1920 appeared THE AGE OF INNOCENCE, perhaps her best combination of the novel of manners and the ethical-psychological novel. This won a Pulitzer prize in 1921. *The Glimpses of the Moon* (1922) is an international novel of manners; New York in the 1840's–70's is depicted in the four novelettes collected in OLD NEW YORK (1924): *False Dawn*, THE OLD MAID, *The Spark*, *New Year's Day;* the best of these, *The Old Maid*, was the basis for a Pulitzer prize-winning play (1935) by ZOË AKINS. Family problems are treated in *The Mother's Recompense* (1925), *Twilight Sleep* (1927), and *The Children* (1928). *Hudson River Bracketed* (1929), another major work, and its sequel, *The Gods Arrive* (1932), contrast the cultural values of the Middle West, New York, England, and the Continent. In addition Mrs. Wharton published several volumes of poetry, travel, and short stories, of which *Xingu and Other Stories* (1916) is probably the most important (see XINGU). Her novels concentrate on the presentation of character and are tragic; her stories emphasize situation and are satiric. Her aloof, ironic point of view is well brought out in the clarity of her composition and her elegant prose style.

In *The Writing of Fiction* (1925) Mrs. Wharton acknowledged her debt to her great friend and literary mentor, Henry James. Like him, she took complex moral values to be the only proper background for fiction; her psychological probings and her keen sense of social gradations are reminiscent of James, though Mrs. Wharton's writing is always more direct and often more conventional. In her evocative, urbane autobiography, *A Backward Glance* (1934), she attempted to analyze her creative processes.

Percy Lubbock wrote *Portrait of Edith Wharton* (1947); Blake Neivus made a close analysis of her writings in *Edith Wharton* (1953). *The Best Short Stories of Edith Wharton* (1958) was edited by Wayne Andrews. Marilyn Jones Lyde's *Edith Wharton: Convention and Morality in the Work of a Novelist* (1959) contains a useful bibliography.

What Is Man? (1906), a platonic dialogue by MARK TWAIN. Written in 1898 and published anonymously, this dialogue between an Old Man and a Young Man embodies Twain's philosophy, a bleakly mechanistic determinism. Free will, genius, virtue, and vice are all dismissed as delusions of the human mind, which is the passive subject of inexorable natural laws. These ideas sprang in part from the intense personal despair and skepticism of Twain's old age and represent his attempt to free "the damned human race" from moral responsibility. In THE MYSTERIOUS STRANGER (also written in 1898) these ideas are transformed into literature far superior to *What Is Man?*

What Maisie Knew (1897), a novel by HENRY JAMES. Always interested in the "small expanding consciousness" of a child, James deals in this novel with twelve-year-old Maisie Farange, whose parents were divorced when she was six; both subsequently remarried. Because custody of the child had been awarded to each of the parents for alternating periods of six months, Maisie presently learns that her stepfather and her stepmother are having an adulterous affair, just as she had become aware of her own parents' earlier infidelities. Instead of corrupting Maisie, this knowledge enables her to make the decision, based on psychological rather than moral maturity, to live with her old governess, Mrs. Wix, instead of with either of her parents. In *Henry James and the Expanding Horizon* (1948) Osborn Andreas summarizes the theme of the novel as "the value to life of the greatest expansion of consciousness possible."

What Makes Sammy Run? (1941), a novel by BUDD SCHULBERG. The hero, Sammy Glick, is a tough New York youth who works his way into a position of power in the motion-picture industry, where his harshness and crude manners are not out of place. The novel is filled with much realistic detail of life in the movie colony, and was not well received in Hollywood, though extremely successful with the public.

What's the Matter with Kansas? (Emporia *Gazette*, Aug. 15, 1896), an editorial by WILLIAM ALLEN WHITE. An ardent but liberal Republican, White was outraged in the summer of 1896 by the arguments which followers of WILLIAM JENNINGS BRYAN were presenting in their campaign for the Presidency against WILLIAM McKINLEY, and he composed his editorial as a reply. He answered the question of his title in a heavily ironical portrait of his state, condemning his fellow Kansans for their shortsighted lust for "money power." The editorial was reprinted all over the country and helped McKinley win, although Kansas went for Bryan.

What Was It? A Mystery (*Harper's Magazine*, March, 1859), a short story by FITZ-JAMES O'BRIEN. This was perhaps O'Brien's most sensational tale, but it lacks the professional competence of Edgar Allan Poe's somewhat similar stories. The setting is a boarding house in which the presence of an invisible but horrible something is felt. The story was included in O'Brien's *Poems and Stories* (1881).

Wheatley, Phillis (b. Africa, c. 1753—d. Dec. 5, 1784), poet. Phillis Wheatley was the first distinguished Negro poet in America. Kidnaped and sold to a Boston merchant, John Wheatley (1761), she was educated by his family. She was a precocious child, learning English in little more than a year and presently reading Greek, Latin, and contemporary English literature. Her first published poem, *An Elegiac Poem on the Death of . . . John Whitefield* (1769), was, like most of her poetry, indebted to Pope and the neoclassical tradition. On a brief visit to England (1773) she was the pet of London society. Her *Poems on Various Subjects, Religious and Moral* (1773) appeared while she was still abroad. After the death of Mr. and Mrs. Wheatley, Miss Wheatley, who had been manumitted (1771),

married a free Negro, John Peters. Her three children died in infancy, and she lived alone and impoverished in Boston until her death. In her poetry, which is generally objective and impersonal, she rarely refers to her own life or to her lot as a slave. Two later collections of her

writings were *Memoir and Poems of Phillis Wheatley* (1834) and *The Letters of Phillis Wheatley, The Negro-Slave Poet of Boston* (1864).

Wheeler, Edward L. ([?]–[?]), late 19th-century dime novelist. Little is known of Wheeler except that he wrote a great many dime novels and created three of the most famous dime-novel characters, DEADWOOD DICK, Hurricane Nell, and CALAMITY JANE. Deadwood Dick was a distinctive Western hero, an exemplar of the American self-made man; he was married several times but fruitlessly courted Calamity Jane, who first appeared in stories about him. Hurricane Nell, a wild-west Amazon, appeared simultaneously with Deadwood Dick. Sample titles of Wheeler's are *Nobby Dick of Nevada* (1880); *Sierra Sam* (1882); *Deadwood Dick in Leadville* (1885); *Corduroy Charlie* (1885); *Colorado Charlie's Detective Dash* (1890).

Wheeler, Post (b. Oswego, N.Y., Aug. 6, 1869—d. Dec. 23, 1957), diplomat, editor, explorer, poet, memoirist. After doing newspaper work in New York, Wheeler began serving in American embassies abroad. He married the Kentucky novelist Hallie Erminie Rives. Among his books were *Love-in-a-Mist* (poems, 1901); *Russian Wonder Tales* (1910); *Albanian Wonder Tales* (1936); *The Golden Legend of Ethiopia* (1936); *India Against the Storm* (1944); *Hawaiian Wonder Tales* (1946); *The Sacred Scriptures of the Sun-Folk* (1948). In collaboration with Mrs. Wheeler he wrote *Dome of Many-Coloured Glass* (1955).

Wheelock, John Hall (b. Far Rockaway, N.Y., Sept. 9, 1886—   ), poet. Educated at Harvard University and the Universities of Göttingen and Berlin, Wheelock became associated with the publishing house of Charles Scribner's Sons in 1911, serving as editor, director, and treasurer. With his friend and Harvard classmate VAN WYCK BROOKS, he published his first book, *Verses of Two Undergraduates* (1905). Other books of poetry are *The Human Fantasy* (1911); *The Beloved Adventure* (1912); *Love and Liberation* (1913); *Dust and Light* (1919); *The Black Panther* (1922); and *The Bright Doom* (1927). His *Collected Poems* (1936) won the Golden Rose Award of the New England Poetry Society (1937). His *Poems Old and New* appeared in 1956 and *The Gardener and Other Poems* in 1961. Wheelock's prose works include *Alan Seeger: Poet of the Foreign Legion* (1918); *A Bibliography of Theodore Roosevelt* (1920); *Editor to Author* (1950), a selection of the letters of Maxwell E. Perkins; and *Poets of Today* (v. 1–8, 1954–61). Although Alfred Kreymborg complains that Wheelock's poetry has "too much talk about Beauty, the poet and his art, God and His Art," William Rose Benét asserts: "Few of our American poets have written more naturally or with more deftly concealed art." Mr. Wheelock was awarded the Bollingen Prize in Poetry in 1962.

When Johnny Comes Marching Home (1863), a famous marching song written by Patrick Sarsfield Gilmore (1829–1892), the official bandmaster of the Union army. The song was used in later wars, and its tune is echoed in several serious compositions, notably Roy Harris's overture, *When Johnny Comes Marching Home* (1934).

When Knighthood Was in Flower (1898), a novel by CHARLES MAJOR. An amateur enthusiast of English history, Major in his light-hearted romance cast a rosy glow over the love of Henry VIII's sister Mary Tudor for the valiant Duke of Suffolk. The book's high-flown sentimentality made it an instant best seller in the unsophisticated early 1900's. A dramatization in 1900 proved a very successful vehicle for JULIA MARLOWE. The book started, as Frank Luther Mott said in *Golden Multitudes* (1947), a "parade of historical romance."

When Lilacs Last in the Dooryard Bloom'd (published in *Sequel to Drum-Taps*, 1865–66, and later included in 1867 edition of LEAVES OF GRASS), a poem by WALT WHITMAN. An elegy on the death of Abraham Lincoln, *Lilacs* is considered one of Whitman's finest poems and one of the greatest elegies in world literature. The first four sections of the poem comprise the first cycle, which presents the grief of the poet over the death of Lincoln and introduces the symbols of the lilac with its blossoms and heart-shaped leaves (love and rebirth), the western star (Lincoln, the beloved comrade), and the hermit thrush (the soul, the poet). The second cycle (sections five through nine) presents the journey of the coffin, first the coffin of Lincoln

and then all coffins. Moving from the particular death to universal death, the poet covers the coffins with lilacs, placing the symbol of ever-returning spring over the symbol of death. The tension between grief and the spiritual knowledge to be found in death is built up, to be continued in cycle three (sections ten through thirteen). Cycle four (sections fourteen through the end) is a celebration of the mystery and glory of death, a reconciliation of the tension of cycle three, in which "lilac and star and bird [are] twined with the chant of [the poet's] soul."

When the Frost Is on the Punkin (1882), a poem in Hoosier dialect by JAMES WHITCOMB RILEY.

When the Great Gray Ships Come In (1898), a poem by GUY WETMORE CARRYL. It was suggested by the sight of an American fleet in New York harbor during the Spanish American War.

When You and I Were Young, Maggie (1866), a lyric by George W[ashington] Johnson (1838–1917), with music by James Austin Butterfield. Johnson, a Canadian, wrote the lyric about a girl named Maggie Clark, near whose home in Canada there flowed the creek mentioned in the poem. But the rest is imaginary, since Maggie died soon after she and Johnson were married in 1865. The song continues to be popular.

Where the Blue Begins (1922), a novel by CHRISTOPHER MORLEY. The fantastic plot is concerned with Gissing, a dog who acquires enough human personality to become a part of the business and social life of New York City. He becomes a floorwalker in a large department store, and through him Morley preaches a satirical and philosophical lesson that home is, after all, the best place to be.

Where the Cross Is Made (produced, 1918; published in THE MOON OF THE CARIBBEES AND SIX OTHER PLAYS OF THE SEA, 1919), a one-act play by EUGENE O'NEILL. Capt. Isaiah Bartlett is obsessed with the idea that he has discovered a chest of gold on a desert island in the Pacific. This obsession, despite all his efforts to resist it, is inherited by his son Nat. Some of the characters of the play reappear in GOLD (1920).

Whiffenpoof Song. A famous Yale college song whose origin is somewhat obscure. The words undoubtedly owe something to Rudyard Kipling's *Gentleman Rankers*. MEADE MINNIGERODE and George S. Pomeroy are usually credited with the Yale verses. For a time Tod Galloway was believed to have composed the tune, but Sigmund Spaeth stoutly maintains that the melody was really composed by Guy Scull, a Harvard graduate. Rudy Vallee made his own version of the song (1936).

Whilomville Stories (1900), short stories by STEPHEN CRANE. These thirteen stories, which Crane wrote during his last years in England, have their setting in a town usually associated with Port Jervis, New York. Whilomville is any boy's town, and Jimmie Trescott is as much Tom Sawyer as he is Stephen Crane. The hair-cutting incident of "An Angel Child" and the comedy of "Lynx-Hunting," where

Jimmie shoots a cow, are based on Crane's childhood. The farmer in "Lynx-Hunting" (like the hero in "The Veteran") is Henry Fleming of THE RED BADGE OF COURAGE now grown old, and Dr. Trescott is transposed from THE MONSTER. Although not Whilomville stories, the baby sketches Crane did in 1893 belong in the same category—particularly "A Dark Brown Dog" and "An Ominous Baby." They too deal with the cruelty of children, as here in "Shame," "The Lover and the Telltale," and "The Fight." In "Shame" Crane alludes to "the jungles of childhood, where grown folk seldom penetrate." Crane's *Whilomville Stories* are only partly in the tradition of previous childhood literature, for they are less nostalgic and they depict children as "little blood-fanged wolves." Realistic and unsentimental, they are akin to the writings of later authors like Ernest Hemingway, Sherwood Anderson, and J. D. Salinger.

Whipple, E[dwin] P[ercy] (b. Gloucester, Mass., March 8, 1819—d. June 16, 1886), lecturer, essayist, critic. Whipple first attracted attention with his critical essay on T. B. Macaulay, published in the Boston *Miscellany* (1843). While working regularly in a Boston bank, then in a brokerage house, and later as superintendent of the Merchants' Exchange, he lectured frequently and published many popular books, most of them based on his lectures. Among his titles: *Essays and Reviews* (2 v., 1848; 1849); *Literature of the Age of Elizabeth* (1869); *Recollections of Eminent Men* (1887); *Outlooks on Society, Literature, and Politics* (1888). Whipple is described by Thomas Wentworth Higginson in *Short Studies of American Authors* (1906) and by William D. Howells in *Literary Friends and Acquaintance* (1900).

Whispering Smith (1906), a popular western novel by Frank H. Spearman. It is a story of a railroad worker in Wyoming who is fired and joins a band of outlaws who prey on railroads. It has been filmed three times.

Whistler, James [Abbott] McNeill (b. Lowell, Mass., July 10, 1834—d. July 17, 1903), painter, etcher, writer. Whistler went to Paris in 1855, and moved to England in 1860 where his life turned into a series of battles in the cause of art against philistines, the bourgeoisie, and those who failed to recognize him as a great genius. His picturesque appearance and bohemian way of life were excellent publicity for him. His most famous literary and legal battle was with the celebrated English art critic John Ruskin (1819–1900). Ruskin, in *Fors Clavigera* (1877), sneered elaborately at Whistler's paintings. Whistler sued for libel, but received only a farthing in damages. Immediately after the case closed he published a vituperative pamphlet entitled *Whistler v. Ruskin; Art and Art Critics*. In 1890 he gave a fuller report of the case in THE GENTLE ART OF MAKING ENEMIES, which is frequently inaccurate. When George du Maurier's *Trilby* was first serialized in *Harper's Magazine* (January–June, 1894), Whistler appeared in caricature as Joe Sibley. The satire was mild, but Whistler protested furiously to

Harper's, and du Maurier subsequently omitted the offending passages.

As an artist Whistler was one of the greatest and most influential of his generation. He followed the Impressionist movement in its earlier phases; he also greatly admired Japanese and Chinese art and was a pioneer in expressing that admiration. He was a master of haziness and mistiness in some of his celebrated drawings, and despised those who claimed only to imitate nature, although his portraits, especially that of Carlyle, are extraordinarily good likenesses. His most famous painting is *The Artist's Mother: Arrangement in Grey and Black;* his *Nocturnes* and *Girl in White* are also well known.

Elizabeth and Joseph Pennell, who wrote an authorized life of Whistler (2 v., 1908), were able to secure for their magnificent edition of *The Whistler Journal* (1921), with its numerous illustrations, the legal papers in the Whistler *v.* Ruskin action. Hesketh Pearson wrote a biography, *The Man Whistler* (1952).

Whitcher, Frances Miriam [Berry] (b. Whitesboro, N.Y., Nov. 1, 1814—d. Jan. 4, 1852), humorist. Mrs. Whitcher published a series of popular sketches called *The Widow Bedott's Table-Talk* in the *Saturday Gazette and Lady's Literary Museum* (1846–50). She also contributed *Aunt Magwire's Experiences* and *Letters from Timberville* to *Godey's Lady's Book,* illustrating many of the sketches herself. *The Widow Bedott Papers* (1856; frequently reissued) and *Widow Spriggins, Mary Elmer, and Other Sketches* (1868) are collections that fully reveal her skill at droll caricature, faithful reproduction of colloquial speech, and incisive satire of small-town life. Mrs. Whitcher's sketches are the earliest extensive treatment of the humorous female character in American literature. Petroleum V. Nasby based his comedy *Widow Bedott, or, A Hunt for a Husband* (1879) on her sketches.

White, Andrew (b. England, 1579—d. Dec. 27, 1656), Jesuit missionary. White was educated on the Continent and taught for a while in Spain and Flanders. In 1633 he headed a mission of three Jesuit priests to Maryland, and in the same year published a *Declaration of the Lord Balteemore's [sic] Plantation,* in which he urged that missionary work be done among the natives and spoke enthusiastically of the resources of the country. In L. C. Wroth's facsimile edition (1929) of the *Declaration* he describes White as "a fervid, naive writer, gifted with an unconscious capacity for picturesque expression." Father White also kept a journal, it is suggested by Jarvis M. Morse (*American Beginnings,* 1952), which formed the basis for his *Relatio Itineris in Marilandiam* (pub. in part 1634, as *A Relation of the Successful Beginnings of the Lord Baltemore's Plantation in Maryland*). Again White gives much information about the natives and local products and praises the friendliness of the Virginian colonists. Yet in the course of later disputes with some of the Virginians, Father White found himself in difficulties, was imprisoned and sent to England

(1645), tried for treason and banished to the Low Countries. He seems to have returned, however, and died in London.

White, Andrew D[ickson] (b. Homer, N.Y., Nov. 7, 1832—d. Nov. 4, 1918), educator, historian, diplomat. A leader in nonsectarian higher education, White began his academic career as professor of history at the University of Michigan. His father's death left him with a comfortable private income; when he was elected to the New York legislature (1864), he joined with his fellow senator Ezra Cornell to found Cornell University. White, who had planned a modern, liberal curriculum, became the school's first president (1868), attracting to the faculty as nonresident teachers James Russell Lowell, Louis Agassiz, G. W. Curtis, Bayard Taylor, and other prominent scholars.

Attacks upon Cornell as a "godless" institution evoked White's *The Warfare of Science* (1876), the liberal tenets of which were further developed in the *History of the Warfare of Science with Theology in Christendom* (2 v., 1896) and *Seven Great Statesmen in the Warfare of Humanity with Unreason* (1910). Another early work, *Paper-Money Inflation in France* (1876), he revised and reissued as *Fiat Money in France* (1896).

White helped found the American Historical Association (1884) and became its first president. Appointed minister to Germany (1878–81), he also served as minister to Russia (1892–94), and later as ambassador to Germany (1896–1902). He headed the American delegation to the Hague Conference (1899) and persuaded his friend Andrew Carnegie to build the Palace of Justice at the Hague. As a personal document his *Autobiography of Andrew Dickson White* (2 v., 1905) is interesting, while a useful account of White's role as educator is found in W. P. Rogers' *Andrew D. White and the Modern University* (1942).

White, E[lwyn] B[rooks] (b. Mt. Vernon, N.Y., July 11, 1899—   ), humorist, essayist. White received his A.B. at Cornell University, then worked as reporter for the Seattle *Times*. According to JAMES THURBER's classic account, White reported a husband identifying his wife's body in the municipal morgue as crying, "My God, it's her!" The city editor changed the quote to "My God, it is she," whereupon White resigned to become mess boy on a ship bound for Alaska.

As production assistant in a New York advertising agency, White began sending manuscripts to the recently founded NEW YORKER. Editor Harold Ross spotted a new and rare talent and soon had him on the staff. He had a finger in every *New Yorker* pie, including writing cartoon captions. But his chief contribution was the witty and urbane "Notes and Comment" column which set the tone for which the magazine is so well-known. He married a *New Yorker* editor, Katharine Angell, in 1929, and later moved to North Brooklin, Me., remote from social chit-chat and reasonably close to animals

and other natural phenomena, remaining, however, a *New Yorker* staff member and continuing his work for the magazine.

He conducted the "One Man's Meat" department for *Harper's* in 1938–43, and continued to contribute to *The New Yorker*, occasionally in

"Talk of the Town" and in more serious pieces dealing with national and international affairs. *The Lady Is Cold* (poems) and *Is Sex Necessary?* (a collaboration with James Thurber) both appeared in 1929, followed by *Alice Through the Cellophane* (1933); *Every Day is Saturday* (1934); *The Fox of Peapack, and Other Poems* (1938); *Quo Vadimus?* (1939). In 1941 Mr. and Mrs. White compiled *A Subtreasury of American Humor*. Then came *One Man's Meat* (1942, enlarged ed., 1944); *The Wild Flag* (1946); *Here Is New York* (1949); *The Second Tree from the Corner* (1953). In 1962 appeared *The Points of My Compass; Letters from the East, the West, the North, the South*, a collection of articles that originally appeared in *The New Yorker*. His revision of William Strunk, Jr.'s *The Elements of Style* (1959), which became a best seller. He also wrote two highly acclaimed children's books: *Stuart Little* (1945) and *Charlotte's Web* (1952). White is recognized as one of America's most incisive and witty essayists.

White, Edward Lucas (b. Bergen, N.J., May 18, 1866—d. March 30, 1934), author, teacher. White received his B.A. at Johns Hopkins University in 1888 and spent the rest of his life teaching Greek and Latin at secondary schools in or near Baltimore. He was a splendid classics scholar, mocked for his old-fashioned eccentricities, but respected and well-liked by his students. Despondent over continued ill health, he ended his life by suicide. White's published works include *Narrative Lyrics* (1908); EL SUPREMO (1916); *The Unwilling Vestal* (1918); *The Song of the Sirens and Other Stories* (1919); *Andivius Hedulio* (1921); *Helen* (1925); *Lukundoo and Other Stories* (1927); *Why Rome Fell* (1927); *Matrimony* (autobiography, 1932). He is best known today for *El Supremo,* an excellent novel of a 19th-century Paraguayan dictator, and for *The Unwilling Vestal* and *Andivius Hedulio,* two lively novels of Roman life.

White, John Williams (b. Cincinnati, Ohio, March 5, 1849—d. May 9, 1917), classical scholar, teacher. White, a member of the Harvard faculty from 1884 to 1909, was one of the most eminent scholars of his day, especially in the field of ancient Greek languages and literatures. Along with J. B. GREENOUGH he founded the *Harvard Studies in Classical Philology.* His best known work was *The Verse of Greek Comedy* (1912). He was considered an authority on Aristophanes.

White, Nelia Gardner (b. Andrews Settlement, Pa., Nov. 1, 1894—d. June 12, 1957), novelist. The daughter of a minister, Mrs. White wrote her most successful novel about a young clergyman, *No Trumpet Before Him* (1948). Also based in part on her own experiences was *The Fields of Gomorrah* (1935), the story of a minister's wife. *Daughter of Time* (1942) is a fictionalized biography of Katherine Mansfield. Among her other books: *David Strange* (1928); *Hathaway House* (1931); *Brook Willow* (1934); *The Pink House* (1950); *The Thorn Tree* (1955).

White, Pearl (b. Green Ridge, Mo., March 4, 1897—d. Aug. 4, 1938), circus performer, actress. At the age of six Miss White appeared as Little Eva in *Uncle Tom's Cabin;* at thirty-three she retired with 2 million dollars. As a circus performer she was a bareback rider and accustomed to taking chances. In the movies she gave thrilling performances, not all of them as hazardous as they seemed. Miss White was especially famous in the movie serials *The Exploits of Elaine* and THE PERILS OF PAULINE.

White, Richard Grant (b. New York City, May 23, 1821—d. April 8, 1885), journalist, scholar. White began his career as a lawyer and worked for some years in a customhouse. He was co-editor of the short-lived humorous paper *Yankee Doodle* (1846), wrote music, art, and literary criticism for the *Morning Courier* and *New-York Enquirer* and contributed to numerous other magazines. He is remembered primarily as a Shakespearean scholar and in this capacity wrote *Shakespeare's Scholar* (1854) and *Studies in Shakespeare* (1886) and edited *The Works of William Shakespeare* (12 v., 1857–66; republished as *The Riverside Shakespeare,* 3 v., 1883). He also wrote *Handbook of Christian Art* (1853); *Words and Their Uses* (1870); *Every-day English* (1880); *England Without and Within* (1881); and an unsuccessful novel, *The Fate of Mansfield Humphreys*

(1884). Willard Thorp called White "a gentleman always, a critic occasionally."

White, Stanford (b. New York City, Nov. 9, 1853—d. June 25, 1906), architect. White was a leading American architect, responsible for such familiar structures in New York City as the George Washington Arch, the old Madison Square Garden, and the Tiffany Building. His full and colorful career ended abruptly when he was shot to death by Harry Thaw in a roofgarden theater; it was charged that White had been overfriendly with Thaw's wife. The story, a nation-wide sensation in its day, is told fully in F. L. Collins' *Glorious Sinners* (1932; reissued as *The Girl in the Red Velvet Swing,* 1954); C. C. Baldwin wrote a biography, *Stanford White* (1931).

White, Stewart Edward (b. Grand Rapids, Mich., March 12, 1873—d. Sept. 18, 1946), novelist, writer on spiritualism. The author of more than fifty books, White chiefly wrote novels based on his own adventures. He was educated at the University of Michigan and Columbia Law School. Prospecting for gold in South Dakota during a summer vacation gave him the background for his first novels, *The Westerners* (1901) and *The Claim Jumpers* (1901). An arduous winter in a Hudson Bay lumber camp produced *The Riverman* (1908). *The Pass* (1906) and *The Cabin* (1910) were based on camping and hunting trips in the West. From two visits to Africa White obtained material for *The Land of Footprints* (1912), *African Camp Fires* (1913), and *Lions in the Path* (1926).

White also did extensive research for two series of historical novels. A trilogy entitled *The Story of California* (1927) consists of GOLD (1913), *The Grey Dawn* (1915), and *The Rose Dawn* (1920). Four novels set in the days of Daniel Boone are *The Long Rifle* (1932); *Ranchero* (1933); *Folded Hills* (1934); *Stampede* (1942). THE BLAZED TRAIL (1902) is often considered his best novel.

White and his wife Betty had been interested in spiritualism for many years. One of the books that they published together on this subject was *The Betty Book* (1937), which was dictated by her while in a trance. After Betty's death in 1939 White published several other books which he claimed Betty dictated from the other world. These are: *The Unobstructed Universe* (1940), which received excellent critical reviews; *The Road I Know* (1942); and *Job of Living* (1948).

White, Theodore H. (b. Boston, Mass., May 6, 1915—   ), correspondent, author. White graduated from Harvard in 1938, and became chief of the China Bureau of Time, Inc., from 1939 to 1945. He was editor of *The New Republic* in 1947, and shortly thereafter returned to Europe as a correspondent during the postwar years. *Thunder Out of China* (1946), written with Mrs. Annalee Jacoby, is an account of the war in China and the rise of Communist power there. *Fire in the Ashes: Europe in Mid-*

Century (1953) was a widely acclaimed presentation of postwar Europe. White's treatment is objective and thorough, giving Americans perhaps their first clear impression of the Continent's progress since the war. *The Making of the President, 1960* (1961) records the events of President Kennedy's campaign for the Democratic nomination and his subsequent election to the Presidency. White's other books include: *The Stillwell Papers* (1948); *The Mountain Road* (1958); *The View from the Fortieth Floor* (1960). *The Making of the President* (1960) won the first Pulitzer award in the general nonfiction category in 1962.

White, Walter [Francis] (b. Atlanta, Ga., July 1, 1893—d. March 21, 1955), novelist, writer on race problems, memoirist. White was long associated with the National Association for the Advancement of Colored People, first as an active member, later as executive secretary (1931). His first novel, *Fire in the Flint* (1924), deals with lynching in a small Southern town. A second novel, *Flight* (1926), is a study of the middle-class Negro of Atlanta. *Rope and Faggot—A Biography of Judge Lynch* (1929) is a nonfiction treatment of the subject of his first novel, and *A Rising Wind* (1945) is a report on the Negro soldier in Europe during World War II. Perhaps the most popular of White's books was the autobiographical *A Man Called White* (1948). White, only five thirty-seconds Negro, was fair-skinned, blond, and blue-eyed, but always insisted on being classified a Negro. His wife, Poppy Cannon, wrote *A Gentle Knight: My Husband, Walter White* (1956).

White, William Allen (b. Emporia, Kans., Feb. 10, 1868—d. Jan. 29, 1944), journalist, writer. White became a newspaperman after attending (but never graduating from) two colleges. He worked for the Kansas City *Star* for a while, then bought the EMPORIA GAZETTE. He made that paper and himself famous with his scathing editorial entitled WHAT'S THE MATTER WITH KANSAS? (Aug. 15, 1896). White was an interpreter of most of the changes that transformed America during his lifetime. His editorials represented the viewpoint of a small town and were devotedly Republican. He had an almost mystic faith in the middle class and hated corruption—as when he spoke in torrid terms of the Harding administration. In 1922 he won a Pulitzer prize for an editorial containing this statement: "You can have no wise laws nor free enforcement of wise laws unless there is free expression of the wisdom of the people—and, alas, their folly with it. But if there is freedom, folly will die of its own poison and the wisdom will survive."

White tried writing poetry as a young man, but without success. His novels were moderately popular: A CERTAIN RICH MAN (1909); *In the Heart of a Fool* (1918); *The Martial Adventures of Henry and Me* (1918). His short stories of life on the plains were collected in *The Court of Boyville* (1899) and *In Our Town* (1906). Some of his editorials and essays were collected in *The Old Order Changeth* (1910), *Politics:*

The Citizen's Business (1924), and other volumes. Probably his most widely circulated piece of writing was his editorial tribute to his daughter Mary, who died as the result of a riding accident. Many papers reprinted the editorial, and it has often appeared in anthologies. White also wrote *Woodrow Wilson: The Man, The Times, and His Task* (1924); *Calvin Coolidge, the Man Who Is President* (1925); and A PURITAN IN BABYLON: *The Story of Calvin Coolidge* (1938). Walter Johnson says that the latter volume is "also an excellent autobiography of White." Johnson made a fine collection from White's voluminous correspondence, *Selected Letters of William Allen White* (1946); White's letters to an aspiring artist, Gil Wilson, were collected in *Letters of William Allen White and a Young Man* (1948).

White, William L[indsay] (b. Emporia, Kans., June 17, 1900—   ), newspaperman, author. A graduate of Kansas State and Harvard universities, White—son of WILLIAM ALLEN WHITE—worked on his father's paper, went into politics briefly, made trips to Europe, and later served on the Washington *Post* and on *Fortune.* He was a war correspondent during World War II; one of his most popular books was *Journey for Margaret* (1941), the story of how he and Mrs. White adopted a three-year-old war orphan. *They Were Expendable* (1942), an account of the heroism of a motor torpedo squadron in the Philippines, was an immediate best seller. *Lost Boundaries* (1948), the true story of the "passing" of a Negro family as white, was made into a successful movie. In 1944 he became publisher and editor of the Emporia *Gazette. Land of Milk and Honey* (1949) is the story of a young Russian who manages to escape his native land. Other books include *Bernard Baruch: Portrait of a Citizen* (1950); *Back Down the Ridge*, on the Korean War (1953); *The Captives of Korea* (1957).

White Buildings (1926), a volume of poems by HART CRANE. Crane's first collection, which contains some of his finest poems, is perhaps most notable for the six-poem suite called "Voyages" and "For the Marriage of Faustus and Helen," both treating themes which recur in his major work, THE BRIDGE [2]. Many of the poems in *White Buildings* deal with the sea as a symbol of integration, with the division between imagination and reality, or with the artist as the isolated individual who can "still love the world" even though it rejects him. Crane's interest in the "logic of metaphor" and the "illogical impingements of the connotations of words" results in tight, multi-level poetry which often requires close reading.

White Fang (1905), a novel by JACK LONDON. Written as a sequel to THE CALL OF THE WILD, which describes the reversion of a tame dog to a wild state, *White Fang* tells of a wild wolf-dog who is gradually domesticated. After being brutally treated by his first owner to make him ferocious for dog fights, White Fang is rescued by Weedon Scott, a mining engineer, who tames the dog by his patience and kindness. Scott takes

White Fang from the Yukon to his home in California, where the dog dies while defending his master's family against an escaped convict.

Whitehead, Alfred North (b. England, Feb. 15, 1861—d. Dec. 30, 1947), mathematician, philosopher. A graduate of Trinity College, Cambridge University, Whitehead lectured on mathematics there and taught applied mathematics and mechanics at University College, London, and at the Imperial College of Science and Technology. After moving to the United States (1924), he served as professor of philosophy at Harvard University. The British government gave him one of its highest awards, the Order of Merit.

Whitehead approached philosophy through the medium of mathematics. His earliest writings were *A Treatise on Universal Algebra* (1898); *The Axioms of Projective Geometry* (1906); *The Axioms of Descriptive Geometry* (1907); and *An Introduction to Mathematics* (1911). With his friend Bertrand Russell he wrote *Principia Mathematica* (3 v., 1910–13), a rigorous development of pure mathematics through formal logic. The evolution of Whitehead's philosophy may be traced through *The Organization of Thought* (1916); the popular *Science and the Modern World* (1925); *Religion in the Making* (1926); *Process and Reality* (1929); *The Function of Reason* (1929); *Adventures of Ideas* (1933); *Nature and Life* (1934); *Modes of Thought* (1938); and *Essays in Science and Philosophy* (1947).

Whitehead's use of the technique of "extensive abstraction," the derivation of concepts from conscious perception, gave his writings what Victor Lowe in *Whitehead and the Modern World* (1950) calls his "unique combination of theory and concreteness." Whitehead was influenced by Henri Bergson. Like other modern philosophers, he rejected mechanical materialism for a subjective idealism and in his attempt to reconcile science and metaphysics viewed the universe as "organic." *Dialogues of Alfred North Whitehead* was published in 1954.

White Jacket, or The World in a Man-of-War (1850), a novel by HERMAN MELVILLE. As in earlier volumes, Melville turned to his own experiences in the Pacific and narrated, with semiautobiographical accuracy, his voyage from Hawaii to the Atlantic coast as a member of the U.S. Navy. Most of the book describes in realistic detail life on a man-of-war, and reveals Melville's dislike of brutality and inhumanity. The dramatic scenes of flogging, in addition to their artistic value, were also useful as propaganda and led to the eventual abandonment of that practice. Melville, however, could not entirely constrain himself from symbolic composition. The subtitle suggests the theme of the ship as an analogue of the world, a theme that Melville was to drive home in the final chapter. The description of the fall from the mast, the dramatic and stylistic high point of the book, may be regarded as the loss of innocence, and the jacket itself can be interpreted as a symbol of the innocence Melville finally succeeds in

shedding. The most memorable character is Jack Chase, captain of the foretop, a tough-minded sailor with the soul of a poet. He is the one ideal figure in all Melville's works, a man equally of the head and the heart.

Whiteley, Opal (b. [?], Wash., [?]—   ), author. In September, 1919, a young woman calling herself Opal Whiteley called on ELLERY SEDGWICK, editor of the *Atlantic Monthly,* and proposed that he reissue a book she had had published in Los Angeles, *The Fairyland Around Us,* all about animals, flowers, and birds. Instead Sedgwick set her to work piecing together her fragmentary diary, large portions of which he published in his magazine. It appeared in book form as *The Story of Opal: The Journal of an Understanding Heart* (1920), with an introduction by Sedgwick, and became a best seller. In these memoirs Opal claimed to be a changeling, really the daughter of Prince Henry of Orléans. The book was obviously written by a lover of the outdoors and appealed deeply to readers of a naturalistic bent. Opal went on to live in England, then France, then India; finally she disappeared from public view.

Elbert Bede, editor of the Cottage Grove (Ore.) *Sentinel,* made painstaking investigations of Opal's story and decided that her book lacked authenticity. But he concluded that her intellect was an extraordinary one and that her breadth of reading was remarkable. Writing about Opal in *The Happy Profession* (1946), Sedgwick still had considerable faith in her genuineness. An account of her is given in Curtis D. MacDougall's *Hoaxes* (1940).

White Rose of Memphis, The (1882), a novel by William C. Falkner, the great-grandfather of WILLIAM FAULKNER, whose family spells the name both ways. His book was one of the most popular novels of the South after the Civil War, ran through 36 editions and sold around 200,-000 copies, and continued to be reprinted up to the time of World War I. In 1953 it was reprinted with an introduction by Robert Cantwell, who called the novel "a thriller, with much in common with the novels of William Faulkner himself."

Whitfield, James M. (b. Boston, [?], 1830—d. [?], 1870), poet, antislavery agitator. Early in life Whitfield moved to Buffalo, then a center of abolitionist agitation, and earned a living for a while as a barber. When his collection *America and Other Poems* appeared in 1853, he gave up this trade and seems to have become a lecturer and free-lance writer. He joined Martin Delaney in believing that emigration was the solution of the Negro problem and urged Central America as a haven. His poetry shows the influence of Byron and Scott.

Whitlock, Brand (b. Urbana, Ohio, March 4, 1869—d. May 24, 1934), reporter, lawyer, public official, writer. Whitlock had a long and varied career, serving as reform mayor of Toledo, Ohio, and as minister and ambassador to Belgium. He also aspired to be a successful writer. Under the influence of William Dean Howells' literary realism and the social criticism of the muckrakers, his first novel, *The Thirteenth District* (1902), dealt with the corruption of a Congressman. But none of his seven novels was truly successful, although *The Turn of the Balance* (1907) was admired by Jack London and Upton Sinclair, and *J. Hardin & Son* (1923) was called by Allan Nevins "probably the most perfect study of the small middlewestern town yet written in America." Whitlock's experiences in Belgium during World War I are to be found in *Belgium: A Personal Narrative* (1919), but perhaps the most engaging of his nonfiction books is his autobiographical *Forty Years of It* (1914). Allan Nevins edited *The Letters and Journal of Brand Whitlock* (2 v., 1936).

Whitman, Albery A[llson] (b. Hart Co., Ky., May 30, 1851—d. June 29, 1901), poet, clergyman. A slave until the age of twelve, Whitman became an itinerant preacher for the African Methodist Episcopal Church and financial agent for Wilberforce College. His was the most ambitious poetry attempted by an American Negro in the 19th century. *Not a Man and Yet a Man* (1877) is a long narrative poem; *The Rape of Florida* (1884; reissued with changes as *Twasinta's Seminoles,* 1893), is a poem in Spenserian stanzas. Other poems by Whitman are *Leelah Misled* (1873), a distinctly Byronic poem, and *The Octoroon* (1901).

Whitman, Sarah Helen [Power] (b. Providence, R.I., Jan. 19, 1803—d. June 27, 1878), poet, critic. Mrs. Whitman, early a widow, was one of the numerous sentimental female poets who became popular in the mid-19th century; sometimes she collaborated with her sister Anna Power. In 1853 she published *Hours of Life and Other Poems;* a complete edition of her *Poems* appeared in 1879. Critics of her day found in her poems "a rare passionate beauty," along with some sensitive pictures of nature.

One of her admirers was EDGAR ALLAN POE, whose work she praised warmly. He wrote in her honor his second poem entitled To HELEN, also wrote her a series of letters, collected by James A. Harrison in *Last Letters of Edgar Allan Poe to Sarah Helen Whitman* (1909). Poe tried to persuade Mrs. Whitman to marry him, but her relatives and friends advised her against the match.

After Poe's death his alleged friend, the Rev. Rufus W. Griswold, made many slanderous charges against him. His strictures finally led Mrs. Whitman to make a vigorous and effective reply, *Poe and His Critics* (1860). Her book was more than a defense of Poe; it was a brilliant critical analysis of his writings and genius. A new edition appeared in 1949, with an introduction by Oral Sumner Coad.

Whitman, Walt[er] (b. West Hills, N.Y., May 31, 1819—d. March 26, 1892), poet, journalist, essayist. Of mixed Dutch and English ancestry, Walter Whitman was the second son of Louisa Van Velsor and Walter Whitman. To distinguish the son from the father, his family called him "Walt," a nickname which the poet later adopted for his literary name. The Whit-

mans had once owned five hundred acres of Long Island farmland, but the poet's father, a carpenter and occasional farmer, could not support his family on the small farm he inherited at West Hills, near Huntington. In 1823 he moved

the family to Brooklyn, where he built and sold houses, but without financial success. Mrs. Whitman was a genial mother, adored by her children, though they disliked their father; but poverty and the bearing of nine children exhausted her. Her husband was a friend of the notorious Deist Tom Paine and the schismatic Quaker Elias Hicks, whom Mrs. Whitman also admired.

In Brooklyn the future poet attended public school for five or six years, then studied the printing trade, which he practiced in Brooklyn and New York. Unemployed in 1835 because of a great fire in New York, he returned to Long Island as a country schoolteacher. For a year (1838–39) he edited and printed a newspaper at Huntington, the *Long Islander*. From 1840 to 1845 he worked as a printer in New York, edited newspapers for brief periods, and wrote sentimental poems and stories for popular magazines, such as the *Democratic Review.* Late in life he collected a few of these in an appendix to SPECIMEN DAYS AND COLLECT (1882). Emory Holloway has salvaged these early poems, some of the fiction, and many essays and editorials, which he has reprinted in several volumes. The most useful of these is *The Uncollected Poetry and Prose of Walt Whitman* (2 v., 1921), which also contains Whitman's temperance novel, FRANKLIN EVANS, OR, THE INEBRIATE (1842). Thomas Ollive Mabbott has edited other short stories in *The Half-Breed and Other Stories* (1927) (see THE HALF-BREED). Copies of the New York *Aurora*, which Whitman edited for about two months in the spring of 1842, have survived, and J. J. Rubin and C. H. Brown have edited a selection of his editorials and sketches in *Walt Whitman and the New York*

Aurora (1950). These throw light on the personal, vindictive, and violent journalism of the times, but give no promise of the future poet.

In 1845 Whitman returned to Brooklyn as a reporter on the *Star*, for which he had earlier set type, but in March, 1846, he became editor of the Brooklyn *Daily Eagle*. Like the other papers he had edited (he was never entrusted with the editorship of the Whig *Star*), the *Eagle* was Democratic. Early in 1848 he lost this position because his editorial support of the "Free-Soil" movement offended the conservatives who dominated the Democratic party in New York State. Thwarted in plans to found a "Free-Soil" newspaper, Whitman accepted a position on the editorial staff of a paper soon to begin publication in New Orleans under the name of the *Crescent*. After an arduous trip by train, stage, and steamboat, he arrived in New Orleans on February 25, 1848, but stayed only until May 27 because of friction with the owners of the paper. He returned home by way of the Mississippi, the Great Lakes, and the Hudson River. Although there is no evidence at all for a love affair in New Orleans which several biographers have hypothecated, the trip did give Whitman intimate knowledge of the expanding nation and a lifelong sympathy for the South. However, his opposition to the extension of slavery into the now Territories was unshaken, and he now carried out his earlier plan to found a "Free-Soil" paper, which he called the *Freeman*, and published from September 9, 1848, until September 11, 1849. Once more he was defeated by the conservative Democrats, who almost ended his journalistic career. After several years of odd jobs, including the operation of a printing office and building houses as a contractor and speculator, he edited one more paper, the Brooklyn *Times*, from 1857 to 1859.

Meanwhile one of the major events in American literary history had taken place early in July, 1855, when a thin quarto book called LEAVES OF GRASS, printed in Brooklyn at Whitman's own expense, was placed on sale in Brooklyn and New York. Whitman had been working on this collection of poems since the failure of the *Freeman*. The title was a multiple-symbol of fertility, universality, and cyclical life. The book contained twelve untitled poems, preceded by a preface (see LEAVES OF GRASS, PREFACE TO) which ultimately became as famous and influential as Wordsworth's Preface to *Lyrical Ballads*. The unconventional form of the verse, without rhyme or meter, the realistic—sometimes physiological—imagery, and the personal tone of the first poem (later called SONG OF MYSELF) shocked the few people who read the book. An exception was Ralph Waldo Emerson, who greeted the author "at the beginning of a great career." Despite the fact that the book did not sell, Whitman published an expanded edition the following year, omitting the 1855 Preface but adding a long open letter to Emerson.

After the interlude as editor of the Brooklyn *Times* Whitman returned to *Leaves of Grass*

with renewed vigor, determined to make the growth of the book his lifework. This was also the period of his association with the Bohemian crowd at PFAFF'S CELLAR, a restaurant on lower Broadway. He was discouraged in the autumn of 1859, but the offer of Thayer and Eldridge in Boston to publish a new edition of *Leaves of Grass* revived his ambition. This third edition (1860) contained many new poems, notably three groups, "Chants Democratic," "Enfans d'Adam," and CALAMUS, representing the tripartite program of nationalism, sex, and love-friendship. In later editions Whitman broke up and redistributed the nationalistic poems, but he kept the CHILDREN OF ADAM (revised title) and "Calamus" groups, with minor revisions.

At the outbreak of the Civil War Whitman wrote the recruiting poem "Beat! Beat! Drums!" and his younger brother, George, enlisted. He himself continued to lead a Bohemian life, loafing at Pfaff's, riding the Broadway omnibuses with his friends the drivers, and hobnobbing with ferryboat pilots. Late in 1862, however, learning that George had been wounded in the battle near Fredericksburg, Walt rushed down to Virginia to nurse his brother. He found George not seriously hurt, but the sight of the other sick and wounded men so aroused his compassion that he volunteered his services in the military hospitals. The Army provided doctors and nurses, though not always in adequate numbers, and almost no provisions had been made for personal services and sympathetic attention. This was exactly the kind of service that Whitman could best render, and he stayed on in Washington throughout the war (except for sick leave) in order to make his trips through the hospital wards, distributing tobacco and reading matter, writing letters, cheering up the depressed, sometimes assisting the physicians. The poem entitled "THE WOUND DRESSER" conveys the spirit of these experiences, though the wounds he "dressed" were mainly mental. The collection of poems published as DRUM-TAPS (1865) is not actually autobiographical, but gives vignettes of sights, sounds, and moods experienced by Whitman during the war years. A "Sequel" contained the great Lincoln elegy, "WHEN LILACS LAST IN THE DOORYARD BLOOM'D." Whitman also published his diary notes and sketches as *Memoranda During the War* (1875), later incorporated into the first part of *Specimen Days and Collect* (1882).

During 1863–64 Whitman supported himself by working part time in the Army Paymaster's Office, and at the beginning of 1865 he obtained a clerkship in the Department of the Interior. The new Secretary of the Interior, James Harlan, discharged him on June 30, apparently for being the author of *Leaves of Grass*, but friends obtained a similar position for him next day in the Attorney General's office. One of the poet's friends, WILLIAM DOUGLASS O'CONNOR, wrote a vehement condemnation of Harlan and a vindication of Whitman in THE GOOD GRAY POET (1866). The first biography of Whitman was written by his friend John Burroughs, and was called *Notes on Walt Whitman as Poet and Person* (1867; rev. 1871). But one of the poet's most intimate friends during this period was Peter Doyle, a young ex-Confederate soldier, employed in Washington as a streetcar conductor. His letters to Doyle were published under the title of *Calamus . . .* (1897) by Dr. R. M. Bucke, who also edited *The Wound Dresser: A Series of Letters Written from the Hospitals in Washington During the War of the Rebellion by Walt Whitman* (1898).

In 1868 William Rossetti published a selected edition, *Poems of Walt Whitman,* which made Whitman known in England and started a reputation that grew steadily for several decades. One of the British readers was Mrs. ANNE GILCHRIST, who fell in love with the poet through his poems and proposed marriage, which was tactfully declined by Whitman. Thomas B. Harned edited *The Letters of Anne Gilchrist and Walt Whitman* (1918).

Still his own publisher of *Leaves of Grass,* Whitman issued a fifth edition in 1870–71, containing a major new poem, PASSAGE TO INDIA. Also in 1871 he published a philosophical essay on democracy called DEMOCRATIC VISTAS (rev. after serial publication in the *Galaxy* in 1867–68), which anticipated the PRAGMATISM of William James and John Dewey. Whitman regarded democracy less as a political system than as a "training school" for producing men and women of superior character.

A paralytic stroke on January 23, 1873, forced Whitman to leave Washington and live with his brother George in Camden, N.J. The death of his mother on May 23 severely depressed him and made this the darkest year of his life. Three years later he began to recuperate on the Stafford farm near Camden, and he recovered sufficiently to give his first Lincoln lecture in New York on April 14, 1879, to make a trip to Colorado the following autumn, and to visit Dr. Bucke in Canada in 1880.

In 1881 James R. Osgood published a new edition of *Leaves of Grass* in Boston, but stopped distribution the following year when threatened with prosecution unless several poems were removed, which Whitman refused to do. Publication was resumed, however, by Rees Welsh in Philadelphia, who also published a volume of collected prose called *Specimen Days and Collect* (1882), subsequently and misleadingly entitled *Complete Prose* (1892). Later in 1882 David McKay, another Philadelphia publisher and a personal friend of Whitman's, took over both *Leaves of Grass* and *Specimen Days;* he was to remain the poet's publisher. The publicity resulting from the Boston suppression gave *Leaves of Grass* the best sale it had ever had, and the royalties enabled Whitman to buy a modest house on Mickle Street in Camden, where he lived at first alone and later with a motherly housekeeper, Mrs. Mary Oakes Davis, until his death.

In his Mickle Street house Whitman was visited by many prominent people, especially from England. These included Oscar Wilde, Sir Edwin Arnold, Edmund Gosse, Lord Houghton (Richard Monckton Milnes), and many others. He was painted by Herbert Gilchrist (son of Mrs. Anne Gilchrist), J. W. Alexander, and Thomas Eakins, and sculptured by Sidney Morse. In 1890, angered by Symonds' belief that the "Calamus" poems had homosexual implications, Whitman claimed that he had fathered six unacknowledged children. These children have never been identified, and most Whitman scholars doubt that they ever existed. Although gravely ill, Whitman managed, with the help of HORACE TRAUBEL, to publish a final edition of *Leaves of Grass* in 1892, which his friends called the "deathbed edition." He died on March 26, 1892, and was buried in Harleigh Cemetery, Camden, N.J., in a tomb which he had already had constructed from his own design. He had also prudently appointed his literary executors, Horace Traubel, Thomas B. Harned, and DR. R. M. BUCKE, who edited the *Complete Writings of Walt Whitman* (10 v., 1902). (A newer, more "complete" edition is now being published—see below.)

Whitman was already a legend when he died in 1892, and so many myths about him have flourished since his death that it is difficult to distinguish fact from fiction. More important, the legends and myths have interfered with the understanding and appreciation of his poems. And Whitman himself was the first myth-maker. Wishing to be a prophet, in the sense of moral and spiritual leader speaking through his poems, he acted the role of poet-prophet until perhaps he seemed at times even to himself to be superhuman. His rough clothes, shaggy beard, slouch hat, and affection for uneducated artisans symbolized his identification with the common people. And yet there was also a paradox, for this superdemocrat loved Italian opera, recited Shakespeare and Homer from memory, and spent many hours in the New York libraries and the Egyptian Museum. In fact, he educated himself in the major works of world literature.

For many years critics, even some of the most friendly to the poet, regarded *Leaves of Grass* as the spontaneous product of an untutored genius, and Whitman's own impatient remarks about artistry encouraged this opinion. The exact prosodic sources of Whitman's verse are still not definitely known, nor even that there were specific sources. The Bible has been suggested, and Whitman's parallelism does resemble the "thought rhythm" (repetition of statement) of Hebraic poetry, which survives in the English translations. Actually, whatever the means by which he achieved this feat, Whitman rediscovered poetic techniques as ancient as those of the old Babylonian-Chaldean epic, *Gilgamesh,* or the Hymns of the Egyptian *Book of the Dead.*

In these ancient poems the line (or verse) is the unit, and much use is made of repeated phrases and clauses, which create both rhetorical and rhythmical patterns. Though Whitman is often regarded as one of the originators of "FREE VERSE," in the French *vers libre* and most of the later American attempts at "free verse" the phrase (not the line, as in *Leaves of Grass*) is the rhythmical unit. But there is a similarity in the disregarding of meter and the production of variable musical effects. Whitman himself said that his rhythms were influenced by Italian opera, and many of his poems do contain passages resembling the aria (singing passage) and the recitative (talking passage) of the Italian opera.

The themes of *Leaves of Grass* have also been interpreted in many ways, but some which he emphasized both in his prefaces and in his "program" poems (such as "Inscriptions," "STARTING FROM PAUMANOK," and "BY BLUE ONTARIO'S SHORE") are: (1) the sacredness of the self; (2) the equality of all things and beings; (3) love and companionship as a force stronger than social compacts; (4) cosmic evolution; and (5) the beauty of death (a Lucretian theme), or death as part of the cycle of birth, life, death, and resurrection. Faith in the immortality of the soul runs throughout *Leaves of Grass*. In Whitman's own interpretations he usually regarded his poems either as preparing his nation for world leadership in spiritual democracy or as teaching the "love of comrades." The former has enabled socialists and Communists to exploit his poetry and prose for political use, while the latter has subjected him to homosexual interpretations. While there is no real evidence of perversion in Whitman's personal life, some of the "Calamus" poems do seem homoerotic, though others merely convey an exalted ideal of friendship. But the frequent sexual imagery in Whitman's poems more often symbolizes the fecundity of nature, cosmic energy, and the promise of rebirth in death. Thus Whitman has become more important as a cosmic than as a national poet. He is a true poet when he images the concrete objects of nature, as in "Song of Myself," or symbolizes the cycles of life, death, and resurrection, as in "OUT OF THE CRADLE ENDLESSLY ROCKING" and the Lincoln elegy, "When Lilacs Last in the Dooryard Bloom'd."

Recent critics have begun to rescue Whitman, to use the words of Leslie Fiedler (Introduction to *Selections from Leaves of Grass*, 1959), "from parody as well as apotheosis." In 1951 the Italian critic Cesare Pavese rejected the image of Whitman as "a bearded centenarian intent on contemplating a butterfly and gathering into his mild eyes the final serenity of all the joys and miseries of the universe . . . the legend of Whitman as a seer, an illuminee, the founder of new religions." He was something better, an artist, but his early poems were his best. "He did not write the primitive poem of which he dreamed, but the poem of that dream." Whitman, then, is losing his appeal as a prophet and *the* poet of democracy, but he has gained almost universal acceptance as a major poet, not only of the United States but also of world literature. *Leaves of Grass* has been translated into nearly every literary language of the world, completely into French, German, Spanish, Italian, and Japanese, in part into the other languages. In Russia selections from his poems and

prose have gone through many editions, but there is not yet a complete Russian version of *Leaves of Grass*. In India selected poems are being translated into the fourteen major languages of the nation. An anthology of foreign criticism of Whitman has been edited in translation by G. W. Allen in *Walt Whitman Abroad* (1955).

There is no definitive bibliography of Whitman, but Carolyn Wells and Alfred Goldsmith compiled *A Concise Bibliography of the Works of Walt Whitman* (1922). Roger Asselineau has a useful check list in *L'Évolution de Walt Whitman Après la première Édition des Feuilles d'herbe* (1954). Evie Allison Allen has compiled a check list of Whitman publications (by and about Whitman) from 1945 to 1960 for Gay Wilson Allen's *Walt Whitman as Man, Poet, and Legend* (1961).

The *Complete Writings of Walt Whitman*, edited by his literary executors (10 v., 1902), is not complete and will be superseded by *The Collected Writings of Walt Whitman*, now in process of publication, under the general editorship of Gay Wilson Allen and Sculley Bradley. The first two volumes, *The Correspondence of Walt Whitman (1842–1875)*, edited by Edwin H. Miller, have been published (1961). When completed, this edition will contain all of Whitman's writings that can be salvaged for publication. The first edition of *Leaves of Grass* (1855) has been reprinted with a valuable critical introduction by Malcolm Cowley (1959); and the third (1860) edition has been reprinted with an introduction by Roy Harvey Pearce (1961). There have been many editions of the 1892 *Leaves of Grass*, such as Everyman (1947), Modern Library (1950), Rinehart (1951), Mentor (1958), and Signet (1960). *Walt Whitman's Poems: Selections with Critical Aids* (1955, 1959), edited by G. W. Allen and Charles T. Davis, contains the 1855 Preface, the first text of "Song of Myself," and bibliographical notes on all poems included. James E. Miller, Jr., has edited a compact volume of *Complete Poetry and Selected Prose* (1959). Walter Lowenfels' *Walt Whitman's Civil War* (1960) contains nearly all the poet's writings about the Civil War in poetry and prose.

The fullest biography is *The Solitary Singer: A Critical Biography of Walt Whitman* (1955), by G. W. Allen, but Roger Asselineau's *The Evolution of Walt Whitman* (1960) is also excellent for interpretation and details. *Walt Whitman* (Evergreen Profile No. 19) by G. W. Allen is a brief illustrated biography with selected bibliography. Of the older biographies, the most important are: Henry B. Binns, *A Life of Walt Whitman* (1905); Bliss Perry, *Walt Whitman: His Life and Works* (1906); Emory Holloway, *Whitman: An Interpretation in Narrative* (1926); Henry S. Canby, *Walt Whitman: An American* (1943).

A quarterly magazine, the *Walt Whitman Review*, publishes scholarly articles, reviews, and lists Whitman publications in all languages. See also: AMERICAN PRIMER; A BACKWARD GLANCE

O'ER TRAVEL'D ROADS; CHANTING THE SQUARE DEIFIC; COME UP FROM THE FIELDS, FATHER; CROSSING BROOKLYN FERRY; DEATH in the SCHOOLROOM; GIVE ME THE SPLENDID SILENT SUN; I HEAR IT WAS CHARGED AGAINST ME; I SING THE BODY ELECTRIC; MIRACLES; THE MYSTIC TRUMPETER; NOVEMBER BOUGHS; O CAPTAIN! MY CAPTAIN!; ONCE I PASS'D THROUGH A POPULOUS CITY; PIONEERS! O PIONEERS!; POETRY IN THE U.S.; SALUT AU MONDE; SONG OF THE BROAD-AXE; SONG OF THE OPEN ROAD; THERE WAS A CHILD WENT FORTH.

GAY WILSON ALLEN

Whitney, William Dwight (b. Northampton, Mass., Feb. 9, 1827—d. June 7, 1894), philologist, teacher, editor. Whitney was a brother of Josiah Dwight Whitney (1819–1896), noted geologist and author of several works in that field. He graduated from Williams College, worked in a bank, thereafter studied Sanskrit, becoming professor of that subject at Yale in 1853, and of comparative philology in 1870. Many of his books deal with Sanskrit, but he also wrote *Language and the Study of Language* (1867); *A German Grammar* (1869); *The Life and Growth of Language* (1875); *The Essentials of English Grammar* (1877); *A French Grammar* (1886). He was editor of the 1864 edition of *Webster's Dictionary*, editor-in-chief of the *Century Dictionary and Cyclopedia* (6 v., 1889–91).

Whitson, John Harvey ["Lieut. A. K. Sims"] (b. Seymour, Ind., Dec. 28, 1854—d. May 2, 1936), dime novelist. Whitson wrote many western stories under his pen name. No record of them is available, but among the titles were *Captain Cactus; Huckleberry the Foot Hills Detective; With Frémont the Pathfinder; The Rainbow Chasers.*

Whittemore, Reed (b. New Haven, Conn., Sept. 11, 1919—   ), poet. A witty, self-limited poet, Whittemore is sharp, cultivated, funny. His work is distinguished by hints of genuine lyric power and submerged, deeper feeling. Among his volumes are *Heroes and Heroines* (1946), *An American Takes a Walk* (1956), and *The Self-Made Man* (1959).

Whittier, John Greenleaf (b. East Haverhill, Mass., Dec. 17, 1807—d. Sept. 7, 1892), poet, editor. "Plain living and high thinking" were Whittier's characteristics from first to last. Poverty, preoccupation with social reform, and sectarian differences—he was an earnest Quaker—combined to keep him a bachelor all his life. MAUD MULLER, a poem marred by sentimentality, contains a famous couplet which may be autobiographical: "Of all sad words of tongue and pen/ The saddest are these: It might have been."

The poet's formal education was limited to a district school and two terms at the Haverhill Academy. At home, however, he was an assiduous reader; the Bible, Robert Burns, and John Woolman were apparently his favorites,

although he knew the English poets too. Before he was twenty he had written and published verse which attracted the attention of editors and readers, among them WILLIAM LLOYD GARRISON, who enlisted Whittier in the antislavery cause. The poet became, successively, editor of *The American Manufacturer,* the Haverhill *Gazette,* and the *New England Weekly Review.* His first book, *Legends of New England in Prose and Verse,* was published in 1831, and he issued many critical essays during this period. Until the outbreak of the Civil War he wrote eagerly and vehemently in favor of abolition, and though most of this work possesses less artistic merit than his later poems, he himself was best pleased with his humanitarian writings.

The Civil War evoked one especially memorable poem, the familiar BARBARA FRIETCHIE (1864), and the ratification of the Emancipation Proclamation inspired LAUS DEO! The end of hostilities marked a turning point in the poet's career. From 1865 until his death Whittier shifted his attention from political issues to religion, nature, and New England life. He preceded Robert Frost as the chief poet of the rural scene in his region. Unlike Emerson, Longfellow, Holmes, and Lowell, he was representative of the uncultured country folk. His poems, often far from polished, contain much vigorous rural speech, colloquialisms used as the natural diction of verse. SNOW-BOUND (1866) is probably Whittier's most characteristic poem of country life and one of his best. As the record of a vanished life, it is a significant document as well as a work of art. An American classic, the poem contains passages of descriptive writing of an authenticity not equaled by any other 19th-century poet.

As Whittier's genius matured, he began more and more to write poems on religious themes. No other American poet possessed more of the lofty devotion characteristic of the ancient psalmist. Even in *The Meeting,* a poem presenting the distinctive tenets of Quakerism, Whittier makes no dogmatic insistence on creed. Orthodox and heterodox alike can accept *The Vandois Teacher, Our Master,* and *The Eternal Goodness* as expressions of the spirit of "pure religion and undefiled." Though he had the orthodox Quaker's attitude toward music and did not write sacred songs, Whittier nevertheless made a great contribution to hymnology, many of the hymns sung in churches today being excerpted from Whittier's longer poems. *Dear Lord and Father of Mankind* and *We May Not Climb the Heavenly Steeps* are notable examples.

But Whittier did not achieve his faith easily. In such poems as *My Soul and I, Questions of Life, The Shadow and the Light,* and *Adjustment* he shows that he did not escape the questioning spirit of his age. The mysteries of life weighed on him heavily, and he attained belief only through a struggle. At last, however, he resigned himself to a large trust in the goodness of the Eternal, singing, "I know not where His islands lift/ Their fronded palms in air;/ I only know I cannot drift/ Beyond His love and care."

Whittier's works include: *Lays of My Home and Other Poems* (1843); *Voices of Freedom* (1846); *Old Portraits and Modern Sketches* (1850); SONGS OF LABOR AND OTHER POEMS (1850); *The Chapel of the Hermits and Other Poems* (1853); *The Panorama and Other Poems* (1856); *Home Ballads and Poems* (1860); *In War Times and Other Poems* (1864); *Snow-Bound* (1866); *The Tent on the Beach and Other Poems* (1867); AMONG THE HILLS AND OTHER POEMS (1869); *Miriam and Other Poems* (1871); *Hazel-Blossoms* (1875); *The Vision of Echard and Other Poems* (1878); *Saint Gregory's Guest and Recent Poems* (1886); *At Sundown* (1890). His *Complete Poetical Works* was edited by H. E. Scudder (1894). His *Writings* were gathered in seven volumes (1888–89). Among books devoted to his life, writings, and ideas are: Mary B. Claflin's *Personal Recollections of John G. Whittier* (1893); Mrs. J. T. Fields' *Whittier: Notes of His Life and Friendships* (1893); Samuel T. Pickard's *Life and Letters of John Greenleaf Whittier* (1894); T. W. Higginson's *John Greenleaf Whittier* (1902); G. R. Carpenter's *John Greenleaf Whittier* (1903); C. J. Hawkins's *The Mind of Whittier* (1904); Paul Elmer More's *Whittier the Poet* (in *Shelburne Essays*, III, 1906); Bliss Perry's *John Greenleaf Whittier* (1907); J. Albree's *Whittier Correspondence from the Oak Knoll Collection* (1911); Iola K. Eastburn's *Whittier's Relation to German Life and Thought* (1915); Marie V. Denervaud's *Whittier's Unknown Romance* (1922); Frances Sparhawk's *Whittier at Close Range* (1925); Frances M. Pray's *Study of Whittier's Apprenticeship as a Poet* (1930); Albert Mordell's *Quaker Militant: John Greenleaf Whittier* (1933); T. F. Currier's *A Bibliography of J. G. Whittier* (1937) and *Elizabeth Lloyd and the Whittiers* (1939); John A. Pollard's *John Greenleaf Whittier, Friend of Man* (1949). Lewis Leary wrote a critical study, *John Greenleaf Whittier* (1961). Donald Hall wrote an excellent introduction to his selection of Whittier's poems in the Laurel Poetry Series (1961). See also BARCLAY OF URY; THE BAREFOOT BOY; CASSANDRA SOUTHWICK; ICHABOD; LEAVES FROM MARGARET SMITH'S JOURNAL; MASSACHUSETTS TO VIRGINIA; MEMORIES; MOGG MEGONE; THE PENNSYLVANIA PILGRIMS; A SABBATH SCENE; TELLING THE BEES.

ELDON C. HILL

Who's Who in America. A series of biographical dictionaries published biennially since 1899, presenting abbreviated biographies of living eminent Americans. The project was begun in Chicago by A. N. Marquis and has been continued since his death by Wheeler Sammons and members of his family. It was modeled on the British *Who's Who*, but differs from it in the kind of information provided. The volumes present abbreviated biographies of living eminent Americans. Inclusion is automatic for government officials of a certain rank, important educational administrators, first-rate authors and art-

ists, editors and publishers, leaders in business, industry, science, etc. Cedric Larson wrote the history of the project in *Who; Sixty Years of Eminence* (1958).

A great many imitations of *Who's Who in America* have been published by other firms: *Who's Who in American Art; Who's Who in Chicago and Illinois; Who's Who in the United States; Who's Who in the Theater.*

In 1954 the Sammons family made arrangements for continuing the publication of *Who's Who in America* and other volumes of a similar nature as a perpetual public trust.

Whyte, William H[ollingsworth] (b. West Chester, Pa., Oct. 1, 1917—   ), writer on corporate business and social subjects. Whyte joined FORTUNE magazine in 1946, became assistant managing editor in 1953. His first book, *Is Anybody Listening: How and Why U. S. Business Fumbles When It Talks With Human Beings* (1952), stemmed from a study of communications conducted by the editors of *Fortune* from 1949 to 1951 under Whyte's direction. Much of the material in his well-known *The Organization Man* (1956) also originally appeared in *Fortune* under the pen name Otis Binet Stanford. This book anatomized the new American corporate worker. This man may be found in any large organization—"industrial, governmental, scientific, military, even academic." Primarily a "member of the team" he has substituted what the author calls a "Social Ethic" for the traditional American "Protestant Ethic" of individualistic striving. Whyte's thesis was presented in a nonacademic, easy reportorial style which is only occasionally marred by sociological jargon. Whyte contributed two articles and the preface for the *Fortune* editors' study *The Exploding Metropolis* (1958). *Men at Work* appeared in 1961.

Wickenden, [Leonard] Dan[iel] (b. Tyrone, Pa., March 24, 1913—   ), novelist, short-story writer, newspaperman. Wickenden, known chiefly as a writer of fiction, worked on the staff of the Columbia Broadcasting Co. and was a reporter on the Grand Rapids *Press.* He traveled widely, and wrote *The Dry Season* (1950) as the result of a trip to Guatemala. Of all his novels *Tobias Brandywine* (1948) made the deepest impression. Among his other novels: *The Running of the Deer* (1937); *Walk Like a Mortal* (1940); *The Wayfarers* (1945); *The Red Carpet* (1952). *Amazing Vacation* (1956) is a fantasy for children.

Wickford Point (1939), a novel by JOHN P. MARQUAND. In this story of an upper-class family that has gone downhill, Marquand may have portrayed some members of his own family. The family in the novel is maintained in tarnished elegance by a trust fund, and their creditors do not press them hard. They live not far from Boston, depend completely on their vanished distinction, and are arrogant and indolent.

Widdemer, Margaret (b. Doylestown, Pa., 1890—   ), poet, teacher, novelist. Miss Widdemer's first poem to win fame, *The Fac-*

tories, denounces child labor; it was reprinted in *The Factories and Other Poems* (1915). She issued several other collections of verses, the best of which were gathered in *Collected Poems* (1928) and *Collected Poems* (1957). She wrote the "Winona" series of books for girls and numerous romantic and historical novels. The backgrounds of some are small American towns. She makes these towns attractive and stresses wholesome ideals. Her first book, *The Rose-Garden Husband* (1915), the story of a young librarian, was a best seller. She also wrote a verse play, *The Singing Wood* (1926), and two manuals for beginning writers, *Do You Want to Write?* (1937) and *Basic Principles of Fiction Writing* (1953). *Red Cloak Flying* (1950) and *The Golden Wildcat* (1954) concern Sir William Johnson of colonial New York. *Buckskin Baronet* and *Stronger Woman's Son* both appeared in 1960.

Wide, Wide World, The (1850), a novel by SUSAN BOGART WARNER. It was published under the pseudonym Elizabeth Wetherell and immediately became a best seller here and in England. Its emphasis on religion and its mawkish sentimentality appealed to the taste of the day.

Wide Awake. A magazine for young people, founded July, 1875, by Daniel Lothrop and absorbed by ST. NICHOLAS in 1893. During its distinguished career it enlisted the services of some of the best-known writers of the day, among them James Whitcomb Riley, Edward Everett Hale, Sarah Orne Jewett, Charles Egbert Craddock, Louise Imogen Guiney. HARRIET MULFORD STONE LOTHROP, wife of the publisher, contributed to the magazine, under the pseudonym Margaret Sidney, her famous story called THE FIVE LITTLE PEPPERS AND HOW THEY GREW, published as a book in 1880.

Widow Bedott, The. See FRANCES M. WHITCHER.

Wieland; or, The Transformation (1798), a novel by CHARLES BROCKDEN BROWN. Set in Pennsylvania, the novel, Brown's first, deals with the baleful influence of a ventriloquist named Carwin upon the family of a German mystic, the Wielands. The plot is based on the history of an actual religious fanatic of Tomhannock, N.Y., who murdered his wife and children at the command of imaginary voices. *Wieland* is the first American novel in the tradition of the Gothic romance, fusing melodramatic improbabilities with quasi-scientific phenomena and exploring the twilight regions of the human mind.

Wiener, Leo (b. Poland, July 26, 1862—d. Dec. 12, 1939), philologist. Wiener came to the United States in 1882. He won a reputation as a scholar in the field of Slavic languages and literature, also in the neglected field of Judaeo-German (Yiddish). He taught these subjects at Harvard University from 1886 until his retirement. But he was also a noted authority in other fields, as his published writings testify. Among them: *The History of Yiddish Literature in the 19th Century* (1899); *An Interpretation of the Russian People* (1915); *Africa and the Dis-*

covery of America (3 v., 1919); and *Mayan and Mexican Origins* (1926). He also compiled an *Anthology of Russian Literature* (2 v., 1902–03) and translated Tolstoy.

Wiener, Norbert (b. Columbia, Mo., Nov. 26, 1894—d. March 18, 1964), teacher, mathematician. Wiener, the son of LEO WIENER, was a noted "infant prodigy" because of his extraordinary linguistic and scientific ability at an early age. He entered Tufts College at the age of eleven, and after graduation studied at Harvard, Cornell, Cambridge, Göttingen, and Columbia universities. He taught for a while at Harvard and the University of Maine, then became a staff writer for the *Encyclopedia Americana* and worked for a year on the Boston *Herald.*

In 1919 he was appointed to teach mathematics at the Massachusetts Institute of Technology. He served as a visiting lecturer in many other universities, including Peiping. His books include some important works in technical fields, also some reminiscences. Among them are: *The Fourier Integral and Certain of Its Applications* (1933); *Fourier Transforms in the Complex Domain* (1934); *Cybernetics* (1948); *The Human Use of Human Beings* (1950); *Ex-Prodigy* (1953); *I Am a Mathematician* (1956); *Nonlinear Problems in Random Theory* (1958).

"Cybernetics" is a word Wiener invented, using the Greek word for the steersman of a ship as a basis, to designate the science of organizing information by means of devices such as computing machines. His ideas brought him the title "the legitimate father of automation."

Wiese, Kurt (b. Germany, April 22, 1887 —   ), author, illustrator. Wiese's first book, *You Can Write Chinese* (1945), intended primarily for children, explained several of the Chinese characters entertainingly. His later books, also containing his illustrations, were for children up to the age of ten. These are: *Fish in the Air* (1948); *Happy Easter* (1952); *The Fox, the Dog and the Fleas* (1953); *The Cunning Turtle* (1956); *The Groundhog and His Shadow* (1959).

Wiggin, Kate Douglas (b. Philadelphia, Sept. 28, 1856—d. Aug. 24, 1923), teacher, writer for children. A lifelong student of child education, Mrs. Wiggin organized in San Francisco the first free kindergarten in the West. She also joined her sister NORA ARCHIBALD SMITH in founding a kindergarten training school. In order to raise funds for her kindergarten she began writing children's books, the best known of which are THE BIRDS' CHRISTMAS CAROL (1887); *The Story of Patsy* (1889); REBECCA OF SUNNYBROOK FARM (1903); and *Mother Carey's Chickens* (1911). Her understanding of children and her homespun humor show to best advantage in *Rebecca,* whose delightfully precocious heroine is at least partly autobiographical. *The Birds' Christmas Carol,* a tale of a child too good for this earth, exhibits too much sweetness and light for modern tastes.

Mrs. Wiggin also published several adult seminovels, the travel accounts of a heroine named Penelope based on Mrs. Wiggin's own travels in

England. With her sister she wrote books on education (among them *Children's Rights*, 1892, and *Froebel's Gifts*, 1895) and edited collections of children's poems and stories. Some of her novels were dramatized in the 1910's. Her autobiography, *My Garden of Memory*, was published in 1923.

Wigglesworth, Michael (b. England, Oct. 18, 1631—d. May 27, 1705), theologian, poet. Wigglesworth came to America at the age of seven, graduated from Harvard in 1651. He became minister of the Congregational church at Malden, Mass., where he remained for fifty years, practicing medicine on the side. His chief claim to fame lies in his long didactic poem THE DAY OF DOOM (1662), which sets forth relentlessly the Puritan dogmas of predestination, original sin, and punishment in ballad stanzas whose thumping meter and internal rhymes are inappropriately reminiscent of W. S. Gilbert's much more polished jingles. In its day, however, *The Day of Doom* was assiduously studied and memorized by countless Puritan children and their elders and was republished in the United States as late as 1867. Another long poem, MEAT OUT OF THE EATER (1669), which deals with "the necessity and usefulness of afflictions unto God's children," was almost equally successful. Briefer poems include *A Short Discourse on Eternity, Vanity of Vanities* and *A Postscript Unto the Reader.* These were theological treatises in rhyme annexed to *The Day of Doom. God's Controversy with England* (pub. 1871) was occasioned by the 1662 drought. Wigglesworth was personally a humble and generous man, beloved by his flock. Today he is best known for the aged Harvard College dormitory that bears his name.

Wigwam and Cabin (1845–46), stories by W. G. SIMMS. These are mainly ingenious stories of horror and the grotesque, with Negro characters in one of the tales dealing with voodoo. In his preface Simms remarked, "The material employed will be found to illustrate, in large degree, the border history of the South. The life of the planter, the squatter, the Indian, and the Negro—the bold and hardy pioneer and the vigorous yeoman—these are the subjects. In their delineations, I have mostly drawn from living portraits and, in frequent instances, from actual scenes and circumstances within the memories of men." Edgar Allan Poe reviewed the collection and praised it highly, one story in particular: "*Murder Will Out* . . . we have no hesitation in calling the best ghost story we have ever read. It is full of the richest and most vigorous imagination."

Wilbur, Homer. See BIGLOW PAPERS.

Wilbur, Ray Lyman (b. Boonesboro [now Boone], Iowa, April 13, 1875—d. June 26, 1949), physician, government official, teacher, educational administrator, author. Wilbur was a graduate of Stanford University and of Cooper Medical College and also studied abroad. He became a teacher of medicine, in 1900 became assistant professor of physiology at Stanford, and in 1909 full professor. He was appointed dean of

the School of Medicine there in 1911, in 1916 was made president of the university, in 1943 its chancellor. Meanwhile he had interrupted his service at Stanford to serve as Secretary of the Interior under President Hoover (1929–33). He wrote several books, among them *Stanford Horizons* (1936); *March of Medicine* (1938); *Human Hopes* (1940); and in collaboration with A. M. Hyde, *Hoover Policies* (1937).

Wilbur, Richard (b. New York City, March 1, 1921—), poet. Wilbur studied at Harvard University, taught there for some years, and then began teaching at Wesleyan University in 1957. His poetry, which owes something to Marianne Moore as well as to the metaphysical school, is formal, polished, yet lively, witty, and full of ingratiating detail. His collections are *The Beautiful Changes* (1947); *Ceremony and Other Poems* (1950); *Things of This World* (1956); *Poems* (1957); and *Advice to a Prophet and Other Poems* (1961). He also translated Molière's *The Misanthrope* (1955), and provided songs for the Broadway production of Voltaire's *Candide* (1957).

Wilcox, Ella Wheeler (b. Johnstown Center, Wis., Nov. 5, 1850—d. Oct. 30, 1919), poet, novelist. Mrs. Wilcox, whose work is rife with platitudes and sentimentality, was in her day an extremely "marketable" poetess. Lloyd Morris gave the most effective description of her in *Postscript to Yesterday* (1947): "A stately figure, Mrs. Wilcox was softly enveloped by plumes, chiffons, and Oriental metaphysics. Her life was blameless, but her imagination simmered. Over the land millions of women throbbed to her verses." She wrote a sentimental novel when she was ten, her first essay was published when she was fourteen, and her first poem not long after. She tried college for a while, but didn't like it and turned to newspaper work. When her *Poems of Passion* (1876) appeared, the work became famous overnight, because of its "daring" quality, and her reputation was made. Mrs. Wilcox published more than forty volumes, from *Drops of Water* (1872) to *The Worlds and I* (1918). Most of these were verse, some were fiction, two were autobiographical. The most famous of her poems is *Solitude*, which begins: "Laugh and the world laughs with you,/ Weep and you weep alone." See THE EROTIC SCHOOL.

Wilde, Percival (b. New York City, March 1, 1887—d. Sept. 19, 1953), playwright, novelist. Wilde, a Columbia graduate, was a skilled writer of one-act plays, many of which appeared in collections: *Dawn and Other One-Act Plays of Life Today* (1915); *Confessional and Other American Plays* (1916); *Comrades in Arms and Other Plays for Little Theaters* (1935). He also wrote a manual, *The Craftmanship of the One-Act Play* (1923), which he later (1951) revised to include a discussion of radio and television plays. In his later years he wrote several mystery stories; the one called *Inquest* (1940) won special praise.

Wilde, Richard Henry (b. Ireland, Sept. 24, 1789—d. Sept. 10, 1847), lawyer, legislator, poet. Wilde's father was an Irish patriot who came to America on a visit but remained when his business in Ireland was confiscated. Wilde became a lawyer in Georgia and was elected to Congress. In Italy he made some studies of Italian literature and translated from the Italian poets. Then he returned to Georgia to practice law, later became professor of constitutional law at the University of Louisiana. He wrote a long poem called *Hesperia*, which his son edited and published in 1867; the poem, never completed, obviously shows the influence of Byron. Wilde is remembered today for a single poem, MY LIFE IS LIKE THE SUMMER ROSE.

Wilder, Laura Ingalls (b. Lake Pepin, Wis., Feb. 7, 1867—d. Jan. 10, 1957), author. The author of *The Little House Books* for children, Mrs. Wilder spent her life in the Wisconsin and Dakota country she wrote about. *The Little House Books* are autobiographical, and their popularity with children lies in their vivid portrayals of a family's life on the frontier. The books in the series are: *Little House in the Big Woods* (1932); *Farmer Boy* (1933); *Little House on the Prairie* (1935); *On the Banks of Plum Creek* (1937); *By the Shores of Silver Lake* (1939); *The Long Winter* (1940); *Little Town on the Prairie* (1941); *These Happy Golden Years* (1943).

Wilder, Thornton (b. Madison, Wis., April 17, 1897—   ), teacher, novelist, playwright. Reared in China and the United States, Wilder graduated from Yale in 1920. He was recalled from archaeological studies in Rome to teach French at the Lawrenceville School (N.J.), going on for an M.A. in French at Princeton University. In 1926 he wrote *The Cabala*, an ironic novel of decadent Italian nobility, and had his first play, *The Trumpet Shall Sound*, produced at a little theater. THE BRIDGE OF SAN LUIS REY (1927), a novel tracing the lives of a number of people killed in a South American bridge catastrophe, was his first popular success and won a Pulitzer prize. *The Woman of Andros* (1930), a story based on a play by Terence (*Andria*), was another success, enabling Wilder to give up his position at Lawrenceville and travel in Europe.

From 1930 to 1936 Wilder taught creative writing and "The Classics in Translation" at the University of Chicago, where his students found him a dramatic and stimulating lecturer. He also published collections of one-act plays in *The Angel That Troubled the Waters* (1928) and *The Long Christmas Dinner* (1931), and a comic novel, *Heaven's My Destination* (1934). Influenced by his friend Gertrude Stein's ideas about America and universality, he wrote OUR TOWN (1938), a beautiful and moving drama which won a Pulitzer prize. A farcical play, *The Merchant of Yonkers*, also appeared in 1938; it was revived more successfully as *The Matchmaker* (1955). THE SKIN OF OUR TEETH, which *Time* described as "a sort of Hellzapoppin with brains," was produced in 1942 and promptly won its author a third Pulitzer prize. It made use of some unique theatrical techniques, as did *Our Town*. Wilder served as an intelligence

officer with the air force in Italy during World War II and wrote THE IDES OF MARCH (1948), a witty and learned epistolary novel about Julius Caesar. He is presently at work on a cycle of fourteen plays. The first three, *Someone from*

G. D. Hackett

Assisi, Infancy, and *Childhood,* have been produced in New York City, Jose Quintero directing, under the collective title *Plays for Bleecker Street.*

Wilder is a curious anomaly in the American literary scene, a widely cultured man who writes as he pleases and yet has managed to captivate the masses in his best known works. Certainly he is no ivory-tower philosopher; he deals with the actual scene in most of his works. Scholars have sometimes criticized his imitativeness, notably the similarities between *The Skin of Our Teeth* and James Joyce's *Finnegans Wake.* To this Wilder admits: "My writing life is a series of infatuations for admired writers." Actually his constant experiments in unconventional literary and theatrical forms place him among our most original writers. Add to this an impeccable prose style and a deeply philosophical vein that often transcends plot and character; as Fred B. Millett says, "He is primarily intent on communicating his own sense of life's values through the complex disguise of fiction." See also MICHAEL GOLD.

Wildfire, Colonel Nimrod. A character in THE LION OF THE WEST (1830), a play by James K. Paulding. A congressman from Kentucky, Wildfire is regarded as the first uncouth frontiersman in American drama.

Wild Honey Suckle, The (1786), a poem by PHILIP FRENEAU. This pleasant but conventional lyric was possibly the first that took as its theme an American flower.

Wild Palms, The (1939), a novel by WILLIAM FAULKNER. *The Wild Palms* contains two narratives which alternate with each chapter—the title piece and a contrasting story later published separately in the *Viking Portable Faulkner* (edited by Malcolm Cowley, 1954) under the title "Old Man." Each is a study of society versus nature, of order juxtaposed with chaos. *The Wild Palms* deals with a young intern who falls in love with a married woman; in their attempt to escape from the civilization that they fear will kill their love, they flee to different parts of the country, but are never able to remain for long. They seek refuge from the world in a mining camp in an isolated part of Utah, but even there they are confronted with the effects of commercial exploitation. Finally the woman dies as a result of the unsuccessful abortion performed on her by her lover, who is imprisoned for life.

"Old Man" begins in prison, from which a tall convict is sent to do rescue work during the great Mississippi flood of 1927. Finding a pregnant woman stranded by the rising water, he takes her into his boat and attempts to deliver himself and his charge back to the authorities—a task which, because of the violence of the flood, takes him almost three months. His stoical, uncommunicative endurance in the face of the flood and his unquestioning sense of obligation to fulfill his mission and return to prison are implicitly contrasted with the fruitless and frantic efforts of the young intern to escape from the world.

Wild Party, The (1928), a narrative poem by JOSEPH MONCURE MARCH. This poem created a considerable stir in the 1920's. It is a story in irregular but effective rhymed verse of an orgy in which participate small-time actors, big-time vaudevillians, prize fighters, and others.

Wilkins, Mary E[leanor]. See MARY E[LEANOR] WILKINS FREEMAN.

Wilkinson, James (b. Benedict, Md., [?], 1757 —d. Dec. 28, 1825), soldier, public official, traitor, memoirist. A captain in the Continental Army, Wilkinson was a masterly intriguer who participated in the "Cabal" against Washington, tried to stir up the West against the central government, and at one point was unofficial governor of Louisiana. He escaped trial several times, but was finally tried and acquitted. He sought to defend himself in *Memoirs of My Own Times* (3 v., 1816). Accounts of Wilkinson include R. O. Shreve's *The Finished Scoundrel* (1933); J. R. Jacobs' *Tarnished Warrior* (1938); T. R. Hay and M. R. Werner's *The Admirable Trumpeter* (1941). He appears in fiction in E. E. Hale's *Philip Nolan's Friends* (1877) and Constance Skinner's *The White Leader* (1926).

Wilkinson, Marguerite (b. Halifax, N. Scot., Nov. 15, 1883—d. Jan. 12, 1928), poet, writer on poets and poetry. She came to the United States when she was very young. She loved poetry and wrote profusely. Among her books: *In Vivid Gardens* (1911); *The Dingbat of Arcady* (1922); *Citadels* (1928). In addition, she wrote *Contemporary Poetry* (1923) and compiled some anthologies.

Willard, Emma Hart (b. Berlin, Conn., Feb. 23, 1787—d. April 15, 1870), teacher, writer. Mrs. Willard as a child taught herself many subjects that were barred from the curricula of the female seminaries. When in 1814 she opened a school for women in Vermont, she began introducing such subjects; in 1818 she sent Governor DeWitt Clinton her *Proposing a Plan for Improving Female Education*. In 1821 her school was moved to Troy, N.Y., where it was called the Troy Female Seminary, later the Emma Willard School. She also founded the Willard Association for the Mutual Improvement of Female Teachers (1837). She wrote accounts of her travels, advanced a theory of blood circulation later generally accepted, and wrote verse. One of her poems became famous, ROCKED IN THE CRADLE OF THE DEEP, the title poem of an 1830 collection. It was set to music by Joseph P. Knight.

Willard, Frances Elizabeth [Caroline] (b. near Rochester, N.Y., Sept. 28, 1839—d. Feb. 18, 1898), temperance reformer, school administrator, writer. From 1871 to 1874 Miss Willard presided over the Evanston College for Ladies, meanwhile lecturing successfully on some trips to Europe she had made. In 1874 she started on a temperance crusade that made her famous, especially when in 1879 she became president of the Women's Christian Temperance Union. She wrote a volume on *Woman and Temperance* (1883), and *Glimpses of 50 Years* (1889).

Willard, Josiah Flynt ["Josiah Flynt"] (b. Appleton, Wis., Jan. 23, 1869—d. Jan. 20, 1907), hobo, sociologist. Willard, nephew of temperance reformer FRANCES WILLARD, took to the road in the United States and Europe as a tramp, and not only acquired the special language of vagrants but even adopted their philosophy. He refused to condemn the denizens of the underworld; they were, he believed, creations of a corrupt police system. In Europe he studied at the University of Berlin and met some noted authors, but preferred his friends at the bottom. Among his books: *Tramping with Tramps* (1899); *Notes of an Itinerant Policeman* (1900); *The World of Graft* (1901); *The Little Brother* (1902); *My Life* (1908).

Williams, Bert [Egbert Austin] (b. Bahamas, 1875—d. March 4, 1922), comedian, song writer. While still a child Williams left the Bahamas for the United States and joined a minstrel troupe. In 1895 he and George Walker formed a popular vaudeville team. In 1902 he wrote and produced an all-Negro musical show, *In Dahomey*, in which he and his partner appeared with great success. He continued to write similar shows—*Abyssinia* (1906), *Bandanna Land* (1907), and others—until the death of Walker in 1909. In that year Williams joined the Ziegfeld Follies, for which he wrote his own songs and other material. Sigmund Spaeth holds that Williams was "unquestionably one of the supreme comedians of all time."

Williams, Blanche Colton (b. Attala Co., Miss., Feb. 10, 1879—d. Aug. 9, 1944), teacher, biographer, critic, authority on the short story. Dr. Williams, who took her higher degrees at Columbia University, taught in Mississippi, then at Columbia Teachers College, becoming a full professor in 1917 and chairman of the English department in 1926. She made a specialty of the short story. She prepared *A Handbook on Story Writing* (1917; rev., 1930) and other books in the same field, including anthologies; she also wrote biographies of George Eliot (1936), Clara Barton (1941), and John Keats (1943).

Williams, Eleazar (b. New York State[?] Canada[?], 1789[?]—d. Aug. 28, 1858), Indian scout, missionary, pretender to the French throne. Williams claimed to be the son of Thomas Williams, a half-breed Oneida Indian who was a descendant of Eunice Williams, a white woman taken captive in the Deerfield Raid (1704). He wrote a biography of his reputed father, *Life of Te-ho-ra-gwa-ne-gen, Alias Thomas Williams* (1859). But in 1853 he also claimed to be the son of Louis XVI, and therefore the dauphin and Louis XVII. J. H. Hanson wrote an article for *Putnam's Magazine* (February, 1853) entitled *Have We a Bourbon Among Us?* This roused much interest and controversy; Hanson later expanded his query into a book, *The Lost Prince* (1854). The controversy continued for close to a century: in 1934 Meade Minnegerode published *The Son of Marie Antoinette* on Williams' claim. Williams himself wrote *The Salvation of Sinners Through the Riches of Divine Grace* (1842) and is believed to have simplified the Mohawk alphabet by dropping several letters when he was translating the *Book of Common Prayer* for use by Indians. Williams is the subject of a romance, *Lazarre* (1910), by Mary Hartwell Catherwood.

Williams, Garth Montgomery (b. New York City, April 16, 1912—   ), illustrator, author of books for children, stage designer. Williams attended the Royal College of Art in London, and worked in advertising, also as a stage designer, mural painter and sculptor. Among his many books: *The Tall Book of Make Believe* (1950); *The Adventures of Benjamin Pink* (1951); *The Rabbit's Wedding* (1958).

Williams, Gluyas (b. San Francisco, July 23, 1888—d. Aug.[?], 1960), cartoonist. One of the most subtle of mid-20th century cartoonists, Williams illustrated many of ROBERT BENCH-LEY's books and was a contributor to *The New Yorker*. He made several collections of his own, including *The Gluyas Williams Book* (1929); *Fellow Citizens* (1940); *The Gluyas Williams Gallery* (1957). A famous Williams cartoon showed a "Crisis in Washington—Mr. Coolidge Refuses Point Blank to Vacate the White House Until His Other Rubber Is Found."

Williams, Henry. See IN THE SHADE OF THE OLD APPLE TREE.

Williams, Jesse Lynch (b. Sterling, Ill., Aug. 17, 1871—d. Sept. 14, 1929), newspaperman, short-story writer, novelist, playwright. Williams was a writer with a good sense of humor and ingenious ideas for plots. He began by writing amusing tales of his alma mater, *Princeton Stories* (1895), while he was a reporter for the New York *Sun*. *The Stolen Story* (1899) was a collection based on his newspaper experiences. Leaving the *Sun*, Williams joined the staff of *Scribner's Magazine*, then became the first editor of the *Princeton Alumni Weekly*. He began writing and publishing some amusing novels: *The Married Life of the Frederic Carrolls* (1910); *And So They Were Married* (1914); *Not Wanted* (1923); *They Still Fall in Love* (1929); and *She Knew She Was Right* (1930).

While at Princeton, Williams and Booth Tarkington had founded the Triangle Club and had helped write its musical revues. In 1906 Williams dramatized his newspaper yarn, *The Stolen Story*, which had some thrilling scenes. Later he made a novel out of the story and the play, calling it *The Day Dreamer* (1906). Much more successful was the comedy *Why Marry?* (1917), based on *And So They Were Married*. It was awarded a Pulitzer prize, the first ever given. Later plays were *Why Not?* (1922) and *Lovely Lady* (1925).

Williams, John (1664–1729), Congregational clergyman. After graduation from Harvard, Williams was given a charge at Deerfield, Mass. During the disastrous Indian massacre (1704) he and his family were captured; they were held for two years. At the request of Cotton Mather he then wrote what became a popular book, THE REDEEMED CAPTIVE RETURNED TO ZION (1707). He gave an impressive account of the massacre and of his sufferings at the hands of the Indians. For his daughter Eunice, see ELEAZAR WILLIAMS.

Williams, John ["Anthony Pasquin"] (b. England, April 28, 1761—d. Oct. 12, 1818), newspaper writer, satirist. Williams, an inveterate controversialist, was first a painter, then a translator, then made connections with several Dublin papers. He worked as a drama critic in England for a while, but was soon embroiled in various difficulties and decided to go to America. His pet aversion was Alexander Hamilton, and he directed against him a virulent verse satire, *The Hamiltoniad* (1804). He also wrote *The Children of Thespis* (1792) and *The Pin-Basket to the Children of Thespis* (1797).

Williams, Michael (b. Halifax, N. Scot., Feb. 5, 1878—d. Oct. 12, 1950), newspaperman, writer. Williams worked on newspapers in Boston, New York City, and San Francisco, and in 1919–20 edited a *National Catholic Bulletin*. In 1922 he became the first editor of THE COMMONWEAL, which developed into a renowned liberal Catholic weekly. He wrote a number of books, among them *The Book of the High Romance* (1918); *American Catholics in the War* (1921); *The Little Flower of Carmel* (1926); *Little Brother Francis of Assisi* (1926); *Catholicism and the Modern Mind* (1928); *The Catholic Church in Action* (1935).

Williams, Oscar (b. New York City, Dec. [?],

1900—d. Oct. 10, 1964), poet, anthologist. Williams, who never finished high school, was educated in Brooklyn public schools. For a number of years he was a successful advertising man, but abandoned that profession to write poetry. His first two collections of poems, *The Golden Darkness* and *In Gossamer Grey*, were published in 1921; then, after a long interval, *The Man Coming Toward You* appeared in 1940, followed by *That's All That Matters* (1945) and *Selected Poems* (1947). Williams' principal subject is the menace and disorder of urban life, mirrored in verse which, if frequently vivid and original, may also be strident and overblown.

He became probably the most successful modern American anthologist of poetry. The general good taste and balance of his *Little Treasury* series, in particular, have made them virtually the standard anthologies of a generation. Among his collections are *New Poems* (a series, 1940, 1942, 1943, 1944); *The War Poets* (1945); *A Little Treasury of Modern Poetry* (1946); *A Little Treasury of Great Poetry* (1947); *A Little Treasury of American Poetry* (1948); *A Little Treasury of British Poetry* (1951); *Immortal Poems of the English Language* (1952); Palgrave's *Golden Treasury* (ed., 1953); *The Pocket Book of Modern Verse* (1954).

Williams, Roger (b. England, 1603[?]—d. March [?], 1683), clergyman, colonist, writer. A highly educated man of deep religious and civic feeling, Williams at first took orders in the Church of England, then became a Puritan and emigrated to Massachusetts. He became pastor at Salem, removed to Plymouth, then returned to Salem. Because of his opposition to authoritarianism the Massachusetts General Court sentenced him to exile (1635). He sought refuge in what is now Rhode Island, where some of his followers joined him, and founded the city of Providence. He established freedom for all creeds in his colony, treated the local Indians well, and in 1639 founded the first Baptist Church in America, but soon became "a Seeker" rather than the follower of any particular creed. He negotiated a charter for PROVIDENCE PLANTATIONS in 1644, and served as governor for several terms. His last years were clouded because of trouble with the Indians; during King Philip's War Providence was burnt to the ground.

Williams contributed enormously to the establishment of religious freedom as a fundamental doctrine. Passionately religious, as Perry Miller calls him in *Roger Williams: His Contribution to American Tradition* (with many selections from Williams, 1953), he was equally passionate in demanding that society respect sincerely held opinions, no matter how bizarre. He was the first to welcome Jews to any American colony. He opposed the Quakers because, according to Miller, they were then "not the sober citizenry of today but a mob of crassly assertive, ignorant, and reckless fanatics."

Williams was an active writer; his work was gathered in *The Writings of Roger Williams* (6 v., 1866–74). Among his separate publications the most remarkable is *A Key into the Language of America* (1643; reprinted, 1936). His most famous production was THE BLOUDY TENE[N]T OF PERSECUTION, FOR CAUSE OF CONSCIENCE, DISCUSSED (1644). His other writings included: *Mr. Cotton's Letter Lately Printed, Examined and Answered* (1644); *Queries of Highest Consideration* (1644); *The Bloudy Tene[n]t Yet More Bloudy* (1652); *The Hireling Ministry None of Christ's* (1652); *Experiments of Spiritual Life and Health* (1652); and *George Fox Digged Out of His Burrowes* (1676). The *Experiments* was reprinted in 1951, and was described by *Time* as containing "some of the most beautiful devotional passages ever written by an American."

Among the volumes devoted to Williams are: J. D. Knowles' *Memoir of Roger Williams* (1834); William Gammell's *Life of Roger Williams* (1846); Oscar S. Strauss' *Roger Williams: The Pioneer of Religious Liberty* (1894); Mary E. Hall's *Roger Williams* (1917); J. E. Ernst's *The Political Thought of Roger Williams* (1929) and *Roger Williams: New England Firebrand* (1932); S. H. Brockunier's *The Irrepressible Democrat, Roger Williams* (1940); Ola E. Winslow's *Master Roger Williams* (1957). Williams appears as a fictional character in Daniel P. Thompson's *The Doomed Chief* (1860) and in W. D. Schofield's *Ashes in the Wilderness* (1942).

Williams, Tennessee [Thomas Lanier] (b. Columbus, Miss., March 26, 1914—   ), playwright, short-story writer, poet, novelist. During his early years Williams held many different jobs to support himself while writing short stories

Angus McBean, London

and plays that did not sell. He worked his way through the University of Iowa, and in 1940 was awarded a $1,000 Rockefeller fellowship to work on a play, *Battle of Angels* (1940), which was produced in Boston and closed after a few weeks. Williams later rewrote the play as *Orpheus Descending* (1957). His first successful play was THE GLASS MENAGERIE (1945), which won the New York Drama Critics Circle Award, and established him as a major American playwright. It is one of the most tender of Williams' plays, and establishes the theme of illusion versus reality—particularly of a lonely woman inhabiting a world of dreams—which recurs frequently in his work. A STREETCAR NAMED DESIRE (1947), which won a Pulitzer prize, repeats this theme and introduces the atavistic hero, as well as scenes of violence and intimations of sexual aberrations. *Summer and Smoke* (1948) combines some of the sexual emphasis of *Streetcar* with the wistfulness of *The Glass Menagerie* in a story of a soulful but repressed woman who is unable to respond to the vitality of the man she loves and is driven, by her dreams of purity, into lonely spinsterhood. THE ROSE TATTOO (1951) deals with Gulf Coast Sicilians with roisterous humor and sympathy. In *Camino Real* (1953) Williams experimented with literary and stage dream techniques. CAT ON A HOT TIN ROOF (1955), which also won a Pulitzer prize, deals with the tensions and pretensions in a wealthy Southern family, and especially with the strained relationship between Maggie and her alcoholic husband, Brick. *Suddenly, Last Summer* (1958) was produced with *Something Unspoken* under the title *Garden District*. It concerns a possessive mother and homosexual son to whom others are merely objects to feed their monstrous self-centeredness. Sebastian, the son, is killed and devoured by a mob of starving children and his cousin, Catherine, whom he has used as bait to lure young men, witnesses his death and is driven almost insane. His mother attempts to commit Catherine to an institution so that she cannot reveal the truth about Sebastian's death. Williams' latest plays are *Sweet Bird of Youth* (1959), *Period of Adjustment* (1960), and *The Night of the Iguana* (1961), the last based on a short-story in *One Arm and Other Stories* (1948).

Williams has often been attacked for the violence and sexual disorder present in a large part of his work, and accused of writing merely shocking sensationalism. Williams, however, feels that beneath the thin veneer of civilization there lies present in all men a primitivism that cannot be ignored. Some of his characters, in one sense, are types—the savage, the degenerate, the weak, the dreamer unable to face reality—that attain to something approaching universal significance. His modified realistic settings are a functional part of the atmosphere created in each play, and he frequently uses physical objects such as the animals in *The Glass Menagerie*, the dressmaker's dummies in *The Rose Tattoo*, and the angel of the fountain in *Summer and Smoke* as symbols of the plight of the main character. His language is poetic

and highly evocative, and contributes much to his dramatic force.

Other work by Williams includes *The Roman Spring of Mrs. Stone* (1950), a novel, and *Hard Candy* (1954), a collection of short stories. He collected several short plays in *Twenty-Seven Wagons Full of Cotton and Other One-Act Plays* (1946), and, with DONALD WINDHAM, wrote *You Touched Me!* (1947), a three-act comedy based on the short story by D. H. Lawrence. He published one volume of poems, *In the Winter of Cities* (1955), and wrote the screenplay for the motion picture *Baby Doll* (1956), based on his *Twenty-Seven Wagons Full of Cotton*. Benjamin Nelson wrote *Tennessee Williams: The Man and His Work* (1961). Nancy Tischler wrote *Tennessee Williams, Rebellious Puritan* (1961), a biography and critique.

Williams, William Carlos (b. Rutherford, N.J., Sept. 17, 1883—d. March 4, 1963), poet, novelist, short-story writer, translator. physician. Dr. Williams was born of an English father and a Puerto Rican mother. He at-

Charles Sheeler

tended Swiss and Parisian lycées, the Horace Mann School, and the University of Pennsylvania Medical School; his internship was at the French Hospital and the Nursery and Child's Hospital in New York; in 1909 he set up a general practice in Rutherford and in the same year his first book, *Poems*, appeared. His published works since then include forty volumes of prose and poetry.

Williams remained apart from literary movements, although his work is influenced by several. He was an early friend of Ezra Pound and Hilda Doolittle (H. D.), and IMAGISM undoubtedly contributed to the formation of his lucid, precise, lyrical style. His poetry is without rhyme or conventional meter, usually written in short graceful lines and in what the poet calls an "American rhythm." His patriotism, as opposed to the sour anti-Americanism of many of his contemporaries who became expatriates, motivated much of his work, especially IN THE AMERICAN GRAIN (1925), a book of prose reconstructions of American cultural history and a volume that Hart Crane found indispensable.

Williams became the poet of everyday life; his passion for the details of existence, presented barely and without moralizing, attracted many followers among younger writers, some of whom organized themselves during the 1930's and 1940's as the Objectivists. None, however, achieved Williams' power to evoke deep feeling from the simplest objects. "No ideas but in things"—this he reiterated in PATERSON, his most ambitious work, which appeared in four books from 1946 to 1951, with a fifth book, a kind of postscript, appearing in 1958. *Paterson* is an attempt to apprehend the essence and the experience of his city and at the same time to use its river as an entrance into the general stream of time.

Williams has been accused by Yvor Winters and others of lacking depth, of cutting poetry off from any possible content other than discrete images without history or intention. He sometimes seems not in full control of his motives as a poet. Yet his work is remarkably unified, deriving from the poet's unaltering emotional center. His point of view, as Louise Bogan has remarked, is "at once archaic and humane; but his straightforward anger at injustice always remains that of the detached observer." In this Dr. Williams combined the sensitivity and linguistic skill of the poet with the observational powers of the physician, and the result is consistently vigorous and acute.

A recent checklist of Williams' poems was compiled by Francis Cheney and included in Allen Tate's *Sixty American Poets, 1896–1944* (1945). Williams' poems have been collected twice (1934, 1938) and re-collected as *The Collected Earlier Poems of William Carlos Williams* (1951) and *The Collected Later Poems of William Carlos Williams* (1950). *The Great American Novel* (1923); *A Voyage to Pagany* (1928); *The Knife of the Times and Other Stories* (1932); *A Novelette, and Other Prose, 1921–1931* (1932); *White Mule* (1937); *Life Along the Passaic River* (1938); *In the Money: White Mule, Part II* (1940); *Make Light of It* (1950); and *The Build Up* (1952) comprise his fiction. *A Dream of Love* (1948) is a representative play. *The Autobiography of William Carlos Williams* appeared in 1951 and *Selected Essays* in 1954. There is an important collection of his letters and manuscripts in the Lockwood Memorial Library at the University of Buffalo. *The Desert Music and Other Poems* (1954); *The Lost Poems of William Carlos Williams or The Past Recaptured* (1957); *Journey to Love* (1955); and *Sappho* (1957) are later verse publications. *The Selected Letters of William Carlos Williams* appeared in 1957.

Many poets and critics have given attention to Williams' work since the early days of the 20th-century poetic "revolution." His friend Ezra Pound wrote a number of perceptive essays. The only full-length critical study, however, is Vivienne Koch's *William Carlos Williams* (1950). An interesting bibliography, which lists all Williams' publications with his oral comments on each work, is *I Wanted to Write a Poem* (1958), edited by Edith Heal.

WILLIAM B. GOODMAN

Williamson, Thames [Ross] ["S. S. Smith"] (b. Nez Percé Indian Reservation, Ida., Feb. 7, 1894—   ), novelist, writer of travel books. As a young man, Williamson followed a variety of occupations—cabin boy, circus hand, sheepherder, teacher, newspaperman, sociologist, fingerprint expert. A prolific fiction writer, he employed five pseudonyms. His earliest novel was *Run, Sheep, Run* (1925); two later ones are *Christine Roux* (1945) and *The Gladiator* (1948). He also wrote juveniles and mysteries. He wrote a book about Alaska, *Far North Country* (1944); and several textbooks, among them *Introduction to Sociology* (1926). During the 1920's he taught economics at Simmons and Smith colleges.

William Wilson (*Burton's Gentleman's Magazine*, October, 1839), a short story by EDGAR ALLAN POE, included in *Tales of the Grotesque and Arabesque*. An allegory of the double personality, this story has been called one of Poe's greatest tales. An alter ego begins to haunt William Wilson at a boys' school, not unlike the English school Poe attended at Stoke Newington, and pursues him like a conscience through all his adventures as a young man. Their conflict leads to a duel in which Wilson, who narrates the story, kills his alter ego. From the story Robert Louis Stevenson derived the idea for his *The Strange Case of Dr. Jekyll and Mr. Hyde* (1885).

Willingham, Calder (b. Atlanta, Ga., Dec. 23, 1922—   ), novelist, short story writer. The violent and occasionally garish realism of Willingham's fiction has disturbed many reviewers. Even the unfavorable critics, however, have generally been impressed by the color and vitality of his style, his ability to create individual scenes and conversations of great reality and power, and the intense conviction which informs much of his work, notably *End As a Man* (1947), which was made into a successful play and movie. Willingham is the author of four other novels—*Geraldine Bradshaw* (1950); *Reach to the Stars* (1951); *Natural Child* (1952); and *To Eat a Peach* (1955)—and a collection of short stories, *The Gates of Hell* (1951).

Willis, Nathaniel Parker (b. Portland, Me., Jan. 20, 1806—d. Jan. 20, 1867), editor, writer. Willis won literary fame while still at Yale, was a skillful writer of all kinds of prose and verse, but retains only small shreds of his reputation. Soon after leaving Yale he began editing literary magazines, one of which, *The Token*, attained considerable success. As foreign correspondent for the New York *Mirror* he sent home lively sketches of travel abroad and meetings with notable personages. On his return Willis took to writing plays in blank verse, one of which, TORTESA, OR, THE USURER (1839), was highly admired by Edgar Allan Poe. Willis encouraged

Poe to write for the *Mirror,* and likewise persuaded Thackeray to do columns for that paper. In 1846 he and GEORGE POPE MORRIS put out the HOME JOURNAL, which changed its name in 1901 to TOWN AND COUNTRY.

Willis has been described as an arrant sentimentalist and something of a fop. He was a strenuous advocate of the American language, which he sought to embellish with words of his own invention. He was sometimes involved in the hot-tempered literary quarrels of the day. When Captain Frederick Marryat, then editor of the London *Metropolitan Magazine,* reviewed Willis' *Pencillings by the Way* (3 v., 1835) by making a personal attack on Willis, the latter challenged him to a duel and shots were exchanged.

Of all Willis' writings only one piece keeps some popularity: the moralistic poem called *Unseen Spirits.* All the rest of his work has perished, even though some of his prose still retains its sparkle. Sometimes a special plea has been made for Willis as a pioneer in the field of the short story. F. L. Pattee, in his *Development of the American Short Story* (1923), tells how when Willis was in England he "poured into the English magazines a series of short stories under the pseudonym 'Philip Slingsby.'" In 1836 thirteen of these were published as *Inklings of Adventure.* In 1840 Willis made another collection, alternately called *Romance of Travel: Comprising Tales of Five Lands* and *Loiterings of Travel.* In 1845 came *Dashes at Life with a Free Pencil.* He wrote one novel, *Paul Vane, or, Parts of a Life Else Untold* (1857). Pattee considers Willis lacking in dramatic sense and truthfulness; he anticipated O. Henry in his fondness for the surprise ending. Other literary historians

have found Willis, in his European stories, not only a romantic pilgrim but also occasionally a keen critic of social snobbery.

Among Willis' other books these may be mentioned: *Poetical Scripture Sketches* (1827); *Fugitive Poetry* (1829); *Melanie and Other Poems* (1835); *A l'Abri* (1839); *Poems of Passion* (1843); *Lecture on Fashion* (1844); *Poems Sacred, Passionate, and Humorous* (1845); *People I Have Met* (1850); *Hurry-Graphs* (1851); *Famous Persons and Places* (1854); *The Convalescent* (1859). During his lifetime he published *The Complete Works of N. P. Willis* (1846; reissued, 13 v., 1849–59). In London appeared *The Poetical Works of N. P. Willis* (1888). A selection of his *Prose Writings* was compiled (1885) by H. A. Beers, who also wrote his biography (1885). Willis' sister, SARA PAYSON WILLIS, drew an unflattering portrait of him in her novel *Ruth Hall* (1855). See KNICKERBOCKER SCHOOL; THE AMERICAN MAGAZINE; THE YOUTH'S COMPANION.

Willis, Sara Payson ["Fanny Fern"] (b. Portland, Me., July 9, 1811—d. Oct. 10, 1872), essayist, author of children's books, free-lance writer. Fanny Fern, the sister of N. P. WILLIS, married three times and led a varied literary career. She reached the height of her success with *Fern Leaves from Fanny's Portfolio* (1853), which sold 70,000 copies within a year. A second series of *Leaves* appeared in 1854, *Fresh Leaves* in 1857. Fanny Fern was no namby-pamby sentimentalist. She had a gift for tart satire and by no means accepted the ideal of a meek and submissive womanhood. The only one of her novels to attract attention, *Ruth Hall* (1855), presumably depicts her own family, mostly in highly unflattering terms. She also wrote *A New Story Book for Children* (1864); *Folly as It Flies* (1868); *Ginger Snaps* (1870); and *Caper-Sauce: A Volume of Chit-Chat about Men, Women, and Things* (1872). See ETHEL PARTON; JAMES PARTON.

Willison, George F[indlay] (b. Denver, Colo., July 24, 1896—   ), historian, nonfiction writer, public official. Willison was originally trained as a classical scholar at the universities of Colorado, Oxford, and Harrison. Later his interest increasingly turned to the history of the American people and to contemporary problems. He joined the Federal Writers' Project in 1934, where he worked on the American Guide series and became national editor-in-chief. In *Here They Dug the Gold* (1936, rev. 1946) he chronicled the Colorado gold rush and the early boom towns. Later, while doing research for several books, he worked with the Department of Commerce, the Democratic National Committee, Senator Kefauver's presidential campaign staff, the United Nations Department of Public Information and the New York City Commission on Inter-Group Relations. He also contributed many articles to national magazines and critical journals. Among his books: *Why Wars Are Declared* (1936); *Let's Make a Play* (1940); *Saints and Strangers* (1945), a group biography of the PILGRIMS; *Behold Virginia* (1951), a history of the dominion to 1776; *The Pilgrim Reader* (1953).

Willkie, Wendell L[ewis] (b. Elwood, Ind., Feb. 18, 1892—d. Oct. 8, 1944), lawyer, business administrator, Presidential candidate. Willkie's parents were both lawyers; after he had taken a B.A. and a law degree at Indiana University, he joined his parents' firm. He was in the army during World War I, then practiced law at Akron, Ohio, and in New York City. In 1929 he became counsel for an important utilities firm, the Commonwealth & Southern, and in 1933 its president. As the New Deal policies toward public utilities developed, Willkie became an outspoken critic of FRANKLIN D. ROOSEVELT. His particular battle ended when the Tennessee Valley Authority paid Commonwealth & Southern 78 million dollars for its Tennessee properties. Meantime Willkie's skill as a debater and critic turned Republican favor toward him, and he won the 1940 Republican Presidential nomination. He made a spectacular, unusual, and almost successful campaign. He supported Roosevelt on his foreign policies, did not deny the value of many of his social reforms, but attacked him mainly because of his attitude toward private enterprise.

After his defeat Willkie resumed the practice of law. In 1942 he was made a special emissary by President Roosevelt and made a tour of Europe and Asia in which he made some shrewd observations, reported in his widely read book *One World* (1943). "Peace must be planned on a world basis," he argued. He continued to hope for another nomination, but his consistent honesty about major issues lost him the adherents he needed. Raymond J. Clapper, an admirer of Willkie, said: "The Republican party was unable to recognize a real leader when it had the luck to find one on its doorstep." Joseph Barnes wrote a biography, *Willkie* (1952), and Muriel Rukeyser wrote another, *One Life* (1957).

Will of Charles Lounsbury, The (1897). See WILLISTON FISH.

Will to Believe, The, and Other Essays in Popular Philosophy (1897), ten essays by WILLIAM JAMES. The title essay of the collection immediately aroused wide discussion and much vehement dissent and affected theological as well as metaphysical circles, the latter less favorably than the former. It restated some of the ideas already expressed in an article, *Reflex Action and Theism*, published in the *Unitarian Review* (1881), in which James said: "The willing part of our nature . . . dominates both the conceiving department and the feeling department; in other words, perception and thinking are only there for behavior's sake." James was making his way toward his philosophy of PRAGMATISM. But *The Will to Believe*, according to Herbert W. Schneider (*History of American Philosophy*, 1946), repelled even his friends, who regarded the essay as a defense of action for action's sake. However, F. C. S. Schiller defended James for

"his much misconstrued doctrine of the 'Will to Believe.' It is not so much exhortation of what we *ought to do* in the future as analysis of what *we have done* in the past." Yet taking the essay as a whole, readers—especially Protestant theologians—noted with gratification that James was justifying religious faith and was asserting the need to accept hypotheses which are not susceptible of experimental proof. Faith, James argued, was completely justified by its results. Ettie Stettheimer made a critical study of *The Will to Believe as a Basis for the Defense of Religious Faith* (1907).

Wilson, Alexander (b. Scotland, July 6, 1766 —d. Aug. 23, 1813), ornithologist, teacher, editor, poet. Although he had some schooling in Scotland, Wilson was largely a self-taught man. He thought of himself first as a poet, one who admired Burns and followed in his footsteps. He published two volumes: *Watty and Meg* (1782) and *Poems, Humorous, Satirical, and Serious* (1789). He emigrated to America in 1793, worked for a while as a weaver, but gave himself enough education to become a teacher in New Jersey and Pennsylvania. His deep interest in nature was fostered by WILLIAM BARTRAM, who gave him the free use of his library.

In 1806 Wilson became assistant editor of an encyclopedia. He interested his employer in the idea of a book on *American Ornithology*, of which the first volume appeared in 1808, the ninth and last in 1814. He made many tours of the country, during the first of which he met J. J. AUDUBON; the two naturalists thereafter engaged in a jealous and petty feud. Wilson is agreed to be almost as good a writer as Audubon and both more original and more accurate in his research. In 1844 his *Poetical Works* appeared, but they are of minor importance. James S. Wilson wrote *Alexander Wilson, Poet-Naturalist* (1906).

Wilson, Augusta. See AUGUSTA JANE EVANS.

Wilson, Charles Morrow (b. Fayetteville, Ark., June 16, 1905—　　　), newspaperman, free-lance writer. Wilson's specialty is rural problems, both at home and abroad. He worked for a number of newspapers, including the *Christian Science Monitor* and *The New York Times*. Among his books: *Backwoods America* (1934); *Meriwether Lewis of Lewis and Clark* (1934); *Roots of America* (1936); *Country Living: Plus and Minus* (1938); *Landscape of Rural Poverty* (1940); *Challenge and Opportunity: Central America* (1941); *Ambassadors in White: The Story of American Tropical Medicine* (1942); *Middle America* (1944); *Oil Across the World* (1945); *The Tropics: World of Tomorrow* (1951); *Aged in Ozark Wood* (1953); *Bodacious Ozarks: True Tales of the Backhills* (1959); *Let's Try Barter* (1960).

Wilson, Earl (b. Rockford, Ohio, May 3, 1907 —　　　), columnist. Night-club editor of the New York *Post*, Wilson conducts a widely syndicated column called "It Happened Last Night"; several books have been made from material originally published in the column: *I Am Gazing into My Eight-Ball* (1945); *Pike's Peek or Bust* (1947); *Let 'Em Eat Cheesecake* (1949); *Look Who's Abroad Now* (1953).

Wilson, Edmund (b. Red Bank, N.J., May 8, 1895—   ), critic, novelist, poet, editor. One of the ablest intellects and writers of our times, Wilson produced books in many fields. At Princeton he served as editor of the *Nassau Literary Magazine*, with JOHN PEALE BISHOP as his assistant and successor. In 1922 the two collaborated on a volume of prose and verse called THE UNDERTAKER'S GARLAND. After graduation Wilson became a reporter on the New York *Sun;* in World War I he was a worker in a French hospital and then in the U.S. intelligence forces; on his return to New York he became managing editor of *Vanity Fair*. In 1926 he was on the staff of the *New Republic* as book review editor, later as associate editor, but resigned to do more writing. In 1944–48 he was regular book reviewer for *The New Yorker* and continued afterward to contribute long critical essays and other pieces to that magazine. He also employed his gifts for scholarship in many other fields, as in his studies of Hebrew and Biblical manuscripts, and wrote on abstruse subjects with critical insight and reportorial skill. His *The Dead Sea Scrolls* (1955) has been the most popular and one of the best considerations of the recently discovered Biblical materials from the Near East.

Wilson's many works include criticism, travel books, novels, verse, and plays, and he edited a valuable anthology of criticism, THE SHOCK OF RECOGNITION (1943), and *The Crack-Up* (1945), a volume of uncollected pieces of F. Scott Fitzgerald. *Memoirs of Hecate County* (1946), a collection of short stories, was banned after publication because of the candid treatment of sex in one story. In reviewing *The Shores of Light* (1952), a collection of some of Wilson's literary essays, Alfred Kazin said: "Wilson is not like other critics: some critics are boring even when they are original; he fascinates even when he is wrong."

Wilson's critical interest has always extended to the social and political implications of literature and a deep concern for moral values. His first critical work, AXEL'S CASTLE (1931), deals with symbolism as an international movement. *To the Finland Station* (1940) gives an authoritative account of the background of the Russian revolution. His earliest travel book, *Travels in Two Democracies* (1936), relates experiences in Russia, where he enjoyed a greater opportunity than most visitors to move about freely. In 1956 he reprinted part of this book in *Red, Black, Blond, and Olive*, where "blond" refers to Russia, the other adjectives to the Zuñi Indians, Haitians, and Israelis.

Wilson wrote several plays. One, *The Little Blue Light* (pub., 1950; prod., 1951), is a sardonic forecast of America in the "not-too-remote future." In 1937 Wilson had collected three plays in book form; these were republished, along with *Blue Light* and *Cyprian's Prayer,* as *Five Plays* (1954). Among his other

books: *Poets, Farewell!* (verse, 1929); *I Thought of Daisy* (novel, 1929); THE WOUND AND THE BOW (1931); *The American Jitters: A Year of the Slump* (1932); *Notebooks of Night* (prose and verse, 1942); *Europe Without Baedeker: Sketches Among the Ruins of Italy, Greece, and England* (1947); *Classics and Commercials* (1950); *A Piece of My Mind: Reflections at 60* (1956); *The American Earthquake* (1958); *Apologies to the Iroquois* (1960); *Night Thoughts* (1961); *Patriotic Gore* (1962). At one time Wilson was married to the distinguished writer MARY MCCARTHY. See F. SCOTT FITZGERALD.

Wilson, Ethel Davis [Bryant] (b. South Africa, 1890—   ), novelist. Mrs. Wilson was educated in England and taught for several years in Vancouver before her marriage there to Dr. Wallace Wilson in 1920. She learned her craft by writing short stories for magazines; her first novel, *Hetty Dorval,* did not appear until 1947. This began a series of sensitive, sophisticated novels: *The Innocent Traveler* (1949), based on the life of Topaz Edgeworth; *The Equations of Love* (1952), a group of three short novels; *Swamp Angel* (1954); *Love and Salt Water* (1956).

Wilson, [Robert] Forrest (b. Warren, Ohio, Jan. 20, 1883—d. May 9, 1942), newspaperman, biographer, novelist. Wilson was a newspaperman in Cleveland, then a Washington correspondent. With Benedict Crowell, he wrote *How America Went to War* (6 v., 1921). For a time he worked in Paris, and wrote *Paris on Parade* (1925), giving his impressions. His most important publication was a biography of HARRIET BEECHER STOWE, *Crusader in Crinoline* (1941), which won a Pulitzer prize. He also wrote *Living Pageant of the Nile* (1924).

Wilson, Francis (b. Philadelphia, Feb. 7, 1854—d. Oct. 7, 1935), actor, playwright, writer. Wilson took to the stage early, appearing in several musical plays, later in straight drama. In 1913 he became the first president of the Actors' Equity Association. He was an intelligent man who liked books and wrote capably; his authorship took the form mainly of reminiscences. Among his books: *Recollections of a Player* (1897); *The Eugene Field I Knew* (1898); *Joseph Jefferson* (1906); *Francis Wilson's Life of Himself* (1924); *John Wilkes Booth* (1929). His best known play was *The Bachelor's Baby* (prod., 1909).

Wilson, H[alsey] W[illiam] (b. Wilmington, Vt., May 12, 1868—d. March 1, 1954), bookseller, publisher, editor. His firm, the H. W. Wilson Co., has published many important indexes and works of reference in literature. The first, the *Cumulative Book Index,* began in 1898. Other indexes, together with the dates on which they were begun, are: READERS' GUIDE TO PERIODICAL LITERATURE (1901); *Book Review Digest* (1905); *International Index to Periodicals* (1907); *Index to Legal Periodicals* (1908); *Industrial Arts Index* (1913); *Agricultural Index* (1916); and others. In addition Wilson issued many important single reference books: *The Junior Book of Authors* (1934; rev., 1951); *British Authors of the 19th Century* (1936) and *British Authors Before 1800* (1952); *American Authors 1600–1900* (1938); *Twentieth-Century Authors* (1942) and *First Supplement* (1955); also a series called *Current Biography* (from 1940). On the company's fiftieth anniversary in 1948 the *Saturday Review of Literature* commented: "The name H. W. Wilson is to bibliography what Webster is to dictionaries, Bartlett to quotations." In 1950 the University of Minnesota Press published *The H. W. Wilson Company: Half a Century of Bibliographic Publishing*, by John Lawler.

Wilson, Harry Leon (b. Oregon, Ill., May 1, 1867—d. June 28, 1939), humorist, novelist, playwright, short-story writer, editor. As a young man Wilson went west, lived in a mining camp, and began writing humor for the old Puck. His work was well liked and in 1892 he was asked to join the staff. He succeeded H. C. Bunner as editor in 1896, left the magazine in 1902. He began writing stories and novels, and turned out many titles. His first success was *The Boss of Little Arcady* (1905), which was followed by four outstanding best sellers: *Bunker Bean* (1912); *Ruggles of Red Gap* (1915); *Ma Pettingill* (1919); Merton of the Movies (1922). His last book, not a success, was *Two Black Sheep* (1931). Wilson and Booth Tarkington were fast friends and collaborated on a play, The Man from Home (1907), which ran for nearly six years. Several of Wilson's books were made into popular motion pictures, and he was one of the first authors to receive a fortune for the motion-picture rights to a book (for his *Merton of the Movies*). *Ruggles of Red Gap* is probably his most enduring work.

Wilson, James (b. Scotland, Sept. 14, 1742—d. Aug. 21, 1798), lawyer, patriot. Wilson had a deep and lasting influence on the founding and early development of the American republic. Educated in Scottish universities, he emigrated to America in 1765, studied law in Philadelphia, and was admitted to the bar in November, 1767. He took a leading role in the controversy with England, publishing in 1774 a widely read essay, *Considerations on the Nature and Extent of the Legislative Authority of the British Parliament*. He served as a delegate to the Continental Congress, signed the Declaration of Independence, served in the Continental Army, and when the war closed became one of the most persuasive members on the side of those who favored a strong central government. He helped draw up a somewhat conservative constitution for Pennsylvania. In 1789 Washington appointed Wilson to the Supreme Court, and he did much to guide its first steps.

Wilson's *Works* were edited by Bird Wilson (3 v., 1804), and again by James De W. Andrews (2 v., 1896). R. G. Adams compiled *Selected Political Essays of James Wilson* (1930). Charles Page Smith wrote a biography, *James Wilson, Founding Father* (1956).

Wilson, John (b. England, 1591[?]—d. August 7, 1667), Congregational minister, poet.

Wilson entered the ministry, emigrated to America because of his nonconformity, and served a church in Boston for the rest of his life. Before leaving England he had published a long poem for children, *A Song or Story, for the Lasting Remembrance of Divers Famous Works Which God Hath Done in Our Time* (1626); a second edition, with a somewhat altered title, appeared in Boston in 1680. Cotton Mather wrote a life of him in 1695; later this was part of Mather's *Magnalia Christi Americana* (1702).

Wilson, Margaret (b. Traer, Iowa, Jan. 16, 1882—   ), missionary, teacher, novelist. Miss Wilson found missionary work disturbing because of the demands it made on her compassion, returned to the United States to teach for a while, and then began writing novels. Both *The Able McLaughlins* (1923), a Pulitzer prize winner for 1924, and *Law and the McLaughlins* (1936), a sequel, deal with the life of Scots pioneers in Iowa. Miss Wilson wrote frankly from a woman's viewpoint for women readers. Among her other novels were *The Kenworthys* (1925); *Daughters of India* (1928); *One Came Out* (1932); *The Valiant Wife* (1933); *Devon Treasury Mystery* (1939). In 1923 Miss Wilson married Colonel G. D. Turner of Oxford, and moved to England.

Wilson, Sloan (b. Norwalk, Conn., May 8, 1920—   ), author. Wilson was graduated from Harvard University in 1942. Though he taught at the University of Buffalo and served as assistant director of the White House Conference on Education, 1955–56, Wilson has declared himself "a professional novelist—a rare breed." His *The Man in the Gray Flannel Suit* (1944), a widely read portrayal of the "Madison Avenue type" executive and suburbanite, established him as a novelist. *A Summer Place* (1958) and *A Sense of Values* (1961) were also best sellers commenting on contemporary mores. Wilson also wrote *Voyage to Somewhere* (1946).

Wilson, [Thomas] Woodrow (b. Staunton, Va., Dec. 28, 1856—d. Feb. 3, 1924), lawyer, teacher, university administrator, writer, public official, 27th President. Wilson took his B.A. at Princeton University, then studied law at the University of Virginia. He practiced law briefly, then went on to obtain a Ph.D. in history and political science at Johns Hopkins University. After teaching there, at Bryn Mawr College, and at Wesleyan University, he accepted a full professorship at Princeton. He was an excellent teacher, and in 1902 was unanimously chosen president of the university. While there he did much to improve its academic standards and to democratize its social system.

Always keenly interested in politics, Wilson left Princeton to run for Democratic governor of New Jersey in 1910. His outstanding oratorical ability, his profound knowledge of American political aims and institutions, and his genuine democratic feeling carried him to victory, and while governor he carried through some remarkable political and economic measures. In 1911 he made his most powerful friend, Col. E.

M. House of Texas; for many years House was his *alter ego*, apparently until Wilson suspected him of making important decisions without consulting him. At the Democratic Presidential convention in 1912 Wilson was nominated after WILLIAM JENNINGS BRYAN threw his support to him and won the election as the result of a political feud between THEODORE ROOSEVELT and WILLIAM H. TAFT, which split the opposition.

Wilson was a middle-of-the-road man in political and economic measures, but his banking and tariff reforms were regarded as radical; the former have withstood the test of time. He gave new meaning to the "general welfare" clause, supplied vigorous executive leadership to Congress and to his party, and fought privilege. But he was unable to complete his projects for domestic reform because of the outbreak of the European war. Our entry into it pushed the country into a position of leadership in international affairs. Wilson chose General J. J. PERSHING as United States military leader. His pronouncements aroused wide comment, such as his address to the Senate on Jan. 22, 1917, in which he declared that the United States must seek "a peace without victory," and his address to Congress (April 2, 1917) asking for a declaration of war: "The world must be made safe for democracy." His program of the *Fourteen Points* (Jan. 8, 1918) exerted a tremendous influence on world opinion. In the midst of this turmoil he had conducted a successful Presidential campaign against CHARLES E. HUGHES.

With the end of the war Wilson began his last and greatest battle in favor of the United States entrance into the League of Nations. The Paris Peace Conference which followed World War I met in the Hall of Mirrors in the famous royal chateau at Versailles in France; there on Jan. 18, 1919, the treaty of peace between the Allies and Germany, known as the Treaty of Versailles, was signed. This treaty provided for a League of Nations, took away some German territory, limited her armament, and included an acknowledgement of war guilt. But the United States refused to sign the treaty, ratification of which was defeated in the Senate because of the provision for a League of Nations. Woodrow Wilson made a strenuous campaign to obtain ratification. The battle turned into a personal quarrel with Senator Henry Cabot Lodge of Massachusetts, mostly over details. Wilson was subject to an immense amount of personal vituperation and controversy. He suffered a stroke; the country remained outside the League, and Wilson ended his days in physical breakdown and defeat.

As a writer, Wilson always knew how to turn a phrase and his love of epigrams and a good story kept his style above the usual professorial level. His CONGRESSIONAL GOVERNMENT (1885) was reprinted several times. *The State* (1889) was revised and rewritten in 1898 and again (by Edward Elliott) in 1918. *Division and Reunion* (1893) was brought up to date by Ed-

ward S. Corwin in 1924. Two collections of essays and lectures were *An Old Master and Other Political Essays* (1893) and *Mere Literature and Other Essays* (1896). *George Washington* (1897) and *A History of the American People* (5 v., 1902) were both reissued. *Constitutional Government* (1908) was reprinted up to 1921; in 1916 one chapter was separately issued as *The President of the U.S.* A collection of most of Wilson's addresses was made by Ray Stannard Baker and William E. Dodd in *The Public Papers of Woodrow Wilson* (6 v., 1925–27). Selections from his writings were made by Richard Linthicum (1916); A. O. Lovejoy (1919); Saul K. Padover (1942); Arthur B. Tourtellot (1945); August Heckscher (1956); and others.

The basic biography of Wilson is RAY STANNARD BAKER's *Woodrow Wilson, His Life and Letters* (8 v., 1927–39). Arthur S. Link engaged in another multivolume endeavor to present the life of Wilson, the first volume of which is *Woodrow Wilson and the Progressive Era* (1954). Other works on Wilson are James Kerney's *Political Education of Woodrow Wilson* (1926); Ruth Cranston's *The Story of Woodrow Wilson* (1945); David Loth's *Story of Woodrow Wilson* (1956); E. B. Alsop's symposium *The Greatness of Wilson* (1956); Herbert Hoover's *The Ordeal of Woodrow Wilson* (1958); Arthur Walworth's *Woodrow Wilson* (2 v., 1958). In 1922 the Woodrow Wilson Foundation was established to further public understanding of international problems and the Wilsonian ideals of world cooperation. It distributes much useful literature and issues some of its own. Howard Koch and John Huston based a play, *In Time to Come* (1942), on Wilson's life, and an earnest movie biography with screenplay by Lamar Trotti was produced in 1944.

Winchell, Walter (b. New York City, April 7, 1897—   ), actor, columnist, broadcaster. Winchell was a child actor, and in 1917 was doing his own vaudeville act. In 1922 he began writing a theatrical column for the New York *Vaudeville News*, two years later was a columnist for Bernarr Macfadden's New York *Graphic*, then became known as a gossip columnist and broadcaster. His early theatrical background undoubtedly influenced his histrionic presentation of material. He is known for his pitiless invasion of other people's privacy, is often involved in feuds and occasionally in libel suits. When asked to compose an epitaph for himself, Winchell proposed: "Here he lies—in the dirt he loved so well."

Although he erred constantly against good taste, Winchell performed some important public services, notably in war bond campaigns during World War II. He also formed the Damon Runyon Memorial Fund for Cancer. His style has vitality if nothing else; *Time* once said that Winchell "spits epithets like an angry alley cat when he is out to claw somebody." His undoubted gift for epigram is shown in such remarks as: "She's been on more laps than a napkin." His fondness for inventing words produced such terms as *lohengrinned* (for wedded), *Reno-vated* (for divorced), *infanticipating* (about to have a child), *pash* (passion), *debu-tramp*, the *Hardened Artery* (Broadway). The authorized biography of Winchell is Ed Weiner's *Let's Go to Press: A Profile of Walter Winchell* (1955).

Winchevsky, Morris (b. Lithuania, Aug. 9, 1856—d. March 18, 1932), poet, editor, trans-lator. Winchesvky's real name was Ben-Zion Novachovitch, and he also used the pen name Leopold Benedict. He was a radical in politics, a writer on proletarian themes, but was best known for his poetry and was called "the Ghetto poet." He lived in New York City for many years; previously he had lived in Denmark, Ger-many, France, and England. In 1919 he col-lected his verse in *Lider un Gedichte, 1871-1910;* in 1920 his *Gezamelte Schriftn* (3 v.) ap-peared. Some of his poems were translated into English. He himself was a skilled translator and rendered Hugo's *Les Misérables*, Ibsen's *Doll's House,* and Hood's *Song of the Shirt* into Yid-dish.

Windham, Donald (b. Atlanta, Ga., July 2, 1920—   ), novelist, playwright, short-story writer. Windham's schooling did not go past the Boys High School in his native Atlanta. From then until he was able to concentrate on his writing as a full-time job he held a variety of jobs, ranging from working in a barrel factory to editing *Dance Index* magazine. In 1947 he collaborated on a play with Tennessee Williams, *You Touched Me!,* based on the short story by D. H. Lawrence. His first book was *The Dog Star* (1950), a novel depicting the effect of a friend's suicide on a sensitive youth living on the seamy side of life. It was praised by E. M. For-ster, André Gide, and Thomas Mann. Other books include: *The Hero Continues* (1960), a novel, and *The Warm Country: Stories* (1960; with an introduction by E. M. Forster). His autobiography, *Emblems of Conduct,* appeared serially in *The New Yorker* magazine (1961).

Windy McPherson's Son (1916), a novel by SHERWOOD ANDERSON. The hero, Sam McPher-son, grows up to hate his squalid home in Cax-ton, Iowa, where his father, a drunken boaster, is a completely dominating force.

Wine of Wizardry, A (*Cosmopolitan*, Septem-ber, 1907), a poem by GEORGE STERLING. It gave its title to Sterling's third collection, *A Wine of Wizardry and Other Poems* (1909). The poem depicts visions seen in a goblet of wine and is composed in an artificial style em-ploying much imagery of light and a resonant diction.

Winesburg, Ohio (1919), a book of twenty-three sketches by SHERWOOD ANDERSON. An-derson, in his best known work, exhibits a typi-cal Middle Western town with its narrow hori-zons and ingrown passions; he does so through the lives of various inhabitants—"grotesques," he calls them. The young reporter George Wil-lard, groping to find himself and achieve "the sadness of sophistication," forms the connecting link among these fragmentary lives. The sketches

are written in simple language, straightforwardly realistic; they were considered a radical venture in the new literature at the time of their publi-cation. At their best the sketches do approach the work of the author with whom Anderson has been most often compared, the Russian, Che-khov. It is generally believed that Winesburg is really Clyde, Ohio, a small town where An-derson lived during his boyhood. An artist from *Life* visited the town (June 10, 1946) and in his report and pictures showed that it has not changed much from the time when Anderson wrote about it.

Winfield, Arthur M. Pen name of EDWARD STRATEMEYER.

Wing-and-Wing (1842), a novel by JAMES FENIMORE COOPER. The merits of this novel have been much disputed. It is a mixture of sea story and historical novel, set in the period when England and France fought the Napoleonic Wars. In the novel appears an important his-torical character, Admiral Caraccioli, whom Lord Nelson executed. Cooper presents an imaginary granddaughter, a devout Catholic who finds herself in love with a French privateer who is an infidel. The plot is complex; there are wild sea chases, attempted rescues, etc. Most critics today disparage the work, but H. W. Boynton, in his biography of Cooper (1931), thought it one of the author's best.

Wings of the Dove, The (1902), a novel by HENRY JAMES. James, somewhat hampered by the prudery imposed on him by English social conventions, devised a complicated and rather bizarre plot. Kate Croy is in love with a journalist, Merton Densher, but will not marry him until he is financially secure. She becomes acquainted with Milly Theale, an American heiress, and learns that an ailment from which Milly is suffering dooms her to an early death. Kate concocts a fantastic scheme; without re-vealing her motive she tells Densher to take an interest in Milly, who promptly falls in love with him and makes a will leaving him all her money. But an English lord, who himself had the notion of marrying Milly and inheriting her wealth, learns of the scheme and reveals it to Milly. She dies soon after and Densher receives a large check for his legacy. He offers to marry Kate if she will consent to let him destroy the check, but she demands a recompense: he must swear he is not in love with Milly's mem-ory. This he refuses to do; and the deal is off. The book is regarded as a culmination of James's final style, along with THE AMBASSADORS and THE GOLDEN BOWL; for many readers its diffi-culties are redeemed by Milly's charm and fortitude. An opera based on the novel was produced in New York (1961) with libretto by Ethan Ayer and music by DOUGLAS MOORE.

Winkle, Rip van. See RIP VAN WINKLE.

Winnebago Indians. A Sioux tribe, originally inhabitants of Wisconsin in the region south of Green Bay. Many are still found here, others on a Nebraska reservation. They were often friendly to white men, and helped in such cam-paigns as the ones against Black Hawk. The greatest authority on the tribe was Paul Radin, who discussed them in his report, *The Winnebago Tribe* (1923), for the Bureau of American Ethnology, and also in *The World of Primitive Man* (1953). Radin showed that a Winnebago chieftain performed many other functions than those commonly assigned to him. His lodge was an asylum for wrongdoers, and he acted as intercessor between wrongdoers and their victims; in general he was a symbol of peace rather than war. Radin also prepared an account of *Winnebago Hero Cycles* (1948).

Winner, Septimus ["Alice Hawthorne"] (b. Philadelphia, May 11, 1827—d. 1902), song writer, music publisher, author. Winner compiled instruction books for playing musical instruments, wrote for *Graham's Magazine*, composed or arranged pieces for the violin and piano, and was a member of the publishing firm of Winner & Shuster. Several of his pieces he published under the pseudonym Alice Hawthorne—among them his most famous song, *Listen to the Mocking Bird* (1855).

Winner Take Nothing (1933), fourteen short stories and sketches by ERNEST HEMINGWAY. Few of the stories in this volume have attracted much attention. Characteristic is *A Natural History of the Dead*, a bitter attack on war which recalls a scene near Milan in World War I. Characters in other stories are prostitutes, neurotics, American tourists, gamblers.

Winning of Barbara Worth, The (1911), a novel by HAROLD BELL WRIGHT. The scene is Rubio City, a recently founded town in Colorado. In a sand storm nearby many travelers die, including a beautiful woman, near whom is found a girl, still living. The girl is adopted by Jefferson Worth and grows up to be an intelligent and beautiful young woman. She falls in love with Willard Holmes, a young engineer from New York but their marriage is opposed by his wealthy guardian. Of course the solution is inevitable. A casket is found with documents establishing Barbara's identity; she is the daughter of Willard's guardian's brother. The book's initial sales were tremendous and it became Wright's most popular work.

Winning of the West, The (4 v., 1889–96), a historical study by THEODORE ROOSEVELT. Using original sources, Roosevelt gave a detailed account of the expansion of our country following the Revolution and at the same time showed the immense significance of this expansion as determining the entire character of the United States. He was undoubtedly influenced in viewpoint and style by the writings of FRANCIS PARKMAN.

Winslow, Edward (b. England, Oct. 18, 1595—d. May 8, 1655), government official, colonist, author. Winslow came to New England on the MAYFLOWER, several times returned to England and then came back to the colonies, was governor of Plymouth in 1633, 1636, and 1644. He was appointed by Oliver Cromwell commissioner of an expedition to the West Indies (1655) which took Jamaica away from

Spain; he died at sea on the trip home. He was a skillful and vivid writer. Along with WILLIAM BRADFORD [1] he wrote the book, called in error *Mourt's Relation* (1622), which is the first account of the Plymouth settlement. On his own he wrote GOOD NEWS FROM NEW ENGLAND (1624), a lively account of personal experiences; *Hypocrisy Unmasked* (1646); *The Glorious Progress of the Gospel Amongst the Indians in New England* (1649); *Platform of Church Discipline* (1653). See GEORGE MORTON.

Winslow, Ola Elizabeth (b. Sheepscot, Me., 1885[?]—   ), biographer, historian, teacher. Miss Winslow studied at Stanford and Johns Hopkins universities and the University of Chicago. She was a professor of English at Wellesley, Radcliffe, and Goucher colleges from 1914 until her retirement in 1950. Her biographies established her as an authority on American colonial religious history. *Jonathan Edwards 1703–1758* (1940) won a Pulitzer prize in biography; it presented a vivid account of the life and times of one of America's early poets and clergymen. Miss Winslow also wrote *American Broadside Verse* (1930); *Meetinghouse Hill* (1952); *Master Roger Williams* (1957); *John Bunyan* (1961).

Winslow, Thyra Samter (b. Fort Smith, Ark., March 15, 1893—d. Dec. 2, 1961), short-story writer, novelist, screen scenarist. Mrs. Winslow, an adept storyteller with a strong sense of character, set some of her stories in Arkansas; others are about the New York theater. Among her books: *Picture Frames* (1923); *Show Business* (1926); *People Round the Corner* (1927); *Blueberry Pie* (1932); *My Own, My Native Land* (short stories, 1939); *Window Panes* (short stories, 1946); *Divorcée* (1953); *The Sex Without Sentiment* (short stories, 1954). She wrote several books on weight reduction, among them *Think Yourself Thin* (1952) and *Be Slim, Stay Slim* (1955).

Winsor, Justin (b. Boston, Jan. 2, 1831—d. Oct. 22, 1897), historian, librarian, editor. This eminent scholar studied abroad, then joined the staff of the Boston Public Library in 1866; he became superintendent in 1868 and instituted many reforms. In 1877 he became librarian of Harvard University. He was a founder of the American Library Association (1876), its president from 1876 to 1885; also a founder of the *Library Journal*. He edited THE NARRATIVE AND CRITICAL HISTORY OF AMERICA (8 v., 1884–89); and he also published a *Reader's Handbook of the American Revolution* (1879); *Christopher Columbus* (1891); *Cartier to Frontenac* (1894); *The Mississippi Basin* (1895); *The Westward Movement* (1897).

Winsor, Kathleen (b. Olivia, Minn., Oct. 16, 1919—   ), novelist. Miss Winsor fared badly with critics, profitably with readers. Her first book, FOREVER AMBER (1944), is set in Restoration England, and centers on a country girl who goes to London and eventually becomes Charles II's mistress. The heroine's sexual activities attracted many readers, and the book was an enormous best seller. Later novels are *Star Money* (1950), *The Lovers* (1952), and *America Without Love* (1957).

Winter, William (b. Gloucester, Mass., July 15, 1836—d. June 30, 1917), drama critic, essayist, poet. While still a student at Harvard Law School, Winter published his first book, *Poems* (1855). Encouraged by Longfellow to devote himself to literature, Winter never practiced law; after a brief stint as reviewer for the Boston *Transcript* he moved to New York, where he joined the "Bohemians" who met in PFAFF'S CELLAR on Broadway. He worked on the *Saturday Press*, then became drama critic for the New York *Albion* and the New York *Tribune*. By temperament and training a romanticist, he could not accept the new realistic drama of such playwrights as Ibsen and Pinero. After his resignation from the *Tribune* he continued to write reviews for *Harper's Weekly*. H. L. Mencken called him "the greatest bad critic who ever lived."

Among Winter's many books are biographies of Henry Irving (1885) and Edward Booth (1893); also *Shakespeare's England* (1886); *Gray Days and Gold* (1892); *Shadows of the Stage* (1892–95); *Shakespeare on the Stage* (2 v., 1911–15). He continued to write verse: *My Witness* (1871); *Thistle-Down* (1878); *Wanderers* (1892); *Poems* (a collected edition, 1909). *The Wallet of Time* (1913) is a collection of *Tribune* pieces. Volumes of reminiscence are *Other Days* (1908); *Old Friends* (1909); *Vagrant Memories* (1915).

Wintergreen, John P. The leading character in OF THEE I SING (1932), a musical comedy of political satire. Wintergreen runs for President on a platform of love. During a whirlwind campaign he publicly proposes marriage in forty-eight states to Mary Turner, a campaign worker who can bake wonderful corn muffins.

Winterich, John T[racy] (b. Middletown, Conn., May 25, 1891—   ), editor, bibliophile, writer. In *Another Day, Another Dollar* (1947), his autobiography, Winterich discusses the vocations he pursued as a youth—from reader of gas-meters to trolley conductor and book peddler. Only the last led to his real vocation—the study of books. He became an authority on first editions and book collecting. A graduate of Brown University, Winterich taught English there in 1912–13, then worked on the Springfield (Mass.) *Republican*, later served as editor for various magazines: *Stars and Stripes, Home Sector, American Legion Weekly, Colophon, New Colophon, Saturday Review*. Among his books: *A Primer of Book Collecting* (1927); *Collector's Choice* (1928); *Books and the Man* (1929); *Early American Books and Printing* (1935); *Twenty-Three Books* (1938); *Three Lantern Slides* (1949); *The Grolier Club* (1950).

Winters, [Arthur] Yvor (b. Chicago, Oct. 17, 1900—d. Jan. 25, 1968), poet, critic, teacher. Winters attended the University of Chicago and received his M.A. degree from the University of Colorado. He taught English at Stanford University, and was well known both as poet and critic. Although his work is often considered to be a part of the NEW CRITICISM, his critical theory is distinctly individual and often at variance with more prevalent opinions. He maintained that the critic should be concerned with the moral evaluation of a work of art, and that a poem should be a rational statement about human experience in which the poet is "seeking to state a true moral judgment." His books of criticism include *Primitivism and Decadence* (1937), *Maule's Curse* (1938), and *The Anatomy of Nonsense* (1943), all of which are collected in *In Defense of Reason* (1947); *Edward Arlington Robinson* (1946); *The Function of Criticism: Problems and Exercises* (1957); *The Poetry of W. B. Yeats* (1960); and *The Poetry of J. V. Cunningham* (1961).

In his poetry, which is of a traditional nature, Winters adhered to his critical theories on the necessity of balance between reason and emotion; his verse was awarded the Bollingen Prize in 1960. His books of poetry include *The Immobile Wind* (1921); *The Magpie's Shadow* (1922); *The Bare Hills* (1927); *The Proof* (1930); *The Journey* (1931); *Before Disaster* (1934); *Poems* (1940); *The Giant Weapon* (1943); *Collected Poems* (1952). He edited and contributed to *Twelve Poets of the Pacific* (1937).

Winterset (1935), a tragedy in verse. See MAXWELL ANDERSON.

Winthrop, John (b. England, Jan. 12, 1588—d. March 26, 1649), colonial official. Winthrop attended Trinity College, Cambridge, and was admitted to the Inner Temple. A man of con-

sequence and intensely religious, he was elected governor of the Massachusetts Bay Co., superintended the arrangements for departure, and arrived in Salem on June 12, 1630. For the greater part of his life thereafter he was either governor or deputy governor of the colony, and was always recognized as its leading citizen. He did not believe in democracy and presented proof against it from the Bible by saying there was "no such government in Israel."

Winthrop's *A Model of Christian Charity* (1630) was first published in full (1838) by the Massachusetts Historical Society. He also wrote *A Short Story of the Antinomians* (1644). His *Journal* was first published, with James Savage as editor, as the *History of New England, 1630–49* (2 v., 1825), and was reprinted, with J. K. Hosmer as editor, as *Winthrop's Journal* (2 v., 1908). His *Papers* were edited by A. B. Forbes (5 v., 1929–47, with others to follow). R. C. Winthrop's *Life and Letters* (2 v., 1869) gives other materials. The Rev. J. H. Twichell, Mark Twain's friend, wrote *John Winthrop* (1891) and edited *Some Old Puritan Love-Letters: John and Margaret Winthrop, 1618–38* (1893). Winthrop has appeared occasionally in fiction, for example in Catherine M. Sedgwick's HOPE LESLIE (1827) and Irving Bacheller's *A Candle in the Wilderness* (1930). He is also portrayed in *The Scarlet Letter* (1850) by Nathaniel Hawthorne.

Winthrop, Theodore (b. New Haven, Conn., Sept. 22, 1828—d. June 10, 1861), poet, novelist, businessman. Winthrop was a descendant of both JOHN WINTHROP and JONATHAN EDWARDS. He traveled for his health in Europe, became acquainted with Panama in connection with his work for a steamship line, also toured extensively in the Northwest. For a time he practiced law, then determined to devote himself to writing. When the Civil War broke out he enlisted and was killed while leading a charge at the Battle of Big Bethel, Va.

His books were all published posthumously, one of them, *Mr. Waddy's Return*, as late as 1904. For a time these books, mostly novels, won him wide renown. In 1884 his sister edited *The Life and Poems of Theodore Winthrop*. His three most important works were novels: *Cecil Dreeme* (1862), the story of a mysterious painter done in the style of Charles Brockden Brown and Nathaniel Hawthorne; *John Brent* (1862), one of the earliest novels of the West; and *Edwin Brothertoft* (1862), a romance of the American Revolution. Winthrop's style was somewhat esoteric and strained, perhaps too literary. However, in two volumes of personal reminiscence, *The Canoe and the Saddle* (1863) and *Life in the Open Air* (1863), Winthrop wrote vivaciously and attractively.

Winwar, Frances (b. Italy, May 3, 1900—), novelist, biographer, critic. Miss Winwar's family name was originally Vinciguerra; she adopted an English translation of this for her writings. She is chiefly known for her biographies of famous people; her books, though sometimes sentimentalized, are historically sound.

Among them: *The Ardent Flame* (1927), about Francesca da Rimini; *Poor Splendid Wings* (1933), about the Pre-Raphaelite group; *The Romantic Rebels* (1935), concerning Keats, Shelley and Byron; *Oscar Wilde and the Yellow '90s* (1940); *American Giant: Walt Whitman and His Times* (1941); *The Life of the Heart* (1945), about George Sand; *The Saint and the Devil: Joan of Arc and Gilles de Rais* (1948); *Immortal Lovers* (1950), about the Brownings; *The Haunted Palace* (1959), about Edgar Allan Poe. Among her novels: *The Sentimentalist* (1943) and *The Last Love of Camille* (1954).

Wirt, William (b. Bladensburg, Md., Nov. 8, 1772—d. Feb. 18, 1834), essayist, lawyer. A Southern gentleman of the old school, Wirt combined polite literature with a legal career. He practiced law in Richmond, gaining fame as

prosecutor in the trial of Aaron Burr. He was appointed attorney-general by President Monroe (1817–29). Wirt also practiced law in Baltimore and ran unsuccessfully as Presidential candidate of the Anti-Masonic party against ANDREW JACKSON (1832). His earliest writing was a popular series of essays, THE LETTERS OF THE BRITISH SPY, printed anonymously in the Richmond *Argus* (1803). These were leisurely descriptions of Southern scenes in a style reminiscent of Addison. Wirt also published *The Rainbow* (1804) and *Sketches of the Life and Character of Patrick Henry* (1817).

Wise, Henry Augustus ["Harry Gringo"] (b. Brooklyn, N.Y., May 24, 1819—d. April 2, 1869), naval officer, memoirist, novelist. Wise became a midshipman at an early age; he served in the Mexican and then in the Civil War. After the war he served in the Bureau of Ordnance and became a captain. In the meantime he had traveled widely, publishing accounts of his war experiences in *Los Gringos, or, An Inside View of Mexico and California, with Wanderings in Peru, Chile, and Polynesia* (1849). Apparently it was from the title of this book that Wise derived his pen name, under which he wrote some unimportant fiction. He also wrote *Tales for the Marines* (1855).

Wise, Isaac Mayer (b. Bohemia, March 29, 1819—d. March 26, 1900), rabbi, editor, historian. Wise came to the United States in 1846, serving congregations at Albany and Cincinnati. In the latter city he organized a new group, breaking away from strict orthodoxy, called Reform Judaism. He became editor of a magazine called *The American Israelite* in English and *Die Deborah* in German, in which he expounded his views. He also wrote numerous books, among them *History of the Israelitish Nation from Abraham to the Present Time* (1854); *The Cosmic God* (1876); and *Reminiscences* (1901). His *Selected Writings* appeared in 1900.

Wise, John (b. Roxbury, Mass., Aug. [?], 1652—d. April 8, 1725), Congregational clergyman, writer. This courageous, witty, and foresighted clergyman served as minister of various churches in Connecticut and Massachusetts and finally was called to Ipswich, Massachusetts. He was also chaplain in two military expeditions, including that against Quebec. He was a leader in protests against arbitrary taxation and was tried for his protests on orders by Sir Edmund Andros, condemned, and imprisoned, but later restored as minister. He boldly presented a petition in behalf of the victims of the Salem witchcraft trials and defended government in church and state in THE CHURCHES' QUARREL ESPOUSED (1710).

Most influential of his writings was a continuation of the argument in the 1710 book in *A Vindication of the Government of New England Churches* (1717), in which he expounds, in direct opposition to the Calvinist doctrine of the "elect," ideas of human equality that undoubtedly influenced the writing of the Declaration of Independence; it was reprinted in 1772 and widely read in the colonies. Wise had great literary gifts, including a robust humor as a controversialist. George Allan Cook wrote a biography of Wise that involved close analysis of his writing, *John Wise, Early American Democrat* (1952).

Wise, Stephen S[amuel] (b. Hungary, March 17, 1874—d. April 19, 1949), rabbi, editor, writer on ethical and social problems. The son of Aaron Wise (1844–1896), an eminent rabbi who came to the United States in 1874, Stephen Wise likewise entered the ministry and in 1907 founded a separate Jewish group which centered in what he called a "Free Synagogue." The freedom consisted largely in the latitude allowed the rabbi in expression of views on all topics, social and political as well as spiritual, and in the refusal to sell pews to members. Wise was an exciting speaker and drew large audiences, and some branches of the Free Synagogue were founded elsewhere. One of the founders of the Zionist Organization of America, he founded also the liberal Jewish Institute of Religion and was active in war relief. Among his writings: *How to Face Life* (1917); *Child Versus Parent* (1922); *The Great Betrayal* (1930). He founded (1936) and edited a magazine, *Opinion: A Journal of Jewish Life and Letters.* Justine Wise Polier and James Waterman Wise edited *The Personal Letters of Stephen Wise* (1956).

Wissler, Clark (b. near Cambridge City, Ind., Sept. 18, 1870—d. Aug. 25, 1947), anthropologist, psychologist, teacher, museum administrator. Wissler, after graduation from Indiana State University, taught psychology at Columbia University, where he took his doctorate. In later years he became an authority in the study of mental growth and development, particularly as related to education. He joined the staff of the American Museum of Natural History in 1902 and was regularly promoted until he became curator. He also taught at Columbia, New York University, and the Institute of Human Relations at Yale. His interest in psychological problems led Wissler into anthropological research; he conducted field studies among Indian tribes and made extensive ethnographical collections for the Museum. He made a systematic summary of American Indian life in his classic volume, *The American Indian: An Introduction to the Anthropology of the New World* (1917). Among his other books: *North American Indians of the Plains* (1912); *Man and Culture* (1922); *Social Anthropology* (1929); *Indians of the United States* (1940).

Wister, Owen (b. Philadelphia, July 14, 1860—d. July 21, 1938), novelist, short-story writer, essayist, biographer. Wister, the grandson of the actress Fanny Kemble, attended St. Paul's School, Concord, N.H., where his first literary appearance was made in *Horae Scholasticae*, and Harvard University, where Theodore Roosevelt became his lifelong friend. Wister was at first a student of music, then of the law, but when illness led him to the ranches of Wyoming he was so impressed with the country that he was inspired to write his stories of the West, laid mainly in that state and of much higher literary merit than most of the numerous "westerns" that have appeared since. Wister's most famous story was THE VIRGINIAN (1902). The book was dedicated to Roosevelt and contained a number of portraits drawn from actual persons (cf. Earle F. Walbridge, *Do Novelists Use Real People?*, *Golden Book*, June, 1928). The book sold more than 1,600,000 copies in English, many more in other languages, ran as a stage medium for Dustin Farnum for many years, and was the basis for four motion pictures.

Wister's PHILOSOPHY FOUR (1903) is a story of undergraduate life at Harvard. *U. S. Grant* (1900) and *The Seven Ages of Washington* (1907) are biographies. He also wrote *Red Men and White* (1895); *Lin McLean* (1898); *LADY BALTIMORE* (1906); *The Pentecost of Calamity* (1915); *When West Was West* (1928); *Roosevelt: The Story of a Friendship* (1930); and other books. Because he was opposed to making war on Germany and because he shared Roosevelt's strong antipathy for Woodrow Wilson, he wrote a denunciatory sonnet on the latter President which aroused wide criticism.

Unquestionably *The Virginian,* a pioneer in

its field, gave great impetus to Western novels. Wister is sometimes criticized for the saccharinity of some of his work, but parts of *The Virginian* are in the tradition of the new realism; indeed, at the request of Roosevelt, Wister excised an eye-gouging episode as too offensive. Recent writers of westerns do not in general follow Wister, although they usually make a point of introducing women characters like Wister's schoolteacher heroine.

One of Wister's severest critics was Alexander Woollcott, who called him "Owen Wisteria," but Van Wyck Brooks found both poetry and truth in Wister's treatment of the West. *Owen Wister Out West: His Journals and Letters* (1958), illuminatingly edited by Fanny Kemble Wister, the novelist's daughter, contains some fine descriptions of scenery, travel, people, and the changing Western life.

Witching Hour, The (1907), a play by AUGUSTUS THOMAS. As far back as 1890 Thomas became interested in "mental telepathy" as a basis for dramatic treatment. In this successful psychological drama about a gambler he also included hypnotism; there were so many sensational incidents that he didn't bother with feminine interest.

Witherspoon, John (b. Scotland, Feb. 5, 1723—d. Nov. 15, 1794), clergyman, teacher, college administrator. Witherspoon served as a

minister in Scotland, became a follower of the exiled Stuarts, and engaged actively in theological controversy. His *Ecclesiastical Characteristics* (1753), directed against religious liberals, was a bitter satire and a best seller. Another satire, *History of a Corporation of Servants* (1765), was less successful. From 1756 to 1768 he published sermons and essays that were widely read.

Witherspoon was elected president of the College of New Jersey at Princeton, and came to this country in 1768 to assume his duties. Besides his administrative functions, he also taught several subjects and was considered a great teacher by such undergraduates as James Madison. He became an ardent patriot, was elected to the New Jersey Constitutional Convention, the Continental Congress (where in 1776 he signed the Declaration of Independence), and to numerous Congressional committees. He continued to act as president of the college until his death.

One of Witherspoon's later writings was *Considerations on the Nature and Extent of the Legislative Authority of the British Parliament* (1774). He was always interested in the linguistic peculiarities of the colonists, coined numerous words, and in an article published in the *Pennsylvania Journal and Weekly Advertiser* (May 9, May 16, May 23, May 30, 1781) he first used the term *Americanism.* V. Lansing Collins wrote *President Witherspoon* (2 v., 1925), and T. J. Wertenbaker contributed an account of him to *The Lives of 18 from Princeton* (1946).

Within the Law (1912), a play by BAYARD VEILLER. Veiller, a very able theatrical craftsman, called his play a "melodrama" and did not hesitate to use most of the sensational devices associated with that type. His heroine, Mary Turner, is a poor working girl who is railroaded to prison by a wealthy scoundrel who accuses her of theft from his department store. When she gets out she contrives a clever blackmailing scheme, within the law, and manages to get revenge. She finally marries the scoundrel's son. The play was a great hit.

Wizard of Oz. See L. F. BAUM; WONDERFUL WIZARD OF OZ.

Wolcott, Roger (b. Windsor, Conn., Jan. 4, 1679—d. May 17, 1767), soldier, public official, poet. Wolcott, a man of many talents and interests, was deputy governor of Connecticut (1741–50), a major general, then governor of Connecticut (1751–54). His verse, rather uninspired, appeared in *Poetical Meditations* (1725).

Wolfe, Bertram D. (b. Brooklyn, N.Y., January 19, 1896—   ), writer. Wolfe studied at the College of the City of New York, the University of Mexico, and Columbia University. His early writings dealt with the history, culture, art, and literature of Spain and Mexico. In 1939 he turned to the history and culture of Soviet Russia, in which field he established a distinguished reputation. Not only was his subject matter topical, but the accuracy of his predictions revealed a thorough comprehension of

Soviet motivations and communist ideology. Wolfe's books include: *Portrait of Mexico* (1937); *Diego Rivera, His Life and Times* (1939); *Three Who Made a Revolution* (1948); *Khrushchev and Stalin's Ghost* (1956); *Six Keys to the Soviet System* (1956); *Communist Totalitarianism* (1961).

Wolfe, Nero. See REX STOUT.

Wolfe, Thomas [Clayton] (b. Asheville, N.C., Oct. 3, 1900—d. Sept. 15, 1938), novelist, short-story writer, playwright. Wolfe's father, a stonecutter, liked to recite Shakespeare to his son and encouraged him to read histories that

UPI

glorified the United States. His mother operated a boardinghouse in Asheville, where young Wolfe attended first the local public school and later a private school. He entered the University of North Carolina at fifteen and showed a deep interest in literature and particularly in drama; he was encouraged to pursue the latter subject by Frederick Koch. Two of Wolfe's plays, *The Return of Buck Gavin* (1924), in which he played the leading role, and *The Third Night* (1938), were produced by Koch's Carolina Playmakers. After graduation Wolfe went to Harvard, largely because of the fame of GEORGE PIERCE BAKER's course in playwriting, "Workshop 47." Under Baker's tutelage he wrote *Welcome to Our City* (produced at Harvard, 1923), in which he created a southern city named "Altamont," based on his native Asheville—the same Altamont that provides the background for his first novel, *Look Homeward,*

Angel. Baker, however, who became the prototype for Professor Hatcher in Wolfe's second novel, OF TIME AND THE RIVER, discouraged Wolfe's ambitions as a playwright.

After receiving his M.A. from Harvard, Wolfe went to New York, where he became an instructor of English at New York University, a position he held intermittently from 1924 to 1930. While trying to find a producer for his play, MANNERHOUSE (1948), he met the gifted stage designer and writer, Aline Bernstein, whom he tempestuously adored for some years, and who appears as Esther Jack in THE WEB AND THE ROCK and *You Can't Go Home Again.* Mrs. Bernstein's novel *The Journey Down* (1938) deals with her relationship with Wolfe.

Wolfe made several trips to Europe, less for enjoyment than for the leisure to write without interruptions. By the end of the 1920's he had completed the vast manuscript of his first novel. His literary agent, Madeline Boyd, took the manuscript to MAXWELL PERKINS, a senior editor of Charles Scribner's Sons, who recognized immediately both the greatness of the work and the impossibility of publishing it as it was. LOOK HOMEWARD, ANGEL: A STORY OF THE BURIED LIFE (1929) was the first product of the six-year-long "creative partnership" between Wolfe and Perkins, whose judicious editing and cutting were largely responsible for turning the large and somewhat chaotic manuscript into a finished and excellent work. The novel, largely autobiographical, deals with the young manhood of Eugene Gant, his life in the southern city of Altamont, and his journey to New York. Although the book was generally well received on publication, citizens of Asheville were scandalized by what they considered to be unfriendly revelations of their lives.

In 1930 Wolfe again left for Europe, where he continued to write. *A Portrait of Bascom Hawke,* a short novel, was published in 1932 and tied for first place in Scribner's short novel contest. Meanwhile Wolfe had completed another massive manuscript dealing again with his own experiences; in 1933 he brought it to Perkins, and the two set out to reduce to order its multiplicity of episodes. *Of Time and the River* (1935) was somewhat less successful than Wolfe's first novel, primarily because of its lack of structure and the tenuous connections between episodes.

Although Wolfe's "partnership" with Perkins came to an end after the publication of this novel, Wolfe spoke warmly of him and acknowledged his help in the preparation of the book at a lecture for the Writer's Conference at Boulder, Colo., in the summer of 1935. The lecture was published in 1936 as *The Story of a Novel.* Also in 1935 Wolfe published a collection of short stories, *From Death to Morning.* He began work on a new novel which would deal with a different autobiographical hero, George Webber, and turned over the partially completed manuscript to Harper and Brothers in 1938 before going on a vacation in the West. In July he developed pneumonia and was hospitalized in Seattle; he was operated on because of a brain infection and died in Johns Hopkins Hospital in Baltimore in September.

At Harper's another devoted and capable editor, Edward C. Aswell, brought order to the eight-foot pile of manuscript Wolfe had left behind and published it as two separate novels and a book of short stories: *The Web and the Rock* (1939); *You Can't Go Home Again* (1940); and *The Hills Beyond* (1941). Maxwell Perkins appears as Foxhall Edwards in the first two of these.

In general, Wolfe's novels have been received with great enthusiasm. Young readers continue to devour his books for their lyrical and expansive echoing of their own aspirations; and even the most hardened Jamesian must admit Wolfe's genius for satire. Hamilton Basso and others have stressed the way in which Wolfe refused to accept the Marxist disillusionment of the 1920's and 1930's and held to faith in America, as in his famous line in *You Can't Go Home Again:* "I believe we are lost here in America, but I believe we shall be found," and in his ecstatic delight in the grandeur of American scenery.

Wolfe's *Letters to His Mother* (1943) were edited by John Terry, and a further collection of *Letters* was made (1956) by Elizabeth Nowell. Books about Wolfe include Herbert Muller's *Thomas Wolfe* (1947); Pamela Hansford Johnson's *Hungry Gulliver* (1948); Richard Walser's *The Enigma of Thomas Wolfe: Biographical and Critical Selections* (1953); Louis D. Rubin, Jr.'s *Thomas Wolfe: The Weather of His Youth* (1955); F. C. Watkins' *Thomas Wolfe's Characters: Portraits from Life* (1957); and Elizabeth Nowell's *Thomas Wolfe* (1960). William B. Wisdom's collection of Thomas Wolfe material, presented to the Harvard College Library, was described in the *Harvard Alumni Bulletin* as being "in its size and completeness a record of a man and a man's mind probably without parallel." *Thomas Wolfe and His Family* by Mabel Wolfe Wheaton (one of Wolfe's sisters) and LeGette Blythe (1961) gives what purports to be an unfictionalized account of some of the events and characters in *Look Homeward, Angel.* See also LOST GENERATION.

Wolfert's Roost (1855), nineteen stories and sketches by WASHINGTON IRVING. These miscellaneous pieces, first published in the *Knickerbocker Magazine,* take their title from the "doughty and valorous little pile," first erected in 1656, which Irving purchased and reconstructed as his beloved Sunnyside. Charming descriptions of scenes in and around Westchester County alternate with lighthearted fables of the American past and tongue-in-cheek Spanish romances. The book was widely popular when first published, and modern critics compare it favorably with Irving's best early works.

Wolff, Mary Evaline [Sister Mary Madeleva] (b. Cumberland, Wis., May 24, 1887—d. July 25, 1964), teacher, poet, essayist, medievalist. Sister Mary Madeleva became a member of the Order of the Sisters of the Holy Cross in 1908. She then began a distinguished career as an English teacher, scholar, and poet. In 1934 she became president of St. Mary's College in Notre Dame, Ind. She wrote many books, mainly in verse. Among them are *Knights Errant and Other Poems* (1923); *Gates and Other Poems* (1938); *Christmas Eve and Other Poems* (1938); *Selected Poems* (1939); *Collected Poems* (1947). Among her prose writings: *Chaucer's Nuns and Other Essays* (1925); *The Pearl—A Study in Spiritual Dryness* (1925); and *The Lost Language and Other Essays on Chaucer* (1951).

Wolfville (1897, 1923), a collection of stories by ALFRED HENRY LEWIS (Dan Quin). These became so popular that they were followed by three other collections: *Wolfville Days* (1902); *Wolfville Nights* (1902); *Wolfville Folks* (1908). Wolfville is supposedly a frontier town in Arizona, the inhabitants of which are miners and cattle raisers. The stories are told by an "Old Cattleman" whom J. Frank Dobie calls "a substantial and flavorsome creation."

Woman's Home Companion. A monthly magazine founded (1873) in Cleveland as the *Ladies' Home Companion,* a magazine for children. It was bought by *Farm & Fireside* in 1884 and the place of publication was changed to Springfield, Ohio. Like *Farm & Fireside* it became part of the Crowell-Collier chain, with editorial offices in New York. It published both fiction and nonfiction, and had for a time a circulation above 4 million. It ceased publication in 1956.

Women, The (1937), a play by CLARE BOOTHE LUCE. A viperish, all-female production, *The Women* concerns Mary Haines, whose marriage is threatened by the middle-aged philandering and maliciousness of her wealthy New York friends; only when she herself adopts the rules of the Park Avenue jungle is she able to retrieve her husband. Critics found the work insubstantial, but audiences of both sexes found it amusing—it ran well over a year. It was made into a movie in 1939, again in 1956.

Wonder-Book for Girls and Boys, A (1852), a collection of Greek myths retold for children by NATHANIEL HAWTHORNE. Here Hawthorne divested his mind of the moral conflict and dark fantasy that he applied to so much of his adult fiction, and wrote simply, charmingly, and even a little naively. The myths are carefully purged of all elements Hawthorne thought unsuitable for children; the book was followed by a similar collection, TANGLEWOOD TALES, in 1853.

Wonderful One-Hoss Shay, The. See THE DEACON'S MASTERPIECE.

Wonderful Wizard of Oz, The (1900), a story for children by L. FRANK BAUM. It is a fairy tale that uses American materials. Dorothy and her dog Toto journey from Kansas to the imaginary realm of Oz, meeting on the way such marvelous creatures as the Scarecrow, the Tin Woodman, the Cowardly Lion, and others. In the end they return to Kansas. In 1902 the book became a successful musical extravaganza, starring David Montgomery and Fred Stone. It was made into a silent film in 1925, broadcast as a radio drama in 1938, turned into a Technicolor musical in 1939. Baum was much plagued by his publishers and admirers to produce sequels, and he wrote a number of them: *The New Wizard of Oz* (1903); *Ozma of Oz* (1907); *Dorothy and the Wizard of Oz* (1908); *The Road to Oz* (1909); *The Emerald City of Oz* (1910); *The Patchwork Girl of Oz* (1913). After Baum's death the series was carried on, virtually *ad infinitum*, by Ruth Plumly Thompson and others. Martin Gardner and Russel B. Nye wrote *The Wizard of Oz and Who He Was* (1957).

Wonders of the Invisible World, The (1693), by COTTON MATHER. This tract is an account of witches and their alleged misdeeds, together with a general discussion of the supernatural. It contains an account of the SALEM WITCHCRAFT TRIALS. ROBERT CALEF replied to Mather in MORE WONDERS OF THE INVISIBLE WORLD, which was ready for publication in 1697; no Boston publisher dared to issue it until 1700. It greatly angered the Mathers, and Increase Mather had Calef's book burnt in Harvard Yard.

Wonder-Working Providence of Sion's Saviour (1654), a history of Massachusetts from 1628 to 1651 by EDWARD JOHNSON.

Wood, Charles Erskine Scott (b. Erie, Pa., Feb. 20, 1852—d. Jan. 22, 1944), soldier, lawyer, writer. A graduate of West Point, Wood helped explore Alaska, also took part in several wars against the Indians. But he was finally so outraged by injustices against the red man that he resigned from the army with the rank of colonel. While still in the army he had studied law, which he practiced in Oregon. Later he removed to California, with which many of his writings deal. His second wife was the poet Sara Bard Field, who after his death edited, in collaboration with Genevieve Taggard, his *Collected Poems* (1949).

Wood's writings, all marked by poetic sensitivity and a gift for phrase, show his keen, almost exacerbated sense of justice. His best known book, *The Poet in the Desert* (1915), was enlarged and rewritten in 1930. He also wrote *Maia* (1918); *Circe* (1919); *Poems from the Ranges* (1929); *Sonnets to Sappho* (1940). His best known prose writings are *Heavenly Discourse* (1927), a satire on war, injustice, and other social evils, and *Earthly Discourse* (1937); he also wrote *A Book of Tales, Being Myths of the North American Indians* (1901).

Wood, Clement (b. Tuscaloosa, Ala., Sept. 1, 1888—d. Oct. 26, 1950), lawyer, teacher, anthologist, author. Out of all Wood's immense literary and other activities little is remembered. He was deeply interested in Negro songs and did much to increase appreciation of them. His own poetry was skillful but rarely inspired. He was also interested in religion, was of a romantic bent, and a bitter, voluble opponent of racial and social injustice. His most famous poem, *De Glory Road*, was the title poem in a 1936 collection; another of his

gatherings was *The Greenwich Village Blues* (1926). He published several novels. In 1929 *Hunters of Heaven*, a discourse on American poetry, was published. Two useful manuals he compiled were *The Complete Rhyming Dictionary and Poet's Craft Book* (1936) and *Poet's Handbook* (1940). He taught in several private schools in New York City and New Jersey, and versification at the Washington Square Writing Center of New York University.

Wood, Grant (b. Anamosa, Iowa, Feb. 13, 1892—d. Feb. 12, 1942), painter. Wood was a Middle-Westerner whose realistic works are indigenously American. His paintings have a startling, sometimes humorous quality that sets him off from other important American artists. Trained at the Minneapolis Handicraft Guild, the Art Institute of Chicago, and the Academy Julian of Paris, he began his career as a metal craftsman and as a teacher in Iowa public schools. His popular satiric painting, *American Gothic* (1930), won a prize at the American exhibit of the Chicago Art Institute. Among other famous paintings by Wood are *Young Corn, Woman with Plants, Victorian Survival,* and the famous satirical painting *Daughters of Revolution* (1932), which created a spirited controversy. In a short book entitled *Revolt Against the City* (1935) Wood argued that the true America to which artists must turn for inspiration is that of the small town and the farm village. Darrell Garwood wrote a good account of Wood in *Artist in Iowa* (1944).

Wood, Sarah Sayward [Barrell] Keating (b. York, Me., Oct. 1, 1759—d. Jan. 6, 1855), novelist. Probably the earliest of Maine fiction-writers, "Madam Wood" wrote *Julia and the Illuminated Baron* (1800), *Amelia, or, The Influence of Virtue* (1802), *Ferdinand and Elmira* (1804), and *Tales of the Night* (1827).

Wood, William. See NEW ENGLAND'S PROSPECT.

Woodberry, George E[dward] (b. Beverly, Mass., May 2, 1855—d. Jan. 2, 1930), critic, poet, teacher. Remembered as a literary critic and scholar and a popular, inspiring teacher rather than as a poet, Woodberry himself conceded that his poetic genius was "less than it should have been." He was educated at Harvard University, studying there under such eminent teachers as Henry Adams, James Russell Lowell, and C. E. Norton. After a brief period as professor of English at the University of Nebraska, he taught comparative literature at Columbia University. He frequently lectured in later years at other institutions and traveled much in Europe.

Except for his first book, *A History of Wood-Engraving* (1883), Woodberry's writings were chiefly literary. His own poetry includes *The North Shore Watch* (1890), a traditional elegy; *Wild Eden* (1899); *Ideal Passion* (1917), a collection of sonnets; and *The Roamer, and Other Poems* (1920). Among Woodberry's critical works are *Makers of Literature* (1900); *America in Literature* (1903); *The Appreciation of Literature* (1907); *Great Writers*

(1907); and *The Inspiration of Poetry* (1910). His biographies of Hawthorne (1902) and Emerson (1907) were followed by *The Life of Edgar Allan Poe* (2 v., 1909), an excellent study based on an earlier shorter biography (1885) and on *The Works of Edgar Allan Poe* (10 v., 1894–95), edited by Woodberry and E. C. STEDMAN.

In spite of his interest in American literature, Woodberry disliked the contemporary scene among American writers and thought that Americans had no chance of competing with Europeans in the creation of fine art. His greatest service was in stimulating the study of comparative literature, a new subject in American universities in his time.

Woodbridge, F[rederick] J[ames] E[ugene] (b. Windsor, Ont., March 26, 1867—d. June 1, 1940), teacher, philosopher, educational administrator. Woodbridge was a highly esteemed teacher of philosophy at the University of Minnesota and then at Columbia University, where he became dean of the graduate faculties. He was a founder (1923) of the *American Journal of Philosophy* and its first editor. Herbert W. Schneider, in his *History of American Philosophy* (1946), stresses the fact that it was Woodbridge, more than C. S. Peirce, who "encouraged Dewey to think naturalistically, to take metaphysics empirically, and to write *Experience and Nature.*" Among Woodbridge's principal works: *The Purpose of History* (1916); *The Realm of Mind* (1926); *The Son of Apollo: The Themes of Plato* (1929); *Nature and Mind* (1937); *An Essay on Nature* (1940).

Woodhull, Victoria [Claflin] (b. Homer, Ohio, Sept. 23, 1838—d. June 10, 1927), reformer, lecturer. Victoria Woodhull began her lively career by giving spiritualistic performances, telling fortunes, and selling patent medicines with her family. Twice married, she moved with her sister Tennessee Celeste Claflin to New York, where they were befriended by Cornelius Vanderbilt, Sr. The two sisters founded *Woodhull and Claflin's Weekly* (1870–76), a periodical devoted to social and political reform in which they advocated women's rights, free love, etc. Both the story of the notorious Beecher-Tilton affair (see HENRY WARD BEECHER) and the first English translation of the *Communist Manifesto* appeared in its pages (1872). The Equal Rights party nominated Victoria for President (1872), with Frederick Douglass as her running mate. Moving to England, Victoria married the scion of a wealthy banking family, and her sister married a baronet. With her daughter Zulu Maud Woodhull, Victoria published a periodical entitled *Humanitarian* (1892–1901).

Among the articles and pamphlets she wrote are *Origin, Tendencies and Principles of Government* (1871); *Stirpiculture* (1888); *The Alchemy of Maternity* (1889); *The Human Body the Temple of God* (with Tennessee, 1890); *And The Truth Shall Make You Free* (1894). The fullest biography is Emanie L. Sachs' *The Terrible Siren* (1928). Victoria and her sister are regarded as the models for Audacia Dangereyes in Harriet Beecher Stowe's novel *My Wife and I* (1871).

Woodman, Spare That Tree! (the opening line, now usually the title, of a poem called *The Oak*, first printed in the New York *Mirror,* Jan. 7, 1837; later included in *The Deserted Bride and Other Poems*, 1838), a poem by GEORGE POPE MORRIS. It immediately became famous and has been used as propaganda for the preservation of trees and forests.

Woodson, Carter Godwin (b. New Canton, Va., Dec. 19, 1875—d. April 3, 1950), historian, editor. Woodson devoted himself to writing chronicles and providing material about members of his own race. Among his books: *The Education of the Negro Prior to 1861* (1915); *History of the Negro Church* (1921); *The Negro in Our History* (1922); *Negro Orators and Their Orations* (1925); *African Heroes and Heroines* (1939). He founded and edited the *Journal of Negro History* (1916).

Woodward, William E. (b. Ridge Spring, S.C., Oct. 2, 1874—d. Sept. 27, 1950), editor, banker, writer. In his autobiography, *The Gift of Life* (1947), Woodward zestfully described his long and varied career as a cotton picker, copyreader, editor of subscription books, advertising agent, newspaperman, banker, and writer in various fields. He wrote two "debunking" (a word of his own invention) biographies, *George Washington, The Image and the Man* (1926) and *Meet General Grant* (1928), as well as a more sympathetic one, *Tom Paine: America's Godfather* (1945), and several novels. *A New American History* (1936) and *The Way Our People Lived* (1944) give his own view of the way this country has developed, and are both informative and amusing.

Woodworth, Samuel (b. Scituate, Mass., Jan. 13, 1784—d. Dec. 9, 1842), poet, editor, playwright. Woodworth was a skillful miscellaneous writer who caught the popular fancy with one poem, THE OLD OAKEN BUCKET. His verses were collected in *Poems, Odes, Songs, and Other Metrical Effusions* (1818). His best known play was THE FOREST ROSE (prod., 1825). He also wrote *The Widow's Son* (prod., 1825). *The Forest Rose*, one of the early Yankee plays, held the stage for forty years. F. A. Woodworth, his son, edited his *Poetical Works* (1861). See KNICKERBOCKER SCHOOL.

Woolf, S[amuel] J[ohnson] (b. New York City, Feb. 12, 1880—d. Dec. 3, 1948), painter, cartoonist, interviewer. Woolf was a striking combination of artist and journalist. He worked mainly for *The New York Times*, and at one time as a cover artist for *Time*. During World War I he scored a great success with his paintings of battlefields. In 1927 he hit on the idea of doing a portrait of each person whom he interviewed as a newspaperman. The writing and the art work were equally good, and these sketches (of which he did about 500 for the *Times* Sunday section) became famous. A number of the best were collected in *Drawn from Life* (1931). *Here Am I* (1941) is an autobiography. He also wrote *A Short History of Art* (1909).

Woollcott, Alexander [Humphreys] (b. Phalanx, N.J., Jan. 19, 1887—d. Jan. 23, 1943), newspaperman, drama critic, radio broadcaster, writer, anthologist. Woollcott was born in the Utopian colony the NORTH AMERICAN PHALANX, founded in 1843; his family lived in an eighty-five-room building, the last remnant of the colony. Woollcott graduated from Hamilton College, then became a bank clerk. He secured a job on *The New York Times,* where he switched from straight reporting to drama reporting. When the war came his physique and eyesight made direct service impossible, but he managed to get into the medical corps, and later went on the staff of *The Stars and Stripes.* After the war he went back to the *Times,* then worked for the *Herald,* later for the *World,* with which he remained until 1928. His personality and renown blossomed; he became perhaps the leading member of the famous ROUND TABLE group that assembled daily at the Algonquin Hotel. In 1929 he went on the air with a program called "The Town Crier." He told stories and boosted favorite causes; his praise or blame of a play or book was enough to make or break it. He never neglected the main chance and saw to it that his services were adequately rewarded. His magazine work (including that for *The New Yorker*) is said to have brought in a sum well over $125,-000, for example.

It is unlikely that anybody ever surpassed Woollcott in the cruelty of his insults, some of them not at all funny. Yet at the same time he was an arrant sentimentalist. He constantly referred in his radio storytelling to happenings, some of them purely imaginary, which left "an honorable moisture" on his "old lashes." A typical remark was his comment about a robust baritone that he sang a battle song in the manner of a germ going to war. He called Eugene O'Neill's *Strange Interlude* "the *Abie's Irish Rose* of the intelligentsia."

Woollcott was also the butt of others' wit. In his later years his appetite for rich foods grew unchecked until it was said of him that he was "all Woollcott and a yard wide." Walter Winchell held that Woollcott always praised the first production in any season—he was reluctant to "stone the first cast." He was the acknowledged model for Sheridan Whiteside, a detestable egomaniac in THE MAN WHO CAME TO DINNER (1939), a play by George S. Kaufman and Moss Hart, but instead of taking offense, Woollcott accepted the characterization as a tribute and played the role himself in a touring company.

Woollcott's books include *Mrs. Fiske—Her Views on Acting, Actors, and the Problems of the Stage* (1917); *The Command Is Forward* (1919); *Shouts and Murmurs* (1923); *Enchanted Aisles* (1924); *The Story of Irving Berlin* (1925); *Going to Pieces* (1928); *Two Gentlemen and a Lady* (1928); *While Rome Burns* (1934); and such anthologies as *The Woollcott Reader* (1935) and *Woollcott's Second Reader* (1937). *The Portable Woollcott* (1946) was edited by Joseph Hennessy, who with Beatrice Kaufman edited Woollcott's *Let-*

ters (1944). *Long, Long Ago* (1943) is a posthumous collection of Woollcott's fugitive essays. Woollcott's stay at Neshobe Island is described in Charles Brackett's novel *Entirely Surrounded* (1934). An odd, scurrilous publication was *Alec the Great: An Account of the Curious Life and Extraordinary Opinions of the Late Alexander Woollcott* (1943), by "Philistina." Samuel Hopkins Adams wrote an admirable biography, *A. Woollcott: His Life and His World* (1945).

Woolman, John (b. Northampton Township, N.J., Oct. 19, 1720—d. Oct. 7, 1772), Quaker leader, abolitionist. The eldest son of Samuel and Elizabeth Burr Woolman, John Woolman was brought up in an atmosphere of earnest piety and was educated chiefly by his parents and through his own wide reading in the libraries of his father's friends. At the age of sixteen he experienced a mystical conversion during a severe illness, as a result of which he later testified: "I was early convinced in my mind that true religion consisted of an inward life. I found no narrowness respecting sects and opinions, but believed that sincere, upright-hearted people in every society, who truly love God, were accepted by him." This spirit of tolerance dominated the rest of Woolman's life as a leader among the Quakers.

Until he was twenty Woolman "wrought on the plantation" of his father, but he apparently did not take well to farming and in 1740 became apprentice to a shopkeeper and baker who also carried on a tailoring business; Woolman set himself to learn the trade of tailor. During this period he became increasingly active in Friends' meetings, and shortly undertook his first independent preaching tour, a journey of six weeks through Pennsylvania and western Virginia. What he saw of slavery during this journey of 1756 prompted him to the writing of an essay, *Some Considerations upon the Keeping of Negroes,* printed eight years later. "I saw in these Southern Provinces," he wrote, "so many Vices and Corruptions increased by this trade and this way of life, that it appeared to me as a dark gloominess hanging over the land." He spoke so pointedly of the inevitable outcome of traffic in human lives that abolitionists a century later found in his words a forecast of the Civil War.

Meanwhile Woolman set up his own tailoring and general merchandise shop in Mount Holly, N.J., and married a "well inclined" Quaker girl, Sarah Ellis. The remaining years of his life were filled with quiet but incessant activity. In 1752 he was made Clerk of the Burlington Quarterly Meeting of Ministers and Elders, a position he held for seventeen years, and became a regular and faithful representative of his district at yearly meetings of his fellow religionists at Philadelphia and elsewhere. For weeks at a time, year in and year out, he traveled among his Quaker friends, exhorting them and counseling with them, particularly attempting to arouse turgid consciences against "reaping the unrighteous profits of that iniquitous practice of dealing in Negroes." Many of his journeys were made on foot to New York and Connecticut, to Newport and Nantucket, slave ports where his word was most greatly needed. In 1763 he held meetings among the Indians, whom he also accepted humbly as fellow aspirants toward the goodness of God. During the next several years he traveled often to the South and visited Friends in eastern New Jersey and Pennsylvania. In the intervals of his tours, while still carrying on his tailoring business, he conducted school in Mount Holly, preparing his own primers. The strain of all these activities, among which must be included the keeping of his *Journal* and his other writings, so told on him that he collapsed with pleurisy in 1770, and his life was despaired of. Nevertheless the next year he undertook a voyage to visit friends in England with whom he had long corresponded. There he died of smallpox, contracted, it is supposed, while ministering among the poor of the manufacturing districts. He was buried in the Bishophill graveyard at York.

Woolman was a man of infinite humility and selflessness. He consistently "studied to be quiet" and to live according to the dictates of the inner light which he sought in himself and which he recommended that all men seek. When, as was often the case, his principles brought him into opposition with the prevailing notions of his time, he governed himself by "passive obedience," which allowed him to follow the letter while disregarding the spirit of oppressive laws. "Woolman's saintliness," said John Greenleaf Whittier, a later Quaker, "was wholly unconscious. He seems never to have thought himself any nearer to the tender heart of God than the most miserable sinner for whom his compassion extended. As he did not live, so he did not die for himself. His prayer on his death bed was for others rather than for himself."

The life of John Woolman is best mirrored in the *Journal* (1774) which he began in his thirty-sixth year. Containing only a slender thread of personal history, introduced as necessary for a background, the *Journal* records Woolman's "inward life, wherein the Heart doth Love and Reverence God the Creator, and learn to Exercise true Justice and Goodness, not only toward all men, but also toward the Brute Creatures." The style of the *Journal* has been widely praised by many generations of critics for its sweetness and lucidity, yet the concreteness with which it reveals a mystical personality has commended it equally to common readers in search of realistic consolation. The *Journal* is, indeed, a chief classic of American spiritual experience.

Woolman's other writings were few, but they too have been often reprinted. The most important among them are *Considerations on Pure Wisdom and Human Policy* (1758); *A Plea for the Poor* (1763); *Considerations on the True Harmony of Mankind* (1770). These and other writings were posthumously collected as *The Works of John Woolman* (2 v., 1774), of which the first volume contained the *Journal*. The best modern edition of his works is *The Journals and Essays of John Woolman* (1922), edited with a biographical introduction by Amelia Mott Gummere; however, that most often reprinted is

based on the text edited in 1871 by Whittier. Janet Whitney prepared a new edition of the *Journal* in 1950, with additions and corrections from the original manuscript in the Swarthmore College Library.

LEWIS LEARY

Woolrich, Cornell ["George Hopley," "William Irish"] (b. New York City, Dec. 4, 1903—d. Sept. 25, 1968), writer. After graduating from Columbia University in 1925, Woolrich tried his hand at fiction with *Cover Charge* (1926) and was so successful that he continued writing at the rate of about one book a year. He is best known for *Rear Window* and for his own film adaptation of the story, which received a citation from the Screen Writers' Guild in 1954. In it a newspaper photographer confined to his Greenwich Village apartment with a broken leg boredly watches his neighbors through his rear window —and gradually becomes suspicious that a murder has been committed. The story demonstrates Woolrich's particular brand of mystery: suspenseful and neatly melodramatic. Among his books: *The Time of Her Life* (1931); *Rendezvous in Black* (1948); *Dead Man Blues* (1948); *Strangler's Serenade* (1951); *Eyes That Watch You* (1952); *Nightmare* (1956); *Hotel Room* (1958).

Woolsey, Sarah Chauncey ["Susan Coolidge"] (b. Cleveland, Ohio, Jan. 29, 1835—d. April 9, 1905), poet, author of books for girls, editor. The niece of THEODORE DWIGHT WOOLSEY began as a poet, went on to write popular books for girls, particularly the "What Katy Did" series, which began (1872) with a story by that name and closed (1886) with *What Katy Did Next*. Under her pen name Miss Woolsey became known for her pleasant verse, for her editions of the letters of several famous women, and for *A Short History of Philadelphia* (1887).

Woolsey, Theodore Dwight (b. New York City, Oct. 31, 1801—d. July 1, 1889), teacher, educational administrator, writer. Woolsey started out as a student of law, then became a theological student, but decided he was unfit for the pulpit and accepted an appointment to teach Greek at Yale University. He edited a series of Greek texts and in 1846 was made president of Yale. Under his administration the university greatly expanded its faculties in arts and sciences, while Woolsey himself took up the study of political science and international law and became an outstanding authority. Among his books: *Introduction to the Study of International Law* (1860); *Essay on Divorce and Divorce Legislation* (1869); *Religion of the Present and the Future* (1871); *Helpful Thoughts for Young Men* (1874); *Political Science* (2 v., 1878); *Communism and Socialism* (1880).

Woolson, Constance Fenimore (b. Claremont, N.H., March 3, 1840—d. Jan. 24, 1894), novelist, short-story writer. Miss Woolson, whose great-uncle was James Fenimore Cooper, traveled a good deal in America, lived for a while in the South, and spent the remainder of her life in England and Europe. A sensitive analyst of human nature and a pioneer regionalist, Miss Woolson was much impressed by Bret Harte's writings. She herself wrote *Two Women* (1862), a long narrative poem; *Castle No-*

where (1875), a collection of stories about French settlers in the Great Lakes region; *Rodman the Keeper* (1880), sketches about the South; *Anne* (1883), a novel about a Mackinac Island girl; *For the Major* (1883), *East Angels* (1886), *Jupiter Lights* (1889), and Horace Chase (1894), novels about the South; *The Front Yard* (1895) and *Dorothy* (1896), stories about Americans in Italy; *Mentone, Cairo and Corfu* (1895), descriptive sketches. Much of her work, which was praised by Henry James, first appeared in the *Atlantic Monthly, Harper's,* and *Century.*

Worcester, Joseph Emerson (b. Bedford, N.H., Aug. 24, 1784—d. Oct. 27, 1865), lexicographer, geographer, historian. A graduate of Yale, Worcester taught in Salem, Mass., where Hawthorne was briefly one of his students. At Salem, Worcester wrote *A Geographical Dictionary, or Universal Gazetteer, Ancient and Modern* (1817). Similar works were his *Gazetteer of the United States* (1818); *Elements of Geography* (1819); *Sketches of the Earth and Its Inhabitants* (1823); *Elements of History, Ancient and Modern* (1826).

With his edition of *Johnson's English Dictionary . . . with Walker's Pronouncing Dictionary, Combined* (1828), Worcester began his career as lexicographer. A *Comprehensive Pronouncing and Explanatory Dictionary of the English Language* (1830), the first of his own dictionaries, marked the beginning of a long and bitter rivalry between Worcester and Noah Webster. In reply to Webster's charge of plagiarism, Worcester published *A Gross Lit-*

erary Fraud Exposed (1853). His dictionaries, which were more conservative and closer to British usage than those of Webster, were preferred by the New England literati, especially his influential *Dictionary of the English Language* (1860), the first illustrated dictionary, which has since ceased publication.

Words for the Wind (1958), a collection of poems by Theodore Roethke. This book, which includes a number of early poems, is written in a variety of styles and covers several subjects, most notably childhood and love. Although some critics find Roethke's work tends to be too subjective, he is acknowledged to be one of the leading poets of his generation. The book was awarded a Bollingen Prize.

Work, Henry Clay (b. Middletown, Conn., Oct. 1, 1832—d. June 8, 1884), song writer. Work was a printer by trade and a specialist in setting up musical scores; sometimes he set up his own songs as he composed them—with no intervening manuscript or piano. His strong political interests on the side of abolitionism, Unionism, and prohibition to some extent determined the content of his songs, among them Marching Through Georgia (1865), which was preceded by other Civil War songs. One of his most successful songs was Grandfather's Clock (1876). He was also the author of the temperance song beginning, "Father, dear father, come home with me now."

Workman, Fanny [Bullock] (b. Worcester, Mass., Jan. 8, 1859—d. Jan. 22, 1925), explorer, writer of travel books. Mrs. Workman was the wife of William Hunter Workman (1847–1937), with whom she explored many countries. She wrote accounts of their experiences in *Algerian Memories* (1895); *Sketches Awheel in Modern Iberia* (1897); *Peaks and Glaciers of Nun Kun* (1909); *Two Summers in the Ice Wilds of Eastern Karakoram* (1917); and other books.

Workshop 47. See George Pierce Baker.

Works Progress Administration [WPA]. At the height of the depression which began in 1929, the Roosevelt administration secured the appropriation of huge sums of money and set up widespread measures for the immediate relief of economic and social distress. The work was placed (May 6, 1935) under a Works Progress (later called Projects) Administration, with an initial appropriation of $4,880,000,000, which was spent on all kinds of projects—highway building, lumber camps, rural rehabilitation, reforestation, electrification, health projects, student aid. The WPA also took into its ranks writers, actors, musicians, and artists of all kinds. The achievement of many of these persons was notable, especially in the Federal Theater. The WPA produced much literary material, notably the "American Guide Series," the volumes of which were produced, with the collaboration of many local groups, for all the states of the Union and outlying territories. See Federal Theater Project and Federal Writers' Project.

World Almanac. A compendious manual of miscellaneous historical and contemporary information, published annually since 1868. It was for many years issued by the New York *World*, first as a reference source for its own reporters and copy editors, later for the general public. It is now published by the *World-Telegram & Sun*. In recent years it has been edited by Harry Hansen.

World Enough and Time (1950), a novel by ROBERT PENN WARREN. The murder in Kentucky of Col. Solomon P. Sharp by Jeroboam O. Beauchamp, whose trial was the sensation of 1826, has been a popular theme for novelists ever since. Warren's version in this novel is based on *The Confession* which Beauchamp himself published in 1826. Warren introduced many variations, however, and his quotations from documents are his own inventions. *Time* commented: "[Warren is] still burrowing into his favorite theme: the corrosive corruption of power politics." See also BEAUCHAMPE.

World Wars I and II, and the Korean War. World War I began with Austria-Hungary's declaration of war on Serbia on July 28, 1914, exactly a month after the Archduke Francis Ferdinand of Austria and his wife had been assassinated by a Serbian nationalist. The causes of the war extended back to the Franco-German War of 1870–71, to French and British colonialism, and to the desire of the larger nations for control of the Balkans.

Russia, Britain, and France promised Serbia aid; Germany, an ally of Austria-Hungary, declared war on Russia, and invaded Belgium and France; and Great Britain, an ally of France, declared war on Germany. In the east the Germans smashed the Russian armies. Italy, an ally of Germany and Austria, abandoned them and joined the Allies; Turkey came into the war on the German side, thus extending the area of conflict to the eastern Mediterranean. Meanwhile, German submarines sank the *Lusitania* (May 7, 1915), a passenger ship carrying many American citizens, and feeling in the United States ran strongly in favor of the Allies. When, after an interval of nonbelligerency toward America, Germany resumed unrestricted submarine warfare in February, 1917, the United States severed diplomatic relations with the Kaiser's government; in April war was declared. The entrance of American troops on the western front ended the stalemate. After a series of reverses the German armies retreated, the Berlin government fell, rebellion broke out in Germany, an armistice was negotiated (Nov. 11, 1918). The war killed millions in battle, through disease and food shortages, and through predatory actions against civilians; it impoverished most of the world; it created a number of new nations when the German, Austrian, and Turkish empires were dismembered; and it hastened the Russian Revolution (1917).

The causes of World War II were intimately connected with those of World War I and with the unfavorable conditions which remained after the Treaty of Versailles. Economic distress together with the unpopularity and weakness of the Weimar Republic in Germany led the way

to the growth of fascism and the rise of Adolf Hitler. The League of Nations, the first world organization established to maintain peace and settle international disputes, was drastically weakened by the refusal of the United States to join. When the League did nothing but formally condemn Japan for its invasion of Manchuria in 1931–32, many countries felt the need to protect themselves by building up armaments. In 1935, the League failed to prevent Italy's invasion of Ethiopia. Under Hitler, Germany began to rearm, and sent troops into the Rhineland (1936) in violation of the Versailles treaty; she seized Austria in 1938, and in August, 1939, entered into a non-aggression pact with Russia. The war officially began with the German invasion of Poland on Sept. 1, 1939. Poland was crushed, Norway and Denmark were seized by the Nazis, the British army was driven off the Continent, and France fell.

On December 7, 1941, the Japanese bombed Pearl Harbor in Hawaii and destroyed the greater part of the United States fleet there. The declarations of war by the United States that followed included Germany and Italy as well as Japan. The latter country followed up her Pearl Harbor attack with others in the Pacific region, and the war became one that involved all the continents and all the oceans. The Japanese captured Wake, Guam, the Philippines, and other strategic islands before the Allied offensive, begun in the fall of 1942, began to dislodge them. However, it was not until President HARRY S. TRUMAN authorized the dropping of the first atomic bombs (on Hiroshima, Aug. 6, 1945; on Nagasaki, Aug. 9, 1945) that Japan was forced to surrender (Sept. 2, 1945).

After an allied invasion of southern Italy the Italian army and navy surrendered (Sept. 3, 1943), but German forces in Rome and to the north were not dislodged until the summer of 1944. On June 6, 1944, immense reinforcements of men and supplies, under the direct supervision of General Dwight D. Eisenhower, had landed in France and forced the Germans to retreat across the Rhine. Germany surrendered unconditionally on May 7, 1945.

The treaties that followed the war set up the organization of the United Nations as an instrument to prevent future aggression by any nation. This instrument was tested and found only partially effective when communist North Korean troops invaded South Korea (June 25, 1950) in an attempt to overthrow the government there. The United Nations took action under United States leadership and forces, for the most part American, were sent to Korea to stop the invasion from the north. In October of that year Chinese Communists from Manchuria crossed the Yalu River to aid the North Koreans, and on November 26–27 four Red Chinese armies attacked and repulsed United Nations troops along their farthest line of advance in North Korea.

Major offensives did much to drive the North Koreans back toward the 38th parallel, and on March 15, 1951, the Allies recaptured Seoul.

The following month a controversy arose between President Truman and General Douglas MacArthur, the commanding general in Korea, as a result of which MacArthur was recalled. On July 27 (Far Eastern Time), 1953, a truce was finally signed, after much futile negotiating, with provisions for the exchange of prisoners and for a cease-fire. Korea remained a divided country.

Nonfiction books dealing with World War I include the following: CHRISTIAN F. GAUSS, *Why We Went to War* (1918); Robert Lansing, *The Peace Negotiations* (1921) and *War Memoirs* (1935); and NORMAN THOMAS, *The Conscientious Objector* (1923). E. E. Cummings' THE ENORMOUS ROOM (1922), an account of the author's term in a French prison camp, was one of the finest works of literature to come out of the war. A number of novels were written about it, among them DOROTHY CANFIELD FISHER'S *Home Fires in France* (1918); John Dos Passos' THREE SOLDIERS (1918) and *1919* (*q.v.*) (1932); Willa Cather's ONE OF OURS (1922); EDITH WHARTON'S *A Son at the Front* (1923); William Faulkner's *Soldier's Pay* (1926); ERICH MARIA REMARQUE'S *All Quiet on the Western Front* (1929); Ernest Hemingway's A FAREWELL TO ARMS (1929).

The Second World War is discussed in BERNARD BARUCH'S *American Industry in the War* (1941); Alexander P. de Seversky's *Victory Through Air Power* (1942); W. L. White's *They Were Expendable* (1942), and *Queens Die Proudly* (1943); Ira Wolfert's *Battle for the Solomons* (1943); Robert L. Scott's *God Is My Copilot* (1943); ERNIE PYLE'S *Brave Men* (1944); George C. Marshall's *The Winning of the War in Europe and the Pacific* (1945); Stewart Alsop and Thomas Braden's *Sub Rosa: O.S.S. and American Espionage* (1946); John Hersey's HIROSHIMA (1946); Samuel Eliot Morison's *History of U.S. Naval Operations in World War II* (the first of fourteen volumes appeared in 1947; the last, in 1961); George S. Patton, Jr.'s *The War As I Knew It* (1947); Dwight D. Eisenhower's *Crusade in Europe* (1948); Lucius D. Clay's *Decision in Germany* (1950); Omar N. Bradley's *A Soldier's Story* (1951); SUMNER WELLES' *Seven Decisions That Shaped History* (1951); WILLIAM L. SHIRER'S *The Rise and Fall of the Third Reich* (1960). World War II novels include Harry Brown's *A Walk in the Sun* (1944); John Hersey's *A Bell for Adano* (1944); THOMAS HEGGEN'S *Mr. Roberts* (1946); John Horne Burns' THE GALLERY (1947); JAMES GOULD COZZENS' *Guard of Honor* (1948); Norman Mailer's THE NAKED AND THE DEAD (1948); Irwin Shaw's *The Young Lions* (1948); James Jones' FROM HERE TO ETERNITY (1951); Herman Wouk's THE CAINE MUTINY (1951); Lionel Shapiro's *The Sixth of June* (1955).

Books on the Korean War include Walter Karig's *War in Korea* (1952); Samuel L. Marshall's *Pork Chop Hill: The American Fighting Man in Action* (1956); Carl Berger's *Korea Knot* (1957); Malcolm Cagle and Frank Manson's *Sea War in Korea* (1957); John Spanier's *Truman-MacArthur Controversy and the Korean War* (1959). The war produced several personal narratives: Clay Blair, Jr.'s *Beyond Courage* (1955); Ward Millar's *Valley of the Shadow* (1955); Martin Russ' *Last Parallel: A Marine's War Journal* (1957). Novels dealing with the war include James A. Michener's *The Bridges at Toko-ri* (1953); Duane Thorin's *Ride to Panmunjom* (1956); A. M. Harris' *Tall Man* (1958); Ernest Frankel's *Band of Brothers* (1959); Quentin Reynolds' *Known But to God* (1960).

In the theater the two wars had a curiously different effect; fiction showed the same trends, but not so emphatically. After World War I American drama attacked the war and patriotism, as in Maxwell Anderson's and Laurence Stallings' *What Price Glory?* (1924). But during World War II many of the same playwrights bitterly attacked fascism and Nazism. Robert E. Sherwood represented the evolution of this point of view in IDIOT'S DELIGHT (1936) and THERE SHALL BE NO NIGHT (1940). Less ideological were the plays that came after World War II, notably the dramatizations of *Mr. Roberts* (1948) and *The Caine Mutiny* (1954). Hollywood made many spectacular documentaries, such as *Victory at Sea* (1954).

One poem that came out of World War I attained wide popularity, Alan Seeger's I HAVE A RENDEZVOUS WITH DEATH (1916). With the rising menace of fascism, Archibald MacLeish became a poet laureate of democracy in his indignant radio plays THE FALL OF THE CITY (1937) and AIR RAID (1938). World War I songs of American origin were George M. Cohan's OVER THERE and Irving Berlin's "Oh, How I Hate to Get Up in the Morning."

Wouk, Herman (b. New York City, May 27, 1915—   ), novelist, playwright. After graduation from Columbia College in 1934, Herman Wouk toiled as a radio scriptwriter for comedian Fred Allen. At the outbreak of World War II he entered the Navy as a line officer, serving four years and winning four campaign stars. His first novel, AURORA DAWN (1947), was an ironic treatment of big business. CITY BOY (1948), an amusing story of youth, became a motion picture. His next novel, THE CAINE MUTINY (1951), a gripping account of Navy life during World War II, had a spectacular impact on the public, selling almost two million copies by 1953. It became a motion picture, then part of it formed a play, *The Caine Mutiny Court Martial*. MARJORIE MORNINGSTAR (1955) also became a best seller, despite sharply divided critical reaction. Among his other works: *The Traitor* (1949, a play); *Slattery's Hurricane* (1948, a movie script; 1949, a novelette; 1956, a novel); *Nature's Way* (1958); *This Is My God* (1959). At his best Wouk has an intelligent narrative style and an awareness of dramatic plot technique.

Wound and the Bow, The (1941), a volume of literary criticism by EDMUND WILSON. The title is derived from Sophocles' play *Philoctetes*, where a warrior exiled to an island because of his foul-smelling wound is yet sought out by his fellows, who need his magic bow to win the Trojan War. To Wilson this is a symbol of the modern artist, who pays for his creative abilities by his sickness. The same society which rejects him needs the restorative powers of his art. Using a psychological and mythological approach, Wilson thus explains the imagination of Dickens as a result of the psychic wounds produced by his father's imprisonment for debt. The volume includes similar essays on Rudyard Kipling, Edith Wharton, and Ernest Hemingway.

Wound Dresser, The (1898), letters written by WALT WHITMAN to his mother from hospitals in Washington, D.C., during the Civil War. When his brother George was wounded in battle, Whitman set out to look for him, then took up residence in Washington and spent much of his time there in visiting army hospitals. In his letters he condemned the bad conditions in the hospitals, praised some of the doctors and nurses, and called himself a "self-appointed missionary" to the wounded.

Wounds in the Rain: A Collection of Stories Relating to the Spanish-American War of 1898 (1900), by STEPHEN CRANE. Of these short pieces *The Nation* said "The manner in which these sketches and memories of the Spanish-American war are written is that of a clever and vivacious journalist, tempered by afterthought and softened by the desire to give literary effectiveness to descriptions of episodes in which the note of life is distressing or violent or brutal. The volume contains some of the best work that Mr. Crane has left behind him."

WPA and **WPA Guides.** See WORKS PROGRESS ADMINISTRATION.

Wreck of the Hesperus, The (1841), a ballad by HENRY WADSWORTH LONGFELLOW. In his *Journal* for Dec. 17, 1839, Longfellow recorded his horror at having read an account of the wreck of a schooner named the *Hesperus* off Norman's Reef near Gloucester. Twenty bodies were washed ashore, one of them lashed to a piece of wreckage. On December 30 Longfellow sat by the fire until midnight smoking, when suddenly it came into his head to write *The Ballad of the Schooner Hesperus;* "It hardly cost me an effort." Obviously there rang in his head the lines of the old Scottish ballad *Sir Patrick Spens*, with which his poem has unmistakable affinities. Posterity finds Longfellow's poem a little naive, but the lines have delighted several generations of readers.

Wright, Fanny [Frances] (b. Scotland, Sept. 6, 1795—d. Dec. 13, 1852), reformer, editor. Miss Wright toured the United States several times, finally settled here in 1829. She was an outspoken freethinker in religion, a crusader for the more equitable distribution of property, as well as for women's rights, free public education, and the abolition of slavery. With the approval of Jefferson and Madison she attempted to solve the slavery problem in the NASHOBA COM-

MUNITY. Her *Views of Society and Manners in America* (1821) was so enthusiastic about this country and so disparaging in its references to England that it was condemned roundly overseas. She also wrote *A Few Days in Athens* (1822), *A Course of Popular Lectures* (1829, v. 2, 1836), and a play about the fight for independence in Switzerland, *Altorf* (1819), produced and published in New York. Throughout her career she was associated with ROBERT DALE OWEN and his father's ideas. She edited with him the *New Harmony Gazette* and the *Free Enquirer*, the latter begun by her in 1829 in New York. She is the subject of W. R. Waterman's *Frances Wright* (1924) and A. J. G. Perkins' and Theresa Wolfson's *Frances Wright, Free Enquirer* (1939). Her views greatly influenced Walt Whitman.

Wright, Frank Lloyd (b. Richland Center, Wis., June 8, 1869—d. April 9, 1959), architect. Wright studied civil engineering but quit before graduation to move to Chicago and begin a career in architecture. He became the assistant of LOUIS SULLIVAN, then the most creative spirit in architecture in Chicago. After a disagreement with Sullivan, Wright left him and started his own practice in Chicago; later he moved back to Wisconsin and built his home and studio which he called Taliesin (a Welsh word meaning "shining brow"). Wright's buildings brought him fame as one of the giants of modern architecture and, despite a dearth of commissions from the late twenties to the middle thirties when his buildings seemed to go out of style, when he died he was regarded as the greatest architect in American history.

Never content to restrict himself to the drafting board, Wright wrote extensively about what he called "organic architecture." His many books include *Experimenting with Human Lives* (1923); *Modern Architecture* (1931); *The Disappearing City* (1932); *An Autobiography* (1932; brought up to date in 1943); *On Architecture* (1941); *When Democracy Builds* (1945, drastically rev. as *The Living City*, 1958); *Genius and the Mobocracy* (1949); *Testament* (1957); and *Drawings for a Living Architecture* (1959). Ayn Rand used Wright as a model for the protagonist in THE FOUNTAINHEAD (1943).

Some of his best known buildings are the Imperial Hotel in Tokyo (successfully designed to withstand severe earthquakes), the Millard House in Pasadena, Calif. (constructed of precast concrete blocks), the Johnson Wax Building, Racine, Wis., Taliesin West (his winter home near Phoenix, Ariz.), and the Solomon R. Guggenheim Museum in New York. Hundreds of private dwellings attest to his mastery of that form of architecture.

Wright, Harold Bell (b. Rome, N.Y., May 4, 1872—d. May 24, 1944), clergyman, novelist. Wright was an extraordinarily successful writer despite the disesteem of literary critics. During most of his life he suffered from tuberculosis. He tried various trades, but while living in the Ozarks for his health he began to preach, and later spent ten years as a pastor in the Church of the Disciples, but never attended either a college or a seminary. He turned to novel writing, and when he attained success with *The Shepherd of the Hills* (1907) he retired from the ministry, due to ill health. Thereafter he wrote a new best seller approximately every two years.

Wright is less meretricious than he seems; he tries to be wholesome and helpful and tells his stories well, if sometimes unbelievably. Among his books: *That Printer of Udell's* (1903); *The Calling of Dan Matthews* (1909); THE WINNING OF BARBARA WORTH (1911); *The Eyes of the World* (1914); *When a Man's a Man* (1916); *The Mine with the Iron Door* (1923); *A Son of His Father* (1925); *Ma Cinderella* (1932); *The Man Who Went Away* (1942). *To My Sons* (1934) is an autobiography.

Wright, Louis B[ooker] (b. Greenwood Co., S.C., March 1, 1899—   ), newspaperman, teacher, historian, library director. Wright worked for newspapers, then taught English at various universities, finally turned to research and library administration. He became director of the Folger Shakespeare Library on July 1, 1948. His books cover a wide range of subjects: *Middle-Class Culture in Elizabethan England* (1935); *The First Gentlemen of Virginia* (1940); *Religion and Empire* (1943); *The Atlantic Frontier* (1947); *Conservation of Culture on the Moving Frontier* (1955); *William Byrd of Virginia, The London Diary* (1958). He also edited numerous writings of historical and literary interest. In his book on frontier culture Wright spiritedly defended a novel thesis—that the colonists and their descendants who moved westward had a deep love of culture, especially British culture. The men and women of the frontier, Wright notes, built schools and churches before they paved streets.

Wright, Orville. See WILBUR WRIGHT.

Wright, Richard [Nathaniel] (b. near Natchez, Miss., Sept. 4, 1908—d. Nov. 28, 1960), novelist, social critic. An uneven but gifted writer, Wright's first important publication was a collection of four novellas, *Uncle Tom's Children* (1938). His biggest success from both a critical and a financial point of view was NATIVE SON (1940). This brutal novel became a best seller and, in a stage version written with Paul Green, was produced by Orson Welles in 1941, with the late Canada Lee in the leading role of Bigger Thomas. The book had a large sale in the United States and abroad and won acclaim from critics. Peter Munroe Jack called it the "Negro 'American Tragedy.'" The story is partly based on Wright's own experiences in the Chicago slums and partly on the case of Robert Nixon, a Chicago Negro who was electrocuted in 1938 for the murder of a white girl. A film was made in Argentina in 1950 with Wright playing the lead.

Another novel which approached the literary quality and commercial success of *Native Son* was *Black Boy* (1945), an autobiography of Wright's youth. His novel *The Long Dream*

(1958) was dramatized by Ketti Frings in 1960. While unemployed and living on relief in the early 1930's he joined the Communist Party; he tells of his disillusionment with it in a chapter of *The God That Failed*

(1950). At this time he moved to Paris with his wife and remained there the rest of his life. He is considered by many the most eloquent spokesman for the American Negro in his generation. He also wrote *12 Million Black Voices* (1941); *Bright and Morning Star* (1941); *The Outsider* (1953), a philosophical novel; *Black Power* (1954), his impressions of the Gold Coast of Africa; *The Color Curtain* (1956), a report on the Bandung Conference in Java; *Pagan Spain* (1957), his severely critical personal observations of Spain; *White Man, Listen!* (1957), a lecture on the evils of racial injustice; and *Eight Men* (1961).

Wright, Richardson Little (b. Philadelphia, June 18, 1886—d. Aug. 6, 1961), newspaperman, historian, editor, garden authority. Wright worked for papers in Albany, New York City, Chicago, and London, at times as literary and theatre critic, also as a special correspondent in the Far East. In 1914 he became editor of *House and Garden,* serving for more than forty years and making that magazine one of the most widely known in its field. Wright wrote books on his observations abroad as well as on gardens and homes. Among his publications: *Through Siberia* (1913); *Inside the Home of Good Taste* (1915); *House & Garden's Book of Houses* (1919; many similar volumes in later years); *Truly Rural* (1922); *The Gardener's Bedbook* (1929); *Revels in Jamaica* (1937); *The*

Gardener's Tribute (1949); A Book of Days for Christians (1951). Wright also composed several books that examined some of the less well-known aspects of the American past: Hawkers and Walkers in Early America (1927); Forgotten Ladies (1928); and Grandfather Was Queer (1939).

Wright, Wilbur (b. Millville, Ind., April 16, 1867—d. May 30, 1912) and **Wright, Orville** (b. Dayton, O., Aug. 19, 1871—d. Jan. 30, 1948), inventors. These brothers were perhaps the most literate of American inventors since Morse. Orville became a printer; Wilbur published a weekly paper. For a while the brothers manufactured bicycles, then became interested in the problem of flight. They studied experiments being conducted in the United States and Europe, and then built gliders which were put into flight at Kill Devil Hill, a sand bar near Kitty Hawk, N.C. They made the first successful heavier-than-air machine flights at Kitty Hawk on Dec. 17, 1903. Their first flights were made in a biplane powered with a four-cylinder motor and launched by a catapult. They were the first to supply the War Department with practical flying machines. In 1915, after they had endured a number of irritating patent suits, the Wright Company took over their patents, with Orville continuing to act as consultant.

F. C. Kelly, their authorized biographer, wrote The Wright Brothers (1943), and also edited and wrote an introduction and commentary for Orville Wright's How We Invented the Airplane (1953). An important collection of papers belonging to the Wright brothers was placed in the Library of Congress and formed the basis for The Papers of Wilbur and Orville Wright (2 v., 1953). Wilbur Wright is one of the quartet treated in Gertrude Stein's Four In America (1947), in which Miss Stein tried to imagine what would have happened if Wilbur had become a painter.

Wright, Willard Huntington ["S. S. Van Dine"] (b. Charlottesville, Va., June 18, 1888—d. April 11, 1939), critic, editor, novelist. Wright began as a reporter for the Los Angeles Times and played an important role in art and drama criticism in the 1920's. He helped as editor (1912–14) to make SMART SET a leading magazine, also served on the staffs of Town Topics, The Forum, International Studio, and other magazines. Under his own name he wrote Songs of Youth (1913); The Creative Will (1916); and The Future of Painting (1923); also a novel, The Man of Promise (1916). During a nervous breakdown in 1923 he read a great many detective stories, then under an old family name he began writing detective novels. His sleuth, PHILO VANCE, is a clever, learned, rather bored dilettante of great ingenuity and insight. The Benson Murder Case (1926) made an immediate hit, The "Canary" Murder Case (1927) broke all records for sales of crime fiction at that time, and Wright went on to even larger sales with many similarly entitled narratives, the last of which, The Winter Murder Case (1939), appeared posthumously.

Wrong, George Mackinnon (b. Gravesend, Ontario, June 25, 1860—d. June 29, 1948), historian, teacher. Wrong taught for a while at the University of Toronto and made many contributions to a better understanding of Canadian history and the relations of that country to the United States. He and others edited the monumental Review of Historical Publications Relating to Canada (22 v., 1896–1918). Among his other publications: The Fall of Canada, 1759–60 (1914); Conquest of New France (1918); Washington and His Comrades in Arms (1920); The United States and Canada (1928); Canada and the American Revolution (1935); The Canadians: The Story of a People (1938).

Wroth, Lawrence Counselman (b. Baltimore, Md., Jan. 14, 1884—   ), historian, biographer, librarian. Wroth served as librarian in various institutions, and became librarian of the John Carter Brown Library at Brown University in 1923. In 1932 he became a research professor in American history at Brown. His publications include Parson Weems (1911); William Parks, Printer and Journalist (1926); The Colonial Printer (1931); An American Bookshelf (1934); The Way of a Ship (1937); The First Century of the John Carter Brown Library (1946); Typographic Heritage (1946); Abel Buell of Connecticut: Silversmith, Type Founder and Engraver (1958).

Wurdemann, Audrey [May] [Mrs. Joseph Auslander] (b. Seattle, Wash., Jan. 1, 1911—d. May 18, 1960), poet, novelist. Miss Wurdemann began writing verse at an early age, publishing her first collection, The House of Silk, in 1926. Her second collection, Bright Ambush (1934), won a Pulitzer prize; she was the youngest poet ever to win the prize. Among her other collections: The Seven Sins (1935); Splendor in the Grass (1936); The Testament of Love (1938). In collaboration with her husband she wrote two novels, My Uncle Jan (1948) and The Islanders (1951).

Wyandot Indians. See HURON INDIANS.

Wyandotté, or, The Hutted Knoll (1843), a novel by JAMES FENIMORE COOPER. In this story about New York state during the Revolution Cooper again treats a favorite theme, a family rift in which one member favors England, another the colonies; in between is Captain Willoughby. Alexander Cowie (Rise of the American Novel, 1948) regards the account of how Willoughby develops his "patent" of land as the best part of the book.

Wyckoff, Walter (b. India, April 12, 1865—d. May 15, 1908), teacher, economist, sociologist, writer. The son of an American missionary, Wyckoff studied in America, specialized in economics and sociology, became professor of sociology at Princeton University. He frequently went to live with workers and the unemployed, recording his experiences in The Workers (1897, 1898) and A Day with a Tramp and Other Days (1901).

Wyeth, Nathaniel Jarvis (b. 1802—d. 1856), ice-dealer, explorer. Wyeth was an ice-dealer in Cambridge, Mass., who was fascinated by the fur trade in the Far West. In 1832 he led an expedition to the coast. One of the members of the company, his cousin John Wyeth, wrote, with the assistance of Dr. Benjamin Waterhouse, a book about the trip called *Oregon, or, A Short History of a Long Journey* (1833), which Wyeth described as a book of "little lies told for gain." Another member of the expedition, John Kirk Townsend, wrote an account entitled *Narrative of a Journey Across the Rocky Mountains to the Columbia River* (1839). The expedition did not fulfill Wyeth's hope of making a fortune, but he did establish a fur post at Fort Hall. His own *Correspondence and Journals, 1831–36* was published by the Oregon Historical Society in *Sources of the History of Oregon* (Nos. 3–6, 1899). Wyeth plays a considerable role in Irving's ADVENTURES OF CAPTAIN BONNEVILLE (1837).

Wyeth, N[ewell] C[onvers] (b. Needham, Mass., Oct. 22, 1882—d. Oct. 19, 1945), artist, illustrator, editor. Wyeth was particularly noted for his illustrations for children's books, and his concepts of Sherwood Forest, Treasure Island, and Camelot ruled the juvenile imagination for more than a generation. His only rival as an illustrator was his teacher HOWARD PYLE. Like Pyle, Wyeth became a teacher and reckoned many noted names among his pupils. In addition to his illustrations he painted easel works in egg tempera on wood and prepared murals for buildings of all kinds. His son, **Andrew Wyeth** (b. Chadds Ford, Pa., July 12, 1917—   ), made a name for himself as a realistic painter whose detailed canvases evoke somber or nostalgic moods.

Wylie, Elinor [Hoyt] (b. Somerville, N.J., Sept. 7, 1885—d. Dec. 16, 1928), poet, novelist. Beautiful, impulsive, and gifted, Miss Hoyt married Philip Hichborn, a wealthy Washingtonian, later eloped to Europe with Horace Wylie, whom she married after her first husband committed suicide. Divorcing Wylie, she married the poet WILLIAM ROSE BENÉT. Lloyd Morris said "her beauty aroused more commotion than her fine poems or the delicate fantasies she called novels" (*Incredible New York*, 1951).

Like Shelley, whom she had admired since the age of seven, Mrs. Wylie had a creative period in poetry as rich as it was brief. *Incidental Numbers* (1912), an early volume, was published anonymously. Her first important book of poems was NETS TO CATCH THE WIND (1921), a collection containing some of her loveliest and most characteristic poems. Her genius for communicating sensuous moods is revealed in *Velvet Shoes* and *August*, while her aristocratic pride is voiced in THE EAGLE AND THE MOLE, in which she writes: "Avoid the reeking herd,/ Shun the polluted flock,/ Live like that stoic bird,/ The eagle of the rock." Two later volumes of poetry, *Black Armour* (1923) and *Trivial Breath* (1928), are considered inferior to *Angels and Earthly Creatures* (1929), which contains a sonnet sequence entitled *One Person* and many intensely mystical poems of rare beauty. Some new poems appeared in *Col-*

lected Poems of Elinor Wylie (1932) and *Last Poems of Elinor Wylie* (1943). Her poetry, influenced by the English Elizabethan and metaphysical poets, is considered among the best by women in the 20th century.

Her novels, JENNIFER LORN (1923); THE VENETIAN GLASS NEPHEW (1925); THE ORPHAN ANGEL (1926); and *Mr. Hodge and Mr. Hazard* (1928), all have a historical background for which she performed extensive research. *The Collected Prose of Elinor Wylie* (1933) contains the four novels, ten short stories, and several of her essays. *The Orphan Angel* (1926) is an extraordinary story of Shelley, based on the invention that he had escaped drowning and had come to America.

A slight but useful critical study is William Rose Benét's *The Prose and Poetry of Elinor Wylie* (1934). Nancy Hoyt, Mrs. Wylie's sister, wrote *Elinor Wylie: The Portrait of an Unknown Lady* (1935). The poet wrote a verse "Profile" of herself for *The New Yorker* (March, 1927), entitled *Portrait in Black Paint, With a Very Sparing Use of Whitewash*.

Wylie, Philip [Gordon] (b. Beverly, Mass., May 12, 1902—   ), novelist, essayist, short-story writer. Wylie's clever and penetrating surveys of American mores and behavior have engaged him in various crusades; the best known is that against the American mother and what he terms "momism" in *Generation of Vipers* (1942). In the *Essay on Morals* (1947), Wylie makes an indignant attack on organized religion, as well as on American ethics. *Opus 21* (1949), a series of fictional dialogues between the author and various people, expresses his views of the problems of American society, with emphasis on its sexual ills. His fiction varies from excellent stories of fishing in Florida (*The Big Ones Get Away!*, 1940) to gloomy predictions of the future (*Tomorrow!*, 1954) in which he describes in detail the horrors of atomic war. Among his other books: *Heavy Laden* (1928); *Finnley Wren* (1934); *Night Unto Night* (1944); *Disappearance* (1951); *The Answer* (1956).

Wynn, Dudley (b. Cooper, Texas, Oct. 2, 1904—   ), educator, editor. Wynn began teaching English at New York University, and joined the staff of the University of New Mexico in 1934, becoming a professor in 1944. He edited the *New Mexico Quarterly Review* from 1940 until 1947, when he was appointed chairman of the humanities staff at the University of Colorado. In 1950 he founded the *Colorado Quarterly,* and edited it until 1953, when he returned to the University of New Mexico as dean of the College of Arts and Sciences.

Wynne, Hugh. See HUGH WYNNE, FREE QUAKER.

X

Xingu (*Scribner's Magazine*, December, 1911), a story by EDITH WHARTON. It is a satire on a snobbish and ignorant group of women in a luncheon club. To expose their stupidity one of the women, more intelligent than the rest, introduces for discussion Xingu, which the others pretend to be well acquainted with, only to discover later that it is the name of a Brazilian river.

Y

Yaddo. This fifty-five room mansion at Saratoga Springs, N.Y., was donated by Mrs. Katrina Nichols Trask Peabody as a haven for creative artists. Guests usually come during the summer, about twenty at a time, and remain there for a month or two free of charge. James T. Farrell, Katherine Anne Porter, and Aaron Copland were among the many beneficiaries of this kindly art colony.

Yaffe, James (b. Chicago, March 31, 1927—   ), author, critic. A graduate of Yale University, Yaffe began his literary career at the age of fifteen with a short story for *Ellery Queen's Mystery Magazine.* After a collection of short stories, *Poor Cousin Evelyn* (1951), he turned to the novel, writing *The Good for Nothing* (1953); *What's the Big Hurry?* (1954); and *Nothing But the Night* (1957). The latter, like Meyer Levin's *Compulsion,* was based upon the Loeb-Leopold case. Laying aside the novel temporarily, Yaffe wrote his first drama, *The Deadly Game* (1960), an adaptation of Friederich Duerrenmatt's *Traps;* it was produced on Broadway in 1960.

Yale Review. This quarterly of high quality is issued by the Yale University Press and was founded in 1911. Its first editor, WILBUR L. CROSS, was a professor of English and for a time governor of Connecticut. See THE NEW ENGLANDER.

Yale Series of Younger Poets. This series has been intended to encourage writers under forty who have not yet had a volume published. The best manuscript received each year is published by the Press. These collections, restricted to a moderate size, have revealed some excellent poets to the public, among them Harold Vinal, Shirley Barker, Paul Engle, and Muriel Rukeyser. STEPHEN VINCENT BENÉT was editor from 1918 to 1941; the present editor is W. H. AUDEN.

Yank. An army weekly that began publication in the summer of 1942 and continued till the end of World War II. It had reporters in every part of the globe, was uninhibited, served only the GI, and made a remarkable reputation. Its contents were miscellaneous but interesting —stories, pictures, letters, poetry, and doggerel. The anthology *The Best from Yank* (1945) constituted a vivid history of the war. Within its pages appear contributions from such well-known authors and cartoonists as Marion Hargrove, Irwin Shaw, Harry Brown, William Saroyan, and Dave Berger. Two noted characters made their initial appearance in *Yank*—the Sad Sack and ARTIE GREENGROIN.

Yankee Doodle. Both the tune and several of the stanzas of *Yankee Doodle* were current early in the British colonies; the catchy tune seems to have inspired innumerable verses. Both words in the title have significance. The genealogy of *Yankee* has never been satisfactorily determined. A *doodle* is a colloquial expression for "a trifler, a dolt," but the verb *to doodle* means "to make a fool of, to cheat," according to the *Merriam-Webster New International.* The song seems to have been deliberately used by the British to provoke the American troops during the Revolutionary War. Like the wise fool suggested by the title, however, the Americans adopted the song as their own and deliberately created an image of the American in a rustic mold. The song was first printed in America as part of an instrumental medley, *The Federal Overture* (1795), arranged by Benjamin Carr. No one knows who composed the words, although Edward Everett Hale attributed them to Edward Bangs, a Harvard graduate of 1777. The fullest research on the song was done by O. G. T. Sonneck in his *Report on "The Star-Spangled Banner," "Hail Columbia," "America," and "Yankee Doodle"* (1909).

Yankee from Olympus (1944), a biography by CATHERINE DRINKER BOWEN. Mrs. Bowen wrote this well-founded account of Justice Oliver Wendell Holmes with all the skill of a novelist and many novelistic techniques. She makes much of Holmes' irritation at his father's eccentricities including the elder Holmes' oversolicitude for him. Emmet Lavery dramatized the book as *The Magnificent Yankee* (1946).

Yankee in American language and literature. The word *Yankee* and the etymological puzzles it presents have already been discussed in part in the entries on HUMOR IN AMERICA, JAMES RUSSELL LOWELL, and NEW ENGLAND. Whatever the origin of the word, Yankee by the middle of the 18th century had become a term of derision for New Englanders, who by 1775, with characteristic irony, adopted the name as a term connoting distinction. The term is used now to apply to all Northerners and occasionally to all Americans. In the song YANKEE DOODLE the Yankee chose to paint himself as a naive, raw, bumptious character. Out of the Yankee concept emerged many familiar figures of folklore and fiction, two in particular—Brother Jonathan and Uncle Sam. The homely and comic Jonathan was highly popular for a while, then was superseded by the more elderly figure whose initials represent the United States. Jeanette Tandy, in *Cracker-Barrel Philosophers* (1925), describes Uncle Sam as "that strange being who embodies our sardonic truthfulness, our matter-of-fact idealism, our exuberance, and our Puritanism." Commercial genius, dry humor, ingenuity, and reforming zeal also characterize the Yankee stereotype. Often his brashness concealed a heart of gold and his wisdom hid behind tomfoolery. Often, too, he engaged in political and social satire. He was the first of the literary cracker-barrel philosophers. An outstanding trait of the Yankee, then and now, is his choice of words, his pronunciation, and the character of his voice. Best-known and most ridiculed by irreverent persons living in other parts of the country is the English spoken in Boston, noteworthy for its aversion to the letter *r*. Constance Rourke, in *American Humor* (1931, 1953), describes "Yankee speech with its slow-running rhythms and high pitch." She found that "its sound was subtly varied; the cautious drawl seemed to find a way among the listeners." It was perfectly suited to the many humorists who used it on the lecture platform. Yankeeism has extended far beyond New England, as Stewart H. Holbrook demonstrated in *The Yankee Exodus: An Account of Migration from New England* (1950).

Walter Blair, in *Native American Humor* (1937), lists the chief exponents of Yankee humor in the early 19th century: SEBA SMITH, THOMAS C. HALIBURTON, J. R. LOWELL, FRANCES M. WHITCHER, BENJAMIN P. SHILLABER. From 1830 to 1865–67 appeared a number of historically significant political caricatures of some literary merit. The greatest of these were of course the BIGLOW PAPERS of Lowell. JOSH BILLINGS and ARTEMUS WARD excelled in social caricatures.

Starting in the 1830's, many novels with Yankee characters were published. Sometimes the novel, as was the fashion of the day, took the form of a sequence of letters, as in Ann Sophia Stephens' *High Life in New York* (1843). Possibly the most artistic work that Harriet Beecher Stowe did may be found in her OLD-TOWN FOLKS (1869) and other New England stories, written under the strong influence of her husband Calvin Stowe, a skillful mimic who reproduced for his amused wife New England backgrounds, characters, and dialect. The best-known Yankee character was Ichabod Crane in Washington Irving's LEGEND OF SLEEPY HOLLOW (*The Sketch Book*, 1820). JAMES FENIMORE COOPER too had his Yankees—in THE SPY (1821), THE PIONEERS (1823), and THE PILOT (1823), for example. Of our writers of first rank the one who was most successful in creating a memorable New England character and interpreting him sympathetically and imaginatively was MARK TWAIN, in whose CONNECTICUT YANKEE IN KING ARTHUR'S COURT (1889) the Yankee reaches his apotheosis. The spilling over of Yankees into northern New York produced a magnificent portrait of a many-sided Yankee, Edward Noyes Westcott's DAVID HARUM (1898).

The Yankee legend was early fostered through a series of humorous "courtin'" poems, beginning with Thomas Green Fessenden's THE COUNTRY LOVERS, OR, JONATHAN'S COURTSHIP (1795). One of Lowell's best products in dialect was THE COURTIN' (1867). In modern poetry ROBERT P. TRISTRAM COFFIN was frequently the enlightened Yankee speaking. ROBERT FROST'S poems are overflowingly rich in Yankee char-

acterizations, the most famous and obdurate of which appears in MENDING WALL (1914). WALTER HARD, less well known, is a free-verse poet who has only one subject—rural life in Vermont. Richard M. Dorson, in analyzing his work (*Jonathan Draws the Long Bow*, 1946), says that "varieties of shiftless, cunning, and stingy Yankees parade through his poems."

The stage Yankee first made his appearance in Royall Tyler's THE CONTRAST (1787). Though the Yankee came into the act quite incidentally, he soon captured the center of the stage. The character was a marvelous opportunity for actors of the time who, even in connection with plays that had nothing to do with Yankees, would stray out between the acts and deliver monologues in Yankee dialect. On the stage the Yankee wasn't always a farmer. He might be a peddler, a sailor, a trader, a Vermont wool dealer, a lawyer. He loved to make wisecracks, to indulge in practical jokes, to boast about the United States. Usually he had a repertoire of songs, mostly variations on *Yankee Doodle*. Among the numerous plays in which Yankee types appeared were David Humphreys' *The Yankey in England* (1805[?]); A. B. Lindsay's *Love and Friendship, or, Yankee Notions* (1809); Mordecai M. Noah's SHE WOULD BE A SOLDIER (1819); Samuel Woodworth's THE FOREST ROSE (1825); Joseph S. Jones' *Green Mountain Boy* (1833), SOLON SHINGLE, OR, THE PEOPLE'S LAWYER (1839), and *The Silver Spoon* (1852); James A. Herne's HEARTS OF OAK (1879); Denman Thompson's *The Old Homestead* (1885); Lottie Blair Parker's WAY DOWN EAST (1899); Owen Davis' ICEBOUND (1923); Sidney Howard's *Ned McCobb's Daughter* (1926). In addition plays were inspired by Sam Patch, JACK DOWNING, MRS. PARTINGTON, the Widow Bedott, and other characters who appeared in humorous sketches and stories in the 1820's and thereafter.

The Yankee has been treated in numerous anthologies and nonfiction works, including B. A. Botkin's *Treasury of New England Folklore* (1947); Dirk J. Struik's *Yankee Science in the Making* (1948); Arthur Mann's *Yankee Reformers in an Urban Age* (1954); Chard Powers Smith's *The Yankees and God* (1954); Constance Winsor Green's *Eli Whitney and the Birth of American Technology* (1956); in addition to volumes mentioned above. See also EDWARD SYLVESTER MORSE.

Yankee in Canada, A (pub. in part in *Putnam's Monthly Magazine*, 1853; in full posthumously, 1866, as part of *Anti-Slavery and Reform Papers*), a travel journal by HENRY DAVID THOREAU. This was intended originally as a lecture, although Thoreau was not a good platform performer. He apparently also intended it to be a fuller and more rounded treatment, since on his return he did some reading on the history of Canada for inclusion in the informal narrative; the Pierpont Morgan Library contains a mass of disorderly notes on the subject that Thoreau never used. The journey was made in 1850, in company with ELLERY CHANNING. The book, as Constance Rourke noted, is another of his Yankee monologues. H. S. Canby called it a guide book to France in America. Thoreau was impressed by the cathedrals and their rituals, but objected to the presence of priests! He also gives impressions of the French Canadians and compares French Canada with New England.

Yankee [or **Yankey**] **in London** (1809), a series of letters by ROYALL TYLER. These letters supposedly came from London and deceived many readers of the day. Tyler joked about the American use of "I guess" and the invariable habit in New England of answering a question by asking another.

Yates, Elizabeth (b. Buffalo, N.Y., Dec. 6, 1905—), novelist, author of children's books. Miss Yates' work includes several books for adults, among them *Wind of Spring* (1945) and *Guardian Heart* (1950), but she is best known for her children's books, excellent stories imbued with sound moral values. Among them: *Under the Little Fir* (1942); *Patterns on the Wall* (1943); *Mountain Born* (1943); *Nearby* (1947); *Rainbow Round the World* (1954). *Pebble in a Pool* (1958) is a biography of Dorothy Canfield Fisher.

Ybarra, Thomas R[ussell] (b. Boston, Oct. 8, 1880—), newspaperman, author. Ybarra, whose father was a Venezuelan, studied in the United States, Europe, and South America, became a reporter on *The New York Times,* and later Sunday editor. His first book was a collection of humorous verses, *Davy Jones's Yarns* (1908). As a correspondent for the *Times* and *Collier's,* Ybarra saw many parts of the world. He wrote lives of Bolívar, Hindenburg, Cervantes, Caruso, and Verdi, also a volume entitled *America Faces South* (1939). But his best books are his accounts of his own life in the United States and Venezuela: *Young Man of Caracas* (1941, 1956) and *Young Man of the World* (1942). He also wrote *Lands of the Andes* (1947); *Caruso: The Man of Naples and the Voice of Gold* (1953); *Verdi: Miracle Man of Opera.* See also LAY OF ANCIENT ROME.

Yearling, The (1938), a novel by MARJORIE KINNAN RAWLINGS. Years after coming to settle in the scrub country of northern Florida, Marjorie Kinnan Rawlings wrote her Pulitzer prize-winning novel, laid in this setting. *The Yearling* recounts one year in the lives of a Florida backwoodsman, his wife, and his young son Jody. The plot is simple: a boy grows into awareness of how cruel adult life can be. Lonely Jody adopts and cares for an orphaned fawn, finding in the animal all the love and companionship he craves. When the fawn starts eating the Baxter family's precious crops, Jody must shoot him, because "love's got nothin' to do with corn." The tragedy lifts Jody out of his boyhood and into a more mature relationship with his hard-working parents. *The Yearling* reflects Mrs. Rawlings' deep understanding of her neighbors, her sensitive ear for their speech, her feeling for nature. The book was made into a movie in 1946.

Yesterdays with Authors (1872), a series of gossipy essays by JAMES T. FIELDS. Fields, as a publisher, had known many prominent writers. The essays appeared originally in the *Atlantic Monthly* in 1871.

Yezierska, Anzia (b. Russia, 1885—), short-story writer, memoirist. Miss Yezierska created something of a sensation with her honest and sympathetic stories of life on New York City's lower East Side. The best known of her early books are *Hungry Hearts* (1920); *Salome of the Tenements* (1922); *Children of Loneliness* (1923); and *Bread Givers* (1925). She received offers from Hollywood and spent some time there, but found existence in the movie colony unpalatable. She wrote an affecting semiautobiographical novel, *All I Could Never Be* (1932), and *Red Ribbon on a White Horse* (1950), an autobiography.

Yoknapatawpha. An imaginary county in Mississippi which serves as a setting for many stories by WILLIAM FAULKNER.

You Can't Go Home Again (pub. posthumously, 1940), a novel by THOMAS WOLFE. The sequel to THE WEB AND THE ROCK, this novel deals again with the experiences of George Webber, Wolfe's semiautobiographical hero, during the 1920's and '30's. Webber, now an author of some renown, revisits his home town and is disillusioned both by what he sees and by the reception he meets with. This episode parallels Wolfe's own experience in his home town of Asheville, North Carolina, after the publication of LOOK HOMEWARD, ANGEL. Webber sojourns for a while in New York, where he is involved with Esther Jack (modeled on Mrs. Aline Bernstein), a talented stage designer, and then travels to Europe. Like the majority of Wolfe's work, the novel is uneven in quality, sometimes massive and overpowering, sometimes turgid; the section generally most admired is that dealing with Esther Jack. Wolfe's description of Webber's meeting with the novelist Lloyd McHarg, for whom Sinclair Lewis was the prototype, was also highly praised. MAXWELL PERKINS, Wolfe's one-time mentor and the editor responsible for the publication of Wolfe's first two novels, appears as Foxhall Edwards.

You Can't Take It With You (1936), a comedy by Moss HART and GEORGE KAUFMAN. Grandpa Vanderhof, the hero of this 1937 Pulitzer prize winner, is the amiable autocrat of a bizarre but supremely happy family. Right in the middle of New York City the Vanderhofs make fireworks in the cellar, write plays, practice ballet, and print anarchistic leaflets "just for practice." Alice, the only conventional member of the family, becomes engaged to her boss's son, Tony Kirby. The clash between the stuffy Kirby family and the flamboyant Vanderhofs nearly spoils the romance, but Grandpa puts all to rights.

You Know Me Al: A Busher's Letters (1916), the first collection of stories by RING LARDNER. Lardner wrote this series of baseball stories while conducting the sports column on the Chicago *Tribune.* Cleverly written as a series of letters from a "busher" (see JACK KEEFE) to his best friend, *You Know Me Al* captures perfectly the half-literate middle-western speech of its protagonist. The Popular Hero reveals himself as a conceited, irresponsible, stingy, gullible sorehead too dumb to resent an insult, with a fantastic ability to pull the wool over his own eyes and eat his words, without even realizing it. Hilarious from start to finish, the story can also sicken the reader at the childish ignobility of the human race. It is an excellent example of Lardner's characteristic mixture of humor and misanthropy.

Youma (1890), a novel by LAFCADIO HEARN. Hearn lived in Martinique during 1887–89, and became familiar with some of the facts regarding the slave insurrection (1848) on that island. His novel, based on an actual occurrence, describes the devotion of a Negro girl to the daughter of her deceased mistress, whom she had promised that she would never desert.

Young, Art[hur] (b. near Orangeville, Ill., Jan. 14, 1866—d. Dec. 29, 1943), cartoonist, writer. Young studied in New York and abroad, returned to the United States to work for Chicago newspapers, then for various weekly magazines, including one or two of radical trend. His cartoons, which often evoked more than a superficial smile, were collected in *Trees at Night* (1927), *The Best of Art Young* (1936), and several other volumes. He wrote two autobiographical books, *On My Way* (1928) and *Art Young: His Life and Times* (1939). In 1918 Young was brought to court on the ground that some of his cartoons were subversive. His reply was: "I drew them for the public good." The jury disagreed. Some of his best cartoons were nonideological, merely revelations of human absurdities.

Young, Brigham (b. Whitingham, Vt., June 1, 1801—d. Aug. 29, 1877), Mormon leader. This remarkable man was in early life a carpenter and painter who lived at Mendon, N.Y., not far from Palmyra, where JOSEPH SMITH published *The Book of Mormon* (1830). In 1832, with his baptism, Young officially became converted to the Mormon creed, and soon became a preacher and leader of the group. When Smith was killed (1844) at Carthage, Ill., Young succeeded him as president of the Mormon Church and conducted the successful migration to Deseret (1847). President Fillmore made him governor of the Utah Territory (1850). In 1852 Young announced the doctrine of polygamy and was removed from public office. In 1871 he was indicted for polygamy, but was never convicted.

Young was skilled in diplomatic negotiations and prevented the complete suppression of Mormonism. He turned his church into a sound social and economic unit and Utah into a prosperous, self-reliant, conservative community. His *Journal of Discourses* were published in 1854–1886 (26 volumes). Among the books written about Young are: *Brigham Young and His Mormon Empire* (1913), by F. J. Cannon and G. L. Knapp; *Brigham Young* (1925), by M. R. Werner; *Brigham Young, The Man and His Work* (1936), by Preston Nibley; *Brigham*

Young (1956), a juvenile by Olive Burt; *Kingdom of the Saints* (1957), by Ray B. West. He was a pet theme of cowboy minstrelsy. The trek to Utah is described in two novels, Harry Leon Wilson's *The Lions of the Lord* (1903) and Vardis Fisher's *Children of God* (1939). He also appears in Robert Lewis Taylor's *The Travels of Jaimie McPheeters* (1958), and in the opera *Deseret* (1961), composed by Leonard Kastle, libretto by Ann H. Bailey.

Young, David (b. Pine Brook, N.J., Jan. 27, 1781—d. Feb. 13, 1852), astronomer, almanac maker, poet, teacher, lecturer. Young turned his deep interest in astronomy into a vocation. He lectured on the subject and prepared almanacs in which much astronomical information was given. *The Citizens' & Farmers' Almanac* appeared in 1814; the *Family Almanac; Harper's U.S. Almanac; Knickerbocker's Almanac;* the *Methodist Almanac;* the *N.Y. Almanac; Paul Pry's Almanac;* and others followed. The *Farmers' Almanac* continued to be published for many decades after Young's death. He also wrote two poems on astronomy—*The Contrast* (1804) and *The Perusal* (1818). He exposed a mining hoax in *The Wonderful History of the Morristown Ghost* (1826).

Young, Philip (b. Boston, May 26, 1918—   ), teacher, critic. Holder of a doctoral degree from the University of Iowa, Young has taught at New York University and at Pennsylvania State University. His *Ernest Hemingway* (1952) is a critical analysis of the writer's work. Articles by Young have appeared in several periodicals, including *American Literature* and *The Kenyon Review.*

Young, Stark (b. Como, Miss., Oct. 11, 1881—d. Jan. 6, 1963), playwright, poet, novelist, essayist. Young's description of the University of Mississippi, from which he received his Bachelor of Arts degree in 1901, as a rural and pleasant place belies the interest in learning which he acquired there. Love of learning and intelligence shaped his career and characterized all his writings. He took a Master's degree at Columbia University in 1902 and spent the following six months in a hut in North Carolina writing poetry and studing Dante and Catullus.

Until World War II, Young spent summers traveling in Italy and winters teaching. He taught English (1904–1907) at the University of Mississippi, during which time he published a book of poems (*The Blind Man,* 1906) and a verse drama (*Guenevere,* 1906); he taught at the University of Texas (1907–1915) and published a book of plays (*Addio, Madretta and Other Plays,* 1912); and he was a professor at Amherst (1915–1921) and published a series of plays in 1919. After this period he left teaching to write for *The New Republic.* He became its drama editor, and also wrote dramatic criticism of enduring value during the '20's for both *Theatre Arts Monthly* and *The New York Times.* In 1923 he wrote *The Flower in Drama,* a series of essays on the theater. Of his later desertion of dramatic criticism, Eric Bentley noted that the theatre had lost an important critic.

In the '20's also, Young saw two of his plays produced in New York City and in London, and he directed Eugene O'Neill's *Welded* for the THEATER GUILD. But the theater was not the only genre in which he worked. He wrote a series of novels: *Heaven Trees* (1926); *The Torches Flare* (1927); *River House* (1929); and his most important success, *So Red the Rose* (1934), a novel of life in Mississippi during the Civil War. This book has often been hailed as a great southern novel and its crisp prose makes it immediately attractive.

Young was one of the twelve southern writers who published in a magazine called *The Fugitive*, a manifesto citing the position of the new southern agrarianism (see THE FUGITIVES). His essay in I'LL TAKE MY STAND (1930) was called "Not in Memoriam, but in Defense" and was more objective than many of the others. He saw the South as a victim of the Civil War, poverty, mishandling from Washington, and bad methods in local administration; he felt that southerners suffered from "a sort of mad self respect and honor complex." He also saw the tragic meaning that southern life assumed in the hands of its most gifted novelists.

All through his life Young has issued books of poetry of high seriousness and profound feeling; he is, thus, somewhat at odds with many modern American poetic tendencies. Lately his expression has taken the form of painting and he has had several professional exhibitions, but his strongest love is still the theater. *Immortal Shadows*, his last book on the subject, was published in 1948, but he has issued a book of reminiscences more recently. During the 1950's several successful productions were given off Broadway of his admirable translations of Chekhov's plays.

Young Goodman Brown (*New England Magazine*, 1835; in *Mosses from an Old Manse*, 1846), a story by NATHANIEL HAWTHORNE. A young Puritan leaves his pretty wife and goes walking gloomily in the forest. He sees or dreams a Witches' Sabbath in which his wife Faith seems to be concerned; in his dream—or in reality—he sees a pink ribbon fluttering down from a treetop, a ribbon like those his wife wore in her hair. He comes home in the morning, and his wife hurries out to meet him, but he repulses her; for the rest of his life he lives in gloom and desperation, thinking there is no good on earth. The story has had various interpretations. Henry James called it a "magnificent little romance," but denied it any depth or moral significance. Mark Van Doren in his *Nathaniel Hawthorne* (1949) thought otherwise; he called it "one of the world's great tales."

Young Lions, The (1948), a novel by IRWIN SHAW. This first novel is one of the host of novels that attempted to find meaning in the experiences of World War II. Beginning on New Year's Eve, 1937, the book is built around the stories of three men who meet only in a final climactic scene. Diestl, a ski instructor and ex-Communist Nazi, looks to Germany for the future of both himself and his country. Bitter but not yet corrupt, he epitomizes the decay of his nation. Michael Whitacre, the stage manager of a frivolous Broadway play, drinks his way into the new year worrying about his wife's infidelity; though aware of world problems, he cannot come to grips with his own. Homeless Noah Ackerman spends New Year's Eve waiting for his father to die in a cheap hotel in California.

Of the three he is the most sympathetically created and the most successful as a literary character. His marriage to a New England girl, her family's treatment of him, and their short happiness are well described, though his persecution as a Jew in a southern regiment is less well written.

The novel overwhelms the reader with shifting scenes, although it has little of the violent but controlled passion of Hemingway's best work and falls short of the emotional strength of Norman Mailer's *The Naked and the Dead*. Its architectural contrivance too often shows through and, finally, the characters seem unreal.

Young Lonigan (1932), a novel by JAMES T. FARRELL. This opening book of the Lonigan trilogy is called in a subtitle "A Boyhood in Chicago," and it is a gloomy, even if impressively related story of the baneful effects of a big-city environment on a boy living in the early 20th century. It was followed by *The Young Manhood of Studs Lonigan* (1934) and *Judgment Day* (1935).

Youth and the Bright Medusa (1920), eight short stories by WILLA CATHER. These brief narratives deal mainly with artists of all types and with sophisticates. The influence of Henry James and Edith Wharton is obvious. "Paul's Case," a famous story of a neurotic boy, is in this collection. Part of the collection is a reprint of four of the seven stories from *The Troll Garden* (1905).

Youth's Companion, The. A magazine for young people founded in Boston, April 16, 1827, by NATHANIEL WILLIS and Asa Rand. It had at the beginning a circulation of several thousand, but the enterprise of some later publishers pushed the list of subscribers up to half a million by 1899. In 1857 it became a magazine for adults as well as children and obtained such distinguished contributors as Harriet Beecher Stowe, Lord Tennyson, John Greenleaf Whittier, William Dean Howells, Jules Verne and Jack London. In the 20th century the magazine began to encounter financial difficulties, merged with THE AMERICAN BOY in 1929, and passed out of existence in 1941. In 1954 four of its former editors—Lovell Thompson, M. A. DeWolfe Howe, Arthur Stanwood Pier, and Harford Powel—compiled an anthology, *Youth's Companion*.

Z

Zara, Louis (b. New York City, Aug. 2, 1910—   ), novelist. Zara's first job was in a law printshop in Chicago. He began writing at an early age, and had his first story accepted by H. L. Mencken for the *American Mercury*. Some of his early novels deal with the Jewish immigrant in the United States—among them *Blessed Is the Man* (1935) and *Give Us This Day* (1936). Later Zara turned to historical settings, and his best-known novel is THIS LAND IS OURS (1940), which tells the story of the Old Northwest and the beginnings of Chicago. Among his other books: *Rebel Run* (1951); *Blessed Is the Land* (1954); and *Dark Rider* (1961).

Zaturenska, Marya (b. Russia, Sept. 12, 1902—   ), poet, historian, biographer. Miss Zaturenska came to the United States in 1909, was naturalized in 1912, and began writing in 1919. She married the poet and critic HORACE GREGORY. In 1924 her poems won the John Reed Memorial Award given by *Poetry*, in 1935, the Shelley Award, in 1936, *Poetry's* Guarantor's Prize, and in 1938 a Pulitzer prize for *Cold Morning Sky* (1937), a collection. Other volumes include *Threshold and Hearth* (1934); *The Listening Landscape* (1941); *The Golden Mirror* (1944); *Selected Poems* (1954); *Terraces of Light* (1960). She wrote a life of Christina Rossetti (1949) and, with her husband, *A History of American Poetry, 1900–1940* (1946).

Zaza (1898), a play adapted by DAVID BELASCO from the French of Pierre Berton and Charles Simon. It portrays a love affair between a married man and a music hall entertainer. The play became the symbol for extreme naughtiness at the turn of the century. Ruggiero Leoncavallo made the play into an opera (premiere, 1900) in which Geraldine Farrar frequently sang the title role.

Zenger, John Peter (b. Germany, 1697—d. July 28, 1746), printer, newspaper publisher. Zenger came to this country at the age of thirteen, and at the age of twenty-nine had a printing business of his own in New York City. In 1733 he began publishing the New York *Weekly Journal*, which became the organ of a group opposed to the arbitrary rule of Governor William Cosby. In 1734 Zenger criticized the removal from office of Chief Justice Lewis Morris and was arrested for libel, but he was defended by Andrew Hamilton and acquitted. The verdict was a great victory for freedom of the press, particularly as Zenger published *A Brief Narrative of the Case and Trial of John Peter Zenger* (1736), which had a wide circulation.

In his career as a printer Zenger published several tracts, some in Dutch, also the first arithmetic textbook in New York. He was made public printer for the colony of New York (1737) and of New Jersey (1738). Livingston Rutherford wrote his biography (1904), Vincent Buranelli an account of his trial (1957), Kent Cooper a novel, *Anna Zenger* (1946).

Zenith. The imaginary Middle-Western town which Sinclair Lewis used as a background for his novel BABBITT (1922), and partially for DODSWORTH (1929).

Zenobia. An exotic character in Nathaniel Hawthorne's THE BLITHEDALE ROMANCE (1852). She was modeled on MARGARET FULLER and FANNY KEMBLE.

Zenobia, or, The Fall of an Empire (1838), a historical romance by William Ware. It was originally (1837) called *Letters of Lucius M. Piso from Palmyra, to His Friend Marcus Curtius, at Rome*. It dealt with the struggles of the early Christians and became a best seller. See HENRY WARE.

Zinsser, Hans (b. New York City, Nov. 17, 1878—d. Sept. 4, 1940), bacteriologist, sanitary commissioner, teacher, author. This remarkable man worked out with his colleagues an active immunization method against certain types of typhus, taught at Stanford University and the Harvard Medical School, and served in several hospitals. He reached the rank of colonel in the Medical Corps of the American Expeditionary Forces (1917–19). To explain new concepts of science and sanitation he wrote a widely read book, *Rats, Lice, and History* (1935). His autobiography was related in the third person in *As I Remember Him* (1940).

Zolotow, Maurice (b. New York City, Nov. 23, 1913—   ), novelist, biographer. Zolotow attended the University of Wisconsin and received his B.A. there in 1936. At various times he was a theatrical press agent, on the editorial staff of *The Billboard*, and drama critic for *Theatre Arts* magazine. His novels and biographies emerge from his intimate knowledge of the theatrical world. He said of his work that it tended "to divide itself into theatrical biography written in a vein of sardonic social comment and involving psychological insights, on the one hand, and into the genre of comic novels on the other." He deplores the fact that theatrical biographies are regarded "as a branch of Hollywood publicity," and are therefore not judged on the same basis as political, scientific, or historical biographies. Among his books: *Never Whistle in a Dressing Room* (1944); *Dr. William and Dr. Sun* (1945); *The Great Balsamo* (novel, 1946); *No People Like Show People* (1951); *It Takes All Kinds* (1952); *Oh Careless Love* (novel, 1959); *Marilyn Monroe, a Biography* (1960).

Zubly, John Joachim (b. Switzerland, Aug. 27, 1724—d. July 23, 1781), clergyman, agitator against British tax laws, advocate of the British constitution. Zubly was a Presbyterian clergyman of Swiss birth who became pastor of a church in Savannah, Ga. When the Stamp Act agitations began he was firmly on the side of the colonists, published a sermon called *The Stamp-Act Repealed* (1766) and *An Humble Inquiry into the Nature of the Dependency of the American Colonies* (1769). Elected to the provincial congress of Georgia, he was delegate to the Continental Congress in Philadelphia. He was one of the representatives from Georgia to the Continental Congress at Philadelphia. However, he was unwilling to support what he felt to be radical demands for independence, and when accused of disloyalty, he returned to Georgia, but was banished in 1777. Later, when the royal government was re-established, he returned to Georgia to preach.

Zuñi Indians. The largest of the group of Indian pueblos in western New Mexico, the Zuñis speak a distinct language of their own and are noted for their tenacious faith in ancient rituals. Ruth Bunzel studied Zuñi ceremonials and poetry in several publications of the American Bureau of Ethnology. Three excellent books on the Zuñis are F. H. Cushing's *Outlines of Zuñi Creation Myths* (1896), *Zuñi Folk Tales* (1901, 1931), and *Zuñi Breadstuff* (1920).

Zury, The Meanest Man in Spring County (1887), a novel by JOSEPH KIRKLAND. In this story of Zury Prouder, a native of rural Illinois, and Anne Sparrow, a New England schoolteacher, three elements are combined: the tradition of the frontier, the faint foreshadowings of naturalism, and romance so unlikely that Henry Nash Smith calls the marriage between Anne and Zury one of the strangest in all literature. *The McVeys* (1888) is a sequel.

GLOSSARY OF
LITERARY TERMS

Glossary of Literary Terms

This glossary includes terms most frequently used in *The Reader's Encyclopedia of American Literature.* An asterisk (°) indicates that a fuller discussion may be found under the same term in the Encyclopedia. *Italicized* terms other than book titles may be found elsewhere in the glossary.

accentual meter. A metrical structure based on the number of accents, or stresses, in a verse line, regardless of the number of syllables or the foot patterns. See *meter.*

action. (1) An event or series of events. (2) Occasionally used as a synonym for *plot.*

adage. A short saying become familiar and esteemed through long use. See *aphorism.*

aesthetics. That branch of knowledge concerned with the beautiful, especially the standards of taste in reactions to the beautiful. Thus, the **aesthetic** appeal of a work of literature is distinguished from its claims as amusing, pleasing, moral, instructive, or useful.

alexandrine. A verse line of iambic hexameter.

allegory. *Metaphor* extended into a narrative, usually with a moral purpose; a story in which the surface plot and characters may have some interest, but in which the real significance depends on understanding each character and action to stand for something else, usually more abstract, as in Nathaniel Hawthorne's "The Birthmark." *Fable* and *parable* are forms of allegory. See *figure of speech.*

alliteration. Repetition of a consonant sound at the beginning of words or syllables that are close, although not necessarily adjacent: "And the silken, sad, uncertain rustling of each purple curtain."

anachronism. Any error in chronology, but especially the incongruous appearance of someone or something at a time when it could not have existed.

analogy. (1) Similarity in apparently dissimilar things, as expressed in *simile* and *metaphor.* (2) The inference that if two things are alike in one respect, they will be alike in another respect. See *figure of speech.*

anapest. A metrical foot consisting of two short (unaccented) syllables followed by a long (accented) one. See *meter.*

aphorism. A brief statement of a general truth. An aphorism usually has a specific author, while a *proverb* and an *adage* come anonymously from folk tradition. A proverb may, like an aphorism, express an abstract truth, or it may have the practical application of a *maxim.* All refer to a succinct and striking observation and are sometimes used interchangeably.

apology. In its literary use, a defense or vindication that describes or explains with no implied confession of guilt or expression of regret. An apology for someone's life, for instance, is simply a personal history.

assonance. Vowel rhyme; a form of half-rhyme with agreement of the vowel sounds in accented syllables without agreement of the following consonants, as in "shape" and "wait." See *rhyme.*

°ballad. (1) A folk song characterized by direct, simple, impersonal narrative of a dramatic event, often romantic or adventurous, usually in a number of short stanzas sung to a repetition of the same melody. (2) A narrative lyric by a known author imitating the form or the style of the traditional ballad.

blank verse. Poetry written in unrhymed lines of iambic pentameter. Occasionally used to refer to unrhymed verse in other metrical patterns.

bombast. Derived from "cotton padding," refers to inflated, pompous, excessively ornate language.

bowdlerize. To expurgate a written work by deleting or paraphrasing words, phrases, or allusions considered obscene, indelicate, or otherwise offensive. Usually implies prudery.

broadsides. Large sheets of paper printed on one side only, used for cheap popular distribution of ballads, political comment, advertising, etc.

burlesque. Grotesque mockery. Extravagant and incongruous imitation, such as treating a trivial subject in a lofty style or a serious subject in a flippantly humorous style. See *humor.*

cadence. (1) Synonymous with *rhythm;* the patterns of rise and fall in emphasis. (2) The sense of rhythmical movement and flow, concerned with sentences, stanzas, and paragraphs as opposed to the smaller patterns of metrical feet. (3) **Cadenced verse** refers specifically to poetry that seeks to use a variety and balance of natural speech rhythms as opposed to the traditional metrical patterns. See *free verse* and *meter.*

caricature. Distortion by exaggeration of characteristic and recognizable parts or qualities. See *humor.*

classic. (1) Any book considered to be of

enduring value and worthy of careful study. (2) **The classics.** Specifically, the best literature of ancient Greece and Rome. (3) Anything considered an excellent and familiar example of its kind, as a play that is a classic of expressionism or a poem that is a classic of tedious rhetoric. (4) As an adjective, may pertain to any of the above, or to *classicism.*

classicism. (1) Aesthetic theory which stresses the importance of harmony and proportion; that is, that all parts of a work must be appropriate to each other and to the purpose of the work, in a coherence which is the idea of perfection. Thus, works of classicism are characterized by rational conception, lucidity, formal elegance, dignity, balance. See comparison with *romanticism.* (2) Synonymous with *traditionalism.*

cliché. A phrase or expression that has been repeated so often that it has lost all originality and force of meaning. The term derives from the stereotype printing process, implying mechanical reproduction without thought or variation. Compare *platitude.*

colloquialism. A word, phrase, or expression considered good usage in conversation or informal writing, although incorrect for formal speech or writing. Its appropriate usage does not necessarily imply lack of culture or education.

comedy. (1) Strictly, a form of drama that amuses and provokes laughter, using any of the forms of *humor,* although its theme may be serious. Comedy deals with man's weaknesses, while *tragedy* shows the limitations of his strengths, so that the division between the highest forms of each is difficult to define. Their traditional forms, however, demand wide divergence in characters and mood, comedy dealing with ordinary people and sustaining a lighthearted manner to a happy ending. (2) By extension, any play or narrative with a happy ending, regardless of characters or treatment. (3) Any event marked by comic or humorous incongruity.

connotation. An implication or suggested meaning of a word or phrase, arising from personal or public association with some experience or literary allusion. The connotations of any given word may be both suggested and limited by context. Their multiple possibilities are distinguished from *denotation,* a precise definition. "Mother" denotes "female parent," but may in context connote love, protection, guidance—or nagging, orders, punishment.

consonance. (1) Any agreement or harmony of sounds. (2) Specifically, consonant rhyme; a form of half-rhyme with agreement of the final consonant sounds in accented syllables without agreement of the vowel sounds. The initial consonants may also, but not necessarily agree. For example: "mail," "meal," "foal"; "calling," "killing," "spelling." See *rhyme.*

couplet. Two successive verse lines with rhyming end-words, usually of corresponding length and rhythm.

criticism. (1) The analysis, evaluation, and judgment of a work of literature. (2) Discus-

sion of the methods and standards for such analysis and evaluation. (3) Discussion of the nature and value of literature in general; aesthetic theory in general. See LITERARY CRITICISM in the Encyclopedia.

dactyl. A metrical foot consisting of one long (accented) syllable followed by two short (unaccented) ones. See *meter.*

denotation. The specific meaning of a word or phrase as determined by good usage and common definition. Its exactness is distinguished from the associative significance of *connotation.*

dénouement. The final event in a plot. The word means the "unknotting" of the complication of conflicting forces. The resolution of conflict may be effected by a victory, a compromise, a realization, or some other change, including an internal change of character. See *plot.*

deus ex machina. Any person, thing, or situation introduced unexpectedly to resolve the complication of a plot, with the usually unfavorable implication of being an accidental and artificial imposition of the author rather than a necessity arising from the plot and characters. The Latin term means "the god from the machine" and refers to a technique in Greek theater of using stage machinery to lower a god onto the scene to untangle the plot.

°dialect. (1) Any form of a language recognizable by its characteristics of pronunciation and vocabulary as belonging to a specific regional, cultural, or social group. (2) Especially, any such form that is markedly different from the dialect considered standard or literary, such as the Cape Cod dialect, the Gullah Negro dialect.

diatribe. A lengthy, informal discourse, usually bitter and abusive in its argument, often characterized by lack of judgment or restraint in thought and language.

diction. (1) The use of words, the deliberate choice of words as appropriate to the subject, theme, mood, etc. (2) **Poetic diction** now refers specifically to the language of poetry characterized by archaisms, inversions, personifications, elevation, and formality, usually as a term of disparagement.

didactic. (1) Having an obvious purpose to instruct and improve, often with a moral lesson, such as H. W. Longfellow's "Psalm of Life." (2) As a derogatory term, having an excessively self-righteous attitude in preaching, or an emphasis on the lesson to the exclusion of pleasing literary qualities.

dimeter. A verse line of two metrical feet. See *meter.*

doggerel. (1) Undignified, trivial, or nonsense verse. (2) Verse that is jingling because of excessive regularity of meter and rhyme, or jerky because of excessive irregularity; often used as a humorous device. (3) Hence, a derogatory term for unsuccessful serious poetry.

°drama. (1) The literary form meant, or written as if meant, to be presented to its audience by actors; in prose unless qualified as "poetic drama" or "verse drama." (2) A play; a composition written in dialogue to be spoken and

acted. (3) Specifically, a play, usually realistic, that is neither a *tragedy* nor a *comedy*, although using some elements of both. See also *melodrama* and *farce*.

dramatic. (1) Pertaining to or having the qualities of *drama*. (2) Characterized by significant conflict, as "a dramatic situation."

elegy. (1) Any poem in a pensive, mournful mood, especially a lamentation on unrequited love or on death. (2) Now usually a lamentation on death in an elevated style.

epic. (1) A long narrative, episodic in structure, treating the adventurous career of a larger-than-life national hero in a serious and elevated style. (2) Hence, any grand narrative chronicling and glorifying a period in a nation's history; for example, a novel may be said to be an epic of the Civil War. (3) As an adjective, on a grand scale, larger-than-life-sized.

epigram. (1) Originally a short poem dealing tersely with a single thought or observation, usually ending with a surprising turn of thought, often satiric. (2) Hence, any concise and witty expression, usually barbed, frequently depending on a paradox, or apparent contradiction. Usually of more specific application than a *proverb* or *aphorism*, and more concerned with ingenuity than universal truth, although a proverb, etc., may be said to be **epigrammatic**.

epigraph. A quotation placed at the beginning of a work or one of its divisions to suggest or comment upon the theme of what follows.

epistolary. Pertaining to the writing of letters. Said of novels that purport to be a series of letters. Also said of letters, as from a distant traveler, that do not actually have the informal style of personal correspondence between intimates, but are obviously written for publication, being noticeably formal, didactic, or elegant.

epitaph. (1) An inscription on a tomb. (2) Hence, any brief poem, epigram, or other form written as if to be inscribed at a place of burial.

epithet. (1) Any descriptive term characterizing a person or thing, often embodying or implying a metaphor, especially one that is used so frequently that it becomes by association a name for that person or thing, such as "the Father of our Country" for George Washington. (2) Frequently, an uncomplimentary descriptive term used in abusive invective.

*****essay.** (1) A brief prose composition discussing a limited subject in almost any manner. (2) Occasionally, a book-length treatise or discourse.

eulogy. A composition in any form praising a person's life, character, or services.

euphemism. An indirect allusion substituted for direct expression of the offensive or indelicate. Speaking pleasantly of something disagreeable. Often used with an implication of evasion, insincerity, or prudery.

*****expressionism.** A literary technique which seeks the essential qualities of things and depicts them to the senses, thus distorting the ordinary external appearance of things. On the stage, for instance, two actors may be used to express the split personality of a single character. Often

merges with *symbolism*. Contrast *impressionism*.

fable. (1) A brief tale which illustrates a moral or a principle of behavior, using animals or inanimate objects that reveal their natural qualities while engaging in human activities and speech, such as J. C. Harris' Uncle Remus stories. (2) Any fictional narrative, especially one with allegorical significance. (3) A fiction or falsehood (said of something held to be true).

farce. (1) "Low" or "broad" comedy; buffoonery; unsubtle humor; tricks or gags provoking laughter with little or no mental effort. (2) Hence, a *comedy* with no serious theme; a play with improbable action and characters depending for effect upon extreme incongruity of situation and farcical devices.

fiction. (1) Any work drawn from imagination rather than fact. (2) Usually, a prose narrative, especially the *novel, short story, romance,* and related forms, as distinguished from *poetry* or *drama*, which are listed by booksellers and reviewers as non-fiction.

figure of speech. Any use of a word or expression other than according to its ordinary definition or meaning. *Irony* implies a meaning opposite to what is actually said. *Analogy* makes striking use of points of comparison between essentially unlike things; it is expressed in several ways: *simile* makes the comparison directly; *metaphor* implies it, often making the second term a vivid *image* for the first, and *allegory* extends such imagery into a narrative. But whereas an *image* suggests only one associative use, readily identifiable, a *symbol* suggests a complex of associations, some of which can only be felt or sensed rather than completely analyzed and understood.

*****folklore.** (1) The stories, songs, dances, customs, beliefs, sayings, etc., preserved traditionally by a people, usually orally, but including that part of the body of written literature which is commonly known by all members of a culture. For example, H. W. Longfellow's account of "The Midnight Ride of Paul Revere" has become a part of American folklore. (2) The comparative study of such traditions and their patterns to reveal the characteristics of a people's life and culture, often associated with the interests of anthropology and sociology.

foot. A unit in the measure of rhythm; in general, a group of syllables with one major stress or accent. See *meter*.

free verse. Poetry whose structure depends on *cadence* rather than regular metrical patterns of rhythm, and on *assonance, consonance,* and *alliteration* rather than traditional rhyme schemes. It may be characterized by irregularly varying line lengths, or by *accentual* or *syllabic meter*. Named in reference to the attempt to "free" poetry from excessive restriction by or dependence on strict forms, it has developed new patterns that permit the poet to take advantage of modern natural speech rhythms without abandoning that sense of rhythm and form which is the essence of poetry.

hack writing. Writing done according to an assignment and primarily for financial return.

The term derives from a horse that is hired out and worn down by service; hence, implies drudgery for the author, mediocrity in the work. Compare *potboiler*.

half-rhyme. See *assonance, consonance, rhyme*.

heptameter. A verse line of seven metrical feet. See *meter*.

hero. (1) The chief sympathetic character in a plot, usually noted for nobility, courage, and other admirable qualities. Often, but not necessarily, the *protagonist*. (2) Any person or character noted for active proof of his courage or nobility. (3) Loosely used, a synonym for *protagonist*.

heroic couplet. Two successive verse lines of iambic pentameter with rhyming end-words.

hexameter. A verse line of six metrical feet. See *meter*.

hudibrastic. Mock-heroic, said of verse that burlesques the epic style, such as the Hartford Wits' *The Anarchiad*.

***humanism.** (1) Stress on the interests or importance of man as opposed both to the divine and to the naturalistic and animalistic. (2) **The New Humanism.** A philosophical and literary movement stressing the dominance of man's free will over his instincts, the universal elements in a changing world, and *classicism* and *traditionalism* as critical standards.

***humor.** In general, that which appeals to man's disposition to laugh, arising from his perception of the incongruous and the ridiculous. As distinguished from *wit*, humor is less an intellectual response and more a sympathetic one. As distinguished from *satire*, humor is more good-natured, even kindly, and less obviously corrective in intent. But such distinctions are difficult, for satire and wit both depend on a sense of humor, whether their purpose is primarily to entertain or to instruct. All three seek to capitalize on the incongruous, finding similarity, or a common denominator, between things commonly considered unlike. Since the discovery is usually of the reality of human weakness beneath the appearance of human civilization, the result is the exposure of pretense, the deflation of the dignified, etc. Thus, humor recognizes human nature, satire criticizes it, and wit aids both, especially in the realm of ideas and words.

In order to deflate by mockery and ridicule, any of the three may employ a number of literary techniques. *Irony* poses hidden meanings. *Parody, caricature, lampoon,* and *burlesque* are all mocking imitations. Parody and caricature mock specific people or works, parody by making them trivial, caricature by exaggeration and distortion. A lampoon maliciously satirizes with parodic caricature. Burlesque trivializes, but is usually less specifically directed than parody, and less frequently used satirically. All these terms overlap considerably, and are often used almost interchangeably.

***hymn.** (1) A lyrical song or poem expressing religious emotion in praise of a god, a hero, nature, etc. (2) By extension, any expression of strong praise, as "The novel is a hymn to the glory of America."

hyperbole. Exaggeration beyond possibility for emphasis, humor, etc., as "I'm as high as a flag on the Fourth of July."

iamb[us]. A metrical foot consisting of one short (unaccented) syllable followed by one long (accented) one. See *meter*.

image. (1) A picture, or anything that appeals to sensory perception. (2) A mental representation of anything not actually present to the senses, as in memory. (3) Anything, sensory or conceptual, used to stand for or suggest something else which it resembles or embodies, such as the "ship" of state on whose deck Walt Whitman's "captain" (Abraham Lincoln) "lies fallen cold and dead."

***imagism.** A literary movement which stressed precision of *images*, or pictures, exactness and concision of language, complete freedom in choice of subject, and *cadenced*, rather than metrical rhythms.

***impressionism.** A literary technique that depicts things as they impress themselves upon the sensory perceptions of the observer (usually the author), without the study or inference of details not included in this impression. Thus it is a *subjective* approach to external experience on the part of the author, as distinguished from *expressionism*, which seeks to externalize the subjective state or essence of the person or thing being described.

internal rhyme. Any rhyme in poetry other than end-rhyme. See *rhyme*.

irony. (1) The quality of an expression whose implied meaning is quite different from and usually opposite to the apparent sense of the words. (2) The quality of a situation that is contrary to prior expectation, usually implying a double significance (the difference between appearance and reality) in all things and events, and implying a mocking design on the part of some power, such as fate. (3) Called "dramatic irony" when the reader or audience is aware of the multiple interpretations of a speech or situation, and one or more of the characters involved are not. See *humor*.

lampoon. A malicious and abusive *satire* directed against a particular person or institution. See *humor*.

legend. (1) Any tale come down from the past, usually in the *folklore* of a people, especially one of a quasi-historical nature, accepted uncritically although authenticated only in part or not at all. When distinguished from *myth*, legend has less of the supernatural and more of the historical. (2) Hence, any literary work by a specific author which appears to retell such a tale, whether original or not, such as Washington Irving's "The Legend of Sleepy Hollow." (3) For further extensions of meaning, see *myth*.

legitimate theater. The spoken drama performed by live actors, as distinguished from the revue, musical comedy, pantomime, radio play, television play, or screenplay.

limerick. A verse form used exclusively for light and nonsense verse, containing five anapestic lines. The first, second, and fifth lines are in trimeter and have rhyming end-words; the third and fourth lines are in dimeter and have rhyming end-words.

local color. The emphasis and detailed description of the characteristics of a specific geographic locale and its inhabitants, including landscape, dress, and traditions, and purporting to reproduce typical lives and native dialectal speech forms. See REGIONALISM in the Encyclopedia.

lyric or **lyrical.** (1) Having a melodic quality, as of song. (2) Personal, *subjective*, a response of and appeal to the emotions. (3) Hence, a lyric, as a noun, is a fairly short poem, melodic in sound or even meant to be sung, creating and sustaining a single effect of imaginative, subjective, emotional quality. It refers to an attitude, a manner of treatment, not to a specific form.

lyrics. The words of a song, such as a musical comedy number. (Always used in the plural in this sense.)

malapropism. Ludicrous misuse of a word (usually polysyllabic) by substitution for another word similar in sound. Mrs. Malaprop (Fr. *mal à propos*, "out of place"), a character in Sheridan's *The Rivals*, was noted for this type of blunder: "As headstrong as an *allegory* on the banks of the Nile."

maxim. A pithy expression of a practical truth or guide to conduct. See *aphorism*.

melodrama. (1) A form of drama in which the conflict is simple, typically between an all-virtuous hero and an all-wicked villain; in which action is sensational and romantic; and in which the ending, usually happy, does not depend on plot or character, but on accident (see *deus ex machina*). See DRAMA in the Encyclopedia. (2) Hence, as a term of disparagement, any play which depends on thrills rather than organic unity for effect, whose characters lack depth, and whose emotional appeal is superficial.

metaphor. An implied expression of comparison, as in "Law, say the gardeners, is the sun." See *figure of speech*.

metaphysical poetry. (1) Originally, poetry dealing with a philosophical subject. (2) Usually, poetry characterized by intellectual and psychological analysis rather than lyrical feeling, extensive use of boldly unusual and elaborate metaphors, and deliberate roughness and irregularity in the rhythms of traditional forms.

metaphysics. (1) The study of the first principles of being. (2) In general, philosophy. (3) Hence, any study or discussion dealing with abstract ideas: morals, ethics, truth, divinity, etc.

meter. (1) The patterns of *rhythm* in poetry, analyzed by *prosody* through *scansion*. (2) Any particular pattern, classified according to the kind of foot and the length of the line.

A recurrent pattern of accent or stress within a line of poetry is called a foot; it usually consists of one long (accented, stressed) syllable (´) and one or two short (unaccented, unstressed) syllables (˘), such as the

iambic (˘´):

And fired | the shot | heard round | the world.

trochaic (´˘):

Once u | pon a | midnight | weary

anapestic (˘˘´):

Of the beau | tiful Ann | abel Lee

dactylic (´˘˘):

This is the | forest pri | meval. The | murmuring | pines and the | hemlocks

Most poetry does not repeat one kind of foot throughout a poem without variation; the meter takes its name from the prevailing pattern. Modulations of rhythm are achieved by variation, and some are very common: for instance, the use of a trochee at the beginning of an iambic line:

Daughters | of Time, | the hyp | ocrit | ic Days

or the use of an iamb in an anapestic line:

It was man | y and man | y a year | ago

A spondee (″) is a foot rarely used as a prevailing pattern, even for a single line, but common as a variant in other meters for effects of slowness, length, or emphasis:

There with | vast wings | across | the can | celed skies

The length of a line is measured by the number of feet, regardless of pattern or number of syllables. Dimeter has two feet:

This knight | so bold →

Trimeter has three feet:

But I | with mourn | ful tread

Tetrameter has four feet:

Ye who | love a | nation's | legends

Pentameter has five feet:

I lift | mine eyes, | and all | the win | dows blaze

Hexameter has six feet:

Black were her | eyes as the | berry that |
grows on the | thorn by the | wayside

Thus, the description of a meter gives the length of the line and its dominant pattern; for instance, blank verse uses iambic pentameter:

And millions in those solitudes, since first
The flight of years began, have laid them
down . . .

When unqualified otherwise, "meter," "metric," and "metrical" are understood to refer to regular patterns of rhythm as described above; occasionally they also imply excessive regularity, unvarying, constricting, and dull. Modern prosody, however, recognizes new verse forms, which permit the freer and longer, more varying and more natural, patterns of *cadence*.

In **syllabic meter,** the line is measured by the number of syllables, regardless of accent pattern. Hence, "decasyllabic" may be preferable to "iambic pentameter" to describe a line in which there are fewer than five stressed syllables, or in which several feet are not iambs. Of course, any number of syllables may be used as the line unit:

The apple on its bough is her desire,—
Shining suspension, mimic of the sun.

In **accentual meter,** the line is measured by the number of strong accents, regardless of the number of syllables, such as a four-beat or a five-beat line. An accentual foot, then, has one accented syllable and zero to four unaccented syllables, the divisions between feet being marked by the pauses:

they sowed | their isn't | they reaped |
their same
sun | moon | stars | rain

In **cadenced meter** the lines are not measured in any way, and are usually of widely varying length, being determined by breath groupings and thought groupings:

A poem should be palpable and mute
As a globed fruit.

*muckraking literature. Literature of social protest that exposes real or alleged corruption in public institutions and leaders, industries, businesses, and the like.

mysticism. Any doctrine or belief that depends on the possibility of union with or knowledge of a force or spirit greater than man, such as nature, absolute truth, or a divinity, through some form of direct intuition, such as religious faith or poetic insight, rather than through reason based on empirical observation.

myth. (1) A tale of primitive origin in the culture of a people, usually dealing with racial heroes and with the supernatural as explanation of natural forces and origins; hence, **mythology** is considered a part of religion. (2) Loosely, myth and *legend* are used to refer to any story or idea that is unauthenticated, but accepted uncritically by some group of people, usually in explanation of an existing institution, custom, or tradition, as "the myth of male superiority," "the legend of the haunted house." (3) Loosely, mythical and legendary refer to any *folklore* tradition, especially one whose form or subject resembles that of the older myths and legends, as "Paul Bunyan is a legendary hero." (4) Both often imply the purely imaginary and unfactual, as, "A liar's exploits are simply mythical adventures."

*naturalism. The literary movement that used the techniques of *realism* to illustrate the deterministic theory that character and behavior are governed by heredity and environment. Emphasizing the instinctual and social forces that restrict human freedom of will and intellect, it is most often associated with the sordid and pessimistic.

neo-classicism. A movement of the 17th and 18th centuries that attempted to recapture and codify the spirit of *classicism*, stressing logic, wit, restrained emotion, formality, "correctness," and "good taste."

*new criticism. A school of *criticism* which demands that literature, especially poetry, be approached not through biographical and historical considerations, but through analytical study of the text itself.

*novel. A long prose fictional narrative, usually characterized by a complication of the *plot* (and usually also subplots) leading to a *dénouement,* and by revelation or development of character. It may make important use of *setting,* mood, and point of view, as opposed to looser forms which present a series of events impersonally and episodically (without causal or motivational relationship). See *romance.*

objective. (1) Pertaining to the object; descriptive of reality as it is rather than as perceived or felt. Contrast *subjective*. (2) Hence, impersonal; free from any prejudice or bias which might prevent or distort such description.

objective correlative. A term used by T. S. Eliot in his essay on Hamlet (1919) to refer to the object, situation, or chain of events an author must use to externalize a subjective experience, such as an emotion, so that the same emotion is evoked in the reader.

occasional verse. Verse written for a specific personal or public occasion, or on a currently topical subject. Usually light verse, frequently satirical, often ephemeral, although some is serious and lasting poetry, such as J. R. Lowell's "Harvard Commemoration Ode."

ode. A lyrical poem of elevated purpose, mood, language, and style, usually characterized by a complex stanza form.

onomatopoeia. An effect of language in which the sound echoes or supports the sense. Some words are in themselves onomatopoeic, such as "hiss," "moan," "humming." Repetition of certain sounds, as in *assonance, consonance,* and *alliteration,* can be used onomatopoeically:

In the ghoul-haunted woodland of Weir . . .

Even metrical patterns and their variations can reinforce meaning, as the trochees of H. W. Longfellow's *Hiawatha* suggest the beating of Indian drums:

Sáng thĕ | Sóng ŏf | Híă | wáthă

or the insertion of an anapest in iambic meter can slow down a line:

Slŏw trác | ĭng dówn | thĕ thíck | ĕnĭng ský

oxymoron. A combination of apparently contradictory words to evoke an unusual twist of thought, such as "wise innocence," "cruel kindness." The term literally means "pointedly foolish." Compare *paradox.*

panegyric. A composition in any form for public and formal praise of someone or something. Sometimes implies excessively elaborate style and insincere sentiment.

pantheism. In general, the idea that all is God, that there is no divinity except as expressed in all the natural objects and forces of the universe, and nothing in the universe except as an expression of the idea of divinity.

parable. A brief and simple tale that illustrates a moral or spiritual truth, using commonly familiar objects and incidents with allegorical significance.

paradox. Any statement or situation that appears to contradict itself or common sense, especially one which is nevertheless actually true. Compare *oxymoron.*

paraphrase. Restatement of a passage or work to give the meaning in different words and form, usually to explain, clarify, or shorten it.

parody. Ridiculing imitation of a well-known work or style, mimicry of its manner and mannerisms in the treatment of an incongruous, usually trivial, subject. See *humor.*

pastiche. A work piecing together excerpts or imitations from various sources. Frequently done humorously, the device is occasionally used in a serious work, such as T. S. Eliot's "The Waste Land."

pentameter. A verse line of five metrical feet. See *meter.*

persona. (1) Any character in a poem, play, or prose fiction. (2) A mask; hence, (*a*) any character who serves as a disguise for the author or his ideas, or (*b*) the projection of any aspect of the author or a character into a separate role.

picaresque novel. A type of fiction consisting of loosely related episodes in the life and wanderings of a rogue or vagabond.

platitude. A dull commonplace or truism; the term is usually used to refer to a flat or trite statement given with undue solemnity, as if it were profound. Compare *cliché.*

plot. An interconnected series of events which has internal unity usually achieved by the resolution of a conflict (see *dénouement*). A plot uses *action* involving its *subject* to express a *theme.* For example, the subject of Herman Melville's *Moby Dick* is a whale hunt; the plot connects a series of incidents (action) in the pursuit of the white whale; a major theme of the book is the relationship between the forces of good and evil.

poetic diction. See *diction.*

poetry. (1) Synonymous with *verse:* a form of literature marked by a certain regularity of rhythm and musicality of sound (see *meter* and *rhyme*), as distinguished from *prose.* (2) When distinguished from verse, and without regard to form, the imaginative and *subjective* response to experience which relies on figurative language more than facts to attain some kind of truth, often an emotional or religious one.

polyphonic prose. A literary form using the characteristic devices of poetry, but printed as prose. Developed by Amy Lowell and defined by her in 1918: "'Polyphonic' means—many voiced—and the form is so called because it makes use of all the 'voices' of poetry, namely: metre, vers libre, assonance, alliteration, rhyme, and return."

portmanteau word. A word formed by the combination of two or more others in order to suggest some of the meaning of each. "Brunch" is eaten between the times for breakfast and lunch; "chortle" is a cross between a chuckle and a snort. Often used as a humorous device.

potboiler. A work written primarily for financial return, often by implication hastily done, intended for immediate popular appeal, and of no lasting value. Compare *hack writing.*

prose. (1) The ordinary language of men in everyday speech. (2) Literary, or careful, expression that does not have the conspicuous rhythm and form of *poetry.* As to content, prose is considered to be used for description, exposition (explanation), argument, and narration; poetry for *subjective* expression of truth through density of connotation and frequent use of *figures of speech.* But obviously, many novels and essays are poetic in their figurative use of language, their impressionistic response to experience, etc., and many poems have simple narrative and descriptive elements. **Prosaic,** however, does not mean having the qualities of good prose, but implies unimaginative, purely factual, ordinary, or dull.

prosody. The art and theory of versification; the analysis of accent and rhythm by *scansion.* See *meter.*

protagonist. (1) The major or central character in a plot. Distinguished from *hero* in that he need not be admirable or sympathetic. (2) The chief advocate or champion of a cause or movement.

proverb. A terse and striking well-known saying that sums up a general truth or observation, usually characterized by a vivid metaphor, a play on words, or apt repetitions of sound. See *aphorism.*

psalm. A lyrical poem in praise of God.

quatrain. A poem or stanza of four lines.

*__realism.__ A literary technique that attempts to present honestly and accurately the realities of characters, social milieus, physical environments, etc. (2) Especially a literary movement which stresses the importance of *objective* representation of ordinary people and their lives in reaction to *romance,* which demands a fanciful and pleasant unreality. Compare *naturalism.*

rhyme. (1) Rhymed verse. (2) Agreement of the final vowel and consonant sounds in the last accented syllables of two or more lines of verse. Full, or perfect, rhyme follows unlike consonants: "ran" and "man"; "remaining" and "explaining."

Listen, my children, and you shall *hear*
Of the midnight ride of Paul Re*vere.*

Half-rhyme includes *assonance* and *consonance,* the agreement of vowels or consonants, but not both:

I never spoke with G*od,*
Nor visited in h*eaven;*
Yet certain am I of the sp*ot*
As if the chart were g*iven.*

Unless otherwise qualified, rhyme is assumed to mean end-rhyme, in which all the rhyming words are the last words in their lines. Internal rhyme refers to rhyming words in any other position, although one of the set may be final:

That the wind came out of the cloud, ch*illing*
And k*illing* my Annabel Lee.

Internal rhyme, assonance, and consonance are frequently used, as well as *alliteration,* to provide harmonies within lines, often in order to achieve *onomatopoeia.*

rhythm. (1) The alternations of stress in recurrent patterns at regular intervals. (2) A particular example or form of such a pattern. See *cadence, meter.*

romance. (1) A fictional narrative in prose or poetry characterized by an air of unreality, usually picturesque, adventurous, supernatural, or sentimental. A *novel* is usually considered to be more concerned with presenting a recognizable imitation of reality, but a novel may also be a romance, such as Nathaniel Hawthorne's *The House of the Seven Gables.* (2) The quality of being highly fanciful, improbable, picturesque, exciting, exotic, etc., as "ambitions full of romance," "a romantic mystery."

romanticism. (1) A tendency toward unrealistic *romance.* (2) Aesthetic theory that stresses imagination, feeling, and individuality. As opposed to *classicism,* it tends toward individuality of expression rather than imitation of accepted standards or obedience to authority, feeling rather than reason, *subjective* response rather than *objective* presentation, the unusual rather than the conventional, excess rather than restraint, inclusion of the common and ordinary rather than selection of the noble and elevating, fantasy rather than order and control, and specifically, revolt against what it considers the excessive restrictions of conventional metrical forms. These distinctions, however, are difficult to draw in practice, because of the changing applications of both terms; and both must be considered only as tendencies, since all the best works of literature synthesize elements of both. It is also important to distinguish among all the possible connotations of these words, and of *classic* and *romance.* For instance, a book may be a classic of romance; and *realism,* which is opposed to romance, is an outgrowth of romanticism.

satire. The use of ridicule to censure human weaknesses and vices, usually with the implied purpose of provoking reform. See *humor.*

scansion. The process of analyzing the rhythmical form of a poem by indicating accents and pauses and identifying the recurrent patterns and their modifications. Verse is said to **scan** if it holds to a specific meter. See *meter.*

setting. The background or environment of an action, with reference to the culture and the moral and social habits of the characters involved, as well as to time and place. The setting may assume great or even the greatest importance in works such as a historical novel, a comedy of manners, a novel of social protest, *local color* writings, etc.

*__short story.__ A brief prose fictional narrative. When distinguished from the *tale,* it uses more of the techniques of the *novel,* although on a small scale, usually achieving a single intensive effect through a densely knit complication of plot.

simile. A direct expression of comparison, usually with "as" or "like," such as "The wind tapped like a tired man." See *figure of speech.*

solecism. A usage or construction of language that violates the rules of grammar or idiom, such as "he don't."

sonnet. A lyric poem of fourteen lines, usually in iambic pentameter. Strictly, the sonnet should follow one of a number of prescribed rhyme and stanza schemes, but experimenters have made innumerable variations.

spondee. A metrical foot consisting of two long (accented) syllables. See *meter.*

stanza. (1) A group of verse lines, usually three to nine, the metrical pattern and rhyme scheme of which follow a pattern repeated throughout the poem as a unit of organization.

*__stream-of-consciousness.__ (1) The flow of thoughts and impressions through a person's mind. (2) A literary technique presenting such a flow in a fictional character. Marked by associations, digressions, and much detail, it makes a human consciousness central to the narrative and emphasizes its approach to experience and its speculations on life rather than the actual external events.

style. (1) Manner of expression, as distinguished from the content or sense of what is being expressed, as "every author has his own personal style." (2) A specific manner of expression, as characterized, such as concrete or figurative style, colonial, western, rhetorical, impressionistic, or lyrical style, etc. (3) The quality of excellence in writing, regardless of manner; that facility and felicity of language that makes a work both effective and pleasurable to read; it has never been defined, but is usually thought to be associated with a perfect unity of content and manner of expression.

subject. (1) A person, thing, event, or idea used as the matter presented. (2) Occasionally used as a synonym for *theme*. See also *plot*.

subjective. (1) As seen, felt, or experienced by the subject. Hence, (a) descriptive of something in terms of its impression on the author or his response to it (see *impressionism*), or (b) descriptive of a character in terms of that character's self-awareness or response to experience, as seen extensively in *stream-of-consciousness* and *expressionism*. (2) Personal, individual, as opposed to common or universal. Contrast *objective*.

*surrealism. (1) A movement in art and literature which seeks to break through the limitations of conscious awareness and rationality, and present the material and activities of the subconscious mind, using the distorted images and apparently illogical sequences of dreams. (2) Any attempt to present a truth or reality by a startling, often violent, distortion or unreality of appearance.

syllabic meter. A metrical structure based on the number of syllables in a verse line, regardless of the foot patterns or the number of accents. See *meter*.

symbol. (1) A sign, something which stands for or suggests something else by arbitrary association rather than intrinsic resemblance, as a cross is a symbol for Christianity. (2) Loosely, an *image*, something which stands for or suggests something else because of some intrinsic similarity or because it embodies a more general or abstract idea. (3) Specifically, an image with more than one identifiable level of meaning in context, aside from the surface meaning, and giving in addition an indefinable sense of further significances, such as the glass unicorn in Tennessee Williams' *The Glass Menagerie*. See *figure of speech*.

*symbolism. (1) In general, the extensive use of images and situations as *symbols*. (2) Specifically, a literary movement seeking to present abstract ideas and moods through sensory perceptions, depending on the suggestion and *connotation* values of words, sounds, and rhythms.

synaesthesia. Interaction of response among the senses; for example, identification or description of a sound in terms of color. Such appeal is common in familiar idioms, such as a "loud red," "a sweet sound," "a cool blue." More complex uses provide literature with fresh images:

> What words
> Can strangle this deaf moonlight?

tale. A story; a short, simple, direct, fictional narrative. When distinguished from the *short story*, it has a less complex structure and less unity of effect and is often more concerned with plot.

tercet. A three-line stanza.

terza rima. A verse form of interlocking three-line stanzas, in which the end-word of the second line rhymes with the end-words of the first and third lines in the following stanza:

> Dance for this music, Mistress to music dear,
> more, that full storm through the disordered
>   *wood*
> ravens at midnight of my thirtieth year
>
> and only the trial of our music *should*
> still this irresolute air, only your voice
> spelling the tempest may compel our *good:*

tetrameter. A verse line of four metrical feet. See *meter*.

theme. An idea present in a subject or plot, although frequently never directly discussed. See *plot*.

traditionalism. (1) Acceptance and imitation of the beliefs, practices, or conventions of the past; conservatism, opposition to change. (2) In literature, respect for and imitation of the touchstones of taste, the past works that have become standards of the best in literature, especially those adhering to the theory of *classicism*. (3) In poetry, specifically, the use of regular metrical patterns and conventional poetic forms. (4) Hence, sometimes a term of disparagement for regularity and balance that is excessive to the point of jingling or dullness, or for preference of older ideas or forms, even if outdated, to modern ideas and their new modes of expression.

tragedy. (1) Strictly, a form of drama whose subject and theme are serious and significant, involving the emotions of pity and fear through the fall of a larger-than-life noble character in a plot governed by internal necessity. (2) By extension, any play or narrative with an unhappy ending deriving from necessity of plot and character. (3) Loosely, any unhappy event with unhappy consequences, such as a flood, a murder, the death of a loved one, as "The disease which blinded her was her personal tragedy." Note that the occurrence of such an event does not necessarily make a play or novel a tragedy in form. Compare *comedy*.

*transcendentalism. (1) In general, the philosophic idea that *a priori* conditions govern the knowledge of empirical experience. (2) In its American form, it emphasized the importance of the individual soul's intuition of truth through its participation in the "Oversoul," or idea of divinity. It was associated with *pantheism* in that all natural objects and forces were seen either as a part of or as an expression of the idea of divinity.

trimeter. A verse line of three metrical feet. See *meter*.

trochee. A metrical foot consisting of one

long (accented) syllable followed by one short (unaccented) one. See *meter*.

trope. (1) Literally, a "turning" of a word or expression from its ordinary meaning or usage to some other use. (2) Any specific type of such use. See *figure of speech*.

verse. (1) Synonymous with *poetry*: a form of literature marked by a certain regularity of rhythm and musicality of sound (see *meter* and *rhyme*), as distinguished from *prose*. (2) When distinguished from poetry, literature which observes the metrical conventions, but whose subject and style do not conform to the idea of seriousness and aesthetic beauty associated with poetry; such as light, humorous, or nonsense verse, doggerel, limericks, epigrams, etc. (3) Occasionally (although disapproved by the best usage), synonymous with *stanza*, especially with reference to a song or ballad.

vers libre. See *free verse*.

wit. (1) Mental ability, especially agility of intellectual perception and analysis. (2) Verbal expression of this agility, especially in a turn of phrase that amuses by finding surprising and thought-provoking associations among words and ideas. See *humor*.